Your beautiful destination

CAMPING
PLAYA JOYEL

E-39180 NOJA

SANTANDER ~ CANTABRIA

TEL. (34) 942 63 00 81

FAX (34) 942 63 12 94

- Only 40 km from Santander (ferry) and 70km from Bilbao (ferry), easily and quickly reached along the magnificent, new, toll-free autovia and the coast roads.
- A 25 ha. holiday site with a large (4 ha) recreation and sports area and a precious, 8 ha natural park with animals in semiliberty.
- Modern, first category installations. Beautifull surroundings with direct access to wide, clean beaches. Surrounded by meadows and woods.
- Service and comfort for the most exacting guests.Properly marked pitches.
- English spoken.
- Open from Easter to 30th September.

Caravan Europe 2008

Explanation of a Campsite Entry

The town under which the campsite is listed, as shown on the relevant Sites Location Map at the end of each country's site entry pages

Distance and direction of the site from the town the site is listed under in kilometres (or metres), together with site's aspect

Site Location Map grid reference

Campsite name

Telephone and fax numbers including national code

Contact email address and website address

Campsite address, including post code

Description of the campsite and its facilities

Directions to the campsite

Comments and opinions of caravanners who have visited the site

The year in which the site was last reported on by a visitor

Opening dates – if the site is open all year there will be a ⊞ symbol in front of the name of the town under which the site is listed, and no opening dates will be given

Charge per night in high season for car, caravan + 2 adults (in local currency) as at year of last report

Reference number for a site included in the Caravan Club's Advance Booking Service

MUIDES SUR LOIRE *4G2* (1km SE Rural) Camping Le Château des Marais, 27-29 Rue de Chambord, 41500 Muides-sur-Loire [02 54 87 05 42; fax 02 54 87 05 43; info@chateau-des-marais.com; www.chateau-des-marais.com] Exit A10 at junc 16 sp Chambord & take N152 sp Mer, Chambord, Blois. At Mer take D112 & cross Rv Loire. After 300m site on L on edge of vill. Well sp. Lge, mkd pitch, pt sl, shd; htd wc; chem disp; mv service pnt; all serviced pitches; baby facs; shwrs inc; el pnts (6-10A) €5-7 (poss rev pol); gas; lndtte; shop; rest; snacks; bar, BBQ; playgrnd; 3 pools (1 htd, covrd); waterslides; fishing; tennis; cycle hire; games area; entmnt; internet; TV; 10% statics (tour ops); dogs €5; Eng spkn; adv bkg fee & deposit; cc acc; CCI. "Excel, modern facs; v well-run site; friendly recep staff; plenty of gd quality children's play equipment; gd for visiting chateaux & Loire; mkt Sat am Blois." ♦ 12 May-14 Sep. € 32.00 ABS - L10   2007*

⊞ FAGERNES *2F1* (500m N Rural) NAF Camping Fagernes, Tyinvegen 23, 2900 Fagernes (Oppland) [tel 61 36 05 10; fax 61 36 07 51; post@fagernes-camping.no; www.fagernes-camping.no] Site on N side of Fagernes on E16. Lge, some hdg pitch, pt sl, pt shd; htd wc; chem disp; mv service pnt; baby facs; shwrs NOK10; el pnts (10A) NOK30; lndtte; shop; rest; snacks; bar; playgrnd; lake sw; activity cent; cycling; skiing; fishing; car wash; TV; 50% statics; phone; poss cr; Eng spkn; quiet low ssn; cc acc; CCI. "Sep area for tourers by rv; Valdes folk museum park adj highly rec." ♦ NOK 165 (CChq acc)   2007*

Unspecified facilities for disabled guests

The site accepts Camping Cheques - see the chapter *Continental Campsites* for details

Caravan Europe 1

© The Caravan Club Limited 2008
Published by The Caravan Club Limited
East Grinstead House, East Grinstead,
West Sussex RH19 1UA

General Enquiries: 01342 326944
Travel Service Reservations: 01342 316101
Brochure Requests: 01342 327410
General Fax: 01342 410258
Website: www.caravanclub.co.uk
Email: enquiries@caravanclub.co.uk

Editor: Bernice Hoare
Email: bernice.hoare@caravanclub.co.uk

Printed by Elanders Hindson Ltd,
Newcastle-upon-Tyne

Maps and distance charts generated from Collins Bartholomew
Digital Database.

Maps © Collins Bartholomew Ltd 2007, reproduced by
permission of HarperCollins Publishers

ISBN 978 1 85733 455 5

Front cover photo: Oranges at Pollença market, Spain,
kindly supplied by Paul Shawcross Photography.
www.paulshawcross.co.uk

Contents

Contents

During Your Stay

Countries

See also alphabetical index at the back of the guide

THE
CARAVAN
CLUB

Welcome to the 50th edition of **Caravan Europe**. This year also marks something of a personal celebration - I am proud to have been Editor of Caravan Europe for the last ten years.

The Caravan Club published its first members' guide to Continental caravanning in 1959. It ran to 70 pages and contained details of fewer than 400 campsites in 14 countries. Now it's a whopping 1500 pages and contains nearly 8000 sites in 22 countries. Remarkably, 150 of those in the first edition are still going strong today.

Since 1959 the caravanning experience has changed beyond recognition – for example, does anyone remember having their caravan hoisted aboard a cross-Channel ferry? So too, have campsites: private bathrooms on pitches, satellite television and wifi connections, cabaret-style entertainment, waterslides and saunas – all unheard of 50 years ago. But there are still thousands of delightful, away-from-it all sites, and **Caravan Europe** lists many of them too. In short, it has something for everyone.

And to encourage you, the caravanner, to tell us about the sites you visit, anyone sending in site reports during 2008 will be entered into a prize draw to win a ferry crossing to France for a car, caravan or motor caravan and two adults. See page 11 for more details.

Now, as in 1959, **Caravan Europe is** a unique guide and an essential travelling companion for anyone heading to the Continent on holiday. Enjoy!

Bernice Hoare

Bernice Hoare
Editor

www.caravanclub.co.uk

The Caravan Club's Travel Service in Europe

We offer our members a comprehensive Travel Service to the highest professional standards for which **The Caravan Club** is renowned. All aspects, from Continental site and ferry booking to a superb travel insurance scheme, are handled with the customer-friendly approach you would expect from The Club. If you're travelling abroad, this service really is a good enough reason on its own to join **The Caravan Club**.

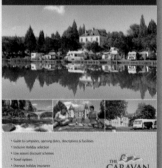

Holidaying with confidence

Over 100,000 members use our popular service each year, testament to the confidence members have in the organisation. Our financial security is one good reason for this trust, coupled with the dedication and efficiency of our staff. Many of our members use our services time and time again and become old friends with the site owners they meet on their travels, and our people too.

Saving money with The Club

We have long established relationships with most of the major ferry operators and many overseas sites, which means we not only obtain very favourable rates but also, and perhaps of even more significance, can work with them to ensure you get the best possible holiday experience. As a mutual organisation The Club is able to pass on considerable savings to its members, an option not available to solely commercial operators.

With respected ferry companies such as Brittany Ferries, Stena Line, P&O Ferries, Norfolk Lines, SeaFrance and Eurotunnel all represented by The Club, you can be sure that almost any combination of route, time and destination will be available to you. Booking through us will ensure that you will be offered the most appropriate crossing at a keen price every time.

Ferry fares can vary considerably by day of week and time of day, so even greater savings can be made if you are willing to be flexible in your travel arrangements. We are only too happy to discuss alternatives on the phone, so you can compare the cost of various options. If you choose to book on The Club's website, the systems are specifically designed to make these comparisons easy.

Keeping up standards

Over 200 sites in Europe are regularly inspected and monitored by The Club's experienced team of site inspectors. They are all members of The Caravan Club and regular overseas caravanners, so they really know what to look for, having a vested interest in maintaining high standards.

Sites in The Club's Travel Service brochure are all pre-bookable by phone, with many also available on The Club website **www.caravanclub.co.uk**

Well connected

We are agents for all the major car ferry operators to the Continent, Ireland and Scandinavia and we can make bookings for all their services. Special package fares are available to those members booking seven nights or more on one or more sites, including 'Camping Cheques'. These fares are often, but not always, cheaper than standard prices, but of course The Club will always offer its members the most suitable option for their circumstances.

Booking early is one of the best ways to ensure you achieve the lowest fare for your chosen sailing. Good planning is essential to take up any of our offers, so deciding your itinerary at the earliest possible date will bring appropriate rewards.

Low season discounts

If you really want to save money then it makes sense to tour abroad out of season, not in the peak months of July and August. We have two discount schemes on offer. Members may pay in advance for a minimum of seven nights with 'Camping Cheque', which also enables members to take advantage of our specially negotiated inclusive tour ferry fares.

Alternatively members may purchase the ACSI Camping Directory and discount card, which offers discounted rates at any of over 600 participating sites. You only need purchase the Directory, which costs a just few pounds, and pay for the site when you arrive. The cost of staying at these sites varies through three categories, but all are very reasonably priced. Remember, however, that this option is only available in conjunction with a ferry crossing.

The ACSI Directory option is particularly appealing to those who wish to tour in less popular areas and who may not want to commit in advance to seven nights' pre-purchase of pitches.

Overseas Holiday Insurance designed for caravanners

The Club's Red Pennant Overseas Holiday Insurance, designed by caravanners for caravanners, motor caravanners and trailer tenters, is believed by many to be the best insurance package on the market for caravanners. Launched in 1967, Red Pennant was designed specifically to protect Club members while caravanning on the Continent. The original concept remains true today and it is the only holiday insurance that really considers the needs of the caravanner in trouble abroad.

Many holidaymakers believe, mistakenly, that breakdown cover alone, or insurance offered with credit cards, will protect their holiday plans in case of problems. As a caravanner, however, taking your accommodation with you, this is far from the case. Would you know who to call should you have the misfortune to have an accident with your car and caravan damaged and the only driver competent at towing injured?

That's when The Club's cover comes into its own, with our multi-lingual staff on a 24-hour freephone helpline ready to take your call to sort out your problem. What could be more reassuring?

There is a range of options, such as Single-trip, Annual multi-trip and Long Stay cover. Cover can also be taken to include breakdown roadside assistance, repatriation, continuation of holiday travel and/or accommodation, cancellation cover, medical cover and ski cover.

How to get on board

For the latest Travel Service brochure simply phone us on **01342 316101** or go online to **www.caravanclub.co.uk**

If you're not a member yet and would like to join The Caravan Club, simply phone **0800 328 6635** quoting TS07 or visit our website **www.caravanclub.co.uk**

THE CARAVAN CLUB

Introduction

The information contained in this guide is presented in the following major categories:

Handbook

General information about touring in Europe, including legal requirements, advice and regulations, appears in the Handbook chapters at the front of the guide under the following section headings:

PLANNING AND TRAVELLING

DURING YOUR STAY

These two sections are divided into chapters in alphabetical order, not necessarily the order of priority. Where additional information is provided in another chapter, cross-references are provided.

Country Introductions

Following on from the Handbook chapters are the individual Country Introduction chapters containing information, regulations and advice specific to each country featured in the guide. These Country Introductions should be read carefully in conjunction with the Handbook chapters before you set off on holiday. Cross-references to other chapters are provided where appropriate.

Campsite Entries

After each Country Introduction you will find pages of campsite entries which are shown within an alphabetical list of towns and villages near which they are situated. Where several campsites are shown in and around the same town, they are given in clockwise order from the north.

A cross-reference system is incorporated within the campsite listings. Simply look for the name of the town or village where you wish to stay. If a campsite is not shown under the name of the particular town or village in which it is situated, then a cross-reference should indicate an alternative village or town name under which it may be found in the guide. For example, for Domme (France) the cross-reference will point you to the campsites listed under Sarlat-la-Canéda, or for San Felice del Benaco (Italy), look at the sites listed under Gardone Riviera.

To maintain consistency throughout the site entries listed in the guide, local versions of town or city names are used, eg:

Bruxelles instead of **Brussels**

Den Haag instead of **The Hague**

Dunkerque instead of **Dunkirk**

Firenze instead of **Florence**

Lisboa instead of **Lisbon**

Praha instead of **Prague**

Except in the case of those campsites marked ABS at the end of their site entries, the Caravan Club has no contractual arrangements with any of the sites featured in this guide. Furthermore, even in the case of sites with which the Club is contracted, it has no direct control over day-to-day operations or administration. Only those sites marked ABS have been inspected by Caravan Club staff.

It is assumed by the Caravan Club Ltd, but not checked (except in the case of sites marked ABS), that all campsites fall under some form of local licensing, which may or may not take account of matters of safety and hygiene. Caravanners will be aware of the varying standards between countries and are responsible for checking such matters to their own satisfaction.

Campsite Fees

Campsite entries show high season charges per night in local currency for a car, caravan + 2 adults, as at the year of last report. A deposit or booking fee may be charged and this may be non-refundable. You are advised to check fees when booking, or at least before siting, as those shown can be used only as a guide. Fees shown do not necessarily include electricity or showers unless indicated, or local taxes.

Sites Location Maps

For all countries, each town and village listed alphabetically in the site entry pages has a map reference number, which relates to a Sites Location Map at the end of that country's site entries. Place names are shown on the maps in two colours; red where there is a site open all year (or for approximately eleven months of the year), or black where only seasonal sites have been reported. **Please note: these maps are for general campsite location purposes only; a detailed road map or atlas is essential for planning your route and touring.**

The scale used for Sites Location Maps means that it is not possible to pinpoint on them every town or village where a campsite exists. Where we cannot show an individual town or village on a Sites Location Map for reasons of space, we list it under another nearby town which then acts as a central point for campsites within that particular local area. With rare exceptions, such as Paris or Berlin, sites are listed under towns up to a maximum of 15 kilometres away. The place names used as a central point are usually, but not always, the largest towns in each region; some may be only small villages. See the paragraph about cross-references earlier in this chapter.

Site Report Forms

With the exception of campsites in our Advance Booking Service network, the Caravan Club does not inspect sites listed in this guide, nor, with a few exceptions, does it ask individual sites to update their own entries. Virtually all the site reports in these guides are submitted by caravanners, whether or not members of the Caravan Club, during the course of their own holidays.

Sites which are not reported on for five years may be deleted from the guide. We rely very much, therefore, on you, the users of this guide, to tell us about old favourites re-visited, as well as new discoveries.

You will find a small number of blank site report forms towards the back of the guide which we hope you will complete and return to us. An abbreviated site report form is also provided if you are reporting no changes, or only very insignificant changes, to a site entry. Additional loose forms are available on request, including a larger A4 version.

You can now complete both the full and abbreviated versions of site report forms online on our website. Simply go to www.caravanclub.co.uk/europereport and fill in the form – abbreviated and full versions are available. Or visit www.caravanclub.co.uk to download blank forms for later completion and posting to the club.

For an explanation of abbreviations used in site entries, refer to the following chapter *Explanation of a Site Entry* or use the tear-out bookmark at the front of the guide which shows the most common abbreviations used.

Please submit reports as soon as possible. Information received by **September** will be used, wherever possible, in the compilation of next year's edition of Caravan Europe. Reports received after that date are still very welcome and will be retained for entry in a subsequent edition. The editor is unable to respond individually to site reports submitted or to process information contained in a batch of receipts.

Win a Ferry Crossing

Anyone submitting site reports to the editor during 2008 — whether by post, email or online — will have his or her name entered into a prize draw to win a return Dover-Calais ferry crossing for a car, caravan or motor caravan and two adults during 2009 (terms and conditions apply), together with a copy of Caravan Europe 2009.

Tips for Completing Site Report Forms

- Try to fill in a form while at the campsite or shortly after your stay. Once back at home it can be difficult to remember details of individual sites, especially if you visited several during your trip.

- When giving directions to a site, remember to include the direction of travel, eg 'from north on N137, turn left onto D975 signposted Combourg' or 'on N83 from Poligny turn right at petrol station in village'. Where possible give road numbers together with junction numbers and/or kilometre post numbers where you exit from motorways or main roads. It is also helpful to mention useful landmarks such as bridges, roundabouts, traffic lights or prominent buildings, and whether the site is signposted.

- When noting the compass direction of a site **this must be in the direction FROM THE TOWN the site is listed under, TO THE SITE and not the compass direction from the site to the town.** Distances are measured in a straight line and may differ significantly from the actual distance by road.

- If you are amending only a few details about a site there is no need to use the longer version form. You may prefer to use the abbreviated version but, in any event, do please remember to give the campsite name and the town or village it is listed under.

- If possible, give precise opening and closing dates, eg 1 April to 30 September. This information is particularly important for early and late season travellers.

The editor very much appreciates the time and trouble taken in submitting reports on campsites you have visited; without your valuable contributions it would be impossible to update the guide.

Every effort is made to ensure that information contained in this publication is accurate and that details given in good faith by caravanners on site report forms are accurately reproduced or summarised. The Caravan Club Ltd has not checked these details by inspection or other investigation and cannot accept responsibility for the accuracy of these reports as provided by caravanners,

or for errors, omissions or their effects. In addition The Caravan Club Ltd cannot be held accountable for the quality, safety or operation of the sites concerned, or for the fact that conditions, facilities, management or prices may have changed since the last recorded visit. Any recommendations, additional comments or opinions have been contributed by caravanners and are not necessarily those of the Caravan Club.

The inclusion of advertisements or other inserted material does not imply any form of approval or recognition, nor can The Caravan Club Ltd undertake any responsibility for checking their accuracy.

Acknowledgements

The Caravan Club's thanks go to the AIT/ FIA Information Centre (OTA), the Alliance Internationale de Tourisme (AIT), the Fédération International de Camping et de Caravaning (FICC) and to the national clubs and tourist offices of those countries who have assisted with this publication.

How to Use this Guide

Explanation of a Campsite Entry

The town under which the campsite is listed, as shown on the relevant Sites Location Map at the end of each country's site entry pages

Distance and direction of the site from the town the site is listed under in kilometres (or metres), together with site's aspect

Site Location Map grid reference

Campsite name

Telephone and fax numbers including national code

Contact email address and website address

Campsite address, including post code

Description of the campsite and its facilities

Directions to the campsite

Comments and opinions of caravanners who have visited the site

The year in which the site was last reported on by a visitor

Opening dates – if the site is open all year there will be a ⊞ symbol in front of the name of the town under which the site is listed, and no opening dates will be given

Charge per night in high season for car, caravan + 2 adults (in local currency) as at year of last report

Reference number for a site included in the Caravan Club's Advance Booking Service

MUIDES SUR LOIRE *4G2* (1km SE Rural) Camping Le Château des Marais, 27-29 Rue de Chambord, 41500 Muides-sur-Loire [02 54 87 05 42; fax 02 54 87 05 43; info@chateau-des-marais.com; www.chateau-des-marais.com] Exit A10 at junc 16 sp Chambord & take N152 sp Mer, Chambord, Blois. At Mer take D112 & cross Rv Loire. After 300m site on L on edge of vill. Well sp. Lge, mkd pitch, pt sl, shd; htd wc; chem disp; mv service pnt; all serviced pitches; baby facs; shwrs inc; el pnts (6-10A) €5-7 (poss rev pol); gas; lndtte; shop; rest; snacks; bar, BBQ; playgrnd; 3 pools (1 htd, covrd); waterslides; fishing; tennis; cycle hire; games area; entmnt; internet; TV; 10% statics (tour ops); dogs €5; Eng spkn; adv bkg fee & deposit; cc acc; CCI. "Excel, modern facs; v well-run site; friendly recep staff; plenty of gd quality children's play equipment; gd for visiting chateaux & Loire; mkt Sat am Blois." ♦ 12 May-14 Sep. € 32.00 ABS - L10   2007*

Unspecified facilities for disabled guests

⊞ FAGERNES *2F1* (500m N Rural) NAF Camping Fagernes, Tyinvegen 23, 2900 Fagernes (Oppland) [tel 61 36 05 10; fax 61 36 07 51; post@fagernes-camping.no; www.fagernes-camping.no] Site on N side of Fagernes on E16. Lge, some hdg pitch, pt sl, pt shd; htd wc; chem disp; mv service pnt; baby facs; shwrs NOK10; el pnts (10A) NOK30; lndtte; shop; rest; snacks; bar; playgrnd; lake sw; activity cent; cycling; skiing; fishing; car wash; TV; 50% statics; phone; poss cr; Eng spkn; quiet low ssn; cc acc; CCI. "Sep area for tourers by rv; Valdes folk museum park adj highly rec." ♦ NOK 165 (CChq acc)   2007*

The site accepts Camping Cheques - see the chapter *Continental Campsites* for details

13

Site Description Abbreviations

Each site entry assumes the following unless stated otherwise:

Level ground, open grass pitches, drinking water on site, clean wc unless otherwise stated (own sanitation required if wc not listed), site is good and suitable for any length of stay within the dates specified.

aspect
> **urban** – within a city or town, or on its outskirts
> **rural** – within a village or in open countryside
> **coastal** – within one kilometre of the coast

size
> **sm** – max 50 pitches
> **med** – 51 to 150 pitches
> **lge** – 151 to 500 pitches
> **v lge** – 501+ pitches

levels
> **sl** – sloping site
> **pt sl** – sloping in parts
> **terr** – terraced site

shade
> **shd** – plenty of shade
> **pt shd** – part shaded
> **unshd** – no shade

pitches
> **hdg pitch** – hedged pitches
> **mkd pitch** – marked or numbered pitches
> **hdstg** – hard standing or gravel

Site Facilities Abbreviations

ABS
> Advance Booking Service (pitch reservation can be made through the Caravan Club's Travel Service)

adv bkg
> Advance bookings are accepted;
> **adv bkg rec** – advance bookings recommended
> **bkg fee** – booking fee may be required

baby facs
> Nursing room/bathroom for babies

beach
> Beach for swimming nearby;
> **1km** – distance to beach;
> **sand beach** – sandy beach
> **shgl beach** – shingle beach

bus/metro/tram
> Public transport within an easy walk of the site

CCI or CCS
> Camping Card International or Camping Card Scandinavia accepted

chem disp
> Dedicated chemical toilet disposal facilities;
> **(wc)** – no dedicated point; disposal via wc only

CL-type
> Very small, privately-owned, informal and usually basic, farm or country site similar to those in the Caravan Club's network of Certificated Locations

dogs
> Dogs allowed on site with appropriate certification (a daily fee may be quoted)

el pnts
> Mains electric hook-ups available for a fee;
> **inc** – cost included in site fee quoted
> **10A** – amperage provided
> **conn fee** – one-off charge for connection to metered electricity supply
> **rev pol** – reversed polarity may be present
> (see *Electricity and Gas* in the section *DURING YOUR STAY*)

Eng spkn
> English spoken by campsite staff

entmnt
> Entertainment facilities or organised entertainment;
> **child entmnt** children's club/ entertainment

fam bthrm
> Bathroom for use of families with small children

gas
> Supplies of bottled gas available on site or nearby

ice
> Ice delivery or ice machine and/or freezer/ fridge available

internet
> Internet point for use by visitors to site;
> **wifi** – wireless local area network available

lndtte
> Washing and drying machines, sometimes other equipment available;
> **lndry rm** – laundry room with only basic clothes washing facilities

Mairie
> Town hall (France); will usually make municipal campsite reservations

mv service pnt
> Special low level waste discharge point for motor caravans; fresh water tap and rinse facilities should also be available

NH
Suitable as a night halt

noisy
Noisy site with reasons given;
quiet – peaceful, tranquil site

open 1 Apr-15 Oct
Where no specific date is given, opening
dates are assumed to be inclusive, ie
Apr-Oct – beginning April to the end of
October
**(NB: opening dates may vary from those
advertised; check in advance before
making a long journey, particularly
when travelling out of the main holiday
season.)**

phone
Public payphone on or adjacent to site

playgrnd
Children's playground

pool
Swimming pool (may be open high
season only);
htd – heated pool
covrd – indoor pool or with retractable
cover

poss cr
During high season site may be crowded
or overcrowded and pitches cramped

red 10 days
Reduction for stays longer than specified
number of days

red CCI/CCS
Reduction in fees on production of a
Camping Card International or Camping
Card Scandinavia

rest
Restaurant
bar – bar
BBQ – barbecues allowed
cooking facs – communal kitchen area
snacks – snack bar, cafeteria or takeaway

serviced pitch
Electric hook-ups and mains water inlet
and grey water waste outlet to pitch;
all – to all pitches
50% – percentage of pitches

shop(s)
Shop on site;
adj – shops next to site
500m – nearest shops
supmkt – supermarket hypmkt –
hypermarket
tradsmn – tradesmen call at the site, eg
baker

shwrs
Hot showers available for a fee;
inc – cost included in site fee quoted

ssn
Season
high ssn – peak holiday season
low ssn – out of peak season

50% statics
Percentage of static caravans/mobile
homes/chalets/fixed tents/cabins or long
term seasonal pitches on site, including
those run by tour operators

sw
Swimming nearby
1km – nearest swimming
lake – in lake
rv – in river

TV rm
TV room
cab/sat – cable or satellite connections
to pitches

wc
Clean flushing toilets on site
(cont) – continental type with floor-level
hole
htd – sanitary block centrally heated
in winter
own san – use of own sanitation facilities
recommended

Other Abbreviations

AIT	Alliance Internationale de Tourisme
a'bahn	Autobahn
a'pista	Autopista
a'route	Autoroute
a'strada	Autostrada
adj	Adjacent, nearby
alt	Alternative
app	Approach, on approaching
arr	Arrival, arriving
avail	Available
bdge	Bridge
bef	Before
bet	Between
C	Century, eg 16thC
c'van	Caravan
cc acc	Credit cards accepted (check with site for specific details)
cent	Centre or central
clsd	Closed
conn	Connection

cont	Continue or Continental (wc)		rd	Road or street
conv	Convenient		rec	Recommend/ed
covrd	Covered		recep	Reception
dep	Deposit		red	Reduced, reduction (for)
diff	Difficult, with difficulty		req	Required
dir	Direction		rlwy	Railway line
dist	Distance		rm	Room
dual c'way	Dual carriageway		rndabt	Roundabout
E	East		rte	Route
ent	Entrance/entry to		rv/rvside	River/riverside
ess	Essential		S	South
excel	Excellent		san facs	Sanitary facilities, wc,
facs	Facilities			showers, etc
FIA	Fédération Internationale de		sep	Separate
	l'Automobile		sh	Short
FICC	Fédération Internationale de		sp	Sign post, signposted
	Camping & de Caravaning		sq	Square
FKK/FNF	Naturist federation, ie naturist site		ssn	Season
foll	Follow		stn	Station
fr	From		strt	Straight, straight ahead
g'ge	Garage		thro	Through
gd	Good		traff lts	Traffic lights
hr(s)	Hour(s)		twd	Toward(s)
immac	Immaculate		unrel	Unreliable
immed	Immediate(ly)		vg	Very good
inc	Included/inclusive		vill	Village
indus est	Industrial estate		W	West
INF	Naturist federation, ie naturist		w/e	Weekend
	site		x-ing	Crossing
int'l	International		x-rds	Cross roads
junc	Junction			
km	Kilometre			

L	Left
ltd	Limited
mkd	Marked
mkt	Market
mob	Mobile (phone)
m'van	Motor caravan
m'way	Motorway
N	North
narr	Narrow
nr, nrby	Near, nearby
opp	Opposite
o'fits	Outfits
o'look(ing)	Overlook(ing)
o'night	Overnight
o'skts	Outskirts
PO	Post office
poss	Possible, possibly
R	Right

◆ Unspecified facilities for disabled guests - check before arrival

⊞ Open all year

* Last year site report received (see Campsite Entries in Introduction)

Caravanning Abroad – Advice For First-Timers

You're seasoned caravanners around Britain and you've probably been caravanning for a few years. Now the time has come to make that trip you've been dreaming of, but understandably you feel a little apprehensive at the thought of taking your caravan or motor caravan across the Channel for the first time.

The advice in this chapter is a summary of the comprehensive information contained elsewhere in this guide, and is designed to give you the confidence to take that first trip, and make it one of many enjoyable and rewarding holidays. Laws, customs, regulations and advice differ from country to country and you are strongly advised to study all the chapters in this Handbook section carefully, together with the relevant Country Introductions for the countries you are planning to visit.

Before You Travel

Choosing Your Campsite

The golden rule is not to be too ambitious. The south of France or southern Spain are exciting destinations but on your first visit you will probably not want to travel too far from your port of arrival and there are many good quality sites near the main French Channel ports. If France does not appeal, think about Belgium or the Netherlands where English is especially widely spoken.

The golden rule is not to be too ambitious

If you use a daytime ferry crossing it may be a good idea to spend your first night at a campsite relatively near the port of arrival in order to give yourself a little time to get used to driving on the right. You will then be fresh for an early start the next morning when traffic is relatively light.

Decide whether you want a site near the seaside or in the country, quiet or lively, with facilities for children or near specific interests, such as vineyards, chateaux, sports facilities, etc. During the peak holiday season the volume of traffic and tourists might be daunting, but remember that in low season not all site facilities will be open. Advance booking is recommended if you do travel during the peak school holiday period in July and August, or over Easter, and this is particularly true if you are visiting a popular tourist resort.

The chapter in this guide entitled Continental Campsites tells you what to expect and has suitably-worded letters in five languages to help you make your own campsite bookings. For peace of mind you may prefer to use the Caravan Club's Advance Booking Service which offers Club members a booking service to over 200 Continental campsites throughout Europe. This service gives freedom and flexibility of travel while eliminating any language problems, expensive international deposit payments or waiting for replies by letter or email. Furthermore, you will have the reassurance of a confirmed pitch reservation and pitch fees paid in advance.

All the sites in the Club's Advance Booking Service are listed in this guide and are marked 'ABS' in their site entries. The Caravan Club cannot make advance reservations for any other campsites.

The Travel Service in Europe brochure gives full details of the ABS and of those sites to which it applies, as well as information on special offers with ferry operators, the Club's range of 'package' inclusive holidays for caravanners and Red Pennant Motoring & Personal Holiday Insurance. Telephone 01342 327410 to request a copy or see www.caravanclub.co.uk

Choosing Your Ferry Crossing

There is a wide choice of ferry operators and routes to the Continent and the use of long or short ferry crossings, or the Channel Tunnel, is a matter of personal preference and convenience. The Channel Tunnel and crossings from Dover to Calais are the quickest, but if you have a long drive from home to your departure port, you may prefer the chance to relax for a few hours and enjoy a meal on an overnight crossing, which means you arrive fresh at the other end. The chapter *Ferries and the Channel Tunnel* contains a list of ferry routes and additional information.

Make sure you know the overall length as well as the height of your vehicle(s); vehicle decks on some ferries have areas where height is restricted, and this should be checked when making your booking.

The Club's website, www.caravanclub.co.uk, has a direct link through to a number of the most popular ferry operators' reservations systems and Club members can make their own reservations while still taking advantage of the Club's negotiated offers and the ferry companies' own early booking offers.

Insurance

All UK motor vehicle policies give you the legal minimum of insurance for EU countries, but it is important to check whether your comprehensive cover becomes third-party only when you leave the UK. It may be necessary to pay an additional premium for comprehensive cover abroad.

Having insurance for your vehicles does not cover other risks which may arise on holiday, for example, emergency medical and hospital expenses, loss or theft of personal effects. The Caravan Club's Red Pennant Motoring & Personal Holiday Insurance gives you maximum protection from a variety of mishaps which might otherwise ruin your holiday and is tailor-made for the caravanner and motor caravanner. This is backed by the Club's own helpline with multi-lingual staff available 24 hours a day, 365 days a year.

If you are going to leave your home unoccupied for any length of time, check your house and contents insurance policies regarding any limitations or regulations.

You will find further details, information and advice in the chapter *Insurance*.

Documents

All members of your party should have a valid passport, including children under 16 who are not already included on a parent's passport. The chapter *Documents* sets out the requirements and explains how to apply for a passport.

In some countries passports must be carried at all times as a form of photographic identification

---

A photocard driving licence or the pink EU version of the UK driving licence is universally acceptable. However, holders of an old-style green UK licence or a Northern Irish licence issued prior to 1991 are recommended to update it to a photocard licence, or obtain an International Driving Permit (IDP) to accompany their old-style UK licence in order to avoid any local difficulties.

In some countries passports must be carried at all times as a form of photographic identification. In any event you should keep a separate photocopy of your passport details and leave a copy of the personal details page with a relative or friend.

You should also carry your Vehicle Registration Certificate (V5C), insurance certificate and MOT roadworthiness certificate, if applicable, together with a copy of your CRIS document in respect of your caravan.

*See the chapter **Documents** in the section **PLANNING AND TRAVELLING** for full details.*

Vehicles and Equipment

Ensure your car and caravan are properly serviced and ready for the journey, paying particular attention to tyres and tyre pressures. Ensure caravan tyres are suited to the maximum weight of the caravan and the maximum permitted speed when travelling abroad – see the chapter *Motoring – Equipment* and the Technical Information chapter of the Caravan Club's UK Sites Directory and Handbook.

Take a well-equipped spares and tool kit. Spare bulbs, a warning triangle (two are required in some countries), a fire extinguisher and a first-aid kit are legal requirements in many European countries. In some countries drivers who leave their vehicle when it is stationary on the carriageway must wear a reflectorised waistcoat, but it is sensible to do so in any country. A second jacket is a common-sense requirement for any passenger who also gets out of your vehicle to assist. A spare tyre for car and caravan and nearside and offside extending mirrors are essential.

If they are likely to dazzle other road users, headlights must be adjusted to deflect to the right instead of the left using suitable beam deflectors or (in some cases) a built-in adjustment system. Even when not planning to drive at night, you will need to switch your headlights on in tunnels or if visibility is poor. Some countries require dipped headlights to be used during daylight hours. Bulbs are more likely to fail with constant use and you are recommended to carry spares.

Money

It is a good idea to carry a small amount of foreign currency, including loose change, for countries you are travelling through in case of emergencies, or when shopping. In addition you may take travellers' cheques, a travel money card or use your credit or debit card on arrival at your destination to obtain cash from cash dispensers, which are often found in supermarkets as well as outside banks. The rate of exchange is often as good as anywhere else; look for the same symbol on the machine as on your debit or credit card.

Travellers' cheques are not welcome in some countries and credit cards issued by British banks may not be universally accepted, so it is wise to check before incurring expenditure. In some countries you may be asked to produce your passport for photographic identification purposes when paying by credit card. See the chapter *Money* and Country Introductions for further information.

On the Journey

Ferries

Report to the check-in desk at the ferry port or Eurotunnel terminal allowing plenty of time, say an hour, before the scheduled boarding time. As you approach the boarding area after passport control and Customs, staff will direct you to the waiting area or the boarding lane for your departure. As you are driving a 'high vehicle' you may be required to board first, or last. While waiting to board stay with your vehicle(s) so that you can board immediately when instructed to do so. Virtually all ferries operate a 'drive on – drive off' system and you will not normally be required to perform any complicated manoeuvres, nor to reverse.

Eurotunnel will not accept vehicles powered by LPG or dual-fuel vehicles

---

While waiting, turn off the 12v electric supply to your fridge to prevent your battery going flat. Most fridges will stay adequately cool for several hours, as long as they are not opened. If necessary, place an ice pack or two (as used in cool boxes) in the fridge. You may be required to show that your gas supply has been turned off correctly.

Neither the ferry companies nor Eurotunnel permit you to carry spare petrol cans, empty

or full, and Eurotunnel will not accept vehicles powered by LPG or dual-fuel vehicles. However Eurotunnel will accept vehicles fitted with LPG tanks for the purposes of heating, lighting, cooking or refrigeration, subject to certain conditions.

If your vehicle has been converted and is powered by LPG, some ferry companies require a certificate showing that the conversion has been carried out to the manufacturer's specification.

You will be instructed when to drive onto the ferry and, once on board, will be directed to the appropriate position. Treat ferry access ramps with caution, as they may be steep and/or uneven. Drive slowly as there may be a risk of grounding of any low point on the tow bar or caravan hitch. If your ground clearance is low, consider whether removing your stabiliser and/or jockey wheel would help.

Once boarded apply your car and caravan brakes. Vehicles are often parked close together and many passengers leaving their vehicles will be carrying bags for the crossing. It may, therefore, be wise to remove extended rear view mirrors as they may get knocked out of adjustment or damaged.

Make sure your car and caravan are secure and that, wherever possible, belongings are out of sight. Ensure that items on roof racks or cycle carriers are difficult to remove – a long cable lock may be helpful. In view of recent problems with stowaways on cross-Channel ferries and trains, check that your outfit is free of unexpected guests at the last practical opportunity before boarding.

Note the deck and staircase numbers for when you return; there is nothing more embarrassing than to discover, when you eventually find them, that your vehicles are blocking other irate motorists in! You will not usually be permitted access to your vehicle(s) during the crossing so take everything you require with you, including passports, tickets and boarding cards. On those ferry routes on which it is possible to carry pets, animals are usually required to remain in their owners' vehicles or in kennels on the car deck. On longer ferry crossings you should make arrangements at the on-board Information Desk for permission to visit your pet at suitable intervals in order to check its well-being.

*See also **Pet Travel Scheme** under **Documents** in the section **PLANNING AND TRAVELLING**.*

If you have booked cabins or seats go to the Information Desk immediately after boarding to claim them. Many ferries have a selection of restaurants and cafés, a children's play area, even a cinema, disco or casino as well as a shop, to while away the time during the crossing. If you wish to use the main restaurant it may be advisable to make an early reservation.

Listen carefully to on-board announcements, one of which will be important safety information at the time of departure. A further announcement will be made when it is time to return to your vehicle(s). Allow plenty of time to get down to the car deck. Don't start your engine until vehicles immediately in front of you start to move. Once off the ferry you may want to pull over into a parking area to allow the queue of traffic leaving the ferry to clear.

Eurotunnel

On arrival at the Eurotunnel terminal, approach one of the toll booths displaying a car/caravan or motor caravan sign and produce your ticket. If you paid for the ticket with a credit card you will also have to produce the card. Having checked in you may, if you wish, visit the terminal to make any last minute purchases etc, and then follow signs to passport control and Customs. Your gas valves will be closed and sealed as a safety precaution and you will be asked to open the roof vents.

You will then join the waiting area allocated for your departure and will be directed onto the single-deck wagons of the train and told to park in gear with your brake on. You then stay in or around your car/motor caravan for the 35-minute journey but will not be allowed to use your caravan until arrival. Useful information and music are supplied via the on-board radio station. On arrival, close the roof vent and release the caravan brake and, when directed by the crew, drive off – remembering to drive on the right!

Motoring on the Continent

The chapters *Motoring – Advice* and *Motoring – Equipment* and the Country Introductions cover all aspects of motoring on the Continent, but the following additional points may be helpful for nervous 'first-timers'.

Most roads are not as busy as those in the UK, but avoid rush hours in larger towns. There are fewer lorries on the roads at weekends and in France in particular, roads are quieter between noon and 2pm, and good progress can often be made.

You are most likely to forget to drive on the right when pulling away from a parked position. It may be helpful to make yourself a sign and attach it to the dashboard to remind you to drive on the right. This can be removed before driving and replaced each time you stop. Alternatively, make a member of your party responsible for reminding the driver every time you start the car. Pay particular attention when turning left or when leaving a rest area, service station or campsite, and after passing through a one-way system.

Don't attempt long distances in a single stint

Make sure the road ahead is clear before overtaking. Stay well behind the vehicle in front and, if possible, have someone with good judgement in the left-hand seat to give you the 'all clear'.

In your eagerness to reach your destination, don't attempt long distances in a single stint. Share the driving, if possible, and plan to break your journey overnight at a suitable site. There are thousands of sites listed in this guide and many are well-situated near motorways and main roads.

Remember speed limit signs are in kilometres per hour, not miles per hour.

You will be charged tolls to use many European motorways. Credit cards are widely accepted in payment, but not always. The Country Introductions provide full details. Motorways provide convenient service stations and areas for a rest and a picnic en-route but, for your own safety, find a proper campsite for an overnight stop.

Beware STOP signs. You will encounter more of them than you find in the UK. Coming to a complete halt is compulsory in most Continental countries and failure to do so may result in a hefty fine.

The maximum legal level of alcohol in the blood in most Continental countries is much lower than that permitted in the UK. It is better not to drink at all when driving, as offenders are heavily fined.

During Your Stay

Arriving at the Campsite

Go to the site reception and fill in any registration forms required. You may need to leave your Camping Card International/

Camping Card Scandinavia or passport. In some countries where you must carry your passport at all times as a form of photographic identity, a CCI is essential.

If you have not booked in advance it is perfectly acceptable to ask to have a look around the site before deciding whether to stay or accept a particular pitch.

Pitches are usually available when the site re-opens after the lunch break and not normally before this time. Aim to arrive before 7pm or you may find site reception closed; if this is the case you will probably find a member of staff on duty in the bar. It is essential to arrive before 10pm as the gates on most sites are closed for the night at this time. If you are delayed, remember to let the site know so that they will keep your pitch. When leaving, you will usually need to vacate your pitch by midday at the latest.

If you have any complaints, take them up with site staff there and then

---

Many sites offer various sporting activities, such as tennis, fishing, watersports, horseriding and bicycle hire, as well as entertainment programmes for children and/or adults in high season. Many also have a snack bar, restaurant or bar. Restrictions may apply on the use of barbecues because of the risk of fire; always check with site staff before lighting up.

Dogs are welcome on many campsites but some sites will not allow them at all, or during the high season, or will require them to be on a lead at all times. Check in advance. In popular tourist areas local regulations may ban dogs from beaches during the summer months.

If you have any complaints, take them up with site staff there and then. It is pointless complaining after the event, when something could have been done to improve matters at the time.

Electricity and Gas

Calor Gas is not available on the Continent. Campingaz is widely available but, unless your caravan is new and already fitted with a special bulkhead-mounted regulator, you will need an adaptor to connect to a Calor-type butane regulator. Alternatively carry sufficient gas for your stay, subject to the cross-Channel operator's regulations which may restrict you to three, two or even only one gas cylinder. Check when making your booking.

Voltage on most sites is usually 220v or 230v nominal but may be lower. Most UK mains appliances are rated at 220v to 240v and usually work satisfactorily. You will need your mains lead that you use in the UK as many sites have the European standard EN60309-2 connectors, (formerly known as CEE17) which your UK 3-pin connector will fit. On some sites you may need a Continental 2-pin adaptor available from UK caravan accessory shops.

Caravanners may encounter the problem known as reverse polarity. This is where the site supply's 'live' line connects to the caravan's 'neutral' and vice versa and is due to different standards of plug and socket wiring that exist in other countries. The Club, therefore, recommends checking the polarity immediately on connection, using a polarity tester, obtainable from a caravan accessory shop before you leave home.

The caravan mains electrical installation should not be used while a reversed polarity situation exists. Ask the site manager if you can use an alternative socket or bollard, as the problem may be restricted to that particular socket only. Frequent travellers to the Continent who are electrically competent often make themselves up an adaptor, clearly marked reversed polarity with the live and neutral wires reversed. This can be tried in place of the standard connector, to see if the electricity supply then reverts to 'normal'.

*See the chapter **Electricity and Gas** and **Country Introductions** for further information.*

Food and Water

There is a limit to the amount of food which may be imported into other countries, although Customs will rarely be interested unless their attention is drawn to it. But in the light of recent animal health concerns in the UK, authorities abroad will understandably take a cautious approach and there is no guarantee that meat and dairy products, if found, will not be confiscated by Customs officers.

You should, therefore, be reasonable in the amount of foodstuffs you take with you. Experience of foreign cuisine is part of the enjoyment of a Continental holiday and there is little point in taking large supplies of food other than basics or children's special favourites.

In remoter parts of some countries the choice of items in food shops may be limited, compared to most British supermarkets, and you will usually find local markets to be a good source of fresh fruit, vegetables, cheese, fish and meat. When shopping it may be helpful to take your own supply of plastic carrier bags and a cool box in hot weather.

On the Continent generally it is sometimes difficult to obtain supplies of fresh milk, bread and cereals at campsite shops, particularly outside the summer season. It may be useful to pack a supply of basic items such as tea, coffee, fruit squash, cereals and powdered or long-life milk.

In the countries covered by this guide drinking water is clean and safe, but you may find the taste different from your own local mains supply. Bottled water is cheap and widely available.

Insect Control

Mosquitoes and flies can be a serious nuisance as well as a danger to health. Although an effective insect repellent is essential as the simplest form of protection, insect screens on windows, door and roof vents will provide complete protection. Most modern caravans have fly screens installed as part of the window roller-blind system. Older caravans may be equipped using DIY kits available from most caravan accessory shops or DIY stores.

There are numerous sprays on the market to kill flies, ants and mosquitoes and insect repellent coils left burning at night are also an effective preventative device, as are anti-insect tablets which slot into a special electric heating element. These are available from High Street chemists and caravan accessory outlets.

Medical Matters

Before you leave home obtain a booklet T7.1 from your local post office and complete the application form for a European Health Insurance Card (EHIC) which entitles you to emergency health care in the EU and some other countries. An EHIC is required by each individual family member, so allow enough time before your departure to obtain them.

Check with your GP the generic name of any prescription medicines you are taking. If you need more or lose your supply, the generic name will help a doctor or pharmacist to identify them. Keep receipts for any medication or treatment purchased abroad, plus the labels from the medicines, as these will be required if you make a claim on your travel insurance on returning home.

If you are unfortunate enough to have an accident, take some photographs to back up the written description on your claim form.

For further advice and information see the chapter Medical Matters.

Safety and Security

Everyone wants you to relax and enjoy your holiday. Safety is largely your own responsibility – taking sensible precautions and being aware of possible hazards won't spoil your holiday, but a careless attitude might.

A comprehensive chapter entitled Safety and Security, together with specific information relevant to particular countries in the appropriate Country Introductions, covers all aspects of your own and your family's personal safety while on holiday. You are strongly advised to read these sections carefully and follow the advice contained in them.

Other Information

Most European countries maintain tourist offices in the UK which will supply information on their respective countries. In addition, a great deal of information can be obtained from tourist boards' websites. Address and contact details are given in each Country Introduction.

The AA Information Centre provides traffic information on UK motorways and A roads including routes to ferry ports on 09003 401100 (calls charged at 60p per minute) or dial 401100 only from a mobile telephone. Both the AA and RAC have useful websites with access for non-members: www.theaa.com and www.rac.co.uk

Checklist

It is assumed that users of this guide have some experience of caravanning and are well aware of the domestic and personal items necessary for trips away in their caravans, and of the checks to be made to vehicles before setting off. The Caravan Club's Technical Office will supply a copy of a leaflet 'Things to Take' on request to Club members, or see www.caravanclub.co.uk

The following is intended merely as an 'aide memoire' and covers some of those necessary items:

Car

Extending mirrors

Fire extinguisher

First aid kit

Fuses

Headlight converters/deflectors

Jack and wheelbrace

Mobile phone charger

Nationality stickers – GB or IRL (car and caravan)

Puncture kit

Radiator hose

Reflectorised safety jacket(s)

Snow chains (if winter caravanning)

Spare bulbs

Spare key

Spare parts, eg fan belt

Spare wheel/tyre

Stabiliser

Tool kit

Tow ball cover

Tow rope

Warning triangle (2 for Spain)

Caravan

Awning and groundsheet

Bucket

Chemical toilet and fluid/sachets

Corner steady tool and pads

Coupling lock

Electrical extension lead and adaptor(s)

Extra long motor caravan water hose pipe

Fire extinguisher

Gas cylinders

Gas regulator (Campingaz)

Gas adaptor and hoses (where regulator is fitted to the caravan)

Hitch and/or wheel lock

Insect screens

Levelling blocks

Mains polarity tester

Nose weight gauge

Peg mallet

Spare bulbs, fuses and lengths of wire

Spare key

Spare 7-pin plug

Spare water pump

Spare wheel/tyre

Spirit level

Step and doormat

Submersible water pump

Water containers - waste/fresh

Water hoses – waste/fresh

Wheel clamp

Documents and Papers

Address book, contact telephone numbers

Camping Card International/Camping Card Scandinavia

Car/caravan/motor caravan insurance certificates

Campsite booking confirmation(s)

Caravan Club membership card

Caravan Europe guide book

Copy of your CRIS document

Credit/debit cards, contact numbers in the event of loss

Driving licence (photocard or green/pink EU version)

European Health Insurance Card

European Accident Statement

Ferry ticket or booking reference and timetable

Foreign currency

Holiday travel insurance documents (Red Pennant)

International Driving Permit (if applicable)

International Motor Insurance Certificate, ie Green Card (if applicable)

Letter of authorisation from vehicle owner (if applicable)

Maps and guides

MOT roadworthiness certificate (if applicable)

NHS medical card

Passport (+ photocopy of details page) and visas (if applicable)

Pet's passport and addresses of vets abroad

Phrase books

Telephone card

Travellers' cheques and/or travel money card

Vehicle Registration Certificate V5C

Continental Campsites

Introduction

Finding a campsite on the Continent is not usually difficult. Many excellent sites belong to local municipalities; others are run by families or private companies, or by camping, touring or automobile clubs. Although these private sites are usually open to non-members who hold a Camping Card International, some are reserved for their own members.

Compared with Caravan Club sites in the UK, pitches may be small and 80 square metres is not uncommon, particularly in Spain, Italy, Germany, Portugal and Switzerland. This may present problems for large outfits and/or with the erection of awnings. Elsewhere, for example in the south of France in summer, it may be difficult to erect an awning because of hard ground conditions.

Generally the approaches and entrances to campsites are well signposted, but often only with a tent or caravan symbol or with the word 'Camping', rather than the full site name.

There are usually sinks for washing-up and laundry and many sites provide washing machines and dryers. Most have a shop in high season, even if only for basic groceries, but many stock a wide variety of items. Often they have a restaurant or snack bar and sometimes a swimming pool, leisure facilities, TV and games room. Occasionally there may be a car wash, petrol pumps, hairdresser, sauna, solarium, internet access point or wifi availability, bureau de change or a tourist information office.

In the high season all campsite facilities are usually open and some sites offer organised entertainment for children and adults as well as local excursions. However, bear in mind that in the months of July and August, toilets, washing facilities and pitch areas will be under the greatest pressure.

Booking A Campsite

It is now normal practice to pre-book pitches on campsites during the high season months of July and August and this is now possible via many campsites' own websites. Some sites impose a minimum length of stay during this time in order to guarantee their business. Usually there are one or two unreserved pitches available for overnight tourers.

Pre-booking sites en route to holiday destinations is not essential, but if you do not book ahead you should plan to arrive for the night no later than 4pm (even earlier at popular resorts), in order to secure a good pitch, since after that time sites fill up rapidly. If you are planning a long stay it is advisable to contact campsites early in the year (January is not too early). Often it is possible to book directly via a campsite's website. Otherwise write, enclosing an International Reply Coupon, obtainable from main post offices and valid virtually all over the world, or letters may be ignored. Not all campsites accept advance bookings.

To assist you, suitably-worded letters in English, German, French, Spanish and Italian are provided at the end of this chapter. Responses are also provided, in the same five languages, which should encourage site operators to reply. In any event it is worth remembering that rarely will a site reserve a special place for you. The acceptance of a reservation merely means you will be guaranteed a space to park; the best pitches are allocated first.

Campsites that accept advance bookings may also require a deposit and this should be sent by credit card, by bank draft or by means of the post office's international registered service. A word of warning: **some campsites regard the deposit as a booking fee and will not deduct this amount from your final bill.**

Caravan Club Advance Booking Service

The Caravan Club's Travel Service offers Club members a campsite advance booking service (to which terms and conditions apply) to over 200 campsites throughout Europe. This service gives freedom and flexibility of travel but with the reassurance of a confirmed pitch reservation and pitch fees paid in advance. Full details of this service, plus information on special offers with ferry operators, the Club's range of 'package' Inclusive Holidays for caravanners and details of Red Pennant

Motoring & Personal Holiday Insurance appear in the Travel Service in Europe brochure — telephone 01342 327410 to request a copy, or visit www.caravanclub.co.uk

Booking an ABS site through the Caravan Club gives you a price guarantee — whatever happens to exchange rates, there will be no surcharges.

All ABS sites are listed in this guide and are marked 'ABS' in their site entries. Many of them can be booked via the Club's website, www.caravanclub.co.uk. **The Caravan Club cannot make advance reservations for any other campsites listed in this guide.**

Camping Cheques

The Caravan Club operates a low season scheme in association with Camping Cheques offering Club members flexible touring holidays. The scheme covers approximately 580 sites in 21 European countries.

Camping Cheques are supplied as part of a package which includes return ferry fare and a minimum of seven camping cheques. Each Camping Cheque is valid for one night's low season stay for two people, plus car and caravan/motor caravan/trailer tent and electricity. Full details are contained in the Club's Travel Service in Europe brochure.

Those sites which feature in the camping cheques scheme and which are listed in this guide are marked 'CChq' in their site entries.

Caravan Storage Abroad

The advantages of storing your caravan on a campsite on the Continent are obvious, not least being the avoidance of the long tow to your destination, and a saving in ferry and fuel costs. Some campsites advertise a long-term storage facility or you may negotiate with a site which appeals to you.

However, there are pitfalls and understandably insurers in the UK are reluctant to insure a caravan which will be out of the country most of the time. There is also the question of invalidity of the manufacturer's warranty for caravans less than three years old if the supplying dealer does not carry out annual servicing.

See also **Insurance** in the section **PLANNING AND TRAVELLING.**

Electricity Supply

For your own safety you are strongly advised to read the chapter *Electricity and Gas* under *PLANNING AND TRAVELLING*

Many campsites now include electricity and/ or shower facilities in their 'per night' price and where possible this has been included in site entries. Where these are not included, a generous allowance should be made in your budget. It is not unknown for sites to charge up to the equivalent of £4 per night or more for electric hook-ups and £2 per shower. In winter sports areas, charges for electricity are generally higher in winter.

The system for charging for electricity varies from country to country and you may pay a flat daily rate or, notably in Germany and Austria, a connection charge plus a metered charge for electricity consumed. The Country Introductions contain specific information on electricity supply.

Facilities and Site Description

Information is given about the characteristics of the campsite and availability of facilities on site or within a reasonable distance, as reported to the editor of this guide. Comments (in inverted commas) are those of caravanners visiting the site and it must be understood that people's tastes, opinions, priorities and expectations differ. Please also bear in mind that campsites change hands, opening dates change and standards may rise or fall, depending on the season.

Facilities Out of Season

During the low season (this can be any time except July and early August) campsites may operate with limited facilities and shops, swimming pools, bars and restaurants may be closed. A municipal site warden may visit only to collect fees which are often negotiable during the low season.

Sanitary Facilities

Facilities normally include toilet and shower blocks with wash basins and razor sockets but toilets are not always fitted with seats, for ease of cleaning. The abbreviation 'wc' indicates the normal, pedestal type of toilet found in the UK. Some sites have footplate 'squatter' toilets and, where this is known, this is indicated by the abbreviation 'cont', ie continental.

It is recommended that you take your own universal flat plug (to fit all basin sizes) and toilet paper. During the low season it is not uncommon for only a few toilet and shower cubicles to be in use on a 'unisex' basis and they may not be cleaned as frequently as they are during the site's busy season. Hot water, other than for showers, may not be generally available.

While many campsites have in recent years upgraded their sanitary facilities in line with visitors' expectations, you may find that some are still unheated and may not offer items such as pegs to hang clothes/towels on, or shelves for soap and shampoo. Rarely, there may be no shower curtains or shower cubicle doors and hence little or no privacy.

Waste Disposal

Site entries in this guide indicate (when known) where a campsite has a chemical disposal facility and/or motor caravan service point, which is assumed to include a waste (grey) water dump station and toilet cassette-emptying point.

Continental caravanners in general tend to prefer to use a site's toilet and shower facilities, together with its dishwashing and vegetable preparation areas, more than their British counterparts who prefer to use their own. Caravanners used to the level of facilities for the disposal of waste water on Caravan Club sites may well find that facilities on Continental campsites are not of the same standard.

Wastemaster-style emptying points are not common

Chemical disposal points are occasionally difficult to locate and may be fixed at a high level requiring some strenuous lifting of cassettes in order to empty them. Or disposal may simply be down a toilet – continental or otherwise. Wastemaster-style emptying points are not common and you may have to empty your Wastemaster down the drain under a drinking water tap. On rare occasions, this is also the only place to rinse a toilet cassette! You may like to carry a bottle of disinfectant spray to use on water taps if necessary.

Formaldehyde-based chemical cleaning products are banned in many countries. If in doubt about the composition of the product you use and its use abroad, it is probably wiser to buy products which are commonly available in caravan accessory shops at your destination.

At some campsites, notably in Switzerland and Germany, you may have to purchase special plastic bags for the disposal of rubbish, or pay a daily 'rubbish' charge or 'environmental' charge. You may also find that you are expected to use recycling bins placed around the campsite.

Lunch Breaks

Some campsites close for a lengthy lunch break, sometimes as long as three hours, and occasionally there is no access for vehicles during this period. In addition, use of vehicles within the site may be restricted during certain hours to ensure a period of quiet. Check individual campsite regulations on arrival.

Motor Caravanners

Increasingly towns and villages across Europe are providing dedicated overnight or short stay areas specifically for motor caravanners, many with good security, electricity, water and waste facilities. These are known as 'Aires de Service' or 'Stellplatz' and are usually well-signposted with a motor caravan pictogram.

Likewise, to cater for this growing market, many campsites in popular tourist areas have separate overnight areas of hard standing with appropriate facilities often just outside the main campsite area. Fees are generally very reasonable. See the Country Introduction chapters for more information.

A number of organisations, for example ADAC (Germany), the Fédération Française de Camping et de Caravaning and Bel-air Camping-Caravaning (France) publish guides listing thousands of these sites in several countries. A new publication, 'All the Aires — France' lists 600 'aires' in towns and villages throughout France and is available from the Club's book shop for £11.99 + p&p.

Where known, information on the availability of public transport within easy reach of a campsite, as supplied by caravanners, is given in the site entries in this guide.

Municipal Campsites

For value for money, municipal sites are usually hard to beat and in France in particular, they are found in many towns and villages. However, you may find that sanitary facilities are basic and old-fashioned, even though they may be clean. Bookings for a municipal site can usually be made through the local town hall (Mairie) during office hours.

Outside the high season you may find significant numbers of workmen, market traders and itinerants resident on municipal sites – sometimes in a separate, designated area. Where their presence is not welcome some sites refuse entry to caravans with twin-axles ('deux essieux' in French) or restrict entry by caravan height, weight or length or charge a hefty additional fee. Check if any restrictions apply if booking in advance. Recent visitors report that bona fide caravanners with twin-axle or over-height/ weight/length caravans may be allowed entry, and/or may not be charged the higher published tariff, but this is negotiable with site staff at the time of arrival.

When approaching a town you may find that municipal sites are not always named and signposts may simply state 'Camping' or show a tent or caravan symbol.

Naturist Campsites

Several naturist sites are included in the guide, mainly in France, Spain, Germany and Croatia, and they are shown with the word 'naturist' after their site name. Some, shown as 'part naturist' simply have separate beach areas for naturists. Visitors to naturist sites aged 16 and over usually (but not always) require an INF card or Naturist Licence and this is covered by membership of British Naturism (tel 01604 620361 or www.british-naturism.org.uk). Alternatively, holiday membership is available on arrival at any recognised naturist site (a passport-size photograph is required). When looking for a site you will find that recognised naturist campsites generally display the initials FNF, INF or FKK on their signs.

Opening Dates

Opening dates (where known) are given for campsites in this guide, many of which are open all year. Sometimes sites may close without notice for refurbishment work or because of a change of ownership or simply because of a lack of visitors. When a site is officially closed, owners who live on site may accept visitors for an overnight or short stay if, for example, they are working on site.

Outside the high season it is always best to contact campsites in advance as owners, particularly in Spain and the south of France, have a tendency to shut campsites when business is slack. Otherwise you may arrive to find the gates of an 'all year' campsite very firmly

closed. Municipal campsites' published opening dates cannot always be relied on at the start and end of the season. It is advisable to phone ahead or arrive early enough to be able to find an alternative site if your first choice is closed.

Pets on Campsites

See also Pet Travel Scheme under Documents and Holiday Insurance for Pets under Insurance in the section PLANNING AND TRAVELLING.

Dogs are welcome on many Continental campsites provided they conform to legislation and vaccination requirements, and are kept under control. There is usually a daily charge, but this may be waived in low season. Dog owners must conform to site regulations concerning keeping dogs on a lead, dog-walking areas and fouling and may find restricted areas within a site where dogs are not permitted. There may also be limits on the number of dogs – often one per pitch – or type or breed of dog accepted. Some campsites will not allow dogs at all, or will require them to be on a lead at all times, or will not allow them during the peak holiday season. Be prepared to present documentary evidence of vaccinations on arrival at a campsite. In popular tourist areas local regulations may ban dogs from beaches during the summer.

Think very carefully before taking your pet abroad. Dogs used to the UK's temperate climate may find it difficult to cope with prolonged periods of hot weather. In addition, there are diseases transmitted by ticks, caterpillars, mosquitoes or sandflies, particularly in southern Europe, to which dogs from the UK have no natural resistance. Consult your vet about preventative treatment well in advance of your planned holiday. You need to be sure that your dog is healthy enough to travel and, if in any doubt, it may be in its best interests to leave it at home.

Think very carefully before taking your pet abroad

Visitors to southern Spain and Portugal, parts of central France and northern Italy from mid-winter onwards should be aware of the danger to dogs of pine processionary caterpillars. Dogs should be kept away from pine trees if possible or fitted with a muzzle that prevents the nose and mouth from touching the ground. This will also protect against poisoned bait sometimes used by farmers and hunters.

In the event that your pet is taken ill abroad, a campsite, will usually have information about local vets. Failing that, most countries have a telephone directory similar to the Yellow Pages, together with online versions such as www.pagesjaunes.fr for France or www.paginas-amarillas.es for Spain.

Most European countries require pets to wear a collar at all times identifying their owners. If your pet goes missing, report the matter to the local police and the local branch of that country's animal welfare organisation.

Prices

Campsite prices per night (for a car, caravan and two adults) are shown in local currencies. In the newest EU Member States included in this guide – Czech Republic, Hungary, Poland, and Slovakia – together with Croatia, euros are not yet the official currency but are usually readily accepted for payment of campsite fees and other goods and services.

If you stay on site after midday you may be charged for an extra day

---

Payment of campsite fees should be made at least two hours before departure. Remember that if you stay on site after midday you may be charged for an extra day. Many campsites shown in this guide as accepting credit card payments may not do so for an overnight or short stay because of high commission charges. Alternatively, a site will impose a minimum limit, or will accept credit cards only in the peak season. It is always advisable to check the form of payment required when you check in.

It is common for campsites to impose extra charges for the use of swimming pools and other leisure facilities, for showers and laundry facilities and for the erection of awnings.

Registering on Arrival

It is usual to have to register in accordance with local police requirements, and to produce an identity document which the campsite office may retain during your stay. Most campsites now accept the Camping

Card International (or Camping Card Scandinavia) instead of a passport and, where known, their sites entries are marked CCI or CCS. Alternatively, a photocopy of your passport may be acceptable and it is a good idea to carry a few copies with you to avoid depositing your passport and to speed up the check-in process.

If you do deposit your passport, make sure you have sufficient money for your stay if you are relying on travellers' cheques, as a passport must be produced when cashing them. Cash may be required on arrival as a deposit on a barrier 'swipe' card. The amount will vary from site to site; €25 or €30 is usual.

Telephone Numbers

These are given for most campsites listed in the guide, together with fax numbers and website and email addresses where known. The telephone numbers assume you are in the country concerned and the initial zero should be dialled, where applicable. If you are telephoning from outside the country the initial zero is usually (but not always) omitted. For more details see individual Country Introductions or the chapter Keeping in Touch.

General Advice

- Most campsites close from 10pm until 7am or 8am. However, late night arrival areas are sometimes provided for late travellers. Motor caravanners, in particular, should check the gate/barrier closing time before going out for the evening in their vehicle.

- If possible inspect the site and facilities before booking in. If your pitch is allocated at check-in, ask to see it first, checking conditions and access, as marked or hedged pitches can sometimes be difficult for large outfits. Riverside pitches can be delightful but keep an eye on water levels; in periods of heavy rain these may rise rapidly and the ground become boggy.

- It is usual for campsites to make a daily charge for children. It is quite common for site owners, particularly in France, to charge the full adult daily rate for children from as young as three years.

- Local authorities in some countries impose a tourist tax on all people staying in hotels and on campsites. This averages around the equivalent of 50 pence per night per person. Similarly, VAT may be payable on top of your campsite fees. These charges may not be included in prices listed in this guide.

- Speed limits on site are usually restricted to 10 km/h (6 mph). You may be asked to park your car in an area away from your caravan. At some sites if you return after 10pm you may have to park your car by an entrance barrier or overnight parking area.

- French regulations ban the wearing of boxer shorts-style swimming trunks in pools on the grounds of hygiene. This rule may be strictly enforced by inspectors who have the power to close a site's swimming pool. As a result site owners may insist on the wearing of conventional (brief-style) swimming trunks.

- The use of the term 'statics' in the campsite reports in this guide may, in many instances, refer to long-term seasonal pitches, chalets, cottages and cabins as well as mobile homes.

Complaints

If you have a complaint, take it up with site staff or owners at the time, so that it can be dealt with promptly. It is pointless complaining after the event, when action could have been taken at the time to improve matters. In France, if your complaint cannot be settled directly with the campsite, and if you are sure you are within your rights, you may take the matter up with the Préfecture of the local authority in question.

The Caravan Club has no control or influence over campsite operations or administration except in the case of a small number of sites with which it is contracted (marked ABS in site entries) and on which it has made a booking for you. It cannot intervene in any dispute a visitor may have with a particular site.

Specimen Site Booking Letters

See the following pages and *Booking a Campsite* earlier in this section. The website www.babelfish.altavista.com allows simple translations into a number of languages which may be useful when communicating with campsites.

Site Booking Letter – English

Date: .... Address (block caps)..

....

....

Tel No: (0044) ....

Fax No: (0044) ....

Email ....

Dear Sir/Madam

I wish to make a reservation as follows:

Arriving (date and month)................ **Departing** (date and month)................ (........nights)

Adults .... **Children (+ ages)** ....

Car ☐   **Caravan** ☐   **Motor Caravan** ☐   **Trailertent** ☐

Electrical Hook-up ☐   **Awning** ☐   **Extra tent** ☐

I look forward to an early reply and enclose an International Reply Coupon and addressed envelope. When replying please advise all charges and deposit required. I look forward to meeting you and visiting your site.

Yours faithfully,

[Name in block capitals after signature]

Caravan Club Membership No.........................

✂ --

Reply

Date: .... Address...

....

....

Dear Mr/Mrs/Ms ....

Thank you for your reservation from .... to .... (........ nights).

- **YES, OK** - I am pleased to confirm your reservation (with/without electrical hook-up) and look forward to welcoming you.

- **NO, SORRY** - I regret that the site is fully booked for the dates you request.

Yours faithfully

....

Date: Adresse (lettres majuscules)...

....

....

Tél   : (0044)..

Fax   : (0044)..

Email...

Monsieur/Madame

J'aimerais désire effectuer la réservation suivante :

Arrivée (jour et mois) .... **Départ** (jour et mois)...................... (........nuits)

Adultes .... **Enfants (+ âges)** ....

Voiture ☐ **Caravane** ☐ **Camping car** ☐ **Tente-remorque** ☐

Branchement électrique ☐ **Auvent** ☐ **Tente supplémentaire** ☐

Ci-joint un coupon-réponse international et une enveloppe avec mon adresse. En vous remerciant par avance pour votre réponse je vous demanderais de bien vouloir me communiquer vos tarifs complets ainsi que le montant des arrhes à verser.

En attendant le plaisir de faire votre connaissance et de séjourner sur votre terrain, je vous prie de croire, Monsieur/Madame, à l'assurance de mes sentiments les meilleurs.

(Nom en lettres majuscules après la signature)

No. d'adhérent du Caravan Club ....

✂--

Réponse

Date: Adresse ....

....

....

Monsieur/Madame/Mademoiselle

J'accuse réception de votre bulletin de réservation pour la période

du...................... au ....(........nuits).

- **OUI** - Je confirme votre réservation (avec/sans branchement électrique) en attendant le plaisir de faire votre connaissance.
- **NON** - Je suis au regret de vous informer que le terrain est complet pendant la période de votre choix.

Veuillez croire, Monsieur/Madame/Mademoiselle, à l'assurance de mes sentiments les meilleurs.

....

Datum: Anschrift (in Großbuchstaben)..…................

....…................

....…................

Telefonnummer.: (0044)...

Faxnummer: (0044)........................…...

Email ....…..

Sehr geehrter Herr/sehr geehrte Dame

Ich möchte wie folgt reservieren:

Ankunft (Tag und Monat) .... **Abreise** (Tag und Monat)................... (... Nächte)

Erwachsene   ....   Kinder (in Alter von) ....

Auto ☐   **Caravan** ☐   **Wohnmobil** ☐   **Klappwohnwagen** ☐

Strom ☐   **Vordach** ☐   **Extra Zelt** ☐

Ich sehe einer baldigen Antwort entgegen und lege einen internationalen Antwortschein und addressierten Umschlag bei. Bitte führen Sie in Ihrem Antwortschreiben sämtliche erforderlichen Gebühren und Anzahlungen an. Ich freue mich auf den Aufenthalt auf Ihrem Campingplatz und hoffe, Sie dort zu treffen.

Mit freundlichen Grüßen

(Unterschrift und Name in Großbuchstaben)

Caravan Club Mitgliednummer ....

✂--

Antwort

Datum: Anschrift: ....

....

....

....

Herrn/Frau/Fräulein...

Vielen Dank für Ihre Reservierung von .... bis .... (......Übernachtungen).

• **JA, OK** - Ich kann Ihre Reservierung (mit/ohne elektr. Anschluß) bestätigen und freue mich, Sie hier zu begrüßen.

• **NEIN, LEIDER** - Ich bedaure, daß der Campingplatz für die von Ihnen gewünschte Zeit voll belegt ist.

Mit freundlichen Grüßen

....

Fecha: Dirección (letra de imprenta)..…......

....…...

....…........

N° de tel.: (0044) ....……

N° de fax: (0044) ....…......………

Email ....……..……………..………………………......…....…………

Estimado Sr/Estimada Sra/Srta

Deseo realizar la siguiente reserva:

Llegada (fecha y mes) .... **Salida** (fecha y mes) .... (.......... noches)

Adultos ....   **Niños** (+ edades) ....

Coche ☐   **Caravana** ☐   **Caravana de motor** ☐   **Tienda con remolque** ☐

Enganche eléctrico ☐   **Toldo** ☐   **Tienda adicional** ☐

Espero con interés recibir su confirmación y tengo el gusto de adjuntar un cupón de respuesta internacional y un sobre con mi dirección. Cuando responda tenga la amabilidad de indicar todos los recargos y depósitos necesarios. Espero con ilusión conocerle y visitar su cámping.

Atentamente:

[Nombre en letra de imprenta después de la firma]

No de socio del Caravan Club ....

✂---

Respuesta

Fecha: Dirección..

....

....,..........................

Estimado Sr/Estimada Sra/Srta

Agradecemos su reserva del .... al .... (.......... noches).

• **SI** - Tenemos el gusto de confirmar su reserva (con/sin enganche eléctrico) y esperamos con ilusión darle la bienvenida.

• **LO SENTIMOS** - Desafortunadamente le cámping está lleno durante las fechas que ha solicitado.

Atentamente:

....

Data: Indirizzo (stampatello)..

....

....

N? Tel: (0044)..

N? Fax: (0044)...

Email...

Egregio Signore/Signora

Desidero fare una prenotazione come segue:

Arrivo (giorno e mese)..................... **Partenza** (giorno e mese).......................(...notti)

Adulti.............. **Bambini** (+ età)..............................

Automobile ☐ **Roulotte/Caravan** ☐ **Camper** ☐ **Tenda a rimorchio** ☐

Allacciamento elettrico ☐ **Tendone** ☐ **Tenda addizionale** ☐

Attendo un sollecito riscontro ed allego un Coupon di Risposta Internazionale con busta indirizzata. Quando risponde, la prego di farmi sapere tutte le tariffe ed il deposito richiesti. Attendendo di incontrarla e di visitare il suo campeggio, la prego di gradire i miei distinti saluti.

[Nome in stampatello dopo la firma]

No d'associazione al Caravan Club.........................

✂--

Risposta

Data: Indirizzo..

....

....

Egregio Signore/Signora..............

La ringrazio per il modulo di prenotazione da............a.............. (......notti).

• **SI, OK** - Sono lieto di confermare la sua prenotazione (con/senza allacciamento elettrico) e attendo di incontrarla.

• **NO, MI DISPIACE** - Mi dispiace ma il campeggio è completamente prenotato per le date da lei richieste.

Distinti saluti.

....

Planning and Travelling

Customs Regulations

Travelling Within the European Union

On entry into the UK no tax or duty is payable on goods you have bought tax-paid in other European Union countries which are for your own use, and which have been transported by you. VAT and duty are included in the price of goods purchased and travellers can no longer buy duty-free or tax-free goods on journeys within the EU. Customs allowances for outside the EU apply to Gibraltar, the Channel Islands and the Canary Islands.

The following are guidance levels for the import of alcohol and tobacco based on European law, but Customs do not enforce any absolute limits. No one under 17 years is entitled to the tobacco or alcohol allowances.

3,200 cigarettes
400 cigarillos
200 cigars
3kg tobacco
10 litres of spirits
20 litres of fortified wine (such as port or sherry)
90 litres of wine
110 litres of beer

However, for an interim period the UK is maintaining limits on the amount of cigarettes that travellers are able to import into the UK for their own use from ten of the new EU member states, without paying UK duty, namely Bulgaria, the Czech Republic, Estonia, Hungary, Latvia, Lithuania, Poland, Romania, Slovakia and Slovenia. The limit is 200 cigarettes from all these countries.

No one under 17 years is entitled to the tobacco or alcohol allowances

---

If you are suspected of having more than the permitted amounts you may be stopped and questioned by a Customs officer. If you are unable or refuse to provide a satisfactory response, the officer may well conclude that the goods are for a commercial purpose or for payment or re-sale (including to family members) and you risk having them seized, together with any vehicle used to transport them, and they may not be returned.

When entering the UK from another member state of the EU without having travelled to or through a non-EU country, you should use the blue channel or exit reserved for EU travellers, provided your purchases are within the limits for imports from that country and you are not importing any restricted or prohibited goods, details of which are given later in this chapter. See individual Country Introductions for further information.

Travelling Outside the European Union

Duty-free goods may be purchased if travelling from the UK direct to a country outside the EU. The allowances for goods you may take into a non-EU country are shown in the relevant Country Introductions.

Duty-free allowances for travellers returning to the UK from a non-EU country are as follows. No one under 17 years is entitled to the tobacco or alcohol allowances.

200 cigarettes, or 100 cigarillos, or 50 cigars, or 250 gms tobacco

1 litre of spirits, or 2 litres of fortified wine, sparkling wine or other liqueurs

2 litres of still table wine

60 cc of perfume, 250 cc of toilet water

£145 worth of all other goods including gifts and souvenirs

When entering the UK from a non-EU country, or having travelled to or through a non-EU country, you should go through the red Customs channel or use the telephone at the Red Point if you have exceeded your Customs allowances, or if you are carrying any prohibited, restricted or commercial goods. Use the green channel if you have 'nothing to declare'.

All dutiable items must be declared to Customs on entering the UK; failure to do so may mean that you forfeit them and your vehicle(s). Customs officers are legally entitled to examine your baggage and your vehicles and you are responsible for packing and unpacking. Whichever channel you use, you may be stopped by a Customs officer and searched. If you are caught with goods that are prohibited or restricted, or goods in excess of your Customs allowances, you risk heavy fines and possibly a prison sentence.

For further information contact HM Revenue & Customs National Advice Service on 0845 010 9000 (+44 2920 501261 from outside the UK) or see www.hmrc.gov.uk for email options.

Boats

Virtually all boats of any size taken abroad, except for very small craft, must carry registration documents when leaving UK waters. Contact the Maritime and Coastguard Agency on 0870 6006505 or www.mcga.gov.uk for details. The Royal Yachting Association recommends that all boats have marine insurance and can provide details of the rules and regulations for taking a boat to countries bordering the Atlantic Ocean, and the Baltic, Mediterranean and Black Seas – tel 0845 345 0400, www.rya.org.uk. Some countries require owners of certain types of vessels to have an International Certificate of Competence and information is contained in RYA publications.

If planning to take a boat abroad check with the appropriate tourist office before departure, as rules and regulations for boat use vary from country to country. Third party insurance is compulsory in most European countries and is advisable elsewhere.

Currency

There is no limit to the amount of sterling notes you may take out of the country. Some countries apply limits to the import and export of their own currencies.

New legislation on the control of funds entering or leaving the EU was introduced in 2007. Any person entering or leaving the EU will have to declare the money that they are carrying if this amounts to €10,000 (or equivalent in other currencies) or more. This includes cheques, travellers' cheques, money orders etc. This ruling does not apply to anyone travelling via the EU to a non-EU country, as long as the original journey started outside of the EU, nor to those travelling within the EU.

Food

Travellers from within the EU may bring into the UK personal imports of food without restriction. Andorra, the Canary Islands, the Channel Islands, the Isle of Man, Norway and San Marino are treated as part of the EU for these purposes. However, there are strict controls on bringing meat, meat products, milk, dairy products, fish, fish products, shellfish, eggs, honey and plants into the UK from outside the EU, including Liechtenstein and Switzerland, as these items can carry animal or plant pests and diseases which may damage our environment or public health.

HM Revenue & Customs publish a leaflet broadly setting out the rules, entitled 'If in Doubt, Leave it Out!' obtainable from their website, www.hmrc.gov.uk or telephone the National Advice Service on 0845 010 9000. Information can also be obtained from The Food Standards Agency on 020 7276 8018, www.food.gov.uk/import or from DEFRA (Department for Environment, Food & Rural Affairs) on 08459 335577, www.defra.gov.uk

If you do bring meat or food into the UK, or are simply unsure of the rules, you must go to the Customs red channel/point or the phone provided at the red point to speak to a Customs officer. All prohibited and restricted meat and food items will be taken away and destroyed. No further action will be taken.

In the light of recent animal health concerns in the UK, authorities abroad will understandably take a cautious approach to the import of foodstuffs. There is no guarantee that such products, if found, will not be confiscated by Customs officers.

Medicines

If you intend to take medicines with you when you go abroad you should obtain a copy of HMRC Notice 4, 'Taking Medicines With You When You Go Abroad', from HM Revenue & Customs National Advice Service on 0845 010 9000 or from www.hmrc.gov.uk. Alternatively contact the Drugs Enforcement Policy Team, HM Revenue & Customs, New King's Beam House, 22 Upper Ground, London SE1 9PJ, tel 020 7865 5767, fax 020 7865 5910.

There is no limit to the amount of medicines obtained without prescription, but medicines prescribed by your doctor may contain controlled drugs (ie subject to control under the Misuse of Drugs legislation) and you should check the allowances for these – in good time – in case you need to obtain a licence from the Home Office. In general, the permitted allowance for each drug is calculated on an average 15 day dose.

Motor Vehicles and Caravans

Travellers between member states of the EU are entitled to import temporarily a motor vehicle, caravan or trailer into other member states without any Customs formalities.

Motor vehicles and caravans may be temporarily imported into non-EU countries generally up to a maximum of six months in any twelve month period, provided they are not hired, sold or otherwise disposed of in that country. Temporarily imported vehicles should not be left behind after the importer has left, should not be used by residents of the country visited and should not be left longer than the permitted period.

Anyone intending to stay longer than six months, take up employment or residence, or dispose of a vehicle should seek advice well in advance of their departure, for example from one of the motoring organisations. Anyone temporarily importing a vehicle which does not belong to them – either hired or borrowed – should carry a letter of authority from the vehicle owner.

See the chapter Documents in the section
PLANNING AND TRAVELLING for further details.

Use Of Caravan By Persons Other Than The Owner

Many caravan owners reduce the cost of a holiday by sharing their caravan with friends or relatives. Either the caravan is left on the Continent on a campsite or it is handed over at the port. In making these arrangements it is important to consider the following:

- The total time the vehicle spends in the country must not exceed the permitted period for temporary importation.

- The owner of the caravan must provide the other person with a letter of authority. It is forbidden to accept a hire fee or reward.

- The number plate on the caravan must match the number plate on the tow car used.

- Each driver's motor insurer must be informed if a caravan is being towed and any additional premium must be paid. Both drivers' International Motor Insurance Certificates (if applicable) must be annotated in the recognised way to show that a caravan is being towed.

- If using the Caravan Club's Red Pennant Motoring & Personal Holiday Insurance, both drivers must be members of the Caravan Club and both must pay for a Red Pennant premium.

Personal Possessions

Generally speaking, visitors to countries within the EU are free to carry reasonable quantities of any personal articles, including valuable items such as jewellery, cameras, etc required for the duration of their stay. It is sensible to carry sales receipts for new items, particularly of a foreign manufacture, in case you need to prove that tax has already been paid.

Visitors to non-EU countries may temporarily import personal items on condition that the articles are the personal property of the visitor and that they are not left behind when the importer leaves the country.

Plants and Plant Products

You may bring in any plants or plant products from another EU country, provided they were grown in those countries. Andorra, the Channel Islands, the Isle of Man, San Marino and Switzerland are treated as part of the EU for these purposes. Restrictions apply to other non-EU countries and countries in the Euro-Mediterannean area including Croatia, Gibraltar, Liechtenstein and Norway. A leaflet detailing allowances and restrictions entitled 'If in Doubt, Leave it Out!' is available from HM Revenue & Customs. See www.hmrc.gov.uk or telephone the National Advice Service on 0845 010 9000.

Prohibited and Restricted Goods

Just because something is on sale in another country does not mean it can be freely brought back to the UK. The importation of some goods is restricted or banned in the UK, mainly to protect health and the environment. These include:

- Endangered species, including birds and plants, whether alive or dead (eg stuffed), and goods made from them such as spotted cat furs, ivory, reptile leather, hides, tortoiseshell, teeth, feathers, and coral.

- Controlled, unlicensed or dangerous drugs eg opium, cannabis, LSD, morphine etc.

- Counterfeit or pirated goods such as fake watches, CDs and sports shirts; goods bearing a false indication of their place of manufacture or in breach of UK copyright.

- Offensive weapons such as flick knives, knuckledusters, push daggers or knives disguised as everyday objects.

- Indecent and obscene material depicting extreme violence or featuring children, such as DVDs, magazines, videos, books and software.

This list is by no means exhaustive; if in doubt contact HM Revenue & Customs National Advice Service for more information or, when returning to the UK, go through the red Customs channel and ask a Customs officer. It is your responsibility to make sure that you are not breaking the law. Never attempt to mislead or hide anything from Customs officers; penalties are severe.

Documents

Camping Card International (CCI)

The Camping Card International (CCI) is a plastic identity card for campers and is valid worldwide (except in the USA and Canada). It is available to members of the Caravan Club and other clubs affiliated to the international organisations, the AIT, FIA and FICC. It is regarded as a camper's identity document and may be deposited with a campsite manager in place of a passport. A CCI is, therefore, essential in those countries where a passport must be carried at all times, and is recommended elsewhere. However, it is not a legal document and campsite managers are within their rights to demand other means of identification. More than 1,100 campsites throughout Europe give a reduction to holders of a CCI, although this may not apply if you pay by credit card.

The CCI is provided automatically, free of charge, to Caravan Club members taking out the Club's Red Pennant Motoring & Personal Holiday Insurance, otherwise there is a small fee. It provides extensive third party personal liability cover and is valid for any personal injury and material damage you may cause while staying at a campsite, hotel or rented accommodation. Cover extends to the Club member and his/her passengers (maximum eleven people travelling together) and is valid for one year. The policy excludes any claims arising from accidents caused by any mechanically-propelled vehicle, ie a car. Full details of the terms and conditions and level of indemnity are provided with the card.

When leaving a campsite, make sure it is your card that is returned to you, and not one belonging to someone else.

The CCI is no longer accepted at a number of campsites in Sweden.

*See individual **Country Introductions** for more information and www.campingcardinternational.com*

Driving Licence & International Driving Permit (IDP)

Driving Licence

A full, valid driving licence should be carried at all times when travelling abroad as it must be produced on demand to the police and other authorities. Failure to do so may result in an immediate fine. If your driving licence is due to expire while you are away it can normally be renewed up to three months before the expiry date. If you need to renew your licence more than three months ahead of the expiry date write to the DVLA and they will try to help.

All European Union countries should recognise the pink EU-format paper driving licence introduced in the UK in 1990, subject to the minimum age requirements of the country concerned (18 years in all countries covered by this guide for a vehicle with a maximum weight of 3,500 kg and carrying not more than 8 people). However, there are exceptions, eg Slovenia, and the Country Introduction chapter contains details.

Holders of an old-style green UK paper licence or a licence issued in Northern Ireland prior to 1991, which is not to EU format, are strongly recommended to update it to a photocard licence before travelling in order to avoid any local difficulties with the authorities. Alternatively, obtain an International Driving Permit. A photocard driving licence is also useful as a means of identification in other situations, eg when using a credit card, when the display of photographic identification may be required.

If you have a photocard driving licence, remember to carry both the card and its paper counterpart as you will need both parts if, for any reason, you need to hire a vehicle.

Application forms are available from most post offices or directly from the DVLA Swansea on 0870 240 0009, email: drivers.dvla@gtnet.gov.uk or, if you live in Northern Ireland, the DVLA Coleraine on 028 70341469. When applying, allow enough time for your application to be processed and do not apply if you plan to hire a car in the near future. Selected post offices and DVLA local offices offer a premium checking service for photocard applications; details on www.dvla.gov.uk or telephone 08457 223344.

International Driving Permit (IDP)

If you hold a British photocard driving licence, no other form of photographic identification is required to drive in any of the countries covered by this guide. If you plan to travel further afield then an IDP may still be required and you can obtain one over the counter at many post offices and from motoring organisations, namely the AA, Green Flag or the RAC, whether or not you are a member. An IDP costs £5.50 and is valid for a period of 12 months from the date of issue but may be post-dated up to three months in advance. To apply for an IDP you will need to be resident in Great Britain, have passed a driving test and be over 18 years of age. When abroad you should always carry your national driving licence with you as well as your IDP.

European Health Insurance Card — Emergency Medical Benefits

For information on how to apply for a European Health Insurance Card (EHIC) and the medical care it entitles you to, see the chapter *Medical Matters* in the section *DURING YOUR STAY.*

MOT Certificate

You are strongly advised to carry your vehicle's MOT certificate of roadworthiness (if applicable) when travelling on the Continent as it may be required by the local authorities if an accident occurs, or in the event of random vehicle checks. If your MOT certificate is due to expire while you are away you should have the vehicle tested before you leave.

Passport

The following information applies only to British citizens and subjects holding, or entitled to hold, a passport bearing the inscription 'United Kingdom of Great Britain and Northern Ireland'. British subjects, British overseas citizens and British dependent territories citizens may need visas that are not required by British citizens. Check with the authorities of the country you are due to visit at their UK Embassy or Consulate. Citizens of other countries should apply to their Embassy, Consulate or High Commission for information.

Each person must hold or be named on a valid passport. Children, including babies, who are not already included on a valid passport need to hold their own passport if they are to travel abroad. It is not now possible to add or include children on a parent's British passport. A standard British passport is valid for ten years, but if issued to children under 16 years of age it is valid for five years.

Children who are already included on a parent's existing passport (one issued before October 1998) may continue to travel with the passport holder until either the child reaches the age of 16, or the passport on which the child is included expires or needs to be amended, whichever comes first. Children aged 16 and over (aged 15 if entering the Czech Republic) must hold their own passport.

Full information and application forms are available from main post offices or from the Identity & Passport Service website, www.passport.gov.uk where you can complete an on-line application. Allow at least three weeks for an application for a renewal passport (four weeks if pre-applying on-line) and at least one week for the replacement of a lost, stolen or damaged passport. There is the option of a guaranteed same-day premium service for passport renewals, amendments or extensions, or a one-week fast track service for replacement of lost, stolen or damaged passports. Additional fees are payable for these services which are available to personal callers at IPS regional offices in Belfast, Durham, Glasgow, Liverpool, London, Newport and Peterborough, but you will need an appointment – telephone the 24-hour Passport Adviceline on 0870 5210410 to arrange one.

All new UK passports are now biometric passports, also known as ePassports, which feature additional security features including a microchip with the holder's unique facial biometric features. Existing passports will remain valid until their expiry date and holders will not be required to exchange them for biometric passports before then. If you are applying for a passport for the first time you are now required to attend an interview at one of a national network of interview offices, and should allow a minimum of six weeks to obtain your passport. The fast track service is no longer available for first-time applicants.

The IPS has arranged for main post offices and branches of WorldChoice travel agents to accept passport applications on their behalf by means of a 'Check and Send' service. For a £7 handling charge staff will check the forms and supporting documents for completeness and forward the application securely to the designated regional IPS office. The passport is then sent directly to the applicant from the issuing office. Priority is given to applications made using this service.

Although the United Kingdom is part of the European Union, you must still carry a full, valid passport with you every time you travel within Europe, including on day trips and via Eurostar. Many countries no longer routinely check passports at frontiers, but visitors must still be able to produce a valid form of identity and nationality at all times and, in the case of British travellers, this is a passport. Many countries require you to carry your passport at all times and immigration authorities may, of course, check your passport on return to the UK. While abroad, it will help gain access to assistance from British Consular services and to banking services.

Your passport is a valuable document - look after it

It is advisable to enter next-of-kin details in the back of your passport and to keep a separate record of your passport details and leave a copy of it with a relative or friend at home. In order to avoid any possible local difficulties with immigration authorities, it is advisable to ensure that your passport has at least three months' validity left after your planned return travel date from most countries in the EU, and six months' validity elsewhere. You may renew your passport up to nine months before expiry, without losing the validity of the current one.

Some countries require documentary evidence of parental responsibility from single parents or other adults travelling alone with children before allowing lone parents to enter the country or, in some cases, before permitting children to leave the country. For further information on exactly what will be required at immigration, contact the Embassy or Consulate of the countries you intend to visit before you travel.

Last but not least: your passport is a valuable document – look after it! Replacing a lost or stolen passport can be time-consuming and expensive.

Pet Travel Scheme (PETS)

The Pets Travel Scheme (PETS) allows pet dogs, cats and a number of other animals from qualifying European countries to enter the UK without quarantine, providing they have an EU pet passport, and it also allows pets to travel from the UK to another EU qualifying country. All the countries covered by this guide (including Gibraltar and Liechtenstein) are qualifying countries. However, the procedures to obtain the passport are lengthy and the regulations of necessity strict. If you are proposing to take your pet abroad you should check the latest available information from your vet or the PETS Helpline on 0870 2411710, email: pets.helpline@defra.gsi.gov.uk. More information is available from the website for the Department for Environment, Food & Rural Affairs (Defra), www.defra.gov.uk

The scheme operates on a number of ferry routes between the Continent and the UK as well as on Eurotunnel services and Eurostar passenger trains from Calais to Folkestone. Some routes may only operate at certain times of the year; routes may change and new ones may be added – check with the PETS Helpline for the latest information.

Adequate travel insurance for your pet is essential

Pets normally resident in the Channel Islands, Isle of Man and the Republic of Ireland can also enter the UK under PETS from qualifying countries if they comply with the rules. Pets resident anywhere in the British Isles (including the Republic of Ireland) will continue to be able to travel freely within the British Isles and will not be subject to PETS rules. Owners of pets entering the Channel Islands or the Republic of Ireland from outside the British Isles should contact the appropriate authorities in those countries for advice on approved routes and other requirements.

It is against the law in the UK to possess certain types of dogs (unless an exemption certificate is held) and the introduction of PETS does not affect this ban. Some European countries have laws about certain breeds of dogs and about transporting dogs in cars and, where known, this is covered in the relevant Country Introductions.

For a list of vets near Continental ports, look in the local equivalent of the Yellow Pages telephone directory, eg www.pagesjaunes.fr for France or www.paginas-amarillas.es for Spain. Or use the links on the Defra website. Last but not least, adequate travel insurance for your pet is essential in the event of an accident abroad requiring extensive veterinary treatment, emergency repatriation or long-term care if treatment lasts longer than your holiday. Travel insurance should also include liability cover in the event that your pet injures another animal, person or property while abroad. Contact the Caravan Club on 0800 0151396 or visit www.caravanclub.co.uk for details of its Pet Insurance scheme, specially negotiated to take into account Club members' requirements both at home and abroad.

See **Holiday Insurance for Pets** under Insurance in the section **PLANNING AND TRAVELLING**.

Vehicle Excise Licence

While driving abroad it is necessary to display a current UK vehicle excise licence (tax disc). If your vehicle tax disc is due to expire while you are abroad you may apply to re-license the vehicle at a post office, or by post, or in person at a DVLA local office up to two months in advance. If you give a despatch address abroad the licence can be sent to you there.

Vehicle Registration Certificate

Your Vehicle Registration Certificate, V5C should always be carried when travelling abroad. If you do not have one you should apply to a DVLA local office on form V62. If you need to travel abroad during this time you will need to apply for a Temporary Registration Certificate if you are not already recorded as the vehicle keeper. There is a fee for this service. Telephone DVLA Customer

Enquiries on 0870 240 0009 for more information.

Caravan – Proof of Ownership (CRIS)

Britain and Ireland are the only European countries where caravans are not formally registered in the same way as cars. This may not be fully understood by police and other authorities on the Continent. You are strongly advised, therefore, to carry a copy of your Caravan Registration Identification Scheme (CRIS) document.

Hired or Borrowed Vehicles

If using a borrowed vehicle you must obtain from the registered owner a letter of authority to use the vehicle. You should also carry the Vehicle Registration Certificate (V5C).

In the case of hired or leased vehicles, when the user does not normally possess the V5C, ask the company which owns the vehicle to supply a Vehicle On Hire Certificate, form VE103B, or telephone the AA's Information Line on 0800 551188 to request an application form for a Certificate. Alternatively, you can download a form from the RAC's website, www.rac.co.uk, or call their Travel Sales on 0800 550055.

Visas

British citizens holding a full UK passport do not require a visa for entry into any of the countries covered by this guide. EU countries normally require a permit for stays of more than three months and these can be obtained during your stay on application to the local police or civic authorities.

Planning And Travelling

Ferries and the Channel Tunnel

Planning Your Trip

If travelling in July or August, or over peak weekends during school holidays, such as Easter and half-term, it is advisable to make a reservation as early as possible, particularly if you need cabin accommodation.

Space for caravans on ferries is usually limited especially during peak holiday periods. Off-peak crossings, which may offer savings for caravanners, are usually filled very quickly.

When booking any ferry crossing, account must be taken of boats, bicycles, skylights and roof boxes in the overall height/length of the car and caravan outfit or motor caravan, as ferry operators require you to declare total dimensions. It is important, therefore, to report dimensions of outfits accurately when making ferry bookings, as vehicles which have been under-declared may be turned away at boarding.

Individual ferry companies may impose vehicle length or height restrictions according to the type of vessel in operation, ie catamarans, fast-craft or conventional ferries. On some routes more than one kind of vessel may be operating. Always check when making your booking.

Report dimensions of outfits accurately when making ferry bookings

---

Advise your booking agent at the time of making your ferry reservation of any disabled passengers, or any who have special needs. Ferry companies can then make the appropriate arrangements for anyone requiring assistance at ports or on board ships.

For residents of both Northern Ireland and the Republic of Ireland travelling to the Continent via the British mainland, Brittany Ferries, Irish Ferries and P & O Irish Sea offer special 'Landbridge' or 'Ferrylink' through-fares for combined crossings on the Irish Sea and the English Channel or North Sea, although the Club's own individually booked offers are often better value.

The table on the following page shows current ferry routes from the UK to the Continent and Ireland. Some ferry routes may not be operational all year and during peak holiday periods the transportation of caravans or motor caravans may be restricted. Current information on ferry timetables and tariffs can be obtained from the Caravan Club's Travel Service or from a travel agent, or from the appropriate ferry operators' websites.

Booking Your Ferry

The Caravan Club is an agent for most major ferry companies operating services to the Continent, Scandinavia and Ireland, and each year provides thousands of Club members with a speedy and efficient booking service. The Club's Travel Service in Europe brochure (available from November) features a range of special offers with ferry operators (some of them exclusive to the Caravan Club), together with full information on the Club's Continental campsite Advance Booking Service, its range of 'package' Inclusive Holidays, and Red Pennant Motoring & Personal Holiday Insurance. Telephone 01342 327410 for a brochure or see www.caravanclub.co.uk

In addition, during the course of the year, new special offers and promotions are negotiated and details of these are featured regularly on the Travel Service News page of The Caravan Club Magazine and on the Club's website.

The Club's website has a direct link through to a number of the most popular ferry operators' reservations systems and Club members can make their own reservations and still take advantage of the Club's negotiated offers and the ferry companies' own early booking offers. The requisite deposit is taken by credit card and the balance collected ten weeks prior to departure date.

Reservations may be made by telephoning the Caravan Club's Travel Service on 01342 316101 or on www.caravanclub.co.uk

43

Route	Operator	Approximate Crossing Time	Maximum Frequency
Belgium			
Hull – Zeebrugge	P & O Ferries	12½ hrs	Daily
Ramsgate – Ostend†	Transeuropa Ferries	4½ hrs	4 daily
Rosyth – Zeebrugge	Superfast Ferries	18 hrs	3 weekly
Denmark			
Harwich – Esbjerg	DFDS Seaways	18 hrs	4 weekly
France			
Dover – Boulogne*†	SpeedFerries	50 mins	5 daily
Dover – Calais	P & O Ferries	1¼ hrs	25 daily
Dover – Calais	SeaFrance	1¼ / 1½ hrs	15 daily
Dover – Dunkerque	Norfolkline	1¾ hrs	12 daily
Folkestone – Calais	Eurotunnel	35 mins	3 per hour
Newhaven – Dieppe	Transmanche Ferries	4 hrs	3 daily
Newhave – Le Havre	LD Lines	5 hrs	Daily (May to Sep)
Plymouth – Roscoff	Brittany Ferries	6 / 8 hrs	3 daily
Poole – Cherbourg	Brittany Ferries	2¼ hrs / 6½ hrs	3 daily
Poole – St Malo (via Channel Islands)	Condor Ferries	4½ hrs	Daily (May to Sep)
Portsmouth – Caen	Brittany Ferries	3¾ / 7 hrs	4 daily
Portsmouth – Cherbourg*	Brittany Ferries	3 hrs	2 daily
Portsmouth – Cherbourg	Condor Ferries	5½ hrs	Weekly (Jul to Sep)
Portsmouth – Le Havre	LD Lines	7½	Daily
Portsmouth – St Malo	Brittany Ferries	10¾ hrs	Daily
Weymouth – St Malo (via Channel Islands)	Condor Ferries	5¼ hrs	Daily
Ireland – Northern			
Cairnryan – Larne	P & O Irish Sea	1 / 1¾ hrs	7 daily
Fleetwood – Larne	Stena Line	8 hrs	3 daily
Liverpool (Birkenhead) – Belfast††	Norfolkline	8 hrs	2 daily
Stranraer – Belfast	Stena Line	1¾ / 3¼ hrs	8 daily
Troon – Larne	P & O Irish Sea	1 hr 50 mins	2 daily
Ireland – Republic			
Cork – Roscoff	Brittany Ferries	13 hrs	Weekly
Fishguard – Rosslare	Stena Line	2 / 3½ hrs	4 daily
Holyhead – Dublin	Irish Ferries	1¾ hr / 3¼ hrs	4 daily
Holyhead – Dublin	Stena Line	1½ / 3¼ hrs	3 daily
Holyhead – Dun Loaghaire	Stena Line	1½ / 3¼ hrs	3 daily
Liverpool – Dublin	P & O Irish Sea	8 hrs	2 daily
Liverpool (Birkenhead) – Dublin†	Norfolkline	7 hrs	2 daily
Pembroke – Rosslare	Irish Ferries	3¾ hrs	2 daily
Rosslare – Cherbourg	Irish Ferries	18½ hrs	3 weekly
Rosslare – Roscoff	Irish Ferries	17 hrs	2 weekly
Netherlands			
Harwich – Hook of Holland	Stena Line	6¼ hrs	2 daily
Hull – Rotterdam	P & O Ferries	10 hrs	Daily
Newcastle – Amsterdam (Ijmuiden)	DFDS Seaways	15 hrs	Daily
Norway			
Newcastle – Bergen	DFDS Seaways	26 hrs	2 weekly
Newcastle – Haugesund	DFDS Seaways	21½ hrs	2 weekly
Newcastle – Stavanger	DFDS Seaways	18½ hrs	3 weekly
Spain			
Plymouth – Santander	Brittany Ferries	20½ hrs	2 weekly
Portsmouth – Bilbao	P & O Ferries	29 / 35 hrs	3 weekly

* *Cars and small motor caravans only.*

** *NB For technical reasons it is sometimes necessary to reverse outfits off ferries on these routes.*

† *Not bookable through the Club's Travel Service.*

Channel Tunnel

The Channel Tunnel operator, Eurotunnel, accepts cars, caravans and motor caravans (except those running on LPG and dual-fuel vehicles) on their service between Folkestone and Calais. While they accept traffic on a 'turn up and go' basis, they also offer a full reservation service for all departures with exact timings confirmed on booking.

All information was current at the time this guide was compiled in the autumn of 2007 and may be subject to change during 2008.

Gas – Safety Precautions and Regulations on Ferries and in the Channel Tunnel

- Gas cylinders should be of a type specifically recommended by the Department for Business, Enterprise and Regulatary Reform.

- UK-based cross-Channel ferry companies usually allow up to three gas cylinders per caravan, including the cylinder currently in use. However some, eg Brittany Ferries, DFDS Seaways, SeaFrance and Stena Line restrict this to a maximum of two cylinders, providing they are securely fitted into your caravan. It is advisable to check with the ferry company before setting out.

- Cylinder valves should be fully closed and covered with a cap, if provided, and should remain closed during the crossing. Cylinders should be fixed securely in or on the caravan in the manner intended and in the position designated by the caravan manufacturers. Ensure gas cookers and fridges are properly turned off.

- Ships' crew may wish to inspect each cylinder for leakage before shipment and to reject leaking cylinders. If cylinders are likely to be inaccessible within an unaccompanied vehicle, arrangements should be made for the shipper to observe this precaution.

- Eurotunnel will allow vehicles fitted with LPG tanks for the purpose of heating, lighting, cooking or refrigeration to use their services but regulations stipulate that a total of no more than 73 litres or 47 kg of gas can be carried through the Channel Tunnel. Tanks must be disconnected and no more than 80% full. Eurotunnel security staff carry out safety inspections on all vehicles carrying LPG. The caravan door will be sealed by a sticker. **Vehicles**

powered with LPG or equipped with a dual-fuel system cannot be carried through the Channel Tunnel.

- Most ferry companies are willing to accept LPG-powered vehicles provided they are advised at the time of booking. During the crossing the tank must be no more than 75% full and it must be turned off. In the case of vehicles converted to use LPG, some ferry companies also require a certificate showing that the conversion has been carried out to the manufacturer's specification.

- The carriage of spare petrol cans, whether full or empty, is not permitted on ferries or through the Channel Tunnel.

Pets on Ferries and Eurotunnel

It is possible to take your pet on a number of ferry routes to the Continent and Ireland as well as on Eurotunnel services and on Eurostar passenger trains from Folkestone to Calais. At the time this guide was compiled the cost of return travel for a pet was between £30 and £50, depending on the route used. Advance booking is essential as restrictions apply to the number of animals allowed on any one departure. Make sure you understand the carrier's terms and conditions for transporting pets.

Ensure that ferry staff know that your vehicle contains an animal

---

On arrival at the port ensure that ferry staff know that your vehicle contains an animal. Pets are normally required to remain in their owners' vehicle or in kennels on the car deck and, for safety reasons, access to the vehicle decks while the ferry is at sea may be restricted. On longer ferry crossings you should make arrangements at the on-board Information Desk for permission to visit your pet at suitable intervals in order to check its well-being. Information and advice on the welfare of animals before and during a journey is available on the website of the Department for Environment, Food and Rural Affairs (Defra), www.defra.gov.uk

*See also **Pet Travel Scheme** under **Documents** and **Holiday Insurance for Pets** under **Insurance** in the section **PLANNING AND TRAVELLING**.*

Caravan Club Sites Near Ports

Once you have chosen your ferry crossing and worked out your route to the port of departure you may like to consider an overnight stop at one of the following Club sites, especially if your journey to or from home involves a long drive. Prior to the opening before Easter of seasonal sites,

you can book by using the Club's Advance Booking Service on 01342 327490 or book online at www.caravanclub.co.uk. Otherwise contact the site direct. Advance booking is recommended, particularly if you are planning to stay during July and August or over Bank Holidays.

Port	Nearest Site and Town	Tel No.
Cairnryan Stranraer	New England Bay, Drummore	01776 860275
Dover, Folkestone, Channel Tunnel	Black Horse Farm*, Folkestone,	01303 892665
	Daleacres, Hythe,	01303 267679
	Fairlight Wood	01424 812333
Fishguard, Pembroke	Freshwater East, Pembroke	01646 672341
Harwich	Colchester Camping*, Colchester	01206 545551
Holyhead	Penrhos, Brynteg, Anglesey	01248 852617
Hull	Beechwood Grange, York	01904 424637
	Rowntree Park*, York	01904 658997
Newcastle upon Tyne	Old Hartley, Whitley Bay	0191 237 0256
Newhaven	Sheepcote Valley*, Brighton	01273 626546
Plymouth	Plymouth Sound, Plymouth	01752 862325
Poole	Hunter's Moon*, Wareham	01929 556605
Portsmouth	Rookesbury Park, Fareham	01329 834085
Rosslare	River Valley, Wicklow	00353 (0)404 41647
Weymouth	Crossways, Dorchester	01305 852032

* Site open all year

When seasonal Club sites near the ports are closed, the following, which are open all year or most of the year (but may not be 'on the doorstep' of the ports in question) may be useful overnight stops for early and late season travellers using cross-Channel or Irish Sea ports. All 'open all year' sites offer a limited supply of hardstanding pitches.

Port	Nearest Site and Town	Tel No.
Dover, Folkestone, Channel Tunnel	Abbey Wood, London	020 8311 7708
	Alderstead Heath, Redhill	01737 644629
	Amberley Fields, Crawley	01293 524834
	Crystal Palace, London	020 8778 7155
Fishguard, Pembroke,Swansea	Pembrey Country Park, Llanelli	01554 834369
Portsmouth	Abbey Wood, London	020 8311 7708
	Alderstead Heath, Redhill	01737 644629
	Amberley Fields, Crawley	01293 524834
	Crystal Palace, London	020 8778 7155

NB Amberley Fields, Daleacres, Fairlight Wood, Hunter's Moon, Old Hartley and Rookesbury Park are open to Caravan Club members only. Non-members are welcome at all the other Caravan Club sites listed above.

Alternatively consider an overnight stay at a CL (Certificated Location) site within striking distance of your port of departure, many of which are open all year.

Full details of all these sites can be found in the Caravan Club's Sites Directory & Handbook 2007/08.

Insurance

Car, Motor Caravan and Caravan Insurance

Insurance cover for motor car, motor caravan and caravan while travelling abroad is of the utmost importance. Travel insurance, such as the Caravan Club's Red Pennant Motoring & Personal Holiday Insurance (available to members only), not only minimises duplicate cover offered by normal motor and caravan insurance, but also covers contingencies which are not included, eg despatch of spare parts, medical and hospital fees, hire vehicles, hotel bills, vehicle recovery etc.

See **Holiday Insurance** later in this section.

In order to be covered for a period abroad the following action is necessary:

- **Caravan** — Inform your caravan insurer/broker of the dates of your holiday and pay any additional premium required. The Caravan Club's 5Cs Insurance gives free cover for up to 182 days.

- **Motor Car or Motor Caravan** — If your journey is outside the EU or EU Associated Countries inform your motor insurer/broker of the dates of your holiday, together with details of all the countries you will be visiting, and pay any additional premium. Also inform them if you are towing a caravan and ask them to include it on your Green Card if you need to carry one.

The Caravan Club's Car Insurance and Motor Caravan Insurance schemes extend to provide full policy cover for European Union or Associated Countries free of charge, provided the total period of foreign travel in any one annual period of insurance does not exceed 180 days. It may be possible to extend this period, although a charge will be made. The cover provided is the same as a Club member enjoys in the UK, rather than just the minimum legal liability cover required by law in the country visited.

Should you be delayed beyond the limits of your insurance you must, without fail, instruct your insurer/broker to maintain cover.

For full details of the Caravan Club's car, caravan and motor caravan insurance products, telephone 0800 0284809 or visit our website, www.caravanclub.co.uk

Green Card – International Motor Insurance Certificate

All countries oblige visiting motorists to have motor insurance cover for their legal liability to third parties. An International Motor Insurance Certificate, commonly known as a Green Card, is evidence of compliance with this requirement. However, motorists visiting European Union and Associated Countries (listed on the next page) do not need an actual Green Card as, under EU legislation, a UK Certificate of Motor Insurance is now accepted in all such countries as evidence that the obligatory motor insurance cover is in force.

Travellers outside the European Union and Associated Countries will need to obtain a Green Card document, for which insurers usually make a charge. If a Green Card is issued, your motor insurers should be asked to include reference on it to any caravan or trailer you may be towing. If you do not have evidence of the obligatory insurance cover, you may have to pay for temporary insurance at a country's border.

Irrespective of whether a Green Card is required, it is still normally necessary for you to notify your insurer/broker of your intention to travel outside the UK and obtain confirmation that your policy has been extended to include use of the insured vehicle abroad. Because of the high cost of claims that can arise on the Continent, your insurer may not automatically provide full policy cover when abroad. You should ensure that your vehicle and caravan policies provide adequate cover for your purposes, rather than the limited cover that the country you are visiting obliges you to have.

European Accident Statement

You should also check with your motor insurer/broker to see if they provide a European Accident Statement to record details of any accident in which you may be involved with your motor vehicle. Travelling with your vehicle registration certificate, MOT certificate (if applicable), certificate of motor insurance, copy of your CRIS document, European Accident Statement and valid pink EU-format or photocard UK driving licence should be sufficient should you be stopped by a routine police check or following an accident while travelling within the EU or an Associated Country. These documents should not be left in your vehicle when it is unattended.

European Union and Associated Countries

European Union: Austria, Belgium, Bulgaria, Cyprus, Czech Republic, Denmark, Estonia, Finland, France, Germany, Greece, Hungary, Ireland, Italy, Latvia, Lithuania, Luxembourg, Malta, Netherlands, Poland, Portugal, Romania, Slovakia, Slovenia, Spain, Sweden and the United Kingdom.

Associated EU Countries (ie non-EU signatories to the motor insurance Multilateral Guarantee Agreement): Croatia, Iceland, Norway, Switzerland and Liechtenstein.

In spite of the foregoing, you may wish to obtain an actual Green Card if visiting Bulgaria or Romania so as to avoid local difficulties which can sometimes arise in these countries. If you do not take a Green Card you should carry your certificate of motor insurance. **Visitors to countries outside the European Union and Associated Countries, and in particular eastern European countries, should check that their motor insurer will provide the necessary extension of cover.**

If you are driving to or through Bosnia and Herzegovina (for example along the 20 km strip of coastline at Neum on the Dalmatian coastal highway to Dubrovnik) you should ensure that you have obtained Green Card cover for Bosnia and Herzegovina. If you have difficulties obtaining such cover before departure contact the Club's Travel Service Information Officer for advice. Alternatively, temporary third-party insurance can be purchased at the country's main border posts, or in Split and other large cities. It is understood that it is not generally obtainable at the Neum border crossing itself. For Club members insured under the Caravan Club's Car Insurance and Motor Caravan Insurance schemes full policy cover is available for the 20 km strip of coastline from Neum.

Bail Cover for Spain

Although Spain's incorporation into the European Union has removed the need to provide this cover, as a precautionary measure bail cover will continue to be provided with the Caravan Club's Red Pennant Motoring & Personal Holiday Insurance.

Caravans Stored Abroad

Caravan insurers will not normally insure caravans left on campsites or in storage abroad. In these circumstances specialist policies are available from Towergate Bakers on 01242 528844, www.towergatebakers. co.uk, email bakers@towergate.co.uk or Drew Insurance, tel 0845 4565758, www. drewinsurance.co.uk, email mail@kdib.co.uk

Legal Costs Abroad

A person who is taken to court following a road traffic accident in a European country runs the risk of having to pay legal costs personally, even if (s)he is cleared of any blame.

Motor insurance policies in the UK normally include cover for legal costs and expenses incurred with the insurer's consent and arising from any incident that is covered under the terms and conditions of the policy. The Caravan Club's Car Insurance and Motor Caravan Insurance schemes incorporate such cover and, in addition, offer an optional legal expenses insurance that may be able to help you recover any other losses that are not covered by your motor insurance policy. Similar optional legal expenses insurance is also offered as an addition to the Club's 5Cs Caravan Insurance scheme.

Holiday Travel Insurance

Having insured your vehicles, there are other risks to consider and it is essential to take out adequate travel insurance. The Caravan Club's Red Pennant Motoring & Personal Holiday Insurance is designed to provide as full a cover as possible, in keeping with a reasonable fee. The Club's scheme is tailor-made for the caravanner and motor caravanner and includes cover against the following:

- Recovery of vehicles and passengers
- Towing charges
- Emergency labour costs
- Chauffeured recovery
- Storage fees
- Spare parts location and despatch
- Continuation of holiday travel, ie car hire etc
- Continuation of holiday accommodation, ie hotels etc
- Emergency medical and hospital expenses
- Legal expenses
- Emergency cash transfers

- Loss of deposits/cancellation cover
- Personal accident benefits
- Personal effects and baggage insurance
- Loss of cash or documents
- Cost of telephone calls

If you are prroposing to participate in dangerous sports activities such as skiing, hang-gliding or mountaineering, check that your personal holiday insurance includes cover for such sports and that it incorporates mountain rescue and helicopter rescue costs.

Look carefully at the exemptions to your insurance policy, including exemptions relating to pre-existing medical conditions or the use of alcohol. Be sure to declare any pre-existing medical conditions to your insurer.

Club members can obtain increased cover by taking out Red Pennant **Plus** cover. The Club also offers a range of annual multi-trip and long stay holiday insurance schemes for Continental and worldwide travel. For more details and policy limits refer to the Travel Service in Europe and/or Overseas Holiday Insurance brochures from the Caravan Club. Alternatively see www.caravanclub.co.uk for details or telephone 01342 336633.

Holiday Insurance for Pets

The Club's Red Pennant Motoring & Personal Holiday Insurance covers extra expenses in respect of your pet that may arise as part of a claim for an incident normally covered under the Red Pennant policy. It does not, however, cover costs arising from an injury to, or the illness of your pet, or provide any legal liability cover to you as a pet owner.

See our website, www. caravanclub.co.uk for details of our Pet Insurance scheme

---

It is a wise precaution, therefore, to ensure that you have adequate travel insurance for your pet in the event of an incident or illness abroad requiring extensive veterinary treatment, emergency repatriation or long-term care if necessary treatment lasts longer than your holiday. Contact the Caravan Club on 0800 0151396 or see our website, www.caravanclub.co.uk for details of our Pet Insurance scheme, specially negotiated to take into account Club members' requirements both at home and abroad.

Home Insurance

Most home insurers require advance notification if you are leaving your home empty for 30 days or more. They often require that mains services (except electricity) are turned off, water drained down and that somebody visits the home once a week. Check your policy documents or speak to your insurer/broker.

The Caravan Club's Home Insurance policy provides full cover for up to 90 days when you are away from home, for instance when touring, and requires only common sense precautions for longer periods of unoccupancy. Contact 0800 0284815 or see www.caravanclub.co.uk for details of our Home Insurance scheme, specially negotiated to suit the majority of Club members' requirements.

Marine Insurance

Car Ferries

Vehicles accompanied by the owner are normally conveyed in accordance with the terms of the carrying companies' published bye-laws or conditions, and if damage is sustained during loading, unloading or shipment, this must be reported at the time to the carrier's representative. Any claim arising from such damage must be notified in writing to the carrier concerned within three days of the incident. It is unwise to rely on being able to claim from the carrier in respect of damage etc, and transit insurance is advised.

The majority of motor policies cover vehicles during short sea crossings up to 65 hours' normal duration – check with your insurer. The Caravan Club's 5Cs policy automatically covers you for crossings of any length within the area covered by Red Pennant Motoring & Personal Holiday Insurance.

Boats

The Royal Yachting Association recommends that all boats have marine insurance. Third party insurance is compulsory for some of the countries covered by this guide, together with a translation of the insurance certificate into the appropriate language(s). Check with your insurer/broker before taking your boat abroad.

Medical Insurance

*See the chapter **Medical Matters** in the section* ***DURING YOUR STAY***.

Personal Effects Insurance

The majority of travellers are able to cover their valuables such as jewellery, watches, cameras, bicycles and, in some instances, small craft under the All Risks section of their Householders' Comprehensive Policy.

Vehicles Left Behind Abroad

If you are involved in an accident or breakdown while on the Continent which requires you to leave a vehicle behind when you return home, you must ensure that your normal insurance cover is maintained to cover the period that the vehicle remains on the Continent, and that you are covered for the journey back to your home address.

You should remove all items of baggage and personal effects from your vehicle before leaving it unattended. If this is not possible you should check with your insurer/broker to establish whether extended cover can be provided. In all circumstances, you must remove any valuables and items which might attract Customs duty, including wines, beer and spirits.

International Holidays 2008

International Holidays, Important Dates & UK Bank Holidays

January	1	Tuesday	New Year's Day
	6	Sunday	Epiphany
	10	Thursday	Al Hijra – Islamic New Year*
February	6	Wednesday	Ash Wednesday
	7	Thursday	Chinese New Year*
March	1	Saturday	St David's Day
	16	Sunday	Palm Sunday (start of Holy Week)
	17	Monday	St Patrick's Day
	21	Friday	Good Friday, Bank Holiday UK
	23	Sunday	Easter Day
	24	Monday	Easter Monday, Bank Holiday UK
	30	Sunday	British Summer Time begins
April	23	Wednesday	St George's Day
	27	Sunday	Christian Orthodox Easter Day
May	1	Thursday	Ascension Day
	5	Thursday	May Bank Holiday UK
	11	Sunday	Whit Sunday (Pentecost)
	22	Thursday	Corpus Christi
	26	Monday	Spring Bank Holiday UK
August	15	Friday	Assumption
	25	Monday	Bank Holiday UK
September	1	Monday	First day of Ramadan
	30	Tuesday	Jewish New Year (Rosh Hashanah)
October	1	Wednesday	Ramadan ends*
	9	Thursday	Jewish Day of Atonement (Yom Kippur)
	26	Sunday	British Summer Time ends
	31	Friday	Halloween
November	1	Saturday	All Saints' Day
	9	Sunday	Remembrance Sunday
	30	Sunday	St Andrew's Day
December	8	Monday	Immaculate Conception
	25	Thursday	Christmas Day
	26	Friday	St Stephen's Day; Boxing Day UK

* Subject to the lunar calendar

NOTES   1) When a holiday falls on a Sunday it will not necessarily be observed the following day.

               2) Public holidays in individual countries are listed in the relevant Country Introductions.

Money

Take your holiday money in a mixture of cash, credit and debit cards and travellers' cheques or pre-paid travel cards. Do not rely exclusively on only one method of payment.

See **Customs** in the section **DURING YOUR STAY** for information about declaring the amount of cash you carry when entering or leaving the EU.

Local Currency

Take sufficient foreign currency in the form of cash for your immediate needs on arrival, including loose change if possible. Even if you intend to use credit and debit cards for most of your holiday spending, it makes sense to take some cash to tide you over until you are able to find a cash machine (ATM) and you may need change for parking meters or the use of supermarket trolleys.

Many High Street banks, exchange offices and travel agents offer commission-free foreign exchange, whereas some will charge a flat fee which makes it more economic to change large amounts of cash, and some offer a 'buy back' service. Most stock the more common currencies, but it is wise to order in advance in case demand is heavy or if you require an unusual currency.

Shop around and compare commission and exchange rates

Currency can also be ordered by telephone or online for delivery to your home or office address on payment of a handling charge. For example, the Post Office allows you to order currency by telephone (08458 500900) or online for collection at any post office the next day, see www.postoffice.co.uk. There are a number of other online suppliers, eg www.travelex.co.uk, and most of the High Street banks offer their customers an online ordering service. It can pay to shop around and compare commission and exchange rates, together with minimum charges.

If you pay for your currency with a credit/debit card the card issuer may charge a cash advance fee, in addition to the commission and/or handling charge. Maestro cards do not incur a cash advance fee.

Visitors have reported that banks and money exchanges in eastern Europe may not be willing to accept Scottish and Northern Irish bank notes and may be reluctant to change any sterling which has been written on, is creased or worn or is not in virtually mint condition.

Exchange rates (as at September 2007) are given in the Country Introductions in this guide. Up to date currency conversion rates can be obtained from your bank or national newspapers. Alternatively, www.oanda.com updates currency rates around the world daily and allows you to print a handy currency converter to take with you on your trip.

Travellers' Cheques

Travellers' cheques can be cashed or used as payment for goods or services in almost all countries, and are the safest way of carrying large sums of money. They can be replaced quickly — usually within 24 hours — in the event of loss or theft. Travellers' cheques may be accepted where credit cards are not and are useful if you are travelling off the beaten track or in far-flung locations, but bear in mind that small bank branches may not offer foreign exchange services. Commission is payable when you buy the cheques and/or when you cash them in. See the Country Introductions for more information.

While it is now possible to buy euro travellers' cheques for use within the euro zone, in practice their use can be limited. Recent visitors report difficulties in finding a bank that will cash them for non-account holders, and where they are accepted high commission charges may be incurred. In addition retailers are often unwilling to handle them, many preferring debit or credit cards.

American Express (www.americanexpress.co.uk) publishes a list of European banks which should provide fee-free encashment of their travellers' cheques. Information on where to cash MasterCard and Visa travellers' cheques, and the fees charged, can be found on www.cashmycheques.com

US dollar travellers' cheques or, more recently, euro travellers' cheques can be used for payment in countries which have a 'soft' currency, ie one which cannot be traded on the international markets. Your bank will advise you.

Travel Money Cards

An increasingly popular and practical alternative to travellers' cheques is a pre-paid, PIN protected travel money card, offering the security of travellers' cheques with the convenience of plastic. Load the card with the amount you need (in euros, sterling or US dollars) before leaving home, and then simply use cash machines to make withdrawals and present it to pay for goods and services in shops and restaurants as you would a credit or debit card. You may obtain a second card so that another user can access the funds and you can also top the card up while abroad over the telephone or the internet.

These cards, which work like a debit card – except there are usually no loading or transaction fees to pay – can be cheaper to use than credit or debit cards for both cash withdrawals and purchases. They are issued by the Post Office, Travelex, Lloyds Bank, American Express, and Cash2Go (www.cash2go.com) amongst others. For a comparison table see www.which-prepaid-card.co.uk

Credit and Debit Cards

Credit cards and debit cards are a convenient and safe way of spending abroad and increasingly holidaymakers use them for the bulk of their purchases. In addition to using a card to pay for goods and services wherever your card logo is displayed, you can obtain cash advances at most banks, and money can be obtained from cash machines with the same PIN as you use in the UK. MasterCard and Visa list the location of their cash dispensers in countries throughout the world on www.mastercard.com and http://visa.via.infonow.net/locator/eur

For credit card use abroad most banks impose a foreign currency conversion charge (up to 2.75% per transaction) which is usually the same for both credit and debit cards. If you use your credit card to withdraw cash there will be a further commission charge of up to 2% and you may also be charged

a higher interest rate. In line with market practice, Morgan Stanley, which issues the Caravan Club's credit card, charges a 2.75% fee for all card transactions outside the UK. Cash withdrawals abroad are subject to a 2% handling charge as in the UK, with a minimum charge of £2.

When paying with a credit or debit card retailers may offer you the choice of currency for payment, ie a euro amount will be converted into sterling and then charged to your credit card account. You will be asked to sign an agreement to accept the conversion rate used and final amount charged and, having done so, there is no opportunity to change your mind or obtain a refund. This is known as a 'dynamic currency conversion' but the exchange rate used is unlikely to be as favourable as that used by your credit/debit card issuer. You may also find retailers claiming that a sterling bill will automatically be generated when a UK-issued credit card is tendered and processed. If this is the case, then you may prefer to pay cash.

Contact your credit card issuer before you leave home to warn them that you are travelling abroad

---

Check the expiry date of your cards before you leave and memorise the PIN for each one. If you have several cards, take at least two in case you come across gaps in acceptance of certain cards, eg shops which accept only MasterCard. If you are planning an extended journey, it is possible to arrange for your credit or charge card account to be cleared each month by variable direct debit, ensuring that bills are paid on time and no interest is charged.

Credit and debit 'chip and PIN' cards issued by UK banks may not be universally accepted abroad and it is wise to check before incurring expenditure. For example, 'chip and PIN' cards have been in use in France for a number of years. However, the French system has had to be modified to make it compatible with that used in the rest of Europe and, until its system is modified across the whole country, on occasion you may still be required to sign a receipt.

Contact your credit card issuer before you leave home to warn them that you are travelling abroad. In the battle against credit card fraud, card issuers are frequently likely to query transactions which they regard as unusual or suspicious. This may result in a cash withdrawal from an ATM being declined, or a retailer at the point of sale having to telephone for authorisation and/or confirmation of your details. Difficulties can occur if there is a language barrier or if the retailer is unwilling to bother with further checks and your card may be declined or, worse still, temporarily stopped. In this instance you should insist that the retailer contacts the local authorisation centre but, in any event, it may also be helpful to carry your card issuer's helpline number with you.

Emergency Cash

If an emergency or robbery means that you need cash in a hurry, then friends or relatives at home can use the Post Office's secure, instant money transfer service. This MoneyGram service, which does not necessarily require the sender to use a bank account or credit card, enables the transfer of money to over 70,000 locations around the world. Transfers take approximately ten minutes; charges are levied on a sliding scale.

As a last resort, go to the nearest British Embassy or Consulate for help

---

Western Union operates a similar secure, worldwide service and has offices located in banks, post offices, travel agents, stations and shops. You can also transfer funds instantly by telephone on 0800 833833 (lines are open 24 hours) or online at www.westernunion.co.uk

As a last resort, go to the nearest British Embassy or Consulate for help. The Foreign & Commonwealth Office in London can arrange for a relative or friend to deposit funds which will be authorised for payment by embassy staff. See individual Country Introductions for embassy and consulate addresses abroad.

Most travel insurance policies will cover you for only a limited amount of lost or stolen cash (usually between £250 and £500) and you will probably have to wait until you return home for reimbursement.

The Euro

The euro is now the only legal tender in the following countries covered by this guide: Austria, Belgium, Finland, France, Germany, Greece, Italy, Luxembourg, the Netherlands, Portugal, Slovenia and Spain. In addition, the Republic of Ireland, Cyprus, Malta and the states of Andorra, Monte Carlo, San Marino and the Vatican City have also adopted the euro. Each country's versions of banknotes and coins are valid in all the countries of the euro zone.

Of the twelve new member states which joined the EU in 2004 and 2007 only Cyprus, Malta and Slovenia have secured agreement to join the single currency. In the meantime, you will usually find euros readily accepted in the other new member states in payment for goods and services. Denmark, Sweden and the UK, although member states of the EU, do not currently participate in the euro.

Police have issued warnings that counterfeit euro notes are in circulation on the Continent. You should be aware and take all precautions to ensure that €10, €20 and €50 notes and €2 coins you receive from sources other than banks and legitimate bureaux de change, are genuine.

Holiday Money Security

- Treat your cards and travellers' cheques as carefully as you would cash. Use a money belt, if possible, to conceal cards and valuables and do not keep all your cash, credit cards and travellers' cheques in the same place. Split cash and travellers' cheques between members of your party.

- If you keep a wallet in your pocket, place a rubber band around it, as it is then more difficult for a pickpocket to slide the wallet out without your noticing.

- To avoid credit or debit card 'cloning' never let your card out of your sight — in restaurants follow the waiter to the till or insist that the card machine is brought to your table. This is particularly important as you may frequently find that a signature on a transaction slip is not checked against the signature on your card. If you do allow your card to be taken and it is gone for more than a minute, become suspicious.

- If a manual card machine is used always check that your credit/debit card vouchers are properly filled in and in the correct currency. Take the black carbon sheets and destroy them, but always keep a copy of the voucher. It has been known for unscrupulous retailers to add a nought after a customer has signed a voucher.

- If you suspect your card has been fraudulently used, or if your card is lost or stolen, or if a cash machine retains it, call the issuing bank immediately. All the major card companies and banks operate a 24-hour emergency helpline. If you are unlucky enough to become a victim of fraud your bank should refund the money stolen, provided you have not been negligent or careless.

- Keep your card's magnetic strip away from other cards and objects, especially if they are also magnetic. If the card is damaged in any way, electronic terminals may not accept your transaction.

- Keep your travellers' cheques and sales advice slip separate so that you have a record of the numbers in case of loss. Keep a record of where and when you cash your travellers' cheques and the numbers. If they are lost or stolen, contact the appropriate refund service immediately.

- Join a card protection plan (the Caravan Club offers one to its members) so that in the event of loss or theft, one telephone call will cancel all your cards and arrange replacements. Carry your credit card

issuer/bank's 24-hour UK contact number with you.

- Take care when using cash machines. If the machine is obstructed or poorly lit, avoid it. If someone near the machine is behaving suspiciously or makes you feel uneasy, find another one. If there is something unusual about the cash machine do not use it and report the matter to the bank or owner of the premises. Do not accept help from strangers and do not allow yourself to be distracted.

- Be aware of your surroundings and if someone is watching you closely do not proceed with the transaction. Shield the screen and keyboard so that anyone waiting to use the machine cannot see you enter your PIN or transaction amount. Put your cash, card and receipt away immediately. Count your cash later and always keep your receipt to compare with your monthly statement.

- If you bank over the internet and are using a computer in a public place such as a library or internet café, do not leave the PC unattended and ensure that no-one is watching what you type. Always log off from internet banking upon completion of your session to prevent the viewing of previous pages of your online session.

*See also **Security and Safety** in the section **DURING YOUR STAY**.*

With over 200 inspected sites on offer, and great ferry deals, you won't be disappointed when you tour with our experts.
Visit: www.caravanclub.co.uk or call 01342 327410 to order a brochure.

Planning And Travelling

Motoring – Advice

Preparing For Your Journey

Caravanning is first and foremost a relaxation and to arrive at your holiday destination on edge — or worse still, not at all because of an accident on the road — is not a good way to start a holiday. Adequate and careful preparation of your vehicles should be your first priority to ensure a safe and trouble-free journey.

Make sure your car and caravan are properly serviced before you depart and take a well-equipped spares kit and a spare wheel and tyre for your caravan; the lack of this is probably the main single cause of ruined holidays.

Re-read the Technical Information section of your UK Sites Directory & Handbook as it contains a wealth of information which is relevant to caravanning anywhere in the world.

The Caravan Club offers a free advice service to Club members, whether newcomers to caravanning or old hands, on technical and general caravanning matters and publishes information sheets on a wide range of topics, all of which members can download from the Club's website. Alternatively, write to the Club's Technical Department or telephone for more details. For advice on issues specific to countries other than the UK, Club members should contact the Travel Service Information Officer.

Driving On The Continent

Probably the main disincentive to travelling abroad, particularly for caravanners, is the need to drive on the right-hand side of the road. However, for most people this proves to be no problem at all after the first hour or so. There are a few basic, but important, points to remember:

Buy a good road map or atlas and plan ahead to use roads suitable for towing. See *Route Planning and GPS* in the chapter *Motoring-Equipment.*

- In your eagerness to reach your destination, don't attempt vast distances in a single stint. Share the driving, if possible, and plan to break your journey overnight at a suitable site. There are thousands of sites listed in this guide and many are well situated near motorways and main roads.

- Adjust all your mirrors for maximum rear-view observation.

- Make sure the road ahead is clear before overtaking. Stay well behind the vehicle in front and, if possible, have someone with good judgement in the left-hand seat to give you the 'all clear'.

- If traffic builds up behind you, pull over safely and let it pass.

- Pay particular attention when turning left, when leaving a rest area/service station/campsite, or after passing through a one-way system to ensure that you continue to drive on the right-hand side of the road.

- If your headlights are likely to dazzle other road users, adjust them to deflect to the right instead of the left, using suitable beam deflectors or (in some cases) a built-in adjustment system. Some lights can have the deflective part of the lens obscured with tape or a pre-cut adhesive mask, but check in your car's handbook if this is permitted or not. Some lights run too hot to be partially obscured.

- While travelling, particularly in the height of the summer, it is wise to stop approximately every two hours (at the most) to stretch your legs and take a break.

- In case of breakdown or accident, use hazard warning lights and warning triangle(s).

Another disincentive for caravanners to travel abroad is the worry about roads and gradients in mountainous countries. Britain has worse gradients on many of its main roads than many other European countries and traffic density is far higher.

The chapter *Mountain Passes and Tunnels* under *PLANNING AND TRAVELLING* gives detailed advice on using mountain passes.

Another worry involves vehicle breakdown and language difficulties. The Caravan Club's comprehensive and competitively priced Red Pennant Motoring & Personal Holiday Insurance is geared to handle all these contingencies with multi-lingual staff available at the Club's headquarters 24 hours a day throughout the year.

Some Final Checks

Experienced caravanners will be familiar with the checks necessary before setting off, and the following list is a reminder:

- All car and caravan lights are working and a set of spare bulbs is packed.
- The coupling is correctly seated on the towball and the breakaway cable is attached.
- All windows, vents, hatches and doors are shut.
- All on-board water systems are drained.
- Car wing mirrors are adjusted for maximum visibility.
- Corner steadies are fully wound up and the brace is handy for your arrival on site.
- Any fires or flames are extinguished and the gas cylinder tap is turned off. Fire extinguishers are fully charged and close at hand.
- The over-run brake is working correctly.
- The jockey wheel is raised and secured, the handbrake is released.

Driving Offences

You are obliged to comply with the traffic rules and regulations of the countries you visit. Since March 2007 there has been no escaping fines for motoring offences in another EU country. The registration number of an offender's vehicle will be sent to the DVLA and you will eventually receive a penalty notice and demand for payment. Failure to pay will result in court proceedings.

Some foreign police officers can look rather intimidating to British visitors used to unarmed police. Needless to say, they expect you to be polite and show respect and, in return, they are generally helpful and may well be lenient to a visiting motorist. Never consider offering a bribe!

The authorities in many countries are hard on parking and speeding offenders. In Scandinavia, for example, fines for speeding are spectacularly high and speed traps so frequent that it is not worth taking the risk of driving over the speed limit. Visiting motorists should not be influenced by the speed at which locals drive; they often know where the speed traps are and can slow down in time to avoid being caught! In addition, driver education in some European countries — and consequently driving standards — is still poor.

In general, it is no use protesting if caught, as those who refuse to pay may have their vehicle impounded.

Many police forces are authorised to carry out random breath tests

---

The maximum legal level of alcohol in the blood in most Continental countries is lower than that in the UK, and many police forces are authorised to carry out random breath tests. It is wise to adopt the 'no drink when driving' rule at all times; offenders are heavily fined all over Europe and penalties can include confiscation of driving licence, vehicle(s) and even imprisonment.

Be particularly careful if you have penalty points on your driving licence. If you commit an offence on the Continent which attracts penalty points, local police may well do checks on your licence to establish whether the addition of those points would render you liable to disqualification. You will then have to find other means to get yourself and your vehicle(s) home.

On-the-Spot Fines

Many countries allow their police officers to issue fines which must be paid on-the-spot, up to certain limits. These may be a deposit for a larger fine which will be issued to your home address. In most countries credit cards are not accepted in payment of on-the-spot fines and you may find yourself accompanied to the nearest cash machine. Always obtain a receipt for money handed over.

Fuel

During ferry crossings make sure your petrol tank is not over-full. Don't be tempted to carry spare petrol in cans; the ferry companies and Eurotunnel forbid this practice and even the carriage of empty cans is prohibited.

Grades of petrol sold on the Continent are comparable to those sold in the UK with the same familiar brands on sale; 3 Star is frequently known as 'Essence' and 4 Star as 'Super'. Diesel is sometimes called 'Gasoil' and is available in all the countries covered by this guide. The fuel prices given in the table at the end of this chapter were correct according to the latest information available in September 2007. Fuel prices and availability can be checked on the AA's website, www.theaa.com

In sparsely populated regions, such as northern Scandinavia, it is a sensible precaution to travel with a full petrol tank and to keep it topped up. Similarly in remote rural areas of any country you may have difficulty finding a petrol station open at night or on Sunday.

Automotive Liquified Petroleum Gas (LPG)
The increasing popularity of LPG and use of dual-fuelled vehicles means that the availability of automotive LPG has become an important issue for some drivers, and the Country Introductions in this guide provide more information. There is a European guide published by EuroGeografiche Mencattini in Italy, listing approximately 13,000 LPG refuelling stations in 26 European countries. Contact EGM, Via Po, 52100 Arezzo, Italy, tel 0039 0575 900010, fax 0039 0575 911161, http://new. eurogasauto.egm.it/en, email eurogeo@egm.it. The website www.cfbp.fr allows you to search on a map of Europe for LPG sales outlets in all the countries covered by this guide.

There are different tank-filling openings in use in different countries. Pending the adoption of a common European filling system, the Liquid Petroleum Gas Association and the major fuel suppliers recommend the use of either of the two types of Dutch bayonet fitting. The LPGA also recommends that vehicle-filling connections requiring the use of adaptors in order to fill with the Dutch bayonet filling guns, should not be used. However, the Club recognises that in some circumstances it may be necessary to use an adaptor and these are available from Autogas 2000 Ltd on 01845 523213, www.autogas.co.uk

Lead Replacement Petrol
Leaded petrol has been withdrawn from sale in many countries in Europe and, in general, is only available from petrol stations as a bottled additive. Where lead replacement petrol is still available at the pump it is generally from the same pumps previously used for leaded petrol, ie red or black pumps, and may be labelled 'Super Plus', 'Super 98' or 'Super MLV', but it is advisable to check before filling up if this is not clear from information at the pump.

See the **Fuel Price Guide Table** at the end of this chapter.

Motor Caravans Towing Cars

A motor caravan towing a small car is illegal in most European countries, although such units are sometimes encountered. Motor caravanners wishing to tow a small car abroad should transport it on a braked trailer so that all four of the car's wheels are off the road.

Motorway Tolls

For British drivers who may never, or rarely, have encountered a toll booth, there are a couple of points to bear in mind. First of all, you will be on the 'wrong' side of the car for the collection of toll tickets at the start of the motorway section and payment of tolls at the end. If you are travelling without a front seat passenger, this can mean a big stretch or a walk round to the other side of the car. Most toll booths are solidly built and you should be careful of any high concrete kerbs when pulling up to them.

On entering a stretch of motorway you will usually have to stop at a barrier and take a ticket from a machine to allow the barrier to rise. Avoid the lanes dedicated to vehicles displaying electronic season tickets. You may encounter toll booths without automatic barriers where it is still necessary to take a ticket and, if you pass through without doing so, you may be fined. On some stretches of motorway there are no ticket machines as you enter and you simply pay a fixed sum when you exit.

Your toll ticket will indicate the time you entered the motorway. Be warned that in some countries electronic tills at exit booths calculate the distance a vehicle has travelled and the journey time. The police are automatically informed if speeding has taken place and fines are imposed.

Payment can be made by credit cards in most, but not all countries covered by this guide.

See **Country Introductions** for specific information.

Parking

Make sure you check local parking regulations, as heavy fines may be imposed and unattended vehicles towed away. Look out for road markings and for short-term parking zones. Big cities often have special parking regulations and it is best to ask about them on arrival. Ensure you are in possession of parking discs in towns where they are required. As a general rule, park on the right-hand side of the road in the direction of traffic flow, avoiding cycle and bus lanes and tram tracks. Vehicles should not cause an obstruction and should be adequately lit when parked at night.

No parking on Monday, Wednesday, Friday or Sunday

No parking on Tuesday, Thursday or Saturday

Fortnightly parking on alternative sides

No parking from the 1st-15th of the month

No parking from the 16th-end of the month

In parts of eastern Europe car theft may be a problem and you are advised to park only in officially designated, guarded car parks whenever possible.

Parking Facilities for the Disabled

The Blue Badge is recognised in most European countries and it allows disabled motorists to use the same parking concessions enjoyed by the citizens of the country you are visiting. Concessions differ from country to country, however, and it is important to know when and where you can and importantly, can not park. If you are in any doubt about your rights, do not park.

An explanatory leaflet 'European Parking Card for People with Disabilities' describes what the concessions are in 29 countries and gives advice on how to explain to police and parking attendants in their own language that, as a foreign visitor, you are entitled to the same parking concessions as disabled residents. It is obtainable from the Department for Transport's publications centre on 0870 1226236 (national call rate), email dft@ twoten.press.net or write to the Department for Transport (Free Literature), PO Box 236, Wetherby LS23 7NB. You may also download it from www.dft.gov.uk or www.iam.org.uk

Priority And Roundabouts

See also **Country Introductions**.

When driving on the Continent it is essential to be aware of other vehicles which may have priority over you, particularly when they join the road you are using from the right. Road signs indicate priority or loss of priority and motorists must be sure that they understand the signs.

Care should be taken at intersections and

you should never rely on being given right of way, even if you have priority, especially in small towns and villages where local, often slow-moving, traffic will take right of way. Always give way to public service and military vehicles and to buses, trams and coaches.

Never rely on being given right of way, even if you have priority

Generally, priority at roundabouts is given to vehicles entering the roundabout unless signposted to the contrary, for example in France (see Country Introduction). This is a reversal of the UK rule and care is needed when travelling anti-clockwise round a roundabout. Keep to the outside lane, if possible, to make your exit easier.

Road Signs And Markings

See also **Country Introductions**.

You will often encounter STOP signs in situations which, in the UK, would probably be covered by a Give Way sign. Be particularly careful; coming to a complete halt is usually compulsory, even if local drivers seem unconcerned by it, and failure to do so may result in a fine. Be careful too in areas where maintenance of roads may be irregular and where white lines have worn away.

A solid single or double white line in the middle of the carriageway always means no overtaking.

Direction signs in general may be confusing, giving only the name of a town on the way to a larger city, or simply the road number and no place name. They may be smaller than you expect and not particularly easy to spot. The colours of signs indicating different categories of road may differ from those used in the UK. For example, motorway signs may be green (not blue) and non-motorway signs may be blue, rather than green as they are in the UK. This can be particularly confusing, for example when crossing from France where motorway signs are blue, into Switzerland or Italy where they are green.

Across the EU you will find that major routes have not only an individual road number, such as A6, but also a number beginning with an 'E' on a green and white sign. Routes running from east to west have even 'E' numbers, whereas routes running from north to south have odd 'E' numbers. This can be helpful when planning long-distance routes across international frontiers. In some countries through routes may only show the 'E' road numbers, so it would be advisable to make a note of them when planning your route.

Pedestrian Crossings

Stopping to allow pedestrians to cross the road at zebra crossings is not nearly as common a practice on the Continent as it is in the UK. Pedestrians often do not expect to cross until the road is clear and may be surprised if you stop to allow them to do so. Check your mirrors carefully when braking as other drivers behind you, not expecting to stop, may be taken by surprise. The result may be a rear-end shunt or, worse still, vehicles overtaking you at the crossing and putting pedestrians at risk.

Speed Limits

Remember speed limit signs are in kilometres per hour, not miles per hour. General speed limits in each country are given in the table at the end of this chapter. Refer to individual Country Introductions for details of any variations.

Radar-detection devices, whether in use or not, are illegal in many countries on the Continent and should not be carried in your vehicle.

Speed cameras are becoming more widespread throughout Europe but you should not expect them to be highly visible,

as they are in the UK. In many instances, for example on the German motorway network, they may be hidden or deliberately inconspicuous. The use of unmarked police cars is common.

Traffic Lights

Traffic lights may not be placed as conspicuously as they are in the UK and you may find that they are smaller, differently shaped or suspended across the road, with a smaller set on a post at the roadside. You may find that lights change directly from red to green, bypassing amber completely. Flashing amber lights generally indicate that you may proceed with caution but must give way to pedestrians and other vehicles. A green filter light should be treated with caution as you may still have to give way to pedestrians who have a green light to cross the road.

You may find that drivers are not particularly well-disciplined about stopping as they approach a light as it turns red and if they are behind you in this situation, they will expect you to accelerate through the lights rather than brake hard to stop. Therefore be cautious when approaching a green light, especially if you are in a relatively fast-moving stream of traffic. Similarly, be careful when pulling away from a green light and check left and right just in case a driver on the road crossing yours jumped a red light.

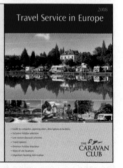

Fuel Price Guide

Country	Unleaded			Diesel
	Price and Octane Rating Available		Translation of Unleaded	
Andorra	72.0	95, 98	Sans plomb or sin plomo	58.0
Austria	80.2	95, 98	Bleifrei	73.2
Belgium	97.9	95, 98	Sans plomb or loodvrije	78.4
Croatia	73.0	95, 98	Eurosuper or bez olova	67.0
Czech Republic	78.7	95, 98	Natural or bez olova	73.3
Denmark	94.7	95, 98	Blyfri	84.3
Finland	91.6	95, 98	Lyijyton polttoaine	69.8
France	88.7	95, 98	Essence sans plomb	76.1
Germany	93.1	91, 95, 98	Bleifrei	79.7
Gibraltar	67.0	95		67.0
Greece	72.0	95, 100	Amoliwdi wensina	68.8
Hungary	77.8	95, 98	Olommentes uzemanyag	70.5
Italy	90.8	95, 98	Sensa piombo	85.7
Luxembourg	77.2	95, 98	Sans plomb	64.3
Netherlands	101.6	95, 98	Loodvrije	75.9
Norway	106.6	95, 98	Blyfri	95.1
Poland	80.0	95, 98	Bezolowiu	68.5
Portugal	96.8	95, 98	Sem chumbo	76.3
Slovakia	80.6	91, 95, 98	Natural or olovnatych prisad	77.7
Slovenia	72.3	95, 98	Brez svinca	68.9
Spain	73.7	95, 98	Sin plomo	67.9
Sweden	87.6	95, 98	Blyfri normal, premium	81.6
Switzerland	73.8	95, 98	Bleifrei or sans plomb or sensa piomba	76.0

Fuel prices courtesy of the Automobile Association (Aug 2007)

Prices shown are in pence per litre and use currency exchange rates at the time this guide was compiled. They should be used for guideline comparison purposes only. Differences in prices actually paid may be due to currency and oil price fluctuations as well as regional variations within countries.

In many countries leaded petrol has been withdrawn and Lead Replacement Petrol (LRP) is becoming more difficult to find. Alternatively a lead substitute additive can be bought at petrol stations and added to the fuel tanks of cars which run on leaded petrol. It is understood that it is the same additive as used in the UK and that 10ml will treat 10 litres of petrol.

Speed Limits

Country	Built-Up Areas	Open Road		Motorways		
		Solo	Towing	Solo	Towing	Minimum Speed
Andorra	40	70	70	n/a	n/a	n/a
Austria*	50	100	80	110-130	100	60
Belgium*	30-50	90	90	120	120	70
Croatia*	50	90-100	80	110-130	80	40
Czech Republic*	50	80-90	80	130	80	80
Denmark*	50	80-90	70	110-130	80	40
Finland*	50	80-100	80	100-120	80	-
France* Normal	50	90	90	110-130	110-130	80
France* Bad Weather	50	80	80	110	110	-
Germany*	50	100	80	130**	80	60
Greece	50	90-110	80	120	80	-
Hungary	50	90-110	70	130	80	-
Italy*	50-70	90-110	70	130	80	40
Luxembourg*	50	90	75	130	90	-
Netherlands*	50	80-100	80	120	80	60
Norway*	50	80	80	90-100	80	-
Poland*	50-60	90-110	70-80	130	80	40
Portugal*	50	90-100	70-80	120	100	50
Slovakia*	60	90	80	130	80	50
Slovenia*	50	90-100	80	130	80	-
Spain*	50	90-100	70-80	120	80	60
Sweden*	50	70-90	70-90	90-110	80	-
Switzerland*	50	80	80	100-120	80	60

Kilometres per hour (see Conversion Table below for equivalent miles per hour)

Converting Kilometres to Miles

km/h	20	30	40	50	60	70	80	90	100	110	120	130
mph	13	18	25	31	37	44	50	56	62	68	74	81

NOTES: 1) * See Country Introductions for further details, including special speed limits, eg for motor caravans, where applicable.

2) ** No upper limit on some limited sections.

3) In some countries speed limits in residential areas may be as low as 20 or 30 km/h

Motoring – Equipment

Bicycle and Motorbike Transportation

Regulations vary from country to country and, where known, these are set out in the relevant Country Introductions. As a general rule, however, separate registration and insurance documents are required for a motorbike or scooter and these vehicles, as well as bicycles, must be carried on an approved carrier in such a way that they do not obscure rear windows, lights, reflectors or number plates. Vehicles should not be overloaded, ie exceed the maximum loaded weight recommended by the manufacturer.

Car Telephones

In the countries covered by this guide it is illegal to use a hand-held car phone or mobile phone while driving; hands-free equipment should be fitted in your vehicle.

First Aid Kit

A first aid kit, in a strong dust-proof box, should be carried in case of emergency. This is a legal requirement in several countries.

See *Essential Equipment Table* at the end of this chapter and the chapter *Medical Matters*.

Fire Extinguisher

As a recommended safety precaution, an approved fire extinguisher should be carried in all vehicles. It is a legal requirement in several countries.

See *Essential Equipment Table* at the end of this chapter.

Glasses

It is a legal requirement in some countries, eg Spain, for residents to carry a spare pair of glasses if they are needed for driving and it is recommended that visitors also comply. Elsewhere, if you do not have a spare pair, you may find it helpful to carry a copy of your prescription.

Lights

When driving on the Continent headlights need to be adjusted to deflect to the right, if they are likely to dazzle other road users, by means of suitable beam deflectors or (in some cases) a built-in adjustment system. Even if you do not intend to drive at night, it is important to ensure that your headlights will not dazzle others as you may need to use them in heavy rain or fog and in tunnels. If using tape or a pre-cut adhesive mask remember to remove it on your return home. It is no longer necessary to tint headlamps yellow when visiting France.

Remember also to adjust headlights according to the load being carried and to compensate for the weight of the caravan on the back of your car.

Dipped headlights should be used in poor weather conditions such as fog, snowfall or heavy rain and in a tunnel even if it is well lit, and you may find police waiting at the end of a tunnel to check vehicles. In some countries dipped headlights are compulsory at all times, in others they must be used in built-up areas, on motorways or at certain times of the year.

Take a full set of spare light bulbs. This is a legal requirement in several countries.

See *Essential Equipment Table* at the end of this chapter.

On the Continent headlight flashing is used as a warning of approach or as an overtaking signal at night, and not, as in the UK, an indication that you are giving way, so use with great care in case it is misunderstood. When another driver flashes you, make sure of his intention before moving.

Hazard Warning Lights

Generally hazard warning lights should not be used in place of a warning triangle, but they may be used in addition to it.

Nationality Plate

A nationality plate of an authorised design must be fixed to the rear of the car and caravan on a vertical or near-vertical surface. Checks are made and a fine may be imposed for failure to display a correct nationality plate. These are provided free to members taking out the Caravan Club's Red Pennant Motoring & Personal Holiday Insurance.

Regulations allow the optional display of the GB or Euro-Symbol – a circle of stars on a blue background, with the EU Member State's national identification letter(s) below – on UK car registration number plates and, for cars with such plates, the display of a conventional nationality sticker or plate is unnecessary when driving within the EU. However, it is still required when driving outside the EU (except in Switzerland) even when number plates incorporate the Euro-Symbol, and it is still required for all vehicles without Euro-Symbol plates. Registration plates displaying the GB Euro-Symbol must comply with the appropriate British Standard. GB is the only permissible national identification code for cars registered in the UK.

Rear View/Wing Mirrors

In order to comply with local regulations and avoid the attention of local police forces, ensure that your vehicle's external wing mirrors are adjusted correctly to allow you to view both sides of your caravan or trailer – over its entire length – from behind the steering wheel. Some countries stipulate that wing mirrors should extend beyond the width of the caravan but should be removed or folded in when travelling solo, and this is common-sense advice for all countries.

Reflectorised Jackets

Legislation has been introduced in some countries in Europe (see individual Country Introductions) requiring drivers to wear a reflectorised jacket or waistcoat if leaving a vehicle which is immobilised on the carriageway outside a built-up area (day or night). This is a common-sense requirement which will probably be extended to other countries and which should be observed wherever you drive. A second jacket is also recommended for a passenger who may need to assist in an emergency repair. Carry the jackets in the passenger compartment of your vehicle, rather than in the boot. The jackets are widely available from motor accessory shops and should conform to at least European Standard EN471, Class 2.

Route Planning and GPS

The AA Information Centre provides information on UK roads including routes to ferry ports on 09003 401100 or 401100 from a mobile phone (calls charged at 60p per minute). Both the AA and RAC have useful websites with access for non-members: www.theaa.com and www.rac.co.uk

Detailed, large-scale maps or atlases of the countries you are visiting are essential. Navigating your way around other countries can be confusing, especially for the novice, and the more care you take planning your route, the more enjoyable your journey will be. Before setting out, study maps and distance charts.

There are a number of websites offering a European routes service and/or traffic information, such as www.theaa.com, www. viamichelin.com and www.mappy.com which, amongst other things, provides city centre maps for major towns across Europe. If you propose travelling across mountain passes check whether the suggested route supplied by the website takes account of passes or tunnels where caravans are not permitted or recommended.

See the chapter Mountain Passes and Tunnels.

Before setting out, study maps and distance charts

GPS systems are obviously a great help to drivers in directing them to their destination. Co-ordinates are not yet given in site entries in this guide (although this is planned) but wherever possible full street addresses are given enabling you to programme your GPS unit as accurately as possible. Continental postcodes do not, on the whole, pinpoint a particular street or part of a street in the same way that the system in use in the UK does, and a French or German five-digit postcode, for example, can cover a very large area of many square kilometres.

Seat Belts

The wearing of seat belts is compulsory in all the countries featured in this guide. On-the-spot fines will be incurred for failure to wear them and, in the event of an accident and insurance claim, compensation for injury may be reduced by 50% if seat belts are not worn. As in the UK, legislation in most countries covered by this guide requires all children up to a certain age or height to use a child restraint appropriate for their weight or size and, in addition, some countries' laws prohibit them from sitting in the front of a car. Where local regulations differ from UK law, information is given in the relevant Country Introductions.

Rear-facing baby seats must never be used in a seat protected by a frontal airbag unless the airbag has been deactivated manually or automatically.

Snow Chains

Snow chains may be necessary on some roads in winter. They are compulsory in some countries during the winter where indicated by the appropriate road sign, when they must be fitted on at least two drive-wheels. Polar Automotive Ltd sells and hires out snow chains, tel 01892 519933, fax 01892 528142 (20% discount for Caravan Club members), www.snowchains.com, email: sales@snowchains.com

Spares

Caravan Spares

On the Continent it is generally much more difficult to obtain spares for caravans than for cars and it will usually be necessary to obtain spares from a UK manufacturer or dealer.

Car Spares Kits

Some motor manufacturers can supply spares kits for a selected range of models; contact your dealer for details. The choice of spares will depend on the vehicle, how long you are likely to be away and your own level of competence in car maintenance, but the following is a list of basic items which should cover the most common causes of breakdown:

- Radiator top hose
- Fan belt
- Fuses and bulbs
- Windscreen wiper blade
- Length of 12v electrical cable
- Tools, torch and WD40 or equivalent water repellent spray

Spare Wheel

Your local caravan dealer should be able to supply an appropriate spare wheel. If you have any difficulty in obtaining one, the Caravan Club's Technical Department will provide members with a list of suppliers' addresses on request.

Tyre legislation across Europe is more or less fully harmonised and, while the Club has no specific knowledge of laws on the Continent regarding the use of space-saver spare wheels, there should be no problems in using such a wheel provided its use is strictly in accordance with the manufacturer's instructions.

Towing Bracket

The vast majority of cars registered after 1 August 1998 are legally required to have a European Type approved towing bracket (complying with European Directive 94/20) carrying a plate giving its approval number and various technical details, including the maximum noseweight. The approval process includes strength testing to a higher value than provided in the previous British Standard, and confirmation of fitting to all the car manufacturer's approved mounting points. Your car dealer or specialist towing bracket fitter will be able to give further advice. Checks may be made by foreign police. This requirement does not currently apply to motor caravans.

Tyres

Safe driving and handling when towing a caravan or trailer are very important and one major factor which is frequently overlooked is tyre condition. Your caravan tyres must be suitable for the highest speed at which you can legally tow (up to 81 mph in France), not for any lower speed at which you may choose to travel. Some older British caravans (usually over six years old) may not meet this requirement and, if you are subject to a police check, this could result in an on-the-spot fine for each tyre, including the spare. Check your tyre specification before you leave and, if necessary, upgrade your tyres. The Caravan Club's technical advice leaflet 'Tyres and Wheels', available to members on the Club's website or by post, explains how to check if your tyres are suitable.

Most countries require a minimum tread depth of 1.6 mm over the central part of the whole tyre, but motoring organisations recommend at least 3 mm across the whole tyre. If you plan an extended trip and your tyres are likely to be more worn than this before you return home, replace them before you leave.

Winter tyres should be used in those countries with a severe winter climate to provide extra grip on snow and ice. If you intend to make an extended winter trip to alpine or Scandinavian areas or to travel regularly to them, it would be advisable to buy a set of winter tyres. Your local tyre dealer will be able to advise. For information on regulations concerning the use of winter tyres and/or snow chains, see the appropriate Country Introductions.

Sizes

It is worth noting that some sizes of radial tyre to fit the 13" wheels commonly used on UK caravans are virtually impossible to find in stock at retailers abroad, eg 175R13C.

Tyre Pressure

Tyre pressure should be checked and adjusted when the tyres are cold; checking warm tyres will result in a higher pressure reading. The correct pressures will be found in your car handbook, but unless it states otherwise it is wise to add an extra four to six pounds per square inch to the rear tyres of a car when towing to improve handling and to carry the extra load on the hitch.

Make sure you know what pressure your caravan tyres should be. Some require a pressure much higher than that normally used for cars. Check your caravan handbook for details.

After a Puncture

The Caravan Club does not recommend the general use of liquid sealants for puncture repair. Such products should not be considered to achieve a permanent repair, and may indeed render the tyre irreparable. If sealant is used to allow the vehicle to be removed from a position of danger, eg motorway hard shoulder, the damaged tyre should be removed from the vehicle as soon as is practical.

Following a caravan tyre puncture, especially on a single-axle caravan, it is advisable to have the opposite side (non-punctured) tyre removed from its wheel and checked inside and out for signs of damage resulting from overloading during the deflation of the punctured tyre. Failure to take this precaution may result in an increased risk of a second tyre deflation within a very short space of time.

Warning Triangles

In almost all European countries it is a legal requirement to use a warning triangle in the event of a breakdown or accident; some countries require two. It is strongly recommended that approved red warning triangles be carried as a matter of course.

A warning triangle should be placed on the road approximately 30 metres (100 metres on motorways) behind the broken down vehicle on the same side of the road. Always assemble the triangle before leaving your vehicle and walk with it so that the red, reflective surface is facing oncoming traffic. If a breakdown occurs round a blind corner, place the triangle in advance of the corner. Hazard warning lights may be used in conjunction with the triangle but they do not replace it.

See Essential Equipment Table at the end of this chapter.

Technical information compiled with the assistance of the Automobile Association.

Essential Equipment

See also the information contained in this chapter and in the
relevant Country Introductions

Country	Warning Triangle	Spare Bulbs	First Aid Kit	Additional Equipment to be Carried/Used
Andorra	Yes	Yes	Rec	Dipped headlights in poor daytime visibility.
Austria	Yes	Rec	Yes	Dipped headlights at all times. Reflectorised jacket.*
Belgium	Yes	Rec	Rec	Dipped headlights in poor daytime visibility. Reflectorised jacket.*
Croatia	Yes (2 for vehicle with trailer)	Yes	Yes	Dipped headlights at all times. All cars must have a towbar or carry a towrope. Reflectorised jacket.*
Czech Rep	Yes	Yes	Yes	Dipped headlights at all times. Wearers of glasses to carry a spare pair. Reflectorised jacket.*
Denmark	Yes	Rec	Rec	Dipped headlights at all times. Use indicators on motorways when overtaking or changing lanes & use hazard warning lights when queues or danger ahead.
Finland	Yes	Rec	Rec	Dipped headlights at all times. Winter tyres December to February.
France	Yes (2 rec)	Yes	Rec	Dipped headlights recommended at all times. Reflectorised jacket highly rec.*
Germany	Yes	Rec	Yes	Dipped headlights recommended at all times. Winter tyres.
Greece	Yes	Rec	Yes	Fire extinguisher. Dipped headlights in towns at night and in poor daytime visibility.
Hungary	Yes	Rec	Yes	Dipped headlights at all times outside built-up areas and in built-up areas at night.
Italy	Yes	Rec	Rec	Dipped headlights at all times outside built-up areas. Reflectorised jacket.*
Luxembourg	Yes	Rec	Rec	Dipped headlights at night in built-up areas and in daytime in bad weather
Netherlands	Yes	Rec	Rec	Dipped headlights at night and in bad weather.
Norway	Yes	Rec	Rec	Dipped headlights at all times. Vehicles over 3,500 kg must use snow chains in winter. Reflectorised jacket.*
Poland	Yes	Rec	Rec	Dipped headlights at all times.
Portugal	Yes	Rec	Rec	Dipped headlights in poor daytime visibility, in tunnels and on main road linking Aveiro-Vilar Formoso at Spanish frontier (IP5). Reflectorised jacket.*
Slovakia	Yes	Yes	Yes	Dipped headlights at all times between 15 Oct and 15 March. Reflectorised jacket.*
Slovenia	Yes (2 for vehicle with trailer)	Yes	Yes	Dipped headlights at all times. Hazard warning lights when reversing. Use winter tyres between 15 Nov and 15 March or carry snow chains.
Spain	Yes (2 Rec)	Yes	Rec	Dipped headlights in tunnels and on 'special' roads (roadworks).* Wearers of glasses used for driving rec to carry a spare pair. Reflectorised jacket.*
Sweden	Yes	Rec	Rec	Dipped headlights at all times. Winter tyres from 1 Dec to 31 March.
Switzerland (inc Liechtenstein)	Yes	Rec	Yes	Dipped headlights recommended at all times and in tunnels.

NOTES: 1)   All countries: seat belts (if fitted) must be worn by all passengers.

2)   Rec: not compulsory but strongly recommended.

3)   Headlamp converters, spare bulbs, fire extinguisher, first aid kit and reflectorised waistcoat are recommended for all countries.

*   See Country Introduction for further information.

European Distances

Distances are shown in kilometres and are calculated
from town/city centres along the most practical roads,
although not necessarily taking the shortest route.

1 km = 0.62 miles

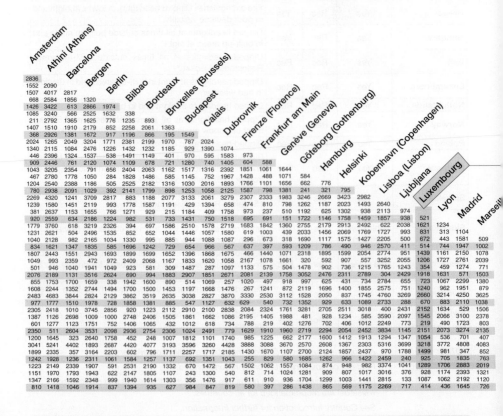

City labels (diagonal headers):
Amsterdam · Athini (Athens) · Barcelona · Bergen · Berlin · Bilbao · Bordeaux · Bruxelles (Brussels) · Budapest · Calais · Dubrovnik · Firenze (Florence) · Frankfurt am Main · Genève (Geneva) · Göteborg (Gothenburg) · Hamburg · Helsinki · København (Copenhagen) · Lisboa (Lisbon) · Ljubljana · Luxembourg · Lyon · Madrid · Marseille

2836																							
1552	2090																						
1507	4017	2817																					
668	2584	1856	1320																				
1426	3422	613	2866	1974																			
1085	3240	566	2525	1632	338																		
211	2792	1365	1625	776	1235	893																	
1407	1910	2179	852	2258	2061	1363																	
368	2926	1381	1672	917	1196	866	195	1549															
2024	1265	2049	3204	2381	2199	1970	787	2024															
1340	2115	1084	2476	1226	1432	1232	1185	929	1390	1074													
446	2396	1324	1537	538	1491	1149	401	970	595	1583	973												
909	2446	761	2120	1074	1109	678	721	1280	740	1405	604	588											
1043	3205	2354	791	656	2404	2063	1162	1517	1316	2392	1851	1061	1644										
467	2780	1778	1050	284	1828	1446	585	1145	752	1967	1428	488	1071	584									
1204	2540	2388	1186	505	2525	2182	1316	1030	2016	1893	1766	1101	1656	662	776								
780	2938	2091	1029	392	2141	1799	898	1253	1058	2125	1587	798	1381	241	321	795							
2269	4320	1241	3709	2817	883	1188	2077	3133	2061	3279	2333	1983	3246	2669	3423	2982							
1239	1580	1451	2119	993	1778	1587	1191	429	1394	658	474	810	798	1262	1187	2023	1493	2640					
381	2637	1153	1655	766	1271	929	215	1184	409	1758	973	237	510	1192	625	1302	938	2113	974				
920	2559	634	2186	1224	982	531	733	1431	750	1518	695	691	151	1722	1146	1758	1459	1857	938	521			
1779	3760	618	3219	2326	394	697	1586	2510	1578	2719	1683	1842	1360	2755	2179	2913	2492	622	2038	1621	1234		
1231	2621	504	2496	1535	852	652	1044	1446	1057	1580	619	1003	439	2033	1456	2069	1769	1727	993	831	313	1104	
1040	2128	982	2165	1034	1330	995	885	944	1088	1087	296	673	318	1690	1117	1575	1427	2205	500	672	443	1581	509
834	1621	1347	1835	585	1696	1242	729	654	966	567	637	397	593	1209	786	490	946	2570	411	514	744	1947	1002
1807	2443	1551	2943	1693	1899	1699	1652	1396	1868	1675	466	1440	1071	2318	1895	1599	2054	2774	951	1439	1161	2150	1078
1049	993	2359	472	972	2409	2068	1167	1833	1620	1058	2167	1078	1661	320	592	907	557	3252	2055	1206	1727	2761	2039
501	946	1040	1941	1049	923	581	309	1487	287	1097	1133	575	504	1478	902	736	1215	1765	1243	354	459	1274	771
2076	2189	1131	3516	2624	690	994	1883	2907	1851	2671	2081	2139	1758	3052	2476	2311	2789	304	2429	1918	1631	571	1503
855	1753	1700	1659	338	1942	1600	890	514	1069	257	1020	497	918	997	625	431	734	2784	655	723	1067	2299	1380
1608	2244	1352	2744	1494	1700	1500	1453	1197	1668	1476	267	1241	872	2119	1696	1400	1855	2575	751	1240	962	1951	879
2483	4683	3844	2824	2129	3862	3519	2635	3038	2827	3870	3330	2530	3112	1528	2050	837	1745	4760	3269	2660	3214	4250	3625
977	1777	1510	1978	728	1858	1381	885	547	1127	632	629	540	732	1352	929	633	1089	2733	288	670	883	2110	1038
2305	2418	1010	3745	2856	920	1223	2112	2910	2100	2838	2084	2324	1761	3281	2705	2511	3018	400	2431	2152	1634	529	1506
1387	1126	2698	1009	1000	2748	2406	1505	1861	1662	1086	2195	1405	1988	481	928	1234	585	3590	2097	1545	2066	3100	2378
601	1277	1123	1751	752	1406	1065	432	1012	618	734	788	219	402	1276	702	406	1012	2249	773	219	490	1723	803
2350	511	2604	3531	2098	2936	2754	2306	1024	2491	779	1629	1910	1960	2719	2294	2054	2452	3834	1145	2151	2073	3274	2135
1200	1645	323	2640	1758	452	248	1007	1812	1101	1740	985	1225	662	2177	1600	1412	1913	1294	1347	1054	536	701	407
3041	5241	4402	1893	2687	4420	4077	3193	3596	3260	4428	3888	3088	3670	2570	2608	1367	2303	5316	3699	3218	3772	4808	4083
1899	2335	357	3164	2203	602	796	1711	2257	1717	2185	1430	1670	1107	2700	2124	1857	2437	970	1788	1499	981	347	852
1242	1928	1236	2311	1061	1584	1257	1137	692	1351	1043	255	829	580	1685	1262	966	1422	2459	240	925	705	1835	763
1223	2149	2339	1907	591	2531	2190	1332	670	1472	567	1502	1062	1557	1084	874	948	982	3374	1041	1289	1706	2883	2019
1151	1970	1793	1943	622	2147	1805	1107	243	1300	540	812	714	1024	1281	909	807	1017	3016	376	928	1174	2393	1321
1347	2166	1592	2348	999	1940	1614	1303	356	1476	917	611	910	936	1704	1299	1003	1441	2815	133	1087	1062	2192	1120
810	1418	1046	1914	837	1394	935	627	984	847	819	580	397	286	1438	865	569	1175	2269	717	414	436	1645	726

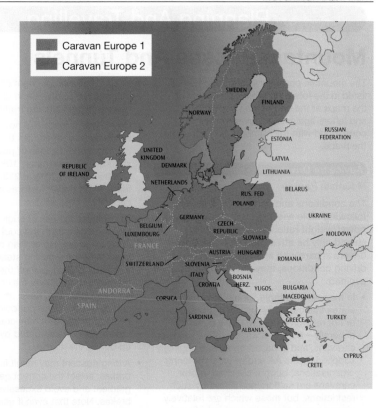

Caravan Europe 1
Caravan Europe 2

Luxembourg - Warszawa (Warsaw) = 1289 km

Distance table (diagonal labels, in order): Marseille, Milano (Milan), München (Munich), Napoli (Naples), Oslo, Paris, Porto, Praha (Prague), Roma (Rome), Rovaniemi, Salzburg, Sevilla (Seville), Stockholm, Strasbourg, Thessalonika, Toulouse, Tromso, Valencia, Venzia (Venice), Warszawa (Warsaw), Wien (Vienna), Zagreb, Zürich

```
509
1002  497
1078  763  1104
2039  1707 1525 2634
771   847  834  1600 1483
1503  1979 2344 2548 3057 1572
1380  868  379  1487 1313 1026 2592
879   564  905  217  2435 1402 2350 1288
3625  3159 2684 3817 1560 2941 4581 2505 3604
1038  544  139  1096 1668 990  2508 372  897  2821
1506  1982 2348 2551 3286 1801 626  2700 2352 4733 2510
2378  2033 1553 2662 538  1823 3398 1341 2463 1170 1697 3627
803   488  359  1255 1293 490  2056 595  1056 2742 516  2124 1619
2135  1642 1577 2116 3035 2426 3655 1688 1903 4197 1446 3631 3082 1952
407   883  1249 1452 2182 696  1102 1601 1253 3748 1411 1228 2520 1026 2508
4083  3717 3242 4375 1720 3499 5139 3063 4162 597  3385 5291 1719 3300 4755 4306
852   1328 1694 1897 2705 1387 925  2046 1698 4189 1857 663  3044 1471 2949 637  4767
763   269  472  722  2001 1110 2234 808  523  3178 433  2237 2029 740  1392 1137 3736 1582
2019  1516 994  1969 1400 1606 3181 612  1770 3340 1456 852  1234 1702 2240 3274 2685 1264
1321  827  398  1279 1597 1231 2797 284  1080 2797 291  2794 1625 760  1376 1694 3355 2140 575  686
1120  626  556  1078 2020 1407 2590 661  879  3184 428  2593 2048 933  1013 1493 3742 1939 374  993  374
726   280  312  1047 1455 586  2044 680  848  2933 437  2047 1782 230  1930 947  3491 1392 532  1319 730  806
```

Mountain Passes And Tunnels

The mountain passes, rail and road tunnels listed in the following tables are shown on the maps at the end of the chapter. Numbers and letters against each pass or tunnel correspond with the numbers and letters on the maps.

Advice for Drivers

Mountain Passes

The conditions and comments in the following table assume an outfit with good power/weight ratio. Mountain passes should only be attempted by experienced drivers in cars with ample power in good driving conditions; they should otherwise be avoided.

- In the following table, where the entry states that caravans are not permitted or not recommended to use a pass, this generally – but not always – refers to towed caravans, and is based on advice originally supplied by the AA and/or local motoring organisations, but not checked. Motor caravans are seldom prohibited by such restrictions, but those which are relatively low powered or very large should find an alternative route. Always obey roads signs at the foot of a pass, especially those referring to heavy vehicles, which may apply to some large motor caravans.

- Do not attempt to cross passes at night or in bad weather. Before crossing, seek local advice if touring during periods when the weather is changeable or unreliable. Warning notices are usually posted at the foot of a pass if it is closed, or if chains or snow tyres must be used.

- Caravanners are obviously particularly sensitive to gradients and traffic/road conditions on passes. Take great care when negotiating blind hairpins. The maximum gradient is usually on the inside of bends but exercise caution if it is necessary to pull out. Always engage a lower gear before taking a hairpin bend and give priority to vehicles ascending. Give priority to postal service vehicles – signposts usually show their routes. Do not go down hills in neutral gear.

- Keep to the extreme right of the road and be prepared to reverse to give way to descending/ascending traffic.

- On mountain roads it is not the gradient which taxes your car but the duration of the climb and the loss of power at high altitudes; approximately 10% at 915 metres (3000 feet), and 23% at 2133 metres (7000 feet). Turbo power restores much of the lost capacity.

- To minimise the risk of engine-overheating, take high passes in the cool of the day, don't climb any faster than necessary and keep the engine pulling steadily. To prevent a radiator boiling, pull off the road, turn the heater and blower full on and switch off airconditioning. Keep an eye on water and oil levels. Never put cold water into a boiling radiator or it may crack. Check the radiator is not obstructed by debris sucked up during the journey.

- A long descent may result in overheating brakes; select the correct gear for the gradient and avoid excessive use of brakes. Note that even if using engine braking to control the outfit's speed, the caravan brakes may activate due to the action of the overrun mechanism, causing them to overheat. Use lay-bys and lookout points to stop and allow brakes to cool.

- Snow prevents road repairs during the winter resulting in increased road works during the summer which may cause traffic delays. At times one-way traffic only may be permitted on some routes. Information will be posted at each end of the road.

- Precipitous road sides are rarely totally unguarded; on older roads stone pillars are placed at close intervals. However, those without a good head for heights should consider alternative routes.

- In mountainous areas always remember to leave the blade valve of your portable toilet open a fraction whilst travelling. This avoids pressure build-up in the holding tank. Similarly, a slightly open tap will avoid pressure build up in water pipes and fittings.

Tunnels

British drivers do not often encounter road tunnels but they are a common feature on the Continent, for example, along stretches of Italian coastline and lakes, and through mountain ranges. Tolls are usually charged for use of major tunnels.

Ensure you have enough fuel before entering a tunnel. Emergency situations often involve vehicles stranded because of a lack of fuel.

In bright sunshine when approaching a tunnel, slow down to allow your eyes to adjust and look out for poorly-lit vehicles in front of you and for cyclists. Take off sunglasses before entering a tunnel and take care again when emerging into sunshine at the other end.

Signposts usually indicate a tunnel ahead and its length. Once inside the tunnel, maintain a safe distance from the vehicle in front in case the driver brakes sharply.

Dipped headlights are usually required by law even in well-lit tunnels. Switch them on before entering a tunnel. Some tunnels may be poorly lit or unlit.

Snow chains, if used, must be removed before entering a tunnel in lay-bys provided for this purpose.

Minimum and maximum speed limits usually apply. 'No overtaking' signs must be strictly observed. Never cross central single or double lines. If overtaking is permitted in twin-tube tunnels only, bear in mind that it is very easy to under-estimate distances and speed when driving in a tunnel.

In order to minimise the effects of exhaust fumes close all car windows and set the ventilator to circulate the air, or operate the air conditioning system coupled with the recycled air option.

Watch out for puddles caused by dripping or infiltrating water.

If there is a traffic jam, switch your hazard warning lights on and stop a safe distance from the vehicle in front. Sound the horn only in a real emergency. Never change driving direction unless instructed to do so by tunnel staff or a police officer.

If you break down, try to reach the next lay-by and call for help from the nearest emergency phone. Modern tunnels have video surveillance systems to ensure prompt assistance in an emergency. If you cannot reach a lay-by, place your warning triangle at least 100 metres behind your vehicle. Passengers should leave the vehicle through doors on the right-hand side only.

Mountain Pass Information

- The dates of opening and closing given in the following table are approximate and inclusive. Before attempting late afternoon or early morning journeys across borders, check their opening times as some borders close at night.

- Gradients listed are the maximum at any point on the pass and may be steeper at the inside of curves, particularly on older roads.

- Gravel surfaces (such as dirt and stone chips) vary considerably; they are dusty when dry and slippery when wet. Where known to exist, this type of surface has been noted.

- In fine weather wheel chains or snow tyres will only be required on very high passes, or for short periods in early or late summer. In winter conditions you will probably need to use them at altitudes exceeding 600 metres (approximately 2000 feet).

Abbreviations

MHV	Maximum height of vehicle
MLV	Maximum length of vehicle
MWV	Maximum width of vehicle
MWR	Minimum width of road
OC	Occasionally closed between dates stated
UC	Usually closed between dates stated
UO	Usually open between dates stated, although a fall of snow may obstruct the road for 24-48 hours.

Mountain Passes and Tunnels Report Form

The Caravan Club welcomes up-to-date information on mountain passes and tunnels from caravanners who use them during the course of their holidays — use the report forms at the end of this chapter. Please complete and return as soon as possible after your journey.

Converting Gradients

20% = 1 in 5	11% = 1 in 9
16% = 1 in 6	10% = 1 in 10
14% = 1 in 7	8% = 1 in 12
12% =1 in 8	6% =1 in 16

Much of the information contained in the following tables was originally supplied by The Automobile Association and other motoring and tourist organisations. Additional updates and amendments have been supplied by caravanners using the passes and tunnels. The Caravan Club has not checked the information contained in these tables and cannot accept responsibility for their accuracy, or for errors, omissions or their effects.

Alpine Mountain Passes

Pass Height In Metres (Feet)	From To	Max Gradient	Conditions and Comments
1 Achenpass (Austria – Germany) 941 (3087)	Achenwald Glashütte	4%	UO. Well-engineered road, B181/307. Gradient not too severe.
2 Albula (Switzerland) 2312 (7585)	Tiefencastel La Punt	10%	UC Nov-early Jun. MWR 3.5m (11'6") MWV 2.25m (7'6") Inferior alternative to the Julier; tar and gravel; fine scenery. Not rec for caravans. Alternative rail tunnel. See *Rail Tunnels* in this section.
3 Allos (France) 2250 (7382)	Colmars Barcelonette	10%	UC early Nov-early Jun. MWR 4m (13'1") Very winding, narrow, mostly unguarded pass on D908 but not difficult otherwise; passing bays on southern slope; poor surface, MWV 1.8m (5'11"). Not rec for caravans.
4 Aprica (Italy) 1176 (3858)	Tresenda Edolo	9%	UO. MWR 4m (13'1") Fine scenery; good surface; well-graded on road S39. Narrow in places; watch for protruding rock when meeting oncoming traffic. Easier E - W.
5 Aravis (France) 1498 (4915)	La Clusaz Flumet	9%	OC Dec-Mar. MWR 4m (13'1"). Fine scenery; fairly easy road – D909. Poor surface in parts on Chamonix side. Some single-line traffic.
6 Arlberg (Austria) 1802 (5912)	Bludenz Landeck	13%	OC Dec-Apr. MWR 6m (19'8"). Good modern road B197/E60 with several pull-in places. Steeper fr W easing towards summit; heavy traffic. Pass road closed to caravans/trailers. Parallel road tunnel (tolls) available on E60 (poss long queues). See *Road Tunnels* in this section.
7 Ballon d'Alsace (France) 1178 (3865)	Giromagny St Maurice-sur-Moselle	11%	OC Dec-Mar. MWR 4m (13'1") Fairly straightforward ascent/descent; narrow in places; numerous bends. On road D465.
8 Bayard (France) 1248 (4094)	Chauffayer Gap	14%	UO. MWR 6m (19'8") Part of the Route Napoléon N85. Fairly easy, steepest on the S side with several hairpin bends. Negotiable by caravans from N-to-S via N75 and Col de la Croix Haute, avoiding Gap.
9 Bernina (Switzerland) 2330 (7644)	Pontresina Poschiavo	12.50%	OC Dec-Mar. MWR 5m (16'5") MWV 2.25m (7'6") Fine scenery. Good with care on open narrow sections towards summit on S-side; on road no. 29.
10 Bracco (Italy) 613 (2011)	Riva Trigoso Borghetto di Vara	14%	UO. MWR 5m (16'5") A two-lane road (P1) more severe than height suggests due to hairpins and volume of traffic; passing difficult. Rec cross early to avoid traffic. Alternative toll m'way A12 available.
11 Brenner (Europabrucke) (Austria – Italy) 1374 (4508)	Innsbruck Vipiteno/Sterzing	14%	UO. MWR 6m (19'8") On road no. 182/12. Parallel toll m'way A13/A22/E45 (6%) suitable for caravans. Heavy traffic may delay at Customs. Pass road closed to vehicles towing trailers.

	Pass Height In Metres (Feet)	From To	Max Gradient	Conditions and Comments
12	Brouis (France) 1279 (4196)	Nice *Col de Tende*	12.50%	UO. MWR 6m (19'8") Good surface but many hairpins on N204/S20. Steep gradients on approaches. Height of tunnel at Col de Tende at the Italian border is 3.8m (12'4) Not rec for caravans.
13	Brünig (Switzerland) 1007 (3340)	Brienzwiler Station *Giswil*	8.50%	UO. MWR 6m (19'8") MWV 2.5m (8'2") An easy but winding road (no. 4); heavy traffic at weekends; frequent lay-bys.
14	Bussang (France) 721 (2365)	Thann *St Maurice-sur-Moselle*	7%	UO. MWR 4m (13'1") A very easy road (N66) over the Vosges; beautiful scenery.
15	Cabre (France) 1180 (3871)	Luc-en-Diois *Aspres-sur-Buëch*	9%	UO. MWR 5.5m (18') An easy pleasant road (D93/D993), winding at Col de Cabre.
16	Campolongo (Italy) 1875 (6152)	Corvara in Badia *Arabba*	12.50%	OC Dec-Mar. MWR 5m (16'5") A winding but easy ascent on rd P244; long level stretch on summit followed by easy descent; good surface. Fine scenery.
17	Cayolle (France) 2326 (7631)	Barcelonnette *Guillaumes*	10%	UC early Nov-early Jun. MWR 4m (13'1") Narrow, winding road (D902) with hairpin bends; poor surface, broken edges with steep drops. Long stretches of single-track road with passing places. Caravans prohibited.
18	Costalunga (Karer) (Italy) 1745 (5725)	Bolzano *Pozza di Fassa*	16%	OC Dec-Apr. MWR 5m (16'5") A good well-engineered road (S241) but mostly winding with many blind hairpins. Caravans prohibited.
19	Croix (Switzerland) 1778 (5833)	Villars-sur-Ollon *Les Diablerets*	13%	UC Nov-May. MWR 3.5m (11'6") A narrow and winding route but extremely picturesque. Not rec for caravans.
20	Croix-Haute (France) 1179 (3868)	Monestier-de-Clermont *Aspres-sur-Buëch*	7%	UO on N75. MWR 5.5m (18') Well-engineered road (N75); several hairpin bends on N side.
21	Falzárego (Italy) 2117 (6945)	Cortina d'Ampezzo *Andraz*	8.50%	OC Dec-Apr. MWR 5m (16'5") Well-engineered bitumen surface on road R48; many hairpin bends on both sides.
22	Faucille (France) 1323 (4341)	Gex *Morez*	10%	UO. MWR 5m (16'5") Fairly wide, winding road (N5) across the Jura mountains; negotiable by caravans but probably better to follow route via La Cure-St Cergue-Nyon.

	Pass Height In Metres (Feet)	From To	Max Gradient	Conditions and Comments
23	Fern (Austria) 1209 (3967)	Nassereith Lermoos	10%	UO. MWR 6m (19'8"). Obstructed intermittently during winter. An easy pass on road 179 but slippery when wet; heavy traffic at summer weekends. Connects with Holzleiten Sattel Pass at S end for travel to/from Innsbruck – see below.
24	Flexen (Austria) 1784 (5853)	Lech Rauzalpe (nr Arlberg Pass)	10%	UO. MWR 5.5m (18') The magnificent 'Flexenstrasse', a well-engineered mountain road (no. 198) with tunnels and galleries. The road from Lech to Warth, N of the pass, is usually closed Nov-Apr due to danger of avalanche. Not rec for caravans.
25	Flüela (Switzerland) 2383 (7818)	Davos-Dorf Susch	12.50%	OC Nov-May. MWR 5m (16'5") MWV 2.3m (7'6") Easy ascent from Davos on road no. 28; some acute hairpin bends on the E side; bitumen surface.
26	Forclaz (Switzerland – France) 1527 (5010)	Martigny Argentière	8.50%	UO Forclaz; OC Montets Dec-early Apr. MWR 5m (16'5") MWV 2.5m (8'2") Good road over the pass and to the French border; long, hard climb out of Martigny; narrow and rough over Col des Montets on N506.
27	Foscagno (Italy) 2291 (7516)	Bormio Livigno	12.50%	OC Nov-May. MWR 3.3m (10'10") Narrow and winding road (S301) through lonely mountains, generally poor surface. Long winding ascent with many blind bends; not always well-guarded. The descent includes winding rise and fall over the Passo d'Eira 2,200m (7,218'). Not rec for caravans.
28	Fugazze (Italy) 1159 (3802)	Rovereto Valli del Pasubio	14%	UO. MWR 3.5m (11'6") Very winding road (S46) with some narrow sections, particularly on N side. The many blind bends and several hairpin bends call for extra care. Not rec for caravans.
29	Furka (Switzerland) 2431 (7976)	Gletsch Realp	11%	UC Oct-Jun. MWR 4m (13'1") MWV 2.25m (7'6") Well-graded road (no. 19) with narrow sections and several hairpin bends on both ascent and descent. Fine views of the Rhône Glacier. Beware of coaches and traffic build-up. Not rec for caravans. Alternative rail tunnel available. See *Rail Tunnels* in this section.
30	Galibier (France) 2645 (8678)	La Grave St Michel-de-Maurienne	12.50%	UC Oct-Jun. MWR 3m (9'10") Mainly wide, well-surfaced road (D902) but unguarded and narrow over summit. From Col du Lautaret it rises over the Col du Telegraphe then 11 more hairpin bends. Ten hairpin bends on descent then 5km (3.1 miles) narrow and rough; easier in north to south direction. Limited parking at summit, controlled by traffic lights; caravans are not permitted. (There is a single-track tunnel under the Galibier summit. Not rec for caravans.
31	Gardena (Grödner-Joch) (Italy) 2121 (6959)	Val Gardena Corvara in Badia	12.50%	OC Dec-Jun. MWR 5m (16'5") A well-engineered road (S243), very winding on descent. Fine views. Caravans prohibited.

	Pass Height In Metres (Feet)	From / To	Max Gradient	Conditions and Comments
32	Gavia (Italy) 2621 (8599)	Bormio Ponte di Legno	20%	UC Oct-Jul. MWR 3m (9'10") MWV 1.8m (5'11") Steep, narrow, difficult road (P300) with frequent passing bays; many hairpin bends and gravel surface; not for the faint-hearted; extra care necessary. **Not rec for caravans.** Long winding ascent on Bormio side.
33	Gerlos (Austria) 1628 (5341)	Zell-am-Ziller Wald im Pinzgau	9%	UO. MWR 4m (13'1") Hairpin ascent out of Zell to modern toll road (no. 165); the old, steep, narrow and winding route with passing bays and 14% gradient is not rec but is negotiable with care. Views of Krimml waterfalls. **Caravans prohibited.**
34	Gorges du Verdon (France) 1032 (3386)	Castellane Moustiers-Ste Marie	9%	UO. MWR probably 5m (16'5") On road D952 over Col d'Ayen and Col d'Olivier. Moderate gradients but slow, narrow and winding. Poss heavy traffic.
35	Grand St Bernard (Switzerland – Italy) 2469 (8100)	Martigny Aosta	11%	UC Oct-Jun. MWR 4m (13'1") MWV 2.5m (8' 2") Modern road to entrance of road tunnel on road no. 21/E27 (UO), then narrow but bitumen surface over summit to border; also good in Italy. Suitable for caravans using tunnel. Pass road feasible but not recommended. See *Road Tunnels* in this section.
36	Grimsel (Switzerland) 2164 (7100)	Innertkirchen Gletsch	10%	UC mid Oct-late Jun. MWR 5m (16'5") MWV 2.25m (7'6") A fairly easy, modern road (no. 6) with heavy traffic at weekends. A long winding ascent, finally hairpin bends; then a terraced descent with six hairpins into the Rhône valley. Good surface; fine scenery.
37	Grossglockner (Austria) 2503 (8212)	Bruck-an-der-Grossglocknerstrasse Heiligenblut	12.50%	UC late Oct-early May. MWR 5.5m (18') Well-engineered road (no. 107) but many hairpins; heavy traffic; moderate but very long ascent. Negotiable preferably S to N by caravans. Avoid side road to highest point at Edelweissspitze if towing, as road is very steep and narrow. Magnificent scenery. Tolls charged. Road closed from 2200-0500 hrs (summer). Alternative Felbertauern road tunnel between Lienz and Mittersil (toll). See *Road Tunnels* in this section.
38	Hahntennjoch (Austria) 1894 (6250)	Imst Elmen	15%	UC Nov-May. A minor pass; caravans prohibited.
39	Hochtannberg (Austria) 1679 (5509)	Schröcken Warth (nr Lech)	14%	OC Jan-Mar. MWR 4m (13'1") A reconstructed modern road (no. 200). W to E long ascent with many hairpins. Easier E to W. **Not rec for caravans or trailers.**
40	Holzleiten Sattel (Austria) 1126 (3694)	Nassereith Obsteig	12.50%	(12.5%), UO. MWR 5m (16'5") Road surface good on W side; poor on E. Light traffic; gradients no problem but not rec for caravans or trailers.
41	Iseran (France) 2770 (9088)	Bourg-St Maurice Lanslebourg	11%	UC mid Oct-late Jun. MWR 4m (13'1") Second highest pass in the Alps on road D902. Well-graded with reasonable bends, average surface. Several unlit tunnels on N approach. **Not rec for caravans.**

	Pass Height In Metres (Feet)	From To	Max Gradient	Conditions and Comments
42	Izoard (France) 2360 (7743)	Guillestre Briançon	12.50%	UC late Oct–mid Jun. MWR 5m (16'5"). Fine scenery. Winding, sometimes narrow road (D902) with many hairpin bends; care required at several unlit tunnels near Guillestre. Not rec for caravans.
43	Jaun (Switzerland) 1509 (4951)	Bulle Reidenbach	14%	UO. MWR 4m (13'1") MWV 2.25m (7'6") A modern but generally narrow road (no. 11); some poor sections on ascent and several hairpin bends on descent.
44	Julier (Switzerland) 2284 (7493)	Tiefencastel Silvaplana	13%	UO. MWR 4m (13'1") MWV 2.5m (8'2") Well-engineered road (no. 3) approached from Chur via Sils. Fine scenery. Negotiable by caravans, preferably from N to S. Alternative rail tunnel from Thusis to Samedan. See *Rail Tunnels* in this section.
45	Katschberg (Austria) 1641 (5384)	Spittal an der Drau St Michael	20%	UO. MWR 6m (19'8") Good wide road (no. 99) with no hairpins but steep gradients particularly from S. Suitable only light caravans. Parallel Tauern/Katschberg toll motorway A10/E55 and road tunnels. See *Road Tunnels* in this section.
46	Klausen (Switzerland) 1948 (6391)	Altdorf Linthal	10%	UC late Oct–early Jun. MWR 5m (16'5") MWV 2.25m (7' 6") Narrow and winding in places, but generally easy in spite of a number of sharp bends; no through route for caravans as they are prohibited from using the road between Unterschächen and Linthal (no. 17).
47	Larche (della Maddalena) (France – Italy) 1994 (6542)	La Condamine-Châtelard Vinadio	8.50%	OC Dec–Mar. MWR 3.5m (11'6") An easy, well-graded road (D900); long, steady ascent on French side, many hairpins on Italian side (S21). Fine scenery; ample parking at summit.
48	Lautaret (France) 2058 (6752)	Le Bourg-d'Oisans Briançon	12.50%	OC Dec–Mar. MWR 4m (13'1") Modern, evenly graded but winding road (N91), and unguarded in places; very fine scenery; suitable for caravans but with care through narrow tunnels.
49	Leques (France) 1146 (3760)	Barrême Castellane	8%	UO. MWR 4m (13'1") On Route Napoléon (N85). Light traffic; excellent surface; narrow in places on N ascent. S ascent has many hairpins.
50	Loibl (Ljubelj) (Austria – Slovenia) 1067 (3500)	Unterloibl Kranj	20%	UO. MWR 6m (19'8") Steep rise and fall over Little Loibl pass (E652) to 1.6km (1 mile) tunnel under summit. Caravans prohibited. The old road over the summit is closed to through-traffic.
51	Lukmanier (Lucomagno) (Switzerland) 1916 (6286)	Olivone Disentis	9%	UC early Nov–late May. MWR 5m (16'5") MWV 2.25m (7'6") Rebuilt, modern road.
52	Maloja (Switzerland) 1815 (5955)	Silvaplana Chiavenna	9%	UO. MWR 4m (13'1") MWV 2.5m (8'2") Escarpment facing south; fairly easy, but many hairpin bends on descent; negotiable by caravans but possibly difficult on ascent. On road no. 3/S37.

	Pass Height In Metres (Feet)	From To	Max Gradient	Conditions and Comments
53	**Mauria** (Italy) 1298 (4258)	Lozzo di Cadore *Ampezzo*	7%	UO. MWR 5m (16'5") A well-designed road (S52) with easy, winding ascent and descent.
54	**Mendola** (Italy) 1363 (4472)	Appiano/Eppan *Sarnonico*	12.50%	UO. MWR 5m (16'5") A fairly straightforward but winding road (S42), well-guarded.
55	**Mont Cenis** (France – Italy) 2083 (6834)	Lanslebourg *Susa*	12.50%	UC Nov-May. MWR 5m (16'5") Approach by industrial valley. An easy highway (N6/S25) with mostly good surface; spectacular scenery; many stopping places. Alternative Fréjus road tunnel available. See *Road Tunnels* in this section.
56	**Monte Croce di Comélico** (Kreuzberg) (Italy) 1636 (5368)	San Candido *Santo Stefano di Cadore*	8.50%	UO. MWR 5m (16'5") A winding road (S52) with moderate gradients, beautiful scenery.
57	**Montgenèvre** (France – Italy) 1850 (6070)	Briançon *Cesana Torinese*	9%	UO. MWR 5m (16'5") An easy, modern road (N94/S24) with some tight hairpin bends on French side; road widened & tunnels improved on Italian side. Much used by lorries; may be necessary to travel at their speed and give way to oncoming large vehicles on hairpins.
58	**Monte Giovo (Jaufen)** (Italy) 2094 (6870)	Merano *Vipiteno/Sterzing*	12.50%	UC Nov-May. MWR 4m (13'1") Many well-engineered hairpin bends on S44; good scenery. **Caravans prohibited.**
	Montets (See Forclaz)			
59	**Morgins** (France – Switzerland) 1369 (4491)	Abondance *Monthey*	14%	UO. MWR 4m (13'1") A lesser used route (D22) through pleasant, forested countryside crossing French/Swiss border. **Not rec for caravans.**
60	**Mosses** (Switzerland) 1445 (4740)	Aigle *Château d'Oex*	8.50%	UO. MWR 4m (13'1") MWV 2.25m (7'6") A modern road (no. 11). Aigle side steeper and narrow in places.
61	**Nassfeld (Pramollo)** (Austria – Italy) 1530 (5020)	Tröpolach *Pontebba*	20%	OC Late Nov-Mar. MWR 4m (13'1") The winding descent on road no. 90 into Italy has been improved but not rec for caravans.
62	**Nufenen (Novena) (Switzerland)** 2478 (8130)	Ulrichen *Airolo*	10%	UC Mid Oct-mid Jun. MWR 4m (13'1") MWV 2.25m (7'6") The approach roads are narrow, with tight bends, but the road over the pass is good; negotiable with care. Long drag from Ulrichen.

	Pass Height In Metres (Feet)	From To	Max Gradient	Conditions and Comments
63	Oberalp (Switzerland) 2044 (6706)	Andermatt Disentis	10%	UC Nov-late May. MWR 5m (16'5") MWV 2.5m (8'2") A much improved and widened road (no. 19) with modern surface; many hairpin bends, but long level stretch on summit. Alternative rail tunnel during the winter. See *Rail Tunnels* in this section. Caravans not permitted.
64	Ofen (Fuorn) (Switzerland) 2149 (7051)	Zernez Santa Maria-im-Münstertal	12.50%	UO. MWR 4m (13'1") MWV 2.25m (7'6") Good road (no. 28) through Swiss National Park.
65	Petit St Bernard (France – Italy) 2188 (7178)	Bourg-St Maurice Pré-St Didier	8.50%	UC mid Oct-Jun. MWR 5m (16'5") Outstanding scenery, but poor surface and unguarded broken edges near summit. Easiest from France (N90); sharp hairpins on climb from Italy (S26). Closed to vehicles towing another vehicle.
66	Pillon (Switzerland) 1546 (5072)	Le Sépey Gsteig	9%	OC Jan-Feb. MWR 4m (13'1") MWV 2.25m (7'6") A comparatively easy modern road.
67	Plöcken (Monte Croce-Carnico) (Austria – Italy) 1362 (4468)	Kötschach Paluzza	14%	OC Dec-Apr. MWR 5m (16'5") A modern road (no. 110) with long, reconstructed sections; OC to caravans due to heavy traffic on summer weekends; delay likely at the border. Long, slow, twisty pull from S, easier from N.
68	Pordoi (Italy) 2239 (7346)	Arabba Canazei	10%	OC Dec-Apr. MWR 5m (16'5") An excellent modern road (S48) with numerous hairpin bends; fine scenery. Long drag when combined with Falzarego pass.
69	Pötschen (Austria) 982 (3222)	Bad Ischl Bad Aussee	9%	UO. MWR 7m (23') A modern road (no. 145). Good scenery.
70	Radstädter-Tauern (Austria) 1738 (5702)	Radstadt Mauterndorf	16%	OC Jan-Mar. MWR 5m (16'5") N ascent steep (road no. 99) but not difficult otherwise; but negotiable by light caravans using parallel toll m'way (A10) through tunnel. See *Road Tunnels* in this section.
71	Résia (Reschen) (Italy – Austria) 1504 (4934)	Spondigna Pfunds	10%	UO. MWR 6m (19'8") A good, straightforward alternative to the Brenner Pass. Fine views but no stopping places. On road S40/180.
72	Restefond (La Bonette) (France) 2802 (9193)	Barcelonnette St Etienne-de-Tinée	16%	UC Oct-Jun. MWR 3m (9'10") The highest pass in the Alps. Rebuilt, resurfaced road (D64) with rest area at summit. Winding with hairpin bends. **Not rec for caravans.**
73	Rolle (Italy) 1970 (6463)	Predazzo Mezzano	9%	OC Dec-Mar. MWR 5m (16'5") A well-engineered road (S50) with many hairpin bends on both sides; very beautiful scenery; good surface.
	Rombo (See Timmelsjoch)			

	Pass Height In Metres (Feet)	From To	Max Gradient	Conditions and Comments
74	St Gotthard (San Gottardo) (Switzerland) 2108 (6916)	Göschenen Airolo	10%	UC mid Oct-early Jun. MWR 6m (19'8") MHV 3.6m (11'9") MWV 2.5m (8'2") Modern, fairly easy two- to three-lane road (A2/E35). Heavy traffic. Alternative road tunnel. See *Road Tunnels* in this section.
75	San Bernardino (Switzerland) 2066 (6778)	Mesocco Hinterrhein	10%	UC Oct-late Jun. MWR 4m (13'1") MWV 2.25m (7'6") Easy modern road (A13/E43) on N and S approaches to tunnel, narrow and winding over summit via tunnel suitable for caravans. See *Road Tunnels* in this section.
76	Schlucht (France) 1139 (3737)	Gérardmer Munster	7%	UO. MWR 5m (16'5") An extremely picturesque route (D417) crossing the Vosges mountains, with easy, wide bends on the descent. Good surface.
77	Seeberg (Jezersko) (Austria – Slovenia) 1218 (3996)	Eisenkappel Kranj	12.50%	UO. MWR 5m (16'5") An alternative to the steeper Loibl and Wurzen passes on B82/210; moderate climb with winding, hairpin ascent and descent. **Not rec for caravans.**
78	Sella (Italy) 2240 (7349)	Selva Canazei	11%	OC Dec-Jan. MWR 5m (16'5") A well-engineered, winding road; exceptional views of Dolomites; **caravans prohibited.**
79	Sestriere (Italy) 2033 (6670)	Cesana Torinese Pinarolo	10%	UO MWR 6m (19'8") Mostly bitumen surface on road R23. Fairly easy; fine scenery.
80	Silvretta (Bielerhöhe) (Austria) 2032 (6666)	Partenen Galtur	11%	UC late Oct-early Jun. MWR 5m (16'5") Mostly reconstructed road (188); 32 easy hairpin bends on W ascent; E side more straightforward. Tolls charged. **Caravans prohibited.**
81	Simplon (Switzerland – Italy) 2005 (6578)	Brig Domodóssola	11%	OC Nov-Apr. MWR 7m (23') MWV 2.5m (8'2") An easy, reconstructed, modern road (E62/S33), 21km (13 miles) long, continuous ascent to summit; good views. Surface better on Swiss side. Alternative rail tunnel fr Kandersteg in operation from Easter to September.
82	Splügen (Switzerland – Italy) 2113 (6932)	Splügen Chiavenna	13%	UC Nov-Jun. MWR 3.5m (11'6") MHV 2.8m (9'2") MWV 2.25m (7'6") Mostly narrow, winding road (S36), with extremely tight hairpin bends, not well guarded; care also required at many tunnels/galleries. **Not rec for caravans.**
83	Stelvio (Italy) 2757 (9045)	Bormio Spondigna	12.50%	UC Oct-late Jun. MWR 4m (13'1") MLV 10m (32') Third highest pass in Alps on S38; 40-50 acute hairpin bends either side, all well-engineered; good surface, traffic often heavy. Hairpin bends too acute for long vehicles. **Not rec for caravans.**
84	Susten (Switzerland) 2224 (7297)	Innertkirchen Wassen	9%	UC Nov-Jun. MWR 6m (19'8") MWV 2.5m (8'.2") Very scenic and well-guarded road (no. 11); easy gradients and turns; heavy traffic at weekends. Negotiable by caravans with care, but not for the faint-hearted.

	Pass Height In Metres (Feet)	From To	Max Gradient	Conditions and Comments
85	Tenda (Tende) Italy – France 1321 (4334)	Borgo S Dalmazzo Tende	9%	UO. MWR 6m (19'8") Well-guarded, modern road (S20/N204) with several hairpin bends; road tunnel (height 3.8m) at summit narrow with poor road surface. Less steep on Italian side. Caravans prohibited during winter.
86	Thurn (Austria) 1274 (4180)	Kitzbühel Mittersill	8.50%	UO. MWR 5m (16'5") MWV 2.5m (8' 2") A good road (no. 161) with narrow stretches; N approach rebuilt. Several good parking areas.
87	Timmelsjoch (Rombo) (Austria – Italy) 2509 (8232)	Obergurgl Moso	14%	UC mid Oct-Jun. MWR 3.5m (11'6") Border closed at night 8pm to 7am. The pass (road no 186/S44b) is open to private cars without trailers only (toll charged), as some tunnels on Italian side too narrow for larger vehicles. Easiest N to S.
88	Tonale (Italy) 1883 (6178)	Edolo Dimaro	10%	UO. MWR 5m (16'5") A relatively easy road (S42); steepest on W; long drag. Fine views.
89	Tre Croci (Italy) 1809 (5935)	Cortina d'Ampezzo Auronzo di Cadore	11%	OC Dec-Mar. MWR 6m (19'8") An easy pass on road R48; fine scenery.
90	Turracher Höhe (Austria) 1763 (5784)	Predlitz Ebene-Reichenau	23%	UO. MWR 4m (13'1") Formerly one of the steepest mountain roads (no. 95) in Austria; now improved. Steep, fairly straightforward ascent followed by a very steep descent; good surface and mainly two-lane; fine scenery. Not rec for caravans.
91	Umbrail (Switzerland – Italy) 2501 (8205)	Santa Maria-im-Münstertal Bormio	9%	UC Nov-early Jun. MWR 4.3m (14'1") MWV 2.25m (7'6") Highest Swiss pass (road S38); mostly tarmac with some gravel surface. Narrow with 34 hairpin bends. Not rec for caravans.
92	Vars (France) 2109 (6919)	St Paul-sur-Ubaye Guillestre	9%	OC Dec-Mar. MWR 5m (16'5") Easy winding ascent and descent on D902 with 14 hairpin bends; good surface.
93	Wurzen (Koren) (Austria – Slovenia) 1073 (3520)	Riegersdorf Kranjska Gora	20%	UO. MWR 4m (13'1") Steep two-lane road (no. 109), otherwise not particularly difficult; better on Austrian side; heavy traffic summer weekends; delays likely at the border. Caravans prohibited.
94	Zirler Berg (Austria) 1009 (3310)	Seefeld Zirl	16.50%	UO. MWR 7m (23') South facing escarpment, part of route from Garmisch to Innsbruck; good, modern road (no. 171). Heavy tourist traffic and long steep descent with one hairpin bend into Inn Valley. Steepest section from hairpin bend down to Zirl. Caravans not permitted northbound and not rec southbound.

Technical information by courtesy of the Automobile Association

Major Alpine Rail Tunnels

	Tunnel	Route	Journey Time	General Information and Comments	Contact
Ⓐ	Albula (Switzerland) 5.9km (3.5 miles)	Chur-St Moritz Thusis-Samedan	90 mins	MHV 2.85m Up to 11 shuttle services per day all year; advance booking required. Journey time 1 hour 20 minutes.	Thusis (081) 2884716 Samedan (081) 2885511 www.rhb.ch
Ⓑ	Furka (Switzerland) 15.4km (9.5 miles)	Andermatt-Brig Realp-Oberwald	15 mins	Hourly all year from 6am to 9pm weekdays; half-hourly weekends. Journey time 15 minutes.	Realp (027) 9277676 Oberwald (027) 9277666 www.fo-bahn.ch
Ⓒ	Oberalp (Switzerland) 28km (17.3 miles)	Andermatt-Disentis Andermatt-Sedrun	60 mins	MHV 2.5m 2-6 trains daily (Christmas-Easter only). Advance booking compulsory. Journey time 60 minutes.	Andermatt (027) 9277707 Sedrun (027) 9277740 www.mgbahn.ch/
Ⓓ	Lotschberg (Switzerland) 14km (8.7 miles)	Bern-Brig Kandersteg-Goppenstein	15 mins	MHV 2.9m Frequent all year half-hourly service. Journey time 15 minutes. Advance booking unnecessary; extension to Hohtenn operates when Goppenstein-Gampel road is closed.	Kandersteg (0900) 553333 www.bls.ch
Ⓔ	Simplon (Switzerland –Italy)	Brig-Domodossola Brig-Iselle	20 mins	10 trains daily, all year.	(0900) 300300 www.sbb.ch
Ⓕ	Lotschberg/Simplon Switzerland – Italy	Bern-Domodossola Kandersteg-Goppenstein	75 mins	Limited service Easter to mid-October up to 3 days a week (up to 10 times a day) for vehicles max height 2.5 m, motor caravans up to 5,000 kg. Advance booking required. Journey time 1 hour.	(033) 6504150 www.bls.ch
Ⓖ	Vereina (Switzerland) 19.6km (11.7 miles)	Klosters-Susch Selfranga-Sagliains	17 mins	MLV 12m Half-hourly daytime service all year. Journey time 18 minutes. Restricted capacity for vehicles over 3.3m high during winter w/ends and public holidays. Steep approach to Klosters.	(081) 2883737 (recorded) www.rhb.ch

NOTES: *Detailed timetable and tariff lists are available from the appropriate tourist offices.*

Major Alpine Road Tunnels

	Tunnel	Route and Height above Sea Level	General Information and Comments
G	Arlberg (Austria) 14km (8.75 miles)	Langen to St Anton 1220m (4000')	On B197 parallel and to S of Arlberg Pass which is closed to caravans/trailers. Motorway vignette required; tolls charged. www.arlberg.com
H	Bosruck (Austria) 5.5km (3.4 miles)	Spital am Pyhrn to Selzthal 742m (2434')	To E of Phyrn pass; with Gleinalm Tunnel (see below) forms part of A9 a'bahn between Linz & Graz. Max speed 80 km/h (50 mph). Use dipped headlights, no overtaking. Occasional emergency lay-bys with telephones. Motorway vignette required; tolls charged.
I	Felbertauern (Austria) 5.3km (3.25 miles)	Mittersill to Matrei 1525m (5000')	MWR 7m (23'), tunnel height 4.5m (14'9"). On B109 W of and parallel to Grossglockner pass; downwards gradient of 9% S to N with sharp bend before N exit. Wheel chains may be needed on approach Nov-Apr. Tolls charged.
J	Frejus (France – Italy) 12.8km (8 miles)	Modane to Bardonecchia 1220m (4000')	MWR 9m (29'6"), tunnel height 4.3m (14'). Min/max speed 60/70 km/h (37/44 mph). Return tickets valid until midnight on 7th day after day of issue. Season tickets are available. Approach via A43 and N6; heavy use by freight vehicles. Good surface on approach roads. Tolls charged. www.sftrf.fr
K	Gleinalm (Austria) 8.3km (5 miles)	St Michael to Fiesach (nr Graz) 817m (2680')	Part of A9 Pyhrn a'bahn. Motorway vignette required; tolls charged.
L	Grand St Bernard (Switzerland – Italy) 5.8km (3.6 miles)	Bourg St Pierre to St Rhémy (Italy) 1925m (7570')	MHV 4m (13'1"), MWV 2.55m (8'2.5"), MLV 18m (60'). Min/max speed 40/80 km/h (24/50 mph). On E27. Passport check. Customs & toll offices at entrance; breakdown bays at each end with telephones; return tickets valid one month. Although approaches are covered, wheel chains may be needed in winter. Season tickets are available. Motorway vignette required; tolls charged. For 24-hour information tel: (027) 7884400 (Switzerland) or 0165 780902 (Italy). www.sitrasb.it
M	Karawanken (Austria – Slovenia) 8km (5 miles)	Rosenbach to Jesenice 610m (2000')	On A11. Motorway vignette required; tolls charged.

Major Alpine Road Tunnels

	Tunnel	Route and Height above Sea Level	General Information and Comments
N	**Mont Blanc** (France – Italy) 11.6km (7.2 miles)	**Chamonix to Courmayeur** 1381m (4530')	MHV 4.7m (15'5"), MWV 6m (19'6") On N205 France, S26 (Italy). Max speed in tunnel 70 km/h (44 mph) – lower limits when exiting; min speed 50 km/h. Leave 150m between vehicles; ensure enough fuel for 30km. Return tickets valid until midnight on 7th day after issue. Season tickets are available. Tolls charged. www.tunnelmb.net
O	**Munt La Schera** (Switzerland – Italy) 3.5km (2 miles)	**Zernez to Livigno** 1706m (5597')	MHV 3.6m (11'9"), MWV 2.5m (8'2"). Open 8am-8pm; single lane traffic controlled by traffic lights; roads from Livogno S to the Bernina Pass and Bormio closed Dec-Apr. On N28 (Switzerland). Tolls charged Tel: (081) 8561888
P	**St Gotthard** (Switzerland) 16.3km (10 miles)	**Göschenen to Airolo** 1159m (3800')	Tunnel height 4.5m (14'9"), single carriageway 7.5m (25') wide. Max speed 80 km/h (50 mph). No tolls, but tunnel is part of Swiss motorway network (A2). **Motorway vignette** required. Tunnel closed 8pm to 5am Monday to Friday for periods during June and September. Heavy traffic and delays high season. www.gotthard-strassentunnel.ch; www.astra.admin.ch
Q	**San Bernardino** (Switzerland) 6.6km (4 miles)	**Hinterrhein to San Bernadino** 1644m (5396')	Tunnel height 4.8m (15'9"), width 7m (23'). On A13 motorway. No stopping or overtaking; keep 100m between vehicles; breakdown bays with telephones. Max speed 80 km/h (50 mph). **Motorway vignette** required.
R	**Tauern and Katschberg** (Austria) 6.4km (4 miles) & 5.4km (3.5 miles)	**Salzburg to Villach** 1340m (4396') & 1110m (3642')	The two major tunnels on the A10. Both tunnels height 4.5m (14'9"), width 7.5m (25'). **Motorway vignette** required; tolls charged.

Technical information compiled with the assistance of the Automobile Association

NOTES: Dipped headlights should be used (unless stated otherwise) when travelling through road tunnels, even when the road appears to be well lit. In some countries police make spot checks and impose on-the-spot fines.

During the winter wheel chains may be required on the approaches to some tunnels. These must not be used in tunnels and lay-bys are available for the removal and refitting of wheel chains.

For information on motorway vignettes, see the relevant Country Introductions.

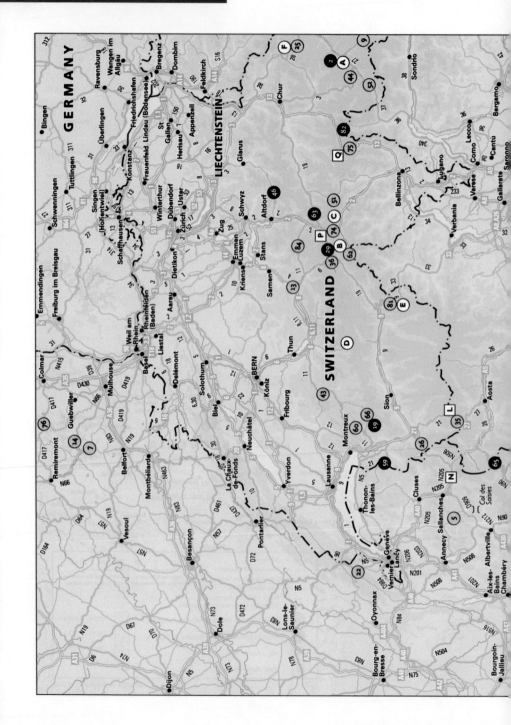

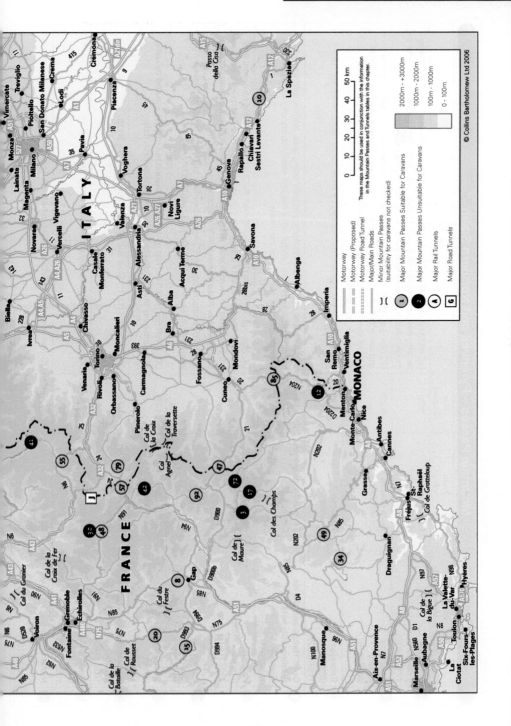

Mountain Passes – Pyrenees and Northern Spain

Pass				
Height In Metres (Feet)	**From** **To**	**Max Gradient**	**Conditions and Comments**	
101 **Aubisque** (France) 1710 (5610)	Eaux Bonnes *Argelés-Gazost*	10%	UC mid Oct-Jun. MWR 3.5m (11'6") Very winding; continuous on D918 but easy ascent; descent incl Col de Soulor 1450m (4757 feet); 8km (5miles) of very narrow, rough, unguarded road with steep drop. Not rec for caravans.	
102 **Bonaigua** (Spain) 2072 (6797)	Viella (Vielha) *Esterri d'Aneu*	8.5%	UC Nov-Apr. MWR 4.3m (14'1") Twisting, narrow road (C1412) with many hairpins and some precipitous drops. Not rec for caravans. Alternative route to Lerida (Lleida) through Viella (Vielha) Tunnel is open all year. See *Pyrenean Road Tunnels* in this section.	
103 **Cabrejas** (Spain) 1167 (3829)	Tarancon *Cuenca*	14%	UO. On N400/A40. Sometimes blocked by snow for 24 hours. MWR 5m (16')	
104 **Col d'Haltza and Col de Burdincurutcheta** (France) 782 (2565) and 1135 (3724)	St Jean-Pied-de-Port *Larrau*	11%	UO. A narrow road (D18/D19) leading to Iraty skiing area. Narrow with some tight hairpin bends; rarely has central white line and stretches are unguarded. Not for the faint-hearted. Not rec for caravans.	
105 **Envalira** (France – Andorra) 2407 (7897)	Pas de la Casa *Andorra*	12.5%	OC Nov-Apr. MWR 6m (19'8") Good road (N22) with wide bends on ascent and descent; fine views. MHV 3.5m (11'6") on N approach near l'Hospitalet. Early start rec in summer to avoid border delays. Envalira Tunnel (toll) reduces congestion. See *Pyrenean Road Tunnels* in this section.	
106 **Escudo** (Spain) 1011 (3317)	Santander *Burgos*	17%	UO. MWR probably 5m (16'5") Asphalt surface but many bends and steep gradients. Not rec in winter. On N632; A67/N611 easier route.	
107 **Guadarrama** (Spain) 1511 (4957)	Guadarrama *San Rafael*	14%	UO. MWR 6m (19'8") On NVI to the NW of Madrid but may be avoided by using AP6 motorway from Villalba to San Rafael or Villacastin (toll).	
108 **Ibañeta (Roncevalles)** (France – Spain) 1057 (3468)	St Jean-Pied-de-Port *Pamplona*	10%	UO. MWR 4m (13'1") Slow and winding, scenic route – N135.	
109 **Manzanal** (Spain) 1221 (4005)	Madrid *La Coruña*	7%	UO. Sometimes blocked by snow for 24 hours. On NVI.	
110 **Navacerrada** (Spain) 1860 (6102)	Madrid *Segovia*	17%	OC Nov-Mar. On M601/CL601. Sharp hairpins. Possible but not rec for caravans.	

	Pass Height In Metres (Feet)	From To	Max Gradient	Conditions and Comments
111	**Orduna** (Spain) 900 (2953)	Bilbao *Burgos*	15%	UO. On A625/BU556 – sometimes blocked by snow for 24 hours. Avoid by using AP68 motorway.
112	**Pajares** (Spain) 1270 (4167)	Oviedo *Léon*	16%	UO. On N630 – sometimes blocked by snow for 24 hours. **Not rec for caravans.** Avoid by using AP66 motorway.
113	**Paramo de Masa** (Spain) 1050 (3445)	Santander *Burgos*	8%	UO. On N623 – sometimes blocked by snow for 24 hours.
114	**Peyresourde** (France) 1563 (5128)	Arreau *Bagnères-de-Luchon*	10%	UO. MWR 4m (13'1") D618 somewhat narrow with several hairpin bends, though not difficult. Not rec for caravans.
115	**Picos de Europa or Puerto de San Glorio** (Spain) 1609 (5279)	Unquera *Riaño*	12%	UO. MWR probably 4m (13'1") N621 good condition but narrow and winding with some hairpin bends, especially over Puerto de San Glorio.
116	**Piqueras** 1710 (5610)	Logroño *Soria*	7%	UO. On N111 – sometimes blocked by snow for 24 hours.
117	**Port** (France) 1249 (4098)	Tarascon-sur-Ariège *Massat*	10%	OC Nov-Mar. MWR 4m (13'1") A fairly easy, scenic road (D618), but narrow on some bends.
118	**Portet d'Aspet** (France) 1069 (3507)	Audressein *Fronsac*	14%	UO. MWR 3.5m (11'6") Approached from W by the easy Col des Ares and Col de Buret; well-engineered but narrow road (D618); care needed on hairpin bends. **Not rec for caravans.**
119	**Pourtalet** (France – Spain) 1792 (5879)	Laruns *Biescas*	10%	UC late Oct-early Jun. MWR 3.5m (11'6") A fairly easy, unguarded road, but narrow in places. Easier from Spain (A136), steeper in France (D934). **Not rec for caravans.**
120	**Puymorens** (France) 1915 (6283)	Ax-les-Thermes *Bourg-Madame*	10%	OC Nov-Apr. MWR 5.5m (18') MHV 3.5m (11'6") A generally easy, modern tarmac road (N20). Parallel toll road tunnel available. See *Pyrenean Road Tunnels* in this section.
121	**Quillane** (France) 1714 (5623)	Axat *Mont-Louis*	8.5%	OC Nov-Mar. MWR 5m (16'5") An easy, straightforward ascent and descent on D118.
122	**Somosierra** (Spain) 1444 (4738)	Madrid *Burgos*	10%	OC Mar-Dec. MWR 7m (23') On A1/E5 – may be blocked following snowfalls. Snow-plough swept during winter months but wheel chains compulsory after snowfalls. Well-surfaced dual carriageway, tunnel at summit.

Planning & Travelling
MOUNTAIN PASSES & TUNNELS – Pyrenees/Spain Passes

	Pass Height In Metres (Feet)	From To	Max Gradient	Conditions and Comments
123	**Somport** (France – Spain) 1632 (5354)	Accous Jaca	10%	UO. MWR 3.5m (11'6") A favoured, old-established route; generally easy but narrow with many unguarded bends on French side (off N134); excellent road on Spanish side (GR653). Use of road tunnel advised – see *Pyrenean Road Tunnels* in this section.
124	**Toses (Tosas)** (Spain) 1800 (5906)	Puigcerda *Ribes de Freser*	10%	UO MWR 5m (16'5") A fairly straightforward, but continuously winding, two-lane road (N152) with many sharp bends; some unguarded edges.
125	**Tourmalet** (France) 2114 (6936)	Ste Marie-de-Campan *Luz-St Sauveur*	12.5%	UC Oct-mid Jun. MWR 4m (13'1") The highest French Pyrenean route (D918); approaches good, though winding, narrow in places and exacting over summit; sufficiently guarded. Rough surface & uneven edges on west side. Not rec for caravans.
126	**Urquiola** (Spain) 713 (2340)	Durango (Bilbao) *Vitoria/Gasteiz*	16%	UO. Sometimes closed by snow for 24 hours. On BI623/A623. Not rec for caravans.

Major Pyrenean Road Tunnels

	Tunnel	Route and Height Above Sea Level	General Information and Comments
AA	**Bielsa** (France – Spain) 3.2km (2 miles)	**Aragnouet to Bielsa** 1830m (6000')	Open 24 hours but possibly closed October-Easter. On French side (D173) generally good road surface but narrow with steep hairpin bends and steep gradients near summit. Often no middle white line. Spanish side (A138) has good width and is less steep and winding. Used by heavy vehicles. No tolls.
BB	**Cadi** (Spain) 5km (3 miles)	**Bellver de Cerdanya to Berga** 1220m (4000')	W of Toses (Tosas) pass on E9/C16; link from La Seo de Urgel to Andorra; excellent approach roads; heavy traffic at weekends. Tolls charged.
CC	**Envalira** (France – Spain via Andorra) 2.8km (1.75 miles)	**Pas de la Casa to El Grau Roig** 2000m (6562')	Tunnel width 8.25m. On N22/CG2 France to Andorra. Tolls charged.
DD	**Puymorens** (France-Spain)	**Ax-les-Thermes to Puigcerda** 1915m (6000')	MHV 3.5m (11'6") Part of Puymorens pass on N20/E9. Tolls charged.
EE	**Somport** (France – Spain) 8.6km (5.3 miles)	**Urdos to Canfranc** 1190m (3904')	Tunnel height 4.55m (14'9"), width 10.5m (34'). Max speed 90 km/h (56 mph); leave 100m between vehicles. On N134 (France), N330 (Spain). No tolls.
FF	**Vielha (Viella)** (Spain) 5km (3.1 miles)	**Vielha (Viella) to Pont de Suert** 1635m (5390')	Single carriageway on N230; gentle gradients on both sides. Some rough sections with pot holes on the approaches and in the tunnel. No tolls.

© Collins Bartholomew Ltd 2006

Insurance Expertise at home and abroad!

All our insurance policies are designed with caravanners and motor caravanners in mind so, whether you're at home or away touring, you can rely on The Club to be sure you are fully covered.

Caravan Insurance

Our competitive policies offer comprehensive and flexible cover, based on more than 35 years' experience operating the UK's largest Caravan insurance scheme for our members.
Call on **01342 336610** or get a quote & buy online at **www.caravanclub.co.uk**

UK Breakdown & Recovery

The Club's Mayday UK vehicle rescue is provided in conjunction with Green Flag and offers fast and reliable rescue and recovery, whether you're towing or not.
Call on **0800 731 0112** or get a quote & buy online at **www.caravanclub.co.uk**

Car Insurance

Competitive Car insurance from a name you can trust, with a guarantee of a lower premium than your current insurer*.
Call on **0800 028 4809**

Home Insurance

Our Home insurance protects your buildings and/or contents against a wide range of risks and offers additional benefits.
Call on **0800 028 4815**

Pet Insurance

Be sure your pets are protected at home or when away touring in the UK or abroad, no matter how many trips you take.
Call on **0800 015 1396**

Motor Caravan Insurance

Another Club speciality, with wide cover at competitive rates and a guarantee to beat the renewal premium offered by your present insurer*.
Call on **0800 028 4809**

Overseas Holiday Insurance

When you travel abroad, take The Club's Red Pennant Holiday Insurance with you. Our own 24-hour emergency team helps you relax, knowing you're in experienced hands.
Call on **01342 336633** or get a quote & buy online at **www.caravanclub.co.uk**

To find out more, please call us stating reference CE08.
We look forward to hearing from you!

THE **CARAVAN CLUB**

Sorry, our policies are only available to Caravan Club members. Why not join us? You could easily save the cost of your subscription. Call **0800 328 5535** quoting ref. INM08

* Conditions apply

Mountain Passes and Tunnels

Passes/Tunnel Report Form)

Name of Pass/Tunnel ....

To/From ....

Date Travelled...

Comments (eg gradients, traffic, road surface, width of road, hairpins, scenery)

....

....

....

....

ARE YOU A: Caravanner	Motor caravanner	Trailer-tenter?

===

Passes/Tunnel Report Form

Name of Pass/Tunnel ....

To/From ....

Date Travelled...

Comments (eg gradients, traffic, road surface, width of road, hairpins, scenery)

....

....

....

ARE YOU A: Caravanner	Motor caravanner	Trailer-tenter?

Mountain Passes and Tunnels

Passes/Tunnel Report Form)

Name of Pass/Tunnel ....

To/From ....

Date Travelled...

Comments (eg gradients, traffic, road surface, width of road, hairpins, scenery)

....

....

....

....

| *ARE YOU A*: Caravanner | Motor caravanner | Trailer-tenter? |

Passes/Tunnel Report Form

Name of Pass/Tunnel ....

To/From ....

Date Travelled...

Comments (eg gradients, traffic, road surface, width of road, hairpins, scenery)

....

....

....

| *ARE YOU A*: Caravanner | Motor caravanner | Trailer-tenter? |

Conversion Tables

Length & Distance

Centimetres/Metres	Inches/Feet/Yards	Inches/Feet/Yards	Centimetres/Metres
1 cm	0.4 in	1 in	2.5 cm
5 cm	2 in	6 in	15 cm
10 cm	4 in	1 ft	30 cm
25 cm	10 in	3 ft/1 yd	90 cm
1 m	3 ft 3 in	10 yds	9 m
100 m	110 yds	100 yds	91 m
Kilometres	Miles	Miles	Kilometres
1	0.6	1	1.6
5	3.1	5	8.1
10	6.2	10	16.1
25	15.5	25	40.2
50	31.1	50	80.5
100	62.2	100	160.9

Weight

Grams/Kilograms	Ounces/Pounds	Ounces/Pounds	GramsKilograms
10 gm	0.3 oz	1 oz	28 gm
100 gm	3.5 oz	8 oz	226 gm
1 kg	2 lb 3 oz	1 lb	453 gm
10 kg	22 lb	10 lb	4.54 kg
25 kg	55 lb	50 lb	22.65 kg

Capacity

Millilitres/Litres	Fluid Ounces/Pints/Gallon	Fluid Ounces/Pints/Gallon	Millilitres/Litres
10 ml	0.3 fl oz	1 fl oz	28 ml
100 ml	3.5 fl oz	20 fl oz/1 pint	560 ml
1 litre	1.8 pints	1 gallon	4.5 litres
10 litres	2.2 gallons	5 gallons	22.7 litres
50 litres	11 gallons	10 gallons	45.5 litres

Area

Hectares	Acres	Acres	Hectares
1	2.5	1	0.4
5	12.4	5	2
10	24.7	10	4
50	123.5	50	20.2
100	247.1	100	40.5

Tyre Pressures

Bar	PSI (lb/sq.in)	Bar	PSI (lb/sq.in)
1.0	15	2.0	29
1.5	22	2.5	36

Map Scales

Scale	Equivalent Distance	
1:15 000	1 cm = 0.15 km	1 in = ¼ mile
1: 50 000	1 cm = 0.5 km	1 in = ¾ mile
1:100 000	1 cm = 1 km	1 in = 1¾ miles
1: 200 000	1 cm = 2 km	1 in = 3¼ miles
1: 400 000	1 cm = 4 km	1 in = 6¼ miles
1: 500 000	1 cm = 5 km	1 in = 8 miles
1: 750 000	1 cm = 7.5 km	1 in = 12 miles
1:1 000 000	1 cm = 10 km	1 in = 16 miles
1:1 250 000	1 cm = 12.5 km	1 in = 20 miles
1: 2 000 000	1 cm = 20 km	1 in = 32 miles

Electricity and Gas

Electricity—General Advice

The nominal voltage for mains electricity has been 230 volts across the European Union for more than ten years, but varying degrees of 'acceptable tolerance' have resulted in significant variations in the actual voltage to be found. Harmonisation of voltage standards remains an on-going project. Most appliances sold in the UK are rated at 220-240 volts and usually work satisfactorily. Some high-powered equipment, such as microwave ovens, may not function well—consult the manufacturer's literature for further information.

Appliances which are 'CE' marked should work acceptably, as this marking indicates that the product has been designed to meet the requirements of relevant European directives.

The Country Introductions in this guide contain information on amperage supplied in individual countries (where known). Frequently you will be offered a choice of amperage and the following table gives an approximate idea of which appliances can be used (erring on the side of caution) – you can work it out more accurately by noting the wattage of each appliance in your caravan. The kettle given is the caravan type, not a household kettle which usually has at least a 2000 watt element. Note that each caravan circuit also has a maximum amp rating which should not be exceeded.

Electrical Connections—EN60309-2 (CEE17)

Whilst there is a European Standard for connectors, EN60309-2, (formerly CEE17), this is not retrospective so you may find some Continental campsites where your UK 3-pin connector, which is to European Standard, will not fit. Accurate information is not easy to come by, but in Austria, Belgium, Denmark, Germany, Luxembourg, and the Netherlands most sites are fitted with CEE17 hook-ups, but not necessarily to all pitches. Spain, France, Italy and Switzerland are gradually changing over, but older style hook-ups may still be encountered. In some countries in Scandinavia and eastern Europe there may be few, if any CEE connections. See Country Introductions for more information.

Different connectors may be found within one campsite, as well as within one country. If you find your CEE17 connector does not fit, apply to campsite staff to hire an adaptor.

Different connectors may be found within one campsite

Even with European Standard connections, poor electrical supplies are possible; the existence of the EN60309-2 (CEE17) standard should not be taken as an automatic sign of a modern system.

Amps	Wattage (Approx)	Fridge	Battery Charger	Air Conditioning	Colour TV	Water Heater	Kettle (750W)	Heater (1KW)
2	400	✓	✓					
4	800	✓	✓		✓	✓		
6	1200	✓	✓	*	✓	✓	✓	
8	1600	✓	✓	✓**	✓	✓	✓	✓**
10	2000	✓	✓	✓**	✓	✓	✓	✓**
16	3000	✓	✓	✓	✓	✓	✓	✓**

*   Possible, depending on wattage of appliance in question

**   Not to be used at the same time as other high-wattage equipment

Site Hook-up Adaptor

(MAINS CONTINENTAL)

ADAPTATEUR DE PRISE AU SITE (SECTEUR)   CAMPINGPLATZ-ANSCHLUSS (NETZ)

16 amp 230 volt AC

Other Connections

French — a 2-pin plus earth socket. Adaptors available from UK caravan accessory shops.

German — the 2-pin plus 2 earth strips, found in Norway and Sweden and possibly still Germany.

If the campsite does not have a modern EN60309-2 (CEE17) supply, ask to see the electrical protection for the socket outlet. If there is a device marked with $I_{\Delta n} = 30mA$, then the risk is minimised.

Hooking Up to the Mains

Connection

Connection should always in the following order:

- Check your caravan isolating switch is at 'off'.
- Uncoil the connecting cable from the drum. **A coiled cable with current flowing through it may overheat.** Take your cable and insert the connector (female end) into the caravan inlet.
- Insert the plug (male end) into the site outlet socket.
- Switch caravan isolating switch 'on'.
- Preferably insert a polarity tester into one of the 13-amp sockets in the caravan to check all connections are correctly wired. **Never leave it in the socket.** Some caravans have these devices built in as standard.

It is recommended that the supply is not used if the polarity is incorrect *(see **Reversed Polarity** overleaf)*.

WARNING

In case of doubt or, if after carrying out the above procedures the supply does not become available, or if the supply fails, consult the campsite operator or a qualified electrician.

From time to time, you may come across mains supplies which differ in various ways from the common standards on most sites. The test equipment built into your caravan or readily available for everyday use may not be able to confirm that such systems are satisfactory and safe to use. While it is likely that such systems will operate your electrical equipment adequately in most circumstances, it is feasible that the protective measures in your equipment may not work effectively in the event of a fault. To ensure your safety, the Club recommends that unless the system can be confirmed as safe, it should not be used.

Disconnection

- Switch your caravan isolating switch 'off'.
- At the site supply socket withdraw the plug.
- Disconnect the cable from the caravan.
- Motor caravanners—if leaving your pitch during the day, do not leave your mains cable plugged into the site supply, as this creates a hazard if the exposed live connections in the plug are touched or if the cable is not seen during grass-cutting.

Reversed Polarity

Even when the site connector is to European Standard (CEE17), British caravanners are still likely to encounter the problem known as reversed polarity. This is where the site supply's 'live' line connects to the caravan's 'neutral' and vice versa. The Club strongly recommends that you always check the polarity immediately on connection, using a polarity tester available from most caravan accessory shops (see illustration overleaf).

The caravan mains electrical installation **should not be used** while reversed polarity exists. Try using another nearby socket instead, which may cure the problem. Frequent travellers to the Continent who are electrically competent often make up an adaptor themselves, clearly marked reversed polarity, with the live and neutral wires reversed. (The 'German' plug can simply be turned upside down, so no further adaptor is required.) If these steps do not rectify the reversed polarity, the site supply may be quite different from that used in the UK and we recommend, for your own safety, that you disconnect from the mains and **do not use the electrical supply.**

Always check the polarity immediately on connection

Using a reversed polarity socket will probably not affect how an electrical appliance works BUT your protection in the event of a fault is greatly reduced. For example, a lamp socket may still be live as you touch it while replacing a blown bulb, even if the light switch is turned off.

Even when polarity is correct, it is always a wise precaution to check that a proper earth connection exists. This can be done with a proprietary tester such as a live-indicating neon screwdriver. If there is any doubt about the integrity of the earth system, DO NOT USE THE SUPPLY.

Kew Technik produces a UK/Europe mains electricity testing kit which includes adaptors/ conversion leads for Continental site sockets; telephone their Helpline on 01256 864100 (office hours), www.kewtechnik.co.uk, email: sales@kewt.co.uk

Shaver Sockets

Most campsites provide shaver sockets on which the voltage is generally marked as either 220V or 110V. Using an incorrect voltage may cause the shaver to become hot or to fail. The 2-pin adaptor obtainable in the UK is sometimes too wide for Continental sockets. It is advisable to buy 2-pin adaptors on the Continent, where they are readily available. Many shavers will operate on a range of voltages and these are most suitable when travelling abroad.

Gas—General Advice

As a guide, plan to allow 0.45 kg of gas a day for normal summer usage. This should be quite sufficient unless you use gas for your refrigerator.

With the exception of Campingaz, LPG cylinders normally available in the UK cannot be exchanged abroad. If possible take sufficient gas with you for your holiday and bring back the empty cylinder. If an additional cylinder is required for a holiday, and it is returned within one year of hire date, then part of the the hire charge will be refunded.

It is preferable to purchase a Campingaz regulator to use with Campingaz cylinders while you are abroad, especially if you are taking a long holiday. It is also wise to hold a spare Calor gas container in reserve in case you experience difficulty in renewing Campingaz supplies locally. With 130,000 stockists in 100 countries, however, these occasions should be rare, but prices may vary considerably from country to country. Alternatively, adaptors are available from Campingaz/Calor stockists to enable use of the normal Calor 4.5 kg regulator with a Campingaz cylinder.

Take sufficient gas with you for your holiday

Campingaz is marketed in the UK by The Coleman Company, Gordano Gate, Portishead, Bristol BS20 7GG tel. 01275 845024, www.campingaz.com. This product is widely available on the Continent

BP Gaslight cylinders, which have been gaining in popularity in the UK, are available in several European countries. BP has a European exchange programme in which the UK does not yet participate. Morever,

Gaslight cylinders use different regulator fittings, depending on the country in which they are supplied. For news of further developments check the BP Gaslight website, www.bpgaslight.com

Cylinder gas under other brand names is widely distributed and is obtainable in most European countries. During winter touring it is advisable to use propane gas and it may be necessary to purchase a cylinder of gas, plus the appropriate regulator or adaptor hose, in the country being visited. It is also advisable to compare prices carefully between the different brands and to check that cylinders fit into your gas cylinder locker.

When using other brands of gas a loan deposit is required, and when buying a cylinder for the first time you should also purchase the appropriate regulator or adaptor hose, as European pressures vary considerably. As in the UK, some operate at 28mbar for butane and 37mbar for propane; others at 30 or 50mbar for both products, and in some parts of France and Belgium at even higher pressures.

The use of 30mbar is being standardised for both types of gas. On the latest model caravans (2004 and later) a 30m bar regulator suited to both propane and butane use is fitted. This is connected to the cylinder by an adaptor hose, and different hoses may be needed for different brands of gas. Availability of hoses and adaptors on the Continent is variable at present, and owners of new caravans may find it prudent to buy a Campingaz adaptor in the UK, to ensure at least that this commonly available make of gas can be used. Hoses and adaptors for other brands of gas used on the Continent are not currently available in the UK.

WARNING

Refilling your own UK standard cylinder is prohibited by law in most countries, unless it is carried out at certain designated filling plants. Since these plants are few and far between, are generally highly mechanised and geared for cylinders of a particular size and shape, the process is usually impracticable. Nevertheless, it is realised that many local dealers and site operators will fill your cylinders regardless of the prohibition.

The Caravan Club does not recommend this practice; there is real danger if cylinders are incorrectly filled.

- Cylinders must never be over-filled under any circumstances.
- Butane cylinders should only be filled with butane and not propane, which is a commonly used gas in Europe.
- Regular servicing of gas appliances is important. A badly adjusted applicance can emit carbon monoxide, which could prove fatal.
- Never use a hob or oven as a space heater.

*For information about the carriage of gas cylinders on ferries and in the Channel Tunnel, including safety precautions and regulations see the chapter **Ferries and Channel Tunnel** in the section **PLANNING AND TRAVELLING**.*

The Editor of Caravan Europe welcomes information from members on the availability (or otherwise) of gas cylinders, especially in eastern Europe and Scandinavia.

Keeping in Touch

Emails and Text Messages

There are numerous hand-held mobile phone devices available equipped with a keyboard which enable the sending and receiving of emails and website browsing. They also have a number of other functions, eg organiser, address book and instant messaging.

Many campsites now have computer rooms or facilities for their guests to access the internet. Wifi hotspots are widespread and are easy to use with a modern laptop computer.

There are internet cafés all over the world where you can log onto the internet and collect and send emails. This is a quick and easy way to keep in touch with family, friends and business at home. You will be charged for the time you are logged on. You can find the location of internet cafés in countries around the world on www.world66.com/netcafeguide. Public libraries in many countries offer free internet access.

Using a mobile phone to send text messages is a cost-effective way of keeping in touch. A number of websites offer a free SMS text message service to mobile phones, eg www.cbfsms.com. No pre-registering is required.

International Direct Dial Calls

The international access code for the UK from anywhere in the world is 0044. International access codes for all the countries in this guide are given in the Country Introductions. To make an IDD call, first dial the international access code from the country you are, in followed by the local number you wish to reach including its area code (if applicable), eg from the UK to France, dial 0033 – the international access code for France – then the local ten-digit number omitting the initial 0.

Most, but not all, countries include an initial 0 in the area code when telephone numbers are quoted. With the exception of Italy where the 0 must be dialled, this initial 0 should not be dialled when calling from outside the country in question. Area codes in Spain do not have an initial 0 but have an initial number 9 which should always be dialled.

Ring tones vary from country to country and the UK's double ring is not necessarily used in other countries. For example when dialling a number in France you will hear long, equal on and off tones, slower than the UK's engaged tone, and in Germany and Spain you will hear short, single tones separated by longer pauses.

International calls can be made from call boxes in countries covered by this guide using coins or, more commonly, phonecards or credit cards, and often instructions are given in English. When telephoning, allow for time differences between countries.

International Telephone Cards

Global calling cards offer rates for international calls which are normally cheaper than credit card or local phonecards. Payment methods vary, but are usually by monthly direct debit from your credit card or bank account. Also widely available are pre-paid international phonecards which are available on-line or locally from post offices, newsagents, kiosks or shops, and rechargeable cards which require a credit card top-up when your credit reduces to a certain level. There are many websites selling international phonecards for use all over the world, eg www.planetphonecards.com or www.1st4phonecards.com

Radio and Television

Radio and Television Broadcasts

The BBC World Service broadcasts radio programmes 24 hours a day from a worldwide network of FM and short wave transmitters, via satellite and via the internet on www.bbc.co.uk/worldservice. Short wave transmissions in English have been reduced in recent years in response to listeners' trends.

Listeners in Belgium, the Netherlands, Luxembourg, north-west Germany and northern France may listen to BBC Radio 5 Live on either 693 or 909 kHz medium wave or BBC Radio 4 on 198 kHz long wave. The BBC World Service is also available in these areas on DRM digital radio.

In addition, many local radio stations broadcast BBC World Service programmes in English on FM frequencies. You can find programme details, plus internet broadcast schedules and links to a weekly email newsletter, at www.bbc.co.uk/worldservice

BBC News Online is available on WAP-compatible mobile phones, palmtop computers and other wireless handheld devices – see www.bbc.co.uk/mobile for set-up information. Mobile phone network providers also have links to the BBC or Sky News from their own portals for breaking news and headlines.

Television Equipment

UK specification televisions are designed to receive only UK analogue transmissions using the PAL 1 system, so if you wish to receive Continental programmes in sound and vision you will need a multi-standard television set. UK-only specification televisions receive vision only.

The most widely used system in western Europe is PAL B/G. France, Luxembourg and Monaco use a different system called SECAM L. Eastern Europe uses SECAM D/K. Most specialist suppliers will stock multi-standard television sets that accommodate all these variations, but just about any television set can be used to receive digital or satellite transmissions.

Satellite Television

Satellite dishes are becoming an increasingly common sight on caravans both at home and abroad. A satellite dish mounted on the roof or clamped to a pole fixed to the hitch or draw bar, or one mounted on a foldable, free-standing tripod, will provide good reception and minimal interference. Remember, however, that mountains or tall trees in the immediate vicinity of your dish, or heavy rain, may interfere with signals. As dishes become smaller and easier to use, numerous methods of fixing them have become available and a specialist dealer will be able to advise you. You will also need a receiver, sometimes called a digibox, and ideally a satellite-finding meter. Many satellite channels are 'free-to-air' which means they can be received by any make of receiver, but others are encrypted and require a viewing card and a Sky digibox. A number of portable systems are available which are suitable for the caravan market; contact a caravan accessory dealer or specialist electrical retailer. Note that these

are 'free-to-air' systems only and will not take a viewing card, for which a Sky digibox is needed.

There are hundreds of TV stations accessible both in the UK and in Europe, together with dozens of English-language radio stations including BBC broadcasts. The BBC's and ITV's satellite signals, while not as widespread throughout Europe as they used to be, are now 'free-to-air' and can be watched without the need for a viewing card throughout most of France, Belgium and the Netherlands, together with those parts of Germany, Switzerland and Spain bordering them. You should need only a 60 cm dish to access these 'free-to-air' channels but a larger dish will enable you to pick up the signals further afield.

In order to watch any encrypted channels you will need a Sky viewing card and, strictly speaking, it is contrary to Sky's terms and conditions to take it outside the UK. However, you are entitled to take your digibox because it is your personal property. Furthermore it will work perfectly well without the card as long as you restrict yourself to the 'free-to-air' channels such as those offered by the BBC and ITV.

If you prefer to have a second digibox for use in your caravan, Sky now offers a non-subscription digital satellite service for a one-off charge covering a digibox, dish, viewing card and installation – further details from www.freesatfromsky.com or on www. satelliteforcaravans.co.uk

In spring 2008 the BBC, in partnership with ITV, plans to launch its own non-subscription Freesat service, called PSB Freesat, carrying all the BBC and ITV digital channels, together with many other independent 'free-to-air' channels and most national radio channels.

See the website www.satelliteforcaravans. co.uk (operated by a Caravan Club member) for the latest changes and developments and for detailed information on TV reception throughout Europe, plus sections on emailing via a mobile phone network and a mine of other information.

Television via a Laptop Computer

With a modern laptop, this should be reasonably straightforward. In order to process the incoming signal the computer must, as a minimum, be fitted with a TV tuner and a 'TV-in connector' – basically an aerial socket. Some modern laptops have them built in, but if not you can obtain a plug-in USB adaptor. An alternative connection is the HDMI socket (High Definition Multimedia Interface) which is fitted to some of the more expensive laptops, for which you will need an HD digital receiver.

Using Mobile Phones Abroad

Mobile phones have an international calling option called 'roaming' which will automatically search for a local network when you switch your phone on, wherever you are in Europe. You should contact your service provider to obtain advice on the charges involved as these are partly set by the foreign networks you use and fluctuate with exchange rates.

There are no further formalities and the phone will work in exactly the same way as in the UK. When calling UK landline or mobile phone numbers prefix the number with +44 and drop the initial 0 of the area code. Format telephone numbers in your phone's memory in this way, and you will get through to those numbers when dialling from the memory, whether you are in the UK or abroad.

Because mobile phones will only work if within range of a base station, reception in some rural areas may be patchy, but coverage is usually excellent in main towns and near main roads and motorways. Approximate coverage maps can be obtained from many dealers.

If you are making calls to numbers within the country you are visiting, just dial the standard dialling code but not the international code – rather like using your phone in the UK. To make a call to a country other than the UK from abroad, simply replace the +44 country code with the applicable country code, eg +33 for France.

Users should note that if you receive an incoming call while abroad, the international leg of the call will be charged to your mobile phone account because the caller has no way of knowing that (s)he is making an international call. It is possible to bar or divert incoming calls when abroad and your service provider will supply a full list of options.

Mobile service providers have responded to pressure from the EU to reduce roaming charges but, in the meantime, it is possible to

reduce costs further by means of 'bolt-ons', on payment of a monthly fee. This may be an option if you travel frequently abroad or intend to be away for a long time. While mobile phone charges are coming down, sending and receiving video messages is still every expensive – check with your network provider.

Alternatively, it is possible to buy a global SIM card which will enable your mobile phone to operate on a foreign mobile network more cheaply. You simply replace the SIM card in your phone with the new card when you go abroad, remembering to leave a voicemail message on the old card telling callers that you have temporarily changed number. This service is offered by a number of companies such as www.roameo.co.uk, www.SIM4travel.co.uk and www.0044.co.uk, or you may find it simpler to buy a SIM card abroad. Before doing this, check with your UK service provider whether it has locked your phone against the use of a different SIM card and what, if anything, it will charge to unlock it. The website www.0044.co.uk has instructions on how to unlock your phone.

As technology advances VoIP (voice-over internet protocol) permits you to be contacted on your usual mobile phone number via a local number while abroad – see www.awayphone.com for more details.

Increasingly legislation in Europe forbids the use of mobile or car phones while driving except when using hands-free equipment. **If you are involved in an accident while driving and, at the same time, using a hand-held mobile phone, your insurance company may refuse to honour the claim.**

Make a note of your mobile phone's serial number, your own telephone number and the number of your provider's customer services and keep them in a safe place separate from your mobile phone. Remember to pack your charger and travel adaptor. Charging packs, available from major mobile phone retailers, which provide a power source to recharge your phone if you do not have access to a mains supply. Whichever network you use, check that you have the instructions for use abroad.

During Your Stay

Medical Matters

Travel abroad is now so common that it is easy to forget potential health risks and the fact that very few countries offer such easy access to medical facilities as Britain. Obtaining medical treatment abroad may seem complicated to UK residents used to the NHS. In most countries around the world you will have to pay, often large amounts, for relatively minor treatment.

This chapter offers advice and information on what to do before you travel, how to avoid the need for health care when away from home and what to do when you return. Specific advice on obtaining emergency medical treatment in the countries covered by this guide is contained in the relevant Country Introductions.

You are also recommended to obtain a copy of the Department of Health's leaflet, T7.1 Health Advice for Travellers which is downloadable from www.dh.gov.uk, email: dh@prolog.uk.com or call 08701 555455.

Before You Travel

If you have any pre-existing medical conditions it is wise to check with your GP that you are fit to travel. If your medical condition is complex then ask your doctor for a written summary of your medical problems and a list of medications currently used, together with other treatment details, and have it translated into the language of the country you are visiting. This is particularly important for travellers whose medical conditions require them to use controlled drugs or hypodermic syringes, in order to avoid any local difficulties with Customs. The Caravan Club does not offer a translation service.

See Customs Regulations in the section PLANNING AND TRAVELLING.

Check the health requirements for your destination; these may depend not only on the countries you are visiting, but which parts, at what time of the year and for how long. If you are travelling to an unusual destination or heading well off the beaten track, or if you simply want to be sure of receiving the most up-to-date advice, the Medical Advisory Service for Travellers Abroad (MASTA) can supply you with a written personal Health Brief covering up to ten countries and designed to meet your specific travel needs, together with information on recommended health products. To obtain a Health Brief, which costs £3.99, log on to www.masta-travel-health.com or telephone 0113 2387500.

Carry a card giving your blood group and details of any allergies

---

Always check that you have enough of your regular medications to last the duration of your holiday, and carry a card giving your blood group and details of any allergies or dietary restrictions. A translation of these may be useful when visiting restaurants. Your doctor can normally prescribe only a limited quantity of medicines under the NHS so if you think you will run out of prescribed medicines while abroad, ask your doctor for the generic name of any drugs you use, as brand names may be different. If you don't already know it, find out your blood group. In an emergency this may well ensure prompt treatment.

If you have any doubts about your teeth or plan to be away a long time, have a dental check-up before departure. An emergency dental kit is available which will allow you temporarily to restore a crown, bridge or filling, or to dress a broken tooth until you can get to a dentist. For further information see www.dentanurse.com or telephone 01981 500135.

European Heath Insurance Card (EHIC)

UK residents who are temporarily visiting another EU member state, as well as Iceland, Liechtenstein, Norway or Switzerland, are entitled to receive any necessary state-provided emergency treatment during their stay, on the same terms as an 'insured' resident of the country being visited. As well as treatment in the event of an emergency, this includes on-going medical care for a chronic disease or pre-existing illness, ie medication, blood tests and injections.

Before leaving home you will need to obtain a European Health Insurance Card (EHIC). Post offices hold application forms for the EHIC but the cards are issued by a central processing agency. You can also apply by telephoning 0845 6062030 or online on www.dh.gov.uk. An EHIC is required by each individual family member, so allow enough time before your departure to obtain them. The EHIC is free of charge and is valid for three to five years. The card is plastic and shows name and date of birth and a personal identification number. It holds no electronic or clinical data.

Private treatment is generally not covered by your EHIC and state-provided treatment may not cover everything that you would expect to receive free of charge from the NHS. If charges are made, these cannot be refunded by the British authorities and **it is strongly recommended that you arrange additional travel insurance before leaving home (see below) regardless of the cover provided by your EHIC.**

An EHIC issued in the UK is valid provided the holder remains ordinarily resident in the UK and eligible for NHS services. Restrictions may apply to nationals of other countries resident in the UK. For full details see the Department of Health's website, www.dh.gov.uk or call EHIC Enquiries on 0845 6050707, email: dhmail@dh.gsi.gov.uk

Health care entitlement under the EHIC does not cover visits abroad specifically to obtain medical treatment, such as a hip replacement, or any other medical treatment, operations or consultations.

Holiday Travel Insurance

Despite the fact that you have an EHIC you may incur thousands of pounds of medical costs if you fall ill or have an accident, even in countries with which Britain has reciprocal health care arrangements. The cost of bringing a person back to the UK, in the event of illness or death, is never covered by reciprocal arrangements. Therefore, separate additional travel insurance adequate for your destination is essential, such as the Caravan Club's Red Pennant Motoring & Personal Holiday Insurance, available to Club members.

First Aid

A first aid kit containing at least the basic requirements is an essential item and in some countries it is compulsory to carry one in your vehicle (see the *Essential Equipment Table* in the chapter *Motoring — Equipment*). Ready-made kits are available from most large chemists or direct from the British Red Cross, and should contain items such sterile pads, assorted dressings and plasters, crepe/elastic bandages, hypo-allergenic tape, antiseptic wipes or cream, painkillers, gauze, cotton wool, scissors, finger stall, eye bath and tweezers. Add to that travel sickness remedies, a triangular bandage, a pair of light rubber gloves and a pocket mask in case you ever find yourself in a situation where you need to give mouth-to-mouth resuscitation. Above all, carry something for the treatment of upset stomachs, which spoil more holidays than anything else.

It is always wise to carry a good first aid manual containing useful advice and instructions. The British Red Cross publishes a comprehensive First Aid Manual in conjunction with St John Ambulance and St Andrew's Ambulance Association, which is widely available. First aid essentials are also covered in a number of readily-available compact guide books. RTFB Publishing produces a useful quick reference health guide for travellers, entitled What Should I Do? priced £4.99, plus health phrase books in French and Spanish for £2.99 each. Telephone 023 8022 9041 or see www.whatshoulddido.com for further details and orders.

Emergency Multilingual Phrasebook

The British Red Cross, with the advice of the Department of Health, produces an Emergency Multilingual Phrasebook covering the most common medical questions and terms. It is aimed primarily at health professionals but the document can be downloaded as separate pages in a number of European languages from the Department of Health's website, www.dh.gov.uk/publications

Vaccinations

It is advisable to ensure your tetanus and polio inoculations are up-to-date before going on holiday, ie booster shots within the last ten years.

Hikers and outdoor sports enthusiasts planning trips to forested, rural areas in some parts of central and eastern Europe should seek medical advice well ahead of their planned departure date about preventative measures and immunisation against tick-borne encephalitis which is transmitted by the bite of an infected tick. TBE is a potentially life-threatening and debilitating viral disease of the central nervous system, although the risk is largely confined to late spring and summer when ticks are active in long grass, bushes and hedgerows in forested areas and along forest paths or animal trails. It is endemic in 16 countries in Europe. For more information see www.masta-travel-health.com/tickalert or telephone 0113 2387500.

The Department of Health advises long stay visitors to some eastern European countries to consider vaccination against hepatitis A. See the relevant Country Introductions.

Avian Influenza

The severe form of H5N1 – bird flu – has now been diagnosed in birds in a number of western European countries. If you are concerned about contact with birds or poultry you can obtain a factsheet from the Foreign & Commonsealth Office's website, www.fco.gov.uk (click on Travel Advice) or by telephoning 0845 8502829.

During Your Stay

When applying for medical treatment in a non-EU country, you may be asked for your NHS Medical Card. You are advised to take this with you if visiting a non-EU country. Residents of the Republic of Ireland should apply to their Regional Health Service Executive. Residents of the Isle of Man and Channel Islands, which are not members of the EU, should check with their own health authorities about reciprocal arrangements with other countries.

If you require treatment in an EU country but do not have an EHIC or are experiencing difficulties in getting your EHIC accepted, you may telephone the Department for Work & Pensions in Newcastle-upon-Tyne for assistance on 0191 218 1999. The office is open from 8am to 8pm Monday to Friday. The department will fax documents if necessary.

Claiming Refunds

If you are entitled to a refund from the authorities of the country in which you received treatment you should make a claim in that country either in person or by post. You must submit the original bills, prescriptions and receipts (keep photocopies for your records). The booklet T7.1 contains details of how to claim refunds, or visit the Department of Health's website, www.dh.gov.uk/travellers

If you cannot claim until your return home you should contact the Department for Work & Pensions on 0191 218 1999. The DWP will liaise with overseas authorities on your behalf to obtain a refund, which may take some time.

Accidents and Emergencies

If you are unfortunate enough to be involved in, or witness a road accident, or become involved in an emergency situation, firstly summon help early by any means available, giving the exact location of the accident or emergency and the number of casualties. Notify the police; most police officers have first aid training. The local numbers to contact police, fire service or ambulance are listed in each Country Introduction.

If you witnessed an accident the police may question you about it. Tell them exactly what you saw and do not venture opinions of any kind or seek to apportion blame. Give your name and address to all parties involved.

Before leaving the scene, make a brief note and a rough sketch to indicate details of the time you arrived and left, the position of the vehicles and the injured, the surface of the road, camber, potholes, etc, the weather at the time of the accident, skid marks and their approximate length — in fact anything you feel might be relevant — then date it and sign it. You may never be called on to use these notes, but if you are, you have a written record made at the time and of great value. Trying to recall details of the event several weeks, even months later can be difficult.

Insect Bites

Most of the temperate parts of Europe have their fair share of nuisance insects, particularly near lakes, and it is wise to carry insect repellant devices as mosquitoes and midges may be a problem. A number of products are available including impregnated wrist and ankle bands and insect repellant sprays and coils. Check with your chemist for suitable products. Covering exposed skin with long trousers and long-sleeved shirts is recommended after dark.

Pollution

Pollution of sea water at some Continental coastal resorts, including the Mediterranean, may still present a health hazard, although within the EU the general situation is improving. In many popular resorts where the water quality may present risks, eg in rivers and lakes as well as at the coast, signs are erected which forbid bathing:

French: Défense de se baigner or Il est défendu de se baigner

Italian: Vietato bagnarsi or Evietato bagnarsi

Spanish: Prohibido bañarse or Se prohibe bañarse

Rabies

Rabies is a serious hazard in many countries, including parts of Europe, and is usually fatal unless treatment is given immediately, before symptoms develop. However, it is extremely rare in domestic animals in the EU and the chances of being bitten or scratched by a rabid animal during the course of a European holiday are remote.

However, you should be aware that you can contract rabies if you are bitten, scratched or even licked by an infected dog, cat, fox, bat or other animal. Rabies-infected wild animals often appear to be tame. **Do not approach or touch animals, particularly if they are behaving oddly, and instruct children not to do so.** If you are bitten or scratched by an animal while abroad, the Department of Health recommends that you should wash the wound and seek medical attention immediately. Inform the local police of the incident and tell your GP as soon as you return home.

The UK is still rabies free; **DO NOT** bring any animals into the UK without first complying with the legal requirements. To do so could endanger lives.

Sun Protection

For many people, getting a good suntan is an essential part of a holiday, but too much sun can also cause sunburn which may ruin it. Never underestimate how ill careless exposure to the sun may make you. Use a good quality, broad-spectrum sun cream with balanced UVA/UVB protection suitable for your skin type and a high sun protection factor (SPF). Re-apply it frequently, especially if you are perspiring heavily or swimming. Avoid sitting in the sun during the hottest part of the day between 11am and 3pm. Take extra care when at high altitude especially in the snow, and in windy conditions.

Children need extra protection as they burn easily, tend to stay out in the sun longer and are unaware of the dangers of over-exposure. Most skin damage is caused in childhood. Put children in sunsuits and hats. Use a total sun block cream and apply liberally half an hour before going out in the sun to allow time for it to develop. Keep babies out of the sun at all times.

If you are not used to the heat it is very easy to fall victim to heat exhaustion or heat stroke. When first in a warm country it is very important that the whole family drinks more fluid than at home. If you feel thirsty, or your urine is very dark yellow, then you are becoming dehydrated and need to increase your fluid intake. The symptoms of sunstroke include headache, tiredness, weakness and thirst, leading to confusion, disorientation and, in very extreme cases, coma and even death. Avoid strenuous exercise, drink plenty of water or soft drinks — alcohol, tea and coffee only increase dehydration.

Precautions

- Wear a broad-brimmed sun hat and light, loose-fitting clothing made of tightly woven fabrics. Swimming in shallow water does not protect from the sun as water and sand reflect rays onto your skin. Cover up with a cotton T-shirt when swimming. Wear good quality sunglasses which filter UV rays.

- If possible store sun cream or lotion in a cool place or at least in the shade. Exposure to heat may damage it and it is probably not a good idea to use last year's leftover cream.

- Anyone showing signs of serious over-exposure to the sun should be placed indoors or in the shade, encouraged to sip water and kept cool by fanning or sponging down with cool water. Call a doctor if the patient becomes unconscious.

Water and Food

Water from mains supplies throughout Europe is generally good but the level of chemical treatment may make it unpalatable and you may prefer to use bottled water. In doubtful cases, where water is cloudy or not clear of all particles, water should be boiled, or water sterilisation tablets used. These are obtainable from most UK chemists and may be used for washing vegetables and fresh fruit. Always boil or sterilise water if it does not come from the mains, or preferably use bottled water from sealed containers.

Food poisoning is a potential risk anywhere in the world, but in extremely hot conditions a common-sense approach is called for. It is wise to protect food being left for any length of time with a fly net and to avoid food that has been kept warm for prolonged periods or left unrefrigerated for more than two to four hours. If the source is uncertain, do not eat unpasteurised dairy products, ice-cream, under-cooked meat, fish or shellfish, salads, raw vegetables or dishes containing mayonnaise.

Returning Home

If you become ill on your return do not forget to tell your doctor that you have been abroad and which countries you have visited. Even if you have received medical treatment in another country, always consult your doctor if you have been bitten or scratched by an animal while on holiday.

If you were given any medicines in another country, it may not be legal to bring them back into the UK. If in doubt, declare them at Customs when you return.

If you develop an upset stomach while away or shortly afterwards, and your work involves handling food, tell your employer immediately.

Claim on your travel insurance as soon as possible for the cost of any medical treatment. Holders of an EHIC should put in a claim for a refund as soon as possible – see *Claiming Refunds* earlier in this chapter.

Safety and Security

Britain has strong and effective safety legislation and a tradition of closely following the law, which is sometimes not the case in other countries. The Caravan Club gives safety a high priority at its UK sites but visitors to Europe often find that sites do not always come up to Club standards on electrical safety, hygiene and fire precautions.

Everyone wants to relax and enjoy their holiday. Safety is largely your own responsibility; taking sensible precautions and being aware of possible hazards won't spoil your holiday, but a careless attitude might. Take a few minutes when you arrive on site to ensure that everyone, from the youngest upwards, understands where everything is, how things work and where care is needed to avoid an accident. The following advice will help you and your family have a safe and trouble-free holiday.

Overnight Stops

The Caravan Club strongly recommends that overnight stops should always be at campsites and not at motorway service areas, ferry terminal car parks or isolated 'aires de service' or 'aires de repos' on motorways where robberies, muggings and encounters with asylum-seekers are occasionally reported. If you ignore this advice and decide to use these areas for a rest during the day or overnight, then you are advised to take appropriate precautions, for example, shutting all windows, securing locks and making a thorough external check of your vehicle(s) before departing.

Having said that, there is a wide network of 'Stellplätze' and 'Aires de Services' in cities, towns and villages across Europe, many specifically for motor caravanners, and many with good security and overnight facilities. It is rare that you will be the only vehicle staying on such areas, but avoid any that are isolated, take sensible precautions and trust your instincts. For example, if there is a site for 'travellers' nearby or if the area appears run down and there are groups of young men hanging around, then you are probably wise to move on.

Around the Campsite

- Once you've settled in, take a walk around the site to familiarise yourself with its layout and ensure that your children are familiar with it and know where their caravan is. Even if you have visited the site before, layout and facilities may have changed. Make sure that children are aware of any places where they should not go.

- Locate the nearest fire-fighting equipment and the nearest telephone box and emergency numbers.

- Natural disasters are rare, but always think what could happen. A combination of heavy rain and a riverside pitch could lead to flash flooding, for instance, so make yourself aware of site evacuation procedures.

- Be aware of sources of electricity and cabling on and around your pitch. Advice about electrical hook-ups is given in detail in the chapter *Electricity and Gas* in the section *DURING YOUR STAY* and it is recommended that you read it carefully.

- If staying at a farm site, remember that the animals are not pets. Do not approach any animal without the farmer's permission and keep children supervised. Make sure they wash their hands after touching any farm animal. Do not approach or touch any animal which is behaving oddly or any wild animal which appears to be tame. While avian influenza cases are rare in Europe, it is wise to avoid close contact with poultry or wild birds.

- A Club member has advised that, on occasion, site owners and/or farmers on whose land a site is situated, use poison to control rodents. Warning notices are not always posted and you are strongly advised to check if staying on a rural site and accompanied by your dog.

- Common sense should tell you that you need to be careful if the site is close to a main road or alongside a river. Remind your children about the Green Cross Code and encourage them to use it. Adults and children alike need to remember that traffic is on the 'wrong' side of the road.

- Incidents of theft from visitors to campsites are rare but when leaving your caravan unattended make sure you lock all doors and shut windows. Conceal valuables from sight and lock bicycles to a tree or to your caravan.

Children at Play

- Watch out for children as you drive around the site and observe the speed limit (walking pace).

- Children riding bikes should be made aware that there may be patches of sand or gravel around the site and these should be negotiated at a sensible speed. Bikes should not be ridden between or around tents or caravans.

- Children's play areas are generally unsupervised. Check which installations are suitable for your children's ages and abilities and agree with them which ones they may use. Read and respect the displayed rules. Remember it is your responsibility to know where your children are at all times.

- Be aware of any campsite rules concerning ball games or use of play equipment, such as roller blades and skateboards. Check the condition of bicycles which you intend to hire.

- When your children attend organised activities, arrange when and where to meet afterwards.

Fire

Caravans are perfectly safe provided you follow a few basic safety rules. Any fire that starts will spread quickly if not properly dealt with. Follow these rules at all times:

- Never use portable paraffin or gas heaters inside your caravan. Gas heaters should only be fitted when air is taken from outside the caravan.

- Never search for a gas leak with naked light. If gas is smelt, turn off the cylinder immediately, extinguish all naked flames and seek professional help.

- Never change your gas cylinder regulator inside the caravan. In the event of a fire starting in your caravan turn off the gas cylinder valve immediately.

- Never place clothing, tea towels or any other items over your cooker or heater to dry.

- Never leave children alone inside a caravan. Never leave matches where they can reach them.

- Never leave a chip pan or saucepan unattended.

- Keep heaters and cookers clean and correctly adjusted.

- Know where the fire points and telephones are on site and know the site fire drill. Establish a family fire drill. Make sure everyone knows how to call the emergency services.

Where regulations permit the use of barbecues, take the following precautions to prevent fire:

Never locate a barbecue near trees, hedges or accommodation. Have a bucket of water to hand in case of sparks.

Only use recommended fire-lighting materials.

Do not leave a barbecue unattended when lit and dispose of hot ash safely.

Do not let children play near a lit barbecue.

Swimming Pools

Make the first visit to the pool area a 'family exploration' not only to find out what is available, but also to identify features and check information which could be vital to your family's safety. Even if you have visited the site before, the layout may have changed, so check the following:

- Pool layout – identify shallow and deep ends and note the position of safety equipment. Check that poolside depth markings are accurate and whether there are any sudden changes of depth in the pool. The bottom of the pool should be clearly visible.

- Are there restrictions about diving and jumping into the pool? Are some surfaces slippery when wet? Ensure when diving into a pool that it is deep enough for you to do so safely.

- Check opening and closing times. For pools with a supervisor or lifeguard, note any times or dates when the pool is not supervised, eg lunch breaks, low season. Read safety notices and rules posted around the pool. Check the location of any rescue equipment.

- Establish your own rules about parental supervision. Age and swimming ability are important considerations and at least one responsible adult who can swim should accompany and supervise children at the pool. Remember that even a shallow paddling pool can present a danger to young children. Even if a lifeguard is present, you are responsible for your children and must watch them closely.

- Do not swim just after a meal, nor after drinking alcohol.

Water Slides

- Take some time to watch other people using the slides so that you can see their speed and direction when entering the water. Find out the depth of water in the landing area. Ensure that your children understand the need to keep clear of the landing area.

- Consider and agree with your children which slides they may use. Age or height restrictions may apply.

- Check the supervision arrangements and hours of use; they may be different from the main pool times.

- Check and follow any specific instructions on the proper use of each slide. The safest riding position is usually feet first, sitting down. Never allow your children to stand or climb on the slide.

- Do not wear jewellery when using slides.

Beaches, Lakes and Rivers

- Check for any warning signs or flags before you swim and ensure that you know what they mean. Check the depth of water before diving and avoid diving or jumping into murky water, as submerged swimmers or objects may not be visible. Familiarise yourself with the location of safety apparatus and/or lifeguards.

- Children can drown in a very short time and in relatively small amounts of water. Supervise them at all times when they are in the water and ensure that they know where to find you on the beach.

- Use only the designated areas for swimming, windsurfing, jetskiing etc. Use life jackets where appropriate. Swim only in supervised areas whenever possible.

- Familiarise yourself with tides, undertows, currents and wind strength and direction before you or your children swim in the sea. This applies in particular when using inflatables, windsurfing equipment, body boards or sailing boats. Sudden changes of wave and weather conditions combined with fast tides and currents are particularly dangerous.

- Establish whether there are submerged rocks or a steeply shelving shore which can take non-swimmers or weak swimmers by surprise. Be alert to the activities of windsurfers or jetskiers who may not be aware of the presence of swimmers.

On the Road

- Do not leave valuable items on car seats or near windows in caravans, even if they are locked. Ensure that items on roof racks or cycle carriers are difficult to remove – a long cable lock may be helpful.

- In view of recent problems with stowaways on cross-Channel ferries and trains, check that your outfit is free from unexpected guests at the last practical opportunity before boarding.

- Beware of a 'snatch' through open car windows at traffic lights, filling stations, in traffic jams or at 'fake' traffic accidents. When driving through towns and cities keep your doors locked. Keep handbags, valuables and documents out of sight at all times.

- If flagged down by another motorist for whatever reason, take care that your own car is locked and windows closed while you check outside, even if someone is left inside. Be particularly careful on long, empty stretches of motorway and when you stop for fuel. Even if the people flagging you down appear to be officials (eg wearing yellow reflective jackets or dark, 'uniform-type' clothing) show presence of mind and lock yourselves in immediately. They may appear to be friendly and helpful, but may be opportunistic thieves prepared to resort to violence. Have a mobile phone to hand and, if necessary, be seen to use it. Keep a pair of binoculars handy for reading registration numbers too.

- Road accidents are a significant risk in some countries where traffic laws may be inadequately enforced and roads may be poorly maintained, road signs and lighting inadequate and driving standards poor. The traffic mix may be more complex with animal-drawn vehicles, pedestrians, bicycles, cars, lorries, and perhaps loose animals, all sharing the same space. In addition you will be driving on the 'wrong' side of the road and should, therefore, be especially vigilant at all times. Avoid driving at night on unlit roads.

- Pursuing an insurance claim abroad can be difficult and it is essential, if you are involved in an accident, to take all the other driver's details and complete a European Accident Statement supplied by your motor vehicle insurer.

- It's a good idea to keep a fully-charged mobile phone with you in your car with the number of your breakdown organisation saved into it.

Personal Security

There is always the risk of being the victim of petty crime whichever country you are in and, as a foreigner, you may be more vulnerable. But the number of incidents is very small and the fear of crime should not deter you from caravanning abroad.

The Foreign & Commonwealth Office's Consular Division produces a range of material to advise and inform British citizens travelling abroad about issues affecting their safety, including political unrest, lawlessness, violence, natural disasters, epidemics, anti-British demonstrations and aircraft safety. Contact the FCO Travel Advice Unit on 0845 8502829, fax 020 7008 0155, email: traveladvicepublicenquiries@fco.gov.uk or see BBC2 Ceefax. The full range of notices is also available on the FCO's website, www.fco.gov.uk

Specific advice on personal security relating to countries covered by this guide is given in the relevant Country Introductions, but the following are a few general precautions to ensure that you have a safe and problem-free holiday:

- Leave valuables and jewellery at home. If you do take them, fit a small safe in your caravan and keep them in the safe or locked in the boot of your car. Do not leave money or documents, such as passports, in a car glovebox, or leave handbags and valuables on view. Do not leave bags in full view when sitting outside at cafés or restaurants. Do not leave valuables unattended on the beach.

- When walking be security conscious. Avoid unlit streets at night, walk well away from the kerb and carry handbags or shoulder bags on the side away from the kerb. The less of a tourist you appear, the less of a target you are. Never read a map openly in the street or carry a camera over your shoulder.

- Carry only the minimum amount of cash. Distribute cash, travellers' cheques, credit cards and passports amongst your party; do not rely on one person to carry everything. Never carry a wallet in your back pocket. A tuck-away canvas wallet, moneybelt or 'bumbag' can be useful and waterproof versions are available. It is normally advisable not to resist violent theft.

- Do not use street money-changers; in some countries it is illegal.

- Keep a separate note of bank account and credit card numbers and serial numbers of travellers' cheques. Join the Club's Credit Card Protection Plan (Club members only) or other credit card protection scheme so that, in the event of theft, one phone call will cancel all cards and arrange replacements.

- Keep a separate note of your holiday insurance reference number and emergency telephone number.

- Keep a separate record of your passport details, preferably in the form of a certified copy of the details pages. Fill in the next-of-kin details in your passport. A photocopy of your birth certificate may also be useful.

- Many large cities have a drug problem with some addicts pickpocketing to fund their habit. Pickpockets often operate in groups, including children. Stay alert, especially in crowds, on trains and stations, near banks and foreign exchange offices, and when visiting well-known historical and tourist sites.

- Beware of bogus plain-clothes policemen who may ask to see your foreign currency and passport. If approached, decline to show your money or to hand over your passport but ask for credentials and offer instead to go with them to the nearest police station.

- Laws vary from country to country and so does the treatment of offenders; find out something about local laws and customs and respect them. Behave and dress appropriately, particularly when visiting religious sites, markets and rural communities.

- Do respect Customs regulations. Smuggling is a serious offence and can carry heavy penalties. Do not carry parcels or luggage through Customs for other people and do not cross borders with people you do not know, such as hitchhikers. If you are in someone else's vehicle do not cross the border in it – get out and walk across; you do not know what might be in the vehicle. Do not drive vehicles across borders for other people.

- Hobbies such as birdwatching and train, plane and ship-spotting, and the use of cameras or binoculars may be misunderstood (particularly near military installations) and you may risk arrest. If in doubt, don't.

- In the event of a natural disaster or if trouble flares up, contact family and friends to let them know that you are safe, even if you are nowhere near the problem area. Family and friends may not know exactly where you are and may worry if they think you are in danger.

The Risk of Terrorism

There is a global risk of indiscriminate terrorist attacks but it is important to remember that the overall risk of being involved in a terrorist incident is very low. Injury or death is far more likely through road accidents, swimming, alcohol-related occurrences, health problems or natural disasters.

Most precautions are common sense. Make sure you are aware of the situation in the country you are visiting and keep an eye on the news. Report anything you think is suspicious to the local police. The FCO Travel Advice for each country in this guide is summarised in the Country Introductions, but situations can change so make a point of reading the FCO's advice before you travel.

British Consular Services Abroad

Consular staff offer practical advice, assistance and support to British travellers abroad. They can, for example, issue replacement passports, contact relatives and friends in the event of an accident or death, provide information about transferring funds and provide details of local lawyers, doctors and interpreters. But there are limits to their powers and a British Consul cannot, for example, give legal advice, intervene in court proceedings, put up bail, pay for legal or medical bills, or for funerals or the repatriation of bodies, or undertake work more properly done by banks, motoring organisations and travel insurers.

Most British Consulates operate an answerphone service outside office hours giving opening hours and arrangements for handling emergencies. If you require Consular help outside office hours you may be charged a fee for calling out a Consular Officer. In countries outside the European Union where there are no British Consulates, you can get help from the Embassies and Consulates of other EU member states.

If you have anything stolen, eg money or passport, report it first to the local police and insist on a statement about the loss. You will need this in order to make a claim on your travel insurance. In the event of a fatal accident or death from whatever cause, get in touch with the nearest Consulate at once.

If you commit an offence you must expect to face the consequences. If you are charged with a serious offence, insist on the British Consulate being informed. You will be contacted as soon as possible by a Consular Officer who can advise on local procedures, provide access to lawyers and insist that you are treated as well as nationals of the country which is holding you. However, (s)he cannot get you released as a matter of course.

British and Irish Embassy and Consular Addresses

These can be found in the relevant Country Introductions.

Andorra

Andorra is an isolated, mountainous, landlocked principality on the southern slopes of the Pyrenees whose seven parishes are administered jointly by France and Spain. In recent years it has achieved considerable prosperity, largely due to its tourist industry – particularly winter sports – and its tax-free status. Its dramatic scenery and opportunities for hiking and birdwatching mean that Andorra merits more than merely a one-night shopping stop en route to France or Spain.

Essential Facts

Capital: Andorra-la-Vella (population 20,400)

Area: 468 sq km

Bordered by: France, Spain

Terrain: Rugged mountains dissected by narrow valleys

Climate: Temperate with cold, snowy winters and warm, dry summers; snow on the highest peaks often until July

Highest Point: Coma Pedrosa 2,942 m

Population: 76,875

Languages: Catalan (official), French, Spanish

Religion: Predominantly Roman Catholic

Government: Parliamentary democracy

Local Time: GMT or BST + 1, ie 1 hour ahead of the UK all year

Currency: Euro divided into 100 cents; £1 = €1.43, €1 = 70 pence*

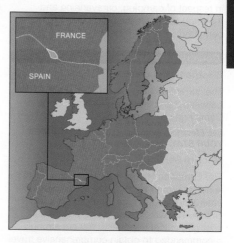

Tourist Information

ANDORRAN EMBASSY
63 WESTOVER ROAD
LONDON SW18 2RF
Tel: 020 8874 4806 (office hours)
Fax: 020 8874 4806
www.andorraonline.ad or www.andorra.ad

Opening Hours

Banks – Mon-Fri 9am-1pm & 3pm-5pm; Sat 9am-12 noon.

Post Offices – Mon-Fri 8.30am-2.30pm; Sat 9am-12 noon; extended opening hours in July and August at the main French post office in Andorra-la-Vella.

Shops – Mon-Sat 9am-8pm/9pm; Sun 9am-7pm; small shops may close between 1pm and 4pm.

Public Holidays 2008

Jan 1, 6; Mar 14 (Constitution Day); Mar 21, 24; May 1, 12; Jun 24 (St John's Day); Aug 15; Sep 8 (National Day); Nov 1, 4 (St Charles's Day); Dec 8, 25, 26, 31. Individual parishes celebrate other holidays and festivals in the summer months.

Telephoning

From the UK dial 00376 for Andorra plus the 6-digit number in full. To call the UK from Andorra dial 0044, omitting the initial zero of the area code.

Mobile phones – use of hand-held phones prohibited when driving.

Emergency numbers – Police 110; Fire brigade 118; Ambulance 118. From a mobile phone dial 112 for any service.

* Exchange rates as at September 2007

The following introduction to Andorra should be read in conjunction with the important information contained in the Handbook chapters at the front of this guide.

Camping and Caravanning

There are 25 campsites in Andorra and, in general French and Spanish regulations in respect of camping, caravanning and motoring apply. Casual/wild camping is not permitted.

Country Information

Electricity and Gas

The current on campsites is generally between 3 and 10 amps. All types of Campingaz are available.

See **Electricity and Gas** in the section **DURING YOUR STAY.**

Medical Services

The European Health Insurance Card (EHIC) is not accepted as there are no reciprocal emergency health care arrangements with Britain. You will be required to pay the full cost of medical treatment. You are strongly recommended to obtain comprehensive travel and medical insurance before travelling, such as the Caravan Club's Red Pennant Motoring & Personal Holiday Insurance.

See **Medical Matters** in the section **DURING YOUR STAY**.

Safety and Security

Street crime is almost unknown but you should take the usual common-sense precautions with passports and money.

If you are planning a skiing holiday it is advisable to contact the Andorran Embassy for advice on safety and weather conditions before travelling. All safety instructions should be followed meticulously given the dangers of avalanches in some areas. See www.andorra.com or www.goski.com for more information.

Your visit to Andorra is likely to be trouble-free but Andorra shares with the rest of Europe a threat from international terrorism, which could be indiscrimate and against civilian targets.

See **Safety and Security** in the section **DURING YOUR STAY.**

British Embassy

There is no British Embassy or Consulate-General's office, or Irish Embassy in Andorra.

There is a British Honorary Consul in La Massana, under the supervision of the British Consulate-General in Barcelona:

AVINGUDA SANT ANTONI 23
CAL SASTRE VELL 1R
AD-400 LA MASSANA
Tel/Fax: 839840
britconsul@andorra.ad

Customs Regulations

Andorra has two 24-hour border posts, one on the French side at Pas de la Casa on the N22, and the other on the Spanish side at La Farga de Moles on the N145. There are no Customs formalities on entering Andorra and no restrictions on imports.

Andorra is well-known for its duty-free shopping opportunities, but visitors must be aware that strict limits apply to goods taken into France or Spain on leaving Andorra and it is understood that Customs checks may be made. The limits are:

1.5 litres of spirits
5 litres of table wine
300 cigarettes or 150 cigarillos or 75 cigars or 400 gm of tobacco
75 gm of perfume and 375 ml of eau de toilette
Other items up to the value of €525
Alcohol and tobacco allowances apply only to persons aged 17 or over.

Documents

You are required to carry your passport at all times.

An International Motor Insurance Certificate (Green Card) is necessary when driving in Andorra.

See also **Documents and Insurance** in the section **PLANNING AND TRAVELLING.**

Motoring

Alcohol

The maximum permitted level of alcohol in the blood is 0.05%, ie lower than in the UK. Penalties for exceeding this limit are severe.

Fuel

Diesel is available but there are no LPG suppliers. Credit cards are accepted at most filling stations.

See **Fuel** under **Motoring** – Advice in the section **PLANNING AND TRAVELLING.**

Roads

Main roads are prefixed 'CG' (Carretera General) and side roads are prefixed 'CS' (Carretera Secundaria). CG road signs are white on red and CS are white on green.

The pass from the French border at l'Hospitalet and Port d'Envalira on the N22/CG2 is well engineered with a maximum gradient of 12.5% (1 in 8), but the gradient is very extensive. It is the highest pass in the Pyrenees, reaching 2,407 metres (7,897 feet). Except for short periods following heavy snowfalls, it is open all year. The 2.8 km Envalira Tunnel connects Pas de la Casa and El Grau Roig and avoids the highest part of the pass.

The main road to Barcelona from Andorra is the C14/C1412/N141b via Ponts and Calaf. It is continually being improved and has a good surface throughout. This road avoids any high passes.

The N260 along the south side of Andorra via Bourg Madame, Puigcerda and La Seo de Urgel has been re-made and has a good surface.

The N152/C26/A26 from Andorra to Gerona via the Toses Pass, Ripoli and Olot is an extremely scenic route but the Toses Pass can be difficult in winter. The road surface is excellent and the maximum gradient is 10% (1 in 10) up to a height of 1,800 metres (5,906 feet).

See **Mountain Passes – Pyrenees and Northern Spain** and **Major Pyrenean Road Tunnels** in the section **PLANNING AND TRAVELLING**.

It is advisable to stick to main roads when towing and not to attempt the many unsurfaced roads.

Travellers to Andorra via France should be aware that conditions on the road from Toulouse to Andorra (N20) can quickly become difficult in severe winter weather and vehicles might be delayed. Ensure that you have water, food, warm clothing and any medical requirements readily to hand.

Speed Limits

All vehicles are restricted to 70 km/h (44 mph) on the open road and to 40 km/h (25 mph) in built-up areas.

Traffic Jams

There is heavy traffic in Andorra-la-Vella on most days of the year.

During the peak summer holiday period you are likely to encounter queues of traffic on the Envalira pass from France into Andorra on the N22. Traffic is at its worst in the morning from France and in the afternoon and evening from Andorra. The Envalira Tunnel has reduced congestion and travel time on this busy route. However, in the peak summer season an early start is recommended from both the French and Andorran sides to avoid possible traffic congestion.

Traffic Regulations

French traffic regulations are in force (see **France** Country Introduction). Warning triangles and spare bulbs are required. It is also recommended that a first aid kit be carried.

Police are empowered to impose on-the-spot fines for violations of traffic regulations.

Winter Driving

Winter tyres and snow chains can be hired or purchased from Polar Automotive Ltd, tel 01892 519933, fax 01892 528142, www.snowchains.com, email: sales@snowchains.com (20% discount for Caravan Club members).

Motorways

There are no motorways in Andorra.

Touring

- Andorra is a shopper's paradise and claims to have more than 4,000 shops. It is a 'free' territory and there are no Customs formalities to worry about on entry but checks will be made on returning to the European Union (see **Customs Regulations** in this section). Some of the cheapest buys are spirits, sports goods, electrical and camera equipment, jewellery and clothing.

- There are tourist offices situated in all the main towns. In Andorra-la-Vella the tourist office is on Plaça de la Rotonda, tel 827 117.

- BBC World Service radio may be heard in English on local frequencies 89.0 and 89.5 FM.

⊞**ANDORRA LA VELLA** *8G3* (7km NE Urban) Camping Internacional, Ctra de Vila s/n, AD200 Encamp [tel/fax 831 609; info@camping internacional.com; www.campinginternacional. com] On rd thro Encamp turn at traff lts & motor museum. Med, mkd pitch, pl sl, pt shd; wc; chem disp; mv service pnt; shwrs inc; el pnts (6A) €3.50; lndtte; shop; supmkt 100m; tradsmn; snacks; bar; htd pool; TV rm; 40% statics; phone; bus; adv bkg; poss v cr; Eng spkn; quiet; CCI. "Sm pitches; gd rests nr; friendly, family-run." € 17.00   2004*

⊞**ANDORRA LA VELLA** *8G3* (600m S Urban) Camping Valira, Ave de Salou, AD500 Andorra-la-Vella [tel/fax 722 384; www.campvalira.com] Site on E site of main rd S fr Andorra-la-Vella; behind sports stadium; clearly sp. Lge, hdstg, terr, pt shd; htd wc; chem disp; mv service pnt; shwrs inc; el pnts (3-10A) €3-5.35 (no earth); gas; lndtte; ice; shop; rest; snacks; bar; playgrnd; covrd pool; Eng spkn; adv bkg; quiet; CCI. "Conv NH for shopping; excel facs; vg rest; beware of sudden storms blowing up." ♦ € 21.40   2006*

⊞**ANDORRA LA VELLA** *8G3* (3km SW) Camping Huguet, Ctra de Fontaneda, AD600 St Julia de Loria [tel 843 718; fax 843 803] Site at S end of St Julia. NE fr Spain site 2km fr frontier. After petrol stn & Mamot supmkt turn L over sm rv bdge. Sp & visible fr main rd. Sm, pt shd; wc; chem disp; shwrs inc; el pnts (6A) inc (no earth); lndtte; shop high ssn; supmkt 100m; rest, snacks, bar 1km; playgrnd; rv fishing; Eng spkn; adv bkg; quiet; CCI. "Excel facs; take care with el pnts; poor value for money high ssn." € 23.50   2005*

As soon as we get home I'm going to post all these site report forms to the editor for inclusion in next year's guide. I don't want to miss the September deadline.

⊞**CANILLO** *8G3* (Urban) Camping Pla, Ctra General s/n, AD100 Canillo [tel 851 333; fax 851 280; campingpla@cyberandorra.com; www. campingpla.cyberandorra.com] App Canillo fr S, pass petrol stn on R; take 1st exit at rndabt, over bdge & turn L to site. Med, mkd pitch, pt shd; htd wc; chem disp; baby facs; shwrs inc; el pnts (5-10A) €2.50; gas; lndtte; rest, snacks in town; bar; playgrnd; htd, covrd pool & sports facs in town; skilift 100m; 75% statics; dogs; bus adj; Eng spkn; adv bkg. "Excel location for skiing." € 14.50   2005*

MASSANA, LA *8G3* (2km N Rural) Camping Borda d'Ansalonga, Ctra del Serrat, AD400 Ordino [tel 850 374; fax 735 400; campingansalonga@ andorra.ad; www.campingansalonga.ad] Fr Andorra-la-Vella foll sp La Massana & Ordino. Turn L twd El Serrat, site on R, well sp. Lge, pt shd; htd wc; chem disp; baby facs; shwrs inc; el pnts (10A) €4.80; gas; lndtte; shop; tradsmn; rest; bar; BBQ; playgrnd; pool; games rm; winter statics for skiers; dogs; phone; Eng spkn; quiet; CCI. "Statics moved to storage area in summer; excel tourist info; quieter than sites on main thro rte." 27 Oct-1 May & 15 Jun-15 Sep. € 17.50   2007*

Did you know you can fill in site report forms on the Club's website — www.caravanclub.co.uk?

⊞**MASSANA, LA** *8G3* (2km NW Rural) Camping Xixerella, Crta de Pal, AD400 Erts [tel 836 613; fax 839 113; c-xixerella@campingxixerella.com; www.campingxixerella.com] Fr Andorra la Vella take rd for La Massana; fr there foll sps for Xixerella & vill of Pal. Site on L. Med, terr, pt shd; htd wc; chem disp; htd shwrs; el pnts (3-6A) €4.70; lndtte; shop; rest; bar; playgrnd; pool; crazy golf; entmnt; some statics; dogs €3.10; phone; Eng spkn; adv bkg; quiet; cc acc; red long stay; CCI. "Lovely site; clean, modern facs; gd mountain walks." ♦ € 19.80   2007*

France

France is the largest country in Western Europe and undoubtedly the most diverse. In terms of landscape, art, architecture, culture and history it is unsurpassed, reflecting the influence of centuries of civilisation and balancing the traditional and modern in a lifestyle that others can only envy. Not surprisingly, it is the favourite destination for British caravanners.

Essential Facts

Capital: Paris (population 13 million)

Area: 547,030 sq km

Bordered by: Andorra, Belgium, Germany, Italy, Luxembourg, Monaco, Spain, Switzerland

Terrain: Mostly flat plains or gently rolling hills in north and west; mountain ranges in south and east

Climate: Temperate climate with regional variations; generally warm summers and cool winters; harsh winters in mountainous areas; hot summers in central and Mediterranean areas

Coastline: 3,427 km

Highest Point: Mont Blanc 4,807 m

Population: 61.2 million

Language: French

Religion: 90% Roman Catholic

Government: Republic

Local Time: GMT or BST + 1, ie 1 hour ahead of the UK all year

Currency: Euro divided into 100 cents; £1 = €1.43, €1 = 70 pence*

Public Holidays 2008

Jan 1; Mar 24; May 1, 8 (VE Day); Jul 14 (Bastille Day); Aug 15; Nov 1, 11 (Armistice Day); Dec 25. School summer holidays extend over July and August.

Tourist Information

FRENCH TOURIST BOARD
MAISON DE LA FRANCE
178 PICCADILLY
LONDON W1J 9AL
Tel: 09068 244123
Personal visits/written requests preferred
www.franceguide.com
info.uk@franceguide.com

Opening Hours

Banks – Tues-Sat 9am-1pm & 3pm-5pm; in Paris Mon-Fri 10am-5pm; in busy centres some banks open on Saturday & close on Monday. Early closing the day before a public holiday.

Museums – Daily 10am-5pm; closed Monday or Tuesday, check locally. In Paris many have late opening once a week.

Post Offices – Mon-Fri 8am-7pm; Sat 8am-12 noon

Shops – Mon-Sat 9am/10am-7pm/8pm (supermarkets to 9pm/10pm); food shops generally close all or half-day on Monday; in small towns shops close for lunch from noon to 2 pm.

Telephoning and the Internet

From the UK dial 0033 for France and omit the initial 0 of the 10-digit number. Mobile phone numbers start 06. The international dialling code for Monaco is 00377. To call the UK from France or Monaco dial 0044, omitting the initial zero of the area code.

Mobile phones – use of mobile phones is prohibited while driving and at petrol stations.

Public phones – operated with telephone cards.

Internet – cyber cafés in most towns; public terminals in post offices (pre-paid card) and France Telecom kiosks in major cities.

Emergency numbers – Police 17; Fire brigade 18; Ambulance 15. Or dial 112 and request the service you require; from a mobile phone dial 112 for any service.

* Exchange rates as at September 2007

The following introduction to France should be read in conjunction with the important information contained in the Handbook chapters at the front of this guide.

Camping and Caravanning

Affiliated National Club

FEDERATION FRANCAISE DE CAMPING ET DE CARAVANING
78 RUE DE RIVOLI
F-75004 PARIS
Tel: 01 42 72 84 08, Fax: 01 42 72 70 21
www.ffcc.fr
info@ffcc.fr

General Information

There are approximately 9,000 campsites throughout France classified from 1 to 4 stars, together with almost 2,000 small farm sites. All classified sites must display their classification, current charges, capacity and site regulations at the site entrance. Some sites have an inclusive price per pitch, whereas others charge per person + vehicle(s) + pitch. It is worth remembering that if you stay on site after midday you may be charged for an extra day.

In terms of site tariffs, high season dates and the qualifying age for charging for children vary from site to site and it is quite common for site owners to charge the full adult daily rate for children from seven years and sometimes from as young as three years of age.

Visitors are usually required to pay a tourism tax (taxe de séjour) which is imposed by the local authority and varies from 15 cents to over €1 per person per day, according to the quality and standard of accommodation. Where the tourism tax is not at a flat rate, children under 4 years of age are exempt and children under 10 are charged half the rate. This tax is collected by campsite owners and will be included in your bill.

Casual/wild camping is prohibited in many state forests, national parks and nature reserves. It is also prohibited in all public or private forests in the départements of Landes and Gironde, along the Mediterranean coast including the Camargue, parts of the Atlantic and Brittany coasts, Versailles and Paris, and along areas of coast that are covered by spring tides.

A Camping Card International is recommended and accepted by most sites in lieu of a passport. Holders of a CCI may enjoy discounted fees at campsites.

The Camping Club de France owns a number of sites in France (some of which are listed in this guide and marked CC de F in their site entries) and has partnership agreements with others including the Campéole and Huttopia chains. Members of the CC de F enjoy a 20% reduction with a CCI at these sites. Caravanners wishing to join the CC de F pay an annual fee of €44 per family (2007). Contact the CC de F at 5 bis Rue Maurice Rouvier, 75014 Paris, tel (0)1 58 14 01 23, email secretariat@campingclub.asso.fr, www.campingclub.asso.fr. In addition there are sites managed by, or operating in association with, the Fédération Française de Camping & de Caravaning (marked FFCC in their site entries) which give a 5-10% discount to holders of a CCI.

July and August are the busiest holiday months and campsites in popular tourist areas, such as the Atlantic Coast, Brittany or the south of France, may be crowded. To be certain of a pitch, make an early booking yourself or use the Caravan Club's Advance Booking Service covering approximately 140 French sites. For details see the Travel Service in Europe brochure or visit www.caravanclub.co.uk. Campsites included in the Advance Booking Service network are marked ABS in their site entries in this guide. **The Caravan Club cannot make advance reservations for any other campsites listed in this guide.**

Many French campsites ban the wearing of boxer-style shorts in swimming pools on hygiene grounds. Visitors are advised to ensure that all male members of their party wear proper, brief-style swimming trunks. Many sites also require swimmers to wear swimming caps.

During the low season it is not uncommon for only a few toilet and shower cubicles to be in use on a 'unisex' basis and they may not be cleaned as frequently as they are during the site's busy season. Hot water, other than for showers, may not be available.

Many sites are increasing their proportion of statics – bungalows, chalets and mobile homes – and these are often situated in premium positions, thus reducing the choice of pitches for touring caravanners. However, in many instances these statics are only occupied during the main French holiday season.

Following incidents in recent years, some authorities in southern France have introduced more severe regulations concerning sites which are potentially liable to flooding. It is understood many have been advised to limit their opening dates to mid-April/early May until end August/mid-September. **Low season visitors are recommended to telephone ahead to sites they plan to visit, particularly in the south of France, to check if they are open on the dates required.**

Recently certain areas of southern France have experienced severe water shortages, with a consequent increased fire risk. This may result in some local authorities imposing restrictions on the use of barbecues at short notice. When they are used, you should be vigilant in ensuring that they do not pose a fire risk.

Motor Caravanners

There is a wide network of 'aires de services' in cities, towns and villages across France, many with good security and electricity, water and waste disposal facilities (called 'bornes'). Many 'aires' are specifically for motor caravanners. It is rare that yours will be the only motor caravan ('camping-car' in French) staying on such areas, but take sensible precautions and avoid any that are isolated.

*See **Safety and Security** later in this chapter and in the section **DURING YOUR STAY.***

The Fédération Française de Camping et de Caravaning (FFCC) publishes a 'Guide Officiel Aires de Services Camping-Car', listing 'aires' and stopping places in France and a number of other countries specifically set aside for motor caravans. Bel-air Camping-Caravaning (France) also publishes a guide entitled 'Evasion Camping-Car' covering several countries. The website www.airecampingcar.com lists hundreds of 'aires' by French region and includes their GPS co-ordinates.

A new publication, 'All the Aires France' lists 600 'aires' in towns and villages throughout France and is available from the Club's book shop for £11.99 + p&p.

Many campsites in popular tourist resorts have separate overnight areas of hardstanding with appropriate facilities often just outside the main campsite area. Fees are generally very reasonable.

Motor caravanners are also welcome to free overnight parking at approximately 840 vineyards and farms throughout France through an organisation called France Passion. Your motor caravan must be completely self-contained and you must have your own sanitation. In addition you must arrive and depart in daylight hours. Membership costing €28 runs from Easter to Easter and is open to motor caravanners only. Write for an application form to France Passion, BP 57, 84202 Carpentras or email: info@france-passion.com or visit www.france-passion.com

Municipal Campsites

Municipal campsites are found in most towns and many villages in France. These can usually be booked in advance through the local town hall ('Mairie') during normal office hours. Their published opening dates cannot always be relied on at the start and end of the season and it is advisable to phone ahead or arrive early enough to be able to find an alternative site if your first choice is closed.

In order to deter itinerants and market traders, some municipal sites are restricting entrance by caravan height or length and some refuse to accept caravans with twin-axles ('deux essieux'), or make a large additional charge for them possibly as high as €45 a night. It is advisable to check for restrictions when booking in advance and/or on arrival. Recent visitors report that bona fide caravanners with twin-axle caravans or over-height/weight/length caravans may be allowed entry, and/or may not be charged the higher published tariff, but this is negotiable with site staff at the time of arrival. When approaching a town you may find that municipal sites are not always named. Signposts may simply state 'Camping' or show a tent or caravan symbol.

Security at municipal sites is often rudimentary; at best there may be a barrier at the main entrance which is lowered at night. Occasionally a warden lives on site or nearby but more often (s)he will only call for an hour or so each morning and evening to clean and collect fees. When selecting a municipal site, therefore, try to take account of the character of the area in which it is situated – evident 'problem' urban areas are probably best avoided, as are isolated sites where yours is the only caravan.

France

Naturism

The French Tourist Office, Maison de la France, has links to naturists centres approved by the French Federation of Naturism, or visit www.naturisme.fr and www.france4naturisme.com for details of naturist centres throughout the country. Visitors aged 15 and over are recommended to have a Naturist Licence, although this is no longer compulsory at many naturist centres. A licence can be obtained in advance from British Naturism (tel 01604 620361, www.british-naturism.org.uk, email Headoffice@british-naturism.org.uk) or on arrival at any recognised naturist campsite. For further details contact the FFN at 5 Rue Regnault, 93500 Pantin, fax (0)1 48 45 59 05, email fedenat@ffn-naturisme.org, www.ffn-naturisme.com

Country Information

Cycling

A number of French towns, including Rennes, Strasbourg and Nantes are actively promoting the use of bicycles. Initiatives include increasing the number of cycle paths, providing parking space for bicycles and constructing shelters and cycle hire points in car parks. You may hire bicycles at many local tourist offices and from some railway stations. The French Tourist Office has information on cycle routes and tours throughout France.

In Paris bicycles, known as 'Les Vélibs', are available to hire at very reasonable rates at approximately 750 self-service stations.

The wearing of cycle safety helmets is not yet officially compulsory, but is highly recommended.

Transportation of Bicycles

Transportation on a support fixed to the rear of a vehicle is permitted provided the rear lights and number plate are not obscured.

Electricity and Gas

Current on campsites is usually between 6 and 20 amps. Plugs have two round pins. Most campsites now have CEE connections. Visitors from the UK should be aware of the problem of reversed polarity which may be found on sites in France. If embarking on a tour of several campsites it may be useful to take two differently wired electric adaptors, one wired normally and one for reversed polarity.

The full range of Campingaz cylinders is widely available from large supermarkets and hypermarkets, although recent visitors report that at the end of the holiday season stocks may be low or shops may have run out altogether. Other popular brands of gas which visitors have found to be economical and easy to use are Primagaz, Butagaz, Totalgaz and Le Cube. A loan deposit is required, and caravanners who are purchasing a cylinder for the first time should also purchase the appropriate regulator or adaptor hose, as cylinder connections vary considerably. It is advisable to compare prices carefully between the different brands and to check that cylinders fit into your gas cylinder locker.

*See **Electricity and Gas** in the section **DURING YOUR STAY**.*

Entry Formalities

British and Irish passport holders may stay in France for up to three months. Visitors remaining more than three months must obtain a 'carte de séjour' (residence permit) from the police station or town hall of their French place of residence.

On arrival at a hotel visitors are usually asked to complete a form for identification purposes. At campsites visitors presenting a Camping Card International do not have to complete such a form.

Regulations for Pets

*See **Pet Travel Scheme** under **Documents** in the section **PLANNING AND TRAVELLING**.*

Campsites may impose a restriction of only one dog per pitch and in popular tourist areas local regulations may ban dogs from beaches during the summer months.

In preparation for your return home with your dog you can find the names and addresses of vets in France in the equivalent of the Yellow Pages on www.pagesjaunes.fr or use the link under Animal Health & Welfare on the website of the Department for Environment, Food & Rural Affairs, www.defra.gov.uk

Medical Services

British nationals requiring emergency treatment can take advantage of the French health services on production of a European Health Insurance Card (EHIC) which will cover you for around 70% of standard doctors' and dentists' fees and between 35% and 65% of the cost of most prescribed medicine. For the address of a doctor 'conventionné', ie working within the French health system, ask at a pharmacy. After treatment you should be given a signed statement of treatment (feuille de soins) showing the amount paid. You will need this in order to claim a refund.

Pharmacies dispense prescriptions and are able to dispense first aid, but will charge a fee. Your prescription will be returned to you and you should attach this, together with the stickers (vignettes) attached to the packaging of any medication or drugs, to the 'feuille de soins' in order to obtain a refund. Applications for refunds should be sent to a local sickness insurance office (Caisse Primaire d'Assurance-Maladie) and you will receive payment at your home address within about two months.

You must pay for out-patient treatment at an approved hospital and then claim a partial refund of the costs at the CPAM office. If you are treated as an in-patient you will receive a refund of 75% of the costs. There is also a fixed daily charge which is not refundable.

All visitors should take out comprehensive travel insurance to cover all eventualities, such as the Caravan Club's Red Pennant Motoring & Personal Holiday Insurance. For sports activities such as skiing and mountaineering, travel insurance must include provision for mountain rescue services and helicopter use. Visitors to the Savoie and Haute-Savoie areas should be aware that an accident or illness may result in a transfer to Switzerland for hospital treatment. There is now a reciprocal health care agreement for British citizens in Switzerland, but you will be required to pay the full costs of treatment and afterwards apply for a refund.

RTFB Publishing produces a useful quick reference health guide for travellers, entitled What Should I Do? priced £4.99, plus health phrase books in French and Spanish, price £2.99 each. Telephone 023 8022 9041 or see www.whatshoulddido.com for further details and orders.

Rabies cases occasionally occur in France, and you should therefore avoid contact with cats and dogs.

See *Medical Matters* in the section *DURING YOUR STAY.*

Safety and Security

See *Safety and Security* in the section *DURING YOUR STAY.*

In and around Calais and Dunkirk British-owned cars have been targetted by thieves, both while parked and on the move, eg by thieves flagging drivers down for a lift or indicating that a vehicle has a flat tyre. In some cases tyres have been punctured at service stations forcing drivers to stop soon afterwards on the road or motorway. If you decide or need to stop in such circumstances, be extremely wary of anyone offering help, ensure that car keys are not left in the ignition and that vehicle doors are locked while you investigate.

Pedestrians should beware of bag-snatchers operating on foot and from motorbikes. Avoid carrying passports, credit cards and money all together in handbags or pockets. Do not leave bags in full view when sitting outside at cafés or restaurants. Do not leave valuables unattended on the beach. Valuables, including tobacco and alcohol, should not be left unattended in parked cars and should be kept out of sight at all times.

Thieves and pickpockets operate on the Paris metro and RER (regional suburban network), especially RER line B, and you should be especially vigilant. Be particularly careful in and around shopping centres and car parks and if possible avoid illegal street vendors, many of whom employ persistent and often intimidating techniques to sell their wares, and who are now to be found at many tourist sites and attractions in Paris.

Visitors to Commonwealth War Graves Commission cemeteries in northern France, many of which are in isolated areas, are advised not to leave handbags or other valuables in parked cars as they can be a target for thieves.

The Caravan Club strongly recommends that overnight stops should always be at campsites and not at motorway service areas, ferry terminal car parks or 'aires de service' or 'aires de repos' along motorways where robberies, muggings and encounters with asylum-seekers are occasionally reported. This advice applies to all motorways, but particularly to isolated rest areas (those without petrol stations or caféterias), especially those on the A10 between Paris

France

and Bordeaux, the A16 between Calais and Dunkirk and the A25 between Dunkirk and Lille. There have been several cases of burglary during the night while travellers are asleep inside their caravans, the victims first being rendered unconscious by the thieves using gas. If you ignore this advice and decide to use these areas for a rest during the day or overnight, then you are advised to take appropriate precautions, for example, avoiding parking in isolated or dark areas, shutting all windows, securing locks and making a thorough external check of your vehicle(s) before departing. Consider fitting an alarm to your caravan.

France shares with the rest of Europe a threat from international terrorism. Attacks could be indiscriminate and against civilian targets, including tourist attractions. The French authorities have raised their level of security, particularly at airports and on public transport.

The South of France and Corsica

Always keep car doors locked and windows closed when driving in populated areas of the south of France and especially in the Marseille to Menton area. It is common for bags to be snatched from a front passenger seat, usually by individuals on motorbikes, often when the vehicle is stationary at traffic lights. Conceal bags and purses when driving and never leave valuables in a vehicle, even for a short period of time or when you are nearby.

There have been a number of bomb and other attacks on public buildings by the Corsican nationalist group, the FLNC. Restaurants, a discotheque and holiday villages and chalets have also been targetted. All the buildings were closed at the time of the attacks and no injuries have been reported. While there is no specific threat to British tourists, visitors should take care, particularly in town centres and near public buildings, and be wary of unattended packages.

Fires can be a regular occurrence in forested areas along the Mediterranean coast and in Corsica during summer months. They are generally extinguished quickly and efficiently but short-term evacuations are sometimes necessary. Visits to forested areas will generally be trouble-free, but if you plan to

stay in a forested area you should familiarise yourself with local emergency procedures in the event of fire.

You are advised to avoid leaving your vehicle(s) unattended by the roadside, especially on coastal/beach roads, as thefts are frequent.

Visitors to Corsica are warned that most road accidents occur during the tourist season. Many roads in Corsica are mountainous and narrow, with numerous bends. Drivers should be extra vigilant and beware of wandering animals.

British Embassy

35 RUE DU FAUBOURG ST HONORE
F-75383 PARIS CEDEX 08
Tel: 01 44 51 31 00
www.amb-grandebretagne.fr
webmaster.paris@fco.gov.uk

British Consulates-General

353 BOULEVARD DU PRESIDENT WILSON
F-33073 BORDEAUX CEDEX
Tel: 05 57 22 21 10
postmaster.bordeaux@fco.gov.uk

11 SQUARE DUTILLEUL, F-59000 LILLE
Tel: 03 20 12 82 72
postmaster.lille@fco.gov.uk

24 RUE CHILDEBERT, F-69002 LYON
Tel: 04 72 77 81 70
postmaster.lyon@fco.gov.uk

24 AVENUE DE PRADO, F-13006 MARSEILLES
Tel: 04 91 15 72 10
MarseilleConsular.marseille@fco.gov.uk

There are also Honorary Consulates in Amiens, Boulogne-sur-Mer, Calais, Cherbourg, Clermont-Ferrand, Dunkirk, Le Havre, Lorient, Monaco, Montpellier, Nantes, Nice, St Malo, Toulouse and Tours.

Irish Embassy

4 RUE RUDE, F-75116 PARIS
Tel: 01 44 17 67 00 Fax: 01 44 17 67 60
www.embassyofireland.fr

There is also an Irish Consulate-General in Cannes, and Honorary Consulates in Cherbourg and Monaco.

Customs Regulations

Alcohol and Tobacco

There are no limits on the importation of goods into France which have been purchased in an EU country, provided that these goods are for the importer's personal use. However, the Customs authorities have fixed indicative limits on alcohol and tobacco as follows:

10 litres of spirits
20 litres of fortified wine
90 litres of wine
110 litres of beer
800 cigarettes
400 cigarillos or 200 cigars or 1 kg of tobacco

Duty-Free Imports from Andorra

Duty-free shopping is permitted in Andorra, which is not a member of the EU, but there are strict limits on the amount of goods which can be imported from there into France, and Customs checks are frequently made. Each person is permitted to import the following items from Andorra free of duty or tax:

1.5 litres of spirits or 3 litres fortified wine
5 litres of table wine
300 cigarettes or 150 cigarillos or 75 cigars or 400 gm of tobacco
75 gm of perfume and 375 ml of eau de toilette
Other items up to the value of €525

Alcohol and tobacco allowances only apply to persons aged 17 or over.

Caravans and Motor Caravans

A caravan, motor caravan or trailer imported into France from an EU country may remain indefinitely. The importer must be in possession of the purchase invoice showing that tax (VAT) has been paid in the country of origin. The temporary importation of a caravan by persons other than the owner requires written authorisation from the owner.

Maximum permitted vehicle dimensions are: height 4 metres, width 2.55 metres, length 12 metres excluding the towbar, and total combined length of car + caravan 18.75 metres. In addition, caravans, trailers and motor caravans must not exceed the maximum authorised laden weight displayed on the vehicle's registration certificate.

There are no Customs controls at the borders with EU countries, but border police may carry out identity checks. Some border crossings in the Alps to Italy and in the Pyrénées to Spain close in winter. Border crossing posts with Germany are open continuously, except for those on ferries crossing the Rhine. Customs offices on main tourist traffic routes to Switzerland are permanently open.

See also Customs Regulations in the section PLANNING AND TRAVELLING.

Documents

Driving Licence

You should carry your driving licence at all times when driving, together with original vehicle registration document, insurance certificate and MOT certificate (if applicable), together with a letter of authority from the owner of the vehicle if it is not registered in your name. A copy of your CRIS document is also advisable.

Passport

Everyone, whether French or foreign, must carry identity papers, ie a passport, at all times as the police are empowered to check a person's identity at any time.

See Documents in the section PLANNING AND TRAVELLING.

Money

See Money in the section PLANNING AND TRAVELLING.

It is understood that French banks will not cash travellers' cheques for non-account holders. Therefore, their use is not recommended as your only means of obtaining cash. You may be able to cash them at some post offices but handling charges and rates of commission for exchanging both travellers' cheques and bank notes may vary considerably and it is recommended that you check such charges before the transaction goes through. Pre-loadable travel money cards are a realistic alternative, offering the security of travellers' cheques with the convenience of a cash card.

Regular visitors to France may wish to consider opening a euro bank account in France in order to obtain a French credit/debit card. This will then avoid the problem of using credit cards at automated petrol stations and means that you will not have to pay any exchange rate fees or commission charges to withdraw euros from cash machines or to use the card in shops, restaurants, campsites etc. Britline, a branch of Crédit Agricole is one bank which provides an English-speaking French banking service to residents of the UK and Ireland, tel 0033 231 55 67 89 or see www.britline.com

Major credit cards are widely accepted and cash dispensers are widespread – many allowing users to choose instructions in English. VISA cards are displayed as 'Carte Bleue'.

France

'Chip and PIN' cards have been in use in France for a number of years. However, the French system has had to be modified to make it compatible with that used in the rest of Europe and, until the modifications are completed across the whole country, you may still be required on occasion to sign a receipt.

Cardholders are recommended to carry their credit card issuer/bank's 24-hour UK contact number in case of loss or theft.

Motoring

Alcohol

The maximum legal level of alcohol in the blood is less than in the UK, at 0.05%. It is advisable to adopt the 'no drink and drive' rule at all times. The police carry out random breath tests and penalties are severe.

Breakdown Service

Breakdown and accident assistance on motorways and on motorway service and rest areas must be obtained by contacting the police. They can be called from one of the orange emergency telephones placed approximately every 2 km or, if in a service area, by asking service station staff to contact the police for you. The police will arrange breakdown and towing assistance. No breakdown vehicle will enter a motorway without police authority.

Charges for motorway assistance are fixed by the government. The tariff (2007) for breakdown service is €107 on a motorway or express road equipped with emergency telephones. This covers the cost of up to 30 minutes repairing your vehicle on the spot. The cost of towing it up to 5 km beyond the next motorway exit is €107 for vehicles up to 1,800 kg and €132 for vehicles between 1,800 and 3,500 kg. Higher fees are charged for breakdown assistance between 6pm and 8am and at weekends and public holidays. Charges are subject to change.

In the event of an accident off the motorway where people are injured or emergency assistance is required, dial 17 (police) from any phone. A European Accident Statement form should be completed and signed by all persons involved in an accident.

Essential Equipment

*See **Motoring Equipment** in the section **PLANNING AND TRAVELLING.***

Lights

The use of dipped headlights is recommended at all times, day and night, but has not yet been made compulsory. Headlights must be adjusted for driving on the right if they are likely to dazzle other road users. Bulbs are more likely to fail with constant use and you are required to carry spares at all times. Drivers able to replace a faulty bulb when requested to do so by the police may not avoid a fine, but may avoid the expense of calling out a garage.

If a driver flashes his headlights in France, he is generally indicating that he has priority and you should give way, contrary to standard practice in the UK.

Reflectorised Waistcoat

You are strongly recommended to wear a reflectorised jacket when getting out of a vehicle which is stationary on the carriageway or on the side of the road outside a built-up area. While not yet a legal requirement, reports have been received recently of over-zealous police officers fining motorists for not having such a waistcoat or jacket in their vehicle.

Warning Triangles

Temporarily imported vehicles must be equipped with either hazard warning lights or a warning triangle (compulsory for cars towing a caravan or trailer, and for vehicles over 3,500 kg). You are recommended to carry warning triangles, as breakdown may affect a vehicle's electrics. The Tourist Office recommends carrying two triangles.

A warning triangle must be placed on the carriageway 30 metres from the obstacle so that it may be seen at a distance of 100 metres in clear weather by drivers approaching along the same lane of traffic.

Fuel

Unleaded petrol pumps are marked Essence Sans Plomb. Diesel pumps are marked Gas Oil or Gazole. There is no leaded petrol but lead replacement petrol is sold under the name of Supercarburant or Super ARS.

LPG (also called Gepel or GPL) is widely available in petrol stations across the whole of France, especially on motorways. Maps showing their company's outlets are issued free by most LPG suppliers, eg Shell, Elf etc. A list of their locations is available on-line on www.gpl.fr which also has information on retail outlets across the whole of Europe.

Filling stations often close on Sundays and those at supermarkets, where petrol is generally cheaper, may close for lunch. At supermarkets it is advisable to check the height and width clearance before towing past the pumps, or alternatively fill up when travelling solo.

Credit cards are generally accepted at filling stations. Some automatic pumps are operated by credit cards but these may not yet accept credit cards issued outside France. A sign on the petrol pump usually indicates this.

To find the cheapest fuel in any area log on to www.zagaz.com. Simply click on the département you want on the map of France on the home page to find the locations of fuel stations across the country, together with their prices.

*See also **Fuel** under **Motoring Advice** in the section **PLANNING AND TRAVELLING**.*

Mountain Passes and Tunnels

*See the chapter **Mountain Passes and Tunnels** in the section **PLANNING AND TRAVELLING**.*

Following fires in 1999 and 2005, safety features in both the Mont Blanc and Fréjus tunnels have been significantly overhauled and improved. Both tunnels are heavily used by freight vehicles and traffic is subject to a number of restrictions including minimum and maximum speed limits. In the Fréjus tunnel vehicles over 3,500 kg are subject to one-hour alternate traffic flows, starting at 8am leaving France. All drivers should listen to the tunnels' radio stations and if your vehicle runs on LPG you should tell the toll operator before entering the tunnel. See www.tunnelmb.net and www.tunneldufrejus.com

Overtaking and Passing

Overtaking where there is a solid single or double centre line is heavily penalised.

On steep gradients, vehicles travelling downhill must give way to vehicles travelling uphill. If one vehicle must reverse, it is the vehicle without a trailer (as opposed to a combination of vehicles) or the lighter weight vehicle which must do so. If both vehicles are of the same category the vehicle travelling downhill must reverse, unless it is clearly

easier for the vehicle travelling uphill, eg if there is a convenient passing place nearby.

Outside built-up areas, outfits totalling more than 3,500 kg or more than 7 metres in length are required by law to leave at least 50 metres between themselves and the vehicle in front. They are only permitted to use the two right-hand lanes on roads with three or more lanes and, where overtaking is difficult, should slow down or stop to allow other smaller vehicles to pass.

Parking

As a general rule, all prohibitions are indicated by road signs or by yellow markings on the kerb. Stopping or parking on the left-hand side of the road is prohibited except in one-way streets. Parking meters and 'pay and display' machines are commonplace and in Paris machines do not take coins, only the 'Paris Carte' card available from tobacconists, or in some cases, you can pay with credit or debit cards. On public holidays and during August you can sometimes park free of charge in certain streets; this is indicated by yellow stickers placed on parking meters. Street parking is limited to two hours.

If you need to stop on the open road ensure that your vehicle(s) are driven off the road. It is illegal to spend the night in a caravan at the roadside.

In Paris two red routes have been created on which stopping and parking are absolutely prohibited. The east-west route includes the left banks of the River Seine and the Quai de la Mégisserie; the north-south route includes the Avenue du Général Leclerc, part of the Boulevard St-Michel, the Rue de Rivoli, the Boulevards Sebastopol, Strasbourg, Barbes and Ornano, Rue Lafayette and Avenue Jean Jaures.

Caravans and motor caravans are prohibited from parking in the area from the Champs Elysées to the Place de la Concorde, in the Champs de Mars (Eiffel Tower) area, in the Bois de Boulogne (outside the campsite), in the Bois de Vincennes and, in general, near historic monuments. Elsewhere, caravanners must observe parking restrictions indicated by signs.

In Paris it is prohibited to leave a parked vehicle in the same place for more than 24 consecutive hours. This provision also

France

applies to the following départements which surround Paris: Haut-de-Seine (92), Seine-St Denis (93) and Val-de-Marne (95).

Illegally parked vehicles, even if registered abroad, may be towed away, impounded or immobilised by wheel clamps.

Parking for the Disabled

The leaflet 'European Parking Card for People with Disabilities' describes the concessions available under the Blue Badge scheme and gives advice on how to explain to police and parking attendants in their own language that, as a foreign visitor, you are entitled to the same parking concessions as disabled residents.

See also **Parking Facilities for the Disabled** under *Motoring Advice* in the section **PLANNING AND TRAVELLING**.

Priority

In France, although the old rule of 'priority from the right' no longer applies at major junctions and roundabouts, it is still advisable to be watchful, particularly in some towns where the yellow lozenge signs still exist. Outside built-up areas, all main roads of any importance have right of way, indicated by:

A red-bordered triangle showing a black arrow with horizontal bar on a white background.

A yellow diamond within a white diamond.

On entering towns, the same sign will often have a line through it, warning that vehicles may pull out from a side road on the right and will have priority.

Priority road

End of priority road

Traffic on the roundabout has priority

Roundabouts

At roundabouts, drivers must give way to traffic already on the roundabout. This is indicated by a red-bordered triangular sign showing a roundabout symbol with the words 'Vous n'avez pas la priorité' or 'Cédez le passage' underneath. However, in a few areas the old ruling of priority given to traffic entering the roundabout still applies and where the sign is not present you should approach with care.

See **Priority and Roundabouts** under **Motoring Advice** in the section **PLANNING AND TRAVELLING**.

Roads

France has a very extensive network of good quality roads falling into three categories: autoroutes (A) ie motorways; national (N) roads; and departmental (D) roads. There are over 8,000 kilometres of motorways, on most of which tolls are levied. British motorists will find French roads relatively uncongested. Lorries are not allowed on the road for a 24-hour period from 11pm on Saturdays and the eve of public holidays.

Re-Numbering of French Roads

The French government has decided to transfer the administration of approximately 18,000 kilometres of national roads to local authorities, resulting in the significant re-classification and re-numbering of roads. For example, the N21 has become the D821 and a part of the N20 is now the D820. The process started in January 2006 and will take several years to complete as each local authority chooses its own re-numbering system and changes road signs.

Where known at the time this guide was compiled, such road number changes have been incorporated into the directions contained in the campsite entries which follow.

Road Signs and Markings

Directional signposting on major roads is generally good. Signs may be placed on walls pointing across the road they indicate and this may be confusing at first until you get the feel for them. The words 'tout droit' have nothing to do with turning right they mean 'go straight ahead' or 'straight on'.

Although roads are well-numbered, it is not advisable to plan your route by road numbers as road signs on approach to roundabouts and at junctions usually do not show road numbers, merely the destination, numbers being displayed once you are on the road itself. Make sure you know the names of places along your proposed route, and not just the road numbers. Once you have seen your destination town signposted continue along the road until told otherwise. Intermediate junctions or roundabouts where you do not have to turn usually omit the destination name if it is straight on.

Lines on the carriageway are generally white. A yellow zigzag line indicates a bus stop, blue markings indicate that parking is restricted and yellow lines on the edge of the roadway indicate that stopping and/or parking is prohibited. A solid single or double white line in the centre of the road indicates that overtaking is not permitted.

STOP signs mean stop. Creeping slowly in a low gear will not do, even if local drivers do so. You must come to a complete halt otherwise you may be liable to a fine.

Whilst road signs conform to international standards, some other commonly used signs you may see include:

RAPPEL		i Information Bison Futé
Continuation of restriction	Alternative holiday routes	Information centre for holiday route

Attention – *Caution*
Bouchon – *Traffic jam*
Chausée deformée – *Uneven road*
Chemin sans issue – *No through road*
Créneau de dépassement – *2-lane passing zone, dual carriageway*
Déviation – *Diversion*
Fin d'interdiction de stationner – *End of prohibited parking*
Gravillons – *Loose chippings*
Itineraire bis – *Alternative route*
Nids de poules – *Potholes*
Péage – *Toll*
Poids lourds – *Lorries*
Ralentissez – *Slow down*
Rappel – *Continued restriction (eg no overtaking or speed limit)*
Rétrécissement – *Narrow lane*
Route barrée – *Road closed*
Sens interdit – *No entry*
Sens unique – *One-way street*
Sortie d'usine – *Factory exit*
Stationnement interdit – *No parking*
Tout droit – *Straight on*
Toutes directions – *All directions*
Travaux – *Road works*
Virages – *Bends*

Traffic Lights

- There is no amber light after the red light in the traffic light sequence.

- Flashing amber light indicates caution, slow down, proceed but give way to vehicles coming from the right.

- Flashing red light indicates no entry; it is also used to mark level crossings, obstacles, etc.

- A yellow arrow at the same time as a red light indicates that drivers may turn in the direction of the arrow, traffic permitting, and providing they give way to pedestrians.

- Watch out for traffic lights which may be mounted high above the road and hard to spot.

Speed Limits

See **Speed Limits Table** under **Motoring Advice** in the section **PLANNING AND TRAVELLING.**

Speed limits on motorways (in dry weather) are higher than in the UK, although they are lower on ordinary roads, and the accident rate is greater. Drivers undertaking long journeys in or through France should plan carefully and take sufficient breaks; a minimum of 15 minutes every two hours is recommended.

Motorists should be aware that non-GPS radar detectors, laser detectors or speed camera jammers are illegal in France, whether in use in your vehicle or not. If caught, you are liable to both a fine up to €1,500 and confiscation of the device, and possibly confiscation of your vehicle if unable to pay the fine. Such devices should be removed from your vehicle before travelling to France. GPS devices which pinpoint the position of speed cameras are legal, but be warned that local law enforcement officers may not be aware of the difference between legal and illegal devices. The website http://english.controleradar.org allows you to look up the location of fixed speed cameras throughout France.

The use of mobile speed cameras and radar traps is frequent, even on remote country roads. These may be operated from parked camera vans or motor bikes, or they may be hand-held. Most static cameras are hidden, or at best inconspicuous, in the form of brown/beige boxes mounted just off the ground. Oncoming drivers may flash warnings, but headlight-flashing for this purpose is itself illegal, so do not be tempted to do it yourself.

Inside Built-up Areas

The general speed limit is 50 km/h (31 mph) which may be raised to 70 km/h (44 mph) on

France

important through-roads or as indicated by the appropriate sign. The beginning of a built-up area is marked by a road sign giving the name of the town or village in black letters on a light background with a red border. The end of the built-up area is indicated by the same sign with a red diagonal line through it – see below. Signs showing the name of a locality in white letters on a blue background do not indicate a built-up area for the purpose of this regulation.

Therefore, when you enter a town or village, even if there is no actual speed limit warning sign, the town sign itself indicates that you are entering a 50 km/h (31 mph) zone. This is the point at which you may encounter the flash of a hidden speed camera, even as you attempt to slow down. The end of the 50 km/h zone is indicated by the place name sign crossed out, as described above. The word 'rappel' on a speed limit sign is a reminder of that limit.

The speed limit on stretches of motorway in built-up areas is 110 km/h (68 mph), except the Paris ring road where the limit is 80 km/h (50 mph).

Outside Built-up Areas

General speed limits are as follows:

- On normal roads 90 km/h (56 mph)
- On dual-carriageways separated by a central reservation 110 km/h (68 mph)
- On motorways 130 km/h (81 mph)

These limits also apply to private cars towing a trailer or caravan, provided the total weight does not exceed 3,500 kg. Vehicles over 3,500 kg are classed as goods vehicles and the speed limit on motorways is 100 km/h (56 mph) while on dual carriageways it is 80-100 km/h (50-62 mph) and on other roads 80 km/h (50 mph).

In case of rain or adverse weather conditions, the speed limits are lowered as follows:

- On motorways 110 km/h (68 mph)

- On urban motorways and dual carriageways 100 km/h (62 mph)
- Outside built-up areas 80 km/h (50 mph)

A speed limit of 50 km/h (31 mph) applies on all roads in foggy conditions when visibility is less than 50 metres.

In long road tunnels there are lower maximum speed limits; in addition, minimum speeds are enforced.

Recently-Qualified Drivers

The minimum age to drive in France is 18 years. Driving on a provisional licence is not allowed. Visiting motorists who have held a full driving licence for less than two years must comply at all times with the wet weather speed limits shown above.

Rumble Strips and Sleeping Policemen

These means of slowing vehicles are becoming more prevalent, particularly, it is reported, in the Massif Central. They are much more offensive than the British versions and should be shown the greatest respect. The advance warning sign shows 'Ralentissez' (slow down).

Traffic Jams

The busiest motorways in France are the A6 and the A7 (the Autoroute du Soleil) from Paris via Lyon to the south. Travelling from the north, bottlenecks are often encountered at Auxerre, Chalon-sur-Saône, Lyon, Valence and Orange. An alternative route to the south is the A20, which is largely toll-free, or the toll-free A75 via Clermont-Ferrand.

During periods of severe congestion on the A6, A7 and A10 Paris-Bordeaux motorways, traffic police close off junctions and divert holiday traffic onto alternative routes or 'Itinéraires Bis' which run parallel to main roads. Yellow and black signs indicate these routes. For a summer traffic calendar, indicating when certain areas are most prone to traffic jams, together with a real-time congestion map and regional telephone numbers to call for traffic and travel information, see www.bison-fute. equipement.gouv.fr (in French only).

Bison Futé information centres located on main national roads are open during the peak summer holiday traffic period, either daily or at weekends, and on public holidays. These centres offer free up-to-date information about the current traffic situation and possible alternative routes. In addition, travel information may be obtained from orange emergency call boxes located every 4 km on main roads and every 2 km on motorways. Calls are free.

In general, Friday afternoons and Saturday mornings are busiest on roads leading to the south, and on Saturday and Sunday afternoons roads leading north may well be congested.

It is still generally true that many French people drop everything for lunch and, therefore, between noon and 2pm roads are quieter and good progress can often be made.

At the start of the school holidays in early July, at the end of July and during the first and last few days of August roads are particularly busy. Avoid driving on these days if possible and avoid the changeover weekend at the end of July/beginning of August when traffic both north and southbound can be virtually at a standstill. Traffic can also be very heavy around the Christmas/New Year period and on the weekend of any public holiday.

For traffic reports tune into Autoroute-Info on 107.7 FM for updates on traffic and weather, roadworks and safety, as well as information on tourist attractions. Information on traffic conditions on autoroutes may be obtained on www.autoroutes.fr, www.cofiroute.fr or www. bison-fute.equipement.gouv.fr

Violation of Traffic Regulations

Severe fines and penalties are in force for motoring offences and the police are authorised to impose and collect fines on the spot. Violations include minor infringements such as an excess at a parking meter, not wearing a seat belt or not respecting a STOP sign. More serious infringements such as dangerous overtaking, crossing a continuous central white line and driving at very high speeds, can result in confiscation of your driving licence.

Police are particularly strict about speeding and many automatic speed controls and speed cameras have been introduced and more are planned. Motorists caught doing more than 40 km/h (25 mph) over the speed limit face immediate confiscation of their driving licence. No distinction is made between French and foreign drivers. British motorists without a co-driver could be left stranded and face heavy costs to get their vehicle(s) home, which would not be covered by insurance.

A new category of offence has been created for drivers who deliberately put the lives of others in danger, with a maximum fine of €15,000 and a jail sentence. Failure to pay may result in your car being impounded. Your driving licence may also be suspended for up to five years.

Computerised tills at motorway toll booths tell the cashier not only how much a driver needs to pay, but also whether he has been speeding. By calculating the distance a vehicle has travelled and the journey time, the computer will indicate by means of a red light whether the speed limit has been exceeded, prompting the cashier to call the police who will impose a heavy on-the-spot fine.

By paying fines on the spot or within 24 hours, motorists can avoid court action and even reduce the fine. These fines must be paid in euros, though in some cases travellers' cheques may be accepted. Cheques and credit cards are not accepted. A receipt should be requested showing the full amount paid.

In some cases instead of, or in addition to, a fine or prison sentence, a vehicle may be confiscated. Although this measure is not often taken, the main offences for which it may be applied are hit and run, refusal to stop when requested, or driving under the influence of alcohol. In such a case, the vehicle becomes the property of the French Government.

A driver involved in an accident, or who has committed a traffic offence such as speeding or not wearing a seatbelt, must take a saliva drugs test.

The authorities are concerned at the serious overloading of many British-registered vehicles touring in France. Drivers of overloaded vehicles may be prosecuted and held responsible for any accident in which they are involved.

Winter Driving

Snow chains must be fitted to vehicles using snow-covered roads in compliance with the relevant road signs. Fines may be imposed for non-compliance. Winter tyres and snow chains can be hired or purchased from Polar Automotive Ltd, tel 01892 519933, fax 01892 528142, www.snowchains.com, email: sales@snowchains.com (20% discount for Caravan Club members).

France

Motorways

France has over 8,000 kilometres of excellent motorways and more are under construction or planned. Tolls are payable on most routes according to distance travelled and category of vehicle(s) and, because motorways are privately financed, prices per kilometre in different parts of the country vary.

Emergency telephones connected to the police are located every 2 km.

Motorway Service Areas

Stopping is allowed for a few hours at the service areas of motorways, called 'aires', and some have sections specially laid out for caravans. All have toilet facilities and a water supply but at 'aires' with only basic facilities, water may not be suitable for drinking, indicated by a sign 'eau non potable'. In addition 'aires de repos' have picnic and play areas, whereas 'aires de service' resemble UK motorway service areas with fuel, shop, restaurant and parking for all types of vehicle. It should be noted that toll (péage) tickets are only valid for 24 or 48 hours depending on the particular autoroute – used check your ticket for details.

Michelin's Motorway Atlas of France gives the location of 'aires' throughout the country. **'Aires' are not campsites and, for reasons of security, the Caravan Club recommends that when seeking an overnight stop, you should leave the motorway system and find a suitable campsite.**

See Safety and Security earlier in this chapter.

Motorway Tolls

Class 1 – Vehicle up to 2 m in height (measured from the ground) with or without caravan/trailer up to 2 m (excluding roof rack/antennae etc), and with total weight up to 3,500 kg.

Class 2 – Vehicle with height between 2 m and 3 m and total weight up to 3,500 kg; vehicles in Class 1 towing a caravan or trailer with height between 2 m and 3 m.

Class 3 – Vehicle with 2 axles and height over 3 m, or with total weight over 3,500 kg.

Class 4 – Vehicle or combination of vehicles with 3 axles or more, with height over 3 m, or with total weight over 3,500 kg.

Road	Total Journey	Class 1	Class 2	Class 3	Class 4
A1	Paris to Lille* (Autoroute du Nord)	10.50	14.90	22.50	29.40
A2	Combles (Junc A1) to Belgian border	1.00	1.40	1.80	2.80
A4	Paris to Reims (Autoroute de l'Est)	8.70	13.10	19.30	25.10
	Paris to Metz	20.30	30.50	45.10	59.40
	Metz to Strasbourg	10.30	15.50	21.70	29.10
	Paris to Strasbourg	30.90	46.60	67.80	89.90
A5	Melun to Langres	13.50	17.70	32.20	44.50
A6	Paris to Lyon (Autoroute du Soleil)	28.20	36.90	66.10	91.30
	Paris to Beaune	17.00	19.50	39.70	54.20
A7	Lyon to Marseille (Autoroute du Soleil)	17.70	27.50	36.50	49.50
A8	Aix-en-Provence to Menton (Italian Border)	17.40	26.30	36.00	49.70
A9	Orange (A7) to Le Perthus (Spanish Border)	19.50	30.30	41.80	55.00
A10	Paris to Poitiers (Autoroute Aquitaine)	29.50	46.50	64.20	87.90
	Poitiers to Bordeaux	17.00	26.20	36.20	48.70
A11	Paris to Le Mans West (Autoroute L'Océane)	16.50	28.80	34.50	48.60
	Le Mans to Nantes	7.00	16.60	25.80	33.10
A13	Paris to Caen (Autoroute de Normandie)	12.30	19.20	32.20	36.20
A16	Paris to Boulogne	16.90	25.30	36.60	53.50
A20	Gignac to Montauban Nord	10.00	15.50	21.00	30.30
A26/A1	Paris to Calais (A26/A1)	18.30	28.20	38.50	53.30
	Calais to Reims	16.70	26.10	36.70	47.90
	Reims to Troyes (A5)	8.20	12.10	19.50	25.70

Road	Total Journey	Class 1	Class 2	Class 3	Class 4
A28	Rouen to Alençon Nord	11.40	19.10	26.50	35.40
	Alençon Nord to Tours	7.80	11.40	15.30	20.10
A29	Le Havre (A13) to St Saëns (A28)	6.10	9.20	12.00	16.80
A31	Beaune to Metz (Luxembourg Border)	12.90	18.00	30.70	42.30
A36	Beaune to Mulhouse (German Border)	13.20	17.30	31.90	44.00
A39	Dijon to Bourg-en-Bresse	7.50	9.90	17.80	24.60
A40	Macon to Genève (Swiss Border)	13.70	20.70	33.50	43.80
A41	Grenoble to Scientrier (A40)	12.50	18.40	24.50	34.00
A42	Lyon to Pont d'Ain (A40)	3.30	4.30	8.00	11.00
A43	Lyon to Chambéry	9.40	15.10	20.00	26.30
	Chambéry to St Michel-de-Maurienne	10.10	15.30	28.10	37.90
A48	Bourgoin (A43) to Grenoble	4.50	7.20	9.30	12.20
A49	Grenoble to Valence	5.50	8.30	11.10	15.20
A50	Aix-en-Provence to Toulon	6.40	9.70	13.40	18.40
A51	Aix-en-Provence to Sisteron	9.30	14.20	19.50	26.80
A52	Chateauneuf-le-Rouge (A8) to Aubagne	3.10	4.70	6.50	9.00
A54	Arles to Nîmes	1.30	2.00	2.90	3.70
A57	Toulon to Le Cannet-des-Maures (A8)	1.90	2.90	4.00	5.50
A61	Toulouse to Narbonne Sud	10.60	17.30	22.90	30.10
A62	Bordeaux to Toulouse	15.80	24.50	33.30	44.60
A63	Bordeaux to Spanish Border	6.20	9.60	11.50	16.00
A64	Bayonne to St Gaudens	12.10	18.60	25.50	34.30
A66	Toulouse to Pamiers	4.30	6.80	9.00	12.20
A68	Toulouse to Montrastruc	1.20	1.90	2.70	3.70
A71	Orléans to Clermont Ferrand	20.40	28.60	47.40	64.90
A72	Clermont Ferrand to St Etienne	9.20	14.30	20.30	26.50
A77	Dordives (A6) to Nevers	4.10	5.40	10.10	13.90
A81	Le Mans to Laval	8.30	12.00	18.20	23.60
A83	Nantes to Niort	9.80	15.00	21.20	28.00
A85	Angers to Tours	5.30	7.40	10.80	13.90
A89	Bordeaux (Arveyres) to Mussidan	8.00	12.40	16.60	24.40
	Tulle (St Germain) to Le Sancy	8.20	12.60	17.40	24.60

Toll charges in euros

* Different charge bands apply at different times and on Sundays and public holidays

France

The table provides a guide to motorway tolls between main towns. These were in effect in autumn 2007 and are subject to change during 2008. A more detailed list of toll charges is available to Caravan Club members from the Club's Travel Service Information Officer. There are numerous stretches of motorway, particularly around large cities, where no tolls are levied.

Payments may be made in cash, by credit card, or by euro travellers' cheques but be aware that when paying with a credit card you will not be asked for a signature or required to key in a PIN. Pay booths marked as accepting credit cards only are usually geared to Class 1 vehicles and will have a height restriction which does not permit the passage of caravans.

On less frequently-used motorways toll collection is increasingly by automatic machine equipped with 'magic-eye' height detectors. It is probably simplest to pay with a credit card but there should be a cash/change machine adjacent. Avoid 'télépéage' toll booths which are for residents with pre-paid window stickers.

Motorists driving Class 2 vehicles adapted for the transport of disabled persons pay the toll specified for Class 1 vehicles. Holding a disabled person's Blue Badge does not automatically entitle foreign motorists to pay Class 1 charges, and the decision whether to downgrade from Class 2 to 1 will be made by the person at the toll booth, based on experience of similar vehicles registered in France.

Toll Bridges

Tolls are charged across the Pont de Tancarville on the River Seine estuary near Le Havre (A15) and the Pont de Normandie near Honfleur. Current charges are €2.90 and €5.80 respectively for car/caravan outfits and motor caravans.

The Pont de l'Ile d'Oléron and Pont de la Seudre (linking La Tremblade with Marennes) south-west of Rochefort are toll-free, but a return charge is made on the Pont de l'Ile de Ré from La Rochelle to the Ile de Ré of €9-16.50 for a car or a motor caravan and €15-27 for a car plus caravan, depending on the time of year.

The 2.5 km long Millau Viaduct opened in December 2004 on the A75 autoroute between Clermont-Ferrand and Béziers. Charges (2007) in summer are €10.60 for a car and caravan, or a motor caravan; lower charges apply in winter see www.leviaducdemillau.com

Touring

- France is divided administratively into 'régions', each of which consists of several 'départements'. There are 95 départements in total including Corsica, and these are approximately equivalent to our counties, although with more autonomy.

- Paris, the capital and hub of the region known as the Ile de France, remains the political, economic, artistic, cultural and tourist centre of France.

- Visit www.parisinfo.com for a wealth of information on what to see and do in the city. A Paris Pass, valid for 1 to 5 days, entitles you to free entrance (ahead of the queues) to over 60 Paris attractions and free unlimited public transport and a range of discounts see www.paris-pass.com

- Under 18's are admitted free and visitors over 60 years old are entitled to reduced price entrance to national museums; show your passport as proof of age. National museums, including the Louvre, are closed on Tuesday with the exception of Versailles and the Musée d'Orsay which are closed on Monday. Entrance to national museums, including the Louvre, is free on the first Sunday of every month. Municipal museums are usually closed on Monday and most museums close on public holidays.

- Ferry services operate for cars and passengers between Poole and Portsmouth and St Malo via Jersey and Guernsey. Caravans and motor caravans are permitted to enter Jersey between May and September, subject to certain conditions, including pre-booking direct with a registered campsite. For further information and a list of campsites on Jersey where caravans are permitted, please see www.jersey.com or contact the Club's Travel Service Information Officer.

- There are three campsites on Guernsey but, for the moment, caravans are not permitted to enter the island. However, motor caravans may be accepted providing permission is first obtained from the Island Development Committee.

  For further details contact the Club's Travel Service Information Officer.

- Sunday lunch is an important occasion for French families; if you have found a restaurant that appeals to you it is advisable to book in advance. Many restaurants are not open on Sunday evening. Restaurants must display priced menus outside and most offer a set menu 'plat du jour' or 'table d'hôte' which usually represents good value. A service charge of 15% is included in restaurant bills but if you have received good service a tip may be left. Smoking is not allowed in bars and restaurants.

- Pasteurised milk is available everywhere; ask for 'lait frais pasteurisé'. When water is not drinkable there is usually a notice EAU NON-POTABLE.

- Information on shopping in Calais, including tips on where best to buy wine, beer, cigarettes etc and DIY supplies, as well as opening hours and price comparisons, can be found on www.day-tripper.net

Local Travel

Several towns in addition to Paris have metro or tram systems and most offer a comprehensive bus network. The Paris metro network comprises 15 lines and around 300 stations in eight zones, and has many connections to the RER (regional suburban network) and the SNCF national railway system. For tourists Paris Visite travel passes are available allowing unlimited travel for one to five days across some or all of the travel zones and on the Montmartre funicular. For further information see www.ratp.fr

Senior citizens aged 60 and over are entitled to a 25% discount when using French railways. Show your passport as proof of age.

Car ferry services operate all year across the Gironde estuary between Royan and Le Verdon (approximately €50 for car, caravan and 2 adults), and between Blaye and Lamarque north of Bordeaux.

Ferry services operate from Marseille, Nice and Toulon to Corsica. For information contact:

SOUTHERN FERRIES
30 CHURTON STREET
LONDON SW1V 2LP
Tel: 020 7976 6340
www.sncm.fr

Much of France remains undiscovered because visitors lack the time, inclination or courage to deviate from the prescribed checklist of what-to-see. Often it's just a question of taking N and D roads instead of autoroutes; many of the country's most appealing treasures whether man-made or natural features are sometimes within easy reach of more familiar sights. Ask at local tourist information offices and Syndicats d'Initiative for leaflets about routes connecting points of interest and discover some of those 'off the beaten track' places. 'Bison futé' or 'bis' routes tend to follow more scenic roads; see www.bison-fute. equipement.gouv.fr

All place names used in the Site Entry listings which follow can be found in Michelin's France Atlas, scale 1:200,000 (1 cm = 2 km).

France

CAMPING-ATTITUDE

Because vacation should always really feel like vacation!
Village Center invites you to discover one of its 27 destination campsites spread over the whole of France and proposes you to enjoy your holidays by three different formulas: Zen, leisure and discovery in close contact with the water and the sun.

Information and reservations:

▶ +33 (0)4 99 57 21 21

www.village-center.com

Village center

VACATIONS SHOULD ALWAYS
BE VACATIONS

www.village-center.com
contact@village-center.com

ABBEVILLE *3B3* (14km SE Rural) **Camp Municipal La Peupleraie, 80510 Long [03 22 31 84 27 or 03 22 31 80 21; fax 03 22 31 82 39; bacquet. lionel@free.fr; www.long.fr]** Exit A16 at junc 21 for D1001 (N1) N then turn L at Ailly-le-Clocher onto D32 for Long & foll sp. Med, mkd pitch, pt shd; wc (some cont); chem disp; shwrs inc; el pnts (6A) inc (long lead req); lndry rm; tradsmn; shop, rest, snacks, bar in vill; BBQ; playgrnd; fishing adj; 90% seasonal statics; dogs; phone adj; poss cr; adv bkg; cc not acc; CCI. "V attractive area beside Somme; many places of interest to visit; gd walking/cycling by rv; vg site; site busy 1st week Sep - flea mkt in town; office open 0800-1100 but warden lives on site." 15 May-31 Oct. € 10.00   2005*

> The opening dates and prices on this campsite have changed. I'll send a site report form to the editor for the next edition of the guide.

ABBEVILLE *3B3* (5km S Urban) **Camp Municipal Le Marais Communal, Rue de Marais-Tulsac, 80132 Mareuil-Caubert [03 22 31 62 37 or 03 22 24 11 46; fax 03 22 31 34 28; mairie-mareuilcaubert@wanadoo.fr]** Leave A28 at junc 3. At T-junc turn L onto D928; foll camping sp. In 4km turn sharp R onto D3 into Mareuil-Caubert. In 1km turn L thro houses to site by stadium. Well sp. Med, mkd pitch, hdstg, pt shd; wc; chem disp; mv service pnt; shwrs; el pnts (6A) €2.55 (poss rev pol); shop & 5km; rest 5km; playgrnd; 25% statics; CCI. "V quiet, clean site; friendly; no twin-axles or vans over 8m; new hdstg for m'vans stony (2006); barrier open 0800-2000, 0800-0900 & 1900-2000 low ssn; interesting area; vg NH to/fr Calais." 1 Apr-30 Sep. € 10.30   2007*

ABBEVILLE *3B3* (10km SW Rural) **Camping Le Clos Cacheleux, Route de Bouillancourt, 80132 Miannay [03 22 31 48 88; fax 03 22 31 35 33; raphael@camping-lecloscacheleux.com; www. camping-lecloscacheleux.com]** Fr A28 exit junc 2 onto D925 sp Cambron. In 5km at Miannay turn S onto D86 sp Bouillancourt. Site thro vill on L adj Camping Le Val de Trie. Sm, mkd pitch, pt shd; wc; chem disp; baby facs; shwrs inc; el pnts (10A) inc; lndtte; shop 1km; tradsmn; rest 1km; snacks; bar; BBQ; htd pool; paddling pool; sand beach 20km; fishing pond; tennis 3km; games area; entmnt; child entmnt; farm animals; TV rm; dogs €1.30; Eng spkn; adv bkg; red low ssn; quiet; cc acc; CCI. "Pleasant, peaceful, wooded site; helpful staff; gd walking & cycling."♦ 1 Apr-15 Oct. € 23.60   2007*

See advertisement on next page

ABBEVILLE *3B3* (10km SW Rural) **Camping Le Val de Trie, Bouillancourt-sous-Miannay, 80870 Moyenneville [03 22 31 48 88; fax 03 22 31 35 33; raphael@camping-levaldetrie.fr; www.camping-levaldetrie.fr]** Fr A28 exit junc 2 onto D925 sp Cambron. In 5km at Miannay turn S onto D86 sp Bouillancourt. Site thro vill on L. Site sp fr A28. NB Last part of app narr & bendy. Med, hdg/mkd pitch, hdstg, pt sl, pt shd; htd wc; chem disp; mv service pnt; baby facs; shwrs inc; el pnts (6A) €4 (poss rev pol); gas; lndtte; ice; shop; tradsmn; rest; snacks; bar; BBQ; playgrnd; htd pool; htd paddling pool; sand beach 20km; lake fishing; games rm; entmnt; child entmnt; TV rm; 1% statics; dogs €1.30; phone; Eng spkn; adv bkg; quiet; cc acc; red long stay/low ssn; CCI. "Beautiful, well-run site; pleasant reception; v helpful owner; excel clean san facs; poss boggy after heavy rain; gd family site - farm animals to see; woodland walks; interesting area; conv Calais." ♦ 21 Mar-15 Oct. € 19.60 (CChq acc)   2007*

See advertisement on next page

France

Last year of report

ABBEVILLE *3B3* (8km NW Rural) **Camping Le Château des Tilleuls**, 80132 Port-le-Grand [03 22 24 07 75 or 03 22 24 23 80; fax 03 22 24 23 80; contact@campingtilleuls.com; www.campingtilleuls.com] Fr N on A16 join A28 dir Rouen. At junc 1 take D40 dir St Valery-sur-Somme, site on R in approx 3km. Sm, hdg/mkd pitch, sl, pt shd; wc; chem disp; shwrs; el pnts (16A); shop & 1.5km; snacks; lndtte; pool; playgrnd; beach 10km; tennis; fishing 1km; 5% statics; dogs €1; phone; adv bkg; Eng spkn; red 15+ days; quiet but some rd & rlwy noise; CCI. "Quaint site; lge pitches; facs converted fr old farm buildings - shabby but clean; water fill down steps, you may need to take your car; ltd/poor facs low ssn; warning - poss v hot water in basins; gd for children/dogs; basic NH/sh stay only." 1 Mar-1 Nov. € 17.80   2006*

ABILLY see Descartes *4H2*

ABJAT SUR BANDIAT see Nontron *7B3*

ABRESCHVILLER *6E3* (Urban) **Camp Municipal du Moulin**, 6 Rue du Moulin, 57560 Abreschviller [03 87 03 70 32; fax 03 87 03 75 90; http://pagesperso-orange.fr/abreschviller] Exit N4 opp junc with D955 onto D41/D44 to Abreschviller. Or S fr Sarrebourg on D44 to Abreschviller. Sm, pt shd; wc (own san); chem disp; shwrs inc; el pnts €3; dogs. "Tourist train stn adj; walks; fishing; vg." ♦ ltd. 1 Apr-30 Oct. € 9.70   2007*

ABRETS, LES *9B3* (2km E Rural) **Camping Le Coin Tranquille**, 6 Chemin des Vignes, 38490 Les Abrets [04 76 32 13 48; fax 04 76 37 40 67; contact@coin-tranquille.com; www.coin-tranquille.com] Fr N exit A43 at junc 10 Les Abrets & foll D592 to town cent. At rndbt at monument take D306 (N6) twd Chambéry/Campings; cont for 500m then turn L sp Le Coin Tranquille; cross level x-ing & cont for 500m; site at end of rd. Fr S on A48 exit junc 10 at Voiron onto D1075 (N75) to Les Abrets; turn R at rndabt twd Le Pont-de-Beauvoisin, then as above. Lge, hdg/mkd pitch, pt shd; wc (some cont); chem disp; mv service pnt; baby facs; shwrs inc; el pnts (6A) inc (poss rev pol & long lead poss req); gas; lndtte; ice; shop; tradsmn; rest; snacks; bar; BBQ; playgrnd; pool + paddling pool in ssn; cycle hire; archery; horseriding & fishing 7km; golf 15km; games area; entmnt; TV rm; dogs €1; Eng spkn; adv bkg ess high ssn; noisy high ssn; red low ssn; cc acc; CCI. "Lovely walks; lge indiv, narr pitches; poss flooding in wet weather; clean san facs; gd, well-organised site but a dist to travel to many places of interest; local tourist info avail fr recep; excel rest; v helpful & friendly staff; well-maintained facs; although a busy/noisy site, some quiet pitches are avail - request bkg; excel activities for children; excel." ♦ 22 Mar-1 Nov. € 31.00 (CChq acc) ABS - M05   2007*

ABRETS, LES *9B3* (3km S Rural) **Camp Municipal Le Calatrin, 38850 Paladru [04 76 32 37 48; fax 04 76 32 42 02; lecalatrin@wanadoo.fr; www. paladru.com]** S on D1075 (N75) turn R onto D50 to Paladru; site 1km beyond vill on L on brow of hill. Med, mkd pitch, some terr, mainly sl, pt shd; wc (some cont); chem disp; shwrs inc; el pnts (5A) €2 (long lead poss req); gas; lndtte; ice; shops 500m; BBQ; playgrnd; lake sw & shgl beach adj; fishing; watersports; TV; 50% statics; dogs €1; adv bkg; quiet; CCI. "Attractive site; v helpful staff; gd lake access & recreational facs." 1 Apr-30 Sep. € 12.50   2007*

ABRETS, LES *9B3* (8km S Rural) **Camping International Le Lac, La Véronniere, 38620 Montferrat [04 76 32 31 67; fax 04 76 32 38 15; www.camping-dulac.com]** D1075 (N75) 5km S of Les Abrets turn R onto D50 dir Paladru. Turn L sp La Véronniere/Charavines, site on R on lakeside. Lge, mkd pitch, pt shd; wc; chem disp; shwrs inc; el pnts (6A) inc; lndtte; tradsmn; rest; snacks; bar; BBQ; playgrnd; lake sw & shgl beach; fishing; sailing; 25% statics; dogs €1.20; phone; Eng spkn; adv bkg; quiet; cc acc; CCI. "Lovely lake with gently shelving beach; supervised high ssn; gd touring base." ♦ 14 Apr-30 Sep. € 16.50   2005*

ABRETS, LES *9B3* (11km SW) **Camp Municipal du Bord du Lac, 38850 Bilieu [04 76 06 67 00 or 04 76 06 62 41 (Mairie); fax 04 76 06 67 15; mairie. bilieu@pays-voironnais.com]** S on D1075 (N75) fr Les Abrets. Turn R onto D50. Just bef Paladru, turn L to Charavines. site on R on ent Bilieu, by lakeside. Med, mkd pitch, pt sl, terr, pt shd; htd wc; chem disp; shwrs inc; el pnts (10A) €3.95; lndtte; tradsmn; playgrnd; 70% statics; poss cr; quiet; CCI. "Nice site by lake; san facs v gd; staff v helpful; no sw in lake fr site, only boat launch; pitch access poss diff; gd." 15 Apr-30 Sep. € 5.50   2007*

Before we move on, I'm going to fill in some site report forms and post them off to the editor, otherwise they won't arrive in time for the deadline at the end of September.

ABZAC see Coutras *7C2*

ACCOUS *8G2* (Rural) **Camping Despourrins, Route du Somport, 64490 Accous [05 59 34 71 16]** On N134 rte to & fr Spain via Somport Pass. Site sp on main rd. Sm, pt shd; wc (some cont); chem dis (wc); shwrs inc; el pnts (6A) €2.60; lndry rm; shop, rest, snacks, bar nrby; BBQ; 10% statics; dogs free; quiet but some rd noise. "Clean, tidy NH conv Col de Somport." 1 Mar-8 Nov. € 8.20   2007*

⊞ACY EN MULTIEN *3D3* (700m SE Rural) **Caravaning L'Ancien Moulin (CC de F), 60620 Acy-en-Multien [tel/fax 03 44 87 21 28; ccdf_ acy@cegetel.net; www.campingclub.asso.fr]** Leave A4 at junc 19 & turn L onto D401 to Lizy-sur-Ourcq. Cross rv & turn R then L onto D147 dir May-en-Multien. 1km then L onto D14 dir May. Cross D405 onto D420 (becomes D332) dir Rosoy-en-Multien & site is on L 2km after Rosoy, 500m bef Acy-en-Multien. Med, mkd pitch, pt shd; htd wc; chem disp; shwrs inc; el pnts (6A) inc; lndtte; shops, rest, snacks, bar, playgrnd 1km; fishing; games area; entmnt; TV rm; 90% statics; dogs €2; Eng spkn; adv bkg; quiet but poss aircraft noise; CCI. "V helpful, friendly staff; pitches by mill pool; 30km fr Disneyland Paris & nr 2 other theme parks; vg." ♦ € 20.30   2006*

ADRETS DE L'ESTEREL, LES see Napoule, La *10F4*

AGAY *10F4* (700m E Coastal) **Camping Agay Soleil, Route de Cannes, 83700 Agay [04 94 82 00 79; fax 04 94 82 88 70; camping-agay-soleil@wanadoo.fr; www.agay-soleil.com/fr]** E fr St Raphaël on D559 (N98) site on R after passing Agay dir Cannes. Or (to avoid busy St Raphaël) fr A8 exit junc 38 on D37 & foll sp St Raphaël, then Agay/Valescure on D100 for approx 8 km; L at rndabt by beach in Agay; site far side of bay immed after watersports club. Med, mkd pitch, hdstg, pt sl, terr, pt shd; wc; chem disp; mv service pnt; baby facs; shwrs inc; el pnts (6A) €3.30; gas; lndtte; shop 500m; rest, snacks, bar high ssn; playgrnd adj; sand beach adj; watersports; games area; some statics; dogs €2 (not acc high ssn); phone adj; train & bus 500m; poss cr; Eng spkn; adv bkg ess Easter to Aug; CCI. "Superb location on sea front; excel modern facs; many pitches too sm for awning; extra charge beach pitches; excel. " ♦ 23 Mar-4 Nov. € 26.50 (3 persons)   2006*

AGAY *10F4* (4km E Coastal) **Camping Azur Rivage, Blvd Eugène Brieux, 83530 Anthéor [04 94 44 83 12; fax 04 94 44 84 39; info@ camping-azur-rivage.com; www.camping-azur-rivage.com]** On D559 (N98) heading NE dir Cannes pass Agay. Opp sandy cove at Anthéor, turn L under viaduct. Med, mkd pitch; wc (mainly cont); chem disp; mv service pnt; shwrs; el pnts €4; gas; lndtte; ice; shop; rest; snacks; bar; cooking facs; BBQ; playgrnd; pool; paddling pool; dir access to sand beach across rd; fishing; wifi internet; some statics; poss cr; adv bkg (dep req); some rlwy noise. "Site virtually under rlwy viaduct; pitches sm." 1 Apr-30 Sep. € 35.00 (4 persons) (CChq acc)   2007*

AGAY *10F4* (1.5km S Coastal) **Royal Camping, Plage de Camp-Long, 83530 Agay [tel/fax 04 94 82 00 20]** On D559 (N98) twd St Raphaël. Turn at sp Tiki Plage & site. Stop in ent rd at recep bef ent site. Sm, mkd pitch, hdstg, pt shd; wc; chem disp; shwrs inc; el pnts (6A) inc; gas; lndtte; ice; shops; tradsmn; rest, snacks, bar 300m; sand beach adj; dogs; phone; bus 200m; poss cr; Eng spkn; adv bkg €63 dep & €17 bkg fee; quiet but some rd/rlwy noise; CCI. "Gd walks; some pitches adj to beach in sep area; vg". ♦ ltd. 15 Mar-31 Oct. € 30.50   2005*

> There aren't many sites open this early in the year. We'd better phone ahead to check that the one we're heading for is actually open.

AGAY *10F4* (600m NW Coastal) **Camping des Rives de l'Agay, Ave de Gratadis, 83530 Agay [04 94 82 02 74; fax 04 94 82 74 14; reception@ lesrivesdelagay.fr; www.lesrivesdelagay.fr]** Fr Agay take D100 dir Valescure, site in 400m on L. NB Dangerous bend & steep ent. Med, hdg/mkd pitch, shd; htd wc; chem disp; baby facs; shwrs inc; el pnts (6A) inc; gas; lndtte; ice; shop & 1km; rest; snacks; bar; htd pool (Mar-Nov); sand beach 500m; dogs €2; poss cr; Eng spkn; adv bkg; poss noisy; CCI. "San facs & pool v clean; gd pool with shade; easy walk to Agay; excel site." ♦ 1 Mar-2 Nov. € 31.00 (3 persons)   2005*

AGAY *10F4* (5km NW Rural) **Esterel Caravaning, Ave des Golfs, 83530 Agay [04 94 82 03 28; fax 04 94 82 87 37; contact@esterel-caravaning.fr; www.esterel-caravaning.fr or www.les-castels. com]** Fr A8 foll sps for St Raphaël & immed foll sp 'Agay (par l'interieur)/Valescure' into Ave des Golfs, approx 6km long. Pass golf courses & at end of rd turn L at rndabt twds Agay. Site 800m on L. Lge, hdg/mkd pitch, hdstg, terr, pt shd; htd wc (some cont); chem disp; mv service pnt; shwrs inc; baby facs; indiv san facs to some pitches (extra charge); el pnts (6A) inc (poss rev pol); gas; lndtte; shop; rest; snacks; bar; no BBQ; playgrnd; htd pools; waterslide; sand beach 3km; lake sw 20km; tennis; mini-golf; squash; cycle hire; archery; games rm; fitness rm; entmnt; underground disco; wifi internet; TV rm; 50% statics; dogs €2; poss cr; Eng spkn; adv bkg; red low ssn/long stay; cc acc; CCI. "Superb site; conv Gorges du Verdon, Massif de l'Estérel, Monaco, Cannes & St Tropez; gd for families - excel leisure activities; min stay 1 week high ssn; ltd lge pitches avail; excel rest; mkt Wed." ♦ 15 Mar-27 Sep. € 47.00 ABS - C21   2007*

See advertisement

AGDE *10F1* (4.5km SE Coastal) **Camping de la Clape, 2 Rue du Gouverneur, 34300 Agde [04 67 26 41 32; fax 04 67 26 45 25; contact@ camping-laclape.com; www.camping-laclape. com]** Foll sp Cap d'Agde, keep L at 1st gantry, L at 2nd gantry foll camping sp. Turn R at rndabt. Camp ent by lge free car pk. Lge, pt shd, mkd pitch; wc; mv service pnt; baby facs; shwrs; el pnts (10A) €3.70; lndtte; ice; shop; rest; snacks; BBQ; pool adj; paddling pool; sand beach adj; games area; entmnt; some statics; dogs €2.65; poss cr; quiet; cc acc; red low ssn; CCI. ♦ 1 Apr-30 Sep. € 21.80   2006*

AGDE *10F1* (1km S Rural) **FFCC Domaine des Champs Blancs, Route de Rochelongue, 34300 Agde [04 67 94 23 42; fax 04 67 21 36 75; champs-blancs@wanadoo.fr; www.champs-blancs.fr]** Exit fr A9 & foll sps to Agde (not Cap d'Agde). Thro cent of Agde foll sps to campsite & Rochelongue. Site on R after bdge over dual c'way. V lge, hdg pitch, shd; wc; chem disp; mv service pnt; individ san facs on pitches (extra charge); shwrs inc; el pnts inc (poss rev pol); gas; lndtte; ice; shop, rest, snacks, bar adj; playgrnd; 2 htd pools; waterslide; sand beach adj; tennis; games area; golf 2km; 10% statics; dogs €2; adv bkg; quiet; CCI. "Friendly site; excel san facs; hot water to shwrs only; vg." ♦ 7 Apr-30 Sep. € 40.00 (CChq acc)   2007*

> Did you know you can fill in site report forms on the Club's website — www.caravanclub.co.uk?

AGDE *10F1* (4km S Coastal) **Camping de la Tamarissière, 4 Rue du Commandant Malet, 34300 Agde [04 67 94 79 46; fax 04 67 94 78 23; contact@camping-tamarissiere.com; www. camping-tamarissiere.com]** At Agde bdge take D32E on R bank of Rv Hérault to La Tamarissière; sp. V lge, mkd pitch, pt sl, shd; wc; shwrs; el pnts (6A) €3.90; lndtte; ice; shop; rest; snacks; bar; playgrnd; sand beach adj; games area; cycle hire; entmnt; harbour nr for boat owners; mkt every morning at site ent; 5% statics; dogs €3; adv bkg; quiet; cc acc; red long stay; CCI. "Sandy site under pines; ferry across rv; ltd facs on site & in vill; lge areas flood after heavy rain; gate shut 2200-0700." ♦ 15 Apr-15 Sep. € 21.00   2007*

AGDE *10F1* (2km SW Rural) **Camping Le Neptune, 46 Boulevard du St Christ, 34300 Agde [04 67 94 23 94; fax 04 67 94 48 77; info@campingleneptune.com; www.campingle neptune.com]** Fr A9 exit junc 34 onto N312, then E on D612 (N112). Foll sp Grau d'Agde after x-ing bdge. Site on D32E on E bank of Rv Hérault on 1-way system. Lge, hdg/mkd pitch, pt shd; wc (some cont); chem disp; baby facs; fam bthrm; shwrs inc; el pnts (6-10A) inc; gas; lndtte; shop & bar in ssn; hypmkt 3km; rest 2km; bar; BBQ; playgrnd; htd pool; paddling pool; sand beach 2km; tennis; games area; entmnt; internet all pitches; TV; 40% statics; dogs €3 (no Pitbulls or Rottweillers); phone; bus 2km; poss cr; Eng spkn; adv bkg rec; quiet; cc acc; red low ssn; CCI. "Peaceful, pleasant & clean site; helpful owners; modern facs; liable to flood after heavy rain; easy rvside walk/cycle to vill; gd cycleways; rv cruises avail; boat launch/slipway 500m." 1 Apr-29 Sep. € 27.20 (CChq acc) 2007*

AGDE *10F1* (3km SW Coastal) **Camping Les Romarins, Le Grau d'Agde, 34300 Agde [04 67 94 18 59; fax 04 67 26 58 80; contact@ romarins.com]** Fr Agde take rd to Grau d'Agde, site at ent to Grau d'Agde adj Rv Hérault. Med, mkd pitch, pt hdg pitch, shd; wc; shwrs inc; el pnts (6A) inc; lndtte; shop 500m; rest; snacks; bar; playgrnd; pool; sand beach 1km; cycle hire; 10% statics; dogs €2.20; poss cr; Eng spkn; adv bkg; quiet; CCI. "Pleasant town with many bars, rests; shops; helpful owner." ♦ ltd. 1 May-15 Sep. € 23.20 2004*

⊞**AGEN** *8E3* (12km SE Rural) **Camping au Lie, 47220 Caudecoste [05 53 87 42 93 or 01473 832388 (UK); td.smith@tiscali.fr; www. aulie.co.uk]** Fr N113 dir Toulouse, turn off sp Layrac approx 8km SE of Agen. Do not use bdges across Rv Garonne at St Nicholas-de-la-Balerme (shut) or Sauveterre-St Denis (width restrict). Fr A62 exit junc 7 & turn R at 1st rndabt sp Layrac. Drive thro vill & turn L at 2nd traff lts (sharp turn) sp Caudecoste, cross bdge over Rv Gers & Caudecoste sp 1st R (silver horse at junc). In Caudecoste take D290 sp Miradoux, cross m'way in approx 1km, on L is farmhouse with pond, turn L just after this onto sm rd with grass growing in middle. At T-junc turn R, site on R. Sm, pt shd, wc; chem disp (v basic); shwrs inc; el pnts (6A) inc; shops, rest, bar in vill; pool; dogs €1; c'van storage avail; quiet; some m'way noise. "V sm CL-type site in owner's garden; sm pitches; san facs clean but dated & ltd; welcoming British owners; lndry facs & use of bikes inc; excel meals avail at farm house, inc coeliac & vegetarian; peaceful countryside; delightful vill; gd cycling area; excel." ♦ ltd. € 18.00 2007*

AGEN *8E3* (8km NW) **Camping Le Moulin de Mellet, Route de Prayssas, 47490 St Hilaire-de-Lusignan [05 53 87 50 89; fax 05 53 47 13 41; moulin.mellet@wanadoo.fr; www.camping-moulin-mellet.com]** NW fr Agen on N113 twd Bordeaux for 5km. At traff lts just bef Colayrac-St Cirq take D107 N twd Prayssas for 3km. Site on R. Sm, pt shd; wc; chem disp; baby facs; shwrs inc; el pnts (10-16A) €2.50; gas; lndry rm; ice; shop 3km; tradsmn high ssn; rest; snacks; BBQ; snacks; playgrnd; pools; dogs €1; adv bkg; quiet; Eng spkn; CCI. "Delightful site; v helpful & friendly Dutch owners; lge pool; small children's farm; RVs & twin-axles phone ahead." ♦ 1 Apr-15 Oct. € 15.50 2005*

This guide relies on site report forms submitted by caravanners like us; we'll do our bit and tell the editor what we think of the campsites we've visited.

AGNAC see Eymet *7D2*

AGON COUTAINVILLE *1D4* (NE Urban/ Coastal) **Camp Municipal Le Martinet, Blvd Lebel-Jehenne, 50230 Agon-Coutainville [02 33 47 05 20; fax 02 33 47 31 95; martinet marais@wanadoo.fr]** Fr Coutances take D44 to Agon-Coutainville; site sp nr Hippodrome. Med, pt shd; wc; mv service pnt; shwrs inc; el pnts (5A) €2.30; lndtte; shop 250m; playgrnd; sand beach 1km; 55% statics; dogs €2.50; bus; poss cr; CCI. "V pleasant site; touring pitches ltd; ltd facs low ssn." ♦ 1 Apr-30 Oct. € 11.20 2006*

AGON COUTAINVILLE *1D4* (600m NE Urban/ Coastal) **Camp Municipal Le Marais, Blvd Lebel-Jehenne, 50230 Agon-Coutainville [02 33 47 05 20; fax 02 33 47 31 95; martinet marais@wanadoo.fr]** Fr Coutances take D44 to Agon-Coutainville. Site sp adj Hippodrome. Lge, unshd; wc; chem disp; shwrs inc; el pnts (5-10A) €2.30; lndtte; shops adj; tradsmn; playgrnd; sand beach 600m; sailing; fishing; dogs €2.50; adv bkg; quiet. ♦ 1 Jul-1 Sep. € 11.80 2006*

AGUESSAC see Millau *10E1*

AIGLE, L' *4E2* (5km NW Rural) **Camp Municipal des Saints-Pères, 61550 St Evroult-Notre-Dame-du-Bois [02 33 34 81 97 or 02 33 34 93 12 (Mairie)]** Fr L'Aigle on D13, on ent vill site on L by lake. Sm, terr, pt shd; wc; chem disp (wc); shwrs; el pnts (10A) €2.50; shop, rest, snacks, bar 500m; playgrnd; lake sw adj; watersports; fishing; mini-golf; dogs; no adv bkg; poss noisy; CCI. "Pleasant lakeside vill; facs v tired low ssn; barrier ent, recep 0800, 1400 & 1800." ♦ 1 Apr-30 Sep. € 6.00 2006*

AIGNAN *8E2* (600m S Rural) **Camping Le Domaine du Castex, 32290 Aignan [05 62 09 25 13; fax 05 62 09 24 79; info@gers-vacances.com; www. gers-vacances.com]** Fr N on N124 turn S on D20 thro Aignan, site on L. Fr S on D935 turn E at Monplaisir onto D3/D48 to Aignan, then onto D20 S. Sm, hdg/mkd pitch, shd; wc; chem disp; shwrs inc; el pnts (10A) €3; lndtte; ice; shop 500m; tradsmn; rest; snacks; bar; BBQ; playgrnd; pool; lake sw 4km; tennis & squash adj; TV rm; 4% statics; dogs €4; phone; poss cr; Eng spkn; adv bkg; quiet; CCI. "Lovely site in grnds of beautiful medieval farmhouse; helpful Dutch owners; new san facs (2008); excel pool & rest; nice little town; mkt Mon; vg." ♦ ltd. 1 Apr-31 Oct. € 15.00   2007*

AIGREFEUILLE D'AUNIS *7A1* (2km N Rural) **Camp Municipal de la Garenne, Route de la Mazurie, 17220 St Christophe [05 46 35 51 79 or 05 46 35 16 15 (LS); fax 05 46 35 64 29; saintchristophe@mairie17.com]** Fr Aigrefeuille-d'Aunis take D112 2.5km N to vill of St Christophe, site sp. Sm, hdg, mkd pitch, pt shd; wc; chem disp; mv service pnt; shwrs inc; el pnts (4A) €2.50; ice; lndry rm; shop 250m; playgrnd; ake fishing 3km; tennis; horseriding; ldogs €0.85; quiet; CCI. "V clean site in sm vill; unreliable opening dates, phone ahead low ssn." ♦ 1 May-15 Sep. € 8.60   2007*

AIGREFEUILLE D'AUNIS *7A1* (500m SE Rural) **Camping La Taillée, 3 Rue du Bois Gaillard, 17290 Aigrefeuille-d'Aunis [tel/fax 05 46 35 50 88; vacances@lataillee.com; www.lataillee.com]** Exit D939 sp Aigrefeuille & fork R immed to 1st major R turn sp 'Equipement'. Take 1st L at mini-rndabt to site on L in 100m. Take care over hump. Med, pt shd; wc; chem disp; baby facs; shwrs inc; el pnts (6A) €3.10; lndtte; ice; shops 500m; bar; BBQ; playground; pool adj; lake 900m; games rm; mini-golf; dogs €2.10; quiet; CCI. "V pleasant, clean site; ltd facs low ssn; excel pool adj; vg security; phone ahead low ssn to check open." ♦ 1 Jun-15 Sep. € 13.50   2007*

AIGUES MORTES See also sites listed under La Grande Motte and Le Grau du Roi.

AIGUES MORTES *10F2* (5km N) **Camping Fleur de Camargue, 30220 St Laurent-d'Aigouze [04 66 88 15 42; fax 04 66 88 10 21; sarlaccv@aol. com; www.fleur-de-camargue.com]** Exit A9 junc 26 dir Aigues-Mortes; go thro St Laurent cent; turn R at junc with D46; site on R in 2km. Or N fr Aigues-Mortes at junc with D58 over high-level bdge on D46, site 3km on L on D46. Med, mkd pitch, pt shd; wc; chem disp; mv service pnt; shwrs inc; el pnts (10A) €4; gas; lndtte; ice; shops 2km; tradsmn; rest, snacks & bar (high ssn); playgrnd; pool; paddling pool; sand beach 11km; rv & fishing 3km; entmnt; TV rm; 40% statics; dogs €4; phone; adv bkg; quiet; cc acc; CCI. "Nice, quiet, relaxing site; lge pitches; v pleasant owners; v clean facs; gd." ♦ 8 Apr-29 Sep. € 22.00 (CChq acc)   2007*

AIGUES MORTES *10F2* (4km E Rural) **Camping à la Ferme (Loup), Le Mas de Plaisance, 30220 Aigues-Mortes [04 66 53 92 84 or 06 22 20 92 37 (mob)]** Site sp in Aigues-Mortes or foll D58 E dir Stes Maries-de-la-Mer, then R along farm road (v narr & potholed) at end of rv bdge. NB Fr town narr rd with much traff calming & sharp bends. Fr D58 4-5km potholed farm rd. Either way for v sm o'fits only. Sm, pt shd; wc; chem disp; mv service pnt; shwrs inc; el pnts inc; lndry rm; BBQ; quiet; CCI. "Excel CL-type site; v peaceful; superb san facs; v helpful owners; set in marshes - gd birdwatching; rec not to use water at m'van service point as off irrigation system - other water points avail." 1 Apr-30 Sep. € 17.00   2007*

AIGUES MORTES *10F2* (3.5km W Rural) **Yelloh! Village La Petite Camargue, 30220 Aigues-Mortes [04 66 53 98 98; fax 04 66 53 98 80; info@yellohvillage-petite-camargue.com; www. yellohvillage-petite-camargue.com]** Heading S on N979 take D62 bef Aigues-Mortes & go over canal bdge twd Montpellier; site on R in 3km; sp. V lge, mkd pitch, pt shd; wc; mv service pnt; chem disp (wc); some serviced pitch; baby facs; shwrs inc; el pnts (10A) inc; gas; lndtte; ice; shop; rest; snacks; bar; playgrnd; pool; paddling pool; jacuzzi; sand beach 3km; tennis; horseriding; cycle hire; entmnt; child entmnt; games rm; wifi internet; many statics; dogs €3; bus to beach high ssn; Eng spkn; adv bkg; red low ssn; cc acc; CCI. "Returnable dep req for ent token; lively, busy, youth-orientated commercial site with lots of sports facs; well-run & clean; some sm pitches; conv Nîmes, Pont du Gard, Camargue, Cévennes; mkt Wed & Sun; gd cycling (map fr recep); take care overhead branches." ♦ 26 Apr-20 Sep. € 43.00 ABS - C04   2007*

AIGUEZE see Pont St Esprit *9D2*

AIGUILLES *9D4* (1km NE Rural) **Camp Municipal Le Gouret, 05470 Aiguilles-en-Queyras [04 92 46 74 61 or 04 92 46 70 34; fax 04 92 46 79 05]** Fr Aiguilles on D947 dir Abriès, sp to site on R across rv bdge. Lge, shd; wc; chem disp; shwrs; el pnts (3-10A) inc; lndtte; shop, rest, snacks, bar 700m; dogs; phone; bus 100m; quiet. "Site on bank of Rv Guil; random pitching in lge area of larch forest; excel cent exploring Queyras National Park; vg." 15 Jun-15 Sep. € 10.00   2006*

AIGUILLON *7D2* (E Rural) **Camp Municipal du Vieux Moulin, Route de Villeneuve, 47190 Aiguillon [05 53 79 61 43; fax 05 53 79 82 01; mairie@ville-aiguillon.fr]** On ent town on N113, turn E onto D666 to site on bank of Rv Lot. Clearly sp. Or exit junc 6 dir Damazan fr A62 onto D8 to Aiguillon. Med, mkd pitch, shd; wc (cont); shwrs; el pnts (10A) €1.40; ice; shops adj; tradsmn; rest, bar 1km; rv sw; playgrnd; quiet. "Site adj old mill house." 1 Jul-31 Aug. € 4.00   2005*

France

AIGUILLON SUR MER, L' *7A1* (S Coastal) **Camp Municipal du Lotissement de la Baie, Blvd du Communal, 85460 L'Aiguillon-sur-Mer [02 51 56 40 70; fax 02 51 97 11 57; camping. delabaie@aiguillonsurmer.fr]** On D46 fr La Tranche, cross bdge into Aiguillon-sur-Mer onto D746a. Foll rd to R; after it turns L site on R in 100m. Lge, pt shd; wc; shwrs inc; el pnts (6A); lndtte; playgrnd; pool 500m; waterslide; sand beach 1km; TV; poss cr; adv bkg; quiet; red long stay/low ssn. "Gd beaches in area." 1 Apr-30 Sep. 2006*

AIGUILLON SUR MER, L' *7A1* (1km W Coastal) **Camp Municipal La Côte de Lumière, Place du Dr Pacaud, 85460 La Faute-sur-Mer [02 51 97 06 16; fax 02 51 27 12 21]** On D46 E of La Tranche, thro town. Site bef bdge over rv. Lge, shd; wc (some cont); shwrs inc; el pnts (6A) €3; lndtte; shop; snacks; playgrnd; sand beach 300m; dogs; quiet; cc acc; CCI. "Naturist beach adj; bird sanctuary, oyster/mussel beds adj; poss prob with insects; facs poss ltd and run down low ssn." ♦ 1 Apr-15 Oct. € 13.50 (3 persons) 2007*

AIGURANDE *7A4* (14km SW Rural) **Camp Municipal Fontbonne, Le Bourg, 23160 Crozant [05 55 89 80 12 or 06 85 96 53 79 (mob); fax 05 55 89 83 80]** Fr A20 take D36 to Eguzon R on D973 after 11km L on D30 to Crozant. Site sp in vill. Sm, mkd pitch, pt sl, pt shd; wc; shwrs inc; el pnts (6A) inc; lndry rm; shops, rest, snacks, bar 500m; BBQ; playgrnd; lake sw 7km; dogs €0.50; adv bkg; quiet; cc not acc. "Attractive vill on Lake Chambon; rvside walk." 1 May-30 Sep. € 9.20 2006*

AILLY SUR NOYE *3C3* (1km S Rural) **Camp Municipal du Val de Noye, 80250 Ailly-sur-Noye [03 22 41 02 11]** Fr Amiens take D7 S thro St Fuscien to Ailly-sur-Noye, then D193 SW for 1km to Berny-sur-Noye & lakeside. Or fr D1001 (N1) turn E onto D920 to Ailly-sur-Noye. Med, mkd pitch, shd; wc; own san rec; chem disp; mv service pnt; shwrs inc; el pnts (3A) €2.20; tradsmn; shops 1km; playgrnd; lake sw, fishing, boating adj; 20% statics; dogs; some rlwy noise; 15% red 3+ days & 5% red low ssn; CCI. "Pleasant NH; fishing fr site free; leisure park adj; ltd facs low ssn." 1 Apr-31 Oct. € 7.00 2004*

⊞**AIME** *9B3* (5km NE Rural) **Camping de Montchavin, 73210 Bellentre [04 79 07 83 23; fax 04 79 07 80 18; montchavin@wanadoo.fr; www. montchavin-lescoches.com]** On N90 fr Moûtiers to Bourg-St Maurice (ignore site sps on N90); at 20km turn R onto D87E sp Landry & Montchavin-les-Coches; in 1km turn R D220 in 500m turn L D225; site in 7km on L at Montchavin. Med, mkd pitch, terr, pt shd; htd wc; mv service pnt; shwrs inc; el pnts (4-10A) €3.50-€7.10; gas; lndtte; ice; shops 500m; 60% statics; adv bkg (ess Jul/Aug & winter); quiet; cc not acc. "Site at 1200m; steep hill to shops; walking in summer, skiing in winter; magnificent setting, great views; cent for mountain activities; site clsd Oct." € 11.75 2005*

AINHOA *8F1* (2.5km SW) **Camping Xokoan, Quartier Dancharia, 64250 Ainhoa [05 59 29 90 26; fax 05 59 29 73 82]** Fr St Jean-de-Luz take D918 to St Pée-sur-Nivelle. Shortly after St Pée take D3 sp Dancharia then turn L at Spanish border post. Site is 25m on R. Long ent is narr & tortuous, poss diff for long o'fits. Sm, pt sl, pt shd; wc; shwrs inc; el pnts (6A) inc; lndtte; shop nr; rest; snacks; bar; playgrnd; adv bkg; quiet; CCI. "Conv for Spain & Pyrenees; gd walks, lovely scenery; site in grounds of sm hotel." 1 Mar-30 Nov. € 14.00 2004*

AINHOA *8F1* (NW) **Aire Naturelle Harazpy, 64250 Ainhoa [tel/fax 05 59 29 89 38]** Take D918 E fr St Jean-de-Luz sp Espelette: in approx 29km turn R on D20 sp Ainhoa. App church in Ainhoa turn R thro open car park to rd at rear. Sh distance to site (sp). Sm, mkd pitch, terr, pt sl, pt shd; wc; mv service pnt; shwrs; el pnts (10A) inc; lndtte; sm shop; tradsmn; lake sw 10km; dogs; phone; adv bkg; quiet; cc not acc; CCI. "Conv Spanish border; helpful warden; excl walking area." ♦ 15 Jun-30 Sep. € 13.50 2004*

AIRE SUR LA LYS *3A3* (2km NE Urban) **Camp Municipal de la Lys, Rue de Fort Gassion, 62120 Aire-sur-la-Lys [03 21 95 40 40; fax 03 21 95 40 41]** Fr town cent, find main sq & exit to R of town hall. Thro traff lts turn R into narr lane just bef rv bdge dir of Hazebrouck. Site poorly sp. Sm, hdg/mkd pitch, hdstg, unshd; wc; chem disp (wc); shwrs inc; some el pnts inc; quiet. "Ltd touring pitches; ltd but clean san facs; not suitable lge o'fits; emergency NH only." € 5.00 2004*

AIRE SUR L'ADOUR *8E2* (Urban) **Camping Les Ombrages de l'Adour, Rue des Graviers, 40800 Aire-sur-l'Adour [tel/fax 05 58 71 64 70 or 05 58 71 75 10; hetapsarl@yahoo.fr; www. camping-adour-landes.com]** Turn E on S side of bdge over Rv Adour in town. Site close to bdge & sp, past La Arena off rd to Bourdeaux. Med, pt shd; wc; chem disp; mv service pnt; shwrs inc; el pnts (10A) €2.80; ice; lndtte; shop; snacks; playgrnd; pool 500m; sports area; canoing, fishing, tennis 500m; dogs €1.50; poss cr; red low ssn. "Vg; boil water or use bottled; v clean facs; mkt Tues." 1 Apr-28 Oct. € 11.00 2005*

⊞**AIRE SUR L'ADOUR** *8E2* (9km E Rural) **Camping Le Lahount, Hameau de Lahount, 32400 Lelin-Lapujolle [tel/fax 05 62 69 64 09 or 06 81 52 39 15 (mob); camping.de.lahount@ wanadoo.fr; http://pagesperso-orange.fr/ camping.de.lahount]** SE fr Aire-sur-l'Adour on D935, turn L in St Germé dir Lelin-Lapujolle. In 1.5km turn L, site on R, sp. Med, mkd pitch, terr, pt shd; wc; mv service pnt; baby facs; shwrs inc; el pnts (10A) inc; lndtte; ice; shop; rest; snacks; bar; BBQ; playgrnd; pool; paddling pool; lake fishing; games area; cycle hire; entmnt; 60% statics; dogs; phone; adv bkg; cc acc; CCI. € 14.50 2006*

AIRES, LES see Lamalou les Bains *10F1*

⊞AIRVAULT *4H1* (1km N Rural) **Camping de Courte Vallée, 8 Rue de Courte Vallée, 79600 Airvault [05 49 64 70 65; fax 05 49 94 17 78; info@caravanningfrance.com; www.caravanning france.com]** Fr N, S or W leave D938 sp Parthenay to Thouars rd at La Maucarrière twd Airvault & foll lge sp to site. Site on D121 twd Availles-Thouarsais N of town. NB If app fr NE or E c'vans not permitted down main street of Airvault & should watch carefully for sp R at Gendarmerie. Well sp fr all dirs. Med, hdg/mkd pitch, some hdstg, pt sl, pt shd; wc; chem disp; mv service pnt; shwrs inc; el pnts (8A) inc; gas; lndtte; shop; tradsmn; rest/bar in town; snacks; bar; BBQ; playgrnd; pool; internet; fishing; cycling; walking; c'van storage; internet; games/TV rm; 8% statics; dogs; recep 0900-2200 high ssn; adv bkg; quiet; cc not acc; red long stay; CCI. "Popular, peaceful, well-maintained site; excel, clean facs; extremely helpful, pleasant British owners; conv Loire, Futuroscope; wine-tasting visits; mkt Sat; walking dist to town." ♦ € 32.00 ABS - L14   2007*

⊞AIX EN PROVENCE *10F3* (9km E Rural) **Camping Ste Victoire, La Paradou, 13100 Beaurecueil [04 42 66 91 31; fax 04 42 66 96 43; campingvictoire@aol.com; www.campingsainte victoire.com]** Exit A8/E80 junc 32 onto D7n (N7) dir Aix, then R onto D58 & foll sp for 3km. Sm, hdg/mkd pitch, hdstg, shd; htd wc (some cont); chem disp; mv service pnt; shwrs inc; el pnts (4-6A) €2.20-3.10 (some rev pol & poss no neutral); lndtte; ice; shop 3km; tradsmn; playgrnd; pool 9km; rv 1km; archery; cycle hire; TV; dogs €1; phone; bus; site clsd mid-Dec to mid-Jan; some Eng spkn; adv bkg; quiet, some rd noise; red low ssn/long stay; no cc acc; CCI. "Lovely site in attractive hilly, wooded country; v friendly, helpful owners; clean, basic san facs, ltd low ssn; variable pitch sizes; lge o'fits poss diff manoeuvring; gd walking & climbing." ♦ € 13.60   2007*

AIX EN PROVENCE *10F3* (1km SE Urban) **Camping L'Arc-en-Ciel, Ave Henri Malacrida, Pont des 3 Sautets, 13100 Aix-en-Provence [04 42 26 14 28; www.campingarcenciel.fr]** Exit A8/E80 at junc 31 onto D7n (N7) dir SE; pass under a'route, R at 1st island, R again at next island, pass under m'way; site ent immed on R; sp. Take care at ent. NB Access easier if go past site for 1km to rndabt, turn round & app fr S. Sm, hdg/mkd pitch, terr, shd; htd wc; chem disp; shwrs inc; el pnts (6A) €3.10 (poss rev pol); gas; lndtte; shops 500m; rest, snacks, bar 100m; BBQ; playgrnd; lge pool; fishing; canoeing; games area; golf 1km; TV; dogs; phone; bus; Eng library; poss cr; Eng spkn; adv bkg; m'way noise not too intrusive; cc not acc; CCI. "Delightful, clean site; vg, friendly, helpful staff; well supervised; pitches poss sm; clean, modern facs; baker & grocer within 100m; superb pool; gd dog walk adj; conv bus to town cent & to Marseille; conv NH a'route; highly rec." 1 Apr-30 Sep. € 17.80   2007*

⊞AIX EN PROVENCE *10F3* (3km SE Urban) **Airotel Camping Chantecler, Val-St André, 13100 Aix-en-Provence [04 42 26 12 98; fax 04 42 27 33 53; info@campingchantecler.com; www.campingchantecler.com]** Fr town inner ring rd foll sps Nice-Toulon, after 1km pass sp for s on R look for sp Chantecler to L of dual c'way. Foll camp sp past blocks of flats. Well sp in Val-St André. If on A8 exit at junc 31 sp Val-St André; site sp. Lge, hdg pitch, hdstg, sl, pt terr, pt shd; htd wc; chem disp; mv service pnt; shwrs inc; el pnts (6A) €3.70; gas; lndtte; ice; shop; tradsmn; rest in ssn; snacks; bar; BBQ; playgrnd; pool; entmnt; TV; dogs €3.10; bus; poss cr; adv bkg; some rd noise; cc acc; red long stay; CCI. "Lovely, well maintained, wooded site in urban area; excel san facs at top of site; gd pool; facs ltd low ssn; some site rds steep - gd power/weight ratio rec; access poss diff some pitches; rec request low level pitch & walk to pitch bef driving to it; vg touring base." ♦ € 18.90   2006*

As soon as we get home I'm going to post all these site report forms to the editor for inclusion in next year's guide. I don't want to miss the September deadline.

AIX LES BAINS *9B3* (3km N) **Camp Municipal Roger Milesey, 73100 Grésy-sur-Aix [04 79 88 28 21 or 04 79 34 80 50 (Mairie)]** Site on N201 bet Aix-les-Bains & Albens-Annecy in vill of Grésy; exit A41 at Aix N; turn L at supmkt flag sp to N201; turn R & site on L in approx 1km. Sm, pt shd; wc (some cont); chem disp; 70% seviced pitches; shwrs; el pnts (10A) €3; gas 1km; ice; lndtte, shop & rest in vill; lake sw 3km; tennis adj; dogs €1.30; quiet; adv bkg; CCI. "Higher charges for 1 night only; unreliable opening, rec phone ahead low ssn; vg." ♦ 1 Jun-30 Sep. € 8.70   2007*

AIX LES BAINS *9B3* (7km SW Rural) **Camping International de l'Ile aux Cygnes, La Croix Verte, 501 Blvd Ernest Coudurier, 73370 Le Bourget-du-Lac [04 79 25 01 76; fax 04 79 25 32 94; camping@ bourgetdulac.com; www.bourgetdulac.com]** Fr N foll Bourget-du-Lac & Lac sp soon after Tunnel Le Chat. Fr Chambéry take N504 dir Aix-les-Bains; foll sp to Le Bourget-du-Lac & Le Lac, bear R at Camping/Plage sp to site at end of rd. Lge, shd; wc (cont); baby facs; shwrs inc; el pnts (6A) €3.35; gas; lndtte; ice; shop; tradsmn; rest; snacks; bar; playgrnd; lake beach & sw; waterslide; boating; watersports; entmnt; TV; some statics; dogs €1.30; phone; bus; adv bkg; quiet; red low ssn; CCI. "On beautiful lake; mountain scenery; old facs, need modernising; ground stoney." ♦ 1 May-30 Sep. € 16.70   2005*

AIX LES BAINS *9B3* (3km W Rural) **Camping International du Sierroz, Blvd Robert Barrier, Route du Lac, 73100 Aix-les-Bains [tel/fax 04 79 61 21 43; campingsierroz@aixlesbains.com; www.aixlesbains.com/campingsierroz]** Fr Annecy S on N201, thro Aix-les-Bains, turn R at site sp. Keep to lakeside rd, site on R. Nr Grand Port. Lge, hdg/mkd pitch, shd; htd wc; chem disp; mv service pnt; baby facs; shwrs inc; el pnts (6-10A) €2.30-4.30; gas; lndtte; ice; shop; tradsmn; rest; snacks; bar; playgrnd; pool 1km; games area; golf 4km; TV; 5% statics; dogs €1.50; bus (ask at recep for free pass); poss cr; no adv bkg; quiet; cc acc; CCI. "Pleasant location; lake adj for watersports; lge pitches; vg san facs." ♦ 15 Mar-15 Nov. € 14.90   2007*

AIXE SUR VIENNE *7B3* (Urban) **Camp Municipal Les Grèves, Ave des Grèves, 87700 Aixe-sur-Vienne [tel/fax 05 55 70 12 98 or 05 55 70 77 00 (Mairie); camping@mairie-aixesurvienne.fr; www.mairie-aixesurvienne.fr]** 13km SW fr Limoges, on N21 twds Périgueux, cross bdge over Rv Vienne & in about 600m turn to R (site sp) by rv. Steep down hill app & U-turn into site - take care gate posts! Med, shd; wc (some cont); chem disp; mv service pnt; shwrs inc; el pnts (10A) €2.30; lndtte; shops adj; tradsmn; rest, snacks, bar 500m; playgrnd; pool adj; fishing; quiet; poss cr; adv bkg; dogs free; "Conv touring Limoges area & Vienne valley; several chateaux easy reach; on banks of rv with public path; excel rv bank pitches; v clean site & san facs; gd disabled facs; no twin-axles; vg." ♦ 1 Jun-30 Sep. € 11.00   2007*

AIZELLES *3C4* (Rural) **Aire Naturelle Camping du Moulin (Bartholomé), Rue du Moulin, 02820 Aizelles [03 23 22 41 18]** Fr Laon take D1044 (N44) dir Reims; in 13km turn L on D88 to Aizelles; site sp in vill 'Camping à la Ferme'. Fr Reims on D1044 turn R to Aizelles on D889 past Corbeny (lge outfits use D88 only). Turn onto Rue du Moulin & site on R in 250m. Camping sp at church says 100m but allow 300m to see ent. Sm, pt sl, pt shd; wc; chem disp; shwrs €1; el pnts (4-6A) €3.50 (poss rev pol); shop 2km; tradsmn; playgrnd; several statics; poss cr; some Eng spkn; quiet but poss noisy w/e; cc not acc; CCI. "Clean, tidy, beautifully kept CL-type farm site; friendly helpful owner; lovely quiet vill nrby; gates clsd 2200-0700; facs ltd but adequate; conv for ferry - Calais 3 hrs; wonderful site; excel." 15 Apr-15 Oct. € 14.50   2007*

AIZENAY *2H4* (1.5km SE Rural) **FFCC Camping La Forêt, Route de la Roche, 85190 Aizenay [tel/fax 02 51 34 78 12; rougier.francoise@wanadoo.fr; www.camping-laforet.com]** Exit Aizenay on D948 twd La Roche-sur-Yon. Site 1.5km on L. Med, mkd pitch, pt shd; wc; chem disp; mv service pnt; shwrs inc; el pnts (6A) €2.60; gas; lndtte; ice; shop 1km; rest 1.5km; snacks; bar; BBQ; playgrnd; htd pool; lake beach & sw 1km; tennis; cycle hire; 10% statics; dogs €1.20; phone; adv bkg (dep req); quiet; cc acc; red low ssn/CCI. ♦ ltd. Easter-30 Sep. € 15.50   2006*

AIZENAY *2H4* (6km NW Rural) **Camping La Résidence du Lac, Chemin du Village Vacances, 85190 Maché [tel/fax 02 51 55 20 30; laresidencedulac@libertysurf.fr; www.residence-du-lac.com]** Fr Aizenay take D948 twds Challans. Take D40 to Maché, pass church & sw pool, site sp. Med, hdg pitch, hdstg, pt sl, pt shd; wc; chem disp; mv service pnt; baby facs; shwrs inc; el pnts (16A) €3; gas; lndtte; ice; shop; snacks; bar; playgrnd; htd pool; sand beach 20km; lake sw adj; tennis 200m; fishing; watersports; games area; entmnt; 97% statics; dogs; Eng spkn; adv bkg; quiet; CCI. "Space for only 2-4 touring c'vans on rough ground." ♦ 15 Jun-15 Sep. € 16.00   2005*

AIZENAY *2H4* (6km NW Rural) **Camping Val de Vie, Rue du Stade, 85190 Maché [tel/fax 02 51 60 21 02; campingvaldevie@aol.com]** Fr Aizenay on D948 dir Challans. After 5km turn L onto D40 to Maché. Fr vill cent cont twd Apremont. Sm, blue site sp 100m on L. Med, hdg/mkd pitch, pt sl, pt shd; wc; chem disp; 10% serviced pitches; playgrnd; fam bthrm; shwrs inc; el pnts (4-10A) €2.90-3.50; lndtte; ice; shops 200m; BBQ; playgrnd; pool; beach 20km; tennis adj; lake 300m; fishing; boat hire; cycle hire; 10% statics; dogs €2; phone in vill; adv bkg (dep); quiet; red low ssn; CCI. "Lovely well-run site; v clean facs; friendly British owners; peaceful, pleasant rural location in pretty vill; gd touring cent; gd cycling; steel pegs useful." ♦ 1 May-30 Sep. € 18.00   2007*

ALBAN *8E4* (Rural) **Camp Municipal La Franquèze, 81250 Alban [05 63 55 91 87 or 05 63 55 82 09 (Mairie); fax 05 63 55 01 97; mairie.alban@wanadoo.fr]** W of Albi on D999 turn L at ent to Alban. Site 300m on R, sp. Sm, hdg pitch, terr, pt sl, pt shd; wc; shwrs; el pnts (6A) €1.80; ice; lndtte; playgrnd; rv fishing; adv bkg; quiet; CCI. "In beautiful country conv Tarn Valley; friendly warden; excel." 1 Jun-30 Sep. € 6.30   2005*

ALBERT *3B3* (500m N Urban) **Camp Municipal du Vélodrome, Rue Henry Dunant, 80300 Albert [03 22 75 22 53; fax 03 22 74 38 30; mairie@ville-albert.fr; www.ville-albert.fr]** Fr town cent take Rue Godin E adjacent to Basilica & foll sp for site. Easiest access fr Bapaume (N) towards Albert; turn R at camping sp on edge of town. Med, mkd pitch, unshd; wc; chem disp; mv service pnt; shwrs €1.70; el pnts (4-10A) €2.10-3.40 (rev pol); shop 1km; 40% statics; dogs; poss cr in high ssn; Eng spkn; poss rwly noise; poss disco noise late Fri & Sat high ssn; adv bkg; CCI. "Clean, well-run site with excel facs; ideal for WWI battlefields & memorials; fishing adj; recep 0800-1200 & 1700-1900 gates locked outside these times but key available; friendly, helpful warden; excel." ♦ 31 Mar-30 Sep. € 8.20
                2007*

ALBERT *3B3* (5km NE Rural) **International Camping Bellevue, 25 Rue d'Albert, 80300 Authuille** [03 22 74 59 29; fax 03 22 74 05 14] Take D929 Albert to Bapaume rd; in 3km turn L at La Boiselle, foll sp to Aveluy cont to Authuille. Site on R in vill cent. Med, hdg pitch, pt sl, pt shd; wc; chem disp; shwrs; el pnts (5A) inc (rev pol); ice; rest; shop 7km; tradsmn; playgrnd; rv fishing 500m; 80% statics; adv bkg; quiet, poss noisy at w/e; CCI. "Helpful owner; gd, clean, quiet site; useful touring Somme WW1 battlefields; walking dist of Thiepval Ridge; gd NH." 1 Mar-31 Oct. € 17.20   2006*

ALBERT *3B3* (10km SE Rural) **Camp Municipal Les Charnilles, 80340 Cappy** [03 22 76 14 50; fax 03 22 76 62 74] Fr Albert S on D329 to Bray-sur-Somme; turn L in Bray onto D1; 100m after vill sp Cappy, turn R (opp D197 to Lille). Site in 500m at end of lane. Med, hdg/mkd pitch, hdstg, pt shd; htd wc; chem disp; shwrs; el pnts (6A) inc; lndry rm; shops 1km; tradsmn; quiet; cc not acc; CCI. "Clean, well-laid out site; owner friendly & helpful; conv A1 a'route; pretty vill on Rv Somme; ltd touring pitches." 15 Mar-31 Oct. € 10.00   2004*

ALBERT *3B3* (10km SW Rural) **FFCC Camping Les Puits Tournants, 6 Rue du Marais, 80800 Sailley-le-Sec** [tel/fax 03 22 76 65 56; camping.puitstournant@wanadoo.fr; www.camping-les-puits-tournants.com] Fr Bapaume on D929 dir Amiens, at Albert take D42 S to Sailly-Laurette then turn R onto D223 to Sailly-le-Sec & foll sp. Or fr A1 junc twd Albert onto N29. At Lamotte-Warfusée R onto D42 to Sailly-Laurette, turn L to Sailley-le-Sec. Med, some hdg pitch, some hdstg, pt shd; htd wc; chem disp; mv service pnt; shwrs inc; el pnts (4A) €2.60; gas; lndtte; ice; shop; tradsmn; BBQ; playgrnd; htd pool; lake & rv sw; fishing; sports area; canoe & cycle hire; tennis 2km; horseriding 5km; TV rm; 60% statics; dogs; adv bkg; quiet; cc acc. "Pleasant site & owners; san facs basic but clean; grass pitches muddy when wet; tight ent, lge o'fits poss diff; excel." 1 Apr-31 Oct. € 16.50 (3 persons) (CChq acc)   2007*

ALBERTVILLE *9B3* (3km NE Rural) **Camping Les Marmottes, 73200 Venthon** [04 79 32 57 40] Fr Albertville take N90 SE, exit junc 32 for Tours-en-Savoie on D990. Drive thro vill, site on R outside vill limits sign. Med, pt sl, pt shd; htd wc (some cont); chem disp; mv service pnt; shwrs inc; el pnts (3-10A) inc; lndry rm; shops 3km; poss cr; adv bkg; no cc acc; quiet. "Gd views of Alps in all dirs." Easter-15 Sep. € 13.40   2005*

ALBERTVILLE *9B3* (2km SE Urban) **Camping La Maladière, 2263 Route de Tours, 73200 Albertville** [tel/fax 04 79 37 80 44] SE fr cent Albertville take N90 twds Moûtiers. After approx 4km turn off sp La Bâthie & Tours-en-Savoie. Turn L under D90 & left onto D990 thro Tours-en-Savoie. Site 300m after exit sp on R. Sm, pt shd; htd wc; shwrs inc; el pnts (10A) €4,30; ice; playgrnd; 50% statics; poss cr; adv bkg; quiet. "Gd NH." 15 Feb-15 Nov.   2005*

ALBERTVILLE *9B3* (W Urban) **Camp Municipal Les Adoubes, Ave du Camping, 73200 Albertville** [04 79 32 06 62 or 04 79 32 04 02; fax 04 79 32 87 09; sylvaine.bouchet@albertville.com; www.albertville.com] 200m fr town cent; over bdge on banks of Rv Arly. Med, unshd; wc (cont); own san; chem disp (wc); shwrs inc; el pnts (3A) €3; ice; gas; lndtte; shop 200m; tradsmn; rest, bar 200m; playgrnd; pool 1km; entmnt; dogs €0.80; poss cr; Eng spkn; adv bkg; some rd noise; 20% red CCI. "Fair NH; v helpful warden." 28 Apr-23 Sep. € 8.50   2006*

ALBI *8E4* (1.5km E Urban) **FFCC Camping Caussels, Allée du Camping, Caussels, 81000 Albi** [tel/fax 05 63 60 37 06 or 05 63 76 78 75] Fr Albi head twd Millau on D999 sp Lacaune/St Juéry & Camping for about 1.5km; at hypmkt immed turn L into rd to site. Fr W round ring rd to D999 sp Millau foll picture camping/piscine sp. Med, mkd pitch, pt terr, shd; wc (some cont); chem disp; shwrs inc; el pnts (4-10A) €3-4.80; lndtte; ice; supmkts adj; snacks; BBQ; playgrnd; pool adj; 5% statics; poss cr; bus; adv bkg; quiet; red CCI. "Conv position; helpful staff; basic, clean facs; pitches unlevelled - soft in wet & some poss diff lge o'fits due trees; gd walk by rv to town cent; Albi cathedral; Toulouse Lautrec exhibitions; 2km walk to town cent; fair NH." 1 Apr-15 Oct. € 12.00   2007*

ALBIAS see Montauban *8E3*

⊞**ALBIES** *8G3* (Rural) **Camp Municipal La Coume, 09310 Albiès** [tel/fax 05 61 64 98 99; camping.albies@wanadoo.fr] Site sp fr N20 in vill. Med, hdg pitch, pt sl, terr, pt shd; htd wc; chem disp (wc); shwrs inc; el pnts (10A) inc; lndtte; shop, rest in vill; BBQ; Rv Ariège 100m; fishing; games area; some statics; quiet. "Gd san facs." ♦ € 10.10   2006*

ALBINE *8F4* (Rural) **Camping de l'Estap, Le Suc, 81240 Albine** [05 63 98 34 74; enquiries@campinglestap.com; www.campinglestap.com] Fr Mazamet on N112 dir Béziers exit on R (D88) sp Albine. Site in 2km. Sm, hdg/mkd pitch, hdstg, terr, pt shd; wc; chem disp; baby facs; shwrs inc; el pnts (6A) €3.30; lndtte; tradsmn; snacks; bar; BBQ (gas); playgrnd; pools; fishing; games area; dogs €1.50; poss cr; Eng spkn; adv bkg (dep req); quiet; cc acc; CCI. "Excel base for Haute Languedoc; superb views; v friendly, helpful British owner; vg." ♦ 1 Apr-31 Oct. € 17.00   2007*

ALBON see St Rambert d'Albon *9C2*

ALBOUSSIERE *9C2* (300m Rural) **Camp Municipal La Duzonne, 07440 Alboussière** [04 75 58 20 91; alboussiere@camping-la-duzonne.com] App fr Valence on D533 (Valence-Lamastre) turn L on ent vill of Alboussière onto D219 sp Vernoux. (Do not take D14 which is 1st Vernoux turn). Site sp. Med, pt shd; wc; shwrs inc; el pnts (15-20A) €2.30-€3.05; ice; lndry rm; shops 1.2km; playgrnd; tennis; rv fishing; lake sw adj; dogs; adv bkg; quiet. 1 Apr-30 Sep. € 8.00   2006*

France

CAMPING MUNICIPAL DE GUERAME ★★

65, rue de Guerame • F-61014 ALENÇON
Phone: +33 (0)2 33 26 34 95 – Fax: +33 (0)2 33 26 34 95

83 pitches, all for caravans; water and electricity; showers and washing-up basins with warm water; washing machine and dryer, ironing; meeting room (with barbecue), TV room; games for children, tennis, table tennis on site; as well: canoe-kayak. Very shady, on the banks of the river "La Sarthe". Village centre, shopping centre, swimming pool nearby; horse riding, forests in the surroundings.

▬ ▬ ▬ ▬ ▬ ▬ ▬ Open from 1st April till 30th September ▬ ▬ ▬ ▬ ▬ ▬ ▬ ▬

ALENCON *4E1* (1km SW Rural) **Camp Municipal de Guéramé**, 65 Rue de Guéramé, 61000 Alençon [tel/fax 02 33 26 34 95; campingguerame@villealencon.fr] Located nr town cent. Fr N on D38 (N138) take N12 W (Carrefour sp). In 5km take D1 L sp Condé-sur-Sarthe. At rndabt turn L sp Alençon then R immed after Carrefour supmkt, foll site sp. Site is sp fr D112 inner ring rd. Med, hdg pitches, hdstg, pt shd; htd wc (some cont); chem disp; mv service pnt; baby facs; shwrs inc; baby facs; el pnts (5A) €2.95 (long cable for some pitches); lndtte; ice; shop, snacks, bar adj; BBQ; playgrnd; pool complex 700m; tennis; boating; rv fishing; canoeing; cycle hire; horseriding; entmnt; TV rm; dogs €1.75; poss cr; Eng spkn; adv bkg; quiet but w/e disco noise; no cc acc; CCI. "Sm pitches, some poss flooded in heavy rain; helpful warden; gd, clean san facs; o'night area for m'vans at site ent; barrier/recep clsd 1800 low ssn; gd rvside walk to town; low ssn phone ahead to check site open; arboretum nrby." ♦ 1 Apr-30 Sep. € 9.70
2007*

See advertisement

ALES *10E1* (13km SE Rural) **Camping Les Vistes**, 30360 St Jean-de-Ceyrargues [04 66 83 29 56 or 04 66 83 28 09; info@lesvisites.com; www.lesvistes.com] Fr Alès take D981 sp Uzès. After 12km take D7 S sp Brignon. At St Jean-de-Ceyrargues foll sp. Site S of vill on D7. Med, hdg/mkd pitch, pt sl, pt shd; wc; chem disp; baby facs; fam bthrm; shwrs inc; el pnts (4A) €2.30; lndtte; shops, rest, bar 2km; tradsmn high ssn; playgrnd; pool; TV rm; Eng spkn; quiet; CCI. "Excel views; excel pools; conv for Pont du Gard, Uzès; diff access some pitches." ♦ 1 Apr-30 Sep. € 15.00
2005*

ALES *10E1* (6km S Rural) **Camping Mas Cauvy**, 30380 St Christol-lès-Alès [tel/fax 04 66 60 78 24; maurin.helene@wanadoo.fr; http://fermemascauvy.free.fr] Fr Alès on D6110 (N110) S sp Montpellier. At S end of Christol-lès-Alès take 2nd rd on L after stone needle. Foll sp to site. Site in 1.5km. Sm, pt terr, pt shd; wc; chem disp (wc); shwrs inc; el pnts (6A) €2.50; gas 1.5km; lndtte; ice; shop 1.5km; tradsmn; BBQ; playgrnd; pool; tennis 3km; bus (1km); dogs €2; poss cr; adv bkg (dep req); quiet; 20% red low ssn/CCI. "V attractive, CL-type site with lovely views; friendly & helpful owner; book early for shd pitch; 10% red on local attractions." 1 Apr-30 Sep. € 12.00
2007*

> The opening dates and prices on this campsite have changed. I'll send a site report form to the editor for the next edition of the guide.

ALES *10E1* (5km NW Rural) **Camping La Croix Clémentine**, Route de Mende, 30480 Cendras [04 66 86 52 69; fax 04 66 86 54 84; clementine@clementine.fr; www.clementine.fr] N fr Alès on N106, in 4 km turn L sp Cendras; site sp. Lge, pt sl, terr, pt shd; wc (some cont); chem disp (wc); mv service pnt; baby facs; shwrs inc; el pnts (10A) €4; gas; lndtte; ice; shop; rest; snacks; bar; BBQ (gas); playgrnd; 3 pools (1 htd); rv sw 3km; tennis; games area; cycle hire; mini-golf; games rm; entmnt; wifi internet; TV rm; some statics; dogs €3; phone; bus adj; poss cr; Eng spkn; adv bkg rec high ssn (dep req); ltd facs low ssn; quiet; cc acc; CCI. "Excel family-run site; friendly, helpful staff; wooded site; tourers on flat, lower level; gd value winter storage avail." ♦ 31 Mar-16 Sep. € 21.60
2007*

⊞ALET LES BAINS 8G4 (Rural) Camping Val d'Aleth, Chemin de la Paoulette, 11580 Alet-les-Bains [04 68 69 90 40; fax 04 68 69 94 60; info@valdaleth.com; www.valdaleth.com] Fr Limoux S on D118 twd Quillan; in approx 8km ignore 1st L turn over Aude bdge into vill but take alt rte for heavy vehicles. Immed after x-ing rv, turn L in front of casino & ent town fr S; site sp on L. Sm, hdg/mkd pitch, hdstg, pt sl, shd; htd wc; chem disp; mv service pnt; shwrs inc; el pnts (4-10A) €3-5 gas; lndtte; ice; shop adj; BBQ (gas only); playgrnd; pool 1km; rv/beach adj; cycle hire; dogs €1.35 phone; poss cr; adv bkg (dep req); some rd & train noise, church bells; cc not acc; red low ssn/long stay; CCI. "British-owned, rvside site in attractive vill; gd modern san facs; sm pitches (lge o'fits will need to book); awnings extra; conv Carcassonne & wine cellars of Limoux." € 13.00   2007*

ALEX see Annecy 9B3

ALLANCHE 7C4 (2km SE Rural) Camp Municipal du Camp Vallat, 15160 Allanche [04 71 20 45 87; fax 04 71 20 49 26; mairie.allanche@wanadoo.fr] Fr Clermont-Ferrand on A75 take exit Massiac, site on N side of D679. Med, pt sl, pt shd; htd wc (some cont); chem disp; mv service pnt 1km; shwrs; el pnts (6A) €1.85; lndtte; shops 2km; rest; snacks; bar; playgrnd; rv 5km; v quiet; CCI. "Steep steps to san facs; attractive rural surroundings; mkt Tues." ♦ 15 Jun-15 Sep. € 4.10   2007*

ALLAS LES MINES see Sarlat la Canéda 7C3

ALLEGRE 9C1 (N Rural) Camp Municipal La Pinède, Le Chier, 43270 Allègre [04 71 00 76 79 or 04 71 00 71 21 (Mairie); mairie.allegre@wanadoo.fr] N on D13 fr Allègre site visible on N edge of Allègre. Sm, pt shd; wc (some cont); shwrs; el pnts (3-6A) €1.70-2.50; gas; lndtte; shop in vill; playgrnd; dogs €0.80; poss cr; quiet; adv bkg. 15 Jun-15 Sep. € 8.30   2005*

ALLEGRE LES FUMADES 10E2 (2km NE Rural) Camping Le Château de Boisson, 30500 Allègre-les-Fumades [04 66 24 85 61 or 04 66 24 82 21; fax 04 66 24 80 14; reception@chateaudeboisson. com; www.chateaudeboisson.com or www. les-castels.com] Fr Alès NE on D904, turn R after Les Mages onto D132, then L onto D16 for Boisson. Fr A7 take exit 19 Pont l'Esprit, turn S on N86 to Bagnols-sur-Cèze & then D6 W. Before Vallérargues turn R onto D979 Lussan, then D37 & D16 to Boisson. Lge, hdg/mkd pitch, pt sl, shd; wc; chem disp; shwrs inc; el pnts (5-6A) inc; gas; lndtte; shop; tradsmn; rest; snacks; bar; no BBQ; playgrnd; 2 pools (1 htd & covrd); tennis; mini-golf; cycle hire; entmnt; 80% statics; no dogs Jul/Aug; phone; poss cr; Eng spkn; adv bkg (dep req + bkg fee); quiet; 15% red 15+ days, red low ssn; cc acc. "Vg, well-run site; peaceful." ♦ 7 Apr-29 Sep. € 33.00
                                            2007*

ALLEGRE LES FUMADES 10E2 (2km S) Camping Le Domaine des Fumades, 30500 Allègre-les-Fumades [04 66 24 80 78; fax 04 66 24 82 42; domaine.des.frumades@wanadoo.fr; www. domaine-des-fumades.com] Take Bollène exit fr A7 m'way, foll sps to Bagnols-sur-Cèze, take D6 twd Alès; 10km bef Alès turn R sp Allègre-les-Fumades on D7 to site in 5km. Easy to find fr Alès ring rd. Med, mkd pitch, pt shd; wc; chem disp; baby facs; shwrs inc; el pnts (4A) inc; gas; lndtte; shop; rest; bar; playgrnd; htd, covrd pool; paddling pool; waterslide; tennis; games rm; entmnt; golf & watersports nr; dogs €4; adv bkg. "V pleasant location; friendly staff; beautiful site; well-run." ♦ 15 Apr-3 Sep. € 31.00   2006*

ALLEMANS DU DROPT see Miramont de Guyenne 7D2

ALLEMONT see Bourg d'Oisans, Le 9C3

ALLES SUR DORDOGNE see Bugue, Le 7C3

ALLEVARD 9B3 (11km S Rural) Camp Municipal Neige & Nature, Chemin de Montarmand, 38580 La Ferrière-d'Allevard [tel/fax 04 76 45 19 84; contact@neige.nature.fr; www.neige-nature.fr] Fr Allevard take D525A S to La Ferrière; foll sp Collet & Le Pleynet. Sm, hdg/mkd pitch, pt sl, terr, pt shd; htd wc; chem disp; baby facs; shwrs; el pnts (10A) €3.80; gas 200m; lndtte; ice; shop 200m; snacks; bar; playgrnd; rv & lake fishing; games area; entmnt; TV; dogs free; Eng spkn; adv bkg (dep req); quiet; red long stay. "Outstanding site in wonderful scenery; many mkd walks, some strenuous; excel." ♦ ltd. 15 May-15 Sep. € 14.70   2007*

ALLONNES see Saumur 4G1

ALTKIRCH 6F3 (1km SE Rural) Camping Les Acacias, Chemin de Hirtzbach, 68130 Altkirch [03 89 40 69 40] Sp on D419 on app to town fr W. Sp in town. Sm, mkd pitch, shd; htd wc (some cont); chem disp; baby facs; shwrs inc; el pnts (10A) €3; shop in ssn & 1km; rest; snacks; bar; playgrnd; pool 1km; dogs €0.80; Eng spkn; adv bkg rec high ssn; quiet; CCI. "Gd, clean facs; office clsd until 1700 in afternoon - site yourself & pay later; gd NH." 15 Apr-15 Oct. € 8.50   2005*

ALTKIRCH 6F3 (12.5km SW Rural) Camping Les Lupins, Rue de l'Ancienne Gare, 68500 Seppois-le-Bas [08 10 12 28 13; fax 03 99 57 21 22; contact@village-center.com; www.village-center. com] SW fr Altkirch on D432, after 3km turn R to Hirtzbach on D17 foll sp to Seppois-le-Bas. Site sp in vill. Med, mkd pitch, pt shd; htd wc; chem disp; shwrs inc; baby facs; el pnts (6A) inc; ice; lndtte; shop 500m; supmkt nrby; tradsmn; rest, snacks, bar 100m; BBQ; playgrnd; pool; paddling pool; games area; TV; walking; fishing; golf 5km; 60% statics; dogs €3; phone; adv bkg; quiet midwk; noisy w/e; cc acc; 10% red CCI. "Excel mod facs; Belfort worth visit; stork sanctuary adj; 1 hour Germany; 30 mins Switzerland; lge groups w/e." ♦ 7 Apr-16 Sep. € 18.00   2007*

France

ALZONNE *8F4* (3km N Rural) **Camping à la Ferme, Domaine de Contresty, 11170 Raissac-sur-Lampy [04 68 76 04 29; jh_cante@club.fr; www.aude-tourisme.com]** Take D6113 (N113) W fr Carcassonne; after 12km in Alzonne take 2nd R after traff lts, sp Camping à la Ferme. In 2km turn L sp Contresty. Sm, pt shd; wc; chem disp (wc); shwrs inc; el pnts (6A) €3; lndtte; ice; tradsmn; BBQ; playgrnd; pool; no dogs; bus 2km; adv bkg; v quiet; CCI. "CL-type site on hilltop; views of Pyrenees; excel for Carcassonne (18km); Cathar castles; gd birdwatching; helpful, friendly owner." ♦ 1 Apr-30 Oct. € 17.00   2005*

AMBAZAC *7B3* (1.8km NE Rural) **Camp Municipal de Jonas, 87240 Ambazac [05 55 56 60 25]** Fr A20 foll sp to Ambazac; site on D914. Med, terr, pt shd; wc (mainly cont); shwrs inc; el pnts (10A) €2.05; ice; shop & 2km; playgrnd; lake sw, fishing, watersports & shgl beach adj; quiet but some noise at night. "Friendly staff; excel waterside site; san facs clean." 1 Jun-15 Sep. € 6.70   2007*

AMBERT *9B1* (1km S Urban) **Camping Les Trois Chênes, Rue de la Chaise-Dieu, 63600 Ambert [04 73 82 34 68 or 04 73 82 23 95 (LS); fax 04 73 82 44 00; tourisme@ville-ambert.fr]** On main rd D906 S twd Le Puy bet Leisure Park & Aquacentre. Med, hdg/mkd pitch, pt shd, serviced pitch; wc (some cont); chem disp; shwrs inc; el pnts (10A) €2.90; gas 400m; lndtte; ice; supermkt adj; tradsmn; rest nrby; playgrnd; htd pool adj; waterslide; dogs €1; poss cr; adv bkg (dep €22.90); quiet but some traff noise; cc not acc; CCI. "Clean san facs; vg; steam train adj, steam museum & working paper mill nr; pretty rvside walk to town; rec arrive bef noon in peak." ♦ 8 May-29 Sep. € 11.10   2005*

AMBERT *9B1* (9km S Rural) **Camp Municipal La Gravière, 63940 Marsac-en-Livradois [04 73 95 60 08 or 04 73 95 61 62 (Mairie); fax 04 73 95 66 87]** Ent vill fr Ambert foll sp to camp, turn L off N106. Med, pt shd; wc; shwrs inc; el pnts (5A) inc (long lead poss req); ice; lndry rm (no hot water); shop 500m; tennis; playgrnd; fishing adj; quiet. "Warden calls; unreliable opening dates, phone ahead." 15 May-15 Oct. € 8.10   2004*

AMBERT *9B1* (10km W Rural) **Camp Municipal Saviloisirs (formerly Village Camping), 63890 St Amant-Roche-Savine [tel/fax 04 73 95 73 60 or 04 73 95 70 22 (Mairie); saviloisirs@wanadoo. fr; www.saviloisirs.com]** W fr Ambert on D996 to St Amant, turn R onto D37 into vill. In vill cent turn R & foll site sp. Bear L at lge building facing, site on L. Sm, hdg/mkd pitch, pt shd; wc; shwrs inc; el pnts (16A) (rev pol); ice; lndtte; rest 300m; shops adj; playgrnd; rv 1km; lake 1km; fishing 1km; cycle hire; horseriding; archery; entmnt; TV; dogs; quiet; CCI. "Tranquil vill site in beautiful area; spotless, modern facs; pleasant staff; easy walk to town; woodland walks." 1 May-30 Oct. € 8.50   2007*

AMBLETEUSE see Wimereux *3A2*

AMBOISE *4G2* (Rural) **Camp Municipal L'Ile d'Or, 37400 Amboise [02 47 57 23 37 or 02 47 23 47 38 (Mairie); fax 02 47 23 19 80; sports. loisirs@ville-amboise.fr; www.ville-amboise.fr]** On island in Rv Loire; access fr bdge spanning rv; fr A10 exit junc 21. Take D751 dir Blois. In Amboise get in L lane to cross bdge to site on lge wooded island. Easiest access fr N side of bdge. Site sp. Lge, mkd pitch, pt shd; wc; chem disp; mv service pnt; shwrs inc; el pnts (6A) €2 (poss rev pol); lndtte; ice; rest; snacks; bar; playgrnd; pool & waterslide 2km (high ssn); tennis; fishing; crazy golf; entmnt; TV; no statics; dogs €1.05; phone; poss cr; Eng spkn; rd noise if pitched nr rd; cc acc; CCI. "Lovely location adj Rv Loire & opp 2 chateaux; clean facs but clsd afternoons low ssn; short walk to interesting old town with gd rests; vg dog walking; recep 0700-2130 high ssn; conv Amboise Château Royal & Loire Valley; Château du Clos Lucé & Parc Léonardo Da Vinci (last place he lived); midsummer week music festival in adj park (v noisy) - check date; no twin-axles; m'van o'night area; highly rec." ♦ 30 Mar-30 Sep. € 8.15   2007*

AMBOISE *4G2* (4km N Rural) **Camp Municipal des Patis, 37530 Nazelles-Négron [02 47 57 71 07 or 02 47 23 71 71; mairie.nazelles-negron@ wanadoo.fr; www.ville-amboise.fr]** Fr Amboise, take N152 twd Tours & turn R (N) onto D5 to Nazelles-Négron. Foll sp to vill. Site N of bdge over Rv Cisse, on R immed after x-ing bdge. Med, mkd pitch, pt shd; wc (some cont); chem disp; shwrs inc; el pnts (3-5A) €1.94-2.83 (check with warden if 3A or 5A) (long lead poss req); lndry rm; shops 100m; playgrnd; dogs €0.90; poss cr; quiet; CCI. "Peaceful, clean, well-kept site; some lge pitches; gd facs; low ssn open only 0900-1000 & 1800-1900 - unsuitable for m'vans; no lge vans or twin-axles; boggy in wet weather; v ltd off-site parking for car+van; excel." 17 Apr-9 Sep. € 7.08   2007*

⊞**AMBOISE** *4G2* (6km NE Rural) **Camping Le Jardin Botanique, 9 bis, Rue de la Rivière, 37530 Limeray [02 47 30 13 50; fax 02 47 30 17 32; info@ camping-jardinbotanique.com; www.camping-jardinbotanique.com]** Fr Amboise on D952/N152 on N side of Rv Loire dir Blois, site sp in Limeray. Med, hdg/mkd pitch, hdstg, pt shd; htd wc; chem disp; mv service pnt; baby facs; fam bthrm; shwrs inc; el pnts (10A) €3.50 (poss rev pol); gas; lndtte; shop 2km; tradsmn; rest; snacks; bar; BBQ; playgrnd; pool; sand beach 15km; tennis; games area; cycle hire; TV; 20% statics; dogs €1.50; Eng spkn; adv bkg; rd & rlwy noise; red long stay/ CCI. "Gd touring base Loire chateaux & vineyards; 500m fr rv; no lighting on roadways; new san facs 2007; v friendly & helpful owner; gd for children; site v muddy when wet; gd cycle rtes." ♦ € 15.50   2007*

See advertisement opposite

AMBOISE *4G2* (3km E Rural) **Camp Municipal Le Verdeau, 37530 Chargé [02 47 57 04 22 or 02 47 57 04 01 (Mairie); fax 02 47 57 41 52]** Fr Amboise take D751 twd Blois, site sp on L. Med, pt shd; wc; chem disp; shwrs inc; el pnts (5A); lndtte; tradsmn; playgrnd; rv fishing & boating; tennis; dogs; no twin-axle c'vans; adv bkg rec high ssn; quiet; CCI. "Gd cent for Loire Valley; site barrier clsd 1100-1600." ♦ 1 Jul-31 Aug.   2004*

AMBON PLAGES see Muzillac *2G3*

AMBRIERES LES VALLEES *4E1* (1km S Rural) **FFCC Camp Municipal de Vaux, Rue des Colverts, 53300 Ambrières-les-Vallées [02 43 04 90 25; fax 02 43 08 93 28; otsiambrieres@wanadoo.fr]** Fr S on D23 turn R at sp 'Parc de Loisirs de Vaux'. Site in approx 400m on bank Rv Varenne. Check in at Office de Tourisme bef park ent. Med, hdg pitch, some hdstg, pt sl, pt shd; wc; shwrs inc; el pnts (10A) €2.70 (poss long lead req) (poss rev pol); lndtte; ice; shops 2km; tradsmn; bar; BBQ; playgrnd; htd pool; canoe hire; fishing; crazy golf inc; tennis; TV rm; adv bkg; quiet; red long stay; CCI. "Excel site; facs ltd low ssn; pitches poss uneven; poor security; san facs v clean; beautiful surroundings." 1 Apr-30 Sep. € 11.10   2007*

AMIENS *3C3* (6km N Rural) **FFCC Camping du Château, Rue du Château, 80260 Bertangles [tel/fax 03 22 93 68 36; camping@chateaubertangles.com; www.chateaubertangles.com]** Foll N25 N of Amiens; after 8km turn W on D97 to Bertangles. Well sp in vill. Sm, hdg pitch, pt shd; wc; chem disp; shwrs inc; el pnts (5A) €2.60 (poss rev pol); ice; tradsmn; tabac/bar in vill; bus; poss cr; quiet but slight rd noise; red 8+ days; no cc acc; CCI. "V pleasant, quiet site by chateau wall; gd site & facs; gd value; early arr rec; spotless san facs; vg warden; ltd recep hrs, pitch yourself; gates open 0800-2200; Amiens v attractive city & cathedral; conducted tours of chateau high ssn; gd walks." ♦ 22 Apr-10 Sep. € 12.40   2007*

AMIENS *3C3* (8km NW Rural) **Camping Parc des Cygnes, 111 Rue de Montières, 80080 Amiens-Longpré [03 22 43 29 28; fax 03 22 43 59 42; camping.amiens@wanadoo.fr; www.parcdescygnes.com]** Exit A16 junc 20 or fr ring rd Rocade Nord exit junc 40. Foll sp Amiens, Longpré D412 & site. Med, mkd pitch, pt shd; htd wc; chem disp; baby facs; shwrs inc; el pnts (6A) inc; gas; lndtte; shop; snacks; bar; BBQ; playgrnd; fishing nrby; kayaking; cycle hire; games rm; internet; TV; dogs €2; bus; adv bkg; quiet; cc acc. "Lovely area; v pleasant, well-kept site in parkland; well laid-out; clean, modern facs; helpful, welcoming staff; ltd facs low ssn; office open 0830-2000 high ssn - ring bell by recep if clsd; gd canal-side cycling to city; Amiens cathedral worth visit (sound & light show in summer) & floating gardens; conv Somme battlefields; bus to city cent adj; excel." ♦ 1 Apr-15 Oct. € 20.10 ABS - P11   2007*

See advertisement on next page (top)

AMPILLY LE SEC see Châtillon sur Seine *6F1*

ANCENIS *2G4* (12km E Rural) **Camping de l'Ile Batailleuse, St Florent-le-Vieil, 44370 Varades [02 40 83 45 01]** On Ancenis-Angers rd N23 turn S in Varades onto D752 to St Florent-le-Vieil. After x-ing 1st bdge over Loire site on L on island immed bef 2nd bdge. Med, pt shd; wc; chem disp; shwrs inc; el pnts (10A) €2; shops 1km; rest 20m; playgrnd; pool 1km; tennis 1km; cycle hire; games area; dogs €1; poss cr; Eng spkn; quiet but poss road noise; CCI. "Basic, clean site; main shwr facs up stone staircase; facs for disabled on grnd floor; panoramic views of Loire in town; gd cycle rtes along Loire." ♦ 28 Apr-9 Oct. € 11.00   2005*

France

ANCENIS 2G4 (5km SW Rural) **Camping La Pêche** (formerly Camp Municipal de Beauregret), 49530 Drain [02 40 98 20 30; fax 02 40 98 23 29] Fr Ancenis take D763 S for 2km, turn R onto D751 & cont for 3km. Site on R bef vill of Drain on L. Sm, hdg pitch, pt shd; wc; own san rec; chem disp; mv service pnt; shwrs inc; el pnts (6-10A) €1.80-2.20 (poss rev pol); ice; lndtte; shop nr; BBQ; playgrnd; lake nrby; games area; entmnt; TV rm; phone; adv bkg; quiet. "Secluded site; gd fishing; san facs up steel steps, poss poor low ssn; poss not suitable lge o'fits." ♦ 1 May-30 Sep. € 6.50   2005*

ANCENIS 2G4 (1km W Rural) **FFCC Camping de l'Ile Mouchet**, La Davrays, 44150 Ancenis [02 40 83 08 43 or 06 83 52 73 44 (mob); fax 02 40 83 16 19; efberthelot@wanadoo.fr; www.camping-estivance.com] Fr S turn L immed after x-ing Rv Loire & foll sp; site on banks of Loire. Med, mkd pitch, pt shd; wc; chem disp; mv service pnt; shwrs inc; el pnts (6-10A) €2.30; lndtte; gas; shops adj; rest, snacks, bar high ssn; playgrnd; pool; rv sw nr; tennis 50m; games rm; TV; 12% statics; dogs; Eng spkn; adv bkg; quiet; cc acc; red low ssn/CCI. "Warden calls am & pm; rvside walk; ltd facs low ssn; excel." ♦ 1 Apr-7 Oct. € 11.50   2006*

ANDELOT BLANCHEVILLE 6F1 (1km W Rural) Camping du Moulin, Rue du Moulin, 52700 Andelot-Blancheville [03 25 01 60 50 or 03 25 01 33 31 (Mairie); fax 03 25 03 77 54; mairie. andelot@wanadoo.fr] Fr N on D974 (N74) site on ent Andelot-Blancheville. Foll sp & turn L onto D147. Site on R in 1km. Med, hdg/mkd pitch, pt shd; wc; chem disp; shwrs inc; el pnts (9A) inc (poss rev pol); lndry rm; ice; shop 1km; tradsmn; bar; playgrnd; lake/ rv fishing; games area; TV rm; dogs; phone; Eng spkn; quiet; CCI. "Peaceful, quiet site by rv; gd NH on journey S." ♦ 1 Jun-31 Aug. € 10.20   2007*

ANDELYS, LES 3D2 (1km S Urban) **Camping de l'Ile des Trois Rois**, 27700 Les Andelys [02 32 54 23 79; fax 02 32 51 14 54; campingtroisrois@aol.com; www.camping-troisrois.com] Fr Louviers after x-ing bdge over Seine, R at junc of D135 & D313 S of Les Andelys. Site on R in 100m. Lge, pt shd; htd wc (some cont); chem disp; mv service pnt; shwrs inc; el pnts (6A) €3; lndtte; shop; tradsmn; rest; snacks; bar; BBQ; playgrnd; htd pool; paddling pool; fishing; bowling alley; 25% statics sep; dogs €2; phone; poss cr; Eng spkn; quiet; red CCI. "Gd position on Rv Seine; ruins of Châteaux Gaillard opp; well cared for; clean facs; recep 0900-1800; conv for Rouen, Evreux, Giverny; excel." ♦ 15 Mar-15 Nov. € 16.00   2007*

See advertisement below

⊞**ANDERNOS LES BAINS** *7D1* (3km NE Rural) **Camping Les Arbusiers, 134 Ave de Bordeaux, 33510 Andernos-les-Bains [05 56 82 12 46; fax 05 56 26 15 21; lesarbousiers@yahoo.fr; www.camping-les-arbousiers.fr]** 7km E of Arès fr Bordeaux on D106, take D215 sp Andernos. Site on L in 2km, ent rd to airport. Lge, hdg/mkd pitch, pt shd; htd wc; chem disp; baby facs; shwrs inc; el pnts (6A) inc (poss rev pol); Indtte; shop 2km; snacks; bar; BBQ; pool; sand beach 3km; 50% statics; dogs €1; Eng spkn; quiet; cc acc. "Friendly staff; pleasantly situated site." € 19.50   2007*

ANDERNOS LES BAINS *7D1* (3km NE Rural) **Camping Pleine Forêt, Ave de Bordeaux, 33510 Andernos-les-Bains [05 56 82 17 18; fax 05 56 26 01 65; pleine.foret@wanadoo.fr; www. campingpleineforet.com]** Take D106 fr Bordeaux, & app Andernos on D215 site on R opp sm airfield. Lge, shd; wc; shwrs; el pnts (6A) €3; Indtte; playgrnd; pool; beach 2.5km; sailing 2.5km; entmnt; mostly statics; dogs; poss cr; quiet. "Tourers put on edge of site, app rds narr within site, care needed; recep clsd 1230-1500." 1 Apr-30 Sep. € 20.00   2005*

ANDERNOS LES BAINS *7D1* (2.5km SE Coastal) **Camping Fontaine Vieille, 4 Blvd du Colonel Wurtz, 33510 Andernos-les-Bains [05 56 82 01 67; fax 05 56 82 09 81; contact@ fontaine-vieille.com; www.fontainevieille.com]** Take D106 fr Bordeaux then D215 on L after 40km sp Andernos. Well sp. Site situated 600m off D3. V lge, hdg/mkd pitch, pt shd; wc (some cont); chem disp; mv service pnt; baby facs; shwrs inc; el pnts (5A) inc; gas; Indtte; shop & 3km; rest; snacks; bar; pool/waterpark; sand beach adj; watersports inc windsurfing; games area; tennis; entmnt; TV; dogs €3; adv bkg rec high ssn; quiet; cc acc; red long stay/low ssn. "Organised bus trips & sports; some pitches sea view (extra charge); excel for families." ♦ 1 Apr-30 Sep. € 24.50   2007*

See advertisement on previous page (top)

⊞**ANDERNOS LES BAINS** *7D1* (5km SE Coastal) **Camping Domaine du Roumingue, 60 Ave de la Libération, 33138 Lanton [05 56 82 97 48; fax 05 56 82 96 09; info@roumingue.fr; www. roumingue.fr]** Approx 7km SE of Andernos-les-Bains on D3 bet Cassy & Lanton. Lge, hdg/mkd pitch, pt shd; htd wc (some cont); mv service pnt; chem disp; serviced pitches; shwrs inc; el pnts (6A) €3.90; gas; ice; Indtte; shop; tradsmn; rest; snacks; bar; playgrnd; pool; guarded private sand beach adj; lake sw; fishing; windsurfing; tennis; games/sports area; cycle hire; entmnt; sat TV; 30% statics; dogs €2.60; phone; Eng spkn; adv bkg (dep req); cc acc; red low ssn/long stay; CCI. "Excel family site; lge entmnt complex; many facs/ activities; helpful, friendly staff; vg." ♦ € 24.20   2007*

See advertisement on previous page (bottom)

ANDERNOS LES BAINS *7D1* (5km SE Coastal) **Camping Le Coq Hardi, Cassy, 33138 Lanton [05 56 82 01 80; fax 05 56 82 16 11; Violesgalyon@ aol.com; www.campingcoq-hardi.com]** At Facture on N250 fr Bordeaux turn R on D3 twd Andernos. Site on L at Cassy. Lge, pt shd; wc (cont); chem disp; mv service pnt; shwrs inc; el pnts (6-10A) €3.70-4.70 (poss rev pol); gas; ice; shop high ssn; snacks; playgrnd; htd pool; paddling pool; sand beach adj; indoor sports hall; entmnt; 15% statics; dogs €2.20; phone; bus adj; adv bkg (fee €16); quiet low ssn; CCI. "Gd rests, shops nrby; pleasant view; peaceful low ssn; v helpful owners; gd pitches." 1 Apr-30 Sep. € 18.00   2007*

ANDERNOS LES BAINS *7D1* (6km W Coastal) **Airotel Camping Les Viviers, Route de Cap-Ferret, Claouey, 33950 Lège-Cap-Ferret [05 56 60 70 04; fax 05 57 70 37 77; reception@ lesviviers.com; www.airotel-les-viviers.com]** Exit A10/A630 W for airport & Bordeaux-Mérignac. Take D106 (sp Cap-Ferret), on exit vill of Claouey (on W side of Bassin d'Arcachon). Camp sp as being 1km away but ent on L after LH bend. V lge, hdg/mkd pitch, pt shd; htd wc; mv service pnt; chem disp; baby facs; sauna; shwrs inc; el pnts (10A) €7; gas; Indtte; supmkt; rest; snacks; bar; BBQ (gas/elec); playgrnd; htd, covrd pool; paddling pool; waterslide; sea water lagoon with private sand beach adj; fishing; sailing; windsurfing; tennis; cycle hire; mini-golf; games area; games rm; cinema; entmnt; child entmnt; TV rm; 27% statics; dogs €3; bus; Eng spkn; adv bkg ess (bkg fee); quiet; cc acc; red long stay/low ssn/CCI. "Sand pitches, variable position & price; v clean san facs; free night bus along peninsular; vg." ♦ 31 Mar-30 Sep. € 37.00   2007*

See advertisement on previous page (middle

ANDERNOS LES BAINS *7D1* (6km W Coastal) **Camping Brémontier, Le Grand Crohot Océan 33950 Lège-Cap-Ferret [tel/fax 05 56 60 03 99; www.campingbremontier.fr]** Fr Andernos NW on D3 to Arès. Take Cap Ferret rd D106. 1km after turn R on D106E sp Le Crohot. Site at end of rd in 5km. Fr Bordeaux stay on D106 thro Arès & Lège & on D106E. Site at end of rd in 6km. Med, shd; wc; shwrs inc; el pnts (5A) €3.30; gas; shop; sand beach 500m; no statics; dogs; quiet. "Simple site in pine woods; gd cycling." 1 Jun-30 Sep. € 15.00   2007*

ANDERNOS LES BAINS *7D1* (5km NW Coastal) **Camping La Cigale, Route de Lège, 33740 Arès [05 56 60 22 59; fax 05 57 70 41 66; camping lacigaleares@wanadoo.fr; www.camping-lacigale-ares.com]** Fr Andernos proceed NW on D3 to Arès. Take Cap-Ferret rd D106. Site on L in 1km. Med, mkd pitch, shd; wc; shwrs inc; el pnts (6A) €5; gas; Indtte; shop; tradsmn; rest; snacks; bar; BBQ; playgrnd; pool; beach 900m; games area; entmnt; TV; some statics; poss cr; adv bkg rec high ssn; quiet. "Excel family-run site." ♦ 4 May-30 Sep. € 29.00   2007*

ANDERNOS LES BAINS *7D1* (5km NW Coastal)
**Camping Les Abberts, Rue des Abberts, 33740
Arès [tel/fax 05 56 60 26 80; campinglesabberts@
wanadoo.fr]** Fr town sq in Arès, take D106 twd
Cap Ferrat, turn 1st L to site in 100m. Med, hdg/
mkd pitch, pt shd; wc; chem disp; shwrs inc; el
pnts (6A) €4.40; gas; lndtte; snacks; shops 400m;
rest; snacks; playgrnd; pool; sand beach 600m;
25% statics; dogs €2; poss cr; adv bkg; quiet;
CCI. "New young owners 2006; improvements
in hand; nr cycle paths to Arès; mkt Tues; gd." ♦
1 May-30 Sep. € 22.00   2006*

> Before we
> move on, I'm going to
> fill in some site report forms
> and post them off to the editor,
> otherwise they won't arrive in
> time for the deadline at the
> end of September.

ANDERNOS LES BAINS *7D1* (5km NW Coastal)
**Camping Les Goëlands, Ave de la Libération, 33740
Arès [05 56 82 55 64; fax 05 56 82 07 51; camping-
les.goelands@wanadoo.fr; www.goelands.com]**
Fr Bordeaux m'way by-pass take D106 for Cap-
Ferret. At Arès take D3 SE twd Andernos. Site
on R 200m after end of Arès town sp. Site sp.
Lge, mkd pitch, shd; wc; chem disp; shwrs inc; el
pnts (6A) inc; gas; lndtte; ice; shop; rest; snacks;
bar; playgrnd; sand beach 200m; seawater lake
200m; 90% statics; dogs; poss cr; adv bkg; poss
noisy; red low ssn; CCI. "Many gd beaches." ♦
1 Mar-31 Oct. € 21.00   2006*

ANDERNOS LES BAINS *7D1* (5km NW Coastal)
**Camping Pasteur Vacances, 1 Rue du Pilote,
33740 Arès [05 56 60 33 33; pasteur.vacances@
wanadoo.fr; www.atlantic-vacances.com]** Take
D106 Bordeaux-Arès. At rndabt in Arès cent take
D3 twd Andernos. Turn R at camp sp, site on L. Sm,
pt shd; wc; mv service pnt; shwrs inc; el pnts (10A)
€3.50; lndtte; snacks; shop adj; playgrnd; sm pool;
beach adj & lake sw; dogs €2; poss cr; quiet; adv
bkg; Eng spkn. "Friendly owners; cycle path round
Arcachon Basin." ♦ 1 Apr-30 Sep. € 23.50
                                                  2006*

ANDERNOS LES BAINS *7D1* (5km NW Coastal)
**FLOWER Camping La Canadienne, 82 Rue du
Général de Gaulle, 33740 Arès [05 56 60 24 91;
fax 05 57 70 40 85; info@lacanadienne.com; www.
lacanadienne.com or www.flowercampings.com]**
N fr town sq at Arès on D3 (Rue du Général de
Gaulle) dir Cap Ferret. Site on R after 1km. Med,
shd; wc; baby facs; shwrs inc; el pnts (15A) inc;
gas; lndtte; ice; shop; rest; snacks; bar; sand beach
2km; playgrnd; pool; paddling pool; cycle & canoe
hire; fishing, sailing & windsurfing 1km; tennis;
archery; entmnt; games/TV rm; dogs €2.50; adv bkg
rec high ssn; quiet, but some rd noise; red low ssn.
♦ 1 Feb-30 Nov. € 30.90   2007*

⊞ANDERNOS LES BAINS *7D1* (7.5km NW
Rural) **Camping La Prairie, 93 Ave du Médoc,
33950 Lège-Cap-Ferret [tel/fax 05 56 60 09 75;
camping-la-prairie@wanadoo.fr; www.camping
laprairie.com]** Site 1km N of Lège-Cap-Ferret
on D3 dir Porge. Med, pt shd; htd wc; chem disp;
shwrs inc; el pnts (10A) €3; lndtte; shop; snacks;
BBQ; playgrnd; sand beach 5km; games area;
games rm; entmnt; some statics; dogs €1.60;
Eng spkn; adv bkg; quiet; CCI. "Poss run down &
unclean low ssn; friendly owner; long distance cycle
paths; gd baker nrby." € 14.00   2007*

ANDERNOS LES BAINS *7D1* (8km NW Rural)
**FFCC Camping Mer et Forêt, 101 Ave du Médoc,
33950 Lège-Cap-Ferret [05 56 60 18 36 or
05 56 60 16 99; fax 05 56 60 39 47]** Fr Bordeaux
take D106 W dir Arès. Fr cent Arès take D3 N sp
Lège-Cap-Ferret. Site on L in 5km adj 'Camping
Prairie'. Med, mkd pitch, pt shd; wc; chem disp; mv
service pnt; shwrs €0.75; el pnts (3-6A) €1.25-2.50;
shop 2km; tradsmn; sand beach 6km; dogs; phone;
quiet; CCI. "Gd for Arcachon Basin; excel, clean
san facs; v friendly owner; gd value for area; vg."
♦ ltd. 1 Jun-30 Sep. € 8.50   2007*

ANDOUILLE see Laval *2F4*

ANDRYES see Clamecy *4G4*

ANDUZE *10E1* (5km E Rural) **Camping du
Domaine de Gaujac, 30140 Boisset-et-Gaujac
[04 66 61 80 65; fax 04 66 60 53 90; gravieres@
clubinternet.fr; www.homair.com or www.
domaine-de-gaujac.com]** Foll sp fr Alès take N110
S & turn R at D910 dir Anduze. At Bagard (3km bef
Anduze) turn L at mini rndabt onto D264 dir Boisset
& Gaujac. At next rndbt turn R, then immed L. Foll
vill & camping sp. Lge, pt terr, shd; htd wc (some
cont); chem disp; mv service pnt; some serviced
pitches; shwrs inc; baby facs; el pnts (4-6A)
€3-3.50; gas; lndtte; ice; shop; rest; snacks; bar;
BBQ; playgrnd; 2 htd pools; rv sw adj; fishing; tennis;
cycle hire; games area; games rm; entmnt; internet;
TV; 30% statics; dogs €2.50; Eng spkn; adv bkg
rec high ssn; quiet; red low ssn. "V tranquil; helpful,
friendly family owners; Trabuc caves, Tarn gorges
nrby. ♦ 1 Apr-30 Sep. € 18.50 (CChq acc)   2004*

ANDUZE *10E1* (2.5km SE Rural) **Camping
Le Bel Eté (formerly Le Malhiver), Route de
Nîmes, 30140 Anduze [tel/fax 04 66 61 76 04;
campingmalhiver@wanadoo.fr; www.camping
malhiver.com]** S fr Alès on N110; W on D910 to
Anduze. In Anduze take D907 SE twds Nîmes. Site
on L, 200m after riv bdge. Med, mkd pitch, pt shd;
wc; chem disp; serviced pitches; shwrs inc; el pnts
(6A) €3.80; gas; lndtte; shop 2km; tradsmn; rest;
playgrnd; pool; rv adj; 10% statics; dogs €1.50;
phone; adv bkg ess; quiet but some rd noise; CCI.
"Delightful, well-kept site in superb location; vg
facs but v ltd low ssn; v helpful owner; gd base for
Cévennes area." ♦ 8 May-17 Sep. € 21.50
                                                  2006*

ANDUZE *10E1* (5km SE Rural) **Camping Le Fief, 195 Chemin du Plan d'Eau, 30140 Massillargues-Attuech [04 66 61 81 71 or 04 66 61 87 80; fax 04 66 61 81 71; natbrunel@cegetel.net; www. campinglefiefdanduze.com]** Leave Anduze S on D982 dir Nîmes; site on L on leaving Attuech; sp. Med, mkd pitch, shd; wc; chem disp; baby facs; shws inc; el pnts (6A) €2.60 (poss no earth); lndtte; shops; tradsmn; rest; snacks; bar; playgrnd; pool; rv sw adj, shgl beach; 10% statics; dogs €1.50; phone; poss cr; adv bkg (dep req); quiet; cc acc; CCI. "Clean facs; gd for cycling." 1 Apr-30 Sep. € 16.90   2006*

> There aren't many sites open this early in the year. We'd better phone ahead to check that the one we're heading for is actually open.

ANDUZE *10E1* (1.4km NW) **Camping Castel Rose, 30140 Anduze [04 66 61 80 15; castel.rose@wanadoo.fr; www.castelrose.com]** Fr Alès S on N110 W on N910A to Anduze. Foll sp Camping L'Arche. Lge, shd; wc; shwrs inc; el pnts (6-10A) €3.20-3.70; gas; lndtte; shop; rest; snacks; bar; pool; rv sw; fishing; boating; entmnt; TV; dogs €2.20; poss cr; adv bkg rec high ssn. "Gd cent touring Cévennes; attractive countryside." 8 Apr-17 Sep. € 17.00   2006*

ANDUZE *10E1* (1.7km NW Rural) **Camping Les Fauvettes, 1030 Route de St Jean-du-Gard, Quartier Labahou, 30140 Anduze [tel/fax 04 66 61 72 23; camping-les-fauvettes@wanadoo.fr; www.camping-les-fauvettes.fr]** Site sp fr D907 to St Jean-du-Gard. Med, mkd pitch, pt sl, terr, pt shd; wc; baby facs; shwrs inc; el pnts (6A) €2.60; gas; ice; shop; snacks; bar; playgrnd; pool; paddling pool; waterslide; fishing; entmnt; TV; some statics; dogs; adv bkg; quiet. 24 Apr-25 Sep. € 15.25   2006*

ANDUZE *10E1* (2km NW Rural) **Camping L'Arche, Quartier de Labahou, 30140 Anduze [04 66 61 74 08; fax 04 66 61 88 94; camping.arche@wanadoo.fr]** Fr Alès S on N110/D910A to Anduze. On D907; sp on R. Access poss dff lge o'fits/m'vans. Lge, mkd pitch, shd; htd wc; chem disp; mv service pnt; baby facs; shwrs inc; el pnts (6-10A) €1.70; gas; lndtte; shop; tradsmn; rest; snacks; bar; BBQ; playgrnd; rv sw; entmnt; TV; dogs €2.70; Eng spkn; adv bkg; quiet; red long stay; CCI. "Well-run site; gd san facs; beautiful area; bamboo gardens worth visit; 24hr security patrols." ◆ 21 Mar-30 Sep. € 22.90   2005*

ANDUZE *10E1* (4km NW Rural) **Camping Cévennes-Provence, Corbes-Thoiras, 30140 Anduze [04 66 61 73 10; fax 04 66 61 60 74; marais@camping-cevennes-provence.fr; www.camping-cevennes-provence.fr]** Fr Anduze D907 & D284 along rvside after bdge, site sp. Diff ent espec for lge o'fits. Lge, mkd pitch, terr, shd; wc (mainly cont); chem disp; some serviced pitches; mv service pnt; baby facs; shwrs inc; el pnts (3-15A) €3-4.30; gas; lndtte; ice; shop, rest, snacks, bar; playgrnd; shgl beach & rv sw adj; games area; games rm; internet; TV; some statics; dogs €2; Eng spkn; adv bkg; quiet; red low ssn; CCI. "Variable pitch sizes; ideal base for area; helpful recep; gd walking; vg site." ◆ 20 Mar-1 Nov. € 18.90
                        2006*

ANET *3D2* (500m N Urban) **Camp Municipal, Rue des Cordeliers, 28260 Anet [02 37 41 42 67 or 02 37 62 55 25 (Mairie); fax 02 37 62 20 99; martine.desrues@cegetel.net]** Take D928 NE fr Dreux; in Anet thro town & take 1st L after chateau; turn L on rd to Ezy & Ivry (camp sp on corner), site in 150m N of rv. Lge, pt shd; htd wc; chem disp (wc); mv service pnt; 75% serviced pitches; shwrs €0.90; el pnts (5A) inc; lndry rm; supmkt 1km; playgrnd; rv adj; lake sw & fishing 2km; tennis; 80% statics; dogs €0.80; poss cr at w/e; Eng spkn; cc not acc; CCI. "Rvside pitches; ground v soft in wet; nice walks in forest; lovely chateau in vill; level walk to town; easy drive to Paris; peaceful site; helpful warden; v clean, basic facs; excel & conv NH." 1 Apr-31 Oct. € 7.30
                        2007*

ANET *3D2* (1km N Urban) **Camp Municipal Les Trillots, Chemin des Trillots, 27530 Ezy-sur-Eure [02 37 64 73 21 or 02 37 64 73 48 (Mairie)]** N fr Dreux on D928/D143. Site on N site of Rv Eure. Med, unshd; htd wc; shwrs inc; el pnts (4-8A) €1.78-2.68; lndtte; supmkt nr; rest, snacks, bar 1km; BBQ; 90% statics; dogs; quiet, "Pleasant rvside walk." 1 May-15 Nov. € 3.50   2005*

ANGERS *4G1* (10km SE Rural) **Camping Caroline, Route de la Bohalle, 49800 Brain-sur-l'Authion [02 41 80 42 18 or 04 99 57 20 25; fax 04 99 57 21 22; caroline@village-center.com; www.village-center.com/caroline]** Turn off N147 onto D113, site sp E of Angers at ent to vill. Med, hdg/mkd pitch, hdstg, pt shd; htd wc; chem disp; shwrs inc; el pnts (10A) inc; lndtte; ice; shop 300m; snacks; BBQ; playgrnd; htd pool; paddling pool; tennis; fishing nrby; games area adj; games rm; skateboarding; entmnt; child entmnt; TV rm; 5% statics; dogs €3; adv bkg; some rd & rlwy noise (& owls, woodpeckers); cc acc. "Gd touring base." ◆ 16 Jun-2 Sep. € 12.00   2007*

France

ANGERS *4G1* (5km S Urban) **Camp Municipal de l'Ile du Château, 49130 Les Ponts-de-Cé** [tel/fax 02 41 44 62 05; ile-du-chateau@wanadoo.fr; www.camping-ileduchateau.com] Fr Angers take N160 (sp Cholet) to Les Ponts-de-Cé. Turn R at traff lts in town opp Hôtel de Ville, & site in 500m. Med, hdg pitch, pt shd; wc; chem disp; mv service pnt; child/baby facs; shwrs inc; el pnts (6A) €2.90; lndtte; ice; shops 1km; tradsmn; snacks; bar; BBQ; playgrnd; pool, waterslide adj; sand beach 500m; tennis; mini-golf; golf 5km; TV; dogs €1.50; phone; poss cr; Eng spkn; quiet; red low ssn; cc acc; CCI. "Well-kept site adj Rv Maine; excel views; access to site warden-controlled, off ssn recep opening times vary; excel pool adj; gd touring base for chateaux, vineyards; gd dog walking; open all year for m'vans; highly rec." ♦ 6 Apr-29 Sep. € 13.00   2007*

⊞ANGERS *4G1* (6km SW Rural) **Camping Aire d'Accueil de Camping Cars, 25 Rue Chevrière, 49080 Bouchemaine** [02 41 77 11 04 or 02 41 22 20 00 (Mairie); adm.generale@ville-bouchemaine.fr; www.ville-bouchemaine.fr] Fr Angers take N160 S, at intersection with D112 W sp Bouchemaine. Cross Rv Maine via suspension bdge. At rndabt on W bank turn L, site in 100m dir La Pointe adj rv. Fr Château-Gontier take N162, then D106, then D102E. Bouchemaine well sp. Sm, pt shd; wc; mv service pnt; shwrs inc; el pnts (16A) €2.55 (poss rev pol); lndtte; shops 1km; rest 500m; pool 500m; games area; dogs; phone; bus; poss cr; adv bkg quiet; CCI. "M'vans & tents only; warden calls am & pm; no el pnts avail mid-Sep to end May." € 10.00   2007*

ANGERS *4G1* (5km W Urban) **Camping du Lac de Maine, Ave du Lac de Maine, 49000 Angers** [02 41 73 05 03; fax 02 41 73 02 20; camping@lacdemaine.fr; www.lacdemaine.fr] W fr Angers on N23, exit at 'Quartier du Lac de Maine then foll sp to site & Bouchemaine. After 4 rndabts site on L; sp W of Rv Maine. Fr S on N160 or A87, turn onto D4 at Les Ponts-de-Cé. In 6km, cross Rv Maine to Bouchemaine & turn R to Pruniers dir Angers. Site on R at Pruniers town exit sp. Lge, hdg/mkd pitch, hdstg, pt shd; htd wc; chem disp; mv service pnt; serviced pitches; baby facs; shwrs inc; el pnts (10A) €3.40 (rev pol); gas; lndtte; shop 1.5km; tradsmn; hypmkt 2km; rest, snacks & bar in ssn; BBQ; playgrnd; htd pool; paddling pool; sand beach 800m; fishing; boating; windsurfing 500m; tennis 800m; games area; cycle hire; wifi internet; TV rm; 10% statics; dogs €2; bus; phone; Eng spkn; adv bkg rec high ssn (dep req); quiet but some rd noise; cc acc; red low ssn/long stay; 10% red CCI. "Excel site in leisure park; in wet weather check stability of hdstg pitches; height barrier at ent 3.20m; some pitches suitable v l'ge o'fits; conv Loire chateaux; excel facs; v helpful managers; conv bus to Angers cent; vg." ♦ 25 Mar-10 Oct. € 17.00 (CChq acc)   2007*

See advertisement

ANGOULEME *7B2* (15km N Rural) **FFCC Camp Municipal Les Platanes, 16330 Montignac-Charente** [05 45 39 89 16 or 05 45 39 70 09 (Mairie); fax 05 45 22 26 71] Fr N, on N10, turn W on D11 then N on D737 thro vill onto D15. Narr rds on app, site on R by Rv Charente. Med, pt shd; wc (cont); chem disp; shwrs inc; el pnts (6-12A) €2.30-€4.25 (poss rev pol); gas 2km; lndry rm; ice; shop 800m; rest, snacks in vill; bar; rv sw & fishing adj; canoeing; direct access to rv; dogs; poss cr; quiet; 25% red 16 days; cc not acc; CCI. "Pleasant vill; grassy site in gd position; excel clean facs; v friendly staff; many trees; no twin-axles; ltd access times for m'vans - height barrier; office 0700-1130 & 1700-2000 - but someone available to let you in; excel." ♦ 1 Jun-31 Aug. € 7.20   2007*

ANGOULEME 7B2 (10km NW Rural) **Camping Marco de Bignac (formerly Les Sablons), Chemin de la Résistance, 16170 Bignac [05 45 21 78 41; fax 05 45 21 52 37; camping.marcodebignac@ wanadoo.fr; www.camping-marco-bignac.com]** Fr N10 approx 14km N Angoulême take exit La Touche & foll D11 W thro Vars; at Basse turn R onto D117 & foll sp in Bignac. Med, mkd pitch, pt shd; htd wc; chem disp; mv service pnt; shwrs inc; child/ baby facs; el pnts (3-6A) €2-3; gas; ice; shops 3km; tradsmn; rest; snacks; bar high ssn; playgrnd; htd pool high ssn; tennis; mini-golf; lake adj, fishing & watersports; children's zoo; fishing; tennis; pedalos; badminton; few statics; dogs; phone; poss cr; adv bkg (dep req + bkg fee); quiet; red long stay/ low ssn; cc acc; 5% red CCI. "Attractive, peaceful, shady lakeside site; scenic area; gd rest; v helpful & welcoming British owners; clean san facs; library of Eng books; no lndtte but owner takes washing in high ssn; conv Charente region; highly rec - worth long drive." ♦ 15 May-15 Sep. € 22.00   2007*

This guide relies on site report forms submitted by caravanners like us; we'll do our bit and tell the editor what we think of the campsites we've visited.

ANGOULINS SUR MER see Rochelle, La 7A1

ANNECY 9B3 (8km SE Rural) **Camping La Ferme de Ferrières, 74290 Alex [04 50 02 87 09; fax 04 50 02 80 54; campingfermedesferrieres@ voila.fr; www.camping-des-ferrieres.com]** Take D909 on E side of lake out of Annecy twds Thônes; look out for sp on L after turn off to Château de Menthon. Med, pt sl, terr, pt shd; wc (cont); chem disp; baby facs; shwrs inc; el pnts (6A) €2.40; lndtte; shop & 2km; tradsmn; snacks; playgrnd; lake sw 6km; dogs €0.80; poss cr; quiet; phone; adv bkg; CCI. "Spectacular views; friendly owner; away fr crowds; v clean; mostly tents; pitches v muddy when wet." ♦ ltd. 1 Jun-30 Sep. € 10.00   2006*

ANNECY 9B3 (8km SE Rural) **Camping Le Clos Don Jean, 74290 Menthon-St-Bernard [tel/fax 04 50 60 18 66; jacob@nwc.fr]** Fr N site clearly sp fr vill of Menthon. L uphill 400m. Med, mkd pitch, pt sl, pt shd; wc (some cont); chem disp; shwrs inc; el pnts (3-10A) €2-2.45; gas; lndtte; shop; playgrnd; lake sw 900m; dogs €0.60; poss cr; Eng spkn; quiet; CCI; "Excel site; san facs spotless; fine views of chateau & lake; orchard setting." ♦ ltd. 1 Jun-15 Sep. € 15.00   2004*

ANNECY 9B3 (9km SE Urban) **Camp Municipal Les Champs Fleuris, 631 Voie Romaine, Les Perris, 74410 Duingt [04 50 68 57 31 or 04 50 68 67 07 (Mairie); fax 04 50 77 03 17; contact@duingt.fr; www.camping-duingt.com]** Fr Annecy take N508 sp Albertville. Site on R bef Duingt vill (2km after St Jorioz). Site poorly sp - foll sp Camping Le Familial, over cycle path & turn L. Med, mkd pitch, pt sl, terr, pt shd; htd wc; chem disp; mv service pnt; shwrs inc; el pnts (3-10A) €2.25-4.80; gas 1km; lndtte; ice; shops 1km; tradsmn; rest; snacks; bar; BBQ; playgrnd; lake sw 750m; 3% statics; dogs €1.65; phone; bus 200m; poss cr; Eng spkn; adv bkg; quiet; CCI. "Gd mountain scenery; gd for walking, touring, cycling (excel cycle rte to Annecy); vg lakeside beach; v friendly, helpful warden; gd." ♦ 28 Apr-8 Sep. € 13.80   2007*

ANNECY 9B3 (10km SE Rural) **Camping Le Familial, Route de Magnonnet, 74410 Duingt [tel/fax 04 50 68 69 91; camping.lefamilial@ laposte.net; www.annecy-camping-familial. com]** Fr Annecy on N508 twd Albertville. 5km after St Jorioz turn R at site sp Entrevernes onto D8, foll sp past Camping Champs Fleuris. Sm, mkd pitch, some hdstg, pt sl, pt shd; wc; shwrs inc; el pnts (5-6A) €2.80-3; lndtte; tradsmn; playgrnd; lake & shgl beach 500m; TV rm; dogs €1.50; some Eng spkn; adv bkg rec Jul/Aug (dep req); quiet but rd noise; CCI. "Gd site in scenic area; generous pitches; poss ltd facs high ssn; friendly owner; gd atmosphere; communal meals & fondu evenings; conv lakeside cycle track." ♦ ltd. 1 Apr-20 Oct. € 12.00   2007*

ANNECY 9B3 (10km SE Rural) **Camping Le Solitaire du Lac, 615 Route de Sales, 74410 St Jorioz [tel/fax 04 50 68 59 30 or 06 88 58 94 24 (mob); campinglesolitaire@ wanadoo.fr; www.campinglesolitaire.com]** Exit Annecy on N508 twd Albertville. Site sp on N o'skts of St Jorioz. Med, hdg/mkd pitch, pt shd; wc (some cont); chem disp; mv service pnt; shwrs inc; el pnts (5A) €3.50 (poss rev pol); gas; lndtte; ice; supmkts 2km; tradsmn; rest; snacks; bar & 2km; BBQ; playgrnd; lake sw; boat-launching; games areas; cycle track; 10% statics; dogs €2.20; poss v cr high ssn; Eng spkn; adv bkg (dep req); v quiet; red low ssn/long stay; cc acc; CCI. "Conv touring Haute Savoie; san facs dated & too few high ssn; sh walk to public beach on lake & water bus to Annecy; cycle path nr site; poss muddy after heavy rain." 14 Apr-15 Sep. € 16.00   2007*

ANNECY *9B3* (12km SE Rural) **Camping Le Lac, Angon, 74290 Talloires [04 50 60 73 16; fax 04 50 60 72 99; camping@lelaccamping.com; www.lelaccamping.com]** Take D909 fr Annecy to Talloires. Site on R off D909A S of Talloires on lakeside. Use most S of 2 ent with long o'fit. Med, mkd pitch, pt sl, pt shd; wc; chem disp (wc); shwrs inc; el pnts (4A) €2.50; lndry rm; ice; shops, rest, bar 1km; BBQ; playgrnd; lake sw adj; boat-launching facs; 10% statics; dogs €1.10; poss cr; some rd noise; cc acc; CCI. "Magnificent views, quiet & tranquil in low ssn; beware grounding at ent; basic facs." 1 Jun-30 Sep. € 19.00   2006*

ANNECY *9B3* (14km SE Rural) **Aire Naturelle Le Combarut (Cottard), Chef-Lieu Le Verger, 74410 St Eustache [04 50 32 00 20]** Take N508 S fr Annecy to Sévrier, turn R onto D912, site on farm just bef St Eustache. Sm, shd; wc (cont); mv service pnt; shwrs €1.20; el pnts (4A) €1.80; shop 5km; pool 15km; dogs €0.80; quiet. "Basic facs but spotless; gd mountain views; tortuous access on winding rds, but not diff with care." 1 Jun-30 Sep. € 9.60   2006*

ANNECY *9B3* (1.5km S Rural) **Camp Municipal Le Belvédère, 8 Route du Semnoz, 74000 Annecy [04 50 45 48 30; camping@ville-annecy.fr]** Fr A41 take N508 at junc 16 & foll sp to Albertville & hospital thro Annecy, turn L at traff lts & up hill. Where main rd bends sharp L downhill bear R (hospital on L). Take next R up hill, Rte du Semnoz (D41); bear R then L & site on R in 250m. Lge, mkd pitch, pt sl, terr, pt shd; htd wc; chem disp; shwrs inc; el pnts (10A) inc (poss rev pol); gas; lndtte; ice; shop; rest; snacks; playgrnd; cycle hire; sailing; fishing; forest walks; excursions; TV; dogs; phone; Eng spkn; adv bkg; poss noisy; cc acc; CCI. "Lovely, tidy site in beautiful setting; well lit at night; staff helpful; v steep footpath to town but easy walking dist; simple but gd food in rest; excel." ♦ 2 Apr-10 Oct. € 21.10   2007*

ANNECY *9B3* (5km S Urban) **Camping au Coeur du Lac, Les Choseaux, 74320 Sévrier [04 50 52 46 45; fax 04 50 19 01 45; info@aucoeurdulac.com; www.campingaucoeurdulac.com]** S fr Annecy on N508 sp Albertville. Pass thro Sevrier cent. Site on L at lakeside 1km S of Sevrier. 300m after MacDonald's. Med, mkd pitch, terr, pt sl, pt shd; some hdstg; wc (some cont); chem disp; mv service pnt; shwrs inc; el pnts (4-13A) €3.20-7.20, long cable rec; lndtte; shop; supmkt with petrol 2km; snacks; playgrnd; lake sw; yachting; grass & shgl beach; cycle/boat hire; entmnt; dogs €1 (low ssn only); bus nrby; info office 1km N; poss cr; some Eng spkn; adv bkg ess high ssn; quiet but some rd noise; red low ssn; cc acc; CCI. "Excel location; gd views fr upper terr overlooking Lac Annecy; tight for lge o'fits as sm, sl pitches; gd san facs; gd info points; busy; excel, esp low ssn." ♦ 1 Apr-30 Sep. € 19.50   2007*

ANNECY *9B3* (6km S Rural) **Camping Le Panoramic, 22 Chemin des Bernets, Cessenaz, 74320 Sévrier [04 50 52 43 09; fax 04 50 52 73 09; info@camping-le-panoramic.com; www.camping-le-panoramic.com]** Exit A41 junc 16 Annecy Sud onto N508 sp Albertville. Thro Sévrier to rndabt at Cessenaz (ignore all prior sp to site) & take 1st R onto D10. In 200m turn R up hill to site in 2km. Lge, mkd pitch, pt sl, terr, pt shd; wc; chem disp; shwrs inc; el pnts (4-6A) €3.10-4.10 (some rev pol); lndtte; ice; shop; supmkt 2km; tradsmn; rest; snacks; bar; playgrnd; pool; beach 2km; lake sw; TV; dogs €1.60; poss cr; Eng spkn; adv bkg; quiet; cc acc; CCI. "Rec for families; lovely views of lake & mountains; blocks/wedges ess for sl pitches; fantastic pool." ♦ ltd. 1 May-30 Sep. € 18.20
2006*

ANNECY *9B3* (6.5km S Urban) **Camping de l'Aloua, 492 Route de Piron, 74320 Sévrier [tel/fax 04 50 52 60 06 or 04 50 52 64 54 (LS); camping.aloua@wanadoo.fr; http://campingaloua.free.fr]** Foll sp for Albertville N508 S fr Annecy. Site on E side, approx 1.4km S of Sevrier vill. Turn L at Champion supmkt rndabt & foll sp twd lake. Lge, pt hdg/mkd pitch, shd; wc (some cont); chem disp; mv service pnt; shwrs inc; el pnts (2-6A) €2.20-3.20; gas 400m; lndtte; ice; shop; supmkt 400m; tradsmn; rest; snacks; bar; playgrnd; shgl beach 300m; lake sw, fishing, boating & watersports adj; archery; entmnts; TV; sm dogs only €2; phone; poss cr; quiet; Eng spkn; adv bkg (dep req); CCI. "Gd base for lake (no dir access to lake fr site); cycle track around lake; night security; poss noisy at night with youths & some rd noise; basic san facs; pleasant owners; gd takeaway." ♦ ltd. 20 Jun-10 Sep. € 16.50   2007*

ANNECY *9B3* (6.5km S) **FFCC Camping Les Rives du Lac, Parc Claude Gelain, 331 Chemin du Communaux, 74320 Sévrier [04 50 52 40 14; fax 04 50 51 12 38; lesrivesdulac.sevrier@ffcc.fr; www.camp-in-france.com]** Take N508 S fr Annecy sp Albertville, thro Sévrier sp FFCC. Turn L 100m past (S) Lidl supmkt, cross cycle path & turn R & foll sp FFCC keeping parallel with cycle path. Site on L in 400m. Med, mkd pitch, pt shd; wc; chem disp; mv service pnt; baby facs; shwrs inc; el pnts (6A) €3.40; lndtte; shops 500m; BBQ; playgrnd; shgl beach; lake sw; sailing; fishing; walking; entmnt; wifi internet; 10% statics; dogs €0.95; bus nr; poss cr; Eng spkn; adv bkg; quiet; red CC members (not Jul/Aug); CCI. "Beautiful situation; generous pitches; v helpful staff; recep clsd 1200-1400; water bus to Annecy nr; gd touring base; gd walking, sailing & cycling; cycle rte adj; excel." ♦ 10 Apr-15 Oct. € 19.90   2007*

France

ANNECY *9B3* (9km S Rural) **Camping International du Lac d'Annecy, 1184 Route d'Albertville, 74410 St Jorioz.** [tel/fax 04 50 68 67 93; www.campannecy.com] Fr Annecy take N508 sp Albertville. Site on R just after St Jorioz. Med, mkd pitch, some hdstg, pt shd; wc; chem disp; mv service pnt; shwrs inc; el pnts (6A) inc; gas; ice; BBQ; lndtte; shop 2km; tradsmn; snacks; bar; playgrnd; pool; lake sw; cycle hire; games area; TV rm; 30% statics; dogs €2; poss cr; rd noise; phone; Eng spkn; CCI. "Friendly owner; excel for touring lake area; gd rest nrby." 1 Jun-15 Sep. € 21.00   2004*

ANNECY *9B3* (9km S Rural) **Village Camping Europa, 1444 Route d'Albertville, 74410 St Jorioz** [04 50 68 51 01; fax 04 50 68 55 20; info@ camping-europa.com; www.camping-europa. com] Fr Annecy take N508 sp Albertville. Site on R 800m S of St Jorioz dir Albertville. Look for lge yellow sp on o'skirts of St Jorioz. Lge, hdg/mkd pitch, pt shd, wc; chem disp; mv service pnt; some serviced pitches; baby facs; shwrs inc; el pnts (6A) €3.80; lndtte; tradsmn; rest; snacks; bar; BBQ (gas); playgrnd; htd pool; waterslides; jacuzzi; beach (lake) 700m; windsurfing; boat hire; fishing; tennis 700m; cycle hire; cycle track adj; child entmnt; wifi internet; TV rm; dogs €3; Eng spkn; adv bkg; quiet but main rd adj; cc acc; red long stay/low ssn; CCI. "Quiet site in beautiful area; friendly staff; facs stretched high ssn; vg rest; excel for m'vans; conv Chamonix & Mont Blanc; variable pitch prices; some pitches tight lge o'fits; gd tourist base; excel." ♦ 30 Apr-13 Sep. € 28.00   2007*

ANNECY *9B3* (7km SW) **Aire Naturelle La Vidome (Lyonnaz), 74600 Montagny-les-Lanches** [tel/fax 04 50 46 61 31; j.lyonnaz@wanadoo.fr] Exit Annecy on N201 sp Aix-les-Bains/Chambéry; after 6km at Le Treige turn R sp Montagny-les-Lanches. In 1km turn R in Avulliens; site on R in 100m. Sm, pt sl, pt shd; wc; chem disp; shwrs; el pnts (3-10A) €2.10-3.50; lndtte; meals avail; hypermkt 3km; playgrnd; pool 3km; beach & mini-golf 10km; fishing 1km; horseriding 1km; dogs €0.80; quiet but some rd noise; adv bkg; gd views; CCI. "Excel site; friendly owners; excel san facs; access poss tight for lge o'fits; gd touring base." 1 May-30 Sep. € 9.40   2006*

ANNECY *9B3* (9km SW Rural) **Aire Naturelle Le Pré Ombragé (Bodard), 74600 Montagny-les-Lanches** [04 50 46 71 31; fax 04 50 57 20 04; montagnardise@aol.com] Exit Annecy on N201 sp Aix-les-Bains/Chambéry, after 8km at Le Treige turn R sp Montagny-les-Lanches; site sp in vill. Sm, pt sl, pt shd; wc; chem disp; shwrs inc; el pnts €2; shops 3km; playgrnd; pool 3km; lake sw 12km; dogs €1; Eng spkn; adv bkg; quiet; CCI. "Friendly, family-run farm in orchard; excel views; produce avail." 15 Jun-30 Sep. € 9.50   2005*

ANNECY *9B3* (12km SW Rural) **Aire Naturelle Jouvenod (Mercier), 460 Route de Jouvenod, 74540 Alby-sur-Chéran** [04 50 68 15 75] Take A41 SW fr Annecy, turn off at junc 15 twds Alby-sur-Chéran. Foll sp in vill. Sm, pt sl, pt shd; wc; chem disp; mv service pnt; shwrs inc; el pnts (10A) €2; shop 3km; playgrnd; beach & boating 13km; lake sw & fishing 8km; tennis; 10% statics; dogs; phone; Eng spkn; cc not acc. "Farm site; 20 pitches; gd views & hill/woodland walks; Alby pretty medieval town." 15 Jun-15 Sep. € 7.50   2004*

ANNECY *9B3* (8km NW Rural) **Camping La Caille, 18 Chemin de la Caille, 74330 La Balme-de-Sillingy** [04 50 68 85 21; fax 04 50 68 74 56; contact@aubergedelacaille.com; www.auberge delacaille.com] Fr Annecy take N508 dir Bellgarde-sur-Valserine. Strt on at rndabt at end of La Balme-de-Sillingy, foll sp. At mini rndabt strt on, site on R in 1km. Sm, hdg/mkd pitch, pt sl, shd; wc; chem disp; el pnts (4-12A) €3-5; ice; lndtte; shop 750m; tradsmn; rest; snacks; bar; playgrnd; pool; 25% statics; dogs €3; adv bkg; quiet; CCI. "Gd, well-kept site." ♦ 1 May-30 Sep. € 18.00   2006*

ANNET SUR MARNE see Meaux *3D3*

ANNEYRON *9C2* (3km S Rural) **FLOWER Camping La Châtaigneraie, Route de Mantaille, 26140 Anneyron** [tel/fax 04 75 31 43 33; contact@ chataigneraie.com; www.chataigneraie.com] Exit A7 junc 12 onto N7 S avoiding St Rambert; at La Creux de la Thine rndabt take D1 sp Anneyron; site sp at end of vill on D161. 3km S of Anneyron via narr, winding rd - poss diff lge o'fits. Med, hdg/mkd pitch, pt sl, terr, pt shd; wc; chem disp; fam bthrm; shwrs inc; el pnts (6-10A) €3.90-€4.50 (poss rev pol); lndtte; shop; tradsmn; rest; snacks; bar; BBQ (gas/elec); playgrnd; pool; tennis; games area; games rm; entmnt; 40% statics; dogs €2; phone; Eng spkn; adv bkg; quiet; cc acc; red low ssn/CCI. "Attractive, peaceful site o'looking Rhône valley; friendly, helpful owner; gd size pitches; gd for children; recep clsd 1130-1730; gd walk to historic castle ruins." ♦ ltd. 1 Apr-30 Sep. € 17.60   2007*

ANNONAY *9C2* (Urban) **Camp Municipal de Vaure, 07100 Annonay** [04 75 32 47 49 or 04 75 33 46 54; fax 04 75 32 28 22; www.mairie-annonay.fr] Sp fr o'skts of town & foll sp St Etienne. Fr St Etienne & NW turn L at 1st rndabt & pass Intermarché, foll camping/piscine sp to site. Sm, pt shd; wc (some cont); shwrs inc; el pnts (6-10A) €1.85-2.80; lndtte; snacks; bar; supmkt adj; htd, covrd pool; games area; few statics; dogs €1.15; cr; quiet. "Helpful staff; poss itinerants; barrier key dep; gd." 1 Apr-31 Oct. € 8.25   2006*

Camping Le Rossignol ★★★

Ideally situated between Cannes and Nice, at 1200 m from the beaches and Marineland; in green, quiet and nice settings, the campsite Le Rossignol offers you marked pitches and chalets to let.

2074, av.Jean Michard Pelissier 06600 Antibes
Tél : 00 33 4 93 33 56 98 - Fax : 00 33 4 92 91 98 99
E-mail : campinglerossignol@wanadoo.fr

Antibes - Riviera Côte d'Azur

www.campingrossignol.com

ANNOT *10E4* (1km N Rural) **Camping La Ribière,** 04240 Annot [04 92 83 21 44] On N202 exit at Les Scaffarels to Annot on D908. Site 1km beyond vill on L bank of rv. Med, mkd pitch, pt shd; wc; chem disp; shwrs €0.80; el pnts (5A) inc; lndtte; shops 1km; rest; snacks; playgrnd; fishing; 30% statics; adv bkg; quiet. "New owner Feb 2006 will improve; interesting medieval vills in rural setting; conv for exploring adj gorges." 15 Feb-5 Nov. € 12.90
2006*

ANOULD see Corcieux *6F3*

ANSE see Villefranche sur Saône *9B2*

ANTIBES *10E4* (2km N Urban) **Camping Caravaning Le Rossignol,** Ave Jean Michard- Pelissier, Juan-les-Pins, 06600 Antibes [04 93 33 56 98; fax 04 92 91 98 99; campinglerossignol@wanadoo. fr; www.campingrossignol.com] Turn W off N7 Antibes-Nice at sp to Hospitalier de la Fontonne then bear L along Chemin des Quatres past hospital & traff lts junc. In 400m turn R at rndabt into Ave Jean Michard Pelissier, site 200m on R. NB Narr ent off busy rd. Med, hdg/mkd pitch, hdstg, terr, shd; wc; chem disp; mv service pnt; baby facs; shwrs inc; el pnts (10A) €4.50; gas; lndtte; ice; shop 400m; tradsmn; bar; BBQ (gas/ elec); playgrnd; htd pool; paddling pool; shgl beach 1.2km; games area; games rm; entmnt; TV rm; dogs €3; Eng spkn; adv bkg; quiet; cc acc; red long stay/CCI. "Conv Antibes & surrounding area; peaceful site." ♦ 16 Mar-27 Sep. € 22.40   2007*

See advertisement

ANTIBES *10E4* (3.5km N Coastal) **Camping Antipolis,** Ave du Pylone, La Brague, 06600 Antibes [04 93 33 93 99; fax 04 92 91 02 00; contact@camping-antipolis.com; www.camping-antipolis.com] Exit A8 at Biot dir Marineland. In 800m turn R & foll site sp. Lge, hdg/mkd pitch, shd; wc (some cont); chem disp; shwrs; el pnts (10A) inc; gas; lndtte; ice; shop; tradsmn; rest; snacks; bar; BBQ; playgrnd; 2 pools (1 htd); shgl beach 800m; tennis; games area; entmnt; 30% statics; dogs €3.50; phone; train 1km; adv bkg (dep req & bkg fee); quiet; cc acc; CCI. "Situated beside m'way, but pitches away fr rd; sm pitches; walk to beach along busy rds & across dual c'way; excel pool complex & activities." ♦ Easter-30 Sep. € 28.00   2006*

> As soon as we get home I'm going to post all these site report forms to the editor for inclusion in next year's guide. I don't want to miss the September deadline.

ANTIBES *10E4* (3.5km N Coastal) **Camping Les Embruns,** 63 Route de Biot, La Brague, 06600 Antibes [04 93 33 33 35; fax 04 93 74 46 70; www. campinglesembruns.com] Fr Antibes take N7 sp Nice, after 3.5km at rmdabt with palm trees turn inland into Route de Biot; site sp on L. Sm, pt shd; wc; baby facs; shwrs inc; el pnts (5) €3.05; lndtte; ice; snacks; bar; shop; shgl beach adj; fishing & watersports adj; cycle hire; tennis; mini-golf; TV; dogs €1; bus & metro nrby; adv bkg; poss noise fr adj rd & rlwy; poss fairgrnd adj (Sep 2007); 5% red low ssn; cc acc. "Lovely site; gd-sized pitches; well-supervised by owner; v easy walking dist beach, bus & metro; no turning space - not suitable lge o'fits; some pitches waterloged in wet weather." 1 Jun-20 Sep. € 21.00   2007*

France

ANTIBES *10E4* (5km N Coastal) **Camping Les Frênes, Route du Pylone, La Brague, 06600 Antibes [04 93 33 36 52; fax 04 93 74 66 00; contact@camping-lesfrenes.com; www.camping-lesfrenes.com]** Fr Antibes on D6007 (N7), turn inland opp Biot rlwy, Rte de Biot. In approx 100m turn L, then R at T-junc, then L in approx 400m. Site 1st on R. Do not take coast rd fr Antibes/Nice, low bdge. Med, mkd pitch, shd; wc; chem disp; shwrs inc; el pnts (6A) inc; lndtte; ice; shop (high ssn); tradsmn; rest; snacks; pizzaria; bar; lndtte; playgrnd; pool; paddling pool; sand beach 600m; entmnt; TV; 10% statics; dogs €1.80; train 600m; poss cr; Eng spkn; adv bkg; quiet but some m'way noise; cc acc. "V friendly, helpful owner; conv Aquasplash & Marineland; conv train to Nice, Monte-Carlo, Monaco etc." 2 May-20 Sep. € 24.00   2007*

ANTONNE ET TRIGONANT see Périgueux *7C3*

APREMONT *2H4* (2km N Rural) **Camping Les Charmes, Route de la Roussière, 85220 Apremont [02 51 54 48 08 or 06 86 03 96 93 (mob); fax 02 51 55 98 85; lescharmes@cer85.cernet.fr; www.lescharmes.fr]** Fr D948 Challans to Aizenay turn W onto D94 sp Commequiers; after 2km L, sp Les Charmes. Med, mkd pitch, pt shd; wc (some cont); chem disp; 70% serviced pitches; fam bthrm; shwrs inc; el pnts (6-10A) €2.60-3; gas; lndtte; ice; shop; tradsmn; playgrnd; pool; lake sw with beach 3km; sand beach 18km; TV rm; 4% statics; dogs €2; poss cr; Eng spkn; adv bkg (dep req); quiet; red long stay; cc acc; CCI. "Beautiful site; generous pitches; mod & v clean san facs; v helpful, friendly owners; immaculate; well appointed site." ♦ 1 Apr-30 Sep. € 13.70   2005*

APREMONT *2H4* (2km E) **Camping Les Prairies du Lac, Route de Maché, 85220 Apremont [02 51 55 70 58; fax 02 51 55 76 04; infos@les-prairies-du-lac.com]** Fr Apremont take D40 twd Maché to site on N side of rd in 2km. Fr Aizenay D107 to Maché then D40 twd Apremont to site in 5km. Lge, mkd pitch, pt shd; wc (some cont); chem disp; 15% serviced pitches; shwrs inc; el pnts (6-10A) €3-5; gas; lndtte; ice; tradsmn; snacks; bar; 2 htd pools; sand beach 17km; playgrnd; rv & lake sw/fishing 2km; mini-golf; entmnt in ssn; TV; dogs €2; phone; 60% statics; Eng spkn; adv bkg; quiet. "Friendly owners; facs v clean, poss ltd low ssn; access to cycle paths; many local attractions." 26 Jun-30 Aug. € 17.00   2004*

APT *10E3* (3km N Rural) **Aire Naturelle La Clé des Champs (Mayer-Abdallah), Quartier des Puits, 84400 Apt [04 90 74 41 41; fax 04 90 04 73 13]** Turn N off N100 in Apt by post office onto rd sp 'Camping La Clé des Champs/Résidence St Michel'. Care req not to miss sudden turnings. Access via steep, winding rd - not suitable lge o'fits. Sm, pt shd; wc; chem disp; shwrs; el pnts (6-10A) inc; gas 3km; lndtte; shop 3km; 10% statics; dogs; adv bkg; quiet; CCI. "Pleasant, off-the-beaten-track site with nice views; v peaceful; vg." 1 Apr-30 Sep. € 10.60   2005*

APT *10E3* (9km N Rural) **Camping Les Chênes Blancs, Route de Gargas, 84490 St Saturnin-les-Apt [04 90 74 09 20; fax 04 90 74 26 98; robert@les-chenes-blancs.com; www.les-chenes-blancs.com]** Exit A7 at Avignon-Sud, take D22-N100 twd Apt, at NW o'skts of Apt turn N on D101, cont approx 2km turn R on D83 into Gargas; thro Gargas & in 4km turn L at camp sp; site on R in 300m. Lge, shd; wc; mv service pnt; shwrs inc; el pnts (6A) €4.90; lndry rm; shop; rest; snacks; bar; playgrnd; htd pool; lake fishing 5km; games area; entmnt; TV rm; dogs €2.20; poss cr; Eng spkn; adv bkg rec; quiet; red low ssn; cc acc. "Stony ground; need steel pegs for awnings; lge pitches amongst oaks poss diff lge outfits; san facs poss stretched in high ssn; friendly staff; gd location; excel touring base." ♦ 15 Mar-3 Nov. € 15.80 (CChq acc)   2006*

APT *10E3* (500m NE Urban) **Camp Municipal Les Cèdres, Ave de Viton, 84400 Apt [tel/fax 04 90 74 14 61; camping-apt@wanadoo.fr]** In town turn N off N100 onto D22 twd Rustrel, site sp. Site on R in 200m immed after going under old rlwy bdge. Med, mkd pitch, pt shd; htd wc; chem disp; mv service pnt; shwrs inc; el pnts (6-10A) €3-4; gas; lndtte; ice; shop & snacks (high ssn); cooking facs; playgrnd; entmnt; dogs €1.20 (high ssn); poss cr; adv bkg; cc acc; CCI. "Excel, friendly site; clean san facs; sm pitches; lovely location; easy 5-10 mins walk to town; cycle tracks E & W; conv Luberon vills & ochre mines; lge mkt Sat." ♦ 1 Mar-10 Nov. € 10.00   2007*

APT *10E3* (2km SE Rural) **Camping Le Luberon, Route de Saignon, 84400 Apt [04 90 04 85 40; fax 04 90 74 12 19; leluberon@wanadoo.fr; www.camping-le-luberon.com]** Exit Apt by D48 sp Saignon & site on R in 2km. Med, mkd pitch, pt sl, pt shd; wc; chem disp; baby facs; shwrs inc; el pnts (6A) €4.50; gas; lndtte; ice; shops 2km; tradsmn; rest; snacks; bar; BBQ; playgrnd; pool (proper sw trunks only); fishing, sailing 3km; TV; 20% statics; dogs €2; phone; poss cr; Eng spkn; adv bkg (dep req); quiet; red low ssn; cc acc; CCI. "Pitches well laid out in natural woodland; v helpful owners; well-run, clean site; gd." ♦ ltd. 1 Apr-5 Nov. € 18.65   2006*

⊞**ARAGNOUET** *8G2* (Rural) **Camp Municipal du Pont de Moudang, 65170 Aragnouet [05 62 39 62 84 or 05 62 39 62 63 (Mairie); fax 05 62 39 60 47; infos@piau-engaly.com]** Site on L of D929, 9km SW fr St Lary, on rvside. Med, mkd pitch, hdstg, terr, pt shd; htd wc; chem disp; shwrs; el pnts (4-10A) €2.45-6.90; lndtte; shop 500m; playgrnd; TV rm; 25% statics; site clsd Oct; poss cr; quiet; CCI. "Jetons needed for use of hot water (no charge); superb surroundings; excel mountain walking area; conv for Aragnouet/Bielsa tunnel." € 9.00   2006*

★CAMPING MUNICIPAL LES VIGNES ★★★

Three-star campsite surrounded by vineyards

139 pitches, rated "great comfort". In pastoral surroundings.
Capital of the reputed Jura wines. Quiet and shady site.
Adjacent swimming pool with terrace, bar and fast food restaurant. Food shop. Games for children,
French boules ground, meeting room, television, library, washing machines and dryer, phone box, etc.
Mountains, forests, fishing, hiking paths, tennis, etc... close by.

OPEN: 1.5 – 30.9

WARM WELCOME AND QUALITY ASSURED

Avenue du Général Leclerc – 39600 Arbois

Phone/fax: 00 33 (0)3 84 66 14 12 Mayor's office : Phone : 00 33 (0)3 84 66 55 55 Fax : 00 33 (0)3 84 66 25 50

ARAMITS *8F1* (1km SW Rural) **Camping Baretous-Pyrénées, Quartier Ripaude, 64570 Aramits [05 59 34 12 21; fax 05 59 34 67 19; atso64@ hotmail.com; www.camping-baretous-pyrenees. com]** SW fr Oloron-Ste Marie take D919 sp Aramits, Arette. Fr Aramits cont on D919 sp Lanne; site on R; well sp. Sm, mkd pitch, pt shd; wc; chem disp; mv service pnt; serviced pitches; shwrs inc; el pnts (10A) €3.50; Indtte; ice; supmkt 500m; tradsmn; snacks, bar high ssn; playgrnd; htd pool high ssn; cycle hire; games rm; TV; 50% statics; dogs €2.50; poss cr; Eng spkn; adv bkg; CCI. "Friendly, helpful owner; well-kept, clean gem of a site; barrier clsd 2230-0800; twin-axles €9.15 extra per day; gd base for Pyrenees; easy day's journey into N Spain; poss unreliable opening dates - phone ahead low ssn." ♦ ltd. 1 Feb-15 Oct. € 19.00 (CChq acc) 2007*

ARBOIS *6H2* (1.5km E Urban) **Camp Municipal Les Vignes, Ave du Général Leclerc, 39600 Arbois [tel/fax 03 84 66 14 12 or 03 84 66 55 55 (Mairie); camping@arbois.fr; www.camping.arbois.fr]** Fr N or S, ent town & at rndabt in cent foll camp sp. Site located next to stadium & municipal pool. NB Steep slopes to terr & narr ent unsuitable lge o'fits. Med, some hdg pitch/mkd pitch, some hdstg, pt sl, terr, pt shd; wc; chem disp; serviced pitches; shwrs inc; el pnts (10A) €3.20; gas; Indtte; shop & 1km; rest; snacks; bar; playgrnd; htd pool adj (sw trunks ess); tennis; fishing 1km; entmnts; TV; dogs €1; poss cr; Eng spkn; adv bkg; quiet; cc acc; CCI. "Beautiful setting; some pitches no elec; spotless san facs but poss stretched high ssn; site clsd 2200-0800 in low ssn; free use of excel pool; ltd facs low ssn; wine-growing area; pleasant sm town with vg rests, home of Louis Pasteur; Roman salt works, grottoes nr; lge fair 1st w/e in Sep; excel." ♦ 1 May-30 Sep. € 12.00 2007*

See advertisement

ARC EN BARROIS *6F1* (W Rural) **Camp Municipal Le Vieux Moulin, 52210 Arc-en-Barrois [03 25 02 51 33 (Mairie); fax 03 25 03 82 89; mairie.arc.en.barrois@wanadoo.fr]** Fr Chaumont exit (24) on A5 take D10 S & site on L on exit vill. Or turn L onto D6 about 4km S of Châteauvillain fr D65. Site on R on D3 at ent to vill, adj rv. Sm, pt shd; htd wc; chem disp; mv service pnt; shwrs inc; el pnts (6A) €2; gas in vill; shops 500m; BBQ; sm playgrnd; tennis adj; TV; dogs; phone in vill; quiet; cc not acc; CCI. "Well-kept, attractive site adj vill sports field; basic, immac san facs; warden calls pm; gd rests in beautiful vill; conv NH fr A5; gd." 1 Apr-30 Sep. € 8.10 2007*

ARCACHON *7D1* (10km E Coastal) **Camp Municipal de Verdalle, 2 Allée de l'Infante, La Hume, 33470 Gujan-Mestras [tel/fax 05 56 66 12 62]** Fr A63 take A660 twd Arcachon. Turn R at rndabt junc with D652 sp La Hume. In vill at junc with D650 turn L, then R at rndabt; then 3rd turning on R after rlwy line. Med, hdg pitch, pt shd; wc (some cont); chem disp (wc); shwrs inc; el pnts (4A) inc; Indtte; BBQ; sand beach adj; dogs; phone; poss cr; v little Eng spkn; CCI. "Excel position; friendly staff; cycling/walking; conv local attractions; vg." ♦ 1 May-15 Sep. € 18.00 2007*

⊞**ARCACHON** *7D1* (2km S Coastal) **Camping Club d'Arcachon, 5 Allée de la Galaxie, Les Abatilles, 33120 Arcachon [05 56 83 24 15; fax 05 57 52 28 51; info@camping-arcachon.com; www.camping-arcachon.com]** Exit A63 ont A660/ N250 dir Arcachon. Foll sp 'Hôpital Jean Hameau' & site sp. Lge, terr, pt shd; htd wc; chem disp; mv service pnt; shwrs inc; el pnts (10A) €3-4; gas; Indtte; shop; tradsmn; rest; snacks; bar; BBQ some pitches; playgrnd; pool; sand beach 1.5km; lake sw 10km; cycle hire; entmnt; child entmnt; TV rm; 40% statics; dogs €4; site clsd 12 Nov-11 Dec; adv bkg; Eng spkn; quiet; cc acc; CCI. "Vg site in pine trees; excel touring base; gd network cycle tracks." ♦ € 29.00 2007*

France

ARCHIAC *7B2* (400m W Urban) **Camp Municipal, Rue des Voituriers, 17520 Archiac [05 46 49 10 46 or 05 46 49 10 82 (Mairie); fax 05 46 49 84 09; archiacmairie@free.fr]** Site sp fr D731 100m past sw pool. Sm, mkd pitch, terr, pt sl, pt shd; wc; shwrs €0.68; el pnts (3A) €2.45; lndtte; tradsmn; shops 400m; 2 pools adj; tennis; games rm; dogs; some noise fr local joinery works. "On arr check list on office door for allocated/free pitches; warden calls." 15 Jun-15 Sep. € 4.95   2007*

ARCIS SUR AUBE *4E4* (300m N Urban) **Camping de l'Ile, Rue des Châlons, 10700 Arcis-sur-Aube [03 25 37 98 79; fax 03 25 82 94 18; camping-arcis@hermans.cx; www.arcis-sur-aube.com]** Fr A26 junc 21 foll sp to Arcis. Fr town cent take D677 (N77) dir Châlons-en-Champagne. Turn R after rv bdge, site sp. Med, mkd pitch, shd, wc (some cont); chem disp; shwrs inc; el pnts (4-10A) inc (poss rev pol); rest, bar & shops 500m; playgrnd; rv adj; fishing; dogs €1.60; Eng spkn; poss cr w/e & noisy; no cc acc; CCI. "Well-maintained; owners v friendly & helpful; gd san facs; narr site rds - diff to manoeuvre lge o'fits; gd local rest; popular NH, rec arr early." ♦ ltd. 15 Apr-30 Sep. € 15.00   2007*

⊞**ARCIS SUR AUBE** *4E4* (8km S Rural) **FFCC Camping La Barbuise, 10700 St Remy-sous-Barbuise [03 25 37 50 95 or 03 25 37 41 11]** Fr Arcis-sur-Aube, take D677 (N77) twd Voué; site on L bef vill of Voué, sp. Fr S exit A26 junc 21 onto D441 W; then onto D677 S twd Voué & as bef. Sm, pt sl, pt shd; wc; chem disp; shwrs inc; el pnts (4A) €1.50 (poss rev pol); lndtte; ice; tradsmn; snacks & bar (high ssn); pool 8km; dogs; phone; adv bkg; quiet but some rd noise; red facs low ssn; cc not acc; CCI. "Peaceful, relaxed site; v friendly owners; spacious CL-type site; mixed reports on basic san facs; early arr rec; el heaters not allowed; site yourself & owner collects payment in eve (cash only); open all night; pleasant views; gd dog-walking; conv NH/sh stay for Troyes & Champagne rtes/region." ♦ ltd. € 6.20   2007*

ARDRES *3A3* (500m N Urban) **Camping Ardresien, 64 Rue Basse, 62610 Ardres [03 21 82 82 32]** Fr St Omer on D943 (N43) to Ardres, strt on at lights in town onto D231; site 500m on R - easy to o'shoot; v narr ent, not suitable twin-axles. Sm, hdg pitch, pt shd; wc; shwrs; el pnts (16A) inc; 95% statics; dogs; CCI. "Basic site; v tidy; poss unkempt low ssn; friendly warden; lge lakes at rear of site - fishing; v ltd touring pitches; conv local vet; NH only." 1 May-30 Sep. € 9.90   2007*

ARDRES *3A3* (9km NE Rural) **Camp Municipal Les Pyramides, Rue Nord Boutillier, 62370 Audruicq [03 21 35 59 17 or 03 21 46 06 60 (Mairie)]** Fr Calais take A16 dir Dunkerque, after 8km exit S at junc 21 onto D219 to Audruicq; foll camp sp. Fr Ardres NE on D224 to Audruicq. Site on NE side of Audruicq nr canal. Med, hdg pitch, unshd; wc; chem disp; shwrs inc, el pnts (6A) inc; gas; lndtte; tradsmn; playgrnd; 80% statics; no cc acc; quiet; CCI. "Conv Calais; few sm pitches for tourers; rec phone ahead." ♦ ltd. 1 Apr-30 Sep. € 18.80   2006*

> The opening dates and prices on this campsite have changed. I'll send a site report form to the editor for the next edition of the guide.

ARDRES *3A3* (9km SE) **Camping Le Relaxe, 318 Route de Gravelines, 62890 Nordausques [tel/fax 03 21 35 63 77; camping.le.relax@cegetel. net]** Fr N on D943 (N43) in vill 25km S of Calais at beginning of vill, turn L at sp. Site 200m on R. Or fr S on A26, leave at junc 2 & take D943 S for 1km into Nordausques, then as above. Med, hdg pitch, pt shd; wc; chem disp; shwrs €1.50; el pnts (6A) €2.20 (poss rev pol); lndry rm; shop 200m; tradsmn; snacks; playgrnd; 90% statics; poss cr; adv bkg ess; quiet; CCI. "Owner v obliging; v conv for A26 & Calais; not suitable lge o'fits as diff to manoeuvre." 1 Apr-30 Sep. € 10.80   2006*

ARDRES *3A3* (10km SE Rural) **Hôtel Bal Caravaning, 500 Rue du Vieux Château, 62890 Tournehem-sur-la-Hem [03 21 35 65 90 or 03 21 35 18 57; fax 03 21 35 18 57]** Fr S on A26 leave at exit 2; turn R onto D217 then R onto D943 (N43) dir St Omer. Turn R in Nordausques onto D218 (approx 1km), pass under A26, site is 1km on L - ent thro Bal Parc Hotel gates. Fr N or S on N43, turn R or L in Nordausques, then as above. Med, hdg/mkd pitch, hdstg, pt sl, pt shd; htd wc (in hotel in winter); chem disp; shwrs inc; el pnts (10A) inc (poss rev pol); gas; tradsmn; rest, snacks, bar in adj hotel; playgrnd; sand beach 20km; sports ground & leisure cent adj; tennis; entmnt; 80% statics; poss cr; Eng spkn; adv bkg; quiet; cc acc; red low ssn/CCI. "25km Cité Europe shopping mall; owner v helpful & friendly; low ssn poss open w/e only & poss clsd during bad weather; v ltd pitches low ssn; gd rest adj; gd NH." ♦ 25 Feb-11 Nov. € 20.00   2007*

⊞ *Site open all year*   166   *Tell us about the sites you visit*

ARDRES *3A3* (1km S Rural) **Camping St Louis, 223 Rue Leulène, 62610 Autingues [03 21 35 46 83; fax 03 21 00 19 78; domirine@aol.com; www. campingstlouis.com]** Fr Calais S on D943 (N43) to Ardres; fr Ardres take D224 S twd Licques, after 2km turn L on D227; site well sp in 100m. Or fr junc 2 off A26 onto D943 dir Ardres. Turn L just after Total g'ge on R on app to Ardres. Well sp. If app fr S via Boulogne avoid Nabringhen & Licques as narr, steep hill with bends. NB Street mkt Sun am - avoid R turn when leaving site. Med, hdg/mkd pitch, pt shd, some hdstg; wc; chem disp; mv service pnt; baby facs; shwrs inc; el pnts (6-10A) €3-3.50 (50m lead req some pitches)(poss rev pol); gas; lndtte; sm shop & 1km; supmkt 3km; rest; snacks; bar; BBQ; playgrnd; lake 1km; games rm; entmnt; 60% statics; dogs free; phone; poss cr; Eng spkn; adv bkg ess high ssn; quiet; cc acc; CCI. "Peaceful, well-maintained, clean site 30 mins fr Calais; gd NH; pleasant welcome; vg san facs (disabled facs need refurb); nice rest; ltd touring pitches high ssn - phone ahead to check any avail; avoid oak trees in Sep due falling acorns; early dep/late arr area; vg." ♦ 17 Mar-13 Oct. € 17.00   2007*

ARES see Andernos les Bains *7D1*

ARFEUILLES see Châtel Montagne *9A1*

ARGELES GAZOST *8G2* (500m N Rural) **Camping Sunêlia Les Trois Vallées, Ave des Pyrénées, 65400 Argelès-Gazost [05 62 90 35 47; fax 05 62 90 35 48; 3-vallees@wanadoo.fr; www. camping-les-3-vallees.fr]** S fr Lourdes on D821 (N21), turn R at rndabt sp Argelès-Gazost on D821A. Site off next rndabt on R. Lge, mkd pitch, pt shd; htd wc; chem disp; sauna; shwrs inc; el pnts (6A) inc (poss rev pol); lndtte; supmkt opp; tradsmn; bar; playgrnd; htd pool; waterslide; games rm; cycle hire; games area; golf 11km; entmnt; TV rm; 30% statics; dogs €2; poss cr; adv bkg ess high ssn; some rd noise nr site ent; cc acc. "Interesting area; views of Pyrenees; conv Lourdes; excel touring base; red facs low ssn." ♦ 10 Mar-1 Nov. € 29.00   2006*

ARGELES GAZOST *8G2* (1km N Rural) **Camping La Bergerie, 54 Ave des Pyrénées, 65400 Ayzac-Ost [tel/fax 05 62 97 59 99; info@camping-labergerie. com; www.camping-labergerie.com]** Sp off D821 (N21). Sm, pt shd; wc; shwrs inc; el pnts (2-6A) €1.80-5.40; lndtte; rest, bar 100m; BBQ; playgrnd; htd pool; games area; entmnt; some statics; dogs €1; Eng spkn; adv bkg; quiet. "V clean, friendly site." ♦ 1 May-30 Sep. € 14.10   2006*

ARGELES GAZOST *8G2* (2km N Rural) **Camping Bellevue, 24 Chemin de la Plaine, 65400 Ayzac-Ost [tel/fax 05 62 97 58 81]** Fr Lourdes S on D821 (N21), foll sp for Ayzac-Ost then sp for 'Camping La Bergerie' but cont past ent for 200m. Site on R behind farm buildings. Sm, pt shd; wc; chem disp; mv service pnt; shwrs inc; el pnts (2-6A) €2; lndtte; shop, rest, snacks, bar 1km; tradsmn; playgrnd; fishing 300m; 2% statics; dogs €1; phone; quiet; CCI. "Surrounded by fields; gd san facs block; could be muddy; gd." ♦ 1 Jun-30 Sep. € 8.40   2007*

⊞ARGELES GAZOST *8G2* (4km N Rural) **Camping Soleil du Pibeste, 65400 Agos-Vidalos [05 62 97 53 23; fax 05 61 06 67 73; info@ campingpibeste.com; www.campingpibeste. com]** On D821 (N21), S of Lourdes. Exit at rndabt sp Agos-Vidalos, site on R on ent vill. Med, terr, pt shd; htd wc; chem disp; mv service pnt; shwrs inc; el pnts (3-6A) €3; gas; lndtte; ice; shops adj; lndtte; tradsmn; rest; snacks; bar; playgrnd; sm pool; rv sw 500m; entmnt; TV; 10% statics; dogs €2; bus; Eng spkn; adv bkg rec high ssn; some rd noise; CCI. "Open outlook with views; beautiful area; warm, friendly welcome; guided mountain walks; excel, family-run site." ♦ ltd. € 20.00   2005*

ARGELES GAZOST *8G2* (5km N Rural) **Camping Le Viscos, 16 Route de Préchac, 65400 Beaucens [05 62 97 05 45]** Fr Lourdes S twd Argelès-Gasost on D821 (N21). Cont twd Luz & Gavarnie to L of Argelès town, & turn L within 500m, sp Beaucens. Turn R to D13, site 2.5km on L. Med, pt sl, shd; wc; chem disp; shwrs inc; el pnts (2-10A) €2-4 (rev pol); gas; ice; lndtte; shops 5km; tradsmn high ssn; rest in hotel adj; snacks; BBQ; playgrnd; pool 4km; lake fishing 500m; dogs €1; quiet; adv bkg ess Jul-Aug; red long stay; cc not acc; CCI. "Sparkling san facs; landscaped grounds; delightful rural site." 15 May-30 Sep. € 10.50   2007*

Before we move on, I'm going to fill in some site report forms and post them off to the editor, otherwise they won't arrive in time for the deadline at the end of September.

ARGELES GAZOST *8G2* (1km S Rural) **Camping Les Frênes, 46 Route des Vallées, 65400 Lau-Balagnas [05 62 97 25 12; fax 05 62 97 01 41; http://campinglesfrenes.fr]** Site on R of D821 (N21) twd S. Med, pt terr, pt shd; htd wc; chem disp; baby facs; shwrs inc; el pnts (2-12A) €1.80-10.80; gas; lndtte; ice; shop 100m; BBQ; playgrnd; pool; rv sw & fishing 1km; entmnt; TV; some statics; adv bkg rec; quiet; red long stay. ♦ 15 Dec-15 Oct. € 12.90   2005*

France

⊞ARGELES GAZOST *8G2* (2km S Rural) **Camp Le Lavedan, 44 Route des Vallées, 65400 Lau-Balagnas [05 62 97 18 84; fax 05 62 97 55 56; michel.dubie@wanadoo.fr; www.lavedan.com]** Fr Lourdes S on D821 (N21) dir Argelès-Gazost/Cauterets; 2km after Argelès on D921 site on R after vill of Lau-Balagnas. Med, pt shd; htd wc (some cont); chem disp; baby facs; shwrs inc; el pnts (2-6A) €2-6 (poss rev pol); gas; ice; lndtte; lndry rm; shops 2km; rest; snacks; bar; BBQ; playgrnd; htd, covrd pool; paddling pool; TV rm; 30% statics; dogs €2; site clsd Nov-mid Dec; Eng spkn; adv bkg; rd noise if pitched adj to rd. "In beautiful green valley; v friendly, relaxed staff; san facs basic but clean; excel cycle rte to Lourdes." ♦ ltd. € 19.00 (CChq acc) 2006*

ARGELES GAZOST *8G2* (2.5km S Rural) **Camping du Lac, 29 Chemin d'Azun, 65400 Arcizans-Avant [tel/fax 05 62 97 01 88; campinglac@campinglac65.fr; www.campinglac65.fr]** Fr Lourdes S thro Argelès-Gazost on D821 (N21) & D921. At 3rd rndabt take exit for St Savin/Arcizans-Avant. Cont thro St Savin vill & foll camp sp; site on L just thro Arcizans-Avant vill. NB: Dir rte to Arcizans-Avant is prohibited to c'vans. Med, hdg/mkd pitch, pt sl, pt shd; wc; chem disp; baby facs; shwrs inc; el pnts (5A) €4.30; gas; lndtte; ice; shop; tradsmn; rest 500m; snacks; playgrnd; htd pool; games rm; cycle hire; TV rm; dogs €2; Eng spkn; adv bkg; quiet; red low ssn; CCI. "Excel, peaceful site; gd size pitches; lovely views; v clean san facs; gd for touring; gd rest in vill; vg." ♦ 15 May-30 Sep. € 21.80 2007*

ARGELES GAZOST *8G2* (2km SW Rural) **Camping L'Idéal, Route de Val d'Azun, 65400 Arras-en-Lavedan [05 62 97 03 13 or 05 62 97 02 12; info@camping-ideal-pyrenees.com; www.camping-ideal-pyrenees.com]** Leave Argelès Gazost SW on D918. Site on N side of rd on E o'skts of Arras-en-Lavedan. Ent on bend. Med, terr, pt shd; wc; chem disp; shwrs inc; el pnts (3-10A) €2.85-€9.50; sm shop; playgrnd; pool high ssn; tennis 1km; adv bkg; quiet; CCI. "Friendly owner, vg clean site/facs; steel awning pegs rec; mountain views; cooler than in valley." ♦ 1 Jun-15 Sep. € 12.00 2006*

ARGELES GAZOST *8G2* (10km SW Rural) **Camping Pyrénées Natura, Route du Lac, 65400 Estaing (Hautes-Pyrénées) [05 62 97 45 44; fax 05 62 97 45 81; info@camping-pyrenees-natura.com; www.camping-pyrenees-natura.com or www.les-castels.com]** Fr Lourdes take D821 (N21) to Argelès Gazost; at 1st rndabt ('Champion' supmkt rndabt) foll sp Col d'Aubisque onto D918; after approx 6km turn L onto D13 to Bun; after Bun cross rv & turn R onto D103; site in 3km - rd narr. Med, hdg/mkd pitch, pt shd; htd wc; chem disp; mv service pnt; baby facs; sauna; shwrs inc; el pnts (10A) inc; gas; lndtte; ice; shop; tradsmn; snacks; bar; BBQ (gas/elec/charcoal); playgrnd; pool 4km; solarium; mini-golf; internet; games/TV rm 15% statics; dogs €2; Eng spkn; adv bkg; quiet; red low ssn; cc acc; CCI. "V well-kept, superb site; immac facs; no plastic ground-sheets allowed; friendly, helpful owners; wonderful scenery; adj National Park; bird viewing area; organised walks; excel." ♦ 1 May-20 Sep. € 27.50 ABS - D22 2007*

ARGELES SUR MER *10G1* (N Coastal) **Camping Les Marsouins, Ave de la Retirada, 66702 Argelès-sur-Mer [04 68 81 14 81; fax 04 68 95 93 58; marsouin@campmed.com; www.campmed.com]** Fr Perpignan take exit 10 fr D914 (N114) & foll sp for Argelès until Shell petrol stn on R. Take next L just bef rv into Allée Ferdinand Buisson to T-junc, turn L at next rndabt dir Plage-Nord. Take 2nd R at next rndabt, site on L opp Spanish war memorial. V lge, hdg/mkd pitch, shd; wc; chem disp; mv service pnt; shwrs inc; el pnts (5A) inc; gas; lndtte; ice; shops; rest; snacks; bar; BBQ; playgrnd; htd pool; sand beach 800m; sailing & windsurfing 1km; cycle hire; games area; entmnt; some statics; dogs €2; poss cr; Eng spkn; adv bkg (acc in writing Jan-May); quiet; red low ssn; cc acc. "Excel, well-run site; busy rd to beach, but worth it; many sm coves; tourist office on site; gd area for cycling." Easter-22 Aug. € 29.00 2007*

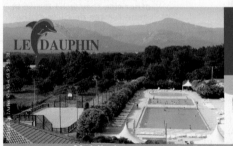

France

ARGELES SUR MER *10G1* (1km N Coastal) **Camping Le Pujol, Route du Tamariguer, 66700 Argelès-sur-Mer [04 68 81 00 25; fax 04 68 81 21 21; www. campingdepujol.com]** Fr Perpignan on D914 (N114) exit junc 10 dir Argelès. L off slip rd foll sp Pujol, site on R - wide entrance. Lge, mkd pitch, pt shd; wc (some cont); chem disp; mv service pnt; baby facs; shwrs inc; el pnts (3-6A); gas 2km; lndtte; ice; shop; rest; snacks; bar; playgrnd; pool; paddling pool; sand beach 1km; rv sw 1km; mini-golf; car wash; entmnt; 30% statics; dogs; phone; poss cr; Eng spkn; adv bkg rec high ssn; quiet but poss noisy disco; CCI. "Vg san facs but poss cold water shwrs only low ssn; vg pool; excel cycling." ♦ ltd. 1 Jun-30 Sep. € 24.00   2007*

There aren't many sites open this early in the year. We'd better phone ahead to check that the one we're heading for is actually open.

ARGELES SUR MER *10G1* (1km N Rural) **Camping Les Galets, Route de Taxo d'Avall, Plage Nord, 66701 Argelès-sur-Mer [04 68 81 08 12; fax 04 68 81 68 76; lesgalets@campinglesgalets. fr; www.campmed.com]** Fr Perpignan take D914 (N114) dir Elne, Argelès, 4km after Elne pass Municipal Camping on L, sp listing many camp sites. Lge, pt shd; wc; baby facs; shwrs inc; el pnts (10A) inc; gas; ice; lndtte; shop; rest; snacks; bar; playgrnd; htd pool; paddling pool; sand beach 1.5km; fishing; sailing & windsurfing 1.5km; rv sw 3km; equestrian cent nr; games area; entmnt; TV rm; 90% statics; dogs €4; poss cr; adv bkg rec all year; quiet; red low ssn. "Ltd touring pitches; gd for families." ♦ 1 Apr-30 Sep. € 33.00   2007*

ARGELES SUR MER *10G1* (2km N Rural) **Camping Le Dauphin, Route de Taxo à la Mer, 66701 Argelès-sur-Mer [04 68 81 17 54; fax 04 68 95 82 60; info@campingledauphin.com; www.campingledauphin.com]** Fr Perpignan take D914 (N114) sp Elne & Argelès-sur-Mer. 4km after Elne, sp on L to Taxo d'Avall, turn L, site 2km on R. Lge, hdg/mkd pitches, shd; wc; chem disp; some serviced pitches; baby facs; shwrs inc; el pnts (10A) €4.10; gas; ice; lndtte; shop; rest; snacks; bar; playgrnd; 2 pools; paddling pool; sand beach 3km; fishing; sailing; windsurfing; tennis; games area; games rm; internet; entmnt; TV rm; 80% statics; dogs €3.50; extra for serviced pitches or with private san facs; adv bkg (dep & bkg fee); quiet. "Gd for families; free transport to beach high ssn; helpful staff; vg site." 17 May-20 Sep. € 25.90   2007*

See advertisement opposite

ARGELES SUR MER *10G1* (2km N Rural) **Camping L'Hippocampe, La Honors, Route de Taxo d'Avall, 66701 Argelès-sur-Mer [04 68 81 10 10; fax 04 68 81 40 97; contact@camping-lasirene. fr; www.camping-lasirene.fr]** Exit junc 10 fr D914 (N114) onto Rte de Taxo. Camp about 1km on L adj lge campsite La Sirène. Med, shd; wc; baby facs; shwrs inc; el pnts (6A) €3; lndtte; shop; rest; snacks; bar; playgrnd; pool; waterslide; sand/shgl beach 900m; entmnt; TV rm; poss cr; adv bkg; quiet. Easter-29 Sep. € 40.00 (3 persons)   2006*

ARGELES SUR MER *10G1* (2km N Coastal) **Camping Paris Roussillon, Route de Tamariguer, Quartier   Pujol,   66700   Argelès-sur-Mer [04 68 81 19 71; fax 04 68 81 68 77; contact@ parisroussillon.com; www.parisroussillon.com]** Fr Perpignan, take D914 (N114), junc 10 twds Pujol. Site 2km on R. Lge, mkd pitch, shd; wc, chem disp; shwrs inc; baby facs; el pnts (6A) €3.50; lndtte; shop 1km; rest; snacks; bar; BBQ; playgrnd; pool; beach 1.5km; tennis; games area; some statics; dogs €2.50; Eng spkn; quiet. ♦ 15 May-30 Sep. € 23.60   2007*

ARGELES SUR MER *10G1* (2km NE Coastal) **Camp Municipal Roussillonnais, Blvd de la Mer, 66700 Argelès-sur-Mer [04 68 81 10 42; fax 04 68 95 96 11; contact@le-roussillonnais.com; www.le-roussillonnais.com]** S fr Perpignan on D914 (N114) thro Elne to Argelès-sur-Mer, turn L in Argelès-sur-Mer foll coast rd & site on R in 1.5km. V lge, hdg/mkd pitch, pt shd; wc (some cont); chem disp; mv service pnt; baby facs; shwrs inc; el pnts (6A) €3.50; gas; lndtte; ice; shop; rest; snacks; bar; playgrnd; sand beach 800m; boating; watersports; tennis; games area; entmnt; some statics; dogs €1.50; shuttle bus to beach; poss cr; Eng spkn; adv bkg; quiet; cc acc; CCI. "Test for firm sand on beach pitches; ltd facs low ssn." 15 Apr-30 Sep. € 20.80   2006*

ARGELES SUR MER *10G1* (2km NE Coastal) **Camping du Stade, Ave du 8 Mai 1945, 66702 Argelès-sur-Mer [04 68 81 04 40; fax 04 68 95 84 55; info@campingdustade.com; www.campingdustade.com]** S on D914 (N114) thro traff lts at Argelès; turn L after 400m at clearly mkd turn sp 'A la Plage'. Site 800m on L. Lge, shd; wc; baby facs; shwrs inc; el pnts (6A) inc; lndtte; shop 500m; rest; snacks; bar; playgrnd; sand beach 800m; sports complex adj; entmnt & child entmnt; TV rm; some statics; dogs €2; poss cr; adv bkg rec high ssn; quiet; red low ssn. "Lge pitches; gd walking area; nice mountain views; friendly owners." 1 Apr-30 Sep. € 23.00   2007*

ARGELES SUR MER *10G1* (2km NE Coastal) **Camping La Marende, Chemin de la Salanque, 66702 Argelès-sur-Mer [tel/fax 04 68 81 03 88; info@marende.com; www.marende.com]** Fr Perpignan S on D914 (N114) exit junc 10 Argelès-sur-Mer; foll sp Plage Nord; after 2km at rndabt turn L sp St Cyprian; at next rndabt turn R sp Plages Nord & Sud; site on L in 800m. L onto unmade rd. V lge, hdg/mkd pitch, shd; wc; chem disp; some serviced pitches; mv service pnt; baby facs; shwrs inc; el pnts (6-10A) inc; gas; lndtte; ice shop; rest & snacks (high ssn); bar; BBQ (el/gas); playgrnd; pool & paddling pool; jacuzzi; games area; sand beach adj; aquarobics, scuba-diving lessons Jul & Aug; internet; TV; 12% statics; dogs €2.50; phone; poss cr; Eng spkn; quiet; adv bkg; cc acc; CCI. "Beautiful site; lge pitches; friendly helpful family owners; 1st class facs; excel pool; recep clsd 1300-1430; many static tents high ssn; gd area for cycling & walking." ♦ 1 May-30 Sep. € 26.00   2007*

> Did you know you can fill in site report forms on the Club's website — www.caravanclub.co.uk?

ARGELES SUR MER *10G1* (2km NE Rural) **Camping La Sirène, Route de Taxo, 66701 Argelès-sur-Mer [04 68 81 04 61; fax 04 68 81 69 74; contact@camping-lasirene. fr; www.camping-lasirene.fr]** Take D914 (N114) fr Perpignan twd Argelès. Cross Rv Tech & take 1st L twd Taxo d'Avall, site 1 of many about 2.5km on R. V lge, shd; wc; baby facs; shwrs inc; el pnts (5A) €3; gas; lndtte; ice; shop; rest; snacks; bar; BBQ; cooking facs; playgrnd; pool; waterslide; sand beach 1.5km; fishing, sailing & windsurfing 1km; tennis; mini-golf; horseriding; archery; cycle hire; games area; dogs €4; adv bkg; quiet; red low ssn. Easter-30 Sep. € 40.00   2004*

ARGELES SUR MER *10G1* (2km NE Coastal) **Camping Le Neptune, Chemin de Tamariguer, Plage Nord, 66700 Argelès-sur-Mer [04 68 81 02 98 or 04 99 57 20 25; fax 04 68 81 00 41; neptune@village-center.com; www.village-center.com/neptune]** Fr Argelès Plage take D81 coast rd to Argelès-Plage Nord & site sp on L. Lge, hdg/mkd pitch, hdstg, pt shd; wc; chem disp; baby facs; shwrs inc; el pnts (6A); gas; lndtte; shop; tradsmn; rest; snacks; bar; BBQ (gas); playgrnd; pool; paddling pool; waterslide; sand beach 350m; golf 7km; entmnt; dogs €3.50; golf 7km; cycle hire; entmnt; 60% statics; dogs; €3; poss cr; Eng spkn; adv bkg; cc acc; red low ssn; CCI. "Busy, well-maintained site; gd san facs; vg." ♦ 21 Apr-16 Sep. € 38.00   2007*

ARGELES SUR MER *10G1* (2km NE Coastal)
Camping Le Soleil, Route du Littoral, Plage-Nord, 66700 Argelès-sur-Mer [04 68 81 14 48; fax 04 68 81 44 34; camping.lesoleil@wanadoo.fr; www.campmed.com] Exit D914 (N114) junc 10 & foll sp Argelès Plage-Nord. Turn L onto D81 to site. Site sp among others. V lge, mkd pitch, pt shd; wc (some cont); chem disp; mv service pnt; baby facs; shwrs inc; el pnts (6A) €3.10; gas; lndtte; ice; shop; rest; snacks; bar; no BBQ; playgrnd; pool; paddling pool; sand beach adj; rv fishing adj; tennis; cycle hire; horseriding; mini-golf; games area; entmnt; TV; 50% statics; no dogs; adv bkg (ess Aug); noisy nr disco; red low ssn; cc acc. "Lovely views; excel site suitable for partially-sighted & handicapped; tel & fax nos swap when site clsd; visit to Collioure a must." ♦ 17 May-20 Sep. € 27.50   2005*

ARGELES SUR MER *10G1* (3km NE Coastal)
Camping Beauséjour, Ave de Tech, Argelès-Plage, 66700 Argelès-sur-Mer [04 68 81 10 63; fax 04 68 95 75 08; contact@camping-lebeausejour.com; www.camping-lebeausejour.com] Fr Perpignan, foll D914 (N114) to Argelès-sur-Mer. Turn L after Champion supmkt & Shell g'ge; foll sp to Plage Nord. At coast rd turn R to Argelès-Plage cent. Site on R shortly after supmkt. Lge, mkd pitch, shd; wc; chem disp; shwrs inc; el pnts (4A) inc; lndtte; shop adj; snacks, playgrnd; 2 pools; paddling pool; waterslide; jacuzzi; sand beach 300m; entmnt; 50% statics; dogs; phone; poss cr; Eng spkn; adv bkg rec; CCI. "Walking dist to beach; lots of shops, rests, takeaways nr." ♦ ltd. 1 Apr-30 Sep. € 34.00 (3 persons)   2006*

ARGELES SUR MER *10G1* (500m E Coastal)
Camping La Massane, Ave Molière (Zone Pujol), 66700 Argelès-sur-Mer [04 68 81 06 85; fax 04 68 81 59 18; camping.massane@infonie.fr; www.camping-massane.com] Fr D914 (N114) exit junc 10, at traff island take 2nd exit, site sp further down rd. Site just bef municipal stadium on L Lge, hdg/mkd pitch, pt shd; wc (some cont); chem disp; baby facs; shwrs inc; el pnts (6A) inc; gas; lndtte; ice; shop & 500m; snacks; bar; BBQ (gas/elec only); playgrnd; htd pool; paddling pool; sand beach 1km; mini-golf; tennis adj; entmnt, excursions high ssn; dogs €2; poss cr; Eng spkn; adv bkg rec high ssn; red long stay/low ssn; quiet; cc acc; CCI. "Vg site; friendly welcome; steel pegs req." ♦ 15 Mar-15 Oct. € 24.00   2006*

ARGELES SUR MER *10G1* (1km E Coastal)
Camping Europe, Ave du Général de Gaulle, 66700 Argelès-sur-Mer [04 68 81 08 10; fax 04 68 95 71 84; camping.europe@wanadoo.fr; www.camping-europe.net] Fr Perpignan take D914 (N114) to Argelès-sur-Mer. Exit junc 12 to Argelès. At rndabt take last exit L to Argelès Ville. At next rndabt turn R, site on L after Dyneff g'ge. Med, mkd pitch, shd; wc; chem disp; baby facs; shwrs inc; el pnts (3-10A) €2.75-3.20; gas; lndtte; shop; tradsmn; rest; snacks; bar; BBQ; playgrnd; pool 800m; sand beach 300m; 10% statics; dogs €1.60; phone; bus adj; poss cr; Eng spkn; adv bkg; quiet; CCI. "Friendly family-run; gd san facs." 1 Apr-15 Oct. € 17.00   2004*

ARGELES SUR MER *10G1* (2km E Urban/Coastal)
Camping La Chapelle, Place de l'Europe, 66702 Argelès-sur-Mer [04 68 81 28 14; fax 04 68 95 83 82; campinglachapelle@free.fr; www.camping-la-chapelle.com] Fr A9 exit junc 42 onto D900 (N9)/D914 (N114) to Argelès-sur-Mer. At junc 10 cont thro Argelès vill & foll sp Argelès-Plage. In 2.5km tun L at rndabt, bear L at Office de Tourisme, site immed L. Lge, hdg/mkd pitch, shd; wc (mainly cont), shwrs inc; el pnts (4-6A) €3.50; lndtte; shop; rests, snacks, bar 100m; playgrnd; pool 2km; beach 200m; tennis 200m; entmnt; 30% statics; dogs €2.50; poss cr; Eng spkn; adv bkg; quiet; CCI. "Ltd facs low ssn; gd." ♦ 1 May-25 Sep. € 21.00   2004*

This guide relies on site report forms submitted by caravanners like us; we'll do our bit and tell the editor what we think of the campsites we've visited.

ARGELES SUR MER *10G1* (3km SE Coastal)
Camping La Coste Rouge, Route de Collioure, Zone La Racou, 66700 Argelès-sur-Mer [04 68 81 08 94; fax 04 68 95 94 17; info@lacosterouge.com; www.lacosterouge.com] Exit junc 13 fr D914 (N114) dir Port-Argelès. At 2nd rndabt foll D114 to Racou, site on L. Med, pt sl, terr, shd; wc (some cont); chem disp; baby facs; shwrs inc; el pnts (6A) inc; lndtte; ice; shop; rest; snacks; bar; no BBQ; playgrnd; pool; paddling pool; sand beach 1km; games rm; entmnt; some statics; dogs €2.30; phone; adv bkg; quiet.cc acc. "Beautiful pool; gd cent for sea, Pyrenees & trips to Spain; aquarium at Banyuls-sur-Mer; cloisters at Elne." ♦ 1 Jun-15 Sep. € 25.80   2007*

France

ARGELES SUR MER *10G1* (4km SE Coastal) Camping Les Criques de Porteils, Corniche de Collioure, 66701 Argelès-sur-Mer [04 68 81 12 73; fax 04 68 95 85 76; info@ lescriques.fr; www.lescriques.com] Fr N on A9/ E15 take exit junc 42 onto D914 (N114) Argelès-sur-Mer. Fr S exit junc 43 onto D914. At exit 13 leave D914 sp Collioure & foll site sp. Site by Hôtel du Golfe 1.5km fr Collioure. Lge, hdg/mkd pitch, pt sl, terr, pt shd; htd wc (some cont); chem disp; mv service pnt; baby facs; shwrs inc; el pnts (5A) €4; gas; lndtte; ice; shop; rest; snacks; bar; playgrnd; htd pool; sand/shgl beach adj; boat excursions; fishing; watersports; scuba-diving; organised walks; games rm; games area; internet; TV rm; 15% statics; dogs €2; phone; Eng spkn; adv bkg; quiet; red low ssn/CCI. "Variable size pitches - not all suitable for lge o'fits; steps to beach; much improved/refurbished site." ♦ 5 Apr-28 Sep. € 32.00   2007*

See advertisement

ARGELES SUR MER *10G1* (2.5km SW Rural) Camping Le Romarin, Route de Sorède, 66702 Argelès-sur-Mer [04 68 81 02 63; fax 04 68 56 62 33; contact@camping-romarin.com; www.camping-romarin.com] S fr Perpignon on D914 (N114); at rndabt junc with D618 foll sp St André on minor rd; in 500m L & immed L & foll sp to site. Or fr A9 exit junc 43; foll D618 to rndabt junc with D914; then as above. Med, pt sl, shd; wc (some cont); shwrs inc; el pnts (4-6A) €2-3.50; gas; lndtte; shop; rest; snacks; bar; playgrnd; pool; waterslide; beach 4km; sports activities; entmnt; dogs €3; Eng spkn; adv bkg; quiet; red low ssn. "V pleasant site; conv Spanish border." 15 May-30 Sep. € 25.00   2005*

As soon as we get home I'm going to post all these site report forms to the editor for inclusion in next year's guide. I don't want to miss the September deadline.

ARGELES SUR MER *10G1* (5km SW Urban) Camping Les Micocouliers, Route de Palau, 66690 Sorède [04 68 89 20 27; fax 04 68 89 25 61; contact@camping-les-micocouliers.com; www. camping-les-micocouliers.com] A9 S dir Le Boulou exit junc 43 onto D618 dir Argelès-sur-Mer; R onto D11 to Sorède, sp to site. Lge, hdg/mkd pitch, pt sl, shd; wc; chem disp; shwrs inc; el pnts (6A) €3.80; gas; lndtte; ice; shops & in vill; tradsmn; snacks; bar; BBQ; playgrnd; pool; beach 20km; tennis adj; cycle hire; TV rm; 5% statics; dogs €2.10; poss v cr; ess adv bkg Jul-Aug (dep & bkg fee). "Lge pitches; conv N Spain eg Figueres, Dali museum." ♦ ltd. 26 Jun-15 Sep. € 22.00   2007*

ARGELES SUR MER *10G1* (8km W Urban) Camp Municipal Le Vivier, 31 Rue du Stade, 66740 Laroque-des-Albères [04 68 89 00 93 or 04 68 89 21 13; fax 04 68 95 42 58; camping.des. alberes@wanadoo.fr; www.campin-des-alberes. com] D2 fr Argelès-sur-Mer to Laroque-des-Albères; foll sp in cent of vill. Lge, mkd pitch, pt sl, pt shd; wc; chem disp; shwrs inc; el pnts (6A) €4; lndtte; ice; shop 300m; 5% statics; dogs €3; bus 300m; adv bkg; quiet; CCI. "Peaceful, simple site at edge of Pyrenees, in pleasant vill with shops & rests; vg." ♦ 15 Jun-15 Sep. € 22.00   2006*

ARGELES SUR MER *10G1* (8km W Rural) Camping Les Albères, 66740 Laroque-des-Albères [04 68 89 23 64; fax 04 68 89 14 30; camping-des-alberes@wanadoo.fr; www.camping-des-alberes.com] Fr A9 exit junc 43 onto D618 dir Argelès-sur-Mer/Port Vendres. Turn R onto D50 to Laroque-des-Albères. In vill at T-junc turn L, then turn R at rndabt & foll sp to site on D11. Lge, mkd pitch, terr, pt shd; wc (some cont); chem disp; mv service pnt; baby facs; shwrs inc; el pnts (6-10A) €4; lndtte; shop; rest; snacks; bar; BBQ (gas only); playgrnd; pool; sand beach 8km; tennis; TV; rm; entmnt; 5% statics; dogs €3; phone; quiet; poss cr; CCI. "V attractive site under slopes of Pyrenees; gd walking area; peaceful (apart fr cockerel!); friendly owners; excel." ♦ ltd. 1 Apr-30 Sep. € 21.00

                2006*

ARGELES SUR MER *10G1* (8km W Rural) Camping-Caravaning Las Planes, 117 Ave du Vallespir, 66740 Laroque-des-Albères [04 68 89 21 36 or 04 68 95 43 76 (LS); fax 04 68 89 01 42; info@lasplanes.com; www. lasplanes.com] Fr Argelès take D914 (N114), D2 twd Sorède, thro Laroque-des-Albères on D11, site sp. Med, pt sl, shd, mkd pitch; wc; chem disp; shwrs inc; el pnts (4-6A) €3.50; gas; lndtte; ice; shop; snacks; bar; BBQ (el/gas); playgrnd; 2 pools; sand beach 8km; cycle hire; dogs €2.50; poss cr; adv bkg rec high ssn; quiet. "V friendly owners & staff." 15 Jun-31 Aug. € 19.00   2007*

ARGELES SUR MER *10G1* (2km NW Rural) Camping Etoile d'Or, Route de Taxo d'Avall, 66701 Argelès-sur-Mer [04 68 81 04 34; fax 04 68 81 57 05; info@aletoiledor.com; www. aletoiledor.com] Fr D914 (N114) exit junc 10 dir Taxo-Plage. Site in 1km on R. Lge, mkd pitch, shd; wc (cont); baby facs; shwrs inc; el pnts (4A) inc; gas; lndtte; ice; shop; rest; snacks; bar; el/gas BBQ; playgrnd; pool; sand beach 2.5km; tennis; mini-golf; games rm; entmnt; TV rm; many statics; dogs €3; adv bkg; quiet. ♦ 15 Mar-15 Sep. € 31.00

                2007*

Les Criques de Porteils

- Exceptional position with direct access to private coves
- 4 stars classification pending
- Heated pool, children's play area, facilities open all season
- Ideal for daytrips, within walking distance of Collioure
- Emplacements for tents, camping cars
- Mobile homes and bengali tents to rent

Corniche de Collioure - FR-66701 Argelès-sur-Mer - ☎ +33 (0)4 68 81 12 73 - www.lescriques.com

France

ARGENTAN *4E1* (500m SE) **Camp Municipal du Parc de la Noë, 34 Rue de la Noë, 61200 Argentan [02 33 36 05 69; fax 02 33 36 52 07; tourisme.argentan@wanadoo.fr]** S fr Caen on N158/D958 foll camping sp fr by-pass. Sm, shd; htd wc; chem disp; mv service pnt; shwrs; el pnts (10A) €2.20; ice; Indtte; shop 1km; playgrnd; pool 1km; rv & pond; sports area; TV; few statics; poss cr; adv bkg ess high ssn; quiet. "Vg clean & tidy site adj town park; v helpful warden; spotless san facs; gd disabled facs." ♦ 1 Apr-30 Sep. € 8.00
2006*

⊞ARGENTAN *4E1* (2km S Rural) **FFCC Aire Naturelle du Val de Baize (Huet des Aunay), 18 Rue de Mauvaisville, 61200 Argentan [02 33 67 27 11; fax 02 33 35 39 16]** Take D958 (N158) fr Argentan twd Sées & Alençon & take 1st or 2nd R to Mauvaisville (not sp), site adj T-junc N of farm buildings. Sm, pt shd; wc; chem disp; mv service pnt; shwrs inc; el pnts (3-6A) €2.50-4.60; gas; shops 1.5km; snacks; playgrnd; pool 2.5km; B&B; 10% statics; dogs; Eng spkn; adv bkg; quiet; cc not acc; CCI. "Lge pitches in orchard; pleasant, well-kept site with clean but v dated facs, ltd low ssn; friendly welcome; NH only." € 9.50   2007*

ARGENTAT *7C4* (10km N Rural) **Camp Municipal La Croix de Brunal, 19320 St Martin-la-Méanne [05 55 29 11 91 or 05 55 29 12 75 (Mairie); fax 05 55 29 28 48]** Fr Argentat take D18 to St Martin-la-Méanne. Site well sp on ent to vill. Sm, hdg pitch, pt shd; wc; shwrs inc; el pnts (5A); gas, Indtte; shop 1km; rest, snacks, bar 1km; BBQ; htd pool 1km; sand beach 15km; rv sw 8km; tennis 1km; games area; some statics; dogs; phone; quiet. "Simple country site; warden calls am & pm; gd walking; fishing, horseriding, canoe hire, watersports within 15km." ♦ ltd. 15 Jun-15 Sep.   2006*

ARGENTAT *7C4* (1km NE Urban) **Camp Municipal, Le Longour, Route d'Egletons, 19400 Argentat [05 55 28 13 84; fax 05 55 28 81 26; mairie. argentat@wanadoo.fr]** 1km fr cent of Argentat heading N dir Egletons on D18. Med, pt shd; wc; chem disp; shwrs inc; el pnts €2.80; Indtte; ice; shops 1km; tradsmn; playgrnd; htd pool & sports complex adj; tennis; fishing; dogs; phone; poss cr; quiet. "Excel, clean site; pleasant rvside walk to old quay & cafés; gd touring base for Dordogne." 15 Jun-14 Sep. € 10.40   2006*

Site report forms at back of guide   173

ARGENTAT *7C4* (4km NE Rural) **Camping Château de Gibanel, 19400 St Martial-Entraygues [05 55 28 10 11; fax 05 55 28 81 62; contact@camping-gibanel.com; www.camping-gibanel.com]** Exit Argentat on D18 twd Egletons & fork R on lakeside past hydro-electric dam. Sp fr all dir. Site in grounds of sm castle on N bank of Rv Dordogne. App rd narr but satisfactory. Lge, mkd pitch, pt sl, pt shd; wc (some cont); chem disp; child/baby facs; fam bthrm; shwrs inc; el pnts (6A) €3.20; gas; lndtte; ice; shop; tradsmn; rest; snacks; bar; BBQ; playgrnd; pool; paddling pool; lake sw; sports area; boating; fishing; entmnt; games rm; TV; 15% statics; dogs €1.50 (free low ssn); Eng spkn; adv bkg; quiet; red low ssn; cc acc; CCI. "Excel, well-managed site; v helpful owner; beautiful location, lovely sm town with gd rests; gd san facs, ltd low ssn; variable sized pitches." ♦ ltd. 1 Jun-8 Sep. € 17.20

2007*

ARGENTAT *7C4* (3km SW Rural) **Camping Europe, Le Chambon, 19400 Monceaux-sur-Dordogne [05 55 28 07 70; fax 05 55 28 19 60; camping-europe@wanadoo.fr; http://perso.wanadoo.fr/camping-europe]** Fr Argentat take D12 twd Beaulieu-sur-Dordogne. Site in 2km fr N120. Ent on L by awkward RH bend in Le Chambon. Med, mkd pitch, pt sl, pt shd; wc; chem disp; mv service pnt; shwrs inc; el pnts (5A) €2.70; gas; lndtte; shops 1km; rest 500m; snacks 1km; playgrnd; pool; tennis; games area; entmnt; child entmnt; some statics; dogs €1.50; poss cr; quiet. "Lovely rvside site; interesting town." 1 Apr-30 Oct. € 14.80

2005*

ARGENTAT *7C4* (4km SW Rural) **Camping Sunêlia au Soleil d'Oc, 19400 Monceaux-sur-Dordogne [05 55 28 84 84 or 05 55 28 05 97 (LS); fax 05 55 28 12 12; info@dordogne-soleil.com; www.dordogne-soleil.com]** Fr N exit A20 junc 46a dir Tulle, then D1120 (N120) to Argentat. Fr Argentat take D12 sp Beaulieu. In 4km in Laygues turn L over bdge x-ing Rv Dordogne, site in 300m. Med, hdg/mkd pitch, terr, pt shd; wc (some cont); chem disp; mv service pnt; baby facs; shwrs inc; el pnts (6A) €3; gas; lndtte; tradsmn; rest; snacks; bar; BBQ; playgrnd; pool & paddling pool; rv sw & shgl beach; canoeing; games area; games rm; cycle hire; mini-golf; archery; entmnt; child entmnt; wifi internet; sat TV; some statics; dogs €3 (free low ssn); phone; Eng spkn; adv bkg; quiet; red low ssn/long stay/CCI. "Ideal family site high ssn & quiet, peaceful low ssn; some pitches on rv bank; gd walking & other activities; many beautiful vills in area; tours arranged." ♦ 20 Mar-16 Nov. € 19.80 (CChq acc) 2007*

See advertisement

ARGENTAT *7C4* (6km SW Rural) **Camping du Saulou, Vergnolles, 19400 Monceaux-sur-Dordogne [05 55 28 12 33; fax 05 55 28 80 67; le.saulou@wanadoo.fr; www.saulou.net]** S on N120, turn R at N o'skts of Argentat on D12, sp Beaulieu. Foll rv L sp Vergnolles & camp sp. Lge, hdg/mkd pitch, pt shd; wc (some cont); chem disp; shwrs inc; el pnts (4-13A) €2.60-3.55; gas; lndtte; ice; shop & 1km; tradsmn; rest; snacks; bar; playgrnd; htd pool; paddling pool; boating; fishing; games area; entmnt; TV rm; 10% statics; dogs €2.05; phone; poss cr; Eng spkn; adv bkg; quiet low ssn; red low ssn; cc acc; CCI. "Early dep arrange el pnts disconnect night bef; facs constantly cleaned; v friendly, helpful owners." 1 Apr-30 Sep. € 18.65

2007*

ARGENTAT *7C4* (9km SW Rural) **Camping Le Vaurette, 19400 Monceaux-sur-Dordogne [05 55 28 09 67; fax 05 55 28 81 14; info@vaurette.com; www.vaurette.com]** SW fr Tulle on N120; fr Argentat SW on D12 sp Beaulieu; site sp on banks of Rv Dordogne. Med, mkd pitch, pt shd; wc (some cont); chem disp; mv service pnt; baby facs; shwrs inc; el pnts (6A) €3; gas; lndtte; ice; shop; snacks; bar; BBQ; playgrnd; pool; shgl beach & rv sw adj; tennis; badminton; fishing; canoe expeditions; games area; games rm; TV rm; statics; dogs €2.50; Eng spkn; adv bkg; quiet; cc acc; red low ssn; CCI. "V helpful, friendly owners; lovely setting; many sports avail." ♦ 1 May 21 Sep. € 20.00 2005*

ARGENTIERE LA BESSEE, L' *9C3* (4km N Rural) **Camping Le Couroumba, 05120 Les Vigneaux [04 92 23 02 09 or 04 92 20 03 00 (LS); fax 04 92 23 04 69; cplcourounba@atciat.com; www.campeole.com]** Take N94 S fr Briançon to L'Argentiere-la-Bessee, turn R onto D994E dir Vallouise. Site on L over bdge. Lge, pt shd; wc; shwrs inc; el pnts €2.74; shop 500m; rest; snacks; bar; htd pool; waterslide; tennis; playgrnd; fishing; walking; adv bkg; quiet; "Beautifully situated in woods by rv in mountains." 7 Apr-23 Sep. € 16.30 2007*

ARGENTIERE LA BESSEE, L' *9C3* (6km N Rural) **Camping de l'Iscle de Prelles, Hameau de Prelles, 05120 St Martin-de-Queyrieres [04 92 20 28 66; contact@camping-iscledeprelles.com; www.camping-iscledeprelles.com]** S fr Briançon on N94; in 5km turn L opp Intermarché supmkt, go over unguarded level x-ing (quiet line), track turns R & site in 500m. Foll sp. Med, mkd pitch, pt shd; (htd winter) wc (some cont); chem disp; baby facs; shwrs inc; el pnts (4-10A) €3.70-7.10; gas; lndtte; ice; sm shop; rest; snacks; bar; BBQ; playgrnd; htd pool; shgl beach 400m; rv sw adj; climbing; gd walking; skiing; quad bikes; rafting; horseriding; games area; tennis; paint ball; entmnt; child entmnt; internet; 25% statics; no twin axles; TV; dogs €1.60; phone; train 5km; Eng spkn; adv bkg; quiet; no cc acc; CCI. "Attractive mountain aspects; cable car; gd long stay for children; new owners 2007 with plans; vg." ♦ ltd. 1 Dec-30 Sep. € 17.00 2007*

ARGENTIERE LA BESSEE, L' 9C3 (2.5km S Rural) Camp Municipal Les Ecrins, 05120 L'Argentière-la-Bessée [04 92 23 03 38; fax 04 92 23 07 71; contact@camping-les-ecrins.com; www.camping-les-ecrins.com] Fr L'Argentière on N94, turn R onto D104, site sp. Med, some mkd pitch, pt shd, htd wc (some cont); shwrs inc; el pnts (10A) €2.40; lndtte; shop; snacks; playgrnd; walking; kayaking; games area; dogs €1; phone; adv bkg; rd/rlwy noise. "Mountain scenery." ♦ 18 Apr-15 Sep. € 12.50 2006*

⊞ARGENTIERE LA BESSEE, L' 9C3 (5km S Rural) FFCC Camping Le Verger, 05310 La Roche-de-Rame [tel/fax 04 92 20 92 23; info@campingleverger.com; www.campingleverger.com] S fr Briançon on N94; site 500m L of road bef vill; sp. Sm, hdg pitch, terr, shd; wc; chem disp; mv service pnt; shwrs inc; el pnts (3-10A) €2.10-3.60; lndtte; shop 5km; rest, snacks, bar 1km; lake sw 1km; TV; 25% statics; dogs; phone; bus 5km; Eng spkn; adv bkg; quiet. "Grass pitches in orchard; excel, well-maintained facs; excel." € 14.00 2006*

⊞ARGENTIERE LA BESSEE, L' 9C3 (8km NW Rural) Camping Les Chambonnettes, 05290 Vallouise [tel/fax 04 92 23 30 26 or 06 82 23 65 09 (mob); camping.vallouise@free.fr] Take N94 Briançon-Gap, on N o'skts of L'Argentière-la-Bessée take D994 W dir Vallouise. In cent of Vallouise turn L over bdge & immed L, site in 200m. Lge, mkd pitch, pt sl, pt shd; htd wc (some cont); chem disp; shwrs inc; el pnts (3-6A) €2.90; gas 1.5km; lndtte; shops 200m; tradsmn, rest, snacks, bar 500m; playgrnd; pool 3km; tennis; boules; TV; 10% statics; phone; poss cr; Eng spkn; adv bkg; quiet; red low ssn "Magnificent mountain scenery; basic facs; gd cent for walking, skiing, canoeing; white-water rafting at nrby rv; interesting vill." € 12.35 2005*

ARGENTON CHATEAU 4H1 (1km W Urban) Camp Municipal du Lac d'Hautibus, Rue de la Sablière, 79150 Argenton-Château [05 49 65 95 08 or 05 49 65 70 22 (Mairie); fax 05 49 65 70 84] Well sp in town, on lakeside. Med, hdg pitch, pt sl, terr; wc (some cont); chem disp; shwrs inc; el pnts (10A) €2.10; lndtte; shops in town; playgrnd; pool 100m; lake sw 500m; quiet; CCI. "Interesting town; excel site." ♦ 1 Apr-31 Oct. € 6.75 2004*

ARGENTON SUR CREUSE 7A3 (6km NE Rural) Camp Municipal des Rives de la Bouzanne, 36800 Le Pont Chrétien-Chabenet [02 54 25 80 53 or 02 54 25 81 40 (Mairie); fax 02 54 25 87 59] Fr St Gaultier on D927 to Argenton-sur-Creuse, turn R in Le Pont Chrétien-Chabenet, bef rv bdge, 50m on L. Med, pt shd; wc (some cont); chem disp (wc); shwrs inc; el pnts €2.50; lndtte; shop, bar adj; playgrnd; rv sw adj; dogs €0.50; adv bkg rec; quiet; CCI. "Picturesque, clean site; gd, drained pitches." 15 Jun-15 Sep. € 7.00 2007*

ARGENTON SUR CREUSE 7A3 (12km SE) La Chaumerette Camping Club à Tou Vert, 36190 Gargilesse-Dompierre [02 54 47 73 44; A.TOU.VERT@net-up.com] Fr A20 take exit 17 for D48 to Badecon-le-Pin then R onto D40. Turn R sp Barsize then foll sp to site. Sm, shd; wc; chem disp; baby facs; shwrs inc; el pnts (6A) inc; tradsmn; snacks; bar; playgrnd; rv sw; fishing; adv bkg; quiet; CCI. "Superb location in wooded valley adj rv; additional overflow area when site full; poor san facs." 1 Apr-31 Oct. € 14.50 2006*

ARGENTON SUR CREUSE 7A3 (12km SW Rural) Camping La Petite Brenne (Naturist), La Grande Metairie, 36800 Luzeret [02 54 25 05 78; fax 02 54 25 05 97; www.lapetitebrenne.com] Fr A20 exit junc 18 sp Luzeret/Prissac; foll D55 to Luzeret vill. After bdge in vill turn L, then next L to site. Lge, pt sl, unshd; wc; chem disp (biodegradable only); sauna; shwrs inc; el pnts (6A) €4 (long leads poss req); lndtte; ice; shop 12km; tradsmn; rest; bar; playgrnd; 2 pools (1 htd); horseriding; no dogs; Eng spkn; adv bkg rec high ssn; quiet; cc acc; red long stay/low ssn; INF card. "V friendly Dutch owners; ideal for children; gd san facs; lge pitches; excel." 27 Apr-30 Sep. € 22.00 2007*

France

ARGENTON SUR CREUSE *7A3* (1km NW) **Camp Municipal Les Chambons, Route des Chambons, 36200 Argenton-sur-Creuse [02 54 22 26 61; fax 02 54 22 58 80]** Fr N exit A20 junc 17 onto D137 dir Agenton; turn R at 1st junc sp St Marcel / Argentomagus, then R at mini rndabt nr supmkt; foll rd downhill over rlwy bdge; then 1st R in 100m. But best app fr N of town on D927 to avoid traff calming rd humps; at town sp cross rlwy bdge & turn R immed past LH turn for Roman archaeological museum; foll camping sp on narr, busy app rd. Med, mkd pitch, some hdstg, pt sl, shd; wc; chem disp; shwrs inc; el pnts (5A) €3.20 (poss long lead req); gas; shop 1.5km; tradsmn; bar; rest 1km; playgrnd; quiet but some rd noise. "Beautiful site by rv; well-kept & peaceful; v muddy after heavy rain & poss uneven pitches by rv; easy rvside walk into old town; archaeological Roman site nrby; no need to unhitch so useful for early start; helpful warden." 15 May-15 Sep. € 12.15   2007*

ARLANC *9C1* (1km W Rural) **Camping Le Metz, 63220 Arlanc [04 73 95 15 62; fax 04 73 95 15 62; jardin-terre.arlanc@wanadoo.fr]** Fr Ambert on D906 to Arlanc, turn R (W) onto D999A dir St Germain-l'Herm. Site on R in 800m, sp. Med, some hdg pitch, pt shd; wc (some cont); chem disp (wc); shwrs inc; el pnts (6A) inc (long lead poss req); lndry rm; shop 800m; rest, snacks, bar 150m; playgrnd; pool 100m; games area; mini-golf; 10% statics; dogs; phone; adv bkg; quiet. "Lace-making museum in Arlanc." ♦ 1 May-30 Sep. € 11.40   2005*

ARLES *10E2* (8km NE Rural) **Camp Municipal des Pins, Rue Michelet, 13990 Fontvieille [04 90 54 78 69; fax 04 90 54 81 25; campmunicipal.lespins@wanadoo.fr]** Take D570 (N570) fr Arles to Avignon; in 2km turn R on D17 to Fontvieille; at far end of vill turn R & foll sp. Med, pt sl, shd; wc; shwrs inc; el pnts (6A) €2.30; gas fr Shell g'ge in vill; shops 1km; pool 500m high ssn; dogs €1.30; poss cr; Eng spkn; adv bkg; quiet; red long stay: CCI. "Delightful, quiet site; friendly staff; vg facs; 20 mins walk to vill & shops; quiet forest walks." 1 Apr-30 Sep. € 10.00   2007*

ARLES *10E2* (7km E Rural) **Camping La Bienheureuse, 13280 Raphèle-les-Arles [04 90 98 48 06; fax 04 90 98 37 62; contact@labienheureuse.com; www.labienheureuse.com]** Fr Arles E on D453, site on L 5km after Pont-de-Crau. W fr Salon-de-Provence on D113 or A54 (exit junc 12) to St Martin-de-Crau & take D453 dir to site. Med, hdg pitch, pt shd; wc; chem disp; shwrs inc; el pnts (10A) €3.50; lndtte; tradsmn; snacks; bar; playgrnd; pool; paddling pool; tennis; horseriding nr; entmnt; some statics; dogs €2.50; phone; bus adj; Eng spkn; adv bkg (dep req); quiet; CCI. "Pleasant, renovated site; gd facs." ♦ 1 Mar-30 Sep. € 14.50   2006*

ARLES *10E2* (2km SE Urban) **Camping Le City, 67 Route de la Crau, 13200 Arles [04 90 93 08 86; fax 04 90 93 91 07; contact@camping-city.com; www.camping-city.com]** Fr town cent foll rd to Pont-de-Crau. Site well sp on L in 2km. Or exit N113 at junc 7 sp Arles & Pont de Crau; at rndabt go R alongside arches; site on R in 350m; well sp. Med, mkd pitch, pt shd; wc (some cont); chem disp; mv service pnt; baby facs; shwrs inc; el pnts (5A) €4; gas 1km; lndtte; shop; supmkt 1km; tradsmn; rest; snacks; bar; playgrnd; pool; paddling pool; sand beach 25km; tennis; cycle hire; entmnt; TV; many statics; dogs €2; bus; some Eng spkn; quiet; CCI. "Vg; 20 min walk to Arles town cent; clean, basic san facs long walk fr some pitches." 1 Mar-30 Oct. € 17.00   2007*

⊞**ARLES** *10E2* (4km SE Urban) **Camping Les Rosiers, Pont-de-Crau, 13200 Arles [04 90 96 02 12; fax 04 90 93 36 72; lesrosiers.arles@wanadoo.fr; www.arles-camping-club.com]** Exit Arles E by D453 sp Pont-de-Crau or junc 7 fr N113 dir Raphèle-les-Arles; 200m after exit vill take 1st exit at rndabt then R at Flor Hotel sp on D83E. Site in 50m on R adj hotel. Med, pt shd; htd wc (some cont); mv service pnt; shwrs inc; chem disp; el pnts (6A) €4; lndtte; shop 500m; rest; bar; playgrnd; pool; games area; entmnt; TV; dogs €1.50; bus fr rndabt; no vans over 5.50m allowed (but poss not enforced); poss cr; Eng spkn; some rd & rlwy noise; red facs low ssn. "Many mosquitoes; v muddy after rain; visit Les Baux citadel early morning bef coach parties arr; gd birdwatching." € 16.00   2006*

ARLES *10E2* (14km W Rural) **Camping Caravaning Crin-Blanc, Hameau de Saliers, 13123 L'Albaron [04 66 87 48 78; fax 04 66 87 18 66; camping-crin.blanc@wanadoo.fr; www.camping-crin-blanc.com]** E fr St Gilles on N572 twd Arles; in 3km turn R onto D37 sp Saliers; site sp. Lge, pt shd; wc; chem disp; mv service pnt; baby facs; shwrs; el pnts (10A) inc; gas; lndtte; shop; tradsmn; rest; snacks; bar; playgrnd; htd pool; paddling pool; tennis; horseriding; 70% statics; dogs €2; Eng spkn; adv bkg; quiet; red low ssn; cc acc; CCI. "Poss muddy; mosquitoes; park with bird reserve."♦ 1 Apr-30 Sep. € 23.00   2006*

ARLES SUR TECH *8H4* (2km NE Rural) **Camping Le Vallespir, Route d'Amélie-les-Bains, 66150 Arles-sur-Tech [04 68 39 90 00; fax 04 68 39 90 09; info@campingvallespir.com; www.campingvallespir.com]** Site on D115 mid-way between Amélie-les-Bains & Arles-sur-Tech. Clearly sp on RH side of rd. Avoids narr vill. Med, some hdg pitch, pt shd; wc; chem disp; mv service pnt; child/baby facs; shwrs inc; el pnts (6-10A) €3.10-4.60; lndtte; tradmn; rest; snacks; bar; playgrnd; pool; paddling pool; tennis; entmnt; golf 2km; TV rm; 50% statics; dogs €2; phone; poss cr; poss noisy by rd. "V pleasant site; well-organised & maintained; lovely area for hiking & cycling; some facs poss clsd low ssn." ♦ 1 Apr-31 Oct. € 17.10   2007*

⊞ARLES SUR TECH *8H4* (1km W Urban) Camping du Riuferrer, 66150 Arles-sur-Tech [04 68 39 11 06; fax 04 68 39 12 09; pascal.larreur@campingduriuferrer.fr; www.campingduriuferrer.fr] Take D115 fr Le Boulou thro Arles-sur-Tech (v narr but poss). Twd town exit just bef rv bdge, turn R. Foll sp 500m to site. Ent across narr footbdge. O'fits width across wheels over 2.19m ask for guidance to rear ent. Med, pt sl, shd, mkd pitch, hdstg; wc (some cont); chem disp; shwrs inc; el pnts (4-6A) €2.50-2.80; gas; lndtte; rest, snacks, bar in ssn; shops 500m; tradsmn; ice; playgrnd; pool adj; poss cr; adv bkg; 20% statics; dogs €1; quiet; cc not acc; red low ssn/long stay; Eng spkn; red CCI. "Helpful owner; some sm pitches diff for manoeuvring; beautiful area; vg." ♦ € 13.00   2006*

ARNAY LE DUC *6H1* (1km E Rural) Camping L'Etang de Fouché, Rue du 8 Mai 1945, 21230 Arnay-le-Duc [03 80 90 02 23; fax 03 80 90 11 91; info@campingfouche.com; www.campingfouche.com] App by D906 (N6) to Arnay (site sp); turn E onto D17, site on R in 2km. Lge, hdg/mkd pitch, hdstg, pt shd; htd wc; chem disp; baby facs; shwrs inc; el pnts (6A) €4; lndtte; shop; tradsmn; rest; snacks; bar; BBQ; playgrnd; htd pool; paddling pool; waterslide; lake sw & beach adj; waterslide; tennis; cycle hire; games rm; TV; entmnt; child entmnt; internet; TV rm; dogs €2; Eng spkn; adv bkg; quiet; cc acc; red low ssn; CCI. "Excel site with pleasant view & surroundings; clean, with lge pitches; gd san facs; friendly staff; sh dist to attractive sm town; gd lakeside situation with fishing, pedalos & walks; gd touring base S Burgundy; gd for young families." ♦ 15 Apr-15 Oct. € 17.80   2007*

ARRADON see Vannes *2F3*

The opening dates and prices on this campsite have changed. I'll send a site report form to the editor for the next edition of the guide.

⊞ARMENTIERES *3A3* (3km E) Camping L'Image, 140 Rue Brune, 59116 Houplines [tel/fax 03 20 35 69 42 or 06 81 61 56 82 (mob); campimage@wanadoo.fr; www.campingimage.com] Exit A25 junc 8 sp Armentières, onto D945 N twd Houplines. After 4km at traff lts go strt on & take 1st R, site in 1km on R. Ent not v clearly sp. Med, hdg pitch, shd; htd wc; chem disp; mv service pnt; serviced pitches; shwrs inc; el pnts (10A) €3; lndtte; shop high ssn & 4km; snacks; playgrnd; tennis; entmnt; 90% statics; poss cr; adv bkg; quiet; 5% red low ssn; CCI. "Turn R at ent for neighbouring site 'Les Alouettes' (more pitches for tourers)." € 9.50   2005*

ARRAS *3B3* (12km SE Rural) Camping Paille Haute, 145 Rue de Seilly, 62156 Boiry-Notre-Dame [03 21 48 15 40; fax 03 21 22 07 24; lapaillehaute@wanadoo.fr; www.la-paille-haute.com] Fr Calais take A26/A1 twd Paris, exit junc 15 onto D939 twd Cambrai; in 3km take D34 NE to Boiry-Notre-Dame & foll camp sp. Fr D950 (N50) Douai-Arras rd, at Fresnes turn S onto D43, foll sp to Boiry in 7km, site well sp in vill. Med, pt hdg pitch, hdstg, terr, pt shd; wc; chem disp; mv service pnt; shwrs inc; el pnts (6A) €3 (poss rev pol); lndtte; shop 500m; rest, snacks high ssn; bar; BBQ; playgrnd; htd pool; lake fishing; mini-golf; tennis; games rm; entmnt; internet; 60% statics; dogs; site open w/ends in winter; Eng spkn; quiet; red long stay/low ssn; cc acc; CCI. "Popular NH; pretty site with lovely views; rec arr early; lge pitches; gd for children; facs stretched high ssn, basic low ssn; friendly management; trout-fishing locally; Calais under 2hrs; conv WW1 sites; excel." ♦ 1 Apr-31 Oct. € 21.50   2007*

See advertisement

France

⊞ARREAU 8G2 (Urban) Camp Municipal Beuse Debat, 65240 Arreau [05 62 98 65 56 (Mairie); fax 05 62 98 68 78] Foll sp fr D929 across bdge (D618 sp Luchon) immed turn E on D19 & foll sp into site on banks of Rv Neste. Sm, terr, pt shd; htd wc; chem disp; shwrs; el pnts (4-10A) €2.80-4.10 (rev pol); lndtte; shops 1km; rest; snacks; playgrnd; rv fishing adj; tennis; entmnts; some statics; dogs €1; site clsd Oct; poss cr; adv bkg; quiet. € 11.90   2004*

⊞ARREAU 8G2 (7km N Rural) Camp Municipal d'Esplantas, 65410 Sarrancolin [tel/fax 05 62 98 79 20 or 06 07 09 35 65; camping. esplantas.sarrancolin@wanadoo.fr; http:// pagesperso-orange.fr/camping.international. arreau] Site on E side of D929 at N end of vill; ent by Total petrol stn, sp. Med, mkd pitch, pt shd; htd wc; mv service pnt; shwrs inc; el pnts (6-10A) €4-5.50 (long lead poss req); shops; rest & gas in vill; pool; dogs; quiet. "Site on rv bank; warden calls am & pm; wc blocks (1 modern) v clean, gd facs for disabled." ♦ € 9.50   2006*

⊞ARREAU 8G2 (12km SE Rural) FLOWER Camping Pène Blanche, 65510 Loudenvielle [05 62 55 68 85; fax 05 62 99 98 20; info@ peneblanche.com; www.peneblanche.com] S fr Arreau on D618 in dir of Avajan. Take D25 thro Genos. Site on W of D25 just bef turn over bdge to Loudenvielle. Avoid app fr E over Col de Peyresourde. Med, some mkd pitch, terr, pt shd; htd wc; chem disp; shwrs inc; el pnts (5-10A) €3.15-7; lndtte; shop 500m; rest; snacks; bar; BBQ; playgrnd; htd pool opp; lake 1km; 20% statics; dogs €1.90; clsd Nov; adv bkg; cc acc. "Lge sports/ recreational complex opp; quiet out of main period." ♦ € 21.50   2006*

⊞ARRENS MARSOUS 8G2 (800m E Rural) Camping La Hèche, 54 Route d'Azun, 65400 Arrens-Marsous [05 62 97 02 64; laheche@free. fr; www.campinglaheche.com] Fr Argelès-Gazost foll D918. Site on L immed bef Arrens. If towing c'van do not app fr Col d'Aubisque. Lge, pt shd; wc; shwrs inc; el pnts (3-6A) €2-3; gas; lndtte; ice; shops 500m; tradsmn; playgrnd; pool in vill high ssn; waterslide; tennis; 10% statics; dogs €0.50; phone; quiet; CCI. "Gd for wintersports; beautiful location; in low ssn only oldest facs block in use - own san rec; other facs block new & immac." € 6.10   2004*

ARROMANCHES LES BAINS 3D1 (3km E Coastal) Camp Municipal Quintefeuille, 14960 Asnelles [02 31 22 35 50] Site sp, but visible fr vill sq in Asnelles. Med, unshd; wc; chem disp; shwrs; el pnts; lndtte; shops adj; rest; snacks; bar; playgrnd; sand beach 300m; sports area; tennis; fishing 300m; poss cr; quiet. "Facs dated but clean; tatty low ssn." ♦ 15 Jun-15 Sep. € 12.00   2004*

ARROMANCHES LES BAINS 3D1 (W Urban/ Coastal) Camp Municipal, Ave de Verdun, 14117 Arromanches-les-Bains [02 31 22 36 78; fax 02 31 21 80 22; campingarromanches@wanadoo. fr] App fr Bayeux on D516. Turn R on onto D65 on app to Arromanches to site on L. Med, pt sl, terr, pt shd; wc; shwrs inc; el pnts (10A) €3; gas; sand beach 500m; poss cr. "Conv Mulberry Harbour Exhibition & invasion beaches; close to town & rests; levelling blocks req most pitches; ground soft when wet; friendly warden." 1 Apr-3 Nov. € 13.00   2007*

ARROU 4F2 (Rural) Camp Municipal du Pont du Pierre, 28290 Arrou [02 37 97 02 13 (Mairie); fax 02 37 97 10 28] Take D15 fr Cloyes. Site sp in vill of Arrou. Med, hdg/mkd pitch, pt sl, unshd; wc; chem disp; shwrs €0.60; el pnts (6-10A) €2-3; lndry rm; supmkt nr; rest, bar, snacks in vill; BBQ; playgrnd; pool adj; fishing; lake, sand beach; tennis; horseriding; cycle hire; 10% statics; phone; adv bkg; quiet; CCI. "Well-kept, peaceful site; v friendly; gd rvside walks/cycle rides; poss local vill events adj." ♦ 1 May-30 Sep. € 4.60   2007*

ARTAIX see Marcigny 9A1

ARTEMARE see Virieu le Grand 9B3

ARZAL 2G3 (6km W Rural) Camping de Kernéjeune, 56190 Arzal [02 97 45 01 60 or 06 18 79 65 10 (mob); fax 02 97 45 05 42; contact@camping-de-kernejeune.com; www. camping-de-kernejeune.com] Fr E on N165 exit onto D139 sp Arzal. Opp town hall turn L sp Billiers & foll sp to site. Fr W on N165 exit onto D5 sp Billiers. Turn R at traff lts, site sp. Med, mkd pitch, pt shd; htd wc; shwrs; el pnts (6-10A) €2.60; lndtte; ice; shop; tradsmn; BBQ; playgrnd; htd pool high ssn; fishing; games area; entmnt; TV; 30% statics; dogs €1.50; phone; red low ssn; quiet. "Gd touring base for interesting area; helpful, friendly owners; rec." ♦ 1 Apr-1 Oct. € 12.00   2007*

ARZON 2G3 (Coastal) Camp Municipal de Port-Sable, Port Navalo, 56640 Arzon [02 97 53 71 98; fax 02 97 53 89 32; portsable@arzon.fr; www. arzon.fr] On L side of D780 that by-passes Arzon, foll black & white camping sps. Lge, pt sl; wc; shwrs €1.75; el pnts (6A) €2.30; gas; shops 800m; playgrnd; sand beach adj; fishing; sailing school; boat excursions; poss cr; quiet; red low ssn. "Gd beach for children; vg spacious site; gd facs & views." ♦ 1 Apr-15 Oct. € 18.45   2006*

ASCAIN see St Jean de Luz 8F1

ASCOU see Ax les Thermes 8G4

ASNIERES SUR OISE *3D3* (1km NE Rural) **Domaine Les Princes, Route des Princes, 95270 Asnières-sur-Oise [tel/fax 01 30 35 40 92; www.g4s@ residence2000.com]** Site sp fr D909, nr Abbaye de Royaumont. Med, hdg/mkd pitch, pt shd; htd wc; shwrs inc; el pnts (10A) €3.50; playgrnd; fishing 500m; games area, golf, horseriding nr; BBQ; 50% statics; adv bkg; quiet; red long stay. "Pleasant, attractive site; conv Parc Astérix & Paris." 1 Apr-31 Oct. € 13.00   2005*

ASPET *8G3* (Rural) **Camp Municipal Lè Cagire, 31160 Aspet [05 61 88 51 55; fax 05 61 88 44 03; camping.aspet@wanadoo.fr]** Exit A64 at junc 18 St Gaudens & take D5 S. In 14km, site sp on R in vill of Aspet. Sm, mkd pitch, shd; wc; chem disp (wc); shwrs; el pnts (5-10A) €1.70-4.50; lndtte; shop, rest, snacks, bar 500m; pool, tennis 300m; games area; dogs €0.50; quiet; adv bkg; CCI. "Pleasant site nr lively old sm town; rec arr bef 1800 hrs high ssn." 1 Apr-30 Sep. € 7.40   2006*

Before we move on, I'm going to fill in some site report forms and post them off to the editor, otherwise they won't arrive in time for the deadline at the end of September.

ASPRES SUR BUECH *9D3* (3km S) **Camping L'Adrech, Route de Sisteron, 05140 Aspres-sur-Buëch [04 92 58 60 45; fax 04 92 58 78 63; ladrech.camping@wanadoo.fr; http://camping. ladrech.chez-alice.fr]** Site on L of N75 fr Aspres. Med, hdg pitch, hdstg, pt sl, pt shd; wc; chem disp; shwrs; el pnts (3-10A) €2.50-6; gas; lndtte; ice; shop & 1km; tradsmn; snacks; BBQ; playgrnd; fishing; rv/ lake 5km; entmnt; 50% statics; dogs €1; phone; poss cr; Eng spkn; adv bkg; quiet; CCI. "Lge pitches; v helpful American owner; also poss open 21-31 Dec; unkempt & facs unclean Jul 2007; ltd facs low ssn; useful NH." 1 Mar-1 Nov. € 10.00   2007*

ASPRES SUR BUECH *9D3* (8km NW Rural) **FFCC Aire Naturelle La Source (Pardoe), 05140 St Pierre-d'Argençon [tel/fax 04 92 58 67 81; info@lasource-hautesalpes.com; www.lasource-hautesalpes.com]** Fr N75 at Aspres-sur-Buëch turn onto D993 dir Valence to St Pierre-d'Argençon; site sp. Or fr N on D93, cont onto D993 over Col de Cabre; site sp on L bef St Pierre-d'Argençon. Sm, mkd pitch, pt sl, pt shd; wc; chem disp; mv service pnt; shwrs inc; el pnts (10A) €2.50; lndtte; tradsmn; BBQ; playgrnd; dogs €1; adv bkg; quiet; cc acc; red long stay; CCI. "Lovely CL-type site in woodland or open field; lovely views; peace & quiet; v clean; helpful British owners; chambre d'hôte on site; beautiful area for walking, cycling, paragliding; watersports & fishing; highly rec." 15 Apr-15 Oct. € 9.00   2007*

ASSERAC *2G3* (5km NW Coastal) **Camping Le Moulin de l'Eclis, Pont Mahé, 44410 Assérac [02 40 01 76 69; fax 02 40 01 77 75; info@ camping-moulin-de-leclis.fr; www.camping-moulin-de-leclis.fr]** Fr D774 turn N onto D83 to Assérac. Take D82 two coast to Pont Mahé, site sp. Lge, hdg/mkd pitch, pt shd; wc; chem disp; mv service pnt; baby facs; shwrs inc; el pnts (4-10A) €2.80-4; lndtte; ice; shop high ssn; rest 100m; snacks; bar; BBQ (gas/elec only); playgrnd; htd, covrd pool; dir access to sand beach adj; watersports; sailing school; windsurfing; games area; cycle hire; entmnt; TV rm; 20% statics; dogs €2; phone; adv bkg; Eng spkn; quiet; cc acc; . "Excel family site; conv Guérande; vg touring base." ♦ 1 Apr-12 Nov. € 22.00   2006*

⊞**ATTICHY** *3C4* (Rural) **Camp Municipal Fleury, Rue de la Fontaine-Aubier, 60350 Attichy [03 44 42 15 97]** Fr Compiègne E on N31. After 16km turn L at traff lts sp Attichy & site. Over iron bdge & turn R to site on lakeside. Med, hdg pitch, pt shd; wc; chem disp; mv service pnt; shwrs €0.50; el pnts (10A) €2.30-3.50; shop 1km; tradsmn; rests in town; BBQ; playgrnd; fishing; 80% statics; poss cr; quiet; CCI. "Attractive site in pleasant vill; many w/e statics; few touring pitches; shut 1200-1430; facs stretched high ssn." € 7.30   2004*

ATTIGNY see Rethel *5C1*

ATUR see Périgueux *7C3*

AUBAS see Montignac *7C3*

AUBAZINES *7C3* (4km E Rural) **Camping Le Coiroux, Parc Touristique du Coiroux, 19190 Aubazines [05 55 27 21 96; fax 05 55 27 19 16; arepos.coiroux@wanadoo.fr; www.camping-coiroux.com or www.campeole.com]** Fr Brive-La-Gaillarde take N89 NE twd Tulle. At Cornil turn R onto D48 & foll sp. Site in 8km - long, fairly steep climb. Med, pt hdg/mkd pitch, pt shd; wc; chem disp; mv service pnt; shwrs inc; el pnts (5A) €3.40; gas; lndtte; shop; rest; snacks; bar; playgrnd; htd pool; lake sand beach & sw 300m; lake fishing & boating; tennis; golf; cycle hire; entmnt; child entmnt; TV rm; 50% statics; dogs €2.40; poss cr; Eng spkn; adv bkg; quiet; CCI. "Excel, wooded site." ♦ 14 Apr-1 Oct. € 17.20   2006*

AUBENAS *9D2* (3km N Rural) **Camping Domaine de Gil, Route de Vals-les-Bains, 07200 Ucel [04 75 94 63 63; fax 04 75 94 01 95; raf.garcia@ wanadoo.fr; www.domaine-de-gil.com]** Fr Aubenas NE on N304 to St Privat. Cross bdge over Rv Ardèche 1km. At Pont d'Ucel, turn L along D578 twds Ucel; site 3km on L. Med, hdg/ mkd pitch, pt shd; wc; chem disp; mv service pnt; serviced pitch; baby facs; shwrs inc; el pnts (6A) €3.70 (poss rev pol); lndtte; shop; tradsmn; rest; snacks; bar; playgrnd; htd pool; tennis; mini-golf; rv sw; canoeing; TV; entmnt; some statics; dogs €2.50; phone; adv bkg ess in Aug; quiet; red low ssn; cc acc; CCI. "Scenic area; v clean san facs; excel, family site." ♦ ltd. 16 Apr-18 Sep. € 25.00   2005*

AUBENAS *9D2* (7km E Rural) **Ludocamping, Route de Lavilledieu, 07170 Lussas [04 75 94 21 22; fax 04 75 88 60 60; ludocamping@infonie.fr; www. ludocamping.com]** SE fr Aubenas on N102 twd Montélimar. Turn L after 10km in vill Lavilledieu onto D224 sp Lussas. Site sp on R in 4km. Med, mkd pitch, terr, pt shd; wc; chem disp; shwrs inc; el pnts (6A) €3 (poss rev pol); gas; lndtte; ice; shop; rest in vill 600m; bar; playgrnd; htd pool; dogs €1.50; poss cr; Eng spkn; adv bkg; quiet. "Gd walking country; peaceful; facs poss stretched in high ssn; Dutch owned - all notices in Dutch only; excel." ♦ 1 Apr-15 Oct. € 25.00   2006*

AUBENAS *9D2* (2km SE) **Camping La Chareyrasse, Quartier St Pierre, 07200 Aubenas [04 75 35 14 59; fax 04 75 35 00 06; camping-la-chareyrasse@wanadoo.fr; www.camping-la-chareyrasse.com]** On app Aubenas on N102 take 1st turning on L after x-ing suspension bdge & foll sp. Site on R bank of Rv Ardèche, side rd clearly mkd. Narr app rd. Med, pt shd; wc; chem disp; shwrs; el pnts (10A) €3.90 inc; gas; ice; shop; snacks; bar; playgrnd; pool; tennis; TV; entmnt; dogs €1.50; quiet. "Pleasant site; excel clean san facs; watch herons etc in rv; absolutely delightful." 1 Apr-15 Sep. € 22.50   2006*

AUBENAS *9D2* (7km SE Rural) **Camping Les Rives d'Auzon, Route de St Germain, 07170 Lavilledieu [tel/fax 04 75 94 70 64; camping.lesrivesdauzon@ wanadoo.fr; www.camping-rivesdauzon.fr]** Fr Aubenas on N102 turn R immed after Lavilledieu, sp St Germain (D103) site on L. Sm, pt shd; wc (some cont); shwrs; el pnts (4-6A) lndry rm; ice; shop; rest; snacks; bar; playgrnd; pool; TV rm; entmnt; dogs; Eng spkn; adv bkg; some rd noise. "Friendly owner, beautiful location, poss diff for lge o'fits due trees; conv for exploring Ardèche." 1 Apr-15 Sep. € 18.00   2005*

> There aren't many sites open this early in the year. We'd better phone ahead to check that the one we're heading for is actually open.

AUBENAS *9D2* (8km SE Rural) **Camping à la Ferme Le Bardou (Boule), 07170 St Germain [tel/ fax 04 75 37 71 91; info@lebardou.com; www. lebardou.com]** On N102 Aubenas-Montélimar turn S at Lavilledieu on D103, site on L in 2km. Site ent fairly narr bet stone houses in St Germain. Med, unshd; wc (mainly cont); chem disp; shwrs inc; el pnts (6A) €2.80; shops 150m; pool; fishing adj; adv bkg; quiet. "Lovely views; helpful owners; pleasant site low ssn; clean, basic facs but poss inadequate high ssn." 1 Apr-1 Oct. € 12.00   2006*

AUBENAS *9D2* (3km S) **Camping Les Acacias, 07200 St Etienne-de-Fontbellon [04 75 93 67 87; fax 04 75 93 71 77; camping-les-acacias@ wanadoo.fr; http://campinglesacacias.monsite. wanadoo.fr]** Fr Aubenas travel thro cent of St Etienne. Turn 2nd R at rndabt S of Leclerc hypmkt & foll sps. Fr S turn off D104 N of Lachapelle to St Etienne. At next rndabt turn L & foll sp. Sm, mkd pitch, pt shd; wc (cont); chem disp; mv service pnt; baby facs; shwrs inc; el pnts (6A) €2.50; lndtte; ice; shops 1.5km; rest, snacks, bar high ssn; BBQ; playgrnd; pool; wifi internet; entmnt; dogs €0.70; Eng spkn; adv bkg; quiet; red low ssn; CCI. "Gd touring cent." 1 Apr-8 Oct. € 10.50   2007*

AUBENAS *9D2* (8km S Rural) **Camping Les Roches, 07200 Vogué [tel/fax 04 75 37 70 45; camping.les.roches@free.fr; www.campingles roches.fr]** Fr Aubenas take D104 S. Then L onto D579 to Vogué. Site on L 1.5km past Vogué - do not turn twd Vogué, but cont in dir Vogué Gare. Med, pt sl, shd; wc (most cont); mv service pnt; baby facs; shwrs inc; el pnts (6-10A) €3.80; lndtte; ice; shop; rest; snacks; bar; playgrnd; pool; tennis; games area; entmnt; TV; some statics; adv bkg; quiet. "Nice site; pitch yourself, warden calls; rests in old vill by rv." ♦ ltd. 28 Apr-2 Sep. € 19.50
                              2006*

AUBENAS *9D2* (10km S Rural) **Camping Les Peupliers, 07200 St Maurice-d'Ardèche [04 75 37 71 47; fax 04 75 37 70 83; girard.jean-jacques@club-internet.fr; www.campingpeupliers. com]** Fr Aubenas take D104 S twd Alès. In 2km, turn L onto D579 dir Vogué/Vallon Pont d'Arc. In 9km, pass L turn to Vogué. Immed after crossing rv, turn R at rndabt. Site on R in 300m, (2nd site of 3 on rd). Lge, mkd pitch, pt shd; wc (some cont); chem disp; mv service pnt; baby facs; shwrs inc; el pnts (6A) €3.85; gas; lndtte; ice; shop; rest; snacks; bar; BBQ; playgrnd; pool; rv sw & shgl beach adj; entmnt; some statics; dogs €1.40; phone; poss cr; adv bkg (dep & bkg fee); quiet; cc acc; CCI. "Gd touring base; access to rv for canoeing & fishing." 1 Apr-30 Sep. € 19.45   2007*

AUBENAS *9D2* (10km S Rural) **Domaine du Cros d'Auzon, 07200 St Maurice-d'Ardèche [04 75 37 75 86; fax 04 75 37 01 02; camping. auzon@wanadoo.fr; www.camping-cros-auzon. com]** Take D104 S fr Aubenas for 2km; at island turn L onto D579. After 9km, pass L turn to Vogué vill, cross rv & turn R immed. Site 600m on R, 1km fr Vogué stn. Lge, hdg/mkd pitch, pt shd; htd wc; chem disp; mv service pnt; serviced pitch; child/baby facs; shwrs inc; el pnts (4-6A) €4.20; gas; lndtte; ice; shop 1km; tradsmn; rest; snacks; bar; playgrnd; pool; waterslide; fishing; cycle hire; tennis; entmnt; games/TV rm; cinema; 70% statics; dogs €2.50; Eng spkn; adv bkg; quiet; red low ssn/long stay; cc acc; CCI. "Gd touring base; office open 0900-1200 & 1600-1900 high ssn, all other times check in at hotel at top of hill; poss long walk to shwrs; excel." ♦ 3 Apr-11 Sep. € 24.00   2006*

AUBENAS 9D2 (7km NW Rural) **Camp Municipal du Pont des Issoux, Allée de Vals, 07380 Lalevade-d'Ardèche [04 75 94 14 09 or 04 75 38 00 51 (Mairie); fax 04 75 94 01 92]** Fr Aubenas, N102 sp Mende & Le Puy-en-Velay; Lalevade in 10km; R in vill; well sp. Med, mkd pitch, pt shd; wc (mostly cont); chem disp (wc); shwrs inc; el pnts inc (poss rev pol); gas; lndtte; ice; supmkt adj; rest, snacks & bar 250m, playgrnd; lake sw & shgl beach adj; tennis & children's park nrby; dogs; bus 250m; poss cr; Eng spkn; adv bkg (dep req); quiet; CCI. "Quiet, shady beside Rv Ardèche; friendly, helpful warden; san facs dated but clean, poss scruffy low ssn; no twin-axles; many tatty statics; close to vill; conv touring base; nr Jaujac with interesting volcanic remains & gd mkt Tues am; vg." ♦ 1 Apr-15 Oct. € 13.50   2007*

AUBENCHEUL AU BAC 3B4 (500m E Rural) **FFCC Camping Les Colombes, Route de Fressies, 59265 Aubencheul-au-Bac [03 27 89 25 90; fax 03 27 94 58 11]** Fr S on N43 dir Douai, on ent vill of Aubencheul-au-Bac, turn R at camp sp onto D71, site on L down lane. Site app thro housing estate. Med, hdg pitch, pt shd; wc; chem disp; shwrs inc; el pnts (4-6A) €2-€3.45; ice; shops 1km; tradsmn; BBQ; playgrnd; lake fishing; 90% statics; dogs; poss cr; adv bkg; quiet; CCI. "V pretty, clean, tidy site; friendly & helpful staff; excel facs, poss stretched high ssn; ltd touring pitches; poss aircraft noise; gate locked 2200-0700." ♦ 1 Apr-31 Oct. € 12.20   2006*

AUBENCHEUL AU BAC 3B4 (2km W Rural) **Camping aux Roubaisiens, Rue de l'Abbeye, 62860 Oisy-le-Verger [03 21 59 51 54; pascallage@aol.com]** Fr Cambrai take N43 NW twd Douai. In 10km immed bef canal bdge turn L (W) twd Oisy-le-Verger. Go under rlwy bdge after 100m then R in 1km: cross canal & site on L in 200m. Sm, pt shd; wc; own san rec; chem disp; shwrs; el pnts (6A) €2; shop; fishing; 95% statics; quiet. "Run down, NH as last resort." 1 Apr-15 Oct. € 8.40   2006*

AUBERIVE 6F1 **Camp Municipal Les Charbonnières, 52160 Auberive [tel/fax 03 25 86 21 13 (Mairie)]** Leave A31 at junc 6 W twds Châtilion-sur-Seine on D428 for 12km, site on L bef vill. Site sp. Sm, mkd pitch, sl, pt shd; htd wc (some cont); chem disp (wc); shwrs inc; el pnts (6A) €1.60; lndry rm; shops in vill; rest in vill; playgrnd; phone; quiet; CCI. "Pleasant site in forestry area with gd walks; clean, well-maintained; site yourself; friendly warden calls; ltd el pnts; attractive vill adj; music festival in abbey early Jul; gd." 15 Apr-1 Oct. € 7.00   2006*

AUBERIVES SUR VAREZE 9B2 (8km E Rural) **FFCC Camping Le Bontemps, 38150 Vernioz [04 74 57 83 52; fax 04 74 57 83 70; info@campinglebontemps.com; www.campinglebontemps.com]** Take N7 S fr Vienne. After climbing hill & L bend, fork L at camping sp. Foll sps, thro Vernioz, site in approx 9km past Vernioz. Fr S, on N7 N of vill of Auberives R onto D37, site on R in 8km. Tight ent - rec swing wide. NB Also sp Hotel de Plein Air. Med, mkd pitch; terr, pt shd; wc; mc service pnt; shwrs inc; el pnts (6A) €3; lndtte; shop; rest; snacks; bar; playgrnd; pool; games area; kids club high ssn; wildlife sanctuary; 30% statics; dogs €2; adv bkg; quiet; CCI. "Attractive site with lovely trees; peaceful; excel sporting facs; twin-axles welcome; excel." ♦ 1 Apr-30 Sep. € 21.00   2007*

⊞**AUBERIVES SUR VAREZE** 9B2 (1km S Rural) **Camping des Nations, 38550 Clonas-sur-Varèze [04 74 84 95 13 or 04 74 84 97 17; fax 04 74 79 93 75; jacquet.g@wanadoo.fr]** S on W side of N7/E15 fr Vienne for 12km; site sp. Sm, hdg/mkd pitch, shd; htd wc; chem disp; shwrs inc; el pnts (5A) inc; tradsmn; rest nr; snacks & pool high ssn; quiet; adv bkg (ess high ssn); no cc acc; Eng spkn; CCI. "Useful transit site for Spain & Med; clean san facs; manager not always present; gd NH; rec." € 16.00   2006*

AUBETERRE SUR DRONNE 7C2 (200m Urban) **Camp Municipal, Route de Ribérac, 16390 Aubeterre-sur-Dronne [05 45 98 60 17 or 05 45 98 50 33 (Mairie); fax 05 45 98 57 82; mairie.aubeterre-sur-dronne@wanadoo.fr]** On D2 fr Chalais, take D17 around S end of town. Turn R over rv & site on R adj sports ground. Med, pt shd; wc (cont); chem disp (wc); shwrs inc; el pnts (6A) €2.20-2.40; shop 250m; rest in town; café 500m; bar; playgrnd; beach & rv sw adj; fishing & boating adj; tennis; cycle hire; dogs €0.20; poss cr; Eng spkn; quiet. "Excel site; gd for children; friendly staff; picturesque town; conv touring Périgord." 15 Jun-15 Sep. € 9.40   2005*

AUBIGNAN see Carpentras 10E2

AUBIGNY SUR NERE 4G3 (1.5km E Rural) **FLOWER Camping des Etangs, 18700 Aubigny-sur-Nère [02 48 58 02 37 or 02 48 81 50 07 (LS); fax 02 48 81 50 98; camping.aubigny@ orange.fr; www.aubigny-sur-nere.fr or www.flowercamping.com]** D940 fr Gien, turn E in vill of Aubigny onto D923, foll sp fr vill; site 1km on R by lake. Best to avoid town cent due congestion. Med, mkd pitch, pt shd; wc; chem disp; shwrs inc; el pnts (6-10A) €2.62-€4.51; ice; lndry rm; shop, rest & bar 1km; tradsmn; BBQ; playgrnd; fishing; 10% statics; dogs; phone; poss cr; adv bkg; quiet; 10% red CCI. "Excel, well-kept site with lake views; plenty to see & do locally; pretty vill; excel mkt Sat; gd value; plans for development (2008) with rest & statics." ♦ 1 Apr-30 Sep. € 13.90 (3 persons)   2006*

France

AUBURE see Ribeauville *6E3*

⊞**AUBUSSON** *7B4* (10km N Rural) **Camping La Perle (formerly Les Genêts), Fourneaux, 23200 St Médard-la-Rochette [05 55 83 01 25; fax 05 55 83 34 18; info@camping-laperle.nl; www. camping-laperle.nl]** On D942 N fr Aubusson dir Guéret; site on R bef Fourneaux. Sm, hdg/mkd pitch, some hdstg, terr, pt shd; wc; shwrs inc; el pnts (10A) inc; lndtte; shops 10km; tradsmn; rest; bar; BBQ; playgrnd; htd pool; cycle hire; wifi internet; TV rm; some statics; dogs; Eng spkn; adv bkg; quiet; red low ssn; CCl. "Tapestry museum in Aubusson & other historical attractions; vg site." € 18.50   2007*

AUBUSSON *7B4* (1.5km S Urban) **Camp Municipal La Croix Blanche, Route de Felletin, 23200 Aubusson [05 55 66 18 00]** Site on D982 on banks of Rv Creuse; sp fr all dir. Med, shd; wc (some cont); shwrs inc; el pnts (10A) €1.87; lndry rm; tradsmn; snacks; playgrnd; pool 1km; phone; adv bkg; quiet; CCl. "Vg site in pleasant location; excel shwrs; conv tapestry factories; easy walk town cent." 1 Apr-30 Sep. € 9.95   2007*

AUCH *8F3* (7km N Rural) **Camping Le Talouch, 32810 Roquelaure [05 62 65 52 43; fax 05 62 65 53 68; info@camping-talouch.com; www.camping-talouch.com]** Head W on N124 fr Auch, then N on D148 for 7km to site. Med, mkd pitch, pt shd; wc; chem disp; mv service pnt; shwrs; baby facs; el pnts (4-6A) €2.70-7.10; gas; lndtte; ice; shop; rest; snacks; bar; playgrnd; pool; paddling pool; tennis; golf driving range; games area; internet; entmnt; 25% statics; dogs €2.20; adv bkg; quiet; red low ssn; CCl. "Poss liable to flooding; gd walking & nature trails; friendly Dutch owners." ◆ 1 Apr-30 Sep. € 22.05 (CChq acc)   2006*

AUCH *8F3* (1.5km SW) **Camp Municipal d'Ile St Martin, Rue de Mouzon, Parc des Sports, 32000 Auch [05 62 05 00 22]** Fr S on N21 approx 750m after business area, turn R at traff lts into Rue Général de Gaulle which runs into Rue du Mouzon, site in 500m adj rv. NB There is also a Parc des Sports on N side of Auch. Med, hdg pitch, hdstg, shd; wc; shwrs inc; el pnts (6-10A) €2.30-4.60; shops 300m; pool 250m; few statics; poss cr; quiet but some rd noise. "Cathedral, ancient & modern architecture with museum in town; 10 min walk along rv to town; dated san facs; site not suitable for disabled with facs up stairs; rec arr bef 1700 recep & barrier clsd 1200-1400." 15 Apr-15 Oct. € 6.40   2006*

⊞**AUDENGE** *7D1* (1km E Rural) **Camping Le Braou, Route de Bordeaux, 33980 Audenge [tel/ fax 05 56 26 90 03; info@camping-audenge.com; www.camping-audenge.com]** SW fr Bordeaux turn R off N250 twd Andernos onto D3; at traff lts in Audenge turn R; site 750m on R. Lge, mkd pitch, pt shd; wc; mv service pnt; shwrs inc; el pnts (3A) €3.50; ice; lndtte; shops 1km; tradsmn; snacks; pool; beach 1.5km; cycle hire; games area; entmnt; some statics; dogs €3.50; bus 1km; quiet; CCl. ◆ ltd. € 16.50   2006*

> Did you know you can fill in site report forms on the Club's website – www.caravanclub.co.uk?

AUDENGE *7D1* (10km SE Urban) **Camp Municipal de l'Eyre, Allée de la Plage, 33380 Mios [05 56 26 42 04; fax 05 56 26 41 69]** Fr N or S on A63, join A660 sp Arcachon; leave at junc 1 to Mios. After vill turn L after traff lts (sm sp) bet tourist & post offices. Site adj Rv Eyre. Med, mkd pitch, pt shd; htd wc; shwrs inc; el pnts (5A) €3; lndtte; shop 500m; sports hall adj; canoe hire; cycle hire for adj rte; many statics; dogs €1.50; CCl. "Excel touring base; v helpful warden; ltd facs low ssn; park outside site to book in; phone ahead low ssn to check if open; san facs poss stretched if site full; poss noisy at night." ◆ 1 Apr-30 Oct. € 13.00   2006*

AUDENGE *7D1* (5km S) **Camping Marache, 25 Rue Gambetta, 33380 Biganos [05 57 70 61 19; fax 05 56 82 62 60; contact@marachevacances. com; www.marachevacances.com]** Exit A660 junc 2 sp Facture; take D3 dir Audenge, site clearly sp. NB Height restriction 2.6m in Facture, use ring rd. Med, mkd pitch, pt shd; wc; mv service pnt; baby facs; shwrs inc; el pnts (6A) €3.80; lndtte; ice; shops 1km; rest; snacks; playgrnd; htd pool; rv sw & fishing 1km; tennis 1km; entmnt; TV; dogs €3.50; adv bkg; quiet. "Pleasant management; twin-axles pay extra; basic facs, ltd low ssn; NH only." ◆ 1 Mar-31 Oct. € 20.50   2007*

AUDIERNE *2F1* (700m SE Coastal/Rural) **Camping Le Loquéran, Bois de Loquéran, 29770 Audierne [02 98 74 95 06; fax 02 98 74 91 14; campgite. loqueran@free.fr; http://campgite.loqueran.free. fr]** Fr Quimper on D784 thro Plozévet & Plouhinec dir Audierne. Look out for sm, yellow/purple camping sp on R, site 500m on L. Sm, mkd pitch, terr, pt shd; wc; chem disp; shwrs inc; el pnts (6A) €2; lndtte; ice; shop & 600m; playgrnd; beach 1km; dogs €1; cc acc; quiet; CCl. "Gd san facs; peaceful site." 15 May-30 Sep. € 10.50   2007*

AUDIERNE *2F1* (3km SE Coastal) **Camping de Kersiny, 1 Rue Nominoé, 29780 Plouhinec [02 98 70 82 44; mail@camping-kersiny.com; www.camping-kersiny.com]** Fr Audierne on D784 turn R at 2nd traff lts in Plouhinec, cont for 1km; turn L into Rue Nominoé (sp diff to see) for 100m. Or fr Quimper on D784 to Plouhinec, turn L at 1st traff lts & as bef. Med, hdg pitch, terr, pt shd; wc; chem disp; mv service pnt; shwrs; el pnts (8A) €2.60; gas; lndtte; ice; tradsmn high ssn; snacks; BBQ; playgrnd; direct access to beach; dogs €1.50; quiet; barrier clsd 2300-0730; CCI. "Beautiful location; gate to beach, friendly warden; gd." 1 Apr-30 Sep. € 12.50   2006*

AUDIERNE *2F1* (8km W Coastal) **Camp Municipal de Kermalero, 29770 Primelin [tel/ fax 02 98 74 84 75 or 02 98 74 81 19 (LS); campingkermalero@wanadoo.fr]** D784 Audierne-Pointe du Raz, after Ecomarché supmkt at Primelin turn L, site sp. Med, hdg pitch, terr, pt shd; wc; chem disp; mv service pnt; shwrs inc; el pnts (6A) €2.30; lndtte; supmkt 1km; tradsmn; playgrnd; games area; sand beach 1km; tennis; TV; 5% statics; quiet. "Gd outlook/views; helpful warden; pleasant site." ♦ 1 Mar-1 Dec. € 8.50   2005*

AUDRUICQ see Ardres *3A3*

AUGIGNAC see Nontron *7B3*

AUGIREIN *8G3* (S Rural) **Camping La Vie en Vert, 09800 Augirein [05 61 96 82 66; fax 05 61 04 73 00; daffis@lavieenvert.com; www. lavieenvert.com]** Fr St Girons on D618 twd Castillon. On app Castillon turn L foll sp to Luchon. 1km after vill Orgibet turn L into vill of Augirein. Site on L over bdge. Sm, hdg/mkd pitch, pt shd; wc; baby facs; shwrs inc; el pnts (3-10A) €2.50-5; lndtte; ice; shop; tradsmn; rest in vill; BBQ; playgrnd; dogs €1; Eng spkn; adv bkg; quiet; 5% red 5+ days; CCI. "Charming owners who own bar/café in vill; excel little site." ♦ 15 May-15 Sep. € 14.00   2006*

⊞**AULUS LES BAINS** *8G3* (NW Rural) **Camping Le Coulédous, 09140 Aulus-les-Bains [05 61 96 02 26; fax 05 61 96 06 74; couledous@ wanadoo.fr; www.couledous.com]** Take D618 fr St Girons. After 13km cross rv; turn R onto D3 sp Aulus-les-Bains. On app to Oust turn L onto D32, site approx 17km on R at ent to vill on rvside. Med, mkd pitch, hdstg, sl, pt shd; htd wc; chem disp; mv service pnt; shwrs inc; el pnts (6-10A) €4.30-6.30; lndtte; shop 500m; bar 300m, playgrnd; some statics; dogs €4; site clsd last week Nov & 1st week Dec; poss cr; Eng spkn; adv bkg; quiet; CCI. "Gd walking & skiing (16km); sm spa in vill; excel." ♦ € 18.00   2006*

AUMALE *3C3* (1km W) **Camp Municipal Le Grand Mail, 76390 Aumale [02 35 93 40 50; fax 02 35 93 86 79; communeaumale@wanadoo.fr; www.aumale.com]** Clearly sp in town; long steep climb to ent. Med, pt shd; wc; mv service pnt; shwrs €1.60; el pnts (6A) €2.10; lndtte; shops 1km; playgrnd; pool 1km; cycle hire €1; fishing 1km; dogs €1.10; noise fr rd. "Gd site; clean, modern san facs; conv Channel ports; set on valley side above town; gd range of shops in town; 500m walk up steep slope fr town to site." ♦ 14 Apr-30 Sep. € 7.90   2007*

AUNAC see Mansle *7B2*

AUNAY SUR ODON see Villers Bocage *3D1*

AUPS *10E3* (500m W Rural) **International Camping, Route de Fox-Amphoux, 83630 Aups [04 94 70 06 80; fax 04 94 70 10 51; info@internationalcamping-aups.com; www. internationalcamping-aups.com]** Site on L on D60 nr vill cent. Lge, hdg/mkd pitch, pt shd; wc (few cont); chem disp; shwrs inc; el pnts (16A) €4.90; lndtte; shop; tradsmn; snacks & rest high ssn; bar; pool; tennis; games rm; disco; entmnt; many statics; dogs €1; Eng spkn; rec adv bkg high ssn; quiet; cc acc; red low ssn. "Beautiful area; nice site; gd rest; lge pitches; 10 min walk fr town." 1 Apr-30 Sep. € 17.80   2007*

AUPS *10E3* (1km W Rural) **Camping St Lazare, Route de Moissac, 83630 Aups [04 94 70 12 86; fax 04 94 70 01 55]** NW fr Aups twd Régusse on D9, site sp. Med, pt sl, pt shd, hdg/mkd pitch; wc; chem disp; shwrs inc; el pnts (10A) €3; gas; ice; lndtte; shop 1.5km; snacks; pool; playgrnd; dogs €2; phone; TV; entmnts; mountain bike hire; 10% statics; adv bkg rec; CCI. "Excel touring base; vg quiet site." 1 Apr-30 Sep. € 11.00   2005*

AURAY *2F3* (5km SE Coastal) **Camp Municipal Kergouguec, 56400 Plougoumelen [02 97 57 88 74]** Site is S of N165, 13km W of Vannes; sp fr vill sq 500m S on R, nr stadium. Med, pt sl, pt shd; wc (some cont); chem disp; shwrs; el pnts (6A) €2.40; ice; playgrnd; beach & windsurfing 300m; tennis; dogs €1.20; adv bkg; quiet; CCI. "Gd tour base, well-run site." ♦ 15 Jun-15 Sep. € 6.50

2005*

AURAY *2F3* (7km SE Rural) **Aire Naturelle La Fontaine du Hallate (Le Gloanic), La Hallate, 56400 Plougoumelen [02 97 57 84 12; clegloanic@ campinghallate.com; www.campinghallate.com]** Fr N165 Vannes-Lorient, turn S onto D101E to Plougoumelen; watch for sp after Plougoumelen; site in La Hallate. Narr, bumpy app rd. Sm, hdg/mkd pitch, pt sl, pt shd; shwrs inc; el pnts (6A) €2 (rev pol); lndtte; shops 2km; playgrnd; golf/tennis adj; 2% statics; dogs €1; phone; adv bkg ess Jul/Aug; CCI. "Gd alternative to lge/noisier sites; gd coast paths; conv local boat trips & Ste Anne d'Auray; vg." 1 Apr-30 Sep. € 9.00   2007*

AURAY 2F3 (5km S Rural) **FFCC Camping du Parc-Lann, Le Varquez, 56400 Le Bono [02 97 57 93 93 or 02 97 57 83 91; campingduparclann@wanadoo.fr; www.auray-tourisme.com]** S fr Auray on D101 sp Le Bono. Site well sp in Le Bono. Turn R after church; site in 600m after end vill sp on D101E. Med,hdg/mkd pitch, unshd; wc; chem disp; mv service pnt; shwrs inc; el pnts (6A) €2.10; lndtte; shop 2km; tradsm; rest; bar; playgrnd; pool 5km; sand beach 9km; dogs €0.60; phone; Eng spkn; adv bkg; quiet; red low ssn; CCI. "Excel rural site; gd, clean san facs poss stretched high ssn; flat site in pretty area, nr rv & sea; ltd facs low ssn & warden only on site 1800-1900; gd walking." ♦ 30 Mar-30 Sep. € 12.60   2007*

AURAY 2F3 (7km SW) **FFCC Camping Le Kergo, 56400 Ploemel [tel/fax 02 97 56 80 66; campingdekergo@wanadoo.fr]** Fr Auray take D768 SW sp Carnac. After 4km turn NW on D186 twd Ploemel & foll sp. Med, mkd pitch, pt shd; wc; chem disp; shwrs inc; el pnts (6-10A) inc; lndtte; shops 2km; tradsmn; playgrnd; sand beach 5km; dogs €0.70; some statics; adv bkg rec high ssn; red low ssn/CCI. "Lovely, peaceful site, lots of trees; excel san facs, ltd low ssn." ♦ ltd. 1 May-30 Sep. € 15.40   2007*

⊞**AURAY** 2F3 (8km W) **FFCC Camping Le St Laurent, Kergonvo, 56400 Ploemel [tel/fax 02 97 56 85 90; camping.saint.laurent@wanadoo.fr; www.ploemel.com]** Fr Auray on D22 twd Belz/Etel; after 8km turn L on D186 to Ploemel & site on L in 200m. Med, some hdstg, shd; wc; chem disp; mv service pnt; baby facs; shwrs inc; el pnts (10A) €2.30; lndtte; shop & 3km; rest; bar; BBQ; playgrnd; htd pool; sand beach 6km; dogs €0.80; adv bkg; quiet. "Peaceful site; friendly staff; red facs low ssn." € 12.60   2006*

AUREILHAN see Mimizan 7D1

AURIBEAU SUR SIAGNE see Grasse 10E4

AURILLAC 7C4 (2km NE) **Camp Municipal de l'Ombrade, Chemin du Gué Bouliaga, 15000 Aurillac [tel/fax 04 71 48 28 87]** Take D17 N fr Aurillac twd Puy Mary; site on banks of Rv Jordanne. Well sp fr town. Lge, mkd pitch, pt shd; wc; shwrs inc; el pnts (10A) inc; lndry rm; ice; shops adj; TV & games rm; poss cr; quiet. "Well-managed site; generous pitches; facs clean but some need refurb; poss not well-kept low ssn; rec arr early high ssn; interesting lge mkt town with gd rests in walking dist." ♦ ltd. 1 Jul-30 Aug. € 9.80
                           2006*

AURILLAC 7C4 (2km S Urban) **Camp Municipal de la Cère, Rue Félix Ramond, 15130 Arpajon-sur-Cère [tel/fax 04 71 64 55 07; sebastienpradel@yahoo.fr]** Fr Rodez take D920 twd Aurillac. Site sp 2km bef Aurillac on S side of Arpajon. Med, hdg pitch, pt shd; wc; shwrs inc; el pnts (10A) €2; gas; lndtte; shops adj; pool 4km; rv fishing adj; beach 20km; sports facs adj; golf 5km; adv bkg; some rd noise; cc acc; CCI. "Pleasant site in pretty area; public access to site - not secure; generous pitches." ♦ ltd. 1 Jun-30 Sep. € 11.00   2006*

AUSSOIS see Modane 9C4

⊞**AUTERIVE** 8F3 (1km S Rural) **Camp Municipal du Ramier, Allée Ramier, 31190 Auterive [05 61 50 65 73 or 05 61 08 33 98]** Turn E off N20, cross rv bdge & immed turn R. Site on R in 1km. Sm, pt shd; wc (some cont); shwrs; el pnts (6A) €3.50; shop 1km; pool adj; tennis; rv fishing; many statics; quiet but poss noise fr disco. "Recep 0800-1030 & 1700-2000; phone & space found even when 'Complet' sign up; rec arr by 1730; fair NH." € 14.00   2007*

⊞**AUTERIVE** 8F3 (7km NW Rural) **Camp Municipal Le Ramier, 31810 Vernet [05 61 08 33 98 or 05 61 08 50 47 (Mairie)]** Site at S exit of Vernet, sp fr N20 Toulouse-Pamiers rd. Med, shd; wc (some cont); chem disp; shwrs; el pnts (5A); shops adj; quiet. "Conv NH for Andorra; nice location by rv." 2005*

AUTHUILLE see Albert 3B3

AUTRANS 9C3 (E Rural) **Camping au Joyeux Réveil, Le Château, 38880 Autrans [04 76 95 33 44; fax 04 76 95 72 98; camping-au-joyeux-reveil@wanadoo.fr; www.camping-au-joyeux-reveil.fr]** Fr Villard-de-Lans take D531 to Lans-en-Vercors & turn L onto D106 to Autrans. On E side of vill site sp at 1st rndabt. NB App on D531 fr W fr Pont-en-Royans not rec - v narr rd & low tunnels. Med, mkd pitch, pt sl, pt shd; htd wc; chem disp; mv service pnt; baby facs; shwrs inc; el pnts (2-10A) €3.50-8; gas; lndtte; ice; shop 300m; tradsmn; rest 100m; snacks; bar; BBQ; playgrnd; htd pool & paddling pool; waterslide; rv fishing; tennis 300m; cycle hire; golf 20km; games area; TV rm; cab TV to pitches; 60% statics; dogs; bus 300m; phone; quiet; adv bkg; Eng spkn; red low ssn; cc acc; CCI. "Site in Vercors National Park with excel views; winter sport facs, 1050m altitude; modern san facs; excel." ♦ ltd. 1 Dec-30 Sep. € 30.00 (CChq acc)   2007*

AUTRECHE 4G2 **FFCC Camp Municipal de l'Etang, Rue du Général de Gaulle, 37110 Autrèche [02 47 29 59 64 or 02 47 56 22 03 (Mairie)]** Exit A10 junc 18 onto D31 S to Autrèche, turn L into vill for 600m, site sp. Sm, unshd; wc (cont for men); shwrs inc; el pnts inc; playgrnd; tennis; poss cr; quiet; CCI. "Useful/vg NH fr m'way." 1 May-25 Sep. € 7.60   2007*

AUTUN 6H1 (1km N Urban) **Camp Municipal de la Porte d'Arroux, Les Chaumottes, 71400 Autun [03 85 52 10 82; fax 03 85 52 88 56; contact@ camping-autun.com; www.camping-autun.com]** Foll sp fr town on D980 to Saulieu & site on L; only site in Autun. Med, some hdg pitch, some hdstg, pt shd; wc (some cont); mv service pnt; baby facs; shwrs inc; el pnts (6A) €2.95; (poss rev pol); gas high ssn; lndry rm; ice; shop; snacks; rest high ssn; playgrnd; rv sw & fishing; dogs €1.30; phone; Eng spkn; adv bkg; noisy nr rest; cc acc; CCI. "Lovely, quiet, clean site; friendly, helpful staff; sm pitches; no twin-axles; v muddy when wet; gd access to facs in town, inc 2 excel pools (1 covrd); perfect medieval architecture & Roman walls around town - nice views fr some pitches; mkt Wed/Fri; gd rest." 1 Apr-31 Oct. € 13.65   2007*

AUVERS SUR OISE see Pontoise 3D3

AUXERRE 4F4 (3km SE Urban) **Camp Municipal, 8 Rue de Vaux, 89000 Auxerre [03 86 52 11 15; fax 03 86 51 17 54; camping.mairie@auxerre.com]** Exit A6 at Auxerre; at junc N6 ring rd foll sp Vaux & Stadium; site sp by Rv Yonne. Or fr N6 (N) take ring rd, site/stadium sp. Site also well sp fr town cent. Lge, mkd pitch, pt shd; wc; chem disp; mv service pnt; shwrs inc; el pnts (6A) €2.45 (long lead poss req); lndtte; ice; shop; supmkt 400m; bar/café; playgrnd; pool 250m; fishing 300m; TV; 10% statics; dogs; adv bkg; quiet; cc acc; CCI. "Lge pitches; friendly staff; town in walking dist; poss cr & noisy during football ssn; site poss flooded stormy weather; c'vans over 5m not allowed; ltd el pnts for site size; no vehicles 2200-0700; popular NH." 15 Apr-30 Sep. € 8.65   2007*

AUXERRE 4F4 (10km S) **Camping Les Ceriselles, Route de Vincelottes, 89290 Vincelles [tel/fax 03 86 42 39 39; lesceriselles@wanadoo.fr; www. campingceriselles.com]** Leave A6 at Auxerre Sud. Fr Auxerre, take N6 S twd Avallon. 10km fr Auxerre turn L into vill. In 400m immed after 'Maxi Marche', turn L into site access rd, sp as Camping/Base de Loisirs. Site is approx 16km fr a'route exit. Med, mkd pitch, some hdstg, pt shd; htd wc; chem disp; mv service pnt; shwrs inc; el pnts (6-10A) €1-3 (poss rev pol); gas adj; lndtte; ice; sm supmkt adj; tradsmn; rest; snacks; takeaway; bar; BBQ; playgrnd; rv sw adj; cycle hire; TV rm; 10% statics; dogs €1.50; phone; no twin-axles; poss cr; some Eng spkn; adv bkg; quiet but noise fr N6; red long stay/low ssn; CCI. "Excel site by canal in lovely countryside; friendly & helpful owner; gd facs poss stretched high ssn & ltd low ssn; gd cycle tracks; cycle along canal to Auxerre; highly rec." ♦ 1 Apr-30 Sep. € 14.00   2007*

AUXI LE CHATEAU 3B3 (Urban) **Camp Municipal des Peupliers, Rue de Cheval, 62390 Auxi-le-Château [03 21 41 10 79]** Take D928 S fr Hesdin. In 11km take D119 to Auxi-le-Château. Fr Doullens-Abbeville rd D925, turn N onto D933 at Bernaville to Auxi-le-Château, then take D938 twds Crécy, site sp on R in 300m by football stadium. Med, hdg pitch; unshd wc; chem disp; shwrs inc; el pnts (3-6A) €1.50-2.50; lndtte; ice; shops, rest, snacks, bar 500m; playgrnd; fishing; sailing; dir access to rv; 80% statics; poss cr; adv bkg; quiet. 1 Apr-30 Sep. € 7.10   2004*

⊞**AUXONNE** 6G1 (Urban) **Camping L'Arquebuse, Route d'Athée, 21130 Auxonne [03 80 31 06 89; fax 03 80 31 13 62; camping.arquebuse@ wanadoo.fr; www.campingarquebuse.com]** On D905 (N5) Dijon-Geneva, site sp on L bef bdge at ent to Auxonne. Med, pt shd; htd wc (some cont); chem disp; mv service pnt; shwrs inc; el pnts (10A) €3.50; gas; lndry rm; shop 500m; rest; snacks; bar; playgrnd; htd pool adj; rv sw; fishing; sailing; windsurfing; entmnt; wifi internet; TV rm; 20% statics; dogs €1.50; adv bkg; quiet at night but poss noisy during day; clsd 2200-0700; CCI. "Site beside rv; sh walk to interesting town." € 11.90   2007*

AVAILLES LIMOUZINE see Pressac 7A3

AVALLON 4G4 (2km SE) **Camp Municipal Sous Roches, 89200 Avallon [tel/fax 03 86 34 10 39; campingsousroche@ville-avallon.fr]** App town fr a'route or fr SE on N6. Turn sharp L at 2nd traff lts in town cent, L in 2km at sp Vallée du Cousin (bef bdge), site 250m on L. If app fr S care needed when turning R after bdge. Med, some hdstg pitches, terr, pt shd; wc; mv service pnt; shwrs inc; el pnts (9A) €3; ice; lndry rm; shop; tradsmn (to order); BBQ; playgrnd; pool 1km; rv sw & fishing adj; dogs; phone adj; Eng spkn; CCI. "Popular, cheerful site; helpful staff; modern san facs; conv Morvan National Park; poss flood warning after heavy rain; no twin-axles or o'fits over 2,500kg." ♦ 15 Mar-15 Oct. € 10.00   2006*

AVANTON see Poitiers 7A2

AVESNES SUR HELPE 3B4 (300m S Urban) **Camp Municipal Le Champs de Mars/La Rotonde, Rue Léo Legrange, 59440 Avesnes-sur-Helpe [tel/fax 03 27 57 99 04]** On SE edge of town. Sp fr all dir. Sm, pt sl, pt shd; htd wc (some cont); shwrs inc; el pnts (6A) €2 (poss rev pol); lndry rm; shop 500m; tennis; fishing adj; adv bkg; quiet, but some rlwy noise & noise fr peacock!; CCI. "Clean, neat site; well-kept facs; gd facs for disabled; conv Belgian ports." ♦ 15 Apr-30 Sep. € 15.00   2007*

France

AVIGNON *10E2* (2km N Urban) **Camp Municipal La Laune, Chemin St Honoré, 30400 Villeneuve-lès-Avignon [04 90 25 76 06 or 04 90 25 61 33; fax 04 90 25 91 55; campingdelalaune@wanadoo.fr; www.cyber-villeneuvelezavignon.com/camping]** Fr Avignon, take N100 twd Nîmes over rv bdge. At W end of 2nd part of rv bdge, turn R onto N980 sp Villeneuve-lès-Avignon. Site is 3km on R just past old walled town battlements on L. Adj sports complex. Med, hdg/mkd pitch, hdstg, shd; wc; chem disp; mv service pnt; shwrs inc; el pnts (6A) €3 (poss rev pol); lndtte; shop; snacks; bar; pool & sports complex adj (free to campers); dogs €0.90; phone; bus; Eng spkn; quiet but some rlwy noise; cc acc; CCI. "Lovely site; gd, v clean facs; helpful staff; excel security; excel local mkt; Villeneuve lovely vill in walking dist; monuments & museum; sports facs adj; gd walks/cycle rides; rec." ♦ ltd. 1 Apr-15 Oct. € 14.00   2007*

AVIGNON *10E2* (4km NE) **Camping du Grand Bois, Quartier La Tapy, 84130 Le Pontet [04 90 31 37 44; fax 04 90 31 46 53]** Exit A7/E714 at junc 23 onto D53 S. Site in approx 1km on R, sp. Med, hdg pitch, pt shd; wc; chem disp; shwrs inc; el pnts (5A) €2.50; lndtte; shop; hypmkt 3km; tradsmn; rest; snacks; playgrnd; cycle hire; TV; dogs €1.50; phone; Eng spkn; adv bkg; quiet; cc acc; CCI. "Superb location; plenty of rm; family-run alt to main Avignon sites; ltd facs; v helpful staff; insects a problem." ♦ 1 May-15 Sep. € 18.00   2005*

AVIGNON *10E2* (9km NE Rural) **FFCC Camping Flory, Route d'Entraigues, 84270 Vedène [04 90 31 00 51; fax 04 90 23 46 19; infos@campingflory.com; www.campingflory.com]** Nr junc of m'way & D942. After exit m'way NE on D942 twd Carpentras. In 3km foll sp on R for Camping Flory. Med, mkd pitch, pt sl, pt shd; wc (some cont); chem disp; shwrs inc; el pnts (10A) €4 (poss rev pol); gas; ice; lndtte; shop & 1km; tradsmn; rest & 3km; snacks; bar & 3km; playgrnd; pool (high ssn); dogs €2.50; phone; 15% statics; poss cr; quiet; adv bkg; Eng spkn; 10% red low ssn; CCI. "Conv touring base Vaucluse; uneven pitches & paths (2007); facs poss stretched high ssn & ltd low ssn; lovely pool." ♦ 15 Mar-30 Sep. € 18.00   2007*

AVIGNON *10E2* (8km S Urban) **Camping de la Roquette, 746 Ave Jean Mermoz, 13160 Châteaurenard [tel/fax 04 90 94 46 81; contact@camping-la-roquette.com; www.camping-la-roquette.com]** Exit A7/N7 Avignon S to Noves; take D28 to Châteaurenard 4km; foll sp to site & Piscine Olympic/Complex Sportiv. Poss awkward access/exit lge o'fits. Med, hdg/mkd pitch, pt shd; wc; chem disp; some serviced pitches; mv service pnt; baby facs; shwrs inc; el pnts (6A) €2.80; lndtte; ice; shops 1.5km; tradsmn; rest; snacks; bar; playgrnd; pool; paddling pool; tennis; dogs €1; phone; TV; Eng spkn; adv bkg rec; quiet but some rd noise; 5% red 30+ days; cc acc; CCI. "Gd touring cent; owners v kind, friendly & helpful; v clean facs; gd walks." ♦ ltd. 1 Mar-31 Oct. € 14.20   2006*

This guide relies on site report forms submitted by caravanners like us; we'll do our bit and tell the editor what we think of the campsites we've visited.

⊞**AVIGNON** *10E2* (12km W Rural) **Camping Le Bois des Ecureuils, Plateau de Signargues, 30390 Domazan [tel/fax 04 66 57 10 03; infos@boisdesecureuils.com; www.boisdesecureuils.com]** Exit A9/E15 at Remoulins junc 23 twd Avignon on N100. Site on R in 6km. Fr S on N7 foll sp for Nîmes onto N100. Go over 2 lge rndabts, site about 6km on L - need to ent R filter rd to turn safely across traff. Sm, mkd pitch, all hdstg, shd; wc (some cont); chem disp (wc); baby facs; shwrs inc; el pnts (6A) inc; gas; lndtte; lndry area; ice; shop; rest adj; snacks; bar high ssn; BBQ; playgrnd; htd pool; entmnt; TV; 5% statics; dogs; phone; poss cr; Eng spkn; adv bkg (rec high ssn); quiet but some rd noise; red low ssn CCI. "Ideal for touring Avignon & Pont du Gard; friendly owners; spotless facs; steel awning pegs ess; many long-stay residents low ssn." € 18.00   2005*

⊞AVIGNON *10E2* (500m NW Urban) **FFCC Camping Bagatelle, Ile de la Barthelasse, 84000 Avignon** [04 90 86 30 39; fax 04 90 27 16 23; camping. bagatelle@wanadoo.fr; www.camping bagatelle. com] Exit A7 at Avignon Nord. After passing end of old bdge bear L, then onto new Daladier bdge & take immed R turn over bdge foll sp to Barthelasse & Villeneuve-lès-Avignon. Caution - do not foll Nîmes sp at more southerly bdge (Pont d'Europe). Lge, mkd pitch, pt shd; htd wc; mv service pnt; baby facs; shwrs inc; el pnts (6A) €2.60; gas; lndtte; shop; rest; pool 100m; playgrnd; entmnt; TV; boating; fishing; tennis 2km; games area; TV rm; dogs €2.20; some traffic noise at night; cc acc; red CCI. "V helpful staff; on bank of Rv Rhône; sm pitches; sh walk to town, also free ferry; site is low lying & poss damp; poss unkempt low ssn; poss o'night tented school parties; facs dated but clean; facs ltd low ssn; narr rds on site, suggest find pitch bef driving in; if recep unmanned, go to bar or supmkt to check in; poor security." ♦ € 18.62   2007*

As soon as we get home I'm going to post all these site report forms to the editor for inclusion in next year's guide. I don't want to miss the September deadline.

AVIGNON *10E2* (1km NW Urban) **Camping du Pont d'Avignon, 10 Chemin de la Barthelasse, Ile de la Barthelasse, 84200 Avignon** [04 90 80 63 50; fax 04 90 85 22 12; info@ camping-avignon.com; www.camping-avignon. com] Exit A7 junc 23 Avignon Nord dir Avignon Centre (D225) then Villeneuve-les-Avignon. Go round & under Pont d'Avignon; then cross rv dir Villeneuve, Ile de la Barthelasse. Turn R onto Ile de la Barthelasse. Lge, hdg/mkd pitch, mostly shd; wc; chem disp; mv service pnt; shwrs inc; el pnts (6-10A) €2.60; gas; lndtte; shop; rest; snacks; bar; BBQ; cooking facs; playgrnd; pool; paddling pool; tennis; rv adj; games area; games rm; entmnt; internet; TV; statics (sep area); dogs €2.15; phone; car wash; poss cr; Eng spkn; adv bkg ess high ssn; quiet but some rd/rlwy noise; red low ssn/7+ days; cc acc; CCI. "Superb, well-managed site; welcoming; floodlit at night; excel, clean facs but dated; some pitches high kerbs & poss cramped; poss flooded low ssn; extra for c'vans over 5.50m; Avignon festival Jul/Aug; many places of interest; magnificent views city & bdge; free ferry to city; best site for Avignon (20 mins walk); gd pool & rest; highly rec." ♦ ltd. 19 Mar-27 Oct. € 21.90 (CChq acc)   2007*

See advertisement

AVIGNON *10E2* (5km NW Rural) **Camping L'Ile des Papes, Quartier I'Islon, 30400 Villeneuve-lès-Avignon** [04 90 15 15 90; fax 04 90 15 15 91; cpliledespapes@atciat.com; www.avignon-camping.com or www.campeole.com] Fr A9 exit sp Roquemaure; head S on D980. Site adj to rv 2km NW of city. Fr A7 exit Avignon Nord, twds Avignon cent & cross bdge twds Villeneuve. Turn off after x-ing rv before x-ing canal. Site bet rv & canal. Lge, pt shd; wc; shwrs; el pnts (6A) €4; ice; lndtte; cooking facs; rest; supmkt; playgrnd; pool; mini-golf; archery; lake fishing adj; hiking; entmt; TV; statics 35%; dogs €3.50; adv bkg; quiet but some rlwy noise; Eng spkn; red low ssn; cc acc; red CCI. "Lovely area; well-run site; pleasant staff; lge pitches; excel disabled facs & access to pool; gd rest on site; office clsd 1230-1430." ♦ 31 Mar-3 Nov. € 25.10   2007*

AVRANCHES *2E4* (6km S Rural) **Camping Rural Avallonn (Martinet), La Caufetière, 50220 Céaux** [02 33 68 39 47] Fr Avranches on N175 exit La Buvette & W onto D43. Site in approx 2km. Sm, pt shd; wc; shwrs inc; el pnts inc; rest; snacks; sand beach 20km; Eng spkn; adv bkg; quiet. "In sm apple orchard; v helpful owner; rm for 3 c'vans; goats & horses in pens on site; 10km fr Mont St Michel; many activities, museums nrby; steep & narr ent but gd NH." ♦ 7 Jul-25 Aug. € 15.00   2005*

AVRANCHES *2E4* (10km W Rural) **Camping Les Coques d'Or, Route du Bec-d'Andaine, 50530 Genêts** [02 33 70 82 57 or 06 85 21 13 01 (mob LS); fax 02 33 70 86 83; information@campinglescoquesdor.com; www. campinglescoquesdor.com] Fr Avranches foll Granville rd. In 1km L on N911 sp Vains to Genêts. D35E for 500m & site on R. Med, hdg/mkd pitch, pt shd; wc; shwrs inc; el pnts (3-10A) €2-4; lndtte; shops 1km; tradsmn; snacks; bar; playgrnd; sm pool; sand beach 800m; fishing; TV rm; entmnt; 80% statics (sep area); dogs €2; poss cr; Eng spkn; quiet; red low ssn. "Gd views Mont St Michel nrby." ♦ ltd. 1 Apr-30 Sep. € 14.80   2007*

AVRANCHES *2E4* (10km W Rural) **FFCC Camping La Pérame, 50530 Genêts** [02 33 70 82 49] Fr Avranches on N176; in 1km L on D911 thro Genêts. Turn R onto D35 immed after passing thro Genêts, site on R in 1km. Sm, pt shd; wc; shwrs inc; el pnts (10A) €2.50 (rev pol); tradsmn; farm produce; playgrnd; 60% statics; dogs €0.70; phone; poss cr; red low ssn; quiet; CCI. "CL-type site in apple orchard; v pleasant owner; gd views of Mont St Michel fr vill; poss ltd & unkempt low ssn; guided walks to Mont St Michel; rec." 1 Apr-31 Oct. € 10.60   2006*

France

AVRANCHES *2E4* (10km NW Rural) **Camping Le Montviron, La Mésangère, 50530 Montviron [02 33 60 43 26 or 02 33 58 67 02 (LS); lemontviron@aol.com]** Exit N175 sp Granville. On D973 fr Avranches, in 6km turn R sp Montviron. In vill turn L sp Sartilly. Site in 2km on L. Well sp. Sm, hdg pitch, pt shd; wc; some serviced pitches; chem disp; shwrs inc; el pnts (6A) €2; gas; lndtte; shops 500m; tradsmn; snacks; bar; playgrnd; sand beach 10km; golf; TV rm; 95% statics; poss cr; Eng spkn; adv bkg; quiet; CCI. "Gd 1st stop fr pm ferry Cherbourg or Le Havre; friendly staff; basic facs; poss tight pitches; wonderful rest nrby; conv Granville & Mont St Michel; useful NH." ♦ ltd. Easter-30 Sep. € 12.00   2007*

AVRILLE *7A1* (1km E) **Camping Le Beauchêne, Ave du Maréchal de Lattre de Tassigny, 85440 Avrillé [02 51 22 30 49 or 02 51 90 35 97; fax 02 51 90 39 31; www.lebeauchene.com]** On E o'skts of Avrillé, on D949, visible fr rd. Med, mkd pitch, shd, wc; chem disp; shwrs inc; el pnts (6A) inc; ice; lndtte; shops 300m; tradsmn; rest adj; playgrnd; htd pool; sand beach 9km; dogs €1.50; TV rm; poss cr; adv bkg; CCI. "Friendly helpful owners; simple, roomy with gd facs." ♦ Easter-30 Sep. € 14.20   2004*

AVRILLE *7A1* (1km S Rural) **Camping Les Mancellières, Route de Longeville-sur-Mer, 85440 Avrillé [02 51 90 35 97; fax 02 51 90 39 31; camping.mancellieres@tiscali.fr; www.lesmancellieres.com]** Fr Avrillé take D105 S twd Longeville-sur-Mer. Site on L in 1.5km. Med, hdg/mkd pitch, pt sl; wc (some cont); chem disp; baby facs; shwrs inc; el pnts (6A) inc; gas; lndtte; ice; shop; snacks; BBQ (charcoal/gas); playgrnd; htd pool; waterslide; beach 5km; watersports 5km; fishing 2km; tennis 800m; cycle hire, horseriding 3km; games rm; entmnt; 30% statics; recep 0900-1200 & 1400-2000; dogs €1.90; some Eng spkn; adv bkg; quiet; 30% red low ssn; cc not acc. "Friendly owners; peaceful; ent gates set on angle & poss diff lge o'fits." ♦ 1 May-15 Sep. € 18.70   2005*

⊞**AX LES THERMES** *8G4* (2km NE Rural) **FFCC Camp Municipal La Prade, 09110 Sorgeat [05 61 64 36 34 or 05 61 64 21 93; fax 05 61 64 63 38; mairie.sorgeat@wanadoo.fr; www.sorgeat.com]** In cent of Ax-les-Thermes turn E off N20 onto D613. In 5km in Sorgeat turn R & foll sp thro vill to site, 800m on R. Sm, hdg/mkd pitch, terr, pt shd; htd wc (some cont); chem disp; shwrs inc; el pnts (5-10A) €2.70-5.20; gas 5km; lndtte; ice; shop 1km; rest 5km; snacks; playgrnd; pool 5km; 15% statics; dogs €0.60; phone; poss cr; adv bkg; quiet; cc not acc; CCI. "V clean; site is 1,150m high overlooking Ariège valley; ski lifts at Ax; gd walks; not suitable for lge o'fits." € 9.40   2005*

⊞**AX LES THERMES** *8G4* (7km E Rural) **FFCC Camping Ascou La Forge, 09110 Ascou [05 61 64 60 03; fax 05 61 64 60 06; mountain. sports@wanadoo.fr; www.mountain-sports. net]** On N20 S turn L at rndabt by church in Ax sp Ascou. In 4km turn R sp Ascou-Pailhères. Foll site sp to site on R in 3km after lake & hamlet Goulours. Rd narr & mountainous, not rec med/lge o'fits. Sm, mkd pitch, pt sl, pt shd; wc; chem disp; shwrs inc; el pnts (4-10A) €3-5; lndtte; shop & 7km; tradsmn; bar; playgrnd; fishing; entmnt; poss €1.50; adv bkg; CCI. "Beautiful mountain scenery; simple, immac facs; gd walking; friendly, v helpful owners." ♦ € 15.50   2007*

⊞**AX LES THERMES** *8G4* (4km SE Rural) **Camp Municipal d'Orlu, 09110 Orlu [05 61 64 30 09 or 05 61 64 21 70; fax 05 61 64 64 23]** On N20 S foll sp for Spain thro town cent. On exit town turn L immed bef bdge sp Orlu. Site on R in 3km. Med, mkd pitch, pt shd; htd wc; shwrs inc; el pnts (2-10A) €1.85-5.30; gas; lndtte; shop 3km; rest, snacks, bar 500m; playgrnd; pool high ssn; rv adj; fishing; games area; entmnt; 30% statics; dogs €0.95; phone; poss cr; adv bkg; quiet; CCI. "Gd, friendly site; surrounded by beautiful mountain scenery; poss floods in bad weather; excel walks; conv Andorra or Spain." ♦ € 10.80   2006*

⊞**AX LES THERMES** *8G4* (1km NW Rural) **Camping Sunêlia Le Malazeou, 09110 Ax-les-Thermes [05 61 64 69 14; fax 05 61 64 05 60; camping. malazeou@wanadoo.fr; www.campingmalazeou. com]** Sp on N20 to Foix. Lge, hdg pitch, pt sl, shd; htd wc (some cont); chem disp; mv service pnt; baby facs; shwrs inc; el pnts (10A) €1.10; gas; lndry rm; ice; shop 1km; tradsmn; playgrnd; 70% statics; dogs €2; train 500m; site clsd Nov; Eng spkn; adv bkg; quiet but some rd noise; CCI. "Fair NH; lovely scenery & gd fishing; rvside walk to town." ♦ ltd. € 21.00   2006*

⊞**AX LES THERMES** *8G4* (8km NW Rural) **Camp Municipal Le Castella, 09250 Luzenac [05 61 64 47 53; fax 05 61 64 40 59; campingcastella@wanadoo.fr; www.campingcastella.com]** Site on W of N20 bet Ax-les-Thermes & Foix. Med, mkd pitch, terr, pt shd; htd wc; shwrs inc; el pnts (4-10A) €2.05-5.20; ice; lndtte; shop, bar 300m; playgrnd; pool in ssn; fishing; tennis; archery; entmnt; quiet; cc acc. "Gd walking; prehistoric caves at Niaux; mountain views; barrier locked until 0900 when office opens." ♦ € 8.95   2007*

AXAT *8G4* (2km E Rural) **Camping La Crémade, 11140 Axat [tel/fax 04 68 20 50 64]** S fr Quillan on N117, cont 1km beyond junc with N118 twd Perpignan. Turn R into site, sp, narr access. Med, hdg pitch, pt sl, pt shd; wc; shwrs inc; el pnts (6A) inc; lndtte; shop & 3km; 5% statics; dogs €1; Eng spkn; adv bkg; quiet; CCI. "Pleasant, well-maintained site in beautiful location; few level pitches." ♦ Easter-30 Sep. € 12.00   2004*

AYDAT *9B1* (Rural) **Camping du Lac d'Aydat** (formerly Camping Les Chadelas), Forêt du Lot, 63970 Aydat [04 73 79 38 09; fax 04 73 79 34 12; info@camping-lac-aydat.com; www.camping-lac-aydat.com] Exit A75 S fr Clermont-Ferrand at junc 5 onto D13 W. Foll sp Lake Aydat. At x-rds at end of Rouillat Bas, turn L at rndabt & foll site sp. Med, mkd pitch, some hdstg, terr, shd; wc (some cont); chem disp; mv service pnt; serviced pitches; shwrs inc; el pnts (10A) €4; lndtte; shop 1km; tradsmn high ssn; rest 500m; snacks; bar 500m; playgrnd; lake sw 500m; fishing; entmnt; 30% statics; dogs €1.50; phone; poss cr; adv bkg; quiet; red low ssn; CCI. "On shore of Lake Aydat; quiet out of ssn but used as base for field work; gd rest by lake; gd for m'vans." ♦ 1 Apr-30 Sep. € 16.00 2007*

AYDAT *9B1* (3km W Rural) **Camping Les Volcans, La Garandie,** 63970 Aydat [tel/fax 04 73 79 33 90; keith_harvey@compuserve.com] Exit A73 junc 5 onto D213 W. In 16km turn S in Verneuge onto D5. After 2km turn W onto D788 sp La Garandie. In vill turn R just after phone box, site on L in 200m. Sm, mkd pitch, pt sl, pt shd; wc; chem disp; shwrs inc; el pnts (4A) inc; lndtte; ice; sm shop; tradsmn; rest, snacks 4km; bar 3km; lake sw & sand beach 4km; dogs €0.60; phone adj; adv bkg; quiet. "Excel walking & cycle rtes nr; relaxing site; lge pitches; beautiful area; gd touring base." 1 Jun-31 Aug. € 11.20 2005*

AZAY LE FERRON *4H2* (Urban) **Camp Municipal Le Camp du Château, Rue Hersent-Luzarche,** 36290 Azay-le-Ferron [02 54 39 21 91 (Mairie)] D975 Châtillon-sur-Indre to Le Bland rd, turn R in vill onto D925, site on R in 100m. Sm, pt shd; wc (some cont); shwrs inc; el pnts (10A) inc; shops 100m; rest; playgrnd; tennis; fishing; mini-golf; quiet. "Warden calls pm; casino & supmkt adj; san facs refurb planned for 2006 ssn." 1 Apr-1 Oct. € 8.00 2005*

AZAY LE RIDEAU *4G1* (300m N Urban) **FFCC Camp Municipal Le Sabot, Rue du Stade,** 37190 Azay-le-Rideau [02 47 45 42 72 or 02 47 45 42 11 (Mairie); fax 02 47 45 49 11; camping.lesabot@wanadoo.fr] Fr town cent foll D84 (N bank of rv) sp Artannes. After chateau on R, cont to mini rndabt & turn sharp R. Parked cars hide ent to site. Lge, mkd pitch, pt shd; wc (some cont); chem disp; mv service pnt; shwrs inc; el pnts (10A) €3.20 (poss rev pol); gas 1km; ice; shop, snacks, rest in town; BBQ; htd pool adj; playgrnd; fishing; boat & canoe hire; TV; phone; dogs; poss cr fr Son et Lumière in high ssn; Eng spkn; adv bkg rec; quiet, 10-15% red 14-30+ days; cc acc; CCI. "Well-kept, pleasant site by rv & chateau; recep open 0800-1200 & 1330-1930; security system; €20 deposit barrier pass; poss long dist to facs fr some pitches - central facs have steps; red facs low ssn; site prone to flooding; when site clsd m'vans can stay on car park by rv o'night - no facs but well lit (enq at tourist office)." ♦ 15 Apr-2 Oct. € 9.90 2007*

AZAY SUR THOUET see Parthenay *4H1*

AZUR see Soustons *8E1*

BACCARAT *6E2* (1km SE Rural) **Camp Municipal Pré de Hon,** 54120 Baccarat [03 83 75 10 46; fax 03 83 75 36 76] Fr Baccarat take D158 S twd Lachapelle & foll sp Tourist Office past church. Turn L after rv bdge at rndabt, site on L after 500m. Sm, pt shd, wc; chem disp; shwrs; el pnts (10A); shop 200m; pool nr; bus 400m; poss cr; adv bkg; quiet, some rd noise; CCI. "Pleasant, quiet rvside site; if warden absent site yourself; interesting town with crystal factory; gd NH." ♦ ltd. 15 May-15 Sep. € 7.00 2005*

BADEN *2F3* (SW Rural) **Camping Mané Guernehué, 52 Rue Mané er Groëz,** 56870 Baden [02 97 57 02 06; fax 02 97 57 15 43; info@camping-baden.com; www.camping-baden.com] Exit N165 sp Arradon/L'Ile aux Moines onto D101 to Baden (10km). In Baden vill turn R at camp sp immed after sharp L-hand bend. After 200m bear R at junc. Site on R, sp at both ends of vill. Lge, hdg/mkd pitch, terr, pt shd; htd wc; chem disp; mv service pnt; sauna; baby facs; shwrs inc; el pnts (10A) €4.60; gas 1km; lndtte; ice; shop; rest; snacks; bar; BBQ; playgrnd; htd pool complex; waterslide; jacuzzi; sand beach 3km; fishing; tennis 600m; fitness rm; games area; games rm; cycle hire; golf 1.5km; internet; entmnt; TV rm; 35% statics; dogs €3.80; phone; Eng spkn; quiet; cc acc; red long stay. "Vg, mature, v pleasant site; lge pitches; gd views; san facs excel." ♦ 5 Apr-30 Sep. € 39.00 (CChq acc) 2007*

See advertisement on next page

BAERENTHAL *5D3* (Rural) **Camp Municipal Ramstein-Plage, Rue de Ramstein,** 57230 Baerenthal [03 87 96 50 73; fax 03 87 06 50 26; camping.ramstein@wanadoo.fr; www.baerenthal.eu] Fr N62 turn onto D36 sp Baerenthal, site sp on lakeside. Lge, hdg/mkd pitch, pt sl, pt shd; htd wc; chem disp; mv service pnt; baby facs; shwrs inc; el pts (12A) €4.20; lndtte; shop 1km; rest; snacks; bar; playgrnd; htd pool; lake sw, sand beach adj; tennis; games area; entmnt; 60% statics (sep area); dogs €1.10; m'van o'night area; poss cr; Eng spkn; adv bkg; quiet. "Attractive location in important ecological area; generous pitch size; excel clean, modern san facs; gd walks; birdwatching; conv Maginot Line; excel." ♦ ltd. 1 Apr-30 Sep. € 17.10 2007*

BAGNEAUX SUR LOING see Nemours *4F3*

France

Situated in a 10 hectares wooded park
During the season: rental of chalets, cottages and mobile homes
Year-round: rental of gîtes

Mané Guernehué
CAMPING ★★★★
Golfe du Morbihan

52 Rue Mané Er Groëz - 56870 BADEN
Tél. 33 (0)2 97 57 02 06
Fax 33 (0)2 97 57 15 43
www.camping-baden.com
E mail : info@camping-baden.com

INDOOR SWIMMING POOL COMPLEX

Morbihan

BAGNERES DE BIGORRE *8F2* (9km NE Rural) **Aire Naturelle Le Cerf Volant (Dhom), 7 Cami de la Géline, 65380 Orincles [tel/fax 05 62 42 99 32; lecerfvolant1@yahoo.fr]** Fr Bagnères-de-Bigorre on D935; turn L onto D397 dir Lourdes; site on L opp D407. Single track app rd for 150m. Sm, pt shd; wc (cont); chem disp; shwrs inc; el pnts (15A) €1.50; lndtte; tradsmn; playgrnd; no statics; dogs free; poss cr; no cc acc; CCI. "Farm site - farm produce sold Jul-Aug; conv Lourdes & touring Pyrenees gd."♦ 15 May-15 Oct. € 6.70   2007*

⊞**BAGNERES DE BIGORRE** *8F2* (7km S) **Camping Le Layris, Quartier Bourg, 65710 Campan [05 62 91 75 34; lelayris@campan-pyrenees. com]** Fr A64 or Tarbes avoid D935 by taking D938 to Bagnères. Fr Bagnères, take D935 S, site on R after ent to Campan, sp. Sm, mkd pitch, pt shd; htd wc (cont); chem disp; shwrs inc; el pnts (2-10A) €2.15-6.10; lndtte; shops adj; playgrnd; pool 5km; fishing; tennis adj; wintersports 12km; dogs €1; poss cr; adv bkg; quiet; CCI. "Gd site for walkers. " € 10.70   2004*

BAGNERES DE BIGORRE *8F2* (1km E Urban) **Camping Les Fruitiers, 91 Route de Toulouse, 65200 Bagnères-de-Bigorre [tel/fax 05 62 95 25 97; daniellevillemur@wanadoo.fr]** On D938 fr town cent dir Toulouse. Site sp at traff lits at x-rds with D8. Site well sp on app; take care on final app to ent. Med, mkd pitch, pt sl, pt shd; htd wc; chem disp; baby facs; shwrs inc; el pnts (2-6A) €2-5; lndtte; ice; shops 500m; rest 300m; snacks 200m; playgrnd; pool 200m; tennis; dogs €0.80; phone; bus; poss cr; adv bkg; quiet/some traff noise; red low ssn; CCI. "Attractive town; well-kept site; excel facs; helpful warden; sharp bends on site rds & overhanging trees poss diff lge o'fits." ♦ 1 May-30 Oct. € 13.30   2005*

The opening dates and prices on this campsite have changed. I'll send a site report form to the editor for the next edition of the guide.

⊞**BAGNERES DE BIGORRE** *8F2* (3km E Urban) **Camping Le Monloo, Quartier Monloo, 65200 Bagnères-de-Bigorre [tel/fax 05 62 95 19 65; www.lemonloo.com]** Fr A64 exit junc 14 onto D20/D938 to Bagnères-de-Bigorre. At traff lts on ent turn R onto D8, site on R in 1km, sp at ent. Med, sl, pt shd; wc; chem disp; mv service pnt; shwrs inc; el pnts (2-6A) €2-5.50; lndtte; shop 1km; playgrnd; pool (high ssn); waterslide; tennis; TV; entmnt; 30% statics; phone; dogs €0.90; adv bkg; quiet; cc acc; CCI. "Friendly, welcoming patron; tidy, clean site; gd facs, poss stretched high ssn; spacious, tidy & peaceful site away fr rds; pleasant town." € 16.50 (3 persons)   2007*

BAGNOLES DE L'ORNE *4E1* (3km SE Rural) **Camping Le Clos Normand, Route de Bagnoles de l'Orne, 61410 Couterne [02 33 37 92 43 or 06 07 17 44 94 (mob); www.camping-clos-normand.fr]** On D916 approx midway bet Couterne & La Ferté Macé; well sp. Med, hdg/mkd pitch, pt sl, shd; wc; chem disp; shwrs inc; el pnts (5-10A) €2.55-3.40; gas; lndtte; ice; shops 2km; tradsmn; rest, bar 2km; snacks; BBQ; playgrnd; canoeing; entmnt; TV; 20% statics; dogs €0.53; phone; Eng spkn; adv bkg; some rd noise. "Attractive, well-maintained, friendly site; san facs in need of updating; in National Park Normandie-Maine; gd walks; poss long stay workers on site; close to thermal spa & excel sports facs, boating lake & casino; I hour fr car ferry." 1 May-30 Sep. € 7.60   2007*

BAGNOLES DE L'ORNE *4E1* (1.3km SW Rural) Camping de la Vée, Rue du President Coty, 61140 Bagnoles-de-l'Orne [02 33 37 87 45; fax 02 33 30 14 32; camping-de-la-vee@wanadoo.fr; www.bagnoles-de-lorne.com] Access fr D335 in vill of Tessé-la-Madeleine. Or fr La Ferté-Macé on D916 for 6km sp Couterne. Well sp fr all dirs. Lge, hdg/mkd pitch, pt shd; htd wc (some cont); chem disp; mv service pnt; baby facs; shwrs inc; el pnts (6A) €3.15 (poss rev pol); gas 1km; lndtte; ice; shop 1km; tradsmn; rest; snacks; bar; BBQ; playgrnd; htd pool 1.5km; rv & lake nrby; golf, archery, tennis & minigolf nrby; TV; 10% statics; dogs €1.35; phone; free bus to town cent at site ent; poss cr; Eng spkn; no adv bkg; quiet; no cc acc; CCI. "Excel site; vg, clean, refurbished facs; beautiful thermal spa town; excel situation; forest walks." ♦ 10 Mar-27 Oct. € 9.80 2007*

See advertisement below

BAGNOLS SUR CEZE *10E2* (1.5km N Rural) Camping La Coquille, Route de Carmignan, 30200 Bagnols-sur-Cèze [04 66 89 03 05; fax 04 66 89 86 86; jose.gimeno@free.fr; http://campinglacoquille.free.fr] Head N fr Bagnols-sur-Cèze over rv bdge turn R at Total stn, site 2km on RH side. Sm, pt shd; wc (cont); chem disp; shwrs inc; el pnts (3A); inc; gas in town; ice; lndtte; rest; shop 2.5km; pool; canoe hire; fishing; dogs; adv bkg rec high ssn; CCI. "Site under military aircraft flightpath, otherwise gd, friendly, family-run site." Easter-15 Sep. € 21.00 2004*

BAGNOLS SUR CEZE *10E2* (2km NE Rural) Camping Les Genêts d'Or, Route de Carmigan, 30200 Bagnols-sur-Cèze [tel/fax 04 66 89 58 67; info@camping.genets-dor.com; www.camping-genets-dor.com] N fr Bagnols on N86 over rv bdge, turn R into D360 immed after Total stn. Foll sp to site on rv. Med, pt sl, pt shd; wc (some cont); shwrs inc; el pnts (3-8A) €2.86-3.70 (rev pol); gas; lndtte; shop; rest; snacks; bar; pool; playgrnd; sports area; canoeing, fishing 2km; games rm; no dogs Jul/Aug; poss cr; Eng spkn; adv bkg ess; quiet; cc acc. "Excel, v clean site; welcoming Dutch owners; nice pool; wildlife in rv; gd rest; highly rec." ♦ 1 Apr-30 Sep. € 21.20 2006*

⊞**BAGNOLS SUR CEZE** *10E2* (7km S Rural) Camping Le Vieux Verger, Ave des Platanes, 30330 Connaux [04 66 82 91 62; fax 04 66 82 60 02; campinglevieuxverger@wanadoo. fr; www.levieuxverger.fr.st] S fr Bagnols-sur-Cèze on D6086 (N86) to Connaux. Look for green site sp 1km after turn. Med, hdg/mkd pitch, pt sl, terr, pt shd; wc; shwrs; el pnts (10A) inc; lndtte; shop; rest; snacks; bar; playgrnd; 2 htd pools; 25% statics; dogs €1.50; poss cr; adv bkg; quiet. "Excel san facs." ♦ € 17.50 2007*

BAGNOLS SUR CEZE *10E2* (8km NW Rural) Camping Les Cascades, 30210 La Roque-sur-Cèze [04 66 82 72 97; fax 04 66 82 68 51; info@campinglescascades.com; www.campingles cascades.com] Fr Bagnols take D6 W twd Alès. After 4km turn N on D143 & foll sp to La Roque-sur-Cèze. Site on R in 7km. App fr N not rec. Long narr bdge (2.3m). Med, pt sl, pt shd; wc (cont); chem disp; shwrs inc; el pnts (6-10A) €3.30-3.50; gas; lndtte; ice; shop; rest; snacks; bar; playgrnd; pool; shgl beach & rv sw adj; tennis; fishing; boating; mini-golf; internet; entmnt; TV; dogs €1.50; poss cr; adv bkg; quiet. "Tranquil site; poss ltd facs when full." 1 Jan-15 Oct. € 17.80 2007*

BAGUER PICAN see Dol de Bretagne *2E4*

BAIGNES STE RADEGONDE *7B2* (500m SW Rural) Camp Municipal, Le Plein, 16360 Baignes-Ste-Radegonde [05 45 78 79 96 or 05 45 78 40 04 (Mairie); fax 05 45 78 47 41; point.i.baignes@orange.fr; www.baignes-sainte-radegonde.fr] Fr N10 turn W onto D2 to Baignes; site well sp on rvside. Sm, pt shd; wc; chem disp; shwrs inc; el pnts (5A) €1.80; shops 100m; tennis; adv bkg; cc acc. "Warden calls pm; v attractive sm town; quiet; gd." 1 May-30 Aug. € 6.20 2007*

France

Camping de la Vée ★★★

Situated between Paris and Brittany, at approx. 55 miles from the Mont Saint Michel and the landing beaches, in the heart of the Normandy, in green surroundings, with casino, golf, swimming pool, tennis, horseback riding, come and discover the charm of the countryside and the untouched magic of a 19th century touristic and thermal region. Open: April till October

250 pitches on offer.
F-61140 BAGNOLES DE L'ORNE
Phone : +33(0) 233 378 745
Fax : +33(0) 233 301 432
Booking of season : +33(0) 233 307 878
camping-de-la-vee@wanadoo.fr
www.bagnoles-de-lorne.com

BAILLEUL 3A3 (3km N Rural) **Camping Les Saules** (Notteau), 453 Route du Mont Noir, 59270 Bailleul [03 28 49 13 75] N fr Lille on A25 exit junc 10 & head N on D10 to Bailleul. In town at traff lts turn R onto D23/N375. After 2km just bef Belgian border turn L onto D223. Site on L in 300m. Sm, hdstg, pt shd; wc; chem disp; shwrs inc; el pnts (6A) €3; lndtte; sm shop; BBQ; playgrnd; 90% statics; dogs; Eng spkn; quiet; CCI. "Clean, modern san facs; friendly owner; visits to WW1 sites & Ypres; conv Calais & Dunkirk." 1 Apr-31 Oct. € 9.30   2007*

BAILLEUL 3A3 (4km N Rural) **Camping Domaine de la Sablière**, Mont-Noir, 59270 St Jans-Cappel [03 28 49 46 34; fax 03 28 42 62 90] Fr A25 exit junc 10, N on D10 thro Bailleul to St Jans-Cappel. Thro vill turn R at x-rds onto D318 to Mont-Noir. Site on R at top of hill. Med, hdg/mkd pitch, terr, shd; wc; chem disp; some serviced pitches; shwrs inc; el pnts (6A) €3; lndtte; shop, rest & bar 3km; bar; playgrnd; fishing 2km; tennis; mini-golf 100m; 80% statics; phone. "Well-kept site; v clean san facs; pitch access poss diff lge o'fits due steep gradients & tight turns; conv WW1 battlefields; conv Dunkirk & Calais; gd." 15 Mar-15 Oct. € 11.00
                                                                   2007*

BAILLEUL 3A3 (8km NE Rural) **Camping Les 5 Chemins Verts**, 689 Rue des 5 Chemins Verts, 59299 Boeschepe [tel/fax 03 28 49 42 37; christianne.degroote@wanadoo.fr] Fr N exit A25 junc 13 onto D948 W; in 5km turn R onto D10 to Boeschepe; turn R in vill. Or fr S exit A25 at Bailleul; N onto D10 to Boeschepe; turn L in vill. Site sp. Med, pt sl, pt shd; wc (some cont); chem disp; fam bthrm; shwrs inc; gas; el pnts (10A) inc; gas; lndtte; ice; tradsmn; rest; snacks; bar; BBQ; playgrnd; games area; games rm; entmnt; child entmnt; 98% statics; dogs; phone; some Eng spkn; adv bkg; cc acc; CCI. "Well-kept gardens; just a few touring pitches; san facs dated but clean; fishing in pond with ducks; v narr app rds, not suitable lge o'fits; conv WWI sites; gd." ♦ ltd. 15 Mar-31 Oct. € 11.00   2007*

BAIN DE BRETAGNE 2F4 (1km SE Urban) **Camp Municipal du Lac**, Route de Launay, 35470 Bain-de-Bretagne [02 99 43 85 67 or 02 99 43 70 24 (Mairie)] Take N772 E fr Bain-de-Bretagne twd Châteaubriant, foll sp. Site on R 300m down sm rd. Med, hdg/mkd pitch, pt shd; wc; chem disp; shwrs inc; el pnts (10A) inc; shop 1km; tradsmn; rest; snacks; bar; playgrnd; htd pool 500m; lake sw; sailing school nr; statics; phone; poss cr; Eng spkn; quiet; CCI. "Fees collected each eve, go to bar/café if gates locked on arr or phone warden on number displayed at office; poor facs; poss itinerants; attractive sm town; many leisure facs within walking dist; excel value; nice outlook; NH only." 1 Apr-30 Oct. € 8.20   2006*

BAIN DE BRETAGNE 2F4 (11km W Rural) **Camp Municipal, Rue de Camping**, 35480 Guipry [02 99 34 72 90 (Mairie) or 02 99 34 28 26] W fr Bain-de-Bretagne on D772, cross bdge at Messac. Under rlwy bdge, sharp 1st L bef Netto g'ge. Site sp bef ent Guipry. Do not app after dark as rv is at end of app rd. Med, hdg/mkd pitch, pt shd; wc; mv service pnt; shwrs; el pnts (8A) €2.20; rest nrby; shops 250m; lndry rm; playgrnd; pool nrby; fishing; rv walks; cycle paths; train noise; CCI. "Cruising & hire boats avail; warden on duty am & late pm; barrier 1.90m locked at times but phone for help or go to pitch 30; friendly, terrific value & clean; gd supmkt 1km." Apr-1 Sep. € 6.50   2004*

BAINS LES BAINS 6F2 (1km N) **Camping Les Pins**, Rue des Creuses, 88240 Bains-les-Bains [03 29 36 33 51 or 03 29 36 20 49] Fr Neufchâteau on D164, 1st L on ent town by ancient wash house. Ent on L in 400m. Fr S site sp fr town cent. Med, pt shd; wc; shwrs; el pnts (5-10A) €2.20-2.30; rest, snacks, bar 1km; playgrnd; rv & fishing, golf, tennis 2km; dogs €1; quiet. "Fair sh stay; pleasant." 1 May-25 Oct. € 8.00   2004*

BAINS LES BAINS 6F2 (9km SW Rural) **Camping Le Fontenoy**, Route de la Vierge, 88240 Fontenoy-le-Château [03 29 36 34 74 or 03 29 30 43 88; fax 03 29 36 37 26; marliesfontenoy@hotmail. com] SE fr Bains-les-Bains, D434 to Fontenoy-le-Château (6km). In cent of vill turn L onto D40 for 2km to site. Med, mkd pitch, pt shd; wc; chem disp; shwrs inc, el pnts (4-11A) inc; lndtte; ice; tradsmn; rest; snacks; bar; playgrnd; pool 5km; 10% statics; dogs €0.60; poss cr; Eng spkn; adv bkg (dep & €15.20 bkg fee); quiet, cc not acc; red long stay; CCI. "Attractive, country site; lovely area; v tired facs; sh stay only." 15 Apr-30 Sep. € 12.80   2005*

BAIX 9D2 (Rural) **Camping Le Merle Roux**, 07210 Baix [04 75 85 84 14; fax 04 75 85 83 07; lemerleroux@hotmail.com; www.lemerleroux. com] Fr A7/E15 exit junc 16. Foll sp Le Pouzin, x-ing Rv Rhône. Turn L onto N86 (S), go thro Le Pouzin, in 2km immed bef rlwy x-ing, turn R twd Privas; in 500m turn L at sp & foll rd approx 2km. Med, pt sl, terr, pt shd; wc; chem disp; shwrs inc; el pnts (4A); lndtte; shop; tradsmn; rest; snacks; bar; pool; playgrnd; 15% statics; adv bkg; quiet; CCI. "V helpful Dutch owners; gd site rest; excel." 1 Apr-30 Sep.   2005*

BALARUC LES BAINS see Sète 10F1

BALAZUC 9D2 (1km N Rural) **FFCC Camping La Falaise**, Hameau Les Silles, 07120 Balazuc [tel/fax 04 75 37 72 33 or 04 75 37 74 27; camping. falaise@wanadoo.fr] Sp on D579 on rvside. Sm, hdg pitch, pt sl, shd; wc; chem disp; baby facs; shwrs inc; el pnts (6A); lndtte; shop; tradsmn; snacks; bar; playgrnd; rv beach; canoe hire; poss cr; Eng spkn; adv bkg; CCI. "Site beside Rv Arèche; v helpful owners; vg." 1 Apr-30 Sep. € 15.00
                                                                   2006*

BALAZUC *9D2* (2km N Rural) **Camping Le Chamadou, Mas de Chaussy, 07120 Balazuc [04 75 37 00 56; fax 04 75 37 70 61; infos@ camping-le-chamadou.com; www.camping-le-chamadou.com]** Fr Ruoms foll D579 dir Aubenas. After approx 9km turn R under viaduct, site sp. Keep R up narr rd to site. App recep on foot fr car pk. Med, hdg pitch, hdstg, pt sl, pt shd; htd wc; chem disp; baby facs; fam bthrm; shwrs inc; el pnts (5A) €4 (some rev pol); lndtte; ice; shop & 3km; tradsmn; snacks; bar; BBQ; playgrnd; pool; rv sw & beach 1.5km; canoe & kayak hire; entmnt; TV rm; dogs €1.80; phone; poss cr; Eng spkn; adv bkg rec (dep req); v quiet; cc acc; CCI. "Excel, well-run, family site; superb panoramic views; most pitches v spacious." 1 Apr-30 Sep. € 18.50 2006*

BALBIGNY *9B1* (3km NW Rural) **Camping La Route Bleue, Route du Lac de Villerest, 42510 Balbigny [04 77 27 24 97; fax 04 77 28 18 05; camping.balbigny@wanadoo.fr; www. laroutebleu.com]** Fr N on D1082 (N82), take 1st R after a'route (A89/72) junc N of Balbigny onto D56. Fr S on D1082, turn L at RH bend on N o'skirts of Balbigny, D56, sp Lac de Villerest & St Georges-de-Baroille. Well sp. Med, some hdg pitch, pt sl, pt shd; chem disp; mv service pnt; wc; shwrs inc; el pnts (6-10A) €2.80-3.20; lndtte; ice; shops 1.5km; tradsmn; rest; snacks; bar; playgrnd; pool & paddling pool; rv sw adj; fishing; games rm; sports complex adj; adv bkg; quiet; red long stay; cc acc; CCI. "Excel site on rv bank; conv for A72; helpful & welcoming staff; extra for twin-axle vans." ♦ ltd. 15 Mar-30 Sep. € 9.90 2005*

BALLEROY *1D4* (5km SW Rural) **Camping L'Orée du Bois, 14490 Litteau [02 31 22 22 08 or 06 62 54 47 22 (mob); fax 02 31 21 85 65; camping.loreedubois@wanadoo.fr]** Fr St Lô, take D972 to Bayeux. After 14km, at La Malbreche, turn R onto D209 to Litteau. Site on L in approx 500m. Sm, some hdg/mkd pitch, pt sl, unshd; wc; chem disp (wc); baby facs; shwrs inc; el pnts (6A) €2.80; lndtte; ice; shop & 4km; bar; playgrnd; htd pool; lake fishing adj; sand beach 25km; horseriding; dogs €2; adv bkg; quiet; CCI. "Forest adj; conv for D-Day beaches & museums & Bayeux tapestry." 1 Apr-5 Nov. € 12.60 2005*

BANDOL *10F3* (6km NW) **Camping Le Clos Ste Thérèse, Route de Bandol, 83270 St Cyr-sur-Mer [tel/fax 04 94 32 12 21; camping@clos-therese.com; www.clos-therese.com]** Fr Bandol take D559 twd St Cyr & Marseilles. Site on R after 3km. Caution - site rent sharp U turn fr rd. Site service rds steep & narr; not suitable lge vans. Med, terr, shd; htd wc; chem disp; shwrs; el pnts (2-10A) €2.60-4.70; gas; lndtte; ice; supmkt 1km; rest; snacks; bar; playgrnd; 2 pools (1 htd); paddling pool; sand beach 4km; golf, tennis, horseriding nr; entmnt; TV rm; 30% statics; dogs €2.10; adv bkg rec; some daytime rd noise. "Many beaches & beauty spots in area; tractor will site c'vans." ♦ Easter-30 Sep. € 20.00 (CChq acc) 2004*

BANDOL *10F3* (6km NW Coastal) **Camping Les Baumelles, Lecques, 83270 St Cyr-sur-Mer [04 94 26 21 27; fax 04 94 88 76 13; baumellesloisirs@aol.com]** Fr Bandol take coast rd D559 NW to St Cyr. Turn L by statue on rd to La Madrague. Foll this coast rd 1.5km. Site on L at junc of coast rd. V lge, some mkd pitch; pt sl, shd; wc; baby facs; shwrs inc; el pnts (10A) €3.50; gas adj; lndry rm; shop; rest; snacks; bar; playgrnd; sand beach adj; entmnt; TV; 60% statics; dogs €3; poss cr; quiet. "Facs clean but some need refurb." 1 Apr-30 Oct. € 22.00 2005*

BANNALEC see Pont Aven *2F2*

BANNES see Langres *6F1*

BANYULS SUR MER *10H1* (2km S Rural) **Camp Municipal La Pinède, 66650 Banyuls-sur-Mer [04 68 88 32 13 or 04 68 88 00 62 (Mairie); fax 04 68 88 32 48; camp.banyuls@banyulss/mer. com]** On D914 (N114) foll sp to Banyuls-sur-Mer; turn R at camping sp at cent of sea-front by town hall; foll camping sp to site (2km fr sea-front). Care needed, narr access rds with sharp bends & trees. Lge, hdg/mkd pitch, pt sl, pt terr; pt shd; wc; chem disp; mv service pnt; shwrs; el pnts (4A) €1.90; lndtte; snacks; supmkt 100m; playgrnd; shgl beach 2km; Eng spkn; quiet; cc acc; CCI. "Vg, clean facs; busy, friendly site; spacious pitches; gd views fr top; sh walk into Banyuls." ♦ 1 Apr-31 Dec. € 12.40 2005*

BAR LE DUC *6E1* (Urban) **FFCC Camp Municipal Parc de Marbeaumont, Rue de St Mihiel, 55000 Bar-le-Duc [03 29 79 17 33 (Mairie)]** Sm, pt shd; wc; shwrs; el pnts €3.54 (poss long lead req); shops adj. "In grounds of chateau; nice setting; pitch yourself if no warden; friendly & helpful warden locks/unlocks el pnts; clean, modern san facs; poss itinerants low ssn; lovely walk into old town; gd." 1 May-30 Sep. € 4.66 2007*

BAR SUR AUBE *6F1* (500m NW Urban) **Camp Municipal La Gravière, Ave du Parc, 10200 Bar-sur-Aube [03 25 27 12 94]** On D619 (N19) fr Chaumont dir Troyes thro town; on N o'skts turn L into Ave du Parc at sm supmkt on R; site in 100m on rvside. Sm, mkd pitch, some hdstg, pt shd; wc; chem disp; shwrs €1; el pnts (6A) €3.30; gas; shop 500m; tradsmn; rest 1km; playgrnd; 20% statics; dogs; phone; poss cr; quiet; red 5+ days; no cc acc; CCI. "Haphazard pitching when site full; poss shabby low ssn; facs poss stretched high ssn & need refurb; poss itinerants; no vehicle access 2200-0700; conv Champagne area & Parc Regional de la Forêt d'Orient; rec arr early as popular, busy NH." ♦ ltd. 15 Mar-15 Oct. € 5.50 2006*

BAR SUR LOUP, LE see Vence *10E4*

BARBATRE see Noirmoutier en l'Ile *2H3*

BARBIERES *9C2* (1km SE Rural) **Camping Le Gallo-Romain, Route de Col de Tourniol, 26300 Barbières [tel/fax 04 75 47 44 07; info@ legalloromain.net; www.legalloromain.net]** Exit A49 junc 7 onto D149 dir Marches & Barbières. Go thro vill & ascend Rte du Col de Tourniol for 2km, site on R, well sp. Med, mkd pitch, pt sl, terr, pt shd; wc; chem disp; baby facs; shwrs inc; el pnts (6A €2.90); lndry rm; ice; shop & 1km; rest; snacks; bar; BBQ; playgrnd; pool; entmnt; internet; TV; 15% statics; dogs €1.80; phone; Eng spkn; adv bkg; quiet; no cc acc; CCI. "Friendly, helpful Dutch owners; warm welcome; beautiful mountain setting; ltd facs low ssn; gd." ♦ 28 Apr-30 Sep. € 23.00   2007*

Before we move on, I'm going to fill in some site report forms and post them off to the editor, otherwise they won't arrive in time for the deadline at the end of September.

BARBOTAN LES THERMES see Gabarret *8E2*

⊞**BARCARES, LE** *10G1* (1km Coastal) **Camping L'Europe, Route de St Laurent, 66420 Le Barcarès [04 68 86 15 36; fax 04 68 86 47 88; reception@europe-camping.com; www.europe-camping.com]** Exit A9 at Perpignan N & take D83 sp Le Barcarès. After 9km turn R on D81 sp Canet Plage, L on D90 sp Le Barcarès. Site on R. Lge, hdg/mkd pitch, shd; wc; shwrs inc; el pnts (16A) €4.20; gas; lndtte; ice; shop & 2km; rest; snacks; bar; playgrnd; 2 pools high ssn; waterslides; rv & beach 500m; tennis; archery; entmnts; disco; 50% statics; dogs €5.60; Eng spkn; adv bkg; poss noisy; red long stay/low ssn; CCI. "Gd location; all pitches have brick-built individual san facs; resident dogs (& mess) nuisance; gd value low ssn but ltd facs & unkempt pitches; gd cycle rte to beach & shops; vg winter NH/sh stay." ♦ ltd. € 34.00
                                                    2005*

BARCARES, LE *10G1* (1.5km S Coastal) **Camping L'Oasis, Route de St Laurent, 66423 Le Barcarès [04 68 86 12 43; fax 04 68 86 46 83; camping. loasis@wanadoo.fr; www.camping-oasis.com]** Fr N exit A9/E15 junc 40 Leucate onto D627 & D83 twd Le Barcarès. Exit junc 9 dir Canet & take 1st R sp St Laurent-de-la-Salanque. Pass St Laurent & go under bdge dir Le Barcarès, site sp on L. Lge, shd; wc (some cont); chem disp; baby facs; shwrs; el pnts (10A) inc; lndtte; supmkt; rest; snacks; bar; playgrnd; 3 pools; waterslide; sand beach 1km; tennis; games area; internet; entmnt; TV; dogs €4; red low ssn; CCI. ♦ 5 May-15 Sep. € 28.00
                                                    2007*

BARCARES, LE *10G1* (2km S Coastal) **Camping California, Route de St Laurent, 66420 Le Barcarès [04 68 86 16 08; fax 04 68 86 18 20; camping-california@wanadoo.fr; www.camping-california.fr]** Exit A9 junc 41 onto D627 sp Leucate. Ignore sp Le Barcarès & Port Barcarès; exit junc 9 sp Canet onto D81; then at D90 intersection turn R dir St Laurent-de-la-Salangue & go under D81; site on L. Lge, hdg/mkd pitch, shd; wc; chem disp; baby facs; shwrs inc; el pnts (10A) inc; lndtte; supmkt 1km; shop, rest, snacks, bar high ssn; BBQ (gas/elec only); playgrnd; 3 pools; waterslide; paddling pool; sand beach 1.5km; watersports 1km; tennis; games area; entmnt; internet; games/ TV rm; 20% statics; dogs €5; Eng spkn; adv bkg; noisy high ssn; cc acc; red 7+ days in Jun & Sep; CCI. "Various pitch sizes, sm poss diff; busy rd thro site; excel, modern san facs, ltd low ssn; friendly, helpful, hardworking owners; highly rec." ♦ 1 Apr-30 Sep. € 32.00 ABS - C02   2007*

BARCARES, LE *10G1* (1km SW Coastal) **Yelloh! Village Le Pré Catalan, Route de St Laurent, 66420 Le Barcarès [04 68 86 12 60; fax 04 68 86 40 17; info@precatalan.com; www. precatalan.com www.yellohvillage.com]** Exit A9 junc 41 onto D83; app Le Barcarès turn R onto D81, then L onto D90 to Le Barcarès, site sp. Lge, shd; wc; shwrs inc; el pnts (6A) €4; gas; ice; shop; rest; snacks; sand beach 1km; pool; playgrnd; tennis; TV; entmnt; dogs €3; quiet; adv bkg. 30 Apr-20 Sep. € 32.00   2007*

BARCARES, LE *10G1* (1km W Coastal) **Camping Las Bousigues, Ave des Corbières, 66420 Le Barcarès [04 68 86 16 19; fax 04 68 86 28 44; info@camping-barcares.com; www.camping-barcares.com]** Fr N exit A9/E15 junc 40 Leucate onto D627 & D83 twd Le Barcarès & exit junc 10. Turn R at rndabt, site sp on L. Lge, hdg/mkd pitch, shd; wc; chem disp; mv service pnt; individual san facs some pitches (extra charge); baby facs; shwrs; el pnts (6-10A) inc; lndtte; ice; shop; rest; snacks; bar; BBQ; playgrnd; pool; paddling pool; waterslide; sand beach 900; games area; entmnt; car wash; 50% statics; dogs €3.50; phone; poss cr; €3.20; Eng spkn; adv bkg (dep req + bkg fee); quiet; CCI. "No twin-axles; v helpful staff; excel." ♦ ltd. 1 Apr-30 Sep. € 32.00   2007*

BARCELONNETTE *9D4* (2km SE Rural) **Camping La Chaup, Route de Sauze, 04400 Enchastrayes [04 92 81 02 82; fax 04 92 81 30 61]** Fr W, go thro Barcelonnette on D900; just after vill go R onto D9 twds La Sauze & Enchastrayes; site sp. Sm, mkd pitch, sl, unshd; htd wc (some cont); shwrs; el pnts (6A) €3.90; lndtte; shop & snacks nrby; BBQ; playgrnd; rv & lake 2km; dogs €1; poss cr; adv bkg; quiet; CCI. "Relaxing site with mountain views; friendly owners." 1 Jun-15 Sep. € 8.50   2004*

BARCELONNETTE *9D4* (500m S Rural) **Camping du Plan, 52 Ave Emile Aubert, 04400 Barcelonnette [04 92 81 08 11; www. campingduplan.fr]** Exit town on D902 sp Col d'Allos & Col de la Cayolle. Site on R. Sm, pt shd; wc; shwrs inc; el pnts (3-10A) €2.70-4 gas; shop; tradsmn; rest;dogs €1; quiet. "Lovely views; lovely walks; sh walk to town; helpful owners; unisex san facs; refurbed shwrs; excel." 25 May-30 Sep. € 12.45   2005*

BARCELONNETTE *9D4* (6km W Rural) **Camping Le Fontarache, 04580 Les Thuiles [tel/fax 04 92 81 90 42; reception@camping-fontarache. fr; www.camping-fontarache.fr]** Site sp fr D900 on ent Les Thuiles fr Barcelonnette. Lge, mkd pitch, pt shd; wc (some cont); chem disp; mv service pnt; shwrs inc; el pnts (6A) €3; lndtte; shop 100m; tradsmn; snacks; BBQ; playgrnd; htd pool; paddling pool; fishing; kayaking; tennis; games area; entmnt; TV; some statics; dogs €3; poss cr; Eng spkn; adv bkg; quiet. "Pleasant, scenic site." ♦ 2 Jun-2 Sep. € 16.00   2006*

BARCELONNETTE *9D4* (6km W Rural) **Domaine Loisirs de l'Ubaye, Vallée de l'Ubaye, 04340 Barcelonnette [04 92 81 01 96; fax 04 92 81 92 53; info@loisirsubaye.com; www.loisirsubaye.com]** Site on S side of D900. Lge, mkd pitch, terr, shd; wc; shwrs inc; el pnts (6A) €3.50; lndry rm; gas; shop; rest; snacks; bar; playgrnd; htd pool; rv sw adj; watersports; cycle hire; entmnt; TV rm; statics; dogs €3.50; phone; red 7 days; CCI. "Magnificent scenery." ♦ 2 Feb-14 Nov. € 19.00   2006*

BAREGES see Luz St Sauveur *8G2*

⊞**BARFLEUR** *1C4* (500m NW Urban/Coastal) **Camp Municipal La Blanche Nef, 50760 Barfleur [02 33 23 15 40; fax 02 33 23 95 14; infos@ lablanchenef.com; www.lablanchenef.com]** Foll main rd to harbour; half-way on L side of harbour & turn L on mkd gap in car pk; cross sm side-street & foll site sp on sea wall; site visible on L in 300m. Med, pt sl, unshd; htd wc; chem disp; mv service pnt; shwrs inc; el pnts (6-10A) €3.10-4.30; ice; lndtte; shops 1km; tradsmn; snacks; bar; playgrnd; sand beach adj; 45% statics; dogs €1; Eng spkn; quiet; adv bkg; red low ssn; cc acc; CCI. "Gd sized pitches; gd birdwatching, walking, cycling; excel position & facs; fine sea views; gd sandy beach but windy." ♦ € 10.70   2007*

BARJAC (GARD) *9D2* (3km S Rural) **Domaine de la Sablière (Naturist), 30430 St Privat-de-Champclos [04 66 24 51 16; fax 04 66 24 58 69; contact@ villagesabliere.com; www.villagesabliere.com]** Fr Barjac S on D901 twd Bagnols. At 3km R onto D266, foll sp. Steep ent. Lge, hdg/mkd pitch, pt sl, shd; wc; chem disp; sauna; shwrs; el pnts (6-10A) inc; gas; lndtte; shop; rest; snacks; bar; playgrnd; 2 pools (1 htd, covrd); paddling pool; rv sw & beach; fishing; canoeing; tennis; games area; archery; entmnt; internet; TV rm; 40% statics; dogs €2.50; bus; car park; Eng spkn; adv bkg; quiet; red low ssn. "Helpful owners; gd facs; card op barrier (dep req); steep rds, narr bends & sm pitches - poss diff access lge o'fits; risk of flooding after heavy rain; gd shopping & excel local mkt; many naturist trails in forest." 1 Apr-30 Sep. € 32.55 (CChq acc)   2006*

BARJAC (GARD) *9D2* (9km S) **Naturissimo La Génèse (Naturist), Route de la Génèse, 30430 Méjannes-le-Clap [04 66 24 51 73 or 04 66 24 51 82; fax 04 66 24 50 89; lagenese@aol. com; www.lagenese.com]** Fr A7 exit junc 19, take dir Bagnols-sur-Cèze (D994 & N86) then in Bagnols head twd Alès on D6. Exit twd Lusanne onto D979 & foll sp for Méjannes-le-Clap. Site on banks of Rv Cèze. Lge, hdg/mkd pitch, pt sl, shd; wc; chem disp; shwrs inc; el pnts (6A) inc; gas; lndtte; ice; shop & 5km; rest; snacks; bar; playgrnd; pool; rv sw; fishing; sailing; canoe & cycle hire; tennis; archery; entmnt; TV rm; 10% statics; dogs €3.80; phone; adv bkg; quiet; INF card req; cc acc; red low ssn. Easter-9 Oct. € 25.60   2004*

BARJAC (LOZERE) see Mende *9D1*

BARNEVILLE CARTERET *1C4* (6km N Coastal) **Camping Bel Sito, Le Caumont de la Rue, 50270 Baubigny [02 33 04 32 74; fax 02 33 04 02 69; bel. sito@wanadoo.fr]** Fr Cherbourg take D950 twd Coutances thro Les Pieux & on twd Carteret. 10km S of Les Pieux turn R onto D131 sp Baubigny to site 1km on L. Med, pt sl, pt shd; wc; shwrs inc; el pnts (6A) €2.50; gas; ice; shop; sand beach 1km; dogs €2.50; quiet. 15 Apr-13 Sep. € 15.10   2004*

BARNEVILLE CARTERET *1C4* (2.5km S Coastal) **Camping Les Vikings, St Jean-de-la-Rivière, 50270 Barneville-Cartaret [02 33 53 84 13; fax 02 33 53 08 19; campingviking@aol.com; www. campingviking.com]** Fr D650 foll sp dir St Jean-de-la-Rivière. Site well sp. Lge, mkd pitch, pt shd; wc; chem disp; baby facs; shwrs inc; el pnts (4A) €3 (poss rev pol); ice; lndtte; shop; rest; snacks; bar; BBQ; playgrnd; htd pool high ssn; sand beach 500m; games rm; games area; golf, tennis nr; entmnt high ssn; excursions; TV; 50% statics; dogs €1.71; Eng spkn; adv bkg; quiet; red low ssn; cc acc; CCI. "Nice site with v helpful owner; vg touring base; gd walking; vg rest." ♦ 15 Mar-15 Nov. € 23.73   2006*

France

BARNEVILLE CARTERET *1C4* (2.5km SW Coastal) Camping Les Bosquets, Rue du Capitaine Quenault, 50270 Barneville-Plage [02 33 04 73 62; fax 02 33 04 35 82] Fr D950 turn R sp Barneville-Plage onto D903, site sp. Lge, terr, pt shd; wc; chem disp; shwrs inc; el pnts (10A) €3.20; Indtte; ice; shop; bar; playgrnd; htd pool; sand beach 400m; 50% statics; bus; poss cr; adv bkg; quiet; CCI. "Beach ideal for children; pleasant site." ♦ 1 Apr-15 Sep. € 13.60   2004*

There aren't many sites open this early in the year. We'd better phone ahead to check that the one we're heading for is actually open.

BARNEVILLE CARTERET *1C4* (10km SW Coastal) Camping L'Espérance, 36 Rue de la Gamburie, 50580 Denneville-Plage [02 33 07 12 71; fax 02 33 07 58 32; camping.esperance@wanadoo.fr] S fr Cherbourg on D950 thro Barneville-Carteret; in 7km fork R & cont on D650 & then R onto D137 sp Denneville-Plage & camping. Med, hdg/mkd pitch, pt shd; wc; chem disp; shwrs inc; el pnts (6A) €3.40; gas; Indtte; ice; shop; snacks; bar; playgrnd; htd pool; sand beach 300m; tennis; cycle hire; entmnt; 50% statics; dogs €1.60; phone; poss cr; Eng spkn; adv bkg (€100 dep); quiet; cc acc; CCI. "Helpful owners." 1 Apr-30 Sep. € 17.00   2005*

BARNEVILLE CARTERET *1C4* (2.5km W Urban/Coastal) Camping du Bocage, Rue du Bocage, Carteret, 50270 Barneville-Carteret [02 33 53 86 91] Fr Cherbourg take D650 to Carteret, turn R onto D902, site by disused rlwy stn & nr tourist office. Med, hdg pitch, shd; wc (some cont); chem disp; shwrs inc; el pnts (3-6A) €2.10-5; Indtte; shops adj; rest 200m; snacks; playgrnd; sand beach 500m; 20% statics; poss cr; adv bkg; quiet; CCI. "Pleasant seaside resort with excel beaches, daily boat in summer to Guernsey & Jersey; pitches soft in wet weather; well-kept site." 1 Apr-28 Sep. € 16.00   2004*

BARROU *4H2* (Rural) FFCC Camping Les Rioms, Les Rioms, 37350 Barrou [02 47 94 53 07 or 02 47 94 98 43 (LS); campinglesrioms@orange. fr; http://pagesperso-orange.fr/lesrioms] Fr D750 Descartes to La Roche-Posay rd turn R at sp Camping at ent to Barrou vill. Site in 1km. NB Site has barriers, phone if clsd. Sm, hdg/mkd pitch, pt sl, pt shd; wc; chem disp (wc); shwrs inc; el pnts (16A) €2.50; shop; rest; bar; BBQ; playgrnd; sand rv beach 2km; 5% statics; dogs €0.50; bus; poss cr; Eng spkn; adv bkg (dep req); quiet; CCI. "Very pleasant & peaceful site on bank of Rv Creuse; excel." 1 Apr-31 Oct. € 6.50   2007*

BARZAN PLAGE see Cozes *7B1*

BASTIDE DE SEROU, LA *8G3* (1km S Rural) Camping L'Arize, Route de Nescus, 09240 La Bastide-de-Sérou [05 61 65 81 51; fax 05 61 65 83 34; camparize@aol.com; www. camping-arize.com] Fr Foix on D117 on ent La Bastide-de-Sérou turn L at Gendarmerie on D15 sp Nescus, site 1km on R. Med, hdg/mkd pitch, pt shd; wc; chem disp; mv service pnt; baby facs; shwrs inc; el pnts 6A) inc (poss rev pol); gas; Indtte; shop & 2km; tradsmn; rest adj; snacks; playgrnd; pool; lake sw 5km; fishing; golf 5km; horseriding adj; golf nr; 10% statics; dogs €1.50; poss cr; Eng spkn; adv bkg; cc acc; CCI. "V pleasant on bank Rv Arize; wonderful scenery; modern facs; gd walking/ cycle rtes well mkd." ♦ ltd. 10 Mar-6 Nov. € 23.70   2006*

BASTIDE SOLAGES, LA *8E4* (Rural) Domaine de la Libaudié (Wijnen), 12550 La Bastide-Solages [05 65 99 70 33; contact@libaudie.com; www. libaudie.com] Fr Albi take D999 W dir St Sernin-sur-Rance; take D33 N to La Bastide-Solanges; in vill turn L & foll site sp. NB Twisting rds not suitable car+c'vans. Sm, pt shd; wc; chem disp; shwrs; el pnts (16A) €3.50; Indtte; ice; shops 5km; rest; bar; playgrnd; pool; rv sw 500m; canoeing; cycling; walking; TV rm; poss open all year; dogs €2; bus; Eng spkn; adv bkg ess high ssn (dep req); no cc acc. "Stunning views; vg family-run CL-type site; v friendly; conv Tarn valley." 1 May-31 Oct. € 15.50   2007*

BAUBIGNY see Barneville Carteret *1C4*

BAUD *2F3* (1km Urban) Camp Municipal L'Orée du Bois, Ave Corbel du Squirio, 56150 Baud [02 97 39 12 46 or 02 97 51 02 29 (Mairie); fax 02 97 39 07 22; mairie.baud@wanadoo.fr] D768 Auray-Baud; turn L on ent town at RH bend. Well sp. Med, v sl, shd; wc (cont); chem disp; shwrs; el pnts (10A); shops adj. "Poss diff pitching due uneven ground bet trees." 15 Jun-15 Sep.   2005*

BAUD *2F3* (3.5km S Rural) Camp Municipal du Petit Bois, Route de Lambel-Camors, 56330 Camors [02 97 39 18 36 or 02 97 39 22 06; fax 02 97 39 28 99; commune.de.camors@wanadoo.fr; www.camors56.com] S fr Baud on D768 to Camors. Sp in vill on D189. Sm, mkd pitch, pt sl, terr, unshd; wc; chem disp; mv service pnt; shwrs inc; el pnts (6A) €2.20; Indtte; playgrnd; horseriding adj; adv bkg; quiet; CCI. "Pleasant surroundings; vg facs; well-managed site." ♦ 1 Jul-31 Aug. € 8.40   2006*

BAUD *2F3* (7km W Rural) Camping de la Vallée du Blavet, Pont Augan, 56150 Baud [02 97 51 04 74 or 02 97 51 09 37 (LS); fax 02 97 39 07 23] Fr N24 exit onto D172 & foll sp Bubry & Quistinic; fr S on D768 to Baud, turn W onto D3, foll sp Bubry & Quistinic. Sm, hdg/mkd pitch, pt shd; htd wc; chem disp (wc); mv service pnt; baby facs; shwrs inc; el pnts (10A) €2; Indtte; rest, snacks, bar 500m; playgrnd; pool; fishing, canoeing in lake on site or in Rv Blavet adj; dogs; adv bkg; quiet; no cc acc; CCI. "V quiet & peaceful; barrier & office ltd opening hrs but parking area avail." ♦ ltd. 1 Apr-30 Sep. € 6.80   2005*

BAUGE *4G1* (1km E Rural) **Camp Municipal du Pont des Fées, Chemin du Pont des Fées, 49150 Baugé** [02 41 89 14 79 or 02 41 89 18 07 (Mairie); fax 02 41 84 12 19; mairie@ville-bauge.fr; www.ville-bauge.fr] Fr Saumur traveling N N147/D938 turn 1st R in Baugé onto D766. Foll camping sp to site by sm rv; ent bef rv bdge. Sm, hdg pitch, shd; wc; chem disp; shwrs inc; el pnts (4A) €2.20; lndtte; shops 1km; BBQ; 2 pools & 2 tennis courts 150m; fishing; no twin-axles; phone; adv bkg; quiet. "Excel countryside; pleasant, well-kept site; obliging wardens; office open 0700-1100 & 1700-2000." 15 May-15 Sep. € 8.00   2007*

BAULE, LA *2G3* (2km NE) **Airotel Camping La Roseraie, 20 Ave Jean Sohier, Route du Golf, 44500 La Baule-Escoublac** [02 40 60 46 66; fax 02 40 60 11 84; camping@laroseraie.com; www.laroseraie.com] Take N171 fr St Nazaire to La Baule. In La Baule-Escoublac turn R at x-rds by church, site in 300m on R; sp fr La Baule cent. Lge, hdg/mkd pitch, pt shd; wc (some cont); chem disp; mv service pnt; baby facs; fam bthrm; shwrs inc; el pnts (6A) €5; gas; lndtte; shop; tradsmn; rest; snacks; bar; BBQ; playgrnd; htd, covrd pool; paddling pool; waterslide; sand beach 2km; fishing; watersports; tennis; games area; games rm; entmnt; TV rm; 80% statics; dogs €4.50; phone; Eng spkn; adv bkg (dep req); quiet; cc acc; red long stay; CCI. "Well-kept, pleasant site; san facs v clean; gd." ♦ ltd. 1 Apr-30 Sep. € 23.00 (CChq acc)   2007*

See advertisement above

⊞**BAULE, LA** *2G3* (5km NE Rural) **Camping Les Chalands Fleuris, Rue du Stade, 44117 St André-des-Eaux** [02 40 01 20 40; fax 02 40 91 54 24; chalfleu@club-internet.fr; www.chalandsfleuris.com] W fr St Nazaire on N171. Take 1st exit to St André-des-Eaux; fr town cent foll site sp 800m. Lge, hdg/mkd pitch, pt shd, serviced pitch; wc; mv service pnt; chem disp; serviced pitches; shwrs inc; el pnts (3-6A) €2.75-3.30; gas; lndtte; ice, shop, tradsmn high ssn; snacks; bar; playgrnd; htd, covrd pool; sand beach 8km; fishing; tennis; golf 2km; games rm; TV; entmnt; child entmnt; 15% statics; dogs €2.30; adv bkg; quiet; red long stay/low ssn; cc acc; red CCI. "Site adj to 'Village Fleuris', v beautiful display all thro vill." ♦ ltd. € 20.00
2004*

BAULE, LA *2G3* (1km E Coastal) **Camping Le Bois d'Amour, Allée de Diane, 44500 La Baule** [02 40 60 17 40; fax 02 40 60 11 48; campi-boisamour@wanadoo.fr; www.campingdelabaule.com] Fr Ave du Bois d'Amour bear L & immed under rlwy bdge, turn R at traff lts. Ent to site on R. Lge, mkd pitch, pt shd; wc; mv service pnt; shwrs inc; el pnts (6A) inc; gas; ice; lndtte; shops & rest 500m; playgrnd; sand beach 800m; 50% statics; phone; bus & railway adj; no dogs high ssn; 'poss cr; adv bkg; quiet, but some rd/rlwy noise at site perimeter; CCI. "Useful NH, some pitches v sm; sm area for tourers." ♦ 1 Apr-15 Oct. € 22.00   2006*

BAULE, LA *2G3* (1km W Rural) **Camping Les Ajoncs d'Or, Chemin du Rocher, 44500 La Baule-Escoublac** [02 40 60 33 29; fax 02 40 24 44 37; contact@ajoncs.com; www.ajoncs.com] Fr D13 foll sp for La Baule cent & turn L at rndabt nr Champion supmkt, site sp. Lge, mkd pitch, pt shd; wc; chem disp; baby facs; shwrs inc; el pnts inc; lndtte; shop; supmkt 1km; rest; snacks; bar; playgrnd; sand beach 1.5km; games area; entmnt; TV; 25% statics; dogs €0.95; adv bkg; quiet. "Peaceful, well-run site; vg." ♦ 1 Apr-30 Sep.   2007*

See advertisement on next page

CAMPING ★★★ LES AJONCS D'OR

44500 La Baule
Phone: 00 33 2 40 60 33 29
Fax: 00 33 2 40 24 44 37

Nearby the beach and the shops of La Baule in a quiet and shady 6 ha park. With heated swimming pool (2 pools), games for children, snacks, bar, groceries. Open from 1st of April till the 30th of September. Rental of mobile homes.

Internet: http://www.ajoncs.com • E-mail: contact@ajoncs.com

BAUME LES DAMES 6G2 (12km N Rural) **Camping du Bois de Reveuge, Route de Rougemont,** 25680 Huanne-Montmartin [03 81 84 38 60; fax 03 81 84 44 04; info@campingduboisdereveuge. com; www.campingduboisdereveuge.com] Exit A36 junc 5 Baume-les-Dames onto D50 dir Rougemont-Villersexel. Foll sp Huanne & site for 9km. Site is 1km N of Huanne. Lge, mkd pitch, pt sl, terr, pt shd; wc (some cont); mv service pnt; chem disp; baby facs; shwrs inc; el pnts (6A) inc; gas; ice; lndtte; shop & 4km; tradsmn; snacks; pizzeria; bar; playgrnd; 3 htd pools, (1 covrd); waterslides; fishing lake with pedaloes; sand beach 15km; sailing school; mini-golf; cycle hire; archery; horseriding; rockclimbing; games area; entmnt; excursions; TV rm; some statics; dogs €2; Eng spkn; adv bkg; quiet; cc acc; red low ssn; CCI. "Superb staff & management; beautiful site; lge pitches; v clean san facs; wonderful countryside; gd walking, birdwatching, watersports; free activities, many for children; gd touring base." ♦ 23 Apr-15 Sep. € 30.00   2007*

BAUME LES DAMES 6G2 (6km S Rural) **Camping L'Ile, 1 Rue de Pontarlier,** 25110 **Pont-les-Moulins** [03 81 84 15 23; info@campingdelile.fr] S fr Baume-les-Dames on D50, site on L on ent Pont-les-Moulins. Sm, pt shd; wc (some cont); chem disp; shwrs inc; el pnts (6A) €2.20; gas; lndtte; shops 6km; playgrnd; pool 6km; Eng spkn; adv bkg; rd noise; CCI. "Pleasant setting by Rv Cusancin; helpful, friendly owner; clean facs but basic; superb rest La Source Bleu 6km." 15 Apr-15 Sep. € 10.40   2005*

BAUME LES MESSIEURS see Lons le Saunier 6H2

BAUME, LA 9A3 (Rural) **Camp Municipal La Baume,** 74430 La Baume [04 50 72 10 06 (Mairie); fax 04 50 72 10 85] Take D902 twd Thonon-Les-Bains. Site on R after sp to La Baume vill adj Lac du Jotty. Sm, terr, pt shd; wc; shwrs; el pnts (3-10A) €1.50-3.10; shops 5km; playgrnd; dogs €0.80; adv bkg; quiet. "Old but clean facs; gd NH." 1 Jul-31 Aug. € 6.90   2005*

BAYEUX 3D1 (1km N Urban) **Camp Municipal, Blvd Périphérique d'Eindhoven, 14400 Bayeux** [tel/fax 02 31 92 08 43; d.poupinel@libertysurf. fr] Site sp off Périphérique d'Eindhoven (Bayeux by-pass, N13); fr W site almost opp Briconaut DIY store. Fr E turn N of N13 Formigny & immed L over N13 sp Trevières. Site on R. Fr Bayeux, site N off inner ring rd. Lge, pt shd, some hdg pitch, some hdstg; wc (some cont); chem disp; mv service pnt; shwrs inc; el pnts (4-10A) €1.50-3 (poss rev pol); gas; lndtte; ice; shop (Jul/Aug); playgrnd; indoor pool adj; sand beach 10km; dogs; phone; some adv bkg ess high ssn; rd noise; 10% red 5+ days; CCI. "Gd, well-kept site; clean facs; avoid perimeter pitches (narr hdstgs & rd noise); no twin-axles; hdstgs poss prob for lge o'fits; conv for ferries; 10 min walk to town; lge mkt Sat; no access to site 1000-1700 low ssn; Bayeux medieval festival 1st w/e July." ♦ 29 Apr-30 Sep. € 11.90   2007*

BAYEUX 3D1 (6km SE Rural) **Camping Le Château de Martragny, 14740 Martragny** [02 31 80 21 40; fax 02 31 08 14 91; chateau.martragny@ wanadoo.fr; www.chateau-martragny.com or www.les-castels.com] Fr Caen going NW on N13 dir Bayeux/Cherbourg, leave at Martragny/Carcagny exit. Strt on & take 2nd R (past turn for Martragny/Creully) into site & chateau grounds. Fr Bayeux go SE on N13 taking Martragny/Carcagny exit, turn L, cross bridge, then as above. Lge, some mkd pitch, pt sl, pt shd; wc; chem disp (ltd in ssn); baby facs; shwrs inc; el pnts (6A) €3.50 (long lead poss req, poss rev pol); gas; lndtte; shop; snacks; bar; BBQ; playgrnd; htd pool; paddling pool; sand beach 10km; fishing; tennis; mini-golf; cycle hire; horseriding 500m; entmnt; internet; games/TV rm; statics; dogs; recep 0900-1200 & 1400-1900 high ssn; Eng spkn; adv bkg; quiet; red low ssn; cc acc; CCI. "Nice site in attractive surroundings; busy; friendly recep; lovely staff; poss long trek to san facs, stretched high ssn; nr Bayeux Tapestry, Calvados chateaux & D-Day beaches; Sat mkt in Bayeux; vg." ♦ 1 May-15 Sep. € 24.10 (CChq acc) ABS - N06   2007*

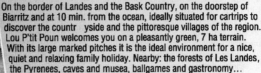

⊞BAYEUX *3D1* (8km SE Rural) **Camping Le Manoir de l'Abbaye (Godfroy), 15 Rue de Creully, 14740 Martragny [tel/fax 02 31 80 25 95; yvette. godfroy@libertysurf.fr;http://pagesperso-orange. fr/godfroy]** Take N13 Bayeux, Caen dual c'way for 7km, fork R sp Martagny. Over dual c'way L at T-junc, then 1st R sp D82 Martragny & Creully site on R 500m. Sm, pt shd; wc; chem disp; shwrs inc; el pnts (15A) €2.80 (poss rev pol); Indtte; tradsmn; dogs €2.30; Eng spkn; adv bkg; CCI. "Peaceful, well-kept site; helpful, friendly, welcoming owners; steps to san facs; meals & wine avail on request; winter storage; conv for tapestry, D-Day museums." ♦ ltd. € 16.10 2007*

BAYEUX *3D1* (6km NW Rural) **Camping La Vignette, Route de Crouay, 14400 Tour-en-Bessin [tel/fax 02 31 21 52 83; relais.vignette@ wanadoo.fr; http://pagesperso-orange.fr/Relais. Vignette/]** Fr Bayeux take N13 sp Cherbourg. Leave at junc 38 sp Tour-en-Bessin. At end of vill turn L sp Crouay, at T-junc turn R & foll sp to site. Sm, unshd; wc; mv service pnt; shwrs inc; el pnts (5A) €2.70; Indry rm; supmkt 8km; rest adj; sand beach 12km; v quiet. "Rustic, clean facs; friendly owners, long lead req (1 el pnts post only); delightful CL-type site." Easter-1 Nov. € 9.30 2005*

BAYEUX *3D1* (9km NW) **Camping Reine Mathilde, 14400 Etréham [02 31 21 76 55; fax 02 31 22 18 33; camping.reine.mathilde@ wanadoo.fr; www.campingreinemathilde.com]** NW fr Bayeux on D6 turn L to Etréham (D100); site 3km (sp). Or W fr Bayeux on N13 for 8km, exist junc 38. At x-rds 1.5km after vill of Tour-en-Bessin turn R on D206 to Etréham & bear L at Etréham church. Med, hdg/mkd pitch, pt shd; wc; chem disp; shwrs inc; el pnts (6A) €4.50; Indtte; ice; shop 4km; rest & snacks (high ssn) playgrnd; pool; htd paddling pool; sand beach 5km; cycle hire; fishing 1km; entmnts; free wifi internet; TV; 15% statics; dogs €2.90; phone; adv bkg; quiet; CCI. "Helpful warden; conv for invasion beaches; basic san facs; site appears rather run down." ♦ 1 Apr-30 Sep. € 17.60 2007*

BAYON *6E2* (Rural) **Camp Municipal du Passetemps, Rue de la Moselle, 54290 Bayon [tel/fax 03 83 72 45 60 or 03 83 72 51 52 (Mairie)]** Fr N57 N fr Charmes or S fr Nancy; turn onto D9 sp Bayon; in 2.5km strt on at x-rds & over bridge; site on L in 500m by Rv Moselle. Med, pt shd; wc (some cont); chem disp; shwrs; el pnts; shop, rest 500m; playgrnd; rv adj & sports facs adj; 50% statics; quiet. "Rv adj liable to dry out & also flood - care in wet weather; barrier clsd 2200-0700; sep area for tourers." 15 Apr-15 Oct. 2005*

> This guide relies on site report forms submitted by caravanners like us; we'll do our bit and tell the editor what we think of the campsites we've visited.

BAYONNE *8F1* (8km NE Rural) **Aire Naturelle L'Arrayade (Barret), 280 Chemin Pradillan, 40390 St Martin-de-Seignanx [05 59 56 10 60]** On D26 midway bet N10 & N117, 3km W of St Martin. (Opp tall crenellated building). Sm, pt sl, pt shd; wc (some cont); shwrs; el pnts €2.30 (long lead rec); Indry rm; BBQ; playgrnd; dogs; quiet. "V helpful owner; gd welcome; simple facs poss stretched high ssn." 1 Jun-30 Sep. € 8.00 2006*

⊞BAYONNE *8F1* (10km NE) **FFCC Camping Le Ruisseau, 40390 St André-de-Seignanx [tel/ fax 05 59 56 71 92; campingle@aol.com; http:// members.aol.com/campingle/ruisseau.htm]** Fr Bayonne, take N117 dir Orthez. Turn L after 10km at traff lts in St Martin & foll sp for 5km to site. Sp fr all dir. Take care on ent - by rd junc. Med, hdg/mkd pitch, terr, pt shd; wc; chem disp; 15% serviced pitches; shwrs inc; el pnts (6A) €3; ice; Indtte; shop; tradsmn; rest, snacks & bar 1km; playgrnd; pool; sand beach 10km; TV; 20% statics; dogs €2; adv bkg; quiet; red long stay/low ssn; CCI ess. "Away fr busy coastal area; owner v helpful; not suitable for long/wide vans." € 13.00 2006*

France

BAYONNE *8F1* (11km NE Rural) **Camping Lou P'tit Poun**, 110 Ave du Quartier Neuf, 40390 St Martin-de-Seignanx [05 59 56 55 79; fax 05 59 56 53 71; contact@louptitpoun.com; www.louptitpoun. com] Fr Bordeaux exit A63 junc 6 dir Bayonne Nord; then take N117 dir Pau & St Martin-de-Seignanx; site sp on R in 7km. Lge, mkd pitch, terr, pt shd; wc; chem disp; mv service pnt; serviced pitch; baby facs; shwrs inc; el pnts (10A) €5; gas; Indtte; ice; shop 4km; tradsmn; rest (high ssn); snacks; bar; BBQ (el/gas); playgrnd; pool; paddling pool; sand beach 10km; tennis; games area; entmnt; child entmnt; games/TV rm; 17% statics; dogs €4.50; phone; Eng spkn; adv bkg; quiet; red low ssn; cc acc; CCI. "V friendly, family-run site; conv Biarritz, St Jean-de-Luz; excel." ◆ 31 May-14 Sep. € 27.50 ABS - A39   2007*

See advertisement on previous page

BAZAS *7D2* (2km E Rural) **Camping Le Grand Pré**, Route de Casteljaloux, 33430 Bazas [05 56 65 13 17; fax 05 56 25 90 52; legrandpre@ wanadoo.fr; http://pagesperso-orange.fr/ legrandpre] Fr Bordeaux on A62 exit junc 3. Turn R onto D932 & R at 3rd rndabt. Then L at next rndabt onto D655 twd Bazas. Cont thro town cent. Site sp on R in 1km. Sm, hdg/mkd pitch, pt sl, pt shd; wc; chem disp; mv service pnt; baby facs; fam bthrm; shwrs inc; el pnts (6-16A) €3.20-4.80; gas; Indtte; ice; shop 2km; tradsmn; bar; playgrnd; htd pool; TV rm; 6% statics; dogs €3 (free low ssn); Eng spkn; adv bkg (dep req); quiet; red long stay/low ssn; CCI. "Friendly, relaxed site nr interesting, walled town; v helpful staff; well-kept; san facs v smart but poss stretched high ssn; breakfast available; pleasant walk to interesting town with cathedral; picturesque location, views of chateau & town; footpath to vill; vineyards nr." ◆ 1 Apr-29 Sep. € 19.00   2007*

BAZINVAL see Blangy sur Bresle *3C2*

BAZOUGES SUR LE LOIR see Flèche, La *4G1*

BEAUCENS see Argelès Gazost *8G2*

BEAUFORT *9B3* (10km SE Rural) **Camping Les Amis**, 73270 Arèches [04 79 38 14 65 or 04 79 38 12 07; info@campinglesamis.com; www. campinglesamis.com] Fr Albertville take D925 to Beaufort cent; turn R onto D218A sp Arèches; site 5km beyond Arèches on rd to Barrage de St Guérin. Narr, winding rds. Sm, pt sl; pt shd, wc (some cont); chem disp (wc); mv service pnt; shwrs inc; el pnts (12A) €2.20; Indtte; tradsmn; shops, rest, snacks & bar 5km; lake fishing 1km; chair lifts to mountains; games rm; TV; 5% statics; dogs free; phone; bus 5km; quiet. "V remote site in mountains; beautiful views; vg walking; gd." ◆ ltd. 20 Jun-15 Sep. € 12.20   2007*

BEAUFORT *9B3* (300m NW Rural) **Camp Municipal Le Domelin**, Domelin, 73270 Beaufort [tel/fax 04 79 38 33 88 or 04 79 38 33 15 (LS)] Fr Albertville take D925 dir Beaufort & Bourg-St Maurice; site on L just bef ent Beaufort 100m up side rd (after passing D218B); clearly sp. NB App fr E (Bourg-St Maurice) rd v diff for towing. Med, mkd pitch, pt shd; htd wc (some cont); chem disp; baby facs; shwrs inc; el pnts (6A) inc; Indtte; shops, rest, snacks & bar 1km; playgrnd; htd pool 1km; dogs; phone; bus 1km; poss cr; adv bkg (dep req); quiet; cc acc; CCI. "Gd base for touring beautiful Beaufortain; vg walking; short walk to attractive town with rests, shops & tourist office." 1 Jun-30 Sep. € 13.55
2007*

BEAUGENCY *4F2* (Urban) **Camp Municipal du Val de Flux**, Route de Lailly-en-Val, 45190 Beaugency [02 38 44 50 39 or 02 38 44 83 12; fax 02 38 46 49 10; mairie.de.beaugency@wanadoo. fr] Exit A10 junc 15 onto N152. In Beaugency turn L at traff lts nr water tower onto D925 & again over rd bdge. Site sp on S bank of Rv Loire. Med, mkd pitch, pt shd; htd wc; chem disp; shwrs inc; el pnts (10A).€3.05; Indry rm; ice; shop & 500m; rest 1km; snacks; bar; playgrnd; sand beach; rv sw forbidden; fishing; watersports; mini-golf; entmnts; 10% statics; dogs €0.55; poss cr w/e in ssn; quiet; Eng spkn; red long stay; CCI. "Basic facs stretched high ssn & poss unclean low ssn; pleasant views over Loire; helpful staff; poss itinerants & unruly youths; free 1 night site for m'vans over rv on other side of town." ◆ 7 Apr-3 Sep. € 5.90   2007*

⊞**BEAUGENCY** *4F2* (8km S Rural) **Camping de l'Amitié**, Nouan-sur-Loire, 41220 St Laurent-Nouan [02 54 87 01 52; fax 02 54 87 09 93; aquadis1@wanadoo.fr; www.aquadis-loisirs. com] On D951 SW fr Orléans cont past power stn into Nouan-sur-Loire. Site on R sp. Med, mkd pitch, pt shd; htd wc; mv service pnt; shwrs; el pnts (10A) inc; Indtte; shop 500m; rest 500m; pools & sports activities nr; direct acc to rv; 50% statics; dogs; adv bkg; quiet; 10% red CCI. "Interesting area; beautiful view of Rv Loire; workers poss resident on site; friendly staff; phone ahead low ssn to check open." € 14.00   2006*

BEAULIEU SUR DORDOGNE *7C4* (Rural) **FLOWER Camping des Iles**, 19120 Beaulieu-sur-Dordogne [05 55 91 02 65; fax 05 55 91 05 19; info@ campingdesiles.fr; www.campingdesiles.fr] On D940 fr Bretenoux, turn R in Beaulieu town sq, site about 200m on island in Rv Dordogne. 3m height limit at ent. Med, shd; wc; baby facs; shwrs inc; el pnts (10A) inc (poss long lead req); Indtte;ice; shops adj; snacks; bar; playgrnd; pool; rv sw; sports area; entmnt high ssn; cycle, canoe hire; archery; 15% statics; dogs €1.50; poss cr; Eng spkn; adv bkg rec; quiet; red long stay/low ssn. "Delightful, wooded site in beautiful surroundings; facs stretched high ssn; sh walk fr cent of attractive vill; highly rec." 5 Apr-11 Oct. € 23.50   2007*

⊞ *Site open all year*   200   *Send in your site reports*

BEAULIEU SUR LOIRE *4G3* (E Rural) **Camp Municipal Touristique du Canal, Route de Bonny,** 45630 Beaulieu-sur-Loire [02 38 35 89 56; fax 02 38 35 86 57; beaulieu-sur-loire@libertysurf. fr] Exit A77 junc 21 Bonny-sur-Loire, cross rv to Beaulieu-sur-Loire on D296. On E o'skirts of vill on D926, nr canal. Sm, hdg/mkd pitch, pt shd; wc; chem disp; shwrs inc; el pnts (6A) €2.50; lndry rm; shop 2km; rest adj; snacks, bar 500m; playgrnd; poss cr; adv bkg; CCI. "Mkt Wed; walking along canal/ Loire; boat trips." ♦ Easter-1 Nov. € 5.60   2005*

BEAUMES DE VENISE see Carpentras *10E2*

BEAUMONT DE LOMAGNE *8E3* (800m E Urban) Camping Le Lomagnol (formerly Municipal Le Lac), Ave du Lac, 82500 Beaumont-de-Lomagne [05 63 26 12 00; fax 05 63 65 60 22; villagedeloisirslelomagnol@wanadoo.fr; www. villagelelomagnol.fr] On SE of D928 at E end of vill. Sp 'Centre de Loisirs, Plan d'Eau'. Med, mkd pitch, pt shd; wc; chem disp; baby facs; sauna; shwrs inc; el pnts (10A) inc; lndtte; ice; shop; rest; snacks; bar; playgrnd; pool; waterslide; jacuzzi; lake sw; fishing; tennis; cycle & canoe hire; golf; sailing; 25% statics; dogs €1.50; poss cr; quiet. "Gd quality, modern site; v interesting old town." ♦ Easter-30 Sep. € 16.00   2006*

BEAUMONT DU PERIGORD *7D3* (6km W Rural) Centre Naturiste de Vacances Le Couderc (Naturist), 24440 Naussannes [05 53 22 40 40; fax 05 53 23 90 98; info@lecouderc.com; www.lecouderc.com] Fr D660 at D25 W thro Naussannes & hamlet of Leydou. Just beyond Leydou turn R into site, well sp. Lge, mkd pitch, pt sl, pt shd; wc; chem disp; sauna; shwrs inc; el pnts (5A) €4.50; shop; rest; snacks; bar; playgrnd; htd pool; paddling pool; jacuzzi; sm lake; cycle hire; entmnt; some statics; dogs €4.50; adv bkg (dep req + bkg fee); quiet; INF card req (can be purchased at site); cc acc; red long stay/low ssn. "Beautiful site; gd san facs spread over 5 camping areas; v friendly & helpful staff; Bastide towns nrby." ♦ 1 Apr-30 Sep. € 25.10   2007*

BEAUMONT HAGUE *1C4* (5km N Rural/Coastal) Camp Municipal du Hable, 50440 Omonville-la-Rogue [02 33 52 86 15 or 02 33 01 86 00; fax 02 33 01 86 01] W fr Cherbourg on D901 to Beaumont-Hague; turn N onto D45 dir Omonville-la-Rogue. Med, hdg/mkd pitch, hdstg, pt shd; wc; chem disp; mv service pnt; shwrs inc; el pnts (5-10A) €2.50-4; lndry rm; shop, gas adj; rest; bar; playgrnd; beach 100m; dogs €0.90; quiet; CCI. "In pretty vill with gd harbour; 30 mins fr Cherbourg; gd NH." 1 Apr-30 Sep. € 8.20   2004*

BEAUMONT SUR OISE *3D3* (8km SW Rural) **Parc de Séjour de l'Etang, 10 Chemin des Bellevues,** 95690 Nesles-la-Vallée [01 34 70 62 89; brehinier1@hotmail.com; www.campingparcset. com] Fr D927 Méru-Pontoise rd, turn L onto D64 at sp L'Isle Adam. After passing thro Nesles-la-Vallée camp sp on L. Med, hdg pitch, pt shd; htd wc (cont); chem disp; serviced pitches (extra charge); shwrs inc; el pnts (3A) €3.15 (rev pol); lndtte; ice; shops 1km; playgrnd; lake fishing adj; 90% statics; dogs €1; Eng spkn; quiet; red CCI. "Lovely, peaceful setting; spacious pitches; friendly, helpful staff; conv day trips to Paris & Versailles." 1 Mar-31 Oct. € 13.50   2007*

BEAUMONT SUR SARTHE *4F1* (E Rural) **FFCC Camp Municipal du Val de Sarthe, 72170 Beaumont-sur-Sarthe** [02 43 97 01 93; fax 02 43 97 02 21; beaumont.sur.sarthe@wanadoo. fr; www.ville-beaumont-sur-sarthe.fr] Fr N138 Alençon-Le Mans, turn L at traff lts in cent of Beaumont & foll site sp twd E of town. Fr Le Mans on A28 exit 21 onto D6, R onto N138 & R at traff lts & foll sp. Med, hdg/mkd pitch, pt shd; wc; chem disp; mv service pnt; shwrs inc; el pnts (6A) €2.40; (long cable poss req); lndtte; shops & rest 500m; playgrnd; pool 500m; rv boating & fishing adj; dogs €0.35; poss cr w/e; adv bkg rec high ssn; cc acc; CCI. "Beautiful, peaceful, well-run site on Rv Sarthe; lge pitches, some right by rv; immac san facs; no twin-axles & poss no c'vans over 2,000 kg; barrier clsd 2200; close to interesting, pretty town; vg value; excel." ♦ 1 May-30 Sep. € 6.20   2007*

BEAUNE *6H1* (1km NE Urban) **Camp Municipal Les Cent Vignes, 10 Rue Auguste Dubois, 21200 Beaune** [03 80 22 03 91; simone.studer.mairie-beaune@wanadoo.fr] Fr N on A31 & fr S on A6 at junc with m'ways A6/A31 take A6 sp Auxerre-Paris; after 1km leave at junc 24 to join D974 (N74) twd Beaune; after approx 1.5km, turn R at 2nd traff lts fr a'route to site (sp) in 200m. Site well sp fr inner ring rd & foll sp to Dijon (not a'route sps) Also sp fr Mersault/L'Hôpital x-rds. Med, hdg/mkd pitch, hdstg, pt shd; htd wc; chem disp; mv service pnt; shwrs inc; el pnts (6-7A) €1.80-3.60 (some rev pol); gas; lndry rm; ice; shop; hypmkt 2km; rest; snacks; bar; playgrnd; pool 800m; tennis; extensive sports facs; cycle hire; TV; dogs; phone; Eng spkn; adv bkg in writing only bef 30 May; quiet; red long stay; cc acc; CCI. "Well-run, clean & busy site; lge pitches - but some tight; no twin-axles; a few pitches with high hdges for lge o'fits; narr access rds, tight turns & low trees poss diff for lge o'fits; san facs poss a bit tired & shwrs cramped; rec arr early even low ssn, site poss full by 1400 high ssn; recep open 0800-1230 & 1330-2200; gd rest/ takeaway; Beaune worth visit - walking dist; gd value." 15 Mar-31 Oct. € 11.40   2007*

France

⊞**BEAUNE** *6H1* (2km NE Rural) **Camping Les Bouleaux, 11 Rue Jaune, 21200 Vignoles** [03 80 22 26 88] Do not leave A6 at new Beaune exit (24) but use old exit (junc 24.1); 500m after toll turn R at rndabt, in 1.5km turn R sp Dole rndabt. Immed after x-ing m'way turn L sp Vignoles. L again at next junc then R & foll camping sp. Site in approx 1.5km in cent Chevignerot; fr town cent take D973 (E) sp Dole. In 2km cross a'route & 1st L (N) sp Vignoles. Sm, hdg/mkd pitch, pt shd; htd wc; chem disp; shwrs inc; el pnts (6A) €2.10 (rev pol altered on request); shop; tradsmn; supmkt 2km; dogs; adv bkg rec; quiet but some rd noise; CCI. "Excel, well-kept, busy site with tree-lined pitches, shrubs & flowers; rec arr early high ssn; some gd sized pitches; helpful & friendly owners; at times staff poss unavailable for checking out; superb clean san facs, poss stretched high ssn; poss muddy after rain - park on rdways; conv Beaune & a'route." ♦ ltd. € 15.20   2007*

BEAUNE *6H1* (8km SW Rural) **Camping La Grappe d'Or, 2 Route de Volnay, 21190 Meursault** [03 80 21 22 48; fax 03 80 21 65 74; info@camping-meursault.com; www.camping-meursault.com] SW on D974 (N74)/D973 fr Beaune, fork R on D973 sp Autun, fork L on D111 sp Monthelie & Mersault; camp at ent to Meursault, 300m past motel; care needed at ent - almost U-turn. Med, mkd pitch; terr, pt shd; wc; chem disp; shwrs inc; el pnts (15A) €3.50 (check pol); gas; lndtte; ice; shop; tradsmn; rest; snacks; bar; playgrnd; pool; tennis; cycle hire; phone; dogs €1.30; poss cr; adv bkg ess in ssn (dep half total charge); some rd noise; red low ssn; CCI. "Basic facs ltd low ssn & well-used - 1 block in need of refurb; busy family site high ssn & busy NH - arr early; superb views over vineyards; conv famous wine vills; gd food adj motel; barrier clsd 2200-0730; some pitches uneven & sm; gd cycle paths." ♦ 1 Apr-15 Oct. € 16.50 (CChq acc)   2007*

BEAUNE *6H1* (5km NW Rural) **FFCC Camping Les Premiers Prés (formerly Municipal), Route de Bouilland, 21420 Savigny-lès-Beaune** [tel/fax 03 80 26 15 06 or 0 6 30 17 98 85 (mob); www.camping-savigny-les-beaune.fr] Fr Beaune ring rd turn N on D974 (N74) sp Dijon; in 200m at traff lts turn L sp Savigny; in 100m ignore camping sp & bear R to Savigny (3km); site 1km thro vill on L. Med, mkd pitch, pt sl, pt shd; wc; chem disp; mv service pnt; shwrs inc; el pnts (10-16A) €3.35 (some rev pol); gas 1.3km; ice; shops 1km; supmkt 3km; tradsmn; BBQ; playgrnd; dogs €1; adv bkg; quiet; CCI. "Pleasant, v busy NH in beautiful area; no twin-axle vans; facs not adequate if site full & ltd low ssn; few water points; pleasant staff; cr after 1700 high ssn; recep 0800-1000 & 1700-2200; conv A6, A31, A36 & Beaune; excel rests in town; chateau has excel motor/motorcyle & aviation museum; poss itinerant workers at grape harvest; privately owned site 2007, changes planned; vg." ♦ ltd. 27 Apr-31 Oct. € 8.20   2007*

BEAURAINVILLE see Hesdin *3B3*

BEAURECUEIL see Aix en Provence *10F3*

BEAUREPAIRE *9C2* (S Urban) **Camp Municipal, Ave Charles de Gaulle, 38270 Beaurepaire** [04 74 84 64 89 or 04 74 84 67 29; fax 04 74 79 24 14; ccpb@pays-de-beaurepaire.com] Sp in town on L of Beaurepaire-Romans rd, adj pool & stadium. Med, shd; wc (some cont); shwrs inc; el pnts (6A) €2; shops 250m; 2 supmkts nr; rv fishing; quiet. 1 May-15 Sep. € 7.00   2007*

BEAUREPAIRE *9C2* (10km S Rural) **Camp Municipal du Château, Route de Romans, 26390 Hauterives** [04 75 68 80 19 or 04 75 68 83 10] Take D538 S to Hauterives, site sp in vill adj Rv Galaure. Med, pt shd; wc; shwrs inc; el pnts (4A); ice; lndtte; snacks; sm supmkt adj; playgrnd; htd pool; rv sw & fishing adj; adv bkg; quiet. "Gd NH; friendly; gd pool." ♦ 1 Apr-15 Oct. € 9.15   2005*

BEAUREPAIRE *9C2* (9km SW Rural) **Camping Château de la Perouze, 26210 St Sorlin-en-Valloire** [04 75 31 70 21 or 06 70 00 04 74 (mob); fax 04 75 31 62 74; georgespont@libertysurf. fr; http://lapeyrouse.free.fr] Exit Beaurepaire on D130/D139 sp Manthes for approx 1km; bef St Sorlin turn L at site sp in 1.5km. Narr site ent. Med, pt shd; shwrs; wc; chem disp; baby facs; sauna; jacuzzi; shwrs inc; chem disp; baby facs; el pnts (6-10A) €2.30-4.20; gas; lndtte; shop; tradsmn; bar; pool; fishing; tennis; 30% statics; no dogs; quiet; adv bkg; CCI. "Friendly, helpful warden in 14thC chateau grounds; sep, shd car park; gates clsd 2100-0900; access to pitches poss diff; c'van storage in winter." 15 Jun-15 Sep. € 18.90   2005*

BEAUVAIS *3C3* (Urban) **Camp Municipal, Rue Camard, 60000 Beauvais** [03 44 02 00 22] On S edge of town. Take Paris rd fr town cent over Pont de Paris; after 200m turn R at lts up Rue Binet (steep). 1st R & site on R. Well sp. Diff steep app but can turn in car park at top of hill. Med, pt sl, pt shd; wc (some cont); shwrs inc; el pnts (4A) €1.25; gas; shops in town; playgrnd; pool; tennis adj; poss cr; quiet; CCI. "Gd value; friendly owner; site self when office clsd; height barrier clsd 1200-1700; phone ahead to check site open low ssn." 1 Jun-30 Aug. € 10.55   2006*

BEAUVAIS *3C3* (6km W) **Camping Le Clos Normand, 1 Rue de l'Abbaye, 60650 St Paul** [03 44 82 27 30] Exit A16 Beauvais Nord & foll green Rouen sp & St Paul Parc onto N31. Drive thro vill, past abbey. Tight R turn into site. Med, pt sl, shd; htd wc; mv service pnt; shwrs inc; el pnts (6A) inc; lndtte; shops 3km; tradsmn; fishing; 80% statics; dogs €2; poss cr; adv bkg; quiet. "Friendly; facs in need of update; poss scruffy/run down low ssn; unreliable opening dates early ssn; NH only." 1 Apr-30 Sep. € 15.00   2005*

BEAUVILLE *7D3* (500m Rural) **Camping Les Deux Lacs, 47470 Beauville [05 53 95 45 41; fax 05 53 95 45 31; camping-les-2-lacs@wanadoo. fr]** Fr D656 S to Beauville, site sp on D122. Med, hdg/mkd pitch, terr, shd; wc; chem disp; mv service pnt; shwrs inc; el pnts (6A) €2.10; lndtte; rest; snacks; bar; shop 600m; playgrnd; lake sw; games area; fishing; watersports; 10% statics; dogs €1.90; Eng spkn; adv bkg; quiet; red long stay/low ssn; cc acc; CCI. "Peaceful; gd fishing; pleasant walk to vill; Eng newspapers avail; vg." ♦ 1 Feb-30 Nov. € 13.20
2005*

BEAUVOIR see Mont St Michel, Le *2E4*

BEAUVOIR EN ROYANS see St Marcellin *9C2*

BEAUVOIR SUR MER *2H3* (4km E Rural) **Camp Municipal St Gervais, 85230 St Gervais [02 51 68 73 14 (Mairie); fax 02 51 68 48 11]** On D948, 1km E of St Gervais on R of rd. Sm, mkd pitch, pt shd; wc; chem disp; shwrs; el pnts inc; gas; lndry rm; shop; BBQ; CCI. "Facs basic but clean." ♦ 1 Jun-30 Sep. € 8.50
2004*

BEAUVOIR SUR MER *2H3* (4km E Rural) **Camping Le Fief d'Angibaud, 85230 St Gervais [02 51 68 43 08; davidleach1522@wanadoo.fr]** Fr Beauvoir-sur-Mer E on D948 to St Gervais turn L after PO/Mairie onto D59 twd Bouin (narr ent easy to miss); in 2km pass sm chapel; take 2nd rd on L; site on R after 500m. Sm, unshd; wc; shwrs inc; chem disp; el pnts (5A) inc; gas 4km; basic lndry rm; ice; shops 2km; tradsmn; sand beach 5km; fishing/golf nrby; adv bkg rec high ssn; quiet; red CCI. "Excel, simple site on farm; v helpful British owners; lge pitches; premium pitches avail; clean facs; variety of bird life; conv Ile de Noirmoutier; ferry to Ile d'Yeu, coastal resorts; free parking close to beach (blue flag); gd cycling area." ♦ Easter-31 Oct. € 15.00
2006*

BEC HELLOUIN, LE see Brionne *3D2*

BEDARIEUX *10F1* (8km N) **FFCC Camping La Sieste, 34260 La Tour-sur-Orb [04 67 23 72 96; fax 04 67 23 75 38; campinglasieste@orange.fr; http://pagesperso-orange.fr/campinglasieste]** Fr Bédarieux, take D35 N twd Lodève; site 3km N of La Tour-sur-Orbe at sm vill of Vereilles. Med, pt shd; wc; chem disp; shwrs inc; el pnts (4-8A) €2.30-4; ice; lndtte; shop; tradsmn; rest; bar; BBQ; pool open June; rv sw; dogs €2.50; phone; adv bkg; Eng spkn; quiet; poss v cr high ssn; cc acc; 20% red low ssn; 5% red CCI. "V well-kept site; charming owners; unspoilt Languedoc countryside." ♦ 1 Jun-31 Aug. € 14.00
2007*

⊞**BEDENAC** *7C2* (1km E Rural) **Camping Louvrignac, 17210 Bedenac [05 46 70 31 88; lcarpenter@freenet.co.uk]** Fr N10 exit sp Bedenac onto D145. Thro Bedenac vill take D158 sp Montguyon & in 500m take 1st L sp Bernadeau. Site on L in 100m - narr rd. Sm, pt shd; own san; chem disp; el pnts (10A) inc; tradsmn; shop, rest, snacks, bar 10km; BBQ; htd pool; adv bkg; quiet. "CL-type site with 5 pitches; friendly British owners; rec phone in advance." € 10.00
2004*

BEDOIN *10E2* (E Rural) **Domaine de Bélézy (Naturist), 84410 Bédoin [04 90 65 60 18; fax 04 90 65 94 45; info@belezy.com; www.belezy. com]** Fr Carpentras D974 to Bédoin. Go thro vill & turn R at rndabt sp Mont Ventoux. In 300m turn L & foll sp to site. Lge, pt sl, shd; htd wc (some cont); chem disp; mv service pnt; sauna; steam rm; shwrs inc; el pnts (12A) €4.50; gas; lndtte; shop; rest; snacks; bar; cooking facs; playgrnd; 2 htd pools; paddling pool; tennis; games area; horseriding 2km; golf 20km; wifi internet; entmnt; child entmnt; TV rm; 20% statics; no dogs; phone; sep car park high ssn; poss cr; Eng spkn; adv bkg (dep req); quiet; red long stay; cc acc; INF card. "Delightful, welcoming, peaceful site; lovely location; extensive facs; some sm & awkward pitches; gd base for Mt Ventoux, Côtes du Rhône." ♦ 19 Mar-6 Oct. € 35.00 (3 persons) (CChq acc)
2007*

BEDOIN *10E2* (1km S Rural) **Camping Ménèque, Chemin de Ménèque, 84410 Bédoin [04 90 65 93 50; fax 04 90 12 83 61; lemeneque@ aol.com; www.lemeneque.eu]** S fr Malaucène on D939, turn E onto D19 to Bédoin. S of Bédoin at fork in rd, bear L. Site on L. Med, pt sl, pt shd; wc; chem disp; shwrs inc; el pnts (6A) €3; gas; lndtte; shop; tradsmn; rest, snacks, bar; BBQ; playgrnd; pool; no statics; dogs €1.50; phone; poss cr; quiet; CCI. ♦ "Basic site; Bédoin v popular & in beautiful area; rec NH." 1 Apr-30 Sep. € 12.00
2006*

BEDOIN *10E2* (1km W Rural) **Camp Municipal de la Pinède, Chemin des Sablières, 84410 Bédoin [04 90 65 61 03; fax 04 90 65 95 22; la-pinede. camping.municipal@wanadoo.fr]** Take D938 S fr Malaucène for 3km, L onto D19 for 9km to Bédoin. Site adj to vill & sp. Med, sl, terr, shd; htd wc; shwrs inc; el pnts (16A) €2.50; lndtte; shops in vill; snacks; playgrnd; pool (high ssn); dogs €1; quiet; cc not acc; CCI. "Pool clsd Mon; office open 0900-1800; 5 min walk to vill & gd mkt on Mon." 15 Mar-31 Oct. € 11.50
2006*

BEDUER see Figeac *7D4*

France

BEGARD *2E2* (2km S Rural) **Camping du Donant, Gwenezhan, 22140 Bégard [02 96 45 46 46; fax 02 96 45 46 48; camping.begard@wanadoo.fr; www.camping-donant-bretagne.com]** Fr N12 at Guingamp take D767 dir Lannion, Perros-Guirec. S of Bégard foll sp Armoripark, site sp. Med, hdg/mkd pitch, hdstg, terr, pt shd; wc; chem disp; mv service pnt; shwrs inc; el pnts €2.60; gas 1km; lndtte; shop & bar adj; BBQ; playgrnd; htd pool & leisure facs adj; tennis adj; TV rm; statics; dogs; Eng spkn; adv bkg; quiet; cc acc. "In v pleasant countryside; conv coast; gd touring base." ♦ Easter-Mid Sep. € 12.10

2005*

As soon as we get home I'm going to post all these site report forms to the editor for inclusion in next year's guide. I don't want to miss the September deadline.

BELCAIRE *8G4* (SW Rural) **Camp Municipal Le Lac, 11340 Belcaire [04 68 20 39 47 or 04 68 20 31 23 (Mairie); fax 04 68 20 39 48; mairie.belcaire@wanadoo.fr]** Site on D613 bet Ax-les-Thermes & Quillan. Sm, mkd pitch, pt sl, shd; wc; chem disp; shwrs inc; el pnts €1,50; gas 1km; lndtte; ice; lake sw adj; dogs; phone; quiet; CCI. "Site by lake; gd cent for walking; tennis & horseriding nrby; historic vill of Montaillou nr; excel." ♦ ltd. 1 Jun-30 Sep. € 10.50   2006*

BELFORT *6G3* (1.5km N Urban) **FFCC Camping de l'Etang des Forges, 11 Rue du Général Béthouart, 90000 Belfort [03 84 22 54 92; fax 03 84 22 76 55; contact@campings-belfort.com; www.campings-belfort.com]** Exit A36 junc 13; go thro cent of Belfort; then foll sp Offemont on D13, then site sp. Or fr W on N19 site well sp. Med, hdg/mkd pitch, pt shd; htd wc; chem disp; mv service pnt; baby facs; shwrs inc; el pnts (6A) €3; lndtte; ice; shop 500m; tradsmn high ssn; rest 200m; snacks, bar high ssn; BBQ; playgrnd; pool; fishing & watersports 50m; archery; internet; entmnt; TV rm; 5% statics; dogs €1.50; extra for twin-axles; Eng spkn; adv bkg (dep req); quiet; red long stay; cc acc; CCI. "Clean modern san facs; friendly recep; conv for Corbusier's chapel at Ronchamp; slightly scruffy & unkempt low ssn; vg rest in Belfort; fair." ♦ 7 Apr-30 Sep. € 16.10 (CChq acc)   2007*

BELLAC *7A3* (Urban) **Camp Municipal Les Rochettes, Rue des Rochettes, 87300 Bellac [05 55 68 13 27; camping.bellac@wanadoo.fr; www.camping-limousin.com]** On N147 ent Bellac fr Poitiers take sharp L at 1st traff lts onto D675. Cont to rndabt & turn L Foll sp, site on L in 400m adj football pitch. Fr Limoges on N147 take R at 3rd traff lts after ent Bellac ont D675 then foll sp as above. Med, mkd pitch, pt sl, pt shd, terr; htd wc; chem disp; mv service pnt; shwrs inc; el pnts (10A) €2.60 (long lead poss req); gas; lndry rm; shops 500m; supmkt 1km; bar 500m; playgrnd; pool & waterslide 1km; games area; dogs €1.10; quiet; red long stay; cc not acc. "Pleasant warden; v spacious, pleasant, clean site but poss diff if wet; able to choose pitch; office clsd 1200-1500; coded barrier clsd 2000-0800; facs poss ltd low ssn; poss run-down low ssn; phone ahead to check site open low ssn; gd NH." € 10.30   2006*

BELLAC *7A3* (9km SE Rural) **Camping Fonclaire, 87300 Blond [tel/fax 05 55 60 88 26; fontclair@neuf.fr; http://limousin-gites.com]** Take D675 S twd St Junien. Site on L in approx 8km, 2km bef Mortemart. Sm, pt shd, wc; chem disp; shwrs inc; (own san facs Nov-Mar) el pnts (6A) €2 (poss rev pol); gas 1km; lndtte; ice; shop 2km; tradsmn; rest & bar 2km; sm htd pool; lake sw; fishing; no statics; dogs; phone 2km; Eng spkn; adv bkg (dep req); quiet; CCI. "CL-type site with v friendly, helpful British owners; gd facs; sm lake on site for carp fishing; close to Oradour-sur-Glane war-time martyr vill; excel base to explore local sights & Futuroscope; excel." ♦ ltd. € 11.00   2007*

BELLEME *4E2* (Urban) **Camp Municipal Le Val, Route de Mamers, 61130 Bellême [02 33 85 31 00 (Mairie); fax 02 33 83 58 85; mairie.bellame@wanadoo.fr]** Fr Mortagne, take D938 S to Bellême; turn R ent town on D955 Alençon rd; site sp on L half-way down hill. Sm, hdg pitch, pt sl, pt shd; wc (some cont); chem disp (wc); shwrs inc; el pnts (10A) inc; shops 1km by footpath; supmkt nrby; playgrnd, pool, fishing; tennis adj; dogs €0.50; adv bkg rec high ssn. "Pretty, well-maintained site; warden visits twice daily; gd san facs; poss long el cables/water hoses req; poss mkt traders; some pitches steep/v sl; some pitches water sodden in wet; steep walk into town." 15 Apr-15 Oct. € 7.40

2007*

BELGENTIER see Cuers *10F3*   **BELLENTRE see Aime** *9B3*

BELLEY 9B3 (8km E Rural) **Camping du Lac du Lit du Roi, La Tuilière, 01300 Massignieu-de-Rives [04 79 42 12 03; fax 04 79 42 19 94;** acamp@wanadoo.fr; www.camping-savoie.com] Fr D1504 (N504) turn E onto D992 to Massignieu-de-Rives, site sp. Site on NE of lake nr Les Mures. Med, hdg/mkd pitch, terr, pt shd; htd wc; chem disp; mv service pnt; shwrs inc; el pnts (10A) €4; gas; lndtte; ice; shop 8km; tradsmn; snacks; bar; BBQ; playgrnd; pool; lake sw & beach; boating; tennis; cycle hire; TV rm; 20% statics; dogs €4; phone; Eng spkn; adv bkg (fee); red long stay; cc acc; CCl. "Many pitches on lake with lovely views; superb site; excel facs." ♦ 14 Apr-30 Sep. € 20.00 (CChq acc)   2007*

BELMONT SUR RANCE 8E4 (Rural) **Camping Val Fleuri du Rance, Route de Lacaune, 12370 Belmont-sur-Rance [05 65 99 95 13; fax 05 65 99 95 82]** On D32 on ent vill fr SW; on L side of rd on sh unmade service rd. Sm, hdg/mkd pitch, pt shd; wc; chem disp; shwrs inc; el pnts (6A); gas; lndry rm; shop 500m; rest; pool 500m; fishing; tennis; adv bkg; quiet; CCl. "Attractive valley setting; helpful staff; easy walk to attract sm town; diff ent/exit to/fr south." ♦ ltd. 1 Jun-15 Sep.
2004*

BELVES 7D3 (4km N) **Camping Le Port, 24170 Siorac-en-Périgord [05 53 28 63 81 or 05 53 31 60 29]** On D25 in vill turn down beside Intermarché supmkt. Site ent strt ahead. Med, mkd pitch, shd; wc; shwrs; el pnts (10A) inc; lndtte; shops 1km; playgrnd; rv beach, sw & fishing; adv bkg rec; quiet. 15 May-30 Sep. € 15.00   2004*

BELVES 7D3 (7km SE Rural) **Camping Les Hauts de Ratebout, 24170 Belvès [05 53 29 02 10; fax 05 53 29 08 28; camping@hauts-ratebout.fr; www.hauts-ratebout.fr]** Turn E fr D710 onto D54 2km S of Belvès & foll camp sp. NB Do not ent Belvès. Lge, pt sl, terr, pt shd; htd wc; chem disp; shwrs inc; el pnts inc (10A) inc; rest; snacks; bar; shop; gas; lndtte; covr'd pool & paddling pool; waterslide; tennis; golf; fishing; horseriding; entmnt; adv bkg Jul/Aug (dep req); Eng spkn; cc acc; CCl. "Excel hilltop site; lge pitches; gd cent for touring." ♦ 13 May-10 Sep. € 33.00 (CChq acc)   2006*

BELVES 7D3 (2km S Rural) **Camping Le Moulin de la Pique, 24170 Belvès [05 53 29 01 15; fax 05 53 28 29 09; camping@perigord.com; www.rcn-campings.fr]** Site sp S of Belvès on L. Med, shd; wc; chem disp; shwrs inc; el pnts (6A) inc; lndtte; shop; rest; snacks; bar; playgrnd; pools (1 htd) & paddling pool; waterslides; boating; fishing; tennis; entmnt; TV; some statics; dogs €2.50; Eng spkn; adv bkg; red low ssn. "Monpazier beautiful; site vg for children; clean & well-maintained site; poss soft in wet weather; gd Sat mkt." ♦ 17 Apr-19 Oct. € 25.00   2004*

BELVES 7D3 (4km SW Rural) **FLOWER Caming Les Nauves, Le Bos-Rouge, 24170 Belvès [05 53 29 12 64 or 05 53 29 07 87; fax 05 53 29 07 87; campinglesnauves@hotmail.com; www.lesnauves.com]** On D53 fr Belvès. Site on L just after junc to Larzac. Med, hdg pitch, pt sl, pt shd; wc; chem disp; mv service pnt; baby facs; shwrs inc; el pnts (6A) inc; lndtte; ice; shop adj; rest; snacks; bar; BBQ; playgrnd; pool; paddling pool; games rm; horseriding; cycle hire; games rm; internet; entmnt; TV; some statics; dogs €2.30; adv bkg; quiet. "Excel site; Belvès lovely town." ♦ 11 Apr-21 Sep. € 16.70   2007*

BELVES 7D3 (8km SW Rural) **Camping Terme d'Astor (Naturist), St Avit-Rivière, 24480 Bouillac [05 53 63 24 52; fax 05 53 63 25 43; termdastor@wanadoo.fr; www.termedastor.com]** Leave D710 at Belvès onto D53; in 4km turn R onto D26 to Bouillac; pass thro vill; then turn 2nd L. Well sp. Med, mkd pitch, pt sl, shd; wc (some cont); chem disp; shwrs inc; el pnts (6A) €4; gas; lndtte; shop; tradsmn; rest; snacks; bar; BBQ; playgrnd; pool; paddling pool; waterslide; excursions; rafting; archery; tennis, horserding & canoeing nrby; games rm; internet; entmnt; TV; 10% statics; dogs free; phone; Eng spkn; adv bkg; quiet; cc acc; INF. "Gd cent for Dordogne rv & chateaux; vg." ♦ ltd. 14 Apr-30 Sep. € 26.00   2007*

BELVES 7D3 (2km NW Rural) **Camping La Lenotte, 24170 Monplaisant [tel/fax 05 53 30 25 80 or 06 89 33 05 60 (mob); campinglanotte@libertysurf.fr; www.la-lenotte.com]** Fr Sarlat take D57 twds Beynac, turn R in vill onto D703, at Siorac turn L onto D710 twd Belvès. Site on L in 2km. Med, hdg/mkd pitch, pt shd; wc; chem disp; mv service pnt; 80% serviced pitches; baby facs; shwrs inc; el pnts (6A) €2.80; gas; lndtte; ice; shop; tradsmn; snacks; BBQ; playgrnd; pool; shgl beach 3km; rv sw & fishing 3km; mini-golf; cycling; 5% statics; dogs €2.50; phone; Eng spkn; adv bkg; quiet but some rd noise; red CCl. "Beautiful scenery; nr old castles & Bastide towns; Belvès magnificent medieval town; helpful owner." ♦ ltd. 1 Apr-31 Oct. € 14.00
2004*

BELZ 2F3 (W Coastal) **Camping St Cado, Port de St Cado, 56550 Belz [02 97 55 31 98; fax 02 97 55 27 52; info@camping-saintcado.com; www.camping-saintcado.com]** W fr Auray on D22 then D16. Well sp fr Belz. Med, hdg pitch, pt shd; wc; el pnts (3-6A) €2.30-3.30; lndtte; tradsmn; shop, rest 300m; playgrnd; tennis; games area; fishing, boat hire 300m; games rm; some statics; dogs €1.40; adv bkg; quiet. 1 Apr-30 Sep. € 11.50   2006*

France

29950 Bénodet   Tel. 00 33 (0)2 98 57 04 69   Direct access to the beach
Bretagne Sud   Fax 00 33 (0)2 98 66 22 56   Caravans for hire
Finistère   www.campingduletty.com

BENODET *2F2* (1.5km E Coastal) **Camping Le Letty, 29950 Bénodet [02 98 57 04 69; fax 02 98 66 22 56; reception@campingduletty. com; www.campingduletty.com]** Fr N ent town on D34, foll sp Fouesnant D44. Le Letty sp R at rndabt. Fr E on N165 take D44 sp Fouesnant & foll rd to outskirts Bénodet. After town sp, site is sp. Lge, hdg/mkd pitches, hdstg, pt shd; wc (some cont); chem disp; mv service pnt; baby facs; sauna; shwrs €0.60; el pnts (5-10A) €3.05-4; gas; lndtte; shop; takeaway snacks; bar; playgrnd; pool 500m; sand beach adj; tennis; squash; games area; games rm; gym; golf, horseriding nr; library; entmnt; wifi internet; TV rm; 2% statics; dogs €2.30; adv bkg; quiet; CCI. "Excel, well-run, well-equipped, beautifully laid out site; v clean; many activities; friendly, helpful staff; highly rec." ♦ 15 Jun-6 Sep. € 24.00   2007*

See advertisement above

BENODET *2F2* (500m SE Coastal) **Camping du Poulquer, Route de Letty, 29950 Bénodet [02 98 57 04 19; fax 02 98 66 20 30; campingdupoulquer@wanadoo.fr; www. campingdupoulquer.com]** Fr N ent town on D34. At rndabt after junc with D44 strt onto Rue Penfoul. At next rndabt (tourist info office on R after rndabt) go strt dir La Plage until reach seafront; turn L at seafront then turn L at end of prom at camping sp; site in 100m on R. Fr E on N165 take D44 sp Fouesnant & foll rd to outskirts Bénodet. After town sp, site is sp. Med, hdg/mkd pitch, pt sl, pt shd; wc; chem disp; baby facs; shwrs inc; el pnts (10A) inc (long lead poss req)(poss rev pol); gas; lndtte; shop, snacks & bar high ssn; BBQ; playgrnd; htd pool & paddling pool; waterslide; aqua park; sand beach adj; tennis; golf nr; cycle hire 1km; entmnt; games/ TV rm; dogs €2; recep 0830-2000; c'vans over 7.50m not acc high ssn; adv bkg; quiet; cc not acc; CCI. "Friendly, helpful owner; easy walk to beach & town; gd base; gd, clean san facs, poss tired end of ssn; pitches tight for lge o'fits; low branches on access rd; gd hotel rest 600m; mkt Mon; ideal for visiting Iles de Glénan." ♦ 15 May-30 Sep. € 26.00 ABS - B16   2007*

BENODET *2F2* (2km SE Coastal) **Camping Sunêlia La Pointe St Gilles, Rue Poulmic, 29950 Bénodet [02 98 57 05 37; fax 02 98 57 27 52; information@ camping-stgilles.fr; www.camping-stgilles.fr]** Fr N ent town on D34. At rndabt after junc with D44 (Pont l'Abbe) strt onto Rue Penfoul. At next rndabt (tourist info office on R after rndabt) go strt dir La Plage until reach seafront. Turn L at end of prom twd Le Letty & L after Les Horizons development into Rue du Poulquer; site in 200m on L. Fr E on N165 take D44 sp Fouesnant & foll rd to outskirts Bénodet. After town sp, site is sp. Lge, hdg pitch, pt shd; wc; shwrs inc; el pnts (10A) inc; gas; lndtte; ice; shop; snacks; htd pool & paddling pool; jacuzzi; waterslide; sand beach adj; 90% statics; no dogs; phone; poss cr; adv bkg; quiet; red long stay; cc acc. "Pleasant town, gd beaches; rv trips; well-run site; helpful staff; ltd touring pitches in sep area." 13 Apr-18 Sep. € 38.00   2005*

> The opening dates and prices on this campsite have changed. I'll send a site report form to the editor for the next edition of the guide.

BENODET *2F2* (7km W Coastal) **Camping Le Helles, 55 Rue du Petit-Bourg, 29120 Combrit-Ste Marine [02 98 56 31 46; fax 02 98 56 36 83; contact@le-helles.com; www.le-helles.com]** Exit D44 S dir Ste Marine, site sp. Med, mkd pitch, pt sl, pt shd; htd wc; chem disp; baby facs; shwrs; el pnts (6-10A) €3.50-4.40; lndtte; tradsmn; snacks; BBQ; playgrnd; htd pool; paddling pool; sand beach 300m; some statics; dogs €2.60; Eng spkn; adv bkg; quiet; cc acc; red low ssn. "Vg site with lge pitches; gd, clean san facs; friendly, helpful staff; excel beach. " ♦ 10 May-15 Sep. € 21.50   2007*

See advertisement opposite

BENODET 2F2 (1km NW Rural) **Yelloh! Village Port de Plaisance, Route de Quimper, Clohars-Fouesnant, 29950 Bénodet [tel/fax 02 98 57 02 38; info@campingbenodet.fr; www.campingbenodet. fr www.yellohvillage.com]** Fr Bénodet take D34 twd Quimper, site on R 200m bef rndabt at ent to town. Lge, hdg pitch, pt sl, pt shd; wc; chem disp; mv service pnt; shwrs inc; child/baby facs; el pnts (6A) inc; lndtte; shop; tradsmn; rest; snacks; bar; playgrnd; htd pool; sand/shgl beach 1.5km; tennis; games area; cycle hire; internet; entmnt; 80% statics; dogs €4.50; phone; poss cr; Eng spkn; poss noisy (disco); adv bkg; red low ssn; cc acc.; CCI. "Many tour ops on site; some pitches poss diff lge o'fits." ♦ ltd. 12 Apr-13 Sep. € 37.00   2007*

BENON see Courçon 7A2

BENOUVILLE see Ouistreham 3D1

BERAUT see Condom 8E2

BERCK 3B2 (4km E Rural) **Camping L'Orée du Bois, 251 Chemin Blanc, 62180 Rang-du-Fliers [03 21 84 28 51; fax 03 21 84 28 56; oree. du.bois@wanadoo.fr; www.loreedubois.com]** Exit A6 junc 25 onto D140 & D917. Thro Rang-du-Fliers, turn R bef pharmacy into Chemin Blanc, site sp. V lge, hdg/mkd pitch, pt shd; wc (some cont); mv service pnt; chem disp; mv service pnt; serviced pitches; shwrs inc; el pnts (6A) inc; gas; shop adj; lndtte; tradsmn; rest; snacks; bar; playgrnd; pools; sand beach 4km; tennis; games area; fishing lake; cycle hire; entmnt; 80% statics; dogs €3; Eng spkn; adv bkg; quiet; cc acc; red low ssn/long stay/CCI. "V conv Le Touquet, Boulogne, Montreuil & Calais; peaceful site in woodland; ltd facs low ssn; ltd space for tourers." ♦ 1 Apr-4 Nov. € 24.00   2007*

See advertisement above

Before we move on, I'm going to fill in some site report forms and post them off to the editor, otherwise they won't arrive in time for the deadline at the end of September.

BERGERAC *7C3* (500m S Urban) **Camp Municipal La Pelouse, 8 bis Rue JJ Rousseau, 24100 Bergerac [tel/fax 05 53 57 06 67; population@ mairie-bergerac.fr; www.ville-bergerac.com]** On S bank of Rv Dordogne 300m W of old bdge opp town cent. Do not ent town, foll camping sp fr bdge, ent on R after L turn opp block of flats. Well sp, on Rv Loire. Med, mkd pitch, pt sl, pt shd; wc; own san; chem disp; mv service pnt; shwrs inc; el pnts (6A) €2.60-3.77; gas; lndtte; ice; shop in town; playgrnd; fishing & rv sw adj; 90% statics; dogs €0.87; dep for barrier; poss cr; adv bkg; Eng spkn; quiet but some rlwy noise; cc not acc; CCI. "Twin-axles & c'vans over 6m not permitted; dated san facs, ltd low ssn; friendly warden; sh walk by rv into attractive old city; poss clsd earlier if weather bad; arr bef 1400 high ssn." ♦ 16 Feb-31 Oct. € 6.98   2007*

BERGERAC *7C3* (8km W Rural) **Camping Parc Servois, 11 Rue du Bac, 24680 Gardonne [05 53 27 38 34]** Fr D936 Bergerac to Bordeaux, R in vill of Gardonne. Site 100m after traff lts. Sm, mkd pitch, pt shd; wc; chem disp; shwrs inc; el pnts (10A) €1.90-2.10; ice; shops 200m; rest 300m; dogs €0.60; phone 200m; quiet; CCI. "Pretty, CL-type site; facs immac but dated & poss stretched in ssn." 1 Apr-30 Sep. € 7.80   2006*

BERGUES *3A3* (500m NE Urban) **Camping Le Vauban, Ave Vauban, 59380 Bergues [03 28 68 65 25 or 03 28 63 07 71; fax 03 28 63 52 60; cassiopee.tourisme@wanadoo. fr; http://cassiopee-tourisme.monsite.wanadoo. fr]** Exit Bergues dir Hoymille; site on L at bottom of ramparts. Well sp. Med, hdg/mkd pitch, pt shd; wc (cont); chem disp; mv service pnt; baby facs; fam bthrm; shwrs €1.10; el pnts (6A) €3.35; lndtte; shop, rest, snacks & bar in town; playgrnd; pool nr; 33% statics; no twin axles; dogs €1.05; poss cr; adv bkg; quiet; no cc acc; CCI. "Lovely fortified town; many shops & rests; conv Dunkerque & Calais; gd NH." ♦ ltd. 15 Apr-30 Oct. € 11.65   2007*

⊞**BERGUES** *3A3* (4km NE Rural) **FFCC Parc Les Résidences La Becque, 791 Rue de l'Est, 59380 Warhem [03 28 62 00 40; fax 03 28 62 05 65; www.residences-la-becque.com]** Exit A25 at junc 16 sp Bergues. At top of slip rd turn L D916 then turn R at rndabt onto D110; L in 4km to Warhem. Site well sp in vill. Med, hdg/mkd pitch, hdstg, pt shd, wc (cont); own san; shwrs €1.50; el pnts (6A) €2.50; gas; lndry rm; shop 1km; supmkt in Hoymille; playgrnd; rv fishing 2km; tennis; 95% statics; dogs €1.50; quiet; CCI. "Gd NH; helpful owner; security barrier." ♦ € 17.00   2007*

BERNAY *3D2* (1.5km S Urban) **Camp Municipal, Rue des Canadiens, 27300 Bernay [02 32 43 30 47; camping@bernay27.fr; www. ville-bernay27.fr]** Site sp fr S'most (Alençon) rndabt off Bernay by-pass N138; twd France Parc Exposition then 1st L & on R. Well sp. Sm, hdg/ mkd pitch, pt shd; wc; chem disp; mv service pnt; shwrs inc; el pnts (10A) inc (poss rev pol); lndry rm; shop 500m; tradsmn; rest, bar 1km; playgrnd; pool 300m; table tennis; TV rm; dogs; phone; adv bkg; no cc acc; CCI. "V nice, quiet, well-maintained site; well set out pitches - diff sizes; gd, clean facs; v helpful & friendly; 20 mins walk to town cent; barrier clsd 2200-0700; excel." ♦ 1 May-30 Sep. € 17.15   2007*

BERNERIE EN RETZ, LA see Pornic *2G3*

BERNEVAL LE GRAND *3B2* (Coastal) **Camp Municipal Le Val Boise, Ave Capitaine Portheous, 76340 Berneval-le-Grand [02 35 85 29 18 or 02 35 06 05 40 (Mairie); camping-berneval@ wanadoo.fr]** Fr Dieppe take D925 for 6km, turn L at Graincourt onto D54 past Silo on R. Site sp. Sm, mkd pitch, hdstg, terr, pt shd; wc; chem disp; mv service pnt; shwrs; el pnts (16A) €2.30; ice; shop 2km; playgrnd; shgl beach 700m; entmnt; some statics; dogs; Eng spkn; adv bkg rec; quiet; CCI. "V hilly area; poss diff lge units; lovely quiet spot." 1 Apr-1 Nov. € 8.00   2005*

BERNY RIVIERE *3C4* (1.5km S Rural) **Camping La Croix du Vieux Pont, Route de Fontenoy, 02290 Berny-Rivière [03 23 55 50 02; fax 03 23 55 05 13; info@la-croix-du-vieux-pont.com; www.la-croix-du-vieux-pont.com]** On N31 bet Soissons & Compiègne. At site sp turn onto D13, then at Vic-sur-Aisne take next R, R again then L onto D91. Foll sp to site on o'skts of Berny. V lge, hdg pitch, hdstg, pt shd; htd wc; chem disp; mv service pnt; some serviced pitch; baby facs; shwrs inc; el pnts (6A) €2.50 (poss rev pol & no earth); gas; lndtte; supmkt; tradsmn; rest; snacks; bar; playgrnd; 4 htd pools (2 covrd); waterslide; tennis; games rm; lake beach & sw; fishing; boating; horseriding; archery; golf; cycle hire; gym; excursions to Paris & Disneyland; internet; TV rm; many tour op statics high ssn; dogs; poss cr; Eng spkn; adv bkg rec; quiet; cc acc; CCI. "V nice site; well-controlled & quiet on rvside pitches; lge pitches; v gd san facs, ltd low ssn; helpful staff; vg rest; wine-growing area; coaches to Disneyland & Paris; popular w/e for Parisians; some sh stay pitches up steep bank; some pitches liable to flood; gd family entmnt; site open all yr but no services avail Nov-Mar; excel." ♦ 20 Mar-31 Oct. € 21.50 (3 persons) (CChq acc)   2007*

⊞BERNY RIVIERE *3C4* (2km W Urban) **Camping La Halte de Mainville, 18 Rue de Routy, 02290 Ressons-le-Long [03 23 74 26 69; fax 03 23 74 03 60; lahaltedemainville@wanadoo. fr]** On L of N31 Soissons to Compiègne rd 10km W of Soissons, clearly sp. Lge, hdg/mkd pitch, pt shd; wc; chem disp; shwrs inc; el pnts (6A) €2.50-5 (poss rev pol); lndtte; shop 4km; tradsmn; playgrnd; htd pool; fishing; tennis; 50% statics; dogs; phone; adv bkg rec; quiet but poss some rd noise; no cc acc; CCI. "Vg, pleasant site; friendly staff; 1 hr fr Disneyland." € 14.50   2006*

BERT see Donjon, Le *9A1*

BERTANGLES see Amiens *3C3*

BESANCON *6G2* (5km NE Rural) **FFCC Camping La Plage, Route de Belfort, 25220 Chalezeule [03 81 88 04 26; fax 03 81 50 54 62; laplage. besancon@ffcc.fr; www.camp-in-france.com]** Exit A36 junc 4; foll sp Montbéliard onto N83. Well sp fr N83. Fr Belfort 2.65m height restriction; foll sp to Chalezeule & 300m after supmkt turn L to rejoin N83, site in 200m. Med, mkd pitch, terr, pt shd; htd wc; chem disp; mv service pnt; shwrs inc; el pnts (6A) €3.50 (poss rev pol); lndtte; supmkt 1km; snacks; playgrnd; htd pool; rv adj; kayaking; 50% statics; dogs €1; bus to city weekdays; poss cr; Eng spkn; quiet but some rd & rlwy noise; cc acc; red CCI. "Rvside site conv for city, local rests & citadel; helpful staff; easy parking in town; twin-axles extra charge." ♦ 1 Apr-30 Sep. € 13.45   2007*

BESANCON *6G2* (11km NW) **Camping Les Peupliers, 25870 Geneuille [03 81 57 72 04]** Fr Besançon take N57 towards Vesoul then take L into D1 & fork R to Geneuille. Site sp thro vill. Sm, mkd pitch, pt shd; wc (some cont); chem disp (wc); el pnts (10A) inc; shops 1km, rest, snacks, bar 500m; rv; 10% statics; quiet; dogs. "Fairly run down, old fashioned but peaceful site; friendly welcome; some refurbed san facs; access to facs by stairs, diff for disabled; conv Besançon; gd." 15 May-30 Sep. € 11.00   2007*

BESSANS *9C4* (800m S Rural) **Camping L'Illaz, Rue de l'Ilette, 73480 Bessans [tel/fax 04 79 05 83 31; bessanscampingillaz@wanadoo.fr; http://pages perso-orange.fr/bessanscampingillaz]** Clearly sp on D902 fr Lanslebourg. Sm, unshd; wc; chem disp; shwrs; no el pnts; shops 1km; fishing; dogs; quiet but some rd noise. "Vg san facs; direct access to rv & lake." 15 Jun-31 Aug. € 13.00   2005*

BESSE SUR BRAYE *4F2* (Rural) **Camping Le Val de Braye, 25 Rue du Val de Braye, 72310 Bessé-sur-Braye [02 43 35 31 13; fax 02 43 35 58 86; mairie-bessesurbraye@wanadoo.fr]** Fr St Calais on D303 turn L in cent of Bessé-sur-Braye sp Troo; turn R immed over rlwy line (disused). Site on L in 300m. Or better rte fr St Calais ignore Centre Ville sp & cont on by-pass. Site on L 300m beyond traff lts. Med, pt shd; htd wc; chem disp; mv service pnt; shwrs inc; el pnts (6A) €2 (some rev pol); lndtte; ice; shop adj; BBQ; playgrnd; htd, covrd pool adj; walking; fishing; TV; adv bkg; quiet; red long stay; CCI; "V helpful resident warden; pitch area ltd low ssn; dep req barrier key; well-kept, excel site." ♦ 15 Apr-15 Sep. € 8.00   2005*

BESSEGES see St Ambroix *9D2*

There aren't many sites open this early in the year. We'd better phone ahead to check that the one we're heading for is actually open.

⊞**BESSINES SUR GARTEMPE** *7A3* (4km N Rural) **Camp Municipal, 87250 Morterolles-sur-Semme [05 55 76 09 28 or 05 55 76 05 09 (Mairie); fax 05 55 76 68 45; ot.bessines@wanadoo.fr]** S on A20 take exit 23.1 sp Châteauponsac. Take 1st turn R, site on L in vill of Morterolles by stadium. N on A20 take exit 24.2 sp Bessines, turn under a'route & take 1st R sp Châteauponsac to Morterolles in 3km. Sm, mkd pitch, pt shd; htd wc; shwrs inc; el pnts (5A) €2.10 (poss rev pol); lndry rm; playgrnd; covrd pool 200m; cycle hire; dogs; poss cr; Eng spkn; quiet; CCI. "Delightful, farm site nr Limoges & a'route; gd low ssn as htd shwr blocks old-fashioned but clean; if warden absent on arr, pitch yourself & will call later; poss itinerants; excel NH." ♦ ltd. € 6.80   2007*

BESSINES SUR GARTEMPE *7A3* (1.5km SW Urban) **Camp Municipal Lac de Sagnat, Route de St Pardoux, 87250 Bessines-sur-Gartempe [05 55 76 17 69 or 05 55 76 05 09 (Mairie); fax 05 55 76 01 24; ot.bessines@wanadoo.fr]** Fr A20 exit sp Bessines-sur-Gartempe onto D220; then D27 sp lake. Foll sp to Bellevue Restaurant. At rest, turn R foll site sp. Med, hdg/mkd pitch, pt sl, terr, pt shd; wc; chem disp; shwrs inc; el pnts inc; lndtte; shops 1km; tradsmn high ssn; rest 500m; snacks high ssn; playgrnd adj; sand beach & lake sw adj; TV rm; Eng spkn; poss cr; quiet. "V friendly staff; lake views; peaceful location; sm boats for children; gd clean san facs." ♦ 15 Jun-15 Sep. € 12.00   2005*

CAMPING CARAVANNING UR-ONEA ★★★

At the entrance of Biarritz, the enchantment of 5 ha terraced terrain, 600 meters from the beaches and the town centre.

A diversity of activities, swimming pool, bar, take away meals, groceries, launderette. Rental of caravans and mobile homes. Rental of chalets all year round.

F-64210 BIDART Phone: 00 33 (0)5 59 26 53 61
Fax: 00 33 (0)5 59 26 53 94
www.uronea.com • uronea@wanadoo.fr

BETHUNE *3B3* (1km E Urban) Camp Municipal, Rue Victor Dutériez, 62660 Beuvry [03 21 65 08 00 or 03 21 61 82 90 (Mairie); fax 03 21 61 82 91] Fr A26 exit junc 6 onto D941 (N41) dir Lille. At junc D94/N943 turn L to Beuvry, sp on R in town as 'Camping', also sp to 'Base de Loisirs'. Med, mkd pitches; some hdstg; pt sl, pt shd; wc (some cont); shwrs €1.10; el pnts (2-6A) €2.30-4.60; lndry rm; shop 500m; tradsmn; snacks nr; htd, covrd pool 500m; fishing adj; 10% statics; adv bkg; cc not acc; CCI. "Basic site; twin-axles prohibited; no recep facs after 1800 tho access allowed; buy jetons for shwrs on arr, as warden often absent; some el pnts not working; conv ferries & WW1 battlefields; poss noise fr football ground adj; san facs rudimentary; gd NH but unreliable opening dates low ssn." 15 May-15 Sep. €6.35　　　　　　　　　　2006*

BEUZEC CAP SIZUN see Douarnenez *2E2*

BEYNAC ET CAZENAC see Sarlat la Canéda *7C3*

BEYNAT *7C4* (4km E) Centre Touristique L'Etang du Miel, 19190 Beynat [05 55 85 50 66; fax 05 55 85 57 96; camping.lac.de.miel@wanadoo. fr] Fr D940 turn W at Quatre Routes onto D921, site sp. Lge, pt sl, pt shd; wc (some cont); chem disp; mv service pnt; baby facs; shwrs; el pnts (6A) inc; lndtte; ice; shop; rest 5km; snacks; bar; BBQ; playgrnd; lake sw & beach; fishing; tennis; games rm; 2% statics; phone; adv bkg; quiet; CCI. ♦ ltd. 15 Apr-15 Sep. €16.00　　　　　　　　　　2004*

⊞**BEZIERS** *10F1* (10km NE Rural) Camping Le Rebau, 34290 Montblanc [04 67 98 50 78; fax 04 67 98 68 63; gilbert@camping-lerebau.fr; www.camping-lerebau.fr] NE on N9 fr Béziers-Montpellier, turn R onto D18. Site sp, narr ent 2.50m. Lge, hdg/mkd pitch, hdstg, pt shd; wc; chem disp; baby facs; shwrs inc; el pnts (5A) €4.50; gas 2km; lndtte; ice; shop in vill; snacks & bar high ssn; playgrnd; pool; fishign; sand beach 13km; entmnt; TV; 10% statics; dogs €2.80; phone; bus 1km; poss cr; Eng spkn; adv bkg (dep req); quiet; red low ssn; CCI. "Gd site; tight ent & manoeuvring onto pitches; some facs old but modern shwr; ltd facs low ssn, but v clean; v helpful owner; gd pool; gd touring base; low ssn phone ahead to check open; excel value low ssn; gd." €19.50　　2007*

BEZIERS *10F1* (4km SE Urban) Camping Les Berges du Canal, 34420 Villeneuve-les-Béziers [04 67 39 36 09; fax 04 67 39 82 07; contact@ lesbergesducanal.com; www.lesbergesducanal. com] Fr A9 exit junc 35 & foll sp for Agde. Exit 1st rndabt for D612 (N112) dir Béziers then 1st L onto D37 sp Villneuve-les-Béziers. Foll site sp. Med, hdg/mkd pitch, shd; wc; chem disp; mv service pnt; baby facs; shwrs inc; el pnts inc (poss rev pol); lndtte; shop; rest; snacks; playgrnd; htd pool; beach 10km; 45% statics; dogs €2; poss cr; Eng spkn; adv bkg dep req; red 5+ days; CCI. "Facs v clean but poss stretched in ssn; some pitches tight lge o'fits; expensive for long family holiday." 15 Apr-15 Sep. €22.00　　　　　　　　　　2005*

⊞**BEZIERS** *10F1* (7km SW Rural) Camping Les Peupliers, 7 Promenade de l'Ancien Stade, 34440 Colombiers [04 67 37 05 26; fax 04 67 37 67 87; contact@camping-colombiers.com; www. camping-colombiers.com] SW fr Béziers on D6009 (N9) turn R on D162E & foll sp to site using heavy vehicle rte. Cross canal bdge & fork R; turn R & site on L. Easier ent fr D11 (Béziers-Capestang) avoiding narr vill rds, turn L at rndabt at end of dual c'way sp Colombiers; in 1km at rlwy bdge, go strt on; in 100m turn L (bef canal bdge) where rd turns sharp R. Med, mkd pitch, pt shd; wc; chem disp; fam bthrm; shwrs inc; el pnts (10A) €3.10 (inc in high ssn); gas; lndtte; ice; shop, rest 1km; snacks; bar; BBQ; playgrnd; sand beach 15km; internet; 10% statics; dogs €2.50; adv bkg; quiet; some rlwy noise; red long stay; CCI. "Nice location nr Canal du Midi away fr busy beach sites; gd san facs; pool planned for 2007; excel walking & cycling; NH only." ♦ €25.00　　　　　　　　　　2007*

BEZINGHEM *3A3* (1km S Rural) FFCC Camping Les Aulnes, Hameau d'Egranges, 62650 Bezinghem [03 21 90 93 88; fax 03 21 86 07 88; campinglesaulnes@orange.fr; www.camping lesaulnes.com] S fr Desvres or N fr Montreuil on D127. Site at S end of vill on W side of rd, v narr app rds. Med, pt shd; wc (some cont); shwrs inc; el pnts (10A) €3; gas; lndtte; ice; shop; snacks; bar; BBQ; playgrnd; fishing; some statics; rd noise; CCI. "Sm pitches." Easter-15 Oct. €14.00　　　　　　　2007*

BIARRITZ *8F1* (3.5km E Rural) **Camping Le Parme, Quartier Brindos, 64600 Anglet [05 59 23 03 00; fax 05 59 41 29 55; campingdeparme@wanadoo. fr; www.campingdeparme.com]** On N10 fr St Jean-de-Luz to Bayonne. Site sp on R bef Biarritz aerodrome, 500m down tarmac app rd. Lge, pt sl, terr, shd; htd wc (some cont); shwrs inc; el pnts (6-10A) €3.70-4; gas; lndtte; ice; shops 3km; rest; snacks; bar; playgrnd; pool; paddling pool; sand beach 2.5km; tennis; entmnt; TV; dogs €3; cc acc. "Diff exit up steep slope & by blind corner - owner will advise alt R-turn rte." ♦ 15 Mar-15 Nov. € 23.00   2005*

BIARRITZ *8F1* (3km S Coastal) **Airotel Camping Résidence des Pins, Ave de Biarritz, 64210 Bidart [05 59 23 00 29; fax 05 59 41 24 59; contact@ campingdespins.com; www.campingdespins. com]** S fr Bayonne on N10, by-pass Biarritz. 1km after A63 junc turn R at rndabt immed after Intermarché on R; sp to Pavillon Royal. Site 1km on R sp. Lge, mkd pitch, pt sl, terr, shd; wc; chem disp; shwrs inc; baby facs; el pnts (10A) €5.10; gas; lndtte; shop; tradsmn; rest & snacks high ssn; bar; playgrnd; htd pool; sand beach 600m; tennis; games area; cycle hire; golf nr; horseriding; child entmnt; internet; TV; many statics & tour ops; dogs €2.50; phone; poss cr; Eng spkn; adv bkg over 15 days & high ssn; red low ssn; cc acc; CCI. "Attractive, mature site; lge pitches; narr access rds poss diff long o'fits; gd san facs; poor night lighting; gd beaches at Bidart, St Jean-de-Luz, Biarritz." ♦ 12 May-29 Sep. € 24.50 (CChq acc)   2007*

Did you know you can fill in site report forms on the Club's website — www.caravanclub.co.uk?

BIARRITZ *8F1* (3km S Coastal) **Village Camping Sunêlia Berrua, Rue Berrua, 64210 Bidart [05 59 54 96 66; fax 05 59 54 78 30; contact@ berrua.com; www.berrua.com]** Exit A63 junc 4 dir Bidart, fr Bidart on N10 sp St Jean de Luz, L at 1st traff lts, site sp. Lge, pt sl, pt shd; wc; chem disp; mv service pnt; shwrs inc; baby facs; el pnts (6-10A) €4.90; (poss long lead req); gas; lndtte; ice; shop; tradsmn; rest; snacks; bar; BBQ; playgrnd; htd pool & paddling pool; waterslides; beach 1km; tennis; cycle hire; archery; golf 2km;TV; 50% statics; dogs €3.40; phone; bus 1km; poss cr; Eng spkn; adv bkg; poss cr & noisy; red 7+ days; cc acc; CCI. "Attractive area; well-maintained site; pitches tight lge o'fits; site rds narr; low trees; some high kerbs; leads poss across rds; excel, clean facs; muddy after rain; gd rest; sh walk to vill." ♦ 31 Mar-14 Oct. € 30.20 (CChq acc)   2007*

BIARRITZ *8F1* (5km S Rural) **Camping Le Ruisseau des Pyrénées, Route d'Arbonne, 64210 Bidart [05 59 41 94 50; fax 05 59 41 95 73; francoise.dumont@wanadoo.fr; www.les-castels. com & www.camping-le-ruisseau.fr]** Exit N10 E in either dir, at Bidart take rd sp Arbonne, site sp. Rds twisty & narr. Lge, some hdg pitch, pt sl, terr, pt shd; wc; chem disp (wc); mv service pnt; shwrs inc; el pnts (6A) inc; gas; lndtte; ice; shop; rest; snacks; bar; playgrnd; 3 pools (1 covrd) & paddling pool; waterslide; lake fishing; boating; sand beach 2.5km; tennis; games area; cycling; mini-golf; 90% statics; dogs €1.50; poss cr; adv bkg ess high ssn; poss noisy; red low ssn; golf nr; CCI. "Steep slope/short run to barrier poss diff; best pitches by lake; site muddy after rain; excel for children & teenagers." 28 Apr-16 Sep. € 30.00   2007*

BIARRITZ *8F1* (5km S Coastal) **Camping Ur-Onéa, Rue de la Chapelle, 64210 Bidart [05 59 26 53 61; fax 05 59 26 53 94; uronea@wanadoo.fr; www. uronea.com]** Exit A63 junc 4 dir Bidart, fr Bidart on N10 sp St Jean de Luz, L at 2nd traff lts nr church, then immed R, site is 500m on L. Access fr main rd a bit tricky, 2nd access further S is easier. Lge, mkd pitch, hdstg, terr, pt shd; wc (some cont); chem disp; serviced pitches; baby facs; fam bthrm; shwrs inc; el pnts (10A) €3.50-5; gas; lndtte; ice; shop high ssn; tradsmn; rest; snacks; bar, BBQ; playgrnd; pool; sand beach 600m; lake sw 12km; entmnt; TV; 20% statics; dogs €2; phone; Eng spkn; adv bkg; quiet, some rail noise; cc acc; red low ssn; CCI. "Conv Pays Basque vills; 600m fr Bidart; staff v friendly & helpful; excel san facs." ♦ 5 Apr-15 Sep. € 24.50   2007*

See advertisement

BIARRITZ *8F1* (2km SW Coastal) **Camping Biarritz, 28 Rue Harcet, 64200 Biarritz [05 59 23 00 12; fax 05 59 43 74 67; biarritz.camping@wanadoo.fr; www.biarritz-camping.fr]** S fr Bayonne on N10, by-pass Biarritz & cont to junc of N10 coast rd sp Bidart & Biarritz; double back on this rd, take 1st exit at next rndabt, 1st L dir Biarritz Cent, foll sp to site in 2km. Lge, mkd pitch, pt sl, terr, pt shd; wc; chem disp; mv service pnt; shwrs inc; el pnts (10A) €4; gas; lndtte; shop; tradsmn; rest; snacks; bar; playgrnd; htd pool; paddling pool; sand beach 1km; tennis 4km; entmnt; 10% statics; no dogs; poss cr; adv bkg (dep req); cc acc; noisy in high ssn; red low ssn/CCI. "One of better sites in area espec low ssn." ♦ ltd. 5 May-15 Sep. € 21.50   2007*

BIARRITZ *8F1* (3.5km SW Coastal) **Camping Pavillon Royal, Ave du Prince-de-Galles, 64210 Bidart [05 59 23 00 54; fax 05 59 23 44 47; info@ pavillon-royal.com; www.pavillon-royal.com]** Leave A63 at junc 4 sp Biarritz. After tolls turn L at rndabt onto N10. In approx 1.5km at 1st rndabt (just past Intermarché store) turn R onto D655 & in 1km turn R at T-junc. Turn L into narr rd & foll site sp. Lge, hdg/mkd pitch, pt sl, pt shd, wc (some cont); chem disp; serviced pitch; baby facs; shwrs inc; el pnts (5A) inc (long lead poss req); gas; lndtte; ice; shop; tradsmn; rest; snacks; bar; BBQ; playgrnd; pool & paddling pool; sand beach adj; tennis & mini-golf nr; games rm; cycle hire; golf 500m; horseriding 2km; wifi internet; 30% statics; no dogs; recep 0800-2100; poss cr; Eng spkn; adv bkg (ess Jul/Aug); dep req & bkg fee €22.87; cc acc; red low ssn. "Direct access via steps to excel beach; clean, well-run, busy, friendly site; various pitch sizes; excel for families; recep 0800-2100; conv Spanish border & Pyrenees; gd rest; mkt Sat." ♦ 15 May-25 Sep. € 45.00 ABS - A06   2007*

BIARRITZ *8F1* (4km SW Coastal) **Camping Erreka, Ave de Cumba, 64210 Bidart [05 59 54 93 64; fax 05 59 47 70 46; campingerreka@laposte.net; www.camping-erreka.com]** Site at junc of N10 Biarritz by-pass & main rd into town cent; well sp. Lge, terr, pt sl, pt shd; wc (some cont); chem disp; mv service pnt; baby facs; shwrs; el pnts (6A) €4; gas; lndtte; shop; snacks; playgrnd; pool; paddling pool; sand beach 800m; wifi internet; entmnt; TV; 75% statics; no dogs; red low ssn; adv bkg; cc acc; quiet; CCI. "Some pitches sl & poss v diff to get into, rec adv bkg to ensure suitable pitch; access rds v steep." 16 Jun-16 Sep. € 22.00   2007*

BIARRITZ *8F1* (5km SW Coastal) **Camping Oyam, Rue d'Eskola, 64210 Bidart [tel/fax 05 59 54 91 61]** Leave A63 at junc 4 onto N10; 150m after Bidart boundary sp, turn L at traff lts sp Arbonne. In 600m at brow of hill turn R & then immed L. Med, pt sl, terr, pt shd, mkd pitch; wc; chem disp; baby facs; shwrs inc; el pnts (3A) €3.50; lndtte; shop; rest; snacks; playgrnd; pool; sand beach 1.2km; mini-golf; 70% statics; Eng spkn; adv bkg; some rd & rlwy noise; CCI. "A well-managed site in lovely surroundings." ♦ 15 Apr-30 Sep. € 22.00   2004*

BIDART see Biarritz *8F1*

BIERT see Massat *8G3*

BIESHEIM see Neuf Brisach *6F3*

BIGANOS see Audenge *7D1*

BIGNAC see Angoulême *7B2*

BILIEU see Abrets, Les *9B3*

BILLOM *9B1* (NE Urban) **Camp Municipal Le Colombier, Allée des Tennis, 63160 Billom [04 73 68 91 50; fax 04 73 73 37 60; billom@billom. com; www.billom.com]** Exit A72 junc 2 onto D906 sp Pont-de-Dore; turn R onto N89; in 1km turn L onto D212/D229 to Billom; at rndabt junc with D997 cont on D229 & take 1st L into Route de Lezoux, then L into Rue des Tennis. Site sp. Sm, hdg/mkd pitch, pt sl, shd; wc (cont); chem disp (wc); shwrs inc; el pnts (10A) €2.70; gas 500m; lndry rm; ice; shop; rest 500m; snacks 200m; bar; BBQ; pool & tennis adj; games rm; entmnt; TV; 30% statics; dogs; phone 200m; no twin axles; adv bkg; quiet; CCI. "Clean, spacious facs; disabled the only non-cont wc (unisex); helpful warden; historic town & interesting area." ♦ ltd. 1 Jun-15 Sep. € 7.00
                                              2007*

BINIC *2E3* (500m NE Urban/Coastal) **Camp Municipal des Fauvettes, Rue des Fauvettes, 22520 Binic [02 96 73 60 83 or 02 96 73 61 15 (Mairie); fax 02 96 73 72 38; ville. binic@wanadoo.fr]** Fr D786 foll sp to Binic & site. Narr ent. Med, mkd pitch, terr, pt sl, pt shd; wc; chem disp (wc); mv service pnt; shwrs €1.50; el pnts (6A) €3.50; lndtte; shop; snacks; BBQ; playgrnd; sand beach adj; some statics; dogs €2; poss cr; Eng spkn; quiet; CCI. "Clifftop site with gd sea views; vg." ♦ 1 Apr-30 Sep. € 18.30   2007*

BINIC *2E3* (1km S Coastal) **Camping Le Panoramic, Rue Gasselin, 22520 Binic [02 96 73 60 43; fax 02 96 69 27 66; camping. le.panoramic@wanadoo.fr; www.lepanoramic. net]** D786 St Brieuc-Paimpol. 1st slip rd for Binic & 1st R up hill 100m, site sp. Med, mkd pitch, pt sl, terr, pt shd; htd wc; chem disp; shwrs; el pnts (10A) €5 (poss rev pol); gas; lndtte; ice; shop; snacks; bar; BBQ; htd pool; paddling pool; sand beach 500m; golf adj; entmnt; many statics; dogs €2; quiet. "V clean facs; pleasant site; coastal path nr." 1 Apr-30 Sep. € 18.50   2007*

See advertisement

BINIC *2E3* (4km S Coastal) **Camping Le Roc de l'Hervieu, 19 Rue d'Estienne d'Orves, 22590 Pordic [02 96 79 30 12; le.roc.de.lhervieu@ wanadoo.fr; www.campinglerocdelhervieu.fr]** Site on E side of vill off N786, Binic-St Brieuc rd. Turn E in cent of vill, sp to Les Madières then sp Le Roc de l'Hervieu. Med, hdg pitch, pt shd; wc (some cont); chem disp; mv service pnt; shwrs inc; el pnts (10A) €3.30; lndtte; shop; playgrnd; sand beach 2km; fishing; some statics; quiet. "Gd walking; pleasant site." ♦ 20 May-30 Sep. € 14.85   2006*

BINIC 2E3 (4km S Coastal) **Camping Les Madières, La Vau Madec, 22590 Pordic [02 96 79 02 48; fax 02 96 79 46 67; campinglesmadieres@wanadoo. fr]** Site at E end of Pordic vill, sp. Med, pt sl, shd; htd wc (mainly cont); shwrs inc; el pnts (10A) €3.50; gas; lndtte; sm shop; rest; snacks; bar; htd pool; shgl beach 800m; sand beach & watersports 3km; entmnt; 10% statics; dogs €1.80; adv bkg; quiet; red CCI. "V pleasant, clean, child-friendly site; immac facs; friendly, helpful owners; poss diff access to shgl beach & not suitable children, Binic beach 3km OK; highly rec." ♦ 1 Apr-3 Nov. € 16.50   2005*

BINIC 2E3 (8km SW Rural) **Camping à la Ferme (Hello), La Corderie, 22170 Plélo [02 96 74 21 21; fax 02 96 74 31 64; hello.odile@22.wanadoo.fr]** Fr Binic take D4 dir Châtelaudren, site on R at La Corderie. Sm, pt shd; wc; chem disp; shwrs inc; el pnts (10A) €2; lndtte; playgrnd; sand beach 8km; 20% statics; quiet. "CL-type site." 25 Jun-10 Sep. € 8.50   2007*

BINIC 2E3 (6km W Rural) **FFCC Camping Les Etangs, Pont de la Motte, Route de Châtelaudren, 22410 Lantic [02 96 71 95 47; contact@campinglesetangs.com; www. campinglesetangs.com]** D786 fr Binic twd Paimpol; turn L approx 1km on D4 sp Châtelaudren & Lantic; in 3km at x-rds turn L foll camping sp; site in 50m on R. Fr N12 Guingamp-St Brieuc take D4 at Châtelaudren. Med, mkd pitch, pt sl, pt shd; wc (cont); chem disp; mv service pnt; shwrs inc; el pnts (6A) €2.60; gas; lndtte; ice; sm shop; tradsmn; snacks; playgrnd; pool; beach 3km; TV; 2% statics; dogs €1.20; phone; poss v cr; Eng spkn; adv bkg (dep req); quiet; cc acc; CCI. "Gd base slightly away fr cr coast sites; helpful, friendly owners; gd pool; boat excursions fr St Brieuc; excel." ♦ 1 Apr-30 Sep. € 17.00   2006*

BIRON 7D3 (4km S Rural) **Camping Le Moulinal, 24540 Biron [05 53 40 84 60; fax 05 53 40 81 49; lemoulinal@perigord.com; www.lemoulinal.com]** Fr Bergerac S dir Agen, then E Issigeac & Villeréal; fr Villeréal dir Lacapelle-Biron, site sp. Fr Monpazier take D104 twd Villeréal; in 4km S on D53 thro Biron & onto Lacapelle-Biron. Head W twd Villeréal for 2km to site. Lge, mkd pitches, terr, pt shd; htd wc (some cont); baby facs; shwrs; el pnts (6A) inc; gas; lndtte; ice; shop; rest; snacks; bar; BBQ; playgrnd; htd pool; sand beach for lake sw; boating; tennis; games area; games rm; internet; entmnt; dogs €5; poss cr; Eng spkn; adv bkg; quiet; cc acc; red low ssn; CCI. "Lovely site; extra for lakeside & 'super' pitches." ♦ 1 Apr-23 Sep. € 35.00 (CChq acc)
                                                     2006*

BIRON 7D3 (4km SW Rural) **Camping Laborde (Naturist), 47150 Paulhiac [05 53 63 14 88; fax 05 53 61 60 23; domainelaborde@wanadoo.fr; www.domainelaborde.com]** Leave Montpazier on D2 sp Monflanquin/Villeréal; in 5.6km at Source de la Brame turn L onto D2E sp Monflanquin. Turn R onto D255 at sp Laborde FFN dir Lacapelle-Born. Med, pt sl, pt shd; wc; chem disp; sauna; shwrs inc; el pnts (3-10A) €3.50-4.50 (poss long lead req); gas; ice; lndtte; tradsmn; shop; rest; snacks; bar; playgrnd; 2 tropical indoor pools & outdoor pool; lake sw adj; tennis; games rm; dogs €3; Eng spkn; adv bkg; quiet; cc acc; INF card not req. "Insensitive over-development has spoilt site." ♦ 31 Mar-1 Oct. € 23.00   2007*

BIRON 7D3 (W Rural) **Aire Communale, Route de Vergt de Biron, 24540 Biron [05 53 63 15 23; fax 05 53 24 28 12]** Fr Villeréal or Monpazier on D104/ D2 turn onto D53 to Biron, foll sp for Information. M'vans only. Sm, unshd; own san; chem disp; mv service pnt; water €2; shop 8km; rest, snacks, bar 100m; dogs; poss cr; quiet. "Extensive views fr site; gd NH." 1 Apr-31 Oct. € 2.00   2006*

France

BISCARROSSE See also sites listed under Gastes, Sanguinet and Parentis en Born.

BISCARROSSE *7D1* (3km N) **Aire Naturelle Camping Les Bruyères, 3725 Route de Bordeaux, 40600 Biscarrosse [05 58 78 79 23]** N fr Biscarrosse on D652 twd Arcachon; site on L behind 2 bungalows (1 new 1 old) 3km fr town; visible fr rd, just bef sm concrete water tower. Sm, shd; wc; chem disp (wc); shwrs €1.10; baby facs; el pnts (3-10A) inc, rev pol; ice; shop adj; cooking facs; BBQ; sand beach 10km; lake sw & watersports 3km; adv bkg; quiet. "Helpful owners; CL-type site; v clean facs; beach 10km excel for surfing; rec Latécoère seaplane museum." Apr-Sep. € 11.00   2005*

BISCARROSSE *7D1* (3km N) **Campéole Navarosse, 712 Chemin de Navarosse, 40600 Biscarrosse [05 58 09 84 32; fax 05 58 09 86 22; cplnavarrosse@atciat.com; www.campeole. com]** Fr Biscarrosse N on D652 dir Sanguinet; 1km beyond turning to L to Biscarosse Plage, turn L onto D305 & foll sp to Navarosse. Lge, pt shd; wc; baby facs; shwrs inc; el pnts (10A) €3.90; ice; tradsmn; supmkt adj; snacks; BBQ: playgrnd; sand beach; lake sailing; tennis; games area; games rm; entmnt; TV; dogs €3.50; poss cr; quiet; some Eng spkn. "Gd." ♦ 26 Apr-21 Sep. € 25.10   2007*

BISCARROSSE *7D1* (5km N Rural) **Aire Naturelle Le Frezat (Dubourg), 2583 Chemin de Mayotte, 40600 Biscarrosse [06 22 65 57 37]** Fr Biscarrosse on D652 dir Sanguinet; after 5km L at water tower onto D333; site 2nd on R in 1km. Med, shd; wc (some cont); chem disp (wc); shwrs €1; el pnts (6A) inc; shops 5km; tradsmn; BBQ; playgrnd; lake & sand beach 3km; dogs; phone 1km; Eng spkn; quiet; adv bkg; CCI. "Vg site; friendly owners; cycle paths." 15 Apr-15 Oct. € 12.50   2005*

BISCARROSSE *7D1* (5km N Rural) **Camping Village Mayotte Vacances, Chemin des Roseaux, 40600 Biscarrosse [05 58 78 00 00; fax 05 58 78 83 91; camping@mayottevacances. com; www.mayottevacances.com]** Twd NE fr Biscarrosse on D652 L sp Navarosse & at 1st fork R to Mayotte, foll camping sp. V lge, mkd pitch, hdstg, pt shd; wc; chem disp; mv service pnt; shwrs inc; el pnts (10A) inc; snacks; gas; lndtte; shop; rest; snacks; BBQ; playgrnd; pool; waterslide; jacuzzi; lake sw adj; sailing school; sand beach 9km; tennis; cycle hire; games rm; entmnt; child entmnt; TV; 25% statics; dogs €5; Eng spkn; adv bkg (ess Jul/Aug); quiet; cc acc; red low ssn/ CCI. "Excel leisure facs; vg for families; rec." ♦ 5 Apr-22 Sep. € 41.00   2007*

See advertisement

BISCARROSSE *7D1* (8km NE Rural) **Camping du Domaine de la Rive, Route de Bordeaux, 40600 Biscarrosse [05 58 78 12 33; fax 05 58 78 12 92; info@camping-de-la-rive.fr; www.larive.fr]** S on D652 fr Sanguinet to Biscarrosse. Site sp on R in 6km nr Lake Cazaux. V lge, hdg/mkd pitch, pt shd; htd wc; chem disp; baby facs; shwrs inc; el pnts (6A) inc; gas; lndtte; ice; shop; rest; snacks; bar; BBQ (gas only); playgrnd; 2 pools (1 htd, covrd); waterslide; jacuzzi; lake sw & private, sand beach adj; ocean beach 18km; watersports; tennis; cycle, canoe, surf hire; archery; games area; organised activities; entmnt; wifi internet; games/ TV rm; 30% statics; dogs €5; poss cr; phone; Eng spkn; adv bkg (dep req); cc acc; red low ssn; CCI. "Lakeside site; delightful area; v well run; some pitches diff lge o'fits due trees." ♦ 5 Apr-7 Sep. € 42.00 (CChq acc) ABS - A38   2007*

⊞**BISCARROSSE** *7D1* (1.5km S Rural) **Camp Municipal de Latécoère, 265 Rue Louis Bréguet, 40600 Biscarrosse [05 58 78 13 01; fax 05 58 78 16 26; latecoere.biscarrosse@wanadoo. fr]** S on D652 Sanguinet-Biscarrosse rd to cent of town. Strt in front of church by mkt sq; site in 1.5km adj lake. Lge, mkd pitch, pt shd; wc; shwrs inc; el pnts inc; lndtte; shop; rest; snacks; bar; BBQ; playgrnd adj; pool; lake sw & sand beach adj; 40% statics; quiet. "Yacht club adj; museums opp; seaplanes." € 12.80   2005*

BISCARROSSE *7D1* (8km NW Coastal) **Camping Le Vivier, 681 Rue du Tit, 40600 Biscarrosse-Plage [05 58 78 25 76; fax 05 58 78 35 23; cplvivier@ atciat.com; www.camping-biscarrosse.info or www.campeole.com]** Fr Arcachon & Pyla-sur-Mer, take D218, D83 to Biscarrosse Plage. Town o'skts site sp to R. Foll sps. Lge, pt shd; wc; chem disp; shwrs; el pnts €3.90; shop; snacks; playgrnd; htd pool; paddling pool; sand beach 800m; tennis; boating; fishing; horseriding nr; cycle hire; entmnt; dogs €3.50; quiet. "Access to beach via path thro dunes." 29 Apr-17 Sep. € 23.10   2006*

BISCARROSSE *7D1* (9km NW Coastal) **Camping Plage Sud, 230 Rue des Bécasses, 40600 Biscarrosse-Plage [05 58 78 21 24; fax 05 58 78 34 23; cplplagesud@atciat.com; www. landes-camping.net or www.campeole.com]** Clearly sp on D146 on ent to Biscarrosse-Plage in pine forest. V lge, mkd pitch, pt sl, pt shd; wc; chem disp; baby facs; shwrs inc; el pnts (6A) €3.90; lndtte; ice; shop adj; tradsmn; snacks; bar; BBQ; playgrnd; htd pool; paddling pool; sand beach 800m; cycle hire; entmnt; 20% statics; dogs €3.50; Eng spkn; adv bkg; noise fr disco high ssn; CCI. "Sm, modern town; lots of rests; gd beach inc surfing." 1 May-17 Sep. € 23.10   2006*

BIZANET see Narbonne *10F1*

BLAIN *2G4* (1km S Rural) **Camp Municipal le Château, Route de St Nazaire, 44130 Blain** [02 40 79 11 00 or 02 40 79 00 08 (Mairie); fax 02 40 78 83 72; www.ville-blain.fr] Fr N on N137 turn W onto N171; fr S on N137 turn W onto D164 to Blain. On app town, take L at rndabt on N171 dir St Nazaire/Bouvron. Immed after x-ing Brest-Nantes canal bdge, site on L adj to chateau. Sm, mkd pitch, pt shd; wc; shwrs; chem disp; el pnts (10A) €2.20; lndry rm; ice; shops 500m; tradsmn; rest, bar 500m; playgrnd; pool 1km; fishing; boating; dogs €0.80; phone adj; Eng spkn; adv bkg; quiet but some rd noise; CCI. "Super, well-managed site; immac san facs; gd pitch size; helpful staff; chateau museum adj; no twin-axles; no vehicular ent after 2000 high ssn." ♦ 1 May-30 Sep. € 6.60   2007*

BLAMONT *6E3* (E Rural) **Camp Municipal de la Vezouze, Route de Cirey, 54450 Blâmont** [03 83 76 28 28 (Mairie)] Fr Sarrebourg on N4 dir Blâmont then D993 dir Cirey-sous-Vezouze & foll sp for site. Sm, pt shd; wc; shwrs inc; el pnts (16A) €2; ice; shop, rest, snacks, bar 300m; playgrnd; sports area; sw, fishing adj. "Gd site beside lake; gd walking, cycling; phone ahead bef arrival." 1 Jun-15 Sep. € 6.50   2004*

BLANC, LE *4H2* (2km E Rural) **Camping L'Ile d'Avant, Route de Châteauroux, 36300 Le Blanc** [02 54 37 88 22; fax 02 54 36 35 42; a.tou.vert@wanadoo.fr; www.atouvert.com] Fr town cent take D951 (N151) twd St Gaultier/Argenton; site on R 1km after supmkt. Med, hdg/mkd pitch, pt shd; wc; mv service pnt; shwrs inc; el pnts (6A) €2.65; lndtte; shops 1km; rest, snacks, bar 2km; BBQ; playgrnd; htd pool adj; rv sw; fishing; tennis adj; adv bkg; quiet but some rd noise. "Poss diff to manoeuvre lge vans; muddy uneven pitches; next to sports field & club house; fair NH only." 1 May-30 Sep. € 11.50
2006*

BLANGY LE CHATEAU *3D1* (Rural) **Camping Le Domaine du Lac, 14130 Blangy-le-Château** [02 31 64 62 00; fax 02 31 64 15 91] Fr Pont-l'Evêque & A13 S on D579 twd Lisieux. In 5km turn L onto D51 to Blangy where at fountain (rndabt) turn L, taking care. In 200m at end of vill turn L onto D140 Rte de Mesnil & site 200m on R. Site is 5km SE of Pont-l'Evêque. Med, pt sl, pt shd; wc; chem disp; baby facs; shwrs inc; el pnts (5A) inc (long lead poss req); gas; lndtte; ice; shop & 1km; rest; snacks; bar; BBQ; beach 22km; lake fishing; tennis; games rm; internet; 70% statics; dogs; recep 0800-2200 high ssn; adv bkg; some rd noise; cc acc; CCI. "Nice, peaceful site in lovely area; friendly British owner; poss uneven pitches & tired facs; access to pitches diff when wet; gd rest; pretty vill; gd local walks; conv Honfleur; allow 1hr to Le Havre for ferry - NH only." 1 Apr-31 Oct. € 20.00 ABS - N03   2007*

BLANGY LE CHATEAU *3D1* (3km SE Rural) **Camping Le Brévedent, 14130 Le Brévedent** [02 31 64 72 88 or 02 31 64 21 50 (LS); fax 02 31 64 33 41; contact@campinglebrevedent.com; www.campinglebrevedent.com or www.les-castels.com] Fr Pont l'Evêque & A13 go S on D579 twd Lisieux; after 5km turn L onto D51 twd Blangy-le-Château. In Blangy bear R at rndabt to stay on D51 & foll sp to Le Brévedent & Moyaux; site on L in 3km. Med, mkd pitch, pt sl, pt shd; htd wc; chem disp; mv service pnt; baby facs; shwrs inc; el pnts (5-10A) inc (poss long leads req); gas; lndtte; ice; shop & 3km; tradsmn; rest; snacks; bar; BBQ (gas/elec); playgrnd; 2 htd pools; paddling pool; sand beach 22km; lake fishing; tennis 100m; sports area; mini-golf; cycle hire; horseriding 2km; golf 11km; entmnt; excursions; wifi internet; games/TV rm; many statics & tour ops; no dogs; sep car park after 2230; poss cr; Eng spkn; adv bkg (dep req); quiet; cc acc; CCI. "Pleasant site in superb setting round lake; v peaceful (Sep); v welcoming & helpful staff; recep 0830-2000 high ssn; some modern san facs, ltd low ssn; sm pitches; poss tour ops tents; popular with rallies; no c'vans over 8m acc; history of chateau given Sun eves; excel." ♦ 26 Apr-28 Sep. € 25.60 (CChq acc) ABS - N01
2007*

France

BLANGY SUR BRESLE *3C2* (2.5km E Rural) **Camp Municipal Les Etangs**, 76340 Blangy-sur-Bresle [02 35 94 55 65; fax 02 35 94 06 14] Leave A28 at junc 5, R at T-junc onto D49, site on L in less than 1km. Med, mkd pitch, unshd; wc; chem disp; shwrs inc (clsd 2100-0700); el pnts (5-10A) €1.40-2.40 (poss rev pol); lndry rm; rest, snacks bar 2km; BBQ; playgrnd; tennis & mini-golf nrby; CCI. "Attractive, peaceful site adj lakes; clean & well-run; gd facs; shwrs poss clsd bef 2100; cramped pitches - narr & long; adv bkg rec lge o'fits high ssn; office clsd 1200-1500 & 1930; rec wait for warden for pitching; poss waterlogged in wet (& entry refused); in walking dist of vill & lge supmkt; conv Calais & A28; excel NH; gd value." ♦ 15 Mar-21 Sep. € 8.25   2007*

BLANGY SUR BRESLE *3C2* (8km W Urban) **Camp Municipal de la Forêt**, 76340 Bazinval [tel/fax 02 32 97 04 01; bazinval2@wanadoo.fr] NW fr Blangy on D49 for 6km, then D149 to Bazinval. Site sp fr rd. Sm, hdg pitch, pt sl, pt shd; wc; chem disp (wc); shwrs inc; el pnts (10A) €4 (poss rev pol); Eng spkn; quiet; CCI. "Beautiful flower beds; early am tractor noise; gd san facs, poss inadequate; site yourself, warden calls early eve; poss itinerants on site; NH only." 1 Apr-30 Oct. € 8.00   2007*

BLAUVAC see Carpentras *10E2*

BLAVOZY see Puy en Velay, Le *9C1*

BLAYE *7C2* (Urban) **Camp Municipal La Citadelle**, 33390 Blaye [05 57 42 00 20 or 05 57 42 16 79 (LS)] Fr N ent town, over x-rds, sp in town; ent thro narr gateways in fortifications; access by narr track, single in places. Fr S on D669 cont thro town passing citadel on L; turn L at mini rndabt, go over bdge & take 1st L; sp strt on thro arches. NB Site access unsuitable m'vans higher than 2.7m due to narr, curved arches. Sm, terr, pt shd; wc (some cont); serviced pitches; shwrs inc; el pnts (10-15A) €2.60; ice; shops 500m; tradsmn high ssn; pool 250m; phone adj; poss cr; quiet; no cc acc. "Lovely site within ancient monument, partly o'lookng rv; pleasant recep; spacious pitches; pitch yourself; warden visits pm; clean but basic san facs; vineyards at Blaye & Bourg." 1 May-30 Sep. € 9.90   2007*

BLAYE *7C2* (5km NE Rural) **Aire Naturelle Les Tilleuls (Paille), Domaine Les Alberts**, 33390 Mazion [05 57 42 18 13; fax 05 57 42 13 01] Fr Blaye D937 N, sp to site on L. Sm, pt sl, pt shd; wc; shwrs inc; el pnts (3-10A) €2.50; ice; BBQ; dogs; rd noise; CCI. "Pleasant, family-run site in cent of vineyards; san facs leave a lot to be desired; wine-tasting; cycle track to Blaye." 15 Apr-15 Oct. € 12.00   2005*

BLENEAU *4G3* (600m N Rural) **Camp Municipal La Pépinière, Rue du Lieutenant Travers**, 89220 Bléneau [03 86 74 93 73 or 03 86 74 91 61 (Mairie); fax 03 86 74 86 74; mairiedebleneau@wanadoo. fr; www.bleneau.fr] At junc of D47/D22 & D90 in Bléneau take D64 twd Champcevrais & site. Sp in Bléneau. Sm, hdg pitch, shd; wc (cont); chem disp; shwrs inc; el pnts (10A) €2; shops, rest, snacks, bar 600m; pool adj; games rm; fishing adj; poss cr; adv bkg; quiet; CCI. "Set in orchard; gd." 1 Apr-30 Sep. € 5.30   2006*

⊞**BLENEAU** *4G3* (12km NE Rural) **Camping Le Bois Guillaume**, 89350 **Villeneuve-les-Genêts** [03 86 45 45 41; fax 03 86 45 49 20; camping@ bois-guillaume.com; www.bois-guillaume. com] Fr W on D965 dir St Fargeau. At Mézilles take D7 twd Tannerre-en-Puisaye & foll sp for site. 2.5km fr Villeneuve-les Genêts. Or fr A6 exit junc 18 onto D16 thro Charny, then turn L onto D119 to Champignelles; take D7 dir Tannere for approx 2km; turn R & foll sp to site. Med, hdg/mkd pitch, some hdstg, shd; htd wc; chem disp; mv service pnt; shwrs inc; el pnts (5-10A) €2.80-3.50; gas; rest; bar; playgrnd; htd pools; sports area; cycle hire; tennis; dogs €1.30; poss cr; Eng spkn; CCI. "Friendly staff; clean, tidy site; facs ltd low ssn; vg rest." € 12.70   2007*

BLERE *4G2* (500m NE Urban) **Camp Municipal La Gâtine, Rue de Cdt Lemaître**, 37150 Bléré [tel/fax 02 47 57 92 60; marie@blere-touraine.com; www. blere-touraine.com] Site adj sports cent on S side of Rv Cher. Lge, mkd pitch, pt shd; wc; chem disp; mv service pnt; shwrs inc; el pnts (6-16A) €3.20-5.50 (poss rev pol & long lead poss req); lndtte; shops 300m; supmkt 400m; htd pool adj; rv fishing adj; 5% statics; dogs €1.90; no adv bkg; quiet; cc acc; CCI. "Vg, well-maintained site; excel san facs; helpful warden; gates clsd 1200-1400 (1530 Sun); sm pitches; sh walk into attractive town; gd dog walks & towpath walks; gd cent for wine rtes (Touraine) & chateaux; excel tourist office in town." ♦ 10 Apr-15 Oct. € 8.80   2007*

BLESLE see Massiac *9C1*

BLET *4H3* (400m S Rural) **Camp Municipal Le Gouffre**, 18350 Blet [tel/fax 02 48 74 78 24 or 02 48 74 71 04 (Mairie)] SE fr Bourges on D2076 (N76). In 35km turn R onto D6 in cent of Blet sp Chalivoy-Milon. Site 400m on R just past sm lake. NB no sp at ent. Med, pt shd; wc; shwrs; el pnts (5A) €2.90; shop 500m; dogs €1; quiet. "Gd NH; facs basic but adequate." ♦ 1 Apr-1 Nov. € 6.30   2006*

BLIGNY SUR OUCHE *6H1* (Rural) **Camp Municipal des Isles**, 21360 Bligny-sur-Ouche [03 80 20 11 21; fax 03 80 20 17 90] On D17/D970 fr Arnay-le-Duc, site on L on ent vill. Med, pt shd; wc; shwrs inc; el pnts (15A) €2.50; shop 500m; rest 300m; playgrnd; quiet. "Site yourself, fees collected each evening; in reach of Côte d'Or wine areas; steam rlwy 100m; peaceful, clean & tidy; noise fr cornmill at harvest time; gd." 15 May-15 Sep. € 13.00   2006*

BLOIS *4G2* (15km NE) **Camping Le Château de la Grenouillère, 41500 Suèvres [02 54 87 80 37; fax 02 54 87 84 21; la.grenouillere@wanadoo.fr; www.camping-loire.com** or **www.les-castels. com]** Exit A10 junc 16 sp Chambord, Mer; take rd to Mer; go thro Mer on N152 dir Blois; site in 5km. (Site 2km NE of Suèvres). Lge, mkd pitch, pt shd; wc; chem disp; mv service pnt; sauna; baby facs; shwrs inc; el pnts (6A) inc; gas; lndtte; ice; shop; pizzeria; snacks; bar; BBQ (gas/charcoal); playgrnd; 2 pools (1 covrd); paddling pool; waterslide; boating; fishing; tennis; cycle hire; entmnt; child entmnt; internet; games/TV; statics (tour ops); dogs €6; Eng spkn; adv bkg (min 3 nts); some pitches some rd & rlwy noise; cc acc; CCI. "Ideal for touring Loire area, particularly visiting chateaux; gates clsd 2230-0700; recep open 0830-2100 high ssn; facs refurbished (2007); facs ltd low ssn; poss narr site lanes due unpruned trees/hedges; gd NH; mkt Tue & Sat Blois. " ♦ 26 Apr-6 Sep. € 35.00 ABS - L04   2007*

BLOIS *4G2* (10km E Rural) **FFCC Aire Naturelle (Delaboissière), 6 Rue de Châtillon, 41350 Huisseau-sur-Cosson [02 54 20 35 26]** Fr Blois cross Rv Loire on D765 dir Vineuil. 1km S turn L onto D33. Site at E end of vill of Huisseau on R. Sm, hdg/mkd pitch, pt sl, pt shd; wc; chem disp; mv service pnt; shwrs inc; el pnts (6A) €3.50 (poss rev pol); gas; shops 400m; supmkt 4km; rv 10km; dogs €1; site clsd 16-22 Jul 08; poss cr; adv bkg; quiet; cc not acc; CCI. "Sm, immac, peaceful garden site; v clean facs; friendly owner; local wine & fruit for sale; conv Loire Valley chateaux; cycle rte thro forest to Chambord Château." ♦ ltd. 1 May-15 Sep. € 10.70   2007*

BLOIS *4G2* (8km S Rural) **Camp Municipal, Rue du Conon, 41120 Cellettes [02 54 70 48 41 or 02 54 70 47 54 (Mairie)]** On D956, Blois to Châteauroux rd, pass almost thro Cellettes, site 120m fr D956 down 1st L after rv bdge, site on L in 100m, well sp. NB Turn-in narr fr v busy main rd. Med, pt shd; wc; chem disp; shwrs inc; el pnts (6-10A) inc; shops, pool, playgrnd & tennis adj; fishing; phone; quiet, some daytime rd noise; cc acc; CCI. "Pleasant rvside location; v friendly warden; poor shwrs; can be boggy after rain; excel for Loire chateaux." ♦ ltd. 1 Jun-30 Sep. € 11.90   2007*

BLOIS *4G2* (6km SW) **FFCC Camping Le Cosson, 1 Rue de la Forêt, 41120 Chailles [02 54 79 46 49]** Fr Blois foll sp dir Montrichard (D751); after x-ing rv bdge at rndabt take 1st exit sp Montrichard/ Chailles (D751); after x-ing sm rv bdge in Chailles take 1st L onto Rue de la Forêt; site in 50m; sm sp easily missed. Sm, hdg pitch, shd; wc; chem disp (wc); shwrs inc; baby facs; el pnts (6A) €3.20; shops 1km; baker 500m; games area; playgrnd; dogs; phone; adv bkg; CCI. "Well-maintained, quiet site nr chateaux; v pleasant, helpful owners; walks & cycle paths in local forest." 15 May-10 Sep. € 10.80   2007*

BOIRY NOTRE DAME see Arras *3B3*

BOIS DE CENE *2H4* (S Urban) **Camping Le Bois Joli, 2 Rue de Châteauneuf, 85710 Bois-de-Céné [02 51 68 20 05; fax 02 51 68 46 40; campingboisjoli@free.fr; www.camping-leboisjoli.com]** Fr D21 turn R at church in cent of vill, site on R in 500m on rd D28. Med, mkd pitch; shd; wc; chem disp; shwrs inc; el pnts (6A) inc; gas; lndtte; ice; shop adj; snacks; playgrnd; pool; sand beach 18km; fishing; tennis; games area; entmnt; some statics; dogs €3.50; Eng spkn; adv bkg; ltd facs low ssn; CCI. "Exceptionally friendly, helpful owner; clean san facs; washing facs for vehicles avail; friendly vill; gd walks." 1 Apr-24 Sep. € 16.90   2006*

Before we move on, I'm going to fill in some site report forms and post them off to the editor, otherwise they won't arrive in time for the deadline at the end of September.

BOISSE PENCHOT see Decazeville *7D4*

BOISSIERE DU MONTAIGU, LA see Montaigu *2H4*

BOLLENE *9D2* (500m Urban) **Camp Municipal du Lez, Quartier des Jardins, 84500 Bollène [tel/fax 04 90 30 16 86; info@bollenetourisme.com; www. bollenetourisme.com]** Exit A7 junc 19 to Bollène town cent; strt on over rv bdge; L & foll sp to site. Sm, hdg/mkd pitch, hdstg, pt shd; wc; chem disp; shwrs inc; el pnts (15A) €2.10; lndtte; shop, rest, snacks & bar 800m; playgrnd; covrd pool 1km; rv sw; dogs €1.10; phone; Eng spkn; adv bkg; quiet; red 15+ days; cc not acc; CCI. "V clean, well-kept site; gd sized pitches; helpful, friendly manager; no twin-axles; office closed 1200-1500; excel touring base; one of best municipal sites in France; Mon am c'van exit poss blocked by mkt stalls; conv supmkt; vg." ♦ ltd. 1 Apr-31 Aug. € 9.00   2007*

⊞**BOLLENE** *9D2* (2.5km N Rural) **Camping Le Barry, 84500 Bollène [04 90 30 13 20; fax 04 90 40 48 64; info@campinglebarry.com; www.campinglebarry.com]** Exit A7 junc 19 at Bollène onto D26 twd Pierrelatte. Foll sp 'Site Troglodytique'. Med, mkd pitch, terr, pt shd; htd wc (some cont); baby facs; shwrs inc; el pnts (6A) €4.50; gas; lndtte; ice; shop; rest; snacks; bar; BBQ (gas); playgrnd; pool; rv 2.5km; lake fishing & watersports 3km; entmnt; TV; dogs €1.50; poss cr; Eng spkn; adv bkg ess; poss noisy; red low ssn. "V ltd facs low ssn; low ssn office open 1030-1200. & 1630-1900 only; access to pool up steep slope; vg." € 17.00   2006*

France

⊞**BOLLENE** 9D2 (5.5km E Rural) **FFCC Camping de la Simioune, Quartier Guffiage, 84500 Bollène [04 90 30 44 62; fax 04 90 30 44 77; la-simioune@wanadoo.fr; www.la-simioune.fr]** Exit A7 junc 19 onto D994/D8 dir Carpentras (Ave Salvatore Allende D8). At 3rd x-rd 900m bef fire stn take L turn (Ave Alphonse Daudet) foll rd 3km to sp for camping on L, then site 1km. Sm, pt sl, shd; wc; chem disp; baby facs; shwrs €1; el pnts (6A) €3.10; lndtte; shops & supmkt 4km; tradsmn; rest; bar; playgrnd; pool; horseriding; BBQ evenings; 10% statics; dogs €1.50; adv bkg rec high ssn; quiet; red CCI. "In pine forest; facs need upgrading - ltd in winter; excel pony club for children & adults; NH only." € 13.00
2004*

BOLLENE 9D2 (7km E) **FFCC Camping Le Lez, La Bourgade, 26790 Suze-la-Rousse [tel/fax 04 75 98 82 83]** E fr Bollène on D94 to Suze-la-Rousse; L in vill sq; R immed bef rv bdge. Sm, pt shd; wc; shwrs inc; el pnts (6-10A) €2.70-3.10 lndtte; shop 300m; snacks; bar; playgrnd; pool; fishing; games area; TV; dogs €1; CCI. "No twin-axle vans; site poss untidy, but facs clean." Easter-30 Sep. € 11.30
2006*

⊞**BOLLENE** 9D2 (6km SW Rural) **Camp Municipal La Pinède, Quartier des Massanes, 84430 Mondragon [04 90 40 82 98; fax 04 90 40 94 82; camping.mondragon@wanadoo.fr]** Exit A7 junc 19 dir Bollène & take D26 S, site 1.5km N of Mondragon. Steep access. Med, mkd pitch, pt sl, terr, pt shd; wc; chem disp; shwrs inc; el pnts (5-8A) inc; lndtte; ice; shop; BBQ; playgrnd; htd, covrd pool 5km; some statics; dogs €1.20; adv bkg; quiet; CCI. "Full by 1700, early arr rec; no twin-axle vans over 6m; gd, clean site but basic facs & poss cold shwrs; code operated barrier; gd touring base; conv Ardèche Gorge." € 11.00
2007*

BONLIEU see St Laurent en Grandvaux 6H2

BONNAC LA COTE 7B3 (1km S Rural) **Camping Le Château de Leychoisier, 1 Route de Leychoisier, 87270 Bonnac-la-Côte [tel/fax 05 55 39 93 43; contact@leychoisier.com; www.leychoisier.com** or **www.les-castels.com]** N'wards on A20 exit junc 27 & L at T-junc onto D220. At rndabt take 3rd exit then 1st L onto D97 after 200m sp Bonnac-la-Côte. Turn L in vill & foll sp to site. Med, mkd pitch, pt sl, shd; wc; chem disp; baby facs; shwrs inc; el pnts (10A) inc; lndtte; shop; rest; snacks; bar; BBQ (gas & charcoal); playgrnd; pool; tennis; internet; games rm/TV; dogs €1; Eng spkn; adv bkg; red low ssn; cc not acc; CCI. "Peaceful site; welcoming, friendly & helpful staff; excel rest; recep 0830-2100; gd san facs; extra for m'vans; conv NH nr m'way." ♦ 15 Apr-20 Sep. € 24.00 ABS - L11   2007*

BONNAL 6G2 (3.5km N Rural) **Camping Le Val de Bonnal, 25680 Bonnal [03 81 86 90 87; fax 03 81 86 03 92; val-de-bonnal@wanadoo.fr; www.val-de-bonnal.com** or **www.les-castels.com]** Leave A36/E60 at junc 5 onto D50 N twd Vesoul. After 11km turn L on D49 then foll sp to Bonnal & site. Lge, mkd pitches, pt shd; wc; chem disp; baby facs; shwrs inc; el pnts (6A) inc; gas; lndtte; shop; rest; snacks; bar; BBQ (charcoal/gas); playgrnd; pool; waterslide; paddling pool; lake sw & sand beach adj; fishing (permit); canoeing; watersports; cycle hire; gym; golf 6km; entmnt high ssn; child entmnt; wifi internet; games/TV rm; 40% statics; dogs free; poss cr; Eng spkn; adv bkg; quiet; red low ssn; cc acc; CCI. "Attractive site; busy & popular high ssn; excel welcome; lge accessible pitches; ultra-modern, clean facs; gd child activities; ltd facs low ssn; tour ops; rest clsd Mon." ♦ 9 May-7 Sep. € 34.20 ABS - J01
2007*

BONNARD see Joigny 4F4

BONNES see Chauvigny 7A3

BONNEUIL MATOURS 4H2 (1km S Rural) **Camp Municipal du Parc de Crémault, 8 Allée du Stade, 86210 Bonneuil-Matours [tel/fax 05 49 85 20 47]** Fr D910 (N10) 20km N of Poitiers take D82 E to Bonneuil-Matours. Site sp in vill next to stadium & Rv Vienne but site ent not well sp. Med, mkd pitch, shd; htd wc; chem disp; mv service pnt; shwrs inc; el pnts €2.70; lndry rm; ice; shops 1km; tradsmn; rest; snacks; bar; BBQ; playgrnd; rv sw & fishing adj; tennis; mini-golf; archery; entmnt; TV; quiet. "Nature reserve adj; clean facs; lovely site." 16 Apr-17 Sep. € 8.70
2007*

BONNEVAL 4F2 (1km SE Rural) **Camp Municipal Le Bois Chièvre, Route de Vouvray, St Maurice, 28800 Bonneval [02 37 47 54 01; fax 02 37 96 26 79; camping-bonneval-28@orange.fr; http://monsite.orange.fr/camping-bonneval-28]** Rec app fr N (Chartres), or SE (D27 fr Patay/Orléans) as app fr S thro town is narr & diff. Fr Chartres take N10 into Bonneval & foll camp sp (mainly to L). Med, mkd pitch, hdstg, pt sl, shd; htd wc; chem disp; mv service pnt; shwrs inc; el pnts (6A) €3.30 (rev pol); lndtte; ice; shop 1km; tradsmn; rest, snacks, bar, BBQ; playgrnd; htd pool adj; some statics; dogs €1; Eng spkn; adv bkg; quiet; red long stay; CCI. "Well-maintained site in woodland; vg facs but poss stretched in ssn; friendly, helpful staff; wooded walk to Rv Loir & picnic site; lge pitches; no twin-axle vans or c'vans over 5.60m; vg NH for Le Havre or Dieppe." ♦ 1 Apr-30 Oct. € 9.90   2007*

BONNEVILLE 9A3 (500m NE Rural) **Camp Municipal Le Bois des Tours, 314 Rue des Bairiers, 74130 Bonneville [04 50 97 03 31 or 04 50 25 22 14 (Mairie)]** Fr A40 junc 16 take N203, or fr Cluses take N205 to Bonneville. Cross rv bdge into town cent; site sp. Med, pt shd; wc (some cont); chem disp; shwrs; el pnts (10A); shops 500m; playgrnd; poss cr; adv bkg; quiet. "Well-maintained, immac site; gd san facs." 15 Jun-15 Sep. € 6.50   2006*

BONNIEUX *10E2* (1km W Rural) **Camp Municipal du Vallon, Route de Ménerbes, 84480 Bonnieux [tel/fax 04 90 75 86 14]** Fr Bonnieux take D3 twd Ménerbes, site sp on L on leaving vill. Med, mkd pitch, terr, pt shd; wc (some cont); shwrs inc; el pnts (10A) inc; lndtte; shop; tradsmn; snacks; bar; playgrnd; dogs €1; quiet; CCI. "Beautiful wooded area; attractive hilltop vill; quaint, 'olde worlde' site in gd touring area; basic facs but very clean; gd walking & moutain bike area." 15 Mar-20 Oct. € 14.30   2007*

This guide relies on site report forms submitted by caravanners like us; we'll do our bit and tell the editor what we think of the campsites we've visited.

BONO, LE see Auray *2F3*

BONZEE *5D1* (E Rural) **Base de Loisirs du Colvert Les Eglantines, 55160 Bonzée [03 29 87 31 98; fax 03 29 87 30 60; blcv@wanadoo.fr; www. campings-colvert.com]** Fr Verdun take D903 twd Metz for 18km; in Manheulles, turn R to Bonzée in 1km; at Bonzée turn L for Fresnes; site on R, adj Camping Marguerites. Or fr A4 exit junc 32 to Fresnes; then foll sp Bonzée. Med, hdg/mkd pitch, pt shd; wc; chem disp; mv service pnt; shwrs inc; el pnts (4-6A) €3.71-5.30; gas & 1km; lndtte; shop & 1km; tradsmn; BBQ; rest; snacks; bar; playgrnd; lake sw & boating adj; waterslide; fishing; tennis 1.5km; many statics; dogs €1.26; phone; extra €14.36 for twin-axles; adv bkg; noisy high ssn; cc acc; CCI. "Spacious pitches in well-planned sites; 2 sites together; facs ltd low ssn." ♦ 1 Apr-30 Sep. € 12.81   2007*

BOOFZHEIM see Rhinau *6E3*

⊞**BORDEAUX** *7C2* (4km S Urban) **Camping Beau Soleil, 371 Cours du Général de Gaulle, 33170 Gradignan [tel/fax 05 56 89 17 66; campingbeausoleil@wanadoo.fr; www.camping-gradignanbeausoleil.fr]** Fr N take exit 16 Bordeaux ring rd-Gradignan (N10). Site S of town on N10 100m on R after Beau Soleil complex. Sm, mkd pitch, hdstg, pt sl, pt shd; htd wc; chem disp; shwrs inc; el pnts (6-10A) inc (poss rev pol); lndtte; ice; shops adj; snacks; bar; gas/elec BBQ; rv/lake sw 2km; 70% statics; dogs €1; bus 100m; poss cr; Eng spkn; adv bkg rec; quiet; CCI. "Pleasant, clean, family-run site; v helpful owners; vg san facs; ltd touring pitches; sm pitches not suitable lge o'fits; adv bkg rec (winter & summer); v conv; excel." ♦ € 16.70   2007*

BORMES LES MIMOSAS see Lavandou, Le *10F3*

BORT LES ORGUES *7C4* (4km N Rural) **Camping La Siauve, Rue du Camping, 15270 Lanobre [04 71 40 31 85 or 05 46 55 10 01; fax 04 71 40 34 33 or 05 46 55 10 10; www.village-center.com]** On D992 Clermont-Ferrand to Bort-les-Orgues, site on R 3km S of Lanobre. Site sp. Lge, hdg/mkd pitch, terr, pt shd; wc; chem disp; mv service pnt; shwrs inc; el pnts (6A) inc; lndtte; shop & 3km; tradsmn; rest; snacks; bar; playgrnd; lake sw adj; fishing; tennis nr; games area; cycle hire; entmnt; TV rm; dogs €3; phone; Eng spkn; adv bkg (dep req); noisy high ssn; cc acc; CCI. "Footpaths (steep) to lake; gd sw, boating etc; excel touring base; v scenic." 16 Jun-2 Sep. € 14.00   2007*

BORT LES ORGUES *7C4* (6km S) **Camp Municipal de Bellevue, 15240 Saignes [04 71 40 68 40 or 04 71 40 62 80 (Mairie); saignes-mairie@wanadoo.fr; www.camping-saignes.com]** Fr Bort-les-Orgues take D922 S twd Mauriac. In 5km, turn L onto D22. Site sp on R after ent vill. Foll sp 'Piscine/Stade'. Sm, hdg/mkd pitch, pt shd; wc (some cont); chem disp; shwrs inc; el pnts (6-10A) €2; lndry rm; ice; shops 500m; snacks; bar; BBQ; playgrnd; 3 pools adj; 2 tennis courts adj; dogs; Eng spkn; adv bkg; quiet; no cc acc; CCI. "Pleasant situation with views, gd for touring area; roomy pitches." 1 Jul-31 Aug. € 5.75   2005*

BORT LES ORGUES *7C4* (7km SW Rural) **Camping à la Ferme (Chanet), Domaine de la Vigne, 15240 Saignes [tel/fax 04 71 40 61 02]** Take D922 S fr Bort sp Mauriac. After 5.5km at junc with D22 take sharp L sp Saignes. In cent of Saignes turn L at T-junc onto D30. After 200m turn L onto C14 sp La Vigne & Camping. Farmhouse on L after 400m, site on R. Sm, pt sl, pt shd; wc; cold shwrs inc; el pnts (6A) €2.30 (rev pol); shops 800m; sm pool; poss cr; adv bkg; quiet. "Beautiful, peaceful setting; CL-type site; friendly owners; ltd facs; san facs poss neglected low ssn." Mar-Nov. € 9.20
                                    2006*

BOUCHEMAINE see Angers *4G1*

BOUGE CHAMBALUD see St Rambert d'Albon *9C2*

BOULANCOURT see Malesherbes *4E3*

BOULOGNE SUR GESSE *8F3* (6km NE Rural) **Camping Le Canard Fou, 31350 Lunax [05 61 88 26 06]** Fr Boulogne-sur-Gesse N on D632 sp Toulouse. In 6km turn L sp Lunax, foll site sp for 1km. Turn L at x-rds, site 300m on R. Sm, pt sl, pt shd; wc; chem disp (wc); shwrs inc; el pnts (9A) inc; gas; lndtte; shop 6km; BBQ; pool 6km; reservoir adj; 40% statics; phone 800m; Eng spkn; adv bkg; quiet. "Peaceful CL-type site; v friendly owners; san facs v clean but open to elements; breakfast & eve meals avail; perfect site for walking, cycling." 15 Mar-15 Dec. € 11.00 (4 persons)   2005*

France

BOULOGNE SUR GESSE *8F3* (1.3km SE) **Camp Municipal du Lac, Ave du Lac, 31350 Boulogne-sur-Gesse [05 61 88 20 54; fax 05 61 88 62 16; villagevacancesboulogne@wanadoo.fr]** Fr Boulogne-sur-Gesse, take D633 for 1km. Foll sp, turn L to site. Lake (watersports cent) adj ent. Lge, mkd pitch, pt sl, pt shd; wc (some cont); chem disp; shwrs inc; el pnts (10A) €3.70; gas; shops 1km; rest; bar; playgrnd; htd pool 300m; boating; fishing; tennis; golf; entmnt; 90% statics; dogs €1; phone; Eng spkn; quiet. "High kerbs mean site poss diff lge o'fits; friendly site; clean facs; sh walk into town; phone ahead to check open early ssn." ♦ 1 Apr-30 Sep. € 10.30   2005*

As soon as we get home I'm going to post all these site report forms to the editor for inclusion in next year's guide. I don't want to miss the September deadline.

⊞**BOULOGNE SUR MER** *3A2* (6km E Rural) **Camping Manoir de Senlecques, 45 Rue de la Fontaine, 62126 Pernes-lès-Boulogne [03 21 83 35 96; fax 03 21 33 83 85; manoirdesenlecques@wanadoo.fr; http://pagesperso-orange.fr/..manoirdesenlecques]** Exit A16 junc 33 sp Wimille; at rndabt turn under m'way onto D233 (pt of rd is narr) to Pernes in 7km & site is on L 1km past vill. Alt rte for longer o'fits (rds wider): exit A16 onto N42 dir St Omer. Turn R for La Capelle, then L on D233E for Pernes; turn R at junc in vill. NB Foll sp 'Manoir de Senlecques' if no 'Camping' sp. Long o'fits take care at ent. Sm, some hdstg, pt shd; wc; chem disp; mv service pnt; shwrs €1; el pnts (6A) €2.50 (some rev pol); lndtte; ice; shop, supmkt 5km; rest in walking dist; BBQ; sand beach 6km; fishing; 10% statics; dogs €1; some Eng spkn; adv bkg; quiet; cc not acc; red CCI. "Beautiful area; warm welcome fr helpful owners; delightful site in manor house grounds; busy NH; dated san facs; B&B also avail; gd vet within 3km; ltd el pnts high ssn; gd cycling; conv Calais, Tunnel & Nausica Seaworld; excel." € 12.50   2007*

BOULOGNE SUR MER *3A2* (8km E) **Camp Municipal Les Sapins, 62360 La Capelle-les-Boulogne [03 21 83 16 61]** Exit A16 junc 31 E onto N42 to La Capelle vill; cont to next rndabt & take sp Crémarest; site on R. Sm, pt shd; wc; shwrs inc; el pnts (4-6A) €3.70-6.70; lndtte; hypmkt, rest, snacks & bar 2km; playgrnd; sand beach 4km; 50% statics; bus 1km; poss cr; adv bkg; poss rd noise & fr adj horseriding school; no cc acc; CCI. " Dated, v basic san facs, poss dirty; hot shwrs; friendly, helpful warden; gd for Calais; gd NH." 15 Apr-15 Sep. € 8.75   2007*

⊞**BOULOGNE SUR MER** *3A2* (16km E Rural) **Camping à la Ferme Le Bois Groult (Leclercq), Le Plouy, 62142 Henneveux [03 21 33 32 16]** Take N42 fr Boulogne twd St Omer, take exit S dir Desvres (D127). Immed at rndabt foll sp Colembert. On ent Le Plouy turn R at the calvary & foll sp to site. Sm, some hdstg, pt sl, pt shd; wc; shwrs €2; el pnts €2 (poss long lead req); shops 6km; dogs; adv bkg; quiet; cc not acc. "Lovely, well-kept CL-type site; pleasant owner; v basic facs ltd in winter; twin-axles acc; no barrier; WWI places of interest; conv for ferries & Channel Tunnel; easy access fr N42; excel." € 6.00   2007*

BOULOGNE SUR MER *3A2* (7km S Urban) **Camping Les Cytises, Rue de l'Eglise, 62360 Isques [tel/fax 03 21 31 11 10]** S fr Boulogne on D901 (N1) to Isques; site 150m fr D901. Or on A16 exit junc 28 & foll sp Isques & camp sp. Med, hdg pitch, terr, pt shd; htd wc; chem disp; baby facs; shwrs inc; el pnts (3-6A) €2.70; gas; lndtte; ice; shop 100m; snacks; playgrnd; pool & sand beach 4km; rv adj; archery; 75% statics; dogs; Eng spkn; adv bkg; some rlwy noise; cc not acc; CCI. "Gd site; v clean san facs; poss sm pitches; informal hedging so more wildlife; poss scruffy & unkempt low ssn; barrier clsd 2300-0700; 30 mins fr Channel Tunnel & 5 mins fr Nausica; vg NH nr m'way." ♦ 1 Apr-15 Oct. € 14.30   2007*

BOULOIRE *4F2* (500m E Rural) **Camp Municipal, Chemin des Ruelles, 72440 Bouloire [tel/fax 02 43 35 52 09 or 02 43 35 40 25 (Mairie); ville. bouloire@wanadoo.fr]** On N157 fr Le Mans. At supmkt in Bouloire turn R onto D34 then L, across N157 at traff lts. Sm, terr, pt sl, pt shd; htd wc; chem disp; shwrs inc; el pnts (3A) €4.30; shops & pizzeria adj; CCI. "Conv Le Mans; excel." Easter-30 Sep. € 6.45   2007*

BOULOU, LE *8G4* (2km N) **Camping Le Mas Llinas, 66160 Le Boulou [04 68 83 25 46; info@ camping-mas-llinas.com; www.camping-mas-llinas.com]** Fr Perpignan, take D900 (N9) S; 1km N of Le Boulou turn R at Intermarché supmkt 100m to mini rndabt, turn L & foll sp to Mas-Llinas to site in 2km. Or fr A9 exit 43 & foll sp Perpignan thro Le Boulou. L at rndabt adj Leclerc supmkt, site well sp. Med, terr, pt shd; wc; shwrs inc; chem disp; el pnts (5-10A) €3.50-4.50; gas; lndtte; shops adj; tradsmn; snacks; playgrnd; pool; some statics; dogs €2; phone; adv bkg; Eng spkn; quiet; red low ssn; CCI. "Friendly, welcoming owners; peaceful in hillside setting with gd views fr top levels; golden orioles on site; beware poss high winds on high plateau pitches; ltd water points at top levels; ltd facs low ssn; facs clean; gd sized pitches." ♦ ltd. 1 Feb-30 Nov. € 18.30   2006*

BOULOU, LE *8G4* (6km E Urban) **Camping Soleil d'Or, Ave des Albères, 66740 Villelongue-dels-Monts [04 68 55 56 62; fax 04 68 55 56 62; alex.toure@laposte.net]** Fr Le Boulou on D618 sp Argelès-sur-Mer; in 7km at rndbt turn R sp Villelongue. Foll yellow camping sp. Sm, hdg/mkd pitch, hdstg, pt sl, pt shd; wc; chem disp; shwrs inc; el pnts (10A) €4; lndtte; ice; shops adj; playgrnd; bus 500m; quiet; no cc acc; CCI. "Helpful owner; ltd pitches for lge o'fits." 15 May-30 Sep. € 13.00

2005*

⊞**BOULOU, LE** *8G4* (1.5km SE Rural) **Camping Les Oliviers, Route d'Argelès-sur-Mer, 66160 Le Boulou [04 68 83 12 86; fax 04 68 87 60 08; campinglesoliviers@wanadoo.fr; http://ot-leboulou.fr/camping-lesoliviers.htm]** Exit A9 junc 43 at Le Boulou. Foll sp onto D618 twds Argelès-sur-Mer. Site on R in 1km, well sp fr D618. Med, mkd pitch, pt shd; htd wc; chem disp; mv service pnt; shwrs inc; el pnts (6A) €2.80; gas 1km; lndry rm; shop & 1km; tradsmn; playgrnd; shgl beach 12km; 10% statics; dogs €1; site clsd mid-Dec to mid-Jan; poss cr; adv bkg; quiet but some rd noise; red low ssn; CCI. "V helpful owner; gd, clean facs & v popular low ssn; dog-friendly; conv juncs of A9 & N9, gd touring base or NH en rte Spain." ♦ ltd. € 13.50

2006*

BOULOU, LE *8G4* (S Urban) **Camping L'Olivette, Route du Perthus, 66160 Le Boulou [04 68 83 48 08; fax 04 68 87 46 00; info@camping-olivette.fr; www.camping-olivette.fr]** D900 (N9) twd Spanish border, site on R alongside main D900, v busy rd. Med, hdg/mkd pitch; pt sl, pt shd; wc; baby facs; shwrs inc; el pnts (10A) €2.40; ice; lndtte; shops; snacks; bar; many statics; dogs €1.60; poss cr; Eng spkn; some rd noise. "Conv for Salvador Dali Museum & ruins at Empurias; security gate; poss tired pitches; clean san facs; v helpful owners; gd NH." 10 Mar-31 Oct. € 13.50   2006*

BOULOU, LE *8G4* (5km S Rural) **Camping Le Congo, Route de Céret, 66480 Maureillas-las-Illas [04 68 83 23 21; fax 04 68 87 47 15; campinglecongo@hotmail.com; www.campinglecongo.com]** Fr Le Boulou take D900 (N9) S, fork R after 2km onto D618 dir Céret. Site on L 500m after Maureillas. Med, hdg pitch, shd; htd wc (cont); chem disp (wc); shwrs inc; el pnts (10A); gas; lndtte; ice; shop 500m; tradsmn; rest; snacks; BBQ; playgrnd; pool; sand beach 20km; 10% statics; dogs; phone; adv bkg; Eng spkn; cc acc. ♦ 1 Feb-30 Nov. € 21.00   2005*

BOULOU, LE *8G4* (4km SW) **Camping de la Vallée/Les Deux Rivières, Route de Maureillas, 66490 St Jean-Pla-de-Corts [04 68 83 23 20; fax 04 68 83 07 94; campingdelavallee@yahoo.fr; www.campingdelavallee.com]** Exit A9 at Le Boulou. Turn W on D115. Turn L after 3km at rndabt, into St Jean-Pla-de-Corts, thro vill, over bdge, site on L. Med, mkd pitch, pt shd, wc; chem disp; mv service pnt; shwrs inc; baby facs; el pnts (5A) €3.90; gas 800m; lndtte; ice; shop 800m; tradsmn; rest; snacks; bar; playgrnd; pool; sand beach 20km; lake sw & fishing 1km; archery; mini-golf; entmnt; TV; phone; dogs €2; 50% statics; poss cr; Eng spkn; adv bkg (bkg fee & dep req); quiet; cc acc; red 10 days CCI. "V well-kept site; easy access lge pitches; excel san facs; owners with gd local info; conv NH fr A9." ♦ 1 Apr-30 Oct. € 16.10   2006*

BOULOU, LE *8G4* (5km SW Rural) **Camping La Clapère (Naturist), Route de Las Illas, 66400 Maureillas-las-Illas [04 68 83 36 04; fax 04 68 83 34 44; info@clapere.com; www.clapere.com]** Exit Le Boulou S on D900 (N9) twd Le Perthus; after 3km take N618 twd Maureillas, D13 for 2km twd Las Illas. Lge, terr, pt shd; wc; chem disp; shwrs inc; el pnts (6-10A) €5-8; lndtte; ice; shop; rest; snacks; bar; playgrnd; pool; rv adj; fishing; tennis; archery; games area; entmnt; TV; dogs €2.50; poss cr; Eng spkn; adv bkg; quiet. "Excel with easy access for c'vans; INF card req or may be purchased; vg for children; friendly recep." ♦ 1 May-30 Sep. € 23.00   2006*

⊞**BOULOU, LE** *8G4* (4km W Rural) **FFCC Camping Les Casteillets, 66490 St Jean Pla-de-Corts [04 68 83 26 83; fax 04 68 83 39 67; jc@campinglescasteillets.com; www.campinglescasteillets.com]** Exit A9 at Le Boulou; turn W on D115; after 3km turn L immed after St Jean-Pla-de-Corts; site sp on R in 400m. NB Narr app last 200m. Med, mkd pitch, pt shd; wc; chem disp; some serviced pitches; shwrs inc; el pnts (6A) €3 (poss rev pol); gas; lndtte; ice; shop; rest; snacks; bar; playgrnd; pool; tennis; sand beach 20km; entmnt; internet; TV; 10% statics; poss cr; Eng spkn; adv bkg ess high ssn; quiet; red low ssn. "Lovely, friendly site; lge pitches; views of mountains; gd rest; conv for touring & en rte NE Spain." ♦ € 16.50

2007*

BOULOU, LE *8G4* (8km W Rural) **Camp Municipal Al Comu, Route de Fourques, 66300 Llauro [04 68 39 42 08; alcomu@wanadoo.fr; www.village-llauro.com/camping]** Fr N on A9 exit junc 43. Take D115 dir Céret. Bef bdge R onto D615 to Llauro. Site on L after vill. Sm, mkd pitch, hdstg, terr, pt shd; wc; chem disp; baby facs; fam bthrm; shwrs inc; el pnts (16A) €2.50; lndtte; ice; shop in vill; tradsmn; playgrnd; pool 10km; lake sw 6km; dogs; Eng spkn; quiet; CCI. "Attractive setting in lower Pyrenees; gd views; friendly & helpful owners live on site; vg." ♦ ltd. 1 Apr-1 Nov. € 12.35

2006*

France

BOURBON LANCY *4H4* (Urban) **Camping St Prix, Rue de St Prix, 71140 Bourbon-Lancy** [tel/fax 03 85 89 20 98 or 03 86 37 95 83; aquadis1@wanadoo.fr; www.camping-chalets-bourbon-lancy.com] Fr N turn L fr D979 on D973 & foll into Bourbon-Lancy. Where D973 veers L (sp Autun) strt on to x-rds in about 100m. Turn R, then next R. Site well sp. Med, hdg pitch, hdstg, terr, pt sl, shd; htd wc; chem disp; shwrs inc; el pnts (10A) inc; lndry rm; ice; shop; snacks; playgrnd; htd pool adj; lake sw/fishing; 25% statics; dogs €3.10; Eng spkn; quiet; CCI. "Well-managed site in gd condition; helpful staff; lovely old town 10 min walk; rec." ♦ 1 Apr-31 Oct. € 18.00   2007*

BOURBON L'ARCHAMBAULT *9A1* (10km NE Rural) **Camping Les Fourneaux (Naturist), Route Limoise, 03160 Couzon** [tel/fax 04 70 66 23 18] Fr Bourbon NE on D139 to Couzon, then L onto D13, site in 2km on L. Med, pt sl, pt shd; wc; chem disp; shwrs el pnts (2-4A) €2.50-4; tradsmn; bar; playgrnd; pool; cycle hire; phone; Eng spkn; quiet; red 3+ days; INF card req. "V lge pitches; helpful Dutch owners; conv touring base." ♦ ltd. 1 Jun-15 Sep. € 22.00   2005*

BOURBON L'ARCHAMBAULT *9A1* (1km W Rural) **Camp Municipal de Bignon, 03160 Bourbon-l'Archambault** [04 70 67 08 83; mairie-bourbon-archambault@wanadoo.fr] Take D953 (sp) to Montluçon fr town cent. Turn R nr top of hill at camping sp bef town cancellation sp. Lge, sl, pt shd; wc (some cont); shwrs inc; el pnts (6-10A) inc; shops 1km; htd pool & waterslide 300m; tennis nr; 75% statics; poss cr; quiet. "Beautifully laid-out in park surroundings; dated san facs; gd pitches; charming town; excel." 1 Mar-31 Oct. € 8.50   2005*

BOURBONNE LES BAINS *6F2* (500m NW Urban) **Camping Le Montmorency, Rue du Stade, 52400 Bourbonne-les-Bains** [03 25 90 08 64; fax 03 25 84 23 74; c.montmorency@wanadoo.fr; www.camping-montmorency.com] Sp on ent town either way on D417. After exit D417, sp at 1st turn L at telephone box. Site adj to pool & stadium. Med, hdg/mkd pitch, pt sl, unshd; wc; mv service pnt; shwrs inc; el pnts (6A) €3; gas; lndry rm; shops 500m; snacks; pool adj; tennis; dogs €0.80; adv bkg; quiet. "Pleasant site; helpful warden; popular with visitors to spa cent; gd NH." 5 Mar-20 Nov. € 9.90   2007*

BOURBOULE, LA *7B4* (1km N Rural) **FFCC Camping Le Panoramique, Le Pessy, 63150 Murat-le-Quaire** [04 73 81 18 79; fax 04 73 65 57 34; camping.panoramique@wanadoo.fr; http://membres.lycos.fr/campingpanoramique] Exit A89 junc 25; cont strt until junc with D922; turn R; in 3km turn R onto D219 dir Mont-Dore; in 5km pass thro Murat-le-Quaire; in 1km turn L in Le Pessy; site on L in 300m. Site well sp fr D922. Med, mkd pitch, terr, pt shd; htd wc; chem disp; mv service pnt; baby facs; shwrs inc; el pnts (6-10A) €4.30-5.60; gas; lndtte; ice; shop & snacks 2km; tradsmn; rest 1km; bar; playgrnd; pool; games rm; 30% statics; dogs €1.70; phone; adv bkg; quiet; CCI. "Site well set out; mountain views; friendly, helpful recep; clean facs; office clsd 1200-1600; pets corner; vg." 15 May-30 Sep. € 14.80   2007*

BOURBOULE, LA *7B4* (500m NE Rural) **Camping Le Poutie, 750 Ave de Maréchal Leclerc, 63150 La Bourboule** [04 73 81 04 54; fax 04 73 81 04 54; campingpoutie@aol.com; www.campingpoutie.com] Fr La Bourboule on D996, 500m past rlwy stn. Med, hdg/mkd pitch, hdstg, terr, pt shd; wc (some cont); chem disp (wc); baby facs; shwrs inc; el pnts (4-10A) €4-5.50 (poss rev pol); gas; lndtte; ice; shop & 500m; tradsmn; rest 500m; snacks; takeaway; playgrnd; htd pool; lge leisure rm; entmnt; wifi internet; 50% statics; dogs €2; phone adj; poss full; adv bkg; quiet; CCI. "Superb views; friendly British owners; san facs need update." ♦ ltd. 15 May-31 Oct. € 12.50   2007*

BOURBOULE, LA *7B4* (3km E) **Camp Municipal des Vernières, Ave de Lattre de Tassigny, 63150 La Bourboule** [04 73 81 10 20 or 04 73 81 31 00 (Mairie); fax 04 73 65 54 98] Fr N on N89 or S on D922 turn E onto D130 dir Le Mont-Dore, site sp. Lge, some hdg pitch; pt terr, pt shd; htd wc (some cont); shwrs inc; el pnts (6-10A) €2.65-5.30; lndtte; supmkt nr; playgrnd; pool nr; fishing nr; dogs €0.95; poss cr; no adv bkg; some rd noise. "Lovely setting in mountains; gd clean facs; short walk to fine spa town; rec." ♦ Easter-30 Sep. € 8.80   2007*

BOURBOULE, LA *7B4* (4km E Rural) **Camping Les Clarines, 1424 Ave Maréchal Leclerc, Les Planches, 63150 La Bourboule** [04 73 81 02 30; fax 04 73 81 09 34; www.camping-les-clarines.com] Fr La Bourboule take D996 (old rd sp Piscine & Gare); fork L at exit fr town. Site sp on R. Lge, terr, pt shd; wc (some cont); baby facs; shwrs inc; el pnts (3-10A) €2.13-€5.79; gas; lndtte; ice; shop & adj; bar; BBQ; htd pool; playgrnd; entmnt; TV; dogs €1; poss cr; adv bkg (ess high ssn); quiet; 15% red low ssn. "Gd winter sports cent (open for ski Xmas-Easter)." ♦ 21 Dec-20 Oct. € 12.95   2005*

BOURDEAU see Yenne *9B3*

BOURDEAUX 9D2 (3km E Rural) **Aire Naturelle Le Moulin (Arnaud), 26460 Bézaudun-sur-Bine** [tel/fax 04 75 53 37 21 or 04 75 53 30 73; arnocampmoulin26@aol.com] Exit A7 junc 16; D104 to Crest then D538 to Bourdeaux; just bef bdge L to Bézaudun-sur-Bine. Site on R in 3km. Sm, pt sl, pt shd; wc; chem disp (wc); shwrs €1; el pnts (6A) €2; lndtte; shop 3km; tradsmn; snacks; bar; pool; no statics; dogs €1; quiet; CCI. "Lovely area; wonderful views; old chateau; pretty vills; gd walking; vg." ♦ ltd. 15 Apr-30 Sep. € 11.00
2006*

BOURDEAUX 9D2 (1.5km SE Rural) **Camping Les Bois du Chatelas, 26460 Bourdeaux** [04 75 00 60 80; fax 04 75 00 60 81; bois.du.chatelas@infonie.fr; www.chatelas.com] A7 m'way exit at Valence Sud, head twd Crest then twd Bourdeaux. In Bourdeaux go Dienlefit, site in 1km on L. Med, mkd pitch, terr, pt shd; htd wc; chem disp; mv service pnt; baby facs; shwrs inc; el pnts (10A) €4.50; gas; lndtte; ice; shop; tradsmn; rest; snacks; bar; cooking facs; playgrnd; htd covrd pool; rv sw 5km; entmnt; TV rm; 30% statics; dogs €4; phone; Eng spkn; adv bkg ess high ssn (dep req + bkg fee); red low ssn; cc acc; CCI. "In lovely area; stunning views; gd walking; on steep slope." 7 Apr-30 Sep. € 23.00
2006*

BOURDEAUX 9D2 (300m S) **FFCC Camp Municipal Le Gap des Tortelles, 26460 Bourdeaux** [tel/fax 04 75 53 30 45; info@campingdebourdeaux.com; www.campingdebourdeaux.com] Foll camping/piscine sp in vill. Gd app fr S via D94 & D70 fr Nyons. Sm, terr, pt shd; wc; mv service pnt; shwrs inc; el pnts (6A) €2.70; lndtte; shop, 600m; rest; bar; playgrnd; sw rv; tennis adj; few statics; dogs €2; adv bkg; quiet. "V attractive area away fr tourist scene; helpful warden; sh path into vill." ♦ 1 Apr-30 Sep. € 10.50
2007*

BOURDEAUX 9D2 (4km NW Rural) **Camping Le Couspeau, Quartier Bellevue, 26460 Le Poët-Célard** [04 75 53 30 14; fax 04 75 53 37 23; info@couspeau.com; www.couspeau.com] Fr D538 Crest-Bourdeaux; pass thro Saou & after several kms turn R over bdge to Le Poët-Célard, site sp in vill. Med, terr, mkd pitch, sl, pt shd; wc; chem disp; serviced pitches; shwrs inc; el pnts (6A) €3 (poss rev pol); gas; lndtte; sm shop; tradsmn; rest, snacks, bar high ssn; playgrnd; 2 htd pools (1 covrd); rv sw & fishing; canoeing; tennis; horseriding 4km; TV rm; 20% statics; dogs €1; Eng spkn; adv bkg; quiet; cc acc; min 6 days high ssn; red low ssn; CCI. "On steep hillside; stunning scenery; peaceful even in high ssn; facs for disabled but site rds steep; tractor assistance avail on arr/dep; red low ssn; fantastic site." ♦ 15 Apr-30 Sep. € 26.00 (CChq acc) 2006*

BOURG see Langres 6F1

BOURG ACHARD 3D2 (1km W) **Camping Le Clos Normand, 235 Route de Pont Audemer, 27310 Bourg-Achard** [02 32 56 34 84 or 06 03 60 36 26 (mob)] 1km W of vill of Bourg-Achard, N175 Rouen-Pont Audemer or exit A13 at Bourg-Achard junc. Med, hdg/mkd pitch, pt sl, pt shd; wc (chem clos); shwrs inc; el pnts (6A) €2.70 (poss rev pol); gas; ice; shop; supmkt nr; pool; playgrnd; mini-golf; 10% statics; dogs €1; poss cr; quiet; adv bkg; cc acc; CCI. "Clean facs; many pitches uneven; walk to vill; gd." ♦ 1 Apr-30 Sep. € 12.70
2007*

BOURG ARGENTAL 9C2 (7km NE Rural) **Camping Le Val de Ternay, Le Pré Battoir, 42220 St Julien-Molin-Molette** [04 77 51 50 76; valduternay@voila.fr; http://valduternay.site.voila.fr] N fr Annonay on D206/N82, turn R onto D306 to vill, site sp. Med, pt shd; wc; baby facs; shwrs inc; el pnts (4-10A) €2-3; lndtte; ice; shop; bar; BBQ; playgrnd; fishing; games area; entmnt; TV; 90% statics; dogs €0.75; adv bkg; quiet; red low ssn. 1 Apr-30 Sep. € 13.00 2005*

⊞**BOURG ARGENTAL** 9C2 (S Rural) **Camp Municipal L' Astrée, Parc Résidentiel de Loisir Les Rivets, 42220 Bourg-Argental** [tel/fax 04 77 39 72 97; PRL@bourgargental.fr] S fr St Etienne on D1082 (N82) to Bourg-Argental, thro town, site well sp on R soon after rndabt & opp filling stn. Fr Annonay or Andance site on L of D1082 at start of Bourg-Argental, adj rv. Sm, pt shd; wc; chem disp (wc); shwrs inc; el pnts (4-6A) €3-4 (long cable poss req); gas; lndtte; shop 250m; snacks; playgrnd; pool 600m; rv sw adj; waterslide; fishing; 60% statics; dogs €1.50; phone; poss cr; some rd noise; red low ssn; cc acc; CCI. "Pleasant site with modern facs; vg." ♦ € 15.00 2006*

BOURG DES COMPTES see Guichen 2F4

BOURG D'OISANS, LE 9C3 (1.5km NE Rural) **Camping à la Rencontre du Soleil, Route de l'Alpe-d'Huez, La Sarenne, 38520 Le Bourg-d'Oisans** [04 76 79 12 22; fax 04 76 80 26 37; rencontre.soleil@wanadoo.fr; www.alarencontredusoleil.com] Fr N91 approx 800m E of town turn on D211, sp Alpe d'Huez. In approx 500m cross sm bdge over Rv Sarennes, then turn immed L to site. (Take care not to overshoot ent, as poss diff to turn back.) Med, mkd pitch, pt shd; htd wc (some cont); chem disp; mv service pnt; baby facs; shwrs inc; el pnts (10A) inc; lndtte; ice; supmkt 300m; tradsmn; rest; snacks; bar; BBQ; playgrnd; htd pool; fishing; tennis; games area; horseriding 1.5km; entmnt; child entmnt; TV/games rm; 45% statics; dogs €0.80; adv bkg ess; rd noise; red low ssn; cc acc; CCI. "Lovely site; wonderful scenery; Ecrins National Park; La Marmotte cycle race (early Jul) & Tour de France usually pass thro area & access poss restricted; excel, inexpensive rest; mkt Sat; organised walks; pitches poss flooded after heavy rain, but staff excel at responding." 3 May-30 Sep. € 29.60 (CChq acc) ABS - M01 2007*

France

BOURG D'OISANS, LE 9C3 (1.5km NE Rural) Camping La Cascade, Route de l'Alpe d'Huez, 38520 Le Bourg-d'Oisans [04 76 80 02 42; fax 04 76 80 22 63; lacascade@wanadoo.fr; http://lacascadesarenne.com] Drive thro Le Bourg-d'Oisans & cross bdge over Rv Romanche. Approx 800m E of town turn onto D211, sp Alpe-d'Huez. Site on R in 600m. Med, mkd pitch, pt shd; htd wc; chem disp; baby facs; shwrs; el pnts (16A) €3.70; lndtte; supmkt 1km; snacks; bar high ssn; playgrnd; htd pool high ssn; some statics; poss cr; Eng spkn; adv bkg; quiet; cc acc; CCI. "Friendly site; discounts for ski passes fr recep; nr Les Deux-Alpes, L'Alpe-d'Huez, Pelvoux National Park." 15 Dec-30 Sep. € 23.30   2005*

⊞**BOURG D'OISANS, LE** 9C3 (1.5km NE Rural) Camping La Piscine, Route de l'Alpe d'Huez, 38520 Le Bourg-d'Oisans [04 76 80 02 41; fax 04 76 11 01 26; infos@camping-piscine.com; www.camping-piscine.com] Fr N91 approx 800m E of town, take D211 sp Alpe d'Huez. After 1km turn L into site. Fountains at ent. Med, mkd pitch, pt shd; htd wc (some cont); chem disp; shwrs inc; el pnts (16A) €3.40; lndtte; ice; shops 1.5km; tradsmn; rest, snacks, bar 1.5km; BBQ; playgrnd; htd pool (summer); rv adj; tennis 2km; entmnts; TV; 10% statics; dogs €1; phone; poss cr; Eng spkn; adv bkg; quiet but with some rd noise; 10% red 7+ days/low ssn; cc acc; CCI. "Excel site; excel lge pool; conv town cent; gd for mountain drives & walks; facs stretched high ssn & when La Marmotte cycle race (early Jul) & Tour de France in area; ski slopes 10-18km." ♦ € 20.00   2004*

BOURG D'OISANS, LE 9C3 (500m SE Rural) Camping Le Colporteur, Le Mas du Plan, 38520 Le Bourg d'Oisans [04 76 79 11 44 or 06 85 73 29 19 (mob); fax 04 76 79 11 49; info@camping-colporteur.com; www.camping-colporteur.com] W fr Briançon on N91 to Le Bourg d'Oisans. Ent town, pass Casino supmkt, site sp on L; 150m to sw pool - 2nd site sp, site 50m - sp on side of house. Fr Grenoble on A480 exit 8 onto N85, cont on N91 to Le Bourg d'Oisans. Foll sp R in cent of town after Total service stn. Med, hdg/mkd pitch, hdstg, shd; htd wc; chem disp; baby facs; shwrs inc; el pnts (6-15A) €4; lndtte; shops 500m; tradsmn; rest; snacks; bar; BBQ; playgrnd; htd pool 150m; waterslide; lake sw 10km; fishing; tennis; squash; mountain bikes; rockclimbing; horseriding; cycle hire 200m; entmnt; games rm; wifi internet; TV; 10% statics; dogs €1.50; Eng spkn; adv bkg (dep req); quiet; red long stay/low ssn; cc acc; red long stay/low ssn; CCI. "Site to v high standard; well-organised; lge indiv pitches; gd security; mountain scenery; many activities; conv National Park des Ecrins." ♦ 10 May-21 Sep. € 24.00   2007*

See advertisement

BOURG D'OISANS, LE 9C3 (13km SE Rural) Camping Le Champ du Moulin, Bourg d'Arud, 38520 Vénosc [04 76 80 07 38; fax 04 76 80 24 44; info@champ-du-moulin.com; www.champ-du-moulin.com] On N91 SE fr Le Bourg d'Oisans sp Briançon for about 6km; turn R onto D530 twd La Bérarde & after 8km site sp. Turn R to site 350m after cablecar stn beside Rv Vénéon. NB Site sp bef vill; do not cross rv on D530. Med, mkd pitch, pt shd; wc; chem disp; baby facs; shwrs inc; el pnts (10A) inc (extra charge in winter; poss rev pol); gas; lndtte; ice; tradsmn; rest; snacks; bar; BBQ; playgrnd nr; htd pool adj; fishing, tennis, rafting, horseriding, archery nr; games/TV rm; wifi internet; 20% statics; dogs €1; recep 0800-1200 & 1400-1900 high ssn; barrier (dep €20 req); poss cr; Eng spkn; adv bkg; quiet; cc acc; red long stay/low ssn; CCI. "Excel, clean site; ideal cent for walking, climbing, touring; telecabins to Les Deux Alpes adj (high ssn); magnificent scenery; beautifully situated by alpine torrent (unguarded); 25% off day ski lift pass for residents; owners friendly & helpful; ltd facs low ssn; ltd bus bet Le Bourg d'Oisans & La Bérarde; mkt Tue Vénosc (high ssn); excel." ♦ 15 Dec-30 Apr & 1 Jun-15 Sep. € 24.80 ABS - M03   2007*

> The opening dates and prices on this campsite have changed. I'll send a site report form to the editor for the next edition of the guide.

⊞**BOURG D'OISANS, LE** 9C3 (4km NW Rural) Camping Ferme Noémie, Chemin Pierre Polycarpe, Les Sables, 38520 Le Bourg d'Oisans [tel/fax 04 76 11 06 14 or 06 87 45 08 75 (mob); sci.smith@libertysurf.fr; www.fermenoemie.com] On N91 Grenoble to Briançon; Les Sables is 4km bef Le Bourg-d'Oisans; turn L next to church, site in 400m. Sm, mkd pitch, unshd; htd wc; chem disp; mv service pnt; shwrs inc; el pnts (16A) €2.50; gas; lndtte; ice; tradsmn; shop, rest, snacks & bar 3km; BBQ (gas communal); playgrnd; rock climbing; skiing; cycling; walking; fishing; pool 3km; games area; internet; 25% statics; dogs free; phone; bus 500m; poss cr; adv bkg; quiet; red long stay; cc acc; CCI. "Superb location for peaceful Alpine holiday; simple site with excel facs; lovely, helpful English owners - quiet, personal service; lots of sports; lakes nrby; gd touring base; conv Ecrins National Park; excel." ♦ € 15.00   2007*

BOURG D'OISANS, LE *9C3* (7km NW Rural) Camping Belledonne, Rochetaillée, 38520 Le Bourg d'Oisans [04 76 80 07 18; fax 04 76 79 12 95; belledon@club-internet.fr; www. le-belledonne.com] Fr S of Grenoble take N85 to Vizille then N91 twd Le Bourg-d'Oisans; about 25km after Vizille in Rochetaillée bef Le Bourg-d'Oisans turn L onto D526 sp Allemont. Site 100m on R. Med, hdg pitch, shd; wc (some cont); chem disp; sauna; baby facs; shwrs inc; el pnts (6A) €4; gas; lndtte; shop; rest; snacks; bar; BBQ; playgrnd; 2 htd pools & paddling pool; tennis; horseriding; fishing 500m; entmnt; games/TV rm; dogs €1.10; recep 0830-2000; Eng spkn; quiet; cc acc; CCI. "Excel mountain scenery; gd recep; La Marmotte cycle race (early Jul) & Tour de France usually pass thro area & access poss restricted; rafting, climbing, paragliding, walks etc. organised by site - gd for families with teenagers; mkt Sat." ♦ 14 May-13 Sep. € 24.20 (CChq acc) ABS - M02 2007*

Before we move on, I'm going to fill in some site report forms and post them off to the editor, otherwise they won't arrive in time for the deadline at the end of September.

BOURG D'OISANS, LE *9C3* (7km NW Rural) Camping Le Château Bourg d'Oisans, Chemin de Bouthéon, 38520 Rochetaillée [04 76 11 04 40; fax 04 76 80 21 23; www.camping-le-chateau. com or www.les-castels.com] On N91 fr Grenoble turn 7km bef Le Bourg d'Oisans onto D526 sp Allemont. Site is 50m on L. Med, pt shd; wc; chem disp; baby facs; shwrs inc; el pnts (6A) inc; lndtte; shop; rest; snacks; bar; BBQ; playgrnd; sports area; pool; dogs €0.80; 5% statics; quiet; CCI. "Vg; san facs clean & new; helpful staff; beautiful mountain views fr site." ♦ 15 May-16 Sep. € 28.80 2007*

⊞BOURG D'OISANS, LE *9C3* (7km NW Rural) Camping Le Grand Calme, Le Plan, 38114 Allemont [04 76 80 70 03; fax 04 76 80 73 13; hotel-ginies@wanadoo.fr; www.hotel-ginies. com] Fr Grenoble on N91, at Rochetailée turn L (N) on D526 to Allemont. Site on R in 1.5km opp Hotel Ginies. Med, pt shd; pt htd wc; chem disp; shwrs €1; el pnts (10A) €3.20; lndtte; shops 500m; tradsmn; rest; bar; playgrnd; 10% statics; dogs €0.50; phone nr; poss cr; Eng spkn; adv bkg; quiet; cc acc; CCI. "Vg, well-maintained site run by hotel opp (gd rest); call at hotel recep if site recep clsd; phone ahead to check site open low ssn; v friendly owner; beautiful, scenic area gd for skiers & walkers." ♦ € 12.00 2007*

BOURG D'OISANS, LE *9C3* (7km NW Rural) Camping Les Bouleaux, La Pernière Basse, 38114 Allemont [04 76 80 71 23; fax 04 76 80 70 75; campinglesbouleaux@wanadoo. fr] Take N91 fr Bourg-d'Oisans, then turn onto D526 dir Allemont/Allemond. After x-ing 2nd bdge, turn immed L down narr lane beside stream to recep on R. Sm, pt shd; wc; chem disp; shwrs inc; el pnts inc; tradsmn; pool 2km; dogs; poss cr; Eng spkn; quiet; red 7+ days & low ssn; CCI. "Vg sheltered, peaceful farm site but basic; v helpful owners." ♦ ltd. 15 Jun-15 Sep. 2006*

BOURG D'OISANS, LE *9C3* (8km NW Rural) Camp Municipal Le Plan, 38114 Allemont [04 76 80 76 88 or 04 76 80 70 30 (Mairie); fax 04 76 79 80 28; info@camping-leplan-allemont. com; www.camping-leplan-allemont.com] At Rochetaillée on N91 fr Grenoble turn N 7km bef Le Bourg-d'Oisans on D526 sp Allemont site on R at N end of vill below dam. Med, mkd pitch, hdstg; pt shd; htd wc; chem disp; shwrs inc; el pnts €2; lndtte; snacks; shops in vill; pool adj high ssn only; no statics; dogs €0.50; adv bkg; quiet; cc acc high ssn; CCI. "In quiet vill with lovely mountain scenery; excel, clean facs; v helpful staff." ♦ 1 May-30 Sep. € 9.20 2007*

BOURG DUN, LE see Veules les Roses *3C2*

France

BOURG EN BRESSE 9A2 (1km NE Urban) FFCC Camp Municipal de Challes, Ave de Bad Kreuznach, 01000 Bourg-en-Bresse [04 74 45 37 21; fax 04 74 22 40 32; camping-municipal-bourgenbresse@wanadoo.fr; www.bourg-en-bresse.org] Fr N or S ON N83 foll sp Camping/Piscine/Stade. Site opp stadium. Med, hdstg, shd; wc (most cont); chem disp; shwrs inc; el pnts (6A) €2.11 (poss rev pol); ice; lndry rm; hypermkt nr; snacks; rest; BBQ; htd, covrd pool & sports ground adj; lake sw 2km; 10% statics; bus adj; poss cr; adv bkg; some rd noise; red long stay; cc acc; 10% red CCI. "Lots of trees; suitable lge o'fits; site poss full by 1800; gd touring base; daytime noise fr stadium; easy walk to town for rests (poss clsd low ssn)." 1 Apr-15 Oct. € 12.30   2007*

BOURG EN BRESSE 9A2 (11km NE Rural) Camp Municipal du Sevron, 01370 St Etienne-du-Bois [04 74 30 50 65 or 04 74 30 50 36 (Mairie); fax 04 74 25 85 72] On N83 at S end of vill of St Etienne-du-Bois on E side of rd. Sm, shd; wc; chem disp; shwrs inc; el pnts (4A) €2.05; ice; shops 300m; tennis; rv fishing; dogs €1.05; Eng spkn; cc not acc. "Gd NH only; clean facs; friendly; sm pitches; late arrivals get v sm pitches; poss rd & rlwy noise." 1 Mar-25 Oct. € 9.90   2006*

BOURG EN BRESSE 9A2 (13km SE) Camp Municipal de Journans, 01250 Journans [04 74 42 64 71 or 04 74 51 64 45; fax 04 74 42 64 83; mairiejournans@wanadoo.fr] Exit A40 junc 7, turn L onto D1075 (N75), then L onto D64 dir Tossiat & Journans. Or SE fr Bourg-en-Bresse on D1075 (N75) for 9.5km E onto D64 to Journans. Site sp on D52 Sm, mkd pitch, sl terr, pt shd; wc (some cont); shwrs inc; el pnts (5-10A) €2.35; shops 1km (Tossiat); dog €1; poss cr; quiet; CCI. "Pleasant setting; helpful warden calls pm; some pitches diff for c'vans; gd views; excel value; v quiet low ssn; poss mkt traders." 1 May-15 Sep. € 6.50   2007*

BOURG EN BRESSE 9A2 (20km SE Rural) Camping de l'Ile Chambod, 01250 Hautecourt-Romanèche [04 74 37 25 41; fax 04 74 37 28 28; camping.chambod@free.fr; www.campingilechambod.com] Fr S exit A42 junc 9 onto D1075 (N75) dir Geneva. In 1km turn L onto N84 dir Nantua. At Poncin turn L at traff lts dir Ile Chambod & site. Fr N turn S off D979 in Hautecourt at x-rds (site sp). Site sp in 4km off D59. At rvside cont for 500m. Med, mkd pitch; pt shd; wc; mv service pnt; baby facs; shwrs inc; el pnts (5-10A) €2.70-3.70 (poss rev pol); gas; lndtte; ice; shop; snacks; BBQ; playgrnd; pool; lake 100m; fishing/boat hire 400m; games area; cycle hire; internet; entmnt; 10% statics; dogs €1.10; Eng spkn; adv bkg; quiet; cc acc; red low ssn. "Gd, clean, picturesque, peaceful site but somewhat remote; superb san facs; helpful manager; conv Geneva; highly rec." ♦ 28 Apr-1 Oct. € 15.30   2007*

BOURG EN BRESSE 9A2 (13km SW) Camp Municipal, 01249 Dompierre-sur-Veyle [04 74 30 31 81; fax 04 74 30 36 61; mairiedompierre@wanadoo.fr] S fr Bourg on N83, fork L after 5km on D22. Site sp on L after 10km on vill o'skts just after vill sign. Sm, pt shd; wc; shwrs inc; el pnts (10A) €1.50; shops 500m; playgrnd; adv bkg. "Gd cent for fishing, birdwatching, many lakes & marshes; pitch yourself, warden calls; v well-maintained site; friendly, helpful warden; facs clean but stretched high ssn; gd cycling; pizza van in vill Tues." 1 Apr-30 Sep. € 6.50   2006*

BOURG EN BRESSE 9A2 (15km SW Rural) Base de Plein Air, Etang du Moulin, 01240 St Paul-de-Varax [04 74 42 53 30; fax 04 74 42 51 57; resa@campingendombes.fr; www.campingendombes.fr/etang_du_moulin] Fr N on N83 fr Bourg-en-Bresse turn L into St Paul-de-Varax under narr rlwy bdge, thro vill on D70B twd St Nizier-le-Désert. In 2km turn L into lane with 45km/h speed limit, site on R in 2km. Lge, hdg/mkd pitch, pt shd; htd wc (some cont); mv service pnt; baby facs; shwrs inc; el pnts (6A) inc; lndtte; ice; shops; rest; snacks; bar; BBQ; playgrnd; pool; paddling pool; waterslide; shgl beach on lake; fishing; watersports; mini-golf; tennis; archery; TV rm; 10% statics; dogs €2.40; quiet low ssn; dep req; cc acc; red 30 days; 10% red CCI. "Many sports & activities; huge pool; excel for bird-watching." 24 May-3 Sep. € 16.00
                    2006*

⊞**BOURG ET COMIN** 3D4 (Rural) Camping de la Pointe, 5 Rue de Moulins, 02160 Bourg-et-Comin [03 23 25 87 52; fax 03 23 25 06 02; michel.pennec@9online.fr; www.tourisme-paysdelaon.com] Leave A26/E17 at junc 14 & turn W along D925 dir Soissons for 15km. Site on R on ent vill. Sm, hdg pitch, pt shd; htd wc; chem disp; shwrs inc; el pnts (5A) €3; lndtte; baker 500m; tradsmn; crêperie adj; rest; bar 500m; BBQ; playgrnd; htd, covrd pool; dogs €2; phone; bus 500m; Eng spkn; adv bkg; quiet; CCI. "CL-type site in orchard; narr ent & acces to pitches poss diff lge o'fits; v sm san facs block; excel rest; gd walking area; 10 mins fr Parc Nautique de l'Ailette with watersports; conv Aisne Valley; gd site-seeing; gd." € 12.00
                    2007*

⊞**BOURG MADAME** 8H4 (1km Urban) Camping Mas Piques, Rue du Train Jaune, 66760 Bourg-Madame [04 68 04 62 11; fax 04 68 04 68 32; campiques@wanadoo.fr] Last camp site in France bef Spain & Cadí Tunnel. App via N20 or N116. Med, pt shd; wc; chem disp; shwrs inc; el pnts (3-10A) €3-7.80; shop 500m; lndry rm; playgrnd; gas; ice; pool 500m; 95% statics; dogs €1.10; poss v cr; adv bkg ess high ssn. "Vg; organised rambling; gd san facs & el pnts." ♦ ltd. € 11.80   2006*

⊞BOURG MADAME 8H4 (200m N) Camping Le Sègre, 8 Ave du Puymorens, 66760 Bourg-Madame [04 68 04 65 87; fax 04 68 04 91 82; camping.lesegre@free.fr] N on N20 site on R immed under rlwy bdge. Med, pt shd; wc; shwrs inc; el pnts (3-6A) €2.25; lndtte; shops adj; playgrnd; sports cent nr; poss cr; some rd & rlwy noise. "V ltd touring pitches in winter, rec arr early." ♦ € 11.50   2006*

⊞BOURG MADAME 8H4 (5km NE Rural) Camping L'Enclave, 66800 Estavar [04 68 04 72 27; fax 04 68 04 07 15; contact@camping-lenclave.com; www.camping.lenclave.com] Leave Saillagouse on D33 sp Estavar vill. Lge, pt sl, terr, pt shd; htd wc; chem disp; mv service pnt; baby facs; shwrs inc; el pnts (3A) inc; gas; lndtte; ice; shop adj; rest adj; snacks; bar; playgrnd; htd, covrd pool; tennis; cycle hire; guided walks; entmnt; dogs €1.52; site clsd 24 Sep-27 Oct; adv bkg; quiet; red low ssn; CCI. "Nr ski resorts & Spanish border, friendly." ♦ € 22.00   2005*

BOURG MADAME 8H4 (7km NE Rural) Camping La Riberette, 20 Rue de la Riberette, 66800 Err [04 68 04 75 60] Fr Bourg-Madame on N116 to Saillagouse turn off onto rd C2 dir Err, site in 300m. Sm, mkd pitch, pt shd; wc (some cont); chem disp; shwrs inc; el pnts (15A) €3.50; lndtte; shop, rest, snacks, bar 300m; playgrnd; fishing, tennis nr; some statics; dogs €1; adv bkg; quiet. "Pleasant owners; simple, quiet site; beautiful situation." ♦ 10 Jun-30 Sep. € 8.70   2004*

⊞BOURG MADAME 8H4 (7km NE Rural) Camping Las Closas, 1 Place St Genis, 66800 Err [04 68 04 71 42; fax 04 68 04 07 20; camping.las.closas@wanadoo.fr; www.camping-las-closas.com] On N116 fr Bourg-Madame immediate after vill of Err take D33A on R. Site well sp. Med, pt sl, unshd; htd wc; shwrs; el pnts (3-10A) €3.70-6.80; gas; lndtte; shop; BBQ; playgrnd; entmnt; dogs €1.30; adv bkg; quiet; red low ssn. € 12.00   2007*

⊞BOURG MADAME 8H4 (11km NE Rural) Camping Le Cerdan, 11 Route d'Estavar; 66800 Saillagouse [04 68 04 70 46; fax 04 68 04 05 26; lecerdan@lecerdan.com; www.lecerdan.com] Fr Mont Louis take N116 twd Bourg Madame; turn R in Saillagouse cent; past church & foll sm sp. Sm, pt sl, shd; htd wc; chem disp; shwrs inc; el pnts (3-6A) €3-3.70; gas; lndtte; shop 250m; playgrnd; BBQ; games area; 10% statics; dogs €1; clsd Oct; Eng spkn; adv bkg rec; quiet; CCI. "Helpful managers; organised walks; orchard site." ♦ € 12.00   2005*

⊞BOURG MADAME 8H4 (6km NW Rural) Camping Le Robinson, Ave Gare Internationale, 66760 Enveitg [tel/fax 04 68 04 80 38; www.robinson-cerdagne.com] Fr Bourg-Madame, take N20 N twd Foix. Thro vill of Enveitg & turn L down Chemin de la Gare & L at camping sp. Lge, mkd pitch, pt sl, shd; wc; chem disp; baby facs; shwrs inc; el pnts (4-13A) €3-9; gas; ice; lndtte; shops adj; tradsmn; rest adj; snacks; BBQ; playgrnd; mini-golf; pool; games rm; entmnt; TV rm; some statics; dogs €1.50; phone; adv bkg; quiet. "Beautiful setting; wintersports cent; conv Barcelona, Andorra; conv scenic rte train (Train Jaune)." ♦ € 16.00   2006*

BOURG ST ANDEOL 9D2 (1.5km N Rural) Camping Le Lion, Chemin du Chenevrier, 07700 Bourg-St Andéol [tel/fax 04 75 54 53 20; contact@campingdulion; www.campingdulion.com] Exit A7 at junc 18 or 19 onto N7. At Pierrelatte turn W on D59 to Bourg-St Andéol. Site sp fr cent town dir Viviers. Med, mkd pitch, shd; wc; own san rec; shwrs inc; el pnts (6A) €3; lndtte; ice; shop; snacks; bar; playgrnd; pool; games area; games rm; dir access to rv; dogs €1.70; poss cr; adv bkg; quiet; red low ssn. "Peaceful site in woodland setting; new modern facs highly rec." 1 Apr-15 Sep. € 16.50   2004*

BOURG ST MAURICE 9B4 (2km NE Rural) Camp Municipal Le Reclus, Pont du Reclus, 73700 Séez [04 79 41 01 05; fax 04 79 40 18 54; campinglereclus@wanadoo.fr] Site on R of N90 bet Bourg-St Maurice & St Bernard Pass, bef vill of Séez. Med, terr, pt sl, shd; htd wc; chem disp; shwrs inc; el pnts (4-10A) €2.50-6.10; lndtte; shops 300m; BBQ; playgrnd; pool 1.5km; site clsd Nov; quiet; CCI. "Diff exit fr site due to slope up to rd & on a bend." ♦ Jan-31 Oct. € 11.50   2006*

BOURG ST MAURICE 9B4 (1km E Rural) Camping Le Versoyen, Route des Arcs, 73700 Bourg-St Maurice [04 79 07 03 45; fax 04 79 07 25 41; leversoyen@wanadoo.fr; www.leversoyen.com] Fr SW on N90 thro town turn R to Les Arcs. Site on R in 1km. Do not app fr any other dir. Lge, hdstg, pt shd; wc; chem disp; mv service pnt; sauna; shwrs inc; el pnts (4-10A) €4.60-5.20; lndtte; shops 200m; playgrnd; 2 pools adj; tennis adj; games area; entmnt; fishing, canoeing; dogs €1; Eng spkn; quiet; red low ssn; red CCI. "Excel for touring mountains & wintersports; mountain views; mkd walks fr site; rvside walk to town; well-organised site; dated but v clean facs; ." ♦ 15 Dec-2 May & 24 May-5 Nov. € 13.90   2007*

France

Camping Municipal DES CHATEAUX ★★★ F-41250

In Sologne, in the heart of the castles region of the Loire: Chambord, Cheverny, Blois, Villessavin region of gastronomy. Relax (rivers, forests), cycling tracks (Velocamp label), hiking tracks. Station verte de vacances (green holidays label). Swimming pool, tennis, fishing All shops at 300 metres. Security surveillance day and night..

Phone: 00.33/02.54.46.41.84
Fax: 00.33/02.54.46.41.21
campingdebracieux@wanadoo.fr
www.campingdeschateaux.com

Rental of chalets and mobile homes.
Open from 17/03 till 13/11

BOURG ST MAURICE 9B4 (8km S Rural) **Camping Les Lanchettes, 73210 Peisey-Nancroix [04 79 07 93 07; fax 04 79 07 88 33; lanchettes@ free.fr; www.camping-lanchettes.com]** Fr Moûtiers foll N90 NE twds Bourg-St Maurice. In 20km turn R sp Landry & Peisey-Nancroix. Up v steep rd with hairpin bends for 6km. Site 1km beyond Nancroix. Long steep ascent with many hairpin bends, not rec for closely rated o'fits. Med, pt sl, terr, pt shd; htd wc; chem disp; mv service pnt; shwrs inc; el pnts (3-10A) €3-7.30; gas adj; lndtte; ice; shop 200m (summer); rest; snacks; bar; playgrnd; tennis 100m; ski cent in winter; dogs €1.20; adv bkg (dep req + bkg fee); CCI. "Lovely setting in National Park; superb location for outdoor pursuits; excel walking." ♦ 17 Dec-30 Sep. € 13.10 (CChq acc) 2006*

BOURG ST MAURICE 9B4 (6km SW Urban) **Camping L'Eden, 73210 Landry [04 79 07 61 81; fax 04 79 07 62 17; info@camping-eden.net; www. camping-eden.net]** Fr N90 Moûtiers to Bourg-St Maurice at 20km turn R onto D87 sp Landry & Mont Chavin; site on L after 500m adj Rv Isère. Med, mkd pitch, hdstg, pt shd; htd wc; chem disp; shwrs inc; el pnts (10A) €4-6; gas; lndtte; shop; tradsmn; snacks; bar; playgrnd; htd pool; dogs €1.50; poss cr; quiet; adv bkg; cc acc; Eng spkn; CCI. "Gd excel mountain sports; helpful, friendly owner; free ski bus." 15 Dec-5 May & 25 May-15 Sep. € 21.40 2006*

BOURG SUR GIRONDE 7C2 (Urban) **Camp Municipal La Citadelle (formerly Halte Nautique), 33710 Bourg-sur-Gironde [05 56 68 40 06; fax 05 57 68 39 84]** Take D669 fr St André-de-Cubzac (off A10) to Bourg. Foll sp Halte Nautique & Le Port into Rue Franklin on L app town cent & foll sp to site. Or fr Blaye, ignore other camping dir sp on app Bourg owing to narr streets & cont to other end of town. Sm, mkd pitch, pt shd; wc; chem disp; shwrs inc; el pnts (3-10A) €4 (poss long lead req); shops in town; BBQ; pool, playgrnd adj; dogs; no statics; adv bkg; CCI. "Quiet, CL-type rvside site; lovely views of rv; well-maintained but basic facs; tourist office in town with Eng info; gd for vineyards; poss variable opening dates; excel." ♦ ltd. 2 May-27 Sep. € 7.00 2007*

BOURGANEUF 7B4 (2km N) **Camp Municipal La Chassagne, Route de Bénévent, 23400 Bourganeuf [05 55 64 07 61 (Mairie); mairie. bourganeuf@wanadoo.fr]** On D912 La Souterraine-Bourganeuf rd. Med, some hdg pitch, pt shd; wc; shwrs inc; el pnts; supmkt 2km; rv sw; quiet. "Situated in pleasant, hilly countryside; office 0900-1200 & 1700-1900." 15 Jun-15 Sep. 2007*

BOURGES 4H3 (1km S Urban) **Camp Municipal Robinson, 26 Blvd de l'Industrie, 18000 Bourges [02 48 20 16 85; fax 02 48 50 32 39; www.ville-bourges.fr]** Exit A71/E11 at junc 7, foll sp Bourges Centre & bear R at 'Autres Directions' sp; foll site sp; site at traff lts on N side of S section of inner ring rd half-way bet junc with D2144 (N144) & D2076 (N76). NB: site access is via a loop - no L turn at traff lts, but rndabt just past site if turning missed. If on outer ring rd D400, app city on D2144 & then as above. Sp on app rds to site gd. Med, hdg/mkd pitch, hdstg, pt shd; htd wc; chem disp; some serviced pitches; shwrs inc; el pnts (6-16A) €3- €7.50 (rev pol); gas 3km; lndtte; playgrnd; pool 300m; dogs; poss cr; Eng spkn; quiet but some rd noise; €25.50 extra twin-axle; cc acc; red long stay; CCI. "Attractive, well-kept, busy, rvside site; v gd location; spotlessly clean; gd facs for disabled; friendly staff; free access to pool; some lge pitches; many sm & poss diff entry; twin-axles extra; poss prob with earwigs; excel NH; 10-15 mins walk to Bourges; chateau & cathedral; museums; excel sightseeing." ♦ 15 Mar-15 Nov. € 12.20 2007*

BOURGET DU LAC, LE see Aix Les Bains 9B3

BOURGUEIL 4G1 (Rural) **Parc Municipal Capitaine, 37140 Bourgueil [02 47 97 85 62 or 02 47 97 25 00 LS]** N on D749 fr junc 5 of A85, site 1km on R. Fr W (Longue) via D10 & by-pass, S at rndabt on D749 to site on L in 200m. Do not app fr N via D749 thro town cent. Med, hdg/mkd pitch, pt shd; wc; chem disp; mv service pnt; shwrs inc; el pnts (10A) €1.85; gas; lndtte; shops 1km; supmkt nrby; playgrnd; sw lake; dogs €1.15; quiet; CCI. "Gd san facs; ideal cent Loire châteaux & wine rtes; long lead pss req some pitches; 2 sites - one on R for tourers." ♦ ltd. 15 May-15 Sep. € 9.40 2006*

BOURNEZEAU *2H4* (500m N Rural) **Camp Municipal Les Humeaux, Rue de la Gare, 85480 Bournezeau [02 51 40 01 31 or 02 51 40 71 20 (Mairie); fax 02 51 40 79 30; mairie@bournezeau.fr]** Exit A83 junc 6 to Bournezeau cent. Take D7 sp St Martin-des-Noyers. Site on R in 500m, well sp. Sm, mkd pitch, pt shd; wc; chem disp; mv service pnt; shwrs; el pnts (6A) €2.70; lndtte; shop, rest, snacks, bar 500m; playgrnd; dogs; adv bkg; quiet. "Vg, conv NH; modern, clean san facs; easy walk to town." 1 Jun-15 Sep. € 8.00   2004*

BOUSSAC *7A4* (2km NE Rural) **Camping Le Château de Poinsouze, Route de la Châtre, 23600 Boussac-Bourg [05 55 65 02 21; fax 05 55 65 86 49; info.camping-de.poinsouze@ orange.fr; www.camping-de-poinsouze.com or www.les-castels.com]** Fr junc 10 on A71/E11 by-pass Montluçon via N145 dir Guéret. After 22km take D917 NW to Boussac, then La Châtre, site 3km on L. Or fr Guéret on N145, exit Gouzon, at rndabt take D997 to Boussac, then as above. Med, mkd pitch, sl, unshd; wc; chem disp; mv service pnt; serviced pitch; baby facs; shwrs inc; el pnts (10A) inc (poss rev pol); lndtte; shop & 3km; tradsmn; rest; snacks; bar; BBQ; playgrnd; pool; paddling pool; waterslide; course-fishing lake; boating; horseriding; golf 20km; cycle hire; entmnt; internet; games/TV rm; 10% statics; dogs €3; Eng spkn; adv bkg ess high ssn & booking fee; quiet; cc acc; CCI. "Super, well-run site; helpful owners; lovely setting; lge pitches, some sl; lake with canoes/windsurfers; immac san facs; excel rest & snacks; pools away fr camp area; v peaceful low ssn; excel." ◆ 10 May-14 Sep. € 33.00 (CChq acc) ABS - L16   2007*

BOUSSAC *7A4* (3km W Rural) **Camping Creuse-Nature (Naturist), Route de Bétête, 23600 Boussac [05 55 65 18 01; fax 05 55 65 81 40; creuse-nature@wanadoo.fr; www.creuse-nature. com]** Fr Boussac take D917 N twd La Châtre. In 500m turn L (W) on D15 sp Bétête. Site on R in 2.5km, clearly sp. Med, hdg/mkd pitch, pt sl, pt shd; wc; shwrs; el pnts (10A) €3.50; lndtte; sm shop; rest; snacks; bar; playgrnd; 2 htd pools (1 covrd); paddling pool; fishing; games area; entmnt; some statics; dogs €5.50; Eng spkn; adv bkg; v quiet; red low ssn; cc acc; INF card req. "Excel site; spotless facs; charming & helpful owners; recep open 1030-1300 & 1500-1900; poss insect prob; interesting château in town." ◆ 14 Apr-31 Oct. € 22.00   2007*

BOZEL see Pralognan la Vanoise *9B4*

BRACH *7C1* (SW Rural) **Aire Naturelle Le Bois de Geai (Douat), 16 Route de Lacanau, 33480 Brach [05 56 58 70 54]** N on D1 fr Bordeaux. At Castelnau-de-Médoc cent turn L onto D207. After 11km in vill of Brach fork L. Sm, mkd pitch; own san; shwrs; el pnts (6A) €2; gas; lndtte; ice; shop; tradsmn; playgrnd; fishing; sailing & beaches nr; some statics; dogs €2; adv bkg; CCI. "Peaceful site; poss v cr with pickers at wine harvest time." 1 May-31 Oct. € 11.50   2007*

BRACIEUX *4G2* (500m N Urban) **Camp Municipal des Châteaux, 11 Rue Roger Brun, 41250 Bracieux [02 54 46 41 84; fax 02 54 46 41 21; campingdebracieux@wanadoo.fr; www. campingdeschateaux.com]** Fr S take D102 to Bracieux fr Cour-Cheverny. Fr N exit Blois on D765 dir Romorantin; after 5km take D923 to Bracieux & site on R on N o'skts of town opp church, sp. Lge, pt hdg/mkd pitch, hdstg, pt shd; wc (some cont); chem disp; shwrs inc; el pnts (3A) €2.60 (poss long lead req); gas 300m; lndtte; shop 300m; supmkt 1km; tradsmn high ssn; rest, snacks 300m; playgrnd; htd pool high ssn; tennis; cycle hire & tracks; games rm; TV; 10% statics; dogs €2.70; Eng spkn; adv bkg; quiet; red long stay; cc acc; CCI. "Peaceful spot; attractive forest area; v busy high ssn; excel disabled facs; gd security; card operated barrier; gd base for touring châteaux; excel." ◆ 28 Mar-30 Nov. € 15.55   2007*

See advertisement

BRAIN SUR L'AUTHION see Angers *4G1*

BRAMANS LE VERNEY see Modane *9C4*

BRANTOME *7C3* (1km E Rural) **Camping Peyrelevade, Ave André Maurois, 24310 Brantôme [05 53 05 75 24 or 04 99 57 20 25; fax 04 99 59 21 22; peyrelevade@village-center.com; www.village-center.com/peyrelevade]** Fr N on D675 foll sp Centre Ville; ent vill & turn L onto D78 Thiviers rd, site sp at turn; in 1km on R past stadium adj g'ge. Fr S D939 foll sp Centre Vill fr rndabt N of town. Then L onto D78 Thiviers rd & foll sp. Do not foll Centre Vill fr rndabt S of town, use by-pass. Site on rvside. Lge, mkd pitch, hdstg, pt shd; wc; chem disp; mv service pnt; baby facs; shwrs inc; el pnts (6A) inc (poss long lead req); lndtte; shop 1km; tradsmn; snacks; bar; BBQ; playgrnd; htd pool; paddling pool; rv sw; tennis nr; games area adj; entmnt; 3% statics; dogs €3; adv bkg; quiet; red low ssn; cc acc; CCI. "Sh walk to pleasant town; interesting abbey & grottoes; beautiful countryside; well laid-out site; spacious pitches; helpful staff; poss unkempt low ssn; excel." ◆ 12 May-16 Sep. € 16.00   2007*

BRANTOME *7C3* (4km SW) **Camping Le Bas Meygnaud, 24310 Valeuil [05 53 05 58 44; camping-du-bas-meygnaud@wanadoo.fr]** Fr Brantôme, take D939 S twd Périgueux; in 4.5km turn R at sp La Serre. In 1km turn L to in 500m, well sp. Winding, narr app thro lanes; poss diff lge o'fits. Sm, pt sl, pt shd; wc; chem disp; shwrs inc; el pnts (6A) inc; gas 4km; ice; lndtte; shop; tradsmn; rest 4km; snacks; bar; BBQ; playgrnd; pool; entmnt; dogs €2; phone; Eng spkn; quiet; CCI. "Helpful & friendly owner; unspoilt countryside; conv for Brantôme." 1 Apr-30 Sep. € 13.50   2004*

France

BRASSAC *8F4* (11km SE Rural) **Camping Le Rouquié, Lac de la Raviège, 81260 Lamontélarie [05 63 70 98 06; fax 05 63 50 49 58; camping. rouquie@wanadoo.fr; www.campingrouquie.fr]** Fr Brassac take D62 to N side of Lac de la Raviège; site on lakeside. Med, mkd pitch, terr, pt shd; wc; baby facs; shwrs; el pnts (3-6A) €4; lndtte; shop; tradsmn; snacks; bar; playgrnd; lake sw; fishing; sailing & watersports adj; games area; cycle hire; entmnt; TV; poss cr; quiet; CCI. "Ltd facs low ssn; gd lake views." 15 Apr-31 Oct. € 11.20   2007*

BRASSAC *8F4* (SW Urban) **Camp Municipal La Lande, Ave de Sidobre, 81260 Brassac [tel/fax 05 63 74 00 82; lalande@sidobretouristique.com]** Fr Castres on D622, turn sharp L just bef rv bdge in Brassac. Sm, pt shd; wc; shwrs inc; el pnts inc; lndtte; ice; shops, rest, bar 500m; BBQ; playgrnd; rv fishing; dogs €1.40; quiet; CCI. "Pleasant site with gd, clean san facs." ◆ ltd. 1 May-30 Sep. € 10.10   2004*

⊞**BRAUCOURT** *6E1* (3km W Rural) **Camping Presqu'île de Champaubert (formerly Municipal), Lac du Der, 52290 Eclaron [03 25 04 13 20; fax 03 25 94 33 51; ilechampaubert@free.fr; http:// lescampingsduder.com]** Fr St Dizier take D384 SW twd Montier-en-Der & Troyes. In Braucourt R onto D153 sp Presq'ile de Champaubert, site on L in 2km. Site situated on Lac du Der-Chantecoq. Lge hdg/mkd pitch, pt shd; wc; chem disp; mv service pnt; serviced pitch; shwrs inc; el pnts (10A) €4 (rev pol); gas; lndtte; ice; basic shop; tradsmn; snacks, bar in ssn; playgrnd; pool; lake sw nrby; sand beach; watersports, boating, fishing, bird-watching; TV; dogs €1; poss cr; quiet; 15% statics; Eng spkn; cc acc; CCI. "Gd watersports; beautiful lge lakeside beach; lge pitches; improved san facs; gates clsd 2230; efficient staff; privately owned fr 2007 - many changes planned." ◆ € 26.00   2007*

⊞**BRAUCOURT** *6E1* (9km W Rural) **Camping Le Clos du Vieux Moulin, 33 Rue du Lac, 51290 Châtillon-sur-Broué [03 26 41 30 43; fax 03 26 72 75 13; eclosduvieuxmoulin@wanadoo. fr; www.leclosduvieuxmoulin.fr]** Fr N take D13 fr Vitry-le-François. Turn R at sp for Châtillion-sur-Broué. Fr S 2nd L fr Giffaumont (1km). Site under 100m on R. Med, hdg/mkd pitch, hdstg, pt sl, pt shd; htd wc; chem disp; baby facs; shwrs inc; el pnts (5A) €3.70; gas; lndtte; ice; shops; tradsmn; rest 400m; snacks; bar; playgrnd; pool; lake 400m; watersports; birdwatching; 50% statics; dogs; phone; quiet; CCI. "Peaceful, green site; gd san facs; paths for disabled." ◆ € 16.00   2006*

BRAY DUNES see Dunkerque *3A3*

BRAY SUR SEINE *4E4* (E Urban) **Camping La Peupleraie, Chemin des Pâtures, 77480 Bray-sur-Seine [01 60 67 12 24 or 06 83 93 33 89 (mob); camping.lapeupleraie@wanadoo.fr]** Exit A5 at junc 18 onto D41, in 20km turn N to Bray. Turn L bef bdge, foll rd down under bdge, cont on rvside to site. Foll 'complex sportif' & camping sp. Lge, hdg/ mkd pitch, pt shd; wc (cont); shwrs inc; el pnts (6A) €3.50; lndtte; supmkt adj; snacks; playgrnd; pool adj; boating; tennis; 40% statics; dogs €1.50; adv bkg; quiet. "Diff to exit bef 0900 when office opens; v clean with helpful warden." ◆ 1 Apr-31 Oct. € 10.00   2005*

BRECEY *2E4* (1km S Rural) **Camp Municipal Le Pont Roulland, 50370 Brécey [02 33 48 60 60; fax 02 33 89 21 09; mairie-brecey@wanadoo.fr]** Fr Villedieu-les-Poêles on D999. In Brécey cont L by church on D911; after 1km turn S on D79 sp Les Cresnays. Site in 50m on L thro car park. Med, terr, pt sl, pt shd; wc; chem disp; shwrs; el pnts (6A) €2; (rev pol); shops 1km; tradsmn; lndtte; tennis; playgrnd; htd pool adj; dogs €0.45; adv bkg; quiet; CCI. "Lovely rural site; well-kept; excel, clean san facs; friendly staff; nr fishing lake; grnd soft after prolonged rain." 1 Jun-30 Sep. € 6.90   2007*

BREHAL *1D4* (4km N Coastal) **Camp Intercommunal de la Vanlée, 50290 Bréhal [02 33 61 63 80; fax 02 33 61 87 18; camping. vanlee@wanadoo.fr]** Turn W off D971 onto D20 thro Bréhal to coast, then N. Site sp, nr 'route submersible'. Lge, mkd pitch, pt sl, unshd; wc; chem disp; mv service pnt; baby facs; shwrs inc; el pnts (6A) €3.15; lndtte; ice; shop high ssn; supmkt nr; rest; snacks; bar; playgrnd; pool; sand beach adj; entmnt; TV rm; dogs; poss cr; Eng spkn; cc acc; quiet; CCI. "Beware soft sand when pitching." ◆ 1 May-30 Sep. € 12.10   2005*

BRENGUES *7D4* (Rural) **Camp Municipal de Brengues, 46320 Brengues [tel/fax 05 65 40 06 82 or 05 65 40 05 71 (Mairie)]** W fr Figeac on D13. After 6km turn L onto D41. After 17km, turn L at x-rds with D38, site ent 100m on R bef bdge over Rv Célé. Sm, mkd pitch, pt shd; wc; shwrs; el pnts (10A) €1.10 (rev pol); ice; lndtte; shop 300m; rest; bar; playgrnd; tennis; CCI. "Warden visits." 15 Jun-30 Sep. € 9.85   2006*

BRENGUES *7D4* (1.5km N Rural) **Camping Le Moulin Vieux, Route de Figeac, 46320 Brengues [05 65 40 00 41; fax 05 65 40 05 65; campingdumoulinvieux@brengues.com; http:// brengues.free.fr]** Fr Figeac on D13, in 6km L onto D41. In approx 17km site well sp on L bef Brengues vill. Med, shd; wc; chem disp; shwrs inc; el pnts (10A) inc; lndtte; ice; shop; rest; bar; playgrnd; pool; rv sw; entmnt; archery; mini-golf; some statics; adv bkg; some rd noise; cc acc; CCI. "Helpful owners; beautiful site; facs stretched high ssn; excel." ◆ 1 Apr-30 Sep. € 14.70   2004*

BRENGUES 7D4 (8km SW Rural) **Camp Municipal de Marcilhac-sur-Célé, 46160 Marcilhac-sur-Célé [tel/fax 05 65 40 77 88]** W fr Figeac on D802; L onto D41; site on L on ent Marcilhac. App fr E, site on R at far end of vill. Med, pt shd; wc; baby facs; fam bthrm; shwrs inc; el pnts €2.35; lndtte; ice; shop 200m; rest; snacks; bar; BBQ; playgrnd; sm play pool; rv sw adj; fishing; canoeing; tennis; cycle hire; games area; games rm; TV; 2% statics; dogs €0.95; phone; Eng spkn; adv bkg (dep req); quiet; CCI. "Vg." ♦ ltd. 1 Apr-15 Oct. € 10.05
2006*

BRENGUES 7D4 (2km W Rural) **Camp Municipal Le Célé, 46160 St Sulpice [05 65 40 78 06 or 05 65 40 64 64 (Mairie); fax 05 65 40 71 17; mairie. saint.sulpice@wanadoo.fr]** Take D13 Figeac to Cahors rd. In 3km turn L on D41. Site on L in St Sulpice on rv bank. Poss diff to turn into site fr dir Figeac. Sm, pt shd; wc; chem disp; shwrs inc; el pnts (4A) €2.60; shop & snacks adj; playgrnd; rv sw; fishing; tennis; phone adj; poss cr; adv bkg; quiet. "Gd base for Figeac, Cahors, Conques, St Céré." 15 Apr-30 Sep. € 8.00
2005*

⊞**BRESSE, LA** 6F3 (3km E Urban) **FFCC Camp Municipal Le Haut des Bluches, 5 Route des Planches, 88250 La Bresse [03 29 25 64 80; fax 03 29 25 78 03; hautdesbluches@labresse.fr]** Leave La Bresse on D34 Rte de la Schlucht. Site on R in 3km. Med, mkd pitch, terr, pt shd; htd wc; chem disp; child/baby facs; shwrs; el pnts (4-13A) €1.50-4.55; lndtte; ice; shop 2km; tradsmn; rest; snacks; bar; BBQ; playgrnd; pool in vill; games rm; TV; 10% statics; dogs; NH area for m'vans; site clsd end Nov-early Dec; Eng spkn; adv bkg; some rd noise; red low ssn; cc acc; red CCI. "Excel site in v attractive setting; excel san facs; many gd walks fr site & further afield; conv winter sports." ♦ € 11.50
2006*

BRESSUIRE 4H1 (S Rural) **Camping Le Puy Rond, Cornet, 79300 Bressuire [05 49 72 43 22 or 06 85 60 37 26 (mob); info@puyrondcamping. com; www.puyrondcamping.com]** Fr N149 foll site sp on rte Poids Lourds to site on D38. V well sp. Fr 'Centre Ville' foll sp for Fontenay-Le-Comte; turn R 100m after overhead bdge & go across junc to site. Sm, mkd pitch, pt sl, pt terr, pt shd; htd wc (some cont); chem disp (wc); mv service pnt; baby facs; shwrs inc; el pnts (10A) €3; gas 1.50m; lndtte; ice; shop & 1.5km; tradsmn; snacks; rest; bar 1.5km; BBQ; playgrnd; pool; fishing 1km; 15% statics; dogs €2; bus 2km; phone 500m; adv bkg (50% dep req); quiet; red long stay; cc acc; CCI. "Gd base for exploring area; British owners; basic facs; adv bkg ess for twin-axles; winter storage avail." ♦ 1 Apr-30 Oct. € 15.50
2005*

BREST 2E2 (4km E Coastal) **Camp Municipal de Camfrout, 29480 Le Relecq-Kerhuon [02 98 28 37 84 or 02 98 28 14 18 (Mairie); fax 02 98 28 61 32; secretariat.mairie@mairie-relecq-kerhuon.fr]** Fr Brest take N165 dir Quimper, at city o'skts becomes Relecq-Kerhuon. In 2km turn L onto D67, site on L opp foreshore. Fr S on N165, cross Rv Elorn twd Brest & R onto D67. Med, hdg pitch, pt shd; wc; chem disp; shwrs; el pnts (6A) €1.65; lndtte; shops 3km; playgrnd; sand beach adj; fishing; boating; dogs €1.25; quiet. "Many places of interest in area." ♦ 24 Jun-10 Sep. € 8.50
2004*

⊞**BREST** 2E2 (6km W Coastal) **Camping du Goulet, Ste Anne-du-Porzic, 29200 Brest [tel/fax 02 98 45 86 84; campingdugoulet@wanadoo.fr; www.campingdugoulet.com]** On D789 turn L at site sp. Approx 4km fr Brest after R bend at T junc, turn L & L again at site sp; down hill to site. Med, pt sl, terr, unshd; htd wc; chem disp; shwrs inc; el pnts (6-10A) €2.50-3; lndtte; shop high ssn; snacks; playgrnd; pool complex; waterslides; sand beach 1km; 15% statics; dogs €1.30; adv bkg; quiet; CCI. ♦ € 15.00
2006*

BRETENOUX 7C4 (Urban) **Camp La Bourgnatelle, 46130 Bretenoux [tel/fax 05 65 38 44 07; bourgnatel@aol.com]** In town 100m fr D940. Lge, pt shd; wc; mv service pnt; shwrs inc; el pnts (5-10A) €2.40; lndtte; ice; shops adj; playgrnd; pool; rv sw & fishing; canoe hire; entmnt; dogs €1; adv bkg; quiet. "Site on banks of Rv Cere; gd fishing; clean site; lovely town." 1 May-30 Sep. € 12.00
2005*

BRETENOUX 7C4 (4km W Rural) **Camping Les Chalets sur La Dordogne, Pont de Puybrun, 46130 Girac [05 65 10 93 33; fax 05 65 38 44 42; contact@camping-leschalets.com; www. camping-leschalets.com]** Fr Bretenoux on D803 dir Puybrun. Site on L on rvside - sp on rd barrier easily missed. Sm, mkd pitch, shd; wc; chem disp; shwrs inc; el pnts (10A) €3; lndtte; ice; shop; tradsmn; rest; snacks; bar; playgrnd; pool; rv sw & shgl beach adj; TV rm; 20% statics; dogs; Eng spkn; quiet. "Gd, clean family site; helpful owners." ♦ 1 May-15 Sep. € 14.00
2005*

BRETIGNOLLES SUR MER 2H3 (Coastal) **Camping La Motine, 4 Rue des Morinières, 85470 Bretignolles-sur-Mer [02 51 90 04 02; fax 02 51 33 80 52; campinglamotine@wanadoo. fr]** Foll sp fr D38 in Bretignolles-sur-Mer dir Plage de la Parée along Ave de la Plage, then turn R into Rue des Morinières. Med, hdg pitch, pt sl, pt shd; wc; chem disp; mv service pnt; serviced pitches; baby facs; shwrs inc; el pnts (6A) inc; lndtte; rest; bar; playgrnd; htd, covrd pool; sand beach 600m; 60% statics; dogs €3; adv bkg; quiet; cc acc; CCI. "Unisex san facs low ssn; vg site." ♦ 1 Apr-30 Sep. € 25.30
2005*

BRETIGNOLLES SUR MER 2H3 (2km N Coastal) Camping Les Vagues, 85470 Bretignolles-sur-Mer [02 51 90 19 48 or 02 40 02 46 10; fax 02 40 02 49 88; les vagues@free.fr] Well sp on D38. Lge, hdg pitch, pt shd; wc; chem disp; shwrs; el pnts (6A) €3.50; lndtte; ice; snacks; playgrnd; pool; waterslide; sand beach 900m; games rm; TV; entmnt; 50% statics; dogs €2.50; adv bkg; red low ssn; CCI. "Gd sized pool; close to town cent with shops & rests; office closes 1830 low ssn." ♦ 1 Apr-30 Sep. € 20.00   2005*

BRETIGNOLLES SUR MER 2H3 (1km E Coastal) Camping La Haute Rivoire, 85470 Bretignolles-sur-Mer [03 76 84 49 59; HauteRivoire@aol.com; www.restandrelaxfrance.com] Fr St Gilles Croix-de-Vie take D38 S twd Les Sables. Cross bdge over Rv Jaunay. Turn L on D12 sp Chaize-Giraud. Site 3rd turning on R sp Chambres. Site in 300m. Take ent after barns. Sm, unshd; wc; chem disp; shwrs inc; el pnts (6A) €4.50 (poss rev pol); snacks; shop 2km; sand beach 2km; pool; golf; fishing; horseriding; watersports adj; sep car park; adv bkg; red low ssn. "British-owned (ex Club member) CL-type farm site; san facs v clean, open 0830-2130; no children under 10yrs/no visitors/no pets; twin-axles extra charge; phone bef arrival to check open; payment on arr." € 28.50   2007*

BRETIGNOLLES SUR MER 2H3 (1km E Urban) CHADOTEL Camping La Trévillière, Route de Bellevue, 85470 Bretignolles-sur-Mer [02 51 90 09 65 or 02 51 33 05 05 (LS); fax 02 51 33 94 04; chadotel@wanadoo.fr; www.chadotel.com] Along D38 fr St Gilles Croix-de-Vie twd Olonne-sur-Mer, site is sp to L in Bretignolles-sur-Mer 1km fr town cent. Sp from town cent. Foll sp 'Ecole'. Lge, hdg/mkd pitch, shd; wc; 50% serviced pitches; baby facs; shwrs inc; el pnts (6A) inc (rev pol); gas; lndtte; shop; tradsmn; snacks; bar; BBQ (charcoal/gas); playgrnd; htd pool; paddling pool; waterslide; sand beach 2km; fishing; watersports 3km; horseriding 5km; mini-golf, cycle hire; entmnt; child entmnt; games/TV rm; 70% statics; dogs €3; phone; recep 0800-2000 high ssn; c'van max 8m high ssn; Eng spkn; adv bkg (dep req); cc acc; red long stay/low ssn; CCI. "Friendly, family site; poss unkempt pitches low ssn; pleasant walk to local shops & rests; mkt Thu & Sun; salt marshes worth a visit." ♦ 5 Apr-27 Sep. € 28.90 ABS - A26   2007*

BRETIGNOLLES SUR MER 2H3 (5km E Rural) Camping L'Evasion, Route des Sables, 85220 Landevieille [tel/fax 02 51 22 90 14; marinette-riv@yahoo.fr] Site sp in Landevieille. Med, hdg/mkd pitch, pt shd; wc; chem disp; baby facs; shwrs inc; el pnts (10A) €3; gas; lndtte; ice; shop; supmkt 750m; rest; snacks; bar; BBQ; playgrnd; 3 htd pools; waterslides; jacuzzi; beach 5km; fishing lake; games area; 75% statics; dogs €2; dog exercise area; phone; some Eng spkn; quiet except for bar/disco high ssn; cc acc; CCI. "Vg." 1 Apr-15 Oct. € 17.00   2006*

BRETIGNOLLES SUR MER 2H3 (5km E Urban) Camping L'Oree de l'Océan, Rue Capitaine de Mazenot, 85220 Landevieille [02 51 22 96 36; fax 02 51 22 29 09] Take D12 fr La Mothe-Achard to St Julien-des-Landes & cont to x-rds bef La Chaize-Giraud. Turn L onto D32, take 1st R in Landevieille to site on L in 50m. Adj Mairie. Med, hdg/mkd pitch, pt sl, pt shd; wc; chem disp; shwrs inc; el pnts (10A) inc; ice; lndtte; lndry rm; shops 500m; bar; playgrnd; htd pool; tennis; sand beach 4km; TV rm; phone; 40% statics; dogs; phone; poss cr; quiet; adv bkg; Eng spkn; 15% red 7+ days; cc acc; CCI. "Gd, friendly, family site; many gd beaches & mkd cycle tracks nr." ♦ 25 Jun-5 Sep. € 22.00
                                                       2004*

BRETIGNOLLES SUR MER 2H3 (5km E) Camping Pong, Rue du Stade, 85220 Landevieille [02 51 22 92 63; fax 02 51 22 99 25; info@lepong.com; www.lepong.com] Fr Challans S on D32. Pass Landevieille church on L, then rd bends R; turn L after sm bdge into Rue de la Stade; foll rd, site on L. Fr Vaire N on D32, soon after ent Landevieille & immed bef sm bdge turn R into Rue de la Stade, then as above. Lge, pt sl, pt shd; wc (some cont); chem disp; serviced pitches; baby facs; shwrs inc; el pnts (6A) inc; gas; lndtte; ice; shop; rest; snacks; bar; BBQ (charcoal/gas); playgrnd; htd pool; paddling pool; waterslide; sand beach 5km; lake 2.5km; fishing; tennis; cycle hire; entmnt; games/TV rm; some statics; dogs €2.50; recep 0900-1300 & 1400-1900; adv bkg; quiet; cc acc. "Beautiful site with great facs; extra charge for lger pitches; v pleasant & extremely helpful staff; Lac d'Apremont with 16thC château 13.5km; vineyards & winetasting in area." ♦ 1 Apr-15 Sep. € 25.70 ABS - A24
                                                       2007*

BRETIGNOLLES SUR MER 2H3 (4km S Coastal) Camping Le Chaponnet, Rue du Chaponnet, 85470 Brem-sur-Mer [02 51 90 55 56; fax 02 51 90 91 67; campingchaponnet@wanadoo.fr; www.le-chaponnet.com] Fr La Roche-sur-Yon on N160 dir Les Sables-d'Olonne. Turn R onto D87 thro St Mathurin vill & take 1st R (just after church) D38 dir L'Ile d'Olonne. Foll sp Brem-sur-Mer, go thro vill & foll sp 'Océan' (nr bakery & bar); turn L opp hairdresser, site in 50m along 1-way rd. Lge, hdg pitch, pt shd; wc; chem disp; baby facs; sauna; shwrs inc; el pnts (6A) inc; gas; lndtte; ice; sm shop; supmkt 200m; rest; snacks; bar; BBQ; playgrnd; htd covrd pool; waterslides; sand beach 1km; jacuzzi; gym; games area; tennis; cycle hire; entmnt; games rm; TV rm; 75% statics; dogs; €3; phone; poss cr; adv bkg; quiet; red low ssn; cc acc; CCI. "Gd beaches adj; vg." ♦ 1 May-15 Sep. € 33.90 (3 persons)   2007*

BRETIGNOLLES SUR MER *2H3* (4km S Coastal) **Camping Les Dunes, 85470 Bretignolles-sur-Mer [02 51 90 55 32; fax 02 51 90 54 85]** Fr N foll D178 fr Nantes as far S as Aizenay. Fr Aizenay foll D6 to Coëx; turn L at Coëx onto D40 & foll sp to Bretignolles-sur-Mer; at Bretignolles turn L onto D38 twd Les Sables d'Olonne; in 3km turn R at sp to Camp Les Dunes; site in 1km. V lge, pt shd; wc (some cont); shwrs inc; el pnts (10A) inc; lndtte; gas; shop; rest; bar; playgrnd; 2 pools; jacuzzi; sand beach 100m; TV; entmnt; 90% statics; bus 1km; poss cr; adv bkg. "Rest, casino in Les Sables; Croix-de-Vie interesting fishing port; tourer pitches scattered among statics; poor disabled facs." ♦ ltd. Easter-11 Nov. € 32.00   2004*

BRETTEVILLE see Cherbourg *1C4*

BREUILLET *7B1* **Camping Transhumance, Route de Royan, 17920 Breuillet [05 46 22 72 15; fax 05 46 22 66 47; contact@transhumance.com; www.transhumance.com]** Fr Saujon take D14 NW dir St Sulphice-de-Royan & La Tremblade. After approx 8km turn L at junc with D140 sp Breuillet & Camping Transhumance; site well sp on L. Or fr Rochefort S on D733; turn R onto D14 to Breuillet & as above. Lge, hdg pitch, unshd; wc; chem disp; baby facs; shwrs inc; el pnts (6A) inc; gas; lndtte; ice; shop; rest; snacks; bar; BBQ; playgrnd; 2 pools; paddling pool; beach 3.5km; watersports 6km; fishing; tennis; games rm; table tennis; cycle hire; archery; horseriding 4km; golf 7km; entmnt; statics; dogs €3; recep 0900-1200 & 1400-2000; adv bkg; quiet; cc acc; CCI. "Facs poss stretched high ssn; vg rest in vill." ♦ 13 May-10 Sep. € 20.50   2005*

BREUILLET *7B1* (1.5km NW Rural) **Camping à la Belle Etoile, 27 Route des Renouleaux, 17920 Breuillet [tel/fax 05 46 02 14 07; camping.a.la.belle.etoile@wanadoo.fr; www.alabelle-etoile.com]** Fr Saujon on D14 W dir La Tremblade, turn L onto D242 dir St Augustin then 1st R after 700m. Site sp. Med, mkd pitch, pt shd; wc (cont); chem disp; mv service pnt; shwrs inc; el pnts (10A) €4; gas; lndtte; ice; shop 1.5km; tradsmn; rest 500m; snacks; bar 1.5km; playgrnd; pool; sand beach 10km; 60% statics; dogs €2; adv bkg; quiet; cc acc; red CCI. "Gd cycle rtes nr; conv Royan, Ile d'Oléron, La Rochelle; insufficient facs for size of site; ." ♦ ltd. 7 Apr-2 Oct. € 15.50   2006*

BREVEDENT, LE see Blangy le Château *3D1*

BREVILLE SUR MER see Granville *1D4*

⊞**BRIANCON** *9C4* (3km NE Rural) **Camping Les Gentianes, La Vachette, 05100 Val-des-Prés [02 92 21 21 41; fax 04 92 21 24 12; camping.lesgentianes@libertysurf.fr]** Fr Briançon take N94 dir Montgenèvre. At La Vachette site sp in vill. Med, pt sl, pt shd; htd wc; chem disp; mv service pnt; shwrs inc; el pnts (6-10A) €3-6; lndtte; shops, rest in vill; snacks; bar; playgrnd; pool; canoeing; fishing; x-country skiing; 40% statics; dogs €1; adv bkg; quiet; CCI. "Renovations poss under way 2006; mountain streams runs thro site; NH only." € 14.10   2006*

BRIANCON *9C4* (5km NE Rural) **Camping de l'Iscle du Rosier, Le Rosier, 05100 Val-des-Prés [04 92 21 06 01; fax 04 92 21 46 46; www.ifrance.com/campingdurosier]** Fr Briançon N94 E & take 3rd L after leaving Briançon (5km) sp Le Rosier. Foll rd thro until Le Rosier, site on L after bdge. Med, pt shd; wc (some cont); chem disp; shwrs inc; el pnts (5A) inc; gas; lndry rm; shops; snacks; bar; BBQ; playgrnd; 5% statics; dogs €1.70; phone; Eng spkn; quiet. "Nice, well-kept site by rv; friendly helpful staff; superb walking, cycling & climbing nrby; conv Col de Montgenèvre rd." ♦ 15 Jun-15 Sep. € 14.50
          2007*

⊞**BRIANCON** *9C4* (6km NE Rural) **Camp Municipal du Bois des Alberts, 05100 Montgenèvre [04 92 21 16 11 or 04 92 21 92 88; fax 04 92 21 98 15]** Take N94/D201 fr Briançon sp Italie. In 4km turn L onto D994, site 200m past Les Alberts vill on L. Lge, hdstg, shd; htd wc (some cont); chem disp; mv service pnt; baby facs; shwrs inc; el pnts (6-10A) inc (rev pol); lndtte; shop; tradsmn; rest, snacks, bar high ssn; playgrnd; tennis; games area; kayak tuition; cycle & walking paths; fishing; x-country skiing; 30% statics; adv bkg; quiet; cc acc; CCI. "Clean site set in pine trees; random pitching in lge forest area; relaxed & friendly; facs dated but v clean, ltd low ssn; lge pinecones can fall fr trees - park away tall ones; gd touring base." ♦ € 12.85   2007*

> There aren't many sites open this early in the year. We'd better phone ahead to check that the one we're heading for is actually open.

BRIANCON *9C4* (2km S Rural) **Camping Les Cinq Vallées, St Blaise, 05100 Briançon [04 92 21 06 27; fax 04 92 20 41 69; infos@camping5vallees.com; www.camping5vallees.com]** S of Briançon by N94 to vill St Blaise. Ent on L. Med, pt shd; wc; shwrs inc; el pnts (10A) inc; lndtte; shop; snacks; playgrnd; htd pool; games rm; TV rm; many statics; some noise fr by-pass. ♦ 1 Jun-30 Sep. € 21.20   2005*

BRIARE *4G3* (7km S) **FFCC Camp Municipal des Combes, 45360 Châtillon-sur-Loire [02 38 31 42 92; mairie-de-chatillon-sur-loire@wanadoo.fr; www.chatillon-sur-loire.com]** SE fr Briare on N7, in 4km turn SW onto D50. Site immed bef rv bdge on R. Care needed over bdge after ent. Med, terr, pt shd; wc (some cont); chem disp; shwrs inc; el pnts (3-6A) inc; gas; lndry rm; shops 2km; playgrnd; fishing; many statics; quiet; CCI. "Lovely location; pleasant, quiet site by Loire; friendly staff; gd san facs; mkt day 2nd Thurs of each month; close to historical canals & Pont-Canal de Briare; no twin-axles; vg sh stay/NH." ♦ 1 Mar-31 Oct. € 11.40   2007*

France

BRIARE 4G3 (W Urban) **Camping Le Martinet, Quai Tchékof, 45250 Briare** [02 38 31 24 50 or 02 38 31 24 51; fax 02 38 31 39 10] Exit N7 into Briare. Fr N immed R after canal bdge; fr S L bef 2nd canal bdge; sp. Lge, mkd pitch, shd; wc (cont); shwrs; el pnts (10A) inc; lndry rm; shops 500m; rest, snacks, bar 500m; fishing adj; poss cr; adv bkg; quiet. "Gd views some pitches; gd walking & cycling; gates close 2200; pretty bars & rests along canal." ♦ 1 Mar-31 Oct. € 16.65   2006*

⊞**BRIENNE LE CHATEAU** 6E1 (6km S Rural) **Camping Le Colombier, 8 Ave Jean-Lanez, 10500 Dienville** [tel/fax 03 25 92 23 47] On D443 S fr Brienne; in Dienville town cent turn L immed after church & bef bdge, site on R thro archway. Sm, hdg pitch, pt shd; htd wc; chem disp; mv service pnt; shwrs inc; el pnts (12A) €3; gas; lndry rm; shop 400m; rest; snacks (high ssn); bar; playgrnd; rv adj; lake 500m; watersports; dogs €1.50; Eng spkn; adv bkg; quiet. "Facs poss stretched high ssn; access poss diff lge vans if site busy; some sm pitches; pretty rvside site - pitches away fr bdge quieter, pitches next to rv extra charge; church clock strikes 24 hrs; rooms avail; excel watersports on lake; red facs low ssn; pleasant, friendly owner." ♦ ltd. € 15.00   2005*

BRIENNE LE CHATEAU 6E1 (6km S Rural) **Camping Le Tertre, Route de Radonvilliers, 10500 Dienville** [tel/fax 03 25 92 26 50; campingdutertre@wanadoo.fr; www.campingdutertre.fr] On D443 S fr Brienne-le-Château; at Dienville cross over rndabt & site on R in 200m, sp. Med, hdg/mkd pitch, hdstg, pt shd; wc; chem disp; 50% serviced pitches; baby facs; shwrs inc; el pnts (6A) €2.80; gas; lndtte; ice; shop; tradsmn; rest; snacks; bar; BBQ; playgrnd; htd pool; paddling pool; sand rv beach 400m; man-made lake with sailing; fishing; gym; games area; games rm; entmnt; internet; TV rm; 10% statics; dogs €1; phone; bus 500m; poss cr; Eng spkn; adv bkg; quiet; cc acc; red low ssn/CCI. "Excel site for all water sports & many other activities; sh walk to lake Amance & marina; vg." ♦ 28 Mar-15 Oct. € 15.60   2007*

See advertisement

BRIENNE LE CHATEAU 6E1 (5km SW Rural) **Camping Le Garillon, Rue des Anciens Combattants, 10500 Radonvilliers** [03 25 92 21 46; fax 03 25 92 21 34] Exit Brienne S on D443 & at Brienne-Le-Ville turn R onto D11B to Radonvilliers. Site well sp. Med, pt shd; wc (some cont); chem disp; shwrs inc; el pnts (3-10A) inc; lndry rm; shops 2km; tradsmn; snacks, bar 2km; playgrnd; pool planned 2007; lake 1.5km; mainly statics; poss cr Jul/Aug; Eng spkn; adv bkg; quiet; red CCI. "Pleasant, friendly, family site in Parc Regional de la Forêt d'Orient; ltd touring pitches; modern, clean facs block but unisex washbasin/wc area; some pitches boggy when wet; 2 golf courses within 40km; Nigoland theme park 5km S; gd cycle track around lake." ♦ ltd. 1 May-15 Sep. € 15.00   2006*

BRIEY 5D2 (1km NW Rural) **Camping Intercommunal Plan d'Eau de la Sangsue, 54150 Briey** [03 82 20 96 22; fax 03 82 21 83 70; marilyne.nicollet@cc-paysdebriey.fr; www.cc-paysdebriey.fr] Exit A4 junction 33 to Briey where sp. Sm, hdstg, terr; wc; chem disp; shwrs inc; el pnts (16A) €1.50; snacks; playgrnd; CCI. "Site adj lake; walks around lake & in woods; gd." 1 May-31 Oct. € 9.00   2007*

BRIGNOGAN PLAGES 1D2 (Coastal) **Camping de la Côte des Légendes, Keravezan, 29890 Brignogan-Plages** [02 98 83 41 65; fax 02 98 83 59 94; camping-cote-des-legendes@wanadoo.fr; www.campingcotedeslegendes.com] Fr Roscoff on D10, fr Brest on D788/770 or fr N12 exit dir Lesneven. In Brignogan foll sp Brignogan-Plages & 'Centre Nautique'. Lge, hdg/mkd pitch, pt shd; wc; chem disp; mv service pnt; baby facs; shwrs inc; el pnts (5-10A) €2.35-3.25 (poss rev pol); lndtte; ice; shop; tradsmn; snacks; BBQ; playgrnd; dir access to sand beach adj; watersports; sailing; entmnt; child ent; site guarded 24 hrs; 10% statics; dogs €1.10; phone; Eng spkn; adv bkg; quiet; cc acc; red long stay/low ssn; red CCI. "Excel san facs; on beautiful sandy cove; some seaview pitches; wonderful site." ♦ Easter-1 Nov. € 13.05   2007*

CAMPING DU PHARE
Plage du Phare 29890 BRIGNOGAN PLAGES

Dogs allowed – Motorhome pitches

Tel.: 00 33 (0)2 98 83 45 06
Fax: 00 33 (0)2 98 83 52 19
www.camping-du-phare.com
camping_du_phare@caramail.com

Direct access to the sandy beach. Hiking trail GR34.
Rental of bungalows. Caravans and mobile homes.

BRIGNOGAN PLAGES *1D2* (1km NW Coastal) **Camping du Phare, Plage du Phare, 29890 Brignogan-Plages** [02 98 83 45 06; fax 02 98 83 52 19; camping_du_phare@caramail. com; www.camping-du-phare.com] Take D770 N fr Lesneven to Brignogan-Plages; take L fork in town cent & foll site sp dir Kerverven. Med, some hdg pitch, pt shd; wc; chem disp; mv service pnt; shwrs €1; el pnts (6A) €2.50; gas; lndtte; shop 1km; tradsmn; snacks; playgrnd; sand beach adj; 10% statics; dogs €1.50; poss cr; adv bkg; quiet; red facs low ssn; CCI. "Next to pretty bay & gd beach; helpful owner; vg site." 1 Apr-30 Sep. € 10.90   2007*

See advertisement

Did you know you can fill in site report forms on the Club's website — www.caravanclub.co.uk?

BRIGNOLES *10F3* (500m E) **Camp Municipal, 786 Route de Nice, 83170 Brignoles** [tel/fax 04 94 69 20 10; campingbrignoles@aol.com; http://campingdebrignoles.ifrance.com] Exit A8 junc 35 onto DN7 (N7) E dir Le Luc/Nice; site just bef Intermarché supmkt rndabt. Med, hdg pitch, pt shd; wc; chem disp; shwrs inc; el pnts (10A) €3; gas; lndtte; supmkt 100m; snacks; playgrnd; municipal pool adj; 10% statics; phone; dogs €1.50; Eng spkn; some rd noise; adv bkg; cc acc; CCI. "NH; well-managed site by friendly family." 15 Mar-15 Oct. € 12.50   2007*

BRIGNOLES *10F3* (9km SE Rural) **Camping La Vidaresse, 83136 Ste Anastasie-sur-Issole** [04 94 72 21 75; fax 04 98 05 01 21; lavidaresse@wanadoo.fr; www.campinglavidaresse.com] On DN7 (N7) 2km W of Brignoles at rndabt take D43 dir Toulon. In about 10km turn L at rndabt to D15. Do not ent vill, go strt & site is approx 250m on R. Med, hdg/mkd pitch, terr, pt shd; wc (some cont); chem disp; mv service pnt; shwrs inc; el pnts (6-10A) €3.50-4.50 (poss rev pol); gas; lndtte; ice; shop in vill 1km & 5km; rest high ssn; snacks & bar (all ssn); BBQ (gas/elec only); playgrnd; htd, covrd pool; paddling pool; sand beach 40km; tennis; games area; fishing 200m; 40% statics; dogs €2; poss cr; adv bkg; red long stay; cc acc; CCI. "Well-managed, family site in lovely area; peaceful; friendly & helpful; facs adequate; excel pool; gd touring base Haute Provence, Gorges du Verdon & Riviera; vineyard adj; gd." ♦ 15 Apr-30 Sep. € 23.00   2007*

BRILLANE, LA *10E3* (8km NE Rural) **Camping Les Matherons, 04700 Puimichel** [tel/fax 04 92 79 60 10; lesmatherons@wanadoo.fr; www.campinglesmatherons.com] Exit N96 or A51 junc 19 at La Brillane. Take D4B across Rv Durance to Oraison. Foll camp sps on D12 twd Puimichel; site on L 6km. Sm, pt sl, terr, pt shd; wc; chem disp; shwrs inc; el pnts (3A) €2.50; shop 6km; tradsmn; rest; snacks; playgrnd; dogs €1.10; Eng spkn; adv bkg ess; quiet; red low ssn; CCI. "Unspoilt natural site in depths of country; gd walks." 20 Apr-30 Sep. € 15.00   2007*

BRILLANE, LA *10E3* (2km E Urban) **Camping Les Oliviers, Chemin St Sauveur, 04700 Oraison** [tel/fax 04 92 78 20 00; camping-oraison@wanadoo.fr; www.camping-oraison.com] Exit A51 junc 19; take rd E to Oraison in 2km; site sp in vill. Med, mkd pitch, pt sl, pt terr, pt shd; wc; chem disp; mv service pnt; baby facs; fam bthrm; shwrs inc; el pnts (16A) €3.50; gas; lndtte; tradsmn (in ssn); shops, snacks & bar (in ssn) or 500m; playgrnd; pool; cycle hire; games area; games rm; TV rm; 10% statics; poss €2.50; Eng spkn; adv bkg (dep req); quiet; cc acc; CCI. "Pleasant, family-run site among olive trees; nice views; friendly, helpful owners; walks fr site; conv Verdon gorge; gd." 15 Apr-15 Oct. € 15.00   2007*

France

BRILLANE, LA *10E3* (3km W Rural) **Camping Le Moulin de Ventre, 04300 Niozelles [04 92 78 63 31; fax 04 92 79 86 92; moulindeventre@aol.com; www.moulin-de-ventre.com]** Leave A51 at La Brillane; in La Brillane turn L onto N100 sp Niozelles & Forcalquier. Site in 2km on L adj Rv Lauzon. Med, mkd pitch, pt sl, pt shd; htd wc; chem disp; mv service pnt; serviced pitches; baby facs; shwrs inc; el pnts (10A) inc; gas; lndtte; ice; shop 2km; tradsmn; rest; snacks; bar; BBQ (gas/elec); playgrnd; pool; rv sw, fishing, boat hire & beach; child entmnt; wifi internet; games/TV rm; 10% statics; dogs €3; phone; Eng spkn; adv bkg (bkg fee + 30% dep); quiet; red long stay; cc not acc; CCI. "Well-run, pleasant site; some pitches adj stream; excel touring base." ♦ 5 Apr-30 Sep. € 26.70 (CChq acc) ABS - M09   2007*

BRIONNE *3D2* (Urban) **Camp Municipal La Vallée, Rue Marcel Nogrette, 27800 Brionne [02 32 44 80 35; fax 02 32 46 25 61]** Fr N138 N or S on by-pass, leave at Champion Supmkt onto D46 past ent to supmkt; turn R, site on L. Sm, hdg pitch, unshd; wc; chem disp; mv service pnt; shwrs inc; el pnts (5A) €3; gas; lndtte; shop, rest etc nrby; BBQ; playgrnd; many statics; dogs; poss cr; quiet; CCI. "Excel site, highly rec; poss ltd facs low ssn; barrier open 1000-1200 & 1700-2000 Tues to Sun only." 1 Apr-30 Sep. € 8.80   2006*

BRIONNE *3D2* (5km N Urban) **Camp Municipal St Nicolas, 15 Rue St Nicolas, 27800 Le Bec-Helluoin [tel/fax 02 32 44 83 55 or 02 32 44 86 40 (Mairie); info@lebec-helluoin.com; www.lebec-helluoin.com]** Exit A28 junc 13 onto D438 (N138) then take D581 to Malleville-sur-le-Bec; site on R 1km after Malleville. Well sp. Med, pt shd; htd wc; chem disp; mv service pnt; shwrs inc; el pnts (10A) inc; lndtte; ice; tradsmn (excel bakeries); rest, snacks, bar in vill; BBQ; playgrnd; tennis, horseriding nr; 50% statics; dogs €0.95; poss cr; Eng spkn; quiet; CCI. "Excel, quiet site in pleasant area - a gem; vg spotless san facs - clean & htd low ssn; spacious pitches; v friendly, helpful warden; gate clsd 2200; cider sold on site; gd cycling; Benedictine abbey & vill 10 mins walk down hill." ♦ ltd. 1 Apr-30 Sep. € 10.80   2007*

⊞**BRIONNE** *3D2* (6km N Rural) **Camp Municipal Les Marronniers, Rue Louise Givon, 27290 Pont-Authou [tel/fax 02 32 42 75 06 or 02 32 42 72 07]** Heading S on N138/E402 take D130 just bef Brionne sp Pont-Audemer (care req at bdge & rndabts). Site on L in approx 5km, well sp on o'skts of Pont-Authou; foll sp in vill. Med, mkd pitch, some hdstg, pt shd; wc; chem disp; mv service pnt; shwrs; el pnts (10A) €2.90 (poss rev pol); lndtte; shops 500m; tradsmn; rest, bar in vill; BBQ; playgrnd; fishing; 50% statics; dogs €1.15; adv bkg; quiet; CCI. "Useful, pleasant, clean stop nr Rouen & m'way; friendly recep; beautiful valley with many historic towns & vills; best pitches far side of lake; excel walking; vg NH." € 8.70   2007*

BRIOUX SUR BOUTONNE see Melle *7A2*

BRISSAC QUINCE *4G1* (2km NE Rural) **Camping de l'Etang, Route de St Mathurin, 49320 Brissac-Quincé [02 41 91 70 61; fax 02 41 91 72 65; info@campingetang.com; www.campingetang.com]** Fr N on A11, exit junc 14 onto N260 passing E of Angers, following sp for Cholet-Poitiers. After x-ing Rv Loire, foll sp Brissac-Quincé on dual c'way way D748. Leave D748 to go into Brissac-Quincé vill. Foll sp for St Mathurin-Domaine de l'Etang & site is on D55 2km fr vill. Med, hdg/mkd pitch, hdstg, pt shd; htd wc; mv service pnt; chem disp; baby facs; some serviced pitches (€3 extra charge); shwrs inc; el pnts (10A) inc; gas; lndtte; ice; shop; tradsmn; rest; snacks; bar; BBQ (charcoal/gas); playgrnd; 2 pools (1 htd, covrd); paddling pool; waterslide; lake fishing; cycle hire; golf 8km; leisure park; poney rides; entmnt; child entmnt; internet; games/TV; dogs €5; recep 0800-1930 high ssn; Eng spkn; adv bkg; quiet; cc acc; red long stay/low ssn; CCI. "Excel, well cared for site amongst vineyards; spotless modern facs; gd disabled facs; staff pleasant & helpful; lge pitches; gd touring base Loire valley; wine-tastings & visits; chateau & grnds interesting; leisure facs gd for children; 15 min rvside walk to Brissac; mkt Thu; vg." ♦ 1 May-15 Sep. € 32.00 ABS - L15   2007*

See advertisement on page 633

BRISSAC QUINCE *4G1* (1km S Rural) **Camping à la Ferme Domaine de la Belle Etoile, La Belle Etoile, 49320 Brissac-Quincé [02 41 54 81 18]** Take D748 S fr Angers to Poitiers. S fr Brissac-Quincé on D748. After D761 rndabt cont on D748 take 3rd rd on L. Site in 500m. Sm, pt shd; wc; chem disp (wc); shwrs €1; el pnts (5A) €2; lndtte; ice; BBQ; playgrnd; quiet. "Vg CL-type site at vineyard with wine-tasting & farm produce; clean, modern facs; troglodyte caves, mushroom farms & Brissac-Quincé Château nrby." 1 Apr-1 Nov. € 7.90   2007*

⊞**BRIVE LA GAILLARDE** *7C3* (8km S Rural) **FFCC Camping à la Ferme (Delmas), Malfarges, 19600 Noailles [tel/fax 05 55 85 81 33]** Fr A20/E9 take exit 52 sp Noailles; immed after tunnel take 1st R at vill café (to avoid steep dangerous hill). Sp fr m'way. Sm, mkd pitch, terr, pt shd; wc; chem disp; mv service pnt; shwrs inc; el pnts (5A) €2.50-5 (poss rev pol); shop 500m; farm meals & produce; rv sw 5km; fishing 200m; dogs €2.50; few statics; adv bkg; quiet; CCI. "V conv NH/sh stay adj to A20; friendly, helpful farmer; gd value; if owner not around choose a pitch; basic san facs, poss unclean; parking on terr poss awkward; fly problem in hot weather; strict silence after 2200; excel." € 7.60   2007*

⊞**BRIVE LA GAILLARDE** *7C3* (6km SW Rural) Camping Intercommunal La Prairie, 19600 Lissac-sur-Couze [05 55 85 37 97; fax 05 55 85 37 11; lecausse.correzien@wanadoo.fr] A20 exit 51; N89 to Larche; L onto D19 sp Lissac; L onto D59 round N side of Lac de Causse, then bear L over dam; R to site in 2km. Site sp as 'Camping Nautica'. Med, mkd pitch, hdstg, terr, pt shd; wc; serviced pitches; shwrs inc; el pnts (16A) €3; gas 4km; lndtte; shop; snacks; bar; playgrnd; pool; lake sw; boating; windsurfing; 5% statics; dogs €3; quiet; adv bkg; no cc acc; CCI. "Beautiful setting o'looking lake; red facs low ssn & poss unclean; recep 1030-1200 & 1700-1900 but poss clsd Tues & Sun - site inaccessible when recep clsed, phone ahead rec; many outdoor activities, gd." ♦ € 14.00   2007*

⊞**BRIVE LA GAILLARDE** *7C3* (10km SW Rural) Camping La Magaudie, 19600 Chartrier-Ferrière [tel/fax 05 55 85 26 06; camping@lamagaudie. com; www.lamagaudie.com] Exit A20 junc 53 onto D19 dir Casteaux. After rlwy bdge take 2nd L to Chartrier & foll blue sps to site. NB Diff app climbing up narr lane with no passing paces for 1km. Sm, mkd pitch, sl, pt shd; htd wc; chem disp; shwrs inc; el pnts (10A) €2.75; lndtte; ice; shop 2km; tradsmn; rest; snacks; bar; gas BBQ; playgrnd; pool; lake sw 3km; 5% statics; dogs €1.25; Eng spkn; adv bkg (dep req); quiet; CCI. "Dutch owners; vg site & facs; rec arr early high ssn." ♦ € 13.25   2005*

BRIVE LA GAILLARDE *7C3* (10km W Rural) Camping La Ferme de Masloup (Fraysse), 19520 Mansac [05 55 85 27 14 & 05 55 85 11 69; masloup@wanadoo.fr] Fr A20 go W on A89; exit junc 18; take D133 sp Mansac. Site sp in 3km. Sm, pt sl, pt shd; wc; shwrs inc; el pnts (5A) €2.50; lndtte; ice; rest; playgrnd; pool; tennis; games area; 10% statics; Eng spkn; adv bkg; quiet; CCI. "Ideal 'get-away-from-it-all' site; gd walking area." 1 Jun-30 Sep. € 12.00   2007*

BROU *4F2* (1.5km W) Parc de Loisirs de Brou, Route des Moulins, 28160 Brou [02 37 47 02 17; fax 02 37 47 86 77] Sp in town on D13. Lge, hdg/ mkd pitch, shd; wc; chem disp; shwrs inc; el pnts (10A) €5.50; lndtte; shops 2km; rest; playgrnd; htd pool; waterslide; lake adj; fishing; golf; many statics; quiet; red low ssn; CCI. "Ent to site by card, so no ent when office clsd (winter office clsd Tues & Wed); excel new san facs 2004." ♦ 16 Feb-14 Dec. € 11.00   2005*

BROUSSES ET VILLARET *8F4* (500m S) Camping Le Martinet Rouge, 11390 Brousses-et-Villaret [tel/fax 04 68 26 51 98; martinet.bv.free.fr] Fr D118 Mazamet-Carcassonne, turn R 3km after Cuxac-Carbades onto D103; turn L in Brousses & foll sp. Sm, pt sl, shd; wc; baby facs; shwrs inc; el pnts €2.50; lndtte; ice; shop; snacks; bar; playgrnd; pool; trout-fishing; horseriding; canoeing; 20% statics; adv bkg; quiet; CCI. "Helpful owners." ♦ 1 Apr-15 Oct. € 12.00   2004*

BRUERE ALLICHAMPS see St Amand Montrond *4H3*

BRUGHEAS see Vichy *9A1*

BRULON *4F1* (Urban) Camping Le Septentrion (formerly Brûlon Le Lac), 72350 Brûlon [02 43 95 68 96; fax 02 43 92 60 36; le.septentrion@wanadoo.ff; www.campingle septentrion.com] Exit A81 junc 1; foll D4 S to Brûlon, site on L on ent town, clearly sp. Sm, pt sl, shd; wc; mv service pnt; shwrs inc; el pnts (6A) €2.50; lndtte; ice; shop 600m; tradsmn; rest; snacks; bar; BBQ; playgrnd; pool; lake sw; boating; fishing; cycle hire; games TV rm; 50% statics; phone; dogs €1; Eng spkn; adv bkg; quiet; red long stay/low ssn. "V spacious pitches; gd welcome fr owners; clean, modern san facs, unisex low ssn; no twin axles; gd cycling & walking area." 7 Apr-30 Sep. € 12.00 (CChq acc)   2007*

BRUNIQUEL *8E3* (4km NW) FFCC Camping Le Clos Lalande, Route de Bioule, 82800 Montricoux [tel/fax 05 63 24 18 89; contact@camping- lecloslalande.com; www.camping-lecloslalande. com] Fr A20 exit junc 59 to Caussade; fr Caussade take D964 to Montricoux where site well sp. Med, hdg/mkd pitch, pt shd; wc; chem disp; mv service pnt; baby facs; shwrs inc; el pnts (6A) €3.30; lndtte; ice; shop 1km; tradsmn; snacks; bar & 1km; BBQ; playgrnd; pool; rv sw; shgl beach 400m; tennis; basketball; fishing; watersports; cycle & canoe hire; internet; TV rm; 10% statics; dogs €1.50; phone; bus 400m; poss full; Eng spkn; adv bkg; CCI. "Quiet site by rv at mouth of Aveyron gorges; beautiful area; clean site; v helpful owners; vg for touring; many attractions; mkt Weds; lovely vill; vg". ♦ 1 May-15 Sep. € 12.70   2007*

BRUSQUE *10E1* (6km W Rural) Aire Naturelle de la Bouyssière de Blanc, 12360 Peux-et-Couffouleux [05 65 49 55 17; vacances@labouyssiere.com; www.labouyssiere.com] Fr N or S on D12 to Brusque. At Brusque cross Rv Dordou & take D119 local rd dir Murat, site in 6km. Sm, mkd pitch, terr, shd; wc (cont); shwrs inc; el pnts (16A) €3; lndtte; tradsmn; rest 6km; snacks; bar; BBQ; playgrnd; pool; no dogs; adv bkg; quiet; red long stay. "Gd walking paths; 9thC vill adj; beautiful, unspoilt location; warm welcome fr British owners." 1 May-30 Sep. € 13.00   2005*

BRUYERES *6E2* (6km SE) Camping Les Pinasses, La Chapelle-devant-Bruyères, 88600 Bruyères [03 29 58 51 10; pinasses@dial.oleane.com; www.camping-les-pinasses.com] Fr Bruyères, take D423 twd Gérardmer. In 3km turn L on D60 sp Corcieux, Site on R in 3km at La-Chapelle- devant-Bruyères. Med, hdg/mkd pitch, pt shd; wc (some cont); chem disp; shwrs inc; el pnts (4-6A) €3.30-4.30; gas; lndtte; shop; tradsmn; rest; snacks; bar; BBQ; playgrnd; entmnt; pool; minigolf; tennis & table tennis; 10% statics; dogs €1.30; adv bkg; some rlwy noise; CCI. "Beautiful area." Apr-15 Sep. € 17.20   2004*

France

BRUYERES *6E2* (6km S Rural) **Domaine des Messires, La Feigne, 88600 Herpelmont [03 29 58 56 29 or 0031 321 331456 (N'lands); fax 03 29 51 62 86; mail@domainedesmessires.com; www.domainedesmessires.com]** SE fr Bruyères on D423; at Laveline turn R sp Herpelmont & foll site sp. Site 1.5km N of Herpelmont. Med, pt shd; wc; mv service pnt; chem disp; serviced pitches; child/baby facs; shwrs inc; el pnts (6A) inc; lndtte; ice; shop; tradsmn; rest; snacks; bar; BBQ; playgrnd; lake sw; fishing; boating; dogs €3; Eng spkn; adv bkg; quiet; cc acc; red low ssn/long stay; CCI. "Attractive, peaceful lakeside site; gd touring base Alsace & Vosges." ♦ 28 Apr-15 Sep. € 24.50
2007*

See advertisement

BUGEAT *7B4* (3km NW Rural) **Camp Municipal Puy de Veix, 19170 Viam [05 55 95 52 05 (Mairie); fax 05 55 95 21 86; viam.mairie@wanadoo.fr]** Fr Bugeat NW on D979; in 4km L onto D160; foll sp to Viam. Sm, mkd pitch, pt sl, terr, pt shd; wc; chem disp; mv service pnt; el pnts (6-10A) €1.80; lndtte; shop 4km; rest 500m; playgrnd; lake sw & shgl beach adj; phone; poss cr; Eng spkn; adv bkg; CCI. "On lakeside; beautiful views; sw, boating, fishing; vg." 15 Jun-30 Sep. € 7.30
2005*

BUGUE, LE *7C3* (4km NE Rural) **Camping La Linotte, Route de Rouffignac, 24260 Le Bugue [05 53 07 17 61; fax 05 53 54 16 96; campinglalinotte@wanadoo.fr]** E off D710 onto D32E after passing thro town heading N twd Périgueux on rd to Rouffignac. Site sp fr D710. Med, hdg pitch, pt sl, terr, pt shd; wc; chem disp; baby facs; fam bthrm; shwrs inc; el pnts (10A) inc; lndtte; shop; rest; snacks; playgrnd; htd pool; entmnt; quiet; adv bkg; CCI. "Splendid views; lovely site; gd mkt Le Bugue Tues." 1 Apr-30 Sep. € 23.65
2004*

BUGUE, LE *7C3* (1km SE Urban) **Camping Les Trois Caupain (formerly Municipal Le Port), 24260 Le Bugue [05 53 07 24 60; info@camping-bugue.com; www.camping-des-trois-caupain.com]** Exit Le Bugue town cent on D703 twd Campagne. Turn R at sp after 400m to site in 600m. Med, mkd pitch, unshd; wc; chem disp; mv service pnt; shwrs inc; el pnts (6-10A) €3-3.60; gas; shops 1km; rest & snacks (high ssn); bar; playgrnd; pool; rv sw & games area adj; wifi internet; 40% statics, sep area; dogs free; adv bkg; quiet. "Pleasant, helpful owners; beautiful site; 15 mins walk to pretty town." 1 Apr-30 Oct. € 16.50
2007*

BUGUE, LE *7C3* (3km SE Rural) **Camping Le Val de la Marquise, 24260 Campagne [05 53 54 74 10; fax 05 53 54 00 70; val-marquise@wanadoo.fr; www.val-marquise.com]** Fr D703 bet Le Bugue & Les Eyzies take D35 at Campagne dir St Cyprien, site sp. Med, mkd pitch, terr, pt shd; wc; chem disp; baby facs; shwrs inc; el pnts (15A) €4; lndtte; shops 4km; tradsmn; snacks; bar; BBQ; playgrnd; pool; paddling pool; fishing lake; games aea; 5% statics; dogs €1.80; phone; Eng spkn; adv bkg; quiet; CCI. "Highly rec; peaceful, friendly esp out of ssn; poss diff access to pitches for lge vans due narr site rds & low terrs; spotless san facs; beautiful pool." 1 Apr-15 Oct. € 16.90
2006*

BUGUE, LE *7C3* (7km SE Rural) **Camping Le Clou, Meynard, 24220 Coux-et-Bigaroque [05 53 31 63 32; fax 05 53 31 69 33; info@camping-le-clou.com; www.camping-le-clou.com]** S fr Le Bugue on D703 twd Belvès; site 8km on R. Med, mkd pitch, pt sl, pt shd; htd wc; chem disp; mv service pnt; serviced pitches; baby facs; fam bthrm; shwrs inc; el pnts (6A) €3.50; gas; lndtte; ice; tradsmn; rest; snacks; bar; BBQ; playgrnd; 2 pools & paddling pool; rv sw 5km; fishing; canoeing; horseriding; entmnt; child entmnt; games rm; TV; phone; 10% statics; dogs €2.50; Eng spkn; adv bkg; quiet; cc acc; red long stay/low ssn/CCI. "Pleasant owners; ideal base for Dordogne; BBQs arranged; lovely wooded site with much wildlife." ♦ 28 Apr-15 Sep. € 19.75
2007*

BUGUE, LE 7C3 (10km SE) Camping La Faval, 24220 Coux-et-Bigaroque [05 53 31 60 44; fax 05 53 28 39 71; www.lafaval.com] On N side of Rv Dordogne at junc of D703 & D710, approx 300m fr rv. Med, shd, mkd pitch; wc; shwrs inc; el pnts (3-6A) €2.60-2.80; lndtte; ice; rest; shop; playgrnd; sm pool; entmnt; golf & tennis adj; TV rm. "Friendly, helpful staff; indiv washrms; gd sized pitches; rd noise but quiet at night." ♦ 1 Apr-30 Sep. € 15.24   2004*

BUGUE, LE 7C3 (8km S Rural) Camping Le Pont de Vicq, 24480 Le Buisson-de-Cadouin [05 53 22 01 73; fax 05 53 22 06 70; le.pont. de.vicq@wanadoo.fr; www.campings-dordogne. com/pontdevicq] Fr Le Bugue foll sp to Le Buisson. Site immed S of bdge over Rv Dordogne on rd D51E. Sp fr all dir in Le Buisson. Med, hdg/ mkd pitch, pt shd; wc; shwrs inc; el pnts (6A) €3 (rev pol); lndtte; shops 1.5km; rest adj; snacks in ssn; playgrnd; shgl beach for rv sw; TV; 60% statics; dogs €1; phone adj; poss cr; adv bkg; quiet; CCI. "Pleasant site on rv but ltd facs; poss mosquitoes." 1 Apr-15 Oct. € 12.70   2005*

BUGUE, LE 7C3 (5km SW Rural) Camping La Ferme des Poutiroux, 24510 Limeuil [05 53 63 31 62; fax 05 53 58 30 84; camping. les.poutiroux@tiscali.fr; www.poutiroux.com] W fr Le Bugue on D703 twd Bergerac; in 2km take D31 S for 4km; bef bdge take R fork twd Trémolat/ Lalinde; in 300m fork R (sp), site well sp. Sm, mkd, pt sl, terr, pt shd; wc; chem disp; mv service pnt; baby facs; shwrs; el pnts (6A) €3.50; lndtte; ice; shops 2km; playgrnd; pool (no shorts); canoes & rv sw nrby; some statics; dogs €1; phone; Eng spkn; adv bkg (dep req); quiet; cc not acc; CCI. "Well-positioned, peaceful, family-run site; friendly, helpful farmer; facs v clean; vg value low ssn; highly rec." ♦ 30 Mar-10 Nov. € 14.00   2007*

BUGUE, LE 7C3 (6km SW Rural) Camping du Port de Limeuil, 24480 Alles-sur-Dordogne [05 53 63 29 76; fax 05 53 63 04 19; didierbonvallet@aol.com; www.leportdelimeuil. com] Exit Le Bugue on D31 sp Le Buisson; in 4km turn R on D51 sp Limeuil; at 2km turn L over rv bdge; site on R after bdge. Med, hdg/mkd pitch, pt sl, pt shd; wc; chem disp; 50% serviced pitches; shwrs inc; el pnts (5A) €3.50; gas; lndtte; shop & 1km; bar; snacks; BBQ; playgrnd; htd pool; shgl beach & rv sw adj; games rm; mini-golf; canoe & cycle hire; 40% statics; dogs €2; poss cr; Eng spkn; adv bkg; quiet; red low ssn; CCI. "Superb location & site for all ages; lge pitches; v clean san facs, ltd low ssn; gd sw in clean rv; conv for exploring region at confluence of Dordogne & Vézère rvs; tour ops." ♦ ltd. 1 May-30 Sep. € 24.90   2007*

BUGUE, LE 7C3 (9km SW Rural) Camping de Trémolat, Centre Nautique, Route de Mauzac, 24510 Trémolat [05 53 22 81 18 or 05 53 05 65 65 (res); fax 05 53 06 30 94; semitour@perigord.tm.fr] Fr Le Bugue, take D703 W twd Pezuls. In vill, turn L onto D30 twd Trémolat. Site 700m N of Trémolat, well sp fr all dir. Med, hdg pitch, pt shd; wc; chem disp; shwrs inc; el pnts (10A) inc; lndtte; ice; shops 700m; rest; snacks; BBQ; pool; rv adj; fishing; canoeing; 20% statics; dogs; phone; poss cr; Eng spkn; adv bkg; quiet; CCI. "Peaceful site; most touring pitches have rv frontage, excel for fishing & canoeing; facs poss stretched high ssn." ♦ ltd. 1 May-30 Sep. € 20.00   2005*

This guide relies on site report forms submitted by caravanners like us; we'll do our bit and tell the editor what we think of the campsites we've visited.

BUGUE, LE 7C3 (10km W Rural) Camping La Forêt, Ste Alvère, 24510 Pezuls [05 53 22 71 69; fax 05 53 23 77 79; camping.laforet@wanadoo.fr; www.camping-la-foret.com] Off D703 fr Le Bugue to Lalinde rd, sp on L 1.5km bef Pezuls. In Le Bugue do not foll sp to Lalinde but cont thro town on D703, turn R, L & R, passing fire stn. Med, pt sl, pt shd; wc; chem disp; baby facs; shwrs inc; el pnts (3A) inc; gas; lndtte; sm shop; snacks; BBQ (gas/charcoal only); playgrnd; pool; tennis; games area; disco weekly high ssn away fr vans; games/TV rm; dogs free; recep 0830-1030 & 1500-1900; no c'vans over 6m high ssn; poss cr; adv bkg; quiet; cc not acc; CCI. "Beautiful, simple, peaceful site; nature lovers' paradise - wild orchids, butterflies, etc; underused low ssn; v helpful & friendly owner; gd san facs, ltd low ssn; mkt Le Bugue Tue; gd touring base; excel." ♦ 1 Apr-15 Oct. € 18.20 ABS - D03   2007*

BUGUE, LE 7C3 (5km NW) Camping St Avit Loisirs, 24260 St Avit-de-Vialard [05 53 02 64 00; fax 05 53 02 64 39; contact@saint-avit-loisirs. com; www.saint-avit-loisirs.com] Leave N89/E70 SE of Périgueux at turn S onto D710. Approx 6km bef Le Bugue turn R onto D42 sp Journiac, then immed L onto C206 for Ste Alvère. In 3km turn R for St Alvère, site on R. Narr, twisting app rd. Lge, hdg pitch, pt sl, pt shd; wc; chem disp; baby facs; shwrs inc; el pnts (6A) inc; gas; lndtte; shop; rest; snacks; bar; BBQ; playgrnd; 2 pools (1 htd, covrd); waterslide; paddling pool; tennis; crazy golf; golf, watersports, archery & horseriding nr; cycle hire; excursions; entmnt; child entmnt; internet; games/ TV rm; dogs €4.70; many static tents/vans; poss cr; adv bkg (bkg fee); quiet; cc acc; CCI. "Excel site & san facs; lovely; friendly welcome; well-run, busy site; conv for mkts, countryside & Lascaux" ♦ 1 Apr-27 Sep. € 38.70 ABS - D10   2007*

France

BUIS LES BARONNIES *9D2* (3km N Rural) Camping Le Romecas (Naturist), 26170 Buis-les-Baronnies [tel/fax 04 75 28 10 78] S fr Nyons on D938, E on D46/D4/D5 to Buis-les-Baronnies. On D546 turn N on D108 sp St Jalle. Site on L bef summit of Col d'Ey. Rd access gd although high altitude. Med, terr, pt shd; wc (some cont); shwrs; el pnts (6A) €2.70; Indtte; shop; rest; playgrnd; pool & paddling pool; TV; some statics; dogs €2.30; no adv bkg; quiet; CCI. "Beautiful situation; gd walking; friendly staff; access round site diff due tight bends & steep hillside." Easter-30 Sep. € 22.70 (3 persons)
2004*

BUIS LES BARONNIES *9D2* (7km E Rural) Camping/Gîte du Lièvre (Taponnier), La Roche-sur-les-Buis, 26170 Buis-les-Baronnies [04 75 28 11 49; fax 04 75 28 19 26; gitedulievre@wanadoo.fr; www.gitedulievre.com] In Buis-les-Baronnies travel N on D546; at edge of town after x-ing rv turn R onto D159; foll for 10km to Poët-en-Percip; site sp on L; 3km down unmade rd. Sm, mkd pitch, hdstg, terr, pt shd; wc (some cont); chem disp (wc); shwrs inc; el pnts (10A) €2 (poss long lead req); tradsmn; rest; snacks; bar; playgrnd; pool; mountain bike trails; horseriding; some statics; adv bkg; quiet; no cc acc; CCI. "Site on farm; scenic but v isolated; 3,000 feet high; views of Mt Ventoux; walks; climbing." May-Oct. € 15.00   2007*

BUIS LES BARONNIES *9D2* (1.5km SW Rural) Camping Les Ephélides, Quartier Tuves, 26170 Buis-les-Baronnies [04 75 28 10 15; fax 04 75 28 13 04; ephelides@wanadoo.fr; www. ephelides.com] Fr S of Vaison D54 or D13 E to Entrechaux, then D5 & D147 to vill. Sp in main rd S across rv, turn R, site in 1.5km. Normal exit in main rd blocked; access fr SW end of town to 'Parking Sud' by Rv L'Ouvèze. Med, pt shd; wc; shwrs; el pnts (3-10A) €2.70-3.30; Indtte; snacks; tennis adj; horseriding; some statics; dogs; phone; adv bkg; quiet; red low ssn; cc acc. "Sited in old cherry orchard; excel views; mkt in town Wed; take care when x-ing bdge." 15 May-1 Sep. € 16.60
2007*

BUIS LES BARONNIES *9D2* (4km SW Rural) Camping La Gautière, La Penne-sur-l'Ouvèze, 26170 Buis-les-Baronnies [04 75 28 02 68; fax 04 75 28 24 11; accueil@camping-lagautiere. com; www.camping-lagautiere.com] On D5 Vaison-la-Romaine to Buis-les-Baronnies rd, on L. Sm, mkd pitch, pt shd; htd wc; shwrs inc; el pnts (3-10A) €2,85-4.50; gas; Indtte; ice; shop & 4km; snacks; bar; BBQ; playgrnd; pool; climbing at Rocher St Julien & Gorges d'Ubrieux; horseriding & fishing nr; games area; games rm; 5% statics; dogs €1.10; phone; bus adj; Eng spkn; adv bkg; quiet; cc acc; CCI. "Beautiful situation; v lge pitches; v nice, helpful owners; one of best sm sites in France; excel." 1 Apr-30 Sep. € 14.90   2007*

BUISSON DE CADOUIN, LE see Bugue, Le *7C3*

BUJALEUF see St Léonard de Noblat *7B3*

BURNHAUPT LE HAUT see Cernay *6F3*

BURTONCOURT *5D2* (1km Rural) FFCC Camping La Croix du Bois Sacker, 57220 Burtoncourt [tel/fax 03 87 35 74 08; camping.croixsacker@wanadoo.fr; www.campingcroixsacker.com] Exit A4 junc 37 sp Argancy; at rndabt foll sp Malroy; at 2nd rndabt foll sp Chieuilles & cont to Vany; then take D3 for 12km dir Bouzonville; turn R onto D53A to Burtoncourt. Lge, hdg/mkd pitch, some hdstg, terr, pt shd; wc; mv service pnt; shwrs €0.90; el pnts (6A) inc; gas; Indtte; ice; shop; tradsmn; rest, snacks 1km; bar; playgrnd; games area; lake sw, sand beach; lake fishing; tennis; entmnt; TV; 2% statics; dogs €1.50; phone; bus 300m; Eng spkn; adv bkg (dep req); quiet; CCI; excel. "Lovely, wooded site in beautiful location; lge pitches; pleasant, v friendly owners; v clean san facs; forest walks; gd security; gd NH or sh stay en rte Alsace/Germany; conv Maginot Line; excel." ♦ 1 Apr-31 Oct. € 14.00
2006*

⊞ *Site open all year*   240   *Help us to update this guide*

BUSSIERE POITEVINE *7A3* (Urban) **Camp Municipal La Croix de L'Hozanne,** 87320 Bussière-Poitevine [05 55 60 08 17 or 05 55 68 40 83 (Mairie); fax 05 55 68 40 72] NW fr Bellac on N147, 8km after St Bonnet-de-Bellac turn R onto D4 sp Bussière-Poitevine. Site 500m on R opp water tower. Sm, hdg pitch, pt shd; htd wc (some cont); shwrs inc; el pnts (10-15A) €1.90-2.80; shops, rest & bar 500m; snacks; playgrnd; CCI. "Gd CL-type site; old but v clean facs; grass pitches poss water-logged in winter but can pitch in rd; ltd facs in low ssn; gd NH." 15 Apr-15 Oct. € 6.00   2005*

BUYSSCHEURE see St Omer *3A3*

BUZANCAIS *4H2* (S Urban) **Camp Municipal La Tête Noire,** 36500 Buzançais [02 54 84 17 27 or 06 15 85 53 04 (mob); fax 02 54 02 13 45; buzancais@wanadoo.fr] D943 (N143) fr Châteauroux thro town cent, cross rv, immed turn R into sports complex. Lge, some hdstg, pt shd; wc (some cont); shwrs inc; el pnts (16A) €2.50; ice; lndtte; shop, rest, snacks, bar 500m; playgrnd; pool 500m; entmnt; some statics; adv bkg; quiet; red 2+ night; CCI. "Pleasant peaceful situation on rv; gd fishing; clean, well-kept site & facs; red low ssn; no twin-axle vans; office clsd 1200-1600 & no access but ample parking; gd disabled facs." ♦ 1 May-30 Sep. € 10.50   2007*

BUZANCY *5C1* (1.5km SW) **Camping La Samaritaine, Rue du Stade,** 08240 Buzancy [03 24 30 08 88; fax 03 24 30 29 39; info@campinglasamaritaine.com; www.campinglasamaritaine.com] Fr Sedan take D977 dir Vouziers for 23km. Turn L onto D12, cont to end & turn L onto D947 for Buzancy. On ent Buzancy in 100m turn 2nd R immed after g'ge on R sp Camping Stade. Foll sp to site on L past football pitches. Med, hdg/mkd pitch, some hdstg; pt shd; wc; chem disp (wc); mv service pnt; 45% serviced pitches; mv service pnt; baby facs; shwrs inc; el pnts (10A) €3.50; lndtte; ice; sm shop; tradsmn; rest 1.6km; snacks, bar high ssn; BBQ (gas/charcoal); playgrnd; lake sw & sand beach adj; fishing; horseriding; tennis; child entmnt; games/TV rm; 10% statics; dogs €2.50; phone; Eng spkn; adv bkg (dep €10 req); quiet; red low ssn; cc acc; CCI. "Beautiful countryside; excel renovated site; no site lighting & ltd san facs low ssn; lovely area for walking/cycling; helpful, pleasant staff." ♦ 30 Apr-28 Sep. € 18.00 ABS - P10   2007*

BUZY see Louvie Juzon *8F2*

CABOURG *3D1* (1km E Coastal) **Camp Municipal Les Tilleuls,** 14160 Dives-sur-Mer [02 31 91 25 21; fax 02 31 91 72 13] Fr Cabourg cross bdge to Dives-sur-Mer, turn R at traff lts (Rue Gaston Manneville) & foll camping sp past church at bottom of hill up to D45. Turn L, site on R in 300m. Or fr A13 take D400 sp Cabourg, pass Super U & Intermarché supmkts & turn R sp Camping Touristique, site on R in 1.2km. Lge, pt sl, pt shd; wc (mainly cont); shwrs inc; el pnts (9A) €3.40; ice; lndry rm; shops 500m; sand beach 1km; horseriding; boules; playgrnd; quiet. Easter-15 Sep. € 10.40   2005*

As soon as we get home I'm going to post all these site report forms to the editor for inclusion in next year's guide. I don't want to miss the September deadline.

CABOURG *3D1* (8km SW) **Camping Le Clos Tranquille,** Gonneville-en-Auge, 14810 Merville-Franceville-Plage [02 31 24 21 36; fax 02 31 24 28 80; contact@campingleclostranquille.fr; www.campingleclostranquille.fr] Fr Cabourg, take D513 twd Caen. 2km after Varaville turn R to Gonneville-en-Auge (by garden cent) D95A. Foll sp to vill, site ent on R after LH bend. Med, pt shd; wc; chem disp; el pnts (4-10A) €3-€5 (poss rev pol & long lead req); shwrs inc; gas; lndtte; tradsmn; snacks; shop; playgrnd; cycle hire; sand beach 5km; 12% statics €2; poss cr; Eng spkn; adv bkg; quiet; cc acc; CCI. "Excel." 24 Mar-29 Sep. € 15.00   2007*

CABOURG *3D1* (1km W Coastal) **Camping La Pommeraie, Le Bas Cabourg,** 14390 Cabourg [02 31 91 54 58] Take D513 fr Cabourg twd Caen. Site on L 1km after Bas Cabourg sp. Med, pt shd; wc; shwrs €1; el pnts (5A) €3.80; gas; lndtte; shop; ice; sand beach 800m; dogs €1.52; adv bkg; cc acc. "Mkt Sat." 9 Apr-19 Sep. € 15.30   2004*

CABOURG *3D1* (2km W Coastal) **Camping Les Peupliers, Allée des Pins,** 14810 Merville-Franceville-Plage [tel/fax 02 31 24 05 07; asl-mondeville@wanadoo.fr; www.aslmondeville.com] Exit A13 to Cabourg, take D514 W, turn R sp Le Hôme, site sp, 2km E of Merville-Franceville. Med, pt sl, unshd; htd wc; chem disp; baby facs; shwrs inc; el pnts (10A) €5.10; lndtte; shop 2km; tradsmn; rest high ssn; snacks; bar; BBQ; playgrnd; htd pool; sand beach 300m; games area; tennis 2km; entmnt; child entmnt; TV; 50% statics; dogs €2.80; phone; poss cr; Eng spkn; adv bkg; quiet; cc acc; red low ssn. "Pleasant, friendly, well-run site; some vg sized pitches; clean, modern san facs; vg facs for children." ♦ 1 Apr-31 Oct. € 20.20   2007*

See advertisement

France

CABOURG *3D1* (6km W Coastal) **Camp Municipal Le Point du Jour, Route de Cabourg, 14810 Merville-Franceville-Plage [02 31 24 23 34 or 02 31 24 21 83 (Mairie); fax 02 31 24 15 54; camp. lepointdujour@wanadoo.fr]** Fr Ouistreham on D514/515 turn E at Bénouville, cross bdge onto D514, site on L dir Cabourg. Med, hdg/mkd pitch, pt sl, pt shd; htd wc; chem disp; baby facs; shwrs inc; el pnts (10A) €5 (poss rev pol); lndtte; shop, rest, snacks, bar 2km; playgrnd; sand beach adj; few statics; no dogs; bus; poss cr; adv bkg; quiet; CCI. "Excel site; easy access D-Day beaches." ♦ 1 May-22 Sep. € 16.40   2005*

CABRERETS *7D3* (1km Rural) **Camping Cantal, 46330 Cabrerets [05 65 31 26 61; fax 05 65 31 20 47]** Fr Cahors take D653 E for approx 15km bef turning R onto D662 E thro Vers & St Géry. Turn L onto D41 to Cabrerets. Site 1km after vill on R. Sm, pt sl, pt shd; wc; chem disp (wc); 50% serviced pitch; shwrs inc; el pnts €2; quiet; CCI. "Superb situation; v peaceful; warden calls; ground conditions rough; new san facs (2008); elec unreliable; not suitable lge o'fits; conv Pech Merle; excel." 1 May-10 Oct. € 9.30   2007*

CABRIERES D'AIGUES see Pertuis *10E3*

CADENET *10E3* (10km NE Rural) **Camping Le Moulin à Vent, Chemin de Gastoule, 84160 Cucuron [04 90 77 25 77; fax 04 90 77 28 12; bressier@aol.com]** Fr A51 exit junc 15 to Pertuis. N on D56 fr Pertuis to Cucuron. Site sp S fr Cucuron vill dir Villelaure. Sm, mkd pitch, terr, pt shd; wc; shwrs inc; el pnts inc (2-10A) €1.60-4; shop; tradsmn; snacks; lndtte; playgrnd; htd pool 4km; 10% statics; dogs €2; Eng spkn; quiet; CCI. "Spacious pitches, but access poss diff; friendly, helpful staff." ♦ 1 Apr-30 Sep. € 13.00   2004*

CADENET *10E3* (10km NE Rural) **Camping Lou Badareu, La Rasparine, 84160 Cucuron [04 90 77 21 46; fax 04 90 77 27 68; contact@ loubadareu.com; www.loubadareu.com]** Take D45 then D27 NE fr Cadenet twds Cucuron. S of Cucuron turn onto D27 (do not go into town), site is E 1km. Well sp fr D27. Sm, mkd pitch, pt sl, pt shd; ltd wc (own san rec); chem disp; shwrs inc; el pnts (4-6A) €3-4 (long lead poss req); lndtte; shop & 1km; playgrnd; pool; 20% statics; dogs €1.50; phone; quiet; CCI. "Pretty, comfortable farm site in cherry orchard; sep access for high vans." ♦ 1 Apr-15 Oct. € 10.60   2006*

CADENET *10E3* (2km SW Rural) **Camping Val de Durance, Les Routes, 84160 Cadenet** [04 90 68 37 75 or 04 42 20 47 25 (LS); fax 04 90 68 16 34; info@homair.com; www.homair.com] Exit A7 at Cavaillon onto D973 dir Cadenet. In Cadenet take D59, site sp. Lge, hdg pitch, pt shd; wc; chem disp; shwrs inc; el pnts (4-10A) inc; gas; lndtte; ice; shop & 2km; rest; snacks; bar; playgrnd; pool; rv sw & beach; archery; canoeing; cycling; games area; entmnt; TV; 70% statics; dogs €5; adv bkg; red low ssn; cc acc; CCI. "Dir access to lake; adj Luberon Park; san facs need update; noisy entmnt till late most evenings high ssn." ♦ 3 Apr-2 Oct. € 37.00   2006*

CADENET *10E3* (5km SW Rural) **Camping Silvacane-en-Provence, Ave de la Libération, 13640 La Roque-d'Anthéron** [04 42 50 40 54; fax 04 42 50 43 75; silvacane@village-centre.com; www.silvacaneenprovence.com www.village-center.com] Fr A7 take Sénas exit onto N7 twd Aix-en-Provence. In 10km take D561 E to La Roque-d'Anthéron. Site sp & visible fr rd. Med, terr, shd; wc; shwrs inc; el pnts (10A) inc; lndtte; shop; supmkt nr; snacks; bar; BBQ; playgrnd; pool; waterslide; fishing; tennis; entmnt; TV; many statics; dogs €3; poss cr; adv bkg; quiet but some rd noise; red low ssn; cc acc; CCI. "Beautiful scenery in Durance Valley." ♦ 16 Jun-2 Sep. € 23.00
2007*

CADENET *10E3* (5km SW Rural) **Caravaning Domaine des Iscles, 13640 La Roque-d'Anthéron** [04 42 50 44 25; fax 04 42 50 56 29; iscles@village-center.com; www.village-center.com/iscles] Fr A7 at junc 26 take N7 sp Lambesc; At Pont Royal turn L onto D561 to La Roque-d'Anthéron at rndabt on edge of vill stay on D561; immed R on slip rd, foll sp thro tunnel under canal. Lge, hdg pitch, pt shd; wc (cont); chem disp; mv service pnt; shwrs inc; el pnts (10A) inc; (long lead poss req); ice; lndtte; shop; tradsmn; rest; snacks; bar; playgrnd; pool; lake adj; fishing; golf; tennis; games area; 10% statics; dogs €3; poss cr; Eng spkn; adv bkg (dep req); red low ssn; CCI. "Gd site for children; lge pitches; pleasant setting; san facs clean." ♦ 21 Apr-16 Sep. € 29.00   2007*

CADENET *10E3* (10km W Rural) **Camping L'Orée du Bois, Ave du Bois, 13350 Charleval** [04 42 28 41 75; fax 04 42 28 47 48; oreedesbois@village-center.com; www.village-center.com/oreedesbois] Fr Cadenet take D561 to La Roque-d'Anthéron, cont to Charleval. Site sp in vill. Lge, hdg/mkd pitch, pt sl, pt shd; htd wc; chem disp; shwrs inc; el pnts (10A) inc; gas; lndtte; shop high ssn; rest, snacks, bar 500m; playgrnd; pool adj; waterslide; entmnt; 30% statics; dogs €3; phone; poss cr; Eng spkn; adv bkg (dep req, bkg fee); poss noisy; cc acc; CCI. 10 Mar-11 Nov. € 23.00
2007*

CAEN *3D1* (14km N Coastal) **Yelloh! Village La Côte de Nacre, Rue Général Moulton, 14750 St Aubin-sur-Mer** [02 31 97 14 45; fax 02 31 97 22 11; camping-cote-de-nacre@wanadoo.fr; www.camping-cote-de-nacre.com or www.yellohvillage.com] Fr Caen on D7 dir Douvres-la-Délivrande, Langrune-sur-Mer & St Aubin. Site in St Aubin-sur-Mer on S side of D514; clearly sp on o'skts. Lge, mkd pitch, hdstg, unshd; wc; chem disp; mv service pnt; baby facs; shwrs inc; el pnts (10A) inc; lndtte; shop high ssn; tradsmn; rest; snacks; bar; BBQ; playgrnd; htd pool; waterslide; sand beach 500m; tennis 200m; cycle hire; games rm; entmnt; TV; internet; 15% statics; dogs €4; quiet; phone; poss cr; Eng spkn; adv bkg rec; cc acc; CCI. "Conv Normandy beaches, Mont St Michel, Honfleur; v helpful staff; vg." ♦ 11 Mar-14 Sep. € 42.00   2007*

See advertisement

CAGNES SUR MER *10E4* (2km N Rural) **Camping Caravaning St Paul, 637 Chemin du Malvan, 06570 St Paul** [04 93 32 93 71; fax 04 93 32 01 97; caravaningstpaul@aol.com] Fr W exit A8 junc 47 dir Vence; fr E exit junc 48; in cent of Cagnes take D36 sp St Paul. At 3rd rndabt in 2km turn R & in 100m L to site in further 1km. Site sp. Med, hdg/mkd pitch, shd; wc; chem disp; mv service pnt; baby facs; shwrs inc; el pnts (6-10A); gas; lndtte; ice; shop 500m; tradsmn; rest; snacks; bar; playgrnd; pool; shgl beach 4.5km; cycle hire; entmnt; dogs €1.50; poss cr; Eng spkn; adv bkg (dep req); quiet; CCI. "Attractive, family-run site; well-kept & clean; conv Côte d'Azur." ♦ 1 May-30 Sep. € 22.00   2005*

CAGNES SUR MER *10E4* (3km N Rural) **Camping Green Park, 159 Vallon-des-Vaux, 06800 Cagnes-sur-Mer** [04 93 07 09 96 or 06 80 48 25 74 (mob); fax 04 93 14 36 55; info@greenpark.fr; www.greenpark.fr] Exit A8 junc 47 onto N7 sp Villeneuve-Loubet, Cagnes-sur-Mer & Nice; at Cagnes at 1st traff lts (do not foll sp Centre Ville) - racecourse on R; go strt for 1.5km (8 sets of traff lts); then turn L onto Chemin du Val Fleuri; cont strt for 4km. Fr Nice take N98 coast rd dir Cannes. Shortly after Cagnes turn R opp Le Port & foll sp Camping. Turn R then L at traff lts, site 3rd on L in 3km. Med, mkd pitch, pt shd; wc; chem disp; mv service pnt; baby facs; shwrs inc; el pnts (16A) inc; gas; lndtte; ice; shop; rest; snacks; bar; BBQ (gas/elec); playgrnd; 2 htd pools; shgl beach 4.3km; fishing 4.5km; horseriding 12km; tennis 400m; sports area; cycle hire; disco; entmnt; wifi internet; games/TV rm; dogs €2.50-3.60; adv bkg; quiet; red low ssn; CCI. "Friendly; well run; rec." ♦ 31 Mar-18 Oct. € 57.90 (4 persons) ABS - C28
2007*

CAGNES SUR MER *10E4* (3km N Rural) Camping Le Todos, 159 Vallon-des-Vaux, 06800 Cagnes-sur-Mer [04 93 31 20 05; fax 04 92 12 81 66; info@letodos.fr; www.letodos.fr] Fr Aix on A8 exit junc 47 & foll dir Cagnes-sur-Mer/Nice on N7 (do not foll sp Centre Ville). After 1st traff lts beside racecourse strt on for 2km, then turn L dir Val Fleuri, site in 3km. Fr Nice take N98 coast rd dir Cannes. Shortly after Cagnes turn R opp Le Port & foll sp Camping. Turn R then L at traff lts, site on L in 3km adj Camping Green Park. Med, mkd pitch, some terr, pt shd; wc; chem disp; mv service pnt; shwrs inc; el pnts (6-10A) €4.10-5.20; lndtte; tradmsn; shop; rest, snacks, bar at adj Camping Green Park; BBQ (gas/elec); playgrnd; pool & use of htd pool at Green Park; sand beach 4.5km; tennis 400m; cycle hire; games area; internet; TV; 10% statics; dogs €3.70; poss cr; adv bkg; quiet; red low ssn. "Owners also own Camping Green Park adj - some facs shared." ♦ ltd. 1 Apr-30 Sep. € 29.20 (CChq acc)   2006*

CAGNES SUR MER *10E4* (3km N Urban) Camping-Caravaning Le Val de Cagnes, 179 Chemin des Salles, 06800 Cagnes-sur-Mer [tel/fax 04 93 73 36 53; valdecagnes@wanadoo.fr; www.camping-leval-cagnes.com] On A8 exit Cagnes sur Mer, foll sp for Centre Ville. In town foll sp 'Haut de Cagnes' to Rue Jean Ferraud, then R fork onto Chemin des Salles & foll for approx 2km to site on L. Sm, hdg/mkd pitch, terr, pt shd; wc; chem disp; shwrs; el pnts (6A) €3.30; lndtte; sm shop; snacks; bar; playgrnd; pool; shgl beach 3.5km; dogs €2.30; Eng spkn; adv bkg (dep req); quiet; red low ssn; CCI. "San blocks v clean but tired; family-run site; v helpful owners; close to beaches & town; trains to Monaco & Italy fr town; sm pitches; v ltd facs low ssn." 10 Jan-27 Oct. € 16.30   2004*

CAGNES SUR MER *10E4* (3.5km N) Camping Le Val Fleuri, 139 Vallon-des-Vaux, 06800 Cagnes-sur-Mer [tel/fax 04 93 31 21 74; valfleur2@wanadoo.fr; www.campingvalfleuri.fr] Fr Nice take D6007 (N7) W twd Cannes. On app Cagnes turn R & foll sp Camping; site on R after 3km, well sp. Sm, terr, pt shd; wc (some cont); shwrs; el pnts (3-10A) €3.60; shop 3km; rest; shgl beach 4km; playgrnd; sm pool; entmnt; dogs €1; poss cr; Eng spkn; adv bkg; red low ssn. "V nice site, divided by rd (not busy); helpful, friendly owners; gd." 11 Feb-31 Oct. € 16.50   2006*

The opening dates and prices on this campsite have changed. I'll send a site report form to the editor for the next edition of the guide.

CAGNES SUR MER *10E4* (8km NE Rural) Camping Magali, 1814 Route de la Baronne, 06700 St Laurent-du-Var [04 93 31 57 00; fax 04 92 12 01 33; www.camping-magali.com] Exit A8 junc 49 to St Laurent-du-Var. Site sp fr town cent. Or fr Digne S on D6202 (N202), turn R onto D2210 at Pont-de-la-Manda; foll sp to St Laurent-du-Var for approx 7km, site on L. Med, mkd, pitch pt shd; htd wc (mainly cont); chem disp; shwrs inc; baby facs; el pnts (2-4A) €2.70-3.20; gas; ice; lndtte; shop; rest; snacks; bar; pool; shgl beach 6km; sailing; fishing; horseriding; tennis; some statics; dogs €1.90; bus nrby; poss cr; adv bkg; quiet; red low ssn; cc acc. "Conv Nice ferry (25 mins to port), Nice carnival/Menton Lemon Fair; sm pitches; v helpful warden." ♦ 1 Feb-31 Oct. € 22.30
2005*

CAGNES SUR MER *10E4* (2km S Coastal) Camping Parc des Maurettes, 730 Ave du Docteur Lefebvre, 06270 Villeneuve-Loubet [04 93 20 91 91; fax 04 93 73 77 20; info@ parcdesmaurettes.com; www.parcdesmaurettes. com] Fr Nice exit A8 junc 47, turn L onto D6007 dir Antibes; foll sp Intermarché, then R into Rue des Maurettes; site in 250m. N fr Cannes on A8 exit Villeneuve-Loubet-Plage junc 46; foll D241 over D6007 (N7) & rwly line, U-turn back over rwly line, then R onto D6007 dir Antibes as above. Med, mkd pitch, terr, pt shd; some serviced pitches; htd wc; chem disp; shwrs inc; el pnts (3-10A) €3-5; gas; ice; lndtte; shops adj; supmkt 100m; snacks; playgrnd; htd, covrd pool; beach 500m; sat TV; dogs €1.75; train Nice 400m; poss cr; Eng spkn; adv bkg; quiet; 10-40% red long stay; cc acc; CCI. "Marineland Zoo 1km; Cannes, Nice 20 mins by train; well-kept site with clean facs; variable pitch size/price." ♦ 10 Jan-15 Nov. € 21.80   2007*

⊞CAGNES SUR MER *10E4* (7km S Rural) Camping La Vieille Ferme, 296 Blvd des Groules, 06270 Villeneuve-Loubet-Plage [04 93 33 41 44; fax 04 93 33 37 28; info@vieilleferme.com; www.vieilleferme.com] Fr W (Cannes) take Antibes exit 44 fr A8, foll D35 dir Antibes 'Centre Ville'. At lge junc turn onto D6007 (N7) twd Biot & Villeneuve-Loubet sp Nice (rlwy line on R). Just after Marineland turn L onto Blvd des Groules. Fr E (Nice) leave A8 at junc 47 to join D6007 twd Antibes, take 3rd turning after Intermarché supmkt; site well sp fr N7. Med, hdg/mkd pitch, pt terr, pt sl, pt shd; htd wc; chem disp; mv service pnt; serviced pitches; baby facs; shwrs inc; el pnts (10A) inc; gas; lndtte; ice; sm shop; supmkt 800m; snacks; BBQ (gas/elec only); playgrnd; 2 pools (1 htd/covrd); shgl beach 1km (busy rd & rlwy to cross); archery; games rm; wifi internet; games/TV; 40% statics; dogs €2; recep 0800-1230 & 1300-2000 high ssn; c'vans over 8m not acc; Eng spkn; adv bkg; some aircraft & rd noise; red long stay & low ssn; cc acc. "Well-kept, family-run site; gd sized pitches; beach not suitable children & non-swimmers; excel pool; gd for walking, cycling & dogs as lge park adj; well-drained, lge pitches; buses & trains for Nice & Cannes/Menton/Monaco 5 min walk; excel." ♦ € 37.00 ABS - C22   2007*

CAGNES SUR MER *10E4* (2km SW Rural) Caravaning L'Oree de Vaugrenier, Blvd des Groules, 06270 Villeneuve-Loubet [tel/fax 04 93 33 57 30] Take N7 fr Antibes, strt over rndabt at Biot & turn L in 500m. Site ent 100m past Camping La Vieille Ferme. C'vans only. Sm, hdg pitch, hdstg, pt shd; chem disp; 75% serviced pitch; wc; shwrs inc; el pnts (2-10A) €2.05-3.25; gas; lndtte; shops 3km; playgrnd; shgl beach 1.5km; dogs €2.80; adv bkg; quiet; cc acc; CCI. "Excel, secure, clean, family-run site; lge pitches; hdstg suitable for awnings; adj Vaugrenier National Park." Easter-15 Oct. € 20.00 (3 persons)   2006*

CAGNES SUR MER *10E4* (4km SW Rural) Parc Saint James Le Sourire, Route de Grasse, 06270 Villeneuve-Loubet [04 93 20 96 11; fax 04 93 22 07 52; info@camping-parcsaintjames. com; www.camping-parcsaintjames.com] Exit A8 at exit 47; take D2 to Villeneuve; at rndbt take D2085 sp Grasse. Site on L in 2km. Sp Le Sourire. Med, hdg pitch, pt shd; wc (some cont); chem disp; mv service pnt; shwrs inc; el pnts (6A) inc; gas; lndtte; ice; shop; tradsmn; rest; snacks; bar; playgrnd; 2 htd pools; shgl beach 4km; tennis, golf & horseriding nr; table tennis; mini-golf; sauna; rv 2km; 70% statics; dogs €5; some rd noise; Eng spkn; adv bkg; 10% red long stay & w/e low ssn; cc acc; CCI. "Vg; red facs low ssn; park in visitors' car park bef registering; conv Nice, Cannes." ♦ ltd. 5 Apr-27 Sep. € 29.00   2007*

See advertisement

CAGNES SUR MER *10E4* (1km NW Urban) Camping Le Colombier, Collines de la Route de Vence, 35 Chemin de Ste Colombe, 06800 Cagnes-sur-Mer [tel/fax 04 93 73 12 77; campinglecolombier06@wanadoo.fr; www. campinglecolombier.com] N fr Cagnes cent foll 1-way system dir Vence. Half way up hill turn R at rndabt dir Cagnes-sur-Mer & R at next island. Site on L 300m, sp fr town cent. Sm, hdg/mkd pitch, pt shd; htd wc; chem disp; mv service pnt; shwrs inc; el pnts (2-6A) €1.80-3.30; lndry rm; shop 400m; rest 800m; snacks; bar; no BBQ; playgrnd, sm pool adj; TV; beach 2.5km; cycle hire; some statics; no dogs Jul/Aug; phone; Eng spkn; quiet; red long stay/CCI. "V friendly, family-run site." 1 Apr-30 Sep. € 22.20   2007*

CAGNES SUR MER *10E4* (4km NW Rural) Camping Le Vallon Rouge, Route de Gréolières, 06480 La Colle-sur-Loup [04 93 32 86 12 or 06 82 90 93 05 (mob); fax 04 93 32 80 08; info@ auvallonrouge.com; www.auvallonrouge.com] Leave A8 at junc 47 Cagnes-sur-Mer, foll dir Cagnes-sur-Mer vill. At vill turn L at traff lts onto D6 to La Colle-sur-Loup & Grasse; site on R. NB Lge o'fits park in lay-by & ask at recep for advice on tackling steep ent driveway. Med, mkd pitch, hdstg, shd; wc; chem disp; mv service pnt; baby facs; shwrs inc; solarium; el pnts (10A) inc; lndtte; ice; rest; snacks; bar; BBQ (gas/elec); playgrnd; pool; paddling pool; shgl beach 9km; rv sw nrby; fishing; games area; entmnt; wifi internet; games/TV rm; 40% statics; dogs €3.50; adv bkg; red low ssn; cc acc; CCI. "Conv Nice, Cannes, St Paul-de-Vence & Grasse; Sat mkt; vg site." ♦ 1 Apr-30 Sep. € 31.80 (CChq acc) ABS - C20   2007*

France

CAGNES SUR MER *10E4* (4km NW) Camping Les Pinèdes, Route de Pont de Pierre, 06480 La Colle-sur-Loup [04 93 32 98 94; fax 04 93 32 50 20; campinglespinedes06@aol. com; www.lespinedes.com] Exit A8 junc 47; take D6007 (N7) dir Nice, then D2 sp Villeneuve-Loubet; turn R at rndabt sp Villeneuve-Loubet & cross rv bdge; go thro sh tunnel, other side is Cagnes-sur-Mer & rndabt; turn L onto D6 to Colle-sur-Loup; site on R sh dist after Colle-sur-Loup. NB Take 2nd turning into site (1st leads to restaurant). Lge, hdg/mkd pitch, hdstg, pt sl, terr, pt shd; wc; chem disp; mv service pnt; serviced pitches; shwrs inc; el pnts (10A) inc; lndtte; shop (high ssn) & 1.5km; tradsmn; rest; snacks; bar; BBQ (gas/elec); playgrnd; pool; paddling pool; solarium; sand beach 3km; rv sw & fishing adj; tennis & horseriding 1.5km; cycle hire; archery; games area; entmnt; child entmnt; wifi internet; games/TV rm; 20% statics; dogs €2.90; c'vans over 6m & m'vans over 8m not acc high ssn; Eng spkn; adv bkg; quiet; cc acc; red long stay/low ssn/CCI. "Excel, family-run site; v helpful & friendly; steep access to pitches but gd rd surface; not suitable for disabled; luxurious san facs; brilliant for touring Côte d'Azur." 15 Mar-30 Sep. € 33.60 ABS - C30   2007*

See advertisement

CAHAGNES see Villers Bocage *3D1*

Before we move on, I'm going to fill in some site report forms and post them off to the editor, otherwise they won't arrive in time for the deadline at the end of September.

CAHORS *7D3* (8km N Rural) Camping Les Graves, 46090 St Pierre-Lafeuille [tel/fax 05 65 36 83 12; infos@camping-lesgraves.com; www.camping-lesgraves.com] Leave A20 at junc 57 Cahors Nord onto D820 (N20). Foll sp St Pierre-Lafeuille; at N end of vill, site is opp L'Atrium wine cave. Med, hdg pitch, pt sl, pt shd; wc; chem disp; mv service pnt; shwrs inc; el pnts (10A) €3.50 (poss rev pol); lndtte; ice; shop 10km; tradsmn; rest; snacks; bar; playgrnd; pool; cycle hire; 5% statics; dogs €1; adv bkg rec high ssn; rd noise; CCI. "V clean; lge pitches; lovely views; guided walks; poss clsd during/after wet weather due boggy ground; disabled facs over stony rd & grass; ltd facs low ssn; poss unkempt & pools dirty low ssn; conv for a'route, Cahors & Lot valley." ♦ 1 Apr-31 Oct. € 13.50   2007*

CAHORS *7D3* (8km N Rural) Quercy-Vacances, Mas de la Combe, 46000 St Pierre-Lafeuille [05 65 36 87 15; fax 05 65 36 02 39; quercyvacances@wanadoo.fr; www.quercy-vacances.com] Heading N on D820 (N20), turn L at N end of St Pierre-Lafeuille turn W at site sp N of vill, site in 700m down lane; new site opened adj so care needed to spot correct sp. Fr A20 exit junc 57 & foll sp N20. Med, pt sl, pt shd; wc; chem disp; baby facs; shwrs inc; el pnts (6-10A) €3.30-5.30; gas; lndtte; shops 10km; tradsmn; rest; snacks; bar; playgrnd; pool; tennis; TV; some statics; dogs €1.50; phone; Eng spkn; adv bkg; quiet; ltd facs low ssn; cc acc; CCI. "Pretty site; most pitches slightly sloping; spotlessly clean; modern san facs; poss unkempt low ssn; v helpful owner; much to do/see locally; conv D820; vg." ♦ 1 Apr-31 Oct. € 18.80   2007*

CAHORS *7D3* (1.5km E Urban) Camping Rivière de Cabessut, Rue de la Rivière, 46000 Cahors [05 65 30 06 30; fax 05 65 23 99 46; camping-riviere-cabessut@wanadoo.fr; www.cabessut. com] Fr N or S on D820 (N20), at S end Cahors by-pass take D911 sp Rodez. At traff lts by bdge do not cross rv but bear R on D911. In 1km at site sp turn L. Site on E bank of Rv Lot, well sp fr town. Med, hdg/mkd pitch, pt shd; wc; chem disp; mv service pnt; some serviced pitches; baby facs; shwrs inc; el pnts (10A) inc; gas; lndtte; ice; shop 2km; tradsmn; rest; snacks; bar; BBQ (gas only); playgrnd; pool (no shorts); rv adj; 5% statics; dogs €2; phone; frequent 'park & ride' bus to Cahors 600m approx; poss cr; adv bkg rec - ess high ssn; quiet (no dawn cockerel 2007); CCI. "Excel, well-managed, clean site; lge pitches; gd san facs, ltd low ssn; efficient & courteous staff; gd for children; rv trips; prehistoric caves & medieval vill nr; cycling rtes; gd mkt Sat." ♦ 1 Apr-30 Sep. € 18.00
                                              2007*

CAHORS *7D3* (7km E) Camp Municipal Lamagdelaine, 46090 Lamagdelaine [05 65 35 05 97 (Mairie); fax 05 65 22 64 93] Fr Cahors take D653 sp Figeac; site on R at Lamagdelaine rndabt. Fr Figeac on D802 (D653) sp Cahors; rndabt is 9km after Vers. Sm, pt shd; wc (some cont); shwrs inc; el pnts €1.80; shops 1.5km; pool 7km; dogs €1; quiet; CCI. "Lovely, quiet site; warden 0800-0930 & 1730-2000, barrier locked outside these hrs; chain across ent 2200; key fr Mairie adj if warden absent, but office infrequently open (3 afternoons pw); rec arrive when warden present." 15 Jun-Aug. € 9.50   2007*

CAJARC *7D4* (300m SW Urban) **Camp Municipal Le Terriol, Rue Le Terriol**, 46160 Cajarc [05 65 40 72 74 or 05 65 40 65 20 (Mairie); fax 05 65 40 39 05] Fr Cahors dir Cajarc on D662 on L foll sp to site. Sm, hdg/mkd pitches, some hdstg, pt shd; wc (cont); chem disp; baby facs; fam bthrm; shwrs inc; el pnts (10A) €2.50 (poss rev pol); lndtte; shop, rest, bar in vill; BBQ; playgrnd; tennis; dogs; phone; poss cr; Eng spkn; adv bkg; some rd noise; CCI. "Gd size pitches; clean, basic facs; lovely sm town on Rv Lot has gd rests & facs." 1 May-30 Sep. € 9.00   2007*

CAJARC *7D4* (6km SW Rural) **Camp Municipal Le Grand Pré**, 46330 Cénevières [05 65 30 22 65 or 05 65 31 28 16 (Marie); fax 05 65 31 37 00] Fr Villefranche on D911 twd Cahors turn R onto D24 at Limogne for Cénevières. Foll sp. Fr St Cirq-Lapopie on D24 thro vill & over rlwy. Sm, hdg/mkd pitch, pt shd; wc; chem disp (wc); mv service pnt; shwrs inc; el pnts (10A) €2.20; rest, snacks, bar 1km; BBQ; rv sw; dogs; bus; phone; quiet. "Peaceful site with vg san facs; site self & warden calls pm; wonderful views of cliffs." Jun-Sep. € 8.80
2005*

CAJARC *7D4* (9km NW Rural) **Camping Mas de Nadal (Naturist)**, 46330 Sauliac-sur-Célé [05 65 31 20 51; fax 05 65 31 20 57; info@masdenadal.com; www.masdenadal.com] Fr Cahors take D653 E. After 35km turn R onto D40 S, sp Blars. Fr Blars cont S for 2km to site ent on R. Sm, mkd pitch, pt sl, pt shd; wc; shwrs inc; el pnts (9A) €3.50; ice; shops 2km; tradsmn; rest; bar; pool; canoe hire; dogs €3.50; phone; poss cr; Eng spkn; adv bkg (dep req €16); quiet; CCI/INF card req. "Secluded wooded hillside; ltd rough pitches not suitable lge o'fits; rec phone ahead to check avail; suitable for m'vans." 1 Apr-1 Oct. € 19.00
2005*

⊞CALAIS *3A3* (8km E Rural) **Camping Bouscarel**, 448 Rue du Lac, 62215 Oye-Plage [03 21 36 76 37; fax 03 21 35 68 19; bouscarel62@aol.com] Fr W exit A16 at junc 49 & foll D940 twd Oye-Plage; at traff lts in cent of Oye-Plage turn L; at junc with D119 turn R, site on R in 200m. Fr E exit A16 junc 50 onto D219 to Oye-Plage. At traff lts strt on then R onto D119, site on R in 200m. Med, hdg/mkd pitch, hdstg, pt shd; wc; chem disp; mv service pnt; shwrs inc; el pnts (4A) €2.90; lndtte; shops 1.5km; playgrnd; sand beach 2km; games rm; 60% statics; dogs €1.90; phone; poss cr; adv bkg rec; cc not acc; CCI. "Friendly owners; gd sized pitches; san facs clean, poss stretched high ssn; neat, well-maintained site but poss untidy low ssn & facs run down; poss noisy high ssn due to constant arr/dep of campers; late arrivals welcome; conv early ferries; conv for Calais & Dunkerque ferries/tunnel/Cité Europe (20 mins to ferry terminal via minor rd) or to tour area." ◆ € 22.30   2007*

There aren't many sites open this early in the year. We'd better phone ahead to check that the one we're heading for is actually open.

CALAIS *3A3* (8km E) **Camping Les Petit Moulins**, 1634 Rue des Petit Moulins, 62215 Oye-Plage [03 21 85 12 94] Fr A16 junc 21 proceed to Oye Plage. Strt thro traff lts & take 2nd L to site past derelict windmill. Sm, unshd; wc (own facs low ssn); chem disp (wc); shwrs inc; el pnts (10A) inc; shops 2km; playgrnd; sw beach 2km; 90% statics; dogs; poss cr; quiet. "Open view; friendly, helpful owner; gd sized pitches; well-kept CL-type site; poss run down low ssn with scruffy, unclean facs; inadequate facs & poss neglected when busy; find pitch, book in house adj; ltd touring pitches; phone ahead." 15 Apr-30 Sep. € 10.00   2007*

France

⊞**CALAIS** *3A3* (12km E Coastal) **Camping Clairette, 525 Route des Dunes, 62215 Oye-Plage [tel/fax 03 21 35 83 51; camping.clairette. sarl@cegetel.net]** Exit A16 junc 50 & foll sp Oye-Plage. At traff lts at D940 cont strt. At junc with D119 turn R then L, site on L in 2km. Foll sp 'Réserve Naturelle'. Med, mkd pitch, pt sl, unshd; htd wc (own san rec); chem disp; mv service pnt; shwrs inc; el pnts (6-10A) €3.20-4; gas 5km; lndtte; shops 5km; tradsmn; BBQ; sm playgrnd; htd, covrd pool 5km; beach 500m; 90% statics; dogs €1.30; clsd 16 Dec-14 Jan; poss cr; Eng spkn; adv bkg; quiet, some rd noise; cc acc; CCI. "Warm welcome; owners v friendly & helpful; nature reserve nrby; conv for ferries; basic, dated facs; security barrier; v ltd touring pitches; fair." € 12.70   2007*

⊞**CALAIS** *3A3* (12km E Rural) **Camping Le Pont d'Oye, Rue de la Rivière, 62215 Oye-Plage [03 21 35 81 25 or 06 67 56 43 46 (mob)]** Exit A16 at junc 50 onto D219 to Oye-Plage; cross rv & turn R sp camping; site on L. Sm, unshd; wc; chem disp (wc); shwrs €0.80; el pnts (6A) €2.20; lndtte; shop 2km; tradsmn; playgrnd; dogs; CCI. "Basic CL-type site; grassed field for c'vans; open views; friendly owners; san facs adj statics park; fair NH." ♦ ltd. € 9.00   2005*

⊞**CALAIS** *3A3* (1km SW Coastal) **Aire Communale, Plage de Calais, Ave Raymond Poincaré, 62100 Calais [03 21 46 66 41; tourisme-patrimonie@ marie-calais.fr]** A16 exit junc 43 dir Blériot-Plage/ Calais cent & foll sp for beach (plage). Site nr harbour wall & Fort Risban. Well sp fr town cent. Med; wc; water; shop, rest nrby; obtain token/ pass fr Camp Municipal adj; wc part-time & have attendant & charge; warden calls to collect fee; m'vans only. € 7.00   2006*

CALAIS *3A3* (1km SW Coastal) **Camp Municipal, Plage de Calais, Ave Raymond Poincaré, 62100 Calais [03 21 34 73 25 or 03 21 97 89 79 (Mairie); tourisme-patrimonie@marie-calais.fr; www. calais.fr]** A16 exit junc 43 dir Blériot-Plage/Calais cent & foll sp for beach (plage). Site nr harbour wall & Fort Risban. If barrier down during day, call at building adj site office. Lge, unshd; wc; own san rec; shwrs; el pnts (10A) €2.05 (poss rev pol); lndtte; sand beach 200m; 70% statics; poss cr; Eng spkn; adv bkg for 5+ nights only; noise fr ferries daytime but quiet at night. "Some sm pitches; rec arr early to secure a pitch high ssn; barrier opens 0600 but poss down low ssn at w/e & warden poss diff to find after 1700 or absent altogether; office clsd 1200-1400; san facs & site poss dirty/scruffy high ssn; security probs (Jul 06) many itinerants; gd rests nr; conv ferries & beach." Easter-31 Oct. € 9.50   2007*

CALAIS *3A3* (4km SW Coastal) **Camp Municipal du Fort Lapin, 62231 Sangatte-Blériot Plage [03 21 97 67 77 or 03 21 97 89 79 (Mairie)]** Fr E exit junc 43 fr A16 to Calais cent, dir beach (Blériot-Plage). Turn L along coast onto D940 dir Sangatte; site on R in dunes shortly after water tower, opp sports cent; site sp fr D940. Fr S exit A16 junc 41 to Sangatte; at T-junc turn R onto D940; site on L just bef water tower. Lge, mkd pitch, pt sl, unshd; htd wc (some cont); own san high ssn; chem disp; baby facs; shwrs inc poss clsd 2130; el pnts (10A) inc (poss rev pol); lndtte; shop 1km; rest; snacks; bar; BBQ; playgrnd; sand beach adj; 50% statics; dogs; phone; bus; poss cr; adv bkg; quiet; CCI. "Warden lives on site - if recep unmanned; rec arr bef 1700 high ssn; recep & gates clsd 1200-1500 & 2300-0700; security code for ent; ltd parking outside espec w/e - phone ahead for access code; poss youth groups high ssn; poor san facs; conv Auchan & Cité Europe shops; conv NH." ♦ 21 May-31 Aug. € 18.60   2007*

CALAIS *3A3* (8km SW Rural) **Camping Les Epinettes, Mont-Pinet, 62231 Peuplingues [03 21 85 22 24 or 03 21 85 21 39; fax 03 21 85 26 95; info@lesepinettes.fr; www. lesepinettes.fr]** A16 fr Calais to Boulogne, exit junc 40 W on D243 sp Peuplingues, go thro vill & foll sp; site on L in 3km. Med, hdg pitch, pt sl, unshd; wc; own san; chem disp; shwrs €1; el pnts (4A) €1.50; lndtte; ice; sm shop & 3km; hypmkt 5km; tradsmn; rest 1.5km; playgrnd; sand beach 3km; 80% statics; dogs €1; phone; poss cr; adv bkg; cc acc; CCI. "Pleasant, quiet site; san facs clean but insufficient for site size; adv bkg doesn't guarantee pitch high ssn; when bureau clsd, site yourself - warden calls eve or call at cottage to pay; if arr late, park on grass verge outside main gate; use facs excl elec - pay half price; some pitches sm; friendly staff; conv NH for ferries & tunnel; conv Calais supmkts & Cité Europe." 1 Apr-30 Oct. € 10.40   2007*

CALAIS *3A3* (5km W Coastal) **Camping Cassiopée/ Les Noires Mottes, Rue Pierre Dupuy, 62231 Sangatte [tel/fax 03 21 82 04 75; cassiopee. tourisme@wanadoo.fr; http://cassiopee-tourisme.monsite.wanadoo.fr]** Fr A16 exit junc 41 sp Sangatte onto D243, at T-junc in vill turn R then R again bef monument. Lge, hdg/mkd pitch, pt sl, pt shd; wc (some cont); chem disp; mv service pnt; shwrs inc (clsd 2130-0800); el pnts (6-10A) €3.20; lndtte; shop 200m; tradsmn; playgrnd; sand beach 500m; many statics; dogs €1.30; poss cr; adv bkg rec high ssn; quiet; red low ssn; cc acc; CCI. "Site smarter (2007); lge pitches, some boggy in wet; conv ferries & Eurotunnel; office clsd 1200-1900 but site yourself; gates clsd 2230-0630 high ssn; poss itinerants low ssn; gd NH." 15 Mar-15 Nov. € 10.80   2007*

CALLAC 2E2 (1km SW Rural) **Camp Municipal La Verte Vallée, Rue de la Verte Vallée, 22160 Callac [02 96 45 58 50 or 02 96 45 81 30 (Mairie); fax 02 96 45 91 70; commune@mairie-callac.fr]** Sp fr all town app rds, on D28 to Morlaix. Off Ave Ernest Renan. Med, mkd pitch, terr, pt shd, unshd; wc; shwrs; el pnts (16A) €1.80; gas; shop 1km; lake sw 500m; fishing; quiet but some traff noise. "One hour to beaches." 15 Jun-15 Sep. € 7.60   2007*

CALLAS see Draguignan 10F3

CALVIAC EN PERIGORD see Sarlat la Canéda 7C3

CAMARET SUR MER 2E1 (500m Urban) **Camp Municipal du Lannic, Rue du Grouanoc'h, 29570 Camaret-sur-Mer [02 98 27 91 31 or 02 98 27 94 22; www.camaret-sur-mer.com]** On ent town foll sp to Port, on quayside to L turn sp Camping-Golf Miniature/m'van parking. Foll sp to site in 500m behind sports cent. Lge, pt sl, pt shd; wc; chem disp; mv service pnt; baby facs; shwrs €2; lndtte; shops 500m; el pnts €2.50; sand beach 1km; some statics; dogs €1; poss cr; quiet. "Excel site bet town & beach; sections for vans & tents." 1 May-30-Sep. € 9.10   2006*

CAMARET SUR MER 2E1 (2km NE Coastal) **Camping Le Grand Large, Lambézen, 29570 Camaret-sur-Mer [02 98 27 91 41; fax 02 98 27 93 72; contact@campinglegrandlarge. com; www.campinglegrandlarge.com]** On D8 bet Crozen & Camaret, turn R at ent to Camaret onto D355, sp Roscanvel. Foll sps to site in 3km. Med, hdg/mkd pitch, pt sl, pt shd; wc; chem disp; baby facs; shwrs inc; el pnts (5A) €3.50; gas; lndtte; shop; snacks; bar; BBQ; playgrnd; htd pool; sandy & shgl beach 450m; tennis; boating; TV; dogs €1.50; Eng spkn; adv bkg; quiet; cc acc; red low ssn. "Superb coastal views some pitches, others countryside; pleasant, helpful owners; cliff top walk to town; excel." ♦ 1 Apr-30 Sep. € 22.40 (CChq acc)   2007*

CAMARET SUR MER 2E1 (3.5km NE Coastal) **Camping Plage de Trez-Rouz, 29160 Camaret-sur-Mer [02 98 27 93 96; fax 02 98 27 84 54; camping-plage-de-trez-rouz@wanadoo.fr; www. trezrouz.com]** Foll D8 to Camaret-sur-Mer & at rndabt turn N sp Roscanvel/D355. Site on R in 3km. Med, hdg/mkd pitch, pt sl, pt shd; wc; chem disp; mv service pnt; baby facs; shwrs inc; el pnts (16A) €3; lndtte; ice; shop; tradsmn; rest; snacks; playgrnd; sand beach; tennis 500m; horseriding 2km; 10% statics; poss cr; adv bkg; poss cr; quiet; CCI. "Great position opp beach; boat trips fr Camaret in ssn; conv for Presqu'île de Crozon; gd facs but stretched high ssn; site scruffy low ssn; friendly owner." 15 Mar-15 Oct. € 15.20   2006*

CAMBIAC see Caraman 8F4

CAMBO LES BAINS 8F1 (10km E) **Camping Chapital, Route de Cambo, 64240 Hasparren [05 59 29 62 94; fax 05 59 29 69 71]** Fr A64 exit onto D21 to Hasparren, site sp off D22/D10 dir Cambo-les-Bains, on L 1km fr Hasparren. Med, mkd pitch, pt sl, shd; wc; chem disp (wc); serviced pitches; shwrs inc; el pnts (10A) inc; gas 500m; lndtte; shop 500m; rest & bar 1km; playgrnd; pool adj; 10% statics; dogs; phone; adv bkg; quiet; cc acc; gd. "Gd for exploring French Basque country & coast nr Biarritz." 1 May-30 Sep. € 9.00   2005*

CAMBO LES BAINS 8F1 (1.3km SW Rural) **Camping Bixta-Eder, Route de St Jean-de-Luz, 64250 Cambo-les-Bains [05 59 29 94 23; fax 05 59 29 23 70; contact@camping-bixtaeder. com; www.camping-bixtaeder.com]** Fr Bayonne on D932 (ignore 1st sp Cambo-les-Bains) exit at junc with D918 L twd Cambo. Site on L nr top of hill (Intermarché supmkt at by-pass junc). Med, mkd pitch, pt sl, pt shd; wc; baby facs; shwrs inc; el pnts (6-10A) €3.50-4; lndtte; shops 500m; rest, bar 100m; sand beach 20km; playgrnd; pool, tennis 400m; TV; dogs €1; poss cr; adv bkg; cc acc. ♦ 15 Apr-15 Oct. € 14.60   2006*

CAMBO LES BAINS 8F1 (3km SW Rural) **Camping L'Hiriberria, 64250 Itxassou [05 59 29 98 09; fax 05 59 29 20 88; hiriberria@wanadoo.fr]** Fr Cambo-les-Bains on D932 to Itxassou. Site on L 200m fr D918. Lge, hdg/mkd pitch, hdstg, pt sl, pt shd; htd wc (some cont); chem disp; mv service pnt; shwrs inc; baby facs; el pnts (5A) €2.50; gas; ice; lndtte; shops 2km; tradsmn; rest, bar 1km; snacks 3km; BBQ; playgrnd; pool; rv 2km; TV rm; 20% statics; dogs €1; Eng spkn; phone; quiet; 10% red 21+ days; CCI. "Popular site, phone ahead rec; gd views Pyrenees; pretty vill in 1km." ♦ 1 Mar-30 Nov. € 15.50   2005*

CAMBO LES BAINS 8F1 (5km W Rural) **Camping Alegera, 64250 Souraïde [05 59 93 91 80; www. camping-alegera.com]** Fr St Jean-de-Luz take D918 to Souraïde, site sp on L on rvside. Lge, hdg/ mkd pitch, pt shd; wc (cont); chem disp; mv service pnt; baby facs; shwrs inc; el pnts (4-10A) €3.10-3.80 (poss rev pol); gas; lndtte; ice, shop (high ssn); snacks; BBQ (gas/elec); playgrnd; pool; fishing 4km; games rm; tennis; golf; dogs €1.20; poss cr; adv bkg; quiet. "Excel for coast & Pyrenees; spacious pitches; v quiet low ssn & red facs; pretty vill." 15 Mar-31 Oct. € 13.80   2006*

CAMBRAI 3B4 (2km SW Urban) **Camp Municipal Les Trois Clochers, 77 Rue Jean Goude, 59400 Cambrai [03 27 70 91 64; mairie@villecambrai. com]** Site sp fr all dirs on ent town. Sm, hdg pitch, unshd; htd wc; chem disp; mv service pnt; shwrs inc; el pnts €2.50; shop, rest adj; playgrnd; Eng spkn; quiet. "Excel in every respect; new site 2005; all new facs & v clean & tidy; v helpful manager; walking dist to town." ♦ 15 Apr-15 Oct. € 12.00   2007*

CAMIERS see Touquet Paris Plage, Le 3B2

CAMON see Mirepoix (Ariege) *8F4*

CAMPAN see Bagnères de Bigorre *8F2*

CAMPOURIEZ see Entraygues sur Truyère *7D4*

CAMPSEGRET *7C3* (Rural) **Camping Le Bourg,** 24140 Campsegret [05 53 61 87 90; fax 05 53 24 22 36] On N21, sp & clearly visible on E of main rd. Sm, mkd pitch, pt shd; wc; shwrs inc; el pnts (10A) €2; shop; playgrnd; paddling pool; fishing; tennis; dogs €0.50; rd & farm noise, church bells. "NH only." ♦ 1 Jun-30 Sep. € 6.40   2007*

CANCALE *2E4* (3km N Coastal) **Camp Municipal a la Pointe du Grouin,** 35260 Cancale [02 99 89 63 79 or 02 99 89 60 15; mairie@ville-cancale.fr; www.ville-cancale.fr] Take D76 twd Cancale & cont on D201 sp Pointe de Grouin; site on R in 3km on cliffs above sea, on N side of Cancale (diff to see, on RH bend mkd with chevrons); sp 'Camp Municipal'. Care req at ent. Lge, pt sl, terr; wc (mainly cont); mv service pnt; shwrs inc; el pnts (5-10A) €3-4 (poss long lead req); lndtte; ice; shop; rest in town; BBQ; playgrnd; rocky beach adj; watersports; fishing; dogs €1.30; Eng spkn; quiet; cc acc. "Well-maintained site in gd location; some pitches uneven; excel san facs; gates clsd 2300-0700; conv Dinan, Mont St Michel, St Malo; sea views; gd walking." 1 Mar-27 Sep. € 11.85   2006*

CANCALE *2E4* (6km S Coastal) **Camp Municipal, Rue Bord de la Mer,** 35114 St Benoît-des-Ondes [02 99 58 65 21; fax 02 99 58 70 30] In vill cent on D155. Med, unshd; wc; chem disp (wc); mv service pnt; shwrs inc; el pnts (6A) €2.31; lndtte; snacks; rest, shop, bar adj; playgrnd; sand/shgl beach adj; dogs €0.82; Eng spkn; phone; CCI. "Gd san facs; gd walking & cycling." 15 Jun-15 Sep. € 11.17   2005*

CANCALE *2E4* (6km S Coastal) **Camping de l'Ile Verte,** 35114 St Benoît-des-Ondes [02 99 58 62 55] Site on S side of vill. Fr Cancale, take D76 SW for approx 4km, then turn L onto D155 into St Benoît. Foll site sp. Sm, hdg pitch, pt shd; htd wc (cont); chem disp; mv service pnt; shwrs inc; el pnts €3 (poss rev pol); gas; lndtte; shop; rest, bar adj; playgrnd; sand beach adj; 3% statics; phone; adv bkg; quiet; CCI "Well-kept site on edge of coastal vill." 31 May-12 Sep. € 17.00   2005*

CANCALE *2E4* (1km W Coastal) **Camping Les Genêts, La Ville Gueurie,** 35260 Cancale [02 99 89 76 17; fax 02 99 89 96 31; les.genets. camping@wanadoo.fr; www.camping-genets. com] Fr Cancale take D355 St Malo rd; go across supmkt rndabt; then take 1st rd on R (about 200m) & site on R in 200m. Med, mkd pitch, pt shd; wc; chem disp (wc); shwrs inc; el pnts (6A) €4; gas 500m; lndtte; ice; shop & supmkt 500m; rest in town; snacks; bar; playgrnd; sand beach 1.5km; 80% statics; dogs €2; phone; adv bkg (bkg fee & dep req); CCI. "V clean, well-kept site; area for tourers on far side of site; v helpful staff; half way bet town & beach; fresh oysters at seafront; gd." ♦ 2 Apr-15 Sep. € 19.00   2007*

CANCALE *2E4* (7km NW Coastal) **Camping Le Bois Pastel, 13 Rue de la Corgnais,** 35260 Cancale [02 99 89 66 10; fax 02 99 89 60 11; camping.bois-pastel@wanadoo.fr; www.camping boispastel.fr.] Fr Cancale take D201 dir Pointe de Grouin & St Malo by Rte Touristique. Site sp on L 2.5km after Pointe du Grouin. Med, pt shd; wc; shwrs inc; mv service pnt; shwrs inc; el pnts (6A) €4; lndtte; ice; shop; bar; BBQ; playgrnd; htd, covrd pool; sand beach 800m; 25% statics; dogs €2.50; adv bkg; quiet; red long stay/low ssn. "Conv Mont St Michel, St Malo; gd touring base." 1 Apr-30 Sep. € 23.00   2007*

See advertisement above

CANCALE 2E4 (2km W Rural) Camping La Ville ès Poulain, 35260 Cancale [02 99 89 87 47; www. ville-cancale.fr] Leave Cancale town cent on D355; after 1km cross D201 & turn immed R by bar & foll sp; site in 1km. Sm, hdg pitch, pt shd; wc; chem disp; shwrs; el pnts (10A) €2.60; lndry rm; supmkt 1.5km; sand beach 2km; dog €1; quiet; no cc acc; CCI. "CL-type site; lge pitches; gd base but no views - entire site surrounded by high hedge; conv St Malo ferry; conv Mont St Michel & oyster beds; excel fish rests in port." 15 Apr-30 Sep. € 13.00   2007*

CANCON 7D3 (5km N) Camp Municipal de St Chavit, 47290 Lougratte [05 53 01 70 05; fax 05 53 41 18 04; mairie.lougratte@wanadoo.fr] N on N21 fr Cancon, site at lake, L turn 50m bef church, site seen fr rd 500m fr turn. Med, hdg pitch, pt shd; wc; chem disp (wc); shwrs; el pnts (6A) €2.50; lndtte; ice; shop 500m; bar; BBQ; playgrnd; games rm; sand beach; boating; fishing; tennis nr; phone; v quiet. "Nice position; v clean san facs high ssn; poss v ltd facs low ssn & unclean; warden calls eves; gd touring base; highly rec." ♦ 15 Jun-15 Sep. € 8.00   2007*

CANCON 7D3 (2km E Rural) Camp Municipal du Lac, 47290 Cancon [05 53 36 54 30 or 05 53 01 60 24 (Mairie); fax 05 53 01 64 70; mairie. cancon@wandado.fr; www.cancon.fr/cancon_cadre.htm] Sp fr N21 on both sides of Cancon & in town. Med, mkd pitch, pt sl, shd; wc; shwrs inc; el pnts (10A) €3.20; shop 2 km; rest, snacks; bar; playgrnd; pool; fishing; games area; dogs €0.90; Eng spkn; CCI. "Gd site; peaceful in beautiful woodland & lake setting; no twin axles; opening dates poss unreliable." 15 Jun-15 Sep. € 8.20   2005*

⊞CANCON 7D3 (8km W Rural) Camping Le Moulin, Lassalle, 47290 Monbahus [05 53 01 68 87; info@lemoulin-monbahus.com; www.lemoulin-monbahus.com] Fr N21 turn W at Cancon on D124 sp Miramont. In 7.5km at Monbahus pass thro vill cent take L turn, still on D124 sp Tomboeuf. In 3km lge grain silos on L, site next on R. Sm, mkd pitch, hdstg, pt shd; wc; chem disp; shwrs inc; fam bthrm; el pnts (10A) €3; lndtte; tradsmn; shop 3km; bistro; snacks & takeaway; BBQ; playgrnd; htd pool; lake 5km; cycle hire; internet; dogs; Eng spkn; adv bkg (dep req); some rd noise; CCI. "CL-type site in garden; friendly British owners; facs spotless; vg pool; excel meals & takeaways; B & B avail; extra for twin-axles over 5m; excel." € 13.00   2007*

CANCON 7D3 (12km NW Rural) Camping La Vallée de Gardeleau, 47410 Sérignac-Péboudou [tel/ fax 05 53 36 96 96; valleegardeleau@wanadoo. fr; http://pagesperso-orange.fr/camping.vallee gardeleau.fr] Fr Cancon take N21 N; turn L twds Montauriol & Sérignac-Péboudou; foll camping sp. Sm, hdg pitch, pt sl, pt shd; wc; chem disp; shwrs inc; el pnts (5A) €3; gas 5km; lndtte; ice; shop & 5km; tradsmn; rest; snacks; bar; playgrnd; pool; lake fishing 2km; entmnt; 8% statics; dogs €2.50; phone; poss cr; Eng spkn; adv bkg (bkg fee & dep req); quiet; poss cr; CCI. "Calm & peaceful atmosphere; friendly owners; close to Bastide towns." ♦ 27 May-15 Sep. € 13.80   2006*

CANDE 2G4 (5km SW) Camp Municipal de l'Erdre, Route de Candé, 44540 St Mars-la-Jaille [02 40 97 00 34; contact@saint-mars-le-jaille.fr] Fr Ancenis N take N23 & N178. In town cent take D33 sp Candé. Site lies immed over bdge on L in St Mars-la-Jaille. Sp on all app rds. Med, pt shd; wc; shwrs inc; el pnts (5A) €1.85; pool 500m; poss noise fr by-pass. "Warden calls daily; ltd facs low ssn." 4 Jun-15 Sep. € 5.25   2005*

CANDE SUR BEUVRON 4G2 (500m S Rural) Camping La Grande Tortue, 3 Route de Pontlevoy,   41120   Candé-sur-Beuvron [02 54 44 15 20; fax 02 54 44 19 45; info@la-grande-tortue.com; www.la-grande-tortue.com] Exit A10 junc 17 at Blois dir Vierzon. Cross rv on D751 (sp Chaumont/Amboise). In 14km cross Rv Beuvron at Candé-sur-Beuvron & 400m after bdge take L fork & site immed on L. Fr Onzain cross rv to Chaumont, then NE on D751; in 4km turn sharp R (S) & site on L. Lge, hdg/mkd pitch, pt sl, pt shd; htd wc; chem disp; mv service pnt; baby facs; shwrs inc; el pnts (10A) inc; gas; lndtte; shop; tradsmn; rest; snacks; bar; BBQ; playgrnd; htd, covrd pool; paddling pool; cycle hire; horseriding; entmnt; internet; TV rm; 20% statics; dogs €3.70; Eng spkn; adv bkg; quiet; cc acc; red low ssn/ CCI. "Excel, rustic site amongst trees; poss diff access due to trees; helpful staff; gd cycling; conv Loire chateaux; gd for children; vg, clean, modern san facs & gd pool." ♦ 5 Apr-20 Sep. € 30.50 (CChq acc)   2007*

See advertisement on next page

CANET DE SALARS see Pont de Salars 7D4

CANET EN ROUSSILLON see Canet Plage 10G1

CANET PLAGE 10G1 (Urban) Camping Domino, Rue des Palmiers, 66140 Canet-Plage [04 68 80 27 25; fax 04 68 73 47 41] Fr Perpignan dir 'Plage'; foll sps to cent; L twds port & 1st L. Med, shd; wc (some cont); shwrs inc; shops adj; el pnts (3-10A) €2.50-3.50; ice; lndtte; snacks (high ssn); bar in town; shop adj; playgrnd; sand beach 50m; dogs €1.52; 20% statics; poss cr; quiet; adv bkg; dep req; red low ssn; 10% red CCI. "Gd long stay." 1 Apr-30 Sep. € 26.00   2004*

France

Loire Valley
3, route de Pontlevoy - 41120 Candé-sur-Beuvron
Tel: 00 33 (0) 2 54 44 15 20-Fax: 00 33 (0) 2 54 44 19 45
info@la-grande-tortue.com - www.la-grande-tortue.com

La Grande Tortue
Camping ★★★★
Caravanning

La Clef Verte

This pleasant,rusticsite has been tastefully developed in an old forest. 169 touring pitches (more than 100 sq.m) set among trees, with some shade and some sunshine. In July and August, the family owners organize a programme of trips including wine and cheese tasting, canoening, and all-day visits to the Loire Valley.

Camping Qualité

3 sanitary blocks - laundry - washing/drying machine - shop - terraced bar and restaurant - trampolines - bouncy castle - ball crawl with slide and climbing wall - table tennis - covered and heated swimming pool - paddling pool. Nearby: golf course, walking, cycling, fishing, horseback riding.

CANET PLAGE *10G1* (4km W Urban) **Camping Ma Prairie, Ave des Coteaux, 66140 Canet-en-Roussillon [04 68 73 26 17; fax 04 68 73 28 82; ma.prairie@wanadoo.fr; www.maprairie.com]** Leave A9/E15 at junc 41, sp Perpignan Centre/Canet-en-Roussillon. Take D83, then D81 until Canet-en-Roussillon. At rndabt, take D617 dir Perpignan & in about 500m leave at exit 5. Take D11 dir St Nazaire, pass under bdge & at rndabt turn R. Site on L. Lge, hdg pitch, shd; wc; serviced pitches; chem disp; baby facs; shwrs inc; el pnts (10A) inc; gas; lndtte; ice; supmkt adj; tradsmn; rest; snacks; bar; BBQ (gas/elec only); playgrnd; pool; paddling pool; waterslide; solarium; sand beach 2km; waterskiing; sailing, canoeing; cycle hire; archery; entmnt; child entmnt; internet; games/TV rm; 20% statics; dogs €3; no c'vans over 7m high ssn; bus to town nr; poss cr; Eng spkn; adv bkg ess Aug; quiet; cc acc; red low ssn; CCI. "Well-kept site; staff friendly & helpful; some pitches sm; san facs gd, one block refurbed (2007); shuttle bus to beach; cycle track to beach & along sea front; recep 0830-1200 & 1400-1930 high ssn; daily mkt Perpignan." ♦ 5 May-25 Sep. € 35.00 (CChq acc) ABS - C05   2007*

CANET PLAGE *10G1* (3km N Coastal) **Yelloh! Village Le Brasilia, 66140 Canet-en-Roussillon [04 68 80 23 82; fax 04 68 73 32 97; camping-le-brasilia@wanadoo.fr; www.brasilia.fr www.yellohvillage.com]** Exit A9 junc 41 sp Perpignan Nord & Rivesaltes onto D83 dir Le Barcarès & Canet for 10km; then take D81 dir Canet for 6km. At Canet go right round 1st big rndabt twd Ste Marie, then foll sp to site. V lge, hdg/mkd pitch, pt shd, wc (some cont); chem disp; baby facs; shwrs inc; el pnts (10A) inc; gas; lndtte; shop; tradsmn; rest; snacks; bar; BBQ (gas/elec); playgrnd; htd pool high ssn; paddling pool; sand beach 150m; fishing; tennis; cycle hire; archery; entmnt; excursions; internet; games/TV rm; 35% statics; dogs €4; recep 0800-2000; bus to Canet; Eng spkn; quiet but poss noisy disco & entmnt on adj campsite; cc acc; CCI. "V well-managed; gardens immac; pool spotless; staff v friendly; excel facs; in Jul & Aug identity card for pool - passport size photo needed; conv day trips to Andorra; daily mkt in Canet except Mon." ♦ 26 Apr-27 Sep. € 44.00 ABS - C01   2007*

CANET PLAGE *10G1* (4km N Coastal) **Camp Municipal de la Plage, 66470 Ste Marie-Plage [04 68 80 68 59; fax 04 68 73 14 70; contact@camping-municipal-de-la-plage.com; www.camping-municipal-de-la-plage.com]** Exit A9 junc 41 onto D83, then D81 to Ste Marie-Plage. Look for sm red sp, site adj Camping La Palais de la Mer. Lge, hdg pitch, pt shd; wc; chem disp; mv service pnt; shwrs; el pnts (6A) €3.30; lndtte; shop; rest; snacks; bar; playgrnd; pool; paddling pool; sand beach adj; games rm; cycle hire; child entmnt; TV; 30% statics; dogs €2.40; poss cr; Eng spkn; adv bkg (dep req); quiet; CCI. "Direct access to beach; v busy high ssn; san facs run down." ♦ ltd. 1 Mar-31 Oct. € 24.00   2006*

CANET PLAGE *10G1* (4km N Coastal) **Camping Le Palais de la Mer, 66470 Ste Marie-Plage [04 68 73 07 94; fax 04 68 73 57 83; contact@palaisdelamer.com; www.palaisdelamer.com]** Exit A9 at Perpignan Nord dir Canet. Fr Canet take D81 N to Ste Marie & foll sp to Ste Marie-Plage. At seafront turn L, site in 300m. Lge, hdg pitch, shd; htd wc (some cont); chem disp; serviced pitches; mv service pnt; baby facs; shwrs inc; el pnts (6A) inc; gas 1km; shop; ice; lndtte; rest; snacks; bar; BBQ; playgrnd; pool; sand beach adj; games area; tennis; entmnt; TV rm; 20% statics; dogs €4; phone; poss cr; Eng spkn; adv bkg (dep & booking fee req); CCI. "Sm pitches poss diff lge o'fits." ♦ 15 May-22 Sep. € 29.50   2005*

CANET PLAGE *10G1* (500m S Coastal) **Camping Club Mar Estang, Route de St Cyprien, 66140 Canet-en-Roussillon [04 68 80 35 53; fax 04 68 73 32 94; marestang@wanadoo.fr; www.marestang.com]** Exit A9 junc 41 Perpignan Nord dir Canet, then foll sp St Cyprien, site sp. V lge, mkd pitch, hdstg, pt shd; wc; chem disp; mv service pnt; baby facs; shwrs inc; el pnts (5A) €7; gas; lndtte; ice; shop; tradsmn; rest; snacks; bar; playgrnd; htd pool; waterslide; private sand beach adj; tennis; cycle hire; fitness rm; TV rm; 50% statics; dogs €4; Eng spkn; adv bkg; quiet; cc acc; red low ssn/long stay/low ssn/CCI. "V conv Spanish border & Pyrenees; gd birdwatching." ♦ 28 Apr-23 Sep. € 30.00   2006*

CANET PLAGE *10G1* (4km W Rural) FFCC Camping Les Fontaines, Route de St Nazaire, 66140 Canet-en-Roussillon [tel/fax 04 68 80 22 57 or 06 77 90 14 91 (mob); campinglesfontaines@ wanadoo.fr; www.camping-les-fontaines.com] Take D11 fr Canet dir St Nazaire; site sp on L in 1.5km. Easy access. Med, hdg/mkd pitch, unshd; wc; chem disp; mv service pnt; baby facs; fam bathrm; shwrs inc; el pnts (10A) €3.50; gas 2km; lndtte; ice; shop & 1km; tradsmn; snacks; bar; BBQ (gas/elec); playgrnd; pool; sand beach 2.5km; 30% statics; dogs €3; bus; phone; Eng spkn; adv bkg (dep req); quiet. "Pitches v lge; Etang de Canet et St Nazaire nature reserve with flamingos; bird watching; excel." 1 May-30 Sep. € 22.00   2006*

CANNES *10F4* (3km NE Urban) Camping Parc Bellevue, 67 Ave Maurice Chevalier, 06150 Cannes [04 93 47 28 97; fax 04 93 48 66 25; contact@parcbellevue.com; www.parcbellevue. com] A8 exit junc 41 twd Cannes. Foll N7 & at junc controlled by traff lts, get in L lane. Turn L & in 100m turn L across dual c'way, foll sp for site. Site in 400m on L after sports complex - steep ramp at ent. Lge, mkd pitch, pt shd; wc; chem disp; shwrs; el pnts (6A) €3; gas; lndtte; shops; rest; snacks; bar; htd pool; sandy beach 1.5km; sat TV; many statics; dogs €2; phone; bus/train nr; poss cr; Eng spkn; adv bkg; rd noise; red low ssn; CCI. "Vg, site on 2 levels; gd security; gd san facs; some pitches long way fr facs; many steps to gd pool; helpful, friendly staff; gd takeaway; conv beaches & A8; green oasis in busy area; gd bus to prom; no m'van facs." ♦ ltd. 1 Apr-30 Sep. € 22.00 (CChq acc)   2007*

CANNES *10F4* (4km NW Urban) Ranch Camping, L'Aubarède, Chemin de St Joseph, 06110 Le Cannet [04 93 46 00 11; fax 04 93 46 44 30; www. leranchcamping.fr] Exit A8 at junc 42 Le Cannet. Foll sp L'Aubarède & then La Bocca. Site well sp via D9. Med, hdg pitch, pt sl, terr, pt shd; htd wc (some cont); baby facs; shwrs inc; el pnts (6A) €3; lndtte; ice; shop; tradsmn; playgrnd; covrd pool; sand beach 2km; wifi internet; 10% statics; dogs €1; bus; adv bkg summer ssn ess by March with deposit; some rd noise; quiet. "Fairly basic site but conv location; pitches at cent or top of site quieter; gd." ♦ 1 Apr-30 Oct. € 25.00   2007*

CANNES *10F4* (5.5km NW Rural) Camping St Louis, Domaine des Chênes, 06550 La Roquette-sur-Siagne [04 92 19 23 13; fax 04 92 19 23 14; caravaning.st-louis@wanadoo. fr; www.homair.com & www.campingsaintlouis. com] Exit A8 at Cannes/Mandelieu & take D6007 (N7) twd Mandelieu. Fr Mandelieu take D109/D9 N twd Grasse. Turn R in Pégomas, site on L on leaving vill. Med, mkd/hdg pitch, v sl, terr, pt shd; wc; chem disp; shwrs inc; el pnts (6A) inc; gas; lndtte; shop; supmkt 100m; pizzeria; snack; bar; pool; waterslide; beach 5km; pool; tennis nr; entmnt; 25% statics; dogs; adv bkg; quiet; red low ssn. "Friendly staff; sm, sl pitches; facs ltd low ssn; conv Nice, Cannes." ♦ 1 Apr-30 Sep. € 37.00 (3 persons)   2007*

CANNES *10F4* (9km NW) FFCC Caravaning Les Mimosas, Quartier Cabrol, 06580 Pégomas [04 93 42 36 11; fax 04 93 60 92 74] Site on L of D109 Mandelieu to Grasse. Exit A8 junc 41 at Mandelieu turn R & foll sp to Pégomas on D9. Turn L immed bef rv bdge app Pégomas. Med, hdg/ mkd pitch, shd; wc; chem disp; mv service pnt; baby facs; shwrs inc; el pnts (5A) inc; lndtte; ice; shop; rest, bar 1km; snacks; playgrnd; pool; sand beach 8km; fishing in rv adj; games area; entmnt; 40% statics; dogs €1.60; adv bkg; quiet; cc acc; CCI. "Pleasant; convenient for Cannes, Côte d'Azur & mountain vills; excel mod shwr block; night security guard in ssn; barrier clsd 2300-0600." ♦ ltd. Easter-31 Oct. € 19.00   2006*

CANNET DES MAURES, LE *10F3* (4km N Rural) FFCC Camping Domaine de la Cigalière, Route du Thoronet, 83340 Le Cannet-des-Maures [04 94 73 81 06; fax 04 94 73 81 06; campinglacigaliere@wanadoo.fr; www.campings-var.com] Exit A8 at Le Cannet-des-Maures onto D17 N dir Le Thoronet; site in 4km on R, sp. Med, hdg/mkd pitch, hdstg, pt shd; wc; baby facs; shwrs inc; el pnts (10A) €3; lndtte; shop; tradsmn; snacks; takeaway; bar; BBQ (gas/elec); playgrnd; pool; paddling pool; games rm; 60% statics; dogs €2; quiet; CCI. "Lge o'fits req movers; v clean unisex facs up steep slope fr touring pitches; St Tropez 44km; gd." ♦ ltd. 1 Apr-31 Oct. € 17.00   2007*

CANOURGUE, LA *9D1* (2km E Rural) Camping Le Val d'Urugne, Route des Gorges-du-Tarn, 48500 La Canourgue [04 66 32 84 00; fax 04 66 32 88 14; lozereleisure@wanadoo.fr; www.lozereleisure. com] Exit A75 junc 40 dir La Canourgue; thro vill dir Gorges-du-Tarn. In 2km site on R 600m after golf clubhouse Sm, hdg pitch, pt sl, pt shd; wc; chem disp; mv service pnt; shwrs inc; el pnts (6A) €3; lndtte; ice; shop (high ssn) & 2km; tradsmn; rest, snacks, bar at golf club; TV rm; some chalets adj; dogs €2; Eng spkn; adv bkg; quiet; cc acc; CCI. "Vg site; golf adj; conv A75 & Gorges-du-Tarn; low ssn stop at golf club for key to site." ♦ ltd. 15 Apr-30 Sep. € 12.50   2006*

CANOURGUE, LA *9D1* (1km SE) Camping La Mothe, 75 Route d'Espagne, 48500 Banassac [04 66 32 88 11 or 04 66 32 97 37; fax 04 66 32 97 37] Leave A75 at junc 40, foll sp D998 La Canourgue. Take 2nd exit at each of 2 rndabts sp St Geniez-d'Olt N9 twds La Mothe. Site on L in 300m immed over Rv Lot. Med, shd; wc (some cont); chem disp (wc); shwrs inc; el pnts (6A) €2.50; lndtte; ice; supmkt 1.5km; rest 2km; snacks; bar; BBQ; playgrnd; pool; rv sw & fishing 1.5km; dogs €0.50; some rd noise; CCI. "Basic site; gd for birdwatchers & fishing; interesting area; phone ahead to check opening dates; no warden on site end ssn." ♦ 1 Apr-30 Oct. € 10.00   2005*

France

In the land of smiles and sunshine
AIROTEL GRAND SUD
Camping-Caravaning ★★★F-11250 PREIXAN
10 minutes away from the medieval center of Carcassonne

Rental of mobile homes & chalets

Phone 00 33 (0)4 68 26 88 18 - Fax 00 33 (0)4 68 26 85 07
E-mail: air.hotel.grand.sud@wanadoo.fr • www.camping-grandsud.com

CANY BARVILLE *3C2* (500m S Urban) **Camp Municipal**, Route de Barville, 76450 Cany-Barville [02 35 97 70 37; fax 02 35 97 72 32; mairie-de-cany-barville@wanadoo.fr] Sp fr town cent, off D268 to S of town, adj stadium. Med, hdg/mkd pitch, hdstg, pt shd; htd wc; chem disp; mv service pnt; shwrs inc; el pnts (10A) €2.80 (poss rev pol); lndtte; shop 500m; playgrnd; pool 1km; lake 2km; 25% statics; dogs €0.95; adv bkg; poss noisy; 10% red 14+ days; cc acc; CCI. "Lovely valley for cycling; excel facs but poss stretched at high ssn; poss no check-in on Sun; within reach of Dieppe & Fécamp Benedictine chateau." ♦ 1 Apr-30 Sep. € 9.65   2006*

CAPELLE LES BOULOGNE, LA see Boulogne sur Mer *3A2*

CAPESTANG *10F1* (Rural) **Camp Municipal**, 34310 Capestang [04 67 49 85 95 or 04 67 93 30 05 (Mairie)] Fr Béziers on D11, turn R twd vill of Capestang, approx 1km after passing supermarket. Site on L in leisure park opp Gendamarie. Med, hdg pitch, pt shd; wc (cont); shwrs; el pnts (6A) €2.85; shops, rest 500m; playgrnd; quiet. "300m fr Canal de Midi, excel walks or cycle rides; lovely rest in vill; low ssn site yourself, fees collected." 1 May-30 Sep. € 11.40   2004*

CAPPY see Albert *3B3*

CAPVERN LES BAINS see Lannemezan *8F2*

CARAMAN *8F4* (5km SE Rural) **FFCC Camping La Ferme du Tuillie**, 31460 Cambiac [05 61 83 30 95 or 06 88 16 27 14 (mob); fax 05 62 18 52 48; www. couleur-lauragais.fr] Fr Toulouse E onto N126; in 30km turn R onto D11 to Caraman; cont thro vill onto D25; in 4km turn L onto D18; site on L in 5km. Sm, hdg/mkd pitch, hdstg, unshd; wc; chem disp; mv service pnt; shwrs inc; el pnts (6A) inc; lndry rm; tradsmn; BBQ; playgrnd; cycle hire; fishing; TV; 5 statics; phone adj; adv bkg; quiet; no cc acc. "Beautiful, remote site by lake; friendly owners; excel." ♦ ltd. 1 Apr-30 Oct. € 12.00   2007*

CARAMAN *8F4* (1.5km S Rural) **Camp Municipal L'Orme Blanc**, 31460 Caraman [05 62 18 81 60 or 05 61 83 10 12 (Mairie); mairie-caraman@ wanadoo.fr] Site sp on D1 & D11 fr all dirs. Steep, narr, unfenced app track & sharp R turn not rec lge o'fits or lge m'vans. Sm, mkd pitch, pt sl, shd; wc; chem disp; shwrs; el pnts €2.50; gas, ice; shop 1km; rest, snacks, bar 1km; BBQ; lake fishing, sw & watersports adj; tennis; phone; adv bkg; quiet; CCI. "Rural site 20km fr Toulouse." ♦ 20 Jun-15 Sep. € 9.00   2004*

CARANTEC see St Pol de Léon *1D2*

CARCANS *7C1* (8km W Rural) **Camping Le Maubuisson**, 81 Ave de Maubuisson, 33121 Carcans [05 56 03 30 12; fax 05 56 03 47 93; camping-maubuisson@wanadoo.fr;   www. camping-maubuisson.com] Fr N215 to Castelnau-de-Médoc turn W onto D207 to Carcans & onto Maubuisson, in vill camp ent on L, sp. V lge, mkd pitch, pt sl, shd; wc; baby facs; shwrs inc; el pnts (5A) €3.50; gas; lndtte; shop; rest; snacks; bar; playgrnd; sand beach 3km; lake sw 100m; fishing; watersports; windsurfing; tennis; mini-golf; some statics; dogs €1.50; poss cr; adv bkg; quiet. "Site in wooded park; conv Médoc wine region & many sandy beaches." ♦ 1 Mar-30 Nov. € 19.60
2007*

CARCASSONNE *8F4* (5km N Rural) **FFCC Camping Das Pinhiers**, 11620 Villemoustaussou [04 68 47 81 90; fax 04 68 71 43 49; campingdaspinhiers@wanadoo.fr] Exit A6 junc 23 Carcassonne Ouest & foll sp Mazamet on D118; R at rndabt with filling stn; turn R & foll camping sp. Med, hdg pitch, pt sl, shd; wc; chem disp; mv service pnt; shwrs inc; el pnts (10A) €3.50; shop (high ssn) & 1km; rest; snacks; bar; playgrnd; pool; 10% statics; dogs; bus 1 km; Eng spkn; adv bkg; quiet; red low ssn; cc acc; CCI. "Diiff to pitch lge vans due to hdg pitches & slope; san facs basic & stretched high ssn; new owners (2006); open all year with ltd facs." ♦ ltd. 1 Mar-15 Nov. € 12.10
2006*

CARCASSONNE *8F4* (10km NE Rural) **Camping Le Moulin de Ste Anne, Chemin de Ste Anne, 11600 Villegly-en-Minervois [04 68 72 20 80; fax 04 68 72 27 15; campingstanne@wanadoo.fr; www.moulindesainteanne.com]** Leave A61 junc 23 Carcassonne Ouest dir Mazamet; after approx 14km onto D620 to Villegly, site sp at ent to vill. NB Turning R off D620 hidden by trees, then over narr bdge; long o'fits need wide swing in. Med, hdg/ mkd pitch, pt l , terr, unshd; htd wc; chem disp (wc); mv service pnt; baby facs; shwrs inc; el pnts (10A) inc; lndtte; shop 300m; tradsmn; snacks; bar; playgrnd; htd pool; sand beach 60km; games area; 25% statics; dogs €2; poss cr; adv bkg; Eng spkn; quiet; red long stay & low ssn; cc acc; CCI. "Pretty, quiet site; lge pitches; v friendly, helpful owner; ltd san facs; pitches poss ltft/muddy in wet; gd touring base; conv Carcassonne; Canal du Midi; vg." ♦ 1 Mar-30 Dec. € 16.00   2007*

CARCASSONNE *8F4* (6km E Rural) **FFCC Camping à l'Ombre des Micocouliers, Chemin de la Lande, 11800 Trèbes [04 68 78 61 75 or 04 68 78 88 77 (LS); fax 04 68 78 88 77; infos@ campingmicocouliers.com; www.campingmicocouliers.com]** Fr Carcassonne, take D6113 (N113) E for 6km to Trèbes; go under rlway bdge; fork L onto D610; turn R immed bef rv bdge; site on L in 200m. Site sp. Med, mkd pitch, shd; wc; chem disp; mv service pnt; shwrs (up steps); el pnts (16A) €3; lndry; shop; rest; snacks; BBQ; htd, covrd pool nr; rv fishing; TV; no statics; dogs €1.50; phone; poss cr; some Eng spkn; red low ssn; CCI. "V sandy site; gd san facs, 1 block poss up steps; walking dist to sm town; gd base Canal du Midi." ♦ 1 Apr-30 Sep. € 16.00   2007*

CARCASSONNE *8F4* (1.5km SE Urban) **Campéole La Cité, Route de St Hilaire, 11000 Carcassonne [04 68 25 11 77; fax 04 68 47 33 13; cpllacite@ atciat.com; www.camping-lacite.com or www. campeole.com]** Fr N & W exit Carcassonne by D6113 (N113) twd Narbonne; cross rv & turn S on D104 foll sp. Fr S (D118) take D104 to E & foll sp. Fr E (D6113) take D342 S to D104; foll sp. NB Site (La Cité) well sp fr all dirs & easy access fr A61 junc 23. Lge, hdg/mkd pitch, pt shd; wc (some cont); chem disp; mv service pnt; shwrs inc; el pnts (10A) €4.10 (poss rev pol); lndry rm; ice; shops 1.5km; tradsmn; rest; snacks; bar; playgrnd; pool (high ssn); tennis; internet; entmnt; some statics; dogs €3.50; Eng spkn; adv bkg (rec high ssn - fewer than 7 days not accepted); quiet with some rd noise; 25% red low ssn; cc acc; CCI. "Delightful site in gd location adj woods; popular - rec arr bef 1600 or earlier; mixed pitch sizes & types; friendly, helpful staff; san facs need refurb & stretched high ssn; poss untidy low ssn; ltd water pnts & waste water pnts; recep clsd 1200-1400; lots of entmnt & facs; reg bus service to town & castle or pleasant walk by stream; no twin-axles or o'fits over 5.50m; high ssn overspill area without el pnts." ♦ 15 Mar-15 Oct. € 23.50   2007*

⊞CARCASSONNE *8F4* (5km S Rural) **Camping à l'Ombre des Oliviers, Ave du Stade, 11570 Cazilhac [tel/fax 04 68 79 65 08 or 06 81 54 96 00 (mob); florian.romo@wanadoo. fr; www.alombredesoliviers.com]** Fr N & W exit Carcassonne by D6113 (N113) dir Narbonne. Cross rv & turn S onto D104, then D142/D56 to Cazilhac, site sp. Sm, pt shd; wc; baby facs; shwrs inc; el pnts (6-10A) €2 (poss rev pol); lndry rm; ice; supmkt in vill; bar; BBQ; playgrnd; pool; tennis; games area; TV; 10% statics; dogs €1.50; poss v cr; adv bkg; quiet; red low ssn. "Site in pleasant position; pitches poss muddy/soft & diff for med/lge o'fits to manoeuvre; few water points; v ltd facs low ssn; long c'vans check with recep, then ent via exit, as corners tight; if office clsd on arr phone owner on mobile, or site yourself; insufficient san facs when site full & ltd other facs; bus to old city nrby; v helpful owners." € 15.00   2006*

CARCASSONNE *8F4* (8km S Rural) **Airotel Camping Grand Sud, Route de Limoux, 11250 Preixan [04 68 26 88 18; fax 04 68 26 85 07; air. hotel.grand.sud@wanadoo.fr; www.campinggrandsud.com]** A61 exit junc 23 at Carcassonne Ouest onto D118 dir Limoux. Site visible fr rd on lakeside. Med, hdg/mkd pitch, hdstg, pt shd; htd wc; chem disp; mv service pnt; baby facs; shwrs inc; el pnts (6A) inc; lndtte; ice; tradsmn; rest; snacks; bar; BBQ; playgrnd; 2 pools high ssn; waterslide; fishing; boating; horseriding; tennis; cycle hire; games area; games rm; internet; entmnt; TV; 50% statics; dogs €4; Eng spkn; adv bkg; quiet; cc acc; CCI. "Pleasant, attractive site; easy access A61; friendly, helpful owners; wild fowl reserve; conv beautiful city of Carcassonne; gd walking; gd rest; excel." ♦ 1 Apr-15 Oct. € 28.00   2007*

See advertisement

CARCASSONNE *8F4* (14km SW Rural) **Yelloh! Village Domaine d'Arnauteille, 11250 Montclar [04 68 26 84 53; fax 04 68 26 91 10; arnauteille@ mnet.fr; www.arnauteille.com www.yellohvillage. com]** Fr Carcassonne take D118 S twd Limoux. Turn R bef end of sm section dual c'way (not 1st section) & foll sp to Montclar. Site approx 3km on L. NB Site app along 3km single track - site ent steep & narr. V lge, hdg/mkd pitch, pt sl, terr, pt shd; htd wc; chem disp; mv service pnt; some serviced pitches; baby facs; shwrs inc; el pnts (6A) €4; gas; lndtte; shop; tradsmn; rest; snacks; bar; playgrnd; pool; waterpark; horseriding; fishing 2km; golf 14km; games rm; games area; entmnt; internet; TV rm; 20% statics; dogs €3; Eng spkn; adv bkg; v quiet; cc acc; red low ssn; CCI. "Huge & impersonal; fabulous pool complex; excel rest; superb facs but siting can be diff in wet weather; muddy after rain; stunning views of Corbières; vg site." ♦ 31 Mar-30 Sep. € 29.00 (CChq acc)   2006*

France

CARCASSONNE 8F4 (4km NW Rural) Camping Château de Pennautier (formerly Les Lavandières), Route de Carcassonne, 11610 Pennautier [tel/fax 04 68 25 41 66; camping@chateaudepennautier.com; www. chateaudepennautier.com] Exit A61 Carcassonne W; site sp on R 4km fr Carcassonne on D6113 (N113) dir of Toulouse. Turn R onto D203 sp Pennautier; site in 500m on rvside. NB Former name 'Les Lavandières' poss still on sp. Sm, hdg pitch, shd; wc; chem disp; mv service pnt; shwrs inc; el pnts (5A) €3 (poss long lead req); lndry rm; ice; shop 1.5km; hypmkt 2km; tradsmn; rest 250m; playgrnd; pool; fishing; lake sw 15km; 11% statics; dogs €1; Eng spkn; adv bkg (25% dep); some rd noise (busy rd adj); cc acc; CCI. "Lovely location; friendly, helpful staff; san facs dated but clean; site poss unkempt & unclean low ssn; barrier clsd 2200-0730; excel vineyards nrby; excel." ♦ 1 May-30 Sep. € 12.50   2007*

CARCES 10F3 (Urban) Camping Les Fouguières, Quartier Les Fouguières, 83570 Carcès [34 94 59 96 28 or 06 74 29 69 02 (mob); fax 34 94 59 96 28; info@camping-les-fouguieres. com; www.camping-les-fouguieres.com] Exit A8 junc 35 at Brignoles onto D554 to Le Val; then take D562 to Carcès. Med, pt shd; wc; mv service pnt; shwrs inc; el pnts (4-12A) €2-2.50; gas; lndry; snacks; playgrnd; pool; Rv Caramy runs thro site; rv sw, fishing & canoeing; TV; dogs €2; phone; bus; Eng spkn; quiet." Excel, friendly site; canoeing & fishing nrby." ♦ 1 Mar-1 Nov. € 15.00   2007*

This guide relies on site report forms submitted by caravanners like us; we'll do our bit and tell the editor what we think of the campsites we've visited.

CARDET 10E1 (500m NW Rural) Camping Beau Rivage, 22 Rue du Bosquet, 30350 Cardet [04 66 83 02 48; fax 04 66 83 80 55; reception@campingbeaurivage.com; www. campingbeaurivage.com] Fr Alès take N106 dir Nîmes. Exit at sp Lédignan onto D982 dir Anduze & cont for 7km & cross D6110 (N110). On app Cardet take 3rd exit to vill avoid narr rds. Med, level, shd; htd wc; chem disp; baby facs; shwrs inc; el pnts (6A) €2.90; gas; lndry rm; ice; tradsmn; rest; snacks; BBQ; playgrnd; pool; rv sw adj; canoe hire; games rm; TV rm; disco; dogs €3; poss cr; Eng spkn; adv bkg ess Jul/Aug; quiet; red low ssn; red CCI. "Pleasant parkland setting by rv; well-organised; v helpful staff; gd pizzeria; if office clsd site yourself; excel." 1 Apr-1 Oct. € 19.75   2007*

CARENTAN 1D4 (10km NE Coastal) Camping Utah Beach, La Madeleine, 50480 Ste Marie-du-Mont [02 33 71 53 69; fax 02 33 71 07 11; utah. beach@wanadoo.fr; www.camping-utahbeach. com] 50km S of Cherbourg on N13 turn L onto D70 to Ste Marie-du-Mont. Foll D913 to coast & sp to Utah Beach Memorial - approx 4km. Site on beach rd D421. Med, hdg/mkd pitch, pt sl, pt shd; wc; chem disp; mv service pnt; shwrs inc; el pnts (6A) €3.70; gas; lndtte; ice; shop; tradsmn; snacks; bar; playgrnd; htd pool; sand beach 50m; water/beach sports; tennis; games rm; mini-golf; archery; entmnt; excursions; 55% statics; dogs €2.90; phone; quiet; adv bkg; red low ssn; cc acc; red low ssn; red CCI. "Well-kept site; gd touring base; site of US landing in 1944; gd birdwatching." 1 Apr-30 Sep. € 16.40
2004*

CARENTAN 1D4 (11km NE Coastal) Camping La Baie des Veys, Le Grand Vey, 50480 Ste Marie-du-Mont [02 33 71 56 90 or 06 09 82 61 82 (mob)] N of Carentan exit N13 onto D913 thro Ste Marie-du-Mont. At lge calvary 2km after vill, turn R onto D115 sp Le Grand Vey. Turn R at sea edge, site on R in 100m. Med, hdg/mkd pitch, pt shd; wc; chem disp (wc); shwrs inc; el pnts (6A) €2.70; lndtte; ice; shop & 6km; BBQ; 10% statics; dogs; adv bkg (dep req); quiet. "Friendly site beside salt flats; gd birdwatching, fishing; conv Utah Beach, D-Day museums etc." ♦ ltd. 1 May-15 Sep. € 10.80
2005*

CARENTAN 1D4 (500m E Urban) Camp Municipal Le Haut Dick, 30 Chemin du Grand-Bas Pays, 50500 Carentan [tel/fax 02 33 42 16 89; lehautdick@aol.com; www.camping-municipal. com] Fr N13 clearly sp in town cent, nr pool, on L bank of canal, close to marina. Med, hdg/ mkd pitch, pt shd; wc; chem disp; mv service pnt; shwrs inc; el pnts (6A) €3.20 (rev pol); gas; ice; shop 500m; tradsmn; rest, snacks, bar 500m; BBQ; playgrnd; htd pool adj; sand beach 10km; cycle hire; mini-golf; games rm; 5% statics; dogs; phone; poss cr; Eng spkn; adv bkg; quiet; cc not acc; CCI. "Immac site; clean san facs, poss ltd in low ssn; some pitches tight for lge o'fits; gd security; gates locked 2200-0700; mkt Mon; conv Cherbourg ferry & D-Day beaches; gd bird-watching on marshes; gd cycling area." ♦ 15 Jan-31 Oct. € 10.00   2007*

CARENTAN 1D4 (6km SE) FFCC Camping à la Ferme (Duval), 50620 Montmartin-en-Graignes [02 33 56 84 87] On N13 by-pass Carantan going S; join N174; site on L in 4km. Sm, unshd; wc; shwrs inc; el pnts inc; chem disp; playgrnd; adv bkg; quiet. "Charming CL-type site; pleasant, obliging owner; also B&B; easy 1 hr drive fr Cherbourg." 15 Jun-15 Sep. € 12.60   2007*

France

CARHAIX PLOUGUER *2E2* (1.5km W Rural) Camp Municipal La Vallée de l'Hyères, Rue de Kerniguez, 29270 Carhaux-Plouguer [02 98 99 10 58; fax 02 98 99 15 92; tourismecarhaix@wanadoo.fr; www.ville-carhaix.com] SE fr Huelgoat on D794 for 17km, sm site sp on all apps to Carhaix Med, pt shd; wc (some cont); chem disp (wc); shwrs inc; el pnts (10A) inc; lndtte; shop 1.5km; tradsmn, snacks; bar; playrnd nr; pool 1.5km; canoe/kayak hire; 5% statics; adv bkg; quiet; CCI. "Pleasantly situated in parkland on rv; muddy after rain, poss waterlogged adj rv." ♦ ltd. 1 Jun-30 Sep. € 9.15   2007*

As soon as we get home I'm going to post all these site report forms to the editor for inclusion in next year's guide. I don't want to miss the September deadline.

CARLEPONT see Noyon *3C3*

CARLUCET *7D3* (1.5km NW Rural) Camping Château de Lacomte, 46500 Carlucet [05 65 38 75 46; fax 05 65 33 17 68; chateaulacomte@wanadoo.fr; www.campingchateaulacomte.com] Fr Gramat SW on D677/D807. After approx 14km turn R onto D32 sp Carlucet, foll site sp (narr rd). Or fr A20 exit junc 56 & foll D802/D807 sp Gramat. In 5km turn L onto D32 as bef. Med, hdg pitch, some hdstg, pt sl, terr, pt shd; wc; chem disp; all serviced pitches; shwrs; el pnts (10A) €4.50; gas 7km; ice; lndtte; shops 12km; rest; snacks; bar; playrnd; 3 pools; tennis; cycle hire; golf 9km; 5% statics; dogs €3; adv bkg; quiet; cc acc; red low ssn/CCI. "British owners; excel facs & rest, superb food; 'freedom' pitches for m'vanners €45 per night inc use of sm car, bookable daily; conv Rocamadour & Lot & A20; excel walking in area." ♦ 15 May-15 Sep. € 20.00   2005*

CARLUX see Sarlat la Canéda *7C3*

CARNAC *2G3* (1km N Rural) **Camping La Grande Métairie, Route des Alignements de Kermario, 56342 Carnac [02 97 52 24 01; fax 02 97 52 83 58; info@lagrandemetairie.com; www.les-castels.com or www.lagrandemetairie.com]** Fr Auray take N768 twd Quiberon. In 8km turn L onto D119 twd Carnac. La Métairie site sp 1km bef Carnac (at traff lts) turn L onto D196 to site on R in 1km. V lge, hdg/mkd pitch, pt shd; htd wc; chem disp; mv service pnt; baby facs; shwrs inc; el pnts (6A) inc; gas; lndtte; ice; shop; rest; snacks; bar; playgrnd; 2 pools (1 htd, covrd); paddling pool; waterslide; sand beach 2.5km; watersports; sailing 2.5km; tennis; mini-golf; entmnt; TV; 80% statics; dogs; Eng spkn; adv bkg; quiet; cc acc; red low ssn. "Excel facs; vg pool complex; friendly, helpful staff; rec." ♦ 31 Mar-8 Sep. € 42.00   2007*

See advertisement

CARNAC *2G3* (1km N Rural) **Camping Les Ombrages, Kerlann, 56340 Carnac [02 97 52 16 52 (Jul & Aug) or 02 97 52 14 06]** Exit Auray SW on N168. After 9.5km L on D119. After 3km R at carwash, site 600m on R sp fr D119. Med, mkd pitch, shd; wc; shwrs; el pnts (6A) €2.50; lndtte; shops 1km; playgrnd; sand beach 3km; tennis; dogs €1; some statics; poss cr; quiet. "Well-kept site in wooded area." 15 Jun-15 Sep. € 13.10   2006*

CARNAC *2G3* (1km N Rural) **Camping Les Pins, Route du Hahon, Kerlann, 56340 Carnac [02 97 52 18 90]** On main Carnac-Auray rd; turn L at alignments; 1st R at fork, site 500m on L. Lge, pt shd; wc; baby facs; shwrs inc; el pnts (6-10A) €3; lndtte; ice; shop; snacks; BBQ; playgrnd; htd pool; sand beach 3km; entmnt; TV; dogs €1; red low ssn. 1 Apr-30 Sep. € 16.50   2006*

Camping de KERVILOR ★★★★
F-56470 La Trinité sur Mer
Tel.: 00 33 (0)2 97 55 76 75
Fax: 00 33 (0)2 97 55 87 26

E-mail : ebideau@camping-kervilor.com
Internet : www.camping-kervilor.com

Close to the harbour and the beaches, rental of mobile homes, heated swimming pools, waterslides, slide with several tracks, thermal waters, bar, animations, tennis, billiards, all services at the site.

CARNAC *2G3* (1km N Rural) **Camping Moulin de Kermaux, Route de Kerlescan, 56340 Carnac [02 97 52 15 90; fax 02 97 52 83 85; moulin-de-kermaux@wanadoo.fr; www.camping-moulin kermaux.com]** Fr Auray take D768 S sp Carnac, Quiberon. In 8km turn L onto D119 twds Carnac. 1km bef Carnac take D196 (Rte de Kerlescan) L to site in approx 500m opp round, stone observation tower for alignments. Med, hdg/mkd pitch, pt shd; htd wc; chem disp; mv service pnt; baby facs; shwrs inc; el pnts (6A) €3; gas; Indtte; ice; shop; snacks; bar; BBQ; playgrnd; htd pool; jacuzzi; sand beach 3km; games area; TV; 30% statics; dogs €3; phone; bus 2km; Eng spkn; adv bkg; quiet; cc acc; CCI. "Well-kept, friendly site; attractive location nr standing stones; quiet & comfortable low ssn; many repeat visitors." ♦ 6 Apr-15 Sep. € 22.00   2005*

CARNAC *2G3* (1.5km NE Rural) **Camping de Kervilor, 56470 La Trinité-sur-Mer [02 97 55 76 75; fax 02 97 55 87 26; ebideau@ camping-kervilor.com; www.camping-kervilor. com]** Sp fr island in cent of Trinité-sur-Mer. Lge, hdg/mkd pitch, hdstg, pt shd; wc; chem disp; mv service pnt; chem disp; shwrs inc; el pnts (6-10A) €3.30-3.80; gas; Indtte; ice; shop; snacks; bar; playgrnd; htd pool & paddling pool; waterslides; solarium; sand beach 2km; tennis; games area; cycle hire; entmnt; internet; 30% statics; dogs €2.80; poss cr; Eng spkn; adv bkg (dep & bkg fee); cc acc; red long stay/low ssn; CCI. "Busy family site; vg facs." ♦ 1 May-10 Sep. € 25.20   2007*

See advertisement

The opening dates and prices on this campsite have changed. I'll send a site report form to the editor for the next edition of the guide.

CARNAC *2G3* (2km NE Rural) **Camping Le Moustoir, 71 Route du Moustoir, 56340 Carnac [02 97 52 16 18; fax 02 97 52 88 37; info@ lemoustoir.com; www.lemoustoir.com]** Fr N165 take D768 at Auray dir Carnac & Quiberon. In 5km take D119 dir Carnac, site on L at ent to Carnac. Lge, hdg/ mkd pitch, pt sl, pt shd; wc; chem disp; mv service pnt; shwrs inc; el pnts (6A) inc; Indtte; ice; shop; tradsmn; snacks; bar; BBQ; playgrnd; 2 htd pools; paddling pool; waterslide; sand beach 3km; tennis; games area; cycle hire; child entmnt; wifi internet; 30% statics; dogs; phone; poss cr & noisy; Eng spkn; adv bkg; red low ssn; cc acc; CCI. "V attractive, friendly, well-run site; facs clean but stretched; tour ops; many megaliths nrby; Sun mkt." ♦ 5 Apr-27 Sep. € 37.00 (4 persons) (CChq acc)   2007*

CARNAC *2G3* (2km N) **Camping L'Etang, 67 Route de Kerlann, 56340 Carnac [02 97 52 14 06; fax 02 97 52 23 19]** Exit Auray on D768 Carnac-Quiberon. In 9.5km L onto D119 & in 3km R immed after petrol stn to site in 700m on R. Sp Les Ombrages, de l'Etang & Les Pins. Lge, hdg/ mkd pitch, hdstg, pt shd; wc (some cont); chem disp; shwrs inc; el pnts (6A) €3; gas; Indtte; ice; shop; tradsmn; snacks; bar; BBQ; playgrnd; htd, covrd pool; waterslide; sand beach 3km; sailing; fishing; tennis; games rm; TV; 10% statics; dogs €1; Eng spkn; adv bkg; quiet; CCI. "Lge pitches; helpful owner; well placed for famous prehistoric 'Alignements'." ♦ 1 Apr-15 Oct. € 16.50   2006*

CARNAC *2G3* (8km NE) **Camping Le Fort Espagnol, Route de Fort Espagnol, 56950 Crac'h [02 97 55 14 88; fax 02 97 30 01 04; fort-espagnol@wanadoo.fr; www.fort-espagnol.com]** Fr Auray take D28 S; in Crac'h turn L at rndabt; site sp in 1km on R. Lge, pt shd; htd wc (some cont); chem disp; baby facs; shwrs inc; el pnts (10A) €3.50; gas; Indtte; shops 1km; tradsmn; snacks; bar; playgrnd; pool; waterslide; sand beach 5km; tennis; sports facs; entmnt; 30% statics; poss cr; adv bkg rec high ssn; quiet; cc acc; CCI. "Helpful, pleasant management; popular with British; some lge pitches." 1 May-10 Sep. € 20.00   2005*

CARNAC 2G3 (2km E Rural/Coastal) **Camping Les Druides, Beaumer, 56340 Carnac [02 97 52 08 18; fax 02 97 52 96 13; campingl-les-druides@ wanadoo.fr]** Go E on seafront Carnac Plage to end; turn N onto Ave d'Orient; at junc with Rte de la Trinité-sur-Mer, turn L, then 1st R; site 1st on L in 300m. Med, hdg pitch, pt sl, pt shd; wc; chem disp; mv service pnt; baby facs; shwrs inc; el pnts (6A) €3.90; lndtte; ice; shop 1km; rest adj; playgrnd; htd pool; sand beach 300m; entmnts; games/TV rm; 5% statics; dogs €2.60; phone adj; Eng spkn; adv bkg; quiet; cc acc; CCI. "Friendly welcome; barrier key dep." ♦ ltd. 9 May-10 Sep. € 27.00   2004*

CARNAC 2G3 (2km E Coastal) **Camping Park Plijadur, 94 Route de Carnac, 56470 La Trinité-sur-Mer [02 97 55 72 05; fax 02 72 68 95 06; parkplijadur@hotmail.com; www.parkplijadur. com]** Take D781 Route de Carnac W fr La Trinité-sur-Mer, site 1km on R. Lge, hdg/mkd pitch, pt shd; wc; chem disp; mv service pnt; baby facs; sauna; shwrs inc; el pnts (6A) €2.75; lndtte; ice; shop; tradsmn; supmkt nr; rest 1km; snacks; bar; BBQ; playgrnd; htd pool; paddling pool; jacuzzi; sand beach 1km; games rm; fitness rm; mini-golf; cycle hire; golf 10km; entmnt; internet; TV rm; 3% statics; dogs €3.05; phone; poss cr; Eng spkn; adv bkg; quiet; cc acc; red low ssn/long stay/CCI. ♦ 1 Apr-30 Sep. € 25.75   2007*

CARNAC 2G3 (3km E) **Camping du Lac, 56340 Carnac [02 97 55 78 78 or 02 97 55 82 60; fax 02 97 55 86 03; camping.dulac@wanadoo.fr; www.camping-carnac.com]** Fr E end of quay-side in La Trinité-sur-Mer take main Carnac rd & in 100m turn R onto D186; in 2km R on C105, R on C131; sp. Fr Auray (by-pass) take D768 sp Carnac; in 4km turn L on D186; after 4km look for C105 on L & foll sp to site. Med, hdg pitch, pt sl, pt shd; wc; chem disp; mv service pnt; serviced pitches; baby facs; shwrs inc; el pnts (6A) €3; gas; lndtte; ice; shop; tradsmn; rest 3km; BBQ; playgrnd; pool; sand beach 3km; cycle hire; exercise equip rm; TV rm; entmnt; 50% statics; dogs €1.50; phone; poss cr; Eng spkn; adv bkg; quiet; cc acc; CCI. "Excel woodland site overlooking tidal lake; v helpful owner; clean, well cared for; superb pool; gd cycling & walking; vg." 15 Apr-20 Sep. € 18.80   2006*

CARNAC 2G3 (2km SE Coastal) **Camping Le Men Dû, Beaumer, 56340 Carnac [02 97 52 04 23; mendu@wanadoo.fr; www.camping-du-mendu. com]** Go E on seafront (Carnac Plage) to end; N on Ave d'Orient; at junc with Rte de la Trinité-sur-Mer turn L & 1st R; 2nd site on R. Med, hdg/mkd pitch, pt sl, pt shd; wc; chem disp; shwrs inc; el pnts (6-10A) €3; gas; lndtte; ice; shop 1km; rest, snacks, bar high ssn; sand beach 200m; 50% statics; bus 100m; poss cr; poss noisy; adv bkg (dep req); some Eng spkn; CCI. "Friendly staff; mkd pitches not rec for manoeuvring twin-axles; manhandling req for long or heavy vans; narr rds on site; yachting (inc school)." ♦ ltd. 1 Apr-30 Sep. € 20.00   2004*

CARNAC 2G3 (3km SE Coastal) **Camping de la Plage, Plage de Kervillen, 56470 La Trinité-sur-Mer [02 97 55 73 28; fax 02 97 55 88 31; laplage@ clubinternet.fr; www.camping-plage.com]** Fr Auray on D28 & D781 dir La Trinite. Foll sp Kervillen Plage to S. Lge, hdg pitch, pt shd; wc; chem disp; mv service pnt; chem disp; serviced pitches; baby facs; shwrs inc; el pnts (6A) €3.10; gas; lndtte; ice; shop 200m; rest; snacks; bar; BBQ; playgrnd; htd pool; waterslide; jacuzzi; sand beach adj; fishing; tennis adj; boat hire; mini-golf; cycle hire; 80% statics; dogs €1.20; poss cr; Eng spkn; adv bkg; quiet; red long stay/low ssn; cc acc; CCI. "Pleasant site; friendly staff; tight ent; variable pitch sizes." ♦ 29 Apr-17 Sep. € 33.70   2006*

CARNAC 2G3 (4km SE Coastal) **Camping La Baie, Plage de Kervillen, 56470 La Trinité-sur-Mer [02 97 55 73 42; fax 02 97 55 88 81; contact@ campingdelabaie.fr; www.campingdelabaie.fr]** Fr Carnac take D186. Turn R after causeway, keep R, past Camping de la Plage site, & site on L. Fr E app vill along seafront sp Carnac, cont strt thro traff lts, after 2nd traff lts take 1st L & foll rd for 1km. Site ent on L. Lge, hdg/mkd pitch, hdstg, pt shd; wc; chem disp; mv service pnt; baby facs; serviced pitches; shwrs inc; el pnts (6-10A) €2.20-3.25; ice; lndtte; shops, snacks, rest, bar 500m; playgrnd; entmnt; htd pool; sand beach 50m; fishing; boat hire, mini-golf & tennis 250m; TV rm; 30% statics; dogs €1.20; phone; poss cr; Eng spkn; adv bkg (dep req & bkg fee); quiet; red low ssn; cc acc. "Excel, well-maintained site in superb location; excel recep & san facs; some narr site rds - pitching poss diff lge o'fits; vg family beach; highly rec." ♦ 20 May-17 Sep. € 35.35   2007*

CARNAC 2G3 (9km SW Coastal) **Camp Municipal Les Sables Blancs, 56340 Plouharnel [02 97 52 37 15 or 02 97 52 30 90 (Mairie); fax 02 97 52 48 49]** Fr Auray take by-pass to Quiberon (clearly mkd), cont thro Plouharnel (D768) twd Quiberon - site clearly mkd after Plouharnel. Lge, unshd; wc; shwrs inc; el pnts (4-13A) €2.45-3.45; gas; lndtte; ice; shops; rest in ssn; sand beach; 30% statics; dogs €1.05; Eng spkn; quiet. "Situated on a sand spit, care needed over soft sand." 31 Mar-30 Sep. € 12.00   2005*

CARNAC 2G3 (1.5km NW Rural) **Camping Les Goélands, Kerbachic, 56340 Plouharnel [02 97 52 31 92; michelinealloux@aol.com]** Take D768 fr Auray twd Quiberon. In Plouharnel turn L at rndabt by supmkt onto D781 to Carnac. Site sp to L in 500m. Med, pt shd; wc (some cont); chem disp; shwrs €0.80; el pnts (3-5A) €1.80-2.80; gas; lndtte; ice; shops 1km; playgrnd; sand beach 3km; dogs €0.80; poss cr; adv bkg. "V friendly owners; excel facs; gd-sized pitches; gate clsd at 2200; nr beaches with bathing & gd yachting; bells fr adj abbey not too intrusive; conv for megalithic sites; high standard." 1 Jun-15 Sep. € 10.30   2005*

CARNAC *2G3* (8km NW Rural) **Camping Kerzerho, 56410 Erdeven [tel/fax 02 97 55 63 16; info@camping-kerzerho.com; www.camping-kerzerho.com]** N fr Carnac on D781, site sp 400m S of Erdeven. Med, hdg/mkd pitch, pt shd; wc; baby facs; sauna; shwrs; el pnts (10A) €5; lndtte; shop; tradsmn; rest; snacks; bar; playgrnd; htd pool; paddling pool; waterslide; beach 2.5km; cycle hire; excursions; entmnt; child entmnt; some statics; dogs €3; adv bkg; quiet; red low ssn. "Busy site; some sm pitches diff lge o'fits." 1 Jun-3 Sep. € 23.00   2006*

CARNAC *2G3* (8km NW Rural) **Camping La Croëz Villieu, Route de Kerhillio, 56410 Erdeven [02 97 55 90 43; fax 02 97 55 64 83; la-croez-villieu@wanadoo.fr; www.la-croez-villieu.com]** Fr Carnac take D781 to Erdeven, turn L opp Marché des Menhirs. Site 1km on R. Med, hdg pitch, pt shd; wc; chem disp (wc); baby facs; shwrs inc; el pnts (4-6A) €2.50-3.50; gas; lndtte; ice; shops 1km; snacks; bar; playgrnd; htd pool; sand beach 2km; 65% statics; dogs €1.65; poss cr; Eng spkn; adv bkg; quiet; red low ssn; CCI. "Friendly & helpful owners." ♦ 1 May-30 Sep. € 17.75   2007*

CARNAC *2G3* (8km NW) **Camping Les Mégalithes, Kerfélicité, 56410 Erdeven [tel/fax 02 97 55 68 76 or 02 97 55 68 09]** Fr Carnac take D781 thro Plouharnel after further 4km; site on L in 500m. Med, hdg/mkd pitch, pt sl, shd; mv service pnt; wc; shwrs inc; el pnts (10A) inc; lndtte; shop high ssn; rest, bar 1km; playgrnd; pool; sand/shgl beach 2km; some statics; dogs €1; quiet. "Nice site with lge pitches but poorly lit; poss diff to manoeuvre lge c'vans; conv for megalithic alignments." 1 May-30 Sep. € 18.00   2005*

The opening dates and prices on this campsite have changed. I'll send a site report form to the editor for the next edition of the guide.

CARNAC *2G3* (8km NW Coastal) **Idéal Camping, Route de la Plage de Kerhilio, Lisveur, 56410 Erdeven [02 97 55 67 66; fax 02 97 55 93 12; contact@camping-l-ideal.com; www.camping-l-ideal.com]** Fr Carnac take D781 to Erdeven, turn L at rndabt. Site 2km on R at hotel/cafe. Sm, hdg pitch, pt shd; wc; chem disp; baby facs; shwrs inc; el pnts (6A) inc; gas; lndtte; rest; ice; shops 500m; tradsmn; rest; snacks; bar; BBQ; playgrnd; htd, covrd pool; sand beach 800m; sailing; fishing; tennis nr; games rm; TV; 90% statics; dogs €4; sep parking area for cars; Eng spkn; no adv bkg; quiet; cc acc; CCI. "Peaceful site nr excel beach & cent of mkt town; gd rest & takeaway." ♦ 1 Apr-30 Oct. € 32.00 (3 persons)   2005*

CARNAC *2G3* (12.5km NW) **Camping Les Sept Saints, 56410 Erdeven [02 97 55 52 65; fax 02 97 55 22 67; info@septsaints.com; www.septsaints.com]** Fr Erdeven on D781 going NW dir Lorient; site on L in 2km. Lge, hdg/mkd pitch, pt sl, pt shd; wc; chem disp; baby facs; shwrs inc; el pnts (10A) inc; gas; lndtte; ice; shop; snacks; bar; BBQ (charcoal/gas); playgrnd; htd pool; paddling pool; waterslide; sand beach 4km; watersports 1.5km; cycle hire; entmnt; internet; games/TV rm; many statics; dogs €5; c'vans over 8m not acc high ssn; adv bkg; quiet; cc acc; red low ssn; CCI. "Lge areas for touring; gd lge pitches; v pleasant site; excursions booked." ♦ 15 May-15 Sep. € 37.50 ABS - B26   2007*

CAROMB see Malaucène *10E2*

CARPENTRAS *10E2* (5km N Rural) **Camping de la Cove le Brégoux, Chemin du Vas, 84810 Aubignan [04 90 62 62 50 or 04 90 67 10 13 (LS); camping-lebregoux@wanadoo.fr; www.camping-lebregoux.fr]** Exit Carpentras on D7 sp Bollène. In Aubignan turn R immed after x-ing bdge, 1st R again in approx 250m at Club de Badminton & foll site sp at fork. Lge, hdg/mkd pitch, hdstg, pt shd; wc; chem disp; mv service pnt; baby facs; shwrs inc; el pnts (6-10A) €3 (poss long lead req); gas 1km; lndtte; ice; shops, rest, bars etc 1km; BBQ; sm playgrnd; pool 5km in ssn; go-karting & golf nrby; entmnt (high ssn); games rm; TV; 2% statics; dogs €1.30; phone; poss v cr; some Eng spkn; adv bkg; poss noisy high ssn; red low ssn; cc acc; CCI. "Populer site in beautiful area; facs need upgrading & stretched when site full; gates clsd 2200-0800; office clsd 1200-1430; poss flooding in heavy rain; prefers stays of 4+ nights; some lge pitches but poss obstructed by lge trees; lge pitches often pre-bkd; poss itinerants; excel walking & cycling nrby." ♦ ltd. 1 Mar-31 Oct. € 9.35   2007*

CARPENTRAS *10E2* (7km N Rural) **Camp Municipal de Roquefiguier, 84190 Beaumes-de-Venise [04 90 62 95 07 or 04 90 62 94 34 (Mairie)]** Leave A7 exit 22, take N7 S then L onto D950 sp Carpentras. At rndabt after Sarrians sp turn L onto D21 to Beaumes-de-Venise. Cross Beaumes & foll site sp. Turn L bef Crédit Agricole to site on R. Med, hdg/mkd pitch, pt sl, terr, pt shd; wc (some cont); chem disp; mv service pnt; shwrs inc; el pnts (6A) €2.30; lndtte; ice; BBQ; pool in vill; wine caves adj; dogs €1.07; phone; no adv bkg; quiet; cc acc; CCI. "Facs clean; steel pegs req for pitches; poss diff access lge o'fits; steep access some pitches; gate clsd 1900-0900, key avail; 5 mins walk to town; gd views; mkd walks & cycle ways; conv for Mt Ventoux, Orange & Avignon." ♦ 1 Mar-10 Nov. € 8.80   2007*

CARPENTRAS *10E2* (7km E Rural) **Camping Le Ventoux, Chemin La Combe, 84380 Mazan [tel/ fax 04 90 69 70 94; info@camping-le-ventoux. com; www.camping-le-ventoux.com]** Take D974 twd Bédoin; after 7km turn R at x-rds on D70 sp Mazan. Site on R in 300m. Sm, mkd pitch, pt shd; wc (some cont); chem disp; mv service pnt; shwrs inc; el pnts (6A) €3.50 (poss rev pol); gas; lndtte; ice; shop (high ssn) & 3km; tradsmn; snacks high ssn; bar; BBQ; playgrnd; pool; lake fishing 4km; some statics; dogs €2.60; phone; poss cr; entmnts; adv bkg (ess high ssn); quiet, poss noise fr farm machinery; cc acc; CCI. "Gd; ltd facs low ssn; friendly staff; wine-tasting area." ♦ ltd 1 Mar-15 Nov. € 18.40   2007*

CARPENTRAS *10E2* (12km E Rural) **Camp Municipal Aéria, Le Portail, 84570 Blauvac [tel/ fax 04 90 61 81 41 (Mairie)]** E fr Carpentras on D942; E of Mazan fork onto D150. Site 100m N of Blauvac vill cent. Sm, mkd pitch, pt shd; wc (some cont); shwrs; el pnts (10A) €2; shop; rest; snacks; bar; playgrnd. "Basic facs on quiet site; gd views; site on hilltop & may be exposed in bad weather; warden calls am & pm." 15 Mar-15 Oct. € 8.00
2006*

CARPENTRAS *10E2* (10km SE Rural) **Camping Font Neuve, Rte de Methamis, 84570 Malemort-du-Comtat [tel/fax 04 90 69 90 00 or 04 90 69 74 86; camping.font-neuve@libertysurf. fr; http://camping.font.neuve.free.fr]** Fr Malemort take Methanis rd D5; as rd starts to rise look for sp on L to site. Med, hdg pitch, terr, pt shd; wc (some cont); chem disp; serviced pitches; baby facs; shwrs inc; el pnts (6A) €3; lndtte; tradsmn; rest; snacks; bar; playgrnd; pool; tennis; entmnt; TV; dogs €1.70; adv bkg req high ssn; quiet. "V friendly, family-run site; gd rest; immac san facs." ♦ 1 May-30 Sep. € 11.50
2006*

CARPENTRAS *10E2* (6km S Urban) **Camp Municipal Coucourelle, Ave René Char, 84210 Pernes-les-Fontaines [04 90 66 45 55 or 04 90 61 31 67 (Mairie); fax 04 90 61 32 46; camping@ville-pernes-les-fontaines.fr; www. ville-pernes-les-fontaines.fr]** Take D938 fr Carpentras to Pernes-les-Fontaines for 6km. Site well sp. Foll sp sports complex, site at rear of sw pool. Sm, hdg/mkd pitch, pt shd; wc; chem disp; mv service pnt; shwrs inc; el pnts (10A) €2.80; gas 1km; lndtte; shops & rests 1km; BBQ; playgrnd; pool, sw & fishing 2.5km; tennis adj; dogs €0.50; Eng spkn; adv bkg (dep req); quiet; cc acc; CCI. "V attractive old town; well-run, pleasant, functional site; some pitches sm & narr; gd clean facs; m'vans can park adj to mv point free when site clsd; gates close 1930; no twin-axle c'vans; free use of adj pool." ♦ 1 Apr-30 Sep. € 10.20   2007*

CARPENTRAS *10E2* (4km SW Rural) **Camp Municipal de Bellerive, 54 Chemin de la Ribière, 84170 Monteux [04 90 66 81 88]** Site on N edge of Monteux cent, sp off ring rd Monteux N, immed after rlwy x-ing. Sm, hdg/mkd pitch, pt shd; some serviced pitches; wc; chem disp; shwrs inc; el pnts (6A) €2; lndry rm; shops 500m; rest, snacks, bar 500m; playgrnd; pool 4km; phone; poss cr; quiet, but poss noise fr park adj (music); CCI. "Excel, gd value site; rec arr early high ssn; warden lives adj; gd security; san facs clean but need refurb; trees a prob for sat TV - choose pitch carefully; park adj gd for children; 5 min walk to vill; gd bus to Avignon & Carpentras; conv wine region; gd for outings to perched vills & Mont Ventoux; Mistral blows early ssn; one of best municipal sites." 1 Apr-31 Oct. € 9.00   2007*

CARPENTRAS *10E2* (11km NW) **Camp Municipal Les Queirades, 84190 Vacqueyras [04 90 65 84 24 (Mairie); fax 04 90 65 83 28; tourisme.vacqueyras@wanadoo.fr; www. vacqueyras.tm.fr]** Site on W of D7 at N end of Vacqueyras, clearly sp. Sm, pt shd, hdg pitch; wc; shwrs inc; el pnts (6-10A) €3; ice; shops 1km; playgrnd; rv sw 3km; tennis adj; Eng spkn; adv bkg; quiet, but some rd noise; CCI. "Clean, popular site; wine caves opp; D7 v fast & busy." 1 Apr-31 Aug. € 9.40   2006*

CARQUEIRANNE see Hyères *10F3*

⊞**CARRY LE ROUET** *10F2* (Coastal) **Camping Lou Souleï, 13620 Carry-le-Rouet [04 42 44 75 75; fax 04 42 44 57 24; lousoulei@wanadoo.fr; www. lousoulei.com]** Fr Martigues take A55 & exit dir Carry-le-Rouet. Site on beach rd. V lge, hdg/mkd pitch, hdstg, pt shd; htd wc; chem disp; serviced pitch; shwrs inc; el pnts (6A) inc; lndtte; shop adj; rest; snacks; bar; playgrnd; htd pool; beach adj; games rm; games area; entmnt; TV rm; 60% statics; dogs; phone; poss cr; Eng spkn; adv bkg; red low ssn. "Gd base for Marseille, Camargue, Aix, etc; red facs low ssn." € 45.00 (4 persons)   2006*

CARSAC AILLAC see Sarlat la Canéda *7C3*

CASSAGNABERE TOURNAS *8F3* (Rural) **Camping Pré Fixe, 31420 Cassagnabère-Tournas [tel/ fax 05 61 98 71 00; camping@instudio4.com; www.instudio4.com/pre-fixe]** Exit A64 at junc 21 onto D635 dir Aurignac. Cont thro vill on D635 sp Cassagnabère for 8km, sp in vill. Sm, hdg/mkd pitch, terr, pt shd; wc (some cont); chem disp; mv disposal; baby facs; shwrs inc; el pnts (6-10A) €2.80-3.40; gas; ice; lndtte; shop 500m; tradsmn; rest; snacks; bar; BBQ; playgrnd; pool; sw 8km; entmnt; TV rm; 10% statics; no dogs; phone; Eng spkn; adv bkg; dep req; quiet; CCI. "V friendly owners; beautiful landscape; gd touring base for Haute-Garonne; excel." ♦ 15 Apr-30 Sep. € 12.80
2005*

France

CASSANIOUZE 7D4 (10km SW Rural) **Camping de Coursavy, 15340 Cassaniouze** [tel/fax 04 71 49 97 70; camping.coursavy@wanadoo.fr; www.campingcoursavy.com] Fr Entraygues (E) foll D107 along Rv Lot dir Conques. 6km after Vieillevie, site on L on rvside. Cont to next rd junc (500m) after site ent to turn & return. Sm, mkd pitch, terr, pt sl, pt shd; wc; chem disp, shwrs inc; el pnts (5A) €2.50; lndtte; ice; shop 2km; tradsmn; rest, snacks, bar 1km; playgrnd; pool; rv sw; fishing; cycle hire; games area; TV rm; dogs €1.50; phone adj; Eng spkn; adv bkg; quiet; red low ssn; CCI. "Excel site in beautiful, unspoilt area; gd touring base; friendly Dutch owners; diff lge m'vans due trees." ♦ 20 Apr-20 Sep. € 17.60   2007*

CASSIS 10F3 (1.5km N Coastal) **Camping Les Cigales, Route de Marseille, 13260 Cassis** [04 42 01 07 34; fax 04 42 01 34 18] App Cassis on D41E, then at 2nd rndabt exit D559 sp Cassis, then turn 1st R sp Les Calanques into Ave de la Marne, site immed on R. Avoid town cent as rds narr. Lge, hgd/mkd pitch, hdstg, pt sl, pt shd; wc (some cont); chem disp; mv service pnt; shwrs inc; el pnts (3A) inc; gas; lndtte; ice; shop; tradsmn; rest; snacks; bar; playgrnd; shgl beach 1.5km; 30% statics; dogs; phone; quiet, but some rd noise; Eng spkn; cc acc; CCI. "Tired san facs end ssn; gd base for Calanques; attractive resort, but steep walk to camp site; poss diff lge o'fits due trees." 15 Mar-15 Nov. € 20.00   2005*

CASTELFRANC 7D3 (9km N Rural) **Camping La Pinède, Le Bourg, 46250 Goujounac** [05 65 36 61 84; camping-goujounac@wanadoo.fr] Fr Gourdon take D673 SW. At Frayssinet-le-Gelet turn L onto D660 for 2.5km. Site on L at ent to vill. Sm, mkd pitch, terr, pt shd; wc; chem disp; shwrs inc; el pnts (20A) €2; lndtte; shop 1km; bar; pool; tennis; quiet. "Attractive vill & site in pine wood; gd rest 1km." 15 Jun-15 Sep. € 14.00   2004*

CASTELFRANC 7D3 (8km E) **FFCC Camping Les Reflets du Quercy, Mas de Bastide, 46150 Crayssac** [05 65 30 00 27; fax 05 65 30 01 43; cplquercy@atciat.com; www.camping-lot.info or www.campeole.com] Take D811 W fr Cahors; 1km after steep winding climb foll camp sp on L sp Luzech for 1km, & R. NB: Do not use D9 to Crayssac. Med, hdstg, pt sl, pt shd; wc; shwrs inc; el pnts; gas; shop; rest; pool; adv bkg; 60% statics; tennis; child entmnt; disco; horseriding; dogs €2.80; quiet; red low ssn. "Beautiful touring area; v pleasant with helpful management." 5 Apr-28 Sep. € 20.30   2007*

CASTELFRANC 7D3 (6km SE Rural) **Camp Municipal de l'Alcade, 46140 Luzech** [05 65 30 72 32 (Mairie); fax 05 65 30 76 80; mairie.luzech@wanadoo.fr; www.ville-luzech.fr] Fr Cahors take D811 NW, turn L onto D8 foll sp to Luzech; cross both bdges in Luzech; site on R in 1km on D8; do not foll camp sp on D88 to Sauzac. Sm, pt shd; wc (cont); sauna; shwrs inc; el pnts (6-10A) €3 (rev pol); shops 1km; bar; playgrnd; dogs €2; some rd noise; red low ssn. "Peaceful site on Rv Lot; rv not suitable for sw, sluice gates of dam upstream liable to be opened, causing rv to rise sharply; warden visits am & pm - arrange for barrier to be open; peaceful site." 1 Jun-30 Sep. € 16.00   2006*

> Before we move on, I'm going to fill in some site report forms and post them off to the editor, otherwise they won't arrive in time for the deadline at the end of September.

CASTELFRANC 7D3 (2km SW Rural) **Camping Base Nautique Floiras, 46140 Anglars-Juillac** [05 65 36 27 39; fax 05 65 21 41 00; info@campingfloiras.com; www.campingfloiras.com] Fr Castelfranc head S on D45; cross rv W on D8; site on W of rd thro Juillac, sp. Or fr W on D811 (formerly D911) turn R at main sq Prayssac sp Mont Cuq. In 2km cross rv at Pont Juillac, turn 1st R & foll sp to site. Sm, pt shd; htd wc; chem disp; mv service pnt; shwrs inc; el pnts (10A) €3 (rev pol); gas; lndtte; ice; shop 3km; tradsmn; rest adj; snacks; sm bar; BBQ; playgrnd; pool 2km; rv sw; cycle & canoe hire; entmnt; TV rm; dogs €1.30; phone adj; poss cr; Eng spkn; adv bkg ess high ssn (bkg fee); quiet but poss youth groups; cc acc; CCI. "Well-kept site on Rv Lot set in vineyards; v lge pitches; no twin-axles; vg, clean san facs; helpful Dutch owner; nr mkts & rests." ♦ 1 Apr-15 Oct. € 16.40   2007*

CASTELJALOUX 7D2 (500m N Urban) **Camp Municipal de la Piscine, Rue du Souvenir Français, Route de Marmande, 47700 Casteljaloux** [05 53 93 54 68; fax 05 53 89 48 07; www.casteljaloux.com] On N side of town on D933 visible fr rd. Sm, pt shd; wc; shwrs inc; el pnts (10A) €2.15; ice; shops 750m; rest; bar; pool adj; rv & lake sw; fishing; rd noise. "Sm park nr; site rather run down (Aug 2007); helpful warden; useful NH." ♦ 1 Apr-11 Nov. € 7.35   2007*

CASTELJALOUX *7D2* (8km SE Rural) **Camping Moulin de Campech, 47160 Villefranche-du-Queyran [05 53 88 72 43; fax 05 53 88 06 52; campech@orange.fr; www.moulindecampech. co.uk]** Fr A62 exit junc 6 (sp Damazan & Aiguillon). Fr toll booth take D8 SW sp Mont-de-Marsan. In 3km turn R in Cap-du-Bosc onto D11 twd Casteljaloux. Site on R in 4km. Or fr Casteljaloux S on D655 then SW on D11 after 1.5km. Site on L after 9.5km. Med, hdg/mkd pitch, pt shd; wc (some cont); chem disp; shwrs inc; el pnts (6A) €3.80; lndtte; sm shop; tradsmn; rest; snacks; bar; BBQ; htd pool; lake fishing; games area; golf nr; guided tours; dogs €2.40; phone; recep 0800-2200; poss cr; British owners; adv bkg; quiet; cc acc; CCI. "Superb, rvside site; interesting & picturesque area; san facs a bit tired end of ssn (2007); diff ent to san facs block poss low ssn only; gd pool; helpful, friendly staff; excel, gd value rest; ideal for nature lovers; excel." 1 Apr-22 Oct. € 21.60 ABS - D16
2007*

CASTELJALOUX *7D2* (2.5km S Rural) **Camping Club de Clarens, Lac de Clarens, Route de Mont-de-Marsan, 47700 Casteljaloux [tel/fax 05 53 93 07 45; location-chalets@cegetel.net; www.castel-chalets.com]** Sp fr D933. Sm, hdg/ mkd pitch, hdstg, pt shd; wc; mv service pnt; shwrs; el pnts (6A) inc; shop, rest nrby; playgrnd; lake sw; fishing; watersports; golf opp; mainly chalets; dogs; Eng spkn; adv bkg; quiet; CCI. "Lakeside pitches in beautiful location; owners making improvements; vg for families & walkers." 1 Apr-30 Nov. € 10.00
2006*

> There aren't many sites open this early in the year. We'd better phone ahead to check that the one we're heading for is actually open.

CASTELLANE *10E3* (1km N Rural) **Camping Le Provencal, Route de Digne, 04120 Castellane [tel/fax 04 92 83 65 50; accueil@camping-provencal.com; www.camping-provencal.com]** Fr N on N85 at foot of Col de Lècques site on R on LH bend. Fr Castellane site on N85 in 1km on L. Med, mkd pitch, pt sl, pt shd; wc; chem disp; baby facs; shwrs inc; el pnts (3-6A) €2-3; lndtte; shop; supmkt 500m; tradsmn; snacks; bar; pool 1.5km; dogs €2; some rd noise; red low ssn. "Gd, clean site; fine scenery, friendly owners; conv Gorges du Verdon." 1 May-15 Sep. € 12.00   2005*

CASTELLANE *10E3* (8km N Rural) **Camping Castillon de Provence (Naturist), La Grande Terre, La Baume, 04120 Castellane [04 92 83 64 24; fax 04 92 83 68 79; info@castillondeprovence.com; www.castillondeprovence.com]** Fr Castellane take D955 at Casino supmkt & after 5km turn L on D402 (up narr mountain rd) site in 7km. NB up access for car & vans only after 1400, down before 1300. Med, pt sl, pt shd; wc (some cont); chem disp (wc); shwrs inc; el pnts (2-6A) €2.20; gas; ice; lndtte; shop; tradsmn; rest; snacks; bar; playgrnd; paddling pool; lake sw, fishing, watersports 2km; TV rm; 20% statics; dogs; phone; poss cr; Eng spkn; adv bkg (dep req); quiet; cc not acc; INF card. "Site 1000m high & cold at night; fantastic mountain views overlooking Lac de Castillon; v lge pitches." ♦ 1 Apr-31 Oct. € 21.00   2004*

CASTELLANE *10E3* (5km SE Rural) **Camping Les Collines de Castellane, Route de Grasse, 04120 Castellane [04 92 83 68 96; fax 04 92 83 75 40; info@rcn-lescollinesdecastellane.fr; www. rcn-campings.fr]** Fr Castellane, take RN85. After 5 km is La Garde, go thro vill & foll sp. Site on R just past this vill. Lge, terr, pt shd; wc; mv service pnt; baby facs; shwrs inc; el pnts inc; gas; lndtte; ice; shop; rest; snacks; bar; playgrnd; pool; lake sw 5km; games area; organised activites inc variety of watersports, rock climbing, paragliding, hiking; entmnt, TV; Eng spkn; adv bkg. "Friendly owners; set on steep hillside with stunning views; peaceful; main site rd v steep; m'vans arr after 1500, dep before 1000; campers arr after 1200, dep bef 1200." ♦ 1 May-15 Sep. € 24.00   2004*

⊞CASTELLANE *10E3* (SW Urban) **Camping Le Frédéric Mistral, Route des Gorges-du-Verdon, 04120 Castellane [04 92 83 62 27]** In town turn onto D952 sp Gorges-du-Verdon, site on L in 100m. Med, mkd pitch, pt shd; htd wc; chem disp; some serviced pitches; shwrs inc; el pnts (6A) €3 (poss earth & polarity probs); gas 200m; shops adj; supmkt nr; rest; bar; snacks; pool 200m; 2% statics; poss cr; adv bkg; quiet; CCI. "Friendly owners; conv town cent; unltd free hot water; gd san facs but poss stretched in ssn; gd base for gorges etc." ♦ € 13.00   2007*

CASTELLANE *10E3* (500m SW Rural) **Camping Notre Dame, Route des Gorges du Verdon, 04120 Castellane [tel/fax 04 92 83 63 02; camping-notredame@wanadoo.fr; www. camping-notredame.com]** N fr Grasse on N85, turn L in Castellane at sq onto D952 to site on R in 500m. Sm, pt shd; wc; chem disp; mv service pnt; shwrs; el pnts (6A) €3.50; gas; ice; lndtte; sm shop; rest 600m; playgrnd; 5% statics; dogs free; phone; poss cr; adv bkg; quiet; red low ssn; CCI. "Immac site early ssn; helpful owners; excel." ♦ ltd. 1 Apr-15 Oct. € 15.00   2007*

CASTELLANE *10E3* (1.5Km SW Rural) **Camping Le Camp du Verdon, Domaine du Verdon, 04120 Castellane [04 92 83 61 29; fax 04 92 83 69 37; contact@camp-du-verdon.com; www.camp-du-verdon.com or www.les-castels.com]** Fr Castellane take D952 SW twd Grand Canyon du Verdon & Moustiers-Ste Marie. After 1.5km turn L into site. (NB To avoid Col de Lèques with hairpins use N202 & D955 fr Barrême instead of N85.) V lge, hdg/mkd pitch; pt shd; wc (some cont); chem disp; mv service pnt; ltd baby facs; shwrs inc; el pnts (6A) inc; gas; lndtte; shop; rest; snacks; bar; BBQ (gas only); playgrnd; 2 pools (1 htd); waterslides; paddling pool; rv fishing adj; canoeing, kayaking, rafting, horseriding nrby; archery; mini-golf; games area; entmnt; wifi internet; games/TV rm; dogs €2.50; poss cr; Eng spkn; poss noisy; cc acc; CCI. Excel site; gd pitches; gd clean facs; many facs high ssn only; quiet, rural walk to town; guided walks to gorge; mkt Wed & Sat am." ♦ 7 May-15 Sep. € 38.00 (3 persons) (CChq acc) ABS - C15   2007*

CASTELLANE *10E3* (2km SW Rural) **Camping de la Colle, Quartier de la Colle, 04120 Castellane [tel/fax 04 92 83 61 57; campinglacolle@tiscali. fr; www.campinglacolle.com]** Leave Castellane on D952 heading W. In 2km, take R fork. Site is on a narr rd, sp. Sm, terr, shd; wc; chem disp; mv service pnt; baby facs; shwrs inc; el pnts (6-10A) €3.90; lndtte; ice; sm shop & 2km; tradsmn; rest; snacks; bar; playgrnd; pool 2km; lake & rv sw 5km; 15% statics; dogs €2.30; phone; adv bkg; quiet; CCI. "Not suitable for v lge c'vans or m'vans; family-run; unspoilt natural setting well above town; dir access to Gorges du Verdon; vg." ♦ 1 Apr-30 Oct. € 16.30   2007*

CASTELLANE *10E3* (8km SW Rural) **FFCC Domaine de Chasteuil-Provence, Route de Moustiers, Chasteuil, 04120 Castellane [04 92 83 61 21; fax 04 92 83 75 62; contact@ chasteuil-provence.com; www.chasteuil-provence.com]** Take D952 W fr Castellane; site by rv on L. Lge, mkd pitch, pt terr, shd; wc; chem disp; shwrs inc; el pnts (10A) inc; gas; lndtte; ice; shop; tradsmn; rest; snacks; bar; playgrnd; htd pool; paddling pool; rv beach; boating; fishing; games area; entmnt high ssn; 10% statics; dogs free; poss cr; adv bkg; quiet; red low ssn; cc acc; CCI. "Excel touring & walking base; beautiful surroundings; more spacious & better located site than some nearer Castellane." 15 May-10 Sep. € 27.20 (3 persons)   2007*

CASTELLANE *10E3* (12km SW Rural) **Camp Municipal de Carajuan, 04120 Rougon [04 92 83 70 94 or 04 92 83 66 32 (Mairie); fax 04 92 83 66 49; camping.carajuan@wanadoo.fr; www.rougon.fr]** S fr Digne on N85 turn R on D952 & foll sps for 16km to rv bank of Gorges du Verdon nr Carajuan bdge; site on L. Med, mkd pitch, pt shd; wc; chem disp; shwrs inc; el pnts (6A) €2.50; lndtte; shop 10km; playgrnd; 10% statics; dogs €1; poss cr; quiet; Eng spkn; CCI. "Natural, unspoilt; basic facs; gd walking; gd." ♦ 1 Apr-30 Sep. € 10.60   2007*

CASTELLANE *10E3* (W Urban) **Camping Les Lavandes, Route des Gorges du Verdon, 04120 Castellane [04 92 83 68 78 or 04 92 78 33 51 (LS); fax 04 92 83 69 92; accueil@camping-les-lavandes.com; www.camping-les-lavandes.com]** Head W on D952 sp Gorges du Verdon to site on R. Med, mkd pitch, pt shd; wc; chem disp; sauna, solarium; baby facs; shwrs €1; el pnts (3-10A) €2.90-3.90; supmkt 500m; playgrnd; entmnt; rv adj; some statics; poss cr; adv bkg; quiet; red low ssn; no cc acc. "Lovely site; sm pitches; beautiful mountain scenery; excel view of Notre Dame du Roc; conv town cent; office open 0900-1000 & 1800-1900, site yourself; poss unkempt low ssn." 1 Apr-15 Oct. € 12.50   2007*

CASTELLANE *10E3* (9km W Rural) **Camp des Gorges du Verdon, Clos d'Aremus, 04120 Castellane [04 92 83 63 64; fax 04 92 83 74 72; aremus@camping-gorgesduverdon.com; www. camping-gorgesduverdon.com]** N85 fr Grasse turn L on D952 in Castellane. Camp in 9km on L. Look for sp Chasteuil on R of rd; camp is 500m further on. Lge, mkd pitch, shd; wc; chem disp; mv service pnt; shwrs inc; el pnts (6A) €4.20; gas; lndtte; ice; sm shop; rest; snacks; bar; playgrnd; htd pool; fishing; boating; canoeing; games area; games rm; entmnt; wifi internet; TV; 10% statics; dogs free; poss cr; Eng spkn; adv bkg ess; red low ssn; CCI. "Some sm pitches; rd along Gorges du Verdon poss diff for lge o'fits; off-rd walk to town; conv town cent." ♦ 28 Apr-16 Sep. € 23.30 (3 persons)   2007*

CASTELLANE *10E3* (2km NW Rural) **FFCC Camping International, Route Napoléon, La Palud, 04120 Castellane [04 92 83 66 67; fax 04 92 83 77 67; info@campinginternational.fr; www.campinginternational.fr]** Site sp fr N85 & D602 Lge, hdg pitch, pt sl, pt shd; wc; chem disp; mv service pnt; serviced pitches; baby facs; shwrs inc; el pnts (6A) €5; gas; lndtte; ice; gd sm supmkt; tradsmn; rest; snacks; bar; playgrnd; pool; lake sw & sand beach 5km; games area; golf; horseriding; entmnt; child entmnt; internet; TV rm; 50% statics; dogs €3; quiet; adv bkg (dep req); Eng spkn; cc acc; red low ssn; CCI. "Friendly, helpful owners; conv Gorges de Verdon; gd walking; dated facs, red low ssn; gd." ♦ 31 Mar-1 Oct. € 21.00 (CChq acc)   2007*

CASTELLANE *10E3* (8km NW Rural) Camping Les Sirènes, Col des Lècques, Route Napoléon, 04120 Castellane [04 92 83 70 56; fax 04 92 83 72 72; accueil@les-sirens.com; www.les-sirenes.com] On N85 8km NW of Castellane. Sm, pt sl, shd; wc; shwrs; el pnts (6A) €3; rest; snacks; bar; BBQ; playgrnd; htd pool; some statics; dogs €1.50; quiet; adv bkg; CCI. "Gd views; scenic walks; conv heritage fossil site." Easter-22 Sep. € 13.50   2007*

CASTELNAU MAGNOAC *8F2* (2km SE Rural) Camping L'Eglantière (Naturist), 65330 Aries-Espénan [05 62 99 83 64 or 05 62 39 88 00; fax 05 62 39 81 44; infos@leglantiere.com; www.leglantiere.com] Fr Castelnau-Magnoac take D929 S sp Lannemezan; in 2.5km L on D9 sp Monléon; in 1km L on unclass rd for 500m; L at T-junc & foll L'Eglantière sp to site; app fr D632 not rec. Lge, hdg/mkd pitch, pt sl, pt shd; wc; chem disp; mv service pnt; serviced pitch; sauna; shwrs inc; el pnts (10A) €4.20 (rev pol); gas; lndtte; ice; shop; tradsmn; rest; snacks; bar; playgrnd; htd pool; paddling pool; rv sw; fishing; canoeing; archery; cycle hire; 15% statics; dogs; adv bkg; Eng spkn; quiet; red low ssn; cc acc; CCI. "Helpful staff; beautiful site on rv; conv Pyrenees; golf courses nrby." ♦ 3 Apr-26 Sep. € 30.00 (CChq acc)
                2005*

CASTELNAUD LA CHAPELLE See Sarlat la Canéda *7C3*

CASTELNAUDARY *8F4* (4km E Rural) FFCC Camping Rural La Domaine de la Capelle (Sabatte), St Papoul, 11400 St Martin-Lalande [04 68 94 91 90; lacapelle1@aol.com; http://la-capelle.site.voila.fr] Fr D6113 (N113), take D103E at rndabt to St Martin-Lalande, foll sp to St Papoul & site in 2km. Sm, pt hdg pitch, pt sl, pt shd; wc; chem disp (wc); mv service pnt; shwrs inc; el pnts (16A) €2; laundry facs; shop 5km; tradsmn; BBQ; playgrnd; no statics; dogs; phone; Eng spkn; quiet; CCI. "Delightful, spacious site; helpful owners; v clean facs, poss stretched when site full; gd walking; abbey at St Papoul; ideal NH for Spain." 1 Apr-30 Sep. € 10.00   2007*

CASTETS *8E1* (1km E Urban) Camp Municipal de Galan, 73 Rue du Stade, 40260 Castets [05 58 89 43 52 or 05 58 89 40 09; fax 05 58 55 00 07; campinglegalan@wanadoo.fr] Site sp N & S of town on N10. Lge, pt sl, shd; wc; hot water & shwrs inc; el pnts (6A) inc; gas; lndtte; shop high ssn & 1km; tradsmn; playgrnd; paddling pool; tennis; few statics; dogs €1.50; bus; adv bkg; quiet but some rd noise; CCI. " Excel, v clean site in nice vill; extra charge for twin-axle; rv walks." ♦ 1 Feb-30 Nov. € 13.60   2005*

CASTIES LABRANDE *8F3* (Rural) Camping Le Casties, Bas de Lebrande, 31430 Casties-Labrande [05 61 90 81 11; fax 05 61 90 81 10; lecasties@wanadoo.fr; www.camping-lecasties.com] S fr Toulouse, exit A64 junc 26 onto D626; after Pouy-de-Touges turn L onto new rd & foll camping sp. Med, hdg pitch, pt shd; wc; chem disp; shwrs inc; el pnts (5A) €1; lndtte; ice; tradsmn; snacks; bar; BBQ; playgrnd; pool; fishing; 10% statics; dogs; phone; Eng spkn; adv bkg; quiet; cc acc; CCI. "In the middle of nowhere!; lge pitches; san facs basic but v clean; staff v friendly & helpful; lovely pool; excel." ♦ ltd. 1 May-30 Sep. € 8.00   2006*

> Did you know you can fill in site report forms on the Club's website — www.caravanclub.co.uk?

CASTILLON LA BATAILLE *7C2* (400m Urban) Camp Municipal La Pelouse, 33350 Castillon-la-Bataille [05 56 40 04 22 or 05 56 40 00 06 (Mairie)] Site in town on N bank of Rv Dordogne; not well sp in town. Sm, shd; wc; shwrs inc; el pnts (15A) inc; shop; rv sw; adv bkg; quiet; CCI. "Conv for wine area; conv St Emillion; clean facs; helpful warden; excel little site; gd NH." 1 May-15 Oct. € 10.00
                2007*

CASTILLONNES *7D3* (300m N Urban) Camp Municipal La Ferrette, Route de Bergerac, 47330 Castillonnès [05 53 36 94 68 or 05 58 36 80 49 (Mairie); fax 05 53 36 88 77; rouquet47@hotmail.fr] On N21, 27km S of Bergerac, on N side of Castillonnès. Easily seen fr main rd. Med, mkd pitch, pt sl, pt shd; wc (cont); el pnts (6A) inc; lndtte; shops 300m; playgrnd; tennis adj; some statics; quiet. "Beautiful situation; interesting town; gd san facs." ♦ 1 Jul-31 Aug. € 11.00   2006*

⊞CASTILLONNES *7D3* (5km NW Rural) Camping Le Bost, Le Bost, 24560 Plaisance [05 53 22 84 98 or 06 75 54 18 44 (mob); camping@lebost.com; www.lebost.com] S fr Bergerac on N21 to Plaisance in 16km; cont thro vill, going up hill, to lane in 500m sp Le Bost; site set back off rd just after sp. Sm, hdstg, pt sl, pt shd; wc; chem disp; shwrs; el pnts (10A) inc; ice; shop 5km; rest, sancks & bar 2km; BBQ; wifi internet; dogs; red long stay. "CL-type site; ideal base for Bergerac wine area; friendly, helpful British owners; gd NH en rte Spain." € 12.00   2007*

CASTRES *8F4* (3km NE Urban) **Camping Gourjade (formerly Municipal), Ave de Roquecourbe, 81100 Castres [tel/fax 05 63 59 33 51; contact@ campingdegourjade.com; www.campingde gourjade.com]** App Castres fr S, after x-ing rv bdge turn NE onto D89 at traff lts sp Rocquecourbe; site after 2km. Well sp. Med, hdg pitch, pt terr, pt shd; wc; chem disp; mv service pnt; shwrs; el pnts (6-10A) €2.50-3.50; gas; lndtte; shop in ssn; rest adj; snacks; bar; BBQ; playgrnd; pool; 9 hole golf course adj; cycling; boat fr site to town; 5% statics; dogs €1; bus; v quiet; cc acc; CCI. "Castres worth visit; lovely site set in beautiful park; big pitches; gd, spotless san facs; gd security; helpful staff, extra charge for twin-axle vans; vg cycling; some lower pitches sl & poss soft; poss groups of workers on site low ssn; walk into town; leisure cent adj; highly rec." ♦ 1 Apr-3 Oct. € 10.50   2007*

⊞**CASTRIES** *10E1* (1.5km NE Rural) **FLOWER Camping Domaine de Fondspierre, 277 Route de Fontmarie, 34160 Castries [04 67 91 20 03; fax 04 67 16 41 48; pcomtat@free.fr; www. campingfondespierre.com]** Fr A9 exit junc 28 dir Castries onto N110; site 1.5km after vill on L. Med, hdg/mkd pitch, hdstg, terr; htd wc; chem disp; mv service pnt; baby facs; shwrs inc; el pnts (10A) inc; gas 5km; lndtte; shops 1.5km; tradsmn; rest, snacks 1.5km; bar; playgrnd; pool; lake sw 5km; tennis adj; golf 2.5km; cycle hire; 20% statics; dogs €3; phone; Eng spkn; quiet; cc acc; red CCI. "Excel touring base; gd walking area; poss itinerants." € 23.00   2007*

CAUDEBEC EN CAUX *3C2* (1km S Rural) **Camping Barre-y-Va, Route de Villequier, 76490 Caudebec-en-Caux [02 35 96 26 38 or 02 35 95 90 10 (Mairie); campingbarreyva@ orange.fr; www.camping-barre-y-va.com]** Fr Caudebec take D81 W twd Villequier & site on R in 1km next to Rv Seine. Med, pt shd; wc (male cont); chem disp; shwrs inc; el pnts (5A) €3.65 (poss rev pol); lndtte; ice; shops 1km; tradsmn; snacks & takeaway; playgrnd; pool 300m; rv fishing & boating adj; cycle hire; games rm; TV; some statics; dogs €2; phone; Eng spkn; some noise fr rd, rv & nrby disco; red CCI. "Interesting area; popular, clean & well-kept site; san block ltd - lights controlled fr outside cubicles & you could be left in the dark!; barrier clsd 2200-0800; recep clsd 1215-1500." 1 Apr-31 Oct. € 13.95   2007*

CAUDEBEC EN CAUX *3C2* (6km S Urban) **Camp Municipal du Parc, Rue Victor Hugo, 76940 La Mailleraye-sur-Seine [02 35 37 12 04; mairie-sg. lamaillerayesurseine@wanadoo.fr]** Fr N on D131/ D490 turn E onto D65. Or fr S on D913. Site sp in cent of town close to rv bank. Sm, hdg pitch, pt sl, pt shd; wc; chem disp; shwrs; el pnts (6A) €3; shop, rest in town; playgrnd; poss cr; quiet. "Site yourself, warden calls; gd walking area; pleasant NH." 1 May-15 Sep. € 6.90   2006*

CAUDECOSTE see Agen *8E3*

CAUNES MINERVOIS *8F4* (1km S Rural) **Camp Municipal Les Courtals, 11160 Caunes-Minervois [04 68 78 07 83 or 04 68 78 00 28 (Mairie); fax 04 68 78 05 78]** Sp fr D620 at stadium & adj rv. Sm, pt shd; wc; shwrs; el pnts (4A) inc; shops adj; playgrnd; pool 6km; games area; rv adj; quiet. "Pleasantly situated site; office opens 1800; gate locked 2100; site self, warden calls; interesting town." 1 Jun-31 Aug. € 12.10   2007*

CAUREL see Mûr de Bretagne *2E3*

CAUSSADE *8E3* (750m NE Urban) **Camp Municipal de la Piboulette, 82300 Caussade [05 63 93 09 07]** S on D820 (N20) fr Cahors (40km), turn L off N20 on ent Caussade onto D17 (Rte de Puylaroque). About 750m turn L (sp), site on R in 100m; lge grass stadium. Med, mkd pitch, pt shd; wc (some cont); chem disp; serviced pitches; shwrs inc; el pnts (3-6A) €1.40-2.80; lndtte; shop 500m; tradsmn; playgrnd; pool on far side of stadium; adv bkg; quiet; CCI. "Spacious pitches; excel san facs; pleasant warden; interesting town; mkt Mon; conv for Gorges de l'Aveyron." ♦ 1 May-30 Sep. € 5.80   2007*

CAUSSADE *8E3* (7km NE Rural) **Camping de Bois Redon, Bonnet, 82240 Septfonds [05 63 64 92 49; info@campingdeboisredon.com; www.camping deboisredon.com]** Exit A20 junc 59 to Caussade, then onto D926 to Septfonds. Site sp to L in vill - lkm. Sm, mkd pitch, pt sl, pt shd; wc; chem disp; baby facs; shwrs inc; el pnts (10A) €3; lndtte; shop; tradsmn; snacks; bar; playgrnd; pool; cycle hire; 10% statics; dogs €1.50; Eng spkn; adv bkg (dep); quiet; CCI. "Refurbished site in ancient oak forest with walks; helpful, enthusiastic owners." ♦ ltd. 1 Apr-1 Oct. € 12.50   2005*

⊞**CAUSSADE** *8E3* (10km NE Rural) **Camping Le Clos de la Lère, Route de Septfonds, 82240 Cayriech [05 63 31 20 41; le-clos-de-la-lere@ wanadoo.fr; www.camping-leclosdelalere. com]** Take D17 fr Caussade. Turn R at junc with D103 (sp Cayriech/Septfonds). In Cayriech will turn R at T-junc by church, site on R. Foll sp only for Camping Le Clos de la Lère. Sm, hdg/mkd pitch, hdstg, pt shd; htd wc; mv service pnt; baby facs; shwrs inc; el pnts (6-10A) €2-3.70; gas; lndtte; shop 4km; tradsmn; snacks; no BBQ; playgrnd; pool; few statics; dogs €1.50; site clsd 20-30 Dec; adv bkg (dep req); quiet; red long stay; cc acc; CCI. "Excel games facs; helpful staff; excel winter site in gd location for touring; ltd facs low ssn; rec arr bef dark." ♦ € 12.00   2007*

CAUSSADE *8E3* (7km S Rural) **Camping de Ferrières (Bergez), 635 Chemin de Ferrières, St Martin-de-Lastours, 82440 Réalville [tel/fax 05 63 31 06 70]** Exit A20 junc 59 onto N20 S to Realville. Cross m'way onto D90 N, site sp in 2.5km. Sm, pt shd; wc; chem disp (wc); shwrs inc; el pnts (10A) €2; Indtte; ice; shop, rest, snacks, bar 3km; dogs €0.50; poss cr; Eng spkn; adv bkg; quiet; CCI. "Gd, basic, CL-type site." ♦ ltd. 15 Apr-15 Oct. € 7.00   2005*

CAUSSADE *8E3* (11km SW) **FFCC Camp Municipal Le Colombier, 82800 Nègrepelisse [05 63 64 20 34; fax 05 63 64 26 24]** Fr A20 exit junc 59 dir Nègrepelisse. Fr Montauban, take D958 to Nègrepelisse, turn L into vill then 1st L after Total/ Citroën g'ge, foll sp to site. Site nr prominent water tower in town. Well sp. Med, mkd pitch, terr, pt shd; wc; mv service pnt; shwrs inc; el pnts (6A) €2.20; supmkt 300m; gas; pool adj; playgrnd; dogs €1.15; quiet. "Pool open school hols - free with 3+ days stay; red long stay." 10 Jun-30 Sep. € 7.00   2007*

CAUSSADE *8E3* (10km NW Rural) **Camp Municipal Le Faillal, 82270 Montpezat-de-Quercy [tel/fax 05 63 02 07 08; montpezat-accueil@wanadoo. fr; www.revea-vacances.fr]** N on N20, turn L onto D20, site clearly sp on R in 2km. (Do not take D38 bef D20 fr S). Med, hdg pitch, pt sl, terr, pt shd; wc; chem disp; shwrs inc; el pnts (6A) €3; Indtte; shops 200m; playgrnd; pool high ssn; few statics; dogs €1.50; phone; adv bkg; quiet; red CCI. "Pretty, well-kept site; gd, clean san facs but poss ltd; v helpful warden; old town a 'must'; rec pay night bef departure; excel." ♦ 31 Mar-28 Oct. € 14.30
                                                                   2007*

⊞**CAUTERETS** *8G2* (500m N Urban) **Camping Les Glères, 19 Route de Pierrefitte, 65110 Cauterets [05 62 92 55 34; fax 05 62 92 03 53; camping-les-gleres@wanadoo.fr; www.gleres.com]** Fr N on N920 ent town; site on R with sharp turn but sp. Narr ent (take care long o'fits). Med, hdg/mkd pitch, hdstg, pt shd; htd wc; chem disp; mv service pnt nr; some serviced pitches; shwrs inc; el pnts (6A) inc; gas; Indtte; rest, snacks, bar, shop, pool 500m; playgrnd; 10% statics; dogs €1.20; phone; site clsd 21 Oct-30 Nov; Eng spkn; quiet; red low ssn; CCI. "Conv town cent; gd walking area with cable car 500m; recep/gate clsd 1230-1500; superb san facs; friendly & helpful; tight access to pitches; municipal m'van site adj; excel." € 17.90   2007*

CAUTERETS *8G2* (1km N Rural) **Camping Le Péguère, Route de Pierrefitte, 65110 Cauterets [tel/fax 05 62 92 52 91; campingpeguere@ wanadoo.fr; www.lescampings.com/peguere]** Fr Lourdes on N21 foll sp for Cauterets. On app Cauterets site on R immed after rv bdge. Med, pt sl, pt shd; wc; mv service pnt; shwrs inc; el pnts (6A) inc; Indtte; ice; tradsmn; snacks; playgrnd; rv fishing adj; entmnt; TV rm; some statics; dogs €0.85; adv bkg; cc acc; CCI. "Clean facs; beautiful setting; ideal base for walking in Pyrenees." ♦ 1 May-30 Sep. € 13.00   2007*

CAUTERETS *8G2* (1.5km N Rural) **Camping Le Cabaliros, Pont de Secours, 65110 Cauterets [tel/fax 05 62 92 55 36; info@camping-cabaliros.com; www.camping-cabaliros.com]** App Cauterests fr Argelès-Gazost on D921/D920, site 1st on R over bdge. Med, pt sl, pt shd wc; chem disp; mv service pnt; shwrs inc; el pnts (3A) €3.15; Indtte; ice; shop 200m; rest; bar; playgrnd; pool 1km; fishing; 10% statics; dogs €0.90; poss cr; adv bkg ess; quiet. "Conv Pyrenees National Park; gd walking." ♦ 1 Jun-30 Sep. € 12.60   2007*

CAVAILLON *10E2* (8km E Rural) **Camp Municipal, 84660 Maubec [04 90 76 50 34; fax 04 90 76 73 14]** Heading E fr Cavaillon on D2, thro vill of Robion, in 400m at end vill sp turn R to Maubec. Site on R in 1km bef old vill. (Avoid any other rte with c'van). Diff access at ent, steep slope. Sm, terr, pt shd; wc (mainly cont); shwrs inc; shops 1km; el pnts (3A) €2.30; Indtte; playgrnd; quiet; secluded; poss cr; 30% statics; CCI. "Awkward site for lge o'fits - otherwise v gd; san facs stretched high ssn; conv A7." 1 Apr-30 Sep. € 14.78   2005*

CAVAILLON *10E2* (10km E Rural) **Camping Les Boudougnes (Guiraud), Les Chênes, Petit-Coustellet, 84580 Oppède [tel/fax 04 90 76 96 10]** Fr N180 in Coustellet, take D2 dir Cavaillon. After 1km turn L onto D3 sp Ménerbes. Site on L in approx 2km just after hamlet of Petit-Coustellet. Take care, hump at ent to lane leading to site; danger of grounding. Sm, pt shd; wc; shwrs inc; el pnts (6A) €1; ice; shop 700m; snacks; playgrnd; adv bkg; CCI. "Pleasant farm site on edge of Luberon National Park; parking among oak trees; levelling blocks req; old facs but spotlessly clean; quiches made to order & fresh fruit fr orchards; close to lavender museum; rec." 10 Apr-1 Oct. € 8.80
                                                                   2007*

CAVAILLON *10E2* (1km S) **Camp Municipal de la Durance, 495 Ave Boscodomini, 84300 Cavaillon [04 90 71 11 78; fax 04 90 71 98 77; camping. cavaillon@wanadoo.fr]** S of Cavaillon, nr Rv Durance. Fr A7 junc 25 foll sp to town cent. In 200m R immed after x-ing rv. Site sp (Municipal Camping) on L. Lge, pt shd; wc; chem disp; shwrs; el pnts (4-10A) €2.40- 6.15; shops 1.5km; snacks; pool 100m; fishing; tennis; TV; some statics; dogs €1.05; poss cr; adv bkg; some noise during early am. "NH only; token for pool at recep." 1 Apr-30 Sep. € 13.20   2006*

⊞**CAVAILLON** *10E2* (7km W Rural) **Camp Municipal St Andiol, 13670 St Andiol [tel/ fax 04 90 95 01 13]** Exit Avignon on N7 & D7n to St Andiol, site on R of D7n past vill. NB No advance warning of site. Sm, hdg pitch, pt shd; wc; shwrs inc; el pnts (6-10A) 3.50-4.50; gas; ice; Indtte; snacks; shop in vill; bar; pool; tennis 1km; golf 15km; dogs €1; some rd noise; CCI. "Facs adequate; unkempt low ssn; NH only." € 13.00
                                                                   2006*

CAVALAIRE SUR MER *10F4* (Urban/Coastal)
Camping La Baie, Blvd Pasteur, 83240 Cavalaire-sur-Mer [04 94 64 08 15 or 04 94 64 08 10; campbaie@club-internet.fr; www.camping-baie.com] Exit A8 sp Ste Maxime/St Tropez & foll D25 & D559 to Cavalaire. Site sp fr seafront. Lge, mkd pitch, pt sl, pt shd; htd wc; baby facs; shwrs inc; el pnts (10A) €4.50; lndtte; ice; shop; rest; snacks; bar; BBQ; playgrnd; htd pool; paddling pool; jacuzzi; sand beach 400m; sailing; watersports; diving 500m; games area; games rm; internet; 10% statics; dogs €3.80; poss cr; Eng spkn; adv bkg; quiet; red low ssn. ♦ 15 Mar-15 Nov. € 38.00 (3 persons)
2006*

CAVALAIRE SUR MER *10F4* (1.5km NE Rural)
Camping/Caravaning Cros de Mouton, Chemin de Cros de Mouton, 83240 Cavalaire-sur-Mer [04 94 64 10 87 or 04 94 05 46 38; fax 04 94 64 10 87; info@crosdemouton.com; www.crosdemouton.com] Exit A8 junc 36 dir Ste Maxime on D125/D25, foll sp on D559 to Cavalaire-sur-Mer. Site sp on coast app fr Grimaud/St Tropez & Le Lavandou; diff access. Lge, mkd pitch, terr, mainly shd; wc; chem disp; mv service pnt; 20% serviced pitches; shwrs inc; el pnts (10A) €4.20; gas; ice; lndtte; shop; rest; snacks; bar; playgrnd; htd pool; paddling pool; sand beach 1.8km; wifi internet; TV; some statics; dogs €2; phone; Eng spkn; adv bkg (ess Jul/Aug book by Jan; bkg fee & dep req); quiet; red low ssn; cc acc; CCI. "Lge indiv pitch; situated in hills behind town; excel, well-run, popular site - rec adv bkg even low ssn." ♦ 15 Mar-4 Nov. € 22.50 (CChq acc) 2007*

CAVALAIRE SUR MER *10F4* (3km NE Coastal)
Sélection Camping, 12 Blvd de la Mer, 83420 La Croix-Valmer [04 94 55 10 30; fax 04 94 55 10 39; camping-selection@wanadoo.fr; www.selection camping.com] Off N559 bet Cavalaire & La Croix-Valmer, 2km past La Croix at rndabt turn R sp Barbigoua, site in 200m. Lge, hdg/mkd pitch, terr, shd; htd wc; chem disp; mv service pnt; baby facs; private bthrms avail; shwrs inc; el pnts (10A) €5; gas; lndtte; shop; tradsmn; rest; snacks; bar; playgrnd; htd pool; paddling pool; sand beach 400m; games area; internet; entmnt; TV rm; 20% statics; dogs (not Jul/Aug) €3.20; phone; bus; poss cr; Eng spkn; adv bkg ess high ssn (dep & bkg fee); quiet. "In excel location; sm pitches; vg san facs; excel pool; vg supmkt." ♦ 15 Mar-15 Oct. € 31.50 (CChq acc)
2007*

CAVALAIRE SUR MER *10F4* (500m SW Coastal)
Camping La Pinède, Chemin des Mannes, 83240 Cavalaire-sur-Mer [04 94 64 11 14; fax 04 94 64 19 25; contact@le-camping-la-pinede.com; www.le-camping-la-pinede.com] Sp on R (N) of N559 on S o'skts of Cavalaire. Lge, mkd pitch, pt sl, shd; wc; shwrs inc; el pnts (5A) €3; shop; gas; ice; lndtte; tradsmn; snacks; playgrnd; sand beach 500m; poss cr; adv bkg ess; quiet but noisy nr rd; red low ssn. "Cavalaire pleasant, lively resort." ♦ 15 Mar-15 Oct. € 21.00 2007*

CAVALAIRE SUR MER *10F4* (1km W Coastal)
Camping Bonporteau, 83240 Cavalaire-sur-Mer [04 94 64 03 24; fax 04 94 64 18 62; contact@ bonporteau.fr; www.camping-bonporteau.com] Sp on S side of N559 Cavalaire-Toulon rd, approx 100m on R after rndabt. Lge, sl, terr, shd; htd wc; shwrs inc; el pnts (10A) €5; gas; ice; lndtte; shop; supmkt 500m; rest; snacks; bar; playgrnd; htd pool; jacuzzi; sand beach 200m; cycle hire; TV; some statics; dogs €4.50; min 1 week's stay Jul/Aug; adv bkg; red low ssn; quiet. 15 Mar-15 Oct. € 28.00 (3 persons) 2006*

CAVALAIRE SUR MER *10F4* (1km W Rural)
Camping La Treille, 83240 Cavalaire-sur-Mer [04 94 64 31 81; fax 04 94 15 40 64; campingdelatreille@wanadoo.fr; www.camping delatreille.com] Fr St Tropez foll promenade into Cavalaire to rndabt. Take Toulon/Lavandou exit, 1 way rd. 50m after passing x-rd sp Pompiers, Camping Pinède, turn R at next junc; phone box on corner. Site on R in 50m. Lge, mkd pitch, terr, pt shd; wc; chem disp; baby facs; shwrs; el pnts (5A) €4; gas; lndtte; shop; supmkt; rest; snacks; bar; BBQ (gas only); playgrnd; pool 2km; sand beach 1.5km; some statics; dogs €2; phone; Eng spkn; adv bkg; poss noisy; red long stay/low ssn; CCI. "Well-run, friendly family site; nr sandy cove & lively town with lots of facs; metal pegs req for awning." ♦ ltd. 15 Mar-15 Oct. € 22.50 2006*

⊞**CAYEUX SUR MER** *3B2* (2km NE Coastal)
Camping Le Bois de Pins, Rue Guillaume-le-Conquérant, Brighton, 80410 Cayeux-sur-Mer [tel/fax 03 22 26 71 04; camping.leboisdepins@ orange.fr] Take D940 out of St Valery to Cayeux, then D102 NE for 2km & foll sp. Lge, mkd pitch, pt shd; htd wc; shwrs; chem disp; mv service pnt; el pnts (6-10A) €3.10-3.87; lndtte; shop; snacks; bar; playgrnd; beach 500m; sailing & fishing adj; cycle hire; mini-golf; horseriding; games rm; entmnt; 50% statics; dogs €1.10; adv bkg. "Gd, clean site." ♦ € 15.90 2007*

See advertisement

CAYEUX SUR MER *3B2* (3km NE Coastal)
Camping Les Galets de la Mollière, Rue Fai-d'Herbe, 80410 La Mollière-d'Aval [tel/fax 03 22 26 61 85] Fr Cayeux-sur-Mer take D102 N along coast for 3km. Site on R. Lge, mkd pitch, pt shd; wc; chem disp; mv service pnt; shwrs inc; el pnts (10A) inc; gas; lndtte; shop; snacks; bar; BBQ; playgrnd; sand beach 500m; games area; games rm; 25% statics; dogs €1.07; phone; adj; quiet; CCI. "Spacious, wooded site with lge pitches; barrier & recep clsd 1230-1500 & 2300-0700; pool & other improvements planned for 2008." 1 Apr-31 Oct. € 20.00 2007*

See advertisement

CAYLAR, LE *10E1* (4km SW Rural) Aire Naturelle Mas de Messier, St Félix de l'Héras, 34520 Le Caylar [tel/fax 04 67 44 52 63] Fr N exit A75 junc 49 onto D9 thro Le Caylar. Turn R sp St Félix & foll sp St Félix de l'Héras. At x-rds in St Félix turn R, site 2.5km on L. Sm, hdg pitch, pt sl, pt shd; wc; chem disp; mv service pnt; shwrs; el pnts (5A) inc; shop 4km; tradsmn; pool; adv bkg; quiet; Eng spkn; CCI. "Friendly & helpful Dutch owner; many; caves, country towns in area; gd walking; excel views; facs fair; adv bkg ess high ssn." ♦ ltd. 15 Apr-15 Oct. € 10.40   2005*

CAYLUS *8E4* (NE Rural) **FFCC Camping La Vallée de la Bonnette**, 82160 Caylus [tel/fax 05 63 65 70 20] In vill by rv. Med, hdg/mkd pitch, pt shd; wc; chem disp; mv service pnt; baby facs; shwrs inc; el pnts (6A) €3.40; lndtte; ice; shop 1km; tradsmn; snacks; BBQ; playgrnd; pool 1km; rv sw & fishing 500m; games area; entmnts; dogs €1.90; Eng spkn; adv bkg (rec high ssn); quiet; red 7 days; CCI. "Nice, tidy site on edge of medieval vill; scenic & historic area; new Dutch owners 2006." ♦ 1 Apr-30 Sep. € 13.50   2006*

CAYRIECH see Caussade *8E3*

CAZALS *7D3* (Rural) **Camp Municipal du Plan d'Eau**, La Cayre, 46250 Cazals [05 65 22 84 45 or 05 65 22 82 84 (Mairie); fax 05 65 22 87 15; mairiecazals@wanadoo.fr] Fr Frayssinet-le-Gélat N on D673 dir Gourdon; site on L immed after ent Cazals. Med, mkd pitch, pt shd; wc; mv service pnt; shwrs; el pnts; lndtte; shops 500m; rest; bar; playgrnd; lake sw; entmnt; some statics; poss cr; quiet. "Basic, clean facs; friendly warden. 1 May-30 Sep.   2006*

CAZOULES see Souillac *7C3*

CELLES SUR BELLE see Melle *7A2*

CELLES SUR PLAINE see Raon l'Etape *6E3*

CELLETTES see Blois *4G2*

This guide relies on site report forms submitted by caravanners like us; we'll do our bit and tell the editor what we think of the campsites we've visited.

CENAC ET ST JULIEN see Sarlat la Canéda *7C3*

CENDRAS see Alés *10E1*

CENEVIERES see Cajarc *7D4*

CERET *8H4* (500m E Urban) **Camp Municipal Bosquet de Nogarède**, Ave d'Espagne, 66400 Céret [04 68 87 26 72] Exit A9 junc 43 onto D115 twd Céret, then foll sp Maureillas D618. Site clearly sp 500m fr cent Céret. Med, mkd pitch, terr, shd; wc; chem disp; mv service pnt; el pnts (6A) €2.80; gas 1km; lndtte; shop 1km; rest; snacks; bar 1km; BBQ; playgrnd; htd, covrd pool 800m; sand beach 27km; 10% statics; dogs; phone; poss cr; some rd noise; CCI. "Céret attractive town with modern art museum; gd san facs; gd NH." ♦ ltd. 1 Apr-30 Oct. € 11.10   2007*

⊞CERET *8H4* (1km E Rural) **Camping Les Cerisiers, Mas de la Toure, 66400 Céret [tel/fax 04 68 87 00 08]** Exit A9 junc 43 onto D115, turn off for cent of Céret. Site is on D618 approx 800m E of Céret twd Maureillas, sp. Tight ascent for lge o'fits. Med, mkd pitch, shd; wc; chem disp; baby facs; fam bthrm; shwrs inc; el pnts (4A) €2.90; gas; lndtte; ice; shop, rest, snacks, bar 1km; playgrnd; pool 600m; lake sw 2km; sand beach 28km; 60% statics; dogs; phone; site clsd Jan; quiet; CCI. "Site in cherry orchard; gd size pitches; facs dated & ltd low ssn; poss seasonal workers & old scrap c'vans; footpath to attractive vill with excel modern art gallery; conv Andorra, Perpignan, Collioure; 1 night stays not allowed." ♦ € 10.80   2006*

CERILLY *4H3* (8km N) **Camping des Ecossais, 03360 Isle-et-Bardais [04 70 66 62 57 or 04 70 67 55 89 (LS); fax 04 70 66 63 99]** Fr Lurcy-Lévis take D978A SW, turn R onto D111 N twd Isle-et-Bardais & foll camp sp. Ent tight. Med, pt sl, pt shd; wc; shwrs inc; el pnts (10A) €2.80; lndtte; playgrnd; rest nr; lake sw; fishing; dogs €0.70; adv bkg; quiet; red low ssn; CCI. "V busy high ssn; ltd facs low ssn; gd cycling; site in oak forest; rec." 1 Apr-30 Sep. € 10.00   2005*

CERILLY *4H3* (11km NW Rural) **Camping de Champ Fossé, 03360 St Bonnet-Tronçais [04 70 06 11 30; fax 04 70 06 15 01]** After 14km on N144 St Amand-Montluçon rd, turn L on D978 sp Forêt de Tronçais; after 8km foll sp to vill of St Bonnet-Tronçais. Med, sl, pt shd; wc (some cont); shwrs inc; el pnts (10A) inc; ice; lndry rm; shops 1km; snacks; playgrnd; sand beach; bathing; boat hire; fishing; walking; dogs €0.80; quiet; adv bkg. "Poor supervision; sl, so blocks req; idyllic location; excel walks; sh walk to vill." 1 Apr-30 Sep. € 10.30   2004*

CERNAY *6F3* (5km N Rural) **Camping Les Sources, Route des Crêtes, 68700 Wattwiller [03 89 75 44 94; fax 03 89 75 71 98; camping. les.sources@wanadoo.fr; www.camping-les-sources.com]** Fr Cernay take D5 NE to Soultz; thro Uffholtz & turn L foll sp to Wattwiller; turn L immed after vill sp & foll camp sp. Park outside bef check-in. Some site rds steep. Lge, mkd pitch, hdstg, terr, pt shd; wc (v steep app to facs - 25% gradient); chem disp; mv service pnt; serviced pitches; baby facs; shwrs inc; el pnts (5A) inc (poss rev pol); gas; lndtte; ice; shop; tradsmn; rest; BBQ (gas/charcoal only); playgrnd; htd, covrd pool; tennis; games rm; games area; badminton; horseriding adj; entmnt; internet; 25% statics; dogs €1.70; recep 0730-1200 & 1300-21.30; barrier pass; Eng spkn; adv bkg ess high ssn (dep req & bkg fee); quiet; cc acc; CCI. "V steep wooded app to site; diff getting on & off some pitches; tractor avail; not suitable lge o'fits; on 'wine rte'; barrier clsd 2200; mkt Tue & Fri Cernay." ♦ 9 Apr-30 Sep. € 25.90   2004*

CERNAY *6F3* (500m S Urban) **FFCC Camping Les Acacias, 16 Rue René Guibert, 68700 Cernay [03 89 75 56 97; fax 03 89 39 72 29; lesacacias. cernay@ffcc.asso.fr; www.camp-in-france.com]** Fr N on N83 by-pass, exit Cernay Est. Turn R into town at traff lts, immed L bef rv bdge, site sp on L; well sp. Lge, mkd pitch, pt shd; wc; mv service pnt; shwrs inc; el pnts (5A) €3.40 (poss rev pol); lndtte; shop, rest, bar & pool (high ssn); entmnt; 25% statics; dogs €1; poss cr; quiet; red long stay; 10% red CCI (pitch only). "Friendly staff; site clean, tidy; dated, clean san facs; €20 dep barrier key; storks nesting over some pitches; sh walk to town." ♦ 1 Apr-10 Oct. € 11.90   2007*

CERNAY *6F3* (6km S Rural) **Camping Les Castors, 4 Route de Guewenheim, 68520 Burnhaupt-le-Haut [03 89 48 78 58; fax 03 89 62 74 68; camping.les.castors@wanadoo.fr]** Exit A36 junc 15 sp Burnhaupt-le-Haut onto N83, then D466 sp Masevaux. Site on R. Med, mkd pitch, pt shd; htd wc; chem disp; baby facs; shwrs inc; el pnts (5-10A) inc; gas; lndtte; ice; tradsmn; rest; bar; BBQ; playgrnd; games rm; 40% statics; dogs €1.20; phone; poss cr; Eng spkn; adv bkg; quiet; CCI. "Conv German & Swiss borders, Black Forest; wine route; Mulhouse motor museum; gd san facs; vg." ♦ 1 Apr-1 Oct. € 16.20   2006*

CESSERAS see Olonzac *8F4*

CEYRAT see Clermont Ferrand *9B1*

CHABANAIS see Rochechouart *7B3*

CHABEUIL see Valence *9C2*

CHABLIS *4F4* (600m W Rural) **Camp Municipal Le Serein, Route des Sept Miraux, 89800 Chablis [03 86 42 44 39; fax 03 86 42 49 71; ot-chablis@ chablis.net; www.chablis.net]** On D965 Tonnerre-Chablis turn L at camping sp bef x-ing Rv Serein. Med, hdg/mkd pitch, shd; wc (some cont); shwrs inc; el pnts (3-5A) €1.80; gas; shops, rest, snacks 1km; playgrnd; rv adj; some statics; no dogs; poss cr; Eng spkn; adv bkg; quiet; CCI. "Vineyards & cellars nrby; facs stretched high ssn; warden calls." ♦ ltd. 1 Jun-20 Sep. € 8.20   2006*

CHAGNY *6H1* (W) **Camp Municipal du Pâquier Fané, Rue du Pâquier Fané, 71150 Chagny [03 85 87 21 42]** Clearly sp in town. Med, hdg pitch, pt shd; wc; chem disp; shwrs; el pnts (6A) €3.60 (rev pol); gas; lndtte; shop; snacks; playgrnd; pool adj; fishing; tennis; dogs €1; adv bkg (Jul/Aug); quiet except rlwy noise adj. "Well laid-out site; poss neglected san facs; gd night lighting; on wine rte; somewhat dictatorial management." ♦ 15 Apr-31 Oct. € 11.40   2005*

CHAGNY *6H1* (6km W Rural) **Camping des Sources, Ave des Sources, 21590 Santenay [03 80 20 66 55; fax 03 80 20 67 36; info@campingsantenay.com; www.campingsantenay.com]** Site sp fr N6 & at D974 (N74) junc, foll sp adverts for Santenay Casino & campsite. Do not drive into Chagny. Med, mkd pitch, pt shd; wc; chem disp; mv service pnt; shwrs inc; el pnts (6A) €3.50 (poss rev pol; long lead poss req); gas; lndtte; shop & 1km; rest; snacks; bar; playgrnd; htd pool adj; tennis adj; 30% statics; dogs €1.30; phone; Eng spkn; adv bkg; cc acc; CCI. "Excel, v popular iste; arr early or bkg rec; no twin-axles; tour ops on site; v clean facs; gates clsd 2200-0730; recep clsd 1100-1400; v helpful owner; vill surrounded by vineyards; lovely walks; wonderful cycle path (Voie Verte)." ♦ 15 Apr-31 Oct. € 19.50 (CChq acc)
2007*

⊞**CHAILLAC** *7A3* (SW Rural) **Camp Municipal Les Vieux Chênes, 36310 Chaillac [02 54 25 61 39; fax 02 54 25 65 41]** Exit N20 S of Argenton-sur-Creuse at junc 20 onto D36 to Chaillac. Thro vill, site 1st L after sq by 'Mairie.' Sm, hdg/mkd pitch, pt sl, pt shd; htd wc (some cont); chem disp; shwrs inc; el pnts (6-16A) €2.50-2.70; lndry rm; BBQ; playgrnd; lake sw adj; waterslide; tennis adj; 35% statics; dogs; phone adj; poss cr; adv bkg; quiet; CCI. "Well-maintained site; beautiful setting with lakes; v clean facs; friendly warden on site; rest within walking dist; conv fr a'route; ideal base for exploring Creuse valley; excel walks. " ♦ € 6.15   2006*

CHAILLES see Blois *4G2*

CHAISE DIEU, LA *9C1* (2km NE Rural) **Camp Municipal Les Prades, 43160 La Chaise-Dieu [04 71 00 07 88; fax 04 71 00 03 43]** Site well sp fr D906. Med, pt sl, shd; wc (some cont); chem disp; shwrs inc; el pnts (10A) €2.80 (long lead poss req); lndtte; shops 2km; playgrnd; lake sw 300m; 10% statics; quiet. "Fair sh stay/NH; tourist info office in vill; 14thC church; vg for mushrooms in ssn!" 1 Jun-30 Sep. € 9.50   2006*

CHALANDRAY *4H1* (Rural) **Camping du Bois de St Hilaire, Rue de la Gare, 86190 Chalandray [tel/fax 05 49 60 20 84 or 01773 873068 (UK); acceuil@camping-st-hilaire.com; www.camping-st-hilaire.com]** Foll N149 bet Parthenay & Vouille; upon ent to Chalandray vill, turn before Spar shop; site 750m on R over rlwy line. Sm, mkd pitch, pt shd; wc; chem disp; shwrs inc; el pnts (10A) €3.10; lndtte; ice; shop; rest, snacks, bar in vill; BBQ; playgrnd; pool; tennis; mini-golf; games rm; TV rm; dogs; bus 750m; c'van storage; adv bkg (25% dep req); cc acc; quiet; CCI. "Friendly, helpful British owners; situated in mature forest area, sh walk fr vill; 20 mins fr Futuroscope; lge pitches; excel, clean site & pool." ♦ 16 Apr-20 Sep. € 14.50 2005*

CHALARD, LE see St Yrieix la Perche *7B3*

⊞**CHALLANS** *2H4* (3km S Rural) **FFCC Camping Le Ragis, Chemin de la Fradinière, 85300 Challans. [tel/fax 02 51 68 08 49; info@camping-leragis.com; www.camping-leragis.com]** Fr Challans go S on D32 Rte Les Sables, turn R onto Chemin de la Fradinière & foll sp. Med, hdg/mkd pitch, pt sl, pt shd; wc; chem disp (wc); baby facs; shwrs inc; el pnts (6A) €2; gas; lndtte; shop; tradsmn, rest, snacks high ssn; bar 3km; playgrnd; htd pool; waterslide; sand beach 12km; mini-golf; games area; entmnt; TV; 60% statics; dogs €2; phone; Eng spkn; adv bkg (dep req); quiet. "Vg." ♦ € 18.00   2007*

CHALLES LES EAUX see Chambéry *9B3*

CHALON SUR SAONE *6H1* (2km E Urban) **Camping du Pont de Bourgogne, Rue Leneveu, 71380 St Marcel [03 85 48 26 86 or 03 85 94 16 90 (LS); fax 03 85 48 50 63; campingchalon71@wanadoo.fr; www.camping-chalon.com]** Fr A6 exit junc 26 (sp Chalon Sud); foll sp Chalon-sur-Saône; at 1st rndabt go strt over (sp Louhans & St Marcel); strt over next rndabt; take 4th exit on next rndabt (sp Roseraie & St Nicolas) - do NOT cross the bdge; foll sp for Camping, turning R at Les Chavannes & turn R at traff lts. Site in 500m. Med, hdg/mkd pitch, hdstg, terr, pt shd; htd wc; chem disp; mv service pnt; shwrs inc; el pnts (6A) inc; gas; lndtte; shop; hypmkt nr; tradsmn; rest; snacks; bar; BBQ; playgrnd; pool 500m; rv fishing; cycle hire; wifi internet; game/TV rm; 20% statics; dogs €2.20; some noise fr rd & rv pathway; CCI. "Charming site by rv; v lge pitches & some by rv; v friendly staff; one san facs block excel, others v basic; ltd facs low ssn; nice rest/bar; rv walks; vg." ♦ 29 Mar-30 Sep. € 18.90 ABS - L17   2007*

CHALON SUR SAONE *6H1* (12km SE Rural) **Mini-Camping Les Tantes, 29 Route de Gigny, 71240 Marnay [03 85 44 23 88]** On D978 SE fr Chalon-sur-Saône, turn R in vill of Ouroux-sur-Saône onto D6 twd Marnay. Over bdge, foll site sp. Sm, hdg pitch, shd; wc; chem disp; el pnts; lndtte; tradsmn; BBQ; sm playgrnd; 50% statics; dogs; phone; quiet. ♦ 1 May-31 Oct. € 10.00   2006*

CHALONNES SUR LOIRE *2G4* (1km E Rural) **Camping Le Candais, Route de Rochefort, 49290 Chalonnes-sur-Loire [02 41 78 02 27 or 04 99 57 20 25; fax 04 99 57 21 22; candais@village-center.com; www.village-center.com/candais]** Turn E in Chalonnes to D751. Site on L in 1km on S bank of Loire. Lge, mkd pitch, hdstg, pt shd; wc; shwrs inc; mv service pnt; el pnts (10A) inc; gas 1km; lndtte; ice; shop adj; snacks; bar; BBQ; playgrnd; pool; fishing; cycle hire; games area; entmnt; TV rm; 2% statics; dogs €3; Eng spkn; adv bkg; quiet; CCI. "Peaceful rvside site in beautiful location; liable to flooding; lge pitches; gd touring base." ♦ 16 Jun-2 Sep. € 12.00   2007*

France

CHALONNES SUR LOIRE 2G4 (8km SE Rural) Camp Municipal Les Pâtisseaux, Route de Chalonnes, 49290 Chaudefonds-sur-Layon [02 41 78 04 10 (Mairie); fax 02 41 78 66 89; mairie.chaudefondsurlayon@wanadoo.fr] Fr Chalonnes on D961 S dir Cholet. Turn L onto D125. At narr rlwy bdge after 3km, foll sp to site on Rv Layon. Sm, mkd pitch, pt shd; wc; shwrs €1; el pnts €2.50; shop, bar 500m; quiet. "V basic, clean site nr rv; lots of interest in area." ♦ 1 May-31 Aug. € 5.50   2006*

As soon as we get home I'm going to post all these site report forms to the editor for inclusion in next year's guide. I don't want to miss the September deadline.

CHALONNES SUR LOIRE 2G4 (9km SE Urban) Camp Municipal du Layon, Rue Jean de Pontoise, 49190 St Aubin-de-Luigné [02 41 78 33 28 (Mairie); fax 02 41 78 68 55; mairie-sg.staubin@wanadoo.fr] Exit N160 Angers-Chemillé at sp St Aubin or turn S off D751 at sp St Aubin. Site sp in vill. Sm, hdg/mkd pitch, pt shd; wc; mv service pnt in adj car pk with access to facs; shwrs inc; el pnts €4.90; shop 150m; playgrnd; rv adj; quiet. "Warden calls - if not pay at Mairie nrby; public footpath thro site; gd walking/wine-tasting area; boats for hire on rv high ssn." ♦ 1 May-30 Sep. € 6.70   2006*

CHALONNES SUR LOIRE 2G4 (9km NW) Camping La Promenade, Quai des Mariniers, 49570 Montjean-sur-Loire [02 41 39 02 68; fax 02 40 83 16 19; efberthelot@wanadoo.fr; www. camping.montjean.net] Exit Angers on N23 twd Nantes. Exit 1km beyond St Germain-des-Prés dir Montjean-sur-Loire. Cross rv then R on D210 to site in 500m. Med, pt shd; wc (some cont); shwrs inc; el pnts (6-9A) €2.60; gas 5km; lndtte; shops adj; rest; snacks; BBQ; playgrnd; pool; sand beach 600m; entmnt; TV; 30% statics; dogs €1.05; Eng spkn; adv bkg; quiet; CCI. "Friendly, young owners; interesting sculptures in vill & at Ecomusée." 1 Apr-7 Oct. € 11.40   2007*

CHALONS EN CHAMPAGNE 5D1 (3km S Urban) Camp Municipal, Rue de Plaisance, 51000 Châlons-en-Champagne [tel/fax 03 26 68 38 00; camping.mairie.chalons@wanadoo.fr; www. chalons-en-champagne.net] Fr N on A26 exit junc 17 take D3 to Châlons, site sp. Fr S exit junc 18 onto D5 & foll sp. Fr N44 S of Châlons sp St Memmie; foll site sp. D977 fr N into Châlons, cont on main rd to traff lts at 6 x-rds & turn R, site well sp. Or exit A4 junc 27 onto N44; turn R at St Memmie; site sp. NB some sps in area still show old town name 'Châlons-sur-Marne'. Med, hdg/mkd pitch, some hdstg (pebbled), pt shd; htd wc; chem disp; mv service pnt; shwrs inc; el pnts (10A) €3.20 (poss long lead req) gas; lndtte; ice; shop 100m; hypmkt 1km; tradsmn; snacks; bar; BBQ; playgrnd; pool 2km; sm lake; TV rm; dogs; bus; c'van cleaning area; poss cr; little Eng spkn; adv bkg; quiet but poss noisy high ssn; cc acc; CCI. "V popular, v clean, tidy site adj park; generous pitches; gd, clean san facs, but stretched if site busy; gd disabled shwr; helpful & efficient management; recep clsd 1200-1315; rec arr early or phone ahead; check barrier arrangements if need early departure; 4.30m height limit at bdge on app to site; gates shut 2130 low ssn & 2300 high ssn; lovely, interesting town; "petit train touristique" daily fr site; excel NH." ♦ 1 Apr-31 Oct. € 17.60   2007*

CHALUS 7B3 (12km S Rural) FFCC Camping Le Périgord Vert, Fardoux, 24450 La Coquille [05 53 52 85 77; fax 05 53 55 14 25; celinelddf@ aol.com] On N21 Périgueux/Châlus rd bet Thiviers & Châlus, turn L in vill of La Coquille at traff lts foll sps for Mialet. In 1.5km turn R, site 500m on L; sp. Sm, pt shd, pt sl; wc; chem disp; mv service pnt; shwrs inc; el pnts (6A) €2; gas; lndtte; shops 2km; tradsmn; rest, snacks, bar high ssn; playgrnd; pool high ssn; free fishing; tennis; 5% statics; dogs; phone; poss cr; Eng spkn; adv bkg; quiet; red low ssn; CCI. "Nice, clean, happy site; helpful staff; choice of meadow or woodland pitch; ltd facs low ssn." ♦ 15 Apr-1 Nov. € 9.00   2006*

⊞**CHALUS** 7B3 (9km NW Rural) Camping Parc Verger, Le Poteau, 87150 Champagnac-la-Rivière [05 55 01 22 83 or 06 72 35 86 88 (mob); info@parcverger.com; www.parcverger.com] N fr Châlus on D901, turn L at sp Champagnac-la-Rivière, site on L in 150m. Sm, hdg/mkd pitch, hdstg, pt shd; htd wc; chem disp; mv service pnt; serviced pitches; shwrs inc; el pnts (16A) €2; gas 1km; lndtte; shop 1km; tradsmn; rest, snacks & bar 1km; BBQ; pool; lake sw & sand beach 10km; dogs; bus 150m; Eng spkn; adv bkg (dep req); quiet; CCI. "Friendly, helpful British owners; lge pitches suitable for RVs; walk/cycle path adj (old rwly track); vg." € 14.00   2006*

CHAMBERY 9B3 (5km E Urban) **Camp Municipal Le Savoy, Parc des Loisirs, Chemin des Fleurs, 73190 Challes-les-Eaux [tel/fax 04 79 72 97 31; camping73challes-les-eaux@wanadoo.fr]** On o'skts of town app fr Chambéry on D306 (N6). Pass airfield, lake & tennis courts on L, L at traff Its just before cent of Challes-les Eaux sp Parc de Loisirs, at Hôtel Les Neiges de France foll camp sp to site in 100m. Fr A41 exit junc 20, foll sp Challes-les-Eaux, then 'Centre Ville', then D306 (N6) N. Med, mkd pitch, hdstg, shd; wc; chem disp; serviced pitches; shwrs; el pnts (6-10A) €2.50-5.05; gas; lndtte; ice; shop, rest adj; snacks in ssn; lake sw, fishing, tennis adj; dogs €0.90; adv bkg; quiet but some rd noise; cc acc. "Well-run, clean site in beautiful setting; friendly, helpful staff; recep clsd 1200-1400; excel walking." 1 May-30 Sep. € 10.55   2006*

CHAMBERY 9B3 (10km SW Rural) **Camping Les Peupliers, Lac d'Aiguebelette, 73610 Lépin-le-Lac [04 79 36 00 48; fax 04 79 44 12 48; info@camping-lespeupliers.net; www.camping-lespeupliers.net]** Exit A43 junc 12 & foll sp Lac d'Aiguebelette (D921). Turn L at rndabt & foll rd on L of lake. Site on R after sm vill. Lge, hdg/mkd pitch, pt shd; wc; chem disp; shwrs inc; el pnts (6A) €3.10; lndtte; shop 3km; tradsmn; rest 3km; snacks; bar; playgrnd; lake sw adj; fishing; dogs €1; poss cr; quiet; cc acc; CCI. "Friendly, helpful owner; beautiful setting, espec lakeside pitches." 1 Apr-31 Oct. € 11.20   2006*

CHAMBERY 9B3 (11km SW Rural) **Camping Le Curtelet, 73610 Lépin-le-Lac [tel/fax 04 79 44 11 22; lecurtelet@wanadoo.fr; www.camping-le-curtelet.com]** Fr A43 E to Chambéry exit junc 12 onto D921 bef Tunnel L'Epine sp Lac d'Aiguebelette. Foll rd round lake, turn L on D921D to Lépin-le-Lac. Site sp after stn on L over level x-ing. Med, mkd pitch, pt sl, pt shd; wc; chem disp; baby facs; shwrs inc; el pnts (2-6A) €2.30-3; lndtte; ice; shop 1km; tradsmn; bar; BBQ; playgrnd; lake sw; sand beach adj; dogs €1.40; Eng spkn; adv bkg; some rlwy noise; red low ssn; CCI. "Beautiful scenery; well-maintained site; poss some rlwy noise at top of site; public beach adj poss scruffy low ssn; poss v quiet low ssn; high rec." 15 May-30 Sep. € 12.00   2007*

CHAMBERY 9B3 (12km W Rural) **Camping Le Sougey, 73610 St Alban-de-Montbel [04 79 36 01 44; fax 04 79 44 19 01; info@camping-sougey.com; www.camping-sougey.com]** Fr A43 E to Chambéry take D921 sp Lac d'Aiguebelette. On W side of lake 3km to site on L. Med, hdg/mkd pitch, some hdstg, pt sl, pt shd; wc; chem disp; 30% serviced pitches; baby facs; shwrs inc; el pnts (6A) inc; gas; lndtte; ice; shop; rest; snacks; bar; playgrnd; lake sw & fishing adj; tennis; horseriding; cycle hire; mini-golf; archery; entmnts; TV; 20% statics; dogs €1.60; Eng spkn; adv bkg rec high ssn; quiet; red low ssn; cc acc. "Attractive area; spacious site; helpful staff." ♦ 1 May-10 Sep. € 19.00   2006*

CHAMBON SUR LIGNON, LE see Tence 9C2

CHAMONIX MONT BLANC 9B4 (2km NE Rural) **Camping Les Rosières, 74400 Chamonix [04 50 53 10 42 or 06 07 44 79 95 (mob); fax 04 50 53 29 55; info@campinglesrosieres.com; www.campinglesrosieres.com]** Fr W on N205 past Mont Blanc tunnel & Chamonix, L 300m bef boundary sp 'Les Praz de Chamonix'. Foll sp Les Rosières. Fr N by N506 turn R 300m after boundary sp to Les Rosières. Thro vill, 1st L after garden cent. Med, shd; htd wc (some cont); baby facs; shwrs inc; el pnts (5-10A) €3.30; gas; lndtte; ice; sm shop adj; supmkt 1.5km; snacks; bar; htd pool 2km; cable cars, rlwy, sports cent nr; some statics; dogs; bus fr ent; phone adj; poss cr; Eng spkn; adv bkg; quiet; red low ssn; CCI. "Gd location with rvside path to town; spectacular views; poor san facs - poss cold shwrs (Jul 2007); all attractions within walking dist; phone ahead to check if open low ssn; gd." ♦ 1 Jun-10 Sep. € 19.40   2007*

CHAMONIX MONT BLANC 9B4 (3.5km NE Rural) **Camping Les Drus, Les Bois, 74400 Les Praz-de-Chamonix [04 50 53 49 20 or 04 50 53 16 59 (LS)]** NE foll by-pass & sps for Argentière & N Suisse. App off Les Praz at x-rds turn R foll sps. SW fr Argentière foll sps for Chamonix. Camp sp at Les Tines vill, level x-ing. Med, unshd; htd wc; shwrs inc; el pnts (3-5A) €2.20-2.70; gas; ice; shop; pool 3km; poss cr; Eng spkn; quiet. "Beautiful views; friendly welcome; helpful owners; san facs basic but clean; gd walking; unreliable opening dates, phone ahead low ssn; gd value; gd for families." 27 May-18 Sep. € 10.80   2005*

CHAMONIX MONT BLANC 9B4 (7km NE Rural) **Camping Le Glacier d'Argentière, Les Chosalets, 74400 Chamonix [04 50 54 17 36; fax 04 50 54 03 73]** On Chamonix-Argentière rd bef Argentière take R fork twd Argentière cable car stn. Site immed on R. Med, pt sl, pt shd; wc; chem disp; shwrs inc; el pnts (2-6A) €2.40-3.60; lndtte; ice; shops 1km; tradsmn; BBQ; dogs; phone adj; poss cr; adv bkg; quiet; CCI. "Alpine excursions; cable cars adj; v beautiful area, mountain views; friendly, helpful owners." ♦ 14 May-30 Sep. € 14.00   2005*

CHAMONIX MONT BLANC 9B4 (1km SW Rural) **Camping Iles des Barrats, 185 Chemin de l'Ile des Barrats, 74400 Chamonix [tel/fax 04 50 53 51 44]** Fr Mont Blanc tunnel take 1st L on app Chamonix, foll sp to hospital, site opp hospital. Do not go into town. Sm, mkd pitch, pt sl, unshd; wc; chem disp; mv service pnt; shwrs inc; el pnts (5-10A) €3.30-4.30; gas; lndtte; shops 1km; sw 250m; €1; poss cr; Eng spkn; adv bkg (dep req); quiet; CCI. "Great little site; immac site with superb mountain views; clean facs; friendly, family owners; 10 mins level walk to town; 10 mins cable car Mont Blanc." 15 May-29 Sep. € 20.20   2007*

France

CHAMONIX MONT BLANC 9B4 (3km SW Rural) Camping Les Ecureuils, Rue Chemin des Deux, Les Bossons, 74400 Chamonix [tel/fax 04 50 53 83 11; roghis@wanadoo.fr] Fr St Gervais on N205 twd Chamonix. L fork to vill. L at x-rd. Under rlwy, sharp R. Site at end of rd. Sm, pt shd, mkd pitch, hdstg; wc; shwrs inc; el pnts (6A) inc; lndtte; shop 3km tradsmn; poss cr; quiet; adv bkg; cc acc; CCI. "Warm welcome; many old c'vans on site; vg." 1 Apr-30 Sep. € 13.90   2004*

CHAMONIX MONT BLANC 9B4 (3.5km SW) Camping Les Cimes, 28 Route des Tissières, Les Bossons, 74400 Chamonix [04 50 53 19 00 or 04 50 53 58 93; infos@ campinglescimesmontblanc.com; www.camping lescimesmontblanc.com] Exit Mont Blanc tunnel foll sps Geneva turn L on N506 (Chamonix-Geneva rd), in 2km turn R for Les Bossons & L under bdge. Fr Sallanches foll sps Chamonix & Mont Blanc tunnel. On dual c/way turn R at sp `Les Bossons' & site after Novotel adj to Les Deux Glaciers site. Med, pt sl, pt shd; wc (cont); shwrs inc; el pnts (3A) €2.50; lndtte; shop 4km; tradsmn; rest 500m; snacks; BBQ; playgrnd; dogs; poss cr; adv bkg; rd noise; CCI. "Fair site; poss diff lge o'fits." 1 Jun-30 Sep. € 13.80   2005*

CHAMONIX MONT BLANC 9B4 (3.5km SW Rural) Camping Les Deux Glaciers, 80 Route des Tissières, Les Bossons, 74400 Chamonix [04 50 53 15 84; fax 04 50 55 90 81; glaciers@ clubinternet.fr] Exit Mont Blanc tunnel foll sps Geneva turn L on N506 (Chamonix-Geneva rd), in 2km turn R for Les Bossons & L under bdge. Fr W foll sps Chamonix & Mont Blanc tunnel. On dual c/way turn R at sp `Les Bossons' & site after Novotel; adj Les Cimes site; site clearly sp from N205. Med, terr, pt shd; htd wc; chem disp; shwrs inc; el pnts (2-10A) €2.50-6.90; shop; lndry rm; rest; snacks; bar; sm shop; tradsmn; playgrnd; pool 4km; Eng spkn; quiet but some rd noise; site clsd 16/11- 14/12; CCI. "Diff site for lge o'fits over 6m; old but v clean facs; pleasant site just under Mont Blanc; funicular adj to Mer de Glace; rec arr early high ssn; gd." ♦ € 12.80   2007*

CHAMPAGNAC LA RIVIERE see Chalus 7B3

CHAMPAGNAT (SAONE ET LOIRE) see Cuiseaux 9A2

CHAMPAGNE SUR LOUE see Mouchard 6H2

CHAMPAGNOLE 6H2 (1km NW Urban) Camp Municipal de Boyse, Rue Georges Vallerey, 39300 Champagnole [03 84 52 00 32; fax 03 84 52 01 16; boyse@free.fr] Turn W onto D5, N of town off main rd to Dijon (N5). Look for sp. Site adj to sw pool. Lge, mkd pitch, pt sl, pt shd; wc (cont); chem disp; shwrs inc; el pnts (5A) inc; lndtte; shops 5km; tradsmn; rest; snacks; bar; sw pools adj; dogs; quiet; adv bkg; phone; free hot water; early arrival rec; barrier card €23; no admissions 1200-1400; cc acc; CCI. "Friendly warden; poss ltd facs low ssn; vg rest." ♦ 1 Jun-30 Sep. € 15.80   2004*

CHAMPANGES see Thonon les Bains 9A3

⊞**CHAMPDOR** 9A3 (Rural) Camp Municipal Le Vieux Moulin, 01110 Champdor [04 74 36 01 72 or 04 74 36 01 79] Exit junc 8 on A404 & foll sp for St-Martin-du-Frêne. At ent to St-Martin-du-Frêne turn R onto D31 twd Brénod. After 10km turn R onto D21. Site 7km on R on o'skts of Champdor. Med, mkd pitch, some hdstg, unshd; wc; chem disp; mv service pnt; shwrs; €0.90; el pnts (4-16A) €1.50; gas; lndry rm; shop, snacks, bar 1km; playgrnd; rv sw & fishing nrby; 20% statics; phone; quiet; CCI. "Modern san facs; gd walks adj; height restricted - 5m." ♦ € 8.70   2004*

CHAMPFROMIER 9A3 (Rural) Camp Municipal Les Géorennes, 01410 Champfromier [04 50 56 92 40 (Mairie); fax 04 50 56 96 05; marire.champfromier@wanadoo.fr] Fr Bellegarde foll D1084 (N84) twds Nantua. In 8km turn sharp R onto D14 sp Pont-des-Pierres/Mont-Rond. Site sp R on ent vill of Champfromier. Sm, terr, pt shd; wc; shwrs; el pnts (16A) €2; shop 500m; playgrnd; fishing; quiet; CCI. "Gd walking & scenery; site yourself, warden calls; excel." ♦ 1 Jun-15 Sep. € 11.00   2007*

CHAMPIGNY SUR MARNE see Paris 3D3

CHAMPS ROMAIN see Nontron 7B3

CHANAC *9D1* (500m S Urban) **Camp Municipal La Vignogue, 48230 Chanac [tel/fax 04 66 48 24 09 or 06 82 93 60 68 (mob)]** Exit A75 junc 39 onto N88 to Chanac; site well sp in vill. Sm, mkd pitch, pt sl, pt shd; htd wc (some cont); chem disp; shwrs inc; el pnts (6A) inc; lndtte; ice; shops, rest, bar 500m; BBQ; pool adj; dogs €1; Eng spkn; adv bkg; quiet. "Excel." ♦ ltd. 16 Apr-30 Sep. € 11.00   2006*

CHANAS see St Rambert d'Albon *9C2*

CHANCEAUX *6G1* (12km SE) **Camp Municipal, Rue de la Foire aux Vaches, 21440 St Seine-l'Abbaye [03 80 35 00 09 or 03 80 35 01 64 (Mairie]** On N71 in vill of St Seine-l'Abbaye, turn N onto D16. Turn R uphill, sp camping & turn R thro gateway in high stone wall. Narr streets in vill. Or fr N on D974 (N74), avoiding Dijon, turn R onto D959 at Til-Châtel, then D6 & D901 Moloy/Lamargelle. Turn L in Lamargelle onto D16 St Seine-l'Abbaye. Turn L uphill at edge of vill & as above (avoids narr streets). Sm, pt sl, unshd; wc (cont); chem disp; shwrs inc; el pnts (10A) €2.50 (rev pol); shops 500m; pool 4km; rv 500m; dogs; v quiet; CCI. "V pleasantly situated site; conv for Dijon or as NH; fees collected at 2000 hrs; basic but immac facs; excel." 1 May-30 Sep. € 8.40   2006*

CHANCEAUX *6G1* (NW Urban) **Camp Municipal, 21440 Chanceaux [03 80 35 06 59 or 03 80 35 02 66 (Mairie)]** Heading SE fr Troyes twd Dijon site on L on N71 on NW o'skts of Chanceaux. Sm, pt shd; wc (some cont); chem disp (wc); shwrs €1; el pnts (4-5A) €2; shop nr; BBQ; games area; quiet tho some rd noise; cc acc; CCI. "Site yourself - warden calls pm; poss itinerants; no security; gd NH." 15 Apr-30 Sep. € 7.00   2005*

CHANTEMERLE LES BLES see Tain l'Hermitage *9C2*

> The opening dates and prices on this campsite have changed. I'll send a site report form to the editor for the next edition of the guide.

CHANTILLAC see Montlieu la Garde *7C2*

⊞**CHANTILLY** *3D3* (5km W) **Camping L'Abbatiale, 39 Rue Salvador Allendé, 60340 St Leu-d'Esserent [tel/fax 03 44 56 38 76; camping-de-l-abbatiale@wanadoo.fr; http://pagesperso-orange.fr/camping.l-abbatiale]** S twds Paris on A1 exit Senlis; cont W fr Senlis on D44 thro Chantilly x-ing Rv Oise to St Leu-d'Esserent; leave St Leu on D12 NW to Cramoisy; foll site sps; avoid rv x-ing on D17 fr SW; v narr bdge. Lge, pt shd; htd wc; shwrs €1; el pnts (3A) €2; lndtte; shop; playgrnd; some statics; dogs €0.50; red long stay. "Chantilly & chateau interesting." € 10.00   2006*

CHANTILLY *3D3* (5km NW Rural) **Camping Campix, 60340 St Leu d'Esserent [03 44 56 08 48; fax 03 44 56 28 75; campix@orange.fr; www.campingcampix.com]** Exit A1 junc 8 to Senlis; cont W fr Senlis on D44 thro Chantilly, x-ing Rv Oise to St Leu-d'Esserent; leave town on D12 NW twd Cramoisy thro housing est; foll site sp for 1km, winding app. Med, mkd pitch, hdstg, terr, shd; htd wc; chem disp; mv service pnt; baby facs; shwrs inc; el pnts (6A) €3.50 (min 25m cable poss req); gas; lndtte; tradsmn; rest & shops 500m; pizza delivery; BBQ; playgrnd; pool complex; sand beach & lake sw 1km; fishing; games rm; some statics; dogs €2; phone; Eng spkn; adv bkg (dep req); quiet; red long stay/low ssn; cc acc; CCI. "Site in former quarry; helpful owner & friendly staff; excel san facs; wide variety of pitches; some pitches narr access & overhanging trees; conv Paris Parc Astérix & Disneyland (Astérix tickets fr recep); sh walk to vill; rec." ♦ 7 Mar-30 Nov. € 16.50 (CChq acc)
      2007*

See advertisement

CHANTONNAY *2H4* (12km NE Rural) **Camping La Baudonnière, Monsireigne, 85110 Chantonnay [02 51 66 43 79; tom.bannigan@wanadoo.fr; www.la-baudonniere.com]** Fr Chantonnay take D960 NE dir St Prouant & Pouzauges. In St Prouant take D23 to Monsireigne. In 1.1km L onto D113; in 400m L onto Rue des Salinières. Site on L in 800m. Sm, pt sl, pt shd; wc; chem disp; shwrs inc; el pnts (10A) inc; shops, rest, snacks, bar 3km; BBQ; pool, tennis 2km; lake 5km; adv bkg; quiet. "V relaxing, CL-type site; friendly Irish owners; site being developed 2006/7; vg." Apr-Sep. € 15.00   2006*

CHANTONNAY *2H4* (4km S Rural) **Camping Les Asphodèles, Le Moulin Neuf, 85110 Chantonnay [02 51 94 30 27; fax 02 51 94 57 76]** Sp as 'Le Moulin Neuf' on D137. App rd winding & narr. Sm, terr, pt shd; wc (cont); shwrs inc; el pnts inc; shop 4km; tradsmn; snacks; playgrnd; pool; lake sw; tennis; quiet. "Logis Hotel adj; excel value; not rec low ssn if site empty - v isolated." 15 May-30 Sep.
      2005*

CHANTONNAY *2H4* (7km NW Rural) **Camp Municipal La Rivière, 25 Rue du Stade, 85110 Ste Cécile [02 51 40 24 07; fax 02 51 40 25 59; mairiestececile85@wanadoo.fr]** Fr Chantonnay NW on D137; in St Vincent-Sterlanges turn onto D39 to Ste Cécile (2.5km); site sp clearly fr main rd. Sm, hdg/mkd pitch, pt shd; wc; shwrs inc; el pnts (10A) €2.50; ice; lndtte; playgrnd; pool; paddling pool; rv fishing adj; tennis; statics; adv bkg rec high ssn; quiet. "Part of larger complex of holiday bungalows; some facs dated & poor." 1 Jun-30 Sep. € 9.00
      2006*

CHAPELLE AUX FILTZMEENS, LA see Combourg *2E4*

France

CHAPELLE D'ANGILLON, LA *4G3* (1 km SE) Camp Municipal Les Murailles, Route d'Henrichemont, 18380 La Chapelle-d'Angillon [02 48 73 40 12 (Mairie); fax 02 48 73 48 67] Fr Bourges or Aubigny-sur-Nère on D940, turn E onto D926; turn onto D12 in vill, site on R, sp. Sm, pt sl, pt shd; wc (some cont); chem disp (wc); shwrs inc; el pnts (6A) €3.20; gas, shop, rest, & bar 1km; BBQ; playgrnd; lake fishing adj; some statics; dogs; cc acc; CCI. "Lake adj with huge castle overlooking; v quiet; facs dated but adequate; site yourself, warden calls; vg." ♦ ltd. 25 Jun-17 Sep. € 7.15
2006*

Before we move on, I'm going to fill in some site report forms and post them off to the editor, otherwise they won't arrive in time for the deadline at the end of September.

CHAPELLE EN VERCORS, LA *9C3* (1km Rural) Camp Municipal Les Bruyères, Ave Bruyères, 26420 La Chapelle-en-Vercors [04 75 48 20 12; fax 04 78 48 10 44] Take D518 N fr Die over Col de Rousset. Fr N on A49 exit 8 to N532 St Nazaire-en-Royans, then D76 thro St Thomas-en-Royans, then D216 to St Laurent-en-Royans. Take D2 round E flank of Combe Laval (2 short 2-lane tunnels). Fr Col de la Machine foll D76 S 1km, then D199 E over Col de Carri to La Chapelle. (D531 fr Villard de Lons, D76 over Combe Laval & D518 Grandes Goulet not suitable for c'vans & diff lge m'vans due narr rds & tunnels & 5km of overhanging ledges.) Med, pt sl, pt shd; wc; chem disp; shwrs inc; el pnts; lndtte; shops adj; rest, snacks, bar 200m; playgrnd; pool 2km; fishing; climbing; horseriding; cycling; TV; adv bkg; quiet; CCI. "Excel base for beautiful Vercors plateau." ♦ 1 May-1 Oct. € 12.00
2004*

CHAPELLE EN VERCORS, LA *9C3* (6.5km N Rural) Camping La Porte St Martin, 26420 St Martin-en-Vercors [04 75 45 51 10; infos@camping-laportestmartin.com; www.camping-laportestmartin.com] Sp 200m N of vill on D103. (D531 fr Villard-de-Lans W not rec for c'vans.) Med, mkd pitch, pt terr, pt shd; wc; shwrs inc; el pnts (6-10A) €2.80; lndtte; shops, rest, snacks & bar 500m; pool; paddling pool; some statics; dogs €2; phone; Eng spkn; quiet; red low ssn; CCI. "Superb mountain views fr most pitches; excel walking." ♦ 1 May-24 Sep. € 13.50
2006*

CHAPELLE EN VERCORS, LA *9C3* (2km E Rural) Camping Les Myrtilles, Les Chaberts, 26420 La Chapelle-en-Vercors [tel/fax 04 75 48 20 89; camping.des.myrtilles@wanadoo.fr] Fr A49/E713 exit 8 to N532 St Nazaire-en-Royans, then D76 thro St Thomas-en-Royans, then D216 to St Laurent-en-Royans. Take D2 around E flank of Combe Laval (2 short 2-lane tunnels). Fr Col de la Machine foll D76 S 1km, then D199 E over Col de Carri to La Chapelle. Fr S fr Die, foll D518 over Col de Rousset. (D76 over Combe Laval, D531 fr Villard-de-Lans & D518 fr Pont-en-Royans over Grandes Goulet not suitable for c'vans.) Med, pt sl, pt shd; wc; chem disp; shwrs inc; el pnts (5A) €2.65; lndtte; shop 1km; snacks; bar; playgrnd; htd pool; rv fishing 2km; 20% statics; dogs €1.30; adv bkg; v quiet; CCI. "Beautiful setting; excel walking, caves & gorges; gates locked 2200-0700." ♦ 1 May-15 Sep. € 12.20
2005*

CHAPELLE HERMIER, LA *2H4* (4km SW Rural) Camping Le Pin Parasol, Châteaulong, 85220 La Chapelle-Hermier [02 51 34 64 72; fax 02 51 34 64 62; campingpinparasol@free.fr; http://campingpinparasol.free.fr] Exit A83 junc 4 onto D763/D937 dir La Roche-sur-Yon. Turn R onto D948 & at Aizenay turn R onto D6 twd St Gilles Croix-de-Vie; after 10km turn L onto D21; in La Chapelle-Hermier foll D42 twds L'Aiguillon-sur-Vie; site sp in 4km. Lge, hdg/mkd pitch, pt sl, terr, unshd; wc; chem disp; mv service pnt; baby facs; shwrs inc; el pnts (10A) inc; gas; lndtte; ice; shop; tradsmn; rest 500m nr lake; snacks; bar; BBQ; playgrnd; 2 pools (1 htd); paddling pool; waterslide; sand beach 12km; lake sw, boating, fishing, canoeing 200m; cycle hire; archery; fitnss rm; games area; entmnt; wifi internet; games/TV rm; 70% statics; dogs €4; poss v cr; Eng spkn; adv bkg; quiet; CCI. "Excel staff & facs; lge pitches; lovely pools; away fr crowds but close to beaches; pleasant walks & cycle tracks around lake; many British tourers." ♦ 25 Apr-25 Sep. € 29.50 ABS - A36
2007*

CHAPELLE TAILLEFERT, LA see Guéret *7A4*

CHARETTE VARENNES *6H1* (500m N Rural) Aire Naturelle Municipale La Jeanette, 5 Rue de la Chapelle, 71270 Charette-Varennes [tel/fax 03 85 76 23 58; mairiecharettevarennes@wanadoo.fr] Exit N73 by bdge at Navilly onto D996. In 3km, turn L onto D73 to Charette-Varennes. Site sp in vill by rv. Sm, pt sl, pt shd; wc (one cont); chem disp (wc); shwrs inc; el pnts (16A) inc; lndry rm; shop 10km; BBQ; dogs €0.80; phone; quiet. "Peaceful CL-type site adj rv; poss problem with flooding in wet weather low ssn." 1 Jun-1 Sep. € 8.75
2006*

CHARITE SUR LOIRE, LA *4G4* (500m W Urban) FFCC Camp Municipal La Saulaie, Quai de la Saulaie, 58400 La Charité-sur-Loire [03 86 70 00 83 or 03 86 70 16 12; fax 03 86 70 32 00; contact@lacharitesurloiretourisme.com] Fr old N7 (Montargis-Nevers) turn W over bdge sp Bourges; take 2nd R bef next bdge. Fr Bourges on N151, turn L immed after x-ing 1st bridge over Rv Loire. Foll sp. NB Take care when turn R over narr rv bdge when leaving site - v high kerb. Med, mkd pitch, pt shd; wc; chem disp; shwrs inc; el pnts (10A) inc; lndtte; ice; shop 500m; tradsmn; snacks; playgrnd & pool adj inc; rv beach & sw adj; sandy rv banks; no twin-axles; cc not acc; CCI. "Rivside site; gd, well-maintained, modern facs, ltd low ssn; gd security; rv views some pitches; helpful staff; sh walk into picturesque old town; low ssn phone to check open." ◆ 15 Apr-30 Sep. € 13.10   2007*

CHARLEVAL see Cadenet *10E3*

CHARLEVILLE MEZIERES *5C1* (500m N Urban) Camp Municipal Mont Olympe, Rue des Pâquis, 08000 Charleville-Mézières [03 24 33 23 60 or 03 24 32 44 80; fax 03 24 33 37 76; camping-charlevillemeziers@wandadoo.fr] Fr N43/E44 head for Hôtel de Ville, with Hôtel de Ville on R, cont N along Ave des Arches, turn R at 'Gare' sp & cont ahead & cross rv bdge. Turn sharp L immed along Rue des Pâquis, site on L in 500m, visible fr rd. Well sp from city centre. Med, hdg/mkd pitch, hdstg, pt shd; htd wc (some cont); chem disp; mv service pnt; all serviced pitches; baby facs; fam bthrm; shwrs inc; el pnts (10A) €3.60; gas; lndtte; ice; shops 500m over suspension bdge; tradsmn; bar; playgrnd; htd covrd pool adj; fishing & boating; TV; some statics; dogs €1.60; poss cr; Eng spkn; quiet; cc acc; CCI. "Next to Rv Meuse; well-kept; excel san facs; vg site." 1 Apr-15 Oct. € 12.10
                    2007*

CHARLEVILLE MEZIERES *5C1* (12km N Urban) Camp Municipal au Port à Diseur, Rue A Combain, 08800 Monthermé [03 24 53 01 21; fax 03 24 53 01 15] Leave Charleville N on N43 turn R sp Nouzonville. Turn on D988 sp Monthermé (D989). In town cross rv bdge, stay on D989 thro town, site 300m on R after supmkt on L. Med, pt sl, pt shd; wc (some cont); chem disp (wc); shwrs inc; el pnts (4-10A) €2.50-3.70; gas 100m; lndtte; ice; shop 100m; rest, snacks, bar 1km; few statics; dogs; phone; poss cr; quiet but some rd noise; CCI. "Pleasant, rvside site; popular with fishermen & canoeists; random pitching; san facs OK; conv location." Easter-28 Aug. € 7.80   2006*

⊞**CHARLEVILLE MEZIERES** *5C1* (12km NE Rural) Camping Departemental d'Haulmé, 08800 Haulmé [03 24 32 81 61; fax 03 24 32 37 66] Fr Charleville, take N43 & turn R at sp to Nouzonville. Turn onto D988, D989 to Monthermé. In town turn R over bdge onto D31. In 5km turn R sp Haulmé, site in 1.5km. Lge, pt shd; wc (cont); shwrs inc; el pnts (10A) inc; gas; ice; tradsmn; rv sw; fishing; tennis; cycle hire; dogs €0.90; poss cr; adv bkg; fairly quiet; cc acc. "Vg; excel for fishing; top end of site noisy due to semi-perm tents for youths; rec pitch mid-site as lower site is adj public park; v wet pitches in rain; vg, modern san facs; sh walk to town cent." ◆ € 11.30   2005*

CHARLIEU *9A1* (Urban) FFCC Camp Municipal de Charlieu, Rue Roittier, 42190 Charlieu [04 77 69 01 70; fax 04 77 69 07 28; camp-charlieu@voila.fr] N fr Roanne on D482 to Pouilly-sous-Charlieu, then E on D487 to Charlieu town cent. site sp in town, by sw pool. NB Do not confuse with Camp Municipal Pouilly-sous-Charlieu which is sp fr main rd. Med, hdg/mkd pitch, pt shd; wc; chem disp; mv service pnt; shwrs inc; el pnts (10A) €4.70; gas; lndtte; ice; shops 1km; snacks; bar; playgrnd; pool adj; sports area; fishing, boating adj; entmnt; 40% statics; poss cr; Eng spkn; adv bkg; CCI. "Gd clean san facs block; ent to adj pool & tennis inc; facs poss stretched high ssn, excel low ssn; vg value." ◆ 1 May-30 Sep. € 10.50   2006*

CHARLIEU *9A1* (4km W Urban) Camp Municipal Les Ilots, Rue de Marcigny, 42720 Pouilly-sous-Charlieu [04 77 60 80 67; fax 04 77 60 79 44; mairie.pouilly-sous-charlieu42@wanadoo.fr] N fr Roanne on D482 sp Poiuilly-sous-Charlieu. Site sp on ring rd 1km N of town, turn E into stadium. Med, mkd pitch, pt shd; wc (cont); mv service pnt; shwrs €1; el pnts (6A) €1.90; gas; lndtte; shops 1km; rest, bar 500m; playgrnd; pool; fishing; games area; 30% statics; poss cr; Eng spkn; quiet; cc not acc. "Lge pitches grouped in circles." 1 May-15 Sep. € 5.10   2005*

CHARLY SUR MARNE *3D4* (S Urban) Camp Municipal Les Illettes, Route de Pavant, 02310 Charly-sur-Marne [03 28 82 12 11 or 03 23 82 00 32 (Mairie); fax 03 23 82 13 99] Exit A4 junc 18 onto N3 dir La Ferté; then take D402/D969 NE to Charly. Site sp in town. Sm, hdg pitch, pt shd; wc; chem disp; shwrs inc; el pnts (5-10A) inc; lndry rm; ice; supmkt adj; quiet; red long stay. "Excel clean site; well-ordered; pleasant warden; conv town cent." ◆ 1 Apr-1 Oct. € 11.25
                    2007*

France

Route Napoleón F-04290 VOLONNE
★★★★
Sunêlia L'Hippocampe
Phone: +33 (0)4.92.33.50.00
Fax: +33 (0)4.92.33.50.49
www.l-hippocampe.com
camping@l-hippocampe.com

In the heart of the Alps of Haute Provence. Near the VERDON and LUBERON PARKS. Unimpeded view onto the lake, in the shade of olive and cherry trees. A site well known for the quality and diversity of its entertainment activities.
Mobile homes and bungalows to let. Open from March 22th till September 30th

CHARMES 6E2 (500m NE Rural) Camp Municipal Les Iles, 20 Rue de l'Ecluse, 88130 Charmes [tel/fax 03 29 38 87 71 or 03 29 38 85 85; andre. michel@tiscali.fr] Exit N57 for Charmes, site well sp on Rv Moselle. Do not confuse with sp for 'Camping Cars'. Med, mkd pitch, pt shd; wc; chem disp (wc); shwrs inc; el pnts (10A) €3; gas; lndtte; ice; shop 300m; tradsmn; rest; snacks; bar; BBQ; playgrnd; fishing; mini-golf; kayak hire; dogs; phone; Eng spkn; adv bkg; quiet; red after 1 night; CCI. "Gd sh stay/NH; pleasant spot." 15 Apr-30 Sep. € 7.90
2005*

CHARMES SUR L'HERBASSE see Romans sur Isère 9C2

CHARNY 4F3 (500m N Rural) FFCC Camping des Platanes, 41 Route de la Mothe, 89120 Charny [tel/fax 03 86 91 83 60; campingdesplatanes@wanadoo.fr; www.campingdesplatanes.com] Exit A6 junc 18 onto D943 to Montargis. Turn S onto D950 dir Charny, site sp. Sm, hdg/mkd pitch, pt shd; htd wc; chem disp; mv service pnt; serviced pitch; shwrs inc; el pnts (10A) €3.50; gas; lndtte; shop 500m; tradsmn; snacks; BBQ; playgrnd; pool; rv fishing 150m; tennis 500m; cycle hire; TV rm; 20% statics; dogs €1; adv bkg; quiet; red low ssn/long stay; CCI. "Pleasant site; gd sized pitches; friendly, helpful owner; excel, clean san facs; short walk to vill; gd walking; gd touring base." ♦ 15 Mar-31 Oct. € 12.50 (CChq acc)   2007*

CHARNY-SUR-MEUSE see Verdun 5D1

CHAROLLES 9A2 (500m E Rural) Camp Municipal, Route de Viry, 71120 Charolles [03 85 24 04 90; fax 03 85 24 08 20; o.t.charolles@wanadoo.fr] Exit N79 at E end of by-pass (Mâcon); sharp R bottom hill bef town; ent town & site on L. Med, hdg/mkd pitch, hdstg, pt shd; wc; chem disp; shwrs inc; el pnts (6A) €1.50; lndtte; shops 300m; rest; snacks; bar; playgrnd; pool adj high ssn (proper sw trunks req); dogs €0.50; adv bkg rec; quiet, but some rd noise; CCI. "Clean, well-maintained site; helpful warden; sm pitches; facs ltd & downstairs under office - but being refurbed (2007); conv Rte des Vins; easy walk to lovely town; nice pool adj; m'van area outside site; gd value; excel." 1 Apr-5 Oct. € 8.00   2007*

CHARRIN see Decize 4H4

CHARTRE SUR LE LOIR, LA 4F2 (500m W Rural) FFCC Camping du Vieux Moulin, Chemin des Bergivaux, 72340 La Chartre-sur-le Loir [02 43 44 41 18 or 02 43 38 16 16 (Mairie); fax 02 43 44 41 18; camping@lachartre.com; www.lachartre.com/campinglachartre.htm] Sp fr D305 in town. Med, hdg/mkd pitch, pt shd; htd wc (some cont); chem disp; mv service pnt; baby facs; fam bthrm; shwrs inc; el pnts (5-10A) €4-5 (poss rev pol); gas 500m; lndtte; ice; sm shop & 500m; tradsmn; snacks; bar; BBQ; playgrnd; htd pool; rv fishing adj; cycle hire; entmnt; TV; 10% statics; dogs €1; poss cr; Eng spkn; adv bkg rec high ssn; red low ssn & CCI. "Beautiful, quiet rvside site; well-kept; gd pitches; helpful, friendly staff; facs gd but stretched high ssn; excel pool; gd for dogs; v lge m'vans acc; gd base for chateaux, forest & Loir Valley; canoes on rv; conv for town & supmkt; gd." ♦ 1 Apr-30 Sep. € 11.00   2007*

CHARTRES 4E2 (1km SE Urban) FFCC Camping Les Bords de l'Eure, 9 Rue de Launay, 28000 Chartres [tel/fax 02 37 28 79 43; camping-roussel-chartres@wanadoo.fr; www.auxbords deleure.com] Exit N123 ringrd at D935, R at T-junc dir Chartres; then R at 2nd traff lts dir Chartres immed after rlwy bdge; site on L in 400m; inside of ring rd. Also sp fr town cent on N154 fr N, foll sp town cent under 2 rlwy bdges, L at traff lts sp Orléans, after 1km site sp. Fr SE on N154 cross ringrd, foll site sp; site on L. Med,some hdg/mkd pitch, pt shd; htd wc (some cont); chem disp; mv service pnt; baby facs; shwrs inc; el pnts (3-10A) €3 (poss rev pol); lndry rm; ice; shop; tradsmn; BBQ; shop in ssn; supmkt 1km; playgrnd; fishing; some statics; dogs €1; poss cr; Eng spkn; adv bkg; quiet; cc acc; CCI. "Spacious, well laid-out, well-maintained, busy site; friendly, helpful staff; facs refurbished (2007), poss stretched high ssn; no water taps except in toilet block; some pitches diff lge o'fits; office shut 1200-1500 low ssn; gates clsd 2200-0800; poss itinerants & long-stay workers; excel walk along rv to Chartres." ♦ 10 Apr-15 Nov. € 10.80   2007*

⊞ Site open all year   278   *Send in your site reports*

CHARTRES *4E2* (9km S Rural) **Camp Municipal, 28630 Morancez [02 37 30 02 80 or 02 37 28 49 71 (Mairie); mairie.morancez@ wanadoo.fr]** S on Chartres by-pass (N123) take exit D935; L at T-junc twd Morancez; R on D114/ Base de Loisirs at S end of vill (abrupt turn); cross bdge; after 200m turn R onto track, site at end of lake 300m. Travelling N on N10 turn R onto D114 sp Morancez. Strt over at x-rds, site down narr track. Sm, hdg/mkd pitch, shd; wc (some cont); chem disp (wc); shwrs inc; el pnts (6A) €2.75 (poss rev pol); shops 2km; playgrnd adj; fishing adj; 20% statics; adv bkg; quiet but some rd noise; CCl. "V nice, peaceful site; surrounded by woods, lakes & rvs; friendly, helpful warden; san facs could be improved; site locked 2200-0700; poss itinerants; excel NH." 1 Jun-30 Aug. € 8.65   2007*

CHASSENEUIL DU POITOU see Jaunay Clan *4H1*

CHASSENEUIL SUR BONNIEURE *7B3* (Urban) **Camp Municipal Les Charmilles, Rue des Ecoles, 16260 Chasseneuil-sur-Bonnieure [05 45 39 55 36; jctelemaque@free.fr]** On N141 Angoulême-Limoges leave by-pass sp Chasseneuil. In town turn L onto D27 sp Mémorial de la Résistance. Turn R at camping sp, site ahead. Med, hdg/mkd pitch, pt shd; wc; chem disp; shwrs inc; el pnts (6A) €2; lndtte; gas 200m; shop; supmkt 100m; rest, snacks, bar 50m; playgrnd; htd, covrd pool adj; dogs; quiet. "Warden calls pm or key fr Office de Tourisme; diff to ent/leave site without key to bollard; gd san facs." ♦ ltd. Easter-1 Nov. € 6.10   2006*

⊞**CHASSENEUIL SUR BONNIEURE** *7B3* (9km E Rural) **Camping Le Paradis, Mareuil, 16270 Mazières [tel/fax 05 45 84 92 06; information@ campingleparadis.fr; www.campingleparadis. co.uk]** Fr Limoges W on N141 twd Angoulême, turn L at La Péruse or Roumazières-Loubert or Fontafie to Mazières, site sp in 7km. Well sp. Sm, hdg/mkd pitch, hdstg, pt shd; htd wc; chem disp; mv service pnt; baby facs; fam bthrm; shwrs inc; el pnts (4-16A) €4-7; gas 3km; lndtte; ice; shop; tradsmn; rest, snacks & bar 3km; BBQ (gas sep area); playgrnd; tennis; watersports nrby; lake sw, sand shore & fishing 5km; games area; internet; 20% statics; dogs €2; phone; bus 1km; Eng spkn; adv bkg; quiet; CCl. "Clean, tranquil site; gd sized pitches; vg, immac san facs; welcoming British owners, v helpful & friendly; Futuroscope nrby; gd touring base; adv bkg rec lge o'fits; excel." ♦ ltd. € 11.50   2007*

CHATAIGNERAIE, LA *2H4* (5km E Rural) **Camping La Viollière, 85120 Breuil-Barret [02 51 87 44 82; familywoodman@aol.com; www. caravancampingsites.co.uk/france/85/violliere. htm]** Take D949 E dir Poitiers thro La Châtaigneraie for 5km. Cont thro Breuil-Barret & site 2nd R after rlwy bdge. Sm, pt sl, pt shd; wc; chem disp; shwrs inc; el pnts €3 (poss long lead req); shop 2km; supmkt 6km; rest, bar 2km; tradsmn; htd, covrd pool 8km; Eng spkn; adv bkg; quiet. "V peaceful & relaxing site; 6 spacious pitches & 4 el pnts only; excel CL-type site with facs; helpful British owners." Apr-Oct. € 11.00   2006*

CHATEAU ARNOUX *10E3* (3km NE Rural) **Camping Sunêlia L'Hippocampe, Route Napoléon, 04290 Volonne [04 92 33 50 00; fax 04 92 33 50 49; camping@l-hippocampe.com; www.l-hippocampe.com]** Exit A51 junc 21 onto N85 12km S of Sisteron twd Volonne vill over rv. Turn R on D4 on ent vill & foll camp sp 1km. Lge, hdg/mkd pitch, hdstg, pt shd; wc; chem disp; mv service pnt; child/baby facs; serviced pitches; shwrs inc; el pnts (10A) inc (poss rev pol); lndtte; ice; shop; tradsmn; rest; bar; BBQ (elec/gas); playgrnd; 2 pools (1 htd); fishing; canoeing; rafting; tennis; cycle hire; games rm; entmnt; internet; TV rm; some statics; dogs €4; Eng spkn; adv bkg; quiet but poss noisy nr recep; red low ssn/long stay; cc acc; red low ssn; CCl. "Excel, busy, well-run site; spacious, well-screened pitches; various pitch sizes/prices; some pitches poss diff due trees; recep open 0700-2000." ♦ 22 Mar-30 Sep. € 39.00 (CChq acc)   2007*

See advertisement

CHATEAU ARNOUX *10E3* (10km SW Rural) **FFCC Camping Les Cigales, Chemin de la Digue-du-Bevon, 04310 Peyruis [tel/fax 04 92 68 16 04; lescigales@mageos.com]** Site sp fr N96. Sm, hdg pitch, terr, pt shd; wc; chem disp; shwrs inc; el pnts (6A) €3.80; lndtte; ice; shop; snacks; bar; BBQ; playgrnd; pool & sports complex nr (tickets fr site recep); entmnt; 5% statics; dogs €1; adv bkg; quiet; 10% red CCl. "Pretty 'garden' site; excel, modern, well-maintained; immac san facs; friendly, helpful manager; interesting old town 15 mins walk; highly rec." ♦ 1 Apr-30 Sep. € 11.55   2004*

CHATEAU CHINON *4H4* (1km S Urban) **Camp Municipal du Gargouillat, Rue de Pertuy d'Oiseau, 58120 Château-Chinon [03 86 85 08 17; fax 03 86 85 01 00]** Sp fr D978 rndabt at E end town. Med, hdg/mkd pitches, sl, pt shd; wc (some cont); shwrs inc; el pnts (10A) inc; shops, rest, bar 1km; tradsmn; poss cr; quiet. "Facs ltd low ssn; poss itinerants; conv Morvan National Park; levelling blocks rec; gd NH." 1 May-30 Sep. € 10.00   2005*

CHATEAU D'OLONNE see Sables d'Olonne, Les *7A1*

CHATEAU DU LOIR *4G1* (6km E Rural) **Camping Le Lac des Varennes, St Lézin, 72340 Marçon [02 43 44 13 72; fax 02 43 44 54 31; camping. des.varennes.marcon@wanadoo.fr; www.ville-marcon.fr]** S on N138 fr Château-du-Loir dir Vendôme for 3km. Turn L onto D305 sp Marçon. In vill turn L onto D61 over bdge. Site on R by lake. NB Sat mkt in Château du Loir makes rec rte v diff. Lge, hdg/mkd pitch, hdstg, pt shd; htd wc (some cont); chem disp; mv service pnt; baby facs; shwrs inc; el pnts (6A) inc (poss rev pol); lndtte; shop high ssn; tradsmn; rest, snacks & bar high ssn; BBQ; playgrnd; lake sw & sand beach adj; boat hire; watersports; tennis; cycle hire; horseriding; mini-golf; cycle hire; entmnt; 15% statics; dogs €1.80; Eng spkn; adv bkg rec; quiet; cc acc; red low ssn; CCI. "Pretty site in lovely situation with lake views; v friendly; gd walks; use of 'loisirs' adj inc in price; gd security; gd rest in vill; gd value." ♦ 21 Mar-11 Nov. € 14.50 2007*

CHATEAU GONTIER *4F1* (1km N Urban) **Camping Le Parc, Route de Laval, 53200 Château-Gontier [02 43 07 35 60; fax 02 43 70 38 94; camping. parc@cc-chateau-gontier.fr; www.sudmayenne. com]** App Château-Gontier fr N on N162, at 1st rndabt on bypass take 1st exit. Site on R in 250m. Sm, mkd pitch, sl, pt shd; wc; chem disp; mv service pnt; shwrs inc; el pnts (10A) €3 (rev pol); lndtte; shops 1km; tradsmn; bar; playgrnd; pool 800m; fishing; tennis; entmnt; games rm; TV; 20% statics; dogs; quiet; red low ssn; cc acc; CCI. "Most pitches sloping; excel san facs; free access to local pool inc; mkt Thurs; easy walk to attractive town via rvside path." ♦ 1 May-30 Sep. € 8.00 2007*

CHATEAU GONTIER *4F1* (11km N Rural) **Camping Village Vacances et Pêche, Rue des Haies, 53170 Villiers-Charlemagne [02 43 07 71 68; fax 02 43 07 72 77; vvp.villiers.charlemagne@ wanadoo.fr; www.sud-mayenne.com]** N fr Château-Gontier on N162; turn R onto D20 to Villiers-Charlemagne; site on R. Sm, pt shd; wc; chem disp; shwrs inc; el pnts (6A) inc; lndtte; playgrnd; cycle hire; lake 200m; fishing; tennis; games rm; entmnt; dogs. 1 Mar-30 Nov. € 17.00 2007*

CHATEAU GONTIER *4F1* (11km SE Rural) **Camping des Rivières, 53200 Daon [02 43 06 94 78 or 02 43 06 94 10; fax 02 43 06 91 35]** On town side of rv bdge, turn down lane & site ent on R at bottom of hill. Med, pt shd; wc; chem disp; shwrs inc; el pnts (10A) inc; lndtte; shop in town; playgrnd; tennis; mini-golf & sw nrby; adv bkg; quiet; CCI. "Vg clean & well cared for site; some pitches diff to access; boating on adj Rv Mayenne." ♦ 1 May-1 Oct. € 18.50 2006*

CHATEAU GONTIER *4F1* (6km S Rural) **Camping du Bac, Rue de Port, 53200 Ménil [tel/fax 02 43 70 24 54 or 02 43 70 25 25; menil@cc-chateau-grontier.fr]** On N162 dir Château-Gontier, turn off at Ménil & foll sp. Sm, hdg pitch, pt shd; wc; shwrs inc; el pnts (10A) €1.75; lndry rm; snacks; bar 250m; playgrnd; 5% statics; dogs; phone; bus; Eng spkn; adv bkg; CCI. "Edge of Rv Mayenne; gd fishing, walks, cycling; lge vans by request." ♦ 15 Apr-15 Sep. € 7.45 2004*

CHATEAU LA VALLIERE *4G1* (Rural) **FFCC Camp Municipal du Val Joyeux, 37330 Château-la-Vallière [02 47 24 00 21 or 02 47 24 04 93; fax 02 47 24 06 13]** Turn L off D959, in vill 1km S on D749. Site on R after x-ing bdge with lake on L. Med, hdg/mkd pitch, pt shd; wc; chem disp; mv service pnt; serviced pitch; shwrs inc; el pnts (5A) €2.50; shops 1km; tradsmn; playgrnd; lake beach & fishing adj; dogs €0.80; Eng spkn; adv bkg rec high ssn; quiet; CCI. "Friendly welcome; handy for Loire chateaux; mkd walks; modern, spotless san facs; v soft ground after heavy rain." ♦ 15 May-15 Sep. € 10.00 2007*

CHATEAU RENAULT *4G2* (6km S Urban) **Camp Municipal du Moulin, Rue du Lavoir, 37110 Villedômer [02 47 55 05 50 or 02 47 55 00 04 (Mairie); fax 02 47 55 06 27; mairie. villedomer@wanadoo.fr]** Fr A10 exit junc 18 onto N10 dir Château-Renault. Turn W onto D73 sp to Auzouer & Villedômer. Fr Château-Renault S on D910 (N10), site sp dir Villedômer. Sm, hdg pitch, shd; wc (male cont); chem disp; shwrs inc; el pnts (10A) €3; shops, rest, bar adj; rv fishing; lake & fishing 2km; dogs €1; adv bkg. "Gd, clean facs but old-fashioned; pitch yourself if warden not present." 15 Jun-15 Sep. € 6.50 2006*

Did you know you can fill in site report forms on the Club's website — www.caravanclub.co.uk?

CHATEAU RENAULT *4G2* (W Urban) **Camp Municipal du Parc de Vauchevrier, Rue Paul-Louis-Courier, 37110 Château-Renault [02 47 29 54 43 or 02 47 29 85 50 (LS); fax 02 47 56 87 50]** At Château-Renault foll sp to site 800m fr D910 (N10). If app fr a'route turn L on ent town & site on R of main rd adj Rv Brenne. Med, mkd pitch, pt shd; wc; chem disp; mv service pnt; shwrs inc; el pnts (6A) inc; shops 800m; rest 600m; bar 300m; playgrnd; htd pool; fishing; tennis; some rd noise; cc acc; CCI. "Part of municipal park; no c'vans over 5.50m; office clsd 1230-1430; v pleasant site & staff; gd san facs; excel NH." ♦ 1 May-31 Aug. € 8.50 2007*

CHATEAU THIERRY 3D4 (E Urban) **Camp Municipal, 70 Ave d'Essomes, 02400 Château-Thierry [03 23 83 48 23]** Fr A4/E50 take junc 20 onto D1 into town. At junc prior to rv bdge, turn R & foll sp Camping/Piscine. Site on L next to McDonalds. Sm, mkd pitch, unshd; wc; chem disp; shwrs inc; el pnts (8A) €2.60; lndtte; BBQ; rest, bar & shops 1.6km; snacks adj; pool adj; 30% statics; dogs €0.84; poss cr; some rd noise; CCI. "Fast-food rest & drive thro immed adj to site - traff noise until 2300; conv trains Paris & Disneyland Paris; gd walks along rv; WW1 US memorial overlooks town; facs clean but worn; phone ahead to check open low ssn; office open 0830-1000 & 1730-2000 - access for vehicles over 1.90m only during these times; gd sh stay/NH." 15 May-30 Sep. € 8.85   2005*

There aren't many sites open this early in the year. We'd better phone ahead to check that the one we're heading for is actually open.

CHATEAUBRIANT 2F4 (1.5km S) **Camp Municipal Les Briotais, Rue de Tugny, 44110 Châteaubriant [02 40 81 14 38 or 02 40 81 02 32; mairie. chateaubriant@wanadoo.fr]** App fr Nantes (D178) site sp on S end of town Or fr Angers (D163) foll sp at 1st rndabt; fr town cent, foll sps thro town. Sm, hdg pitch, pt shd; wc; mv service pnt; shwrs; el pnts inc; shops, rest, snacks, bar 1km; pool in town; games area; dogs; €0.33; quiet. "11thC chateau in town; site locked overnight; site on municipal playing field; gd NH." ♦ 1 May-30 Sep. € 9.50
                                                        2007*

CHATEAUDUN 4F2 (2.5km NW Rural) **Camp Municipal Le Moulin à Tan, Rue de Chollet, 28200 Châteaudun [02 37 45 05 34 or 02 37 45 11 91 (LS); fax 02 37 45 54 46; tourisme-chateaudun@wanadoo.fr]** App Châteaudun fr N on N10; turn R at rndabt (supmkt on L); L at next rndabt & foll site sp. Site adj Rv Loir. Med, mkd pitch, pt shd; wc (some cont); chem disp; mv service pnt; shwrs inc; el pnts (5A) €1.94; lndtte; ice; shops, rest, snacks 2km; playgrnd; htd, covrd pool 2km; fishing; canoeing; games area; TV; 5% statics; CCI. "Continuous traff noise fr N10; gd base for touring; some night flying fr nrby military airfield; security gate 2.10m height; no twin-axle vans; helpful warden." 1 Apr-30 Sep. € 5.80   2006*

CHATEAULIN 2E2 (1.5km S Rural) **La Pointe Superbe Camping, 29150 St Coulitz [tel/fax 02 98 86 51 53; lapointecamping@aol.com; www. lapointesuperbecamping.com]** Fr N165 foll sp to Châteaulin; in town cent, cross bdge & turn L along rv on D770. After approx 750m, turn L at sp for St Coulitz; 100m turn R into site. If travelling N on D770 do not turn R (tight turn), go into town & turn round. Med, hdg/mkd pitch, pt sl, pt shd; wc; chem disp; mv service pnt; baby facs; shwrs inc; el pnts (10A) €2.50; gas 1km; lndry rm; ice; supmkt, rest, snacks & bar 1km; BBQ; playgrnd; covrd pool 1km; games rm; sand beach 15km; rv nr; dogs €1; adv bkg (dep req); quiet; no cc acc. "One of best sites in Brittany if you don't req a pool; gd pitches; immac facs; sm shwr rms; well-organised; delightful, peaceful, rural setting yet close to town; v helpful & friendly British owners; gd base for Crozon peninsula." ♦ 15 Mar-31 Oct. € 15.00 (CChq acc)   2007*

CHATEAULIN 2E2 (500m SW) **Camp Municipal Rodaven, 29150 Châteaulin [02 98 86 32 93 or 02 98 86 10 05 (Mairie); fc-ssport@chateaulin. fr]** Fr canal/rv bdge in town cent take Quai Moulin (SE side of rv) for about 350m & site down track on R opp indoor pool. Med, pt shd; wc; chem disp; shwrs inc; el pnts (10A) €2; shops 200m; playgrnd; htd indoor pool 300m; direct rv access, fishing; sand beah 5km; entmnt; dogs €1; phone; poss cr; adv bkg; quiet; CCI. "Well-managed site; gd touring base; unreliable opening dates." ♦ ltd. 20 Jun-14 Sep. € 10.00   2004*

CHATEAUMEILLANT see Culan 7A4

CHATEAUNEUF D'ILLE ET VILAINE 2E4 (1.5km NE Rural) **Camping Bel Event, 35430 St Père [02 99 58 83 79; fax 02 99 58 82 24; contact@ camping-bel-event.com; www.camping-bel-event.com]** Fr terminal at St Malo, at 1st rndabt foll sp Toutes Directions; at 2nd traff lts turn R & cont foll dir Toutes Directions, then sp Rennes; cont twd Rennes on D937 (N137) for approx 10km & take exit for Dinan/Châteauneuf; take immed L twds Cancale; past an old rlwy stn on R & take 1st little rd on L (500m fr stn) opp rest; site 100m further on L. Fr S on D937 at Châteauneuf junc turn R onto D74 sp Cancale, then as above. Med, mkd pitch, pt sl, pt shd; wc; chem disp; shwrs inc; el pnts (10A) €4.20 (rev pol poss); lndtte; ice; tradsmn; sm shop; snacks; bar; htd pool (Jun-Sep); playgrnd; lake sw, fishing & watersports adj; sand beach 5km; cycle hire; tennis; TV; 75% statics (sep area); dogs €2.10; adv bkg; quiet, some rd noise. "Excel NH for St Malo & ferry; clean & tidy site; immac facs, ltd low ssn; sm pitches - 4 per enclave; recep clsd 1200-1430; gd touring base." 31 Mar-14 Oct. € 16.40   2007*

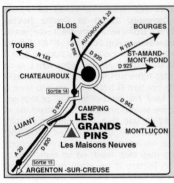

LES GRANDS PINS ★★★

D 920
Les Maisons-Neuves
F-36330 Velles
Tel. 02.54.36.61.93
Fax 02.54.36.10.09

Closed in January and February each year
Weekends closed from November till March

★ PEACE and QUIET. ★ Lots of shadow
★ Bar, Restaurant. ★ Swimming pool, Tennis and Minigolf.
Only 5 min. from the A20, between exits 14 and 15 on the
D 920 road, in "Les Maisons Neuves".
www.les-grands-pins.fr • contact@les-grands-pins.fr
RESERVATION RECOMMENDED FROM NOVEMBER TILL MARCH

CHATEAUNEUF DU FAOU 2E2 (4km SE Rural)
Camp Municipal du Goaker, Moulin du Pré, 29520
St Goazec [02 98 26 84 23; fax 02 98 26 86 48]
D36 fr Châteauneuf-du-Faou, turn L sp St Goazec
& foll sps to site 800m N of vill nr rv. Sm, pt shd;
wc (cont); shwrs inc; el pnts €1.50; shops 2km;
playgrnd; rest; bar 1km; quiet. "Pleasantly situated."
15 Jun-15 Sep. € 6.20   2006*

CHATEAUNEUF LES BAINS see St Gervais
d'Auvergne 7A4

CHATEAUNEUF SUR LOIRE 4F3 (500m S
Urban) Camping La Maltournée, Sigloy, 45110
Châteauneuf-sur-Loire [02 38 58 42 46; fax
02 38 58 54 11; camping-loire-nature@tiscali.
fr] S fr Chateauneuf cent, cross rv on D11; take
1st L, site sp in 1.5km. Lge, pt shd; htd wc; chem
disp; mv service pnt; shwrs inc; el pnts (10A) €3.70;
lndtte; shops 1.5km; tradsmn; snacks; playgrnd;
pool 2km; canoeing; 75% statics in sep area; dogs
€1; security barrier; poss cr; adv bkg; quiet; CCI.
"Well-kept site by rv; clean, modern san facs; m'van
pitches beside rv; helpful, pleasant staff; excel." ♦
1 Apr-30 Oct. € 8.55   2007*

CHATEAUNEUF SUR LOIRE 4F3 (7km W Urban)
Camping de l'Isle aux Moulins, 45150 Jargeau
[02 38 59 70 04; fax 02 38 59 92 62] On D952
thro Châteauneuf & N60 twd Orléans. At St Denis-
de l'Hôtel take sharp L onto D921 to Jargeau over
Loire bdge. Site clearly visible on R of bdge on
W bank. Turn R immed at end of bdge. Lge, shd;
wc (mainly cont); own san rec; chem disp; shwrs
inc; el pnts (10A) inc; gas; ice; lndtte; shops 1km;
tradsmn; playgrnd; pool adj; rv fishing adj; cycle
hire; mini-golf; archery; entmnt; quiet; adv bkg; Eng
spkn; cc acc; CCI. "Poor NH; use only if desperate;
alongside rv; friendly farming family." 1 Mar-31 Oct.
€ 12.70   2005*

CHATEAUNEUF SUR SARTHE 4G1 (E Rural)
Camp Municipal du Port, Rue de la Gare,
49330 Châteauneuf-sur-Sarthe [02 41 69 82 02
or 02 41 96 15 20; fax 02 41 96 15 29;
tourismechateauneufsursarthe@wanadoo.fr]
Site clearly sp in vill, 18km E of Le Lion-d'Angers.
Access to site fr bdge. Sm, pt shd; wc; chem disp;
shwrs inc; el pnts (10A) €2.50 (long lead poss req);
lndtte; shops & rest in vill; playgrnd; rv adj; fishing;
sailing; v quiet but some rd noise; CCI. "Clean facs
but poss stretched high ssn; lge pitches; warden
on site 0900-1200 & 1630-1900; 24-hr access for
cars at rear of site; attractive area." 1 May-30 Sep.
€ 6.65   2006*

⊞CHATEAUPONSAC 7A3 (200m SW Rural)
Camping Le Ventenat (formerly Camp Municipal
La Gartempe), Villages de Vacances, Ave de
Ventenat, 87290 Châteauponsac [05 55 76 55 33
or 05 55 76 31 55 (Mairie); fax 05 55 76 98 05;
chateauponsac.tourisme@wanadoo.fr;   www.
holidayschateauponsac.com] Fr N exit A20 junc
23.1 sp Châteauponsac; go thro vill, well sp on L
on rvside. Fr S exit A20 junc 24 sp Châteauponsac
& then as above. Sm, hdg/mkd pitch, terr, pt shd;
htd wc; chem disp; shwrs inc; el pnts (6A) €3;
lndtte; ice; supmkt 500m; rest, snacks, bar (Jul.
Aug); playgrnd; pool; kayaking; lake 10km; mini-
golf; archery; children's activites; adj to holiday
bungalows/gites; dogs €1; poss cr; Eng spkn; poss
noise fr rest hire parties; adv bkg; red low ssn; CCI.
"Pleasant site; v helpful staff; ltd facs tired; pitches
muddy in wet; not suitable lge m'vans; activities
down steep hill; many sports avail in area; sh walk
to town for shops, museum & historic sites; low ssn
warden visits eves only." € 15.00   2007*

CHATEAURENARD see Avignon 10E2

CHATEAUROUX *4H2* (1km N Rural) **Camp Municipal Le Rochat-Belle Isle, Rue du Rochat, 36000 Châteauroux [02 54 34 26 56 or 02 54 08 33 00; fax 02 54 07 03 11]** Site on banks of Rv Indre, sp in town. Med, pt shd; wc (cont); chem disp; mv service pnt; baby facs; shwrs inc; el pnts (5-10A) €3.30-4.50; gas; lndtte; shops 300m; rest, snacks, bar 100m; playgrnd; Eng spkn. "Leisure park adj with pool & windsurfing on lake; poss music noise till late w/e high ssn; poss itinerants; gd, clean san facs; pleasant walk into town." ♦ 1 May-30 Sep. € 13.00   2006*

CHATEAUROUX *4H2* (9km SW Rural) **Camping Les Grands Pins, Les Maisons-Neuves, 36330 Velles [02 54 36 61 93; fax 02 54 36 10 09; contact@les-grands-pins.fr; www.les-grands-pins.fr]** Fr N exit A20 junc 14 dir Châteauroux; in 500m turn R onto D920 parallel with m'way. Foll sp Maisons-Neuves & site. Fr S exit A20 junc 15, turn R then L onto D920, site on R. Med, pt sl, pt shd; wc (some cont); chem disp; some serviced pitches; shwrs inc; el pnts (10A) €4.20 (poss rev pol) (long lead req if in open field); lndtte; shop 8km; rest; snacks; bar; playgrnd; pool; tennis; mini-golf; entmnt; dogs €1.50; site clsd w/e 1 Oct-30 Dec; Eng spkn; adv bkg; quiet; CCI. "Gd, tidy site in pine forest; clean facs; gd rest; max weight m'van 3,500kg Oct-Apr - heavier acc in summer; no site lighting; phone to check open if travelling low ssn as poss open in winter; vet in Châteauroux; excel NH nr m'way." ♦ 1 Mar-30 Dec. € 14.10   2007*

See advertisement

CHATEL *9A4* (1.5km SW Rural) **Camping Caravaneige L'Oustalet, 1428 Route des Freinets, 74390 Châtel [04 50 73 21 97; fax 04 50 73 37 46; oustalet@valdabondance.com; www.oustalet.com]** Fr Thonon-les-Bains, take D902 & D22 to Châtel. Site sp fr church in cent. Med, hdg/mkd pitch, pt shd; wc; mv service pnt; sauna; shwrs inc; el pnts (10A) inc; gas; lndtte; shop, rest, bar 100m; playgrnd; htd, covrd pool high ssn; tennis; games rm; entmnt; some statics; dogs €2.10; adv bkg rec winter; quiet. "Excel site; conv for ski lifts; gd mountain walks; vg." ♦ 23 Jun-1 Sep & 23 Dec-28 Apr. € 30.00   2007*

CHATEL CENSOIR see Coulanges sur Yonne *4G4*

CHATEL DE NEUVRE *9A1* (N Rural) **Camping Deneuvre, 03500 Châtel-de-Neuvre [tel/fax 04 70 42 04 51; campingdeneuvre@wanadoo.fr; www.deneuvre.com]** S fr Moulins on D2009 (N9); sp N of vill on E side of D2009. Med, mkd pitch, hdstg, pt shd; wc; chem disp; mv service pnt; baby facs; shwrs inc; el pnts (4A) €2.55; ice; gas; lndtte; tradsmn; rest; snacks; bar; playgrnd; rv sw; canoe hire; dogs €1; adv bkg (dep req); Eng spkn; quiet; cc not acc; CCI. "Excel, clean facs; Dutch management; v friendly welcome; at border of Rv Allier in nature reserve; splendid place for walking, fishing, biking & birdwatching; ltd facs low ssn; diff ent/exit for lge o'fits; no twin-axles." ♦ 1 Apr-1 Oct. € 11.85   2006*

⊞**CHATEL DE NEUVRE** *9A1* (400m W Rural) **FFCC Camping de la Courtine, 7 Rue de St Laurant, 03500 Châtel-de-Neuvre [04 70 42 06 21; fax 04 70 42 82 89; camping-lacourtine@club-internet.fr; www.camping-lacourtine.fr]** Fr N on D2009 (N9) to cent of vill, turn L at x-rds onto D32; site in 500m. Sm, mkd pitch, pt shd; htd wc; chem disp; mv service pnt; baby facs; shwrs inc; el pnts (6A) €2 (poss rev pol); lndtte; shop 400m; tradsmn; rest 400m; snacks; bar; playgrnd; wifi internet; dogs €0.50; poss cr; Eng spkn; adv bkg; quiet; CCI. "Friendly welcome; facs poss poorly maintained & site unkempt low ssn; site vulnerable to flooding & poss clsd low ssn, phone ahead to check; access to Rv Allier for canoeing, fishing; walking in nature reserve; NH only." ♦ € 8.70   2006*

CHATEL MONTAGNE *9A1* (10km NE Rural) **Camp Municipal, Laboulère 03120 Arfeuilles [04 70 55 50 11 (Mairie); fax 04 70 55 53 28]** Site off D207 at NE exit to Arfeuilles 50m fr town name sp. 8km fr N7. Sm, pt sl, pt shd; wc; chem disp; fam bthrm; shwrs inc; el pnts (6-10A) €2-2.30; lndry rm; shops, rest, snacks, bar 500m; dogs; Eng spkn; quiet; CCI. "Set in beautiful countryside; local fishing; peaceful." ♦ 1 May-30 Sep. € 6.80   2007*

CHATEL MONTAGNE *9A1* (1km NW Rural) **FFCC Camping La Croix Cognat, 03250 Châtel-Montagne [tel/fax 04 70 59 31 38 or 06 65 53 91 93 (mob); campinglacroixcognat@wanadoo.fr; http://pagesperso-orange.fr/mairie-chatel-montagne]** SW fr Lapalisse on D7; in 15km L on D25 to Châtel-Montagne in 5km & foll sp; site on L bef vill. 'Sleeping policemen' at ent. Sm, mkd pitch, terr, sl, pt shd; wc (some cont); chem disp; mv service pnt; baby facs; shwrs inc; el pnts (6A) €3; gas; lndtte; supmkt 6km; rest; snacks; playgrnd; pool (high ssn); paddling pool; fishing; tennis 100m; mountain bike hire; horseriding & windsurfing adj; 5% statics; dogs €0.50; adv bkg; quiet; CCI. "Sm pitches poss diff o'fits over 6m." 1 May-30 Sep. € 11.00   2006*

CHATELAILLON PLAGE 7A1 (1km N Urban) Camping L'Océan, Ave d'Angoulins, 17340 Châtelaillon-Plage [05 46 56 87 97] Fr La Rochelle take D602 to Châtelaillon-Plage, site sp on L in 300m (after passing g'ge & L'Abbaye camp site). Med, part hdg/mkd pitch, pt shd; wc (some cont); chem disp (wc); mv service pnt; shwrs inc; el pnts (10A) €3.50; lndtte; ice; tradsmn; shops, rest, snacks, bar 1km; BBQ; waterslide; sand beach 500m; dogs €1.60; poss cr. "Gd, clean san facs; daily covrd mkt in town; occasional noise fr rlwy & clay pigeon range." 15 Jun-15 Sep. € 17.40   2006*

⊞**CHATELAILLON PLAGE** 7A1 (2.5km SE Coastal) Camping Port Punay, Les Boucholeurs, Allée Bernard Moreau, 17340 Châtelaillon-Plage [05 46 56 01 53; fax 05 46 56 86 44; camping.port-punay@wanadoo.fr; www.camping-port-punay.com] Exit N137 onto D203 sp Les Boucholeurs; at rndabt in 1km foll site sp to edge of Châtelaillon & turn R, foll sp. Site in 750m. Lge, pt shd; wc; baby facs; shwrs inc; el pnts (6-10A) €4-5; gas; lndtte; lndry rm; ice; shops adj; rest; snacks; bar; playgrnd; pool; sand beach 500m; games area; cycle hire; entmnt; wifi internet; TV; 25% statics; dogs €2; Eng spkn; adv bkg; quiet. "Immac san facs; friendly, helpful owners; steel pegs req; excel." € 21.00 (3 persons)   2007*

CHATELGUYON see Riom 9B1

CHATELLERAULT 4H1 (N Rural) FFCC Le Relais du Miel, Route d'Antran, 86100 Châtellerault [05 49 02 06 27; fax 05 49 93 25 76; camping@lerelaisdumiel.com; www.lerelaisdumiel.com] On A10 exit junc 26 at Châtellerault-Nord. Foll sp twd Antran; site on R fr rndabt, well sp (easy to find). Med, hdstg, terr, shd; wc; chem disp; mv service pnt; serviced pitches; shwrs inc; el pnts (10A) inc; lndtte; ice; shop 400m; tradsmn; bar; BBQ; playgrnd; pool; tennis; dogs €5; Eng spkn; adv bkg; some rd & rlwy noise; red long stay; cc acc; CCI. "Beautifully situated rvside site in Château de Valette park; friendly owners; conv Futuroscope, Chinon, Loches; spotlessly clean san facs; poss unkempt low ssn; san facs ltd low ssn & need updating; conv A10; highly rec." ◆ 12 May-3 Sep. € 21.00   2007*

CHATILLON COLIGNY 4F3 (S Rural) Camp Municipal de la Lancière, Rue André Henriat, 45230 Châtillon-Coligny [02 38 92 54 73 or 06 16 09 30 26 (mob); lalanciere@wanadoo.fr] N fr Briare twd Montargis on N7; E fr Les Bézards on D56 twd Châtillon-Coligny; site sp on ent town on R immed bef canal bdge. Fr town cross Canal de Briare on D93 twd Bléneau; immed turn S along canal rd sp Camping & Marina. Sm, pt shd; wc (some cont); chem disp (wc); shwrs inc; el pnts (3-6A) €1.80-2.80 shops adj; pool high ssn; rv fishing; quiet; 25% statics; no cc acc; CCI. "Clean facs; attractive, peaceful site; excel value; friendly warden; gd walking/cycling along canal; historic town; excel." 1 Apr-30 Sep. € 8.20   2006*

CHATILLON EN DIOIS 9D3 (Urban) Camp Municipal Les Chaussières, 26410 Châtillon-en-Diois [04 75 21 10 30 or 04 75 21 14 44 (Mairie); fax 04 75 21 18 78; camping.chatillonendiois@wanadoo.fr; www.camping-chatillonendiois.com] Fr Die take D93 S for 6km then L on D539 to Châtillon (8km) site sp on R on ent to town. Lge, mkd pitch, pt shd; wc (some cont) chem disp (wc); mv service pnt; shwrs; el pnts (10A) €2.65 ice; shop 200m; snacks; rest, bar 200m; BBQ; playgrnd; pool; canoeing; horseriding; cycling; entmnts; 30% statics; dogs €1.58; phone; Eng spkn; adv bkg; quiet; cc acc; CCI. "On rv bank; attractive old town; gd walking; spectacular mountain scenery; helpful, friendly staff; facs basic but clean; low branches on some pitches." 1 Apr-1 Nov. € 11.98   2007*

CHATILLON EN VENDELAIS see Vitre 2F4

This guide relies on site report forms submitted by caravanners like us; we'll do our bit and tell the editor what we think of the campsites we've visited.

CHATILLON SUR CHALARONNE 9A2 (500m E Urban) FFCC Camp Municipal du Vieux Moulin, Route de Chalamont, 01400 Châtillon-sur-Chalaronne [04 74 55 04 79; fax 04 74 55 13 11] Take D936 SW out of Bourg to Châtillon-sur-Chalaronne. Site clearly sp on ent town. Med, hdg pitch, shd; wc (some cont); baby facs; shwrs inc; el pnts (10A) €3.95 (long lead req on some pitches]; lndry rm; supmkt adj; rest adj; snacks; playgrnd; pool adj; fishing; leisure cent adj; 50% statics; dogs €2; phone; adv bkg; quiet; cc acc; 10% red CCI. "Lovely site; immac facs; helpful warden; red facs low ssn; lovely town; excel." ◆ 15 Apr-15 Sep. € 14.95   2007*

CHATILLON SUR INDRE 4H2 (N Rural) Camp Municipal de la Ménétrie, Rue de Moulin la Grange, 36700 Châtillon-sur-Indre [06 78 27 16 39 or 02 54 38 75 44 (Mairie)] Site well sp in vill. N twd Loches then foll sp. Med, some hdg/mkd pitch, pt shd; wc; shwrs inc; el pnts (6-10A) €1.80; gas, shop & rest 400m; BBQ; playgrnd adj; paddling pool; htd pool adj (proper sw trunks only); dogs; no adv bkg; quiet; CCI. "Lovely relaxed site; well-kept; gd bird-watching area; sh walk to old town; conv Loire chateaux; mkt Fri; recep 0900-1000 & 1900-2000; gd, clean san facs; no twin-axle vans; excel value; vg." ◆ 15 May-15 Sep. € 5.80   2007*

CHATILLON SUR LOIRE see Briare 4G3

CHATILLON SUR SEINE 6F1 (1km Urban) Camp Municipal Louis Rigoly, 21400 Châtillon-sur-Seine [03 80 91 03 05 or 03 80 91 13 19 (LS); fax 03 80 91 21 46; tourism-chatillon-sur-seine@wanadoo.fr] Fr N, cross rv bdge (Seine); cont approx 400m twd town cent; at lge fountain forming rndabt turn L into street with Bureau de Tourisme on corner; foll sp to site. Fr S ignore all camping sp & cont into town cent to fountain, turn R & cont as above. Med, hdg/mkd pitch, pt sl, pt shd; wc; chem disp; shwrs inc; el pnts (4-6A) €2.20-4.40 (rev pol); gas; lndtte; ice; shops 500m; tradsmn; snacks high ssn; playgrnd; htd pool adj; dogs; Eng spkn; quiet; CCI. "Pretty site next to lovely park; clean, tidy, well-spaced pitches; helpful warden; excel, clean san facs; gd rest adj; easy walk to ancient town with museum; ruined chateau; no twin-axles; vg." ♦ ltd. 1 Apr-30 Sep. € 10.60   2007*

⊞CHATILLON SUR SEINE 6F1 (6km S Rural) Camping de la Forge, La Forge, 21400 Ampilly-le-Sec [tel/fax 03 80 91 46 53; campinglaforge@orange.fr; www.campinglaforge.com] S on N71, on leaving Buncey take 1st turn R immed after layby (narr rd). Site on R in 1km, on bend immed bef rv bdge, sp. Sm, pt shd; wc; chem disp; shwrs inc; el pnts (6-16A) €2.20-4; lndtte; ice; shop 2km; tradsmn; rest 2.5km; BBQ; playgrnd; rv sw adj; fishing; dogs; phone; Eng spkn; adv bkg rec high ssn (dep req) ltd facs winter - phone ahead Dec to Feb to check open; quiet; lred long stay; cc acc; CCI. "Beautiful, secluded, CL-type site in woodland setting; helpful & friendly British owners; clean, modern san facs; much bird & wildlife; gd historic area; conv 3 wine-producing areas; area for lge m'vans across rd." ♦ ltd. € 12.00   2007*

CHATONRUPT SOMMERMONT see Joinville 6E1

As soon as we get home I'm going to post all these site report forms to the editor for inclusion in next year's guide. I don't want to miss the September deadline.

CHATRE, LA 7A4 (5km SE Rural) Intercommunal Le Val Vert, Vavres, 36400 La Châtre [02 54 48 32 42 or 02 54 62 10 10; fax 02 54 48 32 87] Fr La Châtre take D943 dir Montluçon. On o'skts La Châtre turn R to Briantes, site sp at this junc. Or fr Montluçon on D943, turn L just bef La Châtre; site sp at this junc. Sm, hdg pitch, terr, pt shd; wc; chem disp; mv service pnt; shwrs inc; el pnts (10A) €2.35; lndry rm; shop 1km; tradsmn; BBQ; playgrnd; htd pool 5km; statics; adv bkg; quiet; cc not acc; CCI. "Spacious, pleasant site; excel grounds; san facs poor quality & looking old; walk/cycle to shops; poss itinerants." ♦ 1 Jun-15 Sep. € 7.80   2006*

CHATRE, LA 7A4 (3km NW) Camp Municipal Solange-Sand, Rue du Pont, 36400 Montgivray [02 54 06 10 34 or 02 54 06 10 36; fax 02 54 06 10 39; mairie.montgivray@wanadoo.fr] Fr La Châtre take rd to Montgivray, foll camping sp. Fr Châteauroux on D943 SE twd La Châtre turn R 2km S of Nohant on D72. Site behind church. Med, mkd pitch, pt shd; wc; chem disp; shwrs inc; el pnts (3-10A) €1.55-5.25 (poss rev pol); lndry rm; BBQ; dogs; quiet; CCI. "Pleasant site in chateau grounds; san facs old but v clean; gd access; warden needs to connect el pnts but not disconnect (calls am & pm); gd rest adj; gd walks." ♦ 15 Mar-15 Oct. € 6.50   2006*

CHATRES SUR CHER see Villefranche sur Cher 4G3

CHAUDEFONDS SUR LAYON see Chalonnes sur Loire 2G4

CHAUDES AIGUES 9C1 (5km N) Camping Le Belvédère, Le Pont-de-Lanau, 15260 Neuvéglise [04 71 23 50 50; fax 04 71 23 58 93; belvedere.cantal@wanadoo.fr; www.campinglebelvadere.com] S on A75/E11 exit junc 28 at St Flour; take D921 S twd Chaudes-Aigues; site at Pont-de-Lanau 300m off D921. Steep acc poss diff lge o'fits. Med, terr, pt shd; wc (some cont); chem disp; baby facs; sauna; shwrs inc; el pnts (6A) inc; gas; lndtte; shop; rest; snacks; bar; BBQ; playgrnd; htd pool; paddling pool; rv sw; canoeing; fishing; sailing 15km; fitness rm; climbing; horseriding 20km; entmnt; child entmnt; internet; games/TV rm; 25% statics; dogs free; adv bkg; quiet; cc acc; CCI. "Views over Rv Truyere; mkt Neuvéglise Fri; v friendly, peaceful, family-run site; steep terrs & tight pitches poss diff; not rec for disabled." ♦ 1 Apr-15 Oct. € 24.00 ABS - D12   2007*

CHAUDES AIGUES 9C1 (3km SW Rural) Camp Municipal Le Château du Couffour, 15110 Chaudes-Aigues [tel/fax 04 71 23 57 08 or 04 71 23 52 47 (Mairie); www.chaudesaigues.com] Sp on L of D921 N dir Laguiole. Lge, pt shd; wc; shwrs inc; el pnts (6A) €2.50; lndtte; shops, rest, snacks, bar 2.5km; BBQ; playgrnd; pool 3km; sports area; tennis; fishing 1km; golf 2km; TV; quiet. "V picturesque area; attractive family-run site with fine views; gd walking; 1000m altitude; thermal spa in town; excel." ♦ 1 May-20 Oct. € 7.70   2007*

CHAUFFAILLES see Clayette, La 9A2

CHAUMARD 4H4 (Rural) Camp Municipal Les Iles, 58120 Chaumard [03 86 78 03 00; fax 03 86 78 05 83] Fr Château-Chinon take D944 dir Pannecière-Chaumard; in 500m turn R onto D37 to Corancy; then D12 to Chaumard; foll camping sp, then turn L into site 100m after cemetary. Sm, hdg pitch, hdstg, pt shd; wc (some cont); chem disp (wc); shwrs €1.20; el pnts €1.50; lake sw adj; fishing; bus 250m. "Access poss diff lge o'fits." € 7.60   2006*

France

CHAUMONT *6F1* (800m NW Urban) **Camp Municipal Parc Ste Marie, Rue des Tanneries, 52000 Chaumont [03 25 32 11 98 or 03 25 30 60 27; fax 03 25 03 92 80; sports@ville-chaumont.fr]** Site on Chaumont W by-pass joining N19 Troyes rd to N67 St Dizier rd. Do not try to app fr town cent. Sm, hdg pitch, pt sl, pt shd; wc (cont); chem disp; shwrs inc; el pnts (10A) €2.20 (poss long lead req); shops 1km; tradsmn; snacks; playgrnd; 20% statics; dogs €1; poss cr; some traff noise; CCI. "Rec arr early; care needed with steep access to some sl pitches; ent barrier under warden control at all times; sh stay/NH." 2 May-30 Sep. € 9.00
2005*

CHAUMONT SUR LOIRE *4G2* (Rural) **Camp Municipal Grosse Grève, Ave des Trouillas, 41150 Chaumont-sur-Loire [02 54 20 95 22 or 02 54 20 98 41 (Mairie); fax 02 54 20 99 61]** Site sp in vill on D751. E of vill, rd to L just bef bdge. Med, terr, pt shd; htd wc; chem disp; shwrs inc; el pnts €1.80; lndry rm; rest & bar 1km; BBQ; playgrnd; fishing; horseriding; canoeing; tennis; cycle hire; quiet; no cc acc; CCI. "Pleasant site by rv; easy walk to vill; interesting chateau; no twin axles." ♦ 15 May-30 Sep. € 7.20   2007*

CHAUNY *3C4* (1km NW Urban) **Camp Municipal, Auberge de Jeunesse, Boulevard de Bad-Köstritz, 02300 Chauny [03 23 52 09 96; fax 03 23 38 70 46; animation@ville-chauny.fr; www.ville-chauny.fr]** Fr S (Soissons) on D1 until junc with D1032 (N32) sp Compiègne. Take D1032 SW until junc with D56. Site sp 100m on L. Sm, hdg/mkd pitch, hdstg, pt sl, pt shd; htd wc (cont); shwrs inc; el pnts (4-10A) €2-50-5.50; ice; shop, rest, bar 1km; playgrnd; sports area; watersports 2km; adv bkg; quiet; cc not acc. "Fair NH; poss itinerant workers on site." ♦ 1 Jul-31 Aug. € 7.00   2006*

The opening dates and prices on this campsite have changed. I'll send a site report form to the editor for the next edition of the guide.

CHAUVIGNY *7A3* (1km E Urban) **Camp Municipal de la Fontaine, Rue de la Fontaine, 86300 Chauvigny [tel/fax 05 49 46 31 94; chauvigny@cg86.fr; www.chauvigny.cg86.fr]** Fr N on D2. On ent vill turn L into Rue Vital Guérin & site on R. Site well sp fr Chauvigny. Med, pt shd; htd wc (some cont); chem disp; mv service pnt; baby facs; shwrs; el pnts (15A) €2.40; lndtte; shop 500m; tradsmn; BBQ; playgrnd; pool & tennis 1km; rv 1km; cycle hire; dogs €1.15; adv bkg; CCI. "Popular site adj park & lake; immac facs; recep clsd 1200-1430; extra for twin-axles; excel views of castle; access to lovely old town via steps." ♦ Apr-Nov. € 7.20
2007*

CHAUVIGNY *7A3* (7km NW Rural) **Camp Municipal, 13 Rue de Varenne, 86300 Bonnes [05 49 56 44 34 or 05 49 56 40 17 (Mairie); fax 05 49 56 48 51; camping_bonnes86@hotmail.com]** Sp fr D951 (N151) & D749. Sp to site easily missed in vill. Site on rvside. Med, hdg pitch, pt shd; wc; chem disp; mv service pnt; shwrs inc; el pnts (10A) inc; lndtte; ice; shop adj in vill; tradsmn; rest & bar 500m; pool adj; waterslide; playgrnd; rv adj; sand beach adj; dogs €1.05; poss cr; adv bkg; quiet; Eng spkn; dogs; CCI. "Old vill, attractive rv; friendly, helpful staff; v clean & welcoming; vg pool; vg value rest adj; poss itinerants." 15 May-15 Sep.
€ 13.90   2006*

CHAVANNES SUR SURAN *9A2* (500m E Rural) **Camp Municipal, 01250 Chavannes-sur-Suran [04 74 51 70 52; fax 04 74 51 71 83]** Turn E off N83 at St Etienne-du-Bois onto D3, cross D52 bef Treffort (v narr rds). Then steep climb & bends & after 6km turn N onto D936 sp Chavannes. Turn E at town hall (Mairie), site sp. Fr Bourg-en-Bresse turn E onto D936 sp Jasseron about 1km aft joining N83 in Bourg. Foll D936 for approx 18km to Chavannes. Sm, hdg/mkd pitch, pt shd; wc; chem disp (wc); shwrs inc; el pnts (5-10A) inc (poss rev pol); shop 500m; BBQ; quiet. "Spotless san facs; excel cycling, fishing; v pretty rvside site; gd touring base; gd walking; attractive vill; site self, warden calls; lge pitches; highly rec." ♦ ltd. 1 May-30 Sep.
€ 8.10   2004*

⊞**CHEF BOUTONNE** *7A2* (2km W Rural) **Camping Le Moulin, Route de Brioux, 79110 Chef-Boutonne [tel/fax 05 49 29 73 46; campinglemoulin.chef@tiscali.fr; www.camping chef.com]** Fr D950 to or fr Poitiers, turn E onto D740 to Chef-Boutonne, site on R. Fr N10 turn onto D948 to Sauzé-Vaussais then L onto D1 to Chef-Boutonne. Sm, hdg/mkd pitch, ltd hdstg, pt shd; htd wc; chem disp; mv service pnt 1km; shwrs inc; el pnts (6-10A) €3.50; lndtte; ice; shop 2km; rest; snacks; bar; playgrnd; pool & terr; entmnt; dogs €1.20; poss cr; adv bkg; quiet; cc acc; red long stay/low ssn; CCI. "Well-maintained; gd, clean facs; friendly, helpful British owners; lge pitches; htd san facs v ltd low ssn (1wc/shwr); gd rest on site (ltd opening in winter); abundance of bird life; conv Futuroscope & La Rochelle; highly rec." ♦ € 14.30
2007*

CHEMERY see Contres *4G2*

CHEMILLE *2G4* (1km SW Rural) **FFCC Camping Coulvée, Route de Cholet, 49120 Chemillé [02 41 30 42 42 or 02 41 30 39 97 (Mairie); fax 02 41 30 39 00; camping-chemille-49@wanadoo. fr; www.camping-coulvee-chemille.com]** Fr Chemillé dir Cholet, 1km on R on N160. Sm, hdg pitch, terr, pt shd; wc; chem disp; mv service pnt; shwrs inc; el pnts (10A) €3.60; lndtte; ice; tradsmn; bar; BBQ on lakeside or on pitch with disclaimer; playgrnd; sm sand beach; lake sw; pedaloes; activities; dogs €1.70; ltd Eng spkn; adv bkg; quiet; cc not acc; 10% red 28 days; CCI. "V clean facs; v helpful staff; lovely pitches; office clsd 1230-1500; mkt Thu; poss unreliable opening dates." ♦ 30 Apr-15 Sep. € 9.90   2007*

CHENAC ST SEURIN D'UZET see Cozes *7B1*

CHENERAILLES *7A4* (2km SW Rural) **Camp Municpal de la Forêt, 23130 Chénérailles [05 55 62 38 26 or 05 55 62 37 22; fax 05 55 62 95 55; mairie.chenerailles@wanadoo.fr]** SW fr Chemillé on D55; site in 2km on R. Sm, mkd pitch, pt sl, pt shd; wc (some cont); chem disp (wc); shwrs inc; el pnts (10A) €2.25; lndry rm; shop, rest, bar 2km; BBQ; lake sw adj; dogs €1.56; Eng spkn; adv bkg; CCI. "Sand beach on lake adj; warden on site 0730-1000 & 1530-1930." ♦ ltd. 15 Jun-15 Sep. € 7.15   2006*

CHENONCEAUX *4G2* (Rural) **Camp Municipal, Fontaine les Prés, 37150 Chenonceaux [02 47 23 90 13 (Mairie); fax 02 47 23 94 46]** In town cent foll sp Château de Chenonceaux & site. Ent as if visiting chateau & attendants will direct you. Site ent narr & twisting, poss not suitable long o'fits. Sm, pt sl, pt shd; wc (some cont); chem disp; mv service pnt; shwrs inc; el pnts (6A) €2.20; shop, rest, bar 500m; BBQ; sm playgrnd; dogs €1; phone; bus adj; poss cr; no adv bkg; some rlwy noise; CCI. "Simple site ideal for visit to chateau." ♦ Easter-30 Sep. € 7.20   2006*

CHENONCEAUX *4G2* (1.5km E Rural) **Camping de l'Ecluse (formerly Municipal), Route de la Plage, 37150 Chisseaux [02 47 23 87 10 or 06 15 83 21 20 (mob); sandrine@campingdelecluse-37.fr; www. campingdelecluse-37.fr]** E fr Chenonceaux on D176; cross bdge; immed hard R & foll rv bank; site in 300m. Med, mkd pitch, pt shd; wc; chem disp; shwrs inc; el pnts (5A) €3.40 (rev pol); lndtte; shop 1km; supmkt 6km; tradsmn; snacks; bar; playgrnd; dogs €1.20; phone; poss cr; Eng spkn; adv bkg; quiet tho some rd/rlwy noise; cc acc; CCI. "Rv trips; fishing; gd walking; well-known Chenonceaux chateau nrby; gd." ♦ 1 Mar-30 Oct. € 10.05
                                                   2004*

CHENONCEAUX *4G2* (1.5km S Rural) **Camping Le Moulin Fort, Pont de Chisseaux, 37150 Francueil [02 47 23 86 22; fax 02 47 23 80 93; lemoulinfort@ wanadoo.fr; www.lemoulinfort.com]** Site on S bank of Rv Cher just off D976 (N76). Fr Tours take D976 signposted Vierzon. Keep on D976 by-passing Bléré. In 5km turn N to cross rv but take sm rd on R to site, bef actually x-ing bdge. Site well sp. Med, hdg/mkd pitch, pt shd; wc; chem disp; baby facs; shwrs inc; el pnts (6A) inc (long lead poss req); gas; lndtte; ice; shop; tradsmn; rest; snacks; bar; BBQ (gas/charcoal); playgrnd; pool; paddling pool; fishing; cycle hire; entmnt; child entmnt; games/TV rm; dogs €3; office clsd 1200-1600 low ssn; Eng spkn; adv bkg ess (min 3 nts); rd noise & a little rlwy noise; red low ssn; cc acc; CCI. "Lovely, well-kept site in beautiful setting; v friendly & helpful British owners; gd san facs; easy access most pitches; some sm pitches & many v shaded; poss security prob due access to site fr rv bank; excel." ♦ 1 Apr-30 Sep. € 26.50 ABS - L08   2007*

CHENONCEAUX *4G2* (2km W Rural) **Camp Municipal de l'Isle, Route de Bléré, 37150 Civray-de-Touraine [02 47 23 62 80 or 02 47 29 90 75 (Mairie); fax 02 47 23 62 88; civraydetouraine@wanadoo.fr]** On D976 (N76) bet Bléré & Montrichard site on N bank of Rv Cher, sp fr both dirs; ent 100m after x-ing narr bdge. V diff for car & c'van to make R turn into ent ent. Instead pass ent, turn around & turn L into ent. Sm, pt shd; wc; chem disp; mv service pnt; shwrs inc; el pnts (5A) €2.50; shop 1km; tradsmn; pool 3km; rv adj; quiet but poss noise fr nrby rd & rlwy; CCI. "Gd well-maintained site; v attractive rv lock & weir 500m." ♦ 19 Jun-31 Aug. € 8.50   2004*

CHENS SUR LEMAN see Douvaine *9A3*

> Before we move on, I'm going to fill in some site report forms and post them off to the editor, otherwise they won't arrive in time for the deadline at the end of September.

CHERBOURG *1C4* (12km NE Coastal) **Camping La Plage, 2 Village de Fréval, 50840 Fermanville [02 33 54 38 84; fax 02 33 54 74 30]** Fr Cherbourg on D116 dir Barfleur, site in 12km on L. Med, some hdg pitch, unshd; wc; chem disp; shwrs inc; el pnts (6A) €3.50; snacks; bar; playgrnd; beach 300m; 70% statics; dogs €1.60; poss cr; adv bkg ess summer, rec winter; quiet. "Friendly owner; conv for ferry & D-Day landing beaches; poss unreliable opening dates." 1 Mar-30 Nov. € 11.50   2004*

France

CHERBOURG *1C4* (5km E Urban/Coastal) **Camping Espace Loisirs de Collignon, Plage Collignon, 50110 Tourlaville [02 33 54 80 68; fax 02 33 20 53 03; camping-collignon@wanadoo.fr]** Foll sp fr ferry terminal for Espace Loisirs Collignon or Tourlaville-Plage; site on D116; turn L at lge rndabt beyond Tourlaville boundary. Med, mkd pitch, unshd; wc; chem disp; shwrs inc; el pnts (10A) inc; gas; lndry rm; shops 1.5km; pool; sand beach adj; fishing, sw & watersports adj; games rm; entmnt; TV; 30% statics; poss cr; adv bkg (rec high ssn); noisy high ssn (youth groups); some rd noise; cc acc; CCI. "Lge landscaped complex; generous pitches; poor security, open to public; conv ferries but check exit barrier key works if leaving early am; NH/sh stay only." ♦ 1 May-30 Sep. € 16.85
2004*

> Did you know you can fill in site report forms on the Club's website — www.caravanclub.co.uk?

CHERBOURG *1C4* (10km E Coastal) **Camp Municipal du Fort, 47 Route du Fort, 50110 Bretteville [02 33 22 27 60]** Immed exit car ferries in Cherbourg, turn L on D116. On leaving Bretteville turn sharp L at junc of D116 & D611, 1st turn R. App poss diff lge o'fits. Med, pt sl, unshd; wc; chem disp; shwrs; el pnts (10A) €2.30; shops 4km; BBQ; playgrnd; shgl beach adj; 90% statics; quiet. "Sep area tourers, sm pitches; some pitches view of coast; locked 2200-0700; poss diff in wet; some pitches diff lge o'fits; sh stay only." 1 May-30 Sep. € 8.50
2006*

> This guide relies on site report forms submitted by caravanners like us; we'll do our bit and tell the editor what we think of the campsites we've visited.

CHERBOURG *1C4* (10km E Coastal) **Camping L'Anse du Brick, 18 L'Anse du Brick, 50330 Maupertus-sur-Mer [02 33 54 33 57; fax 02 33 54 49 66; welcome@anse-du-brick.com; www.anse-du-brick.com]** Temrorary alternative rte fr Cherbourg (due landslide 2007): turn L onto D901 sp Barfleur; go past sm airport; turn L onto D612 sp Fermanville; turn L onto D116; site on L in 3km. Otherwise (when landslide cleared) at rndabt at port take 2nd exit sp Caen, Rennes & Mont St Michel; at 2nd rndabt take 3rd exit sp Caen & Mont St Michel (N13), the sea will be on L; at 3rd rndabt take exit onto dual c'way sp St Lo, Caen (N13), Bretteville-sur-Mer; exit on D116 sp Bretteville-en-Saire; at T-junc turn L onto D116; at rndabt take 2nd exit D116; cont for 4km thro Bretteville-en-Saire (take care massive speed hump); turn R for site just after R-hand blind bend & turning for Maupertus; up v steep incline. Med, hdg/mkd pitch, terr, sl, shd; wc; chem disp; mv service pnt; baby facs; serviced pitches; shwrs inc; el pnts (10A) inc (poss rev pol); gas; lndtte; shop & 3km; tradsmn; rest; snacks; bar; BBQ; playgrnd; 2 htd pools; paddling pool; waterslide; sand beach adj; tennis; cycle hire; archery; wifi internet; games/TV rm; dogs €2.60; poss cr; recep 0800-1300 & 1400-1800 high ssn; adv bkg; quiet; red low ssn; cc acc; CCI. "Attractive, well-kept site in beautiful setting; gd san facs; some pitches for lge o'fits; excel for dogs - allowed on adj beach; cliff behind so no sat TV recep; plenty to do in area; conv Landing Beaches, Barfleur; coastal nature reserve Marais de Cotentin et du Bessin." ♦ 1 Apr-30 Sep. € 35.80 (CChq acc) ABS - N14
2007*

⊞**CHERBOURG** *1C4* (6km S Rural) **Camping Le Village Vert, 50470 Tollevast [02 33 43 00 78; fax 02 33 43 03 38; le-village-vert@wanadoo.fr; www.le-village-vert.com]** S'bound take N13 sp Caen out of town. Cont on N13 fr Auchan rndabt for approx 5km to D56 slip rd sp Delasse. Turn L at x-rds over N13 onto N13 sp Cherbourg. Site on R approx 3.5km, sp nr Auchan hypmkt. N'bound exit sp Tollevast & site. Lge, some hdstg, pt sl, pt shd; wc; chem disp; mv service pnt; shwrs inc; baby facs; el pnts (6A) €1 (check rev pol); gas; sm shop & 1km; tradsmn; rest 200m; playgrnd; tennis; golf & horseriding 2km; 95% statics (sep); dogs €1; Eng spkn; adv bkg; quiet but poss rd noise at front of site; cc acc; red CCI. "Mainly permanent statics; poss itinerants; ltd space for tourers but spacious pitches; woodland setting; coded security barriers; poss waterlogged pitches in wet weather; open san facs block poss cold in winter; friendly & efficient; office closes 1930, night arrivals area; conv NH for ferries." ♦ € 12.50
2007*

⊞CHERBOURG 1C4 (3km NW Coastal) Camp Municipal de la Saline, 50120 Equeurdreville-Hainneville [02 33 93 88 33 or 02 33 53 96 00 (Mairie); fax 02 33 93 12 70; mairie-equeurdreville@dialoleane.com; www. equeurdreville.com] Fr ferry terminal foll D901 & sp Beaumont-Hague. On dual c'way beside sea look out for site sp to L. Med, hdg pitch, hdstg, pt sl, terr, pt shd; htd wc (male cont); chem disp; shwrs inc; el pnts (6A) inc; shop; beach adj; fishing; 30% statics; rd noise; CCI. "Sea view; sandy beach & pier; boules & skateboard park adj; cycle path to town; gd shwrs; site unmanned w/e low ssn." € 12.20   2005*

CHERRUEIX see Dol de Bretagne 2E4

CHERVEUX see Niort 7A2

⊞CHESNE, LE 5C1 (2km NE Rural) Camp Departmental du Lac de Bairon, 08390 Le Chesne [03 24 30 11 66] Leave A203 exit Sedan, W on D764, in 500m L on D977 sp Vouziers. 2km bef Le Chesne R on D12, in 500m L on D312. Site 2km on L. Lge, mkd pitch, some hdstg, pt shd; wc; chem disp; shwrs inc; el pnts (6-10A) €2.60-4.45; ice; lndtte; shop 2km; tradsmn; snacks; bar; playgrnd; tennis; cycle hire; watersports; entmnts; lake sw, sand beach, fishing, boat & canoe hire; TV rm; entmnt; phone; dogs €1.15; poss cr; quiet; CCI. "Excel site; modern, clean san facs; poss diff site ent with lge o'fits; forest walks." ♦ € 13.90   2007*

CHEVENON see Nevers 4H4

CHEVERNY 4G2 (3km N Urban) Camping Essi Le Casseux, 41700 Cour-Cheverny [02 54 79 95 63] Well sp fr all dirs; foll 'camping' sp around Cour-Cheverny. Sm, shd; wc; chem disp; shwrs; el pnts (5A) €1.50; no adv bkg; quiet. "Warden calls am & pm; footpath fr site to town; NH only." 1 Jun-15 Sep. € 6.60   2004*

CHEVERNY 4G2 (1km S Rural) Camping Les Saules, 102 Route de Contres, 41700 Cheverny [02 54 79 90 01; fax 02 54 79 28 34; contact@camping-cheverny.com; www.camping-cheverny.com] Exit A10 junc 17 dir Blois Sud onto D765 to Romorantin. At Cour-Cheverny foll sp Cheverny & chateau. Fr S on D956 turn R onto D102 just N of Contres, site on L just bef Cheverny. Well sp fr all dirs. Lge, mkd pitch, hdstg, shd; htd wc; chem disp; mv service pnt; baby facs; shwrs inc; el pnts (10A) €3.50 (poss long lead req); gas; lndtte; shop; tradsmn; rest; snacks; bar; BBQ; playgrnd; pool; paddling pool; fishing; tennis, golf nr; excursions; games rm; cycle hire; internet; 2% statics; TV; dogs €2; adv bkg rec high ssn; Eng spkn; adv bkg; quiet but some rd noise; cc acc; red long stay/low ssn; CCI. "Well-run site; excel facs; v friendly, welcoming owners; helpful; excel pool; all pitches under trees; in Vallée des Rois & conv many chateaux; muddy after heavy rain; many cycle & walking rtes nr; 18-hole golfcourse nrby; excel." ♦ 28 Mar-30 Sep. € 25.50   2007*

See advertisement

CHEYLARD, LE 9C2 (1km E Rural) Camping La Chèze, Route de St Christol, 07160 Le Cheylard [tel/fax 04 75 29 09 53; mosslercat@wanadoo.fr; www.camping-de-la-cheze.com] Fr Le Cheylard take D264 SE & foll camping sp. App up steep hill & sharp bend into final app. Less steep app fr Valence on N86 & D120. Site 25km fr St Agrève by rd. Med, mkd pitch, terr, pt shd; wc (some cont); chem disp (wc); shwrs inc; el pnts (3-10A) €3-4; lndtte; shops 1.2km; tradsmn; rest; playgrnd; rv sw 2km; some statics; dogs €0.50; phone; security barrier; poss cr; Eng spkn; adv bkg; v quiet; 10% red CCI. "In grounds of château; lovely views over attractive town & mountains; gd walks nrby." ♦ Easter-1 Nov. € 10.50   2007*

CHEZERY FORENS 9A3 (500m S Rural) Camp Municipal de la Valserine, 01410 Chézery-Forens [tel/fax 04 50 56 20 88] Site off D991 on app to vill. Sm, pt shd; wc; chem disp; shwrs inc; el pnts (6-10A) inc; shops adj; rv adj; quiet. "Gd walks." 15 Apr-30 Sep. € 8.60   2004*

France

CHILLY LE VIGNOBLE see Lons le Saunier *6H2*

CHINON *4G1* (500m SW Urban) **Camping de L'Ile Auger, Quay Danton, 37500 Chinon** [02 47 93 08 35; fax 02 47 98 47 92; www.ville-chinon.com] On S side of rv at bdge. Fr S foll sp Chinon St Jacques; when app 2nd bdge on 1-way 'loop', avoid R lane indicated for x-ing bdge & cont strt past S end of main bdge to site on R. Fr N foll sp 'Centre Ville' round castle, cross bdge, site on R. Well sp in town & opp castle. Lge, mkd pitch, pt shd; wc (some cont); chem disp (wc); mv service pnt; baby facs; shwrs inc; el pnts (4-12A) €1.90-3.30 (poss rev pol) lndtte; ice; shop 200m; snacks adj; playgrnd; htd pool 300m; sat TV; dogs €0.90; phone; quiet; cc acc; CCI. "Excel, well-maintained, gd value site; clean san facs; elec connected by warden; twin-axles discretionary; office clsd 1200-1400; poss midge problem; short walk to town; gd base for town, chateaux, wine caves & vineyards; views of chateau." ♦ 15 Mar-15 Oct. € 8.10   2007*

> As soon as we get home I'm going to post all these site report forms to the editor for inclusion in next year's guide. I don't want to miss the September deadline.

CHINON *4G1* (14km NW) **Camping Belle Rive (formerly Intercommunal Bellerive), 37500 Candes-St Martin** [02 47 95 98 11; fax 02 47 95 80 95; cte.de.cnes.RGV@wanadoo.fr; www.cdc-rivegauchevienne.com] Fr Chinon take D751. Site on R bef junc with D7, on S bank of Rv Vienne. Med, mkd pitch, pt shd; wc; shwrs; el pnts (10A) €1.95; lndtte; ice; shops 1km; tradsmn; rvside café; bar; rv sw 1km; playgrnd; fishing adj; dogs €0.90; adv bkg; quiet; CCI. "Pleasant rvside site, conv Saumur & chateaux; poor san facs, on two floors." ♦ Mid Apr-Mid Sep. € 6.50   2007*

CHOLET *2H4* (5km SE Rural) **Camping Village Vacances Le Lac de Ribou, Allée Léon Mandin, 49300 Cholet** [02 41 49 74 30; fax 02 41 58 21 22; info@lacderibou.com; www.lacderibou.com] Fr Cholet ring rd foll sp Parc des Loisirs de Ribou. Sp fr Cholet. Lge, hdg/mkd pitch, hdstg, terr, pt shd; htd wc; chem disp; mv service pnt; serviced pitches; shwrs inc; el pnts (10A) €5.10 (long lead req); lndtte; tradsmn; shop; hypmkt 1.5km; rest; snacks; bar; BBQ; playgrnd; 2 htd pools; waterslides; lake sw & sand beach 500m; fishing; boating; windsurfing; skating; tennis; archery; golf nr; entmnt; child entmnt; TV rm; dogs €1.70; poss cr; Eng spkn; adv bkg ess; quiet; cc acc; 5% red CCI. "Excel touring area; excel site." ♦ 1 Apr-30 Sep. € 18.90   2005*

CHOLET *2H4* (8km SE Rural) **Camping du Verdon, Le Bois Neuf, Route du Verdon, 49280 La Tessoualle** [02 41 49 74 61; fax 02 41 58 21 22; info@lacderibou.com; www.lacderibou.com] D258 fr Cholet ring rd, turn L in 6km. Site well sp at Barrage du Verdon & La Tessoualle vill. Sm, hdg pitch, pt shd; wc; chem disp; shwrs; el pnts (3-5A) €2.05-3 (long lead req some pitches) shop; rest, snacks, bar adj (poss lunchtime only); lake sw & land beach; dogs €1; Eng spkn; adv bkg; quiet; CCI. "Peaceful location, lovely pitches; facs dated but v clean; windsurfing on Lac du Verdon; excel walking, cycling; gd value." 1 Jul-31 Aug. € 9.65   2007*

CHORGES *9D3* (2.5km E Rural) **Camping Le Rio Claret, Les Chabes, 05230 Chorges** [tel/fax 04 92 50 62 16; rio-claret@wanadoo.fr; www.camping-lerioclaret.com] Fr Gap foll N94 E dir Embrun; take main rd by-passing Chorges & 4km past traff lts look for sp to site. Turn L at junc (narr lane), turn R & R again to site. Sm, mkd pitch, pt shd; wc (some cont); chem disp; mv service pnt; shwrs inc; el pnts (3-10A) €2.50-3.80; lndry rm; tradsmn; shop 2.4km; rest; snacks; bar; playgrnd; lake sw & beach 2km; 10% statics; dogs €2; phone; adv bkg; some rd noise at lower level. "Conv touring base; day trip to Italy via Briançon; boat excursions; spectacular views; gd san facs; excel meals; v helpful, pleasant owners." ♦ 1 May-30 Sep. € 12.00   2004*

CHORGES *9D3* (5km E Rural) **Camping Club Le Roustou, 05230 Prunières** [04 92 50 62 63; fax 04 92 50 90 48; info@campingleroustou.com; www.campingleroustou.com] E fr Gap on N94. Site on side of Lac de Serre-Ponçon. Do not attempt to go to Prunières vill, always stay on N94. Lge, mkd pitch, hdstg, terr, pt shd; wc; own san rec; chem disp; mv service pnt; baby facs; shwrs inc; el pnts (4A) inc; lndtte; shops 10km; tradsmn; snacks; bar; playgrnd; pool (no shorts); beach adj; lake sw; canoe hire; tennis; cycle hire; games area; TV; dogs €0.80; poss cr; Eng spkn; quiet; red low ssn; cc acc; CCI. "Beautiful views; excel scenery; relaxing area; always park on E side in case of poss prob with wind; excel." 1 May-30 Sep. € 22.70   2006*

CHORGES *9D3* (6km SE) **Camping Le Nautic, Lac de Serre-Ponçon, 05230 Prunières** [04 92 50 62 49; fax 04 92 53 58 42; campinglanautic@wanadoo.fr; www.campinglenautic.com] Fr Gap or Embrun take N94, site sp bet Savines & Chorges. Med, terr, shd; wc; chem disp; shwrs; el pnts (6A) €3; gas; ice; shop; snacks; playgrnd; pool; shgl beach & lake sw; boating; dogs €1.50; adv bkg; quiet. "Beautiful location, poor pitches; lake sw excel in sheltered bay; vg san facs." 15 May-15 Sep. € 17.80   2006* (CChq acc)

CHORGES *9D3* (10km SW Rural) **Camping La Viste, Le Belvédère de Serre-Ponçon, Rousset, 05190 Espinasses [04 92 54 43 39; fax 04 92 54 42 45; camping@laviste.fr; www. laviste.fr]** N on A51 or N85 twds Gap; take D942 sp Barcelonnette; after Espinasses turn L onto D3 to Barrage de Serre-Ponçon; then L onto D103. Site on L. NB D3 long, v steep climb, hairpin bends. Med, hdg/mkd pitch, pt sl, pt shd; wc (cont); chem disp; mv service pnt; shwrs inc; el pnts (5A) €2.90; gas; lndtte; shop & 4km; tradsmn; rest; snacks; bar; BBQ; playgrnd; pool; lake sw 2km; phone; adv bkg; quiet; cc acc; CCI. "Ltd facs low ssn; site o'looks Lac de Serre-Poncon (amenity area); cool at night; height 770m; gd for walking & touring by rd; site rds narr; access diff lge o'fits." ♦ ltd. 15 May-15 Sep. € 16.60   2005*

CIOTAT, LA *10F3* (2km NE Coastal) **Camping Le St Jean, 30 Ave de St Jean, 13600 La Ciotat [04 42 83 13 01; fax 04 42 71 46 41; stjean@ easyconnect.fr; www.asther.com/stjean]** E on La Ciotat-Plage to far end & foll sp to site on old D559, not new town by-pass. Med, mkd pitch, shd; htd wc; shwrs; mv service pnt; el pnts (2-4A) €3.20-4.50; gas; lndtte; ice; shop; rest; snacks; bar; playgrnd; dir access to beach adj; watersports; tennis; dogs €4.50; poss cr; quiet. "Sm pitches; pleasant site." ♦ 2 Jun-22 Sep. € 27.00 (3 persons)   2007*

CIOTAT, LA *10F3* (4km NE Coastal) **Camping Les Oliviers, Le Liouquet, Route de Toulon, 13600 La Ciotat [04 42 83 15 04; fax 04 42 83 94 43; www. camping-lesoliviers.com]** Fr La Ciotat, foll D559 coast rd sp Bandol & Toulon. Site in 4km, look for lge sp on L. Caution x-ing dual c'way. V lge, pt sl, terr, shd; wc; chem disp; shwrs inc; el pnts (6A) €2.80 (poss rev pol); gas; lndtte; ice; shops 300m; rest, snacks, bar 300m; playgrnd; pool; sand/shgle beach 4km; tennis; 5% statics; dogs €1; bus 300m; poss v cr; Eng spkn; adv bkg; quiet but some noise fr main rd & rlwy adj; cc acc; CCI. "Many pitches have sea views; friendly staff; tired san facs & poss unclean; v sm shwrs; care on ent due to lge boulders; gd touring base." ♦ 15 Mar-15 Sep. € 16.70   2006*

⊞**CIOTAT, LA** *10F3* (3km E Coastal) **Camping Santa Gusta, Domaine de Fontsainte, 13600 La Ciotat [04 42 83 14 17; fax 04 42 08 90 93; santagusta@wanadoo.fr; www.santagusta.com]** Foll D559 coast rd fr La Ciotat twd Les Lecques to Total filling stn on R. Site down by filling stn. Lge, pt sl, pt shd; wc (cont); chem disp (wc); shwrs inc; el pnts (5A) €2.90; lndtte; shop; rest, snacks, bar high ssn; playgrnd; rocky beach adj; boat-launching facs; entmnt; 95% statics; dogs €4; poss cr; quiet; CCI. "San facs open 0730-2000; adj beach not suitable for bathing; ltd facs low ssn; smart card access; NH only." € 18.20   2006*

CIVRAY *7A2* (1km NE Urban) **FFCC Camping Les Aulnes, Les Coteaux de Roche, 86400 Civray [05 49 87 17 24; campingaulnes@yahoo.fr; www. camping-les-aulnes.com]** Civray 9km E of N10 halfway bet Poitiers & Angoulême. Site outside town SE of junc of D1 & D148. Sp on D148 & on S by-pass. Avoid town cent narr rds. Med, pt sl, pt shd; wc (cont); chem disp (wc); shwrs; el pnts (6-10A) €3 (poss long lead req); lndtte; shop 500m; rest; snacks; bar; BBQ; playgrnd; htd pool 1km; rv sw & fishing adj; cycle hire; golf; few statics; dogs €1; Eng spkn; quiet; cc acc; CCI. "V pleasant rvside site; new san facs (2007); pitches soft when wet; vg rest; conv town cent; mkt Wed; vg." 1 Apr-15 Oct. € 7.50   2007*

The opening dates and prices on this campsite have changed. I'll send a site report form to the editor for the next edition of the guide.

CLAIRVAUX LES LACS *6H2* (Rural) **Camp Municipal Le Lac de Narlay, Le Frasnois, 39130 Clairvaux-les-Lacs [03 84 25 58 74 (Mairie)]** On N5 fr Champagnole to St Laurent turn R onto D75 at Pont-de-Chaux; cont to Le Frasnois, site sp in vill. Med, pt sl, pt terr, pt shd; wc (some cont); chem disp (wc); shwrs inc; el pnts inc; lndry rm; snacks; shops 500m; playgrnd; lake sw adj; tennis; cycle hire; 5% statics; dogs; phone; poss cr; Eng spkn; CCI. "Site yourself warden calls each pm; only terr pitches have el pnts; splendid Cascades du Hérisson & gd walks nrby; pizza van calls Wed & Sat; bread avail fr adj farm." 15 May-15 Sep. € 13.00   2004*

CLAIRVAUX LES LACS *6H2* (1.2km SE Rural) **Yelloh! Village Le Fayolan, Chemin de Langard, 39130 Clairvaux-les-Lacs [03 84 25 26 19 or 08 20 00 55 93; fax 03 84 25 26 20; reservation@ rsl39.com; www.campingfayolan.com]** Fr town foll campsite sp, last site along lane adj to lake. V lge, hdg/mkd pitch, terr, pt shd; wc; serviced pitches; chem disp; shwrs inc; el pnts (6A) inc; gas; lndtte; ice; shop; rest; snacks; bar; playgrnd; htd pool; waterslide; sand lake beach adj; games rm; tennis 1km; cycle hire; entmnt; child entmnt; TV; 16% statics; dogs €3.50; Eng spkn; adv bkg rec (dep req + bkg fee); quiet; red low ssn; cc acc; CCI. "Excel, clean site; extra for lakeside pitches high ssn; v pleasant sm town in easy walking dist; lovely area." ♦ 16 May-9 Sep. € 32.00   2007*

See advertisement on next page

France

CLAIRVAUX LES LACS *6H2* (1km S Rural) Camping La Grisière et Europe Vacances, Chemin Langard, 39130 Clairvaux-les-Lacs [03 84 25 80 48; fax 03 84 25 22 34; bailly@la-grisiere.com; www.la-grisiere.com] Turn S off N78 in Clairvaux opp church onto D118 sp St Claude. Fork R in 500m & foll site sps to lake. V lge, mkd pitch, pt sl, pt shd; htd wc (some cont); chem disp; mv service pnt; shwrs inc; el pnts (6-10A) €2.60; gas; lndtte; ice; shop; tradsmn; snacks; bar; BBQ; playgrnd; lake sw & beach adj; rv sw 5km; fishing; watersports; tennis 1km; games rm; cycle hire; internet; TV; 3% statics; dogs €0.90; phone; Eng spkn; no adv bkg; cc acc; red low ssn; CCI. "Lovely views in beautiful area; sm pitches; vg site." ♦ 1 May-30 Sep. € 14.40   2007*

See advertisement opposite

CLAIRVAUX LES LACS *6H2* (1km S Rural) Camping Le Grand Lac, Chemin du Langard, 39130 Clairvaux-les-Lacs [03 84 25 22 14; fax 05 34 25 26 20; reservation@rsl39.com; www.vacances-nature.com] SE on N78 fr Lons-le-Saunier; in Clairvaux vill turn R opp church on L, 1st R then fork R, foll sp. Ent 2.7m wide. Lge, hdg/mkd pitch, terr, pt shd; wc; mv service pnt; baby facs; shwrs inc; el pnts (6A) inc; lndtte; shop; tradsn; BBQ; sand beach; fishing; boating; 30% statics; Eng spkn; cc acc. "Lovely country nr Jura mountains; gd site." ♦ 5 May-4 Sep. € 19.00   2004*

CLAIRVAUX LES LACS *6H2* (10km S Rural) Camping Le Val d'Eté, 100 Rue du Champ-Coubet, 39130 Etival [tel/fax 03 84 44 87 31; camping.etival@cegetel.net] E fr Lons-le-Saunier on N78 to Clairvaux-les-Lacs. In Clairvaux foll camping sp thro town. Then ignore them & take D118 to Châtel-de-Joux & Etival. Site on L on ent to vill. Sm, mkd pitch, terr, pt sl, pt shd; htd wc (cont); chem disp (wc); mv service pnt; shwrs inc; el pnts (6-10A) €2; lndtte, shop & 10km; tradsmn; snacks; bar 10km; playgrnd; lake sw 500m; games area; 30% statics; adv bkg; quiet; red low ssn. CCI. "Lovely position; helpful owner; guided walks - superb wild flowers." 1 Jul-31 Aug. € 12.50 (3 persons)   2007*

CLAIRVAUX LES LACS *6H2* (10km SW Rural) Camping de Surchauffant, Pont de la Pyle, 39270 La Tour-du-Meix [03 84 25 41 08; fax 03 84 35 56 88; info@camping-surchauffant.fr; www.camping-surchauffant.fr] Fr Clairvaux S on D27 or D49 to D470. Foll sp Lac de Vouglans, site sp. Lge, mkd pitch, pt sl, pt shd; wc; shwrs inc; el pnts (5A) inc; lndtte; shops adj; rest, snacks & bar; BBQ; playgrnd; pool; paddling pool; dir access to lake 120m; sailing; watersports; entmnt; TV rm; some statics; dogs €1.55; Eng spkn; adv bkg; quiet; cc acc. "Vg facs; lovely location; hiking trails." ♦ 27 Apr-11 Sep. € 19.35   2007*

See advertisement on page 327

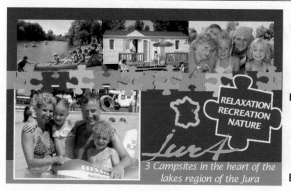

France

CLAIRVAUX LES LACS 6H2 (4km W Rural) Camping Le Moulin, 39130 Patornay [03 84 48 31 21; fax 03 84 44 71 21; contact@ camping-moulin.com; www.camping-moulin. com] Exit A39 junc 9 dir Lons-le-Saunier, on N78 SE to Pont-de-Poitte. After x-ing bdge over Rv Ain, ent to site on L. Lge, hdg/mkd pitch, hdstg, pt terr, shd; wc; chem disp; mv service pnt; baby facs; shwrs inc; el pnts (6A) inc; gas; lndtte; ice; shop; tradsmn; snacks; bar; BBQ; playgrnd; htd pool; waterslide; rv sw & sand beach 5km; fishing; games area; games rm; entmnt; child entmnt; TV; dogs €2; phone; poss cr; Eng spkn; adv bkg; cc acc; red low ssn; CCI. "Site clsd 1200-1400, do not arr during this time as narr app rd poss blocked with queuing traff; excel cent for touring Jura; vg site." ♦ 30 Apr-7 Sep. € 28.00   2007*

See advertisement above

CLAIRVAUX LES LACS 6H2 (7km W Rural) Camping Beauregard, 2 Grande Rue, 39130 Mesnois [tel/fax 03 84 48 32 51; reception@ juracampingbeauregard.com; www.juracamping beauregard.com] Fr Lons on N78 about 1km bef Pont-de-Poitte turn L on D151. Site 1km on L opp rd junc to Pont-de-Poitte. Lge, hdg/mkd pitch, hdstg, pt sl, terr, pt shd; htd wc (some cont); chem disp; baby facs; shwrs inc; el pnts (6A) €3 (poss long lead req); gas; lndtte; shop 1km; tradsmn; rest; playgrnd; htd pool high ssn; sand beach 800m; kayaking nr; tennis; cycle hire; games rm; 10% statics; dogs €2; poss cr; Eng spkn; adv bkg (dep req); quiet; cc acc. "Super site, clean & well-run; gd sized pitches; excel san facs; excel rest; narr site rds; vg info map fr recep for touring many beautiful lakes & waterfalls nrby." ♦ 1 Apr-30 Sep. € 21.50   2007*

See advertisement on next page

Before we move on, I'm going to fill in some site report forms and post them off to the editor, otherwise they won't arrive in time for the deadline at the end of September.

Camping Beauregard ★★★

39130 MESNOIS
Tel/Fax : 00 33 (0) 3 84 48 32 51

Bungalows and
Mobile Homes to let,
Heated swimming pool
Bar, Restaurant.

Open from 1.4 till 30.9

www.juracampingbeauregard.com
reception@juracampingbeauregard.com

CLAMECY *4G4* (5km NE Rural) Camping Le Bois Joli, Route de Villeprenoy, 89480 Andryes [tel/fax 03 86 81 70 48; info@campingauboisjoli.com; www.campingauboisjoli.com] S on N151 fr Auxerre to Coulanges-sur-Yonne. W on D39 sp Andryes, foll sps `Camping Andryes', site 3km after vill. Med, mkd pitch, terr, shd; htd wc; chem disp; baby facs; baby facs; fam bthrm; shwrs inc; el pnts (6A) €3 (poss rev pol); gas; lndry rm; shop; tradsmn; snacks; bar; BBQ; playgrnd; pool inc; rv sw, fishing & boat hire 2km; cycle hire; internet; TV; 10% statics; dogs €2; phone; Eng spkn; quiet; CCI. "Dutch owners; beautiful countryside; gd pitches; muddy in rain; excel facs." ♦ 1 Apr-1 Nov. € 17.75
2007*

CLAMECY *4G4* (8km SE Rural) Camping Municipal Les Fontaines, 58530 Brèves [tel/fax 03 86 24 25 26; mairie-breves@wanadoo.fr; www.vaux-yonne.com] On D985 (Clamecy-Corbigny) at Brèves. Both app clearly sp. Med, pt sl, unshd; wc; chem disp (wc); shwrs inc; el pnts (6A) €2; lndtte; tradsmn; shop; BBQ; playgrnd; 4% statics; dogs; phone. CCI. "Quiet site in pretty area nr Rv Yonne & canal; grnd soft after heavy rain; gd value; vg." ♦ 1 Jun-30 Sep. € 8.00
2007*

CLAMECY *4G4* (S Urban) Camp Municipal du Pont-Picot, Rue de Chevroche, 58500 Clamecy [03 86 27 05 97] Fr S via Nevers, Varzy Nisi turn R immed after level x-ing 1km bef Clamecy. Site sp 2.4km. Fr N Auxerre, Avallon cross rv foll camping sp. Sp but rte takes out of town & doubles back. App satisfactory, but single lane rd. Med, pt sl, pt shd; wc; chem disp; shwrs inc; el pnts (6A) €2.80; lndry rm; shops 1km; tradsmn; playgrnd; sw; poss cr; Eng spkn; quiet; CCI. "Pleasant, quiet site but rv & canal in beautiful location; not rec as NH - access narr; facs poss inadequate when busy; town 10 min walk on towpath; Vézelay (20km) worth a visit; excel." ♦ 1 May-30 Sep. € 10.60
2007*

CLAYETTE, LA *9A2* (8km NE Rural) Camping Château de Montrouant, 71800 Gibles [03 85 84 54 30; fax 03 85 84 52 80; campingdemontrouant@wanadoo.fr] Fr N79 at Trivy take D41 to Dompierre-les-Ormes & Montmelard, then Gibles. Site sp fr Gibles. Sm, mkd pitch, pt sl, pt shd; wc; chem disp; shwrs inc; el pnts (6A); lndry rm; basic shop & 4km; rest 1.5km; snacks; bar; playgrnd; pool; paddling pool; fishing lake; sh tennis; TV; dogs; v quiet. "Vg; v hospitable owners; unsuitable lge o'fits/m'vans due steep rds." ♦ ltd. 1 Jun-8 Sep. (CChq acc)
2007*

CLAYETTE, LA *9A2* (500m E Urban) Camping des Bruyères (formerly Municipal), 9 Route de Gibles, 71800 La Clayette [03 85 28 09 15; fax 03 85 28 17 16; aquadis1@wanadoo.fr; www.aquadis-loisirs.com] Site on D79, 100m fr D987 & lake. Med, hdg/mkd pitch, hdstg, pt sl, shd; htd wc; chem disp; mv service pnt; shwrs inc; el pnts (6A) inc; gas; lndtte; shops adj; tradsmn; snacks; bar 500m; BBQ; playgrnd; htd pool adj Jun-Aug; boating; tennis; games area; mini-golf; entmnt; 10% statics; dogs €1.60; phone; poss cr; adv bkg; quiet; CCI. "Excel site; v clean, pleasant & well-maintained; overlooks lake & chateau; friendly, helpful staff; gd-sized pitches, mostly sloping; attractive sm town in Beaujolais area; 3 min walk fr supmkt; numerous wine cellars." ♦ 1 Apr-31 Oct. € 14.60
2007*

CLAYETTE, LA *9A2* (13km S Rural) FFCC Camp Municipal Les Feuilles, Rue de Châtillon, 71170 Chauffailles [03 85 26 48 12; fax 03 85 26 55 02; st.marie.chauffailles@wanadoo.fr] S fr La Clayette on D985 (dir Les Echarmeaux), turn R at camp sp down hill & cross Rv Botoret to site. Med, mkd pitch, hdstg, pt shd; wc; chem disp; shwrs; el pnts (5-10A) €2.56-5.12; lndry rm; supmkt 500m; playgrnd; pool adj; fishing; tennis; games rm; TV; 30% statics; Eng spkn; adv bkg ess; quiet; 10% red CCI. "Attractive site; walking & wine area, easy walk to interesting town; gd san facs but hot water to shwrs & dishwashing only." 1 May-30 Sep. € 8.20
2007*

CLAYETTE, LA 9A2 (5km NW Rural) **Camping à la Ferme Les Noues, 71800 Vareilles** [03 85 28 09 78] Fr La Clayette on D989 to Vareilles, then foll site sp & sp 'fromage'. Sm, pt sl, pt shd; wc; chem disp; shwrs inc; el pnts; lndtte; quiet. "Excel CL-type site; v friendly, helpful owners." 1 Apr-31 Oct. € 10.00   2006*

CLECY 3D1 (3km N Rural) **Camping Les Rivières, 14570 St Rémy-sur-Orne** [02 31 79 30 84; campingsurorne@tele2.fr] S fr Thury-Harcourt on D562 dir Caumont-sur-Orne & Condé-sur Noireau to St Rémy; garden cent on L, campsite on R. Sm, pt shd; wc; shwrs inc; el pnts inc; lake sw adj; canoeing; walks; dogs; Eng spkn; adv bkg (dep req); quiet. "Situated by rv in heart of Suisse Normandie area; conv Caen ferry." 1 Apr-31 Oct. € 12.00
                                                            2006*

CLECY 3D1 (E Rural) **FFCC Camping Les Rochers des Parcs, La Cour, 14570 Clécy** [02 31 69 70 36; fax 02 31 66 96 08; campingclecy@ocampings. com; www.ocampings.com] Fr Condé take D562 to Caen. R turn sp to Clécy. Foll camp sp. Med, mkd pitch, some hdstg, pt sl, pt shd; wc; shwrs inc; el pnts (6A) €3.15; lndtte; shop 1km; tradsmn; snacks; playgrnd; rv sw; fishing; canoeing; games area; some statics; dogs €1; phone; quiet. "Lovely rvside site; friendly staff; gd facs but ltd low ssn; excel cent for walking." 1 Apr-15 Oct. € 11.30   2006*

CLELLES 9C3 (4km N Rural) **FFCC Camp Municipal de la Chabannerie, 38930 St Martin-de-Clelles** [tel/fax 04 76 34 00 38; camping-chabannerie@wanadoo.fr;   www.camping-chabannerie.eu] D1075 (N75) fr Grenoble, after St Michel-les-Portes look for rest on R. Turn L after 300m to St Martin-de-Clelles, site sp. Site well sp fr N & S. Sm, mkd pitch, hdstg, terr, pt shd; wc; chem disp; shwrs inc; el pnts (10A) €3; gas; lndtte; sm shop; tradsmn; snacks; bar; no BBQs; playgrnd; pool; TV rm; dogs €1.50; phone; Eng spkn; adv bkg; quiet; CCI. "Conv Vercours National Park & mountains; sm pitches & steep site rds, access diff lge o'fits; ltd facs low ssn; gd walking; v quiet site with 38 species of orchids in ssn." ♦ 1 Apr-31 Oct. € 14.00   2007*

> There aren't many sites open this early in the year. We'd better phone ahead to check that the one we're heading for is actually open.

CLELLES 9C3 (6km SE Rural) **Camping à la Ferme (Gabert), 38930 Clelles** [04 76 34 42 51] Fr D1075 (N75) take D526 thro vill of Clelles. At statue turn sharp R then next L in 1km. Farm on L in 200m. Sm, unshd; wc; shwrs inc; el pnts €2; lndry rm; cooking facs; ice; farm produce. "Splendid mountain scenery all round; pleasant town of Mens 14km; gd walking." 1 May-31 Oct. € 10.00   2004*

CLEON D'ANDRAN 9D2 (Rural) **Camp Municipal Les Cigales, Rue de Piscine, 26450 Cléon-d'Andran** [04 75 90 29 51 or 04 75 90 12 73 (Mairie); fax 04 75 90 43 73] Fr A7 leave at junc 16 sp Privas/Crest. S fr Crest on D538. In 5km take D6. In 11km at Cléon-d'Andran turn L in vill, in 100m turn R. Sm, shd; wc (cont); shwrs inc; el pnts €2.50; lndtte; shop 500m; pool; quiet; CCI. 1 Jun-31 Aug. € 10.80   2006*

CLERE SUR LAYON see Vihiers 4G1

CLEREY see Troyes 4E4

CLERGOUX 7C4 (300m E Rural) **Camping La Petite Rivière, 19320 Clergoux** [tel/fax 05 55 27 68 50; jcbakker@xs4all.nl; www. compumess.nl/lapetiteriviere] Site in 20km on D978 fr Tulle, sp. Sm, mkd pitch, pt sl, pt shd; wc; chem disp; mv service pnt; baby facs; shwrs inc; el pnts (6A) €2.20; lndtte; ice; tradsmn; lake sw & sand beach 1.5km; 20% statics; dogs €1.25; Eng spkn; adv bkg (dep req + bkg fee); quiet; CCI. "V helpful Dutch owner; 25 planned walks in area; excel." 1 Apr-30 Sep. € 9.75   2006*

CLERMONT EN ARGONNE 5D1 (6km SW Rural) **Camp Municipal Pierre Cochenet, 55120 Futeau** [03 29 88 27 06 (Mairie)] Leave A4 at Ste Ménéhould & proceed E on N3 for 9km to Les Islettes; turn S on D2 for 4km to Futeau; site behind church. Sm, pt shd; htd wc (some cont); chem disp (wc); shwrs inc; el pnts (10A) inc (poss rev pol); shops 4km; tradsmn; BBQ; dogs; phone; quiet bu church bells early am; CCI. "Site yourself; warden calls; gd for walking; vg NH." ♦ 1 Apr-1 Sep. € 10.00   2007*

⊞**CLERMONT FERRAND** 9B1 (7km SE Rural) **Camping Le Clos Auroy, Rue de la Narse, 63670 Orcet** [tel/fax 04 73 84 26 97; camping.le.clos. auroy@wanadoo.fr; www.camping-le-clos-auroy. com] S on A75 take exit 5 sp Orcet; foll D213 to Orcet for 2km, at rndabt onto D52, take 1st L, site on R, sp. Med, hdg/mkd pitch, hdstg, terr, pt shd; htd wc; chem disp; mv service pnt; shwrs inc; el pnts (5-10A) €3.35-€4.75 (poss rev pol); gas; lndtte; ice; sm shop 500m; tradsmn; snacks; bar; playgrnd; htd pool; paddling pool; rv sw, fishing 500m; tennis; horseriding; entmnt; 15% statics; dogs €2; phone; Eng spkn; adv bkg; quiet but v loud church bells (not at night); red low ssn/long stay; CCI. "Tidy, well-maintained site nr church; easy access; lge pitches, poss v high hedges; pitches by rv poss liable to flood; extra charge for m'vans staying 1-3 nights; ltd fresh water points; ltd facs low ssn; no rests nrby; interesting town; conv touring base Auvergne." ♦ € 16.80   2007*

France

CLERMONT FERRAND 9B1 (9km SE Urban)
Camp Municipal Le Pré des Laveuses, Rue des Laveuses, 63800 Cournon-d'Auvergne [04 73 84 81 30; fax 04 73 84 90 65; camping@cournon-auvergne.fr; www.cournon-auvergne.fr/camping] Fr S o'skts Clermont-Ferrand take D212 E to Cournon & foll sp in town; by Rv Allier, 1km E of Cournon. Lge, mkd pitch, pt shd; wc (some cont); chem disp; baby facs; shwrs inc; el pnts (5-10A) €3-4.55; lndtte; shop; supmkt nrby; snacks; bar; playgrnd; pool nrby; paddling pool; rv sw/lake adj; fishing & boating; dogs €1.75; poss cr; Eng spkn; quiet low ssn; red low ssn; cc acc; CCI. "Well-kept site - even low ssn; lge pitches; helpful manager; sports grnd adj; excel." ♦ 1 Apr-31 Oct. € 11.25
2006*

CLERMONT FERRAND 9B1 (15km SE Rural)
Camping La Font de Bleix, Le Lot, 63730 Les Martres-de-Veyre [04 73 39 26 49; fax 04 73 69 40 27; ailes-libres@infonie.fr] Fr Clermont-Ferrand exit A75 junc 5. Turn E onto D213, then R onto D978 at rndabt. In 1km turn L thro vill. Site on L after traff lts over rlwy x-ing. Sm, mkd pitch, pt sl, unshd; wc (cont); chem disp; shwrs inc; el pnts (10A) €3.50; lndtte; shop 1km; snacks; rv adj; dogs €1.60; quiet; adv bkg; CCI. "Dated facs." ♦ 3 Mar-30 Sep. € 7.80
2006*

⊞**CLERMONT FERRAND** 9B1 (6km SW Urban)
Camp Municipal Le Chanset, Ave Jean-Baptiste Marrou, 63122 Ceyrat [tel/fax 04 73 61 30 73 or 04 73 61 42 55 (Mairie); camping.lechanset@wanadoo.fr; www.ceyrat.com] Exit A75 junc 2 onto D2089 (N189) dir Aubière/Beaumont. Foll sp Beaumont then in approx 7km at rndabt junc foll sp Ceyrat. Uphill into Ceyrat; curve R to traff lts; cross main rd & take L fork up hill. Site at top on R - turn poss diff so cont 50m for U-turn back to site. Lge, hdg/mkd pitch, terr, pt sl, pt shd; htd wc (some cont); chem disp; mv service pnt; baby facs; shwrs inc; el pnts (6-10A) inc (poss rev pol); gas; lndtte; shop; rest; snacks; bar; BBQ; playgrnd; htd pool high ssn; games & TV rm; 10% statics; dogs €1.20; bus; phone; security barrier; poss cr; some Eng spkn; adv bkg; poss noisy when cr; red + 7 days/low ssn; cc acc; CCI. "Excel views; busy site but vg for families; friendly staff; gd bus to Clermont-Ferrand; pool used by public at w/end (poss cr); some sm pitches; gd base for Auvergne, Puy de Dôme & Volcania Park; conv a'route." ♦
€ 17.40
2007*

CLERMONT FERRAND 9B1 (5km W Rural)
Camping Indigo Royat, Route de Gravenoire, 63130 Royat [04 73 35 97 05; fax 04 73 35 67 69; royat@camping-indigo.com; www.camping-indigo.com] Site diff to find fr Clermont-Ferrand cent. Fr N, leave A71 at Clermont-Ferrand. Foll sp Chamalières/Royat, then sp Royat. Go under rlwy bdge & pass thermal park on L. At mini-rndabt go L & up hill. At statue, turn L & go up long hill. Look for site sp & turn R. Site on R. NB Do not go down steep rd with traff calming. Lge, mkd/hdstg pitch, terr, pt shd; htd wc; chem disp; mv service pnt; some serviced pitches; baby facs; shwrs inc; el pnts (6-10A) €4.50-6.20; gas; lndtte; ice; shop; tradsmn; rest, snacks high ssn; bar; BBQ; playgrnd; htd pool; tennis; cycle hire; internet; entmnt; TV rm; some statics; dogs €2.90; phone; Eng spkn; adv bkg; quiet; red low ssn; cc acc; CCI. "Excel, clean site; spacious; lovely views at top levels over Clermont." ♦ 5 Apr-19 Oct. € 19.80 (CChq acc)
2007*

CLERMONT L'HERAULT 10F1 (7km SE Rural)
Camping Les Rivières, Route de la Sablière, 34800 Canet [04 67 96 75 53; fax 04 67 96 58 35; camping-les-rivieres@wanadoo.fr; www.camping-lesrivieres.com] On D2 sp Clermont-l'Hérault/Canet. At Canet foll sp approx 2km. Med, hdg/mkd pitch, pt shd; wc; shwrs inc; el pnts (5A) €4; gas; lndtte; ice; tradsmn; rest; snacks; playgrnd; pool; solarium; rv fishing; TV rm; 5% statics; sm dogs only €5; Eng spkn; adv bkg; quiet. "Well-laid out; nice pool with rest/bar; friendly; young, hardworking & helpful owners; gd area for touring; nr to Lac du Salagou; highly rec." ♦ ltd.
8 Apr-15 Sep. € 22.00
2007*

⊞**CLERMONT L'HERAULT** 10F1 (5km NW Rural) Camp Municipal du Lac du Salagou, 34800 Clermont-l'Hérault [04 67 96 13 13; fax 04 67 96 32 12; centretouristique@wanadoo.fr; www.le-salagou.fr] Fr N9 S take D909 to Clermont-l'Hérault, foll sp to Lac du Salagou 1.5km after town sp. Fr by-pass foll sp Bédarieux. Well sp. Lge, mkd pitch, pt sl, pt shd; htd wc (some cont); chem disp; mv service pnt; shwrs inc; el pnts (6-10A) €2.70-3.30; lndtte; ice; shops 4km; tradsmn; rest; snacks; BBQ; playgrnd; shgl beach & lake 300m; fishing; watersports; entmnt; TV; many statics; dogs €1.55; phone; poss cr; adv bkg; noise fr disco some nights; CCI. "Unique location; poss muddy low ssn & poss windy; facs dated; gd undeveloped beaches around lake." ♦ € 11.40
2007*

CLERY SUR SOMME see Péronne 3C3

CLISSON 2H4 (S Urban) **Camp Municipal du Vieux Moulin, Route de Nantes, 44190 Clisson [02 40 54 44 48 or 02 40 54 02 95 (LS)]** 1km NW of Clisson cent on main rd to Nantes, at rndabt. Look for old windmill nr ent on L of rd. Leclerc hypmkt on opp side of rd; site sp fr town cent. Narr ent. Sm, hdg pitch, pt sl, pt shd; wc; chem disp; shwrs inc; el pnts (10A) inc; hypmkt, rest, snacks, bar 500m; tradsmn; fishing, tennis, horseriding adj; boating; phone (card only); Eng spkn; adv bkg; quiet but some rd noise. "Gd municipal site; v clean facs; lge pitches; gate clsd 1030-1500 (low ssn) but can phone warden; picturesque town 15 min walk fr site; vg." 15 Apr-15 Oct. € 12.50   2007*

CLOHARS CARNOET see Pouldu, Le 2F2

CLOYES SUR LE LOIR 4F2 (1km N Rural) **Parc de Loisirs de Cloyes, Route de Montigny, 28220 Cloyes-sur-le-Loir [02 37 98 50 53; fax 02 37 98 33 84; info@parc-de-loisirs.com]** Located on L bank of Rv Loir off N10; site sp. Med, pt shd; wc (some cont); chem disp; shwrs inc; el pnts (5A) €3.25; ice; shop; rest; snacks; bar; playgrnd; pool; waterslide; cycle hire; 50% statics; dogs €1.65; adv bkg. "Facs gd for children but ltd low ssn; well-run; pleasant & quiet in wooded valley; site fees inc use of sm leisure park, pedaloes & rowing boats on Rv Loir." 15 Mar-15 Nov. € 18.90   2005*

CLOYES SUR LE LOIR 4F2 (2km S Rural) **Aire Naturelle Camping Les Fouquets, 41160 St Jean-Froidmentel [02 54 82 66 97; lesfouquets@aol.com]** Off N10 twd Vendôme. Sp Les Fouquets 200m SE of N10. Sm, shd; wc; shwrs inc; el pnts (4-6A) inc; lndry rm; shop, rest 2km; pool; fishing, tennis & sailing 2km; 10% statics; dogs €1; quiet; CCI. "Lovely family-run site in woodland; v friendly owner; warm welcome." ♦ 1 Apr-30 Sep. € 11.20   2006*

CLUNY 9A2 (E Urban) **Camp Municipal St Vital, Rue de Griottons, 71250 Cluny [tel/fax 03 85 59 08 34; cluny-camping@wanadoo.fr]** Fr Cluny take D15 sp Azé, cross narr rv bdge. Site 1st R adj to pool. Lge, mkd pitch, sl, pt shd; wc; chem disp; shwrs inc; el pnts (6A) €2.75 (poss rev pol); gas; ice; lndtte; shops 500m; playgrnd; pool adj (free to campers); poss cr; adv bkg rec high ssn; frequent rlwy noise daytime (not at night). "V tidy site; clean, well-kept facs (plenty); helpful staff; avoid end Sep/beg Oct when site taken over for dog show (600+ lge dogs!); cycle & walking rte adj (Voie Verte); interesting town & abbey in walking dist." ♦ 1 May-30 Sep. € 11.20   2007*

CLUNY 9A2 (10km S Rural) **Camping Le Lac de St Point-Lamartine, Route Lamartine, 71520 St Point [03 85 50 52 31 or 03 85 50 51 18 (Mairie); fax 03 85 50 51 92; campingstpoint@wanadoo.fr]** Turn S off N79, Mâcon/Paray-le-Monial rd, turn L bef Ste Cécile on D22; site sp at junc; site 100m on R after St Point vill. Med, hdg/mkd pitch, pt terr, pt sl (gd blocks needed), pt shd; wc; chem disp; shwrs inc; el pnts (4-13A) €3-5.50; gas 800m; lndtte; ice; shop 800m; rest; snacks; bar; BBQ; playgrnd; TV; lake sw adj; fishing; boat hire; tennis 4km; 30% statics; dogs €1.50; phone; Eng spkn; adv bkg; quiet; CCI. "Some sm pitches for long o'fits; poss no hot water for washing up; ltd facs low ssn; Cluny attractive town & abbey; lovely scenery & pleasant lake; on edge of Beaujolais; sp walks fr site." 1 Apr-31 Oct. € 12.10 (4 persons)   2006*

Did you know you can fill in site report forms on the Club's website — www.caravanclub.co.uk?

France

CLUNY 9A2 (11km NW Rural) **Camp Municipal de la Clochette, 71250 Salornay-sur-Guye [03 85 59 90 11; fax 03 85 59 47 52; mairie.salornay@wanadoo.fr]** Sp fr N or S on D980; turn E on D14 sp Cormatin & Taizé. Ent opp PO within 300m. Med, mkd pitch, pt shd; wc; shwrs €0.80; chem disp; mv service pnt; el pnts (8-10A) €1.60-2.40; lndry rm; ice; shop adj; BBQ; playgrnd; rv adj; fishing; adv bkg; quiet; CCI. "Pleasant, tidy site on sm rv & mill pond; site yourself, recep open morning & evening; well sp walks around vill; rvside pitches poss subject to flooding if rv rises." 21 May-4 Sep. € 5.20   2005*

CLUSAZ, LA 9B3 (6km N Rural) **Camping Le Clos du Pin, 74450 Le Grand-Bornand [04 50 02 70 57 or 04 50 02 27 61; contact@le-clos-du-pin.com; www.le-clos-du-pin.com]** Foll sps fr La Clusaz &/or St Jean-de-Sixte to Grand Bornand. Thro vill dir Vallée du Bouchet; site on R in 1km. Med, mkd pitch, unshd; htd wc; chem disp; shwrs inc; el pnts (2-10A) €2.90-5; gas 1km; lndtte; ice; shops 1km; BBQ; playgrnd; rv sw & fishing 100m; pool 1km; TV/games rm; 30% statics; dogs €1.30; adv bkg; quiet; cc acc; CCI. "Base for ski stn; ski & boot rm; friendly owner; v clean san facs, shwrs hot; high ssn is Feb when fees are higher; excel." ♦ 15 Jun-20 Sep & 1 Dec-10 May. € 13.00   2007*

CLUSAZ, LA 9B3 (6km N Rural) **Camping L'Escale,** 74450 Le Grand-Bornand [04 50 02 20 69; fax 04 50 02 36 04; contact@campinglescale.com; www.campinglescale.com] Exit A41 junc 17 onto D16/D909 E dir La Clusaz. At St Jean-de-Sixt turn L at rndabt sp Le Grand Bornand. After 1.5km foll camping sp on main rd & at junc turn R sp for site & 'Vallée du Bouchet'. Site is 1st exit R at rndabt at end of this rd. D4 S fr Cluses not rec while towing as v steep & winding. Med, mkd pitch, pt sl, terr, pt shd; htd wc; chem disp; mv service pnt; serviced pitch in summer; baby facs; shwrs inc; el pnts (3-10A) €4.46-6.69 (poss rev pol); gas; lndtte; ice; shop; tradsmn; rest; snacks; bar; BBQ; playgrnd; 2 pools (1 htd, covrd); paddling pool; fishing; wintersports; cycle hire 200m; tennis; archery; wifi internet; games/TV rm; 20% statics; dogs €2.23; skibus; recep 0830-1200 & 1400-1930 high ssn; poss cr; adv bkg ess (dep & bkg fee req); red low ssn; cc acc; CCI. "Scenic area; family-run site; helpful; vg rest; free use htd ski/boot rm in winter; excel sports facs in town; boggy in wet weather; vg mkt Wed." ♦ 22 May-21 Sep & 7 Dec-20 Apr. € 22.50 (CChq acc) ABS - M07   2007*

CLUSAZ, LA 9B3 (2km E Rural) **Camping Le Plan du Fernuy, Route des Confins,** 74220 La Clusaz [04 50 02 44 75; fax 04 50 32 67 02; info@plandufernuy.com; www.plandufernuy. com] Fr Annecy take D909 to La Clusaz (32km). Turn L for Les Confins & site on R in 2km. Med, mkd pitch, pt sl, unshd; wc; chem disp; shwrs inc; baby rm; el pnts (13A) inc; gas; lndtte; shop; snacks; bar; playgrnd; htd, covrd pool; paddling pool; wifi internet; TV; some statics; dogs €2.20; free ski bus; poss cr; quiet. "Site at 1200m alt; excel site & facs; poss diff lge o'fits." ♦ 17 Jun-3 Sep & 17 Dec-30 Apr. € 27.70   2006*

> This guide relies on site report forms submitted by caravanners like us; we'll do our bit and tell the editor what we think of the campsites we've visited.

CLUSES 9A3 (1km N Rural) **Camping La Corbaz, Ave des Glières,** 74300 Cluses [04 50 98 44 03; fax 04 50 96 02 15; camping.lacorbaz@wanadoo. fr; www.cluses.fr] Take N205 W fr Chamonix or fr Annecy N203 NE to Bonneville & N205 E to Cluses; take D902 N dir Taninges; after x-ing rlway turn L onto D19 beside rlwy; site on R in 500m. Med, pt shd; htd wc; chem disp; mv service pnt; shwrs; el pnts (4-10A); ice; shop; rest; bar; playgrnd; pool; lake sw 2km; TV; 70% statics; adv bkg; quiet but some rd & rlwy noise. "Excel base for touring Haute Savoie; lge pitches; helpful owners" 1 May-15 Oct. € 13.15   2007*

⊞CLUSES 9A3 (6km N Rural) **Camp Municipal Essi Les Thézières, Les Vernays-sous-la-Ville,** 74440 Taninges [04 50 34 25 59; fax 04 50 34 39 78; camping.taninges@wanadoo.fr; www.taninges.com] Take D902 N fr Cluses; site 1km S of Taninges on L - just after 'Taninges' sp on ent town boundary; sp Camping-Caravaneige. Lge, pt shd; htd wc (some cont); chem disp; mv service pnt; shwrs inc; el pnts (6-10A) €2.20-6.75; lndtte; ltd shop; shops, rest, snacks, bar 1km; BBQ; playgrnd; pool at Samoens 11km; tennis; TV rm; dogs €1.05; phone; poss cr; Eng spkn; quiet; cc acc; CCI; "Conv for N Haute Savoie & Switzerland to Lake Geneva; splendid site with magnificent views; lge pitches; excel facs; friendly & helpful staff; excel." ♦ € 7.80   2007*

COGNAC 7B2 (200m N Urban) **Aire Communautaire, Place de la Levade, Quartier St Jaques,** 16700 Cognac [05 45 36 64 30; contact@cc-cognac.fr] M'vans only. N fr Cognac, cross rv bdge & foll m'van sp on L. Opp Hennessy Cognac House. Chem disp, mv service pnt, el pnts; lndtte; shop; rest. "Free NH adj rv." 1 Jun-15 Sep.   2006*

COGNAC 7B2 (1km NE Urban) **Camping de Cognac, Blvd de Châtenay, Route de Sainte Sévère,** 16100 Cognac [05 45 32 13 32 or 05 45 36 64 30 (LS); fax 05 45 32 15 82; info@campingdecognac.com; www.camping decognac.com] Foll 'Camping' sp fr town cent, on R of D24 by Rv Charente just S of rv. Take care ent barrier. Med, hdg/mkd pitch, pt shd; wc (some cont); chem disp; mv service pnt; shwrs inc; el pnts (6A) inc (poss long leads req); lndtte; ice; shop high ssn & 2km; tradsmn; rest, snacks high ssn; bar; BBQ; playgrnd; htd pool; rv boating & fishing; dogs €1.50; phone; poss cr; Eng spkn; adv bkg; cc acc; red long stay/low ssn; CCI. "Vg, quiet & clean site; gd value; gates clsd 2200-0700; no twin axles; footpath to town cent along rv; excel lge park with many facs; 30 mins walk along rv; conv Cognac distilleries (ask for free vouchers at site recep)." ♦ 27 Apr-21 Oct. € 17.00   2007*

COGNAC 7B2 (10km E Rural) **Camp Municipal,** 16200 Bourg-Charente [05 45 80 30 25 (Mairie); fax 05 45 81 64 20] Fr Cognac E603, site sp on D158. Sm, pt sl, pt shd; wc (some cont); chem disp; mv service pnt; shwrs €1; el pnts (6A) €1.50; rest, shop 500m; fishing; poss cr; cc acc; red long stay. "Delightful little site on banks of Rv Charente; gd clean facs; gd walks & cycle path to Jarnac & Cognac; poss itinerants; warden calls pm; facs poss stretched in high ssn." 15 Jun-15 Sep. € 6.00   2007*

COGNAC *7B2* (14km E Urban) **Camping de l'Ile Madame**, 16200 Jarnac [05 45 81 18 54 or 05 45 81 68 02; fax 05 45 81 24 98; camping.jarnac@wanadoo.fr; www.camping-jarnac.com] Turn E at S end of rv bdge at S end of town. Lge, pt shd; wc; shwrs inc; el pnts (10A) €2.50 (rev pol); ice; lndtte; shops & rest adj; playgrnd; pool; games area; golf, canoe & cycle hire nrby; entmnt; TV; dogs €0.50; poss cr; adv bkg; poss noise fr adj sports ground & disco; CCI. "Well-run site; clean facs; gd sized pitches; no twin-axles; nr Courvoisier bottling plant." 1 Apr-30 Sep. € 12.10   2006*

⊞COGNAC *7B2* (8km S Rural) **Camping Le Chiron (Chainier), Le Chiron, Celles, 16130 Salles-d'Angles** [05 45 83 72 79; fax 05 45 83 64 80; mchainier@voila.fr] Fr Cognac D731 Barbezieux to Salles-d'Angles, R at bottom hill then in 3km turn L & 1km on R (foll Chambres d'Hôtes sps). Sm, pt sl, pt shd; htd wc (1 cont); chem disp; shwrs inc; el pnts (10A) €4 (rev pol); shop 3km; no dogs; Eng spkn; quiet; cc not acc. "Vg; meals avail at farm." € 9.00   2006*

COGNAC LA FORET *7B3* (1.5km W Rural) **FFCC Camping Les Alouettes, Route des Alouettes, 87310 Cognac-la-Forêt** [03 55 03 26 93; info@camping-des-alouettes.com; www.camping-des-alouettes.com] Fr Aixe on D10, site W of Cognac-la-Forêt on D10, sp to L. Med, hdg/mkd pitch, unshd; wc; chem disp; shwrs inc; el pnts (6A) €2; shop 1.5km; tradsmn; snacks; bar; playgrnd; lake sw 800m; leisure facs 1km; 3% statics; dogs €1; Eng spkn; quiet; CCI. "New Dutch owners 2006; v friendly; conv war vill Oradour-sur-Glane; vg." ♦ ltd. 15 Apr-30 Sep. € 10.50   2006*

COGNIN LES GORGES *9C3* (E Rural) **Aire Naturelle La Chatonnière, Route de Malleval, 38470 Cognin-les-Gorges** [04 76 38 18 76; info@la-chato.com; www.la-chato.com] Exit A49 junc 10 S onto N532, turn 1st L after Cognin-les-Gorges sp at service stn. Fr vill cent, take 1st R past church. In 50m turn L at stop sp, site 100m on L. Sm, pt shd; wc; chem disp; mv service pnt; child/baby facs; shwrs inc; el pnts (10A) €2 (rev pol); ice; shop 500m; tradsmn; pool 6km; rv sw; no statics; dogs; bus; phone 100m; Eng spkn; adv bkg; quiet; red +7 days; CCI. "Welcoming, helpful owners; bread baked on site; meals avail; picturesque mountain setting; conv Grenoble & Vercours." 1 Apr-31 Oct. € 14.00   2005*

COGOLIN see Grimaud *10F4*

COLLE SUR LOUP, LA see Cagnes sur Mer *10E4*

COLLIAS see Remoulins *10E2*

COLMAR *6F3* (2km E Urban) **Camping de l'Ill, Route de Neuf-Brisach, Pont de Harbourg, 68000 Colmar** [tel/fax 03 89 41 15 94; campingdelill@calixo.net] Exit A35 junc 25, foll Freibourg sp. At 2nd rndabt turn L to Colmar cent, site on L bef bdge. Lge, hdg/mkd pitch, hdstg, pt sl, terr, shd; wc; chem disp; mv service pnt; shwrs; el pnts (3-6A) €3.25-4.25 (poss rev pol); lndtte; shop & tradsmn (high ssn); supmkt nr; rest; snacks, bar (high ssn); playgrnd; pool 8km; rv sw adj; 10% statics; dogs €1.75; bus to city cent; poss cr; some Eng spkn; adv bkg; noise fr a'route; cc acc (over €20); CCI. "On rv bank; friendly staff; excel san facs; some pitches req steel pegs; sep area for NH; recep clsd 1200-1400 & 2100-0800; gd rest on site; easy walk to town cent; beautiful city with 'Little Venice' canals; gd art gallery; conv Alsace wine district; gd value; excel." ♦ ltd. 21 Mar-21 Dec. € 11.20
2007*

COLMAR *6F3* (7km S Rural) **Camping Clair Vacances, Route de Herrlisheim, 68127 Ste Croix-en-Plaine** [03 89 49 27 28; fax 03 89 49 21 55; clairvacances@wanadoo.fr; www.clairvacances.com] Exit N83 at sp Herrlisheim onto D1 bis. Take 2nd rd to vill sp camping, foll site sp thro vill. NB Rd thru vill narr with traff calming bollards. Fr A35 turn off at junc 27 sp Herrlisheim/Ste Croix en Plaine onto D1 dir Herrlisheim to site in 1km. Med, hdg/mkd pitch, some hdstg, pt shd; htd wc; chem disp; mv service pnt; baby facs; shwrs inc; el pnts (8-13A) €3-5 (long lead poss req); gas; service wash; shop 2km; tradsmn; snacks high ssn; BBQ; playgrnd; pool; cycle hire; 10% statics; no dogs; phone; poss cr; Eng spkn; adv bkg dep req; quiet; cc acc; red low ssn; CCI. "Well-maintained & supervised; v helpful & friendly owners; gd size pitches; 1st class spotless san facs; barriers in place; gd touring base Alsace wine rte; weekly wine-tasting; excel." ♦ 1 Apr-21 Oct. € 20.00
2007*

COLMAR *6F3* (7km SW Rural) **Camp Municipal Les Trois Châteaux, 10 Rue du Bassin, 68420 Eguisheim** [03 89 23 19 39; fax 03 89 24 10 19] Foll N83 S (Colmar by-pass) R at sp Eguisheim. R into vill to site at top of vill, foll camp sp. Med, mkd pitch, pt sl, terr, pt shd; wc; chem disp; mv service pnt; shwrs inc; el pnts (6A) €3.40 (poss rev pol); gas; lndtte; ice; shops, rest & bars in vill 300m; hypmkt 5km; playgrnd; dogs €1.50; phone adj; poss cr; clsd 1230-1400; adv bkg (tel 2 days bef arr); poss noisy; cc not acc; CCI. "No c'vans over 7m (inc draw bar); sm pitches poss cramped; mv pitches flat but some c'van pitches sl & poss diff; many local attractions; wine-tasting & cellars in vill; rec arr early; stork park adj; delightful area; excel, busy site." ♦ ltd. 1 Apr-30 Sep. € 11.50   2006*

France

COLMAR 6F3 (7km W) **FFCC Camp Municipal Les Cigognes, Quai de la Gare, 68230 Turckheim [03 89 27 02 00; fax 03 89 80 86 93; ot.turckheim@wanadoo.fr www.turckheim-alsace.com]** Fr N83 twd Turckheim turn W onto D11 to Turckheim. On ent vill, turn immed L down 1-way rd after x-ing rlwy lines. Do not cross rv bdge. Site on L bef bdge, adj stadium. Med, hdg pitch, pt shd; wc; chem disp; mv service pnt; baby facs; shwrs inc; el pnts (6-10A) €3.10-5; Indtte; shop 500m; playgrnd; entmnt; TV; 50% statics; dogs €1.10; bus 500m; train 250m; poss cr; quiet; red low ssn; CCI. "Lovely site with spacious pitches; OK san facs, ltd low ssn; office clsd 1100-1400; cycle rtes nr; resident storks; short walk to beautiful old vill with rests; gd wine co-operative 500m; highly rec." ♦ 15 Mar-31 Oct. € 11.10   2007*

COLMARS 9D4 (500m S Rural) **Aire Naturelle Les Pommiers, 04370 Colmars [04 92 83 41 56; fax 04 92 83 40 86]** Fr N on D908 on ent Colmars take 1st R over rd bdge & foll site sp. Sm, pt terr, pt shd; wc (some cont); chem disp (wc); shwrs inc; el pnts (10A) €2; Indry rm; shop 500m; tradsmn; rest, snacks, bar 500m; BBQ; pool 500m; dogs €0.65; phone; adv bkg; CCI. "Beautifully situated, well-maintained CL-type site; friendly owner; Colmars fascinating medieval walled town; ideal for walking in Haute-Provence." ♦ ltd. 14 Apr-30 Sep. € 10.00 | 2005*

COLMARS 9D4 (1km S Rural) **Camping Le Bois Joly, Chemin des Buissières, 04370 Colmars-les-Alpes [04 92 83 40 40; fax 04 92 83 50 60; camping-le-bois-joly@club-internet.fr]** Fr S on D955 & D908 twds Colmars, go thro Beauvezer & Villars-Colmars. Ignore two other sites en rte. Site sp. Sm, mkd, hdstg, shd; wc (some cont); chem disp (wc); mv service pnt; shwrs inc; el pnts (6A) €2.43; gas; Indtte; ice; rest, snacks, bar & shop 1km; BBQ; tradsmn high ssn; rv fishing adj; no dogs; phone; adv bkg; quiet; CCI. "Well-kept wooded site with gd atmosphere; gd facs; ideal base for walking in Haute Provence; friendly owners." 1 May-30 Sep. € 10.40   2006*

COLMARS 9D4 (2km SW Rural) **Camping Le Haut Verdon, 04370 Villars-Colmars [04 92 83 40 09; fax 04 92 83 56 61; campinglehautverdon@wanadoo.fr; www.lehautverdon.com]** Only app fr S on D955 & D908 fr St André-les-Alps thro Beauvezer. Clearly sp on ent Villars-Colmars on R. (Do not confuse with Municipal site approx 5km bef this site). Med, hdg/mkd pitch, pt shd; htd wc; chem disp; mv service pnt; shwrs inc; el pnts (6-10A) €3-4; gas; Indtte; ice; shop & 2km; tradsmn; rest 1km; snacks; bar; playgrnd; pool; rv fishing; TV rm; dogs €2; poss cr; Eng spkn; adv bkg; quiet; CCI. "Superb setting on Rv Verdon; gd, clean san facs; v helpful staff; conv Colmars, flower meadows, Allos Lake." ♦ 3 May-14 Sep. € 25.00   2007*

COMBOURG 2E4 (8km NE Rural) **Camping Le Bois Coudrais, 35270 Cuguen [02 99 73 27 45; fax 02 99 73 13 08; info@vacancebretagne.com; www.vacancebretagne.com]** Fr Combourg take D796 twd Pleine-Fougères, 5km out of Combourg turn L on D83 to Cuguen; 500m past Cuguen, turn L, site sp. Or fr Dol de Bretagne, take D795 then turn L onto D9 to Cuguen. Sm, hdg/mkd pitch, pt sl, pt shd; wc; chem disp; shwrs inc; el pnts (10A) inc ; ice; shop 500m; snacks; bar; BBQ; playgrnd; pool; fishing, watersports, golf, zoo, adventure park nr; cycle hire; dogs €1; Eng spkn; adv bkg (dep req); v quiet; red long stay; no cc acc; CCI. "CL-type site surrounded by fields & trees; friendly British owners; gd facs; great for young children; sm animal-petting area; central to major attractions; gd touring base." ♦ 1 Apr-30 Sep. € 14.50   2007*

COMBOURG 2E4 (1.5km SE Rural) **Camp Municipal Le Vieux Châtel, Route de Lanrigan, 35270 Combourg [02 99 73 07 03; fax 02 99 73 29 66; ot@combourg.org]** Fr W, N & E foll sp fr town cent. Fr S on D795, turn R at lake. Site on L in approx 500m. Med, hdg/mkd pitch, pt shd; wc; chem disp; shwrs; el pnts (5A) €1.85; Indtte; shop, rest, snacks, bar 500m; BBQ; playgrnd; htd pool 1km; lake fishing nrby; phone; Eng spkn; adv bkg; quiet; CCI. "Forests, chateaux & churches nrby; 20 mins to Emerald Coast; castle in Combourg." 1 Jun-15 Sep. € 8.50   2006*

COMBOURG 2E4 (6km SW Rural) **FFCC Camping Domaine du Logis, 35190 La Chapelle-aux-Filtzméens [02 99 45 25 45; fax 02 99 45 30 40; domainedulogis@wanadoo.fr; www.domainedulogis.com]** Fr N176 at junc for Dol-de-Bretagne branch R onto D155 sp Dol & take D795 S to Combourg. Then take D13 twd St Domineuc, go thro La Chapelle-aux-Filtzméens & site on R in 1km. Lge, hdg/mkd pitch, pt shd; wc; chem disp; mv service pnt; shwrs inc; el pnts (10A) €4; gas; Indtte; ice; sm shop & 5km; tradsmn; rest; snacks; bar; BBQ; playgrnd; 2 htd pools; sand beach 20km; fitness rm; canoes 800m; fishing nr; cycle hire; mini-golf; golf 15km; games area; games rm; entmnt; internet;TV rm; 10% statics; dogs €2 (some breeds not acc - check with site); phone; Eng spkn; adv bkg; quiet; cc acc; red low ssn/long stay/CCI. "Helpful staff; mkt in Combourg Mon; conv St Malo, Mont St Michel, Dinan & Channel Islands; excel." ♦ 22 Mar-31 Oct. € 28.00 (CChq acc) ABS - B02

2007*

See advertisement opposite

COMBRIT STE MARINE see Bénodet 2F2

France

COMPREIGNAC *7B3* (2.5km N Rural) **Camp Municipal de Montimbert, 87140 Compreignac [05 55 71 04 49 or 05 55 71 00 23 (Mairie)]** S on A20 to Limoges, turn W at exit 26 Le Crouzill. Foll D5 W to Compreignac, turn N by church onto D60, fork L, foll sp 'Montimbert' for site. Sm, pt sl, pt shd; wc; chem disp; shwrs inc; el pnts (5A) €2.50 (rev pol); shop in vill; playgrnd; lake sw, fishing & boating 1km; CCI. "Facs ltd; unreliable opening dates." 1 Jun-15 Sep. € 6.00   2005*

COMPREIGNAC *7B3* (6km N Rural) **Site de Santrop, Lac de St-Pardoux, 87640 Razès [05 55 71 08 08 or 05 55 71 04 40 (LS); fax 05 55 71 23 93; www.lac-saint-pardoux.com]** N fr Limoges on A20, exit 25 Razès, sp Lac de St Pardoux; foll sp 4km to site. Lge, hdg pitch, pt sl, shd; wc; baby facs; shwrs inc; el pnts (6A) €3; lndtte; shop; rest; bar; playgrnd; pool; waterslide; lake adj; watersports; games area; entmnt; TV rm; dogs €1.10; poss cr; Eng spkn; poss noisy. "Popular, busy site on lake beach; random pitching under trees in woodland; gd rest on lakeside; poss late night noise fr revellers on beach." 4 May-18 Sep. € 15.80   2005*

As soon as we get home I'm going to post all these site report forms to the editor for inclusion in next year's guide. I don't want to miss the September deadline.

CONCARNEAU *2F2* (2km S Coastal) **Camping Le Cabellou Plage, Ave de Cabellou, Kersaux, 29900 Concarneau [02 98 97 37 41; info@ camping-cabellou-plage.com; www.le-cabellou-plage.com]** Turn W off D783 dir Le Cabellou, site sp. Lge, pt shd; wc; shwrs; el pnts (3-6A) €3-6; sand beach adj; dogs €1; adv bkg; quiet. "Pleasant seaside site." 1 Apr-30 Sep. € 16.50   2007*

See advertisement above

CONCARNEAU 2F2 (3km W Coastal) **Camping Les Prés Verts, Kernous-Plage, 29900 Concarneau [02 98 97 09 74; fax 02 98 97 32 06; info@presverts. com; www.presverts.com]** Exit N165 onto D70 dir Concarneau. At rndabt by Leclerc supmkt foll sp 'Centre Ville' (Town Centre) with Leclerc on L. At x-rds with traff lts go strt over, then fork R into Rue de Kerneach & down slope. Bear L at 1st rndabt & R at next. Keep R to join coast rd foll sp La Forêt-Fouesnant; pass Hôtel Océans; site 3rd rd on L in 1.5km. Med, hdg/mkd pitch, pt sl, pt shd; wc; chem disp; mv service pnt; serviced pitch; shwrs inc; el pnts (6A) inc (poss rev pol & long lead req); gas 2km; lndtte; shop; rest 3km; BBQ (charcoal/gas); playgrnd; htd pool; paddling pool; dir access to sand beach 300m; sailing 1km; horseriding 1km; games rm; 10% statics; dogs €1.60; recep 0900-1200 & 1400-2000 high ssn; c'vans over 8m not acc high ssn; poss cr; adv bkg; quiet; red low ssn; cc acc. "Rec; friendly staff; gd facs, ltd low ssn & poss unkempt; dir access to beach; excursions booked; mkt Mon & Fri; gd touring base." 1 May-22 Sep. € 26.90 ABS - B24   2007*

The opening dates and prices on this campsite have changed. I'll send a site report form to the editor for the next edition of the guide.

CONCARNEAU 2F2 (1km NW Urban/Coastal) **Camping Les Sables Blancs, Le Dorlett, 29900 Concarneau [tel/fax 02 98 97 16 44; contact@ camping-lessablesblancs.com; www.camping-lessablesblancs.com]** Exit N165 to Concarneau dir 'Centre Ville'. Then foll sp 'La Côte' 300m after traff lts. Site on R, sp. Med, hdg/mkd pitch, hdstg, pt sl, terr, pt shd; htd wc; chem disp; mv service pnt; baby facs; fam bthrm; shwrs inc; el pnts (10A) €3; lndtte; ice; shop 1.5km; tradsmn; rest; snacks; bar; BBQ; playgrnd; htd pool; paddling pool; sand beach 200m; games area; entmnt; TV rm; 3% statics; dogs €1; phone; poss cr; Eng spkn; adv bkg; quiet; cc acc; red low ssn/long stay; CCI. "Nice, family site in sheltered woodland; v clean; excel san facs; 20 mins walk into town; vg." ♦ 1 Apr-30 Sep. € 17.00   2007*

CONCORET 2F3 (500m S Rural) **Camp Municipal du Val-aux-Fées, 56430 Concoret [02 97 22 64 82 or 02 97 22 61 19 (Mairie); fax 02 97 22 93 17; mairie-concoret@wanadoo.fr]** Site sp fr cent of Concoret. Lge, mkd pitch, pt sl, pt shd; wc; chem disp (wc); mv service pnt; shwrs inc; el pnts (10A) €2.35; ice; shops 500m; playgrnd; fishing; 5% statics; dogs; Eng spkn; quiet. "V basic; san facs clean but dated, poss stretched high ssn; fishing on site €1.50 per day; 'Enchanted Forest' of King Arthur adj; gd." 28 Mar-30 Sep. € 8.60
2007*

CONDAMINE CHATELARD, LA 9D4 (1km W Rural) **Camping Base de Loisirs Champ Félèze, 04530 La Condamine-Châtelard [04 92 84 39 39; fax 04 92 84 37 90; syflor@infonie.fr]** 15 km NE of Barcelonnette on D900. Lge sp on D900 visible fr rd. Sm, pt shd; wc; chem disp; serviced pitch; shwrs inc; el pnts (4-6A) €2.50-3.50; lndtte; shops 1km; rest; snacks; bar; BBQ; playgrnd; lake & rv adj; canoe hire; 5% statics; dogs €0.50; Eng spkn; adv bkg; quiet; CCI. "Gd site; lge pitches; easy access to sm private lake; gd base for touring Alps, fishing & walking." 15 Jun-15 Sep. € 12.70   2006*

CONDE SUR NOIREAU 3D1 (10km E) **Camp Municipal, Route de Flers, 14690 Pont-d'Ouilly [02 31 69 80 20 or 02 31 69 46 12]** Fr Cherbourg take N13 to Vire, D512 for Condé-sur-Noireau & D562/D1 twd Falaise to site in 11km on W side of vill. On ent Pont-d'Ouilly turn R, site bef bdge over rv. Well sp in vill. Med, hdg/mkd pitch, pt sl, pt shd; wc (some cont); own san rec; chem disp; shwrs inc; el pnts (7A) inc; ice; shops, rest, snacks, bar in vill; BBQ; playgrnd; tennis; canoeing & leisure cent adj; phone; poss cr; adv bkg; quiet; CCI. "Gd cent for walking; conv WW2 battle areas; Museum of Automata, Falaise; helpful warden; facs poss stretched high ssn." Easter-15 Sep. € 10.20   2005*

CONDE SUR NOIREAU 3D1 (500m W Urban) **Camp Municipal du Stade, Rue de Vire, 14110 Condé-sur-Noireau [02 31 69 45 24]** On D562 (Flers to Caen rd). In town, turn W on D512 twd Vire. After Zone Industrielle, sports complex on L, no L turn. Go 1 block further & foll lge white sp 'Espace Aquatique' to site. Site 500m on R in grounds of sports cent. Sm, pt shd; wc; chem disp; shwrs inc; el pnts (6-10A) inc; lndry rm; shops, rest, snacks, bar 500m; playgrnd; htd pool adj; tennis; dogs; quiet; CCI. "Well-maintained, clean site in grounds of leisure cent; gd size pitches; vg san facs; staff friendly & helpful; pleasant town; office open 1100-1200 & 1700-1800; gd sh stay/NH." 1 May-30 Sep. € 9.30   2007*

CONDETTE see Hardelot Plage 3A2

CONDOM 8E2 (4km NE Rural) **Camping à la Ferme (Rogalle), Guinland, 32100 Condom [05 62 28 17 85; http://campingdeguinland. monsite.wanadoo.fr]** NE fr Condom on D931, turn R onto D41. Pass water tower on R, site ent on L at bottom of hill just bef sm lake on R. Sm, shd; wc; chem disp; shwrs inc; el pnts inc; shop, rest etc 4km; BBQ; playgrnd; tennis & canoe hire nrby; 10% statics; dogs; quiet. "Vg CL-type site in pine grove; friendly owner; gd value; clean facs." 1 Apr-30 Oct. € 10.00   2005*

⊞CONDOM 8E2 (6km SE Rural) Camping à la Ferme (Vignaux), Bordeneuve, 32100 Béraut [05 62 28 08 41] E fr Condom on D7 to Caussens; far end of vill turn R on D204, sp St Orens; in 1.2km turn R sp Béraut, bear R at fork, site on L in 400m. Also sp fr D654. Sm, pt sl, pt shd; wc; chem disp; shwrs inc; el pnts (12A) €2; lndtte; shops 2.5km; adv bkg; clsd Nov; quiet. "Peaceful & secluded CL-type site; friendly owners; basic san facs; waymkd trails nr." € 6.00   2007*

CONDOM 8E2 (1.5km SW Rural) Camp Municipal de l'Argente, Chemin de l'Argente, Gauge 32100 Condom [tel/fax 05 62 28 17 32] Fr Condom, take D931 twd Eauze; site ent on L opp municipal sports grnd. Med, pt shd, wc; chem disp (wc); baby facs; shwrs inc; el pnts (6A) €3.30; shop 500m; tradsmn; rest & bar adj; playgrnd; pool 200m; fishing; tennis adj; dogs €1.10; phone; red low ssn. "Tidy, well shaded site; friendly staff; excel san facs but ltd low ssn; levelling blocks useful - bumpy surface; lge pitches; no twin-axle c'vans; free access to public pool; lots for older children to do; roomy with lovely walks by rv; unspoilt town; rec visit Armagnac distilleries" Easter-30 Sep. € 10.56   2007*

CONDOM 8E2 (2km SW Rural) Camping La Ferme de Laillon (Danto), Route d'Eauze, 32100 Condom [tel/fax 05 62 28 19 71 or 06 07 69 14 19 (mob); www.calaf32.free.fr/laillon/fr] Site sp fr D931 dir Vopillon. Bumpy lane to site. Sm, pt sl, shd; wc; chem disp; shwrs inc; el pnts inc; lndry rm; farm produce; playgrnd; some statics; dogs; Eng spkn; quiet. "Delightful, wooded site; helpful owner; pleasant area." 21 Mar-19 Dec. € 9.20   2007*

CONDORCET see Nyons 9D2

CONDRIEU 9B2 (4km N Rural) Camping Domaine du Grand Bois (Naturist), Tupin et Semons, 69420 Condrieu [04 74 87 89 00 or 04 74 87 04 29; fax 04 74 87 88 48; domainedugrandbois@free.fr; www.domainedugrandbois.com] Fr Vienne take D502 dir Rive-de-Gier; site well sp after x-ing Rv Rhône. NB Do not app fr Condrieu - v steep with hairpins. Lge, sl, pt shd; wc (most cont); chem disp (wc); shwrs inc; el pnts (6A) €4.50; shop 6km; snacks; bar; playgrnd; pool; TV; 75% statics; phone; poss cr; adv bkg; quiet; INF card. "Spectacular views; v basic san facs." ♦ ltd. 15 Apr-15 Oct. € 16.00   2006*

CONDRIEU 9B2 (1km NE) Camping Belle Rive, Chemin de la Plaine, 69420 Condrieu [tel/fax 04 74 59 51 08] Heading S on D386 (N86) fr Vienne after ent vill turn L immed bef Elf g'ge on R. Site in 600m. NB Headroom under rlwy 2.60m. Alt rte avoiding bdge after vill. Lge, mkd pitch, unshd; wc; shwrs; el pnts (3-6A) €2-4; gas; lndtte; ice; shop; rest adj; snacks; bar; BBQ; playgrnd; pool; paddling pool; waterslide; lake fishing 2km; tennis; cycle hire; games area; 60% statics; dogs €1.20; poss cr; some rlwy noise. "C'vans over 6.50m poss need manhandling." 1 Apr-30 Sep. € 12.40   2005*

CONDRIEU 9B2 (2km SE Rural) Camping Le Daxia, Route du Péage, 38370 St Clair-du-Rhône [04 74 56 39 20; fax 04 74 56 93 46; info@campingledaxia.com; www.campingledaxia.com] S fr Vienne on D386 (N86); turn L in Condieu sp D28 Les Roches-de-Condrieu & Le Péage-de-Roussillon; foll sp A7 Valance & 'Camping' onto D4. Site on L well sp fron Condrieu. Med, hdg/mkd pitch, pt shd; wc; chem disp; mv service pnt; baby facs; shwrs inc; el pnts (5-6A) €2.40-2.85; lndtte; ice; shop 1km; sm rest; takeaway; bar; BBQ; playpark; pool; paddling pool; games rm; table tennis; dogs €1.85; adv bkg; quiet; CCI. "Vg site; on edge of sm rv with beach." ♦ ltd. 1 Apr-30 Sep. € 14.80   2007*

CONFOLENS 7A3 (1km N Rural) Camp Municipal des Ribières, Ave de St Germain, 16500 Confolens [05 45 85 35 27 or 05 45 84 01 97 (Mairie); fax 05 45 85 34 10] Fr N foll D951 dir Confolens turn L sp St Germain-de-Confolens, site on R in 7km at edge of town bet rd & rv. Med, mkd pitch, pt shd; wc (some cont); shwrs inc; gas; ice; el pnts (16A) €2; lndry rm; shop 700m; tradsmn; BBQ; pool 200m; rv sw adj; fishing & boating; no statics; dogs; phone; m'van o'night area outside site; some rd noise; cc & CCI not acc. "Relaxing, clean site by pretty town; ltd facs low ssn & some past their best; warden calls am & pm." ♦ 15 May-1 Sep. € 6.00   2007*

CONFOLENS 7A3 (7km S Rural) Camp Municipal Moulin de la Cour, 16500 St Maurice-des-Lions [05 45 85 55 99; fax 05 45 85 52 89] Fr Confolens take D948 S. In 6.5km turn L thro vill, site 500m, well sp. Sm, hdg/mkd pitch, pt sl, pt shd; wc (some cont); chem disp (wc); shwrs inc; el pnts (6A) €1.60; shop, rest, bar 1km; BBQ; adv bkg; quiet. "Delightful sm site nr pretty vill, 12thC church & old houses; conv Confolens folk festival mid-Aug; warden calls am & pm; pitch yourself; basic facs; v quiet low ssn; height limitations low ssn (see sp at ent to sports cent & site); ent thro stone pillars - care req with wide o'fits." 1 Jun-30 Sep. € 5.34   2004*

CONLIE see Sille le Guillaume 4F1

CONNANTRE see Sézanne 4E4

CONNERRE 4F1 (8km SE) Camp Municipal La Piscine, Rue de la Piscine, 72390 Dollon [02 43 93 42 23; fax 02 43 71 53 88; mairie.dollon@wanadoo.fr] Fr Connerré take D302 sp Vibraye & Thorigné-sur-Dué. In Dollon foll 'La Piscine' sp to sports complex at E end of vill. Sm, pt shd; wc; chem disp; shwrs; el pnts (10A) €3.35; gas; ice; shops 300m; playgrnd; pool; tennis; fishing; adv bkg rec; quiet. "Site part of sports complex; popular - rec arr early high ssn." 15 May-15 Sep. € 6.00   2006*

France

CONQUES *7D4* (8km SE Rural) **Camp Municipal,** 12320 St Cyprien-sur-Dourdou [05 65 72 80 52 or 05 65 69 83 16 (Mairie); fax 05 65 69 89 31; mairie-stcyprien12@wanadoo.fr; www.conques. fr] Fr Conques on D901 S, turn L onto D46 to St Cyprien-sur-Dourdou & foll sp to site. Sm, hdg pitch, shd; wc; shwrs inc (no sep cubicles); el pnts €2; lndry rm; shops, rest, snacks, bar 500m; playgrnd; htd pool & tennis adj; dogs; phone; adv bkg; CCI. "Well maintained; sports field nrby; sh walk to vill; gd shops, bars in vill; gd walking, touring area close to Lot Valley." ♦ 15 Jun-15 Sep. € 7.00   2007*

CONQUES *7D4* (1km W Rural) **Camping Beau Rivage,** 12320 **Conques** [05 65 69 82 23 or 05 65 72 89 29 (LS); fax 05 67 72 89 29; camping. conque@wanadoo.fr; www.campingconques. com] Site on D901 Rodez-Aurillac rd on Rv Dourdou. Med, mkd pitch, pt sl, pt shd; wc (some cont); mv service pnt; shwrs inc; el pnts (6-10A) €3.50; gas; lndry rm; shop; tradsmn; rest; snacks; bar; playgrnd; pool; fishing; rv adj; some statics; adv bkg; quiet; red low ssn; CCI. "Superb position by rv bank & nr medieval town; beautiful but pops run down low ssn; sm pithces; some modern san facs, old still in use; tight for lge o'fits due trees & narr pathways; charming wardens cook evening meals; gd." ♦ 1 Apr-30 Sep. € 16.50   2007*

CONQUES *7D4* (5km NW Rural) **Camping Le Moulin, Les Passes,** 12320 Grand-Vabre [tel/ fax 05 65 72 87 28; contact@grand-vabre.com; www.grand-vabre.com] N fr Conques on D901, site sp on banks Rv Dourdou. Sm, mkd pitch, terr, shd; wc; shwrs; el pnts (10A) €2; tradsmn; snacks; bar; playgrnd; htd pool; tennis 1km; poss cr; quiet. "Pleasant rvside site; gd." 1 Apr-31 Oct. € 11.00
                                                                2006*

CONQUET, LE *2E1* (2km N Coastal) **Camping Les Blancs Sablons (formerly Municipal Le Theven),** 29217 Le Conquet [tel/fax 02 98 89 06 90; www. lescledelles.com] Exit Brest on D789 to Le Conquet. Turn R after 22km (1.8km bef Le Conquet) on D67 twd St Renan, turn L after 700m on D28 twd Ploumoguer. After 2km, turn L at x-rds twd Plage des Blancs Sablons, site on L in 1km. Lge, mkd pitch, unshd; wc; chem disp; mv service pnt; shwrs inc; el pnts (16A) €3 (long lead poss req); lndtte; shop in ssn & 1km; rest, snacks 1km; bar 500m; playgrnd; pool; sand beach 100m; adv bkg; cc acc; CCI. "Vg; excel shwrs; some soft pitches; gd views fr some pitches; lovely old fishing town." ♦ 1 Apr-30 Sep. € 14.50   2005*

⊞**CONQUET, LE** *2E1* (7km SE Coastal) **Camping Les Terrasses de Bertheaume, Route de Perzel,** 29217 Plougonvelin [tel/fax 02 98 48 32 37; camping-lesterrassesdebertheaume@wanadoo. fr] Sp nr town. Sm, mkd pitch, pt sl, terr, unshd; wc (some cont); chem disp (wc); shwrs €1; el pnts €2.50; lndtte; ice; shop 1km; snacks; bar; BBQ; playgrnd; htd pool; sand beach adj; TV rm; 80% statics; dogs €1; poss cr; CCI. "Some sea views & direct access to lovely, quiet beach via steps; Le Fort de Bertheaume 500m interesting; cliff walk; steep access poss diff lge o'fits." ♦ ltd. € 17.00   2006*

CONTIS PLAGE *8E1* (Coastal) **Yelloh! Village Lous Seurrots, 40170 Contis-Plage** [05 58 42 85 82; fax 05 58 42 49 11; info@lous-seurrots.com; www. lous-seurrots.com   www.yellohvillage.com] S fr Mimizan take D652; 14km turn R onto D41 sp Contis-Plage; site on L. Or fr N10/E5/E70 exit junc 14 onto D38/D41 to Contis. V lge, hdg pitch, shd; htd wc; chem disp; baby facs; fam bthrm; shwrs inc; el pnts (6A) €4; gas; lndtte; ice; shop; rest; snacks; bar; playgrnd; pools; sand beach 400m; tennis; cycle hire; games area; entmnt; internet; TV; 30% statics; dogs €3; adv bkg; quiet; Eng spkn; cc acc; red low ssn. "Pitches vary in size, some req levelling blocks; excel." ♦ 5 Apr-6 Sep. € 32.00
                                                                2006*

CONTRES *4G2* (9km S Rural) **Camp Municipal Le Gué, Route de Couddes, 41700 Chémery [02 54 71 37 11 or 02 54 71 31 08; fax 02 54 71 31 08; ot.chemery@wanadoo.fr]** S fr Contres on D956 turn NW in Chémery cent sp Couddes. Site on R over bdge. Med, mkd pitch, pt shd; htd wc; chem disp; mv service pnt; shwrs inc; el pnts (6A) €3.20 (rev pol); ice; shop; tradsmn; rest, bar 500m; playgrnd; pool high ssn; cycle hire; rv fishing adj; dogs €1; quiet; adv bkg; CCI. "Friendly management; gd value; warden only on site Mon-Fri low ssn, ensure arr bef w/e because of ent barrier, otherwise can find warden's home in vill; chateau in vill." 15 Apr-15 Sep. € 10.20   2007*

Before we move on, I'm going to fill in some site report forms and post them off to the editor, otherwise they won't arrive in time for the deadline at the end of September.

CONTRES *4G2* (6km SW Rural) **Camping à la Ferme La Presle (Boucher), 41700 Oisly [02 54 79 52 69; fax 02 54 79 80 44]** Fr Contres take D675 SW for 3km D21 to just past Oisly. Well sp. Sm, pt sl, pt shd; wc; chem disp; shwrs €1; el pnts (4A) €2.20 (poss no earth); shops 1.5km; lake fishing; v quiet. "Excel CL-type site; owner helpful; wine sold on site." Easter-15 Oct. € 6.60   2006*

CONTREXEVILLE *6F2* (1km SW Urban) **Camp Municipal du Tir aux Pigeons, Rue du Onze Septembre, 88140 Contrexéville [03 29 08 15 06]** Off D164. App town fr NW on D164 turn R onto D13 & foll sp. 200m W of level x-ing, adj to stadium. Med, mkd pitch, pt shd; wc; chem disp; shwrs inc; el pnts (5A) €2.30; lndtte; shops 1km; tradsmn; paddling pool; lake fishing 2km; tennis adj; poss cr; some rd noise. "Popular NH." ♦ 1 Apr-31 Oct. € 6.00   2005*

COQUILLE, LA see Chalus *7B3*

CORBIGNY *4G4* (3.5km W Rural) **Camp Intercommunal L'Ardan, Route de Germeney, 58800 Chaumot [03 86 20 07 70; camping delardan@wanadoo.fr]** D977 fr Corbigny to Chaumot. Turn on D130 sp Germenay. Site on R after 50m. Med, shd; wc (some cont); chem disp; shwrs inc; el pnts €2.50; ice; shop 3.5km; rest; bar; playgrnd; lake adj; fishing; boat hire; some statics; adv bkg; quiet. 15 Apr-30 Sep. € 10.50   2005*

CORCIEUX *6F3* (Rural) **Yelloh! Village Le Domaine des Bans, La Rochotte, 88430 Corcieux [03 29 51 64 67; fax 03 29 51 64 65; les.bans@ domaine-des-bans.com; www.domaine-des-bans.com or www.yellohvillage.com]** Fr St Dié by-pass join D415 S to Anould. After approx 10km turn R on D8 & in 5km R on D60 to Corcieux. Or fr S take D8 N fr Gérardmer thro Gerbépal. In 2km turn L onto D60 twd Corcieux, site on L. V lge, hdg/mkd pitch, terr, pt shd; wc; chem disp; baby facs; shwrs inc; el pnts (6A) inc; gas; lndtte; sm shop, rest, snacks, bar high ssn; BBQ; playgrnd; pool high ssn; tennis; games rm; horseriding; sm lake; entmnt; 75% tour ops static tents/vans; dogs; recep 0900-2200; poss cr; Eng spkn; adv bkg ess high ssn (min 7 days); poss noisy; cc acc; CCI. "Pitches by lake quieter than nr vill; gd site with gd facs, poss stretched high ssn; care needed on narr site rds with speed control ditches (warning sps faded); check el pnts; mkt Mon." ♦ 26 Apr-6 Sep. € 30.00

          2004*

CORCIEUX *6F3* (8km NE Urban) **Camping Les Acacias, 191 Rue L de Vinci, 88650 Anould [tel/fax 03 29 57 11 06; contact@acaciascamp.com; www.acaciascamp.com]** Site in vill of Anould sp fr all dir; just off main rd. (Annexe Camping Nature Les Acacias 800m fr this site open 15 Jun-15 Sep, terr in woods.) Med, pt shd; wc (some cont); chem disp; mv service pnt; baby facs; shwrs inc; el pnts (3A) €2.60; gas; lndtte; ice; shops 500m; supmkt 2km; rest; snacks; takeaway; sm bar; playgrnd; sm pool; rv fishing nrby; games rm; tennis & karting 2km; cycle trails; excursions; 10% statics; dogs €1; poss cr; Eng spkn; adv bkg rec; quiet; CCI. "Gd standard; helpful proprietors; excel; san facs clean." ♦ 5 Dec-5 Oct. € 10.80   2005*

CORCIEUX *6F3* (600m E Rural) **Camping Le Clos de la Chaume, 21 Rue d'Alsace, 88430 Corcieux [tel/fax 03 29 50 76 76 or 06 85 19 62 55 (mob); info@camping-closdelachaume.com; www. camping-closdelachaume.com]** Take D145 fr St Dié, then D8 thro Anould onto D60. Site in 3km on R at ent to vill. Med, hdg/mkd pitch, hdstg, pt shd; wc (some cont); chem disp; mv service pnt; some serviced pitches; fam bthrm; shwrs inc; el pnts (6A) €3.60; gas; lndtte; ice; shop 800m; tradsmn, rest, snacks, bar 600m; BBQ; playgrnd; pool; sand beach & lake sw 12km; fishing; cycle hire 800m; games area; games rm; cycle hire 800m; 15% statics; dogs €1.35; phone; Eng spkn; adv bkg; quiet; cc acc; red low ssn/long stay/CCI. "Beautiful area; conv Gérardmer & Alsace wine rte; excel quality site." ♦ 21 Apr-20 Sep. € 13.90

          2007*

See advertisement

France

CORCIEUX 6F3 (1km E Rural) **Camping au Mica,** 8 Route de Gérardmer, 88430 Corcieux [tel/fax 03 29 50 70 07; info@campingaumica.com; www. campingaumica.com] Take D415 fr St Dié, then D8 thro Anould onto D60. Site in 5km on L. Med, hdg/mkd pitch, shd; wc (come cont); chem disp; mv service pnt; serviced pitches; shwrs inc; el pnts (6A) €2.50; gas; ice; Indtte; shop; tradsmn; bar; BBQ; playgrnd; pool 150m; rv fishing adj; games rm; cycle hire; TV; some statics; dogs €1; phone; Eng spkn; adv bkg; quiet; red low ssn/long stay; cc acc; CCI. "Walking rtes; beautiful area in National Park." 15 Apr-1 Nov. € 11.00   2006*

CORDELLE see Roanne 9A1

CORDES SUR CIEL 8E4 (1.5km SE) **Camping Moulin de Julien, Livers-Cazelle, 81170 Cordes-sur-Ciel** [tel/fax 05 63 56 11 10; campingmoulindejulien.com; http://moulin dejulien.free.fr] Exit Cordes E on D600 in Albi dir. Turn R on D922 Gaillac. Site on L in 100m. Fr Gaillac heading N site on R 100m bef junc with D600 & site sp bef red shield on R advertising Hôtel Ecuyer. Med, pt sl, pt shd; wc; chem disp; shwrs inc; el pnts (5A) inc; ice; Indtte; shop 2km; snacks & bar in ssn; playgrnd; 2 pools in ssn; waterslide; lake for fishing; CCI. "V pleasant, peaceful site in interesting area; friendly owners; conv Albi Cathedral, Bastide towns/vills & medieval town of Cordes." 1 May-30 Sep. € 19.00   2005*

CORDES SUR CIEL 8E4 (5km SE Rural) **Camping Redon, Livers-Cazelles, 81170 Cordes-sur-Ciel** [tel/fax 05 63 56 14 64; info@campredon.com; www.campredon.com] Off D600 Albi to Cordes rd. Exit on D107 to E nr water tower. Site sp. Sm, hdg pitch, pt sl, pt shd; wc; chem disp; mv service pnt; baby facs; shwrs inc; el pnts (6-16A) €3.80; gas; Indtte; ice; shops 5km; tradsmn; sm playgrnd; pool; TV rm; dogs €1.25; phone; bus 1km; poss cr; Eng spkn; adv bkg; quiet; red long stay; CCI. "Excel san facs; friendly, helpful Dutch owner; lovely views fr some pitches; conv Bastides in area; highly rec." ♦ 1 Apr-30 Oct. € 17.50   2007*

CORDES SUR CIEL 8E4 (2km W Rural) **Camping Le Garissou, 81170 Cordes-sur-Ciel** [05 63 56 27 14; fax 05 63 56 26 95; legarissou@wanadoo.fr] Take D600 fr Cordes thro Les Cabanes, site sp on L. Med, terr, unshd; wc; shwrs inc; el pnts (5A) inc; Indtte; sm shop; playgrnd; pool complex adj; no dogs; quiet; red low ssn. "Hilltop site; excel views; clean facs." 30 Apr-30 Sep. € 13.00   2006*

CORMATIN 9A2 (500m N Rural) **Camping Le Hameau des Champs, 71460 Cormatin** [03 85 50 76 71; fax 03 85 50 76 98; camping. cormatin@wandoo.fr; www.le-hameau-des-champs.com] Fr Cluny N on D981 dir Cormatin for approx 14km, site N of town sp on L, 300m after chateau. Look for line of European flags. Sm, hdg/ mkd pitch, pt sl, unshd; htd wc; chem disp; mv service pnt; shwrs inc; el pnts (13A) €3.20 (long lead poss req); gas 500m; Indtte; ice; shop 500m; tradsmn; rest; snacks; bar; BBQ (gas/elec); cooking facs; playgrnd; rv sw 1km; shgle beach 7km; cycle hire; TV rm; 10% statics; dogs €1; phone; Eng spkn; adv bkg; dep 25%; quiet; cc acc; CCI. "Clean, secure site; welcoming, friendly resident warden; lge grassy pitches; gd facs, poss stretched high ssn; rest open low ssn; bicycle museum nrby; cycle rte (Voie Verte) Givry to Cluny adj; chateau, church, art gallery, wine rte; entrance to chateau free to campers; beautiful, peaceful surrounding countryside; superb." ♦ 1 Apr-30 Sep. € 12.20
                                                            2007*

CORMATIN 9A2 (6km NW Rural) **Camping Le Gué, Meusseugne, 71460 Savigny-sur-Grosne** [03 85 92 56 86; camping-savigny@wanadoo.fr; www.chalon-sur-saone.net] Fr Cluny N on D981, 2km N of Cormatin fork L sp Malay. Site 3km on R bef rv bdge. Med, mkd pitch, shd; htd wc; chem disp (wc); shwrs €0.80; el pnts €2; tradsmn; snacks; bar; BBQ; playgrnd; games area; dir access to rv; fishing; many statics; dogs; CCI. "Pleasant, friendly site; nr St Genoux-le-National (national monument), Cluny & Taizé; on Burgundy wine rd." 1 May-31 Oct. € 7.10   2007*

CORMEILLES 3D1 (4km E Rural) **Camping Les Pommiers (formerly La Febvrerie), 27260 St Sylvestre-de-Cormeilles** [02 32 42 29 69] Exit A13 junc 28 Beuzeville onto N175 then D27 S sp Epaignes & Bernay twds Lieurey. Cont on D27 for approx 15km & at rndabt with D139 at Epaignes strt on for 5.6km, turn off R down narr lane sp St Sylvestre, Camping. Site on R in 1.5km. Sm, hdg pitch, pt shd; wc; chem disp (wc); shwrs inc; el pnts inc (6A) inc (poss rev pol); Indry rm; shops 4km, rest, snacks, bar 4km; BBQ; playgrnd; some statics; dogs; phone; poss cr; Eng spkn; adv bkg; quiet. "Pleasant, friendly, family-run site in orchard; secluded with excel clean facs; gd rests Cormeilles." 1 Apr-1 Oct. € 10.35   2005*

CORNY SUR MOSELLE see Metz 5D2

CORPS 9C3 (W Rural) **Camping La Rouillière, Route du Coin, 38970 Corps** [04 76 30 03 34; fax 04 76 43 72 34; jeancorporon@club-internet.fr] Sp off D537 dir Veynes. Sm, shd; wc; shwrs €0.20; el pnts (4A) €2.30; shops in town; lake fishing & watersports 3km; quiet. "Gd, basic, clean site." 30 Jun-30 Aug. € 10.00   2005*

France

CORREZE 7C4 (400m E Urban) **Camp Municipal La Chapelle**, 19800 Corrèze [05 55 21 29 30 or 05 55 21 25 21 (Mairie)] N fr Tulle on N89 twd Egletons or halfway fr Seillhac & Tulle on N120, foll sp to Corrèze. Site 400m fr town cent on D143. Med, mkd pitch, pl sl, terr, pt shd; wc; chem disp; shwrs inc; el pnts (5A) €2; gas; lndtte; shop, rest, shops; snacks; playgrnd; htd pool 500m; canoeing & rv fishing; phone; Eng spkn; quiet; CCI. "Lovely area; old vill." ♦ ltd. 15 Jun-15 Sep. € 6.10
2005*

COSNE COURS SUR LOIRE 4G3 (2km S) **Camping de l'Ile**, Ile de Cosne, 18300 Bannay [03 86 28 27 92; fax 03 86 28 18 10; campingile18@aol.com; www.camping-de-l-ile.com] Fr Cosne take Bourges rd, D955, over 1st half of bdge, ent immed on L, 500m strt. On rv island. Lge, shd; htd wc (cont); chem disp; shwrs inc; el pnts (10A) €3.80; lndtte; ice; ltd shop; rest; snacks; bar; BBQ; playgrnd; paddling pool; entmnts; cycle hire; TV; dogs €0.90; quiet; cc acc; CCI. "Helpful staff; gd NH." ♦ 1 Apr-15 Sep. € 13.50   2004*

COUBON see Puy en Velay, Le 9C1

There aren't many sites open this early in the year. We'd better phone ahead to check that the one we're heading for is actually open.

COUCHES see Nolay 6H1

COUCOURDE DERBIERES, LA see Montélimar 9D2

COUHE 7A2 (1km N Rural) **Camping Les Peupliers**, 86700 Couhé [05 49 59 21 16; fax 05 49 37 92 09; info@lespeupliers.fr; www.lespeupliers.fr] Site 35km S of Poitiers on N10 bis (old rd off by-pass); ent by bdge over Rv Dive. Fr N or S on N10 take N exit for Couhé. Site on R in 800m. Lge, hdg/mkd pitch, pt shd; wc; 30% serviced pitch; chem disp; mv service pnt; shwrs inc; el pnts (4-10A) €4.50; gas; lndtte; ice; shop & 1.5km; tradsmn; rest; snacks; bar; BBQ; playgrnd; 3 htd pools & 2 paddling pools high ssn; waterslides; jacuzzis; fishing; sports area; pedaloes; entmnt; child entmnt; games rm; TV rm; some statics; dogs free; Eng spkn; adv bkg; quiet; cc acc; red low ssn/long stay/CCI. "Beautiful, well-organised & maintained; immac san facs; excel site in every way; v friendly; conv & easy access fr N10; conv Futuroscope." ♦ 2 May-30 Sep. € 23.50
2007*

See advertisement

COULANGES SUR YONNE 4G4 (9km E Rural) **Camp Municipal Le Petit Port**, 89660 Châtel-Censoir [03 86 81 01 98 (Mairie) or 03 86 81 06 35; fax 03 86 81 08 05; www.chatel-censoir.com] Fr Auxerre or Clamecy on N151 at Coulanges turn E onto D21, S side of rv & canal to Châtel-Censoir; site sp. Med, pt shd; wc (some cont); chem disp; shwrs €0.75; el pnts (16A) €2 (poss rev pol); lndry rm; shop, rest, & bar 400m; BBQ; playgrnd; rv sw & fishing adj; some statics; phone; some slight rlwy noise; CCI. "V attractive, peaceful site bet rv & canal; beautiful area with gd cycling; superb value; no twin-axles; resident warden." 1 May-30 Sep. € 6.00   2007*

COULANGES SUR YONNE 4G4 (S Rural) **Camping des Berges de l'Yonne**, 89480 Coulanges-sur-Yonne [03 86 81 76 87] On N151 dir Nevers. Med, pt shd; wc; chem disp; shwrs; el pnts (10A) inc; shop; snacks; playgrnd; rv sw; tennis. "V pleasant site in beautiful area; dated facs but v adequate & clean; excel bakery in Coulanges, sh walk fr site; gd." 15 Jun-15 Sep. € 12.20   2006*

COULLONS *4G3* (1km W Rural) Camp Municipal Plancherotte, Route de la Brosse, 45720 Coullons [02 38 29 20 42; fax 02 38 29 23 07] Fr cent of Coullons foll sp twd Cerdon (D51). Bef leaving vill & after passing lake, take 1st rd on L. Site in 500m on L side of lake. Med, pt shd, hdg/mkd pitch; wc (cont); chem disp; some serviced pitches; shwrs; el pnts €2; gas 1km; shop 1km; playgrnd; tennis; 50% statics; phone; adv bkg; CCI. "Vg." ♦ 1 Apr-31 Oct. € 9.00   2005*

Did you know you can fill in site report forms on the Club's website – www.caravanclub.co.uk?

COULON *7A2* (N Rural) Camp Municipal La Niquière, Route de Benet, 79510 Coulon [05 49 35 81 19 or 05 49 35 90 26 (Mairie); fax 05 49 35 82 75; tourisme.coulon79@orange.fr; www.ville-coulon.fr] Fr N148 at Benet take D1 to Coulon to site on L at ent to Coulon. Sm, pt shd; wc (cont); chem disp (wc); shwrs inc; el pnts (15A) €2.80; gas; ice; shops 1km; sports facs adj; boats for hire; poss cr. "Well-kept site; dated but clean san facs; ent only with barrier card; office open 1030-1200 & 1500-1630 low ssn, 0730-2000 Jul/Aug; 10 min walk to vill." 1 Apr-30 Sep. € 6.40
2007*

COULON *7A2* (3km N) Camping à la Ferme La Planche, 79510 Coulon [05 49 35 93 17] Fr N148, foll main rd thro Benet, then foll sp (bus & lorry) Coulon. Take 1st L sp Coulon, then 1st R, site sp. Site on L in 1.5km. Sm, pt shd; wc; shwr; el pnts (10A) inc; supmkt 1.5km; tradsmn; rest 1.5km; BBQ; horse & carriage rides; some statics; adv bkg; quiet. "Excel CL-type farm site; friendly owners; ltd but clean facs; busy high ssn; sm pitches." € 8.20
2004*

COULON *7A2* (2km S Rural) Camping L'Ilot du Chail, Rue des Gravées, 79270 La Garette [05 49 35 00 33; fax 05 49 35 00 31; www.marais-poitevin.com/la-garette] Fr Niort take dir to Coulon & La Venise-Verte; at Coulon rndbt turn L; site thro vill on R. Med, mkd pitch, pt shd; wc; shwrs inc; el pnts (6A) €2.50; rest/bar 300m; shop & 3km; tradsmn; pool; fishing; boat rides; horseriding; minigolf; tennis; games rm; some statics; dogs €0.80; quiet; red long stay; cc acc; CCI. "Many rests within 1km; vg." ♦ 8 Apr-8 Sep. € 12.50   2007*

COULON *7A2* (2km W Rural) Camping La Venise Verte, 178 Route des Bordes de Sèvre, 79510 Coulon [05 49 35 90 36; fax 05 49 35 84 69; accueil@camping-laveniseverte.com; www.camping-laveniseverte.com] Do not app thro Benet. Exit A83 junc 9 onto N148; cont past Benet; at rndabt with D123 turn R to Coulon in 5km; cont thro Coulon; site 1.5km W of vill on R bef bdge. Drive along rv & foll sp to site. Med, mkd pitch, pt shd; wc; chem disp; baby facs; shwrs inc; el pnts (10A) inc (poss rev pol); lndtte; ice; shop; tradsmn; rest, snacks, bar (high ssn); BBQ (charcoal/gas); playgrnd; pool; paddling pool; boating; fishing; canoe/cycle hire; entmnt; wifi internet; 25% statics; dogs €2; phone; Eng spkn; poss cr; adv bkg; poss noisy high ssn; red low ssn; CCI. "Excel site in park-like setting; helpful owner; gd facs; some pitches sm & diff due trees & posts; excel touring base for nature lovers; gd cycle rtes." ♦ 1 Apr-31 Oct. € 27.00 ABS - A37   2007*

COULON *7A2* (6km W Rural) Camping Le Relais du Pêcheur, 85420 Le Mazeau [02 51 52 93 23 or 02 51 52 91 14 (Mairie); fax 02 51 52 97 58] Fr Fontenay-le-Comte take N148 SE. At Benet turn R onto D25 & foll sp to vill. Turn L in vill then R over canal bdge. Site on L in 500m. Med, hdg pitch, pt shd; wc (most cont); chem disp; shwrs inc; el pnts (16A) €2; lndtte; shop 500m; supmkt 5km; playgrnd; paddling pool; boat hire nrby; adv bkg; quiet; CCI. "V pleasant site in delightful location; excel base for Marais Poitevin; gd cyling & walks." ♦ ltd. 1 Apr-15 Oct. € 7.80   2006*

COULONGES SUR L'AUTIZE *7A2* (500m S Rural) Camp Municipal Le Parc, Rue du Calvaire, 79160 Coulonges-sur-l'Autize [05 49 06 27 56; fax 05 49 06 13 26; mcoulonges@cyberscope.fr] Fr Fontenay take D745 sp Parthenay/St Hilaire E to Coulonges, site sp nr 'piscine' on D1. Fr Niort take D744 N to Coulonges. Sm, hdg/mkd pitch, pt shd; wc; chem disp (wc); shwrs inc; el pnts inc; lndry rm; ice; shop adj; tradsmn; playgrnd; pool nr; rv sw & fishing 4km; cycle hire; 80% statics; dogs; phone; quiet; CCI. "Site yourself; warden calls." ♦ Jun-Sep. € 7.40   2004*

⊞ COURBIAC *7D3* (S Rural) FFCC Le Pouchou, 47370 Courbiac [tel/fax 05 53 40 72 68 or 06 80 25 15 13 (mob); camping-le-pouchou@cario; www.camping-le-pouchou.com] S fr Fumel on D102 thro Tournon-d'Agenais; Courbiac sp to L on S side of town. Sm, pt sl, shd; wc; chem disp; mv service pnt; shwrs inc; el pnts (10A) €3 (poss rev pol); lndry rm; ice; shop; snacks; bar; playgrnd; pool & paddling pool; cycle hire; fishing; horseriding; archery; internet; sat TV; some statics; dogs €1.10; site clsd 21 Dec-9 Jan; Eng spkn; adv bkg ess high ssn; quiet; CCI. "Lge pitches each with picnic table; many sl pitches poss diff; gd, v clean facs; gd views; friendly, hospitable owners; gd cycling; vg." ♦ ltd. € 11.50   2007*

COURCON 7A2 (6km N Rural) Camping du Port (Naturist), Rue du Port, 17170 La Ronde [05 46 41 65 58 or 06 26 06 72 37 (mob); jean-jacques.faudoire@wanadoo.fr; www.camping-naturiste-du-port.com] Fr Marans E on D114, bef Courçon head N on D116 dir Maillezais. Site on R after leaving vill of La Ronde. Sm, hdg/mkd pitch, hdstg, pt shd; wc; chem disp; shwrs inc; el pnts (6-10A) €3.50; gas; Indtte; ice; shops adj; BBQ; playgrnd; pool high ssn; sand beach 30km; few statics; dogs €2; poss cr; adv bkg; quiet. "V helpful owner; excel site; well looked-after; facs clean." ♦ 1 May-30 Sep. € 16.00   2007*

COURCON 7A2 (500m SE Rural) Camp Municipal La Garenne, 17170 Courçon [05 46 01 60 19 or 05 46 01 60 50 (Mairie); fax 05 46 01 63 59; mairie.courcon@mairie17.com] Fr N11 Mauzé-La Rochelle turn N at La Laigne on D114 to Courçon. Site on L on app to vill. Sm, pt shd; wc; mv service pnt; shwrs; el pnts (3A) €3.50; Indtte; shops 500m; htd pool adj; rv sw 5km; fishing 5km; dogs €1.50; adv bkg rec high ssn; quiet. 1 Jun-31 Aug. € 8.50
                    2006*

COURCON 7A2 (5km S) Camp Municipal du Château, 17170 Benon [06 66 90 35 59 or 05 46 01 61 48 (Mairie); fax 05 46 01 01 19; benon@mairie17.com; www.smic17.fr/mairie-benon] Fr N11 turn S to Benon onto D116. On S side of Benon turn E onto D206 twd St Georges-du-Bois, site immed on R thro tall, narr, metal gateway; take wide sweep on ent (or use easier access at rear - foll wall round to L). Site also sp in Benon. Sm, pt sl, pt shd; wc; chem disp; shwrs inc; el pnts (10A) €2.20; Indtte; tradsmn; playgrnd; pool 6km; tennis; dogs €1; quiet; adv bkg; cc acc; CCI. "Attractive site with mature trees in walled area adj Mairie; no lighting; site tired/untidy (Aug 2007); excel rest 2km N nr N11 & gd value rest 150m in vill (unreliable opening); oyster beds at Châtelaillon; gd cycling area; Courçon vg; 20 mins La Rochelle; poss itinerants." 1 May-30 Sep. € 8.60   2007*

COURNON D'AVERGNE see Clermont Ferrand 9B1

COURPIERE 9B1 (5km NE Rural) Camping Le Grün du Chignore, Les Plaines, 63120 Vollore-Ville [tel/fax 04 73 53 73 37; camping-du-chignore@hotmail.fr; www.campingauvergne.fr] Fr D906 S fr Thiers, at Courpiere turn L onto D7 dir Vollore-Ville; take D45 N fr vill; site on R in 500m. Sm, hdg/mkd pitch, pt shd; wc (some cont); chem disp (wc); shwrs inc; el pnts (10A) €3.10; Indtte; shop 500m; tradsmn; rest; snacks; bar; BBQ (sep area); playgrnd; shallow pool; games area; some statics; dogs €1.50; a little English spkn; adv bkg (dep req); quiet; cc acc. "Situated above fishing lake; rolling hills; v quiet; lovely owners; gd walks; chateau in Vollore-Ville; bar part of vill life; highly rec." ♦ 1 Apr-31 Oct. € 9.30   2007*

COURSEULLES SUR MER 3D1 (E Coastal) Camp Municipal Le Champ de Course, Ave de la Libération, 14470 Courseulles-sur-Mer [02 31 37 99 26 (Mairie); fax 02 31 37 96 37; camping-courseulles@wanadoo.fr; www.courseulles-sur-mer.com] Fr N814 by-pass thro Caen, take exit 5 onto D7 & D404 dir Courseulles-sur-Mer. On ent to town, foll sp 'Campings' at 1st rndabt, then sp 'Centre Juno Beach'. Site on D514 on R. Lge, hdg/mkd pitch, unshd; wc; chem disp; mv service pnt; baby facs; shwrs inc; el pnts (6-9A) inc; Indtte; tradsmn; rest, snacks, bar adj; BBQ; playgrnd; pool adj; sand beach; sports area; boat hire; tennis, mini-golf & horseriding nr; TV rm; 15% statics; dogs €1.65; phone; poss cr; Eng spkn; adv bkg; quiet; cc acc; CCI. "Friendly staff; recp 0900-1200 & 1400-1900; facs clean; conv Juno (D-Day landings) beach; guided tours; easy walk to town; gd dog walks; oyster beds & daily fish mkt; vg." ♦ 1 Apr-30 Sep. € 17.30   2007*

COURSEULLES SUR MER 3D1 (2km E Coastal) Camping Le Havre de Bernières, Chemin de Quintefeuille, 14990 Bernières-sur-Mer [02 31 96 67 09; fax 02 31 97 31 06; campingnormandie@aol.com] W fr Ouistreham on D514 for 20km. Site well sp. Lge, mkd pitch, pt sl, pt shd; wc; chem disp; 50% serviced pitches; shwrs inc; el pnts (6-10A) €3.90-5.30; Indtte; shop; rest; playgrnd; pool; sand beach adj; tennis; many statics; dogs €3.60; poss cr; Eng spkn; adv bkg; quiet; red low ssn; CCI. "Excel site; gd beaches & watersports; conv Ouistreham ferries; site poss untidy in low ssn; ltd facs low ssn; when site cr c'vans poss need manhandling; gates clsd 2200-0730." ♦ 1 Apr-31 Oct. € 23.80   2005*

COURSEULLES SUR MER 3D1 (8km SW Rural) Camp Municipal des Trois Rivières, Route de Tierceville, 14480 Creully [tel/fax 02 31 80 12 00 or 02 31 80 90 17] Fr Caen ring rd, exit junc 5 onto D7 twd N; at rndabt at Courseulles-sur-Mer turn L onto D12 dir Bayeux. At Tierceville turn S, sp Creully; site 1km on L on D93 to Creully. NB only app is fr Tierceville as c'vans not permitted on other rds. Med, hdg pitch, pt sl, pt shd; htd wc; chem disp (wc); shwrs inc; chem disp; el pnts (6-10A) €3.30-3.70 (long leads adv)(poss rev pol); Indtte; shops, rest, snacks, bar 1km; BBQ; playgrnd; pool 5km; games area; games rm; sand beach 5km; dogs €1; Eng spkn; adv bkg; quiet; cc acc; CCI. "Well-maintained, clean site; super pitches; friendly warden; excel facs, stretched high ssn; conv D-Day beaches, Bayeux; barrier clsd 1200-1500 & at 2200; gd cycling; picturesque vills in area." ♦ 1 Apr-30 Sep. € 9.90   2007*

COURTILS see Mont St Michel, Le 2E4

COURVILLE SUR EURE *4E2* (S Urban) **Camp Municipal, Ave Thier, 28190 Courville-sur-Eure [02 37 23 76 38 or 02 37 18 07 90 (Mairie); fax 02 37 18 07 99; jean-claude.larcher@courville-sur-eure.fr; www.courville-sur-eure.fr]** Turn N off N23 19km W of Chartres. Site on bank of rv. Foll sp. Med, hdg pitch, unshd; wc (some cont); chem disp (wc); shwrs; el pnts (6A) €2.60; shops 2km; rest in town; pool 200m; dogs; poss cr; quiet. "Fair NH; facs tired low ssn & stretched all year; conv Chartres; gd shopping locally; mkt Thurs." 17 May-15 Sep. € 6.50 2007*

⊞**COUTANCES** *1D4* (6km N Rural) **Camping La Raisinière, 50200 Ancteville [02 33 45 50 67; caroline.brooks2@tesco.net]** Fr Cherbourg S on N13, D900 & D2 dir Le Mont-St Michel, 1km S of Montsurvent turn L onto D393 to Ancteville, site 1.5km on L. Sm, some hdstg, pt shd; wc; chem disp; mv service pnt; shwrs inc; el pnts (6A) inc; shop, rest, bar 2km; 1 gite avail; quiet; red long stay. "Gd, clean, simple CL-type site 1 hr fr Cherbourg & 15 mins fr beach; gd san facs; excel walking & cycling; new British owners 2007; in bad weather phone ahead to check open." € 15.00 2007*

COUTANCES *1D4* (9km NE) **Camp Municipal, 50490 St Sauveur-Lendelin [02 33 76 52 00; fax 02 33 76 52 01]** Fr Coutances take D971 NE. Site lies on L of rd bef rd junc on ent vill. Lge o'fits take care at ent. Sm, hdg pitch, pt shd; wc; shwrs inc; el pnts inc; shops & rest 500m; some rd noise. "Warden calls am & pm; generous pitches; basic san facs but clean; 75 min fast rd Cherbourg; conv NH." 1 Jun-15 Sep. € 10.00 2004*

⊞**COUTANCES** *1D4* (1km W Urban) **Camp Municipal Les Vignettes, 27 Rue de St Malo, 50200 Coutances [02 33 45 43 13; fax 02 33 45 74 98]** Fr N on D971 or D2 turn R onto Coutances by-pass, sp St Malo & Avranches. At rndabt turn L. Site 200m on R after Cositel ent. Fr S foll sp for Valognes or Cherbourg. Site in Coutances on L immed after Logis sp. Med, hdg/mkd pitch, pt sl, pt shd; wc (some cont); chem disp; shwrs inc; ltd el pnts (2-6A) €2.30; shops 500m; snacks; bar; BBQ; playgrnd; htd pool adj; sports stadium adj; few statics; dogs €1; poss cr; some rd noise; CCI. "Access poss diff to some pitches; pretty site; san facs poss unclean low ssn; warden calls 0800; gd sh stay/NH for Cherbourg." € 8.60 2006*

COUTRAS *7C2* (Urban) **Camp Municipal Frais Rivage, Route de Guîtres, 33230 Coutras [05 57 49 12 00; fax 05 57 56 09 04]** In Coutras on D674 turn onto D10, over new bdge. Site on R. Fr S on D674 turn L onto D10. Well sp. Sm, pt shd; wc; shwrs; el pnts (6A) €2 (poss rev pol); shop 300m; pool 1km; fishing; quiet. "Pleasant rvside site; rec phone ahead low ssn; clean san facs." ♦ 29 May-12 Sep. € 8.40 2006*

COUTRAS *7C2* (3km SW Rural) **Camping Le Paradis, Port-du-Mas, 33230 Abzac [05 57 49 05 10; fax 05 57 49 18 88; camping leparadis@free.fr]** Fr Coutras on S on D17 to Abzac, site well sp. Sm, pt shd; htd wc; mv service pnt; baby facs; shwrs inc; el pnts (6A) €3; gas; ice; lndtte; shop; rest; BBQ; playgrnd; TV rm; lake sw; fishing; entmnt; 50% statics; dogs €1.30; cc acc; CCI. "Excel site, gd for vineyards; rec long stay." 1 May-15 Sep. € 14.80 2006*

COUTURES *4G1* (1km NE Rural) **Camping Parc de Montsabert, 49320 Coutures [02 41 57 91 63; fax 02 41 57 90 02; camping@parcdemontsabert. com; www.parcdemontsabert.com]** Easy access on R side of Rv Loire bet Angers & Saumur. Take rte D751 to Coutures. Fr town cent foll sp for site. First R after 'Tabac' & foll rd to site (first on R bef chateau). Med, hdg/mkd pitch, hdstg, pt sl, pt shd; htd wc; chem disp; 50% serviced pitches; child/baby facs; shwrs inc; el pnts (5-10A) €2.95-4.10; lndtte; ice; shop 1.5km; tradsmn; rest; snacks; bar; playgrnd; htd, covrd pool; paddling pool with slide; tennis; games area; games hall; cycle hire; crazy golf; gym; entmnt; child entmnt; TV; 15% statics; dogs €3.20; phone; bus 1km; Eng spkn; adv bkg (dep req); quiet; cc acc; CCI. "Ideal for chateaux & wine cellars; lge pitches." ♦ 29 Apr-15 Sep. € 23.80 2006*

COUX ET BIGAROQUE see Bugue, Le *7C3*

COUZON see Bourbon L'Archambault *9A1*

COZES *7B1* (8km NE Rural) **Camping Vacances St Jacques, La Mirolle, 17260 St André-de-Lidon [tel/fax 05 46 90 11 05; vacances_st_jacques@ compuserve.com]** D129 fr St André-de-Lidon dir Montpellier-de-Médillan, just off rd to Cravans. Sm, mkd pitch, pt shd; wc; shwrs; el pnts (16A) inc; gas 7km; lndtte; shops, rest, snacks 2km; bar; BBQ; playgrnd; paddling pool; sand beach 20km; TV rm; quiet; adv bkg (dep req); Eng spkn; no cc acc. "Friendly British owners; CL-type site; gd for disabled; gd cycling; gd rests in vill; nrby beaches, medieval towns." ♦ May-Oct. € 12.00 2004*

COZES *7B1* (9km S Rural) **Camp Municipal St Seurin-d'Uzet, 17120 Chenac-St Seurin-d'Uzet [05 46 90 45 31 or 05 46 90 44 03 (Mairie); fax 05 46 90 40 02]** SE fr Royan take D25/D145 thro St Georges-de-Didonne, Meschers-sur-Gironde & Talmont to St Seurin-d'Uzet. Site sp in vill. Med, hdg/mkd pitch, pt shd; wc; chem disp (wc); shwrs inc; el pnts (5A) inc (poss rev pol & poss long lead req); lndtte; shop 100m; playgrnd; rv sw & sand beach adj; dogs €0.75; adv bkg rec high ssn; quiet. "Rec; pretty, well-maintained site beside creek; lge pitches; gd views & walks; pleasant staff; poss mosquito prob; gd vill shop." ♦ 1 May-30 Sep. € 7.50 2005*

COZES *7B1* (4km SW Rural) **Camping Fleur des Champs, Le Coudinier, 17120 Arces-sur-Gironde [05 46 90 40 11; fax 05 46 97 64 45]** Site on D114 on R 1km fr Arces to Talmont. Sm, mkd pitch, pt sl, pt shd; wc; shwrs inc; el pnts (4-6A) €2-3; gas; ice; tradsmn; lndtte; shop 1km; tradsmn; pool 4km; cycle hire; playgrnd; entmnts; archery; lake beach, sw & fishing 2km; dogs €1.22; 70% statics; quiet. "Gd; nice, quiet rural site; ideal for seaside holiday away fr typical coastal sites." 1 Jun-15 Sep. € 8.70
2004*

COZES *7B1* (10km SW Coastal) **Camping Bellevue, 220 Route Verte, 17120 Barzan-Plage [05 46 90 45 91]** Fr Cozes W D114 thro Arces to Talmont-sur-Gironde L onto D145, site 2km on L. Sm, mkd pitch, pt sl, pt shd; wc (some cont); shwrs; el pnts; lndtte; rest 500m; pool & beach adj; 50% statics; dogs; quiet; CCI. "Fair." ♦ ltd. 15 May-25 Oct.
2005*

COZES *7B1* (W Urban) **Camp Municipal Le Sorlut, Rue de Stade, 17120 Cozes [05 46 90 75 99 or 05 46 90 90 97 (Mairie)]** Clearly sp in Cozes, 150m fr N730. Turn into app rd on R of Champion supmkt. Med, mkd pitch, pt shd; wc; chem disp; shwrs inc; el pnts (5-6A) €2.39; lndry rm; shops adj; supmkt 500m; playgrnd; pool; sand beach 6km; tennis; quiet; CCI. "Helpful warden calls 0830-0930 & 1800-1900 otherwise phone for ent; no twin-axles; v pleasant site close to Royan; ltd facs when only few vans; no arr 1200-1500." 15 Apr-15 Oct. € 6.82
2007*

CRAC'H see Carnac *2G3*

CRAON *2F4* (E Urban) **Camp Municipal du Mûrier, Rue Alain Gerbault, 53400 Craon [02 43 06 96 33 or 02 43 06 13 09 (Mairie); fax 02 43 06 39 20; contact@ville-craon53.fr; www.ville-craon53.fr]** Fr Laval take D771 (N171) S to Craon. Site sp fr town cent. Med, hdg pitch, pt shd; wc; shwrs inc; el pnts (6A) €2; lndtte; snacks; playgrnd; pool 200m; tennis; entmnt; no twin-axles; adv bkg; quiet; 10% red long stays. 1 May-15 Sep. € 9.50   2006*

CRAZANNES see St Savinien *7B2*

CRECHES SUR SAONE see Mâcon *9A2*

CREISSAN *10F1* **Camp Municipal Les Oliviers, 34370 Creissan [04 67 93 81 85 or 04 67 93 75 41 (Mairie); fax 04 67 93 85 28; mairie@creissan.com]** Fr D612 (N112) foll sp Creissan & site. Sm, mkd pitch, pt shd; shwrs inc; el pnts €3; lndtte; shop, rest, bar in vill; BBQ; playgrnd; pool; tennis; entmnt; adv bkg; quiet. "Pleasant site." 1 Apr-30 Sep. € 8.00   2005*

⊞**CREON** *7D2* (3km NW Rural) **FFCC Camping Caravaning Bel Air, 33670 Créon [05 56 23 01 90; fax 05 56 23 08 38; info@camping-bel-air.com; www.camping-bel-air.com]** Fr A10/E70 at junc 24 take D936 E fr Bordeaux sp Bergerac. Approx 15km E turn SE onto D671 sp Créon & cont for 5km. Site on L, 1.5km after Lorient. Med, hdg/mkd pitch, hdstg, pt shd; wc (some cont); chem disp; mv service pnt; shwrs inc; el pnts (5A) €3.50; gas; lndtte; shop high ssn; tradsmn; supmkt 1km; rest; snacks; bar; playgrnd; pool; 10% statics; dogs €2.50; clsd to vehicles 2200-0800; Eng spkn; adv bkg; quiet; red long stay; CCI. "Helpful owners; plenty to do in area; no twin-axle vans; sep car park low ssn; phone ahead to check open low ssn; rest sm & ltd; facs v ltd low ssn; Bordeaux 20km; sh stay/NH only." ♦ ltd. € 13.00   2007*

CREON D'ARMAGNAC see St Justin *8E2*

CRESPIAN *10E1* (Rural) **Camping Le Mas de Reilhe, 30260 Crespian [04 66 77 82 12; fax 04 66 80 26 50; info@camping-mas-de-reilhe.fr; www.camping-mas-de-reilhe.fr]** Exit A9 at Nîmes Ouest N onto N106 dir Alès for 5km. Fork R, then L over bdge onto D999 dir Le Vigan. Foll rd for 24km, R at x-rds onto D6110 (N110) to site on R just on ent Crespian. Take care - ent on a bend on busy rd. Med, mkd pitch, pt sl, terr, pt shd; wc; chem disp; baby facs; shwrs inc; el pnts (6A) inc; lndtte; shop; rest; snacks; bar; BBQ (gas/elec); playgrnd; htd pool & paddling pool; tennis; fishing & horseriding 10km; organised walks; games rm; entmnt high ssn; (wifi planned) internet; TV; dogs €2.60; recep 0830-2000 high ssn; poss cr; Eng spkn; quiet but some rd noise; cc acc; CCI. "Quiet & relaxing; friendly wardens; conv Nîmes, Uzès & Cévennes National Park; excel." ♦ 5 Apr-21 Sep. € 23.40 (CChq acc) ABS - C10   2007*

CREST *9D2* (5km E Rural) **Gervanne Camping, 26400 Mirabel-et-Blacons [04 75 40 00 20; fax 04 75 40 03 97; info@gervanne-camping.com; www.gervanne-camping.com]** Exit A7 junc 16 Loriol onto D104/D164, turn off onto D93. Site 2km E of Mirabel-et-Blacons on both sides or rd. Recep by shop. Med, pt sl, pt shd; htd wc; chem disp; mv service pnt; shwrs inc; baby facs; el pnts (4-6A) €2.80-3.40; gas; lndtte; shop adj; rest; snacks; bar; BBQ (gas/elec); playgrnd; htd pool; rv sw & beach adj; games area; internet; TV; 7% statics; dogs €2; poss cr; Eng spkn; adv bkg (ess high ssn); quiet; cc acc; red low ssn; CCI. "Excel, family-run site in beautiful area on Rv Drôme; v helpful; gd size pitches; lovely pool complex; vg rest." ♦ 1 Apr-31 Oct. € 17.80   2007*

CREST *9D2* (500m S Urban) Camping Les Clorinthes, 26400 Crest [04 75 25 05 28; fax 04 75 76 75 09; lecampinglesclorinthes@minitel.net] S fr Crest twd Nyons on D538 turn L immed after x-ing bdge over rv. Site sp. Lge, hdg/mkd pitch, pt sl, pt shd; wc (some cont); own san rec; chem disp; shwrs; el pnts (6A) €3.60; gas; ice; lndtte; shop & 500m; tradsmn; snacks; bar; pool; rv sw adj; sports complex 500m; TV; entmnt; fishing; 20% statics; dogs €2.10; phone; poss cr; adv bkg; poss cr; quiet, some train noise; CCI. "Well-maintained; security barrier with dep for key; dir access rv; beautiful situation; muddy when wet." ♦ ltd. 1 Apr-30 Sep. € 15.80   2006*

CREST *9D2* (8km W Rural) Camping Les Quatre Saisons, Route de Roche-sur-Grane, 26400 Grane [04 75 62 64 17; fax 04 75 62 69 06; camping.4saisons@wanadoo.fr; www.camping-4saisons.com] Exit A7 at junc for Loriol or Crest, take D104 E for 18km. Turn R thro vill twd Roche-sur-Grane, site well sp. If a lge unit, access thro 4th junc to Grane. Site well sp fr Crest. Med, pt sl, terr, pt shd; wc; chem disp; mv service pnt; baby facs; shwrs inc; el pnts (6-10A) €4; lndtte; ice; shop; tradsmn; snacks; bar; BBQ; pool; tennis; games area; dogs €3; phone; poss cr; adv bkg; quiet; red long stay/low ssn; cc acc; CCI. "Beautiful views; well-run site; friendly owners; sm & lge pitches; nice pool; Grane (supmkt, rest etc.) in walking dist; gd." ♦ € 16.00   2007*

CREULLY see Courseulles sur Mer *3D1*

CREVECOEUR EN BRIE see Fontenay Trésigny *4E3*

⊞**CREVECOEUR LE GRAND** *3C3* (7km SE Rural) Camping à la Ferme (Fontana), 8 Hameau de la Neuve Rue, 60480 Ourcel-Maison [03 44 46 81 55] NE fr Beauvais on D1001 (N1) to Froissy; turn W at traff lts onto D151. Avoid 1st sp to Francastel but cont to x-rds & turn into vill on D11. Francastel adjoins Ourcel-Maison & site at far end. Or fr A16 exit junc 16 W onto D930 & foll sp. Sm, pt shd; wc (some cont); chem disp; shwrs inc; el pnts (5A) inc (rev pol); shop 6km; tradsmn; rest; BBQ; playgrnd; quiet; cc not acc. "Farm produce & occasional eve meals avail; no hdstg & poss muddy/diff in wet weather; san facs need attention; gd NH." € 7.00   2005*

CREYSSE see Martel *7C3*

CRIEL SUR MER *3B2* (2km N Coastal) Camping Les Mouettes, Rue de la Plage, 76910 Criel-sur-Mer [tel/fax 02 35 86 70 73; contact@camping-lesmouettes.fr; www.camping-lesmouettes.fr] Fr D925 take D222 thro Criel to coast, site sp. Care need with narr access. Sm, mkd pitch, terr, unshd; wc; shwrs; el pnts (6A) €3.50; lndtte; ice; shop; supmkt 5km; snacks; bar; BBQ; games area; games rm; TV; some statics; dogs €2; Eng spkn; adv bkg; quiet. "V nice little site; friendly, helpful staff; sea views." Easter-1 Nov. € 12.90   2006*

⊞**CRIEL SUR MER** *3B2* (2km N Coastal) FFCC Camp Municipal Le Mont Joli Bois, 29 Rue de la Plage, 76910 Criel-sur-Mer [02 35 50 81 19; fax 02 35 50 22 37; camping.criel@wanadoo.fr] Fr D925 take D222 into Criel cent. Turn R opp church into D126 for 1.6km to beach. Turn L then immed R & foll beach rd to site in 1.5km. Med, hdg/mkd pitch, pt sl, terr, pt shd; htd wc; chem disp; mv service pnt; shwrs inc; el pnts (4-6A) €3-4.50; lndtte; ice; tradsmn; shops, rest, snacks & bar 2km; playgrnd; shgl beach 500m; TV rm; 50% statics; dogs €1.50; bus; poss cr; quiet; CCI. "Fair." ♦ ltd. € 10.40   2007*

CRIQUETOT L'ESNEVAL see Etretat *3C1*

⊞CROISIC, LE *2G3* (2km S Coastal) **Camping La Pierre Longue, Rue Henri Dunant, 44490 Le Croisic [02 40 23 13 44; fax 02 40 23 23 13; contact@camping-lapierrelongue.com; www.campinglapierrelongue.com]** Turn L off Le Pouliguen-Le Croisic rd at g'ge at Le Croisic sp; foll camp sps. Lge, hdg/mkd pitch, pt shd; htd wc; chem disp; mv service pnt; baby facs; shwrs inc; el pnts (6-10A) €3.50-5; gas; lndtte; ice; shop; rest; snacks; bar; BBQ; playgrnd; htd pool; sand beach 500m; entmnt; TV; 60% statics; phone; dogs €2; Eng spkn; adv bkg; quiet; cc acc; red low ssn; CCI. "Warm welcome; excel facs; excel beaches." ♦ € 19.90   2007*

See advertisement opposite

CROISIC, LE *2G3* (1km W Coastal) **Camping de l'Océan, 15 Route de la Maison Rouge, 44490 Le Croisic [02 40 23 07 69; fax 02 40 15 70 63; info@camping-ocean.com; www.camping-ocean.com]** Foll N171 to Guérande. On D774 to La Baule, Batz-sur-Mer. Back on old N171 to Le Croisic. At rndabt foll site sp. Lge, hdg/mkd pitch, pt shd; wc; chem disp; mv service pnt; serviced pitches; baby facs; shwrs inc; el pnts (6A) inc; gas; lndtte; ice; shop; snacks; playgrnd; 2 htd pools, (1 covrd); waterslide; jacuzzi; sand beach 150m; tennis; games area; fitness rm; entmnt; child entmnt; 40% statics; dogs €6.50; adv bkg; Eng spkn; quiet; red low ssn; cc acc; red low ssn/CCI. "Interesting coast line nr La Baule; caves & rocky headlands; salt flats at ent to Le Croisic; pleasant walk to walled city of Guérande adj; excel pools complex." ♦ 5 Apr-30 Sep. € 40.00   2007*

See advertisement on page 523

CROIX EN TERNOIS see St Pol sur Ternoise *3B3*

CROIXILLE, LA see Ernée *2E4*

CROMARY see Rioz *6G2*

CROTOY, LE *3B2* (Urban/Coastal) **Camping La Prairie, 2 Rue de Mayocq, 80550 Le Crotoy [tel/fax 03 22 27 02 65]** Fr S exit A16 at Abbeville onto D86/D940 to Le Crotoy to rndabt at ent to town. Cont strt for 1.5km then 2nd L, site on L in 500m. Fr N exit A16 for Rue onto D32, then D940, then as above. Lge, hdg pitch, pt shd; wc (some cont); chem disp (wc); shwrs; el pnts (3-6A) €3.30-6.60; tradsmn; playgrnd; sand beach 400m; 90% statics; dogs €1; phone; poss cr; quiet. "Ltd pitches for tourers but conv beach & town; v busy site; gd san facs; excel cycle paths in area." ♦ 1 Apr-30 Sep. € 12.10   2006*

CROTOY, LE *3B2* (1.5km N Rural) **Camping Le Tarteron, Route de Rue, 80550 Le Crotoy [03 22 27 06 75; fax 03 22 27 02 49; contact@letarteron.fr; www.letarteron.fr]** Fr A16 exit junc 24 onto D32, then D940 around Rue twd Le Crotoy. Pass D4 dir St Firmin site on L. Med, hdg/mkd pitch, pt shd; wc; chem disp; shwrs inc; el pnts (4A) €3.40; gas; shop; tradsmn; snacks; bar; playgrnd; htd pool; sand beach 1.5km; many statics; quiet. "Conv Marquenterre bird park & steam train fr Le Crotoy." 1 Apr-31 Oct. € 17.90   2007*

CROTOY, LE *3B2* (3km N Rural) FFCC **Camping Le Ridin, Mayocq, 80550 Le Crotoy [03 22 27 03 22; fax 03 22 27 70 76; contact@campingleridin.com; www.campingleridin.com or www.camphotel.fr]** Fr A16 exit junc 24 dir Rue & Le Crotoy. At ent to Le Crotoy foll sp St Firmin, take 2nd rd to R, site sp. Med, unshd; htd wc; chem disp; baby facs; shwrs; el pnts (6-10A) €2.50-5.50; gas; lndtte; ice; shop; supmkt 1km; rest; snacks; bar; playgrnd; htd pool; paddling pool; sand beach 1.5km; cycle hire; fitness rm; golf 10km; child entmnt; TV rm; 80% statics; dogs €1.50; poss cr; adv bkg; quiet except noise fr adj gravel pit. "Some sm, tight pitches bet statics; narr site rds not suitable lge o'fits; clean san facs; unisex low ssn; bird sanctuary at Marquenterre; Le Crotoy beautiful town." ♦ 1 Apr-4 Nov. € 23.00 (CChq acc)   2007*

See advertisement below

France

CROTOY, LE *3B2* (4km N Coastal) **Camping Les Aubépines, 800 Rue de la Maye, St Firmin, 80550 Le Crotoy [03 22 27 01 34; fax 03 22 27 13 66; contact@camping-lesaubepines.com; www. camping-lesaubepines.com or www.camphotel. fr]** Exit A16 junc 23 to Le Crotoy via D40 & D940; then foll sp St Firmin; site sp. Or exit A16 junc 24 onto D32 dir Rue; by-pass Rue but take D4 to St Firmin; after church look for site sp. Site on rd to beach on W of D4. Med, hdg/mkd pitch, pt shd; htd wc; chem disp; baby facs; shwrs inc; el pnts (3-10A) inc; gas; lndtte; shop; tradsmn; playgrnd; htd pool; sand beach 1km; horseriding; games rm; entmnt; 10% statics; dogs €1.50; phone; poss cr; Eng spkn; adv bkg; quiet; cc acc; red low ssn; CCI. "Well-run site; tourers sited with statics; some pitches sm; gd cyling & walking; Marquenterre ornithological park 3km; steam train 3km; excel." ♦ 30 Mar-4 Nov. € 23.00 2007*

See advertisement on previous page

CROUY SUR COSSON see Muides sur Loire *4G2*

⊞**CROZON** *2E2* (5km E Coastal) **Camping L'Aber, Tal-ar-Groas, Route de la Plage de l'Aber, 29160 Crozon [02 98 27 02 96; fax 02 98 27 28 48; contactcamping-abercom; www.camping-aber. com]** On F887 turn S in Tal-ar-Groas foll camp sp to site in 1km on R. Med, mkd pitch, pt sl, terr, pt shd; wc; shwrs inc; el pnts (5A) €2; gas; lndtte; snacks; bar; htd pool; sand beach 1km; sailing; fishing; windsurfing; adv bkg; quiet. ♦ € 12.60 2007*

CROZON *2E2* (3km SW) **Camping Les Bruyères, Le Bouis, 29160 Crozon [tel/fax 02 98 26 14 87; camping.les.bruyeres@presquile-crozon.com]** Take D887 then D255 SW fr Crozon (sp Cap de la Chèvre). In 1.5km turn R & site on R in 700m. Lge, mkd pitch, pt shd; wc (mainly cont); shwrs inc; gas; ice; shop in ssn; el pnts (5A) €2.80; playgrnd; sand beach 1.8km; dogs €1; Eng spkn; adv bkg; quiet; red 2+ days. "Gd san facs; conv beaches & mkt town." 1 Jun-15 Sep. € 13.00 2006*

CUBJAC *7C3* (1.5km E Rural) **Camping L'Ilot, 24640 Cubjac [05 53 05 53 05; fax 05 53 05 37 82; musitelli@wanadoo.fr]** Take D5 E fr Périgueux to Cubjac (21km). Fork R off D5 into vill. At x-rds in vill E & site on R in 1.5km. Sm, mkd pitch, pt shd; wc (some cont); baby facs; shwrs inc; el pnts (5A) €2.50; ice; lndtte; shop adj; rest; snacks; bar; BBQ; playgrnd; pool 4km; rv sw; fishing; canoes; tennis adj; games area; entmnt; adv bkg. ♦ 1 Apr-30 Sep. € 13.00 2004*

CUCURON see Cadenet *10E3*

CUERS *10F3* (5km SE Rural) **Camping de Déffends, 109 Route de Collobrières, Quarter Bécasson, 83390 Pierrefeu-du-Var [04 94 28 20 62; fax 04 94 48 26 75]** Fr Cuers A57 N exit 10 R onto D14 thro Pierrefeu-du-Var; foll sp E to Collobrières site on L 1km. Med, mkd pitch; terr, pt shd; wc; chem disp; baby facs; shwrs inc; el pnts (6-10A) €3.55-4.60; gas 1km; lndtte; ice; tradsmn; rest, snacks, bar in ssn; playgrnd; pool; sand beach 17km; games area; cycle hire; entmnt; TV; 10% statics; dogs €2; phone; Eng spkn; adv bkg; quiet; CCI. "Some pitches diff for lge o'fits; gates clsd 2200-0800; scenic views in wine-growing area." 15 Apr-15 Sep. € 14.50 2005*

CUERS *10F3* (6km W Rural) **Camping Les Tomasses, 83210 Belgentier [04 94 48 92 70; fax 04 94 48 94 73]** Exit A8 junc 34 St Maximin onto N7. After Tourves take D205 then D5/D554 sp Solliès-Pont. After Belgentier in 1.5km turn R at yellow sp, site in 200m on L. Or N fr Toulon onto D554. Well sp on R in vill. Med, hdg/mkd pitch, pt shd; wc (mainly cont); chem disp (wc); shwrs inc; el pnts (6A) €3.50; gas; lndtte; ice; shop; snacks; bar; BBQ; playgrnd; pool; tennis; entmnt; 10% statics; dogs €2; phone; bus 300m; adv bkg (dep req); quiet, poss dog noise; red low ssn; CCI. "Pretty CL-type site; friendly management; twin-axles welcome; acces poss diff lge o'fits" ♦ ltd. 1 Apr-30 Sep. € 13.30 2006*

CUISEAUX *9A2* (5km SW Rural) **Camping Le Domaine de Louvarel, 71480 Champagnat [tel/ fax 03 85 76 62 71; contact@domainedelouvarel. com; www.domainedelouvarel.com]** Exit A39 junc 9 dir Cuiseaux, then onto N83 dir Louhans, site sp. Med, hdg/mkd, shd (planted 2007); wc; chem disp; mv service pnt; baby facs; shwrs inc; el pnts (10A) €3; lndtte; rest; snacks; bar; BBQ; playgrnd; lake adj; fishing; games area; cycle hire; some statics; dogs €0.50; phone; o'night area for m'vans; adv bkg; quiet; CCI. "Lakeside site; v helpful manager; specially constructed swimming lake; gd walking; gd rest in ssn." 1 Apr-7 Nov. € 13.00 (CChq acc) 2007*

CULAN *7A4* (1km N) **Camp Municipal La Guinguette, 18270 Culan [02 48 56 64 41; fax 02 48 56 67 08]** On D65 1km N of Culan. Sm, hdg pitch, shd; wc; chem disp; 50% serviced pitches; shwrs inc; el pnts (6A) inc; shops 2km; lake sw & fishing 500m; quiet. "Old-fashioned san facs, but clean; pleasant area; chateau worth visit." Easter-15 Sep. € 9.00 2007*

CULAN *7A4* (7km E Rural) **Camp Municipal Les Bergerolles, 18360 Vesdun [02 48 63 03 07 (Mairie); fax 02 48 63 12 62; mairie.vesdun.cher@wanadoo.fr]** Exit Culan S on D943 twd Montluçon; 200m turn L D4 to Vesdun. Site sp in vill adj stadium. Sm, mkd pitch, pt shd; wc; shwrs inc; el pnts; shop, rest, snacks, bar 500m; playgrnd; games area; quiet. "Vill has monument 'Centre of France'; pay site fees at Mairie 300m." Whitsun-30 Sep. 2006*

CULAN *7A4* (12km W Rural) **Camp Municipal L'Etang Merlin,** 18370 Châteaumeillant [02 48 61 31 38; fax 02 48 61 39 89; camping. chateaumeillant.chalets@wanadoo.fr] Rec app fr W to avoid narr town rds. Site sp fr rndabt at W end of town on D80 N of Châteaumeillant on lakeside. Fr Culan by pass town on D943, then as above. Sm, hdg/mkd pitch, pt shd; wc; serviced pitches; chem disp; shwrs inc ; el pnts (5A) €2; lndry rm; shop 3km; playgrnd; lake adj (no sw); fishing; dogs €1; Eng spkn; adv bkg; quiet; no cc acc; CCI. "Superb quality; v clean; v friendly, caring owners; rec arr early high ssn to secure pitch; easy walk to town." ♦ 1 May-30 Sep. € 8.00   2005*

CULOZ see Ruffieux *9B3*

CUVILLY *3C3* (1.5km N Rural) **Camping de Sorel, 24 Rue de St Claude,** 60490 Orvillers-Sorel [03 44 85 02 74; fax 03 44 42 11 65; contact@ aestiva.fr; www.aestiva.fr] Exit A1/E15 at junc 12 (Roye) S'bound or 11 (Ressons) N'bound. Site on E of N17. Med, mkd pitch, pt sl, pt shd; htd wc; chem disp; shwrs inc; el pnts (6A) inc; lndry rm; shop; tradsmn; rest 2km; snacks; playgrnd; games area; TV; 50% statics; poss cr; quiet. "Excel & pleasant situation; conv NH nr a'route; gd facs; friendly staff; rec early arr in ssn; v busy at w/e; 30 mins Parc Astérix. 2 Feb-14 Dec. € 18.00 (CChq acc)   2007*

DABO see Saverne *6E3*

DAGLAN *7D3* (3km Rural) **Camping Le Moulin de Paulhiac,** 24250 Daglan [05 53 28 20 88; fax 05 53 29 33 45; francis.armagnac@wanadoo. fr; www.moulin-de-paulhiac.com] D57 SW fr Sarlat, across rv into St Cybranet & site in 2km. Fr Souillac W on D703 alongside Rv Dordogne; x-ing rv onto D46 (nr Domme) & D50, to site. Med, hdg/mkd pitch, shd; wc (some cont); chem disp; mv service pnt; shwrs; el pnts (6-10A) €3.35-4; gas; lndtte; ice; shop; rest; snacks; bar; playgrnd; 4 htd pools; waterslide; TV rm; entmnt; shgl beach/rv adj with canoeing/fishing; 20% statics; dogs €1.75; Eng spkn; adv bkg; quiet with some rd noise; red low ssn; cc acc; CCI. "V pretty site; vg fruit/ vegetable mkt Sun in vill; v friendly, helpful staff." ♦ ltd. 13 May-16 Sep. € 22.20   2006*

DAMAZAN *7D2* (2km S Rural) **Camp Municipal du Lac, Route de Buzet-sur-Baïse,** 47160 Damazan [05 53 79 40 15; fax 05 53 79 26 92; mairie. damazan@wanadoo.fr] Fr A62 take junc 6, turn R at rndabt. Almost immed take slip rd sp Damazan/ Buzet-dur-Baïse. At top turn R sp Buzet. Site 1km on R (2nd turning goes to lake only). Med, some hdg/mkd pitch, pt sl, pt shd; wc (some cont); chem disp (wc); shwrs inc; el pnts (12A) €2; gas 2km; lndtte; shops, rest, snacks, bar 2km; BBQ; playgrnd adj; lake sw adj; 2% statics; poss cr; adv bkg; quiet but nr a'route; CCI. "Excel NH as 2km fr a'route; next to cricket club!; by pretty lake; v helpful management."♦ ltd. 1 Jun-30 Sep. € 4.00
2007*

DAMBACH *5D3* (Rural) **Aire Naturelle Municipal du Hohenfels,** 67110 Dambach [03 88 09 24 08; fax 03 88 09 21 81] Fr N on D35 turn S onto D853, site sp. Med, pt sl, terr, pt shd; wc; chem disp; shwrs inc; el pnts inc; quiet. "Lovely area; walk fr site to Maginot Line relics; access poss diff lge o'fits." 1 Apr-31 Oct. € 13.30   2006*

DAMBACH LA VILLE see Sélestat *6E3*

DAMGAN see Muzillac *2G3*

DAMPIERRE *6G2* (2km SE) **Camp Municipal, Rue de Gard,** 39700 Fraisans [03 84 71 10 88] Exit A36 junc 2.1 to Dampierre. Fr Dampierre take D73, site sp on R at school bef rv bdge. Sm, mkd pitch, pt shd; wc (some cont); shwrs; el pnts (4A) inc; shops adj; supmkt nr; dir access Rv Doubs; fishing; quiet. "Basic, clean, quiet site; lge pitches; pleasant little town; conv Besançon." 1 May-30 Sep. € 15.00
2005*

DAMPIERRE *6G2* (7km W) **Camp Municipal,** 39700 Orchamps [03 84 81 24 63] N73 Besançon-Dole rd. Turn S at sp in vill. Sm, mkd pitch, pt shd; wc; shwrs inc; el pnts €2 (poss long lead req); lndry rm; shops 500m; rv fishing adj; dogs; quiet. "Excel CL-type site bet Rv Doubs & canal; warden calls each eve; old but v clean facs; vg NH." € 8.00
2004*

DAMPIERRE SUR BOUTONNE *7A2* (Rural) **Camp Municipal,** 17470 Dampierre-sur-Boutonne [05 46 24 02 36 (Mairie); fax 05 46 33 95 49; dampierre-sur-boutonne@mairie17.com] S fr Niort on D150 twds St Jean-d'Angély; in vill of Tout-y-Faut turn E on D115 sp Dampierre; turn N in vill on D127 twds Rv Boutonne, site behind vill hall; well sp. Sm, hdg pitch, shd; wc; shwrs inc; el pnts (6A) inc; shop, rest, snacks, bar 500m; rv fishing; dogs €0.80; quiet. "Clean site; san facs outside camp boundary & open to public; poss noisy, local youths congregate nrby; rec sh stay/NH only." 30 Apr-30 Sep. € 7.90   2007*

DAMVIX see Maillezais *7A2*

DANGE ST ROMAIN *4H2* (3km N Rural) **Camp Municipal, 8 Rue des Buxière,** 86220 Les Ormes [05 49 85 61 30 (Mairie); fax 05 49 85 66 17; les-ormes@cg86.fr; www.lesormes.fr] Turn W off D910 (N10) in cent Les Ormes onto D1a sp Vellèches & Marigny-Marmande, foll site sp to site on rv. Sm, mkd pitch, pt sl, pt shd; wc; chem disp; shwrs inc; el pnts (10A) inc; lndry rm; shop; rest, bar 800m; playgrnd; tennis 100m; dogs €1.20; quiet, but some rlwy noise; adv bkg; Eng spkn; dogs; CCI. "Friendly warden." 1 Apr-30 Sep. € 8.20   2007*

DAON see Château Gontier *4F1*

France

DARBRES *9D2* (Rural) **Camping Les Lavandes, 07170 Darbres [tel/fax 04 75 94 20 65; sarl. leslavandes@online.fr; www.les-lavandes-darbres.com]** SE fr Aubenas on N102 twds Montélimar. Turn L after 10km in vill Lavilledieu onto D224 sp Lussas. Cont 5km to Darbres, site sp. Med, mkd pitch, terr, pt shd; wc; chem disp; baby facs; shwrs inc; el pnts (6A) €3.50; lndtte; ice; shop; rest; snacks; bar; BBQ (gas/charcoal only); playgrnd; pool; waterslide; games area; cycle hire; entmnt; TV; some statics; dogs €2.50; poss cr; Eng spkn; quiet; cc acc. "Attractive site; gd san facs." Easter-30 Sep. € 17.00   2007*

DARDILLY see Lyon *9B2*

DAX *8E1* (3.5km NE Urban) **Camping Les Jardins de l'Adour, 848 Rue de Pouy, 40990 St Vincent-de-Paul [tel/fax 05 58 89 99 60 or 06 03 03 09 77 (mob); info@camping-jardinsdeladour.fr; www.camping-jardins deladour.fr]** NE on N124 fr Dax twd Mont-de-Marsan on dual c'way, take exit to St Vincent-de-Paul at rndabt; site in 200m on L, sp. Med, hdg/mkd pitch, shd; wc; chem disp; shwrs inc; el pnts (6A) €3; gas; lndtte; shop 1km & 5km; rest; snacks; pool; sand beach 30km; 50% statics; dogs €1; phone; barrier clsd 2230-0730; Eng spkn; adv bkg; CCI. "Pretty, well-kept, clean, friendly site; v clean san facs; excel." ♦ 1 Apr-28 Oct. € 12.30   2006*

DAX *8E1* (1.5km W Rural) **Camping Les Chênes, Allée du Bois de Boulogne, 40100 Dax [05 58 90 05 53; fax 05 58 90 42 43; camping-chenes@wanadoo.fr; www.camping-les-chenes. fr]** Fr N124 to Dax, foll sp Bois de Boulogne, cross rlwy bdge & rv bdge & foll camp sp on rv bank. Well sp. Lge, mkd pitch, shd; htd wc (cont); chem disp; some serviced pitches; shwrs inc; el pnts (6A) inc; gas; lndtte; ice; shop; tradsmn; rest; snacks; bar; playgrnd; pool; beach 20km; TV rm; cycle hire; 40% statics; dogs €1; poss cr; Eng spkn; adv bkg; quiet; cc acc; CCI. "Excel position; conv thermal baths at Dax; easy walk along rv into town; excel." ♦ 27 Mar-30 Nov. € 17.50   2005*

DAX *8E1* (6km W) **Camping L'Etang d'Ardy, Route de Bayonne, 40990 St Paul-lès-Dax [05 58 97 57 74; info@etangardy.com; www. etangardy.com]** Fr E on N124 dir Dax; turn R onto D16 dir Magescq; then L sp Ardy; foll camping sp. Fr W leave N124 sp La Pince/Dax/Magescq; at rndabt U-turn onto N124 going E; take 1st exit & foll site sp. Med, hdg pitch, shd; wc; chem disp; shwrs inc; el pnts (5-10A) €2.20-3.15; lndtte; ice; shops; tradsmn; playgrnd; pool; 30% statics; dogs €1.50; adv bkg (dep req); quiet; red long stay. "Many serviced pitches; v friendly; lake fishing; health thermal baths at Dax." ♦ 8 Apr-28 Nov. € 18.20   2006*

DAX *8E1* (9km W Rural) **Camping Lou Bascou, 40180 Rivière-Saas-et-Gourby [05 58 97 57 29; fax 05 58 97 59 52; loubascou@wanadoo.fr; http://pagesperso-orange.fr/loubascou/]** Leave N10 at junc 8 for N124 twd Dax. In 3.5km turn R onto D13 sp Rivière-Saas-et-Gourby. Well sp fr N124. Beware speed humps in Rivière vill. Med, hdg/mkd pitch, pt shd; htd wc; chem disp; shwrs inc; el pnts (6-10A) €3-5; lndtte; shop 300m; tradsmn; snacks; bar; BBQ; playgrnd; pool 9km; sand beach 25km; tennis; entmnt; 50% statics in sep area; dogs €1; Eng spkn; adv bkg; quiet; red long stay/low ssn. "Excel facs; quiet, friendly site; thermal facs in Dax; 60km fr Spanish border; vg NH; nrby wetlands wildlife inc storks worth seeing." ♦ 1 Mar-31 Oct. € 15.00   2007*

⊞**DAX** *8E1* (11km W Rural) **FFCC Camping à la Ferme Bertranborde (Lafitte), 40180 Rivière-Saas-et-Gourby [05 58 97 58 39]** Turn S off N124 5km W of Dax onto D113, sp Angoumé; at x-rd in 2km turn R (by water tower); then immed L; site on R in 100m, well sp. Sm, pt shd, pt sl; wc; chem disp; mv service pnt; shwrs inc; el pnts (4-10A) €2.50-4; lndtte; shops 1km; playgrnd; htd pool 10km; rv sw 7km; dogs €0.50; quiet; adv bkg; CCI. "Peaceful CL-type site; friendly owners; meals on request; excel." € 9.00   2007*

DAX *8E1* (3km NW Rural) **FFCC Camping Les Pins du Soleil, La Pince, 40990 St Paul-les-Dax [05 58 91 37 91; fax 05 58 91 00 24; pinsoleil@ aol.com; www.pinsoleil.com]** Exit N10 sp Dax onto D459. At traff lts turn R sp Bayonne & 3 Campings. In 1.5km turn L sp Dax/La Pince. Site sp in pine forest. Med, hdg/mkd pitch, pt sl, pt shd; htd wc, chem disp; mv service pnt; serviced pitches; baby facs; shwrs inc; el pnts (5A) €2; gas; lndtte; ice; shop; tradsmn; rest 1km; snacks; bar; playgrnd; pool; tennis 2km; cycle hire; entmnt; TV rm; 25% statics; dogs €2; phone; Eng spkn; some rd noise; red long stay/low ssn; cc acc. "Nice, quiet site (low ssn); various pitch sizes, some spacious; soft, sandy soil poss problem when wet; v helpful & friendly; excel pool; spa 2 km; conv Pyrenees & Biarritz; vg." ♦ 10 Mar-10 Nov. € 24.00 (CChq acc)   2007*

DAX *8E1* (12km NW Rural) **FFCC Camping Aire Naturelle Le Toy (Fabas), 40990 Herm [05 58 91 55 16; fax 05 58 91 09 50; vincent. fabas@laposte.net; www.camping-du-toy.com]** Exit N10 junc 11 at Magescq; foll sps for cent vill & then Herm on D150; at Herm x-rds by church turn L onto rd to Castets. Site 1km on R. Sm, hdg/mkd pitch, shd; wc; shwrs inc; el pnts (4-10A) €2.20-4; shops 1km; lndtte; playgrnd; sand beach 20 mins; games area; trampolines; dogs €0.80; Eng spkn; quiet. "Pleasant woodland site; conv Dax ancient Roman settlement town." Easter-31 Oct. € 9.00   2006*

DEAUVILLE *3D1* (2km S Urban) **Camping des Haras, Chemin du Calvaire, 14800 Touques [02 31 88 44 84; fax 02 31 88 97 08; les.haras@ wanadoo.fr]** N on D677 (N177) Pont l'Evêque-Deauville rd, ignore 1st slip rd sp Touques (too narr, vans prohibited); stay on by-pass & turn R at traff lts by g'ge sp Touques then L on D62; fork L to site after church. Also sp fr D513 Deauville-Caen rd. Lge, hdg pitch, pt sl, pt shd; wc; own san; chem disp; shwrs; el pnts (10A) €4.12; gas; lndtte; shop; rest; snacks; bar; playgrnd; pool 2km; sand beach 2km; entmnt; 60% statics; poss cr; adv bkg; red low ssn. "Some pitches poss diff lge o'fits; in winter phone ahead; conv Honfleur & WW2 sites; office clsd fr 1830 low ssn & Sun; san facs run down; c'vans sited nr playgrnd." ♦ 1 Feb-30 Nov. € 16.35   2005*

DEAUVILLE *3D1* (3km S Urban) **Camping La Vallée de Deauville, Route de Beaumont, 14800 St Arnoult [02 31 88 58 17; fax 02 31 88 11 57; campinglavalleededeauville@wanadoo.fr; www. camping-deauville.com]** Fr Deauville take D27 dir Caen, turn R onto D278 to St Armoult, foll site sp. Lge, hdg/mkd pitch, hdstg, pt shd; htd wc (some cont); baby facs; shwrs inc; el pnts (10A) €5.50; gas; lndtte; shop; tradsmn; rest; snacks; bar; playgrnd; htd pool; waterslide; sand beach 4km; fishing lake; games rm; entmnt; child entmnt; 80% statics; dogs €3; phone; Eng spkn; some rlwy noise; red low ssn; cc acc; CCI. "Easy access to beaches & resorts; conv Le Havre using Pont de Normandie; lake walks & activities on site; excel san facs." ♦ 1 Apr-31 Oct. € 26.40   2004*

DEAUVILLE *3D1* (6km S Rural) **Camping du Lieu Rôti, 14800 Vauville [tel/fax 02 31 87 96 22; info@deauville-camping.com; www.deauville-camping.com]** Fr Deauville, take D27 S twd Caen. Site on R 200m after Tourgéville church. Well sp. Med, mkd pitch, pt shd; htd wc; chem disp; shwrs inc; el pnts (5A) €4; lndtte; ice; shop; tradsmn; rest; snacks; bar; playgrnd; htd pool; paddling pool; sand beach 3.5km; games area; 50% statics; dogs €3; phone; Eng spkn; adv bkg; quiet; cc acc; CCI. "Pleasant countryside location; helpful reception; excel." ♦ 15 Apr-15 Oct. € 27.00   2007*

⊞DECAZEVILLE *7D4* (3km NW Rural) **Camping Le Roquelongue, 12300 Boisse-Penchot [tel/ fax 05 65 63 39 67; info@camping-roquelongue. com; www.camping-roquelongue.com]** Fr D963 N fr Decazeville turn W onto D140 & D42 to Boisse-Penchot. Rte via D21 not rec (steep hill & acute turn). Site mid-way bet Boisse-Penchot & Livinhac-le-Haut on D42. Med, hdg/mkd pitch, pt shd; wc; chem disp; shwrs inc; el pnts (6-10A) 3.40-4.10; gas; lndtte; shop; tradsmn; supmkt 5km; snacks; bar; playgrnd; pool; fishing; canoeing; tennis; cycle hire; 10% statics; dogs free; phone; adv bkg; quiet; CCI. "Direct access Rv Lot; pitches gd size; san facs clean; no twin-axles; mkd walks fr site with stunning views." ♦ ltd. € 14.80   2007*

DECIZE *4H4* (500m NE Urban) **Camp Municipal Les Halles, Allée Marcel Merle, 58300 Decize [03 86 25 14 05 or 03 86 25 03 23 (Mairie); fax 03 86 77 11 48; aquadis1@wanadoo.fr; www. aquadis-loisirs.com]** Fr Nevers take N81 to Decize, look for sp for 'Stade Nautique Camping'. Lge, mkd pitch, pt shd; wc (some cont); snacks; shwrs inc; el pnts (6A) inc; gas; ice; shop; sand beach adj; sat TV; dogs €3.10; poss cr; some Eng spkn; quiet; cc acc; CCI. "Lge pitches, some by rv; v helpful staff; gd san facs; extra for twin-axles; poss diff access pitches due trees." ♦ 1 Apr-31 Oct. € 13.00   2007*

DECIZE *4H4* (12km SE Rural) **Camping La Varenne à la Ferme, Rue de Tanjeat, 58300 Charrin [tel/ fax 03 86 50 30 14]** Fr Decize take D979 twd Digoin & foll sp Camping la Ferme; site off to R thro vill of Charrin. In vill foll sp for Chambres d'Hôtes. Sm, pt shd; wc; chem disp; shwrs inc; el pnts inc (long lead req); fishing 2km; adv bkg; quiet. "A lovely, v quiet CL-type site; friendly owners; basic facs; breakfast & some farm produce avail; poss entmnt fr piglets!; gd touring base for Nivernais canal; chambres d'hôtes." 1 Jun-30 Sep. € 8.00   2007*

DELLE *6G3* (5km N Rural) **Camp Municipal du Passe-Loup, Rue des Chênes, 90100 Joncherey [03 84 56 32 63 or 03 84 56 26 07; fax 03 84 56 27 66]** Exit A75 junc 11 Sevenans onto N19 S dir Delle. Turn L onto D3 N dir Boron, site on R in approx 3km. Med, sl, pt shd; wc; chem disp; shwrs inc; el pnts (6A) inc; playgrnd; lake fishing adj; 45% statics; quiet; CCI. "Pleasant, spacious site; basic san facs." 1 Apr-31 Oct. € 13.90   2005*

DENNEVILLE PLAGE see Barneville Carteret *1C4*

DESCARTES *4H2* (5km SE Rural) **Camp Municipal Ile de la Claise, 37169 Abilly [02 47 59 78 01 (Mairie); fax 02 47 59 89 93; mairie.abilly@wanadoo.fr]** Fr Descartes take D750 S for 3km; SE on D42 to Abilly. Site on island in Rv Claise. Sm, shd; wc; shwrs €1.12; el pnts €1.30; shop; rest, snacks, bar 500m; playgrnd; pool 6km; fishing; tennis; dogs; quiet. ♦ 15 May-15 Sep. € 5.10   2006*

DESCARTES *4H2* (S Urban) **Camp Municipal La Grosse Motte, Allée Léo Lagrange, 37160 Descartes [02 47 59 85 90 or 02 47 92 42 20; fax 02 47 59 72 20; otm-descartes@wanadoo. fr; www.ville-descartes.fr]** 500m W of D750 on S side of town on rvside. V narr turn into site due stone house walls. Sm, hdg pitch, pt sl, pt shd; wc (some cont); baby facs; shwrs inc; shops in town; el pnts (rev pol) €1.95; pool adj; playgrnd; tennis, mini-golf nr; boating on rv; dogs €0.90; adv bkg; quiet; cc not acc; CCI. "Beautiful site in historic birth place of Descartes; delightful public gardens adj; spacious pitches; v clean facs; friendly staff; excel value, a real find; popular with school parties; gd NH." 1 Jun-30 Sep. € 6.45   2006*

DEUX CHAISES see Montmarault *9A1*

France

DEVILLAC see Villéreal *7D3*

⊞**DEYME** *8F3* (Urban) **Camping Les Violettes, Porte de Toulouse, 31450 Deyme [05 61 81 72 07; fax 05 61 27 17 31; campinglesviolettes@ wanadoo.fr]** SE fr Toulouse to Carcassonne on N113, sp on L. Med, mkd pitch, pt shd; htd wc; mv service pnt; shwrs inc; el pnts (4-6A) €2.40-3.50; lndtte; shop; rest; snacks; bar; BBQ; playgrnd; TV; 60% statics; dogs €1; poss cr; quiet but rd noise; CCI. "Helpful, friendly staff; poss v muddy in wet weather; 800m fr Canal du Midi & 10km fr Space City." 2006*

DIE *9D2* (N Urban) **Camp Municipal Le Justin (formally de la Piscine), Rue de Chabestar, 26150 Die [04 75 22 14 77; fax 04 75 22 20 42]** Ent town fr W on D93, fork R D751, sp Gap & 'rugby stade' (not football stade); foll sps for Camp Municipal & piscine; site on S of rlwy line bef sw pool 'piscine'. Poss diff bdge for long o'fits. Med, pt sl, pt shd; wc (some cont); chem disp; mv service pnt; shwrs inc; el pnts (10A) €2.75; ice; lndtte; shops, rest 500m; tradsmn; snacks; playgrnd; rv sw adj; entmnts; dogs €1.60; Eng spkn; adv bkg; cc acc; CCI. "Gd facs; site in beautiful setting in Drôme valley; poor security - vehicles use track thro site as short cut; easy walk to Die - interesting town." 1 May-15 Sep. € 10.00 2005*

DIE *9D2* (400m N Urban) **Camping La Riou-Merle, Route de Romeyer, 26150 Die [tel/ fax 04 75 22 21 31]** Fr Gap on D93 heading twd Valence. Cont on D93 twd town cent; R on D742 to Romeyer. Site on L in 200m. On D93 fr Crest foll sp round town cent onto D742. Sharp turn at ent. Med, pt sl, pt shd; wc (some cont); shwrs inc; el pnts (5A) €2.80; lndry rm; shops in town; playgrnd; pool; fishing; 30% statics; dogs €1; quiet; red low ssn. "Site clean but unattractive in wet weather; warden calls am & pm; gd, renovated san facs." Easter-31 Oct. € 10.60 2005*

DIE *9D2* (1km SE Urban) **Camping La Glandasse, Route de Gap, Quartier de la Maladrerie, 26150 Die [04 75 22 02 50; fax 04 75 22 04 91; camping-glandasse@ wanadoo.fr; www.camping-glandasse.com]** Take D93 S twds Gap; site on R 1km outside of Die, under rlwy bdge (3m wide, 2.8m high). Med, hdg pitch, pt sl, pt shd; wc; chem disp; baby facs; shwrs inc; el pnts (10A) inc; gas; lndtte; ice; shop; rest; snacks; bar; playgrnd; pool; paddling pool; shgl rv beach; cycle hire; some statics; dogs €2; poss cr; adv bkg; quiet; CCI. "Gd cent for touring mountains & Parc de Vercours; some noise fr rd, rlwy & air." ♦ 1 Apr-30 Sep. € 19.30 2005*

DIE *9D2* (2km W Rural) **Camping La Pinède, Quartier du Pont Neuf, 26150 Die [04 75 22 17 77; fax 04 75 22 22 73; info@camping-pinede.com; www.camping-pinede.com]** W fr Die on D93 dir Crest, site sp on L. Access diff for lge vans - narr rv bdge 2.75m wide. Med, mkd pitch, terr, pt shd; wc; shwrs inc; el pnts (5-10A) €3.50-5; gas; lndtte; ice; rest; shop; playgrnd; pool; shgl beach & rv sw adj; fishing; canoeing; tennis; mini-golf; entmnt; TV; dogs €2; adv bkg ess; noisy; red low ssn. ♦ 20 Apr-15 Sep. € 24.00 2007*

DIE *9D2* (2km NW Rural) **Camping Le Chamarge, Route de Crest, 26150 Die [tel/fax 04 75 22 14 13 or 04 75 22 06 77]** Foll D93 twd Valence, site on L by Rv Drôme. Med, mkd pitch, shd; wc; shwrs; el pnts (3-6A) €2.45-2.80; gas; shops, rest 1km; bar 2km; playgrnd; rv sw, fishing & canoeing adj; entmnts; TV; dogs €1.10; rec adv bkg high ssn; quiet. "Beautiful mountainous area." ♦ Easter-15 Sep. € 10.20 2006*

DIE *9D2* (12km NW Urban) **Aire Naturelle Le Moulin du Rivet (Szarvas), 26150 St Julien-en-Quint [tel/fax 04 75 21 20 43; contact@ moulindurivet.com; www.moulindurivet.com]** On D93 E fr Crest twd Die, turn L onto D129 dir Ste Croix/St Julien. Foll sp St Julien. Site on L in 9km. Sm, some hdstg, terr, pt shd; wc; chem disp (wc); shwrs inc; el pnts (6A) €3; shop 9km; tradsmn; rest; playgrnd; rv sw adj; dogs; poss cr; Eng spkn; adv bkg; quiet; CCI. "Attractive, peaceful CL-type site on Rv Sûre; gd views; friendly owners." 1 Apr-1 Nov. € 10.00 2007*

DIENVILLE see Brienne Le Château *6E1*

DIEPPE *3C2* (4km S) **Camping Vitamin, 865 Chemin des Vertus, 76550 St Aubin-sur-Scie [02 35 82 11 11; camping-vitamin@wanadoo.fr; www.camping-vitamin.com]** Foll dir to Formule 1 & Hotel B&B. Lge, hdg pitch, unshd; wc; chem disp; mv service pnt; shwrs inc; el pnts (10A) inc; lndtte; shops 1km; bar; playgrnd; pool; shgl beach 2km; adv bkg; 25% statics; dogs €1.50; quiet; CCI. "Lovely, well-maintained site; san facs immac; poss boggy in wet; conv ferries." 1 Apr-15 Oct. € 16.00 (CChq acc) 2007*

DIEPPE *3C2* (5km S Rural) **Camping des 2 Rivières, 76880 Martigny [02 35 85 60 82; fax 02 35 85 95 16; martigny.76@wanadoo.fr; www. camping-2-rivieres.com]** Martigny vill on D154 S fr Dieppe. Med, pt shd; wc; el pnts €2.55; lndtte; shop; playgrnd; covrd pool, watersports, mountain biking, horseriding & Arques forest nrby; dogs €1.30; adv bkg; quiet. "V attractive, spacious site by lge lake; conv Dieppe; highly rec." 30 Mar-14 Oct. € 13.00 2007*

⊞*Site open all year* 318 *Help us to update this guide*

DIEPPE *3C2* (4km SW Rural) **Camping La Source, Le Plessis, Petit-Appeville, 76550 Hautot-sur-Mer** [02 35 84 27 04; fax 02 35 82 25 02; info@camping-la-source.fr; www.camping-la-source.fr] Fr Dieppe ferry terminal foll sp Paris, take D925 W dir Fécamp. In 2km at Petit Appeville turn L, site in 800m on rvside. Med, mkd pitch, hdstg, pt shd; wc (some cont); chem disp; mv service pnt; shwrs inc; el pnts (6A) €3; lndtte; ice; shop 2km; tradsmn; snacks; bar; playgrnd; htd pool; sand beach 3km; rv sw, fishing & boating adj; games area; games rm; cycle hire; golf 4km; entmnt; TV; 30% statics; dogs €1.50; Eng spkn; some rd & rlwy noise; adv bkg; quiet; cc acc; CCI. "Friendly owner; excel sh stay/NH bef or after ferry." ♦ 15 Mar-15 Oct. € 16.60 (CChq acc) 2007*

DIEPPE *3C2* (4km SW Urban) **Camping Relais Motard, Rue de la Mer, 76550 Pourville-sur-Mer** [02 35 83 92 49] Fr Dieppe ferry terminal foll sp Paris. Take D925 W dir Fécamp. In 2km at Petit Appeville turn R, site on R in 600m. Sm, mkd pitch, unshd; wc; chem disp; mv service pnt in nrby g'ge; shwrs inc; el pnts €2; lndry rm; rest 1km; snacks; bar; BBQ; sand beach 1km; dogs; quiet; CCI. "New site 2005 with modern san facs; vg." ♦ 1 May-15 Sep. € 10.40 2005*

DIEPPE *3C2* (6km SW Urban) **Camp Municipal du Colombier, 76550 Offranville** [02 35 85 21 14; fax 02 35 04 52 67] W fr Dieppe on D925, take L turn on D55 to Offranville, site clearly sp in vill to Parc du Colombier. NB Part of site cul-de-sac, explore on foot bef towing in. Med, hdg/mkd pitch, pt shd; wc; chem disp; shwrs inc; el pnts (10A) €2.20; gas; lndtte; shop & supmkt 500m; rest; shgl beach 5km; many statics; ltd Eng spkn; CCI. "Pleasant setting; vg clean site; immac facs; helpful staff; set in ornamental gardens with equestrian cent; security gates clsd 2200-0700; ask warden how to operate barrier in his absence; conv ferries; easy walk to town; rec." ♦ 1 Apr-15 Oct. € 13.80 2007*

DIGNE LES BAINS *10E3* (1km NE) **Camp du Bourg, Route de Barcelonnette, 04000 Digne-les-Bains** [04 92 31 04 87; fax 04 92 34 59 80] Fr rndabt by rv bdge take main st (Boulevard Gassendi) thro cent town, sp D900 La Javie, Barcelonnette. Camp sp on R. Med, pt shd; wc; shwrs inc; el pnts (4A) €2.50; shops 1.5km; pool 1.5km; games area; 95% statics; dogs €1. "Pleasant town with fine scenery; thermal baths; beautiful & fascinating area; poss diff access to some pitches on terraced areas for lge o'fits; recep manned few hrs only." ♦ 15 May-30 Oct. € 11.50 2004*

DIGNE LES BAINS *10E3* (1.5km SE Rural) **Camping Les Eaux Chaudes, 32 Ave des Thermes, 04000 Digne-les-Bains** [04 92 32 31 04; fax 04 92 34 59 80; info@campingleseauxchaudes.com; www.campingleseauxchaudes.com] Fr S foll N85 sp 'Centre Ville' over bdge keeping L to rndabt, turn 1st R sp Les Thermes (D20). Past Intermarché, site on R 1.6km after leaving town. Med, mkd pitch, pt shd; htd wc; chem disp; shwrs inc; el pnts (4-10A) €2-4 (poss rev pol); gas; lndtte; ice; shops 1.5km; snacks; pool 1.5km; pool; lake sw 3km; games area; 30% statics; dogs €1; poss cr; adv bkg; quiet; CCI. "Pleasant site; gd touring base; 500m fr thermal baths; National Geological Reserve in town cent; phone ahead low ssn to check open." ♦ ltd. 1 Apr-30 Oct. € 15.00 2007*

> This guide relies on site report forms submitted by caravanners like us; we'll do our bit and tell the editor what we think of the campsites we've visited.

DIGOIN *9A1* (Urban) **Camping de la Chevrette, Rue de la Chevrette, 71160 Digoin** [03 85 53 11 49; fax 03 85 88 59 70; info@lachevrette.com; www.lachevrette.com] Exit new N79 at junc 24 sp Digoin-la-Grève D994, then on (old) N79 cross bdge over Rd Loire. Take 1st L, sp campng/piscine. Sm, some hdg pitch, terr, pt shd; htd wc (some cont); chem disp; shwrs inc; el pnts (10A) €3.20; tradsmn; lndry rm; shops 500m; rest 500m; snacks; playgrnd; htd pool adj; fishing; dogs €1; sep car park; adv bkg; some rd noise; CCI. "Vg; well-run; gd sized pitches; friendly warden resident on site; barrier clsd 2200-0800; ltd facs low ssn." 1 Mar-31 Oct. € 13.20 2007*

DIJON *6G1* (2km W Urban) **Camping du Lac Kir, 3 Blvd Chanoine Kir, 21000 Dijon** [tel/fax 03 80 43 54 72; campingdijon@wanadoo.fr; www.camping-dijon.com] Site situated nr N5, Lac Kir. Fr Dijon ring rd take N5 exit (W) sp A38 twd Paris. At traff lts L sp A31, site immed on R under 3m high bdge. Do not tow thro town cent. Med, mkd pitch, pt hdstg, pt shd; htd wc (mainly cont); chem disp; shwrs inc; el pnts (6A) inc; (poss rev pol); gas; lndtte; ice; shop; supmkt nr; tradsmn; rest; snacks; sw lake 1km; fishing, sw & boating; dogs €1.50; bus adj; poss cr; Eng spkn; quiet but some rd noise; cc acc; CCI. "Attractive, orderly, busy site adj lake; various pitch sizes; v friendly; 30 min walk to town; attractive rvside path to town cent; gd site but some updating req; poss 'tired' low ssn; gd security; poss flooding; gd." 1 Apr-15 Oct. € 14.40 2007*

DINAN 2E3 (Urban) **Camp Municipal Châteaubriand, 103 Rue Châteaubriand, 22100 Dinan [02 96 39 11 96 or 02 96 39 22 43 (LS); fax 02 96 85 06 97; campingmunicipaldinan@ wanadoo.fr]** Fr N176 (E or W) take slip rd for Dinan cent; at lge rndbt in cent take 2nd R; down hill to site on L (500m). Sm, mkd pitch, pt sl, pt shd; wc; chem disp; mv service pnt; shwrs inc; el pnts (6A) €2.70; gas 500m; lndry rm; shop, rest, snacks 500m; bar adj; BBQ; sand beach 18km; games area; dogs €1.50; phone; poss cr; Eng spkn; adv bkg; daytime rd noise; cc not acc; CCI. "Basic/dated facs poss unclean; pleasant, helpful staff; high kerb onto pitches; poss market traders; opening dates vary each year; check time barrier locked espec low ssn; sh walk to charming town; gd cent for Rance valley, St Malo & coast." 15 Jun-15 Sep. € 9.30   2006*

DINAN 2E3 (3km N Rural) **Camp Municipal Beauséjour, La Hisse, 22100 St Samson-sur-Rance [02 96 39 53 27 or 02 96 39 16 05 (Mairie); fax 02 96 87 94 12; beausejour-stsamson@ orange.fr]** Fr Dinan take D766 N twd Dinard. In 3km turn R onto D12 dir Taden then foll sp thro Plouer-sur-Rance to La Hisse; site sp. Fr N exit N176/ E401 dir Plouer-sur-Rance, then foll sp La Hisse. Med, hdg/mkd pitch, hdstg, pt sl, pt shd; wc; chem disp; mv service pnt; shwrs inc; el pnts (10A) €2.90; lndtte; ice; sm shop; supmkt 5km; tradsmn; rest; snacks; bar; playgrnd; htd pool; tennis; games area; sailing; mini-golf; 50% statics; dogs €2.05; phone; poss cr; Eng spkn; adv bkg; quiet; 1 free night in 5 low ssn; CCI. "No twin-axles; v pleasant, friendly, well-kept, clean site; helpful staff; quiet & spacious Jun/Sep; pitches grouped in 3s & 4s; Dinan worth a visit; excel rv walks. " ♦ ltd. 1 Jun-30 Sep. € 12.20
2007*

DINAN 2E3 (3km NE Rural) **Camp International de la Hallerais, 22100 Taden [02 96 39 15 93 or 02 96 87 63 50 (Mairie); fax 02 96 39 94 64; camping.la.hallerais@wanadoo.fr; www.wdirect. fr/hallerais.htm]** Fr Dinan take D766 N twd Dinard. In 3km turn R onto D12 to Taden. Foll La Hallerais & Taden sp to site. Fr N176 take exit onto D166 dir Taden; turn onto D766 dir Taden, then L onto D12A sp Taden & Camping. At rndabt on ent Taden take 1st exit onto D12 sp Dinan; site rd is 500m on L Do not ent Dinan. Site adj Rv Rance. Lge, mkd pitch, terr, pt shd; wc; chem disp; mv service pnt; serviced pitches; shwrs inc; el pnts (6A) inc (rev pol); gas; lndtte; shop; tradsmn; rest; snacks (high ssn); bar; BBQ; playgrnd; htd pool; paddling pool; shgl beach 10km; tennis; fishing; horseriding 500m; child entmnt; games/TV rm; recep 0900-1200 & 1430-1800 low ssn; statics; dogs; storage facs; Eng spkn; adv bkg; quiet; cc acc. "Pleasant site; excel, clean, spacious san facs; ltd facs low ssn & poss tired; phone ahead if arr late at night low ssn; ltd office hours low ssn - go to bar to check in; mkt Thu am; rv trips; rvside walk to Dinan medieval town; oyster beds at Cancale; rec." ♦
10 Mar-2 Nov. € 19.50 ABS - B01   2007*

DINAN 2E3 (10km NE) **Camping Ville Ger, 22690 Pleudihen-sur-Rance [02 96 83 33 88]** Fr Dinan take D676 in dir Dol de Bretagne; turn L on D29 after 6km; site sp after 4km on L. Sm, mkd pitch; pt shd; wc (cont); rec own san high ssn; shwrs €1; el pnts (3-10A) €1.75-4.30; lndtte; shops 1.5km; rest; bar; playgrnd; dogs; poss cr; adv bkg ess high ssn; quiet; CCI. "Lovely area; close to rv; farm 1km for milk & eggs; local fish; gd for dog-walking." 1 Apr-15 Oct. € 6.80   2004*

DINARD 2E3 (3km S) **Camp Municipal Bellevue, Rue de Bellevue, 35780 La Richardais [02 99 88 50 80 (Mairie); fax 02 99 88 52 12; info@ ville-larichardais.fr;   www.ville-larichardais.fr]** S of Dinard on D114; on ent vill of La Richardais, turn R at traff lts, 1st L into Rue de Bellevue, site on L in 50m. Med, mkd pitch, pt sl, pt shd; wc; chem disp (wc); shwrs inc; el pnts (16A) inc; lndtte; shops, gas adj; BBQ; playgrnd; sand beach 3km; lake/ rv sw 1km; dogs; phone; poss cr; quiet. "Ltd o'fit access low ssn due locked height barriers; recep clsd 1200-1400; park in layby bef booking in." 1 Apr-15 Sep. € 10.20   2005*

DINARD 2E3 (6km S Rural) **Camp Municipal L'Estuaire, Rue Jean Boyer, 35730 Pleurtuit [tel/ fax 02 99 88 44 06; contact@campingdelestuaire. com; www.campingdelestuaire.com]** Fr N on D266 or S on D766 in cent of vill, sp fr each dir. Med, hdg pitch, pt shd; wc; chem disp (wc); baby facs; shwrs inc; el pnts (10A) €3.50; lndtte; shops adj; tradsmn; rest; snacks; bar; playgrnd; sand beach 4km; games area; entmnt; 50% statics; dogs €2.50; quiet. "Friendly site." 1 Apr-30 Sep. € 9.50
2007*

DINARD 2E3 (1.5m W Coastal) **Camping La Touesse, 171 Rue de la Ville Gehan, La Fourberie, 35800 St Lunaire [02 99 46 61 13; fax 02 99 16 02 58; camping.la.touesse@wanadoo. fr; www.campinglatouesse.com]** Exit Dinard on St Lunaire coast rd D786, site sp. Med, mkd pitch, pt shd; wc; mv service pnt; baby facs; shwrs inc; el pnts (5-10A) €3.20-3.60; lndtte; shop; snacks; bar; playgrnd; 2 pools (1 htd, covrd); sand beach 300m; tennis 1.5km; golf 2km; entmnt; TV rm; dog €1.50; adv bkg (dep); quiet, some late night noise; low ssn red; CCI. "Gd beach & rocks nr; friendly recep; clean." ♦ 1 Apr-30 Sep. € 19.00   2007*

See advertisement

DINARD *2E3* (1km W Coastal) **Camp Municipal Le Port Blanc, Rue de Sergent Boulanger, 35800 Dinard [02 99 46 10 74; fax 02 99 16 90 91; camping.municipal@ville-dinard.fr]** Fr Dinard foll sp to St Lunaire on D786 for 1.5km. Turn R at traff lts by football ground to site. Lge, mkd pitch, pt sl, terr, pt shd; wc (some cont); chem disp; child/baby facs; shwrs inc; el pnts (5-10A) €3.30-4.20; lndtte; ice; sm shop; supmkt 800m; rest 500m; snacks; bar; playgrnd; pool; sand beach adj; 40% statics; dogs; phone; bus; poss cr; adv bkg; quiet at night; cc acc; CCI. "Overlooks sand beach; bus fr ent; cr in late May & French holiday ssn." ♦ 1Apr-30 Sep. € 16.80
2004*

As soon as we get home I'm going to post all these site report forms to the editor for inclusion in next year's guide. I don't want to miss the September deadline.

DINARD *2E3* (4km W Coastal) **Camping Longchamp, Blvd St Cast, 35800 St Lunaire [02 99 46 33 98; fax 02 99 46 02 71; contact@ camping-longchamp.com; www.camping-longchamp.com]** Fr St Malo on D168 turn R sp St Lunaire, In 1km turn R at g'ge into St Lunaire, site sp to W of vill on D786 dir St Briac. Lge, hdg/ mkd pitch, pt shd; wc; chem disp; mv service pnt; baby facs; shwrs inc; el pnts (4-10A) €2.80-3.90; gas; lndtte; ice; shop; tradsmn; rest; snacks; bar; BBQ; playgrnd; sand beach 300m; 30% statics; dogs €1.40; phone adj; bus 500m; Eng spkn; adv bkg rec; quietl. "Excel, well-run site; clean facs; v friendly, helpful staff; v clean beach 300m; conv Brittany Ferries at St Malo." ♦ ltd. 17 May-10 Sep. € 20.50
2007*

DIOU see Dompierre sur Besbre *9A1*

DISSAY see Jaunay Clan *4H1*

DIVONNE LES BAINS *9A3* (3km N Rural) **Camping Le Fleutron, Quartier Villard, 01220 Divonne-les-Bains [04 50 20 01 95 or 04 42 20 47 25 (LS); fax 04 50 20 00 35; info@homair.com; www.homair. com]** Exit E62 dir Divonne-les-Bains approx 12km N of Geneva. Fr town on D984, foll sp to site. Lge, hdg/ mkd pitch, pt sl, terr, shd; htd wc; shwrs inc; chem disp; el pnts (4A) €4.20; gas; lndtte; shop, snacks & rest in ssn; bar; supmkts 3km; lake sw 3km; htd pool; paddling pool; lake sw 3km; tennis; games area; entmnt in ssn; TV rm; 50% statics; dogs €3.70; Eng spkn; adv bkg; quiet; red low ssn; cc acc; CCI. "Helpful owner; Lake Geneva 8km." 26 Mar-23 Oct. € 25.80
2005*

DOL DE BRETAGNE *2E4* (6km N Coastal) **Camp Municipal L'Abri des Flots, 35960 Le Vivier-sur-Mer [02 99 48 91 57; fax 02 99 48 98 43; labri.des. flots@free.fr; http://labri.des.flots.free.fr]** On sea front in Le Vivier-sur-Mer at E end of town; sp. Med, mkd pitches, pt shd; wc; mv service pnt; shwrs €1.35; el pnts (6A) €2.30 (long lead poss req); lndtte; sm shop & in vill; tradsmn; dogs €1; poss cr; quiet; no adv bkg; Eng spkn; CCI. "Clean site in vill cent & on sea front; resident warden; friendly; muddy beach not suitable for sw; gd NH to see mussel/ oyster beds; tours fr museum nrby." 25 Apr-30 Sep. € 11.20
2007*

DOL DE BRETAGNE *2E4* (7km NE Coastal) **Camping de l'Aumône, 35120 Cherrueix [02 99 48 95 11; fax 02 99 80 87 37; breizhid@ wanadoo.fr; www.camping-de-laumone.com]** On L of D797, opp rd leading into vill of Cherrueix. Med, unshd; wc; baby facs; shwrs inc; el pnts (10A) €2.50; gas; lndtte; shops 300m; snacks; sand beach 500m (not suitable for bathing); TV; dogs €0.50; adv bkg rec high ssn. "Friendly, sm farm with modern san facs; sand yachting nrby." 15 Jun-15 Sep. € 9.00
2006*

France

DOL DE BRETAGNE *2E4* (8km NE Coastal) Camping Le Teñzor de la Baie (former Municipal), 10 Rue Théophile Blin, 35120 Cherrueix [02 99 48 98 13; www.tenzor-de-la-baie.com] Fr Dol-de-Bretagne, take D155 N to Le Vivier-sur-Mer; turn R onto D797, L onto D82 to Cherrueix; site in vill 150m E of church, just beyond 'Mairie', sp. Sm, pt shd; wc; shwrs; el pnts (6A) €3.50; shop adj; playgrnd; pool; beach 150m; rv fishing & sw 14km; 75% statics; dogs €1.50; poss cr; adv bkg; quiet; cc not acc. "V pleasant, clean, flat site in interesting bay of Mont St Michel; sand yachting, mussel & oyster beds nr; basic facs." 6 Jun-15 Oct. € 14.00   2007*

DOL DE BRETAGNE *2E4* (4km E) **FFCC** Camping du Vieux Chêne, 35120 Baguer-Pican [02 99 48 09 55; fax 02 99 48 13 37; vieux.chene@wanadoo.fr; www.camping-vieuxchene.fr] Leave N176 E of Dol on slip rd sp Baguer-Pican. At traff lts turn L thro vill, site on R of D576 at far end vill adj lake. Lge, hdg pitch, pt sl, pt shd; wc; chem disp; mv service pnt; baby facs; shwrs inc; el pnts (10A) inc (poss rev pol & poss long cable req); gas; lndtte; shop; supmkt nr; rest; snacks; bar; BBQ; playgrnd; 2 htd pools; paddling pool; lake fishing; horseriding; tennis; mini-golf; games area; games rm; entmnt; TV rm; dogs €3; phone; Eng spkn; adv bkg; quiet; red long stay; cc acc; CCI. "Friendly & helpful site; fruit trees on pitches; conv Mont St Michel; basic facs stretched in high ssn; nice clean site; shop & rest ltd low ssn; poss sm pitches; gates & recep clsd 2200-0830; mkt in Dol Sat." ♦ 05 Apr-21 Sep. € 33.40 ABS - B10   2007*

DOL DE BRETAGNE *2E4* (7km SE Rural) Camping Le Domaine des Ormes, 35120 Epiniac [02 99 73 53 60 or 02 99 73 53 01; fax 02 99 73 53 55; info@lesormes.com; www.lesormes.com or www.les-castels.com] Exit N176/E401at W end of Dol-de-Bretagne; then S fr Dol on D795 twd Combourg & Rennes, in 7km site on E of rd, clearly sp. V lge, hdg/mkd pitch, pt sl, pt shd; wc; chem disp; baby facs; shwrs inc; el pnts (6A) inc (poss long lead req); gas; lndtte; ice; shop; tradsmn; rest; snacks; bar; BBQ; playgrnd; htd pool complex; waterslide; paddling pool; lake fishing; canoeing; sand beach 25km; tennis; cycle hire; horseriding; archery; golf course adj (discount to campers); cycle hire; entmnt (child & adult); internet; games/TV rm; 80% statics; dogs €2; poss cr; adv bkg; Eng spkn; poss noisy (disco); red low ssn; cc acc; CCI. "Excel all round; suitable RVs; v helpful staff; few bins or water taps; lots of activities for all ages; pool complex being updated (2007); conv Mont St Michel, St Malo & Dinan; Mecca for golfers; mkt Sat; disco at night." ♦ 17 May-7 Sep. € 44.60 ABS - B08   2007*

DOLE *6H2* (6km NE Rural) **Camping Les Marronniers, Rue Chaux, 39700 Rochefort-sur-Nenon [03 84 70 50 37; fax 03 84 70 55 05]** NE fr Dole on N73 twds Besançon. Turn R on D76 & pass thro vill of Rochefort-sur-Nenon. Site in 2km, well sp. Med, hdg pitch, pt shd; wc; mv service pnt; serviced pitches; shwrs inc; el pnts (6A) €2.50; lndtte; tradsmn; snacks; bar; playgrnd; pool; cycle hire; mini-golf; entmnt; 10% statics; dogs €1; Eng spkn; adv bkg; poss noisy; red low ssn; CCI. "Poss noisy disco; fair sh stay/NH." ♦ 1 Apr-31 Oct. € 17.00   2005*

The opening dates and prices on this campsite have changed. I'll send a site report form to the editor for the next edition of the guide.

DOLE *6H2* (SE Rural) **Camping Le Pasquier, 18 Chemin Thévenot, 39100 Dole [03 84 72 02 61; fax 03 84 79 23 44; lola@camping-le-pasquier.com; www.camping-le-pasquier.com]** Fr A39 foll sp dir Dole & Le Pasquier. Fr all dir foll sp 'Centre ville' then foll site name sp & 'Stade Camping' in town; well sp. Site on rvside private rd. Narr app. Med, hdg/mkd pitch, pt shd; wc (some cont); chem disp; mv service pnt; shwrs inc; el pnts (10A) €3 (rev pol); lndry rm; ice; shop & 1km; tradsmn; snacks; bar; playgrnd; pool; aqua park; dir access rv 500m; rv sw; fishing; entmnt; 10% statics; dogs €1; extra for twin-axle c'vans; poss cr; Eng spkn; quiet; cc not acc; red long stay; CCI. "Well-kept site; generous pitches; friendly recep; san facs ltd low ssn; poss mosquito problem due to rv; nice pool; easy walk by rv into Dole, an interesting old town with many gd rests; rec." 15 Mar-15 Oct. € 13.90   2007*

DOLE *6H2* (8km SE Rural) **Camping Les Bords de Loue, 39100 Parcey [03 84 71 03 82; fax 03 84 71 03 42; contact@jura-camping.com; www.bords-de-loue.com]** Leave A39 at junc 6 onto N5 dir Chalon-sur-Saône. Turn L (SE) at rndabt after going under A39 & in 6km turn R into vill of Parcey at 'Camping' sp. Lge, pt shd; wc; chem disp; 10% serviced pitches; shwrs inc; el pnts (5A) €2.40; lndtte; tradsmn; rest; snacks; bar; BBQ; playgrnd; pool; paddling pool; beach adj; fishing; boating; 20% statics; dogs €1.20; phone; poss cr; Eng spkn; adv bkg; poss some noise when busy; cc acc; CCI. "Pleasant site." ♦ 15 Apr-11 Sep. € 13.50   2007*

See advertisement on page 293

DOLLON see Connerré *4F1*

DOLUS D'OLERON *7B1* (4km SE Coastal) **Camping Ostréa, Route des Huîtres, 17550 Dolus d'Oléron [05 46 47 62 36 or 06 14 35 01 20 (mob); fax 05 46 75 20 01; www.camping-ostrea.com]** After x-ing viaduc bdge to Ile d'Oléron turn R to Château d'Oléron; cont thro vill & foll coast rd Blvd Phillippe Dasté which becomes Route des Huîtres; site on L in 4km. Med, mkd pitch, pt shd; htd wc; chem disp; mv service pnt; baby facs; shwrs (inc); gas; lndtte; el pnts (3-6A) €3.50-4.50; shop, snacks high ssn; tradsmn; BBQ; playgrnd; pool (htd covrd); golf nrby; fishing; archery; games rm; entmnt; TV; dogs €2.30; red low ssn; cc acc; CCI. "Friendly, family-run site in oyster production region; facs immac; vg." ♦ 1 Apr-30 Sep. € 21.00   2007*

DOMAZAN see Avignon *10E2*

DOMFRONT *4E1* (6km N Rural) **Camping La Nocherie, 61700 St Bômer-les-Forges [02 33 37 60 36; fax 02 33 38 16 08]** S fr Flers on D962 1km after Les Forges turn L. Site sp Camping à la Ferme, narr rd with long hill. Sm, pt shd; wc; shwrs inc; el pnts (6A) €1.50; shop 4km; rest; bar; playgrnd; fishing; tennis 3km; quiet. "Farm site in apple orchard; gd walking; gd tourist base." 15 Mar-15 Dec. € 10.50   2006*

DOMFRONT *4E1* (500m S Urban) **Camp Municipal, 4 Rue du Champ Passais, 61700 Domfront [02 33 37 37 66 or 02 33 38 92 24 (LS); mairie@domfront.com; www.domfront.com]** Turn L on ent town when app fr Vire onto D976 (N176), well sp bet old quarter & town cent, dir Mont-St Michel. Sm, hdg/mkd pitch, hdstg, terr, pt shd; wc; chem disp (wc); shwrs inc; el pnts (5-10A) €1.80-3; lndtte; shops, rest, snacks, bar 1km; playgrnd; rv fishing nr; TV rm; dogs €0.60; phone; Eng spkn; some rd noise; red low ssn; CCI. "V pleasant, terr site; helpful, charming staff; site & facs immac; gd security; gd views fr site; sh, steep walk to interesting, medieval town; no twin-axles." ♦ 1 Apr-30 Sep. € 8.30   2007*

DOMFRONT *4E1* (12km SW Rural) **Camp Municipal des Chauvières, 61350 St Fraimbault [02 33 30 69 60 or 02 33 38 32 22 (Mairie); st.fraimbault@wanadoo.fr]** S fr Domfront on D962 sp Mayenne. At Ceaucé turn R on D24 sp St Fraimbault, site on R past lake on ent to vill. Sm, mkd pitch, unshd; wc; mv service pnt; shwrs; el pnts (3A) €2; lndry rm; shop adj; mini-mkt, rest, snacks, bar in vill; playgrnd; lake adj; sw 8km; tennis; cycle hire; games area; some statics; quiet. "Picturesque site in lge park with excel floral displays; warden calls; gd value; super." 20 Mar-31 Oct. € 3.00   2007*

DOMME see Sarlat la Canéda *7C3*

DOMPIERRE LES ORMES *9A2* (Rural) **Camp Municipal Le Village des Meuniers, 71520 Dompierre-les-Ormes [03 85 50 36 60; fax 03 85 50 36 61; levillagedesmeuniers@wanadoo.fr; www.villagedesmeuniers.com]** Fr A6 exit Mâcon Sud onto N79 dir Charolles. After approx 35km take slip rd onto D41 for Dompierre-les-Ormes. Well sp nr stadium. Med, hdg/mkd pitch, terr, pt shd; wc; chem disp; mv service pnt; 50% serviced pitch; shwrs inc; el pnts (16A) €4.50; gas; lndtte; shops 2km; tradsmn; rest; snacks; bar; playgrnd; htd pools; waterslide; cycle hire; mini-golf; tennis; entmnt; child entmnt; dogs €1.50; adv bkg (ess high ssn); quiet; cc acc; red low ssn; CCI. "Excel; elevated position with beautiful views; pitches enormous; scrupulously clean; additional flat field at cheaper rates but with full facs high ssn; facs stretched high ssn; excel site for children; gd sp walks in area; pools, rest, bar etc used by public; free m'van hdstg outside site ent; gd shops, etc in adj vill." ♦ 29 Apr-30 Sep. € 24.00   2006*

DOMPIERRE SUR BESBRE *9A1* (Urban) **Camp Municipal, 03290 Dompierre-sur-Besbre [04 70 34 55 57 or 04 70 48 11 30 (Mairie)]** At E end of town nr rv behind stadium; sp. Med, hdg pitch, pt shd, pt sl; wc (some cont); chem disp; mv service pnt; shwrs inc; el pnts (10A) €1.80; lndtte; shop 500m; BBQ; full sports facs adj; dogs; phone; poss cr; Eng spkn; adv bkg; quiet; CCI. "Smart, well-run, busy site with spotless san facs; vg value; state of the art sports complex; poss stretched high ssn; beautifully maintained; highly rec low ssn; gd for Loire Valley, vineyards & chateaux; excel." ♦ 15 May-15 Sep. € 5.70   2007*

DOMPIERRE SUR BESBRE *9A1* (5km E Rural) **Camping du Gué de Loire, 03290 Diou [03 85 53 11 49 (Mairie); info@lachevrette.com]** Sp in cent of vill in both dirs on rvside, off N79. Sm, hdg/mkd pitch, pt sl, shd; wc; mv service pnt; shwrs inc; el pnts; lndry rm; shop 800m; rest, bar 500m; rd noise; no cc acc; CCI. "Simple site; gd touring base." 1 Jul-15 Sep.   2006*

DOMPIERRE SUR VEYLE see Bourg en Bresse *9A2*

DONJON, LE *9A1* (500m N Urban) **Camp Municipal, Route de Monétay-sur-Loire, 03130 Le Donjon [04 70 99 56 35 or 04 70 99 50 25 (Mairie); fax 04 74 99 58 02]** Fr Lapalisse N on D994. Site sp fr town cent on D166 Rte de Monétay-sur-Loire. Sm, pt sl, pt shd; wc (some cont); mv service pnt; shwrs inc; el pnts (10A) €2; shop 500m; rest, bar 400m; playgrnd; fishing, sailing & windsurfing 900m; quiet; CCI. ♦ 1 May-31 Oct. € 5.50   2006*

DONJON, LE 9A1 (7km SW Rural) **Camp Municipal La Grande Ouche, 03130 Bert [04 70 99 61 92 or 04 70 99 60 90 (Mairie); fax 04 70 99 64 28; mairie-bert@pays-allier.com]** Exit Le Donjon on D989 to NW, after 1km turn L onto D23, after 7km turn L to Bert in 3km. Site on E edge of vill alongside sm lake & Rv Têche. Sm, mkd pitch, pt shd; wc (cont); shwrs inc; el pnts (3-5A) €1.60; ice; shops adj; rest, bar 200m; playgrnd; htd pool adj; tennis; cycle hire; mini-golf adj; lake fishing adj; dogs; quiet. "Clean facs." 1 May-15 Sep. € 6.50   2004*

DONZENAC 7C3 (10km N Rural) **Camp Municipal Les Escures, 19270 St Pardoux-l'Ortigier [05 55 84 51 06 (Mairie); fax 05 55 84 99 79]** Fr A20 take D9 dir Tulle for 2km. Med, mkd pitch, pt sl, pt shd; wc; own san rec; shwrs inc; el pnts €2; gas 1km; shop; rest; playgrnd; lake & fishing adj; adv bkg; CCI. 1 Jun-15 Sep. € 4.60   2005*

⊞**DONZENAC** 7C3 (1km S Rural) **Aire Communale, Route d'Ussac, 19270 Donzenac [05 55 85 72 33 or 06 11 04 28 14 (mob); mairie-donzenac@wanadoo.fr]** Exit A20 at junc 47; take 1st exit at rndabt dir Donzenac; site on L in 3km. NB Avoid app thro Donzenac as narr & diff for lge o'fits. Adj Camping La Rivière. Sm, mkd pitch, hdstg, unshd; wc; chem disp; mv service pnt; el pnts (3A); lndtte; shop & 100m; rest, snacks, bar 100m; bus 100m; phone; quiet. "El pnts not avail Jul/Aug." € 5.80
                    2007*

DONZENAC 7C3 (1km S Rural) **Village de Vacances Municipal La Rivière, Route d'Ussac, 19270 Donzenac [05 55 85 63 95; fax 05 55 98 16 47; www.revea-vacances.fr]** Exit A20 at junc 47; take 1st exit at rndabt dir Donzenac; site on L in 3km. NB Avoid app thro Donzenac as narr & diff for lge o'fits. Med, mkd pitch, pt shd; wc; chem disp; shwrs inc; el pnts (5A) €2.70; lndtte; shops 1km; snacks; bar; htd pool Jul/Aug; rv adj; fishing 5km; cycle hire; dogs €1.10; adv bkg rec high ssn. "Excel facs." ♦ 1 Jun-30 Sep. € 14.00   2007*

DORAT, LE 7A3 (600m S Urban) **Camp Municipal, Route de la Planche des Dames, 87210 Le Dorat [05 55 60 72 20 (Mairie) or 05 55 60 76 81 (TO); fax 05 55 68 27 87]** Site sp fr D675 & in town cent. Sm, hdg/mkd pitch, pt shd; wc; shwrs inc; el pnts €2.30; shop, rest, bar 600m; quiet; CCI. "Clean facs, but ltd & own san rec high ssn; excel, basic site; no barrier; warden calls eves." 1 May-30 Sep. € 4.55
                    2006*

⊞**DORCEAU** 4E2 (2km N Rural) **Camping Forest View, L'Espérance, 61110 Dorceau [tel/fax 02 33 25 45 27 or 06 89 24 49 62 (mob); petej. wilson@wanadoo.fr; www.forestviewleisure breaks.co.uk]** Fr D920 (ring rd) in Rémalard take D38 sp Bretoncelles; site in 2km on corner on L. Sm, pt sl, pt shd; wc; chem disp; shwrs inc; el pnts (10A) inc; lake fishing; painting workshops; adv bkg; quiet; CCI. "Beautiful countryside; new British owners (2006) v friendly & helpful; vill 2km; excel." € 14.00   2006*

DORMANS 3D4 (7km NE Rural) **Camping Rural (Nowack), 10 Rue Bailly, 51700 Vandières [03 26 58 02 69 or 03 26 58 08 79; fax 03 26 58 39 62; champagne.nowack@wanadoo. fr]** Fr N3, turn N at Port Binson, over Rv Marne, then turn W onto D1 for 3km, then N into Vandières. Site on R about 50m fr start of Rue Bailly, sp 'Champagne Nowack' or 'Camping Nowack.' Sm, pt sl, pt shd; wc; shwrs inc; el pnts inc; lndtte; BBQ; playgrnd; pool 8km; fishing 1km; rv sw & boating 6km; tennis 2km; TV; adv bkg; cc acc. "Charming CL-type site in Champagne producer's orchard; quiet & peaceful; friendly owner; facs excel but fresh water tap used for rinsing chem disp; grape pickers on site Sept; excel value." 1 Mar-31 Oct. € 14.00   2007*

DORMANS 3D4 (1km W Urban) **Camping Sous Le Clocher, Route de Vincelles, 51700 Dormans [03 26 58 21 79; fax 03 26 57 29 62; dom.ribaille@ wanadoo.fr]** On D1003 (N3) E fr Château-Thierry; in Dormans foll sp, over Rv Marne; camp site 50m fr end of bdge. Med, hdg pitch, pt shd; wc (some cont); shwrs; el pnts (3-6A) €3 (rev pol); ice; shop 200m; rest, bar 1km; playgrnd; htd pool adj high ssn; games area; TV; some statics; dogs €2; poss cr; rlwy noise & noisy at w/e; cc acc. "Ideal for Champagne area; facs poss stretched high ssn." Easter-15 Sep. € 8.00   2005*

DORTAN 9A3 (3km N Rural) **Camp Municipal Les Cyclamens, La Presqu'île, 01590 Chancia [tel/fax 04 74 75 82 14; campinglescyclamens@ wandadoo.fr]** Fr N on D436 to Dortan; R at traff lts sp Bourg-en-Bresse; in 1.5km R (furniture shop) onto D60 sp Chancia; foll sp. NB go past Camping du Lac. Lge, pt shd; wc; chem disp; mv service pnt; shwrs inc; el pnts (6-10A) €2.40; gas; lndtte; shop 6km; tradsmn; rest 1km; sm bar; playgrnd; lake sw & shgl beach 100m; fishing, tennis, walking & watersports near; 50% statics; dogs; phone; poss cr; adv bkg; quiet; CCI. "Beautiful area; clean, friendly; few tourists; excel." 1 Apr-30 Sep. € 9.60
                    2005*

DOSCHES see Troyes 4E4

DOUAI 3B4 (10km S Rural) **Camp Municipal, Chemin des Bisselles, 59151 Arleux [03 27 89 52 36 or 03 27 93 10 00; fax 03 27 94 37 38; office.tourisme@arleux.com]** Exit A2 junc 14 at Cambrai & take N43 twd Douai, after 5km turn W at Bugnicourt to Arleux. Site sp in vill adj canal La Sensée. Lge, mkd pitch, shd; wc (some cont); el pnts; shop; playgrnd; pool; rv sw & fishing; tennis 200m; games area; entmnt; poss cr; adv bkg; quiet. ♦ 1 Apr-31 Oct.   2007*

⊞ *Site open all year*   324   *Help us to update this guide*

France

DOUAI *3B4* (10km S Rural) **FFCC Camp Municipal de la Sablière, Rue du 8 Mai 1945, 62490 Tortequesne [03 21 24 14 94; fax 03 21 07 46 07; camping@tortequesne.fr; www.tortequesne. fr]** Fr N43 Douai-Cambrai rd; turn S onto D956 to Tortequesne where site sp. Sm, hdg/mkd pitch, hdstg; pt shd; wc (cont); shwrs inc; el pnts (6A) €3; supmkt 5 mins; playgrnd; walking in La Valée de la Sensée; tennis; games area; 30% statics; dogs €0.50; CCI. "Park & fishing adj; gd." 1 Apr-30 Sep. € 11.20   2007*

DOUARNENEZ *2E2* (6km W Rural) **FLOWER Camping Le Pil Koad, Route de Douarnenez, 29100 Poullan-sur-Mer [02 98 74 26 39; fax 02 98 74 55 97; info@pil-koad.com; www. pil-koad.com]** Fr E take circular rd around Douarnenez on D7/D765 dir Audierne. After x-ing rv estuary, turn R at traff lts (D7) sp Poullan-sur-Mer, Tréboul & Pointe-du-Van; at 1st rndabt turn L sp Tréboul onto Blvd Jean Moulin; cont strt over rndabts foll sp Tréboul; at 3rd rndabt turn L sp Poullan-sur-Mer & Beuzec; site off D7 1km fr Poullan-sur-Mer vill on L. Med, hdg/mkd pitch, pt shd; htd wc; chem disp; baby facs; shwrs inc; el pnts (10A) inc; gas; lndtte; ice; shop; rest; snacks; bar; BBQ (charcoal/gas); playgrnd; htd pool; paddling pool; sand beach 5km; watersports 4km; lake fishing; tennis; cycle hire; mini-golf; games area; entmnt; internet; games/TV rm; dogs €3.50; recep 0800-1200 & 1400-2000 high ssn; Eng spkn; adv bkg; quiet; cc acc; CCI. "Tranquil site; staff friendly; UK tour ops use site; ltd facs low ssn; guided walks high ssn; typical Breton ports nr; mkt Mon & Fri." ◆ 21 Mar-28 Sep. € 30.80 ABS - B04   2007*

See advertisement

Before we move on, I'm going to fill in some site report forms and post them off to the editor, otherwise they won't arrive in time for the deadline at the end of September.

DOUARNENEZ *2E2* (2km W Urban) **Camping de Trezulien, 29100 Douarnenez [02 98 74 12 30 or 02 98 92 81 40; fax 02 98 74 01 16; contact@ camping-trezulien.com; www.camping-trezulien. com]** Ent Douarnenez fr E on D7; foll sp 'Centre Ville'; turn L at traff lts sp to Tréboul. Cross rv bdge into Ave de la Gare, at post office turn L, then 1st L. Turn R at island, foll site sp. Lge, pt terr, pt shd; wc; baby facs; shwrs inc; el pnts (6-10A) €2.50-3.10; gas; lndtte; ice; shops 1km; playgrnd; sand beach 1.5km; dogs €1; quiet. "Pleasant, modernised site; steep hill fr ent to recep; 1km by foot to Les Sables Blancs; conv Pointe du Raz." 1 Apr-30 Sep. € 10.50   2006*

DOUARNENEZ *2E2* (11km W Coastal) **Camping Pors Péron, 29790 Beuzec-Cap-Sizun [02 98 70 40 24; fax 02 98 70 54 46; info@ campingporsperon.com; www.camping porsperon.com]** W fr Douarnenez take D7 sp Poullan-sur-Mer. Thro Poullan & in approx 4km turn R sp Pors-Piron, foll site & beach sp. Site bef Beuzec-Cap-Sizun vill. Med, hdg/mkd pitch, pt shd; wc; chem disp; mv service pnt; baby facs; shwrs inc; el pnts (10A) €2.50; gas; lndtte; ice; shop & 3km; snacks; BBQ; playgrnd; sand beach 200m; games area; cycle hire; 5% statics; dogs €1.50; phone 200m; adv bkg; quiet; CCI. "Excel; British owners still improving site (2007); high standards; gd san facs; nr beautiful sandy cove; gd coastal walks." ◆ ltd. 1 Apr-30 Sep. € 10.10   2007*

DOUCIER *6H2* (3km N Rural) **Camping La Pergola, 1 Rue des Vernois, Lac de Chalain, 39130 Marigny** [03 84 25 70 03; fax 03 84 25 75 96; contact@lapergola.com; www.lapergola.com] Fr D471 Lons-le-Saunier to Champagnole rd, turn S on D27 twd Marigny, site on L in 6km on N shore of Lac de Chalain. Lge, hdg/mkd pitch, pt sl, terr, pt shd; wc; chem disp; baby facs; some serviced pitches; shwrs inc; baby facs; el pnts (10A) inc; gas; Indtte; ice; shop; rest; snacks; bar; BBQ; playgrnd; htd pool; paddling pool; lake sand beach 500m; fishing; games rm; games area; entmnt; internet; TV; 50% statics; dogs €4; phone; poss cr; Eng spkn; adv bkg; red long stay; cc acc; CCI. "Beautiful gorges in surrounding area; naturist beach on lake 500m; superb san facs; some sm pitches; busy, popular site." ♦ 1 May-15 Sep. € 36.00 (CChq acc)
2007*

See advertisement above

DOUCIER *6H2* (6km N Rural) **Camping Le Git, 39300 Montigny-sur-l'Ain** [03 84 51 21 17 or 03 84 52 20 81; christian.olivier22@wanadoo.fr] W fr Champagnole on D471 foll sp Monnet-la-Ville & onwards to Montigny-sur-l'Ain, foll camp sp thro vill, turn L at x-rds to church; site immed afterwards on R. Med, mkd pitch, pt sl, pt shd; wc; chem disp; shwrs inc; el pnts (5A) inc; ice; Indtte; Indry rm; supmkt 800m; rest; snacks; bar; playgrnd; lake sw 4km; rv sw 2km; sports area; fishing, kayaking 1.5km; dogs; adv bkg; quiet; CCI. "Tranquil site; beautiful views; excel facs. "♦ 1 Jun-31 Aug. € 12.90
2004*

DOUCIER *6H2* (7km N Rural) **Camping Sous Doriat, 34 Rue Marcel Hugon, 39300 Monnet-la-Ville** [03 84 51 21 43; camping.sousdoriat@wanadoo.fr; www.camping-sous-doriat.com] Take D471 fr Champagnole to Pont-du-Navoy. After 10km fork L to Monnet-la-Ville. Site on L. Sm, unshd; wc; baby facs; shwrs inc; el pnts (10A) €2.50; Indtte; shops 300m; lake sw 6km; some statics; dogs free; adv bkg; quiet. ♦ 1 May-30 Sep. € 13.10
2007*

DOUCIER *6H2* (8km N Rural) **Camping Le Bivouac, Route du Lac de Chalain, 39300 Pont-du-Navoy** [03 84 51 26 95; fax 03 84 51 29 70; gillesferreux@voila.fr] D471 to Pont-du-Navoy, S over bdge & immed fork R onto D27; 2nd site on R. Med, mkd pitch, pt shd; htd wc; chem disp; shwrs inc; el pnts (8A) €2.85 (poss rev pol/no earth); Indtte; shops 1km; tradsmn; rest; snacks; bar; playgrnd; rv adj; lake sw 6km; TV; 20% statics; dogs €1.05; adv bkg; quiet; cc not acc; CCI. "In beautiful countryside, friendly owners; poss unreliable opening dates." 1 May-15 Sep. € 12.55
2005*

DOUCIER *6H2* (3km NE Rural) **Camping Domaine de Chalain, 39130 Doucier** [03 84 25 78 78; fax 03 84 25 70 06; chalain@chalain.com; www.chalain.com] Fr Lons-le-Saunier take D39 E. In Doucier, site sp to L. Fr Champagnole take D471 for 11km, L onto D27 at Pont-du-Navoy to Doucier & foll sp to site. V lge, pt shd; wc (some cont); mv service pnt; chem disp; sauna; shwrs inc; el pnts (7A) €2.80; gas; Indtte; ice; shops; rest; snacks; bar; htd, covrd pools; waterslide & aquatic cent; lake sw adj; boating; fishing; watersports; cycle hire; tennis; horseriding; games area; mini-golf; entmnt; internet; statics; dogs €2.80; poss cr; adv bkg ess. "Extra for lakeside pitches; famous caves Grottes des Beaume adj; vg site." 1 May-20 Sep. € 30.00 (3 persons)
2007*

See advertisement opposite

DOUCIER *6H2* (6km SE Rural) **Camping Le Relais de l'Eventail, Route de la Vallée du Hérisson, 39130 Menétrux-en-Joux** [03 84 25 71 59; fax 03 84 25 76 66; relais-de-leventail@club-internet.fr] Fr Doucier take D326 E (site not accessable fr D39). Med, mkd pitch, pt shd; wc; chem disp; mv service pnt; shwrs inc; el pnts (6A) €2.50 Indtte; rest; bar; tradsmn; pool; dogs €1; quiet. "Site in limestone gorge nr 'Herisson Cascades'; gd walks; lovely, peaceful site; helpful staff." 15 May-15 Sep. € 13.00
2005*

DOUCIER 6H2 (1.5km S Rural) **FFCC Camping Domaine de l'Epinette, 15 Rue de l'Epinette, 39130 Châtillon-sur-Ain [03 84 25 71 44; fax 03 84 25 71 25; info@domaine-epinette.com; www.domaine-epinette.com]** Exit A39 junc 7 to Poligny, then N5 to Champagnole & D471 W. Turn S onto D27 to Lac de Chalain then D39 to Châtillon. Med, mkd pitch, mainly sl, terr, pt shd; wc (some cont); chem disp; shwrs inc; el pnts (6A) inc; lndtte; shop; tradsmn; rest; snacks; bar; playgrnd; pool; paddling pool; rv sw & fishing; canoeing, kayaking & horseriding 3km; games rm; child entmnt; 30% statics; dogs €2; phone; adv bkg; quiet. "Gd base for Jura area; san facs poss tired low ssn." ♦ 9 Jun-17 Sep. € 26.50 (CChq acc)   2007*

See advertisement opposite

DOUE LA FONTAINE 4G1 (N Urban) **Camp Municipal Le Douet, Route d'Angers, 49700 Doué-la-Fontaine [02 41 59 14 47]** Fr Doué N on D761 twd Angers; site in sports ground on o'skts of town; sp. Med, mkd pitch, pt shd; wc; chem disp; shwrs inc; el pnts (6A) inc; lndtte; shop 1km; rests nr; htd pool high ssn adj; tennis; few statics; poss cr; quiet but some factory noise at E end; no cc acc; 5% red CCI. "Clean, well-organised, gd value site; gd san facs; gd, flat pitches; helpful warden; dep req for key to gate; poss itinerant workers in old c'vans low ssn; lovely park & museum; conv Cadre Noir Equestrian Cent." ♦ ltd. 1 Apr-30 Sep. € 11.28   2006*

> There aren't many sites open this early in the year. We'd better phone ahead to check that the one we're heading for is actually open.

France

DOUE LA FONTAINE *4G1* (2km SW Rural) Camping La Vallée des Vignes, 49700 Concourson-sur-Layon [02 41 59 86 35; fax 02 41 59 09 83; campingvdv@aol.com; www.campingvdv.com] D960 fr Doué-la-Fontaine (dir Cholet) to Concourson-sur-Layon; site 1st R 250m after bdge on leaving vill. Or fr Angers foll sp dir Cholet & Poitiers; then foll sp Doué-la-Fontaine. Med, mkd pitch, pt shd; htd wc; chem disp; serviced pitches; baby facs & fam bthrm; shwrs inc; el pnts (10A) €4; gas; lndtte; ice; shop; tradsmn; rest; snacks; bar; BBQ; playgrnd; htd pool; paddling pool; lake sw 10km; mini-golf; cycle hire; entmnt; TV rm; 5% statics; dogs €3.00; bus; poss cr; Eng spkn; adv bkg (dep req); quiet, some rd noise; cc acc; red long stay low ssn; cc acc; CCI. "Peaceful setting amongst vineyards; site poss open all year weather-conditions permitting - phone ahead to check; friendly, helpful British owners; vg, clean, well-maintained facs; pool open & htd early ssn; some pitches diff lge o'fits due overhanging trees; excel rest; conv for Loire chateaux & Futuroscope; wine tasting nr; excel." ♦ 19 Mar-15 Oct. € 22.00 2007*

DOUE LA FONTAINE *4G1* (8km W Rural) Camping Les Grésillons, Chemin des Grésillons, 49700 St Georges-sur-Layon [02 41 50 02 32; fax 02 41 50 03 16; camping.gresillon@wanadoo.fr; www.camping-gresillons.com] Fr Doué-la-Fontaine on D84, site sp. Sm, hdg pitch, hdstg, terr, pt shd; htd wc; chem disp; baby facs; shwrs inc; el pnts (4-10A) €2.45-3.45; lndtte; shop & 500m; rest; snacks; bar 500m; playgrnd; htd pool; rv fishing 200m; games area; entmnt; 28% statics; dogs free; Eng spkn; adv bkg; quiet; cc acc; red long stay/CCI. "Delightful site in area of vineyards." ♦ 1 Apr-30 Sep. € 9.75 2007*

See advertisement

DOUE LA FONTAINE *4G1* (15km W Rural) Camping-KathyDave, Les Beauliers, 49540 La Fosse-de-Tigné [02 41 67 92 10 or 06 14 60 81 63 (mob); bookings@camping-kathydave.co.uk; www.camping-kathydave.co.uk] Fr Doué-la-Fontaine on D84 to Tigne, turn S to La Fosse-de-Tigné. Pass chateau, site sp on R. Sm, pt shd; htd wc; chem disp; shwrs inc; el pnts (8A) inc; lndtte; ice; tradsmn; rest nr; BBQ; adv bkg; quiet; CCI. "Picturesque area; lovely, sm, orchard site; v rural & tranquil; British owners; excel welcome; gd value; adults only preferred; phone ahead rec." 1 May-31 Oct. € 11.00 2007*

DOURDAN *4E3* (700m NE Urban) Camping Les Petits Prés, 11 Rue Pierre Mendès France, 91410 Dourdan [01 64 59 64 83 or 01 60 81 14 17; fax 01 60 81 14 29; loisirs.dourdan@wanadoo.fr] Exit A10 junc 10 dir Dourdan; foll by-pass sp Arpajon; after 5th rndabt site 200m on L. Med, pt sl, pt shd; wc; shwrs; el pnts (4A) €3; gas & supmkt 500m; rest 1km; playgrnd; pool 500m; poss cr; 75% statics; Eng spkn; adv bkg; poss noisy. "Gd NH; ltd facs low ssn; town worth visit." 1 Apr-30 Sep. € 11.25 (3 persons) 2007*

DOUSSARD see Faverges *9B3*

DOUVAINE *9A3* (4km NW) Camp Municipal Le Lémania, Rue du Port, 74140 Chens-sur-Léman [04 50 94 22 43 or 04 76 80 74 71 (LS); fax 04 50 94 22 43; machens@chens-leman.mairies74.org] Fr Geneva to Thonon rd N5 turn L on to D20 dir Touges at Douvaine. Site sp. Med, pt shd; wc (some cont); chem disp; shwrs; el pnts (5A) €2.20; shops 1km; shgl beach on lake 200m; dogs €1; red low ssn. "Gd lake sw nr; rock concert once a year (1 Jul in 2006); gd NH." 1 May-30 Sep. € 13.60 2006*

DOUVILLE *7C3* (2km S Rural) **Camping Lestaubière, Pont-St Mamet, 24140 Douville** [05 53 82 98 15; fax 05 53 82 90 17; lestaubiere@ cs.com; www.lestaubiere.com] Foll sp for 'Pont St Mamet' fr N21; then watch for camping sp. Med, mkd pitch, pt sl, shd; wc; chem disp (wc); baby facs; fam bthrm; shwrs inc; el pnts (4-10A) €2.70-4; gas; lndtte; ice; shop in ssn; tradsmn; rest 5km; bar; playgrnd; pool & lake; fishing; tennis 5km; games area; TV; dogs €0.75; Eng spkn; adv bkg; quiet; CCI. "Run by friendly Dutch couple; superb out of ssn; v lge pitches." ♦ 1 May-30 Sep. € 19.00
2004*

DOUZE, LA *7C3* (3km E Rural) **Camping Laulurie en Périgord (Naturist), 24330 La Douze** [05 53 06 74 00; fax 05 53 06 77 55; toutain@ laulurie.com; www.laulurie.com] Fr Périgueux S on N221; in 8km turn S on D710 twd Le Bugue. Or exit A89 onto D710 S. On ent La Douze turn L & foll arrow signs. Sm, hdg/mkd pitch, pt sl, pt shd; wc (some cont); chem disp; shwrs inc; el pnts (3-10A) €3-6.50; gas; ice; shop; rest; snacks; bar; playgrnd; pool; dogs €3; sep car park; adv bkg; quiet; red low ssn; cc acc. "Excel; friendly owners; gd touring base for Dordogne & Périgueux; INF card req." ♦ ltd. 15 May-15 Sep. € 20.50
2007*

DOUZE, LA *7C3* (4km SW Rural) **Camping La Prade, 24330 La Douze** [tel/fax 05 53 06 73 59] Site sp on N710 adj sm lake. Med, pt sl, pt shd; wc; chem disp; shwrs; el pnts (6A) inc; rest; bar; BBQ; playgrnd; lake fishing; games rm; some statics; dogs; phone; quiet. "V friendly, helpful owners; facs basic but clean." 1 Apr-15 Sep. € 12.40
2006*

DOUZY see Sedan *5C1*

DRAGUIGNAN *10F3* (7km NE Rural) **Domaine de la Haute Garduère (Naturist), Route de Thoronet, 83830 Callas** [tel/fax 04 94 67 95 20] Fr Draguignan D562 NE twd Grasse. After 9km turn R (see sp); site in woodland at end of 3km gravel rd. If poss avoid Draguignan when towing. Lge, hdg pitch, sl, terr, shd; wc; chem disp; shwrs; el pnts (6A) €3; gas; lndtte; shop 10km; tradsmn; rest; snacks; bar; playgrnd; pool; sand beach 30km; golf; archery; 25% statics; dogs €3; phone; Eng spkn; adv bkg quiet "Excel; INF card req; helpful owners; woodland walks." 1 Apr-31 Oct. € 16.00
2004*

DRAGUIGNAN *10F3* (2km S) **Camping La Foux, Quartier La Foux, 83300 Draguignan** [tel/fax 04 94 68 18 27] Fr A8, take Le Muy intersection onto N555 N to Draguignan. Site ent on R at ent to town sp Sport Centre Foux. Fr Draguignan, take N555 S; just after 'End of Draguignan' sp, double back at rndabt & turn R. Lge, pt sl, unshd; wc; shwrs inc; el pnts (4-10A) €2.50-5; lndtte; shop; rest; playgrnd; sand beach 20km; rv adj; fishing; entmnt; TV rm; dogs €2; poss cr; quiet. "V clean san facs; care needed long vehicles on ent site; easy access to Riviera coast." 20 Jun-30 Sep. € 18.00
2005*

⊞**DREUX** *4E2* (6km W Rural) **Camping Les Etangs de Marsalin, 3 Place du Général de Gaulle, 28500 Vert-en-Drouais** [02 37 82 92 23; fax 02 37 82 85 47; camping.etangs.de.marsalin@ wanadoo.fr; www.camping-etangs-de-marsalin. com] Take N12 sp Alençon fr Dreux W & turn R on D152 to Vert-en-Drouais; on ent turn R to church, site on L. NB No access to D152 fr N12 eastbound - go into Dreux & come back westbound. Sm, hdg/ mkd pitch, hdstg, pt sl, pt shd; htd wc (some cont); chem disp; shwrs inc; el pnts (20A) €4 (poss rev pol, long leads poss req, avail at recep); tradsmn; rest 4km; snacks; bar 100m; lake fishing 2km; 90% statics; dogs; poss cr; Eng spkn; quiet; CCI. "Few, sm touring pitches - poss diff for lge vans; peaceful location; v helpful staff; spotless, basic san facs; poss scruffy low ssn; conv NH en rte Spain; gd value." € 9.95
2007*

DUCEY see Pontaubault *2E4*

DUN SUR MEUSE *5C1* (10km SE Rural) **Camping Le Brouzel, 55110 Sivry-sur-Meuse** [03 29 85 86 45] On D964 11km S of Dun twd Verdun, site sp in vill of Sivry. Sm, unshd; wc (cont); chem disp; shwrs €0.80; gas; el pnts (4-6A) €2.60-3.10; shop adj; rest; snacks; bar; playgrnd; games area; dir access to rv; fishing; sailing 2km; 80% statics; adv bkg; quiet. "V clean site." 1 Apr-1 Oct. € 7.50
2004*

DUN SUR MEUSE *5C1* (10km SW Rural) **Camping La Gabrielle, 55110 Romagne-sous-Montfaucon** [03 29 85 11 79; La-Gabrielle@wanadoo.fr; www. antenna.nl/la-gabrielle] Site is on D998, 800m beyond end of Romagne. Well sp. Sm, pt sl, pt shd; wc; chem disp (wc); shwrs inc; el pnts (6A) €2 (rev pol); ice; playgrnd; TV; 10% statics; Eng spkn; adv bkg; quiet; CCI. "Friendly, cheerful Dutch owners; excel evening meals by arrangement; parts of site uneven; close to WW1 historic monuments; gd." ♦ 1 Apr-30 Sep. € 11.00
2007*

DUNKERQUE *3A3* (3km NE Coastal) **Camp Municipal La Licorne, 1005 Blvd de l'Europe, 59240 Dunkerque** [03 28 69 26 68; fax 03 28 69 56 21; campinglalicorne@ville-dunkerque.fr] Leave A16 sp 'Malo'. At end of slip rd traff lts turn L sp Malo-les-Bains. In 2km (at 5th traff lts) turn R at camping sp. At 2nd traff lts past BP G'ge turn L. Site on L (cont strt to rndabt & return on opp side of dual c'way to ent). Lge, mkd pitch, pt sl, unshd; htd wc; chem disp; mv service pnt; shwrs; el pnts (8A) €4.25 (poss long lead); gas; lndtte; ice; sm shop; supmkt 500m; rest; snacks; bar; playgrnd; pool in high ssn; sand beach adj; 80% statics; dogs €0.90; bus fr site ent; clsd 2200-0700; poss cr; adv bkg (dep & bkg fee req); quiet; CCI. "Gd NH for Calais to/fr Belgium; pitches uneven; facs being updated (2007); promenade to town cent; lge supmkts nr with petrol; obliging owners will give code for gate if dep early for ferry; poss dogs roaming site." ♦ ltd. 1 Apr-30 Nov. € 17.10
2007*

France

DUNKERQUE *3A3* (6km NE Coastal) **Camping Mer & Vacances (formerly Les Argousiers), Rue J Baptiste Charcot, 59495 Leffrinckoucke [tel/fax 03 28 20 17 32; info@camping-mer-et-vacances. com; http://camping-mer-et-vacances.com]** Leave A16 at junc 33; foll sp to Leffrinckoucke (cent); go over canal & bear L to cent. Foll sp 'information' & tourist office. Site behind local tourist office & sports facs. Med, mkd pitch, pt sl, pt shd; htd wc; chem disp (wc); shwrs inc; el pnts (10A) €3 (poss rev pol); ice; lndtte; shop & supmkt 1km; rest & bar 500m; playgrnd; sand beach, fishing & watersports 100m; tennis; entmnt; 75% statics; dogs €1.20; phone; bus; adv bkg rec high ssn; some noise at w/e; CCI. "New owner 2006; gates clsd 2200-0700." ♦ 1 Mar-30 Nov. € 15.00
2007*

⊞**DUNKERQUE** *3A3* (11km NE Coastal) **Camp Municipal des Dunes, 222 Rue de l'Eglise, 59123 Bray-Dunes [03 28 26 61 54 or 03 28 26 57 63]** Dunkerque-Ostend on N1, take R slip rd sp Bray-Dunes (approx 100m bef Belgian border), foll rd over N1 for 3km into Bray-Dunes. Foll Camping Municipal sp in town. Or exit A16 junc 36 to Bray-Dunes. V lge, mkd pitch, pt sl, unshd; wc; chem disp (wc); shwrs €1; el pnts (5A) inc (long lead poss req); shop 200m; playgrnd; sand beach 300m; 99% statics; dogs €0.50. "Ltd space for tourers; low ssn untidy & cats roaming site; poss long way to water point; conv for ferry but poss clsd low ssn - phone ahead." € 20.00
2007*

DUNKERQUE *3A3* (12km NE Coastal) **Camping Perroquet Plage Frontière, 59123 Bray-Dunes [03 28 58 37 37; fax 03 28 58 37 01; camping-perroquet@wanadoo.fr]** On Dunkerque-Ostend rd N1, about 100m fr Belgian frontier, thro vill on D947; cont 1km to traff lts, R on D60 thro vill, past rlwy stn to site on L. V lge, pt shd; wc; chem disp; sauna; shwrs inc; el pnts (4-10A) €3.80-4.60; lndtte; shop; rest; snacks; bar; playgrnd; sand beach adj; watersports; tennis; 85% statics; dogs €0.50; poss cr; adv bkg; Eng spkn; quiet; CCI. "Gd site; if parked nr site ent, v long walk to beach; many local attractions." ♦ 1 Apr-30 Sep. € 15.00
2005*

DURAS *7D2* (500m N Rural) **Camping Le Cabri, Malherbe, Route de Savignac, 47120 Duras [05 53 83 81 03; fax 05 53 83 08 91; holidays@lecabri.eu.com; www.lecabri.eu.com]** On ent Duras fr N turn R onto D203. Site well sp fr D708. Sm, pt shd; wc; chem disp; baby facs; shwrs inc; el pnts (4-10A) €3-4; gas 500m; lndtte; shop 500m; rest; snacks; bar; playgrnd; pool; tennis 1km; 50% statics; dogs €1; bus 500m; Eng spkn; adv bkg (dep req); quiet; cc acc; red long stay; CCI. "Excel, clean, spacious site; British owners (Caravan Club members); gd facs." ♦ 1 Mar-2 Dec. € 13.00
2007*

DURAVEL see Puy l'Evêque *7D3*

DURTAL *4G1* (Urban) **Camping L'Internationale, 9 Rue de Camping, 49430 Durtal [02 41 76 31 80; contact@camping-durtal.fr; www.camping-durtal.fr]** Exit A11 junc 11 dir La Flèche, by-passing Durtal. At N23 turn R for Durtal, site on L at ent to town. Med, hdg pitch, pt shd; wc (mainly cont); chem disp; shwrs inc; el pnts (6-10A) inc; gas; lndtte; ice; shops 500m; tradsmn; playgrnd; pool adj; entmnt; TV rm; 5% statics; dogs €1.80; Eng spkn; adv bkg; red long stay; ltd facs low ssn; quiet. "Nice site in pleasant position on Rv Loir; v helpful staff; interesting vill." ♦ 6 Apr-30 Sep. € 12.70
2007*

EAUX BONNES see Laruns *8G2*

⊞**EAUX PUISEAUX** *4F4* (1km S Rural) **Camping à la Ferme des Haut Frênes (Lambert), 6 Voie de Puiseaux, 10130 Eaux-Puiseaux [03 25 42 15 04; fax 03 25 42 02 95; les.hauts.frenes@wanadoo.fr; www.les-hauts-frenes.com]** N fr St Florentin or S fr Troyes on N77. Ignore D374 but take next turning D111 in NW dir. Site in 2km; well sp. Long o'fits take care at ent gate. Med, hdg/mkd pitch, hdstg, pt shd; htd wc; chem disp; shwrs inc; el pnts (10A) €2 (some rev pol); lndtte; shop 2km; tradsmn; rest 3km; BBQ; playgrnd; tennis 3km; TV & games rm; dogs €1.50; poss cr; Eng spkn; adv bkg; quiet; red 10+ days; CCI. "Excel farm site in beautiful setting; clean & well-kept; lge, level pitches; vg, clean san facs poss stretched if site full; helpful owners; meals on request; cider museum in vill." ♦ € 10.00 2007*

EAUZE *8E2* (Urban) **Camp Municipal Le Moulin du Pouy, 32800 Eauze [05 62 09 86 00; fax 05 62 09 79 20; camplinglemoulin@tiscali.fr]** On D931 on N o'skts, sp. Site in 2 parts, connected by bdge. Sm, pt shd; wc (some cont); shwrs inc; el pnts (6-10A) €2.10; rest; snacks; bar; supmkt 500m; pool; TV rm; library; quiet; red CCI. "Noise fr pool during day; gd rest & pool; friendly staff; gd NH/sh stay." 15 May-30 Sep. € 14.70
2006*

EBREUIL see Gannat *9A1*

ECHELLES, LES *9B3* (6km NE Rural) **Camping La Bruyère, Hameau Côte Barrier, 73160 St Jean-de-Couz [tel/fax 04 79 65 74 27; bearob@libertysurf.fr; www.camping-labruyere.com]** Heading S on D306 (N6) Chambéry-Lyon rd, after x-ing Col de Coux 15km S of Chambéry take D45 to St Jean-de-Couz; site sp. Med, pt sl, pt shd; wc (cont); chem disp; shwrs inc; el pnts (6A) €2.90; gas; shop; tradsmn; rest, snacks high ssn; bar; BBQ; playgrnd; TV; 30% statics; dogs €0.90; adv bkg; quiet. "Vg, clean facs; helpful owner; magnificent scenery; peaceful site; Chartreuse caves open to public adj; gd walking area." 1 May-30 Sep. € 12.20
2006*

ECHELLES, LES *9B3* (6km S Rural) **Camp Municipal Les Berges du Guiers, Le Revol, 38380 St Laurent-du-Pont [04 76 55 20 63 or 04 76 06 22 55 (LS); fax 04 76 06 21 21; mairie. st-laurent-du-pont@wanadoo.fr]** On D520 Chambéry-Voiron S fr Les Echelles. On ent St Laurent-du-Pont. R just bef petrol stn on L. Sm, mkd pitch, pt shd; wc; chem disp; baby facs; shwrs; el pnts (5A) €3; shops 1km; rest, bar 600m; playgrnd; pool 200m; rv adj; tennis 100m; dogs €1; cc not acc; CCI. "V clean & well-kept; nice area; gates clsd 1100-1530." 15 Jun-15 Sep. € 11.50
2006*

ECLASSAN see St Vallier *9C2*

ECOMMOY *4F1* (1km NE Urban) **Camp Municipal Les Vaugeons, Rue de la Charité, 72220 Ecommoy [02 43 42 14 14 or 02 43 42 10 14 (Mairie); fax 02 43 42 62 80; mairie.ecommoy@wanadoo.fr]** Heading S on N138 foll sp. Turn E at 2nd traff lts in vill; sp Stade & Camping. Also just off A28. Med, pt sl, pt shd; wc (some cont); chem disp; shwrs €1.30; el pnts (6A) €2.20; lndtte; shops 1km; playgrnd; tennis; poss cr; Eng spkn; adv bkg; quiet; cc not acc; red low ssn; CCI. "Site v full during Le Mans week; close to circuit; friendly; gd ltd facs; recep 1600-2000 low ssn & 1500-2100 high ssn, new arrivals no access when recep clsd; coarse sand/grass surface." ♦ ltd. 30 Apr-30 Sep. € 9.30
2007*

ECOMMOY *4F1* (4km SE Rural) **Camp Municipal Le Chesnaie, 72220 Marigné-Laillé [02 43 42 12 12 (Mairie); fax 02 43 42 61 23; mairie.marigne-laille@wanadoo.fr]** S on N138 Le Mans-Tours, turn E 3km after Ecommoy twds Marigné-Laillé. Site in 1.5km. Sm, pt shd, mkd pitch; wc; shwrs; el pnts (10A) €1.20; shops 300m; playgrnd; pool 5km; lake & fishing adj; tennis; poss cr; v quiet; CCI. "If height barrier down, use phone at ent for vehicles over 2m high; barrier clsd except 1 hr am & pm, w/e open 0900-0930 & 1830-1900; pleasant warden." 1 Apr-1 Oct. € 7.00
2007*

ECOMMOY *4F1* (8km S Rural) **Camp Municipal Plan d'Eau du Fort des Salles, 72360 Mayet [02 43 46 68 72; fax 02 43 46 07 61]** On N138 Le Mans-Tours rd turn W at St Hubert onto D13 to Mayet & site. Sp 'Camping Plan d'Eau'. Or exit A28 sp Ecommoy & then as above. Med, mkd pitch, pt shd; wc, chem disp (wc); shwrs inc; el pnts (10A) €2.32; gas; lndtte; ice; shops 500m; playgrnd; pool nrby; lake fishing; cycle hire; statics; quiet; CCI. "Well-maintained, clean site; mkd walks nrby; card operated barrier; recep open 0830-1130 & 1600-1900; arr only bet these times as no waiting area." ♦ ltd. 15 Apr-17 Sep. € 7.00
2006*

⊞**EGLETONS** *7C4* (2km NE) **Camping Egletons-Lac, 19300 Egletons [tel/fax 05 55 93 14 75]** Site off N89 Clermont-Ferrand-Tulle rd to NE of Egletons; 2km bef Egletons twd Ussel; 300m after Hôtel Ibis on L. Med, mkd pitch, terr, pt shd; wc; chem disp; baby facs; fam bthrm; shwrs inc; el pnts (4-8A); gas; lndtte; shops 2km; tradsmn; rest; snacks; bar; lake sw, fishing & watersports 500m; playgrnd; entmnts; TV; 30% statics; dogs; phone; Eng spkn; quiet; CCI.
2004*

EGUISHEIM see Colmar *6F3*

⊞**EGUZON CHANTOME** *7A3* (300m N Urban) **Camping La Garenne, 1 Rue Yves Choplin, 36270 Eguzon-Chantôme [02 54 47 44 85; info@ campinglagarenne.eu; www.campinglagarenne. eu]** Exit A20 junc 20 onto D36 to Eguzon; on ent vill sq cont strt on, foll sp; site on L in 300m. Med, hdg pitch, pt sl, pt shd; wc; chem disp; baby facs; shwrs inc; el pnts (6A) €3; gas 300m; lndtte; ice; shop & rest 300m; snacks; bar; htd pool; cycling; lake sw & water sports 4km; TV rm; 20% statics; dogs €.1.50; phone; site clsd 16 Dec-14 Jan; poss cr; Eng spkn; adv bkg; quiet; red long stay/CCI. "New owner 2007 & total refurb; all you need on site or in vill; excel." ♦ ltd. € 15.00
2007*

⊞**EGUZON CHANTOME** *7A3* (3km SE Rural) **Camp Municipal du Lac Les Nugiras, Route de Messant, 36270 Eguzon [02 54 47 45 22; fax 02 54 47 47 22]** Fr A20 exit junc 20, E on D36 to Eguzon; in vill turn R & foll site sp. Lge, hdg/mkd pitch, pt sl, terr, pt shd; htd wc; shwrs inc; el pnts (10A) €3.30 (rev pol); lndtte; shop; tradsmn; rest; snacks; bar; playgrnd; sand beach 300m; watersports; waterski school; entmnt; games rm; some statics; security barrier; quiet but poss noise fr statics or entmnt; red low ssn; CCI. "Scenic site & region; ample, clean facs but ltd low ssn; site yourself on arr; warden avail early evening." ♦ € 7.25
2007*

> Did you know you can fill in site report forms on the Club's website — www.caravanclub.co.uk?

ELNE *10G1* (1.8km NE) **Camp Municipal El Moli (Al Mouly), Rue Gustave Eiffel, 66200 Elne [04 68 22 08 46; fax 04 68 37 95 05; contact@ ot-elne.fr]** Exit A9 at Perpignan Sud dir Argelès. Site well sp fr Elne cent in dir St Cyprien on D40. Lge, pt shd; wc; chem disp; baby facs; shwrs inc; el pnts (10A) inc; lndte; shop; rest & snacks high ssn; playgrnd; pool; sand beach 5km; tennis; horseriding; games area; entmnt; TV; poss cr; quiet; adv bkg; CCI. ♦ 1 Jun-30 Sep. € 19.90
2005*

France

ELNE *10G1* (4km S Rural) **Camping Le Haras, Domaine St Galdric, 66900 Palau-del-Vidre [04 68 22 14 50; fax 04 68 37 98 93; haras8@ wanadoo.fr; www.camping-le-haras.com]** Exit A9 junc 42 sp Perpignan S dir Argelès-sur-Mer on D900 (N9) & then D914 (N114); then exit D914 junc 9 onto D11 to Palau-del-Vidre. Site on L at ent to vill immed after low & narr rlwy bdge. Med, shd; wc; chem disp; mv service pnt; baby facs; shwrs inc; el pnts (6A) inc; lndtte; ice; shop; tradsmn; rest, snacks in ssn; bar; BBQ (gas/elec only); pool; sand beach 6km; fishing 50m; tennis 1km; archery; entmnt; internet; games/TV rm; some statics; dogs €3.50; no c'vans over 6.50m acc high ssn; poss cr; Eng spkn; adv bkg; some rlwy noise; 20-30% red low ssn; CCI. "Lovely, peaceful, family site in wooded parkland; helpful, friendly staff; rds around site poss liable to flood in winter; some corners on site rds narr for lge o'fits; staff can tow lge o'fits to pitch; red facs low ssn; gd rest & pool; 5 mins walk to delightful vill with gd rest; Roman remains; guided walks; conv Spanish border; excel." ♦ 20 Mar-20 Oct. € 28.50 (CChq acc) ABS - C26
2007*

EMBRUN *9D3* (6km N Rural) **FFCC Camping Les Cariamas, 05380 Châteauroux-les-Alpes [04 92 43 22 63 or 06 65 00 32 88 (mob); p.tim@ free.fr; http://les.cariamas.free.fr]** Fr Embrun on N94; in 6km slip rd R to Châteauroux & foll sp to site. Site in 1km down narr but easy lane. Med, mkd pitch, pt sl, terr, pt shd; wc; chem disp; mv service pnt; shwrs inc; el pnts (6A) €3.15; lndtte; ice; shop 1km; rest; snacks; bar; BBQ; playgrnd; htd pool; lake sw adj; beach 6km; sailing; rafting; canoeing; tennis 500m; 20% statics; dogs €2.50; phone; Eng spkn; adv bkg; some rd noise; red low ssn; CCI. "Excel for watersports & walking; mountain views; National Park 3km." 1 Apr-31 Oct. € 15.00
2006*

EMBRUN *9D3* (1km S Urban) **Camping de la Vieille Ferme, 05200 Embrun [04 92 43 04 08; fax 04 92 43 05 18; info@campingembrun.com; www.campingembrun.com]** N94 twd Gap, after 2km go strt ahead across rndabt, in 400m turn L (opp Camp Municipal de la Clapière), site sp in 50m on L, leading down narr lane to site. Med, shd; wc; chem disp; shwrs inc; el pnts (6-10A) €3-5; lndtte; rest; snacks; playgrnd; rv 200m, lake 400m; water sports; no statics; dog €2. "Friendly family-run site; poss v busy in French hols; gd facs." 1 May-30 Sep. € 23.00
2007*

⊞EMBRUN *9D3* (4km S Rural) **Camping Le Verger, 05200 Baratier [04 92 43 15 87; fax 04 92 43 49 81; camping.leverger@wanadoo. fr; www.campingleverger.fr]** Fr Embrun N94 twd Gap. L at rndabt onto D40. Ignore 1st sp to Baratier & take 2nd after 1km, thro vill & fork L by monument. Site on R next to trout farm. Med, hdg pitch, hdstg, terr, pt sl, pt shd; htd wc; chem disp; baby facs; shwrs; el pnts (10A) €5.10; lndtte; ice; shop; snacks; bar; BBQ; playgrnd; htd pool; lake 1km; entmnts; TV; 30% statics; dogs €1.50; poss cr; adv bkg; red low ssn; CCI. "Lge pitches, gd views; pleasant site." € 13.00
2007*

EMBRUN *9D3* (4km S Rural) **Camping Les Grillons, Route de la Madeleine, 05200 Embrun [tel/fax 04 92 43 32 75; info@lesgrillons.com; www.lesgrillons.com]** Fr Embrun take N94 twds Gap; over bdge; L at rndabt onto D40. Turn L at 1st sharp bend; site on L in 400m. Med, mkd pitch, pt sl, pt shd; wc; chem disp; shwrs inc; el pnts (3-10A) €2.60-3.96; ice; lndtte; tradsmn; snacks high ssn; playgrnd; 2 pools; tennis; lake sw & fishing 2km; 5% statics; dogs €1.60; Eng spkn; adv bkg (bkg fee & dep req); red low ssn; CCI. "Helpful, pleasant owners." 15 May-6 Sep. € 12.98
2006*

ENTRAIGUES see Mure, La (Isère) *9C3*

ENTRAINS SUR NOHAIN *4G4* (200m N Rural) **Camp Municipal St Cyre, Route d'Etais, 58410 Entrains-sur-Nohain [03 86 29 22 06 (Mairie); fax 03 86 29 25 99; mairie-entrains-sur-nohain@ wanadoo.fr]** On D1 fr Entrains-sur-Nohain, sp on R. Sm, hdg pitch, pt shd; wc (some cont); chem disp (wc); shwrs inc; el pnts (10A) inc; lndry rm; shop, rest, bar 300m; BBQ; htd pool 500m; 1% statics; dogs; phone 300m; quiet; CCI. "Warden calls twice a day; basic, clean san facs." ♦ ltd. 1 Jun-30 Sep. € 5.30
2006*

ENTRAYGUES SUR TRUYERE *7D4* (5km NE Rural) **Camp Municipal du Lauradiol, 12460 Campouriez [05 65 44 53 95; fax 05 65 44 81 37]** On D34, sp on rvside. Sm, hdg/mkd pitch, pt shd; wc; el pnts (6A) inc; lndtte; shop 5km; htd pool; rv adj; quiet; CCI. "Beautiful setting & walks; excel." 1 Jul-31 Aug. € 15.00 (4 persons)
2005*

ENTRAYGUES SUR TRUYERE *7D4* (1.6km S Rural) **Camp Municipal du Val de Saures, 12140 Entraygues-sur-Truyère [05 65 44 56 92; fax 05 65 44 27 21; info@camping-valdesaures. com; www.camping-valdesaures.com]** Fr town cent take D920 & in 200m turn R over narr bdge onto D904, foll site sp. Med, mkd pitch, pt shd; wc; shwrs; el pnts (6A) €3; lndtte; shops in town; playgrnd; pool adj; entmnt; some statics; dogs €1.50; Eng spkn; quiet. "Pleasant, friendly site; direct access to town via footbdge over rv; vg; well-kept san facs; recep clsd Sun & pm Mon low ssn; free use of pool adj; gd touring base." ♦ 1 May-29 Sep. € 15.50
2007*

ENTRECHAUX see Vaison la Romaine *9D2*

ENVEITG see Bourg Madame *8H4*

EPERLECQUES see St Omer *3A3*

EPERNAY *3D4* (1km NW Urban) **Camp Municipal d'Epernay, Allée de Cumières, 51200 Epernay [03 26 55 32 14; fax 03 26 52 36 09; camping. epernay@free.fr]** Fr Reims take N51 twd Epernay, cross rv & turn R at rndabt onto D301 sp Cumières (look for sp 'Stade Paul Chandon'), site sp. Site adj Stadium. Avoid town at early evening rush hour. NB Beware kerb at ent, espec if you have movers. Med, hdg/mkd pitch, pt shd; htd wc; chem disp; mv service pnt; shwrs inc; el pnts (5A) €3; lndtte; tradsmn; supmkt 300m; rest; snacks; bar; BBQ; playgrnd; htd, covrd pool & waterslide 2km; fishing; canoeing; tennis; cycle hire; games area; 3% statics; dogs free; phone; poss cr; Eng spkn; adv bkg; quiet - some rlwy/rd noise; cc acc; red long stay/low ssn/CCI. "On banks of Rv Marne in conv location; attractive site open to public; friendly, helpful staff; clean, modern, spacious san facs; tour ops; conv Champagne area; Mercier train tour with wine-tasting; gd walks; 30 min walk into town centre - gd rests; NB no twin-axles or vans over 6m acc; vg." ♦ 25 Apr-29 Sep. € 13.15
2007*

See advertisement

EPESSES, LES *2H4* (Rural) **FFCC Camping La Bretèche, Zone de Loisirs de la Bretèche, 85590 Les Epesses [02 51 57 33 34; fax 02 51 57 41 98; contact@camping-la-bretache.com; www. camping-la-bretache.com]** Fr Les Herbiers foll sp to Les Epesses. Turn N on D752, site sp on R by lake. Site sp fr cent Les Epesses. Med, hdg/mkd pitch, pt shd; wc, chem disp; mv service pnt; shwrs inc; el pnts (10A) €2.75 (poss rev pol); lndtte; shop 1km; tradsmn; rest; snacks; bar; playgrnd; htd pool adj; tennis; fishing; horseriding; entmnt; TV; dogs €1.75; Eng spkn; adv bkg (fee €8); poss cr; cc acc; red low ssn; CCI. "Clean, well-run site; v busy high ssn; helpful staff; plenty of attractions nr; conv for Puy du Fou." ♦ 1 Apr-20 Sep. € 15.30   2007*

EPINAC *6H1* (Urban) **Camp Municipal Le Pont Vert, 71360 Epinac [03 85 82 00 26 or 03 85 82 10 12 (LS); fax 03 85 82 13 67; mairie-epinac@wanadoo.fr]** D973 Autun to Beaune 16km. L on D43 to Epinac, site on drive to public sports facs, sp in town. Med, pt shd; wc; chem disp; shwrs inc; el pnts (10A) €2.65; lndtte; shops in vill; snacks; rv sw; dogs €0.60; quiet. 15 Jun-15 Sep. € 10.00
2005*

EPINAL *6F2* (1km E) **Camping Parc du Château, 37 Rue du Chaperon Rouge, 88000 Epinal [03 29 34 43 65; fax 03 29 31 05 12; camping. parc.du.chateau@wanadoo.fr]** Sp fr town cent. Or fr N57 by-pass take exit sp Razimont, site sp in 1km. Med, hdg/mkd pitch, some hdstg, terr, pt shd; htd wc (some cont); chem disp; mv service pnt; shwrs inc; el pnts (6A) €4; gas; lndtte; ice; shop; snacks; BBQ; playgrnd; pool; lake sw 8km; tennis; TV; 20% statics; dogs €1.50; Eng spkn; adv bkg; quiet but stadium adj; cc acc; red low ssn/long stay; CCI. "Lge pitches; ltd facs low ssn; slightly run down - like the town!" ♦ 1 Apr-30 Sep. € 15.00
2006*

⊞**EPINAL** *6F2* (8km W Rural) **Camping Club Lac de Bouzey, 19 Rue du Lac, 88390 Sanchey [03 29 82 49 41; fax 03 29 64 28 03; camping.lac. de.bouzey@wanadoo.fr; www.camping-lac-de-bouzey.com]** Fr Epinal take D460 sp Darney. In vill of Bouzey turn L at camp sp. Site in few metres, by reservoir. Lge, hdg/mkd pitch, hdstg, pt sl, terr, pt shd; htd wc (some cont); chem disp; mv service pnt; baby facs; shwrs inc; el pnts (6A) €4; gas; lndtte; ice; shop; tradsmn; rest; snacks; bar; BBQ; playgrnd; htd pool; paddling pool; sand beach & lake dj; fishing; games area; cycle hire; horseriding; child/teenager entmnt; internet; TV rm; 15% statics; dogs €3; phone; adv bkg; Eng spkn; quiet; cc acc; red low ssn/long stay; CCI. "Attractive site; san facs need attention & poss unclean; gd shop & excel pool; excel touring base." ♦ € 25.00 (CChq acc)
2007*

EPINIAC see Dol de Bretagne *2E4*

ERDEVEN see Carnac *2G3*

France

Camping *** LES PINS

Rental, fitness room, Jacuzzi, solarium, bar, pub, restaurant.

ERQUY will change your life!!

yelloh!

22430 Erquy
Phone. : 33 (0) 296 72 31 12
Fax : 33 (0) 296 63 67 94

E-mail: camping.des.pins@wanadoo.fr - Internet: yellohvillage-les-pins.com

ERNEE *2E4* (E Urban) **Camp Municipal d'Ernée,** 53500 Ernée [02 43 05 19 90] Site sp on app to town, off Fougères-Mayenne rd on E side of town. Head for Centre Ville, turn L for Fougères, round rndabt & site on R. Med, pt sl, pt shd, hdg pitch; serviced pitch; wc; shwrs inc; el pnts (6A) inc; shops 300m; pool adj; quiet. 15 Jun-15 Sep. € 12.00
2007*

ERNEE *2E4* (10km SW Rural) **Camping-Caravaning à la Ferme (Jarry), La Lande,** 53380 La Croixille [02 43 68 57 00] SW fr Ernée on D29 to La Croixille. In vill L onto D30 twds Laval. In 2.5km L onto D158, dir Juvigne, then R at next x-rds, sp Le Bourgneuf-le-Forêt. Site in 2km. Fr A81 exit junc 4 onto D30. Sm, pt shd; wc; shwrs €1.20; el pnts (10A) €1.70 (rev pol); lndtte; supmkt 4km; playgrnd; dogs €0.50; Eng spkn. "Excel CL-type farm site with orchard; quiet & beautiful; friendly owners; farm produce for sale; Ernée mkt Tues, Vitré mkt Mon; Laval mkt Sat." 15 May-15 Sep. € 8.00
2007*

ERQUY *2E3* (1km N Coastal) **Yelloh! Village Les Pins, Le Guen, Route des Hôpitaux,** 22430 Erquy [02 96 72 31 12; fax 02 96 63 67 94; camping.des. pins@wanadoo.fr; www.yellohvillage-les-pins. com] Site sp on all app rds to Erquy. Lge, hdg/ mkd pitch, pt sl, pt shd; wc (some cont); chem disp; sauna; baby facs; shwrs inc; el pnts (6A) €2; lndtte; ice; shop; tradsmn; rest; snacks; bar; BBQ; playgrnd; htd pool; waterslide; sand beach 600m; tennis; fitness rm; jacuzzi; games rm; entmnt & child entmnt; TV rm; 40% statics; dogs €2; Eng spkn; adv bkg; quiet; cc acc; CCI. "Gd family holiday site; excel facs." ♦ 1 May-15 Sep. € 33.00
2007*

See advertisement above

ERQUY *2E3* (3km NE Coastal) **Camping Les Hautes Grées, Rue St Michel, Les Hôpitaux,** 22430 Erquy [02 96 72 34 78; fax 02 96 72 30 15; hautesgrees@wanadoo.fr; www.camping-hautes-grees.com] Fr Erquy NE D786 dir Cap Fréhel & Les Hôpitaux sp to site. Med, hdg/mkd pitch, hdstg, pt shd; wc (some cont); chem disp; mv service pnt; shwrs inc; el pnts (10A) €3.60 (rec long lead); gas; lndtte; ice; shop; tradsmn; rest, snacks 2km; bar; BBQ; playgrnd; htd pool; sand beach 400m; fishing; tennis; horseriding; mini-golf; gym; TV rm; some statics; dogs €1.40; adv bkg; red low ssn; cc acc; CCI. "Pleasant, well-run site; helpful staff." ♦ 1 Apr-30 Sep. € 18.30
2007*

See advertisement opposite

ERQUY *2E3* (1km E Coastal) **Camping Le Vieux Moulin, 14 Rue des Moulins,** 22430 Erquy [02 96 72 34 23; fax 02 96 72 36 63; camp.vieux. moulin@wanadoo.fr; www.camping-vieux-moulin.com] Sp fr all dirs on D786. Lge, mkd pitch, sl, pt shd; wc; mv service pnt; shwrs inc; el pnts (6-9A) €4.50-5; gas; lndtte; shop; rest; snacks; bar; htd pools; waterslide; sand beach 1km; games rm; entmnt; TV; statics; dogs €4; poss cr; quiet. "Site set in pine woods; plenty of beaches in 20 mins drive; ideal for family holiday; poss diff access lge o'fits; lower pitches subject to flooding." ♦ Easter-9 Sep. € 29.70
2006*

ERQUY *2E3* (5km S Rural) **Camping Bellevue, Route de Pléneuf-Val-André, La Couture,** 22430 Erquy [02 96 72 33 04; fax 02 96 72 48 03; campingbellevue@yahoo.fr; www.camping bellevue.fr] Fr Erquy, take D786 twd Le Val-André, site sp. Med, hdg/mkd pitch, hdstg, pt shd; wc; chem disp; mv service pnt; baby facs; shwrs inc; el pnts (6-10A) €3.30-4.80; gas; lndtte; ice; shop; tradsmn; snacks; bar; BBQ; 3 playgrnds; htd, covrd pool; paddling pool; sand beach 2km; watersports; tennis 2km; games area; games rm; mini-golf; library; entmnt; child entmnt high ssn; TV rm; 40% statics; dogs €1.70; phone; Eng spkn; adv bkg (dep req); quiet; red low ssn/long stay; cc acc; CCI. "Excel for families; rec." ♦ 12 Apr-15 Sep. € 19.50
2007*

ERQUY *2E3* (700m SW Coastal) **Aire Communale Erquy,** Ave de Caroual, 22430 Erquy [02 96 63 64 64; fax 02 96 63 50 41] Take D786 fr Erquy dir Pleneuf-Val-André. Site on R at Plage de Carouel, sp. Med, chem disp; mv service pnt; el pnts €2; water fill €2 for 100 litres; rest; beach 100m; poss cr; m'vans only. "Rec arr early as full by 1700." Apr-Nov. € 3.00   2005*

This guide relies on site report forms submitted by caravanners like us; we'll do our bit and tell the editor what we think of the campsites we've visited.

ERQUY *2E3* (2.5km SW Coastal) **Camping Les Roches,** Caroual, 22430 Erquy [02 96 72 32 90; fax 02 96 63 57 84; info@camping-les-roches.com; www.camping-les-roches.com] Sp fr D786 fr Erquy or Le Val-André. Med, hdg/mkd pitch, pt sl, pt shd, wc; baby facs; mv service pnt; shwrs inc; el pnts (10A) €3.20; lndtte; sm shop; bar; playgrnd; sand beach 900m; games rm; wifi internet; some statics; dogs €1.20; phone; adv bkg; quiet. "Pleasant site; sea views; gd walking." 1 Apr-15 Sep. € 14.20   2007*

ERQUY *2E3* (4km SW Rural/Coastal) **Camping de la Plage de St Pabu,** 22430 Erquy [02 96 72 24 65; fax 02 96 72 87 17; camping@saintpabu.com; www.saintpabu.com] Sp on D786 bet Erquy & Le Val-André at St Pabu. Narr rd, restricted passing places. Lge, hdg/mkd pitch, hdstg, terr, pt shd; wc; chem disp; mv service pnt; baby facs; shwrs inc; el pnts (6A) €3.50; gas; lndtte; ice; shop; tradsmn; snacks; bar; BBQ; playgrnd; sand beach adj; cycle hire; entmnt; child entmnt; games/TV rm; some statics; dogs €1.50; Eng spkn; adv bkg; quiet; cc acc; red long stay/low ssn; CCI. "Marvellous beach adj; beautifully situated with hills around; vg touring base; conv St Malo, Dinan, Granit Rose coast; upper terraces poss diff lge o'fits; san facs gd; excel." ♦ 1 Apr-10 Oct. € 19.00   2007*

See advertisement below

ERR see Bourg Madame *8H4*

France

ERVY LE CHATEL *4F4* (2km E Rural) **Camp Municipal Les Mottes, 10130 Ervy-le-Châtel [tel/fax 03 25 70 07 96 or 03 25 70 50 36 (Mairie); mairie-ervy-le-chatel@wanadoo.fr]** Exit N77 sp Auxon (int'l camping sp Ervy-le-Châtel) onto D374, then D92; site clearly sp. Med, pt shd; wc; shwrs inc; el pnts (5A) €2.50; lndtte; shops adj; playgrnd; rv fishing 300m; tennis; dogs €1.50; adv bkg; quie; CCI. "Pleasant, well-kept, grassy site; lge pitches; vg facs; friendly, helpful warden; no twin-axles; rests in vill; rec." ♦ 15 May-15 Sep. € 9.00
2007*

ESCALLES see Wissant *3A2*

ESNANDES see Rochelle, La *7A1*

ESPALION *7D4* (300m E Urban) **Camp Municipal Le Roc de l'Arche, 12500 Espalion [tel/fax 05 65 44 06 79; rocher.benoit@wanadoo.fr; http://pagesperso-orange.fr/camping-rocdelarche]** Sp in town off D920 & D921. Site on S banks of Rv Lot 300m fr bdge in town. Med, hdg/mkd pitch, pt shd; wc; mv service pnt; baby facs; shwrs inc; el pnts (6-10A) €2.60; lndtte; shops 250m; snacks; BBQ; playgrnd; pool adj; tennis; fishing; canoeing; dogs €0.50; poss cr; Eng spkn; adv bkg; quiet; red low ssn. "Gd sized pitches; service rds narr; well-kept site; spotless, modern san facs; friendly, helpful warden; in easy reach of town." 15 Mar-1 Nov. € 13.60
2007*

ESPALION *7D4* (4km E Rural) **Camping Belle Rive, Rue de Terral, 12500 St Côme-d'Olt [05 65 44 05 85; bellerive12@voila.fr; http://bellerive.site.voila.fr]** Fr Espalion take D987 E to St Come. Site on N bank of Rv Lot, sp fr vill cent. Med, pt shd; wc; shwrs inc; el pnts (5-10A) €1.95 (poss rev pol & long lead may be req); lndtte; shop, rest in vill; 10% statics; dogs €0.60; poss cr; Eng spkn; quiet. "Pleasant rvside site; v friendly, helpful owner; delightful medieval vill; excel." 1 May-30 Sep. € 9.78
2007*

ESPERAZA see Quillan *8G4*

ESSARTS, LES *2H4* (800m W Urban) **Camp Municipal Le Patis, Rue de la Piscine, 85140 Les Essarts [02 51 62 95 83 or 02 51 62 83 26 (Mairie); fax 02 51 62 81 24; camping.lepatis@wanadoo.fr; www.campinglepatis.com]** Exit A83 junc 5 onto D160. On ent Les Essarts, foll sp to site. Site on L just off rd fr Les Essarts to Chauché. Sm, pt shd; wc; shwrs inc; el pnts (6A) €2.30; supmkt, rests in town; tradsmn; snacks; playgrnd; 2 pools, paddling pool tennis & sports cent adj; 40% statics; dogs €1.60; some statics; cc acc; v quiet. "Gd NH off A83; superb, clean san facs; warden resident; opening dates uncertain - poss open longer." ♦ 1 May-7 Sep. € 10.14
2007*

ESSAY *4E1* (S Rural) **FFCC Camp Municipal Les Charmilles, Route de Neuilly, 61500 Essay [02 33 28 40 52; fax 02 33 28 59 43; sipaysdessay@wanadoo.fr]** Exit A28 junc 18 (Alençon Nord) onto D31 to Essay (sp L'Aigle); turn R in vill dir Neuilly-le-Bisson; site on R in 200m. Sm, hdg pitch, pt shd; wc; shwrs €1.50; el pnts (6A) €1.40; lndry rm; playgrnd; adv bkg. "V quiet on edge of vill; lge pitches; park, then find warden 1st house on L fr site ent; fair NH." 1 Apr-30 Sep. € 5.40
2006*

ESTAGEL *8G4* (6km NE Rural) **Camping Le Priourat, Rue d'Estagel, 66720 Tautavel [tel/fax 04 68 29 41 45; j.ponsaille@libertysurf.fr; www.le-priourat.fr]** W fr Estagel on D117. In 2km turn R onto D611 & keep R onto D9 to Tautavel. Site on R bef cent of vill (2nd rd on R after vill sign). NB Sloping exit fr site onto narr lane. Sm, hdg/mkd pitch, pt sl, pt shd; wc; shwrs inc; el pnts (6A) €3 (rev pol); lndry rm; ice; shop in vill; rest; bar; BBQ; playgrnd; pool high ssn; rv 500m; beach 40km; no statics; Eng spkn; adv bkg ess high ssn; quiet; cc acc; red low ssn; CCI. "Lovely, friendly, sm site; sm pitches; ltd facs low ssn; poss muddy." 1 Apr-30 Sep. € 17.00
2007*

ESTAGEL *8G4* (3km W Rural) **Camping La Tourèze, Route d'Estagel, 66720 Latour-de-France [tel/fax 04 68 29 16 10; camping.latoureze@wanadoo.fr; http://campinglatoureze.monsite.wanadoo.fr]** Fr D117 at Estagel S onto D17 to site. Med, mkd pitch, shd; wc; chem disp; mv service pnt; baby facs; shwrs inc; el pnts (6A) €3; lndtte; ice; tradsmn; shop, rest, bar 500m; playgrnd; htd pool 3km; rv sw adj; 13% statics; dogs €1.80; phone; Eng spkn; adv bkg (dep req); quiet; cc acc. "Pretty vill & wine 'cave' in walking dist; helpful staff; excel." 1 Apr-15 Oct. € 12.00
2006*

ESTAING (AVEYRON) *7D4* (2km N Rural) **Camp Municipal La Chantellerie, 12190 Estaing [05 65 44 72 77 or 05 65 44 70 32; fax 05 65 44 03 20; mairie-estaing@wanadoo.fr]** Fr D920 in Estaing nr rv bdge take D167; fork R onto D97; site on L. Well sp fr Estaing cent adj stadium. Med, hdg/mkd pitch; pt shd; wc (some cont); shwrs inc; el pnts €2; shop 2km; rest, snacks & bar 2km; pool 2km; rv sw 2km; phone; quiet; CCI. "Gd walking country; vg rest in Logis Hotel in Estaing; warden calls am & pm; NH only." 22 May-30 Sep. € 9.10
2007*

ESTAING (HAUTES PYRENEES) see Argelès Gazost *8G2*

ESTAVAR see Bourg Madame *8H4*

ETABLES SUR MER *2E3* (1km S Coastal) **Camping L'Abri Côtier, Rue de la Ville-es-Rouxel, 22680 Etables-sur-Mer [02 96 70 61 57 or 06 07 36 01 91 (mob LS); fax 02 96 70 65 23; camping.abricotier@wanadoo.fr; www.camping-abricotier.fr]** N on N12 around St Brieuc, exit on D786 sp Pordic & St Quay-Portrieux. Foll sp Etables-sur-Mer; drive thro vill & after the turning for Plage du Moulin turn L; site well sp on far side of vill. NB Site app via narr rd & up incline to recep; poss nec to drive across to another section of site and stop on incline to access barrier. Med, mkd pitch, pt sl, pt shd; htd wc; chem disp; mv service pnt; 15% serviced pitch; baby facs; shwrs inc; el pnts (6A) inc; gas; lndtte; shop; tradsmn; snacks; bar; BBQ; playgrnd; htd pool & paddling pool; jacuzzi; sand beach 500m; watersports 2km; tennis in vill; golf 4km; games rm; entmnt; internet; TV; 10% statics; dogs €1.50; British owned; c'vans over 7.50m not acc high ssn; adv bkg; quiet; cc acc; CCI. "Vg, immac site; excel beach; 80% Eng occupied; trips organised; mkt Tue & Sun; entry narr & steep, narr corners on site rds diff lge o'fits; friendly & helpful." ♦ 1 May-9 Sep. € 19.90 ABS - B09   2007*

⊞**ETAMPES** *4E3* (3km S Rural) **FFCC Caravaning Le Vauvert, 91150 Ormoy-la-Rivière [01 64 94 21 39; fax 01 69 92 72 59]** Fr Etampes S on N20 take D49 sp Saclas. Site on L in approx 1.5km. NB acess on a loop to cross rd. Med, hdg pitch, shd; wc; shwrs inc; el pnts (10A) inc; gas; shop 3km; bar; pool 3km; tennis; fishing; rv adj; games area; many statics; quiet; site clsd 15 Dec-14 Jan; red long stay; cc not acc; CCI. "Wcs in touring area clsd winter; gd san facs; if travelling in winter phone to check site open; conv train to Paris; hypmkt 3km; vg." € 17.00   2007*

> As soon as we get home I'm going to post all these site report forms to the editor for inclusion in next year's guide. I don't want to miss the September deadline.

ETANG SUR ARROUX *4H4* (S Rural) **FFCC Camping des 2 Rives, 26 Route de Toulon, 71190 Etang-sur-Arroux [03 85 82 39 73]** Fr Autun on N81 SW for 11km; turn L onto D994 to Etang-sur-Arroux; site on R after passing thro main part of town. Med, shd; wc; chem disp; mv service pnt; shwrs inc; el pnts (6-10A) €3-3.50; lndtte; shop 1km; rest, snacks & bar high ssn or 1km; playgrnd; pool 500m; rv sw adj; canoeing; kayaking; 20% statics; dogs €1.75; phone; Eng spkn; adv bkg; CCI. "Well-kept site bet two rvs; Dutch owners; gd rv sports; ltd opening Jan & Feb." 1 Mar-30 Nov. € 14.50   2006*

ETAPLES *3B2* (2km N) **Camp Municipal La Pinède, Rue de Boulogne, 62630 Etaples [tel/fax 03 21 94 34 51]** Take D940 S fr Boulogne-sur-Mer for 25km, site on R after war cemetary & bef Atac supmkt. Or N fr Etaples for 2km on D940. Med, hdg pitch, terr, pt sl, pt shd; wc; chem disp; mv service pnt; shwrs; el pnts (5A) inc; gas 500m; lndtte; rest, snacks & bar high ssn; shop high ssn 500m & 1km; playgrnd; beach 4km; rv 500m; dogs; phone; 15% statics; adv bkg red high ssn; CCI. "Some rd/rlwy noise; no twin-axles; dated; poss tired san facs; ltd low ssn; office 0800-1200 & 1400-1900; war cemetery adj." ♦ 15 Feb-15 Dec. € 10.40   2007*

ETEL see Plouhinec *2F2*

ETIVAL see Clairvaux les Lacs *6H2*

ETREAUPONT see Vervins *3C4*

ETREHAM see Bayeux *3D1*

ETRETAT *3C1* (4km E Rural) **Camping Hameau Epivent, 76790 Bordeaux-St Clair [02 35 27 12 60]** Sp fr vill on D940 E of Etretat. Med, pt shd; wc; shwrs; el pnts; shop 2km; beach 4km; quiet; adv bkg. "Lovely rural site with pleasant owner." 15 Apr-15 Oct.   2004*

ETRETAT *3C1* (6km E Rural) **FFCC Camping de l'Aiguille Creuse, 24 Rue de l'Aiguille, 76790 Les Loges [02 35 29 52 10; fax 02 35 10 86 64; camping@aiguillecreuse.com; www.camping aiguillecreuse.com]** On S side of D940 in Les Loges; sp. Med, unshd; wc (some cont); chem disp; shwrs inc; el pnts (10A) €4.30; lndtte; shops 500m; bar; BBQ; playgrnd; pool (no shorts); beach 3km; tennis; games rm; dogs €2.50; adv bkg; quiet. "Facs ltd low ssn." ♦ 1 Apr-30 Sep. € 15.10 (CChq acc)   2007*

ETRETAT *3C1* (1km SE Urban/Coastal) **Camp Municipal, Rue Guy de Maupassant, 76790 Etretat [02 35 27 07 67]** Fr Fécamp SW on D940 thro town cent of Etretat & site on L. Or fr Le Havre R at 2nd traff lts; site on L in 1km on D39. Med, mkd pitch, some hdstg, pt sl, pt shd; htd wc (some cont); chem disp; mv service pnt; shwrs inc; el pnts (5-10A) €4-4.80 (poss rev pol); gas; lndtte; shop 1km; BBQ; playgrnd; shgl beach 1km; no statics; phone; poss cr; no adv bkg; quiet; cc acc; CCI. "Busy, well-maintained site; lge pitches; immac san facs; friendly staff; pleasant seaside resort, attractive beach nr; clsd 2200-0730; recep clsd 1200-1500; conv Le Havre ferry; gd clifftop walks nr; level walk to town; m'van o'night area adj (no el pnts); excel." ♦ Easter-15 Oct. € 9.50   2007*

ETRETAT *3C1* (4km S) **Camping Les Tilleuls, Hameau de Grosse Mare, 76790 Le Tilleul [tel/fax 02 35 27 11 61]** Fr Le Havre N on D940 18km to vill of Le Tilleul. Turn R after filling stn. Med, shd; wc (some cont); chem disp; shwrs; el pnts; lndtte; shop; snacks; BBQ; playgrnd; beach 3km; adv bkg; quiet. 1 Apr-30 Sep. € 9.00   2005*

ETRETAT *3C1* (10km SW Rural) **Camping Le Beau Soleil**, 76280 **Criquetot-l'Esneval [02 35 20 24 22; fax 02 35 20 82 09; lebeausoleil@wanadoo.fr; www.etretat.net]** S fr Etretat on D39 to Criquetot-l'Esneval. Site is 3km SW of Criquetot-l'Esneval on D79 twd Turretot. Med, pt shd; wc; chem disp; mv service pnt; shwrs €1; el pnts (2-10A) €1.10-5.50; bar; playgrnd; beach 8km; 70% statics; dogs €0.60; Eng spkn; CCI. "Pleasant site, v friendly owners; conv Le Havre ferry." 1 Apr-30 Sep. € 7.00

2006*

ETRIGNY see Tournus *9A2*

EU *3B2* (Urban) **Camp Municipal du Parc Château**, 76260 Eu **[02 35 86 20 04]** App fr Blangy on D1015 turn L at junc with D925 & foll camp sp to site in grounds of Hôtel de Ville (chateau). Fr Abbeville on D925 fork R at 1st rndabt in town S of rlwy then immed strt on over cobbled rd right up to chateau walls. Turn R at chateau walls. Ignore sp to Stade. Med, some hdg pitch, mainly terr, pt shd; wc; chem disp; shwrs inc; el pnts (6A) inc; gas; lndtte; shops 250m; shgl beach 3km; 10% statics; poss cr. "Louis-Philippe museum in chateau; poss itinerants; vg Fri mkt." 1 Apr-31 Oct. € 15.00

2007*

EVAUX LES BAINS *7A4* (N Urban) **Camp Municipal**, 23110 **Evaux-les-Bains [05 55 65 55 82 or 05 55 65 55 38]** Fr N on D993/D996 sp 'International'. Also site sp fr other dirs. Sm, pt sl, pt shd; wc (some cont); chem disp (wc); shwrs inc; el pnts (3A) €3.20; shops 500m; playgrnd; pool 500m; 10% statics; dogs €0.45; quiet. "Evaux attractive health spa; friendly & informal site; well run; gd facs." ♦ ltd. 1 Apr-31 Oct. € 5.80

2006*

EVAUX LES BAINS *7A4* (5km W Rural) **Camp Municipal La Pouge**, Rue du Stade, 23170 **Chambon-sur-Voueize [05 55 82 13 21]** Take D915 fr Evaux-les-Bains; at ent to Chambon-sur-Voueize turn R bef x-ing rv. Site adj municipal stadium. Sm, mkd pitch, pt shd; wc; chem disp; shwrs inc; el pnts (10A) €1.30; lndtte; shops, rest & bar 150m; BBQ; playgrnd; tennis; games rm; 10% statics; dogs €0.50; phone; bus 1.5km; adv bkg; quiet; no cc acc; CCI. "Pleasant rural area; gd walking & cycling; Evaux-les-Bains a spa town; golf at Gouzon; gd value; vg." 1 Apr-31 Oct. € 6.20

2007*

EVIAN LES BAINS *9A3* (4km E) **Camping de Vieille Eglise**, 21 Ave de Grande Rive, 74500 **Lugrin [04 50 76 01 95; fax 04 50 76 13 12; campingvieilleeglise@wanadoo.fr; www.camping-vieille-eglise.com]** D21 fr Evian via Maxilly, or turn S off N5 at Tourronde, sp. Med, some mkd pitches, pt terr, pt sl, pt shd; wc; chem disp; shwrs inc; el pnts (4-10A) €2.60-3.70; gas; lndtte; supmkt 1km; rest 1km; playgrnd; htd pool; shgl beach 1km; lake 1km; 3% statics; dogs; adv bkg; quiet; 5% red for 15 days; CCI. "View of Lac Léman; poss mkt traders on site." ♦ 1 Apr-15 Oct. € 15.00

2004*

⊞ **EVIAN LES BAINS** *9A3* (3.5km W Rural) **Camping de la Plage**, 305 Rue de la Garenne, Amphion-les-Bains, 74500 **Publier [04 50 70 00 46; fax 04 50 70 84 45; info@camping-dela-plage.com; www.camping-dela-plage.com]** Site sp at rndabt on main lakeside rd (N5) at Amphion-les-Bains. Sm, mkd pitch, pt shd; wc (some cont); chem disp; mv service pnt; baby facs; shwrs inc; el pnts (3-6A) €3-5; gas 500m; lndtte; ice; shop adj; hypmkt 1km; tradsmn; snacks; bar; BBQ; playgrnd; htd, covrd pool; waterslide; jacuzzi; shgl beach & lake sw 150m; sports complex adj; tennis; TV; 20% statics; dogs; phone; poss cr; Eng spkn; adv bkg; site clsd 1 Nov-24 Dec; quiet; CCI. "Helpful owner; excel." ♦ € 22.00

2006*

EVIAN LES BAINS *9A3* (6km W Rural) **FFCC Camping Les Huttins**, Rue de la Plaine, Amphion-les-Bains, 74500 **Publier [tel/fax 04 50 70 03 09; campingleshuttins@club-internet.fr]** Fr Thonon on N5 twds Evian, at start of Amphion turn L onto Rte du Plaine sp; ent 200m on R after rndabt. Fr Evian on N5 twds Thonon, at end of Amphion turn R & foll sp. Med, mkd pitch, shd; wc (some cont); chem disp; mv service pnt; shwrs inc; el pnts (3-6A) €2.30-4; gas; ice; lndtte; shop; hypermkt 300m; rest, bar 400m; BBQ; playgrnd; pool & sports complex 200m; lake sw 400m; tennis adj; TV; 5% statics; Eng spkn; adv bkg; quiet. "Spacious, quiet & restful; simple site with enthusiastic & helpful owners; gd base for Lake Léman area; conv day trips to Mont Blanc; poss unreliable opening dates - phone ahead; vg." 1 May-30 Sep. € 12.00

2007*

EVRON *4F1* (7km SW Rural) **Camp Municipal la Croix Couverte**, La Croix Couverte, 53270 **Ste-Suzanne [02 43 01 41 61 or 02 43 01 40 10 (Mairie); fax 02 43 01 44 09]** Take D7 SW fr Evron sp Ste Suzanne. Site 800m S (downhill) after this sm fortified town. Sm, some hdg/mkd pitch, pt shd; wc; shwrs inc; el pnts (3-5A) €2; shops 800m; playgrnd; htd pool; walking & horseriding adj; some statics; quiet. "V helpful warden; clean, simple site in lovely area; sm pitches; high ssn site facs used by coaches of tourists to vill; unspoilt town & castle with historic Eng connections; excel NH." ♦ 1 May-30 Sep. € 6.00

2006*

⊞ **EVRON** *4F1* (W Urban) **Camp Municipal de la Zone Verte** (formerly du Parc des Loisirs), Blvd du Maréchal Juin, 53600 **Evron [02 43 01 65 36; fax 02 43 37 46 20; camping@evron.fr; www. camping-evron.fr]** Site on ring rd in clockwise dir fr Super-U supmkt; clearly sp fr all rds into town. Med, some hdg pitch, pt shd; htd wc (some cont); chem disp; mv service pnt; shwrs inc; el pnts (6-10A) €1.55-2.40; lndtte; ice; shops 1km; playgrnd; htd pool & sports complex adj; 50% statics; dogs €0.85; adv bkg; quiet. "Triangular hdg pitches - enter tow bar 1st & manhandle; v well-kept; friendly & pleasant site with lots of flowers; v restricted recep hrs in winter - warden on site lunchtime & early eve only; no twin-axle vans." ♦ ltd. € 9.45

2006*

EXCENEVEX see Thonon les Bains *9A3*

EYMET *7D2* (6.5km N Rural) **Camping Lou Tuquet, Le Mayne, 24500 Fonroque [05 53 74 38 32; fax 05 53 27 35 65; olivierbagard@hotmail.com]** Take D933 SW of Bergerac dir Eymet. In vill of Fonroque turn R & foll sp. Site well sp. Sm, mkd pitch, pt sl, pt shd: wc; chem disp (wc); shwrs; el pnts (5A) €2.30; lndry rm; ice; shop, rest, snacks, bar 2km; playgrnd; 15% statics; Eng spkn; quiet; red long stay. "Ideal for walking & cycling on deserted rds; produce avail; basic but peaceful CL-type site." ♦ ltd. 1 May-1 Nov. € 7.80   2004*

EYMET *7D2* (5km SW Rural) **Camping Moulin Brule, 47800 Agnac [tel/fax 05 53 83 07 56; thebeales@wanadoo.fr; www.eymetguide.com]** Fr D933 at Miramont-de-Guyenne (6km S of Eymet) turn E onto D1; in 4km turn L onto C501 dir Eymet; site on L in 2km. Sm, mkd pitch, hdstg, pt shd; wc; el pnts (16A) €3; shwrs inc; lndtte; ice; shops, rest, snacks & bar 6km; BBQ; playgrnd; pool; games area; 2 statics; no twin axles; adv bkg (dep req). "Quiet site with lge grounds; British owners." 1 May-1 Oct. € 12.00   2007*

EYMET *7D2* (500m W Urban) **Camping du Château, Rue de la Sole, 24500 Eymet [05 53 23 80 28; fax 05 53 22 22 19; jean-jacques@eymetcamping. com]** Go thro Miramont onto D933 to Eymet. Turn opp Casino supmkt & foll sp to site. Sp on ent to Eymet fr all dirs. Med, hdg pitch, pt shd, wc; chem disp; mv service pnt; shwrs inc; el pnts (5-10A) €2.50 (poss rev pol); gas; lndtte; ice; shops, rest, snacks, bar 850m; playgrnd; pool 1.5km; lake & rv sw nrby; dogs; poss cr; Eng spkn; adv bkg; quiet; red long stay; CCI. "V pleasant, clean, well-run site behind ruined medieval chateau by rv; lovely old Bastide town but rec not to take car; shops within easy walk; Thurs mkt; don't be deterred by chicane & fire gate at site ent - gate opened on request; v friendly owner." ♦ 1 May-30 Sep. € 12.75   2007*

EYMOUTHIERS see Montbron *7B3*

EYMOUTIERS *7B4* (8km N) **Camp Municipal Les Peyrades, Auphelle, Lac de Vassivière, 87870 Peyrat-le-Château [05 55 69 41 32 or 05 55 69 40 23 (Mairie); fax 05 55 69 49 24]** Fr Peyrat E on D13, at 5km sharp R onto D222 & foll sp for Lac de Vassivière. At wide junc turn L, site on R. Med, pt sl, pt shd; wc cont; shwrs inc; el pnts (5A) €2.30; lndry rm; shop, rest, snacks, bar adj; BBQ; lake sw adj; sand beach adj; dogs; phone; poss v cr; adv bkg; quiet. "Helpful warden; some pitches overlook lake." 2 May-10 Sep. € 8.50
                2006*

EYMOUTIERS *7B4* (8km N Rural) **Camp Municipal Moulin de l'Eau, 87470 Peyrat-le-Château [05 55 69 41 01 or 05 55 69 40 23]** 1.5km N of Peyrat on D940 to Bourganeuf, site on L immed bef bdge. Med, pt sl, pt terr, pt shd; wc; shwrs; el pnts €2.29; shops 2km; fishing; no adv bkg; quiet; CCI. "Pleasant site; beautiful area; pay at Mairie in town." 1 Jul-15 Sep. € 6.00   2006*

EYMOUTIERS *7B4* (2km S) **Camp Municipal, St Pierre-Château, 87120 Eymoutiers [05 55 69 27 81; fax 05 55 69 14 24; OT.eymoutiers@wanadoo.fr; www.mairie-eymoutiers.fr]** On E of D940 S fr Eymoutiers site sp on R. Diff sharp bend bef ent. Sm, pt sl, terr, pt shd; wc; shwrs; el pnts (16A) €2 (long lead poss req); shops 2km; adv bkg; quiet. "Gd views; clean site; site yourself, warden calls; attractive town & area." 1 Jun-30 Sep. € 6.90   2007*

⊞**EYMOUTIERS** *7B4* (10km W Rural) **FFCC Camping Le Cheyenne (formerly Camp Municipal du Lac), Ave Michel Sinibaldi, Rue Torrade, 87130 Châteauneuf-la-Forêt [tel/fax 05 55 69 63 69 or 05 55 69 39 29 (LS); campinglecheyenne@neuf. fr; www.campinglecheyenne.com]** Fr Limoges E on D979 for 33km. Turn R at Lattée D15 & in 4km foll sp to site fr vill of Châteauneuf. Med, mkd pitch, pt shd; htd wc; chem disp; mv service pnt; shwrs inc; el pnts (6A) €3.50; lndtte; ice; tradsmn; bar/ rest; takeaway; lake sw adj; phone; site clsd Feb; Eng spkn. "Lovely position by lake & woods but nr town; gd size pitches; reasonable facs; poss unkempt/untidy low ssn; factory on 24hr shift gives cont background hum, but not obtrusive; gd walks; gd." € 11.00   2007*

EYZIES DE TAYAC, LES *7C3* (4km N Rural) **Camping Bouyssou, Lespinasse, 24620 Tursac [05 53 06 98 08; campingbouyssou@wanadoo.fr; http://pagesperso-orange.fr/campingbouyssou24/]** N fr Les Eyzies on D707, turn L across rv bdge sp La Madelaine. Take R fork, site sp on L. Sm, hdg pitch, pt shd; wc; chem disp; shwrs inc; el pts (10A) €2; shop, rest 1km; playgrnd; pool; paddling pool; rv fishing 200m; some statics; poss cr; adv bkg; quiet. "V pleasant site with gd views; friendly, helpful owner; vg modern, unisex san facs; excel touring base." 2 Jun-29 Sep. € 10.00
                2006*

EYZIES DE TAYAC, LES *7C3* (4km NE Rural) **Camping La Ferme du Pelou, Le Pelou, 24620 Tursac [05 53 06 98 17]** Fr Les Eyzies-de-Tayac take D706 dir Tursac. In 3km turn R, site sp. 1km up hill on L. Ent poss diff for lge o'fits. Sm, hdg pitch, pt shd; wc; chem disp; mv service pnt; shwrs inc; el pnts (6A) €2.60 (long lead poss req); lndtte; shop, rest & bar 4km; BBQ; playgrnd; htd pool; 10% statics; dogs; phone; adv bkg; CCI. "Stunning views across valley; excel, quiet site low ssn; friendly owners; vg san facs & pool; farm produce; nr prehistoric sites; highly rec." ♦ 15 Mar-15 Nov. € 9.90   2007*

EYZIES DE TAYAC, LES *7C3* (5km NE Rural) Camping Le Pigeonnier, Le Bourg, 24620 Tursac [tel/fax 05 53 06 96 90; campinglepigeonnier@ wanadoo.fr] NE fr Les Eyzies for 5km on D706 to Tursac; site is 200m fr Mairie in vill cent; ent tight. Sm, hdg/mkd pitch, pt sl, terr, shd; wc; chem disp in vill; shwrs inc; el pnts (10A) €3; gas; lndtte; ice; tradsmn; shop 5km; snacks; bar; playgrnd; sm pool; shgl beach, rv sw, fishing & canoeing 1km; horseriding; cycle hire; dogs €1; adv bkg (dep req); quiet; no cc acc; CCI. "Welcoming, helpful British owners; freshwater pool on site (v cold); spacious, grass pitches; facs poss stretched high ssn; v quiet hideaway site in busy area; close to prehistoric sites." 1 Jun-30 Sep. € 13.50   2005*

⊞**EYZIES DE TAYAC, LES** *7C3* (6km NE Rural) FFCC Camping Auberge (Veyret), Bardenat, 24620 Marquay [05 53 29 68 44; fax 05 53 31 58 28; contact@auberge-veyret.com; www.auberge-veyret.com] Leave Les Eyzies dir Sarlat on D47; in 4km go L onto D48 (dir Tamniès); in 3.5km turn L & foll sp for Auberge Veyret. Sm, sl, pt shd; wc; chem disp (wc); shwrs inc; el pnts (16A) €2.30; tradsmn; rest; snacks; playgrnd; pool; adv bkg low ssn ess; quiet; CCI. "Excel rest (regional cuisine); views; simple CL-type site with sl grass pitches; conv Sarlat (15km); sells foie gras etc." € 9.15   2006*

EYZIES DE TAYAC, LES *7C3* (2km S Rural) Camping Le Pech Charmant, 24620 Les Eyzies-de-Tayac [05 53 35 97 08; fax 05 53 35 97 09; info@lepech.com; www.lepech.com] Fr D47 Les Eyzies take D706, site sp on L. Med, hdg mkd pitch, terr, pt shd; wc; chem disp; shwrs; el pnts (10A) €3; gas; lndtte; shop; tradsmn; snacks; bar; playgrnd; pool; rv sw 2km; 5% statics; dogs €1; Eng spkn; adv bkg; quiet; cc acc; CCI. ♦ 1 Apr-1 Oct. € 18.35   2005*

EYZIES DE TAYAC, LES *7C3* (2km SW Rural) Camping Le Queylou, 24620 Les Eyzies-de-Tayac [05 53 06 94 71; henri.appels@wanadoo. fr] Take D706 fr Les Eyzies dir Le Bugue; after 2km turn L (after sharp L hand bend) up hill on narr rd to Le Queylou in 1km sp on app. Sm, pt sl, pt shd; wc; shwrs inc; el pnts (16A) inc; ice; shops 3km; BBQ; dogs; poss cr; Eng spkn; adv bkg; quiet; red long stay/CCI. "Helpful owner; pleasant CL-type site; woodland walks." 15 Apr-1 Oct. € 11.25   2005*

EYZIES DE TAYAC, LES *7C3* (1km NW Rural) Camping La Rivière, 24620 Les Eyzies-de-Tayac [05 53 06 97 14; fax 05 53 35 20 85; la-riviere@ wanadoo.fr] Site off D47 Rte de Périgueux. Lge o'fits use 2nd ent by sw pool & walk to recep. Med, hdg/mkd pitch, pt shd; wc; chem disp; mv service pnt; shwrs; el pnts (6A) €3; lndtte; shop; rest; snacks; bar; playgrnd; pool; paddling pool; canoe hire 500m; tennis; internet; TV rm; 5% statics; dogs €1; phone; Eng spkn; adv bkg; quiet; cc acc; CCI. "Pleasant site; facs clean but simple; walking dist many prehistoric caves." ♦ 3 Apr-31 Oct. € 17.20   2004*

FALAISE *3D1* (500m W Urban) FFCC Camp Municipal du Château, Rue du Val d'Ante, 14700 Falaise [02 31 90 16 55 or 02 31 90 30 90 (Mairie); fax 02 31 90 53 38; camping@falaise.fr; www. otsifalaise.com] Fr N on N158, at rndabt on o'skirts of town, turn L into vill; at next rndabt by Super U go strt on; sp R in 200m; then sp on L after housing estate. Or fr S on N158, at 1st rndabt foll sp town cent & site. Cont down hill thro town then turn L (avoid 1st site sp as v narr bdge) foll site sp as rd starts to climb (poss diff for lge o'fits). Cont approx 1km then as above fr castle. Med, hdg/ mkd pitch, pt sl, terr, pt shd; wc (some cont); chem disp; mv service pnt; shwrs inc; el pnts (5A) €2.50; gas 500m; lndry rm; ice; shops, rest, snacks, bar 500m; BBQ; playgrnd; htd pool in town; tennis; TV rm; sat TV some pitches; dogs €1.20; poss cr; some Eng spkn; adv bkg; quiet; cc acc; red long stay & CCI. "Well tended, attractive, clean site in pleasant surroundings; pitches poss diff lge o'fits; clean facs poss ltd low ssn & stretched high ssn & clsd 2200-0800; pitch self & pay later; great view of chateau; interesting old town; birthplace of William the Conqueror; impressive ruined castle; vet in Falaise." ♦ ltd. 1 May-30 Sep. € 10.60   2007*

FANJEAUX *8F4* (2.5km S Rural) FFCC Camping Aire Naturelle Les Brugues (Vialaret), 11270 Fanjeaux [04 68 24 77 37; fax 04 68 24 60 21; lesbrugues@free.fr; http://lesbrugues.free.fr] Exit A61 junc 22 onto D4 to Fanjeaux, then take D119 dir Mirepoix. At top of hill turn L onto D102 sp La Courtète & turn R in 100m to site in 2.5km. Site well sp fr Fanjeaux. Sm, hdg pitch, pt sl, terr, pt shd; wc; chem disp; shwrs; el pnts (15A) inc (rev pol); lndtte; tradsmn; rest, bar 2.5km; playgrnd; htd pool 10km; few statics; dogs; Eng spkn; adv bkg; quiet; CCI. "Delightful, under-used, clean site adj sm lake; v lge pitches; excel touring base; friendly, helpful owners." ♦ 1 Jun-30 Sep. € 14.48   2007*

FAOUET, LE *2F2* (2km SE Rural) Camp Municipal Beg er Roch, Route de Lorient, 56320 Le Faouët [02 97 23 15 11 or 06 89 33 75 70 (mob); fax 02 97 23 11 66; camping.lefaouet@wanadoo.fr] SE fr Le Faouët on D769 site sp on L. Med, hdg/ mkd pitch, pt shd; wc; mv service pnt; chem disp; shwrs inc; el pnts (3-5A) €1.70-3; gas 2km; lndtte; ice; shops, tradsmn, rest, bar 2km; BBQ; playgrnd; htd pool; lake sw 2km; fishing; tennis; games area; golf; games/TV rm; 25% statics; dogs €1.05; Eng spkn; adv bkg; no cc acc; red long stay/CCI. "Pleasant, clean, quiet rvside site with many mkd walks; lovely, historic area; helpful warden." ♦ 15 Mar-30 Sep. € 13.15   2007*

See advertisement

⊞FARAMANS 9C2 (500m E Rural) Camp Municipal des Eydoches, 515 Ave des Marais. 38260 Faramans [04 74 54 21 78 or 04 74 54 22 97 (Mairie); fax 04 74 54 20 00; mairie. faramans@wanadoo.fr] Fr Beaurepaire take D73 to Faramans. Site sp. Med, pt shd; wc; chem disp; mv service pnt; shwrs; el pnts (5A) €3.10; lndtte; shop 500m; rest 100m; snacks; bar 200m; lake sw; fishing; 50% statics; dogs €1.50; adv bkg; quiet. ♦ € 12.50   2007*

FAUTE SUR MER, LA see Aiguillon sur Mer, L' 7A1

FAVERGES 9B3 (2km N Rural) Camp Municipal Les Pins, Le Champ-Canon, 74210 St Ferréol [04 50 32 47 71 or 04 50 44 56 36 (Mairie); fax 04 50 44 49 76; st.ferreol@wanadoo.fr; www. pays-de-faverges.com] Fr N508 nr Faverges go N on D12 for 2km to site on rvside. Med, mkd pitch, pt sl, pt shd; wc (some cont); chem disp; shwrs inc; el pnts (10A) €2.20; gas; lndtte; shop 2km; tradsmn; rest; snacks; bar; playgrnd; dogs €1.10; phone; poss cr; Eng spkn; adv bkg; quiet; cc not acc; CCI. "Well equipped site; gd walking; no twin-axles or 4x4s; poss boggy in heavy rain." ♦ 15 Jun-15 Sep. € 10.30   2007*

FAVERGES 9B3 (6km NW Urban) Camping International de Lac Bleu, 74210 Doussard [04 50 44 30 18 or 04 50 44 38 47; fax 04 50 44 84 35; camping-lac-bleu@nwc.fr; www. camping-lac-bleu.com] S fr Annecy on N508 twd Albertville. Site on L in 20km just past Bout-du-Lac & bef Camp La Nublière. Lge, hdg/mkd pitch, pt sl, pt shd; wc; chem disp; mv service pnt; some serviced pitches; shwrs inc; el pnts (8A) €3.80; gas adj; lndtte; shop 250m; hypmkt 4km; rest & snacks in high ssn; bar; playgrnd; pool; lake beach adj; watersports; dogs €4; poss cr; Eng spkn; rd noise some pitches; red low ssn; cc acc; CCI. "Excel location; rest & shop clsd after 1st week Sep; some lge pitches; gd shops in Doussard 1.5km; gd watersport facs; easy walk for boat trip to Annecy; cycle path into Annecy; ltd facs low ssn; beautiful location beside lake." ♦ 1 Apr-25 Sep. € 25.70   2006*

FAVERGES 9B3 (6km NW Rural) Camping La Nublière, 74210 Doussard [04 50 44 33 44; fax 04 50 44 31 78; nubliere@wanadoo.fr; www. camping-nubliere.com or www.campeole.com] Fr Annecy take N508 twd Albertville, site on L in 20km, 300m after Camp du Lac Bleu. Fr Faverges NW on N508. Lge, mkd pitch, pt shd, wc (some cont); chem disp; mv service pnt; shwrs inc; el pnts (6A) €3.90; gas; lndtte; ice; shop; rest; snacks; bar; playgrnd; lake sw adj; boating; golf; cycle hire; games area; entmnt; dogs €3.50; poss cr; adv bkg; poss noisy; cc acc. "Helpful staff; gd san facs." ♦ 1 May-30 Sep. € 20.30   2006*

The opening dates and prices on this campsite have changed. I'll send a site report form to the editor for the next edition of the guide.

France

FAVERGES 9B3 (6km NW Rural) Camping La Ravoire, Route de la Ravoire, Bout-du-Lac, 74210 Doussard [04 50 44 37 80; fax 04 50 32 90 60; info@camping-la-ravoire.fr; www. camping-la-ravoire.fr] On N508 S fr Annecy twd Doussard, keep lake to your L. Fr Faverges N on N508. Turn at traff lts at Brédannaz then immed L. Site on L in 1km, sp. Med, hdg/mkd pitch, pt shd; wc; chem disp; mv service pnt (poss diff access); serviced pitches; shwrs inc; el pnts (5A) inc (poss rev pol); gas; lndtte; ice; sm shop; tradsmn; supmkt 5km; rest 800m; snacks; bar; playgrnd; htd pool; paddling pool; waterslide; lake sw 800m; fishing; golf, horseriding, sailing & windsurfing adj; cycle hire; games area; TV; some statics; dogs; phone; poss cr; Eng spkn; adv bkg rec Jul/Aug (dep req); quiet; 20% red low ssn; cc acc; CCI. "Mountain views; excel, well-cared for site; immac facs; friendly staff & atmosphere; lake ferry fr Doussard; cycle paths adj; excel." ♦ 15 May-15 Sep. € 29.30 (CChq acc)   2007*

FAVERGES *9B3* (8km NW Rural) **Camping Le Taillefer, 1530 Route de Chaparon, 74210 Doussard [tel/fax 04 50 44 30 30; info@ campingletaillefer.com; www.campingletaillefer. com]** Fr Annecy take N508 twd Faverges & Albertville. At traff lts in Brédannaz turn R, then immed L for 1.5km; site immed on L by vill sp 'Chaparon'. Do NOT turn into ent by Bureau but stop on rd & ask for instructions as no access to pitches fr Bureau ent. Or, to avoid Annecy, fr Faverges, along N508, turn L (sp Lathuile) after Complex Sportif at Bout du Lac. Turn R at rndabt (sp Chaparon), site is on R after 2.5km. Sm, mkd pitch, pt sl, terr, pt shd; wc; chem disp; mv service pnt; shwrs inc; el pnts (6A) inc (check rev pol); lndtte; sm shop & 3km; tradsmn; snacks, bar (high ssn); BBQ (gas/charcoal only); playgrnd; lake sw 1km; shgl beach 3km; tennis 100m; watersports 2km; cycle hire; TV rm; dogs €1.50; Eng spkn; adv bkg (€30.49 dep req); some rd noise; 10% red 1 month; cc not acc. "Lovely area; mains water & waste disp only avail fr wc block at recep; helpful, friendly owners; spotless facs, highly rec; recep 0800-2000 high ssn; vg rest within easy walking dist; excursions organised; mkt Mon." ♦ 1 May-30 Sep. € 18.50 ABS - M06   2007*

FAVERGES *9B3* (8km NW Rural) **Camping L'Idéal, 715 Route de Chaparon, 74210 Lathuile [04 50 44 32 97; fax 04 50 44 36 59; info@ camping-ideal.com; www.camping-ideal.com]** Take Annecy Sud exit fr A41, foll Albertville sp on N508 on W side of lake. In vill of Brédannaz R at traff lts, immed L on narr rd for 100m; site on R after 2km. Lge, mkd pitch, pt sl, pt shd; wc; chem disp; shwrs inc; el pnts (6A) €3.40; gas; lndtte; shop; rest; snacks; bar; BBQ: playgrnd; htd pool; waterslide; lake sw 2km; games area; entmnt; TV; 15% statics; dogs €2; phone; poss cr high ssn; adv bkg (dep & bkg fee); quiet; red long stay; CCI. "Pleasant, family-run site; less cr than lakeside sites; panoramic views of mountains & lake." 1 May-15 Sep. € 20.00
2005*

FAVERGES *9B3* (9km NW Rural) **Camping La Ferme, Chaparon 74210 Lathuile [04 50 44 33 10 or 06 80 72 68 74 (mob); fax 04 50 44 39 50; info@ campinglaferme.com; www.campinglaferme. com]** Fr Annecy take N508 dir Faverges & Albertville; at traff lts in Brédannaz turn R then immed L for 1.5km; site on L by vill sp 'Chaparon' & adj Camping Le Taillefer. Or fr Faverges, along N508, turn L (sp Lathuile) after Complex Sportif at Bout du Lac; turn R at rndabt (sp Chaparon), site is on R after 2.5km. Med, mkd pitch, terr, pt shd; wc (cont); chem disp; baby facs; shwrs inc; el pnts (6-10A) €3.30-4.80; lndtte; ice; sm shop; tradsmn; snacks; takeaway; bar; BBQ; playgrnd; 2 pools (1 htd covrd); lake sw, fishing & watersports 1km; games area; games rm entmnt; wifi internet; doges €2; bus 1km; poss cr; Eng spkn; adv bkg; cc acc; CCI. "Gd views; family-run site; nr beautiful town of Annecy; vg." 28 Apr-30 Sep. € 20.00   2007*

FAVEROLLES *9C1* (S Rural) **Camp Municipal, 15320 Faverolles [04 71 23 49 91 or 04 71 23 40 48 (Mairie); fax 04 71 23 49 65; faverolles.mairie@wanadoo.fr]** Fr A75 exit junc 30 & take D909 S, turn L onto D13 at Viaduct de Garabit & foll sp for Faverolles for 5km, then sp to site dir St Chély-d'Apcher. Sm, mkd pitch, pt sl, pt shd; htd wc (some); chem disp; shwrs inc; el pnts (6A) inc (rev pol); shops 500m; lndtte; playgrnd; some statics; phone; cc not acc; quiet. "Nr pretty lake; vg rest in vill." ♦ 1 Jun-30 Sep. € 10.40
2005*

FAVEROLLES SUR CHER see Montrichard *4G2*

⊞**FAYENCE** *10E4* (3km E Rural) **Camping des Prairies, 83440 Callian [04 94 76 48 36; fax 04 94 85 72 21]** Site on D562 Grasse - Draguignan rd, 3km W fr junc with D37. Site next to Renault g'ge. Fr A8 exit junc 39 onto D37 to D562 (gd rd) & as bef. Med, mkd pitch, hdstg, pt shd; wc; chem disp; shwrs inc; el pnts (4A) inc; ice; lndtte; shops 400m; supmkt 800m; playgrnd; pool; fishing; sailing 5km; 50% statics; dogs €1.50; poss noisy; Eng spkn; adv bkg; CCI. € 19.00   2006*

⊞**FAYENCE** *10E4* (5km E Rural) **FFCC Camp de Loisirs du Lac, Domaine de la Chesnaie, 83440 Montauroux [04 94 76 46 26; fax 04 94 47 66 16; contact@campingdulac.fr; www.campingdulac. fr]** Fr A8 exit junc 39 onto D37; turn L onto D562 sp Draguignan; site on L in 1km soon after rndabt. Lge, hdg pitch, shd; wc (some cont); chem disp; shwrs inc; el pnts (2-10A) inc; gas; lndtte; snacks; bar; BBQ (gas/elec); playgrnd; pool; 40% statics; dogs €2-3; bus; phone; adv bkg; quiet; cc acc; CCI. "Site easy to reach; ltd facs low ssn; poss diff lge o'fits due trees; friendly, helpful staff; vg." € 18.50
2006*

FAYENCE *10E4* (10km S Rural) **Camping Le Parc, Quartier Trestaure, 83440 St Paul-en-Forêt [04 94 76 15 35; fax 04 94 84 71 84; campingleparc@wanadoo.fr; www.camping leparc.com]** Fr D562 midway bet Draguinan & Grasse turn S onto D4. Site sp on L. Exit A8 junc 39, N on D37 for 11km, at junc with D562 turn L for 10km; L onto D4 for 900m; sm sp, L into sm lane, site on bend. Med, mkd pitch, terr, shd; htd wc; chem disp; mv service pnt; shwrs inc; el pnts (10A) inc; gas; lndtte; shop; tradsmn; rest; snacks, bar high ssn; playgrnd; pool; lake 6km; beach 30km; tennis; fishing; lake sw 15km; 10% statics; poss cr; adv bkg; quiet; red low ssn; CCI. "Conv hill vills of Provence; gd rests in St Paul; vg." 1 Apr-30 Sep. € 23.10   2006*

FAYENCE *10E4* (6km W Rural) Camping La Tuquette (Naturist), 83440 Fayence [04 94 76 21 78; fax 04 94 76 23 95; robert@tuquette.com; www.tuquette.com] Fr Fayence take N562. At km 64.2 sp turn R, site ent 100m. Sm, mkd pitch, terr, pt shd; wc; chem disp; shwrs ind; el pnts (6-10A) inc; lndtte; shop 6km; tradsmn; snacks; bar; BBQ; playgrnd; 2 htd pools; some statics; dogs €1.60; poss cr; Eng spkn; adv bkg; quiet; INF card. "Vg site; friendly owners." ♦ 8 Apr-30 Sep. € 29.90
2006*

FECAMP *3C1* (6km SE Rural) Camp Municipal du Canada, 76400 Toussaint [02 35 29 78 34; fax 02 35 27 48 82; mairie.toussaint@wanadoo.fr] On D926 N of Toussaint (sharp turn at side of golf course). Med, hdg pitch, pt sl, shd; htd wc (some cont); shwrs inc; el pnts (4-10A) €2.10-2.65; lndtte; shop; BBQ; playgrnd; games area; 70% statics; dogs €0.35; quiet; CCI. "Gd warden; gd value." ♦ 15 Mar-15 Oct. € 7.35
2006*

FECAMP *3C1* (SW) Camping Le Domaine de Renéville, Chemin de Nesmond, 76400 Fécamp [02 35 28 20 97 or 02 35 10 60 00; fax 02 35 29 57 68; camping-de-reneville@tiscali.fr; http://campingdereneville.free.fr] Site off Etretat rd (D940) on o'skts of Fécamp; sp. NB Steep cliff site, access poss diff lge o'fits; narr bends. NB Lge o'fits best app fr dir Etretat & not Fécamp town. Lge, hdg/mkd pitch, terr, pt sl, shd; htd wc; chem disp; shwrs inc; el pnts (6A) inc (poss long cable req)(poss rev pol); ice; lndtte; shop 1km; tradsmn; rest, snacks & bar in town; playgrnd; pool adj; shgl beach 500m; 15% statics; phone; Eng spkn; CCI. "Fine sea & harbour views; ltd water pnts; poss steep walk to facs; interesting town with excel rests; Benedictine distillery tours; v nice site - can be windy; sep m'van Aire de Service on harbour adj tourist office; highly rec." 31 Mar-12 Nov. € 15.10
2007*

FENOUILLER, LE see St Gilles Croix de Vie *2H3*

FERE, LA *3C4* (Urban) Camp Municipal de la Fère (formerly Marais de la Fontaine), Rue Vauban, 02800 La Fère [03 23 56 82 94; fax 03 23 56 40 04] S on D1044 (N44) (St Quentin to Laon); R onto D338; turn E at rndabt; ignore 1st camping sp; turn N at next rndabt; site sp. Or Exit A26 junc 12 onto D1032 (N32) SW; in 2km turn R onto D35; in 4km pass under D1044; in 400m turn R; in 800m turn R at traff lts; foll over bdge to sports complex. Sm, hdg/mkd pitch, pt shd; wc; chem disp (wc); mv service pnt; shwrs inc; el pnts (15A) €2.70; shop; tradsmn; rest, snacks & bar 1km; BBQ; htd, covrd pool adj; dogs €1.20; adv bkg rec; quiet; red long stay; CCI. "Beautifully kept site adj recreation cent; clean san facs; friendly warden; gates shut 2200-0700 when no vehicle/person access; canals & museums nrby." ♦ ltd. 1 Apr-30 Sep. € 6.60
2007*

FERMANVILLE see Cherbourg *1C4*

FERRIERE AUX ETANGS, LA see Flers *4E1*

FERRIERE D'ALLEVARD, LA see Allevard *9B3*

FERRIERES EN GATINAIS see Montargis *4F3*

FERTE BERNARD, LA *4F2* (1.5km S Rural) Camp Municipal Le Valmer, Espace du Lac, 72400 La Ferté-Bernard [tel/fax 02 43 71 70 03; camping@la-ferte-bernard.com; www.la-ferte-bernard.com] Fr A11/E50 junc 5, take D1 to La Ferté-Bernard. At 1st rndabt in town cent, take 3rd exit. Join N23 & at next rndabt, take 3rd exit. Foll sp Le Valmer. Site off N23 by Rv Huisne & lake. Med, hdg/mkd pitch, pt sl, shd; wc; chem disp; mv service pnt; shwrs inc; el pnts (6A) €2.10; lndry rm; ice; shop 1km; playgrnd; sand beach 500m; watersports; child entmnt Jul/Aug; 10% statics; dogs €1.30; Eng spkn; quiet; CCI. "Vg, friendly, clean site; excel facs; rural but v close to shops & all facs; well lit at night; pitches v soft, wet & muddy after rain; some pitches diff for lge o'fits; no twin-axles; mkt Mon am; vg." ♦ 1 May-15 Sep. € 9.00
2007*

FERTE GAUCHER, LA *4E4* (700m E Urban) Camp Municipal Joël Teinturier, 77320 La Ferté-Gaucher [01 64 20 20 40] On N34 bet Coulommiers & Sézanne; site opp leisure cent. Lge, hdg/mkd pitch, pt shd; htd wc (some cont); chem disp (wc); shwrs inc; el pnts (5A) inc; gas; lndry rm; shop, rest, snacks, bar 700m; playgrnd; htd pool 100m; 30% statics; dogs; bus 500m; phone; adv bkg; quiet; red CCI. "Attractive parkland site by leisure cent; san facs dated but clean; gd touring base." ♦ 1 Mar-31 Oct. € 21.00
2006*

FERTE MACE, LA *4E1* (Urban) Camp Municipal La Saulaie, Blvd Hamonic, 61600 La Ferté-Macé [02 33 37 44 15] Fr town cent foll rd to Flers & turn R onto dual c'way in 500m. Site on L next to stadium. Sp. Sm, pt shd; wc; shwrs inc; el pnts (10A) €1.75; shops 1km; BBQ (gas); playgrnd; rv 2km; dogs; phone; quiet but little rd noise. "Excel little site; key operated gates; call at house adj when recep clsd." ♦ 15 Apr-1 Oct. € 4.90
2005*

FERTE ST AUBIN, LA *4G3* (N Urban) Camp Municipal Le Cosson, Ave Lowendal, 45240 La Ferté-St Aubin [02 38 76 55 90] S fr Orléans on N20; ent on R on N o'skts twd Municipal pool. NB Access fr S poss diff for lge o'fits thro narr rds in business hrs. Sm, pt shd; wc; chem disp (wc); shwrs €1.15; el pnts (2-10A) inc (poss rev pol); shops 1km; tradsmn; rest 100m; pool adj; fishing adj; dogs; some train noise; cc not acc; CCI. "Agreeable, spacious, gd value site; friendly recep; new san facs planned 2008; easy walk to delightful town & gd rests; nr park & chateau; conv A71; gd NH." 1 May-15 Oct. € 10.00
2007*

FEUILLERES see Péronne *3C3*

France

FEURS 9B2 (1km N Urban) **Camp Municipal Le Palais, Route de Civens, 42110 Feurs [tel/ fax 04 77 26 43 41]** Site sp fr D1082 (N82) on N o'skts of town. Lge, pt shd; htd wc; chem disp (wc); mv service pnt; shwrs inc; el pnts (6A) €3; gas; ice; sm shop; tradsmn; snacks; playgrnd; pool adj; 40% statics; dogs €0.50; phone; quiet; CCI. "Spacious, beautifully-kept, busy site; several san facs, all clean." ♦ 1 Mar-31 Oct. € 9.90   2007*

FIGEAC 7D4 (1.5km E Urban) **Camping Les Rives du Célé, Domaine du Surgié, 46100 Figeac [05 65 34 59 00; fax 05 65 34 83 83; surgiecamp. lois@wanadoo.fr; www.domainedesurgie.com]** Fr all dirs foll sp Rodez to site by Rv Célé adj leisure complex. Foll sps 'Base Loisirs de Surgie'. Narr ent, light controlled. NB fr E on N140 v sharp R turn at 1st traff lts. NB Recep at beginning of rd to leisure cent & camping. Med, hdg/mkd pitch, pt shd, wc; chem disp; mv service pnt; chem disp; shwrs inc; el pnts (10A) inc; gas 1km; lndtte; ice; shop; rest; snacks; bar; playgrnd; htd pool & waterslide adj; boating; rv sw adj; tennis; cycle hire; entmnt; 30% statics; dogs €1; Eng spkn; adv bkg; quiet; red low ssn/long stay. "Excel pool complex at leisure cent adj (free to campers); v peaceful low ssn; nice walk to town; vg." ♦ 1 Apr-30 Sep. € 17.50
2007*

FIGEAC 7D4 (7km SE Urban) **Camp Municipal Les Rives d'Olt, Blvd Paul-Ramadier, 12700 Capdenac-Gare [05 65 80 88 87 or 05 65 80 22 22 (Mairie)]** Fr Figeac on N140 dir Rodez; at Capdenac turn R over rv bdge. Site on R in 200m. Med, hdg/mkd pitch, shd; wc; chem disp; mv service pnt; shwrs inc; el pnts (10A) inc; gas adj; lndtte; ice; shop, rest, snacks, bar adj; playgrnd; pool 1km; tennis adj; TV rm; 5% statics; dogs; quiet, a little rd noise; CCI. "Well-cared for site beside Rv Lot; gd fishing, walking & cycling; vg." ♦ 10 Apr-30 Sep. € 9.80   2006*

FIGEAC 7D4 (7km SW Rural) **Camping de Pech-Ibert, Route de Cajarc, 46100 Béduer [05 65 40 05 85; fax 05 65 40 08 33; contact@ camping-pech-ibert.com; www.camping-pech-ibert.com]** SW fr Figeac on D662/D19 twds Cajarc. Site well sp on R after Béduer. Sm, pt shd; wc; chem disp; mv service pnt; baby facs; shwrs inc; el pnts (16A) €3; lndtte; ice; snacks high ssn; BBQ; playgrnd; pool; tennis; cycle hire; fishing & sw 1km; dogs €1.70; Eng spkn; adv bkg ess high ssn; quiet; 5% red 17+ days/low ssn; CCI. "Peaceful CL-type site; pleasant, helpful owners; 2nd san facs block rebuilt (2007) & excel; facs poss ltd low ssn; gd walking fr site (mkd trails); excel." ♦ 15 Mar-31 Dec. € 9.80   2007*

FIGEAC 7D4 (7km W Rural) **Camping La Belle Epoque, Vallée du Célé, 46100 Camboulit [tel/ fax 05 65 40 04 42; julieetpierre@worldonline.fr; www.restaurantlabelleepoque.com]** Take D802 W fr Figeac for 6km, then turn L onto D41 opp viaduct. Site on R in 3km at junc with D211. Sm, mkd pitch, terr, shd; wc (cont); chem disp (wc); shwrs inc; el pnts (10A) inc (long lead poss req); gas 5km; ice; shops 5km; rest; bar; BBQ; pool; some statics; dogs; Eng spkn; adv bkg; quiet; cc acc (long stay only); CCI. "Helpful owners; essentials avail fr rest; acc rd steep with loose surface, help given if req." 15 Jun-15 Sep. € 11.50   2005*

FIQUEFLEUR EQUAINVILLE see Honfleur 3C1

FISMES 3D4 (800m W Urban) **Camp Municipal de Fismes, Allée des Missions, 51170 Fismes [03 26 48 10 26; fax 03 26 48 82 25; mairie-fismes@wanadoo.fr; www.fismes.fr]** Fr Reims NW on N31 (Reims to Soissons). At Fismes do not ent town, but stay on N31 past Champion supmkt on L, under bdge & at rndabt strt on N31 sp Soissons. Site on L in 100m down little lane at end of sports stadium wall. Or exit A4 junc 22 sp Soissons & Fismes & as bef. Sm, hdstg, unshd; wc; chem disp; baby facs; shwrs; el pnts (12A) inc (poss rev pol); shop 250m; supmkt 1km; BBQ (gas & el); playgrnd; horseriding 5km; games rm; dogs; recep 0700-1000 & 1630-1930; no twin-axle vans; Eng spkn; adv bkg; cc not acc; CCI. "Conv for Laon, Epernay, Reims; noisy due to busy rd & position on indus est; san facs usually immac but old; gates locked 2200-0700; warden on site ltd hrs; mkt Sat am; delightful site; vg NH." ♦ 2 May-15 Sep. € 10.00 ABS - P02   2007*

FLAVIGNY SUR MOSELLE see Nancy 6E2

FLECHE, LA 4G1 (10km E Rural) **FFCC Camp Municipal La Chabotière, Place des Tilleuls, 72800 Luché-Pringé [02 43 45 10 00 or 02 43 45 44 50 (Mairie); fax 02 43 45 10 00; lachabotiere@ville-luche-pringe.fr; www.ville-luche-pringe.fr]** SW fr Le Mans on N23 twd La Flèche. At Clermont-Créans turn L on D13 to Luché-Pringé. Site sp. Med, hdg/mkd pitch, pt sl, pt shd; wc (some cont); chem disp; mv service pnt; baby facs; shwrs; el pnts (10A) inc (poss rev pol); lndtte; shops 100m; playgrnd; pool adj high ssn; cycle hire; TV; 10% statics; dogs €1.50; phone; sep car park high ssn; poss cr; Eng spkn; adv bkg; quiet; red low ssn; poss cr; CCI. "Lovely site by Rv Loir; v clean, modern facs; helpful, friendly warden; gd site for children; conv chateaus; excel." ♦ 1 Apr-15 Oct. € 10.00   2006*

FLECHE, LA *4G1* (500m S Urban) **Camp Municipal La Route d'Or, Allée de la Providence, 72200 La Flèche [02 43 94 55 90 or 02 43 48 53 53 (Mairie); fax 02 43 94 33 78; camping@ville-lafleche.fr; www.ville-lafleche.fr]** Fr NW dir Laval D306, keep to W of town, leave S on D306 twd Bauge; site on L after x-ing rv; sp. Fr S take dir for A11 & Laval, site clearly sp on R on rvside. Lge, some hdg pitch, some hdstg, pt shd; htd wc; chem disp; mv service pnt; shwrs inc; el pnts (10A) €3.60 (rec long lead); gas; lndtte; ice; shop 500m; supmkt nr; tradsmn; rest nr; playgrnd; pool; sand beach 1km; canoeing adj; tennis; games area; cycle hire; dogs free; phone; Eng spkn; cc acc; CCI. "Excel facs; warm welcome; busy, well-managed, scenic site; office hrs 0800-1200 & 1500-2030, site yourself if clsd; barrier clsd 2200-0800; helpful staff; lge pitches; facs ltd low ssn; conv ferries: sh walk to interesting town; mkt Wed; excel." ♦ 1 Mar-31 Oct. € 8.75
2007*

FLECHE, LA *4G1* (7km W Rural) **Camp Municipal Le Vieux Pont, 72200 Bazouges-sur-Le Loir [02 43 45 03 91 or 02 43 45 32 20 (Mairie); fax 02 43 45 38 26]** Off N23 fr Le Mans to Angers turn L over rv at 2nd traff lts in cent Bazouges. Sp to site on R after x-ing rv. Sm, hdg pitch, pt shd; wc (some cont); shwrs inc; el pnts (6A) inc; lndtte; playgrnd; pool 7km; fishing, horseriding adj. "Pleasant site on bank of rv." 15 May-30 Oct. € 6.75   2006*

FLERS *4E1* (9km SE Rural) **Camp Municipal Auberge du Lac, Rue de l'Etang, 61450 La Ferrière-aux-Etangs [02 33 96 00 22]** Sp on D18 Flers to La-Ferté-Macé rd on S side of vill adj lake. Foll camping & Auberge du Lac rest sp. Look for sm pond on S side of D18 & E end of vill La Ferrière. Rd on either side of pond goes to site. Sm, mkd pitch, pt shd, pt sl; wc; shwrs inc; el pnts (3-6A) €2; tradsmn; snacks & creperie adj; lake sw adj; adv bkg; quiet but some rd noise. "Pleasant owners; vg small site in attractive setting; v peaceful; area for m'vans just outside main site; recep open v early & after 1700; rec phone bef arr as height bar at ent must be removed." 1 May-30 Sep. € 7.90   2006*

⊞**FLEURAT** *7A4* (500m E Rural) **Camping Les Boueix, Les Boueix, 23320 Fleurat [05 55 41 86 81; info@campinglesboueix.com; www.campinglesboueix.com]** Fr N145 N onto D5 to Fleurat. Foll sp La Boueix & site. Med, hdg/mkd pitch, pt sl, pt shd; wc; chem disp; shwrs inc; el pnts (10A) €3.50; ice; shops, rest, snacks & bar 6km; BBQ; fishing; dogs €1.50; phone; adv bkg; quiet; no cc acc. "Beautiful CL-type site; immac; v helpful British owners; views fr pitches; well-stocked fishing lake nrby; ideal for beautiful Creuse Valley; conv A20; highly rec." € 12.50   2007*

FLEURIE *9A2* (500m SE Rural) **Camp Municipal La Grappe Fleurie, 69820 Fleurie [04 74 69 80 07 or 04 74 04 10 44 (Mairie); fax 04 74 69 85 71; camping@fleurie.org; www.fleurie.org]** S dir Lyon on D306 (N6) turn R (W) at S end of Romanèche onto D32; 4km to vill of Fleurie (beware sharp turn in vill & narr rds) & foll site sp. Med, hdg/mkd pitch, terr, pt shd; wc (some cont); chem disp; mv service pnt; serviced pitches; shwrs inc; baby facs; el pnts (10A) inc; gas; lndtte; tradsmn; shop, rest, snacks, bar 500m; playgrnd; pool; tennis; wifi internet; some statics; poss cr; Eng spkn; adv bkg rec Jul/Aug; cc acc; red CCI. "Clean, well-run, busy site; vg value with 1st class facs; friendly staff; gates & wash rms clsd 2200-0700; lovely pool; gd entmnt & wine-tasting Tue & Sat eves high ssn; excel for touring Beaujolais vills; free, escorted visits to local producers; footpath to town thro vineyards (uphill) with nice rest; mkt Fri; vg." ♦ 25 Mar-23 Oct. € 14.50   2007*

FLORAC *9D1* (1km N) **FFCC Camp Municipal Le Pont du Tarn, Route de Pont de Montvert, 48400 Florac [04 66 45 18 26 or 04 66 45 17 96 (LS); fax 04 66 45 26 43; pontdutarn@aol.com; www.lozere.net]** Exit Florac N on N106 & turn R in 500m by by-pass on D998; site on L in 300m. Lge, pt shd, mkd pitch; htd wc (some cont); chem disp; mv service pnt; shwrs inc; el pnts (10A) €2.95; lndtte; ice; sm shop 2km; tradsmn; rest, snacks, bar 2km; BBQ; playgrnd; pool; rv fishing adj; 60% statics; dogs €1.20; phone; poss v cr; some Eng spkn; adv bkg rec; quiet; red low ssn; CCI. "Nice, well-run site in beautiful area; san facs poor & need update; no twin-axles; gd base for area; mv service pnt poss diff to use; 20 min walk to town, gd shops & lge mkt Thurs; excel." ♦ 1 Apr-30 Sep. € 11.15   2007*

FLORAC *9D1* (4km NE Rural) **Camping Chon du Tarn, 48400 Bédoués [04 66 45 09 14; fax 04 66 45 22 91; info@camping-chondutarn.com; www.camping-chondutarn.com]** Exit Florac N on N106, turn R in 500m onto D998 (sp Pont de Monvert), site on L in 3km in vill. Med, mkd pitch, pt sl, terr, pt shd; wc; chem disp; mv service pnt; shwrs inc; el pnts (6A) inc (poss rev pol); gas; lndtte; ice; shop & 4km; rest, bar adj; playgrnd; rv sw & sand beach; games area; dogs €1; adv bkg (dep req); quiet; cc not acc; CCI. "Gd views; beautiful location; clean san facs, ltd low ssn; helpful staff; conv Tarn Gorges, Causses & Cévennes National Park; excel." ♦ 1 Apr-20 Oct. € 11.70   2007*

FLORAC *9D1* (1km S Urban) **FFCC Camping Velay, Le Pont Neuf, 48400 Florac [04 66 45 19 23 or 04 66 45 12 19]** Site on Rv Tarnon adj to bdge connecting D907 & N106; ent fr N106. Sm, pt sl, pt shd; wc; shwrs inc; el pnts (8A) €2.20; gas; lndtte; shop 300m; tradsmn; rests nr; rv sw & shgl beach adj; 10% statics; dogs €1; some rd noise. "Gd walks; conv Gorges du Tarn & Cévennes National Park." 1 Jul-30 Sep. € 8.70   2007*

France

⊞**FLUMET** *9B3* (1.5km NE Rural) **Camping Le Vieux Moulin, 73590 Flumet [tel/fax 04 79 31 70 06; amrey@hotmail.fr]** Fr Albertville go N on N212 strt to Flumet & cont past Flumet for 1km. Turn R watch for sp. Med, mkd pitch, hdstg, pt shd; htd wc; chem disp; mv service pnt; shwrs inc; el pnts (3-10A) €4.90-8.55; lndtte; tradsmn; rest nr; playgrnd; rv sw; ski lifts 200m; 20% statics; dogs €1.20; phone; poss cr; Eng spkn; some rd noise; CCI. "Superb san block but ltd; friendly staff; gd touring cent for Mont Blanc, Geneva, Annecy etc; highly rec; clsd 15 Apr-30 May." ♦ € 12.90
2006*

⊞**FOIX** *8G3* (2km N Rural) **Camping du Lac, Quartier Labarre, 09000 Foix [05 61 65 11 58; fax 05 61 05 32 62; camping-du-lac@wanadoo.fr; www.campingdulac.com]** Fr N on N20 foll sp for 'Centre Ville', site on R in 2km opp Peugeot g'ge in Labarre. Fr S onto on N20 thro tunnel & take 1st exit N of Foix & foll sp 'Centre Ville', then as above. Lge, mkd pitch, pt shd; wc (some cont); chem disp; mv service pnt; shwrs inc; baby facs; el pnts (6A) inc; lndtte; ice; supmkt adj; tradsmn; rest; snacks; bar; BBQ; playgrnd; pool (high ssn); paddling pool; lake fishing adj; boating; windsurfing; tennis; entmnts; TV; 30% statics; dogs €2; Eng spkn; poss cr; adv bkg rec high ssn; quiet but some rd (N20) noise; red low ssn; cc acc; CCI. "Quiet, spacious pitches on L of camp; facs poss stretched high ssn; gd disabled facs, others need refurb; gates clsd 2300-0700; busy w/e; gd." ♦ € 19.50 (CChq acc)   2006*

FOIX *8G3* (4km S Urban) **FFCC Camping Roucateille, 15 Rue du Pradal, 09330 Montgaillard [tel/fax 05 61 65 22 50; info@roucateille.com]** S on N20 turn L in vill of Montgaillard at Camping-en-Ferme sp; site in 200m. Med, pt shd; wc; chem disp; mv service pnt; shwrs; el pnts (4-10A) €2-5; lndtte; shop 500m, supmkt 2km; playgrnd; pool 3km; some statics in sep area; adv bkg; quiet; 10% red 4+ days; CCI. "Picturesque, informal site; excel facs; charming, helpful owners; garden produce in ssn; gd base for touring; excel." ♦ 1 Apr-30 Sep. € 11.50   2006*

⊞**FOIX** *8G3* (5km NW Rural) **Camp Municipal de Rieutort, 09000 Cos [05 61 02 62 35; fax 05 61 65 39 79]** Fr Foix take D117 dir Tarbes. Foll sp Cos onto D617, site on L in 3km. Sm, pt sl, pt shd; htd wc (some cont); chem disp; 25% serviced pitches; baby facs; fam bthrm; shwrs inc; el pnts (15A) €3.30; lndtte; ice; shop 5km; rest, snacks, bar 5km; playgrnd; pool; tennis; dogs; quiet; CCI. "Site amongst trees with gd views; no c'vans over 6m; sm step into disabled facs." ♦ € 8.00   2007*

FONTAINE DE VAUCLUSE see Isle sur la Sorgue, L' *10E2*

FONTAINE SIMON *4E2* (800m N Rural) **Camp Municipal, Rue de la Ferrière, 28240 Fontaine-Simon [02 37 81 88 11 or 06 81 67 78 79 (mob); fax 02 37 81 83 47; fontaine-simon@wanadoo.fr]** Fr La Loupe on D929 take D25 N to Fontaine-Simon. Med, hdg pitch, pt shd; wc; chem disp; shwrs inc; el pnts inc; lake sw; fishing; 50% statics; dogs €1.10; quiet. "Site at side of lake; excel." 1 Apr-30 Sep. € 13.00   2006*

FONTAINEBLEAU *4E3* (5km NE Rural) **Camp Municipal Grange aux Dîmes, Chemin de l'Abreuvoir, 77210 Samoreau [01 64 23 72 25; fax 01 64 23 98 31; mairie-de-samoreau@wanadoo.fr]** Fr cent of Fontainebleau take D210 (dir Provins); in approx 4km at rndabt cross bdge over Rv Seine; take R at rndabt; sp; site at end of rd thro Samoreau vill. Med, hdg/mkd pitch, pt sl, pt shd; htd wc; chem disp; mv service pnt; shwrs inc; el pnts (10A) inc (poss rev pol); lndtte; shop 250m; snacks & bar 100m; rest 500m; phone; bus; poss v cr; adv bkg; rlwy & barge noise; CCI. "Attractive location by Rv Seine; barges go by site; peaceful; gd sized pitches; v helpful managers; gd, immac san facs; adj vill hall poss noisy w/e; adj café live jazz music Fri nights; conv palace, Paris (gd train service) & Disneyland; clsd 2200-0700; excel, gd value site." ♦ ltd. 15 Mar-30 Sep. € 15.20   2007*

FONTAINEBLEAU *4E3* (12km S Rural) **Camping Les Prés, Chemin des Prés, 77880 Grez-sur-Loing [tel/fax 01 64 45 72 75; camping-grez@wanadoo.fr]** Fr Fontainebleau on N7 twd Nemours (S) for 8km; look for camping sps. At traff island turn L onto D40D, in 1km immed after x-ing bdge turn R; site on L. Do not tow into Grez-sur-Loing. Med, pt shd; wc; chem disp; shwrs inc; el pnts (5A) €2.70; gas; lndtte; ice; shop; rest, bar 200m; snacks; playgrnd; htd, covrd pool 10km; fishing; canoe hire; cycle hire; 60% statics; dogs; phone; poss cr; Eng spkn; adv bkg; quiet; cc acc; 10% red long stay; CCI. "In v attractive area; facs dated but v clean; helpful British manager." ♦ 15 Mar-15 Nov. € 9.70   2007*

FONTENAY LE COMTE *7A2* (7km NE) **FFCC Camping La Joletière, 85200 Mervent [02 51 00 26 87 or 06 14 23 71 31 (mob LS); fax 02 51 00 27 55; camping.la.joletiere@wanadoo.fr; www.campinglajoletiere.fr.st]** Fr Fontenay-le-Comte N on D938; after 6.5km, turn R onto D99; in 3km enter vill of Mervent; site on R. Or fr A83 exit junc 8 & take bypass to W of Fontenay-le-Comte. Med, hdg/mkd pitch, some hdstg, pt sl, pt shd; wc; mv service pnt; shwrs inc; el pnts (5A) €3.60 (rev pol); gas; lndtte; ice; shop 1km; rest; snacks; bar; playgrnd; htd pool high ssn; sw 2km; fishing; boating/windsurfing 2km; forest walks 500m; 25% statics; dogs €1.70; poss cr; adv bkg; cc acc. "Gd lge pitches; quiet & pleasant; v friendly owners; poss ltd facs low ssn." ♦ Easter-1 Nov. € 13.40
2006*

FONTENAY LE COMTE 7A2 (7km NE Rural) FFCC Camping Le Chêne Tord, Route du Chêne-Tord, 85200 Mervent [02 51 00 20 63; fax 02 51 00 27 94] Exit A83 junc 8 & foll D938 N fr Fontenay-Le-Comte twd La Châtaigneraie for 6km to vill of Fourchaud. Turn E to Mervent on D99 & foll camp sps, sharp L turn immed bef vill at stone cross. Med, mkd pitch, pt sl, pt shd; htd wc; chem disp; shwrs inc; el pnts (6-10A) €2.70-3.30; gas; lndtte; shop 1km; rest, snacks, bar 1km; BBQ (gas only); rv/lake sw & fishing 2km; games area; 25% statics; dogs €1.10; phone; Eng spkn; adv bkg rec high ssn; v quiet; red low ssn; CCI. "Nice area; welcoming & friendly; forest location; 30% site forest adventure park - poss noisy high ssn; poss scruffy low ssn; €50 dep req." Easter-31 Oct. € 12.20   2005*

FONTENAY TRESIGNY 4E3 (6km NE Rural) Camping des Quatre Vents, 77610 Crèvecoeur-en-Brie [01 64 07 41 11; fax 01 64 07 45 07; contact@caravaning-4vents.fr; www.caravaning-4vents.fr] At Calais take A26/E15 dir Arras; at Arras take A1/E15 dir Paris; next take A104 dir A4 Metz/Nancy/Marne-la-Vallée, then A4 dir Metz/Nancy, exit junc 13 dir Provins (onto D231); turn R dir Crèvecoeur-en-Brie & foll site sp. Lge, hdg/mkd pitch, pt shd; htd wc; chem disp; serviced pitches; shwrs inc; el pnts (6A) inc; lndtte; shops 2km; tradsmn; snacks; BBQ; playgrnd; pool; horseriding; games area; wifi internet; games/TV rm; 50% statics sep area; dogs €3; poss cr; Eng spkn; adv bkg ess in ssn; quiet but some aircraft noise; CCI. "Friendly, well-run site; gd, lge pitches; san facs clean but v basic; helpful, welcoming staff; excel pool; recep 0830-2300 high ssn; conv Disneyland & Paris by car/train; poss late access to site; superb." ♦ 1 Mar-1 Nov. € 25.00 ABS - P09   2007*

FONTES see Pézenas 10F1

FONTVIEILLE see Arles 10E2

FORCALQUIER 10E3 (500m E Urban) Camping Indigo Forcalquier, Route de Sigonce, 04300 Forcalquier [04 92 75 27 94; fax 04 92 75 18 10; forcalquier@camping-indigo.com; www.camping-indigo.com] Fr town cent foll sp Digne/Sisteron. After 400m turn L at petrol stn, then 1st R. Site on R in 200m. Med, mkd pitch, pt shd; wc; chem disp; mv service pnt; baby facs; some serviced pitches; shwrs inc; el pnts (6-10A) €4.20-6.20; lndtte; shop 500m; tradsmn; rest; snacks; bar; playgrnd; htd pool; paddling pool; games area; internet; TV rm; some statics; dogs €3.30; phone; Eng spkn; adv bkg; quiet; CCI. "V pleasant site in lovely location; san facs ltd/inadequate low ssn; access diff due v narr rds & awkward corners; poss high untrimmed & sharp hedges." ♦ 28 Mar-19 Oct. € 19.50   2007*

FORCALQUIER 10E3 (4km NW Rural) Camping Le Domaine des Lauzons (Naturist), 04300 Limans [04 92 73 00 60; fax 04 92 73 04 31; leslauzons@wanadoo.fr; www.camping-lauzons.com] Exit A51 junc 19 onto N100 dir Avignon; in Forcalquier at rndabt turn L onto D950 sp Banon; site on R in approx 6km. Lge site sp. Diff app. Med, mkd pitch, pt sl, terr, pt shd; wc; chem disp; baby facs; sauna; shwrs inc; el pnts €4.50; gas; lndtte; ice; shop; supmkt 6km; tradsmn; rest; snacks; bar; BBQ; playgrnd; htd pool; pony rides; archery; games area; games rm; many activities; entmnt; child entmnt; internet; TV; 10% statics; dogs €4; phone; poss cr; Eng spkn; adv bkg; quiet; cc acc; INF req. "Pleasant site in wooded valley; wonderful scenery; helpful, friendly staff; vg." ♦ ltd. 1 Apr-30 Sep. € 28.00   2007*

FORET FOUESNANT, LA 2F2 (500m N Rural) Camping Manoir de Penn Ar Ster, 2 Chemin de Penn Ar Ster, 29940 La Forêt-Fouesnant [02 98 56 97 75; fax 02 98 56 80 49; info@camping-pennarster.com; www.camping-pennarster.com] Fr Concarneau take D783 twd Quimper. In 8km after sp Kerlevan L to La Forêt-Fouesnant. After 1km R at bottom of hill opp car pk to site in 100m. Med, hdg pitch, pt sl, terr, unshd; wc (some cont); chem disp; mv service pnt; shwrs inc; el pnts (6-10A) €3.20-3.50; ice; lndtte; shop adj; rest 500m; playgrnd; sand beach 2km; golf adj; entmnt; 60% statics (sep area); dogs €2; adv bkg; fairly quiet; CCI. "Well-kept site; close to gd beaches; nice welcome; conv vill; excel." ♦ 10 Feb-10 Nov. € 22.00   2007*

FORET FOUESNANT, LA 2F2 (2.5km SE Coastal) Camping Club du St Laurent, Kerleven, 29940 La Forêt-Fouesnant [02 98 56 97 65; fax 02 98 56 92 51; saintlaurent@franceloc.fr; www.camping-franceloc.fr] Fr Quimper take D783 SE. Turn R onto D44 to La Forêt-Fouesnant; in vill cent foll sp for Plage de Kerleven; turn L at Kerleven seafront rndabt, cont for 500m & at next rndabt foll site sp. (NB: Camping St Laurent shares same ent with Kéranterec.) Lge, hdg/mkd pitch, pt shd; wc; mv service pnt; chem disp; shwrs inc; el pnts (6A) inc (long lead req); gas; lndtte; ice; shop; tradsmn; snacks; bar; playgrnd; htd pool; paddling pool; waterslide; jacuzzi; sauna; sand beach adj; tennis; gym; entmnt; TV; 50% statics; dogs €2; poss cr; adv bkg; phone; Eng spkn; cc acc; red low ssn; CCI. "V friendly; well-run site with excel facs; lge pitches; many excel, quiet beaches within 10km; beautiful coast, sea views; highly rec. " ♦ 3 May-8 Sep. € 37.00   2007*

See advertisement on next page

FORET FOUESNANT, LA *2F2* (2.5km SE Coastal) Camping de Kéranterec, Route de Port la Forêt, Kerleven, 29940 La Forêt-Fouesnant [02 98 56 98 11; fax 02 98 56 81 73; info@camping-keranterec.com; www.camping-keranterec.com] Fr Quimper take D783 SE. Turn R onto D44 twds La Forêt-Fouesnant; in vill cent foll sp for Beg Menez for 200m, then take 1st R twds Kerleven; turn L at Kerleven seafront rndabt, cont for 500m & at next rndabt foll site sp. (NB: Kéranterec shares same ent with Camping St Laurent.) Lge, hdg/mkd pitch, terr, pt shd; wc; serviced pitches; chem disp; baby facs; shwrs inc; el pnts (6A) €4; gas; lndtte; ice; shop; tradsmn; snacks; bar; playgrnd; htd pool; waterslide; sand beach 400m; tennis; games area; fishing & watersports adj; entmnt; TV; 30% statics; dogs €2.50; adv bkg (ess high ssn); Eng spkn; cc acc; red low ssn/CCI. "Modern san facs; small hdg pitches poss diff lge outfits; lovely views fr higher pitches." ♦ 8 Apr-17 Sep. € 28.00   2006*

⊞FORGES LES EAUX *3C2* (1km S) **Aire de Service (M'vans only), 76440 Forges-les-Eaux** [02 32 89 94 20; mairie@ville-forges-les-eaux.fr] Fr Forges-les-Eaux cent, take D921 S sp Lyons-la-Forêt. In 500m turn R foll sp, camp on L in 250m opp municipal site. Med, hdstg, unshd; mv service pnt; water points; el pnts (poss rev pol). "Free 1st night, 2nd night €5; max 2 nights; warden visits or pay at Municipal site opp; town cent easy walk; views of open countryside; excel."   2007*

FORGES LES EAUX *3C2* (1km S Urban) **Camp Municipal La Minière, 3 Blvd Nicolas Thiese, 76440 Forges-les-Eaux** [02 35 90 53 91] Fr Forges-les-Eaux cent, take D921 S sp Lyons-la-Forêt. In 750m turn R foll sp, camp on R in 150m. Med, hdg pitch, pt sl, pt shd; wc (some cont); mv service pnt opp; shwrs inc; el pnts (4-8A) inc (rev pol); lndry rm; shops nr; htd pool in town; 85% statics (sep area); poss cr; quiet; CCI. "Site well-presented; friendly warden; basic, clean san facs; excel disabled facs; m'van o'night area opp; excel French WWII Resistance Museum in town." ♦ 1 Apr-30 Oct. € 9.95   2007*

FORT MAHON PLAGE *3B2* (1km E Urban) **Airotel Camping Le Royon, 1271 Route de Quend, 80120 Fort-Mahon Plage** [03 22 23 40 30; fax 03 22 23 65 15; info@campingleroyon.com; www.campingleroyon.com] Exit A16 at junc 24 Forest-Montiers onto D32 to Rue, then dir Quend & Fort-Mahon-Plage, site sp. Lge, hdg/mkd pitch, pt shd; wc (some cont); mv service pnt; chem disp; shwrs inc; el pnts (6A); gas; lndtte; shop; tradsmn; snacks; bar; playgrnd; htd, covrd pool; sand beach 2km; games area; sailing, fishing, golf nr; cycle hire; entmnt; child entmnt; 50% statics; dogs €3; phone; Eng spkn; adv bkg; cc acc; red low ssn/long stay/ CCI. "Discount voucher given on departure for next visit; modern san facs; conv Marcanterra nature reserve; site staff connect/disconnect el pnt; vg. ♦ 7 Mar-1 Nov. € 28.00 (3 persons)   2007*

See advertisement opposite (top)

FORT MAHON PLAGE *3B2* (8km S Rural) **FLOWER Camping Les Vertes Feuilles, 25 Route de la Plage, Monchaux, 80120 Quend Plage-les-Pins** [03 22 23 55 12; fax 03 22 19 07 52; contact@lesvertesfeuilles.com; www.lesvertesfeuilles.com or www.camphotel.fr] Exit A16 junc 24 onto D32/D940 N. Turn W dir Quend onto D32, site sp. Med, hdg/mkd pitch, pt shd; wc; baby facs; shwrs inc; el pnts (4A) inc; lndtte; shop; snacks; bar; BBQ; playgrnd; htd, covrd pool; sand beach 3km; games area; entmnt; 40% statics; dogs €1.70; adv bkg; quiet; red low ssn. "Pleasant, family site." 21 Mar-9 Nov. € 24.70   2007*

See advertisement on page 313

FORT MOVILLE see Pont Audemer *3D2*

Enjoy great comfort in a warm environment on the border of a protected nature park. Rental of mobile homes from March till November. Covered and heated swimming pool opened from mid May to mid September. Summer animations.

CAMPING LE ROYON
Loisirs ****
1271, route de Quend
80120 FORT–MAHON–PLAGE
Phone: (0033) 03 22 23 40 30
Fax (0033) 03 22 23 65 15

FOUESNANT *2F2* (3km S Rural) **Camping Les Hortensias, La Grande Allée, 29170 Fouesnant** [02 98 56 52 95; fax 02 98 71 55 07; information@campingleshortensias.com; www.campingleshortensias.com] Fr Quimper on D34 dir Fouesnant, then S twds Mousterlin, site sp. Med, hdg pitch, pt shd; htd wc; chem disp; mv service pnt; baby facs; shwrs; el pnts (6A) €2.90; gas; lndtte; tradsmn; snacks; BBQ; playgrnd; games area; games rm; entmnt; TV; dogs €2; phone; adv bkg; quiet. "Guided walks & cycle rides." Easter-30 Sep. € 13.50   2006*

FOUESNANT *2F2* (4km S Coastal) **Camping Le Kervastard, Hent-Kervastard, Beg-Meil, 29170 Fouesnant** [02 98 94 91 52; fax 02 98 94 99 83; camping.le.kervastard@wanadoo.fr; www.campinglekervastard.com] Foll rd fr Quimper thro Beg-Meil. Site sp on R immed after rd bends sharply to L. Med, hdg/mkd pitch, pt shd; wc; chem disp; mv service pnt; baby facs; serviced pitches; shwrs; el pnts (6-10A) €3.20; gas; lndtte; ice; shops adj; playgrnd; htd pool; paddling pool; sand beach 300m; sailing, watersports nr; entmnt; TV; 30% statics; dogs €2; phone; adv bkg (fee); Eng spkn; quiet; cc acc; red low ssn/CCI. "Quiet part of Brittany with several sheltered coves; boat trips to adj towns & islands; excel site." ♦ 25 May-15 Sep. € 20.60   2005*

FOUESNANT *2F2* (5km S Coastal/Rural) **Camping Le Vorlen, Plage de Kerambigorn, Beg-Meil, 29170 Fouesnant** [02 98 94 97 36; fax 02 98 94 97 23; info@vorlen.com; www.vorlen.com] Fr Fouesnant on D45 to Beg-Meil. Fr cent of Beg-Meil turn R at hotel Bon Acceuil & foll sp Kerambigorn; site 300m W of this beach & sp at most rd juncs. V lge, hdg/mkd pitch, pt shd; wc (some cont); mv service pnt; chem disp; baby facs; shwrs inc; el pnts (5-10A) €3; gas; lndtte; ice; shop; tradsmn; snacks; playgrnd; htd pool & paddling pool; waterslide; sand beach 200m; games area; fishing; watersports; golf nr; TV; 15% statics; dogs €2; phone; Eng spkn; adv bkg (dep & fee req) red low ssn; cc acc; CCI. "Pleasant wooded site; gd, modern san facs; friendly; Beg-Meil excel resort; excel site, espec autumn." ♦ 15 May-20 Sep. € 25.00   2007*

See advertisement below

Before we move on, I'm going to fill in some site report forms and post them off to the editor, otherwise they won't arrive in time for the deadline at the end of September.

France

FOUESNANT 2F2 (3km SW Rural) **Camping La Piscine, 51 Hent Kerleya, 29170 Fouesnant** [02 98 56 56 06; fax 02 98 56 57 64; contact@ campingdelapiscine.com; www.campingdela piscine.com] Turn R off D45 on exit Fouesnant onto D145 sp Mousterlin; In 1km L at site sp. Lge, hdg/mkd pitch, pt shd; wc (some cont); chem disp; mv service pnt; baby facs; shwrs inc; el pnts (3-10A) €3-4.40; gas; Indtte; ice; shop; tradsmn; snacks; BBQ; playgrnd; htd pool; paddling pool; waterslide; sand beach 1.5km; lake adj; golf, tennis, mini-golf nrby; games rm; 15% statics; dogs €1.80; Eng spkn; adv bkg; quiet; cc acc; red low ssn; CCI. "Highly rec family-run site; gd walking, cycling." ♦ 15 May-15 Sep. € 22.00   2005*

FOUESNANT 2F2 (4.5km SW Coastal) **Camping Sunêlia L'Atlantique, Route de Mousterlin, 29170 Fouesnant** [02 98 56 14 44; fax 02 98 56 18 67; information@camping-atlantique.fr; www. camping-atlantique.fr] Exit Quimper on D34 sp Fouesnant, take D45 L to Fouesnant & after lge int'section with D44 look for next R to Mousterlin, site sp. Lge, pt shd; wc (some cont); chem disp; mv service pnt; baby facs; shwrs inc; el pnts (6-10A) inc; gas; Indtte; ice; shop; rest; snacks; bar; playgrnd; htd pool; paddling pool; waterslide; sand beach 400m; watersports; lake fishing 200m; tennis; cycle hire; games rm; games area; golf 12km; internet; entmnt; TV rm; 90% statics; no dogs; phone; poss cr; adv bkg rec; cc acc. "San facs poss stretched high ssn." ♦ 30 Apr-11 Sep. € 38.00 (CChq acc)   2004*

FOUESNANT 2F2 (5km SW Coastal) **Camping Kost-Ar-Moor, Pointe de Mousterlin, 29170 Mousterlin** [02 98 56 04 16; fax 02 98 56 65 02; kost-ar-moor@wanadoo.fr; www.camping-kost-ar-moor.com] S fr Fouesnant on D145, site sp. Lge, pt shd; wc (mainly cont); chem disp; shwrs inc; el pnts (5-10A) €2.80-3.60; Indtte; shop; bar; playgrnd; sand beach 300m; lake adj; games area; entmnt; TV; golf, horseriding nr; 10% statics; dog €1.50; phone; adv bkg; quiet. "V clean; helpful owner; gd beach holiday & walking, cycling." ♦ 1 Apr-15 Sep. € 16.00   2006*

FOUESNANT 2F2 (6km SW Coastal) **Camping Le Grand Large, Route du Grand Large, Mousterlin, 29170 Fouesnant** [02 98 56 04 06 or 04 66 73 97 39; fax 02 98 56 58 26; grandlarge@ franceloc.fr; www.camping-franceloc.fr] Site sp fr D145. Lge, hdg/mkd pitch, pt shd; wc; some serviced pitches; shwrs inc; el pnts (5A) inc; gas; Indtte; ice; shop; tradsmn; rest; snacks; bar; playgrnd; htd pool; waterslide; sand beach adj; tennis; TV; watersports; cycle hire; internet; entmnt; cinema high ssn; 30% statics; dogs €3.50; poss cr; quiet; adv bkg ess Jul & Aug; red low ssn; CCI. "Excel, well-kept site." ♦ 31 Mar-16 Sep. € 37.00   2007*

See advertisement above

There aren't many sites open this early in the year. We'd better phone ahead to check that the one we're heading for is actually open.

FOUGERES 2E4 (1.5km E Urban) **Camp Municipal de Paron, Route de la Chapelle-Janson, 35300 Fougères** [02 99 99 40 81; fax 02 99 94 27 94; campingmunicipal35@orange.fr; www.ot-fougeres.fr] Fr A84/E3 take junc 30 then ring rd E twd N12. Turn L at N12 & foll sp. Site on D17 sp R after Carrefour. Well sp on ring rd. Med, hdg pitch, hdstg, pt sl, pt shd; wc; serviced pitches; chem disp; shwrs inc; el pnts (5-10A) €2.60-3.20 (poss rev pol); Indtte; ice; shops 1.5km; hypmkt 800m; tradsmn high ssn; rest 600m; playgrnd; pool 1km; tennis; horseriding adj; dogs; adv bkg; quiet; red low ssn; cc acc; CCI. "Pleasant area; clean, well-kept site; gd facs; gates clsd to cars 2200-0700; conv town cent; tours of 12thC castle; superb Sat mkt; gd value." 1 May-30 Sep. € 8.40   2007*

FOUILLOUX, LE see Montguyon 7C2

⊞**FOURAS** *7A1* (Coastal) **Camp Municipal du Cadoret, Blvd de Chaterny, 17450 Fouras** [05 46 82 19 19 or 05 46 84 67 31; fax 05 46 84 51 59; campinglecadoret@mairie17.com] Fr Rochefort take N137, L onto D937 at Fouras, fork R at sp to site in 1km. Lge, mkd pitch, pt sl, pt shd; wc (some cont); chem disp; baby facs; shwrs inc; el pnts (6-10A) €2.80-4.60; gas; lndtte; shop, snacks 800m; htd pool; paddling pool; sand beach adj; pool; fishing; boating; tennis 1km; golf 5km; 50% statics; dogs €2.20; bus to La Rochelle, Rochefort, ferry to Ile d'Aix; poss cr; adv bkg; CCI. "Vg site & v clean; poorly lit except for wc block; ltd facs low ssn." ♦ € 18.50   2006*

FOURAS *7A1* (1km E Rural) **Camping Domaine Les Charmilles, Route de l'Océan, 17450 Fouras** [05 46 80 00 05 or 0820 20 23 27; fax 02 46 84 02 84 or 0820 20 19 49; charmilles17@wanadoo.fr; www.domainedescharmilles.com] N fr Rochefort on N137, after 2km L onto D937. Site on L in 2km bef ent Fouras. Lge, hdg/mkd pitch, pt shd; htd wc; chem disp; mv service pnt; shwrs inc; el pnts (6A) €4; gas; lndtte; ice; shop 1km; snacks; bar; BBQ (gas); playgrnd; htd, covrd pool; paddling pool; waterslide; sand beach 3km; cycle hire; entmnt; bus to beach high ssn; 20% statics; no dogs; poss cr; adv bkg; cc acc; red long stay/low ssn; CCI. "Gd; some pitches tight for sm o'fits." ♦ 5 May-22 Sep. € 30.00   2007*

FOURAS *7A1* (3km NW Coastal) **Camp Municipal de la Fumée, Pointe de la Fumée, 17450 Fouras** [05 46 84 26 77 or 05 46 84 60 11 (Mairie); fax 05 46 84 51 59] Fr N137, take D214E twd Fouras. Foll sps La Fumée/Ile d'Aix to end of peninsula. Ent on L immed in front of car park ent for ferry. Med, mkd pitch, pt shd; wc; chem disp; shwrs inc; el pnts (3-6A) €1.50-2.90; gas 3km; lndtte; shop & 3km; rest, bar 100m; snacks; pool 2km; sand beach; tennis 2km; boat excursions; fishing; 10% statics; dogs €1.50; phone; poss cr; Eng spkn; quiet; red long stay; CCI. "Great situation; clean site; vg facs; friendly staff; water on 3 sides; excel beaches; conv La Rochelle, Rochefort; ferry to Ile d'Aix; free NH for m'vans; gd." ♦ 1 Mar-31 Oct. € 8.20   2007*

FOURCHAMBAULT see Nevers *4H4*

FOURMIES see Hirson *3C4*

FRAISSE SUR AGOUT see Salvetat sur Agout, La *8F4*

France

FRANGY *9A3* (4km E Rural) **Camping Le Chamaloup, 74270 Contamine-Sarzin** [04 50 77 88 28 or 06 72 80 09 84 (mob); fax 04 50 77 99 79; camping@chamaloup.com] Exit A40 junc 11 onto N508 dir Annecy, thro Frangy. Site sp on L in 10km. Med, hdg/mkd pitch, pt shd; wc; chem disp; serviced pitches; mv service pnt; baby facs; shwrs inc; el pnts (10A) €3.50; gas; lndtte; shop; tradsmn; snacks; bar; BBQ; htd pool; 20% statics; dogs €1.50; poss cr; Eng spkn; some noise fr bar music; adv bkg; cc acc; CCI. "V friendly owners; rv & fish pond (fenced-off) on site." ♦ 1 Jun-15 Sep. € 16.00   2005*

FREJUS *10F4* (2.5km N Urban) **Aire Naturelle La Bravet, Route de Bagnols, 83600 Fréjus** [04 94 40 85 92; fax 04 94 40 83 85] Fr Fréjus N onto D4 dir Bagnols-en-Forêt, site on R in 2.5km. Sm, pt sl, pt shd; wc; chem disp (wc); shwrs €1.60; el pnts €3.50; shops; rest, bar 500m; snacks; htd pool; sand beach 5km; 20% statics; dogs; Eng spkn; quiet; CCI. "Cold shwrs free; san facs poss stretched." ♦ ltd 15 Apr-30 Sep. € 13.50   2006*

FREJUS *10F4* (2.5km N Urban) **Camping Les Pins Parasols, Route des Bagnols, 83600 Fréjus [04 94 40 88 43; fax 04 94 40 81 99; lespinsparasols@wanadoo.fr; www.lespins parasols.com]** Fr A8 exit junc 38 sp Fréjus cent. Fr E'bound dir foll Bagnols sp at 2 rndabts & Fréjus cent/Cais at 3rd. Fr W'bound dir foll Bagnols at 3 rndabts & Fréjus cent/Cais at 4th. Site on L in 500m. Lge, mkd pitch, terr, pt sl, pt shd, htd wc; chem disp; san facs on individual pitches; baby facs; shwrs inc; el pnts (6A) inc; gas; lndtte; shop; tradsmn; rest; snacks; bar; playgrnd; pool; paddling pool; waterslide; sand beach 6km; tennis; entmnt; TV rm; 30% statics; dogs €2.73; phone; adv bkg; quiet; Eng spkn; cc not acc; CCI. "Pleasant, family-run site; tractor to terr pitches; excel." ♦ 5 Apr-27 Sep. € 26.40

2007*

See advertisement on previous page

FREJUS *10F4* (4km N) **Camping Caravaning de Montourey, Route des Bagnols, Chemin du Reyran, 83600 Fréjus [04 94 53 26 41; fax 04 94 53 26 75; montouray@wanadoo.fr; www. campingmontouray.com]** Fr A8 take exit sp Puget-sur-Argens to DN7 (N7) twd Fréjus. Turn onto D4 twd Bagnols. Site on R. Lge, mkd pitch, shd; wc; chem disp; shwrs inc; el pnts (3A) €3; gas; lndtte; shop; rest; snacks; bar; playgrnd; 2 pools; sand beach 5km; tennis; games area; games rm; entmnt; 80% statics; dogs €3; quiet. "Helpful staff." ♦ 1 Apr-30 Sep. € 18.00 (3 persons) 2005*

FREJUS *10F4* (4km NE Coastal) **Domaine du Colombier, 1052 Rue des Combattants d'Afrique du Nord, Départementale 4, 83600 Fréjus [04 94 51 56 01 or 04 94 51 52 38 (LS); fax 04 94 51 55 57; info@clubcolombier.com; www. clubcolombier.com]** Fr E (Nice) on A8 exit junc 38 sp Fréjus. Go strt over 3 rndabts, turn R at 4th rndabt, then R again at next rndabt, site on R. Fr W (Aix-en-Provence) exit A8 junc 38 & turn R at 1st rndabt, then L at intersection. Site on L. Lge, hdg/mkd pitch, hdstg, terr, pt shd; htd wc (some cont); chem disp; 30% serviced pitches; baby facs; shwrs inc; el pnts (16A) inc; gas; lndtte; ice; supmkt; tradsmn; rest; snacks; bar; BBQ (elec); playgrnd; htd pool & waterslides; sand beach 4km; tennis; sports area; games rm; excursions; entmnt high ssn; internet; TV rm; 85% statics/tour ops; dogs €4; poss cr; Eng spkn; adv bkg (dep req + bkg fee); quiet; red low ssn; cc acc; CCI. "Well-organised site in pine forest with exotic trees; excel." ♦ 15 Mar-19 Oct. € 52.00 (3 persons) (CChq acc) 2007*

FREJUS *10F4* (5km W) **Domaine de la Bergerie, Vallée du Fournel, Route du Col du Bougnon, 83520 Roquebrune-sur-Argens [04 98 11 45 45; fax 04 98 11 45 46; info@domainelabergerie.com; www.domainelabergerie.com]** On DN7 (N7) twd Fréjus, turn R onto D7 sp St Aygulf & Roquebrune; after passing Roquebrune, site sp in approx 6km on R. V lge, hdg/mkd pitch, terr, pt sl, pt shd; wc; chem disp; baby facs; sauna; some serviced pitches; shwrs inc; el pnts (5A) inc; gas; lndtte; ice; supmkt; rest; snacks; bar; BBQ (gas); playgrnd; 2 pools (1 htd, covrd); paddling pool; waterslide; sand beach 10 mins drive; jacuzzi; tennis; creche; archery; entmnt; dogs €3.20; statics in site area; poss cr; Eng spkn; adv bkg (bkg fee); CCI. "Open air cinema twice weekly; ltd facs up to mid-Jun; v well-organised site; masses of entmnt/activities for all ages; early bkg ess for summer; excel site." ♦ 30 Apr-17 Sep. € 39.00 (3 persons) 2006*

FREJUS *10F4* (8km W) **Camping Domaine J Bousquet (CC de F), Route de la Bouverie, 83520 Roquebrune-sur-Argens [04 94 45 42 51; fax 04 94 81 61 06; ccdf_bousquet@cegetel.net; www.campingclub.asso.fr]** Exit A8 at Puget-sur-Argens, onto DN7 (N7) dir Le Muy, R onto minor rd at rndabt in about 2km. Site on R after 'Goelia'. Lge, pt sl, shd; wc (cont); chem disp; baby facs; shwrs inc; el pnts (6A) inc; gas; shop; rest; bar; playgrnd; pool; sand beach 10km; entmnt; statics; dogs €2.10; poss cr; adv bkg; quiet but some rd & rlwy noise; CCI. ♦ 1 Jan-3 Nov. € 22.05 2007*

FREJUS *10F4* (8km W) **Camping Le Moulin des Iscles, 83520 Roquebrune-sur-Argens [04 94 45 70 74; fax 04 94 45 46 09; moulin.iscles@wanadoo.fr; www.provence-campings.com/sttropez/moulin-des-iscles]** Twd Fréjus on DN7 (N7), turn R onto D7 to St Aygulf sp Roquebrune. Site on L after passing thro Roquebrune vill. Med, shd; wc (some cont); baby facs; shwrs inc; el pnts (6A) €2.70; lndtte; ice; shop; rest; snacks; bar; playgrnd; sand beach 12km; games rm; internet; entmnt; TV; 10% statics; dogs €1; adv bkg; quiet; red low ssn/long stay; cc acc. "Gd security; helpful owners; excel family site; clean, well-managed." ♦ 1 Apr-30 Sep. € 18.50 (3 persons) (CChq acc) 2004*

FREJUS *10F4* (8km W Rural) **Camping Leï Suves, Quartier du Blavet, 83520 Roquebrune-sur-Argens [04 94 45 43 95; fax 04 94 81 63 13; camping.lei.suves@wanadoo.fr; www.lei-suves.com]** Exit A8 junc 36 at Le Muy, thro Le Muy twd Fréjus on DN7 (N7). After 5km turn L (under a'route, not into Roquebrune-sur-Argens) at sp. Foll sp to camp 4km N of Roquebrune. Lge, mkd pitch, terr, pt shd; wc; chem disp; mv service pnt; baby facs; shwrs inc; el pnts (6A) €4.50; gas; lndtte; ice; shop; rest; snacks; bar; playgrnd; htd pool; paddling pool; sand beach 14km; lake sw & fishing 3km; tennis; games rm; entmnt; child entmnt; excursions; internet; 50% statics; dogs €3.10; phone; Eng spkn; adv bkg; quiet; cc acc; red low ssn; CCI. "V nice location in pine forest; well-maintained, family-run site; facs v clean; excel pool; some sm pitches; conv Côte d'Azur." ♦ 1 Apr-15 Oct. € 34.50 2007*

See advertisement opposite

FREJUS *10F4* (10km W Rural) **Camping Les Pêcheurs, Quartier Verseil, 83520 Roquebrune-sur-Argens [04 94 45 71 25; fax 04 94 81 65 13; info@camping-les-pecheurs.com; www.camping-les-pecheurs.com]** Exit A8 dir Le Muy, onto DN7 (N7) then D7 sp Roquebrune; camp 800m on L (bef bdge over Rv Argens) at ent to vill. Lge, hdg/mkd pitch, hdstg, pt shd; htd wc; chem disp; mv service pnt; baby facs; sauna; shwrs inc; el pnts (6-10A) €4.20-5.20; gas; lndtte; ice; shop; rest; snacks; bar; BBQ (gas/elec); playgrnd; htd pool; sand beach 12km; lake sw, fishing, canoeing adj; spa & jacuzzi; tennis 2km; mini-golf; horseriding; cycle hire 1km; entmnt; child entmnt; wifi internet; TV rm; 45% statics; dogs €3; phone; Eng spkn; adv bkg; quiet; cc acc; red low ssn/CCI. "Pleasant views; v helpful staff; lovely site but getting tired & in need refurb; most pitches no grass due use; some site rds/pitch access bit tight for lge outfits, OK with mover; organised excursions high ssn; popular with families high ssn; historic vill 1km; conv St Tropez, St Raphaël; gd walking, cycling." ♦ 31 Mar-30 Sep. € 32.50 (CChq acc) 2007*

⊞FREJUS *10F4* (3km NW Rural) **Camping Le Fréjus, Route de Bagnols, 83600 Fréjus** [04 94 19 94 60; fax 04 94 19 94 69; contact@ lefrejus.com; www.lefrejus.com] Exit A8 junc 38, at 1st rndabt turn L, then L at 2nd rndabt & L again at 3rd rndabt, Site on R in 200m. Lge, mkd pitch, pt sl, pt terr, pt shd; wc (some cont); chem disp; mv service pnt; baby facs; shwrs inc; el pnts (6A) inc; gas high ssn; Indtte; ice; shop high ssn & 500m; tradsmn, rest & snacks high ssn; bar; playgrnd; pool; waterslide; sand beach 6km; tennis; games rm; entmnt; internet; 10% statics; dogs; site closed 16 Dec-14 Jan; Eng spkn; adv bkg; quiet; cc acc; red low ssn; CCI. "Ideal position for coast bet Cannes & St Tropez; lge pitches." ♦ € 28.00 2005*

This guide relies on site report forms submitted by caravanners like us; we'll do our bit and tell the editor what we think of the campsites we've visited.

FREJUS *10F4* (4km NW) **Camping Village La Baume, Route de Bagnoles, Rue des Combattants d'Afrique du Nord, 83600 Fréjus** [04 94 19 88 88; fax 04 94 19 83 50; reception@ labaume-lapalmeraie.com; www.labaume-lapalmeraie.com] Fr A8 exit junc 38 sp Fréjus cent. Fr E'bound dir foll Bagnols sp at 2 rndabts & Fréjus cent/Cais at 3rd. Fr W'bound dir foll Bagnols at 3 rndabts & Fréjus cent/Cais at 4th. Site on L in 300m. V lge, pt sl, pt shd; htd wc; shwrs; el pnts (6A) inc; gas; Indtte; ice; shop; rest; snacks; bar; playgrnd; 5 pools (1 htd, 2 covrd); sand beach 5km; waterslide; tennis; horseriding; entmnt; many tour ops statics; dogs €4; adv bkg ess Jul/Aug; quiet (except N part of site adj to m'way); 15% red low ssn. ♦ 1 Apr-30 Sep. € 38.00 (3 persons)   2006*

FREJUS *10F4* (5km NW Rural) **Camping Caravaning des Aubrèdes, 408 Chemin des Aubrèdes, 83480 Puget-sur-Argens** [04 94 45 51 46; fax 04 94 45 28 92; campingaubredes@wanadoo.fr; www. campingaubredes.com] Sp on R of DN7 (N7) W fr Fréjus. Fr A8 exit junc 37 dir Fréjus/Puget-sur-Argens. Lge, mkd pitch, pt sl, pt shd; wc (some cont); chem disp; mv service pnt; shwrs inc; el pnts (8A) €4.50; gas; Indtte; ice; shop; tradsmn, rest, snacks, bar high ssn; playgrnd; pool; sand beach 5km; tennis; games rm; entmnt; 30% statics; dogs €2; poss cr; Eng spkn; adv bkg rec high ssn; quiet; cc acc; red long stay/low ssn; CCI. "Excel, esp low ssn; conv m'way." 1 May-15 Sep. € 25.00   2007*

See advertisement opposite (bottom)

FREJUS *10F4* (6km NW Rural) **Camping La Bastiane, 1056 Chemin des Suivières, 83480 Puget-sur-Argens** [04 94 55 55 94; fax 04 94 55 55 93; info@labastiane.com; www. labastiane.com] Exit A8 at junc 37 Puget/Fréjus. At DN7 (N7) turn R dir Le Muy & in 1km turn R immed after 2nd bdge. Foll sp to site. Fr DN7 turn L at traff lts in Puget, site is 2km N of Puget. Lge, hdg/mkd pitch, pt sl, shd; wc; chem disp; baby facs; fam bthrm; shwrs inc; el pnts (6A) inc; Indtte; ice; shop; tradsmn; rest; snacks; bar; BBQ (elec); playgrnd; htd pool; paddling pool; sand beach 7km; watersports; tennis; cycle hire; games area; games rm; cinema; disco; entmnt; internet; TV; car wash area; 40% statics; dogs €4; phone; poss cr; Eng spkn; adv bkg; quiet; cc acc; red long stay/ low ssn/CCI. "Excel; family-run, friendly site." ♦ 21 Mar-18 Oct. € 37.34   2007*

See advertisement opposite (top)

FREJUS *10F4* (6km NW Rural) **Parc Saint James Oasis, Route de la Bouverie, 83480 Puget-sur-Argens** [04 94 45 44 64; fax 04 94 45 44 99; info@ camping-parcsaintjames.com; www.camping-parcsaintjames.com] Exit A8 at junc 37 for Puget-sur-Argens onto DN7 (N7) dir Le Muy, in 2.5km turn R into Rte de la Bouverie, site in 1km on R. Lge, pt shd; wc; shwrs; el pnts; gas; Indtte; shop; tradsmn; rest; snacks; bar; htd pool; tennis; games area; entmnt; child entmnt; all statics; phone; dogs; adv bkg. 5 Apr-27 Sep.   2007*

See advertisement on page 615

FREJUS *10F4* (7km NW Rural) **Camping La Pierre Verte, Route de Bagnols-en-Forêt, 83600 Fréjus** [04 94 40 88 30; fax 04 94 40 75 41; info@ campinglapierreverte.com; www.campingla pierreverte.com] Exit A8 junc 38 onto D4 dir Bagnols-en-Forêt. Site N of military camp. Lge, mkd pitch, hdstg, pt sl, terr, pt shd; wc; chem disp; baby facs; fam bthrm; shwrs inc; el pnts (6A) €4; gas; Indtte; ice; shop; tradsmn; rest; bar; snacks; no BBQ; htd pool; waterslide; sand beach 8km; tennis; games area; cycle hire; mini-golf; games rm; entmnt; child entmnt; internet; TV rm; 50% statics; dogs €3; phone; adv bkg; quiet; Eng spkn; cc acc; red long stay/low ssn; CCI. "Well-situated for local attractions; vg." ♦ 5 Apr-29 Sep. € 28.00   2007*

See advertisement opposite (middle)

FRELAND see Kaysersberg *6F3*

FRENEUSE see Mantes *3D2*

FRESNAY SUR SARTHE *4E1* (Rural) Camp Municipal Le Sans Souci, Ave Victor Hugo, 72130 Fresnay-sur-Sarthe [02 43 97 32 87; fax 02 43 33 75 72; camping-fresney@wanadoo.fr] Fr Alençon S on N138; in 14km at La Hutte turn R on D310 to Fresnay; sp in town on traff lts bef bdge; fr Beaumont-sur-Sarthe NW on D39 to Fresnay. Med, hdg/mkd pitch, pt sl, terr, pt shd; wc; chem disp; shwrs; el pnts (6A) €2.60 (poss rev pol); lndtte; shops high ssn & 500m; htd pool adj; rv adj; fishing; canoe hire; cycle hire; mini-golf; entmnt; dogs €1.05; Eng spkn; adv bkg; quiet; CCI. "V pleasant, clean site; adj to Rv Sarthe; gd rvside pitches; facs poss stretched high ssn; gd cycling; excel value; vg." 1 Apr-30 Sep. € 9.10   2007*

FRETEVAL see Morée *4F2*

FRONCLES BUXIERES *6E1* Camp Municipal Les Deux Ponts, 52320 Froncles-Buxières [03 25 02 38 35 or 03 25 02 31 20 (Mairie); fax 03 25 02 09 80] Fr Chaumont take N67 twd Joinville, ignore sp to Vouécourt but take R turn E on D253 sp Froncles. Site sp fr main rd. Sm, hdg pitch, pt shd; wc (some cont); chem disp (wc); shwrs; el pnts (6A) inc; shops in vill; fishing; adv bkg; quiet. "Pleasant situation; facs clean; friendly; warden calls pm; gd." 15 Mar-15 Oct. € 10.00   2007*

France

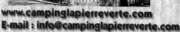

FRONTIGNAN *10F1* (5km NE) **Camping Europe, 31 Route de Frontignan, 34110 Vic La Gardiole** [04 67 78 11 50; europe@village-center.com; www.campingleurope.com www.village-center.com/europe] Exit A9 junc 32 & foll sp N112 dir Sète; in 10km turn L onto D14 to Vic La Gardiole. Lge, pt shd; wc; shwrs inc; el pnts (6A) inc; lndtte; shop; rest; takeaway; bar; playgrnd; 3 pools; aqua gym; beach 2km; archery; games area; games rm; child entmnt; internet; dogs €3; red low ssn. 9 Jun-9 Sep. € 32.00   2007*

> As soon as we get home I'm going to post all these site report forms to the editor for inclusion in next year's guide. I don't want to miss the September deadline.

⊞**FRONTIGNAN** *10F1* (6km NE) **Camping Le Clos Fleuri, 34110 Vic-la-Gardiole** [04 67 78 15 68; fax 04 67 78 77 62; www.camping-clos-fleuri.fr] Fr N9 dir Montpellier take exit 33 for N300 twd Sète. At Sète take N112 for 13 km then R into D114 sp Vic-la-Gardiole. Ignore 1st turn & go round vill & foll sp. Med, hdg/mkd pitch, shd; wc; chem disp; mv service pnt; shwrs inc; el pnts (3-6A) €2.90-3.50; lndtte; shops in ssn or 1km; rest; snacks; bar; pool; shgl beach 2km; 30% statics; dogs €2.20; phone adj; poss cr; adv bkg; quiet but noise fr bar; cc not acc; CCI. "Friendly but not suitable for small children or lge o'fits; cycle hire avail; sheltered fr Mistral." € 15.50 (3 persons)   2004*

FRONTIGNAN *10F1* (1km S Coastal) **Camping Méditerranée, 11 Ave des Vacances, Quartier L'Entrée, 34110 Frontignan-Plage** [tel/fax 04 67 48 12 32 or 04 42 58 11 19 (LS)] 3km fr Sète on N112 to Montpellier, turn R at rlwy bdge, in approx 1km L at x-rds to site. Or on D129 fr Frontignan to Frontignan-Plage site on R 100m past reclamation area. Med, unshd; wc; shwrs inc; el pnts (5-6A) €3.50; lndtte; ice; shop; rest; snacks; bar; playgrnd; pool; sand beach 100m; tennis; lake 500m; games area; entmnt; dogs €1.50; adv bkg rec high ssn; quiet but some rlwy & rd noise. 1 Apr-15 Sep. € 15.00 (3 persons)   2006*

FRONTIGNAN *10F1* (6km S Coastal) **Camping Les Tamaris, 140 Ave d'Ingril, 34110 Frontignan-Plage** [04 67 43 44 77 or 04 78 04 67 92 (LS); fax 04 67 18 97 90; les-tamaris@wanadoo.fr; www.les-tamaris.fr] Fr A9/E15 exit junc 32 St Jean-de-Védas & foll sp Sète. At next rndbt foll sp Sète N112. After approx 8km turn L sp Vic-la-Gardiole onto D114. Cross rlwy & Canal du Rhône. Pass Les Aresquiers-Plages & turn L in 500m, site sp on L in 500m. Fr N on D613 (N113), take N300 to Sète; then N112 to Frontignan-Plage. Lge, hdg pitch, pt shd; wc (some cont); chem disp; mv service pnt; baby facs; shwrs inc; el pnts (10A) inc; lndtte; ice; shop; tradsmn; rest; snacks; bar; BBQ; playgrnd; pool; paddling pool; sand beach adj; watersports; lake fishing; cycle hire; horseriding nrby; archery; weights rm; entmnt; internet; games/TV rm; many statics; dogs €3; phone; poss cr; adv bkg (dep req); quiet; red long stay/low ssn; cc acc; CCI. "Excel, friendly, family-run site on beach; gd san facs; v helpful staff; recep 0800-1900 high ssn; pitches poss tight for lge o'fits; mkt Thu & Sat am." ♦ 1 Apr-27 Sep. € 39.00 (CChq acc) ABS - C11
                                             2007*

FUILLA see Vernet les Bains *8G4*

FUMEL *7D3* (2km E Rural) **FFCC Camping de Condat - Les Catalpas, Route de Cahors, 47500 Fumel** [05 53 71 11 99 or 05 53 71 45 72; fax 05 53 71 36 69] Take D811 fr Fumel E twd Cahors. Clearly sp after Condat. Med, mkd pitch, hdstg, pt sl, pt shd; htd wc; chem disp (wc); mv service pnt; shwrs inc; el pnts (10A) €2; lndtte; ice; shops 1km; rest in vill; snacks; BBQ; playgrnd; pool; fishing adj; entmnt high ssn; 15% statics; dogs; Eng spkn; adv bkg; CCI. "V helpful, friendly owner." ♦ ltd. 1 Apr-31 Oct. € 13.00   2006*

⊞**FUMEL** *7D3* (4km E Rural) **Aire Naturelle Le Valenty (Baillargues), 46700 Soturac** [05 65 36 59 50 or 06 72 57 69 80 (mob); fax 05 65 36 59 50; campingdevalenty@gmail.com; http://members.lycos.nl/brightday] Fr Fumel take D811 dir Cahors. Thro Soturac, site immed on L outside vill. Sm, terr, pt shd; wc; shwrs inc; el pnts (4-10A) inc; gas 3km; ice; lndtte; shops, snacks, bar 2.5km; tradsmn; rest 1km; playgrnd; pool; minigolf; pony rides; games rm; 20% statics; dogs €1; bus 200m; Eng spkn; adv bkg; quiet; CCI. "Delightful CL-type site; helpful owners; tranquil but secure; organic produce for sale." € 13.50   2005*

FUMEL *7D3* (8km E Rural) **Camping Le Ch'Timi, La Roque, 46700 Touzac [05 65 36 52 36; fax 05 65 36 53 23; info@campinglechtimi.com; www.campinglechtimi.com]** Fr N20-E9 at Cahors, turn R at rndabt onto D811 sp Bergerac. In Duravel, take 3rd exit at rndabt, sp Vire-sur-Lot & foll rd to L. After about 3km, cross bdge & turn R at rndabt, sp Touzac. Site on R on rvside, on hill, in about 2km, well sp. Med, mkd pitch, pt sl, pt shd; wc; baby facs; shwrs inc, chem disp; el pnts (6A) inc; gas; lndtte; shop & 700m; tradsmn; rest; snacks; bar; BBQ (charcoal/gas); playgrnd; pool; paddling pool; canoeing; fishing 100m; cycle hire; tennis; archery; games area; entmnt; child entmnt; wifi internet; games/TV rm; 20% statics; dogs €1.70; poss cr; Eng spkn; adv bkg; quiet but poss noisy teenagers high ssn; cc acc; CCI. "Gd position; clean facs, ltd low ssn; Dutch owners; gd local rests; wine-tasting tours; day trips; mkt Puy l'Evêque Tue." 1 Apr-30 Sep. € 20.70 ABS - D05   2007*

FUTEAU see Clermont en Argonne *5D1*

GABARRET *8E2* (E Rural) **Camp Municipal La Chêneraie, 40310 Gabarret [05 58 44 92 62; fax 05 58 44 35 38]** Fr cent of vill take D656 dir Mézin & Nérac. After 300m turn R onto C35, site in 300m on R. Look for bright orange site sp. Sm, hdg pitch, pt sl, pt shd; htd wc; chem disp; shwrs inc; el pnts (10A) €1.70; lndtte; shops, rest, bar 500m; playgrnd; htd pool; adv bkg ess Jul/Aug; quiet; CCI. ♦ 1 Mar-31 Oct. € 8.94   2007*

GABARRET *8E2* (6km SE Rural) **Camping Le Lac de l'Uby, 32150 Barbotan-les-Thermes [05 62 09 53 91; fax 05 62 09 56 97; balia-vacances@wanadoo.fr; www.camping-uby. com]** Fr Eauze take D626 sp Cazaubon, immed bef Intermarché in town, turn R on D656 sp Barbotan. Site on R in 2km. Lge, pt shd; htd wc; chem disp; el pnts (5-10A) €2.50-5; lndtte; ice; shop & 2km; cooking facs; playgrnd; pool; lake sw & beach 300m; fishing; sailing; windsurfing; tennis; games area; cycle hire; entmnt; some statics; dogs €1.80; adv bkg rec; red low ssn; cc acc; CCI. "Lovely lakeside setting; nice pitches nr lake; interesting Bastide towns nrby." ♦ 15 Mar-30 Nov. € 13.00   2007*

⊞**GACE** *4E1* (3km N Rural) **Camping Les Petits Champs, 61230 St Evroult-de-Montfort [tel/fax 02 33 35 67 39; johannes.bouma@wanadoo.fr]** Fr Gacé on D438 (N138) turn L in vill halfway down hill (no L turn but turn R & cross over); site 500m on L, sp. Or fr N turn R at bottom of hill, then as bef. Sm, mkd pitch, terr, unshd; wc; shwrs; el pnts (6A) inc (poss rev pol); tradsmn; playgrnd; Eng spkn; quiet but some rd noise. "Peaceful, welcoming farm site with views; v boggy in wet/winter - pitch at top nr facs block; new san facs planned 2007; gd local walks; gd NH." € 13.00   2007*

GACE *4E1* (200m E Urban) **Camp Municipal Le Pressoir, 61230 Gacé [02 33 35 50 24 or 02 33 35 50 18; fax 02 33 35 92 82; ville.gace@ wanadoo.fr]** Exit A28 junc 16 onto D932/D438; turn off D438 (N138) E opp Intermarché; foll sp. Sm, hdg/mkd pitch, sl, pt shd; wc; chem disp (wc); mv service pnt in vill; shwrs inc; el pnts €2 (poss long lead req); lndry rm; supmkt & rest 100m; playgrnd; rv 500m; poss cr; quiet. "Clean, well-managed site; warden calls am & pm; rec early arrival; sm pitches poss diff for lge vans; ltd el pnts; conv NH fr A28." 1 Jun-1 Sep. € 5.00   2007*

GACILLY, LA *2F3* (200m E Rural) **FFCC Camp Municipal Le Bout du Pont, 35550 Sixt-sur-Aff [02 99 08 10 59 or 02 99 08 10 18 (Mairie); fax 02 99 08 25 38; mairie.lagacilly@wanadoo.fr]** On ent La Gacilly exit rv bdge onto D777 dir Sixt-sur-Aff. Site on L outside town sp. Well sp fr town cent. Sm, mkd pitch, pt shd; wc; mv service pnt; shwrs inc; el pnts (6A) €1.50; shops 500m; tradsmn; rests 200m; playgrnd; rv adj; Eng spkn; quiet. "V pretty town with local artisans; visits to cosmetics factory nrby; vg facs; easy walk to town; poss unreliable opening dates." ♦ ltd. 1 Jun-31 Aug. € 7.50   2006*

GAILLAC *8E4* (8km N Rural) **Camp Municipal au Village, Route de Cordes, 81140 Cahuzac-sur-Vère [05 63 33 91 94 or 05 63 33 90 18 (Mairie); fax 05 63 33 94 03]** Fr Gaillac, take D922 N twd Cordes. Site on L of rd, clearly sp thro vill of Cahuzac. Sm, pt sl, pt shd; wc; shwrs; el pnts (3A) €2.40 (rev pol); shops 500m; rest, snacks, bar nr; playgrnd; pool; tennis; games area; cycle hire; phone; adv bkg; quiet. "Gd, clean site; poss itinerants." 1 Jun-30 Sep. € 8.25   2006*

GAILLAC *8E4* (2km W Urban) **FFCC Camping des Sources, 9 Rue Guynemer, 81600 Gaillac [05 63 57 18 30; fax 05 49 52 28 58]** Exit A68 junc 9 onto D999 then in 3.5km at rndabt turn onto D968 dir Gaillac. In 100m turn R immed past Leclerc petrol stn, then L by Aldi. Site 200m on R, well sp fr town cent. Med, hdg/mkd pitch, hdstg, terr, unshd; htd wc; chem disp; mv service pnt; chem disp (wc); baby facs; shwrs inc; el pnts (10A) €2.50; gas 300m; lndtte; shop 500m; tradsmn; snacks; bar; playgrnd; pool; entmnt; TV; 10% statics; dogs €1; quiet; cc acc (over €15); CCI. "Helpful staff; peaceful site; purpose-made dog-walk area; steep walk to recep & bar but san facs at pitch level; gd touring base Tarn & Albi region; cent of wine area; not suitable lge o'fits; gd." ♦ ltd. 1 Apr-31 Oct. € 12.00   2006*

GALLARGUES LE MONTUEUX see Lunel *10E2*

France

GAMACHES *3B2* (1km NW Urban) **Camping Les Marguerites, Rue Antonin Gombert, 80220 Gamaches [tel/fax 03 22 30 89 51; camping.les. marguerites@wanadoo.fr]** A28 exit 5 onto D1015 dir Eu & Le Treport to Gamaches in 8km. Site sp fr town, 200m fr stadium, Lge, mkd pitch, hdstg, pt shd; wc (cont); chem disp; shwrs inc; el pnts (6-10A) €5-6.50; Indtte; ice; tradsmn; rest; snacks; bar; BBQ; playgrnd; pool; paddling pool; rv adj; games area; 75% statics; dogs; poss cr; quiet; adv bkg; red long stay/CCI. "Run-down & unkempt low ssn; nr forest of Eu, & Somme coast; gd fishing, riding." ♦ ltd. 15 Mar-15 Sep. € 15.00   2006*

GANNAT *9A1* (7km N Rural) **Camp Municipal Champ de la Sioule, Route de Chantelle, 03800 Jenzat [04 70 56 86 35 or 04 70 56 81 77 (Mairie); fax 04 70 56 85 38; mairie-jenzat@pays-allier. com]** D2009 (N9) N fr Gannat for 4.5km, turn L onto D42, site in 3km in Jenzat on R just after rv bdge. Med, pt shd; wc; shwrs inc; el pnts (6-10) €1.90-2.95; ice; Indtte; shops 250m; playgrnd; rv sw adj; Eng spkn; spotless facs; quiet; CCI. "Pleasant site on rv bank; clean facs, poss stretched high ssn; helpful warden; muddy after heavy rain." ♦ ltd. 14 Apr-22 Sep. € 8.60   2007*

GANNAT *9A1* (1km SW Rural) **Camp Municipal Le Mont Libre, 10 Route de la Bâtisse, 03800 Gannat [04 70 90 12 16 or 06 73 86 04 95 (mob); fax 04 70 90 12 16; camping.gannat@wanadoo. fr; www.ville-gannat.fr]** App Gannat fr S on N9, L 2km bef town, 1st R behind Stade, foll sp to L 1st R uphill. Med, pt sl, terr, pt shd; wc; chem disp; mv service pnt; el pnts (10A) €2.25; ice; Indtte; shop & 500m, supmkt 1km; tradsmn; playgrnd; sm pool; rv 5km; games area; games/TV rm; some statics; poss cr; adv bkg; quiet; cc acc. "Delightful situation; pretty site; spotless facs; helpful warden; walking dist to town facs & excel rest; popular, busy NH." ♦ 1 Apr-31 Oct. € 9.70   2007*

> The opening dates and prices on this campsite have changed. I'll send a site report form to the editor for the next edition of the guide.

GANNAT *9A1* (10km W) **Camp Municipal Les Nières, 03450 Ebreuil [04 70 90 70 60 or 04 70 90 71 33 (Mairie); mairie-ebreuil@wanadoo. fr]** Site 1km SW of Ebreuil, sp fr D915. Sm, shd; wc (cont); chem disp; shwrs; el pnts (4-12A) €1.75-4.15; Indtte; shops 1km; snacks; playgrnd; fishing; access to rv; quiet. "NH only; barrier at ent to site locked until 0900; warden calls pm; sh walk into vill." 1 May-30 Sep. € 7.80   2005*

GANNAT *9A1* (10km W Rural) **Camping La Filature de la Sioule, Route de Chouvigny, 03450 Ebreuil [04 70 90 72 01; camping.filature@libertysurf.fr; www.campingfilature.com]** Fr A71 exit 12 (avoid 12.1); foll sp to Ebreuil N 500m, then W for 5km thro vill. Turn W onto D915 dir Chouvigny, site in 1km. Med, hdg/mkd pitch, pt shd; wc (some cont); chem disp; mv service pnt 800m; baby facs; shwrs inc; el pnts (6A) €3; gas; Indtte; shop; tradsmn high ssn; snacks; bar; BBQ; playgrnd; rv sw; tennis 800m; canoes; cycle hire; table tennis; troutfishing; horseriding; TV rm; dogs free; Eng spkn; adv bkg (dep req); v quiet; cc acc; red long stay/ low ssn; CCI. "Nice situation; peaceful site; lge pitches; v helpful British owners; v clean facs, ltd low ssn; vg value take-away (gd home cooking); vg walking area; excel." ♦ 31 Mar-1 Oct. € 17.00   2007*

See advertisement

GAP *9D3* (1.5km N Rural) **Camping Alpes-Dauphiné, Route Napoléon, 05000 Gap [04 92 51 29 95; fax 04 92 53 58 42; info@ alpesdauphine.com; www.alpesdauphine.com]** On N85, sp. Med, mkd pitch, some hdstg, pt sl; terr, pt shd; htd wc; chem disp; mv service pnt; baby facs; shwrs inc; el pnts (6A) €3; gas; Indtte; ice; shop; tradsmn; vg rest; snacks; bar; playgrnd; htd pool; paddling pool; games area; sat TV; 20% statics; dogs €2.10; phone; poss cr; Eng spkn; adv bkg rec high ssn; quiet; cc acc; red low ssn; CCI. "M'vans need levellers; pleasant site; new san facs (2007); excel cent for touring area; gd mountain views; conv NH." ♦ 1 Apr-1 Nov. € 18.10 (CChq acc)   2006*

GAP *9D3* (10km S Rural) **Camp Municipal Le Chêne, Route de Marsailles, 05130 Tallard [04 92 54 10 14 (Mairie)]** Fr S take N85 twds Gap; turn R at traff lts onto D942; site on R after 3km. Fr Gap take N85 S; turn L at traff lts, D942; site on R 3km. Med, hdstg, sl, terr, pt shd; wc (some cont); shwrs inc; el pnts (6A) €4; Indtte; shop 2km; playgrnd; htd pool; tennis; BBQ; entmnts; phone; dogs; adv bkg; CCI. "Poss unsuitable for lgs o'fits, sm pitches." 15 Jun-31 Aug. € 10.00   2005*

GAP *9D3* (8km SW Rural) **Camping Les Bonnets, Le Haut-du-Village, 05000 Neffes [04 92 57 93 89; fax 04 92 57 94 61; www.alpes-campings.com]** N85 SW fr Gap, turn R onto D46, site sp 1km fr vill. Med, mkd pitch, pt shd; htd wc; baby facs; shwrs; el pnts (10A) €3.70; Indtte; shop; supmkt 5km; rest, bar 1km; playgrnd; pool; fishing 3km; games area; entmnt; TV rm; quiet. "Well-maintained farm site in beautiful area; excel pool; friendly owner." 1 May-30 Sep. € 11.00   2004*

GARDONNE see Bergerac *7C3*

GASSIN see St Tropez *10F4*

Camping Filature de la Sioule

F-03450 Ebreuil – Phone + 33 (0)4 70 90 72 01
www.campingfilature.com

Four star campsite in orchard setting beside one of the finest trout rivers in France. Level grassy pitches with good shade. Clean facilities, quiet location. 6 km from exit 12 of A 71 (Paris – Clermond-Ferrand). Shop. Excellent bar and take-away from June onwards. Ideal country for walking and cycling. Fishing, canoeing and swimming in the river. 1 km from Ebreuil town centre (easy walk). Sioule gorges at 5 km. REDUCED LOW SEASON PRICES, UP TO 50% AFTER 6 NIGHTS. SPECIAL RATES FOR DAILY MEALS OVER 4 NIGHTS.

Good starting point to visit Vichy, the volcano park and Vulcania and to explore the Auvergne. Good for long or short stay. Open from 31/03 till 01/10.

GASTES 7D1 (Rural) **FFCC Camping Les Prés Verts**, Ave du Lac, 40160 Gastes [tel/fax 05 58 09 74 11; camping@presverts.net; www. presverts.net] S fr Bordeaux on N10 exit junc 17 & turn W on D43 to Parentis-en-Born & foll D652 to Gastes; site sp in vill. Med, shd; wc; shwrs inc; el pnts (10A) €2.95; gas; lndtte; ice; shop; rest; snacks; bar; playgrnd; htd pool; lake sw; watersports; fishing; cycle hire; tennis; statics; dogs €2; adv bkg; quiet; CCI. "Gd walking; important ecological site." 1 Mar-30 Nov. € 14.30   2005*

GASTES 7D1 (3km SW Rural) **Camping La Réserve**, 1229 Ave Félix Ducourneau, 40160 Gastes [05 58 09 74 79 or 05 58 09 79 23; fax 05 58 09 78 71; lareserve@siblu.fr; www.siblu. com] At traff lts in cent Parentis-en-Born, turn L sp Pontenx & Gastes on D652. After 3km turn R dir Gastes, Ste Eulalie & Mimizan-Plage. Cont onto rndabt & take 2nd exit D652, then turn immed R sp La Réserve. Site sp. V lge, pt shd; wc; chem disp; shwrs inc; el pnts (6A) inc; gas; lndtte; rest; snacks; bar; ice; shop; BBQ (gas only); playgrnd; pools (l htd, covrd); waterslide; lake sw & private beach adj; watersports high ssn; windsurfing; sand beach 25km; cycle hire; tennis; games area; archery; mini-golf; entmnt; child entmnt; 70% statics; no dogs; Eng spkn; adv bkg ess high ssn; cc acc; red low ssn; CCI. "Situated in pine forest & by lakeside; lge pitches; watersports & sailing school avail; children's club inc in site fee." ♦ 29 Apr-23 Sep. € 39.00   2005*

GAUDONVILLE see St Clar 8E3

GAUGEAC see Monpazier 7D3

GAVARNIE 8G2 (2km N Rural) **Camping Le Pain de Sucre**, 65120 Gavarnie [tel/fax 05 62 92 47 55 or 06 75 30 64 22 (mob); info@camping-gavarnie. com; www.camping-gavarnie.com] N of Gavarnie, across rv by sm bdge; clearly visible & sp fr rd. Med, pt shd; wc; mv service pnt; shwrs inc; el pnts (2-10A) €1.75-5.95; ice; lndtte; shops, rest, snacks, bar 3km; BBQ; playgrnd; dogs €1.55; quiet; cc acc. "Gd location; gd facs; access to national park; vg." 1 Jun-30 Sep & 15 Dec-15 Apr. € 11.60   2005*

GEMAINGOUTTE see St Die 6E3

GEMOZAC 7B2 (400m W) **Camp Municipal**, Place de Champ de Foire, 17260 Gémozac [05 46 94 50 16; fax 05 46 94 16 25] Exit A10 junc 36 (or turn W off off N137) onto D732 sp Gémozac. In 7km foll site sp. Turn L immed after Elan/Renault garage at end of vill. Sm, mkd pitch, pt shd; wc; chem disp; mv service pnt adj; baby facs; shwrs inc; el pnts (10A) inc (poss rev pol); ice; lndtte; shop, pizzeria & snacks 500m; tradsmn; rest & bar 100m; BBQ; htd pool adj; dogs; adv bkg; Eng spkn; phone in vill; cc not acc; quiet; CCI. "Excel site; pool free to campers; pleasant sm town; gate clsd 1300-1600; no twin-axles." 15 Jun-2 Sep. € 12.45   2006*

GENETS see Avranches 2E4

GENOUILLE 7A2 (Rural) **Camp Municipal L'Etang des Rosées**, 17430 Genouillé [05 46 27 70 01 or 05 46 27 72 13 (Mairie); fax 05 46 27 89 03] Fr Surgères SW on D911 for 11km. At rndabt turn sharp L D112, site sp on R after 3km. Sm, mkd pitch, pt sl, pt shd; wc; own san; shwrs inc; el pnts (15A) €2.10; lndtte; shops 700m; tradsmn; rest, snacks, bar 1km; playgrnd; lake fishing adj; adv bkg; quiet; CCI. "Rural site away fr main tourist area; facs clean but ltd in number." 21 Jun-11 Sep. € 8.00   2004*

GERARDMER See also sites listed under Corcieux, Granges-sur-Vologne, La Bresse and Le Tholy.

⊞**GERARDMER** 6F3 (3km E Rural) **Camp Municipal du Domaine de Longemer**, 121 Route de la Plage, 88400 Xonrupt-Longemer [03 29 63 07 30; fax 03 29 63 27 10; camping. dudomaine@wanadoo.fr] Fr W thro Gérardmer on D417. immed after sp Xonrupt-Longemer turn R & cont thro vill. Site 1st one; turn L over bdge. App fr E (Colmar), turn L opp Hôtel du Lac de Longemer. Site on both sides of rd. V lge, pt shd; htd wc; mv service pnt; shwrs inc; el pnts (6A) €2.85; shop; rest; snacks; bar; playgrnd; lake sw; fishing; x-country skiing; 10% statics; phone; poss cr; quiet; 5% red for long stays; CCI. "Attractive, clean lakeside site in Vosges; pitches by lake poss unkempt; gd walking." € 10.00   2006*

France

⊞GERARDMER *6F3* (4km E Rural) **Camping La Verte-Vallée, 4092 Route du Lac, Retournemer, 88400 Xonrupt-Longemer [tel/fax 03 29 63 21 77]** Exit Gérardmer on D417 for Colmar/St Dié. After 3km at junc turn R. Cont on D417 for Colmar. After 3km turn R opp Hôtel du Lac on D67 for Retournemer. Keep to N side of lake & site 300m past lake at junc on R. Med, mkd pitch, pt sl, shd; htd wc (some cont); baby facs; shwrs inc; el pnts (2-6A) €3-6.10; gas; lndtte; shops 2km; tradsmn; rest, bar 1km; htd pool; playgrnd; TV; lake sw 300m; fishing; games rm; 50% statics; dogs €1; poss cr; adv bkg; quiet. "Beautiful scenery, many walks." ♦ € 11.00   2004*

GERARDMER *6F3* (6km E) **Camping Belle Rive, 88400 Xonrupt-Longemer [03 29 63 31 12]** W fr Gérardmer on D417 (sp Colmar) in approx 1km over bdge, turn R at T-junc (still on D417). After 2km turn R opp Hôtel du Lac de Longemer & immed R round W side of lake to S bank where site located. Med, mkd pitch, pt sl, terr, pt shd; wc; chem disp; shwrs €0.70; el pnts (1-3A) €1-2; lndry rm; shops adj & 2km; snacks; bar adj; playgrnd; pool 8km; lake sw adj; 10% statics; dogs €0.80; phone adj; quiet. "Clean san facs; lakeside beautiful area; lovely position in heart of Vosges." 15 May-15 Sep. € 8.00   2004*

GERARDMER *6F3* (6km E Rural) **Camping Les Jonquilles, Route du Lac, 88400 Xonrupt-Longemer [03 29 63 34 01; fax 03 29 60 09 28]** Sp off D417 SE of Xonrupt-Longemer. Fr W thro Gérardmer on D417 (sp Colmar) in approx 1km over bdge & turn R at T-junc (still on D417). After 3km turn R opp Hôtel du Lac de Longemer & almost immed R round W end of lake for 500m to T-junc, turn L, site on S bank 1km. Lge, mkd pitch, pt sl, unshd; wc (some cont); chem disp; mv service pnt; baby facs; shwrs inc; el pnts (6-10A) €2.80-4.70; gas; lndtte; shop; rest; snacks; bar; playgrnd; lake beach & sw adj; fishing; sailing; entmnt; TV; few statics; dogs €1.10; phone; bus 1km; Eng spkn; adv bkg (dep req); quiet but some noise fr entmnt at night; cc acc; CCI. "Friendly, well-maintained, family-run site; gd views; poss uneven pitches; excel for Alsace wine region/Colmar." ♦ 15 Apr-10 Oct. € 14.80   2006*

GERARDMER *6F3* (1.5km SW) **Camping Les Sapins, 18 Chemin de Sapois, 88400 Gérardmer [03 29 63 15 01; fax 03 29 60 03 30]** Nr lakeside site Camping Ramberchamp, 150m up C17. Rd sp Col de Sapois. On S side of lake. Med, pt shd; wc; shwrs inc; el pnts (4-6A) €2.80-4.70; ice; sm shop; rest; snacks; bar; playgrnd; games area; TV rm; lake with beach 200m; fishing & watersports adj; quiet; red low ssn; adv bkg rec. "Nice, comfortable site; san facs need refurb; lge pitches but overlooked by sports stadium; no lake views." 1 Apr-30 Sep. € 11.50   2004*

GERAUDOT *6E1* (1km E Rural) **Camp Departmental L'Epine aux Moines, 10220 Géraudot [tel/fax 03 25 41 24 36]** Exit A26 at junc 23 onto D619 (N19) to Lusigny-sur-Barse; foll sp Parc de la Forêt d'Orient. Turn N along lake to site. Or fr Troyes D960 E. At Rouilly head S on D43 sp Géraudot. Site 1km E of vill. Lge, mkd pitch, pt sl, pt shd; htd wc (most cont); chem disp; mv service pnt; shwrs inc; el pnts (4-6A) €3.10 (poss rev pol); lndtte; ice; shop 8km; tradsmn; rest; snacks; bar; playgrnd; lake sw adj; boat hire; dogs €0.90; poss cr; adv bkg; cc acc; CCI. "V quiet, well-maintained site; attractive area; friendly warden; ltd facs low ssn; poss mosquitoes; gd walking & cycle paths; nr bird observatory; lovely vill; conv NH; excel." 15 Mar-15 Oct. € 11.80   2007*

GERE BELESTEN see Laruns *8G2*

GERSTHEIM *6E3* (1km NE Rural) **Camp Municipal au Clair Ruisseau, Rue de Ried, 67150 Gerstheim [03 88 98 30 04; fax 03 88 98 43 26; info@ clairruisseau.com; www.clairruisseau.com]** Site sp on D924. Med, mkd pitch; pt shd; wc; mv service pnt; shwrs inc; el pnts (16A) €3.40; gas; shop; playgrnd; 60% statics; dogs €1; quiet. 30 Mar-28 Oct. € 12.10   2006*

GETS, LES see Morzine *9A3*

⊞ *Site open all year*   *Help us to update this guide*

Les Bois du Bardelet ★★★★

Loire Valley
Poilly - 45500 GIEN
Tel. 00 33/238 67 47 39 - Fax. 00 33/238 38 27 16
Internet: www.bardelet.com
E-mail: contact@bardelet.com

2 lakes, 3 swimming pools, relaxing area
with indoor pool, jacuzzi, fitness room. Children
aquatic play area with paddling indoor pool.
Other activities : fishing, canoe, tennis,
crazy golf, ping pong.

Weekly and weekend-renting. Chalets and mobile-homes.

Sunêlia

France

GEX *9A3* (Urban) **FFCC Camp Municipal Les Genêts, 400 Ave des Alpes, 01170 Gex [04 50 41 61 46 or 04 50 42 63 00 (Mairie); fax 04 50 41 68 77; camp-gex-@cc-pas-de-gex.fr; www.pays-de-gex.org]** Fr all dir head for 'Centre Ville'; at rndabt take D984 twd Divonne/Lausanne. Site sp to R (tight turn) after rlwy sheds (poor sp in town) & Musée Sapeurs Pompiers. Med, hdg pitch, hdstg, pt sl, pt shd; wc (some cont); chem disp; shwrs inc; el pnts (16A) €2.80; gas 500m; lndtte; shops 500m; tradsmn; snacks; bar; playgrnd; htd pool; games area; TV rm; dogs €0.90; phone; gates clsd 2200-0800; dep req for barrier key; Eng spkn; adv bkg; quiet; cc acc; CCI. "Excel site; excel games facs/playgrnd; v friendly, helpful staff; v clean facs; quiet with lots of privacy; conv Geneva." ♦ 1 Jun-19 Sep. € 12.20   2007*

GIBLES see Clayette, La *9A2*

GICQ, LE see Matha *7B2*

GIEN *4G3* (1km SW Urban) **Camping Touristique de Gien, Rue des Iris, 45500 Poilly-lez-Gien [02 38 67 12 50; fax 02 38 67 12 18; camping-gien@wanadoo.fr; www.camping-gien.com]** Off D952 Orléans-Nevers rd; turn R over old rv bdge in Gien & then R again; site on R on Rv Loire. Lge, hdg/mkd pitch, hdstg, pt sl, pt shd; htd wc; chem disp; mv service pnt; baby facs; shwrs inc; el pnts (4-10A) €3.50-5; gas adj; lndtte; shop; rest; snacks; bar adj; BBQ; playgrnd; covrd pool; paddling pool; lake sw 3km; canoeing; tennis; cycle hire; mini-golf; games rm; entmnt; internet; TV rm; 20% statics; dogs €2; phone; adv bkg; Eng spkn; quiet; cc acc; red long stay/CCI. "Lovely rvside site but no sw allowed; porcelain factory 'seconds' in town; gd san facs." ♦ 3 Mar-10 Nov. € 17.50   2007*

See advertisement opposite

GIEN *4G3* (5km SW Rural) **Domaine Les Bois du Bardelet, Route de Bourges, 45500 Poilly-lez-Gien [02 38 67 47 39; fax 02 38 38 27 16; contact@bardelet.com; www.bardelet.com]** Fr Gien take D940 dir Bourges; turn R onto D53 then R again onto unclassified rd to go back across D940; foll sp to site on L side of this rd. Site well sp fr D940. Lge, hdg/mkd pitch, some hdstg, pt shd; htd wc; chem disp; mv service pnt; 50% serviced pitches; baby facs; shwrs inc; el pnts (6A) inc (some rev pol); gas; lndtte; shop; rest; snacks; bar; BBQ; playgrnd; 3 pools (2 htd/covrd); paddling pool; jacuzzi; lake fishing; canoeing; tennis; games area; fitness rm; cycle hire; archery; entmnt; child entmnt; internet; TV; 17% statics; dogs €4; phone; adv bkg (dep req + bkg fee); quiet; cc acc; red snr citizen/low ssn/long stay; red long; CCI. "Friendly welcome; trips & guided walks arranged; modern facs; full site facs all ssn; o'door pools beautiful; v pleasant site." ♦ 1 Apr-30 Sep. € 30.90 (CChq acc) ABS - L05
          2007*

See advertisement above

GIGNAC *10F1* (1km NE Rural) **Camp Municipal La Meuse, Chemain de la Meuse, Route d'Aniane, 34150 Gignac [04 67 57 92 97; camping.meuse@wanadoo.fr; http://ville-gignac.fr]** Exit A75 onto A750 sp Montpellier & Gignac. In Gignac foll D32 sp Aniane. Site on L in 1km just past Aldi supmkt. Med, hdg pitch, pt shd; wc; chem disp; mv service pnt; shwrs inc; el pnts (16A) €2.20; gas 1km; lndtte; shop 1km; bar; rv sw; tennis; dogs €1.50; Eng spkn; adv bkg; quiet; no cc acc; red long stay; CCI. "Easy access; lge pitches; friendly, clean, v pleasant; gd rest in town; excel supmkt in town." ♦ ltd. 1 Jun-30 Sep. € 12.00   2007*

GIGNAC *10F1* (1.5km W Rural) **Camping du Pont, 730 Blvd Moulin, 34150 Gignac [tel/fax 04 67 57 52 40; www.campingdupont.com]** Foll sp fr town cent. Sm, pt shd; wc; chem disp; shwrs inc; el pnts (6A) €2.70; ice; lndtte; shop; tradsmn; rest; snacks; BBQ; playgrnd; pool; fishing; tennis adj; entmnt; 20% statics; dogs €2; adv bkg; quiet. "Friendly welcome." ♦ 1 Apr-30 Sep. € 21.50
          2006*

GIGNAC *10F1* (5km W Rural) **Camping Le Septimanien, Route de Cambous, 34725 St André-de-Sangonis [04 67 57 84 23; fax 04 67 57 54 78; leseptimanien@aol.com; www. camping-leseptimanien.com]** Exit A75 junc 57. At rndabt on E side of a'route take D128 to Brignac. In Brignac turn L at T-junc, then fork R on D4 twd St André-de-Sangonis. Site on R in 3km. Med, hdg pitch, pt shd; wc; chem disp; shwrs inc; el pnts (6A) inc; gas; lndtte; ice; shop & 1km; tradsmn; rest; snacks; bar; playgrnd; pool; paddling pool; entmnt; 15% statics; dogs €1.70; phone; adv bkg; quiet; cc acc; CCI. "Well-organised site; vg sh stay/NH." ♦ ltd. 1 Apr-15 Oct. € 18.00   2005*

GIGNY SUR SAONE see Sennecey le Grand *6H1*

⊞**GISAY LA COUDRE** *3D2* (500m S Rural) **Aire Communale La Villette, 27330 Gisay-la-Coudre [02 32 44 38 86; mairie.gisaylacoudre@wanadoo. fr]** Turn S of N138 at Bernay onto D833 to La Barre-en-Ouche. In town turn R onto D49 dir Broglie & in 200m turn L onto D35, site on R in 3km, sp. M'vans only. Sm, hdstg, unshd; own san; chem disp; mv service pnt; el pnts €2 for 2 hrs; water €2 for 100 litres; shop, rest, snacks, bar 200m; quiet. "Payment for services with jeton obtainable fr Bar-Rest La Tortue 500m further on fr site; car/ c'vans probably acc; vg NH."   2007*

GISORS *3D3* (7km SW Rural) **Camp Municipal de l'Aulnaie, Rue du Fond-de-l'Aulnaie, 27720 Dangu [02 32 55 43 42]** On ent Gisors fr all dirs, take ring rd & exit dir Vernon D10, then L onto D181 dir Dangu. Site on L bef Dangu. Site sp fr D10. NB speed humps. Lge, mkd pitch, pt shd; htd wc; chem disp; mv service pnt; shwrs inc; el pnts (10A) €2.60; gas; lndtte; tradsmn; rest, snacks, bar 800m; playgrnd; lake sw; fishing; 90% statics; office clsd 1200-1500; dogs €2.50; poss cr; adv bkg; some rd noise; CCI. "Conv Giverny & Gisors local attractions; Gisors attractive town; lakeside site." ♦ ltd. 24 Mar-24 Oct. € 12.00   2007*

⊞**GIVET** *5B1* (500m N Urban) **Caravaning Municipal La Ballastière, 16 Rue Berthelot, 08600 Givet [03 24 42 30 20; fax 03 24 40 10 70]** Site at N end of town on lake. Foll 'Caravaning' sp fr W end of rv bdge or Dinant rd. Med, some hdg pitch, hdstg, pt shd; htd wc; chem disp; shwrs; el pnts (10A) inc; lndtte; shop, rest, snacks, bar 1km; pool adj; 70% statics; dogs €0.86; quiet; CCI. "Nr Rv Meuse; adj sports & watersports complex; picturesque town; gd." € 7.92   2006*

GIVET *5B1* (2km SW Rural) **Camping Le Sanglier, Givet-la-Meuse, 08600 Rancennes [03 24 42 72 61]** Off D949 Givet to Beauraing rd. Immed after x-ing rv bdge turn R. Turn R again foll sp to site at end narr access rd on rvside. Sm, pt sl, pt shd; wc; chem disp; shwrs €1.50; el pnts (4A) inc; shop 2km; snacks; rv sw; fishing; watersports; 60% statics; phone; Eng spkn; adv bkg; quiet; CCI. "Gd touring base; clean, basic facs; gd NH." 1 May-30 Sep. € 8.60   2005*

GIVORS *9B2* (7km NW) **Camp Municipal de la Trillonnière, Monts du Lyonnais, Rue de la Loire, 69440 Mornant [04 78 44 16 47 or 04 78 44 00 46 (Mairie); fax 04 78 44 91 70; mairiemornant@wanadoo.fr; www.ville-mornant. fr]** Exit A7 at Givors & foll sp for St Etienne via D488, thro Givors onto D2 till sp seen for Mornant via D34, cont on D34 up hill for 7km, cross D42 & cont 1km to o'skts of Mornant, L at junc island & site on L. Med, pt sl, pt shd; wc; chem disp; shwrs; el pnts (10A) €3.60; shops, rest, snacks bar 500m; pool 250m; dogs €1; adv bkg; some rd noise; access for vans 0815-1015 & 1700-2200. 1 May-30 Sep. € 8.60   2007*

GIVRAND see St Gilles Croix de Vie *2H3*

GIVRE, LE *7A1* (Rural) **Camping Aire Naturelle La Grisse (Martineau), 85540 Le Givre [02 51 30 83 03; lagrisse@wanadoo.fr]** Fr Luçon take D949 & turn L at junc with D747 (La Tranche rd). Turn L in 3km & foll sps. Sm, pt shd; wc; chem disp; shwrs inc; el pnts (5A) €3; lndry rm; sand beach 10km; dogs €2; Eng spkn; adv bkg; cc not acc; CCI. "Peaceful, friendly, farm site; lge pitches; clean, modern facs; beautiful area/beach; gd for dogs." ♦ ltd. 15 Apr-15 Oct. € 13.00   2007*

GIVRY EN ARGONNE *5D1* (N Rural) **Camp Municipal Val d'Ante, 51330 Givry-en-Argonne [03 26 60 04 15 or 03 26 60 01 59 (Mairie); fax 03 26 60 18 22; mairie.givryenargonne@wanadoo. fr]** Exit A4 junc 29 at Ste Menéhould; S on D382 to Givry-en-Argonne; site sp on R. Sm, pt sl, pt shd; wc (some cont); chem disp; shwrs inc; el pnts (3A) €1.41; shops 200m; playgrnd; shgl lake beach sw; boats for hire adj; dogs €0.77; poss cr; quiet; no cc acc. "Attractive site adj to lake; basic but pleasant; san facs old but clean; warden calls am & pm; gd bird-watching; not suitable lge m'vans." 1 May-15 Sep. € 4.95   2005*

GLUIRAS see Ollières sur Eyrieux, Les *9D2*

GONDREXANGE see Héming *6E3*

GONDRIN *8E2* (E Rural) **FFCC Camping Le Pardaillan, Rue du Pardaillon, 32330 Gondrin-en-Armagnac [05 62 29 16 69; fax 05 62 29 11 82; camplepardaillan@wanadoo.fr;www.camping-le-pardaillan.com]** Fr Condom take D931 S for 12km to Gondrin. Site clearly sp. Med, hdg/mkd pitch, hdstg, pt shd; htd wc; chem disp; mv service pnt; baby facs; shwrs inc; el pnts (6-10A) inc; gas; ice; lndtte; shop; tradsmn; rest; snacks; bar; playgrnd; paddling pool; lake sw adj; games rm; entmnt; TV rm; many statics; dogs €2; phone; poss cr; Eng spkn; adv bkg; dep req; CCI. "Excel site; lovely region; red facs & NH only low ssn; highly rec." ♦ 30 Apr-11 Sep. € 21.00   2006*

GORDES *10E2* (2km N Rural) **Camping Les Sources, Route de Murs, 84220 Gordes [04 90 71 12 48; fax 04 90 72 09 43; www. campingdessources.com]** Fr A7 junc 24, E on D973; then D22; then N100 twds Apt. After 18km at Coustellet turn N onto D2 then L on D15 twds Murs; site on L in 2km beyond Gordes. Med, mkd pitch, hdstg, terr, pt shd; wc (some cont); chem disp; mv service pnt; baby facs; shwrs inc; el pnts (6A) €4.10 (long lead poss req); lndtte; shop & 2km; rest; snacks; takeaway; bar; playgrnd; pool; cycles hire; games areas; games rm; entmnt; child entmnt; 25% statics; dogs €4; Eng spkn; adv bkg; quiet; red long stay; cc acc; CCI. "Lovely location & views; access rd narr (300m); modern, spotless san facs; friendly staff; security barriers with 24 hr supervision; sm pitches v diff lge o'fits; ask for easy pitch & inspect on foot; some steep rds to pitches as site on hillside; lovely pool; gd walking; mkt Tues." 1 Apr-30 Sep. € 19.70   2007*

GORDES *10E2* (10km NE Rural) **Camp Municipal Les Chalottes, 84220 Murs [04 90 72 60 84 or 04 90 72 60 00 (Mairie); fax 04 90 72 61 73]** W on N100 fr Avignon, L onto D2 at Coustellet. Do not turn L sp Gordes but cont 3.5km & turn L D102 sp Joucas/Mura. Or fr Apt twd Avignon N100, R to D4 after 4km site sp to Murs. Do not app site thro Gordes. NB 2.5t weight restriction on southern app. Sm, mkd pitch, pt sl, pt shd; wc (some cont); chem disp; shwrs inc; el pnts (16A) €2; tradsmn; playgrnd; dogs; phone; quiet; CCI. "Peaceful, pretty site among pines; gd walks; vill 1.8km." Easter-15 Sep. € 12.00   2007*

GOUAREC *2E3* (3km S Rural) **Camping Tost Aven, Au Bout du Pont, Plélauff, 22570 Gouarec [02 96 24 85 42; baxter.david@wanadoo.fr]** Sp fr town cent on D5 S. Med, mkd pitch, pt shd; wc (some cont); chem disp; shwrs inc; el pnts (10A) €2.25; gas adj; lndry rm; ice; shops adj; supmkt nr; rest, snacks, bar 500m; BBQ; sm playgrnd; sw adj (rv & canal); cycle, canoe hire; entmnt; dogs; bus 200m; poss cr; Eng spkn; adv bkg; quiet. "Helpful, friendly British owners; clean, tidy gem of a site bet canal & rv on edge of vill; Nantes-Brest canal adj; excel towpath for cycling." ◆ ltd. 1 Apr-30 Sep. € 9.45   2006*

GOUDARGUES *10E2* (1km NE Rural) **Camping Les Amarines, La Vérune Cornillon, 30630 Goudargues [04 66 82 24 92; fax 04 66 82 38 64; contact@campinglesamarines.com;   www. campinglesamarines.com]** Fr D928 foll sp onto D23 & site between Cornillon & Goudargues. Med, hdg/mkd pitch, shd; htd wc; baby facs; shwrs inc; el pnts (6A) €3.50; lndtte; ice; snacks; bar; playgrnd; htd pool; rv fishing; entmnt; statics; dogs €1.50; adv bkg; quiet; red low ssn. "Lge pitches; site liable to flood after heavy rain; excel." ◆ 1 Apr-15 Oct. € 17.90   2006*

GOUDELIN *2E3* (3km NE Rural) **Aire Naturelle Kérogel, 22290 Goudelin [tel/fax 02 96 70 03 15; kerogel@wanadoo.fr]** NE fr Guingamp on D9 to Goudelin. Fr cent of vill take rd dir Lanvollon, site sp on R. Sm, pt sl, pt shd; wc; chem disp (wc); shwrs inc; el pnts (10A) inc; lndry rm; tradsmn; rest, snacks, bar 3km; BBQ; playgrnd; games rm; dogs; Eng spkn; adv bkg; CCI. "Well-kept farm site; clean facs; helpful owner; lge pitches; gd touring base away fr cr coastal sites." ◆ 1 Apr-30 Sep. € 9.50   2006*

> *Before we move on, I'm going to fill in some site report forms and post them off to the editor, otherwise they won't arrive in time for the deadline at the end of September.*

GOUEX see Lussac Les Châteaux *7A3*

GOURDON *7D3* (4km E Rural) **Camping Le Rêve, 46300 Le Vigan [05 65 41 25 20; fax 05 65 41 68 52; info@campinglereve.com; www. campinglereve.com]** On D820 (N20), 3km S of Payrac. R onto D673, sp Le Vigan & Gourdon. After 2km turn R onto sm lane, foll camp sp for 2.5km. Med, pt sl, pt terr, pt shd; wc; chem disp; baby facs; shwrs inc; el pnts (6A) €2.60; gas; lndtte; sm shop & 4km; bar; playgrnd; pool & paddling pool; games area; TV rm; entmnt; cycle hire; dogs €0.75; Eng spkn; adv bkg ess Jun-mid Aug (dep req); v quiet; red long stay/low ssn; cc not acc; CCI. "Welcoming, helpful Dutch owners; gd walking; excel." ◆ 25 Apr-15 Sep. € 15.45   2007*

GOURDON *7D3* (11km S Urban) **Camp Municipal Le Moulin Vieux, 46310 St Germain-du-Bel-Air [05 65 31 00 71 or 05 65 31 02 12; makatcho@aol. com]** W fr D820 (N20) Cahors-Souillac rd on D23 sp St Germain-du-Bel Air. On ent vill turn R at camping sp. After 150m turn R & foll narr rd, over sm bdge then imm turn L for site. Lge, shd; wc; chem disp; shwrs; el pnts (6-16A) €3-5; gas; lndtte; rest; shops 1km; pool adj; playgrnd; lake sw & fishing; entmnt; some statics; dogs €2; quiet. "Excel, clean site; vg walks in lovely valley; friendly recep; v helpful warden; pool free for campers; excel value; highly rec." 1 Jun-15 Sep. € 13.00   2007*

GOURDON *7D3* (2km SW Rural) **Aire Naturelle Le Paradis (Jardin), La Peyrugue, 46300 Gourdon [tel/fax 05 65 41 65 01 or 06 72 76 32 60 (mob); contact@campingleparadis.com;   www. campingleparadis.com]** S on D673 Gourdon/ Fumel rd, after Intermarché supmkt on L, turn L onto track sp site. Track shares ent to supmkt. Sm, pt sl, terr, pt shd; wc; shwrs inc; el pnts (6A) €1.60; lndtte; supmkt adj; rest; pool; dogs €2; quiet; adv bkg; gd. "Gd welcome; farm produce; facs poss stretched if full." 1 May-10 Sep. € 8.25   2006*

France

GOURDON *7D3* (5km W Rural) **Camping Le Marcassin de St Aubin (Naturist), 24250 St Aubin-de-Nabirat [tel/fax 05 53 28 57 30; le.marcassin@freesurf.fr; www.best-of-perigord. tm.fr]** Fr Gourdon foll sp for hospital. At hospital take R fork sp Nabirat (D1) & in about 8km turn L at Renault tractor g'ge & foll sp for site in 1.5km. Site on R immed past speed limit sp. Sm, hdg pitch, pt shd; wc; chem disp; shwrs inc; el pnts (6A) €2.50; ice; lndry rm; tradsmn; BBQ gas; pool; TV rm; dogs €2.75/week; Eng spkn; adv bkg (dep req); no cc acc; INF card. "Beautiful area with lots to see; owned by helpful, friendly Dutch couple." ♦ ltd. 28 Apr-15 Sep. € 18.00   2004*

GOURDON *7D3* (10km W Rural) **Camping Calmésympa, La Grèze, 24250 St Martial-de-Nabirat [05 53 28 43 15; fax 05 53 30 23 65; duarte-jacqueline@wanadoo.fr; www.tourisme-ceou.com/calmesympa.htm]** SW fr Gourdon take D673 twd Salviac; at Pont Carrat turn R onto D46 sp Sarlat. Site 1.5km N of St Martial on L. Sm, hdg pitch, pt sl, pt shd; htd wc; chem disp; baby facs; shwrs inc; el pnts (8A) €2.50; lndtte; ice; sm shop; playgrnd; pool; paddling pool; fishing; games area; games rm; entmnt; some statics; dogs €1.50; adv bkg; quiet; CCI. "Off the tourist track; friendly, welcoming owners." ♦ 31 Mar-15 Sep. € 10.50
2007*

GOURDON *7D3* (10km W Rural) **Camping Le Carbonnier, 24250 St Martial-de-Nabirat [05 53 28 42 53 or 0825 13 85 85; fax 05 53 28 51 31 or 02 51 33 91 31; kecarbonnier@aol.com; www.camping-lecarbonnier-dordogne. com]** On D46, sp in St Martial-de-Nabirat. Lge, mkd pitch, pt sl, pt shd; wc; chem disp; shwrs inc; el pnts (6A) inc; lndtte; shop; rest; snacks; bar; playgrnd; htd, covrd pool; waterslides; lake adj; tennis; mini golf; horseriding adj; canoeing 8km; child entmnt; 50% statics; dogs €4.20; poss cr; adv bkg; quiet. "Excel." ♦ 31 Mar-27 Oct. € 26.60
2007*

GOURDON *7D3* (1.5km NW Rural) **Camp Municipal La Quercy, Domaine Ecoute S'il Pleut, 46300 Gourdon [05 65 41 06 19; fax 05 65 41 09 88]** Fr N site on R of D704 1.5km bef Gourdon. Lge, mkd pitch, pt sl, shd; wc; shwrs inc; el pnts (6A) €3; shop & 4km; lndtte; ice; cooking facs; playgrnd; pool; lake beach; fishing; sailing; watersports 200m; tennis; games area; 50% statics; adv bkg rec high ssn; quiet; red low ssn. "50% tented vill; recep clsd 0800-0930, rec pay eve bef dep to avoid waiting; Gourdon attractive town; NH only." 15 Jun-15 Sep. € 10.00   2006*

GOUZON *7A4* (Urban) **Camp Municipal de la Voueize, 23230 Gouzon [05 55 81 73 22]** On E62/ N145 Guéret/Montluçon exit at sp for Gouzon. In cent of vill bear R past church & site is sp on edge of Rv Voueize. Sm, pt shd; wc; chem disp; shwrs inc; el pnts (10A) €2.80 (poss rev pol); gas adj; lndry rm; shop, rest, bar in vill; playgrnd; fishing; cycle hire; golf 2km; birdwatching on lake 8km; adv bkg; quiet. "Friendly recep; clean site & facs; lovely aspect; gd walking & cycling rtes avail fr tourist office in vill; excel touring cent." 1 May-31 Oct. € 11.90   2006*

GRACAY see Vatan *4H3*

⊞**GRAMAT** *7D4* (7km SE Rural) **Camping Le Teulière, L'Hôpital Beaulieu, 46500 Issendolus [05 65 40 86 71; fax 05 65 33 40 89; laparro. mcv@free.fr; http://laparro.mcv.free.fr]** Site on R on D840 (N140) at L'Hôpital, clearly sp. Access fr ent narr & tight corners, not for underpowered. Sm, pt sl, pt shd; wc; shwrs inc; el pnts (20A) €1.90 (poss rev pol); lndtte; shop; rest; snacks; bar; BBQ; playgrnd; pool; tennis; fishing; TV; some statics; poss cr; adv bkg; quiet. "Conv Rocamadour; basic san facs; ltd facs low ssn; site rds unmade, steep & narr - gd traction req; pitches muddy when wet." € 7.50   2005*

GRAND BORNAND, LE see Clusaz, La *9B3*

GRAND LANDES see Legé *2H4*

GRAND PRESSIGNY, LE *4H2* (500m SE Urban) **Camp Municipal Croix Marron, Rue St Martin, 37350 Le Grand-Pressigny [02 47 94 06 55 or 02 47 94 90 37 (Mairie); fax 02 47 91 04 77]** Fr Descartes take D750 S for 3km, L onto D42 to Le Grand-Plessigny. Site at SE end of vill by rv. Sm, mkd pitch, pt shd; wc; chem disp; shwrs inc; el pnts inc; shop, rest, bar in vill; playgrnd; pool adj; quiet. "Pleasant location with lots of places to visit inc prehistoric sites; access to site by key fr Mairie (town hall) in vill, during office hrs." Easter-31 Oct. € 7.00   2006*

GRANDCAMP MAISY *1C4* (500m W Coastal) **Camping Le Joncal, Le Petit Nice, 14450 Grandcamp-Maisy [02 31 22 61 44; fax 02 31 22 73 99; info@campingdujoncal.com; www.campingdujoncal.com]** Ent on Grandcamp port dock area; visible fr vill. Fr N13 take D199 sp Grandcamp-Maisy & foll Le Port & Camping sps. Lge, mkd pitch, unshd; mv service pnt; wc; shops, rest adj; gas; el pnts (3-6A) €2.50-4; many statics; dogs €1; bus; quiet. "Conv for D Day landing beaches." ♦ 1 Apr-30 Sep. € 13.50   2006*

GRANDE MOTTE, LA *10F1* (Coastal) **FFCC Camping La Petite Motte à La Grande-Motte, 195 Allée des Peupliers, 34280 La Grande-Motte [04 67 56 54 75; fax 04 67 29 92 58; camping. lagrandemotte@ffcc.fr; www.camp-in-france. com]** Exit A9 for Lunel or Montpellier Est to La Grande Motte, site sp on D59 coast rd. Lge, shd, wc; shwrs; mv service pnt; el pnts (4A) €4.50; lndtte (no dryer); shop; rest; snacks; bar; playgrnd; sand beach 700m; tennis, horseriding, golf & water sports nrby; games area; entmnt; 10% statics; dogs €1.50; poss cr; adv bkg; red long stay/CCI. "Lovely walk to beach thro ave of trees & footbdge over rds; vg." 1 Apr-30 Sep. € 16.30   2007*

GRANDE MOTTE, LA *10F1* (700m W Coastal/ Urban) **Camping Le Garden, Ave de la Petite Motte, 34280 La Grande-Motte [04 67 56 50 09; fax 04 67 56 25 69; jc.mandel@wanadoo.fr; www.legarden.fr]** Fr La Grande Motte W on D59, site sp. Lge, hdg/mkd pitch, hdstg, pt shd; htd wc; chem disp; mv service pnt; baby facs; fam bthrm; shwrs inc; el pnts (10A) inc; gas; lndtte; ice; shop; rest; snacks; bar; BBQ (gas); pool; paddling pool; sand beach 300m; entmnt; 30% statics; dogs €2; phone; bus; poss cr; Eng spkn; adv bkg; cc acc; CCI. "Lovely place; easy access to beach, town & bus; nearest Grande Motte site to beach; some soft sand on pitches; highly rec." 1 Apr-30 Sep. € 37.50 (3 persons)   2007*

GRANDE MOTTE, LA *10F1* (2km W Coastal) **Camp Intercommunal Les Cigales, Allée des Pins, 34280 La Grande-Motte [tel/fax 04 67 56 50 85; camping.lescigales@wanadoo.fr]** Ent La Grande-Motte fr D62. Turn R at 1st traff lts; 1st on R to site. Lge, mkd pitch, pt shd; htd wc (cont); shwrs inc; el pnts (10A) inc; lndtte; shop 200m; snacks; bar; playgrnd; sand beach 900m; quiet. "One of several sites grouped together in well-planned seaside town; quiet low ssn & ltd facs." Easter-23 Oct. € 16.50   2006*

GRANDPRE *5D1* (300m S Rural) **Camp Municipal, Rue André Bastide, 08250 Grandpré [03 24 30 50 71 or 03 24 30 52 18 (Mairie)]** Fr D946 in Grandpré turn S onto D6 at vill sq by church twd rv, site in 300m on rvside. Med, mkd pitch, pt shd; wc; mv service pnt; shwrs €0.60; el pnts (6-10A) €2.20-3.30; lndtte; shops, rest, bar 300m; playgrnd; rv sw; fishing; dogs €0.50; poss cr; quiet. "Pleasant site." 1 Apr-30 Sep. € 6.70   2006*

GRANE see Crest *9D2*

GRANGES SUR VOLOGNE *6F3* (5km S Rural) **Camping La Sténiole, 1 Le Haut Rain, 88640 Granges-sur-Vologne [03 29 51 43 75; steniole@ wanadoo.fr; www.steniole.fr]** D423 fr Gérardmer NW to Granges-sur-Vologne & foll sp. Well sp. Med, hdg pitch, terr, pt shd; wc (some cont); chem disp; shwrs inc; el pnts (4-10A) €3.05-4; gas; lndtte; shop; supmkt 3km; tradsmn; rest; snacks; bar; BBQ; playgrnd; lake sw & shgl beach adj; fishing, tennis; walking rte; horseriding 4km; games rm; TV rm; 10% statics; dogs €1; Eng spkn; adv bkg rec high ssn; quiet; CCI. "Pleasant, wooded, relaxing site; vg rest." 15 Apr-30 Oct. € 10.00   2007*

There aren't many sites open this early in the year. We'd better phone ahead to check that the one we're heading for is actually open.

GRANGES SUR VOLOGNE *6F3* (200m W Rural) **Camping Les Peupliers, 12 Rue de Pré Dixi, 88640 Granges-sur-Vologne [03 29 57 51 04 or 03 29 51 43 36; fax 03 29 57 51 04]** D423 fr Gérardmer NW to Granges-sur-Vologne. On entering town look for sm park with bandstand on L; shortly after turn L into sm rd just bef rv bdge nr town cent. Well sp. 200m fr D423 & town cent. Sm, mkd pitch, pt shd; wc; chem disp; shwrs €1; el pnts (6A) €3 shop & rest adj; playgrnd; rv sw; fishing; TV rm; dogs €0.70; phone; poss cr high ssn; no Eng spkn; adv bkg; quiet; no cc acc; CCI. "V friendly owner; modern, clean san facs, poss ltd high ssn; site attractively landscaped; gd, peaceful walking area inc farm." ♦ 1 May-15 Sep. € 8.00   2007*

GRANVILLE *1D4* (2km NE Coastal) **Camping L'Ermitage Intercommunal Granville-Donville, Rue de l'Ermitage, 50350 Donville-les-Bains [02 33 50 09 01; fax 02 33 50 88 19; camping-ermitage@wanadoo.fr; www.camping-ermitage. com]** Turn off D971E in Donville at sm rndabt, site sp. Fr Bréhal turn R immed after post office on R. Lge, pt sl, pt shd; wc; chem disp; shwrs; el pnts (10A) €2.90; lndtte; shop 1km; rest, snacks, bar adj; sand beach; tennis adj; 10% statics; dogs €1.90; phone; poss cr; adv bkg; quiet, CCI. ♦ 15 Apr-15 Oct. € 11.90   2007*

GRANVILLE *1D4* (6km NE Coastal) **Camping La Route Blanche, 6 La Route Blanche, 50290 Bréville-sur-Mer [02 33 50 23 31; fax 02 33 50 26 47; larouteblanche@camping-breville.com; www.camping-breville.com]** Exit A84 junc 37 onto D924 dir Granville. Bef Granville turn L onto D971, then L onto D114 which joins D971e. Site on R bef golf club. Nr Bréville sm airfield. Lge, hdg/mkd pitch, hdstg, pt shd; htd wc (some male cont); chem disp; mv service pnt; baby facs; shwrs inc; el pnts (6-10A) €2.60-3.60; gas; lndtte; ice; shop; tradsmn; playgrnd; htd pools; waterpark, waterslide; sand beach 500m; sailing school; golf & tennis nr; games area; entmnt; 40% statics; dogs €2.50; phone; poss cr; Eng spkn; adv bkg; quiet; red long stay/low ssn; cc acc; CCI. "Pleasant, busy site with vg clean facs; staff friendly & helpful; vg disabled facs inc seatlift in pool; gd walking, cycling & beach; pleasant old walled town & harbour; vg." ♦ 1 Apr-31 Oct. € 24.00 (CChq acc)   2007*

See advertisement opposite (top)

GRANVILLE *1D4* (2.5km SE Coastal) **Camping La Vague, St Nicholas, 50400 Granville [02 33 50 29 97]** On D911 coast rd S fr Granville, or on D973 dir Avranches, site sp. Med, hdg/mkd pitch, pt shd; wc; chem disp; mv service pnt; some serviced pitches; shwrs inc; el pnts (4A) inc; gas; lndtte; ice; shop 1km; tradsmn; snacks; playgrnd; sand beach adj; fishing; mini-golf; TV; dogs; poss cr; adv bkg; quiet; CCI. ♦ Easter-30 Sep. € 23.80
                                    2004*

GRANVILLE *1D4* (3km SE) **Camping de l'Ecutot, Route de l'Ecutot, 50380 St Pair-sur-Mer [02 33 50 26 29; fax 02 33 50 64 94; camping. ecutot@wanadoo.fr]** Fr Avranches NW on D973 twds Granville. 5km S of Granville turn onto D309 sp St Pair-sur-Mer; site on R (wide rear ent). Lge, hdg pitch, indiv san facs some pitches; wc; chem disp; shwrs inc; el pnts (2-10A) €1.60-4; lndtte; ice; sm shop; snacks; bar; playgrnd; htd pool; beach 1.2km; games area; entmnt; TV rm; 20% statics; dogs €1; eng spkn; adv bkg; quiet; cc acc. "Beware soft ground early ssn; conv ferry to Channel Is, Bayeux Tapestry, Mont St Michel." 1 Jun-15 Sep. € 17.60   2004*

GRANVILLE *1D4* (3.5km SE) **Camping Angomesnil, 50380 St Pair-sur-Mer [02 33 50 61 41]** Take D973 SE fr Granville twd Avranches. At D154 exit to R sp Kairon-Bourg & site in 1km. Sm, pt sl, pt shd; wc; chem disp; mv service pnt; shwrs inc; el pnts (3A) inc; shops 4km; tradsmn; playgrnd; pool high ssn; sand beach 3.5km; tennis. "Nice little site; helpful warden; roomy pitches." ♦ 20 Jun-10 Sep. € 14.20
                                    2006*

GRANVILLE *1D4* (6km SE Rural) **Camping Le Château de Lez-Eaux, 50380 St Pair-sur-Mer [02 33 51 66 09; fax 02 33 51 92 02; bonjour@ lez-eaux.com; www.lez-eaux.com or www. les-castels.com]** App site on D973 Granville to Avranches rd (not via St Pair). Fr rndabt at Intermarché cont for 2km, site sp on R. Take care not to miss site turning 2km past Intermarché. Med, mkd pitch, pt sl, pt shd; wc; chem disp; mv service pnt; serviced pitches; baby facs; shwrs inc; el pnts (10A) inc; lndtte; ice; shop & 4km; snacks; bar; BBQ; playgrnd; 2 pools (1 htd covrd); paddling pool; waterslide; sand beach 4km; lake fishing; tennis; cycle hire; boat hire 7km; horseriding 4km; child entmnt; wifi internet; games/TV rm; 80% statics; dogs free; poss cr; quiet; cc acc; CCI. "Lovely site; conv Mont St Michel, Dol & landing beaches; gd for children; gd cycling; clean, modern san facs; spacious pitches, various prices; gd cycle rte to beach; mkt Thu St Pair." ♦ 30 Mar-30 Sep. € 43.00 ABS - N02   2007*

See advertisement opposite (bottom)

> Did you know you can fill in site report forms on the Club's website — www.caravanclub.co.uk?

GRANVILLE *1D4* (5km S Coastal) **Camping La Chaussée, 1 Ave de la Libération, 50610 Jullouville [02 33 61 80 18; fax 02 33 61 45 26; jmb@camping-lachaussee.com; www.camping-lachaussee.com]** On coast rd D911 fr Granville to Jullouville. Site on L heading S, sp. Lge, mkd pitch, hdstg, pt shd; wc (some cont); chem disp; mv service pnt; shwrs inc; el pnts (6-10A) €3.60-4; gas; lndtte; ice; shop; snacks; bar; BBQ; playgrnd; htd pool; sand beach 100m; tennis 500m; games area; games rm 400m; archery; games rm; entmnt; internet; TV rm; dogs €1.50; bus; office open 0800-1230 & 1400-2000; Eng spkn; adv bkg; quiet; cc acc; red low ssn; CCI. "V pleasant site on attractive coast; lge pitches; lovely pool; lovely promenade walk; conv Mont St Michel 8 Apr-17 Sep. € 23.00   2005*

GRANVILLE *1D4* (7km S Urban) **Camp du Docteur Lemonnier, 50610 Jullouville [02 33 51 42 60]** S on D911 Granville-Avranches coast rd. On on ent Jullouville turn L in mkt sq. Ent in far L corner. Med, unshd; wc; mv service pnt; shwrs inc; el pnts (6A) inc; gas; lndtte; ice; shop 200m; snacks; BBQ; playgrnd; sand beach 500m; 10% statics; poss cr high ssn; adv bkg; CCI. "Gd." 7 Apr-23 Sep. € 15.90   2006*

GRASSE *10E4* (7km E Rural) **Camping l'Orée d'Azure (formerly Camping Caravan'Inn), 18 Route de Cannes, 06860 Opio** [04 93 77 32 00; fax 04 93 77 71 89; accueil@camping-loreedazur.fr; www.camping-loreedazur.fr] Exit A8 at Cannes/Grasse, foll sp for Grasse & to Valbonne, D3. (Can also exit A8 at Antibes, foll D103 to D3 & Valbonne). On D9 thro Valbonne, R at N end of vill sq. Cont D3 sp Opio. After 3km site on L. Med, low hdg pitch, sl (terr vineyard), shd; wc; chem disp; shwrs inc; el pnts (2-4A) €2.60; shops 1km; gas; lndtte; rest; snacks; bar; playgrnd; pool; sand beach 14km; tennis, horseriding; golf 1km; TV rm; 90% statics; dogs; phone; poss cr; Eng spkn; adv bkg; v quiet; CCI. "Beautiful location conv Côte d'Azur & Provence Alps; v helpful new owner 2007; vg." 1 Jun-1 Sep. € 25.00 2007*

GRASSE *10E4* (8km S Rural) **Camping Le Parc des Monges, 635 Chemin du Gabre, 06810 Auribeau-sur-Siagne** [tel/fax 04 93 60 91 71; contact@parcdesmonges.fr; www.parcdesmonges.com] Exit A8 junc 40 or 41 onto D6007 dir Grasse; then onto D109 becoming D9; foll sp to Auribau-sur-Siagne; site on rd to Le Gabre. Sm, hdg pitch, pt shd; wc (some cont); chem disp; shwrs inc; el pnts (4-10A) €3.50-5.50; gas 1km; lndtte; shop 500m; tradsmn; snacks; bar; playgrnd; pool; activities & entment; 7% statics; dogs €2.20; phone; poss cr; adv bkg (dep req); quiet; CCI. "Vg site by Rv Siagne; rv not accessible fr site." ♦ ltd. 7 Apr-29 Sep. € 22.20 2006*

⊞**GRASSE** *10E4* (8km NW Rural) **Camping Parc des Arboins, 755 Route Napoléon, 06460 St Vallier-de-Thiey** [04 93 42 63 89; fax 04 93 09 61 54; contact@parc-des-arboins.com; www.parc-des-arboins.com] N fr Cannes on D6085 (N85) foll sp thro Grasse for Digne; approx 1.5km bef vill of St Vallier-de-Thiey, site located on R of rd. Med, mkd pitch, hdstg, shd; htd wc; mv service pnt; shwrs; el pnts (3A) €2.40; gas; ice; lndtte; shop; supmkt 1.5km; rest; snacks; bar; playgrnd; htd pool; paddling pool; sand beach 30km; tennis 1.5km; golf 10km; games area; entmnt; TV rm; 95% statics; dogs €1.20; adv bkg; quiet but poss rd noise; CCI. "Lovely position on hillside; ltd touring pitches; ltd space to manoeuvre; 'quaint' san facs (own san rec); vg rest adj." € 17.40 2006*

France

GRAU DU ROI, LE *10F2* (1km N Coastal) Camping Le Boucanet, Route de Carnon, 30240 Le Grau-du-Roi [04 66 51 41 48; fax 04 66 51 41 87; contact@campingboucanet.fr; www.camping boucanet.fr] Fr A9 fr N exit junc 26, fr S exit junc 29 Montpellier Airport dir Aigues-Mortes. Fr Aigues-Mortes take D62/D62A to Le Grau-du-Roi, twd La Grande-Motte. Site clearly sp off rndabt after area called Le Boucanet (on L). Lge, hdg/mkd pitch, some hdstg, pt shd; wc (some cont); chem disp; mv service pnt; shwrs inc; el pnts (6A) inc; gas; lndtte; ice; shop; tradsmn; rest; snacks; bar; no BBQs; playgrnd; htd pool & paddling pool; dir access to sand beach adj; surf school; tennis; horseriding; golf 2km; creche; entmnt; no dogs; Eng spkn; adv bkg; quiet; cc acc; CCI. "Excel, popular site; some sm pitches poss diff lge o'fits; some pitches sandy; m'van parking on rd opp site; no waiting area outside site." ♦ 7 Apr-7 Oct. € 37.70 (CChq acc) 2007*

GRAU DU ROI, LE *10F2* (1km S Coastal) Camping Les Jardins de Tivoli, Route de l'Espiguette, 30240 Le Grau du Roi [04 66 53 97 00; fax 04 66 51 09 81; contact@lesjardinsdetivoli.com; www.lesjardinsdetivoli.com] Fr A9 take exit 26 to Aigues-Mortes. Then foll D979 twds Le Grau-du-Roi, Port Camargue & Espiguette. Site sp. Lge, hdg/mkd pitch, shd; wc; shwrs inc; each pitch has individ san facs inc shwr; el pnts (6-10A) inc; gas; lndtte; ice; shop; rest; snacks; bar; gas; BBQ (gas); playgrnd; 3 pools; paddling pool; waterslides; sand beach 600m; tennis; sports activities; cycle hire; entmnt; TV; 20% statics; dogs €7; phone; adv bkg (dep req); cc acc; red low ssn; CCI. "Excel site; superb individ san facs; lge pitches." ♦ 1 Apr-30 Sep. € 54.00 (4 persons) 2006*

GRAU DU ROI, LE *10F2* (4km SW Coastal) Camping L'Espiguette, 30240 Le Grau-du-Roi [04 66 51 43 92; fax 04 66 53 25 71; reception@ campingespiguette.fr; www.campingespiguette. fr] Fr A9 exit junc 26 onto D979 S to Aigues-Mortes & La Grande-Motte. Foll sps to Port Camargue & L'Espiguette & site sp on R fr rndabt; access via L bank of Le Grau-du-Roi; 3km fr Port Camargue & lighthouse. V lge, pt shd; wc; baby facs; shwrs inc; el pnts (5A) inc; gas; lndtte; shop; rest; snacks; bar; pool; activity pool; watersliges; sand beach adj & access to naturist beach 3km; entmnt; adv bkg; 10% statics; dogs €3; quiet; cc acc; red long stay/ low ssn; CCI. "Some pitches on sand poss diff in wet; caution on app due to height barrier; many facs high ssn; v ltd facs low ssn; poss mosquitoes; beautiful beach adj; helpful staff; gd security; vg." ♦ 8 Apr-5 Nov. € 29.00 2006*

GRAVE, LA *9C3* (1km E Rural) Camping de la Meije, 05320 La Grave [tel/fax 04 76 79 93 34 or 06 08 54 30 84 (mob); nathalie-romagne@ wanadoo.fr; www.camping-delameije.com] On N91 travelling W to E site ent end of vill immed after last building. Site sp easily missed; by stream below vill. Awkward app fr Briançon (sharp L-hand turn) cont & turn in parking area 150m. NB Rec app fr W. Sm, mkd pitch, pt sl, pt shd; wc (cont); chem disp (wc); baby facs; fam bthrm; shwrs €1; el pnts (4A) €3; lndtte; shop 500m; tradsmn; rest, snacks, bar 500m; BBQ; playgrnd; htd pool high ssn; tennis; games area; dogs €1; bus; poss cr; Eng spkn; adv bkg (dep req); quiet; red 5 days+; CCI. "Superb setting; mountain views, walks & excursions; immac kept, beautiful site; poss cr early & mid-July due La Marmotte cycle race & Tour de France." ♦ 15 May-20 Sep. € 11.00 2006*

GRAVE, LA *9C3* (1km W Rural) Camping Le Gravelotte, La Meije, 05320 La Grave [04 76 79 93 14 or 04 76 79 91 34] On N91, 1km W of La Grave. Med, pt sl, pt shd; wc; chem disp; shwrs inc; el pnts (5A) inc; gas 1km; lndtte; shop; tradsmn; bar; htd pool; rv rafting/sw; dogs; poss cr; quiet; CCI. "Friendly welcome; spacious & open situation." 15 Jun-15 Sep. € 13.60 2004*

GRAVELINES *3A3* (1km N Coastal) Camping Les Dunes/Les Navigateurs, Rue Victor-Hugo, Plage de Petit-Fort-Philippe, 59820 Gravelines [03 28 23 09 80 or 03 28 23 29 10; fax 03 28 65 35 99; vpa@club-internet.fr; www. camping-des-dunes.com] E fr Calais on D940 foll sp to Gravelines. Heading W fr Dunkirk exit N1 E of Gravelines foll sp for Petit-Fort-Philippe & foll rd to sp for camping. Site on both sides of rd. Lge, hdg/mkd pitch, pt shd; wc; chem disp; shwrs inc; el pnts (10A) €3.85; lndtte; shop (high ssn); shop, rest, snacks & bar 1km; playgrnd; sand beach nr; entmnt; 90% statics; dogs €1.76; phone; bus; adv bkg; red low ssn; CCI "Site in 2 parts, various prices; gd site rds; helpful, friendly staff; gates locked at night; poss uneven pitches; poss unkempt low ssn; conv Dunkerque ferries (15km)." 1 Apr-2 Nov. € 16.80 2007*

GRAVELINES *3A3* (3km W Coastal) Camping de la Plage, Rue du Maréchal-Foch, 59153 Grand-Fort-Philippe [03 28 65 31 95 or 03 28 23 09 80; fax 03 28 65 47 40; camping.delaplage@wanadoo. fr; www.camping-de-la-plage.info] Exit A16 junc 51 dir Grand-Fort-Philippe; at o'skts of town turn R sp Camping ***; cont into town cent; foll rd along quayside; foll rd to L past lge crucifix; turn R at next x-rds; site on R. Med, mkd pitch, pt shd; htd wc; chem disp; shwrs inc; el pnts (10A) €3.25; lndtte; shops & rest 1km; sand beach 2km; pool 3km; playgrnd; entmnt; 20% statics; dogs €1.73; Eng spkn; adv bkg; quiet. "Various pitch sizes; nice walk to sea front; poss itinerants & circus vans; conv ferries; vg." 1 Apr-31 Oct. € 13.64 2007*

GRAVESON see St Rémy de Provence *10E2*

GRAY *6G2* (1km NE Rural) **Camp Municipal Longue Rive, Rue de la Plage, 70100 Gray** [03 84 64 90 44; fax 03 84 65 46 26; tourisme-gray@wanadoo.fr] S on D67, ent town, cross bdge over rv, L at rndabt, after 300m L at sp for La Plage. Well sp fr all rtes. Med, hdg/mkd pitch, pt shd; wc (mainly cont); mv service pnt; shwrs inc; el pnts (10A) inc; gas; lndtte; ice; shop 1.5km; rest, bar, & pool opp; playgrnd; boating & fishing; tennis; mini-golf; dogs €0.80; poss cr; Eng spkn; poss noisy; cc not acc; CCI. "Friendly recep; 3 supmkts in town; "De la Plage" rest opp site rec; several Bastide vills within cycling dist; many pitches waterlogged early in ssn; facs poss dirty; NH only." 15 Apr-30 Sep. € 11.60   2005*

GRAYAN ET L'HOPITAL see Soulac sur Mer *7B1*

GRENOBLE *9C3* (12km SE) **Camping de Luiset, 38410 St Martin-d'Uriage** [04 76 89 77 98; fax 04 76 59 70 91; camping@leluiset.com] Take D524 SE fr Grenoble to Uriage-les-Bains; turn L on D280 to St Martin-d'Uriage; site behind church in vill; steep climb fr Uriage-les-Bains. Med, pt terr, pt shd; wc (cont); shwrs; el pnts (2-6A) €2-2.60; ice; lndtte; BBQ; playgrnd; sports area; rv fishing 100m. "Beautiful setting; basic facs." ♦ 1 May-30 Sep. € 8.50   2005*

GRENOBLE *9C3* (10km S Rural) **Camping à la Ferme Le Moulin de Tulette (Gaudin), Route du Moulin de Tulette, 38760 Varces-Allières-et-Risset** [04 76 72 55 98; tulette@wanadoo.fr; http://pagesperso-orange.fr/moulindetulette/] Fr A51, exit junc 12 to join D1075 (N75) N, Varces in approx 2km. Turn R at traff lts & foll sp to site, (approx 2km fr D1075). If driving thro Grenoble look for sp Gap - D1075 diff to find; on ent Varce foll site sp. Sm, mkd pitch, pt sl, pt shd; wc; chem disp; baby facs; shwrs inc; el pnts (5-10A) €2.50; shop 1km; tradsmn; dogs €1; poss cr; Eng spkn; adv bkg; quiet; CCI. "Lovely, peaceful site; stunning views; well-maintained; friendly, helpfuly owners; facs ltd but v clean - stretched high ssn; same hose used for disposal point & m'van water top-up; gd base for touring/x-ing Alps; excel rest 1.5km; marvellous." ♦ 1 May-31 Oct. € 12.00   2007*

⊞**GRENOBLE** *9C3* (7km SW Urban) **Camping Caravaning Les 3 Pucelles, Rue des Allobroges, 38180 Seyssins** [04 76 96 45 73; fax 04 76 21 43 73; contact@camping-trois-pucelles.com; www.camping-trois-pucelles.com] On A480 in dir of rocade (by-pass) S exit 5B, on R after supmkt then foll sp to R then L. Clearly sp. Well sp fr m'way. Med, hdg pitch, hdstg, pt shd; htd wc (some cont); chem disp; shwrs inc; el pnts (10A) €2.30; lndtte; ice shop; tradsmn; rest, snacks; bar; playgrnd; pool; 70% statics; phone; bus nr; poss cr; Eng spkn; noise fr indus area; CCI. "Site part of hotel campus; run by friendly family; san facs gd; NH only to explore interesting city; conv Grenoble by bus/tram." € 12.00   2005*

GREOUX LES BAINS *10E3* (600m S Rural) **Yelloh! Village Verdon Parc, La Paludette, 04800 Gréoux-les-Bains** [04 92 78 08 08; fax 04 92 77 00 17; info@yellohvillage-verdon-parc.com; www.yellohvillage-verdon-parc.com] Take D907 over rv R on D4 to Les Hameaux. Turn L on D952. At Gréoux turn R on D8 rd to St Pierre. Cross bdge over Rv Verdon (v narr) take immed rd to L. Site 500m. Lge, mkd pitch, hdstg, terr, pt shd; wc; chem disp; baby facs; fam bthrm; shwrs inc; el pnts (10A) €4; gas 1km; lndtte; shop & 1km; rest; snacks; bar; paddling pool; lake sw & fishing 3km; tennis; star golf; games area; entmnts; internet; TV rm; 60% statics; dogs €2 (low ssn only); phone; bus 1km; Eng spkn; adv bkg; quiet; CCI. "V helpful manager; v clean facs; all gravel standings; barrier clsd 2230-0700; interesting & pleasant spa town; excel." ♦ 1 Apr-27 Oct. € 31.00   2007*

GREOUX LES BAINS *10E3* (1.2km S Rural) **Camping Le Verseau, Route de St Pierre, 04800 Gréoux-les-Bains** [tel/fax 04 92 77 67 10] Fr W on D952 to Gréoux. Go under bdge then bear L just bef petrol stn. Cross rv (narr bdge), site on R in 500m. Med, hdg pitch, pt sl, pt shd; wc; chem disp; mv service pnt; baby facs; shwrs inc; el pnts (10A) €3; lndtte; shop 1km; rest; snacks; bar; BBQ (gas/elec); playgrnd; pool; tennis 1km; entmnt; dogs €1.80; phone; adv bkg; quiet; CCI. "Friendly owners; interesting spa town; great views." 1 Apr-31 Oct. € 16.00   2006*

GREZ SUR LOING see Fontainebleau *4E3*

GRIGNAN see Valréas *9D2*

GRIMAUD *10F4* (2km E Rural) **Aire Naturelle (Gerard), Les Cagnignons, 83310 Grimaud** [04 94 56 34 51; fax 04 94 56 51 26; lyons.cagnignons@wanadoo.fr] Leave A8 at junc 36 onto D125/D25 at Le Muy sp Ste Maxime then onto D559 (N98) dir St Tropez. Take R onto D14 sp Grimaud & 3rd rd on R to site. Sm, terr, shd; wc; chem disp; shwrs inc; el pnts (3-6A) €3-3.50; lndtte; basic playgrnd; pool adj, tennis 500m; sand beach 2km; horseriding 2km; phone; 30% statics; dogs €1.60; adv bkg; quiet; no cc acc; CCI. "V clean; away fr bustle of St Tropez; not rec teenagers; some pitches ltd for long o'fits." ♦ Easter-30 Sep. € 18.00   2006*

GRIMAUD *10F4* (2km E Rural) **Camping Domaine du Golfe de St Tropez, Chemin des Vignaux, 83310 Grimaud** [04 94 43 26 95; fax 04 94 43 21 06; info@golfe-st-tropez.com; www.golfe-st-tropez.com] Sp down lane nr junc of D14 & D61. Med, hdg/mkd pitch, pt shd; wc; chem disp; shwrs inc; el pnts (4-10A) €3-5; rest; snacks; bar; playgrnd; pool; beach 3km; 30% statics; dogs €1.50; phone; cc acc. "Conv for Port Grimaud & beaches; fair." 31 May-28 Aug. € 18.00   2005*

Camping Club Holiday Marina

Holiday Marina is a friendly, safe site ideal for families. Situated at 800 from the centre of Port Grimaud and just 950 from the beach, we are perfectly situated for visiting this famous area of France. Our touring pitches come with their own fully equipped private bathroom, heated in low season with a water and 20 amp electrical hook up. Facilities onsite include pool, Jacuzzi, bar, take-away restaurant, shop, hire shop, kids club, play area. TV & Games room, car wash, WIFI, moorings with access to the Mediterranean & more.
Opening dates March 07 – December 07.

RN98 Le Ginestrel, 83310 Grimaud, France. Tel. + 33 494 56 08 43 Fax + 33 494 56 23 88
Web site: www.holiday-marina.com **Email:** info@holiday-marina.com

As soon as we get home I'm going to post all these site report forms to the editor for inclusion in next year's guide. I don't want to miss the September deadline.

GRIMAUD *10F4* (3km E Coastal) **Domaine des Naïades ACF, St Pons-les-Mûres, 83310 Grimaud** [04 94 55 67 80; fax 04 94 55 67 81; info@ lesnaiades.com; www.lesnaiades.com] Exit A8 junc 36 (for Le Muy) onto D125/D25 dir St Maxime; join D559 (N98) W dir St Tropez & Grimaud. After 5km at rndabt opp Camping Prairies de la Mer turn R sp St Pons-les-Mûres; site sp & ent 500m on L. Lge, terr, shd, mkd pitch; wc (some cont); chem disp; baby facs; shwrs inc; el pnts (10A) inc (poss rev pol); lndtte; ice; shops; rest; snacks; bar; playgrnd; htd pool + paddling pool; waterslides; sand beach 900m; watersports; cycle hire; games area; entmnt; wifi internet; games/TV rm; some statics; dogs €5; poss cr; adv bkg ess; quiet except noisy disco & dog kennels adj; cc acc; red long stay; CCI. "Gd views; vg, clean san facs; 24hr security; gd recep." ♦ 5 Apr-1 Nov. € 48.00 (3 persons) ABS - C27   2007*

GRIMAUD *10F4* (4km E Coastal) **Camping Club Holiday Marina, Le Ginestel, 83310 Grimaud** [04 94 56 08 43; fax 04 94 56 23 88; info@ holiday-marina.com; www.holiday-marina.com] Exit A8 junc 36 onto D125/D25 dir Ste Maxime; turn R onto D559 (N98) dir St Tropez (sea on your L); in approx 6km pass under sm flyover at Port Grimaud. Site on R in approx 500m past flyover just after Villa Verde garden cent. Lge, hdg/mkd pitch, pt shd; htd wc; chem disp; serviced pitches; pitches have private bthrms; shwrs inc; el pnts (20A) inc; gas; lndtte; shop; tradsmn; rest; snacks; bar; BBQ (el only); playgrnd; 2 pools; jacuzzi; sand beach 950m; fishing; cycle & scooter hire; games rm; entmnt; child entmnt; wifi internet; sat TV; 70% statics; dogs €3; €50 dep for barrier card & bathrm; recep 0800-2000 high ssn; sep car park; British owners; poss cr; adv bkg ess high ssn; rd noise; red low ssn/long stay; cc acc; CCI. "Helpful staff; lovely pool area with htd jacuzzi; excel sports facs; touring pitches poss diff manoeuvring for lge o'fits; v conv for all Côte d'Azur." ♦ 1 Mar-31 Dec. € 49.00 ABS - C23   2007*

See advertisement

GRIMAUD *10F4* (4km E Coastal) **Camping de la Plage, 98 Route National, 83310 Grimaud-Cogolin [04 94 56 31 15; fax 04 94 56 49 61; campingplagegrimaud@wanadoo.fr; www.camping-de-la-plage.fr]** Fr St Maxime turn onto D559 (N98) sp to St Tropez; site 3km on L on both sides of rd (subway links both parts). Lge, pt shd; wc; chem disp; mv service pnt; shwrs inc; el pnts (4-10A) €4.40-8.50; gas; lndtte; ice; shop; rest; snacks; bar; playgrnd; sand beach adj; tennis; dogs €1.80; poss cr; some rd noise; adv bkg ess high ssn, rec bkg in Jan (non-rtnable bkg fee); cc acc; CCI. "Pitches nr beach or in shd woodland; excel situation & views; some sm pitches; gd, clean facs; some noise fr disco; little pitch maintanence low ssn; conv for Ste Maxime & Port Grimaud; ferry to St Tropez, Monte Carlo; site poss flooded after heavy rain." ♦ 30 Mar-8 Oct. € 27.00   2007*

GRIMAUD *10F4* (4km E Coastal) **Camping Les Mûres, St Pons-les-Mûres, 83310 Grimaud [04 94 56 16 17; fax 04 94 56 37 91; info@camping-des-mures.com; www.camping-des-mures.com]** Exit Ste Maxime on D559 (N98) twd St Tropez, site in 5km visible on both sides of rd midway bet Ste Maxime & Grimaud. V lge, mkd pitch, pt sl, pt shd; wc (some cont); chem disp; shwrs inc; el pnts (6A) inc; gas; lndtte; ice; shop; rest; snacks; bar; playgrnd; sand beach adj; boat hire; water-skiing; games area; entmnt; some statics; dogs €2; poss cr; quiet but rd noise & disco (high ssn); CCI. "Beach pitches avail; well-run, clean site; v ltd facs low ssn." 1 Apr-30 Sep. € 30.00   2005*

GRIMAUD *10F4* (4km E Coastal) **Camping Les Prairies de la Mer, St Pons-les-Mûres, 83360 Grimaud [04 94 79 09 09; fax 04 94 79 09 10; prairies@campazur.com; www.campazur.com & www.homair.com]** Leave A8/E80 at Ste Maxime/Draguignan exit. Take DD125/D25 twd Ste Maxime. Site on L of D559 (N98) heading SW, 400m bef St Pons-les-Mûres with rndabt at ent. V lge, mkd pitch, pt shd, sm pitch; wc; chem disp; mv service pnt; shwrs inc; el pnts (6-10A) €5; gas; lndtte; ice; shop; supmkt; rest; snacks; bar; playgrnd; sand beach adj; fishing; watersports; entmnt; 60% statics; dogs; adv bkg ess high ssn; red snr citizen low ssn; CCI. "Well organised site; gd recep; poss tatty low ssn; Port Grimaud sh walk." ♦ 1 Apr-8 Oct. € 25.00   2006*

⊞**GRISOLLES** *8E3* (1km NE Rural) **Camping Aquitaine, Route de Montauban, 82170 Grisolles [05 63 67 33 22; campingaquitaine@aol.com]** S on N20, site on L just bef junc N20/N113. Watch for flags at ent. Steep app. Sm, sl, terr, pt shd; wc; shwrs inc; el pnts (10A); gas; ice; lndry rm; sm shop; supmkt 700m; rest, bar 1km; BBQ; playgrnd; rv fishing 1km; lake sw 5km; some statics; dogs €1; no twin-axle vans acc; adv bkg; quiet but some rd & rlwy noise; CCI. "Overlooks valley of Garonne; v steep site; fair NH."   2006*

GRISOLLES *8E3* (4km NW Rural) **FFCC Camping Le Grand Gravier, 82600 Verdun-sur-Garonne [05 63 64 32 44 or 05 63 26 30 64; camping@garonne-gascogne.com; www.garonne-gascogne.com]** Exit A20/E09 at junc 68 onto A72 & exit junc 10 onto N20 S to Grisolles. At rndabt turn R onto N113 NW for 3km, then L at rndabt onto D6 W sp Verdun-sur-Garonne. Cross rv bdge; site sharp R in 500m. Med, hdg pitch, pt shd; wc (mainly cont); shwrs inc; el pnts (6A) €2.80; shop 1km; BBQ; playgrnd; rv fishing; tennis; games rm; dogs €1; adv bkg; quiet; red long stay; CCI. "Pleasant, interesting site; next to fast flowing rv, poss floods in wet weather; boating poss but not sw; gd modern facs; 1km fr town; no access 1400-1600." 26 May-2 Sep. € 9.40   2007*

GROLEJAC see Sarlat la Canéda *7C3*

⊞**GROS THEIL, LE** *3D2* (3km SW Rural) **Camp de Salverte, Route de Brionne, 27370 Le Gros-Theil [02 32 35 51 34; fax 02 32 35 92 79]** Fr Brionne take D26 E twd Le Gros-Thiel. After 10km turn R at Salverte, site sp. Lge, hdg pitch, terr, pt shd; htd wc; shwrs inc; el pnts (3A) inc (poss rev pol); lndry rm; shop; snacks; bar; playgrnd; covrd pool; tennis; mini-golf; entmnt; many statics; quiet; CCI. "Conv NH Le Havre/Caen ferries; attractive site but ltd facs low ssn; sm area for tourers diff when wet." € 13.00   2005*

GRUISSAN *10F1* (5km NE Coastal) **Camping Les Ayguades, 11430 Gruissan [04 68 49 81 59; fax 04 68 49 05 64; loisirs-vacances-languedoc@wanadoo.fr]** Exit A9 junc 37 onto D168/D32 sp Gruissan. In 10km turn L at island sp Les Ayguades, foll site sp. Lge, hdg/mkd pitch, unshd; htd wc; chem disp; mv service pnt; baby facs; shwrs inc; el pnts (6A) inc; lndtte; shop; rest; bar; playgrnd; sand beach adj; entmnt; TV; 25% statics; dogs €2.20; Eng spkn; adv bkg; quiet; cc acc; CCI. ♦ Easter-6 Nov. € 20.00   2004*

GUDAS *8G3* (2km S Rural) **Camping Mille Fleurs (Naturist), Le Tuilier, 09120 Gudas [tel/fax 05 61 60 77 56; info@camping-millefleurs.com; www.camping-millefleurs.com]** Fr S at Foix town on N20, turn R onto D1 at traff lts sp Laroque d'Olmes, Lieurac and l'Herm. In 6.5km sharp bend L onto D13 sp Mirepoix. In 500m fork L at sp Gudas & Varihles. Site in 2km over bdge on L. NB Do not app fr Varilhes thro Dalou & Gudas, rd too narr for c'vans. Sm, hdg/mkd pitch, terr, pt shd; wc; chem disp; mv service pnt; shwrs inc; child/baby facs; fam bthrm; el pnts (4-8A) €2.60-3.25; gas 10km; shop 8km; tradsmn; rest; bar; BBQ; no statics; dogs €1.80; phone; Eng spkn; adv bkg (dep €50); quiet; red low ssn; INF card req. "Excel site; lovely owners; gd pitches; v clean facs; guided mountain walks arranged; gd base Andorra, Toulouse & Carcassonne; gd views; communal meal twice a week in high ssn; adv bkg rec high ssn." ♦ 1 Apr-30 Sep. € 15.75   2006*

France

GUEBWILLER 6F3 (2km E) **Camping Le Florival, Route de Soultz, 68500 Issenheim [tel/fax 03 89 74 20 47; contact@camping-leflorival.com; www.camping-leflorival.com]** Fr Mulhouse take D430 N. Then take D5 twd Issenhiem. Site well sp. Med, hdg/mkd pitch, pt shd; wc; chem disp; shwrs inc; baby facs; el pnts (6A) €3; lndtte, shop & 200m; tradsmn; playgrnd; pool, waterslide 100m; TV rm; 30% statics; dogs €1.50; phone; Eng spkn; quiet; red 7 days; cc acc; CCI. "Vg NH; friendly recep." 1 Apr-31 Oct. € 12.40   2007*

GUEGON see Josselin 2F3

GUEMENE PENFAO 2G4 (1km SE Rural) **Camping L'Hermitage, 36 Ave du Paradis, 44290 Guémené-Penfao [02 40 79 23 48; fax 02 40 51 11 87; contact@campinglhermitage. com; www.campinglhermitage.com]** On D775 fr cent of Guémené-Penfao, dir Châteaubriant for 500m, turn R, site sp. Med, mkd pitch, hdstg, pt shd; wc; chem disp; mv service pnt; baby facs; shwrs inc; el pnts (6A) €2.50; gas; lndtte; ice; shop 1.5km; tradsmn; rest; snacks; bar; BBQ; playgrnd; htd, covrd pool adj; paddling pool; waterslide; jacuzzi; rv sw & fishing 300m; canoeing; tennis; games area; games rm; cycle hire; entmnt; child entmnt; TV; 20% statics; dogs €1; phone; some Eng spkn; adv bkg; quiet; red low ssn; CCI. "Gd walking in area; excel." ♦ 1 Apr-31 Oct. € 10.30   2006*

GUENROUET 2G3 (E Rural) **Camp Municipal St Clair, 44530 Guenrouet [02 40 87 61 52; fax 02 40 87 60 88; www.campingsaintclair.com]** S fr Redon take D164 dir Blain, turn R onto D2 to Guenrouet, over bdge & site directly on L after bdge. Med, hdg/mkd pitch, pt sl, pt shd; wc; chem disp; mv service pnt; 50% serviced pitches; shwrs inc; el pnts (10A) €2.80; gas 1km; ice; shop & 1km; tradsmn; rest 100m; playgrnd; htd pool adj; waterslide; fishing; canoe hire; dogs €1.50; Eng spkn; quiet; CCI. "On banks of canal; special area for late arrivals; excel." ♦ 16 Apr-30 Sep. € 13.00   2005*

GUERANDE 2G3 (2km N Rural) **Camping La Fontaine, Kersavary, Route de St-Molf, 44350 Guérande [02 40 24 96 19 or 06 08 12 80 96 (mob)]** Fr Guérande take N774 N sp La Roche-Bernard; opp windmill, fork L sp St-Molf; site on L in 500m. Med, mkd pitch; pt shd; wc; chem disp (wc); shwrs inc; el pnts (6A) €2.50; lndtte; snacks; shop, rest & bar 4km; playgrnd; sand beach 4km; statics sep; dogs €0.60; phone; adv bkg rec high ssn; quiet; red low ssn; 4% red CCI. "Pleasant, peaceful site in orchard." ♦ ltd. 1 Apr-30 Sep. € 10.00   2006*

GUERANDE 2G3 (2km E Rural) **Camping Domaine de Léveno, Route de Sandun, 44350 Guérande [02 40 24 79 30; fax 02 40 62 01 23; info@camping-leveno.com; www.camping-leveno.com]** Fr Guérande foll sps to l'Etang de Sandun. Med, pt shd; wc; serviced pitches; shwrs; el pnts (6A) inc; gas; lndtte; ice; shop; rest; snacks; bar; BBQ; playgrnd; htd, covrd pool; paddling pool; waterslide; sand beach 5km; tennis; mini-golf; games area; entmnt; TV rm; 60% statics; dogs €4; adv bkg; quiet; red low ssn. "Conv La Baule; vg site in lovely park." 30 Mar-30 Sep. € 30.00
2007*

See advertisement on page 523

GUERANDE 2G3 (7km E Rural) **FFCC Camping de l'Etang en Kerjacob, 47 Rue des Chênes, Sandun, 44350 Guérande [02 40 61 93 51; fax 02 40 61 96 21; camping-etang@wanadoo.fr; www.camping-etang.com]** Fr Guérande take D51 NE for approx 5km, turn R onto D48 for 3km. Turn L to site on lakeside. Sp fr each junc on Guérande by-pass. Med, hdg/mkd pitch, pt shd; wc; chem disp; baby facs; shwrs inc; el pnts (10A) inc; lndtte; shop, rest, snacks, bar high ssn; BBQ; playgrnd; htd pool & paddling pool; sand beach 9km; watersports 9km; lake fishing; cycle hire; games rm; 40% statics; dogs €1.45; poss cr; Eng spkn; adv bkg; cc acc; CCI. "Pleasant, peaceful site; friendly staff; ltd facs low ssn; noisy pool & playgrnd; mkt Wed & Sat." ♦ 15 May-15 Sep. € 20.60   2006*

> The opening dates and prices on this campsite have changed. I'll send a site report form to the editor for the next edition of the guide.

GUERANDE 2G3 (1km S Urban/Rural) **Camping Trémondec, 48 Rue du Château de Careil, 44350 Guérande [02 40 60 00 07; fax 02 40 60 91 10; info@camping-tremondec.com; www.camping-tremondec.com]** Fr Nantes on N175/N171 dir La Baule. Take D192 dir La Baule cent, turn W in 800m dir Brenave, Careil. Site sp. Med, mkd pitch, hdstg, pt sl, pt shd; wc; chem disp; baby facs; shwrs inc; el pnts (6A) €3.80; gas 1km; lndtte; ice; tradsmn; supmkt 900m; rest, snacks, bar high ssn; BBQ; playgrnd; htd pool; sand beach 2km; games area; entmnt; child entmnt; 50% statics; dogs €2.50; adv bkg; Eng spkn; quiet; cc acc; red low ssn/long stay/ CCI. "Château de Careil 200m; Guérande medieval city; lovely beaches & coast; pleasant walks thro salt marshes; cycle rtes; reported unkempt & san facs unclean (Aug 2007)." ♦ 1 Apr-30 Sep. € 20.20
2007*

France

GUERANDE *2G3* (7km W Coastal) **Camp Municipal Les Chardons Bleus, Blvd de la Grande Falaise, 44420 La Turballe [02 40 62 80 60; fax 02 40 62 85 40; camping.les.chardons.bleus@ wanadoo.fr]** Foll D99 to La Turballe. Site well sp fr town cent along D92. Lge, hdg/mkd pitch, unshd; wc; chem disp; mv service pnt adj; shwrs inc; el pnts (6-10A) €2.75-3.70 (poss rev pol, long lead poss req); gas; lndtte; shop; tradsmn; rest in ssn; snacks; bar; playgrnd; htd pool; sand beach adj (pt naturist) & 2km; entmnt; dogs €2.10; phone; Eng spkn; cc acc; CCI. "Well organised site; warm welcome; becoming a little shabby but beach superb; ltd el pnts when full; san facs clean but poss stretched high ssn; variable opening dates - phone ahead to check early ssn; nature reserve adj with bird life." ♦ 30 Apr-30 Sep. € 15.40   2005*

GUERANDE *2G3* (7km NW Coastal) **Camping-Caravaning La Falaise, 1 Blvd de Belmont, 44220 La Turballe [02 40 23 32 53; fax 02 40 62 87 07; info@camping-de-la-falaise.com; www.camping-de-la-falaise.com]** Fr Guérande exit on D99 sp La Turballe/Piriac-sur-Mer; pass La Turballe; site easily seen on L 200m after Intermarché. Med, hdg/ mkd pitch, pt shd; htd wc (some cont); chem disp; some serviced pitches; shwrs inc; el pnts (4-10A) inc; lndtte; ice; shop 200m; tradsmn; rest 100m; bar; BBQ; playgrnd; sand beach adj; watersports; naturist beach 2km; horseriding & mini-golf 3km; entmnts; TV; 5% statics; dogs €2; Eng spkn; adv bkg; quiet (some rd noise); CCI. "V pleasant site." ♦ 25 Mar-31 Oct. € 28.30   2007*

See advertisement above

Before we move on, I'm going to fill in some site report forms and post them off to the editor, otherwise they won't arrive in time for the deadline at the end of September.

GUERANDE *2G3* (8km NW Coastal) **Camping Le Refuge, 56 Rue de Brandu, 44420 La Turballe [02 40 23 37 17; fax 02 40 11 85 10]** On D99 thro La Turballe twd Piriac. Ikm after Intermarché supmkt turn R into Rue de Brandu. Site on R in 800m, sp. Lge, hdg pitch, shd; wc; chem disp (wc); mv service pnt; shwrs inc; el pnts (6A) €3.50; lndtte; ice; shop 1km; tradsmn; BBQ (gas); playgrnd; sand beach 300m; fishing; sailing; tennis; no dogs; adv bkg; quiet; CCI. "Excel, well-kept site; lge pitches; easy access to beach & town; gd cycling area." ♦ 1 Jun-30 Sep. € 17.00   2006*

GUERANDE *2G3* (7km NW Rural) **Camping Le Parc Ste Brigitte, Manoir de Bréhet, 44420 La Turballe [02 40 24 88 91; fax 02 40 15 65 72; saintebrigette@wanadoo.fr; www.camping saintebrigette.com or www.les-castels.com]** Take D99 NW fr Guérande twd La Turballe thro vill of Clis. Sp on R in 900m. Lge, mkd pitch, shd; wc; chem disp; mv service pnt; serviced pitch; shwrs inc; baby facs; el pnts (6-10A) inc; gas; lndtte; ice; shop; rest; snacks; bar; playgrnd; htd, covrd pool; sand beach 2km; fishing; cycle hire; entmnt; TV rm; some statics; dogs €1.50; phone; poss cr; adv bkg (dep req); poss noisy; cc not acc; CCI. "V peaceful; excel rest & bar; some sm pitches; poss unkempt, untidy & poor pitch maintenance low ssn; gd." ♦ 1 Apr-1 Oct. € 28.30   2007*

⊞GUERCHE DE BRETAGNE, LA *2F4* (6km E Rural) **Camp Municipal, 35130 La Selle-Guerchaise [02 99 96 26 81; fax 02 99 96 46 72]** Fr N on D178 Vitré to Châteaubriant rd 3km N of of La Guerche-de-Bretagne; turn L onto D106 to Availles-sur-Seiche, then foll sp La Selle-Guerchaise; site behind Mairie in vill. Sm, hdg/mkd pitch, pt sl, pt shd; htd wc; chem disp (wc); shwrs inc; el pnts (4A) €2; (rev pol, poss long cable req); lndtte; playgrnd; multisports area; mini-golf; fishing adj; 50% statics; dogs; adv bkg; poss noisy; CCI. "Welcoming; excel san facs; site poss untidy low ssn; poss noisy church bells & barking dogs; locked barrier poles OK for cars but too low 4x4s or similar; fair NH." ♦ € 6.80   2006*

villagelaplage.com

Direct access to a sandy beach

Holiday camp   South Brittany   France **yelloh!** VILLAGE

Le Guilvinec Tel : 00 33 (0)2 98 58 61 90 Fax : 00 33 (0)2 98 58 89 06

GUERCHE SUR L'AUBOIS, LA *4H3* (2km SE Rural) Camp Municipal Robinson, 2 Rue Corniche, 18150 La Guerche-sur-l'Aubois [02 48 74 18 86 or 02 48 77 53 53; fax 02 48 77 53 59] Site sp fr D976 opp church in vill cent. Sm, hdg/mkd pitch, pt shd; wc; mv service pnt; shwrs inc; el pnts (6A) €2.20; lndtte; ice; shop; tradsmn; rest, bar 300m; playgrnd; lake sw adj; fishing; pedalo boating; entmnt; poss cr; some rlwy noise; CCI. "Pleasantly situated." ♦ ltd. 1 Jun-30 Sep. 2006*

GUERET *7A4* (8km S Rural) Camp Municipal Le Gué Levard, 5 Rue Gué Levard, 23000 La Chapelle-Taillefert [05 55 51 09 20 or 05 55 52 36 17 (Mairie); www.ot-gueret.fr] Take junc 48 from N145 sp Tulle/Bourganeuf (D33 thro Guéret); S on D940 fr Guéret, turn off at site sp. Foll sp thro vill, well sp. Sm, hdstg, pt sl, terr, shd; wc; mv service pnt; shwrs inc; el pnts (16A) €2; lndtte; shop; tradsmn; rest, snacks, bar 500m; tradsmn; playgrnd; fishing in Rv Gartempe; sports facs nr; some statics; dogs; phone; quiet; cc not acc; CCI. "Attractive, peaceful, well-kept site hidden away; new, vg san facs (2007); trout stream runs thro site; gd walking; ltd facs low ssn; warden calls 1900; gd auberge in vill; phone ahead to check open low ssn." ♦ 1 Apr-1 Nov. € 7.00 2007*

GUERET *7A4* (3km W Rural) Camp Municipal du Plan d'Eau de Courtille, Route de Courtille, 23000 Guéret [05 55 81 92 24 or 05 55 52 99 50 (LS)] Fr W on N145 take D942 to town cent; then take D914 W; take L turn bef lake sp; site in 1.5km along lakeside rd with speed humps. Site sp 'L'Aire de Loisirs de Courtille'. Med, hdg/mkd pitch, pt sl, pt shd; wc (some cont); chem disp; mv service pnt; baby facs; shwrs inc; el pnts (10A) inc; shops 2km; rest, bar 500m; playgrnd; pool 1.5km; sand beach & lake sw; dogs €0.95; phone; poss cr; no adv bkg; quiet; CCI; "Pleasant scenery; well-managed site; narr ent to pitchs; watersports on lake; vg mkd walks nrby; poss noisy w/e." ♦ 1 Jun-30 Sep. € 11.00 2006*

GUERNO, LE see Muzillac *2G3*

GUICHEN *2F4* (8km SE) Camp Municipal La Courbe, 11 Rue du Camping, 35580 Bourg-des-Comptes [06 77 04 37 47 (mob) or 02 99 05 62 62 (Mairie); fax 02 99 05 62 69; bourg-des-comptes@wanadoo.fr] Fr Rennes take N137 S dir Nantes. At Crévin take rd W dir Guichen. Site sp on L bef rv bdge. Sm, pt shd; wc; chem disp; shwrs €0.91; el pnts (10A) €2.20-3.40; shops 1km; playgrnd; lake & rv 100m; fishing; some long-stay statics; dogs €0.53; adv bkg; quiet. "Rough field." 1 Apr-31 Oct. € 5.60 2005*

GUIDEL see Pouldu, Le *2F2*

GUIGNICOURT *3C4* (SE Urban) **Camp Municipal Bord de l'Aisne, Rue des Godins, 02190 Guignicourt [03 23 79 74 58 or 03 23 25 36 60; fax 03 23 79 74 55; mairie-guignicourt@wanadoo. fr]** Exit A26 at junc 14 Guignicourt/Neufchâtel & foll sp for Guignicourt (3km). Site sp in vill on rv bank. Turn R at g'ge down narr rd to site (12% descent at ent & ramp). Med, mkd pitch, pt shd; htd wc (some cont); chem disp; mv service pnt; shwrs; el pnts (6-10A) €2.75-€4.60 (poss rev pol, poss long cable req); shops 300m; tradsmn; rest, bar 300m; snacks; BBQ; playgrnd; fishing; tennis; 50% statics (sep area); dogs €1.50; poss cr; adv bkg; red long stay; cc acc; CCI. "Pretty, tranquil, well-kept rvside site; well guarded; v friendly, helpful staff; v popular NH, conv A26; san facs dated, unisex low ssn & poss unclean; poss muddy when wet; pleasant town; rlwy stn; excel touring base; conv Reims, Epernay; gd cycle tracks; poss itinerants; poss noise & smell fr sugar factory; no twin-axles; easy access despite gradient; office open 0800-2000." 1 Apr-30 Nov. € 9.50   2007*

⊞**GUILLESTRE** *9D4* (1km S Rural) **Camping St James Les Pins, 05600 Guillestre [04 92 45 08 24; fax 04 92 45 18 65; camping@ lesaintjames.com; www.lesaintjames.com]** Exit N94 onto D902A; in 1km foll Camping sps. Med, mkd pitch, shd; wc; chem disp; mv service pnt; shwrs; el pnts (5A) €2.50-4.50; gas; lndtte; ice; sm shop; rest, snacks & bar 1km; playgrnd; pool & tennis 300m; canoeing nrby; games area; games rm; TV rm; 15% statics; dogs €1; phone; CCI. "Vg." € 12.75   2007*

GUILLESTRE *9D4* (2km SW Rural) **Camp Municipal de la Rochette, 05600 Guillestre [tel/fax 04 92 45 02 15; guillestre@aol.com]** On N94 Briançon-Embrun rd take D902 to Guillestre. Fr town on by-pass (D902) turn S at rndabt onto D86 sp Risoul, cross bdge, immed turn W along rv, site in 1km. Lge, wc (some cont); shwrs inc; el pnts (4-10A) €2-3; gas; lndtte; ice; shop; snacks; BBQ; playgrnd; pool; fishing; dir access to rv; sports area; entmnt; poss cr; adv bkg; quiet. "Modern san facs; v helpful, friendly Dutch manager." ♦ 15 May-22 Sep. € 13.50   2005*

⊞**GUILLESTRE** *9D4* (3km W Rural) **Camping Le Villard, 05600 Guillestre [04 92 45 06 54; fax 04 92 45 00 52; camping-le-villard@wanadoo.fr; www.camping-levillard.com]** Exit N94 onto D902 twd Guillestre. Site on R in 1km. Ent few metres down side rd with site sp at corner. Med, mkd pitch, shd; wc (some cont); chem disp; shwrs inc; el pnts (2-10A) €1.40-2.80; gas; lndry rm; shop 500m; tradsmn; rest; snacks; bar; playgrnd; sports area; pool; rv adj; fishing; lake 2km; tennis; mini-golf; wintersports; TV rm; entmnt; 10% statics; dogs €1; adv bkg; red low ssn; CCI. "Poss run down low ssn; vg." ♦ € 16.50   2007*

GUILVINEC *2F2* (2.5km W Coastal) **Yelloh! Village la Plage, 29730 Guilvinec [02 98 58 61 90; fax 02 98 58 89 06; info@yellohvillage-la-plage.com; www.villagelaplage.com]** Fr Pont l'Abbé on D785 SW to Plomeur; cont S on D57 sp Guilvinec. Bear R on app to town & head W along coast rd twd Penmarch. Site on L in approx 1.5km. Lge, pt shd; wc; chem disp; mv service pnt; baby facs; sauna; shwrs inc; el pnts (5A) inc; gas; lndtte; shop; rest; snacks; bar; BBQ; playgrnd; htd pool; paddling pool; waterslide; sand beach adj; tennis; archery; games rm; entmnt (child & adult); mini-golf; cycle hire; wifi internet; 70% statics; dogs €4.50; c'vans over 8m not acc; poss cr; adv bkg; quiet; cc acc. "Spacious pitches; mkt Tue & Sun; excursions booked; ideal for families; site rds poss diff lge o'fits; excel touring base." ♦ 5 Apr-15 Sep. € 40.00 ABS - B15
2007*

See advertisement opposite

GUINES *3A3* (2km W Rural) **Camping La Bien Assise, 62340 Guînes [03 21 35 20 77; fax 03 21 36 79 20; www.camping-bien-assise.fr or www.les-castels.com]** Exit A16 at junc 40 dir Fréthun Gare TGV; turn L onto D215 dir Fréthun Gare TGV; at 1st rndabt take 3rd exit sp Guînes, passing under the TGV; at Féthun take D246 R dir Guînes, St Tricat; at rndabt take exit strt on to Guînes; pass thro vills of St Tricat & Hamas-Boucres (NB 30km/h zone & must give way on your R); at the 'Stop' sp in Guînes vill site opp; turn R dir Marquise & site on L after 130m. NB Arr bet 1000 & 2200 rec; phone ahead if early or late arr anticipated. Lge, hdg/ mkd pitch, pt sl, pt shd; htd wc (some cont); chem disp; mv service pnt; baby facs; shwrs inc; some el pnts (6A) inc (poss rev pol); gas; lndtte; ice; shop; tradsmn; rest (clsd Mon); snacks & bar (high ssn); BBQ; playgrnd; 2 pools (1 htd, covrd); paddling pool; waterslide; beach 15km; tennis; entmnt; cycle hire; library; horseriding 3km; wifi internet; TV/ games rm; many statics; dogs €2; v cr high ssn; Eng spkn; adv bkg; red long stay & low ssn; cc acc; CCI. "In grnds of chateau; v busy high ssn; well-run; lge pitches; beware-soft ground on some pitches low ssn; ask for pitch away fr v busy rd; pleasant, cheerful staff; clean san facs, stretched high ssn; excel rest; own wine sold; Guînes vill worth a visit; vg dog walk; vet in Ardres 9km; conv ferries; late arrivals area - much night movement high ssn; even if notice says 'Complet' worth checking availability for short stay; mkt Fri am; vg." ♦ 12 Apr-30 Sep. € 29.50 ABS - P05   2007*

See advertisement on next page

GUIPRY see Bain de Bretagne *2F4*

France

GUISE *3C4* (SE Urban) **Camp de la Vallée de l'Oise, Rue du Camping, 02120 Guise** [03 23 61 14 86; fax 03 23 61 21 07] Foll Vervin sp in town & camp clearly sp fr all dir in town. Med, pt shd; wc (some cont); shwrs inc; el pnts (3-6A) €3-5 (rev pol); lndry rm; ice; shops 500m; tradsmn; playgrnd; rv fishing & canoe hire adj; cycle hire; games rm; TV; entmnt; 50% statics; dogs; some Eng spkn; adv bkg; v quiet; red low ssn; CCI. "Calm, spacious with mature trees; beautifully kept site on outskirts of town; busy w/e; friendly; basic san facs in need of updating but v clean high ssn - more TLC needed low ssn (2007); supervised fishing; interesting old town with gd rests; if arr late, pitch & pay next morning." 1 Apr-20 Oct. € 10.00 2007*

GUISSENY see Plouguerneau *2E2*

GUJAN MESTRAS see Arcachon *7D1*

GURMENCON see Oloron Ste Marie *8F2*

HAGETMAU *8E2* (200m S Urban) **Camp Muncipal de la Cité Verte, 40700 Hagetmau** [tel/fax 05 58 79 79 79] On D933 S fr Mont-de-Marsan, go thro St Sever & cont on D933 to Hagetmau. Take ring rd & ent town fr S, sp 'Cité Verte'. Heading N fr Orthez on D933, also foll sp 'Cité Verte'. Sm, hdg pitch, pt shd; wc; chem disp (wc); mv service pnt; serviced pitch; fam bthrm; sauna; shwrs inc; el pnts (16A) inc; shops 500m; rest, snacks, bar 1km; BBQ; playgrnd; htd, covrd pool; jacuzzi; gym; dogs; phone; adv bkg ess (dep req); quiet. "A unique site associated with sports cent inc Olympic-sized pool; 24 pitches with personal facs; gd base for touring area; v attractive town; excel." 1 Jun-30 Sep. € 20.00 2006*

HAGUENAU *5D3* (2km S Urban) **Camp Municipal Les Pins, Rue de Strasbourg, 67500 Haguenau** [03 88 73 91 43 or 03 88 93 70 00; fax 03 88 93 69 89; tourisme@ville-haguenau. fr; www.ville-haguenau.fr] N fr Strasbourg; after passing town sp turn L at 2nd set of traff lts; foll camping sp. Med, mkd pitch, terr, pt shd; wc; chem disp; shwrs inc; el pnts (6A) €2.60; gas; lndry rm; shop, rest 2km; bar adj; playgrnd; dogs €0.90; phone; adv bkg; quiet; CCI. "Peaceful; lge pitches; very clean; new facs planned (for 2008); v helpful staff; highly rec." 1 May-30 Sep. € 8.10 2007*

The opening dates and prices on this campsite have changed. I'll send a site report form to the editor for the next edition of the guide.

⊞**HAMBYE** *1D4* (1.5km N Rural) **Camping aux Champs, 1 Rue de la Ripaudière, 50450 Hambye** [02 33 90 06 98; michael.coles@wanadoo.fr] Exit A84 junc 38 to Percy; then turn L at town cent rndabt onto D58 to Hambye; at mkt sq proceed to junc, strt sp Le Guislain, past Mairie; site on R in 1.5 km. Sm, some hdstg, unshd; htd wc; chem disp; fam bthrm; shwrs inc; el pnts (10A) €3; lndtte; shop, rest, snacks, bar 2km; adv bkg; red long stay; quiet; red long stay; CCI. "Friendly, helpful British owners; excel san facs; Abbaye de Hambye nrby; conv ferry ports." € 12.00 2006*

HANNONVILLE SOUS LES COTES *5D2* (3km W Rural) **Camping Le Longeau, Ferm Longeau, 55210 Hannonville-sous-les-Côtes** [03 29 87 30 54; fax 03 29 88 84 40] Fr Hannonville on D908. Foll sp 'Etang du Longeau.' Narr, steep forest tracks to site not rec trailer c'vans. Med, pt shd; wc; chem disp; shwrs inc; el pnts (3-6A) €2.50-4; rest; snacks; bar; fishing; no Eng spkn; quiet. "Gd; several old statics on site (Aug 2007)." Easter-15 Sep. € 8.00 2007*

HARDELOT PLAGE *3A2* (3km NE Urban) **Caravaning du Château d'Hardelot, 21 Rue Nouvelle, 62360 Condette [tel/fax 03 21 87 59 59; campingduchateau@libertysurf.fr; www.camping -caravaning-du-chateau.com]** Take D901 (N1) S fr Boulogne, R turn onto D940 dir Le Touquet; then R at rndabt on D113 to Condette; take 2nd turning to Château Camping, R at next rndabt & site 400m on R. Fr S leave A16 at exit 27 to Neufchâtel-Hardelot then take D940 twd Condette & turn L at 1st rndabt onto D113 then as above. Med, hdg/mkd pitch, pt sl, pt shd; wc; chem disp; mv service pnt; baby facs; shwrs inc; el pnts (10A) €4.50 (poss rev pol); lndtte; shop 500m; playgrnd; sand beach 3km; tennis 500m; sm multi-gym; horseriding; games rm; golf; some statics; dogs free; poss cr; some Eng spkn; adv bkg (rec high ssn); quiet but some rd noise; red low ssn; no cc acc; CCI. "Lovely site in wooded surroundings; well organised; gd value; bar & gd rest walking dist; immac, modern san facs; nr chateau & lake; v helpful & friendly owner; conv for Calais & Cité Europe but barrier only opens at 0800; sm pitches; popular & v busy high ssn; easy cycle ride to beach; excel." ♦ ltd. 1 Apr-31 Oct. € 19.50
2007*

HAULME see Charleville Mézières *5C1*

HAUTECOURT ROMANECHE see Bourg en Bresse *9A2*

HAUTEFORT *7C3* (8km W Rural) **Camping Les Tourterelles, 24390 Tourtoirac [05 53 51 11 17; fax 05 53 50 53 44]** Fr N or S on D704 turn W at Hautefort on D62/D5 to Tourtoirac. In Tourtoirac turn R over rv then L. Site in 1km. Med, hdg/mkd pitch, terr, pt shd; wc; chem disp; mv service pnt; baby facs; shwrs; el pnts (6A) inc; gas; lndtte; shop 2km; rest; snacks; bar; playgrnd; pool; tennis; horseriding; mini-golf; TV rm; 20% statics; dogs €3.50; bus 1km; phone; poss cr; Eng spkn; adv bkg (dep req); quiet; low ssn/snr citizens red; cc acc; CCI. "Beautiful Auvézère valley; rallies welcome; owners v helpful." ♦ Easter-15 Oct. € 20.00
2004*

Before we move on, I'm going to fill in some site report forms and post them off to the editor, otherwise they won't arrive in time for the deadline at the end of September.

HAUTERIVES see Beaurepaire *9C2*

HAUTOT SUR MER see Dieppe *3C2*

HAYE DU PUITS, LA *1D4* (1km N Rural) **Camping L'Etang des Haizes, 50250 St Symphorien-le-Valois [02 33 46 01 16; fax 02 33 47 23 80; info@campingetangdeshaizes.com; www. campingetangdeshaizes.com]** Heading N fr La Haye-du-Puits on D900 under rlwy bdge & site 3rd on L, well sp. Med, hdg pitch, some hdstg, pt sl, pt shd; wc; chem disp; mv service pnt; baby facs; shwrs inc; el pnts (10A) €5; gas; lndtte; supmkt 1km; shop; tradsmn; rest; snacks; bar; playgrnd; htd pool complex; waterslide; beach 15km; archery; fishing; cycle hire; games area; entmnt; TV rm; 50% statics (sep area); dogs €2; bus; phone; poss cr; Eng spkn; adv bkg rec (dep req); quiet; red low ssn; CCI. "Clean, pretty site in Marais du Contentin nature park; barrier clsd 2300-0700; pool area v clean; grounds v well-tended; helpful & pleasant owners; conv vill & Cherbourg ferry (1hr); elec pnts poss insuff - cables across rd; ltd facs low ssn." ♦ 1 Apr-15 Oct. € 26.00 (CChq acc)
2006*

HAYE DU PUITS, LA *1D4* (6km N Urban) **FFCC Camp Municipal du Vieux Château, Ave de la Division-Leclerc, 50390 St Sauveur-le-Vicomte [02 33 41 72 04 or 02 33 21 50 44; fax 02 33 95 88 85; ot.ssv@wanadoo.fr]** Fr Cherbourg on N13/D2 site on R after x-ing bdge at St Sauveur-le-Vicomte, sp. Med, mkd pitch, pt shd; wc; chem disp; shwrs inc; el pnts (6A) €1.75 (rev pol); lndtte; ice; shop 500m; tradsmn; rest at auberge adj; BBQ; playgrnd adj; pool; tennis 1km; games area; games rm; TV; dogs €1; phone; adv bkg; quiet; cc acc; CCI. "Excel site; ideal 1st stop fr Cherbourg; in grounds of old chateau; office open until 2200 & barrier clsd 2200-0800." 15 May-15 Sep. € 8.90
2006*

HEIMSBRUNN see Mulhouse *6F3*

HEMING *6E3* (5km SW) **Camping Les Mouettes, 57142 Gondrexange [03 87 25 06 01; fax 03 87 25 01 13]** Exit Héming on N4 Strasbourg-Nancy. Foll sp Gondrexange & site sp. App fr W on D955 turn to site sp on L about 1km bef Héming. Lge, pt sl, unshd; wc; chem disp; shwrs inc; el pnts (6A) €4 (rev pol) adapter req; lndtte; shop, snacks & rest 1km; bar; playgrnd; lake beach, sw, fishing & sailing adj; cycle hire; tennis; mini-golf; 40% statics; phone; poss cr; quiet; CCI. "Pleasant site by lake; poss noisy w/e; friendly warden; basic facs but immac." 1 Apr-30 Sep. € 11.10
2004*

HENDAYE *8F1* (2km N) **Camping Les Acacias, Route de la Glacière, 64700 Hendaye-Plage [tel/fax 05 59 20 78 76; info@les-acacias.com; www.les-acacias.com]** Exit Hendaye by N10 Rte de la Corniche for St Jean-de-Luz. In 1km turn R on D658. Site sp on R. Caution under rlwy bdge. Lge, sl, shd; wc; shwrs; el pnts (6A) €4.20 (rev pol); gas; lndtte; shop; rest; snacks; bar in high ssn; playgrnd; sand beach 1.4km (free shuttle); lake sw & waterslide 1.5km; poss cr; adv bkg; quiet but some rlwy noise. "Helpful management; 5km to Spanish frontier; many tours in mountains; easy access shops & beaches; own lake for trout fishing." 1 Apr-1 Oct. € 18.00
2004*

France

HENDAYE *8F1* (2km W Urban/Coastal) **Camping Ametza, Blvd de l'Empereur, 64700 Hendaye-Plage [05 59 20 07 05; fax 05 59 20 32 16; contact@camping-ametza.com; www.camping-ametza.com]** Exit A63 junc 2 St Jean-de-Luz S onto D192. Foll sp to site. Turn L on hill down to seafront, cross rlwy, site immed on L. Lge, sl, shd; wc; chem disp; baby facs; shwrs inc; el pnts (6A) €3.90 (poss rev pol); lndry rm; shop; snacks; bar; playgrnd; pool; sand; beach 900m; games area; entmnt; 30% statics; dogs €2; poss cr; Eng spkn; quiet; CCI. "Lovely site, relaxed; gd sized pitches; excel facs; Henday pleasant resort; excel beach in walking dist." 1 Jun-30 Sep. € 21.50   2007*

HENNEBONT see Lorient *2F2*

HENNEVEUX see Boulogne sur Mer *3A2*

HENRIDORFF see Phalsbourg *5D3*

HENVIC see St Pol de Léon *1D2*

HERBIGNAC *2G3* (E Rural) **Camp Municipal de Ranrouet, Rue Cadou, 44410 Herbignac [02 40 88 96 23 or 02 40 91 36 52]** Site at intersection D774 & D33 on E edge of vill. Med, pt shd; wc; chem disp; shwrs; el pnts (6A) inc; lndtte; shop; supmkt adj; playgrnd; beach 10km; entmnt; TV; CCI. "Immac san facs; gd cent for Guérande." Easter-30 Oct. € 12.55   2005*

⊞**HERIC** *2G4* (2km W Rural) **Camping La Pindière, La Denais, Route de la Fay-de-Bretagne, 44810 Héric [tel/fax 02 40 57 65 41; patrick-ara@wanadoo.fr; www.camping-la-pindiere.com]** Exit N137 twd Héric at traff lts in town, leave town & turn W onto D16 (sp Camping). Site on L after rndabt supmkt, turn at sp Notre Dames-des-Landes. Med, hdg pitch, hdstg, pt shd; wc; chem disp; mv service pnt; baby facs; shwrs inc; el pnts (6-10A) €3-4.50; gas; lndtte; ice; shop; tradsmn; rest; bar; playgrnd; htd pool; paddling pool; sports facs; tennis; horseriding 200m; TV; 50% statics; dogs €1.40; phone; Eng spkn; adv bkg rec, site poss clsd w/e low ssn; some noise fr rd on N side; CCI. "Lge, grass pitches, soft in wet weather; v pleasant; warm welcome; gd NH." ♦ € 13.00   2006*

HERICOURT EN CAUX see Yvetot *3C2*

HERISSON *7A4* (W Rural) **Camp Municipal de l'Aumance, Crochepot, 03190 Hérisson [04 70 06 80 45 or 04 70 06 85 93]** Exit A71 junc 9 onto D2144 (N144) N. Turn R onto D11 to Hérisson. Bef vill turn L at blue sp (high on L), site on R down hill. Fr S exit A71 junc 10 onto D94 to Cosne, then D11 to Hérisson. Foll lorry rte to avoid town cent; site on D157 on rv. Med, mkd pitch, pt shd; wc; shwrs inc; el pnts (10A) inc; ice; playgrnd; games area; rv adj; phone. "Idyllic setting; delightful rvside site; warden calls eves; rec." Easter-31 Oct. € 6.94   2007*

HERPELMONT see Bruyères *6E2*

HESDIN *3B3* (6km SE Rural) **Camping de la Route des Villages Fleuris, 98 Rue de Frévent, 62770 St Georges [03 21 03 11 01 or 03 21 41 97 45]** Fr Hesdin, SE on D340 for 5.5km. Site on L in vill, in same rd as Camping St Ladre. Look for correct sp. Med, mkd pitch, pt sl, pt shd; wc (some cont); chem disp; shwrs €1; el pnts (4A) €2.30; gas; shops 6km; tradsmn; BBQ; playgrnd; 90% statics; adv bkg; quiet; CCI. "Space for approx 7 tourers at rear of site; security barrier; friendly warden - can find him in bungalow to L of site ent; gd." 1 Apr-30 Sep.
          2006*

HESDIN *3B3* (6km SE Rural) **Camping St Ladre, 66 Rue Principale, 62770 St Georges [03 21 04 83 34; bd-martin@wanadoo.fr; http://monsite.wanadoo.fr/martinbernard]** Fr Hesdin SE on D340 for 5.5km. Site on L after St Georges, ent narr lane next cottage on bend. Fr W on D939 (N39) or D349 foll sp Frévent, then St Georges. Sp to site poor. Sm, hdg/mkd pitch, pt shd; wc; chem disp; shwrs inc; el pnts (5A) €2.50; lndtte; tradsmn; no statics; adv bkg; quiet; cc not acc; CCI. "Sm family-run, peaceful site in orchard; basic facs but clean; welcoming, pleasant owner; conv Channel ports, Agincourt & Crécy; usual agricultural noises; gd rests in Hesdin." 1 Apr-30 Oct. € 8.00   2006*

⊞**HESDIN** *3B3* (12km NW Rural) **Camp Municipal La Source, Rue des Etangs, 62990 Beaurainville [03 21 81 40 71 or 06 80 32 17 25 (mob); fax 03 21 90 02 88]** Fr Hesdin take D349 NW to Beaurainville. Site on R bef cent of town, 1.5km E of town cent nr lake; sp. Med, mkd pitch, pt shd; htd wc; shwrs inc; el pnts (10A) inc (poss rev pol); lndtte; shop 1km; bar; playgrnd; fishing; boating; games area; horseriding; 90% statics; 10% red long stay; CCI. "Ltd touring pitches; site poss clsd in winter - phone ahead; pleasant area with plenty wildlife; poss cold shwrs low ssn; gd NH." ♦ € 12.60   2006*

HEUDICOURT see St Mihiel *5D2*

HILLION see St Brieuc *2E3*

HIRSON *3C4* (3km N Rural) **FFCC Camp Municipal de la Cascade de Blangy, 02500 Hirson [03 23 58 18 97 or 03 23 58 03 91 (LS); fax 03 23 58 25 39; tourisme.info.hirson@wanadoo.fr]** Exit Hirson W twd La Capelle & turn R on D963; at rndabt (site sp) fork R immed; foll site sp. Long, narr access rd. Med, hdg/mkd pitch, pt sl, pt shd; wc; chem disp; mv service pnt; shwrs inc; el pnts (6-13A) €3-4; lndtte; shop; tradsmn; rest, snacks 2km; bar; BBQ; playgrnd; pool; 25% statics; dogs €0.50; Eng spkn; adv bkg ess high ssn; quiet but some rlwy noise; CCI. "V clean site; 2,500kg weight limit; pitches uneven; rec arr bet 1000-1200 & 1700-1900; immac san facs; popular with youth groups; v helpful; conv N43; gd." ♦ ltd. 15 Apr-15 Sep. € 9.60   2007*

HIRSON *3C4* (10km N) **Camp Municipal des Etangs des Moines, 59610 Fourmies** [03 27 60 04 32 or 03 72 60 03 15; contact@atouvert.com; www.atouvert.com] Fr Hirson head N on D964 to Anor. Turn L to Fourmies, site sp on R on ent town. Med, hdg pitch, hdstg, pt shd; wc; chem disp; shwrs €1; el pnts (10A) €3.20; lndtte; shop 1km; tradsmn; playgrnd; htd pool; 80% statics; dogs €1; no twin-axles; poss cr; Eng spkn; some rlwy noise; CCl. "Textile & eco museum in town; shwrs run down, other facs gd; vg." 1 Apr-31 Oct. € 10.80   2007*

⊞**HOHWALD, LE** *6E3* (1km W Urban) **Camp Municipal Herenhause, 28 Rue du Herrenhaus, 67140 Le Hohwald** [tel/fax 03 88 08 30 90] Site on W o'skts of town on D425 300m fr cent. Med, pt sl, terr, shd; htd wc; shwrs inc; lndtte; shops adj; el pnts (10A) €2-4; snacks; playgrnd; tennis 300m; many statics; dogs €1.65; adv bkg; quiet. "Beautiful setting in pine woodland; san facs dated but immac." € 10.45   2007*

HONFLEUR *3C1* (5km S Rural) **Camping Domaine Catinière, Route d' Honfleur, 27210 Fiquefleur-Equainville** [02 32 57 63 51; fax 02 32 42 12 57; info@camping-catiniere.com; www.camping-catiniere.com] Fr A29/Pont de Normandie (toll) bdge exit junc 3 sp Le Mans, pass under m'way onto D580/D180. In 3km go strt on at rndabt & in 100m bear R onto D22 dir Beuzeville; site sp on R in 500m. Med, hdg/mkd pitch, pt shd; wc (some cont); chem disp; shwrs inc; baby facs; el pnts (4A) inc (long lead poss req)(poss rev pol), extra charge for 8-13A; lndtte; sm shop & 3km; tradsmn; snacks & bar in high ssn; BBQ; snacks; playgrnd; htd pool; games rm; entmnt; wifi internet; TV rm; 60% statics; dogs €2; phone; poss cr; Eng spkn; adv bkg rec high ssn & w/e; (dep req); quiet; cc acc only over €80; CCl. "Attractive, pleasant, well-kept site; lge & sm pitches; gd san facs; gate clsd 2200-0800 (2300 high ssn); 20 mins to Le Havre ferry via Normandy bdge; conv A13; poss school groups; gd walks; Honfleur lovely & interesting; highly rec." ◆ 5 Apr-22 Sep. € 25.00 ABS - N16   2007*

See advertisement below

HONFLEUR *3C1* (2.5km SW Rural) **Camping La Briquerie, 14600 Equemauville** [02 31 89 28 32; fax 02 31 89 08 52; info@campinglabriquerie.com; www.campinglabriquerie.com] Fr E ent town cent keeping harbour on R. Turn L onto D279 then in 2km turn R at rndabt at Intermarché. Site on R, N of water tower, E of Equemauville. Site well sp fr town cent. Fr S take D579 dir Honfleur Centre. At water tower on R turn L at Intermarché rndabt, site on R in 300m. Lge, hdg pitch, pt shd; wc; chem disp; mv service pnt; baby facs; fam bthrm; shwrs inc; el pnts (5-10A) €4-5; gas; ice; lndtte; supmkt adj; rest, snacks & bar (high ssn); BBQ; playgrnd; 3 htd pools; waterslide (high ssn); sand beach 3km; games rm; fitness rm; tennis 500m; TV rm; entmnt; 50% statics; dogs €3; poss cr; Eng spkn; adv bkg (fee for Jul/Aug); quiet; red low ssn; cc not acc; CCl. "Gd pitches; clean facs; staff v helpful late/early ferry arrivals; local vets geared up for dog inspections, etc; gd." ◆ 1 Apr-30 Sep. € 22.80   2007*

See advertisement on next page

HONFLEUR *3C1* (800m NW Coastal) **Camp du Phare, Blvd Charles V, 14600 Honfleur** [02 31 89 10 26 or 02 31 91 05 75 (LS); fax 02 31 24 71 47; vival-cabourg@wanadoo.fr; www.campings-plage.com/phare_honfleur] Fr N fr Pont de Normandie on D929 take D144; at ent to Honfleur keep harbour in R; turn R onto D513 sp Trouville-sur-Mer & Deauville (avoid town cent); fork L past old lighthouse to site entry thro parking area. Or fr E on D180; foll sp 'Centre Ville' then Vieux Bassin dir Trouville; at rectangular rndabt with fountain turn R sp Deauville & Trouville, then as above. Med, hdg pitch, pt shd; wc (some cont); chem disp; mv service pnt; shwrs €1.20; el pnts (2-10A) €3.80-5.75; gas; lndtte; shop 800m; tradsmn; rest 1km; snacks; bar; BBQ; playgrnd; htd, covrd pool nr; sand beach 100m; fishing; 10% statics; dogs €2.50; phone; poss cr; Eng spkn; rd noise; no cc acc; CCl. "Easy walk to delightful town & harbour/beach; m'van pitches narr & adj to busy rd; some surface water after rain; some soft, sandy pitches; facs ltd low ssn; barrier clsd 2200-0700; conv NH Le Havre ferry; sep m'van Aire de Service nr harbour." 1 Apr-30 Sep. € 18.10   2007*

France

CAMPING CARAVANING ★★★★ LA BRIQUERIE
CD62 Equemauville 14600 HONFLEUR - Tel.:02.31.89.28.32 • Fax: 02.31.89.08.52
Internet: www.campinglabriquerie.com • E-mail: Info@campinglabriquerie.com

New: water slide, 3 heated swimming pools and paddling pool

2 km from Honfleur and 12 km from Deauville. 2,5 km to the beach.
Water sports 2,5 km. Heated swimming pools, well equipped bathrooms
(also for disabled), recreation program in July and August, kindergarten, hairdryer.
Baby changing table, fast food, bar, restaurant. Horse riding: 500 m.
Rental of chalets all year. Discounts from 1/04 till 15/05 and from 15/09 till 30/09.

HONNECOURT SUR ESCAUT *3B4* (Rural) Camping de l'Escaut (formerly Municipal), 12 Rue de L'Eglise, 59266 Honnecourt-sur-Escaut [03 27 74 32 22 or 03 27 78 55 34] Fr Cambrai on N44 S twd St Quentin. Turn R onto D16 dir Honnecourt. Or fr A26 exit junc 9 onto D917 then N44. In Honnecourt-sur-Escaut after x-ing canal turn L in 150m; site behind church. Well sp. Med, hdg/mkd pitch, pt shd; wc; chem disp (wc); shwrs €1; mv service pnt; el pnts (6A) €3 (poss rev pol); lndtte; snacks; BBQ; playgrnd; fishing; 80% statics; dogs; adv bkg; noise fr church bells; CCI. "Pleasant, peaceful site on St Quentin canal & stream; lge pitches; san facs still basic (Sep 2007); gd." 1 Feb-30 Nov. € 13.40   2007*

HOSPITALET, L' *8G4* (600m N Rural) Camp Municipal, 09390 L'Hospitalet-près-l'Andorre [05 61 05 21 10; fax 05 61 05 23 08; mairie.lhospitalet-pres-landorre@wanadoo.fr] Site clearly sp on N20 fr Ax-les-Thermes to Andorra. Med, terr, unshd; wc; mv service pnt; shwrs inc; el pnts (5A) €2.30; lndtte; shops 200m; dogs; adv bkg; quiet but some rd noise. "Mainly tents, ltd space for tourers; vg walking; immac facs; conv day trips to Andorra & Spain; friendly warden; excel views." 1 Jun-31 Oct. € 6.70   2007*

HOSSEGOR *8E1* (6km N Rural) Camping Aire Naturelle Loustalet (Bellante), Quartier Lamontagne, Blvd Maritime, 40510 Seignosse [05 58 43 20 20 or 05 58 43 32 19] Exit N10 at St Vincent; turn R onto D33. In Hossegor turn R onto D152/D79. Site on L in approx 6km, after x-rds sp 'Plage de Casernes'. (Ignore no ent sp at site ent.) Sm, pt shd; wc (some cont); chem disp; shwrs inc; el pnts; BBQ; ice; lndry rm; shops 1km; sand beach 1km by foot only (patrolled beach 6km); playgrnd; horseriding; golf; adv bkg; CCI. "Vg long stay; site in Landes forest; v peaceful; family-run; basic facs; helpful, friendly owner." 1 Apr-30 Sep.   2004*

HOSSEGOR *8E1* (6km N Coastal) Village Camping Océliances, Ave des Tucs, 40510 Seignosse [05 58 43 30 30; fax 05 58 41 64 21; oceliances@wanadoo.fr; www.oceliances.com] Take D79 N fr Hossegor. After 6km turn L at rndabt. Site sp. Lge, mkd pitch, pt sl, pt shd; htd wc (some cont); chem disp; mv service pnt; shwrs inc; el pnts (6A) inc; gas; lndtte; ice; shop; rest; snacks; bar; BBQ; playgrnd; pool; paddling pool; sand beach 600m; windsurfing; lake 2km; games area; games rm; 10% statics; dogs €3.10; Eng spkn; adv bkg; quiet; cc acc; red long stay/low ssn. "Pleasant site in pine forest." ♦ 26 Apr-28 Sep. € 28.50   2007*

See advertisement below

VILLAGE CAMPING OCELIANCES

SALE AND RENTAL OF MOBILE HOMES
PITCHES
SWIMMING POOL
BAR - RESTAURANT
SUPERMARKET

OCÉLIANCES
LOISIRS ET RÉSIDENCES

Avenue des Tucs - 40 510 Seignosse
Phone : 33.(0)5.58.43.30.30 - Fax 33.(0)5.58.41.64.21
www.oceliances.com

600 METERS AWAY FROM THE OCEAN
5 MIN AWAY FROM HOSSEGOR

www.campinglavallee.com
tél. : 00 33 2 31 24 40 69
88, rue de la Vallée
14510 HOULGATE - FRANCE

La Vallée
camping & locations
☆☆☆☆

Authentic Normandy…
900 m away from the beaches

Rental of Mobile Homes

France

HOSSEGOR *8E1* (1.5km E Urban) **Camping Le Lac, 580 Routes des Lacs, 40150 Hossegor** [05 58 43 53 14; fax 05 58 43 55 83; info@ camping-du-lac.com; www.camping-du-lac.com] Exit A63 junc 8 or N10 onto D28 sp Hossegor/ Capbreton & foll sp for town cent. Site well sp at Soorts-Hossegor. Lge, hdg/mkd pitch, pt shd; wc (some cont); chem disp (wc); mv service pnt; shwrs inc; el pnts (6A) inc; gas; lndtte; ice; shop; tradsmn; rest; snacks; bar; playgrnd; sand beach 2km; lake 300m; games area; cycle hire; 80% statics; dogs €3; poss cr; Eng spkn; adv bkg; some rd noise; cc acc; CCI. "Ltd space for tourers." ♦ ltd. 1 Apr-30 Sep. € 28.00   2005*

⊞**HOSSEGOR** *8E1* (3km S Coastal) **Camp Municipal Bel Air, Ave de Bourret, 40130 Capbreton** [05 58 72 12 04] Fr N10 or A63, take D28 to Capbreton; turn R onto D152; turn L at 4th rndabt, site on L in 200m. Med, hdg pitch, pt sl, pt shd; wc; chem disp; shwrs; el pnts (10A) €3.15; ice; gas; lndry rm; shops 500m; tradsmn; playgrnd; sand beach 1km; cycle hire adj; dogs €2.05; quiet; 10% red low ssn; CCI. "No arr bef 1500; site office clsd 1200-1500 (1600 in winter); card-op barrier; marina nrby, gd fishing; excel network of cycle paths; excel surfing; conv Biarritz; arr bef 2000 unless late arr agreed in advance; vg winter NH/sh stay but phone ahead to check open." ♦ € 16.85   2006*

HOSSEGOR *8E1* (2km S Coastal) **Camping La Civelle (formerly Municipal), Rue des Biches, 40130 Capbreton** [05 58 72 15 11] Fr N on A63, take exit 8 & foll sps to Capbreton; cont twds cent. At 1st rndabt, turn L past Intermarché. Strt on at 2nd rndabtat. At 3rd rndabt take 3rd exit & foll sp for site. Lge, mkd pitch, shd; wc (some cont); chem disp; 10% serviced pitches; el pnts inc; gas; lndtte; ice; shop 1.5km; snacks; rest; pool; many statics; phone; cc acc; CCI. "Busy site; no arrivals bef 1500 - poss queues lunchtime high ssn; office clsd 1230-1430; some sandy pitches; conv for area; cycle rte dir to beach." 1 Jun-30 Sep. € 20.95
                           2006*

HOSSEGOR *8E1* (4km S Coastal) **Camping de la Pointe, Ave Jean Lartigau, 40130 Capbreton** [05 58 72 14 98 or 05 58 72 35 34; info@camping-lapointe.com; www.camping-lapointe.com www.homair.com]** Fr N10 at Labenne, take D652 twd Capbreton. In 5km turn L at camp sp. Site in 1km on R. Lge, shd; wc; chem disp; shwrs inc; el pnts €3; gas; lndtte; ice; shop; rest; snacks; playgrnd; htd pool; paddling pool; sand beach 800m; entmnt; TV; mini-golf; mainly statics; dogs €2; Eng spkn; quiet; cc acc. 1 Apr-31 Oct. € 23.00   2007*

HOULGATE *3D1* (3.5km NE Coastal) **Camping Les Falaises, Route de la Corniche, 14510 Gonneville-sur-Mer** [02 31 24 81 09; fax 02 31 28 04 11; camping.lesfalaises@voila.fr; www.lesfalaises.com] Fr D513 take D163; site clearly sp close to Auberville. Lge, pt sl, pt shd, wc; chem disp (wc); shwrs inc; el pnts (4-6A) €3.80-4.40 (poss v long lead req); snacks; shop; gas; ice; htd pool; playgrnd; beach reached by cliffs (230 steps); 30% statics; dogs €2.30; poss cr. "Nice site, different areas sep by trees; most pitches sl & poss uneven; gd, clean facs; red facs low ssn; pleasant, helpful staff." ♦ 1 Apr-15 Oct. € 17.00   2007*

HOULGATE *3D1* (1km E Urban) **Camp Municipal des Chevaliers, Chemin des Chevaliers, 14510 Houlgate** [02 31 24 37 93; fax 02 31 28 37 13; houlgate@wanadoo.fr; www.ville-houlgate.fr] Fr Deauville take D513 SW twds Houlgate. Before 'Houlgate' town sp, turn L & foll camping sps to site, 250m after Camping de la Vallée. Lge, mkd pitch, pt sl, pt terr, unshd; wc; shwrs inc; el pnts (10A) €3.90; tradsmn; sand beach 800m; fishing & boating 800m; dogs €0.70; adv bkg (rec high ssn); v quiet. ♦ 1 Apr-30 Sep. € 7.80   2005*

HOULGATE *3D1* (2km E Coastal) **Camping La Vallée, 88 Rue de la Vallée, 14510 Houlgate** [02 31 24 40 69; fax 02 31 24 42 42; camping. lavallee@wanadoo.fr; www.campinglavallee.com] Exit junc 29 or 29a fr A13 onto D45 to Houlgate. Or fr Deauville take D513 W. Before Houlgate sp, turn L & foll sp to site. Lge, hdg/mkd pitch, pt sl, terr, pt shd; wc; chem disp; some serviced pitches; shwrs inc; el pnts (6A) inc; gas; lndtte; ice; supmkt; tradsmn; rest; snacks; bar; playgrnd; htd pool; paddling pool; sand beach 900m; lake fishing 2km; tennis; cycle hire; golf 1km; games rm; entmnt; internet; TV rm; 30% statics; dogs €4; Eng spkn; adv bkg (fee); cc acc; red low ssn; CCI. "Superb, busy site; v clean san facs; friendly recep; some pitches sm for lge o'fits & sl; conv town cent." ♦ ltd. 1 Mar-12 Oct. € 29.00 (CChq acc)   2007*

See advertisement on previous page

HOUMEAU, L' see Rochelle, La *7A1*

HOUPLINES see Armentières *3A3*

HOURTIN *7C1* (1.5km N Rural) **Camping L'Orée du Bois, Route d'Aquitaine, 33990 Hourtin** [tel/fax 05 56 09 15 88 or 06 09 65 48 96 (mob); loree-du-bois@wanadoo.fr; www.camping-loreedubois. fr.st] Fr Hourtin, take D101E twd beach, site in 1.5km. Med, shd; wc; shwrs inc; el pnts (3-6A) €3; gas; lndtte; ice; shop; snacks; bar; playgrnd; pool; sand beach 8km; entmnt; dogs €1.50; adv bkg; quiet; red low ssn. "In Médoc area with its chateaux & wines." May-Sep. € 18.00   2007*

HOURTIN *7C1* (1.5km W Rural) **Camping La Rotonde - Le Village Western, Chemin de Bécassine, 33990 Hourtin** [05 56 09 10 60; fax 05 56 73 81 37; la-rotonde@wanadoo.fr; www. village-western.com] In Hourtin, foll sp Hourtin Port; in 1.5km L at sp; site on L 200m. Lge, pt shd; wc; chem disp; shwrs inc; el pnts (4-6A) €3.80-4.15; gas; lndtte; ice; shop & 2km; Tex-Mex rest; snacks; bar; playgrnd; pool in ssn; lake sw & beach 500m; watersports; tennis; games area; games rm; entmnt; internet; 30% statics; poss €2.05; adv bkg; quiet; cc acc; CCI. "In pine forest nr largest lake in France; gates shut 2230-0730 high ssn. " ♦ 1 Apr-30 Sep. € 24.25   2007*

HOURTIN *7C1* (1.5km W Rural) **Camping Les Ourmes, 90 Ave du Lac, 33990 Hourtin** [05 56 09 12 76; fax 05 56 09 23 90; lesourmes@ free.fr; www.lesourmes.com] Fr vill of Hourtin (35km NW Bordeaux), foll sp Houtin Port. In 1.5km, L at sp to site. Lge; mkd pitch, pt shd; wc; chem disp; mv service pnt; baby facs; shwrs inc; el pnts (6A) inc; gas; lndtte; ice; shops 1.5km; tradsmn; rest; snacks, bar 1.5km; BBQ; playgrnd; pool; lake sw 1km; sand beach (sea) 10km; watersports; fishing; horseriding; games rm; entmnt; TV; 10% statics; dogs €2; phone; bus; poss cr in ssn; Eng spkn; adv bkg (dep req + bkg fee); quiet; CCI. "Excel situation for a family holiday; Lake Hourtin shallow & excel for bathing & sailing dinghies; stunning beaches nrby; nr Les Landes & Médoc Vineyards; conv town cent; gd choice of rests all in walking dist." 1 Apr-30 Sep. € 23.00   2007*

HOURTIN *7C1* (10km W Coastal) **Airotel Camping La Côte d'Argent, Rue de la Côte d'Argent, 33990 Hourtin-Plage** [05 56 09 10 25; fax 05 56 09 24 96; info@camping-cote-dargent.com; www.cca33. com] On N215 at Lesparre-Médoc take D3 Hourtin, D101 to Hourtin-Plage, site sp. V lge, mkd pitch, pt sl, terr, shd; wc (some cont); mv service pnt; chem disp; baby facs; fam bthrm; shwrs inc; el pnts (6A) inc; gas; lndtte; ice; shop; tradsmn; rest; snacks; bar; BBQ playgrnd; 3 htd, pools (1 covrd); waterslide; jacuzzi; sand beach 300m; watersports; lake sw & fishing 4km; tennis; cycle hire; games rm; horseriding; entmnt; internet; TV; 25% statics; dogs €5.50; Eng spkn; adv bkg; quiet; red low ssn; cc acc; CCI. "Pleasant, peaceful site in pine forest & dunes; conv Médoc region chateaux & vineyards; ideal for surfers & beach lovers." ♦ 12 May-16 Sep. € 41.00 (CChq acc)   2007*

HOURTIN PLAGE see Hourtin *7C1*

HUANNE MONTMARTIN see Baume les Dames *6G2*

HUELGOAT *2E2* (3km E Rural) **FFCC Camping La Rivière d'Argent, La Coudraie, 29690 Huelgoat [02 98 99 72 50; fax 02 98 99 90 61; campriviere@ wanadoo.fr; http://larivieredargent.com]** Sp fr town cent on D769A sp Poullaouen & Carhaix. Med, some hdg/mkd pitch, shd; wc; chem disp; shwrs inc; el pnts (6A) inc; lndtte; shops 3km; rest, snacks, playgrnd; pool, tennis & entmnt high ssn; dogs €0.80; adv bkg; quiet; red long stay/low ssn. "Lovely wooded site on rv bank; some rvside pitches; helpful owner; ltd facs low ssn; gd walks with maps provided." 7 Apr-15 Oct. € 14.50
2007*

HUELGOAT *2E2* (1km W Rural) **Camp Municipal du Lac, 29690 Huelgoat [02 98 99 78 80; fax 02 98 99 75 72; mairie.huelgoat@wanadoo.fr]** Fr cent of Huelgoat foll unnumbered rd W sp La Feuillée/Brest; foll site sp. Med, hdg pitch, pt shd; wc; chem disp; shwrs inc; el pnts (10A) €2; lndry rm; shops 2km; playgrnd; htd pool adj; dogs €0.80; no adv bkg; quiet; no cc acc; CCI. "At end of lake (no sw); gd walking; gd san facs; gd size pitches; v peaceful." 15 Jun-15 Sep. € 9.35
2005*

HUELGOAT *2E2* (10km W Rural) **Camp Municipal Nestavel-Bras, 29218 Brennilis [02 98 99 66 57 or 02 98 99 61 07 (Mairie)]** Fr Huelgoat take D764 W for 8km & turn S onto D36. Site sp in Brennilis. Sm, hdg pitch, terr, pt shd; wc (cont); chem disp; shwrs €0.30; el pnts (13A) €0.76; playgrnd; lake sw nrby; fishing; TV rm; entmnt; quiet; CCI. "Lge pitches." 15 Jun-15 Sep. € 5.10
2005*

HUISSEAU SUR COSSON see Blois *4G2*

HUMES JORQUENAY see Langres *6F1*

HYERES *10F3* (4km E Coastal) **Camping Port Pothuau, 101 Chemin des Ourlèdes, 83400 Hyères [04 94 66 41 17; fax 04 94 66 33 09; pothuau@free.fr; www.campingportpothuau.com]** Fr Hyères E twds Nice on D98, turn R on D12 sp Salins d'Hyères. Site 2nd on R. Lge, mkd pitch, shd; wc; some serviced pitches; shwrs; el pnts (6-10A) inc (check rev pol/earth & poss long lead req); gas; lndtte; ice; shop; rest; snacks; bar; playgrnd; pool; sand beach 1km; tennis; games area; cycle hire; mini-golf; child entmnt; TV; 90% statics; dogs €3; red low ssn. "Nr interesting town of Hyères; excursions to peninsula of Giens; basic facs; vg." 1 Apr-22 Oct. € 35.00
2006*

HYERES *10F3* (8km E Rural) **Camping La Pascalinette, 83250 La Londe-les-Maures [04 94 66 82 72 or 04 94 87 46 62; fax 04 94 87 55 75]** Site sp on D98 E of Hyères. Lge, mkd pitch, shd; wc; baby facs; shwrs inc; el pnts (6A) €3.80; gas; lndtte; ice; shop; snacks; playgrnd; sand/shgl beach 3km; games rm; entmnt; TV; adv bkg; CCI. ♦ 1 Jun-15 Sep. € 17.00
2006*

HYERES *10F3* (8km E Coastal) **Camping Les Moulières, Route de Port-de-Miramar, 83250 La Londe-les-Maures [04 94 01 53 21; fax 04 94 01 53 22; camping.les.moulieres@wanadoo. fr]** On D98, in cent La Londe-les-Maures turn S at traff lts. After 1km turn R over white bdge & foll rd for 1km. Camping sp on R. Lge, pt shd; wc; baby facs; shwrs inc; el pnts (6A) inc; lndtte; shop; rest; snacks; bar; playgrnd; sand beach 800m; entmnt; TV; dogs €3; poss cr; adv bkg rec high ssn; quiet. ♦ 14 Jun-6 Sep. € 24.00
2006*

HYERES *10F3* (4km SE Coastal) **Camping Eurosurf, Plage de la Capte, 83400 Hyères [04 94 58 00 20; fax 04 94 58 03 18; cpleurosurf@ atciat.com; www.camping-hyeres.com or www. campeole.com]** Fr A8 take A57 as far as Hyères, foll sps to Giens & Les Iles, site is just outside La Capte vill on L on D97. V lge, mkd pitch, pt sl, pt shd; wc; chem disp; mv service pnt; baby facs; shwrs inc; el pnts (10A) €3.90; gas; lndtte; shop; tradsmn; rest; snacks; bar; no BBQ; playgrnd; sand beach adj; watersports; diving cent; 50% statics; dogs €3.90; phone; poss cr; no adv bkg; some rd noise; cc acc. "Some areas of soft sand & pitches not mkd; excel for watersports; excel location." ♦ ltd. 18 Mar-5 Nov. € 32.50
2006*

HYERES *10F3* (5km SE Coastal) **Camping Domaine du Ceinturon III, Rue du Ceinturon, L'Ayguade, 83400 Hyères [04 94 66 32 65; fax 04 94 66 48 43; ceinturon3@securmail.net; www. provence-campings.com/azur/ceinturon3.htm]** Fr Hyères take L'Ayguade rd sp airport. At T-junc in L'Ayguade turn R. Site 400m twd Hyères harbour & adj airport on D42. Fr NE on D42 drive thro L'Ayguade, turn R at traff lts just after end of vill sp. Lge, mkd pitch, shd; htd wc (some cont); chem disp; serviced pitch; shwrs inc; el pnts (2-10A) €2-3.50; gas; lndtte; ice; shop high ssn; tradsmn; rest; snacks; bar; playgrnd; beach adj; tennis; TV rm; excursions; TV; 15% statics; dogs €3.50; bus; poss cr; Eng spkn; poss ess Jul/Aug; quiet but some daytime noise fr adj airport; no cc acc; CCI. "Excel, popular site; v busy high ssn; sm pitches; helpful owners; smart shwrs; excel cycle paths in area. ♦ 30 Mar-30 Sep. € 16.35
2006*

HYERES *10F3* (5km SE Coastal) **Camping La Bergerie, 4231 Route de Giens, 83400 Hyères [04 94 58 91 75; fax 04 94 58 14 28; info@ camping-de-la-bergerie.com; www.camping-de-la-bergerie.com]** On L of D97 fr Hyères to Giens on Presqu'île de Giens. Med, pt shd; htd wc; mv service pnt; shwrs; el pnts (5A) €6.50; lndtte; shop; tradsmn; snacks (high ssn); bar; playgrnd; sand beach 200m; 50% statics; dogs €3; adv bkg; quiet. "Fair sh stay low ssn." 1 Mar-10 Jan. € 25.50
2007*

France

HYERES *10F3* (8km S Coastal) **Camping La Presqu'île de Giens, 153 Route de la Madrague, Giens, 83400 Hyères [04 94 58 22 86 or 04 94 57 20 18; fax 04 94 58 11 63; info@camping-giens.com; www.camping-giens.com]** Fr Toulon A570 dir Hyères. Thro palm-lined main street in Hyères dir Giens-les-Iles & foll sp to La Capte & Giens past airport on L, thro La Capte, turn R at rndabt to site on L, sp. Lge, pt sl, terr, pt shd; htd wc; mv service pnt; baby facs; shwrs inc; el pnts (6A) €4.50; gas; lndtte; ice; shop; tradsmn; snacks; playgrnd; TV; games rm; entmnt; sand beach 600m; fishing & boat excursions; 75% statics; dogs €2.60; poss cr; adv bkg; quiet. "Access to pitches awkward/steep lge o'fits; sister site La Tour Fondue much better access; ltd water pnts; gd san facs; pleasant, helpful staff." ♦ 1 Apr-1 Oct. € 19.20 (CChq acc) 2006*

HYERES *10F3* (9km S Coastal) **Camping La Tour Fondue, Ave des Arbanais, 83400 Giens [04 94 58 22 86; fax 04 94 58 11 63; info@camping-giens.com; www.camping-giens.com]** D97 fr Hyères, site sp. Med, hdg pitch, pt sl, pt terr, pt shd; wc; chem disp; mv service pnt; shwrs inc; el pnts (6A) €4.50; lndtte; rest; snacks; bar; beach adj; dogs €2.60; no adv bkg; cc acc. "Sister site of Camping Presqu'île de Giens with easier access." 1 Apr-5 Nov. € 19.20 2006*

HYERES *10F3* (13km S Coastal) **Camping International, 1737 Route de la Madrague, 83400 Hyères [04 94 58 90 16; fax 04 94 58 90 50; Thierry.Coulomb@wanadoo.fr; www.international-giens.com]** S fr Hyères on D97 dir Giens, cross past La Capte foll sp La Bergerie & La Madrague, site sp. Lge, mkd pitch, hdstg, terr, pt shd; wc; chem disp; mv service pnt; shwrs inc; el pnts (6A) €5; gas; lndtte; ice; shop; rest; snacks; bar; no BBQ; playgrnd; sand beach 300m; tennis adj; watersports; windsurfing; skin-diving; solarium; horseriding; internet; entmnt; some statics; no dogs; Eng spkn; adv bkg; quiet. "Excel family site; many activities." 1 Apr-31 Oct. € 24.00 2006*

HYERES *10F3* (6km W Rural) **FLOWER Camping Le Beau Vezé, Route de la Moutonne, 83320 Carqueiranne [tel/fax 04 94 57 65 30; info@camping-beauveze.com; www.camping-beauveze.com]** Fr Toulon take D559 E dir Carqueiranne. Approx 2km after Le Pradet turn L onto D76 twd La Moutonne. Site on R in 1.5km. Med, mkd pitch, terr, pt shd; htd wc (some cont); chem disp; baby facs; shwrs inc; el pnts (4A) €4; gas; lndtte; ice; shop; rest; snacks; bar; BBQ (gas only); playgrnd; 2 pools & paddling pool; beach 4km; tennis; mini-golf; cycle hire; entmnt; few statics; dogs €2.50; poss cr; adv bkg; quiet but some rd noise; red low ssn; cc not acc. "Poss diff access some pitches for lge o'fits; no twin-axle c'vans; recep clsd 1300-1500 & after 1600; mkt Thu." 15 May-15 Sep. € 27.00 2006*

IGOVILLE see Pont de l'Arche *3D2*

ILE BOUCHARD, L' *4H1* (Rural) **Camp Municipal Les Bords de Vienne, La Fougetterie, 37220 L'Ile-Bouchard [02 47 95 23 59; fax 02 47 58 67 35; mairie.ilebouchard@wanadoo.fr]** On N bank of Rv Vienne 100m E of rd bdge nr junc of D757 & D760. Med, mkd pitch, pt sl, pt shd; wc; chem disp; shwrs inc; el pnts (6-10A) €2.80; gas; lndtte; supmkt adj; playgrnd; pool; tennis 500m; rv sw adj; dogs €0.80; phone adj; adv bkg (Mairie); CCI. "Lovely, clean rvside site; helpful warden; conv Loire chateaux." ♦ ltd. 17 Jun-15 Sep. € 6.50 2006*

ILLIERS COMBRAY *4E2* (2km SW Rural) **Camp Municipal de Mont Jouvin, Route de Brou, 28120 Illiers-Combray [02 37 24 03 04; fax 02 37 24 16 21]** S on D921 fr Illiers for 2km twd Brou. Site on L. Med, hdg pitch, pt shd; htd wc; chem disp; some serviced pitches; shwrs inc; el pnts (6-8A) €3.10; gas; lndry rm; shop 2km; htd pool 500m; fishing adj; 20% statics; poss cr; adv bkg; quiet; CCI. "Excel san facs; ltd water/el pnts; gd security; many pitches wooded & with flowers; excel cycle path to vill; helpful warden; barrier clsd 1200-1500; 2100-0800 low ssn, 2200-0700 high ssn; office clsd 1800 & all Sun." ♦ 1 Apr-31 Oct. € 8.15 2007*

INGRANDES *4H2* (1km N Rural) **Camping Le Petit Trianon de St Ustre, 1 Rue du Moulin de St Ustre, 86220 Ingrandes-sur-Vienne [05 49 02 61 47; fax 05 49 02 68 81; chateau@petit-trianon.fr; www.petit-trianon.fr or www.les-castels.com]** Leave A10/E5 at Châtellerault Nord exit 26 & foll sp Tours. Cross rv heading N on D910 (N10) twd Tours & Dangé-St Romain. At 2nd traff lts in Ingrandes (by church), turn R. Cross rlwy line & turn L at site sp in 300m. After 1.5km turn R at site sp, site at top of hill. Med, mkd pitch, pt sl, pt shd; wc; chem disp; mv service pnt; baby facs; shwrs inc; el pnts (10A) inc; gas; lndtte; shop; tradsmn; rest & bar 100m; snacks; BBQ; playgrnd; htd pool; paddling pool; games area; cycle hire; mini-golf; tennis 1.5km; rv fishing 3km; internet; games/TV rm; dogs €2.10; quiet; some rlwy noise at night; recep 0900-1300 & 1500-2000; Eng spkn; adv bkg; cc acc; CCI. "Lovely site; charming old buildings; v friendly & helpful; excel facs." ♦ 20 May-20 Sep. € 26.80 ABS - L07 2007*

ISIGNY SUR MER *1D4* (500m NW Rural) **Camping Le Fanal, Rue du Fanal, 14230 Isigny-sur-Mer [02 31 21 33 20; fax 02 31 22 12 00; info@camping-lefanal.com; www.camping-lefanal.com]** Fr N13 exit into Isigny, site immed N of town. Foll sp to 'Stade' in town, (just after sq & church on narr street just bef R turn). Med, hdg/mkd pitch, pt shd; wc; chem disp; mv service pnt; shwrs inc; el pnts (10A) €3.30 (long cable poss req) €3; lndtte; ice; shop; snacks; bar; playgrnd; pool; aquapark; sand beach 10km; lake fishing adj; horseriding; tennis; games area; games rm; entmnt; TV; 50% statics; dogs €4; phone; adv bkg; quiet; cc acc; CCI. "Friendly staff; poss boggy in wet weather; vg site." ♦ 1 Apr-30 Sep. € 25.00 2005*

ISLE ET BARDAIS see Cérilly *4H3*

ISLE JOURDAIN, L' *7A3* (500m N Rural) **Camp Municipal du Lac de Chardes, Rue de Chardes, 86150 L'Isle-Jourdain [05 49 48 72 46 or 05 49 48 70 54 (Mairie); fax 05 49 48 84 19; isle-jourdain@wanadoo.fr]** Fr N147 in Lussac take D11 S to L'Isle-Jourdain. Site sp on R. Sm, mkd pitch, terr, pt shd; wc (some cont); shwrs inc; el pnts; shops, rest, snacks, bar 500m; htd pool 100m; boating; fishing; adv bkg; quiet. "Peaceful; excel san facs; sh walk to Rv Vienne; site yourself; warden calls am & pm." ♦ 15 May-15 Oct.

2007*

ISLE SUR LA SORGUE L' *10E2* (2km E) **Camping La Sorguette, Route d'Apt, 84800 L'Isle-sur-la-Sorgue [04 90 38 05 71; fax 04 90 20 84 61; sorguette@wanadoo.fr; www.camping-sorguette.com]** Fr Isle-sur-la-Sorgue take N100 twd Apt, on L site in 1.5km, sp. Med, hdg/mkd pitch, pt shd; wc (male cont); chem disp; mv service pnt; shwrs inc; el pnts (4-6A) €4.20-4.70; gas; lndtte; shop; tradsmn; rest adj; BBQ; playgrnd; beach adj; trout fishing adj; canoeing; tennis; games area; internet access; adv bkg (dep & booking fee req); 10% statics; dogs €2.70; poss cr; Eng spkn; quiet; cc acc; CCI. "Lovely site; gd facs; poss some pitches bare & muddy; v helpful, friendly staff; high m'vans beware low trees; rvside walk to attractive town surrounded by water; plenty of rests; excel Sun mkt (free shuttle fr site); conv Luberon, Gordes & Fontaine de Vaucluse." ♦ ltd. 15 Mar-15 Oct. € 19.80

2007*

ISLE SUR LA SORGUE L' *10E2* (3km E Rural) **Aire Naturelle de Sorgiack, Route de Lagnes, 84800 L'Isle-sur-la-Sorgue [04 90 38 13 95]** 2.5km E of L'Isle-sur-la-Sorgue on N100; take D99 N twd Lagnes; site sp 500m on L. Sm, mkd pitch, hdstg, pt shd; htd wc; chem disp; shwrs inc; el pnts (10A) inc; lndtte; ice; shop, rest, snacks, bar 2.5km; paddling pool; sw 3km; rv & fishing 500m; games rm; phone; adv bkg; quiet; cc not acc; CCI. "Delightful site in cherry orchard; v friendly hosts; excel facs, inc for disabled; gd mkts in area, esp antiques; excel touring base; gd." ♦ 1 Apr-15 Oct. € 15.75

2007*

⊞**ISLE SUR LA SORGUE L'** *10E2* (5km E Rural) **Aire Communale, Parking Vergnes, 84800 Fontaine-de-Vaucluse [04 90 20 31 79]** D25 fr Isle-sur-la-Sorgue; site on R after vill boundary; or on D24 fr Cavaillon then join D25. Sm, hdstg, unshd; wc; own san; chem disp; shops, rest, snacks & bar 500m; dogs; poss cr; cc acc. "Pleasant location next to rv; mainly for m'vans but spaces for c'vans; gd NH." € 3.00

2005*

ISLE SUR LA SORGUE L' *10E2* (5km NW) **Camping Domaine du Jantou, Chemin des Coudelières, 84250 Le Thor [04 90 33 90 07; fax 04 90 33 79 84; accueil@lejantou.com; www.lejantou.com]** Exit A7 at Avignon Nord onto D942 sp Carpentras. Turn S onto D6; in 8km join N100 E sp Le Thor. Site sp bef vill. App fr E fork R at sharp bend, thro town gate take L turn after passing church & L. Med, hdg pitch, pt shd; wc; chem disp; mv service pnt; shwrs inc; el pnts (3-10A) €2.60-3.40; lndtte; shop; snacks; playgrnd; 2 pools; paddling pool; cycle hire; games rm; entmnt; TV rm; some statics; dogs €1; adv bkg; quiet; cc acc. "Attractive site by Rv Sorgue; sm pitches, ltd access." ♦ ltd. 1 Mar-31 Oct. € 19.00

2005*

ISLE SUR LA SORGUE, L' *10E2* (5km E Rural) **Camping La Coutelière, Route de Fontaine de Vaucluse, 84800 Lagnes [04 90 20 33 97; fax 04 90 20 27 22; info@camping-lacouteliere.com; www.camping-lacouteliere.com]** Leave L'Isle-sur-la-Sorgue by N100 dir Apt, fork L after 2km sp Fontaine-de-Vaucluse. Site on L on D24 bef ent Fontaine. Med, hdg pitch, shd; wc; shwrs inc; el pnts (10A) €4; lndtte; ice; rest; snacks; bar; playgrnd; pool; canoeing nr; tennis; entmnt; 40% statics; dogs €3.10; phone; Eng spkn; adv bkg; quiet; CCI. "Gd site; 2km easy cycle ride to Fontaine." ♦ 1 Apr-15 Oct. € 15.30   2007*

ISLE SUR LE DOUBS, L' *6G2* (400m N Rural) **Camping Les Lumes, Rue des Lumes, 25250 L'Isle-sur-le-Doubs [tel/fax 03 81 92 73 05]** Well sp fr town edge on D83 (N83) bef rv bdge. Med, pt shd; wc; chem disp; shwrs; el pnts (10A) €2.60 (long lead req & poss rev pol); shop; tradsmn; playgrnd; rv sw; dogs; poss cr; Eng spkn; adv bkg; CCI. "Sh walk to town; gd." 1 May-30 Sep. € 11.00

2005*

ISLE SUR SEREIN, L' *4G4* (Rural) **Camp Municipal Le Parc de Château, 89440 L'Isle-sur-Serein [03 86 33 93 50 or 03 86 33 80 74 (Mairie); fax 03 86 33 91 81]** Exit A6 junc 21 or 22 & foll sp Noyers or Montréal & L'Isle-sur-Serein on D117. Or fr Avallon, take D957 twd Sauvigny-le-Bois; then D86 to L'Isle-sur-Serein; site on L on ent to vill. Sm, hdg pitch, pt shd; wc (cont); chem disp; shwrs inc; el pnts (10A) 2.30; lndry rm; ice; shop 1km; rest; bar; BBQ; playgrnd; tennis & boating adj; adv bkg; some rd noise; CCI. "Basic site; tidy; dated facs; attractive area." 1 May-30 Sep. € 6.80   2006*

⊞**ISOLA** *9D4* (1km NW Rural) **Camping Lac des Neiges, Quartier Lazisola, 06420 Isola [04 93 02 18 16; fax 04 93 02 19 40]** SE fr St Etienne-de-Tinée on D2205. site on R after approx 13km, site sp. Med, hdg/mkd pitch, hdstg, pt shd; htd wc; chem disp; mv service pnt; shwrs inc; el pnts (3-6A) €2.80-4.50; lndtte; ice; shops 1km; tradsmn; playgrnd; sw pool 1km; lake adj; ski stn 20 mins; fishing; kayaking; tennis; TV rm; 25% statics; dogs €1; phone; Eng spkn; adv bkg; quiet; cc not acc; CCI. ♦ € 13.50   2007*

France

ISPAGNAC *9D1* (2km E Rural) **Camping de l'Aiguebelle, 48320 Ispagnac [04 66 44 20 26]** N fr Florac on N106 for approx 6km; take turning for Ispagnac & foll sp for site; site on L 1km after Faux bet rd & Rv Tarn. Med, pt sl, pt shd; wc; chem disp; shwrs inc; el pnts (10A) €3.05; lndtte; ice; shop & rest 1km; snacks; bar; BBQ; playgrnd; pool; rv sw; tennis; no statics; dogs; phone; adv bkg; quiet but a little rd noise; CCI. "Uncrowded, shady site; grounds rather unkempt; vg base for Tarn Gorge, Cévennes, etc." 1 Apr-30 Sep. € 11.00   2007*

ISPAGNAC *9D1* (1km W Rural) **FFCC Camp Municipal Le Pré Morjal, 48320 Ispagnac [04 66 44 23 77 or 04 66 44 20 50 (Mairie); fax 04 66 44 23 84; contact@lepremorjal.fr; www. lepremorjal.fr]** 500km on W of town, turn L off D907 & then 200m on R. Med, hdg pitch, pt shd; htd wc; chem disp; mv service pnt; baby facs; shwrs inc; el pnts (10-16A) €3; lndtte; shops 200m; rest; playgrnd; pool 50m; paddling pool; rv sw 200m; games area; games rm; TV; dogs €1; quiet. "Lovely family site on edge of vill; gd size pitches on rocky base; friendly staff; gd rvside walks; interesting old town trail to foll nrby; vg base for Tarn & Joute Gorges; site poss muddy when wet." ♦ 1 Apr-31 Oct. € 16.00   2007*

ISPAGNAC *9D1* (10km W) **Camp Municipal, 48210 La Malène [04 66 48 58 55 or 04 66 48 51 16; fax 04 66 48 58 51]** Site on L of D907 W of Ispagnac in vill of La Malène. Site well sp. Sm, pt sl, pt shd; wc (some cont); chem disp; mv service pnt; shwrs; el pnts (10A) inc; shops, rest, snacks, bar 200m; BBQ; rv sw & fishing; dogs; poss cr; adv bkg; quiet; CCI. "Kayak hire; boat trips fr vill." Easter-30 Oct. € 10.00   2004*

ISQUES see Boulogne sur Mer *3A2*

ISSAMBRES, LES see St Aygulf *10F4*

ISSENDOLUS see Gramat *7D4*

ISSOIRE *9B1* (2.5km E Rural) **Camp Municipal du Mas, Ave du Dr Bienfait, 63500 Issoire [04 73 89 03 59 or 04 73 89 03 54 (LS); fax 04 73 89 41 05; camping-mas@wanadoo.fr; http:// monsite.wanadoo.fr/campingmas]** Fr Clermont-Ferrand S on A75/E11 take exit 12 sp Issoire; turn L over a'route sp Orbeil; at rndabt, take 1st exit & foll site sp. Med, hdg/mkd pitch, pt shd; htd wc (mostly cont); chem disp; shwrs inc; el pnts (10-13A) €2.60 (long lead poss req); gas; lndtte; shops & supmkt 2km; tradsmn; snacks; playgrnd; rv sw; fishing in adj lake; TV rm; 5% statics; dogs free; phone; poss cr; adv bkg (rec high ssn); quiet but some rd noise; red long stay; cc acc; CCI. "Well-run, basic site; san facs to be refurbed (for 2008); v helpful warden; pitches mkd/hdg in pairs; poss boggy after rain; office clsd 1200-1415; supmkt opp exit A75." ♦ 1 Apr-31 Oct. € 12.50   2007*

ISSOIRE *9B1* (10km E) **Camp Sauxillanges, 63490 Sauxillanges [04 73 96 86 26 or 04 73 71 02 43 (HS); fax 04 73 71 07 69; chateau@ grangefort.com]** Exit A75 (E11) at junc 13 to D996, head E twd Sauxillanges. Turn R 100m after Gendarmerie in vill. Sp. Med, mkd pitch, shd; wc; chem disp; some serviced pitches; shwrs inc; el pnts (4A) €2.25 (rev pol); lndtte; ice; playgrnd; pool adj (Jul/Aug); tennis; archery; fishing 50m; no statics; dogs €2.30; Eng spkn; adv bkg ess high ssn; quiet; cc acc. "Adj leisure cent with pool (free to campers); sh walk to charming, interesting town with 3 rests; excel." ♦ 15 Jun-15 Sep. € 13.00
2005*

ISSOIRE *9B1* (6km SE Rural) **FFCC Camping Château La Grange Fort, 63500 Les Pradeaux [04 73 71 05 93 or 04 73 71 02 43; fax 04 73 71 07 69; chateau@lagrangefort.com; www. lagrangefort.com]** S fr Clermont Ferrand on A75, exit junc 13 onto D996 sp Parentignat. At 1st rndabt take D999 sp St Rémy-Chargnat (new rd); at next rndabt take 1st exit onto D34 & foll sp to site on hill-top. Narr app rd & steep ent. Med, hdg/mkd pitch, shd; htd wc; chem disp; mv service pnt; baby facs; sauna; shwrs inc; el pnts (6A) €3; lndtte; gas; ice; shop in vill; tradsmn; rest; snacks; bar; playgrnd; htd, covrd pool; paddling pool; rv fishing; tennis; canoe & mountain bike facs; internet; TV rm; some statics; dogs €3; phone; office clsd 1200-1400; Eng spkn; adv bkg (fee); quiet; cc acc; CCI. "Pleasant, peaceful Dutch-run site in chateau grounds; site on hilltop so excel views; excel san facs; long walk to facs fr some pitches & ltd low ssn; some sm pitches; most pitches damp & gloomy under lge trees; mosquito problem on shadiest pitches; pitches muddy after rain; ltd parking at recep; rest in chateau, adv bkg ess; gd." 10 Apr-15 Oct. € 23.30   2007*

ISSOIRE *9B1* (11km S) **Camping Les Loges, 63340 Nonette [04 73 71 65 82; fax 04 73 71 67 23; camping.les.loges.nonette@wanadoo.fr; www. lesloges.com]** Exit 17 fr A75 onto D214 sp Le Breuil, dir Nonette. Turn L in 2km, cross rv & turn L to site. Site perched on conical hill. Steep app. Med, mkd pitch, pt shd; wc; chem disp; child/baby facs; shwrs inc; el pnts (10A) €3.35; gas; lndtte; shop; tradsmn; rest; snacks; bar; playgrnd; htd pool; rv sw & fishing adj; TV; entmnt; 30% statics; dogs €1.50; quiet; red low ssn; CCI. "Friendly site; conv Massif Central & A75; san facs poss unclean high ssn." Easter-10 Sep. € 15.60   2004*

ISSOUDUN *4H3* (2km N Urban) **Camp Municipal Les Taupeaux, 37 Route de Reuilly, 36100 Issoudun [02 54 03 13 46 or 02 54 21 74 02; tourisme@issoudun.fr; www.issoudun.fr]** Fr Bourges SW on N151, site sp fr Issoudun on D16 nr Carrefour supmkt. Sm, hdg/mkd pitch, pt shd; wc; shwrs inc; el pnts inc; no adv bkg; rd noise. Jun-31 Aug. € 8.00   2007*

ISSY L'EVEQUE *4H4* (S Rural) **Camping L'Etang Neuf, 71760 Issy-l'Evêque [03 85 24 96 05; info@camping-etang-neuf.com; www.camping-etang-neuf.com]** Fr Luzy take D973 S for 2km. Then take D25 to Issy-l'Evêque. Site off D42 well sp in town cent. Med, hdg/mkd pitch, terr, pt shd; wc (some cont); chem disp; mv service pnt; shwrs inc; el pnts (6A) inc; gas; lndtte; shop 800m; tradsmn; rest; bar; playgrnd; pool; paddling pool; lake sw, fishing adj; tennis; wifi internet; TV rm; dogs €2; phone; Eng spkn; adv bkg; quiet; cc acc; CCI. "Nice, peaceful setting in unspoilt area; helpful staff; some san facs a bit run down (2007)." ♦ 28 Apr-15 Sep. € 21.00 (CChq acc)   2007*

ISTRES *10F2* (6km S Coastal) **Camping Félix de la Bastide, Allée Plage d'Arthur, 13920 St Mitre-les-Remparts [04 42 80 99 35; fax 04 42 49 96 85; info@campingfelix.com; www.campingfelix.com]** S fr Istres on D5 to end of built up area. At 2nd rndabt turn L (foll sp); approx 2km on L. Med, hdg/mkd pitch, pt shd; wc; chem disp; shwrs inc; el pnts (6A) €3; gas 2km; lndry service; shop; tradsmn; rest; bar; playgrnd; pool; paddling pool; shgl beach & lake adj; watersports; games area; dogs €1.50; phone; poss cr; Eng spkn; adv bkg. "Spacious pitches; poss strong winds; v friendly Dutch owners; beautiful scenery." 1 Apr-1 Oct. € 16.80   2007*

JABLINES see Meaux *3D3*

JARD SUR MER *7A1* (Coastal) **Camping La Ventouse, Rue Pierre Curie, 85520 Jard-sur-Mer [02 51 33 58 65 or 02 51 33 40 17 (Mairie); fax 02 51 33 91 00; campings-parfums-ete@wanadoo.fr]** Fr Talmont St-Hilaire take D21 to Jard turn R on app & foll sps. Look for blue sp Port de Plaisance; pass Camping Les Ecureuils, site shortly after. Lge, pt sl, pt shd; wc; baby facs; shwrs inc; el pnts (10A) €3 (poss rev pol); gas; lndtte; ice; shops, rest, snacks, bar 500m; playgrnd; sand beach 500m; dogs €1.50; poss cr; quiet. "Gd site with plenty of pine trees; adj vill & harbour." Mid-Jun-15 Sep. € 15.00   2004*

JARD SUR MER *7A1* (Coastal) **Camping Le Bosquet, Rue de l'Océan, 85520 Jard-sur-Mer [02 51 33 56 57 or 02 51 33 06 72; fax 02 51 33 03 69; campings-parfums-ete@wanadoo.fr; www.campings-parfums-ete.com]** Exit D949 at Talmont St Hilaire onto D21 to Jard-sur-Mer. In town look for sp Port de Plaisance, pass Camping Les Ecureuils & La Ventouse on L & take 2nd rd, Rue de l'Ocean, to R. Med, pt sl, shd; wc; baby facs; shwrs inc; el pnts (10A) €3; lndry rm; shops adj; playgrnd; pool 1.5km; sand beach; tennis adj; entmnt; dogs €1.50; adv bkg; quiet. "Picturesque boating cent, with man-made harbour; new prom & sea front under construction 2006." 1 Apr-Oct. € 15.00   2006*

JARD SUR MER *7A1* (Coastal) **Camping Les Ecureuils, Route des Goffineaux, 85520 Jard-sur-Mer [02 51 33 42 74; fax 02 51 33 91 14; camping-ecureuils@wanadoo.fr; www.camping-ecureuils.com]** Fr Talmont St Hilaire take D21 to Jard-sur-Mer. Turn R app vill, site sp. Lge, mkd pitch, shd; wc; chem disp; serviced pitches; baby facs; shwrs inc; el pnts (10A) inc (rev pol); gas; lndtte; ice; sm shop & 1km; snacks; bar; BBQ (gas); playgrnd; htd indoor pool, outdoor pool; rocky beach 400m, sand beach 1km; tennis adj; TV rm; 33% statics; no dogs; poss cr; Eng spkn; adv bkg (dep req); quiet; cc acc; CCI. "Gd rds & lighting; gd, clean san facs; no traffic allowed on site at night; security guard patrols at night; boating cent & man-made tidal harbour 1km." ♦ 1 Apr-30 Sep. € 28.90   2007*

JARD SUR MER *7A1* (Coastal) **CHADOTEL Camping L'Océano d'Or, Rue Georges Clémenceau, 85520 Jard-sur-Mer [02 51 33 65 08 or 02 51 33 05 05 (LS); fax 02 51 33 94 04; chadotel@wanadoo.fr; www.chadotel.com]** D21 & D19 to Jard-sur-Mer. Site sp. Lge, hdg/mkd pitch, pt shd; htd wc; chem disp; baby facs; shwrs inc; el pnts (6A) inc; gas; lndtte; ice; shop; snacks; bar; playgrnd; htd pool; waterslide; sand beach 900m; tennis; mini-golf; cycle hire; entmnt; dogs €2.90; adv bkg; quiet; red long stay/low ssn; CCI. "Vg; gd walking." ♦ Easter-24 Sep. € 28.90   2007*

Did you know you can fill in site report forms on the Club's website — www.caravanclub.co.uk?

JARD SUR MER *7A1* (2km NE Rural) **Camping La Mouette Cendrée, Les Malécots, 85520 St Vincent-sur-Jard [02 51 33 59 04; fax 02 51 20 31 39; camping.mc@free.fr; www.mouettecendree.com]** Fr Les Sables d'Olonne take D949 SE to Talmont-St-Hilaire; then take D21 dir Jard-sur-Mer. Bef ent Jard-sur-Mer turn L onto D19 in NE dir to site in about 1km on L. Or on D949 fr Luçon turn L onto D19 at Avrillé sp Jard-sur-Mer. Site on R in 6km. Med, hdg/mkd pitch, pt shd; wc (some cont); chem disp; shwrs inc; el pnts (10A) €4.10; lndtte; supmkt nr; tradsmn; BBQ (gas/elec); playgrnd; pool; waterslide; paddling pool; sand beach 2km; fishing; windsurfing 2km; table tennis; horseriding 500m; golf 10km; 30% statics; dogs €3; recep 0830-1230 & 1430-1930 high ssn; c'van max 7.50m high ssn; Eng spkn; adv bkg; quiet; cc acc; CCI. "Friendly, peaceful site; v welcoming & helpful owners; gd woodland walks & cycle routes nr; mkt Sun in vill." ♦ Easter-30 Sep. € 21.00 ABS - A20   2007*

France

JARD SUR MER *7A1* (SE Coastal) **CHADOTEL Camping La Pomme de Pin, Rue Vincent Auriol, 85520 Jard-sur-Mer [02 51 33 43 85 or 02 51 33 05 05 (LS); fax 02 51 33 94 04; chadotel@ wanadoo.fr; www.chadotel.com]** Foll sp fr town. Lge, hdg/mkd pitch, shd; htd wc; serviced pitches; baby facs; shwrs inc; el pnts (6A) inc; gas; lndtte; ice; shop; snacks; bar; BBQ (gas); playgrnd; pool; waterslide; sand beach 150m; games rm; TV rm; entmnt; mainly statics; dogs €2.90; Eng spkn; adv bkg; quiet; cc acc; CCI. "Well-maintained; early arrival rec; ltd facs low ssn; vg." ♦ Easter-24 Sep. € 28.90   2007*

JARD SUR MER *7A1* (2km SE Rural) **Camping L'R Pur (Ferret), 85520 St Vincent-sur-Jard [tel/fax 02 51 33 94 32 or 06 15 21 56 17 (mob)]** Fr Talmont-St Hilaire take D21 to Jard-sur-Mer & St Vincent-sur-Jard. Site sp. Sm, hdg pitch, pt shd; wc; chem disp; shwrs; el pnts (10A); playgrnd; sand beach 3km, tennis, fishing, boating 3km; 10% statics; quiet; adv bkg. "CL-type site; friendly owner, lge pitches." 1 Apr-1 Oct.   2004*

JARD SUR MER *7A1* (2km SE Coastal) **CHADOTEL Camping La Bolée d'Air, Le Bouil, Route de Longeville, 85520 St Vincent-sur-Jard [02 51 90 36 05 or 02 51 33 05 05 (LS); fax 02 51 33 94 04; chadotel@wanadoo.fr; www.chadotel.com]** Fr A11 junc 14 dir Angers. Take N160 to La Roche-sur-Yon & then D747 dir La Tranche-sur-Mer to Moutier-les-Mauxfaits. At Moutiers take D19 to St Hilaire-la-Forêt & then L to St Vincent-sur-Jard. In St Vincent turn L by church sp Longeville-sur-Mer, site on R in 1km. Lge, hdg/mkd pitch, pt shd; htd wc; chem disp (wc); serviced pitches; baby facs; sauna; shwrs inc; el pnts (6A) inc; gas; lndtte; ice; shop; snacks; bar; BBQ (charcoal/gas); playgrnd; 2 pools (1 htd covrd); waterslide; paddling pool; sand beach 900m; tennis; cycle hire; entmnt; internet; games/ TV rm; 25% statics; dogs €2; recep 0800-2000 high ssn; no c'vans over 8m high ssn; Eng spkn; adv bkg; quiet; red long stay/low ssn; cc acc; CCI. "Ltd facs fr end Aug; popular, busy site; excel." ♦ 5 Apr-27 Sep. € 28.90 ABS - A31   2007*

JARGEAU see Châteauneuf sur Loire *4F3*

JARNAC see Cognac *7B2*

JAULNY *5D2* (500m S Rural) **Camping La Pelouse, 54470 Jaulny [tel/fax 03 83 81 91 67; lapelouse@ aol.com]** SW fr Metz on N57, cross rv at Corny-sur-Moselle & turn W onto D28 dir Thiaucourt-Regniéville. Site sp, easy to find off D28. Med, sl, pt shd; wc; chem disp; shwrs inc; el pnts (4-6A) €2.05-2.65; lndtte; ice; tradsmn; rest; bar; BBQ; playgrnd; 25% statics; rv sw 100m; fishing; quiet; CCI. "Friendly owner & staff; san facs poss overstretched high ssn; no fresh or waste water facs for m'vans; vg site." 1 Apr-30 Sep. € 8.80   2007*

JAUNAY CLAN *4H1* (1km N Rural) **Camping La Croix du Sud, Route de Neuville, 86130 Jaunay-Clan [05 49 62 58 14 or 05 49 62 57 20; fax 05 49 62 57 20; camping@la-croix-du-sud. fr; www.la-croix-du-sud.fr]** On A10 fr N or S, take Futuroscope exit. Take last exit at rndabt sp Neuville & after 1.5km turn L onto D20/D62. Site on L immed after x-ing m'way. Also clearly sp fr D910 (N10) at traff lts in Jaunay-Clan. Lge, hdg/mkd pitch, pt shd, 20% serviced pitches; wc; chem disp; mv service pnt; shwrs inc; el pnts (10A) €3; gas; lndtte; shop & hypmkt 1km; tradsmn; rest, snacks & bar high ssn; playgrnd; pool; entmnt; 15% statics; dogs; Eng spkn; adv bkg; quiet but some rd noise; cc acc; red low ssn/CCI. "Clean, tidy site; 3km to Futuroscope - mini-bus fr site high ssn; 10km to Poitiers; san facs poss unclean; poss itinerants." ♦ 29 Mar-13 Sep. € 13.70   2006*

JAUNAY CLAN *4H1* (6km NE Rural) **Camp Municipal du Parc, 86130 Dissay [05 49 62 84 29 or 05 49 52 34 56 (Mairie); fax 05 49 62 58 72]** N on D910 (N10) Poitiers dir Châtellerault. At rndabt turn R on D15 sp Dissay. Turn R ent Dissay & site on R 50m. Med, mkd pitch, pt shd; wc; chem disp; shwrs inc; el pnts (10A) €2.50; lndtte; shop 100m; quiet; CCI. "Friendly warden; clean modern facs; conv Futuroscope; 15thC chateau adj; gate locked 2200 but can request key to unlock if later." ♦ 15 Jun-15 Sep. € 9.50   2007*

JAUNAY CLAN *4H1* (7km NE Rural) **Flower Camping du Lac de St Cyr, 86130 St Cyr [05 49 62 57 22; fax 05 49 52 28 58; contact@ lacdesaintcyr.com; www.lacdesaintcyr.com]** Fr A10 take Châtellerault Sud exit & take D910 (N10) dir Poitiers; at Beaumont turn L at traff lts for St Cyr; foll camp sp in leisure complex (Parc Loisirs) by lakeside - R turn for camping. Or fr S take Futuroscope exit to D910. Lge, hdg/mkd pitch, pt sl, pt shd; wc; chem disp; mv service pnt; serviced pitches; shwrs inc; el pnts (10A) inc (poss rev pol); gas; lndtte; shop; rest; snacks; bar; BBQ; playgrnd; sand beach & lake sw; watersports; tennis; mini-golf; boat & cycle hire; fitness rm; games area; golf course adj; entmnt; child entmnt; TV rm; 15% statics; dogs €1.50; poss cr; some Eng spkn; adv bkg (dep req); quiet; red long stay; cc acc; CCI. "Excel, well-maintained site; modern, clean san facs but poss stretched high ssn & ltd low ssn; rec long o'fits unhitch at barrier due R-angle turn; perfect for families; poss school & club groups w/e high ssn; gd golf nr; gd rest; beautiful lake; if late return to site check barrier closing time; public access to site fr lakeside beach; Futuroscope approx 13km; superb site; highly rec." ♦ 1 Apr-30 Sep. € 25.50 ABS - L09   2007*

⊞JAUNAY CLAN *4H1* (2km SE Urban) Camping Le Futuriste, Rue du Château, 86130 St Georges-les-Baillargeaux [05 49 52 47 52; fax 05 49 37 23 33; camping-le-futuriste@wanadoo. fr; www.camping-le-futuriste.fr] On A10 fr N or S, take Futuroscope exit 28; fr toll booth at 1st rndabt take 2nd exit. Thro tech park twd St Georges. At rndabt under D910 (N10) take slip rd N onto D910. After 150m exit D910 onto D20, foll sp. At 1st rndabt bear R, over rlwy, cross sm rv & up hill, site on R. Med, hdg/mkd pitch, pt shd; htd wc; chem disp; mv service pnt; some serviced pitches; shwrs inc; el pnts (6A) €3.70 (check earth & poss rev pol); gas; lndtte; ice; shop; hypmkt 2km; tradsmn; rest; snacks; bar; BBQ; playgrnd; 2 htd pools; waterslide; lake fishing; games area; games rm; entmnt; excursions; TV rm; some statics; dogs €1.90; poss cr; Eng spkn; adv bkg; quiet; red low ssn/long stay; cc acc; CCI. "Excel, vg value, busy site, espec in winter; ltd facs low ssn - facs block clsd 2200-0700; well-drained pitches; friendly, helpful family owners; do not arr bef 1200; ideal touring base for Poitiers & Futuroscope; conv fr a'route; gate opened until 2330; tickets for Futuroscope (2km) avail fr site."
♦ € 20.60 (3 persons) (CChq acc) 2007*

See advertisement

JAUNAY CLAN *4H1* (4km SE Rural) Camp Municipal Parc des Ecluzelles, 86360 Chasseneuil-du-Poitou [05 49 52 77 19; fax 05 49 52 52 23; chasseneuil-du-poitou@cg86. fr] Fr A10 or D910 (N10) N or Poitiers take Futuroscope exit 28/18. Take Chasseneuil rd, sp in town to site. Sm, mkd pitch, some hdstg, pt shd; wc; chem disp; mv service pnt; shwrs inc; el pnts (8A) inc; shop 1km; tradsmn; BBQ; playgrnd; htd pool adj inc; dogs; poss cr; no adv bkg; quiet. "Vg, clean site; v lge pitches; conv Futuroscope; excel." 1 Apr-30 Sep. € 12.85 2006*

JAVIE, LA *10E3* (Rural) Camp Municipal, Route des Prads, 04420 La Javie [04 92 34 91 76; fax 04 92 34 94 81] Sp in vill on D900. Sm, pt shd; wc; shwrs inc; el pnts; dogs; quiet. "Basic, unattended site; clean facs; NH." 15 Jun-15 Sep. € 6.00 2005*

JOIGNY *4F4* (500m N) FFCC Camp Municipal, 68 Quai d'Epizy, 89300 Joigny [03 86 62 07 55; fax 03 86 62 08 03; villedejoigny3@wanadoo.fr] Fr A6 exit junc 18 or 19 to Joigny cent. Fr cent, over brdg, turn L onto D959; turn L in filter lane at traff lts. Foll sp to site. Sm, hdg pitch, hdstg, pt shd; wc; chem disp; mv service pnt; shwrs; el pnts (6A) €1.99; shops 500m; rest, bar 3km; pool 4km; sw 3km; fishing adj; tennis; horseriding; poss cr; quiet; CCI. "Site poss liable to flood in wet weather." 1 Apr-31 Oct. € 4.91 2006*

JOIGNY *4F4* (8km E Urban) Camping Les Confluents, Allée Léo Lagrange, 89400 Migennes [tel/fax 03 86 80 94 55; planethome2003@yahoo. fr; www.les-confluents.com] A6 exit at junc 19 Auxerre Nord onto N6 & foll sp to Migennes & site. Med, hdg/mkd pitch, hdstg, pt shd; htd wc (some cont); chem disp; mv service pnt; baby facs; fam bthrm; shwrs inc; el pnts (6-10A) €2.50-3.50; gas; lndtte; ice; shop; rest; snacks; bar; BBQ; playgrnd; htd, covrd pool; watersports 300m; lake sand beach; canoe, cycle hire; sports area; entmnt; TV rm; 8% statics; dogs €0.50; phone; bus 10 mins; quiet; red long stay; cc acc; CCI. "Friendly, family-run, clean site nr canal & indust area; lge pitches; medieval castle, wine cellars, Puisaye potteries nrby; walking dist to Migennes; lge mkt Thurs; excel." ♦ ltd. 1 Apr-5 Nov. € 10.50 2006*

JOIGNY *4F4* (12km SE Rural) Camp Municipal Le Patis, 28 Rue du Porte des Fontaines, 89400 Bonnard [03 86 73 26 25 or 03 86 73 25 55 (Mairie); mairie.bonnard@wanadoo.fr] Exit A6 junc 19; N on N6 dir Joigny; in 8.5km at Bassou turn R & foll sp Bonnard. Site on L immed after rv bdge. Sm, mkd pitch, shd; wc; chem disp; shwrs inc; el pnts (10A) €2; lndtte; ice; shop 1km; rest 500m; playgrnd; rv sw, fishing, boating, tennis adj; dogs; phone; poss cr; adv bkg; quiet. "Well-kept site on banks of Rv Yonne; friendly, helpful warden; immac san facs; gd security; vg fishing; excel. " ♦ ltd. 15 May-30 Sep. € 7.00 2007*

France

Camping ★★★ Au Bocage du Lac AU BOCAGE DU LAC Hôtel de Plein Air

On the lakeside, in the pretty and historical town of Jugon Les Lacs, for both relaxation and leisure, you will find a wide range of activities : heated pool, water slide, paddling pool, childrens' mini camp, tennis, minigolf, sailing, fishing, walking. New sanitary block includes private cabins, facilities for babies. Rental of Chalets, Mobile Homes with view over the lake.
WELCOME TO BRITTANY!!
22270 Jugon les Lacs / Tél : 02.96.31.60.16
contact@campingjugon.com / www.campingjugon.com

JOIGNY *4F4* (3.5km NW Rural) **Camp Municipal L'Ile de L'Antonnoir, Route de St Aubin-sur-Yonne, 89410 Cézy [03 86 63 17 87 or 03 86 63 12 58 (LS); fax 03 86 63 02 84]** Site sp off N6 N & S-bound (Joigny by-pass). Thro St Aubin vill, cross bdge over Rv Yonne. Site on L bank of rv. Or exit N6 Joigny by-pass at N of rndabt onto N2006 twd St Aubin. After St Aubin turn R to Cézy & site in 1km. Rec app via St Aubin - narr bdge 3.5t weight restriction. Sm, mkd pitch, pt shd; wc; shwrs inc; chem disp; mv service pnt; el pnts (6-10A) €2.20; lndtte; shop 1km; rest, snacks, bar, BBQ; playgrnd; rv sw & beach 100m; dogs €1; Eng spkn; adv bkg; quiet; CCI. "Helpful staff; v pleasant, quiet site; conv Chablis area; barrier clsd 2200." 1 May-31 Oct. € 10.00   2006*

JOINVILLE *6E1* (6km E Rural) **Camp Municipal Poissons, 52230 Poissons** Fr N67 to Joinville 'Centre Ville'; then onto D60 dir Thonnance; after supmkt turn R onto D427 to Poissons; site on L as exit vill. Site sp in vill. Sm, pt sl, pt shd; htd wc (cont); own san; chem disp (wc); shwrs inc; el pnts inc; shop 1km; rest 6km, snacks, bar 1km; BBQ; 20% statics; dogs; quiet; CCI. "V basic, peaceful CL-type site; warden calls evening or call at No 7 same rd to pay; uneven pitches; facs & el pnts poor; san facs poss unclean & need refurb; easy to find; poss open all yr; NH only." € 6.70   2006*

JOINVILLE *6E1* (6km NW) **Camp Municipal Le Jardinot, 52300 Chatonrupt-Sommermont [03 25 94 80 30 or 03 25 94 80 07]** Leave N67 at sp Joinville Centre & cont N on old N67 (now D335) to Chatonrupt. Site on R on ent vill. Sm, pt shd; wc (cont); shwrs; el pnts (6-10A) €1.50; shops 4km; rv sw adj; fishing in rv & canal adj; rd & rlwy noise. "NH only; run down & poss itinerants." 1 May-30 Sep. € 4.00   2004*

JONQUIERES see Orange *10E2*

JONZAC *7B2* **Camp Municipal des Mégisseries, Parc des Expositions, 17500 Jonzac [05 46 48 51 20 or 05 46 48 49 29; fax 05 46 48 51 07; Tourisme. Jonzac@wanadoo.fr; www.jonzac.fr]** Fr A10/N137 to Bordeaux exit D699 to Jonzac, site well sp in all dirs in town past school & sports complex, adj Rv Seugne. Helpful to foll sp to football stadium. Sm, mkd pitch, hdstg, pt shd; wc; own san; mv service pnt; shwrs; el pnts (6-16A) €3.45-5.15; lndtte; shop 2km; tradsmn; pool adj; dogs €1.10; lake fishing 1km; poss cr - pitches close; adv bkg. "Excel situation; pleasant warden; plenty of hot water; facs clean but basic; pitches well-drained in wet at end ssn but site liable to sudden flooding; public footpath thro site; spa town, new leisure complex nr." ♦ 1 Apr-30 Oct. € 8.50   2007*

JONZAC *7B2* (2km SW Rural) **FFCC Camping des Castors, St Simon de Bordes, 17500 Jonzac [05 46 48 25 65; fax 05 46 04 56 76; camping-les-castors@wanadoo.fr; www.campingcastors.com]** Fr Jonzac take D19 S twds Montendre, after approx 2km, immed after ring rd rndabt, turn R into minor rd. Site ent adj. Med, hdg pitch, hdstg, pt shd; wc; chem disp; mv service pnt; shwrs inc; el pnts (6-10A) €4-4.70; lndtte; tradsmn; snacks; bar; playgrnd; covrd pool; rv sw 2km; entmnts; TV; 50% statics; dogs €1.60; some Eng spkn; quiet; CCI. "Peaceful & well-supervised; gd facs; friendly; excel pool; gd ." ♦ 22 Mar-28 Oct. € 12.90

2007*

JOSSELIN *2F3* (2km SW Rural) **FFCC Camp Municipal du Bas de la Lande, 56120 Guégon [02 97 22 22 20 or 02 97 22 20 64; fax 02 97 73 93 85; campingbasdelalande@wanadoo. fr]** Exit N24 by-pass W of town sp Guégon; foll sp 1km; do not attempt to cross Josselin cent fr E to W. Site on D724 just S of Rv Oust (canal). Med, hdg pitch, terr, pt shd; wc; chem disp; baby facs; shwrs inc; el pnts (6-10A) €3.10; lndtte; shops 2km; bar high ssn; playgrnd; mini-golf; quiet but some rd noise; red low ssn; CCI. "Barrier clsd 1200-1400; well-positioned site for walk to Josselin, chateau & old houses; vg, clean san facs; gd cycling." ♦ 1 Apr-31 Oct. € 11.00   2006*

JUGON LES LACS *2E3* (S Rural) **Camping au Bocage du Lac, 22270 Jugon-les-Lacs [02 96 31 60 16; fax 02 96 31 69 08; contact@ campingjugon.com; www.campingjugon.com]** Bet Dinan & Lamballe by N176. Foll `Camping Jeux' sp on D52 fr Jugon-les-Lacs. Situated by lakes, sp fr cent of Jugon. Lge, pt sl, pt shd; wc; mv service pnt; baby facs; shwrs inc; el pnts (5A) €3; lndtte; ice; shops adj; tradsmn; bar; playgrnd; htd pool; waterslide; fishing & watersports in lake/ rv adj; games area; games rm; entmnts; TV; dogs €2.50; adv bkg; red low ssn. "Well-situated nr pretty vill; many sports & activities; vg, attractive site." 14 Apr-22 Sep. € 17.40   2007*

See advertisement

JULLOUVILLE see Granville *1D4*

JUMIEGES *3C2* (1km E Rural) **Camping de la Forêt, Rue Mainberthe, 76480 Jumièges [02 35 37 93 43 or 02 35 02 13 87 (LS); fax 02 35 37 76 48; info@campinglaforet.com; www. campinglaforet.com]** Exit A13 junc 25 onto D313 N to Pont de Brotonne. Cross Pont de Brotonne & immed turn R onto D982 sp Yainville & Jumièges onto D143. Turn L in Jumièges & foll site sp. Turn L at x-rds after cemetary & church, site on R in 1km. NB M'vans under 3.5t & 3m height can take ferry fr Port Jumièges. Med, hdg/mkd pitch, pt shd; wc; chem disp; mv service pnt; baby facs; shwrs inc; el pnts (10A) €4 (poss rev pol); gas; lndtte; shop; supmkt, tradsmn; rest & bar nr; BBQ; playgrnd; htd pool; paddling pool; lake beach 2.5km; watersports; fishing; cycle hire; tennis nrby; games area; child entmnt; internet; games/TV rm; 30% statics; dogs free; phone; poss cr; adv bkg; quiet. "Well-kept, busy site; excel, clean san facs but poss stretched high ssn; nice pitches, some sm, generally tight access; adj Abbey of Jumièges; interesting vill; conv Paris & Giverny; gd walking, cycling; bus to Rouen; excel." ♦ 5 Apr-25 Oct. € 18.50 (CChq acc) ABS - N15   2007*

JUMIEGES *3C2* (3km S Rural) **Camping Boucles de la Seine-Normande, Base de Plein Air du Parc de Brotonne, 76480 Jumièges [02 35 37 31 72; fax 02 35 37 99 97]** E fr Le Havre on N15; foll D131 S fr Yvetot by-pass twd Pont de Brotonne (toll). Bef bdge turn SE on D982, thro Le Trait. Turn S on D143 at Yainville for Jumièges. Cont thro Jumièges on D65, site well sp on R on lake in 3km. Fr S fr Bourg-Achard take D313 twd Pont de Brotonne; turn off after bdge on D982 as above. Med, hdg pitch, pt sl, shd; wc; chem disp; some serviced pitches; shwrs inc; el pnts (6A) inc (check pol); lndtte; shops 3km; tradsmn; rest, snacks, bar 3km; playgrnd; lake sw adj; watersports; tennis; games area; archery; golf, 30% statics; dogs 1.05; barrier clsd 2200-0800; poss cr; adv bkg; quiet; red long stay; CCI. "Lovely area; helpful warden; lge pitches; poss itinerants low ssn; poss youth camps; san facs stretched high ssn; gd." ♦ ltd. 1 Mar-31 Oct. € 17.20   2006*

JUSSAC *7C4* (W Rural) **FFCC Camp Municipal du Moulin, Impasse du Moulin, 15250 Jussac [tel/fax 04 71 46 69 85; s.pradel@laba.fr; www.caba.fr/ camping]** On D922 8km N of Aurillac; on L immed after bdge. Med, mkd pitch, pt shd; wc; chem disp; shwrs inc; el pnts (10A) €2; lndry rm; shop & rest 150m; pool 150m; tennis & riding nr; quiet. "Quiet, country-style site nr lge vill; clean, well-kept, grassy; excel san facs; pleasant, helpful owners; gd walking; interesting countryside; extremely gd value." ♦ 15 Jun-1 Sep. € 8.50   2007*

KAYSERSBERG *6F3* (Urban) **Aire Communale, Rue Rocade, 68240 Kaysersberg [03 89 47 30 60 or 03 89 78 11 12 (Mairie)]** Fr D415 site adj junc with D28. Foll sp, clearly visible. Med, hdstg, unshd; wc; chem disp; mv service pnt; shop, rest, snacks, bar 200m; poss cr; some rd noise. "Gd NH; m'vans only; pay at machine." 15 Mar-31 Dec. € 6.00
               2005*

KAYSERSBERG *6F3* (1km NW) **Camp Municipal, Rue des Acacias, 68240 Kaysersberg [tel/ fax 03 89 47 14 47 or 03 89 78 11 11 (Mairie); camping@ville-kaysersberg.fr; www.kaysersberg. com]** Fr A35/N83 exit junc 23 onto D4 sp Sigolsheim & Kaysersberg; bear L onto N415 bypass dir St Dié; site sp 100m past junc with D28. Or SE fr St Dié on N415 over Col du Bonhomme; turn L into Rue des Acacias just bef junc with D28. Med, hdg/mkd pitch, pt shd; wc; chem disp; shwrs; baby facs; el pnts (8-13A) €3.35-4.25; gas; lndtte; shops 150m; supmkt 700m; pool 1km; playgrnd; TV; fishing, tennis adj; dogs €2 (no dogs Jul/Aug); quiet. "Vg, busy, clean site; rec arr early high ssn; many sm pitches; recep clsd for new arr 1200-1400 & 2000-0700; in heart of Alsace wine region, wine-tasting on site (in ssn); barrier locked 2200; beautiful medieval town on rv; vill is birth place Albert Schweitzer; many mkd walks/cycle rts; Le Linge WWI battle grnd nr Orbey." 1 Apr-30 Sep. € 11.70   2007*

⊞**KAYSERSBERG** *6F3* (7km NW) **Camping Les Verts Bois, 3 Rue de la Fonderie, 68240 Fréland [tel/fax 03 89 71 91 94 or 03 89 47 57 25; lacabane. thai@orange.fr; www.camping-lesvertsbois.com]** Sp off N415 Colmar/St Dié rd bet Lapoutroie & Kaysersberg. Site approx 5km after turn fr main rd on D11 at far end of vill. Turn L into rd to site when D11 doubles back on itself. Sm, pt sl, terr, pt shd; htd wc; chem disp; shwrs inc; el pnts (10A) inc; gas; lndtte; ice; shop & bank in vill; rest; snacks, bar; dogs €0.50; poss cr; Eng spkn; poss cr; adv bkg; quiet; cc acc; CCI. "Beautiful setting adj fast-flowing rv; lovely site; clsd 2230-0700; friendly welcome; eve meals avail - rest open all year; excel." € 13.80
               2007*

France

⊞KESKASTEL *5D3* (700m NE Rural) **Camp Municipal Les Sapins, Centre des Loisirs, 67260 Keskastel [03 88 00 19 25 (Mairie); fax 03 88 00 34 66]** Exit A4 junc 42 fr N or junc 43 fr S dir Sarralbe/Keskastel. In Keskastel cent turn onto D338 twds Herbitzheim. Cont for approx 1km; turn R for approx 400m; site on L, well sp on lakeside. Med, hdg/mkd pitch, pt shd; htd wc; chem disp; shwrs inc; el pnts (10A) €3.60 (poss rev pol); lndtte; shop 1km; tradsmn; rest & snacks (high ssn); bar; BBQ; playgrnd; sand beach adj; lake sw & fishing; tennis nr; 60% statics; dogs; phone; poss cr; some Eng spkn; quiet; adv bkg; cc acc; CCI. "Helpful warden; ltd san facs low ssn; office poss clsd Sun morn; barrier clsd 2300; relaxing location conv m'way; excel." ♦ € 12.45   2007*

⊞**LABENNE** *8E1* (4km S Urban) **Camping du Lac, 518 Rue de Janin, 40440 Ondres [05 59 45 28 45 or 06 80 26 91 51 (mob); fax 05 59 45 29 45; contact@camping-du-lac.fr; www.camping-du-lac.fr]** Fr N exit A63 junc 8 onto N10 S. Turn R just N of Ondres sp Ondres-Plage, at rndabt turn L & foll site sp. Fr S exit A63 junc 7 onto N10 to Ondres. Cont thro town cent & turn L at town boundary, then as above; tight turns thro housing est. Med, hdg/mkd pitch, terr, pt shd; htd wc; chem disp; baby facs; shwrs inc; el pnts (10A) inc; gas; lndtte; ice; shop 500m; rest in ssn; snacks; bar; playgrnd; pool in ssn; sand beach 4km; lake sw adj (not rec); fishing; boating; games area; entmnt; cycle hire; 60% statics; dogs €2.50; phone; Eng spkn; adv bkg (dep); quiet; red long stay/low ssn; CCI. "Peaceful, charming lakeside site; gd welcome; helpful staff; ltd facs low ssn; vg pool; excel." ♦ € 29.00
                2007*

LABENNE *8E1* (4km S Coastal) **Camping Lou Pignada, Ave de la Plage, 40440 Ondres [05 59 45 30 65; fax 05 59 45 25 79; www. loupignada.com]** Turn R off N10 at N end of Ondres vill, sp Ondres-Plage, site immed after rlwy level x-ing on L. Med, shd; wc; baby facs; shwrs; el pnts (6-8A) €6; gas; ice; lndtte; shop; rest; snacks; BBQ; playgrnd; htd, covrd pool; paddling pool; waterslide; spa/jacuzzi; sand beach 500m; games area; tennis; cycle hire; horseriding; golf nrby; entmnts; TV; 50% statics; no dogs; adv bkg; red low ssn; v quiet; cc acc. "Sea bathing unsuitable young children; tight manoeuvring amongst trees." 30 Mar-30 Sep. € 29.00   2004*

LABENNE *8E1* (3km SW Coastal) **Yelloh! Village Le Sylvamar, Ave de l'Océan, 40530 Labenne [05 59 45 75 16; fax 05 59 45 46 39; camping@sylvamar.fr; www.sylvamar.fr or www. yellohvillage.com]** Exit A63 junc 7 onto D85; then take N10 N to Labenne; turn L onto D126; site sp. Lge, hdg/mkd pitch, pt shd; wc; chem disp; serviced pitches; shwrs inc; el pnts (10A) inc; lndtte; shop adj; tradsmn; rest; snacks; bar; pool; waterslide; playgrnd; sand beach 800m; fitness rm; dogs €5.50; adv bkg; quiet; Eng spkn; red low ssn; cc acc; CCI. ♦ 26 Apr-17 Sep. € 40.00   2007*

LABENNE *8E1* (2km W Coastal) **Camping La Côte d'Argent, Ave de l'Océan, 40530 Labenne-Océan [05 59 45 42 02; fax 05 59 45 73 31; info@camping-cotedargent.com; www.camping-cotedargent.com]** Fr N10 take D126 W fr Labenne to Labenne-Plage & site. Lge, hdg/mkd pitch, shd; htd wc; 10% serviced pitches; mv service pnt; chem disp; baby facs; shwrs inc; el pnts (6A) €3.60; gas 300m; lndtte; ice; shop 200m; tradsmn, rest, snacks, bar high ssn; BBQ; playgrnd; pool; paddling pool; sand beach 900m; fishing 300m; games rm; mini-golf; archery; tennis 500m; entmnt high ssn; TV rm; cycle hire; 25% statics; dogs €2.50; poss cr; Eng spkn; adv bkg rec; quiet; cc acc; CCI. "Nice pool area; children's park; gd cycle tracks; ltd facs low ssn; conv Biarritz; excel." ♦ ltd. 1 Apr-31 Oct. € 24.20 (CChq acc)   2006*

LABENNE *8E1* (2km W Coastal) **Camping La Mer, Route de la Plage, 40530 Labenne-Océan [05 59 45 42 09; fax 05 59 45 43 07; campinglamer@wanadoo.fr; www.campinglamer. com]** Turn W off N10 in Labenne at traff lts in town cent onto D126 to Labenne-Plage. Site 2km on L. Lge, shd; wc; baby facs; shwrs inc; el pnts (6A) €3.60; gas; lndtte; shop; rest; snacks; bar; BBQ; playgrnd; htd, covrd pool; jacuzzi; sand/shgl beach 500m; games area; some statics; dogs €2.50; adv bkg; quiet; red long stay/low ssn. 1 Apr-30 Sep. € 17.80   2007*

LAC D'ISSARLES, LE *9C1* (Rural) **Camp Municipal Les Bords du Lac, 07470 Le Lac-d'Issarlès [04 66 46 20 70 or 04 66 46 20 06 (Mairie)]** On N88 S fr Le Puy-en-Velay, take D16 N sp Coucouron. Foll sp for Lac-d'Issarlès. Site on L well sp. Lge, mkd pitch, pt sl, terr, pt shd; wc; chem disp (wc); shwrs inc; el pnts inc; lndtte; lndry rm; shop, rest, snacks, bar 500m; playgrnd; sand beach; lake sw, fishing, boating; dogs; Eng spkn; quiet. "Pleasant views with dir access to lake; poss diff for long o'fits." ♦ 1 May-15 Sep. € 12.10   2004*

This guide relies on site report forms submitted by caravanners like us; we'll do our bit and tell the editor what we think of the campsites we've visited.

LAC D'ISSARLES, LE *9C1* (2km Rural) **Camping La Plaine de la Loire, Pont de Laborie, 07470 Le Lac-d'Issarlès [04 66 46 25 77 or 04 66 46 21 64; fax 04 66 46 21 55]** Fr N102 Aubenas-Le Puy-en-Velay rd going N take D16 sp Le Lac-d'Issarles. After Coucouron (5km) site on R. Med, mkd pitch, pt shd; wc (cont); chem disp; shwrs inc; el pnts (6A) inc; gas; shop; tradsmn; lndtte; playgrnd; rv sw adj; 5% statics; adv bkg; quiet; CCI. "Lovely, tranquil site - a real gem." ♦ 1 Jun-15 Sep. € 12.00   2004*

LACANAU OCEAN *7C1* (1km N Coastal) **Airotel Camping de l'Océan, 24 Rue du Repos, 33680 Lacanau-Océan [05 56 03 24 45; fax 05 57 70 01 87; airotel.lacanau@wanadoo.fr; www.airotel-ocean.com]** On ent town at end of sq in front of bus stn turn R, fork R & foll sp to site (next to Camping Grand Pins). Lge, pt sl, pt shd; wc; chem disp; shwrs inc; el pnts (15A) inc; gas; lndtte; ice; shop; rest; snacks; bar; pool; sand beach 600m; tennis; entmnt; fishing; watersports; cycle hire; TV; statics; dogs €4; poss cr; adv bkg; quiet; red low ssn. "Attractive site/holiday vill in pine woods behind sand dunes & enormous sand beach; care in choosing pitch owing to soft sand." Easter-30 Sep. € 29.50   2006*

As soon as we get home I'm going to post all these site report forms to the editor for inclusion in next year's guide. I don't want to miss the September deadline.

LACANAU OCEAN *7C1* (1km N Coastal) **Yelloh! Village Les Grand Pins, Rue des Pins, 33680 Lacanau-Océan [05 56 03 20 77; fax 05 57 70 03 89; reception@lesgrandspins.com; www.lesgrandspins.com www.yellohvillage.com]** On ent town, by bus stn at sq turn R, fork R & foll sp. V lge, hdg/mkd pitch, terr, pt shd; wc; serviced pitches; chem disp; shwrs inc; el pnts (10A) inc; gas; lndtte; ice; shop; rest; snacks; bar; playgrnd; htd pool; sand beach 500m; TV; cycle hire; entmnt; 20% statics; dogs €4; poss cr; adv bkg red high ssn; quiet; red low ssn. "Excel well organised site; lge pitches; doesn't feel overcr - even when full." 26 Apr-20 Sep. € 33.00   2004*

LACANAU OCEAN *7C1* (7km E Rural) **Camping Talaris Vacances, Route de L'Océan, 33680 Lacanau [05 56 03 04 15; fax 05 56 26 21 56; talarisvacances@free.fr; www.talaris-vacances.fr]** Fr Lacanau-Océan towards Lake Lacanau, site on R. Lge, mkd pitch, hdstg, shd; wc (some cont); chem disp; mv service pnt; baby facs; shwrs inc; el pnts (6A) €3; gas; lndtte; ice; shop; rest; snacks; bar; BBQ area; playgrnd; pool; waterslide; lake sw 2km; tennis; mini-golf; 50% statics; dogs €3; bus adj; Eng spkn; adv bkg (dep req); some rd noise; CCI. "Nr Lake Lacanau, sw & watersports; ideal for cycling, excel network cycle tracks." ◆ 1 Apr-17 Sep. € 26.50   2005*

LACANAU OCEAN *7C1* (5km SE Rural) **Camping Le Tedey, Par Le Moutchic, Route de Longarisse, 33680 Lacanau-Océan [05 56 03 00 15; fax 05 56 03 01 90; camping@le-tedey.com; www. le-tedey.com]** Fr Bordeaux take D6 to Lacanau & on twd Lacanau-Océan. On exit Moutchic take L fork twd Longarisse. Ent in 2km well sp on L. V lge, mkd pitch, shd; wc (some cont); chem disp; mv service pnt; baby facs; shwrs inc; el pnts (10A) €4; gas; lndtte; ice; shop; snacks; bar; playgrnd; lake sw & sand beach adj; boating; cycle hire; golf 5km; entmnt; internet; TV rm; some statics; no dogs; poss cr; Eng spkn; adv bkg (ess Jul/Aug); quiet, but poss live music Sat night high ssn; red low ssn; cc acc; CCI. "Set in pine woods - avoid tree sap; peaceful, friendly, family-run site; golf nr; gd cycle tracks; no el pnts for pitches adj to beach; access diff to some pitches; excel site." ◆ 26 Apr-20 Sep. € 20.50   2007*

LACAPELLE MARIVAL *7D4* (1km NW Rural) **Camp Municipal Bois de Sophie, Route d'Aynac, 46120 Lacapelle-Marival [tel/fax 05 65 40 82 59; lacapelle.mairie@wanadoo.fr; http://lacapelle-marival.site.voila.fr]** NE fr N140 onto D940 dir St Céré; site at far end of Lacapelle-Marival on W side of D940. Visible fr rd. Med, mkd pitch, pt sl, pt shd; wc; chem disp; mv service pnt; shwrs inc; el pnts (10A) €2.75; shops 1km; playgrnd; pool adj; tennis; some statics; quiet; CCI. "Vg sh stay/NH." ◆ 15 May-30 Sep. € 11.00   2007*

⊞**LACAUNE** *8E4* (5km E Rural) **Camping Le Clot, Les Vidals, 81230 Lacaune [tel/fax 05 63 37 03 59; le-clot@worldoline.fr; www.pageloisirs.com/le-clot]** Fr Castres to Lacaune on D622. Cont on D622 past Lacaune then turn R on D62 for Les Vidals. Site sp 500m on L after Les Vidals. Sm, terr, pt shd; htd wc; chem disp; shwrs inc; el pnts (10A) €2.50; lndtte; shop 5km; rest; snacks; playgrnd; lake sw, fishing, sailing, windsurfing 12km; dogs €1.50; Eng spkn; quiet; CCI. "Excel site; gd views; gd walking in Monts de Lacaune; v friendly Dutch owner; excel rest." ◆ € 15.75   2007*

LACAUNE *8E4* (10km SE Rural) **Camping Indigo Rieu-Montagné, Lac du Laouzas, 81320 Nages [05 63 37 24 71; fax 05 63 37 15 42; rieumontagne@camping-indigo.com; www. camping-indigo.com]** E fr Lacaune on D622 for 8km. R on D62 twds Nages. 2km after Nages turn E on shore of Lac de Laouzas. Sp fr junc D662/D62. Lge, hdg/mkd pitch, terr, pt shd; wc (some cont); serviced pitches; baby facs; shwrs inc; el pnts (6-10A) €4-6; gas; lndtte; shop; rest, snacks high ssn; bar; BBQ; playgrnd; htd pool; lake sw; cycle hire, archery, tennis & mini-golf nr; games area; some statics; dogs €3.30; Eng spkn; adv bkg; cc acc; CCI. "Vg rest 100m W of beach; bread made daily on site." ◆ 14 Jun-14 Sep. € 21.70 (CChq acc)   2007*

France

LACELLE *7B4* (Rural) **Camp Municipal, 19170 Lacelle [05 55 95 51 47 or 05 55 46 38 84 (Mairie); fax 05 55 46 03 86]** Fr Bugeat on D979 to Lacelle. Or on D940 15km SE of Eymoutiers. Sm, shd; wc; shwrs; el pnts (6A) €1.50; shop adj; rest; bar; playgrnd; paddling pool; games area; v quiet; adv bkg; phone. "In sm vill with communal fishing pond; v restful; warm welcome fr warden; v cheap!" 15 Jun-15 Sep. € 3.20   2005*

LADIGNAC LE LONG see St Yrieix la Perche *7B3*

LAFFREY see Vizille *9C3*

LAGRASSE *8F4* (1km NE Rural) **Camp Municipal de Boucocers, 11220 Lagrasse [04 68 43 10 05 or 04 68 43 15 18; fax 04 68 43 10 41; mairielagrasse@wanadoo.fr; www.ecamp.com]** 1km on D212 fr Lagrasse to Fabrezan (N). Sm, hdstg, pt sl, pt shd; wc; chem disp; shwrs inc; el pnts (15A) €2.50; shops, rest 500m; rv sw 1km; dogs €1.50; phone; adv bkg; CCI. "Helpful warden; gd walking; o'lookng superb medieval town; 8thC abbey; beautiful area; rec arrive early." ♦ ltd. 1 Mar-31 Oct. € 10.00   2005*

LAGUENNE see Tulle *7C4*

LAGUEPIE *8E4* (1km E Rural) **Camp Municipal Les Tilleuls, 82250 Laguépie [05 63 30 22 32 or 05 63 30 20 81 (Mairie); mairie.laguepie@info82.com; www.laguipie.com]** Exit Cordes on D922 N to Laguépie; turn R at bdge, still on D922 sp Villefranche; site sp to R in 500m; tight turn into narr lane. NB App thro Laguépie poss diff lge o'fits. Med, pt terr, pt shd; wc (some cont); shwrs inc; el pnts (10A) €2.50; shops 1km; playgrnd; pool; 4% statics; dogs; phone; adv bkg; quiet. "V attractive setting on Rv Viaur; Aveyron gorges; pleasant rvside walk to shops." ♦ 3 May-30 Sep. € 8.00   2006*

LAGUIOLE *7D4* (500m NE Rural) **Camp Municipal Les Monts D'Aubrac, 12210 Laguiole [05 65 44 39 72 or 05 65 51 26 30 (LS); fax 05 65 51 26 31]** E of Laguiole on D15 at top of hill. Fr S on D921 turn R at rndabt bef ent to town. Site sp. Med, hdg/mkd pitch, pt sl, pt shd; wc; chem disp; mv service pnt; shwrs inc; el pnts; lndtte; shops, rest, snacks & bar 500m; dogs; phone; quiet; CCI. "Spotless & well-cared for; short walk to pleasant vill; a gem of a site." 15 May-15 Sep. € 9.30   2007*

LAIGNES *6F1* (1km N Urban) **Aire Communale, Le Moulin Neuf, 21300 Laignes [03 80 81 43 03; mairie@laignes.fr]** Fr Châtillon-sur-Seine take D965 16km W to Laignes. Site clearly sp 1km before town. Sm (6 m'vans), pt shd; wc; mv service pnt; water points; el pnts; picnic tables; shops & rest 15 min walk; m'vans only. "Free of charge, delightful site by mill-pond."   2005*

LAISSAC *7D4* (4km N Urban) **Camping Aire de Service Camping Car, 12310 Laissac [05 65 69 60 45; fax 05 65 70 75 14; mairie-de-Laissac@wanadoo.fr]** Exit N88 sp Laissac. Foll sp to site. N of Laissac 4km & site adj live stock mkt. Sm, mkd pitch, hdstg, unshd; wc (some cont); chem disp; mv service pnt; shop, bar 200m; rest, snacks 500m; phone 500m; rd noise. "Gd NH only; clean san facs & washing up facs; room for 6 m'vans only." ♦ ltd. 1 Mar-30 Nov.   2004*

> The opening dates and prices on this campsite have changed. I'll send a site report form to the editor for the next edition of the guide.

LAISSAC *7D4* (3km SE) **FLOWER Camping La Grange de Monteillac, 12310 Sévérac-l'Eglise [05 65 70 21 00; fax 05 65 70 21 01; info@le-grange-de-monteillac.com; www.la-grange-de-monteillac.com]** Fr A75, at junc 42, go W on N88 twds Rodez; after approx 22km; bef Laissac; turn L twds Sévérac-l'Eglise; site sp. Med, hdg/mkd pitch, pt sl, terr, unshd; wc; chem disp (wc); mv service pnt; shwrs inc; el pnts (6A) inc (long lead poss req); ice; lndtte; rest, bar & shops high ssn; playgrnd; 2 pools; archery; horseriding; cycle hire; walking; tennis; entmnts; TV; dogs €1.50; phone; Eng spkn; adv bkg rec high ssn; quiet; CCI. "Beautiful site." ♦ 1 May-15 Sep. € 23.50   2006*

LAIVES see Sennecey le Grand *6H1*

LALINDE *7C3* (1.5km E) **Camping Moulin de la Guillou, Route de Sauveboeuf, 24150 Lalinde [05 53 61 02 91 or 05 53 73 44 60 (Mairie); fax 05 53 57 81 60; la-guillou@wanadoo.fr]** Take D703 E fr Lalinde (Rv Dordogne on R) & keep strt where rd turns L over canal bdge. Site in 300m; sp. Med, shd; wc; shwrs inc; el pnts (6A) €1.85; ice; shops 1km; tradsmn; pool; playgrnd; rv sw & fishing adj; entmnt; tennis adj; dogs €1.10; adv bkg. "Beside Rv Dordogne; basic, clean facs; vg." 1 May-30 Sep. € 10.50   2007*

LALINDE *7C3* (4km E Rural) **Camping Les Bö-Bains, 24150 Badefols-sur-Dordogne [05 53 73 52 52; fax 05 53 73 52 55; info@bo-bains.com; www.bo-bains.com]** Take D29 E fr Lalinde, site sp on L immed after vill sp for Badefols, on rvside. Med, shd, hdg pitch; wc; chem disp; shwrs inc; el pnts (6A) inc; lndtte; shop & 4km; rest; snacks; bar; entmnt; playgrnd; pool; waterslide; rv sw; tennis; games area; canoe hire; mini-golf; archery; boules; entmnt; child entmnt; some statics; dogs €3; quiet; adv bkg; cc acc. "Delightful site on banks of Rv Dordogne." ♦ Easter-30 Sep. € 31.00   2007*

LALINDE 7C3 (8km SE Rural) **Camping La Grande Veyière, 24480 Molières [05 53 63 25 84;** fax 05 53 63 18 25; la-grande-veyiere@wanadoo.fr; www.lagrandeveyiere.com] Fr Bergerac take D660 E for 19km to Port de Couze. Turn SW still on D660 sp Beaumont. In 6km turn L on D27. Site sp fr here. In approx 6km, ent on R. Med, hdg/mkd pitch, pt sl, terr, pt shd; wc (some cont); chem disp; shwrs inc; el pnts (6A) inc; gas; shop; tradsmn; snacks; bar; playgrnd; pool; games/TV rm; some statics; Eng spkn; adv bkg (rec Jul/Aug); phone; CCI. "Off beaten track, worth finding; owners friendly & helpful; staff will help you pitch with tractor in wet weather." ♦ 1 Apr-2 Nov. € 16.48   2004*

LALINDE 7C3 (4km W Urban) **Camping des Moulins, Route de Cahors, 24150 Couze-et-St Front [05 53 61 18 36;** fax 05 53 24 99 72; camping-des-moulins@wanadoo.fr; www. campingdesmoulins.com] Fr Lalinde take D703 dir Bergerac. In 2km turn L on D660 sp Port-de-Couze; over bdge (Dordogne Rv) into Couze. Turn R on D37 sp Lanquais, turn immed L, site sp. (NB Do not take D37E.) Sm, hdg pitch, pt sl, pt shd; wc; chem disp; mv service pnt; shwrs inc; el pnts (10A) €4.50; gas; lndtte; ice; snacks; bar; BBQ; playgrnd; 3 pools; lake sw 3km; games area; games rm; 40% statics; dogs €2; phone adj; poss cr; Eng spkn; adv bkg; quiet; cc acc; CCI. "Generous pitches; v friendly & helpful owner; ltd facs low ssn & poss unclean; gd pools; conv Bergerac; excel." 18 Mar-5 Nov. € 17.00 (4 persons)   2007*

LALLEY 9D3 (300m S Rural) **Camping Belle Roche, 38930 Lalley [tel/fax 04 76 34 75 33 or 06 86 36 71 48 (mob);** gildapatt@aol.com; www. campingbelleroche.com] Off D1075 (N75) at D66 for Mens; down long hill into Lalley. Site on R thro vill. Med, some hdg pitch, hdstg, pt sl, pt shd; wc; chem disp; mv service pnt; baby facs; shwrs inc; el pnts (10A) €3.50 (poss rev pol); gas; lndtte; ice; shop 500m; tradsmn Jul-Aug; rest; snacks; bar; playgrnd; htd pool; tennis 500m; entmnt; TV rm; dogs €1.50; poss cr; adv bkg; quiet; cc acc over €15; CCI. "Fantastic location; spacious pitches; friendly staff; gd clean sans facs, inc for disabled; gd for alpine flowers; excel walks nrby; nr Vercors National Park; highly rec." ♦ Easter-30 Sep. € 14.90 (CChq acc)   2007*

LAMALOU LES BAINS 10F1 (NE Urban) **Camp Municipal Le Verdale, 34240 Lamalou-les-Bains [04 67 95 86 89;** fax 04 67 95 87 70; omt.lamalou@ wanadoo.fr] S fr Bédarieux on D908 twds Lamalou. Turn N off D908 at traff lts into Lamalou. At 2nd rndbt turn E foll sp to site on NE side of town. Med, mkd pitch, pt shd; htd wc; shwrs; el pnts (6A) €2.30; shop, pool, tennis & golf in town; 30% statics; phone; poss cr; adv bkg rec. "San facs clean; helpful, friendly warden; sm pitches; nr thermal baths; easy walk to town & shops." 15 Mar-31 Oct. € 11.20   2005*

LAMALOU LES BAINS 10F1 (2km SE Rural) **Camping Domaine de Gatinié, Route de Gatinié, 34600 Les Aires [04 67 95 71 95 or 04 67 28 41 69 (LS);** fax 04 67 95 65 73; gatinie@ wanadoo.fr; www.domainedegatinie.com] Fr D908 fr Lamalou-les-Bains or Hérépian dir Poujol-sur-Orb, site sp. Fr D160 cross rv to D908 then as above. Med, hdg/mkd pitch, pt sl, pt shd; wc (some cont); chem disp; baby facs; shwrs inc; el pnts (6A) inc; lndtte; ice; tradsmn; rest; snacks; bar; BBQ; playgrnd; pool; paddling pool; rv sw 100m; canoeing; fishing; games area; golf, horseriding, tennis 2km; entmnt; some statics; dogs €2.30; Eng spkn; adv bkg; quiet; red low ssn/long stay/CCI. "Beautiful situation; many leisure activities; vg." ♦ 1 Mar-30 Nov. € 17.00   2005*

LAMASTRE 9C2 (5km NE Rural) **Camping Les Roches, Les Roches, 07270 Le Crestet [04 75 06 20 20;** fax 04 75 06 26 23; camproches@ club-internet.fr; www.campinglesroches.com] Take D534 fr Tournon-sur-Rhône dir Lamastre. Turn R at Le Crestet & foll sp for site, 3km fr vill. Sm, mkd pitch, hdstg, terr, pt shd; wc (some cont); chem disp; mv service pnt; baby facs; shwrs inc; el pnts (4-6A) €2.80-3.50; lndtte; ice; shop; tradsmn; rest; snacks; bar; BBQ; playgrnd; htd pool; rv sw adj; sports area; fishing; TV rm; 30% statics; bus 1km; adv bkg dep req; quiet; cc acc; 5% red CCI. "Family-run site; v clean facs; lovely views; gd base for touring medieval vills; gd walking." ♦ 15 Apr-30 Sep. € 15.00   2004*

LAMASTRE 9C2 (2km NW Rural) **Camping Le Retourtour, 1 Rue de Retourtour, 07270 Lamastre [tel/fax 04 75 06 40 71;** campingderetourtour@ wanadoo.fr; www.campingderetourtour.com] Fr Lamastre take D533 W. Site well sp. Med, mkd pitch, pt shd; wc (some cont); chem disp; mv service pnt; baby facs; shwrs inc; el pnts (4-13A) €2.90-€4.60; gas; lndtte; ice; shop; tradsmn; rest; snacks; bar; BBQ; playgrnd; rv sw 500m; games area; games rm; entmnt; 10% statics; dogs €2; phone; Eng spkn; adv bkg (dep req); quiet; cc not acc; CCI. "V friendly, helpful owners." ♦ 7 Apr-29 Sep. € 14.90   2007*

LAMBALLE 2E3 (700m NE Urban) **Camp Municipal, Rue St Sauveur, 22400 Lamballe [tel/ fax 02 96 34 74 33 or 02 96 50 13 50 (LS)]** NE side of town beyond church; nr water tower. Clearly sp. Sm, terr, pt shd; wc; shwrs inc; el pnts (5A) €3; shops 700m; htd pool 700m; quiet. "Interesting town, historical 17thC church." 1 Jul-4 Sep. € 9.00   2006*

LAMONTELARIE see Brassac 8F4

LANDEBIA see Plancoët 2E3

France

LANDEDA 2E1 (2km NW Coastal) **Camping des Abers, 51 Toull-Tréaz, Plage de Ste Marguerite, 29870 Landéda [02 98 04 93 35; fax 02 98 04 84 35; camping-des-abers@wanadoo.fr; www.camping-des-abers.com]** NW fr Brest on D13/D10 to Landéda via Bourg-Blanc & Lannilis; at church in Landéda (in rndabt) foll sp 'Campings' to NW end of peninsual to Dunes de Ste Marguerite & site. Lge, hdg/mkd pitch, hdstg, terr, pt shd; wc; chem disp; mv service pnt; baby facs; fam bthrm; shwrs €0.80; el pnts (10A) €2.50; gas; lndtte; ice; shop & snacks in ssn; rest 200m; bar 100m; BBQ; playgrnd; sand beach; fishing; cycle hire; entmnt; wifi internet; games/TV rm; 10% statics; dogs €1.80; Eng spkn; adv bkg (rec high ssn); quiet; 20% red low ssn; cc acc; CCI. "Attractive site adj spectacular wild coast; highest pitches have views; site well landscaped with flowers; facs clean & well-maintained; friendly, helpful manager; gd walks, cycling; unspoilt area; shop adj site am only; excel." ♦ 1 May-30 Sep. € 14.50 ABS - B30   2007*

See advertisement

LANDEDA 2E1 (3km NW Coastal) **Camp Municipal de Penn-Enez, 29870 Landéda [02 98 04 99 82; info@camping-penn-enez.com; www.camping-penn-enez.com]** Proceed NW thro Landéda, turn R in 1km sp Penn-Enez then L in 600m. Site sp. Med, pt hdg pitch, pt sl, unshd; wc; chem disp (wc); shwrs inc; el pnts (16A) €2.70; playgrnd; sand beach 500m; 2% statics; dogs €1.30; Eng spkn; quiet. "Friendly, helpful management; grassy headland site; beach views fr some pitches; san facs poss stretched high ssn; site self, warden calls 1100-1200 & 1800-1900; gd walks." ♦ ltd. 25 Apr-30 Sep. € 9.10   2004*

LANDERNEAU 2E2 (SW Urban) **Camp Municipal Les Berges de l'Elorn, Route de Calvaire, 29800 Landerneau [02 98 85 44 94 or 02 98 85 00 66 (Mairie); fax 02 98 85 43 35; tiker-landerne@mairie-landerneau.fr]** Fr main town bdge foll sp to pool, sports stadium & site (200m). Sm, hdg pitch, hdstg, pt shd; wc; chem disp; mv service pnt; shwrs inc; el pnts (7A) €3.10; shops, rest, snacks bar 250m; BBQ; playgrnd adj; pool 500m; tennis; dogs €1.10; phone adj; Eng spkn; adv bkg; quiet, some rd noise; CCI. "Pretty town on rv; pitches all have el pnts & some have water tap; poss itinerants." ♦ 15 May-15 Oct. € 9.10   2005*

LANDEVIEILLE see Bretignolles sur Mer 2H3

LANDIVISIAU 2E2 (7km NE) **Camp Municipal Lanorgant, 29420 Plouvorn [02 98 61 32 40 (Mairie); fax 02 98 61 38 87; commune-de-plouvorn@wanadoo.fr]** Fr Landivisiau, take D69 N twd Roscoff. In 8km turn R onto D19 twd Morlaix. Site sp, in 700m turn R. Sm, hdg/mkd pitch, terr, pt shd; wc (cont for men); mv service pnt; shwrs; el pnts (10A) €2; ice; lndtte; shops, snacks, bar 500m; rest 1km; BBQ; playgrnd; sand beach; lake sw; sailboards & canoes for hire; fishing; tennis; adv bkg; quiet. "Ideal NH for ferries; v diff lge o'fits." 15 Jun-15 Sep. € 8.00   2005*

LANDUDEC 2F2 (2km W Rural) **Domaine de Bel-Air, Route de Quimper-Audierne, Keridreuff, 29710 Landudec [02 98 91 50 27; fax 02 98 91 55 82; camping-dubelair@wanadoo.fr; www.belaircamping.com]** Fr N165 exit dir Quimper Cent. On ring rd foll sp Douarnenez & Audierne & exit ring rd onto D765 immed after Carrefour supmkt sp Douarnenez. Turn L at rndabt onto D784 dir Audierne/Landudec. Strt on at traff lts in Landudec, site on L in 750m. Lge, hdg/mkd pitch, terr, pt shd; wc; chem disp; shwrs inc; el pnts (10A) inc; gas; lndtte; ice; shop; tradsmn; rest; snacks; playgrnd; htd pool; paddling pool; beach 10km; lake adj; waterslide; watersports; tennis; games rm; entmnt; child entmnt; TV; dogs €3; poss cr; Eng spkn; adv bkg; quiet; cc acc; red low ssn; CCI. "Well situated site; excel." ♦ 1 May-30 Sep. € 22.00   2005*

LANGEAC 9C1 (1km N Rural) **Camping Les Gorges de l'Allier, Domaine du Pradeau, 43300 Langeac [04 71 77 05 01; fax 04 71 77 27 34; infos@campinglangeac.com; www.campinglangeac.com]** Site sp on Clermont-Ferrand to Le Puy rd (N102) at D56. Take D56 to Langeac. Site at junc of D590 & D585. Lge, pt shd; wc (some cont); chem disp; mv service pnt; shwrs inc; el pnts (10A) €2.50 (poss long lead req); gas 500m; lndtte; ice; shop 1km; tradsmn; rest 500m; snacks; playgrnd; pool (high ssn); rv sw, fishing, canoeing & walking rtes adj; child entmnt; cycle hire; entmnt; TV rm; some statics; dogs €1; phone; bus 1km; poss cr; Eng spkn; quiet; red low ssn; CCI. "Beautiful location on Rv Allier; tourist train thro Gorges d'Allier fr Langeac to Langogne; gd local mkt; ltd facs low ssn." 1 Apr-31 Oct. € 12.50   2007*

LANGOGNE 9D1 (1km S Urban) **Camp Municipal de l'Allier, 9 Route de St Alban-en-Montagne, 48300 Langogne [04 66 69 28 98]** Fr Le Puy take N88 dir Mende. At Langogne over rv bdge & 1st L. Foll sp, site in 1km. Med, mkd pitch, pt sl, pt shd; wc (some cont); chem disp (wc); shwrs inc; el pnts (6A) €2.40; ice; lndtte; shops 500m; rest; snacks; bar; pool 500m; phone; poss cr; quiet; adv bkg; CCI. "Gd walking area; lake for sailing 2km; close to walking routes." ♦ 1 Jun-15 Sep. € 6.60   2004*

CAMPING DES ABERS★★★

Outstandingly positioned in Brittany, 45 min. West from ROSCOFF - Direct access to a remarkable sandy beach with little islands accessible at low tide. Splendid ocean views. Ideal for families with younger children and nature-lovers. English spoken.

51, Toull-Tréaz, Plage de Sainte-Marguerite
29870 LANDEDA
FINISTERE - BRETAGNE - FRANCE
Phone: 00 33 298 04 93 35 • fax: 00 33 298 04 84 35
camping-des-abers@wanadoo.fr
www.camping-des-abers.com

France

LANGOGNE *9D1* (2km W Rural) **Camping Les Terrasses du Lac, 48300 Naussac [04 66 69 29 62; fax 04 66 69 24 78; info@naussac.com; www.naussac.com]** S fr Le Puy-en-Velay on N88. At Langogne take D26 to lakeside, site sp. Lge, terr, pt shd; wc; chem disp; baby facs; shwrs; el pnts (6A) €2.50; lndtte; lndry rm; shop 2km; rest; snacks; bar; BBQ; playgrnd; pool; lake sw & sand beach adj; watersports adj; sailing school; games area; cycle hire; golf 1km; horseriding 3km; entmnt; excursions; TV rm; 10% statics; dogs €1; phone; Eng spkn; adv bkg (dep req); quiet; red low ssn; CCI. "Vg views; steep hill bet recep & pitches; vg cycling & walking."
♦ 1 Apr-30 Sep. € 13.50 (CChq acc)   2007*

⊞**LANGRES** *6F1* (6km NE Rural) **Camping Hautoreille, 52360 Bannes [tel/fax 03 25 84 83 40; campinghautoreille@free.fr; www.camping hautoreille.com]** N fr Dijon on D974 (N74) to Langres; foll rd around Langres to E; onto D74 NE to Bannes; site on R on ent vill. Or exit A31 junc 7 Langres Nord onto D619 (N19), then D74 NE to Bannes. Med, mkd pitch, some hdstg, pt sl, pt shd; htd wc; chem disp; mv service pnt; shwrs inc; el pnts (6A) €3 (rev pol); lndtte; ice; shops 5km; tradsmn; rest (summer only); snacks; bar; playgrnd; lake sw 2.5km; horseriding & tennis 5km; dogs €1; phone; poss cr; Eng spkn; adv bkg; quiet; CCI. "Peaceful site; basic facs, ltd low ssn & inadequate high ssn; pleasant German owner; gd site rest; v busy NH at w/e; site muddy when wet - parking on hdstg or owner will use tractor; gd NH." ♦ € 13.00
                                             2007*

Before we move on, I'm going to fill in some site report forms and post them off to the editor, otherwise they won't arrive in time for the deadline at the end of September.

LANGRES *6F1* (5km E Rural) **Camping Kawan-Village Le Lac de la Liez, Rue du Camping, 52200 Peigney [03 25 90 27 79; fax 03 25 90 66 79; campingliez@free.fr; www.campingliez.com]** Exit A31 at junc 7 (Langres Nord) onto DN19 sp Langres, Vesoul; at Langres turn L at traff lts onto D74 sp Vesoul, Mulhouse, Le Lac de la Liez; at rndabt go strt on sp Epinal, Nancy; after Champigny-lès-Langres in 60m turn R onto D52 sp Peigney, Lac de la Liez; in 3km bear R onto D284 sp Langres Sud and Lac de la Liez; site on R in 500m. Med, hdg/mkd pitch, some hdstg, terr, pt shd; htd wc; chem disp; mv service pnt; baby facs; sauna; shwrs inc; el pnts (10A) inc; lndtte; ice; shop; tradsmn; rest; snacks; bar; BBQ; playgrnd; 2 pools (1 htd covrd); paddling pool; spa; lake sw & sand beach adj; fishing, windsurfing, sailing & pedaloes; tennis; cycle hire; horseriding; golf 10km; entmnt high ssn; wifi internet; games/TV rm; 15% statics; dogs €3; phone; poss v cr; Eng spkn; quiet; cc acc; CCI. "Lovely, well-run site with lake views fr some pitches; sm pitches; m'van area; modern, v clean facs, ltd low ssn; helpful staff; lovely pool; office clsd 1230-1500 - instruction about barrier on office door; rec arr bef 1600 high ssn; Langres interesting walled Roman town; pleasant rvside walk; excel." ♦ 1 Apr-15 Oct. € 30.00 (CChq acc) ABS - J05   2007*

LANGON *7D2* (4km NE) **Camp Municipal Les Bords de Garonne, 33490 St Pierre-d'Aurillac [05 56 63 39 00 or 05 56 63 30 27 (Mairie); fax 05 56 63 17 39; commune-de-st-pierre-daurillac@wanadoo.fr]** Fr Langon E on N113 thro St Macaire. Site to R in cent of vill of St Pierre-d'Aurillac. Fr E on N113 approx 15km after La Réole site sp L. Easy access. Sm, pt shd; wc (some cont); chem disp; shwrs inc; el pnts 6A) inc; lndtte; shops 500m; quiet; CCI. "Site attended by warden but poss no access 1200-1700; gd fruit & wine region; poor san facs & lndtte low ssn; when leaving with m'van not poss to turn L twd Bordeaux, take alt lanes or turn round in g'ge twd La Réole; poss many itinerants."
1 Jun-31 Oct. € 11.65   2006*

LANGRES *6F1* (5km S Rural) **FFCC Camp Municipal La Croix d'Arles, 52200 Bourg [tel/fax 03 25 88 24 02; croix.arles@wanadoo.fr; www. croixdarles.com]** Site is 4km S of Langres on W side of D974 (N74) S of junc of D974 with D428. Fr Dijon no L turn off N74 - can pull into indust est N of site & return to site. Med, hdg/mkd pitch, ltd hdstg, pt sl, pt shd; wc; chem disp; mv service pnt; shwrs inc; el pnts (10A) €3.50 (poss rev pol) (long cable req); lndtte; shop; tradsmn; rest; snacks; bar; playgrnd; pool; mini-golf; statics; dogs; phone; poss cr; Eng spkn; red low ssn; cc acc; CCI. "Popular site, fills up quickly after 1600; some lovely hidden pitches in woodland; muddy after rain; unkempt low ssn; poss haphazard pitching when full; facs gd; friendly staff; v conv NH; conv Langres historic town." ♦ 15 Mar-31 Oct. € 14.50   2007*

LANGRES *6F1* (500m SW Urban) **Camp Municipal Navarre, Blvd de Lattre de Tassigny, 52200 Langres [03 25 87 37 92; campingnavarre@nomade.fr; http://campingnavarre.com]** Fr D619 (N19) L at sp in town; foll sp to 'Centre Ville'. Site well sp fr town cent; inside old town walls. NB Travelling S ignore 1st sp to town cent, cont to top of hill to rndabt. NB Diff access for lge o'fits thro walled town. Med, pt sl, pt shd; htd wc; chem disp; shwrs inc; el pnts (6A) inc (long cable req & poss rev pol); lndry rm; playgrnd nr; dogs; phone; poss cr in high ssn & w/e; Eng spkn; quiet, some rd noise; cc not acc; CCI. "Popular, gd value site; pleasantly situated; gd views fr some pitches; recep open 1800-2200; on arr site self & see warden at recep; v helpful, polite recep; excel new san facs (2007); no twin-axles; site poss scruffy low ssn; part of site muddy after rain; poss itinerants; Langres interesting Roman walled town; excel Little Train tour of town & walls 1km fr site; excel." ♦ ltd. 15 Mar-30 Nov. € 11.30   2007*

LANGRES *6F1* (4km NW Rural) **Camp Municipal La Mouche, Rue de la Mouche, 52200 Humes-Jorquenay [03 25 87 50 65 (Mairie)]** Exit A31 at junc 7, foll N19 S for 4km; site on W of N19 over rv bdg; sp in vill cent. Or S fr Chaumont on N19, into vill of Humes. Sm, unshd; wc; shwrs inc; el pnts (8A) €1.80 (poss long cable rec); shop in vill; tradsmn; rest 2km; snacks; playgrnd; poss cr; quiet. "Pretty site; basic but busy; early arr rec; no staff on site, fees collected each pm; no apparent security; interesting area; gd NH." 15 Apr-30 Sep. € 7.90   2007*

LANILDUT *2E1* (1km N Coastal) **Camping du Tromeur, 11 Route du Camping, 29840 Lanildut [02 98 04 31 13; tromeur@vive-les-vacances. com; www.vive-les-vacances.com/tromeur]** Exit D205 onto D5 to St Renan; NW on D68; in 9km turn L onto D28 to Brélès; turn R onto D27 to Lanildut. Med; wc; chem disp (wc); shwrs inc; el pnts €2 (poss long lead req & poss rev pol); lndry rm; tradsmn; shop, bar, crêperie & gd rest in vill; BBQ; dogs €1; phone; quiet. "Clean, sheltered site; san facs gd; harbour & sm beach; gd value." 15 May-15 Sep. € 9.00   2007*

LANLOUP *2E3* (W Rural) **FFCC Camping Le Neptune, Kerguistin, 22580 Lanloup [02 96 22 33 35 or 06 75 44 39 69 (mob); fax 02 96 22 68 45; contact@leneptune.com; www. leneptune.com]** Take D786 fr St Brieuc or Paimpol to Lanloup, site sp. Med, hdg/mkd pitch, pt shd; wc (some cont); chem disp; baby facs; shwrs inc; el pnts (6-16A) €3.50; gas; lndtte; ice; shop (high ssn) or 500m; tradsmn; snacks, bar (high ssn) or 500m; BBQ; playgrnd; htd, covrd pool; sand beach 2.5km; tennis 300m; horseriding 4km; cycle hire; mini-golf; TV rm; 15% statics; dogs €2.20; phone; poss cr; Eng spkn; adv bkg; quiet, rd noise some pitches; CCI. "Excel, well-maintained site nr beautiful coast; various pitch sizes; spotless san facs; friendly, helpful owner; highly rec." ♦ 31 Mar-13 Oct. € 19.10 (CChq acc)   2007*

⊞**LANNE** *8F2* (Rural) **Camping La Bergerie, 79 Rue des Chênes, 65380 Lanne [tel/fax 05 62 45 40 05; contact@camping-la-bergerie. com; www.camping-la-bergerie.com]** Fr Lourdes take N21 twd Tarbes. Turn R on D216, site sp. Med, mkd pitch, shd; htd wc; shwrs; el pnts (10A) €2.80 (poss rev pol); gas; ice; shop; snacks & bar (high ssn); playgrnd; pool high ssn; tennis; dogs €0.80; bus 200m; Eng spkn; adv bkg; quiet but some rd noise & some aircraft noise at night; red low ssn; CCI. "Well-run site; friendly owners; gd san facs; recep 0800-1000 & 1800-2000; poss unkempt low ssn; poss flooding wet weather; no turning area." ♦ € 12.50   2007*

LANNEMEZAN *8F2* (6km W Rural) **FFCC Camping Les Craouès, Rue du 8 Mai 1945, 65130 Capvern-les-Bains [tel/fax 05 62 39 02 54; demande@camping-les-craoues.net; www.camping-les-craoues.net]** Exit A64 junc 15. At rndabt at ent to Capvern foll sp Capvern Village, site sp Fr Lannemezan on D817 (N117) site at x-rds with D938. Med, mkd pitch, pt sl, shd; wc; mv service pnt; baby facs; shwrs inc; el pnts (3-8A) €2.75-5; gas; lndtte; ice; shops 500m; playgrnd; pool; paddling pool 100m; games rm; dogs €1; poss cr; adv bkg; red low ssn. "V basic site; not clearly mkd pitches; scruffy overall (low ssn report); NH only." ♦ 1 May-15 Oct. € 12.60   2007*

LANNION *1D2* (2km SE) **Camp Municipal Les Deux Rives, Rue du Moulin du Duc, 22300 Lannion [02 96 46 31 40 or 02 96 46 64 22; fax 02 96 46 53 35; infos@ville.lannion.fr]** SW fr Perros-Guirec on D788 to Lannion; fr Lannion town cent; foll dir Guincamp on D767; site well sp approx 1.5km just bef Leclerc supmkt (do not confuse with hypmkt). Fr S on D767 sp at rndabts; turn L a Leclerc supmkt. Med, mkd pitch, unshd; wc; chem disp; shwrs inc; el pnts (6A) €2; lndtte; shop high ssn & 1km; bar high ssn; playgrnd; security barrier; dogs €1; adv bkg; CCI. "Easy rvside walk to old town; gd san facs but ltd low ssn & poss unclean; phone ahead low ssn to check open; warden lives on site but poss no arrivals Sun." ♦ 1 Apr-30 Sep. € 12.50   2007*

LANNION *1D2* (7km NW Coastal) **FFCC Camping Les Plages de Beg Léguer, Route de la Côte, 22300 Lannion [02 96 47 25 00 or 02 99 83 34 81 (LS); fax 02 96 47 27 77; info@ campingdesplages.com; www.campingdesplages. com]** Fr Lannion take rd out of town twd Trébeurden then twd Servel on D65, then head SW off that rd twd Beg Léguer (sp). Lge, hdg/mkd pitch, pt shd; wc (some cont); chem disp; ltd mv service pnt; baby facs; shwrs inc; el pnts (6-10A) €3-4.50; gas; ice; lndtte; sm shop & 5km; tradsmn; rest; snacks; bar; playgrnd; htd pool; paddling pool; sand beach 350m; fishing; sailing; windsurfing; tennis; mini-golf; TV; 30% statics; dogs €1; phone; bus 400m; Eng spkn; adv bkg; quiet; red long stay/ low ssn; cc acc; CCI. "V pleasant, peaceful site; lge pitches; new san facs (2006); v clean; excel coast." ♦ Easter-1 Nov. € 20.00   2006*

LANOBRE see Bort les Orgues *7C4*

LANSARGUES see Lunel *10E2*

LANSLEBOURG MONT CENIS *9C4* **Camp Municipal Les Balmasses, 73480 Lanslebourg-Mont-Cenis [04 79 05 82 83; fax 04 79 05 91 56; burdin61@club-internet.fr; www.camping-les-balmasses.com]** Fr Modane, site on R on rv on ent to town. Med, mkd pitch, pt shd; wc (some cont); shwrs inc; el pnts (6-10A) €4.30-5; lndtte; ice; shop 500m; rest; snacks; bar; BBQ; playgrnd; dogs; phone; Eng spkn; CCI. "Pleasant, quiet site by rv; v clean facs; lovely mountain views; conv NH bef/after Col du Mont-Cenis." ♦ ltd. 1 Jun-20 Sep. € 12.70   2007*

LANSLEBOURG MONT CENIS *9C4* (2.5km E Rural) **Camp Municipal Caravaneige, 73480 Lanslevillard [tel/fax 04 79 05 90 52 or 06 86 11 66 86 (mob); www.camping-valcenis.com]** Fr Lanslebourg, take sp rd D902 to Lanslevillard. Site on L at ent to vill. Med, mkd pitch, pt sl, unshd; htd wc; chem disp; mv service pnt; shwrs inc; el pnts (6-10A) €5.80-7.80 (ensure staff reset bef connection); gas 500m; lndtte; ice; shops 500m; bar/rest; playgrnd; tennis nr; some statics; phone; poss cr (winter ski); adv bkg only in winter; quiet; CCI. "Winter ski-resort, summer walking & cycling; close to ski-lifts; ltd recep hrs; vg." ♦ 15 Jun-15 Sep & 16 Dec-1 May. € 12.40   2007*

LANVEOC *2E2* (1km N Coastal) **Camping La Cale, 29160 Lanvéoc [tel/fax 02 98 27 58 91]** N fr Crozon dir Roscanvel. After approx 5.5km turn R onto D55 for Lanvéoc. Site sp. Med, terr, unshd; shwrs inc; el pnts (10A) €2.40; lndtte; rest; snacks; bar; dir access to coast; fishing; no statics; quiet; CCI. "Sea views; low ssn unisex san facs." 1 May-15 Sep. € 8.00   2005*

LAON *3C4* (1km NW Rural) **Camp Municipal La Chênaie, Allée de la Chênaie, 02000 Laon [tel/fax 03 23 20 25 56; aaussel@ville-laon.fr; www.ville-laon.fr]** Exit A26 junc 13 onto N2 sp Laon; at junc with D1044 (N44) (rndabt) turn N sp Laon/Semilly, then L at next rndabt. Site well sp. Med, hdg/mkd pitches, pt shd; htd wc (some cont); chem disp; mv service pnt; baby facs; shwrs inc; el pnts (6A) €2.70 (poss rev pol); lndtte; ltd shop & 500m; tradsmn; snacks high ssn; bar; BBQ; playgrnd; fishing lake 500m (no sw); watersports at nrby Parc de l'Ailette; dogs €2; phone; poss cr; Eng spkn; adv bkg; quiet with some rd noise; cc not acc; CCI. "Lovely site; excel, well-mkd pitches; vg, clean san facs; slight uphill access - stop bef ascending; lgest pitches at end of site rd; no twin-axles; gates close 2200; if travelling Sep phone to check site open; shooting club nrby; conv Laon cathedral; m'van parking nr cathedral; busy, popular NH." ♦ 1 May-30 Sep. € 10.00   2007*

LAPALISSE *9A1* (250m S Urban) **Camp Municipal, Rue des Vignes, 03120 Lapalisse [04 70 99 26 31; fax 04 70 99 33 53; office.tourismet@cc-paysdelapalisse.fr; www.ville-lapalisse.fr]** N7 fr Moulins, site on R 50m bef Lapalisse cancellation sp. Med, mkd pitch, pt shd; htd wc (some cont); shwrs inc; el pnts (6-9A) €2.10; lndtte; shops 300m; tradsman; playgrnd; dogs €1; quiet; Eng spkn; cc acc; CCI. "Popular NH; no twin-axle vans." ♦ 1 Apr-30 Sep. € 7.30   2006*

LAPEYROUSE *7A4* (2km SE Rural) **Camp Municipal Les Marins, La Loge, 63700 Lapeyrouse [04 73 52 02 73 or 04 73 52 00 79 (Mairie); fax 04 73 52 03 89; 63lapeyrouse@free.fr; http://63lapeyrouse.free.fr]** Fr Montluçon S on D2144 (N144) sp Montaigut. In 24km turn L on D13 sp Lapeyrouse. In 7km turn R onto D998, site on R at end of vill, well sp. Med, hdg/mkd pitch, pt shd; wc; chem disp; baby facs; shwrs inc; el pnts (10-16A) inc; lndtte; bar nr; playgrnd; lake sw adj; windsurfing; fishing; tennis; games area; cycle hire; TV; adv bkg; quiet; CCI. "Delightful countryside; barrier access." 15 Jun-1 Sep. € 15.00 (3 persons)   2006*

LARGENTIERE *9D2* (4km SE Rural) **Camping Les Châtaigniers, Le Mas-de-Peyrot, 07110 Laurac-en-Vivarais [04 75 36 86 26; chataigniers@ hotmail.com; www.chataigniers-laurac.com]** Fr N on A7, at junc Loriol take N304 via Privas or Aubenas dir Alès. Site sp fr Lachapelle on D104. Sm, mkd pitch, pt sl, pt shd; wc, chem disp (wc); baby facs; shwrs; el pnts (10A) €2.30; lndtte; ice; playgrnd; pool; 10% statics; dogs €1; poss cr; adv bkg; quiet. "Attractive site in S Ardèche, sh walk to vill shops, supmkt & auberge; vg." ♦ 1 Apr-30 Sep. € 18.00   2004*

France

LARGENTIERE *9D2* (1.6km NW Rural) **Camping Sunêlia Les Ranchisses, Route de Rocher, Chassiers, 07110 Largentière [04 75 88 31 97; fax 04 75 88 32 73; reception@lesranchisses.fr; www. lesranchisses.fr]** Fr Aubenas S on D104. 1km after vill of Uzer turn R onto D5 to Largentière. Go thro Largentière on D5 in dir Rocher/Valgorge. DO NOT use D103 bet Lachapelle-Aubenas & Largentière - this rd is too steep & narr for lge vehicles & c'vans. Med, mkd pitch, pt shd; wc; chem disp; baby facs; shwrs inc; el pnts (10A) inc; gas; lndtte; ice; shop; rest; snacks; bar; BBQ (gas/elec only) playgrnd; 2 htd pools (1 covrd); wellness centre; paddling pool; rv sw, fishing; canoeing; tennis; archery; mini-golf; games area; entmnt; internet; games/TV rm; 30% statics; dogs €3; poss cr; adv bkg ess; red low ssn. "Excel rest; noisy rd adj to S end of site, also noisy when site full; lovely, well-managed site adj vineyard; helpful, hard-working staff; close to museums." ♦ 12 Apr-2 Nov. € 34.65 (CChq acc) ABS - C32
2007*

LARGENTIERE *9D2* (8km NW Rural) **Camping La Marette, Route de Valgorge, 07110 Joannas [04 75 88 38 88; fax 04 75 88 36 33; www.lamarette.com]** Fr Aubenas D104 SW to Largentière. Foll D5 3km N of Largentière then W on D24 to Valgorge. Site 3km past vill of Joannas. Med, mkd pitch; pt sl, terr, pt shd; wc; chem disp; mv service pnt; shwrs; el pnts (10A) €3.10; lndtte; shop; tradsmn; snacks; bar; playgrnd; pool; 5% statics; dogs €1.30; quiet; adv bkg; Eng spkn; CCI. "Friendly family-run site; excel for children; organised tours, canoe hire, walking; gd san facs; not rec for lge trailer o'fits." ♦ Easter-15 Sep. € 18.00
2004*

LARNAS *9D2* (2.5km SW Rural) **Camping Le Domaine d'Imbours, 07220 Larnas [04 75 54 39 50; fax 04 75 54 39 20; info@domaine-imbours.com; www.domaine-imbours.com]** Fr Bourg-St. Andéol on N86 take D4 to St Remèze. Do not exit on D462 which has sp for tourists for Imbours site. In St Remèze turn R on D362 to Mas-du-Gras & D262 twd Larnas & site. Do not attempt app to site via D262 thro St Montant. Lge, mkd pitch, some hdstg, pt sl, pt shd; wc; shwrs inc; el pnts inc; lndtte; shop; rest; snacks; bar; playgrnd; htd, pool complex; waterslide; tennis; cycle hire; entmnt; some statics; dogs €4.30; poss cr; adv bkg (ess Jul/Aug); quiet. "Many sports activities; beautiful area." ♦ 31 Mar-6 Oct. € 26.00 (3 persons)
2006*

LAROQUE DES ALBERÈS see Argelès sur Mer *10G1*

⊞**LARUNS** *8G2* (6km N Rural) **Camp Municipal de Monplaisir, Quartier Monplaisir, 64260 Gère-Bélesten [05 59 82 61 18; fax 05 59 82 60 71]** Site sp on E side of D934 S of Gère-Bélesten. Med, mkd pitch, pt shd, htd wc; shwrs €0.82; el pnts (3-16A) €1.95-6.30; tradsmn; shops 4km; rest, bar 100m; playgrnd; htd pool 4km; fishing; TV; 50% statics; adv bkg; quiet. € 8.50
2006*

LARUNS *8G2* (2km E) **Camping Le Valentin, 64440 Laruns [05 59 05 39 33 or 05 59 05 32 80 (LS); fax 05 59 05 65 84; campingduvalentin@wanadoo.fr]** Fr Laruns take D934 dir Col de Pourtalet. Site well sp on L app RH bend. If app fr Col d'Aubisque another site ent is well sp on R at sharp LH bend just bef D934. Med, hdg/mkd pitch, terr, pt shd; wc; shwrs inc; el pnts (3-5A) €2.35-3.20; lndtte; shop; tradsmn; rest, snacks high ssn; bar; playgrnd; pool 3km; 20% statics; dogs €1.10; adv bkg; quiet at night but some rd noise; red low ssn/long stay; CCI. "Extremely pleasant, well-managed site, friendly, helpful management; some pitches cramped if using awning; facs ltd low ssn; conv Spanish border, cable car & mountain train; surrounded by 5 mountain peaks; thermal baths in nrby vill of Eaux-Chaudes; gd sh stay/NH." ♦ 25 Apr-1 Nov. € 14.00
2005*

LARUNS *8G2* (6km SE Rural) **Camping d'Iscoo, 64440 Eaux-Bonnes [05 59 05 36 81; http://iscoo. free.fr]** Site is on R 1.4km fr Eaux-Bonnes on climb to Col d'Aubisque (site sp says Camping * *, no name). Site ent in middle of S-bend so advise cont 500m & turn on open ground on L. Sm, mkd pitch, pt sl, pt shd; wc (some cont); shwrs €0.76; el pnts (2-5A) inc; shops 1.5km; playgrnd; pool 3km; dogs; quiet; cc not acc; CCI. "V pleasant location; site not well maintained low ssn." 1 Jun-30 Sep. € 11.00
2004*

⊞**LARUNS** *8G2* (1km S) **Camping Les Gaves, Pon, 64440 Laruns [05 59 05 32 37; fax 05 59 05 47 14; campingdesgaves@wanadoo.fr]** Site on S edge of town, N of Hôtel Le Lorry & bdge. Fr town sq cont on Rte d'Espagne (narr exit fr sq) to end of 1-way system. After Elf & Total stns turn L at site sp immed bef bdge (high fir tree each side of bdge ent). Ignore 1st site on L. At v constricted T-junc at ent to quartier 'Pon', turn R & foll rd into site. Med, mkd pitch, pt shd; htd wc; chem disp; serviced pitch; shwrs inc; el pnts (10A) €3.20; lndtte; shops 1.5km; bar; playgrnd; pool 1km; fishing; TV; dogs €1.68; rv fishing adj; games area; 75% statics; quiet; CCI. "Beautiful site; excel facs; level walk to vill." € 17.00
2004*

LARUSCADE *7C2* (4km SW Rural) **Aire Naturelle Le Lac Vert (Saumon), 33620 Laruscade [tel/fax 05 57 68 64 43]** N on N10 fr Bordeaux for 28km, about 1km S of Cavignac, sp off to R. Access over narr bdge. Sm, pt shd; wc; chem disp; shwrs inc; ltd el pnts inc (long cable req); shops 1km; rest; snacks; bar; lake sw; playgrnd; dogs; Eng spkn; CCI. "V pretty site by lake; v quiet but some rlwy noise; Auberge rest on site; fair NH." 1 May-30 Sep.
2004*

LATHUILE see Faverges *9B3*

LATTES see Montpellier *10F1*

⊞LAUBERT 9D1 (Rural) Camp Municipal La Pontière, 48170 Laubert [04 66 47 71 37 or 04 66 47 72 09; fax 04 66 47 73 08; pms.laubert@wanadoo.fr] Site on R in hamlet of Laubert on N88. 7% hill descent fr Laubert to Mende. Sm, sl, pt shd; wc; shwrs inc; el pnts inc; lndtte; bar; snacks; quiet. "Peaceful; site at 1000m - can be chilly." ♦ € 10.00
2006*

⊞LAURENS 10F1 (1km S Rural) Camping L'Oliveraie, Chemin de Bédarieux, 34480 Laurens [04 67 90 24 36; fax 04 67 90 11 20; oliveraie@free.fr; www.oliveraie.com] Clearly sp on D909 Béziers to Bédarieux rd. Sp reads Loisirs de L'Oliveraie. Med, mkd pitch, hdstg, terr, pt shd; htd wc; chem disp; baby facs; sauna high ssn; shwrs inc; el pnts (6-10A) €3.20-4.60 (poss rev pol); lndtte; ice; shop high ssn; tradsmn; rest & bar high ssn; snacks; playgrnd; pool high ssn; games rm; beach 30km; TV rm; 30% statics; dogs free, €2 (high ssn); phone; adv bkg; quiet; red low ssn; cc acc; CCI. "Site in wine-growing area nr Haut Languedoc regional park; gd san facs; gd hot shwrs in winter; gd winter NH." ♦ € 23.60
2007*

LAURIERE 7A3 (2km N Rural) Camping du Lac de Pont a l'Age, 87370 Laurière [05 55 71 42 62; fax 05 55 71 49 29] Fr N on A20 turn E at Bessines onto D27; at Bersac-sur-Rivalier turn L on D28 to Laurière. At o'skts of Laurière turn L on D63 (N) sp Folles, in 2km R sp Camping du Lac (17km by rd). Fr S turn E at Chanteloube on D28 to Bersac-sur-Rivalier & Laurière. Med, pt sl, terr, pt shd; wc; shwrs; el pnts inc; ice; lndtte; shop 2km; playgrnd; mini-golf; sand beach; lake sw, fishing & boating adj; poss cr; quiet; adv bkg. 15 Apr-15 Oct. € 11.60
2004*

LAVAL 2F4 (10km N Rural) Camp Municipal Le Pont, Allée des Iles, 53240 Andouillé [02 43 69 72 72 (Mairie); fax 02 43 68 77 77; contact@ville-andouille.fr; www.ville-andouille.com] Fr Laval N on N162; at rndabt in Louverne foll rd to St Jean & then Andouillé; site sp fr vill cent on D104 to N dir St Germain-le-Fouilloux. Sm, hdg pitch, pt shd; wc; chem disp; shwrs inc; el pnts (3A) inc; lndtte; shops 300m; playgrnd; pool 10km; rv adj; 50% statics; poss cr; quiet but some minor rd noise; no cc acc. "Liable to flooding; pretty site, excel value; v busy; excel rest in hotel; superb, spotless shwrs; warden on site 0900-1000 & 1600-1800; code operated barrier - if warden not on site, visit Mairie for access code." 1 Apr-31 Oct. € 5.20
2006*

LAVAL 2F4 (4km S Rural) Camping du Potier, Route d'Angers, 53000 Laval [02 43 53 68 86; office.tourisme@mairie-laval.fr] Fr Laval take N162 S to Thévalles, & on S o'skts of Thévalles turn R onto C35 & foll sps, camp on R. Sm, pt sl, terr, shd; wc (some cont); shwrs inc; el pnts (6A) inc lndtte; ice; shop & 1km; bar; playgrnd; entmnt; TV; dogs €0.80; Eng spkn; adv bkg rec high ssn; quiet; cc not acc; CCI ess. "Excel welcome; helpful staff, local advice given; well-kept facs; elevated pitches o'looking rv; lovely town; poss some rd noise." ♦ 1 Apr-30 Sep. € 10.00
2006*

LAVAL 2F4 (4km W Rural) Camp Municipal Le Moulin de Coupeau, 53940 St Berthevin [02 43 68 30 70; fax 02 43 69 20 88; mairie.saint-berthevin@wanadoo.fr; www.ville.saint-berthevin.fr] Fr Laval W on D57 (N157) twd Rennes. Site sp at St Berthevin. Sm, hdg/mkd pitch, terr, pt shd; wc; shwrs inc; el pnts (10A) €1.40; shops 2km; rest in ssn; bar adj; BBQ; htd pool adj; dogs €1; adv bkg; quiet; no cc acc; CCI. "Attractive, well-maintained site on hillside by rv; gd pool but v steep access; gd walks by rv & in woods; poss diff access lge o'fits." 7 Apr-30 Sep. € 8.60
2007*

> There aren't many sites open this early in the year. We'd better phone ahead to check that the one we're heading for is actually open.

LAVANDOU, LE 10F3 (Urban/Coastal) Camping St Pons, Ave Maréchal Juin, 83960 Le Lavandou [04 94 71 03 93; campingsaintpons@wanadoo.fr] App fr W on D98 via La Londe. At Bormes keep R onto D559. At 1st rndabt turn R sp La Favière, at 2nd rndabt turn R, then 1st L. Site on L in 200m. Med, shd; wc (some cont); shwrs inc; el pnts (6-10A) €3.80-4.40; lndtte; ice; shop; adj; rest, snacks, bar high ssn; sand beach 800m; playgrnd; entmnt; 10% statics; phone; dogs €2.13; poss cr; some rd noise; Eng spkn; red low ssn; CCI. "Much improved site; helpful owner." Easter-10 Oct. € 16.00
2005*

LAVANDOU, LE 10F3 (5km E Coastal) Parc-Camping, Ave Ducourneau, Pramousquier, 83980 Le Lavandou [04 94 05 83 95; fax 04 94 05 75 04; camping-lavandou@wanadoo.fr; www.camping pramousquier.com] At Pramousquier; ent clearly mkd on main rd; awkward bend. Lge, terr on steep hillside, pt shd; wc; shwrs inc; el pnts (6A) €4; gas; lndtte; shop; snacks; bar; playgrnd; sand beach 400m; dog €1.90; Eng spkn. "Relaxing spot; poss cr but pleasant aspects; clean site; camp lighting poor; gd cycle track to Le Lavandou; not rec for disabled; excel." 28 Apr-30 Sep. € 19.70
2007*

France

LAVANDOU, LE *10F3* (2km S Coastal) **Camping du Domaine, La Favière, 2581 Route de Bénat, 83230 Bormes-les-Mimosas [04 94 71 03 12; fax 04 94 15 18 67; mail@campdudomaine.com; www.campdudomaine.com]** App Le Lavandou fr Hyères on D98 & turn R on o'skts of town clearly sp La Favière. Site on L in 1.5km about 200m after ent to Domaine La Favière (wine sales). V lge, sl, shd, 50% serviced pitch; rec long leads; wc; chem disp; shwrs inc; el pnts (10A) inc; (long lead req some pitches) gas; lndtte; ice; shop; supmkt; tradsmn; rest; snacks; bar; BBQ (gas); playgrnd; sand beach adj; dogs, but not in Jul & Aug; phone; poss cr; Eng spkn; adv bkg ess; quiet areas but music fr bar; cc acc; red low ssn. "Lge pitches, some with many trees; well-organised site with excel facs; gd walking & attractions in area." ♦ ltd. 24 Mar-31 Oct. € 29.00   2007*

See advertisement

LAVANDOU, LE *10F3* (2km S Coastal) **Caravaning St Clair, Ave André Gide, 83980 Le Lavandou [04 94 01 30 20; fax 04 94 71 43 64]** N559 thro Le Lavandou twd St Raphaël; after 2km at sp St Clair turn R immed after bend 50m after blue 'caravaning' sp (easy to overshoot). Med, mkd pitch, shd; htd wc (cont); mv service pnt; shwrs inc; el pnts (16A) €3.50 (rev pol); lndtte; shops 100m; rest, bar nrby; playgrnd; sand beach adj; fishing; boat hire; TV rm; dogs €1; no tents; poss cr; adv bkg ess Jul-Aug; some noise fr rd; no cc acc. "Popular with British; pitch & ent screened by trees; conv beach & rests." ♦ Easter-20 Oct. € 25.70 (3 persons)   2006*

LAVANDOU, LE *10F3* (1.5km SW Coastal) **Camping Beau Séjour, Quartier St Pons, 83980 Le Lavandou [04 94 71 25 30]** Take Cap Bénat rd on W o'skts of Le Lavandou. Site on L in approx 500m. Lge, mkd pitch, pt shd; wc; shwrs inc; el pnts (6A); ice; shop; rest; snacks; bar; beach adj; poss cr; no adv bkg; rd noise on W side. "Fixed height barrier 2.60m at ent to site; sm pitches." ♦ Easter-30 Sep.   2006*

⊞**LAVANDOU, LE** *10F3* (9km W) **Camping Manjastre, 150 Chemin des Girolles, 83230 Bormes-les-Mimosas [04 94 71 03 28; fax 04 94 71 63 62; http://manjastre.chez-alice.fr]** App fr W on D98 about 3km NE of where N559 branches off SE to Le Lavandou. Fr E site is 2km beyond Bormes/Collobrières x-rds; sp. Lge, hdg/mkd pitch, v sl, terr, pt shd; wc; chem disp; shwrs inc; el pnts (10A) €3.90; rest; snacks; bar; shop; gas; ice; lndtte; pool; playgrnd; sand beach 8km; 8% statics; poss cr; adv bkg; quiet; Eng spkn; fair long/sh stay; CCI. "Helpful, friendly staff; winter storage; facs poss stretched in ssn; site on v steep hillside - vans taken in & out by tractor; hardwork even walking - not for unfit or disabled; beautiful location in vineyard." € 22.45 (3 persons)
2006*

LAVELANET *8G4* (1km SW Urban) **Camping de Lavelanet, Rue Jacquard, 09300 Lavelanet [tel/ fax 05 61 01 55 54; camping.avelana@wanadoo. fr]** Fr Lavelanet, take D117 twd Foix & foll sp. Adj 'piscine'. Med, mkd pitch, pt shd; wc (mainly cont); chem disp; shwrs; el pnts (16A) inc; lndtte; ice; shops 1km; BBQ; playgrnd; pool adj; sports area; rv 4km; entmnt; TV rm; some statics; adv bkg; quiet; CCI. "Gd sized pitches, some with mountain views; poss open in winter with adv bkg; gates locked 2200; quiet town; vg." ♦ 1 Jun-15 Oct. € 15.00   2005*

⊞**LAVELANET** *8G4* (6km SW) **FFCC Camp Municipal Fount-de-Sicre, 09300 Montferrier [05 61 01 20 97 or 05 61 01 10 08; fax 05 61 01 93 14]** Fr Lavelanet S on D109/D9 twd Montségur. Sm, sl, unshd; htd wc; shwrs; el pnts (6A); shop adj; rest, bar adj; poss cr; adv bkg; quiet. "A bit scruffy; long-stay residents; NH only." € 6.00   2004*

LAVOUTE SUR LOIRE see Puy en Velay, Le *9C1*

Did you know you can fill in site report forms on the Club's website — www.caravanclub.co.uk?

LECTOURE *8E3* (2.5km SE Rural) **Camping Le Lac des Trois Vallées, 32700 Lectoure [05 62 68 82 33; fax 05 62 68 88 82; contact@ lacdes3vallees.fr; www.lacdes3vallees.fr]** Site sp fr N21, on lake between Lectour & Fleurance. Narr app rd with steep gradient. Lge, hdg/mkd pitch, pt sl, pt shd; wc; chem disp; baby facs; shwrs inc; el pnts (10A) inc; gas; lndtte; ice; shop; bar; rest; snacks; bar; BBQ (gas/charcoal only); playgrnd; htd pool; paddling pool; waterslide; lake sw; waterslides; fishing; watersports; tennis; mini-golf; cycle hire; skateboard course; entmnt; child entmnt; internet; games/TV rm; 60% statics; dogs €3; recep 0800-2000 high ssn; poss cr; adv bkg; quiet (some disco noise); red low ssn; cc acc. "Excel lake pool; excursions to Pau, Lourdes, Andorra; mkt Tue Fleurance." ♦ 24 May-7 Sep. € 42.00 ABS - D18   2007*

LEGE *2H4* (7km S Rural) **Camp Municipal de la Petite Boulogne, Rue du Stade, 85670 St Etienne-du-Bois [02 51 34 52 11 or 02 51 34 54 51; fax 02 51 34 54 10; la.petite.boulogne@wanadoo.fr]** S fr Legé on D978 dir Aizenay. Turn E onto D 94 twd St Etienne-du-Bois. Foll sp to site. Sm, mkd pitch, pt sl, terr, pt shd; wc; chem disp (wc); shwrs inc; el pnts (10A) €2.50; gas 7km; lndtte; shops 500m; tradsmn; rest in vill; pool; sand beach 30km; TV rm; dogs €2; Eng spkn; adv bkg (dep req); quiet; CCI. "Excel site; helpful warden; v clean." ♦ 1 May-15 Sep. € 12.00   2004*

Camp du Domaine ★★★★

Var - Provence
Côte d'Azur

**Sea view bungalows
In front of the îles d'Or
(Golden Islands)
Animations
Shops**

**Motor homes
Caravans
Pitches for tents
Mobile homes**

Direct access to one of the most beautiful beaches of the Côte d'Azur

⊞**LEGE** *2H4* (8km SW Rural) **Camping Les Blés d'Or, 85670 Grand'Landes [02 51 98 51 86; fax 02 51 98 53 24; mairiegrandlandes@wanadoo.fr]** Take D753 fr Legé twd St Jean-de-Monts. In 4km turn S on D81 & foll sp. Fr S on D978, turn W sp Grand-Landes. 3km N of Palluau. Sm, pt sl, pt shd; wc; chem disp; shwrs inc; el pnts (5A) €2; gas, shops 3km; playgrnd adj; 30% statics; Eng spkn; adv bkg; quiet; cc not acc. "V pleasant site in tiny vill with helpful staff; gd value; ent barrier clsd 2000 (poss earlier), rec arr early but helpful warden lives in c'van at site ent & will open up; height barrier only, cars 24hr access." € 6.30   2007*

LEGE CAP FERRET see Andernos les Bains *7D1*

LELIN LAPUJOLLE see Aire sur l'Adour *8E2*

LEON *8E1* (6km N Rural) **Camping Sunêlia Le Col Vert, Lac de Léon, 40560 Vielle-St Girons [05 58 42 94 06; fax 05 58 42 91 88; contact@ colvert.com; www.colvert.com]** S fr Bordeaux on N10; at Castets-des-Landes turn R onto D42 to Vielle-St Girons. In turn L onto D652 twd Léon sp Soustons. In 4km, bef Vielle, take 2nd of 2 RH turns twd Lac de Léon. Site on R at end of rd in 1.5km. V lge, shd; wc (some cont); chem disp; baby facs; serviced pitches; shwrs inc; Wellness Beauty Centre; el pnts (3A) inc; gas; lndtte; ice; shop; tradsmn; rest; snacks; bar; BBQ (gas/elec); playgrnd; 2 pools (1 htd, covrd); paddling pool; sand beach 6km; lake sw, fishing, sailing nrby; tennis; fitness rm; mini-golf; archery; horseriding; cycle hire; entmnt; child entmnt; wifi internet; games/TV rm; 60% statics; dogs €4.30; recep 0900-2100 high ssn; max 6m c'van length high ssn; poss cr; adv bkg; poss noisy (nightclub); red for 15+ days; cc acc; CCI. "Lakeside site in pine forest with sailing school; organised tours to Lourdes & Spain; lge site so some pitches 800m fr facs; daily mkt in Léon in ssn; ideal site for children & teenagers." ♦ 8 Apr-21 Sep. € 39.00 ABS - A08   2007*

LEON *8E1* (5km NE Rural) **Camping Aire Naturelle du Cayre (Capdupuy), 40550 St Michel-Escalus [05 58 48 78 15]** Fr N10 exit Castets & St Girons onto D42 sp St Girons/Linxe. In Linxe turn L onto D374 sp Escalus & camping. In 1km R sp Léon, site on L in 1km. Sm, pt shd; wc; shwrs inc; el pnts €2.20; gas; lndtte; shops 4km; playgrnd; pool 5km; sand beach 10km; some statics; dogs €1; poss cr; cc not acc. "In pine forest; friendly & helpful owner; ltd facs low ssn." ♦ 1 Apr-30 Sep. € 10.50
                                           2005*

LEON *8E1* (1.5km NW Rural) **Camping Lou Puntaou, 40550 Léon [05 58 48 74 30; fax 05 58 48 70 42; reception@loupuntaou.com; www.loupuntaou.com]** Site sp fr D142 on Etang de Léon. V lge, mkd pitch, pt shd; wc; chem disp; mv service pnt; shwrs inc; el pnts (15A) inc; lndtte; supmkt; rest 100m; snacks; bar; playgrnd; 3 pools (1 htd, covrd); waterslide; jacuzzi; lake sw 100m; sand beach 5km; tennis; watersports; games area; cycle hire; fitness rm; cash machine; entmnt; child entmnt; 20% statics; dogs €2; adv bkg; quiet. "Excel sports facs; lovely location." ♦ 1 Apr-1 Oct. € 39.00   2005*

LEON *8E1* (10km NW Coastal) **Domaine Naturiste Arna (Naturist), Arnaoutchot, 40560 Vielle-St Girons [05 58 49 11 11; fax 05 58 48 57 12; contact@arna.com; www.arna.com]** Fr St Girons turn R onto D328 at Vielle sp Pichelèbe. Site in 5km on R. Lge, pt sl, shd; wc (some cont); chem disp; baby facs; shwrs inc; Arna Forme Spa; el pnts (3A) inc; gas; lndtte; ice; shop; rest; snacks; bar; BBQ (gas/elec); playgrnd; 2 pools (1 htd covrd); paddling pool; sand beach adj; lake adj; watersports 5km; tennis; cycle hire; golf nr; archery; games area; entmnt; internet; games/TV rm; many statics (sep area); dogs €3.20; recep 0900-2000 high ssn; adv bkg; quiet; red long stay/low ssn; cc acc; INF card req. "In pine forest, some pitches sandy; facs ltd low ssn; c'vans over 6m not acc high ssn; organised excursions; fantastic beach; daily mkt in Léon in ssn; excel naturist site." ♦ 5 Apr-21 Sep. € 39.80 (CChq acc) ABS - A07   2007*

LERAN *8G4* (2km E Rural) **Camping La Régate, 09600 Léran [tel/fax 05 61 01 92 69; contact@ montbel.com.fr; www.montbel.com.fr]** Fr Lavelanet go N on D625, turn R onto D28 & cont to Léran. Site sp fr vill. Ent easily missed - rd past it is dead end. Med, hdg/mkd pitch, terr, shd; wc; chem disp; baby facs; shwrs; el pnts (8A) inc; lndtte; ice; shop 2km; tradsmn; rest; bar; BBQ; playgrnd; pool; leisure cent nr; lake adj; watersports; entmnt; 10% statics; dogs; phone; quiet; adv bkg; cc acc; CCI. "Conv Montségur chateau; v clean san facs." 1 Apr-30 Sep. € 14.00   2004*

LESCAR see Pau *8F2*

LESCHERAINES *9B3* (2.5km SE Rural) **Camp Municipal de l'Ile, Base de Loisirs, 73340 Lescheraines [tel/fax 04 79 63 80 00; contact@ iles-du-cheran.com; www.iles-du-cheran.com]** Fr Lescheraines foll sp for Base de Loisirs. Lge, mkd pitch, pt shd; wc; chem disp; mv service pnt; baby facs; shwrs inc; el pnts (6-10A) €1.75-2.50; gas 1km; lndtte; shop; rest 500m; snacks; bar; BBQ; playgrnd; lake sw; canoe & boat hire; fishing; entmnt; 20% statics; dogs €1.35; phone; Eng spkn; quiet; CCI. ♦ 15 Apr-24 Sep. € 12.20   2006*

LESCONIL see Pont l'Abbé *2F2*

LESCUN *8G2* (1.5km SW Rural) **Camp Municipal Le Lauzart, 64490 Lescun [tel/fax 05 59 34 51 77; campinglauzart@wanadoo.fr]** Turn L (W) off N134 8km N of Urdos on D239 sp Lescun & foll camping sp for 5km; app rd gd but steep with hairpins; foll Camping sp to fork L - do not ent Lescun vill, v narr & steep, unsuitable for c'vans. Sm, mkd pitch, terr, pt shd; htd wc; chem disp; mv service pnt; shwrs inc; el pnts (10A) €2.80; gas; lndtte; ice; shop; rest & bar nr; dogs €0.80; adv bkg; quiet. "Stunning views of mountain peaks of Lescun 'Cirque'; basic san facs, poss stretched high ssn; 20 mins walk to vill; gd walks; vg." ♦ 1 May-30 Sep. € 10.20   2007*

LESPERON *8E1* (4km SW Rural) **FFCC Parc de Couchoy, Route de Linxe, 40260 Lesperon [tel/fax 05 58 89 60 15; info@parcdecouchoy. com; www.parcdecouchoy.com]** Exit N10 junc 13 to D41 sp Lesperon; in 1km turn L, thro vill of Lesperon; L at junc onto D331; bottom of hill turn R & immed L; site on R in 3km dir Linxe. Med, mkd pitch, pt shd; wc; chem disp; child/baby facs; shwrs inc; el pnts (6A) €3; gas; lndtte; shops 3km; tradsmn; snacks; bar; playgrnd; pool; sand beach 8km; lake sw 5km; 10% statics; dogs €1; phone; poss cr; adv bkg; quiet; cc acc high ssn; 10% red long stay; CCI. "Lovely site in lovely location; edge of wine country; gd facs on lakes for sailing, windsurfing; British owners; clean san facs; v isolated; vg." 1 Jun-15 Sep. € 22.00   2007*

LESSAY *1D4* (6km SW Coastal) **Camp Municipal des Dunes, 832 Blvd de la Mer, 50710 Créances [02 33 46 31 86 or 02 33 07 40 42; fax 02 33 07 40 42]** Turn W onto D72/D652 in Lessay, after 3km turn L on D650 at T-junc. After 1.5km turn R at rndabt on D394 sp 'Créances Plage' & site office opp seafront car pk. Med, mkd pitch, pt shd; wc; shwrs inc; el pnts (10A) €2.30; gas; lndtte; shop 3km; tradsmn; rest; snacks; bar; playgrnd; paddling pool; sand beach adj; games area; poss cr; adv bkg; quiet; CCI. ♦ ltd. 19 Jun-5 Sep. € 9.00   2004*

LEUCATE PLAGE *10G1* (200m S Coastal) **Camp Municipal du Cap Leucate, Chemin de Mouret, 11370 Leucate-Plage [04 68 40 01 37; fax 04 68 40 18 34; cap.leucate@wanadoo.fr]** Exit A9 junc 40 onto D627 thro Leucate vill to Leucate-Plage approx 9km. Site sp. Lge, hdg pitch, shd; wc (some cont); chem disp; mv service pnt; baby facs; fam bthrm; shwrs inc; el pnts (6A) inc; lndtte; ice; shop 200m; tradsmn; rest, snacks, bar 300m; BBQ; playgrnd; htd pool 100m; sand beach 100m; games area; entmnt; TV; 60% statics; dogs €2; phone; adv bkg; quiet; CCI. "Sandy site in gd position; popular with surfers; spacious in low ssn; gd NH." 1 Feb-30 Nov. € 15.00   2006*

LEVIER *6H2* (1km NE Rural) **Camping La Forêt, Route de Septfontaine, 25270 Levier [03 81 89 53 46; fax 03 81 49 54 11; camping@ camping-dela-foret.com; www.camping-dela-foret.com]** Fr D72 turn L at rndabt by supmkt onto D41, site on L in 700m. Med, mkd pitch, pt sl, terr, shd; wc; baby facs; shwrs inc; el pnts (6A) €2.30; gas; lndtte; ice; supmkt 500m; snacks; playgrnd; htd pool; poss cr; adv bkg; quiet. ♦ 15 May-15 Sep. € 13.00   2004*

LEVIGNAC DE GUYENNE see Miramont de Guyenne *7D2*

LEVROUX *4H2* (500m N Rural) **Camp Municipal La Piscine, 36110 Levroux [02 54 35 70 54 (Mairie); fax 02 54 35 35 50]** Site on N o'skts of town on W of D956 bet Châteauroux & Valençay. Sm, pt shd; wc; shwrs inc; el pnts (5A); shops 500m; htd pool; playgrnd; htd pool; quiet. "Site yourself, warden calls gates open 0800-1100 & 1600-2100 (Mon-Fri), 0800-1100 & 1800-2100 (Sat & Sun); no twin-axle c'vans." ♦   2004*

⊞**LEZIGNAN CORBIERES** *8F4* (10km S Rural) **Camping Le Pinada, 11200 Fabrezan [04 68 43 61 82; fax 04 68 43 68 61; lepinada@ libertysurf.fr; www.camping-le-pinada.com]** Fr Lézignan-Corbières foll sp to aerodrome & . After airfield, fork L thro Ferrals-les-Corbières on D106 site sp & on L after 4km. Alt rte to avoid narr rd thro Ferrals: exit A61 junc 25 & foll D611 thro Fabrezan. At T-junc turn L onto D613 & after 2km turn L onto D106. Site on R after passing thro Villerouge-la-Crémade. Med, hdg/mkd pitch, pt sl, terr, shd; wc; chem disp (wc); baby facs; shwrs inc; el pnts (6A) €5; ice; lndtte; shop; tradsmn; snacks; bar; playgrnd; pool; rv sw & fishing 3km; tennis; mini-golf; entmnt; TV rm; 25% statics; dogs €1.30; poss cr; Eng spkn; adv bkg, bkg fee; quiet; cc not acc; CCI. "Friendly owners; gd base for Carcassonne & Med coast; well-run site; dated san facs; excel." ♦ € 14.00   2007*

LEZIGNAN CORBIERES *8F4* (500m NW Urban) **Camp Municipal de la Pinède, Ave Gaston Bonheur, 11200 Lézignan-Corbières [tel/fax 04 68 27 05 08; campinglapinede@wanadoo.fr]** On D6113 (N113) fr Carcassonne to Narbonne on N of rd; foll 'Piscine' & 'Restaurant Le Patio' sp. Med, hdg/hdstg pitch, pt sl, terr, pt shd; wc; chem disp; mv service pnt; shwrs inc; el pnts (6A) inc; gas; lndtte; ice; shop 1km; rest; snacks; bar; htd pool adj; tennis; 5% statics; dogs €1.50; adv bkg (dep req); quiet; no cc acc; CCI. "Well-run, clean site; dated san facs; gd m'van facs; superb pool; v pleasant, friendly staff; red low ssn; excel snack bar." ♦ 1 Mar-30 Oct. € 16.10   2006*

France

LICQUES *3A3* (1km E Rural) **Camping Les Pommiers des Trois Pays, 253 Rue de Breuil, 62850 Licques [tel/fax 03 21 35 02 02; denis. lamce@wanadoo.fr; www.pommiers-3pays.com]** Fr Calais to Guînes on D127 then on D215 to Licques. Take D191 fr vill foll sp. Site on L in 1km. NB If joining A26 at junc 2 need €3 in coins (car & c'van) for automatic toll machine. NB sloping ent, long o'fits beware grounding. Med, hdg/mkd pitch, sl, pt shd; wc; chem disp; mv service pnt; baby facs; shwrs inc; el pnts (16A) €4; lndtte; ice; shops 1km; rest; snacks; bar; BBQ; playgrnd; htd, covrd pool; sand beach, golf, sailing 25km; fishing 2km; games area; games rm; TV rm; 65% statics; dogs €0.50; adv bkg; quiet; cc acc; red long stay/low ssn. "High quality facs & lge pitches; friendly, helpful owners; gd walking; gd beaches nr; conv Calais/ Dunkerque ferries." ♦ 1 Apr-31 Oct. € 15.40
2007*

LICQUES *3A3* (2.5km E Rural) **Camping-Caravaning Le Canchy, Rue de Canchy, 62850 Licques [tel/fax 03 21 82 63 41; camping. lecanchy@wanadoo.fr; www.camping-lecanchy. com]** Fr Calais D127 to Guînes, then D215 sp Licques; site sp in vill on D191; site on L in 1km with narr app rd. Or fr Ardres take D224 to Liques then as above. Or A26 fr Calais exit junc 2 onto D217 dir Zouafques/Tournehem/Licques. Foll site sp in vill. Med, hdg/mkd pitch, pt shd; wc (some cont); chem disp; shwrs inc; el pnts (6A) €3.30; lndtte; shops 2km; snacks; bar; BBQ; playgrnd; fishing nrby; entmnt; 50% statics; Eng spkn; adv bkg; quiet; CCI. "Busy site; friendly, helpful staff; san facs ltd low ssn; gd walking/cycling; conv Calais." 15 Mar-31 Oct. € 11.40
2007*

LIEPVRE see Seléstat *6E3*

LIGNIERES *4H3* (N Urban) **Camp Municipal de L'Ange Blanc, Rue de l'Ange Blanc, 18160 Lignières [02 48 60 00 18 (Mairie); fax 02 48 60 18 50]** Site sp in vill at junc of D940 & D925. Sm, mkd pitch, pt shd; wc (some cont); shwrs; el pnts inc; shops adj; quiet. "NH only." 1 Apr-30 Sep. € 9.60
2005*

LIGNY EN BARROIS *6E1* (500m W) **Camp Municipal, Rue des Etats-Unis, 55500 Ligny-en-Barrois [03 29 78 41 33 or 03 29 78 02 22 (Mairie)]** On N4 for Paris sp fr town cent. Leave N4 at Ligny-en-Barrois N exit, turn S twd town. In approx 500m turn R at junc (before rd narr). Foll sm sp, site 500m on L. Sm, hdstg, terr, pt shd; wc (some cont), own san facs; chem disp (wc); shwrs; el pnts inc; ice; shop 500m; pool 1km; rv sw & fishing 500m; dogs; rd noise; Eng spkn; CCI. "Poss diff lge o'fits; gd NH." 1 Jun-15 Sep. € 9.40
2005*

LIGNY LE CHATEL *4F4* (2km W Rural) **Camp Municipal La Noue Marrou, 89144 Ligny-le-Châtel [03 86 47 56 99 or 03 86 47 41 20 (Mairie); fax 03 86 47 44 02]** Exit A6 at junc 20 Auxerre S onto D965 to Chablis. In Chablis cross rv & turn L onto D91 dir Ligny. On ent Ligny turn L onto D8 at junc after Maximart. Cross sm rv, foll sp to site on L in 200m. Sm, mkd pitch, pt shd; wc; chem disp; mv service pnt; shwrs inc; el pnts (10A) €2.70 (poss long lead req); lndtte; ice; shop; rest; snacks; bar; playgrnd; rv sw adj; tennis; dogs; phone; bus 200m; quiet; CCI. "Well-run site; lge pitches; no twin-axles; facs dated but clean; pleasant vill; gd rests; excel." ♦ 1 May-30 Sep. € 9.50
2007*

This guide relies on site report forms submitted by caravanners like us; we'll do our bit and tell the editor what we think of the campsites we've visited.

⊞**LIGUEIL** *4H2* (2km N Rural) **Camping de la Touche, Ferme de la Touche, 37240 Ligueil [02 47 91 94 61 or 06 33 97 02 00 (mob); stuart. may@theloirevalley.com; www.theloirevalley.com]** Fr Loches SW on D31; turn L at x-rds with cross on R 2km after Ciran. In 500m turn R, site on R bef hotel. Fr A10 take exit St Maure. Sm, mkd ptch, pt shd; wc; chem disp (wc); shwrs inc; el pnts €4-5; ice; shop; playgrnd; pool; cycle hire; dogs free; adv bkg (dep req); cc acc; quiet; CCI. "Excel, well-maintained CL-type site; helpful British owners; site ent & surface uneven; c'van storage, B&B & gite avail; ltd facs for size of site; nightingales in trees around site; castles, rvs & wines in area; conv Loire chateaux & m'way." € 12.00
2007*

LIGUGE see Poitiers *7A2*

⊞**LILLEBONNE** *3C2* (4km W Rural) **Camping Hameau des Forges, 76170 St Antoine-la-Forêt [02 35 39 80 28 or 02 35 91 48 30]** Fr Le Havre take rd twds Tancarville bdge, D982 into Lillebonne, D81 W to site on R in 4km, sp. Fr S over Tancarville bdge onto D910 sp Bolbec. At 2nd rndabt turn R onto D81, site 5km on L. Med, pt shd; wc; chem disp; shwrs €1.15; el pnts (5A) €2.50; tradsmn; 90% statics; dogs; poss cr; adv bkg; quiet; no cc acc; CCI. "Basic site but v clean; staff welcoming & helpful; facs ltd low ssn; conv NH for Le Havre ferries late arr & early depart; Roman amphitheatre in town worth visit." € 7.60
2005*

LIMERAY see Amboise *4G2*

LIMEUIL see Bugue, Le *7C3*

LIMOGES 7B3 (10km N Rural) **FFCC Camp Municipal d'Uzurat, 40 Ave d'Uzurat, 87280 Limoges [tel/fax 05 55 38 49 43; contact@ campinglimoges.fr; www.campinglimoges.fr]** Fr N twd Limoges on A20 take exit 30 sp Limoges Nord Zone Industrielle, Lac d'Uzurat; foll sp to Lac d'Uzarat & site. Fr S twd Limoges on A20 exit junc 31 & foll sp as above. Well sp fr A20. Lge, hdstg, pt shd; htd wc (some cont); chem disp; mv service pnt; serviced pitches; baby facs; shwrs inc; el pnts (10A) €3; lndtte; hypmkt 500m; playgrnd adj; lake fishing; some statics; dogs €1; bus; phone; twin-axles acc; Eng spkn; quiet but some rd noise; red low ssn; cc acc; CCI. "Excel, refurbished site; gd sized pitches; gd, clean facs; pitch on chippings; awnings diff; v friendly & helpful; conv martyr vill Oradour-sur-Glane; poss reduced opening dates - phone ahead low ssn; o'night rate for m'vans; poss market traders." ♦ 11 Mar-31 Oct. € 14.00   2007*

LIMOGNE EN QUERCY 7D4 (1km W Rural) **Camp Municipal Bel-Air, 46260 Limogne-en-Quercy [05 65 24 32 75; fax 05 65 24 73 59; camping. bel-air@orange.fr]** E fr Cahors on D911 just bef Limogne vill. W fr Villefranche on D911 just past vill; 3 ents about 50m apart. Sm, mkd pitch, sl, shd; wc; shwrs inc; el pnts (6A) €2; lndtte; shops 1km; pool; quiet; adv bkg rec high ssn. "V friendly welcome; if warden absent, site yourself." 1 Apr-1 Oct. € 11.10   2007*

LIMOGNE EN QUERCY 7D4 (6km NW Rural) **Camping Lalbrade (Naturist), Lalbrade, 46260 Lugagnac [05 65 31 52 35 or 06 20 05 98 57 (mob); fax 05 65 24 36 21; le-camping-de-lalbrade@ wanadoo.fr; http://lalbrade.free.fr/]** Fr D911 Cahors to Villefranche-de-Rouergue rd; at Limogne-en-Quercy take D40 sp Lugagnac (narr rd); site sp after Lugagnac; 2km of single-track ent rd. Diff to find. Sm, pt shd; wc (some cont); shwrs inc; el pnts (10A) €2.50; pool; dogs €3; Eng spkn; quiet. "In interesting area; gd walking within site boundaries." ♦ 31 Mar-30 Sep. € 20.00   2007*

LIMOUX 8G4 (200m SE Urban) **Camp Municipal du Breil, Ave Salvador Allende, 11300 Limoux [tel/fax 04 68 31 13 63]** Site off N118 heading S fr Limoux. Sm, pt sl; wc; shwrs; el pnts (6A) €2.50; shops adj; pool adj; rv sw; fishing; boating; quiet but some rd noise. "Basic rvside site, walking dist pleasant town." 1 Jun-30 Sep. € 7.50   2005*

LINDOIS, LE see Montbron 7B3

LINXE 8E1 (1km N Rural) **Camp Municipal Le Grandjean, 190 Route de Mixe, 40260 Linxe [05 58 42 90 00 or 05 58 42 92 27; fax 05 58 42 94 67; mairie.linxe@wanadoo.fr]** Exit N10 junc 12 dir Castets; take D42 to Linxe; turn R & R into site. Site well sp at N of Linxe cent. Med, mkd pitch, pt shd; wc, chem disp; baby facs; shwrs inc; el pnts (4-6A) inc; lndtte; supmkt 5km; rest, snacks, bar 1km; playgrnd; cycle hire, tennis 1 km; Eng spkn; adv bkg; quiet. "Vg." 1 Jul-31 Aug. € 11.35   2006*

LION D'ANGERS, LE 2G4 (500m N Urban) **Camp Municipal Les Frênes, Route de Laval, 49220 Le Lion-d'Angers [02 41 95 31 56]** On N162 Laval-Angers rd, site on R bef bdge over Rv Oudon app Le Lion-d'Angers, easily missed. Med, pt shd, mkd pitch; wc; chem disp; shwrs inc; el pnts (10A) €2.20; lndry rm; ice; shops adj; rest; BBQ; playgrnd; rv fishing adj; phone; recep open 1000-1200 & 1400-1900 low ssn; card operated barrier (€40 dep); no twin-axle vans; poss cr; Eng spkn; adv bkg; quiet but some rd noise; CCI. "Excel site; friendly staff; gd location; wc block up 2 flights concrete steps; no m'vans; unreliable opening dates - phone ahead." ♦ 15 May-15 Sep. € 5.05   2005*

LISIEUX 3D1 (2km N Rural) **Camp Municipal de La Vallée, 9 Rue de la Vallée, 14100 Lisieux [02 31 62 00 40 or 02 31 48 18 10 (LS); fax 02 31 48 18 11; tourisme@cclisieuxpaysdauge.fr; www.lisieux-tourisme.com]** N on D579 to Lisieux twd Pont l'Evêque. Approx 500m N of Lisieux take L to Coquainvilliers onto D48 & foll sp for Camping (turn L back in Lisieux dir). Site on D48 parallel to main rd. Med, hdstg, pt shd; wc (some cont); chemp disp; shwrs inc; el pnts (6A) €2 gas; shop 1km; rest, snacks, bar 2km; htd pool, waterslide nrby; 20% statics; poss cr; cc not acc; CCI. "Interesting town, childhood home of St Thérèse; gates locked 2200-0700; helpful warden; animal refuge adj - barking of dogs all day; gd." 31 Mar-7 Oct. € 6.90   2007*

As soon as we get home I'm going to post all these site report forms to the editor for inclusion in next year's guide. I don't want to miss the September deadline.

LISIEUX 3D1 (10km NE Rural) **Aire Naturalle Le Mont Criquet (Bernard), Clos du Mont Criquet, 14590 Ouilly-du-Houley [tel/fax 02 31 62 98 98 or 06 08 93 19 63 (mob); bernard.ocjh@wanadoo. fr; http://pagesperso-orange.fr/rmc14/]** Fr D613 (N13) N on D137 to Ouilly-du-Houley. NB App up steep single track rd - owner assists on dep. Sm, pt sl, pt shd; wc; chem disp; shwrs inc; el pnts (2-6A) €2.20; lndtte; ice; tradsmn; BBQ; playgrnd; games area; 60% statics; dogs; poss cr; Eng spkn; adv bkg; quiet; CCI. "Beautiful, peaceful site in orchard setting; gd modern facs; pleasant, helpful owner." 1 May-30 Sep. € 8.50   2006*

LISLE 7C3 **Camp Municipal du Pont, 24350 Lisle [05 53 04 50 02 or 05 53 04 51 76]** W fr Ribérac on D78, site 6km NE of junc with D710 at Tocane-St Apre, on rvside. Sm, mkd pitch, pt shd; wc; shwrs inc; el pnts; lndry rm; shops 500m; rest, bar 800m; playgrnd; tennis; fishing. "Pleasant site." 1 Jun-15 Sep. € 5.00   2004*

France

LIT ET MIXE *8E1* (2km N Rural) **Airotel Camping Les Vignes, Route de la Plage du Cap de l'Homy, 40170 Lit-et-Mixe [05 58 42 85 60; fax 05 58 42 74 36; vignes@village-center.com; www. village-center.com]** N10 S to exit 13 onto D41 twd Lit-et-Mixe. S on D652 dir St Girons. W on D88 twd Cap de l'Homy Plage. Lge, pt shd; wc; chem disp; serviced pitches; shwrs inc; el pnts (10A) inc; gas; lndtte; ice; supmkt; rest; snacks; bar; playgrnd; pool; waterslide; jacuzzi; beach 3km; tennis; minigolf; cycle hire; games rm; fitness rm; entmnt; internet; dogs €3; quiet; adv bkg; red low ssn/CCI. "Wonderful site - everything you need; immac san facs." ♦ 12 May-16 Sep. € 37.00   2007*

LIT ET MIXE *8E1* (8km W Coastal) **Camp Municipal de la Plage du Cap de l'Horny, Ave de l'Océan, 40170 Lit-et-Mixe [05 58 42 83 47; fax 05 58 42 49 79; contact@camping-cap.com; www.camping-cap.com]** S fr Mimizan on D652. In Lit-et-Mixe R on D88 to Cap de l'Homy Plage. Site on R when rd becomes 1-way. Lge, hdg/mkd pitch, pt sl, shd; wc (some cont); chem disp; mv service pnt; shwrs inc; el pnts (10A) inc (poss rev pol); lndtte; shop, rest high ssn; playgrnd; beach 300m; surfing; dogs €1.95; poss cr; quiet. "Site in pine woods on sandy soil; gd walks; interesting flora & fauna; vg." 1 May-30 Sep. € 21.00   2006*

LITTEAU see Balleroy *1D4*

LIVERDUN see Nancy *6E2*

LLAURO see Boulou, Le *8G4*

LOCHES *4H2* (800m S Urban) **Camping de la Citadelle, Ave Aristide Briand, 37600 Loches [02 47 59 05 91 or 06 21 37 93 06 (mob); fax 02 47 59 00 35; camping@lacitadelle.com; www. lacitadelle.com]** Easiest app fr S. Fr any dir take by-pass to S end & leave at Leclerc rndabt for city cent; site well sp on R in 800m. Lge, hdg/mkd pitch, pt shd; htd wc (some cont); chem disp; mv service pnt; serviced pitches extra charge; shwrs inc; el pnts (10A) inc (poss rev pol) (poss long lead req); gas; lndtte; ice; shop & 2km; tradsmn; rests, snacks; bar; BBQ; playgrnd; pool on site & 2 htd pools adj; fishing; boating; games area; tennis nr; cycle hire; golf 9km; entmnt; internet; sat TV rm; 30% statics; dogs €2.30; poss cr; Eng spkn; adv bkg rec (bkg fee); poss night noise fr entmnts; red 7+ days/low ssn; cc acc; CCI. "Attractive, busy site nr beautiful town; chateau & medieval quarter worth visit; gd sized pitches, poss uneven; facs poss stretched high ssn; barrier clsd 2200-0800; no waiting area." ♦ 22 Mar-10 Oct. € 27.50 (CChq acc) ABS - L18   2007*

LOCMARIAQUER *2G3* (1km N Rural) **Camping La Ferme Fleurie, Kerlogonan, 56740 Locmariaquer [tel/fax 02 97 57 34 06; http://pro.pagesjaunes. fr/camping-fleurie]** Sp off D781. Sm, mkd pitch, pt shd; wc; shwrs inc; el pnts (10A) €2.50; shop; lndtte; playgrnd; beach 1km; fishing; sailing; entmnt; some statics; dogs €1; adv bkg ess high ssn; quiet. "Lovely, friendly, CL-type site; coastal path nr; excel, clean facs but poss stretched when site full; midge repellent rec; unreliable opening dates - phone ahead low ssn." 12 Feb-15 Nov. € 11.00   2005*

The opening dates and prices on this campsite have changed. I'll send a site report form to the editor for the next edition of the guide.

LOCMARIAQUER *2G3* (2km S Coastal) **Camp Municipal de la Falaise, Route de Kerpenhir, 56740 Locmariaquer [02 97 57 31 59 or 02 97 57 32 32 (LS); fax 02 97 57 32 85; accueil@ locmariaquer.fr]** Site sp fr Locmariaquer. On ent vill, site sp R avoiding narr cent (also sp fr vill cent). Lge, mkd pitch, pt sl; wc; shwrs; chem disp; mv service pnt; el pnts (5A) €2.40; gas; lndtte; shop 300m; rest 500m; playgrnd; sand beach adj; entmnt (high ssn); dogs €1; poss cr; cc acc. "Gd, quiet site in pleasant countryside; san facs need updating & poss unclean low ssn; archaeological remains; gd fishing, boating,& cycling, coastal walking." ♦ 15 Mar-15 Oct. € 10.00   2006*

LOCRONAN *2E2* (E Urban) **Camp Municipal de Placerhorn, Rue de la Troménie, 29180 Locronan [02 98 91 87 76 or 02 98 51 80 80 (HS)]** Fr Quimper/ Douarnenez foll sp D7 Châteaulin; ignore town sp, take 1st R after 3rd rndabt. Fr Châteaulin, turn L at 1st town sp & foll site sp at sharp L turn. NB Foll gd sp around town, do not enter Locronan. Lge, hdg pitch, steeply terr, pt shd; wc; chem disp (wc); shwrs; el pnts (3-6A) €3.05; shops 1km; playgrnd; sand beach 8km; dogs; phone; quiet; CCI. "Elec hook-up avail fr 1930 on day of arr; gd touring cent; historic town; gd walks, views; gd." 1 Jun-30 Sep. € 10.50   2006*

LOCRONAN *2E2* (5km S Rural) **Camp Municipal de La Motte, 29136 Plogonnec [02 98 91 70 09 or 02 98 91 72 06 (Mairie); fax 02 98 91 83 43]** Fr Locronan take D7 twd Châteaulin. By side of church, foll sp. La Motte at top of hill by La Chapelle Ar-Zonj. Med, mkd pitch, pt sl, terr, unshd; wc; shwrs inc; el pnts; ice; shop 2km; sand beach 10km; poss cr; adv bkg; quiet. 1 Jul-31 Aug.   2004*

LOCUNOLE see Quimperle *2F2*

LODEVE *10E1* (5km NE Rural) **Camping des Sources, Chemin d'Aubaygues, 34700 Soubès [tel/fax 04 67 44 32 02; jlsources@wanadoo.fr; www.campingdessources.cjb.net]** Fr Montpellier take N109 & N9 to Lodève. Take R turn to Soubès; ent Soubès take 1st R in dir Fozières; foll sp. Sm, terr, pt shd; wc; chem disp; shwrs inc; el pnts (6A) €2.50; ice; lndtte; tradsmn; shop 1km; snacks; playgrnd; children pool; rv sw, sailing & fishing adj; no dogs; adv bkg rec high ssn; quiet; cc acc; CCI. "Helpful, pleasant owner; excel, peaceful site; relaxed atmosphere; surrounded by beautiful countryside; not suitable lge o'fits as app rd v narr & some pitches sm; immac facs; gd rest in vill." ♦ 15 May-15 Sep. € 14.00   2006*

⊞**LODEVE** *10E1* (6km SE Rural) **Camping Les Peupliers, Les Casseaux, 34700 Le Bosc [tel/fax 04 67 44 38 08]** Take exit 54 on A75; sp Le Bosc. Med, mkd pitch, pt sl, terr, pt shd; wc (cont); shwrs inc; el pnts (5A) €3 (rev pol); gas; ice; shop 4km; tradsmn Jul-Aug; snacks; bar; playgrnd; pool; sand beach 40km; lake 5km; 50% statics; dogs €0.80; Eng spkn; adv bkg; dep req; quiet; CCI. "Friendly staff; ltd facs low ssn; gd cent for Hérault region; windsurfing Lac du Salagou; winter NH." ♦ ltd. € 11.60   2005*

LODEVE *10E1* (2km S Urban) **Camping Les Vals, Route de Puech, 34700 Lodève [tel/fax 04 67 44 36 57; info@campinglesvals.com; www.campinglesvals.com]** Fr Lodève take D148 along W bank of Rv Lergue, twd Puech; site in 2km on W of rd. Med, pt sl, pt terr, pt shd; wc; chem disp; shwrs; el pnts inc; lndtte; ice; shop; rest; snacks; playgrnd; pool; rv fishing, watersports & sw adj; cycle hire; tennis; mini-golf; TV; entmnt; v ltd facs low ssn; quiet. ♦ 15 Apr-30 Sep. € 16.00   2004*

LODEVE *10E1* (7km S Rural) **Camp Municipal Les Vailhes, Lac du Salagou, 34702 Lodève [04 67 44 25 98]** Fr N exit A75 junc 43 onto D148 dir Octon & Lac du Salagou. Foll site sp. Fr S exit A75 junc 55. Lge, hdg pitch, terr, pt shd; wc; chem disp; shwrs inc; el pnts (6A) €2.50; lndtte; tradsmn; playgrnd; beach by lake; watersports; 20% statics; dogs; poss cr; quiet; CCI. "Peaceful site by lake; excel walks; gd." 1 Apr-30 Sep. € 10.60   2007*

LODEVE *10E1* (5km W Rural) **Camping Domaine de Lambeyran (Naturist), 34700 Lodève [04 67 44 13 99; fax 04 67 44 09 91; lambeyran@wanadoo.fr; www.lambeyran.com]** Fr N or S on N9 take sliprd to Lodève. Leave town on D35 W twd Bédarieux. In 2km take 2nd R, sp L'Ambeyran & St Martin. Foll sp 3.7km up winding hill to site. Lge, hdg/mkd pitch, terr, pt shd; wc; chem disp; 60% serviced pitches; shwrs inc; el pnts (6A) €3.90; gas; lndtte; shop & supmkt 4km, rest, snacks, bar high ssn; BBQ; playgrnd; pool; sailing, windsurfing 10km; 5% statics; dogs; phone; adv bkg (dep req); cc acc; INF card req. "Lge pitches; superb views; gd walking; site ent gate clsd 2000." 15 May-15 Sep. € 18.30   2007*

LODS see Ornans *6G2*

LONG see Abbeville *3B3*

LONGCHAUMOIS see Morez *9A3*

LONGEAU PERCEY *6F1* (3km S Rural) **FFCC Camp Municipal du Lac, 52190 Villegusien-le-Lac [03 25 88 47 25 or 03 25 88 45 24]** Exit A31 junc 6 dir Longeau. Site sp fr both D67 & D974 (N74) S of Longeau. Visible fr D974 & rec app. Med, pt shd; wc; chem disp; mv service pnt; shwrs inc; el pnts (6A) inc; ice; shop; tradsmn; snacks; playgrnd; tennis; fishing, boating & sw in lake; poss cr; adv bkg; rd & rlwy noise; "Conv NH." ♦ 15 Apr-30 Sep. € 19.00   2007*

LONGEVILLE SUR MER *7A1* (1.5km S Coastal) **Camping le Petit Rocher, 85560 Longeville-sur-Mer [02 51 90 31 57; www.camp-atlantique.com]** Fr La Tranche-sur-Mer take D105 N. In 8km site clearly sp 'Le Rocher' at 3rd exit fr rndabt (Ave du Dr Mathevet). Site on R in 1km at beginning of beach rd. Lge, hdg/mkd pitches, pt sl, shd; wc; chem disp; shwrs inc; el pnts (6A) €3; gas; ice; shops adj; rest & snacks nrby; sand beach 300m; adv bkg; quiet; CCI. "Gd beach holiday; gd facs." 15 May-15 Sep. € 12.00

                    2005*

LONGEVILLE SUR MER *7A1* (2km S Coastal) **Camping Le Sous-Bois, La Haute Saligotière, 85560 Longeville-sur-Mer [02 51 33 36 90; fax 02 51 33 32 73]** Sp fr D105 fr La Tranche-sur-Mer. Med, hdg pitch, shd; wc; chem disp; shwrs inc; el pnts (10A) €3.50 (poss rev pol); lndtte; shop; tradsmn; playgrnd; sand beach 1km; tennis; TV; 15% statics; dogs €1.60; phone; quiet; cc not acc; CCI. "Nice, well-managed, family site; pleasant 1km woodland walk to beach; gd walks; cycle track network; excel." ♦ 1 Jun-15 Sep. € 16.88   2007*

LONGEVILLE SUR MER *7A1* (3km S Coastal) **Camping Les Clos des Pins, Les Conches, 85560 Longeville-sur-Mer [02 51 90 31 69; fax 02 51 90 30 68; philip.jones@freesbee.fr; www.efrancevacances.com]** Fr La Tranche-sur-Mer take D105 coast rd N, turn L in Les Conches into Ave de la Plage, site on R in 1km. Med, mkd pitch, pt sl, shd; wc; chem disp; shwrs inc; el pnts (6A) inc; gas; ice; lndtte; shop; rest; snacks; bar; BBQ (gas/elec only); playgrnd; htd pool; waterslide; sand beach 200m; activities inc silk painting, jogging, canoeing, aerobics; entmnt; 60% statics; dogs €2.50; phone; bus; Eng spkn; adv bkg (dep req); quiet except for disco; 20% red low ssn. "Set among pine trees; v helpful owners; some pitches unsuitable for c'vans due to soft sand & diff access - adv bkg rec to ensure a suitable pitch; vg." ♦ ltd. Easter-10 Oct. € 24.00   2004*

France

LONGEVILLE SUR MER *7A1* (3km SW Coastal) Camping Les Brunelles, Le Bouil, 85560 Longeville-sur-Mer [02 51 33 50 75; fax 02 51 33 98 21; camping@les-brunelles.com; www.les-brunelles.com] Site bet Longeville-sur-Mer & Jard-sur-Mer; foll D21. Lge, mkd pitch, pt sl, pt shd; wc; shwrs inc; el pnts (6A) inc; Indtte; shop; rest 500m; snacks; bar; playgrnd; 2 htd pools (1 covrd) & paddling pool; waterslide; sand beach 700m; watersports; tennis; cycle hire; games area; mini-golf; horseriding 2km; golf 15km; internet; entmnt; TV rm; 75% statics; dogs €3; adv bkg; cc acc. ♦ 1 May-18 Sep. € 25.00 (CChq acc)   2004*

LONS LE SAUNIER *6H2* (1km NE) Camping La Marjorie, 640 Blvd de l'Europe, 39000 Lons-le-Saunier [03 84 24 26 94; fax 03 84 24 08 40; info@camping-marjorie.com;   www.camping-marjorie.com] Site clearly sp in town on N83 twd Besançon. Fr N bear R dir 'Piscine', cross under N83 to site. Lge, hdg pitch, some hdstg, pt sl, pt shd; wc; baby facs; chem disp; shwrs inc; el pnts (6A) inc (poss rev pol); gas; Indtte; shop; tradsmn; rest; bar; playgrnd; 2 htd pools (1 covrd) adj; games area; mini-golf; golf 8km; entmnt; child entmnt; dogs €1; phone; Eng spkn; some rd noise; red low ssn; cc acc; CCI. "Beautiful area; gorges, lakes & limestone escarpments nr; walk to pleasant town; excel san facs; friendly staff; conv location; excel." ♦ 1 Apr-15 Oct. € 17.90   2007*

Before we move on, I'm going to fill in some site report forms and post them off to the editor, otherwise they won't arrive in time for the deadline at the end of September.

LONS LE SAUNIER *6H2* (8km NE) Camp Municipal de la Toupe, 39210 Baume-les-Messieurs [03 84 44 63 16; fax 03 84 44 95 40] On D471 Lons-le-Saunier to Champagnole rd, take L onto D4 then D70 to Baume-les-Messieurs. Site 500m thro vill on D70 - narr, steep app rd not suitable lge o'fits. Or, fr N83 turn E onto D120 at St Germain-lès-Arlay to Voiteur then onto D70. Sm, pt shd; wc; shwrs inc; el pnts (9A) €2.80; shops 500m; playgrnd; direct access to lake; dogs; quiet. "New san facs (2007)." 1 Apr-30 Sep. € 7.50   2007*

LONS LE SAUNIER *6H2* (8km SW Rural) Camp Municipal, Grande Rue, 39570 Chilly-le-Vignoble [03 84 43 09 34 or 03 84 43 09 32 (Mairie); fax 03 84 47 34 09] Fr A39 exit junc 8 onto N78. After approx 5km turn R to Courlans & Chilly-le-Vignoble. Site sp 2km. Med, pt shd; wc (most cont); shwrs inc; el pnts (5A) inc; ice; supmkt 3km; tradsmn; rest; snacks; playgrnd; games rm; golf nrby; quiet; CCI. "V pleasant site in quiet vill; ent for c'vans fr 1530 only; gd." 1 Jun-15 Sep. € 12.60   2007*

⊞**LORIENT** *2F2* (6km N Rural) Camping Ty Nénez, Route de Lorient, 56620 Pont-Scorff [02 97 32 51 16; fax 02 97 32 43 77; contact@camping-tynenez.com; www.lorient-camping.com] N fr N165 on D6, look for sp Quéven in approx 5km on R. If missed, cont for 1km & turn around at rndabt. Site sp fr Pont-Scorff. Med, hdg pitch, pt shd; htd wc; chem disp; mv service pnt; baby facs; shwrs inc; el pnts (16A) €2.65; Indtte; supmkt 1km; bar; games area; some statics; dogs €0.65; adv bkg; quiet. "Site barrier locked 2200-0800; zoo 1km; peaceful site." € 7.50   2007*

LORIENT *2F2* (8km N Rural) Camp Municipal St Caradec, 56700 Hennebont [02 97 36 21 73; camping.municipal.stcaradec@wanadoo.fr] Fr Port Louis D781 to Hennebont. L in cent cross bdge, then sharp R along Rv Blavet for 1km. On R on rv bank. Med, mkd pitch, pt shd; wc; chem disp; shwrs inc; el pnts inc; Indtte; shop 2km; playgrnd; sand beach 12km; rv sw; some statics; adv bkg; quiet; CCI. "Pretty site." 1 Jun-15 Sep. € 7.50   2006*

LORIENT *2F2* (3km SW Coastal) Camp Municipal des Algues, 21 Blvd de Port Maria, 56260 Larmor-Plage [02 97 65 55 47; fax 02 97 84 26 27; camping@larmor-plage.com; www.larmor-plage.com] Fr N165, take Lorient exit, foll D29 for Larmor-Plage. Site adj beach, turn R after Tourist Info office. Lge, mkd pitch, pt shd; wc; chem disp; mv service pnt; shwrs inc; el pnts (10A) €3; Indtte; shop adj; rest, playgrnd; sand beach adj; fishing; sailing; dogs €1.20; poss cr; quiet. ♦ 15 Jun-15 Sep. € 13.90   2007*

⊞**LORIENT** *2F2* (4km SW Coastal) Camping La Fontaine, Kerderff, 56260 Larmor-Plage [02 97 33 71 28 or 02 97 65 11 11; fax 02 97 33 70 32; camping-la-fontaine@sellor.com; www.camping-la-fontaine.com] At Larmor-Plage 300m fr D152. Well sp. Med, pt sl; htd wc; mv service pnt; chem disp; shwrs inc; el pnts (10A) (rev pol); Indtte; shop adj; snacks; bar; playgrnd; beach 800m; child entmnt; horseriding; tennis adj; sailing; sports; dogs €1.54; Eng spkn. "Excel site; gd facs." ♦ € 13.50   2005*

⊞**LORIENT** *2F2* (8km W Coastal) FFCC Camping L'Atlantys, Route du Courégant, Fort Bloqué, 56270 Ploemeur [02 97 05 99 81; fax 02 97 05 95 78; camping.atlantys@wanadoo.fr; www.camping-atlantys.com] Fr cent Lorient take rd D162 in dir of Ploemeur then coast rd D152 dir Guidel-Plage. Site ent on R adj to sp Fort Bloqué. Or D29 fr Lorient then onto D152 & site on R at ent Fort Bloqué. Lge, mkd pitch, terr, pt sl, unshd; wc; shwrs inc; el pnts (6-10A) €3-4 (rev pol); ice; Indry rm; shop; snacks; bar; playgrnd; pool, sand beach & golf adj; fishing; horseriding 2km; 85% statics; dogs €2; poss cr; Eng spkn; adv bkg; quiet; CCI. "Sea views fr many pitches - sunsets; ltd facs low ssn; vg." € 17.00   2006*

LORMES *4G4* (500m S Rural) **Camp Municipal L'Etang du Goulot, 2 Rue des Campeurs, 58140 Lormes** [03 86 22 82 37; fax 03 86 85 19 28] Fr Château-Chinon on D944 site on R on lakeside 250m after junc with D17 fr Montsauche, 500m bef town cent. Med, hdg pitch, pt shd, pt sl; wc (some cont); chem disp; mv service pnt; shwrs inc; el pnts (4A) €2.50; shop 500m; snacks; BBQ; playgrnd; lake sw; fishing; 1% statics; dogs €0.50; Eng spkn; adv bkg; quiet; red low ssn; CCI. "O'looking lake with gd walks; friendly, helpful warden." ♦ 1 May-15 Sep. € 12.30   2006*

LOUBRESSAC *7C4* (200m S Rural) **Camping La Garrigue, 46130 Loubressac** [tel/fax 05 65 38 34 88; infos@camping-lagarrigue.com; www.camping-lagarrigue.com] Fr D940 S to Bretenoux, then D14 to Loubressac. Fr cent vill foll sp 200m. Sm, hdg/mkd pitch, pt sl, terr, pt shd; wc; chem disp; shwrs inc; el pnts (6A) €2.80; gas; Indtte; ice; shop; tradsmn high ssn; snacks; bar; BBQ; playgrnd; pool; paddling pool; entmnt; TV rm; 20% statics; dogs €1.20; phone; quiet; Eng spkn; adv bkg; CCI. "Access poss diff for lge vans; walks in pretty vill; vg long stay." ♦ 1 Apr-30 Sep. € 14.00   2007*

LOUDEAC *2E3* (1km E) **Camp Municipal Pont es Bigots, 22600 Loudéac** [02 96 28 14 92 or 02 96 66 85 00 (Mairie); fax 02 96 66 08 93; mairie.loudeac@wanadoo.fr] Fr Loudéac, take N164 twd Rennes, site on L by lake in 1km, sp. Height barrier into site 1.8m. Med, hdg pitch, pt shd; wc; shwrs; el pnts €1.80; ice; shops 1km; playgrnd; entmnt; lake sw; fishing; horseriding; quiet. "V pleasant; site clsd 1100-1700." 15 Jun-15 Sep. € 6.10   2005*

LOUDENVIELLE see Arreau *8G2*

There aren't many sites open this early in the year. We'd better phone ahead to check that the one we're heading for is actually open.

LOUDUN *4H1* (1km W Rural) **Camp Municipal de Beausoleil, Chemin de l'Etang, 86200 Loudun** [05 49 98 14 22; fax 05 49 98 12 88] On main rte fr Poitiers to Saumur/Le Mans; N on D347 (N147) around Loudun, foll sp; turn L just N of level x-ing, then on R approx 250m. Sm, hdg/mkd pitch, terr, pt shd; wc, chem disp; shwrs inc; el pnts €2.90; Indry rm; shop 1km; playgrnd; lake adj for fishing; bus adj; Eng spkn; CCI. "Beautiful, quiet, v well-kept site; low ssn site yourself, warden calls am & pm; friendly, helpful staff; excel." ♦ 15 May-31 Aug. € 10.05   2007*

LOUHANS *6H1* (2km W Urban) **Camp Municipal de Louhans, 10, Chemin de la Chapellerie, 71500 Louhans** [03 85 75 19 02 or 03 85 76 75 10 (Mairie); fax 03 85 76 75 11; mairiedelouhanschateaurenaud@yahoo.fr] In Louhans foll sp for Romenay on D971. Go under rlwy & over rv. Site on L just after stadium. Med, hdg/mkd pitch, hdstg, shd; wc (some cont); chem disp (wc); mv service pnt; shwrs inc; el pnts €3.60; Indtte; ice; snacks; playgrnd; pool & tennis courts adj; sw rv adj; poss cr; adv bkg; some rlwy noise; CCI. "Rv location; clean & well appointed; sports complex adj; lovely cycling area; lge town mkt Mon am; poss itinerants; vg." ♦ ltd. 1 Apr-30 Sep. € 7.40   2007*

LOUPIAC see Payrac *7D3*

LOURDES *8F2* (1km N Urban) **Caravaning Plein-Soleil, Route de Tarbes, 65100 Lourdes** [05 62 94 40 93; fax 05 62 94 51 20; camping.plein.soleil@wanadoo.fr; www.camping-pleinsoleil.com] Fr N site sp on N21. Turn R imm opp aquarium sp. Sm, terr, pt shd; htd wc; chem disp; shwrs inc; el pnts (4A) inc; Indtte; snacks; playgrnd; pool; dogs; poss cr; Eng spkn; adv bkg; poss noise fr adj builders' yard; CCI. "Pleasant site; gd facs; guarded; security lights; helpful staff; ltd access lge o'fits; muddy when wet; 2km walk to grotto at Lourdes; conv hypmkt." Easter-10 Oct. € 21.50   2007*

LOURDES *8F2* (2km N) **FFCC Camping Le Moulin du Monge, Ave Jean Moulin, 65100 Lourdes** [05 62 94 28 15; fax 05 62 42 20 54; camping.moulin.monge@wanadoo.fr] S on N21 fr Tarbes, site on L of rd 2km bef Lourdes, visible fr rd. Med, pt shd; htd wc; mv service pnt; sauna; shwrs inc; el pnts (2-6A) €2-4; ice; Indtte; shops & farm produce; playgrnd; htd, covrd pool; some rd & rlwy noise. "Pleasant site but not well lit at night." 15 Mar-15 Oct. € 13.30   2006*

LOURDES *8F2* (1km S) **Camping du Ruisseau Blanc, Route de Bagnères, 65100 Lourdes** [05 62 42 94 83; fax 05 62 42 94 62] Exit Lourdes on D937 twd Bagnères & foll sp. Site has 2 ents. C'vans ignore 1st sp for site on R & cont on D937 foll next sp. Med, pt shd; wc (most cont); mv service pnt; shwrs; el pnts (2-4A) inc; Indry rm; shop (local produce); playgrnd; TV rm; no dogs; "Gd views; beautiful site but facs poss stretched high ssn." 1 Apr-10 Oct. € 11.10   2004*

LOURDES *8F2* (2.5km W Urban) **Camp du Loup, Route de la Forêt, 65100 Lourdes** [tel/fax 05 62 94 23 60] Fr Lourdes take D937 sp Pau, Bétharram. Turn L at level x-ing into Rue de Pau, then immed R. Foll rd & turn L over rv bdge, site sp. Med, pt shd; wc; chem disp; mv service pnt; shwrs €1; el pnts (6A) €2.50; Indtte; shop 1km; tradsmn; playgrnd; rv 300m; dogs €1; poss cr; adv bkg ess; quiet; CCI. "Excel CL-type site; basic facs; friendly, helpful host; easy rvside walk to shrine; site poss v cr with pilgrims; gd atmosphere; gd site security." ♦ 1 Apr-15 Oct. € 11.00   2007*

LOURDES *8F2* (4km W Rural) **Camping d'Arrouach, 9 Rue des Trois Archanges, Biscaye, 65100 Lourdes [05 62 42 11 43; fax 05 62 42 05 27; camping.arrouach@wanadoo.fr; www.camping-arrouach.com]** Fr Lourdes take D940 twd Pau. As you leave Lourdes take L fork D937 (sp) Bétharram. Site on R 200m. Med, hdg/mkd pitch, hdstg, pt sl, pt shd; wc; chem disp; mv service pnt; shwrs inc; el pnts (3-6A) €2.50-5; gas; lndtte; shop 2km; tradsmn; bar; BBQ; playgrnd; 10% statics; phone; poss cr; quiet; adv bkg; Eng spkn; CCI; red 15 days. "Pleasant, elevated site with mountain views; poss flooding in v wet weather; clean san facs; easy access parking for Lourdes via Rte de Pau." ♦ 15 Mar-31 Dec. € 11.80   2006*

LOURDES *8F2* (4km W Rural) **Camping La Forêt, Route de la Forêt, 65100 Lourdes [05 62 94 04 38 or 05 62 45 04 57 (LS); fax 05 62 42 14 86]** Fr Lourdes take D937 twd Pau; turn L on level x-ing; foll sp to site. Med, mkd pitch, pt shd; wc; mv service pnt; shwrs €1; el pnts (6-10A) €2.60; gas; lndtte; ice; shop; rest; snacks; bar; playgrnd; few statics; dogs €1.30; poss cr; Eng spkn; adv bkg; quiet; CCI. "Lovely site near Pyrenees; helpful owners; conv town cent; 15 mins walk to grotto; poss to stay bef official opening date by arrangement." 1 Apr-31 Oct. € 9.50   2007*

LOURDES *8F2* (6km W Rural) **FFCC Camping Le Prat Dou Rey (formerly Arc en Ciel), 31 Route de Pau, 65270 Peyrouse [05 62 41 81 54; fax 05 62 41 89 76; pradourey@wanadoo.fr; www.pradourey.com]** Take D940 fr Lourdes then in 2km take D937 E sp Bétharram. Cont thro Peyrouse vill & site on L in 500m. Med, pt shd; wc; mv service pnt; shwrs inc; el pnts (6-10A) €2.70-4 inc; lndry rm; shop in ssn & 6km; snacks; BBQ; playgrnd; pool; rv 100m; fishing; 10% statics; CCI. "New, enthusiastic, helpful young owners (2006); immac san facs; various sports activities." 1 Apr-30 Sep. € 10.60   2006*

LOURDES *8F2* (4km NW Rural) **Camping Relais Océan Pyrénées, 3 Rue des Pyrénées, Poueyferré, 65100 Lourdes [05 62 94 57 22 or 05 62 94 95 23]** Fr Pau on D940, site on R at S junc with rd to Poueyferré. Do not take 1st sp for Poueyferré & camp site, as app fr vill not rec. Med, hdg/mkd pitch, terr, pt shd; htd wc; chem disp; shwrs; el pnts (4A) inc; gas; lndtte; shop, tradsmn, snacks, bar in ssn; playgrnd; pool; lake sw 800m; adv bkg (dep req); no cc acc; quiet; CCI. ♦ 15 Mar-15 Sep.   2005*

LOURES BAROUSSE see Montréjeau *8F3*

LOUROUX, LE *4G2* (N Rural) **Camping à la Ferme de La Chaumine (Baudoin), 37240 Le Louroux [06 85 45 68 10; fax 02 47 92 29 24; lachaumine@free.fr]** Fr Tours, take D50 S for 30km. Site immed on R bef Le Louroux. Sm, hdg pitch, shd; wc; chem disp; shwrs inc; el pnts (10A) inc; BBQ; playgrnd; dogs; phone nrby; bus 200m; Eng spkn; adv bkg; quiet. "Superb CL-type site nr quaint vill; excel tourist office in vill; helpful owners; gd, clean san facs; gd walks fr site." 1 May-15 Oct. € 10.00   2006*

> Did you know you can fill in site report forms on the Club's website — www.caravanclub.co.uk?

LOUVIE JUZON *8F2* (1km E) **FFCC Camping Le Rey, Quartier Listo, Route de Lourdes, 64260 Louvie-Juzon [05 59 05 78 52; fax 05 59 05 78 97; campinglerey@club-internet.fr; www.camping-pyrenees-ossau.com]** Site on L at top of hill E fr Louvie; v steep app. Sm, mkd pitch, pt sl, pt shd; htd wc; chem disp; shwrs inc; el pnts (6-1A) €3.30-4.20; lndtte; ice; shops 1km; tradsmn; rest 1km; snacks; bar; playgrnd; sm pool; watersports, fishing nr; games area; entmnt; 50% statics; dogs €2; phone; adv bkg; quiet; CCI. "Fascinating area; chateau nr." ♦ 1 Feb-15 Nov. € 12.10   2005*

LOUVIE JUZON *8F2* (3km S Rural) **Camping L'Ayguelade, 64260 Bielle [05 59 82 66 50; ayguelade@aol.com]** S fr Louvie-Juzon on L of main rd clearly sp. Med, mkd pitch, pt shd; wc; shwrs inc; el pnts (6A); lndtte; shop 4km; tradsmn; rest adj; snacks; bar; 25% statics; Eng spkn; adv bkg; quiet; CCI. "Rv runs thro site, pleasant setting." ♦ ltd. 1 Mar-15 Oct.   2004*

⊞**LOUVIE JUZON** *8F2* (6km NW Rural) **FFCC Aire Naturelle Les Jardins d'Ossau (Dunan), 2 Chemin de Départ, 64250 Buzy [05 59 21 05 71; dunan.pascal@wanadoo.fr]** S fr Pau on N134; approx 12 km past Gan sp Camping; after restaurant at Belair turn L onto D34 sp Buzy; in 2km turn L after going under 1st rlwy bdge. Site on R, sp. Sm, pt shd; wc; chem disp (wc); shwrs inc; el pnts (6A) €2.10; lndtte; ice; games area; games rm; dogs €0.50; Eng spkn; adv bkg (dep req); quiet; no cc acc; CCI. "Peaceful site on fruit farm; lovely views of Pyrenees; easy access; excel touring base; v helpful owners; conv NH en rte Spain; excel." ♦ ltd. € 11.40   2007*

LOUVIERS *3D2* (2km W Rural) **Camping Le Bel Air, Route de la Haye-Malherbe, Hameau de St-Lubin, 27400 Louviers [tel/fax 02 32 40 10 77; contact@camping-lebelair.fr; www.camping-lebelair.fr]** Leave A13 junc 18 sp Louviers; join A154 fr Evreux to Louviers; in cent site sp - foll D81 W for 4km in dir La Haye-Malherbe; twisting rd uphill; site on R. If travelling S leave at junc 19 & foll dirs as bef. NB In town cent look for sm green sp after Ecole Communale (on L) and bef Jardin Public - a v narr rd (1-way) & easy to miss. Med, hdg/mkd/hdstg pitch, pt shd; wc (chem clos); chem disp; mv service pnt; shwrs inc; el pnts (6A) €3.80; gas; lndtte; shop; tradsmn; playgrnd; htd pool; 30% statics; dogs €1.60; poss cr; Eng spkn; adv bkg (dep req); quiet; red low ssn; 10% red CCI. "Pretty site; friendly staff & v helpful owners; will open out of ssn if you phone ahead; barrier clsd at 2200; facs clean but urgently need updating, otherwise vg site; access to pitches diff long o'fits; some pitches sm; conv for Le Havre." 1 Mar-31 Oct. € 14.50 (CChq acc)   2007*

LOYAT see Ploërmel *2F3*

LUBERSAC *7B3* (Urban) **Camp Municipal La Vézénie, 19210 Lubersac [05 55 73 50 14 (Mairie); fax 05 55 73 67 99; mairie.lubersac@wanadoo.fr]** Fr N20 4km N of Uzerche turn W onto D902 to Lubersac. At far end of mkt sq take rd L of Hôtel de Commerce; turn immed L; then 1st L; at T-junc turn R; then L at mini rndabt onto site. Sm, mkd pitch, pt sl, terr, pt shd; wc (some cont); shwrs inc; el pnts; lndry rm; shop adj; rest, snacks; playgrnd; paddling pool; sand beach & lake sw; fishing 400m; tennis; horseriding; poss cr; quiet. "Modern, clean site overlkg lake." 1 Jun-15 Sep. € 8.00   2004*

LUBERSAC *7B3* (2km SE Urban) **Camping Le Domaine Bleu, Bourg, 19210 St Pardoux-Corbier [tel/fax 35 55 73 59 89; www.ledomainebleu.eu]** Exit A20 junc 44; take D920 S for 1.5km; turn W onto D902; in 9km turn S to St Pardoux-Corbier. Sm, pt shd; wc; chem disp; shwrs inc; el pnts (10A) €2.50; lndtte; ice; tradsmn; local rest, snacks, pool & tennis; dogs €1.50; Eng spkn; CCI. "Clean site; Dutch owners; vg." 1 Jun-1 Sep. € 10.00
                2007*

LUC EN DIOIS *9D3* (Rural) **Camp Municipal Les Foulons, 26310 Luc-en-Diois [04 75 21 36 14 or 04 75 21 31 01 (Mairie); fax 04 75 21 35 70; camping.luc@wanadoo.fr]** Sp in vill off D93. Med, pt shd; wc; shwrs; el pnts (6A) inc; lndtte; shops & rest 500m; playgrnd; pool, rv adj; games area adj; tennis; Eng spkn; adv bkg; quiet; CCI. "Excel site; modern & well-maintained; gd walking/cycling; 5 mins walk fr attractive sm town; gates clsd 2200-0700; outstanding scenery; Fri mkt; canoeing, horseriding, hang-gliding avail in area." ♦ 1 Apr-30 Oct. € 13.60   2006*

LUC EN DIOIS *9D3* (6km N Rural) **Camping L'Hirondelle de St Ferréol, Bois de St Ferréol, 26410 Menglon [tel/fax 04 75 21 82 08; contact@campinghirondelle.com; www.camping hirondelle.com]** Foll D93 S twd Luc-en-Diois, in 6km at Pont-de-Quart turn L on D539 sp Châtillon, in 5km turn R on D140 sp Menglon, Recoubeau, site on R in 150m over rv. Med, shd; wc (some cont); baby facs; shwrs inc; el pnts (3-6A) €3-4; lndtte; shop; rest; snacks; bar; playgrnd; htd pool complex; waterslide; rv sw; archery; entmnt; TV rm; 10% statics; dogs €3.15; adv bkg; quiet. "Lovely area." ♦ 1 Apr-15 Sep. € 21.90 (CChq acc)
                2005*

LUC EN DIOIS *9D3* (5km NW Rural) **Camping Le Couriou, 26310 Recoubeau-Jansac [04 75 21 33 23; fax 04 75 21 38 42]** Fr Die on D93 twds Luc-en-Diois for 13 km. Turn R at D140 & foll sp. Med, mkd pitch, some hdstg, terr, pt shd; wc; chem disp; shwrs inc; baby facs; el pnts (6A) €3; gas; lndtte; shop high ssn; rest; snacks; bar; playgrnd; htd pool; 5% statics; dogs; phone; poss cr; adv bkg ess high ssn; quiet; CCI. "Panoramic mountain views." ♦ ltd. 1 May-31 Aug. € 19.00   2004*

LUC SUR MER see Ouistreham *3D1*

LUCAY LE MALE *4H2* (4km SW Rural) **Camp Municipal La Foulquetière, 36360 Luçay-le-Mâle [02 54 40 52 88 or 02 54 40 43 31 (Mairie); fax 02 54 40 42 47; mairie@ville-lucaylemale.fr]** SW fr Valençay & thro Luçay, on D960, then fork L onto D13, site on R in 1km. Sm, hdg/mkd pitch, pt sl, pt shd; htd wc; chem disp; 60% serviced pitch; shwrs inc; el pnts (6A) €1.50; lndtte; shop 3km; rest; snacks; bar; playgrnd; watersports; canoeing; fishing; tennis; mini-golf; games area; Eng spkn; adv bkg; v quiet; CCI. "Excel site but isolated; gd sized pitches; basic facs; gd walking country; by lake in pretty setting; if no one at recep, pay at Mairie or rest." 1 Apr-15 Oct. € 6.50   2005*

LUCENAY L'EVEQUE *6H1* (S Rural) **Aire Naturelle Municipal, 71540 Lucenay-l'Evêque [03 85 82 65 41 (Mairie); fax 03 85 82 65 37; mairie.lucenay.l.eveque@wanadoo.fr]** On D980 Autun to Saulieu rd, 300m S of vill site ent immed bef vill sp. Ent narr; easier when warden opens 2nd gate. Sm, pt shd; wc (some cont); shwrs inc; el pnts; playgrnd; shops 300m; quiet; tennis; cc acc; CCI. "Nice neat site with brook running thro; gd walking country situated in Morvan regional park; v quiet low ssn; warden visits 1730 & 0930; narr ent to pitches with el pnts; site yourself." 1 May-1 Sep.
                2004*

LUCHE PRINGE see Flèche, La *4G1*

France

LUCHON *8G3* (2km N Rural) **Camping Pradelongue, 31110 Moustajon [05 61 79 86 44; fax 05 61 79 18 64; camping-pradelongue@ wanadoo.fr; www.camping-pradelongue.com]** Site is on D125c on W of D125 main rd fr Luchon. Ent at Moustajon/Antignac going S. Site adj Intermarché; sp. Lge, hdg/mkd pitch, pt shd; wc; chem disp; mv service pnt; baby facs; shwrs inc; el pnts (2-10A) €2-4; Indtte; ice; shop 100m; BBQ; playgrnd; htd pool; games area; 10% statics; dogs €2; Eng spkn; adv bkg; quiet; cc acc; CCI. "Excel, well-run site with friendly, helpful owners; excel mountain views; recep clsd 1230-1400; rec." ♦ 1 Apr-30 Sep. € 16.30 2007*

⊞**LUCHON** *8G3* (4km N Rural) **FFCC Camping Le Pyrénéen, 31110 Salles-et-Pratviel [05 61 79 59 19; fax 05 61 79 75 75; campinglepyreneen@wanadoo.fr; www.camping lepyreneen-luchon.com]** Fr Luchon, take N125 twd Montréjeau; in 4km exit on D125 to Salles; thro vill & site sp on R. Med, pt shd; htd wc; chem disp; baby facs; shwrs inc; el pnts (10A) inc; Indtte; ice; shop & 4km; bar; htd pool; paddling pool; games rm; games area; TV; 50% statics; no dogs; adv bkg; quiet. "Some sm pitches; neat, clean site; gd san facs; wintersports." ♦ ltd. € 18.00 (3 persons) 2007*

LUCON *7A1* (11km E Rural) **Camp Municipal Le Vieux Chêne, Rue du Port, 85370 Nalliers [02 51 30 91 98 or 02 51 30 90 71; fax 02 51 30 94 06; nalliers.mairie@wanadoo.fr]** Turn R & foll site sp approx 500m after vill sp on D949 Luçon-Fontenay; site sp easy to miss. Sm, hdg/mkd pitch, pt shd; wc; chem disp; shwrs inc; el pnts (8A) inc; shop 500m; tradsmn; playgrnd; adv bkg; quiet; site yourself on lge pitch; CCI. "Excel site; v clean; plenty hot water; in low ssn contact Mairie for ent to site; lots of interest in area; vg rest nrby; vg NH." 15 May-15 Sep. € 10.20 2006*

⊞**LUCON** *7A1* (10km SW Rural) **Camping La Fraignaye, Rue de Beau Laurier, 85580 St Denis-du-Payré [02 51 27 21 36 or 02 51 27 20 28 (Mairie); fax 02 51 27 27 74; camping.fraignaye@wanadoo.fr; www.camping-lafraignaye.com]** Fr A8 exit junc 7 onto D137 dir La Rochelle. Turn L after Ste Gemme onto D949 to Luçon, then take D746 to Triaize. Take D25 to St Denis-du-Payré, in vill turn L bef church & foll sp. Sm, mkd pitch, pt shd; wc; chem disp; shwrs inc; el pnts (6-10A) €2.50-4; gas; Indry rm; ice; shop & 7km; rest; snacks; bar; playgrnd; sand beach 12km; games rm; cycle hire; TV; 20% statics; dogs €1.50; phone; poss cr; Eng spkn; adv bkg; quiet; cc acc; red long stay/low ssn. "Pleasant owner; nr nature reserve; site liable to flooding." ♦ € 12.00 2006*

LUDE, LE *4G1* (1km NE) **Camp Municipal au Bord du Loir, Route du Mans, 72800 Le Lude [02 43 94 67 70; fax 02 43 94 93 82; camping-lelude@wanadoo.fr]** Fr town cent take D305 (E); in 1km take D307 (N) sp 'Le Mans'; site immed on L. Well sp. Med, hdg/mkd pitch, pt shd; wc; chem disp; mv service pnt; shwrs inc; el pnts (5A) inc; Indtte; shops 300m; tradsmn; rests 100m; snacks adj (high ssn); BBQ (gas only); playgrnd; free pool adj; waterslide; tennis; beach 6km; canoeing; fishing; entmnt; TV; 10% statics; phone; poss cr; Eng spkn; adv bkg; poss traff noise far end of site; cc acc; CCI. "V clean; gd value site; helpful staff; excel rests adj; easy walk to town; Château du Lude worth visit; highly rec." ♦ 1 Apr-30 Sep. € 10.00 2006*

LUGAGNAC see Limogne en Quercy *7D4*

LUGNY see Pont de Vaux *9A2*

This guide relies on site report forms submitted by caravanners like us; we'll do our bit and tell the editor what we think of the campsites we've visited.

LUNEL *10E2* (5km NE Rural) **Camping Les Amandiers, Clos de Manset, 30660 Gallargues-le-Montueux [tel/fax 04 66 35 28 02; camp amandiers@wanadoo.fr; www.camping-les amandiers.com]** Exit A9 at junc 26 Gallargues/Les Plages. Turn R after pool, site in 2km. Med, pt shd; wc; chem disp; mv service pnt; shwrs inc; el pnts (10A) inc; gas; Indtte; ice; shops adj; snacks; bar; playgrnd; pool; sand beach 15km; fishing 800m; tennis; games area; entmnt; TV; 20% statics; dogs €1.50; adv bkg; quiet; cc acc; CCI. "Nr m'way en rte to Spain; gd touring area." ♦ 28 Apr-10 Sep. € 19.10 2005*

LUNEL *10E2* (1km SE Rural) **Camping Le Mas de L'Isle, 85 Chemin du Clapas, 34400 Lunel [04 67 83 26 52; fax 04 67 71 13 88]** Foll D34 twd Marsillargues, site sp on R. Lge, hdg/mkd pitch, pt shd; wc; shwrs inc; el pnts (3A); Indtte; rest; snacks; bar; playgrnd; pool; entmnt; 10% statics; dogs €1.50; adv bkg; quiet; red long stay; CCI. "Conv a'route & Camargue; close to supmkts." 1 Apr-31 Aug. 2006*

LUNEL *10E2* (6km SW) **Camping Le Fou du Roi, Chemin des Cotonniers, 34130 Lansargues [04 67 86 78 08; fax 04 67 86 78 06; lefouduroi@ aol.com]** SW fr Lunel on D24 to Lansargues, 100m past vill turn N. Site 50m on R. Med, hdg pitch, pt shd; wc; chem disp; mv service pnt; shwrs inc; el pnts (5A); Indtte; shop; supmkt 4km; snacks; bar; playgrnd; pool; tennis; horseriding; 75% statics; dogs €2.50; poss cr; adv bkg rec high ssn; quiet; CCI. ♦ ltd. 15 Mar-31 Oct. € 13.00 2004*

LUNEVILLE *6E2* (1km NE Urban) **Camping Les Bosquets (formerly Municipal), Chemin de la Ménagerie, 54300 Lunéville [03 83 73 37 58]** Exit N4 Lunéville by-pass sp `Lunéville-Château' & foll sp to Lunéville. Fr traff lts in sq in front of chateau, take rd to L of chateau (Quai des Bosquets). At sm rndabt do not ent site on R but cont round rndabt to L to yard opp warden's house. Warden will open barrier. Sm, mkd pitch, terr, pt shd; wc; chem disp; shwrs inc; el pnts (10-15A) €2.50; Indtte; shops 500m; tradsmn; pool 200m; playgrnd nrby; dogs; some rd noise; CCI. "Many touring pitches; friendly staff; rec visit adj chateau gardens; vg." ♦ 1 Apr-31 Oct. € 8.55   2007*

LURE *6F2* (1.5km SE Urban) **Camp Intercommunal Les Ecuyers, Route de la Saline, 70200 Lure [03 84 30 43 40 or 03 84 89 00 30; fax 03 84 89 00 31; magalie-sarre@pays-delure.fr]** Well sp fr town cent. Med, hdg pitch, unshd; wc; chem disp; shwrs inc; el pnts (6A) inc; Indtte; ice; supmkt 500m; playgrnd; htd, covrd pool 3km; archery; adv bkg; quiet; no cc acc; CCI. "Le Corbusier church worth visit 8km in Ronchamp; vg clean, well-kept site; rec." ♦ 1 Jun-30 Sep. € 10.00   2005*

LUS LA CROIS HAUTE see St Julien en Beauchêne *9D3*

LUSIGNAN *7A2* (N Rural) **Camp Municipal de Vauchiron, Chemin de la Plage Charles Clerc, 86600 Lusignan [05 49 43 30 08 or 05 49 43 31 48 (Mairie); fax 05 49 43 61 19; lusignan@cg86.fr]** Site sp fr D611 (N411), 22km SW of Poitiers; foll camp sp in Lusignan to rvside. Med, pt shd; wc (some cont); own san; shwrs inc; el pnts (16A) €1.77 (poss rev pol); Indry rm; Indtte; ice; shops 1km; tradsmn; snacks, bar adj; playgrnd; rv adj; fishing; boat hire; entmnt; some statics; CCI. 15 Apr-15 Oct. € 6.50   2005*

LUSSAC LES CHATEAUX *7A3* (6km SW) **Camp Municipal du Moulin Beau, 86320 Gouex [05 49 48 46 14; fax 05 48 84 50 01]** Fr Lussac on N147/E62 dir Poitiers & immed turn L on D25; foll sp to Gouex; site on L. Sm, pt shd; wc (some cont); chem disp; shwrs inc; el pnts (15A) €1.60 (check pol); bakery 500m in vill; pool 300m; v quiet; no cc acc; CCI. "Excel site on bank of Rv Vienne; facs v clean but ltd; friendly; bollards at site ent, care needed if van over 7m or twin-axle; highly rec." 15 Jun-15 Sep. € 4.20   2007*

LUSSAC LES CHATEAUX *7A3* (11km SW Rural) **Camp Municipal du Renard, 86150 Queaux [05 49 48 48 32 or 05 49 48 48 08 (Mairie); fax 05 49 48 30 70; contact@queaux.fr; www.queaux.fr]** Fr Lussac cross rv bdge sp Poitiers & immed turn L. Foll sp to Gouex & Queaux. Site on D25 S of vill. Med, mkd pitch, pt sl, pt shd; wc; mv service pnt; shwrs inc; el pnts (6A) €2.50; tradsmn; shops, rest 500m; bar; playgrnd; paddling pool; quiet. "Lovely rvside site nr pleasant vill; manned high ssn or apply to Mairie." 15 Jun-15 Sep. € 5.50   2006*

LUSSAC LES CHATEAUX *7A3* (3km W Rural) **Camp Municipal Mauvillant, 86320 Lussac-les-Châteaux. [tel/fax 05 49 48 03 32]** Fr Lussac on N147/E62 dir Les Poitiers, bef bdge turn L at Municipal sp & foll to site approx 1.5km on L. Site parallel to Rv Vienne. Exit L turn onto N147 can be diff for lge o'fits Med, hdg/mkd pitch, hdstg, pt shd; wc (mainly cont); chem disp; baby facs; shwrs inc; el pnts (10A) inc; Indtte; BBQ; playgrnd; pool nr; rv 200m; no dogs; Eng spkn; adv bkg; quiet; CCI. "Poss resident workers; warden calls 0800-1000 & 1800-2000, if office clsd site yourself & register later; NH only." 1 Jul-15 Oct. € 10.00   2005*

LUYNES see Tours *4G2*

LUZ ST SAUVEUR *8G2* (1km N Rural) **Airotel Camping Pyrénées, 46 Ave du Barège, La Ferme Theil, 65120 Esquièze-Sère [05 62 92 89 18; fax 05 62 92 96 50; airotel.pyrenees@wanadoo.fr; www.airotel-pyrenees.com]** On main rd fr Lourdes to Luz on L past International Campsite. L U-turn into ent archway needs care - use full width of rd & forecourt. Med, mkd pitch, pt sl, pt shd; htd wc (some cont); mv service pnt; chem disp (wc); sauna; shwrs inc; fam bthrm; el pnts (3-10A) €3.50-6.50 (rev pol); gas; ice; Indtte; shop; supmkt 800m; tradsmn, rest & snacks in high ssn; bar; playgrnd; indoor & o'door pools; ski in winter; fishing; walking; horseriding; rafting; TV; entmnts; dogs €1.50; 30% statics; poss cr; quiet but some rd noise; Eng spkn; adv bkg (dep req); site clsd Oct & Nov; cc acc; CCI. "Beautiful area; facs poss stretched high ssn; excel walking & wildlife; lovely vill." ♦ ltd. 1 Dec-30 Sep. € 24.00   2005*

LUZ ST SAUVEUR *8G2* (1.5km N Rural) **Camping International, Route de Barège, 65120 Esquièze-Sère [05 62 92 82 02; fax 05 62 92 96 87; camping.international.luz@wanadoo.fr]** Alongside D921 on E side, clearly sp. Med, pt sl, pt shd; htd wc; chem disp; shwrs; el pnts (2-6A) €1.85-4.90; rest; snacks; gas; ice; shop; htd pool; playgrnd; 30% statics; adv bkg; rd noise; ltd facs low ssn. "Gd walking." ♦ 20 Dec-Easter & 26 May-30 Sep. € 20.50 (CChq acc)   2007*

LUZ ST SAUVEUR *8G2* (500m E Rural) **Camping Le Bergons, Route de Barègas, 65120 Esterre [05 62 92 90 77; abordenave@club-internet.fr]** On D918 to Col du Tourmalet, site on R. Med, pt sl, pt shd; htd wc; shwrs inc; chem disp; el pnts (3A) €3.50; gas; Indtte; ice; shops adj; BBQ; playgrnd; pool 500m; dogs €0.70; rd noise; 10% red long stay/low ssn; CCI. "Excel site; gd facs; helpful owner; conv for Cirque de Garvanie mountain area; ski at Barèges & walking in Pyrenees National Park with cable cars to peaks." ♦ 15 Dec-15 Oct. € 9.15   2004*

LUZ ST SAUVEUR 8G2 (8km E Rural) **Camping La Ribère, 65120 Barèges [tel/fax 05 62 92 69 01 or 06 80 01 29 51 (mob); contact@laribere.com; www.laribere.com]** On N side of rd N618 on edge of Barèges, site sp as 'Camping Caraveneige'. Phone kiosk at ent. Sm, pt sl, pt shd; htd wc ltd; chem disp; shwrs inc; el pnts (6A) €6; lndtte; shops, tradsmn; rest adj; some statics; dogs €0.95; poss cr; quiet. "V friendly staff; gd facs; magnificent views." 5 May-21 Oct. € 12.80   2006*

LUZECH see Castelfranc 7D3

LUZENAC see Ax les Thermes 8G4

LUZERET see Argenton sur Creuse 7A3

LUZY 4H4 (1km N) **Camp Municipal La Bédure, Route d'Autun, 58170 Luzy [03 86 30 02 34 (Mairie)]** Foll sps on N81 to site. Med, mkd pitch, pt sl, pt shd; wc; shwrs; shops 1km; el pnts €1.50 (rev pol); pool adj; quiet. "Pleasant site; gd walking; poss itinerants; gd touring base." 1 Jul-1 Sep. € 6.00   2006*

LUZY 4H4 (7km NE Rural) **Camping Domaine de la Gagère (Naturist), 58170 Luzy [03 86 30 48 11; fax 03 86 30 45 57; info@la-gagere.com; www. la-gagere.com]** Fr Luzy take N81 dir Autun. In 6.5km over rlwy, turn R onto unclassified rd sp 'La Gagère'. Site at end of rd in 3.5km on L. Med, mkd pitch, pt sl, terr, pt shd; wc; chem disp; mv service pnt; child/baby facs; fam bthrm; sauna; shwrs inc; el pnts (6A) €5; gas 10km; lndtte; ice; sm shop & shops 10km; tradsmn; rest; snacks; bar; BBQ; playgrnd; 2 htd pools; lake, shgle beach 12km; TV rm; entmnt; 20% statics; dogs €3.50; bus 10km; phone; poss cr; Eng spkn; adv bkg (dep req); quiet; cc acc; INF card req. "Excel site; gd touring base; excel san facs; v friendly, helpful owners; set in woodlands overlooking beautiful valley on edge of National Park." ♦ 1 Apr-30 Sep. € 16.00   2005*

LUZY 4H4 (2km SW Rural) **Camping Château de Chigy, 58170 Tazilly [03 86 30 10 80; fax 03 86 30 09 22; reception@chateaudechigy.com. fr; www.chateaudechigy.com.fr]** Fr Luzy take D973 S twd Bourbon-Lancy, in 4km turn L on minor rd sp Chigy, site sp. Fr S turn R onto rd to Chigy. Site is E of D973 - do not take sp rd to Tazilly vill. V lge, pt sl, pt terr, pt shd; wc; chem disp; baby facs; shwrs inc; private san facs some pitches; el pnts (6A) €3.50; gas; lndtte; rest, snacks (high ssn); bar; playgrnd; pool; paddling pool; fishing; games area; entmnt; TV; some statics; dogs €1.50; adv bkg; quiet; red long stay/snr citizens; CCI. ♦ 29 Apr-30 Sep. € 22.35   2006*

LYON 9B2 (12km E Rural) **Camping Le Grand Large, Rue Victor Hugo, 69330 Meyzieu [04 78 31 42 16; fax 04 72 45 91 78; camping. grand.large@wanadoo.fr]** Exit N346 junc 6, E onto D6 dir Jonage. In approx 2 km turn L twd Le Grand Large (lake), site in 1km. Lge, pt shd; wc (most cont); chem disp; mv service pnt; shwrs inc; el pnts (5A) inc; gas; lndtte; ice; shop 2km; snacks; pool 2km; lake sw adj; boating, fishing in lake; games area; entmnt; TV; 90% statics; dogs €1; bus 1km; poss cr; quiet; adv bkg; cc acc; CCI. "Direct access big lake with sm beach; minimal, poss scruffy san facs; stn 2km for trains to Lyon; fair." 1 Apr-31 Oct. € 17.70 (3 persons)   2007*

⊞**LYON** 9B2 (10km SW Urban) **Camping des Barolles, 88 Ave Foch, 69230 St Genis-Laval [04 78 56 05 56; fax 04 72 67 95 01]** Exit A7 at Pierre-Bénite cent onto A450 & exit at Basses Barolles; foll sp. Or fr D42 to St Genis-Laval cent main sq (Place Joffre) then take Ave Foch SW to site. Poorly sp. Sm, hdstg, terr, pt shd; wc (own san rec); shwrs; el pnts (6-10A) €3.30-6.90; gas; lndtte; ice; snacks; bar; playgrnd; dogs €2; quiet. "Ungated; poss itinerants; recep unreliable opening; NH only." € 14.50   2006*

⊞**LYON** 9B2 (8km NW) **Camping Indigo Lyon, La Porte de Lyon, 69570 Dardilly [04 78 35 64 55; fax 04 72 17 04 26; lyon@camping-indigo.com; www. camping-indigo.com]** Fr D306 (N6) Paris rd, take Limonest-Dardilly-Porte de Lyon exit at Auchan supmkt. Fr A6 exit junc 33 Porte de Lyon. Site on W side of A6 adj m'way & close to junc, foll sp (poss obscured by trees) for 'Complexe Touristique'. Fr E take N ring rd dir Roanne, Paris, then as above. Lge, hdg/mkd pitch, hdstg, pt shd; htd wc; chem disp; mv service pnt; serviced pitches; mv service pnt; baby facs; shwrs inc; el pnts (10A) €4-6; gas 100m; lndtte; hypmkt 200m; rest, bar 100m; playgrnd; pool; games rm; TV rm; some statics; dogs €2.40; phone; bus/train to city nr; extra for twin-axle c'vans; Eng spkn; adv bkg; quiet but some rd noise; cc acc; CCI. "Poorly managed site (2007); Lyon easily accessible by bus & metro; gd touring base for interesting area." ♦ € 17.65 (CChq acc)   2007*

LYONS LA FORET 3D2 (500m NE Rural) **FFCC Camp Municipal St Paul, 27480 Lyons-la-Forêt [02 32 49 42 02; camping-saint-paul@wanadoo.fr]** Fr Rouen E on N31/E46 for 33km; at La Feuillie, S on D921/321 for 8km; site on L at ent to town adj Rv Lieure. Med, hdg pitch, pt shd; htd wc; chem disp; shwrs inc; el pnts (6A) inc (poss rev pol); lndtte; shops 1km; tradsmn; rest, snacks, bar 1km; playgrnd; pool adj; fishing; tennis; horseriding; poss cr; 55% statics; dogs €1; adv bkg; quiet; 15% red 7+ days; CCI. "Gd site but liable to flood after heavy rain; lge pitches; facs poss inadequate for site size & ltd low ssn; Lyons-la-Forêt lovely half-timbered town, conv Dieppe ferry; walking & cycling in forested area, gd tour base." 1 Apr-31 Oct. € 17.00   2007*

MACHE see Aizenay 2H4

MACHECOUL 2H4 (500m SE Urban) **Camp Municipal La Rabine, Allée de la Rabine, 44270 Machecoul [tel/fax 02 40 02 30 48; camprabine@ wanadoo.fr]** Sp fr all dirs. Med, pt shd; wc; chem disp; shwrs €0.90; el pnts (4-13A) €1.95-3.15; lndtte; shops 500m; tradsmn; BBQ (gas only) playgrnd; pool adj; sand beach 14km; entmnt; some statics; dogs €0.80; adv bkg; quiet. "V nice site with lge pitches & gd facs; excel base for birdwatching & cycling over marshes; pleasant town; mkt Wed & Sat." 15 Apr-30 Sep. € 7.00   2006*

MACON 9A2 (3km N Urban) **Camp Municipal Les Varennes, 71000 Mâcon [03 85 38 16 22 or 03 85 38 54 08; fax 03 85 39 39 18]** A6 fr S exit Mâcon Sud, thro town on main rd. Pass Auchan hypmkt on L, turn R immed after petrol stn, opp fire stn. Site sp. Fr A40, exit junc 1 & foll sp. Fr N on A6 exit junc 28 & cont S on N6 twd Mâcon. Site on L in approx 3km, sp. Lge, mkd pitch, pt sl, pt shd; htd wc (some cont); chem disp; mv service pnt; shwrs inc; el pnts (6A) inc (rev pol) extra for 10A; gas; lndtte; ice; shop; supmkt nr; hypmkt 1km; rest; snacks; bar; playgrnd; 2 pools; tennis 1km; golf 6km; TV; dogs €0.75; phone; poss cr; Eng spkn; adv bkg; quiet but some noise fr rds & rlwy; cc acc; red 6+ days; CCI. "Well-maintained, busy, cosmopolitan NH nr A6; rec arr early as poss full after 1800; friendly staff; excel rest; superb facs; gd value; gates clsd 2200-0630; poss flooding bottom end of site; twin-axles extra." ♦ 15 Mar-31 Oct. € 14.70   2007*

MACON 9A2 (8km S Rural) **Camp Municipal du Port d'Arciat, Route du Port d'Arciat, 71680 Crêches-sur-Saône [03 85 36 57 91 or 03 85 37 48 32 (LS); fax 03 85 36 51 57; camping-creches.sur.saone@wanadoo.fr; http://membres. lycos.fr/campingduportdarciat]** S fr Mâcon on N6 to Crêches-sur-Saône. Site well sp at 3rd set of traff lts in cent vill on N6, turn E, cross m'way bdge; site on R by rv, sp on rndabt. NB Adj rv bdge has 2.6m height limit. Lge, mkd pitch, pt sl, pt shd; wc (some cont); chem disp; mv service pnt; shwrs inc; el pnts (6A) €3.15; gas; lndtte; ice; shop; supmkt 1km; rest; snacks; bar; playgrnd; pool 1km; lake sw, fishing & boating; entmnt; dogs €1.25; poss cr; gates clsd 2200-0700; some Eng spkn; adv bkg; some noise fr a'route & rlwy; cc acc; CCI. 'Lge pitches; gd facs; gd." ♦ 15 May-15 Sep. € 10.20   2007*

MADIRAN 8F2 (Urban) **Camp Municipal Le Madiran, Route de Vignoble, 65700 Madiran [tel/ fax 05 62 31 92 83 or 06 84 67 26 13 (mob); irma. hofstede@wanadoo.fr]** S fr Riscle on D935 after approx 12km turn R onto D58 to Madiran. Site in middle of town. Sm, mkd pitch, pt sl, unshd; wc; chem disp; shwrs inc; el pnts €2.30; gas, shop, snacks, bar 50m; playgrnd; pool; dogs; Eng spkn; quiet; cc acc; CCI. "Excel site; friendly Dutch warden with gd Eng & extensive knowledge of local wine area." ♦ 15 Jun-30 Aug. € 9.00   2005*

MAGNAC BOURG 7B3 (Urban) **FFCC Camp Municipal Les Ecureuils, 87380 Magnac-Bourg [05 55 00 80 28 (Mairie); fax 05 55 00 49 09; mairie.magnac-bourg@wanadoo.fr]** Leave A20 at junc 41 sp Magnac-Bourg; foll sps to site in vill. Site behind town hall. Sm, pt sl, some hdg pitch, pt shd; wc; shwrs inc; el pnts (5A) €3; supmkt, petrol & rest nr; playgrnd; fishing 2km; CCI. "Quiet & peaceful; coded barrier access if arr at lunchtime; warden calls at 1600; mkt Sat am; gd." 1 Apr-30 Sep. € 9.60   2006*

MAGNIERES 6E2 (Rural) **Camping du Pré Fleury, 54129 Magnières [03 83 72 34 73]** Fr N333 exit junc 4 S onto D914 to Magnières. Site sp. Or on D22 fr Bayon or Baccarat go to Magnières. Site sp. Sm, mkd pitch, hdstg, pt sl, pt shd; wc; chem disp; mv service pnt; shwrs inc; el pnts (10A) €2.50; lndtte; shops 1km; rest, bar adj; playgrnd; fishing; quiet. "Gd site for touring Vosges; gd cycling, birdwatching, walks." ♦ € 7.00   2004*

⊞**MAICHE** 6G3 (1km S Rural) **Camp Municipal St Michel, 23 Rue St Michel, 25120 Maîche [03 81 64 12 56 or 03 81 64 03 01 (Mairie); fax 03 81 64 12 56; camping.maiche@wanadoo.fr; www.mairie-maiche.fr]** Fr S turn R off D437 onto D442. App on D464 L on o'skts of town. Sp fr both dir. Med, hdstg, sl, terr, pt shd; htd wc; chem disp; shwrs inc; el pnts (6A) €2.40; lndry rm + dryer; shops 1km; playgrnd; pool adj; 10% statics; dogs; phone; site clsd 3rd week Nov & Dec; adv bkg; rd noise. "Attractive with gd views & walks in woods; clean, well-run site & facs; phone ahead low ssn to check open." ♦ € 9.80   2006*

MAICHE 6G3 (10km SW Rural) **Camp Municipal Les Sorbiers, Rue Foch, 25210 Le Russey [03 81 43 75 86]** On D437 Maîche-Morteau, 1st R after vill church, site sp on L in 250m. Sm, hdstg, pt shd; htd wc (men cont); chem disp; shwrs €2; el pnts (10A) €2.55; gas; lndtte; ice; shop 1km; rest, snacks, bar 500m; playgrnd; tennis; games rm; 20% statics; adv bkg; quiet; cc not acc. "Excel cent for superb Doubs scenery; high altitude, poss cold nights." 15 Jun-15 Sep. € 6.10   2006*

MAILLE see Maillezais 7A2

MAILLERAYE SUR SEINE, LA see Caudebec en Caux 3C2

MAILLEZAIS 7A2 (Rural) **Camp Municipal de l'Autize, Route de Maillé, 85420 Maillezais [06 31 43 21 33 (mob); fax 02 51 87 29 63; mairie-maillezais@wanadoo.fr; www.maillezais.fr]** Fr Fontenay take D148 twd Niort; after 9km, turn R onto D15 to Maillezais; at church in vill on L, site on R after 200m. Sm, hdg pitch, pt shd; wc; chem disp; shwrs inc; el pnts (5A) €5; lndtte; shops 200m; playgrnd; games area; games rm; TV: 30% statics; adv bkg; quiet; cc not acc; CCI. "Lovely, clean site; spacious pitches; €23 supplement charge for twin-axles; excel san facs, inc for disabled; warden calls am & pm; conv Marais Poitevin area." ♦ 1 Apr-30 Sep. € 9.00   2007*

France

Les îlots de St Val

Caravaning de loisir ★★★ NN

28130 Villiers le Morhier
Tel.: 02 37 82 71 30 - Fax: 02 37 82 77 67

5 km. NW of Maintenon. This calm family site lies on a flat area of 10 ha., with 150 shady and level touring pitches of 120 sq. m., with interesting touristy sites in the surroundings. Within 4 km.: shops, golf course, swimming pool, tennis, fishing in the river (1 km) and pond, pony club, visits to the Castles, the historic city of Chartres and the famous Cathedral, the Royal Chapel in Dreux at 20 km. 5% discount for club card holders, except for rental accommodation

GPS coordinates:
long 1,5476°
lat 48,6089°

1 hour away from Paris by car or train

open all year

www.campinglesilotsdestval.com • e-mail : lesilots@campinglesilotsdestval.com

MAILLEZAIS *7A2* (6km S Rural) **FFCC Camping Les Conches, Le Grand Port, 85420 Damvix** [tel/fax 02 51 87 17 06] Fr Fontenay-le-Comte exit D148 at Benet then W on D25 thro Le Mazeau to sp on L for Damvix. Or exit A83 junc 8 then S on D938 & E on D25 dir Benet. Site 1km thro vill on R over bdge (sp). Med, mkd, shd; wc; chem disp; mv service pnt; shwrs; el pnts (6-8A) €2.50; lndry rm; shops adj; rest adj; playgrnd; pool; tennis; golf; horseriding; rv fishing & boating adj; pedaloes & canoes for hire; dogs €1; adv bkg rec; quiet but some noise fr disco opp high ssn; CCI. "Gd rest; friendly staff; gd cycling." 1 Jun-15 Sep. € 10.00   2006*

MAILLEZAIS *7A2* (5km SW Rural) **Camp Municipal La Petite Cabane, 85420 Maillé** [02 51 87 05 78 (Mairie); fax 02 51 87 02 48; mairiedemaille@wanadoo.fr] Site is 500m W of Maillé, clearly sp. Sm, pt shd; wc; shwrs inc; el pnts (6-15A) inc; gas 500m; lndry rm; shops 500m; playgrnd; paddling pool; boat & canoe hire; adv bkg; quiet; CCI. "Site by canal in cent of Marais Poitevin National Park; gd cycle rtes." 1 Apr-30 Sep. € 11.00   2005*

MAILLY LE CHATEAU *4G4* (S Rural) **Camp Municipal Le Pré du Roi, Pertuis des Bouchets, 89660 Mailly-le-Château** [03 86 81 44 85 or 03 86 81 40 37 (Mairie); fax 03 86 81 40 37; mairie-maillylechateau@wanadoo.fr] NW on N6 fr Avallon twd Auxerre, turn W in Voutenay-sur-Cure on D950 to Mailly-la-Ville. Cross bdge twd Mailly-le-Château, site sp. Heading S fr Auxerre, turn R off N6 SE of Vincelles on D100 to Bazarnes & Mailly-le-Château. Med, mkd pitch, pt shd; wc; shwrs; el pnts (20A) €3; shops 2km; fishing; dogs; quiet. "Pleasant, peaceful situation by Rv Yonne; gd san facs." 25 May-3 Sep. € 8.40   2007*

MAILLY LE CHATEAU *4G4* (5km S Rural) **Camp Municipal Escale, 5 Impasse de Sables, 89660 Merry-sur-Yonne** [03 86 81 01 60; fax 03 86 81 06 14; gite.merrysuryonne@wanadoo.fr] Fr Auxerre, take N151. Turn E onto D21 at Coulanges. Thro Châtel-Censoir turn L over rv into Merry-sur-Yonne. Site sp. Med, mkd pitch, hdstg, pt shd; wc; mv service pnt (some cont); shwrs €2; el pnts (10A) €4; gas; lndtte; shop 5km; rest, bar 500m; rv sw adj; canoe hire, fishing; tennis; dogs €1; phone; quiet; CCI. "Gd site; poss children's groups in adj gite." ♦ ltd. 10 Apr-15 Oct. € 6.70   2007*

⊞**MAINTENON** *4E2* (5km NW Rural) **Camping Les Ilots de St Val, 28130 Villiers-le-Morhier** [02 37 82 71 30; fax 02 37 82 77 67; lesilots@campinglesilotsdestval.com; www.campinglesilotsdestval.com] Take D983 N fr Maintenon twd Nogent-le-Roi, in 5km 2nd L onto D101 sp Néron/Vacheresses-les-Basses/Camping to site in 1km on L at top of hill. NB App fr N on D929 not rec as rds in Nogent-le-Roi narr. Lge, some hdg/mkd pitch, hdstg, pt shd; htd wc; chem disp; baby facs; shwrs inc; el pnts (6-10A) €3.70-6; gas; lndtte; shops 4km; tradsmn; BBQ; playgrnd; pool 4km; rv sw & fishing 1km; tennis; 70% statics; dogs €1.50; train 4km; little Eng spkn; adv bkg; quiet but aircraft noise; red CCI. "V pleasant, peaceful site in open countryside; lge private pitches; some superb, modern san facs, others v dated but clean; helpful staff; take care electrics; muddy after rain; poss itinerants low ssn; conv NH; conv Chartres, Versailles, Maintenon Château & train to Paris." ♦ € 15.60   2007*

See advertisement

MAISONS LAFFITTE see Paris *3D3*

MALARCE SUR LA THINES see Vans, Les *9D1*

MALAUCENE *10E2* (Rural) **Camping Le Bosquet, Route de Suzette, 84340 Malaucène** [04 90 65 24 89 or 04 90 65 29 09; fax 04 90 65 12 52; camping.lebosquet@wanadoo.fr; www.guideweb.com/provence/camping/bosquet] Fr D938 N dir Vaison-la-Romaine turn L onto D90 at Malaucène dir Suzette. Site on R in 300m. Sm, hdg pitch, all hdstg, terr, pt shd; wc; shwrs inc; el pnts (10A) €2.80 (poss rev pol); gas; Indtte; ice; shop 600m; tradsmn; snacks; bar; playgrnd; pool; 2% statics; dogs free; phone; adv bkg; quiet; cc not acc; CCI. "Clean san facs; friendly owner; gd base for touring area & climbing Mt Ventoux." ♦ 1 Apr-30 Sep. € 14.60   2007*

MALAUCENE *10E2* (4km N Rural) **Camping Aire Naturelle La Saousse (Letilleul), La Madelaine, 84340 Malaucène** [04 90 65 14 02] Fr Malaucène take D938 N dir Vaison-la-Romaine & after 3km turn R onto D13 dir Entrechaux where site sp. After 1km turn R,site 1st on R. Sm, hdg pitch, terr, shd; wc; chem disp; shwrs inc; el pnts (5A) €2.20; Indry rm; tradsmn high ssn; shop, rest, snacks, bar, pool 4km; no statics; dogs; adv bkg rec; quiet; cc not acc; CCI. "CL-type site o'looking vineyards with views to Mt Ventoux; some pitches in woods with steep incline to reach; basic, clean facs; friendly, helpful owners; rec pitch on lower level for easy access; excel." 1 Apr-30 Oct. € 13.90   2007*

MALAUCENE *10E2* (8km S Rural) **Camping Le Bouquier, Route de Malaucène, 84330 Caromb** [tel/fax 04 90 62 30 13; lebouquier@wanadoo. fr; www.lebouquier.com] NE fr Carpentras on D974 then D13; site on R 1.5km after Caromb cent. Fr Malaucène S on D938 for 8km; turn L D13 sp Caromb. Site 800m on L just bef vill. Med, hdg/mkd pitch, hdstg, terr, pt shd, htd wc; chem disp; shwrs inc; el pnts (10A) €3; Indtte; ice; shops 1.5km; tradsmn; snacks; bar; BBQ (gas/elec); playgrnd; htd pool; lake sw 1km; gd walking/cycling; 5% statics; dogs; phone; poss cr; Eng spkn; adv bkg (dep req); quiet but some rd noise; CCI. "Well-kept site; attractive scenery; gd touring base; spotless san facs; steps to disabled facs; no twin-axles; vg." ♦ ltd. 31 Mar-15 Oct. € 15.00   2007*

MALBUISSON *6H2* (S Urban) **Camping Les Fuvettes, 25160 Malbuisson** [03 81 69 31 50; fax 03 81 69 70 46; les-fuvettes@wanadoo.fr; www. camping-fuvettes.com] Site 19km S of Pontarlier on N57 & D437 to Malbuisson, thro town, R down rd to Plage. Lge, pt shd; htd wc (some cont); shwrs inc; el pnts (4A) €3.40; gas; Indtte; ice; shop; rest; snacks; bar; playgrnd; shgl beach for lake sw; fishing; boating; 30% statics; dogs €1,50; poss cr; quiet; CCI. "Site alongside lake; mkd walks/cycle paths in adj woods." 1 Apr-30 Sep. € 21.00
2006*

MALBUISSON *6H2* (2km S Rural) **Camping du Lac, 10 Rue du Lac, 25160 Labergement-Ste Marie** [03 81 69 31 24; camping.lac.remoray@wanadoo. fr; www.camping-lac-remoray.com] Exit N57/E23 junc 2 onto D437 thro vill & turn L onto D9 then R to site, sp. Site 300m fr Lake Remoray. Med, mkd pitch, pt shd; wc; chem disp; baby facs; shwrs inc; el pnts (6A) €3.20; gas; Indtte; ice; tradsmn; rest; snacks; bar; playgrnd; beach adj; fishing; walking; cycling; sports area; internet; 10% statics; dogs €1.30; Eng spkn; adv bkg; quiet; cc acc; CCI. "Quiet location with forest views; v kind & helpful owner; excel, roomy site; v clean san facs; vill 500m with gd shops; castles, museums nrby; vg." ♦ 1 May-30 Sep. € 14.50   2006*

MALEMORT DU COMTAT see Carpentras *10E2*

⊞**MALESHERBES** *4E3* (5km S Rural) **FFCC Camping Ile de Boulancourt, 6 Allée des Marronniers, 77760 Boulancourt** [01 64 24 13 38; fax 01 64 24 10 43; camping-ile-de-boulancourt@ wanadoo.fr] Exit A6 at junc 14 Ury & Fontainebleau. SW on N152 to Malesherbes; S on D410 for 5km into Boulancourt. Site sp fr D410 & in vill. Med, pt shd; htd wc (some cont); chem disp; mv service pnt; shwrs inc; el pnts (3-6A) €2; Indtte; ice; shop 3km; rest; BBQ; playgrnd; pool nr; tennis; rv adj; fishing 3km; waterslide 5km; 80% statics; dogs €1; sep field for tourers; Eng spkn; quiet; red low ssn; CCI. "V friendly, helpful staff; attractive rv thro site; golf course in vill; ltd facs low ssn; excel." € 12.50
2006*

MALESTROIT *2F3* (500m E Urban) **Camp Municipal de la Daufresne, Chemin des Tanneurs, 56140 Malestroit** [02 97 75 13 33 or 02 97 75 11 75 (Mairie); fax 02 97 75 06 68; tourisme@malestroit.com; www.malestroit.com] S fr Ploërmel on N166 dir Vannes for 9km. Turn L onto D764 to Malestroit; site sp just off D776 on E bank of Rv Oust. Sm, some hdg pitch, pt shd; wc; chem disp; mv service pnt; shwrs; el pnts (6A) €2.40; Indry rm; shop, rest, snacks, bar 300m; playgrnd; tennis; adv bkg; rv & fishing adj; canoeing nr; CCI. "Great little site in excel location; pleasant, peaceful; spotless facs; v helpful warden; no twin-axle vans; facs stretched high ssn." 1 May-15 Sep. € 6.50   2006*

MALICORNE SUR SARTHE *4F1* (Urban) **Camp Municipal Porte Ste Marie, 72270 Malicorne-sur-Sarthe** [02 43 94 80 14; fax 02 43 94 57 26; mairie. malicorne@wanadoo.fr; www.ville-malicorne.fr] Fr A11/E501 take D306 exit twds La Flèche. Site E onto D23 twds Malicorne. Site across rv on W of town adj stadium. Med, pt shd; wc; chem disp; mv service pnt, shwrs inc; el pnts (4-13A) €1.45-2.50; Indtte; ice; shops, rest, bar 500m; BBQ; playgrnd; pool; tennis adj; dogs €0.50; poss cr; quiet; red low ssn; "Quiet position by rv; gd san facs & Indry facs; no access when recep clsd 1230-1430 & after 1930; poss noise (church bell); no waiting area; diff turning; gd." 1 Apr-31 Oct. € 8.70   2006*

France

MALLEMORT see Salon de Provence *10E2*

⊞**MAMERS** *4E1* (500m N Rural) **Camp Municipal du Saosnois (formerly Camp Municipal La Grille), Route de Contilly, 72600 Mamers [02 43 97 68 30; fax 02 43 97 38 65; camping.mamers@free.fr; www.tourisme-mamers-saosnois.com]** Sp fr D311 (Alençon rd). Best app fr turn to N on N o'skts of town. Foll sp fr E app thro town bit tricky. Sm, hdg pitch, pt sl, terr, pt shd; htd wc; mv service pnt; shwrs inc; el pnts (10A) €2.50 (long lead poss req); lndtte; shop & 500m; snacks; pool 200m; lakeside beach; games area; TV rm; 30% statics; dogs €0.50; poss cr; adv bkg; quiet. "Well-kept, secure site; admittance low ssn 1700-1900 only; Mamers pretty; poss itinerants." ♦ € 7.80
2005*

MANDEURE *6G3* (500m NW Urban) **Camping Les Grands Ansanges, Rue de l'Eglise, 25350 Mandeure [03 81 35 23 79; fax 03 81 30 09 26; ville.mandeure@wanadoo.fr; www.ville-mandeure.com]** Exit A36 sp Exincourt, site sp fr cent Mandeure, adj Rv Doubs. Med, mkd pitch, pt shd; wc; chem disp; shwrs inc; el pnts (4-10A); lndry rm; sm shop; tradsmn; rest; bar; playgrnd; games rm; archery & golf nrby; 10% statics; poss cr; CCI. "Faces open farmland; site barrier operated by token; helpful staff; not suitable disabled as san facs up steps." 1 Apr-31 Oct. € 8.00
2006*

MANDRES AUX QUATRE TOURS *5D2* (1.5km S Rural) **Camp Municipal Orée de la Forêt de la Reine, Route Forêt de la Reine, 54470 Mandres-aux-Quatre-Tours [03 83 23 17 31]** On D958 Commercy to Pont-à-Mousson, sp as Camping Mandres. Turn R at sp in Beaumont & foll sp to vill Mandres-aux-Quatre-Tours. Sm, mkd/hdg pitch, pt shd; wc; chem disp (wc); shwrs inc; el pnts (10A) inc; ice; tradsmn; playgrnd; tennis; mini-golf; watersports, sailing 500m; horseriding adj; some statics; dogs; quiet; CCI. "Gd, peaceful NH; warden calls 0800-1000 & 1800-1900; clean facs but need update; site poss muddy in wet weather; lovely scenery nr Lac de Madine; gd birdwatching, walking, cycling." 1 Apr-31 Oct. € 7.80
2006*

MANOSQUE *10E3* (8.5km NE Rural) **Camp Municipal de la Vandelle, Chemin de Pietramal, 04130 Volx [04 92 79 35 85 or 04 92 70 18 00; fax 04 92 79 32 27; infos@camping-volx.com; www.camping-volx.com]** Fr N96 (Aix-Sisteron) turn W at traff lts in Volx, foll sp to site in 1km. Sm, pt sl, terr, pt shd; htd wc; shwrs inc; el pnts (3A) €3.40; lndtte; shops 1.3km; playgrnd; sm pool; paddling pool; games area; entmnt; dogs free; adv bkg; quiet. ♦ 1 May-30 Sep. € 10.00
2007*

MANOSQUE *10E3* (1.5km W) **FFCC Camping Les Ubacs, 1138 Ave de la Repasse, 04100 Manosque [04 92 72 28 08; fax 04 92 87 75 29; lesubacs.manosque@ffcc.fr; www.camp-in-france.com]** Exit A51 junc 18 onto D907 dir Manosque; then D907 dir Apt; site sp at last rndabt on W side of Manosque. NB easy to overshoot. Med, hdg/mkd pitch, pt shd; wc (cont); mv service pnt; shwrs inc; el pnts (3-9A) €3.45-4.20; lndtte; shop; rest, snacks (high ssn); bar; playgrnd; pool (high ssn); tennis; lake sw 5km; entmnt; dogs €1; cc acc; red long stay/low ssn/CCI. "Conv Gorges du Verdon; helpful." 1 Apr-30 Sep. € 12.65
2007*

MANS, LE *4F1* (9km N Rural) **FFCC Camping Le Vieux Moulin, 72190 Neuville-sur-Sarthe [02 43 25 31 82; fax 02 43 25 38 11; vieux.moulin@wanadoo.fr]** Leave N138 6km N of Le Mans at St Saturnin; turn E onto D197 to Neuville & foll sp for 3km to site. Med, pt shd, hdg/mkd pitch, serviced pitch; wc (some cont); chem disp; mv service pnt; baby facs; shwrs inc; el pnts (10A) €3 (poss rev pol); gas; lndtte; sm shop (high ssn) & 500m; tradsmn; rest adj; playgrnd; sm htd pool; tennis; mini-golf; 5% statics; dogs €1; Eng spkn; adv bkg; quiet; 20% red low ssn; cc acc; 5-10% red CCI. "Lge, well-grassed pitches; friendly, helpful British owner; sm lake & water-mill/rest adj; 5 mins walk to Rv Sarthe; peaceful setting; gd simple hotel rest in vill; clean san facs; gates clsd 2200-0730; highly rec." 1 Jul-31 Aug. € 13.00
2006*

MANSAC see Brive la Gaillarde *7C3*

MANSIGNE *4F1* (Rural) **Camp Municipal de la Plage, Route du Plessis, 72510 Mansigne [02 43 46 14 17 or 02 43 46 10 33 (Mairie); fax 02 43 46 16 65; camping-mansigne@wanadoo.fr; www.ville-mansigne.fr]** N fr Le Lude on D307 to Pontvallain. Take D13 E for 5km to Mansigne, thro vill & foll site sp. Lge, pt shd; wc; chem disp; shwrs inc; el pnts (10A) inc; lndtte; shop 200m; rest; pool; sand beach adj; lake sw adj; dogs €1.45; adv bkg; quiet; red long stay; CCI. "Conv for Loir Valley & Le Mans 24-hour race; v ltd facs & office hrs low ssn." ♦ Easter-15 Oct. € 9.60
2006*

MANSLE *7B2* (NE Urban) **Camp Municipal Le Champion, 16230 Mansle [05 45 20 31 41 or 05 45 22 20 43; fax 05 45 22 86 30; mairie. mansle@wanadoo.fr]** N on N10 fr Angoulême, foll sp Mansle Ville. Leave N10 at exit to N of town, site rd on L, well sp. Rec ent/leave fr N as rte thro town diff due to parked cars. Site beside Rv Charente. Med, mkd pitch, pt shd; wc; chem disp; mv service pnt; shwrs inc; el pnts (16A) €2.50 (poss long lead req); gas in town; lndtte; shops 200m; shop 800m; rest; snacks, bar adj; BBQ; playgrnd; rv sw & boating adj; fishing; mini-golf; entmnt; 5% statics; phone; poss cr; quiet but some rd noise; adv bkg; phone 1km; Eng spkn; cc not acc; CCI. "Well-maintained; lge pitches; immac san facs; choose own pitch; gd rest & bar adj; sm mkt Tues, Fri am; popular, peaceful NH nr N10." ♦ 15 May-15 Sep. € 8.60
2006*

Camping ★★★ Loisirs des Groux

78270 Mousseaux sur Seine
Phone: 00 33 (0)1 34 79 33 86

45 minutes from Paris by A13 : visit of the capital and the Palace of Versailles.

45 minutes from Rouen by A13 : visit of "the town of 100 bell-towers".

15 minutes from Giverny : the road of the impressionists — Monet museum.

At 500 meters : leisure park close to pool and golf 18 holes.

www.loisirsdesgroux.com • infos@loisirsdesgroux.com

France

MANSLE 7B2 (8km NE Rural) **Camp Municipal Le Magnerit, Les Maisons Rouges, 16460 Aunac** [05 45 22 24 38; fax 05 45 22 23 17] N on N10 fr Mansle, exit onto D27 to Bayers & Aunac. Site 1km SE vill, well sp. Sm, pt shd; wc; chem disp; shwrs; el pnts (8A) €2; shop 1km; playgrnd; rv sw adj; fishing; quiet; CCI. "Warden visits; peaceful CL-type site beside Rv Charente; facs ltd but v clean & well-kept; quiet, simple, rural site; vg NH." 15 Jun-15 Sep. € 7.30   2007*

⊞**MANSLE** 7B2 (10km SE Rural) **Camping Devezeau, 16230 St Angeau [tel/fax 05 45 39 21 29; bookings@campingdevezeau. com; www.devezeaucamping.com]** N or S on N10 exit Mansle; in cent vill at traff lts foll sp twd La Rochefoucauld (D6); past Champion supmkt; over bdge; 1st R onto D6. In approx 9km at T-junc turn R, site sp. App down narr rd. Sm, hdstg, pt sl, pt shd; wc; chem disp; 20% serviced pitches; shwrs inc; el pnts (10A) €2; ice; gas; lndtte; shop 1.5km; tradsmn; supmkt in Mansle; rest 5km; snacks & bar 1.5km; BBQ; playgrnd; htd pool; cycling; walking; canoeing; golf 20 mins; fishing; horseriding; 10% statics; no dogs; phone 1km; Eng spkn; adv bkg (dep req); quiet; CCI. "Excel CL-type site; facs exceptionally clean; poss electrics probs; v friendly British owners; traction diff in wet (4x4 avail); gd cycling country; phone ahead in winter." ◆ ltd. € 18.00   2006*

MANTENAY MONTLIN 9A2 (400m W Rural) **Camp Municipal du Coq, 01560 Mantenay-Montlin [04 74 52 66 91or 04 74 52 61 72 (Mairie)]** Exit A40 junc 5 Bourg-en-Bresse Nord onto D975 to Mantenay-Montlin; site sp in vill on D46. Or exit A39 junc 10 to St Trivier-de-Courtes, then S to Mantenay. Sm, hdg/mkd pitch, pt shd; wc; chem disp; shwrs inc; el pnts (6A) €1.70; shop, rest & bar 400m; playgrnd; tennis; dogs €1; bus 400m; quiet; red long stay; cc acc. "Vg rvside site in pretty area; lge pitches; san facs old but clean; warden calls pm; conv NH just off D975." 1 Jun-15 Sep. € 7.50   2007*

MANTES 3D2 (12km NW Rural) **Camping Loisirs des Groux, Chemin de Vetheuil, 78270 Mousseaux-sur-Seine** [01 34 79 33 86; infos@ loisirsdesgroux.com; www.loisirsdesgroux.com] Fr Rouen exit A13 junc 15 onto N13 dir Bonnières. At x-rds with N15 (offset junc) turn R, then L dir Bonnières. Cont thro Bonnières & past commercial cent dir Rolleboise. Turn L at next traff lts onto D37 sp Parc de Loisirs & strt at rndabt onto D124/ D125 dir Mousseaux. Strt at x-rds, site sp at next R. Fr Paris exit A13 junc 13 onto N13 dir Bonnières, N fr Rolleboise on N13 dir Mousseaux, turn R at traff lts onto D37, then as above. Med, hdg/mkd pitch, pt shd; wc (some cont); shwrs inc; mv service pnt; chem disp; el pnts (10A) €1.90; lndtte; BBQ; leisure cent 500m; lake sw & beach 500m; games area; entmnt; 90% statics; dogs; Eng spkn; adv bkg rec; CCI. "Quiet, leafy site; basic, well-maintained san facs; gates locked at 2130 - given key for late entry; friendly, helpful staff; adv bkg rec high ssn; ltd touring pitches; excel walks or cycling along Seine; conv Paris (65km), Versailles, Rouen, Monet's garden at Giverny; gd." ◆ 1 Apr-30 Nov. € 14.20   2007*

See advertisement

As soon as we get home I'm going to post all these site report forms to the editor for inclusion in next year's guide. I don't want to miss the September deadline.

⊞**MANTES** 3D2 (14km NW) **Camping Le Criquet, 42 Rue du Criquet, 78840 Freneuse [tel/fax 01 30 93 07 95; www.camping-le-criquet.fr]** Fr N15 at Bonnières to Freneuse on D37. Thro vill, site sp at end of vill past cemetary. Lge, pt shd; wc; chem disp; shwrs €2.10; el pnts (10A) €2.70; BBQ; playgrnd; games area; mainly statics; adv bkg; quiet. "Monet's garden 12km; pitches poss unkempt low ssn." € 11.40   2007*

MARANS *7A1* (2km N Rural) Camp Municipal Le Bois Dinot, Route de Nantes, 17230 Marans [05 46 01 10 51; fax 05 46 01 01 72; campingboisdinot.marans@wanadoo.fr; www.ville-marans.fr] Heading S, site on L of D137 bef ent Marans. Heading N, site is well sp on R 300m after supmkt on L. Lge, shd; wc; shwrs inc; el pnts (10A) €3; shops adj; rest, snacks, bar 200m; pool adj; fishing; dogs €1; Eng spkn; poss cr; some rd noise; 7+ days/low ssn; CCI. "V clean, well-kept site; quieter pitches at back of site; helpful warden; recep open 1000-1300 & 1500-2000; mkt Tues, Sat; gd cycling area; excel." 1 Apr-30 Sep. € 10.90
2007*

MARCENAY *6F1* (1km N Rural) Camping Les Grèbes du Lac de Marcenay, 5 Route du Lac, 21330 Marcenay [03 80 81 61 72; fax 03 80 81 61 99; info@campingmarcenaylac.com; www.campingmarcenaylac.com] On D965 bet Laignes & Châtillon-sur-Seine. Fr Châtillon sp on R 8km after vill of Cérilly. Foll sp to lake & camp. Med, pt shd; wc; chem disp; shwrs inc; el pnts (6A) €3.10; lndtte; shop; snacks; rest, bar nrby; playgrnd; fishing; watersports; boat & canoe hire; golf; horseriding; games rm; TV rm; dogs; adv bkg rec; quiet; CCI. "Well-run, pleasant, peaceful site in beautiful Burgundy area; well worth finding; excel value; recep clsd 1200-1500; Châtillon museum & Abbey de Fontenay outstanding." 1 May-30 Sep. € 10.15
2007*

MARCHAINVILLE *4E2* (N Rural) Camp Municipal Les Fosses, 61290 Marchainville [02 33 73 69 65 or 02 33 73 65 80 (Mairie); fax 02 33 73 65 80] Fr Verneuil-sur-Avre take D941 S to La Ferté-Vidame & at start of town turn R onto D4/D11 SW to Marchainville; site sp at x-rds in vill on D243. Sm, hdg/mkd pitch, pt sl, pt shd; wc; shwrs; el pnts (10A) €2.20; shop, rest, snacks, bar 8km; tennis; no statics; phone; adv bkg; quiet; CCI. "Warden visits." ♦ ltd. 1 Apr-30 Oct. € 9.70
2005*

MARCIAC *8F2* (1.5km NW Rural) FFCC Camping Le Lac, Bezines, 32230 Marciac [tel/fax 05 62 08 21 19; camping.marciac@wanadoo.fr; www.camping-marciac.com] E fr Maubourguet take D943 to Marciac. Take D3 to lake dir Plaisance. At lake turn R & R again at sp. Site on L in 200m. Fr N exit A62 at junc 3 & foll D932 sp Pau to Aire-sur-Adour then E on D935 & D3 & foll sp. Med, mkd pitch, some hdstg, pt shd; wc chem disp; mv service pnt (also avail to m'vans not staying on site); baby facs; shwrs inc; el pnts (6A) inc; gas; lndtte; ice; shop & 800m; rest 300m; snacks; bar; BBQ; playgrnd; pool; lake adj; internet; 8% statics; dogs €1.50; phone; adv bkg (dep req); red long stay/low ssn; cc acc; CCI. "Friendly British owners improving site; lge pitches with easy access; interesting old town; picturesque area; new disabled facs (2007); busy for jazz festival 1st 2 weeks in Aug; Wed mkt." ♦ 17 Mar-27 Oct. € 20.50
2007*

MARCIGNY *9A1* (7km W Rural) Camping La Motte aux Merles, 71110 Artaix [03 85 25 37 67] Leave D982 (Digoin-Roanne) at Marcigny by-pass. Take D989 twd Lapalisse. In 2km at Chambilly cont on D990, site sp in 5km on L, 200m down side rd. Sm, pt sl, pt shd; wc; shwrs; el pnts (8A) €2.40; lndry rm; snacks; playgrnd; pool (high ssn) fishing, tennis; golf nrby; dogs €1; quiet. " V friendly owners; gd sightseeing in peaceful area; excel." ♦ 1 Apr-30 Oct. € 9.60
2007*

MARCILLAC LA CROISSILLE *7C4* (2km SW Rural) Camp Municipal Le Lac, 28 Route du Viaduc, 19320 Marcillac-la-Croisille [tel/fax 05 55 27 81 38 or 05 55 27 82 05 (Mairie); campingdulac19@wanadoo.fr; www.campingdulac19.com] S fr Egletons on D16 & D18. Site sp at S end of vill at intersection with D978. Lge, pt sl, shd, wc; shwrs; el pnts (6A) €2.40; lndtte; ice; shops 2km; snacks; playgrnd; lake & sand beach adj; tennis adj; entmnt; TV; some statics; dogs €0.80; adv bkg; quiet; red low ssn. 1 Jun-1 Oct. € 10.20
2007*

MARCILLAC ST QUENTIN see Sarlat la Canéda *7C3*

MARCON see Château du Loir *4G1*

MARENNES *7B1* (5km SE Rural) Camping Séquoia Parc, La Josephtrie, 17320 St Just-Luzac [05 46 85 55 55; fax 05 46 85 55 56; info@sequoiaparc.com; www.sequoiaparc.com or www.les-castels.com] Fr A10/E05 m'way exit at Saintes, foll sp Royan (N150) turning off onto D728 twd Marennes & Ile d'Oléron; site sp to R off D728, just after leaving St Just-Luzac. Or fr Rochefort take D733 & D123 S; just bef Marennes turn L on D241 sp St Just-Luzac. Best ent to site fr D728, well sp fr each dir. Lge, hdg/mkd pitch, sl, unshd; wc; chem disp; mv service pnt; baby facs; shwrs inc; el pnts (6A) inc (poss rev pol); gas; lndtte; shop; rest; snacks; bar; BBQ; playgrnd; 3 htd pools; paddling pool; waterslides; sand beach 5km; fishing, watersports 3km; horseriding; tennis; cycle hire; games area; games rm; entmnt; child entmnt; wifi internet; TV rm; 50% statics (tour ops); dogs €5; recep 0830-2000 high ssn; coded barrier, clsd 2230; exchange bureau; adv bkg (bkg fee); cc acc; red long stay/low ssn; CCI. "High standard site; nice, lge pitches; clean san facs; superb pools; excel free club for children; some pitches flood in v heavy rain; wonderful flowers." ♦ 8 May-14 Sep. € 43.00 ABS - A28
2007*

See advertisement

Excellent restaurant and bar

Horseriding centre and Kid's club

Aquapark of 2000 m² and water slides

Lazy river

Cottage mobile homes and large pitches

4 pools

LES CASTELS CAMPING VILLAGE

Online bookings:
www.sequoiaparc.com
Séquoia Parc, 17320 St.Just-Luzac, France
Tel: 00 33 546 85 55 55

MARENNES *7B1* (10.5km SE Rural) **Camping Le Valerick, La Mauvinière, 17600 St Sornin** [tel/fax 05 46 85 15 95; camplevalerick@aol.com] Fr Marennes take D728 sp Saintes for 10km; L to St Sornin; site sp in vill. Fr Saintes D728 W for 26km; turn R to vill. Sm, mkd pitch, pt sl, pt shd; wc; chem disp (wc); shwrs inc; el pnts (4-6A) €2.90-€3.50 (poss rev pol); lndtte; shop; rest; snacks; bar; BBQ; playgrnd; sand beach 18km; entmnt; dogs €1.30; adv bkg; CCI. "Nice site; friendly; refurbished san facs (2007); plenty of bird life - herons, storks etc; poss mosquito probem." 1 Apr-30 Sep. € 11.50
2007*

MARENNES *7B1* (2km SW Coastal) **Camping La Ferme de la Prée, 17320 Marennes** [05 46 85 03 61] On D123 & Marennes N by-pass, foll sps for Ile d'Oléron to concrete water tower. In 150m turn L on C15 (sp Marennes-Plage 2km). Site on L in 1km. Sm, mkd pitch, pt shd; wc (some cont); shwrs €0.80; el pnts (6A) €2.50; gas; lndry rm; shops 2.5km & supmkt 4km; tradsmn; BBQ; sand beach 500m; pool 500m; few statics; adv bkg; v quiet; CCI. "V gd farm site; v flat; friendly & helpful owners; farm produce avail; gd." 15 Jun-15 Sep.
€ 4.40
2006*

MARENNES *7B1* (2km NW Coastal) **Camp Municipal La Giroflée, 17560 Bourcefranc-le-Chapus** [05 46 85 06 43 or 05 46 85 02 02 (Mairie); fax 05 46 85 48 58; camping-lagiroflee-bourcefranc@mairie17.com] Fr S on D26, 2km after junc with rd marked 'Royan par la Côte', turn N at traff lts. Site on L after 1km (after sailing school) opp beach. Med, pt shd; wc (few cont); shwrs €0.80; el pnts (8A) €2.65; lndry rm; shops 2km; snacks; playgrnd; beach adj; poss cr; quiet. 1 May-30 Sep. € 6.65
2005*

MAREUIL *7B2* (5km N Rural) **Camping Les Graulges, Le Bourg, 24340 Les Graulges** [tel/fax 05 53 60 74 73; info@lesgraulges.com] Fr D939 at Mareuil turn L onto D708 & foll sp to Les Graulges in 5km. Sm, mkd pitch, pt sl, terr, pt shd; wc; chem disp (wc); baby facs; shwrs inc; el pnts (6A) €3; lndtte; ice; tradsmn; rest; snacks; bar; BBQ; playgrnd; pool; fishing; dogs €2; phone 300m; poss cr; Eng spkn; adv bkg (dep req); quiet; red 7+ days. "Tranquil site in forested area; superb fishing in lge lake on site; ideal touring base; friendly Dutch owners; excel rest." ♦ 1 Apr-15 Sep. € 13.75
2005*

MAREUIL *7B2* (5km NE) **Camping Corneuil, 24340 St Sulpice-de-Mareuil** [05 53 60 79 48; fax 05 53 60 79 47; campingcorneuil@wanadoo.fr; www.corneuil.com] Fr Brantôme on D939 to Mareuil, turn R onto D708, site in L. Or S fr Nontron on D675/708, thro St Sulpice, site 3km on R, site sp on D708. Med, mkd pitch, terr, pt shd; wc; chem disp; shwrs inc; el pnts (8A) €3; lndtte; shop; rest; snacks; bar; playgrnd; pool; dogs €2; poss cr; adv bkg rec; quiet; red low ssn/red CCI. "Vg san facs; vg NH/sh stay." 14 May-11 Sep. € 22.00
2004*

> The opening dates and prices on this campsite have changed. I'll send a site report form to the editor for the next edition of the guide.

MAREUIL *7B2* (4km SE) **Camping L'Etang Bleu, 24340 Vieux-Mareuil** [05 53 60 92 70; fax 05 53 56 66 66; marc@letangbleu.com; www.letangbleu.com] On D939 Angoulême-Périgueux rd, after 5km turn L cent of Vieux-Mareuil onto D93, foll camping sp to site in 2km. Narr app thro vill. Lge, hdg/mkd pitch, pt shd; wc; chem disp; mv service pnt; baby facs; fam bthrm; shwrs inc; el pnts (10A) inc; gas; lndtte; ice; shop; tradsmn; rest; snacks; bar; BBQ; playgrnd; pool; paddling pool; lake fishing 500m; TV; entmnt; 10% statics; dogs €3; adv bkg €25 dep reqd; 30% red low ssn; cc acc; CCI. "Lovely site in beautiful, unspoilt countryside; v pleasant; gd for lge o'fits; friendly British owners; gd san facs; staff have 'relaxed' attitude; excel." ♦ 31 Mar-19 Oct. € 22.50
2007*

⊞**MAREUIL** 7B2 (6km SE Rural) **Camping La Charrue, Les Chambarrières, 24340 Vieux-Mareuil [tel/fax 05 53 56 65 59; info@la-charruefrance.com; www.la-charruefrance.com]** SE fr Angoulême on D939 sp Périgueux to Mareuil. Fr Mareuil stay on D939 twds Brantôme, thro Vieux-Mareuil then in 2km site immed on L after passing a lge lay-by on R with white stone chippings. Awkward turn. NB Website says 2 ents. Sm, mkd pitch, pt shd; wc; chem disp; shwrs inc; el pnts (4A) €3; gas 3km; lndtte; shop 2km; tradsmn; rest & bar 500m; snacks; BBQ; playgrnd; pool; sand beach, lakes & watersports nr; fishing 3km; cycle hire; table-tennis; dogs (low ssn); adv bkg (full payment req); some rd noise; 10% red +14 days; CCI. "CL-type site; nr many chateaux; v friendly British owners; immac facs; vg rest; golf, walking nr; B&B & gites avail; excel." € 13.00   2006*

MAREUIL 7B2 (500m SW) **Camp Municipal Vieux Moulin, 24340 Mareuil [05 53 60 91 20 (Mairie) or 05 53 60 99 80; fax 05 53 60 51 72]** Fr town cent take D708 (sp Ribérac); after 300m turn L on D99 (sp 'La Tour Blanche'); after 100m turn L opp lge school, site 100m ahead. Sm, mkd pitch, shd; wc; shwrs; el pnts (5A) €1.50; shops, rest, snacks, bar 500m; playgrnd; rv 1km; adv bkg; quiet. "Friendly warden; interesting chateau in vill; vg." ♦ 1 Jun-30 Sep. € 8.00   2004*

MARIGNY see Doucier 6H2

MARNAY (HAUTE SAONE) 6G2 (500m SE Urban) **Camp Municipal Vert Lagon, Route de Besançon, 70150 Marnay [03 84 31 71 41 or 03 84 31 73 16; sidmarnay@wanadoo.fr; www.camping-vertlagon.com]** Fr N stay on D67 Marnay by-pass; ignore old camping sp into town. Proceed to S of town on by-pass then turn L at junc. Bef bdge in 1km take gravel rd on S side, round under bdge to site (app thro town fr N v narr). After heavy rain access to site under rd bdge imposs due rv flooding. Use slip rd at vill end of bdge but fr dir of vill only (turn fr opp dir too acute & nr dangerous corner). Med, some hdg/mkd pitch, pt shd; wc; chem disp (wc); shwrs inc; el pnts (3-5A) €3-4; shops, rest, snacks & bar 500m; snacks (high ssn); BBQ; playgrnd; fishing; canoeing; 20% statics; dogs €1; adv bkg; quiet; cc acc; CCI. "Pleasant site by Rv Ognon; new san facs 2007; lake adj; tree-top walks." 1 May-30 Sep. € 11.40   2007*

MARNAY (SAONE ET LOIRE) see Chalon sur Saône 6H1

MARQUAY see Eyzies de Tayac, Les 7C3

MARQUION 3B4 (2km N Rural) **Camping de l'Epinette, 7 Rue du Calvaire, 62860 Sauchy-Lestrée [03 21 59 50 13; epinette62@wanadoo.com; http://pagesperso-orange.fr/campingepinette/camp.html]** Fr A26 exit junc 8 onto D939 to Marquion. On ent Marquion turn R at x-rds to Sauchy-Lestrée; on ent vill turn R at 1st T-junc & site on L in 100m. Fr Cambrai take D939 twd Arras, then as above. Sm, pt sl, pt shd; wc (own san rec); chem disp; shwrs €1.50; el pnts (4-6A) €2.50-3 (poss rev pol); gas; lndtte; shops 3km; playgrnd; games area; many statics; dogs free; adv bkg; quiet but some military aircraft noise; cc not acc; CCI. "Pretty, well-kept, clean, homely site; simple but adequate facs; ltd facs low ssn; ask recep for key to shwrs; helpful owner; CL-type area for tourers; levelling blocks ess for m'vans; conv Calais/Dunkerque; WW1 cemetary nr." 1 Apr-31 Oct. € 9.00   2006*

Before we move on, I'm going to fill in some site report forms and post them off to the editor, otherwise they won't arrive in time for the deadline at the end of September.

MARQUISE 3A3 (4km S Rural) **FFCC Camping L'Escale, 62250 Wacquinghen [tel/fax 03 21 32 00 69; camp-escale@wanadoo.fr; www.escale-camping.com]** Fr A16 S fr Calais exit junc 34. Fr A16 N fr Boulogne exit junc 33. Foll sp. Lge, shd; wc (cont); chem disp (wc); mv service pnt; shwrs inc; el pnts (4A) €3.20 (poss rev pol); gas; lndtte; shop; supmkt 3km; rest; snacks; bar; playgrnd; 90% statics; dogs; poss cr; quiet; cc acc. "Open 24 hrs; conv NH nr WW2 coastal defences, ferries & Channel tunnel; o'fits staying 1 night pitch on meadow at front of site for ease of exit; m'van 'aire' open all yr; vg." ♦ 15 Mar-15 Oct. € 14.80   2007*

MARSAC EN LIVRADOIS see Ambert 9B1

MARSANNE 9D2 (1km NE Rural) **Camping Les Bastets, Quartier Les Bastets, 26740 Marsanne [04 75 90 35 03; fax 04 75 90 35 05; contact@campinglesbastets.com; www.campinglesbastets.com]** Exit A7 junc 17; pass thro Les Tourettes & La Coucourde to Marsanne; cont on D105 for 1km. Site sp fr D105. App fr N on D57 not rec. Med, hdg/mkd pitch, sl, terr, pt shd; wc; chem disp (wc); mv service pnt; baby facs; shwrs inc; el pnts (10A) €4; lndtte; shop; tradsmn; rest; snacks; bar; BBQ; playgrnd; pool; archery; games area; games rm; entmnt; TV rm; 10% statics; dogs €4; Eng spkn; adv bkg; quiet; red low ssn. "Pleasant site with gd views; beautiful area; vg." ♦ ltd. 1 Apr-31 Oct. € 18.00 (CChq acc)   2007*

MARSEILLAN PLAGE *10F1* (Coastal/Urban)
Camping Beauregard-Est, Chemin de l'Airette,
34340 Marseillan-Plage [04 67 77 15 45; fax
04 67 01 21 78; campingbeauregardest@
wanadoo.fr] On N112 Agde-Sète rd, turn S at
rndabt to Marseillan-Plage onto D51 & foll camping
sp thro town. Site immed on leaving town cent. Lge,
hdg pitch, pt shd; wc; chem disp; mv service pnt;
baby facs; shwrs inc; el pnts (6A) inc; Indtte; shop,
rest, snacks, bar adj; playgrnd; sand beach adj;
entmnt; TV; 5% statics; Eng spkn; adv bkg; poss
cr; quiet. "Superb sand beach sheltered by dunes."
♦ 10 Apr-3 Oct. € 27.50 (CChq acc) 2006*

MARSEILLAN PLAGE *10F1* (1km NE Coastal)
Camping Le Paradou, 2 Impasse Ronsard, 34340
Marseillan-Plage [04 67 21 90 10; info.paradou@
wanadoo.fr; www.paradou.com] Exit A9 junc 34
or 35 onto N113/N312 dir Agde & Sète. Fr Agde foll
sp Sète to Marseillan-Plage. Site well sp on N112.
Med, hdg pitch, pt shd; htd wc; chem disp; baby
facs; shwrs inc; el pnts (10A) €3.20; gas; Indtte;
ice; shop 1km; tradsmn; rest, bar 1km; snacks;
playgrnd; dir access sand beach adj; 5% statics;
dogs; phone; bus 1km; poss cr; CCI. "Gd area
for cycling; Itd pitches avail for long o'fits." ♦ Itd.
26 Mar-29 Oct. € 21.00 2006*

MARSEILLAN PLAGE *10F1* (500m SW Coastal)
Camping Europ 2000, 960 Ave des Campings,
34340 Marseillan-Plage [tel/fax 04 67 21 92 85;
contact@camping-europ2000.com; www.
camping-europ2000.com] Fr cent of Marseillan-
Plage S on coast rd D51e, site on L. Med, hdg/mkd
pitch, hdstg, pt shd; wc; chem disp; mv service pnt;
shwrs inc; el pnts (10A) €3.50; gas; Indtte; shop &
500m; tradsmn; snacks; BBQ; playgrnd; sand beach
adj; games area; 10% statics; dogs €2; phone; poss
cr; Eng spkn; adv bkg; quiet; red low ssn CCI. "Easy
access to beach; v friendly, helpful owner; gd value,
family-run site." ♦ 1 Apr-20 Oct. € 20.50 2005*

MARSEILLAN PLAGE *10F1* (500m SW Coastal)
Camping La Plage, 69 Chemin du Pairollet,
34340 Marseillan-Plage [04 67 21 92 54; fax
04 67 01 63 57; info@laplage-camping.net; www.
laplage-camping.net] On N112 Agde to Sète, turn
S at rndabt dir Marseillan-Plage. Foll sp for site. At
2nd rndabt, take 3rd exit. Site on L in 150m. Med,
hdg pitch, pt shd; wc; chem disp; mv service pnt;
shwrs inc; child/baby facs; el pnts (10A) inc; gas;
Indtte; ice; rest; snacks; bar; BBQ; playgrnd; sand
beach adj; watersports; games area; entmnt;
TV in bar; 1% statics; dogs €3; phone; extra for
beachfront pitches; poss cr; Eng spkn; adv bkg
(dep req+bkg fee); quiet; cc acc, CCI. "Excel family-
run site; superb beach; v popular with gd, friendly
atmosphere." ♦ 15 Mar-5 Nov. € 30.00
2007*

MARSEILLAN PLAGE *10F1* (1km SW Coastal)
Camping La Créole, 74 Ave des Campings,
34340 Marseillan-Plage [04 67 21 92 69; fax
04 67 26 58 16; campinglacreole@wanadoo.
fr; www.campinglacreole.com] Fr Agde-Sète rd
N112, turn S at rndabt onto D51 & foll sp thro town.
Narr ent easily missed among lger sites. Med, hdg/
mkd pitch, hdstg, pt shd; wc; chem disp; mv service
pnt; baby facs; shwrs inc; el pnts (6A) €2.85; Indtte;
shop; rest, snacks, bar adj; playgrnd; sand beach
adj; tennis 1km; games area; entmnt; 10% statics;
dogs €3; phone; adv bkg; quiet; red long stay; CCI.
"Dir access to excel beach; naturist beach 600m;
well-maintained, quiet site." ♦ 4 Apr-8 Oct. € 25.75
2007*

MARSEILLAN PLAGE *10F1* (1.5km SW Coastal)
Camping La Nouvelle Floride, Ave des Campings,
34340 Marseillan-Plage [04 67 21 94 49; fax
04 67 21 81 05; info@yellohvillage-mediterranees.
com; www.yellohvillage-mediterranees.com]
Exit A9 sp Agde/Bessan junc 34 or 35 onto
N312/N112 & foll sps to site. Turn R at traff Its in
Marseillan-Plage, site 1.5km. Lge, shd; htd wc; mv
service pnt; shwrs inc; baby facs; el pnts (6A) inc;
gas; Indtte; ice; supmkt; rest; snacks; bar; BBQ;
playgrnd; htd pool; paddling pool; waterslide;
sand beach adj; games area; horseriding; entmnt;
20% statics; dogs €4; adv bkg; quiet; red long
stay/low ssn; cc acc; CCI. "Excel family site."
♦ 1 Apr-29 Sep. € 44.00 (3 persons) 2007*

MARSEILLAN PLAGE *10F1* (1.5km SW Coastal)
Camping Le Charlemagne, Ave des Campings,
34340 Marseillan-Plage [04 67 21 92 49; fax
04 67 21 86 11; info@yellohvillage-mediterranees.
com; www.yellohvillage-mediterrannes.com]
In Marseillan-Plage, off N112 Sète-Agde rd, take
D51e SW to site. Lge, hdg/mkd pitch, shd; wc;
chem disp; mv service pnt; baby facs; shwrs inc;
el pnts (6A) inc; shop; Indtte; rest; snacks; bar;
playgrnd; 3 htd pools; waterslide; sand beach
200m; games area; golf 5km; entmnt; 50% statics;
dogs €3.50; phone; poss cr; Eng spkn; adv bkg
(dep & bkg fee); red low ssn for 14+ days; quiet.
"Site also owns Nouvelle Floride opp on beach of
similar standard; lge pitches; lots of shops, rests
nrby; many tour operators; poss mosquitoes;
excel." ♦ 1 Apr-29 Sep. € 41.00 (3 persons)
2004*

MARTEL *7C3* (5km SE Rural) **Camping du Port,**
46600 Creysse [05 65 32 20 82 or 05 65 32 27 59;
fax 05 65 38 78 21; contact@campingduport.com;
www.les-campings.com/port] Fr Souillac take
D803 to Martel. On ent Martel turn R on D23 on rd
to Creysee. Alt app via D840 (N140) fr Cressensac
to Martel. Site sp. NB Narr, twisty rd fr Gluges.
Med, pt sl, pt shd by rv; wc (some cont); shwrs inc;
el pnts (6A) €3; ice; Indtte; shops in Martel; rest in
Creysse; playgrnd; pool; canoe & cycle hire; dogs
€1.50; adv bkg; quiet. "Lovely grounds; gd access
to rv; friendly; v peaceful low ssn." 28 Apr-22 Sep.
€ 12.60 2007*

MARTEL 7C3 (500m NW Rural) **Camp Municipal de la Callopie, Ave de Turenne, 46600 Martel [05 65 37 30 03 (Mairie); fax 05 65 37 37 27; mairiedemartel@wanadoo.fr]** On NW o'skts of vill of Martel on D23, 100m fr rndabt on L, ent opp Auberge des 7 Tours. Sm, shd; wc; shwrs inc; el pnts (10A) €1.60; shops, rest, bar 200m; rv 5km; no statics; poss cr; no adv bkg; rd noise. "Attractive site in beautiful medieval vill; gd, clean, modern facs; warden calls or pay at Mairie; gd meals at auberge." 15 Jun-15 Sep. € 6.80
2007*

MARTIGNE FERCHAUD 2F4 (NE Rural) **Camp Municipal Le Bois Feuillet, 35640 Martigné-Ferchaud [02 99 47 84 38; fax 02 99 47 84 65]** After ent Martigné-Ferchaud on E of D178; fr N cross level x-ing, site on L in 400m; fr S, thro vill, site on R after bend at bottom of hill. Site sp fr town cent. Med, terr, unshd; wc; chem disp; shwrs inc; el pnts (16A) €2; lndtte; ice; shop adj; rest, snacks, bar 1km; BBQ; playgrnd; lake sw with sm shgl beach; fishing & boating; sports area; tennis; quiet; CCI. "Attractive site beside picturesque lake; lovely position; in June & Sep barrier opened at 0900 & 1900 - foll instructions in Eng on office door or report to town hall to gain ent (parking diff); lge pitches; gd san facs; 2nd week Aug excel water spectacular." ♦ 1 Jun-30 Sep. € 8.50   2004*

MARTIGUES 10F2 (8km S Coastal) **Camping L'Arquet, Chemin de la Batterie, 13500 Martigues [04 42 42 81 00 or 04 42 44 34 00 (LS); fax 04 42 42 34 50; arquet@semovim-martigues. com; www.semovim-martigues.com]** Exit A55 at Martigues Sud exit for D5 dir Sausset & Carro. In 4km turn R onto rd to La Couronne. Pass under dual c'way. On main rd turn L at church & foll camp sp. Lge, pt shd; wc (cont); chem disp; shwrs; el pnts inc; lndtte; shops 1km; lndtte; playgrnd; sand beach 300m; tennis nr; fishing; boating; diving; cycling; dogs €2.50; adv bkg; quiet. ♦ 6 Mar-30 Sep. € 21.65   2004*

MARTRAGNY see Bayeux 3D1

MARTRES DE VEYRE, LES see Clermont Ferrand 9B1

⊞**MARTRES TOLOSANE** 8F3 (2km E) **Camp Intercommunal Le Plantaurel, 31220 Palaminy [05 61 97 03 71; fax 05 61 90 62 04]** Exit A64 at junc 23 onto D6 to Cazères, cross rv bdge. Turn W (R) on D62, foll rv for 1.5km. Site well sp, Lge, shd; wc; chem disp; shwrs inc; el pnts (10A) inc; gas; ice; BBQ; lndry rm; shop & 2km; snacks; pool; playgrnd; TV; entmnt; many statics; phone; dir access to rv; dogs €0.91; adv bkg; red long stay; CCI. "Poss itinerants; poss noisy; could be better maintained." € 16.77 (4 persons)   2005*

MARTRES TOLOSANE 8F3 (1.5km S Rural) **Camping Le Moulin, 31220 Martres-Tolosane [05 61 98 86 40; fax 05 61 98 66 90; info@ campinglemoulin.com; www.campinglemoulin. com]** Exit A64 junc 21 or 22, site sp adj Rv Garonne. Med, pt sl, pt shd; htd wc (some cont); baby facs; shwrs inc; el pnts (6-10A) €3.50-5; lndtte; shops 1.5km; snacks; bar; playgrnd; htd pool; paddling pool; rv fishing adj; tennis; cycle hire; games area; games rm; entmnt; TV; 20% statics; dogs €2; adv bkg rec high ssn; quiet; red long stay; 20% red low ssn; cc acc; CCI. "Excel, well-maintained site; gd, modern san facs." 15 Apr-30 Sep. € 21.00
2006*

MARTRES TOLOSANE 8F3 (7km SW Rural) **Camp Municipal, 31360 St Martory [05 61 90 44 93 or 05 61 90 22 24; cccsm@wanadoo.fr]** Leave A64 at junc 20. Turn R onto D117 twd St Martory. In 1km turn L (sp) soon after Gendarmerie. Sm, hdg pitch, pt shd; htd wc (some cont); chem disp (wc); shwrs inc; el pnts inc; dogs €1.50; quiet; CCI. ♦ 15 Jun-15 Sep. € 9.90   2006*

MARVAL 7B3 (3.5km N Rural) **Camping La Nozillière, L'Age de Milhaguet, 87440 Marval [05 55 78 25 60; adriaan.von-bekkum@wanadoo. fr; www.nozilliere.nl]** Fr Marval N on D67 sp Milhaguet; take D73 to St Barthélemy, turn L in 500m, site sp. Sm, pt sl, pt shd; wc; chem disp; shwrs inc; el pnts (6A) inc; gas 3.5km; ice; shop 3.5km, rest; snacks, bar 3.5km; tradsmn; BBQ; playgrnd; pool; lake sw 3km; dogs; Eng spkn; adv bkg (dep req); quiet; cc acc; CCI. "Excel." ♦ 1 May-31 Oct. € 18.00   2006*

MARVEJOLS 9D1 (1km NE Rural) **Camp Municipal L'Europe, Quartier de l'Empery, 48100 Marvejols [04 66 32 03 69 or 04 66 32 00 45 (Mairie); fax 04 66 32 43 56]** Exit A75 junc 38 onto D900 & N9. Foll E ring rd onto D999, cont over rv & foll sp to site; no R turn into site, cont 500m to Aire de Retournement, & turn L into site. Med, hdg pitch, pt shd; wc (mainly cont); shwrs inc; el pnts (5A) inc (poss rev pol); lndtte; shop & 1km; playgrnd; pool 1km; rv adj; TV rm; many statics; no dogs; phone; poss cr; adv bkg; quiet. "Interesting walled town; sep area for tourers." ♦ 15 May-15 Sep € 10.30
2006*

MASEVAUX 6F3 (N Urban) **Camp Municipal, 3 Rue du Stade, 68290 Masevaux [tel/fax 03 89 82 42 29; camping@masevaux.fr]** Fr N83 Colmar-Belfort rd take N466 W to Masevaux; site sp. NB D14 fr Thann to Masevaux narr & steep - not suitable c'vans. Med, mkd pitch, pt shd; htd wc; chem disp; baby facs; shwrs inc; el pnts (3-6A) €2.65-5; lndtte; ice; shop 1km; tradsmn; playgrnd; htd pool & sports complex adj; entmnt; TV rm; 40% statics; dogs €0.80; no twin-axles; poss cr; Eng spkn; adv bkg; quiet; some rd noise; cc acc; CCI. "Pleasant walks; interesting town - annual staging of Passion Play; helpful staff; excel facs; in walking dist of town; gd cycle rtes; excel." ♦ 15 Feb-31 Dec. € 10.60
2006*

MASSAT 8G3 (4km W Rural) **Aire Naturelle L'Azaigouat (Gouaze), Route du Col de Saraillé, 09320 Biert [tel/fax 05 61 96 95 03; camping. azaigouat@club-internet.fr; www.azaigouat.com]** Take D618 S fr St Girons dir Massat. At Biert turn R onto D118 dir Oust & Col de Saraille, site sp. Sm, pt sl, pt shd; wc; shwrs inc; el pnts (6-10A) €2.50; lndry rm; ice; shop, rest, snacks 800m; BBQ; games area; games rm; horseriding 3km; fishing nr; dogs; adv bkg; quiet; CCI. "Excel CL-type site beside stream; v friendly owners; gd wildlife walks." 15 Jun-15 Sep. € 10.00   2007*

MASSERET 7B3 (9km N Rural) **Camp Municipal Montréal, 87380 St Germain-les-Belles [05 55 71 86 20 or 05 55 71 80 09 (LS); fax 05 55 71 82 25]** S on N20/A20 fr Limoges, turn L onto D7, junc 42. Vill is 4.5km. Site sp in vill. Care needed due narr rds. Med, terr, unshd, hdg pitch; wc; shwrs inc; el pnts (5A) inc; ice; rest, snacks, bar 250m; sm shop 800m; playgrnd; lake sw adj; fishing; watersports; walks; dogs; phone; poss cr; quiet; adv bkg; CCI. "Peaceful site in attractive setting; excel san facs; warden calls every pm low ssn." ♦ ltd. 1 Jun-15 Sep. € 10.00   2004*

MASSERET 7B3 (5km E Rural) **Camping Plan l'Eau, 19510 Lamongerie [05 55 73 44 57; fax 05 55 73 49 69]** Exit A20 at junc 43 sp Masseret & foll sp Lamongerie. At rndabt turn R, site sp. Site ent bet 2 lge stone pillars. Med, sl, shd; wc; chem disp; shwrs; el pnts (12A) €2 (poss rev pol); lndtte; sm shop; snacks; playgrnd; lake beach & sw; fishing; tennis; golf nrby; fitness course thro woods & round lake; TV; poss cr; quiet. "V pleasant situation; gd NH." ♦ 1 Apr-30 Sep. € 9.20
2007*

MASSEUBE 8F3 (12km NE Rural) **Camping Domaine Naturiste du Moulin de Faget (Naturist), Au Grange, 32450 Faget-Abbatial [05 62 65 49 09; fax 05 62 66 29 21; info@moulin-faget.com]** Fr Masseube D929 for 7 km; in Seissan R on D104 sp Faget-Abbatial; in 8.5km R at T-junc onto D40; site sp on L in 300m; at top of track after 500m. Sm, pt sl, unshd; wc; chem disp (wc); shwrs inc; el pnts (6A) £3.25; lndry rm; tradsmn; rest; bar ltd; 10% statics; Eng spkn; adv bkg; quiet; CCI. "V quiet & rather isolated; gd walks; friendly Dutch owners." ♦ ltd. 1 May-1 Oct. € 18.00   2005*

MASSIAC 9C1 (7km N Rural) **Camp Municipal La Bessière, 43450 Blesle [04 71 76 25 82; fax 04 71 76 25 42; bleslecamping@free.fr]** Fr Massiac take D909 N. In 5km at Babory turn L onto D8. In 2km turn L immed after x-ing rv bdge. Site sp. Sm, some hdg/mkd pitch, terr, pt shd; wc (some cont); chem disp (wc); mv service pnt; shwrs inc; el pnts (10A) €1.50; lndry rm; BBQ; playgrnd; tennis; 30% statics; dogs €0.80; phone 200m; poss cr; CCI. "Blesle one of most beautiful vills in France; attractive site; helpful, friendly warden; gd touring base; vg site." ♦ ltd. 1 May-30 Sep. € 6.00
2006*

MASSIAC 9C1 (800m SW Rural) **Camp Municipal de l'Allagnon, Ave de Courcelles, 15500 Massiac [tel/fax 04 71 23 03 93 or 04 71 23 02 61 (Mairie)]** Take N122 off N9 in Massiac, rte to Murat, site sp on rvside. Med, mkd pitch, shd; wc; shwrs; el pnts (6-10A) inc; gas; lndtte; shops adj; playgrnd; pool adj; fishing; tennis; poss cr; CCI. "Popular site; sh walk to town cent; vg." ♦ 15 May-15 Sep. € 9.00
2006*

MASSIAC 9C1 (6km SW Rural) **Camp Municipal, Pré Mongeal, 15500 Molompize [04 71 73 62 90 or 04 71 73 60 06; fax 04 71 73 60 24; mairie. molompize@wanadoo.fr]** Exit junc 23 fr A75, take N122 twd Aurillac. Site on L just bef Molompize. Med, pt shd; wc; chem disp (wc); shwrs inc; el pnts (10A) €1.65; lndry rm; shops 500m; playgrnd; 6% statics; quiet; CCI. "Rvside site behind stadium; tennis courts; friendly warden; super vill; gd." ♦ ltd. 15 Jun-15 Sep. € 4.90   2006*

MATEMALE 8G4 (1.7km SW Rural) **Camping Le Lac, Forêt de la Matte, 66210 Matemale [04 68 30 94 49; fax 04 68 04 35 16; www. camping-lac-matemale.com]** N on D118 fr Mont Louis, site sp in vill. App rd narr & poss diff lge o'fits. Sm, pt sl, pt shd; htd wc; mv service pnt; baby facs; shwrs; el pnts (3-6A) €2.60-4.20; lndtte; tradsmn; snacks; bar; BBQ; lake 200m; fishing; watersports; games area; games rm; dogs €1; open w/end & school hols rest of yr; quiet. "Friendly site amid pine trees." ♦ 1 Jun-30 Sep. € 13.00
2006*

MATHA 7B2 (9km NE Rural) **Camping La Forge, 10B Rue de la Forge, 17160 Le Gicq [tel/fax 05 46 32 48 42 or 01733 252089 (UK); mail@la-forge-holidays.com; www.la-forge-holidays.com]** Fr Matha take D131 thro Les Touches-de-Périgny. In 5km turn R at x-rds sp Le Gicq & foll sp to site. Sm, hdg pitch, pt shd; wc; chem disp; mv service pnt; shwrs inc; el pnts (10A) €3; gas 5km; lndtte; tradsmn; shop, rest, snacks, bar 5km; BBQ; htd pool; lake sw 10km; no dogs; phone; adv bkg; quiet. "Peaceful CL-type site on farm with added extras; relaxing; v helpful British owners; vg touring base Cognac, La Rochelle & coast; gd cycling area." ♦ 19 May-29 Sep. € 24.00   2007*

MATHA 7B2 (5km S Rural) **Camping Le Relais de l'Etang, Route de Matha, La Verniouze, 17160 Thors [05 46 58 26 81 or 05 46 58 75 36; paysmatha@cc-matha.fr]** Fr Matha take D121 S twd Cognac. Site on L in 5km. Sm, hdg/mkd pitch, pt shd; wc (some cont); chem disp; shwrs inc; el pnts (10A) inc; rest; snacks; bar; playgrnd; lake sw; mini-golf; adv bkg; quiet; CCI. "Gd for visiting Cognac." 1 Jun-30 Sep. € 9.00   2006*

MATHES, LES 7B1 (2.5 N Rural) **FFCC Camping La Palombière, 1551 Route de la Fouasse, 17570 Les Mathes [05 46 22 69 25; fax 05 46 22 44 58; camping.lapalombiere@wanadoo.fr;   www. camping-lapalombiere.com]** Fr La Tremblade bypass foll sp Dirée on D268; site on R in 5km just past Luna Park. Med, pt shd; htd wc; chem disp; mv service pnt; baby facs; shwrs inc; el pnts (6A) €3; gas; lndtte; ice; tradsmn; rest, snacks, bar 500m; BBQ; playgrnd; pool; sand beach 4km; dogs €1.50; bus; Eng spkn; quiet; CCI. "Spacious, tranquil site under oaks & pines; lge pitches; palatial san facs; superb beaches 5km (some naturist); excel." ♦ 1 Apr-31 Oct. € 16.00   2006*

There aren't many sites open this early in the year. We'd better phone ahead to check that the one we're heading for is actually open.

MATHES, LES 7B1 (3.5km N Rural) **Camping L'Orée du Bois, 225 Route de la Bouverie, La Fouasse, 17570 Les Mathes [05 46 22 42 43; fax 05 46 22 54 76; info@camping-oree-du-bois.fr; www.camping-oree-du-bois.fr]** Fr A10 to Saintes, then dir Royan. Fr Royan take D25 thro St Palais & La Palmyre twd Phare de la Coubre. Cont 4km past Phare & turn R on D268 to La Fouasse. Site on R in 4km. Lge, hdg/mkd pitch, hdstg, pt shd; wc (some cont); 40 pitches with own san; chem disp; baby facs; shwrs inc; el pnts (6A) inc; gas; lndtte; ice; shop; rest; snacks; bar; BBQ; playgrnd; 3 htd pools; waterslide; sand beach 4km; tennis; cycle hire; golf 20km; games area; games rm; entmnt/child ent Jul & Aug; internet; sat TV rm; 50% statics; dogs €3.50; Eng spkn; adv bkg rec high ssn; quiet; cc acc; red low ssn/CCI. "Site in pinewood; local beaches ideal for sw & surfing; zoo in La Palmyre worth visit; min stay 7 days high ssn; excel." ♦ 29 Apr-16 Sep. € 32.00 (CChq acc)   2005*

MATHES, LES 7B1 (4km SW Coastal) **Camping Bonne   Anse   Plage,   17570   La   Palmyre [05 46 22 40 90; fax 05 46 22 42 30; contact@ campingbonneanseplage.com;   www.camping bonneanseplage.com]** N fr Royan on D25 thro St Palais-sur-Mer to La Palmyre, after zoo at rndbt site sp; site on L after x-rds D25 & D141 in 600m. Lge, mkd pitch, terr, pt sl, shd; wc; chem disp; mv service pnt; shwrs inc; el pnts (6A) €6; gas; lndtte; ice; shops; rest; snacks; bar; playgrnd; htd pool complex; waterslides; sand beach 500m; games area; cycle hire; internet; entmnt; sat TV; many tour ops statics; no dogs; poss cr; Eng spkn; no adv bkg more than 2 days ahead; some rd noise; cc acc; CCI. "Superb pool complex, friendly, family site; dated but clean san facs; cycle path." ♦ 24 May-1 Sep. € 35.00 (3 persons)   2006*

MATHES, LES 7B1 (6km SW Coastal) **Camping Parc   de   la   Côte   Sauvage,   Phare   de   la Coubre, 17570 Les Mathes [05 46 22 40 18 or 05 49 35 83 60; contact@parc-cote-sauvage.com; www.parc-cote-sauvage.com]** D25 fr Royan, thro La Palmyre, at rndabt foll sp 'Phare de la Coubre'. Turn L at junc sp as bef, turn L on R-hand bend. Lge, mkd pitch, pt terr, pt shd; wc (some cont); chem disp; mv service pnt; shwrs inc; el pnts (6-10A) €4.50-5.50; gas; lndtte; shop; rest/bar adj; snacks; playgrnd; pool complex; sand beach 500m - can be v windy; tennis; cycle hire adj; boating; surf school; entmnt; internet; TV; 25% statics; dogs €2.60 (not acc Jul/Aug); poss cr (NH area); Eng spkn; v cr Jul/Aug; no adv bkg; cc acc; red low ssn; CCI. "Lge pitches; wc facs poss grubby; low ssn expensive for facs provided." ♦ 1 May-15 Sep. € 25.50   2005*

MATHES, LES 7B1 (2km W Rural) **Camping La Pinède, La Palmyre, 17570 Les Mathes [05 46 22 45 13; fax 05 46 22 50 21; contact@ campinglapinede.com;   www.campinglapinede. com]** Fr La Tremblade, take D141 twd Les Mathes. Turn R after vill onto D141 E twd La Fouasse, foll sp. Site in 2km. Lge, mkd pitch, pt shd; wc; chem disp; shwrs inc; el pnts (5A) €6.50; lndtte; ice; shop; rest; snacks; bar; playgrnd; 2 pools (1 htd, covrd); waterslide; sand beach 4km; tennis; cycle hire; archery; mini-golf; games area; games rm; entmnt; child entmnt; mini-farm; many statics; dogs €4.80; private san facs avail for extra charge; adv bkg; quiet. "Dir access to rv; excel for children." 1 May-4 Sep. € 36.80   2005*

MATHES, LES 7B1 (2km NW) **Camping Atlantique Forêt (formerly Le Moulin Rouge), La Fouasse, 17570 Les Mathes [05 46 22 40 46 or 05 46 36 82 77 (LS); www.camping-atlantique-foret.com]** Fr La Tremblade by-pass, foll sp Diree (D268). Drive thro vill & cont for 2km. Site on L. Or fr La Palmyre on D141 twd Les Mathes; at rndabt take dir La Fouasse. Last site on R. Med, pt shd; wc; chem disp; baby facs; shwrs inc; el pnts (6A) €3.90; gas; lndtte; ice; shop; tradsmn; rest, snacks, bar 500m; BBQ (gas only); playgrnd; pool, tennis 300m; beach 2km; 2% statics; dogs free; phone; poss cr; Eng spkn; adv bkg; quiet; CCI. "Roomy, clean & peaceful; gd alt to nrby lge sites; friendly, family-run; excel for young children; cycle paths thro forest; farm produce avail." 15 Jun-15 Sep. € 17.80   2007*

MATHES, LES 7B1 (2.5km NW Rural) **Camping La Clé des Champs, 1188 Route de la Fouasse, 17570 Les Mathes [05 46 22 40 53; fax 05 46 22 56 96; contact@la-cledeschamps.com; www.la-cledeschamps.com]** S of La Tremblade, take D141 twd La Palmyre, site sp. Lge, mkd pitch, pt shd; wc (some cont); chem disp; baby facs; shwrs inc; el pnts (6A) €4; gas; lndtte; shop; rest; snacks; bar; BBQ; playgrnd; htd, covrd pool; sand beach 3.5km; cycle hire; fishing & watersports 3km; cycle hire; games rm; TV rm; entmnt; 30% statics; dogs €2.50; Eng spkn; adv bkg; cc acc; quiet; CCI. "Well-equipped, busy site; many excel beaches in area; local oysters avail; Cognac region; Luna Park nrby - poss noise at night." ♦ 1 Apr-30 Sep. € 19.30   2007*

See advertisement above

MATHES, LES 7B1 (3km NW Rural) **Camping L'Estanquet, 2596 Route de la Fouasse, 17570 Les Mathes [05 46 22 47 32 or 05 46 93 93 51 (LS); fax 05 46 22 51 46; contact@campinglestanquet.com; www.campinglestanquet.com]** Fr Royan take D25 to La Palmyre. Turn R in town cent onto D141 dir Les Mathes; cont on D141 passing racecourse on R; turn L bef Les Mathes along La Fouasse. Site in 2.5km on L. Lge, hdg/mkd pitch, pt shd; wc; chem disp; baby facs; shwrs inc; el pnts (10A) inc; gas; lndtte; ice; shop; rest; snacks; bar; BBQ (gas only) ; playgrnd; pool; paddling pool; waterslide; sand beach 5km; fishing, windsurfing 5km; tennis; mini-golf; cycle hire; horseriding 1km; golf 9km; entmnt; games/TV rm; 85% statics; dogs €3; recep 0900-1930; poss cr; adv bkg; quiet ♦ 1 May-30 Sep. € 29.50   2006*

MATIGNON see St Cast le Guildo 2E3

MATOUR 9A2 (1km W) **Camp Municipal Le Paluet, 71520 Matour [03 85 59 70 58; fax 03 85 59 74 54; mairie.matour@wanadoo.fr; www.matour.com]** On W o'skts of Matour off Rte de la Clayette. Med, hdg/mkd pitch, pt shd; wc; chem disp; shwrs inc; el pnts (10A) inc; lndtte; shop 500m; bar; snacks; BBQ; playgrnd; pool high ssn; waterslide; lake fishing adj; tennis; games area; entmnt; TV; adv bkg; quiet; CCI. "Conv touring vineyards; highly rec; facs poss inadequate high ssn." ♦ 1 May-30 Sep. € 15.90   2006*

MAUBEC see Cavaillon 10E2

MAUBEUGE 3B4 (1km N Urban) **Camp Municipal du Clair de Lune, 212 Route de Mons, 59600 Maubeuge [tel/fax 03 27 62 25 48; camping@ville-maubeug.fr; www.ville-maubeuge.fr]** Fr Mons head S on N2 twd Maubeuge, site on L about 1.5km bef town cent, sp. Med, hdg/mkd pitch, some hdstg, pt shd; htd wc; chem disp; baby facs; shwrs inc; el pnts (6A) inc (rev pol); shops 500m; hypmkt nr; tradsmn; rest, snacks, bar 2km; BBQ; playgrnd; watersports 25km; cycle hire; internet; few statics; dogs; Eng spkn; adv bkg; some rd noise; cc acc. "Attractive, well-kept, busy transit site; gd, modern san facs; pitches spacious; friendly staff; recep 0900-1200 & 1400-1900; some rd noise; mkt Sat am; barrier clsd 2200; vg." ♦ 9 Feb-20 Dec. € 14.95 ABS - P07   2007*

See advertisement on next page

MAUBEUGE 3B4 (8km NE Rural) **Camping Les Avallées, 59600 Villers-Sire-Nicole [03 27 67 92 56 or 03 27 67 98 57; fax 03 27 67 45 18; bauduincaravanes.ludovic@wanaddo.fr]** N fr Maubeuge on N2; in 5km R onto D159 to Villers-Sire-Nicole. Site well sp. Lge, pt sl, terr, pt shd; wc; chem disp; el pnts (4A) €1.60; shwrs inc; shop (high ssn); rest; snacks; bar; BBQ; playgrnd; mainly statics; quiet. "Friendly owners; lake fishing; no twin-axles; site developing (2006); vg." 1 Apr-30 Sep. € 5.80   2006*

MAUBOURGUET *8F2* (SW Urban) Camp Municipal de l'Echez, Rue Jean Clos Pucheu, 65700 Maubourguet [05 62 96 37 44 or 06 12 90 14 55 (mob)] On D935 (NW of Tarbes), sp in Maubourguet, on bank of Rv Echez. Sm, pt shd; wc; shwrs inc; mv service pnt; el pnts; ice; shops 200m; lndtte; playgrnd; TV; rv fishing 300m; quiet. "Pleasantly situated; nice country town." 15 Jun-15 Sep. € 10.40   2006*

MAULEON LICHARRE *8F1* (1km S Rural) Camping Uhaitza Le Saison, Route de Libarrenx, 64130 Mauléon-Licharre [05 59 28 18 79; fax 05 59 28 00 78; camping.uhaitza@wanadoo. fr; www.camping-uhaitza.com] Fr Sauveterre take D936 twd Oloron. In 500m turn R onto D23 to Mauléon, then take D918 dir Tardets, site on R. Sm, hdg/mkd pitch, pt sl, pt shd; wc; chem disp; baby facs; shwrs inc; el pnts (4-6A) €2.50-3.20; lndtte; shops 1.5km; bar high ssn; BBQ; playgrnd; pool 4km; rv fishing adj; some statics; dogs €1; adv bkg; quiet; CCI. "Lovely quiet site beside rv - steep access; friendly owners." ♦ Easter-30 Oct. € 13.20   2006*

MAUPERTUS SUR MER see Cherbourg *1C4*

MAURIAC *7C4* (1km SW Rural) Camping Le Val St Jean, 15200 Mauriac [04 71 67 31 13 or 04 73 34 75 53 (Res); fax 04 71 68 17 34; info@camping-massifcentral.com; www.camping-massifcentral.com] Site in town adj to lake; well sp. Med, hdg/mkd pitch, terr, unshd; wc; chem disp; shwrs inc; el pnts (10A) €3.50; lndry rm; ice; shop; tradsmn; snacks; playgrnd; pool; sand beach &; lake sw adj; fishing; golf adj; some statics; dogs €1.50; adv bkg; quiet; red low ssn; CCI. "Excel site; exceptionally clean & tidy; ltd facs low ssn; gd cent for touring." ♦ 8 Apr-30 Sep. € 18.50   2005*

MAURIAC *7C4* (1.5km SW) Camp Municipal La Roussilhe, 15200 Mauriac [04 71 68 06 99] Foll sp for Ally & Pleux (D681); downhill, past supmkt, sp to R, 1st L. Med, pt shd; wc; 50% serviced pitches; shwrs; el pnts (3A) inc; quiet. "Site situated around perimeter of a football grnd; plenty of shade." 15 Jun-15 Sep. € 6.00   2005*

MAUROUX see St Clar *8E3*

MAURS *7D4* (Urban) Camp Municipal du Vert, Route de Decazeville, 15600 Maurs [04 71 49 04 15; fax 04 71 49 00 81] Fr Maurs take D663 dir Decazeville. Site on L 400m after level x-ing thro sports complex. Narr ent. Med, mkd pitch, shd; wc; chem disp; baby facs; shwrs inc; el pnts (3-5A) inc; lndtte; shops 1km; playgrnd; pool; tennis; rv fishing; poss cr; adv bkg; quiet. "V pleasant on side of rv; sports complex adj." ♦ 1 May-30 Sep. € 9.60   2004*

MAURY see St Paul de Fenouillet *8G4*

MAUSSANE LES ALPILLES see Mouriès *10E2*

MAUZE SUR LE MIGNON *7A2* (1km NW Urban) Camp Municipal Le Gué de La Rivière, Route de St Hilaire-la-Palud, 79210 Mauzé-sur-le-Mignon [05 49 26 76 28 or 05 49 26 30 35 (Mairie); fax 05 49 26 71 13; mairie@ville-mauze-mignon.fr; www.ville-mauze-mignon.fr] Site clearly sp. Sm, hdg pitch, shd; wc; chem disp; shwrs inc; el pnts (2-10A) €1.56-3.16; ice; lndtte; shop 1km; playgrnd; rv fishing; quiet; adv bkg; Eng spkn; CCI. "Pleasant site; excel san facs; warden calls am & pm; gd value." 1 Jun-2 Sep. € 5.71   2007*

MAXONCHAMP see Remiremont *6F2*

⊞**MAYENNE** *4E1* (1km N Rural) Camp Municipal du Gué St Léonard, Route de Brives, 53100 Mayenne [02 43 04 57 14; fax 02 43 30 21 10; tourisme-pays-mayenne@wanadoo.fr; www.paysdemayenne-tourisme.fr] Fr N, sp to E of D23 & well sp fr cent of Mayenne on rvside. Med, hdg/mkd pitch, pt shd; htd wc; chem disp; some serviced pitches; shwrs inc; el pnts (6A) €2; gas 1km; lndtte; BBQ; shop (high ssn) & 1km; tradsman high ssn; snacks; rest 1km; playgrnd; htd pool high ssn; rv fishing adj; 20% statics; phone; adv bkg; some noise fr adj factory; red low ssn; CCI. "Pleasant location adj parkland walks; peaceful; well maintained; clean facs but dated." ♦ € 5.90 (3 persons)   2007*

MAYET see Ecommoy *4F1*

MAYRES *9D1* (500m S Rural) **Camping La Chataigneraie, Hameau de Cautet, 07330 Mayres** [04 75 87 20 40 or 04 75 87 20 97] Fr Aubenas on N102; L after Mayres vill, over Ardèche bdge, up hill in 500m. Sm, mkd pitch, terr, pt shd; wc (cont); shwrs inc; el pnts (3-6A) €2.50-4; tradsmn; rv sw 2km; dogs €1; quiet; cc acc. "Vg CL-type site; secluded by tributary of Rv Ardèche; helpful owners. ♦ ltd. Easter-30 Sep. € 11.50   2005*

> Did you know you can fill in site report forms on the Club's website — www.caravanclub.co.uk?

MAZAMET *8F4* (1km E) **FFCC Camp Municipal de la Lauze, Stade de la Chevalière, 81200 Mazamet** [tel/fax 05 63 61 24 69; camping.mazamet@imsnet.fr] Exit Mazamet on St Pons rd N112, site on R past rugby grnd. Med, hdstg, pt sl, pt shd; wc (mainly cont); chem disp; shwrs inc; el pnts (6-10A) inc; lndry rm; supmkt 300m; BBQ; htd pool adj; tennis; dogs; poss cr; adv bkg; poss some rd noise; 10% red 2 nights / CCI. "San facs excel; gd touring base 'Black Mountain' region." 1 Jun-30 Sep. € 14.00   2006*

MAZAMET *8F4* (8km E Urban) **Camping La Vallée du Thoré, La Lamberthe, 81240 St Amans-Soult** [05 63 98 30 20; camping-valleethore@wanadoo.fr] Fr Mazamet take N112 dir Béziers; site on L in 8km, clearly sp in vill. By Nursery School. Sm, pt sl, pt shd; wc; chem disp; shwrs inc; el pnts (4-6A) €2.70-3.10; gas; lndtte; tradsmn; shops, rest, snacks & bar 500m; 30% statics; dogs free; Eng spkn; adv bkg; quiet; CCI. "Lovely vill site close to rv; conv N112; church bells stop at night; vg." 1 May-30 Sep. € 8.40   2007*

MAZAN see Carpentras *10E2*

MAZERES *8F3* (1km SE Rural) **Camp Municipal La Plage, Ave de Belpech, 09270 Mazères** [05 61 69 38 82 or 05 61 69 42 04 (Mairie); fax 05 61 69 37 97; danielle@camping-mazeres.com; www.camping-mazeres.com] Exit A66 junc 2; foll sp Mazères; on ent vill turn R onto lorry rte; site sp on D11 just bef leaving vill. Med, hdg/mkd pitch, pt shd; wc; chem disp; fam bthrm; shwrs inc; el pnts (10A) inc; lndtte; ice; shop 100m; tradsmn; rest; snacks; bar; playgrnd; 2 pools (1 htd); tennis; fishing & canoeing nr; games rm; entmnt; dogs; phone; adv bkg, dep req; noise fr peacocks; CCI. "Several san blocks, poss not all cleaned regularly low ssn (Jun 2007); gd." ♦ ltd. 26 May-1 Oct. € 14.00   2007*

MAZIERES see Chasseneuil sur Bonnieure *7B3*

MAZURES, LES see Rocroi *5C1*

MEAUDRE see Villard de Lans *9C3*

> This guide relies on site report forms submitted by caravanners like us; we'll do our bit and tell the editor what we think of the campsites we've visited.

MEAULNE *7A4* (S Urban) **Camp Municipal Le Cheval Blanc, Rue de Dr Conquet, 03360 Meaulne** [04 70 06 91 13 or 04 70 06 95 34; fax 04 70 06 91 29; mairie.meaulne@wanadoo.fr] Site off D2144 (N144) on bank Rv Aumance. Sm, mkd pitch, pt shd; wc; chem disp (wc); shwrs inc; el pnts (12A) €2; lndtte; shop, rest, bar 300m; BBQ; playgrnd; rv fishing; canoeing; dogs; phone; some rd noise; CCI. "Basic, pleasant rvside site; warden calls 1300 & 1900 or put money in letterbox; site yourself; poss flooding in high rainfall." ♦ ltd. 1 May-30 Sep. € 8.00   2006*

⊞MEAUX *3D3* (4km NE Rural) **Camping Village Parisien, Route de Congis, 77910 Varreddes [01 64 34 80 80; fax 01 60 22 89 84; leslie@villageparisien.com; www.villageparisien.com]** Fr Meaux foll sp on D405 dir Soissons then Varreddes, site sp on D121 dir Congis. Lge, hdg/mkd pitch, shd; htd wc; chem disp; mv service pnt; baby facs; shwrs inc; el pnts (6A) €2; gas; lndtte; sm shop; tradsmn; rest; snacks; bar; BBQ; playgrnd; pool; paddling pool; waterslide; fishing; tennis; games area; cycle hire; golf 5km; games rm; entmnt; TV rm; 50% statics; dogs free; site clsd mid-Dec to mid-Jan; Eng spkn; adv bkg; quiet; cc acc; red long stay/CCI. "Conv Paris cent (drive to metro), Parc Astérix & Disneyland - tickets avail fr site; lge pitches; friendly, helpful staff." 15 Mar-1 Nov. € 25.00   2007*

See advertisement on previous page

MEAUX *3D3* (10km SW Rural) **Camping International de Jablines, 77450 Jablines [01 60 26 09 37; fax 01 60 26 43 33; welcome@camping-jablines.com; www.camping-jablines.com]** Fr N A1 then A104 exit Claye-Souilly. Fr E A4 then A104 exit Meaux. Fr S A6, A86, A4, A104 exit Meaux. Site well sp 'Base de Loisirs de Jablines'. Lge, mkd pitch, pt sl, pt shd; htd wc; chem disp; mv service pnt; shwrs inc; el pnts (10A) inc; lndtte; ice; shop; tradsmn; rest; snacks; bar; playgrnd; sand beach & lake sw 500m; fishing; sailing; windsurfing; tennis 500m; horseriding; mini-golf; cycle hire; dogs €2; bus to Eurodisney; Eng spkn; adv bkg; quiet; red low ssn; cc acc; CCI. "V clean, well-run site; ideal for Disneyland (tickets for sale on site), Paris & Versailles; well-guarded; pleasant staff." ♦ 29 Mar-26 Oct. € 23.00 (CChq acc)   2007*

See advertisement below

MEAUX *3D3* (14km W Rural) **Camping L'Ile Demoiselle, Chemin du Port, 77410 Annet-sur-Marne [01 60 26 03 07 or 01 60 26 18 15; ile.demoiselle@wanadoo.fr]** Fr Meaux take N3 W, then turn L onto D404 twd Annet. Foll sp to 'Base de Loisirs de Jablines'. Fr Annet take D45 twd Jablines. Site on R immed bef bdge over rv. Med, some hdg pitch, pt shd; wc; chem disp (wc); shwrs €1.50; el pnts (4-6A) inc; gas 4km; lndry rm; shops 1km; BBQ; lake sw, sand beach 1km; 25% statics; dogs; some Eng spkn; adv bkg; rd noise; cc acc; CCI. "V nice site; conv Paris & Disneyland Paris; many other attractions in area; gd sh stay/NH." Apr-Oct. € 16.00   2006*

MEES, LES *10E3* (9km S Rural) **Camping L'Olivette, Hameau Les Pourcelles, 04190 Les Mées [tel/fax 04 92 34 18 97; campingolivette@club-internet.fr; http://campingolivette.free.fr]** Exit A51 junc 20 (fr N) or 19 (fr S) & cross Rv Durance onto D4. Site bet Oraison & Les Mées. Turn onto D754 to Les Pourcelles & foll site sp. Sm, hdg/mkd pitch, pt sl, terr, pt shd; wc; chem disp; shwrs inc; el pnts (6A) €2.80; ice; playgrnd; pool; 5% statics; dogs €1; Eng spkn; adv bkg; quiet. "Views over beautiful area; friendly owners; occasional out of ssn pitches avail; vg." ♦ ltd. 15 Apr-15 Sep. € 13.00   2006*

MEGEVE *9B3* (2km SW) **Camping-Caravaning Gai Séjour, 332 Route de Cassioz, 74120 Megève [tel/fax 04 50 21 22 58]** On N212 Flumet-Megève rd, site on R 1.5km after Praz-sur-Arly, well sp. Med, mkd pitch, sl (blocks needed), pt shd; wc; chem disp; shwrs inc; el pnts (4A) €2.20; lndry rm; ice; shops 1.5km; dogs €0.80; Eng spkn; adv bkg; quiet; CCI. "Pleasant site with gd views, lge pitches; gd walks; 40km fr Mont Blanc; helpful owners." 20 May-15 Sep. € 9.80   2005*

MEHUN SUR YEVRE 4H3 (500m N Urban) **Camp Municipal, Ave Châtelet, 18500 Mehun-sur-Yèvre [02 48 57 13 32 or 02 48 57 30 25 (Mairie); fax 02 48 57 34 16]** Leave A71 junc 6 onto N76 dir Bourges. App Mehun turn L into site at 2nd traff lts. Sm, mkd pitch, pt shd; wc; chem disp; mv service pnt; shwrs inc; el pnts (5-6A) €2.30 (poss rev pol); shop, rest & bar 600m; pizza van Thu & Sun (2007); playgrnd; free pool & tennis adj; quiet with some rd noise; cc not acc. "Excel value NH conv for m'way; v clean, modern san facs; relaxed atmosphere with friendly, helpful warden; water pnts poss long walk; site v quiet when pool clsd; office open 0700-1000 & 1700-2000, gates locked 2200-0700 (high ssn); twin-axles extra charge; 5 min walk to pleasant town; Bourges worth visit - use train; site under-used (Jul 2007)." ♦ 2 Jun-15 Sep. € 6.90   2007*

MEILHAN SUR GARONNE 7D2 (N Rural) **Camp Municipal au Jardin, 47200 Meilhan-sur-Garonne [06 08 03 54 77 (mob) or 05 53 94 30 04 (Mairie); fax 05 53 94 31 27; communedemeilhan.47@wanadoo.fr]** On N side of Canal Latéral, below Meilhan; exit A62 at junc 4 onto D9; or turn off N113 at Ste Bazeille; foll sp. Med, mkd pitch, pt shd; wc; shwrs €1; el pnts (10A) €1.35; lndtte; shops 500m; playgrnd; pool 500m; rv sw; fishing 100m; quiet; CCI. "If barrier down & no warden, key is in elect cupboard." 1 Jun-30 Sep. € 7.00   2007*

MEIX ST EPOING, LE see Sézanne 4E4

MEJANNES LE CLAP see Barjac (Gard) 9D2

MELE SUR SARTHE, LE 4E1 (500m SE Rural) **Camp Intercommunal de la Prairie, La Bretèche, St Julien-Sarthe, 61170 Le Mêle-sur-Sarthe [02 33 27 18 74]** Turn off N12 onto D4 S, site sp. Med, mkd pitch, pt shd; wc; chem disp; mv service pnt; shwrs; el pnts (6A) €2; lndtte; supmkt 300m; playgrnd; sand beach/lake 300m; sailing; tennis; mini-golf; adv bkg; CCI. "Site part of excel municipal sports complex; vg." 1 May-30 Sep. € 8.60   2005*

MELISEY 6F2 (7km E Rural) **Camping La Broche, Route du Mont-de-Vanne, 70270 Fresse [tel/fax 03 84 63 31 40]** Fr Lure head NE on D486 twd Melisey. Fr Mélisey stay on D486 twd Le Thillot, in 2.5km turn R onto D97 dir Plancher-les-Mines. In approx 5.5km site sp on R in Fresse. Sm, pt sl, terr, pt shd; wc; shwrs; el pnts (10A) €2; shop 1km; playgrnd; fishing adj; adv bkg; quiet apart fr double-chiming church bells; CCI. "In regional park, v secluded; friendly owner; great site." ♦ 1 Apr-15 Oct. € 8.00   2005*

MELISEY 6F2 (SE) **Camping La Bergereine, Route de Thillot, 70270 Mélisey [tel/fax 03 84 20 01 57; christiane.caritey@tele2.fr]** Fr Lure (or by-pass) take D486 dir Le Thillot; site sp. Sm, pt shd; wc; chem disp; shwrs; el pnts €2; gas; leisure cent & pool 500m; adv bkg; v quiet; fishing in adj rv; CCI. "Gd NH; simple farm site, friendly owner; attractive scenery, gd rest adj; gd family site." 1 Apr-30 Sep. € 8.00   2005*

MELLE 7A2 (2km N Urban) **Camp Municipal La Fontaine de Villiers, Route de Villiers, 79500 Melle [05 49 29 18 04 or 05 49 27 00 23 (Mairie); fax 05 49 27 01 51]** Fr N on D150 (D950) on ent Melle turn R at 1st rndabt, site is 1km fr Super U, well sp. Sm, hdg/mkd pitch, pt sl, pt shd; wc (some cont); chem disp; mv service pnt; shwrs inc; el pnts (4-10A) €2.40-3.80; shop, rest; snacks, bar 1km; BBQ; playgrnd; htd pool 500m; tennis 1km; phone; adv bkg; quiet; CCI. "NH only." Easter-30 Sep. € 7.65   2004*

As soon as we get home I'm going to post all these site report forms to the editor for inclusion in next year's guide. I don't want to miss the September deadline.

MELLE 7A2 (8km S Rural) **Camping La Maison de Puits, 14 Rue de Beauchamp, 79110 Tillou [05 49 07 20 28; mail@hallmarkholidays.eu; www.hallmarkholidays.eu]** Fr Niort on D948. At Melle foll sp Angoulême, R turn (to ring rd & avoids Melle cent). At Total stn rndabt turn R onto D948 dir Chef-Boutonne. In 3.5km turn R onto D737 sp Chef-Boutonne. After approx 5km at x-rds of D111 & D737, strt over & take 2nd turn R in 1km (sm sp to Tillou) along narr rd sp Tillou. In 1.6km site on L. Sm, sl, unshd; own san; chem disp; el pnts (16A) €3; BBQ; splash pool; adv bkg; quiet. "CL-type site in meadow/orchard (6 vans only); quiet & peaceful; new British owners (2006) plan to develop (shwrs & pool); ring ahead to book; interesting area; a real gem." € 10.00   2006*

MELLE 7A2 (10km SW Urban) **Camp Municipal, Rue des Merlonges, 79170 Brioux-sur-Boutonne [05 49 07 50 46; fax 05 49 07 27 27]** On ent Brioux fr Melle on D150 (D950) turn R immed over bdge; site on R in 100m. Sm, pt shd; wc; shwrs inc; el pnts (6A) €1.80; lndry rm; shops 300m; playgrnd; Eng spkn; quiet. "Pleasant rural setting; tidy, well cared for site; spotless ltd facs; choose own pitch & pay at Mairie on departure if no warden; vg sh stay/NH." 1 Apr-31 Oct. € 6.00   2006*

MELLE 7A2 (6km NW Rural) **Camp Municipal La Boissière, Route de Chizé, 79370 Celles-sur-Belle [05 49 32 95 57 or 05 49 79 80 17 (Mairie); fax 05 49 32 95 10; mairie-cellessurbelle@wanadoo.fr]** Fr Melle or Niort on D948. Exit by-pass into Celles & in town foll sp to Sports Complex & camping. Sm, pt sl, pt shd; htd wc (some cont); shwrs inc; el pnts (6A) €2.10; gas, shop 500m; BBQ; playgrnd; pool adj; rv 200m; lake 400m; tennis; 20% statics; dogs €0.85; adv bkg rec high ssn. "Warden calls am & pm; quiet apart fr football ground adj; gd NH." ♦ 15 Apr-15 Oct. € 6.75   2006*

MELUN *4E3* (3km S Rural) **Camping La Belle Etoile, Quai Joffre, 77000 La Rochette [01 64 39 48 12; fax 01 64 37 25 55; info@campinglabelleetoile. com; www.campinglabelleetoile.com]** On ent La Rochette on N6 fr Fontainbleu pass Total stn on L; turn immed R into Ave de la Seine & foll site sp; turn L at Rv Seine & site on L in 500m. Lge, hdg/ mkd pitch, pt shd; wc; chem disp; mv service pnt; shwrs; el pnts (6A) €3.20; gas; lndtte; shop 1km; snacks (high ssn); bar; playgrnd; htd pool; rv fishing; tennis 500m; golf 8km; internet; 10% statics; phone; dogs €1.40; Eng spkn; cc acc; red low ssn; CCI. "Helpful owners; conv Paris, Fontainebleau & Disneyland (ticket fr recep); gates locked 2300; indus area; sports complex nrby; gd walking & cycling in forest; rlwy noise thro night." ♦ ltd. 1 Apr-22 Oct. € 16.20 (CChq acc)   2006*

MEMBROLLE SUR CHOISILLE, LA *4G2* (Urban) **Camp Municipal, Route de Fondettes, 37390 La Membrolle-sur-Choisille [02 47 41 20 40]** On D938 (N138) Tours to Le Mans rd. Site on L on ent La Membrolle, sp. Med, pt shd; wc (some cont); chem disp; mv service pnt; shwrs inc; el pnts (6A) inc; lndtte; shop 5mins; hypmkt 3km; playgrnd; fishing, tennis, rv walks; dogs; bus 5min; phone; adv bkg; some rd noise; CCI. "Clean, well-maintained; gd san facs; wardens friendly/helpful; office/ent clsd 1300-1500." ♦ 1 May-30 Sep. € 9.30   2005*

MENAT *7A4* (2km E Rural) **Camp Municipal des Tarteaux, 63560 Menat [04 73 85 52 47 or 04 73 85 50 29 (Mairie); fax 04 73 85 50 22]** Heading SE on N144 foll sp Camping Pont de Menat. Exit N144 at Menat opp Hôtel Pinal. Site alongside Rv Sioule. Med, terr, pt sl, shd; wc (cont); shwrs inc; el pnts (5A) €2.40; ice; lndtte; shop 2km; playgrnd; rv adj; fishing & boating 2km; adv bkg; quiet; CCI. "Beautiful position; basic san facs." 1 Apr-30 Sep. € 7.70   2007*

MENDE *9D1* (2km S Rural) **Camping Tivoli, Route des Gorges du Tarn, 48000 Mende [tel/ fax 04 66 65 00 38; tivoli@libertysurf.fr; www.camping-tivoli.com]** Sp fr N88, turn R 300m downhill (narr but easy rd). Site adj Rv Lot. Med, pt shd; htd wc (some cont); chem disp; mv service pnt; shwrs inc; el pnts (6A) inc; lndtte; shop & 1km; bar; playgrnd; pool; rv fishing; TV rm; some statics; dogs €1; quiet; adv bkg. "Gd site nr town." € 17.25   2007*

MENDE *9D1* (8km SW Rural) **Camping Le Clos des Peupliers, 48000 Barjac [04 66 47 01 16]** On N88 in dir of Mende turn N on D142 sp Barjac & Camping. Site ent almost immed on R thro sh narr but not diff tunnel (max height 3.4m), adj Rv Lot. Lge, pt shd; wc; chem disp; shwrs inc; el pnts (6-10A) €2.50-3; lndtte; rest 500m; snacks; shops 500m; rv fishing adj; TV; dogs €1.30; quiet. "Facs clean, ltd low ssn; pleasant rvside site; poss unkempt low ssn; gd walks; helpful warden." 1 May-15 Sep. € 9.00   2005*

MENESPLET see Montpon Ménestérol *7C2*

MENETRUX EN JOUX see Doucier *6H2*

MENGLON see Luc en Diois *9D3*

MENIL see Château Gontier *4F1*

MENITRE, LA see Rosiers sur Loire, Les *4G1*

MENNETOU SUR CHER see Villefranche sur Cher *4G3*

MENTON *10E4* (1km N Urban/Coastal) **Camp Municipal du Plateau St Michel, Route de Mont Gros, 06500 Menton [04 93 35 81 23; fax 04 93 57 12 35]** Fr A8 Menton exit foll sp to town cent. After 2km with bus stn on L & rlwy bdge ahead turn L at rndabt, then R at T-junc. L at next T-junc, foll sp to site & Auberge Jeunesse. Rd is v steep & narr with hairpins - not rec trailer c'vans. Med, mkd pitch, terr, pt shd; wc (some cont); shwrs; el pnts (6A) €2.75; ice; rest; snacks; bar; sand beach 1km; poss v cr with tents; noisy; cc acc; CCI. "V steep walk into town; gd san facs." 1 Apr-31 Oct. € 16.50   2005*

⊞**MEOUNES LES MONTRIEUX** *10F3* (Rural) **FFCC Camping aux Tonneaux, Les Ferrages, 83136 Méounes-lès-Montrieux [04 94 33 98 34]** D554 fr Brignoles to Toulon. Site sp off D554 at exit to vill - busy, narr rd. Sm, mkd pitch, shd; wc; chem disp; shwrs inc; el pnts (3-6A); gas; ice; lndtte; shop; rest; bar; playgrnd; pool; tennis; 20% statics; dogs; Eng spkn; no adv bkg; quiet; 25% red low ssn; CCI. € 15.00   2004*

⊞**MERENS LES VALS** *8G4* (1km W Rural) **Camp Municipal Ville de Bau, 09110 Mérens- les-Vals [05 61 02 85 40 or 05 61 64 33 77; fax 05 61 64 03 83; camping.merens@wanadoo.fr]** Fr Ax-les-Thermes on N20 sp Andorra past Mérens-les-Vals turn R nr start of dual c'way sp Camp Municipal. Site on R in 800m. Med, hdg pitch; wc (some cont); shwrs inc; el pnts (6-10A) €2.30-4 (poss rev pol); shop; playgrnd; pool 8km; 20% statics; dogs €0.50; poss cr; quiet; cc acc; CCI. "Conv Andorra, Tunnel de Puymorens; excel facs; gd walks fr site; vg value." € 10.40   2006*

MERIBEL *9B3* (2km N Rural) **Camping Le Martagon, Le Raffort, Route de Méribel, 73550 Les Allues [04 79 00 56 29; fax 04 79 00 44 92]** Fr Moûtiers on D915 S to Brides-les-Bains then D90 S dir Méribel. Site on L at Le Raffort. Park in public car park & go to rest. Sm, hdstg, terr, unshd; htd wc; chem disp; shwrs inc; el pnts (10A) €5; gas 200m; lndtte; shop 2km; tradsmn; rest; bar; no statics; dogs; adv bkg; rd noise; cc acc. "Ski bus every 20 mins at site ent; skilift 100m; htd boot room; mountain-biking in summer." ♦ 26 Apr-Nov. € 25.00   2007*

MERINCHAL *7B4* (S Urban) **Camp Municipal La Mothe, Château de Mérinchal, 23420 Mérinchal** [05 55 67 25 56 (Tourist Office); fax 05 55 67 23 71; tourisme.merinchal@wanadoo.fr] E fr Pontaumur on D941twds Aubusson. R onto D27 to Mérinchal. Site in vill. Sm, pt sl, pt shd; wc; shwrs inc; el pnts €2; lndtte; shop, rest, bar nr; playgrnd; TV; fishing 500m; quiet. "Excel site in chateau grounds but poss clsd w/e if weddings etc in chateau - phone ahead to check." ♦ 1 May-30 Oct. € 8.50   2007*

MERVANS *6H1* (NE Rural) **Camp Municipal du Plan d'Eau, Route de Pierre-de-Bresse, 71310 Mervans** [03 85 76 16 63 (Mairie); fax 03 85 76 16 93; mairie-de-mervans@wanadoo.fr] E on N78 fr Chalon-sur-Saône. At Thurey fork L onto D204; at x-rds turn L onto D996 to Mervans. In vill take D313 dir Pierre-de-Bresse, site sp by lake. Sm, pt shd; wc (some cont); shwrs inc; el pnts (10A) €1.80; shop, rest adj; fishing nr; quiet; CCI. "Well-kept site, clean facs; lovely countryside; v attractive vill." ♦ 1 Jun-15 Sep. € 6.60   2007*

MERVENT see Fontenay le Comte *7A2*

MERVILLE FRANCEVILLE PLAGE see Cabourg *3D1*

MERY SUR SEINE *4E4* (1km N Rural) **Camp Municipal, 10170 Méry-sur-Seine** [03 25 21 23 72 or 03 25 21 20 42 (Mairie); fax 03 25 21 13 19] Turn N off D619 (N19) Troyes to Romilly onto D373 sp Méry-sur-Seine; in vill turn 1st L after x-ing Rv Seine; site on L in 1km on rv bank. Med, hdg/mkd pitch, hdstg, pt sl, pt shd; wc (some cont); chem disp; shwrs inc; el pnts (3-10A) €1.40-2.70; lndtte; shops 50m; BBQ; playgrnd; fishing; 75% statics; phone; poss cr; Eng spkn; adv bkg; quiet; CCI. "Gd san facs but no tap for attaching hose - poss diff for m'vans to fill tank; friendly warden on site for initial access (0900-1200 & 1700-1900); €25 dep for barrier card; pleasant town with mkt; vg." ♦ ltd. 1 Apr-30 Sep. € 7.00   2007*

MESCHERS SUR GIRONDE see Royan *7B1*

MESLAND see Onzain *4G2*

MESLAY DU MAINE *4F1* (2.5km NE Rural) **Camp Municipal La Chesnaie, 53170 Meslay-du-Maine** [02 43 98 48 08 or 02 43 64 10 45 (Mairie); fax 02 43 98 75 52; camping-lachesnaie@wanadoo.fr] Take D21 SE fr Laval to Meslay. Turn L in cent of vill onto D152. Site on R in 2.5km. Med, hdg/mkd pitch, pt shd; wc (some cont); shwrs inc; el pnts (6-12A) €2.30 (poss long lead req); lndtte; shop 2.5km; rest 200m; snacks; bar; playgrnd; lake adj; watersports, leisure cent adj; 10% statics; poss cr; adv bkg; cc acc; CCI. "Excel; clean & quiet." ♦ Easter-30 Sep. € 8.60   2007*

MESNOIS see Clairvaux les Lacs *6H2*

France

The opening dates and prices on this campsite have changed. I'll send a site report form to the editor for the next edition of the guide.

MESSANGES *8E1* (2km S Coastal) **Camping La Côte, Route de Vieux-Boucau, 40660 Messanges** [05 58 48 94 94; fax 05 58 48 94 44; lacote@wanadoo.fr; www.campinglacote.com] On D652 2km S of Messanges. Med, pt shd; wc; chem disp; mv service pnt; serviced pitches; shwrs inc; el pnts (6-10A) €3.50-4.50; lndtte; sm shop; supmkt 1km; tradsmn; snacks; playgrnd; pool complex; paddling pool; sand beach 1km; horseriding 300m; golf 2km; 5% statics; dogs €2; phone; adv bkg; Eng spkn; quiet; red low ssn; CCI. "Peaceful, clean, tidy site on edge of pine woods; big pitches; gd access to beaches; gd network cycle tracks; excel." ♦ 1 Apr-30 Sep. € 16.20   2007*

MESSANGES *8E1* (2km SW Coastal) **Airotel Camping Le Vieux Port, Plage Sud, 40660 Messanges** [01 72 03 91 60; fax 05 58 48 01 69; contact@levieuxport.com; www.levieuxport.com or www.natureetloisirs.fr] Fr S take D652 past Vieux-Boucau, site sp. V lge, mkd pitch, pt sl, pt shd; wc (some cont); chem disp; mv service pnt; shwrs inc; el pnts (6-8A) €4-7; gas; lndtte; ice; shop; tradsmn; rest; snacks; bar; playgrnd; htd, pt covrd pool + pool complex; paddling pool; waterslide; dir access to sand beach 400m; tennis; games area; cycle hire; horseriding; quadbikes; mini-golf; boules; beach train; entmnt; child entmnt; dogs €4.50; adv bkg, dep req; poss cr; quiet; red low ssn; cc acc; CCI. "Excel touring base; v pleasant site." ♦ 1 Apr-30 Sep. € 39.00 (CChq acc)   2007*

See advertisement on previous page

METZ *5D2* (12km SW) **Camping Le Pâquis, 57680 Corny-sur-Moselle** [03 87 52 03 59 or 03 87 60 68 67; fax 03 87 60 71 96; www.camping-lepaquis.com] SW fr Metz on N57; site sp on ent to vill. Or S on A31 take junc 29 Féy & turn R onto D66 into Corny-sur-Moselle. At rndabt in vill turn R. Site is 300m on L. Lge, shd; wc; chem disp; shwrs inc; el pnts (6A) €2.60 (long cable poss req); lndry rm; gas; ice; snacks; bar; shops 1km; tradsmn; lndtte; playgrnd; rv sw adj; TV; entmnt; dogs €0.92; poss cr; adv bkg; cc acc; CCI. "Gd, well-run site on Rv Moselle; friendly owners; poss rlwy noise; recep 0800-1200 & 1430-1800; rec arr early for quieter pitch at far end site." 1 May-30 Sep. € 9.20
2007*

METZ *5D2* (500m NW Urban) **Camp Municipal Metz-Plage, Allée de Metz-Plage, 57000 Metz** [03 87 68 26 48; fax 03 87 38 03 89; campingmetz@mairie-metz.fr; www.mairie-metz.fr] Exit A31 junc 33 Metz-Nord/Pontiffroy exit. Foll 'Autres Directions' sp back over a'route & Rv Moselle; site sp. Fr S turn R over Rv Moselle & as above. Med, mkd pitch, hdstg, pt sl, pt shd; wc; chem disp; mv service pnt; baby facs; shwrs inc; el pnts (10A) inc (poss rev pol); lndtte; shop, snacks; playgrnd; pool adj (inc); rv fishing adj; internet; dogs €0.50; extra for twin-axles; poss cr; Eng spkn; adv bkg; traff noise fr rv bdge; cc acc; CCI. "Lovely site; views over rv (fenced); some gd sized pitches, most modest & some on sl & poss diff to exit (uphill reverse); facs stretched if site full; early arr ess high ssn; recep open 0700-2030; flood warning area; easy walk to attractive town with cathedral." ♦ 5 May-25 Sep. € 13.30   2007*

MEURSAULT see Beaune *6H1*

MEYRAS see Thueyts *9D2*

MEYRIEU LES ETANGS *9B2* (800m SE Rural) **Camping du Moulin, Route de Châtonnay, 38440 Meyrieu-les-Etangs** [04 74 59 30 34; fax 04 74 58 36 12; contact@camping-meyrieu.com; www.camping-meyrieu.com] Exit A43 at junc 8. Enter Bourgoin & foll sp for La Gare to pick up D522 SW twd St Jean-de-Bournay. Site next to lake 1km fr D522, sp. Med, mkd pitch, hdstg, terr, pt shd; wc; shwrs; el pnts (6-10A) €3.60-4.80; lndry rm; ice; shop; rest; lake sw; pedaloes; fishing; canoeing; archery; mini-golf; games rm; entmnt in ssn; TV; dogs €1.60; phone; adv bkg; quiet. "Lovely views across lake; sm pitches; hdstg on all pitches for car parking; v clean san facs & site; vg." ♦ 15 Apr-30 Sep. € 15.40   2007*

MEYRUEIS *10E1* (3km N Rural) **FFCC Camping La Cascade, Salvinsac, 48150 Meyrueis** [04 66 45 45 45 or 06 85 84 07 15 (mob); fax 04 66 45 48 48; contact@camping-la-cascade.com; www.camping-la-cascade.com] N of Meyrueis on D996, on R. NB Do not app fr N - narr rd. Rec app fr Millau dir only. Sm, mkd pitch, pt sl, terr, pt shd; wc; chem disp; mv service pnt; baby facs; shwrs inc; el pnts (10A) €2.90; gas; lndtte; shop; tradsmn; BBQ; playgrnd; canoeing; fishing; horseriding; walking; 20% statics; dogs; poss cr; Eng spkn; adv bkg; cc acc. "V friendly owners." ♦ 8 Apr-1 Nov. € 12.50   2006*

MEYRUEIS *10E1* (1km NE Rural) **Camping Le Pré de Charlet, Route de Florac, 48150 Meyrueis** [04 66 45 63 65; fax 04 66 45 63 24; contact@camping-lepredecharlet.com; www.camping-lepredecharlet.com] Exit Meyrueis on rd to Florac (D996). Site on R on bank of Rv Jonte. Med, mkd pitch, pt sl, terr, pt shd, pt sl; wc (some cont); chem disp; mv service pnt; baby facs; shwrs inc; el pnts (16A) €2.60; gas; lndtte; shop & 11km; tradsmn; bar; BBQ; playgrnd; pool 400m; rv fishing; phone; adv bkg; phone; quiet; cc acc; CCI. "Friendly owner; excel." ♦ ltd. 15 Apr-10 Oct. € 12.00   2007*

MEYRUEIS *10E1* (500m E Rural) **Camping Le Champ d'Ayres, Route de la Brèze, 48150 Meyrueis** [tel/fax 04 66 45 60 51; campinglechampdayres@wanadoo.fr; www.campinglechampdayres.com] Fr W on D907 dir Gorges de la Jonte into Meyrueis. Foll sp Château d'Ayres & site. Med, hdg/mkd pitch, pt sl, pt shd; wc (some cont); chem disp; mv service pnt; baby facs; fam bthrm; shwrs inc; el pnts (6-10A) €2.50; lndtte; shop; tradsmn; snacks; bar; playgrnd; htd pool; 15% statics; dogs free; phone; poss cr; Eng spkn; adv bkg; red low ssn; cc not acc; CCI. ♦ 9 Apr-25 Sep. € 17.00   2005*

MEYRUEIS *10E1* (800m NW Rural) **Camping Le Capelan, Route de Jonte, 48150 Meyrueis [tel/fax 04 66 45 60 50 or 04 90 53 34 45 (LS); camping. le.capelan@wanadoo.fr; www.campingcapelan. com]** Site sp on D996 on banks of Rv Jonte. Med, mkd pitch, shd; wc; chem disp; mv service pnt; baby facs; fam bthrm; shwrs inc; el pnts (4-10A) €3; gas; lndtte; ice; shop; tradsmn; supmkt 500m; BBQ; rest 1km; snacks; bar; playgrnd; 2 htd pools (no shorts); rv sw; fishing; tennis 1km; games rm; games area; rockclimbing; internet; entmnt; sat TV; 70% statics; private bthrms avail; Eng spkn; adv bkg; quiet; red low ssn; cc acc; CCI. "Gd rvside site; conv touring Gorges du Tarn & Cévennes National Park; beautiful scenery." ♦ 5 May-15 Sep. € 19.00 (CChq acc) 2007*

MEYSSAC *7C3* (2km NE Rural) **Intercommunal Moulin de Valane, Route de Collonges-la-Rouge, 19500 Meyssac [05 55 25 41 59; fax 05 55 84 07 28; mairie@meyssac.fr; www. meyssac.fr]** Well sp on D38 bet Meyssac & Collonges-la-Rouge. Med, mkd pitch, pt sl, pt shd; wc; chem disp; shwrs; el pnts (10A) €2.80; lndtte; shop; rest; snacks; bar; playgrnd; pool; tennis; many statics; adv bkg; CCI. "Within walking dist of attractive vill; fair only." ♦ 1 May-30 Sep. € 13.00 2007*

MEYZIEU see Lyon *9B2*

MEZE *10F1* (1km N Coastal) **Camping Beau Rivage, 113 Route Nationale, 34140 Mèze [04 67 43 81 48; fax 04 67 43 66 70; reception@camping-beaurivage.fr; www.camping-beaurivage.fr]** Fr Mèze cent foll D613 (N113) dir Montpellier, site on R 100m past rndabt on leaving town; well sp. Lge, mkd pitch, pt shd; wc; chem disp; mv service pnt; shwrs inc; el pnts (3-6A) inc; lndtte; shop; supmkt 200m; rest; snacks; bar; BBQ; playgrnd; htd pool & paddling pool; sand beach 700m; fishing; sailing; tennis 900m; entmnt; TV rm; 50% statics; phone; dogs €3; poss cr; Eng spkn; adv bkg; quiet; cc acc; CCI. "Gd rests nr harbour; excel local oysters; conv Sète & Noilly Prat distillery; vg new san facs (2007); trees & narr access rds poss diff lge o'fits." ♦ 7 Apr-22 Sep. € 32.00 (CChq acc) 2007*

MEZE *10F1* (3km N Rural) **Camp Municipal Loupian, Ave de la Gare, 34140 Loupian [04 67 43 57 67]** Fr Mèze tak D613 (N113) & turn L at 1st Loupian sp, then foll sp for site. Med, hdg/mkd pitch, pt shd; wc; shwrs; el pnts (5A) €2; lndtte; snacks; bar; playgrnd; sand beach 3km; poss cr; Eng spkn; adv bkg; quiet; CCI. "Pleasant site in popular area; gd rests near Mèze." ♦ ltd. 1 May-15 Sep. € 10.00 2004*

MEZEL *10E3* (W Rural) **Camp Municipal Le Claus, 04270 Mezel [04 92 35 53 87 (Mairie); fax 04 92 35 52 86]** Sp fr N85 fr both dir. Heading S fr Digne onto D907; turn R to site on L. Sm, pt sl, pt shd; wc (cont); shwrs; el pnts (3-6A); lndtte; snacks nr; poss cr; quiet. "Private rlwy to Nice v nr." 1 Jul-31 Aug. 2004*

MEZIERES EN BRENNE *4H2* (500m E Rural) **Camp Municipal La Cailauderie, 36290 Mézières-en-Brenne [02 54 38 12 24 or 02 54 38 09 23]** On D925 to Châteauroux, sp Stade. Sm, mkd pitch, pt shd; wc; chem disp; shwrs inc; el pnts (6A) inc; shop, rest, bar 500m; playgrnd; rv adj; dogs; quiet; CCI. "Bird-watching; site yourself, warden calls am & pm; rv fishing on site; poss itinerants; poss vicious mosquitoes." 1 May-30 Sep. € 9.00 2004*

MEZIERES EN BRENNE *4H2* (6km E Rural) **Camping Bellebouche, 36290 Mézières-en-Brenne [02 54 38 32 36; fax 02 54 38 32 96; v.v.n@ wanadoo.fr]** Sp on D925. Med, mkd pitch, pt sl, pt shd; wc (cont); chem disp (wc); baby facs; shwrs inc; el pnts inc; lndtte; shop 6km; rest high ssn; bar 6km; playgrnd; lake sw adj; watersports; fishing; no statics; no dogs high ssn; phone; quiet; cc acc; CCI. "In country park; gd walking, cycling, bird-watching; vg." 1 Mar-30 Nov. € 14.00 2006*

MEZOS see St Julien en Born *8E1*

MIANNAY see Abbeville *3B3*

MIGENNES see Joigny *4F4*

France

⊞**MILLAS** *8G4* (3km W Rural) **FLOWER Camping La Garenne**, 66170 Néfiach [04 68 57 15 76; fax 04 68 57 37 42; camping.lagarenne.nefiach@ wanadoo.fr; www.camping-lagarenne.fr] Fr Millas on R of D916, sp. Med, shd; htd wc (some cont); chem disp; baby facs; shwrs inc; el pnts (6-10A) €5; gas; lndtte; shop; snacks; bar; BBQ; playgrnd; pool high ssn; tennis 500m; games area; entmnt; 20% statics; dogs free; adv bkg rec high ssn; quiet but poss noisy disco; red low ssn. "Friendly owners." ♦ € 18.00   2006*

MILLAU *10E1* (1km NE Urban) **Camping du Viaduc, Millau-Cureplat, 121 Ave du Millau-Plage, 12100 Millau** [05 65 60 15 75; fax 05 65 61 36 51; info@ camping-du-viaduc.com;   www.camping-du-viaduc.com] Exit Millau on N991 (sp Nant) over Rv Tarn via Cureplat bdge. At rndabt take D187 dir Paulhe, 1st campsite on L. Lge, hdg/mkd pitch, shd; htd wc (some cont); chem disp; some serviced pitches (extra charge); baby facs; shwrs inc; el pnts (6A) €3 (poss long lead req); gas; lndtte; ice; shop; rest; snacks; bar; BBQ; playgrnd; htd pool; paddling pool; rv sw & private sand beach; entmnt; child entmnt; wifi internet; dogs €2.50; Eng spkn; cc acc; red long stay; CCI. "Well run site; excel san facs; warm welcome; v helpful staff; easy walk to Millau cent; barrier clsd 2200-0700; many sports & activities in area; conv for gorges & viaduct; v quiet low ssn; excel." ♦ 25 Apr-29 Sep. € 23.00   2007*

See advertisement on previous page

MILLAU *10E1* (1km NE Urban) **Camping Larribal, Ave de Millau Plage, 12100 Millau** [05 65 59 08 04; camping.larribal@wanadoo.fr; www.campinglarribal.com] Exit Millau on D991 (sp Nant), cross rv & at rndabt take 3rd exit, site on L. Med, mkd pitch, shd; htd wc; chem disp; shwrs inc; el pnts (6A) inc; gas; lndtte; ice; shop; tradsmn; playgrnd; rv sw adj; shgl beach; TV; 5% statics; phone; adv bkg; red 30+ days; CCI. "Excel, well-kept, quiet site on bank of Rv Tarn; san facs need updating but spotless; recep clsd 1300-1500; lge o'fits poss diff access; high m'vans poss diff under trees; gd access to gorges; severe tree fluff in May." ♦ 1 May-30 Sep. € 12.80   2007*

MILLAU *10E1* (1km NE Urban) **Camping Les Erables, Route de Millau-Plage, 12100 Millau** [05 65 59 15 13; fax 05 65 59 06 59; camping-les-erables@wanadoo.fr; www.campingleserables.fr] Exit Millau on D991 (sp Nant) over Rv Tarn bdge; take L at island sp to Millau-Plage & site on L immed after Camping du Viaduc & bef Camping Larribal. On ent Millau fr N or S foll sps 'Campings'. Med, hdg/mkd pitch, pt shd; wc; chem disp; baby facs; shwrs inc; el pnts (6A) €3 (poss rev pol); lndtte; ice; shop; snacks high ssn; bar; BBQ; playgrnd; direct acc to rv - sw & canoeing; entmnt; TV; dogs €1.20; phone; Eng spkn; adv bkg; some rd noise; cc acc; CCI. "Excel rvside site; v clean; friendly, helpful owners; beavers nrby." ♦ 1 Apr-30 Sep. € 14.90   2007*

MILLAU *10E1* (2km NE Urban) **Camping Côte-Sud, Ave de l'Aigoual, 12100 Millau** [tel/fax 05 65 61 18 83; camping-cotesud@orange.fr; www.campingcotesud.com] Fr N exit A75 junc 45 to Millau. Turn L at 2nd traff island sp 'Camping'. Site on R over bdge in 200m. Fr S exit A75 junc 47 onto N9 & cross rv on by-pass, turn R at 1st traff island sp Nant on D991, cross bdge, site on R in 200m, sp. Site a S confluence of Rv Dourbie & Rv Tarn. Med, mkd pitch, pt sl, shd; wc; chem disp; shwrs inc; el pnts (5A) €3; gas; lndtte; ice; shop; snacks; playgrnd; pool; rv sw adj; fishing, canoe hire & hang-gliding nrby; some statics; dogs €1.50; Eng spkn; adv bkg; red low ssn; CCI. "Lge mkt Fri; conv Tarn Gorges; pleasant, friendly owner; vg." 1 Apr-30 Sep. € 19.00   2007*

MILLAU *10E1* (8km NE Rural) **Camping Les Cerisiers, Pailhas, 12520 Compeyre** [05 65 59 87 96 or 05 65 59 10 35 (LS); contact@campinglescerisiers.com;   www. campinglescerisiers.com] Fr Millau N on N9 for 4km, then D907 to Pailhas; site at exit to vill on R. Med, mkd pitch, pt shd; wc; chem disp; shwrs inc; el pnts (6A) €3; lndtte; shop; tradsmn; snacks; playgrnd; private beach on Rv Tarn; pool 3km; rock climbing; canoeing, mountain biking, paragliding & horseriding nrby; games rm; dogs €1.50; phone; poss cr; Eng spkn; adv bkg; quiet; cc acc; CCI. "Vg, clean site; bird-watching; Millau tourist train; conv Tarn gorges; 1 May-15 Sep. € 12.00   2007*

MILLAU *10E1* (9km NE Rural) **Camp Municipal d'Aguessac, Chemin de Prades, 12520 Aguessac** [05 65 59 84 67; fax 05 65 59 08 72; camping. aguessac@wanadoo.fr] Site on N907 in vill; ent on R v soon after level x-ing when app fr Millau - adj g'ge forecourt. Med, mkd pitch, pt shd; wc; chem disp; shwrs inc; el pnts (6-10A) €2.50; gas; lndtte; shops adj; bar; rv adj; fishing; canoeing; games area; sports grnd adj; entmnt; 10% statics; dogs €1; quiet; red long stay/low ssn; CCI. "Rvside site with mountain views; delightful position; public footpath thro site along rv; gd sized pitches; tourers in lge area under trees; picturesque vill & local viaduct; poss youth groups high ssn - but no problem; excel touring base; unreliable opening dates." ♦ 1 Jun-15 Sep. € 12.00   2007*

MILLAU *10E1* (E Rural) **Camping Club Le Millau-Plage, Route de Millau-Plage, 12100 Millau** [05 65 60 10 97; fax 05 65 60 16 88; info@campingmillauplage.com;   www.camping millauplage.com] Exit Millau on D991 (sp Nant) over Rv Tarn; at rndabt take final exit onto D187 sp Paulhe; site is 4th on L. Lge, mkd pitch, pt shd; wc (some cont); chem disp; shwrs inc; el pnts (5A) inc; gas; lndtte; shop; rest; snacks; bar; playgrnd; pool; multi-sports area; child entmnt; TV; play rm; 10% statics; dogs €3; poss cr; Eng spkn; adv bkg; quiet; red low ssn; cc acc; CCI. "Magnificent scenery." ♦ 1 Apr-30 Sep. € 24.50   2006*

Camping ★★★
La Musardière

Route des Grandes Vallées
F-91490 MILLY LA FORET
TEL/FAX: 00 33 (0) 164 98 91 91

The campsite La Musardière welcomes you on a splendid, 12 ha large, forestry site with its pitches of 200m2. It is the ideal place for all nature, hiking and climbing fans (FONTAINEBLEAU Forest). A large number of parks, castles and museums surround us and Paris is at less than one hour's drive away.
On site, you will find an aquatic park (4 pools), a volleyball pitch, table tennis, French boules ground. Open from 15/2 till 1/12.

lamusardiere@infonie.fr

France

MILLAU *10E1* (1km E Urban) **Camping Les Deux Rivières**, 61 Ave de l'Aigoual, 12100 Millau [05 65 60 00 27 or 06 07 08 41 41 (mob); fax 05 65 60 76 78; camping.deux-rivières@wanadoo. fr; www.ot-millau.fr] Fr N on D911 foll sp for Montpellier down to rv. At rndabt by bdge turn L over bdge, site immed on L well sp. Fr S D992 3rd bdge, sp camping. Med, mkd pitch, shd; htd wc (50% cont); shwrs inc; el pnts (8A) €2.80; gas; lndry rm; shops adj; tradsmn; snacks; playgrnd; fishing; phone; poss cr; quiet; CCI. "Gd base for touring gorges; gd modern san facs." 1 Apr-31 Oct. € 13.90   2006*

MILLAU *10E1* (2.5km E) **FFCC Camping St Lambert**, Ave de l'Aigoual, 12100 Millau [05 65 60 00 48; fax 05 65 61 12 12; camping. saintlambert@free.fr] Fr N on either N9 or D11 foll dir D992 St Affrique/Albi. Turn L at rndabt over bdge onto D991 dir Nant. Site on R, sp. Fr S on D992 turn R at rndabt & dir as above. Med, mkd pitch, shd; wc (some cont); chem disp; mv service pnt; shwrs inc; el pnts (6A) €2.50; gas; lndtte; ice; shop; bar; playgrnd; sand/shgl beach & rv sw adj; 10% statics; dogs €1; poss cr; adv bkg; quiet; CCI. "Particularly gd low ssn; owners helpful; twin-axles not acc." 1 May-30 Sep. € 12.90   2006*

Before we move on, I'm going to fill in some site report forms and post them off to the editor, otherwise they won't arrive in time for the deadline at the end of September.

MILLY LA FORET *4E3* (4km SE Rural) **Camping La Musardière**, Route des Grandes Vallées, 91490 Milly-la-Forêt [tel/fax 01 64 98 91 91; lamusardiere@infonie.fr] Fr S exit A6 junc 14 onto N152 then D16 dir Milly. Fr N exit A6 junc 13 onto D372 to Milly. Site on sm rd joining D16 & D837/ D409. Lge, mkd pitch, hdstg, pt sl, pt shd; htd wc (some cont); chem disp; shwrs inc; el pnts (6A) inc; lndtte; ice; shop 4km; tradsmn (w/e only low ssn); BBQ; playgrnd; htd pool high ssn; paddling pool; 60% statics; dogs free; Eng spkn; adv bkg; quiet; cc acc; red long stay; CCI. "Excel wooded site; excel pool; helpful, friendly staff; gd walks in nrby forest." ♦ 15 Feb-1 Dec. € 20.70   2007*

See advertisement above

MILLAU *10E1* (1km E Urban) **Camping Les Rivages**, Ave de l'Aigoual, 12100 Millau [05 65 61 01 07 or 06 89 78 50 33 (mob); fax 05 65 59 03 56; campinglesrivages@wanadoo.fr; www.campinglesrivages.com] Fr Millau take D991 dir Nant (sp Gorges de la Dourbie & Campings). Cross Rv Tarn & cont on this rd, site is 500m after bdge on R. Lge, pt shd; htd wc (some cont); chem disp (wc); serviced pitches (additional charge); baby facs; shwrs inc; el pnts (6A) inc (poss rev pol); gas; lndtte; ice; sm shop; supmkt 2km; tradsmn; rest; snacks; bar; BBQ; playgrnd; 2 pools; paddling pool; tennis; rv sw; fishing; canoeing; cycle hire; hanggliding; entmnt; child entmnt; wifi internet; games/TV rm; 10% statics; dogs €3; phone; poss cr; Eng spkn; adv bkg; quiet; red low ssn; cc acc over €30; CCI. "V scenic, pleasant site, esp rv/side pitches, in o'standing area; gd security; excursions; v busy high ssn; Gorges du Tarn nr for family canoeing; staff v helpful & friendly; mkt Wed & Fri am; vg rest & bar; san facs clean but need update." ♦ 1 Apr-10 Oct. € 26.60 ABS - D20   2007*

MIMIZAN *7D1* (2km N Rural) **Camping du Lac**, Ave de Woolsack, 40200 Mimizan [05 58 09 01 21; fax 05 58 09 43 06; lac@mimizan-camping.com; www.mimizan-camping.com] Fr Mimizan N on D87, site on L. Lge, mkd pitch; pt shd; wc; chem disp; mv service pnt; baby facs; shwrs inc; el pnts (3A) inc; gas; lndtte; ice; shop; rest; snacks; bar; BBQ; playgrnd; sand beach 6km; lake adj - no sw; boating; fishing; entmnt; some statics; dogs €1.70; poss cr; adv bkg; quiet; red low ssn. "Nice site in lovely location; o'night area for m'vans; rec." ♦ ltd. 30 Mar-30 Sep. € 17.00   2007*

MIMIZAN *7D1* (3km E Rural) **Camping Aurilandes, 1001 Promenade de l'Etang, 40200 Aureilhan [05 58 09 10 88 or 05 46 55 10 01; fax 05 46 55 10 00; aurilandes@village-center.com; www.village-center.com/aurilandes]** Fr N10 S of Bordeaux take D626 W fr Labouheyre twds Mimizan. Site 1km fr D626 by Lake Aureilhan. V lge, mkd pitch, pt shd; wc; mv service pnt; sauna; shwrs inc; el pnts (6-10A) inc; lndtte; shop; tradsmn; rest; playgrnd; htd pool complex; paddling pool; spa; sand beach 10km; dir access to lake; watersports; tennis; games rm; entmnt; child entmnt; statics; dogs €3; Eng spkn; adv bkg; cc acc; quiet; cc acc. ♦ 12 May-19 Sep. € 29.00   2007*

MIMIZAN *7D1* (3km E Rural) **Parc Saint James Eurolac, 1001 Promenade de l'Etang, 40200 Aureilhan [05 58 09 02 87; fax 05 58 09 41 89; info@ camping-parcsaintjames.com; www.camping-parcsaintjames.com]** Fr Bordeaux take N10 S to Labouheyre & cont on D626 W twd Mimizan. Turn R 3km bef Mimizan onto D329 twd Etang d'Aureilhan. Site beside lake. V lge, hdg/mkd pitch, pt sl, pt shd; wc; chem disp; mv service pnt; baby facs; sauna; shwrs inc; el pnts (6-10A) €3; gas; lndtte; ice; shop; supmkt; rest; snacks; bar; BBQ area; playgrnd; htd pool & waterpark; paddling pool; sand beach 10km; lake sw adj; fishing; sailing; canoe hire; windsurfing; tennis; cycle hire; games area; horseriding nr; archery; mini-golf; games rm; golf 2km; entmnt; TV rm; 90% statics; dogs €5; Eng spkn; adv bkg; quiet; cc acc; red low ssn; CCI. ♦ 5 Apr-27 Sep. € 27.00   2007*

See advertisement above

MIMIZAN PLAGE *7D1* (1km E Coastal) **Camp Municipal La Plage, Blvd d'Atlantique, 40200 Mimizan-Plage [05 58 09 00 32; fax 05 58 09 44 94; contact@mimizan-camping.com]** Turn off N10 at Labouheyre on D626 to Mimizan (28km). Approx 5km after Mimizan turn R. Site in approx 500m. V lge, pt sl, shd; wc; mv service pnt; baby facs; shwrs; el pnts (10A) €2; lndtte; ice; shops 500m; playgrnd; sand beach 850m; games area; entmnt; 15% statics; dogs €1.80; poss cr; noisy. Easter-30 Sep. € 16.00   2006*

MIMIZAN PLAGE *7D1* (3km E Coastal) **Club Marina-Landes, Rue Marina, 40202 Mimizan-Plage-Sud [05 58 09 12 66; fax 05 58 09 16 40; contact@clubmarina.com; www.marinalandes. com]** Turn R off N10 at Labouheyre onto D626 to Mimizan (28km). Approx 5km fr Mimizan-Plage turn L at Camping Marina sp on dual c'way. Site sp on S bank of rv. V lge, hdg pitch, hdstg, pt shd; wc; chem disp; mv service pnt; baby facs; shwrs inc; el pnts (10A) inc; gas; lndtte; lndry rm; shop; rest; snacks; bar; BBQ; playgrnd; 2 pools (1 htd, covrd); paddling pool; waterslide; sand beach 500m; tennis; horseriding; games area; mini-golf; cycle hire; games rm; fitness rm; golf 7km; entmnt; child entmnt; internet; TV rm; some statics; dogs €4; poss cr; Eng spkn; adv bkg; cc acc; quiet; red CCI. "Excursions to Dax, Biarritz & Bordeaux areas; excel leisure facs; vg." ♦ 25 Apr-15 Sep. € 42.00 (3 persons)   2007*

See advertisement opposite

There aren't many sites open this early in the year. We'd better phone ahead to check that the one we're heading for is actually open.

MIOS see Audenge *7D1*

⊞**MIRAMBEAU** *7C2* (1km N Urban) **Camp Municipal Le Carrelet, 17150 Mirambeau [05 46 70 26 99 or 05 46 49 60 73 (Mairie)]** Exit 37 fr A10 onto N137 dir Saintes. Site opp Super U supmkt, behind tourist office.. Sm, pt shd; wc; chem disp (wc); washing cubicles; shwrs inc; el pnts (12A) €3; shops, rest adj; mostly statics; dogs €3; quiet. "Basic site; clean facs; obliging warden; site yourself & warden calls evening; v muddy when wet; poss neglected low ssn; conv NH for A10." € 12.00   2007*

France

⊞**MIRAMBEAU** 7C2 (8km S Rural) **Camping Chez Gendron, 33820 St Palais [tel/fax 05 57 32 96 47; info@chezgendron.com; www.chezgendron.com]** N fr Blaye on N137; turn to St Palais, past church 1km; turn L twd St Ciers. Site sp R down narr lane. Or N fr Bordeaux on A10 exit juncs 37 or 38 onto N137 to St Palais & as above. Sm, mkd pitch, terr, pt sl, pt shd; htd wc; chem disp; shwrs; fam bthrm; el pnts (6A) €1.70; lndtte; shops 3km; tradsmn; rest; snacks; bar; BBQ; playgrnd; pool; paddling pool; games area; tennis 3km; TV rm; dogs free; phone; Eng spkn; adv bkg; quiet; red low ssn; CCI. "Friendly Dutch owners; superb facs; great bar; conv NH fr m'way; peaceful, relaxed atmosphere; sep car park high ssn; excel Sun mkt." ♦ € 16.50
2007*

⊞**MIRAMONT DE GUYENNE** 7D2 (13km W Rural) **Camping Parc St Vincent, 47120 Lévignac-de-Guyenne [05 53 83 75 17 or 01425 275080 (UK); sara.psv@wanadoo.fr; www.psv47.com]** Fr Miramont take D668 to Allemans-du-Dropt, then D211. At junc D708 turn S to Lévignac, site sp. Fr Marmande N on D708 sp St Foy & Duras. Turn E at Lévignac church to further green site sp on D228. Sm, pt shd; wc; chem disp; mv service pnt; shwrs inc; el pnts (5A); gas; lndtte; ice; shops 2.5km; tradsmn; rest; snacks; BBQ; playgrnd; pool; lake sw 6km; entmnt; TV rm; 90% statics; dogs; phone; adv bkg; quiet; CCI. "Peaceful site; British owners make visitors welcome." ♦ 2006*

MIRAMONT DE GUYENNE 7D2 (6km NW Rural) **Camp Municipal Le Dropt, Rue du Pont, 47800 Allemans-du-Dropt [05 53 20 68 61 or 05 53 20 23 37 (Mairie); fax 05 53 20 68 91]** Fr D668 site well sp in vill. Sm, shd; wc (some cont); chem disp (wc); shwrs inc; el pnts (20A) €2; shop 400m; rest, snacks & bar 400m; playgrnd; quiet; CCI. "V attractive, grassed site on opp side of Rv Dropt to vill; v quiet; v friendly warden; excel." 1 May-31 Oct. € 7.00
2006*

MIRANDE 8F2 (500m E Rural) **Camp Municipal L'Ile du Pont, 32300 Mirande [05 62 66 64 11; fax 05 62 66 69 86; info@camping-iledupont. com or info@camping-gers.com; www.camping-gers.com]** On N21 Auch-Tarbes, foll sp to site on island in Rv Grande Baise. Med, pt shd; wc (cont); chem disp; mv service pnt; shwrs inc; el pnts (10A) inc; lndtte; tradsmn; snacks; bar; playgrnd; pool; waterslides; canoeing; sailing; windsurfing; fishing; tennis; entmnt; 20% statics; dogs €1; adv bkg rec; quiet; red low ssn; cc not acc; CCI. "Excel site; helpful staff; dep ent gate key; recep/barrier clsd 1200-1500; many sports free." 15 May-15 Sep. € 14.00
2006*

⊞**MIRANDE** 8F2 (4km S Rural) **FFCC Aire Naturelle La Hourguette, 32300 Berdoues [tel/fax 05 62 66 58 47]** Exit Mirande on N21 S dir Tarbes. 1st L after 'Intermarché' onto D524 to Berdoues, sp 'Camping La Ferme'. After 600m, turn R at fork in rd. Site in 2km. Sm, pt sl, pt shd; htd wc; chem disp; shwrs inc; el pnts (10A) €2; lndtte; shop 1.5km; rest, snacks & bar 3km; playgrnd; pool 3km; 10% statics; dogs; Eng spkn; quiet; CCI. "CL-type site; gd san facs; gd." ♦ ltd. € 18.00
2007*

MIRANDOL BOURGNOUNAC 8E4 (5km N Rural) **Camping Les Clots, 81190 Mirandol-Bourgnounac [tel/fax 05 63 76 92 78; campclots@wanadoo. fr; www.campinglesclots.info]** Fr Carmaux N on N88; L onto D905 to Mirandol, site sp; last 2-3km narr private rd - rough with steep hairpin. Sm, terr, pt shd; wc; chem disp; shwrs inc; el pnts (6-10A) €2.80; gas; lndtte; sm shop, tradsmn, bar high ssn; playgrnd; 2 pools; rv sw & fishing adj; games rm; TV; 10% statics; dogs €1; Eng spkn; adv bkg; quiet; red 5+ days; CCI. "V helpful Dutch owners; poss diff ent to site - not rec for towed c'vans; interesting area." 1 May-1 Oct. € 22.00 (3 persons)
2007*

MIREPOIX (ARIEGE) 8F4 (1km E Rural) **Camp Municipal Dynam'eau, Route de Limoux, 09500 Mirepoix [05 61 68 28 63 or 05 61 68 10 47 (Mairie); fax 05 61 68 89 48; www.mirepoix.fr]** E fr Pamiers on D119 to Mirepoix. Site well sp on D626. Med, mkd pitch, shd; wc (some cont); shwrs; el pnts €3; shops 1km; pool; fishing 1km; tennis; dogs €2; quiet. "If warden not present pay at Mairie in town; interesting medieval town; gd mkt Mon; gd facs." ♦ 1 Jul-1 Sep. € 11.00   2007*

MIREPOIX (ARIEGE) 8F4 (10km SE Rural) **Camping La Pibola, Le Cazalet, 09500 Camon [05 61 68 12 14; fax 05 61 68 10 59; marceldesboeufs@aol.com; www.lapibola.com]** E fr Pamiers to Mirepoix. Site on D625 twds Lavelanet. L after 4km sp Lagarde. Foll D7 for 4km sp on R, 1km to site. App is steep & narr. Med, terr, pt shd, mkd pitch; wc; chem disp; shwrs inc; el pnts (5A) €4; lndtte; ice; shop; rest; snacks; BBQ; playgrnd; pool; lake fishing 5km; games area; cycle hire; TV; some statics; dogs €1; adv bkg; quiet; red low ssn. "Gd." 1 May-30 Sep. € 14.00   2006*

MIRMANDE 9D2 (3km SE Rural) **Camping La Poche, 26270 Mirmande [04 75 63 02 88; fax 04 75 63 14 94; camping@la-poche.com; www.la-poche.com]** Fr N on N7, 3km after Loriol turn L onto D57 sp Mirmande. Site sp in 7km on L. Fr S on N7 turn R onto D204 in Saulce & foll sp. Med, hdg/mkd pitch, some hdstg, terr, shd; wc; chem disp; baby facs; shwrs inc; el pnts (6A) €3; lndtte; shop; snacks; rest & bar high ssn; playgrnd; pool; paddling pool; games area; entmnt; TV; poss cr; 90% statics; adv bkg; quiet; red low ssn; CCI. "Pleasant site set in wooded valley; excel scenery; gd walking/cycling area; friendly, helpful owner." 15 Apr-15 Oct. € 17.00   2007*

MITTLACH see Munster 6F3

⊞**MODANE** 9C4 (7km NE Rural) **Camp Municipal La Buidonnière, 73500 Aussois [04 79 20 35 58 or 04 79 20 30 80; fax 04 79 20 35 58; info@aussois.com; www.aussois.com]** Fr Modane on D125 to Aussois; in vill foll sp camping. Lge, mkd pitch, hdstg, pt sl, terr, unshd; htd wc (cont); chem disp; shwrs inc; el pnts (10A) €1.90-5.80; lndtte; shops 500m; playgrnd; 50% statics; adv bkg; CCI. "Mountain views; skiing resort; v exposed site; poss unkempt low ssn; gd rest in vill." ♦ € 10.20   2006*

MODANE 9C4 (10km NE) **Camp Municipal Val d'Ambin, 73500 Bramans-le-Verney [04 79 05 22 88 or 06 16 51 90 91 (mob); fax 04 79 05 23 16; campingdambin@aol.com]** 10km after Modane on D306 (N6) twd Lanslebourg, take 2nd turning R twd vill of Bramans, & foll camping sp, site by church. App fr Lanslebourg, after 12km turn L at camping sp on D306 at end of vill. Med, unshd; wc; shwrs; el pnts (12-16A) €3.30; shops 5km; playgrnd; pool 10km; dogs €1.50; no adv bkg; v quiet. "Away-from-it-all site worth the climb; beautiful area." 15 May-30 Sep. € 9.60   2007*

⊞**MODANE** 9C4 (1km W Rural) **Camping Les Combes, Refuge de La Sapinière, Route de Bardonnèche, 73500 Modane [04 79 05 00 23 or 06 10 16 54 61 (mob); fax 04 79 05 00 23; camping-modane@wanadoo.fr; www.camping-modane.fr.st]** Exit A43 junc 30 twd Modane. Take D216 on R, site on bend on hill. Fr Fréjus tunnel site on L 1km bef Modane. Med, pt sl, pt shd; htd wc (some cont); chem disp; shwrs inc; el pts (6A) €3; lndtte; shop 1km; tradsmn; snacks; bar; playgrnd; pool 1km; tennis; winter sports; 10% statics; dogs €1; quiet. "Excel & conv NH for Fréjus tunnel; warm welcome; superb scenery; low ssn phone ahead." € 15.00   2006*

> Did you know you can fill in site report forms on the Club's website – www.caravanclub.co.uk?

MOELAN SUR MER see Pont Aven 2F2

MOIRANS EN MONTAGNE 9A3 (Rural) **Camping Le Champ Renard, 39260 Moirans-en-Montagne [03 84 42 34 98; fax 03 84 42 60 50; camping.champ.renard@wanadoo.fr]** Fr St Claude foll Lons-Lyon rd (D436 to D470) to Moirans-en-Montagne (approx 25km by rd). Site opp sm indus est. Steep access rds. Med, mainly sl, terr, pt shd; wc; shwrs inc; el pnts (6A) €2.50; shops 2km; tradsmn; snacks; pool; shgl beach & lake 6km; mini-golf; dogs €1.20; adv bkg; some rd noise; CCI. "V friendly & helpful warden; one of nicer sites in area; local town & lake attractive; 15thC church in vill; pleasant sp walks." 15 Mar-15 Oct. € 13.90   2005*

MOIRANS EN MONTAGNE 9A3 (5km NW Rural) **Camping Trélachaume, Lac de Vouglans, 39260 Maisod [tel/fax 03 84 42 03 26; trelachaume@ifrance.com; www.trelachaume.com]** Fr St Claude take D436 NW past Moirans-en-Montagne; turn L onto D301 to Masoud; site well sp. Lge, mkd pitch, pt sl, pt shd; wc; chem disp; baby facs; shwrs inc; el pnts (5A) €2.70; lndtte; ice; shop; tradsmn; rest; snacks; bar; BBQ; adventure playgrnd; paddling pool; lake sw/sand beach 800m; games rm; entmnt; 10% statics; dogs €1.50; phone; poss cr; Eng spkn; adv bkg (dep req); quiet; cc acc; CCI. "Beautiful, uncrowded part of France; v helpful owners; excel." ♦ 22 Apr-9 Sep. € 13.20   2006*

MOISSAC *8E3* (2km S Rural) **Camp Municipal L'Ile de Bidounet**, St Benoît, 82200 Moissac [tel/fax 05 63 32 52 52; info@camping-moissac.com; www.camping-moissac.com] Exit A62 at junc 9 at Castelsarrasin onto N113 dir Moissac, site sp. Or fr N on N113 cross Rv Tarn, turn L at 1st rndabt & foll camp sp, site on L by rv. Med, hdg/mkd pitch, shd; wc (some cont); chem disp; mv service pnt; baby facs; shwrs inc; el pnts (6A) €3; gas 2km; lndtte; ice; shop, rest & snacks 2km; tradsmn; bar; BBQ; playgrnd; pool (high ssn); fishing; watersports; boat & canoe hire; cycle hire; entmnt; 10% statics; dogs €1.50; phone; Eng spkn; adv bkg; quiet; red long stay; cc acc; CCI. "Excel rvside site in lovely area; height restriction 3.05m for tunnel at ent & tight turn lge o'fits; extra charge for twin-axles; pitches tight lge o'fits; recep & barrier clsd 1230-1500; helpful staff; basic, clean san facs; 20 min walk to Moissac; v conv historic abbey & walking/cycling." ♦ 1 Apr-30 Sep. € 15.50   2007*

See advertisement

This guide relies on site report forms submitted by caravanners like us; we'll do our bit and tell the editor what we think of the campsites we've visited.

MOLIERES (DORDOGNE) see Lalinde *7C3*

MOLIERES (TARN ET GARONNE) *8E3* (Rural) **Domaine des Merlanes**, 82220 Molières [05 63 67 64 05; fax 05 63 24 28 96; simone@domaine-de-merlanes.com] Fr N on N20, exit on D20 to Montpezat-de-Quercy & Molières; sp in vill. Sm, terr, pt shd; wc; chem disp; baby facs; shwrs; el pnts (6A) inc; tradsmn; rest; bar; playgrnd; htd pool; 10% statics; poss cr; Eng spkn; quiet; red low ssn; cc acc; CCI. "Pleasant, Dutch owned; clean & well-kept; excel child facs; adv bkg ess high ssn; excel." 1 May-3 Sep. € 16.50   2005*

MOLIETS ET MAA *8E1* (2km W Coastal) **Airotel Camping St Martin**, Ave de l'Océan 40660 Moliets-Plage [05 58 48 52 30; fax 05 58 48 50 73; contact@camping-saint-martin.fr; www.camping-saint-martin.fr] On N10 exit for Léon, Moliets-et-Maa. At Moliets foll sp to Moliets-Plage. Camp site after Les Cigales, by beach. V lge, hdg/mkd pitches, pt sl, terr, pt shd; htd wc (some cont); chem disp; some serviced pitches (surcharge); baby facs; sauna; shwrs inc; el pnts (10A) inc; gas; lndtte; ice; shops; supmkt; rests; snacks; bar; playgrnd; 3 pools (1 htd, covrd); paddling pool; jacuzzi; dir access to sand beach 300m; rv 250m; watersports; tennis; golf nr; games area; cycle paths; entmnt high ssn; TV rm; dogs €3 (free low ssn); Eng spkn; adv bkg rec high ssn (fee); quiet; cc acc; red low ssn; CCI. "Excel family site; vg san facs." Easter-30 Oct. € 32.50   2005*

MOLIETS ET MAA *8E1* (2km W Coastal) **Camping Les Cigales**, Ave de l'Océan, 40660 Moliets-et-Maa [05 58 48 51 18; fax 05 58 48 53 27; reception@camping-les-cigales.fr; www.camping-les-cigales.fr] In Moliets-et-Maa, turn W for Moliets-Plage, site on R in vill. Lge, pt sl, shd; wc; chem disp; mv service pnt; shwrs inc; el pnts (5A) €2.80; lndtte; shop; tradsmn; rest; snacks; bar; BBQ; playgrnd; sand beach 300m; games area; TV; many statics; adv bkg; quiet; cc acc; CCI. "Site in pine wood - sandy soil; narr access tracks; poorly lit at night; excel beach & surfing; many shops, rests 100m." Easter-30 Sep. € 16.00   2005*

MOLOMPIZE see Massiac *9C1*

MOLSHEIM see Obernai *6E3*

MONBALEN 7D3 (Rural) **Ferme Equestre Crinière au Vent, Bouillon, 47340 Monbalen** [05 53 95 18 61; SLX47@wanadoo.fr] Site 15km N Agen & 13km S Villeneuve-sur-Lot. Fr Agen, take N21 N dir Villeneuve-sur-Lot. In approx 15km turn R onto D110 sp Laroque-Timbaut & foll 'Camping' sp. Fr Villeneuve-sur-Lot, take N21 S dir Agen. In approx 10km turn L onto D110 sp Laroque-Timbaut & foll 'Camping' sp. Sm, pt sl, shd; wc (some cont); chem disp; shwrs inc; el pnts (10A) €2; lndry rm; ice; tradsmn; bar (soft drinks only); horseriding; no statics; dogs €1; little Eng spkn; no cc acc; CCI. "Owner v pleasant; horseriding for all ages on site; vg." ♦ 15 Apr-30 Sep. € 8.20   2006*

MONCEAUX SUR DORDOGNE see Argentat 7C4

MONDRAGON see Bollène 9D2

MONESTIER DE CLERMONT 9C3 (700m W Rural) **Camp Municipal Les Portes du Trièves, Chemin de Chambons, 38650 Monestier-de-Clermont** [04 76 34 01 24; fax 04 76 34 19 75; campinglesportesdutrieves@wanadoo.fr] On D1075 (N75), sp in vill. Turn W at traff lts, foll sp to site, 700m up steep hill behind pool. Sm, hdg/mkd pitch, hdstg, pt terr, pt shd; wc; chem disp; shwrs inc; el pnts (6A) €2.70; lndry rm; shop, rest, snacks, bar 800m; playgrnd; htd pool 200m; tennis adj; lake 10km; quiet; adv bkg; CCI. "Immac, well-run site; watersports at lake; spectacular countryside." ♦ 1 May-30 Sep. € 11.10   2006*

MONETIER LES BAINS, LE 9C3 (W Rural) **Camp Municipal Les Deux Glaciers, 05220 Le Monêtier-les-Bains** [04 92 46 10 08 or 06 83 03 70 72; fax 04 92 24 52 18; monetier@monetier.com] On N91 12km NW of Briançon; site at W end of vill. Med, mkd pitch, hdstg, terr, unshd; htd wc; mv service pnt; baby facs; shwrs inc; el pnts (16A) €3.50; lndtte; tradsmn; shop, rest, snacks bar 1km; dogs €1; adv bkg; CCI. "Excel site bef x-ing Montgenèvre pass to Italy; easy access fr N91; vg." ♦ ltd. 15 Dec-Apr & Jun-Sep. € 14.50   2006*

MONFORT 8E3 (Urban) **Camp Municipal de Monfort, 32120 Monfort** [tel/fax 05 62 06 83 26 (Mairie)] SE fr Fleurance on D654 to Monfort, then foll sp to 'Centre Ville' & camping sp. Town has narr rds so foll sp. Sm, hdg pitch, pt sl, pt shd; wc; chem disp (wc); shwrs inc, el pnts (5A) €1.50; shop, rest & bar 200m; BBQ; playgrnd; dogs €0.50; quiet; cc not acc; CCI. "Excel, well-kept CL-type site on ramparts of attractive Bastide town; marvellous views; pitch yourself, warden calls am & pm." 1 May-15 Oct. € 8.00   2006*

MONISTROL D'ALLIER 9C1 (Urban) **Camp Municipal du Vivier, 43580 Monistrol-d'Allier** [04 71 57 24 24 or 04 71 57 21 21 (Mairie); fax 04 71 57 25 03] Fr Le Puy-en-Velay W on D589 to Monistrol d'Allier. Turn L in vill immed after rlwy stn & cont down steep entry rd bef x-ing bdge. Site sp in town cent. Sm, mkd pitch, pt shd; wc; chem disp; shwrs inc; el pnts (5-10A) €2.80; shops, rest, snacks; bar 200m; BBQ; rv sw; no statics; dogs; phone; train 500m; quiet; CCI. "Vg site situated in steep sided rv valley; rv activities avail." ♦ ltd. 15 Apr-15 Sep. € 8.30   2004*

MONISTROL D'ALLIER 9C1 (4km N Rural) **Camp Municipal Le Marchat, 43580 St Privat-d'Allier** [04 71 57 22 13; fax 04 71 57 25 50; info@mairie-saintprivatdallier.fr; www.mairie-saintprivatdallier.fr] Fr Le Puy-en-Velay W on D589. Turn R in cent of vill at petrol stn, site on R in 200m. Sm, hdg pitch, terr, shd; wc; chem disp; shwrs inc; el pnts (10A) €1.10; shops, bar in vill; playgrnd; quiet. "Beautifully kept site; not suitable lge o'fits." ♦ ltd. 1 May-31 Oct. € 6.10   2007*

MONISTROL SUR LOIRE 9C1 **Camp Municipal Beau Séjour, Route de Chaponas, 43120 Monistrol-sur-Loire** [04 71 66 53 90] Site on N88, on W edge of town, sp. Exit by-pass at 1 of exits to Monistrol - head for casino, then Intermarché. Med, hdg pitch, pt sl, shd; htd wc; shwrs inc; el pnts (6A) €2.44; lndtte; supmkt adj; playgrnd; pool; tennis adj; 90% statics; adv bkg; quiet. "Gd NH." ♦ 1 Apr-31 Oct. € 10.00   2004*

MONISTROL SUR LOIRE 9C1 (7km SE Rural) **Camping de Vaubarlet, 43600 Ste Sigolène** [04 71 66 64 95; fax 04 71 66 11 98; camping@vaubarlet.com; www.vaubarlet.com] Fr Monistrol take D44 SE twd Ste Sigolène & turn R into vill. In vill take D43 dir Grazac for 6km. Site by Rv Dunière, ent L bef bdge. Site well sp fr vill. Med, mkd pitch, pt shd; wc; chem disp; mv service pnt; shwrs inc; el pnts (6A) €3 (poss rev pol); lndtte; shop & 6km; tradsmn; rest; snacks; bar; playgrnd; htd pool; paddling pool; rv sw adj; trout fishing; cycle hire; games area; entmnt; TV rm; 15% statics; phone; dogs €1; Eng spkn; adv bkg; quiet; red low ssn; cc acc; CCI. "V friendly & helpful staff; well-run site; excel san facs; snail museum nrby; gd weaving museum in Ste Sigolène." ♦ 1 May-30 Sep. € 18.00 (CChq acc)   2006*

AN OASIS SITUATED ON THE ILE DE FRANCE AND CLOSE TO BEAUCE

LE BOIS DE LA JUSTICE ★★★

91930 MONNERVILLE
Bookings: tel.: 00 33 (0)1 64 95 05 34
Fax: 00 33 (0)1 64 95 17 31

Just off Beauce, in a forest with pine trees and leaf trees. Heated swimming pool – bar – children's games – table tennis – French boules – volleyball.
Many hiking paths and bicycle routes. 50 km from Paris, Versailles and Orléans. Close to Fontainebleau and the Loire Castles. The campsite is ideally situated to visit these cities with their rich history and to return at night to the peace and quiet of the countryside.

Open from 4/02 till 26/11

http://perso.orange.fr/campingboislajustice/

MONNERVILLE *4E3* (2km S Rural) **Camping Le Bois de la Justice, Méréville, 91930 Monnerville** [01 64 95 05 34; fax 01 64 95 17 31; picquetfredo@orange.fr; http://pagesperso-orange.fr/camping boislajustice/] Fr N20 S of Etampes, turn onto D18 at Monnerville, site well sp. Long narr app rd. Med, hdg/mkd pitch, pt sl, pt shd; htd wc; chem disp (wc); shwrs inc; el pnts (5A) €2.50; lndtte; ice; tradsmn; snacks high ssn; bar; BBQ; cooking facs; playgrnd; htd pool high ssn; tennis; games area; TV rm; 50% statics; dogs €1; phone; Eng spkn; adv bkg; quiet; red low ssn; cc acc. "Delightful woodland oasis in open countryside; v pleasant welcome; ideal for Chartres, Fontainebleau, Orléans, Paris." ♦ 4 Feb-26 Nov. € 19.50   2007*

See advertisement

MONPAZIER *7D3* (3km SW Rural) **Camping Moulin de David, Route de Villeréal, 24540 Gaugeac-Monpazier** [05 53 22 65 25 or 04 99 57 20 25; fax 05 53 23 99 76; moulindedavid@village-center.com; www.village-center.com/aurilandes] Fr Monpazier, take D2 SW twd Villeréal, site sp on L after 3km. Narr app rds. Lge, hdg/mkd pitch, pt shd; htd wc; chem disp; mv service pnt; serviced pitches; baby facs; shwrs inc; el pnts (3-10A) inc gas; lndtte; ice; shop; tradsmn; rest; snacks; bar; BBQ; playgrnd; pool; paddling pool; lake sw & waterslide high ssn; fishing adj; tennis; games area; internet; games/TV rm; cycle hire; archery; internet; entmnt; many statics; dogs €3; poss cr; Eng spkn; adv bkg; quiet; cc acc; CCI. "Charming, highly rec site nr lovely town; excel facs; helpful, welcoming owners; recep 0830-1200 & 1400-1900; mkt Thu Monpazier." ♦ 2 Jun-16 Sep. € 27.00   2007*

MONT DORE, LE *7B4* (Urban) **Camp Municipal des Crouzets, 4 Ave des Crouzets, 63240 Le Mont-Dore** [tel/fax 04 73 65 21 60 or 04 73 65 22 00 (Mairie); camping.crouzets@wanadoo.fr; www.mairie-mont-dore.fr] Take D130 fr Bourboule to Le Mont-Dore; site ent just on L after entering town. Poor sps. Lge, mkd pitch, hdstg, pt sl, unshd; htd wc; chem disp; mv service pnt adj; shwrs inc; el pnts (10A) €3.90 (poss rev pol); lndtte; ice; tradsmn; shops & rests adj; BBQ; playgrnd; pool 4km; sports area; dogs €1.45; poss cr; Eng spkn; cc acc. "Cent position in town but quiet; gd sized pitches; well run; excel san facs; helpful warden; cable car to Puy de Sancy; walks to mountain tracks." ♦ 22 Dec-18 Oct. € 9.10   2007*

MONT DORE, LE *7B4* (12km N Rural) **Camp Municipal La Buge, 63210 Rochefort-Montagne** [04 73 65 84 98 or 04 73 65 82 51; fax 04 73 65 93 69; mairie.rochefort@rochefort-montagne.com] Fr NE on N89. Thro vill L after x-ing bdge. Sp 200m R. Med, pt shd; wc; chem disp; shwrs inc; el pnts (15A) €2.65; lndtte; shop adj; playgrnd; rv 500m; tennis; dogs €0.90; adv bkg. 1 Jun-15 Sep. € 8.80 (3 persons)   2006*

MONT DORE, LE *7B4* (1.5km NW Urban) **Camp Municipal L'Esquiladou, Le Queureuilh, Route des Cascades, 63240 Le Mont-Dore** [04 73 65 23 74 or 04 73 65 20 00 (Mairie); fax 04 73 65 23 74; camping.esquiladou@wanadoo.fr] Fr Mont-Dore cent, take D996 dir La Bourboule (not D130). Pass 'La Poste' on L & at rlwy stn app turn R, then L at T-junc onto D996. In Queureuilh fork R at 'Route Cascades' sp, then foll camping sp. Med, hdg/mkd pitch, hdstg, terr, pt shd; htd wc; chem disp; mv service pnt; shwrs inc; el pnts (6-10A) €2.80-5.45; gas; lndtte; shops 1km; tradsmn; BBQ; playgrnd; pool; dogs €1.40; phone; Eng spkn; adv bkg; cc acc; CCI. "V pleasant, quiet site; gd views; well-run; excel san facs; gd mountain walks." ♦ ltd. 1 May-20 Oct. € 8.65   2007*

Renée and Alain Bigrel welcome you to

CAMPING-CARAVANING
AUX POMMIERS ★★★

4 km from
MONT-SAINT-MICHEL

Heated swimming pool
Waterslide

28, Route du Mont Michel 50170 BEAUVOIR
Tel. & Fax: 00 33 (0)2 33 60 11 36

pommiers@aol.com
www.camping-auxpommiers.com

Open from 20 March till 6 November

MONT LOUIS *8G4* (3km N Rural) **Camp Municipal, Place de Barres, 66210 La Llagonne [04 68 04 26 04 or 04 68 04 21 18 (Mairie)]** Leave Mont-Louis on D118 dir Formiguères rd; site sp on L at top of hill; cont for 1km. Lge, pt shd; wc (cont); shwrs; el pnts (10A) €3; playgrnd; paddling pool; rv sw; fishing; quiet. "Most of site in pine forest; ground poss boggy." 15 Jun-30 Sep. € 7.90   2004*

MONT ST MICHEL, LE *2E4* (8km E Rural) **Camping Le St Michel, Route du Mont St Michel, 50220 Courtils [02 33 70 96 90; fax 02 33 70 99 09; infos@campingsaintmichel.com; www.camping saintmichel.com]** Fr E exit A84 junc 33 to N175. Take D43 coast rd fr Pontaubault twds Le Mont St Michel. Site in vill of Courtils on R. Med, mkd pitch, some hdstg, pt shd; wc; chem disp; mv service pnt; baby facs; shwrs inc; el pnts (6A) €2.60; lndtte; shop; rest; bar; playgrnd; htd pool; sand beach 8km; cycle hire; some statics; dogs €1; poss cr; Eng spkn; noisy (farm adj); CCI. "Excel, flat site; v clean facs; helpful owner; no privacy in shwrs/wcs; cycle paths adj; gd NH for St Malo." ♦ ltd." 24 Mar-15 Oct. € 14.50   2005*

MONT ST MICHEL, LE *2E4* (2km S) **Camping du Mont St Michel, 50150 Le Mont St Michel [02 33 60 22 10; fax 02 33 60 20 02; stmichel@ le-mont-saint-michel.com; www.camping-mont saintmichel.com]** Located at junc of D976 (Pontorson/Le Mont St Michel) with D275; on L behind Hotel Vert. Lge, hdg/mkd pitch, pt shd; wc; chem disp; mv service pnt; shwrs inc; baby facs; el pnts (5A) inc (poss long lead req); gas; lndtte; supmkt, rest adj; snacks; bar; playgrnd; mini-golf; sand beach 2km; fishing; TV; dogs; phone; adv bkg; Eng spkn; cc acc; red CCI. "Well-located, well-maintained site; excel san facs, inc for disabled; vg shady pitches behind hotel; poss noisy - m'van area on opp side D275 quieter, closes end Sep; beach at 2km reported unsafe for sw (quicksand); Abbey nrby; pitches poss muddy after heavy rain; diff to get onto some pitches due trees; gd walking & cycling to the mount." ♦ 10 Feb-10 Nov. € 17.20
2007*

MONT ST MICHEL, LE *2E4* (4km S Rural) **Camping aux Pommiers, 28 Route du Mont-St Michel, 50170 Beauvoir [tel/fax 02 33 60 11 36; pommiers@ aol.com; www.camping-auxpommiers.com]** N fr Pontorson foll D976 sp Le Mont St Michel. Site 5km on R on ent vill of Beauvoir. Med, hdg/mkd pitch, hdstg, pt shd; htd wc (some cont); chem disp; mv service pnt; shwrs inc; el pnts (6A) €3; gas; lndtte; ice; shop; supmkt 4km; tradsmn; rest; snacks; bar; BBQ; playgrnd; htd pool; waterslide; sand/shgl beach 2km; tennis 900m; games area; games rm; cycle hire; entmnt; TV; 30% statics; dogs €1.20; Eng spkn; adv bkg; quiet; cc acc; red long stay/low ssn/CCI. "Friendly, helpful staff & owner; clean facs; gd touring base; easy cycle ride to Mont St Michel; poss mosquito prob." 20 Mar-12 Nov. € 14.20   2007*

See advertisement

MONTAGNAC MONTPEZAT see Riez *10E3*

MONTAGNY LES LANCHES see Annecy *9B3*

⊞**MONTAIGU** *2H4* (10km SE Rural) **Camping L'Eden, 85600 La Boissière-de-Montaigu [02 51 41 62 32; fax 02 51 41 56 07; domaine. eden@free.fr; www.domaine-eden.fr]** Fr Montaigu S on D137, in 8km turn E on D62, thro Le Pont-Legé. Site sp on L off D62. Med, mkd pitch, pt shd; wc (some cont); shwrs inc; el pnts (10A) €3; gas; lndtte; shop & 4km; rest; snacks; bar; playgrnd; htd pool; tennis; mini-golf; entmnt; TV; 40% statics; dogs €2; poss cr; adv bkg; red low ssn; CCI. "V nice, quiet site in lovely woodlands; clean facs; excel." ♦ ltd. 1 Mar-15 Nov. € 15.50   2007*

MONTARGIS *4F3* (12km N Rural) **Camp Municipal, Rue du Perray, 45210 Ferrières-en-Gâtinais** [02 38 96 64 68 or 02 38 96 52 96 (Mairie); fax 02 38 96 62 76; ferrieres.mairie@wanadoo.fr; www.ferrieres-en-gatinais.com] N fr Mantargis on N7. R onto D32 sp Ferrières & foll camp sp. Med, mkd pitch, pt shd; wc; chem disp; mv service pnt; shwrs inc; el pnts (10A) €2.50 (poss rev pol); ice; playgrnd; pool & sports facs adj; rv fishing adj; entmnt; 5% statics; quiet. "Vg." 1 Apr-30 Sep. € 6.00   2007*

MONTARGIS *4F3* (2km NE Urban) **Camp Municipal de la Forêt, 38 Ave Chautemps, 45200 Montargis** [02 38 98 00 20] Heading N on N7 at town boundary take R fork sp Paucourt/camping symbol. Or head E on N60, take 2nd L to site in 1km. Med, mkd pitch, hdstg, shd; htd wc (some cont); shwrs inc; el pnts (5A) €2.60; shop 200m; playgrnd; pool adj; 50% statics; quiet. "Site with spacious pitches & oak trees; conv for train to Paris; pleasant views; lovely old vill, abbey & church; nice walks; no vans over 6m; poss muddy in wet weather; facs dated but clean; gate/recep closes 1900; NH only." 1 Feb-30 Nov. € 10.80   2006*

MONTARGIS *4F3* (10km W Rural) **Camping du Huillard, La Garenne, 45700 St Maurice-sur-Fessard** [02 38 97 85 32 or 02 38 97 81 99 (LS); sylvie-taillandier@wanadoo.fr] On N side of N60 by-pass bet Ladon & Montargis Well sp twd St Maurice-sur-Fessard on rvside. Sm, pt shd; wc; chem disp (wc); mv service pnt; shwrs inc; el pnts (6-10A) €2-2.50 (poss rev pol); gas; ice; shop; playgrnd; fishing; 50% statics; dogs €1; some rd noise; adv bkg. "Delightful site; poss resident workers." 15 Apr-15 Oct.   2006*

MONTAUBAN *8E3* (10km NE) **Camping La Forge, 85 Route de Nègrepelisse, 82350 Albias** [tel/fax 05 63 31 00 44 or 06 76 38 81 22 (mob); contact@camping-laforge.com] Fr S turn R at traff lts on N20 in Albias onto D65 sp Nègrepelisse. Site clearly sp 1km on L adj cemetary extension. Sm, pt shd; wc; chem disp; shwrs inc; el pnts (3-6A) €1.85-3.65; lndtte; shops 500m; tradsmn; sm pool; 10% statics; dogs €0.75; adv bkg; quiet; red low ssn; CCI. "Quiet, unpretentious woodland site; helpful & friendly owner; facs dated; poss unsuitable for sm children due to v steep bank to fast-flowing rv; no twin-axles; excel rest in vill." 1 Apr-30 Sep. € 11.00   2007*

MONTAUBAN DE BRETAGNE *2E3* (500m Urban) **Camp Municipal de la Vallée St Eloi, 35360 Montauban-de-Bretagne** [02 99 06 42 55; fax 02 99 06 59 89] 25km NW of Rennes on N12. Fr N12 foll sp to Montauben cent. Site in 500m on R at ent to town by sm lake. Sm, mkd pitch, pt shd; wc; shwrs inc; el pnts (6A) €1.90; shop 500m; quiet; no statics; CCI. "Basic but clean san facs; picturesque location; unreliable opening dates; phone ahead." 1 Jul-31 Aug. € 8.25   2004*

MONTAUROUX see Fayence *10E4*

MONTBARD *6G1* (1km W Urban) **Camp Municipal, Rue Michel Servet, 21500 Montbard** [tel/fax 03 80 92 21 60; camping.montbard@wanadoo.fr; www.montbard.com] Lies off N side D980. Camping sp clearly indicated on all app including by-pass. Turn onto by-pass at traff lts at rndabt at junc of D905 & D980. Site nr pool. Med, hdg pitch, pt shd, wc; chem disp; shwrs inc; el pnts (16A) inc; lndry rm; shop 1km; supmkt 300m; tradsmn; BBQ; snacks; playgrnd; cycle hire; rv sw 100m; dogs €1; phone; poss cr; quiet but rd/rlwy noise at far end; CCI. "V clean, well-kept but poss shabby low ssn; gd pitches; v quiet low ssn; poss a few contract worker campers; lge, smart san facs; interesting area; excel." ♦ 1 Mar-27 Oct. € 16.50   2007*

MONTBAZON *4G2* (300m N Rural) **Camping de la Grange Rouge, 37250 Montbazon** [02 47 26 06 43; fax 02 47 26 03 13; infos@camping-montbazon.com; www.camping-montbazon.com] On D910 (N10) site clearly visible & clearly sp on W side of rd at N end of town. Med, mkd pitch, shd; wc (some male cont); chem disp; shwrs inc; el pnts (6A) €3.60; lndtte; shops 300m; tradsmn; rest & bar adj; playgrnd; htd pool; fishing; tennis; TV rm; some statics; dogs €1; Eng spkn; adv bkg; quiet; cc acc; CCI. "Lovely, rvside site; helpful, friendly owner; conv Tours." ♦ 28 Apr-15 Sep. € 12.10   2007*

MONTBAZON *4G2* (2km E Rural) **Camping de la Plage, 37250 Veigné** [02 47 26 23 00; fax 02 47 73 11 47; campingveigne@wanadoo.com; www.touraine-vacance.com] Exit A10 junc 23 dir Montbazon onto D910 (N10). N of Montbazon after 'Les Gues' turn SE onto D50 to Veigné & site. Site in 2km on R at rvside. Med, mkd pitch, pt shd; htd wc; chem disp; baby facs; shwrs, el pnts (6-10A) €3.60-3.90; gas 200m; lndtte; ice; shop 200m; rest; snacks; BBQ; playgrnd; htd pool high ssn; canoeing; fishing; mini-golf; games area; entmnt; child entmnt; 13% statics; dogs €1; phone; Eng spkn; adv bkg; quiet, some rd/rlwy noise; red long stay; cc acc; CCI. "Lovely rvside site; friendly, helpful owners; nr vill; ideal for Loire chateaux & Tours; gd walking & cycling; excel." ♦ 10 Apr-3 Oct. € 9.50   2006*

MONTBERT *2H4* (500m SE Rural) **Camping Le Relais des Garennes, La Bauche Coiffée, 44140 Montbert** [tel/fax 02 40 04 78 73; phgendron@wanadoo.fr] Fr Nantes on N937 dir La Roche, at Geneston turn L dir Montbert & foll site sp. Or fr Nantes on N137 dir La Rochelle turn R at Aigrefeuille-sur-Maine for Montbert. Sm, mkd pitch, pt shd; htd wc; serviced pitches; baby facs; fam bthrm; shwrs inc; el pnts (10A) inc; lndry rm; ice; htd pool 1km; tennis; sports facs nrby; sm lake; lake fishing adj; dogs; Eng spkn; adv bkg; quiet; CCI. "V peaceful & picturesque; immac facs; friendly owners; rabbits & hens on site; toys for children; many attractions nrby; nice walk to town; highly rec." ♦ 1 Jun-30 Sep. € 10.00   2006*

France

MONTBLANC see Béziers *10F1*

⊞**MONTBOUCHER** *7B4* (Rural) **Camping La Chassagne, 23400 Montboucher [05 55 64 22 87; jonesca@wanadoo.fr; http://pagesperso-orange.fr/cp23400]** Montboucher is 5km E of Bourganeuf on D941. Sm, hdg, sl, pt shd; htd wc; chem disp; fam bthrm; shwrs inc; el pnts (10A) inc; lndtte; ice; shops & rest 5km; fishing, tennis & golf 5km; dogs; adv bkg (dep req); quiet; CCI. "Well-kept CL-type site in beautiful area; friendly British owners; excel touring base; mv service pnt in vill; excel." € 10.00
2007*

MONTBRISON *9B1* (2km S) **Camp Municipal Le Surizet, Route de St Etienne, Moingt, 42600 Montbrison [04 77 58 08 30; fax 04 77 58 00 16]** Fr St Etienne on D8, at rndabt junc with D204 turn L sp St Anthème & Ambert. Cross rlwy & turn R in 400m, site sp. Med, pt shd; wc; shwrs; el pnts (5-10A) €2.60-4.65; shop 1km; playgrnd; pool; fishing; pool, tennis 2km; 60% statics; dogs €0.85; quiet; adv bkg. "No twin-axle vans." 15 Apr-15 Oct. € 8.30
2005*

MONTBRISON *9B1* (2km W Rural) **Camping Le Bigi, Vinols, 42600 Bard [tel/fax 04 77 58 06 39; eric.drutel@laposte.net; http://campinglebigi.site.voila.fr]** Fr Montbrison cent take D113 twd Bard, site sp. Sm, hdg/mkd pitch, sl, terr, pt shd; wc; chem disp; mv service pnt; shwrs inc; el pnts (5A) inc; lndtte; tradsmn; playgrnd; pool; 60% statics; dogs €1; poss cr; CCI. "V helpful owner; well-run; delightful site in landscaped former nursery garden nr medieval town; no twin-axle c'vans." ♦ 31 May-15 Sep. € 13.20
2007*

MONTBRON *7B3* (11km NE Rural) **Camping de l'Etang, Les Geloux, 16310 Le Lindois [05 45 65 02 67; fax 05 45 65 08 96]** Fr S take D16 N fr Montbron, in 9km turn R onto D13, in 3km turn R onto D27. Site sp in vill opp lake. Sm, hdg/mkd pitch, pt sl, pt shd; htd wc; chem disp; baby facs; shwrs inc; el pnts (16A) €3.35; lndtte; ice; small shop; rest; snacks; bar; playgrnd; lake sw adj; fishing; sand beach adj; dogs €1.55; Eng spkn; adv bkg rec high ssn; cc acc; quiet; CCI. "Beautiful, peaceful, wooded site by sm lake; lge pitches in mild clearings in trees; friendly Dutch owners; excel." 1 Apr-1 Nov. € 14.20
2005*

MONTBRON *7B3* (500m E Urban) **Camp Municipal Les Moulins de Tardoire, Route de Limoges, 16220 Montbron [05 45 70 74 67 or 05 45 63 15 15 (Mairie); info@ot-montbron.com; www.ot-montbron.com]** On D699, foll sp fr vill cent. Sm, hdg pitch, pt shd; wc (cont); chem disp; shwrs inc; el pnts (16A) €2.50: shop 500m; pool 100m; playgrnd; dogs free; quiet; adv bkg; Eng spkn; CCI. "Within walking dist of shops/rests in vill; basic site but OK sh stay." 15 May-15 Sep. € 6.30
2007*

MONTBRON *7B3* (6km SE Rural) **Camping Les Gorges du Chambon, Le Chambon, 16220 Eymouthiers [05 45 70 71 70; fax 05 45 70 80 02; gorges.chambon@wanadoo.fr; www.gorgesdu chambon.fr or www.les-castels.com]** Fr N141 turn onto D6 at La Rochefoucauld; cont on D6 out of Montbron; after 5km turn L at 'La Tricherie' onto D163; foll camp sp to site in approx 1.6km. Med, mkd pitch, pt sl, pt shd; htd wc; chem disp; mv service pnt; baby facs; shwrs inc; el pnts (6A) inc; gas; lndtte; ice; shop; tradsmn; rest; snacks; bar; BBQ (gas/charcoal only); playgrnd; pool; paddling pool; sand/shgl beach 15km; rv sw; fishing, canoe hire; tennis; cycle hire; mini-golf; walking; horseriding, golf nrby; entmnt; child entmnt; internet; games/TV rm; 25% statics; no dogs; Eng spkn; adv bkg; quiet; red long stay/low ssn; cc acc; CCI. "Beautiful, 'away from it all' site; exceptional staff - v welcoming, helpful & friendly; big pitches but some sl; gd walks & bird-watching; gd views; excel." ♦ 19 Apr-20 Sep. € 27.20 (CChq acc) ABS - D11
2007*

See advertisement

MONTBRUN LES BAINS *10E3* (500m Rural) **Camp Municipal Le Pré des Arbres, 26570 Montbrun-les-Bains [04 75 28 85 41 or 04 75 28 82 49; fax 04 75 28 81 16]** Site well sp in Montbrun. Sm, mkd pitch, terr, pt shd; wc; shwrs; el pnts (15A) €3.25; pool, tennis adj; some statics; dogs; quiet. "Gd, clean site; walking dist to pleasant town & spa; thermal baths; interesting area; warden visits." 1 Apr-31 Oct. € 9.20
2006*

MONTCABRIER *7D3* (2km NE Rural) **Camping Le Moulin de Laborde, 46700 Montcabrier [05 65 24 62 06; fax 05 65 36 51 33; moulindela borde@wanadoo.fr; www.moulindelaborde.com]** Fr Fumel take D673 NE & site 1km past Montcabrier on L. Med, hdg pitch, pt shd; wc; chem disp; baby facs; shwrs inc; el pnts (6A) €2.60; gas; ice; lndtte; shop; tradsmn; snacks; bar; playgrnd; pool; sm lake; games area; cycle hire; entmnt; TV rm; no dogs; phone; poss cr; Eng spkn; adv bkg (dep req); quiet; red low ssn. "Pleasant, peaceful site; gd facs; many attractions & activities nrby; vg." 1 May-15 Sep. € 19.60
2005*

MONTCLAR (ALPES DE HAUTE PROVENCE) *9D3* (2km N Rural) **Yelloh! Village Etoile des Neiges, St Jean, 04140 Montclar [04 92 35 01 29 or 04 92 35 07 08; fax 04 92 35 12 55; contact@etoile-des-neiges.com; www.etoile-des-neiges.com www.yellohvillage.com]** On D900 turn S at St Vincent-les-Forts twd Col St Jean & Digne, site sp at the Col. Med, terr, shd; htd wc; some serviced pitches; shwrs; el pnts (6A) inc; lndtte; rest; bar; snacks; playgrnd; htd pool; tennis; rv fishing; games area; entmnt; TV; dogs €2; adv bkg rec winter & summer. "Ski stn in winter; steep access rds to pitches poss diff; site 1300m above sea level; excel." ♦ 21 May-30 Sep. € 25.00 (CChq acc)
2004*

MONTCLAR (AUDE) see Carcassonne *8F4*

GORGES DU CHAMBON ★★★★

F-16220 MONTBRON

In the PERIGORD VERT, at the doors of the Dordogne. Site is situated on an inclination of 28 hectares, in the curve of a river. Come and discover the tranquillity, the freedom of REAL untouched nature and enjoy our spacious pitches.

Many activities possible on the premises: Swimming pool – Entertainment – Mini-golf – Tennis – Bathing in the river – Fishing – Canoes – Games for children – Library – Playroom – Space for teenagers – Rock climbing – Mountain bikes – Hiking – Horse riding – Archery.

Complete service – Restaurants - Bar – Take away – Grocery – Change – Credit cards.

Jacques and Jean-Louis will be happy to welcome you.

Tel.: 00 33 (0) 5 45 70 71 70
Fax: 00 33 (0) 5 45 70 80 02
www.gorgesduchambon.fr
gorges.chambon@wanadoo.fr

MONTCUQ 7D3 (Rural) **Camp Municipal St Jean, 46800 Montcuq [05 65 22 93 73 or 05 65 31 80 05 (Mairie); communaute.communes-montcuq@wanadoo.fr]** Fr Cahors on N20 twd Montauban. 3km S take D653 sp to vill. Site sp on R in vill. Sm, mkd pitch, shd; wc; mv service pnt; shwrs inc; el pnts (10-15A); lndtte; supmkt; rest 300m; bar 200m; playgrnd; pool, tennis adj; lake fishing, lake sw & watersports 800m; tennis; horseriding; adv bkg rec high ssn; quiet.
♦ 15 Jun-15 Sep. € 6.00   2004*

⊞**MONTDIDIER** 3C3 (1km W Urban) **Camping Le Pré Fleuri, 46 Route d'Ailly-sur-Noye, 80500 Montdidier [03 22 78 93 22]** App Montdidier fr Breteuil (W) on D930; on W o'skts, foll site sp & turn L onto D26. Site 1km on R. Or leave A1 at junc 11 onto D935 Montdidier. In town foll sp for Breteuil until rlwy x-ing & turn R onto D26. Sm, hdg/mkd pitch, pt sl, pt shd; wc (some cont); chem disp; mv service pnt; shwrs inc; el pnts (6-10A) inc (poss rev pol); gas; lndtte; shop 1km; tradsmn; rest, snacks, bar 1km; playgrnd; pool 1km; fishing, tennis nr; horseriding; 75% statics; dogs; adv bkg; rd noise; red long stay; CCI. "V helpful, friendly owners; guided walks; insufficient san facs; diff to level m'van; conv Amiens, Compiègne & Somme; vg."
♦ € 16.00   2006*

⊞**MONTELIMAR** 9D2 (12km N Rural) **Camping Floral, 26740 La Coucourde-Derbières [04 75 90 06 69; info@campingfloral.com; www. campingfloral.com]** Exit A7 at junc 17 Montélimar Nord, S on N7 for 4km. Site sp S of vill. NB Across rv fr power station cooling towers. Sm, mkd pitch, hdstg, pt sl, pt shd; wc; mv service pnt; shwrs inc; el pnts (6A) inc; gas; lndtte; sm shop; rest; snacks; bar; playgrnd; pool; entmnt; dogs €0.50; Eng spkn; quiet but some rlwy & rd noise; red low ssn; CCI. "Welcome drink on arr; v friendly owners; clean & tidy site; gd home cooked rest food; facs poss stretched high ssn; vg." € 16.00   2007*

MONTELIMAR 9D2 (3km NW Rural) **Camping L'Ile Blanc, Ancône, 07400 Rochemaure [tel/ fax 04 75 51 20 05; ile.blanc@wanadoo.fr; www. camping-montelimar.com]** Fr Montélimar take N7 N dir Valence (E bank of Rv Rhône) & foll sp Ancône. Site sp nr aviation museum. Med, hdg/mkd pitch, hdstg, pt shd; wc; chem disp (wc); baby facs; shwrs inc; el pnts (10A) €4; gas; lndtte; tradsmn; bar; BBQ; playgrnd; lake sw, boating, fishing; tennis; 10% statics; dogs; adv bkg; quiet; red long stay; CCI. "V friendly staff; gd cent for day trips."
♦ ltd. 1 Apr-30 Sep. € 16.50   2005*

> The opening dates and prices on this campsite have changed. I'll send a site report form to the editor for the next edition of the guide.

MONTERBLANC see Vannes 2F3

MONTESTRUC SUR GERS 8E3 (2km NE Rural) **Camping en Saubis (Daguzan), Route de Céran, 32390 Montestruc-sur-Gers [05 62 62 26 12; vacances_gers@hotmail.com; http://vacances-gers.chez.tiscali.fr]** S fr Fleurance on N21; after Montestruc-sur-Gers (immed past level x-ing) turn L onto D240; then turn R onto D251 for 1.5km, take R fork. Farm ent on L in 500m with conifer drive, site on L 50m. Sm, shd; wc; chem disp (wc); shwrs inc; el pnts (6A) €2.50 (long cable poss req); shops 2km; BBQ; playgrnd; golf 4km; 2 statics; poss cr; quiet. "Gd CL-type site with gd facs; peaceful farm with pleasant walks; farmer v friendly." 1 Jun-30 Sep. € 6.50   2006*

MONTEUX see Carpentras 10E2

France

MONTFAUCON 7D3 (2km N Rural) **FFCC Domaine de la Faurie**, 46240 Séniergues [05 65 21 14 36; fax 05 65 31 11 17; contact@camping-lafaurie.com; www.camping-lafaurie.com] Fr N20 turn E onto D2 sp Montfaucon, or fr A20 exit junc 56. In 5km site sp. Rd to site (off D2) is 500m long, single-track with passing places & steep but passable. Med, mkd pitch, pt sl, pt shd; wc; chem disp; mv service pnt; shwrs inc; el pnts (6A) €3.50; lndtte; ice; shop; rest; playgrnd; pool; paddling pool; cycle hire; games area; a few statics; dogs €2; Eng spkn; adv bkg; quiet; cc acc. "Superb, pretty site in lovely location; quiet & peaceful; lge pitches; v welcoming owners; excel facs & rest; gd touring base; narr, slightly steep site rds - some pitches poss diff l'ge o'fits; many walks; conv A20." ♦ 7 Apr-28 Sep. € 16.50 (CChq acc) 2007*

MONTFERRAND 8F4 (2km N Rural) **FFCC Domaine St Laurent (Naturist)**, Les Touzets, 11320 Montferrand [tel/fax 04 68 60 15 80; naturisme-st-laurent@wanadoo.fr; www.naturisme-st-laurent.com] S fr Toulouse on N113/D1113 past Villefranche-de-Lauragais. Turn L onto D43 for 4.2km; then R to St Laurent. Or turn L onto D218 bypassing Montferrand & cont directly to St Laurent; turn R at church. Site well sp. Sm, some hdg pitch, pt shd; wc; chem disp; shwrs inc; el pnts (3-6A) €4-5; lndtte; shop; rest; snacks; bar; playgrnd; pool; tennis; archery; cycle hire; entmnt; TV rm; dogs €2.50; Eng spkn; adv bkg; quiet; cc not acc; red low ssn; INF card req. "Attractive, peaceful, well-kept site; clean san facs; friendly owners; gd views; woodland walks; goats & ducks." 1 May-30 Sep. € 23.00 2006*

MONTFERRAND 8F4 (6km SE Rural) **Camping Le Cathare**, Château de la Barthe, 11410 Belflou [04 68 60 32 49; fax 04 68 60 37 90; info@auberge-lecathare.com; www.auberge-lecathare.com] Fr Villefranche-de-Lauragais on N113/D6113, foll D622 sp Toulouse/Carcassonne over rlwy, , canal, then immed L on D625 for 7km. Thro St Michel-de-Lanes then take D33 to Belflou; foll sp to Le Cathare. Sm, mkd pitch, pt shd; wc (some cont); chem disp; shwrs inc; el pnts (3A) €2.50; shops 12km; tradsmn; rest in ferme auberge; snacks, bar 4km; lake sw 3km; sand/shgl beach; some statics; dogs €0.50; v quiet; CCI. "Poss long walk to san facs & poss sh timer for lts at san facs; Centre Nautique on lake." 1 May-30 Oct. € 9.50 2006*

MONTFERRAT see Abrets, Les 9B3

MONTFERRIER see Lavelanet 8G4

MONTGAILLARD see Foix 8G3

MONTGEARD see Villefranche de Lauragais 8F3

MONTGENEVRE see Briançon 9C4

MONTGUYON 7C2 (3km E Rural) **Aire Naturelle La Motte**, La Motte, 17270 Le Fouilloux [05 46 04 08 39; enquiries@lamottecamping.com; www.lamottecamping.com] Exit N10 at Montlieu-la-Garde onto D730 to Montguyon where site sp. La Motte bet vills Le Gat & Lampiat on D270. Sm, mkd pitch, shd; wc; chem disp; mv service pnt; shwrs inc; el pnts €4.50; lndtte; ice; shop; BBQ; playgrnd; games area; cycle hire; conv Montguyon medieval castle; twin-axles by prior arrangement; dogs €1.80; quiet; adv bkg. "Excel." ♦ 1 Apr-30 Sep. € 13.60 2007*

MONTHERME see Charleville Mézières 5C1

⊞**MONTIGNAC** 7C3 (5km SE Rural) **Camping La Tournerie Ferme**, La Tournerie, 24290 Aubas [05 53 51 04 16; la-tournerie@orange.fr; www.montignac-camping.com] Fr Montignac on D704 dir Sarlat-la-Canéda; in 5.5km turn L onto C1 sp St Amand-de-Coly; in 1.6km at x-rds turn L sp Malardel & Drouille; in 400m at Y-junc foll rd to R sp Manardel & La Genèbre; cont on this rd ignoring minor rds; in 1.6km at elongated junc take rd to R of post box; immed after passing Le Treuil farm on R turn R at x-rds La Tournerie. Site opp farm. Sm, terr, hdstg, terr, sl, pt shd; htd wc; chem disp; shwrs inc; el pnts (6A) inc; dogs; adv bkg ess (dep req); v quiet. "Fantastic area, superb views; lge pitches; new facs (2007); no children; British owners; dog pitches sep; sun shelters on all pitches; excel touring base; highly rec." ♦ € 20.00 2007*

MONTIGNAC 7C3 (500m S Urban) **Camping Le Moulin du Bleufond**, Ave Aristide Briand, 24290 Montignac [05 53 51 83 95; fax 05 53 51 19 92; le.moulin.du.bleufond@wanadoo.fr; www.bleufond.com] S on D704, cross bdge in town & turn R immed of rv on D65; site sp in 500m nr stadium. Med, hdg pitch, pt shd; wc (some cont); shwrs inc; el pnts (10A) €3; ice; shops 500m; rest; snacks; bar; BBQ; htd pool high ssn; paddling pool; tennis adj; fishing; entmnt; dogs €1.52; poss cr; quiet; cc acc. "V pleasant site; poss diff lge o'fits due trees; pleasant, helpful owners; conv Lascaux caves & town; gd walking area; helpful staff, facs excel." Easter-15 Oct. € 14.80 2005*

MONTIGNAC 7C3 (7km S Rural) **FFCC Camping La Fage**, 24290 La Chapelle-Aubareil [05 53 50 76 50; fax 05 53 50 79 19; camping.lafage@wanadoo.fr; www.camping-lafage.com] Fr Montignac take D704 twd Sarlat. In approx 7km turn R to La Chapelle-Aubareil & foll camp sp to site ent 1km bef La Chapelle. Long winding drive thro woods to site. Med, pt sl, pt shd; wc; mv service pnt; baby facs; shwrs inc; el pnts (10A) inc; lndtte; shop; snacks; bar; playgrnd; pool; games area; entmnt; TV; 30% statics; dogs €1.50; adv bkg; red CCI. "Owner & facs v gd; excel site; red facs low ssn." 1 May-30 Sep. € 19.50 (CChq acc) 2006*

MONTIGNAC 7C3 (8km SW Rural) **Camping La Castillonderie, 24290 Thonac [05 53 50 76 79; fax 05 53 51 59 13; castillonderie@wanadoo.fr; www.castillonderie.nl]** Take D706 dir Les Eyzies. At Thonac take D65 sp Fanlac in 1km after x-rd take R, site is sp 2km. Med, mkd pitch, pt shd; wc; chem disp; mv service pnt; shwrs inc; el pnts (16A) €3; gas 5km; lndtte; lndry rm; ice; sm shop & 2km; tradsmn; rest; snacks; bar; BBQ; playgrnd; pool; paddling pool; canoeing 3km; TV rm; some statics; dogs; Eng spkn; adv bkg (dep req); quiet; 20% red low ssn; CCI. "Dutch owners v friendly & helpful; excel for relaxation; gd cent for historic visits; designated pitches with water & elec avail low ssn." ♦ Easter-30 Sep. € 15.00   2004*

MONTIGNAC 7C3 (9km SW Rural) **Camping Le Paradis, 24290 St Léon-sur-Vézère [05 53 50 72 64; fax 05 53 50 75 90; le-paradis@perigord.com; www.le-paradis.com]** On W bank of Rv Vézère on D706 Montignac-Les Eyzies rd, 1km fr Le Moustier. D706 poss rough rd. Med, hdg pitch, pt shd; htd wc; chem disp; mv service pnt; baby facs; shwrs inc; el pnts (10A) €3.50; lndtte; ice; shop; tradsmn; rest; snacks; bar; BBQ; playgrnd; htd, covrd pool; paddling pool; beach adj; boat hire; rv sw & fishing; tennis; cycle hire; games area; entmnt; wifi internet; TV rm; 25% statics; dogs €2; phone; poss cr; Eng spkn; adv bkg (dep req); poss rd noise; cc acc; red low ssn; CCI. "Gd site in gd location; vg for families; immac san facs & gd pool; rest & take-away vg; tropical vegetation around pitches; excel, esp low ssn." ♦ 1 Apr-25 Oct. € 26.00 (CCHq acc)   2007*

MONTIGNAC CHARENTE see Angoulême 7B2

MONTIGNY EN MORVAN 4H4 (2km E Rural) **Camp Municipal Plat du Lac, Bonin, 58120 Montigny-en-Morvan [tel/fax 03 86 84 73 05 or 03 86 84 71 77; montignyenmorvan@free]** N fr Château-Chinon on D944. At Montigny take D303 on R sp Barrage de Pannecière. Foll sp Bonin & site. Access fr D303 narr & not rec lge o'fits. Med, pt sl, shd; wc; chem disp; shwrs; el pnts (10A) inc (poss rev pol); tradsmn; lake sw; fishing; CCI. "Pitches poss soft after rain; helpful, friendly warden." 1 May-30 Sep. € 11.30   2005*

MONTIGNY LE BRETONNEUX see Versailles 4E3

MONTIGNY LE ROI 6F2 (1km N Rural) **Camping du Château, Rue Hubert Collot, Val-de-Meuse, 52140 Montigny-le-Roi [tel/fax 03 25 87 38 93]** Fr A31 junc 8 for Montigny-le-Roi. Site well sp in cent vill on D74. Med, terr, pt shd; htd wc; chem disp; baby facs; shwrs inc; el pnts (5A) €2; ice; shop; snacks; playgrnd; tennis; cycle hire; fishing 5km; entmnt. "Modern facs; steep ent; rests & shops in vill." ♦ 15 Apr-15 Oct. € 11.00   2005*

MONTJEAN SUR LOIRE see Chalonnes sur Loire 2G4

MONTLIEU LA GARDE 7C2 (8km N Rural) **Camp Municipal Bellevue, 17210 Chevanceaux [05 46 04 60 03 or 05 46 04 60 09 (Mairie)]** N fr Montlieu on N10, site by church in vill of Chevanceaux. Sm, mkd pitch, pt sl, pt shd; wc; chem disp (wc); mv service pnt; shwrs inc; el pnts inc; shops, rest, bar in vill; playgrnd; pool adj; tennis; quiet; CCI. "Excel, peaceful, clean site in pleasant vill, highly rec." 1 Apr-31 Oct. € 10.10   2007*

⊞**MONTLIEU LA GARDE** 7C2 (9km N Rural) **Camping Chez Frapier, 16360 Chantillac [05 45 79 00 53; momorley@hotmail.com]** Fr N10 ent Chevanceaux & leave vill on D156 dir Chatenet. Turn R at x-rds sp La Ferme Auberge. Site in 1km on L. Narr, single track app rd. Sm, pt shd; no san facs - own san req; chem disp (septic tank); el pnts (10A) €3; rest nrby; BBQ; sm splash pool; riding school, sw lakes picnic area 1.5km; no dogs; Eng spkn; adv bkg rec; quiet. "British-owned, basic, peaceful CL-type site in secluded countryside; poss diff access when wet; gd base for Cognac, Bordeaux & Médoc wine country, Atlantic coast, La Rochelle." € 12.00   2006*

MONTLIEU LA GARDE 7C2 (1km NE Rural) **Camp Municipal des Lilas, 17210 Montlieu-la-Garde [05 46 04 44 12 (Mairie); fax 05 46 04 50 91; montlieulagarde@mairie17.com]** On L N10 sp Montlieu-la-Garde; take D730 into vill. Turn L at multiple sp on corner (diff to see) & in 1km turn R & foll site sp. Site along vill lane. Sm, pt sl, pt shd; wc; shwrs; el pnts €2.10; tradsmn; shop in vill; pool 1km; quiet. "Vg NH; clean san facs; some rd noise." 1 May-30 Sep. € 5.70   2005*

MONTLUCON 7A4 (12km NW Rural) **Camp Municipal Le Moulin de Lyon, 03380 Huriel [06 11 75 05 63 or 04 70 28 60 08 (Mairie); fax 04 70 28 94 90; mairie.huriel@wanadoo.fr; http://huriel.planet-allier.com]** Exit A71 junc 10 & foll sp Domérat, then D916 to Huriel. Site well sp. Or fr N D943 turn SW at La Chapelaude to Huriel on D40, foll sp to site. Last km single track (but can pass on level grass) with steep incline to site ent. Site adj Rv Magieure. Med, hdg pitch, pt sl, pt shd; wc (some cont); chem disp; shwrs; el pnts (10A) €2.15 (poss rev pol); gas; lndry rm; shops, tradsmn; snacks, bar 1km; BBQ; playgrnd; lake/rv fishing; tennis; TV; few statics; Eng spkn; quiet. "V peaceful, clean, friendly, wooded site; site yourself, warden calls am & pm; no apparent security; 10 mins walk to vill; excel value." 15 Apr-15 Oct. € 4.90   2007*

France

⊞**MONTMARAULT** *9A1* (5km N Rural) **Camping La Ferme La Charvière, 03390 St Priest-en-Murat [04 70 07 38 24; fax 04 70 02 91 27; robert.engels@wanadoo.fr]** Exit A71 junc 11 at Montmarault onto D68 dir Sazeret/Chappes. Site 4km beyond Sazeret, sp. Sm, pt shd; wc; shwrs inc; el pnts (10A) €2.50; lndtte; ice; rest; playgrnd; pool; adv bkg; quiet; red low ssn; CCI. "Helpful Dutch owner; v peaceful & quiet at night; ltd facs low ssn & poss run down; san facs, stretched if busy; poss clsd winter - phone ahead; easy access to m'way." € 15.00   2005*

MONTMARAULT *9A1* (4.5km NE Rural) **Camping La Petite Valette, La Vallette, 03390 Sazeret [04 70 07 64 57 or 06 80 23 15 54 (mob); fax 04 70 07 25 48; la.petite.valette@wanadoo.fr; www.valette.nl]** Leave A71 at junc 11 & take 3rd exit at 1st rndabt onto D46; after 400m turn L at next rndabt, site sp on L in 3km. Or N of Montmarault in vill of Sazeret site well sp. Narr rd fr vill to site Med, hdg/mkd pitch, pt shd; htd wc; chem disp; shwrs inc; el pnts (6A) €2.85; gas; lndtte; lndry rm; ice; tradsmn; rest (high ssn); bar; playgrnd; htd pool & paddling pool; cycle hire; fishing; entmnt; dogs €1.70; Eng spkn; adv bkg, bkg fee req; quiet; red low ssn. "Run down appearance (Sep 07); gd, clean facs; pleasant walks." ♦ 1 Apr-31 Oct. € 17.40   2006*

MONTMARAULT *9A1* (9km NE) **Camp Municipal, 03240 Deux-Chaises [04 70 47 12 33]** Fr A71 in Montmarault take 2nd rndabt to Deux-Chaises; site on R in vill; well sp. Sm, hdg pitch, terr, pt sl, unshd; wc; shwrs; el pnts (16A) €2; shop; rest & bar 200m; playgrnd; tennis; lake fishing adj. "Clean, well-maintained site; warden calls for fees pm; phone to check opening bef arr, esp low ssn; vg rest nrby; gd NH." 25 Mar-15 Oct. € 6.50   2006*

MONTMAUR see Veynes *9D3*

MONTMEDY *5C1* (NW Urban) **Camp Municipal La Citadelle, Rue Vauban, 55600 Montmédy [03 29 80 10 40 (Mairie); fax 03 29 80 12 98; mairie.montmedy@wanadoo.fr]** Fr D643 (N43) foll sp to Montmédy cent & foll site sp. Steep app. Sm, hdg pitch, pt sl, pt shd; wc; chem disp; shwrs inc; el pnts (5-10A) €2.80-3.97; lndry facs; shops 1km; tradsmn; playgrnd; dogs €1.90; phone; quiet; red long stay; CCI. "Warden calls am & pm; facs v clearn; nr Montmedy Haut, old fortified town with ramparts & dry moat, excel views all round; 10A hook-up not avail in high ssn; office open 0730-0800 & 1930-2000 but not reliable; vg." 1 May-30 Sep. € 8.00   2007*

MONTMELIAN *9B3* (5km SE Rural) **FFCC Camping L'Escale, 73800 Ste Hélène-du-Lac [tel/fax 04 79 84 04 11; campingescale@aol.com; www.camping-savoie-escale.com]** Exit A43 junc 22 onto D923 dir Pontcharra & Les Mollettes; after x-ing A43 site on R. Med, hdg pitch, pt shd; wc; baby facs; shwrs inc; el pnts (6A) inc; gas; lndtte; rest; snacks; bar; BBQ; playgrnd; pool; 30% statics; dogs €1; poss cr; adv bkg; some rd & rlwy noise; CCI. "Gd san facs." 15 Feb-15 Oct. € 14.00   2006*

MONTMEYAN *10E3* (500m S Rural) **Camping Le Château de L'Eouvière, 83670 Montmeyan [tel/fax 04 94 80 75 54; leouviere@wanadoo.fr; www.leouviere.com]** Fr Montmeyan take D13 dir Fox-Amphoux; site 500m on R out of Montmeyan. Med, mkd pitch, terr, pt shd; wc; chem disp; shwrs inc; el pnts (10A) €4; lndtte; ice; shop; tradsmn; rest; snacks; bar; BBQ (el only on pitch); playgrnd; pool; tennis; games rm; TV rm; no statics; dogs €4; Eng spkn; adv bkg (dep req); Eng spkn; quiet; red low ssn; no cc acc. "Peaceful site in lovely area; diff access; steep slopes/uneven steps poss diff for disabled; poorly lit; adequate san facs." ♦ 15 Apr-15 Oct. € 23.00   2006*

MONTMIRAIL *3D4* (1km E) **Camp Municipal Les Châtaigniers, Rue du Petit St Lazare, 51210 Montmirail [03 26 81 25 61; fax 03 26 81 14 27; mairie.montmirail@wanadoo.fr]** Site opp junc of D933 & D373 at E o'skts of town. Sm, mkd pitch, pt shd; wc (cont); own san rec; shwrs inc; el pnts (20A) €4; shops 500m; playgrnd; pool 500m; tennis; golf; cc not acc; CCI. "Gd, clean, peaceful site approx 1 hr fr Paris; warm welcome tho late arr; fees collected each pm; call at warden's house L of ent for removal of barrier; lots of hot water." 1 Apr-31 Oct. € 4.35   2007*

MONTMORILLON *7A3* (500m E Urban) **Camp Municipal de l'Allochon, Ave Tribot, 86500 Montmorillon [05 49 91 02 33 or 05 49 91 13 99 (Mairie); fax 05 49 91 58 26; montlorillon@cg86.fr]** On D54 to Le Dorat, approx 400m SE fr main rd bdge over rv at S of town. Site on L. Fr S v sharp RH turn into site. Med, mkd pitch, terr, pt shd; htd wc (some cont); mv service pnt; shwrs inc; el pnts (6-10A) €1.57-2.68; lndtte; shop 1km; rest, snacks, bar 500m; BBQ; playgrnd; htd, covrd pool 300m; fishing; games area; TV; poss cr; adv bkg; some rd noise; CCI. "Delightful, clean, friendly & peaceful site; barrier card; gd touring base." ♦ 1 Mar-31 Oct. € 4.00   2007*

MONTOIRE SUR LE LOIR *4F2* (500m S Rural) Camp Municipal Les Reclusages, Ave des Reclusages, 41800 Montoire-sur-le Loir [tel/fax 02 54 85 02 53] Foll site sp, out of town sq, over rv bdge & 1st L on blind corner at foot of old castle. Med, some mkd pitch, pt shd; wc (some cont); chem disp; mv service pnt; shwrs inc; el pnts (10A) €3.30; lndtte; ice; shops 500m; bar; snacks (am only); playgrnd; htd pool adj; playgrnd; canoeing; fishing; mini-golf; 5% statics; adv bkg; quiet; no cc acc; CCI. "Well situated, peaceful, well-kept, secure site bet wooded hill & Rv Loir; friendly & helpful warden; excel clean san facs, v ltd low ssn; conv troglodyte vills; pleasant walk over bdge to town cent; gd cycling." ♦ 8 May-20 Sep. € 6.55   2006*

Before we move on, I'm going to fill in some site report forms and post them off to the editor, otherwise they won't arrive in time for the deadline at the end of September.

MONTPELLIER *10F1* (8km N Rural) Camping Sunêlia Le Plein Air des Chênes, Route de Castelnau, 34830 Clapiers [04 67 02 02 53; fax 04 67 59 42 19; pleinairdeschenes@free.fr; www.pleinairdeschenes.net] Exit A9 junc 28 onto N113/D65 twd Montpellier. Leave at junc with D21 sp Jacou & Teyran, site sp on L. Tight ent. Med, mkd pitch, pt sl, terr, pt shd; wc (cont); shwrs inc; private san facs some pitches (extra charge); el pnts (10A) inc; gas; lndtte; shops 800m; rest (high ssn); snacks; bar; playgrnd; pool (high ssn); paddling pool; waterslides; sand beach 16km; tennis; games area; horseriding; 60% statics; dogs €6; quiet; red long stay/low ssn. "Ongoing improvements 2007; site rds tight for lge o'fits; pitches muddy in wet." ♦ 1 Mar-31 Dec. € 37.00 (CChq acc)   2007*

MONTPELLIER *10F1* (6km SE) Camping Le Parc, Route de Mauguio, 34970 Lattes [04 67 65 85 67; fax 04 67 20 20 58; camping-le-parc@wanadoo.fr; www.leparccamping.com] Exit A9 junc 29 for airport onto D66. In about 4km turn R onto D172 sp Lattes & campings, cross over D21. Site ent in 200m on R. Med, hdg pitch, shd; wc; chem disp; shwrs inc; el pnts (10A) inc; gas; lndtte; ice; sm shop; huge shopping cent 1km; tradsmn; snacks high ssn; playgrnd; pool; sand beach 4km; 15% statics; dogs €2.80; Eng spkn; adv bkg (dep); quiet; CCI. "V friendly, helpful owners; lge pitches but dusty; gd facs, excel pool & snack bar; conv Cévennes mountains, Montpellier & Mediterranean beaches; sporting activities organised, eg hiking & mountain biking; barrier locked 2200." ♦ 25 Mar-11 Nov. € 23.40   2006*

MONTPELLIER *10F1* (4km S Rural) Camping L'Oasis Palavasienne, Route de Palavas, 34970 Lattes [04 67 15 11 61; fax 04 67 15 10 62; oasis.palavasienne@wanadoo.fr; www.oasis-palavasienne.com] Leave A9 at exit Montpellier Sud. Take D986 sp Palavas. About 1.5km after Lattes take slip rd sp Camping; turn under dual c'way. Site opp. Lge, hdg pitch, pt shd; wc; gym & sauna; shwrs inc; el pnts inc; lndtte; ice; shop; rest; snacks; bar; playgrnd; pool; rv adj; sand beach, watersports 4km; cycle hire; horseriding 2km; entmnt; disco; TV; free bus to beach; Eng spkn; adv bkg ess; some traff noise; CCI. "Bus to Palavas & Montpellier." 1 May-31 Aug. € 26.00   2004*

MONTPEZAT DE QUERCY see Caussade *8E3*

MONTPON MENESTEROL *7C2* (300m N Rural) Camping Port Vieux, 1 Rue de la Paix, Route de Ribérac, 24700 Montpon-Ménestérol [05 53 80 22 16; daniel.taillez455@orange.fr] Fr Montpon town cent traff lts take D730 N to Ménestérol. Site on L bef bdge beside Rv Isle. Med, hdg/mkd pitch, pt shd; wc; chem disp; shwrs inc; el pnts (10A) €3; gas 500m; lndtte; ice; shop 100m; tradsmn; rest; snacks; bar; BBQ; playgrnd; lake sw 200m; boat hire; fishing; tennis 200m; cycle hire 500m; leisure park nrby; child entmnt; TV rm; 2% statics; dogs; Eng spkn; adv bkg (30% dep); quiet; cc acc; CCI. "Gd touring base for St Emilion region; gd walking, cycling; vg." ♦ 1 Apr-30 Sep. € 9.00   2007*

MONTPON MENESTEROL *7C2* (10km SE) Domaine de Chaudeau (Naturist), 24700 St Géraud-de-Corps [05 53 82 49 64; fax 05 53 81 18 94; chaudeau.naturiste@wanadoo.fr; www.domainedechaudeau.com] Fr Montpon take D708 S; after 8km turn E on D33 for St Géraud-de-Corps; foll black & white sp Chaudeau. Fr St Foy-la-Grande take D708 N; after 11km on exit St Méard-de-Gurçon turn E & foll sp as above. Med, hdg/mkd pitch, shd; wc; chem disp; shwrs inc; el pnts (5A) €3.20; lndtte; ice; shop; snacks; bar; pool; fishing; entmnt; child entmnt; some statics; dogs €2.30; phone; quiet; red low ssn. "An excel naturist site; INF card req but holiday membership avail; v lge pitches." 1 Apr-30 Sep. € 18.00   2005*

MONTPON MENESTEROL *7C2* (4km S Rural) Caravaning La Tuilière, 24700 St Rémy-sur-Lidoire [tel/fax 05 53 82 47 29 or 06 87 26 28 04 (mob); la-tuiliere@wanadoo.fr; www.campinglatuiliere.com] On W side of D708 4km S of Montpon-Ménestérol. Med, hdg/mkd pitch, shd; wc; chem disp; shwrs inc; el pnts (5-10A) €2.50-3.20; gas; lndtte; ice; sm shop 3km; tradsmn; rest; snacks; bar; playgrnd; pool; tennis; crazy golf; boating; lake on site; 20% statics; dogs €1.20; poss cr; Eng spkn; adv bkg; quiet; red long stay; cc acc; CCI. "Gd value; excel rest." ♦ 1 May-16 Sep. € 12.00   2006*

France

⊞**MONTPON MENESTEROL** *7C2* (9km W Rural) **Camping Les Loges, 24700 Ménesplet [05 53 81 84 39; fax 05 53 81 62 74]** At Ménesplet turn S of N89 onto D10 sp Minzac. Turn L after level x-ing, foll sp. Sm, hdg pitch, pt shd; wc; mv service pnt; shwrs inc; el pnts (16A) inc (take care electrics); gas 7km; lndtte; shops 2.5km; playgrnd; rv sw 5km; games area; 5% statics; dogs €2; adv bkg; quiet; CCI. "V quiet site in pleasant countryside." ♦ € 17.00   2006*

MONTREAL *8E2* (2km NW Rural) **FFCC Camping Rose d'Armagnac, Moulierous, 32250 Montréal [tel/fax 05 62 29 47 70; campingrosedarmagnac@ free.fr;   http://campingrosedarmagnac.free.fr]** Exit Montréal in dir of Fources; L turn to Sos, v sharp turn off D29; after sm bdge 1st L, uphill 1km. Sm, some mkd pitch, pt terr, pt shd; wc; chem disp; mv service pnt; shwrs inc; el pnts (6A) €2.50; gas; lndtte; ice; tradsmn; BBQ; rest, snacks & bar 2km; sm playgrnd; unhtd paddling pool; waterslide & sand beach 2km; dogs €0.50; poss cr; adv bkg; quiet; cc not acc; CCI. "V quiet, relaxing site; choice of pitches in woods or on open terr; British owners; gd san facs; picturesque area; Roman villa nr; Bastide vill." ♦ ltd. 1 Apr-31 Oct. € 9.50   2007*

⊞**MONTREJEAU** *8F3* (1.5km N Rural) **Camping Midi-Pyrénées, Route de Cuguron, Quartier Loubet, 31210 Montréjeau [05 61 95 86 79; fax 05 61 95 90 67; camping-midi-pyrenees@ wanadoo.fr;   www.campingmidipyrenees.com]** N fr Montréjeau on D34 on terr hillside, well sp. Med, hdstg, pt sl, some terr, pt shd; htd wc; shwrs inc; el pnts (6A) €3; ice; rest; snacks; bar; playgrnd; pool; rv & lake 2km; mini-golf; entmnts; 60% statics; dogs €1; quiet; CCI. "Excel views Pyrenees; gd welcome; gd san facs; gd." € 12.00   2007*

⊞**MONTREJEAU** *8F3* (7km S Rural) **Camping Es Pibous, Chemin de St-Just, 31510 St Bertrand-de-Comminges [05 61 94 98 20 or 05 61 88 31 42; fax 05 61 95 63 83]** Turn S fr D817 (N117) onto N125 sp Bagnères-de-Luchon & Espagne. Foll past 'Super U' to lge rndabt & turn R sp St Bertrand-de-Comminges/Valcabrère then at 1st traff lts turn R & foll sp for St Bertrand & site. Or exit A64 junc 17 onto A645 sp Bagnères-de-Luchon to lge rndabt, then as above. Med, hdg/mkd; pt shd; wc; chem disp; mv service pnt; shwrs inc; el pnts (6A) €3.50; gas; lndtte; shop; rest, bar 300m; playgrnd; pool; fishing, tennis 3km; TV; 10% statics; dogs; poss cr; adv bkg; quiet; cc acc. "Excel, friendly, peaceful site; lge pitches among cherry trees; ltd facs low ssn, poss stretched high ssn; gd touring area nr mountains; prehistoric caves; picturesque town with cathedral in walking dist." ♦ € 11.22   2007*

MONTREJEAU *8F3* (8km S Rural) **Camp Municipal Bords de Garonne, Chemin du Camping, 65370 Loures-Barousse [05 62 99 29 29]** Exit A64 junc 17 onto A645 by-passing Montréjeau. Or fr Montréjeau take N125 to Luchon & 'Espagne'. In 5km cont onto D33. Site on R in 3km, visible fr rd. Access fr D122 sp Loures-Barousse across rv bdge. Med, shd; htd wc (some cont); chem disp (wc); shwrs; el pnts (4A) €2.50; rest & snacks in adj hotel; shops 500m; 80% statics; adv bkg; some Eng spkn; quiet but some rd noise; CCI. "Touring pitches on rvside; clean san facs but site looking run down; friendly, helpful staff; ideal for exploring Pyrenees or as NH to/fr Spain; pleasant site; easy walk to vill." ♦ 1 Mar-31 Oct. € 6.35   2005*

MONTREJEAU *8F3* (6km W Rural) **Camping de la Neste, 65150 St Laurent-de-Neste [05 62 39 73 38 or 05 62 99 01 49]** Exit A64/E80 junc 17 to Montréjeau or S fr Toulouse on N117. At W end of Montréjeau keep L on D938 sp La Barthe-de-Neste; in 6km turn S in vill of St Laurent-de-Neste & immed W on N bank of rv at camp sp; site on L in 1km. Sm, pt shd, mkd pitch; wc; chem disp; mv service pnt; shwrs inc; el pnts (6A) €3; lndry rm; shop 1km; playgrnd; rv sw & beach; phone; dogs; quiet; adv bkg; CCI. 1 May-30 Sep. € 10.00   2004*

MONTRESOR *4H2* (3km NE Rural) **Camping Les Coteaux du Lac, 37460 Chemillé-sur-Indrois [02 47 92 77 83; fax 02 47 92 72 95; lescoteauxdulac@wanadoo.fr;   www. lescoteauxdulac.com]** Fr Loches on D764; then D10 dir Montrésor; cont to Chemillé-sur-Indrois. Med, pt sl; wc; chem disp; baby facs; shwrs inc; el pnts (6A) €3.70; lndtte; sm shop; rest & bar 200m; playgrnd; htd pool; lake fishing & boating; trekking in Val d'Indrois; child activities; games rm; internet; TV rm; dogs €1.50; phone; v quiet. "Excel new site (2006) by lake; clean san facs." ♦ 7 Apr-30 Sep. € 16.50   2006*

⊞**MONTREUIL** *3B3* (500m N Rural) **FFCC Camping La Fontaine des Clercs, 1 Rue de l'Eglise, 62170 Montreuil [tel/fax 03 21 06 07 28; desmarest.mi@ wanadoo.fr;   www.campinglafontainedesclercs. com]** Fr N or S turn W off D901 (N1) at traff lts on D939 dir Le Touquet. Turn R after rlwy x-ing & in 100m fork R to site, site sp on Rv Canche. Med, mkd pitch, hdstg, pt sl, terr, pt shd; wc; chem disp; mv service pnt; shwrs inc; el pnts (6A) €3.50; lndtte; shops 500m; tradsmn; pool 1.5km; rv adj; fishing; games rm; dogs €1; adv bkg rec high ssn; quiet; red 4+ days; no cc acc; CCI. "V helpful owner; excel, generous pitches beside rv; some on steep terr with tight turns; dated san facs but clean; attractive, unusual site nr interesting, historic town & area; conv NH Le Touquet, beaches & ferry; lovely rvs nrby - Canche & Authie. € 12.70   2007*

TOURAINE VACANCES

10 % off-season discount

The campsite is situated in the region of the Loire and Cher castles; supermarket Champion 50 m, family campsite, restaurant, animation during high season. Directions: direction Bordeaux – Blois Sud – follow N76 Vierzon – Montrichard direction Loches, the camping is situated at the roundabout (bas de Montparnasse) next to the Champion supermarket.

Rental of chalets and mobile homes, sale and rental for a whole year of mobile homes.

**Bas de Montparnasse . 41400 Faverolles sur Cher. Tel. : +33 (0) 2 5432 0608 .
Fax : +33 (0) 2 5432 6135. info@tourainevacances.fr . www.tourainevacances.fr**

France

MONTREUIL *3B3* (7km SW Rural) **Camping à la Ferme, 14 Rue Verte, 62170 Wailly-Beaucamp** [03 21 81 26 29] Fr Montreuil take D901 (N1) S to Wailly-Beaucamp. In Wailly turn L along side of lge car park. Site within 500m at fork in rd. Sm, pt shd; wc; shwrs; el pnts (4A) €2; shop 800m; playgrnd; sand beach 12km; poss cr; adv bkg; quiet. "Beautiful CL-type site; friendly owners; basic but clean san facs; Montreuil interesting walled town." € 14.00   2007*

> There aren't many sites open this early in the year. We'd better phone ahead to check that the one we're heading for is actually open.

⊞**MONTREUIL BELLAY** *4H1* (4km E Rural) **FFCC Camping Le Thouet, Les Côteaux-du-Chalet, 49260 Montreuil-Bellay** [02 41 38 74 17; fax 02 41 50 92 83; Brian.Senior@wanadoo.fr; www. camping-le-thouet.co.uk] Fr N147 N of Montreuil-Bellay take dir 'Centre Ville'; turn L immed bef rv bdge & foll sp to Les Côteaux-du-Chalet. Access via narr, rough rd for 1km. Sm, mkd pitch, pt shd; wc; chem disp (wc); mv service pnt; shwrs inc; el pnts (10A) inc; gas; Indtte; shop 4km; tradsmn; bar; BBQ; playgrnd; pool; fishing; boating; dogs; phone; 5% statics; adv bkg; quiet but some rlwy noise; cc acc; red long stay; cc acc; CCI. "Quiet, peaceful; gd, spacious, British-owned site; lge area grass & woods surrounded by vineyards; pitches in open grass field; gd walks; vill not easily accessed by foot; unguarded rv bank poss not suitable children; excel." ♦ € 18.50   2006*

MONTREUIL BELLAY *4H1* (1km W Urban) **Camping Les Nobis, Rue Georges Girouy, 49260 Montreuil-Bellay** [02 41 52 33 66; fax 02 41 38 72 88; campinglesnobis@wanadoo.fr; www.campinglesnobis.com] Fr S on D938 turn L immed on ent town boundary & foll rd for 1km to site; sp fr all dir. Fr N on N147 ignore 1st camping sp & cont on N147 to 2nd rndabt & foll sp. Fr NW on D761 turn R onto N147 sp Thouars to next rndabt, foll site sp. Lge, hdg/mkd pitch, pt shd; wc (some cont); chem disp; mv service pnt; shwrs inc; el pnts (10A) €2.90 (poss long cable req); gas; Indtte; ice; shop; tradsmn; rest; snacks; bar; playgrnd; htd pool; cycle hire; TV rm; 7% statics; dogs; phone; poss cr; Eng spkn; adv bkg (dep req) quiet; 10% red 15+ days/low ssn; cc acc; CCI. "Spacious site between castle & rv; gd position; san facs run down low ssn (Apr 2007); vg rest; local chateaux & town worth exploring; 'aire de service' for m'vans adj." ♦ 31 Mar-30 Sep. € 19.00   2007*

MONTREVEL EN BRESSE *9A2* (500m E Rural) **Camping La Plaine Tonique, Base de Plein Air, 01340 Montrevel-en-Bresse** [04 74 30 80 52; fax 04 74 30 80 77; plaine.tonique@wanadoo.fr; www.laplainetonique.com] Exit A40 junc 5 Bourg-en-Bresse N onto D975 N dir Montrevel-en-Bresse; foll sp Marboz. Or exit A6 junc 27 Tournus S onto D975. V lge, hdg/mkd pitch, shd; wc; chem disp; mv service pnt; baby facs; shwrs inc; el pnts (10A) inc; Indtte; ice; shop; rest; snacks; bar; BBQ; playgrnd; 3 htd, covrd pools; 2 paddling pools; 2 waterslides; lake beach & sw adj; watersports; fishing; tennis; cycle hire; games area; archery; mountain biking; entmnt; child entmnt; TV; dogs €2; Eng spkn; adv bkg; quiet; cc acc. "Lovely, very busy lakeside site; superb leisure facs & excursions - something for everyone; vg clean san facs; gd rests & shops in vill; excel family site; some pitches boggy after rain." ♦ 8 Apr-21 Sep. € 22.60   2007*

MONTRICHARD *4G2* (1km S Rural) **Camping Touraine Vacances, Bas de Montparnasse, 41400 Faverolles-sur-Cher [02 54 32 06 08; fax 02 54 32 61 35; touraine-vacances@wanadoo. fr; www.tourainevacances.fr]** E fr Tours on N76 thro Bléré; at Montrichard turn S on D764 twd Faverolles-sur-Cher, site 200m fr junc, adj to Champion supmkt. Med, mkd pitch, hdstg, pt shd; wc; chem disp; baby facs; shwrs inc; el pnts (10A) €3.50 (rev pol); lndtte; supmkt; rest; snacks; bar; BBQ; playgrnd; pool; beach & sw 600m; games area; entmnt; 5% statics; dogs €2; Eng spkn; adv bkg (dep req); quiet, but some rd noise; gate clsd 2200-0800; cc acc; red low ssn/CCI. "Busy rds nrby; gd hypermkt adj; gd sports activities; vg site; conv many chateaux." ♦ 19 Apr-1 Oct. € 19.00
2007*

See advertisement on previous page

MONTRICHARD *4G2* (1km W Urban) **Camp Municipal L'Etourneau, 41400 Montrichard [02 54 32 10 16 or 02 54 32 00 46 (Mairie); fax 02 54 32 05 87]** Fr D150 site sp twd rv. Med, mkd pitch, pt shd; wc; chem disp; mv service pnt; shwrs inc; el pnts (13A) inc (poss long leads req); supmkt & shops, rest, snacks 1km; bar; playgrnd; pool 2km; rv sw 2km; poss cr; Eng spkn; CCI. "Well-run site; helpful staff; card operated barrier." 1 Jun-15 Sep. € 12.00
2004*

MONTRIGAUD *9C2* (3km E) **Camping La Grivelière, 26350 Montrigaud [tel/fax 04 75 71 70 71; courrier@lagriveliere.com; www. lagriveliere.com]** Fr Romans-sur-Isère take D538 N 13km to La-Cabaret-Neuf, then NE on D67 to Montrigaud. Nr vill take D228 & foll sp to site. Med, hdg pitch, pt shd; wc (some cont); shwrs inc; el pnts (4A) inc; lndtte; ice; sm shop; tradsmn; rest; snacks; bar; BBQ; playgrnd; pool; sports area; lake sw, fishing 2km; entmnt; 50% statics; dogs €1.40; phone; adv bkg 25% dep + booking fee; quiet, but some noise fr disco; CCI. "Many activities avail; key operated barrier, dep req." ♦ ltd. 1 Apr-15 Sep. € 14.50
2004*

MONTSALVY *7D4* (800m S) **Camp Municipal de la Grangeotte, Route d'Entraygues, 15120 Montsalvy [04 71 49 26 00 or 04 71 49 20 10 (Mairie); fax 04 71 49 26 93; mairie-montsalvy@wanadoo.fr]** On W of D920 behind sports complex. Sm, pt sl, pt shd; wc; shwrs; el pnts (3-6A) €2.50-3.70; lndtte; shops in vill; rest; snacks; bar; playgrnd; sports area; htd pool adj (Jun-Aug) free to campers; fishing 2km; adv bkg; quiet but some rd noise. "Pleasant vill; entmnt; panoramic views fr some pitches; friendly warden." 4 Jun-15 Sep. € 12.10
2004*

MONTSAUCHE LES SETTONS *4G4* (4km SE Rural) **FFCC Camping de la Plage des Settons, Rive Gauche, Lac des Settons, 58230 Montsauche-les-Settons [03 86 84 51 99; fax 03 86 84 54 81; camping@settons-tourisme.com]** Fr Montsauche foll sp Château-Chinon. In 500m fork L to Les Settons. After 2km foll sp for Rive Gauche, after 1km L at bend for site. Med, hdg/mkd pitch, terr, pt shd; wc; chem disp; shwrs inc; el pnts (3-10A) €2.60-4.50; lndtte; ice; shops 500m; tradsmn; playgrnd; pool nrby; sand/shgl lake beach adj; fishing; pedaloes; lake sw; cycle hire; Eng spkn; poss noisy; cc acc; CCI. "In cent of Parc du Morvan; direct access to Lac des Settons; long elec cable rec; access rd busy pm." ♦ ltd. Easter-15 Oct.
€ 11.20
2005*

MONTSAUCHE LES SETTONS *4G4* (5km SE Rural) **Camp Municipal de la Baie de la Faye, Lac des Settons, 58230 Montsauche-les-Settons [03 86 84 55 83; fax 03 86 84 54 99; mairie-de-montsauche-les-settons@wanadoo.fr]** Foll sp 'Rive Droite' off D193 fr Montsauche-les-Settons. Sm, hdg pitch, terr, pt shd; wc; chem disp (wc); shwrs inc; el pnts (6A) €3; lndry rm; tradsmn; lake sw; watersports; boat hire 1km; 3% statics; dogs; poss cr; adv bkg; quiet; CCI. "Lake-side access dir fr site; Morvan National Park; gd." ♦ ltd. 1 Jun-15 Sep. € 11.00
2006*

MONTSAUCHE LES SETTONS *4G4* (5km SE) **Camping L'Hermitage de Chevigny, 58230 Moux-en-Morvan [03 86 84 50 97]** Fr Montsauche take D520 S & after approx 5km turn L on D290; at T-junc in 3km turn L & in further 800m turn L into Chevigny & foll sp to L'Hermitage. App rds narr & twisting. Med, hdg/mkd pitch, pt shd; wc (mainly cont); chem disp; shwrs inc; el pnts (3-6A) €3.20; gas; lndtte; sm shop; tradsmn; snacks; bar; playgrnd; lake sw; watersports; fishing; games area; dogs €1.80; adv bkg; Eng spkn; quiet; cc not acc; CCI. "Peaceful, secluded woodland site; spotless facs; v friendly, helpful owner; gd cycling & walking; less well-known part of France - a real gem; excel." 1 Apr-30 Sep. € 15.60
2007*

MONTSAUCHE LES SETTONS *4G4* (5km SE Rural) **FFCC Camping Les Mésanges, 58230 Montsauche-les-Settons [tel/fax 03 86 84 55 77 or 03 86 84 54 74]** Fr Montsauche take D193 to Les Settons, then D520 dir Chevigny. Foll sp to site on W side of lake. Med, mkd pitch, terr, pt sl, pt shd; wc (some cont); chem disp; mv service pnt; baby facs; shwrs inc; el pnts (4A) €3.20; gas; ice; shop; rest 1km; snacks; playgrnd; lake sw; fishing; games area; dogs €0.80; poss cr; Eng spkn; quiet; adv bkg; CCI. "Beautiful, lakeside site; well maintained; gd for families - lge play areas; excel." ♦ 1 May-15 Sep.
€ 13.00
2006*

MONTSAUCHE LES SETTONS *4G4* (7km SE Rural) **Camping Plage du Midi, Lac des Settons Les Branlasses, 58230 Montsauche-les-Settons [03 86 84 51 97; fax 03 86 84 57 31; campplagedumidi@aol.com; www.settons-camping.com]** Fr Salieu take D977 bis to Montsauche, then D193 'Rive Droite' to Les Settons for 5km. Cont a further 3km & take R fork sp 'Les Branlasses' Centre du Sport. Site on L after 500m at lakeside. Med, mkd pitch, terr, pt shd; wc (few cont); chem disp; baby facs; shwrs inc; el pnts (10A) €3.40; gas; shop; rest; snacks; bar; playgrnd; lake sw; sand beach adj; watersports; horseriding 2km; entmnt; dogs €1; phone; poss cr; Eng spkn; adv bkg; poss noisy; red low ssn; cc acc; CCI. "Slopes slippery when wet." ♦ Easter-15 Oct. € 13.90 (CChq acc) 2007*

MONTSOREAU *4G1* (Rural) **Airotel Camping L'Isle Verte (formerly Municipal), Ave de la Loire, 49730 Montsoreau [02 41 51 76 60 or 02 41 67 37 81; fax 02 41 51 08 83; isleverte@wanadoo.fr; www.campingisleverte.com]** Fr S at Saumur turn R immed bef bdge over Rv Loire; foll sp to Chinon. Fr N foll sp for Fontevraud & Chinon fr Rv Loire bdge; site on D947 in vill on banks of Loire opp Traiteur. Med, mkd pitch, pt shd; wc; chem disp; mv service pnt; shwrs inc; el pnts (16A) €3 (poss long lead req); gas; lndry rm; shops 200m; tradsmn; ice; rest 100m; snacks; bar; playgrnd; pool; paddling pool; rv fishing/watersports; tennis; games area; golf 13km; entmnt high ssn; TV rm: poss cr; Eng spkn; adv bkg rec high ssn; rd noise; red low ssn; cc acc; CCI. "Simple, fair rvside site - no frills; sandy pitches; v clean san facs; chem disp diff to access; ltd power pnts; barrier clsd 2100-0700; extra charge for twin-axles; 10 min rvside walk to vill; gd wine caves & chateaux." ♦ 1 Apr-30 Sep. € 17.50 (CChq acc) 2006*

MONTSURS *4F1* (500m N Rural) **Camp Municipal de la Jouanne, Rue de la Jouanne, 53150 Montsûrs [02 43 01 00 31 (Mairie); fax 02 43 02 21 42; commune.montsurs@wanadoo.fr]** Well sp fr town cent. Med, pt shd; wc; chem disp (wc); shwrs inc; el pnts (2-10A); lndry rm; shop, rest, snacks, bar 500m; playgrnd; rv fishing adj; phone; adv bkg rec; quiet; no cc acc; CCI. "Pretty, well-kept rvside site; pleasant situation; conv many medieval vills; barrier (dep req) open approx 0930-1030 & 1630-1730, ask at house opp if clsd." 1 Jun-30 Sep. 2006*

MONTVIRON see Avranches *2E4*

MOOSCH see Thann *6F3*

MORCENX *8E1* (3km SE Rural) **Camping Le Clavé, 40110 Morcenx [58 07 83 11; contact@camping-leclave.com; www.camping-leclave.com]** Exit junc 14 fr N10 onto D38 thro Morcenx. Site on o'skts of vill on D27 bordering rv in chateau grounds. Med, pt sl, pt shd; wc; shwrs; el pnts (10A) €3; lndtte; ice; shop; snacks; supmkt 2km; BBQ; sm pool; cycle hire; nr National Park; mini-golf; games rm; dogs €1.50; quiet. 1 Apr-31 Oct. € 18.00 2007*

MORCENX *8E1* (2km S Rural) **Camping Fortanier, 40110 Morcenx [05 58 07 82 59]** Fr N10 turn E at junc 14 onto D38 dir Mont-de-Marsan. At Morcenx turn R on D27. Site on R 1km past Camping Le Clavé. Well sp. Sm, hdg/mkd pitch, shd; wc; chem disp (wc); shwrs inc; el pnts (6A) €2.50-3.50; gas; lndtte; shop, rest, bar 1km; playgrnd; pool, lake 3km; BBQ; 5% statics; dogs; phone 500m; dv bkg; quiet; cc not acc; CCI. "Friendly owners; well-kept site, clean & tidy; peaceful & relaxing; flat, excel." May-Oct. € 8.00 2004*

MORCENX *8E1* (7km W Rural) **Aire Naturelle La Réserve (Lemercier), 1870 Ave de l'Océan, 40110 Garrosse [dlemercier@club-internet.fr; www.camping-lareserve.com]** Exit N10 junc 14 onto D38 dir Morcenx; foll camping sps for 5km; site on L. Sm, pt sl, shd; wc; chem disp (wc); shwrs inc; el pnts (6-10A) €4; playgrnd; sm pool; snacks; games area; dogs €1; quiet. "Site in pine trees; conv N10." ♦ 1 Apr-30 Sep. € 9.10 2007*

MOREE *4F2* (S Rural) **Aire Naturelle Municipale du Plan d'Eau, 41160 Morée [02 54 82 06 16 or 02 54 89 15 15; fax 02 54 89 15 10]** W fr Orléans on N157 or N fr Vendôme on D910 (N100 & foll sp in vill onto D19 to site. Sm, pt shd; wc; chem disp; mv service pnt; shwrs inc; el pnts (8A) inc; ice; gas, shops 400m; snacks; bar; playgrnd; lake sw & beach adj; fishing; canoeing; tennis 500m; golf 5km; adv bkg (dep req); red long stay; CCI. "Lovely, lakeside site; ltd san facs stretched if site full; popular with school parties high ssn." 15 Jun-10 Sep. € 14.50 2005*

MOREE *4F2* (2km W Rural) **Camp Municipal, Rue de l'Etang, 41160 Fréteval [02 54 82 63 52 (Mairie); fax 02 54 82 07 15; freteval.mairie@wanadoo.fr]** Site 100m fr N157 by Rv Loir in vill cent, 500m fr lake. NB Chicane ent/exit thro concrete posts & fencing. Med, mkd pitch, pt shd; wc; shwrs inc; el pnts inc; shops 500m; playgrnd; fishing; quiet. "Diff ent/exit esp med/lge o'fits; lovely, peaceful location on bank of Rv Loir; conv beautiful town of Vendôme; conv N10; excel value; vg." 15 Mar-15 Oct. € 6.85 2007*

MOREE *4F2* (3km NW Rural) **Camping La Maladrerie, 41160 Freteval [tel/fax 02 54 82 62 75]** Fr Le Mans on N157, turn L in vill. Fr D910 (N10) site nr Le Plessis. Foll sp. Med, pt shd; wc; chem disp; shwrs inc; el pnts (4-6A) €1.55-2.30; gas; lndtte; shops 1km; bar; playgrnd; pool; 75% statics; cc acc; CCI. "V ltd facs low ssn; site was a medieval leper colony!!" ♦ 15 Mar-31 Oct. € 8.45 2005*

France

⊞ **MORESTEL** *9B3* (8km S Urban) **Camping Les Epinettes, 6 Rue du Stade, 38630 Les Avenières [tel/fax 04 74 33 92 92; infos@camping-les-avenieres.com; www.camping-les-avenieres.com]** S fr Morestel on N74, turn onto D40 to Les Avenières, site well sp. Med, hdg/mkd pitch, pt shd; wc; chem disp; mv service pnt; baby facs; shwrs inc; el pnts (10A) inc; lndtte; ice; shop; tradsmn; rest; snacks; bar; BBQ; playgrnd; pool adj; rv sw 2km; entmnt; TV rm; 35% statics; dogs €1.95; phone; adv bkg; noise fr adj stadium; red low ssn; cc acc; CCI. "Phone ahead low ssn to check open." ♦ € 17.10   2005*

MORESTEL *9B3* (NW Urban) **Camp Municipal La Rivoirette, Rue François Perrin, 38510 Morestel [04 74 80 14 97; mairie@morestel.com; www. morestel.com]** Foll camping sps in town. Site by sports complex on D517. (NB No ent sps do not apply to campers). Med, pt shd; wc; shwrs inc; el pnts (8A) €2.50; supmkt 1km; pool & sports complex adj; dogs; quiet. "Sm, poss awkward pitches; ent barrier operated by adj sw pool staff; pleasant NH." 1 May-30 Sep. € 9.30   2006*

MORET SUR LOING *4E3* (2km NW Urban) **Camping Les Courtilles du Lido, Chemin du Passeur, 77250 Veneux-les-Sablons [01 60 70 46 05; fax 01 64 70 62 65; jack.richard@wanadoo.fr]** Use app fr N6 sp Veneux-les-Sablons & foll sp. 1km fr N6. Or fr Moret foll sp; long, tortuous rte; narr streets; 35m, 1-width tunnel. NB sp say 'Du Lido' only. Lge, mkd pitch, pt shd; wc; chem disp; shwrs; el pnts (6-10A) €3; gas; lndtte; ice; shops 1km; tradsmn; rest; snacks; bar; playgrnd; sm pool; tennis; table tennis; mini-golf; 75% statics; dogs €1; poss cr; Eng spkn; adv bkg; rlwy noise at night; CCI. "Early arr advised; conv Fontainebleau; lge pitches; v clean facs but poss insufficient high ssn; friendly owners; vg for children; lovely old town; conv for train to Paris; excel." 3 Apr-20 Sep. € 13.75   2005*

MOREZ *9A3* (3km N Rural) **Camp Municipal La Bucle, 54 Route Germain Paget, 39400 Morbier [tel/fax 03 84 33 48 55; info.bucle@wanadoo.fr; www.euro-tourisme.com/pub/bucle]** Fr N on N5 look for sps 10km after St Laurent. Pass supmkt & lge car pk on R, take sharp L turn after L bend in rd. Fr S turn R 50m past bdge. Med, some hdstg, pt sl, pt terr, unshd; wc; shwrs inc; el pnts (10A) €2.30; shops 1km; pool; dogs €0.60; quiet; red low ssn; gd NH. "Lovely site & town but poss slightly unkempt." 1 Jun-15 Sep. € 14.50   2006*

MOREZ *9A3* (9km S Rural) **Camping Le Baptaillard, 39400 Longchaumois [03 84 60 62 34; camping-lebaptaillard@orange.fr]** Foll D69 S, site sp on R. Med, mkd pitch, pt sl, pt shd; htd wc; chem disp; shwrs inc; el pnts (6A) €2.50; lndtte; shop; rest, snacks, bar 3km; playgrnd; paddling pool; fishing 3km; tennis; mini-golf; skiing; games rm; some statics; adv bkg essential winter; quiet. "Beautiful CL-type site; lovely views; lge pitches." 1 Jan-30 Sep & Dec. € 12.30   2007*

MORHANGE *5D2* (6.5km N Rural) **Camp Municipal La Mutche, Harprich, 57340 Morhange [03 87 86 21 58; fax 03 87 86 24 88; mutche@ wanadoo.fr; www.morhange.fr]** Fr N74 turn N onto D78 sp Harprich, site sp on shore of Etang de la Mutche. Med, mkd pitch, hdstg, pt sl, pt shd; htd wc; chem disp; shwrs €0.70; el pnts (16A) €2.80; lndtte; shop 2km; tradsmn; rest 2km; bar; BBQ; playgrnd; pool; sand beach; lake sw; watersports; fishing; tennis; games area; entmnt; 20% statics; Eng spkn; adv bkg; quiet; red long stay. ♦ ltd. 1 Apr-31 Oct. € 11.20   2007*

MORLAIX *2E2* (6km N Rural) **Camping La Ferme de Keroyal, Le Bois de la Roche, 29610 Garlan [02 98 79 12 54]** Fr Morlaix take D786 dir Lannion. Foll blue & white camping sps. At app 6km turn R, farm on L. Sm, some hdg pitch, pt shd; wc; chem disp (wc); shwrs inc; el pnts inc; beach 20km; dogs; quiet. "Gd sh stay; CL-type site." ♦ Easter-31 Oct. € 11.00   2005*

MORLAIX *2E2* (11km E Rural) **Camping Aire Naturelle la Ferme de Croas Men (Cotty), Garlan, 29610 Plouigneau [tel/fax 02 98 79 11 50; croasmen@wanadoo.fr; http://pagesperso-orange. fr/camping.croamen]** Fr D712 rndabt W of Plouigneau twd Morlaix (exit from N12) 2km R sp Garlan; thro Garlan site 1km on L, well sp. Sm, hdg pitch, pt shd; wc; 50% serviced pitches; chem disp; baby facs; shwrs; el pnts (10A) €3; playgrnd; horseriding 200m; farm museum; donkey/tractor rides; some statics; dogs €1; quiet; CCI. "Super CL-type site; clean, well-presented; ideal for children - welcome to visit farm & see animals; excel facs; produce avail inc cider & crêpes." ♦ 1 Apr-31 Oct. € 10.80   2007*

MORLAIX *2E2* (15km S Rural) **Aire Naturelle Les Bruyères, 29410 Le Cloître-St Thégonnec [02 98 79 71 76 or 01736 362512 (England)]** Fr Morlaix take D769 S twd Huelgoat/Carhaix & Le Cloître-St Thégonnec. At Le Plessis after 14.5km turn L for Le Cloître-St Thégonnec. When ent vill, take L fork at Musée des Loups, 1st L, 500m then R to camp. Sm, mkd pitch, pt sl, pt shd; wc; chem disp; shwrs inc; lndry rm; shop 500m; rest; bar; BBQ; playgrnd; dogs €2; quiet; adv bkg; CCI. "Helpful British owners; NB no electricity/el pnts; water htd by gas; oil lamps in san block; camp fires; for stays outside of Jul/Aug tel to request." 1 Jul-31 Aug. € 13.00   2004*

MORMOIRON *10E2* (4km E Rural) **Camp Municipal, Route de la Nesque, 84570 Villes-sur-Auzon [04 90 61 82 05]** E on D942 fr Carpentras; at T-junc in Villes-sur Auzon turn R; foll sp Gorge de la Nesque & sports complex 400m. R into site. Med, pt shd; wc; shwrs inc; el pnts (5A) €2.30; shop nrby pool 500m; playgrnd; quiet. "Friendly, helpful owners; spotles facs; gd walking & choice of local wines." 1 Apr-30 Sep. € 9.70   2004*

⊞ *Site open all year*   458   *Send in your site reports*

MORMOIRON *10E2* (4km E Rural) **Camping Les Verguettes, Route de Carpentras, 84570 Villes-sur-Auzon** [04 90 61 88 18; fax 04 90 61 97 87; info@provence-camping.com; www.provence-camping.com] E on D942 fr Carpentras dir Sault. Site at ent to Villes-sur-Auzon beyond wine cave. Or at Veulle-les-Roses turn E onto D68. Cont thro Sottenville-sur-Mer. Site on L in 2km. Lge, hdg/mkd pitch, pt sl, pt shd; wc; chem disp; shwrs inc; el pnts (6A) inc; lndry rm; shops 1km; rest; pool; tennis; games rm; mini-golf; fishing 300m; internet; dogs €2.50; adv bkg rec all times; quiet; red low ssn. "Lovely location, view of Mont Ventoux; gd walking; friendly & helpful owner; families with children sited nr pool, others at end of camp away fr noise; poss muddy when it rains; sm pitches & poor access, not suitable lge o'fits; red facs low ssn; poss unkempt low ssn; pretty village." ♦ 1 Apr-15 Oct. € 21.90 (CChq acc)   2006*

MORMOIRON *10E2* (2km SE Rural) **Camping de l'Auzon, 84570 Mormoiron** [tel/fax 04 90 61 80 42] Fr Carpentras or Sault on D942, turn S of D942 onto D14. Foll sp. Sm, terr, shd; wc; chem disp (wc); shwrs inc; el pnts (6A) €2.50; lndtte; shop, rest, snacks, bar 1km; playgrnd; 50% statics; dogs €1.20; quiet "Asparagus fair last w/e in Apr; m'van could be charged extra." ♦ Easter-15 Oct. € 7.80   2004*

MORNAS *10E2* (2km E Rural) **Camping Beauregard, Route d'Uchaux, 84550 Mornas** [04 90 37 02 08; fax 04 90 37 07 23; beaurega@wanadoo.fr; www.camping-beauregard.com] Exit A7 at Bollène, then N7 twd Orange. On N end of Mornas turn L on D74 to Uchaux, site after 1.7km, sp. Lge, pt sl, shd; htd wc (some cont); chem disp; mv service pnt; shwrs inc; el pnts (6-10A) €3.30-4.40; gas; lndtte; shop; rest; snacks; bar; playgrnd; 3 htd pools; games rm; tennis; golf; horseriding; cycle hire; entmnt; dogs €4.15; 80% statics; adv bkg rec high ssn; quiet; Eng spkn; cc acc; red CCI. "Open until 2230; phone ahead to check open low ssn; gd san facs; many derelict vans; poorly maintained & ltd facs low ssn" ♦ 25 Mar-4 Nov. € 21.00 (3 persons)   2006*

MORNAY SUR ALLIER see St Pierre le Moûtier *4H4*

⊞**MORTAGNE SUR GIRONDE** *7B2* (1km SW Coastal) **Aire Communale Le Port, 17120 Mortagne-sur-Gironde** [05 46 90 63 15; fax 05 46 90 61 25; mairie-mortagne@smic17.fr] Fr Royan take D730 dir Mirambeau for approx 28km. Turn R in Boutenac-Touvent onto D6 to Mortagne, then foll sp Le Port & Aire de Camping-Car. M'vans only. Sm, unshd; chem disp; mv service pnt; el pnts (10A) inc; shop 500m; rest, snacks, bar 600m; dogs; poss cr; quiet. "Car/c'vans poss acc; shwrs & mv service pnt 800m fr site; fees collected 0900; gd." € 6.00   2006*

⊞**MORTAIN** *2E4* (8km S Rural) **Camping Les Taupinières, La Raisnais, 50140 Notre-Dame-du-Touchet** [tel/fax 02 33 69 49 36; kevin.gimbert@wanadoo.fr; http://lestaupinieres.mysite.wanadoo-members.co.uk] Fr Mortain S on D977 sp St Hilaire-du-Harcouet; shortly after rndabt take 2nd L at auberge to Notre-Dame-deTouchet. In vill turn L at post office, sp Le Teilleul D184, then 2nd R sp La Raisnais. Site at end of lane on R (haycart on front lawn). Sm, pt sl, pt shd; wc; chem disp; shwrs inc; el pnts (10A) inc; shop, rest 1km; htd pool 8km; dogs; adv bkg; quiet. "Tranquil CL-type site next to farm; lovely outlook; friendly, helpful British owners; adults only; excel." € 12.00   2007*

MORTAIN *2E4* (500m W Urban) **Camp Municipal Les Cascades, Place du Château, 50140 Mortain** [06 23 90 42 65; mairie.de.mortain@wanadoo.fr] On D977 S fr Ville twd St Hilaire-du-Harcoueu; site in cent of Mortain, sp to R. Sm, pt shd; wc; chem disp; mv service pnt; shwrs inc; el pnts (6A) €2; shop 200m; sm playgrnd; no statics; dogs; m'van parking area outside site; CCI. "Sm extra charge for twin-axles." ♦ Easter-1 Nov. € 6.00   2006*

MORTEAU *6H3* (Urban) **Camping Le Cul de la Lune, Rue du Pont Rouge, 25500 Morteau** [03 81 67 17 52 or 03 81 67 18 53; fax 03 81 67 62 34; otsi.morteau@wanadoo.fr; www.morteau.org] Fr Besançon take N57 E then D461. In Morteau foll sps to Pontarlier then 'Toutes Directions'. Site on R over rlwy/rv bdge sp Montlebon (D48). Clearly sp on brown sps thro'out town. Across rv bdge. Sm, pt shd; wc (some cont); shwrs inc; el pnts (10A) €3; ice; shops 300m; tradsmn; rv sw, fishing & boating; cycling; dogs €1; poss v cr; adv bkg; noise fr rd & rlwy; "In beautiful countryside on rv bank; facs basic & need renovation; warden visits; helpful local tourist office; poss cold at nights (altitude)." 1 Jun-15 Sep. € 13.00   2007*

MORZINE *9A3* (7km SW Rural) **Camping La Grange au Frêne, Les Cornuts, 74260 Les Gets** [04 50 79 70 64 or 04 50 75 80 60; fax 04 50 75 84 39] Fr Morzine go S on D902 to Les Gets. Site sp at end of vill. Sm, hdg/mkd pitch, terr, pt sl, pt shd; htd wc; 50% serviced pitches; baby facs; shwrs inc; el pnts (2-4A) €2-4; lndtte; shop 3km; tradsmn; rest, snacks & bar 3km; playgrnd; lake sw nr; TV rm; dogs; phone; Eng spkn; adv bkg (dep req); quiet. "Vg; golf, climbing, fishing, tennis, bowling, walking, adventure park & watersports nrby." 24 Jun-15 Sep. € 15.00   2005*

France

MORZINE 9A3 (3km NW Rural) **Camping Les Marmottes, 74110 Essert-Romand [tel/fax 04 50 75 74 44 or 06 12 95 00 48 (mob); camping. les.marmottes@wanadoo.fr]** Exit A40 junc 18 or 19 onto D902 twd Morzine, then turn L onto D328 to Essert-Romand. Fr A40 take junc 18 to Morzine. Sm, hdstg, unshd; wc; chem disp; serviced pitches; shwrs inc; el pnts (3-10A) €3.50-6.50; lndtte; ice; shop 2km; tradsmn; playgrnd; lake sw 3km; TV; dogs €1; Eng spkn; adv bkg (dep req); quiet; red long stay; CCI. "Specialises in winter c'vanning for skiers; tractor to tow to pitch in snow." ♦ 22 Jun-15 Sep & 15 Dec-15 Apr. € 14.50   2005*

Did you know you can fill in site report forms on the Club's website — www.caravanclub.co.uk?

MOSNAC 7B2 (Rural) **Camp Municipal Les Bords de la Seugne, 17240 Mosnac [05 46 70 48 45; fax 05 46 70 49 13]** Fr Pons, S on N137 for 4.5km; L on D134 to Mosnac; foll sp to site behind church. Sm, pt shd; wc; shwrs inc; el pnts (3A) €2; gas; shop 100m; 10% statics; dogs; Eng spkn; adv bkg; no cc acc; poss noisy; red long stay; CCI. "Excel facs; charming, clean, neat site in sm hamlet; helpful staff; site yourself, warden calls; conv Saintes, Cognac & Royan; bakery nr." 1 Apr-31 Oct. € 6.00   2005*

MOSTUEJOULS see Peyreleau 10E1

MOTHE ACHARD, LA 2H4 (1km S) **Camping Le Pavillon, Rue des Sables, 85150 La Mothe-Archard [02 51 05 63 46; fax 02 51 09 45 58; campinglepavillon@wanadoo.fr]** Foll D160 by-pass twd Les Sables-d'Olonne. Site on R on S app. Med, pt shd; wc; shwrs inc; el pnts (10A) inc; lndtte; ice; shops 1km; tradsmn; snacks; bar; playgrnd; 2 pools; waterslide; sand beach 15km; lake fishing; games area; entmnt; quiet; cc acc; CCI. "Gd facs for children." ♦ 31 Mar-30 Sep. € 16.70   2005*

MOTHE ACHARD, LA 2H4 (5km NW Rural) **Camping Domaine de la Forêt, Rue de la Forêt, 85150 St Julien-des-Landes [02 51 46 62 11; fax 02 51 46 60 87; camping@domainelaforet; www. domainelaforet.com]** Take D12 fr La Mothe-Achard to St Julien. Turn R onto D55 at x-rds & site sp on L. Med, hdg/mkd pitch, pt shd; wc; all serviced pitches; shwrs inc; el pnts (6A) €3.80; gas; ice; lndtte; shop & in vill; rest; snacks; bar; BBQ; 2 htd pools (no shorts); gd playgrnd; games rm; sand beach 12km; cycle hire; tennis; mini-golf; lake fishing adj; entmnt; dogs €2.60; 60% statics; poss cr; adv bkg rec high ssn; quiet; red low ssn; CCI. "Part of private chateau estate, popular with British visitors; gd for families; excel facs; gates clsd 2200-0800." 15 May-15 Sep. € 28.00 (3 persons)   2006*

MOTHE ACHARD, LA 2H4 (5km NW Rural) **Camping La Guyonnière, 85150 St Julien-des-Landes [02 51 46 62 59; fax 02 51 46 62 89; info@ laguyonniere.com; www.laguyonniere.com]** Leave A83 junc 5 onto D160 W twd La Roche-sur-Yon. Foll ring rd N & cont on D160 twd Les Sables-d'Olonne. Leave dual c'way foll sp La Mothe-Achard, then take D12 thro St Julien-des-Landes twd La Chaize-Giraud. Site sp on R. Lge, hdg pitch, pt sl, pt shd; wc; chem disp; shwrs inc; el pnts (6A) inc (long lead rec); gas; lndtte; shop; tradsmn; rest; snacks; bar; BBQ; playgrnd; 2 pools (1 htd, covrd); waterslide; sand beach 10km; lake fishing, canoe hire, windsurfing 400m; cycle hire; internet; cab/sat TV rm; some statics; dogs; phone; Eng spkn; adv bkg (dep req); cc acc; red low ssn. "V lge pitches; friendly owners; gd walking area." ♦ 15 Apr-28 Sep. € 28.00   2004*

MOTHE ACHARD, LA 2H4 (6km NW Rural) **FLOWER Camping La Bretonnière, 85150 St Julien-des-Landes [02 51 46 62 44; fax 02 51 46 61 36; camp.la-bretonniere@wanadoo. fr; www.la-bretonniere.com]** Fr La Roche-sur-Yon take D160 to La Mothe-Achard, then D12 dir St Gilles-Croix-de-Vie. Site on R 2km after St Julien. Med, mkd pitch, pt sl, pt shd; wc; chem disp (wc); baby facs; shwrs inc; el pnts (6-10A) €1.50-3; lndtte; ice; shops, bar 1km; BBQ; playgrnd; pool; sand beach 14km; fishing, sailing, lake sw 3km; 20% statics; dogs €2; Eng spkn; adv bkg; quiet; CCI. "Excel friendly site; adj working dairy farm, elec extension cables avail; 10 mins fr Bretignolles-sur-Mer sand dunes." ♦ ltd. 1 Apr-15 Oct. € 26.00   2007*

This guide relies on site report forms submitted by caravanners like us; we'll do our bit and tell the editor what we think of the campsites we've visited.

MOTHE ACHARD, LA 2H4 (7km NW) **Camping La Garangeoire, 85150 St Julien-des-Landes [02 51 46 65 39; fax 02 51 46 69 85; info@ garangeoire.com; www.camping-la-garangeoire. com or www.les-castels.com]** Site sp fr La Mothe-Achard. At La Mothe-Achard take D12 for 5km to St Julien, D21 for 2km to site. Or fr Aizenay W on D6 turn L dir La Chapelle-Hermier. Site on L, well sp. Lge, hdg/mkd pitch, pt sl, shd; serviced pitch; wc; chem disp; mv service pnt; shwrs inc; el pnts (6A) inc; gas; lndtte; ice; shop; rest; snacks; bar; playgrnd; htd pool complex; waterslide; lake fishing; sand beach 12km; horseriding; tennis; 50% statics; dogs €3; phone; poss cr; adv bkg (ess Aug); cc acc; red low ssn; CCI. "Busy site; many tour ops' static tents & vans; vg, clean facs; lge pitches; gd for families & all ages; pleasant friendly owners; super site." ♦ 31 Mar-29 Sep. € 34.50 (CChq acc)   2007*

MOUCHAMPS *2H4* (1km SE Rural) **Camp Municipal Le Hameau du Petit Lay, Route de St Prouant**, 85640 Mouchamps [tel/fax 02 51 66 25 72 or 02 51 66 28 02] Fr Chantonnay to D137 NW; 1km past St Vincent-Sterlanges turn R sp Mouchamps; turn R onto D113 sp St Prouant & camping; site on L in 1 km. Sm, hdg/mkd pitch, pt shd; wc, chem disp; shwrs inc; el pnts €2; shop, rest, snacks & bar 1km; playgrnd adj; htd pool adj; quiet, but traff noise am; CCI. "Next to sm chalet complex with pool (free) & playgrnd; barrier clsd 2200-7000; vg." ♦ € 9.90   2006*

MOUCHARD *6H2* (8km N Rural) **FFCC Camp Municipal La Louve, Rue du Pont**, 39600 Champagne-sur-Loue [tel/fax 03 84 37 69 12; camping.champagne@valdamour.com] Fr Mouchard NW on D121 to Cramans then NE on D274. Sm, shd; wc (some cont); mv service pnt; shwrs inc; el pnts (6A) €2.50; shops 2km; tradsmn; rest 1km; BBQ; playgrnd; fishing; dogs €0.80; adv bkg; quiet; CCI. "Beautiful situation on rv; all grass, poss diff m'vans if wet; nr historic Salines at Arc-et-Senans; vd." ♦ 1 Apr-30 Sep. € 6.30   2007*

MOULIHERNE see Vernantes *4G1*

MOULINS *9A1* (500m SW Rural) **Camping de la Plage**, 03000 Moulins [04 70 44 19 29] Fr Moulins turn W across Rv Allier at town bdge sp Clermont-Ferrand. Turn L on D2009 (N9) & in 100m turn L & foll sp to site. Med, some hdstg, pt shd; wc; own san facs rec high ssn; chem disp (wc); shwrs inc; el pnts (10A) inc (poss rev pol); gas; lndtte; ice; shop 500m; rest adj; snacks; bar; playgrnd; pool 1km; rv fishing & boat hire; entmnt; TV; phone; poss cr; poss noisy high ssn; cc acc; CCI. "Lovely, spacious site on rv bank; ltd water pnts; basic san facs, poss ltd low ssn & stretched high ssn; site poss unkempt low ssn; helpful staff; 10 min stroll to medieval town; gates clsd 2200-0700." 1 May-15 Sep. € 8.50   2007*

MOURIES *10E2* (2km E Rural) **Camping à la Ferme Les Amandaies (Crouau)**, 13890 Mouriès [04 90 47 50 59; fax 04 90 47 61 79] Fr Mouriès take D17 E sp Salon-de-Provence. Site sp 200m past D5 rd to R. Foll site sp to farm in 2km. Sm, pt shd; wc; shwrs inc; el pnts €2.50 (rec long lead) (poss rev pol); tradsmn; dogs; quiet. "Simple CL-type site; a few lge pitches; friendly owners; dated, dimly-lit san facs; conv coast & Avignon; book in using intercom on LH wall at ent to shwr block." 15 Mar-10 Oct. € 11.00   2006*

MOURIES *10E2* (2km NW Rural) **Camping Le Devenson, Route du Férigoulas**,13890 Mouriès [04 90 47 52 01; fax 04 90 47 63 09; devenson@libertysurf.fr; www.camping-devenson.com] Exit St Rémy by D5 for Maussane-les-Alpilles, turn L on app to vill onto D17 (sps), after 5km (NW edge of vill) bef g'ge on o'skts of Mouriès, sharp L to D5, site on R, approach narr. Med, hdstg, pt sl, terr, pt shd; wc; chem disp; shwrs inc; el pnts (5A) €3 (rec long cable); lndtte; ice; shop; BBQ (gas); pool; playgrnd; TV; dogs €1.80; Eng spkn; adv bkg; quiet; red low ssn; CCI. "Tractor tow to pitch if necessary; simple, spotless facs; min 1 week stay high ssn; attractive situation in pine & olive trees; simple but v special site; gd pool." 1 Apr-15 Sep. € 14.50   2006*

MOURIES *10E2* (7km NW) **Camp Municipal Les Romarins, Route de St Rémy-de-Provence**, 13520 Maussane-les-Alpilles [04 90 54 33 60; fax 04 90 54 41 22; camping-municipal-maussane@wanadoo.fr; www.maussane.com] Fr Mouriès on D17 NW, turn onto D5 on o'skts of vill dir St Rémy-de-Provence, turn immed L site on R adj municipal pool. Med, hdg pitch, pt shd; wc (some cont); chem disp; baby facs; shwrs inc; el pnts (4A) €3.20; gas 200m; lndtte; shops 200m; BBQ; playgrnd; pool adj; tennis free; cycle hire; internet; TV; dogs €2.10; adv bkg rec (dep req); quiet, but some rd noise; 10% red for 8+ days; cc acc; CCI. "Well-managed, clean site in lovely area; office clsd 1200-1500 & 2200-0700; some pitches diff m'vans due low trees; vg shops & rests within 5 min walk; Eng library; excel." ♦ 15 Mar-15 Oct. € 16.00   2007*

MOUSSEAUX SUR SEINE see Mantes *3D2*

MOUSTERLIN see Fouesnant *2F2*

MOUSTIERS STE MARIE *10E3* (6km N) **Camping à la Ferme Vauvenières (Sauvaire)**, 04410 St Jurs [04 92 74 72 24; fax 04 92 74 44 18; contact@ferme-de-vauvenieres.fr; www.ferme-de-vauvenieres.fr] Fr Riez take D953 N to1km beyond Puimoisson then fork R onto D108 sp St Jurs & site sp. Sm, pt shd; wc; chem disp; shwrs; el pnts €2.60; shops 2km; lake sw 2.5km; sports area; dogs €0.65; Eng spkn; adv bkg; quiet; CCI. "Peaceful & quiet; off beaten track; wonderful views; v clean san facs; gd for mountain walking; lavender production area; gd Sunday mkt in Riez." 1 Apr-1 Oct. € 9.60   2007*

France

MOUSTIERS STE MARIE *10E3* (300m S Rural) Camping Le Vieux Colombier, Quartier St Michel, 04360 Moustiers-Ste Marie [04 92 74 61 89 or 04 92 74 61 82 (LS); fax 04 92 74 61 89; camping. vieux.colombier@wanadoo.fr; www.lvcm.fr] Fr Moustiers go E on D952 dir Castellane. Site on R in 300m opp garage. NB Steep, winding access rd. Med, mkd pitch, sl, terr, pt shd; htd wc; 80% serviced pitches; chem disp; mv service pnt; baby facs; shwrs inc; el pnts (3-6A) €2.70-3.30 (rev pol); gas; lndtte; shop 600m; snacks; bar; BBQ; playgrnd; lake sw 5km; dogs €1.60; Eng spkn; adv bkg ess high ssn; quiet; cc acc; CCI. "V helpful staff; steep terrs, park at top & walk down; gd, clean san facs; well-situated for Gorges du Verdon & conv for town/ shops; gd walking; canoeing; windsurfing; Moustiers v attractive; vg." ♦ ltd. 1 Apr-30 Sep. € 12.80
2007*

MOUSTIERS STE MARIE *10E3* (1km SW Rural) Camping St Jean, Route de Riez, 04360 Moustiers-Ste Marie [tel/fax 04 92 74 66 85; camping-saint-jean@wanadoo.fr] On D952 opp Renault g'ge. Med, some hdg pitch, pt sl, pt shd; wc (some cont); mv service pnt; shwrs inc; el pnts (3-6A) €2.60-3.30; gas; lndtte; ice; shop 700m; tradsmn; sand beach & lake sw 4km; 3% statics; dogs €1.40; poss cr; Eng spkn; adv bkg (dep req for 7+ days); quiet; cc acc; CCI. "Excel site in lovely location; conv Gorges du Verdon." ♦ ltd. 1 Apr-29 Oct. € 12.90
2007*

MOUSTIERS STE MARIE *10E3* (500m W Rural) Camping Manaysse, 04360 Moustiers-Ste Marie [04 92 74 66 71; fax 04 92 74 62 28; camping-manaysse@aol.com; www.camping-manaysse. com] Fr Riez take D952 E, pass g'ge on L & turn L at 1st rndabt for Moustiers; site on L off RH bend; strongly advised not to app Moustiers fr E (fr Castellane, D952 or fr Comps, D71) as these rds are diff for lge vehicles/c'vans - not for the faint-hearted. Med, mkd pitch, pt sl, pt shd; wc (some cont); chem disp; shwrs inc; el pnts (6-10A) €2.50-3.50; shops 500m; tradsmn; playgrnd; sand/ shgl beach; rv or lake sw; dogs €0.50; adv bkg; quiet; CCI. "Welcoming, family-run site; super views; gd san facs; cherry trees on site - avoid parking during early Jun; steep walk into vill; lge o'fits do not attempt 1-way system thro vill, park & walk." ♦ ltd. 25 Mar-2 Nov. € 9.30   2007*

MOUTIERS *9B3* (3km N Rural) Camping Eliana, 205 Ave de Savoie, 73260 Aigueblanche [tel/fax 04 79 24 11 58] Fr Albertville take N90 S & exit 38 for Aigueblanche. Foll sp in vill for 'Camping' on D97 dir La Léchère. Site on L 700m after supmkt; well sp. NB Final L turn from D97 is through a NO ENTRY sign. Sm, mkd pitch, terr, shd; htd wc; chem disp; mv service pnt; shwrs inc; el pnts (4-10A) €1.90-3.50; gas 1km; lndtte; ice; shop 1km; tradsmn; rest; snacks; bar; BBQ; htd pool 500m; phone; dogs €0.30; quiet; CCI. "Well-managed site; friendly warden; facs vg & v clean; warden calls 1800 - lives nr; excel centre for Alps, walking & cycling; sm pitches poss diff lge o'fits; beautiful location in orchard." ♦ ltd. 1 Apr-31 Oct. € 8.50
2006*

> As soon as we get home I'm going to post all these site report forms to the editor for inclusion in next year's guide. I don't want to miss the September deadline.

MOUTIERS *9B3* (4km S Urban) Camping La Piat, Ave du Comte Greyfié de Brides-les-Bains, 73570 Brides-les-Bains [04 79 55 22 74; fax 04 79 55 28 55] Fr Moûtiers on D90 fr dual c'way foll sp for 'Vallée du Bozel' then take D915 to Brides-les-Bains into town cent. Turn R onto Ave du Comte Greyfié de Brides-les-Bains & foll sp to site. Med, mkd pitch, some hdstg, pt sl, terr, pt shd; wc (some cont); chem disp; mv service pnt; baby facs; shwrs inc; el pnts (30-16A) €1.50-3.60; gas; lndtte; lndry rm; shops, rest, snacks, bar 500m; tradsmn; playgrnd; pool adj; 10% statics; dogs €0.70; phone adj; poss 500m; poss cr; Eng spkn; adv bkg; quiet but some rd noise; cc acc; CCI. "Gd base for valleys, mountain biking, walking; ski lift 500m; Brides-les-Bains is thermal spa town specialising in obesity treatments; some pitches v muddy in wet weather." ♦ 21 Apr-27 Oct. € 9.50   2004*

> The opening dates and prices on this campsite have changed. I'll send a site report form to the editor for the next edition of the guide.

MOUTHIER HAUTE PIERRE see Ornans *6G2*

MOUTIERS EN RETZ, LES see Pornic *2G3*

France

F-14590 MOYAUX
Phone : 33 (0) 231 63 63 08 - Fax : 33 (0) 231 63 15 97
www.camping-lecolombier.com • mail@camping-lecolombier.com
Roadmap Michelin Number 55 Section 4

LES CASTELS
★★★★

Château - Camping
LE COLOMBIER
★★★★

"Le Colombier" is situated between Deauville and Lisieux, it is the perfect place to discover the attractions and charm of Normandy. A campsite with a great atmosphere and excellent facilities where you will enjoy the rest and space without the presence of mobile homes or bungalows. The facilities are fully operative during the whole season: 01/05 – 21/09/08

MOYAUX 3D1 (3km NE Rural) Camping Château Le Colombier, Le Val Séry, 14590 Moyaux [02 31 63 63 08; fax 02 31 63 15 97; mail@camping-lecolombier.com; www.camping-lecolombier.com or www.les-castels.com] Fr Pont de Normandie (toll) on A29, at junc with A13 branch R sp Caen. At junc with A132 branch R & foll sp Lisieux to join A132, then D579. Turn L onto D51 sp Blangy-le-Château. Immed on leaving Moyaux turn L onto D143 & foll sp to site on R in 3km. Lge, mkd pitch, pt shd; wc; chem disp; mv service pnt; baby facs; shwrs inc; el pnts (10A) inc (poss lead req); gas; lndtte; shop; tradsmn; rest; snacks; bar; BBQ; playgrnd; htd pool (high ssn); tennis; mini-golf; cycle hire; excursions; games area; library; entmnt; internet; games/TV rm; some static tents/tour ops; dogs €4; phone; recep open 0800-2230 high ssn; Eng spkn; adv bkg; quiet; 10% red long stay; cc acc; CCI. "Beautiful, spacious, well-kept, family-run site in chateau grounds; nice pitches; vg for children; friendly, helpful staff; gd shop & crêperie; vg takeaway; excel rest in chateau; shgl paths poss diff some wheelchairs etc; mkt Sun; barrier closed at 2230-0800; excel." ♦ 1 May-21 Sep. € 33.00 ABS - N04   2007*

See advertisement

MOYENNEVILLE see Abbeville 3B3

> Before we move on, I'm going to fill in some site report forms and post them off to the editor, otherwise they won't arrive in time for the deadline at the end of September.

MUIDES SUR LOIRE 4G2 (6km E Rural) Camp Municipal du Cosson, 41220 Crouy-sur-Cosson [02 54 87 08 81 or 02 54 87 50 10; fax 02 54 87 59 44] Fr Muides-sur-Loire, take D103 E dir Crouy-sur-Cosson. In vill, turn R onto D33 dir Chambord. Site 200m fr village, well sp. Med, mkd pitch, pt shd; wc; shwrs inc; el pnts (5A) €3.15 (poss rev pol); lndry rm; shops 500m; tradsmn; rest 300m; snacks; bar 300m; BBQ; playgrnd; rv fishing nr; few statics; dogs; adv bkg; quiet; CCI. "Pleasant, gd value site; woodland setting; nr Rv Loire; 10km to Chambord, 26km to Blois; poss long-stay workers; barrier clsd until 1730 high ssn." Easter-1 Nov. € 6.85   2006*

MUIDES SUR LOIRE *4G2* (1km SE Rural) **Camping Le Château des Marais, 27 Rue de Chambord, 41500 Muides-sur-Loire [02 54 87 05 42; fax 02 54 87 05 43; info@chateau-des-marais.com; www.chateau-des-marais.com]** Exit A10 at junc 16 sp Chambord & take N152 sp Mer, Chambord, Blois. At Mer take D112 & cross Rv Loire onto D103; at Muides-sur-Loire x-rds cont strt on for 800m; then turn R at Camping sp; site on R in 800m. Lge, mkd pitch, pt sl, shd; htd wc; chem disp; mv service pnt; all serviced pitches; baby facs; shwrs inc; el pnts (6-10A) €5-7 (poss rev pol); gas; lndtte; shop; rest; snacks; bar, BBQ; playgrnd; 3 pools (1 htd, covrd); waterslides; water park; fishing; tennis; cycle hire; games area; wifi internet; TV; 10% statics (tour ops); dogs €5; Eng spkn; adv bkg fee & deposit; cc acc; CCI. "Excel, modern facs; v well-run site; friendly recep staff; plenty of gd quality children's play equipment; gd for visiting chateaux & Loire; mkt Sat am Blois." ♦ 16 May-30 Sep. € 34.00 ABS - L10   2007*

See advertisement

MUIDES SUR LOIRE *4G2* (W Rural) **Camp Municipal Belle Vue, Ave de la Loire, 41500 Muides-sur-Loire [02 54 87 01 56 or 02 54 87 50 08 (Mairie); fax 02 54 87 01 25; mairie.muides@wanadoo.fr; http://pagesperso-orange.fr/mairie-muides]** Fr A10/E5/E60 exit junc 16 S onto D205. Turn R onto N152 then D112 over rv. Site on S bank of rv on D112 W of bdge. Tight U-turn into site fr N. Med, mkd pitch, pt shd; wc; chem disp/mv service pnt; shwrs inc; el pnts (5A) €2.10-2.55 (poss long lead req)(poss rev pol); gas in vill; lndtte; ice; shops 200m; rest, snacks adj; playgrnd; rv fishing adj; sw 4km; cycling; dogs €1.30; vehicle barrier; quiet; no cc acc; CCI. "Lovely neat & clean basic site; gd views over rv; pitches by rv; plenty of rm; little shade; office open 0800-0930 & 1700-2000 low ssn, clsd 1200-1500 high ssn; excel for cycing; gd rest in vill; vg value." ♦ 30 Apr-15 Sep. € 7.10   2007*

⊞**MULHOUSE** *6F3* (4km NE Urban) **Camping Le Safary, 35 Rue de la Forêt-Noire, 68390 Sausheim [tel/fax 03 89 61 99 29; contact@campinglesafary.com; www.campinglesafary.com]** Exit A36/E54 junc 20 onto D201 N dir Battenheim & Baldersheim, site on E of D201, sp. Med, hdg/mkd pitch, pt shd; wc; chem disp; shwrs inc; el pnts (6-10A) €3; lndtte; shops 2km; bar; 60% statics; dogs €1; CCI. "Barrier clsd 2200-0800; few facs for size of site, poss inadequate if site full; poss itinerants." € 11.00   2006*

MULHOUSE *6F3* (2km SW) **Camping de l'Ill, 1 Rue de Pierre Coubertin, 68100 Mulhouse [03 89 06 20 66; fax 03 89 61 18 34; campingdelill@aol.com; www.camping-de-lill.com]** Fr A36 take Mulhouse/Dornach exit & foll sp Brunstatt at 1st traff lts. At 2nd traff lts turn R, foll University/Brunstatt/Camping sps, site approx 2.5km. Lge, some mkd pitch, pt sl, pt shd; wc; chem disp; mv service pnt; shwrs inc; el pnts (5A) €3.60; gas; supmkt & rest 1km; tradsmn; snacks; pool adj; dogs €1; quiet but some rlwy noise; 10% red CCI. "Welcoming recep; facs a little unkempt even high ssn (2007); day pass for bus to gd museums in town; superb sw complex & park adj; OK NH." 1 Apr-25 Oct. € 14.40   2007*

⊞**MULHOUSE** *6F3* (10km SW Rural) **FFCC Camping Parc La Chaumière, 62 Rue de Galfingue, 68990 Heimsbrunn [tel/fax 03 89 81 93 43 or 03 89 81 93 21; accueil@camping-lachaumiere.com; www.camping-lachaumiere.com]** Exit A36 junc 15; turn L over m'way; at rndabt exit on N466 sp Heimsbrunn; in vill turn R at rndabt; site end of houses on R. Med, hdg pitch, hdstg, pt sl, shd; htd wc; chem disp; mv service pnt; shwrs inc; el pnts (10A) €2.50 (rev pol); lndry rm; ice; shop 1km; tradsmn; snacks; playgrnd; pool; 50% statics; dogs €1; quiet; cc acc; CCI. "Sm pitches not suitable long o'fits; beautiful wine vills on La Route des Vins; museum of trains & cars in Mulhouse." € 9.50   2007*

MUNSTER *6F3* (10km N Rural) **Camp Municipal Lefebure, 68370 Orbey [tel/fax 03 89 71 37 42 or 03 89 71 33 18; jmiclo@aol.com; www.camping-orbey.com]** Fr Colmar take N415 to St Dié. At rndabt just beyond Hachimette, turn L onto D48 to Orbey. Turn R after supmkt at site sp. Site on L after 2km climb. Med, mkd pitch, terr, pt shd; wc; chem disp (wc); mv service pnt; shwrs inc; el pnts (5-10A) inc (long cable req some pitches); lndtte; shops 1km; tradsmn; snacks; playgrnd; 5% statics; dogs €1; phone; quiet; cc not acc; CCI. "Peaceful site 300m above Rhine valley; helpful staff; gd value." 1 May-30 Sep. € 12.20   2007*

MUNSTER *6F3* (1km E Rural) **Camping Le Parc de la Fecht, 68140 Munster [03 89 77 31 68 or 08 10 12 21 83 (LS); www.village-center.com]** Clear site sp on all app to Munster & in town. Site on D10. Lge, hdg/mkd pitch, pt shd; wc; chem disp; shwrs inc; el pnts (6A) inc; lndtte; shops adj; rest; snacks; bar; BBQ; playgrnd; htd pool, waterslide adj; entmnt; child entmnt; TV; some statics; dogs €3; Eng spkn; quiet; CCI. "Pleasant site within sh walk of town; friendly & helpful; gd sightseeing area with mountains & lakes; gd walking & cycling; o'night waiting area." ♦ 12 May-16 Sep. € 16.00   2007*

MUNSTER *6F3* (3km E) **Camping Beau Rivage, 8 Rue des Champs, 68140 Gunsbach [03 89 77 44 62; fax 03 89 77 13 98]** Site on rv off D417 Colmar to Munster rd. Med, pt shd; htd wc; chem disp; shwrs inc; el pnts (6A) €3.10; gas; lndtte; ice; shop (high ssn); supmkt 2.5km; snacks; bar; playgrnd; rv adj; fishing; sports area; 50% statics; dogs €0.65; adv bkg; quiet; CCI. "Excel for visiting Albert Schweitzer house & memorial." 1 Apr-20 Oct. € 11.30   2004*

MUNSTER *6F3* (4km E Rural) **Camping La Route Verte, Rue de la Gare, 68230 Wihr-au-Val [03 89 71 10 10; info@camping-routeverte.com; www.camping-routeverte.com]** Take D417 out of Colmar twd Munster & turn R int Wihr-au-Val. Site on L 800m. Well sp. Med, mkd pitch, pt sl, shd; wc; chem disp; mv service pnt; shwrs inc; el pnts (4-6A) €2.65-3.75; ice; lndtte; shops, rest, bar 50m; pool 4km; games rm; dogs €1.20; phone; poss cr; adv bkg; quiet; 10% red long stay; CCI. "Delightful site; owner v helpful & friendly; not suitable for lge c'vans (6m max); excel san facs; gd touring base Alsace; forest walks; winemaker 100m; site surrounded by vineyards." ♦ 30 Apr-30 Sep. € 9.00   2006*

MUNSTER *6F3* (2km SW Rural) **FFCC Camping Les Amis de la Nature, 4 Rue du Château, 68140 Luttenbach [03 89 77 38 60; fax 03 89 77 25 72; camping.an@wanadoo.fr]** Fr Munster take D27 sp Luttenbach, site sp. Lge, pt shd; htd wc; mv service pnt; baby facs; shwrs inc; el pnts (6A) €3.05; lndtte; ice; shop; rest; snacks; playgrnd; pool 2km; dir access to rv; tennis 1km; games area; golf; entmnt; TV; 50% statics; dogs €1.25; poss cr; quiet. 1 Feb-30 Nov. € 9.40   2005*

MUNSTER *6F3* (9km SW Rural) **Camp Municipal de Mittlach Langenwasen, 68380 Mittlach [03 89 77 63 77; fax 03 89 77 74 36; mairiemittlach@wanadoo.fr]** Fr Munster on D10 to Metzeral then R onto D10. Site at end rd in 6km. Med, hdg/mkd pitch, pt sl, pt shd, serviced pitch; wc; chem disp; shwrs inc; el pnts (4A) €1.15: gas; lndtte; ice; sm shop & 6km; tradsmn; playgrnd; 10% statics; dogs €0.75; adv bkg; quiet; CCI. "Peaceful location in mountains; wooded site at bottom of valley; local walks; helpful staff; san facs gd & v clean." ♦ ltd. 1 May-30 Sep. € 8.90   2005*

⊞**MUR DE BRETAGNE** *2E3* (6km N Rural) **Camping Le Boterff d'en Haut, 22320 St Mayeux [02 96 24 02 80; victor.turner@wanadoo.fr; www.holidayinbrittany.net]** N fr Mur-de-Bretagne on D767 to St Mayeux. Turn R into vill & R after vill hall (Salle Municipal); to T-junc, turn R & site on L. App via 750m single-track lane. Car parking in rd outside. Sm, unshd; wc; chem disp; shwrs inc; el pnts (6A) inc; gas 8km; shops, rest, bar 2km; lake sw & watersports 8km; adv bkg; v quiet; cc not acc; red low ssn. "Excel, v remote site; gd touring cent; gd walks & cycling; excel san facs; v friendly British owners (C'van Club members) will cook eve meal." € 18.00   2007*

MUR DE BRETAGNE *2E3* (6km SE Rural) **Camping Le Cosquer, 22530 St Connec [tel/fax 02 96 28 55 88 or 01432 880597 (UK); lecosquer@compuserve.com; www.lecosquer.co.uk]** Fr N164 turn S onto D81 sp St Connec, then L at Quatre rtes, 1st L Lanrivault, then R at cross in rd, 1st house on R at rdside. Sm, pt sl, pt shd; wc; chem disp; shwrs inc; el pnts (10A) inc; lndtte; shop 1km; rest, bar 1km; playgrnd; pool; sand beach 10km; lake sw, fishing 10km; horseriding 8km; golf 20km; gites avail; adv bkg; quiet; CCI. "In remote, pleasant countryside; friendly." 1 May-30 Sep. € 16.25   2005*

MUR DE BRETAGNE *2E3* (2km SW Rural) **Camp Municipal Le Rond Point du Lac, Rond-Point de Guerlédan, 22530 Mur-de-Bretagne [02 96 26 01 90 or 02 96 28 51 32 (LS); fax 02 96 26 09 12]** Fr Mur-de-Bretagne take D18 & foll site sp; ent opp view point of Lake Guerlédan. Med, terr, pt sl, pt shd; wc (mainly cont); chem disp; shwrs inc; el pnts €2.20; lndry rm; shops, rest1.5km; bar 50m; playgrnd; sand beach/lake 500m; poss cr; quiet; CCI. "Gd walking & watersports." ♦ 15 Jun-15 Sep. € 7.10   2004*

MUR DE BRETAGNE *2E3* (4km NW Rural) **Camping Beau Rivage Les Pins, 22530 Caurel [02 96 28 52 22]** Fr Mur-de-Bretagne foll Caurel sp W on N164. Turn L off Caurel by-pass onto D111. Fork L after church in Caurel & foll sp to site. Med, pt sl, pt shd; wc; chem disp; shwrs inc; el pnts (6A) €2.20; lndtte; ice; shop; playgrnd; lake sw; boating; watersports; dogs €1; adv bkg; quiet. "Attractive countryside; friendly owners; san facs dated." 1 Apr-30 Sep. € 11.90   2005*

France

MUR DE BRETAGNE 2E3 (4km NW Rural) **Camping Le Guerlédan, 22530 Caurel [02 96 26 08 24; fax 02 96 26 08 24]** Fr Mur-de-Bretagne head W on D164 & foll sp to Caurel. L off Caurel by-pass onto D111. L after church in town & foll sp to site on lakeside. Med, mkd pitch, pt sl, pt shd; wc; shwrs inc; el pnts (poss rev pol); gas; playgrnd; lake sw adj; quiet; CCI. "Vg; attractive lakeside setting; friendly, helpful owners." 1 Jul-31 Aug. € 10.80
2006*

MUR DE BRETAGNE 2E3 (4km NW) **Camping Nautic International, Route de Beau Rivage, 22530 Caurel [02 96 28 57 94; fax 02 96 26 02 00; contact@campingnautic.fr; www.campingnautic.fr]** App Caurel fr Loudéac on N164, turn L off new Caurel by-pass onto D111, fork L 100m past church, site is 1st on L, beside Lac de Guerlédan. NB App fr Pontivy on D767 via Mur-de-Bretagne v steep in places & not rec when towing. Med, mkd pitch, terr, pt shd; wc (some cont); chem disp; baby facs; shwrs inc; el pnts (10A) inc; lndtte; shop; BBQ; playgrnd; htd pool; paddling pool; jacuzzi; lake fishing; watersports & horseriding nr; cycle hire; tennis; games/TV rm; dogs €1.60; recep 1000-2100 high ssn; adv bkg; quiet; cc acc; CCI. "Excel position in attractive countryside; facs poss stretched when site full; dated san facs; poss diff lge o'fits; peaceful site & set up; nice pitches; wonderful pool & lake." ♦ 15 May-25 Sep. € 27.40
ABS - B22   2007*

MURAT 7C4 (1km SW Urban) **Camp Municipal de Stalapos, 8 Rue de Stade, 15300 Murat [04 71 20 01 83 or 04 71 20 03 80; fax 04 71 20 20 63; ville.murat@wanadoo.fr]** Fr N122 site sp fr cent of Murat dir Aurillac, adj Rv Alagnon. Lge, some hdstg, pt sl, pt shd; wc (cont); chem disp; shwrs inc; el pnts (10A) €3.80; lndtte; ice; shops 1km; playgrnd; rv fishing adj; poss cr; no adv bkg; quiet; CCI. "Wonderful, peaceful location amidst extinct volcanoes; gd value; busy high ssn; basic but clean san facs; warden lives on site; excel touring base; gd views medieval town." ♦ 1 May-30 Sep. € 5.50   2006*

MURAT 7C4 (5km SW Rural) **Camping Les Trois Pierres, Le Bourg, 15300 Albepierre-Bredons [04 71 20 12 23]** Fr Murat take D39 sp Prat de Bouc. Site sp fr cent of vill of Albepierre-Bredons. Sm, pt sl, pt shd; wc; chem disp (wc); shwrs inc; el pnts inc; shop, rest, bar 500m; dogs; Eng spkn; adv bkg; quiet; CCI. "Excel, peaceful location for Cantal mountains, touring or walking; v helpful owner." ♦ ltd. 1 Jul-30 Aug. € 9.00   2006*

MURE ARGENS, LA see St André les Alpes 10E3

MURE, LA (ISERE) 9C3 (13km E Rural) **Camp Municipal Les Vigneaux, 38740 Entraigues [04 76 30 24 44 or 06 10 78 16 36 (mob); fax 04 73 60 20 18]** S on N85 fr La Mure, turn L on D114, fork R on D26 to Valbonnais. This rd becomes D526. Site on L on ent Entraigues, 4km beyond Lake Valbonnais. Ent on bend in rd, more diff if ent fr Bourg d'Oisans. Sm, mkd pitch, pt shd; wc; mv service pnt; shwrs inc; el pnts (5A) inc (poss rev pol); shops 100m; rv 100m; lake 3km; fishing; 15% statics; dogs; adv bkg; quiet; red long stay; CCI. "Clean facs; mountainous National Park adj; warden visits am & pm." ♦ 1 May-30 Sep. € 12.00
2007*

There aren't many sites open this early in the year. We'd better phone ahead to check that the one we're heading for is actually open.

MURE, LA (ISERE) 9C3 (7km SE Rural) **Camping Belvédère de l'Obiou, Les Egats, 38350 St Laurent-en-Beaumont [tel/fax 04 76 30 40 80; info@camping-obiou.com; www.camping-obiou.com]** Clearly sp on N85. Sm, pt sl, pt terr, pt shd; htd wc; chem disp; mv service pnt; shwrs; el pnts (4-10A) €3-5 (poss rev pol); lndtte; ice; shop 7km; tradsmn; rest; snacks; playgrnd; htd, covrd pool; cycle hire; internet; TV; English library; 5% statics; dogs €2; poss cr; Eng spkn; rd noise; 10% red long stay/low ssn; CCI. "Superb, immac, family-run site; excel facs; v helpful owners; picturesque & interesting area; guide given for local walks." 1 Apr-30 Sep. € 18.50 (CChq acc)   2006*

MUROL 7B4 (1km S Rural) **Camping Sunêlia La Ribeyre, Route de Jassat, 63790 Murol [04 73 88 64 29; fax 04 73 88 68 41; laribeyre@free.fr; www.camping-laribeyre.com]** Exit 6 fr A75 onto D978 S sp Champeix/St Nectaire, then D996 to Murol. In Murol take D5 S sp Besse-et-St Anastaise. In approx 500m take D618 twd Jassat & site in 500m on rvside. Sp fr Murol. Lge, mkd pitch, pt shd; wc (some cont); baby facs; shwrs inc; el pnts (6A) €5.40 (poss rev pol); gas; lndtte; ice; shop 1km; tradsmn; snacks & creperie; bar; BBQ; playgrnd; pools (1 htd, covrd) & aqua park; waterslides; lake sw & sand beach adj; fishing; boat hire; tennis; horseriding; hiking; games area; games rm; entmnt; TV rm; 25% statics; dogs €2.40; Eng spkn; adv bkg (dep req + bkg fee); quiet; red low ssn; CCI. "Ideal touring base & family site; spacious pitches; immac san facs; excel scenery & mountains nr; great walks fr site; activities for all ages; barrier operated 2300-0700; groups welcome low ssn." ♦ 7 May-15 Sep. € 22.95 (CChq acc)
2007*

See advertisement opposite

MUROL *7B4* (1km S Rural) **FFCC Camp Le Repos du Baladin, Groire, 63790 Murol** [04 73 88 61 93; fax 04 73 88 66 41; reposbaladin@free.fr; http://reposbaladin.free.fr] Fr D996 at Murol foll sp 'Groire' to E, site on R in 1.5km just after vill. Med, hdg/mkd pitch, pt sl, shd; wc (some cont); chem disp; shwrs inc; el pnts (5A) €4; lndtte; shop 1.5km; tradsmn; snacks; playgrnd; htd pool; lake sw 5km; dogs €2; poss cr; poss noise high ssn; Eng spkn; CCI. "Lovely site with immac san facs; friendly & helpful owners." 1 May-22 Sep. € 16.90   2006*

MUROL *7B4* (2km W Rural) **Camping La Plage du Lac Chambon, 63790 Murol** [04 73 88 60 04; fax 04 73 88 80 08; lac.chambon@wanadoo.fr; www.lac-chambon-plage.com] Exit A75 junc 6 sp Champeix/St Nectaire; cont for 34km thro St Nectaire to Murol on D996; 1km past Murol turn L sp Lac Chambon/Centre Touristique; bear L past lge car park to site ent. Lge, hdg/mkd pitch, terr, pt shd; htd wc; chem disp; shwrs inc; baby facs; el pnts (6-10A) €2.80; gas & 2km; lndtte; ice; shop & 2km; rest, snacks, bar at hotel; playgrnd; lake sw & fishing adj; tennis; mini-golf; cycle hire; entmnt; TV; statics; dogs €0.50; phone; Eng spkn; adv bkg; quiet; cc acc; CCI. "Gd birdwatching & walking."
♦ ltd. 1 May-30 Sep. € 13.70   2005*

MUROL *7B4* (2km W Rural) **Camping Le Pré Bas, 63790 Chambon-sur-Lac** [04 73 88 63 04; fax 04 73 88 65 93; prebas@lac-chambon.com; www.campingauvergne.com] Take D996 W fr Murol twd Mont-Dore. Site 1.5km on L, immed after lake. Lge, hdg/mkd pitch, pt sl, pt shd; wc; chem disp; mv service pnt; serviced pitches; baby facs; shwrs inc; el pnts (6A) €4.40; gas 1km; lndtte; ice/freezer; shop & 1km; tradsmn; snacks; bar (high ssn); BBQ; playgrnds; 2 pools (l htd, covrd); waterslides; lake sw; games area; library; entmnt; TV rm; 40% statics; dogs €2; phone; poss cr; Eng spkn; adv bkg; quiet; CCI. "Excel, friendly, family-run site; v helpful staff; superb views; immac san facs; excel walking area; access to sm pitches poss diff lge o'fits."
♦ 15 Apr-30 Sep. € 19.90   2006*

MUROL *7B4* (5km W Rural) **Camp Municipal Les Bombes, 63790 Chambon-sur-Lac** [04 73 88 64 03 or 04 73 88 61 21 (Mairie); fax 04 73 88 62 59; les-bombes-camping@orange.fr] Site is on D996. Nr exit fr vill Chambon. Well sp. Med, mkd pitch, pt shd; wc (some cont); chem disp; mv service pnt; shwrs; el pnts (3-6A) €2.60-3.80; lndtte; ice; shops; tradsmn; rest 500m; snacks; bar; BBQ; playgrnd; pool; lake sw 1km; TV rm; 5% statics; dogs €0.60; phone; quiet; Eng spkn; adv bkg (dep req); cc acc; CCI. "Beautiful area; gd, clean, well-maintained facs; v lge pitches; friendly, helpful warden; gd for touring volcanic park; open views of countryside; lake 1km with usual facs."
♦ 15 Jun-15 Sep. € 10.20   2006*

> Did you know you can fill in site report forms on the Club's website — www.caravanclub.co.uk?

MUY, LE *10F4* (3km W Rural) **Camping Les Cigales, 721 des Oliviers, 83490 Le Muy** [04 94 45 12 08; fax 04 94 45 92 80; contact@les-cigales.com; www.les-cigales.com] Exit A8 at Le Muy, keep in L hand lane & take 1st L across dual c'way after Péage (toll), foll lge sp at sm lane ent to site. Fr DN7 (N7) W of Le Muy take A8 access rd, turn R into lane 250m bef toll booth & foll lane past toll to site in 1km. Lge, hdg/mkd pitch, hdstg, pt sl, terr, shd; wc (some cont); chem disp; mv service pnt; shwrs inc; el pnts (6-10A) €3-4.50; gas; lndtte; ice; sm shop & 3km; rest; snacks; bar; playgrnd; htd pool; sand beach 20km; rv sw 2km; tennis; games area; horseriding; entmnt; TV rm; 20% statics; dogs free; Eng spkn; adv bkg (rec); quiet; red long stay; cc acc; CCI. "Conv for St Raphaël & a'route to Nice; beautiful, clean facs blocks; excel pool; helpful staff; some pitches diff for lge o'fits but tractor avail; peaceful site; nightingales!" ♦ 31 Mar-28 Sep. € 29.50   2007*

See advertisement on next page

France

MUZILLAC *2G3* (12km N) **Camp Municipal de l'Etang de Célac, Place du Général de Gaulle, 56230 Questembert [02 97 26 11 24 or 02 97 26 11 38 (LS)]** Site on D7 W of Questembert on o'skts of town. Med, mkd pitch, pt shd; wc (some cont); chem disp; mv service pnt; shwrs; el pnts (12A) €2.25; shop; rest; tradsmn; lndry rm; playgrnd; TV; beach 25km; fishing; dogs €1.05; CCI. "V clean facs, attractive location by lake; Monday mkt sp fr vill; no twin-axles; diff access lge o'fits as ent zig-zags around concrete flower tubs." 15 Jun-15 Sep. € 7.60   2006*

MUZILLAC *2G3* (5km NE) **Camping Le Moulin de Cadillac, Route de Beric, 56190 Noyal-Muzillac [02 97 67 03 47; fax 02 97 67 00 02; infos@moulin-cadillac.com; www.moulin-cadillac.com]** Fr N165 take D140 N to Noyal-Muzillac, turn R at x-rds, site well sp; care on LH hairpin at rd junc 100m fr site. Sh app rd but steep & sharp bends. Med, hdg pitch, terr, shd; wc; chem disp; mv service pnt; baby facs; shwrs inc; el pnts (4A) inc; gas; lndtte; ice; shop; tradsmn; rest; bar; playgrnd; htd pool; waterslide; beach 15km; fishing lake; tennis; games area; pets corner; golf 15km; TV rm; 30% statics; dogs €1; phone; adv bkg rec high ssn; quiet; "In pleasant wooded valley away fr cr coastal sites; relaxing site." ♦ 1 May-30 Sep. € 13.60   2004*

MUZILLAC *2G3* (7km NE) **Camp Municipal Borgnehue, 56190 Le Guerno [02 97 42 99 38 or 02 97 42 94 76 (Mairie); fax 02 97 42 84 36; mairie-leguerno@wanadoo.fr]** Exit N165 onto D139 dir Questembert. In 5km turn L onto D20 dir Muzillac then in 2km R onto D139A to Le Guerno. Just pass vill sp do not foll rd round to R into vill but take C104 strt for 100m, then foll camping sp. Site on R just after leaving Le Guerno. When turning R into site, keep to L. Med, pt shd; wc; chem disp (wc); mv service pnt; baby facs; shwrs inc; el pnts (6-10A) €2.04-3.09; lndtte; playgrnd; phone; adv bkg; quiet. "Warden high ssn only; book in & obtain gate card fr vill shop or Mairie (clsd 1300-1600); pitches lge but poss diff lge o'fits - need to unhitch; gd site." 1 Apr-31 Oct. € 7.65   2006*

MUZILLAC *2G3* (E Urban) **Camp Municipal, Rue de Stade, 56190 Muzillac [02 97 41 67 01 or 02 97 41 66 25 (Mairie); fax 02 97 41 41 58; marie.muzillac@wanadoo.fr; www.muzillac.fr]** N165 Nantes-Vannes rd, site sp in Muzillac cent. Med, level, pt shd, hdg pitch; wc (some cont); chem disp; baby facs; shwrs inc; el pnts (10A) €2.75; lndtte; shop, rest, snacks, bar 500m; playgrnd; TV; dogs €1.30; poss cr; adv bkg (dep req); Eng spkn; CCI. "Delightful, quiet site in early ssn; school coaches drive thro site daily; gd sh stay/NH." ♦ 15 Apr-30 Sep. € 8.45   2007*

MUZILLAC *2G3* (8km SW Coastal) **Camping Ty Breiz, 15 Grande Rue, 56750 Kervoyal-Damgan [tel/fax 02 97 41 13 47; info@campingtybreiz.com; www.campingtybreiz.com]** Fr Muzillac on D153 dir Damgan, turn S for Kervoyal; site on L opp church. Med, hdg/mkd pitch, pt shd; wc; shwrs inc; el pnts (6-10A) €2.90-3.50; lndtte; shop adj; playgrnd; sand beach 300m; dogs €1.50; Eng spkn; adv bkg rec high ssn; quiet; cc acc; CCI. "Gd welcome; v happy, family-run site; excel shellfish in Damgan; mkt on Wed (high ssn)." 28 Apr-30 Sep. € 16.50   2006*

MUZILLAC *2G3* (4km W Coastal) **Camping Le Bédume, Bétahon-Plage, 56190 Ambon-Plages [02 97 41 68 13; fax 02 97 41 56 79; campingdubedume@free.fr; www.bedume.com]** Fr N165 take D20 W dir Ambon, foll to Bétahon, site sp. Lge, hdg pitch, pt shd; wc; chem disp; baby facs; shwrs inc; el pnts (5A) inc; lndtte; ice; shop; tradsmn; snacks; bar; BBQ; playgrnd; htd pools; waterslide; sand beach adj; games area; games rm; TV rm; 75% statics; dogs €4.20; Eng spkn; adv bkg req; quiet; cc acc; red low ssn. ♦ 1 Apr-30 Sep. € 34.10   2006*

MUZILLAC *2G3* (10km NW Rural) **Camp Municipal de Lann Floren, Rue des Sports, 56450 Surzur [02 97 42 10 74; fax 02 97 42 03 54; mairie-surzur@wanadoo.fr]** Sp fr vill cent. Med, hdg/mkd pitch, pt shd; htd wc; chem disp; baby facs; shwrs inc; el pnts (10A); lndtte; shop, rest, bar 500m; playgrnd; sand beach 4km; bus 1km; adv bkg; quiet; CCI. "Attractive site." ♦ ltd. 25 Jun-31 Aug. € 4.42   2005*

NAGES see Lacaune *8E4*

NAJAC *8E4* (Rural) **Camping Le Païsserou, 12270 Najac** [05 65 29 73 96; fax 05 65 29 72 29; info@camping-massifcentral.com; www.camping-massifcentral.com/Najac.htm] Take D922 fr Villefranche-de-Rouergue. Turn R on D39 at La Fouillade to Najac. Site by rv, sp in vill. Or fr A20 exit junc 59 onto D926. At Caylus take D84 to Najac. Med, hdg pitch, shd; wc; chem disp; shwrs inc; el pnts €3; ice; lndtte; shops & rest in vill; tradsmn; snacks; bar; htd, covrd pool adj (free); rv sw; tennis adj; some statics; dogs €1.50; phone; poss cr; Eng spkn; adv bkg (dep req, bkg fee); quiet; red low ssn; CCI. "Conv for Aveyron gorges; ltd facs low ssn; friendly owners; lovely vill." 30 Apr-1 Oct. € 22.00   2007*

NALLIERS see Luçon *7A1*

⊞**NAMPONT ST MARTIN** *3B3* (2km NE Rural) **Camping Auberge des Etangs, 91 Rue Vallée de l'Authie, 62870 Roussent** [03 21 81 20 10; www.auberge-des-etangs.fr] 11km S of Montreuil on D901 (N1), take D139E to Roussent, site on R in vill. Med, mkd pitch, pt sl, pt shd; wc; chem disp; shwrs inc; el pnts (6A) inc; gas; lndtte; ice; shop; rest; snacks; playgrnd; entmnt; rv fishing 2km; TV; mostly statics; site clsd Jan; quiet but noise fr hotel (disco); sm space for tourers; NH only. € 13.00   2006*

NAMPONT ST MARTIN *3B3* (3km W Rural) **Camping La Ferme des Aulnes, 1 Rue du Marais, Fresne-sur-Authie, 80120 Nampont-St Martin** [03 22 29 22 69 or 06 22 41 86 54 (mob LS); fax 03 22 29 39 43; contact@fermedesaulnes. com; www.fermedesaulnes.com] D901 (N1) S fr Montreuil 13km thro Nampont-St Firmin to Nampont-St Martin; turn R in vill onto D485; site in 3km; sp fr D901. Med, some hdg pitch, pt sl, pt shd; htd wc; chem disp; mv service pnt; shwrs inc; el pnts (6-10A) €6-12; lndry rm; shop 5km; tradsmn, rest, snacks, bar high ssn; BBQ (not elec); playgrnd; htd, covrd pool; beach 10km; games area; golf 1km; entmnt; TV & cinema rm; mostly statics; dogs €4; poss cr; adv bkg; CCI. "Gd, modern san facs; v friendly staff; new area for tourers (2007); gd rest; gd pool; some pitches v sl; clsd 2200-0800." ◆ ltd. 1 Apr-4 Nov. € 21.00 (3 persons) (CChq acc)   2007*

NANCAY *4G3* (Rural) **Camp Municipal des Pins, Route de Salbris, La Chaux, 18330 Nançay** [02 48 51 81 80 or 02 48 51 81 35 (Mairie); fax 02 48 51 80 60] Site on N944 fr Salbris twd Bourges clearly sp on L immed bef ent Nançay. Med, mkd pitch, shd, hdstg; htd wc; chem disp; shwrs inc; el pnts (6-12A) €3.80-€6.90; gas; lndtte; shops 1km; playgrnd; tennis; golf 2km; fishing; 50% statics; adv bkg; quiet; CCI. "Lovely setting in pine woods; friendly recep; facs basic but clean; no twin-axles; poor site lighting; beautiful vill; gd walking." 1 Apr-2 Nov. € 6.10   2007*

NANCY *6E2* (12km S Rural) **Camping du Chaubourot,   54630   Flavigny-sur-Moselle** [03 83 26 75 64; fax 03 83 26 74 76] Take A33 then A330 S fr Nancy sp Flavigny-sur-Moselle; on N570 in vill on bank of Rv Moselle; sm sp in main st. Sm, mkd pitch, pt shd; wc; chem disp; shwrs €1; el pnts (4-6A) inc; shops adj; playgrnd; sand/shgl beach 250m; fishing; pedalo hire; mini-golf; few statics; adv bkg; CCI. "No rv view; fair NH only." 1 May-30 Sep. € 12.50   2006*

NANCY *6E2* (6km SW Urban) **Camping Le Brabois, Ave Paul Muller, 54600 Villers-lès-Nancy** [03 83 27 18 28; fax 03 83 40 06 43; campeoles. brabois@wanadoo.fr;   www.camping-brabois. com or www.campeole.com] Fr A33 exit junc 2b sp Brabois onto D974 dir Nancy; after 400m turn L at 2nd traff lts; at sliprd after 2nd further traff lts turn R on slip rd & site on R; site well sp. Lge, mkd pitch, pt shd; htd wc (some cont); chem disp; mv service pnt; shwrs inc; el pnts (5-15A) €3.90-5.25 (poss rev pol); gas; lndtte; ice; shop; tradsmn; supmkt & petrol 2km; rest; snacks (high ssn); bar; BBQ; playgrnd; games area; TV; dogs €2.60; bus (tickets fr recep); poss cr; Eng spkn; adv bkg; quiet; red low ssn; cc acc; CCI. "Nice setting; v helpful staff; well-run site with lge pitches; gd, clean san facs; less pitch care low ssn; comfortable club rm; no twin-axle c'vans over 5.50m (m'vans OK); interesting town; arr early - site v popular NH; bus tickets to town fr recep." ◆ 1 Apr-15 Oct. € 12.90   2007*

NANCY *6E2* (10km NW Rural) **Camping de Liverdun (formerly Municipal Defranoux), 54460 Liverdun** [tel/fax 03 83 24 43 78] Fr A31 take Frouard exit. In Frouard bear L onto D90 to Liverdun; cross rv bdge (sp Liverdun); under rlwy bdge L at traff lts, thro town, fork L & foll sp to site by sports area. Do not turn L at site exit when towing. Lge, pt shd; htd wc; own san; shwrs (0730-1000) inc; el pnts (6A) €2.90; lndtte; shop & 1.5km; rest; snacks; bar Aug; playgrnd; paddling pool; entmnt; 80% statics; dogs; quiet except rlwy noise; cc not acc; CCI. "Lovely site & area; helpful staff; beautiful city of Nancy worth visit; situated in Lorraine National Park; basic facs; fair sh stay/NH." May-Sep. € 10.20   2005*

NANS LES PINS *10F3* (1km N Rural) **Camping Village Club La Sainte Baume, Quartier Delvieux Sud, 83860 Nans-les-Pins** [04 94 78 92 68; fax 04 94 78 67 37; ste-baume@wanadoo.fr; www. saintebaume.com] Exit A8 junc 34 dir St Maximin onto N560. Cross N7 & at next lge junc turn R onto D560 then immed L onto D80. Site 600m after sp Nans-les-Pins, then up private rd to site. Lge, mkd pitch, pt sl, shd; wc; chem disp; baby facs; shwrs inc; el pnts (6A) inc; gas; lndtte; ice; shop; rest; snacks; bar; playgrnd; 3 pools; waterslide; jacuzzi; sand beach 35km; horseriding; 90% statics; dogs €5; adv bkg; red low ssn. "Friendly staff; path into pleasant vill; noise fr pool till late; modern facs; excel." ◆ 1 Apr-30 Sep. € 30.00 (CChq acc)   2006*

France

NANS LES PINS *10F3* (1.5km S Rural) **Camp Municipal La Petite Colle, 83860 Nans-les-Pins [04 94 78 65 98 or 06 62 58 83 76 (mob); fax 04 94 78 95 39; camping.denis@club-internet.fr]** Exit A8/E80 at junc 34 onto N560 dir St Maximin. Foll sp St Zacharie, then in approx 8km fr leaving m'way, turn L onto D80 sp Nans-les-Pins. Foll sp to site thro village into woods. Rough rd on L to site. Med, hdstg, terr, shd; wc; chem disp; serviced pitch; baby facs; shwrs inc; el pnts (6A) €3.50; lndtte; tradsmn; snacks; bar; many statics; dogs €1.50; phone; Eng spkn; adv bkg; quiet; red long stay/low ssn; CCI. "Mkd woodland walks & to vill; san facs poss stretched if busy; helpful owner; NH only." 15 Mar-15 Oct. € 14.00   2005*

NANT *10E1* (2km N Rural) **Camping Le Roc Qui Parle, Les Cuns, 12230 Nant [tel/fax 05 65 62 22 05; contact@camping-roc-qui-parle. com; www.camping-roc-qui-parle-aveyron.com]** Fr Millau take D991E to site passing Val de Cantobre. Fr La Cavalerie take D999E to Nant & at T-junc on o'skts of Nant turn N; Millau & Les Cuns approx 2km; site on R. NB Steep decent into site. Med, hdg/mkd pitch, pt sl, pt shd; wc; serviced pitches; chem disp; mv service pnt; shwrs inc; el pnts (6A) €2.90; lndtte; ice; shop; BBQ; playgrnd; rv sw & fishing on site; dogs free; adv bkg; quiet; no cc acc; CCI. "Magnificent surroundings; excel, well-run site; v lge pitches with views; excel facs; friendly & helpful; v warm welcome; pool in Nant opens 1 Jul; rv walk; shop sells farm produce; rec." ♦ ltd. 1 Apr-30 Sep. € 13.00   2007*

NANT *10E1* (4km N Rural) **Camping Le Val de Cantobre, Domaine de Vellas, 12230 Nant [05 65 58 43 00 or 06 80 44 40 63 (mob); fax 05 65 62 10 36; info@rcn-valdecantobre.fr; www. rcn-campings.fr]** Exit A75 junc 47; foll sp D999 E to Nant for 12 km. At Nant at T-junc turn L onto D991 sp Val de Cantobre. Site on R in 4km - steep access rd, care req. Lge, mkd pitch, hdstg, terr, pt shd; wc (some cont); chem disp; mv service pnt; baby facs; shwrs inc; el pnts (6A) inc; gas; lndtte; shop; rest; snacks; bar; BBQ; playgrnd; htd pool; paddling pool; waterslide; tennis; games rm; rv sw; mini-golf; organised walks; entmnt; wifi internet; games/TV rm; some tour op statics & tents; dogs €4; poss cr; Eng spkn; adv bkg ess; quiet; red low ssn; cc acc. "Lovely position & outstanding scenery; lovely views most pitches; busy & popular site; new Dutch owners (2007); excel welcome; v helpful staff; excel amenities; san facs immac; gd disabled facs; steep site rds & too many steps - not gd disabled; long walk to san facs fr most pitches; many pitches sm with no privacy; recep clsd 1200-1500 low ssn; mkt Tue; excel." ♦ 12 Apr-11 Oct. € 45.50 (CChq acc) ABS - C19   2007*

NANT *10E1* (1km S Rural) **Camping Les Deux Vallées, 12230 Nant [05 65 62 26 89 or 05 65 62 10 40; fax 05 65 62 17 23; www. lesdeuxvallees.com]** Exit A75 junc 47 onto D999 for 14km to Nant; site sp. Med, mkd pitch, pt shd; wc (some cont); own san; chem disp; mv service pnt; some serviced pitches; shwrs inc; el pnts (6A) €2 (poss rev pol); lndtte; tradsmn; rest; snacks; bar; shop 1km; pool 500m; playgrnd; entmnts; rv fishing; TV; dogs €1; phone; quiet; adv bkg; CCI. "Peaceful, well-kept, friendly site; ltd facs low ssn; 15 mins walk fr vill cent; rests in vill; gd walking; stunning scenery; rec." ♦ 1 Apr-31 Oct. € 14.00   2007*

NANT *10E1* (2.5km S Rural) **Camping Castelnau (Gely), 12230 Nant [05 65 62 25 15; isaetdom@ aliceadsl.fr]** Fr Nant take D999 E twds Le Vigan; site is sp on L in 2.5km. Last 200m rough rd. Sm, pt shd; wc; chem disp (wc); shwrs inc; el pnts (11A) €2.50 (poss long lead req); lndtte; shop, rest, snacks, bar 2.5km; playgrnd; pool 3km; sw & fishing nr; some statics; dogs free; poss cr; adv bkg; quiet; cc not acc; CCI. "Nice CL-type site with plenty of space; lovely location; v clean facs; conv Roquefort." 1 Apr-31 Oct. € 8.00   2007*

NANT *10E1* (500m SW Rural) **Camping Les Vernèdes, Route St Martin-Le Bourg, , 12230 Nant [05 65 62 15 19]** Site sp fr vill cent. Sm, shd; wc (some cont); chem disp; shwrs inc; el pnts (10A) €2 (long lead req); gas 500m; lndtte; ice; rest adj; BBQ; playgrnd; dogs; Eng spkn; adv bkg; quiet; CCI. "Orchard site - many low branches make access to pitches poss diff; scruffy & unkempt low ssn; boggy after rain; pleasant stroll to Nant cent; gd trout rest adj; gd touring base; helpful owners." 1 Mar-31 Oct. € 8.00   2007*

⊞**NANTES** *2G4* (3km N Urban) **Camping Le Petit Port, 21 Blvd de Petit Port, 44300 Nantes [02 40 74 47 94; fax 02 40 74 23 06; camping-petit-port@nge-nantes.fr; www.nge-nantes.fr]** Fr ring rd exit Porte de la Chapelle & foll sp Centre Ville, Camping Petit Port or University when ent o'skts of Nantes; site ent opp Hippodrome. Site nr racecourse & university; well sp. Fr S keep on ring rd & exit Porte de la Chapelle, then as before. Lge, hdg/mkd pitch, all hdstg, shd; wc; serviced pitches; chem disp; mv service pnt; shwrs inc; el pnts (10A) €3.50; gas; lndtte; ice; shop; tradsmn; snacks, rest & bar 100m; BBQ; playgrnd; htd, covrd pool adj; waterslide; cycle hire; TV; 30% statics; dogs €1.50; twin-axles acc (extra charge); m'van area; poss cr; Eng spkn; adv bkg (groups); quiet; red long stay; cc acc; CCI. "Vg, well-equipped, functional site; access to san facs by security code; trams fr site ent to town; ice skating adj." ♦ € 16.00   2007*

See advertisement

⊞**NANTES** *2G4* (6km E Rural) **Camping Belle Rivière, Rue des Perrières, 44980 Ste Luce-sur-Loire [tel/fax 02 40 25 85 81; belleriviere@wanadoo.fr; www.camping-belleriviere.com]** Fr 'Nantes Périphérique Est' take exit 42 thro St Luce on D68 twds Thouaré; at traff lights turn S & foll sp over rlwy bdge. Fr E via D68, thro Thouaré twd Ste Luce. At traff lts nr g'ge, S over rlwy bdge twd rv (sp). Med, hdg/mkd pitch, hdstg, pt shd; wc (50% cont); chem disp; shwrs inc; el pnts (3-10A) €2.45-3.50 (extra charge in winter); gas; lndry rm; shops 3km; rest; snacks; bar; BBQ; playgrnd; 50% statics; dogs €1.20; poss cr; Eng spkn; adv bkg; quiet; red low ssn/CCI. "Gd value site; office clsd 1230-1630 (1530 Jul/Aug); spotless, modern san facs; v helpful owners; conv for Nantes Périphérique & city cent; pleasant rvside walks; excel." ♦ € 12.40   2007*

NANTES *2G4* (7km S Urban/Rural) **Camp Municipal du Loiry, Blvd Guiche-Serex, 44120 Vertou [tel/fax 02 40 80 07 10]** Exit Nantes ring rd junc 47 sp Porte de Vertou. Strt at 1st rndabt & cont along rd, which becomes Blvd Guiche-Serex. Site on L, well sp. Med, hdg/mkd pitch, pt shd; wc; chem disp; shwrs inc; el pnts (6-10A) €2.25-3.60; lndtte; rest, snacks, bar, fishing, entmnt adj; no statics; dogs €1; phone; Eng spkn; adv bkg; quiet; CCI. "No twin-axles; site adj parkland, rvside walks." ♦ 1 Apr-30 Sep. € 8.75   2005*

NANTIAT *7B3* (Rural) **Camp Municipal Les Haches, 87140 Nantiat [05 55 53 42 43 (Mairie); fax 05 55 53 56 28]** Turn E off N147 at x-rds in Chamboret, site 1km on L, sp fr N147. Sm, pt sl, pt shd; wc; chem disp; shwrs inc; el pnts €1.40; shops 1km; fishing; train noise & kennels opp; CCI. "Gd facs; poss lukewarm water when site busy; v clean; lovely setting o'looking lake; conv 'Martyr Village' at Oradour-sur-Glane; gd rest at hotel in vill; phone ahead as opening dates not reliable; height barrier 2.50m; gd sh stay/NH." 15 Jun-15 Sep. € 10.24   2005*

NANTUA *9A3* (1km W Urban) **Camp Municipal Le Signal, 17 Ave du Camping, 01130 Nantua [04 74 75 02 09 or 04 74 75 20 55 (Mairie)]** E on D1084 (N84) fr Pont d'Ain, rd passes alongside Nantua lake on R. At end of lake bef ent town turn R & foll sps. Med, mkd pitch, shd; wc; shwrs inc; el pnts inc; ice; shops 200m; rest; snacks; playgrnd; lake sw 300m; sports cent nr; poss cr; quiet. "V attractive site." 1 Jun-30 Sep. € 13.20   2006*

This guide relies on site report forms submitted by caravanners like us; we'll do our bit and tell the editor what we think of the campsites we've visited.

⊞**NAPOULE, LA** *10F4* (2km N Coastal) **Camping Les Cigales, 505 Ave de la Mer, Quartier d'Etang, 06210 Mandelieu-la-Napoule [04 93 49 23 53; fax 04 93 49 30 45; campingcigales@wanadoo.fr; www.lescigales.com]** Take Mandelieu exit junc 40 fr A8 & turn R twice in Mandelieu cent into Ave des Ecureuils, sp Campings. Pass under a'route & in 1km turn L at T-junc into Ave de la Mer. Site in 50m on L. Or on DN7 fr Fréjus turn R at rndabt with fountains app Mandelieu. Or fr coast rd turn inland at bdge over Rv La Siagne into Blvd de la Mer & site in 1km on R. Med, mkd pitch, shd; htd wc; baby facs; shwrs inc; el pnts (6A) €4; lndtte; ice; shop 1.5km; rest; snacks; bar; playgrnd; pool; sand beach 800m; solarium; dir access to rv; fishing, sailing & other watersports 800m; entmnt; dogs €1; poss cr; Eng spkn; quiet; red low ssn/long stay. "High quality site in excel location; gd san facs; ltd facs low ssn; excel site." ♦ € 38.00   2005*

France

NAPOULE, LA *10F4* (2km N Urban) **Camping Les Pruniers, 18 Rue de la Pinéa, 06210 Mandelieu-la-Napoule [04 92 97 00 44 or 04 93 49 99 23; fax 04 93 49 37 45; contact@bungalow-camping. com; www.bungalow-camping.com]** Fr A8 exit junc 40 & turn R twice in Mandelieu cent into Blvd des Ecureuils sp 'Sofitel Royal Casino'. Pass under a'route & in 1km turn L at T-junc into Ave de la Mer. At rndabt bear R & next R sp Pierre-Vacances. Turn R in 50m, site at end of rd. On DN7 fr Fréjus, turn R at rndabt with fountains app Mandelieu. Fr coast rd take slip'rd for Mandelieu. Sm, mkd pitch, hdstg; shd; wc; chem disp (in cont wc); shwrs inc; el pnts (5-20A) €4.40; lndtte; shop (high ssn) & 1.2km; snacks, bar in vill; playgrnd; htd pool; sand beach 500m; sea & rv fishing; entmnt; 60% statics (sep area); dogs €5; no twin-axle c'vans & max length c'van 6m, m'van 7m; poss cr; Eng spkn; adv bkg; quiet; red low ssn; cc acc; CCI. "Delightful, peaceful site on rv & facing marina; dated clean san facs; friendly recep; excel base for area; easy cycling to beach & Cannes." 1 Apr-15 Oct. € 23.00   2006*

As soon as we get home I'm going to post all these site report forms to the editor for inclusion in next year's guide. I don't want to miss the September deadline.

NAPOULE, LA *10F4* (3km N Urban) **Camping de la Ferme, 06210 Mandelieu-la-Napoule [04 93 49 94 19; fax 04 93 49 18 52]** Fr A8 exit junc 40 & turn L in Mandelieu cent sp Fréjus; 200m after rndabt with palm tree centre, fork R into Ave Maréchal Juin & strt into Bvd du Bon Puits. Avoid La Napoule vill when towing. Med, shd; wc; shwrs €0.50; el pnts (6-10A) €2.50-€3.00; gas; ice; lndtte; shops; snacks; sand beach 650m; dogs; adv bkg; quiet. "Helpful staff; nice atmosphere; mobile bank; facs looking old & tired; some pitches v sm; cr high ssn." ♦ 25 Mar-3 Oct. € 13.80   2004*

⊞**NAPOULE, LA** *10F4* (5km N Urban/Coastal) **Camping L'Argentière, 264 Blvd du Bon-Puits, 06210 Mandelieu-la-Napoule [tel/fax 04 93 49 95 04; www.campingdelargentiere.com]** Fr A8 turn L in Mandelieu cent (sp Fréjus). At rndabt with fountains take 2nd exit, at next rndabt take 2nd exit to L of BP stn, at next rndabt take 2nd exit, site on R in 150m. Avoid La Napoule vill when towing. Med, hdg/mkd pitch, hdstg, pt shd; wc; chem disp; mv service pnt; shwrs inc; el pnts (6A) €3.20; ice; lndtte; shop; hypmkt 1km; rest; snacks; bar; sand beach 800m; fishing; entmnt; TV rm; 80% statics; dogs €3; bus; Eng spkn; adv bkg ess in ssn; poss cr; quiet; CCI. "Clean san facs; lovely local beaches." € 21.00   2007*

NAPOULE, LA *10F4* (10km W Rural) **Camping Les Philippons, 83600 Les Adrets-de-l'Esterel [04 94 40 90 67; fax 04 94 19 35 92; info@ philipponscamp.com; www.philipponscamp.com]** Exit A8 at junc 39 Les Adrets (14km fr Cannes). Foll sp Les Adrets on D837 S. In 2km turn L on D237 thro vill, site on L; sm ent. Sm, pt sl, terr, shd; wc; shwrs inc; el pnts (3-9A) €2.70-5; shop; snacks; bar; playgrnd; pool; sand beach 9km; poss cr; 90% statics; dogs €2; m'van height limit 2.80m; adv bkg; quiet. "Attractive site; diff access for towed c'van with steep, narr & twisty rd, v ltd turning space; not rec for c'vans, adequate for m'vans & tents only." 1 Apr-30 Sep. € 19.00   2006*

NARBONNE *10F1* (10km N Rural) **Camp Municipal, Rue de la Cave Coopérative, 11590 Sallèles-d'Aude [04 68 46 68 46 (Mairie); fax 04 68 46 91 00; ot.sallelesdaude@wanadoo.fr; www.salleles-daude.com]** Fr A9/E15 exit junc 36 onto D64 N & in approx 4km turn L to join D11 W. Cont on this rd for approx 18km, then turn L onto D13 S to Ouveillan. In vill, turn R onto D418 SW to Sallèles-d'Aude. Site in vill. NB Nr Canal du Midi some narr app rds. Sm, hdg/mkd pitch, pt shd; wc; chem disp; el pnts €2.50; shops 1km; BBQ; no statics; dogs; adv bkg; quiet. "Quite rural location; v clean site; 16 pitches; adj canal; excel." 1 Jun-30 Sep. € 10.80   2006*

NARBONNE *10F1* (6km S Rural) **Camping Les Mimosas, Chaussée de Mandirac, 11100 Narbonne [04 68 49 03 72; fax 04 68 49 39 45; info@lesmimosas.com; www.lesmimosas.com]** Leave A9 junc 38 at Narbonne Sud & at rndabt foll sp La Nautique. Turn L opp ent to Camping La Nautique & foll sp Mandirac & site. Lge, hdg/ mkd pitch, hdstg, pt shd; wc; chem disp; some serviced pitches (extra); baby facs; sauna; shwrs inc; el pnts (6A) inc; gas; lndtte; ice; shop; rest; snacks; bar; no BBQ; playgrnd; 3 pools (1 htd); 4 waterslides; jacuzzi; sand beach 6km; watersports; rv fishing adj; fishing lake 300m; tennis; cycle hire; table tennis; mini-golf; horseriding adj; games aea; internet; entmnt high ssn; TV rm; some statics; dogs €3; adv bkg; Eng spkn; some rd/rlwy noise; cc acc; red low ssn/long stay; CCI. "Excel touring base in lovely, historic area; gd choice of pitches; gd for birdwatching; cycle path into Narbonne; gd san facs; vg for children; recep clsd 1200-1400; friendly, helpful staff." ♦ 21 Mar-1 Nov. € 30.00 (CChq acc)   2007*

See advertisement opposite (bottom)

France

NARBONNE *10F1* (4km SW Urban) **Camping La Nautique**, 11100 Narbonne [04 68 90 48 19; fax 04 68 90 73 39; info@campinglanautique.com; www.campinglanautique.com] Exit junc 38 fr A9 at Narbonne Sud. After toll take last rndabt exit & foll sp La Nautique. Site on R 2.5km fr A9 exit. Lge, hdg/mkd pitch, some hdstg, pt shd; chem disp; mv service pnt; all serviced pitches; individ wash cubicles (wc, shwr) on each pitch inc; el pnts (10A) inc; gas; Indtte; ice; shop high ssn & 3km; tradsmn; rest, snacks & bar high ssn; BBQ (elec only); playgrnd; htd pool; waterslide; paddling pool; sand beach 10km; lake sw adj; tennis; entmnt; 30% statics; dogs €3.50; Eng spkn; adv bkg; quiet with some rd noise; cc acc; red low ssn/long stay; CCI. "Excel site; spotless facs; caution - hot water v hot; some pitches lge but v narr; pitches sheltered, can be windy and some muddy after rain; special pitches for disabled; excel rest; helpful, friendly Dutch owners; many sports activities avail; guided walks; recep clsd 1200-1400 low ssn." ♦ 15 Feb-15 Nov. € 37.00   2007*

See advertisement above

⊞NARBONNE *10F1* (12km SW Rural) **Camping La Figurotta**, Route de Narbonne, 11200 Bizanet [tel/fax 04 68 45 16 26 or 06 88 16 12 30 (mob); info@figurotta.eu; www.figurotta.eu] Exit A9 at Narbonne Sud onto slip rd N9/D6113 (N113) twd Lézignan-Corbières; in 3km at new rndabt head L twd D613 & then D224 sp Bizanet & site. App fr W not rec due narr D rds. Sm, mkd pitch, hdstg, pt sl, pt terr, shd; htd wc; chem disp; shwrs €0.50; el pnts (4-5A) €2.50 (poss long lead req); gas; Indtte; sm shop & 2km; tradsmn; rest; snacks; bar; playgrnd; sm pool; sand beach 20km; games area; no dogs; phone; Eng spkn; adv bkg; rd noise; up to 50% red low ssn; 10% red 7+ days; red low ssn; CCI. "Superb, well-managed, simple site; excel facs, ltd low ssn; gd pool; helpful & friendly Dutch owners; gd views most pitches; a gusty & stony site in beautiful location - steel pegs req; gd walks; conv Corbières & Minervois wine areas; gd NH en rte Spain; rec." ♦ ltd. € 15.00   2007*

> The opening dates and prices on this campsite have changed. I'll send a site report form to the editor for the next edition of the guide.

NARBONNE PLAGE *10F1* (Coastal) **Camp Municipal La Falaise, 8 Ave des Vacances, 11000 Narbonne-Plage [04 68 49 80 77 or 04 68 49 83 65 (LS); fax 04 68 49 40 44; resacamp@wanadoo.fr; www.campinglafalaise. com]** Exit A9 at Narbonne Est junc 37 onto D168 for 10km to Narbonne-Plage. Site on L at ent to vill. Lge, hdg pitch, shd; wc; chem disp; shwrs inc; el pnts (6A) €3; gas; Indtte; ice; shop; rest; snacks; bar; playgrnd; beach 300m; waterslide 1.5km; games area; cycle hire; TV; some statics; dogs €2; poss cr; adv bkg; poss noise r open air theatre; red low ssn. "Gd for beach holiday; run down low ssn & v ltd facs." 1 Apr-30 Sep. € 19.00   2006*

NARBONNE PLAGE *10F1* (8km NE Coastal) **Camping La Grande Cosse (Naturist), St Pierre-sur-Mer, 11560 Fleury-d'Aude [04 68 33 61 87; fax 04 68 33 32 23; contact@grandecosse.com; www.grandecosse.com]** Exit A9 junc 36 onto D64 twd Béziers. Turn L onto D14 to Lespignan then L on D14 to Fleury. L on D718 sp 'Les Cabanes de Fleury' to site. Avoid Vendres - v narr & diff. Lge, hdg/mkd pitch, pt shd; wc; chem disp; serviced pitches; chem disp; mv service pnt; shwrs inc; el pnts (10A) €3.50; gas; Indtte; ice; shop; rest; snacks; bar high ssn; playgrnd; htd pool; sand beach 300m; tennis; games area; games rm; gym; entmnt; boat hire; fishing; TV rm; 20% statics; dogs €3; phone; poss cr Aug; Eng spkn; adv bkg (dep req); red long stay/low ssn; cc acc; INF card req. "Excel site; helpful, friendly staff; high quality san facs; naturist walk to beach thro lagoons & dunes; mosquitoes poss problem Jun-Sep; flood risk after heavy rain; gd." ♦ 30 Mar-7 Oct. € 29.00   2006*

NASBINALS *9D1* (1km N Rural) **Camp Municipal, Route de St Urcize, 48260 Nasbinals [02 46 32 51 87 or 04 66 32 50 17]** Fr A75 exit 36 to Aumont-Aubrac, then W on D987 to Nasbinals. Turn R onto D12, site sp. Med, pt sl, pt shd; htd wc; chem disp; mv service pnt; shwrs inc; el pnts (16A) €2.30; shop, rest in vill; BBQ; dogs; quiet; red CCI. "Excel long/sh stay." ♦ ltd 25 May-30 Sep. € 6.00   2007*

NAUCELLE *8E4* (Rural) **FLOWER Camping du Lac de Bonnefon (FFCC), L'Etang de Bonnefon, 12800 Naucelle [05 65 69 33 20; fax 05 65 69 33 20; camping-du-lac-de-bonnefon@ wanadoo.fr; www.camping-du-lac-de-bonnefon. com]** N fr Carmaux turn L off N88 Albi-Rodez rd at Naucelle Gare onto D997, sp Naucelle Centre. Site sp in 2km. Med, mkd pitch, pt sl, pt shd; htd wc; chem disp; mv service pnt; shwrs inc; el pnts (6A) inc; Indtte; shop 1.5km; rest; snacks; bar; playgrnd; pool; TV; many statics; dogs €2.50; poss cr; quiet; CCI. "Pleasant, clean site adj lge fishing lake; gd san facs; conv Sauveterre-de-Rouergue." ♦ 1 Apr-24 Oct. € 22.90 (CChq acc)   2007*

NAUSSANNES see Beaumont du Périgord *7D3*

NAVARRENX *8F1* (200m S Rural) **Camping Beau Rivage, Allée des Marronniers, 64190 Navarrenx [05 59 66 10 00; curtisrw@free.fr; www. beaucamping.com]** Fr E exit A64 junc 9 at Artix onto D281 dir Mourenx, then Navarrenx. Fr N exit junc 7 Salies-de-Béarn onto D933 to Sauveterre-de-Béarn, then D936 to Navarrenx. Med, hdg/mkd pitch, terr, pt shd; htd wc; chem disp; mv service pnt; shwrs inc; el pnts (8-10A) €3.50; gas; Indtte; ice; shop, rest, snacks & bar 300m; BBQ; playgrnd; htd pool & paddling pool adj; tennis; 13% statics; dogs €1.50; phone; Eng spkn; adv bkg; quiet; CCI. "Peaceful, well-run site bet town & rv; helpful, friendly, British owners; clean san facs; pool planned 2007; gd area for walking, fishing, cycling; lovely, interesting town in walking dist; conv for Biarritz & Spain; gd value; rec." ♦ 15 Mar-15 Oct. € 12.50   2006*

NEBOUZAT *9B1* (1km W Rural) **Camping Les Domes, 4 Route de Nébouzat, 63210 Nébouzat [04 73 87 14 06 or 04 73 93 21 02 (LS); fax 04 73 87 18 81; camping-les-domes@wanadoo. fr; www.les-domes.com]** Exit 5 fr A75 twd Col de la Ventouse; turn L on N89 sp Tulle. Do not ent vill of Nébouzat but cont for 1km. Take L onto D216 sp Orcival then immed L. Site on L in 100m. Med, mkd pitch, hdstg, pt shd; wc (mainly cont); chem disp; baby facs; shwrs inc; el pnts (10-15A) €5 (poss long lead req); gas; Indtte; ice; shop; tradsmn; snacks; playgrnd; htd covrd pool; boules areas; walking; sailing; windsurfing; entmnt; TV rm; phone; dogs; Eng spkn; adv bkg; quiet; cc not acc; 10% red CCI. "V friendly, helpful staff; gd welcome; sm pitches; basic san facs - dep req for key; max 6m height; in volcanic region, conv Volcania." 9 May-16 Sep. € 15.50   2005*

NEMOURS *4F3* (5km S Urban) **FFCC Camping de Pierre Le Sault, Chemin des Grèves, 77167 Bagneaux-sur-Loing [01 64 29 24 44]** Well sp bef town fr both dir off N7. Med, hdg/mkd pitch, pt shd; wc; shwrs inc; el pnts (3-6A) €1.90-2.95; gas 2km; Indtte; shop 2km; tradsmn; playgrnd; tennis; rv sw; 90% statics; poss cr; some Eng spkn; ent barrier clsd 2200-0700; no adv bkg; some rd noise; red low ssn; no cc acc; CCI. "Lovely site by canal & rv; excel clean facs." ♦ 1 Apr-31 Oct. € 7.10   2007*

NERAC *8E2* (800m SW Rural) **Aire Naturelle Les Contes d'Albret, 47600 Nérac [05 53 65 18 73; fax 05 63 65 66 97; sylvie.fagalde@wanadoo.fr; www.albret.com]** Exit A62 junc 7 onto D931 to Laplume. Then turn W onto D15 & D656 to Nérac. Cont on D656 dir Mézin & foll site sp to end of rd in 3km. Sm, pt sl, pt shd; htd wc; chem disp; baby facs; shwrs inc; el pnts €2; BBQ; farm shop, other shops in vill; rest; rv sw; kayaking; crazy golf; Eng spkn; adv bkg; quiet. "Vg CL-type site; excel views; glorious garden." 1 May-30 Sep. € 13.00   2005*

NERIS LES BAINS 7A4 (1km N Urban) Camping du Lac (formerly Municipal), Ave Marx Dormoy, 03310 Néris-les-Bains [04 70 03 17 59 or 04 70 03 24 70 (recep); fax 04 70 03 79 99; neris-les-bains@wanadoo.fr; www.ville-neris-les-bains.fr] Site on N side of Néris off D2144 (N144). Turn at rndabt by blue tourist office, opp park, & foll sp round 1 way system to site in 500m. Med, hdg/mkd pitch, pt sl, terr, pt shd; wc (some cont); chem disp; shwrs inc; el pnts (10A) inc; gas; shops 1km; tradsmn; snacks; bar; playgrnd; covrd pool 500m; some statics; dogs €0.95; quiet; red long stay. "6 pitches for m'vans at ent to site, charge for el pnts (10A) & water only; lovely walks nrby; spa town - thermal baths, theatre & parks etc; vg." 1 Apr-22 Oct. € 12.86   2007*

NESLES LA VALLEE see Beaumont sur Oise 3D3

NESMY see Roche sur Yon, La 2H4

NEUF BRISACH 6F3 (6km NE) Camping de L'Ile du Rhin, Zone Touristique 68, 68600 Biesheim [03 89 72 57 95; fax 03 89 72 14 21; camping@shn.fr; www.campingiledurhin.com] On rte Colmar to Freiburg (Germany). Site on island in Rv Rhine, on R after French Customs point off N415. Lge, hdstg, pt shd; wc; shwrs inc; el pnts (4-10A) €4-5.75; Indtte; ice, snacks & shop (high ssn); htd, covrd pool adj; tennis; rv fishing 100m; 50% statics sep area; poss cr Jul-Aug; Eng spkn; cc acc. "Excel facs; gates clsd 1200-1400 & 2000-0700; €10 dep barrier card; vg." ◆ 18 Mar-1 Oct. € 13.36

2005*

NEUF BRISACH 6F3 (1.2km E Urban) Camp Municipal Vauban, 68600 Neuf-Brisach [tel/fax 03 89 72 54 25 or 03 89 72 51 68 (Mairie)] Fr N415 (Colmar-Freiburg) at E of Neuf-Brisach turn NE on D1 bis (sp Neuf-Brisach & Camping Vauban). At next junc turn L & immed R into site rd. Med, pt shd; wc; mv service pnt; shwrs €1; el pnts (6A) €2.50; ice; shops in town; playgrnd; pool 3km; 40% statics; dogs; adv bkg; quiet; CCI. "Fascinating ramparts around town; no new arr 1200-1400." 1 Apr-1 Oct. € 9.60   2007*

NEUF BRISACH 6F3 (6km SE Rural) FFCC Camping L'Orée du Bois, 5 Rue du Bouleau, 68600 Geiswasser [03 89 72 80 13; fax 03 89 72 80 13; valerie.schappler@wanadoo.fr] Site in vill cent; street name on bungalow; ent bet bungalow & vegetable garden - tight turn, watch out bungalow gutters. Sm, hdg pitch, pt shd; htd wc; chem disp; shwrs inc; el pnts (10A) €2.50; Indtte; BBQ; playgrnd; dogs; Eng spkn; adv bkg (dep req); quiet; CCI. "Gd touring base; v friendly owner; vg." ◆ ltd. 1 May-31 Oct. € 6.60   2006*

NEUFCHATEAU 6E2 (10km N Rural) Camp Municipal, Chemin de Santilles, 88630 Domrémy-la-Pucelle [03 29 06 90 70; fax 03 29 94 33 77] Take D164 fr Neufchâteau, site in cent of Domrémy vill, clear sp by stadium, nr Rv Meuse. Sm, pt shd; wc (some cont); chem disp; shwrs €0.80; el pnts (16A) €2.30; shops adj; rest, bar 500m; tennis; pool nrby; quiet. "Site yourself, warden calls (not Sun); nr birthplace of Joan of Arc." 1 Jun-31 Aug. € 7.00   2007*

NEUFCHATEAU 6E2 (NW Urban) Camp Municipal, Rue de Moulinot, 88300 Neufchâteau [03 29 94 19 03 or 03 29 94 14 75 (Mairie); fax 03 29 94 33 77; contact@neufchateau-tourisme.com; www.neufchateau-tourisme.com] Clear sp on ent town next to sports stadium. Sm, pt shd; wc; chem disp; shwrs inc; el pnts (10A) inc; Indry rm; shops 500m; htd pool nr; poss cr; some rlwy noise. "Sh walk to town; gd san facs, ltd low ssn; poss unkempt low ssn; no twin-axles; gd value." ◆ 15 Apr-30 Sep. € 13.00   2007*

France

Before we move on, I'm going to fill in some site report forms and post them off to the editor, otherwise they won't arrive in time for the deadline at the end of September.

NEUFCHATEL EN BRAY 3C2 (1km NW Urban) Camping de Ste Claire, Route Ste Claire, 76270 Neufchâtel-en-Bray [02 35 93 03 93 or 06 20 12 20 98 (mob); fancelot@wanadoo.fr; www.camping-sainte-claire.com] Fr S exit A28 junc 9 sp Neufchâtel. In 1.9km at bottom hill, immed after rv bdge (easily missed) turn L into Rue de la Grande Flandre, strt on into Rue Ste Claire. Cont past Leclerc supmkt on L. Or Fr N exit A28 junc 7 dir Neufchâtel. In approx 5km turn R onto D1 for Dieppe & in approx 1km turn L at site sp. Med, hdg/mkd pitch, hdstg, pt sl, pt shd; wc (some cont); chem disp; shwrs inc; el pnts (6-10A) €4-6; sm shop; supmkt 500m; tradsmn; bar/rest; snacks; playgrnd; few statics; dogs; phone adj; bus 1km; Eng spkn; adv bkg; quiet; no cc acc; red long stay; CCI. "Pretty, v pleasant, well-kept, family site by rv in parkland; roomy layout; facs dated but clean; gd wheelchair access / easy walking; friendly, helpful owner; gd rest; easy walk into town; cycle rte adj; Sat mkt; conv Le Havre/Dieppe ferries & a'route; poss occasional smell fr sewage works in hot weather! (reported OK Aug 2007)." 1 Apr-31 Oct. € 9.45   2007*

NEUILLY SUR MARNE see Paris 3D3

NEUNG SUR BEUVRON *4G3* (500m NE Rural) **FFCC Camp Municipal de la Varenne, 34 Rue de Veillas, 41210 Neung-sur-Beuvron [tel/ fax 02 54 83 68 52 or 06 76 80 88 41 (mob); camping.lavarenne@wanadoo.fr; www.neung-sur-beuvron.fr/camping]** On A10 heading S take Orléans Sud exit & join N20 S. At end of La Ferté-St Aubin take D922 SW twd Romorantin-Lanthenay. In 20km R onto D925 to Neung. Turn R at church pedestrian x-ing in cent of vill ('stade' sp), R at fork (white, iron cross) & site on R in 1km. Site by rvside. Fr A71 exit junc 3 onto D923; turn R onto D925 & as above. Sm, hdg/mkd pitch, pt sl, pt shd; wc; chem disp; mv service pnt; shwrs inc; el pnts (10A) €2.50; gas; lndtte; ice; shops 1km; tradsmn; rest, bar 500m; playgrnd; tennis; few statics; dogs; poss cr (Aug); adv bkg; v quiet; cc acc. "Friendly, helpful warden; barrier clsd 2200-0800; recep clsd 1200-1400; immac facs; lge pitches, levelling boards poss req; Sat mkt; vg cent for hiking, cycling, birdwatching." Easter-30 Sep. € 7.10
2007*

NEUVE LYRE, LA *3D2* (Rural) **Camp Municipal La Salle, Rue de l'Union, 27330 La Neuve-Lyre [02 32 60 14 98 or 02 32 30 50 01(Mairie); fax 02 32 32 30 22 37; mairie.la-neuve-lyre@wanadoo. fr]** Fr NE on D830 into vill turn R at church (sp not visible), fr S (Rugles) foll sp. Well sp fr vill. Med, pt shd; wc (some cont) ltd; chem disp (wc); shwrs €0.75; el pnts (5A) €1.70 (poss long lead req); shops 500m; fishing; 40% statics; dogs; quiet; CCI. "Delightful quiet & clean site; site yourself, warden calls; friendly, helpful warden; excel sh stay/NH." ♦ 15 Mar-15 Oct. € 3.20
2006*

NEUVEGLISE see Chaudes Aigues *9C1*

NEUVIC (CORREZE) *7C4* (4km N Rural) **Camping Domaine de Mialaret, Route d'Egletons, 19160 Neuvic [05 55 46 02 50; fax 05 55 46 02 65; info@ lemialaret.com; www.lemialaret.com]** Fr N on A89 exit 23 twds St Angel then D171 to Neuvic or foll sp fr Neuvic on D991. Med, some hdg pitch, pt sl, pt shd; htd wc; chem disp; mv service pnt; baby facs; shwrs inc; el pnts (6A) inc; ice; lndtte; shop; tradsmn; rest in chateau fr May; snacks high ssn; bar; playgrnd; pool; 2 carp fishing pools; watersports nrby; mini-farm; mountain bike routes; walking tours; games rm; entmnt; child entmnt; internet; 30% statics (sep area); dogs; phone; bus 4km; poss cr; quiet; adv bkg; Eng spkn; red 7 days/ low ssn; CCI. "Excel site in grounds of chateau; excel welcome pack; children's mini-zoo & rare sheep breeds nrby; charming owner; friendly staff; facs ltd low ssn." 1 Apr-1 Nov. € 25.00 (CChq acc)
2006*

NEUVIC (CORREZE) *7C4* (4km N Rural) **Camping du Président Queuille, Antiges, 19160 Neuvic [05 55 95 81 18; fax 05 55 46 02 50]** Fr Neuvic, D982 N twd Ussel. In 3km turn R onto D20 sp Antiges. Site in 1km. Or fr N/S A89 exit 23 then foll St Angel & take D171. Foll sp. Med, pt sl, pt shd; wc; shwrs; el pnts (10A) €1.49; lndtte; snacks; rest; sand beach; lake sw adj; adv bkg; red low ssn; quiet. "Gd site but basic; pleasant views on lake." 1 May-30 Sep. € 10.82
2004*

NEUVIC (CORREZE) *7C4* (4km N Rural) **Camping Le Soustran, Pellachal, 19160 Neuvic [05 55 95 03 71 or 06 47 94 89 34 (mob); info@ lesoustran.com; www.lesoustran.com]** N fr Neuvic on D982 dir Ussel for 4km; site on L 300m after bdge. Ent steepish & rough. Med, mkd pitch, terr, pt shd; wc; chem disp; shwrs inc; el pnts (6A) €2.50; lndtte; snacks; bar; BBQ; playgrnd; lake sw 300m; TV rm; dogs €1; Eng spkn; quiet; CCI. "No twin-axles." ♦ ltd. 1 May-30 Sep. € 11.00
2006*

NEUVIC (CORREZE) *7C4* (7km NW Rural) **Camping Le Vianon, Les Plaines, 19160 Palisse [05 55 95 87 22; fax 05 55 95 98 45; camping. vianon@wanadoo.fr; www.levianon.com]** Fr Neuvic take D47 twd Pallisse. Site well sp. Med, mkd pitch, pt sl, pt shd; htd wc; chem disp; mv service pnt; baby facs; shwrs inc; el pnts (6A) €3.80; lndtte; ice; shops; tradsmn; rest; snacks; bar; BBQ; playgrnd; pool; sports activities; tennis; child entmnt; watersports; TV rm; 15% statics; dogs €2; poss cr; Eng spkn; adv bkg (dep req); quiet; red 7+ days; CCI. "Woodland walks & great scenery; v friendly Dutch owners; vg rest & bar; spotless facs; fully equipped chalets avail." ♦ ltd. 10 Apr-16 Oct. € 19.10
2005*

NEUVIC (DORDOGNE) *7C3* (500m N Rural) **Camping Le Plein Air Neuvicois, Ave de Planèze, 24190 Neuvic [05 53 81 50 77; fax 05 53 80 46 50; camp.le.plein.air.neuvicois@libertysurf.fr]** On N89, 26km SW fr Périgueux (Mussidan-Bordeaux rd). After 24km, turn R (D44) at Neuvic. Site clearly sp thro vill, by rv bef bdge, on both sides of rv. Med, pt shd; htf wc; baby facs; shwrs inc; el pnts (6-10A) €3-4; lndtte; ice; shop; tradsmn; snacks; bar; pool; fishing; tennis; games rm; some statics; dogs €0.50; phone; adv bkg; quiet. "Charming owners; beautiful location; vg." 1 Jun-15 Sep. € 11.50
2007*

NEUVILLE SUR SARTHE see Mans, Le *4F1*

NEVACHE *9C3* (6km W Rural) **Camp Municipal de Foncouverte, 05100 Névache [04 92 21 38 21 or 04 92 21 31 01]** Fr Briançon take N94 NE twd Italian border dir Turin, then L onto D994 sp Névache. Rd is narr with passing places. Site is 2nd in vill. Med, pt sl, pt shd; wc; shwrs €1.20; lndry rm; shop; tradsmn; Eng spkn; quiet. "Vg for walkers; lovely alpine flowers; diff lge o'fits; no c'vans or m'vans allowed W of Névache 0900-1800 in summer." 1 Jun-28 Sep. € 9.50
2006*

⊞ *Site open all year*   *Send in your site reports*

NEVERS *4H4* (Urban) **Camping de Nevers, Rue de la Jonction, 58000 Nevers [06 84 98 69 79; info@ campingnevers.com; www.campingnevers.com]** Exit A77 junc 37 dir Centre Ville. Site on L immed after bdge over Rv Loire. Med, mkd pitch, hdstg, pt shd; htd wc; chem disp; mv service pnt; baby facs; shwrs inc; el pnts (6-10A) €2.50-4.30; lndtte; ice; supmkt 2km; tradsmn; rest 500m; snacks; bar; playgrnd; pool 200m; sand beach 200m; rv fishing;cycle hire; internet; TV; 3% statics; dogs €2; phone; bus 20m; poss cr; Eng spkn; adv bkg; rd noise; red low ssn; cc acc; CCI. "Nice site, on bank of Rv Loire; stunning view of Nevers & cathedral across rv; sh walk to town cent; cycle rides along Loire; barrier clsd 1200-1400; san facs poss stretched high ssn; site poss unkempt low ssn & ltd/ mixed san facs; poss noisy if site used by parties attending events at Nevers Magny-Cours racing circuit; excel." ♦ 13 Apr-15 Oct. € 16.00 (CChq acc) 2007*

⊞**NEVERS** *4H4* (10km SE Rural) **Camp Municipal Plan d'Eau Bagnade, Route de Magny-Cours, 58160 Chevenon [03 86 68 71 71 or 03 86 68 72 75; fax 03 86 38 30 33]** Fr N7 site sp at Magny-Cours turn R fr S (L fr N) onto D200, site ent on R just bef Chevenon. Or fr N exit N7 junc 37 to Chevernon; site sp. Med, hdg pitch, terr, pt sl, pt shd; htd wc; shwrs inc; el pnts (6A) inc; lndry rm; shops 1km; playgrnd; lake sw adj; fishing; mini golf; many statics; quiet; cc acc; CCI. "Pleasant, peaceful site nr lakes & close to French Grand Prix circuit; site yourself if warden not present; gd, clean san facs; facs & pitches unkempt low ssn." ♦ ltd. € 12.90 2006*

NEVERS *4H4* (7km NW Urban) **FFCC Camping La Loire, 2 Rue de la Folie, 58600 Fourchambault [03 86 60 81 59; fax 03 86 60 96 24; http:// membres.lycos.fr/campingloire]** Fr Nevers on D40 thro town, site on L bef rv bdge. Med, pt shd; wc; chem disp; mv service pnt; shwrs inc; el pnts (6-20A) €3-7; lndtte; shop 500m; rest 100m; snacks; bar; BBQ; htd, covrd pool; rv adj; dogs €1; bus; red long stay/CCI. "Friendly, helpful; san facs need update & poss unclean." ♦ ltd. 1 Apr-30 Oct. € 9.00 2006*

NEVEZ see Pont Aven *2F2*

NEXON *7B3* (3km S) **Camp Municipal de l'Etang de la Lande, 87800 Nexon [05 55 58 35 44 or 05 55 58 10 19 (Mairie); fax 05 55 58 33 50]** Exit Nexon by D11 spf Ladignac & Camping, site 3km S at junc with D17. Fr W on D15 take D15A nr Nexon & foll sp. Sm, sl, pt shd; wc; shwrs; el pnts (5-10A) inc; ice; lndtte; shops 3km; lake sw adj; playgrnd; cycle hire; entmnts; TV rm; Eng spkn; quiet. "Excel base for Limoges; site open to adj leisure pk; warden visits 3-4 times day; arrive & site self." 1 Apr-30 Sep. € 10.00 2004*

NEYDENS see St Julien en Genevois *9A3*

NIBELLE *4F3* (2km E Rural) **Parc de Nibelle, Route de Boiscommun, 45340 Nibelle [02 38 32 23 55; fax 02 38 32 03 87; contact@caravaningnibelle. com; www.parc-nibelle.com]** Fr N60 turn N onto D114 dir Nibelle. Turn R onto D9, site sp. Med, pt shd; wc; shwrs inc; el pnts inc; lndtte; shop; tradsmn; rest; snacks; bar; BBQ; playgrnd; htd, covrd pool; paddling pool; tennis; games area; games rm; cycle hire; entmnt; statics; dogs €3; Eng spkn; adv bkg; quiet; red low ssn. "Excel site; nr Etang de la Vallée; poss facs ltd low ssn - no facs for water tank filling etc." ♦ 1 Mar-30 Nov. € 31.00 2007*

NICE *10E4* (14km NE Rural) **Camping La Laune, Moulin de Peillon, Blvd de la Vallée, 06440 Peillon [06 75 69 97 00 (mob); campingdelalaune@yahoo. fr]** Leave A8 junc 55 (Nice Est); foll D2204 twds Sospel; cont until R turn at rndbt sp D21 Peillon/ Peille; site on R in vill in approx 4km. Sm, mkd pitch, pt shd; wc; chem disp; mv service pnt; shwrs inc; el pnts (12-4A) €2.50-3.50 (rev pol); lndtte; shop, rest, bar in vill; tradsmn; shgl beach 14km; dogs €2.50; phone adj; adv bkg; quiet; no cc acc; CCI. "Sm family-run site; v helpful owner; conv for Monaco, Monte Carlo, Nice; sm pitches; some rd/ rlwy noise; ltd facs low ssn." May-Sep. € 21.00 2007*

NIEDERBRONN LES BAINS *5D3* (3.5km N Rural) **Camping Heidenkopf, Route de la Lisière, 67110 Niederbronn-les-Bains [tel/fax 03 88 09 08 46; heidenkopf@tiscali.fr]** Fr Niederbronn NW on N62 & foll sp rd R into forest fr mineral spring. Med, pt sl, terr, pt shd; htd wc (some cont); chem disp; mv service pnt; baby facs; shwrs inc; el pnts (6A) €2.90; gas; lndtte; shops 3km; tradsmn; BBQ; playgrnd; pool 1km; dogs €1.25; adv bkg; quiet. "Forest walks; 20 mins walk to town." ♦ 1 Apr-31 Oct. € 10.50 2005*

NIEDERBRONN LES BAINS *5D3* (1.5km SW Rural) **Camp Municipal L'Oasis, 3 Rue de Frohret, 67110 Oberbronn [03 88 09 71 96; fax 03 88 09 97 87; oasis.oberbronn@laregie.fr]** Fr N62 turn S on D28 away fr Niederbronn; thro Oberbronn, site sp. Lge, mkd pitch, pt sl, pt shd; wc; chem disp; mv service pnt; sauna; shwrs inc; el pnts (6A) €3.70; lndtte; shop & 1.5km; tradsmn; rest; snacks; bar; BBQ; playgrnd; htd, covrd pool high ssn; paddling pool; tennis; fitness rm; walking, cycling, horseriding rtes; golf; games rm; fishing 2km; 20% statics; dogs €1.80; clsd 1200-1300; poss cr; adv bkg rec high ssn; quiet; red long stay/low ssn; cc acc; CCI. "Vg site with lovely views; part of leisure complex; v quiet low ssn; sm, sl area for tourers; some san facs tired; site gravel paths not suitable wheelchair users." ♦ ltd. 12 Mar-11 Nov. € 13.40 2007*

France

⊞NIMES *10E2* (7km NE) **Camping Les Cyprès, 5 Rue de la Bastide, 30320 Bezouce** [04 66 75 24 30; fax 04 66 75 64 78] Sp on N86 Nîmes-Avignon rd. Site not well sp in Bezouce - sign high on wall. Narr site access. Sm, pt shd; wc; chem disp; shwrs; el pnts (4-6A) €3.70; shop, rest, bar in vill; sm pool; mostly statics; dogs; poss cr; adv bkg; rd noise & cockerels. "Facs rustic & v basic but clean; v friendly & helpful owners; basic meals in hotel adj; conv Pont-du-Gard, Nîmes, Arles; not rec lge o'fits; closes early evening low ssn; NH only." € 12.00   2005*

⊞NIMES *10E2* (7km S Rural) **Domaine de la Bastide, Route de Générac, 30900 Nîmes** [tel/fax 04 66 38 09 21] Site well sp fr town cent. Lge, hdg/mkd pitch, pt shd; wc; chem disp; mv service pnt; serviced pitches; shwrs inc; el pnts (15A); gas; lndtte; shop; tradsmn; hypmkt nr; rest; bar; TV rm; 10% statics; dogs €2; phone; bus; Eng spkn; adv bkg; some rd noise; CCI. "Lge pitches; friendly recep; gd base Nîmes, 20 mins by bus fr site; site poss unkempt; poss no lighting after dark; poss itinerants." ♦ ltd. € 22.40 (4 persons)   2005*

NIORT *7A2* (13km NE Rural) **Camp du Plan d'Eau de St Christophe, St Christophe-sur-Roch, 79410 Cherveux** [05 49 05 21 38 or 05 49 75 01 77 (Mairie); fax 05 49 75 86 60] Exit A83 junc 10 onto D743. Turn E onto D6 sp Augé. Turn R at 3rd set of x-rds onto D122, site on R in 1km on lake, 2km fr Cherveux. Med, mkd pitch, pt sl, pt shd; wc; shwrs inc; el pnts (6A) €2.60; lndry rm; ice; shop 3km; tradsmn; rest; bar; playgrnd; lake sw; sand beach; boating; fishing; mini-golf; dogs €1.15; CCI. "Gd rest & bar; clean san facs; friendly." 1 Apr-15 Oct. € 7.15   2006*

NIOZELLES see Brillane, La *10E3*

NOAILLES see Brive la Gaillarde *7C3*

NOCLE MAULAIX, LA *4H4* (W Rural) **Camp Municipal du l'Etang Marnant, Route de Decize, 58250 La Nocle-Maulaix** [tel/fax 03 86 30 84 13] Fr Luzy twd Fours on N81, turn L on D3 & foll sp. Site in 5km at La Nocle-Maulaix by junc with D30. Sm, mkd pitch, pt sl, pt shd; wc; shwrs; el pnts; shops 400m; lndtte; playgrnd; sports area; fishing; adv bkg; quiet. "Take 2nd ent to site; site yourself & warden calls; watersports on lake." 15 May-15 Sep. € 9.90   2004*

NOGENT L'ARTAUD *3D4* (1km S Rural) **Camp Municipal des Monts, 56237 Nogent-l'Artaud** [03 23 70 01 18] Site sp W of D222/D11, 1km S fr Nogent-l'Artaud. Sm, hdg/mkd pitch, terr, pt shd; wc; chem disp (wc); shwrs inc; el pnts (6A) inc; shop 1.5km; playgrnd; table tennis, games area adj; 25% statics; dogs €0.60; phone; quiet; CCI. "Helpful; gd views fr site; wc old but clean; beautiful garden-type site." 30 Mar-29 Sep. € 9.20
2004*

NOGENT SUR SEINE *4E4* (500m NE Rural) **Camp Municipal, Rue Villiers-aux-Choux, 10400 Nogent-sur-Seine** [tel/fax 03 25 39 76 67 or 03 25 39 42 00 (Mairie)] Fr Troyes site sp fr D619 (N19) on app to town & fr S ring rd, Site on rvside. Med, mkd pitch, some hdstg, pt shd; htd wc; shwrs; mv service pnt; el pnts; shop 500m; rest 100m; playgrnd; pool adj; tennis; quiet. "Pleasant site; poss many long-stay residents; gd NH." 1 Apr-5 Oct. € 11.22   2006*

NOGENT SUR SEINE *4E4* (10km NE Rural) **Aire Naturelle Municipale (Cunin), 10400 Pont-sur-Seine** [03 25 21 43 44 or 03 25 39 42 00 (Mairie); fax 03 25 21 45 66; mairie.pontseine@wanadoo.fr] Fr Nogent-sur-Seine (N19) twd Romilly-sur-Seine. In 10km turn L on D52 to Pont-sur-Seine. Site on L thro vill. Med, unshd; wc; chem disp (wc); el pnts (6A) inc; rest, shop 750m; quiet; adv bkg; phone. "Peaceful site nr rv; pitch yourself, warden calls; excel value; gd facs poss stretched if busy." ♦ 1 May-17 Sep. € 9.00   2006*

NOIRETABLE *9B1* (1km S Rural) **Camp Municipal de la Roche, Route de la Roche, 42440 Noirétable** [04 77 24 72 68; fax 04 77 24 92 20] Leave A72/E70 junc 4 sp Noirétable; thro toll & turn SW onto D53. Ignore narr tourist rte sp to W; cont downhill to T-junc & turn R onto D1089 (N89). Take next L & site on R in 750m. Sm, mkd pitch, hdstg, pt terr, pt sl, pt shd; wc (cont); shwrs; el pnts (10A) inc; snacks, bar nr; playgrnd; lake adj; cc not acc. "V friendly warden." 1 Apr-1 Nov. € 8.20   2006*

NOIRMOUTIER EN L'ILE *2H3* (2km E Coastal) **Camp Municipal Le Clair Matin, Les Sableaux, 85330 Noirmoutier-en-l'Ile** [02 51 39 05 56; fax 02 51 39 74 36] Ent Noirmoutier on D948 & foll sp to Les Sableaux. Site well sp. Med, mkd pitch, terr, pt shd; wc; shwrs €1; el pnts (10A) €3.30; lndtte; shop; playgrnd; pool 2.5km; sand beach adj; fishing; dogs €1.20; adv bkg rec; quiet. "Gd; clean facs; excel cycle paths & beach fishing." ♦ Easter-30 Oct. € 13.00 (3 persons)   2005*

NOIRMOUTIER EN L'ILE *2H3* (2km E Coastal) **Camping Indigo Noirmoutier, 23 Rue des Sableaux, 85330 Noirmoutier-en-l'Ile** [02 51 39 06 24; fax 02 51 35 97 63; noirmoutier@ camping-indigo.com; www.camping-indigo.com] Ent Noirmoutier on D948, turn R at quay bdge, E on dyke for 2km to site on R. Lge, pt shd; mv service pnt; shwrs inc; el pnts (6-10A) €2.90-4.50; lndtte; ice; tradsmn; rest; snacks; bar; playgrnd; sand beach adj; fishing; boat-launching; some statics; dogs €2.40; phone; poss cr; adv bkg; quiet; red low ssn; CCI ess. "Gd for children; shellfish at low tide; set in pine forest & nr salt water marshes." 28 Mar-28 Sep. € 17.30 (CChq acc)   2007*

NOIRMOUTIER EN L'ILE *2H3* (10km SE Coastal) **Camp Municipal du Midi, Fief du Moulin, 85630 Barbâtre** [02 51 39 63 74; fax 02 51 39 58 63; camping-du-midi@wanadoo.fr] Cross to island by Passage du Gois D948 (low tide - 2.5 hrs per day) or bdge D38. Turn L after 2.5km off dual c'way to Barbâtre. Site sp N thro vill. V lge, pt sl, shd; wc; baby facs; shwrs; el pnts (5A) inc; gas; lndtte; ice; shop; rest; snacks; bar; BBQ (gas/elec); htd pool; sand beach adj; tennis; mini-golf; entmnt; poss cr; no adv bkg; quiet; cc acc; red low ssn. ♦ Easter-16 Sep. € 28.00 (3 persons)   2006*

NOIRMOUTIER EN L'ILE *2H3* (4km S Coastal) **Camping Le Caravan'île, 1 Rue de la Tresson, 85680 La Guérinière** [02 51 39 50 29; fax 02 51 35 86 85; contact@caravanile.com; www. caravanile.com] Cross to island on D38, at rndabt foll sp La Guérinière. Site on L. Lge, hdg pitch, pt shd; wc; shwrs; el pnts (5A) inc; lndtte; shop; rest 1km; snacks; playgrnd; 3 pools (1 covrd); waterslide; beach adj; games rm; fitness rm; TV; 50% statics; dogs €2.90; adv bkg (dep req); quiet; cc acc; CCI. "Well-run, popular site; conv for cycling, birdwatching, watersports, fishing etc." ♦ 1 Mar-15 Nov. € 22.00   2007*

NOIRMOUTIER EN L'ILE *2H3* (3.5km SW Coastal) **Camp Municipal La Bosse, 85740 L'Epine** [02 51 39 01 07] Fr bdge take D38 to La Guérinière: turn W along D38 to L'Epine & foll camp sp to La Bosse. Lge, pt sl, pt shd; wc; chem disp; shwrs inc; el pnts (5A) €2.50-3; ice; lndtte; BBQ; playgrnd; sand beach, boat hire, sw & fishing 100m; entmnt; quiet; adv bkg. "Cheap & cheerful; many pitches v sl & others permanently occupied; can get v windy; sand dunes poor for pegs; san facs just OK." ♦ 1 Apr-30 Sep. € 15.00   2007*

There aren't many sites open this early in the year. We'd better phone ahead to check that the one we're heading for is actually open.

NOIRMOUTIER EN L'ILE *2H3* (8km W Coastal) **Camp Municipal La Pointe, L'Herbaudière, 85330 Noirmoutier-en-l'Ile** [02 51 39 16 70; fax 02 51 39 74 15; info@noirmoutier-camping. com; www.noirmoutier-campings.com] Fr bdge to island foll sp to Noirmoutier town, then to L'Herbaudière & port. At port turn L, 500m to site. Med, mkd pitch, unshd; wc (some cont); chem disp; mv service pnt; shwrs €1; el pnts (10A) €3.50 (long leads poss req); gas; lndtte; shop; rest, snacks & bar in town; beach adj; dogs €1.50; adv bkg; quiet; CCI. "Beautiful location; gd, open, sometimes windy site with sea on 2 sides; adequate facs; helpful staff; gd rests nr; excel cycle rtes on island; highly rec." 31 Mar-4 Nov. € 13.10   2007*

NOLAY *6H1* (500m S Rural) **Camp Municipal Les Chaumes de Mont, Route de Couches, 21340 Nolay** [03 80 21 79 61; fax 03 85 91 14 13; contact@campingnolay.com] Exit A6 at junc 24.1 at Beaune & take D973 sp Nolay, Autun. Vill in 20km. Turn by Hôtel de Ville onto D33a dir Couches, site sp. Med, pt sl, terr; pt shd; wc; chem disp (wc); shwrs inc; el pnts (6A) inc; lndtte; shops 500m; snacks; BBQ (gas); playgrnd; lake sw; fishing; tennis; dogs €0.60; phone; quiet; cc not acc; CCI. "Lovely site; ideal stop en rte S; gates clsd 2200-0730; sm, interesting town; lake is meeting point for local youngsters - poss noisy." 1 May-15 Sep. € 12.80   2005*

NOLAY *6H1* (9km SW Rural) **Camp Municipal La Gabrelle, La Varenne, 71490 Couches** [03 85 45 59 49 or 03 85 98 19 20 (Mairie); fax 03 85 98 19 29; danielemaire@aol.com] Exit A6 at junc 25 Chalon-sur-Saône Nord onto D978 sp Autun. In 26km at Couches, site W of vill. Sm, hdg pitch, terr, pt shd; wc; shwrs inc; el pnts (6A) inc; lndtte; supmkt 5km; snacks; bar; playgrnd; lake adj; some daytime rd noise. "Attractive countryside nr wine area." ♦ 1 Jun-15 Sep. € 7.60   2005*

⊞**NOLAY** *6H1* (1km NW Rural) **Camping La Bruyère, Rue du Moulin Larché, 21340 Nolay** [tel/fax 03 80 21 87 59; camping.labruyere@nolay. com; www.nolay.com] Fr Beaune take D973 W dir Autun. In approx 20km, arr in vill of Nolay & cont on D973 thro vill. Site on L in 1km after vill, opp supmkt. Sm, hdg pitch, terr, pt shd; htd wc; chem disp; mv service pnt; shwrs inc; el pnts (10-16A) €3.30; lndry rm; dogs; no Eng spkn; quiet; cc acc. "Lovely site in quiet, hidden valley in wine area; gd, clean san facs; v friendly owner; Nolay bustling town with lots of rests; excel." ♦ € 12.90   2007*

NONANCOURT *4E2* (4km E Urban) **Camp Municipal du Pré de l'Eglise, Rue Pré de l'Eglise, 28380 St Rémy-sur-Avre** [02 37 48 93 87 or 02 37 62 52 00; fax 02 37 48 80 15; mairiesaintremy2@wanadoo.fr; www.ville-st-remy-sur-avre.fr] Fr Dreux take N12 W to St Rémy; at E end of by-pass, at rndabt with traff lts, turn L & then immed R at end of rv bdge. Foll camping sp. NB Speed ramps on app rd. Sm, hdg/mkd pitch (some grouped x 4), pt shd; wc; chem disp; shwrs inc; el pnts (10A) €2.66 (rev pol); lndtte; ice; shop; tradsmn; rest 500m; snacks; playgrnd; tennis & trout fishing adj; sat TV; dogs; phone; poss cr; Eng spkn; adv bkg rec high ssn; factory adj poss noisy; CCI. "Pleasant, well-maintained, popular NH; spotless facs, some modern; shwrs need update; facs ltd low ssn; friendly warden; no twin-axles (but negotiable); some pitches diff access; excel NH." ♦ 1 Apr-30 Sep. € 8.87   2007*

NONETTE see Issoire *9B1*

France

⊞**NONTRON** 7B3 (7km NE Rural) **Camping Manzac Ferme, Manzac, 24300 Augignac [05 53 56 02 62; info@manzac-ferme.com; www. manzac-ferme.com]** Fr Nontron take D675 N dir Rochechouart & after 7km on ent Augignac turn R sp Abjat-sur-Bandiat then immed R sp Manzac. Site on R 3.5km Sm, mkd pitch, pt hdstg, sl, pt shd; htd wc; chem disp; shwrs inc; el pnts (6A) inc; gas 6km; ice; shops, rest, bar 5km; BBQ; dogs by arrangement; adv bkg; quiet. "Adults only, relaxing site; ideal for birdwatching & wildlife; v helpful British owners; excel." ♦ ltd. € 18.00   2006*

NONTRON 7B3 (8km NE Rural) **Camping La Ripole, Route du Stade, 24300 Abjat-sur-Bandiat [tel/fax 05 53 56 38 81 or 06 11 51 90 25 (mob); camping. la.ripole@wanadoo.fr; www.campingripole.info]** Exit D675 at Nontron onto D707 then L onto D85; in 8km turn L onto D96 dir Abjat-sur-Bandiat; in 3km turn L into Route du Stade. Site on L in 2km. Sm, hdg pitch, pt shd; wc; chem disp (wc); shwrs inc; el pnts (6A) €3; lndtte; tradsmn; snacks; bar; BBQ (gas/elec); playgrnd; pool; lake sw; fishing; games area; games rm; entmnt; 60% statics; dogs €1.10; bus 2km; Eng spkn; adv bkg; quiet; cc acc; CCI. "Execl touring base." ♦ ltd. 15 Jun-15 Sep. € 11.30   2007*

NONTRON 7B3 (11km NE) **Camping Le Château Le Verdoyer, 24470 Champs-Romain [05 53 56 94 64; fax 05 53 56 38 70; chateau@ verdoyer.fr; www.verdoyer.fr]** Fr Limoges on N21 twd Périgueux. At Châlus turn R sp Nontron (D6 bis-D85). After approx 18km turn L twd Champs Romain on D96 to site on L in 2km. Med, terr, pt shd; wc; chem disp; baby facs; shwrs inc; el pnts (5A) inc; gas; lndtte; ice; shop; rest, B&B in chateau; bistro Jul/Aug; snacks; bar; BBQ (charcoal/ gas); playgrnd; 2 pools (1 covrd); paddling pool; waterslide; lake fishing; tennis; mini-golf; cycle hire; golf 25km; child entmnt (4-13yrs) high ssn; crèche (0-4yrs); wifi internet; games/TV rm; 20% statics; dogs €4; phone; recep 0830-2000 high ssn; poss cr; Eng spkn; adv bkg; quiet; cc acc; CCI. "Excel, peaceful site; friendly staff; superb facs; poss steep access some pitches; excursions booked in high ssn; highly rec." ♦ 26 Apr-6 Oct. € 29.00 (CChq acc) ABS - D21   2007*

⊞**NONTRON** 7B3 (1km S) **Camping de Nontron (formerly Camp Municipal Masviconteaux), 24300 Nontron [05 53 56 02 04; fax 06 30 66 25 74; terry.homain@club-internet.fr; www.campingdenontron.com]** Thro Nontron S twd Brantôme on D675. Site on o'skts of town on L nr stadium. Sp. Med, hdg/mkd pitch, pt shd; wc; mv service pnt; shwrs; el pnts (10A) inc; gas; ice; lndtte; shops adj; tradsmn; rest, snacks, bar 600m; playgrnd; pool adj; paddling pool; games area; games rm; entmnt; TV rm; statics; dogs; poss cr; Eng spkn; quiet; CCI. "V helpful staff; gd san facs; gd touring base." € 11.00   2006*

NORDAUSQUES see Ardres 3A3

NORT SUR ERDRE 2G4 (1.5km S) **Camp Municipal du Port Mulon, 44390 Nort-sur-Erdre [02 40 72 23 57; fax 02 40 72 16 09; acceuil@ mairie-nort-sur-erdre.fr; www.nort-sur-erdre.fr]** Sp fr all ents to town; foll 'Camping' & 'Hippodrome' sp. NB: C'vans banned fr town cent, look for diversion sp. Med, shd; wc; chem disp; shwrs inc; el pnts (6A) €2; lndtte; ice; supmkt 1.5km; playgrnd; tennis; fishing; boating; dogs €0.65; adv bkg; quiet; CCI. "Delightful site but area not v interesting." 1 Mar-31 Oct. € 8.00   2005*

NOTRE DAME DE MONTS 2H3 (600m N Coastal) **FFCC Camping Le Grand Jardin, 50 Route de la Barre-de-Monts, 85690 Notre-Dame-de-Monts [02 28 11 21 75; fax 02 51 59 56 66]** Fr Notre-Dame-de-Monts heading N on D38 site on R. Med, pt shd; wc; mv service pnt; baby facs; shwrs inc; el pnts (10A) €3.40; ice; lndtte; shop; rest; snacks; bar; BBQ; playgrnd; htd pool; sand beach 900m; games area; entmnt; TV; 90% statics; dogs €1.50; adv bkg; quiet. ♦ 1 Apr-31 Oct. € 19.50   2005*

> Did you know you can fill in site report forms on the Club's website — www.caravanclub.co.uk?

NOTRE DAME DE RIEZ 2H3 (1km N) **Domaine des Renardières, Route des Garateries, 85270 Notre-Dame-de-Riez [02 51 55 14 17 or 06 20 98 37 46 (mob); fax 02 51 54 96 13; caroline. raffin@free.fr; www.camping-renardieres.com]** On D38 to Notre-Dame-de-Riez. Thro vill, over rv & 1st L over rlwy to site in 1km. Med, pt shd; wc; chem disp; baby facs; shwrs inc; el pnts (6A) inc; gas; ice; lndtte lndry rm; tradsmn; rest; bar; snacks; BBQ; pool; playgrnd; sand beach 5km; TV rm; 20% statics; dogs €3; Eng spkn; adv bkg; quiet phone; 15% red low ssn; cc not acc; CCI. "Gd picturesque site; helpful owner; poss cash only; rec." ♦ ltd. 1 May-2 Sep. € 17.50   2006*

NOTRE DAME DE RIEZ 2H3 (2km SW Rural) **Camping Fonteclose, Route de Commequiers, 85270 Notre-Dame-de-Riez [02 51 55 22 22; fax 02 51 55 91 98; la.fonteclose@wanadoo. fr; www.fonteclose.com]** Sp fr D83 & D32. Med, pt shd, wc; baby facs; shwrs inc; el pnts (6A) €3; lndtte; ice; shop; rest; bar; BBQ; BBQ; playgrnd; htd pool; fishing 100m; tennis; games area; entmnt; TV; 60% statics; dogs €2; adv bkg. "Friendly site." 1 Jun-30 Sep. € 15.00   2006*

NOTRE DAME DU TOUCHET see Mortain 2E4

NOUAN LE FUZELIER *4G3* (Urban) **Camping La Grande Sologne, 1 Ave Cauchoix, 41600 Nouan-le-Fuzelier [02 54 88 70 22; fax 02 54 88 41 74; camping-lagrande-sologne@wanadoo.fr; www. nouan-le-fuzelier.fr/camping.html]** On E side of N20, at S end of Nouan opp rlwy stn. Sp fr town cent. NB Lge site sp on W side of N20 opp main ent. Lge, mkd pitch, pt shd; wc (some cont); chem disp; mv service pnt; baby facs; shwrs inc; el pnts (6-10A) €4; gas; lndtte; shops 800m; tradsmn; rest; snacks; bar; playgrnd; htd pool adj; tennis; games area; fishing; mini-golf; golf 15km; dogs €1; poss cr; Eng spkn; adv bkg; quiet; red long stay; CCI. "Pretty site with lge lake but no sw allowed; some pitches boggy in wet weather; spotless san block; ltd facs end of ssn & poss unclean; recep clsd 1200-1330; excel rest in vill; nr chateaux country; rec arr early; easy to locate fr a'route; excel." 1 Apr-2 Oct. € 14.40   2007*

NOUATRE MARCILLY see Ste Maure de Touraine *4H2*

NOUVION EN THIERACHE, LE *3B4* (1km S Urban) **Camp Municipal du Lac de Condé, Promenade Henri d'Orléans, Rue de Guise (Le Lac), 02170 Le Nouvion-en-Thiérache [03 23 98 98 58; fax 03 23 98 94 90; mairie.nouvion@wanadoo.fr; www.lenouvion.com]** Sp fr cent of Le Nouvion fr D1043 (N43) on D26, dir Guise opp chateau. Med, hdg/mkd pitch, some hdstg, pt sl, pt shd; wc; chem disp; shwrs inc; el pnts (4-8A) €2.80-3.50; ice; shop 1km; tradsmn; rest, snacks, bar 1km; BBQ; playgrnd; htd pool adj; tennis, mini-golf, canoe hire, horseriding nrby; 5% statics; dogs €0.70; phone; Eng spkn; red long stay/CCI; cc acc. "Beautiful, old-fashioned, lakeside site; gd value; warm welcome; friendly, helpful warden; gd san facs; gd for families - lots of space/play areas; gd cent for Picardy area; not suitable m'vans due sloping pitches; muddy when wet; excel." ♦ 15 Apr-15 Oct. € 8.00
                 2007*

NOYERS *4G4* (200m S Rural) **Camping Rurale, 89310 Noyers [03 86 82 83 72; fax 03 86 82 63 41; mairie-de-noyers@wanadoo.fr]** Exit A6 at Nitry & turn R onto D944. In 2km at N edge of Nitry, turn R onto D49 sp Noyers. In 10km in Noyers, turn L onto D86 sp Centre Ville/Camping. Immed after crossing rv & bef gate, turn L bet 2 obelisks. Site at end of track. Sm, mkd pitch, terr, shd; wc; own san; chem disp; shwrs inc; el pnts €1.05; shop, rest, snacks, bar 200m; BBQ; playgrnd; dogs; quiet. "Only 6 pitches; v attractive, secluded site nr Rv Serein; ent key obtained fr Mairie on R after going thro town gate, on 1st floor (€15 dep req); ltd san facs." € 4.30   2006*

⊞**NOYON** *3C3* (4km E Rural) **FFCC Camping L'Etang du Moulin, 54 Rue du Moulin, 60400 Salency [tel/fax 03 44 09 99 81 or 03 44 43 06 78]** Take D1032 (N32) fr Noyon dir Chauny. On ent Salency turn L & foll site sp. Site in 1km. Sm, pt sl, shd; htd wc; chem disp; mv service pnt; shwrs €1.50; el pnts (10A) €1.60; gas; shop, rest 4km; tradsmn; bar; BBQ; playgrnd; fishing; tennis; mini-golf; 60% statics; dogs €0.90; quiet; CCI. "San facs need maintenance & unclean (Sep 2007)." ♦ € 10.50   2007*

NOYON *3C3* (8km S Rural) **Camping Les Araucarias, 870 Rue du Général Leclerc, 60170 Carlepont [03 44 75 27 39; fax 03 44 38 12 51; camping-les-araucarias@wanadoo.fr; www. les-araucarias.com]** Fr S, fr A1 exit junc 9 or 10 for Compiègne. There take D130 sp Tracy-le-Val & Carlepont. Site on L 100m fr Carlepont vill sp. Or fr N on D934 Noyon-Soissons rd take D130 dir Carlepont & Tracy-le-Val. Site on R after vill on SW twd Compiegne. Sm, mkd pitch, pt sl, pt shd; wc; chem disp; mv service pnt; baby facs; shwrs inc; el pnts (6-10A) €2.95 (poss rev pol); gas; lndtte; ice; shop, rest, bar 1km; BBQ; playgrnd; 20% statics; dogs €1; poss cr; Eng spkn; adv bkg (dep req); quiet; CCI. "V secluded site, previously an arboretum; poss diff when wet; close Parc Astérix & La Mer-de-Sable (theme park); 85km Disneyland; vg." ♦ ltd. 21 Mar-21 Dec. € 9.00   2006*

NOZAY *2G4* (8km NW Rural) **Camp Municipal La Roche, 44170 Marsac-sur-Don [02 40 87 54 77 (Mairie); fax 02 40 87 51 29; mairie.marsacsurdon@wanadoo.fr]** Fr N137 turn W onto D124 to Marsac-sur-Don. Fr vill take D125 W dir Guénouvry, site sp. Sm, mkd pitch, pt sl, pt shd; wc; shwrs; el pnts €2.10; rest, bar nrby; playgrnd; fishing; games area; walking circuit; quiet; CCI. "Gd basic site; own san rec; vg value." 1 May-30 Sep. € 5.00   2006*

NUITS ST GEORGES *6G1* (3km SW Urban) **Camping Le Moulin de Prissey, 21700 Premeaux-Prissey [03 80 62 31 15; fax 03 80 61 37 29]** Exit Beaune on D974 (N74) twd Nuits-St Georges & Dijon; app Premeaux-Prissey turn R soon after vill sp, under rlwy bdge & foll site sp. Fr A31 exit at Nuits-St Georges & foll camp sp for Saule-Guillaume, thro Premeaux-Prissey & foll site sp. Sm, mkd pitch, pt sl, pt shd; wc (some cont); chem disp (wc); mv service pnt; shwrs inc; el pnts (6A) €3.50; gas; lndtte; ice; shops 3km; tradsmn; snacks; rest, bar 4km; BBQ; playgrnd; dogs €0.90; poss cr; adv bkg; noisy rlwy adj; cc not acc; CCI. "Arr early; popular NH; sm pitches; access poss diff for lge o'fits; gd cent Beaune wine area; lots of quiet minor rds for cycling." ♦ ltd. 1 Apr-15 Oct. € 13.35
                 2007*

France

NUITS ST GEORGES *6G1* (6km SW Rural) Camp Intercommuncal Saule Guillaume, 21700 Premeaux-Prissey [03 80 62 30 78 or 03 80 61 27 99 (LS); fax 03 80 61 35 19] Fr A31 to 1st rndabt & foll sp for camping via Quincey. Med, hdg pitch, pt shd; wc (some cont); shwrs inc; el pnts (6-12A) €2.80-4.30; ice; shop & 7km; tradsmn; playgrnd; lake beach, fishing, boating & sw adj; dogs €2; poss cr; Eng spkn; adv bkg; quiet but some rd & rlwy noise; CCI. "Facs poss unclean; helpful staff; gd rest; fair." 14 Jun-1 Sep. € 9.10
2004*

NYOISEAU see Segré *2F4*

This guide relies on site report forms submitted by caravanners like us; we'll do our bit and tell the editor what we think of the campsites we've visited.

NYONS *9D2* (1km NE Rural) Camping Les Clos, Route de Gap, 26110 Nyons [04 75 26 29 90; fax 04 75 26 49 44; camping-les-clos@clario. fr; www.campinglesclos.com] Fr rndabt in town cent take D94 sp Gap & site on R in 1km. Med, hdg/mkd pitch, hdstg, pt shd; wc; chem disp; shwrs inc; baby facs; el pnts (6A) inc; gas; lndtte; ice; shop; rest 1km; snacks; bar; BBQ (gas/elec only); playgrnd; pool; shgl rv beach & fishing; entmnt (ltd); 20% statics; dogs €2; phone; poss v cr; Eng spkn; adv bkg (dep & fee req) red low ssn; cc acc; CCI. "Excel site in lovely area; beautiful scenery; v quiet; clean & well-kept; friendly, helpful staff; excel touring cent for Drôme Provençale." ♦ 24 Mar-21 Oct. € 18.50
2007*

NYONS *9D2* (3km NE Rural) Camping L'Or Vert, 26110 Aubres [04 75 26 24 85; fax 04 75 26 17 89; camping-or-vert@wanadoo.fr; www.camping-or-vert.com] Fr Nyons take D94 twd Serre, site on R of rd on rvside. Med, hdg/mkd pitch, hdstg, pt sl, pt shd; wc (cont); chem disp; shwrs inc; el pnts (6A) €3.60; gas; lndtte; ice; shop; snacks; playgrnd; pool 3km; rv adj; fishing; tennis 600m; games area; entmnt; TV; some statics; dogs €1.80 (not acc Jul/Aug); quiet; cc not acc. "Interesting scenic countryside; min stay 10 days Jul-Aug; nice rv site; ltd facs low ssn; phone ahead to check opening dates low ssn; v clean facs." 1 Apr-1 Oct. € 13.30
2006*

NYONS *9D2* (10km NE Rural) Camping Le Chambron, Route de St Pons, 26110 Condorcet [tel/fax 04 75 27 70 54] Fr Nyons on D94 dir Serres. In 7km turn L onto D70 to Condorcet & foll site sp. Med, shd; wc; shwrs inc; el pnts (6A) €2.50; lndry rm; tradsmn; bar; playgrnd; pool; tennis; 10% statics; dogs €1; quiet. 1 Apr-30 Sep. € 10.50
2005*

NYONS *9D2* (12km NE Rural) Camping de Trente Pas, 26110 St Ferréol-Trente-Pas [04 75 27 70 69; contact@campingtrentepas.com; www.camping trentepas.com] Exit A7 junc 19 Bollène onto D994 & D94. L on D70 to St Ferréol-Trente-Pas. Site 100m fr vill on banks of stream. Med, shd; wc; shwrs; el pnts (6A) €2.80; lndry rm; shop & snacks high ssn; playgrnd; pool; games rm; tennis; cycle hire; horseriding 4km; entmnt; TV; 20% statics; dogs €1.60. "Lovely area with beautiful scenery; v quiet low ssn; excel value; gd, v clean san facs; gd views & pool; rec." 1 May-31 Aug. € 13.20
2007*

NYONS *9D2* (12km NE Rural) FFCC Camping Le Pilat, 26110 St Ferréol-Trente-Pas [04 75 27 72 09; fax 04 75 27 72 34; info@ campinglepilat.com; www.campinglepilat.com] Fr D94 N or Nyons turn N at La Bonté onto D70 to St Ferréol, site sp 1km N of vill. Med, hdg pitch, shd; wc (some cont); chem disp; shwrs inc; el pnts (6A) €3; lndtte; shop high ssn & 3km; tradsmn; snacks; playgrnd; covrd pool; paddling pool; lake sw adj; games area; entmnt; TV; 25% statics; dogs €1.30; phone; Eng spkn; quiet; CCI. "Site among lavender fields; beautiful area; Thurs mkt Nyons; v pleasant, helpful owners; clean facs; gd walking & off-rd cycling; excel." ♦ 1 Apr-30 Sep. € 16.10
2006*

NYONS *9D2* (12km E Rural) Camp Municipal Les Cigales, Allée des Platanes, 26110 Ste-Jalle [04 75 27 34 88 or 04 75 27 32 78 (mairie)] Fr Nyons take D94 dir Serres; in 10 km at Curnier turn R onto D64 to Ste-Jalle. In vill turn R onto D108 dir Buis-les-Baronnies. Site on R in 300m. NB Dist by rd fr Nyons is 20km. Sm, hdg pitch, pt shd; wc; chem disp; shwrs inc; el pnts (10A) €2.20; ice; shop, rest, snacks, bar 300m; playgrnd; 15% statics; dogs; adv bkg. "V quiet in attractive old vill with gd rests; vg." 1 May-30 Sep. € 7.40
2006*

⊞**NYONS** *9D2* (6km SW Rural) Camping Domaine Le Sagittaire, Le Pont de Mirabel, 26110 Vinsobres [04 75 27 00 00; fax 04 75 27 00 39; camping.sagittaire@wanadoo.fr;www.le-sagittaire. com] Fr Nyons on D94, sp Orange, site on L just after junc with D4, well sp. Lge, hdg pitch, pt shd; htd wc; chem disp; shwrs inc; el pnts (6-10A) €3.40-4,40; gas; lndtte; shop; tradsmn; rest, snacks, bar in ssn; playgrnd; htd, covrd pool; waterslide; cycle hire; entmnt; TV; 25% statics; dogs €4.10; poss cr; adv bkg (bkg fee & dep req) quiet but some rd noise on edge of site; red long stay/low ssn; cc acc; CCI. "Part of holiday complex in attractive, uncommercialised area." € 25.50
2005*

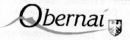

NYONS *9D2* (7km SW Rural) **Camp Municipal Chez Antoinette, Champessier, 26110 Vinsobres** [04 75 27 61 65 or 04 75 27 64 49 (Mairie); fax 04 75 27 59 20; camping-municipal@club-internet.fr] Fr Nyons on D94 sp Orange. Turn R 500m after junc with D4 twd Vinsobres vill. Site 500m on L bef vill. Sm, mkd pitch, pt shd; htd wc; chem disp; shwrs inc; el pnts (6A) €2.70; lndry rm; BBQ; playgrnd; adv bkg; quiet; cc acc; CCI. "Peaceful, v popular site; cramped san facs; steep unhill walk to vill; excel touring area." ♦ Easter-30 Oct. € 8.20   2006*

NYONS *9D2* (4km NW Urban) **Camping Les Terrasses Provençales, Les Barroux-Novezan, 26110 Venterol** [tel/fax 04 75 27 92 36; novezan@lesterrassesprovencales.com; www.lesterrassesprovencales.com] Exit A7/E15 at junc 18 sp Nyons. Join D541 E twd Nyons. Site in Venterol, sp bet Valréas & Nyons. Med, hdg/mkd pitch, hdstg, terr, pt shd; wc; chem disp; baby facs; fam bthrm; shwrs inc; el pnts (10A) €3.70 (poss rev pol); gas; lndtte; shop 6km; tradsmn; rest, bar 2km; playgrnd; pool; dogs low ssn only €1.85; poss cr; some Eng spkn; quiet; cc acc; CCI. "Owner will tow c'van onto terr pitch; pizza delivery twice weekly; excel." ♦ 1 Apr-30 Sep. € 16.00   2007*

OBERNAI *6E3* (10km N Urban) **Camp Municipal de Molsheim, 9 Rue des Sports, 67120 Molsheim** [03 88 49 82 45 or 03 88 49 58 58 (LS); fax 03 8 49 58 59; www.mairie-molsheim.fr] On ent town fr Obernai on D1422 (D422) site sp on R immed after x-ing sm rv bdge. Med, mkd pitch, pt shd; wc; chem disp; mv service pnt; shwrs inc; el pnts €2.50; lndtte; tradsmn; BBQ; pool adj; cycle hire; dogs €1.10; train to Strasbourg 700m; poss cr; Eng spkn; adv bkg; quiet; CCI. "Easy walk to town cent & shops." ♦ 1 May-30 Sep. € 11.30   2007*

⊞**OBERNAI** *6E3* (1km W Urban) **Camp Municipal Le Vallon de l'Ehn, 1 Rue de Berlin, 67210 Obernai** [03 88 95 38 48; fax 03 88 48 31 47; camping@obernai.fr; www.obernai.fr] Fr Strasbourg SW on D1422 (D422)/A35; leave at junc 11 sp Obernai; on ent town, turn L at 2nd rndabt (McDonalds) sp D426 Ottrott; in 3km after 3rd rndabt turn R at T-junc sp Obernai then almost immed L at camping sp; site on L in 200m, sp but obscure. Look for sp Camping VVF. Fr S on A35, exit at junc 12 sp Obernai. Foll sp Obernai, then Centre Ville, then site. Lge, mkd pitch, hdstg, pt sl, pt shd; htd wc; chem disp; mv service pnt; 75% serviced pitches; baby facs; shwrs inc; el pnts (16A) €3.70; gas 1km; ice; lndtte; sm shop & 1km; tradsmn; BBQ; playgrnd; pool 200m, tennis, horseriding adj; cab TV; internet; dogs; bus; train; poss cr; Eng spkn; adv bkg; quiet; cc acc; 5% red C'van Club members; cc acc; red CCI. "Attractive, busy, well-run site; well-maintained; superb clean facs; sm pitches; warm welcome; v friendly & helpful staff; recep clsd 1230-1400; rec arr early high ssn; c'vans, m'vans & tents all sep areas; bus to Obernai adj, bus to Strasbourg 500m; easy walk to attractive old town; highly rec." ♦ € 12.70   2007*

See advertisement

OCTON *10F1* (Rural) **Camping Le Village du Bosc (Naturist), Ricazouls, 34800 Octon** [04 67 96 07 37; fax 04 67 96 35 75; www.villagedubosc.net] Exit 54 or 55 fr N9/A75 dir Octon onto D148, foll sp to Ricazouls/site. Med, terr, pt shd; wc; chem disp; shwrs; el pnts (6A) inc; rest; snacks; bar; shop; lndtte; playgrnd; htd pool; lake sw; watersports; 20% statics; dogs €1.90; poss cr; Eng spkn; adv bkg; CCI. "Tight turns on terr access for lge o'fits; v pleasant naturist site (INF card reqd) with wooded walks on site; Octon vill pretty." ♦ ltd. 1 Apr-30 Sep. € 23.20   2007*

France

OCTON 10F1 (4km E Rural) **Aire Naturelle Les Arcades (Gros-Fromenty), Lac-de-Salagou, 34800 Octon [04 67 96 99 13]** Sp fr Octon. Sm, pt shd; wc; chem disp (wc); shwrs inc; no el pnts; BBQ; fishing nrby; quiet. "Excel clean & tidy; lge pitches under acacia trees; gd views; no el pnts; vg." 15 May-30 Sep. € 14.50   2007*

The opening dates and prices on this campsite have changed. I'll send a site report form to the editor for the next edition of the guide.

OCTON 10F1 (600m SE Rural) **Camping Le Mas des Carles, 34800 Octon [04 67 96 32 33]** Leave A75 at junc 54, foll sp for Octon, 100m after vill sp turn L & foll white site sp keeping L. Ent on L opp tel kiosk (sharp turn). Sm, some hdg/mkd pitch, pt sl, terr, pt shd, pt shd; wc; chem disp; shwrs inc; el pnts (6-10A) inc; lndtte; lndry rm; ice; shop 500m; rest adj; playgrnd; pool; boating/watersports in lake 800m; 30% statics; dogs; phone; poss cr; adv bkg; quiet; cc not acc; CCI. "Lovely views, v pleasant site; facs a little tired; helpful owner; take care low branches on pitches - diff for c'vans; Lac de Salagou with abandoned vill of Celles 1km." 1 Apr-15 Oct. € 21.40   2007*

OFFRANVILLE see Dieppe 3C2

OLARGUES 8F4 (N Rural) **Camp Municipal Le Baoüs, 34390 Olargues [04 67 97 71 26 or 04 67 97 71 50; otsi.olargues@wanadoo.fr; www. olargues.org]** Take D908 W fr Bédarieux, site immed bef ent Olargues. Site sp over sm bdge on L. At end of bdge turn R to site. Last 50m rough track & narr turn into site. Sm, pt shd; wc (cont); chem disp; shwrs inc; el pnts (6A) €2.20; shop 300m; playgrnd; canoeing; cycle hire; internet; adv bkg Jul/Aug; quiet. "Helpful warden; hill climb to services block; site poss flooded by Rv Jaur in spring; lovely mountain area." 15 May-15 Sep.
2006*

OLLIERES SUR EYRIEUX, LES 9D2 (Rural) **Camping Le Chambourlas, 07360 Les Ollières-sur-Eyrieux [04 75 66 24 31; fax 04 75 66 21 22; lechambourlas@aol.com; www.chambourlas. com]** Fr Aubenas take N304 dir Privas. At Privas, turn R at 1st traff lts twd Le Cheylard (D2). Site on R in 14km at Les Ollières. Steep site ent. Med, mkd pitch, shd; wc; chem disp; baby facs; shwrs inc; el pnts (10A) inc; gas; lndtte; ice; shop; rest; snacks; bar; BBQ; playgrnd; pool; paddling pool; lake sw & fishing; canoe hire; sports area; organised excursions; TV rm; 10% statics; dogs €2.50; adv bkg; cc acc. "Warm welcome; some v lge pitches; gd nature walks fr site." ♦ Easter-2 Oct. € 23.50 (CChq acc)   2005*

OLLIERES SUR EYRIEUX, LES 9D2 (Rural) **Camping Le Domaine des Plantas, 07360 Les Ollières-sur-Eyrieux [04 75 66 21 53; fax 04 75 66 23 65; plantas.ardeche@wanadoo. fr; www.domainedesplantas.com or www. campings-franceloc.com]** Exit A7 junc 16, cross Rv Rhône on N304 to Le Pouzin, then turn N thro La Voulte-sur-Rhône. Then take D120 sp St Fortunat, 20km to Les Ollières; over bdge, turn L & foll site sp. Med, hdg/mkd pitch, hdstg, terr, pt shd; wc; chem disp; mv service pnt; baby facs; shwrs inc; el pnts (10A) inc; gas; lndtte; ice; shop & 2km; rest; snacks; bar; playgrnd; htd, covrd pool; rv sw & sand beach adj; fishing; hiking; games rm; child entmnt; 30% statics; dogs €3; Eng spkn; adv bkg ess; quiet; cc acc; red low ssn; CCI. "Beautiful site in wondrous setting; well wooded; warm-hearted owners; gd san facs; v highly rec; interesting rest; c'vans can only leave when accompanied 0800, 0930 & 1100; 4x4 used to take c'vans up v steep exit; excel." ♦ 5 Apr-4 Oct. € 31.00 (CChq acc)
2007*

OLLIERES SUR EYRIEUX, LES 9D2 (Rural) **Camping Le Mas de Champel, Route de La Voulte-sur-Rhône, 07360 Les Ollières-sur-Eyrieux [04 75 66 23 23; fax 04 75 66 23 16; masdechampel@wanadoo.fr; www.masde champel.com]** Fr N86 W on D120 at La Voulte-sur-Rhône or D21 at Beauchastel. Rds join at St Laurent-du-Pape. Cont on D120, turn R soon after D2 on ent Les Ollières bef descent into vill. Site sp. Med, terr, unshd; wc; chem disp; shwrs inc; el pnts (10A) inc; lndtte; shops 1km; rest; snacks; bar; playgrnd; pool; paddling pool; rv sw; fishing; canoeing; guided walks; cycle hire; archery; solarium; entmnt; some statics; poss cr; adv bkg; quiet. "Pleasant site in lovely countryside." ♦ 28 Apr-22 Sep. € 24.00   2005*

Before we move on, I'm going to fill in some site report forms and post them off to the editor, otherwise they won't arrive in time for the deadline at the end of September.

OLLIERES SUR EYRIEUX, LES 9D2 (Rural) **Eyrieux Camping, La Fereyre, 07360 Les Ollières-sur-Eyrieux [04 75 66 30 08; fax 04 75 66 63 76; blotjm@aol.com]** Exit N86 at Beauchastel via D21 to D120. In 15km site on L bef ent Les Ollières. App via 500m of steep, unmade single track rd with unexpected hairpin bend at bottom. For sm vans & experienced drivers only. Med, pt sl, terr, pt shd; wc; chem disp; shwrs inc; baby facs; el pnts (6A) inc; ice; shop & 500m; rest; snacks; bar; playgrnd; pool; rv sw & fishing adj; tennis; games area; cycle hire; mini-golf; entmnt; dogs €2.30; adv bkg; quiet. ♦ Easter-17 Sep. € 21.50   2006*

OLLIERES SUR EYRIEUX, LES *9D2* (10km NW Rural) **L'Ardechois Camping, Le Chambon, 07190 Gluiras [04 75 66 61 87; fax 04 75 66 63 67; ardechois.camping@wanadoo.fr; www.ardechois-camping.fr]** Exit A7 junc 15 or 16 & cross rv onto N86. Turn W at Beauchastel onto D120 dir Le Cheylard to St Sauveur. In St Sauveur foll D102 dir Mézilhac & St Pierreville. Site approx 8km on bank Rv Glueyre. Med, hdg/mkd pitch, terr, shd; htd wc (mainly cont); chem disp; mv service pnt; shwrs inc; el pnts (6-10A) inc; gas; lndtte; shop & 8km; tradsmn; rest high ssn; snacks; bar; playgrnd; htd pool; paddling pool; rv & sand beach adj; cycle hire; games area; internet; TV rm; 70% statics; dogs €4; Eng spkn; adv bkg ess in ssn; cc acc; red low ssn/snr citizens; CCI. "Wonderful, friendly, family site in glorious countryside; organised walks, picnics; excel rest; v helpful Dutch owners." ♦ 27 Apr-30 Oct. € 26.50 (CChq acc)
2006*

There aren't many sites open this early in the year. We'd better phone ahead to check that the one we're heading for is actually open.

OLONNE SUR MER see Sables d'Olonne, Les *7A1*

OLONZAC *8F4* (6km N Rural) **Camping Le Mas de Lignières (Naturist), Montcélèbre, 34210 Cesseras-en-Minervois [tel/fax 04 68 91 24 86; mas.lignieres@tiscali.fr; www.languedoc-naturisme.com/mdl]** Fr Olonzac go N on D182 thro Cesseras & cont N dir Fauzan. Site sp. Access narr last 4km after Olonzac, care needed thro Cesseras. Sm, hdg/mkd pitch, hdstg, pt sl, pt shd; wc (some cont); chem disp; baby facs; fam bthrm; shwrs inc; el pnts (6-10A) €3-4.50; gas; lndtte; sm shop & 2km; tradsmn; covrd pool; tennis; library; TV rm; 5% statics; dogs €1.50; phone; poss cr; adv bkg; red 10 days; quiet; cc acc; INF card ess & avail at site. "Magnificent scenery, gorges; well-run site; lge pitches; gd san facs; wonderful walks." ♦ ltd 1 Apr-15 Oct. € 23.00
2005*

⊞**OLONZAC** *8F4* (9km E Rural) **Camping Les Auberges, 11120 Pouzols-Minervois [tel/fax 04 68 46 26 50; vero.pradal@neuf.fr; http://pagesperso-orange.fr/xanne/camping/]** Fr D5 site 500m S of vill of Pouzols. Sm, mkd pitch, pt shd; wc; chem disp (wc); shwrs inc; el pnts (6A) €5; gas adj; lndtte; ice; shop adj; playgrnd; pool; 30% statics; dogs; poss cr; Eng spkn; adv bkg rec; quiet; CCI. "V popular site; friendly owners; sm Sat mkt at 'cave' opp." € 10.00
2006*

OLORON STE MARIE *8F2* (6km S Rural) **Camping Val du Gave d'Aspe, 6 Rue de Lazères, 64400 Gurmençon [05 59 36 05 07; fax 05 59 36 00 52; chalet.aspe@wanadoo.fr; www.chalet-aspe.com]** Fr Oloron on N134 sp in 10km vill of Gurmençon. L past church then immed R (to avoid diff ent). Site in 100m. Sm, hdg pitch, terr, pt shd; wc; shwrs inc; el pnts (10A) inc; lndtte; tradsmn; shop & rest 200m; bar; playgrnd; pool; cycle hire; mostly statics; dogs; phone 100m; poss cr; adv bkg (dep req); quiet; red low ssn; CCI. "Excel site on Col du Somport rte to Spain; gd clean facs; helpful & friendly warden; ltd touring pitches, espec low ssn; low hanging trees; poss diff access." ♦ 1 Apr-1 Nov. € 15.00
2005*

Did you know you can fill in site report forms on the Club's website — www.caravanclub.co.uk?

France

OLORON STE MARIE *8F2* (2km W Urban) **Camping-Gîtes du Stade, Chemin de Lagravette, 64400 Oloron-Ste Marie [05 59 39 11 26; fax 05 59 36 12 01; camping-du-stade@wanadoo.fr]** Fr N on ring rd foll sp to Sarragosse (Spain); at rndabt take 2nd exit onto D6 still sp Sarragosse, site sp on R just after sports field. Med, hdg/mkd pitch, pt shd; wc; chem disp; shwrs inc; el pnts (6-10A) €3-5.50 (some rev pol); lndry rm; ice; tradsmn; supmkt 1km; rest; snacks; playgrnd; pool adj; rv fishing & sw 1km; tennis; cycle hire; entmnts; TV; dogs €1.20; adv bkg; CCI. "Well-maintained, v quiet site; lge pitches; spotless facs but stretched in ssn; barrier clsd 1200-1500; excel base for Pyrenees; open for wintersports; gd walking." 1 May-30 Sep. € 14.00
2005*

OMONVILLE LA ROGUE see Beaumont Hague *1C4*

ONESSE ET LAHARIE *8E1* (Rural) **Camp Municipal Bienvenue, 259 Route de Mimizan, 40110 Onesse-et-Laharie [05 58 07 30 49 or 05 58 07 30 10; fax 05 58 07 30 78]** On N10 Bordeaux-Bayonne rd, turn W onto D38 at Laharie. Site in 5km. Med, mkd pitch, pt shd; wc (some cont); chem disp; shwrs inc; el pnts (6A) €2.60; lndtte; shop 100m; rest, bar adj; playgrnd; beach 20km; quiet; adv bkg; red long stay; CCI. "Well-run, family site." 15 Jun-15 Sep. € 12.55
2004*

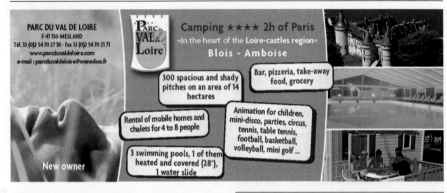

ONZAIN *4G2* (4km N Rural) **Camping Domaine de Dugny, 45 Route de Chambon-sur-Cisse, 41150 Onzain** [02 54 20 70 66; fax 02 54 33 71 69; info@ dugny.fr; www.camping-de-dugny.fr] Exit A10 junc 17 Blois onto N152 dir Tours. After 16km at rndabt at bdge to Chaumont, turn N dir Onzain. Take D45 N dir Chambon-sur-Cisse to Cabinette. Site sp on a minor rd to L, beside sm lake. Site well sp fr Onzain cent. Lge, hdg/mkd pitch, hdstg, pt sl, pt shd; htd wc; chem disp; mv service pnt; serviced pitches; baby facs; fam bthrm; shwrs inc; el pnts (6-10A) €5.50; gas; lndtte; ice; shop; tradsmn; rest; snacks; bar; BBQ; playgrnd; htd pool & paddling pool; waterslide; lake sw & 10km; fishing; cycle hire; games rm; games area; golf 8km; boules; boat hire; entmnt high ssn; ultra-light flights; TV rm; internet; 10% statics; dogs €4.50; train 4km; Eng spkn; adv bkg; quiet; cc acc; red low ssn; CCI. "Peaceful site; v welcoming; clean san facs but ltd low ssn; chateaux close by - World Heritage site; gd facs for children; new management 2007; ideal NH." ♦ 31 Mar-29 Sep. € 40.00 (CChq acc)   2007*

ONZAIN *4G2* (6km W Rural) **Camping Le Parc du Val de Loire, 155 Route de Fleuray, 41150 Mesland** [02 54 70 27 18; fax 02 54 70 21 71; parcduvaldeloire@wanadoo.fr; www.parcdu valdeloire.com] Fr Blois take N152 SW twd Amboise. Approx 16km outside Blois turn R to Onzain & foll sp to Mesland; go thro Mesland vill & turn L dir Fleuray; site on R after 1.5km. Lge, hdg/mkd pitch, pt sl, pt shd; wc; chem disp; mv service pnt; serviced pitches; baby facs; shwrs inc; el pnts (10A) inc; gas; lndtte; shop; tradsmn; rest; snacks; bar; BBQ; playgrnd; 2 pools (1 htd, covrd); paddling pool; waterslide; tennis; games area; mini-golf; cycle hire; wine-tasting; entmnt; child entmnt; wifi internet; games/TV rm; 30% statics; dogs €5; Eng spkn; adv bkg; cc acc; red low ssn/ CCI. "Secluded site; conv Loire chateaux; visits arranged to vineyards; mkt Thu Onzain; excel." ♦ 5 Apr-27 Sep. € 30.50 ABS - L02   2007*

See advertisement

OPIO see Grasse *10E4*

OPPEDE see Cavaillon *10E2*

ONZAIN *4G2* (1.5km SE) **Camp Municipal, Ave Général de Gaulle, 41150 Onzain** [02 54 20 85 15 or 02 54 51 20 40 (Mairie); fax 02 54 20 74 34; marie@ville-onzain.fr; www.ville-onzain.fr] Fr N of Chaumont-sur-Loire, at rndabt at junc N152 & D1 take D1 N twds Onzain then take 1st turn on R. Foll sp. Sm, hdg pitch, pt sl, pt shd; wc (some cont); chem disp; shwrs inc; el pnts (10A) €1.84; gas; lndtte; ice; shops 500m; playgrnd; dogs €1.53; no twin-axle vans; gates locked 2000-0800; poss cr; some rd & rlwy noise; cc not acc; CCI. "Rlwy service to Paris; central for Loire chateaux; clsd 2200-0800." ♦ 1 May-31 Aug. € 6.42   2007*

ORANGE *10E2* (6km N Rural) **Camping La Ferme de Rameyron (Pellegrin), Chemin de Roard, Route de Camaret-sur-Aigues, 84830 Sérignan-du-Comtat** [04 90 70 06 48] Fr Orange on N7 dir Bollène turn R sp Sérignan-du-Comtat. In town cent turn R at x-rds sp Camaret. Turn 3rd R into Chemin de Roard. Site on L in 100m. Sm, pt shd; wc (some cont); chem disp; mv service pnt; shwrs inc; el pnts (10A) €1.50; gas, shops, rest, bar 800m; playgrnd; pool; dogs; poss cr; quiet; cc acc. "CL-type site; clean, pleasant site but poss run down low ssn & cold shwrs; close to historic vill; 5km fr m'way." 1 Jun-31 Aug. € 10.00   2006*

ORANGE *10E2* (10km NE Rural) **Aire Naturelle Domaine des Favards, Route d'Orange, 84150 Violès [04 90 70 90 93; fax 04 90 70 97 28; favards@free.fr]** Fr N exit A7 junc 19 Bollène. Foll D8 dir Carpentras & Violès. In Violès foll dir Orange & look for camp sp. Fr S exit A7 junc 22 sp Carpentras, take dir Avignon, then dir Vaison-la-Romaine to Violès. Avoid cent of Orange when towing. Sm, hdg/mkd pitch, unshd; htd wc (some cont); baby facs; shwrs inc; el pnts (6-10A) €3 (poss rev pol); lndry rm; tradsmn; snacks; bar; playgrnd; pool; dogs €1; poss cr; Eng spkn; adv bkg; quiet; no cc acc; red low ssn; CCI. "Well-maintained site; excel pitches - some v lge; superb shwr block & laundry; facs poss stretched; wine-tasting on site high ssn; gd touring base; dust clouds fr Mistral wind; gd." ♦ 26 Apr-1 Oct. € 14.00   2007*

ORANGE *10E2* (8km SE Urban) **Camp Municipal Les Peupliers, Ave Pierre-de-Coubertin, 84150 Jonquières [04 90 70 67 09; fax 04 90 70 59 01]** Exit junc 22 fr A7 onto N7 S. In 2km turn L (E) onto D950. In 5km at rndabt turn L onto D977. In 200m turn L sp Jonquières, site on L in 2km, sp in vill. Site behind sports complex. Sp not obvious. Med, mkd pitch, pt shd; wc; chem disp; shwrs inc; el pnts (10A) inc; gas 500m; lndtte; ice; shop, rest, snacks, bar 500m; playgrnd; pool; tennis adj; dogs €2.65; phone; poss cr; Eng spkn; adv bkg; noise fr airfield (week days); cc not acc; CCI. "Excel site; friendly & welcoming owners; v well-run, busy site; v clean san facs; shwrs excel; need care with high o'fits due trees; arr bef 1600; gates close 2200; extensive Roman ruins nrby; popular long stay." 1 May-30 Sep. € 10.55   2007*

ORANGE *10E2* (1.5km NW Urban) **Camping Le Jonquier, 1321 Rue Alexis Carrel, 84100 Orange [04 90 34 49 48; fax 04 90 51 16 97; info@campinglejonquier.com; www.camping lejonquier.com]** Site N of Arc de Triomphe off N7; turn W at traff lts to site in 500m & foll site sp across rndabt, R at next rndabt. Med, hdg/mkd pitch, mostly unshd; wc (some cont); chem disp; mv service pnt; baby facs; shwrs inc; el pnts (3A) inc; lndtte; ice; supmkt 500m; bar; playgrnd; htd pool; tennis; mini-golf; pony rides; some statics; dogs €4.50; poss cr; Eng spkn; quiet; cc acc; CCI. "1.5km walk into historic town; helpful staff; unkempt low ssn; san facs poss stretched high ssn; lge mkt Thurs." ♦ 31 Mar-30 Sep. € 27.00   2007*

ORBEC *3D1* (Urban) **Camp Municipal les Capucins, 14290 Orbec [02 31 32 76 22]** Exit A28 junc 15 to Orbec; on ent town foll site sp. If app fr D519 or D819 steep drag up to site & care req down to town. Sm, pt shd; wc; chem disp; shwrs inc; el pnts (10A) €2; shops 800m; playgrnd; quiet. "Sm immac site; san facs old but clean; no twin-axles; delightful countryside." 24 May-8 Sep. € 7.40
          2007*

ORBEY see Munster *6F3*

ORCET see Clermont Ferrand *9B1*

ORCHAMPS see Dampierre *6G2*

⊞**ORCIVAL** *7B4* (6km NE Rural) **FFCC Camping La Haute Sioule, 63210 St Bonnet-près-Orcival [04 73 65 83 32; fax 04 73 65 85 19; hautesioule@ wanadoo.fr; www.camping-hautesioule.com]** Fr Clermont-Ferrand take N89 S then W twds La Bourboule for approx 20km. At junc with D216 turn L twds Orcival. Site in 4km. Foll site sp. Med, sl, pt shd; wc; mv service pnt; shwrs inc; el pnts (4-13A) €2.30-5.50; gas; lndtte; shops 250m; snacks; playgrnd; rv sw adj; golf; fishing adj; games rm; entmnt; 50% statics; poss cr; Eng spkn; CCI. "Owners friendly; v pleasant late ssn but poss untidy; poss diff for lge o'fits; ltd facs low ssn & no recep, site self; fair NH." € 12.70   2006*

> As soon as we get home I'm going to post all these site report forms to the editor for inclusion in next year's guide. I don't want to miss the September deadline.

⊞**ORGEVAL** *3D3* (2km N Rural) **Caravaning Club des Renardières, Route Vermouillet, 78670 Villennes-sur-Seine [01 39 75 88 97]** E on A13 twd Paris take exit sp Poissy. Foll Orgeval & Centre Commercial sp at rndabt. In approx 2km turn R immed after lge green Habitat warehouse. Site 1km on L after 2nd x-rds. No site sp so look for title on wall of white building on L. Or W on A13, foll sp to Poissy & Villennes, & immed after a'route turn L (over dual c'way), as above. Steep access, narr gate; check on foot bef ent site. Lge, mkd pitch, pt sl, terr, shd; htd wc (some cont); shwrs inc; el pnts (6A) (rev pol); gas; shops 4km; 90% statics; dogs; Eng spkn; adv bkg (dep req); quiet; CCI. "Conv Paris by RER fr Poissy; friendly recep open Mon-Fri 1000-1800 & clsd for lunch 1200-1400; do not rec arr/depart Sat/Sun; simple, spacious site; basic but clean htd facs; twin-axle vans over 8m not acc." ♦ ltd. € 11.50   2006*

ORINCLES see Bagneres de Bigorre *8F2*

ORLEANS *4F3* (10km E Rural) **Camp Municipal Les Pâtures, 55 Chemin du Port, 45440 Chécy [02 38 91 13 27]** Take D960 E twd Châteauneuf. In Chécy, foll site sp. Access thro town v narr streets. Med, hdg pitch, pt shd; wc; chem disp; mv service pnt; shwrs €0.30/3 mins; el pnts (16A) inc; lndtte; ice; shop 1km; BBQ; tennis; fishing; golf 5km; no statics; dogs; Eng spkn; adv bkg; some noise fr adj site; CCI. "Superb, refurbished site on banks of Rv Loire; helpful warden; gd clean san facs; gd walking; conv Orléans." ♦ 28 May-3 Sep. € 12.90
          2006*

ORLEANS *4F3* (4km S Urban) **Camp Municipal d'Olivet, Rue du Pont-Bouchet, 45160 Olivet [02 38 63 53 94 or 02 38 63 82 82 (Mairie); fax 02 38 63 58 96; campingolivet@wanadoo.fr; www.camping-olivet.org]** N on N20 bef Orléans sp on RH side turn R opp Auchan supmkt foll sp; at 1km turn R at rndabt over rv bdge (3,500 kg weight limit/3.1m height restriction) over rv bdge & L at traff lts on D14 & L down Rue de Pont-Boucher; narr app rd. To avoid height restriction, fr A71 exit junc 2 onto N271 dir Orléans-La Source. Cont on N271 until rd crosses N20 keeping L at all forks until Rue de Bourges. Turn L at 2nd traff lts into Rue de Châteauroux, turn L at traff lts onto D14, Rue de la Source then in 500m R into Rue to Pont-Boucher (narr rd). Sp from Olivet but sps diff to pick out (sm, green). NB Beware height restrictions on junc underpasses in Orléans cent. Med, hdg pitch, pt sl, pt shd; htd wc (some cont); chem disp; shwrs inc; el pnts (16A) inc; lndtte; ice; shop 500m; tradsmn; snacks; playgrnd; dogs €2; bus/tram 200m (secure car park); poss cr; Eng spkn; adv bkg rec, confirm by tel bef 1800 (booking fee & dep); quiet - poss noisy at w/e; red long stay; CCI. "Well-run, busy, friendly site by Rv Loiret; vg san facs; excel tram service into town; vineyards nr; gd walking." ♦ 1 Apr-31 Oct. € 15.68   2007*

ORLEANS *4F3* (10km SW Rural) **Camping Fontaine de Rabelais, Chemin de la Plage, 45130 St Ay [02 38 88 94 35 or 02 38 88 65 56; fax 02 38 88 82 14]** Exit A10/E60 at junc 15 Meung-sur-Loire onto N152 dir Orléans; site sp on app to St Ay on N bank Rv Loire. Fr A71 exit junc 1 dir Blois & Beaugency onto N152. Lge, pt sl, pt shd; wc; chem disp; mv service pnt; shwrs inc; el pnts (6A) inc (poss rev pol); gas; shops 500m; tradsmn; rest 500m; BBQ; playgrnd; rv fishing & boating adj; dogs; phone; bus 500m; no twin-axles; dep for ent barrier; adv bkg; quiet; cc not acc; CCI. "Friendly, helpful staff; pleasant, clean, tidy site on bank of Rv Loire; excel modern facs for sm site but poss stretched high ssn; conv Orléans; gd base for chateaux." ♦ 15 Apr-31 Oct. € 15.50   2007*

ORLEANS *4F3* (3km W Urban) **Camping Gaston Marchand, Rue de la Roche, 45140 St Jean-de-la-Ruelle [02 38 88 39 39; fax 02 38 79 33 62; sports@ville-saintjeandelaruelle.fr]** On ent Orléans fr S take N152 to Blois W. Site sp on L after 2nd set of traff lts on N bank of rv. On N152 fr Blois turn R immed at Gaston Marchand sp. Med, mkd pitch, pt sl, pt shd; wc (some cont); chem disp; shwrs inc; el pnts (6A) €2.60; gas; shops 2km; pool 1.5km; dogs €1.10; bus; poss cr; adv bkg; some rd noise. "On bank of Rv Loire; clean, well-maintained site; gd value; conv Orléans." 1 Jul-31 Aug. € 9.80
                     2005*

ORLEAT see Thiers *9B1*

ORNANS *6G2* (6km SE Rural) **Camp Municipal Le Pré Bailly, 25840 Vuillafans [03 81 60 91 52 or 03 81 60 92 36; fax 03 81 60 95 68; mairie.vuillafans@wanadoo.fr; www.vuillafans.fr]** Site sp fr D67 adj Rv Loue. Sm, mkd pitch, terr, pt shd; htd wc; shwrs inc; el pnts (4-16A) €1.65-6.30; shop 300m; rest, bar 200m; playgrnd; fishing; canoeing; phone adj; quiet. "Simple site; pleasant situation in pretty vill; gd walks; site yourself, warden calls." 15 Mar-30 Sep. € 7.60   2006*

ORNANS *6G2* (10km SE Rural) **Camping Essi Les Oyes, 25920 Mouthier-Haute-Pierre [03 81 60 91 39]** SE fr Ornans on D67. Site 1.5km on R past Lods. Site sp & easily visible fr rd. Sm, pt shd; wc (some cont); shwrs; el pnts; shops 1.5km; playgrnd; rv sw, fishing, canoeing & shgl beach; quiet; CCI. "Fair NH; warden collects fees each pm; magnificent views; area of interest to archaeologists & geologists; take care at exit; no water point." 1 Apr-15 Sep.   2005*

ORNANS *6G2* (11km SE Rural) **Camp Municipal, Champaloux, 25930 Lods [03 81 60 90 11 (Mairie); fax 03 81 60 93 86; mairie.lods@wanadoo.fr]** Fr Ornans SE on D67. In Lods turn R across Rv Loue. Site in 150m beside rv. Or N fr Pontarlier on N57/E23 to St Gorgon then W on D67 to Lods. Med, pt shd, hdstg; wc; shwrs inc; el pnts (5A) €2.50; shop 1.5km; playgrnd; fishing; quiet. "Lovely, peaceful sity by rv; nice views; on disused rlwy stn in attractive area; woodland walk; excel shwrs; friendly, helpful warden; vg value." 15 Jun-15 Sep. € 10.60   2007*

> The opening dates and prices on this campsite have changed. I'll send a site report form to the editor for the next edition of the guide.

ORNANS *6G2* (1km S Rural) **Camping Domaine Le Chanet, 9 Chemin de Chanet, 25290 Ornans [03 81 62 23 44; fax 03 81 62 13 97; contact@lechanet.com; www.lechanet.com]** Fr Besançon take D67 25km to Ornans. In Ornans at rndabt cont to town cent. Take 1st R, cross Rv Loue then turn R. Foll sp to site in 1km. Look for R turn after school. Med, hdg pitch, steep sl & terr, pt shd; htd wc; chem disp; mv service pnt; baby facs; shwrs inc; el pnts (3-10A) €3-3.50; ice; lndtte; shop; tradsmn; snacks; bar; BBQ; sm playgrnd; htd pool 500m; rv 1km; games area; child entmnt; many statics; dogs €1.50; phone; poss cr; adv bkg; quiet; red low ssn. "Picturesque site; sm pitches; facs poss stretched in ssn; new owner improving (2007)." ♦ 24 Mar-4 Nov. € 16.40   2007*

ORPIERRE *9D3* (500m E Rural) **Camping Les Princes d'Orange, Flonsaine, 05700 Orpierre [04 92 66 22 53; fax 04 92 66 31 08; campingorpierre@wanadoo.fr; www.camping orpierre.com]** N75 S fr Serres for 11km to Eyguians. Turn R in Eyguians onto D30, 8km to Orpierre, turn L in vill to site (sp). Med, mkd pitch, hdstg, pt sl, terr, pt shd; wc; chem disp; mv service pnt; baby facs; shwrs inc; el pnts (4A) €3.10; gas; lndtte; ice; shop; snacks; bar; playgrnd; htd pool; waterslide; tennis; games area; entmnt; TV; fishing; some statics; dogs €1.50; adv bkg; red low ssn. "Rock-climbing area; gd walking; beautiful vill." ♦ 1 Apr-28 Oct. € 20.00 (3 persons)   2007*

Before we move on, I'm going to fill in some site report forms and post them off to the editor, otherwise they won't arrive in time for the deadline at the end of September.

ORTHEZ *8F1* (1.5km SE Rural) **Camping La Source, Blvd Charles de Gaulle, 64300 Orthez [05 59 67 04 81; fax 05 59 67 02 38; info@ camping-orthez.com; www.camping-orthez. com]** Leave Orthez on N117 twd Pau, turn L at sp Mont-de-Marsan & site on R in 300m. Sm, pt sl, some hdstg, pt shd; wc; mv service pnt; shwrs inc; chem disp; el pnts (10A) €2.70; tradsmn; snacks; playgrnd; pool 2km; fishing; some statics; phone; v quiet; CCI. "Walking dist fr interesting town; some pitches soft in wet weather; helpful staff; gd security." 1 Apr-31 Oct. € 12.40   2006*

OUILLY DU HOULEY see Lisieux *3D1*

OUISTREHAM *3D1* (1km S Urban) **Camp Municipal Les Pommiers, Rue de la Haie Breton, 14150 Ouistreham [tel/fax 02 31 97 12 66]** Fr ferry terminal foll sp Caen on D84 (Rue de l'Yser / Ave du Grand Large); in approx 1.5km site sp at rndabt; take 3rd exit. Lge, hdg pitch, pt shd; htd wc; chem disp; mv service pnt; shwrs inc; el pnts (6-10A) €2.90-4.50 (poss no earth); gas; lndry rm; ice; shop 500m; tradsmn; playgrnd; pool 1km; sand beach 1.8km; tennis; rv 200m; 80% statics; poss cr; Eng spkn; no adv bkg; some rd noise; cc acc; CCI. "Conv for late or early ferry (5 mins to ferry terminal); sep section for 'Brittany Ferries' tourers; gates open 0700-2300 (open automatic outgoing at other times); friendly, efficient recep - late arrivals welcome; basic facs, stretched high ssn; v nice walk/cycle ride along Caen canal to Ouistreham; rests by harbour; no twin-axles; mkt Thu; excel supmkt 3 min walk; vg NH." 15 Feb-15 Dec. € 11.00   2007*

⊞**OUISTREHAM** *3D1* (6km S Rural) **FFCC Camping des Capucines, 14860 Ranville [02 31 78 69 82; fax 02 31 78 16 94]** App Caen fr E or W, take Blvd Péripherique Nord, then exit 3a sp Ouistreham car ferry (D515). In approx 8.5km turn R onto D514 sp Cabourg, cross Pegasus Bdge & cont to sp rndabt. Take exit Ranville, at x-rds in 500m turn L, site 300m on L. Fr Ouistreham foll D514 dir Caborg to Pegasus Bdge, then as above. Med, hdg/mkd pitch, terr, pt shd; htd wc (some cont); chem disp; mv service pnt; shwrs inc; el pnts (6-10A) €2.35-3 (poss rev pol); gas; lndtte; sm shop; supmkt 2km; rest, bar 1km; playgrnd; sand beach 3km; 20% statics; dogs €1.80 (not German Shepherds or other 'dangerous' breeds); phone; bus 500m; poss cr; some Eng spkn; adv bkg if arr late; quiet; cc acc; red low ssn/ CCI. "Excel site in pleasant position; some pitches sm for lge o'fits; gd san facs; helpful, friendly owner; barrier open 0600-2400; late arr use intercom at recep; take care overhanging trees; conv ferries (if arr late fr ferry, phone in advance for pitch number & barrier code); conv Pegasus Bdge, museum, war cemetery; vg." € 14.80   2007*

There aren't many sites open this early in the year. We'd better phone ahead to check that the one we're heading for is actually open.

OUISTREHAM *3D1* (3km SW Urban) **Camping Les Hautes Coutures, Route de Ouistreham, 14970 Bénouville [02 31 44 73 08 or 06 07 25 26 90 (mob LS); fax 02 31 95 30 80; info@campinghautescoutures.com; www. campinghautescoutures.com]** Leave Ouistreham ferry & foll sp Caen & A13 over 2 rndabts. After 2nd rndabt join dual c'way. Leave at 1st exit (D35) sp St Aubin d'Arquenay & ZA de Bénouville. Turn R at end of slip rd, then L at T-junc; site in 200m uphill on R. Or fr Caen twd port on dual c'way, site has own exit shortly after Pegasus Memorial Bdge exit; site clearly visible on R of dual c'way. Med, hdg pitch, pt sl & uneven, pt shd; wc; chem disp; baby facs; shwrs inc; el pnts (6A) inc (rev pol) (adaptors provided free); lndtte; sm shop; hypmkt at Hérouville; tradsmn; rest, snacks; bar; BBQ; playgrnd; htd pool; beach 2km; fishing; tennis; mini-golf; horseriding, windsurfing 1km; golf 4km; entmnt; wifi internet; games/TV rm; 60% statics; dogs; recep 0900-2300 high ssn; poss cr; Eng spkn; adv bkg; cc acc; CCI. "Friendly staff; v clean san facs; pos tired end of ssn; conv for ferry; sm pitches; tourist info at recep; access code req for fishing (fr recep); gates clsd 2200-0630 but staff will open gate for late ferry arrivals; busy, poss noisy site; overlooks Caen Canal; Caen-Ouistreham cycle path; daily mkt in Ouistreham; NH only." ♦ 1 Apr-31 Oct. € 30.10 ABS - N05   2007*

France

OUISTREHAM *3D1* (7km W Coastal) **Camping des Hautes Sentes, Chemin des Hautes Sentes, 14880 Hermanville [02 31 96 39 12; fax 02 31 96 92 98; leshautessentes@yahoo.fr; www.campingdeshautessentes.fr]** Well sp on D514 fr Ouistreham. Med, mkd pitch, pt shd; wc; chem disp; shwrs inc; el pnts (6A) €5.50; Indtte; tradsmn; rest; snacks; bar; playgrnd; beach 700m; games area; TV rm; 30% statics; bus 400m; quiet; Eng spkn. "Extremely friendly; rec sh stay." 1 Apr-30 Sep. € 17.10   2004*

This guide relies on site report forms submitted by caravanners like us; we'll do our bit and tell the editor what we think of the campsites we've visited.

OUISTREHAM *3D1* (12km NW Coastal) **Camp Municipal Capricieuse, 2 Rue Brummel, 14530 Luc-sur-Mer [02 31 97 34 43; fax 02 31 97 43 64; info@campinglacapricieuse.com; www.camping lacapricieuse.com]** Fr ferry terminal turn R at 3rd traff lts (D514) into Ave du G. Leclerc. Cont to Luc-sur-Mer; 1st turn L after casino; site on R in 300m. Ave Lecuyer is sp & Rue Brummel is off that rd. Lge, hdg/mkd pitch; terr, pt shd; wc; mv service pnt; chem disp; shwrs inc; el pnts (6-10A) €4.20-5.70; gas; Indtte; shop 300m; tradsmn; playgrnd; sand beach adj; tennis; games rm; entmnt; child entmnt; excursions; TV rm; dogs €2.30; Eng spkn; adv bkg; quiet; cc acc; red low ssn; CCI. "Some lge pitches with easy access; gd position - conv WW2 beaches; v clean; ltd facs low ssn; excel site." ♦ 1 Apr-30 Sep. € 13.90   2007*

See advertisement below

OUNANS *6H2* (1km N Rural) **Camping La Plage Blanche, 3 Rue de la Plage, 39380 Ounans [03 84 37 69 63; fax 03 84 37 60 21; reservation@ la-plage-blanche.com; www.la-plage-blanche. com]** Exit A39 junc 6 sp Dole Centre. Foll N5 SE for 18km dir Pontarlier. After passing Souvans, turn L on D472 sp Mont-sous-Vaudrey. Foll sp to Ounans. Site well sp in vill. Lge, mkd pitch, hdstg, pt shd; wc; chem disp; mv service pnt; shwrs inc; el pnts (10A) €4 (poss rev pol); gas 1km; Indtte; ice; shop 1km; supmkt 4km; tradsmn; rest; snacks; bar; playgrnd; pool; paddling pool; shgl rv beach & sw 500m; trout & carp fishing lake; canoeing; horseriding; entmnt; TV rm; 1% statics; dogs €1.50; Eng spkn; adv bkg rec (bkg fee); quiet; red low ssn; cc acc; CCI. "V friendly reception; excel san facs; superb rvside pitches; rest v gd." ♦ 31 Mar-12 Oct. € 18.00 (CChq acc)   2007*

See advertisement opposite

OURSEL MAISON see Crèvecoeur le Grand *3C3*

OUSSE see Pau *8F2*

As soon as we get home I'm going to post all these site report forms to the editor for inclusion in next year's guide. I don't want to miss the September deadline.

OUST *8G3* (2km N Rural) **Camp Municipal La Claire, Rue La Palere, 09140 Soueix-Rogalle [05 61 66 84 88; campinglaclaire@aol.com]** S fr St Girons take D3/D618; in 13km just bef rndabt turn R onto D32 sp Soueix. Turn L at vill sq & site in 200m. Sm, pt shd; wc (cont); shwrs inc; el pnts (10A) €3.15; Indtte; shop 1.5km; rest 200m; playgrnd; paddling pool; fishing; 10% statics; dogs €1; phone; quiet; CCI. "Pleasant, well-maintained rvside site; gd hiking & touring cent." 1 Apr-31 Oct. € 7.00   2005*

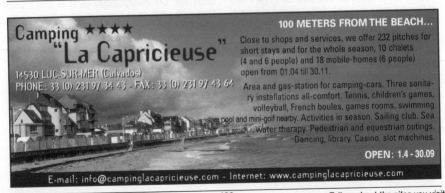
⊞ *Site open all year*   490   *Tell us about the sites you visit*

France

⊞**OUST** *8G3* (9km SE Rural) **Camping Le Montagnou, Route de Seix, Le Trein-d'Ustou, 09140 Ustou** [05 61 66 94 97; fax 05 61 66 91 20; campinglemontagnou@wanadoo.fr; www.lemontagnou.com] Fr Oust SE on D3 & D8 (via Seix) dir Aulus, approx 13km by rd. Site sp. Med, hdg pitch, pt shd; htd wc; chem disp; shwrs inc; el pnts (6-10A) inc; lndtte; mini shop, tradsmn & snacks (Jul/Aug); rest nr; playgrnd; fishing; rv sw 3km; tennis; 15% statics; dogs €1.50; phone; poss cr; Eng spkn; adv bkg (dep req); quiet; CCI. "Beautifully situated rvside site surrounded by mountains; well-managed; v friendly owners; gd walking; skiing 9km; highly rec." ♦ € 14.80

2007*

OUST *8G3* (S Rural) **Camping Les Quatre Saisons, Route d'Aulus-les-Bains, 09140 Oust** [05 61 96 55 55; camping.ariege@gmail.com; www.camping4saisons.com] Take D618 S fr St Girons; then D3 to Oust; on N o'skts of town turn L (sp Aulus) onto D32; site 150m on R nr Rv Garbet. Med, hdg pitch, pt shd; htd wc; chem disp; shwrs inc; el pnts (5-10A) €2.80-5.60; lndtte; shop 200m; bar; playgrnd; pool; games area; TV; 25% statics; dogs €1.50; phone; Eng spkn; adv bkg rec; quiet; cc acc; CCI. "In beautiful, unspoilt area; friendly site; footpath to vill; excel." 15 Mar-15 Dec. € 17.00

2007*

OUST *8G3* (1km S Rural) **Camp Municipal La Côte, 09140 Oust** [05 61 95 50 53 or 05 61 66 81 12 (Mairie); fax 05 61 66 86 95; camping-oust@tiscali.fr] Take D618 fr St Girons; after 13km cross rv; turn R onto D3 sp Aulus-les-Bains; site in 4km on R after passing Oust on L, adj Rv Salat. Med, hdg/mkd pitch, pt shd; wc; chem disp; shwrs inc; el pnts (6-10A) €1.55-€3.05 (rev pol); ice; lndtte; shop 1km; playgrnd; BBQ; tennis; fishing; dogs €1; 25% statics; adv bkg; quiet. "Easy access to site & pitches; hot water poss unreliable early am & eves." ♦ 1 Mar-31 Oct. € 10.60

2005*

⊞**OUST** *8G3* (2.5km S Rural) **Camping Le Haut Salat, La Campagne, 09140 Seix** [05 61 66 81 78; fax 05 61 66 94 17; camping.le-haut-salat@wanadoo.fr; www.camping-haut-salat.com] Take D618 S fr St Girons, at Oust take D3 twds Seix. Site well sp just N of vill nr rv. Med, hdg/mkd pitch, pt shd; htd wc (some cont); chem disp; baby facs; shwrs inc; el pnts (6A) inc; lndtte; shops 500m; bar; BBQ; htd pool; rv sw; fishing; games area; games rm; entmnt; TV; 60% statics; dogs; adv bkg; quiet; CCI. "Gd facs; gd walking area; pitches poss not open winter, phone ahead." € 16.90   2007*

OYE PLAGE see Calais *3A3*

OYONNAX *9A3* (8km E Rural) **Camping Les Gorges de l'Oignin, Rue du Lac, 01580 Matafelon-Granges [04 74 76 80 97; camping. lesgorgesdeloignin@wanadoo.fr; www.gorges-de-loignin.com]** Exit A404 junc 11, take D13/D18 to Matafelon-Granges; foll sp. NB Fr Oyonnax 22km by rd. Med, hdg/mkd pitch, hdstg, terr, pt shd; htd wc; chem disp; baby facs; shwrs inc; el pnts (10A) inc; lndtte; ltd shop or 5km; rest; snacks; bar; BBQ; playgrnd; 3 pools; lake sw adj; games area; TV rm; 10% statics; dogs €1; phone; Eng spkn; adv bkg; quiet; CCI. "Beautiful site on lake; walks around lake; Jura National Park; Rv Ain gorges; friendly, helpful staff; excel." 1 Apr-30 Sep. € 19.00
2006*

PACAUDIERE, LA *9A1* (200m E Rural) **Camp Municipal Beausoleil, 42310 La Pacaudière [04 77 64 11 50 or 04 77 64 30 18 (Mairie); fax 04 77 64 14 40]** NW on N7 Roanne to Lapalisse; turn R in La Pacaudière, D35; site well sp; fork R in 50m; site ent in 400m. Sm, hdg pitch, hdstg, sl, unshd; wc; chem disp; shwrs inc; el pnts (10A) inc; gas; lndtte; shop; playgrnd; public pool; crazy golf; TV rm; quiet. "Pleasant site; gd base for interesting area; ideal NH & gd sh stay; ltd facs low ssn; Sat mkt in town." 15 May-30 Sep. € 10.30
2005*

⊞**PAIMBOEUF** *2G3* (Urban/Coastal) **Camp Municipal de l'Estuaire, 44560 Paimboeuf [02 40 27 52 12; fax 02 40 27 61 14; info@camping-lestuaire.com; www.camping-lestuaire.com]** Fr St Nazaire on D77; turn L at rndabt imm after town sp; site on L in 300m.. Med, pt shd; htd wc; shwrs inc; el pnts (10A) €3.85 (poss rev pol & poss long lead req); lndtte; supmkt 3km; bar; crêperie rest adj; playgrnd; pool; rv adj; cycle hire; entmnt; dogs €1.25; adv bkg; red low ssn; CCI. "Poss itinerants." € 11.50
2007*

PAIMPOL *1D3* (2km SE Coastal) **Camp Municipal Crukin, Ave Crukin, Kérity, 22500 Paimpol [02 96 20 78 47 or 02 96 55 31 70 (Mairie); fax 02 96 20 75 00; camping.cruckin@wanadoo.fr]** On D786 fr St Brieuc/Paimpol, site sp in vill of Kérity 80m off main rd. Med, hdg pitch, pt shd; htd wc; chem disp; mv service pnt; shwrs inc; el pnts (6-12A) €2.40-2.69; lndtte; shops 1km; playgrnd; shgl beach 250m; rv sw; fishing; watersports; TV rm; 10% statics; dogs €1.12; bus 100m; poss cr; quiet; CCI. "Clean & tidy; friendly warden; excel sh stay/NH." ◆ 1 Apr-30 Sep. € 12.20
2006*

> The opening dates and prices on this campsite have changed. I'll send a site report form to the editor for the next edition of the guide.

PAIMPOL *1D3* (5km SE Coastal) **Camping Le Cap Horn, Port-Lazo, 22470 Plouézec [02 96 20 64 28; fax 02 96 20 63 88; lecaphorn@hotmail.com; www.lecaphorn.com]** Foll D786 fr Paimpol or Plouézec. Site sp 3km NE of Plouézec dir Port-Lazo. Med, hdg/mkd pitch, pt sl, terr, pt shd; wc; chem disp; baby facs; shwrs inc; el pnts (6A) €3.50 (poss rev pol); gas; lndtte; ice; shop; rest 1km; snacks; bar; playgrnd; htd pool; paddling pool; direct access to shgl beach 500m; boating; games rm; entmnt; 5% statics; dogs €2; adv bkg; quiet; cc acc; red low ssn/long stay; CCI. "On 2 levels in valley & hillside with beautiful sea views; steep path to beach; gd facs." ◆ 1 Apr-30 Sep. € 18.10
2007*

See advertisement

PAIMPONT see Plélan le Grand *2F3*

PALAU DEL VIDRE see Elne *10G1*

⊞**PALAVAS LES FLOTS** *10F1* (500m N Coastal) **Aire Communale/Camping-Car Halte, Base Fluviale Paul Riquer, 34250 Palavas-les-Flots [04 67 07 73 45 or 04 67 07 73 48; fax 04 67 50 61 04]** Fr Montpellier on D986 to Palavas. On ent town at 1st rndabt 'Europe' foll sp Base Fluviale & site sp. Med, mkd pitch, hdstg, pt shd; wc; chem disp; mv service pnt; shwrs inc; el pnts (16A) €2; lndtte; shop, rest, snacks, bar adj; sand beach 500m; phone; bus 200m; poss cr; some rd noise; cc acc; CCI. "M'vans only; special elec cable req - obtain fr recep (dep); some pitches along marina quayside; conv Montpellier, Camargue; 3 night max stay." € 10.00   2005*

PALAVAS LES FLOTS *10F1* (1km NE Coastal) **Camping Montpellier Plage, 95 Ave St Maurice, 34250 Palavas-les-Flots [04 67 68 00 91; fax 04 67 68 10 69; camping.montpellier.plage@wanadoo.fr; www.domaine-saint-maurice.com]** Site on D21ES on o'skts of vill twd Carnon. V Lge, pt mkd pitch, pt shd; wc (some cont); shwrs inc; mv service pnt; el pnts (4A) inc; gas; lndtte; ice; shops; tradsmn; rest; snacks; bar; BBQ; playgrnd; pool with spa facs; paddling pool; sand beach adj; games area; 50% statics; dogs; poss cr; Eng spkn; adv bking; noisy; CCI. "Gd location; basic san facs but lge pitches & friendliness of site outweigh this; easy walk into Palavas - interesting sm port; flamingoes on adjoining lake; gd." ◆ 14 Apr-9 Sep. € 30.30   2007*

PALAVAS LES FLOTS *10F1* (2km E Urban/Coastal) **Camping Les Roquilles, 267b Ave St Maurice, 34250 Palavas-les-Flots [04 67 68 03 47; fax 04 67 68 54 98; roquilles@wanadoo.fr; www.camping-les-roquilles.fr]** Exit A9 junc 30 onto D986 dir Palavas. In Palavas foll sp Carnon-Plage on D62, site sp. V lge, mkd pitch, hdstg, pt shd; wc (mainly cont); chem disp; mv service pnt; serviced pitches; shwrs inc; el pnts (6A) €3.20; gas 100m; lndtte; ice; rest; snacks; bar; playgrnd; 3 pools (1 htd); waterslide; sand beach 100m; entmnt; 30% statics; no dogs; phone; bus; poss cr; Eng spkn; adv bkg (dep req + bkg fee); poss noisy high ssn; cc acc; CCI. 15 Apr-15 Sep. € 26.30   2007*

PALINGES *9A2* (1km N Rural) **Camp Municipal du Lac, 71430 Palinges [03 85 88 14 49; jeroenvs@wxs.nl; http://home.planet.nl/~jeroenvs]** N70 Montceau-les-Mines dir Paray, turn L onto D92 into Palings cent (4km). By church turn L church onto D128. Site in 1km. Sm, hdg/mkd pitch, pt sl, pt shd; htd wc; chem disp; baby facs; shwrs inc; el pnts (10A) inc; lndtte; ice; shop 1km; rest 1km; snacks; bar; playgrnd; lake fishing adj; cycle hire; tennis; dogs €1.50; adv bkg; Eng spkn; quiet; no cc acc; CCI. "Excel site; friendly; kept immac; highly rec." ◆ Apr-Sep. € 16.00   2007*

PALME, LA see Sigean *10G1*

PALMYRE, LA see Mathes, Les *7B1*

PALUD SUR VERDON, LA *10E3* (1km E Rural) **Camp Municipal Le Grand Canyon, Route de Castellane, 04120 La Palud-sur-Verdon [tel/fax 04 92 77 38 13 or 02 92 77 30 87 (Mairie); campinglapalud@wanadoo.fr]** W on D952 fr Castellane, site on L (S) of rd just bef vill La Palud (30km W of Castellane, max gradient 1-in-8). Or on D952 fr Moustiers-Ste-Marie site on R (S) after leaving vill La Palud (also with steep & narr sections). App fr Moustiers easier. Med, mkd pitch, pt sl, pt shd; wc (some cont); chem disp; mv service pnt; baby facs; shwrs inc; el pnts (10A €3 (poss rev pol); gas 800m; lndtte; shops, rest, snacks, bar 500m; dogs €0.50; phone; poss cr; quiet; cc not acc. "Basic facs but well-kept; helpful staff; interesting area; many activities nrby; conv Gorge du Verdon." ◆ ltd. 15 Apr-30 Sep. € 9.70   2007*

PAMIERS *8F3* (800m N Rural) **Camping L'Apamée, Route d'Ecosse, 09100 Pamiers [tel/fax 05 61 60 06 89; contact@flowercampingsariege.com; www.flowercampingsariege.com]** Fr N on D820 (N20), at traff lts turn R & cross narr bdge over Rv Ariège, Pont du Jeu du Mail, site sp. Med, shd; wc; chem disp; baby facs; shwrs inc; el pnts (6A) inc; lndtte; shop 800m; tradsmn; snacks; bar; BBQ; playgrnd; htd pool; rv fishing; games rm; cycle hire; TV rm; 5% statics; dogs €2; phone; o'night area for m'vans; Eng spkn; adv bkg; quiet; red low ssn; CCI. "New owners (2006) making big improvements; clean, modern facs; excel." ◆ Easter-31 Oct. € 22.00   2006*

PAMPELONNE *8E4* (2km NE Rural) **Camping Thuries, 81190 Pampelonne [05 63 76 44 01; fax 05 63 76 92 78; campthuries@wanadoo.fr]** N fr Carmaux on N88 turn L onto D78 sp Pampelonne. Site sp & 2km fr town over narr bdge; steep, winding rd. Or S fr Rodez on N88 turn R onto D17 sp Pampelonne. Site bef rv bdge on L. Sm, mkd pitch, shd; htd wc; chem disp; mv service pnt; shwrs inc; el pnts (6A) €2.60; lndtte; ice; shop & 3km; tradsmn; rest, snacks 3km; dogs €1; phone; poss cr; Eng spkn; quiet; CCI. "Pleasant site; conv Albi & Rodez." 15 Jun-1 Sep. € 11.60   2005*

PARAY LE MONIAL *9A1* (1km NW Urban) **Camping de Mambré, Route du Gué-Léger, 71600 Paray-le-Monial [03 85 88 89 20; fax 03 85 88 87 81]** Fr N79 Moulin to Mâcon; site at W end of town; just after level x-ing turn NE into Rte du Gué-Léger. Turn R into site after x-ing rv; well sp. Lge, hgd/mkd pitch, pt shd; wc; chem disp; shwrs inc; el pnts (10A) inc; lndtte; sm shop & 500m; rest; snacks in high ssn; bar; playgrnd; pool 200m high ssn; dogs; quiet, but some rd noise; CCI. "Paray is pilgrimage cent; walking dist town; ltd facs low ssn & poss poorly maintained." 15 May-30 Sep. € 18.20

2006*

PARCEY see Dole *6H2*

France

PARENTIS EN BORN *7D1* (2km W Rural) FFCC Camp Municipal Pipiou, Route du Lac, 40160 Parentis-en-Born [05 58 78 57 25; fax 05 58 78 93 17; pipiou@parentis.com] Site on D43 rd twds lake beach. In vill foll sp 'Lac'. After 2km where rest on R, turn R. Site is 150m on R. Lge, hdg/mkd pitch, pt shd; wc; chem disp; mv service pnt; 100% serviced pitches; baby facs; shwrs inc; el pnts (10A) €2.75 (poss rev pol); gas high ssn; lndtte; ice; shop; rest; snacks; bar; playgrnd; lake sw & sand beach adj, fishing & watersports adj; entmnts; TV; 25% statics; dogs €1.15; phone; poss cr; adv bkg; quiet but pitches adj rd noisy; cc acc; red long stay & CCI. "Swipe card barrier (refundable dep €20 - check office hrs as clsd w/e low ssn); phone to check open in low ssn; lovely location on lakeside; some pitches tight; smart shwr facs stretched high ssn; cycle tracks thro vill & woods; dogs beware lge, hairy caterpillars (cause acid burns); excel." 15 Feb-10 Nov. € 16.00   2006*

PARENTIS EN BORN *7D1* (3km W Rural) Camping La Forêt Lahitte, Route des Plages, 40160 Parentis-en-Born [05 58 78 47 17 or 06 81 25 74 26 (mob); fax 05 58 78 43 64; contact@ camping-lahitte.com; www.camping-lahitte.com] Fr Biscarrosse on D652, site sp adj lake. Fr N10 turn W onto D43 at Liposthey (junc 17), thro Parentis-en-Born, site sp. Med, pt shd; wc; shwrs; el pnts (6-10A) €3; lndtte; shop; snacks; bar; playgrnd; child club; pool; jacuzzi; lake sw; sailing; fishing; entmnt; games/ TV rm; statics; dogs €2; adv bkg; red low ssn; quiet. 14 Apr-28 Aug. € 24.00   2004*

PARENTIS EN BORN *7D1* (3km NW Rural) Camping Calède, Quartier Lahitte, 40160 Parentis-en-Born [05 58 78 44 63; fax 05 58 78 40 13; contact@ camping-calede.com; www.camping-calede. com] Exit N10 junc 17 onto D43 to Parentis-en-Born; then take D652 dir Biscarrosse; site in 3km on L. Sp adj lake. Med, hdg pitch, pt shd; wc; chem disp; baby facs; shwrs inc; el pnts (5A) €3.15; gas; lndtte; ice; shop 3km; tradsmn; snacks; bar; BBQ; playgrnd; lake sw & sand beach adj; sailing; fishing; dogs €0.50; phone; poss cr; Eng spkn; quiet; adv bkg; CCI. "Superbly maintained pitches & san facs; excel." ♦ 1 May-1 Oct. € 16.70   2006*

PARIS *3D3* (12km E) Camp Municipal La Haute Ile, Rue de l'Ecluse, 93330 Neuilly-sur-Marne [01 43 08 21 21; fax 01 43 08 22 03; campingmunicipal.nsm@wandadoo.fr] Fr Périphérique (Porte de Vincennes) foll N34 sp Vincennes. Shortly after passing Château de Vincennes on R, L at fork, sp Lagny. At next major x-rds sharp L (still N34) sp Chelles. Thro Neuilly-Plaisance to Neuilly-sur-Marne. In cent lge x-rds turn R sp N370 Marne-la-Vallée & A4 Paris. In 200m, bef rv bdge, foll Camping Municipal sp (no tent or c'van symbols on this or previous sp) turn L. Site at junc of rv & canal. Lge, mkd pitch, pt shd; wc (some cont); shwrs inc; el pnts (10A) inc (check rev pol); gas; lndtte adj; ice; shop; rest adj; BBQ; playgrnd; rv fishing; 25% statics; dogs €2.85; bus/ train; poss cr; Eng spkn; adv bkg (rec high ssn); quiet. "Lovely location; wooden posts on pitches poss diff manoeuvring lge o'fits; some sm pitches; soft after rain; gd base & transport for Paris; poss unkempt low ssn; gd NH." 1 Apr-30 Sep. € 18.70   2007*

⊞**PARIS** *3D3* (15km SE Urban) Camping Paris Est Le Tremblay, Blvd des Alliés, 94507 Champigny-sur-Marne [01 43 97 43 97; fax 01 48 89 07 94; champigny@campingparis.fr; www.campingparis. fr] Rec rte for c'vans. Fr A4 (Paris-Reims) exit 5 sp Nogent/Champigny-sur-Marne. D45 dir Champigny to end of dual c'way at traff lts go R on N303 dir St Maur. Join N4 after 1km (traff lts) & take 2nd R (200m). Site sp. NB site also known as 'Camping de Champigny' or 'Camping International/IDF'. Med, hdg/mkd pitch, pt shd; htd wc (some cont); chem disp; mv service pnt; shwrs inc; el pnts (10A) inc; gas; lndtte; shop; rest; snacks; bar; games rm; TV; playgrnd; 20% statics; dogs €2.60; adv bkg; some rd noise; red low ssn; cc acc; CCI. "Vg site conv for Paris, easy parking nr metro or bus fr camp to rlwy stn direct to city & Disneyland; twin-axle c'vans book ahead or poss extra charge; take care to avoid grounding on kerb to pitches; clsd to cars 0200-0600." ♦ € 29.90   2007*

⊞PARIS *3D3* (10km W Urban) **Camping Bois de Boulogne, 2 Allée du Bord de l'Eau, 75016 Paris [01 45 24 30 81; fax 01 42 24 42 95; camping-boulogne@stereau.fr; www.campingparis.fr or www.hotelparispleinair.com]** Site bet bdge of Puteaux & bdge of Suresnes. App fr A1: take Blvd Périphérique W to Bois de Boulogne exit at Porte Maillot; foll camp sp. App fr A6: Blvd Périphérique W to Porte Dauphine exit at Porte Maillot; foll camp sp. App fr Pont de Sèvres (A10, A11): on bdge take R lane & take 2nd rd R mkd Neuilly-sur-Seine; rd runs parallel to Seine; cont to site ent. App fr A13: after St Cloud Tunnel, foll sp twd Paris; immed after x-ing Rv Seine, 1st turn on R sp Bois de Boulogne; foll camp sps; traff lts at site ent. NB Sharp turn to site, poorly sp fr N - watch for lge 'Parking Borne de l'Eau 200m'. V lge, hdg/mkd pitch, hdstg, pt sl, pt shd; htd wc (some cont); chem disp; mv service pnt; baby facs; shwrs inc; el pnts (10A) inc; gas; Indtte; shop in ssn; rest, bar, pool 1km; TV; Metro Porte Maillot 4km; shuttle bus (Apr-Sep) to & fr site morn/eve to 2300; some statics; dogs €2; phone; extra €26 per night for twin-axles; poss cr; Eng spkn; adv bkg rec high ssn; rd noise; red low ssn; cc acc; CCI. "Excel location, easy access A13; conv cent Paris; some sm pitches; walk over Suresne bdge for shops, food mkt, supmkt etc; some v sm pitches; some commercial units on site; excel." € 35.70   2007*

PARIS *3D3* (20km NW Urban) **Camping International Maisons Laffitte, Ile de la Commune, 1 Rue Johnson, 78600 Maisons-Laffitte [01 39 12 21 91; fax 01 39 12 70 50; ci.mlaffitte@wanadoo.fr; www.campint.com]** Easy access fr A13 sp Poissy; take N308 to Maisons-Laffitte; foll site sp bef town cent. Fr A15 take N184 S fr Poissy, foll sp St Germain; approx 6km after x-ing Rv Seine & approx 300m after x-ing lge steel bdge, take L lane ready for L turn onto D308 to Maison-Laffitte; foll camp sp. Or A1 to St Denis, then A86 exit Bezons, then dir Poissy, Noailles, Sartrouville & Maisons-Laffitte. NB Narr app rd diff due parked cars & high kerbs. Lge, hdg/mkd pitch, pt shd; htd wc; chem disp; mv service pnt; shwrs inc; el pnts (6A) €3 (poss rev pol); gas; Indtte; sm shop; tradsmn; hypmkt 5km; rest; snacks; bar; BBQ; playgrnd; games area; TV rm; 50% statics; dogs €2.50; RER stn 1km; poss cr; Eng spkn; adv bkg (dep req & bkg fee); some noise fr rlwy & rv traff; cc acc; CCI. "Site on island in Rv Seine; ideal for visiting Paris (20 min by RER), Disneyland & Versailles; Mobilis ticket covers rlwy, metro & bus for day in Paris; friendly, v helpful staff; busy tourist site; ltd facs low ssn; vg." ♦ 16 Mar-31 Oct. € 26.00   2007*

See advertisement

PARRANQUET see Villeréal *7D3*

PARTHENAY *4H1* (1km SW Urban) **FFCC Camping du Bois Vert, 14 Rue de Boisseau, 79200 Parthenay [tel/fax 05 49 65 78 43; bois-vert@wanadoo.fr; www.camping-boisvert.com]** Site on D743 to Niort. Sp fr N & S. Fr S 1km bef town turn L at sp La Roche-sur-Yon immed after rv bdge turn R; site on R in 500m. Med, hdg/mkd pitch, some hdstg, pt sl, pt shd; htd wc (some cont); chem disp; mv service pnt; baby facs; shwrs inc; el pnts (10A) €3.50; Indtte; shops 1km; tradsmn; rest; snacks; bar; playgrnd; pool; boating; fishing; tennis; games rm; TV; 10% statics; phone; poss cr; adv bkg; noisy nr main rd & bar; cc not acc; red low ssn; CCI. "Conv Futuroscope; pleasant, riverside walk into interesting old town; dated facs ltd low ssn, tired high ssn; some pitches a bit close; new owner, improvements in hand (2007); m'van o'night area adj; Wed mkt; gd NH to Spain." ♦ 1 Apr-30 Sep. € 17.50 (CChq acc)   2007*

PARTHENAY *4H1* (9km W Urban) **Camp Municipal Les Peupliers, 79130 Azay-sur-Thouet [05 49 95 37 13 (Mairie); fax 05 49 70 36 14; mairie-azaysurthouet@cc-parthenay.fr]** Fr Parthenay take D949 dir Secondigny to Azay-sur-Thouet; turn L onto D139 dir St Pardoux; site on L in 200m. Site adj stadium on rvside. Sm, mkd pitch, pt shd; wc; shwrs inc; el pnts (10A) €2.65; shop 500m; BBQ; playgrnd; dogs €1.55; quiet. "V Pleasant, peaceful site; barrier poss clsd to exclude itinerants, key fr Mairie 200m." 15 Jun-30 Sep. € 7.75   2007*

PARTHENAY *4H1* (10km W Rural) **Camping La Chagnée (Baudoin), 79450 St Aubin-le-Cloud [05 49 95 31 44; fax 06 71 10 09 66; gerard.baudoin3@wanadoo.fr; www.cc-parthenay.fr/la-chagnee]** Fr Parthenay on D949 dir Secondigny. Turn R in Azay-sur-Thouet onto D139 dir St Aubin, site on R in 2km, look for 'Gîte' sp. Sm, pt shd; wc; mv service pnt; shwrs el pnts €2.90; Indtte; shops 1km; pool 1km; fishing; dogs; Eng spkn; quiet. "Charming CL-type farm site; v friendly owners; meals avail; beautiful setting o'looking lake; spotless facs; open all yr providing use own san in winter; excel." ♦ 1 Apr-31 Oct. € 10.30   2007*

PASSY see Sallanches *9A3*

PATORNAY see Clairvaux les Lacs *6H2*

⊞PAU *8F2* (8km E) **FFCC Camping Les Sapins, Route de Tarbes, 64320 Ousse [05 59 81 74 21]** Site alongside Hôtel des Sapins on S side of N117 (Pau-Tarbes rd) at Ousse. Sm, pt shd; wc; mv service pnt; shwrs inc; el pnts (4-6A) €2-3; ice; shop adj; rest in hotel adj; fishing; poss cr; noisy; some rd noise. "Popular NH; red facs low ssn; hot water in shwrs but no heating; pleasant site; helpful owners; NH only." € 9.50   2006*

PAU *8F2* (10km S) **Camping à la Ferme (André), Chemin de Castagnet, Haut de Gan, 64290 Gan [05 59 21 51 84]** S fr Pau on N134 dir Oloron-Ste Marie; approx 8km past Gan turn L sp 'Camping Paysan'; site on R in 150m. Sm, pt shd; wc; chem disp; shwrs; el pnts inc; lndry rm; tradsmn; shop 8km; horseriding nrby; quiet. "Peaceful site in orchard; views of fields & Pyrenees; facs clean; excel touring base inc Lourdes; conv NH to Spain; helpful, friendly owners." € 14.20   2006*

⊞**PAU** *8F2* (6km W Urban) **Camping Le Terrier, Ave du Vert-Galant, 64230 Lescar [05 59 81 01 82; fax 05 59 81 26 83; camping.terrier@wanadoo.fr; www.camping-terrier.com]** Fr N117 at Lescar foll sp S dir Artiguelouve, site at rv bdge. Access via narr lane - no parking or turning space. Med, hdg/mkd pitch, pt shd; wc (own san rec); chem disp; baby facs; shwrs inc; el pnts (3-6A) €2.20-3.10; gas; lndtte; shop 500m; tradsmn; hypmkt 2km; rest, snacks, bar high ssn; playgrnd; htd pool high ssn; rv fishing adj; tennis; car wash; 10% statics; dogs €1.50; poss cr; Eng spkn; adv bkg; quiet; 30% red 30+ days; CCI. "Gd base for Pau & district; some permanent residents; 2 gd golf courses nr; gd value; reported run-down, unclean May 06." € 12.00
                    2006*

PAUILLAC *7C2* (1km S Urban) **FFCC Camp Municipal Les Gabarreys, Route de la Rivière, 33250 Pauillac [05 56 59 10 03 or 05 56 73 30 50; fax 05 56 73 30 68; camping.les.gabarreys@wanadoo.fr; www.pauillac-medoc.com]** On ent Pauillac on D206, turn R at rndabt, sp site. On app Quays, turn R bef 'Maison du Vin'. Site on L in 1km. Med, hdg/mkd pitch, hdstg, pt shd; wc; chem disp; mv service pnt; shwrs inc; el pnts (5-10A) €3.70-5; lndtte; ice; shop 1km; tradsmn; BBQ; playgrnd; htd, covrd pool 1km; mini-golf; games rm; TV; 6% statics; dogs €1.80; Eng spkn; adv bkg; quiet; red low ssn; cc acc; CCI. "On bank of estuary in peaceful situation; excel, well-kept, well-equipped site; helpful warden; immac san facs; short walk to town; conv major wine chateaux; cycle rtes; mkt Sat." ♦ 2 Apr-6 Oct. € 12.80   2007*

PAULHAGUET *9C1* (500m SE Urban) **Camping La Fridière, 6 Route d'Esfacy, 43230 Paulhaguet [04 71 76 65 54; campingpaulhaguet@wanadoo.fr; www.campingfr.nl]** On SE side of town on D4. Sm, hdg/mkd pitch, pt shd; htd wc; chem disp; mv service pnt; shwrs inc; el pnts (16A) €3.50; gas 500m; lndtte; shop, snacks 500m; tradsmn; bar; playgrnd; rv fishing; internet; dogs €1; Eng spkn; quiet; CCI. "Useful NH; vg, immac san facs; lge pitches; friendly owners; popular with young Dutch families; Château Lafayette nr; 10 min stroll to town; gd mkt Mon; excel." ♦ 1 Apr-15 Oct. € 13.00
                    2006*

PAULHIAC see Biron *7D3*

⊞**PAYRAC** *7D3* (1km N Rural) **Camping Panoramic, Route de Loupiac, 46350 Payrac-en-Quercy [05 65 37 98 45; fax 05 65 37 91 65; camping.panoramic@wanadoo.fr; www.camping panoramic.com]** N fr Payrac, site W of D820 (N20) at start of dual c'way, foll sp Loupiac, then site. Sm, pt sl, hdstg pt shd; htd wc; chem disp; baby facs; shwrs inc; el pnts (5A) €2.50; gas; lndtte; ice; shop 1km; tradsmn; rest high ssn (15 Mar-7 Sep in 2007); snacks; bar; BBQ; playgrnd; pool 400m; rv sw 5km; canoe hire; walking; table tennis; TV rm; cycle hire; 10% statics; phone; poss cr; Eng spkn; adv bkg; v quiet; CCI. "Well-run, clean, busy site with excel san facs; poss v muddy in bad weather; friendly, helpful Dutch owner; organised canoe trips & entmnt; excel winter NH." ♦ € 9.60   2007*

PAYRAC *7D3* (6km N Rural) **Camping à la Ferme Le Treil (Gatignol), 46350 Loupiac [05 65 37 64 87; francis.gatignol@wanadoo.fr]** Fr N or S on D820 (N20), sp 'A la Ferme'. Sm, sl, pt shd; wc; chem disp (wc); shwrs inc; el pnts (4A) €2 (long lead poss req); lndtte; shops 2km; tradsmn; bar; playgrnd; pool; fishing; boating; tennis; golf 3km; TV; BBQ; poss cr; Eng spkn; adv bkg; quiet; 10% red low ssn. "Pleasant site; mkd ent for c'vans poss diff long o'fits - rec use ent for tents if gd power/weight ratio; v friendly owner." 1 May-30 Oct. € 10.00   2006*

PAYRAC *7D3* (6km N Rural) **Camping Les Hirondelles, Al Pech, 46350 Loupiac [05 65 37 66 25; fax 05 65 37 66 65; camp.les-hirondelles@orange.fr; www.les-hirondelles.com]** Fr Souillac foll D820 (N20) for about 12km. Site on R bef dual c'way. Sm, hdg/mkd pitch, pt sl, shd; htd wc; chem disp; baby facs; shwrs inc; el pnts (6A) inc (poss rev pol); gas; lndtte; ice; shop; tradsmn; rest; snacks; bar; playgrnd; htd pool; cycle hire; entmnt; TV; 40% statics; dogs €1.20; phone; poss cr w/e; Eng spkn; adv bkg (dep req); quiet; CCI. "Vg friendly, helpful owners; clean site; gd views fr some pitches; excel." ♦ 1 Apr-15 Sep. € 15.00   2006*

PAYRAC *7D3* (500m S Rural) **FLOWER Camping Les Pins, 46350 Payrac-en-Quercy [05 65 37 96 32; fax 05 65 37 91 08; info@les-pins-camping.com; www.les-pins-camping.com]** Exit A20 junc 55 dir Souillac onto D820 (N20) dir Cahors. Foll sp Payrac 12km S of Souillac on D820, site sp & clearly visible as climb hill. Med, hdg/mkd pitch, hdstg, terr, pt shd; wc; chem disp; mv service pnt; serviced pitches; shwrs inc; el pnts (10A) inc; gas 1km; lndtte; ice; shop; rest; snacks; bar; BBQ; playgrnd; 2 htd pools; waterslide; paddling pool; tennis; entmnt; child entmnt; wifi internet; games/TV rm; many statics; dogs €2.50; some rd & disco noise; adv bkg; Eng spkn; rd noise; cc acc; red low ssn; CCI. "Gd, clean site; friendly staff; vg pool; most pitches shd with high firs; trees make access to some pitches diff; low ssn not suitable disabled unless sited nr recep; v boggy in wet; v interesting area; Rocamadour & Lacave worth visit." ♦ 5 Apr-14 Sep. € 26.90 ABS - D25   2007*

PAYRAC *7D3* (5km NW Rural) **Camping Les Grands Chênes (Naturist), Le Peyronnet, 46350 Lamothe-Fénelon (Postal address 46300 Fajoles) [tel/fax 05 65 41 68 79; camping@les-grands-chenes.com; www.les-grands-chenes.com]** Fr N exit A20 junc 55 onto D820 (N20) dir Payrac; turn R onto minor rd to Lamothe-Fénelon; site on D12, sp in vill; turn R in Payrac onto D36 (best route). Fr S exit junc 56 onto D80, then turn R onto N20/D820. Sm, mkd pitch, pt sl, pt shd; wc; chem disp; baby facs; shwrs inc; el pnts (6A) €3 (long lead poss req); lndtte; shop; tradsmn; rest 6km; snacks; bar; playgrnd; pool; games area; canoe hire, golf, horseriding nrby; 2% statics; dogs €1.50; poss cr; little Eng spkn; adv bkg (dep req); quiet; INF card req. "Beautiful situation, charming & peaceful site; attractive & unusual architecture on site; excel san facs; green toilet chem only; v beautiful & historic area; v friendly staff; close to Rv Dordogne & attractions; excel." ♦ ltd. 13 May-25 Sep. € 19.20 2006*

PEGOMAS see Cannes *10F4*

PEIGNEY see Langres *6F1*

PEILLAC *2F3* (1km N Rural) **Camp Municipal du Pont d'Oust, 56220 Peillac [02 99 91 39 33 or 02 99 91 26 76 (Mairie); fax 02 99 91 31 83]** Fr La Gacilly on D777, turn L onto D14 sp Les Fougerêts. Thro vill, site on R opp canal. Med, pt shd; htd wc; shwrs €1.16; el pnts (10A) €2.33; lndtte; shops 1km; rest, bar 300m; BBQ; pool adj; rv adj; child entmnt; quiet. "Vg site; within walking dist of pretty vill; gd shops; v flat, ideal for cycling." 1 May-30 Sep. € 5.75 2006*

PEILLON see Nice *10E4*

PEISEY NANCROIX see Bourg St Maurice *9B4*

PENESTIN *2G3* (1.5km N Coastal) **Camping Les Pins, Route de La Roche-Bernard, 56760 Pénestin [tel/fax 02 99 90 33 13; camping.lespins@wanadoo.fr; www.camping-despins.com]** Fr Roche-Bernard take D34 to Pénestin. 2km bef Pénestin take L turn sp Camping Les Pins. Site on R in 1km. Med, pt sl, pt shd; wc (some cont); chem disp; shwrs inc; el pnts (5A) €2.50; gas; lndtte; shop & 2km; tradsmn; bar; BBQ; htd pool; paddling pool; waterslide; playgrnd; sand beach 1km; games area; entmnt; TV; statics; dogs €1; adv bkg; red long stay/CCI. "Sunday mkt at Pénestin." ♦ 1 Apr-22 Oct. € 13.10 2006*

PENESTIN *2G3* (1.5km E Rural) **Camping Le Cénic, 56760 Pénestin-sur-Mer [02 99 90 45 65; fax 02 99 90 45 05; info@lecenic.com; www.lecenic.com]** Fr La Roche-Bernard take N774 sp La Baule. In 1.5km turn R onto D34. At Pénestin turn L opp Intermarché & foll sp to site in 800m. Lge, mkd pitch, pt sl, pt shd; wc; chem disp; mv service pnt; shwrs inc; el pnts (4-6A) €4; lndtte; shop adj; snacks; bar; playgrnd; htd, covrd pool/aquatic park; waterslides; beach 3km; lake fishing; tennis; sports cent; games rm; few statics; dogs €2.50; Eng spkn; adv bkg rec high ssn; poss noisy high ssn; red low ssn; CCI. "Vg rural site nr unspoilt coastline; pleasant staff; take care when pitching due trees." ♦ 9 Apr-18 Sep. € 22.00 2005*

PENESTIN *2G3* (2km S) **Camping Domaine d'Inly, Route de Couarne, 56760 Pénestin [02 99 90 35 09; fax 02 99 90 40 93; inly-info@wanadoo.fr; www.camping-inly.com]** Fr Vannes or Nantes on N165, exit junc 15 W onto D34 fr La Roche-Bernard to Pénestin, then onto D201, site sp on L. Lge, hdg pitch, hdstg, pt shd; wc; chem disp; shwrs inc; el pnts (10A) €3.30; lndtte; shop; rest; snacks; bar; playgrnd; htd pool; paddling pool; waterslide; sand beach 1.5km; tennis; TV; entmnt; child entmnt; horseriding; 20% statics; dogs €2.10; Eng spkn; adv bkg; cc acc; red long stay/low ssn; cc acc; CCI. "V pleasant site." ♦ 7 Apr-23 Sep. € 30.80 2005*

PENESTIN *2G3* (3km S Coastal) **Camping des Iles, La Pointe du Bile, 56760 Pénestin [02 99 90 30 24; fax 02 99 90 44 55; contact@camping-des-iles.fr; www.camping-des-iles.fr]** Fr La Roche Bernard take D34 to Pénestin; cont on D201 for 2.5km & foll site sp. Lge, hdg/mkd pitch, pt shd; wc; chem disp; some serviced pitches; baby facs; shwrs inc; el pnts (6A) inc; gas; lndtte; shop; tradsmn; rest; snacks; bar; BBQ (elec/charcoal); playgrnd; htd pool & paddling pool; waterslide; sand beach adj; fishing adj; tennis; cycle hire; horseriding; entmnt; child entmnt; internet; games/TV rm; some tour op statics; no c'vans over 7m high ssn; dogs €2.50; poss cr; Eng spkn; adv bkg; quiet but noisy nr rd; cc acc; CCI. "Gd clean, quiet site; gd san facs; v helpful staff; lovely cliff-top walks & clean beach; boat trips fr Vannes; mkt Sun (also Wed in Jul/Aug)." ♦ 4 Apr-18 Oct. € 38.50 ABS - B06 2007*

PENNAUTIER see Carcassonne *8F4*

PENNE SUR L'OUVEZE, LA see Buis les Baronnies *9D2*

PENVINS see Sarzeau *2G3*

PERASSAY see Ste Sévère sur Indre *7A4*

France

Camping du Port de Plaisance ★★★
★★★
80200 Peronne Tel. : 33 (0) 03 22 84 19 31 – Fax : 33 (0) 03 22 73 36 37
Open: 01/03 - 31/10
> Heated swimming pool
Internet : www.camping-plaisance.com – E-mail : contact@camping-plaisance.com

PERIERS *1D4* (5km SE Rural) **Aire Naturelle Municipale Le Clos Vert, 50190 St Martin-d'Aubigny [02 33 46 57 03 or 02 33 07 73 92 (Mairie); fax 02 33 07 02 53; mairie-st-martin-daubigny@wanadoo.fr]** E fr Périers on D900 twd St Lô; site sp 1km on R; behind church in vill. Sm, pt shd; wc; shwrs inc; el pnts (10A) €2; shop 1km; playgrnd; fishing, tennis & golf 2km; quiet; red low ssn. "Easy 70km run to Cherbourg." ♦ 15 Apr-15 Oct. € 6.60   2007*

⊞**PERIGUEUX** *7C3* (12km NE Rural) **Camping Le Bois du Coderc, Route des Gaunies, 24420 Antonne-et-Trigonant [05 53 05 99 83; fax 05 53 05 15 93; info@le-bois-du-coderc.com; www.le-bois-du-coderc.com]** NE fr Périgueux on N21 twd Limoges, thro Antonne approx 1km turn R at x-rds bet car park & Routiers café. Site in 500m. Sm, pt shd; wc; chem disp; baby facs; shwrs inc; el pnts (6-10A) €3-5; gas 5km; ice; lndtte; shop 4km; tradsmn; rest 1km; snacks; bar; BBQ; playgrnd; htd, covrd pool 12km; rv sw & shgl beach adj; some statics; dogs; Eng spkn; adv bkg (dep req); quiet; cc not acc; red low ssn/CCI. "Helpful owners, quiet, secluded site; most pitches spacious; excel san facs; rallies welcome; ent for o'fits over 11m poss diff - suggest inspect pitch 1st." ♦ ltd. € 11.00
2006*

PERIGUEUX *7C3* (1.5km E Urban) **Camping de Barnabé, 80 Rue des Bains, 24750 Boulazac [05 53 53 41 45; fax 05 53 54 16 62; contact@barnabe-perigord.com; www.barnabe-perigord.com]** 1.5km E on rd to Brive, sp to L. Sp not clear - 2 bdges, site across 2nd bdge. Med, hdg/mkd pitch, pt shd; htd wc; chem disp; shwrs inc; el pnts (4-6A) €2.80-3.20; ice; shops 500m; supmkt 1km; rest; snacks; bar; rv fishing; no statics; dogs €1.20; poss cr; Eng spkn; adv bkg; quiet; red long stay/low ssn; cc acc. "Pleasant rvside site; facs dated but clean; pitches cramped for lge o'fits; poss noise fr busy café/bar; rvside cycle track; pleasant walk to town cent; poss clsd low ssn - phone ahead." 1 Mar-31 Oct. € 14.20   2006*

PERIGUEUX *7C3* (10km E Rural) **FFCC Camping au Fil de l'Eau, 6 Allée des Platanes, 24420 Antonne-et-Trigonant [05 53 06 17 88; fax 05 53 08 97 76; campingaufildeleau@wanadoo.fr; http://camping-aufildeleau.monsite.wanadoo.fr]** E fr Périgueux on N21 twd Limoges; sp on R at end of vill; camp 350m along rd to Escoire. Well sp. Sm, pt shd; wc; chem disp; shwrs inc; el pnts (5A) €2.70; lndtte; shops 1km; tradsmn; snacks; playgrnd; lake sw; canoe hire; fishing; cycle hire; some statics; adv bkg (dep req); CCI. "Pleasant, quiet site; woods, birds & wildlife around; gd base for area; helpful owners; v clean facs; red facs low ssn; excel." ♦ 15 Jun-15 Sep. € 10.80   2006*

PERIGUEUX *7C3* (7km S Rural) **Camping Le Grand Dague, 24750 Atur [05 53 04 21 01; fax 05 53 04 22 01; info@legranddague.fr; www.legranddague.fr]** Fr cent Périgueux, take N21 & A89 twd Brive. Fork L onto D2 to Atur (main rd bears R). In Atur turn L after bar/tabac; foll site sp for 2.5km. Med, pt sl, shd; wc; chem disp; baby facs; shwrs inc; el pnts (6A) €3.50; lndtte; ice; ltd shop; tradsmn; rest; snacks; bar; playgrnd; pool; games rm; entmnt; mini-golf; TV; dogs €1.75; phone; Eng spkn; adv bkg; quiet; red low ssn; cc acc; CCI. "Gd family site; friendly owners; lots to do."♦ 28 Apr-15 Sep. € 21.25   2007*

> There aren't many sites open this early in the year. We'd better phone ahead to check that the one we're heading for is actually open.

PERNES LES BOULOGNE see Boulogne sur Mer *3A2*

PERNES LES FONTAINES see Carpentras *10E2*

CAMPING LA TORTILLE
80200 CLÉRY-SUR-SOMME
Phone: 00 33 (0)3 22 83 17 59.
Phone low season: 00 33 (0)3 22 84 10 45
5 km from the motorway exit A1 (Paris-Lille no. 13-1)

Open: 1 April till 31 October
Rental of mobile homes

Camping Château de L'OSERAIE***
3 km from the motorway exit A1 (Paris-Lille no. 13-1). Only 50 minutes away from EuroDisney. 10 minutes from l'Historial Museum of The First World War
Telephone high season: 00 33 (0)3 22 83 17 59
Telephone low season: 00 33 (0)3 22 84 10 45
Fax: 03 22 83 04 14 jsg-bred@wanadoo.fr

Open: 1 April till 30 October. Rental of mobile homes.
Web: www.camping-chateau-oseraie.com

PERONNE *3C3* (Urban) **Camp Municipal du Brochet, Rue Georges Clémenceau, 80200 Péronne [03 22 84 02 35 or 03 22 73 31 00; fax 03 22 73 31 01]** Fr N on D1017 (N17) turn R into town. L at lights & L immed after footbdge. 1st R & site on L. Well sp fr all dirs. Go to town cent then foll 'Intn'l Camping Site' sps. Sm, hdstg, pt sl, terr, pt shd; wc; mv service pnt; shwrs €1.10; el pnts (5A) €2.20; Indtte; shops 500m; tradsmn; playgrnd; bus 500m; phone; poss cr; Eng spkn; adv bkg; quiet; CCI. "Basic but clean site; san facs need refurb; grass v soft when wet; town in walking dist; arr early high ssn; conv WWI museum & tour; lots of tourist info avail; poss itinerants." ♦ ltd. 1 Apr-1 Oct. € 10.70   2007*

⊞**PERONNE** *3C3* (11km SE Rural) **Camping Les Hortensias, 22 Rue Basse, 80240 Vraignes-en-Vermandois [03 22 85 64 68; fax 03 22 85 63 20; campinghortensias@free.fr; www.campinghortensias.com]** Fr N on A1/E15 take exit 13 onto N29 sp St Quentin; strt rd 16km until rndabt, take D15 (Vraignes) exit; site sp 1st on R in vill. Or fr S & A26, take junc 10 onto N29 sp Péronne; after 15km at rndabt take D15 as bef. Sm, hdg pitch, hdstg, pt shd; htd wc; chem disp; shwrs €1.10; el pnts (4-8A) €2.50-4; Indtte; ice; shop 1km; tradsmn; red 5km; snack, bar 1.5km; BBQ; 50% statics; dogs €1.10; quiet; red long stay; CCI. "Excel site; v quiet; v gd clean san facs; v helpful & friendly couple; conv for Somme battlefields." € 9.00   2007*

PERONNE *3C3* (Urban) **Camping du Port de Plaisance, Route de Paris, 80200 Péronne [03 22 84 19 31; fax 03 22 73 36 37; contact@camping-plaisance.com; www.camping-plaisance.com]** Site on L when ent town fr S on D1017 (N17), sp 500m after 1st traff lts, o'looking canal. Well sp fr all dirs. Med, mkd pitch, pt shd; htd wc; chem disp; mv service pnt; shwrs inc; el pnts (6-10A) €3.70-6.35 (some rev pol & long lead poss req); Indtte; ice; sm shop; tradsmn; snacks high ssn; bar; playgrnd; htd pool high ssn; jacuzzi; lake fishing; dogs €1.20; poss v cr; Eng spkn; poss some rd noise; red low ssn/long stay; cc acc. "Helpful owners; popular NH; san facs adequate; supmkt walking dist; gd play park & pool; gd rest nr; gates locked 2200-0800; when clsd - park outside; nr visit to war museum in Péronne castle; WW1 cemeteries & battlefields; popular with ralliers; no twin-axles; excel." ♦ 1 Mar-31 Oct. € 21.00 (3 persons)   2007*

See advertisement opposite

PERONNE *3C3* (8km W Rural) **Camping Château de l'Oseraie, 10 Rue du Château, 80200 Feuillères [03 22 83 17 59 or 03 22 84 10 45 (LS); fax 03 22 83 04 14; jsg-bred@wanadoo.fr; www.camping-chateau-oseraie.com]** Fr A1/E15 exit 13.1 Maurepas, R onto D938 & then L onto D146; R at staggered x-rds in Feuillères (by church) & site on R in 500m. Med, hdg/mkd pitch, hdstg, pt shd; wc; chem disp; mv service pnt; shwrs €1.10; el pnts (6A) €2.90; gas 100m; Indtte; ice; tradsmn; supmkt 10km; snacks; bar; BBQ; playgrnd; htd pool 8km; fishing; tennis; games area; games rm; internet; entmnt high ssn; 2% statics; dogs €1.10; Eng spkn; adv bkg rec high ssn; red long stay; CCI. "Excel, well-run site; immac san facs; friendly staff; in Vallée de la Haute Somme; conv WW1 battlefields & Disneyland Paris." ♦ 1 Apr-30 Oct. € 13.20   2007*

See advertisement above

PERONNE *3C3* (2km NW Rural) **Camping La Tortille, L'Orgibée, 80200 Cléry-sur-Somme [03 22 83 17 59 or 03 22 84 10 45; fax 03 22 83 04 14; jsg-bred@wanadoo.fr]** Exit A1/E15 junc 13.1 onto D938 to Cléry, dir Peronne. Site sp on rvside in 4km. Med, hdg pitch, hdstg, pt shd; wc; shwrs €1.10; el pnts (6A) €2.85; shop 4km; BBQ; playgrnd; rv fishing; games area; 80% statics; dogs €1; adv bkg; quiet; red long stay; CCI. "Peaceful site; sm pitches poss bet statics; conv for m'way." ♦ 1 Apr-31 Oct. € 12.20
2007*

See advertisement on previous page

PERPIGNAN *8G4* (6km S Rural) **Camping Les Rives du Lac, Chemin de la Serre, 66180 Villeneuve-de-la-Raho [04 68 55 83 51; fax 04 68 55 86 37; camping.villeneuveraho@wanadoo.fr]** Fr A9 exit Perpignan Sud, dir Porte d'Espagne. In 3km turn R onto N9 dir Le Boulou. In 1km after Auchan supmkt take slip rd to N91 dir Villeneuve-de-la-Raho. In 2km rd becomes D39, turn R to site, site on L in 1km. Beware ford on D39 in v wet weather (usually dry). Med, mkd pitch, pt sl, hdstg, pt shd; htd wc; chem disp; mv service pnt; shwrs inc; el pnts (6A) €3; lndtte; shop; supmkt 3km; rest; snacks; bar; BBQ (elec/gas); playgrnd; htd pool; lake sw, beach, fishing & watersports 1.5km; tennis 2km; some statics; dogs €1.60; phone; Eng spkn; adv bkg; quiet; red low ssn; cc acc; CCI. "Lovely site by lake; lovely lake views fr most pitches; conv trips to Spain; busy public beach nr; gd for families." ♦ Mar-Nov. € 13.60
2007*

PERROS GUIREC *1D2* (10km E Coastal/Rural) **FFCC Camping de Port l'Epine, 10 Venelle de Pors-Garo, 22660 Trélévern [02 96 23 71 94; fax 02 96 23 77 83; camping-de-port-lepine@wanadoo.fr; www.camping-port-lepine.com]** N fr Guingamp on D767 dir Lannion; fr Lannion take D788 dir Perros-Guirec; at rndabt on sea front just outside Perros-Guirec turn R onto D6 dir Louannec & Trélévern; at rndabt after Louannec turn L to Trélévern; in vill go strt over x-rds & foll sp Camp Municipal & beach; site on L at bottom of hill opp municipal site. (Site is on a headland at end of D73). On arr at sea front park in public car park & walk to site recep to register. Med, hdg/mkd pitch, pt sl, pt shd; wc; chem disp; serviced piches; shwrs inc; el pnts (16A) inc (poss rev pol); gas; lndtte; shop; tradsmn; rest; snacks; bar; BBQ; playgrnd; htd pool; paddling pool; dir access shgl beach; cycle hire; games rm; entmnt; 30% statics; no dogs; c'vans over 8m not acc high ssn; poss cr; Eng spkn; adv bkg; quiet; cc acc; red long stay/low ssn; CCI. "Quiet, pleasant site; friendly, family-run; facs poss stretched in high ssn; narr site rds; gd touring base; recep 0930-1800; mkt Perros-Guirec Fri; deluxe or beach front pitches avail at extra cost; NB site clsd/locked up 2230-0730." ♦ 5 Apr-20 Sep. € 30.00 (CChq acc) ABS - B18
2007*

PERROS GUIREC *1D2* (1km SE Coastal) **Camp Municipal Ernest Renan, 22700 Louannec [02 96 23 11 78; fax 02 96 23 35 42; mairie-louannec@wanadoo.fr]** 1km W of Louannec on D6. Lge, unshd; wc; chem disp; mv service pnt; shwrs inc; el pnts (6A) inc; gas; ice; shop high ssn; rest; bar; playgrnd; htd pool; sand beach adj; fishing & watersports adj; games rm; TV; dogs €1; poss cr; adv bkg; Eng spkn; traff noise early am (minimal away fr rd). "Well-kept site; pitches right on seashore; marvellous views; clsd 1200-1530, little parking space outside." ♦ 1 Jun-30 Sep. € 16.00
2006*

> Did you know you can fill in site report forms on the Club's website — www.caravanclub.co.uk?

PERROS GUIREC *1D2* (1km W Urban) **Camping La Claire Fontaine, Tour ar Lann, 22700 Perros-Guirec [02 96 23 03 55; fax 02 96 49 06 19]** Fr Lannion N on D788 twd Perros-Guirec. At 2nd rndabt W on D11, then N on D6, L fork sp. Med, pt sl, pt shd; wc (some cont); chem disp; shwrs inc; baby facs; el pnts (4-6A) inc; ice; lndry rm; tradsmn; shops 800m; sand beach 800m; playgrnd; TV rm; dogs €0.95; quiet; adv bkg rec high ssn; Eng spkn. "Helpful staff." 1 May-15 Sep. € 21.96
2004*

PERROS GUIREC *1D2* (3km NW Coastal) **Camping Le Ranolien, Ploumanac'h, 22700 Perros-Guirec [02 96 91 65 65; fax 02 96 91 41 90; leranolien@yellohvillage.com; www.yellohvillage.com]** At Perros-Guirec harbour turn R at Marina foll sp Trégastel. Up hill above coast into Perros Guirec town. Cont strt thro traff lts & into La Clarté vill; strt at traff lts & sharp R at Camping & Le Ranolien sp. Ent shortly on L. Foll Trégastel sp all way. Lge, pt sl, pt shd; wc; mv service pnt; baby facs; shwrs inc; el pnts (16A) inc; lndtte; shop; rest; snacks; bar; 2 pools; waterslide; sand & rock beach; fishing; tennis; golf; horseriding; entmnt; many tour op statics; dogs €2; poss cr; Eng spkn; adv bkg; cc acc. "Excel for Corniche Bretonne beaches; wonderful coastal walks within 250m." ♦ 5 Apr-14 Sep. € 39.00
2006*

PERTRE, LE *2F4* (1km W Rural) **Camp Municipal Le Chardonneret, Route des Martyres, 35370 Le Pertre [02 99 96 99 27; fax 02 99 96 98 92; marieleperte@wandadoo.fr]** 25km W of Laval on N157 or A81; sp Le Pertre. Sm, hdg pitch, pt sl, pt shd; wc; shwrs; el pt (16A) inc; lndry rm; BBQ; 20% statics; dogs; phone; quiet. "Warden calls am/pm; o'night area for m'vans outside site; vg sh stay/NH." ♦ ltd. € 8.00
2005*

⊞**PERTUIS** *10E3* (8km N Rural) **Camping Etang de la Bonde, 84730 Cabrières-d'Aigues [04 90 77 63 64 or 04 90 77 77 15 (HS); fax 04 90 07 73 04; campingdelabonde@wanadoo. fr; www.campingdelabonde.com]** NE fr Pertuis on D956, fork L onto D9 (sp Cabrières & Etang de la Bonde). At x-rds in 8km turn R onto D27. Site on L in 200m. Med, pt shd; wc (some cont); shwrs; el pnts (6A) €3; gas; ice; shop; rest; snacks; playgrnd; pool 8km; games area; lake sw, watersports & fishing; tennis; many statics; dogs €1.60; poss cr; adv bkg; quiet; cc acc; CCI. "Lovely lakeside & beach; ltd facs low ssn - phone ahead to check open." € 10.50   2004*

PERTUIS *10E3* (2km E) **FFCC Camp Municipal Les Pinèdes, Quartier St Sépulcre, 84120 Pertuis [04 90 79 10 98; fax 04 90 09 03 99; campinglespinedes@free.fr; www.camping lespinedes.com]** Exit Pertuis on D973 twd Manosque. After 1km fr cent of Pertuis turn R foll sp Camping & Piscine. In 2km pass pool to site 100m on brow of hill. Lge, hdg pitch, pt sl, terr, pt shd; wc (some cont); chem disp; mv service pnt; baby facs; shwrs inc; el pnts (6-10A) €2-3.50; gas; lndry rm; ice; shop & 2km; playgrnd; pool 200m; entmnt; 5% statics; dogs €2; phone; quiet; red long stay; cc acc (high ssn); CCI. "Spacious, attractive site; clean & well-run; gates clsd 2200-0700; no twin-axle c'vans; vg." 15 Mar-15 Oct. € 9.30   2007*

PERTUIS *10E3* (6km SW Rural) **Camping Messidor (Naturist), Route de St Canadet, 13610 Le Puy-Ste Réparade [04 42 61 90 28; fax 04 42 50 07 08; messidor@online.fr; www.messidor.fr]** S fr Pertuis on D956/D556 twds Aix-en-Provence; after 5km turn R onto D561 twds Le Puy-Ste Réparade & Silvacane. At ent to vill take sp Aix-en-Provence via St Canadet (D13). Cross canal & turn immed 2nd R. Med, terr, pt sl, pt shd; wc; shwrs inc; el pnts (4A) €2.80; lndtte; ice; shop 3km; tradsmn; rest; snacks; bar; pool; rv fishing & watersports; tennis; 50% statics; dogs €2; Eng spkn; adv bkg; quiet; INF card req. "Gd facs & pool; lovely views fr some pitches; sh walk to bus stop for Aix." 1 Apr-30 Sep. € 18.00   2006*

PESMES *6G2* (500m S Rural) **Camp Municipal La Colombière, Route de Dole, 70140 Pesmes [03 84 31 20 15; fax 03 84 31 20 54; campcolombiere@aol.com]** On D475 halfway bet Gray & Dole. S fr Pesmes immed on L after x-ing rv bdge. N fr Dole, site sp on R immed bef rest at rv bdge. Med, some hdg pitch, pt shd; wc; own san rec high ssn; chem disp (wc); shwrs; el pnts (6-10A) €2.30-3.60; lndtte; shop 500m; rest adj; snacks; bar; cycle hire; dogs €1; phone; Eng spkn; adv bkg rec high ssn; quiet; no cc acc. "Picturesque vill; helpful, friendly management; vg." 1 Apr-30 Sep. € 8.30   2007*

PETIT PALAIS ET CORNEMPS see St Médard de Guizières *7C2*

PEUPLINGUES see Calais *3A3*

PEYNIER see Trets *10F3*

PEYRAT LE CHATEAU see Eymoutiers *7B4*

PEYRELEAU *10E1* (1km N Rural) **Camp Municipal de Brouillet, 48150 Le Rozier [05 65 62 63 98; fax 05 65 62 60 83; contact@camping-lerozier. com]** Fr Millau take N9 N to Aguessac, onto D907; in Le Rozier, x bdge over Rv Tarn onto D996 & in 200m (opp church); take rd on R to site; sp. Lge, mkd pitch, pt shd; wc; chem disp (wc); baby facs; shwrs inc; el pnts (6A) €2.70-3.10; lndtte; ice; shop 200m; playgrnd; htd pool; poss cr; adv bkg rec high ssn; quiet; red low ssn; CCI. "V pleasant, busy site; friendly recep; vg base for Tarn Gorges; gd area walking & birdwatching; conv, spacious site adj to rv; vg for m'vans; facs stretched when site full & poss poor cleaning; vg." ♦ ltd. 8 Apr-20 Sep. € 13.50   2006*

PEYRELEAU *10E1* (1km W Rural) **Camping Saint Pal, Route des Gorges du Tarn, 12720 Mostuéjouls [tel/fax 05 65 62 64 46 or 05 65 58 79 82 (LS); saintpal@wanadoo.fr; www.campingsaintpal.com]** Exit A75 exit junc 44.1 onto D29 to Aguessac then L onto D907 to Mostuéjouls. Or fr Millau take N9 N to Aguessac, turn R onto D907 to Mostuéjouls. Site in 10km 500m fr Rozier bdge. Med, hdg/mkd pitch, shd; wc (some cont); chem disp; mv service pnt; baby facs; fam bthrm; shwrs; el pnts (6A) €3; gas; lndtte; shop & 1km; tradsmn; snacks; bar high ssn; BBQ; playgrnd; pool; rv sw & beach adj; games rm; organised walks; TV; 20% statics; dogs €2; phone; poss cr; Eng spkn; adv bkg; quiet; cc acc; red low ssn/CCI. "Gd walks, canoeing, fishing & bird watching; v helpful owner; vg info rm; excel facs; poss diff for lge o'fits." ♦ 1 May-30 Sep. € 20.00   2007*

See advertisement on next page

PEYRIGNAC *7C3* (1km W Rural) **Camping La Garenne, La Brousse, 24210 Peyrignac [tel/ fax 05 53 50 57 73; s.lagarenne@wanadoo.com; http://membres.lycos.fr/campinglagarenne]** E fr Périgueux on A89. At Peyrignac foll site sp. Narr, steep rd poss diff lge o'fits. Med, mkd pitch, pt sl, shd; htd wc; chem disp; mv service pnt; baby facs; shwrs inc; el pnts (3-5A) €3.50-€5 (poss rev pol); gas; lndtte; ice; shop; tradsmn; snacks; bar; playgrnd; sm pool; games area; 50% statics; dogs €1.50; poss cr; adv bkg (dep req); quiet; CCI. "Gd touring base; gd size pitches; clean san facs." ♦ Mar-Nov. € 12.00   2006*

PEYRILLAC ET MILLAC see Souillac *7C3*

PEYRUIS see Château Arnoux *10E3*

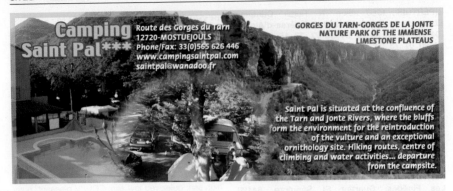

Camping Saint Pal***

Route des Gorges du Tarn
12720-MOSTUEJOULS
Phone/Fax: 33(0)565 626 446
www.campingsaintpal.com
saintpal@wanadoo.fr

GORGES DU TARN-GORGES DE LA JONTE
NATURE PARK OF THE IMMENSE
LIMESTONE PLATEAUS

Saint Pal is situated at the confluence of
the Tarn and Jonte Rivers, where the bluffs
form the environment for the reintroduction
of the vulture and an exceptional
ornithology site. Hiking routes, centre of
climbing and water activities... departure
from the campsite.

PEZENAS *10F1* (1km NE Urban) **Camping St Christol, Chemin de St Christol, 34120 Pézenas [04 67 98 09 00 or 06 11 39 59 17 (mob); fax 04 67 98 89 61; info@campingsaintchristol. com; www.campingsaintchristol.com]** Exit A75 junc 59 Pézenas N onto N9 by-pass for town cent; turn R immed bef bdge; sp on R in 200m. NB app rds narr. Med, hdg/mkd pitch, hdstg, shd; wc (some cont); chem disp (wc); baby facs; shwrs inc; el pnts (10A) €2.60; gas; lndtte; shop; tradsmn; rest; snacks; BBQ area; playgrnd; pool; fishing; games rm; entmnt; TV; some statics; dogs €1.30; poss cr; adv bkg rec Jul/Aug; quiet; cc acc; CCI. "Vg, friendly, lively site; lge gravel pitches but hard & dusty; diff to manoeuvre onto most pitches due trees; vg renovated san facs; rest rec; easy walk to historic town." ♦ 15 Apr-15 Sep. € 14.70   2006*

PEZENAS *10F1* (5km NE Urban) **Camp Municipal La Piboule, 34530 Montagnac [04 67 24 01 31]** Fr Pézenas on N9 dir Clermont-'Hérault, in approx 1km turn R onto N113 sp Montagnac. Site sp. Narr app unsuitable lge o'fits. Med, hdg/mkd pitch, pt sl, pt shd; wc (cont); shwrs inc; el pnts (10A) €3.20; lndry; shop, rest, snacks, bar 800m; playgrnd; phone; CCI. "Clean san facs; short walk to pretty vill; poss diff lge o'fits." 15 Mar-15 Dec. € 8.00
2006*

PEZENAS *10F1* (5km NE Rural) **Domaine St Martin-du-Pin (Crebassa), 34530 Montagnac [04 67 24 00 37; fax 04 67 24 47 50; elise_crebassa@yahoo.fr; www.saint-martin-du-pin.com]** Exit A75 junc 59 onto D113 to Montagnac. 2km past Montagnac turn R immed past picnic site at end of dual c'way, site sp. Sm, hdg pitch, pt sl, pt shd; wc; chem disp; baby facs; shwrs inc; el pnts €3; lndtte; ice; shop 2.5km; tradsmn; BBQ; playgrnd; pool; sand beach 9km; few statics; no dogs; Eng spkn; adv bkg (dep req); quiet; CCI. "Friendly owners; delightful site; spotless facs; lge pitches; gd touring base." May-30 Sep. € 20.00
2007*

PEZENAS *10F1* (8km S Rural) **Camping Le Pin Parasol, 34630 St Thibéry [tel/fax 04 67 77 84 29]** Fr A9 exit junc 34 onto D13 & foll Pézenas sps; in 2.5km turn R to St Thibéry & site 150m on R. Med, mkd pitch, pt shd; wc; shwrs inc; el pnts (10A) €3.40; snacks; supmkt 200m; tradsmn; playgrnd; pool; sand beach 10km; tennis 1km; games rm; rv sw 1km; fishing; entmnt; TV; 30% statics; poss cr; adv bkg (dep req); rd noise; cc not acc; CCI. "Vg san facs; lovely pool but site poss run down low ssn; interesting vill." ♦ 1 Jun-15 Sep. € 14.40
2007*

PEZENAS *10F1* (1km SW Urban) **Camp Municipal de Castelsec, Chemin de Castelsec, 34120 Pézenas [04 67 98 04 02; fax 04 67 90 72 47]** Fr Béziers take N9 to Pézenas. At rndabt turn L towards Centre Ville; in 300m turn L at ent HyperChampion supmkt & foll Campotel sp. Sm, mkd pitch, pt sl, pt terr, pt shd; wc; shwrs inc; el pnts (10A) €2.50; lndtte; shops 500m; playgrnd; pool 1km; tennis adj; TV; 30% statics; dogs; adv bkg; quiet; red low ssn; CCI. "V friendly staff; pleasant, functional site; clean, dated facs; sh walk into lovely town; NH only." ♦ 1 Apr-10 Oct. € 18.70
2007*

⊞**PEZENAS** *10F1* (10km NW) **Camping Les Clairettes, 34320 Fontès [04 67 25 01 31; fax 04 67 25 38 64; camping-clairettes@wanadoo.fr]** Sp both ways on N9. Turn onto D128 sp Adissan, Fontès. Fr A75 exit junc 58. Foll sp for Fontès. Med, hdg/mkd pitch, pt shd; wc; chem disp; serviced pitches; shwrs inc; el pnts (6A) inc; gas; lndtte; sm shop, rest, snacks, bar in ssn; BBQ; playgrnd; pool; entmnt; TV; 50% statics; adv bkg; red low ssn. "V quiet; friendly owners; ltd facs low ssn." ♦ ltd.
€ 20.50   2004*

PEZENAS *10F1* (10km NW Rural) **FFCC Camping L'Evasion, 34320 Fontès [04 67 25 32 00; fax 04 67 25 31 96; campingevasion34@yahoo.fr]** Fr A75 exit junc 59 (Pézenas). At rndabt take D124 to Lézignan-la-Cèbe then fork L, cont on D124 to Fontès. In vill foll sp to site. Sm, hdg/mkd pitch, pt sl, pt shd; wc; chem disp; mv service pnt; baby facs; showrs inc; el pnts (6A) €1.80; gas; lndtte; rest; snacks; bar; BBQ; playgrnd; pool; beach 30km; 20% statics; dogs €2.60; phone; adv bkg; quiet; CCI. "Excel san facs; gd value." ♦ ltd. 1 Apr-30 Oct. € 11.50   2006*

PEZULS see Bugue, Le *7C3*

PHALSBOURG *5D3* (2km N Rural) **FFCC Camping de Bouleaux (CC de F), Route des Trois Journeaux, 57370 Vilsberg [03 87 24 18 72; fax 03 87 24 46 52; ccdf_vilsberg@cegetel.net; www.campingclub.asso.fr]** Fr A4 exit dir Phalsbourg, then take N61 dir Sarreguemines. Site on R in 2km. Med, pt shd; wc; chem disp; baby facs; shwrs inc; el pnts (6A) inc; lndry rm; shop; tradsmn; playgrnd; 80% statics; dogs €2; red low ssn; CCI. "Gd facs; clean." ♦ 1 Apr-31 Oct. € 17.80   2006*

PHALSBOURG *5D3* (6km SW Rural) **Camping du Plan Incliné, Hoffmuhl, 57820 Henridorff [tel/fax 03 87 25 30 13 or 06 71 21 86 91 (mob); campingplanincline@wanadoo.fr; www.camping planincline.com]** Exit A4 at junc 44. In Phalsbourg take D38 twds Lutzelbourg; turn R onto D98 dir Arzviller & foll sp to Henridorff & site on R adj rv (narr ent). Med, some hdg/hdstg pitches, pt shd; wc; chem disp; shwrs inc; el pnts (6A) €3; gas; lndtte; ice; shop 2km; tradsmn; rest; snacks; bar; playgrnd; pool high ssn; rv sw, fishing & boating adj; entmnts; 30% statics; dogs €1; phone; Eng spkn; adv bkg; rlwy noise & some rd & boat noise; red low ssn; cc not acc; CCI. "In wooded valley; friendly warden; cycle path to Strasbourg; many local attractions." ♦ 1 Apr-20 Oct. € 12.50   2006*

PICQUIGNY *3C3* (Urban) **Camp Municipal, 66 Rue du Marais, 80310 Picquigny [03 22 51 25 83 or 03 22 51 40 31 (Mairie); fax 03 22 51 30 98]** Site sp fr town cent. Med, unshd; wc; chem disp; shwrs inc; el pnts (10A) €4; lndry rm; shop nr; rv & fishing; mainly statics; dogs €1.35; quiet; occasional noise fr rlwy line; adv bkg rec high ssn. "V nice site; modern san facs; WW1 war cemetery nr town; shops nrby." 1 Apr-1 Oct. € 10.00   2005*

PIERRE BUFFIERE *7B3* (1.5km S Rural) **Camp Intercommunal Chabanas, 87260 Pierre-Buffière [tel/fax 05 55 00 96 43]** Approx 20km S of Limoges on A20, take exit 40 onto D420 southbound; site on L in 500m. Foll sps for 'Stade-Chabanas'. Med, hdg/mkd pitch, pt sl, pt shd; htd wc; chemp disp (wc); shwrs inc; el pnts €2.30 (poss rev pol); lndtte; ice; shop & snacks 2 km; playgrnd; fishing; dogs €0.76; phone; adv bkg; quiet but some rlwy noise; red low ssn; CCI. "V clean & quiet site; v helpful staff; excel san facs; some pitches diff for lge o'fits; no twin-axles; warden on site 1600-2200, but gate poss locked all day low ssn (code issued); phone ahead; conv Limoges; excel NH fr A20." ♦ 15 May-30 Sep. € 10.00   2007*

This guide relies on site report forms submitted by caravanners like us; we'll do our bit and tell the editor what we think of the campsites we've visited.

PIERREFITTE SUR SAULDRE *4G3* (6km NE Rural) **Yelloh! Village Parc des Alicourts, Domaine des Alicourts, 41300 Pierrefitte-sur-Sauldre [02 54 88 63 34; fax 02 54 88 58 40; info@yellohvillage-parc-des-alicourts.com; www.sologne-parc-des-alicourts.com]** Fr S of Lamotte-Beuvron, turn L on D923. After 14km turn R on D24E sp Pierrefitte. After 750m turn L, foll sp to site approx 750m on R. Med, pt shd; wc; mv service pnt; chem disp; baby facs; shwrs inc; el pnts (6A) inc; gas; lndtte; shop; rest; snacks; bar; BBQ; playgrnd; 3 pools; waterslide; tennis; lake sw; kayak/pedalo hire; skating rink; mini-golf; cycle hire; games rm; entmnt; child entmnt; some statics; dogs €7; extra for lakeside pitches; poss cr (but roomy); Eng spkn; adv bkg (bkg fee); quiet; red low ssn; cc acc; CCI. "Excel, peaceful site; gd, clean facs; v lge pitches." ♦ 30 Apr-10 Sep. € 42.00   2007*

See advertisement on next page (top)

PIERREFONDS *3D3* (500m N Urban) **Camp Municipal de Batigny, Rue de l'Armistice, 60350 Pierrefonds [03 44 42 80 83]** Take D973 fr Compiegne; after 14km site on L adj sp for Pierrefonds at ent to vill. Med, hdg pitch, pt shd; htd wc; chem disp; mv service pnt; 90% serviced pitches; shwrs inc; el pnts (8A) €1.90; lndtte; shops 800m; rest in vill; 80% statics; dogs €1; poss cr; adv bkg; quiet; cc not acc; CCI. "Attractive site; well-maintained; facs stretched high ssn; much bird song; nr Armistice train & museum; Château Pierrefonds nr; red price 2nd night onwards; excel." 31 Mar-15 Oct. € 6.25   2007*

PIERREFORT *7C4* (7km SW Rural) **FLOWER Camping La Source, Presqu'île de Laussac, 12600 Thérondels [05 65 66 05 62; fax 05 65 66 25 07; info@camping-la-source.com; www.camping-la-source.com]** Fr A75 at St Flour, take D921 to Les Ternes, then D990 thro Pierrefort. Approx 2km after Pierrefort, turn L onto D34. Go thro Paulhenc, site on L after approx 7km. Med, hdg pitch, terr, pt shd; wc; chem disp; mv service pnt; baby facs; shwrs inc; el pnts (6-10A) €3-5; gas; lndtte; ice; shop; tradsmn; rest; snacks; bar; playgrnd; htd pool; paddling pool; waterslide; lake sw adj; fishing; watersports; games area; entmnt; TV; dogs €1.50; 20% statics; quiet; adv bkg (dep req) rec high ssn; CCI. "Excel lakeside site; boats for hire etc; poss diff lge o'fit due many lge trees." ♦ 12 May-9 Sep. € 25.90 (CChq acc) 2007*

⊞**PIEUX, LES** *1C4* (6km SE Rural) **Camp Municipal, 2 Route du Rozel, 50340 St Germain-le-Gaillard [02 33 52 55 64]** Take D650 fr Cherbourg. 3km beyond Les Pieux turn R sp Le Rozel. Site on R 100m. Sm, hdg pitch, some hdstg, unshd; htd wc; chem disp; shwrs inc; el pnts (15A) €2.50; 4 water stand pnts; lndry rm; shop; playgrnd; pool & sand beach 3km; 85% statics (sep area); dogs €1.05; poss cr; adv bkg. "Modern, clean, well-kept san facs; rec arr early high ssn - ltd touring pitches; poss diff in wet." ♦ € 6.10 2004*

PIEUX, LES *1C4* (3km SW Coastal) **Camping Village Le Grand Large, 50340 Les Pieux [02 33 52 40 75; fax 02 33 52 58 20; le-grand-large@wanadoo.fr; www.legrandlarge.com]** Fr ferry at 1st rndabt take 1st exit sp Centre Ville. Closer to town cent foll old N13 sp Caen. In about 1.5km branch R onto D900 then L onto D650 sp Carteret. Foll this rd past Les Pieux, cont on D650 to sp Super U. Turn R & foll site sp onto D517, then D117 for 3km until reaching beach rd to site, site on L in 2km. Lge, hdg/mkd pitch, pt shd; htd wc; chem disp; mv service pnt; baby facs; shwrs inc; el pnts (6A) inc; gas; lndtte; ice; shop; tradsmn; rest, snacks high ssn; bar; BBQ; playgrnd; htd pool; paddling pool; sand beach adj; horseriding 4km; tennis; entmnt; wifi internet; games/TV rm; 50% statics; dogs; phone; recep 0900-2100 high ssn; poss cr; Eng spkn; adv bkg; quiet; cc acc; CCI. "Dir access to superb beach; v clean facs; friendly staff; barrier clsd 2100-0900; outside pitches avail for early dep for ferries; coastal footpath; rec for families; great sunsets; mkt Fri." ♦ 12 Apr-21 Sep. € 34.00 (CChq acc) ABS - N07 2007*

See advertisement below

France

PIEUX, LES *1C4* (4km SW Coastal) **Camping Le Ranch, 50340 Le Rozel [02 33 10 07 10; fax 02 33 10 07 11; contact@camping-leranch.com; www.camping-leranch.com]** S fr Cherbourg on D650 & turn R to Les Pieux, then take D117 to Le Rozel. Turn L thro Rozel, foll sps to site. Site is on R at end rd. Med, pt sl, unshd; wc; chem disp; baby facs; shwrs inc; el pnts (3A) €4.20; lndtte; ice; shop; rest; snacks; bar; playgrnd; htd pool; waterslide; sand beach adj; fishing; watersports; games area; wifi internet; entmnt; 40% statics; dogs €2.30; quiet; red low ssn/long stay; CCI. 1 Apr-31 Oct. € 25.40
2007*

⊞**PIEUX, LES** *1C4* (6km NW Coastal) **Camp Municipal Clairefontaine, 5 Rue Alfred Rossel, 50340 Siouville-Hague [02 33 52 42 73]** Take D650 S fr Cherbourg, just bef Les Pieux turn R onto D23 Siouville-Hague, site sp fr beach rd. Lge, mkd pitch, pt shd; wc; shwrs; el pnts (6A) €2.19; ice; lndtte; shops, rest, bar 500m; playgrnd; sand beach 300m; rv adj; mini-golf; quiet.
2004*

PINSAC see Souillac *7C3*

PIRIAC SUR MER *2G3* (Coastal) **Camping Le Pouldroit, Route de Mesquer, 44420 Piriac-sur-Mer [02 40 23 50 91; fax 02 40 23 60 77; pouldroit@domaines-pleinair.com]** Foll coast rd fr La Baule to Guérande D99, NW to La Turballe & Piriac; on ent Piriac turn R & site 1km on L, on D52; sp. Lge, mkd pitch, pt shd; wc; shwrs inc; el pnts (10A) €1.98; gas; lndtte; shop; rest; snacks; bar; BBQ; playgrnd; htd pool; sand beach 300m; tennis; entmnt; many statics; phone; bus 100m; adv bkg; cc acc; CCI. "Conv Guérande, La Baule, St Nazaire." ♦ ltd. 1 Apr-12 Nov.
2005*

PIRIAC SUR MER *2G3* (3.5km E Coastal/Rural) **Camping Parc du Guibel, Route de Kerdrien, 44420 Piriac-sur-Mer [02 40 23 52 67; fax 02 40 15 50 24; camping@parcduguibel.com; www.parcduguibel.com]** Fr Guérande take D99 to La Turballe, D333 to St Sébastien. In St Sébastien turn R to Kerdrien over x-rds & site on R in approx 500m. Lge, mkd pitch, hdstg, pt sl, pt shd; wc (some cont); chem disp; mv service pnt; serviced pitches; shwrs inc; el pnts (3-10A) €2.90-4.30 (poss rev pol); gas; lndtte; shop; rest; snacks; bar; BBQ; playgrnd; htd pool high ssn; paddling pools; mini-waterslide; sand beach 1km; tennis; games area; cycle hire; entmnt; TV rm; 30% statics; dogs €2; phone; adv bkg; cc acc; CCI. "Helpful owner; lovely, quiet location in woods; gd touring base." ♦ 22 Mar-21 Sep. € 19.50
2006*

See advertisement above

As soon as we get home I'm going to post all these site report forms to the editor for inclusion in next year's guide. I don't want to miss the September deadline.

PIRIAC SUR MER *2G3* (1km S Rural) **Camping Amor-Héol, Route de Guérande, 44420 Piriac-sur-Mer [02 40 23 57 80; fax 02 40 23 59 42; armor-heol@wanadoo.fr; www.camping-armor-heol.com]** Fr Guérande on D90 & D33, site sp. Lge, mkd pitch, pt shd; wc; chem disp; baby facs; shwrs inc; el pnts (5A) €3.50; gas; lndtte; ice; shops 1km; rest; snacks; bar; BBQ; playgrnd; htd, covrd pool; waterslide; sand beach 700m; tennis; games area; games rm; fitness rm; 40% statics; dogs €4; adv bkg; quiet. "Attractive, well-maintained site; lge pitches." 5 Apr-21 Sep. € 29.75
2007*

See advertisement on next page

⊞**PITHIVIERS** *4F3* (1km SW Urban) **Camping Les Peupliers, Rue de Laas, 45300 Pithiviers [tel/fax 02 38 30 76 96; lespeupliers45@aol.com]** Fr town cent take rd sp Jargeau/Montargis. Turn R at 'Camping' sp on R in about 1km on L-hand bend into Rue de Laas. Site on R in approx 750m down narr, rough track on rvsite. Ring bell at barrier. Fr S on D921 at rndabt where D950 joins, take exit sp 'Centre Ville, Faubourg du Gâtinais, site sp on L. Sm, some hdg pitch, pt shd; htd wc (some cont); chem disp; shwrs inc; el pnts (10A) €3; gas; lndtte; shops 800m; snacks, bar high ssn; playgrnd; pool 500m; dogs €1; adv bkg; quiet but some rd noise; 10% red long stay. "Picturesque setting; pleasant town; welcoming owner; tourist steam rlwy (Suns) & museum nr; gd rest in vill; some permanent residents; ltd facs & rough pitches - NH only." € 10.00   2006*

PLAINE SUR MER, LA see Pornic *2G3*

PLAISANCE (GERS) *8F2* (500m Urban) **Camping de l'Arros, Allée de Ormeaux, 32160 Plaisance [05 62 69 30 28; infos@plaisance-evasion.com; www.plaisance-evasion.com]** N from Tarbes on D935, approx 25 km N of Maubourguet turn R onto D946 to Plaisance. Foll sp to site on o'skts of town. Sm, mkd pitch; pt sl, pt shd; wc; chem disp; shwrs inc; el pnts (2-5A); lndtte; shops 500m; rest; snacks; bar; gas BBQ only; playgrnd; pool; 40% statics; dogs €2; phone; adv bkg ess high ssn; red low ssn; cc acc; CCI. "Close to rv; canoes avail." ♦ ltd. 1 Apr-30 Sep. € 21.00   2006*

PLANCOET *2E3* (Urban) **Camp Municipal du Verger, 22130 Plancoët [02 96 84 03 42 or 02 96 84 39 70 (Mairie); fax 02 96 84 19 49; mairie.plancoet@wanadoo.fr;   www.mairie-plancoet.fr]** On D974 fr Dinan descend to bdge over rlwy lines & site well sp. Med, mkd pitch, pt shd; wc; chem disp; shwrs inc; el pnts (5A) inc; lndtte; shops 50m; sand beach 13km; rv fishing; cycle hire; TV; some statics; adv bkg rec high ssn; quiet; CCI. "Excel sand beach at Pen Guen; adj pleasant park & rv with canoeing & close to rests/bars; poss itinerants/mkt traders." 1 Jun-15 Sep. € 8.60   2006*

PLANCOET *2E3* (4km SW Rural) **Camping Pallieter (Naturist), Le Ville Menier, Bourseul, 22130 Plancoët [02 96 83 05 15; fax 02 96 83 06 13; mail@pallieter.fr; www.pallieter.fr]** NW fr Dinan on D794 to Plancoët. In Plancoët turn L at rndbt opp Hotel Relais de la Source onto D19 dir Plélan-le-Petit. Site in 3km, sp. Med, unshd, mkd pitch; wc; chem disp; shwrs inc; el pnts (6A) €3.50; lndtte; shop 4km; tradsmn; snacks; bar; playgrnd; pool; some statics; dogs €5; Eng spkn; adv bkg; quiet. "Gd naturist site; min stay 3 nights high ssn; INF card req." 28 Apr-30 Sep. € 25.00   2007*

PLANCOET *2E3* (8km W Rural) **Camping à la Ferme (Robert), Le Pont-à-l'Ane, 22130 Landébia [tel/fax 02 96 84 47 52]** Fr Plancoët, take D768 twd Lamballe; in 8km turn L at 1st sp to Landébia, farm in 800m on R, sp fr Plancoët. Sm, pt shd; wc; own san; shwrs inc; el pnts (10A) €2.70; shops 1km; tradsmn; playgrnd; dogs €0.50; some Eng spkn; quiet; cc not acc. "CL-type in old orchard; nice rural site but facs v basic/primitive; owners v helpful & friendly; gd base for N coast beaches; poss mosquitoes." 1 Apr-31 Oct. € 8.40   2005

PLELAN LE GRAND *2F3* (400m S Urban) **Camp Municipal, Rue de l'Hermine, 35380 Plélan-le-Grand [02 99 06 81 41 (Mairie)]** Fr Rennes on N24. Leave N24 at town sp. Site sp on L at W end of town. Sm, shd; wc (some cont); chem disp (wc); mv service pnt; shwrs inc; el pnts €2.35; lndtte; shops 400m; playgrnd; htd pool; rv 2km; tennis; dogs; quiet but some traff noise. "Well-organised, gd facs for municipal site; warden calls am & pm, site yourself; gd NH." 15 Apr-15 Sep. € 8.40   2004*

PLELAN LE GRAND *2F3* (7km SW Rural) **Camping du Château d'Aleth, Rue de l'Ecole, 56380 St Malo-de-Beignon [02 99 80 96 96 or 06 78 96 10 62 (mob) or 06 08 32 98 81 (mob); contact@camping-aleth.com;   www.camping-aleth.com]** Fr N24 twds Rennes exit N onto D773 to St Malo-de-Beignon in 5km, site L by church. Sm, pt sl, pt shd; wc; chem disp; mv service pnt; shwrs; el pnts (10A) €2.50; lndtte; shop; rest, bar 300m; BBQ; playgrnd; dogs; Eng spkn; quiet. "Pleasant site by lake with boats for children; clean site & facs." ♦ 1 May-30 Sep. € 9.50   2006*

PLELAN LE GRAND *2F3* (8km NW Rural) **Camp Municipal Brocéliande, Rue du Chevalier Lancelot du Lac, 35380 Paimpont [02 99 07 89 16 or 02 99 07 81 18 (Mairie); fax 02 99 07 88 18; mairie.paimport@wanadoo.fr]** Sp on N edge of Paimpont vill. On D773 dir St Méen-le-Grand/Concoret, 500m fr Paimpont. Med, hdg/mkd pitch, pt shd; wc (some cont); chem disp; shwrs inc; el pnts (5A) €2.50; gas 500m; lndtte; playgrnd; rv & lake sw & fishing adj; cycle hire; tennis; entmnts; phone; bus in vill; quiet; CCl. "V pleasant site, spacious & clean; friendly; conv NH; excel touring base; sh walk to attractive vill with shops & gd rest."
♦ 1 May-30 Sep. € 8.55   2006*

PLESTIN LES GREVES *2E2* (2km NE Coastal) **Camp Municipal St Efflam, Rue Lan-Carré, 22310 Plestin-les-Grèves [02 96 35 62 15; fax 02 96 35 09 75; campingmunicipal@plestingreves. com; www.camping-municipal-bretagne.com]** Fr Morlaix D786 thro Plestin, on R at foot of hill, well sp. Lge, mkd pitch, pt sl, terr, pt shd; wc; chem disp; mv service pnt; shwrs inc; el pnts (7A) €2.40; gas; lndry rm; lndtte; tradsmn; rest; bar; BBQ; playgrnd; sand beach 150m; sw, fishing, boating adj; dogs €1.20; Eng spkn; adv bkg ess high ssn; red low ssn; cc acc; CCl. "Excel; v helpful recep."
♦ ltd. 1 Apr-30 Sep. € 10.60   2007*

PLEUBIAN see Tréguier *1D3*

PLEUMEUR BODOU see Trégastel *1D2*

PLEUVILLE see Pressac *7A3*

PLEYBEN *2E2* (5km S Rural) **Camp Municipal de Pont-Coblant, 29190 Pleyben [02 98 73 31 22 or 02 98 26 68 11 (Mairie); fax 02 98 26 38 99; communedepleyben@wanadoo.fr]** On D785 Quimper rd. Turn L immed by phone box on ent Pont-Coblant. Med, mkd pitch, pt shd; wc; shwrs inc; el pnts (6-10A) €3; shop 4km; rest, bar adj; rv sw; canoe & cycle hire; poss cr; some rd noise. "Beautiful, quiet site beside rv/canal; charming; spacious pitches; clean facs; tow-path walks; warden visits twice daily (or call at Mairie); rec 400 yr old vill church calvaries." 15 Jun-15 Sep. € 9.00
2007*

PLOBANNALEC see Pont l'Abbé *2F2*

PLOEMEL see Auray *2F3*

PLOEMEUR see Lorient *2F2*

PLOERMEL *2F3* (3km N Rural) **Camping du Lac, Les Belles Rives, 56800 Taupont-Ploërmel [tel/fax 02 97 74 01 22; camping-du-lac@wanadoo.fr; www.camping-du-lac-ploermel.com]** Fr Ploërmel cent, take D8 twds Taupont; under narr bdge; foll sp to Lac-au-Duc 3km. Site clearly sp on R on edge of lake. Med, hdg/mkd/hdstg pitch, terr, pt shd; htd wc; mv service pnt; chem disp; shwrs inc; el pnts (5A) €2.10; gas; lndtte; ice; shop; tradsmn; snacks; bar; BBQ; playgrnd; pool & waterslide nrby; sand beach & lake sw adj; watersports adj; cycle hire nrby; tennis; 10% statics; dogs €0.60; Eng spkn; adv bkg; quiet; cc acc high ssn; red low ssn; CCl. "V pleasant site; golf & horseriding 1km; interesting area; vg." ♦ 1 Apr-30 Sep. € 9.40 2007*

See advertisement below

⊞**PLOERMEL** *2F3* (6km N Rural) **FFCC Camping Parc Merlin l'Enchanteur, 8 Rue du Pont, Vallée de l'Yvel, 56800 Loyat [02 97 93 05 52 or 02 97 73 89 45; fax 02 97 60 47 77; camelotpark@wanadoo.fr; www.campingmerlin.com]** Fr Ploërmel take D766 N sp St Malo. In 5km turn L to Loyat. Site on L on ent vill opp garage. Med, hdg/mkd pitch, pt shd; htd wc; chem disp; mv service pnt; shwrs inc; el pnts (6-10A) €3-4 (poss rev pol); gas; lndtte; ice; sm shop & other shops 600m; tradsmn high ssn; rest, bar 200m; BBQ; sand beach/lake sw with watersports 4km; fishing; tennis; games area; cycle hire; 10% statics; dogs €1; phone 1km; adv bkg; v quiet; red long stay; cc acc; red CCl. "Peaceful atmosphere; sm lake adj; spacious pitches but poss soggy in winter; vg clean facs; welcoming British owners; excel rest in vill; conv Château Josselin, Lizio & Brocéliande forest with legend of King Arthur; pool planned for 2008; vg." ♦ € 9.50   2007*

France

PLOERMEL *2F3* (10km S Urban) **Camp Municipal du Pont Salmon, Rue Général de Gaulle, 56460 Sérent [02 97 75 91 98; fax 02 97 75 98 35]** Fr N166 Vannes-Rennes take D10 W 5km to Sérent. At N end of vill turn L at Pont Salmon, site on R. Med, hdg pitch, pt sl, pt shd; htd wc (male all cont); chem disp; mv service pnt; shwrs inc; el pnts (10A) €2.15 (poss rev pol); lndtte; shops 300m; playgrnd; htd pool; 5% statics; adv bkg; quiet. "Excel, well-kept site; Resistance Museum at St Marcel-Malestroit; gd san facs." ♦ ltd. 1 May-15 Sep. € 6.60   2004*

PLOERMEL *2F3* (7km NW Rural) **Camping La Vallée du Ninian, Route du Lac, Le Rocher-Taupont, 56800 Ploërmel [02 97 93 53 01; fax 02 97 93 57 27; infos@camping-ninian.com; www.camping-ninian.com]** Fr Ploërmel cent foll sp to Taupont or Lac au Duc; N on D8. Thro vill Taupont take L hand turn sp La Vallée du Ninian; site on L 1km fr Helléan. Sm, hdg pitch (lge), pt shd; wc; chem disp; shwrs inc; baby facs; el pnts (3-6A) €1.80-3.30; ice; lndtte; shop; bar; playgrnd; htd pool; paddling pool; lake sw & watersports 4km; sand beach 4km; entmnt; dogs €1; quiet; adv bkg. "Farm produce; helpful owners; v peaceful; singing rd campfire some nights; gd facs for children; vg." ♦ 15 Apr-30 Sep. € 12.10   2005*

PLOGONNEC see Locronan *2E2*

PLOMBIERES LES BAINS *6F2* (10km S Rural) **Camp Municipal Le Val d'Ajol, Chemin des Oeuvres, 88340 Le Val-d'Ajol [03 29 66 55 17]** Fr N on N57 after Plombières-les-Bains turn onto D20 sp Le Val-d'Ajol. Site sps in vill. Sm, hdg pitch, pt shd; wc; chem disp; shwrs inc; el pnts (6A) €2.20; shop 1km; pool adj; TV; dogs; phone; adv bkg; quiet; CCI. "Clean facs; gd for touring Vosges & walking; one of best municipal sites seen." ♦ 15 Apr-30 Sep. € 8.10   2006*

PLOMBIERES LES BAINS *6F2* (4km W Urban) **Camp Municipal du Fraiteux, 81 Rue du Camping, Ruaux, 88370 Plombières-les-Bains [03 29 66 00 71 or 03 29 66 00 24 (Mairie); fax 03 29 30 06 64; campingdufraiteux@tiscali.fr; http://campingdufraiteux.chez-alice.fr]** Turn W fr N57 in cent of Plombières-les-Bains onto D20, foll sp to Epinal for 2km then L onto D20B to Ruaux, site on L. Sm, mkd pitch, pt sl; wc; shwrs inc; el pnts (4-10A) €2.70-4; gas; lndtte; ice; shops adj; playgrnd; pool 3km; some statics; dogs €0.70; poss cr; quiet; 20% red CCI. 1 Mar-31 Oct. € 10.60   2007*

PLONEOUR LANVERN see Pont l'Abbé *2F2*

The opening dates and prices on this campsite have changed. I'll send a site report form to the editor for the next edition of the guide.

PLONEVEZ PORZAY *2E2* (4km W Coastal) **Camping de Tréguer Plage, Ste Anne-la-Palud, 29550 Plonévez-Porzay [02 98 92 53 52; fax 02 98 92 54 89; camping-treguer-plage@wanadoo.fr; www.camping-treguer-plage.com]** On D107 S fr Châteaulin. After 8km turn R to Ste Anne-la-Palud & foll sp. Lge, hdg/mkd pitch, hdstg, pt shd; wc (some cont); chem disp; mv service pnt; shwrs inc; el pnts (6A) €2.80; gas; lndtte; ice; shop; tradsmn; snacks; bar; BBQ; playgrnd; sand beach adj; games area; games rm; entmnt; child entmnt; TV rm; some statics; dogs €1.60; Eng spkn; adv bkg; cc acc; CCI. "Well-situated touring base; vg, friendly site; excel beach." 7 Apr-29 Sep. € 14.10   2007*

See advertisement below

A campsite on an untouched beach for unique holidays.

LA PLAGE DE TRÉGUER   Tel + 33 (0)2 98 92 53 52
Reservation on
www.camping-treguer-plage.com

France

PLONEVEZ PORZAY *2E2* (4km W Coastal) Camping Domaine de Kervel, 29550 Plonévez-Porzay [02 98 92 51 54; fax 02 98 92 54 96; camping.kervel@wanadoo.fr; www.camping-franceloc.fr] Fr Douarnenez take D107 twd Châteaulin. After 8km turn L to Plage de Kervel & foll sp. Lge, hdg/mkd pitch, hdstg, pt shd; htd wc; chem disp; mv service pnt; baby facs; shwrs inc; el pnts (10A) €3.50; gas; lndtte; ice; shop; rest; snacks; bar; BBQ (gas/charcoal); playgrnd; 3 htd pools (1 covrd); waterslide; sand beach 800m; tennis; games rm; mini-golf; entmnt (Jul & Aug); child entmnt; 30% statics; dogs €5; poss cr; Eng spkn; adv bkg (rec in high ssn); cc acc; 5% red CCI. "Gd touring base for lovely area; helpful staff; excel, clean san facs." ♦ 28 Apr-30 Sep. € 23.50 2007*

See advertisement above

PLONEVEZ PORZAY *2E2* (4km W Coastal) Camping Trezmalaouen, 20 Route de la Baie, 29550 Plonévez-Porzay [tel/fax 02 98 92 54 24; contact@campingtrezmalaouen.com; www.camping-trezmalaouen.com] Fr Douarnenez take D107 N dir Plonévez-Porzay, site sp. Med, hdg/mkd pitch, some hdstg, pt shd; wc; chem disp; mv service pnt; shwrs inc; el pnts; lndtte; BBQ; playgrnd; sand beach adj; 75% statics; dogs €1.70; 2 mobile homes for disabled; dogs; adv bkg; cc acc; red long stay/low ssn/CCI. "Sea views; vg touring base." 15 Mar-15 Oct. € 13.00 2006*

PLOUAY *2F2* (4km NW Rural) Camping Bois des Ecureuils, 29300 Guilligomarc'h [tel/fax 02 98 71 70 98; bois-des-ecureuils@tiscali.fr; www.bois-des-ecureuils.fr] N fr Plouay on D769 dir Faouet, for 5km; turn L to Guilligomarc'h; site sp. Sm, mkd pitch, pt sl, shd; wc (some cont); chem disp; shwrs inc; el pnts (5A) €2.40; gas; lndtte; ice; shop 3km; tradsmn; playgrnd; rv sw 3km; lake 6km; sand beach 25km; cycle hire; dogs €1; poss cr; Eng spkn; adv bkg; quiet; no cc acc; CCI. "Friendly British owners; conv touring Brittany; gd walking; excel peaceful site; lge pitches." ♦ ltd. 15 May-15 Sep. € 10.00 2005*

PLOUESCAT *2E2* (2km W Coastal) Camping La Baie de Kernic, Rue de Pen-an-Théven, 29430 Plouescat [02 98 69 86 60 or 04 99 57 20 25; fax 04 99 57 21 22; kernic@village-center.com; www.village-center.com/kernic] Site sp W of Plouescat fr D10. Lge, hdg/mkd pitch, hdstg, pt shd; wc; chem disp; mv service pnt; sauna; shwrs €2; el pnts (8A) inc; lndtte; shop; rest; tradsmn; snacks; bar; BBQ; playgrnd; htd pools (1 covrd); paddling pool; sand beach adj; watersports; tennis; games area; internet; entmnt; child entmnt; dogs €3; Eng spkn; adv bkg; red low ssn. "Pleasant resort; well-run site." ♦ 7 Apr-16 Sep. € 29.00 2007*

PLOUEZEC see Paimpol *1D3*

PLOUGASNOU *1D2* (1.5km SE Rural) Camping Le Trégor, Route de Morlaix, Kerjean, 29630 Plougasnou [02 98 67 37 64; bookings@campingdutregor.com; www.campingdutregor.com] At junc of D46 to Plougasnou. Site is on L just bef town sp. Sm, hdg/mkd pitch, pt shd; wc; chem disp (wc); shwrs inc; el pnts (6-10A) inc; gas; ice; lndtte; shop 1km; BBQ; playgrnd; sand beach 1.2km; lake sw & watersports 3km; 10% statics; dogs €0.80; poss cr; adv bkg; quiet; CCI. "British owners; ideal for walking, cycling & fishing; beautiful countryside & beaches nrby; convenient for Roscoff ferries & Morlaix town; phone if req NH after end Oct." Easter-31 Oct. € 13.00 2005*

PLOUGASNOU *1D2* (3km NW Coastal/Urban) Camp Municipal de la Mer, 29630 Primel-Trégastel [tel/fax 02 98 72 37 06 or 02 98 67 30 06; primel-tregastel.camping-de-la-mer@wanadoo.fr] Fr Morlaix take D46 to Plougastel on to Primel-Trégastel. Bear R in vill & 1st L opp cafe to site on R in 100 m. Med, unshd; wc; chem disp; mv service pnt; shwrs (with token); el pnts (10A) inc; gas 1.5km; lndtte; shops 1.5km; tradsmn high ssn; playgrnd; sand beach 500m; dogs; phone; poss cr; quiet; no cc acc; CCI. "Fine coastal views; gd walking & cycling; ltd facs low ssn." ♦ ltd. 1 Jun-30 Sep. € 15.30 2005*

⊞**PLOUGASTEL DAOULAS** 2E2 (4.5km NW Coastal) **Camping St Jean, 29470 Plougastel-Daoulas [02 98 40 32 90; fax 02 98 04 23 11; campingstjean@wanadoo.fr; www.camping saintjean.com]** Fr Brest, take N165 E for approx 12km then leave m'way after Plougsatel exit & foll sp. Site in 2km at end of rd by rv. Med, pt sl, terr, pt shd; wc; mv service pnt; shwrs; el pnts (6-10A) €2.50-€3 (poss rev pol); lndtte; ice; shop & 5km; snacks; playgrnd; htd, covrd pool; TV; dogs €1; poss cr; quiet; red low ssn. "Nice site by rv; steep in places; gd facs; €20 dep for security barrier." € 15.00   2006*

PLOUGONVELIN see Conquet, Le 2E1

PLOUGOULM see Roscoff 1D2

Did you know you can fill in site report forms on the Club's website — www.caravanclub.co.uk?

PLOUGRESCANT see Tréguier 1D3

PLOUGUERNEAU 2E2 (2km N Coastal) **Camping La Grève Blanche, St Michel, 29880 Plouguerneau [02 98 04 70 35 or 02 98 04 63 97 (LS); fax 02 98 04 63 97; lroudaut@free.fr]** Fr Lannilis D13 to Plouguerneau, D32 sp La Grève, St Michel (look out for lorry rte sp). Avoid Plouguerneau vill when towing - tight RH bend. Med, pt sl, terr, unshd; wc; shwrs €1; el pnts (9A) €2.30; bar; shops 3km; playgrnd; sand beach; dogs €1.80; Eng spkn; adv bkg; 10% red low ssn; CCI. "Gd views over sea & islands; in fog lighthouse sounds all night otherwise quiet; facs clean & well-kept; low ssn recep open eves only; helpful staff." ♦ ltd. 15 May-10 Oct. € 10.00   2006*

PLOUGUERNEAU 2E2 (6km N Coastal) **Camping du Vougot, Route de Prat-Leden, 29880 Plouguerneau [tel/fax 02 98 25 61 51; campingduvougot@hotmail.fr; www.camping plageduvougot.com]** Fr N12 at Landerneau exit N onto D770 to Lesneven, then D28/D32 to Plouguerneau. Fr Plouguerneau take D10 dir Guissény then turn W onto D52 dir Grève du Vougot, site sp. Med, hdg/mkd pitch, pt shd; wc; chem disp; shwrs €1; el pnts (10A) €3.30; lndtte; ice; shop 6km; tradsmn; snacks; playgrnd; sand beach 250m; watersports nr; entmnt; 30% statics; dogs €2.60; adv bkg; red long stay; CCI. "Gd walking; interesting area; excel touring base." ♦ 1 Apr-15 Oct. € 16.00   2007*

See advertisement below

PLOUGUERNEAU 2E2 (5km NE Coastal) **Aire Naturalle de Keralloret (Yvinec), 29880 Guissény [02 98 25 60 37; fax 02 98 25 69 88; auberge@keralloret.com jiesan@davidryan@ wanadoo.co.uk; www.keralloret.com]** On D10 dir Plouguerneau, site 2.5km after Guissény. Sm, pt shd; wc; chem disp (wc); shwrs inc; el pnts (6A) €2.40 (v long lead req most pitches); tradsmn; rest; snacks; beach 5km; Eng spkn; adv bkg; quiet; cc acc; CCI. "Delightful CL-type site with pitches around a sm lake; spacious & peaceful; pleasant owners; ltd hook-ups; sm, dated but clean san facs; vg rest; excel." Easter-1 Nov. € 9.50   2007*

PLOUHA 2E3 (Rural/Coastal) **Camping Domaine de Kerjean, 22580 Plouha [02 96 20 24 75]** Exit N12 at Les Rampes onto D786 N to Plouha. Site sp fr town cent. Lge, mkd pitch, hdstg, pt shd; wc; shwrs inc; el pnts €4; ice; shop 3km; snacks; bar; BBQ (gas/elec); playgrnd; htd, covrd pool nr; sand beach 1km; fishing, sailing 10km; tennis 4km; horseriding 2km; dogs; adv bkg; Eng spkn; quiet. "Well-situated for beautiful local beaches; gd walking area; vg." ♦ 15 May-15 Sep. € 18.00
                                                2007*

Le camping du Vougot** 29880 PLOUGUERNEAU • Phone/Fax 02 98 25 61 51
www.campingplageduvougot.com • campingduvougot@hotmail.fr

Protected and quiet campsite. Spacious beautifully landscaped pitches. 250 m from a fine sandy beach and a turquoise bleu sea - many tourist pitches. **Phone / fax: 0033 (0)2 98 25 61 51**

Situated at Bréhec, at 600 m from the beach, on a 2 ha surface with 73 pitches, at 100 m from the Customs Officers' trail G34, the campsite Le Varquez will accommodate you in a family atmosphere and green surroundings.
You will get a warm welcome, quality services and our full commitment for great holidays.

CAMPING LE VARQUEZ-SUR-MER ★★★

5, route de la Corniche BREHEC PLAGE
F-22580 PLOUHA Phone: +33 (0)2.96.22.34.43
Fax: +33 (0)2.96.22.68.87 • www.camping-le-varquez.com

France

⊞PLOUHA 2E3 (5km NE Coastal) **Camping Le Varquez-sur-Mer, 5 Route de la Corniche, Bréhec-Plage, 22580 Plouha** [02 96 22 34 43; fax 02 96 22 68 87; campinglevarquez@wanadoo.fr; www.camping-le-varquez.com] Sp bet St Quay-Portrieux & Paimpol fr D786. Med, hdg/mkd pitch, hdstg, pt sl, pt shd; wc; chem disp; shwrs; el pnts (6-10A) €3.60; gas; lndtte; shop 4km; tradsmn; snacks; bar; BBQ; playgrnd; htd pool; paddling pool; sand beach 600m; cycle hire; entmnt; TV; 30% statics; dogs €1.80; Eng spkn; quiet cc acc; CCI. "Lovely coast; peaceful, family-run site; adj walking rte G34." ♦ € 17.30   2007*

See advertisement above

PLOUHARNEL see Carnac 2G3

PLOUHINEC 2F2 (1km SE Coastal) **Camping Le Moténo, Route du Magouër, 56680 Plouhinec** [02 97 36 76 63; fax 02 97 85 81 84; camping-moteno@wanadoo.fr; www.camping-le-moteno.com] App Auray on D22, take 2nd turn L after Pont Lerois & foll sps. Lge, hdg/mkd pitch, pt shd; wc; chem disp; shwrs; el pnts (6A) €3.50; gas; lndtte; ice; shop; rest; snacks; bar; playgrnd; pool; waterslide; rv sw, beach 800m; fishing & watersports 100m; cycle hire; games area; games rm; entmnt; TV; some statics; dogs €3.80; Eng spkn; adv bkg; quiet; red low ssn. "Pleasant site; gd base for visiting Carnac & Quiberon Peninsula." ♦ 15 Apr-15 Sep. € 22.90   2007*

PLOUHINEC 2F2 (5km S Coastal) **Camp Municipal de la Falaise, Rue de la Barre, 56410 Etel** [02 97 55 33 79; fax 02 97 55 34 14] Fr L'Orient, take D781 twd Carnac, turn R to Etel (sp) after x-ing bdge over Rv Etel. Foll sp for La Plage or Camping. Or fr Carnac, exit D781 at Erdeven on D105 to Etel. Med, mkd pitch, pt sl, pt shd; wc; shwrs inc; el pnts (poss rev pol); lndtte; ice; shop 500m; sand beach; lake sw; boat trips; windsurfing & canoes; quiet; CCI. 15 May-15 Sep.   2005*

PLOUVORN see Landivisiau 2E2

PLOZEVET 2F2 (500m W) **Camping de la Corniche, Route de la Corniche, 29710 Plozévet** [02 98 91 33 94 or 02 98 91 32 93; fax 02 98 91 41 53; infos@campinglacorniche.com; www.campinglacorniche.com] Fr N165 foll sp Audierne onto D784 to Plozévet & foll sps to site. Med, hdg pitch, pt shd; wc; chem disp; mv service pnt; baby facs; shwrs inc; el pnts (6A) €3; lndtte; shop; tradsmn; playgrnd; pool; beach 2km; 10% statics; dogs €2; red low ssn; CCI. "Lge pitches; helpful owner; excel facs; gd." ♦ 1 Apr-30 Sep. € 16.20   2006*

PLUMERGAT see Ste Anne d'Auray 2F3

POET LAVAL, LE 9D2 (E Rural) **Camp Municipal Lorette, 26160 Le Poët-Laval** [04 75 91 00 62 or 04 75 46 44 12 (Mairie); fax 04 75 46 46 45; camping.lorette@wanadoo.fr] Site 4km W of Dieulefit on D540. Med, mkd pitch, pt shd; wc; chem disp (wc); mv service pnt; shwrs inc; el pnts (10A) €1.85; lndtte; ice; shop; tradsmn; rest 500m; snacks; playgrnd; pool; tennis; no statics; dogs €0.90; bus; phone; quiet; CCI. "Nr lavender fields (Jun/Jul); views; well-kept; v lge pitches; clean, modern facs; mkt in Dieulefit Fri; excel." ♦ 1 May-30 Sep. € 19.15   2006*

POET LAVAL, LE 9D2 (8km W Rural) **Camping à la Ferme des Roures (Gontard), Route de St Gervais, Les Roures, 26160 La Bégude-de-Mazenc** [04 75 46 21 80; gitesfrance@ferme-des-roures.com] Fr Montélimar E on D540 for 15km. Turn L onto D74 dir St Gervais. Foll sp for site. Sm, pt sl, shd; wc; chem disp; shwrs inc; el pnts (10A) €2.20 (poss rev pol); lndtte; gas & shop 4km; dogs €0.75; quiet; CCI. "Site in wood in pleasant area; friendly, helpful owners; clean facs; fridge hire." ♦ 1 May-30 Sep. € 8.00   2006*

POILLY LEZ GIEN see Gien 4G3

POITIERS For sites convenient for Futuroscope, also see listings under Châtellerault and Jaunay Clan.

POITIERS *7A2* (10km N Rural) **Camping du Futur, 1 Rue des Bois, 86170 Avanton [05 49 54 09 67; fax 05 49 54 09 59; contact@camping-du-futur. com; www.camping-du-futur.com]** Exit A10 junc 28. After toll take 1st exit at rndabt sp Avanton. Site well sp fr Avanton, but care needed thro Martigny & hotel complex. Med, hdg/mkd pitch, pt shd; wc; chem disp (wc); mv service pnt; shwrs inc; el pnts (10A) €3; lndtte; tradsmn; bar; playgrnd; pool high ssn; mini-golf; TV; dogs €1.50; c'van storage; adv bkg; quiet; red low ssn; CCI. "Lovely site & well-managed; v helpful British owners; modern, clean, excel facs; 5 mins Futuroscope & A10; excel site." ♦ 1 Apr-30 Sep. € 18.00   2007*

POITIERS *7A2* (8km S Urban) **Camp Municipal, Ave de la Plage, 86240 Ligugé [05 49 55 29 50; fax 05 49 55 38 45; liguge@cg86.fr; www.liguge. fr]** E of N10; site sp & off D4 Poitiers-Vivonne rd (not N10) in Ligugé. Sm, mkd pitch, pt shd; wc; chem disp; shwrs; el pnts (8A) inc; ice; tradsmn; shops 2km; playgrnd; rv fishing 200m; football stadium adj; TV; Eng spkn; quiet; CCI. "V pleasant & helpful resident wardens; ample san facs; barrier unlocked for each ent/exit; some rd & rlwy noise; public access to stadium thro site; twin-axle extra charge." 15 Jun-15 Sep. € 7.50   2006*

POITIERS *7A2* (1.5km NW Urban) **Camp Municipal du Porteau, Rue du Porteau, 86000 Poitiers [05 49 41 44 88; fax 05 49 46 41 91; rebeilleau@ agglo-poitiers.fr; www.mairie-poitiers.fr]** Sp off D910 (N10) Rocade Quest. Sm, unshd; wc; chem disp; mv service pnt; shwrs; el pnts inc €2.50; bus adj; CCI. "Basic but OK; gd facs; conv for bus to Poitiers." 1 Jun-17 Sep. € 11.60   2006*

POIX DE PICARDIE *3C3* (300m SW Rural) **Camp Municipal Le Bois des Pêcheurs, Route de Forges-les-Eaux, 80290 Poix-de-Picardie [03 22 90 11 71 or 03 22 90 32 90 (Mairie); fax 03 22 90 32 91; mairie@ville-poix-de-picardie.fr; www.ville-poix-de-picardie.fr]** Fr town cent by D901 dir Beauvais, turn R onto D919 sp Camping. Fr Beauvais, turn L at bottom of steep hill opp Citroen agent, site 500m on R. Med, hdg/mkd pitch, hdstg, pt shd; wc; chem disp; shwrs inc; el pnts (10A) €3.80; gas 300m; lndtte; ice; shops, supmkt adj; rest, bar 500m; BBQ; playgrnd; htd, covrd pool 800m; rv & fishing adj; tennis 800m; games rm; cycle hire; TV; dogs €1.30; tourist info; poss cr; Eng spkn; adv bkg; quiet; red long stay; CCI. "Pleasant, peaceful site in delightful area; friendly; clean facs; gd touring base; vg walking & cycling; train to Amiens; mkt Sun." ♦ 1 Apr-30 Sep. € 11.00   2007*

See advertisement below

POLIGNY *6H2* (1km SW Rural) **Camp Communautaire de la Croix du Dan, 39800 Poligny [03 84 37 01 35; fax 03 84 73 77 59; villedepoligny.jura@wanadoo.fr]** Fr SW on N83 site on R immed bef town sp Poligny. Fr N & NW take N5 into & thro town cent (no L turn on N83 S of Poligny), then foll sp Lons-Le Saunier. Site on L bef sportsgrnd - look for m'van sp. Do not overshoot ent, as diff to see. N5 fr E not rec as steep & hairpins. Med, mkd pitch, pt shd; wc (mainly cont); chem disp; shwrs inc; el pnts (10A) inc; lndtte; shops 1km; tradsmn; playgrnd; no statics; dogs; phone; poss cr; Eng spkn; quiet; CCI. "Excel, clean, tidy site; helpful warden; gates open 24hrs; welcome aperitif every Sat in Jul/Aug; extra charge twin-axle c'vans; v pretty, friendly town." ♦ ltd. 15 Jun-30 Sep. € 10.80   2006*

POMMEROL see Rémuzat *9D2*

POMMEUSE *4E4* (1km SW Rural) **Camping Le Chêne Gris, 24 Place de la Gare de Faremoutiers, 77515 Pommeuse [01 64 04 21 80; fax 01 64 20 05 89; info@lechenegris.com; www.lechenegris.com]** Fr A4, take N34 SE dir Coulommiers, turn R onto D25 sp Pommeuse & Faremoutiers. Site on R after stn at Faremoutiers. Well sp. Lge, hdg pitch, hdstg, terr, pt shd; htd wc; chem disp; mv service pnt; baby facs; shwrs inc; el pnts (10A) inc; lndtte; shop; tradsmn; rest; snacks; bar; playgrnd; 2 pools (1 htd, covrd); paddling pool; games rm; internet; 60% statics; dogs €2.50; phone; Eng spkn; adv bkg; quiet; red low ssn; CCI. "Conv Paris cent, Disneyland & Parc Astérix; walking dist to trains - direct line to Paris; excel new san facs; vg." ♦ 25 Apr-9 Nov. € 37.00   2007*

PONCIN see Pont d'Ain *9A2*

As soon as we get home I'm going to post all these site report forms to the editor for inclusion in next year's guide. I don't want to miss the September deadline.

PONS (CHARENTE MARITIME) *7B2* (W Urban) **Camp Municipal Le Paradis, Ave de Poitou, 17800 Pons [05 46 91 36 72; fax 05 46 96 14 15; ville.pons@smic17.fr]** Well sp fr town o'skts. Med, mkd pitch, pt shd; wc; shwrs inc; el pnts (6-10A) inc; shops adj; tradsmn; pool, waterslide 100m; fishing; TV; dogs €1.76. "Excel; attractive grounds; interesting town; conv for Saintes, Cognac, Royan; helpful warden." ♦ 1 May-30 Sep. € 15.00   2004*

⊞**PONS (CHARENTE MARITIME)** *7B2* (1km N Rural) **Camping Les Moulins de la Vergne, 9 Route de Colombiers, 17800 Pons [tel/fax 05 46 90 50 84 or 05 46 49 11 49; uffelen@wanadoo.fr; www. moulinsdelavergne.nl]** Exit A10 junc 36 onto D732 sp Pons. Take N137 N in 3km then turn R in 4km onto D125 (E2). Site sp on L on D234 - visible & sp fr N137. Fr town cent foll yellow sps in Pons - do not confuse with municipal site Le Paradis. NB c'vans not allowed thro Pons & should stay on by-pass. Site is sp fr N137 dir Saintes. Med, mkd pitch, pt shd; wc; chem disp; shwrs inc; el pnts (10A) €2.90; lndtte; shops 1km; tradsmn; rest; snacks; bar; BBQ; playgrnd; pool; wifi internet; dogs €1.76; adv bkg; Eng spkn; rd noise; cc acc; CCI. "Relaxed, friendly & helpful Dutch owners; info fr site re local vet; vg, modern facs; grass pitches soft in wet weather - park on site roads off ssn; conv touring base or NH nr A10 en rte Spain." ♦ € 13.20   2007*

⊞**PONS (CHARENTE MARITIME)** *7B2* (2km W Rural) **FFCC Aire Naturelle de Camping (Chardon), 13 Route des Bernards, 17800 Pons [50 46 95 01 25 or 06 62 34 39 44 (mob); jacques. bier@cegetel.net; www.camping-chardon.fr]** Fr N or S on A10, exit junc 36 onto D732 (take care as heavy, fast traff). Site sp on R in 1km. Narr ent to rd. Or fr N or S on N137 take D732 twd Gémozac, site on L 2km fr Pons. Site lies to S of D732, bet N137 & A10. Foll yellow Camping Chardon sp (easily missed). Sm, hdg pitch, pt shd; wc; chem disp; serviced pitch; shwrs; el pnts (10A) €3; gas 2km; lndtte; shops 1km; tradsmn; rest; pizzeria; bar; playgrnd; pool 1km; 25% statics; dogs €1.50; adv bkg (20% dep req); quiet; no cc acc. "Excel basic site; quaint & rustic; v friendly owners; basic, open-air san facs, ltd low ssn; poor facs for disabled; vg rest; accomm at farm; conv Cognac, Saintes & Royan; low ssn phone ahead to check if open; conv NH if using A10 or N137." ♦ ltd. € 12.00   2007*

PONT AUDEMER *3D2* (8km W Rural) **Camping La Lorie (Lehaye), 5 La Lorie, 27210 Fort-Moville [02 32 57 15 49]** Fr A13 exit junc 28 Beuzeville onto D27 S dir Bernay. Immed on x-ring m'way turn L onto D623 to Fort-Moville. Site sp just bef vill on farm. Sm, pt shd; wc; chem disp (wc); shwrs inc; el pnts (10A) inc; BBQ; rest, snacks, bar 2km; 10% statics; dogs; quiet; CCI. "CL-type site in attractive countryside; basic facs; conv Le Havre, Honfleur; own cider & eggs for sale." Easter-1 Nov. € 13.50   2006*

PONT AUDEMER *3D2* (2km NW Rural) **Camp Municipal Risle-Seine Les Etangs, 19 Route des Etangs, 27500 Toutainville [02 32 42 46 65; fax 02 32 42 24 17; camping@ville-pont-audemer.fr; www.ville-pont-audemer.fr]** Fr Le Havre on A131/E05 cross rv at Pont de Normandie (toll). Take D580 & at junc 3 branch R & take 2nd exit sp Beuzeville. At edge of Fiquefleur take D180, then N175 dir Pont-Audemer. In Toutainville foll site sp, turn L just bef A13 underpass, then immed R. Site approx 2km on R. Med, hdg/mkd pitch, pt shd; wc; chem disp; mv service pnt; serviced pitches; shwrs inc; el pnts (10A) inc; lndtte; ice; shop 1.5km; tradsmn; snacks; bar; BBQ; playgrnd; pool 1.5km; paddling pool; htd pool & tennis 2km; fishing; canoeing, watersports; cycle hire; games area; games rm; wifi internet; games/ TV rm; dogs free; bus; Eng spkn; adv bkg; quiet; red long stay/low ssn; cc acc. "Lovely, well-run, immac site; poss school groups at w/e; helpful warden; barrier clsd 2200-0830 but flexible for ferry; recep opening erractic low ssn; many leisure activities; vg for dogs; 1hr Le Havre ferry; pitches poss v soft early ssn; Fri mkt Pont-Audemer; vg NH; excel." ♦ 15 Mar-15 Nov. € 16.70 ABS - N13   2007*

PONT AUTHOU see Brionne *3D2*

France

PONT AVEN *2F2* (10km N Rural) **Camping Les Genêts d'Or, Kermerour 29380 Bannalec [tel/fax 02 98 39 54 35; info@holidaybrittany.com; www.holidaybrittany.com]** Fr Pont Aven/Bannalec exit on N165 N to Bannalec on D4; after rlwy x-ing turn R sp Quimperlé. In 1km turn R, sp Le Trévoux; site on L 500m. Sm, hdg/mkd pitch, pt sl, pt shd; wc; chem disp; shwrs inc; el pnts (6A) €3; lndtte; sm shop; supmkt 1km; tradsmn; rest; snacks; bar; playgrnd; pool 10km; sand beach 15km; games rm; cycle hire; some statics; dogs €1; Eng spkn; adv bkg; quiet; 10% red 7 days; CCI. "Well-kept, clean, peaceful site in orchard; lge pitches; friendly, helpful, welcoming British owners; excel touring base." ♦ ltd. 1 Apr-30 Sep. € 11.50   2005*

PONT AVEN *2F2* (7km SE Rural) **Camping La Grande Lande, 7 Rue de Grande Lande, Kergroës, 29116 Moëlan-sur-Mer [02 98 71 00 39; fax 02 98 71 00 19; camping.grande.lande@wanadoo.fr]** Exit N165/E60 dir Pont Aven. Then D783 & D24 to Moëlan. Fr Quimperlé S on D16 to Clohars-Carnoët W on D24 to Moëlan-sur-Mer; thro town on rd to Kerfany Plage site on R in vill of Kergroës. Med, mkd pitch, pt sl, pt shd; wc (mainly cont); chem disp (wc); baby facs; shwrs inc; el pnts (3-10A) €2.80-3.80; lndtte; ice; shop in vill; tradsmn; rest; snacks; bar; BBQ; playgrnd; pool; sand beach 2km; tennis; games area; mini-golf; cycle hire; horseriding; archery; entmnt; TV rm; 6% statics; dogs €1; phone; some Eng spkn; adv bkg; quiet. "Gd touring base; Port-du-Bélon (2km) boat trips; scuba diving; fishing." ♦ Easter-30 Sep. € 16.00   2005*

PONT AVEN *2F2* (8km SE Coastal) **Camping de l'Ile Percée, Plage de Trénez, 29350 Moëlan-sur-Mer [02 98 71 16 25; contact@camping-ilepercee.com; http://camping-ilepercee.ifrance.com]** App thro Moëlan-sur-Mer, 6km SE of Pont-Aven or 6km SW of Quimperlé - watch for R turn after Moëlan. Take D116 sp to Kerfany. Keep strt at Kergroës, turn L after 500m sp L'Ile Percée. Med, pt sl, unshd; wc (some cont); baby facs; shwrs; el pnts (4-6A) €2.40-3.25; lndtte; ice; snacks; bar; BBQ; playgrnd; sandy/rocky beach adj; sw, fishing & watersports 50m; games area; entmnt; TV; some statics; dogs €1; poss cr; adv bkg; v quiet. "Well-run site; superb sea views some pitches; rent narr & winding; sm pitches; san facs poss stretched high ssn." Easter-17 Sep. € 14.50   2006*

PONT AVEN *2F2* (8km S Coastal) **Camping Les Chaumières, Kerascoët, 29920 Névez [02 9806 73 06; fax 02 98 06 78 34; campingdeschaumieres@wanadoo.fr]** S fr Pont-Aven thro Névez to Kerascoët. Med, hdg/mkd pitch, pt shd; wc; chem disp; mv service pnt; serviced pitches; shwrs inc; el pnts (4-10A) €2.70-3.60; gas 3km; lndtte; ice; shop 3km; tradsmn high ssn; rest, snacks, bar adj; playgrnd; sand beach 800m; dogs €1; Eng spkn; adv bkg ess; quiet; red low ssn; CCI. "Excel site; many diff kinds of pitch; well-organised recep; facs poss stretched high ssn; gd play & games areas; lovely sandy bay/beaches; cliff walks." ♦ 15 May-15 Sep. € 14.70   2006*

PONT AVEN *2F2* (10km S Coastal) **Camping Le St Nicolas, Port Manec'h, 29920 Névez [02 98 06 89 75; fax 02 98 06 74 61; info@campinglesaintnicolas.com; www.campinglesaintnicolas.com]** Take D783 W fr Pont-Aven for 2km, turn L onto D77 S thro Névez to Port Manech. Site well sp. Narr app to site. Lge, hdg/mkd pitch, pt sl, pt shd; wc (some cont); chem disp; shwrs inc; el pnts (6A) €3.30; gas; lndtte; ice; tradsmn high ssn; rest, snacks, bar in vill; playgrnd; htd pool; paddling pool; sand beach 200m; watersports; games area; games rm; tennis, horseriding nrby; entmnt; TV rm; dogs €1.50; Eng spkn; adv bkg; quiet; cc acc; red low ssn; CCI. "Pleasant, wooded site; friendly owners; cliff walks; gd touring base." ♦ 1 May-14 Sep. € 18.70   2007*

See advertisement opposite

PONT AVEN *2F2* (3km SW Rural) **Domaine de Kerlann, Land Rosted, 29930 Pont Aven [02 98 06 01 77; fax 02 98 06 18 50; reservations@ledomainedekerlann.fr; www.siblu.fr/domaine dekerlann]** Fr Pont Aven foll sp twd Concarneau. After 1.5km, turn L onto D77 twd Névez. Site approx 1.5km on R. V lge, hdg/mkd pitch, hdstg, pt sl, pt shd; wc; chem disp; baby facs; shwrs inc; el pnts (8A) inc; gas; lndtte; shop; rest; snacks; bar; playgrnd; htd pools (1 covrd); waterslide; sand beach 3km; tennis; cycle hire; entmnt; child entmtn; TV rm; 85% statics; Eng spkn; adv bkg ess high ssn; cc acc; red low ssn/low ssn; CCI. "Wooded site & areas poss muddy after rain; children's club all ssn; teenagers' club Jul/Aug; sports pitch; all facs open all ssn." ♦ ltd. 31 Mar-27 Oct. € 37.00   2006*

PONT AVEN *2F2* (5km SW Rural) **Camping Les Genêts, Route St Philibert, 29920 Névez [02 98 06 86 13 or 02 98 06 72 31; campinglesgenets@aol.com; www.campinglesgenets-nevez.com]** Turn S off D783 onto D77 to Névez. At church in town, bear R & turn immed R to exit Névez with post office on R. Site on L, clearly sp. Med, hdg/mkd pitch, pt shd; wc (some cont); shwrs inc; el pnts (3-10A) €2.10-4.40; gas 500m; lndtte; ice; shops 500m; playgrnd; sand beach 5km; 10% statics; dogs €1; some Eng spkn; adv bkg; quiet; CCI. "Choice of excel beaches adj; vg." 1 Jun-15 Sep. € 10.00   2005*

PONT AVEN *2F2* (6km SW Coastal) **Camping Les Deux Fontaines, 29920 Raguenès [02 98 06 81 91; fax 02 98 06 71 80; info@les2fontaines.fr; www.les2fontaines.fr]** Leave N165/E60 at Kérampaou foll sp D24 twds Pont Aven. In approx 4.5km turn R (S) foll sp Névez then Raguenès. Site 3km fr Névez. Lge, mkd pitch, pt shd; wc (some cont); shwrs inc; baby facs; el pnts (6A) €3.40; lndtte; shop; rest; bar; sand beach 800m; htd pool; tennis; 80% statics; dogs €2.40. "Holiday camp atmosphere high ssn; many tour operator statics, popular with British families." ♦ ltd. 15 May-15 Sep. € 18.70   2005*

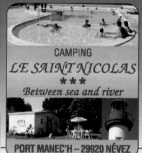

PONT AVEN *2F2* (8km SW Coastal) **Airotel Camping Raguenès-Plage, 19 Rue des Iles, 29920 Raguenès-en-Névez [02 98 06 80 69; fax 02 98 06 89 05; info@camping-le-raguenes-plage.com; www.camping-le-raguenes-plage.com]** Fr Pont-Aven take D783 dir Trégunc; in 2.5km turn L for Névez, foll sps to Raguenès fr Névez. Or fr N165 take D24 at Kérampaou exit; in 3km turn R to Nizon; at church in vill turn R onto D77 to Névez; site on L 3km after Névez. Lge, mkd pitch, shd; wc (some cont); chem disp; mv service pnt; baby facs; sauna; shwrs inc; el pnts (2-10A) €3.20-4.60; gas; lndtte; ice; shop; rest; snacks adj; bar; BBQ; playgrnd; htd pool & paddling pool; waterslide; sand beach adj; watersports school adj; tennis nr; games rm; trampoline; games area; horseriding; entmnt; 20% statics (sep area); dogs €2.50; adv bkg rec (dep req); quiet; red low ssn; cc acc; CCI. "Pretty, wooded, family-run site; private path to lge, sandy beach; v clean facs; 1st class site." ♦ Easter-1 Oct. € 28.00   2007*

See advertisement below

The opening dates and prices on this campsite have changed. I'll send a site report form to the editor for the next edition of the guide.

PONT AVEN *2F2* (8km SW Coastal) **Camping Le Vieux Verger - Ty Noul, Raguenès-Plage, 29920 Névez [02 98 06 86 08 or 02 98 06 83 17 (LS); fax 02 98 06 76 74]** Fr Pont-Aven take D783 dir Concarneau; in 2.5km L onto D77 to Névez; foll sp Raguenès-Plage; 1st site on L. NB Le Vieux Verger (open Jul/Aug) & Ty Noul are adj sites, same owner. Med, hdg/mkd pitch, pt shd; wc; chem disp (wc); shwrs inc; el pnts (4-10A) €2.90-3.90; shop (high ssn); rest 500m; playgrnd; sand beach 500m; no statics; phone; poss cr; quiet; CCI. "Ty Noul excel, well-kept site; highly rec low ssn." 15 Apr-30 Sep. € 14.30   2006*

PONT D'AIN *9A2* (6km NE Rural) **Camping Vallée d'Ain, Allée Terres de l'Ain, 01450 Poncin [tel/fax 04 74 37 20 78; camping-vallee-de-lain@laposte.net; www.chez.com/campingponcin]** Fr Pont-d'Ain cent foll D1075 (N75) S & when exit Pont-d'Ain turn L on N84 (sp 300m fr vill); site on D81 off D91. Med, pt shd; wc; chem disp; mv service pnt; shwrs inc; el pnts (5-16A) €2.80-4; gas; ice; lndtte; shops adj; rest; snacks; bar; BBQ; playgrnd; htd pool; entmnt; rv adj; canoe, cycle hire; some statics; dogs €1.10; quiet, but some m'way noise; CCI. "Walks by rv, helpful staff; gd san facs." 1 Apr-30 Sep. € 12.20   2007*

France

PONT D'AIN 9A2 (3km E Urban) **Camping de l'Oiselon, 01160 Pont-d'Ain [tel/fax 04 74 39 05 23; campingoiselon@libertysurf.fr]** Fr A42 exit Pont-d'Ain foll D90 to vill. In vill cent turn R on D1075 (N75). Turn L immed after x-ing Rv L'Ain. Foll rd passing tennis club on L. Site on L. Lge, pt shd; wc; chem disp; shwrs inc; el pnts (6-10A) €2.20-3.05 (poss rev pol); shops; rest; snacks; BBQ; playgrnd; pool; rv sw & beach; fishing; canoeing; tennis adj; horseriding 5km; cycle loan; many statics; poss cr; adv bkg; quiet (some noise fr disco). "V helpful, friendly staff; fair NH." 17 Mar-14 Oct. € 11.10   2007*

PONT DE L'ARCHE 3D2 (Urban) **Camp Municipal Eure et Seine, Quai du Maréchal-Foch, 27340 Pont-de-l'Arche [02 35 23 06 71 or 02 32 98 90 70 (Mairie); fax 02 35 23 90 88]** Fr N15 turn E at S end of rv bdge, drive downhill then under bdge & strt on for 300m, site on R. Restricted width on app. Med, mkd pitch, unshd; wc; chem disp; shwrs inc; el pnts (6-10A) inc; lndtte; shop 200m; rest; bar; playgrnd; rv fishing adj; some statics; dogs; phone; poss v cr; rd noise; cc not acc; CCI. "V pleasant, clean, peaceful rvside site in attractive, medieval town; sm pitches; san facs need updating & poss stretched high ssn." ♦ 1 Apr-30 Oct. € 9.75
2007*

⊞PONT DE L'ARCHE 3D2 (3km N) **Camping Les Terrasses, 2 Rue de Rouen, 27460 Igoville [tel/fax 02 35 23 08 15]** Site sp fr N15 in both dirs. Fr A13 take exit sp Pont-de-l'Arche D321, pass thro town & at intersection of D321 & N15 turn L. Cross Seine to Igoville & cont up N15 & foll site sp. App hill may cause problems heavy/lge vans. Sm, mkd pitch, hdstg, sl, terr, pt shd; wc; chem disp; shwrs €1; el pnts (6-10A) inc; lndtte; supmkt 1km; playgrnd; 80% statics; dogs €1.10; bus to Rouen; adv bkg; quiet; red low ssn; CCI. "Suitable m'van or sm van & 4x4 only - steep, bumpy access rd poss diff towed vehicles; not rec as NH; site clsd Xmas & New Year; excel views Seine valley; warm welcome; v sm shwr cubicles; san facs poss unclean high ssn." € 10.40   2006*

⊞PONT DE L'ARCHE 3D2 (10km S Rural) **FFCC Camping Le St Pierre, 1 Rue du Château, 27430 St Pierre-du-Vauvray [tel/fax 02 32 61 01 55; eliane.darcissac@wanadoo.fr; www.lecamping desaintpierre.com]** Fr S exit N154 junc 3 or A13 junc 18 (Louviers) onto N155 E until junc with N15. Turn L & in 4km turn R to St Pierre. Fr N on N15 after x-ing Rv Seine at Pont-de-l'Arche cont for approx 6km & turn L to St Pierre. Do not ent St Pierre fr E on D313 due low bdge under rlwy line. Med, hdg/mkd pitch, pt shd; wc; chem disp; shwrs inc; el pnts (6-10A) €2.30; lndry rm; shop 1km; BBQ; playgrnd; htd pool; 25% statics; dogs €1.10; site clsd 2 weeks at Xmas/New Year; adv bkg rec; noise fr rlwy adj; CCI. "Main Paris/Le Havre TGV rlwy line adj site; in grnds sm chateau; conv Giverny; walks by Seine; friendly staff; ltd facs; NH only." € 8.20
2006*

PONT DE SALARS 7D4 (1.5km N Rural) **Parc Camping du Lac, 12290 Pont-de-Salars [05 65 46 84 86; fax 05 65 46 60 39; camping. du.lac@wanadoo.fr]** Fr Rodez on D911 La Primaube-Millau rd, turn L bef ent Pont-de-Salars. Site sp. Lge, mkd pitch, pt sl, terr, pt shd; wc (some cont); chem disp; shwrs inc; el pnts (3-6A) €2-3.50; gas; lndtte; ice; shop & 1km; tradsmn; rest; snacks; bar; BBQ; playgrnd; pool; lake sw; sailing; fishing; entmnt; TV; 5% statics; no dogs; phone; poss cr; Eng spkn; adv bkg (dep req & bkg fee); noisy nr entmnt area; red low ssn. "Site has own slipway & landing stage; beautiful situation; poss unkempt & ltd facs low ssn; san facs clean & well-kept but poss stretched high ssn; fair sh stay/NH." ♦ ltd. 15 Jun-15 Sep. € 15.50   2005*

PONT DE SALARS 7D4 (4km N Rural) **FLOWER Camping Les Terrasses du Lac, Route du Vibal, 12290 Pont-de-Salars [05 65 46 88 18 or 06 72 89 84 34 (mob); fax 05 65 46 85 38; campinglesterrasses@wanadoo.fr; www. campinglesterrasses.com]** Dir Albi fr Rodez N88 to La Primaube. Turn L in La Primaube on D911 for Pont-de-Salars. Turn L on D523 by timberyard to Le Vibal & foll sp to site approx 4km fr vill cent. Lge, terr, pt shd; wc; chem disp; shwrs inc; el pnts (10A) €3.75; gas; lndtte; ice; shop; rest; snacks; bar; BBQ; playgrnd; htd pool; sand beach & lake sw; boating; fishing; entmnt; TV; dogs €1.35; Eng spkn; adv bkg; quiet; cc acc; CCI. "Well laid-out site overlooking lake; gd touring area." ♦ 1 Apr-30 Sep. € 19.95
2005*

> Before we move on, I'm going to fill in some site report forms and post them off to the editor, otherwise they won't arrive in time for the deadline at the end of September.

PONT DE SALARS 7D4 (7km SE Rural) **Camping Le Caussanel, Lac de Pareloup, 12290 Canet-de-Salars [05 65 46 85 19; fax 05 65 46 89 85; info@ lecaussanel.com; www.lecaussanel.com]** Exit A75 junc 44.1 onto D911 dir Pont-de-Salars, then D993 Salles-Curan & D538 Canet-de-Salars, dir Lac de Pareloup. In 6km fork R to Le Caussanel: in 100m fork L to site. Fr N88 exit at La Primaube then D911 to Pont-de-Salars, then as above. Lge, mkd pitch, hdstg, pt sl, terr, pt shd; wc; mv service pnt; chem disp; baby facs; shwrs inc; el pnts (5A) inc; shop; tradsmn; rest; snacks; bar; playgrnd; htd pools; waterslide; fishing; windsurfing & sailing; boat & cycle hire; games rm; entmnt; internet; 20% statics; dogs €3.60; Eng spkn; adv bkg; quiet; CCI. "Beautiful situation; friendly owner; vg." ♦ 26 Apr-13 Sep. € 31.10 (CChq acc)   2007*

PONT DE SALARS 7D4 (8km S Rural) **Camping Le Soleil Levant, Lac de Pareloup, 12290 Canet-de-Salars [05 65 46 03 65; fax 05 65 46 03 62; contact@camping-soleil-levant.com; www.camping-soleil-levant.com]** Exit A75 junc 44.1 onto D911 to Pont-de-Salars, then S on D993 dir Salles-Curan. Site in 8km bef bdge on L. Lge, mkd pitch, terr, pt sl, pt shd; htd wc (some cont); chem disp; baby facs; shwrs inc; el pnts (6A) €2; gas; lndtte; ice; shop 4km; tradsmn; snacks; bar; BBQ; playgrnd; lake sw & sand/shgl beach adj; fishing; watersports; games area; games rm; internet; entmnt; internet; TV rm; 10% statics; dogs €2; Eng spkn; adv bkg; quiet; cc acc; red low ssn; CCI. "Lovely site; beautiful location on lakeside; excel san facs." ♦ 1 Apr-30 Sep. € 18.50   2007*

See advertisement

There aren't many sites open this early in the year. We'd better phone ahead to check that the one we're heading for is actually open.

PONT DE VAUX 9A2 (4km NE Rural) **Camping Les Ripettes, Chavannes-sur-Reyssouze, 01190 St Bénigne [03 85 30 66 58; info@camping-les-ripettes.com; www.camping-les-ripettes.com]** Take D2 fr Pont-de-Vaux sp St Trivier-des-Courtes for 3km. Immed after water tower on R turn L onto D58 sp Romenay, then immed L. Site well sp on L in 100m. Med, hdg/mkd pitch, pt sl, pt shd; htd wc; chem disp; mv service pnt; shwrs inc; el pnts (10A) €2.50; lndtte; shop & 4km; tradsmn; snacks; playgrnd; 2 pools; games area; cycle hire; 2 statics; dogs €1.50; phone; Eng spkn; adv bkg; quiet; cc acc; CCI. "Pleasant, popular site in beautiful location; spacious pitches, some poss diff when wet; friendly, v helpful British owners; immac facs; if planning to stay in Oct, make an adv bkg or phone ahead bef arr; excel touring base; gd NH en rte S France; excel." ♦ ltd. 1 Apr-30 Sep. € 13.50   2007*

PONT DE VAUX 9A2 (5km W) **Camping aux Rives du Soleil (formerly Les Peupliers), 01190 Pont-de-Vaux [tel/fax 03 85 30 33 65; info@rivesdusoleil.com; www.rivesdusoleil.com]** On D306 (N6) bet Mâcon & Tournus. Cross Rv Saône on D933A at Fleurville. Lge, pt shd, wc; mv service pnt; baby facs; shwrs inc; el pnts (6A) €3; gas; lndtte; ice; shop; rest adj; snacks; bar; BBQ; playgrnd; pool; paddling pool; rv beach adj; fishing; boating; entmnts; TV; 15% statics; dogs €2; poss cr; Eng spkn; adv bkg; some rlwy noise; red long stay. "Beautiful site, almost surrounded by rv/stream & canal; lots of wildlife; Dutch owners; san facs & rest undergoing refurb (2006); excel NH fr A6 - NH pitches on sep area; excel location in wine area; gd." 28 Apr-30 Sep. € 16.00   2007*

PONT DE VAUX 9A2 (15km W Rural) **Camp Municipal St Pierre, 71260 Lugny [03 85 33 20 25 or 03 85 33 21 96 (Mairie); fax 03 85 33 00 58]** W of A6/N6; take C7 off D56 N out of Lugny; foll sp for Rest St Pierre; site adj & sp fr town. Diff app for lge o'fits. Sm, mkd pitch, pt shd; wc; shwrs inc; el pnts inc; lndry rm; shop 1.5km in Lugny; rest & 1.5km; v quiet; cc not acc. "Beautiful panoramic views of vineyards; simple site; warden calls am & pm; facs v clean; v steep ascent to site fr town; excel cent for touring vineyards; gd local walks; vg rest adj." 1 May-30 Sep.   2007*

PONT D'OUILLY see Condé sur Noireau 3D1

PONT DU NAVOY see Doucier 6H2

PONT EN ROYANS 9C2 (Rural) **Camp Municipal Les Seraines, 38680 Pont-en-Royans [04 76 36 06 30 or 04 76 36 03 09 (Mairie); fax 04 76 36 10 77; mairie.pont.en.royans@wanadoo.fr]** App on D531 fr St Nazaire or D518 fr St Marcellin, site on R on ent to town. Sm, hdg pitch, hdstg, pt terr, pt shd; wc (mainly cont); chem disp; shwrs inc; el pnts (4A) inc; gas in town; ice; shops 500m; lake 8km; rv adj; tennis; entmnts; poss cr; statics; quiet but some rd noise; CCI. "Site in 2 adj parts; helpful warden; rvside walk to Pont-en-Royans." 15 Apr-30 Sep. € 12.00   2004*

PONT EN ROYANS *9C2* (4km E Rural) **FFCC Camping Le Gouffre de la Croix, 38680 Choranche** [tel/fax 04 76 36 07 13; camping. gouffre.croix@wanadoo.fr; www.camping-choranche.com] App fr Pont-en-Royans only. Site at far end of vill. Ent over narr bdge, OK with care. Sm, mkd pitch, terr, pt shd; wc; chem disp; fam bthrm; shwrs inc; el pnts (6A) €3.50; gas; lndtte; ice; shop 4km; tradsmn; rest 100m; snacks; bar; playgrnd; rv sw; TV; 4% statics; dogs €1.50; phone; Eng spkn; adv bkg (dep req); quiet; CCI. "Lovely, friendly site on trout rv; views fr most pitches; excel walking area; excel." 27 Apr-16 Sep. € 15.50
2007*

PONT FARCY *1D4* (E Rural) **Camp Municipal Pont-Farcy, Quai de la Vire, 14380 Pont-Farcy** [02 31 68 32 06; fax 02 31 67 94 01; pontfarcy@ free.fr; http://pontfarcy.free.fr/] Leave A84 junc 39 onto D21 to Pont-Farcy vill cent; site on L 50m. Med, hdg/mkd pitch, terr, pt shd; wc; chem disp; mv service pnt; shwrs inc; baby facs; el pnts (15A) €1.85; shop, rest & bar 500m; playgrnd; rv fishing & boating adj; cycle hire; 30% statics; dogs; phone; adv bkg; quiet; CCI. "Gates pass locked periods during day but plenty of parking space; helpful, friendly warden; spotless facs." ♦ 1 Apr-30 Sep. € 9.00
2007*

PONT L'ABBE *2F2* (6km S Rural/Coastal) **Camping des Dunes, 67 Rue Paul Langevin, 29740 Lesconil** [02 98 87 81 78; fax 02 98 82 27 05] Fr Pont l'Abbé, S on D102 for 5km to Plobannelec; over x-rds; in 1km turn R, 100m after sports field; green sp to site in 1km. Med, hdg/mkd pitch, pt shd; wc (few cont); chem disp; mv service pnt; baby facs; shwrs inc; el pnts (6-10A) inc; gas 1km; lndtte; ice; shop 1km; tradsmn; snacks; bar; playgrnd; sand beach 200m; trampolines; games rm; games area; dogs €3.15; poss cr high ssn; adv bkg (dep req); cc acc; CCI. "Helpful owner; 800m fr fishing port; ltd rests & bars etc; facs poor low ssn; dune & heathland conservation area; gd walking, cycling & birdwatching; site ideal for children." ♦ 3 Jun-9 Sep. € 23.30
2006*

PONT L'ABBE *2F2* (7km S) **Yelloh! Village Le Manoir de Kerlut, 29740 Plobannalec** [02 98 82 23 89 or 04 66 73 97 39; fax 02 98 82 26 49; info@campingsbretagnesud. com; www.campingsbretagnesud.com or www. yellohvillage.com] Fr Pont l'Abbé S on D102 to Plobannalec & head for Lesconil; site on L after supmkt. Lge, hdg/mkd pitch, pt shd; wc; serviced pitches; mv service pnt; chem disp; sauna; shwrs inc; el pnts (5A) inc; gas; lndtte; ice; shop; tradsmn; rest; snacks; bar; playgrnd; htd pool; waterslide; sand beach 2km; fitness rm; tennis; games area; 30% statics; dogs €3.50; phone; Eng spkn; adv bkg; quiet; red long stay; cc acc; CCI. ♦ 5 Apr-14 Sep. € 37.00
2005*

PONT L'ABBE *2F2* (5km SW) **Camping Caravaning Pointe de la Torche, 29120 Plomeur** [02 98 58 62 82; fax 02 98 58 89 69; info@ campingdelatorche.fr; www.campingdelatorche. fr] Fr Quimper take D785 to Pont l'Abbé & on to Plomeur. After Plomeur turn W twd La Pointe de la Torche & foll sps. Lge, pt shd; mkd pitch; wc; chem disp; shwrs inc; baby facs; el pnts (5A) €3.20; ice; gas; lndtte; shop; rest; bar; sand beach 1.5km; pool; playgrnd; tennis; horseriding; fishing; golf; surfing adj; dogs €1.40; Eng spkn; adv bkg. "V quiet off ssn." 1 Apr-30 Sep. € 19.00
2006*

PONT L'ABBE *2F2* (5km NW) **Camp Municipal de Mariano, 29720 Plonéour-Lanvern** [02 98 87 74 80; fax 02 98 82 66 09; mairie@ ploneour-lanvern.fr; www.ploneour-lanvern.fr] Fr Pont l'Abbé, take D2 to Plonéour-Lanvern, site sp fr cent town; fr cent L of church & strt to T-junc, turn R 2nd on L. Med, hdg pitch, pt shd; wc; shwrs inc; el pnts (5A) inc; lndtte; shops 400m; pool 6km; playgrnd; sand beach 13km; tennis adj; adv bkg; quiet. ♦ 15 Jun-15 Sep. € 12.50
2006*

Did you know you can fill in site report forms on the Club's website — www.caravanclub.co.uk?

PONT L'ABBE *2F2* (10km NW Rural) **Camping Kerlaz, Route de la Mer, 29670 Tréguennec** [tel/ fax 02 98 87 76 79; contact@kerlaz.com; www. kerlaz.com] Fr Plonéour-Lanvern take D156 SW to Tréguennec. Med, pt shd; wc; chem disp; mv service pnt; shwrs inc; el pnts (3-10A) €2.40-3.20; lndry rm; shop 300m; tradsmn; snacks; playgrnd; htd, covrd pool; sand beach 2km; tennis; 10% statics; dogs €1.20; adv bkg; quiet; cc acc. "Nice, friendly site." 1 Apr-30 Sep. € 12.00
2005*

PONT L'ABBE D'ARNOULT *7B1* **Camping Parc de la Garenne, 24 Ave Bernard Chambenoit, 17250 Pont-l'Abbé-d'Arnoult** [05 46 97 01 46 or 06 09 43 20 11 (mob); info@lagarenne.net; www.lagarenne.net] N fr Saintes on N137. In 18km turn L onto D18 to Pont-l'Abbé. In town turn L, foll camp sp to site adj sw pool. Med, shd; wc; chem disp; mv service pnt 150m; baby facs; shwrs inc; el pnts (6-10A) €3.90-4.20; gas; lndtte; ice; shop, rest, snacks & bar 500m; snacks; BBQ (elec only); playgrnd; pool adj; tennis; games area; TV rm; 10% statics; dogs €2; phone; Eng spkn; adv bkg; quiet; CCI. "Well-run site, conv coast, inland touring; gd san facs; late night rock restival last w/e Jul – vg value; €50 dep for barrier disk, cash only; gd." ♦ 15 May-25 Sep. € 15.00
2006*

PONT LES MOULINS see Baume les Dames *6G2*

PONT L'EVEQUE *3D1* (500m NW Urban) **Camping du Stade, Rue de Beaumont, 14130 Pont l'Evêque [02 31 64 15 03]** Fr town cent take N175 W twd Caen, turn R at traff lts bef town o'skts to site in 300m. Site sp on R in 300m on D118. Med, mkd pitch, pt shd; wc (some cont); chem disp; shwrs inc; el pnts (6A) inc (poss rev pol); lndry rm; shops in town; tradsmn; playgrnd; beach 12km; rv fishing; tennis; 2% statics; quiet; cc not acc; CCI. "Basic, clean site; dated san facs; staff v friendly & helpful; site poss waterlogged after heavy rain." ♦ ltd. 1 Apr-30 Sep. € 13.00   2007*

PONT ST ESPRIT *9D2* (5km W Rural) **Camping Les Oliviers, Chemin de Tête Grosse, 30130 St Paulet-de-Caisson [04 66 82 14 13]** Exit A7 at Bollène-Pont-St Esprit. Foll D994 to Pont-St Esprit, then sp to St Paulet-de-Caisson. Turn R into vill & foll sp to St Julien-de-Peyrolas on D343, site sp 1.5km off narr rd - unsuitable lge o'fits. Sm, hdg/mkd pitch, terr, pt shd; wc; chem disp; shwrs inc; el pnts (4A) inc; lndtte; ice; shops 2km; tradsmn; rest; snacks; bar; pool; playgrnd; rv sw 5km; Eng spkn; adv bkg; quiet; CCI. "Ardèche, Rhône Valley, Roman sites nr; v helpful Dutch owners; gd rest; guided walks; painting tuition; ltd water points & long way fr lower levels." 1 Apr-1 Oct. € 21.00   2004*

PONT ST ESPRIT *9D2* (6km NW Rural) **Camping Le Pontet, 07700 St Martin-d'Ardèche [04 75 04 63 07 or 04 75 98 76 24; fax 04 75 98 76 59; contact@campinglepontet.com; www.campinglepontet.com]** N86 N of Pont-St Esprit; turn L onto D290 at sp Gorges de l'Ardèche & St Martin-d'Ardèche, site on R after 3km, lge sp. Med, mkd, pt shd; wc; chem disp; mv service pnt; shwrs inc; el pnts (6A) €3.50 (rev pol); gas; lndry rm; ice; tradsmn; shop, rest high ssn; snacks; bar; playgrnd; pool; rv sw 1km; 5% statics; dogs €1; phone; Eng spkn; adv bkg; quiet (poss noisy w/e); cc not acc; CCI. "Vg; helpful owners; entmnts some evenings; beware low tree branches & falling fruit; access disabled facs thro passage bet shwrs; peaceful & gd value out of ssn." ♦ 2 Apr-28 Sep. € 18.90   2007*

PONT ST ESPRIT *9D2* (7km NW) **Camping Les Cigales, 30760 Aiguèze [04 66 82 18 52; fax 04 66 82 25 20; striducette@aol.com]** N fr Pont-St Esprit on N86 take D901 NW twd Barjac & D141 to St Martin-d'Ardèche. Site on L bef rv bdge. Avoid app fr St Martin-d'Ardèche over narr suspension bdge. Care at ent. Sm, shd; wc; mv service pnt; shwrs inc; el pnts (4-6A) €2.30-2.75; gas; lndtte; ice; shops, rest 500m; tradsmn; BBQ; htd pool, caps ess; rv sw 500m; 25% statics; dogs €1.25; poss cr; adv bkg; rd noise; cc not acc; CCI. "Helpful owner; easy walk to rest in St Martin-d'Ardèche." 15 Mar-15 Oct. € 13.00   2004*

PONT ST ESPRIT *9D2* (7.5km NW Urban) **Camp Municipal Le Village, Rue du Nord, 07700 St Martin-d'Ardèche [04 75 04 65 25 or 04 75 04 66 33; fax 04 75 98 71 38]** N on N86 fr Pont-St Esprit, turn L onto D290 at St Just. Foll D290 around St Martin-d'Ardèche, turn L at sp Le Castelas & immed L into Chemin La Joyeusse, site on L in 300m. Med, mkd pitch, pt shd; wc; chem disp; shwrs inc; el pnts (4-13A) €1.70-2.80; lndtte; shop, rest, snacks, bar 200m; playgrnd; rv beach adj; fishing; tennis; adv bkg; quiet. "Excel facs; quiet, lovely vill." Easter-30 Sep. € 11.50   2005*

PONT ST ESPRIT *9D2* (7.5km NW Urban) **Camping Le Castelas, Chemin de Tabion, 07700 St Martin-d'Ardèche [tel/fax 04 75 04 66 55; camping-le-castelas@wanadoo.fr;www.camping-le-castelas.com]** N fr Pont-St Esprit on N86. At St Just turn W onto D290 sp Ardèche Gorges, St Martin. In 4km take 2nd L sp St Martin-de l'Ardèche & site. In 50m turn R at site sp; site on R in 150m. Med, hdg/mkd pitch, sl, shd; wc; chem disp; shwrs inc; el pnts (3-4A) €1.80-1.90; lndtte; ice; shops 300m; tradsmn; rest, bar 500m; snacks; BBQ; playgrnd; rv sw; canoeing; fishing; dogs inc; poss cr; Eng spkn; adv bkg (ess Jul/Aug - bkg fee); noisy; red low ssn. "V shd pitches; position van with door to S or E in case Mistral blows; helpful, friendly owner; delightful site with beautiful views over gorge; gd NH." 12 Mar-12 Nov. € 10.50   2006*

PONT ST ESPRIT *9D2* (8km NW) **Camp Municipal Le Moulin, 07700 St Martin-d'Ardèche [04 75 04 66 20; fax 04 75 04 60 12; contact@camping-lemoulin.com]** Exit A7 junc 19 to Bollène, then D994 to Pont-St Esprit & N86 to St Just. Turn L onto D290 to St Martin in 4km. Site on L on rvside. Med, pt sl, pt shd; htd wc; chem disp; mv service pnt; shwrs inc; el pnts (6A) €3; lndtte; ice; shop; rest 5km; snacks; bar; playgrnd; rv sw adj; fishing; canoeing; tennis 500m; 5% statics; dogs €1.50; phone; Eng spkn; no adv bkg; cc acc; quiet. "Super place & site; friendly; san facs ltd low ssn; footpath to vill; rec." ♦ Easter-30 Sep. € 15.50   2007*

PONT ST ESPRIT *9D2* (8km NW Rural) **Camping Le Peyrolais, Route de Barjac, 30760 St Julien-de-Peyrolas [04 66 82 14 94; fax 04 66 82 31 70; contact@camping-lepeyrolais.com; www.camping-lepeyrolais.com]** N fr Pont-St. Esprit on N86 turn L onto D901 sp Barjac. In 2.5km turn R at site sp, site in 500m up narr track on bank of Rv Ardèche. Med, mkd pitch, pt shd; wc; chem disp; mv waste; shwrs inc; el pnts (3-10A) €2.30-3.80; lndtte; ice; shop & 3km; tradsmn; rest; bar; playgrnd; rv sw adj; fishing; kayaking; cycle & canoe hire; games area; hiking; horseriding; entmnt; disco; TV rm; dogs €1.60; phone; poss cr; adv bkg; quiet; cc acc; CCI. "Attractive, well-maintained site in beautiful location; v clean facs; friendly owners; vg." ♦ 8 Apr-29 Sep. € 15.80   2005*

⊞**PONT ST ESPRIT** 9D2 (8km NW Rural) **FFCC Camping Les Truffières, Route de St Ramèze, 07700 St Marcel-d'Ardèche [04 75 04 68 35 or 06 82 01 28 30 (mob); fax 04 75 98 75 86]** S fr Bourg-St Andéol, turn W on D201; in vill foll sp to site located approx 3km W of vill. Med, mkd pitch, terr, pt shd; htd wc; mv service pnt; shwrs inc; el pnts (3-6A) €3.50-4.40 (poss rev pol); gas; lndtte; ice; shops 3km; rest; snacks; bar; playgrnd; pool; entmnt; 70% statics; dogs €1.50; adv bkg; quiet; red low ssn; CCI. "Friendly owners; glorious views; gd location for Ardèche, away fr crowds along gorge; gd clean san facs; gd NH nr A7." ♦ € 10.10
2005*

PONT SUR SEINE see Nogent sur Seine 4E4

PONTAILLER SUR SAONE 6G1 (750m E Rural) **Camping La Chanoie, 46 Rue de la Chanoie, 21270 Pontailler-sur-Saône [03 80 36 10 58; fax 03 80 47 84 42; tourisme-canton-pontailler. com; www.tourisme-canton-pontailler.com]** E fr Pontailler-sur-Saône on D959; pass town hall & tourist office on R; after bdg take 1st L sp Camping; site in 500m. Fr W on D959 turn R bef bdg & bef ent town. Med, hdg/mkd pitch, pt shd; htd wc (some cont); chem disp (wc); mv service pnt; baby facs; shwrs inc; el pnts (6-10A) €2.85-4.10; gas 1km; lndtte; ice; shops 750m; rest; snacks; bar; BBQ; playgrnd; rv sw, water sports & fishing adj; tennis; games area; games rm; dogs €1.55; bus; poss cr; adv bkg; quiet; poss noisy if busy; red long stay; CCI. "In walking dist of attractive sm town; polite & helpful owner; modern & dated clean san facs; poss stretched high ssn; vg." ♦ ltd. 15 Apr-15 Oct. € 9.30
2007*

PONTAIX 9D2 (2km E Rural) **Aire Naturelle La Condamine (Archinard), 26150 Pontaix [04 75 21 08 19; fax 04 74 04 46 12; aurelie. goderiaux@laposte.net]** W fr Die on D93; site on R just after D129. Fr E, 2km after Pontaix on L. Sm, unshd; wc; chem disp; shwrs inc; el pnts (10A) €2; lndry rm; ice; shop 8km; rest, snacks, bar 1km; BBQ; rv sw adj; dogs €1.50; adv bkg; quiet; CCI; excel. "New CL-type site by Rv Drôme (2006); will have shd when trees grow." ♦ 15 Apr-15 Oct. € 8.10
2006*

PONTARLIER 6H2 (1km SE Rural) **FFCC Camping Le Larmont, Rue du Toulombief, 25300 Pontarlier [03 81 46 23 33; fax 03 81 46 23 34; lelarmont. pontarlier@ffcc.fr; www.camp-in-france.com]** Leave N57 at Pontarlier Gare & foll site sp. Site uphill, turning nr Nestlé factory. Med, some hdstg, terr, unshd; htd wc; chem disp; mv service pnt; shwrs inc; el pnts (10A) €3.05; gas; lndtte; sm shop; tradsmn; snacks; bar; playgrnd; pool 2km; horseriding adj; skiing winter; 10-20% statics; dogs €1; Eng spkn; adv bkg; red CCI. "Friendly; easy access; immac san facs; ltd pitches for awnings; battery-charging; pitch yourself out of office hrs." ♦ ltd. 1 Apr-1 Nov. € 14.80
2006*

PONTARLIER 6H2 (12km S Rural) **Camp Municipal, 8 Rue du Port, 25160 St Point-Lac [03 81 69 61 64 or 03 81 69 62 08 (Mairie); fax 03 81 69 65 74; camping-saintpointlac@ wanadoo.fr; www.camping-saintpointlac.com]** Exit Pontarlier on N57 dir Lausanne, turn R on D437, after further 6km turn R on D129. Site on L in sm vill St Point-Lac. Med, mkd pitch, hdstg, unshd; htd wc; chem disp; mv service pnt; chem disp; shwrs inc; el pnts (16A) inc; lndtte; shops, rest, snacks, bar 100m; BBQ; 10% statics; dogs €1; adv bkg rec high ssn; quiet; cc acc; CCI. "Pleasantly situated base for local nature reserves; beautiful views; on edge of lake, shgl landing for boats; well-kept site; vg san facs; a great site for birdwatching, fishing, walking; v friendly staff; excel local cheesemaker; vg meals at hotel at ent; rec adv bkg for lakeside pitches; sm pitches; o'night parking area across rd fr site for m'vans with water, waste, wc etc; vg value." ♦ 1 May-30 Sep. € 14.50
2007*

This guide relies on site report forms submitted by caravanners like us; we'll do our bit and tell the editor what we think of the campsites we've visited.

PONTAUBAULT 2E4 (Urban) **Camping La Vallée de la Sélune, 7 Rue Maréchal Leclerc, 50220 Pontaubault [tel/fax 02 33 60 39 00; campselune@ wanadoo.fr; www.caravancampingsites.co.uk/ france/50/selune.htm]** Foll sp to Pontaubault (well sp fr all dirs). In vill head twd Avranches. Turn L immed bef bdge over Rv Sélune. In 100m turn L, site strt in 100m, well sp. Med, mkd pitch, pt sl, pt shd; wc; chem disp; shwrs inc; el pnts (8-10A) €3; lndtte; ice; shop; tradsmn; supmkt 6km; snacks; bar high ssn; playgrnd; pool 7km; sand beach 10km; tennis adj; fishing adj; horseriding, cycling & golf nrby; 10% statics; dogs €1.30; poss cr; British owners; adv bkg rec; rd/rlwy noise; cc acc; red long stay/CCI. "Relaxing site; v friendly owner; san facs vg & v clean; conv Mont St Michel, Avranches, St Malo & Cherbourg ferries; highly rec." ♦ 1 Apr-20 Oct. € 12.00
2006*

PONTAUBAULT 2E4 (4km E Rural) **Camp Municipal La Sélune, Rue de Boishue, 50220 Ducey [02 33 48 46 49 or 02 33 48 50 52; fax 02 33 48 87 59; ducey.tourisme@wanadoo.fr]** Exit A84 junc 33 onto N176 E fr Pontaubault. In Ducey turn R onto D178 twd St Aubin-de-Terregatte. Ent to site at municipal sports ground in 200m. Sm, hdg pitch, pt sl, shd; wc; chem disp; shwrs inc; el pnts (10A) (rev pol) €1.64; gas; lndtte; shop; rest, snacks, bar in vill; playgrnd; pool nr; sand beach 25km; tennis adj; 10% statics; dogs €1.30; phone; bus; poss cr; Eng spkn; adv bkg; quiet; CCI. "Poss diff to manoeuvre onto pitches due sl, soft ground & ruts." 1 Apr-30 Sep. € 7.10
2007*

PONTAUBAULT 2E4 (6km SW Coastal) **Camping St Grégoire, Le Haut Bourg, 50170 Servon** [02 33 60 26 03; fax 02 33 60 68 65; www. normandie-camping.net or www.campeole. com] Foll N175 fr Pontaubault twd Pontorson. After 6km site sp on R twd Servon vill. Med, pt shd; wc; shwrs; el pnts (6A) €2.90; lndtte; sm shop; playgrnd; pool; games rm; TV; 30% statics; dogs €2.60; adv bkg; quiet but some rd noise on S side of site; cc acc; CCI. "Conv ferries." 1 Apr-15 Oct. € 14.00
2006*

PONTCHATEAU 2G3 (4km W Rural) **Camping Le Château du Deffay, 18 Ste Reine-de-Bretagne, 44160 Pontchâteau** [02 40 88 00 57; fax 02 40 01 66 55; campingdudeffay@wanadoo. fr; www.camping-le-deffay.com] Leave N165 at junc 13 onto D33 twd Herbignac. Site on R approx 1.5km after Le Calvaire de la Madeleine x-rds. Site sp fr by-pass. Med, mkd pitch, pt terr, pt shd; wc; chem disp; mv service pnt; serviced pitches; baby facs; shwrs inc; el pnts (6A) inc; lndtte; shop; rest; snacks; bar; BBQ (charcoal/gas); playgrnd; htd, covrd pool; paddling pool; lake fishing; tennis & pedaloes; cycle hire; woodland walks; golf 10km; entmnt; internet; games/TV rm; dogs €2; recep 0830-2000 high ssn; adv bkg (dep req); red low ssn; cc acc (not in rest); CCI. "Friendly owners; lovely site, well worth 4-star designation; lakeside pitches not fenced; staff v welcoming & helpful; insufficient water taps; weekly chateau dinners high ssn; rest gd value; mkt Mon; vg." ♦ 1 May-30 Sep. € 25.80 (CChq acc) ABS - B25
2007*

See advertisement

PONTCHATEAU 2G3 (2km NW Rural) **Camping Le Bois Beaumard, 1 Rue de la Beaumard, 44160 Pontchâteau** [tel/fax 02 40 88 03 36; obocamp@ aol.com; www.campingbeaumard.com] Fr Nantes on N165 by-pass; ignore sp Pontchâteau Est, take 2nd sp & foll site sp. Fr Vannes NW of town exit sp Beaulieu; foll site sp. Site also sp bef Pontchâteau on D773 S fr Redon. Sm, hdg/mkd pitch, pt shd; wc; chem disp; shwrs inc; el pnts (10-12A) €3; lndtte; ice; shops 2km; tradsmn; BBQ; playgrnd; TV rm; dogs €1; Eng spkn; adv bkg; some rd noise; CCI. "Delightful, immac site in orchard; wooded setting; red squirrels, bird song; calm & quiet low ssn; friendly, helpful owners; on edge of Brière regional nature park with gd walking & birdwatching." 1 Apr-1 Oct. € 9.50
2007*

⊞**PONTENX LES FORGES** 7D1 (1km S Rural) **Camp Municipal Le Guilleman, 645 Route de Guilleman, 40200 Pontenx-les-Forges** [05 58 07 40 48; contact@leguilleman.com; www. leguilleman.com] Exit N10 at Labouheyre onto D626 W for 16km. Ent vill, sp to L, foll sm lane for 1km, clearly sp. Med, mkd pitch, pt shd; wc (some cont); chem disp; shwrs inc; el pnts (10A) inc (poss rev pol); lndtte; shop; snacks; bar; pool 1km; sand beach 15km; 10% statics; dogs €1; poss cr; adv bkg; poss noisy at times; CCI. "Relaxed, spacious site away fr cr coastal sites; esp gd for children; friendly management; san facs being renovated (2007)." ♦ € 15.00
2007*

PONTET, LE see Avignon 10E2

PONTGIBAUD 7B4 (3km NE Rural) **Camping Bel-Air, 63230 St Ours** [04 73 88 72 14; camping. belair@free.fr; http://camping.belair.free.fr] Exit A89 junc 26 to Pontgibaud onto D941 N, site sp. Med, mkd pitch, pt sl, shd; wc; chem disp; mv service pnt; baby facs; shwrs inc; el pnts (6A) €3.20; gas; lndry rm; ice; shop 1.5km; tradsmn; rest; snacks; bar; BBQ; playgrnd; golf; dogs €1; Eng spkn; adv bkg; quiet, but some rd noise; CCI. "Beautiful area with panoramic views of Puy-de-Dome volcanic mountains fr site ent; peaceful site; spotless facs; vg facs for disabled; gd walking; v helpful owners; ltd facs low ssn." ♦ 28 Apr-30 Sep. € 13.00
2006*

France

PONTGIBAUD 7B4 (200m S Rural) **Camp Municipal La Palle, Route de la Miouze, 63230 Pontgibaud [04 73 88 96 99 or 04 73 88 70 42 (LS); fax 04 73 88 77 77]** At W end of Pontgibaud turn S over bdge on D986 & site in 500m on L. Med, hdg/ mkd pitch, hdstg, pt shd; htd wc (some cont); chem disp; mv service pnt; shwrs inc; el pnts (6-10A) €2.50-2.90; gas 400m; lndtte; ice; shops 400m; tradsmn; rest; BBQ; playgrnd; lake sw & beach 4km; games area; tennis, cycle hire 400m; entmnt; 5% statics; dogs; Eng spkn; adv bkg; quiet; red long stay/low ssn; CCI. "Pleasant site; helpful staff; gd touring base; conv Vulcania." ♦ 13 May-15 Oct. € 11.40   2006*

PONTOISE 3D3 (6km E Urban) **Camp Municipal Bellerive, Chemin de Bellerive, 95430 Auvers- sur-Oise [01 34 48 05 22; fax 01 30 36 70 30; www.auvers-sur-oise.com]** Exit N184 junc 7 sp Méry & Auvers-sur-Oise; in Méry foll sp to Auvers; immed on ent Auvers turn L sp Parking; foll rd (narr in places) to T-junc; turn L; foll Camping sp. Site 300m on L along rvside. Sm, shd; wc (some cont); chem disp (wc); shwrs inc; el pnts (6A) inc (poss rev pol); lndry rm; shop, rest, snacks & bar 1km; BBQ; adv bkg; quiet; CCI. "Easy access to Paris & Disneyland; shops etc sh walk along rvside; Van Gogh buried here; gd." 15 Jun-15 Sep. € 14.30   2007*

The opening dates and prices on this campsite have changed. I'll send a site report form to the editor for the next edition of the guide.

PONTORSON 2E4 (400m Urban) **Camping Haliotis, Chemin des Soupirs, 50170 Pontorson [02 33 68 11 59; fax 02 33 58 95 36; info@ camping-haliotis-mont-saint-michel.com; www. camping-haliotis-mont-saint-michel.com]** Turn N off N176 at W end of town cent (well sp); take L turn to site. Med, hdg pitch, pt sl, pt shd; htd wc (cont); chem disp; mv service pnt; baby facs; sauna; shwrs inc; el pnts (10-16A) €3; gas; lndtte; ice; shop; supmkt 400m; tradsmn; rest; snacks; bar; BBQ; playgrnd; htd pool; paddling pool; spa; rv fishing; boating; tennis; cycle hire; games games area; games rm; child entmnt; wifi internet; 25% statics; dogs €0.50; phone; bus 400m; poss cr; Eng spkn; adv bkg rec; quiet; red low ssn; cc acc; CCI. "V popular; modern & well-maintained; immac san facs; friendly, helpful, interested owners; lovely pool & bar; locked at night till 0730; 9km to Mont St Michel - bus nrby & cycle rte; lovely rv walk fr site to sm town with rests; gd touring base; gd value; highly rec." ♦ ltd. 31 Mar-5 Nov. € 19.00 (CChq acc)   2007*

PONTRIEUX 2E3 (4km E Rural) **Camp Municipal du Bois d'Amour, 22260 Quemper-Guézennec [02 96 95 13 40 or 02 96 95 62 62; fax 02 96 95 36 07]** Exit N12 at Guincamp Est; D787 twds Pontrieux. At rndabt ent to Pontrieux, turn R & foll rd to indus est over level x-ing. Turn R along rv front, site in approx 200 yrds. Sm, pt shd, mkd pitch; wc; shwrs; el pnts (15A) inc; lndry rm; ice; sm shop; tradsmn; playgrnd; fishing; cc not acc; quiet; CCI. "Pay at Marie in Quemper-Guézennec; gd touring base; best pitches overlook Rv Trieux; clean & roomy san facs; excel." ♦ 15 Jun-15 Sep. € 12.00   2006*

Before we move on, I'm going to fill in some site report forms and post them off to the editor, otherwise they won't arrive in time for the deadline at the end of September.

⊞**PONTRIEUX** 2E3 (500m W Urban) **Camping de Traou Mélédern (Thomas), 22260 Pontrieux [02 96 95 68 72 or 02 96 95 69 27; http:// campingpontrieux.free.fr]** N on D787 fr Guingamp; on ent town square turn sharp L sp Traou Mélédern, cross rv bdge & turn R alongside church. Site in 400m. Access poss diff for lge o'fits; steep exit on 1-way system. Med, hdg/mkd pitch, pt sl, pt shd; wc; chem disp; shwrs inc; el pnts (8A) €3; lndtte; shops, supmkt 1km; tradsmn; playgrnd; BBQ; dogs; €0.90; phone; poss cr; Eng spkn; adv bkg; quiet but some daytime factory noise; CCI. "Among apple trees; gd for touring Pink Granite coast; Pontrieux attractive sm town; conv Bréhat & train to Brest, WW2 museum Fort Montbarey, Allée Bir Hakiem; friendly owner; steep junc nr site poss problem for lge o'fits; gd." ♦ € 9.40   2007*

PONTS DE CE, LES see Angers 4G1

PORDIC see Binic 2E3

PORGE, LE 7C1 (9km W Coastal) **Camp Municipal La Grigne, Ave de l'Océan, 33680 Le Porge [05 56 26 54 88; fax 05 56 26 52 07; campingduporge@wanadoo.fr]** Fr Bordeaux ring rd take N215 twd Lacaneau. In 22km at Ste Hélène D5 to Saumos & onto Le Porge. Site on L of rd to Porge-Océan in approx 9km. V lge, mkd pitch, terr, pt sl, shd; wc; chem disp; shwrs; el pnts (10A) €3.60; gas; shop; lndtte; ice; bar; snacks; playgrnd; beach 600m; tennis; games area; TV; poss cr; adv bkg; quiet. "Unreliable opening/closing dates - phone ahead." ♦ 1 Apr-30 Sep. € 17.00   2006*

France

PORNIC Caravans are prohibited in Pornic. If app fr E on D751 or fr SE on D13 remain on by-pass to N of Pornic & take D286/D13 exit.

PORNIC *2G3* (10km N Urban) **Camp Municipal Le Grand Fay, Rue du Grand Fay, 44320 St Père-en-Retz** [02 40 21 72 89; fax 02 40 82 40 27; legrandfay@aol.com; www.camping-grandfay.com] Fr Mairie in cent St Père-en-Retz take D78 E twds Frossay. After 500m turn R into Rue des Sports, after 200m turn L into Rue du Grand Fay. Site on L in 200m adj sports cent. Med, mkd pitch, pt sl, pt shd; wc (some cont); shwrs inc; el pnts (10A) €3.80; lndry rm; ice; tradsmn; supmkt nrby; playgrnd; htd pool; beach 8km; lake fishing adj; games areal some statics; dogs €1.60; quiet; CCI. "Pleasant site nr sandy beaches." ♦ 1 Apr-15 Nov. € 13.30   2007*

PORNIC *2G3* (9km NE) **Camping La Renaudière, 44770 La Plaine-sur-Mer** [02 40 21 50 03; fax 02 40 21 09 41; camping.la.renaudiere@wanadoo.fr; www.campinglarenaudiere.com] S fr St Nazaire on D213 twd Pornic, turn onto D96 twd Préfailles. Fr Nantes D751 W to Pornic then D13, dir La Plaine-sur-Mer, then Rte de la Prée. Med, pt shd; wc; chem disp; baby facs; shwrs; el pnts (10A) €3.10; gas; ice; lndtte; shop adj; rest; snacks; bar; BBQ; playgrnd; htd pool; beach & watersports 2km; entmnts; TV; some statics; dogs €2; adv bkg; CCI. ♦ 1 Apr-30 Sep. € 14.50   2004*

PORNIC *2G3* (3km E Rural) **Camping La Chênaie, 36 Rue du Patisseau, 44210 Pornic** [02 40 82 07 31; fax 02 40 82 62 62; la.chenaie@free.fr; www.campinglachenaie.com] Fr Nantes on D751 to Pornic, at 1st rndabt turn R. Fr St Nazaire on D213, foll sp Nantes & Le Clion-sur-Mer to avoid Pornic cent. Med, hdg/mkd pitch, hdstg, pt sl, terr, pt shd; wc; chem disp; mv service pnt; serviced pitch; child/baby facs; shwrs inc; el pnts (6A) €3.50; lndtte; ice; shop; tradsmn; snacks; bar; BBQ; playgrnd; 3 pools; sand beach 2.5km; horseriding; golf; cycle hire; entmnt; child entmnt; 37% statics; dogs €2; Eng spkn; adv bkg; quiet; cc acc; red low ssn; CCI. "Nice, lge pitches; friendly site; gd walking." ♦ 8 Apr-30 Sep. € 18.00   2005*

PORNIC *2G3* (4km E Rural) **Camping Sunêlia Le Patisseau, 29 Rue de Patisseau, 44210 Pornic** [02 40 82 10 39; fax 02 40 82 22 81; contact@lepatisseau.com; www.lepatisseau.com] Fr N or S on D213, take slip rd D751 Nantes. At rndabt take exit sp to Le Patisseau, foll sp. Lge, hdg/mkd pitch, hdstg, pt sl, pt shd; htd wc; chem disp; mv service pnt; sauna; shwrs inc; el pnts (6A) inc; gas; lndtte; ice; shop; tradsmn; rest; snacks; bar; BBQ; playgrnd; 2 htd pools (1covrd); 2 htd paddling pools (1 covrd); 2 waterslides; sand beach 2.5km; jacuzzi; fitness rm; tennis 1km; games area; games rm; golf 2km; entmnt; child entmnt; TV; 35% statics; dogs €5; Eng spkn; adv bkg rec high ssn; quiet; red low ssn; cc acc. "Excel, modern, family site; modern htd san facs block; poss groups at w/ends." ♦ 31 Mar-11 Nov. € 34.50   2006*

PORNIC *2G3* (5km E Coastal) **Camping Village La Boutinardière, Rue de la Plage, Le Clion-sur-Mer, 44210 Pornic [02 40 82 05 68; fax 02 40 82 49 01; info@laboutinardiere.com; www.camping-boutinardiere.com]** SW fr Nantes on D723; turn L on D751 twd Pornic. Foll dir La Bernerie-en-Retz & site sp. Lge, hdg pitch, pt sl, pt shd; wc (some cont); chem disp; mv service pnt; serviced pitches; baby facs; shwrs inc; el pnts (6-10A) €3.50-5 (poss rev pol); gas; lndtte; ice; shop; supmkt; rest; snacks; bar; BBQ; playgrnd; 2 pools (1 htd, covrd); paddling pool; waterslide; jacuzzi; sand beach 200m; lake sw 3km; tennis; games rm; golf 5km; cycle hire; entmnt & activities; TV rm; 15% statics; dogs €4; poss cr; Eng spkn; adv bkg; quiet; red low ssn; cc acc; red long stay/low ssn; CCI. "Excel family site; v busy high ssn; Pornic interesting town; 8 min walk to bus in vill." ♦ 5 Apr-28 Sep. € 34.00   2007*

See advertisement on previous page

There aren't many sites open this early in the year. We'd better phone ahead to check that the one we're heading for is actually open.

PORNIC *2G3* (6km SE Rural/Coastal) **Camping Les Ecureuils, 24 Ave Gilbert Burlot, 44760 La Bernerie-en-Retz [02 40 82 76 95; fax 02 40 64 79 52; camping.les-ecureuils@wanadoo.fr; www.camping-les-ecureuils.com]** Fr Pornic take D13 S for 5km, then D66 for 1km; site sp. Lge, hdg pitch, pt sl, pt shd; wc; chem disp; baby facs; shwrs inc; el pnts (6-10A) €4; lndtte; shops 500m; snacks; bar; BBQ area; playgrnd; htd pool; paddling pool; waterslide; sand beach 400m; tennis; golf 5km; entmnt; children's club; 30% statics; dogs (up to 10kg only) €3; Eng spkn; adv bkg; quiet; cc acc; red low ssn/CCI. "Excel." ♦ 12 Apr-17 Sep. € 29.00   2007*

See advertisement below

PORNIC *2G3* (7km SE Coastal) **Camping de la Plage, 53 Route de la Bernerie, 44580 Les Moutiers-en-Retz [02 40 82 71 43; fax 02 40 82 72 46; bernard.beaujean@wanadoo.fr; www.camping-la-plage.com]** SE fr Pornic dir Bourgneuf, in 5km turn R for La Bernerie. 1st L after church. Site on R in 2km. Foll sps fr cent Les Moutiers. Lge, hdg/mkd pitch, pt sl, pt shd; wc; chem disp; shwrs inc; el pnts (10-16A) €3.60; lndtte; shop; snacks; bar; BBQ; playgrnd; htd pool; beach adj; entmnt; TV; some statics; dogs €1; Eng spkn; adv bkg; red low ssn; cc acc; CCI. "Vg; diff access to some pitches - manhandling poss req." 1 Apr-30 Sep. € 21.00   2006*

Did you know you can fill in site report forms on the Club's website — www.caravanclub.co.uk?

PORNIC *2G3* (9km SE Coastal) **Camping Le Village de la Mer, 18 Rue de Prigny, 44760 Les Moutiers-en-Retz [02 40 64 65 90; fax 02 51 74 63 17; info@village-mer.fr; www.village-mer.fr]** Site sp on D97 dir Bourgneuf, site is 100m to SE of Les Moutiers-en-Retz. Lge, hdg/mkd pitch, pt shd; mv service pnt; chem disp; baby facs; shwrs inc; el pnts (8A) inc; gas; lndtte; shop adj; snacks; bar; BBQ; playgrnd; htd pool; waterpark; sand beach 300m; watersports; tennis; games rm; entmnt; internet; excursions; 50% statics; dogs €3; Eng spkn; adv bkg; red low ssn; cc acc; CCI. "Quiet; ideal for families." ♦ 15 Jun-15 Sep. € 26.00   2005*

PORNIC *2G3* (600m W Coastal/Urban) **Camping du Golf, 40 Rue de la Renaissance, 44210 Pornic [02 40 82 41 18 or 06 09 71 23 92 (mob LS); fax 02 51 74 06 62; campingdugolf@yahoo.fr or cledelles@aol.com; www.camping-du-golf.com or www.lescledelles.com.fr]** Fr Nantes, take D751 W dir Ste Marie. App Pornic, take D213 dir St Nazaire & foll sp Ste Marie & site; well sp. Med, mkd pitch, hdstg, pt shd; wc; chem disp (wc); baby facs; fam bthrm; shwrs inc; el pnts (6-10A) €5-6; gas; lndtte; ice; shop 600m; tradsmn; rest, snacks, bar high ssn; BBQ; htd pool high ssn; playgrnd; sand beach 600m; lake sw 200m; tennis; games rm; golf 1km; cycle hire; entmnt; child entmnt; TV; 90% statics; dogs €2.20; Eng spkn; adv bkg; quiet; red low ssn/long stay; cc acc; CCI. "Conv coastal path; 40 mins walk to Pornic; twin-axles not acc; gd san facs poss unclean; ltd space for tourers." ♦ 1 Apr-30 Sep. € 22.00   2005*

PORNIC *2G3* (1km W Coastal) **Camping La Madrague, Chemin de la Madrague, Ste Marie, 44210 Pornic [02 40 82 06 73; fax 02 51 74 11 93; info@madrague.net; www.madrague.net]** Fr Pornic on D213 foll sp Ste Marie-sur-Mer. Foll D286 then R on D13. Turn L into Rue du Moulin Neuf, then R into Rue des Bougrenets. Cont on Rue Yves Ponceau, then Chemin de la Madrague to site. Lge, hdg/mkd pitch, pt sl, pt shd; htd wc; chem disp; mv waste; baby facs; fam bthrm; shwrs inc; el pnts (3-6A) €3-3.50; gas; lndtte; ice; shop; tradsmn; rest; snacks; bar; playgrnd; dir access to sand beach 500m; games area; entmnt; 60% statics; dogs €2; phone; bus; poss cr; adv bkg; quiet. "V clean, well-organised site; helpful staff; excel coastal path walks; gd for dog owners; sea views." ♦ 1 Apr-15 Oct.   2005*

PORNIC *2G3* (2km W Urban) **Camping Les Coeurés, 28 Rue des Coeurés, Ste Maire, 44210 Pornic [06 87 29 33 62 (mob)]** S fr St Nazaire on D213; turn R bef Pornic onto D286 to Ste Marie; turn R at rndabt onto D13, then 1st L. Site on L in 100m. Med, pt shd; wc (some cont); chem disp (wc); shwrs inc; el pnts (10A) inc; shop 300m; sand beach 3km; 10% statics; dogs €0.60; poss cr; quiet. "Excel." 1 May-30 Sep. € 13.50   2006*

PORNIC *2G3* (5km W Coastal) **Camping Le Ranch, Chemin des Hautes Raillères, 44770 La Plaine-sur-Mer [02 40 21 52 62; fax 02 51 74 81 31; info@camping-le-ranch.com; www.camping-le-ranch.com]** S fr St Nazaire on D213 twd Pornic, turn onto D96 twd Préfailles. Site between Tharon-Plage & La Plaine-sur-Mer on D96. Lge, hdg/mkd pitch, pt shd; wc; chem disp; baby facs; shwrs; el pnts (6A) €3.80; gas; lndtte; shop; tradsmn; snacks; bar; BBQ; playgrnd; htd pool; paddling pool; waterslide; sand beach 800m; tennis; games rm; games area; entmnt; dogs €2.50; Eng spkn; adv bkg; quiet; red low ssn; CCI. "Excel, family site." ♦ 1 Apr-30 Sep. € 23.00   2007*

This guide relies on site report forms submitted by caravanners like us; we'll do our bit and tell the editor what we think of the campsites we've visited.

PORNIC *2G3* (5km W Rural) **FFCC Camping La Tabardière, 44770 La Plaine-sur-Mer [02 40 21 58 83; fax 02 40 21 02 68; info@camping-la-tabardiere.com; www.camping-la-tabardiere.com]** Take D13 out of Pornic sp Préfailles & La Plaine-sur-Mer. In about 5.5km turn R (nr water tower) & site sp on D213. Foll sps to site, about 1km fr main rd. Lge, hdg/mkd pitch, hdstg, terr, pt shd; htd wc (some cont); chem disp; mv service pnt; baby facs; shwrs inc; el pnts (8A) inc; gas; lndtte; ice; shop & 3km; tradsmn; snacks; bar; BBQ; playgrnd; htd, covrd pool & paddling pool; waterslides; sand beach 3km; tennis; mini-golf; fishing 3km; horseriding 5km; games area; games rm; entmnt; TV rm; 40% statics; dogs €3; Eng spkn; adv bkg; quiet; cc acc; red low ssn; CCI. "Excel, peaceful site; office open 0830-1230 & 1430-2000; gates clsd 2230-0800; children's club Mon-Fri mornings." ♦ 5 Apr-30 Sep. € 30.50 (CChq acc) ABS - B31   2007*

See advertisement below

France

PORNIC 2G3 (8km W Coastal) **Camping Eléovic, Route de la Pointe St Gildas, 44770 Préfailles** [02 40 21 61 60; fax 02 40 64 51 95; contact@camping-eleovic.com; www.camping-eleovic.com] W fr Pornic on D13 to La Plaine-sur-Mer, turn S to Préfailles, cont twds Pointe-St Gildas 1km, L site sp. Med, hdg pitch, terr, pt shd; htd wc; chem disp; mv service pnt; serviced pitches; baby facs; shwrs inc; el pnts (6A) €4.15; lndtte; tradsmn; rest; snacks; bar; BBQ; htd, covrd pool; waterslide; playgrnd; sand beach adj; fishing; sailing; TV; entmnt; child entmnt; 20% statics; dogs €3-5.40; phone; Eng spkn; adv bkg; red low ssn/long stay/CCI; cc acc. "Dir access to coast path; barrier clsd 2200-1000; recep opens 1000; vg." ♦ 31 Mar-30 Sep. € 31.10   2006*

PORNIC 2G3 (8km NW Coastal) **Camping Clos Mer et Nature, 103 Rue Tharon, 44730 St Michel-Chef-Chef** [02 40 27 85 71; fax 02 40 39 41 89; info@camping-clos-mer-nature.com; www.camping-clos-mer-nature.com] Take D213 fr Mindin. After 11km R on D77 sp St Michel-Chef-Chef 2nd R after cent of vill sp Tharon-Plage site on L after 1.5km. Lge, pt sl, pt shd; htd wc; mv service pnt; baby facs; shwrs inc; el pnts (6-16A) €3.50; lndtte; ice; shop; supmkt 300m; snacks; playgrnd; pool; waterslide; sand beach 400m; fishing; sailing; windsurfing; tennis; cycle hire; games area; entmnt; some statics; dogs €2; adv bkg; quiet. "Vg, modern san facs." ♦ 1 Apr-Oct. € 17.00   2007*

See advertisement

PORNIC 2G3 (8km NW Coastal) **Camping Le Vieux Château, Ave du Vieux-Tharon, Tharon-Plage, 44730 St Michel-Chef-Chef** [02 40 27 83 47 or 02 33 65 02 96; camping.duvieuxchateau@wanadoo.fr] Fr Pornic dir St Nazaire, turn W twd Tharon-Plage, site sp. Med, hdg/mkd pitch, terr, pt shd; wc; chem disp; shwrs inc; el pnts (6A) €3.50; lndtte; ice; shop; tradsmn; snacks; bar; BBQ; playgrnd; htd pool; paddling pool; sand beach 400m; playgrnd; games rm; many statics; dogs €1.50; poss cr; Eng spkn; adv bkg; quiet; cc acc; red long stay; CCI. "Unkempt low ssn; clean facs." ♦ 1 May-15 Sep. € 17.00   2006*

PORNIC 2G3 (7km NW Coastal) **Camping Bel Essor, Rue de Bel Essor, 44730 St Michel-Chef-Chef** [02 40 27 85 40 or 02 47 38 89 07 (LS); www.campingbelessor.com] Take D123 fr Pornic sp St Nazaire. After 8.5km for R onto D78 sp St Michel-Chef-Chef. At rndabt turn L, at next rndabt turn L. Strt on at traff lts, then fork R. Site on R in 300m, sp. Lge, mkd pitch, pt sl, pt shd; wc (some cont); chem disp (wc); shwrs inc; el pnts (6A) €3.20; lndtte; supmkt opp; tradsmn; snacks; bar; playgrnd; sand beach 400m; some statics; dogs €1.30; phone adj; poss cr in high ssn; Eng spkn; adv bkg; CCI. "10 min walk to beach fr rear ent of site; vg & clean facs; helpful owners." ♦ 1 May-15 Sep. € 12.50   2005*

PORNIC 2G3 (10km NW Coastal) **Camping Bernier, 56 Rue de la Cormorane, 44770 La Plaine-sur-Mer** [02 40 21 04 31; fax 02 40 21 08 12; gegene.jolivet@free.fr] S fr St Nazaire bdge on D213 twd Pornic, turn R, S of St Michel-Chef-Chef on D96. Cont to junc, turn R, cont to x-rd, turn L. In 500m on R. Or thro La Plaine-sur-Mer on D13, turn R on leaving vill past g'ge twd Port Guraud. Site on L in 1km. Med, some hdg pitch, pt shd; wc; chem disp; some serviced pitches; shwrs inc; el pnts (6A) €3.50; ice; lndtte; shop 300m; snacks; playgrnd; sand beach 600m; some statics; dogs €2.50; adv bkg; quiet; 40-50% red low ssn; 5% red CCI. "Excel family site site nr gd beaches." ♦ 1 Apr-30 Sep. € 15.00   2005*

PORNICHET *2G3* (2km E Coastal) **Camping Bel Air,
150 Ave de Bonne Source, Ste Marguerite, 44380
Pornichet [02 40 61 10 78; fax 02 40 61 26 18;
reception@bel-air-pornichet.com; www.
belairpornichet.com]** On coast rd fr Pornichet to
Ste Margarite; sp. Lge, hdg/mkd pitch, pt sl, pt shd;
htd wc; chem disp; mv service pnt; baby facs; fam
bthrm; shwrs inc; el pnts some (10A) €4; gas; lndtte;
ice; shop; tradsmn; snacks; rest; snacks; bar; BBQ;
playgrnd; htd pool; sand beach 50m; multi-sport
area; fishing; sailing; cycle hire; internet; TV rm;
50% statics; dogs €1.50; no twin-axles; Eng spkn;
adv bkg; quiet; cc acc; red long stay/low ssn. "Easy
access to lge sand beach 50m; close to shopping
area; pleasant town; St Nazaire shipyards worth
visit." ♦ 28 Apr-16 Sep. € 35.00   2007*

PORNICHET *2G3* (2km E Urban/Coastal) **Camping
du Bugeau, 33 Ave des Loriettes, 44380 Pornichet
[02 40 61 02 02 or 02 40 61 15 44 (LS); fax
02 40 61 22 75; campingdubugeau@wanadoo.fr;
http://campingdubugeau.free.fr]** W fr St Nazaire
on D92 then L at rndabt at St Marguerite by car
showrm; site sp 2nd L, site 500m on L. Med, hdg/
mkd pitch, pt shd; htd wc; chem disp; mv service
pnt; shwrs inc; el pnts (4-10A) €2.90-3.80; lndtte;
ice; shop & 500m; tradsmn; snacks; BBQ; playgrnd;
htd, covrd pool; sand beach & watersports 500m;
tennis 500m; cycle hire 1km; child entmnt; TV;
30% statics; dogs; Eng spkn; adv bkg; cc acc.
"Gd." ♦ 1 Jun-15 Sep. € 19.10   2007*

⊞**PORNICHET** *2G3* (4km E Rural) **Camping au
Repos des Forges, 98 Route Villès-Blaise, 44380
Pornichet [02 40 61 18 84; fax 02 40 60 11 84;
camping@campinglesforges.com; www.
campinglesforges.com]** To N of D92 halfway bet
St Nazaire & Pornichet. Accessible also fr N171; sp.
Med, pt sl, pt shd; wc; chem disp; shwrs inc; el pnts
(6-10A) inc; gas; lndry rm; ice; shop in ssn; snacks;
playgrnd; pool; beach 3km; games rm; 70% statics;
Eng spkn; adv bkg; quiet; CCI. "Friendly reception;
barrier clsd 2300-0700; excel san facs." ♦ € 17.00
                                        2004*

PORT DES BARQUES see Rochefort *7B1*

PORT EN BESSIN HUPPAIN *3D1* (500m W
Coastal) **Camping Port'land, Chemin de Castel,
14520 Port-en-Bessin [02 31 51 07 06; fax
02 31 51 76 49; campingportland@wanadoo.fr;
www.camping-portland.com]** Site sp fr D514
W of Port-en-Bessin. Lge, hdg/mkd pitch, pt shd;
wc; mv service pnt; chem disp; shwrs inc; el pnts
(15A) €5; gas 1km; lndtte; shop; tradsmn; rest;
snacks; bar; BBQ; playgrnd; htd, covrd pool; sand
beach 4km; tennis 500m; games area; entmnt; child
entmnt; games rm; TV; 20% statics; dogs €3; Eng
spkn; adv bkg; red long stay/low ssn; cc acc; red
CCI. "Conv D-Day landing beaches & US cemetery,
Bayeux; many activities; extra charge for lger
pitches; v friendly & helpful; excel touring base." ♦
1 Apr-5 Nov. € 32.30   2006*

PORT LA NOUVELLE see Sigean *10G1*

PORT SUR SAONE *6F2* (800m S Rural) **Camp
Municipal Parc de la Maladière, 70170 Port-sur-
Saône [03 84 91 51 32 or 03 84 78 18 00 (Mairie);
fax 03 84 78 18 09; tourisme.portsursaone@
wanadoo.fr]** Take D619 (N19) SE fr Langres or
N19 NW fr Vesoul. Site sp in vill bet rv & canal off
D6 at municipal bathing area. Med, hdg pitch, pt
shd; wc (mainly cont); own san facs; chem disp;
shwrs inc; el pnts (6A) €2.50 (poss rev pol); lndry
rm; shops 1km; tradsmn high ssn; rest, bar; in vill;
playgrnd; pool adj; tennis; fishing; adv bkg; cc acc;
quiet; CCI. "Gd walks; 48km rvside cycle path;
peaceful site on isle bet canal & Rv Saône; sports
facs, sm pool & deer park adj; conv touring Franche
Comté; golf 40km at Cubrial; gd sh stay/NH." ♦ ltd.
15 May-15 Sep. € 7.50   2006*

> The opening dates and prices
> on this campsite have changed.
> I'll send a site report form to the
> editor for the next
> edition of the guide.

⊞**PORT VENDRES** *10G1* (500m W Urban)
**Aire Communale des Tamarins, Route de la
Jetée, 66660 Port-Vendres [04 68 82 01 03; fax
04 68 82 22 33]** Fr D914 (N114) at Port-Vendres
at Banyuls side of town turn N on D86B sp Port de
Commerce & Aire de Camping-Cars. Foll sp to site
on R in 700m. Sm, hdstg, pt shd; chem disp; mv
service pnt; wc (part cont); own san; gas 1km; shop
1km; rest 500m; snacks, bar 1km; playgrnd adj;
shgl beach 100m. "Vg NH m'vans only; walking dist
rlwy stn; poss cr even low ssn." € 7.50   2005*

PORT VENDRES *10G1* (2km NW Coastal) **Camping
Les Amandiers, Plage de l'Ouile, 66190 Collioure
[04 68 81 14 69; fax 04 68 81 09 95; contact@
camping-les-amandiers.com; www.camping-les-
amandiers.com]** On D914 (N114) SE fr Perpignan,
leave at junc 13 sp Collioure. After rndabt foll rd to
Collioure. Climb coastal rd; site on L, steep descent,
not rec lge o'fits. Med, mkd pitch, pt sl, terr, shd;
htd wc (some cont); chem disp; mv service pnt;
shwrs inc; el pnts (5A) €4; lndtte; gas; sm shop;
tradsmn; sm rest, bar high ssn; sm playgrnd; shgl
beach 200m; 10% statics; dogs €3; poss cr; Eng
spkn; adv bkg; (rec high ssn); some rlwy noise; cc
not acc; CCI. "Site access v diff, esp for lge/med
o'fits, manhandling prob req - rec investigation bef
ent; sm pitches; facs stretched high ssn; many
trees - dusty site; steep site rds; v friendly & helpful
owners; Collioure historic port; gd." ♦ 1 Apr-30 Sep.
€ 22.00   2007*

France

PORTIRAGNES PLAGE *10F1* (Coastal) **Camping Les Sablons, Plage-Est, 34420 Portiragnes-Plage [04 67 90 90 55; fax 04 67 90 82 91; les.sablons@wanadoo.fr; www.les-sablons.com]** Fr A9 exit Béziers Est junc 35 onto N112. Then take D37 S to Portiragnes-Plage & foll sp. V lge, mkd pitch, shd; wc; chem disp; mv service pnt; baby facs; shwrs inc; el pnts (6A) inc; gas; lndtte; ice; shop; rest; snacks; bar; BBQ; playgrnd; 2 htd pools; waterslide; sand beach adj; diving; boating; fishing; tennis; games area; cycle hire; entmnt; 50% statics; dogs €4; phone; poss cr; Eng spkn; adv bkg (dep & bkg fee, min 3 wks Jul/Aug); cc acc; quiet. "Gd site on beach; modern san facs; nightly disco but quiet after midnight; grottoes & local excursions." ♦ ltd. 1 Apr-30 Sep. € 46.00   2007*

Before we move on, I'm going to fill in some site report forms and post them off to the editor, otherwise they won't arrive in time for the deadline at the end of September.

PORTIRAGNES PLAGE *10F1* (2km NE Coastal) **Camping Les Mimosas, Port Cassafières, 34420 Portiragnes [04 67 90 92 92; fax 04 67 90 85 39; info@mimosas.fr or les.mimosas.portiragnes@wanadoo.fr; www.mimosas.com]** Exit A9 junc 35 Béziers Est & take N112 sp Vias, Agde. After 3km at rndabt foll sp Portiragnes & cont along side of Canal du Midi. Cross canal, site sp. Lge, mkd pitch, hdstg, pt shd; wc; sauna; private san facs avail; shwrs inc; el pnts (6-10A) €4; gas; lndtte; ice; shop; supmkt; rest; snacks; bar; BBQ area; playgrnd; pools; paddling pool; waterslide; jacuzzi; sand beach 1km; cycle hire; games area; fitness rm; entmnt; 50% statics; dogs €5.50; Eng spkn; adv bkg; quiet; cc acc. "Excel touring base in interesting area; friendly welcome; vg water park; gd for families." ♦ 24 May-6 Sep. € 32.00   2007*

See advertisement

POUANCE *2F4* (1.5km NW Urban) **Camp Muncipal La Roche Martin, 23 Rue des Etangs, 49420 Pouancé [02 41 92 43 97; fax 02 41 92 62 30]** Take D6 (sp St Aignan) N fr town. After level x-ing turn L onto D72 (sp La Guerche-de-Bretagne). In 300m, site on L. Sm, pt terr, pt sl; wc; shwrs; el pnts (10A) €1.65; gas; ice; shops 1km; playgrnd; sports area; tennis; direct access to lake; watersports; poss cr; adv bkg. "Well-kept, friendly site overlooking lge lake; noise fr rd & sailing school; low ssn facs inadequate & in need of refurb." 1 May-30 Sep. € 6.20   2004*

POUGUES LES EAUX *4H4* (1km N Urban) **Camp Municipal Les Chanternes, Ave du Paris, 58320 Pougues-les-Eaux [03 86 68 86 18 or 03 86 90 96 00 (Mairie); www.ville-pouguesleseaux.fr]** On side of D907 (N7) in Pougues-les-Eaux at rear of open-air pool & thro same ent. Med, mkd pitch, pt shd; htd wc (some cont); mv service pnt; shwrs inc; el pnts; shops, rest & snacks in vill; pool adj; adv bkg; rd & rlwy noise; CCI. 1 Jun-30 Sep.   2006*

POUILLY EN AUXOIS *6G1* (Urban) **FFCC Camping Le Vert Auxois, Voute du Canal du Bourgogne, 21320 Pouilly-en-Auxois [03 80 90 71 89; fax 03 80 90 77 58; vert.auxois@wanadoo.fr; http://camping.vertauxois.free.fr]** Exit A6 at Dijon/Pouilly-en-Auxois onto A38. Exit A38 at junc 24. Thro vill & turn L after church on R, site sp adj canal. Med, hdg pitch, pt shd; wc; mv service pnt; shwrs inc; el pnts (6-10A) €3-4; gas; lndtte; ice; shop 400m; tradsmn; rest 400m; snacks, bar high ssn; playgrnd; rv fishing adj; lake 5km; quiet; bus 300m; cc not acc; CCI. "Beautiful position; gd facs; gd cycling; boat trips on Burgundy canal; conv NH - rural but in urban situation." Easter-30 Sep. € 9.20   2007*

⊞ *Site open all year*

Help us to update this guide

POUILLY SUR LOIRE *4G3* (1km N Urban) **Camp Municipal Le Malaga, Route des Loges, 58150 Pouilly-sur-Loire [tel/fax 03 86 39 14 54 or 03 86 58 74 38 (LS); www.ot-pouillysurloire.fr]** Fr N7 go to town cent & take D59/D4289 W. Bef rv bdge turn R along Rv Loire, site in 1km on rv. Med, pt sl, terr, pt shd; wc; chem disp; shwrs inc; el pnts (10A) €2.40 (poss long lead req); lndry rm; ice; shop & 1km; tradsmn; snacks; bar; BBQ; playgrnd; rv sw; dogs €1; phone; Eng spkn; quiet, some rlwy noise. "Excel, spacious site; lge pitches; immac san facs high ssn; twin-axle c'vans not acc; beautiful area; wildlife reserve adj; vg value." ♦ 1 Jun-1 Sep. € 9.80   2007*

POULDU, LE *2F2* (N Urban/Coastal) **Camping Les Embruns, Rue du Philosophe Alain, Clohars-Carnoët, 29360 Le Pouldu [02 98 39 91 07; fax 02 98 39 97 87; camping-les-embruns@wanadoo. fr; www.camping-les-embruns.com]** Exit N165 dir Quimperlé Cent, onto D16/D24 to Clohars-Carnoët. Foll sp Le Pouldu & site on R on ent 1-way traff system. Lge, hdg/mkd pitch, hdstg, terr, pt shd; wc; chem disp; mv service pnt; all serviced pitches; baby facs; fam bthrm; shwrs inc; el pnts (10A) inc; gas; lndtte; ice; shop; rest; snacks; bar; BBQ; playgrnd; 2 pools (1 htd, covrd); sand beach 200m; watersports; tennis 200m; fishing; cycle hire; horseriding nr; games area; games rm; TV rm; 50% statics; dogs €1; adv bkg (dep req + bkg fee); quiet; cc acc; red low ssn; CCI. "Gd location - town was home of Paul Gauguin; luxury pitches extra charge; well-appointed & spotless san facs; card-op barrier; gd walking along coastal paths." ♦ 7 Apr-15 Sep. € 28.20   2006*

POULDU, LE *2F2* (2km N) **Camping du Quinquis, 29360 Clohars-Carnoët [02 98 39 92 40; fax 02 98 39 96 56; andrew.munro@clara.co.uk; www.campingquinquis.com]** On D16 fr Quimperlé, 2km S of x-rds with D224. Or fr N165 exit Guidel junc 45; foll sps to Le Pouldu & zoo adj to site. Med, hdg pitch, pt sl, pt shd; wc; shwrs; el pnts (10A) inc; gas; lndtte; ice; sm shop; snacks; bar; playgrnd; pool & paddling pool; sand beach 2km; games rm; entmnt; child entmnt; TV; 80% statics; dogs; phone; poss cr; Eng spkn; quiet. "Vg site." ♦ 1 Apr-30 Sep. € 23.00   2005*

POULDU, LE *2F2* (500m NE Rural) **Camping Keranquernat, Le Pouldu, 29360 Clohars-Carnoët [02 98 39 92 32; fax 02 98 39 99 84; camping.keranquernat@wanadoo.fr; www. camping-keranquernat.com]** Fr Quimperlé D16 to Clohars-Carnoët D24 to Le Pouldu - twd port. Turn R at x-rds nr Ar Men Résidence. Site ent immed on R. Med, hdg/mkd pitch, pt shd; wc (some cont); chem disp; baby facs; shwrs; el pnts (5A) €3; gas; lndtte; ice; shops 300m; tradsmn; snacks; playgrnd; htd pool; paddling pool; sand beach 800m; fishing; sailing; tennis; cycle hire; games rm; TV; dogs; Eng spkn; adv bkg; quiet; red low ssn; CCI. "Beautifully-kept site; lots to do in area; excel." 10 May-9 Sep. € 15.20   2007*

POULDU, LE *2F2* (2km E Rural/Coastal) **Camping Les Jardins de Kergal, 56520 Guidel [tel/fax 02 97 05 98 18; jardins.kergal@wanadoo.fr]** Fr N165 Brest-Nantes take Guidel exit; thro Guidel & onto Guidel-Plages; camp sp in 1km. Lge, hdg/mkd pitch, pt sl, pt shd; wc; chem disp; baby facs; shwrs inc; el pnts (10A) inc; lndtte; ice; shops 2km; tradsmn high ssn; snacks; bar high ssn; BBQ; playgrnd; pool; sand beach 1.5km; tennis; entmnt; cycle hire; games area; 75% statics; dogs €2; adv bkg; quiet but poss noisy youth groups high ssn; red low ssn; CCI. "Friendly, helpful, welcoming wardens; well-run peaceful site; conv beaches & touring; most pitches triangular - poss diff." ♦ 19 Apr-14 Sep. € 26.80   2004*

POULE LES ECHARMEAUX *9A2* (1.5km W Rural) **Camp Municipal Les Echarmeaux, 69870 Poule-les-Echarmeaux [06 89 90 33 64 or 04 74 03 64 48 (LS); fax 04 74 03 68 71]** Turn E off D385 to Poule-les-Echarmeaux. 'Poule Camping' sp. Sm, hdg pitch, terr, pt shd; wc; shwrs inc; el pnts inc; ice; shop 500m; snacks; bar; playgrnd; adv bkg. "Beautifully situated; excel NH." ♦ ltd. 15 Apr-15 Oct. € 9.00   2007*

> There aren't many sites open this early in the year. We'd better phone ahead to check that the one we're heading for is actually open.

POULIGUEN, LE *2G3* (Urban/Coastal) **Camp Municipal Les Mouettes, 45 Blvd de l'Atlantique, 44510 Le Pouliguen [02 40 42 43 98 or 02 40 15 08 08 (Mairie); fax 02 40 15 08 03; lesmouettes@mairie-lepouliguen.fr]** Fr La Boule (W end) take coast rd to Le Pouliguen & foll sps. Lge, unshd; wc; baby facs; shwrs; el pnts (6A) €2; shop, supmkt 200m; rest; snacks; bar; playgrnd; sports area; & beach 1km; fishing; sailing; cycle hire 200m; entmnt; TV; dogs €1.50 "Poss workers residing on site." 1 Apr-15 Oct. € 12.80   2005*

POULLAN SUR MER see Douarnenez *2E2*

⊞**POUZAUGES** *2H4* (1.5km W Rural) **Camping du Lac, L'Espérance, 85700 Pouzauges [02 51 91 37 55; fax 02 51 57 07 69; camplac@ aol.com; www.campingpouzauges.com]** W fr Pouzauges on D960, turn R in 1km onto unclass rd, site in 1km. Sp fr all dir. Sm, hdg/mkd pitch, pt sl, shd; wc; shwrs; el pnts (6-10A) €3.50 (poss rev pol); lndtte; shops 1.5km; tradsmn; snacks; rest, bar 1.5km; lake sw & fishing adj; boat hire; play & picnic area adj; dogs €3; c'van storage; poss cr; adv bkg; quiet; CCI. "Excel site in idyllic setting; lake adj with footpath around; poss poor san facs; friendly, helpful British owners; gd local walks & cycling." ♦ € 13.00   2006*

PRADEAUX, LES see Issoire *9B1*

PRADES *8G4* (500m N Urban) **Camp Municipal Plaine St Martin, 66500 Prades [04 68 96 29 83 or 04 68 05 41 00 (Mairie); prades-conflent@ wanadoo.fr]** Site sp on ent town on N116 fr both dirs. Med, hdg/mkd pitch, pt sl, shd; wc (some cont); chem disp; 50% serviced pitches; shwrs inc; el pnts (6-10A) inc; gas 500m; lndtte; ice; shop, rest, snacks & bar 500m; playgrnd; htd, covrd pool; fishing; 30% statics; dogs €1.10; phone; poss cr; adv bkg; quiet; cc acc; CCI. "Lge pitches; facs old but clean; poss unkempt low ssn; excel area for walking & sightseeing; conv Pyrenees & Perpignan; music festival in Jul; mkt Tues; NH." 1 Apr-30 Sep. € 12.50   2006*

PRADES *8G4* (7km E Rural) **Camping Le Canigou, 66320 Espira-de-Conflent [04 68 05 85 40; fax 04 68 05 86 20; canigou@yahoo.com; www. canigou-espira.com]** On N116 Andorra-Perpignan, 2km after Marquixanes, R at sm site sp also sp 'Espira-de-Conflent'. Or, fr Perpignan on N116, turn L 7km bef Prades onto D25 & foll sp for 3.5km. Med, hdg/mkd pitch, pl sl, terr, shd; wc; chem disp; mv service pnt; shwrs inc; el pnts (6A) €3; lndtte; shop; tradsmn; rest; snacks; bar; playgrnd; rv pool; lake & watersports 5km; 5% statics; dogs €1.50; Eng spkn; adv bkg; quiet; red long stay/low ssn; cc acc; CCI. "Beautiful rvside site in foothills of Pyrenees; youth groups in summer; some noise; narr site rds - not rec for lge o'fits." ♦ ltd. 1 Mar-31 Oct. € 17.00   2006*

PRADES *8G4* (4km W Rural) **Camping Bellevue, Rue de St Jean, 66500 Ria-Sirach [tel/fax 04 68 96 48 96]** W on N116 fr Perpignan, thro Prades. In 1km at far edge of vill of Ria, turn L on D26A & foll sps to site. Access steep. Med, mkd pitch, pt sl, terr, shd; wc; baby facs; shwrs inc; el pnts (3-6A) €2.15-2.80; lndtte; shop 500m; bar; playgrnd; rv sw & fishing 600m; dogs €0.85; adv bkg; quiet. "Site formerly cherry orchard; peaceful with gd valley outlook." ♦ 1 Apr-30 Sep. € 9.00   2005*

PRADES *8G4* (5km W Rural) **Camping Mas de Lastourg, Serdinya, 66500 Villefranche-de-Conflent [04 68 05 35 25; maslastourg@aol.com; www.camping-lastourg.com]** W fr Prades on N116. Site on L of main rd 2km after Villefranche. U-turn at end of dual c'way to rtn. Med, hdg/mkd pitch, pt shd; wc; chem disp (wc); baby facs; shwrs inc; el pnts (6-10A) €3-5; lndtte; sm shop & 2km; tradsmn; rest; snacks; bar; BBQ; playgrnd; sm pool; a few statics; dogs €1; phone; poss cr; Eng spkn; adv bkg; quiet but some rd/rlwy noise; cc acc; CCI. "Lovely site; easy access; nice pitches; keen, new helpful owners (2007); conv 'Little Yellow Train'; excel." ♦ 1 Apr-15 Nov. € 17.30   2007*

PRALOGNAN LA VANOISE *9B4* (8km N Rural) **Camp Municipal Le Chevelu, 73350 Bozel [04 79 22 04 80 or 04 79 55 03 06 (LS); fax 04 79 22 01 47; wadelle-camping@wanadoo.fr]** Foll D915 thro Bozel dir Pralognan. Site on R immed beyond vill. Lge, mkd pitch, terr, shd; wc; shwrs inc; el pnts (6-10A) €2.60-4.40; lndtte; ice; shops 1km; playgrnd; lake fishing & sw 300m; adv bkg (dep req); quiet; CCI. "In wood by rv; excel walking & climbing; vg." 15 Jun-31 Aug. € 9.60   2004*

PRALOGNAN LA VANOISE *9B4* (500m S Rural) **Camp Municipal Le Chamois, Route de l'Isertan, 73710 Pralognan-la-Vanoise [04 79 08 71 54; fax 04 79 08 78 77; camping@pralognan.com]** Fr Moûtiers take D915 to Pralognan. Pass under concrete bdge, turn SW & foll camping sp; keep L past recep of bigger Iseran site. Lge, mkd pitch, terr, pt sl, unshd; htd wc (some cont); chem disp (wc); shwrs inc; el pnts (2-10A) €2.30-3.90; lndtte; shops 500m; htd pool 300m; rv fishing; dogs; poss cr; quiet. "Marvellous scenery; v peaceful; wonderful walks; v friendly staff; lots of free hot water; cable car up mountain." 1 Jun-15 Sep & 15 Dec-8 May.   2006*

PRALOGNAN LA VANOISE *9B4* (500m S Rural) **Camping Le Parc Isertan, Route de l'Isertan, 73710 Pralognan-la-Vanoise [04 79 08 75 24; fax 04 79 08 76 13; camping@camping-isertan. com; www.camping-isertan.com]** Fr Moûtiers, take D915 E to Pralognan. Pass under concrete bdge & foll camping sp. Site behind pool adj municipal site. Lge, hdstg, terr, pt shd; htd wc; chem disp; mv service pnt; baby facs; shwrs inc; el pnts (10A) €5.50; gas 500m; tradsmn; shop 500m; rest; snacks; bar; BBQ; playgrnd; htd, covrd pool, sports cent adj; horseriding 500m; some statics; dogs €1; phone; poss cr; Eng spkn; adv bkg; quiet; cc acc; red low ssn/CCI. "Superb scenery; wonderful walking; cable car in vill; v peaceful." ♦ 23 Dec-21 Apr & 26 May-23 Sep. € 18.00   2007*

PRATS DE CARLUX see Sarlat la Canéda *7C3*

PRATS DE MOLLO LA PRESTE *8H4* (11km E Rural) **Camp Municipal Verte Rive, Place de l'Ile, 66260 St Laurent-de-Cerdans [04 68 39 54 64 or 04 68 39 50 04 (Mairie); fax 04 68 39 59 59; contact@ville-saint-laurent-de-cerdans.fr; www. ville-saint-laurent-de-cerdans.fr]** Fr Le Boulou, take D115 twd Prats-de-Mollo, turn L on D3 twd St Laurent. Site 4km fr Spanish border. Med, mkd pitch, pt sl, pt shd; htd wc; shwrs inc; el pnts (5A) €2.75; lndtte; shop 1.5km; playgrnd; pool adj; some statics; poss cr; adv bkg; CCI. "Conv NH." ♦ 1 May-31 Oct. € 5.40   2006*

PRATS DE MOLLO LA PRESTE *8H4* (12km E Rural) **Camping Domaine Le Clols (Naturist), 66260 St Laurent-de-Cerdans** [tel/fax 04 68 39 51 68; info@leclols.com; www.leclols.com] Fr A9 at Le Boulou take D115 dir Prats-de-Mollo; 6km past Arles-sur-Tech take D3 on L sp St Laurent-de-Cerdans; at La Forge-del-Mitg turn sharp L sp Le Clols; site on R in 3km. Sm, pt sl, pt shd; wc (some cont); chem disp (wc); shwrs inc; el pnts (4A) €3; gas; lndtte; ice; shop; snacks; playgrnd; pool; TV; dogs €1.50; Eng spkn; adv bkg; quiet; red 10+ days; CCI. "Spectacular views; friendly British owners; narr winding rd fr La Forge-del-Mitg, but easily navigable; walks fr site." ♦ ltd. 1 May-30 Sep. € 19.00　　　　　　　　　　　　2005*

PRE EN PAIL *4E1* (200m N Urban) **Camp Municipal Alain Gerbault, Rue des Troènes, 53140 Pré-en-Pail** [02 43 03 04 28; camping.preenpail@wanadoo.fr] Fr E on N12, tunr R at major rnabt (D976 (N176) Domfront). Turn R twd sports cent & well sp fr there. Sm, mkd pitch, pt shd; wc (some cont); chem disp; shwrs inc; el pnts (16A) €2.60; shop 250m; rest; snacks; bar; playgrnd; htd pool adj; dogs €1.10; phone; CCI. "Pleasant wooded region; places of historical interest; poss mkt traders on site on mkt day; OK as touring base." Easter-30 Sep. € 7.40　　　　　　　　2006*

PRECY SOUS THIL *6G1* (Rural) **Camp Municipal, Rue de l'Hôtel de Ville, 21390 Précy-sous-Thil** [03 80 64 43 32 or 03 80 64 57 18 (Mairie); fax 03 80 64 43 37] Exit A6 at Bierre-lès-Semur exit, turn R at camping sp. Sp in vill, 6km fr . Sm, pt sl, pt shd; wc; shwrs inc; el pnts (4A) €2.40; lndtte; ice; shops adj; playgrnd; rv adj; horseriding; entmnt; TV; dogs €1.30; quiet. 19 Apr-2 Nov. € 9.00　　2004*

PRECY SOUS THIL *6G1* (8km S Rural) **Camping Le Village, 21210 La Motte-Ternant** [tel/fax 03 80 84 30 11; campinglamotteternant@wanadoo.fr; www.campinglamotteternant.eu] Exit A6 junc 23 onto D980 to Précy-sous-Thil; then take D36 to Fontangy; then turn R onto D26 to La Motte-Ternant. Sm, pt sl, shd; wc (cont); chem disp (wc); shwrs inc; el pnts (16A) €3; tradsmn; shop & bar 800m; tradsmn; BBQ; 5% statics; dogs free; Eng spkn; adv bkg; quiet; cc acc. "Within Morvan Natural Park; friendly site; Dutch owners; nr wine areas; gd." 1 Apr-1 Nov. € 10.50　　　　　　　　　　　　　2007*

PREFAILLES see Pornic *2G3*

PREIXAN see Carcassonne *8F4*

PREMEAUX PRISSEY see Nuits St Georges *6G1*

PREMERY *4G4* (500m NW) **Camp Municipal Les Prés de la Ville, 58700 Prémery** [03 86 37 99 42 or 03 86 68 12 40 (Mairie); fax 03 86 37 98 72; mairie-premery@wanadoo.fr] N fr Nevers L off D977, turn R approx 500m after 2nd rndabt at Prémery. Med, pt shd; wc (some cont); chem disp (wc); shwrs inc; el pnts (8-10A) €1-1.70; shops 500m; lake & rv adj with sand beach, sw, fishing & boating; tennis adj; adv bkg; quiet; 10% red 10+ days. "Lovely site; a well-run & popular NH; poss market traders; excel value." ♦ 1 May-30 Sep. € 7.60　　　　2007*

PREMIAN see St Pons de Thomières *8F4*

PRESILLY LA TUILIERE see St Julien en Genevois *9A3*

PRESSAC *7A3* (7km E Urban) **FFCC Camp Municipal Le Parc, 86460 Availles-Limouzine** [05 49 48 51 22; fax 05 49 48 66 76] Fr Confolens N on D948 & turn R on D34 to Availles-Limouzine. Site on rv by town bdge. Med, pt shd; wc; chem disp; mv service pnt; shwrs inc; el pnts (10A) €2; gas; shops 750m; playgrnd; paddling pool; rv sw; dogs €2.65; poss cr; Eng spkn; adv bkg; quiet; CCI. "Attractive site on Rv Vienne; well-run; barrier clsd 2200-0800; excel san facs; warden lives on site; delightful old vill; excel." ♦ 1 May-30 Sep. € 7.80　　　　　　　　　　　　　2006*

⊞**PRESSAC** *7A3* (6km SW Rural) **Camping Rural des Marronniers, La Bussière, 16490 Pleuville** [05 45 31 03 45; ssmpooleman1@tiscali.fr; www.conkertreefarmcampsite.bravehost.com] S fr Poitiers on D741 to Pressac; turn R onto D34 to Pleuville; site on D30 dir Charroux. Sm, terr, pt shd; htd wc; chem disp; fam bathrm; shwrs inc; el pnts (6A) €2; gas; lndtte; ice; shop 1km; rest 8km; snacks; bar 1km; BBQ; playgrnd; pool; games rm; dogs; adv bkg; quiet. "CL-type site; farm animals on site; garden produce & free range eggs; British owners; conv numerous attractions in Poitou-Charentes area; excel." ♦ ltd. € 8.00　　2006*

PRESSIGNAC see Rochechouart *7B3*

PREUILLY SUR CLAISE *4H2* (SW Urban) **Camp Municipal, 37290 Preuilly-sur-Claise** [02 47 94 50 04; fax 02 47 94 63 26] Fr E on D725 descend hill into vill. At T-junc opp town hall turn R & in 30m take 2nd L sp Camping & Piscine - poss diff turn long o'fits due narr rd. Site adj pool in 300m. Sm, hdg pitch, pt shd; wc; chem disp (wc); shwrs inc; el pnts (5A) inc; lndry rm; shop, rest in vill; BBQ; htd pool adj; rv fishing adj; poss cr; quiet. "No twin-axles allowed." 1 May-15 Sep. € 10.20　　　　　　　　　　　　　2005*

PRIVAS *9D2* (8km NE Rural) **Camping L'Albanou (formerly Pampelonne), Quartier Pampelonne, 07000 St Julien-en-St Alban [04 75 66 00 97; camping.albanou@wanadoo.fr; http://camping. albanou.free.fr]** Fr A7 exit junc 16 at Loriol dir Le Pouzin, go thro Le Pouzin on N304 (N104) dir Privas/Aubenas. Site in 6km on L just bef vill of St Julien-en-St Alban. Med, hdg/mkd pitch, pt sl, pt shd; wc; chem disp; mv service pnt; baby facs; shwrs inc; el pnts (6A) €3.50; lndtte; ice; shops 1km; tradsmn; snacks; playgrnd; pool; rv fishing adj; some statics; dogs €2; Eng spkn; adv bkg; quiet; CCI. "Friendly welcome; helpful owners; v clean, well-run site by rv; gd size pitches." 28 Apr-22 Sep. € 15.00   2005*

PRIVAS *9D2* (3km E Rural) **Camping Le Moulin d'Onclaire, 07000 Coux [04 75 64 51 98; michelelampe@voila.fr]** Fr Privas take N304 E twds Le Pouzin, sp Valence. Site on R after passing narr bdge to Coux. Sm, pt shd; wc; shwrs inc; el pnts (5A) €2.60; ice; shop; snacks; rest & bar adj; BBQ; pool 3km; tennis; Eng spkn; adv bkg; CCI. "Somewhat run-down; site rds not suitable for disabled; poss itinerants; owner's dog roaming site; helpful staff; NH only." 1 Apr-15 Oct. € 11.50
                                            2004*

PRIVAS *9D2* (8km SE Rural) **FFCC Camp Municipal Les Civelles d'Ozon, 07210 St Lager-Bressac [04 75 65 01 86; fax 04 75 65 13 02; camping@ saintlagerbressac.fr; www.saintlagerbressac. com]** S fr Privas on D2 dir Montélemar; site well sp on L. S fr Valence on N86; turn R onto D22; site sp to L, narr rd - or cont to rndabt, turn L onto D2 to Montélimar & as above. Sm, hdg/mkd pitch, pt sl, pt shd; serviced pitches; wc; chem disp; shwrs inc; el pnts (10A) €3 (poss rev pol); lndtte; ice; tradsmn; shops 1.5km; playgrnd; pools & paddling pool adj inc; tennis; games rm; dogs €2; adv bkg; quiet; CCI. "V helpful warden; excel." ♦ ltd. 1 May-30 Sep. € 10.00   2006*

PRIVAS *9D2* (10km SE Rural) **Camping Le Rieutord, 07210 St Vincent-de-Barrès [04 75 65 07 73; moncamping@wanadoo.fr; www.ardeche-sud-camping.com]** Fr N exit A7 junc 16 Loriol onto N304 & foll sp Le Pouzin then Chomérac (do not foll 1st sp St Vincent-de-Barrès - narr rd). At rndabt foll D2 dir Le Teil-Montélimar for 6km. When arr at St Vincent (vill on L), turn R & foll site sp for 1.5km. Fr S exit junc 18 Montélimar Sud, foll sps Montélimar then Privas. Cross Rv Rhône, go thro Rochemaure sp Privas. At Meysse turn L after bdge dir Privas. Foll D2 for 4.5km then turn L dir St Bauzile to site in 3km. Med, hdg pitch, pt sl, pt shd; htd wc; shwrs inc; el pnts (16A) €3; lndtte; shop; snacks; bar; cooking facs; playgrnd; pool; paddling pool; waterslide; games area; some statics; €2; no c'vans over 6m or twin-axles; Eng spkn; adv bkg; quiet CCI. "Tranquil site in beautiful setting; pleasant owners; St Vincent old walled town; gd touring base." 28 Apr-30 Sep. € 15.00
                                            2006*

PRIVAS *9D2* (1km S Urban) **Ardèche Camping, Blvd de Paste, Quartier Ouvèze, 07000 Privas [04 75 64 05 80; fax 04 75 64 59 68; jcray@ wanadoo.fr; www.ardechecamping.fr]** Exit A7 junc 16 dir Privas. Fr Privas take D22 twd Montélimar on Rte de Chomérac. Site sp. Lge, mkd pitch, pt sl, pt shd; wc (some cont); chem disp; mv service pnt; baby facs; shwrs inc; el pnts (5-10A) €3.50; lndtte; ice; shops adj; supmkt 100m; rest; snacks; bar; BBQ; playgrnd; htd pool; rv fishing; tennis adj; entmnt; TV rm; 80% statics; dogs €2; Eng spkn; adv bkg; some rd noise fr D2; red low ssn; cc acc; CCI. "Excel management; conv for town; gd touring base; m'vans beware low canopy on service stn at Intermarche opp." ♦ 1 Apr-30 Sep. € 18.00 (CChq acc)   2005*

PRIVEZAC *7D4* (1km E Rural) **Aire Naturelle Municipale Les Malénies, Plan d'Eau, 12350 Privezac [05 65 81 92 80; fax 05 65 81 96 77]** N fr Villefranche-de-Rouergue on D1 dir Rodez, at Lanuéjouls turn onto D614 & D48 to Privezac. In vill foll sp 'Plan d'Eau', site sp in 1km by lake. Sm, hdg pitch, pt shd; wc; shwrs inc; el pnts €1.50; bar; playgrnd; sand beach & lake sw adj; fishing; canoeing; 10% statics; dogs; quiet. "Fair sh stay." ♦ 1 Jun-15 Sep.   2006*

PROISSANS see Sarlat la Canéda *7C3*

PROVINS *4E4* (1km NE Rural) **Camping MJC de Fontaine Riante, Route de la Ferté Gaucher, 77483 Provins [01 64 00 53 62; fax 01 64 00 57 55; camping.mjc.provins@free.fr; http://mjc.provins. free.fr/camping]** App Provins fr N D403, foll sp at rndabt NE of town. After 200m turn R for site. Sm, pt sl, terr, pt shd; wc; own san; chem disp (wc); shwrs inc; el pnts (4-6A) €3-4; gas, lndtte, shop, rest ctr 1km; dogs €1.60; poss cr; quiet. "Facs old & poss used by itinerants fr adj field; avoid town cent narr rds; sh, steep gravel slopes bet terr levels." 1 Apr-31 Oct. € 9.40   2006*

PRUNIERES see Chorges *9D3*

PUGET SUR ARGENS see Fréjus *10F4*

PUGET THENIERS *10E4* (9km E Rural) **Camping L'Amitie, 06710 Touët-sur-Var [tel/fax 04 93 05 74 32; camping-de-lamitie@wanadoo.fr]** Site sp at both end of vill on N202. Fr Nice turn L off N202, site in 800m immed after x-ing rv & sp fr town cent. App v difficult - rv bdge v narr & site ent req tight turn; imposs for vans +6m long. Sm, mkd pitch, pt shd; wc; chem disp; mv service pnt; shwrs €1.30; el pnts (3-16A) inc; gas; lndtte; shop; tradsmn; snacks; bar; BBQ; playgrnd; rv sw & fishing adj; horseriding; cycle hire; games area; entmnts; TV; dogs €2; 30% statics; adv bkg (ess high ssn); CCI. "Fair NH; steam train ride down valley to coast." ♦ 1 Apr-30 Sep. € 16.40
                                            2007*

PUGET THENIERS *10E4* (8km W Rural) **Camping Le Brec, 04320 Entrevaux [tel/fax 04 93 05 42 45; camping.dubrec@wanadoo.fr;http://pagesperso-orange.fr/camping.dubrec/]** Site sp on R just after bdge 2km W of Entrevaux on N202. Rd (2km) to site narr with poor surface, passing places & occasional lge lorries. Med, mkd pitch, pt shd; htd wc; chem disp; baby facs; shwrs inc; el pnts (10A) €3; Indtte; ice; tradsmn; snacks; BBQ; site watersports centre; rv sw, fishing & boating adj; wifi internet; TV; 10% statics; dogs €1; phone; Eng spkn; adv bkg; quiet; cc acc; red CCl. "In beautiful Alpes-Maritimes area; friendly Dutch owners; popular with canoeists; easy rv walk to town." 15 Mar-31 Oct. € 16.00
2007*

PUGET THENIERS *10E4* (2km NW Rural) **Camping L'Origan (Naturist), 06260 Puget-Théniers [04 93 05 06 00; fax 04 93 05 09 34; origan@wanadoo.fr; www.origan-village.com]** On N202 fr Entrevaux (dir Nice) at Puget-Théniers, immed turn L at rlwy x-ing (sp), site approx 1km up track. Med, hdg/mkd pitch, hdstg, pt sl, terr, pt shd; htd wc; sauna; shwrs inc; el pnts (6A) €4; gas 2km; Indtte; ice; shop; tradsmn; rest; snacks; bar; BBQ; playgrnd; htd pool; white water rafting adj; fishing; tennis; archery; internet; TV rm; 50% statics; dogs €2.30; phone; adv bkg (dep req); Eng spkn; cc acc; INF card. "Sm pitches not suitable o'fits over 6m; gd position; hilly site but pitches level; tourist train to Nice fr Puget-Théniers; interesting area." ♦ Easter- Oct. € 31.50 (CChq acc)
2005*

PUIVERT *8G4* (500m S Rural) **Camping de Puivert (formerly Camp Municipal de Fontclaire), Fontclaire, 11230 Puivert [04 68 20 00 58; fax 04 68 20 82 29; camping-de-puivert@orange.fr; www.puivert.net]** Take D117 W fr Quillan twd Lavelanet for 16km. Site by lake well sp. Med, hdg pitch, pt sl, pt shd; wc; chem disp (wc); mv service pnt; shwrs; el pnts inc; Indtte; shops in vill 500m; snacks; lake adj; fishing; entmnt; internet; quiet. "Attractive scenery & lake sw, poss diff lge c'vans." 27 Apr-30 Sep. € 12.00
2007*

PUTANGES PONT ECREPIN *4E1* (1km W Rural) **Camp Municipal Le Val d'Orne, Le Friche, 61210 Putanges-Pont-Ecrepin [02 33 35 00 25 (Mairie); fax 02 33 35 49 50]** S fr Falaise on D909 to Putanges. Ent Putanges cross Rv L'Orne & ignore camping sp immed on L (Grand Rue). Go thro vill for approx 1km, turn L sp camping 200m. Site on R. Sm, hdg/mkd pitch, pt shd; wc; shwrs inc; el pnts (6A) inc; shops & rest 5 mins walk via rv bank; rv fishing; playgrnd; dogs €0.85; adv bkg; quiet. "Site yourself, warden visits am & pm; excel rvbank site; ltd facs but clean & well-run." 1 Apr-30 Sep. € 7.70
2006*

PUY EN VELAY, LE *9C1* (500m N Urban) **Camping Bouthezard (formerly Camping du Puy-en-Velay), Chemin de Bouthezard, Ave d'Aiguilhe, 43000 Le Puy-en-Velay [04 71 09 55 09 or 06 15 08 23 59 (mob); www.ot-lepuyenvelay.fr]** Fr Le Puy heading NW on N102 to city cent; look for sp Clermont & Vichy; turn R at traff lts in Place Carnot at sp for Valence; site on L on bank of rv. Site ent immed opp Chapel St Michel & 200m fr volcanic core. Med, some hdg pitches, pt shd; wc; chem disp; mv service pnt; shwrs inc; el pnts (6A) €3.10 (rev pol); Indtte; shop 200m & supmkt 500m; snacks; playgrnd adj; pool & tennis adj; games rm; dogs €0.85; poss cr; Eng spkn; adv bkg; noise of church bells (not nighttime); cc not acc; CCl. "V popular, busy site - rec arr early; efficient & helpful staff; gd facs; gates clsd 2100-0700 low ssn; recep clsd 1230-1500; no twin axles; may flood in v heavy rain; excursions to extinct volcanoes high ssn; sh walk to cathedral & old Le Puy; on pilgrim rte to Santiago de Compostela; vg." ♦ ltd. 15 Mar-31 Oct. € 10.10
2007*

PUY EN VELAY, LE *9C1* (9km N) **Camp Municipal Les Longes, Route des Rosières, 43800 Lavoûte-sur-Loire [04 71 08 18 79; fax 04 71 08 16 96; mairie.lavoutesurloire@wanadoo.fr; www.cc-emblavez.fr]** Fr Le Puy take N on D103 sp Lavoûte & Retournac. In Lavoûte turn R onto D7 bef rv bdge, site on L in 1km. Med, mkd pitch, pt shd; wc; shwrs €1; el pnts (6A) €1.90; Indtte; shops 9km; bread 1km; tradsmn (high ssn); playgrnd; pool 1km; rv sw 50m; tennis; dogs €1.50; quiet. "On banks of Loire; fishing; walking; scenic views." ♦ 1 May-15 Sep. € 8.25
2007*

PUY EN VELAY, LE *9C1* (3km E Urban) **Camp Municipal Audinet, Ave des Sports, 43700 Brives-Charensac [tel/fax 04 71 09 10 18; camping.audinet@wanadoo.fr; www.brives-charensac.fr]** Fr Le Puy foll green sp E twd Valence. Fr S on N88 foll sp twd Valence & on E side of town foll white sp. Lge, pt shd; wc (mostly cont); chem disp; mv service pnt; baby facs; shwrs inc; el pnts (6A) €2.50; Indtte; sm shop & shops 500m; supmkt 1.5km; rest; snacks; bar; BBQ; playgrnd; rv & lake sw/fishing; quiet. "Nice, spacious, relaxed site on rvside; friendly, helpful staff; poss itinerants - but not a prob; san facs only adequate - stretched high ssn; no twin-axles; reg bus into town." ♦ 1 Apr-30 Sep. € 10.40
2007*

PUY EN VELAY, LE *9C1* (9km E Rural) **Camping Le Moulin de Barette, Le Pont de Sumène, 43540 Blavozy [04 71 03 00 88; fax 04 71 03 00 51; lemoulindebarette.com; www.lemoulindebarette.com]** Take N88 dir St Etienne. Exit after 7km at D156 Blavozy. At rndabt foll sp for Rosières & 1st L to Moulin-de-Barette. Med, mkd pitch, pt sl, pt shd; wc; chem disp; shwrs inc; el pnts €3; Indtte; shop; rest; pool; playgrnd; tennis; cycle hire; TV rm; few statics; dogs €1; quiet; 10% red low ssn/long stay; cc acc. "Part of hotel complex; san facs block old but gd; facs poss stretched in high ssn; poss elect probs." ♦ Easter-15 Oct. € 13.60
2004*

France

PUY EN VELAY, LE *9C1* (7km S Rural) **Camping Comme au Soleil, Route du Plan d'Eau, 43700 Coubon [tel/fax 04 71 08 32 55; dumoulin-patrick@club-internet.fr]** S fr Puy-en-Velay on N88, turn E onto D38 to Coubon, site sp. Sm, pt shd; wc; baby facs; shwrs; el pnts (10A) €3; lndtte; ice; tradsmn; rest; snacks; bar; playgrnd; pool; rv sw; games area; cycle hire; 5% statics; dogs €1; bus; Eng spkn; adv bkg; red long stay; CCI. ♦ 15 Apr-15 Oct. € 13.00   2007*

PUY EN VELAY, LE *9C1* (11km S Rural) **Camp Municipal, Le Monastier, 43370 Solignac-sur-Loire [04 71 03 11 46 (Mairie); fax 04 71 03 12 77; maire.solignacsurloire@wanadoo.fr]** Fr Le Puy S on N88 twd Mende; after about 7km at Les Baraques turn L on D27 dir Solignac & foll camping sp. Sm, hdg/mkd pitch, pt shd, pt sl; wc; shwrs inc; el pnts (6-10A) €2.06; lndry rm; shops 1km; playgrnd; quiet; CCI. "Site yourself; warden calls am & pm; gd views Valley of Volcanoes; excel facs; clean & tidy; no twin-axle c'vans, but mkt traders sometimes tolerated." ♦ 15 Jun-15 Sep. € 7.80   2006*

⊞**PUY GUILLAUME** *9B1* (6km SW Rural) **Camping à la Ferme (Lehalper), Les Marodons, 63290 Noalhat [04 73 94 11 68; l.lehaper@libertysurf.fr]** Fr D906 turn W at La Croix-St Bonnet onto D44 to Noalhat, site sp. Sm, shd; wc; shwrs; el pnts €2; lndtte; games area; fishing, rv sw nr; dogs; quiet. "San facs gd; c'vans phone ahead to ensure access." € 2.00   2007*

PUY GUILLAUME *9B1* (1km W Rural) **Camp Municipal de la Dore, Rue Joseph Claussat, 63290 Puy-Guillaume [04 73 94 78 51 or 04 73 94 70 49 (Mairie); fax 04 73 94 78 51; mairie.puyguillaume@wanadoo.fr]** N fr Thiers by D906A join D906 as far as Puy-Guillaume. Ent vill, turn L at rndabt onto D343 which joins D63, then L again at 3rd rndabt. Site on R by rv. Med, pt shd; wc (some cont); chem disp; some serviced pitches; shwrs inc; el pnts (6A) €2.50; lndtte; shops 500m; playgrnd; pool (high ssn) adj; rv fishing adj; dogs; adv bkg rec high ssn. "Neat, tidy site; v clean san facs; pleasant location by Rv Dore; facs poss used by locals; helpful wardens." ♦ ltd. 1 May-30 Sep. € 10.50   2005*

PUY L'EVEQUE *7D3* (3km E Rural) **FFCC Village-Camping Les Vignes, Le Meoure, 46700 Puy-l'Evèque [tel/fax 05 65 30 81 72; villagecamping.lesvignes@wanadoo.fr]** On D811 dir Villeneuve-sur-Lot, just bef ent Puy-l'Evèque turn L, foll sp for 3km. Site adj Rv Lot. Avoid town cent while towing. Med, shd; wc; baby facs; shwrs; el pnts; (6A) €2.50; gas; lndtte; shops 3km; tradsmn; snacks; bar; playgrnd; pool; tennis; rv sw; games area; fishing; cycle hire; entmnt high ssn; TV; dogs €1; quiet; red over 55s/low ssn. "Beautiful countryside; gd san facs; friendly owners." 1 Apr-30 Sep. € 12.85   2006*

PUY L'EVEQUE *7D3* (6km W Urban) **Club de Vacances Duravel, Route de Vire, 46700 Duravel [05 65 24 65 06 or 0031 74 2666499 (LS-N'lands); fax 05 65 24 64 96 or 0031 74 2668205 (LS-N'lands); clubduravel@aol.com; www.clubde vacances.net]** Fr D811 Puy-l'Evèque to Fumel rd at Duravel town cent, opp Mairie turn S onto D58 sp Vire-sur-Lot. Site in 2.5km. Lge, hdg/mkd pitch, pt sl, pt shd; wc (some cont); chem disp; mv service pnt; shwrs inc; el pnts (10A) €3.15; gas; lndtte; ice; shop; tradsmn; rest; snacks; bar; playgrnd; 2 pools (1 htd); waterslide; beach nr; tennis; games area; guided walks; canoeing; fishing; cycle hire; entmnt; 12% statics; poss cr; Eng spkn; adv bkg (dep req); quiet; 10% red low ssn; cc acc; CCI. "Vg site; v friendly staff; lovely situation; conv Cahors; all signs & notices on site in Dutch - enquire at recep for info in Eng on excursions/activities etc." ♦ ltd. 29 Apr-23 Sep. € 23.35   2006*

PUYCELCI *8E3* (4km W Rural) **Centre Naturiste Le Fiscalou (Naturist), 1 Route de Montclar, 81140 Puycelci [05 63 30 45 95; fax 05 62 30 32 88; fiscalou@wanadoo.fr;   www.fiscalou.com]** Fr Bruniquel D964 S twd Castelnau. Take D1 sp Monclar-de-Quercy. Site on L after 4km. Sm, pt sl, pt shd; wc; chem disp; shwrs inc; el pnts (6A) inc (poss long lead req); tradsmn; rest; bar; playgrnd; pool; Eng spkn; adv bkg; quiet. "A pleasant, rustic site; excel cent for touring area." 1 May-30 Sep. € 17.00   2004*

PYLA SUR MER *7D1* (7km S Coastal) **Camping La Dune, Route de Biscarrosse, 33115 Pyla-sur-Mer [tel/fax 05 56 22 72 17; reception@ campingdeladune.fr; www.campingdeladune.fr]** Fr Bordeaux app Arcachon; at rndabt foll sp Dune du Pilat & 'campings'; at T-junc turn L & foll 'plage' & camping sp on D218; site on R. Lge, pt sl, pt shd; htd wc (some cont for men); shwrs inc; el pnts inc; gas; lndtte; ice; shop; rest; snacks; bar; playgrnd; pool; sand beach 500m; tennis; cycle hire; entmnt; TV rm; dogs €4; poss cr; adv bkg (ess Jul/Aug); quiet; "Poss diff pitches for c'vans; sm, unlevel, narr access; dominated by Europe's largest sand dunes." 1 May-30 Sep. € 32.00   2006*

PYLA SUR MER *7D1* (7km S Coastal) **Camping La Forêt, Route de Biscarosse, 33115 Pyla-sur-Mer [05 56 22 73 28; fax 05 56 22 70 50; camping.foret@wanadoo.fr;   www.campinglaforet.fr]** Fr Bordeaux app Arcachon on A660 by-pass rd; at La Teste-de-Buch at rndabt foll sp for Dune du Pilat & 'campings'. At T-junc in 4km turn L; foll 'plage' & camping sp on D218. Site on R. Lge, hdg/mkd pitch, pt sl, shd; wc; chem disp; mv service pnt; shwrs inc; el pnts (6A) inc; lndtte; shop; rest; snacks; bar; BBQ; playgrnd; pool; sand beach 600m; solarium; tennis; cycle hire; child entmnt; some statics; dogs €2; adv bkg; red low ssn; cc acc; CCI. "Forest setting at foot of lgest sand dune in Europe; well organised; many facs; hang-gliding, surfing, sailing nrby." ♦ 7 Apr-5 Nov. € 32.00   2005*

PYLA SUR MER *7D1* (7km S Coastal) **Camping Le Petit Nice, Route de Biscarosse, 33115 Pyla-sur-Mer [05 56 22 74 03; fax 05 56 22 14 31; info@petitnice.com; www.petitnice.com]** Fr Bordeaux on app Arcachon foll sp for Dune-du-Pilat & 'campings'. At T-junc turn L; foll 'plage' & camping sp on D218. Site on R. Lge, pt sl, shd; wc; chem disp; mv service pnt; baby facs; shwrs inc; el pnts (5A) inc; gas; lndtte; ice; shop; rest; snacks; bar; playgrnd; htd pool; paddling pool; sand beach adj tennis; TV rm; entmnt; TV rm; 50% statics; dogs €3; poss cr; adv bkg; quiet but poss noisy disco; red low ssn. "Open beach with steep wooden steps." 1 Apr-30 Sep. € 32.00 (CChq acc) 2005*

PYLA SUR MER *7D1* (7km S Coastal/Rural) **Yelloh! Village Panorama du Pyla, Route de Biscarosse, 33115 Pyla-sur-Mer [05 56 22 10 44; fax 05 56 22 10 12; mail@camping-panorama.com; www.camping-panorama.com; www.yellohvillage.com]** App Arcachon fr Bordeaux on A63/660, at rndabt foll sp for Dune-du-Pilat & 'campings'. Foll sp for 'plage' & 'campings' on D218. Site on R next to Camping Le Petit Nice. Lge, mkd pitch, pt sl, terr, pt shd; wc (some cont); chem disp; mv service pnt; sauna; shwrs inc; el pnts (3-10A) inc; gas; rest; snacks; bar; shop; playgrnd; htd pool; sand beach adj; tennis; mini-golf; TV; entmnt; dogs €5; Eng spkn; adv bkg; quiet; red low ssn; CCI. "Pleasant site on wooded dune; direct steep access to excel beach; site rd v narr; varying pitch size, poss none for v lge o'fits; some pitches sandy & unsuitable m'vans; gd facs; paragliding adj." ♦ 20 Apr-15 Sep. € 40.00 2007*

QUEAUX see Lussac les Châteaux *7A3*

QUESTEMBERT see Muzillac *2G3*

QUETTEHOU *1C4* (8km NE Coastal) **Camping Municipal le Jonville, 50760 Réville [02 33 54 48 41; camping-joinville@saint-vaast-reville.com]** S fr Barfleur on D1 twd Quettehou & turn L in Réville. Foll sp. Med, hdg pitch, pt sl, pt shd; wc; shwrs inc; el pnts (6A) €3.50; lndry rm; shops 1km; snacks; beach adj; phone; dogs; poss cr; adv bkg; quiet; CCI "Gd site; gd boating & sw." 1 Apr-30 Sep. € 10.00 2004*

QUETTEHOU *1C4* (2.5km E Urban/Coastal) **Camping La Gallouette, Rue de la Gallouette, 50550 St Vaast-la-Hougue [02 33 54 20 57; fax 02 33 54 16 71; contact@camping-lagallouette.fr; www.lagallouette.com]** E fr Quettehou on D1, site sp in St Vaast-la-Houge to S of town. Lge, hdg/mkd pitch, pt shd; wc; chem disp; mv service pnt; baby facs; shwrs; el pnts (6-10A) €3.70-4.50; gas; lndtte; ice; shop; tradsmn; rest; snacks; bar; BBQ; playgrnd; htd pool; sand beach 300m; games area; games rm; child entmnt; 10% statics; dogs €1.60; phone; poss cr; adv bkg; quiet; CCI. "Sh walk to interesting town; rec ferry trip to Ile de Tatihou; some lge pitches; gd range of facs; recep 0800-2200 high ssn, 0815-1230 & 1400-1930 low ssn; excel site." ♦ 1 Apr-30 Sep. € 22.00 2007*

See advertisement above

QUETTEHOU *1C4* (2km S Coastal) **Camping Le Rivage, Route de Morsalines, 50630 Quettehou [02 33 54 13 76; fax 02 33 43 10 42; info@camping-lerivage.com]** Fr Quettehou on D14, sp on L. Med, unshd; wc; shwrs inc; el pnts (6A) €3.90; lndtte; shop; snacks; bar; BBQ; playgrnd; htd pool; paddling pool; sand beach 400m; 50% statics; dogs €2; Eng spkn; adv bkg rec high ssn; quiet. "Gd base for Normandy beaches, boating, shrimping & seafood; gd clean site." 1 Apr-30 Sep. € 18.00 2006*

QUIBERON *2G3* (1.5km N Coastal) **Camping Do Mi Si La Mi, St Julien-Plage, 56170 Quiberon [02 97 50 22 52; fax 02 97 50 26 69; camping@domisilami.com; www.domisilami.com]** Take D768 down Quiberon Peninsular, 3km after St Pierre-Quiberon & shortly after sp for rlwy level x-ing turn L into Rue de la Vierge, site on R in 400m. Lge, hdg/mkd pitch, pt sl, pt shd; wc (some cont); chem disp; mv service pnt; baby facs; shwrs inc; el pnts (3-10A) €2.70-4.20; gas; lndtte; shop; snacks; bar adj; BBQ; playgrnd; sand/shgl beach 100m; games area; cycle hire; sailing, horseriding, tennis nr; 40% statics; dogs €2.30; poss cr; Eng spkn; quiet; red low ssn; cc acc; CCI. "Gd touring base; vg." ♦ 22 Mar-2 Nov. € 20.60 2007*

See advertisement on next page

QUIBERON 2G3 (2.5km N Coastal) **Camping Beauséjour, St Julien-Plage, 56170 Quiberon** [tel/fax 02 97 30 44 93; info@campingbeausejour. com; www.campingbeausejour.com] On D768 S, turn L at camping sp & L onto coast rd. Site on L facing sea. Lge, hdg/mkd pitch, pt sl, pt shd; wc (mainly cont); chem disp; shwrs inc; el pnts (3-6A) €3-4.20; gas; lndtte; shop; snack bar; playgrnd; sand beach adj; 5% statics; dogs €2; Eng quiet; spkn; red low ssn; CCI. 15 May-15 Sep. € 18.20
2004*

This guide relies on site report forms submitted by caravanners like us; we'll do our bit and tell the editor what we think of the campsites we've visited.

QUIBERON 2G3 (SE Urban) **Camping Les Joncs du Roch, Rue de l'Aérodrome, 56170 Quiberon** [02 97 50 24 37 or 02 97 50 11 36 (LS)] Foll sp to aerodrome. Site ent opp. Lge, pt shd; wc (some cont); chem disp; shwrs inc; el pnts (4-10A) €2.70-3.70; gas; ice; shops 1km; sand beach 1km; dogs €2; poss cr; quiet, but minimal aircraft noise; 15% red Sep. "Vg, clean,well-maintained, friendly site in sheltered position; gd facs; conv; easy access town/beach." 3 Apr-25 Sep. € 20.00   2007*

QUIBERON 2G3 (1.5km SE Coastal/Rural) **Camping Le Bois d'Amour, Rue St Clément, 56170 Quiberon** [02 97 50 13 52 or 04 42 20 47 25 (LS); fax 02 97 50 42 67; info@homair.com; www. homair.com] Exit N165 at Auray onto D768. In Quiberon foll sp 'Thalassothérapie', site sp. Lge, hdg/mkd pitch, pt shd; wc; mv service pnt; chem disp; baby facs; shwrs inc; el pnts (10A) €5; gas; lndtte; ice; shop; rest; snacks; bar; BBQ; playgrnd; htd pool; beach 200m; games area; tennis; horseriding; cycle hire; entmnt; dogs €5; adv bkg; quiet; Eng spkn; red low ssn; cc acc; CCI. ♦ 3 Apr-2 Oct. € 36.00   2006*

QUIBERON 2G3 (1.5km SE Coastal) **Camping Le Conguel, Blvd de la Teignouse, 56175 Quiberon** [02 97 50 19 11; fax 02 97 30 46 66; info@campingduconguel.com; www.camping duconguel.com] On D768 fr N, turn E at rlwy stn on ent Quiberon, foll sps for Pointe du Conguel, site sp. Lge, mkd pitch, pt sl, unshd; wc; baby facs; sauna; shwrs; el pnts €3.65; gas; lndtte; ice; shop; rest; snacks; bar; playgrnd; htd pool; paddling pool; waterslide; sand beach adj; watersports; tennis; games area; games rm; fitness rm; cycle hire; entmnt; child entmnt; internet; TV rm; adv bkg; quiet; red low ssn. "Beautiful, varied coastline; watersports & boat trips; excel family site." ♦ 5 Apr-31 Oct. € 43.25   2007*

See advertisement on page 561

QUIBERON 2G3 (1km S Coastal) **Camp Municipal Le Goviro, Blvd du Goviro, 56170 Quiberon** [02 97 50 13 54] Fr D768 at Quiberon foll sp Port Maria & 'Centre Thalassothérapie'. Site 1km on L. Lge, hdg/mkd pitch, terr, pt shd; wc; chem disp; mv service pnt; shwrs; el pnts (13A) €3; gas; ice; lndtte; rest adj; playgrnd; sand beach, fishing & watersports adj; dogs €1.60; poss cr. "Gd sea views & coastal path; gd san facs, ltd low ssn; quiet; clean; vg sh stay." ♦ ltd. 1 Apr-15 Oct. € 12.60
2006*

QUIBERVILLE PLAGE see Veules les Roses 3C2

QUILLAN 8G4 (6km N Rural) **Camp Municipal de la Salle, Rue des Jardins, 11260 Espéraza** [04 68 74 08 60; fax 04 68 74 07 48] Site clearly sp fr D118 & in vill. Sm, pt shd; wc; own san; shwrs inc; el pnts (6A) €2; shops 500m; rv sw; quiet; CCI. "NH only." 15 Apr-30 Sep. € 8.40   2005*

QUILLAN *8G4* (1km W Urban) **Camp Municipal La Sapinette, 11500 Quillan [04 68 20 13 52; fax 04 68 20 27 80]** Foll D118 fr Carcassonne to Quillan; turn R at 2nd traff lts in town cent; site sp in town. Med, sl, terr, pt shd; wc; shwrs inc; el pnts (6A) €2.80; shops 400m; playgrnd; pool & leisure cent 500m in town; dogs €1; poss cr; adv bkg; quiet; cc acc; red CCI. "Excel site; gd touring base; sm pitches; low tree branches; basic san facs; early arr rec; helpful staff; town nr, gd mkt Wed; vet adj; rec." 1 Apr-31 Oct. € 13.20   2005*

QUILLAN *8G4* (8km NW Rural) **Camping Le Fontaulié-Sud, 11500 Nébias [tel/fax 04 68 20 17 62; lefontauliesud@free.fr; www.fontauliesud.com]** In Quillan take D117 twd Foix. Turn L at sp immed after leaving Nébias vill. Site in 1km. NB Steep rd to site. Med, pt sl, pt shd; wc; chem disp; shwrs inc; el pnts (4A) inc; lndtte; ice; shop; snacks; bar; playgrnd; pool; paddling pool; tennis, horseriding, watersports nr; TV rm; some statics; adv bkg; quiet; CCI. "Beautiful scenery & many mkd walks; owners friendly, helpful; ltd facs low ssn; gd touring base." 1 May-15 Sep. € 16.00
                     2005*

QUIMPER *2F2* (9km SE Rural) **Camping Vert de Creac'h-Lann (Hemidy), Créach Lann, 29170 St Evarzec [02 98 56 29 88 or 06 68 46 97 25 (mob); contact@campingvertcreachlann.com;   www. campingvertcreachlann.com]** S fr Quimper on D783, 1.5km fr St Evarzec rndabt at brow of hill (easily missed). Sm, hdg pitch, pt sl, pt shd; wc; chem disp; shwrs; el pnts (4-13A) €2.50-3.50; lndtte; shop, rest, snacks & bar 3km; playgrnd; sand beach 5km; 10% statics; dogs; poss cr; Eng spkn; adv bkg; quiet. "V friendly, helpful owner; site being developed (2006); v lge pitches; gd playgrnd; poss to stay after end Sep by arrangement; lovely old town; gd shopping & daily covrd mkt; excel." 1 May-15 Sep. € 9.70   2007*

QUIMPER *2F2* (2km S Rural) **Camping L'Orangerie de Lanniron, Château de Lanniron, 29336 Quimper [02 98 90 62 02; fax 02 98 52 15 56; camping@ lanniron.com; www.lanniron.com or www.les-castels.com]** Fr Rennes/Lorient: on N165 Rennes-Quimper, Quimper-Centre, Quimper-Sud exit, foll dir Pont l'Abbé on S bypass until exit sp Camping de Lanninon on R. At top of slip rd turn L & foll site sp, under bypass then 2nd R to site. Lge, pt shd; wc; chem disp; some serviced pitches; baby facs; shwrs inc; el pnts (10A) inc; gas; lndtte; shop; supmkt adj; rest; snacks; bar; BBQ; playgrnd; htd pool & paddling pool; aquatic park; fishing; beach 12km; tennis; cycle hire; mini-golf; entmnt; child entmnt; wifi internet; games/TV rm; 25% statics; dogs €4; bus; phone; recep 0800-2100 high ssn; poss cr; Eng spkn; adv bkg; 10% red low ssn due ltd facs; cc acc; CCI. "Family-run site with excel facs; well-spaced pitches; vg san facs; vg rest; excursions booked; 30 mins walk town cent; recep at Old Farm 500m before site; excel." ♦ 15 May-15 Sep. € 39.90 (CChq acc) ABS - B21   2007*

QUIMPERLE *2F2* (7km NE Rural) **Camping Le Ty-Nadan, Route d'Arzano, 29310 Locunolé [02 98 71 75 47; fax 02 98 71 77 31; info@tynadan-vacances.fr; www.camping-ty-nadan.fr]** To avoid Quimperlé cent exit N165 dir Quimperlé. As ent town turn R onto D22 dir Arzano. In 9km turn L in Arzano (un-numbered rd) sp Locunolé & Camping Ty Nadan; site on L just after x-ing Rv Elle. Or fr Roscoff on D69 S join N165/E60 but take care at uneven level x-ing at Pen-ar-Hoat 11km after Sizun. Lge, hdg/mkd pitch, shd; htd wc; chem disp; mv service pnt; sauna; serviced pitches; baby facs; shwrs inc; el pnts (10A) inc (long lead poss req); gas; lndtte; ice; shop; rest; snacks; bar; BBQ; playgrnd; htd pools (1 covrd); waterslides; paddling pool; sand beach 18km; rv fishing, canoeing adj; tennis; cycle hire; horseriding; archery; rock-climbing; excursions; adventure park nrby; games area; entmnt; wifi internet; sat TV/games; 40% statics; dogs €5.90; c'vans over 8.50m not acc high ssn; Eng spkn; adv bkg; cc acc; red CCI. "Excel touring base; peaceful site; excel." ♦ 28 Mar-4 Sep. € 46.90 (CChq acc) ABS - B20   2007*

See advertisement below

France

QUIMPERLE *2F2* (1.5km SW Urban) **Camp Municipal de Kerbertrand, 29300 Quimperlé [02 98 39 31 30 or 02 98 96 01 41 (Mairie); fax 02 98 96 37 39]** Exit N165 at Kervidanou junc SW of town. Foll sp 'Centre Ville' along Rue de Pont-Aven. In 1km turn L bef supmkt, sp v sm. Sm, hdg pitch, pt shd; wc; shwrs; el pnts €1.50; ice; playgrnd; TV. "Delightful site; helpful warden; conv for old town." 1 Jun-15 Sep. € 8.00   2005*

QUINGEY *6H2* (Urban) **Camp Municipal Les Promenades, 25440 Quingey [03 81 63 74 01 or 03 81 63 63 25 (Mairie); fax 03 81 63 63 25; mairie-quingey@wanadoo.fr]** Site sp off N83 by-pass, then in Quingey. Thro vill, immed on L after bdge over Rv Loue. Sm, pt shd; wc (some cont); chem disp; shwrs inc; el pnts (6A) €2.70; lndtte; ice; shop; snacks; rest; playgrnd; rv sw; fishing, sailing; canoeing, tennis, cycle hire & archery adj; dogs €0.80; quiet but some daytime rd noise. ◆ 1 May-30 Sep. € 11.10   2007*

QUINSON *10E3* (Rural) **Camping Les Prés du Verdon, 04500 Quinson [0810 122 813 0r 04 99 57 21 21; presduverdon@village-center. com; www.village-center.com/presverdon]** Site sp fr D11. Lge, mkd pitch, pt shd; wc; shwrs inc; el pnts (6A) inc; lndtte; shop; snacks; bar; playgrnd; pool; paddling pool; lake fishing adj; entmnt; child entmnt; statics; dogs €3; Eng spkn; adv bkg; cc acc. "Beautiful area; vg site." ◆ 12 May-16 Sep. € 16.00   2007*

QUINTIN *2E3* (NE Urban) **Camp Municipal Le Vélodrome, Route de la Roche Longue, 22800 Quintin [02 96 74 92 54 or 02 96 74 84 01 (Mairie); fax 02 96 74 06 53]** Site on D790, N (100m) of town gardens & boating lake. Sm, pt sl, pt shd; wc (some cont); mv service pnt; shwrs; el pnts (6A) €2.60; BBQ; shops, rest, snacks, bar 500m; playgrnd; fishing; quiet. "Fair sh stay; interesting town with gd tourist office." ◆ Easter-30 Sep. € 7.80   2006*

RABASTENS *8E3* (2km NW Rural) **Camp Municipal des Auzerals, Route de Grazac, 81800 Rabastens [05 63 33 70 36 or 06 12 90 14 55 (mob); fax 05 63 33 64 05; mairie.rabastens@libertysurf.fr]** Exit A68 junc 7 onto D12. In Rabastens town cent foll sp dir Grazac, site sp. Sm, hdg/mkd pitch, pt sl, terr, pt shd; wc (mainly cont); chem disp; shwrs inc; el pnts (10-12A) inc; lndtte; ice; shop 2km; rest 2km; playgrnd; pool adj high ssn; adv bkg ess high ssn; CCI. "V attractive lakeside site; facs old but spotless; highly rec; friendly warden on site 0800-1100 & 1700-2000 otherwise height barrier in operation; conv m'way NH." 1 Apr-31 Oct. € 10.30   2007*

RAGUENES see Pont Aven *2F2*

RAMATUELLE see St Tropez *10F4*

RAMBOUILLET *4E3* (3km SE Rural) **Camping Huttopia Rambouillet, Route du Château d'Eau, 78120 Rambouillet [01 30 41 07 34; fax 01 30 41 00 17; rambouillet@huttopia.com; www. huttopia.com]** Fr S on N10 (sp Camping) twd Paris, turn onto D906 dir Chevreuse & foll sm white sp to site. Fr N on N10 go past D906 junc, take next slip rd, stay in inside lane & foll sp Rambouillet, Les Eveuses. Avoid Rambouillet town cent. Lge, hdg pitch, pt shd; htd wc (some cont); mv service pnt; chem disp; baby facs; shwrs inc; el pnts (6-10A) €4.20-6.20 (poss rev pol); lndtte; shop; tradsmn, rest; snacks; bar; BBQ (gas/elec); playgrnd; fishing adj; some statics; dogs €3.50; phone; sep car park; Eng spkn; adv bkg (rec high ssn); quiet; red low ssn; cc acc; CCI. "Excel, busy, wooded site; conv Paris by train - parking at stn 3km; gd cycling routes inc path to town; interesting town & gd tourist office." ◆ 28 Mar-2 Nov. € 22.00 (CChq acc)   2007*

RANG DU FLIERS see Berck *3B2*

RANVILLE see Ouistreham *3D1*

RAON L'ETAPE *6E3* (10km NE Rural) **Camping des Lacs, 88110 Celles-sur-Plaine [03 29 41 28 00; fax 03 29 41 18 69; camping@sma-lacs-pierre-percee.fr; www.sma-lacs-pierre-percee.fr]** Fr Raon L'Etape turn onto D392A to Celles-sur-Plaine, site sp. Med, hdg/mkd pitch, hdstg, pt sl, pt shd; wc (some cont); solarium; chem disp; shwrs inc; el pnts (4-10A) €2.60-4; lndtte; shop; tradsmn; snacks; bar; playgrnd; htd pool; sand beach (lake) 400m; tennis; fishing; sports; windsurfing; 10% statics; dogs €1.30; Eng spkn; adv bkg (dep req); quiet; red low ssn/long stay; cc acc; CCI. "Beautiful location; vg site." ◆ 1 Apr-30 Sep. € 15.45   2005*

RAON L'ETAPE *6E3* (10km E Rural) **Camping des 7 Hameaux, Chez Fade, Ban-de-Sapt, 88210 Senones [03 29 58 95 75; camping7hameaux@ wanadoo.fr; http://camping7hameaux.monsite. orange.fr]** Fr St Dié NE on D49 to St Jean-d'Ormont (turn R after cathedral in St Dié). Then D32 sp 'Saales' to Ban-de-Sapt. Turn L onto D49 to La Fontenelle. Site on R 1km past sp to military cemetery. Or fr N59 take D424 sp Senones. In 3.3km in Moyenmoutiers turn R onto D37 sp Ban-de-Sapt. In 6.1km join D49. site on L in 1.3km. Sm, pt sl; wc; chem disp; shwrs €1; el pnts (6A) €2; rest, bar & shop 1km; tradsmn; pool 7km; quiet; adv bkg; cc not acc; CCI. "Walks, cycle rtes; farm prod; friendly; tourist info on site; vg." 15 Mar-15 Nov. € 5.20   2004*

⊞**RAON L'ETAPE** *6E3* (4km SE) **Camping Beaulieu-sur-l'Eau, Rue de Trieuche, 88480 Etival-Clairefontaine [tel/fax 03 29 41 53 51]** SE fr Baccarat on N59 turn R in vill of Etival-Clairefontaine on D424 sp Rambervillers & Epinal & foll sp for 3km. Ent on L in front of Epicurie. Med, terr, pt shd; wc; shwrs inc; el pnts (6A) €2.90; gas; ice; shop; playgrnd; rv sw & beach 400m; 10% statics; adv bkg rec high ssn; quiet; CCI. "Vg sh stay/NH." € 10.00   2004*

⊞**RAON L'ETAPE** *6E3* (5km SE) **Camping Vosgina, 1 Rue la Cheville, St Blaise, 88420 Moyenmoutier [tel/fax 03 29 41 47 63; camping-vosgina@wanadoo.fr; www.vosges-camping.com]** On N59 St Dié-Lunéville rd, take exit mkd Senones, Moyenmoutier. At rndabt take rd twd St Blaise & foll camping sp. Site is on minor rd parallel with N59 bet Moyenmoutier & Raon. Med, hdg pitch, terr, shd; wc; shwrs inc; el pnts (4-10A) €2.20-5.50; gas; lndtte; sm shop & 3km; tradsmn; snacks; bar; 20% statics; dogs €1.50; Eng spkn; quiet but some rd noise; CCI. "Gd site for quiet holiday in a non-touristy area of Alsace; friendly recep; lovely countryside; many cycle/walking routes in area; barrier clsd 2200-0700." € 12.30   2006*

RAUZAN *7D2* (200m N Rural) **Camping du Vieux Château, 33420 Rauzan [05 57 84 15 38; fax 05 57 84 18 34; hoekstra.camping@wanadoo.fr; www.vieux-chateau.com]** Fr Libourne S on D670, site is on D123 about 1.5km, off D670, sp. Sm, mkd pitch, pt shd; wc; chem disp; baby facs; shwrs inc; el pnts (6-10A) €3-4; gas; lndtte; ice; shop, tradsmn; rest 200m; snacks; sm bar & in 200m; playgrnd; pool; tennis; rv/lake 5km; cycle hire; horseriding; wine-tasting; entmnt; TV; 10% statics; dogs €1.20; poss cr; Eng spkn; adv bkg; quiet; red low ssn; cc acc; CCI. "Conv vineyards; helpful owners; view of ruined chateau fr site; lovely site but care as some pitches badly pitted due lge tree roots; poss ltd facs low ssn." ♦ 1 Apr-30 Sep. € 16.00   2006*

RAVENOVILLE PLAGE see Ste Mere Eglise *1C4*

REALMONT *8E4* (2km SW Rural) **Camp Municipal de la Batisse, Route de Graulhet, 81120 Réalmont [05 63 55 50 41 or 05 63 45 50 68; fax 05 63 55 65 62; camping-realmont@wanadoo. fr; www.realmont.fr]** On N112 fr Albi heading S thro Réalmont. On exit turn R on N631 where site sp. Site 1.5km on L on Rv Dadou. Sm, pt shd; wc; shwrs; el pnts (3A) inc; gas; shops, rest, snacks, bar 2km; playgrnd; rv adj; fishing; some statics; quiet. "Pleasant, well-kept site; friendly warden; excel value; gd." 1 Apr-30 Sep. € 9.00   2007*

RECOUBEAU JANSAC see Luc en Diois *9D3*

REDON *2F3* **Camp Municipal de la Goule d'Eau, Rue de la Goule d'Eau, 35600 Redon [02 99 72 14 39 or 02 99 71 05 27 (Mairie)]** Foll sp in town. Sm, shd; wc; shwrs inc; el pnts; ice; shop; playgrnd; fishing; sailing; quiet; CCI. 15 Jun-15 Sep.   2004*

REGUINY *2F3* (1km S Urban) **Camp Municipal de l'Etang, 56500 Réguiny [02 97 38 61 43 or 02 97 38 66 11; fax 02 97 38 63 44]** On D764 fr Pontivy to Ploërmel, turn R into D11 to Réguiny then foll sp. Med, pt shd; wc; chem disp; mv service pnt; baby facs; shwrs inc; el pnts (10A) €2; lndtte; shop 2km; rest, bar 1km; playgrnd; htd pool 500m; no statics; dogs; phone; Eng spkn; quiet; cc acc. "Gd facs; gd touring base." 1 Jun-15 Sep. € 10.60   2004*

REGUSSE *10E3* (1.5km NW Rural) **Village-Camping Les Lacs du Verdon, Domaine de Roquelande, 83630 Régusse [04 94 70 17 95; fax 04 94 70 51 79; info@leslacsduverdon.com; www.leslacsduverdon.com]** Fr W exit A8 junc 34 at St Maximin onto D560 Barjols, Tavernes, Montmeyan then D30 to Régusse. At rndabt in Régusse turn L twd St Jean & foll sp. Fr E exit A8 junc 36 Le Muy then Draguignan then D557 to Villecroze, Aups & Régusse. At rndabt turn R twd St Jean & foll sp. Lge, mkd pitch, pt shd; wc; chem disp; mv service pnt; shwrs inc; el pnts (6A) €4; gas; lndtte; ice; shop; rest; snacks; bar; BBQ; playgrnd; pool; tennis; mini-golf; entmnt; internet; TV rm; 10% statics; dogs €3; poss cr; Eng spkn; adv bkg ess high ssn; quiet; cc acc; CCI. "Beautiful area; lake 20 mins drive; mainly gravel pitches under pine trees; diff lge outfits without mover due to trees; gd facs slightly scruffy low ssn; recep closes 1800." ♦ 29 Apr-23 Sep. € 27.00 (CChq acc)   2006*

As soon as we get home I'm going to post all these site report forms to the editor for inclusion in next year's guide. I don't want to miss the September deadline.

REHAUPAL see Tholy, Le *6F3*

REILLANNE *10E3* (2km W Rural) **Camping le Vallon des Oiseaux (Naturist), 04110 Reillanne [04 92 76 47 33; fax 04 92 76 44 64; info@levallon. com; www.levallon.com]** Fr Apt take N100 twd Céreste. Approx 2km after Céreste sharp turn L onto minor rd. Site sp. Med, pt sl, pt shd; wc; chem disp; shwrs inc; el pnts (4A) €3; lndtte; shop 2km; tradsmn; rest; snacks; bar; playgrnd; pool; TV rm; 5% statics; dogs €3; phone; poss cr; Eng spkn; adv bkg; quiet; INF card. "V friendly & helpful staff; office clsd 1300-1600." ♦ 1 Apr-14 Oct. € 22.00   2006*

REIMS *3D4* (16km SE Rural) **Camp Municipal, 8 Rue de Routoir Courmelois, 51360 Val-de-Vesle [03 26 03 91 79; fax 03 26 03 28 22]** Fr Reims twd Châlons-en-Champagne on D944 (N44), turn L by camp sp on D326 to Val-de-Vesle, foll camp sp; look for tall grain silos by canal. NB do not turn L bef D326 due narr lane. Sm, shd; wc; chem disp; shwrs inc; el pnts (6-10A) inc (long lead poss req); gas; lndtte; tradsmn; BBQ; playgrnd; rv fishing; 30% statics; dogs €0.60; poss cr; adv bkg; quiet; cc acc; CCI. "V popular, busy site; friendly staff; vg, immac san facs; office open 1400-2000; informal pitching; gd off-lead dog-walking adj; poss mosquito problem; poss grapepickers; excel for visiting Reims; gd value; rec NH." ♦ 1 Apr-15 Oct. € 10.90   2007*

REMIREMONT *6F2* (8km SE Rural) **Camping Le Pont de Maxonchamp, Rue du Camping, 88360 Maxonchamp [03 29 24 30 65]** Fr Remiremont on N66 twrds Maxonchamp; site clearly sp to L; also visible 300m down lane. Sm, pt shd; wc; chem disp; shwrs €1; el pnts (10A) €2; shop 3km; playgrnd; rv sw adj; 20% statics; dogs €0.50; poss cr; quiet; CCI. "Vg, attractive site on rv; conv S Vosges area" ♦ 1 Apr-31 Oct. € 6.00   2007*

The opening dates and prices on this campsite have changed. I'll send a site report form to the editor for the next edition of the guide.

REMIREMONT *6F2* (3.5km W Rural) **Camping de Ste Anne, Fallières, 88200 Remiremont [03 29 62 20 98]** Fr Epinal on N57 foll sp for Remiremont. After turning for N66/D3 foll sp for Fallières & Camping Ste Anne. Sm, pt sl, pt shd; wc; shwrs inc; el pnts (6A) inc; no dogs; quiet; no cc acc; CCI. "10 pitches only; spotless, attractive site with modern facs; peaceful." € 10.00   2004*

REMOULINS *10E2* (1.5km S Rural) **Camping Domaine de la Soubeyranne, Route de Beaucaire, 30210 Remoulins [04 66 37 03 21; fax 04 66 37 14 65; soubeyranne@franceloc.fr; www.soubeyranne.com]** Exit A9 for Remoulins onto D986. On D6086 (N86) Remoulins to Nîmes rd turn L after x-ing bdge fr Remoulins. Site on L in 1km. Lge, hdg pitch, shd; wc; chem disp; baby facs; shwrs inc; el pnts (6A) €3.40; gas; ice; lndtte; shop; rest; snacks; bar; BBQ; playgrnd; pool; paddling pool; fishing; tennis; TV rm; some statics; dogs €4.15; adv bkg; some rd & rlwy noise; CCI. "Gd site; plenty hot water." 25 Mar-23 Sep. € 21.00 (CChq acc)   2006*

Before we move on, I'm going to fill in some site report forms and post them off to the editor, otherwise they won't arrive in time for the deadline at the end of September.

REMOULINS *10E2* (2km NW Rural) **Camping La Sousta, Ave du Pont de Gard, 30210 Remoulins [04 66 37 12 80; fax 04 66 37 23 69; info@lasousta.fr; www.lasousta.fr]** Fr A9 exit Remoulins, foll sp for Nîmes, then sp 'Pont du Gard par Rive Droite' thro town. Immed over rv bdge turn R sp 'Pont du Gard etc'; site on R 800m fr Pont du Gard. Lge, mkd pitch, shd; wc (some cont); chem disp; mv service pnt; baby facs; shwrs inc; el pnts (6A) €3; gas; lndtte; shop; tradsmn; rest adj; snacks; bar; BBQ in sep area; playgrnd; pool; tennis; rv sw adj; watersports; fishing; cycle hire; mini-golf; wifi internet (free); entmnt; child entmnt; TV; 20% statics; dogs €2; poss cr; Eng spkn; adv bkg; quiet; cc acc; CCI. "Friendly, helpful staff; poss diff for lge o'fits due trees; best pitches o'look rv; interesting area; excel touring base; walking dist of Pont-du-Gard." ♦ 1 Mar-31 Oct. € 20.00   2007*

See advertisement below

France

REMOULINS *10E2* (4km NW Rural) **Camping International Les Gorges du Gardon, Chemin de la Barque Vieille, Route d'Uzès, 30210 Vers-Pont-du-Gard [04 66 22 81 81; fax 04 66 22 90 12; camping.international@wanadoo.fr; www. le-camping-international.com]** Exit A9 junc 23 Remoulins & head NW twd Uzès on D981. Pass turn for Pont-du-Gard & site on L in 1.5km. Or fr E on N100 turn N onto D6086 (N86) then D19A to Pont-du-Gard (avoiding Remoulins cent). Lge, hdg/mkd pitch, pt shd; wc; chem disp; mv service pnt; baby facs; shwrs inc; el pnts (6A) €3.20; gas; lndtte; ice; shop; tradsmn; rest; snacks; bar; playgrnd; htd pool; rv sw & private beach adj; boating; fishing; tennis; games area; games rm; entmnt; internet; TV rm; 10% statics; dogs €2; twin-axles not allowed; Eng spkn; adv bkg; quiet; cc acc; red low ssn/long stay; CCI. "Friendly, cheerful owners; gd san facs; beautiful location; some lge pitches to back of site; cycle track to Roman aquaduct at Pont-du-Gard 2km down stream; conv Avignon, Nîmes; site poss subject to flooding & evacuation; excel." ♦ 15 Mar-31 Oct. € 18.50   2007*

See advertisement above

REMOULINS *10E2* (7km NW Rural) **Camping Le Barralet, 30210 Collias [04 66 22 84 52 or 04 66 22 80 40 (LS); fax 04 66 22 89 17; camping@barralet.fr; www.barralet.fr]** W off A9 on D981 to Uzès; thro Remoulins; foll camp sp; turn S on D112 D3 to Collias; sp in 4km on L past quarry on bend; turn L up narr rd & site in 50m on R. Med, pt shd; wc; shwrs inc; el pnts €3.50 (adaptors supplied free); lndtte; shop; rest; snacks; bar; pool; playgrnd; volleyball; fishing & canoe/kayak hire adj; tennis & horseriding in vill; dogs €2; phone; quiet; cc acc; CCI. "Excel site; gd rvside walks; sm pitches; lge youth groups use this activity cent." ♦ 1 Apr-20 Sep. € 17.00   2006*

REMUZAT *9D2* (8km N Rural) **Camp Municipal Le Village, Chemin du Piscine, 26470 La Motte-Chalancon [04 75 27 22 95 or 04 75 27 20 41 (Mairie); fax 04 75 27 20 38; mairie@lamotte chalancon.com; www.lamottechalancon.com]** S fr Die on D93 dir Luc-en-Diois for 18km, turn R onto D61 S twd La Motte-Chalancon for 19km. In La Motte, just bef rv bdge & Citroën garage on L, turn sharp L. Site sp in 500m on L adj Rv L'Oule. Med, pt shd; wc (cont); chem disp; mv service pnt; shwrs inc; el pnts (5-10A) inc; lndtte; shops, rest 500m; snacks; bar; playgrnd; pool; paddling pool; rv sw, beach 2km; dogs €0.80; phone; poss noisy; cc acc; CCI. "Beautiful views fr site; attractive vill." Easter-30 Sep. € 14.00   2007*

REMUZAT *9D2* (9km NE Rural) **Aire Naturelle de Pommerol (Morin), Quartier Lemoulin, 26470 Pommerol [04 75 27 25 63 or 04 75 98 26 25 (LS); fax 04 75 27 25 63; camping.pommerol@wanadoo.fr]** Fr Rémuzat, take D61 N dir La Motte-Chalancon. In vill, turn R & cont on D61 for 6km dir La Charce, then turn R onto D138 sp Montmorin/Pommerol. In 1km bear R onto D338 to Pommerol. Site sp in 2km on R. Sm, terr, pt shd; htd wc; chem disp; shwrs inc; el pnts €2 (long lead req); gas 10km; lndtte; shops 10km; rest, snacks, bar, (high ssn only or 10km); BBQ; playgrnd; htd pool 10km; lake sw, beach 12km; dogs €2; Eng spkn; adv bkg (dep req); quiet; CCI. "Superb views fr site; situated in Pommerol Gorge adj to stream; access diff for lge o'fits; adv bkg ess high ssn." 1 Apr-30 Oct. € 10.00   2006*

REMUZAT *9D2* (S Rural) **Camp Municipal Les Aires, 26510 Rémuzat [04 75 27 81 43 or 04 75 25 85 78 (Mairie); www.remuzat.com]** Fr Rosans take D994 W for approx 10km & then R on D61 to Rémuzat. Site on rvside. Sm, hdg/mkd pitch, pt shd; wc; baby facs; shwrs inc; el pnts (4-10A) €1.50-2.50; lndtte; shop nr; BBQ; dogs €1; quiet; CCI. "Beautiful site, vill & area; v helpful warden." ♦ Mid May-30 Sep. € 7.30   2007*

REMUZAT 9D2 (10km W Rural) **Camp Municipal Les Oliviers, Quartier St Jean, 26510 Sahune [04 75 27 40 40; fax 04 75 27 44 48]** Take N94 fr Nyons dir Serres. In 16km at Sahune turn R over bdge & foll sp to site. Sm, pt shd; wc; chem disp (wc); shwrs inc; el pnts (4-10A) €1.70-2.70; gas 500m; lndtte; shop, rest, snacks, bar 500m; rv sw; Eng spkn; quiet; CCI. 5 May-15 Sep. € 8.90   2004*

REMUZAT 9D2 (10km W Rural) **Camping La Vallée Bleue, La Plaine-du-Pont, 26510 Sahune [tel/fax 04 75 27 44 42; www.lavalleebleue.com]** On D94 well sp. Med, pt shd; wc; chem disp; shwrs; el pnts (6A) €3; lndtte; shop 500m; tradsmn; rest; snacks; bar; playgrnd; pool; 5% statics; dogs €1.50; phone; poss cr; adv bkg; quiet; CCI. "Golf & fishing nrby."
♦ 1 Apr-30 Sep. € 16.00   2004*

⊞**RENNES** 2F4 (2km NE Urban) **Camp Municipal des Gayeulles, Rue du Professeur Maurice Audin, 35700 Rennes [02 99 36 91 22 or 02 99 65 01 11; fax 02 23 20 06 34; www.camping-rennes.com]** Fr Fougères, exit A84 at junc 25 sp dir Thorigny Fouillard. Join N12 for approx 10km to city ring rd. At rndabt La Gayeulles (Elf g'ge), turn R to 'Centre Loisirs' & university campus. Site sp on R. Med, mkd pitch, hdstg, pt sl, pt shd; wc; chem disp; mv service pnt; baby facs; shwrs; el pnts (10A) €3; lndtte; shops 500m; tradsmn; snacks; BBQ; playgrnd; pool 500m; tennis, archery & mini-golf nrby; internet; dogs €1; phone; bus; Eng spkn; adv bkg; quiet; red low ssn; cc acc; CCI. "Excel, clean, well-kept site; friendly staff; lge pitches; slight sl for m'vans; 1st class facs; office open 0800-0900 & 1800-2000 winter; magnificient park adj; narr app to site; frequent bus to city cent; Rennes well worth a visit." ♦ € 15.10   2007*

RENNES LES BAINS 8G4 (S Rural) **Camping La Bernède, 11190 Rennes-les-Bains [04 68 69 86 49; fax 04 68 74 09 31; camping. renneslesbains@wanadoo.fr]** S fr Carcassonne or N fr Quillan on D118, turn E at Couiza on D613. In 5km turn R onto D14 to Rennes-les-Bains in 3km. Site at far end of vill on L. Sm, mkd pitch, pt shd; wc; chem disp (wc); shwrs inc; el pnts (5A) €2.55; lndtte; ice; shop; tradsmn; rest in vill; bar; playgrnd; rv adj; fishing; 10% statics; dogs €1.15; adv bkg; quiet; CCI. "10 mins walk into town with thermal spa; vg." ♦ 10 May-30 Sep. € 11.55   2007*

REOLE, LA 7D2 (S Urban) **Camp Municipal La Rouergue, Bords de Garonne, 33190 La Réole [05 56 61 13 55; fax 05 56 61 89 13; lareole@ entredeuxmers.com; www.entredeuxmers.com]** On N113 bet Bordeaux & Agen or exit A62 at junc 4. In La Réole foll sps S on D9 to site on L immed after x-ing suspension bdge. Med, pt shd; wc; shwrs inc; el pnts (3A) €3; gas; shop; tradsmn; snacks; pool 500m; fishing, boating; dogs €2; some rd noise. "Resident warden; 2m barrier clsd 1200-1500; poss itinerants & facs dirty; Sat morning mkt on rv bank; conv for historical, cultural & gastronomic Entre-Deux-Mers area." 15 May-15 Oct. € 8.60   2007*

RETHEL 5C1 (14km E Urban) **Camp Municipal Le Vallage, 38, Chemin de l'Assaut, 08130 Attigny [03 24 71 23 06 or 03 24 71 20 68; fax 03 24 71 94 00]** E on D983 fr Rethel to Attigny; fr town cent take D987 twd Charleville; over rv bdge; 2nd turn on L; sp. Med, hdg/mkd pitch, hdstg, unshd; wc; chem disp; shwrs inc; el pnts (10A) inc; lndry rm; shop 1km; tradsmn; sw adj; playgrnd; fishing; tennis; 50% statics; dogs; phone; quiet; CCI. "Park & sports stadium adj with sw pool, tennis etc." Easter-30 Sep. € 8.10   2005*

REVEL 8F4 (500m E Urban) **Camp Municipal Le Moulin du Roy, Rue de Sorèze, 31250 Revel [05 61 83 32 47 or 05 62 18 71 40 (Mairie)]** Fr Revel ring rd take D85 dir Sorèze, site sp. Med, hdg pitch, pt shd; shwrs inc; el pnts €2.30; shop 500m; supmkt nr; playgrnd; pool; lake sw & beach 2.5km; tennis adj; dogs €0.50; phone; bus; Eng spkn; quiet. "Pleasant, helpful staff; Sat mkt in Revel; vg site." 18 Jun-2 Sep. € 6.80   2004*

REVEL 8F4 (5.5km E Urban) **Camping Saint Martin, 81540 Sorèze [tel/fax 05 63 73 28 99; mary@campingsaintmartin.com; www.camping saintmartin.com]** Fr Revel take D85 sp Sorèze; site sp outside vill; turn L at traff lts; site on R in 100m. Sm, hdg/mkd pitch; pt shd; wc; chem disp; shwrs inc; el pnts (4-13A) €3.15-6.12; ice; sm shop & rest 500m; snacks; bar; playgrnd; pool; lake sw 3km; TV; 20% statics; dogs €1; quiet; CCI. "Fascinating medieval town; nr Bassin de St Ferréol; friendly staff; barrier clsd 2230-7000; excel mkt in Revel; vg." 15 Jun-15 Sep. € 14.30   2006*

REVEL 8F4 (8km SE Rural) **Camping La Rigole, 81540 Les Cammazes [tel/fax 05 63 73 28 99; mary@campingdlr.com; http://campingdlr.free. fr]** Fr Revel take D629 E to Les Cammazes. Thro vill 300m take 1st L. Site well sp, 1km fr vill. Med, mkd pitch, pt sl, terr, pt shd; wc; chem disp; shwrs inc; el pnts (4-13A) €3.15-6.12; lndtte; ice; shop &1km; rest 1km; playgrnd; pool; lake sw 400m; TV rm; dogs €1; phone; poss cr; Eng spkn; adv bkg; quiet; 20% red low ssn; CCI. "Pretty & pleasant site; help req to access some pitches; gd san facs; gd disabled facs but wheelchair movement on site impossible unaided & diff at best; gd walks adj; phone ahead to check open low ssn." ♦ 15 Apr-15 Oct. € 14.30   2006*

REVEL 8F4 (4km S Rural) **Camping En Salvan, 31350 St Ferréol [05 61 83 55 95; lvt-en-salvan@ wanadoo.fr;   www.camping-ensalvan.com]** Fr Revel head S on D629 up long hill. At lake at top turn R for 2km. site on R. Sm, mkd pitch, hdstg, shd; shwrs; mv service pnt; el pnts (10A) €3.90; lndtte; shop; BBQ; playgrnd; games area; 20% statics; dogs €1.20; quiet. "V pleasant." 1 Apr-31 Oct. € 10.15   2006*

France

REVIGNY SUR ORNAIN *5D1* (S Urban) **Camp Municipal du Moulin des Gravières, Rue du Stade, 55800 Revigny-sur-Ornain [tel/ fax 03 29 78 73 34 or 03 29 70 50 55 (Mairie); contact@ot-revigny-ornain.fr; www.ot-revigny-ornain.fr]** N fr Bar-le-Duc on D994 to Revigny-sur-Ornain; fr town cent take D995 twd Vitry-le-François. Site on R, sp. Sm, hdg/mkd pitch, pt shd; wc (some cont); chem disp; mv service pnt; shwrs inc; el pnts (5-16A) €2.65-3.65; ice; lndry rm; supmkt 500m; snacks; playgrnd; TV rm; 40% statics; dogs; Eng spkn; adv bkg; v quiet; cc not acc; CCI. "V pleasant, clean, beautifully maintained site; excel value; v lge pitches but poss mkt traders/itinerants spread over lgest pitches; superb facs; weekly mkt (Wed am) at sports complex adj; trout stream running thro site; conv centre sm town; v highly rec." ♦ 1 May-30 Sep. € 9.10   2007*

REVIN *5C1* (500m Urban) **Camp Municipal Les Bateaux, Quai Edgar Quinet, 08500 Revin [03 24 40 15 65 or 03 24 40 19 59 (LS); fax 03 24 40 21 98; camping.les.bateaux-revin@ wanadoo.fr; www.ville-revin.fr]** Fr Fumay take D988 to Revin, or fr Charleville take D989/988 (23km) or take rte D1 E fr Rocroi. On ent Revin turn L after narr bdge (1-way) over Rv Meuse. Fr cent of Revin foll sp Montherme; at Total g'ge R fork, then 1st L. At rv turn L, 500m to site. Med, hdg/ mkd pitch, pt shd; htd wc; chem disp; baby facs; shwrs; el pnts (6A) €2.65 (poss rev pol); ice; lndtte; shop; supmkt 1km; tradsmn; playgrnd; rv fishing; paragliding nrby; games rm; TV rm; 5% statics; dogs €0.90; adv bkg; quiet; CCI. "Peaceful, beautiful, rvside site; clean & modern; lge pitches; excel san facs, inc for disabled; if office clsd site self & book in later; helpful warden; easy walk to town cent; gd walking & lovely walks by rvside; gd cent for Ardennes region; excel." ♦ Easter-30 Oct. € 8.55   2007*

RHINAU *6E3* **Camping Ferme des Tuileries, 67230 Rhinau [03 88 74 60 45]** S on D468 at Boofzheim, turn L at sp Rhinau, D5. Site 2.4km after L turn. Ent Rhinau site 3rd turn R. Med, some hdstg; shd; wc; chem disp; shwrs inc; el pnts (2-6A) €1.40- 3.20; lndtte; gas; ice; shops 500m; tradsmn; sm htd pool; tennis; 50% statics; dogs; poss cr; quiet. "Extended site; spacious with excel facs; regimented; barrier key req; free ferry adj for x-ing Rhine. " 1 Apr-30 Sep. € 9.60   2004*

RHINAU *6E3* (2.5km NW Rural) **Camping du Ried, 1 Rue du Camping, 67860 Boofzheim [03 88 74 68 27; fax 03 88 74 62 89; info@ camping-ried.com; www.camping-ried.com]** Site sp fr D5, 1km E of Boofzheim. Lge, hdg/mkd pitch, pt shd; htd wc; mv service pnt; shwrs; el pnts (5A) €4; lndtte; shop 200m; snacks; bar; BBQ; playgrnd; 2 htd pools (1 covrd); paddling pool; lake sw; watersports; fishing; games area; mini-golf; cycle hire; entmnt; TV rm; 20% statics; dogs €4; phone; adv bkg; quiet; red low ssn; cc acc. "Conv Strasbourg, Colmar & Europa Park theme park; vg site." ♦ 1 Apr-30 Sep. € 17.50   2007*

See advertisement

RIBEAUVILLE *6E3* (2km E Urban) **Camp Municipal Pierre-de-Coubertin, Rue de Landau, 68150 Ribeauville [tel/fax 03 89 73 66 71; camping. ribeauville@wanadoo.fr; www.camping-alsace. com]** Exit N83 at Ribeauville, turn R on D106 & foll rd to o'skts, at traff lts turn R & then immed R again. Site on R in 750m. Camp at sports grnd nr Ribeauville Lycée. Lge, mkd pitch, pt sl, pt shd; htd wc; chem disp; baby facs; shwrs inc; el pnts (2-6A) €2.50-4 (rev pol & poss long lead req); gas; lndtte; sm shop; pool adj; dogs €1; poss cr; quiet; CCI. "Well-run site; friendly, helpful managers; recep clsd 1200-1400; on arr park outside site bef registering at recep; spotless san facs; resident storks; easy walk to attractive, historical town on Rte des Vins; mkt Sat; excel." ♦ 15 Mar-15 Nov. € 11.60

2007*

RIBEAUVILLE *6E3* (4.5km S Rural) **Camp Intercommunal, 1 Route des Vins, 68340 Riquewihr [03 89 47 90 08; fax 03 89 49 05 63; camping.riquewihr@tiscali.fr]** Fr Strasbourg on N83/E25, take junc 21 (fr opp dir take junc 22) to Blebenheim/Riquewihr. D416 & D3 thro Blebenheim. At T-junc turn R onto D1B, site on R at rndabt. Lge, hdg/mkd pitch, pt sl, pt shd; htd wc; chem disp; mv service pnt; baby facs; shwrs inc; el pnts (6A) €3.50 (poss rev pol); gas; lndtte; ice; shops 5km; tradsmn in ssn; snacks; playgrnd; games area adj; dogs €1.20; poss cr; adv bkg; noise fr main rd; cc acc; CCI ess. "Register 1st with recep, open 0830-1200 & 1300-2100 high ssn, 0830-1200 & 1330-1900 low ssn; rec arr early; friendly staff; san facs clean; gd for sm children; Riquewihr lovely town in cent of wine region; m'van o'night area." ♦ Easter-31 Dec. € 12.00   2006*

RIBEAUVILLE *6E3* (8km W Rural) **FFCC Camp Municipal de la Ménère, 68150 Aubure [03 89 73 92 99; aubure@cc-ribeauville.fr]** Take D416 W fr Ribeauville for 7km, then turn L to Aubure; foll rd to vill for 5km; site 200m S of vill. Or take D416 E fr Ste Marie-aux-Mines; then turn R onto D11to Aubure (gd rd, resurfaced 2007). For info: D11 gd rd S fr Aubure over hills to N415. Med, mkd pitch, terr, pt shd; wc; chem disp; mv service pnt; shwrs inc; el pnts (6A) €2.65; gas; lndry rm; ice; shops 12km; playgrnd 50m; no statics; dogs €0.50; phone; Eng spkn; adv bkg (dep req); quiet; CCI. "Highest vill in Alsace (800m) & former medical spa; fresh & pleasant site in mountains; walking & cycling rtes nrby; peaceful & friendly." 8 May-15 Sep. € 10.55   2007*

RIBERAC *7C2* (500m N Urban) **Camp Municipal La Dronne, Route d'Angoulême, 24600 Ribérac [05 53 90 50 08 or 05 53 90 03 10; fax 05 53 91 35 13; ot.riberac@perigord.tm.fr]** Site on L of main rd D709 immed N of bdge over Rv Dronne on o'skts of Ribérac. Med, some hdg pitches, pt shd; wc (cont for men); shwrs inc; el pnts €2; lndtte; supmkt 500m; tradsmn; snacks; playgrnd; sw pool 1km; lake sw 10km; no twin-axles; quiet. "Vg, well-run site; pitches in cent hdgd & shady; facs gd & clean but inadequate, poss overstretched high ssn; walking dist town cent; kingfishers on rv; lge Fri mkt in Ribérac." ♦ 1 Jun-15 Sep. € 10.00   2007*

RICHELIEU *4H1* (S Urban) **Camp Municipal, 6 Ave de Schaafheim, 37120 Richelieu [02 47 58 15 02 or 02 47 58 10 13 (Mairie); fax 02 47 58 16 42; commune-de-richelieu@wanadoo.fr]** Fr Loudun, take D61 to Richelieu, D749 twd Châtellerault; site sp. Sm, hdg/mkd pitch, pt shd; wc; chem disp; shwrs inc; el pnts (5-15A) €1.50-3.10; shop 1km; playgrnd; pool 500m; fishing; tennis; quiet; CCI. "Phone ahead to check site open as open dates may vary; clean, gd facs but may need updating; poss itinerants; conv Loire châteaux & gardens of Richelieu; bureau open 0930-1030 & 1830-1930 low ssn & all day high ssn; €30 dep req for barrier key." ♦ 15 May-15 Sep. € 6.70   2006*

RIEL LES EAUX *6F1* (2km SW Rural) **Camp Municipal du Plan d'Eau, 21570 Riel-les-Eaux [tel/fax 03 80 93 72 76; bar-camping-du-marais@wanadoo.fr]** Fr Châtillon-sur-Seine on D965 NE twd Chaumont: after 6km turn N onto D13 thro Belan-sur-Ource. Turn R onto D22 to Riel-les-Eaux, site well sp. Sm, hdg pitch, pt shd; wc; chem disp; shwrs inc; el pnts (6A) €2.50; tradsmn; snacks; bar; playgrnd; lake adj; fishing; Eng spkn; quiet; CCI. "Conv Champagne area; excel." ♦ 1 Apr-31 Oct. € 7.50   2006*

RIEZ *10E3* (500m E Urban) **Camping Rose de Provence, Rue Edouard Dauphin, 04500 Riez [tel/fax 94 92 77 75 45; info@rose-de-provence.com; www.rose-de-provence.com]** Exit A51 junc 18 onto D82 to Gréoux-les-Bains then D952 to Riez. On reaching Riez strt across rndabt, at T-junc turn L & immed R, site sp. Med, mkd pitch, pt shd; wc; chem disp; shwrs inc; el pnts (6A) €2.95; lndtte; rest, snacks, bar 500m; playgrnd; jacuzzi; lake sw 10km; tennis adj; 5% statics; dogs €1.40; phone; adv bkg (dep & bkg fee req); red low ssn; CCI. "V clean site; helpful, friendly owners; conv Verdon Gorge." ♦ ltd. 31 Mar-1 Oct. € 13.20   2007*

RIEZ *10E3* (10km S Rural) **Camping Le Côteau de la Marine, 04500 Montagnac-Montpezat [04 92 77 53 33; fax 04 92 77 59 34; contact@village-center.com; www.village-center.com]** A51 exit 18, D82 to Gréoux-les-Bains, then D952 & D11 & Montagnac, Montpezat & site sp. (Steep incline bef ent to site) Lge, hdg/mkd pitch, hdstg, pt sl, terr, pt shd; wc; chem disp; mv service pnt; 50% serviced pitch; shwrs inc; el pnts (10A) inc; gas; lndtte; ice; shop; tradsmn; rest; snacks; bar; playgrnd; pool; fishing; boating; tennis; games area; games rm; entmnt; internet & wifi; TV; dogs €3; statics; Eng spkn; adv bkg ess high ssn; quiet but poss noise fr night-flying helicopters in gorge; cc acc; CCI. "Mountainous scenery; v helpful staff; gd facs; gravel pegs req for awnings; excel." ♦ 21 Apr-16 Sep. € 30.00   2007*

RILLE *4G1* (4km W Rural) **Camping Huttopia Rillé, Base de Loisirs de Pincemaille, Lac de Rillé, 37340 Rillé [02 47 24 62 97; fax 02 47 24 63 61; rille@huttopia.com; www.huttopia.com]** Fr N or S D749 to Rillé, foll sp to Lac de Pincemaille, site sp on S side of lake. Med, shd; htd wc; chem disp; mv service pnt; baby facs; fam bthrm; shwrs inc; el pnts (6-10A) €4.20; ice; shop; rest; snacks; bar; playgrnd; htd pool; lake sw & beach adj; fishing; watersports; tennis; games rm; some statics; dogs €3.50; sep car park; adv bkg. "Peaceful site; conv Loire chateaux; vg walking; excel." 28 Mar-2 Nov. € 22.00 (CChq acc)   2007*

RIOM *9B1* (5km NW) **Camping de la Croze (formerly Municipal), St Hippolyte, 63140 Châtelguyon [04 73 86 08 27 or 06 87 14 43 62 (mob); fax 04 73 86 08 51; info@campingcroze.com; www.campingcroze.com]** Fr A71 exit junc 13; ring rd around Riom sp Châtelguyon to Mozac, then D227. Site L bef ent St Hippolyte. Fr Volvic on D986 turn L at rndabt after Leclerc supmkt & L again to D227. NB Avoid diff ent to site by going ahead 1km, doing U-turn in St Hippolyte & then R turn to site. Not rec to tow thro Riom. Lge, mkd pitch, pt sl, pt shd; wc; chem disp; shwrs inc; el pnts (6-10A) €2.50; lndtte; ice; shops 2km; tradsmn; playgrnd; pool 3km; 10% statics; dogs €1.30; quiet; CCI. "€20 dep for barrier key; gd sightseeing area; poss diff for British vans on sl pitches; vg." 1 May-20 Oct. € 9.00
2006*

RIOM *9B1* (6km NW) **Camping Clos de Balanède, Route de la Piscine, 63140 Châtelguyon [04 73 86 02 47; fax 04 73 86 05 64; clos-balanede.sarl-camping@wanadoo.fr; www.balanede.com]** Fr Riom take D985 to Châtelguyon, site on R on o'skts of town. Tight turn into ent. Lge, pt sl, pt shd; wc; shwrs inc; el pnts (5-10A) €2.50-3.90; gas; lndtte; shop; rest; snacks; bar; playgrnd; 3 pools; tennis; dogs €1.50; poss cr; Eng spkn; adv bkg; quiet. "Nice, v clean, well organised site; 15 mins walk to town with gd rest; poss some itinerants; excel." ♦ 15 Apr-2 Oct. € 13.10
2007*

RIOM ES MONTAGNES *7C4* (E Urban) **Camp Municipal Le Sédour, 15400 Riom-ès-Montagnes [04 71 78 05 71]** Site on W of D678 Riom N to Condat rd, 500m out of town over bdge, sp fr all dirs, opp Clinique du Haut Cantal. Med, pt shd; wc; shwrs inc; el pnts (2-10A) €2.10; lndtte; supmkt 200m; playgrnd; pool 5km; games area; TV rm; Eng spkn; adv bkg; some rd noise top end of site. "V helpful staff; vg." 1 Jun-30 Sep. € 6.00   2004*

RIOM ES MONTAGNES *7C4* (10km SW Rural) **Camp Municipal Le Pioulet, 15400 Trizac [04 71 78 64 20 or 04 71 78 60 37 (Mairie); fax 04 71 78 65 40]** D678 W fr Riom-ès-Montagnes to Trizac. Site on R after leaving vill S twd Mauriac. Sm, hdg pitch, pt sl, pt shd; wc; chem disp; el pnts (2-5A) €2; gas, tradsmn, rest, bar, shops 1km; BBQ; lndtte; playgrnd; tennis nr; sand beach; lake sw; quiet; Eng spkn; adv bkg; phone; CCI. "Friendly site; spotless facs; vg walking area, lovely scenery." ♦ 16 Jun-15 Sep. € 7.00   2004*

RIOZ *6G2* (Rural) **Camp Municipal du Lac (formerly Camp Municipal Les Platanes), Rue de la Faïencerie, 70190 Rioz [03 84 91 91 59 or 03 84 91 84 84 (Mairie); fax 03 84 91 90 45; mairiederioz@wanadoo.fr]** Site off D5 in vill of Rioz. Med, some hdg pitch, some hdstg, pt shd; htd wc; baby facs; shwrs inc; el pnts (6A) €2.40; gas; shops 500m; rests in vill; playgrnd; pool adj; dogs €1.50; quiet. "Site yourself, warden calls; v friendly; gd facs; pool free to campers; friendly vill." 1 Apr-30 Sep. € 10.40   2007*

RIOZ *6G2* (7km S Rural) **Camping L'Esplanade, Rue du Pont, 70190 Cromary [03 84 91 82 00 or 03 84 91 85 84 (LS); benttom@hotmail.com; www.lesplanade.nl]** Fr S on N57 take D14 E thro Devecey. At Vielley turn L onto D412. Site on L over rv. Fr N on N57 by-pass Rioz & take slip rd onto D15 sp Sorans. Turn L in vill, pass under N57 to They, then foll sp Cromary & site. Sm, hdg/mkd pitch, pt shd; wc (some cont); chem disp; shwrs inc; el pnts (4-8A) €2.10-3.10; lndtte; ice; shop 3km; tradsmn; snacks; BBQ; playgrnd; rv sw adj; 40% statics; dogs €0.50; Eng spkn; adv bkg; quiet; cc acc. "Welcoming Dutch owners; well-kept site." ♦ ltd. 1 Apr-30 Nov. € 10.30   2007*

RIQUEWIHR see Ribeauville *6E3*

RISCLE *8E2* (500m N Urban) **FFCC Camp Municipal Le Pont de l'Adour, 32400 Riscle [05 62 69 72 45 or 06 08 55 36 89 (mob); fax 05 62 69 72 45; camping.dupondeladour@wanadoo.fr]** On ent Riscle fr N on D935, site on L immed after x-ing Rv Adour. Med, pt shd, hdg pitch; wc (some cont); chem disp; mv service pnt; shwrs inc; el pnts (5-6A) inc; lndtte; ice; shop; rest; snacks; pool adj; playgrnd; entmnt; TV; dogs €1.52; quiet; red low ssn; CCI. "V quiet low ssn with slightly scruffy san facs - but v hot water." ♦ ltd. 1 Apr-15 Oct. € 15.00   2006*

RIVIERE SAAS ET GOURBY see Dax *8E1*

RIVIERE SUR TARN *10E1* (Rural) **Camping du Moulin de la Galinière, Boyne, 12640 Rivière-sur-Tarn [05 65 62 65 60 or 05 65 62 61 81; fax 05 65 62 69 84; moulindelagaliniere@wanadoo.fr; www.moulindelagaliniere.com]** Exit A75 junc 44.1 La Gamasse onto D29 & foll sp Gorges du Tarn. Site ent bef Boyne vill, other side of bdge to Camping Le Pont, bef R turn. Site on bank Rv Tarn. Med, pt shd; wc; baby facs; shwrs inc; el pnts (6A) €3; lndtte; ice; shops adj; snacks; playgrnd; shgl beach; rv sw; fishing (permit req'd); birdwatching; dogs €1; quiet. "Excel, v clean facs, poss tired low ssn; no hand-rail up steps to san facs; no lights on site low ssn; pleasant owner." 1 Jul-31 Aug. € 12.00   2006*

RIVIERE SUR TARN *10E1* (Rural) **FFCC Camping Le Pont, Boyne, 12640 Rivière-sur-Tarn [05 65 62 61 12]** Fr Millau head N on N9, R after 7km onto D907 sp Gorges du Tarn, site in 9km on R on ent to vill. Sm, pt shd; wc (some cont); chem disp; mv service pnt; shwrs inc; el pnts (6A) €2.50; lndry rm; shops, rest adj; playgrnd; sw pool 2km; rv sw & fishing adj; dogs €1; quiet; CCI. "Gd base for Tarn gorges; canoeing & climbing nrby; facs dated but spotlessly clean; helpful owner has tourist info; excel." 1 Jun-30 Sep. € 9.00   2006*

France

RIVIERE SUR TARN *10E1* (2km E Rural) **FLOWER Camping Le Peyrelade, Route des Gorges du Tarn, 12640 Rivière-sur-Tarn [05 65 62 62 54; fax 05 65 62 65 61; campingpeyrelade@wanadoo.fr; www.campingpeyrelade.com]** Exit A75 junc 44.1 to Aguessac, then take D907 N thro Rivière-sur-Tarn to site in 2km. Fr Millau drive N on N9 to Aguessac, then onto D907 thro Rivière-sur-Tarn, & site sp on R. Lge, hdg/mkd pitch, terr, shd; wc; chem disp; mv service pnt; baby facs; shwrs inc; el pnts (6A) €3; gas; lndtte; shop; tradsmn; rest; snacks; bar; BBQ; playgrnd; htd pool; rv beach & sw adj; canoeing; games rm; cycle hire 100m; entmnt; child entmnt; TV; dogs €2; adv bkg; quiet; cc acc; red low ssn; CCI. "Excel touring base in interesting area." ♦ 15 May-15 Sep. € 24.00
2006*

> There aren't many sites open this early in the year. We'd better phone ahead to check that the one we're heading for is actually open.

RIVIERE SUR TARN *10E1* (2km SE Rural) **Camping Le Papillon, Les Canals, 12640 La Cresse [tel/fax 05 65 59 08 42; canal2@wanadoo.fr; http://campsitelepapillon.monsite.wanadoo.fr]** Fr N on A75 exit junc 44.1 onto D29 dir Aguessac. Cross rv & take D187 N, site in 1.5km on R. Sm, hdg/mkd pitch, terr, shd, pt shd; htd wc; chem disp; baby facs; fam bthrm; shwrs inc; el pnts (10A) €3; gas; lndtte; ice; shop; tradsmn; rest; snacks; bar; BBQ (not charcoal); sm playgrnd; rv sw 150m; entmnt; TV; 5% statics; dogs €1; Eng spkn; adv bkg (dep req); quiet; red 30+ days; CCI."Quiet & pleasant; vg." 25 Apr-3 Oct. € 14.50
2005*

RIVIERE SUR TARN *10E1* (SW Rural) **Camping Les Peupliers, Rue de la Combe, 12640 Rivière-sur-Tarn [05 65 59 85 17; fax 05 65 61 09 03; lespeupliers12640@wanadoo.fr; www.camping lespeupliers.fr]** Heading N on N9 turn R dir Aguessac onto D907 twd Rivière-sur-Tarn. Site on R bef vill. Or fr A75 exit junc 44.1 sp Aguessac/Gorges du Tarn. In Aguessac, foll sp Rivière-sur-Tarn for 5km, site clearly sp. NB Take care speed humps bet main rd & site. Med, hdg/mkd pitch, some hdstg, pt shd; wc (some cont); chem disp; mv service pnt; baby facs; shwrs inc; el pt (6A) €4; gas; lndtte; ice; shop 200m; tradsmn; rest; snacks, bar high ssn; BBQ; playgrnd; pool; waterslide; rv sw & shgl beach adj; fishing; canoeing; watersports; horseriding; games area; entmnt; child entmnt; wifi internet; TV rm; some statics; dogs €2.50; phone; Eng spkn; adv bkg (rec high ssn); quiet; red low ssn; cc acc; CCI. "Beautiful, peaceful, well-run site; busy low ssn; lge, well-shaded pitches, but some sm pitches diff lge o'fits; spotless san facs; excel pool area; friendly staff; beavers in rv; superb." ♦ 1 Apr-30 Sep. € 24.00 (CChq acc)
2007*

ROANNE *9A1* (12km S Rural) **Camping Le Mars, 42123 Cordelle [tel/fax 04 77 64 94 42; baznew@wanadoo.fr]** On D56 fr Roanne foll dir Lac Villarest; cross barrage & site 4.5km S of Cordelle well sp just off D56. Fr junc 70 on N7 to St Cyr-de-Favières. Foll sp to Château de la Roche on D17 & site on D56. Fr S take D56 immed after Balbigny; single track app, with restricted visibility. Or fr N82 exit for Neulise onto D26 to Jodard, then D56 twd Cordelle. Site on L in 11km. Med, pt sl, terr, pt shd, hdg pitch; wc; chem disp; serviced pitch; mv service pnt; shwrs; child/baby facs; el pnts (6A) inc; lndtte; ice; shop; tradsmn; snacks; bar; playgrnd; pool; lake sw, fishing & watersports 500m; mini-golf; entmnts; 40% statics; Eng spkn; adv bkg rec high ssn; quiet; red long stay; CCI. "Peaceful; lovely views; poss run down, scruffy low ssn." ♦ ltd. 2 Apr-30 Sep. € 19.50
2005*

ROANNE *9A1* (5km SW Rural) **Camping L'Orée du Lac, Le Barrage, 42300 Villerest [tel/fax 04 77 69 60 88; camping@loreedulac.net; www.loreedulac.net]** Take D53 SW fr Roanne to Villerest; site sp in vill. Sm, mkd pitch, pt sl, pt shd; wc; chem disp (wc); shwrs inc; el pnts (6A) €2.80; ice; shop 400m; rest; bar; playgrnd; pool; rv 300m; lake 100m; fishing; watersports; mini-golf; entmnt; TV; dogs €1.50; phone; adv bkg rec high ssn; quiet; CCI. "Attractive site; nr medieval vill; gd local wine." Easter-30 Sep. € 11.60
2006*

ROCAMADOUR *7D3* (1km E Rural) **Camping Les Cigales, L'Hospitalet, Route de Rignac, 46500 Rocamadour [05 65 33 64 44; fax 05 65 33 69 60; camping.cigales@wanadoo.fr; www.camping-cigales.com]** Fr N on D840 (N140) Brive-Gramat turn W on D36 approx 5.5km bef Gramat; in 3km site on R at L'Hospitalet. Med, mkd pitch, shd; wc (some cont); chem disp; mv service pnt; baby facs; shwrs inc; el pnts (6A) €3; gas; lndtte; shop; rest; snacks; bar; playgrnd; pool & paddling pool; rv, canoeing 10km; mini-golf; games rm; entmnt; TV; dogs €2; adv bkg dep & booking fee req; CCI. "Busy, family site; facs poss stretched; gd pool." ♦ 1 Apr-31 Oct. € 15.50
2007*

ROCAMADOUR *7D3* (1km E Rural) **Le Relais du Campeur, L'Hospitalet, 46500 Rocamadour [05 65 33 63 28; fax 05 65 10 68 21; contact@relais-du-campeur.com; www.relais-du-campeur.com]** Fr S exit D820 (N20) (Brive-la-Gaillarde to Cahors) at Payrac; R on D673, 21km to L'Hospitalet. Fr N exit D820 at Cressensac for D840 (N140) to Figeac & Rodez; turn R at D673; site at x-rds after 4km; site behind grocer's shop on L. Avoid app fr W & coming thro Rocamadour (acute hair-pin & rd 2.2m wide). Med, pt sl, pt shd; wc (some cont); shwrs inc; el pnts (6A) €2.50; gas; ice; shops; tradsmn; BBQ; playgrnd; pool; cycling; sailing; dogs €1; adv bkg; quiet; cc acc. "Ideal for Rocamadour (walking); friendly recep; dated facs, insufficient high ssn; gd rests adj; vg." 1 Apr-30 Sep. € 11.00
2007*

ROCAMADOUR *7D3* (1km NW Rural) **FFCC Aire Naturelle (Branche), Route de Souillac, 46500 Rocamadour** [05 65 33 63 37] Site on D247, 1km N of Rocamadour. Sm, pt shd; wc; (some cont); mv service pnt; shwrs inc; el pnts (6A) €1.80; lndtte; shop 1km; BBQ; playgrnd; dogs; phone; quiet. "Lovely, open site; gd, clean facs; spacious; friendly; easy walk to Rocamadour; gd for dogs; gd value." 1 Apr-15 Nov. € 6.60   2007*

Did you know you can fill in site report forms on the Club's website — www.caravanclub.co.uk?

ROCHE BERNARD, LA *2G3* (500m S Urban) **Camp Municipal Le Pâtis, Chemin du Patis, 56130 La Roche-Bernard** [02 99 90 60 13 or 02 99 90 60 51 (Mairie); fax 02 99 90 88 28; mairie-lrb@wanadoo.fr; www.camping-larochebernard.com] Leave N165 junc 17 (fr N) junc 15 (fr S) & foll marina sp. Med, mkd pitch, hdstg, pt shd; wc; chem disp; mv service pnt; shwrs inc; el pnts (6A) €3; lndtte; ice; shops & snacks 500m; playgrnd; pool 1km; sand beach 1km; rv adj; sailing, boating at marina adj; dogs €1; m'van o'night area; poss cr; Eng spkn; adv bkg; quiet but some rd noise; red low ssn; cc acc. "Lovely & conv location; excel clean site; v helpful staff; facs poss stretched high ssn; grass pitches poss v soft; heavy o'fits phone ahead in wet weather; recep 0830-1130 & 1600-1800, pitch self & pay am; beautiful sm town; Thurs mkt day - do not exit/arr." ♦ 1 Apr-30 Sep. € 10.00
2007*

ROCHE CHALAIS, LA *7C2* (500m S Rural) **Camp Municipal Gerbes, Rue de la Dronne, 24490 La Roche-Chalais** [05 53 91 40 65; fax 05 53 90 32 01; camping.la.roche.chalais@wanadoo.fr] Fr S on D674 turn sharp L in vill at site sp. Site on R in 500m. Fr N take Coutras-Libourne rd thro vill; site sp on L beyond sm indus est. Med, mkd pitch, terr, pt shd; wc; shwrs inc; el pnts (5-10A) €2.20-3.20; ice; lndtte; tradsmn; shops 500m; playgrnd; pool, tennis, cinema 800m; rv sw, fishing, boating & canoeing adj; leisure pk 5km; poss cr; adv bkg; rlwy & factory noise; CCI. "Pleasant, clean & well-run site; day free per week; farm produce avail; spotless san facs; some terr plots leading down to rv; pitch N-side of site to avoid factory noise/smell; sh rvside walks; vg value; excel; rec." ♦ 15 Apr-30 Sep. € 7.10   2006*

ROCHE DE GLUN, LA see Valence *9C2*

ROCHE DES ARNAUDS, LA see Veynes *9D3*

ROCHE POSAY, LA *4H2* (1.5km N Rural) **Camp Municipal Le Riveau, Route de Lésigny. 86270 La Roche-Posay** [05 49 86 21 23] Fr both E & W take new by-pass around N of town on D725; turn N onto D5; foll 'Hippodrome & Camping' sp; site on R 100m after D5/D725 junc; avoid town cent. Fr S bear L in town bef arch & foll sp. Lge, hdg/mkd pitch, shd; htd wc; mv service pnt; shwrs inc; el pnts (16A) inc (check pol); gas; lndtte; ice; shops 1km; rest; snacks; bar; BBQ (gas/elec); playgrnd; pool; rv sw & fishing 1.5km; tennis; cycle hire; entmnt; 10% statics; poss cr; Eng spkn; adv bkg; quiet; red long stay; CCI. "Excel, popular site; well-maintained; 1st class facs; barrier locks automatically 2300; parking avail outside; gd rests nrby; spa town." ♦ 31 Mar-22 Oct. € 15.20
2005*

ROCHE POSAY, LA *4H2* (3km E Rural) **Camp Municipal Les Bords de Creuse, Rue de la Baignade, 37290 Yzeures-sur-Creuse** [02 47 94 48 32 or 02 47 94 55 01 (Mairie); fax 02 47 94 43 32] Fr Châtellerault take D725 E twds La Roche-Posay; after x-ing Rv Creuse, turn L onto D750 twds Yzeures-sur-Creuse; at traff lts in vill turn S onto D104; site on R in 200m at T-junc. Med, pt sl, pt shd; wc; chem disp; shwrs inc; el pnts (10A) inc; lndtte; shops, pool, rv sw; tennis adj. ♦ 15 Jun-31 Aug.   2005*

ROCHE SUR YON, LA *2H4* (8km S Rural) **Camping La Venise du Bocage, Le Chaillot, 85310 Nesmy** [tel/fax 02 51 98 01 20; contact@la-venise-du-bocage.com; www.la-venise-du-bocage.com] Fr N take D747 dir La Tranche-sur-Mer. Take D36 twd Nesmy & site sp on R after 500m. Sm, mkd pitch, pt shd; wc (some cont); chem disp; baby facs; shwrs inc; el pnts (6-10A) €2.80-3.70; lndtte; shop, rest, bar 3km; playgrnd; pool; tennis; horseriding; golf 3km; 25% statics; dogs €1.50; phone; poss cr; adv bkg; quiet; red low ssn. "Helpful, friendly owner; many games/sports avail." ♦ 1 Apr-30 Sep. € 10.60
2006*

ROCHEBRUNE *9D3* (S Rural) **Camping Les Trois Lacs, Les Plantiers, 05190 Rochebrune** [04 92 54 41 52; fax 04 92 54 16 14; direction@campingles3lacs.com; www.campingles3lacs.com] On D900b fr Serre-Ponçon to Tallard, 2km after Espinasses turn L onto D951 & look for site sp. Turn R onto D56 after x-ing Rv Durance. Site on R in 2km. Sm, mkd/hdstg pitch, pt sl, shd; wc (some cont); chem disp; baby facs; shwrs inc; el pnts (2-6A) €2.50-4.70; gas; lndtte; ice; shop 5km & supmkt 8km; tradsmn high ssn; rest; snacks; bar; playgrnd; lake sw adj; fishing; tennis nrby; paragliding; go-karting; entmnt; 20% statics; dogs €3; poss cr; adv bkg; quiet; red long stay/low ssn; cc acc high ssn only; CCI. "Site among pine trees, poss diff for lge o'fits; lake access via security gate. ♦ 1 Apr-30 Oct. € 15.00   2007*

France

ROCHECHOUART *7B3* (3km S Rural) **Camp Municipal Lac de Bois Chenu, 87600 Rochechouart [05 55 03 65 96]** S fr Rochechouart on D675. Turn R onto D10 them immed L by lake into park. Site ent at far end of park by snack bar. Med, mkd pitch, pt sl, terr, shd; wc; shwrs; el pnts (5A) inc (long cable req some pitches); gas; shops 3km; rest adj; lake sw; 10% statics; poss cr; adv bkg; quiet. "Shady site in v nice area; open plan under trees, o'looking lake; poss busy w/e due to fishing; basic, clean san facs; ltd facs low ssn & could be cleaner (Sep 2007)." 1 Jun-15 Sep. € 10.80   2007*

ROCHECHOUART *7B3* (4km SW Rural) **Camping des Lacs, Le Guerlie, 16150 Pressignac [05 45 31 17 80; fax 05 56 70 15 01; aquitaine@relaisoleil.com;www.relaisoleil.com/pressignac]** W fr Rochechouart on D161, then D160 dir La Guerlie & lake. Lge, hdg/mkd pitch, terr, pt shd; wc; chem disp; mv service pnt; el pnts (10A) €3.70; gas; lndtte; ice; sm shop & 4km; rest 100m; bar; playgrnd; 2 pools (1 htd, covrd); paddling pool; lake sw 500m; watersports; games area; games rm; wifi internet; entmnt; 5% statics; dogs €3.15; adv bkg; Eng spkn; cc acc; red low ssn; CCI. "Peaceful site; superb walking; excel touring base." ♦ 28 Jun-30 Aug. € 20.20   2007*

See advertisement

⊞**ROCHECHOUART** *7B3* (13km SW Rural) **Camping Chez Rambaud, 87440 Les Salles-Lavauguyon [05 55 00 08 90; fax 05 55 00 08 90; camping@chez-rambaud.com; www.chez-rambaud.com]** Fr Rochechouart on D10 to Verneuil, turn L sp Les Salles-Lavauguyon for 2km. Sm, hdg/mkd pitch, pt sl, pt shd; htd wc; chem disp; shwrs inc; el pnts (10A) inc; lndtte; ice; shop 2km; rest, snacks & bar 1km; BBQ; lake sw & sand beach 10km; dogs €1.50; Eng spkn; adv bkg; no cc acc; CCI. "Queit, CL-type site in National Park with lovely views over wooded valley; enthusiastic, friendly & helpful British owners; gd base for region; gd walking & cycling; horseriding & kayaking nrby; extensive site library; easy walk to vill; quite a way to shops; Richard The Lion Heart rte in vill; mkt in Rochechouart Sat; excel." ♦ ltd. € 14.50   2007*

ROCHECHOUART *7B3* (6km NW Rural) **Camp Municipal, Rue de Collège, 16150 Chabanais [05 45 89 03 99 (Mairie); fax 05 45 89 13 83]** D54/D29 NW fr Rochechouart to Chabanais. Sp fr town cent. Sm, pt shd; htd wc; shwrs inc; el pnts (16A) €2.30; shop, rest, snacks, bar 200m; rv adj. 15 Jun-15 Sep. € 4.40   2004*

ROCHEFORT *7B1* (1.5km N Coastal) **Camping Le Bateau, Rue des Pêcheurs d'Islande, 17300 Rochefort [05 46 99 41 00; fax 05 46 99 91 65; lebateau@wanadoo.fr; www.campinglebateau.com]** Exit A837/E602 at junc 31 & take D733 dir Rochefort. At 1st rndabt by McDonalds, take D733 dir Royan. At next rndabt 1st R onto Rue des Pêcheurs d'Islande. Site at end of rd on L. Med, hdg pitch, pt shd; wc; chem disp; shwrs inc; el pnts (8A) inc; lndtte; shop; tradsmn; rest; snacks; bar; playgrnd; pool; waterslide; watersports; fishing; tennis; games rm; entmnt; 25% statics; dogs €1.70; quiet; CCI. "Helpful staff; no twin-axles; lovely location o'looking estuary; ideal touring base; gd cycling, walking; easy access to Rochefort on bikes." Jan-Oct. € 17.00   2005*

ROCHEFORT *7B1* (8km W Coastal) **Camp Municipal de la Garenne, Ave de l'Ile-Madame, 17730 Port-des-Barques [05 46 84 80 66 or 06 08 57 08 75 (mob); fax 05 46 84 98 33; camping@ville-portdesbarques.fr; http://pages perso-orange.fr/recard/camping/]** Fr Rochefort S on D137, cross Rv Charente bdge & take 1st exit sp Soubise & Ile Madame. Cont strt thro Port-des-Barques, site on L opp causeway to Ile Madame. Lge, mkd pitch, unshd; wc; chem disp; mv service pnt; baby facs; shwrs inc; el pnts (10A) €3.20; lndtte; shop 1km; rest 500m; snacks; bar 1km; playgrnd; htd pool; sand/shgl beach adj; 25% statics; dogs €0.95; phone; bus adj; poss cr; adv bkg; quiet; cc acc; CCI. "Pleasant site; lge pitches; v clean facs." ♦ ltd. 15 Mar-15 Oct. € 10.30   2006*

ROCHEFORT EN TERRE 2F3 (600m Rural) **Camping du Moulin Neuf, Chemin de Bogeais, Route de Limerzel, 56220 Rochefort-en-Terre [02 97 43 37 52; fax 02 97 43 35 45]** Fr Redon W on D775 twd Vannes, approx 23km turn R onto D774 sp Rochefort-en-Terre at rlwy x-ing; immed after vill limit sp, turn sharp L up slope to ent; avoid vill. Med, hdg/mkd pitch, terr, pt sl, pt shd; mv service pnt; wc; chem disp; shwrs inc; el pnts ltd (10A) €4.50 (check rev pol); lndtte; ice; shops in vill; tradsmn; rest nr; BBQ; play area; htd pool high ssn; lake beach & sw 500m; some statics; dogs €3; poss cr; adv bkg; quiet; cc acc; CCI. "Well-run; peaceful base for touring area; easy walk to lovely town; no vehicle movements 2200-0700; British owners strictly maintain site; no twin-axles." ♦ ltd. 13 May-13 Sep. € 20.60   2007*

ROCHEFORT EN TERRE 2F3 (8km NE) **Camp Municipal La Digue, 56200 St Martin-sur-Oust [02 99 91 55 76 or 02 99 91 49 45; fax 02 99 91 42 94; st-martin-oust@wanadoo.fr]** On D873 14km N of Redon at Gacilly, turn W onto D777 twd Rochefort-en-Terre; site sp in 10km in St Martin. Med, pt shd; wc; shwrs; el pnts (3-5A) €2.20; lndtte; ice; shops adj; BBQ; playgrnd; rv fishing 50m; dogs €0.30; adv bkg; quiet. "Towpath walks to vill & shops; clean facs but ltd low ssn; well-maintained site; site yourself, warden calls am & eve." 1 May-30 Sep. € 6.70   2006*

ROCHEFORT MONTAGNE see Mont Dore, Le 7B4

ROCHEFORT SUR NENON see Dole 6H2

ROCHEFOUCAULD, LA 7B2 (500m N Urban) **Camping des Flots, 16110 La Rochefoucauld [05 45 63 10 72 or 06 81 28 28 45 (mob); fax 05 45 62 14 55]** Foll camping sp on app to Rochefoucauld; site next to rv. Sm, shd; wc (cont); chem disp; shwrs inc; el pnts €1.50; shops 500m in town; playgrnd; pool & tennis 300m; rv fishing 200m; adv bkg; quiet; CCI. "Site run by fire brigade, use adj phone to ring fire stn for site key if no-one on site; pitch near recep as other end adj to sewage plant; excel clean san facs; chateau & cloisters worth visit." 15 May-15 Sep. € 6.50   2004*

⊞**ROCHEFOUCAULD, LA** 7B2 (6km E Rural) **Camping La Rose Blanche (Gannicott), 16110 Yvrac-et-Malleyrand [tel/fax 05 45 63 07 56; gannicott@wanadoo.fr]** Take D13 E fr La Rochefoucauld, after 7km turn R onto D62 sp Malleyrand. Site in vill cent L past fire hydrant 100m. Sm, hdstg, pt sl, unshd; wc; chem disp; shwrs inc; el pnts (16A) inc; BBQ; lake sw nr; dogs (on lead only); adv bkg; quiet. "V friendly, helpful British owners; phone ahead rec; CL-type site with vg views; vg san facs." € 15.00   2007*

ROCHELLE, LA 7A1 (Urban/Coastal) **Camp Municipal Le Soleil, Ave Marillac, 17000 La Rochelle [05 46 44 42 53 or 05 46 51 51 25 (Mairie)]** App La Rochelle on N11, prepare to take L turn sp Port des Minimes when 2 lge concrete water towers come into view. Foll Port des Minimes to rlwy stn (clock tower). Turn R for site over mini-rndabt then L, then L again onto Quai Georges Simenon. Turn L onto Rue Sénac de Meilan, then turn onto Ave Michel Crépeau, site on L, sp. Or fr S on N137 take D937 sp Port des Minimes & rest as above. Lge, mkd pitch, unshd, some hdstg; wc; chem disp; mv service pnt adj; shwrs inc; el pnts (6A) €3.20; shops 1km; tradsmn; BBQ area; beach 1km; some Eng spkn; adv bkg; some noise fr rd & port; CCI. "Easy walking dist cent La Rochelle & lge new yachting marina; sm pitches, facs basic; ltd space for tourers; free m'van o'night area immed opp camp ent; daily cover'd mkt in town; site poss full by 1400 - rec arr early; NH only." 15 May-15 Sep. € 10.75   2006*

Did you know you can fill in site report forms on the Club's website — www.caravanclub.co.uk?

ROCHELLE, LA 7A1 (12km N Rural/Coastal) **Camp Municipal Les Misottes, Rue de l'Océan, 17137 Esnandes [05 46 35 04 07 or 05 46 01 32 13 (Mairie); lesmisottes@yahoo.fr; www.campinglesmisottes.blogspot.com]** Fr N on D938 or N1327 turn W at Marans onto D105. In 7.5km turn S onto D9 then D202 to Esnandes. Enter vill, at x-rds strt, site on R in 200m adj Maison de la Mytiliculture. Fr La Rochelle D105 N to cent Esnandes, site sp. Med, mkd pitch, pt shd; wc; shwrs inc; el pnts (10A) €2.80; lndtte; shops 500m; rest, bar 200m; snacks; playgrnd; pool; shgl beach 2km; canal fishing; 5% statics; dogs €1.60; Eng spkn; adv bkg; quiet; CCI. "Vg; liable to flood." 10 Apr-10 Oct. € 7.50   2007*

ROCHELLE, LA 7A1 (3km S Coastal) **Camping de la Plage, La Lizotière, 66 Route de la Plage, 17440 Aytré [05 46 44 19 33; fax 05 46 45 78 21; contact@campingdelaplage17.com; www.campingdelaplage17.com]** S fr La Rochelle on N137 twd Rochefort; take exit sp Aytré & head for coast rd. Med, shd; wc; baby facs; shwrs inc; el pnts (6A) €3.50; lndtte; snacks; playgrnd; htd, covrd pool; sand beach adj; games area; entmnt; some statics; dogs €2; poss cr; quiet. "Some sm pitches; gd cycling." 1 Feb-30 Nov. € 17.00   2006*

Les Chirats-La Platère ★★★

Tel: 00 33.5.46.56.94.16 - Fax: 00 33.5.46.56.65.95
Owner: Marc Nadeau • Web: www.campingleschirats.fr

Campsite Les Chirats-La Platère is situated at 8 km of La Rochelle, at 100 m of a small sandy beach and at 3 km of the big beaches of Aytré and Châtelaillon. It has all modern facilities that one can expect to find on a 3 star campsite. You can enjoy the pleasures of several swimming pools with water slide with free entry for all ages. The sports and health centre (hammam, sauna, jacuzzi, solarium, heated swimming pool) as well as the 18 holes mini golf course have paid access. Angoulins sur mer has a wonderful micro climate that will provide your vacation with lots of sunshine. The village is situated in the heart of a wonderful holiday region (La Rochelle, Le Marais Poitevin, Rochefort, Saintes, Cognac and the islands of Ré and Oléron). The big playing area is situated directly on the seaside: on the top of the cliffs one can oversee the natural harbour of the Basque area (Fouras, Île d'Aix, Fort Boyard and Fort Enet). 4 hectares, 230 pitches. Tents, caravans, camping-cars, rental of chalets / Plane, grassy, lighted/ Electricity/ Hot showers, facilities equipped for disabled people / Restaurant, bar, grocery store, snacks/ TV/ Animations/ Fishing/ horse riding at 1 km/ Tennis at 0,5 Km/ Open from 01.04 till 30.09

ROCHELLE, LA *7A1* (8km S Coastal) **Camping Les Chirats-La Platère, Route de la Platère, 17690 Angoulins-sur-Mer** [05 46 56 94 16; fax 05 46 56 65 95; contact@campingleschirats.fr; www.campingleschirats.fr] Turn off N137 S of La Rochelle & go thro Angoulins-sur-Mer. Foll site sp fr vill N twd Aytré. After 300m turn L across rlwy at stn. Foll sp 'plage' & site. Lge, hdg/mkd pitch, hdstg, pt sl, pt shd; wc (some cont); chem disp; sauna; serviced pitches; shwrs inc; el pnts (6-10A) inc; gas; lndtte; shop & 2km; tradsmn; rest; snacks; bar; playgrnd; pools (1 htd, covrd); paddling pool; waterslide; jacuzzi; sand beach adj; fishing; fitness rm; games area; horseriding 1km; tennis 500m; TV rm; 10% statics; dogs €2.30; phone; poss cr; Eng spkn; adv bkg; quiet; cc acc; CCI. "Gd facs; well-run extended site; aquarium worth a visit." ♦ Easter-30 Sep. € 23.50   2007*

See advertisement above

⊞**ROCHELLE, LA** *7A1* (2km W) **Camp Municipal de Port Neuf, Blvd Aristide Rondeau, Port Neuf, 17000 La Rochelle** [05 46 43 81 20 or 05 46 51 51 25 (Mairie)] On ring rd fr N on N11 turn R onto N237 sp Ile-de-Ré, after sp to city cent, foll sp 'Pont Neuf & Ile-de-Ré' & site. Well sp on promenade rd on N side of harbour. If app fr airport side take care to avoid Ile-de-Ré tollbooth. Lge, some hdstg, pt shd; wc; chem disp; baby facs; shwrs inc; el pnts (6-16A) €3.90-4.50 (poss rev pol); gas; lndttes nr; pool 2km; sand beach 1.5km; dogs €2.25; bus; poss cr; Eng spkn; rd noise; red low ssn; CCI. "Busy, poss shabby site; clean facs but poss ltd low ssn; phone ahead to check open low ssn; office open 0900-1200 & 1700-1900 - some parking along rd adj football pitch; min stay 2 nights high ssn; m'vans not allowed in old part of town; cycle path along seafront to old town; bus stop on 1-way system; walking dist to lovely beach." € 11.20   2007*

ROCHELLE, LA *7A1* (3km NW) **Camp Municipal Le Parc, Rue du Parc, 17140 Lagord** [05 46 67 61 54 or 05 46 00 62 12 (Mairie); fax 05 46 00 62 01; contact@marie-lagord.fr] On ring-rd round NW of La Rochelle, take exit for Lagord onto D105. Ignore 2 sps to site & take 3rd L (sharp turn). Pass sm rndabt & turn R in 100m, site on L, well sp. Fr N take sp to Lagord. At Lagord ignore 1st sp & go to rndabt sign. Turn L at mini rndabt & R at traff lts, site 50m on L. Med, hdg/mkd pitch, pt shd; wc; chem disp; shwrs inc; el pnts (3-10A) €2.20-4.30 (poss rev pol); lndtte; supmkt 2km; BBQ (gas only); playgrnd; beach 4km; few statics; dogs €1.10; bus; Eng spkn; adv bkg; quiet; CCI. "Gd facs & pitches; red facs low ssn; v helpful staff; conv Ile de Ré; conv bus & cycle path to La Rochelle; twin axles extra charge; excel." ♦ 1 Jun-29 Sep. € 8.15   2007*

ROCHELLE, LA *7A1* (5km NW Rural) **Camping au Petit Port de l'Houmeau, Rue des Sartières, 17137 L'Houmeau** [05 46 50 90 82; fax 05 46 50 01 33; info@aupetitport.com; www.aupetitport.com] On ring rd N237 twd Ile-de-Ré, take exit Lagord, across rndabt, after 300m turn R onto D104 to L'Houmeau. At T-junc in L'Houmeau turn R on D106, at 2nd boulangerie turn L & foll 1-way system/sp 'camping' thro vill (modern housing est). Site on L immed after sharp R-hand bend. Med, hdg/mkd pitch, hdstg; shd; wc; chem disp; mv service pnt; baby facs; shwrs inc; el pnts (5-10A) €3.50-4.20; lndtte; ice; shops 800m; bar; BBQ (gas); playgrnd; shgl beach 1.5km; cycle hire; games rm; dogs €2; bus nr; poss cr; Eng spkn; adv bkg rec; quiet; red low ssn; cc acc; CCI. "Pleasant, friendly site; walking dist of boulangerie & rest; helpful owners; no vehicle access 2200-0800; lovely cycling fr site; vg." ♦ 30 Mar-30 Sep. € 16.00   2007*

See advertisement opposite

ROCHETTE, LA (SAVOIE) *9B3* (2km S Rural) **Camp Municipal Le Lac St Clair, Chemin de la Plaine, 73110 Détrier [04 79 25 73 55 or 04 79 25 50 32 (Mairie); fax 04 79 25 50 32; larochettesavoie.mairie@wanadoo.fr]** Exit A41 at Pontcharra junc 22; foll D925 NE sp La Rochette & Albertville. Take 1st sp turn to La Rochette on R. Pass supmkt & boating pool. Site 300m on R. Med, pt sl, pt shd; wc (some cont); baby facs; shwrs inc; baby facs; el pnts (5-10A) €2.50; ice; lndtte; shop; tradsmn; bar; children's pool adj; playgrnd; cycle hire; some statics; poss cr; dogs €0.95; some rd noise. "Gd base for W Alps." ♦ ltd. 1 Jun-30 Sep. € 11.95   2005*

⊞**ROCROI** *5C1* (3km SE Rural) **Camping La Murée, Rue Catherine-de-Clèves, 08230 Bourg-Fidèle [tel/fax 03 24 54 24 45]** Site sp fr Rocroi on R. Sm, some hdstg, pt shd; wc; chem disp; shwrs inc; el pnts (10A) €3.80; lndtte; shops 3km; rest; bar; playgrnd; lake sw 4km; 40% statics; dogs €1.60; some Eng spkn; adv bkg; quiet; cc acc; CCI. "Two lakes on site for fishing; pleasant site; gd sh stay/NH." ♦ € 16.00   2005*

> The opening dates and prices on this campsite have changed. I'll send a site report form to the editor for the next edition of the guide.

⊞**ROCROI** *5C1* (8km SE) **Camp Départemental du Lac des Vieilles Forges, 08500 Les Mazures [tel/fax 03 24 24 40 17 31]** Fr Rocroi take D1 & D988 for Les Mazures/Renwez. Turn R D40 at sp Les Vieilles Forges. Site on R nr lakeside with lake views fr some pitches. Lge, mkd pitch, hdstg, pt sl, shd; wc; shwrs inc; el pnts (6-10A) €2.50-4.30; lndtte; ice; shop; tradsmn; snacks; playgrnd; shgl beach by lake; boating, fishing & sw; tennis; cycle hire; entmnts high ssn; TV; 20% statics; dogs €1; poss cr; adv bkg; quiet. "Attractive walks; tennis & watersports lessons avail; vg site." ♦ € 9.30
2005*

ROCROI *5C1* (S Urban) **Camp Municipal Les Remparts, Ave du Général de Gaulle, 08230 Rocroi [03 24 54 10 22 (Mairie)]** Fr N foll N51 thro town over bdge, site sp in 200m to R bef junc; site R 200m fr sp. Site outside town wall, v sm sp at rndabt. Sm, pt sl, pt shd; wc; shwrs; el pnts (10A) €3 (check rev pol & earth); lndry rm; shops 500m; quiet; CCI. "Pleasant sm town nr for meals & shops; ground v soft after heavy rain; poss itinerants; no twin-axles." 1 May-15 Sep. € 6.00   2004*

RODEZ *7D4* (1km NE Urban) **Camp Municipal de Layoule, 12000 Rodez [05 65 67 09 52; fax 05 65 67 11 43; contact@mairie-rodez.fr; www.mairie-rodez.fr]** Clearly sp in Rodez town cent & all app rds. Access at bottom steep hill thro residential area. Med, hdg/mkd pitches, hdstg, pt shd; wc (poss cont only low ssn); chem disp; mv service pnt; shwrs inc; el pnts (6A) €3; lndry rm; shop 1km; tradsmn; playgrnd; pool, golf, tennis nrby; no statics; no dogs; phone; quiet; CCI. "Ideal for exploring Cévennes; adj rv with footpath; clean facs; helpful warden; historic town of interest; 20-25 min steep walk town cent with gd shops & numerous rests; gates clsd 2000-0700; 2 exits fr site, one uphill & poss v diff; excel." ♦ 1 Jun-30 Sep. € 12.00 (3 persons)   2007*

ROESCHWOOG *5D3* (Rural) **Camping du Staedly, 30 Rue de l'Etang, 67480 Roeschwoog [03 88 86 42 18]** Fr traff lts in cent of Roeschwoog go W sp Luttenheim twd rlwy stn, cross rlwy turn L immed to site. Med, mkd pitch, pt shd; htd wc; chem disp; shwrs inc; el pnts (6A) €3.10; gas; snacks; bar; shop & 1.5km; lake sw; many statics; adv bkg; noisy Fri & Sat (bar). "Cars parked outside." 1 Apr-31 Oct. € 9.00   2005*

ROMAGNE SOUS MONTFAUCON see Dun sur Meuse *5C1*

France

ROMANS SUR ISERE *9C2* (10km N Rural) **FFCC Camping Les Falquets, Route de Margès, 26260 Charmes-sur-l'Herbasse [04 75 45 75 57 or 04 75 45 27 44 (LS); fax 04 75 45 66 17; info@ lesfalquets.com; www.lesfalquets.com]** Exit A7 junc 13 onto D532 to Romans-sur-Isère. At Curson turn N onto D67 to Charmes, then D121 dir Margès. Site sp in vill. Med, pt shd; wc (some cont); chem disp; shwrs inc; el pnts (6-10A) €2.80-3.50 (poss rev pol); lndtte; ice; shop 3km; tradsmn; bar; playgrnd; lake sw, waterslide, windsurfing & tennis 3km; 25% statics; dogs free; phone; Eng spkn; adv bkg rec high ssn; quiet; CCI. "Pleasant, well-kept, country site; old facs but clean; helpful warden; sm rv on 1 side; red squirrels; gd rest in St Donat; gd." ♦ 1 May-2 Sep. € 12.00   2007*

ROMANS SUR ISERE *9C2* (3km NE Rural) **Camp Municipal des Chasses, 26100 Romans-sur-Isère [04 75 72 35 27]** Fr W take D532 thro town, then D1092 (N92), at sp for airport turn L, sp fr Thors. Fr E take A49, then D1092 (N92), turn R at airport rndabt. Sm, hdg pitch, pt shd; wc (mainly cont); chem disp; mv service pnt; shwrs inc; el pnts (6-10A) €2.56-3.30 (poss rev pol); ice; gas; lndtte; sm shop; supmkt 1km; tradsmn; bar; pool 2km; tennis; 10% statics; dogs €1.10; phone; Eng spkn; adv bkg rec; quiet; CCI. "Fantastic views of Vercors mountains; friendly staff; sm private airport adj (no night flights); lax security." ♦ ltd. 1 Apr-15 Oct. € 7.80   2007*

ROMANSWILLER see Wasselonne *6E3*

ROMIEU, LA *8E2* (Rural) **Le Camp de Florence, 32480 La Romieu [05 62 28 15 58; fax 05 62 28 20 04; info@lecampdeflorence.com; www.lecampdeflorence.com]** Take D931 N fr Condom & turn R onto D41, where La Romieu sp next to radio mast. Go thro La Romieu & turn L at sp just bef leaving vill. Lge, hdg pitch, some hdstg, pt shd; wc; chem disp; mv service pnt; baby facs; shwrs inc; el pnts (6A) inc (poss rev pol); lndtte; shops in vill; tradsmn; rest in 16thC farmhouse; snacks; bar; BBQ; playgrnd; pool; paddling pool; waterslide; jacuzzi; leisure complex 500m; tennis; cycle hire; games area; archery; clay pigeon-shooting; wifi internet; entmnt, excursions high ssn; TV/games rm; many statics; dogs €2.10; Eng spkn; adv bkg ess; quiet; red low ssn; cc acc; CCI. "Lovely, peaceful Dutch-run site; helpful, friendly staff; gd size pitches poss muddy wet weather, most with views; clean facs; some noise fr disco, ask for pitch away fr bar; facs some dist fr touring pitches; nice pool but take care sl ent; sh walk to historic La Romieu & Arboretum Coursiana; mkt Wed Condom." ♦ 1 Apr-11 Oct. € 30.90 (CChq acc) ABS - D19   2007*

⊞**ROMILLY SUR SEINE** *4E4* (4km W Rural) **Camping La Noue des Rois, Chemin des Brayes, 10100 St Hilaire-sous-Romilly [03 25 24 41 60; fax 03 25 24 34 18; michele.desmont@wanadoo. fr; www.lanouedesrois.com]** Site sp fr D619 (N19), on rvside. Med, mkd pitch, pt shd; htd wc; mv service pnt; baby facs; shwrs; el pnts (16A) €3.50-5; gas; lndtte; shop; tradsmn; rest; bar; playgrnd; htd, covrd pool; paddling pool; waterslide; fishing; sailing; watersports; tennis; games area; entmnt; 10% statics; dogs (on lead) €3; Eng spkn; adv bkg; quiet; cc acc; red long stay; CCI. "Gd situation in lovely wooded area; conv Paris & Disneyland." ♦ € 19.00   2007*

ROMORANTIN LANTHENAY *4G2* (E Urban) **Camping de Tournefeuille, Rue de Long-Eaton, 41200 Romorantin-Lanthenay [02 54 76 16 60; fax 02 54 76 00 34; camping.romo@wanadoo. fr; www.ethicetapes-romorantin.com]** Fr town cent on D724 to Salbis, foll sp thro several traff lts over bdge turn R into Rue de Long-Eaton, sp. Med, pt shd; htd wc; shwrs inc; el pnts (6A) €2.50; gas; ice; shop 500m; snacks; pool adj; playgrnd; fishing; cycle hire; quiet. "Rv walk to town rec; office closed 1130-1700 but code is req for barriers. NB: May close earlier in ssn if quiet." 1 Apr-30 Sep. € 13.00 (3 persons)   2007*

RONCE LES BAINS see Tremblade, La *7B1*

RONDE, LA see Courçon *7A2*

ROQUE D'ANTHERON, LA see Cadenet *10E3*

⊞**ROQUE ESCLAPON, LA** *10E4* (Rural) **Camp Municipal Notre Dame, Quartier Notre Dame, 83840 La Roque-Esclapon [04 94 76 83 18 or 04 94 50 40 50 (Mairie); fax 04 94 50 40 51]** Fr Castellane, take N85 for approx 14km & turn R onto D21 twd Comps-sur-Artuby. Turn L at sp for La Roque-Esclapon & foll sp to site. Sm, pt sl, pt shd; htd wc; chem disp; shwrs inc; el pnts (6A) €3; ice; lndtte; shop, rest, bar 500m; BBQ; pool; playgrnd; tennis; games area; 65% statics; dogs €2; phone adj; poss cr; quiet; CCI. "Gd site in scenic area; gd for walks." € 8.40   2005*

ROQUE GAGEAC, LA see Sarlat la Canéda *7C3*

ROQUEBRUN *10F1* (Rural) **Camp Municipal Le Nice, Rue du Temps Libre, 34460 Roquebrun [04 67 89 61 99 or 04 67 89 79 97; fax 04 67 89 78 15; otroquebrun@bechamail.com]** N112 to St Chinian & take D20 dir Cessenon-sur-Orb, turn L onto D14 twd Roquebrun; site on L bef bdge over rv. Sm, mkd pitch, some hdstg, pt sl, terr, pt shd; wc (some cont); chem disp; mv service pnt; shwrs inc; el pnts (6A) €2.20; lndtte; ice; shops, rest, snack, bar 1km; playgrnd; rv sw & shgl beach adj; rv sw, fishing, sailing, canoe hire adj; tennis; entmnt; 15% statics; dogs €1.30; phone; poss cr; adv bkg; quiet; cc acc; CCI. "Excel cent for walking & cycling; beautiful scenery; ltd touring pitches." 1 Mar-30 Nov. € 12.00   2006*

ROQUEBRUNE SUR ARGENS see Fréjus *10F4*

ROQUEFORT *8E2* (2.5km S Rural) **Camp Municipal, Route de Pau, 40120 Sarbazan [05 58 45 64 93 (Mairie); fax 05 58 45 69 91]** Fr Roquefort take D934 S twd Villeneuve-de-Marsan & Pau. In 2km camp sp on L in Sarbazan. Sm, mkd pitch, pt sl, shd; wc (some cont); shwrs inc; el pnts (5A) €1.60-2.40; lndtte; shops 2.5km; tradsmn; BBQ; playgrnd; tennis; dogs; quiet; red low ssn; CCI. "Peaceful, friendly; site yourself, warden calls am & pm; dated san facs; sports cent/health club adj; highly rec." ♦ ltd. 1 Apr-30 Oct. € 9.00   2006*

ROQUELAURE see Auch *8F3*

ROQUES see Toulouse *8F3*

ROQUETTE SUR SIAGNE, LA see Cannes *10F4*

ROSANS *9D3* (1.5km N Rural) **Camping Tamier Naturiste (Naturist), Route du Col de Pomerol, 05150 Tamier [04 92 66 61 55 or 04 92 87 47 24 (LS); fax 04 92 87 47 24; tamier@wanadoo.fr; www.alpes-campings.com]** On D94/D994 Serres to Nyons rd, turn N onto D25 at Rosans. Site sp in vill. Med, mkd pitch, terr, pt shd; wc; chem disp; shwrs inc; el pnts (6A) inc; lndtte; ice; shop; tradsmn; rest; snacks; bar; playgrnd; pool; some statics; adv bkg; quiet. "Wonderful scenery; v friendly owners; v steep access rd; suggest park in upper car park nr ent bef going to recep." 1 May-15 Sep. € 19.65   2004*

ROSANS *9D3* (4km W Rural) **Aire Naturelle Le Gessy (Cagossi), 26510 Verclause [tel/fax 04 75 27 80 39 or 06 84 14 69 01 (mob); legessy@hotmail.com]** Site sp fr vill; 2km up steep, narr, winding rd. Sm, hdstg, sl, terr, pt shd; wc; chem disp (wc); shwrs inc; el pnts (6-10A) €2.50; supmkt & rest 2km; snacks; playgrnd; pool; 10% statics; dogs €2; Eng spkn; adv bkg; quiet; CCI. "Spacious pitches; wonderful views of Southern Alps; Dutch owner; vg." 1 Apr-15 Oct. € 12.50   2006*

ROSCANVEL *2E1* (500m S Coastal) **Camp Municipal Le Kervian, Route du Camping, 29570 Roscanvel [02 98 27 43 23 or 02 98 27 48 51 (Mairie); fax 02 98 27 41 10]** Fr Crozon foll D355 dir Le Fret/Roscanvel. After Le Fret x-rds foll Municipal sp. Turn L just bef Roscanvel. Sm, mkd pitch, terr, unshd; wc (some cont); chem disp (wc); shwrs inc; el pnts (10A) €3.18; gas 1km; lndry rm; shop & bar 1km; tradsmn; playgrnd; sand beach 800m; horseriding nrby; some statics; dogs €1.06; phone adj; Eng spkn; quiet; cc not acc; CCI. "Panoramic views across valley to sea; gd." 15 Jun-15 Sep. € 8.00   2006*

ROSCOFF *1D2* (7km SW Coastal/Rural) **Camp Municipal du Bois de la Palud, 29250 Plougoulm [02 98 29 81 82 or 02 98 29 90 76 (Mairie); mairie-de-plougoulm@wanadoo.fr]** Fr D58 turn W on D10 sp Cléder/Plouescat; after 3km on ent Plougoulm foll sp to site. Sm, hdg/mkd pitch, terr, pt shd; wc; chem disp; shwrs inc; el pnts (6A) €3; lndry rm; shop 800m; sand beach 500m; playgrnd; phone; some Eng spkn; adv bkg; quiet; CCI. "If arr late, site yourself; warden calls am & pm; clean, tidy site; recep 0930-1030 & 1745-1845; conv ferry; sh walk to vill; excel." ♦ ltd 15 Jun-15 Sep. € 11.00   2007*

ROSCOFF *1D2* (10km SW Coastal) **Camping Village de Roguennic, 29233 Cléder [02 98 69 63 88; fax 02 98 61 95 45; semcleder@wanadoo.fr; www.campingvillageroguennic.com]** Fr D10 bet St Pol-de-Léon & Lesneven, take coast rd at either Plouescat or Cléder, foll Camping sp twd sea. Site sp. Lge, mkd pitch, pt sl, pt shd; wc; mv service pnt; shwrs inc; el pnts (6A) €2.15; gas; lndtte; shop, rest, snacks, bar (high ssn); playgrnd; htd pool (high ssn); sand beach; tennis; games area; sailing school nr; entment; statics sep area; dogs €1; phone; bus; adv bkg; quiet; cc acc; CCI. "Big holiday vill, lovely early ssn; direct access to fine sand beach." ♦ 1 May-15 Sep. € 13.10   2006*

ROSCOFF *1D2* (3.5km W) **Camping des Quatre Saisons (formerly Camp Municipal de Perharidy), Perharidy, Le Ruguel, 29680 Roscoff [02 98 69 70 86; fax 02 98 61 15 74; camping.roscoff@wanadoo.fr; www.camping-aux4saisons.com]** Fr dock foll exit & camping sps; at rndbt exit N on D169 twd cent ville; in 800m turn W dir Santec, foll camping sps, pass travellers' site. Lge, hdg pitch, unshd; wc; chem disp; shwrs inc; baby facs; el pnts (4-8A) €2.50-4; lndtte; ice; shops 2km; BBQ; playgrnd; sand beach; windsurfing; fishing; sailing; entmnt; dogs €1; poss cr; adv bkg rec high ssn; red low ssn; quiet. "Will open low ssn if bkd in adv; conv for ferry; cheap & cheerful." ♦ 1 Apr-14 Oct. € 12.20   2006*

ROSIERS SUR LOIRE, LES *4G1* (1km N Rural) **Camping Val de Loire, 6 Rue Ste Baudruche, 49350 Les Rosiers-sur-Loire [02 41 51 94 33; fax 02 41 51 89 13; contact@camping-valdeloire.com; www.camping-valdeloire.com]** Take D952 fr Saumur in dir Angers. Site on D59 1km N vill cent on L dir Beaufort-en-Vallée. Med, hdg/mkd pitch, hdstg, pt shd; wc; chem disp; mv service pnt; baby facs; 50% serviced pitch; shwrs inc; el pnts (10A) €4; gas; lndtte; ice; tradsmn; rest; snacks; bar; BBQ; playgrnd; htd pool; paddling pool; lake sw 15km; waterslide; tennis; games rm; internet; entmnt; TV rm; 15% statics; dogs; Eng spkn; adv bkg; quiet; red long stay/low ssn; CCI. "Close to Rv Loire; gd touring base for chateaux & Loire region; friendly & helpful staff; lge pitches; excel facs." ♦ 1 Apr-30 Sep. € 20.00   2007*

See advertisement on next page

France

ROSIERS SUR LOIRE, LES *4G1* (1km S Urban) Camping Le Bord de Loire, Ave Cadets-de-Saumur, 49350 Gennes [02 41 38 04 67 or 02 41 38 07 30; fax 02 41 38 07 12; auborddeloire@free.fr; www.cfp-gennes.com] At Rv Loire bdge cross S to Gennes on D751B. Site on L. Ent to site thro bus terminus/stop on ent to Gennes. Lge, mkd pitch, pt sl, pt shd; wc (some cont); chem disp; shwrs; el pnts (10A) €2.50; lndry rm; rest; bar; shop in vill; playgrnd; htd pool in vill; dogs €0.60; rd noise; CCI. "Well-maintained site; excel san facs." 1 May-30 Sep. € 7.50   2005*

Before we move on, I'm going to fill in some site report forms and post them off to the editor, otherwise they won't arrive in time for the deadline at the end of September.

ROSIERS SUR LOIRE, LES *4G1* (6km NW) Camp Municipal Port St Maur, 49250 La Ménitré [02 41 45 60 80; fax 02 41 45 65 65; info@loiredelumiere.com] Exit Les Rosiers on D952 sp Angers. Site on L by rv. Med, mkd pitch, pt shd; wc; shwrs inc; el pnts (5A); lndtte; shops 1km; rest; snacks; bar; playgrnd; games area; entmnt; boat trips on Loire; some rd & rlwy noise. "Access to san facs by steps; height barrier at ent; helpful warden." ♦ 1 Jun-15 Sep.   2004*

⊞**ROSNAY** *4H2* (500m N Rural) Camp Municipal Les Millots, Route de St Michel-en-Brenne, 36300 Rosnay [02 54 37 80 17 (Mairie); fax 02 54 37 02 86; rosnay-mairie@wanadoo.fr] NE on D27 fr Le Blanc to Rosnay; site sp 500m N of Rosnay on D44. Med, some mkd pitch, pt shd; htd wc; chem disp; baby facs; shwrs inc; el pnts (3-6A) €1.90-3.20 (rev pol); lndry rm; rest & shop 500m; BBQ; playgrnd; fishing; cycling; tennis; dogs; phone; poss cr; adv bkg; quiet; CCI. "Lovely, well-kept, tranquil site by lake; populer; excel, clean san facs; warden collects fees twice daily; superb area for bird-watching; lakeside walks in National Park; excel." ♦ € 7.50   2007*

ROSPORDEN *2F2* (1km N Urban) Camp Municipal de Roz an Duc, Route de Coray, 29140 Rosporden [02 98 59 90 27 or 02 98 66 99 00 (Mairie); fax 02 98 59 92 00; mairie.rosporden@oleane.fr] At Rosporden, take D36 N dir Châteauneuf-du-Faou. Site in leisure complex 500m fr rlwy stn. Sm, hdg/mkd pitch, pt sl, terr, pt shd; wc; chem disp; shwrs inc; el pnts (3-6A) €2.30 (rev pol); gas; lndtte; shop, rest, snacks, bar in town; tradsmn; playgrnd; pool, tennis 100m; sand & shgl beach 15km; dogs €0.55; phone; poss cr; adv bkg; quiet; CCI. "Vg, well laid-out site; excel facs; conv to shops, etc." ♦ 13 Jun-4 Sep. € 8.00   2005*

ROSPORDEN *2F2* (12km NE Rural) Camp Municipal de Kérisole, Rue Pasteur, 29390 Scaër [02 98 59 42 10 or 02 98 57 60 91; fax 02 98 57 66 89; mairie.scaer@altica.com; www.ville-scaer.fr] Fr N165 take D70 to Rosporden, then N on D782, well sp in Scaër. Thro town foll sp to site. Med, mkd pitch, pt shd; wc; chem disp; mv service pnt; baby facs; shwrs; el pnts (13A) €2.60; lndtte; ice; shop; tradsmn; rest; snacks; bar 250m; playgrnd; pool; few statics; dogs; phone; Eng spkn; adv bkg; quiet; CCI. "This is a gem at ent to forest with mkd walks; vill has great rests; excel san facs." ♦ 15 Jun-15 Sep. € 8.10   2004*

ROSPORDEN *2F2* (8km W) Camp Municipal du Bois de Pleuven, 29140 St Yvi [02 98 94 70 47; www.village-center.com] Site sp fr Rosporden-Quimper D765, or Concarneau-Quimper D783. Turn S at St Yvi & turn R at x-rds; foll site sp. Lge, mkd pitch, shd; wc; baby facs; shwrs inc; el pnts (6A) inc; gas; lndtte; ice; shop; snacks; bar; playgrnd; htd pool; beach 5km; tennis; mini-golf; cycle hire; entmnt; TV rm; 90% statics; dogs €0.50; adv bkg; red low ssn; quiet. "Site in woodland." 1 Apr-15 Oct. € 20.00   2007*

⊞ROSTRENEN *2E2* (2km S Rural) **Camping Fleur de Bretagne, Kerandouaron, 22110 Rostrenen** [02 96 29 15 45; fax 02 96 29 16 45; info@fleurdebretagne.com; www.fleurdebretagne.com] Fr Rostrenen town cent foll dir Intermarché & take next R turn sp D31 Silfiac. In approx 1km turn L, site sp. Med, mkd pitch, pt sl, terr, pt shd; wc; chem disp; mv service pnt; shwrs inc; el pnts (6A) €3.50; lndry rm; shop 2km; snacks; bar; BBQ; playgrnd; pool; fishing lake; watersports, horseriding nr; dogs €1; phone; Eng spkn; adv bkg; quiet; red long stay; CCI. "V helpful British owners; wooded walks; ltd opening Nov-Mar - phone ahead." ♦ € 12.00   2005*

> There aren't many sites open this early in the year. We'd better phone ahead to check that the one we're heading for is actually open.

⊞ROUEN *3C2* (4km N Urban) **Camp Municipal, Rue Jules Ferry, 76250 Déville-lès-Rouen** [02 35 74 07 59] Fr Rouen take N15 N twd Dieppe (avoid); in Déville turn L at traff lts immed after Hôtel de Ville, foll sp to site. Fr Le Havre at Barentin, turn R onto old N15, thro Maromme, turn R after 3 traff lts. Med, unshd, gravel pitch; wc; chem disp; mv service pnt; shwrs inc; el pnts (10A) €2.15; supmkt 500m; playgrnd; pool 300m; some statics; dogs €0.90; poss cr; adv bkg; some noise fr adj factory & rd. "Excel bus service to Rouen; facs need update & poss tired/unclean; narr pitches; site office clsd Sat, Sun, local & national holidays; poss mkt traders on site; phone ahead to check site open low ssn." € 11.35   2007*

⊞ROUEN *3C2* (6km E) **Camping L'Aubette, 23 Rue du Vert Buisson, 76160 St Léger-du-Bourg-Denis** [tel/fax 02 35 08 47 69] Fr N31 Darnétal dir Beauvais. Site well sp as 'Camping' fr Rouen cent. Med, pt sl, terr, pt shd; wc (mainly cont); shwrs €1.60; el pnts (3-10A) €1.50-5; shops 400m; sw pool in Rouen; 50% statics; poss cr. "Helpful, friendly staff; basic facs; most pitches sl & muddy when wet; poss untidy low ssn; extra charge for m'van water tank fill-up; in attractive rv valley; conv city cent; arrange with owner if req to leave early; NH only." € 9.10   2007*

ROUFFACH *6F3* (S Urban) **Camp Municipal, 68250 Rouffach** [03 89 49 78 13; fax 03 89 78 03 09] On N83 S fr Colmar bet Colmar & Cernay. Sm, pt shd; wc; chem disp; shwrs €1.50; el pnts (4A) inc; lndry rm; shop 500m; cc not acc; CCI. "Clean site at start Alsace wine rte; ring bell on wall nr san facs block for warden; sh walk to town cent; vg NH." Easter-30 Sep. € 8.90   2004*

ROUFFIGNAC *7C3* (300m N) **Camping Bleu Soleil, Domaine Touvent, 24580 Rouffignac** [05 53 05 48 30; fax 05 53 05 27 87; infos@bleusoleil.com; www.camping-bleusoleil.com] On D6 in Rouffignac, take D31 NE twd Thenon. Site clearly sp on R after 300m. Med, hdg/mkd pitch, pt sl, terr, pt shd; wc; chem disp; 75% serviced pitches; shwrs inc; el pnts (6-10A) €2.90; lndtte; ice; shop; tradsmn; rest, snacks & bar high ssn; BBQ; playgrnd; htd pool; tennis; games rm; TV rm; 10% statics; dogs €1.50; phone; Eng spkn; adv bkg (dep req); quiet; red low ssn; cc acc; CCI. "Amazing views & scenery; relaxing site; v friendly, helpful owners; ltd facs low ssn; caves nrby; poss diff for lge o'fits; pretty vill; excel." ♦ ltd. 1 Apr-30 Sep. € 16.10   2007*

ROUFFIGNAC *7C3* (6km SW Rural) **Camping Le Coteau de l'Herm (Naturist), 24580 Rouffignac** [05 53 46 67 77; fax 05 53 05 74 87; info@naturisme-dordogne.com; www.naturisme-dordogne.com] Fr N89 (E70) 1.5km fr Thenon twd Périgueux, take D31 sp Rouffignac & Château de l'Herm, site well sp. In approx 10km turn R & after 3km site on L. Sm, mkd pitch, terr, pt sl, pt shd; htd wc; chem disp; shwrs inc; el pnts (4-10A) €3.20-4.20; gas; ice; lndtte; shop; tradsmn; bar; snacks; BBQ; playgrnd; pool; cycle hire; dogs €3; quiet; adv bkg (dep req, bkg fee); Eng spkn; red 14 days; CCI. "Excel naturist site; excel facs; gd access; helpful Dutch owners; prehistoric sites; delightful location." 15 May-16 Sep. € 21.00   2006*

ROUSSET, LE *9A2* (Rural) **Camping du Lac de Rousset, 71220 Le Rousset** [03 85 24 68 74; fax 03 85 24 68 00] Fr Montceau-les-Mines S on D980; in 10 km turn R onto D33; well sp. Sm, mdk pitch, pt sl, pt shd; wc, chem disp; shwrs inc; el pnts (6A) €2; snacks (high ssn); playgrnd; lake sand shore adj; no statics; quiet; CCI. "Lakeside, CL-type site in beautiful location; basic facs; fair." 3 Mar-10 Oct. € 9.00   2007*

ROUSSILLON *10E2* (2.5km SW Rural) **Camping L'Arc-en-Ciel, Route de Goult, 84220 Roussillon** [04 90 05 73 96] Take N100 W out of Apt, then R on D201 sp Roussillon, then R on D4 for 1.5km, then L on D104 twd Roussillon. Take L fork twd Goult, site well sp 2.5km on L. No access for c'vans & m'vans in Roussillon vill. Med, mkd pitch, hdstg, terr, pt shd; wc; chem disp; serviced pitch; shwrs inc; el pnts (4-6A) inc; gas; lndtte; ice; sm shop & 2.5km (uphill); tradsmn; snacks; playgrnd; children's pool; phone; adv bkg; quiet; CCI. "V helpful staff; tranquil, gd value site in old wooded ochre quarry; full of character; beware rd humps & drainage channels on site access rds; v quiet; lovely vills within easy reach; worth a detour." ♦ 15 Mar-31 Oct. € 11.90   2004*

ROYAN *7B1* (Coastal) **Camping Les Catalpas, 45 Chemin d'Enlias, 17110 St Georges-de-Didonne** [05 46 05 84 97 or 04 99 57 20 25; fax 04 99 57 21 22; catalpas@village-center.com; www.village-center.com/catalpas] Site sp in St Georges-de-Didonne. Med, mkd pitch, pt shd; wc; chem disp; baby facs; shwrs; el pnts (6A) inc; gas; lndtte; ice; shop; tradsmn; supmkt 500m; rest; snacks; bar; playgrnd; htd pool; sand beach 1.5km; entmnt; 7% statics; dogs €3; Eng spkn; adv bkg; quiet. ♦ 28 Apr-16 Sep. € 23.00   2007*

ROYAN *7B1* (6km NE Rural) **FFCC Camping Le Bois Roland, 82 Route de Royan, 17600 Médis** [tel/fax 05 46 05 47 58; bois.roland@wanadoo.fr; www.le-bois-roland.com] On N150 Saintes-Royan rd, site sp on R 100m beyond Médis vill sp. Med, pt shd; wc (some cont); chem disp; shwrs inc; el pnts (5A) €4; gas; ice; lndtte; ice; shop & 600m; tradsmn; snacks; bar; playgrnd; pool; sand beach 4km; entmnt; TV; dogs €2.50; phone; poss cr; adv bkg; Eng spkn; quiet; cc acc; CCI. "Attractive wooded site; family-run; friendly; facs poss stretched high ssn; barrier key €10 dep; vg." ♦ 1 May-30 Sep. € 17.00   2006*

ROYAN *7B1* (5km E Rural) **Camping Le Clos Fleuri, 8 Impasse du Clos Fleuri, 17600 Médis** [05 46 05 62 17; fax 05 46 06 75 61; clos-fleuri@wanadoo.fr; www.le-clos-fleuri.com] On N150 Saintes-Royan rd turn S in Médis twd Semussac. Well sp. Med, pt sl, shd; wc; baby facs; sauna; shwrs inc; el pnts (5-10A) €4.40-5.60; lndtte; shop in ssn & 6km; tradsmn; rest, snacks & bar in ssn; playgrnd; pool; sand beach 4km; games area; mini-golf; entmnt; TV; some statics; dogs €3.30; Eng spkn; adv bkg (dep req); quiet; cc acc; red low ssn; CCI. "Peaceful, family-run site; lge indiv pitches; san facs clean but dated; rec for young families; access poss diff lge o'fits; nr local air field; excel." ♦ 1 Jun-15 Sep. € 25.50   2007*

⊞**ROYAN** *7B1* (2km SE Coastal) **Camping La Triloterie, 44 ter, Ave Aliénor d'Aquitaine, 17200 Royan** [05 46 05 26 91; fax 05 46 06 20 74; triloterie@iroyan.com; www.iroyan.com/triloterie] Fr Royan PO, foll sp Bordeaux N730, on E of rd. Med, shd; htd wc; chem disp (wc); baby facs; shwrs inc; el pnts (4-12A) €3-5 (poss rev pol); shops 500m; waterslide; sand beach 900m; dogs €1; phone; poss cr/noisy high ssn; some rd noise; red low ssn. € 16.00   2006*

ROYAN *7B1* (4km SE Coastal) **Camping Idéal, Ave de Suzac, 17110 St Georges-de-Didonne** [05 46 05 29 04; fax 05 46 06 32 36; info@ideal-camping.com; www.ideal-camping.com] Fr Royan foll coast rd sp St Georges-de-Didonne. Site sp on D25 2km S of St Georges. Lge, mkd pitch, shd; wc (some cont); chem disp; shwrs inc; el pnts (6-10A) €4-4.80; gas; ice; lndtte; shop; tradsmn; rest; snacks; bar; playgrnd; pool; paddling pool; waterslide; jacuzzi; sand beach 200m; tennis 500m; games area; games rm; cycle hire; horseriding 300m; entmnt; phone; no dogs; poss noisy (bar); cc acc; red low ssn; CCI. ♦ 28 Apr-9 Sep. € 24.50 (3 persons)   2007*

ROYAN *7B1* (8km SE Coastal) **Camping Bois-Soleil, 2 Ave de Suzac, 17110 St Georges-de-Didonne** [05 46 05 05 94; fax 05 46 06 27 43; camping.bois.soleil@wanadoo.fr; www.bois-soleil.com] Fr A10 exit junc 35 dir Saintes & Royan. Fr Royan foll seafront rd to S thro St Georges-de-Didonne, where rd turns inland, turn R in 100m sp Meschers. In 500m turn R into Ave Suzac & site ent on R, but recep on L. Site well sp. Lge, hdg/mkd pitch, hdstg, terr, pt shd; htd wc (some cont); chem disp; mv service pnt; baby facs; shwrs inc; el pnts (6A) inc (poss rev pol); gas; lndtte; ice; shop; tradsmn; rest; snacks; bar; BBQ (gas); playgrnd; htd pool; paddling pool; dir access to sand beach adj; tennis; games area; wifi internet; entmnt; child entmnt; TV rm; 30% statics; dogs €3 (not acc end Jun-Aug inc); phone; poss cr; Eng spkn; adv bkg (ess Jul/Aug); cc acc; red low ssn; CCI. "Superb wooded site in wonderful location; popular/busy; 3 sep areas to site low ssn; pitches sm & poss tight for lge o'fits; excel, clean san facs; vg shop & rest; war-time bunkers nrby; gd value." ♦ 4 Apr-2 Nov. € 34.00 (3 persons) (CChq acc)   2007*

See advertisement

ROYAN *7B1* (10km SE) **Camping Soleil Levant, Allée de la Langée, 17132 Meschers-sur-Gironde** [05 46 02 76 62; fax 05 46 02 50 56; soleil.levant.ribes@wanadoo.fr; www.les-campings.com/camping-soleillevant] Take D145 coast rd fr Royan to Talmont. At Meschers turn R foll camp sp twd port; sp. Med, pt shd; wc (some cont); chem disp; shwrs inc; el pnts (10A) €4.50; gas 1km; lndtte; ice; snacks; bar; shop; playgrnd; sand beach 1.5km; free pool & paddling pool; watersports & horseriding adj; 20% statics; dogs €2.90; adv bkg; quiet; cc acc; CCI. "Gd, busy site; sm pitches, some diff to get into; port & rest 300m; vill shop & daily mkt 500m; visits to Cognac & Bordeaux distilleries." 1 Apr-30 Sep. € 16.90   2007*

France

ROYAN 7B1 (2km NW Urban) **Camping Le Royan, 10 Rue des Bleuets, 17200 Royan** [05 46 39 09 06; fax 05 46 38 12 05; camping.le.royan@wanadoo.fr; www.le-royan.com] Take D25 by-pass fr Royan dir La Palmyre. Site sp. Lge, mkd pitch, hdstg, pt sl, pt shd; wc (some cont); chem disp; mv service pnt; baby facs; some serviced pitches; shwrs inc; el pnts (10A) inc; gas; Indtte; ice; shop; rest; snacks; bar; BBQ; playgrnd; htd pool; paddling pool; waterslide; spa; sand beach 2.5km; lake sw 3km; solarium; games area; games rm; cycle hire; entmnt; child entmnt; TV; 25% statics; dogs €3; poss cr; adv bkg; quiet; cc acc; red low ssn/long stay/CCI. "Friendly, helpful owners; excel pool complex." ♦ 1 Apr-10 Oct. € 30.50 (3 persons)   2006*

ROYAN 7B1 (4km NW Urban/Coastal) **Camping Clairefontaine, Allée des Peupliers, Pontaillac, 17200 Royan** [05 46 39 08 11; fax 05 46 38 13 79; camping.clairefontaine@wanadoo.fr; www.camping-clairefontaine.com] Foll Pontaillac sp fr Royan. Site sp in Clairefontaine (& Pontaillac). Lge, mkd pitch, pt shd; wc (some cont); chem disp; mv service pnt; fam bthrm; serviced pitches; shwrs inc; el pnts (5A) €4; gas; Indtte; tradsmn; ice; shop; rest; snacks; bar; BBQ; playgrnd; 2 pools; sand beach 300m; tennis; TV rm; phone; Eng spkn; adv bkg; quiet; cc acc; CCI. "Gd family holiday; site patrolled; attentive staff." ♦ 20 May-15 Sep. € 32.00 (3 persons)   2004*

ROYBON 9C2 (1km S) **Camping de Roybon (formerly Camp Municipal Aigue Noire), Route de St Antoine, 38940 Roybon** [04 76 36 23 67; fax 04 76 36 33 02; info@campingroybon.com; www.campingroybon.com] Fr Roybon go S on D71 & foll sp. Med, mkd pitch, pt sl, pt shd; wc; chem disp; shwrs inc; el pnts (6A) €3.50; shops 1km; playgrnd; sw & watersports in lake adj; dogs €2; adv bkg; quiet. "V peaceful; walks adj; facs new & on solar power; vg." ♦ 15 Apr-15 Oct. € 14.00
2006*

ROYERE DE VASSIVIERE 7B4 (6km SW Rural) **Camping Les Terrasses du Lac, Vauveix, 23460 Royère-de-Vassivière** [05 55 64 76 77; fax 05 55 64 76 78; http://lesterrasses.camping.free.fr] Fr Eymoutiers take D43 for approx 10km then take D36 to Vauveix & foll sp. Med, hdg/mkd pitch, terr, pt shd; htd wc; chem disp; shwrs inc; el pnts (10A) €3 (poss rev pol); Indtte; rest, bar 300m; snacks 500m; sand beach, sw & watersports adj; horseriding; walking; cycling; TV rm; dogs; phone 50m; quiet; CCI. "Helpful staff; lovely setting." ♦ 1 Apr-15 Oct. € 12.50   2006*

RUE 3B2 (7km N Rural) **Camping du Val d'Authie, 20 Route de Vercourt, 80120 Villers-sur-Authie** [03 22 29 92 47; fax 03 22 29 92 20; camping@valdauthie.fr; www.valdauthie.fr] Best access via Rue or via D85/D485 fr D1001 (N1). Rd fr Vron to Villers-sur-Authie is narr single track across fields. Lge, hdg/mkd pitch, pt sl, pt shd; htd wc; chem disp; mv service pnt; sauna; steam rm; shwrs inc; baby facs; el pnts (6-10A) €5-8 (rev pol); gas; Indtte; ice; shop; tradsmn; rest; snacks; bar; playgrnd; htd, covrd pool; paddling pool; sand beach 10km; tennis; games area; games rm; fitness rm; internet; entmnt; TV rm; 60% statics; dogs €1.50; phone; poss cr; Eng spkn; adv bkg; quiet but poss noise fr chalets/statics; cc acc; CCI. "Set in pleasant countryside; helpful, friendly owners; v clean, unisex facs & spacious shwrs; sep area for tourers; gd pool; poss diff for lge o'fits; v cr & noisy high ssn." ♦ 29 Mar-12 Oct. € 25.00 (3 persons) (CChq acc)   2007*

⊞**RUFFEC** *7A2* (5km NE Rural) **Camping Rural La Renardière, 16700 Taizé-Aizie [05 45 71 74 59; la-renardiere@club-internet.fr; www.la-renardiere. eu]** Fr N fr Civray on D1/D8 pass L turn sp Lizant; take next L turn (dir Le Gros Chêne) bef x-ing Rv Charente; foll sm rd up hill; site in 1km on R bef hamlet of Le Gros Chêne. Sm, some hdg/mkd pitch, hdstg, pt shd; htd wc; shwrs inc; el pnts (10A) €3.50; lndtte; ice; shop & 5km; rest, snacks & bar 2km; BBQ; playgrnd; pool; lake sw & fishing 3km; tennis; cycle hire; games area; games rm; wifi internet; dogs €1; adv bkg (dep req); quiet. "Beautiful views; vg pool; British owners; site being developed (2007)." ♦ ltd. € 10.00   2007*

RUFFEC *7A2* (3km SE Rural) **Camping Le Réjallant, Les Grands Champs, 16700 Condac [05 45 31 29 06 or 05 45 31 07 14; fax 05 45 31 34 76; cdc-ruffec-charente@wanadoo. fr]** Site sp fr N10 & fr town. App 1km fr turn-off. Med, hdg/mkd pitch, pt sl, shd; wc; chem disp (wc); shwrs inc; el pnts (10A) €2; lndtte; tradsmn; snacks; rest & bar 100m; sm playgrnd; rv sw, fishing 100m; dogs; Eng spkn; quiet; cc not acc; CCI. "Some pitches v lge; v clean facs - water poss v hot; shwrs ltd; gates open 0700-2100 high ssn; no entry/exit 1100-1600 low ssn; rv 100m; great for families." 15 May-15 Sep. € 8.10   2007*

⊞**RUFFEC** *7A2* (10km W Rural) **Camping à la Ferme (Peloquin), Chassagne, 16240 Villefagnan [05 45 31 61 47; fax 05 45 29 55 87]** Exit N10 onto D740 W to Villefagnan. Site 1.8km SE of vill on D27. Sm, pt sl, pt shd; wc; chem disp (wc); shwrs; el pnts (10A) inc; lndtte; ice; farm produce; shop, rest, snacks, bar 1.8km; playgrnd; pool high ssn; gites avail; dogs; poss cr; adv bkg; quiet. "Vg CL-type site; excel pool." ♦ ltd. € 12.50   2005*

As soon as we get home I'm going to post all these site report forms to the editor for inclusion in next year's guide. I don't want to miss the September deadline.

RUFFIEUX *9B3* (S Rural) **Camping Le Saumont, 73310 Ruffieux [04 79 54 26 26; fax 04 79 54 24 74; camping.saumont@wanadoo.fr; www.campingsaumont.com]** N fr Aix-les-Bains take D991 N to Ruffieux, sp just bef Ruffieux at junc with D904. Sm, hdg/mkd pitch, pt shd; wc; chem disp; serviced pitch; shwrs; el pnts (6-10A) €1.80-2.50; lndtte; ice; shop 1.5km; snacks; bar; BBQ; playgrnd; 2 pools (no shorts); watersports; lake & rv sw 2.5km; tennis; cycle hire; 10% statics; dogs €1.20; adv bkg; quiet; red low ssn. "Dusty rd thro site when hot & dry; muddy after rain; sm pools." Easter-30 Sep. € 13.50   2005*

RUFFIEUX *9B3* (4km W Rural) **Camping Le Colombier, Ile de Verbaou, 01350 Culoz [tel/fax 04 79 87 19 00; camping.colombier@free.fr; http://camping.colombier.free.fr]** W fr Ruffieux or N fr Belley on D904, site sp off rndabt 1km E of Culoz. Med, hdg/mkd pitch, hdstg, pt shd; wc (some cont); chem disp; mv service pnt; baby facs; shwrs inc; el pnts (10A) €3; lndtte; shop 1km; tradsmn; rest; snacks; bar; playgrnd; lake sw adj; tennis; mini-golf; cycle hire; TV; some statics; dogs €1; phone; Eng spkn; adv bkg; quiet; cc acc; red CCI. "Gd touring base; conv Annecy." ♦ 14 Apr-23 Sep. € 15.00   2007*

RUMILLY *9B3* (4km N Rural) **Camping Les Charmilles, Route de Seyssel, 74150 Vallières [04 50 62 10 60; fax 04 50 62 19 45; lescharmilles.camping@wanadoo.fr; www. campinglescharmilles.com]** Exit A41 junc 15 at Alby onto D3 to Rumilly; 4km N of Rumilly in Vallières exit D910 on D14 sp Seyssel. Site on L in 500m. Med, mkd pitch, pt shd; wc; baby facs; shwrs inc; el pnts (6A) €3.50; gas; lndtte; shops 500m; tradsmn; rest; snacks; bar; BBQ; playgrnd; pool; paddling pool; games area; entmnt; TV; dogs €1.50; phone; adv bkg; quiet; red low ssn. "Gd, modern san facs; pleasant situation." ♦ 1 Apr-30 Oct. € 15.00   2007*

RUMILLY *9B3* (5km NE Rural) **Camping à la Ferme Fleurie (André), Route de Rumilly, 74150 Marcellaz-Albanais [04 50 69 70 36]** Fr Rumilly take D16 N thro Marcellaz-Albanais. Site sp 600m past vill on rd to Annecy. Sm, pt sl, pt shd; wc; chem disp (wc); mv service pnt; shwrs inc; el pnts (5A); shop & 5km; tradsmn; playgrnd; beach 10km; no statics; quiet; adv bkg; cc not acc; CCI. "Excel activities & visits to local attractions; farm produce avail; mountain hikes; fondue nights; family atmosphere; poss diff access some pitches; service block across minor rd - poss unsuitable sm children." 15 Apr-15 Oct. € 11.80   2004*

RUOMS *9D2* (2km N Rural) **Camping Les Coudoulets, 07120 Pradons [04 75 93 94 95; fax 04 79 39 65 89; camping@coudoulets.com; www. coudoulets.com]** Site sp fr D579. Med, mkd pitch, shd; wc; chem disp; mv service pnt; shwrs inc; el pnts (6A) €3.60; lndtte; shop 300m; rest; snacks; bar; playgrnd; htd pool; rv fishing nr; games area; 5% statics; dogs €2; Eng spkn; adv bkg; quiet. "Site o'looks Rv Ardèche; v friendly, careful owners; excel pool." ♦ 1 May-8 Sep. € 20.00   2005*

⊞**RUOMS** *9D2* (1km S Rural) **FFCC Camping Le Mas du Barry, Bevennes, 07120 Ruoms [04 75 39 67 61; fax 04 75 39 76 33]** By-pass Ruoms on D579 sp Vallon-Pont-d'Arc. On D579, 100m N of junc with D111. Site on R 2km S of Ruoms. Med, mkd pitch, sl, pt shd; wc; baby facs; shwrs; el pnts (6A) inc; gas; lndtte; ice; shop; snacks; rest in ssn; bar; playgrnd; pool; some statics; poss cr; Eng spkn; adv bkg; rd noise; cc acc; CCI. "Quiet site in busy area; clean facs; helpful, welcoming manager." ♦ € 20.00   2004*

RUOMS *9D2* (3km S Rural) **Yelloh! Village La Plaine**, 07120 Ruoms [04 75 39 65 83; fax 04 75 39 74 38; camping.la.plaine@wanadoo.fr; www.camping-la-plaine.com www.yellohvillage.com] Exit Ruoms S on D579 dir Vallon-Pont-d'Arc; at junc in 2km turn S onto D111 dir St Ambroix. Site on L. Lge, mkd pitch, pt sl, pt shd; wc; baby facs; shwrs inc; el pnts (6A) inc; lndtte; ice; shop; rest; snacks; bar; BBQ; playgrnd; rv sw, fishing & private beach; dogs €5; red low ssn; CCI. 5 Apr-14 Sep. € 40.00   2007*

The opening dates and prices on this campsite have changed. I'll send a site report form to the editor for the next edition of the guide.

RUOMS *9D2* (4km SW) **Camping La Chapoulière**, 07120 Ruoms [tel/fax 04 75 39 64 98 or 04 75 93 90 72; camping@lachapouliere.com; www.lachapouliere.com] Exit Ruoms S on D579. At junc 2km S, foll D111 sp St Ambroix. Site 1.5km fr junc. Med, mkd pitch, pt sl, shd; wc; mv service pnt; baby facs; shwrs inc; el pnts (6A) €4; gas; ice; lndtte; shop in ssn & 3km; rest; snacks; bar; pool; paddling pool; rv sw & fishing adj; tennis 2km; games area; entmnts; TV; dogs €2; Eng spkn; adv bkg rec high ssn; quiet. "Beautiful pitches on rv bank; friendly; ltd facs low ssn; vg." ♦ 23 Mar-10 Sep. € 26.00   2007*

RUOMS *9D2* (7km SW) **Camping Sunêlia Le Ranc Davaine**, 07120 St Alban-Auriolles [04 75 39 60 55; fax 04 75 39 38 50; camping.ranc.davaine@wanadoo.fr; www.camping-ranc-davaine.fr] Leave A7/E15 at Montélimar/Aubenas exit, foll sp twd Aubenas on N102. Just past Villeneuve-de-Berg turn L onto D103, thro St Germain, then join D579 to Ruoms. S of Ruoms leave D579 sp Gorges de l'Ardèche & join D111 twd Grospierres. At Les Tessiers turn R onto D246, sp St Alban-Auriolles. After x-ing Rv Chassezac turn L twd Chandolas. Ignore D246 turn to R, site after this turn on R. Lge, shd; wc; chem disp; baby facs; sauna; steam rm; shwrs inc; el pnts (6-10A) inc; lndtte; shop; rest; snacks; bar; BBQ (el only); playgrnd; pool complex (inc 1 htd, covrd); waterslide; paddling pool; rv sw; fishing; tennis; archery; fitness cent; entmnt; wifi internet; games/TV rm; 75% statics; dogs €4.65; recep 0800-1930 high ssn; adv bkg; quiet; cc acc. "Helpful staff; conv Gorges de l'Ardèche; public rd divides site; excel pool complex; playgrnd with many facs; mkt St Alban Mon; guided walks." ♦ 15 Mar-14 Sep. € 41.00 (CChq acc) ABS - C16   2007*

RUSSEY, LE see Maîche *6G3*

RUYNES EN MARGERIDE *9C1* (Rural) **Camp Municipal du Petit Bois**, 15320 Ruynes-en-Margeride [tel/fax 04 71 23 42 26; info@camping-massifcentral.com; www.camping-massifcentral.com] Fr St Flour S on N9. After 7km turn L onto D4. Site in 7km, sp. Or exit junc 30 fr A75, turn R into vill & foll sp. Lge, pt sl, pt shd; wc (some cont); chem disp; mv service pnt; baby facs; shwrs inc; el pnts (6-10A) €3.50; gas; lndtte; ice; shops, rest, bar 500m; playgrnd; pool adj; some log cabins; dogs €1.50; phone; Eng spkn; adv bkg; quiet; cc acc; CCI. "Excel scenery; v few flat pitches; gd cent for walking, horseriding, fishing; used as field work cent in term time; excel san facs." ♦ 28 Apr-30 Sep. € 14.50 (CChq acc)   2007*

RUYNES EN MARGERIDE *9C1* (4km E Rural) **Camping à la Ferme (Rolland)**, 15320 Clavières [04 71 23 45 50] Fr St Flour, S on N9. After 7km turn L onto D4 thro Clavières & foll sps. Site in Chirol, foll Chirol sp. Sm, wc; shwrs inc; el pnts; farm food avail; shops 2.5km; playgrnd; rv 2.5km; pool, tennis, golf, horseriding 10km; sailing, fishing 15km; quiet. "Isolated, with beautiful views, gd facs for a basic site; long el lead req; pay at old white house in Chirol." 1 Jun-30 Sep. € 4.57   2006*

SAALES *6E3* (W Rural) **Camp Municipal Rové**, Route de la Grande Fosse, 67420 Saales [03 88 97 70 26 (Mairie); fax 03 88 97 77 39; www.mairie-saales.fr] Fr St Dié take D420 twd Strasbourg, turn onto D32 in vill. Site on R just bef football pitch, well sp. Med, pt sl, terr, pt shd; wc; chem disp; shwrs inc; el pnts inc; shop & rest 500m; tennis, fishing adj; 40% statics; quiet. "Site yourself, warden calls." ♦ ltd. 15 Jun-15 Sep.   2007*

SABLE SUR SARTHE *4F1* (10km NE Rural) **Camp Municipal des Deux Rivières**, 72430 Avoise [02 43 95 32 07 or 02 43 92 76 12; fax 02 43 95 62 48] Fr Sablé take D309 twd Le Mans, after 10km thro vill of Parcé-sur-Sarthe, cont twds Le Mans & cross bdge over Sarthe; sp for Avoise & camping sp on L, in cent Avoise on L 3rd car park. Site adj Rv Sarthe. Sm, hdg pitch, pt shd; wc; shwrs inc; el pnts inc (poss rev pol); gas; ice; shops adj; Eng spkn; adv bkg; quiet; CCI. "Pleasant, clean site, off beaten track; vg." 4 Jun-4 Sep. € 6.30   2006*

SABLE SUR SARTHE *4F1* (S Urban) **Camp Municipal de l'Hippodrome, Allée du Québec**, 72300 Sable-sur-Sarthe [02 43 95 42 61; fax 02 43 92 74 82; camping-sable@wanadoo.fr; www.sable-sur-sarthe.com] W fr town cent (dir Angers) on Rue St Denis, Ave de Montreaux & Ave de la Vaige, sp in town (foll sm, white sp with c'van symbols or Hippodrome). Med, hdg pitch, pt shd; wc; shwrs inc; el pnts (15A) €2.20; gas; ice; BBQ; lndry rm; sm shop; tradsmn; snacks; playgrnd; pool; rv fishing; boat & cycle hire; canoeing; entmnt; TV rm; Eng spkn; quiet; cc acc; red long stay/low ssn. "Excel site; gd, clean facs; helpful staff; some pitches by rv, some diff for lge fits; sh walk to town; vg value." ♦ 31 Mar-7 Oct. € 8.68   2007*

France

SABLES D'OLONNE, LES *7A1* (4km N Rural)
Camping de Sauveterre, 3 Rue des Amis de la
Nature, 85340 Olonne-sur-Mer [02 51 33 10 58;
fax 02 51 21 33 97] Fr Les Sables-d'Olonne take
D32 N to Olonne-sur-Mer; then D80 twds St Gilles-
Croix-de-Vie for 3.5km; after 2nd rndabt site is on L.
Med, mkd pitch, pt shd; wc (some cont); chem disp;
shwrs inc; el pnts (6A) €2.10; gas; ice; lndtte; shop;
rest; snacks; bar; playgrnd; pool; sand beach 3km;
many statics; dogs €1.20; poss cr; adv bkg rec high
ssn; quiet; CCI. "Poss no water points; water avail
fr sinks; site poss untidy; gd walking/cycling; conv
sandy beaches." 1 Apr-30 Sep. € 14.50   2004*

SABLES D'OLONNE, LES *7A1* (4km N Rural)
Camping Nid d'Eté, 2 Rue de la Vigne Verte, 85340
Olonne-sur-Mer [02 51 95 34 38; fax 02 51 95 34 64;
info@leniddete.com; www.leniddete.com] Fr Les
Sables-d'Olonne take D32 N to Olonne-sur-Mer. L
onto D80 twd St Gilles-Croix-de-Vie. Immed over
rlwy bdge turn L, site on L. Med, pt hdg/mkd pitch, pt
shd; wc; chem disp; baby facs; shwrs inc; el pnts (6A)
€3; lndtte; ice; shop & 2km; snacks; playgrnd; htd,
covrd pool high ssn; beach 3km; entmnt; few statics;
dogs €2; c'van winter storage; adv bkg; v quiet; CCI.
"Pleasant site; surfing at La Plage Sauveterre 4km."
1 Apr-30 Sep. € 21.50   2007*

SABLES D'OLONNE, LES *7A1* (5km N Urban)
Airotel Camping Le Trianon, 95 Rue du Maréchal
Joffre, 85340 Olonne-sur-Mer [02 51 23 61 61; fax
02 51 90 77 70; campingletrianon@free.fr; www.
camping-le-trianon.com] S on D160 La Roche-
sur-Yon twd Les Sables-d'Olonne; at Pierre Levée
turn R onto D80 sp Olonne-sur-Mer. Also sp fr D80
N. V lge, hdg/mkd pitch, pt shd, serviced pitches;
wc; chem disp; shwrs inc; el pnts (6A) inc (extra
for 10-16A); lndtte; ice; shop; rest; snacks; bar;
playgrnd; htd, covrd pool; waterslide; sand beach
5km; fishing & watersports 4km; tennis; golf; games
area; entmnt; 40% statics; dogs €3.90; poss cr; adv
bkg; quiet; red low ssn. "Pleasant situation; high
kerbs into sm pitches; friendly, helpful staff; excel
facs for families." ♦ 31 Mar-29 Sep. € 32.10   2007*

See advertisement above

SABLES D'OLONNE, LES *7A1* (5km N Coastal)
Camping La Loubine, 1 Route de la Mer,
85340 Olonne-sur-Mer [02 51 33 12 92; fax
02 51 33 12 71; camping.la.loubine@wanadoo.fr;
www.la-loubine.fr] Fr Les Sables-d'Olonne take
D32 N to Olonne-sur-Mer then D80 dir St Gilles-
Croix-de-Vie for 3.5km; turn L at junc to Plage-
de-Sauveterre; ent to site immed on L after turn.
Lge, hdg/mkd pitch, pt sl, pt shd; wc; chem disp;
serviced pitches; shwrs inc; el pnts (5A) €3.65; ice;
gas; lndtte; shop; rest; snacks; bar; playgrnd; 2 htd
pools (1 covrd); sand beach 1.8km; tennis; entmnt;
TV; 50% statics; no dogs; poss cr; Eng spkn; adv
bkg; noise fr rd & nightclub; cc acc; CCI. "Site lit
& guarded at night; lge car park for late arrivals;
excel." ♦ 5 Apr-30 Sep. € 27.00   2007*

See advertisement opposite

SABLES D'OLONNE, LES *7A1* (8km N Rural)
Camping Domaine de l'Orée, Route des Amis de
la Nature, 85340 Olonne-sur-Mer [02 51 33 10 59;
fax 02 51 33 15 16; loree@free.fr; www.l-oree.
com] Fr Les Sables-d'Olonne take D80 twd
St Gilles-Croix-de-Vie for 4km - site on L after
traff lts in Olonne-sur-Mer, well sp. Lge, hdg/mkd
pitch, pt shd; wc; baby facs; shwrs inc; el pnts (6A)
€4; gas; lndtte; ice; shop; snacks; bar; playgrnd;
htd pool; waterslide; sand beach 3km; tennis;
horseriding; cycle hire; games area; games rm;
entmnt; 90% statics; dogs €2.50; phone; Eng spkn;
adv bkg; quiet; CCI. "Pleasant walk (30-40 mins)
thro forest to vg beach; c'vans & tents for hire;
helpful owner." ♦ 1 Apr-30 Nov. € 25.00
          2007*

France

SABLES D'OLONNE, LES 7A1 (2km E Rural) Camping Le Puits Rochais, 25 Rue de Bourdigal, 85180 Château-d'Olonne [02 51 21 09 69; fax 02 51 23 62 20; bhjmp@wanadoo.com; www. puitsrochais.com] Fr Les Sables-d'Olonne take D949 twd La Rochelle. Pass rndabt with lge hypermrkt 'Magasin Géant' & turn R at 1st traff lts at Mercedes g'ge, then 1st L to site. Med, mkd pitch, pt shd; wc; chem disp; baby facs; shwrs inc; el pnts (6-10A) inc; lndtte; shop; rest; snacks; bar; BBQ; playgrnd; htd pool; paddling pool; waterslide; sand beach 2km; tennis; cycle hire; games area; games rm; entmnt; child entmnt; internet; TV; 60% statics; dogs €3.10; phone; adv bkg; quiet; cc acc; red CCI. "Friendly, welcoming site; gd for families." ♦ 1 Apr-30 Sep. € 29.95   2007*

See advertisement on next page

SABLES D'OLONNE, LES 7A1 (SE Urban/Coastal) CHADOTEL Camping Les Roses, Rue des Roses, 85100 Les Sables-d'Olonne [02 51 95 10 42 or 02 51 33 05 05 (LS); fax 02 51 33 94 04; chadotel@ wanadoo.fr; www.chadotel.com] Fr town cent foll dir Niort, turn down Blvd Ampère by Total petrol stn to Rue des Roses. Site opp trave-away cafe & adj to hospital, lying bet D949 & sea front. Lge, hdg/mkd pitch, pt shd; htd wc; chem disp; shwrs inc; el pnts (6A) inc; gas 1.5km; ice; lndtte; tradsmn; rest 500m; snacks (high ssn); bar; BBQ (gas); playgrnd; htd pool; waterslide; sand beach 500m; entmnt; cycle hire; games rm; TV rm; 70% statics; dogs €2.90; phone; poss cr; Eng spkn; adv bkg; quiet; cc acc; CCI. "Conv for town & beach; close by harbour, shops, museums, salt marshes, shuttle buses; excel." ♦ Easter-4 Nov. € 28.90   2006*

SABLES D'OLONNE, LES 7A1 (3km SE) Camping Les Fosses Rouges, La Pironnière, 85180 Château-d'Olonne [02 51 95 17 95; info@ camping-lesfossesrouges.com; www.camping-lesfossesrouges.com] Take D949 La Rochelle. At lge rndabt turn R, sp La Pironnière. Camp clearly sp on L in 1km. Lge, mkd pitch, shd; wc; shwrs inc; el pnts (10A) €3.50; gas; lndtte; shop & 500m; snacks; bar; playgrnd; htd pool; sand beach 1.5km; cycle hire; entmnt; internet; TV; 70% statics; dogs €1.30; poss cr; adv bkg; quiet; red low ssn. "Attractive site on o'skts town; interesting fishing port; some pitches poss diff lge o'fits; gd pool." ♦ 8 Apr-30 Sep. € 15.90   2007*

SABLES D'OLONNE, LES *7A1* (4km SW Coastal) **CHADOTEL Camping La Dune des Sables, La Paracou, 85100 Les Sables-d'Olonne** [02 51 32 31 21 or 02 51 33 05 05 (LS); fax 02 51 33 94 04; chadotel@wanadoo.fr; www. chadotel.com] Foll D160 to Les Sables-d'Olonne. Fr town foll sps to La Chaume & Les Dunes. Lge, mkd pitch, pt sl, unshd; htd wc; serviced pitches; shwrs inc; el pnts (6A) inc; gas; lndtte; ice; shop; snacks; bar; BBQ (gas); playgrnd; pool; waterslide; sand beach 100m; tennis; cycle hire; games rm; entmnt; 75% statics; dogs €2.90; Eng spkn; adv bkg rec high ssn; red low ssn; CCI. "Helpful warden; great for family beach holiday." ♦ Easter-24 Sep. € 28.90   2006*

SABLES D'OR LES PINS *2E3* (4km NE Coastal) **Camp Municipal Pont de l'Etang, Pléhérel-Plage, 22240 Fréhel** [02 96 41 40 45 or 02 96 41 40 12; campingfrehel:free.fr] Best app fr D786 via D34 to Sables d'Or; then D34A to Pléhérel-Plage; just N of vill, sp. Lge, pt sl, pt shd; wc; chem disp; mv service pnt; shwrs inc; el pnts (6A) €1.90; lndry rm; mobile shops in high ssn; tradsmn; snacks; playgrnd; horseriding, tennis adj; sand beach 200m; v few statics; dogs €0.70; phone; poss cr; Eng spkn; poss noisy; CCI. "Lovely natural site amongst sand dunes leading to beach; ideal for children; ltd facs low ssn; gd shops & rests in vill; gd." ♦ 1 Apr-30 Sep. € 10.71   2006*

SABLES D'OR LES PINS *2E3* (1.2km NW Coastal/Rural) **Camp Municipal La Saline, Rue du Lac, 22240 Plurien** [02 96 72 17 40 or 02 96 72 17 23 (Mairie)] Fr D786 turn N at Plurien onto D34 to Sables-d'Or. In 1km turn L & site on L after 200m. Med, pt sl, terr, pt shd; wc (some cont); chem disp; shwrs inc; el pnts (6A) €2.15; lndtte; ice; shops 500m; playgrnd; sand beach 400m; dogs €0.50; phone; poss cr; Eng spkn; adv bkg; quiet; CCI. "Lovely hillside, family site; some pitches with sea views; vg san facs; office open 0800-1200 & 1400-2000 (high ssn), no pitching outside these hrs; gates clsd 2200-0700." ♦ 1 Jun-15 Sep. € 9.05   2006*

SACQUENAY *6G1* (500m S Rural) **Aire Naturelle La Chênaie (Méot), 16 Rue du 19 Mars, 21260 Sacquenay** [eric.meot@wanadoo.fr] S on D974 (N74) turn L onto D171A sp Occey & Sacquenay, site sp. Sm, pt sl, pt shd; wc; shwrs inc; el pnts (6A); ice; shop 400m; lndtte; playgrnd; poss cr; Eng spkn; adv bkg; quiet; red 10+ days; CCI. "Peaceful site amongst apple orchards." 1 Apr-1 Oct. € 12.20   2007*

SAHUNE see Rémuzat *9D2*

SAILLAGOUSE see Bourg Madame *8H4*

SAILLANS *9D2* (Rural) **Camping Les Chapelains, 26340 Saillans** [04 75 21 55 47; info @camping. saillans.com] Fr Crest to Die on D93 turn onto D493. Site just bef Saillans vill boundary, well sp adj Rv Drôme. Sm, hdg/mkd pitch, pt shd; wc; shwrs inc; el pnts (4-10A) €2.30-4; gas; lndtte; ice; sm shop; rest; tradsmn; snacks; bar; playgrnd; shgl beach; rv sw; dogs €1; Eng spkn; adv bkg; quiet; cc not acc; CCI. "Attractive, well-run site by rv in area of stupendous beauty; some v sm pitches; san facs need updating; friendly, helpful warden; rv walk to vill; rest open low ssn." 1 Apr-30 Sep. € 7.50   2006*

SAILLANS *9D2* (4km NE Rural) **Camping Les Tuillères, Route de Die, 26340 Vercheny** [04 75 21 18 86; fax 04 75 21 29 34; bbouillie@ neuf.fr; www.camping-les-tuilleres.com] On D93, 1km E of Vercheny. Med, pt shd; wc; chem disp; shwrs inc; el pnts (6A) €3; lndtte; ice; shop 6km; tradsmn; rest & bar 1km; snacks; playgrnd; pool; rv sw adj; dogs €1.60; phone; Eng spkn; adv bkg (dep req); quiet; red low ssn; cc acc; CCI. "In beautiful location by rv; v relaxed site; helpful owner; highly rec." ♦ ltd. 24 Apr-30 Sep. € 13.50   2007*

SAILLANS *9D2* (3km E Rural) **Camping Le Pont d'Espénel, 26340 Espénel** [04 75 21 72 70; fax 04 75 21 71 10; reservation@camping-du-pont. com; www.camping-du-pont.com] Fr Crest dir Die on D93, dir access to site on R, adj Rv Drôme. Med, mkd pitch, pt sl, pt shd; wc; chem disp; shwrs inc; el pnts (6A) €2.60; lndtte; rest; bar; playgrnd; rv sw adj; canoeing; dogs €1.40; phone; Eng spkn; cc acc; CCI. "Excel." 1 Apr-15 Oct. € 9.80   2006*

SAILLANS 9D2 (8km E Rural) Camp Municipal La Colombe, 26340 Aurel [04 75 21 76 29 or 04 75 21 71 88; fax 04 75 21 71 89] E of Saillans on D93, in vill of Vercheny turn S onto D357. Bef vill of Aurel turn R by war memorial. Sm, mkd pitch, terr, shd; wc (cont); shwrs inc; el pnts; lndtte; shops 4km; rest; snacks; bar; playgrnd; pool; rv sw & fishing 5km; games area; some statics; v quiet. "Peaceful, mountain site, beautiful views." 1 May-30 Sep. 2006*

SAILLY LE SEC see Albert 3B3

SAINTES 7B2 (1km N Urban) Camp Municipal au Fil de l'Eau, 6 Rue de Courbiac, 17100 Saintes [05 46 93 08 00; fax 05 46 93 61 88; info@ campingsaintes.com; www.camping-saintes-17. com] Well sp as 'Camping Municipal' fr rndbts on by-pass N & S on D150 & D137 (thro indus area), adj rv. Lge, hdg/mkd pitch, pt shd; wc; chem disp; shwrs inc; el pnts (10A) €3.50; lndtte; ice; shop; snacks; rest high ssn; bar; playgrnd; sm pool; rv sw, fishing & boating; mini-golf; some statics; dogs €0.85; cc acc; red low ssn; CCI. "Excel site; interesting Roman ruins in Saintes; rvside walk to town; easy walk to town; guided tours around Cognac distilleries; ground poss v wet; main san facs need TCL; gd tourng base; poss itinerants." ♦ 1 May-30 Oct. € 12.90 2007*

ST AFFRIQUE 8E4 (1km E Urban) Camp Municipal, Parc des Sports, La Capelle Basse, 12400 St Affrique [05 65 98 20 00; fax 05 65 49 02 29] Site on D99 Albi-Millau rd to St Affrique sp fr all dir in E end of town. Nr stn & sports complex. Med, pt shd; wc (some cont); shwrs; el pnts; ice; shop 1km; rest, snacks, bar 1km; pool; rv fishing & sw; tennis; adv bkg; quiet. 15 Jun-15 Sep. € 8.85 2006*

ST AGNAN 4G4 (Rural) Camping du Lac, Le Château, 58230 St Agnan [03 86 78 73 70 or 01772 700531 (UK tel LS); fax 03 86 78 74 94; info@campingburgundy.co.uk; www.camping burgundy.co.uk] Exit A6 junc 22 onto N146 then N6 dir Saulieu; at La Roche-en-Brenil turn R to St Agnan. Med, pt sl, pt shd; wc; chem disp; shws inc; el pnts €3; lndtte; ice; shop; tradsmn; rest; snacks; bar; BBQ; playgrnd; lake sw adj; kayak & pedalo hire nr; games rm; dogs €1; Eng spkn; adv bkg; quiet; cc acc. "Pretty site in grnds of chateau, next to lake; children's craft mornings." 15 Apr-15 Oct. € 12.90 2006*

ST AGREVE 9C2 (2km N Rural) Camping La Licorne (formerly Château Lacour), Route de Chomette, 07320 St Agrève [tel/fax 04 75 30 27 09 or 04 75 30 60 45 (LS); jacqueline. halatsis@wanadoo.fr] Clearly sp in town. Med, mkd pitch, pt sl, pt shd; wc (cont); shwrs; el pnts; lndtte; ice; shops 1km; playgrnd; tennis 1km; horseriding, quiet. "Spacious site; lge pitches; basic facs." 1 Jun-30 Sep. 2005*

ST AIGNAN SUR CHER 4G2 (2km SE Rural) Camping Les Cochards, 1 Rue du Camping, Seigy, 41110 St Aignan-sur-Cher [02 54 75 15 59 or 06 83 79 45 44 (mob); fax 02 54 75 44 72; camping@lescochards.com; www.lescochards. com] On D17 heading SE fr St Aignan twd Seigy on S bank of Rv Cher. Lge, mkd pitch, pt shd; htd wc; chem disp; mv service pnt; baby facs; shwrs inc; el pnts (5A) €3.40; lndtte; ice; shop 3km; rest; snacks; bar; BBQ; playgrnd; pool; rv sw adj; rv fishing; canoeing; horseriding 3km; archery; entmnt; TV rm; 20% statics; dogs €1.20; phone; quiet; red low ssn; cc acc; CCI. "Nr several châteaux; fishing & boating; young, enthusiastic owners v helpful; gd, modern san facs; recep clsd 2000; excel." ♦ ltd. 30 Mar-15 Oct. € 17.50 (CChq acc) 2007*

ST AIGNAN SUR CHER 4G2 (4km NW Rural) Camp Municipal Le Port, Place de l'Eglise, 41110 Mareuil-sur-Cher [tel/fax 02 54 32 79 51 or 02 54 75 21 78; leportdemareuil@orange.fr; www.campingleportdemareuil.com] Fr St Aignan take D17 twd Tours (on S bank of Cher); site in 4km in vill of Mareuil-sur-Cher behind church, thro new archway, on Rv Cher. By Mareuil chateau. Sm, mkd pitch, pt shd; htd wc; chem disp; shwrs inc; el pnts (10A) €3.20; ice/gas 50m; shop & baker 100m; supmkt adj; rest 4km; playgrnd; rv sw (shgl beach); fishing; dogs €1; quiet, but poss events in chateau; red CCI; no cc acc; CCI. "Beautiful, rvside site; simple & quiet; spotless san facs but poss ltd low ssn; friendly staff; opening/closing dates variable, phone ahead to check; if office clsd enquire at supmkt adj (same owners); no twin-axles; m'vans extra charge; wine-tasting nr; gd touring area; vg. ♦ 7 Apr-30 Sep. € 8.00 2007*

ST ALBAN AURIOLLES see Ruoms 9D2

ST ALBAN DE MONTBEL see Chambéry 9B3

ST ALBAN SUR LIMAGNOLE see St Chély d'Apcher 9D1

ST AMAND EN PUISAYE 4G4 (500m NE Urban) Camp Municipal La Vrille, Route de St Sauveur, 58310 St Amand-en-Puisaye [03 86 39 72 21 or 03 86 39 63 72 (Mairie); fax 03 86 39 64 97; saintam.mairie@wanadoo.fr] Fr N7 take D957 Neuvy-sur-Loire to St Amand, at rd junc in vill take D955 sp St Sauveur-en-Puisaye, site on R in 500m; clearly sp on all app to vill. Sm, mkd pitch, pt shd; wc (some cont); shwrs inc; el pnts inc; shop, rest, bar 500m; sailing & fishing in adj reservoir. "Vg simple site; gates closd 2200-0700." 1 Jun-30 Sep. € 10.60 2005*

France

ST AMAND LES EAUX *3B4* (3.5km SE Rural) Camping du Mont des Bruyères, 806 Rue Basly, 59230 St Amand-les-Eaux [tel/fax 03 27 48 56 87] Exit A23 m'way at junc 5 or 6 onto ring rd D169, site sp. Fr N exit E42 junc 31 onto N52/N507 then D169. Avoid St Amand cent. Med, hdg/mkd pitch, pt sl, terr, shd; htd wc; shwrs inc; el pnts (6A) inc; lndtte; ice; shop; bar; playgrnd; pool 7km; 60% statics; adv bkg; quiet; CCI. "Attractive site on forest edge; most touring pitches under trees; access to some pitches diff due slopes; dated facs clean but tired; gd cycling; excel birdlife on site; ltd facs & poss unkempt low ssn; fair." 15 Mar-15 Nov. € 13.40
2007*

ST AMAND LES EAUX *3B4* (7km NW Rural) Camping La Gentilhommière, 905 Rue de Beaumetz, 59310 Saméon [tel/fax 03 20 61 54 03] Fr A23 Paris-Lille, exit junc 3, sp St Amand, then L at rndabt foll sp Saméon. Site on R 300m. Med, hdg pitch, shd; htd wc; chem disp; shwrs inc; el pnts (3A) inc; gas; lndtte; ice; shop 8km; tradsmn; snacks; bar; BBQ; playgrnd; fishing; tennis; 90% statics; dogs €0.80; poss cr; quiet; CCI. "Well-maintained site; 5 touring pitches only; gd for Lille (park & ride fr a'route); gd local rest." ♦ 1 Apr-30 Sep. € 11.00
2005*

ST AMAND MONTROND *4H3* (3km SW Rural) Camp Municipal La Roche, Chemin de la Roche, 18200 St Amand-Montrond [tel/fax 02 48 96 09 36; ot-sam@wanadoo.fr; www.st-amand-tourisme.com] Exit A71/E11 junc 8 twd St Amand-Montrond on D300. Turn R at rndabt on top of canal. Site sp. Med, shd, pt sl; wc (some cont); shwrs inc; chem disp (wc); el pnts (5A) €2.50; ice; lndry rm; shops 900m; playgrnd; pool nr; rv fishing; tennis; entmnt; dogs; phone; quiet; CCI. "Spotless facs; helpful, pleasant warden; twin-axles extra charge; nice town; popular NH, rec arr by 1700 high ssn; gd." ♦ 1 Apr-30 Sep. € 9.20
2007*

ST AMAND MONTROND *4H3* (8km NW) **FFCC** Camping Les Platanes, 18200 Bruère-Allichamps [02 48 61 06 69 or 02 48 61 02 68 (Mairie)] Site on N edge of town on rvside. Sm, pt shd; wc; chem disp; shwrs €1; el pnts (10A) €1.50; ice; shops adj; tradsmn; snacks; playgrnd; rv fishing; quiet. "Relaxing rvside site in lovely surroundings; san facs dated but spotless; friendly staff; v cent of France; level walk to interesting vill; excel." 1 Apr-30 Sep. € 4.20
2007*

ST AMANS DES COTS *7D4* (5km S Rural) Camping Les Tours, 12460 St Amans-des-Cots [05 65 44 88 10 or 04 99 57 20 25; fax 05 65 44 83 07; lestours@village-center. com; www.village-center.com/lestours or www.camping-les-tours.com] Foll D34/D97 fr Entraygues to St Amans, sp in vill. Site on Lac de la Selves. Or fr S, D97 fr Estaing. V lge, hdg/mkd pitch, hdstg, terr, pt shd; wc (some cont); chem disp; mv service pnt; serviced pitches; baby facs; fam bthrm; shwrs inc; el pnts (6A) inc; gas; lndtte; sm shop & 5km; rest; snacks; bar; BBQ; playgrnd; htd pool complex; paddling pool; waterslide; lake (shgl) & rv sw; windsurfing, boating on lake; tennis; horseriding; fishing; golf; gym; entmnt; TV; 20% statics; dogs €3; adv bkg; quiet; red low ssn; cc acc. "Beautiful site on lake shores; some unshd pitches - book early (Xmas) for shd pitch; 600m altitude so cold mornings & evenings; gd rest; steep slope to san facs." ♦ 12 May-9 Sep. € 37.00 (CChq acc)
2007*

Did you know you can fill in site report forms on the Club's website — www.caravanclub.co.uk?

See advertisement

ST AMANT ROCHE SAVINE see Ambert *9B1*

ST AMBROIX *9D2* (3km S Rural) **Camping Beau Rivage, Route de Uzès, 30500 St Ambroix [04 66 24 10 17; fax 04 66 24 21 37; marc@ camping-beau-rivage.fr]** N on D904, after Les Mages in 5km. Camping sp on R. Foll sp approx 2-3km. Site off D37 twd Le Moulinet. Med, hdg/mkd pitch, pt sl, terr, pt sl, shd; wc (some cont); chem disp; shwrs inc; el pnts (2-6A); €2.20-2.80; gas; lndtte; ice; shop 1km; tradsmn; rest, snacks 2km; bar 1km; playgrnd; pool 3km; paddling pool; rv sw; canoeing; dogs €2.50; poss cr; adv bkg; quiet; CCI. ♦ ltd. 1 Apr-15 Sep. € 15.00   2005*

ST AMBROIX *9D2* (200m W) **Camping Le Clos, Place de l'Eglise, 30500 St Ambroix [04 66 24 10 08; fax 04 66 60 25 62]** Fr S on D904, in St Amboix turn L immed bef church. Site in 300m. Foll intn'l camping sp. Sm, pt shd; wc; chem disp; shwrs inc; el pnts (10A) €3.05; lndtte; rest; playgrnd; cycle hire; rv sw; fishing; sailing; TV rm; 20% statics; adv bkg. "Well-kept san facs; access poss diff for lge o'fits." ♦ 1 Apr-31 Oct. € 12.20   2004*

ST AMBROIX *9D2* (12km NW Rural) **Camping des Drouilhedes, Peyremale-sur-Cèze, 30160 Bessèges [04 66 25 04 80; fax 04 66 25 10 95; joost.mellies@wanadoo.fr;   www.camping-drouilhedes.com]** Leave D904 at St Ambroix onto D51 sp Bessèges. In Bessèges turn L over bdge sp Peyremale & in approx 1km turn R & foll camping sp. Med, hdg/mkd pitch, pt shd; wc (some cont); chem disp; baby facs; shwrs inc; el pnts (6A) €3.40; gas; lndtte; ice; shop; tradsmn; rest; snacks; bar; BBQ (gas only); playgrnd; rv sw adj; tennis; games area; TV rm; 10% statics; dogs; phone; poss cr; Eng spkn; quiet; cc acc; CCI. "Well-run, scenic site with excel facs; ideal for children; v helpful Dutch owners." ♦ 1 Apr-30 Sep. € 17.70   2004*

ST AMOUR *9A2* (Urban) **Camp Municipal, Ave des Sports, 39160 St Amour [03 84 48 71 68 or 03 84 44 02 00; fax 03 84 48 88 15]** Sp S & N of vill. Ent by pool & tennis courts. Narr app. Med, pt sl, pt shd, some hdstdg; wc; chem disp; el pnts (6A) €4.50; shwrs; shops 400m; playgrnd; pool adj; tennis; rv 5km; quiet. "Office open ltd hrs, site yourself, no barriers; effectively in public park; well-kept san facs; gd cycling; some rlwy noise at night; gd NH or longer." 1 Apr-30 Sep. € 12.30   2007*

STE ANASTASIE SUR ISSOLE see Brignoles *10F3*

ST ANDIOL see Cavaillon *10E2*

ST ANDRE D'ALLAS see Sarlat la Canéda *7C3*

ST ANDRE DE CUBZAC *7C2* (4km NW Rural) **FFCC Camping Le Port Neuf, 33240 St André-de-Cubzac [tel/fax 05 57 43 16 44; camping. port.neuf@wanadoo.fr]** Fr A10 or N10 take exit sp St André. Well sp fr St André (narr rds) on D669. Med, pt shd; wc; chem disp; mv service pnt; shwrs inc; el pnts (10A) €2 (poss long lead req); ice; bar; playgrnd; pool; cycle hire; trout-fishing & boating in sm lake + rv 100m; many statics; dogs €1; quiet; Eng spkn. "San facs clean; gd NH only." 1 May-1 Oct. € 11.00   2007*

ST ANDRE DE LIDON see Cozes *7B1*

ST ANDRE DE SEIGNANX see Bayonne *8F1*

ST ANDRE DES EAUX see Baule, La *2G3*

ST ANDRE LES ALPES *10E3* (500m Urban) **Camp Municipal Les Iscles, Rue de Nice, 04170 St André-les-Alpes [04 92 89 02 29; fax 04 92 89 02 56; mairie.st-andre-les-alpes@ wanadoo.fr; www.saint-andre-les-alpes.fr]** Exit St André-les-Alpes SE on N202 to Nice turn E at edge of vill on wide service rd. Site almost immed on L fronted by lge car-park. Med, mkd pitch, shd; wc (some cont); chem disp; serviced pitches; shwrs inc; el pnts (4A) €2; lndtte; supmkt adj; BBQ; TV/ games rm; Eng spkn; quiet. "Gd welcome; gd site in scenic area in pine woods on rough stony ground; lovely mountains & lakes; trains to Nice; Verdon Gorge & several Provence vills within reach." 1 May-30 Sep. € 10.90   2007*

⊞**ST ANDRE LES ALPES** *10E3* (6km NE Rural) **Camping L'Adrech, Route du Pont d'Allons, 04170 La Mure-Argens [04 92 89 18 12; contact@ adrech.com; www.adrech.com]** Fr E or W on N202 to St André-les-Alpes, turn N onto D955 dir Colmars, Site on R. Do not app fr N fr Barcelonette via Col d'Allos. Sm, mkd pitch, pt sl, pt shd; wc; chem disp (wc); shwrs inc; el pnts (3-6A) €3; snacks; bar; BBQ; watersports, lake sw nrby; 25% statics; dogs €1; Eng spkn; adv bkg; cc acc; CCI. "Family-run site; helpful, friendly owners; gd touring base in interesting area." € 13.50   2005*

ST ANGEAU see Mansle *7B2*

STE ANNE D'AURAY *2F3* (Rural) **Camp Municipal du Motten, Allée des Pins, 56400 Ste Anne-d'Auray [02 97 57 60 27]** Fr W on N165 take D17bis N to St Anne-d'Auray; then L onto D19 to town. This rte avoids Pluneret. Foll site sp. Med, pt shd; wc; chem disp; mv service pnt; shwrs inc; el pnts (10A) €2.50; lndtte; shops 1km; snacks; playgrnd; sand beach 12km; sports area; tennis; TV adv bkg; poss cr; quiet; "Clean, peaceful & well-maintained; best pitches immed R after ent; san facs poss stretched high ssn; office open 0800-1000 & 1600-1900." ♦ 1 Jun-30 Sep. € 7.90   2005*

France

STE ANNE D'AURAY 2F3 (6km N Rural) **FFCC Aire Naturelle Nerhouit, 56400 Plumergat [02 97 57 70 62; nerhouit@tromp.net]** Fr N165 turn N on D17 to Plumergat; site 3km W of Plumergat, sp. Sm, pt shd; wc; chem disp (wc); shwrs €0.50; el pnts (6A) inc (poss long lead req); lndry rm; shop, rest, bar 3km; playgrnd; dogs; Eng spkn; adv bkg; quiet; CCI. "Pitches on lge grassy area; v friendly Dutch owner; own cider avail; gd touring base." ♦ ltd. 1 Jun-15 Sep. € 12.50   2006*

As soon as we get home I'm going to post all these site report forms to the editor for inclusion in next year's guide. I don't want to miss the September deadline.

ST ANTOINE D'AUBEROCHE see Thenon 7C3

ST ANTOINE DE BREUILH see Ste Foy la Grande 7C2

ST ANTONIN NOBLE VAL 8E4 (Rural) **Camping Ponget, Route de Caylus, 82140 St Antonin-Noble-Val [05 63 68 21 13 or 05 63 30 60 23 (Mairie); fax 05 63 30 60 54; camping-leponget@wanadoo.fr]** Fr Caylus take D19 S to St Antonin; site on R just bef vill bef x-ing rv bdge; well sp. Sm, hdg pitch, pt shd; wc (some cont, own san rec); shwrs inc; el pnts (3-6A) €2.50-3.60; gas; lndtte; shops, rest, snacks, bar 1km; playgrnd; sw 1km; phone; quiet; cc not acc; CCI. "Well-maintained site adj sports field; sh walk into medieval town; canoeing on Rv Aveyron; gd walking; modern san facs; poss diff lge o'fits." ♦ 1 May-30 Sep. € 12.10   2004*

ST ANTONIN NOBLE VAL 8E4 (6km N Rural) **FFCC Camping Les Trois Cantons, Vivens, 82140 St Antonin-Noble-Val [05 63 31 98 57; fax 05 63 31 25 93; info@3cantons.fr; www.3cantons. fr]** Fr Caussade take D926 dir Villefranche (do not take D5 or D19 sp St Antonin.) Site is on C5, sp. Fr St Antonin foll dir Caylus on D19. Just outside vill, after sm bdge where rd turns to R, turn L up hill. Foll this rd for 6km - narr rd. NB Hill steep & continuous. Med, mkd pitch, hdstg, pt sl, pt shd; htd wc (some cont); chem disp; mv service pnt; shwrs inc; el pnts (3-10A) €2.65-6.70; gas; lndtte; ice; shop; supmkt 8km; BBQ; playgrnd; htd, covrd pool; rv sw 8km; tennis; cycle hire; horseriding nr; canoeing; entmnt; child entmnt; TV rm; dogs €1.25; poss cr; Eng spkn; adv bkg; quiet; cc acc; red low ssn; CCI. "Peaceful, family holiday site in oak forest in unspoilt region; clean & well-managed; clean san facs; v helpful Dutch owners; gravel pitches muddy in wet; gd." ♦ 15 Apr-30 Sep. € 19.35 (CChq acc)   2007*

ST ANTONIN NOBLE VAL 8E4 (1km E Rural) **FLOWER Camping des Gorges de L'Aveyron (formerly Camping d'Anglars), Marsac Bas, 82140 St Antonin-Noble-Val [05 63 30 69 76; fax 05 63 30 67 61; www.camping-gorges-aveyron. com]** Fr Cassade on D926 dir Caylus for approx 5km, after Septfords take D5 then D958 twd St Antonin Noble-Val. Cont over rv & L thro tunnel then onto D115. Site in 1.5km on L twd Féneyrols & Cordes-sur-Ciel. Med, hdg pitch, pt shd; wc; chem disp; mv service pnt; shwrs inc; el pnts (3-10A) €2.50-4.50; lndtte; ice; shops; tradsmn; snacks; bar; playgrnd; sw & fishing rv adj; 5% statics; dogs €1.30; adv bkg; quiet; red long stay/low ssn; CCI. "Lge pitches with trees; shady; neat & tidy; new san facs planned for 2008; friendly owners; best in area." ♦ 15 Apr-15 Sep. € 16.00   2007*

ST ANTONIN NOBLE VAL 8E4 (12km E Rural) **Camping Pech Contal, Arnac, 82330 Varen [tel/ fax 05 63 65 48 34; contact@campingpechcontal. com; www.campingpechcontal.com]** 8km fr St Antonin-Noble-Val on D115 Montauban-Cordes rd, turn L sp Arnac. Turn L in sq at Arnac, site 1.5km on R. App rd steep - poss diff lge o'fits. Sm, hdg/mkd pitch, hdstg, pt sl, pt shd; wc; chem disp; 50% serviced pitches; baby facs; shwrs inc; el pnts (10A) €3.50; gas; lndtte; ice; shop; tradsmn; rest; snacks; bar; playgrnd; pool; rv sw & fishing 1km; entmnt; some statics; dogs €1.50; adv bkg; quiet; red long stay/snr citizens/CCI. "V quiet, immac, peaceful in beautiful area; gd cycling; Albi, Najac, Cordes & Gorges d'Aveyron nrby; golden orioles on site." ♦ 1 Apr-30 Sep. € 14.50   2006*

ST ARNOULT see Deauville 3D1

ST ASTIER 7C3 (600m E Rural) **Camp Municipal Le Pontet, Route de Montanceix, 24110 St Astier [05 53 54 14 22; fax 05 53 04 39 36; camp. lepontet@wanadoo.fr; www.ville-saint-astier.fr]** Take D6089 (N89) SW fr Périgueux; in 14km turn R sp St Astier; site on R on D41 on banks of Rv Isle. Med, mkd pitch, shd; wc; chem disp; shwrs inc; el pnts (6A) €2.55; gas; lndtte; shops 400m; snacks; BBQ; playgrnd; pool; paddling pool; sand beach adj; fishing; canoeing; entmnt; statics; dogs; poss cr; adv bkg; v quiet; CCI. "Some areas soft in wet weather." 1 Apr-30 Sep. € 12.00   2007*

ST AUBAN 10E4 (300m S Rural) **Camping La Pinatelle, 06850 St Auban [04 93 60 40 46; fax 04 93 60 42 45]** Fr D6085 (N85) take D2211, site well sp on R just bef vill. Sm, mkd pitch, pt shd; wc; chem disp (wc); shwrs; el pnts €3.50; lndtte; supmkt 1km; tradsmn; rest; snacks; bar; playgrnd; sm pool; games area; dogs; phone; Eng spkn; adv bkg; quiet; CCI. "Friendly, helpful, family-run site; in beautiful countryside; easy access to gorges, coast & fishing." 1 Apr-30 Sep. € 11.40   2005*

ST AUBAN *10E4* (4km NW Rural) **Camping Le Haut Chandelalar (Naturist), 06850 Briançonnet [04 93 60 40 09; fax 04 93 60 49 64; info@le-haut-chandelalar.com; www.le-haut-chandelalar.com]** Exit D6085 (N85) Gasse-Castellane rd onto D2211; site bet St Auban & Briançonnet. Or fr Nice on N202 dir Digne-les-Bains; at Puget-Théniers turn L onto D2211 dir St Auban; 1.5km after Briançonnet turn R at site sp; site on L in 900m. Med, mkd pitch, hdstg, pt sl, terr, pt shd; wc (some cont); chem disp (wc); baby facs; shwrs inc; el pnts (4A) inc; gas; lndtte; ice; shop; tradsmn; rest; snacks; bar; BBQ; playgrnd; htd pool; entmnt; internet; TV rm; some statics; no dogs; phone; poss cr high ssn; adv bkg (dep req); Eng spkn; quiet; cc acc; CCI. "V peaceful, quiet, secluded site; stunning views; gd touring base; gd walking; v pleasant owners; some pitches poss diff access for lge o'fits - steep site rds with sharp bends; excel." ♦ ltd. 1 May-30 Sep. € 27.30
2006*

ST AUBIN DE LUIGNE see Chalonnes sur Loire *2G4*

ST AUBIN DU CORMIER *2E4* (Urban) **Camp Municipal, Rue de l'Etang, 35140 St Aubin-du-Cormier [06 83 38 93 63 (mob) or 02 99 39 10 42 (Mairie); fax 02 99 39 23 25; mairie@ville-staubinducormier.fr]** NE fr Rennes on A84; in 20km exit junc 28 dir St Aubin-du-Cormier. Foll sp 'Centre Ville' then site sp. Poss diff for lge o'fits - narr app. Sm, pt sl, pt shd; wc; shwrs €1.05; el pnts (6-10A) inc; ice; shops adj; forest walks; lake fishing; 10% statics; dogs; poss cr; adv bkg; quiet; CCI. "Nice site beside lake; pretty vill in walking dist; lovely walks around lake; gd." 1 Apr-30 Sep. € 9.55
2007*

ST AUBIN SUR MER see Caen *3D1*

ST AUGUSTIN (CHARENTE MARITIME) see St Palais sur Mer *7B1*

ST AVERTIN see Tours *4G2*

ST AVIT DE VIALARD see Bugue, Le *7C3*

ⓘ**ST AVOLD** *5D2* (1km N Urban) **FFCC Camping Le Felsberg, Centre de Rencontre International, 57500 St Avold [03 87 92 75 05; fax 03 87 92 20 69; cis.stavold@wanadoo.fr; www.camping-moselle.com]** Fr A4 exit 39 & go S to St Avold, stay in L hand lane at 2nd traff lts & turn L; pass under N4 for 2km & turn R. Site well sp in & around town; app up steep incline. Sm, hdg/mkd pitch, hdstg, pt sl, pt shd; wc; chem disp; mv service pnt; shwrs inc; el pnts (6-10A) €3-5; lndtte; tradsmn; hypmkt 1.5km; rest, bar high ssn; playgrnd; 50% statics; dogs €1; poss cr; adv bkg; poss noisy youth groups; cc acc; red long stay; CCI. "German border 10km; coal mine & archaeological park nrby worth visit; heavy duty security gate at site ent - awkward; close to m'way; sm pitches; gd sh stay/NH." ♦ ltd. € 12.40
2004*

ST AYGULF *10F4* (N Coastal) **Camping de St Aygulf Plage, 270 Ave Salvarelli, 83370 St Aygulf [04 94 17 62 49; fax 04 09 81 03 16; camping.cote.d.azur.plage@wanadoo.fr; www.camping-cote-azur.com]** Fr Roquebrunne on D7 at rndabt 100m after vill sp St Aygulf take 3rd exit leading to Rue Roger Martin du Gard. Keep turning L. Fr Fréjus on D559 (N98), rd bends R after bdge over beach access, turn R bef rd climbs to L. V lge, mkd pitch, shd; wc; chem disp; shwrs inc; el pnts (5A) €3.50; gas; lndtte; ice; shop; rest; snacks; bar; playgrnd; sand beach adj; watersports & sports facs nr; fishing; games area; entmnt; statics; dogs €3-3.50; adv bkg (dep & bkg fee); cc acc; red 28+ days; CCI. "Nr town & direct access to beach; facs dated but v clean; gd." 28 Apr-30 Sep. € 26.00
2007*

ST AYGULF *10F4* (4km S Coastal) **Camping Le Pont d'Argens, 83370 St Aygulf [04 94 51 14 97; fax 04 94 51 29 44]** Well sp fr D559 (N98) bet Fréjus & St Aygulf. Situated by Rv Argens. If app fr W pass site on R & return via next rndbt, Lge, mkd pitch, pt shd; htd wc; chem disp; mv service pnt; baby facs; shwrs; el pnts (5A) €3.50; gas; lndtte; ice; shop; tradsmn; rest; snacks; bar; playgrnd; pool; sand beach adj; cycle hire; TV rm; 5% statics; dogs €2.50; €30 dep barrier card; poss cr; Eng spkn; adv bkg; quiet, some rd noise; cc acc; CCI. "Excel, well-run site by rv & 10 mins walk to uncrowded beach (pt naturist). "Excel facs & pool." 1 Apr-20 Oct. € 24.00
2006*

The opening dates and prices on this campsite have changed. I'll send a site report form to the editor for the next edition of the guide.

ST AYGULF *10F4* (2km W Rural) **Camping Les Lauriers Roses, Route de Roquebrune, 83370 St Aygulf [04 94 81 24 46 or 04 94 81 03 58 (LS); fax 04 94 81 79 63; lauriersroses@cs.com; www.info-lauriersroses.com]** Exit A8 at junc 37 Puget-sur-Argens onto DN7 to Fréjus. At 1st rndabt after Fréjus town sp, turn R to St Aygulf at junc immed after rndabt. Pass under rlwy bdge & turn R onto D8. After bdge with traff lts foll rd up to junc & turn L onto D7, site in 1.5km on R. Med, mkd pitch, pt sl, terr, pt shd; wc; chem disp; baby facs; shwrs inc; el pnts (6A) €3.50; gas; lndtte; ice; shop 500m; snacks; bar; BBQ (gas only); playgrnd; htd pool & paddling pool; sand beach 2km; games rm; entmnt; internet; 10% statics; dogs €1.85; Eng spkn; adv bkg; quiet; cc not acc; CCI. "Excel, family-run site site on hillside amongst trees; diff acc some pitches for lge o'fits (max 8m) - owner assists with siting c'vans; mkt Tue & Fri; no arrivals bet 1230-1500." ♦ ltd. 19 Apr-27 Sep. € 27.50
2007*

France

ST AYGULF *10F4* (2.5km W Coastal) **Camping Au Paradis des Campeurs, La Gaillarde-Plage, 83380 Les Issambres [04 94 96 93 55; fax 04 94 49 62 99; www.paradis-des-campeurs. com]** Exit A8/E80 junc 37 at Puget-sur-Argens onto DN7 to by-pass Fréjus, then onto D559 (N98) twd Ste Maxime. Site on R 2km after passing thro St Aygulf, on LH bend bef hill. Or exit junc 36 onto D125 to Ste Maxime, then D559 dir Fréjus. Site on L after ent Les Issambres. Med, mkd pitch, hdstg, pt sl, terr, pt shd; htd wc; chem disp; mv service pnt; baby facs; fam bthrm; 30% serviced pitches (extra charge); shwrs inc; el pnts (6A) €4 (poss rev pol); gas 2km; lndtte; ice; shop; tradsmn; rest; snacks; bar; BBQ; playgrnd; sand beach adj; cycle hire; golf 4km; games rm; internet; TV rm; dogs €3; poss cr; Eng spkn; quiet; cc acc; red low ssn; CCI. "V popular low ssn; direct access via underpass to beach; excel san facs; superb views fr top level pitches - worth extra; gates shut at night & guarded; helpful owners; old rd to St Aygulf suitable for cycling; gd walks in wooded area behind site; excel." ♦ 25 Mar-16 Oct. € 23.00
2007*

See advertisement above

ST AYGULF *10F4* (5km NW Rural) **Camping L'Etoile d'Argens, Chemin des Etangs, 83370 St Aygulf [04 94 81 01 41; fax 04 94 81 21 45; info@etoiledargens.com; www.etoiledargens. com]** Exit A8 at junc 37 Puget-sur-Argens onto DN7 to Fréjus & D559 (N98) to St Aygulf, or fr DN7 take D7 to St Aygulf by-passing Fréjus & turn onto D8 to site. Lge, hdg/mkd pitch, shd; 25% serviced pitches; wc; chem disp; baby facs; shwrs inc; el pnts (10A) inc; gas; lndtte; ice; shop; tradsmn; rest; snacks; bar; no BBQ; playgrnd; htd pool; sand beach 3km; rv fishing; tennis; mini-golf; archery; golf 1.5km; entmnt; 40% statics; dogs €4; poss cr; Eng spkn; adv bkg; quiet; cc acc; red low ssn; CCI. "Standard, Comfort or Luxury pitches avail; busy low ssn; ferry down Rv Argens to beach in ssn; friendly, helpful owners; well-organised; gd facs; excel pool complex." ♦ 1 Apr-30 Sep. € 46.00
2006*

⊞**ST BEAT** *8G3* (500m S Rural) **Camp Municipal Clef de France, 31440 St Béat [05 61 94 35 39]** On N125 at S exit to town, sp on L on rvside. Med, mkd pitch, pt shd; htd wc; shwrs inc; el pnts (5A) inc; ice; shops, rest, bar 500m; playgrnd; pool 200m; fishing; boating; 95% statics; dogs free; quiet. "Facs ltd low ssn; long walk to san facs; site bet two rvs & close to Spanish border; NH/sh stay only." € 10.45
2006*

ST BENOIT DES ONDES see Cancale *2E4*

ST BENOIT SUR LOIRE *4F3* (1.5km SE Rural) **FFCC Camping Le Port, Rue du Port, 45730 St Benoît-sur-Loire [02 38 35 79 00; fax 02 38 35 77 19; ostbenoitsurloire-maisonmaxjacob@wanadoo.fr; www.st-benoit-sur-loire.fr]** Fr Orléans take N60 & bypass Châteauneuf-sur-Loire. Take D60 twd Sully-sur-Loire to St Benoît-sur-Loire. Foll sp fr vill, site in 1.5km on L side of 1-way street. Sm, pt sl, shd; wc; mv service pnt; shwrs inc; el pnts (13A) €2.50; gas 4km; shop, rest 1.5km; BBQ; playgrnd; sand beach adj; rv sw, fishing, canoeing adj; dogs; phone; poss cr; Eng spkn; quiet; CCI." ♦ 1 Apr-30 Sep. € 11.00
2007*

ST BERTRAND DE COMMINGES see Montréjeau *8F3*

ST BOIL *6H1* (Rural) **Camping Moulin de Collonge, Route des Vins, 71940 St Boil [03 85 44 00 40 or 03 85 44 00 32; fax 03 85 44 00 40; millofcollonge@wanadoo.fr; www.moulindecollonge.com]** S on A6 take N80 at Chalon-Sud; W dir Le Creusot; 9km turn S on D981 thro Buxy to St Boil; sp on L thro vill. Sm, hdg/mkd pitch, pt shd; wc (few cont); baby facs; shwrs inc; el pnts (6A) €3.50; gas; lndtte; ice; shop & 2km; tradsmn; rest; snacks; bar; BBQ; playgrnd; htd, covrd pool; lake fishing; cycle hire; entmnt; some statics; dogs; v cr high ssn; some Eng spkn; adv bkg; quiet; cc acc; CCI. " Busy but v quiet site away fr it all; v clean; modern facs; friendly owner; gd snacks; gd cycle ways nrby; two sm ponds with free fishing; excel vineyards on Bourgogne rte." ♦ 1 Apr-30 Sep. € 19.00 (CChq acc)
2007*

ST BOMER LES FORGES see Domfront *4E1*

ST BONNET DE CHAVAGNE see St Marcellin *9C2*

ST BONNET EN CHAMPSAUR *9D3* (800m SE Rural) **Camp V V F Le Roure, 05500 St Bonnet-en-Champsaur [04 92 50 01 86; fax 04 92 50 11 85]** On N85 Route Napoléon (90km S of Grenoble) exit for St Bonnet & site, foll VVF sp. Note St Bonnet 8km N of Col Bayard with 16% gradient. Sm, pt sl, shd; wc; shwrs inc; el pnts (6A) €3.50; ice; lndtte; shops 600m; snacks; bar; BBQ; playgrnd; htd pool; rv 1km; lake 4km; fishing 2km; games area; entmnt; dogs €8; poss cr; adv bkg; quiet; red low ssn. 1 May-30 Sep. € 12.50 2004*

ST BONNET PRES ORCIVAL see Orcival *7B4*

ST BONNET TRONCAIS see Cérilly *4H3*

⊞**ST BREVIN LES PINS** *2G3* (N Coastal) **Camp Municipal Le Mindin, 32-40 Ave du Bois, 44250 St Brévin-les-Pins [02 40 27 46 41; fax 02 40 39 20 53; info@camping-de-mindin.com; www.camping-de-mindin.com]** On beach rd at N end of St Brevin. Med, shd; htd wc; chem disp; baby facs; shwrs inc; el pnts (6A) €4.20; lndtte; shop; rest; snacks; bar; playgrnd; paddling pool; sand beach adj; mainly statics; dogs €2; poss cr; adv bkg; cc acc; red low ssn; CCI. "Sm, sandy pitches; gd san facs." € 12.80 2005*

⊞**ST BREVIN LES PINS** *2G3* (1km S Coastal) **Camp Municipal La Courance, 100-110 Ave Foch, 44250 St Brévin-les-Pins [02 40 27 22 91; fax 02 40 27 24 59; francecamping@wanadoo. fr; www.campinglacourance.fr]** Take Ave Foch fr cent of St Brevin, site on R, clearly sp. Lge, pt sl, shd; htd wc; baby facs; shwrs inc; el pnts (5A) €3.25 (poss long lead req); gas; lndtte; ice; shops 1km; rest; snacks; bar; beach adj; 90% statics; dogs €1.50; quiet; red low ssn. "Unkempt low ssn; steep, poss slippery paths." € 11.90 2006*

ST BREVIN LES PINS *2G3* (2km S Coastal) **Camping Les Rochelets, Chemin des Grandes Rivières, 44250 St Brévin-les-Pins [02 40 27 40 25; fax 02 40 27 15 55; rochelets@ wanadoo.fr; www.rochelets.com]** Fr N or S on D213 exit sp Les Rochelets, site sp. Lge, hdg/mkd pitch, pt shd; wc (some cont); shwrs; el pnts (6A) €4; lndtte; ice; tradsmn; rest; snacks; bar; playgrnd; htd pool; beach 100m; games area; games rm; entmnt & child entmnt; 30% statics; dogs €2.05; adv bkg; quiet; cc acc; red low ssn. "Gd site for families." 1 Apr-30 Oct. € 19.00 2006*

ST BREVIN LES PINS 2G3 (2.4km S Coastal) Camping Le Fief, 57 Chemin du Fief, 44250 St Brévin-les-Pins [02 40 27 23 86; fax 02 40 64 46 19; camping@lefief.com; www.lefief. com] Fr Nantes dir St Nazaire. After St Nazaire bdge S on D213. Pass Leclerc & exit sp St Brévin-l'Océan/La Courance. At rndabt foll sp Le Fief. Lge, hdg/mkd pitch, pt shd; wc; chem disp; baby facs; sauna; shwrs inc; el pnts (5A) €5; gas; lndtte; ice; shop; tradsmn; rest; snacks; bar; BBQ (gas/charcoal); playgrnd; htd, covrd pool; jacuzzi; sand beach 800m; waterpark & waterslide etc adj; tennis; gym; games area; cycle hire nr; entmnt; 30% statics; dogs €5; Eng spkn; adv bkg; quiet; cc acc; red low ssn. "Excel for families; vg leisure facs." ♦ 31 Mar-14 Oct. € 35.00   2007*

See advertisement on previous page

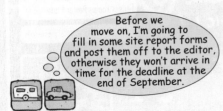

Before we move on, I'm going to fill in some site report forms and post them off to the editor, otherwise they won't arrive in time for the deadline at the end of September.

ST BREVIN LES PINS 2G3 (5km S Coastal) Camping Village Club Les Pierres Couchées, Ave des Pierres Couchées, L'Ermitage, 44250 St Brévin-les-Pins [02 40 27 85 64; fax 02 40 64 97 03; contact@pierres-couchees. com; www.pierres-couchees.com] Sp fr D213 in St Brévin-l'Ermitage. Lge, mkd pitch, terr, pt shd; htd wc (some cont); baby facs; shwrs inc; el pnts (10A); lndtte; shop & 3km; tradsmn; rest; snacks; bar; BBQ; playgrnd; htd pool; paddling pool; waterslide; sand beach 300m; tennis; games area; games rm; fitness rm; cycle hire; horseriding 300m; golf 12km; child entmnt; TV; 75% statics; dogs €3.05; Eng spkn; adv bkg; quiet; cc acc; red low ssn; CCI. "Vg facs for families; friendly, helpful staff." ♦ 31 Mar-9 Oct. € 24.00   2005*

ST BRIAC SUR MER 2E3 (Urban/Coastal) FFCC Camping Emeraude, 7 Chemin de la Souris, 35800 St Briac-sur-Mer [tel/fax 02 99 88 34 55; camping.emeraude@wanadoo.fr; www.camping-emeraude.com] SW fr Dinard to St Lunaire on N786, after passing Dinard golf course, site is sp to L. Lge, pt shd; wc; chem disp; shwrs inc; el pnts (6A) €3.80; gas; lndtte; ice; sm shop & 200m; tradsmn; snacks; bar; playgrnd; htd pool & paddling pool; water park; beach 700m & sand beach 1.5km; mini-golf; games area; entmnt; 40% statics; dogs €2.30; poss cr; adv bkg. "Excel, well-run & established site; close to sm vill with gd facs; many beaches adj; St Briac noted for its bathing, yachting & sports facs." ♦ 3 Apr-29 Sep. € 19.00   2006*

There aren't many sites open this early in the year. We'd better phone ahead to check that the one we're heading for is actually open.

ST BRIAC SUR MER 2E3 (400m S Coastal) Camping Le Pont Laurin, La Vallée Gatorge, 35800 St Briac-sur-Mer [02 99 88 34 64 or 06 03 60 67 64 (mob); fax 02 99 16 38 19; lepontlaurin@ouest-camping.com; www.ouest-camping.com] Fr St Briac, 500m S on D3. Lge, hdg/mkd pitch, hdstg, pt shd; wc (some cont); serviced pitches; chem disp; mv service pnt; shwrs inc; el pnts (10A) €3.60 (poss rev pol); lndtte; ice; shop & 400m; tradsmn; rest; snacks; playgrnd; sand beach 900m; sailing; canoe hire; sports cent adj; some statics; dogs €1.50; Eng spkn; adv bkg; quiet; CCI. "Welcoming, helpful staff; peaceful site; clean modern san facs; excel beaches; gd walking; sh walk to interesting vill; conv for St Malo, Mont St Michel; highly rec." Easter-30 Sep. € 15.40   2007*

See advertisement below

⊞ Site open all year

Help us to update this guide

ST BRIAC SUR MER 2E3 (1km SW Coastal) **Camp Municipal des Mielles, Rue Jules Jeunet, 22770 Lancieux [02 96 86 22 98 or 02 96 86 22 19; fax 02 96 86 28 20; marie.lancieux@wanadoo.fr; www.mairie.lancieux.fr]** Fr S on D786 at 500m past windmill turn L into Rue du Fredy. Site on R in 300m, sp. Lge, mkd pitch, unshd; wc (some cont); chem disp; shwrs inc; el pnts (6A) €2.90; lndtte; ice; shop 500m; playgrnd; sand beach 150m; watersports 150m; tennis; entmnts; 2% statics; dogs €1.55; poss cr; CCI. "Well-managed, & guarded in ssn; hot water ltd low ssn; excel facs; popular site." ♦ 1 Apr-30 Sep. € 9.70   2007*

ST BRICE SUR VIENNE see St Junien 7B3

ST BRIEUC 2E3 (5km E Coastal) **FFCC Camping Bellevue, Pointe de Guettes, 22120 Hillion [02 96 32 20 39 or 02 96 31 25 05 (HS); fax 02 96 32 20 39; contact@bellevuemer.com; www.bellevuemer.com]** Fr St Brieuc twds Dinan on N12 turn N at exit St René onto D712 to Hillion, then rd to Lermot. Site well sp. Narr, winding app rd. Med, unshd; wc; chem disp; mv service pnt; shwrs €0.15; el pnts (4-10A) €2-3 (poss rev pol); lndtte; shops 1.5km; tradsmn; bar; playgrnd; dogs free; quiet; red low ssn. "Vg sea views fr most pitches; coastal paths; well-maintained site; friendly owners; facs basic; narr site rds poss diff lge o'fits; vg." 1 Apr-30 Sep. € 12.30   2007*

ST BRIEUC 2E3 (3km S Urban) **Camping des Vallées, Parc de Brézillet, 22000 St Brieuc [tel/fax 02 96 94 05 05]** Fr N12 take exit sp D700 Tregeux, Pleufragan & foll sp 'Des Vallées' for 3km. Med, hdg pitch, some hdstg, pt shd; wc (some cont); chem disp; mv service pnt; baby facs; shwrs inc; el pnts (10A) €3.80; lndtte; shop; snacks; bar; playgrnd; htd pool, waterslide adj; sand beach 3km; 25% statics; dogs €2; adv bkg; cc not acc; CCI. "High kerb on ent to pitches." ♦ Easter-15 Oct. € 13.90   2004*

ST CALAIS 4F2 (500m N Urban) **Camp Municipal du Lac, Rue du Lac, 72120 St Calais [02 43 35 04 81]** Leave N157 at R angle bend by Champion supmkt; site in 100m. Site by lake on N edge of town, well sp fr cent. Ent easy to miss. Med, hdg/mkd pitch, pt shd; wc; chem disp; mv service pnt; shwrs inc; el pnts (3-6A) inc; lndtte; shops 500m; rest; snacks; bar adj; BBQ; playgrnd; pool adj; lake sw adj; dogs; poss cr; adv bkg; quiet; no cc acc; CCI. "Site v clean, pleasant, well-kept; warden friendly & helpful; spacious pitches esp nr lake; plenty for children; gd situation bet Le Mans & Vendôme, close to Loire; gd touring base." ♦ 1 Apr-15 Oct. € 10.77   2007*

ST CANNAT 10F2 (3km NW Rural) **Provence Camping, Chemin des Ponnes, 13410 Lambesc [04 42 57 05 78; fax 04 42 92 98 02; provence.camping@wanadoo.fr; www.provencecamping.com]** Fr N on D7n (N7), at end of Lambesc by-pass turn R onto D15; site on L in 150m. Sm, mkd pitch, pt sl, terr, shd; wc; mv service pnt; shwrs inc; el pnts (5-10A) €2.50-3.50; gas; lndtte; ice; shop; bar; playgrnd; pool; games area; horseriding; entmnt; TV; some statics; dogs €2; red low ssn; CCI. "Kerbs to pitches; stays of 3+ nights preferred to o'nighters." ♦ 1 Apr-15 Oct. € 15.00   2007*

ST CAST LE GUILDO 2E3 (Coastal) **Camping Les Mielles, Blvd de la Vieux Ville, 22380 St Cast-le-Guildo [02 96 41 87 60; fax 02 96 41 98 08; info@campingsvert-bleu.com]** Fr D786 at Matignon turn onto D13 into St Cast. Cross over staggered x-rds foll site sp down long gentle hill. R at next x-rds & site on R in 200m. Lge, unshd; wc (mainly cont); chem disp; baby facs; shwrs inc; el pnts (5-6A) €4.16-5.80; ice; lndtte; shop; snacks; bar; playgrnd; htd pool; sand beach 350m; entmnt; 95% statics; dogs €1.85; poss cr; poss noisy. "Plenty of facs for teenagers." 15 Mar-13 Nov. € 16.00   2006*

ST CAST LE GUILDO 2E3 (500m N Coastal) **Camping La Crique, Rue La Mare, 22380 St Cast-Le-Guildo [02 96 41 89 19; fax 02 96 81 04 77; info@campings-vert-bleu.com; www.campings-vert-bleu.com]** On ent town foll site sp. Med, mkd pitch, unshd; wc; chem disp; shwrs inc; el pnts (6A) €3.85; lndtte; snacks; bar; playgrnd; beach 200m; some statics (sep area); dogs €1.85; poss cr; adv bkg; quiet; CCI. "Site on top of low cliff with path to beach; vg." 15 Jun-15 Sep. € 14.60   2006*

ST CAST LE GUILDO 2E3 (500m N Coastal) **Camping Le Chatelet, Rue des Nouettes, 22380 St Cast-le-Guildo [02 96 41 96 33; fax 02 96 41 97 99; chateletcp@aol.com; www.lechatelet.com]** Site sp fr all dir & in St Cast but best rte via D13 fr Matignon into St Cast, turn L after passing Intermarché supmkt on R; foll sm site sp. Or app on D19 fr St Jaguel. Care needed down ramp to main site. (NB Avoid Matignon cent Wed due to mkt.) Lge, hdg/mkd pitch, pt sl, terr, pt shd; wc; chem disp; mv service pnt; baby facs; shwrs inc; el pnts (8A) €5.60 (50m cable req); gas; lndtte; ice; shop; snacks; bar; BBQ (gas/elec); playgrnd; htd pool & paddling pool; dir access sand beach 300m (via steep steps); fishing; tennis; cycle hire 500m; games rm; golf 2km; internet; entmnt; TV; 10% statics (tour ops); dogs €4.60; adv bkg; red low ssn; cc acc. "Overlkg sea & beautiful coast; extra for sea view pitches; gates clsd 2230-0730; helpful staff; acc to some pitch diff for lge o'fits; steep climb to beaches; mkt Mon." ♦ 28 Apr-12 Sep. € 32.00 ABS - B11   2007

France

ST CAST LE GUILDO *2E3* (1km S Coastal) **Camping Les Blés d'Or, La Chapelle, 22380 St Cast-le-Guildo** [02 96 41 99 93; fax 02 96 81 04 63; camping-les-bles-dor@wanadoo.fr; www.camping-les-bles-dor.com] App St Cast fr S on D19. Site sp opp beach N of Pen-Guen. Med, hdg/mkd pitch, pt shd; wc; chem disp; 30 pitches with individ san facs €25 per night, el pnts inc; shwrs inc; el pnts (10A) €3; gas; lndtte; ice; supmkt 900m; tradsmn; rest 700m; snacks high ssn; bar; BBQ; playgrnd; htd pool; sand beach 700m; games rm; 30% statics; dogs free; phone; adv bkg; quiet; red low ssn; cc acc; CCI. "Excel site; warm welcome." ♦ 1 Apr-31 Oct. € 15.00
2007*

ST CAST LE GUILDO *2E3* (3.5km S Rural) **Camping Le Château de Galinée, 22380 St Cast-le-Guildo** [02 96 41 10 56; fax 02 96 41 03 72; chateaugalinee@wanadoo.fr; www.chateaude galinee.com or www.les-castels.com] Fr St Malo take 2nd exit (Toutes Direction) & branch R at junc with D301, sp Rennes, Dinard. At next rndabt take 2nd exit onto D168. At Ploubalay go thro vill & turn L at rndbt onto D768. Branch onto D786 at La Ville-es-Comte & foll D786 thro Notre Dame-du-Guildo. Approx 2km after leaving Notre Dame-du-Guildo turn 3rd L into Rue de Galinée & foll sp to site. Med, hdg/mkd pitch, pt shd; wc; chem disp; baby facs; fam bthrm; shwrs inc; el pnts (10A) inc; lndtte; sm shop; snacks; bar; BBQ; playgrnd; htd pool complex inc covrd pool; waterslide; new covrd pool; paddling pool; sand beach 4km; fishing pond; tennis; games area; mini-golf; horseriding 6km; golf 3km; entmnt; wifi internet; games/TV rm; 30% statics; dogs €3.50; recep 0900-1200 & 1400-1900; Eng spkn; adv bkg; red long stay; quiet; cc acc; CCI. "Excel, peaceful, family site; friendly, helpful staff; gd, clean facs; pitches poss muddy after rain; mkts Fri (& Mon high ssn); excursions to Jersey." ♦ 3 May-13 Sep. € 34.20 (CChq acc) ABS - B27
2007*

See advertisement

ST CAST LE GUILDO *2E3* (6km SW) **Camping Le Vallon aux Merlettes, Route de Lamballe, 22550 Matignon** [02 96 41 11 61 or 06 70 31 03 22 (mob); giblanchet@wanadoo.fr; www.camping-matignon.com] Fr E & W take D786 to Matignon; 500m fr town cent turn SW on D13 twds Lamballe. Med, pt sl, pt shd; wc (cont); chem disp; mv service pnt; shwrs inc; el pnts (8A) €2.50; gas; lndtte; shop; snacks; playgrnd; pool 4km; tennis; sand beach 6km; some statics; dogs €0.50; adv bkg rec; quiet; cc not acc; CCI. "Lovely site on playing fields outside attractive town; vg clean facs." ♦ Easter-30 Sep. € 11.50
2005*

STE CATHERINE DE FIERBOIS see Ste Maure de Touraine *4H2*

STE CECILE see Chantonnay *2H4*

ST CERE *7C4* (SE Rural) **Camping Le Soulhol, Quai Salesses, 46400 St Céré** [tel/fax 05 65 38 12 37; info@campinglesoulhol.com; www.campinglesoulhol.com] Fr S on D940 twds St Céré turn onto D48 (Leyme); in 300m turn L (sp not easily seen); site in 200m. Site sp fr all dirs to St Céré. Lge, pt shd; wc; chem disp; mv service pnt; baby facs; shwrs; el pnts (10A) €2.90; gas; lndtte; ice; sm shop, tradsmn (high ssn); shops, rests in town 1km; snacks; pool; tennis; internet; entmnts; TV rm; 10% statics; dogs €1; phone; Eng spkn; red low ssn; cc not acc; CCI. "Charming site; lge pitches; friendly, helpful staff; vg san facs; far end of site bet 2 rvs v quiet; poss flooding after heavy rain; severe speed ramps; excel walks in pleasant area; sh walk to town; gd for cycling; gd." ♦ 1 May-30 Sep. € 13.40
2007*

ST CHELY D'APCHER *9D1* (N Rural) **Camp Municipal Croix des Anglais, 48200 St Chély-d'Apcher** [04 66 31 03 24 or 04 66 31 00 67 (Mairie); fax 04 66 31 30 30; contact@ot.saintchelydapcher.com; www.ot-saintchely dapcher.com] On E side of D809 (N9) to N end of town. Med, hdg pitch, unshd; wc; shwrs; el pnts (10A) inc; shops, rest bar 2km; playgrnd; htd pool 1km; TV; some statics; dogs €1; poss cr; Eng spkn; adv bkg; quiet. "Friendly site; gd walks; gd NH." 15 Jun-15 Sep. € 10.00
2007*

ST CHELY D'APCHER *9D1* (8km E Rural) **FFCC Camping Le Galier, Route de St Chély, 48120 St Alban-sur-Limagnole [04 66 31 58 80; fax 04 66 31 41 83; campinglegalier48@wanadoo.fr]** Exit A75 junc 34 onto D806 (N106), then E on D987. Site 1.5km SW of St Alban on rvside. Sm, mkd pitch, pt sl; htd wc (some cont); shwrs inc; el pnts (6A) €3.70; lndtte; shop 1.5km; snacks; bar; BBQ; playgrnd; pool; some statics; dogs €1.50; poss cr; adv bkg; quiet; red low ssn/CCI. "Clean san facs; friendly owners; gd walking, fishing; vg NH to/fr S." ♦ 1 Mar-15 Nov. € 13.20   2007*

ST CHERON *4E3* (3km SE Rural) **Camping Héliomonde (Naturist), La Petite Beauce, 91530 St Chéron [01 64 56 61 37; fax 01 64 56 51 30; helio@heliomonde.fr; www.heliomonde.fr]** N20 S to Arpajon; then D116 to St Chéron. Site bet Arpajon & Dourdan. Sp in town. Med, shd; wc; chem disp; sauna; shwrs inc; el pnts €3.30; lndtte; shop; rest; htd pool; paddling pool; games area; fitness rm; entmnt; some statics; adv bkg; quiet. 7 Mar-12 Nov. € 22.90 (CChq acc)   2005*

ST CHERON *4E3* (3.5km SE Rural) **Camping Le Parc des Roches, La Petite Beauce, 91530 St Chéron [01 64 56 65 50; fax 01 64 56 54 50; contact@parcdesroches.com; www.parcdesroches.com]** N20 S to Arpajon; then D116 to St Chéron. Site bet Arpajon & Dourdan. Sp in town. Lge, hdg/mkd pitch, hdstg, pt shd; htd wc; chem disp; baby facs; shwrs inc; el pnts (4A) €2.60; gas 200m; lndtte; ice; shop 3lkm; tradsmn; rest; snacks; bar; BBQ; playgrnd; htd pool; paddling pool; tennis; solarium; games area; games rm; 70% statics; dogs €1.70; train 3km; Eng spkn; adv bkg; quiet but poss noisy high ssn; cc acc; CCI. "Pleasant, wooded site; v helpful, friendly owner; o'night pitches lge & nr ent; some san facs new; train to Paris 3km; historical sites; châteaux; gd walking." ♦ 1 Apr-15 Oct. € 20.80   2006*

ST CHINIAN *10F1* (1km W) **Camp Municipal Les Terrasses, Route de St Pons, 34360 St Chinian [04 67 38 28 28 (Mairie); fax 04 67 38 28 29; mairie@saintchinian.fr]** On main Béziers-St Pons rd, D612 (N112), heading W on o'skts of St Chinian. Site on L. Med, terr, unshd; wc; shwrs inc; el pnts €2; shops 1km; poss cr; quiet. "Attractive site with gd views; sm pitches; diff access some pitches." 15 Jun-31 Aug. € 6.90   2006*

⊞**ST CIRQ LAPOPIE** *7D3* (2km N Rural) **Camping La Plage, 46330 St Cirq-Lapopie [05 65 30 29 51; fax 05 65 30 23 33; camping.laplage@wanadoo.fr; www.campingplage.com]** Exit Cahors on D653, in Vers take D662 sp Cajarc. In 20km turn R at Tour-de-Faure over narr bdge, sp St Cirq-Lapopie, site 100m on R beside Rv Lot. Med, mkd pitch, shd; wc; baby facs; shwrs inc; el pnts (6-10A) €4-5; lndtte; shop; rest; snacks; bar; BBQ; playgrnd; pool; rv sw; canoeing; watersports; entmnt; 5% statics; dogs €2; adv bkg; quiet; CCI. "Low ssn site yourself, pay later; clean, tidy site (Sep 2007); gd rest in town; gd walking; excel." ♦ € 17.00   2007*

ST CIRQ LAPOPIE *7D3* (9km E Rural) **Camping Ruisseau de Treil, 46160 Larnagol [05 65 31 23 39; fax 05 65 31 23 27; lotcamping@wanadoo.fr; www.lotcamping.com]** Exit A20 junc 57 onto D49 sp St Michel; in 4km turn R onto D653; after 5.5km in Vers at mini-rndabt turn L onto D662; site on L immed after leaving Larnagol. Or fr Figeac foll D19 thro Cajarc. At top of hill leaving Cajarc turn R onto D662 sp Cahors & Larnagol. Site sp on R 300m bef Larnagol on blind bend. Sm, mkd pitch, pt sl, pt shd; wc; chem disp; baby facs; shwrs inc; el pnts (6A) €3.60; lndtte; ice; tradsmn; rest; snacks; bar; BBQ; playgrnd; 2 pools; rv sw, fishing, canoeing adj; horseriding; cycle hire; TV rm; 4% statics; dogs €2.80; poss cr; Eng spkn; adv bkg; quiet; 20-30% red low ssn & snr citizen; CCI. "Lovely, spacious, British-owned site in valley; friendly, helpful owners; spotless san facs but inadequate when site full; beautiful area; guided walks; conv many tourist attractions; pitches poss uneven; excel." ♦ ltd. 12 May-15 Sep. € 19.30   2007*

ST CIRQ LAPOPIE *7D3* (2.5km S Rural) **FFCC Camping La Truffière, Route de Concots, 46330 St Cirq-Lapopie [05 65 30 20 22; fax 05 65 30 20 27; contact@camping-truffiere.com; www.camping-truffiere.com]** Take D911, Cahors to Villefranche, then turn N onto D42 at Concots dir St Cirq for 8km - site clearly sp. Med, pt sl, terr, shd; htd wc; chem disp; mv service pnt; shwrs inc; el pnts (6A) €3.50; lndtte; ice; ltd shop & 4km; rest; snacks; bar; playgrnd; htd pool; paddling pool; rv sw & fishing 3km; cycle hire; entmnt; TV; dogs €1.50; phone; Eng spkn; adv bkg; quiet; 10% red low ssn; cc acc; CCI. "Well-kept; hospitable site but rather isolated low ssn; excel facs but ltd low ssn; most pitches in forest clearings - pitches in open with temp el pnts (no earth); site & rds not suitable v lge o'fits; some pitches steep; gd rest; lovely pool." ♦ 1 Apr-30 Sep. € 15.50 (CChq acc)   2007*

ST CIRQ LAPOPIE *7D3* (7km W Rural) **Camp Municipal, 46330 St Géry [05 65 31 40 08 (Mairie); fax 05 65 31 45 65]** Fr St Cirq foll N side Rv Lot on D662. Thro St Géry & after rlwy x-ing turn R bef petrol stn. Sp. Sm, pt sl, shd; wc (cont); el pnts (10A) inc (poss long lead req); shop 2km; rv & fishing adj; quiet. "V clean facs; warden calls 2000." 1 Jul-5 Sep. € 8.80   2006*

ST CLAR *8E3* (4km NE Rural) **Camping Les Roches (Naturist), 32380 Mauroux [tel/fax 05 62 66 30 18; campinglesroches@wanadoo.fr; www.campinglesroches.net]** Fr Fleurance take D953 to St Clar then D167 for 3km to site on L. Sm, hdg pitch, pt sl, pt shd; wc; chem disp; mv service pnt; sauna; shwrs; el pnts (6A) €3.80; lndtte; shops; tradsmn; rest; snacks; bar; pool; fishing; entmnt; TV rm; some statics; dogs €1.50; phone; adv bkg; Eng spkn; INF card. "Beautiful site in remote location; pleasant owners; fishing in lake; gd sized pitches." ♦ ltd. 1 May-30 Sep. € 17.50   2007*

France

⊞ST CLAR *8E3* (8km E Rural) **FFCC Centre Naturiste de Devèze (Naturist)**, 32380 Gaudonville [05 62 66 43 86; fax 05 62 66 42 02; camping. deveze@wanadoo.fr; www.deveze.eu] Fr Fleurance to St Clar on D953, then D167 to site 4km on L. Lge, hdg pitch, pt sl, terr, pt shd; wc; chem disp; mv service pnt; 80% serviced pitches; shwrs inc; el pnts (5A) €4; ice; gas; lndtte; shop; tradsmn; rest, snacks high ssn; bar; playgrnd; pool; lge lake; fishing; tennis; cycle hire; entmnt; TV rm; 15% statics; dogs €1.60; phone; site clsd 1 Jan-14 Feb; Eng spkn; adv bkg; quiet; cc acc; INF card req. "Excel site; excursions arranged. "♦ € 17.50   2006*

ST CLAUDE *9A3* (2km SE Rural) **Camp Municipal du Martinet, Route de Genève**, 39200 St Claude [03 84 45 00 40 or 03 84 41 42 62 (LS); fax 03 84 45 11 30] On ent town foll 1-way, under bdge mkd 4.1m high, then take R turn 'Centre Ville' lane to next traff lts. Turn R then immed L sp Genève, turn R 300m after Fiat g'ge onto D290, site on R. Med, pt shd; wc (cont); chem disp; shwrs inc; el pnts (5A) €2.30; gas; ice; shops 1km; rest; htd pool adj; tennis; fishing; poss cr; adv bkg; quiet; red low ssn; CCI. "In Jura mountains; warden am & pm only low ssn; ltd facs low ssn; smoking pipe factory & museum nrby; excel walking; v attractive town; gd." 1 May-30 Sep. € 9.70   2006*

ST COLOMBAN DES VILLARDS *9C3* (700m SW Rural) **Camping La Perrière, Route du Col du Glandon**, 73130 St Colomban-des-Villards [04 79 59 16 07; fax 04 79 59 15 17; camping. laperriere@wanadoo.fr] Exit A43 junc 26 onto D927. Site at end of vill. Access rd narr & winding in places - not rec long o'fits. Sm, mkd pitch, hdstg, terr, pt shd; w; mv service pnt; shwrs inc; el pnts €4; lndtte; shop 200m; BBQ; playgrnd; games area; phone; quiet. "Excel."♦ 10 Jun-9 Sep. € 15.00   2006*

ST CONNEC see Mur de Bretagne *2E3*

ST COULOMB see St Malo *2E4*

ST CREPIN ET CARLUCET see Sarlat la Canéda *7C3*

STE CROIX EN PLAINE see Colmar *6F3*

ST CYBRANET see Sarlat la Canéda *7C3*

ST CYPRIEN *7C3* (1km S) **Camping du Garrit, Le Garrit**, 24220 St Cyprien [tel/fax 05 53 29 20 56; pbecheau@aol.com; www. campingdugarritendordogneperigord.com] Fr W on D703 turn R bef town sp; cross rlwy & bear R; then sharp R at rv. Sp on D703 fr St Cyprien as 'Le Garrit'. Med, hdg/mkd pitch, pt shd; wc; chem disp; baby facs; shwrs inc; el pnts (6A) €3; BBQ; lndtte; ice; shop; playgrnd; pool; canoeing; sailing; boat hire; fishing; rv adj; dogs €1; phone; Eng spkn; adv bkg (dep req); quiet; CCI. "Lovely rvside site; highly rec; friendly owner; lge pitches; excel san facs; easy walk to town; gd touring base for prehistoric caves; excel. 1 May-1 Oct. € 15.00   2007*

ST CYPRIEN PLAGE *10G1* (3km S Coastal) **Camping Cala Gogo, Ave Armand Lanoux, Les Capellans**, 66750 St Cyprien-Plage [04 68 21 07 12; fax 04 68 21 02 19; camping.calagogo@wanadoo. fr; www.campmed.com] Exit A9 at Perpignan Nord onto D617 to Canet-Plage, then D81; site sp bet St Cyprien-Plage & Argelès-Plage dir Les Capellans. V lge, hdg/mkd pitch, pt shd; htd wc (some cont); chem disp; mv service pnt; baby facs; shwrs inc; el pnts (6A) €3.40; lndtte; ice; supmkt; rest; snacks; bar; playgrnd; 2 pools; paddling pool; sand beach adj; tennis; games area; entmnt; TV rm; 30% statics; dogs €3.70; Eng spkn; adv bkg; red low ssn; cc acc; CCI. "Suitable for partially-sighted." ♦ 10 May-20 Sep. € 29.80   2007*

ST CYPRIEN PLAGE *10G1* (1.5km SW Urban/ Coastal) **CHADOTEL Camping Le Roussillon, Chemin de la Mer**, 66750 St Cyprien [04 68 21 06 45 or 02 51 33 05 05 (LS); fax 02 51 33 94 04; chadotel@wanadoo.fr; www. chadotel.com] Exit A9 junc 42 Perpignan Sud onto D914 (N114) to Elne, D40 to St Cyprien. Site sp. Lge, hdg/mkd pitch, unshd; htd wc; baby facs; shwrs inc; el pnts (6A) inc; gas; lndtte; shop; snacks; bar; BBQ (gas); playgrnd; htd pool; waterslide; sand beach 1km; cycle hire; games rm; TV rm; entmnt; bus to beach; dogs €2.90; Eng spkn; adv bkg; red long stay/low ssn; cc acc. "Vg family site; gd touring base." ♦ Easter-24 Sep. € 28.90   2006*

ST CYPRIEN SUR DOURDOU see Conques *7D4*

ST CYR (VIENNE) see Jaunay Clan *4H1*

ST CYR SUR MER (VAR) see Bandol *10F3*

ST DENIS DU PAYRE see Luçon *7A1*

ST DIE *6E3* (10km E Urban) **Camp Municipal Le Violu**, 88520 Gemaingoutte [03 29 57 70 70 (Mairie); fax 03 29 51 72 60; mairiegemaingoutte@wanadoo.fr] Take D459 (N59) Rte du Col fr St Dié twd Ste Marie-aux-Mines. Site on L at ent to Gemaingoutte, 1km after junc with D23 Sm, pt sl, pt shd, mkd pitch; wc (some cont); chem disp; shwrs inc; el pnts (5A) €2.20; lndtte; ice; shops 2.5km; tradsmn; playgrnd; rv adj; dogs €0.80; quiet; CCI. "Peaceful site on Rte du Vin; office only open 1900-2030 daily."♦ 1 Apr-31 Oct. € 8.50   2007*

⊞ST DIE *6E3* (1km SE Urban) **Camping La Vanne de Pierre, 5 Rue du Camping**, 88100 St Dié-des-Vosges [03 29 56 23 56; fax 03 29 42 22 23; vannedepierre@wanadoo.fr; www.vannedepierre. com] Fr any dir twd town cent foll 'Stade du Breuil Camping' sp. Med, hdg/mkd pitch, terr, pt shd; htd wc (some cont); chem disp; shwrs inc; el pnts (10A) inc; lndtte; shops 2km; tradsmn; rest in town; snacks; bar; playgrnd; htd pool; rv fishing; tennis 500m; entmnt; internet; TV rm; 2% statics; dogs €3; poss cr; adv bkg rec; quiet but some rd noise; cc acc; CCI. "Gd, clean san facs; lge pitches; well-kept site; office open 0900-1300 & 1500-2000; helpful staff."♦ € 28.00 (CChq acc) ABS - J06   2007*

ST ELOY LES MINES *7A4* (S Rural) **Camp Municipal La Poule d'Eau, Rue de la Poule d'Eau, 63700 St Eloy-les-Mines [04 73 85 45 47; fax 04 73 85 07 75]** On D2144 (N144) fr S turn W at 1st rndabt at St Eloy-les-Mines (Vieille Ville) onto D110; site 200m clearly sp. Fr Montluçon/Montaigut, last rndabt; site by 2 lakes. Med, mkd pitch, pt sl, shd; wc; shwrs; el pnts (6A) €2.16; ice; shop adj; tradsmn; playgrnd; lake sw, fishing & watersports adj; entmnt; adv bkg; quiet. "For security san facs open at set times, site ent barrier clsd 1200-1600; nice location; warden v proud of his site; excel sh stay/NH." 1 Jun-30 Sep. € 7.35   2007*

ST EMILION *7C2* (3km N Rural) **Camping Domaine de la Barbanne, Route de Montagne, 33330 St Emilion [05 57 24 75 80; fax 05 57 24 69 68; barbanne@wanadoo.fr; www.camping-saint-emilion.com]** NB: Trailer c'vans not permitted in cent of St Emilion. Fr A10 exit junc 39a sp Libourne onto D670. In Libourne turn E on D243 twd St Emilion. On o'skts of St Emilion turn L onto D122 dir Lussac & Montagne, site on R by lake in 3km. Or fr S, foll site sp off D670 to Libourne, nr Les Bigaroux. NB D122 S of St Emilion unsuitable for c'vans. Lge, hdg/mkd pitch, shd; wc; chem disp; mv service pnt; baby facs; shwrs inc; el pnts (10A) inc; gas; lndtte; ice; sm shop; tradsmn; rest, snacks high ssn; BBQ; playgrnd; htd pools inc; paddling pool; waterslide; fishing; watersports nr; tennis; mini-golf; cycle hire; horseriding 8km; children's club; excursions high ssn; internet; games/TV rm; 20% statics; dogs €3.50; phone; poss cr; Eng spkn; adv bkg; quiet; red low ssn; cc acc; CCI. "Well-run, peaceful site; owners friendly & helpful; clean, dated facs poss stretched high ssn & ltd low ssn; activities inc in site fee; vg family site; beautiful lake with walk around; lakeside pitches muddy when wet; facs used by long-dist coach firms; shop sells wine at château prices; free bus/taxi service to St Emilion; tree fluff a minor irritation in May (gone by Jun); wine-tasting tours; gd cycle rtes; excel." ♦ 7 Apr-23 Sep. € 28.00 (CChq acc) ABS - D08   2007*

⊞**ST EMILION** *7C2* (4km SE Rural) **Aire St Emilion Domaine du Château Gerbaud, 33000 St Peu-d'Armens [06 03 27 00 32 (mob); fax 05 57 47 10 53; contact@chateau-gerbaud.com; www.chateau-gerbaud.com]** Fr Libourne SE on D670/D936 dir Castillon-la-Bataille. In St Pey-d'Armens at bar/tabac foll sp Château Gerbaud vineyard. Parking & service pnt for m'vans for max 48 hours; no charge if wine purchased; friendly, Eng-speaking owners.   2006*

STE ENGRACE *8F1* (5km NW Rural) **FFCC Camping Ibarra, Quartier Les Casernes, 64560 Ste Engrâce [05 59 28 73 59; maryse@ibarra-chantina.com; www.ibarra-chantina.com]** D918 S fr Tardets-Sorholus; in 2km turn R onto D26; in 6km to L onto D113 sp Ste Engrâce; site on R in 5km. Site clearly sp just bef La Caserne. NB not suitable car+c'van. Sm, mkd pitch, pt shd; wc (some cont); chem disp; shwrs inc; el pnts (5A) €1.70; lndry rm; tradsmn; snacks 500m; bar; BBQ (sep area); playgrnd; dogs; quiet; CCI. "On rv bank; scenic views; spectacular Kakuetta gorges nrby; vg." ♦ ltd. Easter-1 Nov. € 9.60
                        2007*

STE ENIMIE *9D1* (1.5km SW Rural) **Camp Couderc, Route de Millau, 48210 Ste Enimie [04 66 48 50 53; fax 04 66 48 58 59; campingcouderc@wanadoo.fr; www.campingcouderc.fr]** Leave Ste Eminie on D9078 in dir Millau, site on L bank of Rv Tarn. Med, mkd pitch, pt sl, terr, pt shd; wc; chem disp; mv service pnt; baby facs; shwrs inc; el pnts (6A) €3; gas; shop; snacks; bar; playgrnd; pool; canoeing; dogs free; Eng spkn; quiet; red low ssn; CCI. "Rd along gorge narr & twisting; busy, friendly site." ♦ 1 Apr-30 Sep. € 16.00   2007*

ST ETIENNE DE BAIGORRY *8F1* (500m N Rural) **Camp Municipal L'Irouleguy, 64430 St Etienne-de-Baïgorry [05 59 37 43 96 or 05 59 37 40 80; fax 05 59 37 48 20; comstetiennebaigorry@wanadoo.fr]** W on D15 fr St Jean-Pied-de-Port to St Etienne-de-Baigorry. Site on R, sp 300m past rlwy x-ing. Ent next to wine co-operative. Fr N on D948, on ent St Etienne-de-Baïgorry turn L onto D15; site in 300m on L. Med, shd; wc; chem disp; shwrs inc; el pnts (13A) €2.70; lndtte; gas; shop 100m; htd pool adj; tennis adj; troutfishing; birdwatching; poss cr; adv bkg; quiet. "V scenic; gd hill walking cent; out of ssn call at Mairie who will open site for NH." ♦ 1 Mar-15 Dec. € 10.80   2007*

ST ETIENNE DE CROSSEY see Voiron *9C3*

ST ETIENNE DE FONTBELLON see Aubenas *9D2*

⊞**ST ETIENNE DE MONTLUC** *2G4* (E) **Camp Municipal de la Colleterie, Blvd de Tivoli, 44360 St Etienne-de-Montluc [02 40 86 97 44; fax 02 40 86 98 78]** Well sp fr N165 (E60) in both dirs. Sm, hdg/mkd pitch, pt sl, pt shd; htd wc; chem disp; shwrs inc; baby facs; el pnts (20A) €3.20; lndtte; shop, rest, bar 500m; playgrnd; fishing; dogs €0.75; adv bkg rec; CCI. ♦ € 6.60   2005*

ST ETIENNE DE VILLEREAL see Villeréal *7D3*

ST ETIENNE DU BOIS (VENDEE) see Legé *2H4*

ST ETIENNE DU GRES see St Rémy de Provence *10E2*

France

STE EULALIE EN BORN *7D1* (W Rural) **Le Camping du Lac, 1590 Route du Lac, 40200 Ste Eulalie-en-Born** [05 58 09 70 10; fax 05 58 09 76 89; contact@lecampingdulac.com; www.lecampingdulac.com] N fr Mimizan on D87/D652. Pass Ste Eulalie & turn W at water tower, site sp. Med, mkd pitch, pt shd; wc; chem disp; mv service pnt; shwrs inc; el pnts (6A) €3.90; gas; lndtte; snacks; bar; pool; lake sw & beach adj; boat hire; games area; some statics; dogs €2; phone; poss cr; Eng spkn; adv bkg; quiet; cc acc; CCI. "Friendly site on Lake Biscarrosse; vg for familes; do not confuse with site of similar name on Lac Aureilhan, 2km N of Mimizan." 1 Mar-30 Oct. € 11.55   2005*

ST EUSTACHE see Annecy *9B3*

ST EVARZEC see Quimper *2F2*

ST EVROULT NOTRE DAME DU BOIS see Aigle, L' *4E2*

ST FARGEAU *4G4* (6km SE Rural) **Camp Municipal La Calanque, 89170 St Fargeau** [tel/fax 03 86 74 04 55] Fr St Fargeau take D85 dir of St Sauveur-en-Puisaye. In 4.5km turn R sp Lac/Réservoir de Bourdon. Site on N shore of lake, well sp. Lge, mkd pitch, shd; htd wc (some cont)(own san rec Jul 2007); shwrs inc; el pnts (6-10A) €2-2.60; lndtte; ice; shop, rest, snacks, bar adj; playgrnd; lake & sand beach adj; fishing; 10% statics; poss cr; quiet (noisy nr lake); adv bkg rec high ssn; CCI. "Pleasant site in birch woods; tight manoeuvring round trees; sm pitches; cycling, canoeing, horseriding nr; gd lake sw; recep clsd 1200-1500; gd." ♦ 15 Apr-30 Sep. € 8.20
2007*

ST FERREOL TRENTE PAS see Nyons *9D2*

ST FLORENT SUR CHER *4H3* (7km SE Rural) **Camp Intercommunal, 6 Rue de l'Abreuvoir, 18400 Lunery** [02 48 68 07 38 or 02 48 23 22 08; fax 02 48 55 26 78; fercher@fr-oleane.com] Fr N151 turn S onto D27 at St Florent-sur-Cher, cont for 7km, site in vill cent of Lunery. Sm, hdg/mkd pitch, pt shd; wc; chem disp; mv service pnt; shwrs inc; el pnts (6A) €1 (poss rev pol); ice; shop, rest in vill; playgrnd; fishing; tennis nr; no statics; bus 200m, train in vill; phone 100m; Eng spkn; red long stay; CCI. "Charming, friendly site in peaceful location; friendly welcome; gd clean san facs; on banks of Rv Cher; liable to flooding low ssn; phone ahead to check open low ssn; gd." ♦ 15 May-15 Sep. € 14.00   2007*

ST FLORENTIN *4F4* (1km S Urban) **Camping L'Armançon, 89600 St Florentin** [tel/fax 03 86 35 11 86; ot.saint-florentin@wanadoo.fr] N fr Auxerre on N77 site on R app rv bdge S of town. Fr N pass traff islands, exit town up slope, x-ing canal & rv. Site immed on S side of rv bdge - turn R immed at end of bdg then under bdg to site, sp. Lge, pt sl, pt shd; wc (cont); shwrs inc; el pnts inc; gas; lndtte; shop; café/bar; snacks; playgrnd; rv sw; fishing; dogs €0.20; poss cr; some rd noise at night. "Friendly manager; excel pitches; site well kept; dated but clean san facs; small town worth visit; wine-growing area; diff, steep exit to main rd; gd." 8 Apr-1 Oct. € 10.10   2007*

ST FLOUR *9C1* (3km N Rural) **Camping International La Roche Murat, 15100 St Flour** [04 71 60 43 63; fax 04 71 60 02 10; courrier@camping-saint-flour.com; www.camping-saint-flour.com] Fr N or S on A75 exit junc 28; sp off rndabt on St Flour side of m'way. Site ent visible 150m fr rndabt. Med, hdg/mkd pitch, terr, pt shd; htd wc; chem disp; mv service pnt; shwrs inc; el pnts (10A) inc; gas; lndry rm; shops 4km; tradsmn; playgrnd; pool 2km; dogs; Eng spkn; adv bkg; quiet but some rd noise; cc not acc; CCI. "Busy, agreeable site; conv NH fr A75; v helpful warden; gd views; sunny & secluded pitches; gd, clean facs; some pitches sm; when pitches waterlogged - use site rds; excel touring cent." ♦ 1 Apr-1 Nov. € 13.20
2007*

ST FLOUR *9C1* (SW Urban) **Camp Municipal Les Orgues, 19 Ave Dr Maillet, 15100 St Flour** [04 71 60 44 01] On A75 to St Flour, foll sps for 'ville haute'; at x-rds in town cent turn L (dir Aurillac). Ent in 250m, narr & steep on L bet houses, site sp opp poss obscured by parked cars. NB Site ent is on busy main rd & has 2m high barrier. If c'van over 2m, stop at barrier (c'van sticking out into rd), walk down to office & ask warden to unlock barrier - poss v dangerous. Med, mkd pitch, pt sl, pt shd; wc; shwrs inc; el pnts (6A) €2.40; ice; shops, rest; bar 1km; playgrnd; covrd pool 1km; tennis; quiet; poss cr; CCI. "Facs need updated; Gd NH." ♦ 15 May-15 Sep. € 9.60   2005*

ST FORT SUR GIRONDE *7B2* (4km SW Rural) **Camping Port Maubert, 8 Rue de Chassillac, 17240 St Fort-sur-Gironde** [05 46 04 78 86; fax 05 46 04 16 79; bourdieu.jean-luc@wanadoo.fr; www.campingportmaubert.com] Exit A10 junc 37 onto D730 dir Royan. Foll sp Port Maubert & site. Sm, hdg/mkd pitch, shd; wc (some cont); chem disp; mv service pnt; shwrs inc; el pnts (10A) €3.50; gas; lndtte; ice; shop 4km; tradsmn; bar; BBQ; playgrnd; pool; sand beach 25km; cycle hire; games rm; TV; some statics; dogs €2; Eng spkn; adv bkg; quiet; cc acc; red long stay/CCI. "Pleasant, well-run site." 1 May-30 Sep. € 12.20   2005*

STE FOY LA GRANDE 7C2 (1.5km NE Rural) Camping de la Bastide (formerly Camp Municipal La Tuilerie), 2 Les Tuileries-Pineuilh, 33220 Ste Foy-la-Grande [tel/fax 05 57 46 13 84; contact@camping-bastide.com; www.camping-bastide.com] Fr W go thro town & turn off at D130 to site, sp on Rv Dordogne. Med, mkd pitch, pt shd; wc; chem disp; mv service pnt; baby facs; shwrs inc; el pnts (5-10A) inc (rev pol); lndtte; ice; tradsmn; shops, snacks & bar 500m, playgrnd; pool; fishing, canoeing; games rm; wifi internet; 10% statics; dogs; phone; poss cr; Eng spkn; adv bkg; v quiet; cc acc; CCI. "Well-cared for & pretty site; immac, modern san facs; nice pool; charming young enthusiastic owners; high kerb stones onto pitches - poss diff lge o'fits; no twin-axles; gd street mkt Sat; vg." ♦ 1 Apr-27 Oct. € 19.00   2007*

This guide relies on site report forms submitted by caravanners like us; we'll do our bit and tell the editor what we think of the campsites we've visited.

STE FOY LA GRANDE 7C2 (6km W Rural) Camping La Rivière Fleurie, 24230 St Antoine-de-Breuilh [tel/fax 05 53 24 82 80; info@la-riviere-fleurie.com; www.la-riviere-fleurie.com] Turn S off D936 in St Antoine-de-Breuilh, site 2.7km fr main rd exit. Well sp adj Rv Dordogne. Med, mkd pitch, pt shd; wc; chem disp; baby facs; shwrs inc; el pnts (4-10A) €3.10-€4.50; gas; lndtte; ice; shops 4km; hypmkt 5km; tradsmn; bar; BBQ; playgrnd; pool; games rm; rv sw adj; tennis, horseriding; golf; canoeing & fishing nrby; 10% statics; dogs €2; phone; Eng spkn; adv bkg; quiet except for church bells; red long stay; CCI. "Site & facs excel; v friendly, helpful owners; high kerb stones to pitches; v gd cycling area; mkt Sat in Ste Foy; gets better every year; poss unreliable opening dates." ♦ 2 Apr-30 Sep. € 18.00   2007*

STE FOY LA GRANDE 7C2 (10km W Rural) Camping de La Plage, 24230 St Seurin-de-Prats [tel/fax 05 53 58 61 07; info@camping-in-france.net; www.camping-in-france.net] Fr D936 W of Ste Foy take D11 at Les Réaux twrds Pessac. Site on R of D11 immed bef x-ing Rv Dordogne into Pessac. Med, pt hdg/mkd pitch, pt sl, pt shd; wc; chem disp; mv service pnt; shwrs inc; el pnts (15A) €4; lndtte; ice; shops 500m; rest; snacks; bar; BBQ; playgrnd; pool; rv sw & shgl beach adj; boating; fishing; tennis; games area; games rm; sat TV; 4% statics; dogs €1.80; Eng spkn; adv bkg; quiet; CCI. "Beautiful rvside site; British owners; san facs a bit dated, could be cleaner; canoeing & kayaking, golf course, aquapark, go-carting, bowling & animal pk nrby." 1 May-15 Sep. € 18.50   2007*

STE FOY L'ARGENTIERE 9B2 (7km SE Rural) Camp Municipal Les Verpillières, Les Plaines, 69850 St Martin-en-Haut [04 78 48 62 16] Fr Craponne on W o'skts of Lyon SW on D11 to cent of St Martin-en-Haut. W of St Martin dir St Symphorien turn L dir Ste Catherine, site on L in 3km. Fr Ste Foy take D489 SE to Duerne, D34 to St Martin-en-Haut, then as above. This app not for lge o'fits, two 7-12% climbs out of Ste Foy & hairpins after Duerne. Med, pt sl, shd; htd wc; shwrs; el pnts (10A) €3.75; lndtte; shops 4km; snacks; playgrnd; tennis 300m; entmnt; 75% statics; poss cr; adv bkg; quiet. "Lovely wooded site with red squirrels; busy at w/e." 1 Apr-31 Oct. € 4.55   2006*

ST FRAIMBAULT see Domfront 4E1

ST GALMIER 9B2 (2km E Rural) Camping Val de Coise, 42330 St Galmier [04 77 54 14 82; fax 04 77 54 02 45; cplvaldecoise@atciat.com; www.camping-valdecoise.com or www.campeole.com] Fr St Etienne take D1082 (N82) N. In 7km turn R onto D12 sp St Galmier; after x-ing rv bdge on outskirts of vill turn R & foll Camping sp for 2km. Or fr N on D1082 look for sp to St Galmier about 1.5km S of Montrond-les-Bains & turn L onto D6 to St Galmier. On D12 in St Galmier at floral rndabt with fountain if app fr N go L & fr S go R, uphill & foll site sp. Site approx 1.5km fr rndabt. Med, mkd pitch, terr, pt shd; wc; chem disp; shwrs inc; el pnts (10A) €4; gas; lndtte; ice; sm shop; tradsmn; rest & snacks 2km; BBQ; playgrnd; htd pool; paddling pool; tennis 2km; fishing; cycle hire; TV rm; 50% statics; dogs €2.60; phone; Eng spkn; adv bkg; v quiet; cc acc; CCI. "Pretty hilltop town, off beaten track; pleasant site by sm rv; access rd and site rds a little steep; helpful staff; facs stretched high ssn; scenic walks & cycle rtes; highly rec." ♦ ltd. 1 Apr-30 Sep. € 15.00   2007*

ST GAUDENS 8F3 (1km W Rural) Camp Municipal Belvédère des Pyrénées, Rue des Chanteurs du Comminges, 31800 St Gaudens [05 62 00 16 03; www.st-gaudens.com] Foll camping sp fr St Gaudens town cent on N117 dir Tarbes. Site ent at top of hill on N side. Last rd sp is 'Belvédère'. Med, pt shd; htd wc; mv service pnt; shwrs inc; el pnts (4-13A) €2.75-5.35; gas; ice; rest nrby; playgrnd; dogs €1.50; no adv bkg; some rd noise; cc not acc. "Pleasant site; facs clean; gates clsd 2300-0700, need key after; phone to check opening in low ssn; gd views of Pyrenees in gd weather." 1 Jun-30 Sep. € 14.70   2007*

ST GAULTIER 4H2 (S Rural) Camp Municipal L'Illon, Rue de Limage, 36800 St Gaultier [02 54 47 11 22 or 02 54 01 66 00 (Mairie); fax 02 54 01 66 09] Site well sp in town. Med, mkd pitch, pt sl, pt shd; wc; shwrs inc; el pnts; ice; gas; shops 500m; playgrnd; rv & fishing 50m; quiet. "Lovely, peaceful setting; pitch yourself, warden calls; S edge of Brenne National Park; v quiet." Easter-30 Sep. € 7.20   2006*

France

ST GENIEZ D'OLT *9D1* (1km NE) **Camping La Boissière, Route de la Cascade, 12130 St Geniez-d'Olt** [05 65 70 40 43; fax 05 65 47 56 39; cplboissiere@atciat.com; www.camping-aveyron.info or www.campeole.com] Site 500m off D988 on D509; sp on D988 E of town. Lge, mkd pitch, pt sl, pt shd; wc (cont); baby facs; shwrs inc; el pnts (6A) €3.90; lndtte; shop & supmkt 1km; rest; snacks; bar; playgrnd; pool; paddling pool; tennis adj; fishing & canoeing nrby; games area; games rm; entment; dogs €2.80; fairly quiet. "Pleasant town in Lot Valley." ♦ 22 Apr-24 Sep. € 18.90
2006*

ST GENIEZ D'OLT *9D1* (1.8km W Rural) **Camping Marmotel, 12130 St Geniez-d'Olt** [05 65 70 46 51; fax 05 65 47 41 38; info@marmotel.com; www.marmotel.com] Exit A75 at junc 41 onto D37 dir Campagnac. Then onto D202, D45 & D988. Site situated on W of vill by rv on D19. Lge, hdg pitch, pt shd; wc; chem disp; mv service pnt; some pitches with individual san facs; baby facs; sauna; shwrs inc; el pnts (10A) inc; gas; lndtte; shop 500m; tradsmn; rest, bar high ssn; BBQ; playgrnd; htd pool; paddling pool; waterslide; tennis; games area; cycle hire; entmnt; TV rm; some statics; dogs €1.50; Eng spkn; adv bkg; quiet; red low ssn; cc acc; CCI. "Highly rec; some pitches poss tight lge o'fits; poss muddy when wet; gd pool & rest; easy walk into St Geniez medieval town; lovely countryside around." ♦ 1 May-19 Sep. € 23.50 (CChq acc)
2004*

ST GENIS LAVAL see Lyon *9B2*

ST GEORGES (PAS DE CALAIS) see Hesdin *3B3*

ST GEORGES DE DIDONNE see Royan *7B1*

As soon as we get home I'm going to post all these site report forms to the editor for inclusion in next year's guide. I don't want to miss the September deadline.

ST GEORGES DE LEVEJAC *9D1* (1.5km N Rural) **Aire Naturelle de Camping à la Ferme (Bonnal), Le Bouquet, 48500 St Georges-de-Lévéjac** [04 66 48 81 82; http://cardoule.com/lebouquet] Exit A75 junc 42 onto D955 to Le Massegros; turn L onto D32 sp La Canourgue; at next x-rds turn L to Le Bouquet. Site sp at x-rds. Sm, pt sl, pt shd; wc; chem disp (wc); shwrs inc; el pnts (10A) €2.30; dogs; phone; adv bkg; quiet. "Site is a huge field on a farm; v peaceful, nr Gorge du Tarn; all basic facs; owners v helpful." ♦ 1 May-30 Sep. € 9.00
2006*

ST GEORGES DU VIEVRE *3D2* (Rural) **Camp Municipal du Vièvre, Route de Nouards, 27450 St Georges-du-Vièvre** [02 32 42 76 79 or 02 32 56 34 29 (LS); fax 02 32 57 52 90; camping.stgeorgesduvievre@wanadoo.fr; www.camping-normand.com] Fr traff lts on D130 in Pont Authou turn W onto D137 to St Georges-du-Vièvre; in town sq at tourist info turn L uphill sp camping; site 200m on L. If app fr S on N138 at Bernay take D834 sp Le Havre to Lieurey. Turn R onto D137 to St Georges, then turn R at camping sp by sw pool. Sm, hdg pitch, pt shd; wc; chem disp; serviced pitches; shwrs inc; el pnts (5A) inc; gas 200m; lndry rm; shops 200m; playgrnd; pool 150m; tennis 50m; sw 100m; cycle hire; dogs; Eng spkn; adv bkg (rec high ssn); quiet; CCI. "Peaceful; gd facs & pitches; well-run site; v interesting area; gd cycling; vg." ♦ 1 Apr-30 Sep. € 12.50
2007*

ST GEORGES DU VIEVRE *3D2* (3km E Rural) **Camping La Brettonnière (Séjourne), 27450 St Grégoire-de-Vièvre** [02 32 42 82 67; www.stgeorgesvievre.fr] At traff lts on D130 in Pont Authou turn W onto D137 twd St Georges-du-Vièvre; after 7km turn L, sp Camping Rural; site in 1km. NB Steep rdway down & narr terrs poss unsuitable for c'vans. Sm, mkd pitch, terr, shd; wc; chem disp; shwrs inc; el pnts €4; shop 1km; playgrnd; pool 4km; adv bkg; quiet; CCI. "Eggs & cider for sale; CL-type farm site; vg." 1 May-31 Oct. € 14.60
2007*

ST GEORGES LE GAULTIER *4E1* (2km W Rural) **Camping La Gendrie, 72130 St Georges-le-Gaultier** [tel/fax 02 43 33 87 21; info@frenchadventures.co.uk; www.frenchadventures.co.uk] 50km NW fr Le Mans; 8km W N138. In vill take rd by cafe, site 2km on L, dir St Mars-du-Désert. Sm, hdg pitch, pt sl, pt shd; wc; chem disp; shwrs inc; el pnts inc; gas; lndtte; BBQ; shop, rest, snacks, bar, 2km; covrd pool; playgrnd; sand beach 15km; fishing 3km; cycle hire; games rm; adv bkg (dep) - tel 01925 630757 (UK); quiet. "British-owners; conv National Park; beautiful countryside; phone site for rd map; 2 hrs fr Caen ferry." ♦ ltd. Easter-31 Oct. € 17.00
2004*

ST GEORGES SUR LAYON see Doué la Fontaine *4G1*

ST GEOURS DE MAREMNE *8E1* (500m W Rural) **Camping Les Platanes, 3 Route de Lecoume, 40230 St Geours-de-Maremne** [tel/fax 05 58 57 45 35; info@platanes.com; www.platanes.com] Fr N10 take junc sp St Geours-de-Maremne. Site sp fr town cent. Med, pt sl, pt shd; htd wc; chem disp; shwrs inc; el pnts (6A) €4.10; gas; lndtte; ice; shop nr; tradsmn; rest; snacks; bar; BBQ; playgrnd; pool (high ssn); sand beach 8km; tennis; games area; wifi internet; TV; 50% statics; dogs €1.40; phone; poss cr; adv bkg; quiet; cc acc; red low ssn/long stay; CCI. "Great beaches, surfing & rafting nr; friendly British owners; diff to site on lower level; OK upper level; low ssn poss long walk to san facs in dark; muddy pitches if wet; useful NH on N10." 1 Mar-15 Nov. € 17.95
2006*

ST GERAUD DE CORPS see Montpon Ménestérol *7C2*

ST GERMAIN see Aubenas *9D2*

ST GERMAIN DU BEL AIR see Gourdon *7D3*

ST GERMAIN DU BOIS *6H1* (1km S Rural) **Camp Municipal de l'Etang Titard, Route de Louhans, 71330 St Germain-du-Bois [03 85 72 06 15; fax 03 85 72 03 38; mairie-71330-saint-germain-du-bois@wanadoo.fr]** Fr Chalon-sur Saône E on N78, exit at Thurey onto D24 to St Germain. Site sp on D13 adj lake. Sm, mkd pitch, terr, pt shd; wc; chem disp; mv service pnt; shwrs inc; el pnts (6A) €1.85; lndry rm; shops 1km; BBQ; playgrnd, pool in sports grnd adj; fishing; dogs; adv bkg; quiet; CCI. "Lge pitches; friendly warden; no sw in lake; pleasant town; gd cycling area." ♦ 15 May-15 Sep. € 6.00   2005*

ST GERMAIN LES BELLES see Masseret *7B3*

ST GERMAIN L'HERM *9B1* (500m Rural) **Camping St Eloy, 63630 St Germain-l'Herm [04 73 72 05 13 or 04 73 34 75 53 (LS)); fax 04 73 34 70 94; sogeval@wanadoo.fr; www.camping-massif central.com]** Take D906 S fr Ambert to Arlanc, turn R onto D999A to St Germain, site sp on app to vill. Med, mkd pitch, pt sl, terr, pt shd; wc (some cont); chem disp; mv service pnt; el pnts (8A) €3; lndry rm; shop 500m; tradsmn; rest 500m; BBQ; playgrnd; pool; 10% statics; dogs €1.50; phone; adv bkg; quiet. "Pleasant views; cycle & walking tracks fr vill; vg." ♦ ltd. 1 Jun-15 Sep. € 12.00   2004*

ST GERVAIS D'AUVERGNE *7A4* (N Rural) **Camp Municipal L'Etang Philippe, 63390 St Gervais-d'Auvergne [tel/fax 04 73 85 74 84; camping. stgervais-auvergne@wanadoo.fr]** Fr N144 3km S of St Eloy-les-Mines, take D987 S to St Gervais. Site on R just bef town. Lge, hdg pitch, pt shd; wc; chem disp; mv service pnt; shwrs inc; el pnts (10A) inc; lndtte; ice; shop 500m; tradsmn (Jul/Aug); playgrnd; lake sw & beach adj; cycle hire; tennis; mini-golf; archery; entmnt; some statics; dogs €0.50; Eng spkn; adv bkg; quiet; CCI. "Popular, well-maintained site; v clean facs; poss untidy low ssn & ltd facs; lovely setting by sm lake; many activities in town & on site in Jul/Aug; vg." ♦ Easter-30 Sep. € 8.90   2006*

ST GERVAIS D'AUVERGNE *7A4* (8km E Rural) **Camp Municipal Les Prés Dimanches, 63390 Châteauneuf-les-Bains [04 73 86 41 50 or 04 73 86 67 65 (LS); fax 04 73 86 41 71; mairie-chat-les-bains@wanadoo.fr]** Fr Montaigut take N144 S twd Riom & Clermont-Ferrand. In 9km at La Boule S onto D987 to St Gervais. Take D227 E to Chateuneuf-les-Bains. In 7km L onto D109. Site thro vill on R. Sm, pt shd, hdg/mkd pitch; htd wc; shwrs inc; el pnts (6A) inc; lndtte; shop 250m; rest adj; playgrnd; quiet; adv bkg; excel; CCI. "Nrby fishing, tennis, boules, canoeing, spa baths 500m; helpful warden; beautiful countryside." ♦ ltd. 15 May-15 Oct. € 10.00   2005*

ST GERVAIS LES BAINS *9B4* (10km SE Rural) **Camping Le Pontet, Route de Notre-Dame-de-la-Gorge, 74170 Les Contamines-Montjoie [04 50 47 04 04; fax 04 50 47 18 10; campingdupontet@wanadoo.fr; www.camping lepontet.com]** Fr St Gervais take D902 to Les Contamines-Montjoie (sp); go thro vill & foll sp to Notre Dame-de-la-Gorge; site in 2km on L, clearly sp. Lge, mkd pitch, hdstg, pt shd; htd wc; chem disp; baby facs; shwrs inc; el pnts (2-10A) €2.70-9.90; lndtte; shops 2km; tradsmn; rest; snacks; playgrnd; fishing; lake adj; leisure/sports park adj; tennis; mini-golf; horseriding; phone; Eng spkn; adv bkg; quiet. "Alpine walking on mkd walks in area; in winter ski lift 200m fr site." ♦ 1 Dec-30 Sep. € 15.00   2005*

> The opening dates and prices on this campsite have changed. I'll send a site report form to the editor for the next edition of the guide.

ST GERVAIS LES BAINS *9B4* (1.2km S Rural) **Camping Les Dômes de Miage, 197 Route des Contamines, 74170 St Gervais-les-Bains [04 50 93 45 96; fax 04 50 78 10 75; info@ camping-mont-blanc.com; www.camping-mont-blanc.com]** Fr N thro St Gervais, at fork take L sp Les Contamines onto D902, site 2km on L. Med, mkd pitch, pt shd; htd wc (some cont); chem disp; mv service pnt; baby facs; shwrs inc; el pnts (3-10A) €2.90-3.90; gas; lndtte; ice; shop; tradsmn; rest adj; snacks; bar; BBQ; playgrnd; pool, tennis 800m; fishing 1km; cycle hire; internet; TV rm; dogs €2; bus; Eng spkn; adv bkg (bkg fee); quiet; cc acc; red low ssn; CCI. "Superb, family-owned site; beautiful location; warm welcome, friendly; vg walking in area; immac san facs; poss long walk to san facs; excel." ♦ 1 May-21 Sep. € 20.50 (CChq acc)   2007*

See advertisement on next page

ST GERY see St Cirq Lapopie *7D3*

ST GILLES *10E2* (Urban) **Camping de la Chicanette, Rue de la Chicanette, 30800 St Gilles [04 66 87 28 32; fax 04 66 87 49 85; camping. la.chicanette@libertysurf.fr]** Site on D6572 (N572) W fr Arles, sp in cent of town, behind Auberge de la Chicanette. Narr app rd, tight turn to ent. Med, hdg pitch, pt shd; wc; chem disp; shwrs inc; el pnts (6A) inc (rev pol); lndtte; shop adj; snacks; bar; playgrnd; pool; entmnt; 20% statics; dogs €2; poss cr; quiet; red low ssn; CCI. "Sm pitches; site poss unkempt low ssn; interesting old town; birdwatching; cycling; facs poss stretched high ssn; bus to Nîmes." 1 Apr-Nov. € 21.00   2007*

France

ST GILLES CROIX DE VIE *2H3* (3km NE Rural)
**Camping Aire Naturelle Le Petit Beauregard,
Rue du Petit Beauregard, 85800 Le Fenouiller
[02 51 55 07 98]** N fr Les Sables d'Olonne take D38
twd St Gilles Croix-de-Vie. Turn R onto D754 sp Le
Fenouiller for 3km. Turn R; site well sp in 500m. Sm,
mkd pitch, pt shd; wc; chem disp; shwrs inc; el pnts
(6A) €2.50; lndtte; shop 1km; tradsmn; rest nr; BBQ;
playgrnd; sand beach 3km; few statics; dogs; quiet;
Eng spkn; adv bkg; CCI. "V friendly & helpful owner;
excel san facs & v clean; gd beaches nrby; gd value
long stay; St Gilles v busy & cr." ♦ 1 May-30 Sep.
€ 11.00   2005*

ST GILLES CROIX DE VIE *2H3* (3km NE) **Camping
Le Chatelier, Route de Nantes, 85800 Le
Fenouiller [tel/fax 02 28 10 50 75]** Fr St Gilles-
Croix-de-Vie D754 NE, sp to Le Fenouiller, site on L.
Med, mkd pitch, pt shd; wc; chem disp; shwrs inc;
baby facs; el pnts (6A) (rec long lead); gas; lndtte;
tradsmn; shops 2km; snacks; bar; BBQ; playgrnd;
htd pool high ssn; sand beach 3km; entmnt adj;
TV rm; 50% statics; dogs €2.20; quiet. "Friendly
owners; area for tourers far fr pool; sm san facs
block; 10 mins cycle to town." ♦ ltd. Easter-15 Oct.
€ 18.50   2006*

ST GILLES CROIX DE VIE *2H3* (5km E) **Camping
Europa, Le Bois Givrand, 85800 Givrand
[02 51 55 32 68; fax 02 51 55 80 10; mayer@club-
internet.fr; www.europacamp.com]** App site
fr 'Leclerc' rndabt at St Gilles-Croix-de-Vie, take
D6 exit dir Coëx & Aizenay; at 1st & 2nd rndabts go
straight on; at 3rd rndabt take 1st exit; site on right
in 150m, opp boat builders. Lge, mkd pitch, pt shd;
wc (some cont); chem disp; serviced pitches; baby
facs; shwrs inc; el pnts (6-10A) inc; gas; lndtte; shop
3km; rest, snacks, bar high ssn; BBQ; playgrnd;
pool complex; waterslide; sand beach 5km; rv
fishing, boat hire adj; fishing, watersports, cycle hire
& horseriding 5km; golf nr; tennis; mini-golf; entmnt;
wifi internet; games/TV rm; 60% statics (sep area);
recep 0900-1900; dogs €2.70; adv bkg; cc acc.
"Vg; pleasant site but facs stretched high ssn." ♦
1 Jun-20 Sep. € 28.00 ABS - A13   2007*

ST GILLES CROIX DE VIE *2H3* (8km E Rural)
**Camping Le Pont Rouge, Ave Georges
Clémenceau, 85220 St Révérend [tel/fax
02 51 54 68 50; camping.pontrouge@wanadoo.
fr; www.camping-lepontrouge.com]** W fr Aizenay
on D6 rd for St Gilles-Croix-de-Vie, turn R just past
water tower into St Révérend. Foll sp to site. Med,
hdg pitch, pt sl, pt shd; htd wc; chem disp; mv
service pnt; baby facs; shwrs inc; el pnts (6A) €3;
lndtte; ice; shop 1km; tradsmn; rest 3km; snacks;
playgrnd; htd pool; sand beach 8km; games area;
entmnt; TV; 50% statics; dogs €2.25; poss cr; Eng
spkn; adv bkg; quiet; red low ssn; CCI. "Attractive,
secluded site; gd." ♦ 1 Apr-31 Oct. € 18.50
                                                          2006*

ST GILLES CROIX DE VIE *2H3* (4km SE Urban/
Coastal) **CHADOTEL Le Domaine de Beaulieu,
Route des Sables, 85800 Givrand [02 51 55 59 46
or 02 51 33 05 05 (LS); fax 02 51 33 05 06;
chadotel@wanadoo.fr; www.chadotel.com]** S on
D38 fr St Gilles Croix-de-Vie, site sp on L. Lge, hdg/
mkd pitch, pt shd; htd wc; serviced pitches; baby
facs; shwrs inc; el pnts (6A) inc; gas; lndtte; ice;
shop; snacks; bar; BBQ (gas); playgrnd; 2 pools;
waterslide; sand beach 1km; tennis; entmnt; mini-
golf; golf 5km; TV; dogs €2.90; adv bkg; quiet; red
long stay/low ssn; cc acc; CCI. "Lots to do on site
- gd for families; red facs low ssn." ♦ 1 Apr-23 Sep.
€ 27.90   2006*

ST GILLES CROIX DE VIE *2H3* (9km SE) **Camping
Les Alouettes, Route de St Gilles, 85220 La
Chaize-Giraud [02 51 22 96 21; fax 02 51 22 92 68;
pascal.chaillou@free.fr; www.lesalouettes.com]**
Take D38 S fr St Gilles dir Sables-d'Olonne: in
2.5km take D12 to La Chaize-Giraud. Site on L
in 5km. Med, pt sl, pt shd; wc (some cont); chem
disp; shwrs inc; el pnts (6A) €3; gas; lndtte; shop;
tradsmn; snacks; playgrnd; htd pool; sand beach
5km; lake sw 14km; games area; 75% statics; dogs
€1.70; adv bkg; quiet; cc acc; CCI. "Few touring
pitches; gd san facs." ♦ ltd. 18 Apr-14 Sep. € 14.30
                                                          2004*

ST GILLES CROIX DE VIE *2H3* (1km S Coastal) **Camping Les Cyprès, 41 Route du Pont Jaunay, 85800 St Gilles-Croix-de-Vie [02 51 55 38 98; fax 02 51 54 98 94; camping@free.fr]** Site on S end of St Gilles-Croix-di-Vie off D38, after rndabt sp Le Jaunay turn sharp L - hard to spot. Lge, hdg pitch, shd; wc; chem disp; mv service pnt, shwrs inc; el pnts (10A) inc; gas; ice; lndtte; shop, tradsmn; rest; snacks; bar; playgrnd; htd, covrd pool & jacuzzi; sand beach 600m; 12% statics; dogs €3.50; rv 100m; Eng spkn; adv bkg €7.62 fee; quiet; cc acc; red long stay/low ssn; CCI. "Excel for family hols; family-run site; some facs poss clsd low ssn." ◆ 1 Apr-15 Sep. € 23.00   2007*

ST GILLES CROIX DE VIE *2H3* (2km S Coastal) **CHADOTEL Camping Le Bahamas Beach, 168 Route des Sables, 85800 St Gilles-Croix-de-Vie [02 51 54 69 16 or 02 51 33 05 05 (LS); fax 02 51 33 94 04; chadotel@wanadoo.fr; www.chadotel.com]** S fr St Gilles-Croix-de-Vie on Rte des Sables (D38), sp. Lge, hdg/mkd pitch, unshd; wc; chem disp (wc); shwrs inc; el pnts (6A) €4.70; gas; lndtte; ice; sm shop (high ssn) & 3km; tradsmn; rest, snacks & bar (high ssn); BBQ (gas); playgrnd; htd covrd pool; waterslide; sand beach 800m; watersports; excursions; cycle hire; games area; games rm; entmnt; internet; TV rm; many statics; dogs €3; phone; poss cr; Eng spkn; adv bkg; quiet; red long stay/low ssn; cc acc; CCI. "Gd holiday site for children; superb pool; san facs need update - low ssn ltd & poss unclean; facs far fr some pitches; site can be very wet in heavy rain; excel cycle rtes along coast." ◆ ltd. 7 Apr-24 Sep. € 24.20
2007*

ST GIRONS *8G3* (3km N Rural) **Camping Audinac, 09200 Audinac-les-Bains [tel/fax 05 61 66 44 50; accueil@audinac.com; www.audinac.com]** E fr St Girons take D117 twd Foix; after 2km uphill turn L onto D627; foll sp. Med, terr, pt shd; wc; chem disp (wc); mv service pnt; shwrs inc; el pnts (10A) €3; gas; lndtte; ice; shops 5km; tradsmn; rest in ssn; playgrnd; pool high ssn; no statics; dogs €1; no twin-axles; Eng spkn; adv bkg ess; quiet; cc acc; red low ssn; CCI. "Spacious, attractive, well appointed site; not all pitches are level; facs ltd low ssn." ◆ 1 May-30 Sep. € 14.00   2004*

ST GIRONS *8G3* (3km SE Rural/Urban) **Camping du Pont du Nert, Route de Lacourt, 09200 Encourtiech [05 61 66 58 48; dmmadre@aol.com]** On E bank of Rv Salat at junc D33 & D3. Fr St Girons by-pass foll D618 sp Aulus-les-Bains. Site on L at junc to Rv Nert. Sm, pt sl, pt shd; wc; shwrs inc; el pnts (8A) €2; playgrnd; fishing; tennis; quiet; CCI. 1 Jun-15 Sep. € 9.00   2004*

ST GIRONS PLAGE *8E1* (Coastal) **Camping Eurosol, 40560 St Girons-Plage [05 58 47 90 14 or 05 58 56 54 90; fax 05 58 47 76 74; contact@camping-eurosol.com; www.camping-eurosol.com & www.homair.com]** Turn W off D652 at St Girons on D42. Site on L in 4km. Lge, pt sl, pt shd; wc; chem disp; baby facs; shwrs inc; el pnts (6-10A) inc; gas; lndtte; ice; shop; rest; snacks; playgrnd; 2 pools; paddling pool; sand beach 700m; tennis; games area; games rm; horseriding adj; cycle hire; entmnt; TV rm; some statics; dogs €2.50; poss cr; red low ssn; quiet. "Pitches poss tight for long vans." ◆ 12 May-15 Sep. € 31.50
2007*

ST GIRONS PLAGE *8E1* (Coastal) **Camping Les Tourterelles, 40560 St Girons-Plage [05 58 47 93 12; www.camping-tourterelles.com or www.campeole.com]** Exit N10 at Castets & take D42 W to St Girons, then to St Girons-Plage. Lge, pt sl, shd; wc; shwrs inc; el pnts (6A) €3.90; lndtte; ice; shops 1km; BBQ; playgrnd; sand beach 200m; games area; games rm; entmnt; dogs €1; poss cr; quiet. "Situated among pine trees; footpath to dunes & beach; sw restricted to area with lifeguards." 1 May-30 Sep. € 20.20   2007*

STE HERMINE *2H4* (11km NE Rural) **FFCC Camping Le Colombier (Naturist), 85210 St Martin-Lars [02 51 27 83 84; fax 02 51 27 87 29; lecolombier.nat@wanadoo.fr; www.lecolombier-naturisme.com]** Fr junc 7 of A83 take D137 N thro Ste Hermine (do not foll sp for town cent.) Just past town limit turn R onto N148 sp Niort & Thiré. In 2km turn R sp Thiré & in 500m turn R onto D8. Turn L onto D10 sp St Martin-Lars. 150m past St Martin-Lars turn R sp Le Columbier. Site ent on L in 200m. Med, pt sl, pt shd; wc; chem disp; shwrs inc; el pnts (6A) €3.60; lndtte; ice; shops 2km; tradsmn; rest; snacks; bar; playgrnd; new pool; lake sw; 2% statics to let; dogs €3.60; poss cr; Eng spkn; adv bkg; quiet; cc acc; INF card req. "Excel, well-run site; lge pitches; vg facs; friendly Dutch owners; conv Mervent National Park; excel." ◆ ltd. 1 Apr-31 Oct. € 18.50   2007*

STE HERMINE *2H4* (500m SW Rural) **Camp Municipal La Smagne, 85210 Ste Hermine [02 51 27 35 54]** On D137 500m S of vill cent. Med, mkd pitch; pt shd; wc; chem disp; serviced pitches; mv service pnt; shwrs inc; el pnts (5A) €1.50; gas; lndtte; shops 500m; playgrnd; pool adj; tennis; quiet but some rd noise. "Nice site; pleasant vill; conv location just off A83; phone ahead to check open low ssn." 15 Jun-15 Sep. € 4.50   2004*

ST HILAIRE DE LUSIGNAN see Agen *8E3*

France

ST HILAIRE DE RIEZ 2H3 (Coastal) **Camp Municipal de La Plage de Riez, Ave des Mimosas, 85270 St Hilaire-de-Riez [02 51 54 36 59; fax 02 51 60 07 84; riez85@free.fr; www.souslespins. com]** Fr St Hilaire take D6A sp Sion-sur-l'Océan. Turn R at traff lts into Ave des Mimosas, site 1st L. V lge, mkd pitch, pt sl, shd; wc; some serviced pitch; shwrs inc; el pnts (10A) €3.40; gas; lndtte; ice; shop; rest; snacks; bar; playgrnd; pool 5km; sand beach adj; cycle hire; internet; entmnt; TV; 30% statics; dogs €3.90; poss cr; Eng spkn; red low ssn. "Vg for dogs; exceptionally helpful manager." 30 Mar-31 Oct. € 21.80   2007*

Before we move on, I'm going to fill in some site report forms and post them off to the editor, otherwise they won't arrive in time for the deadline at the end of September.

ST HILAIRE DE RIEZ 2H3 (Coastal) **Camping La Ningle, Chemin des Roselières, 85270 St Hilaire-de-Riez [02 51 54 07 11 or 02 51 54 16 65 (LS); fax 02 51 54 99 39; campingdelaningle@wanadoo. fr; www.campinglaningle.com]** Fr St Hilaire, take rd sp Sion-sur-l'Océan. At traff lts/rndabt, foll sp 'Autres Campings' until site sp is seen. Med, hdg/ mkd pitch, pt shd, wc; chem disp; serviced pitches; shwrs inc; el pnts (6A) inc; gas; lndtte; shop; tradsmn; bar; playgrnd; pool; sand beach 500m; tennis; fitness rm; poss cr; adv bkg (dep req) & bkg fee; dogs €1.90; Eng spkn; red low ssn; CCI. "Highly rec; v friendly & personal; helpful; gd sized pitches; well-maintained; excel." ♦ ltd. 20 May-10 Sep. € 24.40   2006*

ST HILAIRE DE RIEZ 2H3 (2km N Urban/Coastal) **Camping Cap Natur (Naturist), 151 Ave de la Faye, 85270 St Hilaire-de-Riez [02 51 60 11 66; fax 02 51 60 17 48; info@cap-natur.com; www. cap-natur.com]** Ent St Hilaire fr N via D69, turn R at 1st rndabt; R at next rndabt; fork R in approx 300m; site on L approx 600m. Med, hdg/mkd pitch, pt sl, pt terr, pt shd; htd wc; chem disp; mv service pnt; baby facs; sauna; shwrs inc; el pnts (10A) €4.40; gas; lndtte; ice; shop & 1km; tradsmn; rest; snacks; bar; BBQ; playgrnd; 2 htd pools (1 covrd); sand/shgl beach 800m (naturist beach 6km); games area; games rm; cycle hire; golf 10km; entmnt; many statics; dogs €2.50; poss cr; Eng spkn; adv bkg (dep req); quiet; 20% red 20+ days/low ssn; cc acc; INF card req (can purchase on site). "Excel site in gd location; sm pitches; gd facs; v friendly staff; gd base for interesting area; can be busy." ♦ 31 Mar-14 Oct. € 28.70   2007*

ST HILAIRE DE RIEZ 2H3 (6km N Rural) **Camping La Puerta del Sol, Les Borderies, 85270 St Hilaire-de-Riez [02 51 49 10 10; fax 02 51 49 84 84; info@campinglapuertadelsol. com; www.campinglapuertadelsol.com]** N on D38 fr Les Sables-d'Olonne; exit on D69 sp Soullan, Challans, Le Pissot. At next rndabt take 3rd exit & foll lge sp to site. Site on R in 1.5km. Lge, hdg/ mkd pitch, pt sl, pt shd; wc; chem disp; serviced pitches; baby facs; shwrs inc; el pnts (6A) inc (poss rev pol); lndtte; ice; shop, rest, snacks, bar high ssn; BBQ (gas/elec); playgrnd; htd pool; paddling pool; waterslide; sand beach 4.5km; watersports 5km; fishing 2km; tennis; horseriding; golf; cycle hire; games area; entmnt; wifi internet; games/TV rm; 50% statics; dogs €4; Eng spkn; adv bkg; quiet; cc acc; CCI. "Vg; red facs low ssn; sm pitches not rec twin-axles." ♦ 1 Apr-30 Sep. € 29.00 ABS - A19   2007*

ST HILAIRE DE RIEZ 2H3 (1km W Coastal) **Camp Municipal de Sion, Ave de la Forêt, Sion-sur-l'Océan, 85270 St Hilaire-de-Riez [02 51 54 34 23; fax 02 51 60 07 84; sion85@free.fr; www. souslespins.com]** Fr St Hilaire, take D6A sp Sion-sur-l'Océan, strt at traff lts. Site 200m on R. Lge, mkd pitch, pt shd; wc; chem disp; mv service pnt; shwrs inc; el pnts (10A) inc; lndtte; ice; shop, rest, snacks, bar 400m; BBQ; playgrnd; pool 1km; sand beach adj; games rm; 15% statics; dogs €2.70; phone; Eng spkn; adv bkg rec high ssn; quiet; CCI. "Gd for family holidays." ♦ 30 Mar-31 Oct. € 26.90   2007*

There aren't many sites open this early in the year. We'd better phone ahead to check that the one we're heading for is actually open.

ST HILAIRE DE RIEZ 2H3 (2km NW) **Camping Les Chouans, 108 Ave de la Faye, 85270 St Hilaire-de-Riez [02 51 54 34 90 or 02 51 54 33 87; fax 02 51 55 33 87; leschouans@free.fr or idees@ sunmarina.com; www.sunmarina.com]** Take main rd fr St Gilles-Croix-de-Vie to St Hilaire. At rndabt foll sps for St Hilaire to 2nd rndabt. Foll sps for Sion cont for La Pege. Pass 2 sites, Les Chouans is 3rd. Lge, pt shd; wc; baby facs; shwrs inc; el pnts (6-10A); lndtte; lndry rm; shop; rest; snacks; bar; BBQ (gas); playgrnd; htd pool; beach & waterslide 1.3km; games area; fitness rm; child club; entmnt; TV; 70% statics; dogs €3; quiet. "Lge pitches." ♦ 15 May-15 Sep. € 29.00 (3 persons)   2004*

ST HILAIRE DE RIEZ *2H3* (5km NW Coastal)
Camping La Parée Préneau, 23 Ave de la Parée
Préneau, 85270 St Hilaire-de-Riez [02 51 54 33 84;
fax 02 51 55 29 57; camplapareepreneau@
wanadoo.fr; www.campinglapareepreneau.com]
Fr N on D38; on reaching St Hilaire-de-Riez at
1st rndabt take 1st exit sp Sion-sur-l'Océan and
St Hilaire-de-Riez centre. At next rndabt take 1st exit
(petrol station on R) sp La Parée Préneau & bear R
soon after rndabt again sp La Parée Préneau; site on
L in 2km. Or fr Les Sables-d'Olonne N on D38, go
thro St Gilles-Croix-de-Vie & pass St Hilaire-de-Riez;
at rndabt turn L sp Sion-sur-l'Océan & St Hilaire-de-
Riez centre, then as above. Lge, mkd pitch, pt sl,
shd; wc (some cont); baby facs; shwrs inc; el pnts
(6A) inc; Indtte; sumpkt nrby; tradsmn; bar; BBQ
(charcoal/gas); playgrnd; 2 pools (1 htd/covrd);
paddling pool; jacuzzi; sand beach 1km; fishing 1km;
windsurfing 5km; entmnt; TV/games rm; dogs €2.10;
recep 1000-1900 high ssn; c'vans over 7m not acc;
Eng spkn; adv bkg; red low ssn; cc acc high ssn (not
Amex); CCI. "Gd, simple site; v shaded; pool poss
unsupervised at times, care req with young children;
some pitches poss tight lge o'fits; mkt Thu & Sun." ♦
19 May-7 Sep. € 22.00 ABS - A29   2007*

ST HILAIRE DU HARCOUET *2E4* (1km W Urban)
FFCC Camp Municipal de la Sélune, 50600
St Hilaire-du-Harcouët [02 33 49 43 74 or
02 33 49 70 06; fax 02 33 49 59 40; info@st-hilaire.
fr; www.st-hilaire.fr] Sp on N side of N176 twd
Mont St Michel/St Malo/Dinan, on W side of town;
well sp. Med, hdg pitch, pt sl, pt shd; wc; chem
disp; shwrs inc; el pnts (6A) €1.85; Indry rm; shops
1km; snacks 500m; playgrnd; pool 300m; dogs;
gate locked 2200-0730; 15% red 20+ days; 10%
red CCI. "Easy access; v helpful & pleasant warden;
vet practice on corner with N176; poss lge groups
of noisy youths; excel." 1 Apr-15 Sep. € 7.85
                                              2007*

ST HILAIRE LA FORET *7A1* (4km SW Rural)
Camping Les Batardières, Rue des Bartardières,
85440 St Hilaire-la-Forêt [02 51 33 33 85]
Fr Sables d'Olonne take D949 twd Avrillé. 7km after
Talmont-St-Hilaire fork R on D70 to St Hilaire-la-
Forêt. In 3km turn R on ent vill. Site 70m on L. Med,
hdg pitch, pt shd; wc; chem disp; serviced pitches;
shwrs inc; el pnts (6A) €3.50; Indtte; ice; shop adj;
playgrnd; sand beach 5km; free tennis; cycling; no
statics; dogs €1.50; adv bkg; quiet; CCI. "Excel;
spacious pitches; wide choice of beaches; excel for
children & families; rec." 1 Jul-2 Sep. € 19.50
                                              2006*

ST HILAIRE LA FORET *7A1* (1km NW Rural)
Camping La Grand' Métairie, 8 Rue de la
Vineuse-en-Plaine, 85440 St Hilaire-la-Forêt
[02 51 33 32 38; fax 02 51 33 25 69; info@
camping-grandmetairie.com; www.la-grand-
metairie.com] Fr D949 turn S onto D70, sp
St Hilaire-la-Forêt, or fr Avrillé take D19. Site at
ent to vill. Lge, hdg/mkd pitch, hdstg, pt shd; wc;
chem disp; serviced pitches; sauna; shwrs inc; el
pnts (6A) inc; gas; Indtte; ice; shop; tradsmn; rest;
snacks; bar; playgrnd; htd, covrd pool; paddling
pool; sand beach 3km; tennis; jacuzzi; fitness
rm; play rm; cycle hire; golf 15km; entmnt & child
entmnt; 80% statics; dogs €3; Eng spkn; adv bkg
(dep req + bkg fee); quiet; red low ssn/long stay; cc
acc; red CCI. "Gd base for beaches, La Rochelle,
Ile de Ré; friendly & helpful owners; excel." ♦
31 Mar-30 Sep. € 27.00   2007*

See advertisement

ST HILAIRE ST FLORENT see Saumur *4G1*

ST HONORE LES BAINS *4H4* (150m Rural) **Camp Municipal Plateau du Guet, 13 Rue Eugène Collin, 58360 St Honoré-les-Bains [03 86 30 76 00 or 03 86 30 74 87 (Mairie); fax 03 86 30 73 33; mairie-de-st-honore-les-bains@wanadoo.fr]** On D985 fr Luzy to St Honoré-les-Bains. In cent vill turn L on D106 twd Vandenesse. Site on L in 150m. Or N fr Château-Chinon 27km. Then D985 to St Honoré. Med, pt hdstg, pt terr, pt shd; wc; shwrs inc; el pnts (10A) €2.50; lndry rm; shop; snacks 100m; playgrnd; pool 1km; adv bkg; quiet; CCI. "V clean facs; pleasant, conv site but town rather run down." ♦ 1 Apr-10 Oct. € 8.10   2005*

> Did you know you can fill in site report forms on the Club's website — www.caravanclub.co.uk?

ST HONORE LES BAINS *4H4* (1km W Rural) **Camping Les Bains, 15 Ave Jean Mermoz, 58360 St Honoré-les-Bains [03 86 30 73 44; fax 03 86 30 61 88; camping-les-bains@wanadoo. fr; www.campinglesbains.com]** Fr St Honoré-les-Bains foll site sp as 'Village des Bains' fr town cent on D106 twd Vandenesse. Med, hdg/mkd pitch, some hdstg, pt sl, shd; wc (some cont); chem disp; baby facs; shwrs inc; el pnts (6A) inc; gas; lndtte; shop 1km; rest; snacks; bar; BBQ; playgrnd; pool; waterslide; paddling pool; fishing; tennis, mini-golf; horseriding 300m; cycle hire; entmnt; internet; games/TV rm; dogs €1.50; recep 0830-2200; c'vans over 8m not acc; Eng spkn; adv bkg; quiet low ssn; cc acc; CCI. "Helpful staff; adj Morvan Regional National Park; gd walking; sm pitches & poss waterlogged in wet weather; mkt Thu am." ♦ 1 Apr-31 Oct. € 16.00 (CChq acc) ABS - L01   2007*

ST JACQUES DES BLATS *7C4* (Rural) **Camp Municipal des Blats, Route de la Gare, 15800 St Jacques-des-Blats [04 71 47 06 00 or 04 71 47 05 90 (Mairie); fax 04 71 47 07 09; i-tourisme-st-jacques@wanadoo.fr]** L of N122 Murat to Aurillac; 3km W of Horan Tunnel in vill of St Jacques-des-Blats; 300m fr N122 down steep app rd; sp in vill. Sm, hdg pitch, pt shd; wc; chem disp; shwrs; el pnts (10A) €2.40; lndtte; ice; shops 500m; BBQ; playgrnd; mini-golf; TV; 30% statics; quiet; CCI. "Gd British-owned hotel for meals & bar nrby; 4 rests within walking dist; gd walking & VTT trails fr site; lift to summit Plomb de Cantal; vg mountain walks." 1 May-30 Sep. € 8.80   2005*

ST JANS CAPPEL see Bailleul *3A3*

ST JEAN D'ANGELY *7B2* (500m W Rural) **Camping du Val de Boutonne, Quai de Bernouet, 17400 St Jean-d'Angély [05 46 32 26 16; fax 05 46 32 29 54; info@valba.net; www.valba.net]** Exit A10 at junc 34; head SE on D939; turn R at 1st rndabt into town. Site sp. Med, mkd pitch, shd; wc (some cont); chem disp; mv service pnt; shwrs inc; el pnts (6A) €3; lndtte; ice; sm shop; tradsmn; rest, snacks, bar 200m; playgrnd; htd covrd pool 500m; TV rm; 10% statics; dogs €1.20; phone adj; Eng spkn; adv bkg (dep req); quiet; cc acc; CCI. "Pleasant, friendly, clean site by Rv Boutonne; v helpful owners; gd san facs; park with boating lake & rv adj; poss open Apr-Oct - phone ahead; vg." ♦ 1 Apr-30 Sep. € 12.00   2007*

ST JEAN DE CEYRARGUES see Alès *10E1*

ST JEAN DE COUZ see Echelles, Les *9B3*

ST JEAN DE LOSNE *6H1* **Camping Essi Les Herlequins, 21170 St Jean-de-Losne [03 80 39 22 26; fax 03 80 29 05 48; www. saintjeandelosne.com]** Site sp on ent town fr N on D968. Access fr town on Quai National & Rue du Port-Bernard on N bank of Rv Saône. Med, hdg/mkd pitch, hdstg, pt shd; wc (some cont); shwrs; el pnts (10A); ice; rest; snacks; BBQ; playgrnd; sand beach; rv sw; dogs €1.14; poss cr; adv bkg; quiet. "Fair for sh stay; 10 mins walk fr town cent; v helpful, friendly owners." 1 May-30 Sep. € 13.60   2005*

ST JEAN DE LUZ *8F1* (3km N Coastal) **Camping Bord de Mer, Erromardie, 64500 St Jean-de-Luz [tel/fax 05 59 26 24 61]** Exit A63 junc 3 onto N10 dir St Jean-de-Luz. In 1km cross rlwy & immed turn sharp R sp Erromardie. Site on sharp turn L bef beach. Ent by plastic chain fence bef ent to prom, but easy to miss. Med, hdg pitch, pt sl; terr; wc (mainly cont); chem disp; mv service pnt; shwrs inc; el pnts (4-10A) €3; lndy rm; tradsmn; snacks; bar; BBQ; sand beach adj; dogs; quiet. "Nice site in excel position; v basic facs in basement need update but clean; friendly owner; recep clsd 1300-1600; cliff walk to town; superb, clean beach; gd sh stay en route Spain; rec." ♦ ltd. 1 Mar-30 Oct. € 20.50   2007*

ST JEAN DE LUZ *8F1* (3km N Coastal) **Camping de la Ferme Erromardie, 64500 St Jean-de-Luz [05 59 26 34 26; fax 05 59 51 26 02]** Exit A63 junc 3 onto N10 sp St Jean-de-Luz. After 1km x rlwy and turn immed sharp R sp Erromardie. Site ent on R in 1km just bef rest/bar. Lge, hdg/mkd pitch, shd; wc; chem disp; mv service pnt; baby facs; shwrs inc; el pnts (4-6A) €2.30-3; gas; lndtte; tradsmn; rest; snacks; bar; playgrnd; beach adj; dogs €0.60; poss cr; Eng spkn; adv bkg; CCI. "Ideal for coastal walk into St Jean-de-Luz; Basque museum nrby; san facs down steps & poss stretched high ssn." 15 Mar-15 Oct. € 18.50   2005*

ST JEAN DE LUZ 8F1 (3km N Urban/Coastal) Camping International Erromardie, Ave de la Source, 64500 St Jean-de-Luz [05 59 26 07 74; fax 05 59 51 12 11; camping-international@ wanadoo.fr; www.erromardie.com] Fr A63 exit junc 3 sp St Jean-de-Luz. At traff lts at end of slip rd turn L onto N10 sp St Jean; in 1km cross rlwy & immed turn sharp R sp Erromardie, site on R in 1km opp beach. Lge, hdg/mkd pitch, pt sl, shd; wc (some cont); chem disp (wc); shwrs inc; el pnts (5A) inc; lndtte; shop; rest; snacks; bar; BBQ (charcoal); playgrnd; pool; sand/shgl beach adj; fishing 2km; watersports 3km; golf, entmnt; TV rm; many statics; dogs €3; c'vans over 7m not acc high ssn; adv bkg; quiet; cc acc. "Mkt Tue & Fri am; some facs poss clsd & office clsd after 1800 low ssn; poss poor security; twin-axle c'vans acc." 7 Apr-30 Sep. € 29.00 ABS - A17   2007*

ST JEAN DE LUZ 8F1 (1.5km NE Coastal) Camping Iratzia, Chemin d'Erromardie, 64500 St Jean-de-Luz [05 59 26 14 89; fax 05 59 26 69 69] Fr A63 exit St Jean-de-Luz Nord. Join N10 twds St Jean; after Shell g'ge cross rlwy bdge & immed turn R sp Erromardie. Site on R in 500m. Lge, pt terr, pt sl, pt shd; wc; shwrs inc; el pnts (6A) €3.50; lndry rm; ice; shop; rest; bar; playgrnd; sand beach 300m; TV; entmnt; dogs €1; phone; poss cr; adv bkg; red low ssn; CCI. "Poss some noise fr young tenters & chalets; many pitches diff access for long o'fits; friendly, well-kept, clean site." 1 May-30 Sep.
2006*

ST JEAN DE LUZ 8F1 (3km NE Coastal) Camping Itsas-Mendi, Acotz, 64500 St Jean-de-Luz [05 59 26 56 50; fax 05 59 26 54 44; itsas@ wanadoo.fr; www.itsas-mendi.com] Exit A63 junc 3 sp St Jean-de-Luz; take N10 dir Biarritz; in 3km turn L sp Acotz Plage & Camping; site well sp. Lge, hdg pitch, pt sl, terr, shd; htd wc; chem disp; mv service pnt; sauna; shwrs inc; fam bthrm; el pnts (10A) inc; lndtte; ice; shop; rest; snacks; bar; playgrnd; htd pools; waterslides & aquatic area; paddling pool; tennis; games area; beach 500m; internet; TV rm; dogs €2.20; phone; poss cr; Eng spkn; quiet but rlwy adj; red low ssn; CCI. "Excel." ♦ 30 Mar-30 Sep. € 32.50   2007*

ST JEAN DE LUZ 8F1 (3km NE Coastal) Camping Le Maya, Quartier Acotz, 64500 St Jean-de-Luz [05 59 26 54 91; CampingMaya@aol.com] Fr N exit A63 at Biarritz Sud onto N10 head SW. After passing thro Guéthary turn W off N10 sp Acotz, foll camping sp. Or fr S exit junc 3 sp St Jean-de-Luz onto N10, as above. Med, mkd pitch, terr, pt shd; wc; chem disp; shwrs; el pnts (6A) €3; gas; shops adj; hypmkt 1km; rest, snacks 300m; bar; playgrnd; sand beach 500m; dogs €2; adv bkg; quiet; Eng spkn; CCI. "Gd long stay/NH." 25 Jun-25 Sep. € 17.80   2004*

ST JEAN DE LUZ 8F1 (4km NE Rural) Camping Atlantica, Quartier Acotz, 64500 St Jean-de-Luz [05 59 47 72 44; fax 05 59 54 72 27; camping@ club-internet.fr; www.campingatlantica.com] Exit A63 at junc 3 sp St Jean-de-Luz-Nord. Take (N10) twd Biarritz at top of hill sp Acotz Plage; site well sp. Lge, mkd pitch, pt sl, pt shd; wc; mv service pnt; shwrs inc; baby facs; el pnts (6A) €3.80; lndtte; shop; rest; snacks; bar; playgrnd; pool; beach 500m; entmnt; games/TV rm; 35% statics; dogs €2.30; bus; poss cr; Eng spkn; adv bkg (dep €61 + bkg fee €15); quiet but some rd & train noise; cc acc; CCI. "Excel pool; facs ltd low ssn; excel all stays." ♦ 15 Mar-15 Sep. € 23.00   2004*

ST JEAN DE LUZ 8F1 (4km NE Coastal) Camping Duna-Munguy, Rue Mer, Acotz Plages, 64500 St Jean-de-Luz [05 59 47 70 70; fax 05 59 47 78 82; www.camping-dunamunguy. com] Exit A63 at junc 3 St Jean-de-Luz Nord. Take N10 twd Biarritz, turn L at 2nd rise then R at T-junc & down hill under rlwy bdge sp Acotz Plages. Site well sp. NB Steep downhill app. Sm, mkd pitch, hdstg, pt shd; htd wc; chem disp; shwrs inc; jacuzzi; el pnts (10A) €4 (poss rev pol); lndtte; playgrnd; sm pool; sandy beach 300m; golf 5km; TV; 80% statics; dogs €3; phone; bus 1km (at top of hill); site clsd 15 Dec-15 Jan; poss cr; Eng spkn; adv bkg; quiet but rlwy noise; cc not acc; CCI. "Steep app poss diff long o'fits & ltd space on site; gd san facs with smart shwrs; v helpful owner; conv on way to Spain; site 1 of 10 in area; no sea views but sheltered in storms; gd coastal walks; pitches have patio, table/chairs & washing line; excel & rec." ♦ ltd. 3 Feb-17 Nov. € 25.00   2007*

ST JEAN DE LUZ 8F1 (4km NE Coastal) Camping Merko Lacarra, Plage d'Acotz, 64500 St Jean-de-Luz [05 59 26 56 76; fax 05 59 54 73 81; contact@ merkolacarra.com; www.merkolacarra.com] Exit A63 at junc 3 St Jean-de-Luz Nord. Take N10 twd Biarritz, turn L at 2nd rise then R at T-junc & down hill under rlwy bdge sp Acotz Plages, site on L. NB steep downhill app. Med, pt sl, pt shd; wc; chem disp; shwrs; el pnts (16A) £3.80; lndtte; shop; snacks; bar; sand beach over rd; 15% statics; dogs €1.50; m'van o'night sep area; Eng spkn; quiet; cc acc; CCI. "Lovely walking/cycling along coast; poss cr high ssn; conv foothills Pyrenees." ♦ 27 Mar-30 Oct. € 23.00   2005*

ST JEAN DE LUZ 8F1 (4km NE Coastal) Camping-Plage Soubelet, Quartier Acotz, 64500 St Jean-de-Luz [05 59 26 51 60] Fr St Jean take N10 twd Biarritz. Bef Guéthary turn L to Acotz/Plages. Turn R down hill, under rlwy bdge & turn L. Site on R in 300m. Lge, mkd pitch, hdstg, pt shd; htd wc; chem disp; baby facs; shwrs inc; el pnts (12A) €2.75; lndtte; shop; snacks; playgrnd; sand beach adj; 5% statics; poss cr; Eng spkn. "Gd sea views; peaceful, poss ltd san facs in low ssn & stretched high sssn, rec own san facs; poss unkempt; conv Bidart for rests, shops etc." Easter-30 Oct. € 16.60
2004*

France

ST JEAN DE LUZ *8F1* (5km NE Coastal) **Camping Les Tamaris Plage, 64500 St Jean-de-Luz [05 59 26 55 90; fax 05 59 47 70 15; contact@ tamaris-plage.com]** Fr A63 take St Jean-de-Luz Nord exit. Turn R sp Guéthary. After 1km turn L sp Acotz, Campings-Plages. Then foll sps to Tamaris Plage. Med, mkd pitch, pt sl, pt shd; wc; chem disp; baby facs; shwrs inc; el pnts (5A) inc; gas; lndtte; ice; shop, rest, snacks, bar 1.5km; BBQ; playgrnd; beach adj; child club; entmnt; TV rm; phone; poss cr; poss noisy; Eng spkn; red low ssn; CCI. "Under personal supervision of owner; do not arrive bet 1200-1400; luxurious facs block has fountain & flowers; excel." ♦ 1 Apr-30 Sep. € 29.00   2004*

ST JEAN DE LUZ *8F1* (5km NE Coastal) **Caravaning Playa, Quartier Acotz, 64500 St Jean-de-Luz [tel/fax 05 59 26 55 85; www.camping-playa.com]** Fr St Jean-de-Luz take N10 twd Biarritz. Before Guéthary turn L at sp Acotz-Plages. Turn L at T-junc & foll rd to site. Med, mkd pitch, terr, pt shd; wc; chem disp; shwrs inc; el pnts (6A) €3; lndtte; shop; rest; snacks; bar; sand/shgl beach adj; fishing; boating; many statics; dogs €1.80; poss cr; noisy nr rd; cc acc; CCI. "V pretty site o'looking lovely beach." ♦ 1 Apr-30 Oct. € 22.00   2006*

ST JEAN DE LUZ *8F1* (6km SE Urban) **Camping Chourio, Luberriaga, 64310 Ascain [05 59 54 06 31 or 05 59 54 04 32]** Fr St Jean-de-Luz take D918 sp Ascain. In 6km turn R at traff lts, in 250m over rv bdge & turn L at mini-rndabt. Site sp in town. Med, pt shd; wc; chem disp; shwrs €1; el pnts (6A) €2.40; tradsmn; rest, snacks, bar 1km; poss cr; quiet; CCI. "Conv Spanish border; facs tired but clean & adequate." 1 Apr-31 Oct. € 9.50   2004*

ST JEAN DE LUZ *8F1* (10km SE Rural) **Camping d'Ibarron, 64310 St Pée-sur-Nivelle [05 59 54 10 43; fax 05 59 54 51 95; camping.dibarron@wanadoo.fr; www.camping-ibarron.com]** Fr St Jean take D918 twd St Pée, site 2km bef St Pée on R of rd. Lge, shd; wc (mainly cont); chem disp; mv service pnt; shwrs inc; el pnts (6A) €3.90; gas 3km; lndtte; shop, tradsmn, snacks high ssn; supmkt adj; playgrnd; pool; sand beach 10km; tennis; 5% statics; dogs €1.60; phone; Eng spkn; adv bkg; quiet; CCI. "Helpful, pleasant owner; ltd facs low ssn; on main rd & no footpath to walk to vill; excel." ♦ 1 May-30 Sep. € 18.70   2007*

ST JEAN DE LUZ *8F1* (10km SE Rural) **Camping Goyetchea, Route d'Ahetze, 64310 St Pée-sur-Nivelle [05 59 54 19 59; info@camping-goyetchea.com; www.camping-goyetchea.com]** Fr St Jean-de-Luz take D918 twd St Pée-sur-Nivelle. Turn L at Hotel Bonnet at Ibarron D855. Site on R in 800m. Med, pt shd; wc (some cont); chem disp; baby facs; shwrs inc; el pnts (6A) €3.50; gas; lndry rm; ice; shop; supmkt 800m; tradsmn; rest; snacks; BBQ; playgrnd; pool; sand beach 10km; lake sw 4km; games area; entmnt; TV rm; 10% statics; dogs €1.50; adv bkg; quiet; cc acc; red low ssn; CCI. "Pleasant, quiet site; vg." ♦ 3 Jun-16 Sep. € 18.50   2006*

> This guide relies on site report forms submitted by caravanners like us; we'll do our bit and tell the editor what we think of the campsites we've visited.

⊞**ST JEAN DE LUZ** *8F1* (3km SW Rural) **Camping Larrouleta, 210 Route de Socoa, 64122 Urrugne [05 59 47 37 84; fax 05 59 47 42 54; info@ larrouleta.com; www.larrouleta.com]** Exit A63 junc 2 St Jean-de-Luz Sud. Pass under N10 & take 1st L sp Urrugne. Loop back up to N10 & turn R, site sp in 500m. Or fr S on N10, 2km beyond Urrugne vill (by-pass vill), turn L into minor rd, site 50m on R. Lge, hdg/mkd pitch, hdstg, pt shd; htd wc; chem disp; baby facs; shwrs inc; el pnts (5A) €2.50 (poss rev pol); gas; lndtte; ice; shop; hypmkt 1.5km; tradsmn; rest (Jul/Aug); snacks; bar; playgrnd; htd, covrd pool; lake sw, fishing & boating; sand beach 3km; tennis; games; wifi internet; entmnt; no statics (2007); dogs €2; phone; bus; poss cr; some Eng spkn; adv bkg ess high ssn; rd/rlwy noise & poss noise fr disco; red low ssn; cc acc; CCI. "Pleasant, well-maintained, clean site nr lake; excel san facs (but unisex low ssn) & pool; v friendly & helpful (ask for dir on dep to avoid dangerous bend); gd hdstg; some pitches unreliable in wet but can park on site rds/hdstg; poss ltd facs low ssn; poor facs for disabled; conv a'route, Biarritz & en rte Spain; vg all ssns." ♦ € 16.00   2007*

ST JEAN DE LUZ *8F1* (4km SW Coastal) **Camping Juantcho, Route de la Corniche, Socoa, 64122 Urrugne [tel/fax 05 59 47 11 97; camping.juantcho@wanadoo.fr; www.camping-juantcho.com]** Leave A63 at junc 2. Keep to L lane & immed after passing toll booth take exit to Socoa, site on R on cliff top rd - busy & steep. Lge, mkd pitch, terr, pt shd; wc; chem disp; shwrs inc; el pnts (5A) €3.80; lndtte; ice; shop & snacks in ssn; playgrnd; beach 500m; fishing; watersports; entmnts 500m; some statics; dogs €2; poss cr; quiet; CCI. "V helpful staff; beautiful beach; ferry fr Socoa to St Jean; ltd facs low ssn." 1 May-30 Sep. € 16.80   2006*

Camping du Col d'Ibardin

Basque Country

Located between Biarritz (25 kms) and San Sebastian (25kms), our campsite will please the chidren as much as their parents

Swimming Pool / Tennis / Playground / Bar/ Snack / Take Away / Launderette / Kid's Club / Mobil homes to rent...

Tél. : (00 33) 559 54 31 21 • Fax : (00 33) 559 54 62 28 • 64122 Urrugne • www.col-ibardin.com • info@col-ibardin.com

ST JEAN DE LUZ *8F1* (7km SW Rural) **Camping Aire-Ona, 64122 Urrugne** [tel/fax 05 59 54 30 32] S fr Bayonne on N10, take A63 by-passing St Jean-de-Luz. Take Urrugne exit, immed E sp Ascain & camping sp. Fr St Jean-de-Luz exit by N10, turn R sp 'Frontière par Béhobie' past m'way access & turn R in 1km. Site in 1km. Last 500m of app narr but surface gd. Med, pt sl, pt shd; wc; shwrs inc; el pnts (4A) inc; gas; lndtte; ice; shop & 4km; BBQ; playgrnd; sand beach, sailing, watersports 5km; cycle hire; adv bkg; quiet. "Pleasant owners resident; gd views of Pyrenees foothills; La Rhune funicular 10km." 1 Jun-30 Sep. € 15.00   2004*

> As soon as we get home I'm going to post all these site report forms to the editor for inclusion in next year's guide. I don't want to miss the September deadline.

ST JEAN DE LUZ *8F1* (7km SW Rural) **Camping Sunêlia du Col d'Ibardin, Route d'Ascain, 64122 Urrugne** [05 59 54 31 21; fax 05 59 54 62 28; info@col-ibardin.com; www.col-ibardin.com] Turn L off N10 onto D4; at rndbt foll sp Col d'Ibardin Ascain; site on R immed past minor rd to Col d'Ibardin. Med, hdg/mkd pitch, pt sl, pt terr, pt shd; 5% serviced pitch; wc; chem disp; baby facs; shwrs inc; el pnts (5A) inc (poss rev pol); gas; lndtte; ice; shop; tradsmn; supmkt 5km; rest, snacks & bar in ssn; BBQ; playgrnd; htd pool; paddling pool; sand beach 6km; tennis; TV; 5% statics; dogs €2.50; phone; Eng spkn; adv bkg; quiet; cc acc; CCI. "Well-run; helpful, friendly owner; mountain rlwy nr; excel san facs; gd walking; gd touring base for Pyrenees & N Spain; excel." ♦ 21 Mar-30 Sep. € 30.00   2007*

See advertisement

ST JEAN DE MAURIENNE *9C3* (Urban) **Camp Municipal des Grands Cols, Ave du Mont-Cenis, 73300 St Jean-de-Maurienne** [tel/fax 04 79 64 11 44 (Mairei); campinglesgrandscols@tele2.fr] Site sp fr D306 (N6) in St Jean-de-Maurienne; site behind shops 100m fr town cent behind trees/parking. Med, hdg/mkd pitch, hdstg, pt sl, pt shd; wc; chem disp; mv service pnt; 20% serviced pitches; shwrs inc; el pnts (16A) €3; lndtte; ice; supmkt 1km; tradsmn; snacks; bar; playgrnd; pool 1.5km; lake 3km; games rm; TV; dogs €1; Eng spkn; quiet; red low ssn; CCI. "Warm welcome; v helpful staff; clean san facs; gd mountain views; interesting town cent; gd NH for Fréjus tunnel; excel." 15 May-30 Sep. € 14.00   2006*

ST JEAN DE MONTS *2H3* (Coastal) **Camping Les Places Dorées, Route de Notre Dame de Monts, 85160 St Jean-de-Monts** [02 51 59 02 93 or 02 40 73 03 70 (LS); fax 02 51 59 30 47; abridespins@aol.com; www.placesdorees.com] Fr Nantes dir Challons & St Jean-de-Monts. Then dir Notre Dame-de-Monts. Med, pt sl, shd; wc; chem disp; shwrs inc; el pnts (2-10A); gas; lndtte; ice; shop adj; tradsmn; rest; snacks; sand beach 800m; htd pool; waterslides; sports area; games rm; entmnt; dogs €2.80; Eng spkn; adv bkg; quiet; CCI. "Vg; free entmnt children/adults; organised excursions; friendly family-run site; mountain views." ♦ 1 Jun-10 Sep. € 30.00 3 persons   2004*

ST JEAN DE MONTS *2H3* (2km Urban) **Camping Le Bois Dormant, 168 Rue de Sables, 85167 St Jean-de-Monts** [02 51 58 01 30; fax 02 51 59 35 30; boisdormant@siblu.fr; www.siblu.com] Fr Challans pass thro Le Perrier & on coming to St Jean-de-Monts, at 1st rndabt take last exit dir Les Sables d'Olonne. Foll Les Sables dirs to 4th rndabt, turn R, site on L. V lge, hdg/mkd pitch, pt shd; htd wc; chem disp; mv service pnt; serviced pitches; baby facs; shwrs inc; el pnts (6A) inc; gas; lndtte; ice; shop; tradsmn; rest; snacks; bar; playgrnd; htd pool; waterslide; sand beach 2.5km; tennis; sports area; entmnt; child entmnt; TV/games rm; statics; no dogs; poss cr; Eng spkn; adv bkg; red low ssn; CCI. "Excel; access to sister site with disco & entmnt; various sports facs; children's club." ♦ 29 Apr-9 Sep. € 144.00 (7 nights)   2005*

ST JEAN DE MONTS *2H3* (2km N Coastal) Camping La Davière Plage, Route de Notre Dame, 85160 St Jean-de-Monts [tel/fax 02 51 58 27 99; daviereplage@wanadoo.fr; www. daviereplage.com] Site on L off D38 Rte de Notre Dame fr St Jean & 2km W of Notre Dame. Well sp. Med, hdg/mkd pitch, pt shd; wc; chem disp; shwrs; el pnts (10A) €3.90; gas; lndry rm; ice; shops adj; tradsmn; rest; snacks; bar; playgrnd; sand beach; watersports 700m; sports area; entmnt; TV rm; dogs €3.15; CCI. "Gd value, family site close to amenities; mkd cycle & walking trails; o'night area for m'vans." 1 May-30 Sep. € 18.65   2007*

The opening dates and prices on this campsite have changed. I'll send a site report form to the editor for the next edition of the guide.

ST JEAN DE MONTS *2H3* (SE Urban/Coastal) Camping Les Sirènes, Ave des Demoiselles, 85160 St Jean-de-Monts [02 51 58 01 31; fax 02 51 59 03 67; cplsirenes@atciat.com; www. vendee-camping.info or www.campeole.com] Site in town cent; ent town on D753 fr Challans, turn R at junc, then 1st L at church. Take 2nd L (Ave des Demoiselles). Site on L. V lge, pt sl, shd; wc (some cont); chem disp; shwrs inc; el pnts (10A) inc; gas; lndtte; ice; sm shop adj or 2km; rest; snacks; bar; playgrnd; pool; sand beach 500m; fishing, watersports 500m; cycle hire; games area; entmnt; dogs €2.50; adv bkg ess high ssn; quiet. "Sh walk thro pines to beach; vg." ♦ 1 Mar-30 Sep. € 20.30   2007*

ST JEAN DE MONTS *2H3* (2km SE Urban) Camping Le Bois Masson, 149 Rue des Sables, 85167 St Jean-de-Monts [02 51 58 62 62; fax 02 51 58 29 97; boismasson@siblu.fr; www. siblu.com] Fr Challans pass thro Le Perrier & on ent to St Jean-de-Monts, at 1st rndabt take last exit dir Les Sables d'Olonne. Foll Les Sables at next rndabts & 4th rndabt turn R, site on R shortly after Camping Le Bois Dormant. V lge, hdg/mkd pitch, pt shd; htd wc; chem disp; baby facs; shwrs inc; el pnts (6A) inc; gas; lndtte; shop; rest; snacks; bar; BBQ (gas); playgrnd; 2 htd pools (1 covrd); waterslide; sand beach 2.5km; fishing, windsurfing, watersports nrby; entmnt; child entmnt; internet; TV; 4% statics; no dogs; Eng spkn; adv bkg; quiet; 20% red low ssn. "Busy, popular site with narr access rds; excel family site; mkt Sat." ♦ 8 Apr-16 Sep.   2005*

ST JEAN DE MONTS *2H3* (6km SE Coastal) Camping La Yole, Chemin des Bosses, Orouët, 85160 St Jean-de-Monts [02 51 58 67 17; fax 02 51 59 05 35; contact@la-yole.com; www. la-yole.com] Take D38 S fr St Jean-de-Monts dir Les Sable d'Olonne & Orouet. At Orouet turn R at L'Oasis rest dir Mouette; in 1.5km turn L at campsite sp; site on L. Situated bet D38 & coast, 1km fr Plage des Mouettes. On arr, park in carpark on R bef registering. Lge, hdg/mkd pitch, shd; wc; chem disp; serviced pitch; baby facs; jacuzzi; shwrs inc; el pnts (10A) inc; lndtte; ice; shop; rest; snacks; bar; BBQ (gas only); playgrnd; 2 pools (1 htd covrd); paddling pool; waterslide; jacuzzi; sand beach 2km; tennis; fishing; horseriding 3km; watersports 6km; entmnt; games/TV; some statics (tour ops); sm dogs €5; recep 0800-1830 high ssn; c'vans over 6m not acc high ssn; poss cr; Eng spkn; adv bkg ess; cc acc; CCI. "Gd, well-run, v busy site; reasonable pitches; facs clean but need update; friendly staff; close to gd beaches; excel cycle paths; mkt Wed & Sat am." ♦ 5 Apr-26 Sep. € 30.00 (CChq acc) ABS - A23   2007*

ST JEAN DE MONTS *2H3* (2km S Rural/Coastal) Camping Les Verts, 177 Ave Valentin, 85160 St Jean-de-Monts [tel/fax 02 51 58 47 63] Sp on D38 & coast rd. Lge, hdg/mkd pitch, pt sl, pt shd; wc; shwrs inc; el pnts (3-6A) inc; gas; lndtte; shop high ssn; rest 2km; snacks; bar; playgrnd; TV; htd pool; sand beach 1.6km; 10% statics; dogs €1.50; poss cr; adv bkg; red low ssn; CCI. "Excel beach, v welcoming; ltd facs low ssn; some pitches narr & rough." ♦ 1 May-30 Sep. € 18.90 (3 persons)   2006*

Before we move on, I'm going to fill in some site report forms and post them off to the editor, otherwise they won't arrive in time for the deadline at the end of September.

ST JEAN DE MONTS *2H3* (1km W Coastal) Camping Le Bois Joly, 46 Route de Notre Dame-de-Monts, 85165 St Jean-de-Monts [02 51 59 11 63; fax 02 51 69 11 06; boisjoly@ compuserve.com; www.camping-leboisjoly.com] N on D38 circular around St Jean-de-Monts; at rndabt past junc with D51 turn R dir Notre Dame-de-Monts, site on R in 300m. Lge, hdg/mkd pitch, pt shd; wc; chem disp; baby facs; sauna; shwrs inc; el pnts (6A) inc; lndtte; shops 1km; rest, snacks, bar high ssn; playgrnd; 2 pools (1 htd, covrd); waterslide; sand beach 1km; games area; entmnt; TV rm; 25% statics; dogs €2.50; phone; poss cr; Eng spkn; adv bkg; cc acc; CCI. "Ideal for families; gd san facs; lge pitches; coastal & inland cycleways nrby; excel." ♦ 1 Apr-30 Sep. € 26.00   2006*

France

ST JEAN DE MONTS 2H3 (1km NW Rural) Camping La Buzelière, 79 Rue de Notre Dame, 85169 St Jean-de-Monts [02 51 58 64 80; fax 02 28 11 03 61; buzeliere@aol.com; www. buzeliere.com] Take D38 fr St Jean-de-Monts to Notre Dame-de-Monts. Site on L. Med, hdg/mkd pitch, pt sl, pt shd; wc; chem disp; baby facs; fam bthrm; shwrs inc; el pnts (10A) inc; gas; lndtte; ice; shop 1km; tradsmn; snacks; bar; BBQ; playgrnd; htd pool; sand beach 1km; games area; games rm; TV; 20% statics; dogs €1.50; phone adj; Eng spkn; adv bkg; quiet; cc acc; CCI. "Many sports inc golf nr; san facs spotless; red facs low ssn; excel." ♦ 1 May-30 Sep. € 24.40   2007*

ST JEAN DE MONTS 2H3 (4km NW Coastal) Camping aux Coeurs Vendéens, 251 Route de Notre Dame-de-Monts, 85160 St Jean-de-Monts [02 51 58 84 91; fax 02 28 11 20 75; infocoeursvendeens.com;www.coeursvendeens. com] Take D38 fr St Jean-de-Monts to Fromentine, site on L after 4km. Med, hdg pitch, shd; wc; shwrs inc; el pnts (10A) €3.30; lndtte; ice; shop; rest; snacks; bar; playgrnd; htd pool; sand beach 700m; cycle hire; mini-golf; sailing & windsurfing 700m; entmnt; TV rm; 10% statics; dogs €2.90; late night car park; poss cr; adv bkg rec high ssn; quiet; red low ssn. ♦ 1 May-30 Sep. € 25.50   2007*

There aren't many sites open this early in the year. We'd better phone ahead to check that the one we're heading for is actually open.

Did you know you can fill in site report forms on the Club's website — www.caravanclub.co.uk?

ST JEAN DE MONTS 2H3 (3.5km NW Urban/ Coastal) Camping Les Amiaux, 223 Rue de Notre-Dame-de-Monts, 85160 St Jean-de-Monts [02 51 58 22 22; fax 02 51 58 26 09; accueil@ amiaux.fr; www.amiaux.fr] Site on D38 mid-way bet St Jean-de-Monts & Notre-Dame-de-Monts. V lge, hdg/mkd pitches, pt shd; htd wc; chem disp; serviced pitches; baby facs; shwrs inc; el pnts (10A) inc; gas; lndtte; ice; sm shop; rest; snacks; bar; BBQ (gas & elec); playgrnd; htd, covrd pool; waterslides; sand beach 700m; tennis; cycle hire; horseriding 2km; golf 4km; games area; games rm; entmnt; TV rm; 50% statics; dogs €2.50; Eng spkn; adv bkg; cc acc; red low ssn; CCI. "Excel site; gd facs; conv Océanile water park & Puy du Fou theme park; rec long stay." ♦ 1 May-30 Sep. € 32.60
2007*

See advertisement

ST JEAN DE MONTS 2H3 (6km NW Coastal) Camping La Forêt, Chemin de la Rive, 85160 St Jean-de-Monts [02 51 58 84 63; www.chez. com/campinglaforet] Fr St Jean-de-Monts, take D38 twd Notre-Dame-de-Monts for 6km, over rndabt then turn L (last turning bef Notre-Dame-de-Monts) sp Pont d'Yeu, then immed L, site on L in 200m, on parallel rd to main rd. Med, hdg/mkd pitch, pt shd; wc; chem disp; shwrs inc; el pnts (6A) €3.80; gas; lndtte; shop; tradsmn; snacks; pool; playgrnd; htd pool; sand beach 500m; TV; 30% statics; dogs €2; phone; poss cr; Eng spkn; adv bkg; quiet; Eng spkn; BBQ; CCI. "Track thro pine forest to beach in 500m; cycle tracks; not suitable twin-axles; some pitches diff c'vans." ♦ ltd. 15 May-15 Sep. € 23.50   2005*

ST JEAN DE MUZOLS see Tournon sur Rhône 9C2

ST JEAN DU GARD *10E1* (1.5km N) **Camping Les Sources, Route du Mialet, 30270 St Jean-du-Gard [04 66 85 38 03; fax 04 66 85 16 09; www. camping-des-sources.fr]** Fr Alès take D907 twd Anduze & St Jean-du-Gard. Take by-pass twd Florac. R at traff lts on D983, foll camp sp. NB: Do not enter town cent when towing - v narr streets. Med, hdg pitch, terr, shd; htd wc; chem disp; shwrs inc; el pnts (6A) inc; gas; ice; shop; tradsmn; snacks; bar; playgrnd; pool; rv sw; dogs €1.50; Eng spkn; adv bkg ess Jul/Aug; quiet. "Lovely, well laid-out site; pitches sm, not rec for lge o'fits; friendly family owners; steam rlwy nrby; conv National Park of Cévennes." ♦ 1 Apr-30 Sep. € 17.25   2004*

ST JEAN DU GARD *10E1* (5km N Rural) **Camping La Forêt, 30270 Falguières [04 66 85 37 00; fax 04 66 85 07 05; laforet30@aol.com; www. campingalaforet.com]** Fr D907 turn N fr by-pass onto D983, then D50. Foll sp to Falguières & site sp on narr winding rd for 2.5km. Med, pt sl, pt shd; wc; baby facs; shwrs inc; el pnts (4-6A) €2.70-3.70; gas; lndtte; ice; shop; rest 5km; bar; playgrnd; pool; paddling pool; rv sw 400m; 15% statics; adv bkg; quiet. "Site in wooded hill country; friendly family owners; walking rtes fr site." 1 May-15 Sep. € 18.10   2006*

ST JEAN DU GARD *10E1* (2km W Rural) **Camping Le Petit Baigneur (Rossel), Les Deux Chemins, 30270 St Jean-du-Gard [04 66 85 32 05; fax 04 66 85 35 48; http://pagesperso-orange.fr/le-petit-baigneur]** Site on S side of D907 at W end of St Jean-du-Gard by-pass & 250m beyond D907/260 junc. If app fr W go past site ent & make U turn at layby opp D907/260 junc - due acute angle of site ent. Sm, pt shd; wc; chem disp (wc); shwrs inc; el pnts (6A) €1.50; lndtte; ice; shop 1.5km; tradsmn; rest, snacks, bar 1.5km; BBQ; playgrnd; rv sw & shgl beach adj; fishing; TV; no statics; dogs; phone; some rd noise; CCI. "Beautiful, family-run site by rv; lovely quiet spot; vg facs; tourist steam train 1.5km; conv town; Bambouseraie nature park rec; gd base for Cévennes area; vg mkt Tues." ♦ Easter-15 Sep. € 11.85   2007*

ST JEAN EN ROYANS *9C2* (Rural) **Camp Municipal, Ave de Provence, 26190 St Jean-en-Royans [04 75 47 74 60]** Exit A49 junc 8 onto D1532 (N532) to St Nazaire-en-Royans. Shortly after passing under high rlwy arch in St Nazaire turn R on D76 to St Jean-en-Royans. Site at S end of St Jean; sp (different site fr Camp Municipal St Nazaire). Med, hdg pitch, pt shd; wc; chem disp; shwrs inc; some el pnts (10A) €2; shops 500m; playgrnd; rv fishing 50m; some statics; dogs €1; daytime factory noise. "V pleasant, under-used site in semi-parkland but dated san facs (clean); lge pitches; no twin-axle vans; rec use drinking water fr san facs, not fr old water pumps; gd supmkt in vill; spectacular mountain rds & gd walking; vg site in excel area." 1 Apr-30 Sep. € 8.60   2007*

ST JEAN EN ROYANS *9C2* (6km NE Rural) **Camp Municipal, 26190 St Nazaire-en-Royans [04 75 48 41 18 or 04 75 48 40 63 (Mairie); fax 04 75 48 44 32]** Exit A49 onto D1532 (N532) to St Nazaire-en-Royans, site is on W edge of vill on D76, 700m fr cent, well sp. Med, hdg pitch, pt sl, pt shd; wc (some cont); chem disp; shwrs inc; el pnts (3-6A) €2.60-3.50; lndtte; shops & rest 700m; playgrnd; dogs €1.22; quiet; CCI. "Immac facs but need updating; helpful warden; gate clsd 2200-0700; excel rest in vill; ideal for mountains of Vercors; aquaduct on Rv Isère a tourist attraction; excel." ♦ 1 May-30 Sep. € 8.10   2005*

ST JEAN FROIDMENTEL see Cloyes sur le Loir *4F2*

ST JEAN LE CENTENIER *9D2* (Rural) **Camping Les Arches, 07580 St Jean-le-Centenier [tel/fax 04 75 36 75 45]** Situated midway Aubenas & Montélimar. Leave N102 just after St Jean-le-Centenier dir Mirabel, site in 500m (D458). Sm, hdg pitch, pt sl, terr, pt shd; wc; baby facs; shwrs; el pnts (10A) €3; lndtte; rest; snacks; bar; playgrnd; rv sw; fishing; canoeing; dogs €1.50; Eng spkn; quiet. "Vg site; simple & immac; peaceful location; helpful owner." ♦ Easter-15 Sep. € 14.00   2005*

ST JEAN PIED DE PORT *8F1* (Urban) **Camp Municipal de Plaza Berri, 64220 St Jean-Pied-de-Port [05 59 37 11 19]** Fr N on D933 thro town & cross rv. In 50m bear L at sm rndabt, site in 200m, sp. Enquire at Hôtel de Ville (Town Hall) off ssn. Some care needed on app as narr rds. Med, some mkd pitch; pt sl, pt shd; wc; chem disp; mv service pnt; shwrs inc; el pnts (5A) €2.50 (poss rev pol); shops 400m; pool 500m; quiet; CCI. "Busy site - arr early; if no-one at recep, take numbered pitch & contact recep later; facs well-kept & clean; lovely old walled town on rv; street mkt Mon; poss open until mid-Nov; gd NH - used by walkers on pilgrim rte." ♦ Easter-30 Sep. € 8.00   2007*

ST JEAN PIED DE PORT *8F1* (3km E Rural) **Aire Naturelle La Paix des Champs (Jasses), Ferme Asoritzia, Route de Jaxu, 64220 St Jean-le-Vieux [05 59 37 02 63]** E fr St Jean-Pied-de-Port on D933. In 2km turn L onto D22 sp Jaxu, site on R in 1km. Sm, pt shd; wc; chem disp (wc); shwrs inc; el pnts (3A) €1.80; lndry facs; supmkt 1km; playgrnd; pool 2km; trout-fishing; dogs €0.50; quiet; CCI. "Tranquil & beautiful; mountain views; san facs poss stretched high ssn; site needs maintenance (09/07) & poss run down low ssn; interesting old town on pilgrim rte to Santiago de Compostela." ♦ ltd. 15 Apr-30 Sep. € 8.70   2007*

ST JEAN PIED DE PORT *8F1* (1.5km W Rural) Europ Camping, 64220 Ascarat [05 59 37 12 78; fax 05 59 37 29 82; europcamping64@orange. fr; www.europ-camping.com] Site on D918 bet Uhart-Cize & Ascarat. Well sp. Med, hdg/mkd pitch, pt shd; wc; chem disp; serviced pitch; sauna; shwrs inc; el pnts (6A) €4 (check pol); lndtte; shop 2km; tradsmn; rest; snacks; bar; playgrnd; pool; paddling pool; games area; games rm; 30% statics; dogs €2; adv bkg; quiet; cc acc; CCI. "Vg; helpful staff; beautiful location; ltd facs low ssn; ground v soft when wet." ♦ Easter-30 Sep. € 19.00   2007*

ST JEAN PIED DE PORT *8F1* (3km W Rural) Camping Narbaitz, Route de Bayonne, 64220 Ascarat [05 59 37 10 13 or 05 59 37 09 22 (LS); fax 05 59 37 21 42; camping-narbaitz@wanadoo. fr; www.camping-narbaitz.com] Site on L of D918 St Jean to Bayonne 3km fr St Jean, sp. Med, hdg/ mkd pitch, pt sl, pt shd; wc (some cont); chem disp; mv service pnt; baby facs; shwrs inc; el pnts (6A) €3 (poss rev pol); lndry rm; shop, snacks & bar in ssn; tradsmn; playgrnd; pool; trout-fishing; canoeing; kayaking; cycling; entmnt; 5% statics; dogs free; phone; poss cr; Eng spkn; adv bkg (dep req); quiet; cc acc high ssn; red low ssn; CCI. "Attractive, clean, gd value, family-run site; gd facs; helpful owners; rec m'vans use top end of site when wet; nr Spanish border (cheaper petrol); lovely views; guided walks." ♦ 10 Mar-29 Sep. € 19.00 (CChq acc)   2007*

ST JODARD *9B1* (Rural) Camp Municipal, 42590 St Jodard [04 77 63 42 42; fax 04 77 63 40 01] Fr Roanne take N7 S then N82 to Neulise. Exit at junc 72 & turn R onto D26 to St Jodard. Site in 6km on ent vill, sp. Sm, shd; htd wc (mainly cont); shwrs inc; el pnts (5A) €3.37; ice; shops, rest, bar etc in vill; playgrnd; pool high ssn; lake 1.5km; fishing; boat hire; tennis; mini-golf; quiet; red low ssn; CCI. "Pleasant site; pretty, rural vill; site yourself - warden calls am & pm." 1 May-30 Sep. € 5.70
                                                          2006*

ST JORIOZ see Annecy *9B3*

ST JORY DE CHALAIS see Thiviers *7C3*

ST JOUAN DES GUERETS see St Malo *2E4*

ST JOUIN DE MARNES *4H1* (Rural) Camping Clos-aux-Pères, 18 Rue des Gentils-Lieux, 79600 St Jouin-de-Marnes [05 49 67 44 50; fax 05 49 67 47 89; p.panneau@tiscali.fr; www.clos-aux-peres.fr.st] S of Thouars on D37 in dir Poitiers, site on L on ent to vill. Sm, hdg pitch, pt shd; wc; chem disp; shwrs inc; el pnts (10A) €2.50; lndtte; tradsmn; shop, rest, bar in vill; BBQ; playgrnd; pool; lake nr; phone; quiet; CCI. "Welcoming, CL-type site." 1 Jun-30 Sep. € 12.00   2006*

ST JULIEN DE LAMPON see la Canéda *7C3*

ST JULIEN DE PEYROLAS see Pont St Esprit *9D2*

ST JULIEN DES LANDES see Mothe Achard, La *2H4*

ST JULIEN EN BEAUCHENE *9D3* (7km N Rural) Camp Le Champ La Chèvre, 26620 Lus-La-Croix-Haute [04 92 58 50 14; fax 04 92 58 55 92; info@campingchamplachevre.com; www. campingchamplachevre.com] Turn E off D1075 (N75) thru Lus vill, site SE of vill nr sw pool on D505. Med, mkd pitch, pt sl, terr, pt shd; wc; chem disp; shwrs €1; el pnts (6A) €3.40; gas; lndtte; ice; shops 300m; snacks; playgrnd; htd pool adj; fishing; some statics; dogs €1.60; poss cr; adv bkg; quiet; cc acc; CCI. "Excel mountain views; helpful staff; excel pool; many waymkd walks; gd NH; vg." ♦ ltd. 28 Apr-30 Sep. € 12.50   2007*

This guide relies on site report forms submitted by caravanners like us; we'll do our bit and tell the editor what we think of the campsites we've visited.

ST JULIEN EN BORN *8E1* (1.5km N Rural) Aire Naturelle (Daret), Marregue, 40170 St Julien-en-Born [tel/fax 05 58 42 72 35] Foll D652 N fr St Julian-en-Born, site 400m N of Cusson x-rd. Sm, shd; wc; shwrs inc; el pnts; lndtte; shop 2km; playgrnd; sand beach 10km; fishing, sailing, horseriding 1km; Eng spkn; quiet. "Poss need long elec lead; vg." 15 Jun-30 Sep.   2004*

ST JULIEN EN BORN *8E1* (6km NE Rural) Le Village Tropical Sen Yan, 40170 Mézos [05 58 42 60 05; fax 05 58 42 64 56; reception@sen-yan.com; www.sen-yan.com] Fr Bordeaux on N10 in 100km at Laharie turn W onto D38 dir Mimizan; in 12km turn L onto D63 to Mézos; turn L at mini-rndabt; site on L in approxd 2km. Site 1.5km fr D63/D38 junc NE of Mézos. Lge, hdg/ mkd pitch, shd; wc (some cont); chem disp; baby facs; sauna; shwrs inc; el pnts (6A) inc; gas; lndtte; shop; rest; snacks; bar; BBQ (gas only); playgrnd; 3 pools (1 htd & covrd); paddling pool; waterslides sand beach 12km; rv adj; fishing; canoe hire 1km; watersports 15km; tennis; mini-golf; cycle hire; many sports & games; fitness cent; entmnt; wifi internet; games/TV (cab/sat) rm; 80% statics; dogs €4; phone; recep 0900-1230 & 1330-1930 high ssn; max c'van 7m high ssn; Eng spkn; adv bkg; quiet; cc acc; CCI. "Pleasant & restful; excel facs for families; lively atmosphere with music in bar - but not audible fr camping area; mkt Mimizan Fri." ♦ 1 Jun-15 Sep. € 35.50 ABS - A09   2007*

ST JULIEN EN GENEVOIS *9A3* (5km SE Rural) Camping La Colombière, Chef-Lieu, 74160 Neydens [04 50 35 13 14; fax 04 50 35 13 40; la.colombiere@wanadoo.fr; www.camping-la-colombiere.com] Fr A40 junc 13 take N201 twd Annecy. Site is sp after approx 1.75km at Neydens. NB: Do not go into St Julien-en-Genevois when towing. Med, hdg/mkd pitch, pt sl, pt shd; htd wc; chem disp; mv service pnt; baby facs; shwrs inc; el pnts (6A) €5, extra for 15A; gas; lndtte; ice; shops 500m; farm produce; rest; snacks; bar; BBQ (gas/elect/charcoal); playgrnd; 2 pools (1 htd); paddling pool; lake fishing 1km; cycle hire; archery; entmnt; child entmnt; wifi internet; games/TV rm; 30% statics; dogs €2; park & ride bus; poss cr; Eng spkn; quiet; cc acc; CCI. "Excel, clean, family-run site; vg san facs; helpful staff; conv Swiss border & Lake Geneva; lovely vill walks; vg rest; excel tour of Geneva inc vineyard & wine-tasting; friendly & helpful staff; gd NH." ♦ 20 Mar-12 Nov. € 25.50 (CChq acc) ABS - M08   2007*

ST JULIEN EN GENEVOIS *9A3* (6km S Rural) Camping Le Terroir, 118 Chemin de Clairjoie, 74160 Présilly-la-Tuilière [04 50 04 42 07; fax 04 50 04 55 53; camping.le.terroir@wanadoo.fr] Fr St Julien-en-Genevois S on N201 for 5km. At traff lts after rndabt turn R twd Présilly. Site on L past vill on D18. Sm, mkd pitch, pt shd; htd wc; chem disp; shwrs inc; el pnts (5-10A) €2.80-3.50; lndtte; tradsmn; rest 5km; snacks, bar 2km; BBQ; playgrnd; htd pool 6km; TV rm; some statics; dogs; poss cr; Eng spkn; adv bkg; quiet; CCI. "Gd touring base." 1 Jun-30 Sep. € 10.10   2005*

> As soon as we get home I'm going to post all these site report forms to the editor for inclusion in next year's guide. I don't want to miss the September deadline.

ST JULIEN EN ST ALBAN see Privas *9D2*

ST JULIEN MOLIN MOLETTE see Bourg Argental *9C2*

ST JUNIEN *7B3* (500m Urban) Camp Municipal de la Glane, Allée des Pommiers, Ave Corot, 87200 St Junien [05 55 02 34 86; fax 05 55 02 34 88; sports@mairie-saint-junien.fr; www.mairie-saint-junien.fr] Fr Limoges take N141 W to St Junien. Or 9km NE Rochechouart on D675. Site in town, sp. Med, hdg pitch, sl, shd; wc; chem disp; mv service pnt; shwrs inc; el pnts (10A) €3.30; ice; playgrnd; htd pool 300m; rv fishing 200m; dogs; adv bkg (dep req). "Modern san facs; many sloping pitches, some can be v wet in rain; excel shwrs; vg." 15 May-19 Sep. € 6.75   2007*

ST JUNIEN *7B3* (4km E Rural) Camping de Chambery, 87200 St Brice-sur-Vienne [05 55 02 18 13; mairie-brice@wanadoo.fr] Fr Limoges on N141 turn L at rndabt 5km fr St Junien sp St Brice. In vill turn L onto D32; in 1.5km (on outskirts of vill) turn L & foll site sp; site on L in 500m. Sm, hdg/mkd pitch, hdstg, pt sl, pt shd; htd wc; chem disp; shwrs inc; el pnts (10A) €3.10; lndtte; shop in vill; playgrnd; rv nr; dogs; adv bkg; CCI. "V nice site; lovely location in municipal park; pitches overlook lake & countryside; site yourself, lge hdstg pitches; helpful warden calls early eve; barrier clsd 2200-0700; conv Oradour-sur-Glane." ♦ 26 Apr-15 Sep. € 11.00   2007*

ST JURS see Moustiers Ste Marie *10E3*

ST JUST (CANTAL) *9C1* (Urban) Camp Municipal, 15320 St Just [04 71 73 72 57; fax 04 71 73 71 44; commune.stjust@wanadoo.fr; www.saintjust.com] Exit junc 31 fr A75, foll sp St Chély-d'Apcher D909; turn W onto D448 twds St Just (approx 6km); sp with gd access. Med, mkd pitch, pt sl, terr, pt shd; htd wc; chem disp; shwrs inc; el pnts (10A) €2; lndtte; ice; shop; snacks; bar; pool high ssn; fishing; tennis; cycle hire; v quiet. "Friendly warden; ltd facs low ssn; gd touring base; gd rest in vill." Easter-30 Sep. € 9.00   2006*

ST JUST EN CHEVALET *9B1* (Urban) Camp Municipal Le Verdille, 42430 St Just-en-Chevalet [04 77 65 02 97] Exit A72 at junc 4, join D53 NE twd St Just-en-Chevalet. Foll sp in town to camping/piscine. Due to steep gradients avoid D1 when towing. Med, hdg pitch, pt sl, pt shd; wc (mainly cont); chem disp shwrs inc; el pnts (16A) €2.20; lndtte; shops & supmkt 500m; rest 500m; snacks, bar adj; pool & tennis adj; 10% statics; phone; Eng spkn; adv bkg; quiet; CCI. "Friendly proprietors; v quiet site." 15 Apr-30 Sep. € 7.70   2004*

ST JUST LUZAC see Marennes *7B1*

ST JUSTIN *8E2* (11km E Rural) Aire Naturelle Municipal, 40240 Créon d'Armagnac [05 58 44 81 07 (Mairie); mairie.creon-armagnac@wanadoo.fr] Fr Roquefort take D626 dir La Bastide, turn L onto D933. After 500m turn R onto D35, site on L after 11km on ent vill of Créon d'Armagnac. Sm, pt sl, pt shd; wc; chem disp; shwrs inc; no el pnts; shop 1km; playgrnd; sports area; fishing; horseriding; quiet; CCI. "Gd NH." 1 May-30 Oct. € 4.00   2006*

ST JUSTIN *8E2* (2km NW) Camping Le Pin, Route de Roquefort, 40240 St Justin [tel/fax 05 58 44 88 91; campinglepin@wanadoo.fr] Fr St Justin D933, take D626 twd Roquefort. Site on L in 2km, well sp fr town. Sm, shd; wc; shwrs inc; el pnts (6A) €3; lndtte; shop & 2km; rest; snacks; bar; playgrnd; pool; cycle hire; horseriding; rv fishing 2km; dogs €1.50; poss cr; Eng spkn; adv bkg; quiet; CCI. "Helpful owner; facs poss stretched when site full; ongoing improvements; gd rest; beautiful vill." ♦ 1 Apr-30 Oct. € 17.20   2004*

ST LAMBERT DU LATTAY *4G1* FFCC Camp Municipal La Coudraye, Rue de la Coudray, 49190 St Lambert-du-Lattay [02 41 78 49 31 or 02 41 78 44 26 (Mairie); miche.rip@wanadoo. fr] Fr Angers on N160 thro vill cent & foll N160 sp Chemillé. Site sp on L adj wine museum in 200m. Poor sp fr N. Sm, hdg pitch, pt sl, pt shd; wc (some cont); chem disp; shwrs inc; el pnts (10A) €2.40-4.20; gas; lndry rm; ice; playgrnd; rv 500m; fishing 50m; entmnt; dogs €0.70; adv bkg. "Lovely, quiet site; wine museums worth visiting; site yourself, warden comes am & pm; gd walking; fair NH." ♦ 26 Apr-30 Oct. € 6.90   2007*

ST LARY SOULAN *8G2* (Rural) Camp Municipal La Lanne, 65170 St Lary-Soulan [05 62 39 41 58 or 05 62 40 87 85 (LS); fax 05 62 40 01 40; camping@ saintlary-vacances.com] On Bielsa-Aragnouet rd, sp on on ent vill. Site in side street E of main rd & ent not sp. Look for ent with tall trees at each side. Med, mkd pitch, pt sl, shd; htd wc; chem disp; shwrs inc; el pnts (6-10A) €5; gas; lndtte; shop 250m; rest, snacks, bar 400m; playgrnd; htd pool adj; TV rm; adv bkg; quiet; red low ssn. "Office clsd 1200-1430; vg san facs." ♦ 5 Dec-1 Oct. € 14.40   2005*

⊞ST LARY SOULAN *8G2* (2km N Rural) Camping Le Rioumajou, 65170 Bourisp [tel/fax 05 62 39 48 32; lerioumajou@wanadoo.fr; www. camping-le-rioumajou.com] On W side of D929 2km N of St Lary-Soulon & 500m N of Bourisp. Lge, hdg/mkd pitch, hdstg, shd; wc; chem disp; shwrs inc; el pnts (4-10A) €3.50-6; gas; lndtte; shop; tradsmn; rest; snacks; bar; htd pool; playgrnd; tennis; entmnt; TV rm; phone; dogs €1; poss cr; Eng spkn; adv bkg; quiet; CCI. "Conv National Park & Bielsa tunnel; lots to do in area; St Lary-Soulan attractive; gd walking & watersports." € 14.00   2004*

⊞ST LARY SOULAN *8G2* (4km NE Rural) Camping Le Lustou, Agos, 65170 Vielle-Aure [05 62 39 40 64; contact@lustou.com; www. lustou.com] Exit A64 junc 16 & head S on D929. Thro Arreau & Guchen turn R onto D19 dir Vielle-Aure. Site on R just bef Agos. Med, mkd pitch, pt sl, pt shd; htd wc; chem disp; baby facs; shwrs inc; el pnts (6-10A) €5.50-6.50; gas; lndtte; ice; shop 2km; snacks; bar; playgrnd; htd, covrd pool; fishing, canoeing, tennis nrby; TV rm; dogs €1.60; phone; adv bkg; some rd noise; CCI. "Family-owned site; excel walking, skiing; immac facs." ♦ € 12.20 (3 persons)   2007*

ST LAURENT DE CERDANS see Prats de Mollo la Preste *8H4*

ST LAURENT DE NESTE see Montréjeau *8F3*

ST LAURENT DU PAPE see Voulte sur Rhône, La *9D2*

ST LAURENT DU PONT see Echelles, Les *9B3*

ST LAURENT DU VAR see Cagnes sur Mer *10E4*

ST LAURENT DU VERDON *10E3* (1.5km N Rural) Camping La Farigoulette, Lac de St Laurent, 04500 St Laurent-du-Verdon [04 92 74 41 62; fax 04 92 74 00 86; info@camping-la-farigoulette. com; www.camping-la-farigoulette.com] Fr Riez SE on D11; in 15km turn L onto D311 to St Laurent-du-Verdon; on ent vill turn L at shrine onto C1 dir Montpezat; site on R in 1km. Fr Quinson take D11 & in 2km turn R onto D311; cont thro vill & take R fork at shrine onto C1 dir Montpezat, site on R in 1km. Lge, pt sl, shd; wc; mv service pnt; shwrs inc; el pnts (5A) €3.50; lndtte; ice; shop; rest; snacks; bar; BBQ; playgrnd; 2 pools; lake sw adj; canoeing, watersports; fishing; tennis; mini-golf; cycle hire; entmnt; TV; some statics; dogs €2; poss cr; red low ssn. 15 May-30 Sep. € 20.00   2007*

ST LAURENT DU VERDON *10E3* (2km W Rural) Domaine Naturiste d'Enriou (Naturist), 04500 St Laurent-du-Verdon [04 92 74 41 02; fax 04 92 74 01 20; domaine.enriou@voila.fr] Fr Riez foll D11 S, site on D311 to St Laurent-du-Verdon & sp fr D11/D311 junc immed N of Quinson. Med, shd; wc; chem disp; shwrs inc; el pnts (3-6A) €2.60-3.60; gas; ice; shops; rest; snacks; playgrnd; 2 pools; sw lake 500m; canoes; archery; fishing; entmnt; TV; few statics; adv bkg; v quiet; INF card req. "Vg, friendly, peaceful site; excel for Gorges du Verdon." 15 May-30 Sep. € 26.50   2005*

ST LAURENT EN BEAUMONT see Mure, La (Isere) *9C3*

ST LAURENT EN GRANDVAUX *6H2* (SE Urban) Camp Municipal Le Champs de Mars, Rue du Camping, 39150 St Laurent-en-Grandvaux [03 84 60 19 30 or 06 03 61 06 61; fax 03 84 60 19 72; champmars.camping@wanadoo. fr; www.st-laurent39.fr] E thro St Laurent on N5 twd Morez, site on R, sp 'Caravaneige' at ent. Med, mkd pitch, hdstg, pt sl, pt shd; htd wc; chem disp; mv service pnt; shwrs inc; some serviced pitches; el pnts (6A) €2; lndtte; ice; shops & Super U supmkt in vill (900m); playgrnd; TV rm; 20% statics; dogs; phone; adv bkg; quiet; CCI. "Gd site, pleasantly quiet in May; no dog walk area." ♦ 16 Dec-30 Sep. € 8.10   2007*

ST LAURENT EN GRANDVAUX *6H2* (10km W Rural) Camping L'Abbaye, Route du Lac, 39130 Bonlieu [03 84 25 57 04; fax 03 84 25 50 82; camping.abbaye@wanadoo.fr] Site on L of N78, 1km bef vill of Bonlieu, sp. Med, mkd pitch, pt sl, pt shd; wc; chem disp; baby facs; shwrs inc; el pnts (6A) €2.70; lndtte; shop 4km; rest; snacks; bar; BBQ; playgrnd; lake sw nr; games area; dogs €0.80; Eng spkn; adv bkg; quiet; CCI. "Gd walks; gd dog walks; attractive area with Lac de Bonlieu 1km; bar/rest open low ssn; access to san facs poss diff elderly/disabled fr lower terraces." ♦ 1 May-30 Sep. € 12.10   2005*

France

ST LAURENT MEDOC 7C1 (2km N Rural) Camping Le Paradis, 8 Rue Fournon, 33112 St Laurent-Médoc [tel/fax 05 56 59 42 15 or 06 87 73 66 36 (mob); leparadismedoc@free.fr; www.leparadismedoc.com] On W side of N215 at Ballac. Med, mkd pitch, pt shd; wc; chem disp; mv service pnt; baby facs; shwrs inc; el pnts (10A) €4; lndtte; tradsmn; snacks; bar; playgrnd; pool; paddling pool; games area; entmnt; TV; some statics; dogs €2.60; adv bkg; quiet. "Excel site; helpful staff." 1 Apr-17 Sep. € 14.00   2006*

ST LAURENT NOUAN see Beaugency 4F2

ST LAURENT SUR SEVRE 2H4 (5km S Rural) Camp Municipal La Vallée de Poupet, 85590 St Malô-du-Bois [02 51 92 31 45; fax 02 51 92 38 65; camping@valleedepoupet.com; www.valleedepoupet.com] Fr N on N149 turn S onto D752 at La Malô-du-Bois (4km) foll sp for 4.5km. Fr S fr Mauléon on N149 turn L onto D11 twd Mallièvre; 4km after Mallièvre turn R onto D752. After 2.5km turn R & foll sp. Steep app to site. Med, mkd pitch, pt shd; wc; chem disp; mv service pnt; baby facs; shwrs inc; el pnts (6A) €2.60; lndtte; shops 2km; tradsmn; rest; bar 500m; playgrnd; htd; covrd pool; rv sw & fishing; entmnt inc theatre; 10% statics; dogs €1; phone adj; Eng spkn; adv bkg (dep req); quiet; CCI. "Excel rvside site in depths of country; nr Puy du Fou Grand Parc; rds poss busy on Wed & Sat evening for theatre entmnt." ♦ 15 May-15 Sep. € 14.00   2006*

⊞**ST LAURENT SUR SEVRE** 2H4 (1km W Rural) Camping Le Rouge Gorge, Route de la Verrie, 85290 St Laurent-sur-Sèvre [02 51 67 86 39; fax 02 51 67 73 40; info@lerougegorge.com; www. lerougegorge.com] Fr Cholet on N160 dir La Roche-sur-Yon; at Mortagne-sur-Sèvre take N149 to St Laurent-sur-Sèvre. In St Laurent foll sp La Verrie on D111. Site on R at top of hill. Or take 762 S fr Cholet to St Laurent. Med, hdg/mkd pitch, pt sl, pt shd; htd wc; chem disp; mv service pnt; baby facs; shwrs inc; el pnts (4-13A) €2-5; lndtte; shop; snacks; bar; playgrnd; pool; paddling pool; rv & lake fishing 800m; games area; golf 15km; 30% statics; dogs €1.60; adv bkg; quiet; CCI. "Peaceful family site; woodland walks & mountain biking; conv Parc de Puy du Fou; attractive sm town." ♦ € 15.60 (CChq acc)   2006*

⊞**ST LEGER LES MALEZES** 9D3 (Rural) Camping La Pause, 05260 St Léger-les-Mélèzes [04 92 50 44 92; fax 04 92 50 77 59; valerie. portier@wanadoo.fr; www.camping-la-pause. com] Fr N85 Route Napoléon turn E onto D14 St Laurent-du-Cros. At La Plaine take D113 to St Léger, site sp. Med, pt shd; htd wc; baby facs; chem disp; mv service pnt; shwrs inc; el pnts (2-10A) €2-10; gas; lndtte; shop 100m; rest; snacks; bar; BBQ; playgrnd; htd pool; tennis; horseriding; games area; games rm; wintersports; entmnt; 60% statics; dogs €1.50; adv bkg; quiet. € 13.00   2006*

ST LEGER SOUS BEUVRAY 4H4 (1km N Rural) Camping La Boutière, 71990 St Léger-sous-Beuvray [03 85 82 48 86 or 03 85 82 39 73 (LS); camping@la-boutiere.com; www.la-boutiere. com] Take N81 SW fr Autun dir Bourbon-Lancy & in approx 10km, turn R onto D61 to St Léger. Site sp in vill. Sm, mkd pitch, pt sl, pt shd; wc; chem disp; shwrs inc; el pnts (6-10A) €3-3.50; shops 1km; 5% statics; dogs €1.50; phone; twin-axle c'vans €75; poss cr; quiet; CCI. "Simple, quiet site; in Morvan Regional Park; renovated facs; Mt. Beuvray 3km; museum 3km." 1 Apr-30 Sep. € 13.40   2007*

ST LEON SUR VEZERE see Montignac 7C3

ST LEONARD DE NOBLAT 7B3 (12km N) Camp Municipal du Pont du Dognon, 87240 St Laurent-les-Eglises [05 55 56 57 25 or 05 55 56 56 13; fax 05 55 56 55 17] Take N141 fr St Léonard-de-Noblat; after 1.5km turn L (N) on D19 thro Le Chatenet-en-Dognon. Site in approx 4km, bef St Laurent-les-Eglises. Med, mkd pitch, terr, pt shd; htd wc; shwrs inc; el pnts (4A) €2.40; gas; lndtte; shop & 3km; rest; snacks; pool; rv sw; shgl beach; canoeing; tennis; cycle hire; entmnt; dogs €0.90; adv bkg; quiet. 15 Apr-15 Oct. € 10.20   2004*

ST LEONARD DE NOBLAT 7B3 (9km SE Rural) Camp Municipal du Lac, Ste Helène, 87460 Bujaleuf [tel/fax 05 55 69 54 54; tourisme@ bujaleuf.fr] Fr St Léonard take D13, D14 to Bujaleuf. Site 500m N of town on D16. Med, terr, pt shd; htd wc; shwrs inc; el pnts (5A) €2; lndtte; shops 1km; tradsmn; playgrnd; rv sw; poss cr; adv bkg; quiet; red low ssn. "No warden Sun or Mon; el pnts on terr below; modern san facs; Bujaleuf sm mkt town." 15 May-30 Sep. € 8.00   2007*

ST LEONARD DE NOBLAT 7B3 (2km S Rural) Camp Municipal Beaufort, 87400 St Léonard-de-Noblat [05 55 56 02 79; fax 05 55 56 98 01; mairie-st-leonard-de-noblat@wanadoo.fr] Leave A20 S-bound at junc 34 dir St Léonard, onto N141. In 18km on ent St Léonard, 300m after x-ing Rv Vienne, fork R (sp). Site on R in 2km. Med, hdg pitch, pt sl, pt shd; htd wc; chem disp (wc); shwrs inc; el pnts (5A) inc; ice; lndtte; shop & 4km; tradsmn; bar; playgrnd; rv sw; fishing; dogs; phone; poss cr & noisy; adv bkg; CCI. ♦ 15 Jun-15 Sep. € 12.40   2005*

ST LEONARD DES BOIS 4E1 (Rural) Camp Municipal des Alpes Mancelles, 72130 St Léonard-des-Bois [02 43 33 81 79; fax 02 43 34 49 02; campalpesmancelles@free.fr] SW of Alençon on D1/D121 to Gesvres; turn L onto D149 to St Léonard-des-Bois; site sp on Rv Sarthe. Med,mkd pitch, pt sl, pt shd; wc; shwrs inc; el pnts (6-16A) €2.10-3.10; lndry rm; shop, snacks & bar nrby; playgrnd; dogs €0.50; phone; CCI. "Pretty location by rv in Sarthe valley; basic but spotlessly clean; inadequate facs high ssn; gd touring base; gd walking; interesting vill; watersports on rv; vg." 1 Apr-31 Oct. € 7.10   2007*

ST LEU D'ESSERENT see Chantilly *3D3*

ST LO *1D4* (500m NE Urban) **Camp Municipal de Ste Croix, Ave de Paris, 50000 St Lô** [02 33 55 16 14 or 02 33 57 10 25; fax 02 33 57 27 52; sport.stlo@wanadoo.fr] On D972 on L exit St Lô on Bayeux rd climbing hill. Site on L at pedestrian traff lts. Sharp turn into site. Sm, hdg pitch, pt sl, pt shd, wc; chem disp; shwrs inc; el pnts (6-10A) €1.22-2.45; lndry rm, shop 500m; tradsmn; rest, snacks, bar 500m; BBQ; playgrnd; htd pool 1km; sand beach 25km; dogs €0.45; adv bkg; quiet; CCI. "Well-kept site; warden present 0730-1200 & 1730-2030, barrier poss clsd other times." 1 Jun-12 Sep. € 8.90   2005*

ST LOUIS *6G3* (2km N) **Camping au Petit Port, 8 Allée des Marronniers, 68330 Huningue** [tel/fax 03 89 69 05 25; www.tourisme-alsace.info] Exit N66 Mulhouse-Basel in St Louis. Foll sps to Huningue & strt, after level x-ing, site sp. Sm, shd; wc; shwrs inc; el pnts (4A) €1.50; shop 1km; htd pool 2km; 50% statics; bus to Basle; poss cr; quiet. "Poss diff access lge o'fits; v helpful warden; gd." ♦ 15 Apr-15 Oct. € 10.00   2007*

ST LUNAIRE see Dinard *2E3*

ST LYPHARD *2G3* (500m W Rural) **Camping Les Brières du Bourg, Route d'Herbignac, 44410 St Lyphard** [02 40 91 43 13 or 01 40 33 93 33 (LS); fax 02 51 74 06 62; cledelles.reservations@wanadoo.fr; www.lescledelles.com] Fr Nantes on N165 dir Vannes, exit junc 15 dir La Roche-Bernard then in 2km turn L onto D574 then D774 sp Herbignac, Guérande. At Herbignac fork L onto D47. Pass 1st sp on R to St Lyphard, site on L in 1km. Med, hdg/mkd pitch, pt sl, shd; wc; chem disp; mv service pnt; baby facs; serviced pitch; shwrs inc; el pnts (6A) €5; gas; lndtte; ice; shops 1km; tradsmn; rest 1km; snacks; bar; playgrnd; pool; lake sw adj; fishing; sand beach 10km; tennis; cycle hire; mini-golf; games rm; entnmt; child entnmt; TV; 10% statics; dogs €2.30; phone; Eng spkn; adv bkg; quiet; red long stay/low ssn; CCI. "Delightful vill; beautiful National Park; sports complex adj." ♦ 1 Apr-30 Sep. € 15.00   2007*

ST MAIXENT L'ECOLE *7A2* (SW Urban) **Camp Municipal du Panier Fleuri, Rue Paul Drévin, 79400 St Maixent-l'Ecole** [05 49 05 53 21 or 05 49 76 13 77 (Mairie)] Take D611 (N11) twd Niort, at 2nd set of traff lts nr top of hill out of town turn L. Foll camping sps into ent. Med, mkd pitch, pt sl, pt shd; wc (some cont); mv service pnt; shwrs inc; el pnts (10A) €1.45-5; tradsmn; rest, snacks, bar 1km; playgrnd; pool adj (proper sw trunks only); tennis; dogs €0.55; quiet; cc not acc. "Helpful warden on site 0930-1200 & 1700-2130, if locked for security go to house nr wc block; ltd/basic facs low ssn in Portakabin; poss itinerants; interesting town; medieval houses, abbey church & crypt adj; NH en rte Spain." 1 Apr-31 Oct. € 7.30   2006*

> The opening dates and prices on this campsite have changed. I'll send a site report form to the editor for the next edition of the guide.

ST MALO *2E4* (500m Urban/Coastal) **Camp Municipal Cité d'Alet, Rue Gaston Buy, 35400 St Malo** [02 99 81 60 91 or 02 99 40 71 11 (LS); fax 02 99 40 71 37; camping@ville-saint-malo.fr; www.ville-saint-malo.fr/campings/] Fr ferry terminal go twd St Malo, site sp at rndabt immed past docks. Fr all other dir foll sp for port/ferry, then site sp. Site off Place St Pierre, St Servan-sur-Mer. App thro old part of city poss diff for lge o'fits. Lge, mkd pitch, pt sl, pt shd; wc; chem disp; mv service pnt; shwrs inc; el pnts (10A) inc (poss rev pol & long elec cable poss req); lndtte; shops, tradsmn, rest, snacks 500m; bar; playgrnd; sand beach 500m; dogs €2.25; bus; phone; poss v cr; Eng spkn; adv bkg; quiet; cc acc; CCI. "Staff helpful & courteous; sm pitches; WW2 museum on site; nice views; conv for St Malo & ferries; gd views over harbour to old city; noise fr harbour, esp when foggy; gd shwr block; gd mkt Fri." ♦ ltd. 27 Apr-30 Oct. € 16.00   2006*

France

ST MALO *2E4* (2km NE Coastal) **Camp Municipal du Nicet, Ave de la Varde, 35400 St Malo** [02 99 40 26 32; fax 02 99 21 92 62; camping@ ville-saint-malo.fr] Fr St Malo take coast (busy & narr) rd Ave JF Kennedy twd Cancale; pass Camping Nielles on L bef district of Rotheneuf; turn L at camping sp just after sm g'ge on L; turn L at T-junc; site in view. Lge, mkd pitch, pt sl, pt terr, unshd; wc; chem disp, shwrs inc; el pnts (5-10A) inc (rev pol); lndtte; shops 800m; tradsmn; playgrnd; sand beach adj; dogs €2.20; poss cr & noisy high ssn; Eng spkn; adv bkg (dep req;) cc acc; CCI. "Clean, well-run site on cliff top; secluded beach via steep steps; can be exposed if pitched nr edge with sea view; some pitches sm; recep clsd 1200-1630 low ssn." ♦ 1 Jul-1 Sep. € 15.50   2006*

ST MALO *2E4* (4km NE Coastal) **Camping des Chevrets, Plage de Chevrets, La Guimorais, 35350 St Coulomb** [02 99 89 01 90; fax 02 99 89 01 16; campingdeschevrets@wanadoo. fr; www.campingdeschevrets.fr] St Malo to Cancale coast rd D201; La Guimorais on L 3km E of Rotheneuf, strt thro vill; fairly narr app. V lge, hdg/mkd pitch, pt sl, pt shd; wc; chem disp; mv service pnt; baby facs; shwrs €1.50; el pnts (6A) €3.35; gas; lndtte; shop; rest; snacks; bar; BBQ; playgrnd; sand beach adj; games area; cycle hire; internet; entmnt; 50% statics; dogs; poss cr; Eng spkn; adv bkg; quiet; cc acc; red low ssn/long stay; CCI. "Conv St Malo, Mont St Michel; vg site." ♦ 6 Apr-1 Nov. € 21.95   2007*

See advertisement on previous page

ST MALO *2E4* (1km E Coastal) **Camp Municipal Les Nielles, 47 Ave du Président Kennedy, 35400 St Malo** [02 99 40 26 35 or 02 99 40 71 11 (LS); fax 02 99 40 71 38; camping@ville-saint-malo. fr] Fr cent of St Malo (avoiding old walled town) E on D201 parallel & adj to coast; few site sp & poss not easy to find. Med, mkd pitch, unshd; wc (some cont); shwrs inc; el pnts (10A) inc; ice; shop 900m; rest, bar 500m; playgrnd; beach adj; fishing; dogs €2.15; poss cr; some rd noise. "Excel for beach & ferry; pitches nr beach v exposed if weather bad." 1 Jul-31 Aug. € 15.50   2005*

ST MALO *2E4* (5km SE Rural) **Camping Le P'tit Bois, La Chalandouze, 35430 St Jouan-des-Guérets** [02 99 21 14 30; fax 02 99 81 74 14; camping.ptitbois@wanadoo.fr; www.ptitbois. com] Fr St Malo take D937 (N137) dir Rennes; after o'skts of St Malo turn R twd St Jouan-des-Guérets, site sp. Lge, hdg/mkd pitch, pt shd; wc (some cont); chem disp; mv service pnt; baby facs; shwrs inc; el pnts (10A) €4; gas; lndtte; shop; rest; snacks; bar; BBQ (gas/elec); playgrnd; 2 htd pools; (1 covrd); waterslides; paddling pool; jacuzzi; turkish bath; sand beach 2km; tidal rv sw, fishing, watersports 2km; tennis; mini-golf; entmnt & child entmnt; internet; games/TV rrm; 50% tour ops/ statics; dogs €6 (1 only per pitch); adv bkg; cc acc; red low ssn/CCI. "30 mins fr port/ferries; well-run, gd quality site; friendly & helpful recep; gd for families; conv Le Mont St Michel." ♦ 5 Apr-13 Sep. € 35.00 ABS - B03   2007*

See advertisement above

ST MALO *2E4* (3km S) **Camping Domaine de la Ville Huchet, Rue de la Passagère, Quelmer, 34500 St Malo** [02 99 81 11 83; fax 02 99 81 51 89; info@lavillehuchet.com; www.lavillehuchet.com] Fr ferry turn R. 1km to traff lts & T-junc, turn R. On D937 (N137) foll sp Rennes. Turn R after 5km to side rd sp Quelmer & La Passagère. Lge, pt sl, pt shd; wc; chem disp; baby facs; shwrs inc; el pnts (4A) inc; lndtte; shop; rest; snacks; bar; playgrnd; pool; waterpark; sand beach 3km; cycle hire; games area; entmnt; TV; 40% statics; dogs €1.30; adv bkg; quiet, but some rd noise; "Spacious site; helpful owner; excel pool." ♦ 19 Apr-13 Sep. € 28.80 ABS - B32   2007*

ST MALO DU BOIS see St Laurent sur Sèvre *2H4*

ST MARCEL D'ARDECHE see Pont St Esprit *9D2*

ST MARCELLIN *9C2* (7km E Rural) **Camping Château de Beauvoir, 38160 Beauvoir-en-Royans [04 76 64 01 79; fax 04 76 38 49 60; jbourgeat2001@yahoo.fr]** On N532 Romans to Grenoble, turn into narr uphill rd to vill; L into site, sp. Care needed on app rd & ent gate narr. Sm, shd; htd wc; shwrs inc; el pnts (10A) €2; lndtte; shop 6km; bar; rest 2km; 10% statics; dogs; quiet. "Vg sm site on château lawn." 1 Apr-31 Oct. € 10.00
2005*

ST MARCELLIN *9C2* (7km SW Rural) **Camping Les Carrets (Farconnet), 38840 St Bonnet-de-Chavagne [04 76 38 41 15]** Fr St Marcellin on D1092 (N92)/D27 to Chatte, then D68 to St Bonnet, keep L below vill about 2km, farm on L. Sm, pt sl, unshd; wc; chem disp (wc); shwrs inc; el pnts (6A) €2 (long lead rec); quiet; adv bkg. "Outstanding farm site; spectacular views of Vercors; farm produce." 15 Mar-15 Nov.
2005*

⊞**STE MARIE AUX MINES** *6E3* (1km E Rural) **FFCC Camping Les Reflets du Val d'Argent, 20 Rue d'Untergrombach, 68160 Ste Marie-aux-Mines [03 89 58 64 83; fax 03 89 58 64 31; reflets@calixo.net; www.valdargent.com]** Fr Sélestat N59 into Ste Marie. Go thro vill to traff lts & turn L. 1km to site; sp. Med, mkd pitch, pt shd; htd wc; chem disp; mv service pnt; shwrs inc; el pnts (5-15A) €3.05-9.15; lndtte; shop & 1km; tradsmn; rest; snacks; bar; BBQ; playgrnd; pool; games rm; TV; 5% statics; dogs €3.50; phone; adv bkg; quiet; red low ssn; CCI. "Lovely peaceful site; skiing in winter 5km." ♦ € 15.80
2007*

Before we move on, I'm going to fill in some site report forms and post them off to the editor, otherwise they won't arrive in time for the deadline at the end of September.

STE MARIE DU MONT see Carentan *1D4*

⊞**STES MARIES DE LA MER** *10F2* (1km E Coastal) **Camping La Brise, Rue Marcel Carrière, 13460 Stes Maries-de-la-Mer [04 90 97 84 67; fax 04 90 97 72 01; labrise@saintesmaries.com; www.saintesmariesdelamer.com]** Sp on o'skts on all rds. Take N570 fr Arles or D58 (N570) fr Aigues-Mortes. V lge, unshd; htd wc (mainly cont); mv service pnt; shwrs inc; el pnts (10A) €4.60; lndtte; ice; shops 500m; 3 htd pools; fishing; entmnt; dogs €4.50; clsd mid Nov to mid Dec; red low ssn. "Under same ownership as Le Clos du Rhône & can use their facs; v cr Aug; poss mosquitoes; m'vans can use free municipal car park with facs; conv Camargue National Park; gd security; poss unkempt low ssn; vg winter NH." ♦ € 19.80
2007*

STES MARIES DE LA MER *10F2* (2km W Coastal) **Camping Le Clos du Rhône, 13460 Stes Maries-de-la-Mer [04 90 97 85 99; fax 04 90 97 78 85; leclos@laposte.net; www.saintesmariesdelamer.com]** Fr Arles take D570 to Stes Maries; fr Aigues Mortes, D58/D570. Lge, unshd; wc; some serviced pitches; chem disp; shwrs inc; el pnts (6-10A) €4.40; gas; lndtte; ice; shop; rest; snacks; playgrnd; pool; sand beach; entmnt; dogs; horseriding adj; poss cr; quiet; adv bkg; cc acc. "Excel pool & facs; san facs poss ltd & stretched low ssn; popular with families; private gate to beach; mosquitoes." ♦ 20 Mar-30 Oct. € 29.20
2006*

ST MARTIAL DE NABIRAT see Gourdon *7D3*

ST MARTIAL ENTRAYGUES see Argentat *7C4*

ST MARTIN D'ARDECHE see Pont St Esprit *9D2*

ST MARTIN DE CRAU *10F2* (W Urban) **Camping La Crau, 170 Ave de la République, Route du Stade, 13310 St Martin-de-Crau [04 90 47 17 09; fax 04 90 47 09 92; camping.lacrau@wanadoo.fr]** Fr W take D453 sp St Martin-de-Crau. L at 1st traff lts. Fr E take D453 thro town & R at traff lts by Hotel. Site behind Hôtel de la Crau, 50m up side rd running N off D453 on D83b. Fr N (St Rémy) on D27 turn R in town & as bef. Med, hdg/mkd pitch, shd; wc (some cont); chem disp; mv service pnt; shwrs inc; el pnts (6A) inc; gas in town; rest; snacks; bar; shop in high ssn & 300m; tradsmn; lndtte; ice; playgrnd; pool (high ssn); beach 35km; TV rm; dogs €1.60; Eng spkn; adv bkg; poss noise fr local airfield; red long stay/low ssn; cc acc (Visa); CCI. "Site run by adj hotel; poss itinerants; facs dated (plans for upgrading); special private pitch extra; noisy nr pool; under-staffed low ssn; conv for Arles, St Rémy, Les Baux; gd for bird watchers (Camargue/Crau plain); excel mkt Fri." ♦ Easter-15 Oct. € 24.00
2006*

ST MARTIN DE LONDRES *10E1* (10km N Rural) **Camping Les Muriers, Chemin de Sauzèdes, 34190 Bauzille-de-Putois [04 67 73 73 63; fax 04 67 73 31 84 (Mairie)]** Fr S on D986 twd Ganges turn L at rndabt on ent Bauzille-de-Putois & foll sp. Site in 500m on L. Med, pt shd; wc (cont); chem disp (wc); mv service pnt; shwrs inc; el pnts (5A) €3; ice; lndtte; tradsmn; snacks; BBQ; playgrnd; sw rv & canoe hire 500m; dogs; phone; bus 500m; poss cr; quiet; cc not acc; CCI. "Coast 45km; gd." 1 May-30 Aug. € 10.00
2007*

France

ST MARTIN DE LONDRES *10E1* (2km E Rural)
FFCC Camping Le Pic St-Loup, 34380 St Martin-de-Londres [04 67 55 00 53; fax 04 67 55 00 04; depelchinp@aol.com] Fr Ganges take D986 S. In St Martin turn L onto D122, site sp. Med, some hdg/mkd pitch, pt sl, pt shd; wc; chem disp; shwrs inc; el pnts (6A) inc; gas; lndtte; shop; ice; rest; snacks; bar; playgrnd; pool (covrd or uncovrd); 10% statics; poss cr; adv bkg; quiet but some rd noise; 10% red for 10+ nights; cc not acc; CCI. "Helpful owner; some pitches v sm for van, awning & car; lger pitches on lower terr, but ltd elec; shwrs awkward to use; dated san facs poss not v clean; site slightly disorganised; OK NH." 1 Apr-30 Sep. € 19.04   2007*

ST MARTIN DE SEIGNANX see Bayonne *8F1*

ST MARTIN DES BESACES *1D4* (W Rural) Camping Le Puits, La Groudière, 14350 St Martin-des-Besaces [tel/fax 02 31 67 80 02; camping.le.puits@wanadoo.fr; www.lepuits.com] Fr Caen SW on A84 dir Rennes, Villers-Bocage & exit junc 41 to St Martin-des-Besaces. At traff lts in vill turn R & foll site sp, site on L at end of vill in 500m. Fr Cherbourg foll sp St Lô onto m'way. After Torini-sur-Vire at junc with A84 foll sp Caen & exit junc 41, then as above. Sm, hdg/mkd pitch, pt sl, pt shd; wc; chem disp; mv service pnt; shwrs inc; el pnts (6A) €4 (poss rev pol); gas; lndtte; ice; shop 500m; tradsmn; rest 500m; snacks; bar; BBQ; sm playgrnd; pool 10km; sand beach 35km; lake adj; fishing; cycling; equestrian trails; entmnt; no statics; dogs; adv bkg (dep req); quiet; red low ssn; cc acc; CCI. "Pleasant CL-type orchard site; v helpful, welcoming, Irish owners; no arr bef 1400; lge pitches with garden; san facs v ltd; B&B in farmhouse; suitable for rallies up to 30 vans; c'van storage; nice local walks; excel war museum in vill; conv for Caen ferries & D-Day beaches." ♦ 1 Mar-31 Oct. € 16.00   2007*

ST MARTIN EN CAMPAGNE *3B2* (3km N Coastal) Camping Domaine Les Goélands, Rue des Grèbes, 76370 St Martin-en-Campagne [02 35 83 82 90; fax 02 35 83 21 79; g4sdomaine@wanadoo.fr; www.lesdomaines.org] Fr Dieppe foll D925 twd Le Tréport & Abbeville. Turn L at rndabt on D113 twd St Martin-en-Campagne. Cont thro vill to St Martin-Plage (approx 3km) & foll 'Camping' sp to site on L. Lge, hdg/mkd pitch, hdstg, pt sl, terr, pt shd, hdstg; htd wc; 100% serviced pitches; chem disp; baby facs; shwrs inc; el pnts (16A) inc (poss rev pol); gas; lndtte; shop 1km; tradsmn; snacks (& in vill), bar high ssn; BBQ; playgrnd; htd pool & waterslide 1km; sand/shgl beach 500m; fishing; tennis; mini-golf; cycle hire; golf 20km; horseriding, archery 15km; TV; 40% statics; dogs €1.50; Eng spkn; adv bkg; quiet; cc acc; red CCI. "Sports complex in St Martin; gd touring area; ltd recep hrs low ssn; no late arrivals area; poss resident workers low ssn; mkt Dieppe Sat am; vg site." ♦ 1 Apr-31 Oct. € 27.00   2006*

ST MARTIN EN HAUT see Ste Foy l'Argentiere *9B2*

ST MARTIN EN VERCORS see Chapelle en Vercors, La *9C3*

ST MARTIN LARS see Ste Hermine *2H4*

ST MARTIN SUR LA CHAMBRE *9B3* (Rural) Camping Le Bois Joli, 73130 St Martin-sur-la-Chambre [04 79 56 21 28; fax 04 79 56 29 95; camping.le.bois.joli@wanadoo.fr; www.camping leboisjoli.com] Leave A43 at junc 26 onto D213 sp La Chambre & Col de la Madeleine; foll camping sp (rd narr & winding in places); site on L. Med, mkd pitch, terr, pt sl, pt shd; wc (some cont); chem disp; baby facs; shwrs inc; el pnts (10A) €3.50; gas; lndtte; ice; shop, snacks, bar 3km; tradsmn; rest; BBQ; playgrnd; pool; fishing; guided walks; entmnt; dogs €1; 20% statics; poss cr; quiet; Eng spkn; adv bkg; red long stay; phone; CCI. "V helpful staff; spectacular mountain scenery; gd location walking rtes & skiing; ltd facs low ssn; conv Fréjus Tunnel." ♦ 15 Apr-30 Oct. € 13.00   2007*

⊞**ST MARTIN SUR LA CHAMBRE** *9B3* (2km N Rural) Camping Le Petit Nice, Notre Dame-de-Cruet, 73130 St Martin-sur-la-Chambre [tel/fax 04 79 56 37 72 or 06 76 29 19 39 (mob); campinglepetitnice@wanadoo.fr; www.camping-petitnice.com] Fr N on A43 exit junc 26 & foll sp to cent of La Chambre, thro town to rndabt & turn R into Rue Notre Dame-du-Cruet. Foll site sp & in 2km turn R thro housing, site on L in 200m. Sm, terr, pt shd; htd wc; chem disp; shwrs inc; el pnts (3-10A) €3-8; lndtte; shop & 2km; rest; snacks; bar; playgrnd; pool; 80% statics; dogs; poss cr; Eng spkn; adv bkg; quiet; CCI. "By stream with mountain views; basic, clean san facs; gd for mountain touring." ♦ € 12.00   2005*

ST MARTIN SUR OUST see Rochefort en Terre *2F3*

ST MATHIEU *7B3* (3km E) Camp Municipal Le Lac, Les Champs, 87440 St Mathieu [05 55 00 30 26 (Mairie); fax 05 55 48 80 62] On D699 heading E in dir of Limoges 1.8km fr vill turn on L (N). Sp fr vill cent. Med, hdg/mkd pitch, pt shd; wc; baby facs; shwrs; el pnts; lndtte; shops 3km; rest adj; playgrnd; lake sw & beach; quiet. "Pleasantly situated nr lake; windsurfing; pedaloes; lge pitches." 1 May-15 Sep.   2004*

STE MAURE DE TOURAINE *4H2* (6km NE Rural) Camping Le Parc de Fierbois, 37800 Ste Catherine-de-Fierbois [02 47 65 43 35; fax 02 47 65 53 75; parc.fierbois@wanadoo.fr; www. fierbois.com] S on D910 (N10) fr Tours, thro Montbazon & cont twd Ste Maure & Châtellerault. About 16km outside Montbazon at vill of Ste Catherine look for site sp. Turn L off main rd & foll sp to site. Lge, hdg/mkd pitch, pt shd; wc; chem disp; mv service pnt; baby facs; shwrs inc; el pnts (4A) €4.30; lndtte; shop; rest; bar; BBQ; playgrnd; htd, covrd pool; paddling pool; waterslide; sand/ shgl beach at lake; boating; fishing; tennis; games area; games rm; entmnt; internet; statics; dogs free; poss cr; Eng spkn; adv bkg; cc acc; red low ssn; CCI. "Helpful staff; peaceful low ssn; check el pnts; rec site." ♦ 28 Apr-12 Sep. € 40.00   2007*

STE MAURE DE TOURAINE *4H2* (1.5km SE Rural) Camp Municipal de Marans, Rue de Toizelet, 37800 Ste Maure-de-Touraine [02 47 65 44 93] Fr A10 take Ste Maure exit junc 25 & foll D760 twd Loches. At 4th rndabt turn L & then immed R. Site on R in 500m. Site sp fr m'way. Med, mkd pitch, pt shd; wc; chem disp; mv service pnt; shwrs inc; el pnts (10A) €2.45 (poss long cables req); supmkt 500m; shops, rest, bar 1km; BBQ; playgrnd; pool 1.5km; fishing; tennis; roller blade court; dogs €1.35; phone; Eng spkn; adv bkg; quiet. "Excel, v clean facs, beautiful & well-kept; facs poss stretched when busy; excel disabled facs; office closed 1100-1200; barrier down 2200-0700; twin-axle vans not allowed; easy walk to town." ♦ 10 Apr-30 Sep. € 7.25   2007*

STE MAURE DE TOURAINE *4H2* (11km SW Rural) Camp Municipal La Croix de la Motte, 37800 Nouâtre-Marcilly [02 47 65 20 38 or 02 47 65 33 56] In Ste Maure, turn W off D910 (N10) onto D760 for 4km, turn L onto D58 twd Pouzay for 4km, turn S onto D18 for 4km, site on L on ent vill adj Rv Vienne. Med, hdg/mkd pitch, pt shd; wc (some cont); chem disp; baby facs; shwrs inc; el pnts (6A) €2.60; lndtte; ice; shop 1km; tradsmn; rest, snacks, bar 4km; playgrnd; rv sw adj; fishing; some statics; some Eng spkn; adv bkg; quiet; CCI. "Helpful warden; clean san facs; pitches private & gd size; v quiet, pleasant site; conv for Loire chateaux; canoes/kayaks for hire; no c'vans over 6m or twin-axles." 15 Jun-15 Sep. € 7.00   2006*

STE MAURE DE TOURAINE *4H2* (6km W Rural) Camping du Château de la Rolandière, 37220 Trogues [tel/fax 02 47 58 53 71; contact@ larolandiere.com; www.larolandiere.com] Exit A10 junc 25 onto D760 dir Chinon. Site sp. Sm, hdg/mkd pitch, pt shd; wc; chem disp; baby facs; shwrs inc; el pnts (10A) €3.50; gas 6km; lndtte; shop & 6km; tradsmn; snacks; bar; BBQ; playgrnd; pool; paddling pool; rv sw & sand beach 4km; games rm; mini-golf; cycle hire; TV rm; dogs €2; Eng spkn; adv bkg; quiet; red low ssn; CCI. "Delightful site; ideal for Loire chateaux." ♦ 1 May-30 Sep. € 21.00
2005*

STE MAURE DE TOURAINE *4H2* (6km W Rural) Camping Parc des Allais, Les Allais, 37220 Trogues [02 47 58 60 60; fax 02 47 95 24 04; contact@parc-des-allais.com; www.parc-des-allais.com] Exit A10 junc 25 onto D760 dir Chinon. At Noyant turn S onto D58 to Pouzay. In Pouzay turn W for 1km to site, sp. Lge, hdg/mkd pitch; pt shd; htd wc; chem disp; mv service pnt; baby facs; shwrs inc; el pnts (10A) inc; lndtte; ice; shop; tradsmn; snacks; bar; BBQ; playgrnd; htd, covrd pool; waterslide; rv sw 2km; fishing; tennis; cycle hire; games area; games rm; fitness rm; internet; entmnt; TV; 40% statics; dogs €3; phone; Eng spkn; adv bkg; cc acc; red long stay/CCI. "V pleasant site; superb pool complex; easy access a'route (10 mins) & Futuroscope (45 mins); conv Loire chateaux." ♦ 5 Apr-13 Sep. € 34.00
2007*

ST MAURICE D'ARDECHE see Aubenas *9D2*

ST MAURICE DE LIGNON *9C1* (1km E Rural) Camping du Sabot, 43200 St Maurice-de-Lignon [04 71 65 32 68; cmegiraud@aol.com] Take N88 N fr Yssingeaux or S fr St Etienne. Site well sp in St Maurice. Med, mkd pitch, part terr, pt shd; htd wc (some cont); chem disp; mv service pnt; shwrs; el pnts (6A) €3.25; lndtte; shops; rest, snacks 250m; BBQ; playgrnd; 50% statics; dogs; phone; poss cr; Eng spkn; adv bkg; quiet. "Much improved site; warm welcome; helpful owner; mkd walks fr site; ltd touring pitches, blocks poss needed." 15 Apr-15 Oct. € 9.75   2005*

⊞**ST MAURICE LES CHARENCEY** *4E2* (Rural) Camp Municipal de la Poste, 61190 St Maurice-lès-Charencey [02 33 25 72 98] Vill on N12 halfway bet Verneuil-sur-Avre & Mortagne-au-Perche. Site in vill cent, adj post office. Sm, mkd pitch, pt sl, pt shd; wc; shwrs inc; el pnts (5A) €2 (poss rev pol); lake adj; fishing; 50% statics; phone; rd noise. "Direct access to lovely fishing lake; phone ahead low ssn to check open; helpful warden; facs basic but adequate; basin only for disabled; gd NH." ♦ ltd. € 6.00   2007*

ST MAURICE SUR FESSARD see Montargis *4F3*

⊞**ST MAURICE SUR MOSELLE** *6F3* (4.5km NE Urban) Camping Domaine de Champé, 14 Rue des Champs-Navets, 88540 Bussang [03 29 61 61 51; fax 03 29 61 56 90; info@ domaine-de-champe.com; www.domaine-de-champe.com] Fr N66/E512 in Bussang, site sp from town sq. Med, hdg/mkd pitch, pt sl, pt shd; wc; chem disp; mv service pnt; baby facs; sauna; shwrs; el pnts (10A) €3.90; lndtte; ice; shop; tradsmn; rest; snacks; bar; BBQ; playgrnd; pool; paddling pool; rv 1km; tennis; cycle hire; games area; games rm; w/e activities; wifi internet; TV; 10% statics; dogs €2.20; phone; bus 1km; poss cr; Eng spkn; quiet; adv bkg; CCI. "Lovely views; v helpful owners; excel walks in Vosges by Rv Moselle; gd rest in vill; san facs shabby low ssn & insufficient for size of site." ♦ € 16.60   2006*

France

ST MAURICE SUR MOSELLE *6F3* (10km E Rural) **Camp Municipal Benelux-Bâle, Rue de la Scierie, 68121 Urbès [03 89 82 78 76 or 03 89 82 60 91 (Mairie); fax 03 89 82 16 61; mairie.urbes@wanadoo.fr]** Site off N66 on N side of rd at foot of hill rising W out of Urbès. At foot of Col de Bessang. Lge, hgd/mkd pitch, pt shd; wc; chem disp; shwrs €0.95; el pnts (4-10A) inc; gas in vill; ice; lndtte; bar; playgrnd; rv & lake sw & fishing adj; dogs €0.35; quiet; adv bkg rec high ssn; 60% statics; CCI. "Gd sh stay/NH; beautiful area nr Col de Bussang." 23 Apr-2 Oct. € 10.35   2005*

ST MAURICE SUR MOSELLE *6F3* (W Rural) **Camping Les Deux Ballons, Ave Pied des Ballons, 88560 St Maurice-sur-Moselle [03 29 25 17 14; fax 03 29 25 27 51; verocamp@aol.com; www.camping-deux-ballons.fr]** On N66 on E side of rd in vill, site on L before petrol stn. Clearly sp. Lge, mkd pitch, pt sl, pt shd; wc; chem disp; mv service pnt; baby facs; shwrs inc; el pnts (4-15A) €4-5; gas; lndtte; ice; shop 500m; snacks; bar; pool; waterslide; tennis; games rm; internet; TV rm; dogs €2; phone; poss cr; Eng spkn; adv bkg; dep req + bkg fee; quiet; red low ssn; cc not acc; CCI. "Cycle path thro countryside fr site; some pitches sm; excel site." ♦ 10 Apr-12 Sep. € 20.50   2004*

STE MAXIME *10F4* (1km N Rural) **Camping La Beaumette-Imbert, 83120 Ste Maxime [04 94 96 14 35 or 04 94 96 10 92; fax 04 94 96 35 38; camping@labeaumette.com; www.labeaumette.com]** Leave Ste Maxime on D25 dir Le Muy, site on L in 1km. Med, shd; wc (own san rec); chem disp; shwrs inc; el pnts (16A) €4; lndry rm; shop 500m; beach 1km; dogs; 50% statics; phone; quiet; adv bkg; CCI. "Security vg but low ssn warden absent; €80 dep security gate; site liable to flooding in severe weather; all facs upstairs inc disabled; cold water only except shwrs; vg." ♦ ltd. Easter-Oct. € 20.00   2004*

STE MAXIME *10F4* (5km NE Coastal) **Camping Les Cigalons, La Nartelle, 83120 Ste Maxime [04 94 96 05 51; fax 04 94 96 79 62; campingcigalon@wanadoo.fr; www.camping cigalon.com]** Site on D559 (N98) E of Ste Maxime, go thro La Nartelle & turn L into lane immed after seafood rest. Site on L after 25m. Med, mkd pitch, pt sl, shd; wc; chem disp; shwrs; el pnts (6A) €3.60; lndtte; sm shop; rest, snacks, bar adj; paddling pool; sand beach 50m; dogs €2.50poss cr; adv bkg; v quiet. "Friendly owners; gd position; sm v hard compacted earth pitches; car parking poss diff." ♦ 1 Apr-13 Oct. € 23.00   2006*

⊞ST MAXIMIN LA STE BAUME *10F3* (3km S Rural) **Camping Caravaning Le Provencal, Chemin de Mazaugues, 83470 St Maximin-la-Ste Baume [04 94 78 16 97; fax 04 94 78 00 22; camping. provencal@wanadoo.fr]** Exit St Maximin on N560 S twd Marseilles. After 1km turn L onto D64. Site on R after 2km. Lge, pt sl, shd; wc; mv service pnt; shwrs inc; el pnts (6-10A) €3.40-4.50; gas; lndtte; shop & 3km; rest high ssn; snacks; bar; playgrnd; pool; TV; some statics; adv bkg; CCI. € 18.30
      2007*

ST MAYEUX see Mur de Bretagne *2E3*

ST MEDARD DE GUIZIERES *7C2* (500m N Rural) **Camp Municipal Le Gua, 33230 St Médard-de-Guizières [tel/fax 05 57 69 82 37]** On N89 bet Libourne & Montpon-Ménestérol; in St Médard foll sp 'Base de Loisirs'; site adj sw pool. Med, mkd pitch, shd; wc (some cont); chem disp (wc); shwrs inc; el pnts €2.60; ice; shop, rest, snacks, bar 500m; playgrnd; pool adj; rv fishing; quiet. "Direct access to rv; conv Bordeaux, St Emillion & vineyards; vg." ♦ ltd. 15 Jun-15 Sep. € 7.00   2006*

ST MEDARD DE GUIZIERES *7C2* (4km S Rural) **FLOWER Camping Le Pressoir, Queyrai, 33570 Petit-Palais-et-Cornemps [05 57 69 73 25; fax 05 57 69 77 36; camping.lepressoir@wanadoo.fr; www.campinglepressoir.com]** Leave A9/E70 junc 11, then N89 Bordeaux-Périgueux rd to St Médard-de-Guizières onto D21 & foll sp, site bef Petit-Palais. Fr Castillon-la-Bataille on D936 Bergerac-Bordeaux rd take D17/D21 sp St Médard & foll site sp. Take care on access & exit. Med, hdg/mkd pitch, pt sl, pt shd; wc; chem disp; shwrs inc; el pnts (6A) inc; lndtte; shop 1.5km; tradsmn; rest; snacks; bar; BBQ; playgrnd; pool; dogs €2; Eng spkn; quiet; cc acc; red CCI. "Barrier card ent, close to vineyards; Belgian owners; basic san facs; site poss unkempt." ♦ 26 Mar-2 Oct. € 26.50 (CChq acc)   2007*

STE MENEHOULD *5D1* (1km E Rural) **Camp Municipal de la Grelette, Chemin de l'Alleval, 51800 Ste Menéhould [03 26 60 80 21 (Mairie); fax 03 26 60 62 54; mairie@ste-menehould.fr; www.ville-sainte-menehould.fr]** E on N3; turn R over 1st bdge after rlwy stn; foll sp for La Piscine; site on R after pool; sp fr town. Sm, mkd pitch, pt sl, pt shd; wc; shwrs inc; chem disp; el pnts (4A) €1.90; tradsmn; supmkt 500m; rest, snacks, bar 1km; pool adj; dogs €0.70; poss cr; adv bkg; Eng spkn; no cc acc; CCI. "Helpful warden on site 0800-1100 & 1800-2000, arrives in mins if absent; do not site self; dated, clean san facs; town run-down." 1 May-30 Sep. € 4.80   2006*

STE MERE EGLISE *1C4* (9.5km NE Coastal) Camping Le Cormoran, 2 Rue du Cormoran, 50480 Ravenoville-Plage [02 33 41 33 94; fax 02 33 95 16 08; lecormoran@wanadoo.fr; www. lecormoran.com] NE on D15 fr Ste Mère-Eglise to Ravenoville, turn L onto D14 then R back onto D15 to Ravenoville Plage. Turn R on D421, Rte d'Utah Beach, site on R in 1km. Or fr N13 sp C2 Fresville & ent Ste Mère-Eglise, then take D15. Lge, hdg/ mkd pitch, some hdstg, unshd; wc; chem disp; mv service pnt; baby facs; shwrs inc; el pnts (6A) €4; gas; lndtte; ice; shop; tradsmn; snacks; bar; BBQ (not elec); playgrnd; htd pool; paddling pool; jacuzzi; sand beach adj; sea fishing; tennis; cycle hire; horseriding; games area; archery; entmnt; wifi internet; TV/games rm; 60% statics; dogs €3; poss cr; recep 0830-1300 & 1500-2000; Eng spkn; adv bkg; quiet; cc acc; CCI. "Excel, family-run site with vg facs for children; places of interest & museums relating to D-Day Landings; warm welcome; helpful reception; lge pitches; poss tired san facs end of ssn; poss v windy; special pitches for early dep for Cherbourg ferry; m'vans o'night rate €13." ♦ 1 Apr-28 Sep. € 28.00 (CChq acc) ABS - N12
2007*

STE MERE EGLISE *1C4* (500m E Urban) Camp Municipal, 6 Rue Airborne, 50480 Ste Mère-Eglise [02 33 41 35 22; fax 02 33 41 79 15; www.sainte-mere-eglise.info/camping.html] Fr Cherbourg S on N13 to cent of Ste Mère-Eglise (avoiding by-pass); at vill sq turn L on D17 to site, next to vill sports ground. Med, some hdstg, pt sl, pt shd, wc (some cont); chem disp (wc); shwrs inc; el pnts (10A) €3 (poss rev pol); gas 500m; lndtte; ice; shop & bar 500m; rest, snacks, BBQ; playgrnd; sand beach 10km; tennis; 5% statics; dogs €1; phone; poss cr; little Eng spkn; adv bkg; CCI. "Nice site; clean facs; conv D-Day beaches, museums & Cotentin Peninsula; conv ferries; gates locked o'night but open 6 am for early departures; 5 min walk to town; access poss if warden absent & pay later." ♦ 15 Mar-30 Sep. € 13.00
2007*

There aren't many sites open this early in the year. We'd better phone ahead to check that the one we're heading for is actually open.

ST MICHEL CHEF CHEF see Pornic *2G3*

ST MICHEL DE MAURIENNE *9C3* (500m SE Rural) Camping Le Marintan, 1 Rue de la Provalière, 73140 St Michel-de-Maurienne [04 79 59 17 36; fax 04 79 59 17 86] Fr N6 foll sp in town to 'Centre Touristique' & 'Maison Retraite'. Sm, hdg pitch, unshd; htd wc; chem disp; shwrs inc; el pnts; shops in town; rest; bar; pool; some statics; quiet. "Excel new site (2006)."
2006*

ST MICHEL EN GREVE *2E2* (1km N Coastal) Camping Les Capucines, Kervourdon, Trédez-Locquémeau, 22300 St Michel-en-Grève [02 96 35 72 28; fax 02 96 35 78 98; les. capucines@wanadoo.fr; www.lescapucines.fr] Fr Lannion on D786 SW twd St Michel-en-Grève, sp Morlaix; approx 700m bef ent St Michel-en-Grève, turn R into narr rd & R again in 100m at x-rds. Fr Roscoff take D58 to join N12 at junc 17; NE of Morlaix at junc 18 turn onto D786 twd Lannion; site down narr app rd on L on leaving St Michel-en-Grève, then R at x-rds. Med, hdg/mkd pitch, pt sl, pt shd; wc; chem disp; 100% serviced pitches; baby facs; shwrs inc; el pnts (7A) inc; gas; lndtte; ice; shop & 1km; tradsmn; rest 2km; snacks; bar; BBQ (charcoal/gas); playgrnd; htd, covrd pool; paddling pool; sand beach 8km; watersports 1km; mini-golf; cycle hire; wifi internet; games/TV rm; 7% statics; dogs €2; phone; c'van max length 8m high ssn; Eng spkn; adv bkg; quiet; 1 night in 7 free; cc acc; CCI. "Excel; well-maintained, peaceful site; immac san facs; gd pool; gd size pitches; exceptionally helpful owners; lovely bays; gd base; mkt in Lannion Thu." ♦ 15 Mar-5 Nov. € 26.60 ABS - B13
2007*

ST MICHEL ESCALUS see Léon *8E1*

ST MIHIEL *5D2* (14km NE Rural) Camp Municipal Les Passons Madine 2, 55210 Heudicourt [03 29 89 36 08; fax 03 29 89 35 60; lacmadine@ wanadoo.fr] Fr St Mihiel, take D901 NE to Chaillon. Turn R on D133 to Heudicourt. Bear L out of vill, still on D133 & after 1km turn R to Nonsard. Site on R in 1.5km, immed after sailing school at N end of Lake Madine. Lge, mkd pitch, pt sl, pt shd; wc (mainly cont); shwrs inc; el pnts £2.50; rest; shop; lndry rm; lake sw adj; nautical sports & fishing; horseriding school & sailing school adj; many statics; CCI. "Gd location by lake Madine; a little run down; sm, cramped pitches; san facs clean but need updating; gd lake for watersports; fair NH - not well looked after low ssn." 1 Apr-30 Sep. € 13.80
2006*

ST MIHIEL *5D2* (2km W Urban) Camping Base de Plein Air, Chemin du Gué Rappeau, 55300 St Mihiel [03 29 89 03 59; fax 03 29 89 07 18; base.de.plein.air@wanadoo.fr] Site on W bank of rv. Sp app St Mihiel. Fr town cent take rd sp Bar-le-Duc (D901) 1st R after rv bdge. Med, mkd pitch, pt shd; wc (mainly cont); chem disp; shwrs inc; el pnts (10A); lndtte; shops 2km; tradsmn; rest, snacks, bar 1km; playgrnd; games area; canoeing & sailing; 10% statics; adv bkg; quiet; CCI; "Site developed as youth cent; facs clean but tired; pleasant scenery; lge pitches." 15 Apr-15 Oct.
2005*

STE NATHALENE see Sarlat la Canéda *7C3*

France

ST NAZAIRE *2G3* (6km SW Rural/Coastal) **Camping Yakudi Village de l'Eve, Route du Fort, St Marc-sur-Mer, 44600 St Nazaire [02 40 91 90 65 or 05 46 22 38 22; fax 02 40 91 76 59 or 05 46 23 65 10; camping-de-leve@wanadoo.fr; www.yukadivillages.com]** At St Nazaire (Ouest) stay on N171 La Baule rd. Exit N171 on D492 (Pornichet/La Baule) & cont to junc with D92 (end of D492); at lge island immed after Géant superstore & Big Mac sp, take 4th exit sp Université/Camping de l'Eve. In 1km turn R at traff lts sp Camping de l'Eve; site on R in 2km. Lge, hdg/mkd pitch, pt sl, shd; wc; chem disp; baby facs; shwrs inc; el pnts (5A) €4.75 (poss rev pol); gas; lndtte; shop; tradsmn; supmkt 2km; snacks; rest, bar high ssn; playgrnd; htd pool; paddling pool; waterslide; sand beach (via subway); tennis; entmnt; child entmnt; 65% statics; dogs €4; bus; poss cr; Eng spkn; adv bkg; quiet; red low ssn; CCI. "Vg facs; few flat pitches; pleasant vill." ♦ 15 May-9 Sep. € 24.00   2006*

> Did you know you can fill in site report forms on the Club's website — www.caravanclub.co.uk?

ST NAZAIRE EN ROYANS see St Jean en Royans *9C2*

ST NECTAIRE *9B1* (1km SE Rural) **Camping Le Viginet, 63710 St Nectaire [04 73 88 53 80 or 08 25 80 14 40; fax 04 73 88 41 93; info@camping-massifcentral.com; www.camping-massifcentral.com]** Exit A75/E11 junc 14 onto D996 dir Mont-Doré. In E side of St Nectaire (opp Ford g'ge) turn sharp L up v steep hill; rd widens after 100m; site on R after bends. Car park at site ent. Med, hdg/mkd pitch, pt sl, pt shd; wc; chem disp; mv service pnt; baby facs; shwrs inc; el pnts (10A) €3.60; gas; ice; lnd rm; shops, rest & bar 1.5km; snacks; playgrnd; pool; 30% statics; dogs €1.50; poss cr; adv bkg; quiet; cc not acc; CCI. "Nice pitches; gd views; maintenance needed (Jun 2007) & san facs scruffy; nice sm pool." ♦ ltd. 7 Apr-30 Sep. € 17.80   2007*

ST NECTAIRE *9B1* (2km SE) **Camping La Hutte des Dômes, Saillant, 63710 St Nectaire [04 73 88 50 22]** Exit 6 fr A75 S of Clermont-Ferrand. Take D978 to Champeix. Turn R onto D996 sp St Nectaire. Site on L in Saillant, ent easily missed. Sm, mkd pitch, pt sl, pt shd; wc (some cont); chem disp; shwrs inc; el pnts (4-6A) €2.50-3; shops 2km; tradsmn; dogs €0.50. "Quiet, peaceful site; exceptionally clean." 1 Jun-31 Aug. € 9.10   2006*

ST NECTAIRE *9B1* (500m S Rural) **Camping La Clé des Champs, Les Sauces, Route des Granges, 63710 St Nectaire [04 73 88 52 33; campingcledechamps@free.fr; www.campingcledeschamps.com]** S bound exit A75 at junc 6 to join D978 sp Champeix; N bound exit junc 14 to join D996 sp Champeix/St Nectaire. In St Nectaire turn L at VW/Audi g'ge on L (site sp); site 300m on L. Med, hdg/mkd pitch, pt sl, pt shd; wc (some cont); chem disp; mv service pnt; shwrs inc; el pnts (2-6A) €2.10-3.50 (rev pol); gas; lndtte; ice; shops 1km; playgrnd; pool; some statics; dogs €1; poss cr; adv bkg (dep req); poss noisy high ssn; CCI. "Well-kept, clean site; helpful owner; facs stretched in high ssn; extra charge for water." ♦ Easter-30 Sep. € 16.00   2007*

ST NIC *2E2* (1.5km SW Coastal) **Camping Ker-Ys, Pentrez-Plage, 29550 St Nic [02 98 26 53 95; fax 02 98 26 52 48; camping-kerys@wanadoo.fr; www.ker-ys.com]** Turn W off D887 onto D108 & into St Nic, & foll sp Pentrez-Plage & site. Lge, pt shd; wc; chem disp; baby facs; shwrs inc; el pnts (10A) €3.20; gas; lndtte; shop; snacks; BBQ; bar; htd pool complex; waterslide; sand beach adj; watersports; tennis; games area; entmnt; child entmnt; TV rm; some statics; dogs €2.50; adv bkg; cc acc; red low ssn. "Gd family site in lovely location; vg beach; friendly, helpful staff." ♦ 1 May-15 Sep. € 22.00   2006*

ST NICOLAS DU PELEM *2E3* (1.5km SW Rural) **Camp Municipal de la Piscine, Goas-Cussuliou, Rue de Rostrenen, 22480 St Nicolas-du-Pélem [02 96 29 51 27; fax 02 96 29 59 73]** Fr Rostrenen, take D790 NE twd Corlay. In 11km, turn L sp St Nicolas-du-Pélem. Site in 500m on R, opp pool. Med, pt shd; wc (some cont); chem disp (wc); shwrs inc; el pnts (5A) €1.45; gas, shops 1.5km; rest, snacks, bar adj; htd pool opp; dogs; quiet; CCI. "V clean, well-kept site; choose own pitch, warden will call." ♦ ltd. 15 Jun-15 Sep. € 4.20   2006*

ST NIZIER LE DESERT *9A2* (Rural) **Camp Municipal La Niziere, 01320 St Nizier-le-Désert [04 74 30 35 16; fax 04 74 30 32 78]** Fr Bourg-en-Bresse take N83 SW for 4km, L onto D22 to Dompièrre-sur-Veyle (13km). Turn R onto D90 at camping sp & site in 2km on R by lakeside. Med, shd; wc; shwrs inc; el pnts (6A) €2; lndry rm; shops 1km; playgrnd; fishing; tennis; 75% statics; quiet. "Unspoilt; rural off beaten track on side of sm lake; v peaceful; site yourself, warden calls each pm; access poss diff for c'vans." 1 Apr-30 Sep. € 9.80   2004*

⊞ *Site open all year*   602   *Send in your site reports*

ST OMER 3A3 (8km NE Rural) **Camping La Chaumière, 529 Langhemast Straete, 59285 Buysscheure** [03 28 43 03 57; camping.la chaumiere@wanadoo.fr; www.campingla chaumiere.com] Take D928 fr St Omer (see NOTE) twd Bergues & Watten & foll sp St Momelin. Stay on rd until Lederzeele & turn R onto D26 twds Cassel. After approx 2km turn R just bef rlwy bdge sp Buysscheure & site. Turn L after church, R, then site on L 500m. Single-track rd after church. NOTE on D928 fr St Omer height limit 3m; use adj level x-ing sp rte for vehicles over 3m. NB appr fr Cassel diff, especially for wide or long o'fits; also rd thro Cassel cobbled & poss more diff to find. Sm, hdg/mkd pitch, hdstg; pt sl, unshd; wc; chem disp; mv service pnt; baby facs; shwrs inc; el pnts (6A) inc; lndry rm; shop 1km; rest; snacks; bar; BBQ; playgrnd; htd pool; paddling pool; fishing lake; cycle hire; archery; entmnt; TV; dogs €1; Eng spkn; adv bkg; quiet, but some rlwy noise; red 10+ days; cc not acc; CCI. "Lovely, clean, well-cared for, family-run site; friendly & helpful; v gd san facs, ltd in number; office open 0800-2100; regional dishes served in rest; in interesting area; close to WW1 battlefields & WW2 sites; owner can advise on local vets & book appointment; excel." ♦ 1 Apr-31 Oct. € 18.00   2007*

ST OMER 3A3 (10km E Rural) **FFCC Camping Le Bloem Straete, 1 Rue Bloemstraete, 59173 Renescure** [03 28 49 85 65; lebloemstraete@ yahoo.fr; www.lebloemstraete.fr] E fr St Omer on N42 thro Renescure dir Hazebrouck; turn L (site sp) onto D406 Rue André Coo on bend on leaving Renescure; over level x-ing; site on L thro gates. Sm, hdg pitch, hdstg, pt shd; htd wc; chem disp (wc); shwrs inc; el pnts (5-10A) €2.50; lndtte; shop, rest, snack & bar 1km; playgrnd; tennis; games rm; 70% statics; dogs; poss cr; Eng spkn; quiet; adv bkg (dep req); CCI. "Lovely, peaceful site; m'van area; conv Calais ferry & tourist sites; excel." ♦ ltd. 15 Apr-15 Oct. € 14.00   2007*

ST OMER 3A3 (3km SE Urban) **Camp Municipal Beauséjour, Rue Michelet, 62510 Arques** [tel/ fax 03 21 88 53 66; mairie@ville-arques.fr; www. ville-arques.fr] Fr junc 4 of A26 foll sp Arques to town cent. Foll sp Hazebrouck. Ater x-ring canal site sp 'Camping ****' on L. Med, hdg/mkd pitch; wc; chem disp; mv service pnt; shwrs €1.10; el pnts (6A) €3; lndtte; shops 1.5km; playgrnd; lake fishing; 75% statics; dogs; phone; adv bkg; rlwy noise; cc not acc; CCI. "Nice, friendly site; lge pitches; excel, clean facs; office open am only low ssn; access poss diff for lge o'fits; site boggy if wet; no twin-axle vans; m'van o'night area; conv visit to Cristal d'Arques; Pas de Calais or Belgium (Ypres 50km); useful NH." ♦ 1 Apr-31 Oct. € 8.95   2007*

ST OMER 3A3 (10km NW Rural) **Camping Château du Gandspette, 133 Rue du Gandspette, 62910 Eperlecques** [03 21 93 43 93 or 03 21 12 89 08 (LS); fax 03 21 95 74 98; contact@chateau-gandspette. com; www.chateau-gandspette.com] Fr Calais SE on A26/E15 exit junc 2 onto D943 (N43) foll sp Nordausques-St Omer. 1.5km after Nordausques turn L onto D221 twd Eperlecques; site about 5km on L. Do not ent Eperlecques. (Larger o'fts should cont on D943 fr Nordausques to Tilques; straight on at rndabt foll sp for Dunkerque (D300) leaving this rd on D221 dir Eperlecques to find site on R. Or leave A16 at junc 24, foll D600 twd St Omer. After about 20km turn R at rndabt onto D207, site sp. Ent on bend. (D300 & D600 are same rd but change number at rndabt.). NB When travelling to Calais fr site toll barriers at junc 2 with A26 are not manned; stay on D943. NB V ltd visibility when leaving site onto main rd. Med, hdg/mkd pitch, pt hdstg, pt sl, pt shd; wc; chem disp; mv service pnt; baby facs; shwrs inc; el pnts (6A) inc (some rev pol); gas; lndtte; ice; supmkt 800m; tradsmn; rest (high ssn); snacks; bar; BBQ (not el); playgrnd; 2 pools (1 htd); fishing 3km; tennis; cycle hire; horseriding; golf 3km; child entmnt; wifi internet; games/TV rm; 40% statics; dogs €1; phone; recep 0800-2000; poss cr; Eng spkn; adv bkg (dep req high ssn + bkg fee); quiet; cc acc; CCI. "Lovely, well-run, efficient, busy site; spacious, mainly sl pitches, various sizes; superb, v clean san facs; charming, v friendly & helpful owners; super pool; excel rest/take-away; gd dog walks; local vet avail; no shade if full; narr app on woodland track to far tourer field; site poss muddy in wet; ltd hdstg; high m'vans take care o'hanging trees on site; conv Calais & Dunkerque; highly rec." ♦ 1 Apr-30 Sep. € 27.00   (CChq acc) ABS - P08   2007*

ST PABU 2E1 (Coastal) **Camp Municipal de L'Aber Benoît, Corn ar Gazel, 29830 St Pabu** [02 98 89 76 25] E fr Ploudalmézeau on D28; in 5km L to St Pabu. Site sp in vill. Med, hdg pitch, pt shd; wc; chem disp (wc); shwrs inc; el pnts (6A) €2.30; lndtte; ice; shop, rest (high ssn); snacks; BBQ; playgrnd; beach 100m; TV rm; 10 statics; dogs €1; poss cr; CCI. "Facs stretched high ssn; vg." Easter-15 Oct. € 9.00   2006*

ST PAIR SUR MER see Granville 1D4

ST PALAIS (GIRONDE) see Mirambeau 7C2

ST PALAIS (PYRENEES ATLANTIQUES) 8F1 (1km S Rural) **Camp Municipal Ur-Alde, 64120 St Palais** [06 73 55 84 48 (mob) or 05 59 65 72 01 (Mairie); camping-ur-alde@wanadoo.fr] Fr S on D933 site bef rv bdge at ent of vill. Or foll sp fr cent St Palais. Med, hdg pitch, pt hdstg, pt terr, pt shd; wc; chem disp; shwrs inc; el pnts €2.60; gas 400m; lndtte; ice; bar sells provisions; shops 400m; playgrnd; pool adj; fishing; horseriding adj; tennis; TV; adv bkg; quiet; CCI. "Lovely area; lge pitches, some with taps." 15 Jun-15 Sep. € 18.00   2005*

France

ST PALAIS SUR MER *7B1* (1km N Rural/Coastal) **Camping Le Logis, 22 Rue des Palombes, 17420 St Palais-sur-Mer [05 46 23 20 23 or 05 46 22 38 22; fax 05 46 23 10 61 or 05 46 23 65 10; lelogis@yukadivillages.com; www.www.yukadivillages.com]** On rd N out of Royan, after vill of St Palais-sur-Mer, site sp on R after petrol stn. V lge, pt sl, shd; htd wc (some cont); chem disp; shwrs inc; el pnts (6A) €5.10; gas 2km; lndtte; ice; shop & 2km; tradsmn; snacks; bar; playgrnd; pool; paddling pool; waterslide; aquapark; shgl beach 1km; tennis; games area; entmnt; child entmnt; TV; 35% statics; dogs €4.60; poss cr; Eng spkn; adv bkg; red low ssn. "La Palmyre zoo & wine-tasting close by; excel water park." 16 May-9 Sep. € 30.00   2006*

ST PALAIS SUR MER *7B1* (7km N Rural) **Camping Le Logis du Breuil, 17570 St Augustin [05 46 23 23 45; fax 05 46 23 23 83; camping. logis-du-breuil@wanadoo.fr; www.logis-du-breuil.com]** N150 to Royan, then D25 dir St Palais-sur-Mer. Strt on at 1st rndabt & 2nd rndabt; at next rndabt take 2nd exit dir St Palais-sur-Mer. At next traff lts turn R dir St Augustin onto D145; site on L. Lge, mkd pitch, pt shd, pt sl; wc (some cont); chem disp; baby facs; shwrs inc; el pnts (6A) inc (50m cable poss req); gas; lndtte; ice; shop; supmkt; rest; snacks; bar; BBQ (gas/elec); playgrnd; pool; paddling pool; sand beach 5km; fishing 1km; tennis; games area; cycle hire; archery; horseriding 400m; golf 3km; excursions; entmnt; internet; games/TV rm; 10% statics; dogs €2.30; phone; recep 0800-2000; barrier, dep req €20; poss cr; Eng spkn; adv bkg; cc acc; CCI. "Lge pitches; gd alt to cr beach sites; san facs gd; friendly." ♦ 15 May-30 Sep. € 24.30 ABS - A04   2007*

ST PALAIS SUR MER *7B1* (8km N Rural) **Camping Les Vignes, 3 Rue des Ardilliers, 17570 St Augustin [tel/fax 05 46 23 23 51; campinglesvignes17@wanadoo.fr]** On app Royan on D733, after x-ing D14 turn R sp St Palais (by-passing Royan cent). At rndabt on D25 foll sp St Augustin. Site on R Med, mkd pitch, pt shd; wc (some cont); shwrs; el pnts (10A) €3.60; gas; lndtte; ice; shop; tradsmn; rest; snacks; bar; playgrnd; 2 pools 200m; cycle hire; entmnt; 70% statics; dogs €1; phone; adv bkg; red long stay/low ssn; CCI. "Excel rest/bar; remote & peaceful; gd value; v welcoming; basic facs, ltd low ssn; site on wine producer's land, own produce sold; immac pools." ♦ ltd. Easter-1 Nov. € 11.00   2005*

ST PALAIS SUR MER *7B1* (NE Coastal) **Parc ACCCF Marcel Taburiaux, 2 Ave de Bernezac, 17420 St Palais-sur-Mer [05 46 39 00 71; fax 05 46 38 14 46; acccf-ber@wanadoo.fr]** Foll sp off Royan-St Palais coast rd. Med, pt shd; wc; chem disp; mv service pnt; 50% serviced pitches; baby facs; shwrs inc; el pnts (6A) €3.25; lndtte; ice; shop; rest; snacks; BBQ; playgrnd; htd pool; beach adj; lake fishing 1km; entmnt; TV; 30% statics; dogs €1; adv bkg; quiet. 15 Mar-15 Oct. € 19.05   2006*

ST PALAIS SUR MER *7B1* (1.5km E Rural/Coastal) **Camping Les Ormeaux, 44 Ave de Bernezac, 17420 St Palais-sur-Mer [05 46 39 02 07; fax 05 46 38 56 66; campingormeaux@tiscali.fr; www. camping-ormeaux.com]** Foll sp fr D25 Royan-St Palais rd. Rec app ent fr R. Ent & camp rds narr. Lge, mkd pitch, pt shd; wc; baby facs; shwrs inc; el pnts (6-10A) €7.50-8.50; gas; lndtte; ice; shop; snacks; bar; playgrnd; htd pool; sand beach 800m; entmnt; TV; some statics; dogs €3.50; quiet; red low ssn. 1 Apr-31 Oct. € 26.00 (3 persons)   2007*

ST PALAIS SUR MER *7B1* (2km E Coastal) **Camping Le Val Vert, 108 Ave Frédéric Garnier, 17640 Vaux-sur-Mer [05 46 38 25 51; fax 05 46 38 06 15; camping-val-vert@wanadoo.fr; www.val-vert.com]** Fr Saintes on N150 dir Royan; join D25 dir St Palais-sur-Mer; turn L at traff lts dir Vaux-sur-Mer, Zone Artisanale & Val Vert; at rndabt 1st exit R to Vaux-sur-Mer; at traff lts turn L; at rndabt 3rd exit, then immed R. Site on R in 500m. Lge, hdg pitch; wc; chem disp; baby facs; shwrs inc; el pnts (10A) inc; gas; lndtte; shop; rest; snacks; bar; gas/elec BBQ (gas/elec); playgrnd; htd pool; paddling pool; sand beach 900m; watersports; fishing; tennis 400m; horseriding, golf 5km; entmnt; games rm; wifi internet; dogs €2.70; recep 0800-2100; no c'vans over 6.50m high ssn; adv bkg; cc acc. "Gd clean site; no twin-axles; gd local shops; daily mkt in Royan." ♦ 5 Apr-28 Sep. € 31.80 (3 persons) ABS - A25   2007*

ST PALAIS SUR MER *7B1* (2km SE Coastal) **Camping Nauzan (formerly Municipal), Ave de Nauzan, 17640 Vaux-sur-Mer [05 46 38 29 13; fax 05 46 38 18 43; camping@vaux-atlantique. com]** Take either coast rd or inland rd fr Royan to Vaux-sur-Mer; site not well sp. Lge, mkd pitch, pt shd; wc; chem disp; baby facs; shwrs inc; el pnts (6A) inc; gas; lndtte; ice; shop; supmkt 1km; rest; snacks; bar; playgrnd; sm pool; sand beach 500m; tennis 200m; 10% statics (sep area) dogs €2.75; adv bkg; quiet; 30% red low ssn; CCI. "Gd site, being improved (2005); helpful staff." ♦ 1 Apr-30 Sep. € 24.40 (3 persons)   2005*

ST PALAIS SUR MER *7B1* (3km NW Coastal) **Camping La Côte de Beauté, Ave de la Grande Côte, 17420 St Palais-sur-Mer [05 46 23 20 59; fax 05 46 23 37 32; phlDct@aol.com]** Fr St Palais-sur-Mer foll sp to La Tremblade & Ronce-les-Bains. Site on D25, 50m fr beach, look for twin flagpoles of Camping Le Puits de l'Auture & lge neon sp on R; site in 50m. Med, shd; htd wc; baby facs; shwrs inc; el pnts (6A) inc; lndtte; supmkt adj; tradsmn; rest; snacks; bar; playgrnd; sand beach 200m across rd; tennis, cycle hire adj; golf 2km; some statics; dogs €2; adv bkg; quiet. "Friendly staff; clean & tidy site; 8km of sand beach; steep descent to beach opp which is covrd at high tide; better beach 600m twd La Tremblade; cycle track to St Palais & Pontaillac." 1 May-30 Sep. € 22.10 (3 persons)   2004*

ST PALAIS SUR MER 7B1 (3km NW Coastal) **Camping La Grande Côte, 157 Ave de la Grande Côte, 17420 St Palais-sur-Mer [tel/fax 05 46 23 20 18]** Fr Royan, take D25 thro St Palais, site on R where rd runs close to sea. Look for flags. Med, mkd pitch, pt shd; htd wc; baby facs; shwrs inc; el pnts (6A) inc; gas; lndtte; ice; rest adj; bar; sand beach 200m; dogs €1.50; bus; quiet; CCI. "Helpful staff; excel site; close to flagged area for safe bathing." ♦ 15 May-15 Jun. € 22.50   2004*

ST PALAIS SUR MER 7B1 (3km NW Coastal) **Camping Le Puits de l'Auture, La Grande Côte, 17420 St Palais-sur-Mer [05 46 23 20 31; fax 05 46 23 26 38; camping-lauture@wanadoo.fr; www.camping-puitsdelauture.com]** Fr Royan take D25 onto new rd past St Palais foll sp for La Palmyre. At 1-way section turn back L sp La Grande Côte & site is 800m; rd runs close to sea, flags at ent. Lge, pt shd; htd wc; serviced pitches; baby facs; shwrs inc; el pnts (10A) inc; gas; lndtte; ice; shop; snacks; bar; playgrnd; htd pool; sand beach opp & 500m; fishing; games area; internet; 25% statics; no dogs; poss cr; Eng spkn; adv bkg rec; quiet; red low ssn; cc acc; CCI. "Well-maintained, well laid-out, excel site; san facs stretched high ssn; poss cr but pitches carefully controlled; friendly, helpful staff." ♦ 1 May-30 Sep. € 31.00 (3 persons)   2007*

ST PALAIS SUR MER 7B1 (4km NW Rural) **Camping Les Côtes de Saintonge, 11 Rue des Sables, 17570 St Augustin [05 46 23 23 48; fax 05 46 39 48 37; lescotesdesaintonge@libertysurf.fr; www.lescotesdesaintonge.com]** Foll rd sp fr Royan to La Tremblade & St Augustin, site on R after sp end St Augustin. Med, shd; wc (some cont); shwrs inc; el pnts (6A) inc; shop & 600m; rest; snacks; bar; playgrnd; pool; sand beach 3km; entmnt; TV rm; many statics; dogs €2.30; quiet. "Amongst oak trees; fine forests & beaches locally; poss clsd low ssn - phone to check." ♦ 1 Apr-15 Sep. € 22.30   2004*

ST PANTALEON 7D3 (4km NE Rural) **Camping des Arcades, Moulin de St Martiel, 46800 St Pantaléon [05 65 22 92 27 or 06 80 43 19 82 (mob); fax 05 65 31 98 89; info@des-arcades.com; www.des-arcades.com]** Fr N20 3km S of Cahors take D653 sp Montcuq, after 17km site in hamlet of St Martial on L. Med, mkd pitch, pt sl, pt shd; wc; chem disp; shwrs inc; el pnts (6A) 3; lndtte; sm shop; tradsmn; rest; snacks; bar; BBQ; playgrnd; htd pool; paddling pool; lake sw & fishing adj; child entmnt; 5% statics; dogs €1.50; Eng spkn; adv bkg; quiet; red low ssn; cc acc; CCI. "Vg Dutch-owned site with restored 13thC windmill; sm lake; lovely countryside; vg rest; clean facs." ♦ 28 Apr-30 Sep. € 20.00   2007*

ST PARDOUX 9A1 (4km SW Rural) **Camping Elan, Route de St Pardoux, 63440 Blot-l'Eglise [04 73 97 44 94 or 06 10 21 40 58 (mob); campingelan@hotmail.com]** Fr N on N144 take D16 to Blot, fr S take D50, foll site sp. Med, hdg/mkd pitch, pt shd; wc; chem disp (wc); shwrs inc; el pnts (5A) €2.25; lndry rm; shop, rest, bar 500m; playgrnd; rv fishing, canoeing 6km; tennis; dogs €1.50; poss cr; Eng spkn; adv bkg; quiet; red long stay; CCI. "New Dutch owners making improvements; new san facs & pool planned for 2006; gd walking area; conv Vulcania; c'van storage avail; site open low ssn by arrangement." 1 Apr-30 Sep. € 10.00   2005*

ST PARDOUX L'ORTIGIER see Donzenac 7C3

ST PAUL DE FENOUILLET 8G4 (7km E Rural) **Camp Municipal Les Oliviers, 66460 Maury [04 68 59 15 24 (Mairie)]** Heading W on D117. Site immed after level x-ing on R 500m bef Maury. Sm, shd; wc (cont); shwrs inc; el pnts; playgrnd; CCI. "Some rd noise fr level x-ing; vineyards & castles to visit." 1 Jun-15 Sep. € 11.00   2004*

⊞ **ST PAUL DE FENOUILLET** 8G4 (S Rural) **Camp Municipal de l'Agly, 66220 St Paul-de-Fenouillet [04 68 59 09 09; fax 04 68 59 11 04; contact@camping-agly.com; www.camping-agly.com]** Heading W on D117; turn L at traff lts in St Paul; site on R in 200m, well sp. Sm, hdg/mkd pitch, pt sl, pt shd; wc; chem disp; shwrs inc; el pnts (16A) €3.70; gas & supmkt 500m; pool 1km; rv sw 500m; quiet; CCI. "Gd site; friendly warden; beautiful mountain scenery; gd climbing & biking; poss unkempt low ssn." ♦ € 13.65   2005*

ST PAUL DE VARAX see Bourg en Bresse 9A2

ST PAUL DE VEZELIN 9B1 (N Rural) **Camping d'Arpheuilles, Lac de Villerest, 42590 St-Paul-de-Vézelin [04 77 63 43 43; arpheuilles@wanadoo.fr; www.camping-arpheuilles.com]** Take D53 fr Roanne 10km. Turn L onto D8 twd St German-Laval. Turn L at Dancé onto D112 to St-Paul-de-Vézelin. Turn L on ent to vill. Or fr A72 exit junc 5 onto D8, then D26. V diff single track fr vill (3km) - v steep in places. Med, mkd pitch, pt sl, pt shd; wc (some cont); chem disp; mv service pnt; shwrs inc; el pnts (5/6A) €3; gas; lndtte; ice; shop; tradsmn; rest; snacks; bar; BBQ; playgrnd; pool; paddling pool; lake sw & sand beach adj; TV; few statics; dogs; phone; Eng spkn; adv bkg (dep req); 20% red 3+ days; quiet. "Beautiful location; helpful owner; well-managed with gd facs; various sports facs." 1 May-10 Sep. € 17.00   2006*

ST PAUL EN FORET see Fayence 10E4

ST PAUL LE GAULTIER 4E1 (S Rural) **Camp Municipal, 72590 St Paul-le-Gaultier [02 43 33 58 55 or 02 43 97 27 55]** Located on D15, St Paul-le-Gaultier is 25km SW of Alençon. Sm; shwrs free; el pnts (4A) inc; playgrnd; rv fishing. "Tranquil site; excel value; site by lake; office open 0900-1000 & 1700-1900." € 6.30   2004*

France

ST PAULIEN *9C1* (2.5km SW Rural) **Camping de la Rochelambert, 43350 St Paulien [04 71 00 54 02; fax 04 71 00 54 32; infos@camping-rochelambert. com; www.camping-rochelambert.com]** Fr St Paulien take D13; turn L onto D25 sp La Rochelambert; site on L in 1.5km. Med, mkd pitch, terr, pt shd; wc (some cont); chem disp; mv service pnt; shwrs inc; el pnts (10A) €2.90; lndtte; shop 3km; tradsmn; snacks; bar; BBQ; playgrnd; pools; paddling pool; tennis; rv sw; 15% statics; dogs; phone; pools cr; Eng spkn; adv bkg (dep req); quiet; CCI. "New, enthusiastic owners (2007) aim to upgrade; gd walking & fishing; app poss diff lge/long o'fits; gd touring base; gd." ♦ ltd. 29 Apr-30 Sep. € 14.95   2007*

ST PEE SUR NIVELLE see St Jean de Luz *8F1*

This guide relies on site report forms submitted by caravanners like us; we'll do our bit and tell the editor what we think of the campsites we've visited.

ST PEREUSE *4H4* (SE Rural) **Camping Le Manoir de Bezolle, 58110 St Péreuse-en-Morvan [03 86 84 42 55; fax 03 86 84 43 77; info@bezolle. com; www.bezolle.com]** 9km W of Château-Chinon on D978 Autun-Nevers. Site sp; ent on N side of D978 on D11. Med, pt sl, pt terr, pt shd; wc; chem disp; mv service pnt; shwrs inc; el pnts (10A) inc (long lead poss req & avail on loan); gas; lndtte; ice; vg shop; rest; snacks; bar; playgrnd; 2 pools; lakeside walks; fishing; tennis; mini-golf; horseriding; entmnt; TV rm; 25% statics; dogs €2; quiet; red low ssn; cc acc; CCI. "Friendly recep; well-kept site; med sized pitches, lge ones avail at extra cost; gd views; lovely situation in National Park; gd for touring Burgundy wine region." ♦ 1 May-15 Sep. € 27.00   2007*

ST PHILBERT DE GRAND LIEU *2H4* (N Rural) **Camping La Boulogne, 1 Ave de Nantes, 44310 St Philbert-de-Grand-Lieu [32 40 78 88 79; fax 32 40 78 76 50; contact@campinglaboulogne.fr; www.campinglaboulogne.fr]** Fr Nantes on A83 exit junc 1 or 2 onto D178 - D117 dir St Philbert; turn L onto D65 (Ave de Nantes) to St Philbert; site on R in 500m adj rv & sp. Or fr Machecoul take bypass to St Philbert & then D65 as narr rds thro town. Med, hdg/mkd pitch, pt shd; wc; chem disp; baby facs; shwrs inc; el pnts (6A) inc; lndtte; ice; shops 500m; tradsmn; snacks; bar; BBQ; playgrnd; htd, covrd pool 200m; lake adj; fishng 4km; entmnt; internet; 10% statics; dogs €1; phone; bus adj; no twin-axles; Eng spkn; adv bkg; quiet; cc acc; CCI. "Gd." ♦ 6 Apr-30 Sep. € 12.50   2007*

ST PIERRE A CHAMP *4H1* (S Rural) **Camping Skorski, 26 Rue de Acacias, 79290 St Pierre-à-Champ [05 49 66 41 28; skorski.anthony@ wanadoo.fr; www.campingalaskorski.com]** Leave Doué-la-Fontaine S on D69/D32; in 15km turn L in St Pierre-à-Champ onto D61 dir Thouars; site in 100m on R. Sm, unshd; wc; chem disp; shwrs inc; baby facs; el pnts (16A) €2; lndtte; tradsmn; rest & bar 200m; BBQ; playgrnd; swimming & fishing nrby; dogs; phone & bus 200m; adv bkg (dep req); will open any time by prior arrangement. "Quiet site for relaxation; British owned; wine tasting; gd cycling; conv Futuroscope, zoo, Puy-du-Fou theme park & Jananese garden; more el pnts & shade planned (2007); gd value; rec." ♦ Easter-31 Oct. € 9.50   2007*

ST PIERRE D'ARGENCON see Aspres sur Buëch *9D3*

ST PIERRE DE CHARTREUSE *9C3* (2km Rural) **Camping de Martinière, Route du Col de Porte, 38380 St Pierre-de-Chartreuse [04 76 88 60 36; fax 04 76 88 69 10; brice.gaude@wanadoo.fr; www.campingdemartiniere.com]** Take D520 S fr Les Echelles to St Laurent-du-Pont, D512 thro Gorge-du-Guiers-Mort to St Pierre-de-Chartreuse. Site clearly sp on D512 rd to Grenoble. Med, mkd pitch, pt shd; htd wc (mainly cont); chem disp; mv service pnt; shwrs inc; el pnts (2-6A) €2-3.90; gas; lndtte; ice; shop; tradsmn; rest; bar; playgrnd; pool; paddling pool; fishing; games area; library; dogs €1; Eng spkn; adv bkg rec (ess in winter ssn); red low ssn; CChq not acc; cc acc; CCI. "Grand Chartreuse Monastery 4km; spectacular mountain scenery; unspoilt vills; friendly owner." 30 Apr-18 Sep. € 15.00 (CChq acc)   2004*

ST PIERRE DU VAUVRAY see Pont de l'Arche *3D2*

ST PIERRE LAFEUILLE see Cahors *7D3*

ST PIERRE LE MOUTIER *4H4* (500m N Urban) **Camp Municipal Le Panama, Rue de Beaudrillon, 58240 St Pierre-le-Moûtier [03 86 90 19 94 or 03 86 37 42 09 (Mairie); fax 03 86 90 19 80]** Site on N7, sp at either ent to town. Sm, hdg pitch, pt sl, pt shd; wc (some cont); chem disp; shwrs inc; el pnts (6A) €2; ice; shop, rest, bar 500m; no adv bkg; quiet, some rd & rlwy noise; CCI. "Modern, clean san facs; warden present 0800-1000 & 1800-2000, otherwise go to Mairie; sh stay/NH nr French Grand Prix circuit; gd cycling area." ♦ 15 May-15 Sep. € 11.00   2005*

ST PIERRE LE MOUTIER *4H4* (7km W) **Camp Municipal de St Mayeul, 03320 Le Veurdre [04 70 66 40 67 (Mairie); fax 04 70 66 42 88]** Fr N7 at St Pierre-le-Moûtier SW onto D978A to Le Veurdre. Site sp on far side of Le Veurdre. Sm, pt shd; wc; shwrs inc; el pnts €3.10; shops 500m; no statics; quiet. "Pleasant quiet spot; site yourself, warden calls; friendly staff; excel rest in vill." 1 Jun-15 Sep. € 6.00   2007*

ST PIERRE LE MOUTIER *4H4* (8km NW Rural) Camp Municipal La Bruyère, 18600 Mornay-sur-Allier [02 48 74 50 75 or 06 32 34 97 15 (mob)] Fr W on D2076 (N76) turn R onto D45 & foll sp. Site just bef x-ing Rv Allier. Sm, pt shd; wc; shwrs inc; el pnts (12A) €1.50; quiet. "V tidy site with clean facs, run by volunteers; pitch self & warden collects fees; excel NH." 1 May-15 Sep. € 6.15   2006*

ST PIERRE QUIBERON *2G3* (1.5km SE Coastal) Camp Municipal du Petit Rohu, Rue des Men-Du, 56510 St Pierre-Quiberon [02 97 50 27 85 or 02 97 30 92 00 (Mairie)] On D768 dir Quiberon, 1km past exit for St Pierre-Quiberon turn L at camp sp. Turn R in 200m & L after 250m at T-junc sp Le Petit Rohu. Site on R in 50m on beach. Well sp. Med, mkd pitch, pt sl, unshd; wc; shwrs; mv service pnt; el pnts (10A) inc; gas; lndtte; ice; shop; snacks adj; playgrnd; sand beach adj; boating; fishing; sports area; some statics; dogs; poss cr; quiet. "Vg, clean site; gd location on beach; gd, clean facs; boat ramp nr; gd cycling country; recep open 1000-1200 & 1700-1900; button on wall to open barrier." ♦ 1 Apr-7 Oct. € 14.00   2007*

ST PIERRE QUIBERON *2G3* (3km SE Coastal) Camp Municipal de Kerhostin, Allée du Camping, 56510 St Pierre-Quiberon [02 97 30 95 25 or 02 97 30 92 00 (Mairie); fax 02 97 30 87 20; mairie.saintpierrequiberon@wanadoo.fr; www.saintpierrequiberon.fr] Off D768 turn SE onto Rue des Goëlettes by rlwy x-ing (no thro rd sp), turn L at 1st sm island, turn L at end, site 300m on R. Med, mkd pitch, pt shd; wc; shwrs inc; el pnts (10A) €1.69; lndtte; shops adj; rest, snacks, bar 500m; playgrnd; pool 2km; sand beach 200m; dogs €0.86; poss cr; no adv bkg; red low ssn. 28 Apr-2 Sep. € 14.38   2006*

ST PIERRE QUIBERON *2G3* (W Coastal) Relais-Camping St Joseph de l'Océan, 7 Ave de Groix, Kerhostin, 56510 St Pierre-Quiberon [02 97 30 91 29; fax 02 97 30 80 18; stjo56@free.fr; www.relaisdelocean.com] S on D768 fr Carnac at traff lts in Kerhostin turn R into Rue de Sombreuil then Ave de Groix, site sp. Lge, hdg/mkd pitch, pt shd; wc; chem disp; baby facs; shwrs inc; el pnts (10A) €3.80; gas; lndtte; shop 1km; tradsmn; rest; snacks; bar; BBQ; playgrnd; sand beach adj; games area; games rm; cycle hire; golf 15km; thelassotherapy 8km; entmnt; TV; 20% statics; dogs €2.15; Eng spkn; adv bkg; quiet; cc acc; red low ssn/CCI. "Pleasant site; gd sized pitches; gd amenities; staff helpful; gd for families; popular with surfers - groups can be noisy; vg." ♦ 1 Apr-5 Nov. € 15.00   2006*

ST POINT see Cluny *9A2*

ST POINT LAC see Pontarlier *6H2*

ST POL DE LEON *1D2* (2km E Coastal) Camping Ar Kleguer, Plage de Ste Anne, 29250 St Pol-de-Léon [02 98 69 18 81; fax 02 98 29 12 84; info@camping-ar-kleguer.com; www.camping-ar-kleguer.com] In St Pol-de-Léon foll Centre Ville sp. At cathedral sq (2 towers), turn R foll sp for Plage. In 150m, bef church with tall belfry, turn L foll Plage & camping sp. On reaching sea turn L (N); site at end, well sp. NB Narr, busy rds in town. Med, mkd pitch, terr, pt shd; wc (some cont); chem disp; mv service pnt; baby facs; shwrs inc; el pnts (10A) €3.60 (long lead poss req); lndtte; shops 500m; tradsmn; snacks; bar; htd pool; waterslide; beach adj; tennis; games rm; 40% statics; dogs €2; poss cr; adv bkg; poss noisy; CCI. "Modern facs; gd views." 1 Apr-30 Sep. € 18.70   2007*

> As soon as we get home I'm going to post all these site report forms to the editor for inclusion in next year's guide. I don't want to miss the September deadline.

ST POL DE LEON *1D2* (2km E Coastal) Camping de Trologot, Grève du Man, 29250 St Pol-de-Léon [02 98 69 06 26 or 06 62 16 39 30 (mob); fax 02 98 29 18 30; camping-trologot@wanadoo.fr; www.camping-trologot.com] Fr E take N12/E50 twd Morlaix & join D58 to St Pol-de-Léon. In St Pol foll 'Campings' & 'Plages' sp along seafront for approx 600m. Site on L after a sharp L-hand bend, opp Grève du Man beach. Fr Roscoff on D58 turn L onto D769 sp St Pol. In town cent pass church on L then in 200m turn L at bell tower sp Morlaix & Carantec. At graveyard turn L & foll sp 'Campings', 'Plage' & 'Mer'; then turn L at seafront and then as above. NB Narr, busy rds in town. Med, hdg/mkd pitch, unshd; wc (some cont); chem disp; mv service pnt; baby facs; shwrs inc; el pnts (10A) inc; lndtte; shop & 600m; tradsmn; snacks; bar; BBQ (gas/charcoal only); playgrnd; htd pool; paddling pool; shgl beach adj; entmnt; games/TV rm; 20% statics; dogs €2; no c'vans over 7m high ssn; poss cr; adv bkg; quiet; cc acc; red long stay/low ssn/CCI. "Ideal NH for Roscoff ferry; excel refurbished site; v clean, modern san facs; boat slipway on adj beach; gd sized pitches; helpful owners; highly rec." ♦ 1 May-30 Sep. € 20.90 (CChq acc) ABS - B29   2007*

ST POL DE LEON *1D2* (2km SE Rural) Camping des Hortensias, Kermen, 29660 Carantec [tel/fax 02 98 67 08 63 or 02 98 67 96 34] Fr Roscoff on D58 dir Morlaix. Turn L after approx 10km on D173, turn R at 1st rndabt for site sp. Sm, unshd; wc; chem disp; mv service pnt; shwrs inc; el pnts (10A) €2; gas 3km; lndtte; shop 3km; playgrnd; beach 3km; dogs €0.80; adv bkg; quiet; CCI. "Gd touring base; conv ferry." ♦ 1 May-30 Sep. € 9.60   2005*

France

ST POL DE LEON *1D2* (5km SE Coastal) **Yelloh! Village Les Mouettes, La Grande Grève, 29660 Carantec [02 98 67 02 46; fax 02 98 78 31 46; camping@les-mouettes.com; www.les-mouettes. com www.yellohvillage.com]** Fr Morlaix take D58 N sp Roscoff; at lge rndabt turn R sp Carantec on D173; turn L at 1st rndabt; strt on at 2nd rndabt; turn L at 3rd rndabt; site on L. Or fr Roscoff take D58 sp Mortaix, then D173 to Carantec; foll sp town cent, then site. Lge, mkd pitch, pt shd; wc; chem disp; mv service pnt; baby facs; shwrs inc; el pnts (6A) inc (poss rev pol); gas; lndtte; ice; shop; snacks; bar; BBQ (charcoal/gas only); playgrnd; htd pool & paddling pool; waterslide; sand/shgl beach 1km; fishing; golf & watersports in town; tennis; entmnt; child entmnt; wifi internet; games/TV rm; 50% statics; dogs €5; poss cr; Eng spkn; adv bkg; noise fr boatyard; red low ssn; cc acc; CCI. "Conv Roscoff ferry; sea views; mkt Carentec Thu." ♦ 17 May-7 Sep. € 44.00 ABS - B14   2007*

ST POL DE LEON *1D2* (6km S Urban) **Camp Municipal de Kerilis, Menez Izella, 29670 Henvic [02 98 62 82 10; fax 02 98 62 81 56; commune-henvic@wanadoo.fr]** Site on R of main rd bet St Pol-de-Léon & Morlaix. Foll sp for Henvic. Site 150m after exit main rd. Med, pt shd; wc; shwrs inc; el pnts €2.50 (poss rev pol) (poss long lead req); lndry rm; supmkt nr; playgrnd; sand beach 8km; quiet; CCI. "Simple, clean well-run site; barrier closes 2200; helpful warden; conv for evening arr fr ferry." 1 Jul-31 Aug. € 8.30   2006*

⊞**ST POL DE LEON** *1D2* (7km W Coastal) **Camp du Theven, Ports Misclic - Moguériec, 29250 Sibiril [02 98 29 96 86; fax 02 98 61 23 30; roudaut. theven.29@wanadoo.fr; http://pagesperso-orange.fr/camping.theven.29]** Fr Roscoff ferry on D58, at junc with D10 take Sibiril/Cléder turn. In Sibiril pass church & turn R past water tower, foll sp Port de Moguériec, site sp. Sm, hdg/mkd pitch, terr, pt shd; wc; shwrs €1; el pnts (4-6A) €3; ice; lndtte; shop; supmkt 5km; snacks; bar; BBQ; playgrnd; sand/rocky beach adj; fishing; boat hire; entmnt; 6% statics; dogs €1; Eng spkn; adv bkg; quiet; CCI. "Friendly, helpful owner; hot water/shwrs coin op; liable to close for 10 day periods low ssn - phone ahead to check open; v ltd facs low ssn, poss no hot water." € 10.90   2004*

⊞**ST POL SUR TERNOISE** *3B3* (5km NW Rural) **Camping du Ternoise (formerly Camp de M. Vigneron), Rue d'en Haut, 62130 Croix-en-Ternois [tel/fax 03 21 03 39 87 or 03 21 03 43 12]** W fr St Pol-sur-Ternoise on D939 (N39) then into Croix-en-Ternois; foll camp sp. Sm, hdg pitch, pt shd; wc; shwrs €1.50; el pnts (6A) inc; ice; shop 5km; bar; BBQ; playgrnd; mini-golf, fishing & horseriding nr; 50% statics; dogs; adv bkg; poss noise fr motorbike circuit. "Pleasant, quiet site; spotless, smart san facs; site yourself; sep area for tourers; gd walks & cycling; vg." ♦ € 20.00   2007*

ST PONS DE THOMIERES *8F4* (4km N Rural) **Aire Naturelle La Borio de Roque, Route de la Salvetat, 34220 St Pons-de-Thomières [04 67 97 10 97; fax 04 67 97 21 61; info@ borioderoque.com; www.borioderoque.com]** On D907, R at sp, foll track for 1.2km to site. Sm, hdg pitch, terr, shd; wc; chem disp; shwrs inc; el pnts (10A) €3; lndtte; ice; tradsmn; bar; playgrnd; pool; Eng spkn; some statics; dogs €2; adv bkg rec high ssn (€15.24 bkg fee); CCI. "Excel, welcoming & spotless site; meals served if req; secluded & peaceful in wooded hills; diff access lge/underpowered o'fits down single, dirt track - no turning/passing." ♦ 15 May-15 Sep. € 20.25   2007*

ST PONS DE THOMIERES *8F4* (8km NE Rural) **Camp Municipal Les Terrasses du Jaur, Chemin de Notre Dame, 34390 Prémian [04 67 97 27 85; fax 04 67 97 06 40]** Go E on D908 fr St Pons-de-Thomières twd Olargues for 8km. Imposs to turn R over rv to site, cont on D908, turn round & app fr E, turn L into site. Sm, hdg pitch, pt sl, terr, pt shd; wc; chem disp; shwrs inc; el pnts (3A) €1.50; lndry rm; shop; rv sw & fishing 100m; quiet; 30% statics; adv bkg; CCI. "Site in full operation bet dates shown, but pitching acc all year - ltd facs." 15 May-15 Oct.   2006*

ST PONS DE THOMIERES *8F4* (1km E Urban) **Camping Village Les Cerisiers du Jaur, Route de Bédarieux, 34220 St Pons-de-Thomières [04 67 95 30 33; fax 04 67 23 09 96; lescerisiersdujaur@orange.fr; www.cerisier dujaur.com]** Fr Castres on N112 go thro town cent under rlwy bdge. Turn L onto D908 sp Olargues. Site on R immed past block of flats. Med, mkd pitch, terr, pt shd; wc; mv service pnt; baby facs; shwrs inc; el pnts (10A) €3.50; ice; lndtte; tradsmn; snacks; bar; playgrnd; pool planned for 2008; dogs €1.50; poss cr; quiet; Eng spkn; phone; cc acc; CCI. "Excel site; warm welcome; friendly, helpful owner; vg san facs inc spacious facs for disabled; sh walk to vill." ♦ 1 Apr-31 Dec. € 20.00   2007*

ST PONS DE THOMIERES *8F4* (11km W Rural) **Camp Municipal de Cabanes, Route de St Pons, 81270 Labastide-Rouairoux [05 63 98 01 26 or 05 63 98 07 58; fax 05 63 98 01 99; tourisme@ labastide-rouairoux.com]** E fr Labastide-Rouairoux twd St Pons on D612 (N112). Site adj D612 immed after leaving Labastide vill. Sm, hdg/mkd, terr, pt shd; wc; chem disp; shwrs €0.76; el pnts inc; shop 1km; tradsmn; ice; adv bkg; some rd noise; CCI. "Lovely site, spotless facs; v pretty; poss diff lge o'fits due to terr." 15 Jun-15 Sep. € 11.00   2005*

France

ST POURCAIN SUR SIOULE *9A1* (E Urban) **Camp Municipal Ile de la Ronde, Quai de la Ronde, 03500 St Pourçain-sur-Sioule [04 70 45 45 43; hdv.st.pourcain.s.sioule@wanadoo.fr; www.ville-saint-pourcain-sur-sioule.com]** On D2009 (N9), 31km S of Moulins; sp in town; bordering rv. Med, hdg pitch; pt shd; wc; chem disp; mv service pnt; shwrs; el pnts (6A) €2.10; lndtte; shops adj; playgrnd; pool 1km; dogs; adv bkg; quiet; CCl. "Clean, well-run site in pretty town; extra charge for lger pitches; barrier clsd 2000-0800; great value; excel." 5 May-30 Sep. € 7.60   2007*

⊞**ST PRIVAT** *7C4* (400m N) **Aire Communale Les Chanoux, 19220 St Privat [tel/fax 05 55 28 28 77 (Mairie); francois-michel.perrier@wanadoo.fr]** Fr Argentat on D980 for 17km dir Pleaux & Mauriac, rd steep & winding in parts. Sm, chem disp; mv service pnt; water fill €2 for 100 litres; el pnts (10A) €2; shops, rests in vill; m'vans only.   2006*

ST PRIVAT D'ALLIER see Monistrol d'Allier *9C1*

ST QUAY PORTRIEUX *2E3* (1km NW Coastal) **Camping Bellevue, 68 Blvd Quay du Littoral, 22410 St Quay-Portrieux [02 96 70 41 84; fax 02 96 70 55 46; campingbellevue@free.fr; www.campingbellevue.net]** Foll D786 thro St Quay-Portrieux twd Paimpol; turn R at traff lts sp St Quay-Portrieux; foll site sp; site in 2.5km. Lge, hdg/mkd/pitch, hdstg, terr, pt shd; wc (some cont); chem disp; mv service pnt; serviced pitch; baby facs; shwrs inc; el pnts (6A) €3; gas; lndtte; ice; shop; tradsmn; snacks; BBQ; playgrnd; htd pool; paddling pool; sand beach 800m; games area; TV; dogs €1; Eng spkn; adv bkg; quiet; red low ssn; cc acc; CCl. "Beautiful position with sea views; direct access to sm cove, main beaches 800m St Quay; friendly staff; gd, clean facs." ♦ 16 Apr-15 Sep. € 17.80   2007*

See advertisement

ST QUENTIN *3C4* (SE Urban) **Camp Municipal, 91 Blvd Jean Bouin, 02100 St Quentin [03 23 06 94 05]** Fr all app rds foll sp Centre Ville/Auberge de Jeunesse (c'van on sign). Press intercom at barrier for ent. Sp 'Terrain de Camping'. Sm, mkd pitch, hdstg, unshd; wc (most cont); chem disp; shwrs; el pnts (6-10A) €2.35-3.70; supmkt 1km; pool adj; dogs; bus adj; some rd noise; CCl. "Easy access to lge, gritty pitches; grounds gd; v helpful staff; san facs run down but clean & functional; pleasant canal walk adj; gates clsd 2200-0700; poss itinerants; gd value; OK NH." 1 Mar-30 Nov. € 10.95   2007*

The opening dates and prices on this campsite have changed. I'll send a site report form to the editor for the next edition of the guide.

ST QUENTIN *3C4* (10km SW Urban) **Camping Le Vivier aux Carpes, 10 Rue Charles Voyeux, 02790 Seraucourt-le-Grand [03 23 60 50 10; fax 03 23 60 51 69; camping.du.vivier@wanadoo.fr; www.camping-picardie.com]** Fr A26 take exit 11 St Quentin/Soissons; S 4km on D1 dir Tergnier/Soissons. Fork R onto D8 to Essigny-le-Grand & in vill foll camping sp W to Seraucourt. Fr St Quentin, S 10km on D930 to Roupy, E on D32 5km to Seraucourt-le-Grand. Site N of Seraucourt on D321. Med, hdg/mkd pitch, some hdstg, pt shd; wc; chem disp; mv service pnt; baby facs; shwrs inc; el pnts (10A) inc (poss rev pol); gas; lndtte; shop & supmkt 200m; tradsmn; snacks; BBQ; playgrnd; pool nr; angling; golf, tennis, horseriding adj; games rm; 20% statics; dogs €0.80; c'van storage; Eng spkn; adv bkg; quiet; CCl. "Pleasant, well-organised, gd value, busy site - rec arr early; peaceful low ssn; gd, immac san facs; lge pitches (but poss flooding); ltd hdstg; friendly, v helpful staff; gd dog walks; can arrange vet for return home; poss mosquito prob late Jun; WW1 cemeteries etc; Disneyland 90 mins; conv Channel ports; warn staff night bef if v early dep; excel." ♦ 1 Mar-31 Oct. € 17.50   2007*

Before we move on, I'm going to fill in some site report forms and post them off to the editor, otherwise they won't arrive in time for the deadline at the end of September.

ST QUENTIN EN TOURMONT 3B2 (500m S Rural) Camping Le Champ Neuf, 8 Rue du Champ Neuf, 80120 St Quentin-en-Tourmont [03 22 25 07 94; fax 03 22 25 09 87; contact@ camping.lechampneuf.com; www.camping-lechampneuf.com] Exit D1001 (N1) or A16 onto D32 to Rue, take D940 around Rue & foll sp St Quentin-en-Tourmont, Parc Ornithologique & Domaine du Marquenterre to site. Site sp fr D204. Lge, hdg/mkd pitch, shd; wc; chem disp; mv service pnt; baby facs; shwrs inc; el pnts (5-10A) €3.40-3.80; lndtte; shop; snacks; bar; BBQ; playgrnd; beach 2km; games area; cycle hire; horseriding 500m; entmnt high ssn; some statics; dogs €1; adv bkg; quiet; cc acc. "Excel Ornithological Park adj; well-kept, pleasant site; friendly, helpful owner." ♦ 1 Apr-31 Oct. € 14.60 2007*

See advertisement

ST QUENTIN EN TOURMONT 3B2 (1km S Rural) Camping Le Bout des Crocs, 2 Chemin des Garennes, 80120 St Quentin-en-Tourmont [03 22 25 73 33; fax 03 22 25 75 17] Exit D1001 (N1) or A16 onto D32 to Rue. When W of Rue turn off onto D4 heading W. In 2km turn R onto D204 & foll sp Le Bout des Crocs, then Parc Ornithologique. Site on R. Med, hdg/mkd pitch, unshd; wc; chem disp; baby facs; shwrs €1; el pnts (6A) €3.50; lndtte; tradsmn; playgrnd; TV rm; 80% statics; dogs; CCI. "Very quiet site; superb area; v nr Marquenterre bird reserve; tourers put at end of site 200m fr san facs; immac facs; excel cycle tracks to beach & inland; mosquitoes poss problem; vg." 1 Apr-1 Nov. € 13.50 2006*

ST QUENTIN LA POTERIE see Uzès 10E2

ST RAMBERT D'ALBON 9C2 (Urban) Camping Les Claires, 26140 St Rambert-d'Albon [tel/fax 04 75 31 01 87; info@camping-des-claires.com; www.camping-des-claires.com] Fr A7 exit junc 12 dir Chanas, turn S onto N7. In 1km turn R to St Rambert, turn R at rndabt by rlwy stn, under rlwy bdge & foll site sp. Med, pt sl, shd; wc; chem disp (wc); baby facs; shwrs inc; el pnts (6A) €3.80; gas; lndtte; ice; tradsmn; rest; snacks; bar in vill; BBQ; playgrnd; pool; sports area; entmnt; 50% statics; dogs €1.40; phone adj; Eng spkn; some rlwy noise; CCI. "Excel NH." 1 Apr-15 Oct. € 14.80 2007*

ST RAMBERT D'ALBON 9C2 (3km N Urban) Camping Beauséjour, Route de Grenoble, 38150 Chanas [04 74 84 21 38 or 04 74 84 31 01; campingvernet@club-internet.fr; www.camping-beausejour.fr] Exit A7 junc 12 onto D519 dir Grenoble; site on R in 3km. Med, mkd pitch; pt sh; wc; chem disp; shwrs inc; lndry rm; el pnts (6A) €3.20; playgrnd; sm pool; shops 1km; games rm; no statics; some rd noise fr D519; red CCI; no cc acc; CCI. "Gd NH off A7/N7; fair." 15 Apr-30 Sep. € 12.40 2007*

ST RAMBERT D'ALBON 9C2 (8km NE Rural) Camping Le Temps Libre, Quartier Font Rozier, 38150 Bougé-Chambalud [04 74 84 04 09; fax 04 74 84 15 71; camping.temps-libre@libertysurf. fr; www.temps-libre.fr] Fr A7 take exit junc 12 Chanas onto D519, dir Grenoble for 8km. Or fr N7 take exit D519 E sp Grenoble. Site sp at 1st rndabt & well sp in vill. Med, hdg/mkd pitch, hdstg, pt sl, terr, pt shd; wc; chem disp; serviced pitches; shwrs inc; el pnts (9A) €4.50 lndtte; shop in ssn & supmkt 10km; tradsmn; rest high ssn; snacks; bar high ssn; playgrnd; 3 htd pools with chutes (1 covrd); tennis; mini-golf; fishing; pedal boats; 50% statics; dogs free; Eng spkn; adv bkg; poss noisy; red low ssn; cc acc; CCI. "Useful NH S of Lyon; ltd facs low ssn; busy w/e; excel sw pools; excel." ♦ 31 Mar-30 Sep. € 20.50 (CChq acc) 2007*

ST RAMBERT D'ALBON *9C2* (5km SE) Camping Le Château de Senaud, 26140 Albon [04 75 03 11 31; fax 04 75 03 08 06; campingdesenaud@liberty surf.fr; www.chateau-de-senaud.com] Exit A7 junc 12 at Chanas. S on N7 twd Valence, in 10km L at sp Camping Senaud onto D132. Foll sp to site (1.5km). access tight for lge o'fits - narr ent & sharp bends. Med, mkd pitch, pt sl, pt shd; wc (some cont); chem disp; mv service pnt; shwrs inc; el pnts (6-10A) inc; lndtte; shop high ssn; rest; snacks; bar; playgrnd; pool; waterslide; fishing; tennis; mini-golf; golf adj; 60% statics; dogs €2; poss cr; some rd noise; cc acc. "Gd site but needs facelift; facs ltd low ssn; poss diff access to some pitches." ♦ 1 Mar-30 Nov. € 25.00   2005*

ST RAPHAEL *10F4* (Coastal) Camping Vallée du Paradis, Route de Gratadis, 83700 St Raphaël [04 94 82 16 00; fax 04 94 82 72 21; info@ camping-vallee-du-paradis.com; www.camping-vallee-du-paradis.fr] Turn off D559 (N98) inland for St Raphaël via Valescure; cont past Le Verlaine site; Vallée du Paradis sp on L. Lge, pt shd; wc; shwrs; el pnts (10A) €4.20; gas; lndtte; ice; shop; rest; snacks; playgrnd; sand/shgl beach 400m; boat-launching; rv fishing adj; entmnts; TV; 50% statics; poss cr; quiet; red low ssn. 15 Mar-15 Oct. € 34.00
                                                                 2004*

There aren't many sites open this early in the year. We'd better phone ahead to check that the one we're heading for is actually open.

ST RAPHAEL *10F4* (4.5km N Rural) Camping Douce Quiétude, 3435 Blvd Jacques Baudino, 83700 St Raphaël [04 94 44 30 00; fax 04 94 44 30 30; info@douce-quietude.com; www.douce-quietude.com] Exit A8 at junc 38 onto D37 then D100 sp Agay. Foll sp Valescure-Boulouris, site sp. NB c'vans not permitted on St Raphaël seafront. Lge, pt sl, pt shd; wc; chem disp; serviced pitches; shwrs; el pnts (6A) inc; gas; lndtte; shop; rest; bar; BBQ (gas only); ice; playgrnd; pool; sand beach 6km; entmnt; excursions; TV; many tour ops statics; dogs €4; phone; poss v cr; cc acc. "Noisy disco nightly high ssn; excel facs; sm touring pitches mostly amongst statics." ♦ 1 Apr-14 Oct. € 49.50 (3 persons) (CChq acc)
                                                                 2007*

ST REMEZE see Vallon Pont d'Arc *9D2*

ST REMY DE PROVENCE *10E2* (500m NE) **FFCC Camping Le Mas de Nicolas (formerly Municipal), Ave Plaisance-du-Touch, Ave Théodore Aubanel, 13210 St Rémy-de-Provence** [04 90 92 27 05; fax 04 90 92 36 83; camping-mas-de-nicolas@ wanadoo.fr; www.camping-masdenicolas.com] S fr Avignon on D571, at rndabt just bef St Rémy turn L onto D99 sp Cavaillon; at next rndabt turn L, site sp on L in 500m. Well sp fr all dirs & in town. Site ent narr. NB Avoid ent St Rémy. Med, mkd/hdg pitch, pt sl, terr, pt shd; wc (some cont); chem disp; baby facs; shwrs inc; el pnts (6A) €3.50 gas 2km; lndtte; ice; sm shop or supmkt 1km, snacks; bar in ssn; BBQ; pool; playgrnd; games area; games rm; internet; sat TV; 20% statics; dogs €1.50; phone 400m; bus 1km; poss cr; Eng spkn; adv bkg ess; quiet; red low ssn; cc acc; CCI. "Family-owned site; v helpful; spotless san facs, being updated; some pitches diff access long o'fits; 25 min walk into town; lovely canal walk behind site; excel base for 'Roman Provence; excel'." ♦ ltd. 15 Mar-13 Oct. € 18.00   2007*

ST REMY DE PROVENCE *10E2* (500m E) Camping Pégomas, Ave Jean Moulin, 13210 St Rémy-de-Provence [tel/fax 04 90 92 01 21; contact@ campingpegomas.com; www.campingpegomas.com] On D99 W dir Cavaillon, ignore R fork to St Rémy. Under aquaduct to next rndabt, turn L (Champion sp). Pass twin stone sculptures on rndabt, at 2nd rndabt turn R, site in 400m - v sharp turn into site - flags flying. Fr E on D99 foll 1st sp to St Rémy along ave of trees; 1st R at mini rndabt (sharp R); then L into site. Med, hdg/ mkd pitch, shd; htd wc (mainly cont); chem disp; mv service pnt; baby facs; shwrs inc; el pnts (6A) €3.20 (poss rev pol & long lead req); gas; lndtte; ice; shop 300m; tradsmn; snacks; bar; playgrnd; pool & paddling pool high ssn; entmnt; TV; dogs €1.50; phone; poss cr; Eng spkn; adv bkg; quiet; red low ssn; cc acc; red long stay; CCI. "Well-run, busy site; lge o'fits poss diff some sm pitches; gd pool; san facs spotless (1 block dated & shwrs cramped); gates clsd 2000/2100-0800 - security code avail; sh walk to lovely town; mkt Wed; gd touring base Provence." ♦ 1 Mar-31 Oct. € 17.00   2007*

ST REMY DE PROVENCE *10E2* (8km SE Rural) **FFCC Camping Les Oliviers, Ave Jean Jaurès, 13810 Eygalières** [04 90 95 91 86; fax 04 90 95 91 86; reservation@camping-les-oliviers.com; www.camping-les-oliviers.com] Exit A7 junc 25; D99 dir St Rémy-de-Provence; in 8km camping sp on L; in vill well sp. Sm, hdg pitch, pt shd; htd wc; el pnts (6A) inc; shop, rest, snacks, bar 250m; BBQ; playgrnd; dogs €1; bus 3km; adv bkg (dep req); quiet. "Site set in olive grove 250m fr scenic vill; gd." 1 Apr-31 Oct. € 12.00
                                                                 2006*

France

Camping MONPLAISIR ★★★

Chemin Monplaisir • F-13210 SAINT-REMY-DE-PROVENCE

PHONE: + 33 (0)4 90 92 22 70 · FAX: + 33 (0)4 90 92 18 57

★ **Overflowing swimming and paddling pool – Snack bar in high season – Laundry**
★ **130 pitches, 2.8 ha of comfort, quietness and garden area.**
★ **Boules, children's games, table tennis, supermarket.**
★ **Chalets and mobile homes to let.**

www.camping-monplaisir.fr · E-MAIL: reception@camping-monplaisir.fr

---

ST REMY DE PROVENCE *10E2* (8km W) **Camp Municipal, Ave Docteur Barberin, 13150 St Etienne-du-Grès [04 90 49 00 03; corinne. gervais@voila.fr]** Fr Arles take N570 dir Avignon D99 E dir St Rémy. Site sp on o'skts of St Etienne. Sm, hdg pitch, pt shd; wc (some cont); chem disp; mv service pnt; shwrs inc; el pnts (6A) €2.50; ice; shop 1km; no statics; quiet; CCI. "Gd, peaceful site; gd grass pitches, poss muddy when wet; ltd wc/ shwr facs - rec own san facs; conv Arles, Avignon & Nîmes." 1 Apr-30 Sep. € 10.20   2005*

ST REMY DE PROVENCE *10E2* (1km NW Rural) **Camping Monplaisir, Chemin Monplaisir, 13210 St Rémy-de-Provence [04 90 92 22 70; fax 04 90 92 18 57; reception@camping-monplaisir. fr; www.camping-monplaisir.fr]** Exit St Rémy NW by D5 to Maillane, in 110m turn L & foll sp in 500m. Med, hdg/mkd pitch, pt shd; htd wc (some cont); chem disp; mv service pnt; baby facs; fam bthrm; shwrs inc; el pnts (6A) €3.50 (poss rev pol); gas; lndtte; ice; shop; supmkt 500m; tradsmn; snacks; bar; BBQ; playgrnd; pool; paddling pool; child entmnt; internet; dogs €1.80; phone; bus 1km; Eng spkn; adv bkg (dep req); quiet; cc acc; red long stay/low ssn; CCI. "Some sm pitches poss diff lge o'fits; immaculate, well-run site; clean, modern san facs; gd touring base; lovely town." ♦ 1 Mar-2 Nov. € 19.50   2007*

See advertisement

ST REMY DE PROVENCE *10E2* (8km NW Rural) **Camping Les Micocouliers, 445 Route de Cassoulen, 13690 Graveson [tel/fax 04 90 95 81 49; micocou@free.fr; http://micocou. free.fr]** Leave A7 junc 25 onto D99 St Rémy-de-Provence then D5 N past Maillane, site on R. Med, hdg/mkd pitch, unshd; wc; chem disp; mv service pnt; shwrs inc; el pnts (4-13A) €2.85-5.20; lndtte; sm shop & 3km; BBQ; pool; 8% statics; dogs €1.60; phone; Eng spkn; adv bkg; CCI. "V helpful owners; immac san facs; gd pool & sun area." ♦ 15 Mar-15 Oct. € 14.30 (CChq acc)   2005*

ST REMY SOUS BARBUISE see Arcis sur Aube *4E4*

ST RENAN *2E1* (2km NW Urban) **Camp Municpal Lokournan, Route de l'Aber, 29290 St Renan [02 98 84 37 67 or 02 98 84 20 08 (Mairie); fax 02 98 32 43 20]** On D27 fr St Renan dir Lanildut, site sp in 2km. Sm, hdg pitch, pt sl, pt shd; wc; chem disp; shwrs; el pnts €2.70; shop 1km; no statics; dogs €0.80; adv bkg; CCI. "Vg." ♦ ltd. 1 Jun-15 Sep. € 7.00   2006*

ST REVEREND see St Gilles Croix de Vie *2H3*

ST ROME DE DOLAN see Severac le château *9D1*

⊞**ST ROME DE TARN** *8E4* (300m N Rural) **Camping La Cascade des Naisses, 12490 St Rome-de-Tarn [05 65 62 56 59; fax 05 65 62 58 62; campingdelacascade@wanadoo. fr; http://campingdelacascade.com]** Fr Millau take D992 to St Georges-de-Luzençon, turn R onto D73 & foll sp to St Rome. Diff, steep app for sm o'fits. Med, hdg/mkd pitch, hdstg, terr, pt shd; wc; own san; chem disp; mv service pnt; shwrs inc; el pnts (6A) inc; lndtte; shop; snacks; playgrnd; pool; tennis; cycle hire; dogs €6; adv bkg; quiet; CCI. "Ideal NH for m'vans - but not rec disabled & lge & underpowered o'fits due v steep rds & bends, particularly after rain; lovely rvside pitches; each level has a wc but steep walk to shwr block; sh walk into beautiful vill; v ltd facs low ssn." ♦ € 25.00   2007*

ST ROME DE TARN *8E4* (10km W Rural) **Camping La Tioule, 12400 St Victor-et-Melvieu [05 65 62 51 93; carriere.nic@wanadoo.fr; http:// pagesperso-orange.fr/campinglatioule/]** Fr Millau or St Affrique on D999 at Lauras take D23 sp Tiergues, then D250/D50 sp St Victor-et-Melvieu. Other app not rec due narr, winding rds. Sm, mkd pitch, pt sl, terr, pt shd; wc; chem disp; shwrs inc; el pnts (16A) €2.80; tradsmn; BBQ; playgrnd; pool; dogs; adv bkg; quiet; CCI. "Beautiful area; vg site." 15 Jun-31 Aug. € 12.00   2005*

ST SATURNIN (PUY DE DOME) *9B1* (Rural) Domaine La Serre de Portelas (Naturist), 63450 St Saturnin [04 73 39 35 25 or 04 73 91 21 31 (LS); fax 04 73 39 35 76; ffn-laserre@ifrance.com] On A75 S fr Clermont-Ferrand exit junc 5 onto D213 W-bound sp Tallende. In 4km turn N on D96 sp Chadrat. Site on L about 3.5km after Chadrat. Turn acute L at end of tel posts. Or take N89 S fr Clermont-Ferrand twd Theix, turn S onto D96 & foll rd to site, sp. Sm, pt sl, pt shd; wc; chem disp; shwrs inc; el pnts (6A) €3; gas; ice; lndtte; sm shop & 6km; BBQ; playgrnd; games area; 35% statics; dogs; quiet; red low ssn; INF card req. "Panoramic views; gd base for Parc des Volcans d'Auvergne." 15 Jun-15 Sep. € 13.85   2005*

ST SATURNIN (PUY DE DOME) *9B1* (9km W Rural) Camping La Clairière, Rouillas-Bas, 63970 Aydat [tel/fax 04 73 79 31 15; info@campinglaclairiere. com] S fr Clermont-Ferrand exit A75 junc 5 onto D213 W & foll sp Lac d'Aydat. At x-rds at end Rouillas-Bas turn L, site 100m on L. Sm, hdg pitch, terr, pt shd; htd wc; chem disp; shwrs inc; el pnts (10A) €3 (poss rev pol); lndtte; shop 600m; rest 250m; snacks high ssn; playgrnd; 10% statics; dogs €1; Eng spkn; adv bkg rec high ssn; quiet; red low ssn. "V pleasant, quiet site; excel walking Puy-de-Dôme area; friendly, helpful owner; clean facs poss stretched when site full." 1 Apr-30 Sep. € 12.00
2005*

ST SAUVEUR EN PUISAYE *4G4* (1km) FFCC Camping Les Joumiers, Route de Mézilles, 89520 St Sauveur-en-Puisaye [03 86 45 66 28 or 03 86 45 46 28; fax 03 86 45 60 27; campingmoteljourniers@wanadoo.fr] Fr A6 S, exit at sp Joigny-Toucy onto D955 thro Aillant-sur-Tholon to Toucy, then cont to St Sauveur. Or N fr St Sauveur on D7 sp Mézilles, site on R in 1.5km. Site well sp at main x-rds in town. Med, hdg/mkd pitch, pt shd; htd wc; chem disp; shwrs inc; el pnts (5-10A) €2.80-3.80; gas; lndry rm; ice; tradsmn; rest; snacks; bar 2km; BBQ; playgrnd; htd pool; lake sw & beach adj; fishing; games area; cycle hire; 6 statics; dogs €1.25; phone; poss cr; no adv bkg; quiet; cc acc; 5% red long stay/CCI. "Helpful staff; lge pitches; lake views fr pitches; sm beach on lakeside." ♦ ltd. 15 Mar-15 Nov. € 12.00
2006*

Did you know you can fill in site report forms on the Club's website — www.caravanclub.co.uk?

ST SAUVEUR LE VICOMTE see Haye du Puits, La *1D4*

ST SAUVEUR LENDELIN see Coutances *1D4*

ST SAVIN *7A3* (1km N Urban) Camp Municipal Moulin de la Gassotte, 10 Rue de la Gassotte, 86310 St Savin-sur-Gartempe [05 49 48 18 02; fax 05 49 48 28 56; saint.savin@ag86.fr] E fr Chauvigny on D951 (N151) to St Savin; fr St Savin N on D11; well sp; flagged ent on R. Fr S on D5 cross rv; meet D951, turn R & camp on R. Fr S on D11 use 'heavy vehicles' rec rte to meet D951. NB There are 3 sites in St Savin. Sm, pt shd; wc (some cont); chem disp; mv service pnt; shwrs inc; el pnts (12A) €2.27-4.53; lndry rm; shop 500m; tradsmn; playgrnd; rv fishing adj; TV; quiet; CCI. "Famous murals in Abbey restored by UNESCO; attractive, peaceful site; old mill converted to social cent; v helpful warden." ♦ 13 May-15 Sep. € 6.11
2006*

ST SAVINIEN *7B2* (1km S Rural) Camping L'Ile aux Loisirs (La Grenouillette), 17350 St Savinien [05 46 90 35 11; fax 05 46 91 65 06; ileauxloisirs@ wanadoo.fr; www.ileauxloisirs.com] Fr St Jean-d'Angély take D18 to St Savinien. Site on S side of town; cross rv bdge in vill; site on L after 300m. Med, pt shd; wc; shwrs inc; el pnts (6A) €4.50; (rev pol); lndtte; shop; bar; snacks; playgrnd; pool adj; tennis & mini-golf nrby; entmnt; dogs €1; adv bkg; quiet; some rd noise; cc acc. "Pleasant, well-run site; short walk to v attractive town." 1 Apr-22 Sep. € 14.50
2007*

ST SAVINIEN *7B2* (5km SW Rural) FFCC Camping du Petit Bonheur, 14 Rue du Port, 17350 Crazannes [tel/fax 05 46 74 44 25 or 06 64 74 71 10 (mob); petit-bonheur@wandadoo. fr] Fr St Savinien take D18 for 1.5km, turn L onto D119. Site on L in 300m. Sm, pt sl, pt shd; wc; chem disp; baby facs; shwrs inc; el pnts (10A) €3; gas; lndtte; shops 300m; tradsmn; rest, snacks, bar 300m; BBQ (gas/elec); playgrnd; pool; rv sw, fishing 100m; dogs €0.80; Eng spkn; quiet; CCI. "Peaceful, CL-type site nr Rv Charente; new san facs planned 2006; gd cycling." Easter-15 Sep. € 8.00
2006*

⊞**ST SEBASTIEN** *7A3* (1km SW Rural) Camp Municipal, 23160 St Sébastien [05 55 63 50 39] Exit A20 junc 20 & foll sp dir La Souterraine on D5. In 4km turn L to St Sébastien. On ent vill turn R, R again, site on L just after equestrian cent. Sm, mkd pitch, pt sl, terr, pt shd; wc; shwrs inc; el pnts inc; shop, rest 500m; quiet. "Gd NH nr A20; gd touring base." € 6.20
2006*

ST SEINE L'ABBAYE see Chanceaux *6G1*

France

ST SERNIN 7D2 (2km N Rural) **Camping du Moulin de Borie Neuve,** 47120 St Sernin [05 53 20 70 73; info@borieneuve.com; www.borieneuve.com] S fr Ste Foy-la-Grande on D708 twd Duras. 2km after Villeneuve turn L, sp St Astier. Site on R in 100m. Sm, pt shd; wc; 60% serviced pitches; shwrs inc; el pnts (5A) €3.50 (poss rev pol); gas 2km; lndry rm; ice; shop 2km; tradsmn; snacks; bar; BBQ; playgrnd; pool; lake sw 4km; dogs €1.60; poss cr; Eng spkn; adv bkg; quiet; 5% red 7+ days; cc not acc; CCI. "Dutch owners v helpful & friendly; excel eve meals cooked by hosts; local wine sold on site; lovely quiet site; lge pitches; superb pool; excel local activities & mkts; tourist attractions in area, castles, vineyards; gd walking/cycling; site will open outside these dates by special arrangement by tel 24 hrs ahead." ♦ ltd. 29 Apr-9 Oct. € 14.30   2006*

ST SEURIN DE PRATS see Ste Foy la Grande 7C2

ST SEVER 8E2 (1km N Urban) **Camp Municipal Les Rives de l'Adour,** Ave René Crabos, 40500 St Sever [05 58 76 04 60 or 05 58 76 34 64; fax 05 58 76 43 55; ot.saintsever-capdegascogne@wanadoo.fr] S on D933 fr Mont de Marsan, cross D924 then bdge over Rv Adour. Look immed for access rd on L bef rlwy x-ing & steep climb up to St Sever. Site sp, easy to find adj Parc des Sports. Med, shd; wc; shwrs inc; el pnts; shops 1km; ice; lndry rm; playgrnd; pool; tennis; sailing; fishing; quiet. "Poss unreliable opening dates." 1 Jul-31 Aug.   2005*

ST SEVER CALVADOS 1D4 (SE Rural) **Camp Municipal, Route du Vieux Château,** 14380 St Sever-Calvados [02 31 68 82 63; fax 02 31 67 95 15] Fr A84 exit junc 37 or 38 E onto D924 or fr Vire W on D524, site sp on SE dir Champ-du-Boult.. Med, pt shd; wc; chem disp; shwrs inc; el pnts (5A) €2.50; shops 500m; snacks; bar; playgrnd; sand beach 30km; fishing; boating; tennis adj; dogs; adv bkg rec high ssn; quiet. "V peaceful, clean site on hill in forested area; gd walking; great for families with young children; barrier open 1200-1330 & 1700-2100 only." Easter-1 Oct. € 6.30   2004*

STE SEVERE SUR INDRE 7A4 (Rural) **Camp Municipal, Route de l'Auvergne,** 36160 Ste Sévère-sur-Indre [02 54 30 50 28 (Mairie); fax 02 54 30 63 39] On D917 fr La Châtre, site on R 200m after g'ge on L. Sm, pt shd; wc (some cont); mv service pnt; shwrs inc; el pnts €1.60; gas, shop, rest, bar 500m; playgrnd adj; fishing; dogs; quiet. "Tiny site in pleasant vill; associations with Jacques Tati & Georges Sand; gd NH." 1 Apr-15 Oct. € 6.40   2005*

⊞**STE SEVERE SUR INDRE** 7A4 (6km SE Rural) **Camping Pérassay, Le Bourg,** 36160 Pérassay [02 54 30 63 25; camping@the-french-connection.net; www.the-french-connection.net] Fr Ste Sévère take D917 S & after approx 6km turn L onto D71 sp Pérassay. Site on R in cent of vill opp tabac. Sm, pt sl, pt shd; wc; chem disp (wc); shwrs inc; el pnts (10A) inc; lndtte; BBQ; lake sw 10km; 1 statics; c'van storage; adv bkg; quiet. "British-owned CL-type site; vg." ♦ € 15.00   2005*

STE SIGOLENE see Monistrol sur Loire 9C1

ST SORNIN see Marennes 7B1

ST SULPICE see Brengues 7D4

ST SYLVESTRE (HAUTE VIENNE) 7B3 (Rural) **Camping Les Roussilles, La Crouzille,** 87240 St Sylvestre [05 55 71 32 54] Fr N on A20 exit junc 25, fr S take exit 26; site approx 1.5km N of Le Crouzille. Med, mkd pitch, pt sl, shd; wc; chem disp; shwrs inc; el pnts (6A) inc; lndtte; shop 5km; tradsmn; rest high ssn; snacks; bar; playgrnd; pool; poss cr; adv bkg; quiet; CCI. "Excel pool; basic facs; conv Limoges; phone ahead low ssn to check open." ♦ ltd. 1 Mar-31 Dec. € 15.00   2006*

ST SYLVESTRE SUR LOT see Villeneuve sur Lot 7D3

⊞**ST SYMPHORIEN** 7D2 (1km S Rural) **FFCC Camping La Hure, Route de Sore,** 33113 St Symphorien [tel/fax 05 56 25 79 54 or 06 86 77 09 27 (mob); campingdelahure@libertysurf.fr] S thro Langon on app to . Foll sp Villandraut, St Symphorien. Sp fr vill 1km S on D220, opp Intermarché. Med, shd; htd wc; chem disp; mv service pnt; shwrs inc; el pnts (5A) €2.40; lndtte; shops; rest; snacks; playgrnd; pool adj; tennis; rv fishing; many statics; dogs €1.30; adv bkg; red low ssn. "Helpful staff; basic facs - poss unclean low ssn (Oct 2007); in beautiful pinewoods; gd cycling, walks, beaches." € 9.80   2006*

ST SYMPHORIEN 7D2 (14km SW Urban) **Aire Naturelle Municipale,** 40430 Sore [05 58 07 60 06; fax 05 58 07 64 72; sore.mairie@libertysurf.fr] Fr St Symphorien, take D220/D43 to Sore, then take D651 sp Mont-de-Marsan. Lane to site on L, nr rv. Sm, pt sl, pt shd; wc; chem disp (wc); shwrs inc; el pnts inc; lndtte; gas, shop, snacks, bar 1km; BBQ; playgrnd; pool, tennis & sports facs adj; dogs; phone; quiet. "Site & san facs open to public; site yourself & warden calls; some el pnts don't work so long lead handy; pleasant wooded area." ♦ ltd. 15 Jun-15 Sep. € 9.50   2005*

ST THEOFFREY 9C3 (E Rural) **Camping Ser-Sirant, Petichet,** 38119 St Théoffrey [04 76 83 91 97; fax 04 76 30 83 69; campingsersirant@wanadoo.fr; www.euro-campsite.com] N fr La Mure on N85 dir Grenoble. At traff lts in Petichet turn E, site on lakeside in 500m. Med, mkd pitch, pt terr, pt shd; wc; chem disp; shwrs inc; el pnts (3-10A) €2.60-5.10; lndtte; shop 8km; tradsmn; rest 1km; lake sw & beach adj; watersports; dogs €2.50; phone; bus 1km; Eng spkn; adv bkg; quiet; CCI. "Lovely views; excel walking & cycling; v helpful owners; highly rec." 28 Apr-30 Sep. € 16.90
                                                        2007*

ST THIBERY see Pézenas 10F1

France

ST TROPEZ *10F4* (6km SE Rural) **Camping Moulin de Verdagne, Route du Brost, 83580 Gassin** [04 94 79 78 21; fax 04 94 54 22 65; info@moulindeverdagne.com; www.moulinde verdagne.com] Foll N559 N fr Cavalaire for 6km. Take 1st R after town traff lts in La Croix-Valmer, site sp on R. Site in 2km, surrounded by vineyards. Rough app rd/track. Med, mkd pitch, terr, pt shd; wc (some cont); chem disp; shwrs inc; el pnts (10A) €4; lndtte; shop 4km; tradsmn; rest; snacks; playgrnd; pool; sand beach 5km; dogs €3; 60% statics; phone; poss cr; Eng spkn; quiet; cc acc. "Pool is 2m deep; tight bends & narr pitches poss diff long o'fits." 1 Apr-5 Nov. € 19.50

2005*

ST TROPEZ *10F4* (6km S Rural) **Parc Saint James Gassin, Route de Bourrian, 83580 Gassin** [04 94 55 20 20; fax 04 94 56 34 77; info@ camping-parcsaintjames.com; www.camping-parcsaintjames.com] Exit A8 at junc 36 St Tropez; after Port-Grimaud foll sp Cavalaire-sur-Mer S on D559 where clearly sp. V lge, hdg/mkd pitch, pt sl, terr, pt shd; wc (some cont); chem disp; shwrs inc; el pnts (6A) inc; gas; lndtte; ice; shop; rest; snacks; bar; BBQ; plagyrnd; htd pool; paddling pool; beach 2.5km; tennis; games area; games rm; solarium; entmnt (child & adult); cable TV; cycle hire; golf 12km; 50% statics; dogs €5; phone; Eng spkn; adv bkg ess high ssn; quiet but some rd noise; cc acc; 10% red + 14 days/low ssn; CCI. "Conv St Tropez; scenic drives; vg." ♦ 12 Jan-22 Nov. € 37.00

2007*

See advertisement

ST TROPEZ *10F4* (7km S Rural) **Camping La Croix du Sud, Loumède, Route des Plages, 83350 Ramatuelle [04 94 79 89 21; fax 04 94 79 89 21; cplcroixdusud@atciat.com; www.camping-saint-tropez.com or www.campeole.com]** App St Tropez fr W on N98A, turn R at traff lts at W o'skts onto D93 sp Ramatuelle. Site on R in 7km opp filling stn. Med, mkd pitch, pt sl, terr, pt shd; wc; baby facs; shwrs; el pnts (3-6A) €3.90; gas; lndtte; ice; shop; tradsmn; rest; snacks; playgrnd; htd pool; sand beach 1.7km; games area; entmnt; TV; 50% statics; dogs €3.90; poss cr; Eng spkn; no adv bkg; quiet; CCI. 1 Apr-15 Oct. € 35.00   2006*

ST TROPEZ *10F4* (7km S Coastal) **Riviera Villages Kon-Tiki, Plage de Pampelonne, 83350 Ramatuelle [04 94 55 96 96; fax 04 94 55 96 95; kontiki@riviera-villages.com; www.riviera-villages.com or www.campazur.com]** Foll Ramatuelle on D93 sp fr St Tropez; site sp on L. V lge, mkd pitch, pt sl, pt shd; wc; chem disp; baby facs; shwrs inc; el pnts (6A) inc; gas; lndtte; ice; shop; rest; snacks; bar; playgrnd; sand beach adj; tennis; archery; entmnt; TV; 50% statics; dogs; poss cr; adv bkg ess high ssn (dep req); quiet; red low ssn; cc acc; CCI. "Some sm pitches; gd rest; ideal beach holiday; all watersports avail; fantastic coastal walks; conv St Tropez & hill vills." 31 Mar-29 Oct. € 40.00   2007*

ST TROPEZ *10F4* (8km S Coastal) **Camping La Cigale, Route de l'Escalet, 83350 Ramatuelle [04 94 79 22 53; fax 04 94 79 12 05; campinglacigale@wanadoo.fr; www.camping-lacigale.fr]** Fr A8 or DN7 at Le Luc take D558 to Grimaud & D61, N98 & N98A to St Tropez. Bef St Tropez take D93 S for 7km minor rd to Plage de l'Escalet. Med, pt shd; wc; shwrs; el pnts (6A) inc; shop; lndtte; rest; snacks; bar; playgrnd; htd pool; paddling pool; sand beach 800m; cycle hire; tennis 800m; golf 8km; 30% statics; dogs €5; no c'vans acc over 5m; poss cr; Eng spkn; quiet. "Gassin, Ramatuelle must see vills; gd rest; gd." 1 Apr-15 Oct. € 30.00   2005*

ST TROPEZ *10F4* (8km S Rural) **Yelloh! Village Les Tournels, Route de Camarat, 83350 Ramatuelle [04 94 55 90 90; fax 04 94 55 90 99; info@tournels.com; www.tournels.com or www.yellohvillage.com]** Exit A8 at Le Muy dir St Maxime, St Tropez. Take D61 dir Ramatuelle then foll sp 'La Plage' & Camarat lighthouse. V lge, mkd pitch, terr, shd; htd wc (some cont); chem disp; mv service pnt; some serviced pitches; sauna; shwrs inc; el pnts (5A) inc; gas; lndtte; shops; rest; snacks; bar; playgrnd; htd pool; paddling pool; sand beach 1.5km; (shuttle bus high ssn); tennis; games area; fitness rm; mini-golf; cycle hire; entmnt; child entmnt; TV; 90% statics; dogs €4; Eng spkn; adv bkg; quiet; cc acc; red low ssn; CCI. "Well-run, peaceful site; v clean & well-maintained; lower pitches full long term winter vans; upper terr levels via v steep, narr rd; poss diff long o'fits; lovely views fr upper level." 15 Mar-9 Jan. € 40.00   2007*

ST VAAST LA HOUGUE see Quettehou *1C4*

ST VALERY EN CAUX *3C2* (500m NE Coastal) **Camp Municipal Falaise d'Amont, Rue Traversière, 76460 St Valery-en-Caux [02 35 97 05 07]** SW fr Dieppe on D925 to St Valery-en-Caux; site sp on R off D925 500m fr town cent. App rd v steep, not rec lge o'fits. Sm, mkd pitch, terr, unshd; wc; chem disp; shwrs inc; el pnts (6A) €2.15; shop & gas 500m; lndtte; playgrnd; shgl beach 500m; quiet; CCI. "Panoramic views; conv WW2 memorials; unsuitable towed c'vans due terrs; v steep app rd poss problem for lge o'fits &/or lge m'vans; 18% gradient on app, risk of grnding." 16 Mar-15 Nov. € 6.00   2006*

⊞**ST VALERY EN CAUX** *3C2* (SW Coastal) **Camp Municipal d'Etennemare, Rue Traversière, 76460 St Valery-en-Caux [tel/fax 02 35 97 15 79; servicetourisme@ville-saint-valery-en-caux.fr]** Fr Dieppe on D925 foll camping sp on ent town. Med, mkd pitch, pt shd; htd wc; chem disp; baby facs; shwrs inc; el pnts (10A) €2.15; lndtte; shop; tradsmn; pool & tennis in town; shgl beach; adv bkg; quiet; cc acc; CCI. "Site poss clsd low ssn - phone to check; nice, v clean & tidy site; conv for town." ♦ € 13.40   2006*

⊞**ST VALERY EN CAUX** *3C2* (W Coastal) **Aire Communale, Plage Ouest, 76460 St Valery-en-Caux [02 35 97 00 63 or 02 35 97 00 22 (Mairie)]** Sp fr cent of St Valery-en-Caux along rv/seafront to harbour. Sm, chem disp; mv service pnt; water fill €3; el pnts €3; lndtte, shops, rests nr; phone; free parking for 48 hrs. M'vans only.   2006*

ST VALERY SUR SOMME *3B2* (2km S Rural) **Camping Le Domaine du Château de Drancourt, 80230 Estréboeuf [03 22 26 93 45; fax 03 22 26 85 87; chateau.drancourt@wanadoo.fr; www.chateau-drancourt.com or www.les-castels.com]** Leave A28/E402 at junc 1 at Abbeville onto D40 twd Noyelles-sur-Mer. At rndabt with D940 turn L sp St Valéry-sur-Somme. Turn S onto D48 dir Estréboeuf. Turn immed L for Château de Drancourt, site sp on L. NB.1-way ent & exit system operates at recep area. Lge, mkd pitch, pt sl, pt shd; wc; chem disp; mv service pnt; baby facs; shwrs inc; el pnts (6A) inc (poss rev pol); gas; lndtte; shop; rest; snacks; bar; BBQ; playgrnd; 2 htd pools + paddling pool; sand beach 8km; fishing adj; watersports 2km; tennis; mini-golf; new games hall (for 2008); cycle hire; horseriding 12km; entmnt; 80% statics; dogs; Eng spkn; adv bkg; cc acc; CCI. "Conv, busy, popular NH; lge allocation of best pitches to tour op statics & fixed tents; friendly, helpful staff; red facs low ssn; chem disp long walk fr site; golf lessons; trips to Paris; excel." ♦ 1 Apr-2 Nov. € 34.00 ABS - P06   2007*

France

ST VALERY SUR SOMME 3B2 (1km SW Urban/ Coastal) **Camping Le Walric, Route d'Eu, 80230 St Valery-sur-Somme** [03 22 26 81 97; fax 03 22 60 77 26; info@campinglewalric. com; www.campinglewalric.com] Ringrd round St Valery D940 dir Le Tréport. Cont to 2nd rndabt (1st rndabt Champion supmkt on L) 3km & take 1st exit (R) sp St Valery & Cap Hornu D3. Site on R in 2km at ent to town sp. Lge, hdg/mkd pitch, pt shd; wc; chem disp; mv service pnt; baby facs; shwrs inc; el pnts (6A) inc; gas; lndtte; ice; shop; tradsmn; bar; BBQ; playgrnd; htd pool; paddling pool; beaches nr; fishing; boat & cycle hire; tennis; games area; games rm; entmnt; child entmnt; 70% statics; dogs €2; phone; Eng spkn; adv bkg; quiet; cc acc; red low ssn; CCI. "Excel location; well-maintained; excel facs; cycle rtes, canal track, steam train; mkt Sun; delightful town." ♦ 1 Apr-1 Nov. € 27.00 (3 persons) 2007*

See advertisement

ST VALERY SUR SOMME 3B2 (3km SW Rural) **Camping de la Baie, Routhiaville, 80230 Pendé** [03 22 60 72 72] Just off D940 twd Tréport, well sp. Sm, hdg pitch; wc (some cont); chem disp; shwrs inc; el pnts (3-6A) inc; lndtte; shop 2km; tradsmn; playgrnd; mini-golf; 95% statics; adv bkg; quiet; red low ssn; CCI. "Friendly, helpful owners; superbly run, clean, tidy site; san facs spotless; low trees in places need care; cycle rte to St Valery." Easter-15 Oct. € 14.50 2007*

ST VALLIER 9C2 (400m N Urban) **Camp Municipal Les Iles de Silon, 26240 St Vallier** [04 75 23 22 17 or 04 73 23 07 66] On N7 just N of town, clearly sp in both dirs. Med, hdg pitch, pt shd; wc; chem disp; shwrs inc; el pnts (6A) €2 (rev pol, adaptor & poss long cable req); lndtte; shop & 500m; snacks; BBQ; playgrnd; pool 1km; watersports; tennis adj; dogs €1; Eng spkn; adv bkg; quiet but some rlwy noise; cc acc; CCI. "Views over rv; v friendly warden; c'vans over 5.50m not admitted; rec arr bef 1600 high ssn; site yourself, office opens eves; immac facs." ♦ ltd. 15 Mar-15 Nov. € 9.00 2004*

ST VALLIER 9C2 (5km W Rural) **Camping L'Oasis, Le Petit Chaléat, 07370 Eclassan** [04 75 34 56 23; fax 04 75 34 47 94; oasis.camp@wanadoo.fr; www.oasisardeche.com] Leave N7 at St Vallier, cross Rhône to Sarras. Then across N86 onto D6 sp St Jeure-d'Ay, in 7km turn R foll sp to site. App rd twisting & narr, many sharp bends & no passing places. Tractor tow available. Sm, hdg/mkd pitch, terr, pt shd, 80% serviced pitch; wc; chem disp; shwrs inc; el pnts (3-6A) €3.10-3.60; gas; lndtte; ice; shop; tradsmn; rest; snacks; bar; playgrnd; pool; rv adj; mini-golf; archery; golf 10km; 20% statics; dogs €2; Eng spkn; adv bkg; quiet; cc not acc; CCI. "In idyllic setting by rv; tractor takes c'vans to pitch; not rec NH due diff approach." 15 Apr-30 Sep. € 18.00 2006*

ST VALLIER DE THIEY see Grasse 10E4

ST VARENT 4H1 (2km S Rural) **Camp Municipal La Grande Versenne, 79330 St Varent** [05 49 67 62 11 (Mairie); fax 05 49 67 67 87; villestvarent@wanadoo.fr] Site sp on D938 at Bouillé-St Varent. Sm, hdg pitch, pt shd; wc; baby facs; shwrs inc; el pnts (10A) €2.50; supmkt nr; playgrnd; rv nrby; no statics; dogs €0.50; adv bkg; quiet. "Friendly staff; gd NH." ♦ 1 Apr-31 Oct. € 9.50 2007*

ST VICTOR ET MELVIEU see St Rome de Tarn 8E4

ST VINCENT DE BARRES see Privas 9D2

ST VINCENT DE COSSE see Sarlat la Canéda 7C3

ST VINCENT DE PAUL see Dax 8E1

ST VINCENT SUR JARD see Jard sur Mer 7A1

ST YORRE 9A1 (5km SE Rural) **Camping des Marants, 70 Ave des Sources, 03270 Mariol** [04 70 59 44 70] Fr Vichy take D906 S & after 13.5 km take L turn sp Mariol. Site on L after 250m. Sm, pt shd; wc; chem disp; shwrs inc; el pnts inc; lndry rm; playgrnd; pools; lake sw; tennis; games area; dogs; CCI. "V pleasant site; friendly staff; excel value." € 9.50 2005*

ST YORRE *9A1* (SW Rural) **Camp Municipal Les Gravières**, 03270 St Yorre [04 70 59 21 00; fax 04 70 59 20 09; mairie.saint-yorre@wanadoo.fr] Fr A71 exit junc 12 sp Gannat. At Bellerive turn R onto D131 sp Hauterive. L over bdge to St Yorre. Foll camping sp. C'vans banned fr St Yorre town cent. Med, hdg pitch, pt shd; wc (some cont); chem disp; baby facs; shwrs inc; el pnts (4-10A) €2.55; lndry rm; shops 1km; tradsmn; snacks; BBQ; playgrnd; pool adj; rv sw & fishing; games area; sports cent adj; dogs; phone adj; Eng spkn; adv bkg; quiet; CCI. "Gd touring base; helpful warden." ♦ 1 May-30 Sep. € 8.85   2006*

ST YRIEIX LA PERCHE *7B3* (1km N Urban) **Camp Municipal d'Arfeuille, Plan d'Eau d'Arfeuille,** 87500 St Yrieix-la-Perche [05 55 75 08 75; fax 05 55 75 26 08; camping@saint-yrieix.com] Site well sp on L on D704 dir Limoges. Med, hdg pitch, terr, pt shd; htd wc; chem disp; baby facs; shwrs; el pnts (10A) inc; playgrnd; lake sw & beach adj; quiet. 1 Jun-15 Sep. € 12.00   2007*

⊞**ST YRIEIX LA PERCHE** *7B3* (8km W Rural) **FFCC Camping Les Vigères,** 87500 Le Chalard [05 55 09 37 22; fax 05 55 09 93 39; lesvigeres@ aol.com; www.lesvigeres.com] Take N20 to Limoges then N704 to St Yrieix. In St Yrieix turn W on D901 to Châlus. 1st vill is Le Chalard & site is 1km after vill. Sm, hdg/mkd pitch, pt shd; wc; chem disp; shwrs inc; el pnts (3-10A) €3-4; lndtte; shops 2km; BBQ; playgrnd; pool; lake sw & sand beach adj; fishing; library; adv bkg; v quiet; 10% red low ssn; CCI. "Vg, peaceful site; welcoming British owners; clean san facs; historic area; rec." ♦ € 12.50   2006*

ST YRIEIX LA PERCHE *7B3* (12km NW Rural) **Camp Municipal (de Bel Air),** 87500 Ladignac-le-Long [05 55 09 39 82 or 05 55 09 30 02 (Mairie); fax 05 55 09 39 80; camping-ladignac@wanadoo. fr] Exit Limoges S on N21 to Châlus. Turn E on D901 sp St Yrieix to Ladignac. Turn N to lakes at sp. Site on R. Med, pt shd, hdg pitch; wc; chem disp; serviced pitch; shwrs inc; el pnts (10A) €2.50; lndtte; shop & 1km; tradsmn; playgrnd; lake sw 500m; 10% statics; dogs; phone; Eng spkn; adv bkg; quiet; red low ssn; CCI. "Beautiful lakeside site; v spacious pitches; spotless san facs; barrier with card operation - early ssn apply to Mairie in vill sq for card; cycling; walking; excel." 1 May-31 Oct. € 9.50   2006*

SALBRIS *4G3* (NE Urban) **Camping de Sologne, 8 Allée de la Sauldre, Route de Pierrefitte,** 41300 Salbris [02 54 97 06 38; fax 02 54 97 33 13; campingdesologne@wanadoo.fr; http://monsite. wanadoo.fr/camping.salbris] Exit A71 junc 4. Take D944 bypass, then take N20 N. Turn E onto D55 sp Pierrefitte; site on R in 200m on rvside. Med, hdg/mkd pitch, pt shd; wc (some cont); chem disp; baby facs; shwrs inc; el pnts (10A) inc (some rev pol); gas; lndtte; shop 200m; hypmkt 1km; tradsmn; rest; snacks; bar high ssn; playgrnd; htd pool nr; lake adj; fishing; boat hire; karting 6km; TV rm; 25% statics; dogs €0.50; phone; poss cr; Eng spkn; adv bkg; some noise fr rlwy, rd & motor circuit; cc acc; CCI. "Excel, well-maintained, lakeside site; friendly, helpful owners; gd san facs but dated & poss stretched if site busy & ltd low ssn; gd dog walks adj; easy walk to town." ♦ 30 Mar-30 Sep. € 15.50   2007*

SALERNES *10F3* (1km N Rural) **Camping Le Relais de la Bresque, Chemin de la Piscine,** 83690 Sillans-la-Cascade [04 94 04 64 89; fax 04 94 77 19 54; info@lerelaisdelabresque.com; www.lerelaisdelabresque.com] Fr W on D560 to Salernes. At vill take D22 N to site, 1km on R. Med, shd, mkd pitch; htd wc; chem disp; mv service pnt; shwrs inc; serviced pitch; el pnts (5-10A) €3-5; lndtte; ice; rest; tradsmn; playgrnd; pool adj; rv 1.5km; cycle hire; horseriding; archery, fitness course; games rm; wifi internet; entmnt; TV; some statics; dogs €1.50; Eng spkn; quiet; adv bkg rec; red low ssn. 1 Apr-31 Oct. € 18.50   2007*

SALERNES *10F3* (4km E Rural) **Camping Club Le Ruou, Les Esparrus,** 83690 Villecroze-les-Grottes [04 94 70 67 70; fax 04 94 70 64 65; camping.leruou@wanadoo.fr; www.leruou.com] Fr Draguignan take D557 thro Flayosc, then D560 dir Salernes. Site sp on L. Med, mkd pitch, terr, shd; htd wc; chem disp; mv service pnt; baby facs; el pnts (6-10A) €4-5; gas; lndtte; ice; shop; rest; snacks; bar; BBQ: playgrnd; pool; paddling pool; waterslides; games area; fishing; archery; games/ TV rm; adv bkg; 35% statics; dogs €2.50; adv bkg; quiet. ♦ 1 Apr-31 Oct. € 18.00 (CChq acc)
                    2004*

SALERNES *10F3* (W Rural) **Camp Municipal Les Arnauds,** 83690 Salernes [04 94 67 51 95; fax 04 94 70 75 57; lesarnauds@ville-salernes.fr; www.ville-salernes.fr] W fr Draguignan on D557 thro Salernes; site sp on L on W o'skts of town; to avoid town cent turn R at rndabt on E o'skts sp Villecroze; take 1st L at next 2 rndabts & foll site sp. Med, hdg/mkd pitch, pt shd; wc; chem disp; baby facs; shwrs; el pnts (10A) inc; lndtte; bar; playgrnd; rv sw adj; tennis; dogs €1.80; Eng spkn; adv bkg; quiet; red low ssn; CCI. "Excel; warm welcome; excel san facs; gd night lighting; pleasant location; some sm pitches poss diff lge o'fits; rvside site; no twin-axle vans; no entry 1200-1500; take torch into shwrs, lights on sh time switch." 2 May-30 Sep. € 22.55   2006*

SALERS 7C4 (800m NE Rural) **Camp Municipal Le Mouriol, Route de Puy-Mary, 15410 Salers [04 71 40 73 09 or 04 71 40 72 33 (Mairie); fax 04 71 40 76 28]** Take D922 SE fr Mauriac dir Aurillac; turn onto D680 E dir Salers; site 1km NE of Salers on D680 dir Puy Mary, opp Hôtel Le Gerfaut; sp fr all dir. Med, hdg/mkd pitch, sl, pt shd, wc; chem disp; shwrs inc; el pnts (16A) inc (long lead poss req); lndtte; shops, rest, snacks & bar 1km; BBQ; playgrnd; tennis; hill-walking; dogs; bus 1km; phone; poss cr; no adv bkg; quiet; 10% red 10 days; CCI. "Beautiful area; Salers o'stndg medieval vill; site within walking dist for rest & museums; generous pitches; san facs stretched if site full; v peaceful low ssn; excel cycling & walking; gd touring base; vg." ♦ 15 May-15 Oct. € 14.00
2006*

SALERS 7C4 (800m W Rural) **Camping à la Ferme (Fruquière), Apcher, 15140 Salers [04 71 40 72 26]** D922 S fr Mauriac for 17km; L on D680 sp Salers; in lane on R sp Apcher - immed after passing Salers town sp. Sm, pt shd; wc (some cont), chem disp (wc); shwrs inc; el pnts (10A) €2.20; shop 300m; dogs; poss cr; quiet; CCI. "Sm farm site conv for Salers & Cantal area; gd." 1 May-30 Sep. € 8.60
2005*

SALIES DE BEARN 8F1 (2km NW Urban) **Camp Municipal de Mosquéros, Ave Al Cartero, 64270 Salies-de-Béarn [05 59 38 12 94]** Leave A64 at exit 7 S onto D430 sp Salies de Béarn. After 500m take D330 on R sp 'Casino' & turn R onto D17 at rndabt. Site sp in town, on D17 Bayonne rd NW of town. NB Avoid town - narr streets & diff when busy. Med, hdg/mkd pitch, pt sl, pt shd; wc; chem disp; shwrs inc; el pnts inc (10A) inc; lndtte; shops 1km; rest 600m; pool; sports facs adj; fishing 1km; golf 2km; horseriding 3km; TV; quiet; "V helpful warden; levelling blocks req some pitches; poss diff lge o'fits; barrier clsd 2200-0700; mkt Thu." ♦ 15 Mar-15 Oct. € 13.60
2007*

SALIES DU SALAT 8F3 (2km S) **FFCC Camp Municipal La Justale, Chemin de St Jean, 31260 Mane [05 61 90 68 18; fax 05 61 97 40 18; contact@village-vacances-mane.com; www.village-vacances-mane.com]** Fr A64 exit 20 onto D117, turn R in vill at sp 'Village de Vacances'. Site on R in approx 500m. Sm, pt shd; wc; mv service pnt; shwrs inc; el pnts (6A) €2.90; lndtte; shops 500m; playgrnd; rv sw adj; fishing; tennis; horseriding; TV rm; dogs €1; adv bkg. "Lovely, sm, peaceful site; lge pitches; helpful staff; excel facs." 1 Apr-31 Oct. € 10.85
2007*

SALIGNAC EYVIGNES see Sarlat la Canéda 7C3

SALINS LES BAINS 6H2 (500m N) **Camp Municipal, 39110 Salins-les-Bains [03 84 37 92 70]** SE fr Besançon on N83. At Mouchard take D472 E to Salins. Turn L at rndabt at N of Salins, well sp. If app fr E take 2nd exit fr rndabt (blind app). Sm, pt shd; wc; shwrs inc; el pnts (10A) €2.80; lndry rm; supmkt 500m; playgrnd; htd pool adj; adv bkg; quiet but some rd noise one end & primary school the other. "Well run site; v clean, modern san facs; excel touring base N Jura; not often visited by British; far end of site quieter." ♦ 1 Apr-30 Sep. € 10.80
2007*

SALLANCHES 9A3 (2km SE Urban) **Camping L'Ecureuil, 490 Route des Follieux, 74700 Sallanches [04 50 58 43 67; fax 04 50 58 44 61; contact@camping-ecureuil.com]** App fr Chamonix on N205, turn R opp Ford g'ge ent Sallanches; strt on thro traff lts, over sleeping policemen, under rlwy bdge & fork R at Braconne rest; strt at next junc to site in 200m. Med, shd; wc; chem disp; mv service pnt; shwrs inc; el pnts (10A) €2.50; gas; lndtte; ice; shops 1km; tradsmn; rest (not every day); bar; playgrnd; pool nr; lake sw & sand/shgl beach; games area; some statics; dogs €1; poss cr; quiet; cc acc; CCI. "Excel, v clean facs; plenty of trees; mountain views inc Mont Blanc." Easter-15 Oct. € 15.60
2007*

SALLANCHES 9A3 (2km SE Rural) **Camping Miroir du Mont Blanc, Chemin de Mont-Blanc-Plage, 74700 Sallanches [04 50 58 14 28 or 04 50 58 12 04 (LS); fax 04 50 93 95 23; beatrice.brosse2@wanadoo.fr]** Fr Geneva on N205 into Sallanches. Take 1st L after 2nd set of traff lts (by post office) sp 'Hôpital'. Foll rd thro traff lits & over rndabt when rd turns sharp R & runs alongside m'way. In 2km site ent on R beside rndabt. Park here & walk to recep to check in. Or exit A41 junc 21 or 22 dir Lac de Passy, site sp. Med, mkd pitch, shd; wc; shwrs inc; el pnts (8A) €2.50; gas 2km; lndry rm; ice; shops 2km; tradsmn; rest; snacks; bar; playgrnd; pool; paddling pool; waterslide; lake sw & sand/shgl beach adj; tennis; fishing; sailing; windsurfing 50m; entmnt; TV rm; adv bkg rec; quiet; red low ssn. "Magnificent views." 15 May-15 Sep. € 13.00
2007*

SALLANCHES 9A3 (4km SE) **Camping des Iles, 245 Chemin de la Cavettaz, 74190 Passy [04 50 58 45 36 or 04 99 57 21 21; www.village-center.com]** On N205 dir Chamonix t turn L (1st into filter to turn L) onto D199 3km after Sallanches. Turn L immed bef level x-ing. Site at end of rd. Lge, hdg/mkd pitch, pt shd; wc (some cont); baby facs; shwrs inc; el pnts (8A) inc; lndtte; shop & 3km; snacks; playgrnd; htd pool; shgl lake beach & sw adj; fishing; entmnt; child entmnt; statics; dogs €3; phone; Eng spkn; adv bkg; quiet; cc acc high ssn; CCI. "Mountain views; conv Mt Blanc, glacier & Chamonix; vg site." ♦ 2 Jun-16 Sep. € 18.00
2007*

SALLELES D'AUDE see Narbonne 10F1

France

SALLES (GIRONDE) *7D1* (Urban) **FFCC Camping Parc du Val de l'Eyre, 8 Route du Minoy, 33770 Salles [05 56 88 47 03; fax 05 56 88 47 27; levaldeleyre@free.fr; www.valdeleyre.com]** Exit junc 21 fr A63, foll dir to Salles on D3. On edge of Salles turn L on D108 at x-rds. Ent to site on L after rv opp Champion supmkt building. Lge, pt shd; wc; chem disp; baby facs; shwrs inc; el pnts (6A) €3.80 (poss rev pol); gas; lndtte; shops adj; supmkt nr; rest; snacks; bar; BBQ; playgrnd; sports area; lake & rv sw; fishing; canoeing; tennis 500m; horseriding 8km; entmnt; dogs €3; quiet but entmnt poss noisy; cc acc; red low ssn. "Attractive site; gd san facs but poss stretched when site busy." ♦ 1 Apr-30 Sep. € 22.00   2007*

SALLES (GIRONDE) *7D1* (8km S Rural) **Camping La Cypréa, 33830 Lugos [05 57 71 93 30]** S fr Bordeaux on N10 to cent Belin-Béliet; turn R onto D110; camp sp on wall facing you; stay on this rd thro pine forest. Camp on L just bef sp for Lugos (Gare). Sm, pt shd; wc; mv service pnt; shwrs €1; el pnts inc (2A) €2.50; lndtte; tradsmn; playgrnd; pool; games area; no dogs; quiet; CCI. "Friendly owner; lovely sm pool." 1 Jul-1 Sep. € 10.00   2006*

⊞**SALLES (GIRONDE)** *7D1* (4km SW Rural) **Camping Le Bilos, 37 Route de Bilos, 33770 Salles [05 56 88 45 14 or 05 56 88 36 53; fax 05 56 88 45 14; http://pageperso.aol.fr/lebilos]** Exit 21 fr A63. Foll sp Salles on D3. Turn L onto D108 sp Lanot, pass Champion supmkt on R; in 2km bear R & site on R in 2km. Med, pt shd; htd wc; chem disp; shwrs inc; el pnts (3-10A) €1.90-5.30; gas; lndtte; shop; supmkt 2.5km; BBQ sep area; playgrnd; 80% statics; dogs; adv bkg; quiet. "Pleasant, peaceful farm in pine forest; not muddy when wet; friendly owners; phone to check open low ssn; conv for Arcachon, Bordeaux, Dune of Pyla; vg NH en rte Spain, especially low ssn, but ltd facs low ssn; cycle lane thro forest; vg value; lovely." € 7.00   2007*

SALLES CURAN *8E4* (Rural) **Camping Les Genêts, Lac de Pareloup, 12410 Salles-Curan [05 65 46 35 34 or 05 65 42 06 46; fax 05 65 78 00 72; contact@camping-les-genets. fr; www.camping-les-genets.fr]** Fr D911 Rodez-Millau rd take D993 S for approx 9km, then R onto D577, site sp on R by lake. Lge, pt sl, shd; wc; shwrs; el pnts (6A) inc; lndtte; shop; rest; pizzeria; bar; htd pool; cycle hire; sailing; fishing; lake sw & beach; child entmnt; 40% statics; dogs €4; adv bkg; red long stay. "On edge of lake in beautiful area; ltd facs low ssn." ♦ 1 Jun-11 Sep. € 28.00   2005*

SALLES LAVAUGUYON, LES see Rochechouart *7B3*

SALLES SUR VERDON, LES *10E3* (500m Rural) **Camping La Source, 83630 Les Salles-sur-Verdon [04 94 70 20 40; fax 04 94 70 20 74; contact@camping-lasource.com; www.provence-campings.com/verdon/lasource]** Fr Moustiers on D957, site sp in vill via rd round vill. Med, hdg/mkd pitch, hdstg, pt terr; pt shd; wc (some cont); chem disp; child/baby facs; serviced pitches; shwrs inc; el pnts (10A) €3.50 (poss rev pol); gas; lndtte; ice; shop, rest, snacks, bar 500m; BBQ;playgrnd; TV rm; dir access to lake; lake sw & shgl beach adj; watersports; canoe hire; dogs €2; phone; Eng spkn; adv bkg; quiet; cc acc; red low ssn; CCI. "Excel facs; superb situation; well-run site conv Gorges du Verdon; direct access to vill square; friendly, helpful owners; gates clsd 2200-0700 & recep clsd 1200-1400 (Jul/Aug)." ♦ 1 Apr-10 Oct. € 15.00
                2007*

> As soon as we get home I'm going to post all these site report forms to the editor for inclusion in next year's guide. I don't want to miss the September deadline.

SALLES SUR VERDON, LES *10E3* (N Rural) **Camp Municipal Les Ruisses, 83630 Les Salles-sur-Verdon [04 98 10 28 15; fax 04 98 10 28 16]** Fr Moustiers foll D957, site on L just bef Les Salles. Lge, mkd pitch, pt shd; wc (some cont); shwrs inc; el pnts (6A) €2.70; ice; lndtte; shop, snacks, bar high ssn; playgrnd; shgl lake 1km; fishing; no adv bkg; quiet; cc acc; CCI. "Pleasant site, easy access to nice lake." ♦ 15 Feb-15 Dec. € 10.50   2004*

SALLES SUR VERDON, LES *10E3* (2km E Rural) **FFCC Camping L'Aigle, Quartier St Pierre, 83630 Aiguines [tel/fax 04 94 84 23 75; www.aiguines. com]** Fr D957 fr Les Salles or Moustiers turn onto D19 & cont for approx 7km. Site sp 1km beyond vill. Rd steep, winding & with hairpins & vill narr for lge o'fits. Med, sl, terr, pt shd; wc; mv service pnt; baby facs; shwrs inc; el pnts (2-10A) €2.50-3.70; lndtte; shops, rest 300m; BBQ; playgrnd; ent barrier; dogs €1.70; phone; Eng spkn; quiet; cc acc; CCI. "Panoramic views of lake; clean, modern facs; steep, twisting access to terr pitches poss diff lge o'fits; highly rec." Easter-30 Sep. € 12.00
                2006*

SALLES SUR VERDON, LES *10E3* (3km E Rural) **Camp Municipal Le Galetas, 83630 Aiguines [tel/fax 04 94 70 20 48; campinglegaletas@aol.com]** Fr S foll D957 twd Moustiers-Ste Marie then take D71 to Aguines & foll sp. Lge, pt shd; wc; chem disp; mv service pnt; shwrs inc; el pnts (6A) €2.50; lndtte; bar; rv sw; watersports. "Site is set back into hills." 1 Apr-15 Nov. € 12.50   2004*

SALLES SUR VERDON, LES *10E3* (W Rural) Camping Les Pins, Lac de Sainte Croix, 83630 Les Salles-sur-Verdon [04 98 10 23 80; fax 04 94 84 23 27; camping.les.pins@wanadoo.fr; www.campinglespins.com] Fr Moustiers on D957 to Les Salles-sur-Verdon. Site clearly sp in vill, via track round vill. Med, hdg/mkd pitch, hdstg, terr, pt shd; wc; chem disp; mv service pnt; serviced pitches; baby facs; shwrs inc; el pnts (6A) inc; gas; lndtte; ice; shop 200m, tradsmn; bar; playgrnd; shgl beach & lake sw 200m; fishing; canoe hire; watersports; dogs €1.80; Eng spkn; adv bkg; quiet; cc acc; red low ssn/CCI. "On shore of Lake of Ste Croix; marvellous views; gd touring base; excel, friendly site." ♦ 1 Apr-18 Oct. € 21.40   2007*

See advertisement

> The opening dates and prices on this campsite have changed. I'll send a site report form to the editor for the next edition of the guide.

SALON DE PROVENCE *10E2* (12km SE) **FFCC** Camping Durance et Luberon, Domaine du Vergon, 13370 Mallemort [04 90 59 13 36; fax 04 90 57 46 62; duranceluberon@aol.com; www. campingduranceluberon.com] Fr Salon take N538 (N) for approx 6km; turn E onto D17/D23 twd Mallemort; go strt at N7 rnabt, into Mallemort cent; site sp fr there. Med, hdg/mkd pitch, pt shd; wc (some cont); chem disp (wc); mv service pnt; shwrs inc; el pnts inc (6-10A) €3-3.60; ice; gas; lndtte; sm shop & 3km; tradsmn; rest adj; snacks; bar; BBQ; playgrnd; htd pool; tennis; cycle hire; horseriding adj; rv fishing 1km; 5% statics; dogs €1.70; phone; Eng spkn; adv bkg; quiet; 10% red long stays; cc not acc; CCI. "Lge pitches; v clean, modern san facs; friendly owners; excel lge pool & baby pool; gd touring base; excel." 1 Apr-15 Oct. € 17.00
2006*

SALON DE PROVENCE *10E2* (3km NW Rural) Camping Nostradamus, Route d'Eyguières, 13300 Salon-de-Provence [04 90 56 08 36; fax 04 90 56 65 05; gilles.nostra@wanadoo.fr; www. camping-nostradamus.com] Exit A54/E80 junc 13 onto D569 N sp Eyguières. After approx 1.5km turn R opp airfield onto D72d, site on R in approx 4km just bef T-junc. Or fr N exit A7 junc 26 dir Salon-de-Provence. Turn R onto D17 for 5km dir Eyguières, then L onto D72, site on L. Med, hdg/mkd pitch, pt shd; wc; chem disp; mv service pnt; baby facs; shwrs inc; el pnts (4-6A) €2.90-5.20; gas; lndtte; ice; shop; tradsmn; rest; snacks; bar; BBQ; playgrnd; pool; paddling pool; games area; entmnt; TV; 15% statics; dogs €2.70; phone; Eng spkn; adv bkg (bkg fee); quiet; cc acc; red low ssn; cc acc; CCI. "Pleasant site; owner v helpful & welcoming, with excel sense of humour!; poss diff access for lge o'fits; gd walking; excel." ♦ 1 Mar-30 Oct. € 16.10 (CChq acc)   2006*

SALORNAY SUR GUYE see Cluny *9A2*

⊞**SALSES LE CHATEAU** *10G1* (1km N Rural) **FFCC** Camp International du Roussillon, 66600 Salses-le-Château [04 68 38 60 72; fax 04 68 52 75 46] Fr N on A9 exit junc 40 on D6009/D900 (N9) dir Perpignan; site on R, N of town. Fr S exit A9 junc 41. Site has hotel, rest & camping. Med, hdg pitch, hdstg, pt shd; wc; chem disp; shwrs inc; el pnts (5-6A) €2.50-4 (poss rev pol); gas; lndtte; ice; shops 2km; tradsmn; rest; snacks; bar; BBQ (no elec); playgrnd; pool; 20% statics; dogs €2; phone; Eng spkn; adv bkg; some rlwy noise; 10% red 15+ days; cc acc; CCI. "Gd local wine sold at recep; red facs low ssn; on wine rte for Languedoc Roussillon & Hérault; sh walk to castle; popular NH." ♦ ltd. € 16.60   2007*

SALVETAT SUR AGOUT, LA *8F4* (N Rural) **Camping de la Blaquière, Route de Lacaune, 34330 La Salvetat-sur-Agout** [tel/fax 04 67 97 61 29 or 04 67 24 71 08; jerome@campingblaquiere.com; www.blaquiere.fr.st] Fr Lacaune S on D607 to site in La Salvetat. Sp on ent to vill. Fr S heading N on D907 foll site sps thro vill, site on L on rvside just after sm supmkt. Med, mkd pitch, shd; wc; chem disp (wc); baby facs; shwrs inc; el pnts €2.80; ice lndtte; shop, rest etc in vill; BBQ; playgrnd; rv sw adj; lake sw, fishing, watersports 3km; tennis; horseriding; 5% statics; adv bkg; quiet; CCI. "Spectacular scenery, esp for walking in Hérault National Park; friendly owner." 1 Jun-31 Aug. € 9.50
2006*

SALVETAT SUR AGOUT, LA *8F4* (4km N Rural) **Camping Goudal, Route de Lacaune, La Gâche, 34330 La Salvetat-sur-Agout** [04 67 97 60 44; fax 04 67 97 62 68; info@goudal.com; www.goudal. com] Fr St Pons-de-Thomières take D907 N dir Lacaune. Go thro La Salvetat, site sp. Med, mkd pitch, pt sl, terr, pt shd; wc; chem disp; mv service pnt; shwrs inc; el pnts (6A) €2.50; gas; lndtte; ice; shop; rest high ssn; BBQ; playgrnd; child entmnt high ssn; some statics; dogs €1.50; poss cr; Eng spkn; adv bkg; quiet; CCI. "Friendly Dutch owners; spacious site in woodland; lovely location; vg." 1 May-30 Sep. € 14.95
2005*

SALVETAT SUR AGOUT, LA *8F4* (10km E Rural) **Camping Le Pioch, 34330 Fraisse-sur-Agout** [04 67 97 61 72; NICO-OUDHOF@wanadoo.fr] Fr Salvetat take D14 E twd Fraisse-sur-Agout. In 6km look for sp on L (2km bef Fraise). Site is up narr, steep rd but with passing places. Med, pt sl, pt shd; wc; shwrs inc; el pnts (6A) €2.50; gas; lndtte; shop; tradsmn; rest; snacks; bar; BBQ; playgrnd; dogs; Eng spkn; adv bkg; quiet; CCI. "Excel walking area." 1 May-1 Oct. € 11.50
2005*

SAMEON see St Amand les Eaux *3B4*

⊞**SAMOENS** *9A3* (750m S Rural) **Camping Caravaneige Le Giffre, La Glière, 74340 Samoëns** [04 50 34 41 92; fax 04 50 34 98 84; camping@ samoens.com; www.camping-samoens.com] Leave A40 at junc 15 sp Fillinges/St Jeoire. Foll D907 thro Taninges E for 11km, sp Samoëns. At W town boundary turn R immed after wooden arch over rd, foll sp to Parc des Loisirs. Site on R after sw pool & park. Lge, mkd pitch, pt shd; htd wc (few cont); chem disp; shwrs inc; el pnts (6-10A) €3-4.50; gas 3km; lndtte; ice; shops 750m; tradsmn; rest, snacks adj; playgrnd; htd pool adj; fishing lake adj; drying rm; ski navette 25m; tennis; 5% statics; dogs €2; phone; poss cr; adv bkg ess high ssn (dep req); quiet; cc acc; red CCI. "Superb situation surrounded by mountains; friendly staff; v quiet; simple but excel snacks & rest; some facs ltd low ssn; on arr, park on rdside - book in bef ent site; recep open 0800-1200 & 1400-1800; gondola stn 400m fr gate." € 16.00
2007*

⊞**SAMOENS** *9A3* (5km W Rural) **Camp Municipal Lac et Montagne, 74440 Verchaix** [04 50 90 10 12; fax 04 50 54 39 60] Fr Taninges take D907 sp Samoëns for 6km, site to R of main rd in Verchaix. Med, shd; shwrs; el pnts (10A) €7.40; lndtte; ice; shops nr; rest, bar adj; playgrnd; rv & lake adj; tennis; mini-golf; some statics; adv bkg; quiet. "Gd base Haute Savoie; recep closd 1230-1430; car park by barrier; dep req for barrier." ♦ € 8.30
2007*

SAMOREAU see Fontainebleau *4E3*

SAMPZON see Vallon Pont d'Arc *9D2*

SANARY SUR MER *10F3* (4km NE) **Campasun Mas de Pierredon, 652 Chemin Raoul Coletta, 83110 Sanary-sur-Mer** [04 94 74 25 02; fax 04 94 74 61 42; pierredon@campasun.com; www.campasun-pierredon.fr] Take D11 fr Sanary, cross m'way & 1st L. Site on R in approx 1km. Med, shd; htd wc; chem disp; mv service pnt; shwrs inc; el pnts (10A) inc; ice; lndtte; shop; supmkt 800m; rest; snacks; bar; playgrnd; htd pool; paddling pool; waterslides; beach 3km; tennis; wifi internet; entmnt; TV; dogs €4; poss cr; adv bkg rec; rd noise; red low ssn; red CCI. "Gd family site." ♦ 1 Apr-30 Sep. € 35.00
2007*

SANARY SUR MER *10F3* (1.5km W Coastal) **Campasun Parc Mogador, Chemin de Beaucours, 83110 Sanary-sur-Mer** [04 94 74 53 16; fax 04 94 74 10 58; mogador@campasum.com; www. campasun-mogador.fr] Fr A50 exit junc 12 dir Bandol. Camping sp on R bef Sanary (for 2 sites). Lge, pt shd; htd wc; mv service pnt; shwrs inc; el pnts (10A) inc; gas; lndtte; shop; rest; snacks; bar; playgrnd; htd pool; paddling pool; shgl beach 800m; fishing, watersports 1km; games area; entmnt; TV; 30% statics; dogs €4 (not acc Jul/Aug); adv bkg rec; quiet; red low ssn. "Excel, modern san facs." 15 Mar-4 Nov & 15 Dec-2 Jan. € 35.00 (CChq acc)
2007*

SANARY SUR MER *10F3* (3km W Coastal) **Camping Les Girelles, 1003 Chemin de Beaucours, 83110 Sanary-sur-Mer** [04 94 74 13 18; fax 04 94 74 60 04; www.lesgirelles.com] Fr Sanary on D559 to Bandols; site on L, well sp. Med, mkd pitch, terr, pt shd; wc; shwrs inc; el pnts (4A) €3.70; gas; lndtte; shop; snacks; bar; no BBQ; playgrnd; paddling pool; shgl beach adj; some statics; dogs €4; poss cr; quiet; CCI ess. "Gd site in 2 parts; lower level overlooks bay but haphazard & dusty; upper level better." Easter-25 Sep. € 23.00
2005*

SANCERRE *4G3* (4km N Rural) **Camping Le René Foltzer**, 18300 St Satur [02 48 54 04 67 or 02 48 54 02 61 (Mairie); fax 02 48 54 01 30; otsi. saint.satur@wanadoo.fr; www.sancerre.net/saint-satur] Fr Sancerre on D955 thro cent St Satur & St Thibault. Turn L immed bef Loire bdge. Site on R in 100m. Med, hdg pitch, shd; wc; chem disp; shwrs inc; el pnts (10A) €2.55; gas; lndtte; shop 500m; rest 500m; playgrnd; pool 500m; rv sw, canoe hire adj; tennis; entmnt; golf 1km; 50% statics; poss cr; some Eng spkn; adv bkg (dep req); quiet; CCI. "Friendly & helpful staff; gd san facs; mixed reports on water temperature - poss lukewarm, poss v hot; some sm pitches & some with rv view; gates clsd 2200-0700; recep clsd 1200-1600; poss itinerants; rvside walks; gd touring cent; vg." ♦ 1 May-30 Sep. € 8.40   2006*

SANCHEY see Epinal *6F2*

SANDUN see Guérande *2G3*

SANGUINET *7D1* (3km N Rural) **Camping Lou Broustaricq**, Route de Langeot, 40460 Sanguinet [05 58 82 74 82; fax 05 58 82 10 74; loubrousta@wanadoo.fr; www.lou-broustaricq.com] Take Arcachon exit off Bordeax-Bayonne m'way. After 5km twd S on D3 & D216 to Sanguinet. Site sp in town off Bordeaux rd. V lge, mkd pitch, pt shd; htd wc (some cont); chem disp; shwrs inc; el pnts (10A) €3.65; lndtte; shop; rest, snacks, bar high ssn; BBQ; playgrnd; pool; waterslide; lake sw & sand beach 500m; watersports; sailing school; tennis; walking tracks; games area; cycle hire; entmnt; child entmnt; golf nr; TV rm; 60% statics; dogs €2.60; Eng spkn; adv bkg (dep req + bkg fee); quiet; red low ssn; cc acc; CCI. "In lovely wooded area; close to freshwater lake with sandy beaches; gd cycle tracks; gd for children; facs poss unclean low ssn; vg." ♦ 16 Mar-15 Nov. € 29.10   2006*

SANGUINET *7D1* (1.5km S Rural) **Camping Le Lac** Sanguinet, 526 Rue de Pinton, 40460 Sanguinet [05 58 82 70 80; fax 05 58 82 14 24; camping. lelac@wanadoo.fr; www.camping-lelac.com or www.campeole.com] Foll Le Lac sp at rndabt in Sanguinet, turn L on lakeside, site on L in 600m. Lge, mkd pitch, pt shd; shwrs inc; el pnts (6-10A) €2.60-3.80; snacks; shops 500m; tradsmn; lndtte; ice; playgrnd; sand beach; lake sw & sailing nrby; dogs €1.85; poss cr; quiet; CCI. "Spacious site in pine woods 2 min walk to lake & beach; cycle path around lake; san facs poss run down low ssn; poss itinerants; friendly, helpful staff." 1 Apr-15 Oct. € 13.25   2006*

SANGUINET *7D1* (2km SW) **Camping Les Grands Pins**, Route du Lac, 40460 Sanguinet [05 58 78 61 74; fax 05 58 78 69 15; info@camping lesgrandspins.com; www.campinglesgrandspins. com] Foll Le Lac sp at rndabt in Sanguinet. Turn L at lakeside. Site on L in 450m opposite yacht club. Lge, hdg pitch, shd; wc; chem disp; (wc); shwrs inc; child/baby facs; el pnts (3-10A) €3.50; lndtte; ice; rest; snacks; bar; playgrnd; pool; sand beach; lake sw; boating; windsurfing; fishing, canoeing; tennis; mini-golf; cycle hire; TV; 50% statics; dogs; poss cr; Eng spkn; adv bkg; poss noisy; CCI. "Clean site, rest & bar poss clsd low ssn; parking for m'vans adj." ♦ 1 Apr-31 Oct. € 28.50   2004*

⊞**SARLAT LA CANEDA** *7C3* (12km N Rural) **Camping Les Tailladis**, 24200 Marcillac-St Quentin [05 53 59 10 95; fax 05 53 29 47 56; tailladis@aol.com; www.tailladis.com] N fr Sarlat on D704 dir Montignac. After 7km turn L & foll sp to site. Med, hdg pitch, pt sl, terr, pt shd; wc; chem disp; mv service pnt; shwrs inc; el pnts (6A) €3.40; gas; lndtte; ice; shop; rest, snacks & bar (Apr-Oct); pool; lake sw; horseriding; fishing; canoeing; 6% statics; dogs €1.95; phone; poss cr; Eng spkn; adv bkg (dep req & bkg fee); cc acc; red low ssn. "Free glass wine on arrival; meals rec; v friendly & helpful Dutch owners; clean san facs; 1 week horseriding course avail." ♦ € 16.50   2006*

SARLAT LA CANEDA *7C3* (5km NE Rural) **Camping Le Val d'Ussel**, 24200 Proissans [05 53 59 28 73; fax 05 53 29 38 25; valdussel@online.fr; www. valdussel.com & www.homair.com] Fr Sarlat, take D704 N & foll sps to Proissans. Fr Périgueux, take N89 to Thenon, D67 to Chambon, D704 to sps to Proissans. Fr Brive, N89 twd Périgueux, D60 S. Med, pt sl, pt shd; wc; chem disp; shwrs inc; baby facs; el pnts (6-10A) €3-3.75; gas; lndtte; ice; tradsmn; rest; snacks; bar; BBQ; playgrnd; 2 htd pools; lake adj; fishing; shgl beach 15km; tennis; games area; child entmnt; TV; statics; dogs €1.75; adv bkg; quiet; red low ssn. 19 May-25 Sep. € 20.00   2004*

SARLAT LA CANEDA *7C3* (8km NE) **Camping La Châtaigneraie**, 24370 Prats-de-Carlux [05 53 59 03 61 or 05 53 30 29 03 (LS); fax 05 53 29 86 16; lachataigneraie@wanadoo.fr; www.lachataigneraie24.com] Avoid app fr Sarlat as rd winds around steep hill. Instead, take D703 W fr Souillac & in 14km turn R onto D61 sp Carlux. On o'skirts of Carlux fork L onto D47B. Site in 6km on R. Med, hdg/mkd pitch, terr, pt shd; wc; chem disp; baby facs; shwrs inc; el pnts (10A) inc (poss rev pol); gas; lndtte; shop; rest; snacks; sm bar; BBQ (gas only); playgrnd; htd covrd pool; paddling pool; waterslide; fishing; tennis; mini-golf; entmnt & child entmnt (Jul/Aug); games/TV rm; dogs €2; max van length high ssn 7m; poss cr; quiet; cc acc. "Excel; friendly & helpful owners; mkt Sarlat Wed & Sat am; some pitches diff due position of trees; vg pool area; vg san facs." ♦ 1 May-15 Sep. € 28.30 ABS - D13   2007*

France

SARLAT LA CANEDA *7C3* (8km NE Rural)
Camping Maillac, Ste Nathalène, 24200 Sarlat-
la-Canéda [05 53 59 22 12; fax 05 53 29 60 17;
campingmaillac@wanadoo.fr; www.camping
maillac.fr] Take D47 out of Sarlat to Ste Nathalène.
After 4km turn L at x-rds (if missed next 2 turnings
also lead to site), v well sp. Med, mkd pitch, pt sl,
pt shd; wc; chem disp; mv service pnt; shwrs inc;
el pnts (6-10A) €3-4.50; gas; Indtte; ice; shop; rest;
snacks; bar; BBQ; playgrnd; pool; paddling pool;
games rm; entmnt; 10% statics; dogs €1.20; poss
cr Jul/Aug; some Eng spkn; adv bkg; quiet; red
low ssn; cc acc; CCI. "Family-run site; spacious
pitches; excel, gd value rest in vill; lovely area."
15 May-30 Sep. € 15.80   2007*

SARLAT LA CANEDA *7C3* (9km NE Rural) Camping
La Palombière, Ste Nathalène, 24200 Sarlat-
la-Canéda [05 53 59 42 34; fax 05 53 28 45 40;
la.palombiere@wanadoo.fr; www.lapalombiere.
fr] Take D47 fr Sarlat to Ste Nathalène, thro vill,
past Mill Rest, fork L on o'skts by cemetary. Site
sp on R in 300m - sharp R turn & access poss diff.
Med, terr, shd; wc; chem disp; baby facs; shwrs
inc; el pnts (10A) €3; Indtte; shop; rest; snacks;
bar; BBQ; htd pools; waterslide; tennis; games rm;
games area; mini-golf; entmnt; TV; 70% statics;
dogs €2; Eng spkn; adv bkg; quiet; 10% red low
ssn. "Lovely, well-run site in beautiful setting;
friendly owners; immac san facs; vg rest with views;
vg sport/play facs; tour ops on site; poss diff for lge
o'fits due trees, narr site rds & pitch sizes; highly
rec." ♦ 27 Apr-15 Sep. € 24.30   2006*

Before we move on, I'm going to fill in some site report forms and post them off to the editor, otherwise they won't arrive in time for the deadline at the end of September.

SARLAT LA CANEDA *7C3* (10km NE Rural)
Camping Les Péneyrals, Le Poujol, 24590
St Crépin-et-Carlucet [05 53 28 85 71; fax
05 53 28 80 99; camping.peneyrals@wanadoo.fr;
www.peneyrals.com] Fr Sarlat N on D704; D60 E
dir Salignac-Eyvignes to Le Poujol; S to St Crépin.
Site sp. Lge, hdg pitch, pt sl, terr, pt shd; htd wc;
chem disp; mv service pnt; all serviced pitch; baby
facs; shwrs inc; el pnts (5-10A) €3.10-3.70; Indtte;
ice; shop; rest; snacks; bar; playgrnd; 4 pools (1 htd,
covrd); paddling pool; waterslide; fishing; tennis;
games area; mini-golf; boules; entmnt; 50% statics;
dogs €2; phone adj; Eng spkn; adv bkg; quiet; red
low ssn; cc acc;red low ssn. "Friendly owners;
superb family & touring site." ♦ 15 May-15 Sep.
€ 25.90   2006*

SARLAT LA CANEDA *7C3* (12km NE Rural) Flower
Camping Le Temps de Vivre, Route de Carlux,
24590 Salignac-Eyvignes [tel/fax 05 53 28 93 21;
contact@temps-de-vivre.com; www.temps-de-
vivre.com] Fr Sarlat N on D704, bear R onto D60
to Salignac-Eyvigues. Fr Salignac take D61 S dir
Carlux, site sp in 1.5km on R. Sm, mkd/hdg pitch,
terr, pt shd; wc; chem disp; mv service pnt; baby
facs; fam bthrm; shwrs inc; el pnts (10A) €3; gas;
ice; Indtte; shop; tradsmn; BBQ; supmkt 2km; rest &
bar (high ssn); snacks; pool; playgrnd; games area;
golf; tennis; fishing; dogs €2; 40% statics; poss cr;
quiet; phone; adv bkg (fee); Eng spkn; cc acc; CCI.
"Attractive, clean, well-kept site; gd touring base
Dordogne; friendly, helpful owners; highly rec." ♦
29 Mar-1 Nov. € 18.50   2007*

SARLAT LA CANEDA *7C3* (1km E) Camping Les
Périères, Rue Jean Gabin, 24200 Sarlat-la-
Canéda [05 53 59 05 84; fax 05 53 28 57 51; les-
perieres@wanadoo.fr; www.lesperieres.com]
Site on R of D47 to Proissans & Ste Nathalène.
NB steep access rds. Med, mkd pitch, terr, pt shd;
wc; mv service pnt; sauna; baby facs; shwrs inc;
el pnts (6A) inc; gas; Indry rm; ice; shop; tradsmn;
bar; BBQ (gas/charcoal); playgrnd; 2 pools
(1 htd covrd); games rm; tennis; Eng spkn; adv bkg;
quiet; cc acc +2% charge. "Walking dist Sarlat; in
grounds of holiday vill; every facility; spotlessly
clean; friendly & helpful; excel sw facs; excel site;
poss not suitable disabled as steep site rds." ♦
Easter-30 Sep. € 34.40 (3 persons)   2007*

SARLAT LA CANEDA *7C3* (6km E Rural) Camping
Les Grottes de Roffy, 24200 Ste Nathalène
[05 53 59 15 61; fax 05 53 31 09 11; roffy@
perigord.com; www.roffy.fr] Fr N end of Sarlat
take D47 NE for Ste Nathalène. Site on R 1km bef
vill. Fr Souillac (E) exit junc 55 onto N703/704 to
Carlux. Turn R onto D61 then D47 to Ste Nathalène,
site thro vill on L. Lge, hdg/mkd pitch, terr, pt shd;
htd wc; chem disp; baby facs; shwrs inc; el pnts
(6A) inc; gas; Indtte; ice; shop 5km; tradsmn; rest;
playgrnd; 4 pools; tennis; entmnt; child entmnt;
40% statics (inc tour ops); dogs €1.90; extra for
'comfort' pitches; Eng spkn; adv bkg (ess Jul/Aug
- write Jan 1); noisy high ssn; CCI. "Excel rest &
shop; helpful staff." ♦ 1 May-18 Sep. € 25.05
                                            2005*

SARLAT LA CANEDA 7C3 (10km E Rural) **Camping Les Ombrages de la Dordogne, Rouffillac, 24370 Carlux [05 53 28 62 17; fax 05 53 28 62 18; ombrages@perigord.com; www.ombrages.fr]** 12km W thro Souillac on D703. Turn L at x-rds in Rouffillac & immed turn L bef rv bdge into site. Med, some mkd pitch, pt shd; wc; chem disp; shwrs inc; el pnts (6-10A) €2.50-3.50; gas 1km; lndtte; ice; shop 1km; tradsmn (high ssn); rest 500m; snacks; bar; BBQ; playgrnd; pool adj; rv sw adj; fishing; tennis; games area; cycle & canoe hire; internet; TV rm; 2% statics; dogs €1.50; phone; poss cr; Eng spkn; adv bkg; quiet but some rd noise; cc acc; CCI. "Pleasant, well-maintained, rvside site; enthusiastic owners live on site; pitching poss diff due trees; facs poss stretched high ssn; canoe trips arranged; cycle track; vg." 1 Apr-28 Oct. € 12.50
2006*

There aren't many sites open this early in the year. We'd better phone ahead to check that the one we're heading for is actually open.

SARLAT LA CANEDA 7C3 (12km E Rural) **Camp Municipal Le Bourniou, 24370 St Julien-de-Lampon [05 53 29 83 39 or 05 53 29 46 11 (Mairie); fax 05 53 59 69 18; camping-le-bourniou@tiscali. fr; www.camping-bourniou.com]** Fr Sarlat-la-Canéda take D704/703 E, cross rv at Rouffillac sp St Julien-de-Lampon. Site on L on rvside 200m after bdge. Med, mkd pitch, pt shd; wc; chem disp; shwrs inc; el pnts (6A) €2.50; lndtte; ice; shop 500m; tradsmn; rest, snacks & bar 200m; playgrnd; rv sw adj; fishing; canoe hire; tennis 500m; some statics; dogs; phone; Eng spkn; quiet; CCI. "Lovely location with mature trees; poss tight pitches for lge o'fits; football stadium on site & public use rest, bar & picnic area; site is NH for canoe safaris; gd walking." 1 Jun-15 Sep. € 12.60
2007*

SARLAT LA CANEDA 7C3 (12km E Rural) **Camping Le Mondou, 24370 St Julien-de-Lampon [tel/fax 05 53 29 70 37; lemondou@camping-dordogne. info; www.camping-dordogne.info]** Fr Sarlat-la-Canéda take D704/D703 E; cross rv at Rouffillac, ent St Julien-de-Lampon & turn L at x-rds; site sp on R in 2km. Med, hdg/mkd pitch, pl, pt shd; wc; chem disp; mv service pnt; baby facs; shwrs inc; el pnts (6-10A) €2.50-3.50; gas 700m; lndtte; shop 2km; tradsmn; rest; snacks; bar; BBQ; playgrnd; pool & paddling pool; rv sw, fishing & watersports 300m; games rm; games area; cycle hire; internet; 10% statics; dogs €1; phone; poss cr; Eng spkn; adv bkg rec, dep req; quiet. "Beautiful views; friendly, helpful owners; sm, uneven pitches; gd cycle paths." ♦ 1 May-15 Oct. € 13.20
2006*

SARLAT LA CANEDA 7C3 (5km SE Rural) **Camping Les Acacias, Route de Cahors, 24200 Sarlat-la-Canéda [05 53 31 08 50; fax 05 53 59 29 30; camping-acacias@wanadoo.fr; www.acacias. fr]** Foll sp La Canéda vill & site fr D704 S fr Sarlat. NB Last few metres of app v narr rd. Med, hdg/ mkd pitch, pt sl, shd; wc; chem disp; mv service pnt; baby facs; shwrs inc; el pnts (6A) €2.80; gas; lndtte; ice; supmkt 3km; tradsmn; rest; snacks; bar; playgrnd; 2 pools; entmnt; some statics; dogs €1.50; phone; bus; adv bkg; quiet; cc acc; CCI. "Clean, modern san facs; helpful, enthusiastic owners; ideal touring base; gd mkt in Sarlat Wed & Sat." 1 Apr-30 Sep. € 13.50
2006*

SARLAT LA CANEDA 7C3 (7km SE Rural) **Camping Aqua Viva, 24200 Carsac-Aillac [05 53 31 46 00 or 04 99 57 20 25; aqua-viva@perigord.com or aquaviva@village-center.com; www.aquaviva.fr or www.village-center.com/aquaviva]** Fr N or S take N20/A20 to Souillac; the foll D703 beside Rv Dordogne twd Sarlat-la-Caneda. Just past Calviac-en-Périgord, turn R onto D704a; site on L in 3km. Ent easily missed; app with care as busy rd. Lge, mkd pitch, pt terr, pt sl, pt shd; wc; chem disp; baby facs; shwrs inc; el pnts (10A) inc (poss rev pol); gas; lndtte; ice; shop; rest; snacks; bar; BBQ; playgrnd; pool; sw & boating in sm lake; fishing; cycle hire; games rm; internet; many statics; dogs €3; recep 0900-1900; poss cr; Eng spkn; adv bkg ess; cc acc; CCI. "Nice, friendly staff; excel, lively site for families; basic but gd value rest; gd sports facs; facs stretched high ssn & ltd low ssn." ♦ 21 Apr-16 Sep. € 30.00
2007*

SARLAT LA CANEDA 7C3 (7km SE Rural) **Camping Le Rocher de la Cave, 24200 Carsac-Aillac [05 53 28 14 26; fax 05 53 28 27 10; rocherdelacave@wanadoo.fr; www.rocher delacave.com]** Fr Sarlat-la-Canéda take D704 S twd Carsac-Aillac & turn L bef vill. Follow sp. Med, hdg/mkd pitch, pt shd; wc; shwrs inc; el pnts (10A) €2.60; gas; lndtte; shops 2km; tradsmn; rest; snacks; bar; playgrnd; pool; rv sw; canoe hire; tennis 500m; 5% statics; dogs; phone; quiet. "Rv site with chalets avail; 20% red low ssn; gd." ♦ ltd. 1 May-15 Sep. € 15.30
2004*

SARLAT LA CANEDA 7C3 (8km SE Rural) **Camping Le Plein Air des Bories, 24200 Carsac-Aillac [tel/ fax 05 53 28 15 67; camping.lesbories@wanadoo. fr]** Take D704 SE fr Sarlat sp Gourdon; diff RH turn to site after Carsac vill. Easier access on D703 fr Vitrac. Med, pt sl, shd; wc (male cont); baby facs; shwrs; el pnts (3-6A) inc; gas; lndtte; sm shop & 1.5km; tradsmn; snacks; bar; htd pool; rv sw, canoe hire, boating & fishing; tennis 700m; dogs €1.30; poss cr; Eng spkn; quiet; CCI. "Clean, shady rvside site; friendly owners." ♦ 1 Jun-15 Sep. € 18.00
2004*

France

SARLAT LA CANEDA *7C3* (8km SE Rural) Camping Les Chênes Verts, Route de Sarlat, 24370 Calviac-en-Périgord [05 53 59 21 07; fax 05 53 31 05 51; chenes-verts@wanadoo.fr; www.chenes-verts.com] S fr Sarlat on A20 leave at Souillac exit. Join D703 heading W twd Sarlat; branch R onto D704a soon after Calviac-en-Périgord, site on R in 2km. Or take D704/704A SE fr Sarlat. Site in 8km on L; clearly sp & flags at ent. Med, hdg/mkd pitch, pt sl, pt shd; wc; chem disp; mv service pnt; baby facs; shwrs inc; el pnts (6A) inc (25m cable rec); gas; lndtte; sm shop; tradsmn; rest; snacks; bar; BBQ (gas/charcoal only); playgrnd; 2 pools (1 htd, covrd); paddling pool; canoeing; cycle hire; golf 7km; games area; games rm; entmnt; TV; 70 statics (sep area); no dogs; recep 0830-1200 & 1400-1900; Eng spkn; adv bkg; quiet but some noise fr bar; red long stay; cc acc; CCI. "Pleasant, peaceful site; gd size pitches but sandy, so muddy when wet; v helpful owners; wine-tastings; excel pool; mkt Sat Sarlat; basic san facs, ltd low ssn; v gd location for Dordogne." ♦ 1 Apr-30 Sep. € 30.30 ABS - D04   2007*

SARLAT LA CANEDA *7C3* (9km SE Rural) Camping La Butte, 24250 La Roque-Gageac [tel/fax 05 53 28 30 28; contact@camping-la-butte.com; www.camping-la-butte.com] On D703 1km fr Vitrac bet Vitrac & Cénac. Med, hdg pitch, shd; wc; shwrs inc; el pnts (4-10A) €2.90-3.50; gas; lndtte; ice; shop; rest; snacks; bar; BBQ; pool; rv sw; fishing; boating; dogs €1/70; poss cr; adv bkg; red low ssn. "Many interesting chateaux & towns in easy reach; in beautiful part of Dordogne." Easter-Oct. € 16.20   2007*

SARLAT LA CANEDA *7C3* (10km SE Rural) Camping Les Granges, 24250 Groléjac [05 53 28 11 15; fax 05 53 28 57 13; contact@lesgranges-fr.com; www.lesgranges-fr.com] Fr Sarlat take D704 SE, sp Gourdon. Site sp nr cent of Groléjac on R. Care on acute corner after rlwy bdge. Med, hdg, terr, pt shd; wc; chem disp; baby facs; serviced pitches; shwrs inc; el pnts (6A) inc; gas; lndtte; shop; rest; snacks; bar; playgrnd; htd pool; paddling pool; cycle hire; entmnt; mini-golf; rv & lake fishing 1km; TV; 40% statics; dogs €3; poss cr; Eng spkn; adv bkg; cc acc; red low ssn; CCI. "Historical & beautiful area; vg site & facs." 28 Apr-16 Sep. € 27.20 (4 persons)
                                                  2007*

See advertisement on page 561

SARLAT LA CANEDA *7C3* (13km SE Rural) Camp Municipal Le Roc Percé, Plan d'Eau, 24250 Groléjac [05 53 59 48 70; fax 05 53 29 39 74] On D704 SE fr Sarlat twd Goudon, Groléjac in 11km. In vill cent, foll sp 'Plan d'Eau'; pass thro vill & turn R in front of Le Marais Rest, in 100m turn L dir Nabirat. Site on L in 500m. Med, hdg pitch, pt shd; wc; chem disp; baby facs; shwrs; el pnts (10A) inc; gas 1km; lndtte; shop 1km; rest 500m; playgrnd; sand beach; lake sw, fishing & watersports; dogs; Eng spkn; adv bkg; quiet; no cc acc CCI. "Popular site on created lake with artificial sand beach; rest walking dist; v quiet (lonely) low ssn." ♦ 15 Jun-15 Sep. € 12.00
                                                  2005*

Did you know you can fill in site report forms on the Club's website — www.caravanclub.co.uk?

SARLAT LA CANEDA *7C3* (13km SE Rural) Camping à la Ferme La Noyeraie, Le Barthe, 24250 Groléjac [05 53 28 14 59] Fr Sarlat SE twds Gourdon on D704; in Groléjac turn L sp Milhac; site well sp in 1km. Access rd steep, narr & winding. Sm, pt sl, pt shd; wc; shwrs inc; el pnts (10A) inc; gas, shop 2km; lndtte; ice; playgrnd; pool; TV rm; dogs €0.50; Eng spkn; adv bkg; quiet; no cc acc; CCI. "Excel; pleasant, tranquil site for touring Dordogne, Cahors; v helpful owners; farm produce avail; v clean facs." ♦ Apr-Sep. € 12.50   2005*

SARLAT LA CANEDA *7C3* (6km S Rural) Camping La Bouysse de Caudon, 24200 Vitrac [05 53 28 33 05; fax 05 53 30 38 52; info@labouysse.com; www.labouysse.com] S fr Sarlat on D46 dir Vitrac. At Vitrac 'port' bef bdge turn L onto D703 sp Carsac. In 2km turn R & foll site sp, site on L. Well sp. Med, hdg/mkd pitch, pt shd; wc; chem disp; baby facs; shwrs inc; el pnts (6-10A) €3.40-3.90; gas; lndtte; shop; rest; snacks; bar; BBQ; playgrnd; pool; rv sw & shgl beach; fishing; canoe hire; tennis; games area; internet; entmnt; 8% statics; dogs €1.70; phone; poss cr; Eng spkn; adv bkg (dep); quiet; cc acc; red low ssn; CCI. "Excel, family-run site on Rv Dordogne; helpful staff; plenty of gd, clean san facs; many Bastides in area." ♦ 1 Apr-30 Sep. € 18.50   2007*

France

SARLAT LA CANEDA *7C3* (8km S Rural) Camping Domaine de Soleil-Plage, Caudon-par-Montfort, 24200 Vitrac [05 53 28 33 33 or 06 07 33 96 54 (mob LS); fax 05 53 28 30 24; info@soleilplage.fr; www.soleilplage.fr] On D46, 6km S of Sarlat twd Vitrac, turn L onto D703, to Château Montfort, R to site dir Caudon, sp. Site beyond Camping La Bouysse on rvside, 2km E of Vitrac. If coming fr Souillac on D703, when app Montfort rd v narr with overhanging rock faces. Narr access rds on site. Med, hdg pitch, pt shd; wc; chem disp; mv service pnt; baby facs; serviced pitches; shwrs inc; el pnts (10A) €3.50; gas; Indtte; ice; shop & 6km; rest; snacks; bar; BBQ; playgrnd; htd pool; paddling pool; waterslide; rv sw & sand beach adj; fishing; canoeing; tennis; cycle hire; mini-golf; golf 1km; horseriding 5km; games rm; child entmnt; internet; TV; 45% statics; dogs €2.50; phone; Eng spkn; adv bkg ess Jul/Aug; quiet; cc acc; red low ssn/groups; CCI. "Lovely site in beautiful location; v friendly, welcoming owner; variety of pitches - extra for serviced/rvside; san facs v clean; superb aquatic complex; v shd pitches by rv; muddy when wet; farm produce avail; excel." ♦ 31 Mar-30 Sep. € 37.00

2007*

See advertisement above

SARLAT LA CANEDA *7C3* (9km S Rural) Camping Beau Rivage, Gaillardou, 24250 La Roque-Gageac [05 53 28 32 05; fax 05 53 29 63 56; camping.beau.rivage@wanadoo.fr; www.camping-beau-rivage.com] On S side of D703, 1km W of Vitrac, E of Elf petrol stn, adj Rv Dordogne. Lge, mkd pitch, shd; htd wc (some cont); chem disp; baby facs; shwrs inc; el pnts (6A) inc; gas; Indtte; ice; shop; rest 200m; snacks; bar; playgrnd; pool; rv sw & beach; canoeing; tennis; games area; cycle hire; horseriding; archery; golf 2km; entmnt; TV; some statics; dogs €1.60; phone; poss cr; adv bkg rec high ssn; quiet. ♦ 1 Apr-30 Sep. € 21.85

2006*

SARLAT LA CANEDA *7C3* (9km S Rural) Camping La Plage, 83 Près La Roque-Gageac, 24220 Vézac [05 53 29 50 83; fax 05 53 30 31 63] On banks of Rv Dordogne, 500m W of La Roque-Gageac on D703. Med, mkd pitch, shd; wc; chem disp (wc); shwrs inc; el pnts (3-10A) €2.10-4.20; gas; sm shop 1km; BBQ; playgrnd; shgl beach & rv sw; fishing; canoeing; poss cr; adv bkg; quiet; CCI. "Attractive site; excel pitches; basic san facs but v clean; ltd facs low ssn; highly rec." 1 Apr-30 Sep. € 13.00

2006*

SARLAT LA CANEDA *7C3* (9km S Rural) Camping Le Pech de Caumont, 24250 Cénac-et-St-Julien [05 53 28 21 63 or 05 53 28 30 67; fax 05 53 29 99 73; jmilhac@pech-de-caumont.com; www.pech-de-caumont.com] D46 fr Sarlat to Cénac, cross rv & cont on D46 thro Cénac; site ent on L 500m past End of Vill sp. Do not go thro Domme. Med, hdg/mkd pitch, pt sl, terr, pt shd; wc; chem disp; shwrs inc; el pnts (6A) €3.10; Indtte; ice; shops 1km; snacks & sm bar (high ssn); BBQ; playgrnd; pool; rv sw 2km; TV rm; 20% statics; dogs; phone; poss cr; Eng spkn; adv bkg; quiet; red low ssn; cc acc; CCI. "Excel views most pitches; tidy site; modern, clean san facs; v helpful owners; family-run site, popular with British; rest & shops in vill; excel." 1 Apr-30 Sep. € 15.45

2007*

SARLAT LA CANEDA *7C3* (10km S Rural) Camp Municipal, 24250 Cénac-et-St Julien [05 53 28 31 91 or 05 53 31 41 31 (Mairie)] D46 fr Sarlat to Vitrac then Cénac; cross rv & site on L on ent Cénac. Med, mkd pitch, pt shd; wc; chem disp; shwrs inc; el pnts (6A) €2.43 (poss long lead req); Indtte; shop, rest, snacks, bar 200m; rv sw, boating & fishing adj; quiet; no cc acc. "V pleasant, rvside site; lovely vill nrby with gd rest, shops etc; site opens earlier if demand; expensive for ltd facs low ssn; facs clean but well-used, superb location compensates." 1 Jun-15 Sep. € 11.06

2007*

SARLAT LA CANEDA *7C3* (10km S Rural) **Camping La Rivière, 24250 Domme [05 53 28 33 46; fax 05 53 29 56 04; contact@camping-riviere-domme.com; www.camping-riviere-domme.com]** Fr Sarlat take D46 to Vitrac. Cross rv bdge on D46E. In 1km at T-junc turn R on D50 & in 1km turn R at sp into site. Sm, pt shd; wc; chem disp; shwrs inc; el pnts (10A) €2.60 (poss rev pol); lndtte; shops 4km; playgrnd; pool; games area; few statics; Eng spkn; adv bkg; quiet; red low ssn. "Generous pitches; v pleasant owner; modern san facs; excel disabled facs; many walks directly fr site." ♦ 30 Mar-30 Sep. € 9.75   2007*

SARLAT LA CANEDA *7C3* (10km S Rural) **Camping Le Bosquet, La Rivière, 24250 Domme [05 53 28 37 39; fax 05 53 29 41 95; info@lebousquet.com; www.lebosquet.com]** Fr Sarlat take D46 S to Vitrac cross rv on D46E. Sp at junc, site 500m on R. Sm, hdg/mkd pitch, pt shd, wc; chem disp; shwrs inc; el pnts (6A) €2.50 (long lead poss req); gas; lndtte; sm shop; tradsmn; snacks; pool; rv sw & fishing 500m; 50% statics; dogs €1; Eng spkn; adv bkg; quiet; CCI. "Friendly, helpful owners; excel clean facs but poss stretched high ssn; gd shd but sm pitches; gd value in popular area." ♦ 1 Apr-30 Sep. € 11.80   2005*

SARLAT LA CANEDA *7C3* (10km S Rural) **Camping Le Perpetuum, 24250 Domme [05 53 28 35 18; fax 05 53 29 63 64; luc.parsy@wanadoo.fr; www.campingleperpetuum.com]** Fr Sarlat take D46 to Vitrac; cross rv bdge to D46E; in 1km turn R onto D50, R again in 1km at site sp. Med, hdg/mkd pitch, pt shd; wc; chem disp; mv service pnt; baby facs; shwrs inc; el pnts (10A) €3.50; lndry rm; lndtte; ice; shop (farm produce); tradsmn; snacks; bar; BBQ; playgrnd; pool; rv sw (Rv Dordogne); canoeing adj; tennis; games area; entmnt; statics; dogs €1; poss cr; Eng spkn; adv bkg (dep req); quiet; red low ssn; cc acc; CCI. "Relaxed, friendly atmosphere; welcoming & helpful owners; conv many tourist attractions; gd local walks." ♦ 1 May-1 Oct. € 16.60   2007*

SARLAT LA CANEDA *7C3* (12km S Rural) **Camping Bel Ombrage, 24250 St Cybranet [05 53 28 34 14; fax 05 53 59 64 64; belombrage@wanadoo.fr; www.belombrage.com]** S on D57 fr Sarlat to Vézac; then turn L to Castelnaud-la-Chapelle; then fork L onto D57 sp St Cybranet; site on L in 800m outside St Cybranet. Lge, hdg pitch, shd; wc; chem disp; shwrs inc; el pnts (10A) inc; gas 800m; lndtte; tradsmn; shop 800m; rest; snacks; bar; BBQ; playgrnd; 3 pools; paddling pool; rv sw & beach; fishing; canoeing; tennis; cycle hire; horseriding 3km; games area; games/TV rm; library; dogs free; c'vans over 8m not acc high ssn; adv bkg; quiet; cc not acc; CCI. "Attractive, well-managed site; beautiful setting; popular with British; recep clsd lunchtime & after 1900; mkt Thu; ideal base for Dordogne." ♦ 1 Jun-5 Sep. € 21.40 ABS - D01   2007*

SARLAT LA CANEDA *7C3* (4km SW Rural) **Camping Domaine de Loisirs Le Montant, Negralot, Route de Bergerac, 24200 Sarlat-la-Canéda [05 53 59 18 50; fax 05 53 59 37 73; contact@camping-sarlat.com; www.camping-sarlat.com]** Leave Sarlat on D57 dir Bergerac. Turn R opp school 'Pré de Cordy', site in 2.3km, sp. Med, hdg/mkd pitch, hdstg, terr, pt shd; htd wc; chem disp; mv service pnt; baby facs; fam bthrm; shwrs inc; el pnts (6A) €3.60; lndtte; ice; shop 3km; tradsmn; rest; snacks; bar; BBQ; playgrnd; htd, covrd pool; paddling pool; jacuzzi; lake/rv sw & sand beach; canoeing; fishing; games area; games rm; golf nr; wifi internet; entmnt; TV; 5% statics; dogs free; Eng spkn; adv bkg rec high ssn; quiet; cc acc; red low ssn; CCI. "Vg, pleasant site set in heart of Périgord Noir; many sports activities & excursions." ♦ 22 Mar-2 Nov. € 17.60   2007*

See advertisement above

MAISONNEUVE

Situated in a beautiful setting at the border of the river Le Céou and 800 m from the castle of Castelnaud.

Swimming pool • mini golf • snacks • bar • take away meals • grocery. Modern installations.

Open: 22 March - 15 October
Discounts of 10-30% in low season.
Interesting prices for caravan groups in May and June.

Mobile homes for hire.

Phone: 00 33 (0) 5 53 29 51 29
Fax: 00 33 (0) 5 53 30 27 06
www.campingmaisonneuve.com
contact@campingmaisonneuve.com

CAMPING ★★★ MAISONNEUVE
24250 CASTELNAUD-LA-CHAPELLE

France

⊞SARLAT LA CANEDA *7C3* (8km SW Rural) Camping Les Deux Vallées, 24220 Vézac [05 53 29 53 55; fax 05 53 31 09 81; les2v@ perigord.com; www.les-2-valees.com] Fr W leave D703 onto D49 - ignore 1st sp to site & cont onto D57 sp Sarlat. 250m fr junc foll 2nd site sp. Fr E leave D703 onto D57; 250m after junc with D49 turn L & foll sp to site. Med, hdg/mkd pitch, shd; htd wc; chem disp; baby facs; shwrs inc; el pnts (6A) €3.50; ice; gas; lndtte; shop; tradsmn; rest; snacks; bar; BBQ; playgrnd; 3 pools; shgl beach 500m; cycle hire; games rm; entmnt July/Aug; 6% statics; dogs €1.50; Eng spkn; adv bkg ess Jul/Aug (dep req + bkg fee); quiet but rlwy adj; cc acc; red low ssn/ long stay; CCI. "Excel site; helpful, friendly Dutch owners; ltd san facs low ssn; poss uneven pitches & muddy when wet; Beynac Château & caves 1km, Castlenau 3km." ♦ € 17.15   2006*

SARLAT LA CANEDA *7C3* (9km SW Rural) Camping Le Tiradou, Chemin du Grand-Fosse, 24220 St Vincent-de-Cosse [05 53 30 30 73; fax 05 53 31 16 24; francis@letiradou.fr; www. letiradou.fr] Take D703 fr La Roque-Gageac thro Beynac & onto St Vincent; site is 2km fr Beynac on R. Med, hdg/mkd pitch, shd; wc; chem disp (wc); shwrs inc; el pnts (6A) inc; ice; BBQ; lndtte; snacks; bar, shop, tradsmn avail high ssn; playgrnd; pool; rv fishing, boating, watersports & beach adj; TV; quiet; phone; Eng spkn; adv bkg; cc acc. "Gd touring base along Dordogne Rv." ♦ Easter 30 Sep. € 12.50   2004*

This guide relies on site report forms submitted by caravanners like us; we'll do our bit and tell the editor what we think of the campsites we've visited.

As soon as we get home I'm going to post all these site report forms to the editor for inclusion in next year's guide. I don't want to miss the September deadline.

SARLAT LA CANEDA *7C3* (9km SW Rural) Camping La Cabane, 24220 Vézac [05 53 29 52 28; fax 05 53 59 09 15; contact@lacabanedordogne. com; www.lacabanedordogne.com] Fr Sarlat-La-Canéda take D57 thro Vézac. On leaving Vézac turn L immed bef rlwy bdge, site sp on R on bank of Rv Dordogne. Lge, hdg/mkd pitch, pt shd; wc; shwrs inc; el pnts (6-10A) €2;60-3.20; gas; lndtte; ice; shop high ssn; rest & snacks 3km; BBQ; playgrnd; htd covrd pool; rv sw & shgl beach adj; TV rm; internet; some statics; phone; poss cr; Eng spkn; adv bkg (dep req); quiet; cc acc; CCI. "Well shd, rvside site; lge pitches; immac facs; friendly owner; conv all attractions; easy rvside walk to Beynac Château; boat trips, light aircraft flights & canoe hire locally; many sports." ♦ ltd. 1 Apr-30 Oct. € 11.60
2007*

SARLAT LA CANEDA *7C3* (10km SW Rural) Camping Le Capeyrou, 24220 Beynac-et-Cazenac [05 53 29 54 95; fax 05 53 28 36 27; lecapeyrou@ wanadoo.fr; www.campinglecapeyrou.com] Fr W on D703 on R (opp new shops) immed past vill of Beynac. Or fr N on D57 fr Sarlat; in vill immed on L on rv. Med, hdg pitch, pt shd; wc; chem disp; mv service pnt; baby facs; shwrs inc; el pnts (6-10A) €3-4; lndtte; shop & rest adj; snacks; bar; playgrnd; pool; dogs €1: poss cr; Eng spkn; adv bkg; quiet; 20% red low ssn; cc acc. "On banks of Rv Dordogne, rvside walk into attractive vill with castle; clean san facs; excel lge pool; v helpful, friendly owners; towpath to Castelnaud with chateau; walnut farm nrby; excel site." ♦ Easter-30 Sep. € 16.70   2006*

SARLAT LA CANEDA *7C3* (10km SW Rural) Camping-Caravaning Maisonneuve, Vallée de Céou, 24250 Castelnaud-la-Chapelle [05 53 29 51 29; fax 05 53 30 27 06; campmaison@aol.com; www.campingmaisonneuve.com] D57 SW fr Sarlat sp Beynac. Cross Rv Dordogne at Castelnaud; site sp 1km on L out of Castelnaud on D57 twd Daglan. Foll narr rd across bdge (or alt ent sp 500m for vans). Med, hdg/mkd pitch, most shd; htd wc (some cont); chem disp; mv service pnt; child/baby facs; fam bthrm; shwrs inc; el pnts (6-10A) €3.60-4.20; gas; lndtte; ice; shop, rest, snacks & bar high ssn; BBQ; playgrnd; pool; paddling pool; rv & shgl beach; fishing; tennis 2km; mini-golf; games rm; wifi internet; TV rm; no statics; dogs €1; Eng spkn; adv bkg ess high ssn; quiet; cc acc; red low ssn/CCI. "Vg, spacious site with modern facs; helpful owners; lovely rural setting in heart of Périgord Noir; gd walking, cycling." ♦ 22 Mar-15 Oct. € 17.80   2007*

See advertisement on previous page

SARLAT LA CANEDA *7C3* (18km SW Rural) Domaine Le Cro Magnon, La Raisse, 24220 Allas-les-Mines [05 53 29 13 70; fax 05 53 29 15 79; contact@domaine-cro-magnon.com; www.domaine-cro-magnon.com] Fr Sarlat on D57/D703 two Le Buisson turn L onto D48 sp site & Berbiguières. Do not foll any earlier sp to site as rds impassable to c'vans & m'vans. App steep, narr & twisting but gd surface. NB App via Berbiguières only. Med, pt shd; wc; chem disp; baby facs; sauna; shwrs inc; el pnts (6A) inc; gas; lndtte; ice; shop; rest; snacks; bar; BBQ; playgrnd; 2 pools (1 htd covrd); paddling pool; rv fishing 800m; watersports; tennis; cycle hire; mini-golf; games area; entmnt; internet; games/TV rm; dogs €3.40; adv bkg; quiet. ♦ 14 Jun-13 Sep. € 28.00 ABS - D24   2007*

SARLAT LA CANEDA *7C3* (9km W Rural) Camping Le Moulin du Roch, Route des Eyzies, St André d'Allas, 24200 Sarlat-la-Canéda [05 53 59 20 27; fax 05 53 59 20 95; moulin.du.roch@wanadoo.fr; www.moulin-du-roch.com] Fr A20 take exit 55 at Souillac dir Sarlat. At rndabt in Sarlat (just under rlwy viaduct) take 1st exit & foll sp thro Sarlat dir Périgueux. As come to end of Sarlat turn L onto D6 dir Les Eyzies (bcomes D47 in 2km). Site on L in approx 11 km on D47. Lge, hdg/mkd pitch, terr, pt shd; htd wc; chem disp; baby facs; some serviced pitches; shwrs inc; el pnts (6A) inc; gas; lndtte; shop; rest; snacks; bar; BBQ (gas/charcoal only); playgrnd; htd pool; paddling pool with mini-waterslide; fishing lake; lake sw 8km; tennis; horseriding; canoeing 10km; wifi internet; entmnt; child entmnt; internet; games/TV rm; 45% static tents/vans; no dogs; Eng spkn; adv bkg rec Jun-Aug; quiet; red low ssn/long stay; cc acc; CCI. "V well-run site; rec arr bef 2000; lge pitches; gd rest & pool; strict rules pool area; v clean facs but poss long, steep walk; mkt Sat; many sports in area; guided walks; m'vans poss not acc after prolonged heavy rain due soft ground." ♦ 30 Apr-13 Sep. € 32.00   (CChq acc) ABS - D02   2007*

See advertisement below

SARZEAU *2G3* (10km E Coastal) Camp Municipal, Rue de la Plage de Rouvran, 56370 Le Tour-du-Parc [02 97 67 30 88; fax 02 97 67 39 02] On N165 fr Vannes dir Nantes, exit sp Sarzeau onto D780. Just S of St Armel turn L onto D199 & in 3km onto D199A for Le Tour-du-Parc, then foll sp for site. Med, mkd pitch, pt sl, pt shd; wc; chem disp (wc); shwrs inc; el pnts (5A) €3; gas; lndtte; lndry rm; ice; tradsmn; shop; rest; snacks 1km; playgrnd; sand beach adj; watersports adj; tennis; cycle hire & routes; 5% statics; dogs €0.80; phone adj; poss cr; Eng spkn; adv bkg; quiet; CCI. "Megaliths & menhirs nrby; medieval city of Vannes 20km; boat trips around Golfe du Morbihan 8km; little shade; new san facs (2006); fair." ♦ ltd. 1 Apr-15 Sep. € 9.00   2007*

⊞ Site open all year   630   *Help us to update this guide*

France

SARZEAU *2G3* (10km E Coastal) **Camping Le Cadran Solaire, Kerjambet, 56370 Le Tour-du-Parc [02 97 67 30 40; fax 02 97 67 40 28; cadransolaire56@yahoo.fr]** Take N165 fr Vannes twds Nantes, turn R for Sarzeau (D780), nr St Armel turn L on D199 & in 3.2km on D199A for Le Tour-du-Parc. In Le Tour-du-Parc turn R at water tower onto D324 sp Sarzeau, site on R in 1km. Med, hdg pitch, pt shd; wc; chem disp; shwrs inc; el pnts (6A) €2.80; lndtte; shop; playgrnd; shgl beach adj; tennis; some statics; phone; poss cr; quiet; cc acc; CCI. "Situated by lake; vg san block." ♦ 1 Apr-30 Sep. € 12.30   2007*

> The opening dates and prices
> on this campsite have changed.
> I'll send a site report form to the
> editor for the next
> edition of the guide.

SARZEAU *2G3* (2.5km S Coastal) **Camping La Ferme de Lann Hoëdic, Route de Roaliguen, 56370 Sarzeau [02 97 48 01 73; fax 02 97 41 72 87; contact@camping-lannhoedic.fr; www.camping-lannhoedic.fr]** Fr Vannes on N165 turn onto D780 dir Sarzeau. Do not ent Sarzeau, but at Super U rndabt foll sp La Roaliguen. After 1.5km turn L to Lann Hoëdic. Med, mkd pitch, pt shd; htd wc; chem disp; mv service pnt; baby facs; fam bthrm; shwrs inc; el pnts (10A) inc; gas; lndtte; ice; shop 800m; tradsmn; rest 2km; snacks; bar 1km; playgrnd; sand beach 800m; cycle hire; 10% statics; dogs €1.70; phone; Eng spkn; adv bkg; quiet; CCI. "Peaceful, well-run site; warm welcome; excel, clean facs & disabled facs; beautiful coastline - quiet beaches, sand dunes; conv St Malo." ♦ 1 Apr-31 Oct. € 19.20 (CChq acc)   2007*

See advertisement above

SARZEAU *2G3* (7km SE Coastal) **Camping Manoir de Ker An Poul (formerly La Madone), Penvins, 56370 Sarzeau [02 97 67 33 30; fax 02 97 67 44 83; info@camping-lamadone.fr; www.camping-lamadone.fr]** Fr E exit N165 1km E of Muzillac, sp Sarzeau D20 & cont approx 20km to junc of D20 & D199, S on D199 sp Penvins. Fr W, 6km E of Vannes, exit N165 onto N780 sp Sarzeau, in 9.5km S onto D199 sp Penvins. Lge, pt sl, pt shd; wc (some cont); chem disp; baby facs; shwrs inc; el pnts (6A) €3.30; gas; lndtte; ice; shop; rest adj; snacks; bar; playgrnd; htd pool; sand beach 700m; games area; entmnt; 10% statics; dogs €3; poss cr; adv bkg; quiet; red low ssn; CCI. ♦ Easter-29 Sep. € 19.50   2006*

SARZEAU *2G3* (4km S Coastal/Rural) **Camping An Trest, Route de la Plage de Roaliguen, 56370 Sarzeau [02 97 41 79 60; fax 02 97 41 36 21; letreste@campingletreste.com; www.camping letreste.com]** Fr E on D780 turn L at 1st rndabt nr Super U supmkt sp Le Roaliguen, site sp on L. NB ignore R turn to Sarzeau after sp Port Navalo. Lge, hdg/mkd pitch, pt sl, pt shd; wc (some cont); chem disp; baby facs; shwrs inc; el pnts (10A) €3.30; gas; lndtte; ice; supmkt 2km; tradsmn; snacks; bar in ssn; playgrnd; htd pool & paddling pool; waterslide; sand beach 800m; tennis, horseriding, golf 3km; TV rm; 5% statics; dogs €1.50; phone; Eng spkn; adv bkg; quiet; 20% red low ssn; cc acc; CCI. "Pleasant, well-run site; gd base for exploring region; lots to do in area; helpful owners." ♦ 24 May-10 Sep. € 20.70   2006*

SARZEAU 2G3 (2km SW Rural) **Camping Domaine Le Bohat, Route d'Arzon, 56370 Sarzeau** [02 97 41 78 68; fax 02 97 41 70 97; www.domainelebohat.com] Fr Vannes on N165, exit onto D780 to Sarzeau. Do not turn off this main rd to Sarzeau but cont twd Arzon; 1km after 2nd rndabt turn L for Le Bohat. Fr Nantes on N165 take D20 at Muzillac, cont to end & join D78. Rest as above. Lge, hdg/mkd pitch, pt shd; wc (some cont); chem disp; mv service pnt; baby facs; shwrs inc; el pnts (10A) inc; gas; Indtte; ice; shop; tradsmn; rest; takeaway; bar; BBQ (gas/charcoal); playgrnd; htd pool & paddling pool; waterslide; sand beach, watersports 4km; cycle hire 2km; golf 6km; horseriding 2km; entmnt; games/TV rm; 4% statics; dogs €3.30; phone; recep 0830-1930 high ssn; c'vans over 7.50m not acc high ssn; poss cr; Eng spkn; adv bkg; quiet; cc acc; CCI. "Busy, family-run site; lge pitches; excel, helpful staff; cycle tracks; Château de Suscinio & local zoo worth visit; boat trips round Golfe du Morbihan & local islands; mkt Thu; vg." ♦ 25 Apr-26 Sep. € 30.40 ABS - B07
2007*

SARZEAU 2G3 (5km SW Coastal) **Camping Saint Jacques, 1 Rue Pratel Vihan, 56370 Sarzeau** [02 97 41 79 29; fax 02 97 48 04 45; info@camping-stjacques.com; www.camping-stjacques.com] Fr Sarzeau on D780, at 2nd rndabt foll dir St Jacques, site sp. Lge, mkd pitch, pt shd; wc (come cont); chem disp; baby facs; shwrs inc; el pnts (4-6A) €2.55; gas; Indtte; ice; shop; snacks; bar; BBQ; playgrnd; sand beach adj; tennis; fishing; sailing school; mini-golf; cycle hire; entmnt; 10% statics; dogs €1; Eng spkn; adv bkg; quiet; red low ssn; cc acc; CCI. "Excel beach & dunes; gd sea sw." ♦ 1 Apr-30 Sep. € 13.20 2006*

SAUCHY LESTREE see Marquion 3B4

SAUGNACQ ET MURET 7D1 (4km W Rural) **Camping Le Muretois, 40410 Saugnacq-et-Muret** [tel/fax 05 58 09 62 14 or 05 58 09 60 45] Exit A63/N10 junc 18 at Le Muret, site within 500m of N10 at junc with D20, sp. Nr Hotel Le Caravaniers. Sm, mkd pitch, pt shd; wc (own san rec); chem disp (wc); shwrs; el pnts (10A) (some rev pol); gas; ice; shop 500m; rest 100m; snacks; bar; playgrnd; rv fishing 3km; tennis; cycle hire; dogs; phone; poss cr; adv bkg rec high ssn; quiet; CCI. "Friendly, basic site; gd NH; watch elec points!" Apr-Sep. 2006*

SAUGUES 9C1 (Urban) **Camp Municipal, 43170 Saugues** [04 71 77 80 62 or 04 71 77 81 21; fax 04 71 77 66 40] 500m W fr Saugues on D589 twd Paulhac, turn R into Ave de Gévaudan. Site on L in 100m. Well sp. Med, mkd pitch, pt shd; wc; chem disp; baby facs; shwrs inc; el pnts (10A) inc; shop; snacks; bar; Indtte; BBQ; rv sw; fishing; boating; canoeing; sports area; adv bkg; cc not acc; CCI. "Gd cent for gorges of Allier & Le Puy-en-Velay; barriers clsd at night; lge grass pitches." 15 Jun-15 Sep. € 13.50 2004*

SAUJON 7B1 (2km N Rural) **Aire Naturelle La Lande (Renouoleau), Route de l'Illate, 17600 Saujon** [05 46 02 84 31; fax 05 46 02 22 47] Fr N150 Saujon by-pass turn onto D1 dir Le Gua. At 1st rndabt turn L, pass fire stn & sports grnd on L. Site on R immed after R bend. Sm, pt sl, pt shd; wc; chem disp; shwrs; el pnts (6A) €2.30; Indry rm; shop, rest, snacks & bar 2km; playgrnd; beach 12km; poss cr. "Excel CL-type site with full facs; v quiet." Apr-Oct. € 9.10 2006*

SAUJON 7B1 (2km N Rural) **FFCC Camping du Lac du Saujon, Aire de la Lande, Voie des Tourterelles, 17600 Saujon** [05 46 06 82 99; fax 05 46 06 83 66; info@campingdulac.net; www.campingdulac.net] Fr N150 Saujon by-pass turn onto D1 dir Le Gua. Foll sp to site. Med, mkd pitch, pt shd; wc; chem disp; mv service pnt; shwrs inc; el pnts (6-10A) €4-6; Indtte; shop & 2km; rest; snacks; bar; playgrnd; htd, covrd pool adj; fishing; tennis; cycle hire; jogging course, horseriding nr; entmnt; 33% statics; dogs €2.60; phone; poss cr; Eng spkn; adv bkg; red low ssn; CCI. "Excel site." ♦ 1 Apr-15 Nov. € 15.80 2006*

SAULCE, LA 9D3 (2km E Rural) **Camping du Lac, Route Napoléon, Curbans, 05110 La Saulce** [04 92 54 23 10] S fr Gap on N85 twd Sisteron for 16km; R to La Saulce over ; in vill turn L onto D19 & over canal. Turn L again. Site 1km on L. Med, pt shd; wc; chem disp; shwrs inc; el pnts (6A) inc; Indtte; shop 2km; tradsmn; rest; playgrnd; pool; paddling pool; walking; cycling; fishing; 10% statics; poss cr; Eng spkn; adv bkg; quiet; CCI. "Enthusiastic family owners; lge pitches." ♦ 1 Apr-10 Oct. € 17.00 2004*

SAULIEU 6G1 (1km N Rural) **Camp Municipal du Perron, Route de Paris, 21210 Saulieu** [tel/fax 03 80 64 16 19 or 03 80 64 09 22 (Mairie); saulieu.tourisme@wanadoo.fr] On D906 (N6) on L of rd on entr fr N. Sp. Lge, hdg/mkd pitch, pt sl, pt shd; htd wc; chem disp; shwrs inc; el pnts (10A) €2.50; gas; Indtte; ice; sm shop; tradsmn; rest in ssn; bar; playgrnd; pool; tennis; dogs €1; adv bkg; quiet, but rd noise; red low ssn; CCI. "No twin-axle vans; gates clsd 2200-0700; office clsd 1200-1500; gd cent touring Morvan Regional Park; many gd rests; fishing in lake; gd walking area." ♦ ltd. 10 Apr-25 Sep. € 12.50 2006*

⊞**SAULXURES SUR MOSELOTTE** 6F3 (1.5km W Rural) **Camping Le Lac de la Moselotte, 336 Route des Amias, 88290 Saulxures-sur-Moselotte** [03 29 24 56 56; fax 03 29 24 58 31; lac-moselotte@ville-saulxures-mtte.fr; www.ville-saulxures-mtte.fr] Sp fr D43. Med, hdg/mkd pitch, pt sl, pt shd; htd wc; chem disp; shwrs inc; el pnts (10A) €5 (poss rev pol); Indtte; shop; tradsmn; snacks; bar; playgrnd; lake sw & sand beach adj; watersports; canoe & cycle hire; fishing; games rm; entmnt; TV; 5% statics; dogs €1; phone; Eng spkn; adv bkg; quiet; cc acc; red long stay/CCI. "Pleasant, beautifully situated site; lake fenced off but v steep shelving in places." ♦ € 15.00 2007*

France

SAUMUR See also sites listed under Bourgueil, Coutures, Doué-la-Fontaine, Montsoreau, Les Rosiers-sur-Loire and Vernantes.

SAUMUR *4G1* (1km N Urban) **Camping L'Ile d'Offard, Rue de Verden, 49400 Saumur** [02 41 40 30 00; fax 02 41 67 37 81; iledoffard@cvtloisirs.fr; www.cvtloisirs.com] Fr N or S on N147 turn off for town cent at rndabt N of Saumur. Ent town past rwly station & cross Rv Loire brdge. Turn L immed over bdge & foll sp Chinon alongside rv & at rndabt turn L & take 1st L to site; foll sp. Lge, hdg/mkd pitch, hdstg, pt sl, pt shd; htd wc; chem disp; mv service pnt; shwrs inc; el pnts (6-10A) €3.50 (poss rev pol); ice; gas; lndtte; shops in ssn; tradsmn; rest; snacks; bar; playgrnd; htd pool; covrd pool; paddling pool; rv sw & fishing, boating adj; tennis; cycle hire; games area; child entmnt; TV rm; 20% tour ops statics; dogs; poss cr; Eng spkn; adv bkg (non-refundable bkg fee); some rlwy noise; red low ssn; cc acc; red CCI. "Pleasant, busy, well-managed site; hdstg pitches in winter; poss unkempt/scruffy low ssn; helpful staff; gd, clean san facs, ltd low ssn; recep open 0800-1900 daily, clsd 1200-1400 or 1600 (w/e), clsd 1200-1700 winter; most pitches lge but some v sm pitches bet statics; can be muddy when wet; lge o'fits check in advance; sh rvside walk to town; gd cycle rtes; gd." ♦ ltd. 1 Mar-16 Nov. € 24.00 (CChq acc)   2007*

SAUMUR *4G1* (8km NE Rural) **Camping Le Pô Doré, 49650 Allonnes** [02 41 38 78 80; fax 02 41 38 78 81; camping.du.po.dore@wanadoo.fr] NE fr Saumur on N147/E60 to D10. Site 3km W of Allonnes on R. Med, hdg/mkd pitch, pt shd; wc; chem disp; shwrs inc; el pnts (6-10A) €2.80-4 (rev pol); gas 3km; lndtte; tradsmn; rest; snacks; bar; playgrnd; htd pool; mountain cycle hire; 10% statics; dogs €1; phone; poss cr; some Eng spkn; some noise fr rlwy; red low ssn; cc acc; CCI. "Run down site; poss unclean facs; access to el pnts diff fr some pitches; conv for wine rtes, caves & museums; barrier clsd 2200-0700; 10 mins fr a'route; NH only." ♦ 1 Apr-31 Oct. € 15.20   2005*

SAUMUR *4G1* (6km E Rural) **Camping L'Etang de la Brèche, 5 Impasse de la Brèche, 49730 Varennes-sur-Loire** [02 41 51 22 92; fax 02 41 51 27 24; mail@etang-breche.com; www.etang-breche.com] Exit Saumur on N152 twd Tours & site sp fr either dir. Site on N side of rd (6km W of Varennes) app fr lge lay-by giving easy ent. Lge, hdg pitch, pt shd; wc; chem disp; mv service pnt; 20% serviced pitch; baby facs; shwrs inc; el pnts (10A) inc; gas; lndtte; ice; shop; tradsmn; rest; snacks; bar; playgrnd; 2 htd pools (no shorts); waterslide; cycle hire; tennis; games rms; entmnt; internet; TV rm; 30% statics; dogs; phone; Eng spkn; adv bkg (ess Jul/Aug), dep req; quiet but rd noise in some areas; 40% red low ssn; cc acc; CCI. "Spacious site, gd, lge pitches; well-organised; excel facs; auto barrier clsd 2300-0700; plenty of space for children's play; easy access; v helpful staff; excel rest; conv Loire chateaux & wine-tastings; gd." ♦ 12 May-15 Sep. € 34.00   2007*

SAUMUR *4G1* (5km NW Rural) **Camping de Chantepie, Route de Chantepie, 49400 St Hilaire-St-Florent** [02 41 67 95 34; fax 02 41 67 95 85; info@campingchantepie.com; www.campingchantepie.com] Take D161, then D751 on S bank of rv sp Gennes. Site is on L of rd bet Le Pointrineau & La Croix, approx 5km fr N147 junc. Or fr N after x-ing rv on N147, take turn sp St Hilaire-St-Florent & join D751 for Gennes; well sp fr D751. NB Easy to miss turning. Lge, hdg/mkd pitch, pt shd; wc; chem disp; mv service pnt; baby facs; shwrs inc; el pnts (10A) €3 (poss rev pol); gas; lndtte; ice; shop; tradsmn; rest/snacks; bar; BBQ; playgrnd; 2 pools (1 htd, covrd); paddling pool; rv beach 200m; fishing; tennis 2km; mini-golf; cycle hire; golf 2km; horseriding, boating 5km; entmnt; internet; games/TV rm; 10% statics; dogs €4; c'vans over 8m not acc; Eng spkn; adv bkg; quiet; red low ssn; cc acc; CCI. "Excel site with lovely view over Rv Loire; well-spaced, lge pitches; friendly, helpful staff; care with access to pitches for lge o'fits; recep 0800-1930 high ssn; excel san facs, inc for disabled; wine-tastings & visits; mkt Sat Saumur." ♦ 1 May-15 Sep. € 29.00 ABS - L06   2007*

See advertisement

SAUMUR *4G1* (8km NW Rural) **Camp Municipal La Croix Rouge, Ave de la Gare, 49160 St Martin-de-la-Place [02 41 38 09 02; fax 02 41 45 65 65]** Fr Saumur, take N147 N then turn L onto D952 dir Angers. At St Martin-de-la-Place foll sp for site. Med, mkd pitch, pt shd; wc; chem disp; mv service pnt; shwrs; el pnts (8A) inc; lndry rm; ice; shop, rest, 600m; bar 200m; playgrnd; rv sw, sailing adj; dogs; bus 150m; Eng spkn; adv bkg; quiet; cc not acc; CCI. "Beautiful, tranquil site on bank of Rv Loire; rv views on some pitches; poor el pnts; no twin-axles." ♦ ltd. 1 Jun-10 Sep. € 9.10   2006*

SAUSHEIM see Mulhouse *6F3*

SAUVETERRE DE BEARN *8F1* (S Rural) **Camping du Gave, Ave de la Gare, 64390 Sauveterre-de-Béarn [05 59 38 53 30; fax 05 59 36 19 88; camping-du-gave@wanadoo.fr]** Site on D933 on S side of town. Ent immed off rndabt at end of rv bdge. Med, mkd pitch, shd; wc (some cont); chem disp (wc); shwrs; el pnts (6A); lndtte; shop & 200m; tradsmn; rest 1km; snacks; bar; playgrnd; rv sw adj; canoeing; 10% statics; dogs; poss cr; adv bkg; quiet. "Facs poss stretched in ssn; friendly management; footpath fr site to lovely medieval town." ♦ 1 Apr-30 Sep. € 11.40   2006*

SAUVETERRE DE GUYENNE *7D2* (8km NW Rural) **Camping Château Guiton (Naturist), 33760 Frontenac [05 56 23 52 79; fax 05 56 23 99 40; accueil@chateau-guiton.com; www.chateau-guiton.com]** N of Sauveterre-de-Guyenne turn W onto D123 sp Frontenac. Turn L just bef vill sp Château Guiton. Sm, mkd pitch, pt sl, pt shd; wc; chem disp; sauna; shwrs; el pnts (6-10A) €3.50; lndtte; ice; shop; tradsmn; rest & bar 4km; playgrnd; pool; gym; TV rm; bus 6km; dogs €1.50; phone; Eng spkn; adv bkg; quiet; cc acc; IFN card req; "V friendly owner; site is converted chateau, pt open, pt wooded; in cent wine region; communal meal twice a week high ssn; close to Bordeaux." 13 May-17 Sep. € 19.50   2006*

SAUVETERRE LA LEMANCE see Villefranche du Périgord *7D3*

SAUVIAN see Valras Plage *10F1*

SAUXILLANGES see Issoire *9B1*

SAUZE VAUSSAIS *7A2* (1km SW Rural) **Camp Municipal Puits d'Anché, Route de Chef Boutonne, 79190 Sauzé-Vaussais [05 49 07 61 33 or 05 49 07 60 53 (Mairie); fax 05 49 07 78 49; mairie-sauze@marcireau.fr; www.mairie-sauze-vaussais.fr]** Fr N10 turn W onto D948 at Les Maisons-Blanches to Sauzé. Site sp in vill. Sm, mkd pitch, pt sl, pt shd; wc (cont); shwrs inc; el pnts (10A) €2.60; shops, rest, snacks, bar 1km; BBQ; playgrnd; 2 htd pools (public); tennis; quiet. "Comfortable, value-for-money; fair sh stay/NH." 1 Jul-31 Aug. € 5.30   2006*

SAVENAY *2G3* (3km E) **Camp Municipal du Lac, La Moëre, 44260 Savenay [02 40 58 31 76; fax 02 40 58 39 35]** Site well sp in Savenay. Med, mkd pitch, terr, pt shd; wc; shwrs inc; el pnts (5A) inc; gas adj; lndtte; ice; tradsmn; snacks; sm playgrnd; free pool adj; fishing; quiet; cc not acc. "Vg, clean site in attractive park adj to lake; lge pitches; conv La Baule, St Nazaire; 45 mins drive to excel beaches." ♦ 1 May-30 Sep. € 11.00   2005*

SAVERNE *6E3* (1.3km SW Urban) **FFCC Camping de Saverne, Rue du Père Libermann, 67700 Saverne [03 88 91 35 65 or 03 88 71 52 82 (Mairie); fax 03 88 91 35 65; camping-saverne@ffcc.fr; www.camp-in-france.com]** Take Saverne exit fr A4, junc 45. Site well sp nr town cent. Med, hdg/mkd pitch, hdstg, pt sl, pt shd; htd wc; chem disp; mv service pnt; shwrs inc; el pnts (16A) €2.40-4.85 (poss rev pol); gas; lndtte; ice; shop 1km; hypmkt 4km; snacks; playgrnd; pool 1km; 30% statics; dogs €1.25; poss cr; Eng spkn; adv bkg; quiet; cc acc; 10% red CCI. "Pleasant, busy, well-run site on edge of lovely town; excel, clean san facs; aire de service nr ent; 30 mins walk into Saverne; hourly trains to Strasbourg; gd." ♦ 1 Apr-30 Sep. € 10.50   2007*

SAVERNE *6E3* (5km SW Rural) **Camping au Paradis Perdu, Rue de Hirschberg, St Gall, 67440 Thal-Marmoutier [03 88 70 60 59]** Fr Saverne, use minor rds rather than by-pass; foll sp Thal-Marmoutier then foll camp sps to St Gall & site; access thro archway - poss tight for lge vans. Sm, pt sl, pt shd; wc; chem disp; shwrs; el pnts (3-6A) €1.85-€3.70; shops 3km; rest; snacks; bar; playgrnd; 30% statics; dogs €1.20; adv bkg; quiet. "Pleasant setting at rear of rest; facs basic but gd." 1 Apr-15 Oct. € 10.30   2006*

SAVERNE *6E3* (13km SW) **Camping du Rocher, 57850 Dabo [03 87 07 47 51; fax 03 87 07 47 73; ot-dabo@claranet.fr; www.ot-dabo.fr]** Fr Saverne take D132 to Lutzelbourg, then D98 to Haselbourg & D45 to Dabo. Go thro vill; site sp on R in 2km. Sm, mkd pitch, pt shd; wc; shwrs €1.50; el pnts (6-10A) €2-3.30; shop 2km; playgrnd; cycling; fishing; quiet. "Site yourself; warden calls; fair sh stay/NH." ♦ ltd. Easter-1 Nov. € 8.30   2004*

SAVIGNY EN VERON *4G1* (W Rural) **FFCC Camping La Fritillaire, Rue Basse, 37420 Savigny-en-Véron [02 47 58 03 79; fax 02 47 58 03 81; lafritillaire.veron@ffcc.fr; www.camp-in-france.com]** Fr Montsoreau on D751 or D7 on S bank of Rv Loire, foll sp to Savigny-en-Véron & site. Med, mkd pitch, pt shd; htd wc; chem disp; mv service pnt; baby facs; some serviced pitches; shwrs inc; el pnts (10A) €2.75; lndtte; rest, snacks & bar 500m; BBQ; playgrnd; htd, covrd pool 4km; games area; tennis; cycle hire; horseriding; some statics; dogs €0.70; Eng spkn; adv bkg; quiet; CCI. "Excel, peaceful site; clean, modern facs; gd touring base Loire chateaux; vg cycle rtes; wine tasting in vill." 1 Apr-15 Sep. € 13.00   2007*

SAVINES LE LAC 9D3 (2km SW Rural) Camp Municipal Les Eygoires, 05160 Savines-le-Lac [04 92 44 20 48 or 04 92 44 20 03 (Mairie); fax 04 92 44 39 71; camping.municipal.savinelelac@wanadoo.fr] Take N94 to Savines. Site on D954 on N side of rd. Lge, terr, pt shd; wc (some cont); baby facs; shwrs; el pnts (5A) €3.30; lndtte; shop; snacks; bar; playgrnd; lake sw & shgl beach; sailing; some statics; dogs €1; adv bkg; quiet. "Security barrier operated by key fr office, clsd 1200-1600." 1 Jun-30 Sep. € 11.60   2006*

SAVINES LE LAC 9D3 (5km SW Rural) Camping La Palatrière, 05160 Le Sauze-du-Lac [tel/fax 04 92 44 20 98; lapalatriere@wanadoo.fr; www.lapalatriere.com] Take N94 fr Gap thro Chorges, turn R after bdge at Savines-le-Lac onto D954 for 5km twds Le Sauze-du-Lac. Sm, mkd pitch, terr, pt shd; wc; shwrs inc; el pnts (6A) inc; lndtte; shop; rest; snacks; bar; BBQ; playgrnd; lake sw; 25% statics; dogs €1; entmnt; TV; cc acc. "Lovely, family-run site on hillside above lake; beautiful views; unsuitable lge o'fits due steep site rds; some newer pitches v soft after rain." 1 May-30 Nov. € 20.00   2007*

SCHOENAU 6E3 (800m S) Camping Schoenau Plage, 67390 Schoenau [03 88 85 22 85] Fr Sélestat take D424 twd German border then L to D20. On D20 turn L just bef Rhône Bdge; site on L. Lge, mkd pitch, pt shd; wc; chem disp; shwrs; el pnts (10A); gas; ice; shops 1km; tradsmn; snacks; bar; playgrnd; lake sw; boating; fishing; 60% statics; poss cr; quiet; red CCI. "V pleasant, friendly site." 1 Apr-30 Sep.   2004*

SECONDIGNY 4H1 (S Rural) Camp Municipal du Moulin des Effres, 79130 Secondigny [05 49 95 61 97 or 05 49 63 70 15 (Mairie); fax 05 49 63 55 48; secondigny@marie-secondigny.fr] D949 to Secondigny, S onto D748. Site sp 800m on L immed after lake. Med, mkd pitch, pt sl, pt shd; wc (some cont); shwrs inc; el pnts (6A) €2.80; rest 400m; snacks; shops 500m; lndry rm; pool; tennis; TV; entmnt; lake fishing adj; poss cr; quiet; CCI. "Warden calls pm; in pleasant surroundings nr attractive vill." 1 Jun-15 Sep. € 8.60   2006*

SEDAN 5C1 (11km SE) Camp Municipal du Lac, Route de Mouzon, 08140 Douzy [03 24 26 31 19 or 03 24 26 31 48 (Mairie); fax 03 24 26 84 01; aubergedulac@free.fr] On N43 fr Sedan-Metz to Douzy. Turn R (S) at traff lts in Douzy & site in 500m on L. Clearly sp. Med, pt shd; few hdstg; wc; 60% serviced pitch; shwrs inc; el pnts (6A) inc; gas 1km; lndtte; shops 1km; tradsmn; rest adj; snacks; bar; playgrnd; shgl beach & lake sw adj; waterslides; tennis; dogs €1.50; poss cr; Eng spkn; adv bkg; 10% red 8+ days; CCI. "V helpful staff; pitches mostly uneven, few have shd; 3 modern san facs blocks; gd site for Ardennes, Verdun; vg." ♦ 1 May-30 Sep. € 15.00   2007*

SEDAN 5C1 (1km W Urban) Camp Municipal de la Prairie, Prairie de Torcy, Blvd Fabert, 08200 Sedan [tel/fax 03 24 27 13 05 or 03 24 27 73 42] Fr A203/E44 exit junc 4 dir Sedan cent. Cont strt thro town & over rlwy bdge; in 500m cont over viaduct, site visible on R, turn R at next traff lts at end of viaduct, site 100m on R. Med, mkd pitch, pt shd; no hdstg; wc (some cont); chem disp; mv service pnt; shwrs inc; el pnts (10A) inc; lndtte; shop 300m; rest 500m; snacks; bar; BBQ; sm playgrnd; pool 500m; rv beach adj; fishing; dogs €1; phone; poss cr; adv bkg; some traff noise; red long stay; CCI. "Pleasant site by rv; friendly, helpful recep; uneven pitches; basic san facs clean, too few & need refurb; poss muddy in wet weather; office open 0800-2200; sh walk into town, interesting with castle (one of largest in Europe); excel medieval festival around Château Fort 2nd half May w/e; poss itinerants; lge, fenced-off itinerant park adj; gd value; vg." ♦ 1 Apr-30 Sep. € 7.95   2007*

SEDERON 9D3 (2km E Rural) Camping Les Routelles (Naturist), 26560 Séderon [04 75 28 54 54; fax 04 75 28 53 14; infos@routelles.com; www.routelles.com] Best app fr E fr Sisteron on D946. Immed bef Séderon turn R onto D225B (opp Renault g'ge), & foll sp 2km. At ent owner will tow up steep track to pitch. Med, sl, terr, pt shd; wc; chem disp; sauna; shwrs inc; el pnts (6A) €2.50; tradsmn; rest; snacks; bar; BBQ (subject to pitch); playgrnd; pool; sw 3km; TV rm; dogs €0.70; quiet; phone; some Eng spkn; adv bkg; red low ssn. "Excel site; v clean san facs; excel rest; v friendly & helpful owner; eagles fly overhead; stunning views; owner pitches vans with 4x4; highly rec; unsuitable for disabled." 1 Apr-1 Nov. € 22.50   2006*

SEES 4E1 (S Urban) Camp Municipal Le Clos Normand, Route d'Alençon, 61500 Sées [02 33 28 87 37 or 02 33 28 74 79 (LS); fax 02 33 28 18 13; office-tourisme.sees@wanadoo.fr] C'vans & lge m'vans best app fr S - twd rndabt at S end of by-pass (rec use this rndabt as other rtes diff & narr). Well sp. Narr ent. Sm, hdg pitch, pt shd; wc; chem disp; mv service pnt; shwrs inc; el pnts (6A) €2.25; gas; lndtte; ice; supmkt opp; snacks & bar 100m; rest 500m; playgrnd; pool 2km; fishing; 10% statics; no twin axles; dogs €1.15; Eng spkn; adv bkg; slight rd noise; CCI. "Pitches spacious & well-cared for; helpful, friendly warden; gd san facs; excel mv service pnt; gates clsd 2100 (2000 low ssn); cathedral nrby." ♦ 1 May-30 Sep. € 10.10   2007*

France

⊞ **SEGRE** *2F4* (5km NW Rural) **Pageant Camping à la Ferme, Le Petit Villeprouve, 49500 Nyoiseau [02 41 61 74 03]** W fr Segré on D775 dir Pouancé. At start dual c'way go under rd bdge & at next rndabt take exit sp Bourg d'Iré, L'Arbre Vert (tractors, cyclists only). In 500m turn R after pond on R, in 500m turn L after 2nd house on L (old rails in rd), sp to site in 200m. Sm, hdstg, pt sl, pt shd; htd wc; shwrs inc; el pnts (10A) inc; lake sw; adv bkg; red long stay. "CL-type site; British owners; 2006 new rds under construction - ring for directions." € 15.00   2006*

SEGRE *2F4* (7km NW Rural) **Camping Parc de St Blaise, 49520 Noyant-la-Gravoyère [02 41 61 75 39; fax 02 41 61 53 25]** Fr Segré take dir Pouancé to Noyant, site/park sp in vill on R. Sm, hdg pitch, terr, pt shd; wc; chem disp (wc); serviced pitches; shwrs inc; el pnts (5A) €2.50; shop & 1km; tradsmn; rest; bar; playgrnd; lake sw adj; entmnt; dogs; phone; CCI. "Clean, well-maintained site in leisure park; gd views; slate mine worth visit (not an eyesore)." ♦ 1 May-30 Sep. € 8.50   2006*

SEIGNOSSE see Hossegor *8E1*

SEILHAC *7C4* (4km SW Rural) **Camp Municipal du Pilard, La Barthe, 19700 Lagraulière [05 55 73 71 04; fax 05 55 73 25 28; mairie. lagrauliere@wanadoo.fr; www.lagrauliere. correze.net]** Exit A20 junc 46 onto D34 to Lagraulière, site sp. NB Lge o'fits rec take D44 & D167E fr Seilhac. Sm, mkd pitch, pt shd; wc; chem disp (wc); shwrs inc; el pnts (3-6A) €2; gas 2km; shop 700m; rest, snacks, bar 1km; BBQ; playgrnd; htd pool adj; tennis; dogs €0.75; phone adj; Eng spkn; quiet; CCI. "V quiet, clean site nr pleasant vill; warden calls; excel value." ♦ ltd. 15 Jun-15 Sep. € 5.80   2007*

SEILHAC *7C4* (2.5km NW Rural) **Camp Municipal Le Lac de Bournazel, 19700 Seilhac. [05 55 27 05 65]** Fr Seilhac W on D1120 (N120) for 1.5km turn R at rndabt for 1km, clearly sp. Lge, mkd pitch, terr, pt shd; wc; chem disp; baby facs; shwrs inc; el pnts (10A) €2.70; lndtte; shop in ssn; rest 1km; snacks & bar 500m; BBQ; playgrnd; lakeside beach sw adj; 25% statics; dogs €1; Eng spkn; adv bkg; CCI. "V lge pitches; v clean; beach surveillance in ssn; pedaloes on lake." 1 Apr-30 Sep. € 12.50   2005*

SELESTAT *6E3* (Urban) **Camp Municipal Les Cigognes, Rue de la 1ère DFL, 67600 Sélestat [03 88 92 03 98 or 03 88 58 87 20; fax 03 88 92 88 63; accueil@selestat-tourisme.com; www.selestat-tourisme.com]** Site sp N83 & D424. Fr S town cent turn E off N83 & foll sps to site adj schools & playing fields. Med, mkd pitch, pt shd; wc; mv service pnt; chem disp; shwrs inc; el pnts (5A) inc; gas; lndtte; ice; shops; rest, snacks, bar 500m; playgrnd; pool 300m; rv & lake nrby; enmnts; dogs €0.85; poss cr; Eng spkn; adv bkg rec high ssn; quiet but some noise fr local football area; CCI. "Helpful staff; gd train service Strasbourg - 10 mins walk to stn." ♦ 1 May-15 Oct. € 15.25   2007*

SELESTAT *6E3* (4km N Rural) **Camping à la Ferme St Paul (Loos), 67600 Ebersheim [03 88 85 71 80; fax 03 88 85 71 05]** Exit Sélestat on N83 to N & site on R in approx 4km, sp. Sm, pt shd; wc; chem disp; mv service pnt; shwrs €1; el pnts €1.50; gas 1km; ice; lndtte; shops 1km; snacks; rest & bar Sat eve; playgrnd; horseriding, tennis 1km; dogs; adv bkg; quiet; CCI. "Working farm with animals; CL-type site; friendly owner; excel bakery in vill." 1 Apr-1 Nov. € 5.50   2007*

SELESTAT *6E3* (5km N Rural) **Camping Rural (Weiss), 17 Rue du Buhl, 67600 Ebersheim [03 88 85 72 97; elizabeth.trau@wanadoo.fr]** Fr S or N on N83 in vill of Ebersheim foll green Camping Rural sps. Sm, pt shd; wc; shwrs inc; el pnts inc; shop 500m; cooking facs; quiet; adv bkg; cc not acc; CCI. "Gd touring base & friendly, helpful warden; wine sold on site." ♦ 15 Jun-15 Sep. € 9.40   2007*

SELESTAT *6E3* (6km N Rural) **Camping Caravaning Les Reflets du Vignoble (formerly Camp Municipal Le Wasen), Route d'Ebersheim, 67650 Dambach-la-Ville [03 88 92 48 60; fax 03 88 92 60 09 (Mairie); info.tourisme@dambach-la-ville.fr]** Exit A35 at junc 16 for D1422 (formerly N422) dir Obernai. After approx 2km take D210 for Dambach-la-Ville & foll sp. Med, mkd pitch, pt shd; wc; chem disp; shwrs inc; el pnts (5A) inc; shop, rest, snacks, bar 1km; BBQ; lndtte; playgrnd; sports area; tennis adj. "Attractive medieval town; recep clsd fr 1200-1430; no access when barrier down as rd too narr for waiting." ♦ 16 Jun-30 Sep. € 14.70   2004*

SELESTAT *6E3* (12km W Rural) **Camping du Haut-Koenigsbourg, 68660 Lièpvre [03 89 58 43 20; fax 03 89 58 98 29; camping.haut-koenigsbourg@ wanadoo.fr]** Fr Sélestat W on N59 twd Lièpvre vill then R at factory car park & site sps. Fr Ste Marie-aux-Mines on N59 turn L at rndabt after tunnel. Med, mkd pitch, pt sl, pt shd; htd wc; mv service pnt; shwrs inc; el pnts (4-8A) €2.50-3.50; lndtte; ice; shop 1km; tradsmn; bar; BBQ; playgrnd; TV rm; 10% statics; dogs €1.50; poss cr; quiet; CCI. ♦ 15 Mar-15 Nov. € 9.50   2004*

SELESTAT *6E3* (5km NW Rural) **Aire Naturelle (Palmer), 11 Rue Faviers 67759 Scherwiller [03 88 92 94 57; fax 03 88 82 05 39]** Fr N foll N83 to Ebersheim then D81 to Scherwiller. Site sp off D35 at N end vill. Sm, pt shd; wc; shwrs €2.05; el pnts €1.60; shop 1km; tradsmn; pool 5km; cc acc; CCI. "Vg; many tourist attractions nr." 15 May-15 Sep. € 8.70   2005*

> Before we move on, I'm going to fill in some site report forms and post them off to the editor, otherwise they won't arrive in time for the deadline at the end of September.

SELONGEY *6G1* (S Rural) **Camp Municipal Les Courvelles, Rue Henri Jevain, 21260 Selongey [03 80 75 52 38 or 03 80 75 70 74 (Mairie); fax 03 80 75 56 65; mairie.selongey@wanadoo.fr; www.selongey.com]** Exit A31 junc 5 N of Dijon onto D974 (N74) N for 3km to Orville: turn W in Orville sp Selongey & site; site in approx 2km. Sm, some hdstg, unshd; wc; shwrs inc; el pnts (6A) €2; shop 1km; tennis; quiet; CCI. "Lovely clean, friendly, gd value site; warden calls 0700-0830 & 1900-2030; rec arr early bef 1700 & site yourself; no twin-axles; patisserie nrby; conv a'rte/NH; excel." ♦ 1 May-30 Sep. € 10.00   2007*

SELTZ *5D4* (1km S Rural) **Camping Die Grune Les Peupliers, 67470 Seltz [03 88 86 52 37]** Fr Seltz on D468, turn L in 1km at sp. Lge, pt shd; wc; chem disp; mv service pnt; shwrs; el pnts (6A) €2.50; rest; bar; playgrnd; lake fishing & boating adj; 85% statics; cc acc; CCI. "Sm pitches; 1 old & 1 modern shwr block; direct access to lake." ♦ € 12.60   2005*

SEMUR EN AUXOIS *6G1* (3.5km S Rural) **Camp Municipal du Lac de Pont, 21140 Pont-et-Massène [03 80 97 01 26 pr 03 80 97 25 72 (Mairie); camping-lac@worldonline.fr; www.lacdepont.com]** Exit A6 junc 23 twd Semur-en-Auxois on D980; after sh dist turn R sp 'Lac de Pont'. Med, some hdg pitch, pt shd; wc; chem disp; shwrs inc; el pnts (6A) €2.50; gas; lndtte; ice; shop; tradsmn; rest 100m; snacks; bar; lake sw; watersports; tennis; games rm; cycle hire; 30% statics; dogs €1.55; phone; poss cr; quiet; CCI. "Watersports on lake; conv ancient town; gd touring base; nr A6 m'way; easy access; vg." 1 May-15 Sep. € 10.80   2006*

SENNECEY LE GRAND *6H1* (6km E Rural) **Camping Domaine du Château de L'Epervière, Rue du Château, 71240 Gigny-sur-Saône [03 85 94 16 90; fax 03 85 94 16 97; info@domaine-eperviere.com; www.domaine-eperviere.com]** Fr N exit A6 junc 26 (Chalon Sud) onto N6 dir Mâcon & Tournus; at Sennecey-le-Grand turn E onto D18 sp Gigny-sur-Saône. Or fr S exit A6 junc 27 (Tournus) onto N6 N to Sennecey-le-Grand, then as above. NB Diff to find signs fr main rd, poss juncs not mkd. Lge, mkd pitch, pt shd; htd wc; chem disp; baby facs; jacuzzi/sauna; shwrs inc; el pnts (10A) inc; gas; lndtte; ice; sm shop; tradsmn; rest; snacks; pizzeria; bar high ssn; BBQ; playgrnd; 2 pools (1 htd, covrd); paddling pool; lake & rv nr; fishing; tennis 400m; cycle hire; entmnt; wifi internet; games/TV rm; tour op statics & chalets; dogs €3; poss v cr; recep 0800-1900; Eng spkn; adv bkg; quiet; cc acc; CCI. "Excel, busy, top-quality site; lge pitches; excel for château visits, wine-tastings, cycling; vg rest & gd value meals; san facs clean & modern; warm welcome, pleasant staff; popular site with tour ops; boggy when wet." ♦ 1 Apr-30 Sep. € 32.00 (CChq acc) ABS - L12   2007*

SENNECEY LE GRAND *6H1* (6km NW Rural) **Camping La Héronnière, Les Lacs de Laives, 71240 Laives [tel/fax 03 85 44 98 85 or 03 85 44 89 67; camping.laives@orange.fr; http://pagesperso-orange.fr/camping.laives]** Turn W off N6 Chalon-Mâcon rd at Sennecey-le-Grand to Laives. Foll sp 'Lacs de Laives'. Sp on D18. Med, hdg/mkd pitch, some hdstg, pt shd; wc; chem disp; shwrs inc; el pnts (6A) €3.90; lndry rm; rest 300m; snacks; shop; playgrnd; htd pool; lake sw & beach nrby; fishing; windsurfing; pedalo; sail boarding; cycle hire; dogs €1.50; Eng spkn; quiet; adv bkg; CCI. "Lakeside location nr a'route; lovely site; excel NH; busy site when fine; may fill up after 1500; popular with bikers; gd shwrs; rest at lakeside; level site, gd for wheelchair users; vg." ♦ 1 May-15 Sep. € 15.50 (CChq acc)   2006*

SENONCHES *4E2* (Urban) **Camp Municipal du Lac, 28250 Senonches [02 37 37 94 63 or 02 37 37 76 76 (Mairie); fax 02 37 37 92 92]** NE on D928, take D25, sp, to Senonches fr cent of La Loupe. Site clearly sp by sports facs & piscine adj to site (by sm lake). Sm, hdg/mkd pitch, pt shd; wc (cont); chem disp (wc); shwrs inc; el pnts (6A) €2.10; shops 100m; pool & lake adj; phone; quiet. "Gd site." 1 May-30 Sep. € 4.20   2005*

SENONES see Raon l'Etape *6E3*

France

SENS 4F4 (1km S Urban) **Camp Municipal Entre Deux Vannes, Ave de Senigallia, 89100 Sens** [03 86 65 64 71; fax 03 86 95 39 41] NW on N6 take rd into Sens; site bet town cent & N6 on E side of N360, 1km to S of town cent; foll sp. Med, mkd pitch, pt shd; wc (some cont); chem disp (wc); mv service pnt; baby facs; shwrs inc; el pnts (16A) €1.30; lndtte; shops 1km; tradsmn high ssn; rest nrby; playgrnd; adv bkg rec; some noise fr rd & commercial premises nrby during day; cc acc; CCI. "Friendly, helpful warden; san facs old but clean; gate locked 2200." 15 May-15 Oct. € 10.20
2006*

SENS DE BRETAGNE 2E4 (Rural) **Camp Municipal La Petite Minardais, Rue du Clos Bertrand, 35490 Sens-de-Bretagne** [02 99 39 51 33 (Mairie)] Take N175 fr Antrain twd Rennes. Turn R at camping sp in Sens-de-Bretagne & foll sp to site. Sm, pt shd; wc; shwrs inc; el pnts (4A); shop 500m; quiet. "CL-type site; pleasant sm park & lake adj." 1 May-30 Sep.
2004*

SEPPOIS LE BAS see Altkirch 6F3

SERAUCOURT LE GRAND see St Quentin 3C4

SERENT see Ploermel 2F3

SERIGNAC 7D3 (5km W Rural) **Camping Le Clos Barrat (Naturist), 46700 Sérignac** [05 65 31 97 93; fax 05 65 31 91 17; contact@leclosbarrat.com; www.leclosbarrat.fr] Fr Fumel by-pass turn S on D139 to Montayral, rd cont but becomes D4. Site sp bet Mauroux & St Matré. Med, pt shd, mkd pitch; wc; chem disp; shwrs inc; el pnts (6A) inc; gas; lndtte; ice; shop; tradsmn; rest; snacks; playgrnd; pool; paddling pool; entmnt; dogs €1.60; quiet; cc acc. "Nr Rv Lot; INF card req - can be bought on site; v helpful staff; excel." 1 Apr-30 Sep. € 22.10
2006*

SERIGNAC PEBOUDOU see Cancon 7D3

SERIGNAN DU COMTAT see Orange 10E2

SERIGNAN PLAGE 10F1 (Coastal) **Camping Domaine de Beauséjour, 34410 Sérignan-Plage** [04 67 39 50 93; fax 04 67 32 01 96; info@camping-beausejour.com; www.camping-beausejour.com] Fr A9/E15, exit Béziers Est junc 35 onto D64 S. In 4km turn L onto D37E to Sérignan-Plage. Site on R just bef shops. Lge, hdg/mkd pitch, pt shd; wc; chem disp; mv service pnt; shwrs inc; el pnts (10A) inc; gas; lndtte; ice; shop; supmkt 8km; rest; snacks; bar; BBQ; playgrnd; sand beach adj; entmnt; 50% statics; dogs €3.50; poss v cr; Eng spkn; adv bkg (dep req + bkg fee); quiet; red low ssn; cc acc; red long stay; CCI. "Direct access to excel beach; weekly mkts in vill; excel hypmkt nrby; vg site." ♦ 1 Apr-30 Sep. € 36.50
2007*

See advertisement

SERIGNAN PLAGE 10F1 (Coastal) **Camping La Maïre, Route de Sérignan-Plage, 34410 Sérignan-Plage** [04 67 39 72 00; fax 04 67 32 56 16; richard.berge@wanadoo.fr; www.camping-lamaire.fr] Exit A9 junc 35 onto D64 dir Sérignan; bef vill turn L onto D37E11 to Sérignan-Page; site on L after ent vill. Lge, hdg/mkd pitch, pt shd; wc; chem disp; shwrs inc; el pnts (6A) inc; gas; lndtte; ice; shop; rest; snacks; bar; BBQ (sep area); playgrnd; pool; sand beach 1km; cycle hire; horseriding adj; games rm; child entmnt; 20% statics; dogs €0.50; phone adj; no twin-axles; poss cr; quiet; cc acc. "V lge pitches; excel, clean san facs; gd beaches adj; excel." 15 Apr-15 Sep. € 30.00
2007*

> There aren't many sites open this early in the year. We'd better phone ahead to check that the one we're heading for is actually open.

SERIGNAN PLAGE 10F1 (Coastal) **Camping Le Clos de Ferrand (Naturist), 33 Ave de Beziers, 34410 Sérignan Plage** [04 67 32 14 30; fax 04 67 32 15 59; centrenaturiste.closferrand@wanadoo.fr; www.leclosferrand-centrenaturiste.fr] Exit A9 junc 35 onto D64 dir Valras-Plage. At Sérignan town turn L on D37E to Sérignan-Plage 5km, site sp. Med, hdg/mkd pitch, pt shd; wc; chem disp; shwrs inc; el pnts (2-6A) €4-5; ice; lndtte; shop; snacks; rest; bar; playgrnd; TV rm; beach adj; rv 1km; fishing; boat hire; quiet; adv bkg; cc not acc; INF card req; CCI. "Direct access to beach; gd sized pitches divided by trees; reported run down (Aug 2007)." ♦ ltd. 10 May-20 Sep. € 38.00
2007*

SERIGNAN PLAGE 10F1 (Coastal) **Camping Le Clos Virgile, 34410 Sérignan-Plage** [04 67 32 20 64; fax 04 67 32 05 42; le.clos.virgile@wanadoo.fr; www.leclosvirgile.com] Exit A9 Béziers Est junc 35 twd Les Plages, turn R onto N112 at Villeneuve-les-Béziers. Foll D37 for 5km to Sérignan-Plage, site sp. Lge, mkd pitch; shd; wc; shwrs inc; el pnts (5A) inc; gas; lndtte; ice; shop & 500m; rest; snacks; bar; playgrnd; htd, covrd pool; paddling pool; waterslide; sand beach & watersports 500m; cycle hire; horseriding; games area; entmnt; 33% statics; dogs €3; phone; adv bkg; cc acc; quiet. "V friendly; constant hot water; money change on site; cycle hire." ♦ 4 May-15 Sep. € 30.00
2004*

SERIGNAN PLAGE *10F1* (Coastal) **Camping Le Sérignan-Plage Nature (Naturist), Les Orpelières, 34410 Sérignan-Plage [04 67 32 09 61; fax 04 67 32 26 36; info@leserignannature.com; www.leserignannature.com]** Exit A9 junc 36 Beziers Est onto D64. At Sérignan town turn L on D37E to Sérignan-Plage. After 4km turn R on single-lane dual c'way. At T-junc turn L & immed L again in 50m to site. Lge, mkd pitch, pt shd; wc (some cont); chem disp; mv service pnt; shwrs inc; el pnts (5A) inc; gas; lndry rm; ice; shop; rest; snacks; bar; playgrnd; pool complex; sand beach; mini-golf; golf 15km; internet; beauty cent; child entmnt; TV rm; 75% statics; dogs €3; poss cr; Eng spkn; adv bkg; quiet but some noise fr disco; red long stay/low ssn; CCI. "Excel, immac san facs; helpful staff; Camping Le Sérignan Plage (non-naturist) adj with use of same private beach & facs; pool also shared - for naturists' use 1000-1200 only." 22 Apr-20 Sep. € 36.00 (CChq acc) 2005*

SERIGNAN PLAGE *10F1* (Coastal) **Yelloh! Village Le Sérignan-Plage, Les Orpelières, 34410 Sérignan-Plage [04 67 32 35 33; fax 04 67 32 26 36; info@leserignanplage.com; www.leserignanplage.com or www.yellohvillage.com]** Exit A9 junc 35. After toll turn L at traff lts onto N112 & at 1st rndabt strt on to D64. In 5km turn L onto D37E Sérignan-Plage, turn R on narr 1-way rd to site. Adj to Camping Sérignan-Plage Nature (Naturist site). V lge, hdg pitch, pt shd; wc (some cont); chem disp (wc); mv service pnt; baby facs; shwrs inc; el pnts (5A) inc; gas; ice; lndtte; shop; hypmkt 6km; rest; snacks; bar; playgrnd; htd, covrd pool; Club Nautique - sw, sailing & water-ski tuition on private beach; tennis; horseriding; disco; entmnt; TV; many statics; dogs €3; use of naturist private beach & facs adj; poss v cr; Eng spkn; adv bkg; poss noisy; red low ssn; no cc acc; CCI. "V busy & tightly packed; busy low ssn: excel pool but poss v cr; some tourers amongst statics & sm sep touring area quite nice." 26 Apr-23 Sep. € 42.00
2006*

SERIGNAN PLAGE *10F1* (5km W Rural) **Camping Le Paradis, Route de Valras-Plage, 34410 Sérignan [tel/fax 04 67 32 24 03; paradiscamping34@aol.com]** Exit A9 junc 35 Béziers Est onto D64 dir Valras-Plage. Site on L on rndabt at S end of Sérignan by-pass, 1.5km S of Sérignan. Med, mkd pitch, pt shd; wc; chem disp; shwrs; el pnts (6A) inc; gas; lndtte; ice; shop; supmkt opp; rest & bar high ssn; snacks; playgrnd; pool (high ssn); sand beach 2km; no dogs; poss cr; Eng spkn; adv bkg rec; quiet except for twice weekly disco to 0030 & some rd noise; red low ssn/CCI. "Excel family-run site; immac san facs; tree planting (2007) making access rds diff." ♦ 1 Apr-30 Sep. € 19.60 (3 persons) 2007*

SERRES *9D3* (2km SE Rural) **Camping Domaine des Deux Soleils, 05700 Serres [04 92 67 01 33; fax 04 92 67 08 02; contact@domaine-2soleils.com; www.domaine-2soleils.com]** Take N75 S fr Serres dir Sisteron, then turn L to Super-Serres thro wood & up winding mountainside rd, site sp. Med, mkd pitch, sl, terr, pt shd; wc; shwrs inc; el pnts (6A) €3.35; lndtte; shop; rest; snacks; playgrnd; pool; paddling pool; waterslide; fishing; horseriding adj; archery; games area; guided walks; entmnt; TV; dogs €2; phone; adv bkg; quiet. "Some lge pitches; pleasant site & area." 1 May-30 Sep. € 19.10
2007*

SERRIERES *9C2* (3km W) **Camping Le Bas Larin, 07340 Félines [tel/fax 04 75 34 87 93 or 06 74 75 96 07 (mob); camping.baslarin@wanadoo.fr; www.bas-larin.com]** Exit A7 junc 12 Chanas or fr N7, exit at Serrières onto N82; cross canal & rv; cont over rndabt up winding hill, camp on L nr hill top. Sp fr N7 & N82, but easily missed - foll sp Safari Peaugres. Med, terr, shd; wc; chem disp; shwrs inc; el pnts (4-10A) €2.50-3.50; lndtte; shops 2km; rest adj; playgrnd; pool; paddling pool; dogs; Eng spkn; some rd noise; CCI. "Friendly, family-run site; helpful staff; easy access pitches; beautiful views; v popular with Dutch; excel." ♦ 1 Apr-30 Sep. € 14.00 2006*

SERVON see Pontaubault *2E4*

France

SETE *10F1* (6km N Coastal) **Camp Municipal Pech d'Ay, Ave de la Gare, 34540 Balaruc-les-Bains [04 67 48 50 34]** Exit N113 to Balaruc-les-Bains; foll sp Centre Commercial & then head for prom. Site on prom. Lge, mkd pitch, pt sl, pt shd; wc; chem disp; mv service pnt; shwrs; el pnts (5A) inc; lndtte, shops, rest bar adj; playgrnd; shgle beaches nrby; bus; poss cr; adv bkg rec (even low ssn); poss noisy; CCI. "Gd site; delightful holiday resort; thermal baths in vill; busy all ssn, rec arr early; when full pitches seem cramped; vg, clean san facs; many gd rests adj; bus to Sete." 28 Feb-12 Dec. € 14.40
2007*

SETE *10F1* (7km N Coastal) **Camping Les Vignes, 34540 Balaruc-les-Bains [04 67 48 04 93; fax 04 67 18 74 32; camping.lesvignes@free.fr; www.camping-lesvignes.com]** Fr N113 take D2 sp Sète, turn W sp Baluruc-les-Bains, after 2nd rndabt turn R, well sp in 100m on R. Med, hdg/mkd pitch, pt shd; wc (some cont); chem disp; mv service pnt; shwrs inc; el pnts (6-10A) €3-3.50; lndtte; shops 1km; snacks; bar; playgrnd; pool; shgl beach 1km; sand beach 7km; fishing, horseriding & tennis nr; 30% statics; dogs €2; poss cr; adv bkg rec high ssn; quiet; cc acc; CCI. "V tight for long o'fits; narr rds on site; Sète worth a visit; gd touring base." ♦ ltd. 1 Apr-31 Oct. € 17.00
2007*

SETE *10F1* (7km NE Coastal) **Camping Le Mas du Padre, 4 Chemin du Mas du Padre, 34540 Balaruc-les-Bains [04 67 48 53 41; fax 04 67 48 08 94; info@mas-du-padre.com; www.mas-du-padre.com]** Fr Sète N on D2. In Balaruc turn R after traff lts 1km fr vill, then 2nd on R onto local rd for 500m. Well sp. Fr A9 exit junc 33 on N300 sp Sète; foll sp Balaruc-les-Bains on D2 for 2 rndabts, then turn R on D2E6 sp campings. Med, hdg/mkd pitch, pt sl, terr, shd; wc; chem disp; baby facs; shwrs inc; el pnts (6A) inc; gas; lndtte; ice; shops 3km; tradsmn; playgrnd; pool; sand beach 8km; lake sw, fishing & boating 2km; tennis; entmnt; TV; 10% statics; dogs €2.10; poss cr; Eng spkn; adv bkg rec high ssn; quiet; cc acc; CCI. "Pretty, well-equipped & well-kept site nr beaches; immac facs; extra for lger pitches; site rds narr; owner v helpful; excel." ♦ 31 Mar-14 Oct. € 23.40   2007*

SETE *10F1* (11km SW Coastal) **Camping Le Castellas, Cours Gambetta, 34200 Sète [04 67 51 63 00; fax 04 67 53 63 01; www.le-castellas.com   www.village-center.com]** SW fr Sète foll sp for La Corniche; pick up N112 & foll sp for 'Plages-Agde'. Lge, hdg pitch, pt shd; wc; chem disp; shwrs inc; el pnts (6A) inc; gas; lndtte; ice; shop; rest; snacks; bar; playgrnd; 2 htd pools; sand beach 150m (across busy rd); tennis; mini-golf; games area; cycle hire; entmnt; dogs €3; poss cr; Eng spkn; adv bkg; rd & rlwy noise; red 7+ days; CCI. "Bull-fighting in ssn; Sète worth visit; superb beach; twin-axles welcome." 21 Apr-16 Sep. € 38.00   2007*

SEURRE *6H1* (500m S Urban) **Camp Municipal du Port, Rue de la Pêche a l'Oiseau, 21250 Seurre [03 80 20 32 63 or 03 80 21 09 11 (Mairie); ot.seurre@wanadoo.fr]** Fr A36 exit 1, foll D976 to Seurre, past supmkt on R, next R, foll sp, site 1km approx. Sm, pt shd; wc (cont); 50% serviced pitches; shwrs inc; el pnts (5A) €1.60; ice; shops 1km; BBQ; statics; playgrnd; rv fishing; dogs €0.50; poss cr; quiet. "Fair NH; beside Rv Saône." 1 May-30 Sep. € 7.00   2005*

SEURRE *6H1* (600m W) **Camp Municipal de la Piscine, 21250 Seurre [03 80 20 49 22 or 03 80 21 15 92 (Mairie); fax 03 80 20 34 01]** Exit Seurre on D973 Dijon/Beaune rd; site on R over bdge adj municipal pool. Lge, hdstg, pt shd; wc; chem disp; shwrs inc; el pnts (10A) inc (rev pol); gas; lndry rm; shops 600m; rest; snacks; bar; playgrnd; pool adj; 25% statics; adv bkg ess high ssn; quiet; CCI. "Vg san facs but inadequate when full; gd rest; twin-axles acc." ♦ ltd. 15 May-15 Sep. € 9.50   2004*

SEURRE *6H1* (3km NW) **Camping Les Sables, Chemin de la Plage, 21250 Pouilly-sur-Saône [03 80 20 43 50; les.sables@tiscali.fr]** Exit A36 at junc 1 onto D976 for Seurre then onto D973 to D996 to Pouilly-sur-Saône. Fr A31 exit junc Nuits-St Georges & take D35 dir Gerland & Bagnot. At D996 turn R for Pouilly in 7km. Site well sp. Sm, mkd pitch, pt shd; wc; chem disp (wc); shwrs inc; el pnts (6A) €2.30; ice; shop 5km; tradsmn; BBQ; playgrnd; pool 2km; fishing adj; dogs €0.80; Eng spkn; adv bkg; quiet; CCI. "Excel CL-type site sh walk fr Rv Saône; v helpful British owners; facs basic but spotless; conv Beaune, Dijon & local mkts." ♦ ltd. 1 May-30 Sep. € 8.50   2004*

SEVERAC LE CHATEAU *9D1* (1km Urban) **FFCC Camping Les Calquières (formerly Municipal), Ave Jean Moulin, 12150 Sévérac-le-Château [05 65 47 64 82; contact@camping-calquieres.com; www.camping-calquieres.com]** Exit A75 junc 42 sp Sévérac & Rodez; foll 'Camping' sps to avoid narr town rds. Site adj sw pool. Med, hdg pitch, pt shd; wc (some cont); 50% serviced pitches; shwrs inc; el pnts (6A) €3; (poss long lead req); lndry rm; shop 250m; tradsmn; snacks; playgrnd; pool adj (inc); games area; fishing; tennis; some statics; dogs €1.50; adv bkg; quiet, but poss noise fr sports facs adj; red long stay; CCI. "Lovely, spacious site with beautiful views; lge pitches; main san facs block vg, other needs updating but clean; friendly owners; office 0800-1000 & 1800-2000, if clsd site self; lovely old town & château; gd hotel rest short walk into town; gd touring base; busy NH, espec w/e; vg." ♦ 4 Apr-30 Sep. € 14.60
2007*

SEVERAC LE CHATEAU *9D1* (12km SE Rural) **Camp Municipal, 48500 St Rome-de-Dolan [04 66 48 87 46 or 04 66 48 83 59; fax 04 66 48 87 46; mairie-stromededolan@wanadoo.fr]** Exit A75 junc 42 to Sévérac, then take D995 fr Sévérac-le-Château then E thro Le Massegros to St Rome-de-Dolan. Site on R at ent to vill. V diff app fr Les Vignes, Gorges du Tarn. Sm, pt sl, pt terr, pt shd; wc; chem disp; shwrs inc; el pnts (6A) €2; Indtte; ice; shop 5km; tradsmn; rest, snacks, bar 5km; BBQ; playgrnd; rv sw 5km; dogs €1; phone 50m; Eng spkn; adv bkg; quiet; CCI. "Delightful, simple site on edge of Gorges du Tarn: stunning views; birdwatching; walking; well-managed; v friendly, helpful warden; basic but spotless san facs; highly rec." ♦ 15 May-15 Sep. € 8.80

2006*

SEVRIER see Annecy *9B3*

SEYNE *9D3* (800m S Rural) **Camping Les Prairies, Haute Gréyère, 04140 Seyne-les-Alpes [04 92 35 10 21; fax 04 92 35 26 96; info@campinglesprairies.com; www.camping lesprairies.com]** Fr Digne-les-Bains, take D900 N to Seyne. Turn L on ent Seyne onto D7, site sp beside Rv La Blanche. Med, mkd pitch, pt shd; htd wc; chem disp; mv service pnt; baby facs; shwrs inc; el pnts (10A) €3.50; gas; Indtte; shop 800m; tradsmn; rest 800m; snacks; BBQ; playgrnd; htd pool; tennis 300m; horseriding 500m; dogs €2; phone; Eng spkn; adv bkg; quiet; cc acc; CCI. "Immac site, v clean & tidy." 14 Apr-15 Sep. € 18.00

2007*

⊞**SEYNE SUR MER, LA** *10F3* (2km W Rural) **Camping St Jean, Ave de la Collégiale, 83140 Six-Fours-les-Plages [04 94 87 51 51; fax 04 94 06 28 23; info@campingstjean.com; www.campingstjean.com]** Fr Toulon exit junc 15 sp La Seyne-sur-Mer. Turn R at 2nd x-rds onto D559, sp Six-Fours. Site sp 1km on R, diff turn. Lge, hdg pitch, shd; wc; shwrs inc; el pnts €3.50; gas; Indtte; ice; shop; snacks; playgrnd; pool; paddling pool; sand beach 3km; games rm; entmnt; TV; some statics; dogs €3; phone; adv bkg rec Jul/Aug; quiet. "Generous pitches; facs clean but a little dated." € 24.00 (3 persons)

2005*

SEYSSEL *9B3* (N Urban) **Camping Le Nant Matraz, 74270 Seyssel [tel/fax 04 50 59 03 68]** Nr town cent on L of D992 N of Seyssel sp Frangy. Lge supmkt on opp side of rd. Med, mkd pitch, pt shd; wc; mv service pnt; shwrs inc; el pnts (3-6A) inc; ice; Indtte; shops adj; snacks; bar; BBQ; playgrnd; pool in town; boat hire; rv fishing; games rm; dogs; adv bkg; quiet; Eng spkn; cc acc. "On banks of Rv Rhône." 1 Apr-31 Oct. € 13.60

2006*

SEZANNE *4E4* (11km E Rural) **Camp Municipal Parc du Château, 51230 Connantre [03 26 81 08 76 or 03 26 81 07 16 (Mairie)]** On N4; site sp both dir. Med, hdg pitch, few hdstg, pt shd; wc; chem disp; shwrs inc; el pnts (5-10A) €1.50-2.30 (rev pol) gas; ice; shops 1km; playgrnd; pool 5km; beach; lake sw 500m; 15% statics; dogs €1.10; adv bkg; some noise fr N4; 20% red 2+ days; CCI. "Clean, neat camp; friendly recep; excel facs; no twin-axles." 1 Apr-31 Oct. € 8.40

2005*

⊞**SEZANNE** *4E4* (6km SW Rural) **Aire de Loisirs La Traconne, 4 Impasse de Rouge Coq, 51120 Le Meix-St Epoing [03 26 80 70 76; fax 03 26 42 74 98; info@camping-traconne.com; www.camping-traconne.com]** Turn S off N4 at Beauvais about 12km W of Sézanne. Foll sp to vill/site on D239, site sp. Exit fr N4 at Moeurs-Verday via v narr rd - not rec. Med, hdg/mkd pitch, pt shd; htd wc; chem disp; mv service pnt; baby facs; shwrs inc; el pnts (6A) €3.50 (poss rev pol); gas; Indtte; ice; shops 5km; tradsmn; BBQ; playgrnd; pool & waterslide 5km; fishing adj; games rm; 30% statics; dogs €2; Eng spkn; adv bkg; quiet; CCI. "Peaceful, restful site in forest but neglected; scruffy; facs unclean; local wine sold on site; excel cycling & walking." ♦ € 12.00 (CChq acc)

2006*

SEZANNE *4E4* (500m NW) **Terrain de Camping Municipal, Route de Launat, 51120 Sézanne [03 26 80 57 00]** W'bound on N4 Sézanne by-pass onto D373 & foll site sp. No access fr N4 E'bound. If app fr S foll camping sps, but avoid town cent, turn L immed after 2nd set of traff lts. Med, mainly sl, pt shd; serviced pitches; wc (some cont); shwrs inc; shop, el pnts (10A) inc; shop 500m; rest in town 1km; sm playgrnd; pool adj; waterslide; dogs €0.90; some rd noise; no cc acc; CCI. "Clean & tidy site; helpful manager; levelling blocks needed; request for gate opening/closing at back bungalow of two opp site (playing field); town in walking dist; vet nr Leclerc supmkt on D373; vg." ♦ 1 Apr-1 Oct. € 9.45

2007*

SIBIRIL see St Pol de Léon *1D2*

⊞**SIGEAN** *10G1* (5km N Rural) **Camping La Grange Neuve, Route de la Réserve Africaine, 11130 Sigean [tel/fax 04 68 48 58 70; info@camping-sigean.com; www.camping-sigean.com]** Exit junc 39 fr A9; pass under A9; foll sp La Réserve Africaine. Med, hdg/mkd pitch, hdstg, pt sl, terr, pt shd; wc; chem disp; shwrs inc; el pnts (6A) €4; Indtte; shop; rest; snacks; bar; playgrnd; pool; waterslide; sand beach 5km; TV rm; 5% statics; dogs €2.50; poss cr; adv bkg; quiet but some rd noise; red low ssn; CCI. "Easy access; san facs dated - tired end of ssn & ltd facs low ssn; phone ahead to check open low ssn; NH only." ♦ € 15.00

2007*

France

SIGEAN *10G1* (8km E Urban) **Camp Municipal du Golfe, 406 Blvd Francis Vals, 11210 Port-la-Nouvelle [04 68 48 08 42; fax 04 68 40 37 90]** Exit A9/E15 junc 39 onto D6139 (N139) to Port-la-Nouvelle; at cement works rndbt R into D709; in 1km L over rlwy; L at rndbt; immed L into site. Lge, some hdg/mkd pitch, pt shd; wc; shwrs inc; el pnts (6A) €2.30; lndry rm; shop 500m; playgrnd; sand beach 1km; dogs €1.20; some rlwy & rd noise; red low ssn; CCI. "Useful NH off A9 or N9." ♦ ltd. 1 Apr-30 Sep. € 13.00   2007*

SIGEAN *10G1* (8km SE) **Camping Le Clapotis (Naturist), 11480 La Palme [04 68 48 15 40; info@leclapotis.com]** On D6009 (N9) Narbonne-Perpignan rd turn L 8km S of Sigean. After 350m turn R at camping sp. Site in 150m. Final app rd narr but negotiable for lge vans. Lge, mkd pitch, pt shd; wc (cont); shwrs inc; el pnts (4-10A) €3.45; gas; ice; rest in ssn; pool; internet; dogs €1.80; poss cr; Eng spkn; adv bkg; quiet; 10% red low ssn; Naturists INF card req; cc acc. "Friendly site; helpful owners; san facs dated but clean; subject to strong winds; gd windsurfing." 15 Mar-31 Oct. € 20.90   2006*

SIGNY L'ABBAYE *5C1* (Urban) **Camp Municipal de l'Abbaye, 08460 Signy-l'Abbaye [03 24 52 87 73]** Take D985 N twd Belgium fr Rethel to Signy-l'Abbaye. Foll sp fr town cent to Stade & Camping. Site by sports stadium. Sm, some hdg/hdstg pitch, pt sl, pt shd; htd wc; chem disp; shwrs inc; el pnts (10A) €2.70 (poss rev pol); lndry rm; shops, rest 500m; playgrnd; rv fishing adj; dogs €0.60; little Eng spkn; adv bkg; v quiet; CCI. "Lovely, gd value site adj to sports cent; gd location; v friendly resident warden; san facs excel (shared with public fr sports cent); gravel surfaced hdg pitches - v strong awning pegs req, or can park on open grassed area; pleasant vill with vg rest; vg." ♦ ltd. 1 May-30 Sep. € 6.00   2007*

SIGOULES *7D2* (1.5km N Rural) **Camp Municipal La Gardonnette, Les Coteaux de Sigoulès, 24240 Sigoulès [tel/fax 05 53 58 81 94; campingdelagardonnette@wanadoo.fr; www.campingdelagardonnette.com]** S fr Bergerac take D933 S. After 6km at top of hill turn R by la Grappe d'Or Rest onto D17 sp Pomport/Sigoulès. Thro Pomport, site at bottom of hill on R by lake. Med, mkd pitch, pt sl, shd; wc; chem disp; shwrs inc; el pnts (6A) €2; lndtte; lndry rm; shop, snacks, bar 1km; playgrnd; lake sw; fishing; canoeing; tennis; games area; entmnt; TV; 25% statics; dogs €1.50; phone; Eng spkn; adv bkg dep req; cc acc; CCI. "Barrier ent; facs clean but well worn & in need of refurb; gd security; gd value." 1 Apr-30 Sep. € 11.50   2005*

SILLE LE GUILLAUME *4F1* (3km N Rural) **FFCC Camping La Forêt, Sillé-Plage, 72140 Sillé-le-Guillaume [02 43 20 11 04; fax 02 43 20 84 82; info@campingsilleplage.com; www.campingsilleplage.com]** Exit Sillé on D304 sp Mayenne. After 2km at x-rds turn R; across next x-rds & turn L at next x-rds; sp Sillé-Plage; site immed on R visible. Sp fr other dir. Lge, pt shd; wc; mv service pnt; shwrs inc; el pnts (10A) €2.50; gas; shop; tradsmn; playgrnd; tennis; boating; lake sw; fishing; 20% statics; dogs €1.10; poss cr; rd noise; CCI. "Pleasant lakeside & forest scenery (some pitches amongst trees); super lake; highly rec." 31 Mar-31 Oct. € 9.00   2007*

Did you know you can fill in site report forms on the Club's website — www.caravanclub.co.uk?

SILLE LE GUILLAUME *4F1* (11km SE Urban) **Camp Municipal de la Gironde, 72240 Conlie [02 43 20 81 07 or 02 43 20 50 35 (Mairie); fax 02 43 20 99 37; camping.conlie@wanadoo.fr]** SE fr Sillé-le-Guillaume on D304 twd Conlie. Ent vill & site sp in vill to R. Sm, hdg/mkd pitch, pt sl, shd; wc; chem disp (wc); shwrs inc; el pnts (6A) €2.50; lndtte; shops 200m; playgrnd adj; pool 5km; dogs; phone; adv bkg, quiet; CCI. "No resident warden, access poss diff; phone ahead to check open if travelling low ssn; v pleasant site." ♦ 1 Apr-31 Oct. € 5.00   2005*

SILLE LE GUILLAUME *4F1* (2km NW Rural) **Camping Les Tournesols, Route de Mayenne, Le Grez, 72140 Sillé-le-Guillaume [02 43 20 12 69; campinglestournesols@wanadoo.fr; www.campinglestournesols.com]** Exit Sillé on D35 Rennes rd (route verte), after 2km at x-rds, turn R to site in 150m on L, easily visible & sp. Sp fr Sillé-Plage. Med, pt sl, pt shd; wc; chem disp; baby facs; shwrs; el pnts (10A) inc; gas; lndtte; ice; shop 2km; rest; snacks; bar; playgrnd; rv/lake sw 2km; 50% statics; dogs €1; adv bkg (fee); CCI. "Beautiful site; lovely lake at Sillé-Plage; nice town." 1 May-30 Sep. € 14.00   2007*

SILLE LE PHILIPPE *4F1* (2km SW Rural) **Camping Le Château de Chanteloup**, 72460 Sillé-le-Philippe [02 43 27 51 07 or 02 43 89 66 47; fax 02 43 89 05 05; chanteloup.souffront@wanadoo. fr; www.chateau-de-chanteloup.com or www. les-castels.com] Leave A11/E50 at junc 7 Sp Le Mans Z1 Nord. After toll turn L onto N138. Foll this & turn L onto D313 sp Coulaines & Ballon. Take D301 (just bef lge supmkt) & approx 13km site is sp just after ent to Sillé-le-Philippe. Avoid ent Sillé-le-Philippe. Med, some mkd pitch, pt sl, pt shd; wc; chem disp; baby facs; shwrs inc; el pnts (6A) €3.70 (poss rev pol); Indtte; ltd shop & 2km; tradsmn; rest high ssn; snacks; bar; BBQ; playgrnd; pool; paddling pool; lake fishing; tennis; horseriding & golf 10km; games area; entmnt; child entmnt; wifi internet; games/TV rm; dogs free; c'vans over 8m not acc; sep o'night area with elec & water; poss v cr; Eng spkn; adv bkg; higher charge during Le Mans events; quiet; cc acc; CCI. "Excel, friendly site; clean facs & gd rest; recep 0815-2300; breakfast avail; gd for Le Mans 24hr car race; rest & shop poss clsd after Le Mans w/e; châteaux & wine tours arranged." 31 May-31 Aug. € 27.50 ABS - L13   2007*

SIMIANE LA ROTONDE *10E3* (4km SE Rural) **Camping Valsaintes Le Château**, 04150 Simiane-la-Rotonde [tel/fax 04 92 75 91 46; agripaulo@ aol.com; www.valsaintes.com] E fr Simiane-la-Rotonde on D18 for 1.5km; at top if hill turn R dir Valsaintes; in 3km (after turning to L'Abbaye de Valsaintes) turn R; in 500m turn L; site on R in 1km. Site ent steep with sharp turn off rd. Sm, pt sl, terr, shd; wc (own san rec); chem disp (wc); shwrs inc; el pnts (6A) €2.80; Indtte; ice; shop (high ssn); snacks; bar; playgrnd; pool; dogs €0.80; quiet. "V isolated; pitches sm clearings in wood/scrub; v basic facs." 1 Apr-15 Oct. € 11.20   2006*

SISTERON *10E3* (1.5km N) **Camp Municipal Les Prés Hauts, 44 Chemin des Prés Hauts**, 04200 Sisteron [tel/fax 04 92 61 00 37 or 04 92 61 19 69; camping.sisteron@wanadoo.fr; www.sisteron. com] On W of D951 3km N of Sisteron. Fr S on N85 take R turn 300m after thro tunnel exit town & cross rv; L after 2km. Lge, hdg pitch, pt sl, pt shd; wc; chem disp; serviced pitches; shwrs inc; el pnts (6A) €3.80 (poss rev pol); Indtte; shop & 1.5km; playgrnd; pool; tennis; fishing; entmnt; dogs €1; Eng spkn; quiet; cc acc; CCI. "Gd views; vg facs; friendly warden; lge pitches; ltd facs low ssn; Citadelle a must; pleasant old town within easy cycling dist; gd local produce mkt; vg." ♦ 1 Mar-31 Oct. € 13.50
                                                          2007*

SIVRY SUR MEUSE see Dun sur Meuse *5C1*

SIX FOURS LES PLAGES see Seyne sur Mer, La *10F3*

SIXT SUR AFF see Gacilly, La *2F3*

SIZUN *2E2* (Rural) **Camp Municipal du Gollen**, 29450 Sizun [02 98 24 11 43 or 02 98 68 80 13 (Mairie); fax 02 98 68 86 56] Fr Roscoff take D788 SW onto D69 to Landivisiau, D30 & D764 to Sizun. In Sizun take D18 at rndabt. At end of by-pass, at next rndabt, take 3rd exit. Site adj pool. Sm, pt shd; wc (some cont); shwrs inc; el pnts (10A) €3 (poss rev pol); Indry rm; shops 500m; playgrnd; htd pool adj high ssn; phone; poss cr; no adv bkg; quiet; cc not acc; CCI. "Site in Armorique Nature Park; friendly recep; site yourself if warden not avail; no twin-axle vans." Easter-30 Sep. € 9.40
                                                          2007*

⊞**SOISSONS** *3D4* (1km N Urban) **Camp Municipal, Ave du Mail**, 02200 Soissons [03 23 74 52 69; fax 03 23 59 67 72; officedetourisme@ville-soissons. fr; www.ville-soissons.fr] Fr N on D1; foll town cent sp to 1st rndabt; turn R, cross rv & immed R into Ave du Mail. Foll sp 'Camping Piscine'. Site well sp beside sw pool. Rd humps & tight ent on last 500m of access rd. (Poss to avoid tight ent by going 150m to rndabt & returning.) Med, hdg/mkd pitch, hdstg, pt shd; htd wc; chem disp (wc); shwrs inc; el pnts (5A) €3-4 (poss rev pol); Indry rm; sm shop 600m; tradsmn; rest; snacks; bar 1km; BBQ; playgrnd; pool adj; excursions; 5% statics; dogs €1; phone; poss cr; quiet; cc acc; CCI. "Well-run, lovely site in interesting area; gd sized pitches; helpful, friendly & efficient staff; gd san facs; rvside walks, cycling, dog walks; flat, easy walk to town; poss itinerants; gate clsd 2200-0700; mkt Wed & Sat; vg winter NH." ♦ € 12.00   2007*

SOLIGNAC SUR LOIRE see Puy en Velay, Le *9C1*

SOLOMIAC *8E3* (W Rural) **Camp Municipal**, 32120 Solomiac [05 62 65 01 02 (Mairie)] S fr Montauban on D928, bet Beaumont-de-Lomagne & Mauvezin; camp sp in vill of Solomiac dir Montfort on D151; foll sp. Sm, pt shd; wc; shwrs; el pnts; sm shop 200m; quiet. "Excel site in historic vill; site yourself, warden on site fr early am; san facs v clean; gd NH." € 9.00   2006*

SOMMIERES *10E1* (2km SE Rural) **Camping Domaine de Massereau, 1990 Route d'Aubais**, 30250 Sommières [04 66 53 11 20 or 06 03 31 27 21 (mob); fax 04 92 46 82 37; info@ massereau.fr; www.massereau.fr or www. les-castels.com] Exit A9 junc 26 at Gallargues, foll sp Sommières. Site sp on D12. NB Danger of grounding at ent fr D12. Med, hdg/mkd pitch; pt shd; wc (some cont); chem disp; mv service pnt; baby facs; shwrs inc; el pnts (16-20A) inc; gas; Indtte; ice; shop; tradsmn; rest; snacks; bar; BBQ (gas/elec only); playgrnd; pool; waterslide; rv sw 500m; tennis; cycle hire; trampoline; games area; games rm; internet; entmnt; TV; 50% statics; dogs €5; phone; poss cr; Eng spkn; adv bkg (dep req); quiet; cc acc; CCI. "Lovely site attached to vineyard; basic san facs; pleasant staff; on a cycle way; vg." ♦ 1 Mar-15 Nov. € 33.00 ABS - C33
                                                          2007*

France

SOMMIERES *10E1* (3km SE Rural) **Camping Les Chênes, Les Teullières Basses, 30250 Junas** [04 66 80 99 07 or 06 03 29 36 32 (mob); fax 04 66 51 33 23; chenes@wanadoo.fr] Fr Sommières take D12 S (sp Gallargues) 3km to junc with D140 L (N) for 1km. Site on R 300m up side rd. Sp. Med, pt sl, shd; wc (cont); chem disp; shwrs inc; el pnts (3-10A) €2.05-3.10 (long lead poss req); lndtte; shops 1km; playgrnd; pool; beach & rv sw 2km; games area; some statics; dogs €2.20; phone; sep car park; security barrier; adv bkg; quiet; CCI. "Gd shade; gd san facs; friendly, helpful staff; vg." Easter-15 Oct. € 9.50   2005*

SOMMIERES *10E1* (500m NW Urban) **Camp Municipal Le Garanel, Rue Eugène Ranché, 30250 Sommières** [tel/fax 04 66 80 33 49] Fr S on A9 exit junc 27 N & foll D34 then take D6110 (N110) twd Sommières. By-pass town on D6110, over rv bdge; turn R for D40. After L turn for Nîmes pull out to make sharp R turn sp 'Camping Arena'. At T-junc turn R, site thro car park. Fr N on D6110 turn L at 4th junc sp 'Ville Vieille' & site adj rv. Site sp fr D6110 fr N. Sm, hdg/mkd pitch, pt shd; wc (some cont); chem disp; mv service pnt; shwrs inc; el pnts (10A) €4; lndtte; shops, rest, snacks 300m; tradsmn; bar 200m; BBQ; beach 25km; tennis adj; bus 500m; twin-axle restrictions; poss cr; Eng spkn; adv bkg; quiet; CCI. "Friendly, helpful warden; some open views; sh walk to historic town; rv walks; Voie Verte cycle rte Sommières to Caveirac; Sat mkt." 1 Apr-30 Sep. € 5.80   2007*

SONZAY *4G1* (W Rural) **Camping L'Arada Parc, 88 Rue de la Baratière, 37360 Sonzay** [02 47 24 72 69; fax 02 47 24 72 70; info@laradaparc.com; www.laradaparc.com] Exit A28 junc 27 to Neuillé-Pont-Pierre; then D766 & D6 to Sonzay; turn R in town cent. Site on R on o'skirts immed past new houses; sp. Med, hdg/mkd pitch, pt sl, pt shd; wc; chem disp; mv service pnt; 20% serviced pitches; child/baby facs; shwrs inc; el pnts (10A) €3.60 (poss rev pol); gas; lndtte; ice; shop; tradsmn; rest; snacks; bar; BBQ; playgrnd; htd pool; paddling pool; tennis; lake sw 9km; rv fishing 500m; mini-golf; cycle hire; games area; entmnt; internet; TV rm; 15% statics; dogs €1.50; phone; bus to Tours; Eng spkn; adv bkg; red long stay/low ssn; cc acc; CCI. "Peaceful, well-maintained site; v quiet; friendly, helpful owners; excel rest & pool; immac modern facs; gd views; poss diff for lge o'fits when site full/cr; various pitch sizes; barrier clsd 2300-0800; conv Loire chateaux & vineyards; 60km fr Le Mans circuit; excel." ♦ 22 Mar-25 Oct. € 20.50 (CChq acc)   2007*

SOREDE see Argelès sur Mer *10G1*

SOSPEL *10E4* (4km NW Rural) **Domaine Ste Madeleine, Route de Moulinet, 06380 Sospel** [04 93 04 10 48; fax 04 93 04 18 37; camp@camping-sainte-madeleine.com; www.camping-sainte-madeleine.com] Take D2566 fr Sospel NW to Turini & site 4km on L; sp fr town. Rd to site fr Menton steep with many hairpins. Med, mkd pitch, pt sl, pt terr, shd; wc; chem disp; mv service pnt; shwrs €0.50; el pnts (10A) €2.90; gas; ice; lndtte; pool; beach 20km; rv 3km; dogs €1.40; Eng spkn; adv bkg rec high ssn; quiet; 10% red low ssn; CCI. "Friendly, busy site; gd facs; gd pool but has no shallow end; stunning scenery." 1 Apr-30 Sep. € 19.00   2006*

SOUBES see Lodève *10E1*

SOUILLAC *7C3* (5km SE Rural) **Camp Municipal, 46200 Pinsac** [05 65 37 85 83 or 05 65 37 06 02] S on D820 (N20) thro Souillac, turn L on o'skts onto D43 immed bef Rv Dordogne. Site in 5km. Sm, pt shd; wc; shwrs inc; el pnts (5A) €2.80; lndry rm; ice; shop 1km; rest & bar 100m; snacks; fishing; Eng spkn; quiet. "Useful NH/sh stay espec low ssn; lovely rvside position; warden calls pm; conv for Rocamadour & local attractions; basic facs." 1 Jun-30 Sep. € 8.40   2007*

SOUILLAC *7C3* (1km S Rural) **Camp Municipal du Pont, 46200 Lanzac** [05 65 37 02 58 or 05 65 37 88 53; fax 05 65 37 02 31] S on D820 (N20) thro Souillac; immed after x-ing Rv Dordogne site visible on R of N20. Sm, shd; wc (mainly cont); chem disp; shwrs inc; el pnts (6-10A) €2.33; gas; shops 1km; tradsmn; snacks; adv bkg; CCI. "Easy stroll into Souillac along rv; lovely location but poss itinerants; facs tired high ssn; haphazard pitching; unreliable opening dates - phone ahead." ♦ 15 Jun-15 Sep. € 13.30   2006*

SOUILLAC *7C3* (5km S Rural) **Camping Verte Rive, 46200 Pinsac** [05 65 37 85 96; fax 05 65 32 67 69; laverterive@online.fr;   http://laverterive.free.fr] Fr Souillac S on D820 (N20). Turn L immed bef Dordogne rv bdge on D43 to Pinsac. Site on R in 2km on rvside. Med, hdg/mkd pitch, shd; wc (some cont); chem disp; baby facs; shwrs inc; el pnts (4-8A) €3-4.20; gas; lndtte; shop & 1km; rest; snacks; bar; playgrnd; pool; rv sw; canoeing; 20% statics; dogs €1; poss cr; Eng spkn; adv bkg ess high ssn (bkg fee & dep req); quiet; CCI. "Friendly, peaceful, wooded site on banks Rv Dordogne; poss mosquitoes by rv; gd pool; helpful staff; beautiful scenery." ♦ Easter-30 Sep. € 15.60   2006*

France

SOUILLAC 7C3 (5km SW Rural) **Camp Municipal La Borgne, 24370 Cazoulès** [05 53 29 81 64 or 05 53 31 45 25 (Mairie); fax 05 53 31 45 26; mairie.cazoules@wanadoo.fr; http://pagesperso-orange.fr/cazoules] Fr Souillac, take D703 twd Sarlat. In 4km in vill of Cazoulès turn L & foll site sps. Site adj Rv Dordogne. Lge, pt shd; wc; baby facs; shwrs inc; el pnts (10A) €2.50; lndtte; sm shop; supmkt 4km; BBQ; playgrnd; pool; paddling pool; rv sw; canoe trips; boat hire; fishing; tennis adj; some statics; dogs €0.80; quiet. "Poss mosquito problem; helpful staff; excel rest in vill." ♦ 4 Jun-8 Sep. € 14.50   2007*

SOUILLAC 7C3 (10km SW Rural) **Camping Le Héron, Mareuil, 46200 Le Roc** [tel/fax 05 65 37 67 38; vpassingham@free.fr; www.heroncamping.com] Fr Souillac, take D804 (D703) W sp Sarlat & in 300m turn L onto D255 (later becomes D43) sp Le Roc, over rv bdge (take care sharp bend & single track). Cont on D43 thro Le Roc. Foll sp L onto D12 sp Gourdon, site in 200m on L. Sm, pt shd; wc; chem disp; fam bthrm; shwrs inc; el pnts (6-10A) inc; gas 6km; lndtte; ice; shop & 4km; tradsmn; rest, snacks, bar 4km; htd pool; rv nr; fishing; watersports; dogs €2; Eng spkn; adv bkg; quiet but some rd/rlwy noise; no cc acc; red long stay/CCI. "Friendly British owners; lge pitches; château & caves nrby; beautiful scenery for walks & cycling." ♦ 1 Apr-31 Oct. € 16.90   2005*

SOUILLAC 7C3 (1km W Urban) **Camping Les Ondines, Ave de Sarlat, 46200 Souillac** [05 65 37 86 44 or 06 33 54 32 00; fax 05 65 32 61 15; mairie@souillac.fr; www.souillac.fr] Turn W off D820 (N20) in cent Souillac onto D703 sp Sarlat. In 200m turn L at sp into narr rd. Ent 400m on R adj rv. Lge, mkd pitch, pt sl, pt shd; wc; chem disp; shwrs inc; el pnts (5A) €2; lndtte; shop; rest 1km; BBQ; playgrnd; htd pool & aquatic park nrby; rv sw; tennis; fishing; canoeing; tennis; minigolf; horseriding; gd walking; entmnt; child entmnt; some statics; dogs; phone; Eng spkn; quiet; CCI. "Clean facs; dedicated staff; conv for Rocamadour & caves; conv NH; vg." ♦ 1 May-30 Sep. € 9.50   2007*

⊞**SOUILLAC** 7C3 (6km W Rural) **Camping à la Ferme (Levet), Le Périgourdine, 24370 Peyrillac-et-Millac** [05 53 29 72 12] Fr cent of Souillac, W on D703 to Peyrillac-et-Millac; in vill turn L at sp to site. Drive past farmhouse, ent 75m on R. Sm, pt shd; htd wc; shwrs inc; el pnts (16A) €2.50; lndry rm; shop, rest, bar etc 5km; BBQ; playgrnd; pool; rv 2km; dogs €1.50; adv bkg; quiet; no cc acc; CCI. "Excel CL-type site; gd touring cent & gd NH en rte Spain; friendly & helpful; ltd facs low ssn; easy to find; not suitable lge o'fits as access narr, sloping & sharp bend." € 10.00   2007*

SOUILLAC 7C3 (6km W Rural) **Camping au P'tit Bonheur, 24370 Peyrillac-et-Millac** [tel/fax 05 53 29 77 93; auptitbonheur@wanadoo.fr; www.camping-auptitbonheur.com] Exit Souillac by D703 sp Sarlat. At Peyrillac turn R to Millac, about 2km on minor & narr rd uphill (13%) to plateau. Well sp fr D703. Med, terr, hdg/mkd pitch, pt shd; wc (some cont); chem disp; shwrs inc; el pnts (10A) €3.50; gas; shops 2km; tradsmn; snacks; bar; playgrndhtd pool; 5% statics; dogs €1.95; Eng spkn; adv bkg; quiet; 10% red low ssn; cc acc high ssn only; CCI. "Peaceful, well-run site with views; owners pleasant; app rd steep mostly single track; many pitches diff for twin-axles & lge o'fits; excel." ♦ 15 Apr-15 Sep. € 15.80   2007*

SOUILLAC 7C3 (7km NW Rural) **Camping La Draille, La Draille, 46200 Souillac** [05 65 32 65 01; fax 05 65 37 06 20; la.draille@wanadoo.fr; www.ladraille.com] Leave Souillac on D15 sp Salignac-Evvigues; at Bourzoles in 6km take D165; site sp in 500m on L. Med, hdg pitch, pt sl, pt shd; wc; chem disp; baby facs; shwrs inc; el pnts (4A) €2.50; lndtte; ice; shop; rest; snacks; bar; BBQ; pool; 25% statics; dogs €2.50; phone; poss cr; Eng spkn; adv bkg; quiet; cc acc; CCI. "Lovely location; v friendly; gd walks; highly rec." ♦ 22 Apr-13 Oct. € 20.50   2007*

SOUILLAC *7C3* (8km NW Rural) **Camping Le Domaine de la Paille Basse, 46200 Souillac [05 65 37 85 48; fax 05 65 37 09 58; info@lapaillebasse.com; www.lapaillebasse.com or www.les-castels.com]** Exit Souillac by D15 sp Salignac, turn onto D165 at Bourzolles foll sp to site in 3km. Steep & narr app, few passing places (not suitable lge o'fits). Lge, hdg pitch, terr, pt shd; wc; chem disp; mv service pnt 800m; shwrs inc; el pnts (3-6A) €4-6; gas; Indtte; shop; rest; snacks; bar; ice; playgrnd; pool; paddling pool; waterslides; games rm; tennis; mini-golf; sports area; golf 5km; organised outdoor activities; entmnt; internet; TV rm; dogs €4; adv bkg; quiet; red low ssn; cc acc;. "Excel site in quiet, remote location; v clean facs; some shwrs unisex; friendly, helpful staff; excel rest & gd shop; restored medieval vill." ♦ 12 May-15 Sep. € 28.80 (CChq acc)   2007*

SOULAC SUR MER *7B1* (1km S Coastal) **Camping Le Palace, 65 Blvd Marsan-de-Montbrun, Forêt Sud, 33780 Soulac-sur-Mer [05 56 09 80 22; fax 05 56 09 84 23; www.camping-palace.com; www.camping-palace.com]** Fr ferry at Le Verdon-sur-Mer S on N215, site sp. Or fr S on D101. V lge, mkd pitch, shd; wc; mv service pnt; baby facs; shwrs inc; el pnts; Indtte; shop; rest; snacks; bar; BBQ; playgrnd; htd, covrd pool; sand beach 400m; entmnt; 65% statics; dogs €2.50; adv bkg; quiet. "Ideal for family beach holiday." 1 Apr-30 Sep. € 25.00   2007*

See advertisement on previous page

SOULAC SUR MER *7B1* (13km S Coastal) **Camp Municipal du Gurp, 51 Route de l'Océan, 33590 Grayan-et-L'Hôpital [05 56 09 44 53; fax 05 56 09 54 73]** Take D101 fr Soulac. Turn R after 5km sp Grayan & R at x-rds. Site clearly sp. V lge, mkd pitch, hdstg, shd; wc; chem disp; shwrs inc; el pnts (4A); Indtte; shop; rest; snacks; bar; playgrnd; sand beach adj; tennis; games area; entmnt; TV; dogs; poss cr; quiet. "In pine forest; gd, vast beaches." 1 Jun-10 Sep. € 10.67   2005*

SOULAC SUR MER *7B1* (13km S Coastal) **Centre Naturiste Euronat La Dépée (Naturist), 33590 Grayan-et-L'Hôpital [05 56 09 33 33; fax 05 56 09 30 27; info@euronat.fr; www.euronat.fr]** Fr Soulac, take D101 twd Montalivet, turn W at camp sp onto rd leading direct to site. Fr Bordeaux, take N215 sp Le Verdon-sur-Mer. Approx 8km after Lesparre-Médoc turn L onto D102. In Venday-Montalivet bear R onto D101. In 7.5km turn L sp Euronat. V lge, mkd pitch, hdstg, shd; wc (some htd); chem disp; shwrs inc; el pnts (10A) inc; gas; Indtte; ice; shop; rest; snacks; bar; BBQ; playgrnd; htd, covrd pool; sand beach adj; tennis; horseriding; cinema; archery; cycle hire; golf driving range; internet; TV; 30% statics; dogs €3; phone; Eng spkn; adv bkg (dep req); quiet; red low ssn; INF card req. "Expensive, but well worth it." ♦ 24 Mar-4 Nov. € 42.00 (CChq acc)   2006*

SOULAC SUR MER *7B1* (1.5km SW Coastal) **Camping Les Sables d'Argent, Blvd de l'Amélie, 33780 Soulac-sur-Mer [05 56 09 82 87; fax 05 56 09 94 82; sables@lelilhan.com; www.sables-d-argent.com]** Drive S fr Soulac twd L'Amélie-sur-Mer. Clearly sp on R. Med, mkd pitch, pt sl, pt shd; wc; shwrs inc; el pnts (10A) €3.95; Indtte; shop; rest; snacks; bar; private sand beach adj; fishing; tennis; internet; entmnt; TV; 60% statics; dogs €2.60; poss cr. "Poss diff lge o'fits; ideal seaside with lge uncr beach & some surf; Soulac sm, lively mkt town." 1 Apr-30 Sep. € 18.95 (CChq acc)   2007*

SOULAINES DHUYS *6E1* (500m Rural) **Camp Municipal de la Croix Badeau, 10200 Soulaines-Dhuys [03 25 92 77 44 or 03 25 92 77 85]** 500m N of junc D960 & D384, behind lge church of Soulaines-Dhuys, well sp. Sm, hdg/mkd pitch, hdstg, pt shd; wc ltd (some cont); chem disp (wc); shwrs inc; el pnts (10A) inc (rev pol); Indry rm; ice; shop 500m; playgrnd; tennis; rv 300m; phone; Eng spkn; quiet; CCI. "Excel, clean site in fascinating vill; twin-axle €25 extra; security gate clsd 24 hrs; resident warden; security card req for facs block; facs stretched if site full; hourly church bells (silent 1930-0900)." 1 May-30 Sep. € 9.13   2006*

SOULLANS *2H3* (500m NE Urban) **Camp Municipal Le Moulin Neuf, Rue St Christophe, 85300 Soullans [02 51 68 00 24 (Mairie); fax 02 51 68 88 66]** Fr Challans ring rd take D69 sp Soullans. Site sp on L just bef town cent. Med, hdg/mkd pitch, pt shd; wc (some cont); shwrs inc; el pnts (4A) inc; gas 500m; Indtte; shop 500m; playgrnd; beach 12km; tennis; phone adj; poss cr; adv bkg; quiet; CCI. "Vg; lovely walks & cycling; simple site." 15 Jun-15 Sep. € 8.80   2005*

SOUPPES SUR LOING *4F3* (1km SW) **Camp Municipal Les Bords du Loing, Chemin des Mariniers, 77460 Souppes-sur-Loing [01 64 29 72 63 or 01 64 78 57 77]** Fr A77 take exit 17 onto N7 dir Nemours, site sp on SW side of rd over rlwy x-ing alongside Loing canal. Lge, pt shd; wc (cont); shwrs inc; el pnts (6A); gas; Indtte; ice; shops 1km; BBQ; playgrnd; child club; sports area; lake 50m; fishing, tennis, kayak 400m; horseriding 3km; golf 7km; entmnt; statics; adv bkg;. "Poss noisy at w/e & hols; fair sh stay." ♦ 1 Apr-31 Oct. € 8.38   2004*

SOURAIDE see Cambo les Bains *8F1*

SOURDEVAL *2E4* (N Urban) **Aire Naturelle de Camp Municipal, 50150 Sourdeval [02 33 59 61 97 or 02 33 79 35 55 (Mairie); fax 02 33 79 35 59; otsourdeval@wanadoo.fr]** Well sp fr all dirs on D977 11km N Mortain. Sm, pt sl, unshd; wc; shwrs; el pnts (10A); playgrnd; fishing; tennis; quiet. "NH only." 1 Jun-30 Sep.   2004*

SOURSAC 7C4 (1km NE) Camp Municipal de la Plage, Centre Touristique du Pont Aubert, 19550 Soursac [05 55 27 55 43 or 05 55 27 52 61 (Mairie); fax 05 55 27 63 31; centrepontaubert@wanadoo.fr] Fr Mauriac take D678 to Chalvignac. Bear R onto D105 at 3km (12% descent) to cross Barrage de l'Aigle & 2km 12% ascent on D105E/D16, winding rd. In further 3km pass junc to Latronche, 1st R to site. Med, terr, pt sl, shd; wc; mv service pnt; baby facs; shwrs inc; el pnts (6A) €2.10; lndtte; ice; shop 1km; rest planned 2006; snacks; playgrnd; pool & waterslide nrby; lake sw; archery; cycle hire; mini golf; games area; TV; adv bkg; quiet; "V gd clean san facs; attractive by lake; well worth detour; excel." ♦ 15 Jun-15 Sep. € 8.80   2005*

SOUSTONS 8E1 (6km NE Rural) Camping Le Tuc, 155 Rue Henri Goalard, 40140 Azur [05 58 48 22 52; fax 05 58 48 33 53; campingletuc@wanadoo.fr; www.campingletuc.fr] Exit N10 junc 11at Magescq onto D150 dir Azur; site on R 1km SE fr Azur. Site sp fr Azur. Med, hdg pitch, pt shd; wc; chem disp; shwrs inc; el pnts (6-10A) €2.30; gas; lndtte; ice; shop, tradsmn (high ssn); playgrnd; pool; tennis; games area; lake water sports & fishing 2km; TV rm; 50% statics; dogs €1.60; poss cr; adv bkg; quiet; red low ssn; CCI. "Woodland walk; excel." ♦ 1 Apr-15 Sep. € 11.50   2006*

SOUSTONS 8E1 (6km NE Rural) Camping Village La Paillotte, 40140 Azur [05 58 48 12 12; fax 05 58 48 10 73; info@paillotte.com; www.paillotte.com] Fr N10 turn W at Magescq onto D150 (site about 8km fr this junc); join D50 to Azur. Turn L at church in Azur; foll site sp. Lge, mkd pitch, pt shd; wc (some cont); chem disp; baby facs; shwrs inc; el pnts (10A) inc; lndtte; shop; rest; snacks; bar; BBQ (gas/elec); playgrnd; htd pool; paddling pool; waterslide; lake sw & sand beach adj; hot springs; dinghy sailing; windsurfing; fishing; cycle hire; tennis; horseriding 7km; entmnt; internet; games/TV rm; statics (tour ops); no dogs; bus; recep 0900-2000 high ssn; adv bkg; cc acc; CCI. "Facs ltd low ssn; lakeside site; mkt Soustons Mon." ♦ ltd. 31 May-20 Sep. € 38.00 ABS - A22   2007*

SOUSTONS 8E1 (6.5km NE) Camping Azu'Rivage, 720 Route des Campings, 40140 Azur [tel/fax 05 58 48 30 72; info@camingazurivage.com; www.campingazurivage.com] Exit m'way A10 at exit Magescq & take D150 W for 8km to Azur, site sp fr church adj La Paillotte. Med, pt shd; wc; baby facs; shwrs inc; el pnts (10A) inc; lndtte; sm shop & 6km; rest; snacks; playgrnd; pool; sand beach & lake sw; tennis; boating; watersports; entmnt; TV rm; dogs €1.65; poss cr; adv bkg; red long stay; quiet. "Delightful forest setting adj lake; rec." ♦ 15 Jun-15 Sep. € 17.40   2005*

SOUSTONS 8E1 (2km W Rural) Camp Municipal L'Airial, 61 Ave de Port d'Albret, Quartier Nicot, 40140 Soustons [05 58 41 12 48; fax 05 58 41 53 83; contact@camping-airial.com; www.camping-airial.com] On D652 (Mimizan/Labenne), opp Etang de Soustons. Foll site sp fr Soustons. Lge, mkd pitch, shd; wc; chem disp; shwrs inc; el pnts (10A) €4.70; lndtte; shop; snacks; bar; playgrnd; htd, covrd pool; sand beach 7km; boating; watersports; fishing; cycle hire; entmnt; TV rm; dogs €3.50; phone; poss cr; adv bkg; quiet; red low ssn. "V pleasant site; gd shade & many birds; gd, clean facs but ltd low ssn." 1 Apr-15 Oct. € 19.80   2007*

⊞SOUTERRAINE, LA 7A3 (2km NE Rural) Camping Suisse Océan, Etang du Cheix, 23300 La Souterraine [05 55 63 33 32 or 05 55 63 59 71; fax 05 55 63 21 82] N145/E62 take D72 sp La Souterraine. Strt over 1st rndabt, at 2nd rndabt turn R, then L to L'Etang de Cheix. Sm, hdg/mkd pitch, hdstg, pt sl, terr, pt shd; htd wc (some cont); chem disp; mv service pnt; shwrs inc; el pnts (10A) €2.80; lndtte; ice; sm shop & 2km; tradsmn; rest; snacks; bar; playgrnd; sand lake beach adj; tennis; fishing, sailing adj; diving (summer); 10% statics; dogs €0.80; poss cr; Eng spkn; adv bkg; quiet but night noise fr factory nrby; CCI. "V attractive site in superb location by lake; v lge pitches; v sl rds on site could ground lge o'fits - walk site bef pitching; san facs in portacabin; ltd facs low ssn inc el pnts & stretched when site full; gd rest; pleasant sm town; mkt Thur & Sat." ♦ € 9.20   2007*

SOUTERRAINE, LA 7A3 (6km E Rural) Camp Municipal Etang de la Cazine, 23300 Noth [05 55 63 72 21; fax 05 55 63 13 12; mairiedenoth@wanadoo.fr] Exit A20 junc 23 onto N145 dir Guéret; turn L on D49 sp Noth. Site opp lake. Sm, shd; wc, chem disp; shwrs inc; el pnts (10A) €1.60; ltd snacks; bar; lake fishing & sw adj; quiet; CCI. "Gd touring base; fishing permits fr bar; gd." 1 Jun-30 Sep. € 7.40   2006*

SOUTERRAINE, LA 7A3 (10km S Rural) Camp Municipal, 23290 St Pierre-de-Fursac [05 55 63 65 69 or 05 55 63 61 28 (Mairie); fax 05 55 63 68 20] Exit A20 at junc 23.1 onto D1 S twd St Pierre-de-Fursac. Site on L at ent to vill dir 'Stade'. Sm, mkd pitch, pt sl, pt shd; wc; shwrs inc; el pnts (6A) €1.20 (poss rev pol); shop 500m; playgrnd; phone; quiet. "Pleasant, well-kept site o'looking vill; well-kept san facs; many walks sp." ♦ ltd. 15 Jun-16 Sep. € 4.00   2007*

STENAY 5C1 (2km W Urban) Camp Municipal Les Pâquis, 55700 Stenay [03 29 80 64 56 or 03 29 80 64 22 (Tourist Office); fax 03 29 80 62 59; otsistenay@wanadoo.fr] App on D964 or D947. Site adj Rv Meuse, sp fr rndabt in cent of Stenay. Lge, mkd pitch, pt shd; wc; own san; chem disp; shwrs; el pnts (6A) €2.50; gas; shop; rv fishing; adv bkg; quiet; CCI. "Museum of Beer in town." 25 May-3 Sep. € 7.00   2007*

France

⊞**STRASBOURG** *6E3* (3km W Urban) **FFCC Camping La Montagne Verte, 2 Rue Robert Forrer, 67000 Strasbourg [03 88 30 25 46; fax 03 88 27 10 15; aquadis1@wanadoo.fr; www. aquadis-loisirs.com]** Fr A35 about 2km S of Strasbourg exit junc 4 for Montagne-Verte. Foll camp sp, 1st R to site on R in approx 1km. Sp off D1004 (N4) & D392 to W of city, 1km fr town side of Boulevard de Lyon. Fr town cent foll sp for St Dié/ Colmar as camp sp intermittent. Height limit 3.3m on app rd. Lge, mkd pitch, pt shd; wc; chem disp; baby facs; shwrs inc; el pnts (6A) inc (poss rev pol); gas; lndry rm; shop 200m; rest 250m; tradsmn; bar; BBQ; playgrnd; covrd pool; tennis; games area; few statics; dogs €3.10; bus/tram to city; Eng spkn; noise fr aircraft, rlwy & church clock; cc acc; 10% red CCI. "Well-maintained site adj rv; poss unkempt low ssn; san facs clean but need refurb; pitches v soft after rain; gates clsd 1900-0700 & 1200-1530 low ssn; easy access to city lge gd cycle tracks by rv; mixed reports early ssn; poss itinerants; gd dog walks." € 19.90   2007*

SUEVRES see Blois *4G2*

⊞**SUHESCUN** *8F1* (Rural) **Camping à la Ferme (Bachoc), Maison Etchemendigaraya, 64780 Suhescun [05 59 37 60 83; bruno.bachoc@ wanadoo.fr; www.chez.com/mendi]** Fr D933 fr St Palais to St Jean-Pied-de-Port, take D22 twd Suhescun. Site sp. Sm, pt sl, pt shd; wc; shwrs inc; el pnts (3A) €2; lndry rm; ice; shop 3km; farm produce for sale; sand beach 45km; watersports nr; cycle hire; statics; adv bkg; quiet; red CCI. "CL-type site on working farm; vg family atmosphere; welcoming owners; conv en rte Spain." € 10.00
                                                    2004*

⊞**SULLY SUR LOIRE** *4F3* (2km N Rural) **Camping Hortus - Le Jardin de Sully, 1 Route d'Orléans, St Père-sur-Loire, 45600 Sully-sur-Loire [tel/ fax 02 38 36 35 94; info@camping-hortus.com; www.camping-hortus.com]** Fr N on D948 to Sully then turn R at rndabt immed bef x-ing bdge over Rv Loire onto D60 in St Père-sur-Loire, dir Châteauneuf-sur-Loire. Sp to site in 200m. Fr S thro Sully on D948, cross Rv Loire & turn L at rndabt onto D60. Well sp fr town. Med, hdg/mkd pitch, hdstg, pt shd; htd wc; chem disp; mv service pnt; serviced pitches; shwrs inc; el pnts (10A) inc (poss rev pol); gas 800m; lndtte; shop; snacks; pizzeria; bar; BBQ; sm pool; playgrnd; rv beach adj; child entmnt; sat TV; 45% statics; dogs €1.60; phone; bus; Eng spkn; adv bkg rec; quiet; cc acc; red CCI. "Nice, well laid out, v organised site on rvside; warm welcome; helpful & friendly; clean facs; some sm pitches; gd cycling; gd dog walks; nature reserve adj; fairy-tale chateau in Sully." ♦ € 19.50   2007*

See advertisement

SURGERES *7A2* (1km S Urban) **Camp Municipal de la Gères, 17700 Surgères [05 46 07 79 97 or 05 46 07 00 23 (Mairie); fax 05 46 07 53 98 (Mairie)]** Site sp in Surgères, on banks of Rv Gères, & fr Surgères by-pass. Sm, pt shd; wc (cont); mv service pnt; shwrs; el pnts (5A) €2.50-3.00; shop 200m; rest, snacks & bar 800m; pool & tennis 800m; dogs €1; phone; poss cr; cc acc; CCI. "Adj to park; m'vans extra charge; poss itinerants; NH only." 1 Apr-30 Oct. € 7.63
                                                    2005*

SURIS *7B3* (1km N Rural) **Camping La Blanchie, 16270 Suris [tel/fax 05 45 89 33 19 or 06 12 15 66 03 (mob); lablanchie@wanadoo. fr; www.lablanchie.co.uk]** Fr N141 halfway bet Angoulême & Limoges take D52 S at La Péruse to Suris. In 2km turn E up a narr lane to site. Sm, some hdstg, pt sl, pt shd; wc; chem disp; shwrs inc; el pnts (10A) €2.50; lndtte; playgrnd; pool; lake/rv sw & sand beach 2.5km; tennis, golf, Futuroscope nrby; some statics; no dogs; c'van storage; adv bkg; quiet; red long stay; CCI. "V welcoming British owners; v clean site in lovely area; ltd facs; gd touring base." ♦ 1 Mar-31 Oct. € 12.50   2007*

⊞**SURTAINVILLE** *1C4* (1km W Coastal) **Camp Municipal Les Mielles, 80 Route des Laguettes, 50270 Surtainville [02 33 10 12 40 or 02 33 04 31 04 (Mairie); mairie.surtainville@ wanadoo.fr; www.surtainville.com]** S fr Cherbourg on D650, take D66 W thro Surtainville, site on R. Med, pt sl, unshd; htd wc (male cont); chem disp; shwrs inc; el pnts (4A) €2.50; lndtte; playgrnd; sand beach 100m; 30% statics; dogs €1; adv bkg; quiet; CCI. "Excel beach." ♦ ltd. € 8.25   2005*

SUSSAC *7B4* (S Rural) **Camp Municipal Beauséjour, Plan d'Eau, 87130 Sussac [05 55 69 62 41; fax 05 55 69 36 80]** Fr Eymoutiers take D30 dir Chamberet & turn R onto D43 at Chouviat for Sussac. Cont for approx 9 km & foll sp. Site adj lake Sm, mkd pitch, terr, pt shd; wc (cont); chem disp; shwrs inc; el pnts €2.30; lndtte; shops 500m; snacks; bar; playgrnd; sw lake adj; Eng spkn; adv bkg; quiet. "Gd site; gd walks, fishing." Jul-Aug. € 8.00   2004*

SUSSAC *7B4* (S Rural) **Camping Les Saules (Naturist), 87130 Sussac [05 55 69 64 36 or 0031-2068-25077 (LS); janjansen@lessaules. com; www.lessaules.com]** SE fr Limoges on D979; in 33km turn R to Châteauneuf-la-Forêt; then sharp L turn onto D39 to Sussac. Site sp. Sm, hdg/ mkd pitch, terr, pt shd; wc; shwrs inc; el pnts (6A) €3.50; lndtte; ice; shop 10km; tradsmn; snacks; bar; BBQ; playgrnd; lake sand beach; games area; dogs free; Eng spkn; adv bkg (dep req); quiet. "Natural site with wild life & flowers; friendly Dutch owners; communal meals twice wk; guided walks; facs poss stretched when full; sep car park; vg." 16 Jun-31 Aug. € 16.60   2007*

SUZE SUR SARTHE, LA *4F1* (Urban) **Camp Municipal Le Port, Ave de la Piscine,** 72210 La Suze-sur-Sarthe [02 43 77 32 74 or 02 43 77 30 49; fax 02 43 77 28 77] Take D23 S of Le Mans fr N226 ring rd for 6.5km. Turn R at sp for La Suze-sur-Sarthe & foll sp for Camping & Piscine. Turn R just bef pool 200m fr rv bdge in vill & adj to pool. Rec use D23 sp for lorries fr E of town. Med, mkd pitch, pt shd; wc; own san; chem disp; mv service pnt (in adj car park); shwrs inc; el pnts (10A) €2.30; shops, snacks 300m; BBQ; playgrnd adj; htd pool adj; rv adj; fishing; boating; tennis; TV; many statics; dogs €0.45; adv bkg; red 7+ days. "Narr gate to site; ample hdstg & ltd free el pnts for m'vans in adj car park." ♦ ltd. 1 May-30 Sep. € 4.50
2005*

This guide relies on site report forms submitted by caravanners like us; we'll do our bit and tell the editor what we think of the campsites we've visited.

TADEN see Dinan *2E3*

⊞**TAIN L'HERMITAGE** *9C2* (5km NE Rural) **Camping Chante-Merle,** 26600 Chantemerle-les-Blés [04 75 07 49 73; fax 04 75 07 45 15; campingchantemerle@wanadoo.fr] Exit A7 at Tain-l'Hermitage. After exit toll turn L twd town, next turn R (D109) to Chantemerle; site sp. Cont for 5km, site on L. Sm, hdg/mkd pitch, pt shd; htd wc; chem disp; serviced pitches; baby facs; shwrs inc; el pnts (6A) €2.60; lndtte; ice; shops 300m; tradsmn; rest & snacks high ssn; bar; playgrnd; pool; tennis 500m; 10% statics; dogs; site clsd Jan; adv bkg ess; quiet but some rd noise; CCI. "Helpful manager; v popular site; excel facs." ♦ € 14.80   2006*

TAIN L'HERMITAGE *9C2* (S Urban) **Camp Municipal Les Lucs,** 24 Ave Roosevelt, 26600 Tain l'Hermitage [04 75 08 32 82 or 04 75 08 30 32; fax 04 75 08 32 06; camping. tainlhermitage@wanadoo.fr; http://pagesperso-orange.fr/leslucs] At S end of town on N7 nr bdge to Tournon. Alongside Rv Rhône via gates (locked o/night). Well sp adj sw pool/petrol stn. Med, hdg/ mkd pitch, pt shd; wc (mainly cont); chem disp; mv service pnt; shwrs inc; el pnts (10A) €1.10 (poss rev pol); lndtte; shops, snacks adj; playgrnd; pool adj high ssn; dogs €1.15; phone; no twin-axles & no access for c'vans or m'vans over 5.50m; Eng spkn; rd/rlwy noise; red low ssn; cc not acc; CCI. "Popular NH; pretty, immac, secure site by Rhône; well-organised & well-controlled; super, friendly staff; excel pool complex adj open 1 Jun; access via barrier code; pleasant walks by rv to Tain & Tournon; no twin-axles & no access for lge m'vans over 6m; highly rec." 15 Mar-15 Oct. € 16.60
2007*

TALLARD see Gap *9D3*

TALLOIRES see Annecy *9B3*

TANINGES see Cluses *9A3*

⊞**TARADEAU** *10F3* (3km S Rural) **Camping La Vallée de Taradeau, Chemin La Musardière,** 83460 Taradeau [tel/fax 04 94 73 09 14; campingdetaradeau@hotmail.com; www. campingdetaradeau.com] Exit A8 at Le Muy W or Le Luc E & take DN7 (N7) to Vidauban. Opp Mairie take D48 twd Lorgues & D73 N twd Taradeau for 1.5km. Site sp - rough app rd - on rvside. Med, mkd pitch, shd; htd wc; mv service pnt; shwrs inc; el pnts (2-10A) €2.30-6.50; lndtte; rest; snacks; bar; playgrnd; pool; caneoing; games area; internet; entmnt; some statics; dogs €2; adv bkg; quiet; CCI. "Pleasantly situated site; friendly, helpful staff." € 17.00   2007*

France

TARASCON *10E2* (6km N Rural) **Camping Lou Vincen, 30300 Vallabrègues [04 66 59 21 29; fax 04 66 59 07 41; campinglouvincen@wanadoo.fr; www.campinglouvincen.com]** N fr Tarascon on D81A, then D183A. Med, hdg/mkd pitch, hdstg, shd; htd wc (some cont); chem disp; mv service pnt; shwrs inc; el pnts (6A) €3.20; gas; lndtte; ice; shop, rest, snacks, bar 100m; playgrnd; pool; tennis; fishing; horseriding 3km; TV; dogs €1; adv bkg; quiet ut noise fr skateboarders opp; cc acc; red long stay/low ssn; CCI. "Hdg pitches poss diff v lge o'fits; v ltd facs low ssn; attractive vill; gd base for Camargue/Nîmes." 2 Apr-20 Oct. € 13.80
2006*

TARASCON *10E2* (5km SE Rural) **Camping St Gabriel, 13150 Tarascon [tel/fax 04 90 91 19 83; contact@campingsaintgabriel. com; www.campingsaintgabriel.com]** Take D970 fr Tarascon, at rndabt take D33 sp Fontvieille, site sp 100m on R. Med, hdg pitch, shd; htd wc; chem disp; shwrs inc; el pnts (6A) €3; gas; lndtte; shop; rest adj; snacks; bar; playgrnd; htd pool; games rm; statics 10%; dogs €1; bus 3km; adv bkg; quiet but some rd noise; CCI. "Excel base for Camague & Arles; not suitable lge o'fits; gd." ♦ ltd. 1 Feb-15 Dec. € 13.50
2006*

TARASCON *10E2* (2km W Rural) **Camp Municipal Le Rhodanien, Ave des Arènes, 30300 Beaucaire [04 66 59 25 50 or 04 66 59 26 57; fax 04 66 59 68 51; beaucair@mnet.fr]** Take D999 W fr Tarascon to Beaucaire, across Rv Rhône. At end of bdge immed turn R at Camping sp to site in 1km. Fr W on D999 turn N on W o'skts of town twd chateau, adj Rv Rhône. Med, mkd pitch, shd; htd wc (some cont); shwrs; gas; ice; el pnts (10A) €3.05; shops 200m; rest, bar 100m; playgrnd; pool; fishing; sailing; windsurfing; tennis; games area; adv bkg; quiet, but some rd noise; CCI. ♦ 15 Jun-15 Sep. € 12.36
2005*

TARASCON SUR ARIEGE *8G3* (4km N Rural) **Camping du Lac, 1 Promenade du Camping, 09400 Mercus-Garrabet [tel/fax 05 61 05 90 61 or 06 86 07 24 18 (mob); info@campinglac.com; www.campinglac.com]** N20 S fr Foix, after 10km exit Mercus over N20 sp, cross rlwy line. At T-junc turn R thro Mercus, site of R over level x-ing. Tight bend into site off long, narr ent drive. Med, hdg/mkd pitch, terr, shd; wc (some cont); chem disp; baby facs; shwrs inc; el pnts (6-10A) €3-4.50; ice; lndtte; shop; tradsmn; rest & bar 1km; supmkt 4km; BBQ; htd pool; rv & lake sw, fishing & watersports adj; games rm; 20% statics; dogs €2; phone; some Eng spkn; adv bkg (fee); slight rd & rlwy noise; red long stay: CCI. "V clean facs; v friendly owners; diff ent for long c'vans; sm pitches; 60km Andorra; a real find; excel." ♦ ltd. Easter-6 Oct. € 23.00
2006*

TARASCON SUR ARIEGE *8G3* (1.5km SE Rural) **FFCC Camping Le Pré-Lombard, Route d'Ussat, 09400 Tarascon-sur-Ariège [05 61 05 61 94; fax 05 61 05 78 93; leprelombard@wanadoo.fr; www. prelombard.com]** Travelling S twd Andorra join N20 to Tarascon. Approx 15km S of Foix after 3 rndabts & x-ing a bdge, at 4th rndabt turn L & foll site sp after rlwy. This rte avoids cent of Tarascon. Lge, mkd pitch, pt shd; htd wc; chem disp; mv service pnt; shwrs inc; el pnts (10A) inc; gas; lndtte; ice; shop & snacks high ssn only; rest & supmkt in town; bar; BBQ (gas/elec/charcoal); playgrnd; htd pool; paddling pool; rv fishing, watersports & sw adj; tennis 1km; archery; entmnt; child entmnt; internet; games/TV rm; 50% statics; dogs €2; Eng spkn; adv bkg rec high ssn; quiet; red low ssn; cc acc; CCI. "Lovely location by rv; spacious pitches; well-run; gd san facs; helpful owner; excel winter NH en rte to Spain; busy family site high ssn; poss noisy at night; gd walks; conv Andorra; prehistoric caves nrby; vg." ♦ 22 Mar-11 Nov. € 29.50 (CChq acc) ABS - D23
2007*

As soon as we get home I'm going to post all these site report forms to the editor for inclusion in next year's guide. I don't want to miss the September deadline.

TARASCON SUR ARIEGE *8G3* (2km S Rural) **Camping Ariège Evasion, 09400 Ornolac-Ussat-Les-Bains [tel/fax 05 61 05 11 11; contact@ ariege-evasion.com; www.ariege-evasion.com]** S on N20 fr Foix to Tarascon-sur-Ariège then 2km to Ornolac-Ussat-Les-Bains. Foll camp sp over narr bdge & R at T-junc. In 750m turn L & immed R at staggered x-rds, site in 100m. Med, hdg/mkd pitch, pt shd; wc (cont); chem disp; mv service pnt; shwrs inc; el pnts (3-10A) €2-4; gas 1km; lndtte; shop 1km; tradsmn; rest; playgrnd; rv sw; trout-fishing; canoe hire; 5% statics; Eng spkn; adv bkg; quiet; red low ssn; CCI. "Prehistoric caves nr; largest cave in Europe in vill; conv Andorra." 1 Mar-15 Oct. € 12.50
2004*

⊞**TARASCON SUR ARIEGE** *8G3* (1.5km NW Rural) **Camping Le Sédour, Florac, 09400 Surba [05 61 05 87 28; fax 05 61 01 49 33; info@ campinglesedour.com; www.campinglesedour. com]** Fr rndbt 1km N of Tarascon take 1st R sp Massat. Turn R in 100m, site on L in Surba vill. Med, hdg/mkd pitch, pt sl, pt shd; wc; chem disp; some serviced pitches; shwrs inc; el pnts (10A) inc; lndtte; supmkt 1km; tradsmn; rest, bar 300m; playgrnd; 60% statics; dogs €1.50; poss cr; some Eng spkn; adv bkg; quiet; red long stay; CCI. "Friendly, helpful owners; gd facs; poss diff access lge o'fits; conv for Ariège valleys & prehistoric park; mountain views." ♦ € 18.00
2005*

LE PANORAMIC**✱✱✱✱**
Campsite of the "SITES et PAYSAGES de FRANCE" chain

Camping LE PANORAMIC
Route de la Plage
29560 TELGRUC SUR MER
Phone: 02 98 27 78 41
Fax: 02 98 27 36 10
Info@camping-panoramic.com
www.camping-panoramic.com

Quiet family camping at the seaside (beach at 700m), in the Regional Natural Park of Armorique. Situated on the peninsula of CROZON where one can discover all the different faces of Brittany: the beaches, the steep cliffs, the dunes, the harbours, the islands, the forests.... 200 pitches, swimming pool, Jacuzzi, tennis, restaurant, bar. Rental of mobile homes.

TARDETS SORHOLUS *8F1* (1km S Rural) **Camping du Pont d'Abense, 64470 Tardets-Sorholus [tel/ fax 05 59 28 58 76; camping.abense@wanadoo. fr; www.camping-pontabense.com]** Take D918 S to Tardets, turn R to cross bdge onto D57. Site sp on R. Tardets cent narr. Med, mkd pitch, shd; wc; chem disp; shwrs inc; el pnts (3A) inc; lndry rm; shop, rest, snacks & bar 500m; tradsmn; rv sw & beach nrby; fishing; some statics; dogs €2; quiet; adv bkg; CCI. "Facs old and poss dirty; 20 mins walk to town with traditional Basque shops; excel gorge walks short drive away." 15 Apr-11 Nov. € 17.90   2007*

TARDETS SORHOLUS *8F1* (1km W) **Camping à la Ferme Carrique (Iriart), 64470 Alos-Sibas-Abense [05 59 28 50 25; carrique64@hotmail.fr; www. valleedesoule.com/MINISITE/camping-carrique. htm]** S fr Mauléon on D918 to Tardets-Sorholus. Turn W on D24 to Alos over single c'way bdge. Site 500m on L after Alos. Sm, pt shd; wc; shwrs inc; el pnts (3A) €2; lndtte; shops 2km; tradsmn; rv sw 2km; dogs €0.50; quiet. "CL-type farm site; friendly family; clean facs; excel." ♦ 1 Jun-31 Oct. € 9.00   2007*

TAUPONT see Ploërmel *2F3*

TAUTAVEL see Estagel *8G4*

TEILLET *8E4* (S Rural) **Camping Le Relais de l'Entre-Deux-Lacs, 81120 Teillet [05 63 55 74 45; fax 05 63 55 75 65; contact@ camping-entredeuxlacs.com; www.camping- entredeuxlacs.com]** Fr Albi by-pass take D81 SE to Teillet. Site on R at S end of vill. Med, hdstg, terr, shd; wc; chem disp; mv service pnt; shwrs inc; el pnts inc (10A) inc (poss no earth & long lead poss req); gas; lndtte; shops 200m; rest, snacks, bar high ssn; BBQ; playgrnd; pool high ssn; games area; archery; guided walks; 10% statics; dogs €2; adv bkg (dep & admin fee); quiet; red 5+ nights Sep-Jun. "Farm welcomes children; friendly; steep site rds; few water points; heavily wooded." ♦ 1 Apr-31 Oct. € 22.00   2007*

TELGRUC SUR MER *2E2* (1km Coastal) **Camping Les Mimosas, 106 Rue de la Plage, 29560 Telgruc-sur-Mer [tel/fax 02 98 27 76 06 or 06 78 02 55 66 (mob); www.campingmimosa. com]** Fr D887 Crozon-Châteaulin rd turn SW onto D208 into Telgruc. Fr town sq foll sp Trez-Bellec-Plage. 300m after exiting town, turn L & L, site clearly sp. Med, hdg/mkd pitch, terr, pt shd; wc; chem disp; shwrs inc; el pnts (10A) €1.80; lndtte; shop 600m; sand beach 1km; playgrnd; tennis; dogs €0.80; poss cr; adv bkg rec high ssn; quiet; CCI. "Gd; excel coastal scenery; lots of trees." 1 Apr-30 Sep. € 9.40   2005*

TELGRUC SUR MER *2E2* (1km S Coastal) **Camping Le Panoramic, 130 Route de la Plage, 29560 Telgruc-sur-Mer [02 98 27 78 41; fax 02 98 27 36 10; info@camping-panoramic.com; www.camping-panoramic.com]** Fr D887 Crozon-Châteaulin rd, turn W on D208 twd Trez-Bellec Plage, site sp on R in approx 1.5km. Med, hdg/mkd pitch, terr, pt shd, wc (some cont); chem disp; mv service pnt; baby facs; shwrs inc, el pnts (6-10A) €3.10-4.50; lndtte; ice; shop; rest; snacks; bar; BBQ; playgrnd; covrd pool; jacuzzi; sand beach 700m; tennis; cycle hire; games rm; TV rm; some statics; dogs €1.60; adv bkg; quiet; cc acc; red low ssn; CCI. "Access to pitches poss diff due trees; vg, well-run, welcoming site." ♦ 1 Jun-15 Sep. € 22.00   2007*

See advertisement

TELGRUC SUR MER *2E2* (1.2km S Coastal) **Camping L'Armorique, Plomodiern, 29560 Telgruc-sur-Mer [02 98 27 77 33; fax 02 98 27 38 38; contact@campingarmorique.com; www.campingarmorique.com]** D887 Châteaulin to Crozon; turn S on D208 at sea end of Telgruc-sur-Mer. Steep hairpins on access rd, poss diff for long/ low powered o'fits. Med, terr, pt shd; wc; shwrs inc; el pnts (5A) €2.80; shop; lndtte; snacks; playgrnd; pool; sand beach 750m; games area; deep-sea diving, climbing, horseriding schools nrby; entmnt; games/TV rm; 20% statics; dogs €1.50; adv bkg; quiet; cc acc; CCI. "Pleasant, well-wooded site." ♦ ltd. 1 Apr-15 Sep. € 18.25   2004*

France

TELGRUC SUR MER *2E2* (2km S Coastal) **Camping Pen-Bellec, Trez Bellec, 29560 Telgruc-sur-Mer [02 98 27 31 87 or 02 98 27 76 55]** Fr D887 turn S onto D208 for Telgruc-sur-Mer. In Telgruc take rd mkd 'Plage Trez Bellec' & cont to far end where rd rises & turns inland. Sm, mkd pitch, unshd; wc; mv service pnt; shwrs €1; el pnts (3A) €2.50; lndtte; ice; shop & 2km; rest 3km; playgrnd; sand beach adj; watersports adj; cycle hire; games area; dogs €1; poss cr; adv bkg; poss noisy. "Conv beach; v clean; in gd position with beautiful views, but exposed in bad weather; gd cliff walking." 15 Jun-15 Sep. € 11.00   2006*

TENCE *9C2* (9km S Rural) **Camping Les Hirondelles, Route de la Suchère, 43400 Le Chambon-sur-Lignon [04 71 59 73 84; fax 04 71 65 88 80; les.hirondelles.bader@wanadoo. fr]** Fr cent of Le Chambon foll site sp S. Cross rv, bear R & after 200m turn L up hill & camp ent 300m on R. Med, hdg/mkd pitch, pt terr, pt shd; htd wc; chem disp; shwrs inc; el pnts (2-6A) inc; lndtte; lndry rm; shop & 1km; rest; snacks; bar; playgrnd; paddling pool; canoeing, horseriding nrby; sports area; games/TV rm; 50% statics; dogs €1.05; adv bkg (ess Jul/Aug); quiet; CCI. ◆ 25 Jun-1 Sep. € 16.00   2004*

TENDE *10E4* (9km S Rural) **Camp Municipal, Quartier Barnabin, 06540 Fontan [04 93 04 52 02 or 04 93 04 50 01 (Mairie); http://fontanaquarum. free.fr/camping]** Site is on N204 200m N of Fontan. Sm, pt sl, pt shd; wc (some cont); shwrs inc; el pnts; lndtte; rshop, est, snacks, bar 200m; dogs; phone; adv bkg; some rd noise; CCI. "Pleasant site close to scenic vill of Saorge; site yourself if recep shut (ltd open hrs)." 1 Apr-30 Sep.   2006*

THANN *6F3* (7km NW) **FFCC Camp La Mine d'Argent, Rue des Mines, 68690 Moosch [03 89 82 30 66 or 03 89 60 34 74; fax 03 89 42 15 12; serge.sorribas@free.fr]** Turn L off N66 Thann-Thillot rd in cent of Moosch opp church; foll sps for 1.5km, ent on R, narr app. Med, mkd pitch, pt sl, pt terr, pt shd; wc; chem disp; shwrs inc; el pnts (4-10A) €2.75-5.25; gas; lndtte; tradsmn; shops 1.5km; playgrnd; 5% statics; dogs €0.60; phone; adv bkg; quiet; red low ssn; no cc acc; CCI. "In heavily wooded valley; v clean & well-kept site; v enjoyable stay; helpful wardens; excel walking; busy w/e; highly rec." 15 Apr-15 Oct. € 10.40   2007*

THARON PLAGE see Pornic *2G3*

THEIX see Vannes *2F3*

THENON *7C3* (3km SE Rural) **Camping Jarry-Carrey, Route de Montignac, 24210 Thenon [05 53 05 20 78; fax 05 67 34 05 00; lejarrycarrey@ aol.com; www.lejarrycarrey.com]** Sp fr A89, take D67 fr Thenon to Montignac. Site on R in 4km. Med, mkd pitch, pt sl, terr, pt shd; wc; chem disp (wc); shwrs inc; el pnts (10A) €3.10; shops 2km; tradsmn; snacks; bar; ice; gas; lndtte; playgrnd; pool; lake fishing; dogs €1.60; adv bkg; quiet; 20% statics; dogs €1.37; Eng spkn; quiet; CCI. "Beautiful setting away fr tourist bustle but easy reach attractions; excel base for area; friendly owners." ◆ 1 Apr-30 Sep. € 13.10   2007*

THENON *7C3* (10km W Rural) **Camping de la Pélonie, La Bourgie, 24330 St Antoine-d'Auberoche [05 53 07 55 78; fax 05 53 03 74 27; lapelonie@aol.com; www.lapelonie.com]** Fr Périgueux on A89 twd Brive; 5km past St Pierre-de-Chignac, site sp on L; turn L at picnic area - go under rlwy bdge; site ent on L. Med, mkd pitch, pt shd; wc; chem disp; shwrs inc; el pnts (6A) €3.10 (poss req long cable); lndtte; gas; ice; shop; rest; bar; playgrnd; htd pool; paddling pool; TV; 10% statics; dogs €1.80; phone; poss cr; Eng spkn; adv bkg; quiet; red low ssn; cc acc; CCI. "A delightful, welcoming site; charming owners; gd facs & v clean; supmkt at Périgueux." ◆ 1 Apr-30 Oct. € 16.20   2007*

THERONDELS see Pierrefort *7C4*

THIEMBRONNE *3A3* (500m NW Urban) **Camping Les Pommiers, 1 Route des Desvres, 62560 Thiembronne [03 21 39 50 19 or 03 21 66 25 47 (LS); fax 03 21 95 79 20]** SW fr St Omer for 25km on D928 to Fauquembergues. NW on D158 for 4km past water tower. Site sp. Med, sl, shd; wc; chem disp; shwrs €0.30; el pnts (4A) €2.60; lndtte; shop 1km; snacks; playgrnd; pool; games area; entmnt; TV; 75% statics; poss cr; adv bkg; quiet. 15 Mar-15 Oct. € 15.40   2006*

THIERS *9B1* (6km NE) **Camp Municipal Les Chanterelles, 63550 St Rémy-sur-Durolle [tel/ fax 04 73 94 31 71; mairie-saint-remy-sur-durolle@wanadoo.fr]** On A72/E70 W dir Clermont-Ferrand, exit at junc 3 sp Thiers. Foll sp twd Thiers on N89 into L Monnerie. Fr vill, take D20 & foll sp St Rémy. In St Rémy, foll 'Camping' sp. Do not app thro Thiers as narr rds v diff for lge o'fits. Med, terr, pt shd; wc; chem disp; mv service pnt; shwrs inc; el pnts (10A) €2.95; gas; lndtte; ice; shops 3km; tradsmn; BBQ; playgrnd; pool & lake 300m; tennis; windsurfing; dogs €0.90; adv bkg; quiet; CCI. "Many attractions by lake with beach; site beautifully situated with lovely views; modern, clean facs; some noise at w/e fr statics; excel." ◆ 1 May-30 Sep. € 9.70   2006*

THIERS *9B1* (8km W Rural) **Camp Municipal Pont Astier, 63190 Orléat [tel/fax 04 73 53 64 40; sogeval@wanadoo.fr]** On A72 take exit 2 onto D906 S. for 2.5km. Turn R on N89 for Clermont-Ferrand. Turn R at Pont-de-Dore onto D224. Site 3km on R. Med, hdg pitch, pt sl, pt shd; wc; chem disp; shwrs inc; el pnts (10A) €3; lndry rm; ice; shop 3km; tradsmn; snacks; bar; BBQ; playgrnd; pool; fishing; tennis; dogs €1.50; Eng spkn; adv bkg; red low ssn; CCI. "Park nrby; by Rv Dore; lge pitches, but some damp; poss mosquito prob; ent poss diff." ♦ 1 Apr-30 Sep. € 12.00   2005*

THIERS *9B1* (4km NW Rural) **Camping Base de Loisirs Iloa, Courty, 63300 Thiers [04 73 80 92 35 or 04 73 80 14 90; fax 04 73 80 88 81]** Exit A72 junc 2 for Thiers; at rndabt turn L sp Vichy but take D44 sp Dorat; pass under m'way, site beyond Courty on L sp Les Rives-de-Thiers. Sm, mkd pitch, pt shd; wc (some cont); chem disp; mv service pnt; some serviced pitches; shwrs inc; el pnts (6A) €2; gas 5km; lndtte; supmkt 5km; tradsmn; playgrnd; pool high ssn adj; lake fishing; tennis; mini-golf; entmnt; TV rm; dogs; noisy; CCI. "Well-maintained; v gd, clean san facs; excel sports facs adj; friendly warden." ♦ ltd. 15 Apr-15 Oct. € 11.00 (3 persons)
                   2005*

THIEZAC see Vic sur Cère *7C4*

⊞**THILLOT, LE** *6F3* (1km NW) **Camp Municipal Clos des Chaume, 88160 Le Thillot [03 29 25 10 30; fax 03 29 25 25 87; campingmunicipal@ville-lethillot.fr]** Site sp on N o'skts of town N on N66, on R behind sports cent. Med, pt sl, pt shd; htd wc; shwrs inc; el pnts (6A) €4.65; gas; lndtte; shops 1km; playgrnd; pool, tennis adj; few statics; adv bkg; quiet. € 5.80
                   2007*

THILLOT, LE *6F3* (2km NW) **Camping Le Clos Martin, 5 Rue du Clos-Martin, 88160 Ramonchamp [03 29 25 05 38]** At Ramonchamp on N66 (travelling E) turn R & foll sp. Sm, pt shd; wc; chem disp; shwrs €1.25; el pnts (6A) €2 (poss rev pol); lndtte; shops, rest 200m; BBQ; playgrnd; rv fishing; dogs €0.50; phone; CCI. "Nice, quiet site; helpful owners; gd walking & cycling." 1 Apr-15 Sep. € 6.80   2005*

THIONVILLE *5C2* (NE Urban) **Camp Municipal, 6 Rue du Parc, 57100 Thionville [03 82 53 83 75; fax 03 82 53 91 27]** Exit A31 at sp Thionville Cent; foll sp 'Centre Ville'; foll site sp dir Manom. Sm, mkd pitch, some hdstg, pt shd; wc; chem disp; mv service pnt; shwrs inc; el pnts (3-10A) €2.15-4.20; shop 250m; rest snacks, bar 250m; playgrnd; pool 1km; boating; fishing; poss cr; Eng spkn; adv bkg; quiet; CCI. "Well-kept site, poss untidy low ssn; helpful & friendly warden; gd san facs; sh rvside walk to quaint town cent, or thro park; some pitches with rvside views; no hdstg until Jun due to rv conditions; rec arr early high ssn; barrier open 0800-1200 & 1600-2000; vg." ♦ 1 May-30 Sep. € 96.00   2007*

⊞**THIVIERS** *7C3* (10km N Rural) **Camping Le Touroulet, Moulin du Tourelet, 24800 Chaleix [tel/fax 05 53 55 23 59; touroulet@hotmail.com; www.camping-touroulet.com]** Fr Limoges on N21 S twd Périgueux, thro vill of La Coquille, in about 4.5km turn R onto D98 twd St Jory-de-Chalais & Chaleix. In 4km turn L to vill & site 1km further on. Take care narr bdge & site ent. Sm, pt sl, some hdstg, pt shd; pt htd wc; chem disp; shwrs inc; el pnts (8A) €3.10; lndtte; ice; shop 1.5km; tradsmn; rest; bar; BBQ; fishing; games rm; entmnt; dogs €0.50; adv bkg; quiet; CCI. "Spacious, attractive rvside site; welcoming, helpful British owners; basic, ltd san facs, stretched high ssn; hdstg pitches sl & uneven; gd rest; weekly BBQs in ssn; excel Xmas package; highly rec." € 10.90   2007*

THIVIERS *7C3* (10km N Urban) **Camping Maisonneuve, 24800 St Jory-de-Chalais [tel/fax 05 53 55 10 63; camping.maisonneuve@wanadoo.fr; www.camping-maisonneuve.com]** N fr Thiviers on N21 for 6km; turn L on D98 thro Chaleix; Maisonneuve on L bef ent St Jory-de-Chalais. Other rtes v narr. Sm, hdg/mkd pitch, hdstg, pt sl, pt shd; wc; chem disp; mv service pnt; sauna; shwrs inc; el pnts (10A) €3.50; lndtte; shop 500m; rest; snacks; bar; playgrnd; pool; fishing lake; games rm; TV; 10% statics; dogs €1; Eng spkn; adv bkg; quiet; red 7+ days; CCI. "Excel; v helpful, welcoming owners; pretty site in attractive countryside; lge pitches." ♦ 1 Apr-31 Oct. € 18.00   2007*

THIVIERS *7C3* (2km SE Urban) **Camp Municipal Le Repaire, Route de Lanouaille, 24800 Thiviers [tel/fax 05 53 52 69 75; mairie-thiviers@wanadoo.fr]** N21 to Thiviers; at traff lts take D707 E twd Lanouaille; site in 1.5km on R. Med, hdg/mkd pitch, pt sl, terr, pt shd; wc; chem disp; mv service pnt; shwrs inc; el pnts (12A) €2.75; lndry rm; shop 2.5km; tradsmn; snacks; playgrnd; pool high ssn; lake fishing; sw 800m; TV rm; 5% statics; dogs €1.60; poss cr; adv bkg; quiet; red 7+ days; CCI. "Many chateaux, museums; walks; gd cent for N Périgord; some pitches unrel in wet weather; vg." ♦ 1 May-30 Sep. € 14.00   2006*

THOISSEY *9A2* (1km S) **Camp-Plage Municipal, 01140 Thoissey [04 74 04 02 97 or 04 74 04 04 25 (LS); fax 04 74 69 76 13; thoissey@wanadoo.fr; www.campingdethoissey.com]** S on D306 (N6) turn L onto D9. Turn sharp R on Plage immed after x-ing Rv Saône. Lge, mkd pitch, pt shd; wc (mainly cont); shwrs inc; el pnts (6-10A) inc; lndtte; shop; rest; snacks; bar; playgrnd; htd pool (high ssn); watersports; rv beach & sw adj; TV; 75% statics; dogs €1.50; poss cr; quiet; CCI. "Excel site for families; lge pitches; full facs for children; helpful staff; san facs due for renewal (2008); v muddy when wet; conv for vineyards." 1 Apr-1 Oct. € 11.00   2007*

France

THOLY, LE 6F3 (6km N Rural) **Camping Le Barba,** Le Village, 88640 Rehaupal [tel/fax 03 29 66 35 57 or 03 29 66 21 17; camping.barba@wanadoo.fr] Fr Gérardmer on D417 after 8km site sp on R 2km bef Le Tholy. Foll sp to Rehaupal, site on R on ent to vill. Sm, mkd pitch, pt shd; wc; chem disp; shwrs inc; el pnts (3-6A) €2-3; gas; lndtte; ice; shop adj; tradsmn; rest; dogs €1; Eng spkn; quiet. "Excel base for Alsace; beautiful scenery; friendly owner." 1 May-30 Sep. € 9.00   2004*

> The opening dates and prices on this campsite have changed. I'll send a site report form to the editor for the next edition of the guide.

THOLY, LE 6F3 (1.3km NW Rural) **Camping JP Vacances (formerly Noir Rupt),** 15 Chemin de L'Etang, 88530 Le Tholy [03 29 61 81 27; fax 03 29 61 83 05; info@jpvacances.com; www. jpvacances.com] Fr Gérardmer, take D417 W, turn R in Le Tholy up hill onto D11. Site on L on secondary rd to Epinal & sp. Med, terr, pt shd; wc (some cont); chem disp; baby facs; sauna; shwrs inc; el pnts (2-6A) €3-5; gas; lndtte; shops 1km; snacks; bar; BBQ; htd pool; lac sw 10km; tennis inc; entmnt; TV rm; some chalets; dogs €1.50; poss cr; some rd noise; red long stay. "Pleasant site; v clean & well presented; sm pitches; vg." 15 Apr-15 Oct. € 19.40   2007*

THONAC see Montignac 7C3

THONNANCE LES MOULINS 6E1 (2km W Rural) **Camping La Forge de Ste Marie,** 52230 Thonnance-les-Moulins [03 25 94 42 00; fax 03 25 94 41 43; la.forge.de.sainte.marie@ wanadoo.fr; www.laforgedesaintemarie.com or www.les-castels.com] Fr N67 exit sp Joinville-Est, foll D60 NE sp Vaucouleurs. In 500m turn R onto D427 sp Poissons & Neufchâteau. Site on R in 11km. NB Swing wide at turn into site fr main c'way, not fr what appears to be a run in. Site ent quite narr. Med, hdg/mkd pitch, pt sl, pt terr, shd; wc; chem disp; serviced pitches; baby facs; shwrs inc; el pnts (6A) inc; gas; lndtte; shop; tradsmn; rest; snacks; bar; BBQ; htd, covrd pool & paddling pool; lake; boating; freshwater fishing; cycle hire; gd walking; entmnt; wifi internet; games/TV rm; 25% statics; dogs €1.50; phone; Eng spkn; adv bkg (dep req); cc acc; CCI. "Vg, clean, well-kept site; v busy high ssn; access diff to some terr pitches; v friendly & helpful owners; sharp bends on app rds to pitches poss diff lge o'fits; muddy after rain; mkt Fri; vg rest." ♦ 27 Apr-13 Sep. € 29.90 (CChq acc) ABS - J04   2007*

THONON LES BAINS 9A3 (3km NE Rural) Camping St Disdille, Vongy, 117 Ave de St Disdille, 74200 Thonon-Les-Bains [04 50 71 14 11; fax 04 50 71 93 67; camping@ disdille.com; www.disdille.com] Fr W on N5 thro Thonon on HGV rte twds Evian; at Vongy rndabt foll sp to site or to St Disdille. Fr E on N5 sp app town; site by Lac Léman. V lge, mkd pitch, shd; wc; shwrs; el pnts (6-10A) €3-4; gas; lndtte; ice; shop; rest; snacks; bar; playgrnd; lake sw 200m; fishing; tennis; games area; 30% statics; dogs €2; adv bkg ess; cc acc; CCI. "Well-situated, well-equipped site." ♦ 1 Apr-30 Sep. € 17.00   2007*

See advertisement

⊞**THONON LES BAINS** *9A3* (9km SE Rural) **Camping La Prairie, Rue de Savoie, 74500 Champanges [04 50 81 02 08; fax 04 50 73 40 68; www.champanges.fr]** Rec rte for c'vans & lge m'vans: D32 fr Thonon & foll sp Marin & Vallée d'Abondance/Champanges. Turn R into vill, site on R. Med, pt sl, terr, pt shd; htd wc; chem disp (wc); mv service pnt; baby facs; shwrs inc; el pnts (6A) €2.75; lndtte; ice; shop 200m; rest; snacks; bar; BBQ; playgrnd; lake sw in Thonon; tennis; games area; entmnt; TV rm; 40% statics; dogs €0.60; CCI. "Gd walking." ♦ ltd. € 8.10   2006*

THONON LES BAINS *9A3* (10km W Rural) **Camping La Pinède, 74140 Excenevex [04 50 72 85 05 or 04 50 72 81 27 (Mairie); fax 04 50 72 93 00; cplpinede@atciat.com; www.camping-lac-leman. info or www.campeole.com]** On N5 to Geneva, 10km fr Thonon, turn R at Camping sp. Lge, shd; htd wc; shwrs inc; chem disp; 2 serviced pitches; el pnts (10A) €3.90; gas; lndtte; ice; shop; rest; snacks; bar; BBQ; playgrnd; sports area; tennis; lake sw, fishing, watersports & sand beach; horseriding 1km; entmnt; TV; 75% statics; dogs €3.50; poss cr; adv bkg; quiet; "Friendly & efficient staff; excel lakeside situation; supmkts close." 14 Apr-23 Sep. € 19.90
                                                     2006*

THONON LES BAINS *9A3* (10km W Rural) **Camping Mathieu Le Léman 1, 74140 Yvoire [04 50 72 84 31; fax 04 50 72 96 33; www. campingsmathieu.com]** Exit N5 at Sciez (bet Geneve & Thonon) onto D25 sp Yvoire; site in 10km; at Yvoire foll camping sp; fr Douvaine foll Lac Léman lakeside sp. NB Narr ent to site. Med, mkd pitch, pt sl, pt shd; wc (mainly cont); chem disp; shwrs inc; el pnts (6A) €2.50; lndtte; ice; tradsmn; shop, snacks & bar 500m; BBQ; playgrnd; lake sw 500m; 75% statics; dogs €1; Eng spkn; adv bkg (dep req); quiet; red low ssn; CCI. "Excel site o'looking medieval vill; v friendly owner; v lge pitches; gd lake sw; adj site Mathieu Le Léman 2 open Jul-Aug only; same ownership, sep recep & facs; conv Geneva & Thonon-les-Bains; vg." 1 Apr-28 Oct. € 14.00   2007*

THORE LA ROCHETTE see Vendôme *4F2*

THORENS GLIERES *9A3* (Rural) **Camp Nantizel, 74570 Thorens-Glières [04 50 22 43 42]** Fr A40/ A41 exit 19. Take N203 twd Annecy. In 10km after S-bend take D5 E to Thorens-Glières & foll camping sp to site. Sm, pt sl, pt shd; wc; own san rec; chem disp; shwrs inc; el pnts (3A) €2; shops 4km; playgrnd; dogs €0.80; v quiet. "CL-type site on alpine farm with superb views; highly rec." 15 Jun-15 Sep. € 10.00   2005*

THORENS GLIERES *9A3* (3km SE Rural) **Camping Rural Les Combes d'Usillon, 461 Chemin des Combes d'Usillon, 74570 Thorens-Glières [04 50 22 81 10; campingville@aol.com]** Fr Thorens-Glières take D5 S twd Aviernoz. In 1km turn L twd La Louvatière. Site sp Camping Rural in 2km on rvside. Sm, pt shd; shwrs inc; el pnts €1.85; lndtte; shop 2.5km; rest; dogs; v quiet. "Pleasant owner; gd walking fr site." 15 May-15 Sep. € 10.00
                                                     2005*

THORENS GLIERES *9A3* (3km NW Rural) **Aire Naturelle Le Moulin Dollay, 206 Rue du Moulin Dollay, 74570 Groisy [tel/fax 04 50 68 00 31]** Fr Annecy take N203 N. At Champion supmkt fork L to Groisy. Thro Groisy & over rv bdge, turn R sp La Roche-sur-Foron, site on L. Sm, mkd pitch, pt shd; htd wc; chem disp; mv service pnt; baby facs; fam bthrm; shwrs inc; el pnts (6A) €3; gas 1km; lndtte; shops 1km; tradsmn; snacks; BBQ; bar 5km; playgrnd; rv sw adj; sand beach 12km; TV rm; no dogs; train 500m; phone; adv bkg 25% dep; quiet; 10% red 8+ days; cc not acc. "Excel site with immac san facs; v friendly owner; highly rec." ♦ 15 May-15 Sep. € 15.00   2004*

THOUARCE *4G1* (SW Rural) **Camp Municipal de l'Ecluse, Ave des Trois Ponts, 49380 Thouarcé [02 41 54 14 36 (Mairie); fax 02 41 54 09 11; mairie.thouarce@wanadoo.fr]** Exit A87 junc 24 onto N160/D55 dir Beaulieu-sur-Layon & Thouarcé. Site sp adj Rv Layon. Sm, pt shd; wc (cont for men); shwrs inc; el pnts €1.70; gas; ice; shops & supmkt 400m; playgrnd; pool; tennis nr; fishing; no adv bkg; quiet; CCI. 15 Apr-15 Sep. € 3.20   2006*

THOUARS *4H1* (500m E Rural) **Camp Municipal Le Clos Imbert, Rue de la Grande-Côte-de-Crevant, 79100 Thouars [05 49 66 17 99 or 05 49 68 22 80 (Mairie); fax 05 49 66 16 09; camping@ville-thouars.fr; www.ville-thouars. com]** Sp fr cent of town & fr D938 Ent down 1 in 5 hill, narr & winding; access diff lge o'fits. Site adj Rv Thouet. Sm, pt shd; wc; shwrs; el pnts (5-10A) €2.15-3.20; snacks; playgrnd; fishing; sports facs nr; quiet. "Pleasant little site." ♦ 1 Jun-30 Sep. € 8.00   2007*

THUEYTS *9D2* (1.5km E Rural) **Camping Le Pont de Mercier, Le Champs de Mercier, 07330 Thueyts [tel/fax 04 75 36 46 08 or 04 75 36 43 83]** Clearly sp fr N102. Narr app rd. Med, mkd pitch, pt sl, terr, pt shd; wc; shwrs inc; el pnts (5A) €2.30; gas; lndtte; ice; shop 1km; playgrnd; rv fishing adj; games area; some statics; dogs €1; adv bkg; quiet but some rd noise; red low ssn. "On banks of Rv Ardèche with gd views & walks; ample shops & rests in Thueyts; Pont de Diable worth visit." ♦ 1 May-10 Sep. € 13.00   2005*

France

THUEYTS 9D2 (4km E Rural) **Camping Le Ventadour, Pont de Rolandy, 07380 Meyras [tel/fax 04 75 94 18 15; info@leventadour.com; www.leventadour.com]** Sp fr N102. Med, pt shd; htd wc; shwrs inc; el pnts (6-10A) €3-3.50 (poss rev pol); lndtte; ice; shop; supmkt 5km; snacks; bar; gas BBQ; playgrnd; rv sw; fishing; some statics; dogs €1.50; Eng spkn; adv bkg; quiet. "Owners v helpful; easy access; gd, clean facs; attractive site; ideal base for touring Cévennes." 1 Apr-30 Sep. € 14.00
2006*

THURY HARCOURT 3D1 (Rural) **Camping de la Vallée du Traspy, Rue du Pont Benoît, 14220 Thury-Harcourt [02 31 79 61 80 or 02 31 52 53 54; fax 02 31 84 76 19]** App fr N on D562 fr Caen, take L fork into town after pool complex. In 100m turn L at Hôtel de la Poste, 1st L to site, clearly sp. Med, mkd pitch, terr, pt shd; wc (some cont); chem disp; serviced pitches; shwrs inc; el pnts (6-10A) €3.70; gas; lndtte; ice; shop 1km; tradsmn; snacks; bar; BBQ; playgrnd; htd pool nr; sauna & spa; rv adj & lake nrby; fishing; entmnt; 20% statics; dogs €2.65; phone; poss cr; Eng spkn; adv bkg rec high ssn; quiet; CCI. "Friendly owners; quiet & close to town; gd for walking & canoeing on Rv Orne; o'night area for m'vans." ♦ 1 Apr-30 Sep. € 13.50   2006*

TIL CHATEL 6G1 (2km E Rural) **Camping Les Sapins, Til-Châtel [03 80 95 16 68]** Leave A31 junc 5 onto D974 (N74) twd Til-Châtel. Site on R in 500m adj Rest Les Sapins. Sm, pt sl, pt shd, serviced pitch; wc (some cont); shwrs inc; el pnts (10A) inc; shops 2km; rest; snacks; bar; poss cr; Eng spkn; adv bkg; rd noise; CCI. "New owners (2007); poss v overcr high ssn; facs need upgrade but v conv NH; no twin-axles." Easter-31 Oct. € 14.00   2007*

TIL CHATEL 6G1 (5km W Rural) **Camp Municipal des Capucins, 21120 Is-sur-Tille [03 80 95 02 08; fax 03 80 95 08 33; mairiedis@wanadoo.fr]** Leave A31 at junc 5 S onto D974 (N74) dir Til-Châtel. Turn R onto D959 to Is-sur-Tille. Site on L at sports grnd. Well sp. Sm, shd; wc (cont); chem disp; shwrs inc; el pnts (3A) inc; lndry rm; shops 1km; tradsmn; pool adj; poss cr; quiet. "Site yourself; warden calls am & pm; facs old but clean, useful NH." 1 Jun-30 Sep. € 7.90   2004*

TINTENIAC 2E4 (Urban) **Camp Municipal du Pont L'Abbesse, Rue du 8 Mai 1945, 35190 Tinténiac [02 99 68 09 91 or 02 99 68 02 15 (Mairie); fax 02 99 68 05 44]** Sp in cent of Tinténiac. Site behind Auberge La Halage, on Canal d'Ille et Rance. Sm, hdg/mkd pitch, pt sl, pt shd; htd wc; shwrs; el pnts €2; shops, rest, snacks & bar adj; playgrnd; 30% statics; quiet; CCI. "Backs on canal with fishing & boating; lovely walk/cycle on canal bank." ♦ 1 Mar-31 Oct. € 7.00   2007*

TINTENIAC 2E4 (2km S Rural) **Camping Les Peupliers, La Besnelais, 35190 Tinténiac [02 99 45 49 75; fax 02 99 45 52 98; camping.les-peupliers@wanadoo.fr; www.les-peupliers-camping.fr]** On D937 (N137) Rennes to St Malo rd; after Hédé foll rd to Tinténiac about 2km; site on main rd on R, sp. Med, hdg/mkd pitch, pt sl, pt shd; wc (some cont); chem disp; mv service pnt; shwrs inc; el pnts (6A) €2.70 (poss rev pol); lndtte; ice; shops 2km; tradsmn high ssn; rest; snacks; bar; playgrnd; htd pool; lake fishing; tennis; games area; TV rm; 30% statics; dogs €1.60; phone; adv bkg; CCI. "Quiet, clean, tidy site amongst fir trees; gd pool & park; on Pilgrim Rte to Santiago de Compostela." ♦ ltd. 1 Apr-30 Sep. € 17.40
2007*

TONNEINS 7D2 (500m SE Urban) **Camp Municipal Le Robinson, 47400 Tonneins [05 53 79 02 28; fax 05 53 79 83 01; tonneins@valdegaronne.com]** On N113, bet Marmande & Agen. Sm, mkd pitch, pt shd, hdstg; wc; shwrs inc; el pnts inc; lndtte; hypermkt 3km; dogs; phone; quiet, some rd & rlwy noise. ♦ 1 Jun-30 Sep. € 10.25   2006*

TONNERRE 4F4 (600m N Urban) **Camp Municipal de la Cascade, Ave Aristide Briand, 89700 Tonnerre [03 86 55 15 44 or 03 86 55 22 55 (Mairie); fax 03 86 55 30 64; ot.tonnerre@wanadoo.fr; www.tonnerre.fr]** Best app via D905 (E by-pass); turn at rndabt twd town cent L after x-ing 1st rv bdge. Foll site sp to avoid low bdge (height 2.4m, width 2m). On banks of Rv Armançon & nr Canal de l'Yonne, 100m fr junc D905 & D944. Med, mkd pitch, pt shd (lge pitches); htd wc; chem disp; mv service pnt; baby facs; shwrs inc; el pnts (6A) €2.50; lndry rm; ice; shops; tradsmn; rest; snacks; bar; playgrnd; htd pool 1km; rv sw adj; fishing; entmnt; TV rm; 5% statics; Eng spkn; adv bkg; quiet, but some rlwy noise (not a problem); cc acc; CCI. "V pleasant, spacious & shady site; excel san facs; lge pitches; no twin-axles; interesting town; excel." ♦ 1 Apr-2 Nov. € 9.90   2007*

Before we move on, I'm going to fill in some site report forms and post them off to the editor, otherwise they won't arrive in time for the deadline at the end of September.

TONNOY 6E2 (500m SW Rural) **Camp Municipal Le Grand Vanné, 54210 Tonnoy [03 83 26 62 36; fax 03 83 26 66 05; mairie-de-tonnoy@wanadoo.fr]** On A330 S fr Nancy sp Epinal, exit junc 7 onto D570 sp Flavigny. Site on L on banks of Rv Moselle in 5km. Med, pt shd; wc (cont); shwrs inc; el pnts (3-6A) inc; ice; shops 500m; snacks; BBQ; playgrnd; rv sw; fishing; 50% statics; dogs; poss cr; quiet. "Gd." 15 Jun-31 Aug. € 11.30   2006*

⊞TORCY *3D3* (3km N Urban) **Camping Le Parc de la Colline, Route de Lagny, 77200 Torcy** [01 60 05 42 32; fax 01 64 80 05 17; camping. parc.de.la.colline@wanadoo.fr; www.camping-de-la-colline.com] Exit A104 junc 10 W onto D10 sp Torcy/Noisiel. Site on L in 1km. Lge, hdg/mkd pitch, terr, pt shd; htd wc (some cont); chem disp; mv service pnt; shwrs inc; el pnts (6A) €3; lndtte; shop; hypmkt 3km; playgrnd; htd pool; waterslide; lake beach & sw 1km; tennis; internet; TV rm; some statics; dogs €4.50; poss cr; adv bkg; cc acc; CCI. "Conv Disneyland, Parc Astérix & Paris; conv RER to Paris or Disneyland by site minibus; v helpful Eng-spkg staff; steep app to pitches but tow avail." ♦ € 24.80   2006*

There aren't many sites open this early in the year. We'd better phone ahead to check that the one we're heading for is actually open.

TORIGNI SUR VIRE *1D4* (1km S Rural) **Camping Le Lac des Charmilles, Route de Vire, 50160 Torigni-sur-Vire** [02 33 56 91 74; contact@ camping-lacdescharmilles.com; www.camping-lacdescharmilles.com] Exit A84 junc 40 onto N174 dir Torigni-sur-Vire/St Lô; site on R in 4km. Opp municipal stadium. Med, mkd pitch, pt shd; wc; chem disp; mv service pnt; baby facs; shwrs inc; fam bthrm; el pnts (10A) €2 (long lead poss req); lndtte; shop; tradsmn; rest; snacks; takeaway; bar; BBQ; playgrnd; lake sw adj; cycle hire; games area; games rm; TV; 10% statics; dogs €1.50; phone; poss cr; Eng spkn; adv bkg (dep req); quiet; cc acc; CCI. "Lovely, well-laid out site; easy access to interesting town, in walking dist; v clean facs; plans for pool (2008); conv St Lô; vg." ♦ 30 Mar-31 Oct. € 13.00   2007*

See advertisement on page 692

TORREILLES PLAGE *10G1* (Coastal) **Camping Le Calypso, 66440 Torreilles-Plage** [04 68 28 09 47; fax 04 68 28 24 76; info@camping-calypso. com; www.camping-calypso.com] Take D617 fr Perpignan sp Canet-Plage & D81 to St Laurent. 1.7km prior to St Laurent on R hand side of rd. 2nd site on L on way to beach. Lge, mkd pitch, shd; wc; chem disp; baby facs; shwrs; el pnts (6A) inc; gas; lndtte; shop adj; snacks; bar; playgrnd; htd pool; sand beach 300m; rv 1km; games area; entmnts; TV; 40% statics; dogs €4.10; poss cr; adv bkg rec high ssn; quiet; cc acc. "Interesting trips to vineyards; many activities." ♦ 1 Apr-30 Sep. € 26.60   2006*

TORREILLES PLAGE *10G1* (Coastal) **Camping Sunêlia Les Tropiques, Blvd de la Méditerranée, 66440 Torreilles-Plage** [04 68 28 05 09; fax 04 68 28 48 90; camping-les-tropiques@ wanadoo.fr; www.camping-les-tropiques.com] Exit A9 junc 41 onto D83 twd Canet-Plage, foll sp Torreilles-Plage & site. Lge, mkd pitch, shd; wc (some cont); chem disp; mv service pnt; shwrs inc; el pnts (6A) inc; gas; lndtte; ice; shop; rest; snacks; bar; playgrnd; pool; sand beach 300m; tennis; archery; games area; entmnt; internet; TV rm; 80% statics; dogs €4; poss cr; Eng spkn; cc acc; red low ssn; CCI. "Gd family-run site; purchase camp bracelet to join in entmnts." ♦ 9 Apr-9 Oct. € 33.00   2005*

TORREILLES PLAGE *10G1* (Coastal) **CHADOTEL Camping Le Trivoly, Blvd des Plages, 66440 Torreilles-Plage** [04 68 28 20 28 or 02 51 33 05 05 (LS); fax 04 68 28 16 48; chadotel@ wanadoo.fr; www.chadotel.com] Torreilles-Plage is sp fr D81, site in vill cent. Lge, hdg/mkd pitch, pt shd; htd wc; serviced pitches; shwrs inc; el pnts (6A) inc; gas; lndtte; ice; shop; snacks; bar; playgrnd; htd pool; waterslide; sand beach 800m; tennis; cycle hire; watersports; games rm; TV rm; entmnt; dogs €2.90; Eng spkn; adv bkg; quiet; cc acc. "Gd walking in Pyrenees; vg." ♦ Easter-24 Sep. € 28.90   2006*

TORREILLES PLAGE *10G1* (8km N Coastal) **Camping La Palmeraie, Blvd de la Plage, 66440 Torreilles-Plage** [04 68 28 20 64; fax 04 68 59 67 41; info@camping-la-palmeraie. com; www.camping-la-palmeraie.com] Exit A9/ E15 junc 41 at Perpignan Nord onto D83 twd Le Barcarès for 10km. At int'chge turn R at junc 9 onto D81 dir Canet-Plage, cont for 3km to lge rndabt & turn L sp Torreilles-Plage, site on R. Lge, hdg/mkd pitch, shd; wc; chem disp; shwrs inc; el pnts (5-10A) €3.50-6.60; gas; lndtte; ice; shop; rest; snacks; bar; BBQ (gas only); playgrnd; pool; sand beach 600m; tennis, horseriding nr; games rm; entmnt; child entmnt; TV rm; some statics; dogs; Eng spkn; adv bkg; quiet; red low ssn; cc acc; CCI. "Attractive site; friendly, helpful staff." ♦ 27 May-30 Sep. € 23.70   2005*

TORTEQUESNE see Douai *3B4*

TOUCY *4F4* (Urban) **Camp Municipal Base de Loisirs Le Pâtis, 89130 Toucy** [03 86 44 13 84 or 03 86 44 28 44; fax 03 86 44 28 42] On D3, 25km SW of Auxerre, Site on S bank of Rv Quanne almost in town cent; sp. Med, pt shd; wc; shwrs inc; el pnts (3A) €2.50; shops 500m; pool; fishing; poss cr; adv bkg; quiet. "Friendly warden; excel rests in town; vg mkt Sat; no twin-axles." 1 May-30 Sep. € 6.00   2004*

France

TOUL *6E2* (7km E Rural) **Camping de Villey-de-Sec, 34 Rue de la Gare, 54840 Villey-le-Sec [tel/fax 03 83 63 64 28; info@campingvilleylesec.com; www.campingvilleylesec.com]** Exit Toul E on D909 or take junc 15 fr A31 onto D909. In vill site S by Rv Moselle. V steep app rd. Med, hdg/mkd pitch, hdstg, pt shd; wc; chem disp; mv service pnt; baby facs; shwrs inc; el pnts (6-10A) €3.50-4.50; gas; lndtte; ice; shop; rest; snacks; bar; BBQ; playgrnd; games area; dogs €1.70; phone; Eng spkn; no adv bkg; quiet; cc acc; red long stay. "Friendly, beautifully-situated, clean site on rvside; arr early rec high ssn & Dutch holidays; cycle path to Maron & Toul; conv Nancy; popular NH; excel." ♦ 1 Apr-30 Sep. € 13.50 2007*

⊞**TOULOUSE** *8F3* (5km N Urban) **Camping Le Rupé, 21 Chemin du Pont de Rupé, 31000 Toulouse [05 61 70 07 35; fax 05 61 70 93 17; campinglerupe31@wanadoo.fr]** N fr Toulouse on N20, sp. Poss tricky app fr N for long vans, suggest cont past Pont de Rupé traff lts to next rndabt & double back to turn. Fr S on ring rd exit junc 33A (after junc 12), turn immed R & foll sp. Lge, hdg/mkd pitch, hdstg, pt shd; htd wc (cont); chem disp; mv service pnt; shwrs inc; el pnts (6-10A) €3.50-4.70; lndtte; shop; rest; snacks; playgrnd; lake fishing; games rm; TV; 90% statics; dogs €1; phone; bus; poss cr (esp public hols); Eng spkn; adv bkg; cc acc; CCI "Poss unkempt & poor facs low ssn; many shabby statics & poss itinerants low ssn; access by barrier card; NH only." € 13.50 2006*

TOULOUSE *8F3* (10km S) **Camp Municipal du Ramier, 31120 Roques [05 61 72 56 07; fax 05 61 72 57 52]** Take Muret exit off A6 S of Toulouse on N117 to Roques. Site on banks of Rv Garonne. Med, pt shd; wc (most cont); shwrs inc; el pnts (6-10A) inc; lndtte; shop; playgrnd; bus to city; poss cr; rd noise. "Grubby facs; poss itinerants & workers on site; poss light aircraft noise; v quiet at night; NH only." 1 May-31 Oct. € 15.50 2004*

TOUQUES see Deauville *3D1*

⊞**TOUQUET PARIS PLAGE, LE** *3B2* (5km N Rural) **Camping La Dune Blanche, Route de Camiers, 62176 Camiers [03 21 09 78 48 or 06 86 15 69 32 (mob); fax 03 21 09 79 59; duneblanche@wanadoo.fr; www.lesdomaines.org]** Leave A16 junc 26 dir Etaples or junc 27 dir Neufchâtel onto D940 dir Etables, Le Touquet. Site well sp. Lge, mkd pitch, pt sl, shd; wc; chem disp; baby facs; shwrs inc; el pnts (6A) €6; gas; lndtte; shops 2km; tradsmn; bar; BBQ; playgrnd; sand beach 3km; entmnt; TV; 90% statics; dogs €2.50; phone; bus to beach at Ste Cécile; poss cr; adv bkg; quiet; red long stay; cc acc; CCI. "Amongst trees; remote, v quiet by rlwy line; staff friendly & helpful; site poss scruffy; san facs need upgrade." ♦ € 15.00 2007*

TOUQUET PARIS PLAGE, LE *3B2* (1km S Coastal) **Camping Caravaning Stoneham, Ave Godin, Paris Plage, 62520 Le Touquet [03 21 05 16 55; fax 03 21 05 06 48; caravaning.stoneham@letouquet.com; www.letouquet.com]** Fr Etaples on D939 (N39); stay in L-hand lane at traff lts dir airport & cont strt on (Ave du Général de Gaulle); L at traff lts sp Golf (Ave du Golf); foll rd to rndabt; turn R (1st exit) onto Ave François Godin (sm campsite sp at rndabt); at next rndabt site ent on R. Lge, hdg pitch, pt shd; wc; shwrs inc; el pnts (6A) €4.60 (poss rev pol); lndtte; shops 1km; tradsmn; playgrnd; htd pool 2km; sand beach 1km; 95% statics; dogs €1.40; poss cr even low ssn; adv bkg rec; CCI. "Pleasant site; excel facs; helpful staff; conv town & beach; Sat gd mkt; sep m'van Aires de Services nr yacht harbour & equestrian cent; gd value; excel." 4 Feb-19 Nov. € 16.00 2007*

TOUQUIN *4E4* (2km W Rural) **Camping Les Etangs Fleuris, Route de la Couture, 77131 Touquin [01 64 04 16 36; fax 01 64 04 12 28; contact@etangs-fleuris.com; www.etangsfleuris.com]** On D231 fr Provins, turn R to Touquin. Turn sharp R in vill & foll sp to site on R in approx 2km. Or fr Coulommiers, take D402 SW twd Mauperthuis, after Mauperthuis L twd Touquin. Foll sp in vill. Med, some hdg pitch, pt shd; wc; chem disp; mv service pnt; shwrs inc; el pnts (10A) inc; gas; lndtte; ice; sm shop; tradsmn; hypmkt nr; snacks; bar; playgrnd; htd pool; paddling pool; lake fishing; minigolf; entmnt; 80% statics; phone; adv bkg; quiet; cc not acc; CCI. "Tour ops on site; no twin-axle c'vans high ssn; v rural & quiet; conv Paris & Disneyland." 1 Apr-18 Sep. € 19.80 2005*

TOUR DU MEIX, LA see Clairvaux les Lacs *6H2*

TOUR DU PARC, LE see Sarzeau *2G3*

TOURCOING *3A4* (5km SW Rural) **Camping Les Ramiers, 1 Chemin des Ramiers, 59910 Bondues [tel/fax 03 20 23 13 42; glepers@aol.com]** A19 junc 2, S on N17 twd Menen & Tourcoing, exit Bondues sp to site. Med, pt shd; wc; chem disp; mv service pnt; shwrs €1; el pnts (4A) €2.50; ice; BBQ; playgrnd; games area; 60% statics; bus 2km; phone adj; adv bkg; quiet; CCI; "Sh stay/NH, conv Lille & TGV 1 hr Paris." 15 Apr-31 Oct. € 7.10 2005*

TOURNAN EN BRIE *4E3* (1km S Rural) **Caravaning Fredland, Parc de Combreux, 77220 Tournan-en-Brie [01 64 07 96 44; fax 01 64 42 00 61; fred.chauvineau@wanadoo.fr]** Foll N4 E fr Paris. 15km beyond junc with N104 turn R onto D10 sp Liverdy. Site immed on R on lakeside Med, mkd pitch, pt sl, pt shd; wc; chem disp; shwrs inc; el pnts (6A) inc; lndtte; rest; snacks; bar; BBQ; playgrnd; htd pool; fishing; games area; 75% statics; poss cr; Eng spkn; adv bkg; quiet. "Conv for Paris visits; 10 min walk to stn; v nice site." 1 Mar-31 Oct. € 21.50 2005*

TOURNEHEM SUR LA HEM see Ardres *3A3*

⊞**TOURNIERES** *1D4* (Rural) **Camping Le Picard, 14330 Tournières [02 31 22 82 44; fax 02 31 51 70 28; paul.palmer@wanadoo.fr; www. camp-france.com]** Fr Bayeux foll D5/D15 W to Tournières, 5km past Le Molay-Littry. Fr N13 Cherbourg-Bayeux, E of Carentan turn S onto N174 then E on D15 to Tournières. Site sp opp Tournières church. Sm, pt shd, hdg pitch; wc; chem disp; serviced pitches; shwrs inc; el pnts (10A) €3.50; lndtte; shop 5km; tradsmn; rest; snacks; bar; playgrnd; htd pool; sand beach 20km; boating; fishing; wifi internet free; no dogs; phone; adv bkg; quiet; cc acc; CCI. "Delightful, British-owned site with rustic atmosphere; conv Normandy beaches, Bayeux Tapestry, Cherbourg ferry; v popular with British tourists; van storage; helpful owners bake croissants & will do laundry; ample hot water." ♦ € 18.00   2007*

⊞**TOURNON SUR RHONE** *9C2* (500m N Urban) **Camping de Tournon HPA, 1 Promenade Roche-de-France, 07300 Tournon-sur-Rhône [tel/fax 04 75 08 05 28; camping@camping-tournon.com; www.camping-tournon.com]** Fr Tain l'Hermitage cross Rhône, turn R onto N86. In approx 1km R at end of car park. Turn L after 50m, site on R on Rv Rhône. Med, shd; htd wc (some cont); chem disp; mv service pnt; shwrs inc; el pnts (6-10A) €2.70-4.60; gas; lndtte; shop, rest, snacks & bar nr; playgrnd; pool 1km; canoeing; internet; some statics; dogs €1; phone; m'van o'night area; c'van storage avail; poss cr; Eng spkn; adv bkg rec; some rlwy noise; red long stay; cc acc high ssn; CCI. "Nice site in beautiful wooded location; views of rv fr some pitches; friendly owners; gd, clean san facs; mainly sm pitches & narr rds poss diff lge o'fits; easy walk into town; nr steam rlwy (adv bkg poss req high ssn); sh walk across Rhône to Tain-l'Hermitage; fr mid-Jun rock concerts poss held nrby at w/e; Mistral can make site v dusty; in need of more TLC (Sep 2007)." ♦ € 12.20   2007*

TOURNON SUR RHONE *9C2* (6km N Rural) **FFCC Camping L'Iserand, Rue Royal, 07610 Vion [04 75 08 01 73; fax 04 75 08 55 82; iserand@ tele2.fr; www.iserandcampingardeche.com]** Take N86 N fr Tournon, site 1km N of Vion on L. Med, hdg/mkd pitch, sl, terr, pt shd; htd wc (some cont); chem disp; mv service pnt; baby facs; shwrs inc; el pnts (10A) €3; ice; gas; lndtte; shop & 1km; tradsmn; rest 1km; snacks; bar; BBQ; playgrnd; pool; beach; cycle hire; canoeing 1km; entmnt; TV rm; 15% statics; dogs €3; bus 1km; phone; poss cr; adv bkg; Eng spkn; quiet but some rd & rlwy noise; red low ssn; CCI. "Steam rlwy to mountains adj; v friendly owner lives on site - & will take low ssn visitors; excel." 1 Apr-30 Sep. € 15.00   2007*

TOURNON SUR RHONE *9C2* (3km SW Rural) **FFCC Camping Le Manoir, 222 Route de Lamastre, 07300 Tournon-sur-Rhône [04 75 08 02 50 or 06 70 00 06 13 (mob); fax 04 75 08 57 10; info@ lemanoir-ardeche.com; www.lemanoir-ardeche. com]** Leave Tournon on D532 just bef x-ing rv, dir Lamastre. Site on R after 3km (4th site). Med, mkd pitch, pt shd; wc (50% cont); chem disp; mv service pnt; shwrs inc; el pnts (10A) €3; ice; BBQ; lndtte; shop 2.5km; tradsmn; snacks; bar; playgrnd; pool; rv sw adj; TV rm; entmnt; 70% statics; dogs; phone; poss cr; adv bkg; quiet but some rd noise; cc acc; red CCI. "Very pleasant, family-run, rvside site; friendly, hard working staff; gd facs; ideal for walking; vineyard tours; vg." ♦ 1 Apr-30 Sep. € 16.00   2007*

TOURNON SUR RHONE *9C2* (2.5km W Rural) **Camping Les Acacias, 07300 Tournon-sur-Rhône [tel/fax 04 75 08 83 90; acacias-camping@ wanadoo.fr]** Fr N86 Tournon turn W onto D532 dir Lamastre, site on R in approx 2km. Med, pt shd; wc (some cont); chem disp; shwrs; el pnts (6A) €3; gas; lndtte; rest; shop 2km; playgrnd; pool; dogs €1.80; poss cr; Eng spkn; rd noise; adv bkg; CCI. "Nr steam rlwy; gd pitches; some noise fr sawmill; friendly; vg site." ♦ 1 Apr-30 Sep. € 14.50   2005*

TOURNON SUR RHONE *9C2* (4km W Rural) **Camping Le Castelet, 113 Route du Grand Pont, 07300 St Jean-de-Muzols [04 75 08 09 48; fax 04 75 08 49 60; courrier@camping-lecastelet. com; www.camping-lecastelet.com]** Exit Tournon on N86 N; in 500m turn L on D532 twd Lamastre; in 4km turn R on D532 over bdge & turn immed R into site. Med, mkd pitch,terr, pt shd; wc (some cont); chem disp; baby facs; shwrs inc; el pnts (5A) €3.20; gas; lndtte; ice; shop & supmkt 4km; tradsmn; bar; playgrnd; pool; paddling pool; rv sw; entmnt; dogs; adv bkg; quiet, but some rd noise; red low ssn; cc not acc. "Steam rlwy adj; owner will arrange to have train stop; spotless san facs." 1 Apr-16 Sep. € 14.50   2007*

TOURNUS *9A2* (1km N Urban) **Camp Municipal en Bagatelle, 71700 Tournus [03 85 51 16 58]** Fr N6 at N of town turn E opp rlwy stn & rest 'Le Terminus;' foll site sp. Med, some mkd pitch, pt sl, pt shd; wc (some cont); chem disp (wc low ssn); mv service pnt; shwrs inc; el pnts (10A) €2.70 (long lead poss req); gas; lndtte; ice; shops; BBQ; playgrnd; htd pools adj high ssn; rv 250m; TV; dogs €0.50; Eng spkn; quiet but some rd & rlwy noise; CCI. "Peaceful site nr rv; popular NH - rec arr early; conv A6; v helpful staff; spotless facs but v stretched high ssn & ltd low ssn; muddy after rain; 15 min walk to interesting old town on rv; gd cycling nrby on the Burgundy Voies Vertes; tourist info in office." ♦ 1 May-30 Sep. € 12.60   2007*

TOURNUS 9A2 (6km S Rural) **Camping Le National 6, 71700 Uchizy [tel/fax 03 85 40 53 90]** Exit A6 junc 27 & foll N6 S; sp on L, turn L over rwly bdge on lane to site on L. Adj Rv Saône. NB Some sp 'Camping d'Uchizy' only. Med, shd; wc; shwrs inc; el pnts (6A) €3.50; gas; shop; snacks; playgrnd; pool; fishing; boat hire; dogs €1; poss cr; adv bkg; quiet; red low ssn. "Lovely, quiet site in attractive setting on bank of Rv Saône; gd new san facs; well-maintained site; helpful staff; soft & muddy in rain: arr early for rvside pitch." 1 Apr-30 Sep. € 13.30
2007*

Did you know you can fill in site report forms on the Club's website — www.caravanclub.co.uk?

TOURNUS 9A2 (10km W Rural) **Aire Naturelle de Camping à la Ferme de Malo (Goujon), Champlieu, 71240 Etrigny [03 85 92 21 47 or 03 85 92 23 40; fax 03 85 92 22 13; fam@aubergemalo.com; www.aubergemalo.com]** S on N6 to Tournus; after rwly stn turn R onto D14; after passing under rlwy DO NOT fork L to foll D14 - cont strt onto D215 dir St Gengoux-le-National. In 8km, in Nogent, turn R at lge stone drinking trough onto D159 (not mkd); at 2nd x-rds turn L onto D459 (sp Champlieu); at 1st x-rds turn L into Champlieu; site on L 500m after vill, bef rv. Sm, pt shd; wc (cont); chem disp (wc); shwrs inc; el pnts (6-10A) €3 (long lead poss req); lndtte; tradsmn; rest 1km; playgrnd; horseriding; sw, fishing & boating 10km; tennis 3km; dogs; adv bkg ess high ssn; quiet; no cc acc; CCI. "Pitch yourself, owner will call 1800; san facs poss stretched high ssn; additional pitches & rv water pool opp main site; farm produce avail; eve meals avail in farmhouse 1km; adj to Rv Grison & close to Maconnais wine rte." 1 May-1 Nov. € 9.80
2006*

⊞**TOURS** 4G2 (6km E Rural) **Camping Les Acacias, Rue Berthe Morisot, 37700 La Ville-aux-Dames [02 47 44 08 16 or 02 62 19 18 08 (LS); fax 02 47 46 26 65; camplvad@.aol.com]** Fr Tours take D751 sp Amboise; after 6km at rndabt where La Ville-aux-Dames sp to R, go strt on for 200m, then turn R, site sp. Med, shd; htd wc; chem disp; mv service pnt; serviced pitch; shwrs; el pnts (4-10A) €2.90-4.60; gas; lndtte; ice; sm shop; supmkt 1km; playgrnd; pool 500m; boules; tennis 600m; fitness trail, mountain bike circuit, fishing 100m; dogs €1.80; adv bkg; quiet, but rd & rlwy noise; CCI. "V helpful owners; excel san facs; gd site; conv town cent; recep clsd at w/e Oct-Apr - no ent without key pass during this period." ♦ € 11.30
2007*

TOURS 4G2 (8km E Rural) **Camping des Peupliers (formerly Municipal), 37270 Montlouis-sur-Loire [02 47 50 81 90 or 03 86 37 95 83; aquadis1@wanadoo.fr; www.camping-de-touraine-loire-et-chateaux.com or www.aquadis-loisirs.com]** On D751, 2km W of vill of Montlouis. Fr N foll sp to Vouvray (keep on N side of Loire to avoid Tours) & cross rv by bdge to Montlouis. Sp at last minute. NB App fr E a 'Q-turn' to get into site. Lge, hdg pitch, pt shd; htd wc; chem disp; mv service pnt; baby facs; shwrs inc; el pnts (6A) €4.10; ice; lndtte; shop 2km; tradsmn; playgrnd; tennis; 12% statics; dogs €1.90; Eng spkn; adv bkg; quiet but some rd & rlwy noise; cc acc; CCI. "Clean & tidy site; lge pitches; conv vineyards & chateaux; gd mkt Sun in Amboise; lge Leclerc supmkt nrby; vg." ♦ 1 Apr-31 Oct. € 13.70
2007*

TOURS 4G2 (5km SE Urban) **Camping Les Rives du Cher, 61 Rue de Rochepinard, 37550 St Avertin [02 47 27 27 60; fax 02 47 25 82 89; contact@camping-lesrivesducher.com; www.camping-lesrivesducher.com]** Fr Tours, take D976 (N76) S of rv sp Bléré/Vierzon into St Avertin vill. Take next L at traff lts over 1st of 2 bdges. Site on R in 450m, not well sp. Med, hdg/mkd pitch, some hdstg, pt shd; wc (some cont); chem disp; mv service pnt; shwrs inc; el pnts (4-10A) €2.85-4.60 (poss rev pol); lndtte; shops 400m; rest, snacks & bar adj; playgrnd; htd pool adj; tennis; fishing; dogs €1.10; phone; adv bkg; quiet; cc acc; CCI. "Friendly owner; camp neat, clean but needs modernising; some resident workers; pitches on rd side of site noisy in morning rush hour; poss late night noise fr adj parks & clubs; conv." ♦ 1 Apr-15 Oct. € 13.25
2005*

This guide relies on site report forms submitted by caravanners like us; we'll do our bit and tell the editor what we think of the campsites we've visited.

TOURS 4G2 (10km SE Rural) **Camp Municipal Les Isles, 37270 Véretz [02 47 50 50 48; fax 02 47 35 70 10; mairie@varetz.com; www.veretz.com]** Exit Tours on D976 (N76) dir Vierzon to Véretz; site 1km past rv bdge on L (S) bank of Rv Cher. Med, hdg/mkd pitch, pt shd; wc (some cont); chem disp; mv service pnt; shwrs inc; el pnts (6A) €3.50; lndtte; ice; supmkt 500m; playgrnd; pool 5km; table tennis; fishing; TV rm; dogs €1; poss cr; Eng spkn; adv bkg ess high ssn; red 14+ days; 10% red CCI. "Vg site; gd welcome; facs adequate, clean; pitches among tall trees by rv overlooking Château Véretz; friendly recep; gd security." ♦ 16 May-9 Sep. € 12.00
2007*

A natural landscaped and shaded family campsite on the banks of the River Loire and on the Loire Chateaux route.

"Les Granges" Camping Caravaning
37230 LUYNES
Tél : 33 1 76 616 594
Fax : 33 2 47 409 243
www.campinglesgranges.fr
Email : reception@campinglesgranges.fr

TOURS *4G2* (8km SW Urban) **Camping La Mignardière, 22 Ave des Aubépines, 37510 Ballan-Miré [02 47 73 31 00; fax 02 47 73 31 01; info@mignardiere.com; www.mignardiere.com]** Fr A10 exit junc 24 onto N585 & D37 by-pass. At exit for Joué-lès-Tours foll sp Ballan-Miré onto D751. Turn R at 1st set traff lts & foll site sp to W of lake. Lge, hdg/mkd pitch, hdstg, pt shd; htd wc; chem disp; mv service pnt; 10% serviced pitch; baby facs; shwrs inc; el pnts (6-10A) €3; lndtte; sm shop; tradsmn; snacks; bar 200m; BBQ; playgrnd; htd pools; windsurfing & fishing 1km; tennis; cycle hire; squash; internet; entmnt; child entmnt; TV rm; dogs; phone; Eng spkn; adv bkg; quiet; red low ssn; CCI. "Conv Loire Valley & chateaux; friendly staff; unisex facs low ssn; gd cycle paths; vg site." ♦ 27 Mar-23 Sep. € 20.00 (CChq acc)   2007*

See advertisement below

TOURS *4G2* (8km W Rural) **Camping L'Islette, 23 Rue de Vallières, 37230 Fondettes [02 47 42 26 42]** Foll D952 (N152) W fr Tours twd Saumur. In approx 6km turn R at traff lts onto D276 at Port de Vallières. Site on L in approx 2km. Sm, hdg pitch, pt shd; wc (some cont); shwrs inc; el pnts (10A) €1.70; shop 2km; playgrnd; pool 4km; dogs; bus; poss cr; adv bkg; quiet; CCI. "V pleasant site; helpful owners; facs poss stretched if site full." ♦ ltd. 1 Apr-30 Oct. € 7.00   2004*

TOURS *4G2* (10km W Rural) **Camping Club Les Granges, Le Bourg, 37230 Luynes [02 47 55 79 05 or 01 76 61 65 94; fax 02 47 40 92 43; reception@campinglesgranges. fr; www.campinglesgranges.fr]** Fr Tours take D952 (N152) twd Saumur. Turn R at Le Port-de-Luynes, sp to Luynes & site on rvside. Med, hdg/mkd pitch, pt shd; htd wc; mv service pnt; baby facs; shwrs inc; el pnts (10A) €1.50; lndtte; shops; tradsmn; snacks; bar; BBQ; playgrnd; pool 800m; fishing 500m; tennis 700m; games area; games rm; wifi internet; TV; some statics; dogs €1; adv bkg; quiet; cc acc. "Pleasant site; gd touring base Loire valley." ♦ 1 May-16 Oct. € 11.00   2007*

See advertisement above

TOURS *4G2* (10km W Rural) **Camping de la Confluence, Route de Bray, 37510 Savonnières [tel/fax 02 47 50 15 71]** Fr Tours take D7 on S of Rv Cher. Site on R on ent Savonnières on rvside. Med, hdg/mkd pitch, hdstg, pt shd; wc (some cont); chem disp; mv service pnt; baby facs; shwrs inc; el pnts (10A) inc; lndtte; ice; shops 500m; tradsmn; rest 100m; bar adj; BBQ; playgrnd; canoe hire; tennis adj; dogs; phone; bus 200m; Eng spkn; adv bkg (dep req); quiet; red 15 days; CCI. "Refurbished 2005; gd views of Rv Cher; gd birdwatching; gd cycling area." ♦ 1 Jun-15 Sep. € 13.00   2005*

TOURY *4F3* **Camp Municipal, Rue de Boissay, 28310 Toury [02 37 90 50 60 (Mairie); fax 02 37 90 58 61; mairie-toury@wanadoo.fr]** Fr Orléans take N20 N. Site well sp. Sm, shd; wc; chem disp; shwrs inc; el pnts (16A) €3; gas 1km; shop 800m; rest 200m; bar 100m; BBQ; playgrnd; dogs; poss cr' rd & rlwy noise. "NH only; warden calls; clean san facs; arrive bef 1600 to ensure pitch." 1 Apr-15 Oct. € 11.60   2007*

As soon as we get home I'm going to post all these site report forms to the editor for inclusion in next year's guide. I don't want to miss the September deadline.

TOUSSAINT see Fécamp *3C1*

TOUSSUIRE, LA *9C3* (1km E Rural) **Camping Caravaneige du Col, Fontcouverte, 73300 La Toussuire [04 79 83 00 80; fax 04 79 83 03 67; campingducol@free.fr]** Fr Chambéry E on A43 to St Jean-de-Maurienne. In St Jean foll sp Vallée de l'Arvan. Site on L after vill of Fontcouverte, 1km bef vill of La Toussuire. Sm, terr, pt shd; htd wc (some cont); chem disp; mv service pnt; baby facs; shwrs inc; el pnts (10A) €4.30; gas; lndry rm; rest; snacks; bar; playgrnd; TV: drying-room & skiboot storage; adv bkg; quiet; 5% red CCI. "Excel welcome; site owner runs navette to vill, 1km fr ski-lifts; clean san facs up external flight of stairs." 11 Jun-4 Sep & 15 Dec-30 Apr. € 10.65   2005*

TOUTAINVILLE see Pont Audemer *3D2*

TOUZAC see Fumel *7D3*

TRANCHE SUR MER, LA *7A1* (500m N Urban/ Coastal) **Camp Municipal Le Vieux Moulin, Ave Maurice Samson, 85360 La Tranche-sur-Mer [02 51 27 48 47]** On ent town foll sp for Gendarmerie, sp adj supmkt. Lge, mkd pitch, some hdstg, pt sl, pt shd; wc (chem closet); own san; chem disp; shwrs inc; el pnts (6A) €1.83; lndry rm; shop 400m; sand beach 500m; 50% statics; poss cr; adv bkg (dep); quiet; CCI. "Some sm pitches; town cent & beach 5 mins walk." 1 Apr-30 Sep. € 14.50   2004*

TRANCHE SUR MER, LA *7A1* (2.6km NE) **Camping Les Blancs Chênes, Route de la Roche-sur-Yon, 85360 La Tranche-sur-Mer [02 51 30 41 70 or 02 51 27 37 80 (res); fax 02 51 28 84 09; info@camping-vagues.oceanes.com; www.camping-vagues-oceanes.com]** Site sp on rd D747 Lge, mkd pitch, pt shd; mv service pnt; wc; baby facs; shwrs inc; el pnts (6A) €5.50 gas; lndtte; shop; tradsmn; rest; snacks; bar; BBQ; playgrnd; htd, covrd pool; paddling pool; waterslide; sand beach 1.8km; tennis; games area; games rm; entmnt; statics; dogs €2.60; shuttle bus to beach; quiet; Eng spkn; adv bkg; cc acc; red low ssn; CCI. "Superb pool complex." ♦ Easter-15 Sep. € 23.00   2006*

TRANCHE SUR MER, LA *7A1* (3km NE Rural) **Camping Les Almadies, La Charrière des Bandes, Route de la Roche-sur-Yon, 85360 La Tranche-sur-Mer [02 51 30 36 94; fax 02 51 30 37 04; info@lesalmadies.com; www. lesalmadies.com]** S fr La Roche-sur-Yon on D747, site sp. Lge, mkd pitch, pt shd; wc; chem disp; baby facs; shwrs; el pnts (10A) €3.65; lndtte; shop; rest; snacks; bar; BBQ; htd pool; paddling pool; waterslides; sand beach 3km; bus to beach high ssn; cycle hire; games area; entmnt; child entmnt; internet; TV; dogs; adv bkg; quiet; red low ssn. "V pleasant site; vg facs for children; helpful, friendly staff." ♦ 5 Apr-27 Sep. € 25.30   2007*

See advertisement on page 561

CAMPING DU JARD ★★★★
123 Bd Mal. de Lattre de Tassigny - La Grière
85360 La Tranche sur Mer
Phone : 0033 02 51 27 43 79
Fax : 0033 02 51 27 42 92

700 meters from a splendid fine sandy beach. Flat and half shaded campsite, 350 clearly marked sites and equipped with European connections. Outdoor swimming pool with water slide, indoor swimming pool with Jacuzzi, children's club, all shops. Guarded night-time car-park at the entrance.

Web: www.campingdujard.fr
Email: info@campingdujard.fr

TRANCHE SUR MER, LA *7A1* (500m E Coastal) Camping Bel, Rue de Bottereau, 85360 La Tranche-sur-Mer [02 51 30 47 39; fax 02 51 27 72 81] Ent La Tranche on D747, take 2nd R at rndabt, R at traff lts, ent on L. Med hdg/mkd pitch, pt shd; wc; chem disp; baby facs; shwrs inc; el pnts (6A) inc; lndtte; shops rest adj; snacks; bar; tradsmn; playgrnd; pool & children's pool; table-tennis; TV; 70% statics; phone; poss cr; Eng spkn; adv bkg; quiet; CCI "Ideal for families with young children; cycle hire nearby." ♦ 25 May-7 Sep. € 20.00   2004*

The opening dates and prices on this campsite have changed. I'll send a site report form to the editor for the next edition of the guide.

TRANCHE SUR MER, LA *7A1* (500m E Coastal) Camping La Baie d'Aunis, 10 Rue de Pertuis, 85360 La Tranche-sur-Mer [02 51 27 47 36; fax 02 51 27 44 54; info@camping-baiedaunis.com; www.camping-baiedaunis.com] App on D747 fr La Roche-sur-Yon, turn 2nd R at rndabt sp 'Centre Ville', strt at traff lts & ent on L. Well sp. Med, hdg/mkd pitch, hdstg, pt shd; htd wc (some cont); chem disp; mv service pnt; baby facs; shwrs inc; el pnts (10A) €4.20; gas; ice; lndtte; shop 600m; tradsmn; rest; snacks; bar; BBQ; playgrnd; htd pool; sand beach adj; sailing; sea-fishing; watersports; tennis 500m; cycle hire adj; games rm; entmnt; TV; 10% statics; dogs (not Jul/Aug) €2.20; Eng spkn; adv bkg (ess Jul/Aug); quiet; cc acc; red low ssn; CCI. "Vg, friendly site; excel facs & rest; lovely area, gd beaches; poss diff ent lge o'fits." ♦ 1 May-14 Sep. € 25.40   2007*

See advertisement opposite

TRANCHE SUR MER, LA *7A1* (3km E Coastal) Camping du Jard, 123 Blvd du Lattre de Tassigny, 85360 La Tranche-sur-Mer [02 51 27 43 79; fax 02 51 27 42 92; info@campingdujard.fr; www.campingdujard.fr] Foll D747 S fr La Roche-sur-Yon twd La Tranche-sur-Mer on D747; at rndabt on outskirts of La Tranche turn L (3rd exit) onto D1046 sp La Faute-sur-Mer; cont for approx 5km. At rndabt turn R (1st exit) sp La Faute-sur-Mer 'par la côte', then R at next rndabt onto D46 sp La Tranche-sur-Mer 'par la côte' & La Grière-Plage (ignore all previous La Grière sp); cont for approx 1km; site on R. Rough app rd. Lge, hdg pitch, unshd; wc (some cont); chem disp; serviced pitch; baby facs; sauna; shwrs inc; el pnts (10A) inc; lndtte; shop; rest; snacks; bar; BBQ; playgrnd; 2 pools (1 htd, covrd); paddling pool; waterslide; sand beach 700m; tennis; games area; fitness cent; mini-golf; cycle hire; horseriding 10km; golf 20km; entmnt; wifi internet; games/TV rm; 30% statics (tour ops); no dogs; c'vans over 10m not acc high ssn; adv bkg; rd noise; red low ssn; cc acc; red CCI. "Clean, tidy, well-run site; pitches liable to flood in wet weather; recep 0800-2100 high ssn; some sm pitches; gd pool; mkt Tue & Sat." ♦ 1 May-15 Sep. € 34.90 ABS - A03   2007*

See advertisement above

TREBES see Carcassonne *8F4*

TREBEURDEN *1D2* (4km N Coastal) Camping L'Espérance, Penvern, 22560 Trébeurden [02 96 91 95 05; fax 02 96 91 98 12; accueil@camping-esperance.com; www.camping-esperance.com] Fr Lannion on D65 to Trébeurden, then D788 sp Trégastel, site in 5km. Med, hdg/mkd pitch, pt shd; wc (some cont); chem disp; mv service pnt; baby facs; shwrs inc; el pnts (5-10A) €2.80-3.50; gas; lndtte; ice; shop 2km; playgrnd; sand beach adj; golf adj; TV; 10% statics; dogs €1.50; bus; Eng spkn; adv bkg; quiet; cc not acc; CCI. "V pleasant site; nr GR34 long dist walking rte." ♦ 1 Apr-30 Sep. € 14.20   2005*

TREBEURDEN *1D2* (1km S Coastal) **Camping Armor Loisirs, Pors-Mabo, Rue de Kernévez, 22560 Trébeurden [02 96 23 52 31; fax 02 96 15 40 36; info@armorloisirs.com or armorloisirs@aol.com; www.armorloisirs.com]** N fr Lannion twds Trébeurden on D65. Turn L at 1st mini rndabt, then immed fork R into Rue de Kernévez, site on R in 800m, foll sp Pors-Mabo. Med, hdg/mkd pitch, pt sl, pt shd; wc; chem disp; baby facs; fam bthrm; serviced pitches; shwrs; el pnts (10A) inc; gas; lndtte; ice; shop; tradsmn; snacks; bar; BBQ; playgrnd; htd pool; sand beach 500m; watersports; fishing; games rm; entmnt; internet; TV; 50% statics; dogs €2; Eng spkn; adv bkg; quiet; cc acc; red low ssn/long stay/ CCI. "Peaceful, well-run site; steep 'sleeping policemen'; some pitches poss diff for long o'fits; gd sea views; vg." ♦ 1 Apr-30 Sep. € 22.50
2007*

See advertisement above

TREDION *2F3* (1.5km S Rural) **Camp Municipal l'Etang aux Biches, Route d'Elven, 56350 Trédion [02 97 67 14 06; fax 02 97 67 13 41]** E fr Vannes on N166 for 15km to Elven; in town foll sps N on D1 for Trédion. Site on L in 5km. Sm, hdg/mkd pitch, pt sl, pt shd; wc; shwrs €1.10; el pnts (3A) €1.90; ice; shop 1.5km; tradsmn; playgrnd; quiet. "V peaceful; inland fr v busy coast; helpful staff." ♦ 1 Jul-31 Aug. € 5.40
2006*

TREGASTEL *1D2* (1.5km N Coastal) **Tourony Camping, Route de Poul Palud, 22730 Trégastel [02 96 23 86 61; fax 02 96 15 97 84; contact@ camping-tourony.com; www.camping-tourony. com]** On D788 fr Trébeurden dir Perros Guirec, site on R immed after exit Trégastel town sp & immed bef bdge over Traouieros inlet, opp Port de Ploumanac'h. Med, hdg/mkd pitch, pt shd; wc (some cont); chem disp; mv service pnt; baby facs; shwrs inc; el pnts (6A) €2.90; gas; ice; lndtte; shop 400m; tradsmn; snacks; bar; BBQ; playgrnd; sand beach adj; lake fishing; tennis; cycle hire; games area; golf, horseriding nrby; entmnt; TV; 15% statics; dogs €1.50; Eng spkn; adv bkg; quiet; cc acc; red long stay/low ssn; CCI. "V pleasant site in gd location; friendly, helpful management; gd touring base Granit Rose coast." ♦ 7 Apr-22 Sep. € 16.50
2007*

See advertisement below

⊞ Site open all year

Tell us about the sites you visit

CAMPING DU PORT ★★★★ Watersports (mooring)

Landrellec
22560 PLEUMEUR-BODOU
Tel.: 02 96 23 87 79 - Fax : 02 96 15 30 40
Web: http://www.camping-du-port.com Mail : renseignements@camping-du-port.com

TREGASTEL *1D2* (4km SW Coastal) **Camp Municipal Le Dourlin, L'Île Grande, 22560 Pleumeur-Bodou [02 96 91 92 41 or 02 96 23 91 17 (Mairie)]** Off D788 SW of Trégastel. Foll minor rd thro vill to site on coast. Well sp. Med, mkd pitch, unshd; wc; chem disp; shwrs inc; el pnts (6-13A) €2.20-4.40; lndtte; ice; shops 500m; rest; snacks; bar; BBQ; playgrnd; sand/shgl beach; sailing; fishing; sports area; dogs; phone; bus; poss cr; Eng spkn; quiet; CCI. "Fine sea views; marina; gd walking, cycling; ornithological cent nr; gd." ♦ 15 May-16 Sep. € 8.05   2006*

TREGASTEL *1D2* (4km W Coastal/Rural) **Camping du Port, Chemin des Douaniers, Landrellec, 22560 Pleumeur-Bodou [02 96 23 87 79; fax 02 96 15 30 40; renseignements@camping-du-port.com; www.camping-du-port.com]** Turn off D788 to Landrellec & foll rd thro vill past shop for 100m, take care tight turn L. Site in 500m. Med, hdg/mkd pitch, pt sl, pt shd; htd wc; chem disp; mv service pnt; serviced pitches; baby facs; shwrs inc; el pnts (10A) €2.60; gas; lndtte; ice; shop; tradsmn; rest; snacks; bar; BBQ; playgrnd; pool 2km; direct access to sandy/rock beach; fishing, boating, waterskiing; cycle hire; games rm; entmnt; internet; TV rm; 25% statics; dogs €2.50; Eng spkn; adv bkg; quiet; cc acc; red low ssn; CCI. "Immac, family-owned site; beautiful location; direct access beach; coastal path runs thro site; narr pitches by shore; telecoms museum worth visit." ♦ 22 Mar-5 Oct. € 16.50   2007*

See advertisement above

TREGUENNEC see Pont l'Abbé *2F2*

TREGUIER *1D3* (8km N Coastal) **Camp Municipal de Beg-Ar-Vilin, 22820 Plougrescant [02 96 92 56 15 or 02 96 92 51 18 (Mairie); fax 02 96 92 59 26]** Take D8 N out of Tréguier to Plougrescant. At St Gonéry/Plougrescant turn R foll sp. Med, pt shd; wc; shwrs inc; lndtte; shops 2km; el pnts €3.15; beach sand/rock adj; phone; quiet. "Gd; busy, cr site high ssn." ♦ 1 Jun-15 Sep. € 8.80
                    2005*

TREGUIER *1D3* (10km N Coastal) **Camp du Gouffre, 22820 Plougrescant [tel/fax 02 96 92 02 95]** On D8 N fr Tréguier to Plougrescant. R at 2nd church & foll site sp. Med, mkd pitch, pt sl, unshd; wc; chem disp; mv service pnt; shwrs inc; el pnts (6-15A) €2.50; lndtte; shop 2km; tradsmn (bread only); ice; playgrnd; sand/shgl beach adj; quiet; adv bkg; cc acc; CCI. "Facs well designed & immac." ♦ 15 Apr-15 Sep. € 10.00
                    2004*

TREGUIER *1D3* (10km N) **FFCC Camping Le Varlen, Route de Pors-Hir, 22820 Plougrescant [02 96 92 52 15; fax 02 96 92 50 34; www.levarlen.com]** Take D8 N out of Tréguier to Plougrescant. Go past old chapel then immed bef church turn R sp Pors-Hir to site in 1km on R. Sm, mkd pitch, pt sl, pt shd; wc; mv service pnt; baby facs; shwrs inc; el pnts (6-10A) €2.80-3.50 (poss rev pol); lndtte; ice; shop; bar; playgrnd; sports area; shgl beach 200m; 90% statics; dogs €1.30; adv bkg; quiet; cc acc. "Shwrs v clean but avoid shwr behind house/bar due dangerous electrics; beautiful coastal walks; some pitches sm & poss diff lge o'fits/m'vans; v helpful owners." 1 Mar-15 Nov. € 13.50
                    2006*

TREGUIER *1D3* (9km NE Coastal) **Camping Port La Chaîne, 22610 Pleubian [02 96 22 92 38; fax 02 96 22 87 92; info@portlachaine.com; www.portlachaine.com]** Fr Paimpol take old D786 W & pick up new D786 over estuary & thro Lézardrieux. After 3km at x-rds turn R (N) onto D33 thro Pleumeur-Gautier; cont for 4.5km to Pleubian; then take D20 twds Larmor-Pleubian; turn L after 2km twd coast & foll site sp. Lge, mkd pitch, pt sl, pt shd; wc (some cont); chem disp; serviced pitch; baby facs; shwrs inc; el pnts (6A) inc; gas; lndtte; ice; shop; tradsmn; rest; snacks; bar; BBQ; playgrnd; pool; paddling pool; shgl beach adj; watersports nr; fishing; cycle hire in vill; child entmnt; internet; games/TV rm; 30% statics; dogs €2.90; poss cr; Eng spkn; adv bkg ess; quiet; cc acc. "Lovely, peaceful site; excel views fr some pitches; gd facs; helpful owners." ♦ 5 Apr-13 Sep. € 25.00
ABS - B23   2007*

France

⊞**TREGUNC** 2F2 (3km SE Rural) **Camping Fleuri, Route de Névez, Kervec, 29910 Trégunc [02 98 96 74 76; ulrike.kuster@orange.fr]** Fr D783 turn S onto D77 dir Névez. At rndabt turn R onto D177, site in 500m on R. Sm, hdg pitch, pt shd; htd wc; chem disp (wc); mv service pnt; shwrs inc; el pnts (6A) €2.20; gas; lndtte; supmkt 500m; playgrnd; sand beach 3km; 70% statics; dogs €1; phone; poss cr; Eng spkn; adv bkg; quiet; cc acc; CCl. "Wooded site; friendly, helpful owners; gd san facs; gd coastal walking & beaches; plants for sale; conv Concarneau & Pont-Aven; gd." ♦ € 9.70
2007*

TREGUNC 2F2 (3km S Coastal) **Camping des Etangs de Trévignon, Kerlin, 29910 Trégunc [02 98 50 00 41; fax 02 98 50 04 09; camp. etangdetrevignon@wanadoo.fr; www.camping-etangs.com]** Exit N165/E60 at Kérampaou. S on D122 to Trégunc, then cont S on D1 to Trévignon. Site in 3km. Foll sp. Lge, hdg/mkd pitch, pt shd; wc (some cont); chem disp; baby facs; shwrs inc; el pnts (5A) €3.10; gas; lndtte; ice; shop 2km; tradsmn; rest 3km; snacks; bar; BBQ; playgrnd; htd, covrd pool high ssn; waterslide; sand beach 800m; mini-golf; cycle hire; TV rm; 5% statics; dogs €1.80; phone; Eng spkn; adv bkg; quiet; red low ssn/ long stay; cc acc; red CCl. "In nature res with bird sanctuary nr; close to fishing ports, islands; excel." ♦ 25 May-15 Sep. € 19.85
2005*

TREGUNC 2F2 (4km S Coastal) **Camping Le Suroît, Plage de Karidan, 29128 Trégunc [tel/ fax 02 98 50 01 76 or 02 98 97 65 42 (LS)]** Fr Concarneau take D783 to Trégunc; D1 S for 3km dir La Pointe de Trévignon & turn L & foll sps for 3.5km. Med, mkd pitch, pt sl, pt shd; wc; chem disp; shwrs inc; el pnts (4-10A) €2.60; lndtte; shop 2km; rest; snacks; bar; BBQ; sand beach ajd; 50% statics; dogs €0.50; poss cr; adv bkg; quiet; CCl. "Simple site; v sm, modern san facs block, poss stretched high ssn; pleasant owner; lovely sand beach across rd; gd." 15 Apr-30 Sep. € 12.50
2007*

TREGUNC 2F2 (5.5km S Coastal) **Camping La Pommeraie, St Philibert, 29910 Trégunc [02 98 50 02 73; fax 02 98 50 07 91; pommeraie@ club-internet.fr; www.campingdelapommeraie. com]** Fr D783 bet Concarneau & Pont-Aven, turn S in Trégunc onto D1 twd Pointe de Trévignon. In 5.5km look for site sp. Turn L to Philibert & Névez. Ent immed on L. Lge, hdg/mkd pitch, pt shd; wc (some cont); chem disp; shwrs inc; mv service pnt; some serviced pitches; el pnts (6-10A) €3.20-4.20; gas; lndtte; ice; shop & 250m; rest; snacks; bar; playgrnd; htd pool; paddling pool; sand beach 1km; boating; fishing; games rm; cycle hire; entmnt; TV; 60% statics; dogs €1.60; Eng spkn; adv bkg; quiet; cc acc; red low ssn; CCl. "Sale of farm produce; pleasant site in apple orchard; warm welcome." ♦ 1 May-4 Sep. € 19.00
2005*

TREGUNC 2F2 (3.5km SW Coastal) **Camping La Plage Loc'h Ven, Plage de Pendruc, 29910 Trégunc [02 98 50 26 20; fax 02 98 50 27 63]** Fr N165 exit at Kérampaou sp Trégunc. At rndbt W of Trégunc foll Loc'h Ven sp thro Lambell, site on coast. Med, hdg/mkd pitch, pt sl, pt shd; htd wc; chem disp; shwrs inc; el pnts (4-6A) €2.60-3.20; gas; lndtte; shop 4km; tradsmn; rest, snacks, bar 4km; playgrnd; sand/shgl beach adj; games area; TV; 40% statics; dogs; poss cr; Eng spkn; adv bkg; quiet. "Easy walk to beach, rock pools & coastal footpath; v helpful owners." 1 Apr-30 Sep. € 12.00
2004*

TREIGNAC 7B4 (4.5km N Rural) **Camping La Plage, Les Barriousses, 19260 Treignac [05 55 98 08 54; fax 05 55 98 16 47; info@ laplagecamping.com; www.laplagecamping. com]** On D940 opp Lac des Barriousses. Med, mkd pitch, pt sl, terr, shd; htd wc; chem disp; mv service pnt; shwrs inc; el pnts (6A) €2.80; lndtte; sm shop & 4.5km; rest 500m; snacks; lake sw, boating, fishing adj; 5% statics; dogs €1.20; poss cr; adv bkg; quiet; CCl. "Beautiful area & outlook; friendly; facs unclean low ssn (Sep 2007)." ♦ 1 May-16 Sep. € 12.70
2007*

TREIGNAC 7B4 (10km SE Rural) **Camping Le Fayard, Cors, 19260 Veix [05 55 94 00 20 or 0031 113301245 (N'lands); veen514@zonnet. nl; www.le-fayard.com]** Fr Treignac take D16 dir Lestards. 1km after Lestards take D32 dir Cors, site sp. Sm, mkd pitch, pt sl, pt shd; wc; chem disp; baby facs; fam bthrm; shwrs inc; el pts (6A) €2.95; lndtte; shop 7km; tradsmn; rest 10km; bar; playgrnd; htd pool; games area; dogs €1.60; adv bkg (dep req); quiet; CCl. "Friendly Dutch owners; relaxing site in National Park of Limousin." ♦ 12 May-1 Oct. € 15.00
2006*

TREIN D'USTOU, LE see Oust 8G3

TRELEVERN see Perros Guirec 1D2

TREMBLADE, LA 7B1 (2km N Rural) **Camping La Clairière, Rue des Roseaux, Ronce-les-Bains, 17390 La Tremblade [05 46 36 36 63; fax 05 46 36 06 74; info@camping-la-clairiere.com; www.camping-la-clairiere.com]** Fr N on A10 exit Saintes, foll sp La Tremblade; site sp. Med, pt shd; wc; baby facs; shwrs; el pnts (6A) €4.80; lndtte; shop; rest; snacks; bar; BBQ (gas); playgrnd; 2 htd pools; paddling pool; waterslide; beach 2.5km; fishing; watersports; tennis; cycle hire; games area; entmnt; TV; statics; dogs €3; poss cr; adv bkg; quiet. 1 May-15 Sep. € 25.00
2007*

TREMBLADE, LA *7B1* (3km W Rural) **Camping La Pacha, Rue Buffard, 17390 La Tremblade** [05 46 36 14 44 or 06 16 38 45 46] App fr Saujon on D14 turn L soon after passing rd sp with name of town. If overshot turn L at 1st traff lts. Foll sps. Site on R after 3km. Med, shd; wc; shwrs inc; el pnts (6A); ice; tradsmn; snacks; bar; playgrnd; pool; beach 5km; entmnt; TV; some statics; dogs; quiet. "Peaceful amongst pine trees." Easter-15 Oct. € 15.00   2005*

TREMOLAT see Bugue, Le *7C3*

TREPORT, LE *3B2* (N Urban) **Camp Municipal Les Boucaniers, Rue des Canadiens, 76470 Le Tréport** [02 35 86 35 47; fax 02 35 86 55 82] Fr Eu take minor rd sp to Le Tréport under low bdge. On ent o'skts of Le Tréport, turn R at traff lts, camp ent 100m on R. Site nr stadium. Lge, pt shd; htd wc; shwrs inc; el pnts (6A) £3.90; lndtte; shop; rest; snacks; bar; playgrnd; sand beach 2km; games rm; entmnt; TV; 10% statics; dogs; quiet; red facs low ssn. "Gd san facs; gd seafood rests 15 mins walk; pebble beach but lots of interest in port; gd." ♦ Easter-30 Sep. € 11.10   2006*

TREPORT, LE *3B2* (1km S Coastal) **Camp International du Golf, 102 Route de Dieppe, 76470 Le Tréport** [02 27 28 01 50; fax 02 27 28 01 51] Fr Dieppe, take D925 NE twd Le Tréport for 20km bef taking D940 sp Floques/Le Tréport. Site on L at top of hill on o'skts of Le Tréport. Foll sp. Lge, mkd pitch, shd; wc; chem disp; mv service pnt; 30% serviced pitches; shwrs inc; el pnts (5A) €4.60; ice; shop 1km; rest, snacks, bar 500m; playgrnd; shgl beach 600m; fishing; sailing; windsurfing; 10% statics; dogs €3; adv bkg; quiet; red low ssn; cc acc; CCI. "Pleasant site; conv town; Le Tréport down fairly steep hill fr site, lovely but poss cr." 1 Apr-20 Sep. € 15.00   2006*

TREPT *9B2* (2.5km E Rural) **Domaine Les Trois Lacs du Soleil, 38460 Trept** [04 74 92 92 06; fax 04 74 92 93 35; info@les3lacsdusoleil.com; www. les3lacsdusoleil.com] Exit A432 at junc 3 or 3 & head twd Crémieu then Morestel. Trept bet these 2 towns on D517, site sp by lakes. Lge, pt shd; wc; baby facs; shwrs inc; el pnts (6A) inc; lndtte; shop; rest; snacks; bar; BBQ (gas); playgrnd; pool complex; waterslides; lake sw & beach adj; fishing; tennis; archery; horseriding 2km; mini-golf; entmnt; internet; TV rm; 5% statics; dogs €1.50; adv bkg; Eng spkn; quiet; cc acc; red low ssn. "Modest rest; OK NH." ♦ 1 May-16 Sep. € 31.00 (CChq acc)
                                          2006*

☐**TRETS** *10F3* (4km SW Rural) **Camping Le Devançon, Chemin de Pourachon, 13790 Peynier** [04 42 53 10 06; fax 04 42 53 04 79; infos@ledevancon.com; www.ledevancon.com] Leave A8 at Canet or Pas-de-Trets or leave D6 at Trets & take D908 to Peynier. In vill cont on D908 sp Marseille. Site on R at end vill after g'ge. Med, mkd pitch, all hdstg, pt sl, shd; htd wc; chem disp; mv service pnt; shwrs inc; el pnts (3-10A) €3-5; gas; ice; lndtte; shop; tradsmn; snacks; rest & bar (high ssn) BBQ; playgrnd; pool; paddling pool; sand beach 30km; tennis; entmnt; TV rm; 50% statics; dogs €2; some Eng spkn; adv bkg; quiet; cc acc; red long stay/CCI. "Excel facs & site; v helpful owner; poss diff manoeuvring onto pitches for lge o'fits; few water points; ltd facs low ssn; gd touring area." ♦ € 19.00   2006*

TREVIERES *1D4* (Rural) **Camp Municipal Sous Les Pommiers, Rue du Pont de la Barre, 14710 Trévières** [02 31 22 57 52 or 02 31 92 89 24; fax 02 31 22 19 49; mairie@ville-trevieres.fr] Turn S off N13 onto D30 sp Trévières. Site on R on ent to vill. Med, hdg pitch, pt shd; wc (cont); chem disp; mv service pnt; shwrs inc; el pnts (10A) €2.60; lndtte; shop 500m; rest; playgrnd; sand beach 10km; rv fishing adj; poss cr; adv bkg rec high ssn; quiet; CCI. "Excel site in apple orchard; lge pitches; ideal for D-Day beaches." ♦ Easter-30 Sep. € 8.60
                                          2006*

TREVIERES *1D4* (3km NE Rural) **Camping La Roseraie, Rue de l'Eglise, 14710 Surrain** [tel/ fax 02 31 21 17 71; camping.laroseraie@neuf. fr] Take N13 fr Bayeux twds Cherbourg. In approx 12km take D208 sp Surrain. Site sp in vill. Med, mkd pitch, pt sl, pt shd; wc; el pnts (6A) €4.10; lndtte; ice; shop; snacks; playgrnd; htd pool; tennis; entmnt; 20% statics; dogs €1.90; Eng spkn; adv bkg; quiet. "Friendly recep; conv Bayeux & D-Day Museums." ♦ Easter-30 Sep. € 15.50   2006*

TREVOUX see Villefranche sur Saône *9B2*

TRIE SUR BAISE *8F2* (2.5km NE Rural) **Camping Fontrailles, Le Quartier Lanorbe, 65220 Fontrailles** [05 62 35 62 52; detm.paddon@free.fr; www.fontraillescamping.com] Fr N on N21 leave Mirande & turn L (S) at end of town sp Trie-sur-Baïse onto D939. After St Michel look out for silos on R after 7km, site sp. Fr S at Miélan turn onto D3/17 sp Trie-sur-Baïse to Fontrailles. Sm, pt sl, pt shd; wc; chem disp (wc); shwrs inc; el pnts (9A) €2; ice; shop, rest, snacks & bar 3km; BBQ; playgrnd; pool; tennis; fishing; dogs; Eng spkn; adv bkg; quiet; red long stay; CCI. "Delightful CL-type site; well-kept in orchard; excel pool & tennis in nrby communal oak wood; gd base for area; gd walking; helpful British owners; conv Lourdes, Pyrenees & Spain; mkt Trie-sur-Baïse Tues." 1 Jul-30 Sep. € 14.00   2005*

TRINITE SUR MER, LA see Carnac *2G3*

TRIZAC see Riom ès Montagnes *7C4*

France

TROCHE see Uzerche *7B3*

TROGUES see Ste Maure de Touraine *4H2*

TROYES *4E4* (2km NE Urban) **Camping de Troyes, 7 Rue Roger Salengro, 10150 Pont Ste Marie [03 25 81 02 64; fax 03 25 42 34 09; info@ troyescamping.net; www.troyescamping.net]** Fr Troyes on D960 twd Nancy, on o'skts of town on L opp Stadium & bet Esso g'ge & car wash. Fr N site on R on N77 just pass junc with D960. Foll sp fr all dirs to Pont Ste Marie & site. To avoid busy town cent when towing, app fr N on by-pass using D960, site on R. Fr S on D26 exit junc 23 onto D619 (N19), then D960 ring rd twd Troyes Cent. Site on R. Well sp fr all dirs & in town. NB Queues form onto rd outside site, use Esso g'ge or supmkt to turn if queue too long. Med, some hdg/mkd pitch, some hdstg, pt shd; wc; chem disp; mv service pnt; shwrs inc; el pnts (6A) €2.70 (long lead poss req); gas; lndtte; ice; shop; tradsmn; supmkt adj; vg rest nrby; snacks; playgrnd; pool 2km; TV; dogs €1; bus opp; poss cr; Eng spkn; adv bkg; cc acc; red 3+ nights low ssn; CCI. "Excel, well-run site in great position; lge pitches; twin-axles acc at recep's discretion; peaceful parkland but v busy, popular site - rec arr early; v friendly, hardworking staff; tourist info office on site (high ssn); gd bus service to town or 20 min easy walk; excel, clean san facs, poss inadequate when site full; red facs low ssn; Troyes Cathedral, museums & old quarter worth visit; lge discount clothing outlet nrby; gd fruit & fish mkts; conv NH." ♦ 1 Apr-15 Oct. € 14.70   2007*

TROYES *4E4* (16km E Rural) **Camping La Fromentelle, 10220 Dosches [tel/fax 03 25 41 52 67]** Exit A26 junc 23 onto D619 (N19) dir Bar-sur-Aube. In 8.5km turn L onto D1 sp Géraudot (take care bends). Site on L in 5km. Sm, mkd pitch, pt sl, unshd; wc; chem disp (wc); mv service pnt; shwrs inc; el pnts (6A) €2.80 (long lead poss req)(poss rev pol); BBQ; playgrnd; sand beach 6km; lake sw 5km; dogs €0.60; adv bkg; quiet, poss noise fr workers in statics leaving for work 6am; CCI. "Clean, pleasant, but remote CL-type site; warm welcome; gd san facs; gd for birdwatching, sailing, watersports on lakes; excel cycle tracks; conv Troyes." ♦ 30 Apr-30 Sep. € 9.50   2007*

TROYES *4E4* (10km SE Rural) **FFCC Camping Plan d'Eau des Terres Rouges, 10390 Clérey [03 25 46 04 45; fax 03 25 46 05 86; terres-rouges@wanadoo.fr; www.terres-rouges. fr.st]** Exit A5 junc 21 onto D671 (N71) S dir Dijon, foll sp Clérey onto D1 in 2km. Or SE fr Troyes on D671 (N71) dir Bar-sur-Seine, foll sp Clérey. Site well sp. NB App to site via unmade rd. Sm, hdstg, pt shd; wc (1 cont); chem disp; shwrs €1; el pnts (5-10A) €2.60 (poss rev pol); shops 4km; tradsmn; rest; snacks; bar; playgrnd; pool; tennis; fishing, waterskiing, boating; 75% statics; dogs; phone; adv bkg; quiet; no cc acc; CCI. "Gd, basic NH; san facs clean; friendly, helpful owners; gate opens 0600; conv fr a'route to Calais." Easter-30 Sep. € 11.00
                                                              2007*

TUFFE *4F1* (1km N Urban) **FFCC Camping du Lac, Plan d'Eau, Route de Prévelles, 72160 Tuffé [02 43 93 88 34; fax 02 43 93 43 54; camping. tuffe@wanadoo.fr; www.camping.tuffe.fr]** Site on D33, sp. Med, hdg/mkd pitch, pt shd; htd wc; chem disp; mv service pnt; baby facs; fam bthrm; shwrs inc; el pnts (6A) €2.50; lndtte; snacks; bar; BBQ; playgrnd; fishing; TV; sw adj; 10% statics; dogs €2; Eng spkn; adv bkg; CCI. "Well-kept, pretty site by lake & adj tourist train; friendly staff." 1 Apr-30 Sep. € 9.30   2007*

TULLE *7C4* (2km NE) **Camp Municipal Bourbacoup, Ave du Lieutenant-Colonel-Faro, 19000 Tulle [05 55 26 75 97 or 06 87 84 90 60 (mob)]** Fr Tulle, take N120 NW dir Limoges. Foll site sp. Med, mkd pitch, pt shd; wc (some cont); shwrs inc; el pnts inc; supmkt 3km; rest, bar 1km; pool 1km; rv adj; dogs; quiet. "Pretty site on bank of rv; easy cycle ride to town; poss itinerants; dated but v clean san facs." ♦ 1 Jul-31 Aug. € 10.50   2005*

TULLE *7C4* (4km SE Rural) **Camping Le Pré du Moulin, 19150 Laguenne [tel/fax 05 55 26 21 96; lepredumoulin@yahoo.fr; http://pagesperso-orange.fr/lepredumoulin]** Exit Tulle on N120 twd Aurillac, pass ATAC commercial cent on R, cross bdge & 1st L to camp site. Last 1km on unmade rd, but not diff. Sm, pt sl, pt shd; wc; chem disp; shwrs inc; el pnts (6A) inc; gas; lndtte; shops 2km; tradsmn; snacks; pool; rv fishing adj; cycle hire; no dogs high ssn, low ssn; €2.30; adv bkg rec high ssn; dep req; quiet; CCI. "Attractive, peaceful, British-owned site; steep climb to adequate san facs - diff for disabled." 15 Apr-30 Sep. € 15.50   2007*

TURBALLE, LA see Guérande *2G3*

TURCKHEIM see Colmar *6F3*

TURSAC see Eyzies de Tayac, Les *7C3*

UCHIZY see Tournus *9A2*

UGINE *9B3* (7km NW Rural) **Camping Champ Tillet, 74210 Marlens [04 50 44 40 07; fax 04 50 32 51 92; cchamptillet@caramail.com; www.champtillet.com]** N508 S fr Annecy after leaving Lake. Take new by-pass past Faverges to Ugine. Look for baker's shop. Sp. Med, pt shd; wc (some cont); chem disp (wc); shwrs inc; el pnts (3-10A) €3.40 (poss rev pol); lndtte; ice; shops adj; supmkts 3km; rest; snacks; bar; playgrnd; pool; rv 500m; some rd noise - adj extensive cycle track; red low ssn; cc acc. "Gd walks, lovely views; barrier clsd 2300-0700." ♦ 1 Apr-30 Oct. € 19.00   2007*

URBES see St Maurice sur Moselle *6F3*

URCAY *4H3* (500m W Rural) **Camp Municipal La Plage du Cher, Rue de la Gare, 03360 Urçay [04 70 06 96 91 or 04 70 06 93 30 (Mairie); fax 04 70 06 96 78; mairie-urcay@pays-allier.com]** S fr Bourges on D2144 or N fr Montluçon to Urçay. Site by rv to W of Urçay, sp fr both N & S. Sm, mkd pitch, pt shd; wc (some cont); shwrs inc; el pnts (5A) €3; shops 500m; rest, snacks & bar in vill; playgrnd; rv sw adj; fishing; phone; train 200m; adv bkg; quiet; cc not acc; CCI. "Clean, basic site by rvside; ltd facs; pleasant situation; site yourself, warden calls; gd cycling; forest with lake sw nrby." 15 May-15 Sep. € 8.00   2007*

URDOS *8G2* (500m N Rural) **Camp Municipal Le Gave d'Aspe, 64490 Urdos [05 59 34 88 26; fax 05 59 34 88 86; legavedaspe@aol.com]** Turn W off N134 onto site access rd by disused Urdos stn approx 1km bef vill, clear sp. Other access rds in vill v diff lge o'fits. Sm, mkd pitch, pt sl, pt shd; wc; chem disp; shwrs inc; el pnts (30A) €2.30; shop, rest, bar 500m; tradsmn; BBQ; playgrnd; paddling pool; rv sw; phone; poss cr; Eng spkn; adv bkg; quiet; cc acc; CCI. "Adj Rv Aspe; 14km fr Col du Somport/Tunnel; surrounded by mountains; conv x-ing into Spain; ltd facs; vg." 1 May-15 Sep. € 9.00   2004*

URRUGNE see St Jean de Luz *8F1*

⊞URT *8F1* (E Rural) **Camping Ferme Mimizan, 64240 Urt [05 59 56 21 51]** E fr Bayonne on A64/E80, exit junc 4 sp Urt; in vill turn sharp R at PO & foll sps; site on R in 1km. Fr N on D12 cross Rv Adour by metal bdge & turn L immed past church, site on R in 1.5km. Med, pt shd; wc; shwrs inc; el pnts (10A) €2.50; playgrnd; pool; 98% statics; adv bkg; poss noise fr static residents; red low ssn; CCI. "Facs old & basic; v peaceful out of ssn; friendly owners; gd walking & cycling; conv coast & Pyrenees; NH only." € 15.00   2005*

URT *8F1* (500m S Rural) **Camping Etche Zahar, Allée des Mesplès, 64240 Urt [05 59 56 27 36; fax 05 59 56 29 62; camping.etche-zahar@wanadoo.fr; www.etche-zahar.fr]** Exit A64 at junc 4 dir Urt. Fr N on N10 exit junc 8 at St Geours-de-Maremne onto D12 S to Urt, site sp. Fr town cent head W, L at rndabt, L again to site. Sm, hdg pitch, pt sl, pt shd; wc; chem disp; shwrs inc; el pnts (10A) €3.20; lndtte; shop 500m; tradsmn; snacks; bar; BBQ; rest 500m; playgrnd; pool & children's paddling pool; fishing; games area; cycle hire; bird sanctuary nrby; entmnt; internet; 25% statics; dogs €2.10; phone; site clsd 1 Jan-7 Feb; Eng spkn; adv bkg; quiet; CCI. "Peaceful site; welcoming, pleasant owners; gd walking & cycling; conv Belloc Abbey & Bayonne." ♦ 24 Mar-5 Nov. € 17.00   2006*

USTOU see Oust *8G3*

UZER *9D2* (3km SE Rural) **Camping La Turelure, Fontanne, 07110 Uzer [04 75 36 87 47; fax 06 87 14 75 46; laturelure@free.fr]** S fr Aubenas on D104, 1km S of Uzer. Site well sp; app rd narr. Sm, hdg/mkd pitch, pt shd; wc (some cont); chem disp; mv service pnt; shwrs; el pnts (3-6A) €2.30-3.50; gas; lndtte; shop 1km; tradsmn high ssn; rest 1km; snacks 5km; BBQ; playgrnd; rv sw; fishing; canoeing; games area; 10% statics; dogs; phone; poss cr; some Eng spkn; adv bkg; quiet; red low ssn; cc not acc; CCI. "V pleasant farm site bet vineyard & rv; situated in cherry orchard; v friendly owner; regional wines & produce avail; excel base for touring S Ardèche; peaceful with beautiful views." ♦ ltd. 1 Apr-31 Oct. € 10.00   2004*

UZERCHE *7B3* (8km NE Rural) **Camping Aimée Porcher (Naturist), 19140 Eyburie [05 55 73 20 97 or 0031 264 436285 (N'lands) (LS); fax 0031 264 436285; info@aimee-porcher.com; www.aimee-porcher.com]** Fr Uzerche take D3 NE to Eyburie & in Eyburie turn R at site sp (Cheyron/Pingrieux). In 1km turn L at site sp; site at end of narr lane. Sm, mkd pitch, terr, pt shd; wc; chem disp; shwrs inc; baby facs; el pnts (6A) €3.50 (poss long lead req); lndtte; ice; tradsmn; snacks; bar; BBQ; playgrnd; lake & rv sw adj; no statics; dogs €2; Eng spkn; adv bkg; quiet; red long stay; CCI. "Beautiful views; friendly & helpful Dutch owners; v lge site with pitches well spread out; basic, clean facs - stretched if site full." ♦ 1 Jun-1 Sep. € 31.50   2006*

UZERCHE *7B3* (200m SE Rural) **Camp Municipal La Minoterie, Route de la Minoterie, 19140 Uzerche [05 55 73 12 75 or 05 55 73 17 00 (Mairie); fax 05 55 98 44 55; www.uzerche.fr]** Fr N exit A20 at junc 44 for Uzerche. After x-ing town bdge turn L & proceed thro tunnel. Site clearly sp on ent to town on rvside. Steep app rd & sharp bend. NB Narr app rd used by lorries fr nrby quarry. Site well sp. Med, mkd pitch, pt sl, shd; wc; chem disp; shwrs inc; el pnts (10A) €2.40; lndtte; shops 200m; tradsmn; playgrnd; fishing; kayak hire; rock-climbing; TV; quiet; CCI. "Rvside site; excel value; poss risk of flooding; not suitable lge o'fits or lge m'vans; sh walk to beautiful old vill; gd local walks; conv NH." 1 May-30 Sep. € 10.00   2007*

UZERCHE *7B3* (9km SW Rural) **Camp Municipal du Lac du Pont-Charal, 19410 Vigeois [05 55 98 90 86 or 05 55 98 91 93 (Mairie); fax 05 55 98 99 79]** Fr A20 exit 45 onto D3 & D7. Med, pt sl, shd; wc; chem disp; shwrs inc; el pnts (15A) €2.60; gas; lndtte; ice; shop; rest; snacks; bar; playgrnd; lake sw & beach; fishing; watersports; sports area; tennis 2km; entmnt; TV; dogs €0.90; adv bkg; quiet. "Delightful, well-kept site; excel san facs." ♦ 1 Jun-15 Sep. € 8.30   2006*

France

UZERCHE *7B3* (9km SW Rural) **Camping à la Ferme Domaine Vert, Les Magnes, 19230 Troche [tel/fax 05 55 73 59 89; www.ledomainevert. nl]** Exit A20 junc 45 onto D3 to Vigeois, 2km after Vigeois turn R onto D50 sp Lubersac. After 5km (ignore sp to Troche) foll site sp to R. Sm, pt shd; wc; shwrs; lndry rm; el pnts €2.50 (poss rev pol); meals avail; fishing 4km; canoeing nr, lake sw; dogs €1.50; Eng spkn; quiet. "Peaceful, farm site; surrounded by woodland; welcoming, friendly Dutch owners; spotlessly clean; adv bkg ess high ssn." 1 Apr-1 Oct. € 16.00   2006*

UZERCHE *7B3* (12km SW Rural) **Aire Naturelle du Bois Coutal (Veysseix), Perpezac-le-Noir, 19410 Vigeois [05 55 73 71 93; fax 05 55 73 27 66; boiscoutal@wanadoo.fr]** Exit A20/E09 S fr Uzerche at junc 46 onto D920 N & foll sp Perpezac le-Noir. Go thro Perpezac on D156 N dir Vigeois & foll site sp. Site in 4km. Sm, sl, pt shd; wc; chem disp; shwrs inc; el pnts inc (6A) €2.50; lndtte; shop, rest, snacks, bar 3km; playgrnd; pool; games rm; entmnt; few statics; dogs; poss cr; Eng spkn; adv bkg; quiet. "Friendly, helpful owner; v clean facs." 15 Jun-15 Oct. € 8.60   2007*

Before we move on, I'm going to fill in some site report forms and post them off to the editor, otherwise they won't arrive in time for the deadline at the end of September.

UZES *10E2* (800m N Urban) **Camping La Paillotte, Mas Franval, Quartier de Grézac, 30700 Uzès [04 66 22 38 55; fax 04 66 22 66 66]** Exit A9 junc 23 sp Remoulins. Fr Remoulins take D981 to Uzès. Aim for town cent 1-way ring rd. Site sp clearly. Narr rds for 800m passing cemetery. Med, mkd pitch, terr, shd; wc; shwrs inc; el pnts (10A) inc; gas; lndtte; shop; tradsmn; rest high ssn; snacks; bar; playgrnd; pool; paddling pool; cycle hire; games area; games rm; entmnt; some statics; adv bkg; quiet; CCI. "Poolside rest; facs clean but water temperature poss variable." 20 Mar-20 Oct. € 35.00   2007*

UZES *10E2* (3km E Rural) **Camping Le Moulin Neuf, 30700 St Quentin-la-Poterie [04 66 22 17 21; fax 04 66 22 91 82; le.moulin.neuf@wanadoo.fr; www.le-moulin-neuf.com]** Take D982 out of Uzès, after 3km turn N, site in 400m. Med, mkd pitch, pt shd; wc; chem disp; shwrs inc; el pnts (5A) inc; lndtte; shop & 2km; snacks; bar; playgrnd; tennis; htd pool; cycle hire; mini-golf; fishing; horseriding; poss cr; v quiet. "Site off beaten track; conv Gorges d'Ardèche, Avignon, Arles & Nîmes; barrier clsd 2230-0700; mosquito problem." ♦ 10 Apr-15 Oct. € 18.20   2004*

UZES *10E2* (3km SW Rural) **Camping Le Mas de Rey, Route d'Anduze, 30700 Arpaillargues [tel/ fax 04 66 22 18 27; info@campingmasderey.com; www.campingmasderey.com]** Sp fr Uzès. Exit by D982 sp Anduze. After 2.5km cross narr bdge, turn L in 100m on site app rd. Med, hdg/mkd pitch, hdstg, pt sl, pt shd; wc; chem disp; fam bthrm; shwrs inc; el pnts (10A) €3 (rev pol); lndtte; ice; shop & 3km; tradsmn; rest, snacks; bar; BBQ; playgrnd; pool; rv sw 6km; TV rm; dogs €1.60; phone; poss cr; Eng spkn; adv bkg (dep req); quiet; red low ssn/ snr citizens; CCI. "Helpful Dutch owners & staff; gd for sm children; some v lge pitches; excel cycling; pleasant town; Uzès interesting." ♦ 1 Apr-15 Oct. € 17.50   2007*

VACQUEYRAS see Carpentras *10E2*

VAISON LA ROMAINE *9D2* (500m Urban) **Camping du Théâtre Romain, Quartier des Arts, Chemin du Brusquet, 84110 Vaison-la-Romaine [04 90 28 78 66; fax 04 90 28 78 76; info@ camping-theatre.com; www.camping-theatre. com]** Fr town cent foll sp for Théâtre Romain & site. Ent to Chemin du Busquet on rndabt at Théâtre Romain. Or site sp off Orange-Nyons rd thro town (do not ent town cent). Med, hdg/mkd pitch, pt shd; wc; chem disp (wc); mv service pnt; serviced pitches; baby facs; shwrs inc; el pnts (5-10A) €2.80-4; gas 500m; lndtte; ice; shop 500m; tradsmn; bar; BBQ; playgrnd; pool; wifi internet; dogs €2; Eng spkn; adv bkg ess high ssn (bkg fee); quiet; cc acc; CCI. "Helpful owner may accept visitors out of ssn - phone ahead; v busy site even low ssn; rec arr early or adv book; poss overcrowded; scrupulously clean & tidy; poss unisex san facs; v attractive Provençal town; Roman remains; summer concerts in amphitheatre; wine tasting; short walk to town; mkt Tues; highly rec." ♦ 15 Mar-15 Nov. € 19.60   2007*

VAISON LA ROMAINE *9D2* (4km NE Rural) **Camping L'Ayguette, 84110 Faucon [04 90 46 40 35 or 06 18 47 33 42 (mob); fax 04 90 46 46 17; info@ayguette.com; www. ayguette.com]** Exit Vaison NE on D938, R on D71, thro St Romain-en-Viennois. Then R onto D86 sp Faucon. Site on R, well sp. Med, mkd pitch, terr, shd; htd wc; chem disp; baby facs; shwrs inc; el pnts (10A) €2.50 (poss long lead req); lndtte; ice; shop, supmkt 4km; tradsmn; snacks; bar; BBQ; playgrnd; htd pool; dogs €1.70; adv bkg; quiet; cc acc; CCI. "Fantastic well-run site in scenic area; relaxed atmosphere; v helpful owners; excel mod facs inc hairdryers & children's shwrs; tractor tow available; excel." 1 Apr-30 Sep. € 20.50   2007*

VAISON LA ROMAINE *9D2* (4km NE Rural) Camping Le Soleil de Provence, Route de Nyons, Quartier Trameiller, 84110 St Romain-en-Viennois [04 90 46 46 00; fax 04 90 46 40 37; info@camping-soleil-de-provence.fr; www.camping-soleil-de-provence.fr] Leave A7 at junc 19 Bollène onto D94 dir Nyons. After Tullette turn R onto D20 & then D975 to Vaison-la-Romaine; fr Vaison take D938 sp Nyons; in 4km R & in 150m L to site; well sp. Lge, terr, hdg/mkd pitch, pt shd; wc; chem disp; some serviced pitches; shwrs inc; el pnts (10A) €3.50; gas; lndtte; ice; shop; tradsmn; rest high ssn; snacks; bar; playgrnd; pool; paddling pool; entmnt; dogs: poss cr; adv bkg; quiet; CCI. "Stunning views; friendly, family-run site; lovely pools; lovely town & countryside; mkt Tues; popular site; excel." ♦ 15 Mar-31 Oct. € 17.00   2007*

VAISON LA ROMAINE *9D2* (800m SE Rural) **FFCC** Camping Club International Carpe Diem, Route de St Marcellin, 84110 Vaison-la-Romaine [04 90 36 02 02; fax 04 90 36 36 90; contact@camping-carpe-diem.com; www.camping-carpe-diem.com] S on A7 exit Orange; foll sp to Vaison; at Vaison on Nyons rd (D938) turn S at rndabt by supmkt dir Carpentras. In 1km turn L at junc to St Marcellin, site immed on L. Lge, hdg/mkd pitch, terr, pt shd; wc (some cont); chem disp; mv service pnt; shwrs inc; el pnts (6-10A) €3.70-4.70; gas; lndtte; shop & 800m; tradsmn; pizzeria, snacks, bar high ssn; playgrnd; 2 pools; paddling pool; waterslide; rv sw 5km; mini-golf; entmnt; internet; TV rm; 10% statics; dogs €4.30; poss cr; Eng spkn; adv bkg (dep req + bkg fee); red low ssn; cc acc; CCI. "Lively site; helpful staff; new owners 2007; poss dust from nrby quarry; bare, poss muddy pitches; basic san facs need refurb & stretched high ssn; conv Roman ruins; summer concerts; gd cent for Provence region." ♦ 24 Mar-1 Nov. € 29.00 (CChq acc)   2007*

VAISON LA ROMAINE *9D2* (6km SE) **Camping Les Trois Rivières, Quarter des Jonches, 84340 Entrechaux [04 90 46 01 72; fax 04 90 46 00 75; www.camping-les3rivieres.com]** Take D938 fr Vaison twd Malaucène for 3.5km. Turn E onto D54 to Entrechaux; site well sp rndabts at both ends of vill. Narr app rd. Med, pt sl, shd; wc; shwrs inc; el pnts (3-10A) €2.50-4; gas; lndtte; ice; shop 2km; rest; snacks; bar; playgrnd; rv shgl beach, sw & fishing; horseriding; some statics; internet; entmnt; TV; dogs €1.50; poss cr; quiet; adv bkg; 20% red Jun & Sep. "Gd clean rv bathing; rds rough & twisty, access v diff for lge o'fits; quiet & shd." 1 Apr-30 Sep. € 12.00   2005*

VAISON LA ROMAINE *9D2* (5km NW Rural) Camping Domaine de La Cambuse, Route de Villedieu, 84110 Vaison-la-Romaine [tel/fax 04 90 36 14 53; brun.pierre@club-internet.fr] Fr Vaison-la-Romaine N on D51 sp Villedieu. After 4km fork R onto D94 sp Villedieu. Site on R after 300m. Sm, terr, pt shd; wc (some cont); chem disp; shwrs inc; el pnts (15A) €2.35; gas 4km; ice; tradsmn; snacks, bar in ssn; pool; 5% statics; phone; poss cr; quiet; CCI. "Site on side of hill within working vineyard; v friendly & helpful owners." 1 May-30 Sep. € 10.60   2004*

VAL ANDRE, LE *2E3* (3km S Coastal) Camping Les Monts Colleux, 26 Rue Jean Le Brun, 22370 Pléneuf-Val-André [02 96 72 95 10; fax 02 96 63 10 49; cplmontscolleux@atciat.com; www.camping-montscolleux.com or www.campeole.com] Site 800m off D786 & off D78, sp fr Pléneuf town cent. Rec app only fr Pléneuf centre; at traff lts turn towards Les Plages, then site sp. Lge, mkd pitch, terr, pt sl, pt shd; wc; chem disp; shwrs inc; el pnts (6A) €2.90 (poss rev pol); ice; lndtte; shops, rest, bar 300m; BBQ; playgrnd; covrd pool nrby; sand beach 300m; entment; dogs €2.60; phone; adv bkg; red low ssn.. "Cliff top walks & mussel fishing; office 0900-1200 & 1400-1800; v pleasant combination of gd beach, port & vill with mkt; many gd rests." 1 Apr-30 Sep. € 14.00

2007*

VAL D'AJOL, LE see Plombières les Bains *6F2*

VAL DE VESLE see Reims *3D4*

VAL D'ISERE *9B4* (1km E Rural) Camping Les Richardes, Le Laisinant, 73150 Val-d'Isère [tel/fax 04 79 06 26 60; campinglesrichardes@free.fr; http://campinglesrichardes.free.fr] Leave Val d'Isère going E twds Col de l'Iseran on D902, site on R 1.5km bef Le Fornet vill. Med, pt sl, unshd; wc; shwrs €1; el pnts (3-6A) €1.90-3.80; pool 1.5km; dogs €0.50; quiet; CCI. "Situated in beautiful mountains; peaceful." 15 Jun-15 Sep. € 9.50

2006*

VALENCAY *4H2* (1km W Urban) Camp Municipal Les Chênes, Route de Loches, 36600 Valençay [tel/fax 02 54 00 03 92 or 02 54 00 32 32] App town fr E on D960 or N/S on D956, foll sp for D960 Luçay-le-Mâle. Ignore 1st sp for camping (Veuil); D960 is next L in town. Foll sp for pool & camping. Site adj pool mkd by flags. Sm, hdg/mkd pitch, pt shd; wc; chem disp; shwrs inc; el pnts (10A) €4 (poss rev pol); lndtte; ice; shop; tradsmn; BBQ; playgrnd; htd pool adj (high ssn); tennis adj; fishing; TV rm; dogs; adv bkg; quiet; 10% red 8+ days; CCI. "Excel site in parkland; gd, clean facs; lge pitches; poss muddy after heavy rain; gate clsd 1200-1500 & 2200-0700; landscaped grounds around lake; gd car museum in town; Son et Lumière at chateau Jul/Aug; day's drive to Calais or Le Havre for ferries." ♦ ltd. 1 May-30 Sep. € 11.30   2007*

France

VALENCE 9C2 (12km SE Rural) **Camping Sunêlia Le Grand Lierne, 26120 Chabeuil [04 75 59 83 14; fax 04 75 59 87 95; contact@grandlierne.com; www.grandlierne.com]** Fr A7 S take Valence Sud exit dir Grenoble. After 8km take D68 on R twd Chabeuil. Turn L at rndabt on o'skts of vill & foll site sp using by-pass; do not go into vill. On arr, park in lay-by at end of appr rd & walk to recep to book in. Or app off D125 NE of Chabeuil. Med, some mkd pitch, shd; wc; chem disp; baby facs; shwrs inc; el pnts (6-10A) €4.70-5.70; gas; lndtte; shop; rest; snacks; bar; BBQ (gas & el only); playgrnd; pool & whirlpool; paddling pool; archery; golf 3km; games area; entmnt; internet; games/TV rm; many statics; dogs €2.50 (no dogs Jul/Aug): poss cr; Eng spkn; adv bkg rec; poss noisy high ssn; cc acc; CCI. "Site set in oak forest; friendly staff; gd facs & all-round entmnt; one half of site some sm pitches - poss diff twin-axle & lge o'fits; gd for families; barrier clsd 2200-0700; mkt Chabeuil Tue; gd but regimented!" ♦ 5 Apr-27 Sep. € 30.90 (CChq acc) ABS - M04
2007*

⊞**VALENCE** 9C2 (1km S Urban) **Camp Municipal de l'Epervière, Chemin de l'Epervière, 26000 Valence [04 75 42 32 00; fax 04 75 56 20 67; eperviere@vacanciel.com]** Exit A7 at Valence Sud & turn N onto N7, site well sp fr N7. When app fr S on N7 turn L at traff lts 500m after Géant supmkt. Fr N on N7 look for R turn 2km S of Valence. Lge, hdg pitch, hdstg, pt shd; htd wc; mv service pnt; shwrs inc; el pnts (10A,) inc; lndtte; supmkt 500m; rest adj; rest; snacks; bar; playgrnd; htd pool; fishing in Rv Rhône; watersports cent adj; games area; TV; 30% statics; site clsd mid-Dec to mid-Jan; poss cr; Eng spkn; no adv bkg; rd noise; cc acc; red low ssn; CCI. "Generous pitches; clean, dated san facs; office opp side of rd behind other buildings & up steps; poss itinerants & unkempt low ssn." ♦ ltd. € 25.00
2007*

VALENCE 9C2 (9km NW Rural) **Camp Municipal Les Vernes, 26600 La Roche-de-Glun [04 75 84 54 11 or 04 75 84 60 52 (Mairie); mairie. rdg@wanadoo.fr]** Turn W off N7 at Pont-d'Isère. On ent La Roche-de-Glun foll camping sp. Sm, hdg/ mkd pitch, pt shd; wc (some cont); serviced pitches; chem disp; shwrs inc; el pnts (10A) inc; lndtte; ice; shop 500m; BBQ; htd pool adj in ssn; sports cent adj; 50% statics; phone; poss cr; adv bkg; quiet; no cc acc; CCI. "V pleasant site; gd & v clean san facs; friendly resident warden; barrier clsd 2200-0700." ♦ 1 May-30 Sep. € 12.90
2006*

VALENCE D'AGEN 8E3 (1km S) **Camp Municipal, Route des Charretiers, 82400 Valence-d'Agen [05 63 39 61 67; tourisme.valencedagen@ wanadoo.fr]** Exit town on D953 sp Auch, turn R after x-ing rv 1st L. Site sp behind sw baths on R. Sm, pt shd; wc (cont); shwrs inc; el pnts; shops 1km; rest, snacks adj; playgrnd; games area; poss cr; quiet. 1 Jul-31 Aug.
2004*

VALLABREGUES see Tarascon 10E2

VALLERAUGUE 10E1 (2km NW Rural) **Camping Le Pied de l'Aigoual, Domaine de Pateau, 30570 Valleraugue [04 67 82 24 40; fax 04 67 82 24 23]** Fr Le Vigan, take D999 E to Pont L'Hérault then take D896 N. Site on R. Well sp. Med, mkd pitch, shd; wc; shwrs inc; chem disp; el pnts (3-6A) €3-5; ice; lndtte; shops in vill; snacks; bar; playgrnd; pool; fishing; tennis 2km; 4% statics; dogs €1.20; phone; bus; Eng spkn; adv bkg; quiet; CCI. "Excel base for Cévennes National Park; 1 hr drive fr Mediterranean; well positioned site in valley; pretty vill." 10 Jun-15 Sep. € 13.50
2006*

VALLET 2G4 (1km N Rural) **Camp Municipal Les Dorices, Route d'Ancenis, 44330 Vallet [02 40 33 95 03; fax 02 40 33 98 58]** Leave Vallet on D763; on R approx 1.2km after last rndabt on by-pass; foll sp. Narr site ent. Med, mkd pitch, pt shd; wc (some cont); shwrs inc; el pnts (6A) inc; lndry rm; shop, rest, snacks, bar 1km; pool 2km; fishing; tennis; gate open 0700-2100; c'vans over 5.50m not acc; some rd noise; CCI. "Clean & comfortable; 20 mins walk to town cent; cent of wine-growing area; gd mkt Sun am." 1 Jul-31 Aug. € 6.00
2005*

VALLIERES see Rumilly 9B3

VALLOIRE 9C3 (500m N Rural) **Camp Caravaneige Municipal Ste Thècle, Route des Villards, 73450 Valloire [04 79 83 30 11; fax 04 79 83 35 13; camping-caravaneige@valloire.net]** Exit A43 junc 29 onto D306 (N6) to St Michel-de-Maurienne, then onto D902 to Valloire. At vill mkt turn R over rv to site. Climb fr valley 15% gradient max. Med, mkd pitch, some hdstg, unshd; htd wc (cont); chem disp; mv service pnt; baby facs; fam bthrm; shwrs €1; el pnts (13A) €2.20; gas 1km; lndtte; shop 300m; rest 500m; bar 200m; playgrnd; skiing, iceskating, pool nr; TV rm; dogs; phone 100m; bus; Eng spkn; adv bkg; quiet; red long stay; cc acc. "Superb mountain scenery for walking & cycling; excel." ♦ ltd. 22 Dec-20 Apr & 1 Jun-30 Sep. € 15.70
2006*

VALLON EN SULLY 7A4 (Rural) **Camp Municipal, Les Soupirs, 03190 Vallon-en-Sully [04 70 06 50 96 or 04 70 06 50 10 (LS); fax 04 70 06 51 18; mairie.vallonensully@wanadoo. fr]** N fr Montluçon on N144; in 23km at traff lts where D11 crosses N144 turn L & foll camping sp for Vallon-en-Sully. After bdge over Rv Cher turn L in 50m. Site in 100m. If N or S on A71 exit at junc 9 Vallon-en-Sully; turn N on N144; in 3km at traff lts turn L. Med, pt shd; wc (cont); chem disp (wc); shwrs; el pnts (6-20A) €2-4; shops 500m; rest, snacks, bar adj; TV rm; dogs; bus 500m; adv bkg; quiet. "On banks of rv & bounded by canal; risk of flooding in wet; lge pitches; gd cycling along canal." 15 Jun-15 Sep. € 6.00
2005*

VALLON PONT D'ARC *9D2* (9km E Rural) **Camping Carrefour de l'Ardèche, Route de Bourg-St Andéol, 07700 St Remèze [04 75 04 15 75; fax 04 75 04 35 05; carrefourardeche@worldonline.fr]** D4 E fr Vallon-Pont-d'Arc. Site on L on bend after St Remèze vill. Med, mkd pitch, pt shd; wc; chem disp; shwrs inc; el pnts (6A) €5; gas; lndtte; ice; snacks; bar; playgrnd; pool; cycle hire; canoeing; fishing 5km; entmnt; TV; dogs €3.50; adv bkg; quiet; cc acc. "On plateau surrounded by vineyards; conv gorges; vg." ♦ 15 Apr-30 Sep. € 22.00   2006*

VALLON PONT D'ARC *9D2* (1.5km SE Rural) **Camping Le Provençal, Route des Gorges, 07150 Vallon-Pont-d'Arc [04 75 88 00 48; fax 04 75 37 18 69; camping.le.provencal@wanadoo. fr; www.camping-le-provencal.fr]** Fr Aubenas take D579 thro Vallon-Pont-d'Arc to S. Turn L on D290 N of rv; site on R in 500m (middle of 3 sites). Fr Alès, N on D904/D104, turn R onto D111 & D579 to Vallon-Pont-d'Arc. Lge, pt shd; htd wc; shwrs inc; el pnts (8A) inc; gas; lndtte; ice; shop; rest; snacks; bar; playgrnd; htd pool; rv sw; canoeing; fishing; sailing; tennis; poss cr; Eng spkn; adv bkg; quiet; cc acc. "Friendly, helpful staff; site at NW end of spectacular Gorges de l'Ardèche." ♦ Easter-20 Sep. € 31.60   2004*

France

There aren't many sites open this early in the year. We'd better phone ahead to check that the one we're heading for is actually open.

VALLON PONT D'ARC *9D2* (1km SE Rural) **Camping L'Ardéchois, Route des Gorges, 07150 Vallon-Pont-d'Arc [04 75 88 06 63; fax 04 75 37 14 97; ardecamp@bigfoot.com; www. ardechois-camping.com]** Fr Vallon take D290 rte des Gorges & site on R bet rd & rv. Lge, mkd pitch, hdstg, pt sl, shd; htd wc; chem disp; mv service pnt; baby facs; fam bthrm; serviced pitch; private bthrm €15 (by reservation); shwrs inc; el pnts (6-10A) inc; gas; lndtte; ice; shop; tradsmn; rest; snacks; bar; BBQ; playgrnd; htd pool & paddling pool; rv sw; tennis; canoeing; games area; cycle hire; internet; entmnt; TV rm; 80% statics; dogs €6.80; Eng spkn; adv bkg; quiet; cc acc; red low ssn; CCI. "Spectacular scenery; excel rvside site; v helpful staff; town 15 mins walk; price depends on size of pitch; gd san facs; excel." ♦ Easter-30 Sep. € 42.00   2007*

See advertisement above

VALLON PONT D'ARC *9D2* (1.5km SE Rural) **Mondial Camping, Route des Gorges, 07150 Vallon-Pont-d'Arc [04 75 88 00 44; fax 04 75 37 13 73; reserv-info@mondial-camping. com; www.mondial-camping.com]** Fr N exit A7 Montélimar Nord junc 17 dir Le Teil, Villeneuve-de-Berg, Vogué, Ruoms then Vallon-Pont-d'Arc. Take D290, Rte des Gorges de l'Ardèche to site in 1.5km. Fr S exit A7 junc 19 at Bollène, dir Bourg-St Andéol, then D4 to St Remèze & Vallon-Pont-d'Arc. Lge, hdg/mkd pitch, shd; htd wc; chem disp; mv service pnt; serviced pitches; baby facs; shwrs inc; el pnts (6-10A) €4.50; gas; lndtte; ice; shop; rest; snacks; bar; playgrnd; 2 htd pools; waterslides & aqua park; rv sw; canoeing; tennis adj; games rm; entmnt; internet; TV; some statics; dogs €4.50; poss cr; Eng spkn; adv bkg; quiet; red low ssn; cc acc; CCI. "Dir access to rv, Ardèche gorges & canoe facs; gd touring base; additional charge for serviced pitches; excel." ♦ 8 Mar-30 Sep. € 32.00   2007*

See advertisement on next page

VALLON PONT D'ARC *9D2* (2km SW Rural) Camping Le Casque Roi, Route de Vallon-Pont-d'Arc, 07150 Salavas [04 75 88 04 23; fax 04 75 37 18 64; casqueroi@aol.com; www. casqueroi.com] Take D579 S fr Vallon-Pont-d'Arc; site on R 500m after bdge over Ardèche. Sm, mkd pitch, shd; htd wc (some cont); baby facs; shwrs inc; el pnts (10A) inc; Indtte; shop; snacks; bar; playgrnd; pool; rv sw 1km; cycle hire; entmnt; 10% statics; dogs €4; poss cr; quiet; CCI. "Gd touring base for Ardèche gorges; canoeing & guided walks." 1 Apr-12 Nov. € 27.00   2007*

VALLON PONT D'ARC *9D2* (800m W Rural) Camping La Roubine, Route de Ruoms, 07150 Vallon-Pont-d'Arc [tel/fax 04 75 88 04 56; roubine.ardeche@wanadoo.fr; www.camping-roubine.com] Site on W side of Vallon-Pont-d'Arc off D579, well sp by rvside. Med, hdg/mkd pitch, pt shd; htd wc; chem disp; mv service pnt; baby facs; shwrs inc; el pnts (10A) €4.50; gas; Indtte; ice; shop; rest; snacks; bar; BBQ (gas/elec) playgrnd; htd pool; sm waterslide; rv sw & sand beach adj; fishing; canoeing; tennis; cycle hire; games area; mini-golf; entmnt; child entmnt; wifi internet; TV rm; some statics; dogs €3.50; Eng spkn; adv bkg; quiet; cc acc. "Excel, well-run site in lovely area." ♦ 21 Apr-13 Sep. € 34.00   2007*

See advertisement opposite

VALLON PONT D'ARC *9D2* (2km W Rural) Camping La Plage Fleurie, Les Mazes, 07150 Vallon-Pont-d'Arc [04 75 88 01 15; fax 04 75 88 11 31; info@laplagefleurie.com; www.laplagefleurie.com] Site on main 'Route Touristique' of Ardèche: D579, 4.5km SE of Ruoms turn R at sp La Plage Fleurie in 1.5km. Fr N sp easily missed; no sp fr S. Lge, mkd pitch, pt sl, terr, shd; wc; baby facs; shwrs inc; chem disp; el pnts (10A) €3.90; gas; Indtte; ice; shop & 1.5km; tradsmn; snacks; rest; bar; BBQ; playgrnd; pool; sand beach & rv sw; canoe hire; fishing; sailing; entmnt; TV rm; 10% statics; dogs €4; Eng spkn; adv bkg rec high ssn; quiet; red low ssn; CCI. "Conv Gorges de l'Ardèche; gd position on rvside; excel san facs." ♦ 28 Apr-28 Aug. € 26.00   2007*

VALLON PONT D'ARC *9D2* (2km W Rural) Camping L'Arc en Ciel, Route de Ruoms, Les Mazes, 07150 Vallon-Pont-d'Arc [04 75 88 04 65; fax 04 75 37 16 99; info@arcenciel-camping.com; www.arcenciel-camping.com] Take D579 W fr Vallon. After 1.1km bear L for Les Mazes. Pass thro vill & in about 1.7km bear L at camp sp. Lge, pt sl, pt shd; wc; baby facs; shwrs inc; el pnts (6A) €3.50; Indtte; ice; shop; rest; snacks; bar; playgrnd; pool; paddling pool; shgl beach & rv sw; fishing; tennis; horseriding nr; games rm; entmnt; some statics; dogs €3; poss cr; adv bkg; quiet; cc acc. "Pleasant site on rv bank; excel." ♦ 16 May-9 Sep. € 23.50   2006*

VALLON PONT D'ARC *9D2* (2km W Rural) Camping Le Beau Rivage, Les Mazes, 07150 Vallon-Pont-d'Arc [tel/fax 04 75 88 03 54; a.massot@worldonline.fr; www.beaurivage-camping.com] Take D579 W fr Vallon. After approx 1km bear L for Les Mazes at rndabt. After 800m turn L down side rd for site. Med, mkd pitch, terr, shd; wc (some cont); baby facs; shwrs; el pnts (6A) €3.50; gas; Indry rm; ice; shop & 2km; tradsmn; rest 2km; bar; BBQ; playgrnd; htd pool; rv sw; fishing; sailing; canoe hire; entmnt; TV rm; 5% statics; dogs €1.60; phone; poss cr; Eng spkn; cc acc; CCI. "Vg quality site; dir access to rv; if site full poss diff access some pitches for lge o'fits due trees; excel." 1 May-15 Sep. € 22.50   2005*

VALLON PONT D'ARC *9D2* (3km W Rural) Camping Le Chassezac, Route d'Alès, 07120 Sampzon [04 75 39 60 71; fax 04 75 39 76 35; info@campinglechassezac.com; www.campinglechassezac.com] Fr Aubenas S on D579. Approx 2.5km past Ruoms at rndabt, turn R onto D111. Foll sp 2km to site on R. Med, mkd pitch, pt shd; wc (some cont); chem disp; baby facs; shwrs inc; el pnts (6A) €3.80; Indtte; ice; shop; rest; snacks; bar; BBQ (gas only); playgrnd; pool; rv sw adj; fishing; cycle & canoe hire; horseriding; TV; 15% statics; dogs €2; phone; poss cr; Eng spkn; adv bkg dep req; quiet; CCI. "Friendly, helpful staff; vg." ♦ ltd. 1 Apr-30 Sep. € 17.00   2004*

VALLON PONT D'ARC *9D2* (5km NW Rural) Camping Soleil Vivarais, 07120 Sampzon [04 75 39 67 56 or 04 66 73 97 39; fax 04 75 39 64 69; info@soleil-vivarais.com; www.camping-soleil-vivarais.fr or www.yellohvillage.com] Take D579 fr Vallon-Pont-d'Arc. After 6km turn L onto D161, cross narr bdge over Rv Ardèche. Site immed on R. Lge, hdg/mkd pitch, shd; wc; chem disp; mv service pnt; baby facs; shwrs inc; el pnts (10A) inc; gas; lndry rm; ice; shop; rest; snacks; bar; playgrnd; htd pool; shgl beach & rv sw 500m; canoe hire; tennis; games rm; entmnt Jul/Aug; TV; 50% statics; dogs €3; poss cr; Eng spkn; adv bkg; quiet; cc acc. "V interesting area; busy site in gd location; sm pitches poss diff lge o'fits; gd entmnt." ♦ 5 Apr-13 Sep. € 38.00   2004*

VALLON PONT D'ARC *9D2* (5km NW Rural) FLOWER Camping Le Riviera, 07120 Sampzon [04 75 39 67 57; fax 04 75 93 95 57; leriviera@wanadoo.fr; www.campingleriviera.com] Take D579 W fr Vallon-Pont-d'Arc. After 6.5km cross narr bdge over Ardèche on D161. Site immed on L. Lge, mkd pitch, pt shd; wc; chem disp; mv service pnt; shwrs inc; el pnts (10A) inc; gas; lndry rm; ice; shop 100m; rest; snacks; bar; BBQ; playgrnd; pool; paddling pool; rv sw adj; shgl beach; tennis; games rm; cycle hire; horseriding; entmnt; TV rm; some statics; dogs €3; poss cr; some rd noise. "Attractive pools." 1 Apr-30 Sep. € 36.00   2007*

VALLON PONT D'ARC *9D2* (6km NW Rural) Camping La Bastide en Ardèche, Route de Gros-Pierres, 07120 Sampzon [04 75 39 64 72; fax 04 75 39 73 28; info@rcn-labastideenardeche.fr; www.rcn-campings.fr] Fr Vallon take D579 W & turn L onto D111. Cross rv, site sp on L. Lge, mkd pitch, pt shd; htd wc; chem disp; sauna; shwrs; el pnts (3-5A) inc; gas; lndtte; shop high ssn; tradsmn; rest, snacks, bar high ssn; BBQ (gas); playgrnd; 2 htd pools; rv sw; canoeing; fishing; sailing; tennis; mini-golf; games area; entmnt; horseriding; entmnt; TV rm; 70% statics; dogs €4; Eng spkn; adv bkg (dep req); quiet; cc acc; red low ssn; CCI. "Lovely scenery nr Ardèche gorge; well-run site." ♦ 1 Apr-27 Oct. € 43.50   2007*

VALLORCINE *9A4* (1km SE Rural) Camping des Montets, Le Buet, 74660 Vallorcine [04 50 54 60 45 or 04 50 54 24 13 (LS); fax 04 50 54 01 34; camping.des.montets@wanadoo.fr; www.vallorcine.com] N fr Chamonix on N506 via Col de Montets; Le Buet 2km S of Vallorcine; site sp nr Le Buet stn. Fr Martigny (Switzerland) cross border via Col de la Forclaz; then N506 to Vallorcine; cont to Le Buet in 1km. Med, hdg/mkd pitch, pt shd; wc; chem disp (wc); shwrs inc; el pnts (3-6A) €2-3; lndtte; shops 1km; tradsmn; no statics; dogs; Eng spkn; quiet; CCI. "Excel walking direct fr site; free train pass to Chamonix; vg." ♦ ltd. 1 Jun-15 Sep. € 13.10   2007*

VALLOUISE see Argentière La Bessée, L' *9C3*

Did you know you can fill in site report forms on the Club's website — www.caravanclub.co.uk?

France

VALOGNES *1C4* (1km N Urban) Camp Municipal Le Bocage, Rue Neuve, 50700 Valognes [02 33 95 82 01 or 06 10 84 59 33 (mob); environement@mairie-valognes.fr; www.mairie-valognes.fr] Off N13 Cherbourg to Carentan take 1st exit to Valonges, turn L just past Champion at Lidl sp; site sp bef & in town. Fr Carentan dir, take 3rd R after 4th set traff lts. Sm, hdg/mkd pitch, hdstg, pt shd; wc (cont); chem disp (wc); shwrs inc; el pnts (6-10A) €2-3.10 (poss rev pol); gas; shop 300m; rest, snacks, bar nr; dogs €0.50; poss cr; quiet; cc not acc; CCI. "Excel, gem of a site; spotless san facs; friendly staff; ideal NH & conv Cherbourg ferries (17km); sh walk to attractive town; poss itinerants; warden calls 1900-2000, site self if office not open." ♦ 1 Apr-15 Oct. € 9.00   2007*

VALRAS PLAGE *10F1* (N Coastal) **Camping L'Occitanie, Chemin de Querelles, 34350 Valras-Plage [04 67 39 59 06; fax 04 67 32 58 20; campingoccitanie@wanadoo.fr; www.camping occitanie.com]** Fr A9/E15 exit junc 35 at Béziers Est & join D64 sp Valras-Plage. Site is immed on L after rndabt at ent to Valras-Plage Est. Lge, hdg/mkd pitch, hdstg, pt sl, shd; htd wc; chem disp; mv service pnt; baby facs; shwrs inc; el pnts (5A) inc (poss rev pol); lndtte; ice; shop 1km; tradsmn; rest; snacks; bar; BBQ (gas/charcoal only); playgrnd; pool; paddling pool; sand beach 1km; sailing; fishing; mini-golf; entmnt; games/TV rm; 25% statics; dogs €3; recep 0800-2100 high ssn; c'van/mvan max 7m Jul/Aug; poss cr; Eng spkn; adv bkg; quiet; cc acc; red low ssn/long stay; CCI. "Lively town; mkt Mon & Fri am; mixed reports 2007." ♦ 31 May-6 Sep. € 29.00 ABS - C12
2007*

This guide relies on site report forms submitted by caravanners like us; we'll do our bit and tell the editor what we think of the campsites we've visited.

VALRAS PLAGE *10F1* (500m N Urban/Coastal) **Camping Le Levant, Ave Charles Cauquil, 34350 Valras-Plage [04 67 32 04 45; fax 04 67 32 06 33; camping.dulevant@free.fr; www.campingdulevant.com]** Exit A9 junc 35 onto D64 twd Valras-Plage. At rndabt junc with D19, turn L into Ave Charles Cauquil, site sp. Med, mkd pitch, pt shd; htd wc; chem disp; mv service pnt; baby facs; shwrs inc; el pnts (10A) inc; lndtte; shops; snacks; bar; BBQ; playgrnd; htd pool; paddling pool; sand beach 800m; games area; 40% statics; dogs €3; adv bkg; quiet. "Pleasant family site; gd facs; friendly, helpful staff." 15 Apr-15 Sep. € 29.00
2007*

See advertisement

VALRAS PLAGE *10F1* (3km SW Coastal) **Camping Domaine de la Yole, 34350 Valras-Plage [04 67 37 33 87; fax 04 67 37 44 89; info@campinglayole.com; www.campinglayole.com]** Leave A9/E15 at Béziers-Ouest; foll D64 twd coast dir Valras-Plage, then Valras-Plage-Ouest & site sp. V lge, hdg/mkd pitch, hdstg, shd; wc (some cont); chem disp; baby facs; shwrs inc; el pnts (5A) inc; gas; lndtte; ice; supmkt; rest; snacks; bar; BBQ (charcoal/gas); playgrnd; 2 pools & paddling pool; waterslide; sand beach 400m; tennis; cycle hire; fishing, horseriding 3km; games area; games rm; entmnt; internet; TV; tour ops statics; dogs €3.90 (not on beach); poss cr; Eng spkn; adv bkg; quiet but some rd noise; cc acc; red low ssn; CCI. "Excel; gd for all age groups; special offers families & children; mkt Mon & Fri." ♦ 26 Apr-20 Sep. € 41.10 ABS - C03
2007*

VALRAS PLAGE *10F1* (3km SW Coastal) **Camping Sunêlia Les Vagues, Chemin des Montilles, 34350 Vendres-Plage [04 67 37 33 12; fax 04 67 37 50 36; lesvagues34@free.fr; www.lesvagues.net]** Exit A9 junc 36 onto D64 to Valras-Plage then Vendres-Plage. Site sp. Lge, pt shd; wc; baby facs; shwrs inc; el pnts inc; lndtte; shop; rest; snacks; bar; playgrnd; htd pool complex; paddling pool; waterslides; jacuzzi; sand beach 300m; games area; horseriding 5km; entmnt; TV rm; 75% statics; dogs €6; adv bkg; red low ssn. "Recep v helpful; 3 sections all with own spotless san facs; excel." ♦ 31 Mar-30 Sep. € 42.00 (CChq acc)
2007*

VALRAS PLAGE *10F1* (2.5km W Urban/Coastal) **Camping Blue Bayou, Vendres-Plage-Ouest, 34350 Valras-Plage [04 67 37 41 97; fax 04 67 37 53 00; bluebayou@infonie.fr; www.bluebayou.fr]** Exit Béziers Ouest fr A9 twd Valras-Plage & Vendres-Plage-Ouest. Lge, mkd pitch, pt shd; wc; baby facs; shwrs inc; el pnts inc; gas; lndtte; shop; rest; snacks; bar; playgrnd; 2 htd pools; waterslide; sand beach 300m; Rv Aude 1km; tennis; games area; games rm; entmnt; 30% statics; dogs €5; adv bkg; quiet; CCI. "Poss dusty/windy end Jul/Aug, gd beach & pool." 1 May-30 Sep. € 38.00
2006*

VALRAS PLAGE *10F1* (3.5km W Rural) **Camping Domaine Les Vignes d'Or, Route de Valras, 34350 Valras-Plage [04 67 32 37 18; fax 04 67 32 00 80; info@vignesdor.com; www.vignesdor.com]** Exit A9 junc 35 Béziers Est onto D64 to Sérignan then dir Valras-Plage; site sp. Med, hdg/mkd pitch, pt shd; wc; baby facs; shwrs inc; el pnts (6A) €3.70; lndtte; tradsmn; rest; snacks; bar; playgrnd; pool; beach 2.5km; games area; entmnt; 95% statics; dogs €4.30; quiet; red long stay; CCI. "Ltd touring pitches; gd NH only." ♦ ltd. 1 Apr-30 Sep. € 26.00
2007*

VALRAS PLAGE *10F1* (5km W Coastal) **Camping Les Foulègues, 34350 Valras-Plage [04 67 37 33 65; info@campinglesfoulegues.com; www.campinglesfoulegues.com]** Exit fr A9 junc 36 onto D64 dir Valras-Plage; then foll sp Valras-Plage Ouest, by-passing town. Site sp. Lge, hdg/mkd pitch, shd; wc (some cont); chem disp; shwrs inc; el pnts (6A) inc; gas; lndtte; ice; shop; snacks; bar; BBQ (sep area); playgrnd; pool; paddling pool; sand beach 500m; watersports; bike hire; tennis; games area; entmnt; child entmnt; internet; 80% statics; dogs €4; phone; bus adj; poss cr; Eng spkn; adv bkg (dep req); cc acc; CCI. "Quiet site opp nature reserve; gd pitches; welcoming owner; excel beaches; popular with French families; mkt 3x wk nrby; gd." 24 Jun-23 Sep. € 37.50
2007*

VALRAS PLAGE *10F1* (5km NW Rural) **Camp Municipal Les Cardonilles, Route des Cardonilles, 34350 Vendres [04 67 39 57 14 or 04 67 32 60 50 (Mairie); fax 04 67 32 60 45; info@vendres.com; www.vendres.com]** Exit A9 junc 36 onto D64 & foll sp Valras-Plage & Vendres; ignore 1st rd to Vendres (D37E)(to avoid narr rds) & cont to rndabt where turn R sp Vendres & site; in 500m at 2nd rndabt turn sharp L. Site on R. Med, mkd pitch, pt shd; wc; shwrs inc; el pnts (5A) €3.55; ice; shop, rest, bar 400m; BBQ; playgrnd; sand beach 4km; dogs; quiet; CCI. "Steel pegs req high ssn." 1 May-30 Sep. € 12.15
2007*

VALRAS PLAGE *10F1* (5km NW Rural) **Camping La Gabinelle, 34410 Sauvian [04 67 39 50 87 or 04 67 32 30 79; info@lagabinelle.com; www.lagabinelle.com]** Exit A9 at Béziers Ouest, turn R twd beaches sp S to Sauvian on D19. Site 500m on L thro town. Med, pt shd; wc; chem disp; shwrs inc; el pnts €3; lndtte; shops, rest, snacks adj; bar; playgrnd; pool; sand beach 5km; fishing 1km; canoeing 2km; games area; games rm; entmnt; TV; dogs €2; adv bkg; quiet. "Friendly; suitable lge m'vans; gd rest in vill." ♦ 26 Apr-13 Sep. € 17.00
2004*

VALREAS *9D2* (1km N Rural) **Camping La Coronne, Route de Pègue, 84600 Valréas [04 90 35 03 78; fax 04 90 35 26 73]** Fr Nyons take D538 W to Valréas. Exit town on D10 rd to Taulignan, immed after x-ing bdge over Rv Coronne turn R into D196 sp Le Pègue. Site on R in 100m on rvside. Sp app fr E but easy to miss; app fr W; well sp in Valréas. Med, hdg/mkd pitch, pt shd; wc (some cont); chem disp; mv service pnt; shwrs inc; el pnts (3-10A) inc; gas; lndtte; ice; shop; tradsmn; rest; snacks; bar; BBQ; playgrnd; pool; paddling pool; fishing; entmnt; TV; dogs €0.80; phone; poss cr; Eng spkn; adv bkg (dep req); quiet; cc acc; CCI. "Sm pitches; excel pool; facs need refurb & poss unclean; site clsd 2200-0700." ♦ ltd. 1 Mar-30 Sep. € 15.00
2006*

VALREAS *9D2* (8km SE) **Camping de l'Hérein, Route de Bouchet, 84820 Visan [04 90 41 95 99; fax 04 90 41 91 72; campingrinaldi@aol.com; www.camping-herein.chez.tiscali.fr]** E fr Bollène on D94/D994 twd Nyons; after Tulette turn L (N) onto D576 dir Visan & Valréas; sp in vill opp PO; turn L onto D161 Bouchet rd; site on L in 800m just over sm bdge. Med, hdg/mkd pitch, pt shd; wc; chem disp; shwrs inc; el pnts (6-10A) €3-3.50; gas; ice; lndtte; shop & 1km; tradsmn; snacks; bar; playgrnd; pool; dogs €1.50; quiet; adv bkg rec; cc acc; CCI. "Lge pitches; well wooded; poss unkempt low ssn; facs poss stretched high ssn; friendly staff; vg." ♦ ltd 15 Mar-15 Oct. € 14.50
2007*

As soon as we get home I'm going to post all these site report forms to the editor for inclusion in next year's guide. I don't want to miss the September deadline.

VALREAS *9D2* (8km W Rural) **Camping Les Truffières, 26230 Grignan [tel/fax 04 75 46 93 62; info@lestruffieres.com; www.lestruffieres.com]** Fr A7 take D133 E twds Grignan. On W o'skts of vill turn S on D71. In 1km turn L at sp. Site is 200m on R. Fr Nyons take D538 W to Grignan. Sm, mkd pitch, shd; wc; chem disp; mv service pnt; shwrs inc; el pnts (10A) €4.30; gas; lndtte; ice; shop 1km; tradsmn, rest, snacks high ssn; bar; communal BBQ only; playgrnd; pool; fishing; 5% statics; Eng spkn; adv bkg; quiet; CCI. "Pleasant owners; 20 min stroll to town; immac san facs; gd pool area; some pitches diff access; well wooded; excel." ♦ 20 Apr-21 Sep. € 16.50
2007*

France

VANDENESSE EN AUXOIS *6G1* (3km NE Rural) Camping Le Lac de Panthier, 21320 Vandenesse-en-Auxois [03 80 49 21 94; fax 03 80 49 25 80; info@lac-de-panthier.com; www.lac-de-panthier.com] Exit A6 junc 24 (A38) at Pouilly-en-Auxois; foll D16/D18 to Vandenesse; turn L on D977bis, corss canal bdge & cont strt for 3km to site on L. Lge, hdg/mkd pitch, pt sl, terr, pt shd; wc; chem disp (wc); sauna; shwrs inc; el pnts (6A) inc (some rev pol); lndtte; shop & 6km; rest; snacks; bar; playgrnd; 2 pools (1 htd, covrd); waterslide; lake beach 50m; fishing; cycle hire; entmnt; sat TV; dogs €3 adv bkg ess; Oct open Fri, Sat & Sun; CCI. "Lovely area; wonderful view higher pitches; well-run site operating with Les Voiliers adj; lge pitches; facs poss stretched high ssn; gd takeaways; gd cycling & walks round lake; popular NH; vg." ♦ 7 Apr-13 Oct. € 25.00 (CChq acc)　　　　2007*

VANDIERES see Dormans *3D4*

⊞**VANNES** *2F3* (5km N Rural) Camping du Haras, Aérodrome Vannes-Meucon, 56250 Monterblanc [02 97 44 66 06 or 06 71 00 05 59 (mob LS); fax 02 97 44 49 41; camping-vannes@wanadoo.fr; http://campingvannes.free.fr] App fr N165 turn L onto D767 sp Airport. Go N for 7km & turn R onto D778 for 1km & turn R again. After 1km approx, turn L onto Airport Perimeter Rd, site sp on W side. App fr N on D767, join D778 & as above. Med, hdg/mkd pitch, hdstg, pt shd; htd wc; chem disp; mv service pnt; fam bthrm; shwrs inc; el pnts (4-10A) €3-6; gas; lndtte; ice; sm shop; tradsmn; snacks; bar; BBQ; playgrnd; htd pools; waterslide; sand beach 12km; lake sw 3km; fishing; tennis; horseriding 300m; trampoline; mini-golf; cycle hire; games rm; entmnt; 60% statics; dogs €4; Eng spkn; adv bkg; quiet with minimal aircraft noise; cc acc; red CCI. "Lovely site; basic facs; ltd space for tourers; pitches soft in wet." ♦ € 18.00　　2007*

See advertisement above

VANNES *2F3* (10km SE Rural) Camping La Peupleraie, Le Marais, 56450 Theix [tel/fax 02 97 43 09 46; contact@camping-lapeupleraie.com; www.camping-lapeupleraie.com] Exit N165 into Theix foll sp dir Trefféan, site off D116/D104 2.5km NE of Theix, well sp. Med, shd; wc; chem disp; shwrs inc; el pnts (5A) €2 (rev pol); lndtte; shops 3km; tradsmn; playgrnd; games area; mainly statids; dogs €1; adv bkg; quiet; 10% red CCI. "Fruit & veg fr farm; san facs in need of update; gd NH for Vannes." 15 Apr-15 Oct. € 11.50　　2006*

VANNES *2F3* (4km S) Camping Moulin de Cantizac, 199 Route de Vannes, 56860 Séné [02 97 66 90 26] S fr Vannes on D199 twds Séné. Site on L at rndabt beside rv. Med, hdg pitch, pt sl, pt shd; wc (some cont); shwrs inc; el pnts (6A) €3; lndtte; tradsmn; ice; sand beach 4km; boating; dogs €1.20; quiet. "Superb cent for bird watching, starting with estuary outside site ent; Vannes of historical interest; poss unkempt; unreliable opening dates." 1 May-15 Oct. € 14.00　　2005*

VANNES *2F3* (3km SW Coastal) Camp Municipal de Conleau, 188 Ave Maréchal Juin, 56000 Vannes [02 97 63 13 88; fax 02 97 40 38 82; camping@mairie-vannes.fr; www.mairie-vannes.fr] Exit N165 at Vannes Ouest junc; look for sp Conleau on R. Site twd end of rd on R. If on N165 fr Auray take 1st exit sp Vannes & at 2nd rndabt R (sp) to miss town cent. C'vans not allowed thro town cent. Lge, mkd pitch, pt sl, pt shd; wc; chem disp; mv service pnt; shwrs; el pnts (6A) €3.50 (some rev pol); lndtte; ice; tradsmn; playgrnd; sea water pool nr; sand beach 300m; entmnt; TV; dogs €1.50; adv bkg; quiet; cc acc. "Lovely walk along shore to interesting town; boat trips around gulf rec; office clsd 1200-1500, but space to wait; sep area for m'vans by rd - little shd & poss long walk to san facs; excel for c'vans." ♦ 1 Apr-30 Sep. € 17.30　　2007*

See advertisement opposite

VANNES 2F3 (5km SW Coastal) **Camping de Penboch, 9 Chemin de Penboch, 56610 Arradon [02 97 44 71 29; fax 02 97 44 79 10; camping. penboch@wanadoo.fr; www.camping-penboch. fr]** Exit Brest-Nantes N165 Vannes by-pass onto D101 & foll sp Arradon. Site well sp. Lge, hdg/mkd pitch, pt shd; wc (some cont); chem disp; mv service pnt; baby facs; shwrs inc; el pnts (6-10A) €3.20-4.20 (poss rev pol); gas; lndtte; ice; sm shop & 2km; tradsmn; snacks; bar; BBQ; playgrnd; htd pool; waterslide; sand beach 200m; games rm; internet; TV rm; some statics; dogs €3.50 (high ssn); Eng spkn; adv bkg rec high ssn; quiet; rcc acc; ed low ssn; CCI. "Boat trips around Morbihan; steel pegs req; overflow has 50 pitches with all facs; plenty of activities for youngsters; excel." ♦ 5 Apr-20 Sep. € 33.80   2007*

> The opening dates and prices on this campsite have changed. I'll send a site report form to the editor for the next edition of the guide.

VANNES 2F3 (6km SW Coastal) **Camping de l'Allée, Rue du Moustoir, 56610 Arradon [02 97 44 01 98; fax 02 97 44 73 74; campingdelallee@free.fr; www.camping-allee. com]** Fr Vannes take D101 & D101A to Arradon. Take by-pass & take 1st exit at rndabt & foll sp. Site to SW of Arradon. Fr Auray on D101 turn R on C203 immed after Moustoir. Med, hdg/mkd pitch, pt sl, pt shd; wc; chem disp; shwrs inc; el pnts (6-10A) €2.80-4.20 (poss long leads req); gas; lndtte; ice; sm shop & 2km; snacks; playgrnd; htd pool (high ssn); shgl beach 600m; games/TV rm; dogs €1.60; poss cr; Eng spkn; quiet; 20% red low ssn; CCI. "Delightful, family-run site in restful area; helpful; new san facs (2007); pitches in apple orchard; site yourself if office clsd; dinghy-launching & boat-mooring nrby; gd rests in Arradon; gd walks." ♦ 1 Apr-30 Sep. € 18.20   2007*

VANS, LES 9D1 (2.5km E Rural) **Camping Domaine des Chênes, 07140 Chassagnes-Haut [04 75 37 34 35; fax 04 75 37 20 10; reception@ domaine-des-chenes.fr; www.domaine-des-chenes.fr]** Fr town cent take D104A dir Aubenas. After Peugeot g'ge turn R onto D295 at garden cent twd Chassagnes. Site on L after 2km; sp adj Rv Chassezac. Med, terr, pt sl, pt shd; wc (some cont); mv service pnt; baby facs; shwrs inc; el pnts (10A) inc; lndtte; shop; rest; snacks; bar; BBQ; playgrnd; pool; rv fishing 500m; 80% statics; dogs €2.50; poss cr; adv bkg; quiet; cc acc; CCI. "Lovely shady site; ideal for birdwatchers." 1 Apr-30 Sep. € 24.00   2007*

VANS, LES 9D1 (5km NW Rural) **Camping Les Gorges de Chassezac, Champ d'Eynes, 07140 Malarce-sur-la-Thines [04 75 39 45 12; campinggorgeschassezac@wanadoo.fr; www. campinggorgeschassezac.com]** Fr Les Vans cent, dir Gravière, approx 5km thro Gravière cont, site on L. Med, mkd pitch, pt sl, terr, shd; wc (many cont); chem disp; shwrs; el pnts (6A) €3; gas; lndtte; ice; shop; tradsmn; snacks; bar; playgrnd; rv sw adj; TV; dogs €1; entmnt; poss cr; Eng spkn; adv bkg; quiet; CCI. "Peaceful site." ♦ ltd. 1 May-31 Aug. € 13.00   2006*

VARADES see Ancenis 2G4

VARCES ALLIERES ET RISSET see Grenoble 9C3

VAREN see St Antonin Noble Val 8E4

VARENNES EN ARGONNE 5D1 **Camp Municipal Le Pâquis, Rue St Jean, 55270 Varennes-en-Argonne [03 29 80 71 01 (Mairie); fax 03 29 80 71 43]** On D946 Vouziers/Clermont-en-Argonne rd; sp by bdge in vill, on banks of Rv Aire, 200m N of bdge. NB Ignore sp by bdge to Camping Lac Vert (not near). Med, pt shd; wc; shwrs inc; el pnts (3-6A) €2.70; ice; lndtte; shops adj; BBQ; playgrnd; rv fishing; dog €0.40; quiet. "Pleasant site with gd facs; nice (hilly) cycle ride taking in US WWI cemetary." 21 Apr-30 Sep. € 7.35   2007*

France

VARENNES SUR ALLIER *9A1* (9km N Rural) **Camp Municipal Le Moullin, 03340 St Gérand-de-Vaux [04 70 45 08 83 (Mairie)]** N on N7 fr Varennes-sur-Allier; turn E onto D32 to St Gérand-de-Vaux, site sp adj fishing lake. Sm, mkd pitch, terr, pt shd; wc; shwrs inc; el pnts (6A); lndry rm; playgrnd; quiet; CCI. "Rec check opening dates." ♦ ltd. May-Sep.
2005*

VARENNES SUR ALLIER *9A1* (3km NW Rural) **Camping Le Château de Chazeuil, 03150 Varennes-sur-Allier [tel/fax 04 70 45 00 10; info@camping-dechazeuil.com; www.camping-dechazeuil.com]** Ent to chateau grounds at traff lts at junc of N7 & D46. Med, pt shd; wc (some cont); mv service pnt; shwrs inc; el pnts (6A) €2.75 (long lead poss req); lndtte; ice; shops, rest, snacks & bar 2km; tradsmn; BBQ; playgrnd; pool; fishing; games rm; games area; horseriding; internet; dogs €1; Eng spkn; adv bkg; quiet; CCI. "Superb, quiet site in grounds of chateau; gd supmkt in Varennes; friendly owners; well off main rds; excel pool & san facs tho shortage of wcs & el pnts." ♦ 1 Apr-15 Oct. € 17.90
2006*

VARENNES SUR LOIRE see Saumur *4G1*

⊞**VARILHES** *8G3* (Urban) **Camp Municipal du Parc du Château, Ave de 8 Mai 1945, 09120 Varilhes [05 61 67 42 84 or 05 61 60 55 54 (Tourist Office); marie-line.bordin165@orange.fr; www.camping-ariege-pyrenees.com]** Exit N20/E9 at sp Varilhes. Turn N in town on D624. Site 250m on L (sp) just bef leisure cent adj Rv Ariège. Med, mkd pitch, terr, pt shd; htd wc; shwrs inc; el pnts (5-10A)€5.90-6.40; lndtte; shops adj & 200m; tradsmn; rest 200m; snacks; bar 300m; playgrnd; pool adj; rv fishing adj; games area; 20% statics; dogs; adv bkg; quiet. € 11.50
2007*

⊞**VARILHES** *8G3* (3km NW Rural) **FFCC Camping Les Mijeannes, Route de Ferriès, 09120 Rieux-de-Pelleport [05 61 60 82 23; fax 05 61 67 74 80; lesmijeannes@wanadoo.fr; www.campinglesmijeannes.com]** Exit N20 sp Varilhes; on app Varilhes cent join 1-way system; 1st R at Hôtel de Ville; over rv bdge; foll camp sps; site 2km on R. Med, hdg pitch, pt shd; wc; chem disp; shwrs inc; el pnts (6-10A)€3.60-4.10; tradsmn; bar; BBQ; playgrnd; pool; fishing; games area; TV; dogs €1.10; some Eng spkn; adv bkg; quiet; CCI. "Peaceful site by rv; v helpful owner; storage & equip hire; gd size pitches; poss ltd facs low ssn; call number on arr; excel." € 16.50
2007*

VARREDDES see Meaux *3D3*

VARZY *4G4* (1.5km N) **Camp Municipal du Moulin Naudin, 58210 Varzy [03 86 29 43 12; fax 03 86 29 72 73]** On D977 fr Clamecy to Nevers, sp. Sm, pt shd; some hdg pitch; wc; shwrs inc; el pnts (5A) €2.10; tradsmn; shops 1.5km; fishing; tennis nrby; quiet. 1 May-30 Sep. € 8.60
2007*

VATAN *4H3* (8km N Rural) **Camp Municipal St Phalier, 2 Chemin Trompe-Souris, 18310 Graçay [02 48 51 24 14 or 02 48 51 42 07 (Mairie); fax 02 48 51 25 92]** Leave A20 at junc 9 & take D83 to Graçay. On o'skts of vill turn L & immed turn L foll sp to Cent Omnisport & site. Sm, mkd pitch, pt shd; wc (some cont); chem disp; shwrs inc; el pnts (10A) €2; rest, bar & shop 1km; tradsmn; playgrnd & pool adj; fishing; dogs €0.56; phone; Eng spkn; quiet; CCI. "Clean site; excel san facs; sm lake & sm park adj; vill in walking dist; plenty of space - site yourself; gd NH for A20." 1 May-15 Sep. € 7.20
2007*

VATAN *4H3* (1km S Rural) **Camping Le Moulin de la Ronde (Naturist), Route de la Ronde, 36150 Vatan [02 54 49 83 28; www.moulindelaronde.com]** Fr town cent take D136 S twds A20; at supmkt turn R; site on L 500m. Sm, hdg/mkt pitch, pt shd; htd wc; chem disp; shwrs inc; el pnts (10A) €2.50; gas 1km; supmkt 400m; tradsmn; snacks; bar; BBQ; playgrnd; pool; games area; games rm; dogs €1.60; adv bkg; quiet; INF card req. "Simple site; dated & modern san facs; take great care with el pnts; gd mkt Wed; gd NH; fair ." 1 Apr-30 Sep. € 15.00
2007*

VATAN *4H3* (W Urban) **Camp Municipal de la Ruelle au Loup, Rue du Collège, 36150 Vatan [02 54 49 91 37 or 02 54 49 76 31 (Mairie); fax 02 54 49 93 72; vatan-mairie1@wanadoo.fr; www.vatan-en-berry.com]** Exit A20 junc 10 onto D922 to town cent. Take D2 dir Guilly & foll site sp - 2nd on L (easily missed). Med, hdg/mkd pitch, pt shd; wc; mv service pnt; shwrs inc; el pnts (6A) €2 (rev pol); lndtte; shops, rests 200m; playgrnd; pool adj; adv bkg; quiet; cc not acc; CCI. "V pleasant, clean & well-kept site in park; spacious pitches; easy access fr a'route; conv Loire chateaux; excel value." ♦ 15 Apr-15 Sep. € 8.00
2006*

VAUVERT *10E2* (5km SE Rural) **FLOWER Camping Le Mas de Mourgues, Gallician, 30600 Vauvert [tel/fax 04 66 73 30 88; info@masdemourgues.com; www.masdemourgues.com]** Exit A9 junc 26 onto N313/D6572 (N572). Site on L at x-rds with D779 sp to Gallician & Stes Marie-de-la-Mer. Med, mkd pitch, pt shd; wc; chem disp; mv service pnt; shwrs inc; el pnts (6A) €2.50; lndtte; ice; shop; snacks; BBQ; pool; games area; 15% statics; dogs €2; phone; Eng spkn; adv bkg (25% dep req); rd & farming noise; cc acc; CCI. "V enthusiastic, helpful British owners; some diff, long narr pitches; ground stony; v clean facs but poss stretched high ssn; excel pool; communal BBQ Thur nights; conv the Camargue; gd." ♦ 1 Apr-30 Sep. € 16.60
2007*

VAUX SUR MER see St Palais sur Mer *7B1*

VEDENE see Avignon *10E2*

VEIGNE see Montbazon *4G2*

VEIX see Treignac *7B4*

VELLES see Châteauroux *4H2*

VENAREY LES LAUMES *6G1* (1km W) **Camp Municipal Alésia, Rue de Docteur-Roux, 21150 Venarey-les-Laumes [tel/fax 03 80 96 07 76 or 03 80 96 01 59 (Mairie); camping.venarey@ wanadoo.fr]** SE fr Montbard on D905, site well sp fr Venarey on D954. Med, hdg/mkd pitch, pt shd, some hdstg; htd wc; chem disp; shwrs inc; el pnts (5A) €2.50; Indtte; shops 1km; tradsmn; BBQ; playgrnd; sand beach 50m; lake sw; cycle hire; TV rm; dogs €0.50; phone; poss cr; Eng spkn; adv bkg; some rlwy noise; red low stay; cc acc; CCI. "V scenic area, much to explore; warden on site am till 0930 & 1800-2000; barrier clsd 2200-0700; friendly staff." ♦ 1 Apr-15 Oct. € 9.00   2006*

VENCE *10E4* (8km SW Rural) **FFCC Camping des Gorges du Loup, Chemin des Vergers, 06620 Le Bar-sur-Loup [04 93 42 45 06; info@ lesgorgesduloup.com; www.lesgorgesduloup. com]** Fr A8 exit junc 47 & foll sp Vence then to Pont-du-Loup. Site well sp. App fr other dirs is diff. Med, mkd pitch, some hdstg, terr, pt shd; wc (some cont); chem disp; shwrs inc; el pnts (4-10A) €2.50-4 (poss rev pol); gas; Indtte; ice: shop; playgrnd; pool; shgl beach; TV rm; 20% statics; dogs €2; phone; bus 1km; Eng spkn; adv bkg 25% dep & bkg fee req; quiet; cc not acc; CCI. "Vg site with helpful, pleasant owners; owner will site c'van; spotless san facs; superb views; not suitable disabled; not suitable lge o'fits; highly rec. " 1 Apr-30 Sep. € 21.40   2006*

Before we move on, I'm going to fill in some site report forms and post them off to the editor, otherwise they won't arrive in time for the deadline at the end of September.

VENCE *10E4* (3km W Rural) **Domaine La Bergerie, 1330 Chemain de la Sine, 06140 Vence [04 93 58 09 36; fax 04 93 59 80 44; info@ camping-domainedelabergerie.com; www. camping-domainedelabergerie.com]** Fr A8 exit junc 47 & foll sp Vence thro Cagnes-sur-Mer. Take detour to W around Vence foll sp Grasse/ Tourrettes-sur-Loup. At rndabt beyond viaduct take last exit, foll site sp S thro La Sine town; long, narr rd to site, up driveway on R. Lge, mkd pitch, hdstg, pt sl, shd; wc; chem disp; mv service pnt; shwrs inc; el pnts (2-5A) inc; gas; Indtte; ice; shop & 5km; tradsmn; rest; snacks; bar; playgrnd; pool; tennis; dogs; poss cr; Eng spkn; no adv bkg; quiet; 5-10% red 10-20+ days; cc acc; CCI. "Office clsd 1230-1500; helpful owner; waiting area if full; access to san facs diff for disabled & many pitches long way fr san facs; Vence lovely & excel touring base; Antibes gd sand beach (30km); Italian border 40km; site poss neglected & scruffy low ssn." 25 Mar-15 Oct. € 29.00 (CChq acc)   2005*

VENCE *10E4* (6km W Rural) **Camping Les Rives du Loup, Route de la Colle, 06140 Tourrettes-sur-Loup [04 93 24 15 65; fax 04 93 24 53 70; info@ rivesduloup.com; www.rivesduloup.com]** Exit A8 junc 47 at Cagnes-sur-Mer. Foll sp La Colle-sur-Loup, then Bar-sur-Loup (D6). Site in Gorges-du-Loup valley, 3km bef Pont-du-Loup. Sm, pt shd; wc; baby facs; shwrs inc; el pnts (5A) €3.50 (poss rev pol); Indtte; ice; shop; rest; snacks; bar; playgrnd; pool; fishing; tennis; guided walks; horseriding 5km; internet; 60% statics; dogs €3.50; adv bkg; quiet. "Many outdoor activities avail; beautiful location." Easter-30 Sep. € 23.50   2006*

VENDAYS MONTALIVET *7C1* (6km NE Rural) **Camping du Vieux Moulin, 15 Route du Moulin, 33590 Vensac [tel/fax 05 56 09 45 98; postmaster@campingduvieuxmoulin.fr; www. campingduvieuxmoulin.fr]** Turn off N215 sp Vensac. Well sp in vill adj windmill. Med, pt shd, mkd pitch; wc; chem disp; shwrs inc; el pnts (10A) €3; Indtte; ice; shop; tradsmn; rest; snacks; bar; playgrnd; pool; sand beach 8km; entmnt; TV; 50% statics; dogs €1.50; Eng spkn; adv bkg; quiet. "Excel ambiance; v friendly site; ltd facs low ssn; tourers in sep field." 1 May-31 Oct. € 13.00

          2007*

VENDAYS MONTALIVET *7C1* (1km S) **Camping Les Peupliers, 17 Route de Sarnac, 33930 Vendays-Montalivet [tel/fax 05 56 41 70 44; lespeupliers33@hotmail.com; www.camping-montalivet-lespeupliers.com]** NW fr Lesparre on N215 for 9km. Then W on D102 to Vendays-Montalivet. In town cent foll D101 twd Hourtin. Turn L in 100m (sp), site on L in 200m. Med, mkd pitch, shd; wc; chem disp; baby facs; shwrs inc; el pnts (4-6A) €2.40-3.50; gas; Indtte; ice; shop 400m; tradsmn; snacks; BBQ; playgrnd; sand beach 10km; entmnt; fitness rm; TV rm; cycle hire; 10% statics; dogs €1.70; phone; adv bkg; quiet; red long stay/low ssn; cc acc; CCI. "Friendly owners; conv Médoc vineyards; excel cycle paths adj; excel san facs; €20 dep barrier key; shortage of el pnts high ssn." ♦ 1 May-30 Sep. € 13.00   2007*

VENDAYS MONTALIVET *7C1* (3km W Rural) **Camping du Mérin, 33930 Vendays-Montalivet [tel/fax 05 56 41 78 64; www.campinglemerin. com]** NW fr Lesparre-Médoc on N215 for 9km; then W on D102 to Vendays-Montalivet. Cont on D102 twds Montalivet-les-Bains. Site on L in 3km. Lge, hdg pitch, pt shd; wc; shwrs; el pnts (6-10A) inc; Indtte; shop 3km; tradsmn in ssn; playgrnd; sand beach 4km; fishing; cycle hire; entmnt; 5% statics; dogs €0.80; adv bkg; CCI. "Working farm; v basic facs." 1 Apr-31 Oct. € 12.65   2006*

France

VENDAYS MONTALIVET *7C1* (6km W Coastal) **Camp Municipal de Montalivet, Ave de l'Europe, 33930 Vendays-Montalivet** [05 56 09 33 45] Take D101 fr Soulac to Vendays, D102 to Montalivet-les-Bains. Site sp bef ent to Montalivet. Turn L at petrol stn, site 500m on L. V lge, mkd pitch, shd; wc; chem disp; mv service pnt; shwrs inc; el pnts inc; lndtte; shop; rest; snacks; bar; playgrnd; paddling pool; beach 700m; dogs €1.80; quiet; adv bkg. "Site in pine forest; gd mkt 1km; naturist beaches N & S of Montalivet." ♦ 1 May-30 Sep. € 14.20   2004*

⊞**VENDAYS MONTALIVET** *7C1* (6km W Coastal) **Camping CHM Montalivet (Naturist), 46 Ave de l'Europe, 33340 Vendays-Montalivet** [05 56 73 26 81 or 05 56 73 73 73; fax 05 56 09 32 15; infos@chm-montalivet.com; www.chm-montalivet.com] D101 fr Soulac to Vendays-Montalivet; D102 to Matalivet-les-Bains; site bef ent to vill; turn L at petrol stn; site 1km on R. V lge, mkd pitch, pt sl, pt shd; wc; chem disp (wc); el pnts €4.70; gas; lndry rm; ice; shop; rest; snacks; bar; playgrnd; htd pool; sand beach adj; 50% statics; dogs €6.70; poss cr; Eng spkn; adv bkg (dep req); quiet; red long stay; cc acc; INF card. "V peaceful; rather dated facs; fine, lge naturist beach adj." ♦ € 30.35   2007*

⊞**VENDOIRE** *7B2* (3km W Rural) **Camping Le Petit Lion, 24320 Vendoire** [05 53 91 00 74; info@dordogne-camping.info; www.self-catering-dordogne.co.uk] S fr Angoulême on D939 or D674, take D5 to Villebois-Lavalette, then D17 to Gurat. Then take D102 to Vendoire, site sp. Sm, hdg pitch, some hdstg, pt shd; htd wc; shwrs inc; el pnts (10A) €2.50; lndtte; shop & 7km; rest; snacks; bar; playgrnd; pool; paddling pool; lake fishing; tennis; 10% statics; dogs €2; rally fields; British owners; adv bkg; quiet; CCI. ♦ ltd. € 10.00   2006*

VENDOME *4F2* (500m E Urban) **Camp Municipal Les Grands Prés, Rue Geoffroy-Martel, 41100 Vendôme** [02 54 77 00 27 or 02 54 89 43 51; fax 02 54 89 41 01; campings@cpvendome.com; www.vendome.eu] Fr N10 by-pass foll sp for town cent. In town foll sp Loisirs & Sports. Site adj to pool 500m. Or fr D957 N of town foll sp to Loisirs & Sports for 2km. Lge, mkd pitch, pt shd; wc; chem disp; baby facs; shwrs inc; el pnts (4-6A) €2.60-3.85; lndtte; shop high ssn; rest in town; snacks; BBQ; playgrnd; htd pool adj; rv fishing adj; entmnt; 5% statics; dogs €0.85; phone; poss cr; adv bkg rec high ssn; quiet but some rd noise; CCI. "Pleasant setting beside rv; friendly staff; v clean san facs a trek fr outer pitches; sports cent, pool & theatre adj; historic town; vg." ♦ 10 Jun-31 Aug. € 11.00   2007*

VENDOME *4F2* (8km W Rural) **Camp Municipal de la Bonne Aventure, 41100 Thoré-la-Rochette** [02 54 72 00 59; fax 02 54 89 41 01; enora. conan@cpvendome.com] Fr Vendôme take D917 twd Montoire. After 6km turn R onto D82 for Thoré; thro vill & cont to vill exit sign, foll site sp. Beware there are 2 rds to Montoire - foll sp to vill. Med, pt shd; wc; chem disp; shwrs; el pnts (5A) €2.20 (long lead poss req); lndtte; shop 2km; tradsmn; snacks; rv sw, fishing & watersports adj; playgrnd; tennis; entmnts; games area; dogs €0.85; Eng spkn; adv bkg; CCI. "Peaceful site; v pretty & quiet setting by Rv Loir; worth effort to find; well-kept facs; helpful warden." 15 May-30 Sep. € 6.15   2006*

VENDRES see Valras Plage *10F1*

VENOSC see Bourg d'Oisans, Le *9C3*

VENSAC see Vendays Montalivet *7C1*

VERCHAIX see Samoëns *9A3*

VERDON SUR MER, LE *7B1* (Rural/Coastal) **Camping Le Royannais, 88 Route de Soulac, 33123 Le Verdon-sur-Mer** [05 56 09 61 12; fax 05 56 73 70 67; camping.le.royannais@wanadoo. fr; www.royannais.com] Fr Bordeaux N215 tw Le Verdon-sur-Mer (Royan), L on D1 twd Soulac then R, site on L. Med, mkd pitch, hdstg, pt shd; htd wc; chem disp; baby facs; serviced pitches; shwrs inc; el pnts (4-6A) €4.50-5.50; gas; lndtte; ice; shop; snacks; bar; BBQ; playgrnd; pool complex; waterslide; beach 400m; cycle hire; 40% statics; dogs €2.50; phone; bus; Eng spkn; adv bkg; quiet; red long stay; CCI. "Conv Soulac; ferry to Royan 30 mins; charming wooded site; gd shwrs." ♦ 1 Apr-15 Oct. € 18.00   2006*

VERDON SUR MER, LE *7B1* (1km Coastal) **Camping La Pointe du Médoc, Ave de la Pointe de Grave, 33123 Le Verdon-sur-Mer** [05 56 73 39 99; fax 05 56 73 39 96; info@camping-lapointedumedoc.com; www.camping-lapointedumedoc.com] App Le Verdon-sur-Mer on N215, site sp. Lge, terr, pt shd; wc (some cont); chem disp; mv service pnt; 30% serviced pitch; shwrs; el pnts (6A) inc; lndtte; shop & 1km; tradsmn; rest; snacks; bar; playgrnd; htd pools; sand beach 1km; watersports; fishing; horseriding; mini-golf; entmnt; TV rm; 20% statics; dogs €5; adv bkg; quiet; red low ssn; cc acc. ♦ 9 Apr-30 Sep. € 26.00   2005*

VERDUN *5D1* (SW Urban) **Camping Les Breuils,** **Allée des Breuils, 55100 Verdun [03 29 86 15 31; fax 03 29 86 75 76; contact@camping-lesbreuils. com; www.camping-lesbreuils.com]** Fr A4/ E50 exit junc 30. Site sp nr Citadel. Avoid Verdun town cent due to 1-way streets. Allée des Breuils runs parallel to D34 on other side of rwly. Site well sp fr N3. Lge, hdg/mkd pitch, some hdstg, pt sl, pt shd; wc; chem disp; mv service pnt; baby facs; shwrs inc; el pnts (6A) €4 (some rev pol); gas; lndtte; shop 3km; tradsmn, rest, snacks & bar (high ssn); playgrnd; pool with flumes high ssn; cycle hire; dogs €1.70; phone; extra for twin-axles; poss cr; Eng spkn; adv bkg (dep req) rec high ssn; cc acc; red 10+ days; CCI. "Pleasant, busy, well-kept site; family-run - helpful & friendly young couple; lovely pitches beside lge pond; some lge pitches; modern san block (locked o'night) but unscreened, outdoor facs for men; facs poss stretched if site full; poss long walk to water taps; some site rds tight for lge o'fits; gd pool; gd rest; easy walking dist to town & citadel; WWI museums local; excel hypmkt 3km fr town twd Metz; excel." ♦ ltd. 1 Apr-30 Sep. € 15.50   2007*

> There aren't many sites open this early in the year. We'd better phone ahead to check that the one we're heading for is actually open.

VERDUN *5D1* (4km NW Rural) **Camp Municipal sous Le Moulin, 55100 Charny-sur-Meuse [03 29 84 28 35 or 03 29 86 67 06 (LS); fax 03 29 84 67 99; mairie.charny.sur.meuse@ wanadoo.fr]** N fr Verdun on D964; turn L onto D115 to Charny-sur-Meuse; site sp. Med, pt shd; wc (all cont) (own san rec); mv service pnt; shwrs inc; el pnts €2.30; CCI. "CL-type site; fishing on site; gd." 1 May-30 Sep. € 6.70   2007*

VERDUN SUR LE DOUBS *6H1* (500m W Rural) **Camp Municipal La Plage, 71350 Verdun-sur- le-Doubs [03 85 91 55 50 or 03 85 91 52 52; fax 03 85 91 90 91; mairie.verdunsurledoubs@ wanadoo.fr]** SE on D970 fr Beaune to Verdun- sur-le-Doubs & foll sp in town. Or on D973 or N73 twd Chalon fr Seurre, turn R onto D115 to Verdun; site on bank of Rv Saône. Lge, mkd pitch, pt sl, shd; wc (some cont); chem disp; shwrs inc; el pnts (15A) €1.80; shops 500m; rest, snacks & bar 500m; BBQ; playgrnd; pool adj; waterslide; gd cycling & fishing; phone; quiet. "Lovely rvside location; interesting sm town; welcoming; lge pitches; excel." 1 May-30 Sep. € 8.10   2006*

VERMENTON *4G4* (500m W Rural) **Camp Municipal Les Coullemières, 89270 Vermenton [03 86 81 53 02 or 03 86 81 50 01 (Mairie); fax 03 86 81 63 95; mairie.vermenton@free.fr; http:// mairie.vermenton.free.fr]** Lies W of N6. Well sp in vill, over rlwy x-ing & site adj to rv. Med, hdg/ mkd pitch, pt shd; htd wc (some cont); chem disp; shwrs inc; el pnts (6A) €2.50; lndtte; shop 500m; rest 200m; playgrnd; tennis; fishing, boating & rv sw 20m; cycle hire; TV rm; dogs €1; bus; Eng spkn; adv bkg rec high ssn; quiet; cc acc. "Peaceful, clean, well-run site; gd facs; no twin-axle vans; weight limit on access rds & pitches; gd location by rv; gd walks & cycling; beautiful town with 12thC church." ♦ 1 Apr-30 Sep. € 10.50   2006*

VERMENTON *4G4* (2km W Rural) **Camp Municipal Le Moulin Jacquot, Route de Bazarnes, 89460 Accolay [tel/fax 03 86 81 56 58 or 03 86 81 56 87 (Mairie); mairie.accolay@ wanadoo.fr]** N fr Vermenton on N6 dir Auxerre; in 2km turn L onto D39 sp Accolay. Cross bdge, turn R thro vill; site on R at 500m adj Canal du Nivernais. Med, mkd pitch, pt shd; wc; chem disp; 4 serviced pitches; shwrs; el pnts (3-10A) €1.22-1.85; gas; lndtte; shops, rest, bar 300m; playgrnd; adv bkg; quiet; cc acc; red long stay; CCI. "Site yourself; grassy pitches poss boggy; beautiful countryside & pleasant sm vill; caves 11km." ♦ ltd. 1 Apr-15 Oct. € 5.60   2006*

⊞**VERNANTES** *4G1* (Rural) **Camping La Sirotière, 49390 Vernoil [02 41 67 29 32; ann.bullock@ orange.fr]** Fr Venantes on D767 take D206 dir Vernoil; turn R at rndabt (Super U on L); in 800m turn R sp La Jametière/La Sablonnière; in 800 turn R at sm x-rds bef post boxes; foll long drive to site. Sm, pt shd; htd wc; chem disp; shwrs inc; el pnts inc; lndtte; ice; shop & bar 1km; rest 2km; cycle hire; dogs; Eng spkn; adv bkg; quiet; no cc acc. "CL-type site; Loire valley châteaux; vineyards; adults only." € 13.00   2006*

VERNANTES *4G1* (2km E Rural) **Camping Intercommunal de la Grande Pâture, Route de Vernoil, 49390 Vernantes [02 41 51 45 39; fax 02 41 51 57 20]** Fr Saumur on N147. Take D767 to Vernantes then D58 dir Vernoil. Site sp. Sm, pt shd; wc; shwrs inc; el pnts (10A) €2.29; shop 200m; playgrnd; tennis; fishing adj; adv bkg; quiet; CCI. 15 Jun-30 Sep. € 7.71   2006*

⊞**VERNANTES** *4G1* (4km NW Rural) **Camping La Fortinerie, 49390 Mouliherne [02 41 67 59 76; john.north@wanadoo.fr]** Fr Vernantes take D58 dir Mouliherne. Opp Château Loroux (Plaissance) turn L. At x-rds turn R, site over 1km on L. Sm, pt shd; wc; chem disp; mv service pnt; shwrs inc; lndtte; ice; pool; no statics; B&B avail; adv bkg; quiet. "El pnts planned for 2007; v helpful, friendly British owners; ideal for Loire valley & surrounding forests; only sound is crickets!" € 10.00   2006*

France

⊞**VERNANTES** *4G1* (9km NW Rural) **Camping Le Chant d'Oiseau, 49390 Mouliherne [02 41 67 09 78; info@loire-gites.com; www.loire-gites.com]** Fr Saumur take D767 twd Noyant. Turn L in Vernantes then R onto D58 twd Mouliherne. Turn off D58 3km SE Mouliherne opp wooden cross. Foll rd for 2km. Site sp on L. Sm, pt sl, pt shd; wc; chem disp; shwrs inc; el pnts €4.50; BBQ; pool; cycle hire; some statics; no dogs; Eng spkn; quiet. "Lovely, clean, CL-type site; helpful & friendly British owners; gd facs; peaceful paradise for birdwatchers; excel." ♦ ltd. € 18.50   2007*

VERNET see Auterive *8F3*

VERNET LES BAINS *8G4* (1km N Rural) **Camping L'Eau Vive, Chemin de St Saturnin, 66820 Vernet-les-Bains [04 68 05 54 14; fax 04 68 05 78 14; info@leau-vive.com; www.leau-vive.com]** On app to town cent on D116 turn R over rv & site 1st R 1km at end of rd. Med, mkd pitch, terr, pt shd; wc; chem disp; serviced pitch; mv service pnt; shwrs inc; el pnts (10A) €1.50; lndtte; shop 1km; tradsmn; rest; snacks; bar; BBQ; playgrnd; lake sw; waterslide; tennis 500m; games area; TV rm; 40% statics; dogs €2.50; site clsd Nov to mid-Dec; Eng spkn; quiet. "V helpful, friendly Dutch owners; beautiful area; gd walking." ♦ 1 Apr-31 Oct. € 22.00 (3 persons) (CChq acc)   2005*

> Did you know you can fill in site report forms on the Club's website — www.caravanclub.co.uk?

VERNET LES BAINS *8G4* (1.2km N Urban) **Camping Del Bosc, 68 Ave Clémenceau, 66820 Vernet-les-Bains [04 68 05 54 54; fax 04 68 05 51 62]** Fr Villefranche to Vernet on D116, site on o'skirts of town on L opp Ecomarché. Med, pt sl, shd; wc; chem disp; shwrs inc; el pnts (3-10A) €1.70-2.20; lndtte; shop; playgrnd; entmnt; Eng spkn; adv bkg rec Jul/Aug; quiet; CCI. "Conv Tet valley & 'Little Yellow Train'; some pitches v sm & some steep; v clean facs; hot water to shwrs only." ♦ 1 Apr-1 Oct. € 9.60   2005*

VERNET LES BAINS *8G4* (2km N Rural) **Camping Les Closes, Route de Fillois, 66820 Corneilla-de-Conflent [04 68 05 64 60 or 04 68 05 64 48]** Fr Villefranche twd Vernet-Les-Bains on D116. Turn L into Corneilla-de-Conflent. Foll sp, site approx 1km. Med, mkd pitch, pt sl, terr, pt shd; wc (some cont); chem disp; shwrs inc; el pnts (10A) €2.30; lndtte; shop 500m; playgrnd; pool; dogs; phone; adv bkg; CCI. "Beautiful views; helpful owners; interesting area." ♦ 1 Apr-30 Sep. € 9.00   2004*

VERNET LES BAINS *8G4* (3km NW Rural) **Camping Le Rotja, Ave de la Rotja, 66820 Fuilla [tel/fax 04 68 96 52 75; camping@camping-lerotja.com; www.camping-lerotja.com]** Take N116 fr Prades dir Mont-Louis, 500m after Villefranche-de-Conflens turn L onto D6 sp Fuilla. In 3km just bef church, turn R at sp to site. Sm, mkd pitch, pt sl, terr, pt shd; htd wc; chem disp; baby facs; shwrs inc; el pnts (10A) inc; gas; lndtte; ice; shop 2km; rest 100m; snacks; BBQ (gas); playgrnd; pool; rv sw adj; 10% statics; dogs €2; phone; Eng spkn; adv bkg (dep req); quiet; cc acc; red long stay; CCI. "Views of Mount Canigou; peaceful site; friendly Dutch owners; gd hiking." ♦ 1 Apr-31 Oct. € 20.50   2007*

VERNET, LE *9D3* (800m N Rural) **Camping Lou Passavous, Route de Roussimat, 04140 Le Vernet [04 92 35 14 67; fax 04 92 35 09 35; loupassavous@wanadoo.fr; www.loupassavous.com]** Fr N on A51 exit junc 21 Volonne onto N85 sp Digne. Fr Digne N on D900 to Le Vernet; site on R. Fr S exit A51 junc 20 Les Mées onto D4, then N85 E to Digne, then as above. Sm, pt sl, pt shd; htd wc; chem disp; baby facs; shwrs inc; el pnts (6A) €3.50; lndtte; shop; tradsmn; rest; snacks; bar; playgrnd; pool; fishing; games area; entmnt; TV; dogs €1; poss cr; Eng spkn; adv bkg; quiet; cc acc; CCI. "Excel scenery; relaxing location; gd walking & other activities; gd facs for size; Dutch owners." ♦ 15 Apr-15 Sep. € 15.00   2007*

⊞**VERNEUIL SUR AVRE** *4E2* (1km W Rural) **Camping Le Vert Bocage, Ave Edmond Demolins, 27130 Verneuil-sur-Avre [02 32 32 26 79]** On ent Verneuil-sur-Avre join ring rd & foll sp for D926 (N26) to L'Aigle & Argentan. Site clearly sp on o'skts on L. Med, hdg/mkd pitch, pt shd; wc; chem disp; shwrs inc; el pnts (6A) inc; lndry rm; shops 1km; rest, snacks, bar & pool 200m; playgrnd; fishing adj; tennis; sports in town; 15% statics; dogs; site clsd Jan; no adv bkg; quiet but some traff noise; CCI. "Expensive for facs avail; clean facs but old & v ltd low ssn; site scruffy low ssn; NH only." € 25.00   2004*

VERNEUIL SUR SEINE *3D3* (NW Rural) **Camping-Caravaning 3* du Val de Seine, Chemin du Rouillard, 78480 Verneuil-sur-Seine [01 39 71 88 34 or 01 39 28 16 20; fax 01 39 71 18 60; contact@valdeseine78.com; www.valdeseine78.com]** Exit A13 junc 8 & foll sp to Verneuil; site sp twd rvside. Med, mkd pitch, hdstg, pt shd; htd wc; shwrs inc; chem disp; mv service pnt; el pnts (6A) €4.25; lndtte; shop & 1km; rest; snacks; BBQ; playgrnd; lake sw & beach 600m; fishing; watersports; horseriding; games area; some statics; dogs €2; Paris 20 mins by train; Eng spkn; quiet; cc acc; red low ssn. "V pleasant site adj Rv Seine; friendly, helpful staff; gd facs & activities." ♦ 15 Apr-30 Sep. € 13.90   2007*

VERNIOZ see Auberives sur Varèze *9B2*

VERNON *3D2* (2km W Rural) **Camping Les Fosses Rouges, Chemin de Réanville, 27950 St Marcel** [02 32 51 59 86; fax 02 32 53 30 45; camping@cape27.fr; www.cape-tourisme.fr] Exit E5/A13 junc 16 dir Vernon onto D181; in 2km at rndabt L onto D64E dir St Marcel; in 2km at rndabt turn R & foll camping sp. Med, mkd pitch, pt sl, pt shd; htd wc (some cont); chem disp (wc); shwrs inc; el pnts (6-10A) €2.50-3.30 (poss rev pol); gas; ice; shops 600m; tradsmn; BBQ; playgrnd; pool 4km; some statics; adv bkg (dep req); quiet; no cc acc; CCI. "Well-maintained site; gd views; clean san facs (modern & dated blocks); friendly owner; parking for m'vans at Giverny - cont past site over rndabt for 900m, turn v sharp L past hotel on R & parking on R; gd dog walking; lovely little vill; gd." ♦ ltd. 1 Mar-31 Oct. € 6.70   2007*

VERRUYES *7A2* (Rural) **Camping Etang de la Fragnée, 79310 Verruyes** [tel/fax 05 49 63 21 37; contact@campinglafragnee.com; www.campinglafragnee.com] Fr D743 S fr Parthenay turn SE onto D24 at Mazières-en-Gâtine for Verruyes; sp `Verruyes Plan d'Eau'. Med, mkd pitch, shd; wc; chem disp; shwrs inc; el pnts (6A) €2.80; lndtte; gas; ice; shop; tradsmn; rest; snacks; bar; playgrnd; sand beach & lake sw; fishing; tennis; cycle hire; entmnt; dogs €1.30; Eng spkn; adv bkg; quiet; cc acc. "Friendly site; pitches muddy when wet." 15 Apr-15 Oct. € 10.60   2006*

VERS *7D3* (Urban) **Camp Municipal de l'Arquette, 46090 Vers** [05 65 31 45 60 or 06 33 65 06 23 (mob); fax 05 65 31 41 94] Fr Cahors foll D653 on N side Rv Lot to Vers; in vill turn R over bdge onto D662 sp St Cirq-Lapopie; turn R in 100m, foll site sp. Use this rte to avoid low bdge 2.9m. Med, mkd pitch, shd; wc; chem disp (wc); shwrs inc; el pnts (10A) €1.80 (rev pol); shop & rest 200m; playgrnd adj; dogs €1; phone; poss cr; Eng spkn; adv bkg; cc not acc; CCI. "Friendly staff; attractive rvside site but poss flood risk; facs basic & dated; gd rests in vill; pleasant, local walks, views; conv Pech-Merle cave paintings." 1 May-30 Sep. € 9.70   2007*

VERS *7D3* (Rural) **Camping La Chêneraie, Le Cuzoul, 46090 Vers** [05 65 31 40 29; fax 05 65 31 41 70; lacheneraie@free.fr; www.cheneraie.com] Exit Cahors on D653 sp Figeac. In Vers turn L at rlwy x-ing, site on R in 50m, clearly sp. App steep & siting lge o'fits poss diff. Sm, mkd pitch, pt sl, pt shd; wc; chem disp (wc); mv service pnt; shwrs inc; el pnts (10A) €4; gas; lndtte; rest 2km; snacks; bar; playgrnd; pool; tennis; entmnt; some statics; dogs; phone; Eng spkn; adv bkg ess high ssn; quiet; cc acc; CCI. "Lovely scenery in Lot Valley; well-run, friendly site." 1 May-31 Oct. € 17.00   2007*

VERS PONT DU GARD see Remoulins *10E2*

VERSAILLES *4E3* (3km E Urban) **Camping Huttopia Versailles, 31 Rue Berthelot, Porchefontaine, 78000 Versailles** [01 39 51 23 61; fax 01 39 53 68 29; versailles@huttopia.com; www.huttopia.com] Foll sp to Château de Versailles; fr main ent take Ave de Paris dir Porchefontaine & turn R immed after twin gate lodges; sp. Lge, mkd pitch, pt sl, pt shd; htd wc; chem disp; mv service pnt; baby facs; shwrs inc; el pnts inc (6-10A) €4.20-6.20; gas; lndtte; shop 500m; tradsmen; rest; snacks; bar; BBQ; playgrnd; htd pool; games area; cycle hire; TV rm; 20% statics; dogs €3.50; bus 500m; Eng spkn; adv bkg (dep req); quiet; cc acc; red low ssn/long stay; CCI. "Pretty, renovated, wooded site; sl, uneven pitches poss diff; friendly, helpful staff; conv Paris (RER stn 400m) & Versailles Château (2km); excel clean san facs; vg management; excel." ♦ 28 Mar-2 Nov. € 29.70 (CChq acc)   2007*

> This guide relies on site report forms submitted by caravanners like us; we'll do our bit and tell the editor what we think of the campsites we've visited.

VERSAILLES *4E3* (7km S Urban) **Camping Le Parc Etang de St Quentin-en-Yvelines, 78180 Montigny-le-Bretonneux** [01 30 58 56 20; fax 01 34 60 07 14] Fr A12, N10 or N286 foll sp for Bois d'Arcy. Then foll Base de Loisirs sp. At rndabt surrounding sm pond & lge blue arch, take exit sp camping, site 200m on R. Lge, hdg pitch, pt shd; wc (some cont); chem disp; mv service pnt; shwrs inc; el pnts (6-10A) €3.90-€4; gas; lndtte; ice; tradsmn; rest; no BBQ; playgrnd; pool; fishing; sailing adj; 20% statics; dogs €2.10; poss cr; Eng spkn; adv bkg (dep req); some rd/rlwy noise; CCI. "Conv Palace Versailles; 10 min walk to rlwy for 40 min to Paris; country park adj; excel shopping cent 5 mins in car; helpful staff; office & gate clsd Sat noon to Mon am low ssn; pitches liable to flood; ageing facs & generally shabby; poss itinerants." ♦ 15 Mar-31 Oct. € 14.95   2006*

VERTEILLAC *7C2* (600m NE Urban) **Camp Municipal Le Pontis Sud-Est, 24320 Verteillac** [05 53 90 37 74; fax 05 53 90 77 13; j-c.rouvel@wanadoo.fr] N fr Ribérac on D708 dir Angoulême; in Verteillac turn R at 'Camping' sp, then L at gendarmerie, then 1st R. Site adj stadiium Sm, hdg pitch, sl, pt shd; wc, chem disp (wc); mv service pnt; shwrs inc; el pnts (5A) €2.70; lndry rm; shop, rest, snacks, bar nrby; BBQ; pool 500m; dogs; quiet; CCI. "Facs modern but poss stretched high ssn; ltd el pnts; leisure cent adj; attractive vill; Ribérac mkt Fri; gd." ♦ 1 Apr-15 Oct. € 9.90
                                      2006*

France

VERTEILLAC *7C2* (8km NW Rural) **Camping Petit Vos, 24320 Nanteuil-Auriac-de-Bourzac [05 53 90 39 46; petitvos@aol.com]** On D674 S fr Angoulême to Libourne, turn L at Montmoreau-St Cybard onto D24 to Salles-Lavalette (11km), then take D1 to Nanteuil-Auriac (4.5km). Go thro vill & foll sp 'Petit Vos' up to x-rds. Turn R sp Vendoire, then 2nd R. Site immed on R. Sm, pt sl, pt shd; wc; chem disp (wc); shwrs inc; el pnts (10A) inc; lndtte; shops & bar 4.5km; rest 2km; BBQ; rv sw & sand beach 15km; dogs €1; lge m'vans & children not acc; adv bkg ess (dep req); quiet; CCI. "CL-type, British owned site; excel facs but ltd; wonderful views fr site; v peaceful." € 8.50   2006*

VERVINS *3C4* (7km N) **FFCC Camping Le Val d'Oise, Route de Mont-d'Origny, 02580 Etréaupont [03 23 97 48 04]** Site to E of Etréaupont off N2, Mons-Reims rd. Site adj football pitch on banks of Rv Oise. Well sp fr main rd. Sm, /hdg/mkd pitches, pt shd; wc (some cont); shwrs inc; el pnts (6A) €3 (poss rev pol); ice; shops 500m; tradsmn; playgrnd; tennis; sports field adj; rv & fishing adj; dogs €0.30; quiet. "Pretty, tidy site; warm welcome; uninspiring vill; supmkt in Hirson; conv rte to Zeebrugge ferry (approx 200km); gd walking & cycling; site self if recep clsd; gd." Easter-30 Oct. € 7.60   2006*

VESOUL *6G2* (1.5km W Rural) **Camping International du Lac, Ave des Rives du Lac, 70000 Vesoul [03 84 76 22 86; fax 03 84 75 74 93; camping_dulac@yahoo.fr; www.camping-vesoul. com]** 2km fr D619 (N19), sp fr W end of by-pass, pass indus est to lge lake on W o'skts. Ent opp Peugeot/Citroën factory on lakeside. Lge, mkd pitch, pt shd; htd wc; mv service pnt; baby facs; shwrs inc; el pnts (10A) €2; gas; lndtte; shops 2km; rest; bar; playgrnd; pool, paddling pool, waterslides 300m; fishing; tennis; games area; some statics; dogs €1.80; adv bkg; cc acc; red CCI. "Super site with gd size pitches & excel aqua park nr with red for campers; screened fr indus est by trees; gd cycle rtes; pitches poss soft after rain." ♦ 1 Mar-31 Oct. € 12.60   2007*

VEULES LES ROSES *3C2* (3.5km E Rural) **Camp Municipal Le Mesnil, 76740 St Aubin-sur-Mer [02 35 83 02 83]** On D68 2km W of St Aubin-sur-Mer. Med, hdg pitch, terr, unshd; mv service pnt; htd wc; shwrs inc; el pnts (10A) €3.70; lndtte; shop; tradsmn; playgrnd; sand beach 1.5km; cc acc; CCI. ♦ 1 Apr-31 Oct. € 16.00   2007*

VEULES LES ROSES *3C2* (6km E Rural) **Camping Les Garennes de la Mer, 76740 Le Bourg-Dun [tel/fax 02 35 83 10 44; didpoulain@spray.fr]** Fr Veules-les-Roses, take D925 twd Dieppe. Site sp in Le Bourg-Dun. Sm, mkd pitch, pt sl, pt shd; wc; shwrs inc; el pnts (16A) €3; gas; lndry rm; shops 250m; supmkt 5km; tradsmn; shgl beach 3km; 60% statics; Eng spkn; poss cr; adv bkg; quiet; cc acc; CCI. "Beautifully laid out; v clean & tidy." ♦ ltd. 1 Apr-15 Oct. € 10.40   2005*

VEULES LES ROSES *3C2* (10km E Coastal) **Camp Municipal de la Plage, Rue de la Saâne, 76860 Quiberville-Plage [02 35 83 01 04 or 02 35 04 21 33 (Mairie); fax 02 35 83 67 33; campingplage@normandnet.fr]** Fr Dieppe on D75, site sp in Quiberville-Plage on D127. Lge, mkd pitch, unshd; wc; mv service pnt; shwrs; el pnts (6-10A) €4-4.70; lndtte; rest in vill; playgrnd; beach 100m; tennis adj; dogs €1.15; adv bkg. "Conv Dieppe ferry." ♦ 1 Apr-31 Oct. € 16.20   2006*

VEULES LES ROSES *3C2* (500m S Coastal) **Camp Municipal des Mouettes, Ave Jean Moulin, 76980 Veules-les-Roses [02 35 97 61 98 or 02 35 97 64 11 (Mairie); fax 02 35 97 33 44; camping-les-mouettes@veules-les-roses.fr]** On ent vill fr Dieppe on D925, turn R onto D68, site in 500m up hill (14%). Med, mkd pitch, pt sl, pt shd; htd wc; shwrs inc; el pnts (6A) €4.30; lndry rm; shops 300m; snacks; bar; pool 7km; beach 300m; games area; TV; 50% statics; dogs €1.05; Eng spkn; quiet. "Immac site & vg facs; interesting/ pleasant area; v helpful warden." 1 Mar-30 Nov. € 14.00   2007*

VEURDRE, LE see St Pierre le Moûtier *4H4*

VEYNES *9D3* (6km NE Rural) **Camping Mon Repos, Le Cadillon, 05400 Montmaur [04 92 58 03 14; campings@alpes-campings. com]** Fr D994 Veynes-Gap rd, foll D937 N, turning R at bdge to keep on D937. Site sp. Sm, pt sl, shd; wc; chem disp; mv service pnt 6km; shwrs inc; el pnts (2-5A) €2-3; gas; ice; lndtte; shop; tradsmn; snacks; playgrnd; pool 6km; rv sw; entmnt; TV rm; 30% statics; dogs €1; quiet; Eng spkn; CCI. "Friendly, family-run site; excel area for walking." ♦ ltd. 1 Apr-30 Sep. € 10.00   2006*

⊞**VEYNES** *9D3* (15km NE Rural) **Camping au Blanc Manteau, Route de Céüse, Mantayer 05400 La Roche-des-Arnauds [02 97 57 82 56]** Take D994 fr Veynes twd Gap; site sp in vill of La Roche-des-Arnauds on D18 in 1km. Sm, pt shd; htd wc (some cont); chem disp; baby facs; shwrs inc; el pnts (10A) €5.35; lndtte; shops 750m; snacks; bar; playgrnd; pool; tennis; adv bkg. "Gd sized pitches; v scenic." ♦ € 16.00   2007*

VEYNES *9D3* (2km SW Rural) **Camping Les Rives du Lac, Les Iscles, 05400 Veynes [04 92 57 20 90; fax 04 92 58 16 82; muretr@aol.com; www. camping-lac.com]** Off D994. Sp on lakeside. Med, mkd pitch, hdstg, pt sl, pt shd; wc; chem disp; mv service pnt; baby facs; shwrs; el pnts (10A) €3l; lndtte; ice; shop; tradsmn; snacks; bar; BBQ; playgrnd; pool; lake sw & beach adj; watersports; mountain biking; climbing; dogs €2; bus 500m; phone; adv bkg; quiet; cc acc; CCI. "V attractive, well-managed, clean site on shore of sm lake; san facs excel; welcoming staff." 14 May-17 Sep. € 16.50   2005*

VEYNES *9D3* (1.5km W) **Camping Solaire du Petit Buëch, Les Iscles, 05400 Veynes [04 92 58 12 34; fax 04 92 58 00 47; contact@camping-solaire. com; www.camping-solaire.com]** Sp fr rndabt at ent to Veynes fr Serres on N994. Lge, shd; wc; chem disp; shwrs inc; el pnts (5A) €3; gas; lndtte; ice; shop; tradsmn; rest; snacks; bar; 2 pools; games area; entmnt; some statics; dogs €2; phone; adv bkg; quiet. "Helpful staff" 1 May-30 Oct. € 13.40   2005*

VEZAC see Sarlat la Canéda *7C3*

VEZELAY *4G4* (3km N Rural) **Camp Municipal Le Pâtis, Route de Givry, 89450 Asquins [03 86 33 30 80; mairie.asquins@wanadoo.fr]** Fr Vézelay take D951 N to Asquins, & turn R to site on rvside - tight turn. Site sp. Sm, pt shd; wc; chem disp (wc); shwrs inc; el pnts €3; ice; shop 500m; BBQ; playgrnd; dogs; poss cr; quiet; CCI. 15 Jun-15 Sep. € 8.00   2005*

VEZELAY *4G4* (2km SE) **Camp Municipal, 89450 St Père [03 86 33 36 58 or 03 86 33 26 62 (Mairie); fax 03 86 33 34 56; mairie-saint-pere@wanadoo. fr]** Fr Vézelay take D957, turn onto D36 to St Père. Site sp. Med, pt shd; wc (cont); shwrs inc; el pnts (10A) inc; ice; shops 500m; playgrnd; rv sw adj; fishing; canoeing; tennis; poss cr; quiet. "Conv Morvan National Park; basic facs but pleasant; san facs poss tired; quiet site with gd walking area." Easter-30 Sep. € 8.10   2006*

VEZELAY *4G4* (600m S Rural) **Camping L'Ermitage, Route de l'Étang, 89450 Vézelay [tel/fax 03 86 33 24 18]** Foll sp fr cent of Vézelay to 'Camping Vézelay' & Youth Hostel. Sm, pt sl, pt shd; wc; some serviced pitches; shwrs inc; el pnts (4-6A) €2.50 (rev pol); shops 500m; tradsmn (high ssn); sw 13km; poss cr; Eng spkn; quiet; no cc acc; CCI. "Very pleasant, peaceful site; beautiful outlook; modern, clean facs; little shade; 10 mins walk to Vézelay with superb abbey church; blocks req; some pitches diff lge o'fits; 1 day free in 10." 1 Apr-31 Oct. € 7.00   2007*

VIAS *10F1* (2km S Coastal) **Camping Cap Soleil, 34450 Vias-Plage [04 67 21 64 77; fax 04 67 21 70 66; cap.soleil@wanadoo.fr; www. capsoleil.fr]** D612 (N112) W fr Agde to Vias. Turn S in town & foll sps for Vias-Plage over canal bdge & sps to site. Lge, mkd pitch; shd; wc; chem disp; mv service pnt; baby facs; shwrs inc; el pnts (10A) €3.50; lndtte; ice; shop in ssn; rest; snacks; bar; BBQ; playgrnd; htd pool; waterslide; naturist pool 1/7-31/8; sand beach 800m; rv sw 600m; tennis; entmnt; TV rm; 90% statics; dogs €5; private washrms avail; adv bkg; quiet; red low ssn. "Sm pitches; open NH winter but v ltd facs & poss unclean." 1 Apr-14 Oct. € 39.00   2007*

VIAS *10F1* (3km S Coastal) **Camping Californie Plage, 34450 Vias-Plage [04 67 21 64 69; fax 04 67 21 54 62; californie-plage@wanadoo. fr; www.californie-plage.fr]** W fr Agde on D612 (N112) to Vias; turn S in town & foll sps 'Mer' over canal bdge & sp to site. Lge, mkd pitch, shd; wc; chem disp; shwrs inc; el pnts (5-10A) €1.60-3.20; gas; lndtte; supmkt; rest; snacks; bar; playgrnd; htd/covrd pool; waterslide; sand beach adj; cycle hire; entmnt; TV rm; 10% statics; dogs €4.60; Eng spkn; adv bkg; CCI. ♦ 1 Apr-15 Sep. € 31.00
                                                        2004*

VIAS *10F1* (3km S Coastal) **Camping Domaine Sainte-Cécile, 34450 Vias-Plage [04 67 21 63 70; fax 04 67 21 48 71; campingsaintececile@ wanadoo.fr; www.camping-sainte-cecile.com]** Exit A9 junc 34 dir Agde on N312, then D612 (N112) to Vias-Plage; at rndabt turn R & foll sp. Med, mkd pitch, hdstg, shd; htd wc (some cont); chem disp (wc); baby facs; shwrs inc; el pnts (3-6A) inc; gas; lndtte; ice; shop; rest; snacks; bar; BBQ; playgrnd; pool; sand beach 500m; 20% statics; dogs €2; phone; poss cr; adv bkg (dep req); quiet; red low ssn; cc acc; CCI. "Well-run, peaceful site; friendly; spacious pitches; gd clean san facs; nr less commercialised beach; gd cycling & walking along Canal du Midi; vg." ♦ 15 Apr-22 Sep. € 26.50
                                                        2006*

VIAS *10F1* (3km S Coastal) **Camping Les Salisses, Route de la Mer, 34450 Vias Plage [04 67 21 64 07; fax 04 67 21 76 51; info@ salisses.com; www.salisses.com]** Turn S off D612 (N112) (Agde-Béziers rd) in Vias & foll sp to Vias-Plage. Cross Canal du Midi bdge & site on R. Lge, mkd pitch, pt shd; wc; chem disp; shwrs inc; el pnts (6A) inc; gas; lndtte; shop; rest; snacks; bar; playgrnd; 3 pools (1 htd, covrd); waterslide; sand beach 1km; tennis; cycle hire; horseriding; TV rm; 80% statics; dogs €5; quiet; cc acc. "Vg family hols; interesting town & mkt in Agde; boat trips avail." Easter-11 Sep. € 31.00 (CChq acc)   2006*

VIAS *10F1* (3km S Coastal) **Yelloh! Village Le Club Farret, 34450 Vias-Plage [04 67 21 64 45; fax 04 67 21 70 49; farret@wanadoo.fr; www. camping-farret.com   www.yellohvillage.com]** Fr A9, exit Agde junc 34. Foll sp Vias-Plage on D137. Sp fr cent of Vias-Plage on L, immed after Gendarmerie. V lge, mkd pitch, pt shd; wc; chem disp; mv service pnt; baby facs; shwrs inc; el pnts (6A) inc; gas; lndtte; ice; shop; rest; snacks; bar; playgrnd; htd pool; sand beach adj; watersports; tennis; cycle hire; fitness rm; games area; games rm; entmnt; child entmnt; TV; 20% statics; dogs €3; Eng spkn; adv bkg; quiet; cc acc; red low ssn; CCI. "Camp guarded at night; excel facs, entmnt & lessons; excursions." ♦ 24 Apr-11 Oct. € 44.00
                                                        2007*

See advertisement on next page

France

L'Esprit de Famille

At Club Farret, the family spirit is allowed free rein. The high quality pitches and accommodations set among tenderly cared-for flowery gardens ensure that you will have a pleasant stay in a comfortable home-from-home. From April to October, everyone can choose their own leisure activities and take full advantage of the pleasures of the pool that is heated in cooler weather, and of course of the beach that is only a stone's throw away. **Request our 2008 brochure as soon as possible by e-mail, telephone or letter!**

NEW 2008 booking for pitches

OPEN FROM 24TH APRIL TO 11TH OCTOBER 2008

Le Club Farret
★ ★ ★ ★
CAMPING PLAGE
Languedoc - Méditerranée
L'Esprit DE Famille

Le Club Farret - 34450 VIAS PLAGE
Tel.: +33 (0)4 67 21 64 45 - Fax: +33 (0)4 67 21 70 49
E-mail : farret@wanadoo.fr
www.camping-farret.com

yelloh! VILLAGE

VIAS *10F1* (5km SW Coastal) **Camping La Carabasse, Route de Farinette, 34450 Vias-Plage** [04 67 21 64 01; fax 04 67 21 76 87; lacarabasse@siblu.fr; www.siblu.com] Fr S on A9 exit 34 & take 1st exit onto N312 sp Vias & Agde. After 8km take RH lane twd Béziers on D612 (N112). Branch R to Vias-Plage & at rndabt foll sp for Vias-Plage on D137. Site 1km on L. V lge, hdg/mkd pitch, pt shd; wc; chem disp; baby facs; shwrs inc; some pitches with indiv san facs; el pnts (6A) inc (poss rev pol); gas; lndtte; ice; shop; rest; snacks; bar; BBQ; playgrnd; 2 htd pools; waterslide; sand beach 600m; tennis; mini-golf; watersports; golf 10km; entmnt; child entmnt; TV; 70% statics; no dogs; Eng spkn; adv bkg ess; quiet but poss noisy high ssn; red low ssn; CCI. "Vg local produce inc wines; organised activities; pitches poss tight med/lge o'fits due trees; excel for young families." ♦ 15 Apr-14 Sep. € 144.00 (7 nights)   2005*

VIAS *10F1* (5km SW Coastal) **Camping Les Flots Bleus, Côte Ouest, 34450 Vias-Plage** [04 67 21 64 80; fax 04 67 01 78 12; campinglesflotsbleus@wanadoo.fr; www.camping-flotsbleus.com] Fr D612 (N112) at Vias, take D137 sp Vias-Plage. After x-ing Canal du Midi turn R sp Côte Ouest, site sp. Lge, some hdg/mkd pitch, hdstg, pt shd; wc (some cont); chem disp; mv service pnt; baby facs; shwrs €0.30; el pnts (6A) inc; lndtte; ice; shop; tradsmn; rest; snacks; bar; playgrnd; htd pool; waterslide; sand beach adj; games area; cycle hire; entmnt; 50% statics; dogs €3.50; adv bkg; quiet; CCI. "Europark 2km; facs clean but poss stretched high ssn; gd." 15 Apr-15 Sep. € 29.00   2005*

As soon as we get home I'm going to post all these site report forms to the editor for inclusion in next year's guide. I don't want to miss the September deadline.

VIAS *10F1* (3km W Rural) **Camping Sunêlia Le Domaine de la Dragonnière, 34450 Vias [04 67 01 03 10; fax 04 67 21 73 39; dragonniere@wanadoo.fr; www.dragonniere.com]** Exit A9 junc 35 onto D64 twd Valras, then D612 (N112) dir Agde & Vias. Site on R bef Vias. Or exit junc 34 onto N312. At Vias turn R onto D612 (N112) sp Béziers, site on L. V lge, hdg/mkd pitch, pt shd; wc; chem disp; mv service pnt; sauna; shwrs inc; el pnts (10A) inc; gas; lndtte; ice; shop; tradsmn; rest; snacks; bar; BBQ; playgrnd; htd pool complex; paddling pool; sand beach 3km (free shuttle high ssn); tennis; games area; cycle hire; entmnt; internet; TV rm; 80% statics; dogs €5; phone; poss cr; Eng spkn; adv bkg; traff & aircraft noise; cc acc; CCI. "Vg site in Rochehaute Botanical Reserve; excel for children & teenagers high ssn; many activities; Canal du Midi nrby; opp Béziers airport; site poss flooded after heavy rain." ♦ 1 Apr-29 Sep. € 39.00 (3 persons) (CChq acc) 2006*

VIC LE COMPT *9B1* (10km N) **Camp Municipal La Croix de Vent, 63270 Vic-le-Comte [04 73 69 22 63 or 04 73 69 02 12 (Mairie)]** Fr N exit A75 junc 5 onto D213/D225 to Vic-le-Comte & foll sp for camping or sw pool, 'piscine'. Fr S exit A75 junc 8 onto D229 to Vic. Sm, pt shd; wc; shwrs; el pnts (16A) €2; lndry rm; shops 500m; pool adj; tennis; adv bkg; quiet. "Friendly, helpful staff; gd san facs; v pleasant old town walking dist; conv Auvergne area; conv NH." 1 Jul-31 Aug. € 10.30 2007*

VIC SUR CERE *7C4* (6km NE Rural) **Camp Municipal La Bédisse, Route de Raulhac, 15800 Thiézac [04 71 47 00 41 or 04 71 47 01 21 (Mairie); fax 04 71 47 02 23; otthiezac@wanadoo.fr]** Sp fr N122 on D59. Med, mkd pitch, pt shd; wc (some cont); shwrs inc; el pnts (10A) €2.20; lndry rm; shops 500m; playgrnd adj; pool 3km; tennis; poss cr; quiet. "Gd walking in Cantal; helpful owner; clean facs." 15 Jun-15 Sep. € 7.80 2007*

VIC SUR CERE *7C4* (1km E Rural) **Camp Municipal du Carladez, Ave des Tilleuls, 15800 Vic-sur-Cère [04 71 47 51 04 or 04 71 47 51 75 (Mairie); fax 04 71 47 50 59; vic-sur-cere@wanadoo.fr; www.vicsurcere.com]** Fr Aurillac on N122 site sp on ent Vic-sur-Cère on R. Lge, pt shd; wc (some cont); shwrs inc; el pnts (6A) €2.50; supmkt 100m; pool 500m; playgrnd, tennis & mini-golf nrby; rv fishing; poss cr; adv bkg; quiet. "Gate clsd 2000; office clsd Sun; no pitching without booking in; plenty of rm high ssn (2007); helpful warden; clean facs; vg value." ♦ 1 Apr-30 Sep. € 8.40 2007*

VIC SUR CERE *7C4* (3km SE) **Camping La Pommeraie, 15800 Vic-sur-Cère [04 71 47 54 18; fax 04 71 49 63 30; pommeraie@wanadoo.fr; www.camping-la-pommeraie.com]** Fr Vic-sur-Cère take D54 twd Pierrefort & Chaudes-Aigues, initially sp Salvanhac. Foll yellow site sp over rv, under rlwy bdge. Foll D154 up steep, narr, winding hill for 1.5km. Foll camp sp R into narr lane. Med, terr, pt shd; wc (some cont); baby facs; serviced pitches; shwrs inc; el pnts (6A) inc; lndtte; ice; shop high ssn; rest; snacks; bar; no BBQ; playgrnd; pool; fishing; tennis; entmnt; many statics; dogs €2; poss cr; adv bkg rec; cc acc. "Peaceful site; best pitches at top of site but v steep access; not suitable elderly or infirm; wonderful views; mkt Tue & Fri." ♦ 1 May-15 Sep. € 21.00 2004*

VICHY *9A1* (1km SW Urban) **Camping Les Acacias, Rue Claude Decloître, 03700 Bellerive-sur-Allier [04 70 32 36 22; fax 04 70 32 88 52; camping-acacias@club-internet.fr; www.camping-acacias.com]** Cross bdge to Bellerive fr Vichy, turn L at 2nd rndabt onto D1083 (past Conforma), then turn L at next rndabt sp 'piscine'. Foll sm camping sps. Or fr S leave D906 at St Yorre & cross Rv Allier, then foll sp to Bellerive. Site so at rndabt on app to Bellerive adj Rv Allier. On final app, at sp showing site in either dir, keep L & foll site sp along rv bank to recep. NB Many other sites in area, foll sp carefully. Med, hdg/mkd pitch, shd; wc; chem disp; baby facs; shwrs inc; el pnts (10A) €3; gas; ice; shops 1km; snacks; BBQ; playgrnd; pool; fishing; boating; TV; 20% statics; adv bkg; quiet; cc acc; CCI. "Helpful owner; gd, modern san facs; easy walk into lovely town." 2 Apr-15 Oct. € 14.40 2006*

VICHY *9A1* (1.5km SW Rural) **Camping Beau Rivage, Rue Claude Decloître, 03700 Bellerive-sur-Allier [04 70 32 26 85; fax 04 70 32 03 94; camping-beaurivage@wanadoo.fr; www.camping-beaurivage.com]** Fr Vichy take N209 dir Gannat. After x-ing bdge over Rv Allier, turn L at rndabt foll sp Camping, sp to Beau Rivage. Site on L on rv bank. Med, shd; wc (mainly cont); chem disp; baby facs; shwrs inc; el pnts (10A) €3; gas; lndtte; ice; shop; supmkt 1km; rest; BBQ; playgrnd; 2 pools & waterslide; tennis 2km; fishing; canoeing; boating; archery; entmnt; TV; poss cr. 1 Apr-30 Sep. € 14.80 (CChq acc) 2006*

VICHY *9A1* (5km SW Rural) **Camping La Roseraie, Route de Randan, 03700 Brugheas [04 70 32 43 33; fax 04 70 32 26 23; campinglaroseraie@wanadoo.fr]** Fr Vichy on D1093, foll sp to Brugheas. Site well sp. Med, hdg/mkd pitch, pt shd; wc; chem disp; baby facs; shwrs inc; el pnts (6A) €2.50; gas; lndtte; ice; shop 3km; tradsmn; snacks; bar high ssn; BBQ; playgrnd; pool; TV rm; games area; mini-golf; 10% statics; dogs; adv bkg; quiet; red long stay; CCI. "Lovely pool; sm chateau in Brugheas; salmon smokerie opp site." ♦ ltd. 1 Apr-30 Oct. € 12.60 2006*

VIEILLE BRIOUDE 9C1 (2km S Rural) **Camping La Bageasse, Route de Puy-en-Velay, 43100 Vieille-Brioude** [04 71 50 07 70; fax 04 73 34 70 94; contact@revea-vacances.com; www.revea-vacances.fr] Off N102 fr S foll camp sps on SE side of town at boundary sp. Narr app rd. Site on Rv Allier. Med, mkd pitch, terr, pt shd; wc (some cont); chem disp (wc); shwrs inc; el pnts (6A) €3.50 (some rev pol); Indtte; ice; sm shop; tradsmn; snacks; bar; BBQ; playgrnd; pool 2km; rv/lake sw, fishing & boating adj; canoe hire; 8% statics; dogs €1.50; phone; Eng spkn; adv bkg; quiet; red long stay; CCI. "V clean site; phone ahead to check open low ssn; interesting basilica." ♦ 2 Jun-30 Sep. € 14.70
2007*

VIELLE ST GIRONS see Léon 8E1

⊞**VIELMUR SUR AGOUT** 8F4 (S Rural) **FFCC Camping Le Pessac, 14 Quartier du Pessac, 81570 Vielmur-sur-Agout** [tel/fax 05 63 74 30 24; info@camping-lepessac.com; www.camping-lepessac.com] W on D112 fr Castres after 13km turn L D92 S. 200m after level x-ing turn L, site in 100m, sp. Sm, mkd pitch, pt shd; wc; mv service pnt; shwrs; el pnts (6-10AA) €3.20-5; Indtte; ice; shop; bar; playgrnd; pool; paddling pool; fishing; tennis nr; entmnt; 20% statics; dogs €1; CCI. € 9.20
2006*

VIERZON 4G3 (2.5km SW Urban) **Camp Municipal de Bellon, Route de Bellon, 18100 Vierzon** [02 48 75 49 10 or 02 48 53 06 11; fax 02 48 71 40 94; campingmunicipal-vierzon@wanadoo.fr; www.ville-vierzon.fr] Fr N on A71 take A20 twd Châteauroux, leave at junc 7 onto D320 & then D27, turn 2nd L off D27 after Intermarché supmkt. Site 1km on R, sp. Med, hdg pitch, pt sl, pt shd; wc (some cont); chem disp; mv service pnt; shwrs inc; el pnts (6A) €2.30 (some rev pol); gas; Indry rm; ice; shop 500m; rest; snacks; playgrnd; fishing; boat hire; internet; phone; poss cr; Eng spkn; adv bkg; quiet; no cc acc; CCI. "Attractive, well-kept site by rv; gd sized pitches but some poss diff to negotiate; clean facs; poss some rlwy noise; gates clsd 2300-0700; warden on site 1700-2200; vg." ♦ 1 May-30 Sep. € 10.80
2007*

⊞**VIERZON** 4G3 (5km NW Rural) **Aire Communale, Place de la Mairie, 18100 Méry-sur-Cher** [02 48 75 38 18; mairie-mery-sur-cher@wanadoo.fr] Fr Vierzon on N76 dir Tours. Site clearly sp on L on ent Méry-sur-Cher. Sm, mkd pitch, hdstg, unshd; wc; chem disp; mv service pnt; el pnts; shop 100m; dogs; phone; bus; rd noise; m'vans only - max 48 hrs. "Excel NH." € 3.00
2007*

VIEUX BOUCAU LES BAINS 8E1 (800m N Coastal) **Camp Municipal Les Sablères, Bldv du Marensin, 40480 Vieux-Boucau-les-Bains** [05 58 48 12 29 0r 05 58 48 13 22; fax 05 58 48 20 70; camping-lessableres@wanadoo.fr; www.les-sableres.com] Foll sps fr cent of vill twd beach, site sp fr D652. V lge, mkd pitch, pt sl, shd; wc (some cont); chem disp; mv service pnt; baby facs; shwrs inc; el pnts (5-10A) €3.10-4.30; Indtte; shops, rest & snack 1km; BBQ; playgrnd; sand beach 300m (sw not rec due dangerous currents; lake sw nrby; games area; 20% statics; dogs €1.80; phone; poss cr; Eng spkn; adv bkg (dep req); quiet; CCI. "Site by lge sand dune; direct access to beach; adj surf beach; vg." ♦ ltd. 1 Apr-15 Oct. € 16.00
2007*

VIGAN, LE (GARD) 10E1 (2km E) **Camping Le Val d'Arre, 30120 Le Vigan** [04 67 81 02 77 or 06 82 31 79 72 (mob); fax 04 67 81 71 23; valdelarre@wanadoo.fr; www.valdelarre.com] E fr Vigan on D999. Turn R at 1st rndabt over bdge. Turn L immed after bdge; site in 400m, well sp. Height limit 2.10m. Lge, mkd pitch, pt sl, pt shd; wc (some cont); chem disp; shwrs inc; el pnts inc (10A) €3.50; gas & 2km; Indtte; ice; tradsmn; shop & 2km; rest; snacks; playgrnd; htd pool; rv sw & fishing 4km; entmnt; games rm; TV; dogs €2; phone; Eng spkn; adv bkg; some traff noise; site poss noisy high ssn; red low ssn; cc acc; CCI. "Friendly & v helpful owners; peaceful, well-run site by river; gd touring base for Les Grand Causses & gorges; rec." ♦ 1 Apr-5 Oct. € 16.00
2007*

VIGAN, LE (GARD) 10E1 (7km S Rural) **Camp Municipal, 30120 Montdardier** [04 67 81 52 16 or 04 67 81 52 46 (Mairie); fax 04 67 81 53 22] Fr D999 in Le Vigan turn S onto D48 dir Aveze, site sp (sm brown) in Mondardier. NB D48 narr & steep with hairpins. Sm, pt sl, pt shd; wc; shwrs; el pnts (6A) €1-1.50; shop 300m; playgrnd; poss cr; quiet; adv bkg. "Quiet, rural site; approaches req care - not suitable lge o'fits; warden calls." 1 Mar-31 Oct.
€ 9.70
2006*

VIGAN, LE (LOT) see Gourdon 7D3

VIGEOIS see Uzerche 7B3

VIGNES, LES 9D1 (6km NE Rural) **Camping La Blaquière, 48210 Les Vignes** [tel/fax 04 66 48 54 93; campingblaquiere@wanadoo.fr; www.campingblaquiere.fr] On Gorges du Tarn D907b fr Le Rozier to St Enimie, camp is on R 6km after Les Vignes on rvside. Sm, mkd pitch, terr, shd; wc; chem disp; baby facs; shwrs inc; el pnts (6A) €2.50; ice; Indtte; shop; tradsmn; rest; snacks; BBQ; playgrnd; rv sw & beach; fishing; entmnt; 50% statics; dogs €1.60; phone; Eng spkn; quiet; red low ssn. "Superb location on rvside." ♦ 1 May-10 Sep. € 12.60
2007*

⊞**VIHIERS** *4G1* (10km SE Rural) **Camping Le Serpolin, St Pierre-à-Champ, 49560 Cléré-sur-Layon [02 41 52 43 08; fax 02 41 52 39 18; info@ loirecamping.com; www.loirecamping.com]** Take D748 S fr Vihiers by-pass sp Argenton Château. In 2km turn L at sp Cléré-sur-Layon onto D54. Cont thro vill to 1st mkd x-rd, turn R, site last house along this lane. Sm, pt shd; htd wc; chem disp; shwrs inc; el pnts (6A) €4; lndtte; ice; BBQ; playgrnd; pool; fishing; cycle hire; dogs free; Eng spkn; adv bkg rec (dep req); quiet; CCI. "Peaceful, CL-type site nr vineyards; v clean san facs; v helpful & enthusiastic young British owners; fruit & vegetables in ssn; rallies by arrangement; conv major towns, chateaux, mkts & attractions inc Futuroscope; Doué-la-Fontaine zoo; Puy du Fou theme park; vg." € 12.00
2007*

VIHIERS *4G1* (1km W Rural) **Camp Municipal le la Vallée du Lys, Route du Voide, 49310 Vihiers [02 41 75 00 14 or 02 41 75 80 60 (Mairie); fax 02 41 75 58 01; ville.vihiers@wanadoo.fr; http:// vihiers.free.fr]** W of Vihiers leave D960 onto D54 twds Valanjou, & within 150m bear L at 1st fork in rd. Sm, mkd pitch, pt shd; wc; shwrs inc; el pnts (6A) €1.91; lndry rm; shop; playgrnd; coarse fishing; games area; 15% statics; some rd noise; CCI. "Surcharge for twin-axles; san facs excel, warden v helpful; narr ent to some pitches; rec." ♦ 25 May-1 Sep. € 6.55
2007*

VILLARD DE LANS *9C3* (800m N Rural) **Camping Caravaneige L'Oursière, 38250 Villard-de-Lans [04 76 95 14 77; fax 04 76 95 58 11; info@ camping-oursiere.fr; www.camping-oursiere.fr]** Site clearly visible on app to town fr D531 Gorges d'Engins rd (13km SW Grenoble). App fr W on D531 not rec for c'vans. Lge, terr, unshd; htd wc (some cont); chem disp; mv service pnt; baby facs; shwrs inc; el pnts (6-10A) €3.50-6; gas; ice; lndtte; shops; snacks; rest; BBQ; playgrnd; pool, waterspark 800m; drying rm; 20% statics; dogs €0.80; poss cr; adv bkg; quiet; cc acc; CCI. "Excel all winter sports; friendly, helpful owners." ♦ 3 Dec-30 Sep. € 21.50
2006*

⊞**VILLARD DE LANS** *9C3* (10km N Rural) **Camping Caravaneige Les Buissonnets, 38112 Méaudre [04 76 95 21 04; fax 04 76 95 26 14; camping-les-buissonnets@wanadoo.fr; www.camping-les-buissonnets.com]** NE o'skts of Méaudre off D106, approx 30km SW of Grenoble by rd & 18km as crow flies. Med, sl, unshd; htd wc; chem disp; mv service pnt; shwrs inc; el pnts (2-10A) €2.20-8; lndtte; shops 500m; snacks; rest 500m; pool 300m; playgrnd; games area; bus to ski slopes; site clsd 5 Nov-mid-Dec; Eng spkn; quiet; higher price in winter. "Gd skiing cent; conv touring Vercours; levellers ess; highly rec." ♦ € 12.00 2007*

VILLARS COLMARS see Colmars *9D4*

VILLARS LES DOMBES *9A2* (Urban) **Camp Municipal Les Autières, Ave des Nations, 01330 Villars-les-Dombes [04 74 98 00 21 or 06 61 70 36 51 (mob)]** N fr Lyon on N83, site in town cent on R by sw pool. Lge, pt shd; wc; shwrs inc; el pnts €3; lndtte; ice; shop; rest; snacks; BBQ; playgrnd; pool adj; tennis; mini-golf; rv adj; entmnts; 50% static. "Popular NH; fine bird park 10 mins walk; tight security, barrier & pedestrian gate." ♦ 1 Apr-25 Sep. € 12.30 2004*

VILLECROZE LES GROTTES see Salernes *10F3*

VILLEDIEU LES POELES *1D4* (500m S Urban) **Camping des Chevaliers, 2 Impasse Pré de la Rose, 50800 Villedieu-les-Poêles [02 33 61 02 44; contact@camping-deschevaliers; www. camping-deschevaliers.com]** Exit A84 junc 38 onto D999 twd Villedieu, then R onto D975 (N175) & R onto D924 to avoid town cent. Foll sp fr car park on R after x-ing rv. Med, hdg/mkd pitch, pt shd; wc (some cont); chem disp; mv service pnt; shwrs inc; baby facs; el pnts (6-8A) €2; lndtte; ice; shop 500m; supmkt 2km; rest, snacks, & bar 500m; playgrnd; rv fishing; boating; tennis; entmnt; TV rm; dogs €1; phone; poss cr; Eng spkn; adv bkg; quiet; red low ssn; CCI. "Peaceful site; sh walk to delightful, historic town founded by Knights of St John; copper, pewter & lace workshops, bell foundry worth visit; mini-train avail Jul/Aug; lge pitches but kerbs poss diff lger o'fits; site gates clsd 2200-0700; site yourself if office clsd; avoid arr Tue am due mkt; conv for Cherbourg ferry." ♦ ltd. 30 Mar-31 Oct. € 13.00 2007*

See advertisement on next page

VILLEFAGNAN see Ruffec *7A2*

VILLEFORT (LOZERE) *9D1* (3.4km N Rural) **Camping Morangiés - Le Lac, 48800 Villefort [04 66 46 81 27; fax 04 66 69 77 49; jo.genti.le@ libertysurf.fr; www.campinglelac.com]** Well sp on D906 nr Villefort dir Pourcharesses. Steep access rd. Med, hdg/mkd pitch, terr, pt shd; wc; chem disp (wc); baby facs; shwrs inc; el pnts inc; lndtte; tradsmn (high ssn); playgrnd; pool (high ssn); lake sw; some statics; dogs €1; poss cr; Eng spkn; adv bkg. "Diff access to terr for lge o'fits; gd." 1 May-30 Sep. € 15.20 2006*

VILLEFORT (LOZERE) *9D1* (600m S Rural) **Camp Municipal Les Sédaries, Route d'Alès, 48800 Villefort [04 66 46 84 33; fax 04 66 46 89 66; sedaries.villefort@wanadoo.fr]** On D906 heading S fr Villefort twd Alès. Sm, terr, pt shd; wc; chem disp (wc); shwrs inc; el pnts (6A) €2; lndtte; shops, rest, bar in town; BBQ; lake sw, fishing 2km; dogs €1; phone; poss cr; quiet; CCI. "Attractive site in beautiful Lozère mountains; bureau clsd 1000-1830; diff access upper terr." 1 Jun-30 Sep. € 7.00
2006*

VILLEFRANCHE DE CONFLENT see Prades *8G4*

France

⊞**VILLEFRANCHE DE LAURAGAIS** *8F3* (8km SW Rural) Camping Le Lac de la Thésauque, Nailloux, 31560 Montgeard [05 61 81 34 67; fax 05 61 81 00 12; camping-thesauque@caramail. com; www.camping-thesauque.com] Fr S exit A61 at Villefrance-de-Lauragais junc 20 onto D622, foll sp Auterive then Lac after Gardouch vill, site sp. Fr N turn off A61 at 1st junc after tolls S of Toulouse onto A66 (sp Foix). Leave A66 at junc 1 & foll sp Nailloux. Turn L on ent vill onto D662 & in 2km turn R onto D25 & immed R to site, sp. Med, mkd pitch, hdstg, terr, pt shd; htd wc; chem disp; shwrs inc; el pnts (6-10A) inc; lndtte; shop; rest; snacks; bar; BBQ; playgrnd; fishing; boating; 70% statics; dogs €1; poss cr; red low ssn; CCI. "Lovely, peaceful location conv for A61; scenic walk around lake; steep app to sm terr pitches poss diff lge o'fits; v ltd facs low ssn & poss cold water only; gd security; gd for m'vans." € 17.70   2007*

VILLEFRANCHE DE ROUERGUE *7D4* (9km SE) Camping Le Muret, 12200 St Salvadou [05 65 81 80 69 or 05 65 29 84 87; info@lemuret. com; www.lemuret.com] Fr Villefranche on D911 twd Millau, R on D905A sp camping & foll camping sp 7km. Sm, hdg/mkd pitch, shd; wc; shwrs inc; el pnts (16A) €4.50; gas & ice at farm; lndtte; shops 9km; tradsmn; rest; snacks; bar; lake adj; fishing; dogs €2; phone; adv bkg; v quiet; red long stay; CCI. "Attractive farmland setting." ♦ 1 Apr-27 Oct. € 14.50   2007*

VILLEFRANCHE DE ROUERGUE *7D4* (1km SW Urban) Camping du Rouergue, 35b Ave de Fondies, Le Teulel, 12200 Villefranche-de-Rouergue [tel/fax 05 65 45 16 24; camping rouergue@wanadoo.fr; www.villefranche.com/ camping] Best app fr N on D922, then D47 dir Monteils & Najac; avoid 1-way system in town; ent thro sports stadium. Site well sp. Med, hdg/ mkd pitch, hdstg, shd; wc (some cont); chem disp; mv service pnt; baby facs; serviced pitches; shwrs inc; el pnts (16A) €3; lndtte; shop; tradsmn; rest; snacks; bar; playgrnd; pool; sports stadium adj; tennis 1km; entmnt; TV rm; 15% statics; dogs €1; extra charge for twin-axles; Eng spkn; adv bkg (30% dep); quiet; cc acc; red low ssn/long stay/CCI. "Clean, well-kept, peaceful, gd value site; friendly owners; excel san facs; lge pitches; v helpful wardens; gd security; m'van services outside site; nr Najac medieval vill; rvside path to beautiful 'Bastide Royal' town 15 mins." ♦ 14 Apr-30 Sep. € 14.00   2007*

See advertisement below

VILLEFRANCHE DU PERIGORD *7D3* (1km E) FFCC Camping La Bastide, Route de Cahors, 24550 Villefranche-du-Périgord [05 53 28 94 57; fax 05 53 29 47 95; campinglabastide@wanadoo. fr; www.camping-la-bastide.com] On N660 fr Villefranche-du-Périgord dir Cahors; site past Post Office on R nr top of hill on town o'skts. Med, hdg/mkd pitch, terr, pt shd; wc; chem disp; mv service pnt; baby facs; shwrs inc; el pnts (6-10A) €3-4; lndtte; ice; shops 300m; rest; snacks; bar; playgrnd; pool; tennis 300m; fishing; entmnt; 25% statics; dogs €1; poss cr; adv bkg; quiet; CCI. "Steep, terr site but easy access; easy walk to vill; charming owners (also gd cooks); excel touring base; vg." ♦ ltd. 31 Mar-10 Nov. € 17.00   2007*

VILLEFRANCHE DU PERIGORD *7D3* (6km SW Rural) Camping Moulin du Périé, 47500 Sauveterre-la-Lémance [05 53 40 67 26; fax 05 53 40 62 46; moulinduperie@wanadoo.fr; www.camping-moulin-perie.com] Fr Périgueux foll dir Brive; after 8km turn R onto D710 & foll rd S. Rd numbers change briefly to D31, D51 & D25 bet Le Bugue & Siorac-en-Périgord & then cont D710. In dir of Fumel after turn off to Villefranche-du-Périgord, in Sauveterre-la-Lémance turn L at traff lts nr PO, over level x-ing. Cont strt down main rd & turn L bef cemetary (sp) & foll camping sp for 3km dir Loubejac to site on R. Tight ent to site. Med, pt sl, pt shd; wc; chem disp; mv service pnt; baby facs; shwrs inc; el pnts (6A) inc (poss rev pol); gas; lndtte; ice; shop; rest; snacks; bar; BBQ; playgrnd; pool; paddling pool; sm lake & beach; trout fishing - current British licence helpful; tennis 3km; horseriding 18km; cycle hire; archery; organised activities; microlight flying; internet; games/TV rm; 25% statics; dogs €2.20-4.20; poss cr; Eng spkn; adv bkg rec; quiet; cc acc; CCI. "Beautiful, extremely well-run site; v warm welcome; friendly family owners; attention to detail maintained even low ssn; san facs spotless; red facs low ssn; poss overhanging bushes; vg rest open all ssn; gd touring base; site rds narr; a bit remote; highly rec." ♦ 7 May-21 Sep. € 26.55 (CChq acc) ABS - D09   2007*

VILLEFRANCHE DU QUEYRAN see Casteljaloux *7D2*

VILLEFRANCHE SUR CHER *4G3* (9km SE) Camp Municipal Val Rose, Rue de Val Rose, 41320 Mennetou-sur-Cher [02 54 98 11 02 or 02 54 98 01 19 (Mairie)] Site sp fr N76 fr Villefranche; site on R at end of vill of Mennetou. Sm, pt shd; wc; chem disp; shwrs inc; el pnts €1.80; lndtte; snacks & shops adj; rest in town; playgrnd; pool adj; rv sw 1km; adv bkg; quiet. "Gem of a site; well-kept & clean; pretty, walled town 5 mins walk along canal; excel san facs; friendly warden; excel baker nr; mkt Thurs; gd." ♦ 2 May-5 Sep. € 5.50   2007*

VILLEFRANCHE SUR CHER *4G3* (10km SE Rural) Camp Municipal Les Saules, 41320 Châtres-sur-Cher [02 54 98 04 55 or 02 54 98 03 24 (Mairie); fax 02 54 98 09 57; chatres-sur-cher@cg41.fr] Site off N76 in Châtres-sur-Cher bet Villefranche & Vierzon. Med, pt shd; wc; shwrs inc; el pnts (5A) €1.80; ice; shops & rests nrby; playgrnd; sand beach adj; rv sw, fishing & watersports adj; 10% statics; adv bkg; quiet; CCI. "Lovely, well-kept site on rv; friendly warden; facs old but v clean; gd NH." 1 May-31 Aug. € 6.25   2007*

VILLEFRANCHE SUR SAONE *9B2* (3km E Urban) Camp Municipal Plan d'Eau (also called La Plage), 2788 Route de Riottier, 69400 Villefranche-sur-Saône [04 74 65 33 48; fax 04 74 60 68 18; campingvillefranche@voila.fr] Exit A6 (Lyon-Paris) junc 31.2 Villefranche. Fr N turn R at rndabt, cross under a'route & str over next rndabt; cont to site on R bef Rv Saône. Or fr S turn R at rndabt & cont to site as above. Look for sp on rndabt. Med, unshd; wc (some cont); chem disp; mv service pnt; shwrs inc; el pnts (6A) inc (poss rev pol); gas; lndry rm; shop 1km; tradsmn; snacks in ssn; bar; lake sw adj; fishing; 10% statics; adv bkg; quiet; cc acc; CCI. "Easy access & nr a'rte but quiet; run down low ssn (Sep 2007); gd walking." ♦ 29 Apr-30 Sep. € 15.30   2007*

VILLEFRANCHE SUR SAONE *9B2* (10km E Rural) Camp Municipal le Bois de la Dame, 01480 Ars-sur-Formans [04 74 00 77 23 or 04 74 00 71 84 (Mairie); fax 04 74 08 10 62; mairie.ars-sur-formans@wanadoo.fr] Exit A6 junc 31.1 or 31.2 onto D131/D44 E dir Villars-les-Dombes. Site 500m W of Ars-sur-Formans on lake, sp. Med, mkd pitch, pt sl, terr, pt shd; wc (cont); chem disp; shwrs inc; el pnts (6A) €2; lndtte; playgrnd; fishing lake; 60% statics; dogs €1.22; poss cr; adv bkg rec high ssn; CCI. "Ltd facs low ssn; twin-axle vans not acc; office clsd 1400-1600; pilgrimage vill with museum; excel." ♦ 1 Apr-30 Sep. € 8.00   2007*

VILLEFRANCHE SUR SAONE *9B2* (6km SE) Camp Municipal La Petite Saône, 01600 Trévoux [tel/fax 04 74 00 14 16 or 04 74 08 73 73 (Mairie)] Fr Villefranche take D306 (N6) S to Anse. Turn L onto D39/D6 for Trévoux, site sp in town, on bank of Rv Saône. Lge, pt shd; wc (mainly cont); shwrs; el pnts (10A); shops 1km; playgrnd; rv fishing & sw adj; entmnts; 75% statics; adv bkg high ssn; quiet; 10% red CCI. "Spacious site; clean facs; some pitches taken up by permanent vans." 1 Apr-30 Sep. € 16.60   2005*

VILLEFRANCHE SUR SAONE *9B2* (5km S Rural) Camping Les Portes du Beaujolais, Chemin des Grandes-Levées, 69480 Anse [04 74 67 12 87; fax 04 74 09 90 97; campingbeaujolais@wanadoo. fr; www.camping-beaujolais.com] Exit A6 junc 31 at Villefranche & foll D306 S to Anse. Site well sp off D39, on banks of Rvs Saône & L'Azergues. Lge, hdg/mkd pitch, hdstg, pt shd; htd wc (some cont); chem disp; mv service pnt; shwrs inc; el pnts (6-10A) inc; lndtte; shop; snacks; bar; playgrnd; pool; lake sw; cycle hire; TV rm; 10% statics; dogs €3; phone; Eng spkn; adv bkg; rd noise fr A6 nrby; CCI. "Friendly site; super pitches but some sm, uneven pitches diff lge o'fits; ltd facs low ssn; gd base for Beaujolais region; Anse 10 mins walk; bus fr Anse to Lyons; narr gauge rlwy adj; conv NH." ♦ 1 Mar-31 Oct. € 18.70 (CChq acc) 2007*

VILLENEUVE DE BERG *9D2* (2km N Rural) **Camping Domaine Le Pommier, 07170 Villeneuve-de-Berg [04 75 94 82 81; fax 04 75 94 83 90; info@campinglepommier.com; www.campinglepommier.com]** Site off rndabt at E end of by-pass to Villeneuve-de-Berg on N102. If app fr Aubenas do not go thro town. Steep incline, poss req tractor. Lge, mkd pitch, hdstg, terr, pt sl, pt shd; htd wc; chem disp; mv service pnt; baby facs; fam bthrm; shwrs inc; el pnts (6A) €4; lndtte; ice; supmkt; rest; snacks; bar; BBQ (gas); playgrnd; htd pools; waterslides; tennis; games area; games rm; cycle hire; wifi internet; entmnt; sound-proofed disco high ssn; TV rm; 30% statics; dogs €4; Eng spkn; adv bkg; quiet; cc acc; red low ssn/long stay; CCI. "Vg Dutch-owned site; superb pool complex; excel san facs; excursions high ssn." ♦ 28 Apr-30 Sep. € 29.50 2007*

See advertisement

VILLENEUVE DE LA RAHO see Perpignan *8G4*

VILLENEUVE LES GENETS see Bléneau *4G3*

VILLENEUVE LOUBET see Cagnes sur Mer *10E4*

⊞**VILLENEUVE SUR LOT** *7D3* (7km E Rural) Camping Le Sablon, 47140 St Sylvestre-sur-Lot [05 53 41 37 74; campinglesablon@wanadoo. fr] Fr Villeneuve E on D911 sp Cahors, after 5km on ent St Sylvestre site on R behind supmkt. Sm, hdg/mkd pitch, shd; htd wc; shwrs; el pnts (6-10A) €2.50-3.50; lndry rm; snacks; playgrnd; pools & paddling pool; waterslide; fishing; mini-golf; 25% statics; quiet. "Pleasant, family-owned site; interesting local sights; gd facs but run down low ssn; muddy when wet - no hdstg; poss itinerants; barrier clsd 1200-1400." € 10.00 2006*

VILLENEUVE SUR LOT *7D3* (8km E Urban) Camping Les Berges du Lot, Place de la Mairie, 47140 St Sylvestre-sur-Lot [05 53 41 22 23 or 05 53 41 24 58 (Mairie)] Exit Villeneuve on D911 sp Cahors. Site in cent of St Sylvestre-sur-Lot. Foll Camping sp to rear of La Mairie (Town Hall) & adj car park supmkt to R of main rd. Sm, mkd pitch, pt shd; wc; chem disp; shwrs inc; el pnts (16A) €2.50; shops adj; rest, bar 1km; sm pool; boating; fishing; birdwatching; Eng spkn; quiet. "Recep open 0800-1000 & 1600-2000; adv bkg rec high ssn; immac, popular site; helpful staff; gd views; Lot Valley cycle rtes." ♦ 15 May-30 Sep. € 6.50 2006*

VILLENEUVE SUR LOT *7D3* (1.5km S Urban) **Camp Municipal du Rooy, Rue de Rooy, 47300 Villeneuve-sur-Lot [05 53 70 24 18 or 05 53 36 17 30; tourisme.villeneuve-sur-lot@wanadoo.fr; www.ville-villeneuve-sur-lot.fr]** Site sp to E of N21. Med, mkd pitch, pt sl, terr, pt shd; wc (some cont); chem disp; shwrs inc; el pnts (6-10A) €1.50-2.30; lndtte; shops 2km; tradsmn; BBQ; pool nrby; rv 5m; 15% statics; dogs €0.30; phone; poss cr; no cc acc; quiet; CCI. "Nice, friendly site; helpful warden; some pitches poss flooded in bad weather (keep to L of site); san facs old but v clean." 15 Apr-30 Sep. € 6.60 2007*

VILLEREAL *7D3* (2km N Rural) **Camping Château de Fonrives, Route d'Issigeac, Rives, 47210 Villeréal [05 53 36 63 38; fax 05 53 36 09 98; contact@campingchateaufonrives.com; www. campingchateaufonrives.com]** Fr Bergerac take N21 S for 8km, turn L onto D14 thro Issigeac; site is just outside vill of Rives in grounds of chateau. Med, pt sl, pt shd; wc; baby facs; shwrs inc; el pnts (6A) €4.50; gas; lndtte; ice; shop; rest; bar; BBQ; playgrnd; pool; waterslide; lake sw; fishing; golf; cycle hire; games rm; entmnt; some statics; dogs €3; Eng spkn; adv bkg; quiet but some noise fr weekly disco; cc acc; CCI. "Spacious site; gd, lge pool; van poss manhandled on some shady pitches; easier access pitches without shade; v friendly owners; B&B avail; interesting town; mkt Sat am." ♦ 1 May-30 Sep. € 24.50   2007*

VILLEREAL *7D3* (7km NE Rural) **Camping Le Moulin de Mandassagne, 47210 Parranquet [tel/ fax 05 53 36 04 02; ipimougu@fr.packardbell.com; www.haut-agenais-perigord.com]** Fr D104/D2 bet Villeréal & Monpazier turn N sp Parranquet, site sp. Sm, mkd pitch, pt shd; wc; chem disp; shwrs inc; el pnts (6A); gas; lndry rm; ice; shop adj; snacks; playgrnd; pool; sand beach 6km; fishing; tennis; entmnt; TV; Eng spkn; adv bkg; v quiet. "Lovely countryside." ♦ 1 May-1 Oct. € 12.80   2004*

VILLEREAL *7D3* (3km SE Rural) **Camping Les Ormes, Fauquié-Haut, 47210 St Etienne-de-Villeréal [05 53 36 60 26; fax 05 53 36 69 90; info@ campinglesormes.com; www.campinglesormes. com]** Take D255 SE fr Villeréal. At fork in rd in 1km, take RH rd sp St Etienne-de-Villeréal. Site on R in 2km. Med, mkd pitch, pt shd; wc; chem disp; baby facs; shwrs inc; el pnts (4A) €3; gas; lndtte; ice; shop; tradsmn; rest; snacks; bar; BBQ; playgrnd; pool; lake fishing; tennis; games rm; entmnt; TV; 10% statics; dogs €3 (not acc high ssn); phone; poss cr; Eng spkn; adv bkg; quiet; red low ssn; CCI. "Excel site; highly rec early & late summer; busy high ssn." 29 Apr-30 Sep. € 22.00   2007*

VILLEREAL *7D3* (10km SE Rural) **Camping Fontaine du Roc, Les Moulaties, 47210 Dévillac [05 53 36 08 16; fax 05 53 61 60 23; fontaine. du.roc@wanadoo.fr; www.fontaineduroc.com]** Fr Villeréal take D255 sp Dévillac, just beyond Dévillac at x-rds turn L & L again sp Estrade; site on L in 500m. Med, hdg/mkd pitch, hdstg, pt shd; wc; chem disp; shwrs inc; el pnts (5A) €3 gas; lndtte; ice; shop 7km; tradsmn; rest; snacks; bar; BBQ; playgrnd; pool; paddling pool; cycle hire; games rm; TV; 2% statics; dogs €3; phone; Eng spkn; adv bkg; quiet; red low ssn/long stay; no cc acc; CCI. "Delightful, peaceful setting; v helpful owner; site v well-cared for; lge pitches; lge pool; views of Château Biron; interesting towns nrby." 1 May-30 Sep. € 17.00   2006*

VILLEREAL *7D3* (3km NW Rural) **Aire Naturelle de Bergougne (Bru), 47210 Rives [05 53 36 01 30; fax 05 53 36 05 41; info@camping-de-bergougne. com; www.camping-de-bergougne.com]** Fr Villeréal, take D207 NW sp Issigeac/Bergerac. In 1km turn L onto D250 W sp Doudrac. Foll sm green sp to site. Sm, hdg pitch, pt sl, unshd; wc; chem disp; shwrs inc; el pnts (6A) inc; lndtte; rest; bar 3km; snacks; playgrnd; pool; fishing; games area; games rm; dogs €2; adv bkg (dep req). 15 May-30 Sep. € 14.70   2007*

VILLERS BOCAGE *3D1* (7km S Urban) **Camp Municipal La Closerie, Rue de Caen, 14260 Aunay-sur-Odon [02 31 77 32 46; fax 02 31 77 70 07; mairie.aunay.sur.odon@wanadoo. fr]** Exit A84 junc 43 sp Villers-Bocage/Aunay & take D6 twd Aunay. In approx 5km bef Aunay town sp, turn L sp 'Zone Industrielle', in 200m turn R at rndabt. Site on R in 100m. Sm, mkd pitch, pt sl, pt shd; wc; chem disp; shwrs inc; el pnts inc; gas; shops 500m; games area; dogs €1.55; quiet; CCI. "Barrier never clsed; warden calls." ♦ ltd. 1 Jul-31 Aug. € 15.00   2007*

VILLERS BOCAGE *3D1* (6km SW Rural) **Camping Vallée de Graham, 14240 Cahagnes [02 31 77 88 18 or 06 72 12 10 40 (mob)]** Fr cent Cahagnes on D54 then take D193 for 2km; sp fr town sq; 1.5km narr app rd is 1-way. Med, pt sl, pt shd; wc; shwrs inc; el pnts (6A) inc; lndry rm; shops 3km; snacks; fishing; boating; quiet. "Excel view over lakes & countryside; poss to stay low ssn; site yourself, warden calls; dated facs; still v peaceful." 1 Jun-30 Sep. € 12.20   2007*

VILLERS COTTERETS *3D4* (7km NE) **Camping Castel des Biches, Parc du Château Alexandre Dumas, 02600 Villers-Hélon [03 23 72 93 93; fax 03 23 72 93 33; acceuil@castel-des-biches.com; www.castel-des-biches.com]** Site S of Soissons bet N2 & D1; exit Soissons S on D1 sp Château-Thierry, turn R sp Villers-Hélon, foll sp. Med, mkd pitch, pt shd; htd wc; shwrs inc; el pnts (10A) €3.90; gas; lndtte; playgrnd; paddling pool; fishing; cycle hire; games area; 80% statics; adv bkg; quiet. 1 Apr-31 Oct. € 13.10   2004*

VILLERS HELON see Villers Cotterêts *3D4*

VILLERS LES NANCY see Nancy *6E2*

VILLERS SIRE NICOLE see Maubeuge *3B4*

VILLERS SUR AUTHIE see Rue *3B2*

VILLES SUR AUZON see Mormoiron *10E2*

France

⊞**VILLEVAUDE** *3D3* (2km E Rural) **Camping Le Parc de Paris, Rue Adèle Claret, Montjay-la-Tour, 77410 Villevaudé [01 60 26 20 79; fax 01 60 27 02 75; camping.leparc@club-internet. fr; www.campingleparc.fr]** Fr N, A1 twds Paris, then A104 to Marne-la-Vallée, exit at junc 6B (Paris Bobigny), then D105 to Villevaudé, then to Montjay & site sp. Fr S exit A104 at junc 8 to Meaux & Villevaudé. Lge, hdg/mkd pitch, pt shd; htd wc; serviced pitches; chem disp; mv service pnt; baby facs; shwrs inc; el pnts (6A) €3; lndtte; shop 5km; tradsmn; rest high ssn; snacks; bar; playgrnd; waterpark; lake sw & sand beach 5km; tennis 200m; games area; TV rm; 30% statics; dogs €1.50; phone; Eng spkn; adv bkg; cc acc; CCI. "V conv Disneyland, Paris, Parc Astérix; gd san facs; twin-axles acc if adv bkg." ♦ € 26.00   2007*

See advertisement

VILLIERS CHARLEMAGNE see Chateau Gontier *4F1*

VILLIERS LE MORHIER see Maintenon *4E2*

⊞**VILLIERS SUR ORGE** *4E3* (600m SE Urban) **Camping Le Beau Village, Voie des Prés, 91700 Villiers-sur-Orge [01 60 16 17 86 or 01 60 16 17 88; fax 01 60 16 31 46; le-beau-village@wanadoo.fr; www.beau-village.com]** Rec app fr N20, exit sp La Ville-du-Bois & Carrefour. Take rd for Villiers-sur-Orge & turn R at traff lts with sm Renault g'ge. Site sp 200m on L. Care needed on app due to narr rds. Med, hdg pitch, pt shd, htd wc; chem disp; shwrs inc; el pnts (10A) €3.50 (poss rev pol); gas; lndtte; shops 1km; tradsmn; bar; playgrnd; kayaking; dogs €2; phone; train 700m; site clsd mid-Dec to mid-Jan; poss cr; quiet; red low ssn. "Well-run site but poss neglected statics; pleasant orchard; train to Paris 25 mins; ltd space for lge o'fits." € 14.50   2005*

VIMOUTIERS *3D1* (700m NW Urban) **Camp Municipal La Campière, Blvd Dentu, 61120 Vimoutiers [02 33 39 30 29 or 02 33 39 18 86 (Mairie); fax 02 33 36 51 43; campingmunicipalvimoutiers@wanadoo.fr; www.mairie-vimoutiers.fr]** App on D579 or D916 or D979 bet Lisieux & Argental. Site nr stadium. Sm, hdg pitch, pt shd; htd wc; chem disp; shwrs inc; el pnts (6A) €2; lndry rm; shop 200m; rest, snacks 800m; playgrnd adj; pool & sports facs 2km; rv fishing, sw & boating 2km; tennis; cycle hire; 10% statics; dogs €1.15; poss cr; adv bkg; noise fr nrby factory; red low ssn; CCI. "Excel, well-maintained, pretty site at cent of Camembert cheese industry; helpful, friendly warden; vg, clean san facs; ent poss tight for lge o'fits; attractive town within easy walk; vg value." ♦ 1 Mar-1 Nov. € 9.70   2007*

VINCELLES see Auxerre *4F4*

VINSOBRES see Nyons *9D2*

VIOLES see Orange *10E2*

VION see Tournon sur Rhône *9C2*

⊞**VIRIEU LE GRAND** *9B3* (5km NE Rural) **Camping Le Vaugrais (formerly Municipal), 01510 Artemare [04 79 87 37 34; fax 04 79 87 37 46; www.camping-le-vaugrais.fr]** N fr Belley on D1504 (N504) then D904 to Artemare; sp in vill. Well sp fr D904 on rvside. Sm, pt shd, hdg pitch; wc (some cont); chem disp (wc); baby facs; shwrs inc; el pnts (5A) €2.40; lndtte; ice; shop 500m; tradsmn; snacks; bar; BBQ; playgrnd; pool; fishing; wifi internet; 1% statics; dogs €1; Eng spkn; adv bkg; quiet; CCI. "Charming site; lge pitches with gd views; v friendly owner; v clean san facs, poss inadequate high ssn; Artemare within walking dist; interesting area; excel." ♦ ltd. € 12.00   2007*

VIRIEU LE GRAND *9B3* (1km S Rural) **Camping du Lac, 01510 Virieu-le-Grand [tel/fax 04 79 87 82 02]** Fr D904 site sp on L 1km past Virieu-le-Grand. Uneven app. Med, terr, hdg pitch, pt shd; wc; mv service pnt; shwrs inc; el pnts (6A) inc; ice; tradsmn; shops 4km; playgrnd; cycle hire; lake beach, sw & fishing; some rd & rlwy noise. "Clean, pleasant lakeside site; v clean facs; helpful owner; views of lake fr most pitches." Jun-15 Sep. € 13.50   2004*

VISAN see Valréas *9D2*

VITRAC see Sarlat la Canéda *7C3*

VITRE *2F4* (N Rural) **Camp Municipal du Lac, 35210 Châtillon-en-Vendelais [02 99 76 06 32 or 02 99 76 06 22 (Mairie); fax 02 99 76 12 39]** Take D178 fr Vitré to Fougères. In 11km branch L onto D108, sp Châtillon-en-Vendelais. Foll sp thro vill for 'Camping du Lac', turning R immed after rlwy level x-ing & bef bdge; site in 1km. Med, pt sl, pt shd; wc; shwrs inc; el pnts (6A) €2.56 (poss rev pol); lndtte; ice; shop & 1km; playgrnd; tennis; lake adj; fishing; 10% statics; quiet; CCI. "Nature reserve (birds) nr; warden on site 0930-1030 only; pleasant site; v quiet low ssn; gd walks, birdwatching; clean vg san facs." 15 May-30 Sep. € 6.67   2006*

VITRE *2F4* (2km SE Urban) **Camp Municipal Ste Etienne, Route d'Argentré-du-Plessis, 35500 Vitré [02 99 75 25 28 or 02 99 74 43 53; fax 02 99 74 04 12]** Exit A11 at junc 5 onto D857 twd Vitré. Take Vitré ring rd twd Rennes; 500m fr ring rd S on D88 twd Argentré-du-Plessis & foll camp sp. Sm, hdg pitch, pt sl, shd; wc (some cont); chem disp (wc); mv service pnt; shwrs inc; el pnts (10A) €2; ice; shop 1km; supmkt 800m; sports complex adj; 25% statics; dogs; quiet; cc not acc; CCI. "Gd size pitches but access to some poss diff; pitch yourself; no security; ltd office hrs; gd rests in town." 1 Apr-31 Oct. € 7.00   2005*

France

VITRY AUX LOGES *4F3* (3.5km N Rural) **Camping Etang de la Vallée**, Seichebrières, 45530 Vitry-aux-Loges [02 38 59 35 77; fax 02 38 46 82 92; canal.orleans@wanadoo.fr; http://canal.orleans.monsite.wanadoo.fr] Fr junc of N60, E60 & D952 N of Châteauneuf-sur-Loire take D10 N. In Vitry-aux-Loges foll sp Seichbrières, site sp of R just outside vill. Lge, mkd pitch, shd; htd wc; chem disp (wc); shwrs inc; el pnts (10A) €3.70; lndtte; tradsmn; snacks, bar 100m; lake sw 100m; phone; adv bkg; quiet; CCI. "Gd forest walking; conv Orléans; fishing & watersports nr." ♦ 1 Apr-1 Oct. € 9.50
2006*

VITRY LE FRANCOIS *6E1* (4km SE Rural) **Aire Naturelle Camping Nature (Scherschell)**, 13 Rue de l'Evangile, 51300 Luxémont-et-Villotte [03 26 72 61 14 or 06 83 42 83 53 (mob)] Fr Châlons sp on N4 at E end of Vitry-le-François by-pass, foll sp to R, then foll 3km to site. Fr S take exit for Vitry & pass lorry park, in approx 1km, turn L at rndabt to site. Sm, pt sl, pt shd; wc (some cont); own san facs; chem disp; mv service pnt; shwrs inc; el pnts (6A) inc (poss rev pol); gas 2km; shop 6km; tradsmn; BBQ; playgrnd; lake sw 500m; fishing; adv bkg; quiet; CCI. "Delightful, quiet site in trees & farmland; well maintained; v helpful & friendly owners; no twin-axles; excel." 1 May-1 Oct. € 12.00
2007*

VITRY LE FRANCOIS *6E1* (2km W Urban) **Camp Municipal La Peupleraie**, Quai des Fontaines, 51300 Vitry-le-François [03 26 74 20 47 or 03 26 41 22 77 (Mairie); fax 03 26 41 22 88] Fr N on N44 turn R at lge gate (sp Paris) & cont on dual c'way for approx 1km. Turn R on side rd, site sp nr lge parking area. Med, hdg pitch, pt shd; wc; shwrs inc; el pnts (5A) inc; gas; shops adj; rest, snacks, bar 500m; dogs €2; quiet, but some rd noise. "Delightful site; tight ent poss diff lge o'fits." 1 Jun-30 Sep. € 9.40
2005*

The opening dates and prices on this campsite have changed. I'll send a site report form to the editor for the next edition of the guide.

VITTEAUX *6G1* (1km W Rural) **Camp Municipal La Gare**, 21350 Vitteaux [03 80 49 60 87 or 03 80 49 61 25 (Mairie)] Sp fr vill nr Hippodrome. Sm, hdg pitch, shd; wc; chem disp (wc); shwrs inc; el pnts (6A) €2.50; lndry rm; rest, snacks & bar 1km; BBQ; playgrnd; htd covrd pool nr; dogs €1; quiet. "In cent Burgundy; part of sports complex; new facs 2005; warden calls am & pm; pick your spot; no security barrier." ♦ 15 Mar-1 Nov. € 6.50
2005*

VITTEL *6F2* (1km NE) **Camping de Vittel, Rue Claude Bassot, 88800 Vittel [03 29 08 02 71; aquadis1@wanadoo.fr; www.aquadis-loisirs. com]** Fr Chaumont/Dijon at traff lts take Epinal/Nancy rd into Place Gen de Gaulle; turn L over bdge & foll sp. Fr Epinal turn R over bdge at Place Gen de Gaulle & foll sp. Med, hdg/mkd pitch, hdstg, pt shd; htd wc (mainly cont); chem disp; shwrs inc; el pnts (6A) inc; lndtte; shop 1km; tradsmn; pool. Tennis 2km; dogs €2; poss cr; Eng spkn; adv bkg; quiet; CCI. "Immac site; friendly warden; sh walk into interesting town with spa/hydro/racecourse park; walking & cycling rtes; recep clsd 1200-1500; excel." 1 Apr-30 Oct. € 18.00   2007*

VIVIER SUR MER, LE see Dol de Bretagne *2E4*

VIVIERS *9D2* (1km N Urban) **Camping Rochecondrie, 07220 Viviers [tel/fax 04 75 52 74 66; campingrochecondrie@wanadoo. fr]** Fr site 1km N of Viviers (dir Le Teil); ent on E side of N86. Fr N ent for S'bound traff tricky - rec cont past site to junc with D107, turn W (dir Aubenas) & turn around; app fr S as bef. Med, mkd pitch, pt shd; wc (some cont); chem disp; el pnts (6A) inc; gas; lndtte; BBQ; rest & bar high ssn; playgrnd; pool high ssn; fishing; 30% statics; dogs €1; phone; Eng spkn; rlwy noise; red low ssn; cc acc; CCI. "Resident llamas; sm shwr cubicles; nr to Ardèche gorges, canoe & raft excursions; Viviers interesting medieval vill with Roman bdge." ◆ ltd. 1 Apr-15 Oct. € 21.50   2005*

VIVONNE *7A2* (500m E Rural) **Camp Municipal, Chemin de Prairie, 86370 Vivonne [05 49 43 41 05 (Mairie); fax 05 49 43 34 87; vivonne@cg86.fr]** Exit N10 where it by-passes Vivonne & ent town. Site in municipal park to E of town. Med, pt shd; wc; shwrs inc; el pnts inc; lndtte; playgrnd; pool; waterslide adj; noisy fr busy rlwy, at w/e & at nights. "Warden resident on site; v welcoming & helpful; v clean facs; gd for wheelchair users." ◆ 15 May-15 Sep. € 9.55   2005*

VIZILLE *9C3* (500m N Urban) **FFCC Camping Le Bois de Cornage (formerly Municipal), Chemin du Camping, 38220 Vizille [tel/fax 04 76 68 12 39; campingvizille@wanadoo.fr; www.campingvizille. com]** Site sp at x-rds of Rte Napoléon (N85) & Rte de Briançon (N91). Site on N outskirts of town. Well sp. Med, hdg/mkd pitch, pt sl, terr, shd; wc; chem disp; mv service pnt; baby facs; shwrs inc; el pnts (6-10A) €2.80-3.30 (long lead poss req); gas 500m; lndtte; shops 200m; supmkt 500m; tradsmn; rest; snacks; bar; playgrnd; htd pool; gd cycling & climbing nrby; 10% statics; dogs €0.80; no vans over 5m permitted; poss v cr; Eng spkn; adv bkg rec high ssn; quiet; red long stay/low ssn; CCI. "V helpful owner; excel clean facs; pizzeria on site; mkd walks nrby; poss mosquitoes; visit Château de Vizille; La Mure tourist rlwy; Grenoble, Vercors & Chartreuse Monastry; excel value; vg." 25 Apr-30 Sep. € 13.90   2007*

VIZILLE *9C3* (7km S) **Camp Municipal Les Grands Sagnes, 38220 Laffrey [04 76 73 10 21 or 04 76 73 11 37]** Exit Grenoble on N85. S thro Vizille to Laffrey. Steep climb on narr rd. Site 200m S of vill at top of steep hill on Rte Napoléon. Site sp fr town. Med, pt sl, pt shd; wc; shwrs inc; el pnts (6A) €3.10; shop in ssn; snacks; sw & watersports in lake; dogs €1; some rd noise. "Gd sized pitches; adj attractive lake with mountain views." 15 Jun-15 Sep. € 10.80   2006*

VOGUE see Aubenas *9D2*

VOIRON *9C3* (4km NE) **Camp Municipal de la Grande Forêt, 38960 St Etienne-de-Crossey [04 76 06 05 67]** Site sp on main rd D520 fr both Voiron & St Laurent-du-Pont bet Voiron & Chambéry. Clearly sp in vill sq. Site also sp fr D1075 (N75) Les Abrets-Voiron rd at Le Fagot. Sm, pt shd; wc; shwrs; el pnts inc (6A); shops 200m; playgrnd; quiet. "Well-laid out & maintained; ltd facs low ssn; but full price; pitches badly worn & muddy end of ssn (Sep)." 15 Jun-15 Sep. € 12.50   2004*

VOIRON *9C3* (10km E Rural) **Camping Le Balcon de Chartreuse, 950 Chemin de la Forêt, 38380 Miribel-les-Echelles [04 76 55 28 53; fax 04 76 55 25 82; balcondechartreuse@wanadoo. fr; www.camping-balcondechartreuse.com]** Fr N520 out of Voiron to St Etienne-de-Crossey. Then take D49 to Mirabel. Do not app with c'van fr Les Echelles. Med, terr, pt shd; wc; chem disp; shwrs inc; el pnts (6A) €4; lndtte; ice; shop 4km; rest; snacks; bar; playgrnd; pool; paddling pool; horseriding; tennis 1km; games area; entmnt; TV; 30% statics; dogs €1.50; poss cr; adv bkg rec; quiet; CCI. "Few touring pitches." 1 Apr-30 Oct. € 14.00   2007*

VOLONNE see Château Arnoux *10E3*

VOLVIC *9B1* (E Urban) **Camp Municipal Pierre et Sources, Rue de Chancelas, 63530 Volvic [04 73 33 50 16; fax 04 73 33 54 98; camping@ ville-volvic.fr; www.ville-volvic.fr]** Exit Riom on D986: foll sp for Pontgibaud & Volvic. Site sp to R on app to town. Sm, shd; htd wc; chem disp; mv service pnt; shwrs inc; e; pnts (10A) €3.50; lndte; sm shop; tradsmn; some statics; dogs €1.50; adv bkg; quiet. 15 Apr-31 Oct. € 13.00   2007*

VONNAS *9A2* (300m W Rural) **Camp Municipal Le Renom, Ave des Sports, 01540 Vonnas [04 74 50 02 75; fax 04 74 50 08 96; mairie@ vonnas.com]** Fr Bourg-en-Bresse take D1079 (N79) W sp Mâcon. In 15km take D26 or D47 S to Vonnas; turn R in town cent (ignore sp on o'skts of town) & site on R in 300m by leisure cent. Med, pt shd; wc; chem disp; baby facs; shwrs inc; el pnts (10A) €2; lndtte; shop 300m; BBQ; htd pool, tennis adj; rv fishing; dogs €0.85; quiet. "Gd mkt Thurs am; interesting, attractive town." ◆ ltd. 15 Apr-15 Oct. € 10.00   2006*

VOREY 9C1 (4km E Rural) **Camping Domaine du Pra de Mars**, 43800 Vorey-sur-Arzon [tel/fax 04 71 03 40 86; leprademars@wanadoo.fr; www. leprademars.com] On D103 dir Retournac. Med, hdg/mkd pitch, pt sl, pt shd; htd wc (some cont); chem disp; some serviced pitches; mv service pnt; baby facs; fam bthrm; shwrs inc; el pnts (5A) €2.90; lndtte; rest; snacks; bar; BBQ; htd pool; rv sw; dogs €1.50; bus; phone; Eng spkn; adv bkg; quiet; cc acc; CCI. "Welcoming owners; beautiful location; gd walking area; vg." 1 Apr-30 Sep. € 13.00
2005*

Before we move on, I'm going to fill in some site report forms and post them off to the editor, otherwise they won't arrive in time for the deadline at the end of September.

VOREY 9C1 (1.5km SW Rural) **Camping Les Moulettes**, Chemin de Félines, 43800 Vorey-sur-Arzon [04 71 03 70 48; fax 04 71 03 72 06; campinglesmoulettes@libertysurf.fr; www. camping-les-moulettes.fr] Fr Le Puy take D103 sp Vorey. Site sp in vill; L in main sq. Sm, hdg pitch, pt shd; wc; shwrs inc; el pnts (10A) €2.90; lndtte; shops in vill; snacks; bar; playgrnd; pool, waterslide adj; fishing adj; games area; some statics; dogs €1.50; Eng spkn; adv bkg; quiet. "Excel rest nrby - site will make res." ♦ 1 May-15 Sep. € 12.50
2006*

VOUECOURT 6E1 (Rural) **Camp Municipal Rives de Marne**, 52320 Vouécourt [03 25 02 44 46 (Mairie); commune-vouecourt@ wanadoo.fr] N fr Chaumont on N67; sp to site in 17km; thro vill by Rv Marne; well sp. Sm, mkd pitch; pt shd; wc (some cont); chem disp; shwr; el pnts (10A) €2.20 (poss rev pol); gas; shop 6km; tradsmn; playgrnd; rv sw; fishing; CCI. "Perfect location on bank of Rv Marne; attractive setting; gd sized pitches; antiquated but adequate san facs; baker calls am; warden calls each evening; rv known to flood in winter; nice forest walks nearby; excel cycling along canal towpath." 12 Apr-16 Oct. € 8.00
2007*

VOUILLE 4H1 (Urban) **Camp Municipal**, Chemin de la Piscine; 86190 Vouillé [05 49 51 90 10 (after 1800) or 05 49 54 20 30 (Mairie); fax 05 49 51 14 47; vouille@cg86.fr] Fr Parthenay take N149 twds Vouillé; go thro Vouillé & turn R onto D43 by Super U. At bottom of hill turn R twds town cent; site sp behind Cheval Blanc rest nr rvside. Sm, mkd pitch, shd; wc; chem disp (wc); shwrs inc; el pnts (3A) €2; ice; lndry rm; shop; supmkt 1km; rest 500m; bar; playgrnd adj; fishing; quiet. "Site yourself; useful NH; excel rest nrby; ideal Futuroscope." ♦ 15 May-30 Aug. € 6.00
2007*

VOULTE SUR RHONE, LA 9D2 (4km N Rural) **Camping La Garenne**, 07800 St Laurent-du-Pape [tel/fax 04 75 62 24 62; campinglagarenne@ freesurf.fr] Well sp fr La Voulte. Fr Valence S on N86 La Voulte, approx 15km turn W onto D120; 300m after St Laurent-du-Pape cent, turn R bef PO. Med, pt terr, pt shd; wc; chem disp; shwrs inc; el pnts (4A) inc; gas; lndtte; ice; shop 1km; rest; snacks; bar; playgrnd; pool; dogs €1.70; poss v cr; Eng spkn; adv bkg; quiet; red long stay; CCI. "V helpful owners; magnificent view fr terr pitches." ♦ 1 Mar-1 Nov. € 28.50
2004*

VOULTE SUR RHONE, LA 9D2 (4km NE Rural) **Camp Municipal Les Voiliers**, 07800 Beauchastel [04 75 62 24 04; fax 04 75 62 42 32] Site 30km S of Tournon on N86, 500m E of Beauchastel sp in town, over canal, past hydro. Med, terr, shd; htd wc (cont); snacks; shwrs inc; el pnts (5A) inc; lndtte; ice; shops 500m; snacks; bar; BBQ; playgrnd; pool; rv sw; 15% statics; dogs €1.07; poss cr; quiet. "V friendly; gd san facs." 1 Apr-31 Oct. € 13.50
2006*

VOUVRAY 4G2 (500m S Urban) **Camp Municipal du Bec de Cisse**, 37210 Vouvray [02 47 52 68 81; fax 02 47 52 67 76] Travelling E on N152 fr Tours for about 6km, turn R at traff lts in Vouvray; site on L in 200m adj to rv bdge & opp tourist office. Do not turn L into town cent. Sm, hdg/mkd pitch, pt shd; wc; chem disp; shwrs; el pnts (10A) €3; gas; lndtte; ice; shop 500m; tradsmn; rest, snacks, bar 300m; playgrnd; sw 1km; dogs €1; Eng spkn; adv bkg rec high ssn; quiet but some traff noise; CCI. "Pleasant, well-run site; modern san facs v clean; bus tours - old town worth a visit; vg." ♦ 1 May-26 Sep. € 11.10
2007*

VRAIGNES EN VERMANDOIS see Péronne 3C3

VUILLAFANS see Ornans 6G2

WACQUINGHEN see Marquise 3A3

There aren't many sites open this early in the year. We'd better phone ahead to check that the one we're heading for is actually open.

WARLINCOURT LES PAS 3B3 (Rural) **Domaine La Kilienne**, 1 Rue du Moulin, 62760 Warlincourt-lès-Pas [03 21 73 03 03; fax 03 21 22 64 14; lakilienne@wanadoo.fr] Fr Arras or Doullens turn S fr N25. Site 2.5km on L, in vill. Lge, hdg/mkd pitch, terr, pt shd; wc; chem disp; mv service pnt; shwrs inc; el pnts (10A) inc; lndtte; ice; tradsmn; snacks; bar; BBQ; htd pool; playgrnd; fishing; mini-golf; TV; entmnt; some statics; dogs €1; poss cr; adv bkg. "Attractive site with watermill; St Kilien Spring & chapel." ♦ 1 Apr-31 Oct. € 15.00
2006*

France

WASSELONNE *6E3* (1km W Urban) **FFCC Camp Municipal, Route de Romanswiller, 67310 Wasselonne [tel/fax 03 88 87 00 08 or 03 88 59 12 27; camping-wasselonne@wanadoo. fr]** Fr D1004 (N4) take D244 to site. Med, mkd pitch, terr, pt shd; wc; mv service pnt; shwrs inc; el pnts (5-10A) €2.30-3.70; gas; lndtte; shop; rest; snacks; bar; playgrnd; htd, covrd pool high ssn; 30% statics; dogs €0.60; quiet; CCI. "Pleasant town; views over hills; facs OK; vg cycle rte to Strasbourg; gd NH." 15 Apr-15 Oct. € 11.10   2007*

WASSELONNE *6E3* (5km NW Urban) **Camp Municipal, 67310 Romanswiller [tel/fax 03 88 87 45 54 or 03 88 87 05 57 (Mairie)]** Fr Saverne take D1004 (N4) twd Strasbourg. 1km N of Wasselonne turn R onto D260 & cont twd town cent, turn R onto D224 sp Romanswiller & 'Camping Piscine'. 2km N at o'skts turn L into 'Centre des Loisirs'. Sm, hdg pitch, pt shd; wc; chem disp; all serviced pitches; shwrs inc; el pnts (10A) inc; lndry rm; ice; shops 2km; rest; snacks; BBQ; playgrnd; htd pool 5km; games area; cycle hire; 90% statics; dogs; poss cr; some Eng spkn; poss noisy; CCI. "V well-kept site; pleasant town; views over hills." 1 May-15 Sep. € 12.00   2006*

WATTEN *3A3* (W Rural) **Camping Le Val Joly, Rue de l'Aa, Wattendam, 59143 Watten [03 21 88 23 26 or 03 21 88 24 75]** NW fr St Omer on D943 (N43); N of Tilques turn N on D300/D600; in 5km turn R to D207 sp Watten; at T-junc turn L; cross rv; thro town; site sp on R nr L'Aa canal. Site sp fr N & S on D943. Med, pt sl, pt shd; wc; chem disp; shwrs €1.75; el pnts (3A) €2.55; shops adj; playgrnd; fishing & cycling along rv/canal; 90% statics; quiet, some rd noise; CCI. "Spacious, attractive, well-kept site; conv ferries & glass works at Arques; gd clean san facs; friendly, helpful warden; call at house, gd welcome; secure gates; conv cycling; vet 20 mins walk; gd." 1 Apr-31 Oct. € 9.00   2007*

WATTWILLER see Cernay *6F3*

⊞**WIMEREUX** *3A2* (5km N Rural) **Camping Le Beaucamp, 10 Rue de Ferquent, Raventhun, 62164 Ambleteuse [03 21 32 62 10; fax 03 21 30 63 77; le-beaucamp@fr.st; www.le-beaucamp.fr.st]** Exit A16 junc 36 onto D191E dir Ambleteuse, site in 6km in R. Lge, hdg pitch, unshd; htd wc; chem disp; shwrs €2.10; el pnts (10A) €3.70; gas; ice; lndtte; shop; rest; snacks; bar; BBQ; playgrnd; htd, covrd; sand beach 1.5km; entmnt; 90% statics; dogs €2.30; quiet; cc acc; CCI. "Gd NH; sep area for tourers but sharp R-angle turns to ent & poss reverse to exit so diff lge o'fits; lge pitches; basic facs; poor value in low ssn." € 19.40   2007*

WIMEREUX *3A2* (1km S Coastal) **Camp Municipal Olympic, 49 Rue de la Libération, 62930 Wimereux [03 21 32 45 63]** A16 exit 32 & foll sp Wimereux Sud to vill; turn R at rndabt to site. Or N fr Boulogne on D940, at vill sp Wimereux & rndabt, turn R. Med, hdg/mkd pitch, pt sl, unshd; wc; chem disp; baby facs; shwrs inc; el pnts (4A) inc (rev pol); BBQ; lndry rm; shop adj; tradsmn; rest; playgrnd; pool 4km; beach 800m; sailing; fishing; 30% statics; dogs €2; Eng spkn; some noise fr rds & rlwy; CCI. "Conv Boulogne & NH; office open fr 0800; ent card dep €5; basic facs; hot water runs out early; sh walk into town; gd vet in town." 15 Mar-28 Oct. € 14.10   2007*

⊞**WIMEREUX** *3A2* (1.5km S Coastal) **Caravaning L'Eté Indien, Hameau de Honvault, 62930 Wimereux [03 21 30 23 50; fax 03 21 30 17 14; eteindien@eracotedopale.com]** Fr Calais A16 SW exit junc 32 sp Wimereux Sud. Thro Terlincthun R after x-ing rlwy, site in 700m on R. Med, mkd pitch, pt sl, unshd; htd wc; chem disp; mv service pnt; serviced pitches; baby facs; shwrs inc; el pnts (6-10A) inc; lndtte; snacks; bar; BBQ (gas); playgrnd; sandy beach 1.5km; 95% statics; dogs; adv bkg; some rlwy noise; red 14+ days. "Conv A16, Calais ferries; rec low ssn phone to check site open; mainly statics but tourers welcome although no dedicated pitches or elec; rlwy runs along one side of site." ♦ € 19.50   2006*

WINGEN SUR MODER *5D3* (W Rural) **Aire Naturelle Municipal, 67290 Wingen-sur-Moder [03 88 89 71 27 (Mairie); fax 03 88 89 86 99; mairie@wingen-moder.com]** W fr Haguenau on D919 to W end Wingen-sur-Moder. Site sp by rlwy arch. Sm, mkd pitch, terr, pt shd; wc; chem disp; shwrs inc; el pnts (13A) €2; rest nr; shop 500m; Eng spkn; adv bkg; quiet; 7th day free; CCI. "Excel site; v peaceful but adj sports field poss used by youth groups/motorbikers high ssn; clean facs; warden calls am & pm; gd walking/cycling." 1 May-30 Sep. € 10.40   2005*

WISSANT *3A2* (Urban/Coastal) **Camp Municipal La Source, Rue de la Source, 62179 Wissant [03 21 35 92 46; fax 03 21 00 19 11; camping. wissant@wanadoo.fr; www.ville-wissant.fr]** Fr Calais exit Wissant. At D940 bear L twd Boulogne. In 1.5km turn R at camping sp into Rue de la Source. Site on L in 300m. Lge, hdg/mkd pitch, pt shd; htd wc; chem disp; shwrs inc; el pnts (5A) €3.52; gas; 500m; ice; lndtte; shops 500m; tradsmn; rest adj; playgrnd; sand beach 500m; entmnt; 80% statics; dogs €0.91; phone; poss cr; quiet; CCI. "Gd location & scenery; scruffy statics area; run down low ssn; path to beach; gd walking/ cycling." 15 Mar-25 Nov. € 12.65   2006*

WISSANT 3A2 (6km NE Coastal/Rural) **Camping Côte d'Opale Le Blanc Nez, 18 Rue de la Mer, 62179 Escalles [tel/fax 03 21 85 27 38; camping. blancnez@laposte.net; http://camping.blancnez. free.fr]** Fr A16 take junc 40 to Cap Blanc-Nez. Site situated on W edge of Escalles on D940 twd sea. Med, mkd pitch, pt sl, pt shd; wc; chem disp; mv service pnt; shwrs €1; el pnts (4A) inc (long lead poss req); gas; lndry rm; ice; shop; tradsmn; rest; snacks; bar; playgrnd; sand/shgl beach 1km; 25% statics; dogs €1.40; phone; bus 100m; poss cr; adv bkg; quiet; cc acc; CCI. "Ltd hot shwrs/ hot water; v clean, basic san facs; diff access for lge o'fits due parked cars; sm pitches; elec linked to pitch number - no choice; excel rest; gd location & walking; security barrier; gd NH." 15 Mar-15 Nov. € 16.50   2007*

WISSANT 3A2 (6km NE Coastal) **Camping Les Erables, 17 Rue du Château d'Eau, 62179 Escalles [03 21 85 25 36; boutroy.les-erables@ wanadoo.fr]** Fr A16 take exit 40 onto D243 thro Peuplingues. Site sp to L on ent Escalles (on sharp R bend). Steep ent. Don't be put off by No Entry signs - one-way system for c'vans on appr rd. Sm, hdg/mkd pitch, terr, unshd; htd wc; chem disp; mv service pnt; shwrs €1; el pnts (6-10A) inc; lndry rm; shop 2km; tradsmn; rest 500m; bar 3km; BBQ; sand beach 3km; dogs; phone; quiet; CCI. "Lovely site with superb cliff views; spacious pitches; well-maintained, family-owned site; warm welcome, helpful & friendly; immac, modern facs; gates open 0600-2200; 2 pitches for disabled visitors; view to Cap Blanc-Nez; ideal for tunnel & ferries; excel." ♦ 1 Apr-1 Nov. € 15.40   2007*

WISSANT 3A2 (4km E Rural) **Camping La Vallée, 901 Rue Principale, 62179 Hervelinghen [03 21 36 73 96 or 03 21 85 15 43]** Fr Calais exit A16 onto D244 & foll sp St Inglevert. Site on L at end Hervelinghen vill. Sm, hdg/mkd pitch, unshd; htd wc; chem disp; shwrs €1; el pnts (6A) €3.30 (poss rev pol); lndry rm; rest; snacks; bar; BBQ; playgrnd; sand/shgl beach 3km; 75% statics; dogs €1; Eng spkn; adv bkg; quiet; CCI. "Family-run site; immac san facs but no stand pipes or waste water emptying point; attractive countryside; conv Calais, Cité Europe; gd walking in area." ♦ ltd. 1 Apr-31 Oct. € 14.50   2005*

XONRUPT LONGEMER see Gérardmer 6F3

YCHOUX 7D1 (10km E Rural) **Camp Municipal du Lac des Forges, 40160 Ychoux [05 58 82 35 57 or 05 58 82 36 01 (Mairie); fax 05 58 82 35 46]** Fr Bordeaux take N10 S & turn onto D43 at Liposthey W twd Parentis-en-Born. Site in 8km on R, past vill of Ychoux. Sm, pt sl, pt shd; wc; chem disp; shwrs; el pnts (rev pol); ice; lndtte; shops 1km; snacks; rest; playgrnd; TV rm; lake adj; fishing; sailing; quiet. "Levelling blocks poss req; unisex, open-plan san facs; pitches nr rd poss noisy." 15 Jun-15 Sep. € 12.00   2005*

YENNE 9B3 (300m N Rural) **Camping Le Flon, Ave du Rhône, 73170 Yenne [04 79 36 82 70 or 04 79 36 90 76; fax 04 79 36 92 72; ccyenne@ wanadoo.fr]** Fr N504 ent Yenne, site visible. E on rd to Tunnel du Chat, site sp on banks Rv Rhône. Med, mkd pitch, shd; wc (cont); shwrs inc; el pnts €2.50; shops 500m; rest, snacks, bar 500m; playgrnd; fishing; canoeing; dogs €1.10; adv bkg; some rd noise. 15 Jun-31 Aug. € 8.85   2004*

YENNE 9B3 (4km E) **FLOWER Camping des Lacs, 73170 St. Jean-de-Chevelu [04 79 36 72 21 or 04 79 36 90 76; camping-des-lacs@wanadoo. fr; www.camping-lacs-savoie.com or www. flowercamping.com]** Fr Yenne, take D504, D210 to St Jean-de-Chevelu. Med, pt shd; wc; mv service pnt; shwrs inc; el pnts (6A) inc; lndtte; ice; shop; rest; snacks; bar; playgrnd; lake sw, sand beach; boating; fishing; games rm; dogs €3; quiet."V peaceful." 2 Jun-1 Sep. € 18.00   2007*

YENNE 9B3 (8km E Rural) **Camp Municipal Le Lamartine, 73370 Bourdeau [04 79 25 03 41 (Mairie); fax 04 79 25 35 73]** N fr Chambéry on N504 sp Bourg-en-Bresse on W side of lake. 2km N of Le Bourget turn R opp g'ge sp Bourdeau. Thro car park in front of Mairie. Fr N or W fr Yenne turn L just after Tunnel du Chat. Sm, pt sl, pt shd; wc (some cont); shwrs inc; el pnts (6A) inc; shop 200m; rest adj; BBQ; lake 1.5km; dogs; adv bkg; quiet; CCI. "Gd views; nice walks nr." 15 Jun-15 Sep. € 10.00   2004*

YPORT 3C1 (1km SW Coastal) **Camping Le Rivage, Rue Hottières, 76111 Yport [tel/fax 02 35 27 33 78]** Fr D940 bet Etretat & Fécamp take D11 2km NE of Les Loges, meeting up with D211 & head twd Yport. Site on D211. Or foll sp fr Yport. Med, pt sl, terr, unshd; wc; chem disp; shwrs; el pnts (6A) inc (poss long lead req); ice; shops 1km; snacks; bar; shgl beach 300m; games rm; TV rm; phone; adv bkg; quiet. "Magnificent situation; views o'looking sea; steep descent to beach; san facs inadequate high ssn & long walk fr most pitches; rec stop at top of site & walk to recep bef pitching, as turning poss diff lge o'fits; conv Etretat, Fécamp & Benedictine palace." 12 Apr-21 Sep. € 14.00   2006*

YSSINGEAUX 9C1 (300m SE Urban) **Camp Municipal de Choumouroux, 43200 Yssingeaux [04 71 65 53 44 or 04 71 59 01 13 (Mairie); fax 04 71 65 19 35]** N88 Le Puy to St Etienne on R bef Yssingeaux; ent next to school, opp petrol stn. Sm, pt shd; wc (cont); chem disp; shwrs inc; el pnts (10A) inc; shops 500m; playgrnd; fishing; dogs €1.20; quiet. "Gd location amongst extinct volcanoes; well-maintained." 1 May-30 Sep. € 9.30   2006*

France

YVETOT *3C2* (10km N Rural) **Camp Municipal de la Durdent, 76560 Héricourt-en-Caux [02 35 96 38 08 or 02 35 96 42 12 (Mairie); fax 02 32 70 02 59; officedetourisme.doudeville@ wanadoo.fr]** Fr Le Havre on N15 L at traff lts in Yvetot on D131 sp Cany to Héricourt. After passing thro vill turn L on D149. Site on L in 300m. Or exit A29 junc 8 dir Fécamp. After 3.5km at rndabt outside Fauville turn R sp Héricourt 10km. Site visible on R below rd on ent vill. Sm, mkd pitch, pt sl, unshd; wc (some cont); shwrs inc; el pnts (6A) €2; lndry rm; shops 500m; poss cr; quiet; cc not acc; CCI. "Site by trout stream, excel rests in vill; pitch yourself; warden calls; pleasantly situated; basic facs but well-maintained." 15 Apr-30 Sep. € 10.00   2005*

YVOIRE see Thonon les Bains *9A3*

YVRAC ET MALLEYRAND see Rochefoucauld, La *7B2*

CORSICA

AJACCIO *10H2* (4km W) **Camping de Barbicaggia, Rue de Sanguinaires, 20000 Ajaccio [04 95 52 01 17]** Fr Ajaccio take D111 twds Iles Sanguinaires. Site on R after 4km. Med, hdg/ mkd pitch, hdstg, terr, shd; wc (some cont); chem disp; shwrs inc; el pnts; lndtte; sand beach 100m; 5% statics; phone adj; bus 200m; poss v cr; Eng spkn. "Sea views over bay; ltd space for vans; steep entry not suitable for lge units; rec check pitch bef ent site." ♦ ltd. € 16.70   2004*

AJACCIO *10H2* (1km NW Coastal) **Camping Les Mimosas, Route d'Alata, 20000 Ajaccio [04 95 20 99 85; fax 04 95 10 01 77]** Foll D194 round N of Ajaccio & then directions to Super U; 1st R off rndabt immed after Super U. Med, hdg/mkd pitch, hdstg, pt sl, shd; wc; chem disp; serviced pitches; shwrs inc; el pnts (5-10A) gas 1km; lndtte; ice; sm shop & 1km; tradsmn; rest; snacks; bar; playgrnd; shgl beach 1km; 5% statics; dogs; phone; adv bkg; quiet; 10% red CCI. "Conv Ajaccio; gd rest on site." ♦ ltd. 1 Apr-15 Oct. € 15.30   2005*

ALERIA *10H2* (7km N Coastal) **Camping-Village Riva-Bella (Naturist), 20270 Aléria [04 95 38 81 10 or 04 95 38 85 97; fax 04 95 31 91 29; riva-bella@wanadoo.fr; www.rivabella-corsica.com]** Fr Bastia S on N198 for 60km, site sp to L. Med, pt shd; wc; mv service pnt; shwrs; el pnts €3.80; shop; lndtte; rest; snacks; bar; playgrnd; sand beach adj; fishing; watersports; tennis; cycle hire; fitness rm; internet; entmnt; excursions; TV rm; 10% statics; dogs €3; adv bkg; quiet; red low ssn; INF card req. 9 Apr-31 Oct. € 31.00 (CChq acc)   2005*

ALERIA *10H2* (3km E Coastal) **Camping Marina d'Aléria, 20270 Aléria [04 95 57 01 42; fax 04 95 57 04 29; info@marina-aleria.com; www. marina-aleria.com]** S fr Bastia on N198; in Aléria turn L at x-rds onto N200 to Plage de Padulone. Lge, hdg pitch, pt shd, wc; mv service pnt; shwrs inc; el pnts (6A) €3.70; lndtte; shop; rest; snacks; bar; BBQ; playgrnd; sand beach adj; tennis; cycle hire; entmnt; TV; some statics; dogs €3; cc acc. "Superb site on sea shore; Roman ruins in Aléria." Easter-15 Oct. € 27.50   2006*

ALGAJOLA *10G2* (800m E Coastal) **Camping de la Plage en Balagne, 20220 Algajola [tel/fax 04 95 60 71 76; campingalgajola@wanadoo.fr; www.camping-de-la-plage-en-balagne.com]** Site 6km W fr L'Ile-Rousse on N197 (D199) dir Algajola. On R opp Hotel Pascal Paoli bef Algajola. Med, pt shd; htd wc (some cont); chem disp; mv service pnt; shwrs inc; el pnts (6A) €3; lndtte; shop; rest; snacks; bar; playgrnd; sand beach adj; games area; gym; entmnt; some statics; dogs €1.50; tram; poss cr; adv bkg; quiet; cc acc. "Rest, snacks & bar on beach - poss clsd low ssn; tram to l'Ile-Rousse & Calvi fr site gd for touring inland; gd." 15 Mar-15 Nov. € 20.60   2007*

BASTIA *10G2* (5km N Coastal) **Camping Casablanca (formerly Les Orangers), Licciola, 20200 Miomo [04 95 33 24 09; fax 04 95 33 23 65]** Foll main coast rd D80 N 4km fr ferry. Site well sp on L of rd. Sm, shd; wc; shwrs; el pnts €2.45-3.10; ice; shop; tradsmn; rest; snacks; bar; TV; sandy/ shgl beach adj; quiet; CCI. "Poss run down low ssn; friendly owners; vg rest; site ent tight for lge o'fits; poss unreliable opening dates." 1 Apr-1 Oct. € 13.10   2004*

BASTIA *10G2* (11km S Coastal) **Camping San Damiano, Lido de la Marana, 20620 Biguglia [04 95 33 68 02; fax 04 95 30 84 10; l.pradier@ wanadoo.fr; www.campingsandamiano.com]** S fr Bastia on N193 for 4km. Turn SE onto Lagoon Rd (sp Lido de Marana). Site on L in 7km. Lge, pt shd; wc; chem disp; baby facs; shwrs inc; el pnts (6A) €3; lndtte; shop; rest; playgrnd; sandy beach adj; cycle path; games area; games rm; dogs €0.50; Eng spkn; cc acc; CCI. ♦ 1 Apr-20 Oct. € 20.00   2005*

BELGODERE see Ile Rousse, L' *10G2*

BIGUGLIA see Bastia *10G2*

BONIFACIO *10H2* (15km N Coastal) **Camping Rondinara, Suartone, 20169 Bonifacio [04 95 70 43 15; fax 04 95 70 56 79; reception@ rondinara.fr; www.rondinara.fr]** Fr Bonifacio take N198 dir Porte-Vecchio for 10km, then turn R onto D158 dir Suartone (lge camp sp at turning). Site in 5km. NB D158 single track, many bends & hills. Med, pt sl, pt shd; wc; mv service pnt; shwrs inc; el pnts (6A) €3.30; lndtte; ice; shop; rest; snacks; bar; BBQ; playgrnd; pool; sand beach 400m; watersports; volleyball; dogs €1.60; poss cr; Eng spkn; no adv bkg; quiet; red low ssn; cc acc; CCI. "Excel rest; idyllic location." 15 May-30 Sep. € 19.70   2005*

BONIFACIO *10H2* (4km NE Rural) **Camping Pian del Fosse, Route de Santa Manza, 20169 Bonifacio [tel/fax 04 95 73 16 34; pian.del.fosse@ wanadoo.fr]** Leave Bonifacio on D58 dir Sta Manza, site on L in 4km. Sm, hdg/mkd pitch, terr, shd; wc; chem disp; shwrs inc; el pnts (4A) €3.80; lndtte; shop; tradsmn; snacks; BBQ; playgrnd; sand/ shgl beach 3km; 20% statics; dogs €3.20; poss cr; Eng spkn; quiet. "Pitches poss diff lge m'vans due overhanging trees; vg." ♦ ltd. Easter-15 Oct. € 21.50   2004*

BONIFACIO *10H2* (4km NE Rural) **Pertamina Village U Farniente, 20169 Bonifacio [04 95 73 05 47; fax 04 95 73 11 42; pertamina@ wanadoo.fr; www.camping-pertamina.com]** Fr Bonifacio take RN198 N, site on R in 4km. Med, hdg/mkd pitch, pt sl, pt shd; wc (some cont); chem disp; mv service pnt; baby facs; shwrs inc; el pnts (6A) inc; gas; lndtte; ice; shop; rest; snacks; bar; playgrnd; htd pool; waterslide; beach 4km; tennis; archery; entmnt; TV rm; 50% statics; dogs; poss cr; adv bkg; cc acc; CCI. "Access to pitches diff; excel." ♦ 1 Apr-15 Oct. € 27.00 (CChq acc)
                                          2005*

CALVI *10G2* (Coastal) **Camping La Pinède, Route de la Pinède, 20260 Calvi [04 95 65 17 80; fax 04 95 65 19 60]** S fr L'Ile-Rousse on N197; well sp ent Calvi; 1st ent on R to Rte de la Pinède, 2nd ent 1km after 1st. Lge, shd; shwrs; el pnts (6A) €3.50; shop; supmkt nrby; rest; pool; superb beach 250m; mini-golf; no dogs; train to Calvi & Ile-Rousse 250m; cc acc. "Too shd; clean facs." 1 Apr-1 Oct. € 22.00
                                          2005*

CALVI *10G2* (1.8km SE Coastal) **Camping Paduella, Route de Bastia, 20260 Calvi [04 95 65 13 20 or 04 95 65 06 16; fax 04 95 65 17 50]** On N197 fr Calvi; on R 200m after rndabt by casino supmkt. Med, mkd pitch, pt sl, terr, pt shd; wc chem disp; baby facs; shwrs inc; el pnts (6A) €3.30; lndtte; ice; shop/supmkt; snacks; bar; playgrnd; sand beach 400m; 25% statics; poss cr; quiet; CCI. "Poss best site at Calvi; immac san facs but slippery when wet, especially disabled ramp; vg." ♦ 10 May-15 Oct. € 18.80   2005*

CALVI *10G2* (4km SE Coastal) **Camping La Dolce Vita, Route de Bastia, 20260 Calvi [04 95 65 05 99; fax 04 95 65 31 25]** N197 twd L'Ile Rousse. Site on L, by rest, immed after x-ing rv bdge. Adj Bastia-Calvi . Lge, shd; wc; shwrs inc; el pnts (10A) €3.50; gas; lndtte; ice; shop; rest; snacks; bar; playgrnd; sand beach 150m; TV rm; dir access to rv; fishing; sailing windsurfing; poss cr; quiet, but some aircraft noise. 1 May-30 Sep. € 21.60   2005*

CARGESE *10H2* (3km N) **Camping Le Torraccia, 20130 Cargèse [04 95 26 42 39 or 04 95 20 40 21 (LS); fax 04 95 20 40 21; contact@ camping-torraccia.com]** N fr Cargèse twd Porto on D81 for 3km. Site on L. Med, terr, pt shd; wc; shwrs inc; ltd el pnts (10A) €2.50; lndry rm; shop; rest; snacks; bar; playgrnd; sports area; sand beach 3km; adv bkg; red low ssn. "Nearest site to Porto without diff traffic conditions." 1 May-30 Sep. € 17.00   2004*

CERVIONE *10G2* (7km NE Coastal) **Camping Merendella, Moriani-Plage, 20230 San Nicolao [04 95 38 53 47 or 04 95 38 50 54; fax 04 95 38 44 01; merendel@club-internet.fr; www. merendella.com]** Site 44km S of Bastia at Moriani-Plage; foll N193 & N198 fr Bastia to Moriani Plage, on E (beach side) of N198, 700m after supermkt. Med, hdg/mkd pitch, shd; wc; chem disp; mv service pnt; shwrs inc; el pnts (5A) €4.30; lndtte; ice; shop & supmkt 1km; rest; bar; playgrnd; dir access to beach adj; tennis 500m; TV rm; no dogs; adv bkg (€15.24 dep req); quiet; cc acc; CCI. "Idyllic beachside pitches; friendly; most helpful & efficient staff; superb pitches; easy access; excel." ♦ 10 May-15 Oct. € 21.95   2007*

CERVIONE *10G2* (6km SE Coastal) **Camping Calamar, Prunete, 20221 Cervione [04 95 38 03 54 or 04 94 38 00 94 (LS); fax 04 95 31 17 09; camille. zucca@wanadoo.fr; www.campingcalamar. com]** On N198 S fr Prunete for 6km. Turn L at x-rds, site in 500m beside beach, sp. Sm, pt shd; wc; shwrs inc; el pnts €2.50; lndtte; shop 500m; tradsmn; snacks; bar; BBQ; sand beach adj; sailing; watersports; games area; dogs free; Eng spkn; adv bkg; quiet; red low ssn. "Friendly owner; pleasant site with trees & shrubs; close to mountains; 30 mins fr Bastia; excel." 1 Apr-31 Oct. € 13.00
                                          2006*

CORBARA see Ile Rousse L' *10G2*

CORTE *10G2* (E Urban) **Camping Le Restonica, Faubourg St Antoine, 20250 Corte [tel/fax 04 95 46 11 59; vero.camp@worldonline.fr]** Fr N193 Ajaccio to Corte, twd cent of town. Pass petrol stn on R then sharp turn R before x-ing bdge (acute angle). Site on R bet rv bdge in 200m. Sharp turn down hill to ent. Med; wc; shwrs inc; el pnts €3.50; gas; ice; shops 200m; rest; sports complex 150m; adv bkg; quiet. "Corte beautiful old town; gd walking & horseriding." 1 May-30 Sep. € 16.00
                                          2004*

France

CORTE *10G2* (500m SW Rural) **Aire Naturelle Camping U Sognu, Route de la Restonica, 20250 Corte [04 95 46 09 07]** At rndabt turn W off N193 sp Centre Ville. Immed L after bdge onto D623 sp La Restonica & site. Site on R in 200m. Med, pt shd; wc; shwrs inc; el pnts (6A); ice; shop; tradsmn; rest; bar; rv & lake 200m; sw & fishing; poss v cr; cc not acc. "Gd views of old university capital town; clean but inadequate facs high ssn; gd rest & bar; conv walking Restonica & Tavignano gorges." 1 Apr-25 Oct. 2007*

> Did you know you can fill in site report forms on the Club's website — www.caravanclub.co.uk?

GHISONACCIA *10H2* (4km E Coastal) **Camping Arinella Bianca, Route de la Mer, Bruschetto, 20240 Ghisonaccia [04 95 56 04 78; fax 04 95 56 12 54; arinella@arinellabianca.com; www.arinellabianca.com]** S fr Bastia on N193/N198 approx 70km to Ghisonaccia. At Ghisonaccia foll sp opp pharmacy to beach (plage) & Rte de la Mer. In 3km turn R at rndabt & site well sp. NB When towing keep to main, coastal rds. Lge, hdg/mkd pitch, shd; wc (some cont); chem disp; mv service pnt; baby facs; shwrs inc; el pnts (6A) €3.50 (rev pol); gas; lndtte; ice; shop; tradsmn; rest; snacks; bar; BBQ; playgrnd; pool; sand beach adj; fishing; watersports & activities; tennis; horseriding adj; cycle hire; games rm; internet; entmnt; TV rm; 45% statics; recep 0830-2100; dogs €2.50; Eng spkn; adv bkg (dep req); barrier (dep €15); red low ssn; cc acc; CCI. "V clean, well-run site; attractive lake in cent; trees make access to pitches diff; v helpful owner & staff." ♦ 16 Apr-30 Sep. € 33.00 (CChq acc) 2005*

GHISONACCIA *10H2* (5km E Coastal) **Camping Marina d'Erba Rossa, Route de la Mer, 20240 Ghisonaccia [04 95 56 25 14 or 04 95 56 21 18; fax 04 95 56 27 23; info@marina-erbarossa.com; www.marina-erbarossa.com]** Drive into town on N198. Site sp down D144 (easy to miss). Take D144 E to coast & site on R after 5km. Lge, hdg/mkd pitch, shd; wc; chem disp; shwrs; el pnts (5-6A) inc (long lead rec); lndtte; ice; shop; rest; pizzeria; snacks; playgrnd; pool; private sand beach; watersports; tennis; cycle hire; mini-golf; horseriding; entmnt; child entmnt; some statics; adv bkg. ♦ 3 Apr-23 Oct. € 31.80 2004*

ILE ROUSSE, L' *10G2* (7km SE Rural) **Camping Le Clos des Chênes, Route de Belgodère, Lozari, 20226 Belgodère [04 95 60 15 13 or 04 95 60 41 27 (LS); fax 04 95 60 21 16; cdc. lozari@wanadoo.fr; www.closdeschenes.fr]** E on fr L'Ile Rousse on N197 E twd Bastia. After 7km turn S at Lozari onto N197 sp Belgodère; site on R after 1.5km. Lge, sl, pt shd; wc; shwrs inc; baby facs; chem disp; el pnts (10A) inc (long cable req); gas; lndtte; ice; shop; tradsmn; rest; bar; pizzeria; BBQ; playgrnd; pool; paddling pool; sand beach 2km; tennis; games rm; 10% statics; dogs €2.70; poss cr; some Eng spkn; adv bkg; red low ssn; cc acc; CCI. "V tranquil, few pitches with view of mountains, most amongst sm oaks haphazardly placed; v ltd facs low ssn; gd touring cent; daily mkt." ♦ Easter-30 Sep. € 26.00 2004*

ILE ROUSSE, L' *10G2* (3km S Urban/Coastal) **Camping Les Oliviers, Route de Bastia, 20220 Monticello [04 95 60 19 92; fax 04 95 60 30 91]** Fr town take rd dir Bastia. Site on L in 800m. Lge, mkd pitch (some), pt sl, pt shd; wc; chem disp; mv service pnt; shwrs inc; el pnts (6A) €3.50; gas 800m; ice; lndtte; shop 800m; tradsmn; rest; snacks; bar; shgl beach 500m; 5% statics; dogs; phone; tram 1km; poss cr; adv bkg; cc acc. "Pleasant site but facs stretched & cr high ssn; ltd el pnts; quiet at night but some rd noise in parts of site; gd location; coastal path to town." ♦ ltd 1 Apr-30 Sep. € 18.00 2004*

ILE ROUSSE, L' *10G2* (6km SW Coastal) **Aire Naturelle Balanéa (Savelli de Guido), Route d'Algajola, 20256 Corbara [tel/fax 04 95 60 06 84 or 04 95 60 11 77 (ssn); contact@balanea. net; www.balanea.net]** Off N197, site sp. Med, pt shd; wc; shwrs inc; el pnts €3; lndtte; shops 5km; snacks; beach 1km; dogs €1.50; CCI. ♦ Easter-30 Sep. € 18.50 2007*

LECCI *10H2* (8km S Rural) **Camping Mulinacciu, 20137 Lecci [04 95 71 47 48; fax 04 95 71 54 82; infos@campingmulinacciu.com; www.camping-mulinacciu.com]** N fr Porto-Vecchio on N198 for approx 10km. Cross double bdge over Rv Oso & turn L onto unmade rd opp D668 dir San Ciprianu. Site sp down this rd. Med, pt shd; wc; shwrs inc; el pnts (5A) €3.50; lndtte; shop; playgrnd; pool; waterslide; sand beach 7km; fishing; tennis; games area; TV; some statics; dogs €2; Eng spkn; quiet. "Access to rv; friendly owners." 15 Jun-15 Sep. € 20.20 2006*

OLMETO *10H2* (3km S Coastal) **Camping Vigna Maggiore, 20113 Olmeto-Plage [04 95 76 02 07; fax 04 95 74 62 02; www.vignamaggiore.com]** Site is approx 5km N of Propriano at junc N196 & D157 Med, terr, pt shd; wc; chem disp; mv waste; shwrs inc; el pnts €3.50; lndtte; rest; bar; playgrnd; pool; sand beach 1km; games area; some statics; poss cr; adv bkg; CCI. 1 Apr-30 Sep. € 18.40 2005*

OLMETO *10H2* (4km SW Coastal) **Camping L'Esplanade, Tour de la Calanca, 20113 Olmeto-Plage [04 95 76 05 03; fax 04 95 76 16 22; infos@camping-esplanade.com; www.campingesplanade.com]** S fr Olmeto on N196 twd Propriano; turn R onto D157; site in 1km. Med, mkd pitch, pt sl, terr, shd; wc; shwrs; el pnts (10A) inc; shop; rest; snacks; ice; tradsmn; playgrnd; lndtte; beach adj; sep car park. 10 Apr-21 Oct. € 20.00
2004*

OLMETO *10H2* (6km SW Coastal) **Camping Abartello, Route Porto Pollo, 20113 Olmeto-Plage [04 95 74 05 12; fax 04 95 74 04 95; jpvogli@aol.com]** Fr Propriano take N196 N & turn onto D157 dir Porto Pollo to site. Med, shd; wc; chem disp; shwrs inc; el pnts (10A) €2.75; ice; lndtte; shop, rest, snacks & bar nrby; tradsmn; supmkt 8km; beach adj; some statics; dogs; phone; poss cr; quiet; CCI. "Excel site for beach sw, exploring megalithic sites & mountain drives; basic facs poss unclean." 1 May-30 Sep.
2005*

PIANA *10G2* (11.5km W Coastal) **Camping Plage d'Arone, 20115 Piana [04 95 20 64 54]** Tho SW of Porto, rec c'vans arr fr Cargèse in S. Fr Cargèse head N on D81 to Piana. Turn L in vill onto D824 (sp), site on R in 11km. Med, pt shd; wc; chem disp; shwrs inc; el pnts inc; lndtte; shop high ssn; supmkt in Piana; tradsmn; playgrnd; sand beach 350m; no statics; quiet; CCI. "Access fr site to excel sandy bay with 2 rests/bars." ♦ 15 May-30 Sep. € 20.60
2004*

PIANOTTOLI CALDARELLO *10H2* (3.5km SE Coastal) **Camping Kevano Plage, 20131 Pianottoli-Caldarello [04 95 71 83 22; fax 04 95 71 83 83]** Turn off N196 in Pianottoli at x-rds onto D122 for 1km. Turn R in Caldarello, site on L in 2km. Med, mkd pitch, pt sl, terr, pt shd; wc; chem disp; mv service pnt; shwrs inc; el pnts (4-6A) €2.50; lndtte; ice; shop; tradsmn; pizzeria; snacks; bar; playgrnd; sand beach 400m; entmnt; TV; phone; poss cr; Eng spkn; adv bkg rec high ssn; quiet; cc acc; CCI. "Site in macchia amongst huge boulders; beautiful site nr gd beaches; family-run site; no dogs on beach Jul/Aug." ♦ ltd. 1 May-30 Sep. € 29.00
2005*

PIETRACORBARA *10G2* (4km SE Coastal) **Camping La Pietra, Marine de Pietracorbara, 20233 Pietracorbara [04 95 35 27 49; fax 04 95 35 28 57; www.la-pietra.com]** Fr Bastia on D80 N. In 20km ent vill & turn L onto D232. Site on R in 1km at marina beach. Well sp. Sm, hdg/mkd pitch, shd; wc; shwrs inc; el pnts (20A) €3.40; lndtte; ice; shop; tradsmn; rest on beach; playgrnd; pool; sand beach 300m; tennis; dogs €2.50; bus nr; Eng spkn; red low ssn; cc acc; CCI. "Excel facs; beautiful pool; generous pitches; helpful owners." ♦ 1 Apr-15 Oct. € 26.00
2007*

PORTO *10G2* (1km E Rural) **Camping Sole e Vista, Rue d'Ota, 20150 Porto [04 95 26 15 71; fax 04 95 26 10 79; fceccaldi@freesurf.fr; www.camping-sole-e-vista.com]** On D81 Ajaccio-Calvi rd, turn E onto D124. Ent thro Spar/Timy supmkt car park in Porto. NB rd fr Calvi diff for c'vans. Lge, mkd pitch, terr, pt sl, shd; wc; chem disp; mv service pnt; shwrs inc; el pnts (16A) €3.80; gas; lndtte; shop adj; snacks; bar; BBQ; playgrnd; shgl beach 1.5km; some statics; poss cr; Eng spkn; adv bkg; quiet; red CCI. "National Parks area; vg." 1 Apr-31 Oct. € 15.50
2006*

PORTO *10G2* (1.5km E Coastal) **Camping Les Oliviers, 20150 Porto [04 95 26 14 49; fax 04 95 26 12 49; www.campinglesoliviers.com]** On D81 fr Porto on R bank of Rv Porto nr Pont de Porto. Site nr rv a sh distance downhill fr Cmp Sole e Vista. Check for access, poss ltd space for c'vans. Lge, terr, shd; wc; baby facs; shwrs; el pnts (5A) inc; lndry rm; ice; shop high ssn; tradsmn; snacks; bar; BBQ; playgrnd; beach 1km; rv sw; sailing & windsurfing 1km; tennis; cycle hire; mini-golf; archery; entmnt; TV; quiet. "Gd, clean, modern facs; dir access to rv; ent to upper levels of site v steep." 1 Apr-31 Oct. € 27.50
2004*

PORTO POLLO *10H2* (Coastal) **Camping Alfonsi-U-Cassedu, Porto-Pollo, 20140 Serra-di-Ferro [04 95 74 01 80; fax 04 95 74 07 67]** Turn W onto D157 off N196 Propriano-Olmeto rd sp Porto-Pollo. After narr rv bdge turn L on D757. Site in 4km on L bef Porto-Pollo vill. Med, pt shd; wc; mv service pnt; shwrs; el pnts (10A) €3.40; lndtte; shop high ssn; supmkt in vill; rest high ssn; snacks; beach; poss cr; poss noisy; CCI. "Pleasant site." ♦ 1 Jun-15 Oct. € 21.40
2006*

PORTO VECCHIO *10H2* (5km N Rural/Coastal) **Camping La Vetta, Ste Trinité, 20137 Porto-Vecchio [04 95 70 09 86; fax 04 95 70 43 21; info@campinglavetta.com; www.campinglavetta.com]** On L (W) of N198 N of Ste Trinité. Sp in advance fr N & S. Med, pt sl, shd; wc; shwrs inc; el pnts €3; gas; lndtte; ice; shop 500m; supmkt 3km; rest; snacks; playgrnd; sports are; sand beach 4km; pool; Eng spkn; quiet but some rd noise. "Excel bay for snorkelling, sw & windsurfing." 15 May-15 Oct. € 19.00
2004*

PORTO VECCHIO *10H2* (5km N Coastal) **Camping Les Ilots d'Or, Ste Trinité, Route de Marina di Fiori, 20137 Porto-Vecchio [04 95 70 01 30 or 04 95 36 91 75; fax 04 95 70 01 30; www.campinglesilotsdor.com]** Turn E off N198 5km N of Porto-Vecchio at Ste Trinité twd San Ciprianu. In 1km fork R, site in 1km. Med, pt terr, shd; wc (cont); shwrs inc; el pnts (6A) €3; gas; ice; shop; poss cr; quiet. "Well organised site with beach on gulf of Porto Vecchio; helpful family owners; lovely part of Corsica with many v gd beaches within easy reach." 15 Apr-15 Oct. € 19.00
2007*

France

PORTO VECCHIO *10H2* (7km SE Rural) **Camping U Pirellu, Route de Palombaggia, 20137 Porto-Vecchio [04 95 70 23 44; fax 04 95 70 60 22; u.pirellu@wanadoo.fr; www.u-pirellu.com]** On N198 fr Porto-Vecchio 2km S, L on rte de Palombaggia & site in 6km. Med, hdg pitch, terr, pt sl, pt shd; wc; chem disp; shwrs; el pnts (6A) €3.50; lndtte; ice; shop; rest; snacks; bar; playgrnd; pool; sand beach 3km; tennis; TV; some statics; no dogs; red low ssn; CCI. "Steep slope fr ent gate; pleasant site amongst oak trees." 15 Apr-30 Sep. € 20.50
2007*

PORTO VECCHIO *10H2* (2km S Rural) **Camping U-Stabiacciu, Route de Palombaggia, 20137 Porto-Vecchio. [04 95 70 37 17; fax 04 95 70 62 59; stabiacciu@wanadoo.fr; www.stabiacciu.com]** Foll ring-rd N198 to S Porto-Vecchio, take 1st L sp Palombaggia. Site in 50m. Med, shd; wc (some cont); mv service pnt; shwrs inc; el pnts (10A) €3; ice; lndtte; shop in ssn; tradsmn; rest; snacks; bar; BBQ; playgrnd; jacuzzis; sand beach 4km; 3% statics; dogs; phone; Eng spkn; cc acc; CCI. "Excel beaches; gd base for exploring region." 1 Apr-14 Oct. € 19.10   2006*

PORTO VECCHIO *10H2* (8km W Coastal) **Club la Chiappa (Naturist), 20137 Porto-Vecchio [04 95 70 00 31; fax 04 95 70 07 70; chiappa@wanadoo.fr; www.chiappa.com]** On N198 fr Bastia heading S thro Porto-Vecchio. 2km S turn L to Pointe de la Chiappa & foll camp sp. Lge, pt shd; wc; chem disp; shwrs; el pnts inc; lndtte; ice; sauna; shop; rest; bar; playgrnd; pool; watersports; sand beach adj; tennis; horseriding; entmnt; TV rm; 10% statics; dogs €5; adv bkg; quiet; red low ssn. "Set in naturist reserve with 3km of private beach; vg facs; lovely setting." 12 May-6 Oct. € 34.00
2007*

SAGONE *10H2* (2km N) **Sagone Camping, Route de Vico, 20118 Sagone [04 95 28 04 15; fax 04 95 28 08 28; sagone.camping@wanadoo.fr; www.camping-sagone.fr]** Fr Sagone dir Cargèse then D70 dir Vico, site sp. Lge, mkd pitch, pt shd; wc; baby facs; shwrs inc; el pnts inc; lndtte; ice; shop; rest; snacks; bar; BBQ; playgrnd; pool; beach 1.5km; tennis 100m; horseriding 1km; entmnt; TV rm; 10% statics; dogs €1.75; adv bkg; quiet. ♦ 1 May-30 Sep. € 24.25 (CChq acc)
2004*

ST FLORENT *10G2* (1km SW Coastal) **Camping U Pezzo, Route de la Roya, 20217 St Florent [tel/fax 04 95 37 01 65; contact@upezzo.com; www.upezzo.com]** Exit St Florent for L'Ile-Rousse on D81 then N199 Route de la Plage. After 2km sharp R immed after x-ing bdge. Med, terr, pt shd; wc; mv service pnt; baby facs; shwrs; el pnts (10A) €3.50; lndtte; shop; rest; snacks; bar; sand beach adj; fishing; sailing; windsurfing; waterslide; horseriding; mini-farm for children; adv bkg; quiet; red low ssn; CCI. "Pleasant site; sh walk to town." 15 Apr-15 Oct. € 17.00   2007*

ST FLORENT *10G2* (2.5km W Coastal) **Camping Kalliste, Route de la Plage, 20217 St Florent [04 95 37 03 08; fax 04 95 37 19 77; www.camping-kalliste.com]** Fr St Florent twd L'Ile-Rousse on N199, after 2km sharp R immed after x-ing bdge. Site sp in 500m. Lge, hdg pitch, unshd; wc; mv service pnt; shwrs inc; el pnts (10A) €3.40; lndtte; ice; shop high ssn; rest; snacks; bar; tennis; horseriding; sand beach adj; fishing; sailing; windsurfing; games area; TV; poss cr; adv bkg; CCI. 1 Apr-30 Sep. € 20.50   2006*

SARTENE *10H2* (5km N Rural) **Camping Olva Les Eucalyptus, Route de la Castagna, 20100 Sartène [04 95 77 11 58 or 04 95 77 14 09; fax 04 95 77 05 68]** Fr Sartène, take D69 twd Ste Lucie, site in 5km. Med, pt sl, ter, pt shd; wc; shwrs; el pnts (6A); gas; lndtte; shop; rest; playgrnd; rv sw 1km; beach 8km; some statics; adv bkg; quiet. "V friendly." 1 Apr-30 Sep.   2005*

SERRA DI FERRO see Porto Pollo *10H2*

VENACO *10G2* (4km E Rural) **Camping La Ferme de Peridundellu, 20231 Venaco [tel/fax 04 95 47 09 89]** S on N200 fr Corte for 15km; R on D143; at bdge keep R towards Venaco; site on L in 1.5km on bend. Sm, pt sl, pt shd; htd wc; chem disp (wc); shwrs inc; el pnts (6-10A) inc; lndtte; ice; shop 2km; tradsmn; rest; snacks & bar 2km; quiet; cc acc; CCI. "CL-type site; beautifully situated; gd walking country; friendly owner whose wife cooks evening meals in rest." € 18.00   2005*

VIVARIO *10G2* (5km N Rural) **Aire Naturelle Le Soleil (Marietti), 20219 Tattone [04 95 47 21 16; www.corte-tourisme.com]** N fr Ajaccio on N193 twds Corte. Well sp by stn in Tattone. Sm, hdstg, terr, shd; wc; chem disp; shwrs; el pnts inc; ice; pizzeria; bar; fishing; quiet. "Nice, clean site; superb views; friendly owners; sm area for tourers; facs poss stretched high ssn; ring ahead low ssn; train to Corte & Ajaccio stops on request; ideal walking." 1 May-15 Oct. € 17.00
2007*

ILE DE RE

ARS EN RE *7A1* (400m S Coastal) **Camping du Soleil, 57 Route de la Grange, 17590 Ars-en-Ré [05 46 29 40 62; fax 05 46 29 41 74; contact@campdusoleil.com; www.campdusoleil.com]** On ent Ars-en-Ré on D735, pass Citroën g'ge & in 700m take 3rd L dir Plage de la Grange. Site sp. Med, hdg/mkd pitch, pt shd; wc; chem disp; mv service pnt; baby facs; fam bthrm; shwrs inc; el pnts (10A) €4.56; lndtte; ice; shop; rest; snacks; bar; BBQ (gas/elec); playgrnd; htd pool; paddling pool; sand beach 400m; tennis; games area; cycle hire; wifi internet; TV rm; 35% statics; dogs €3; phone; adv bkg; CCI. "Pleasant, pretty site; helpful, friendly staff." ♦ 15 Mar-15 Nov. € 30.50   2007*

See advertisement opposite

ARS EN RE 7A1 (800m SW Coastal) **Camping ESSI**, Route de la Pointe de Grignon, 17590 Ars-en-Ré [05 46 29 44 73 or 05 46 29 46 09 (LS); fax 05 46 37 57 78; camping.essi@wanadoo.fr; www.campingessi.com] D735 to Ars-en-Ré; do not enter town; turn L at supmkt. Site sp. Med, hdg pitch, pt shd; htd wc; chem disp; baby facs; shwrs inc; el pnts (5-10A) €3.70-5.25; lndtte; shop; tradsmn; rest; snacks; bar; BBQ; playgrnd; pool; watersports; cycle hire; 7% statics; dogs €2.10; phone; bus 800m; adv bkg (dep req); quiet; red low ssn; CCI. "Attractive waterfront town; excel beaches 2km; gd cycling; gd oysters; vg." ♦ 25 Mar- 31 Oct. € 21.30 (3 persons) 2006*

ARS EN RE 7A1 (300m NW Coastal) **Airotel Camping Le Cormoran**, Route de Radia, 17590 Ars-en-Ré [05 46 29 46 04; fax 05 46 29 29 36; info@cormoran.com; www.cormoran.com] Fr La Rochelle take D735 onto Ile-de-Ré, site sp fr Ars-en-Ré. Med, hdg/mkd pitch, hdstg, pt shd; wc; chem disp; mv service pnt; baby facs; sauna; shwrs inc; el pnts (10A) €5; lndtte; ice; shop 800m; tradsmn; rest; snacks; bar; playgrnd; htd pool; beach 500m; tennis; cycle hire; games area; games rm; golf 10km; entmnt; some statics; dogs €5.50; Eng spkn; adv bkg; quiet; cc acc; red low ssn; CCI. "Delightful vill; vg site." ♦ 1 Apr-30 Sep. € 40.00 (3 persons) 2007*

COUARDE SUR MER, LA see St Martin de Ré 7A1

PORTES EN RE, LES 7A1 (800m E Urban/Coastal) Camping La Providence, Route de la Trousse-Chemise, 17880 Les Portes-en-Ré [05 46 29 56 82; fax 05 46 29 61 80; campingprovidence@wanadoo.fr; www.campingprovidence.com] On N11 & N137 to La Rochelle foll sp to Ile de Ré. Cross toll bdge & foll D735 to Les Portes-en-Ré at far end of island. Site adj to Plage de la Redoute. Lge, hdg/mkd pitch, pt shd; htd wc (few cont); chem disp; mv service pnt; baby facs; shwrs inc; el pnts (10A) €5; gas; lndtte; shop; rest; snacks; bar; playgrnd; sand beach adj; sailing, watersports, tennis, golf nrby; cycle hire; games rm; mini-golf; 50% statics; dogs €4; poss cr; Eng spkn; adv bkg; CCI. "Lge pitches; easy access to beach & town; gd, flat cycling on island & across bdge to mainland." ♦ 1 Apr-15 Oct. € 27.00 (3 persons) 2007*

See advertisement above

RIVEDOUX PLAGE 7A1 (Coastal) Camping Les Tamaris, 4 Rue du Comte-d'Hastrel, 17940 Rivedoux-Plage [05 46 09 81 28; www.rivedoux-plage.fr] Cross bdge to island on D735 & bear L onto D201. Site sp. Med, mkd pitch, pt shd; wc; chem disp; shwrs inc; el pnts (10A) €3.60 (long lead poss req); lndtte; shop, rest, snacks, bar nrby; sand beach adj; sat TV; dogs €1.20; phone; poss cr; quiet; red low ssn; CCI. "Friendly, helpful, unobtrusive owners; facs basic but clean; excel cycling on island." 1 May-30 Sep. € 13.00 2007*

France

Camping *** La Tour des Prises

Ile de Ré

Rental of mobile homes

Route d'Ars – 17670 La Couarde-sur-Mer
Phone: 00 33 (0)5 46 29 84 82 • Fax 00 33 (0)5 46 29 88 99
E-Mail: camping@lesprises.com

Covered and heated swimming pool

ST CLEMENT DES BALEINES *7A1* (Coastal) Camping La Côte Sauvage, 336 Rue de la Forêt, 17590 St Clément-des-Baleines [04 73 77 05 05; fax 04 73 77 05 06; contact@lesbalconsverts. com; www.lesbalconsverts.com] Fr cent of vill, foll sp to site at edge of forest. Lge, mkd pitch, pt sl, pt shd; wc; chem disp; mv service pnt; baby facs; shws inc; el pnts (10A) €3.80; shop 300m; sand beach adj; cycle routes adj; sw; dogs €3; phone; quiet; Eng spkn; CCI. "Gd location; vg san facs; poss unreliable opening dates; gd." ♦ 1 Apr-30 Sep. € 16.00   2007*

ST CLEMENT DES BALEINES *7A1* (500m N Coastal) **Airotel Camping La Plage, 408 Rue du Chaume, 17590 St Clément-des-Baleines** [05 46 29 42 62; fax 05 46 29 03 39; info@la-plage.com; www.la-plage.com] Fr La Rochelle on D735 to far end of Ile de Ré; site 500m fr Baleines lighthouse, sp. Med, hdg/mkd pitch, hdstg, unshd; htd wc (some cont); chem disp; mv service pnt; baby facs; fam bthrm; shwrs inc; el pnts (10A) €5; gas 1km; Indtte; ice; shop 1.5km; tradsmn; rest; snacks; bar; playgrnd; htd pool; paddling pool; sand beach adj; games area; games rm; cycle hire; wifi internet; entmnt; child entmnt; dogs €5.50; Eng spkn; adv bkg; quiet; cc acc; red low ssn; CCI. "Delightful vill; excel facs for families; vg." ♦ Easter-30 Sep. € 40.00 (3 persons)   2007*

STE MARIE DE RE see St Martin de Ré *7A1*

ST MARTIN DE RE *7A1* (4km E Coastal/Urban) **Camp Municipal de Bel Air, Route de la Noué, 17630 La Flotte** [05 46 09 63 10] Fr toll bdge take D735 to La Flotte. Turn R at rndabt to town into Route de la Noué, site sp.. Lge, hdg/mkd pitch, pt shd; wc (some cont); chem disp; mv service pnt; shwrs inc; el pnts (6A) €3.84; Indtte; rest; snacks; bar; playgrnd; beach 800m; tennis; games rm; entmnt; phone; adv bkg; quiet. "Gd value site; walk to shops, harbour, beach etc." ♦ 1 Apr-30 Sep. € 13.64   2007*

ST MARTIN DE RE *7A1* (2km SE Coastal) **FFCC** Camping Les Peupliers, 17630 La Flotte-en-Ré [05 46 09 62 35; fax 05 46 09 59 76; camping@ lespeupliers.com; www.les-peupliers.com] Site sp fr D735, the main rd on Ile-de-Ré. Lge, hdg pitch, pt shd; wc; chem disp; mv service pnt; shwrs inc; el pnts (5A) inc; Indtte; shop; tradsmn; rest; snacks; bar; playgrnd; pool; sand beach 3km; games area; entmnt; internet; TV; 80% statics; dogs €5; phone; Eng spkn; adv bkg; quiet; cc acc; CCI. "Sea views; some pitches sm; crowded in Jun; gd sports facs; island ideal for cycling & swimming." 5 Apr-27 Sep. € 28.00 (3 persons) (CChq acc)
2007*

ST MARTIN DE RE *7A1* (5km SE Coastal) **Camping Antioche, Route de Ste Marie, 17580 Le Bois-Plage-en-Ré** [05 46 09 23 86; fax 05 46 09 43 34; camping.antioche@wanadoo.fr; www.antioche. com] Fr toll bdge fr La Rochelle, at 1st rndabt take D201 sp Le Bois-Plage. In about 9km, site on L. Med, hdg/mkd pitch (sandy), pt shd; wc; chem disp; mv service pnt; shwrs inc; el pnts (6A) inc; Indtte; shop & 3km; playgrnd; snacks; bar; sand beach adj; entmnt; some statics; dogs €4; phone; poss cr; Eng spkn; adv bkg (dep req); cc acc; red long stay/CCI. "Direct access to beach & cycle path; friendly staff; v clean facs." ♦ 9 Apr-24 Sep. € 33.00 (3 persons)
2005*

ST MARTIN DE RE *7A1* (5km SE Rural) **Camping La Grainetière, Route St Martin, 17630 La Flotte** [05 46 09 68 86; fax 05 46 09 53 13; lagrainetiere@ free.fr; www.la-grainetiere.com] 10km W fr toll bdge, site sp on La Flotte ring rd. Med, pt shd; wc; chem disp; mv service pnt; baby facs; shwrs inc; el pnts (10A) €4; gas; Indtte; shop; tradsmn; playgrnd; htd pool; sand beach 3km; cycle hire; TV rm; 70% statics; dogs €3; poss cr; Eng spkn; adv bkg; CCI. "Beautiful wooded site kept spotlessly clean; generous pitches; immac san facs; helpful owners; easy cycle ride to La Flotte with daily mkt." ♦ 1 Apr-30 Sep. € 24.00   2007*

ST MARTIN DE RE *7A1* (7km SE Coastal) **Camp Municipal La Côte Sauvage, La Basse Benée 17740 Ste Marie-de-Ré [05 46 30 21 74; fax 05 46 30 15 64; info@mairie-sainte-marie-de-re. fr; www.mairie-sainte-marie-de-re.fr]** Site sp fr main rd. V narr rds thro town. Med, mkd pitch, pt shd; wc; chem disp; mv service pnt; shwrs inc; el pnts (6A) €2.50; shop; supmkt 2km snacks; bar; playgrnd; sand beach adj; fishing; quiet; CCI. "Excel location; v helpful owners; many cycle tracks; free parking for m'vans adj; windy; highly rec." 1 May-21 Sep. € 13.00   2007*

ST MARTIN DE RE *7A1* (800m S Urban) **Camp Municipal Les Remparts, Rue Les Remparts, 17410 St Martin-de-Ré [05 46 09 21 96; fax 05 46 09 94 18; camping.stmartindere@wanadoo. fr; www.saint-martin-de-re.fr]** Foll D735 fr toll bdge to St Martin; sp in town fr both ends. Med, hdg/mkd pitch, pt sl, pt shd; wc; chem disp; mv service pnt; shwrs inc; el pnts (10A) €3.50; lndtte; shop; snacks; BBQ; playgrnd; pool 3km; sand beach 1.3km; dogs €1.70; Eng spkn; adv bkg; quiet; cc acc; CCI. "Busy site; v clean facs but ltd; some pitches boggy in wet weather; conv lovely port vill; excel cycling on island." ♦ 1 Feb-15 Nov. € 16.00 (3 persons)   2006*

ST MARTIN DE RE *7A1* (3km SW Coastal) **Camping Les Varennes, Raise Maritaise, 17580 Le Bois-Plage-en-Ré [05 46 09 15 43; fax 05 46 09 47 27; les-varennes@wanadoo.fr; www.les-varennes. com]** Fr toll bdge at La Rochelle, foll D201 to Gros-Jonc; turn L at rndabt; after 350m turn R; site on R in 500m. Med, mkd pitch, pt shd; htd wc (some cont); chem disp; mv service pnt; baby facs; shws inc; el pnts (10A) €5.30; lndtte; shop & rest 1km; snacks; bar; BBQ; playgrnd; htd, covrd pool; sand beach 800m; cycle hire; internet; TV; 60% statics; dogs €6; poss cr; Eng spkn; adv bkg; quiet; cc acc; red low ssn/long stay; CCI. "Excel, quiet site; many cycle tracks; vg." ♦ 31 Mar-30 Sep. € 37.00
                                            2006*

ST MARTIN DE RE *7A1* (3km SW Coastal) **Sunêlia Parc Club Interlude, Plage de Gros-Jonc, 17580 Le Bois-Plage-en-Ré [05 46 09 18 22; fax 05 46 09 23 38; infos@interlude.fr; www. interlude.fr]** Fr toll bdge at La Rochelle foll D201 to Gros-Jonc. Turn L at rndabt at site sp. Site 400m on L. Lge, mkd pitch, hdstg, pt shd; htd wc; chem disp; mv service pnt; baby facs; fam bthrm; sauna; some serviced pitches; shwrs inc; el pnts (10A) inc; gas; lndtte; shop; rest; snacks; bar; BBQ; playgrnd; 2 pools (1 htd, covrd); sand beach; watersports; jacuzzi; solarium; tennis nr; games area; boat & cycle hire; fitness rm; child entmnt; TV rm; 45% statics; dogs €7; poss cr; Eng spkn; o'night spaces/facs for m'vans; adv bkg ess; quiet. "Excel, v quiet, relaxing, well-run, busy site; excel location & facs; mature trees & birdsong; some sm, sandy pitches - extra for lger pitches; nrby beaches excel." ♦ 1 Apr-11 Nov. € 42.00
                                            2006*

ST MARTIN DE RE *7A1* (4km SW Coastal) **Camp Municipal des Amis de la Plage, Ave Pas des Boeufs, 17580 Le Bois-Plage-en-Ré [tel/fax 05 46 09 24 01; contact@les-amis-de-la-plage. com; http://les-amis-de-la-plage.com]** Fr toll bdge fr La Rochelle foll D201 to Le Bois-Plage-en-Ré; on ent vill take 1st L sp 'Plage-des-Boeufs' & 'Municipal'. Site on R at end of rd. Lge, pt sl, pt shd; wc; chem disp (wc); mv service pnt; shwrs inc; el pnts (10A) €4; shops & mkt 1km; tradsmn; rest; snacks; bar; BBQ; playgrnd; sand beach nrby; 5% statics; dogs €2; phone; bus 1km; poss cr; Eng spkn; quiet; CCI. "Friendly, easy-going site; gd beach adj; pitches on sand/soil/dry grass; gd." 1 Apr-30 Sep. € 19.00 (3 persons)   2007*

ST MARTIN DE RE *7A1* (6km W Coastal) **Camping de l'Océan, 50 Route d'Ars, 17670 La Couarde-sur-Mer [05 46 29 87 70; fax 05 46 29 92 13; campingdelocean@wanadoo.fr; www.camping ocean.com]** Fr La Rochelle take D735 over bdge to lle de Ré. Past St Martin-de-Re & La Couarde. Site on R, 2.5km after La Couarde. Lge, hdg/mkd pitch, shd; wc; chem disp; mv service pnt; baby facs; fam bthrm; shwrs inc; el pnts (5-10A) €3.50-5.20; lndtte; shop; rest, snacks & bar high ssn; no BBQ; playgrnd; 2 pools (1 htd); paddling pool; sand beach adj; watersports; tennis; games area; cycle hire; horseriding 1.5km; golf 6km; entmnt; wifi internet; 40% statics; dogs €4.55; phone; poss cr; Eng spkn; adv bkg, dep req; rd noisy; CCI. "Spacious site; well-laid out pitches, but site rds & ent to pitches v narr; excel, clean san facs (but 1 block not gd low ssn); twin-axles not rec; friendly staff; busy holiday area; St Martin v pretty; gd walking & cycling; excel." ♦ Easter-23 Sep. € 38.20 (3 persons) (CChq acc)
                                            2007*

France

ST MARTIN DE RE *7A1* (6km W Coastal) **Camping La Tour des Prises, Chemin de la Grifforine, Route d'Ars, 17670 La Couarde-sur-Mer [05 46 29 84 82; fax 05 46 29 88 99; camping@ lesprises.com; www.lesprises.com]** Fr toll bdge foll D735 or D201 to La Couarde, then Rte d'Ars for 1.8km to R turn; site sp & 200m on R. Med, hdg/mkd pitch, pt shd; htd wc (some cont); chem disp; mv service pnt; baby facs; shwrs inc; el pnts (16A) inc; lndtte; ice; shop; tradsmn; snacks; playgrnd; htd, covrd pool; beach 600m; sailing school; games rm; cycle hire; 30% statics; dogs €3; Eng spkn; adv bkg; quiet; cc acc; red low ssn; CCI. "Excel, well-managed, clean site; lge indiv pitches, mixed sizes; helpful owner & staff; many cycle/walking tracks; all watersports on island; beach 10 mins walk; ideal site for families." ♦ 1 Apr-30 Sep. € 34.00 (3 persons)   2007*

See advertisement

BOIS PLAGE EN RE, LE see St Martin lle de Re *7A1*

ILE D'OLERON

BREE LES BAINS, LA *7A1* (Coastal) **Camp Municipal Le Planginot, Allée du Gai Séjour, 17840 La Brée-les-Bains [05 46 47 82 18; fax 05 46 75 90 74; camping.planginot@wanadoo.fr]** N fr St Pierre d'Oléron on D734, turn R for La Brée on D273, site sp. Lge, mkd pitch, pt shd; htd wc; shwrs €0.80; el pnts (5-10A) €2-3.25; lndtte; snacks; rest in high ssn; playgrnd; pool; beach adj; dogs €1.80; adv bkg; quiet. "Immac facs; gd location for beach & cycle path; friendly, helpful staff; excel mkt adj; excel value low ssn." ♦ 15 Mar-15 Oct. € 11.05
2006*

BREE LES BAINS, LA *7A1* (3km NW Coastal) **Camp Municipal, Blvd d'Antioche, 17650 St Denis-d'Oléron [05 46 47 85 62; fax 05 46 47 81 51; camping-municipal-st-denis-doleron@wanadoo. fr]** Clear sp fr D734 in St Denis-d'Oléron town cent. Lge, mkd pitch, pt sl, pt shd; htd wc; chem disp; mv service pnt; shwrs inc; el pnts (6A) €3.50; gas; lndtte; ice; shop; rest; snacks; playgrnd; sand beach adj; fishing; tennis; dogs €1.80; poss cr; Eng spkn; quiet; CCI. "Gd facs; some pitches v soft; ideal for beach holiday with children." 15 Apr-15 Oct. € 12.40 (3 persons)
2006*

CHATEAU D'OLERON, LE *7B1* (Urban/Coastal) **Camping Les Remparts, Blvd Philippe-Daste, 17480 Le Château-d'Oléron [05 46 47 61 93; fax 05 46 47 73 65; camping@les-remparts.com; www.les-remparts.com]** Fr cent Le Château-d'Oléron take D734 dir Dolus d'Oléron rd. After x-ing ramparts/moat turn R at next rndabt, site on R Lge, pt sl, pt shd; wc (maintly cont); mv service pnt; shwrs inc; el pnts (5A) €3.90; lndtte; shop nrby; tradsmn; rest, snacks, bar nrby; playgrnd; sand beach adj; some statics; dogs €2; phone; quiet. "Pleasant site for NH/sh stay." 1 Mar-31 Oct. € 17.90
2006*

CHATEAU D'OLERON, LE *7B1* (1km W Coastal) **Airotel Camping Domaine d'Oléron, Domaine de Montravail, 17480 Le Château-d'Oléron [05 46 47 61 82; fax 05 46 47 79 67; info@camping-airotel-oleron.com; www.camping-airotel-oleron.com]** Clearly sp fr D734 after x-ing bdge. Med, mkd pitch, pt shd; wc; shwrs inc; el pnts (10A) €3.90 (poss rev pol); gas; lndtte; ice; shop & 500m; snacks; bar; BBQ; playgrnd; htd pool; sand beach 1km; fishing; tennis; horseriding; games area; cycle hire; some statics; dogs €2.50; poss cr; Eng spkn; adv bkg; quiet; red low ssn/CCI. ♦ 1 Apr-15 Oct. € 22.00
2006*

CHATEAU D'OLERON, LE *7B1* (2.5km NW Coastal) **Camping La Brande, Route des Huîtres, 17480 Le Château-d'Oléron [05 46 47 62 37; fax 05 46 47 71 70; info@camping-labrande.com; www.camping-labrande.com]** Cross bdge on D26, turn R & go thro Le Château-d'Oléron. Foll Rte des Huîtres to La Gaconnière to site. Lge, shd; wc; mv service pnt; baby facs; sauna; steam room; shwrs inc; el pnts (6-10A) €3.20-4; gas; lndtte; shop; rest in ssn; snacks; bar; BBQ; playgrnd; 3 pools (1 htd, covrd), waterslide; sand beach 300m; tennis; mini-golf; games area; golf 6km; entmnt; wifi internet; TV rm; 60% statics; dogs €2.50; sep car park; Eng spkn; adv bkg; red low ssn. "V pleasant owners; gd rest on site; 10 min cycle ride into town; pitches at far end adj oyster farm - noise fr pumps & poss mosquitoes." ♦ 15 Mar-15 Nov. € 29.00 (CChq acc)
2007*

ST DENIS D'OLERON see Brée les Bains, La *7A1*

ST GEORGES D'OLERON *7A1* (5km E Coastal) **Camping La Gautrelle (CC de F), Plage des Saumonards, 17190 St Georges-d'Oléron [05 46 47 21 57; fax 05 46 75 10 74; lagautrelle. ccdf@wanadoo.fr; www.campingclub.asso.fr]** Fr viaduct, take D734 to St Pierre. At 3rd traff lts, turn R to Sauzelle, thro vill & L for St Georges & immed to R sp CCDF La Gautrelle. Site at end of lane in approx 1.5km & adj to beach. Lge, mkd pitch, shd; wc; shwrs inc; el pnts (6A) inc (long cable req); shops adj; sand beach; fishing; some statics; dogs €2.10; adv bkg; quiet; CCI. "Splendid beaches; forest walks, fishing; ltd el pnts." ♦ 31 Mar-30 Sep. € 18.00
2006*

ST GEORGES D'OLERON *7A1* (6km E Coastal) **Camping Signol, Ave des Albatros, Boyardville, 17190 St Georges-d'Oléron [05 46 47 01 22; fax 05 46 47 23 46; contact@signol.com; www.signol. com]** Cross bdge onto Ile d'Oléron & cont on main rd twd St Pierre-d'Oléron. Turn R at Dolus-d'Oléron for Boyardville & foll sp in vill. Lge, hdg/mkd pitch, pt sl, pt shd; wc (most cont); mv service pnt; chem disp; baby facs; shwrs inc; el pnts (6A) €4.60; gas; lndtte; shops adj; tradsmn; bar; playgrnd; htd pool; paddling pool; sand beach 800m; some statics; no dogs Jul/Aug, low ssn €4; Eng spkn; adv bkg. "San facs inadequate for size of site & v stretched peak times; size & quality of pitches variable, some far fr san facs & some prone to flooding in wet weather." ♦ 1 May-30 Sep. € 29.00
2006*

France

ST GEORGES D'OLERON *7A1* (800m SE Rural) **CHADOTEL Camping Le Domaine d'Oléron, La Jousselinière, 17190 St Georges-d'Oléron [05 46 76 54 97 or 02 51 33 05 05 (LS); fax 02 51 33 94 04; chadotel@wanadoo.fr; www.chadotel.com]** After x-ing Viaduct (bridge) onto island foll sp dir St Pierre d'Oléron & St Georges-d'Oléron on D734; turn R on rndabt immed see Leclerc supmkt on R; at next rndabt turn L sp 'Le Bois Fleury'; pass airfield 'Bois 'Fleury' on R; take next R & then immed L. Site on L in 500m. Med, mkd pitch, terr, pt shd; wc; chem disp; baby facs; shwrs inc; el pnts (6A) inc; gas; lndtte; ice; shop; rest; snacks; bar; BBQ (gas only); playgrnd; pool; waterslide; paddling pool; sand beach 2.5km; cycle hire; games/TV rm; 25% statics; dogs €3; Eng spkn; adv bkg; red long stay; quiet; CCI. "Well-organised, v clean site; v pleasant & helpful; barrier card €15 dep; excel." ♦ 5 Apr-27 Sep. € 28.90 ABS - A41
2007*

ST GEORGES D'OLERON *7A1* (2km SE Rural) **Camping Verébleu, La Jousselinière, 17190 St Georges-d'Oléron [05 46 76 57 70; fax 05 46 76 70 56; verebleu@wanadoo.fr; www.verebleu.tm.fr]** Foll D734 thro St Pierre-d'Oléron. On NW o'skts of town at St Gilles turn R (sp La Jousselinière), cross over D273. After 1km take 1st turn L (sp St Georges, La Jousselinière). Site 500m on L. Lge, hdg/mkd pitch, some hdstg, pt shd; wc (some cont); chem disp; mv service pnt; baby facs; shwrs inc; el pnts (4-8A) €3.50-€6; gas; lndtte; ice; sm shop; supmkt 1.5km; rest; snacks; bar; playgrnd; htd pool; waterslide; sand beach 3km; tennis; entmnt; 30% statics; no dogs; poss cr; adv bkg ess high ssn (30% dep req + bkg fee); quiet; cc acc; CCI. "V efficient management; excel; Oléron is a sm, unspoilt island; lovely beaches; gd for families." ♦ 2 Jun-16 Sep. € 29.00
2007*

ST GEORGES D'OLERON *7A1* (3km W Coastal) **Camping Le Suroit, L'Ileau, 17190 St Georges-d'Oléron [05 46 47 07 25 or 06 80 10 93 18 (mob); fax 05 46 75 04 24; camping@lesuroit.fr; www.camping-lesuroit.com]** Fr Domino cent foll sp for beach, turn L for L'Ileau. Strt at x-rds. Fork L for La Cotinière, 150m site on R. Lge, mkd pitch, shd; htd wc; baby facs; shwrs inc; el pnts (10A) €4; gas; lndtte; ice; shop; rest; snacks; bar; playgrnd; htd, covrd pool; sand beach adj; tennis; games area; cycle hire; entmnt; TV; some statics; dogs €3; adv bkg; quiet; red low ssn. "Excel site." ♦ 1 Apr-30 Sep. € 22.00
2007*

See advertisement

ST GEORGES D'OLERON *7A1* (3km W Coastal) **Camping Les Grosses Pierres, Les Sables Vigniers, 17190 St Georges-d'Oléron [05 46 76 52 19 or 02 51 27 37 80 (reservation); fax 05 46 76 54 85 or 02 51 28 84 09; vagues-oceanes@wanadoo.fr; www.camping-vagues-oceanes.com]** Site sp fr D734. Lge, mkd pitch, terr, pt shd; wc; shwrs inc; el pnts (5A) €6; gas; lndtte; shop; rest; snacks; bar; playgrnd; 2 pools (1 htd, covrd); waterslide; sand beach 900m; 95% statics; dogs €4; Eng spkn; adv bkg; cc acc; CCI. 15 Apr-30 Sep. € 24.00
2006*

ST PIERRE D'OLERON *7B1* (Coastal) **FFCC Camp Municipal La Fauche Prère, Ave des Pins, La Cotinière, 17310 St Pierre d'Oléron [05 46 47 10 53; fax 05 46 75 23 44; camping@saint-pierre-oleron.com; www.saint-pierre-oleron.com]** Fr bdge foll D734 N to St Pierre-d'Oléron. Turn L onto D274 for La Cotinière, site bef vill on L, sp. Med, mkd pitch, pt sl, shd; wc; chem disp (wc); mv service pnt; baby facs; shwrs €0.80; el pnts (12A) €3.10; lndtte; shop; playgrnd; sand beach adj; dogs €1.55; poss cr; CCI. "Direct access to beach; most pitches sandy; gd." 1 Apr-30 Sep. € 12.40 (3 persons)
2006*

ST PIERRE D'OLERON 7B1 (400m N Rural)
**Camping La Pierrière, 18 Route de St Georges,
17310 St Pierre-d'Oléron** [05 46 47 08 29; fax
05 46 75 12 82; info@camping-la-pierriere.com;
www.camping-la-pierriere.com] On island foll sp
into St Pierre. Turn R at 3rd traff lts then L. Sp to La
Pierrière-Piscine are clear. Med, mkd pitch, pt shd;
some serviced pitch; wc; chem disp; shwrs inc, el
pnts (4-10A) €3.50-5; lndtte; ice; rest; snacks; bar;
playgrnd; htd pool; sand beach 4km; some statics;
dogs €2; poss cr; Eng spkn; adv bkg; quiet; cc acc;
CCI. "Gd for cycling; daily mkt in town; some facs
clsd Sep." ♦ 5 Apr-19 Sep. € 22.00   2006*

ST PIERRE D'OLERON 7B1 (3km W Coastal)
**Camping La Perroche Leitner, 18 Rue de
Renclos de la Perroche, 17310 St Pierre-d'Oléron**
[05 46 75 37 33; fax 05 49 85 12 57] Site about
10km fr bdge on W coast of Ile d'Oléron. Fr bdge
foll sp to Grande Village/Vert-Bois/La Remigeasse
& La Perroche. Well sp. Med, hdg/mkd pitch, hdstg,
terr, pt shd; wc; mv service pnt; shwrs inc; el pnts
(5-10A) €4.90-5.90; gas; lndtte; ice; shop; tradsmn;
playgrnd; direct access sand beach 200m; games
area; dogs €2.20; Eng spkn; quiet; cc acc. "Superb
site in all respects; site staff have to connect/
disconnect el pnt." ♦ 1 Apr-15 Sep. € 20.20
                                                          2006*

ST TROJAN LES BAINS 7B1 (1km SW Coastal)
**Camp Municipal Montplaisir, 8 Ave des Bris,
17370 St Trojan-les-Bains** [05 46 76 01 03 or
05 46 47 02 39; fax 05 46 76 42 95; monplaisir@
netcourrier.com] App St Trojan-les-Bains on D126,
strt thro rndabt with figure sculpture & R at next
rndabt, site sp. Site in fork in 1km. Lge, pt sl, pt shd;
wc; chem disp; baby facs; fam bthrm; shwrs inc; el
pnts (6A) €3.25; gas 200m; ice; lndtte; shop 200m;
tradsmn; rest; snacks; bar; BBQ; sm playgrnd; sand
beach 1km; horseriding, tennis, cinema & fun park
nrby; dogs €1.35; phone; no adv bkg; cc acc; CCI.
"Gd value; site in forest; adequate, clean facs." ♦
1 Jul-31 Aug. € 11.80   2005*

ST TROJAN LES BAINS 7B1 (1.5km SW Coastal)
**Camp Municipal Les Martinets, 11 Ave des
Bris, 17370 St Trojan-les-Bains** [05 46 76 02 39;
fax 05 46 76 42 95; lesmartinets@free.fr; http://
monsite.wanadoo.fr/lesmartinets] Fr D26 cont
on toll bdge rd then L onto D126 to St Trojan-les-
Bains. Foll sp for 'Campings' & 'Plage' then sp for
Gatseau Plage. Lge, mkd pitch, pt sl, terr, pt shd;
wc (few cont); chem disp; mv service pnt; shwrs
inc; el pnts (6A) €3.40; gas 500m; lndtte; ice; shops
300m; tradsmn; snacks high ssn; playgrnd; sand
beach 1km; cycle hire; 5% statics; dogs €1.35;
phone; Eng spkn; adv bkg dep req; cc acc; CCI.
"Gd site." ♦ ltd. 15 Jan-15 Nov. € 12.30   2006*

> This guide relies
> on site report forms submitted
> by caravanners like us; we'll do
> our bit and tell the editor what
> we think of the campsites
> we've visited.

ST TROJAN LES BAINS 7B1 (1.5km SW Rural)
**Camping La Combinette, Ave des Bris, 17370
St Trojan-les-Bains** [05 46 76 00 47; fax
05 46 76 16 96; la-combinette@wanadoo.fr; www.
combinette-oleron.com] Fr toll bdge stay on D26
for 1km, L onto D275 & L onto D126 to St Trojan-
les-Bains. Strt ahead at rndabt with figure sculpture,
then R at next rndabt sp Campings. In 1km turn L at
rd fork, site on R in 1km. Lge, shd; wc; baby facs;
shwrs inc; el pnts (5-10A) €3-3.90; gas; lndtte; ice;
shop; rest; snacks; playgrnd; beach 2km; games
area; cycle hire; entmnt; dogs €2.20; poss cr; quiet.
"Gd touring base; facs poss stretched high ssn." ♦
1 Apr-31 Oct. € 15.30   2006*

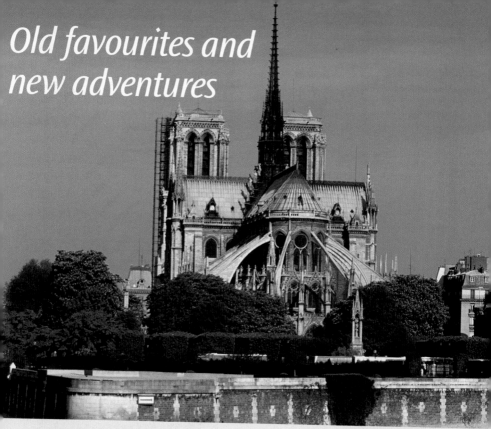

Old favourites and new adventures

The Club's Inclusive Holidays for 2008 feature many of our members' best-loved trips, including walking and gastronomic holidays in France, together with a few new additions and the return of old favourites to tempt you.

Our Grand tour for 2008 will travel north to the Scandinavian capitals and incorporate a rail / hotel short trip from Helsinki to St Petersburg. There will also be a second longer tour to Northern Spain and the Pyrenees.

New sites which can be booked with a ferry crossing for independent travel have been introduced in France, Spain, Germany, Denmark, Slovenia, Hungary and the Czech Republic.

Our Inclusive Holidays can be booked in conjunction with any ferry crossing, other sites en route and The Club's Red Pennant Holiday Insurance, if required.

Find out more in our **Travel Service in Europe** brochure or your copy phone **01342 327410** or visit our website **www.caravanclub.co.uk**

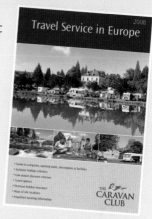

France

Distances are shown in kilometres and are calculated from town/city centres along the most practical roads, although not necessarily taking the shortest route.

1km = 0.62miles

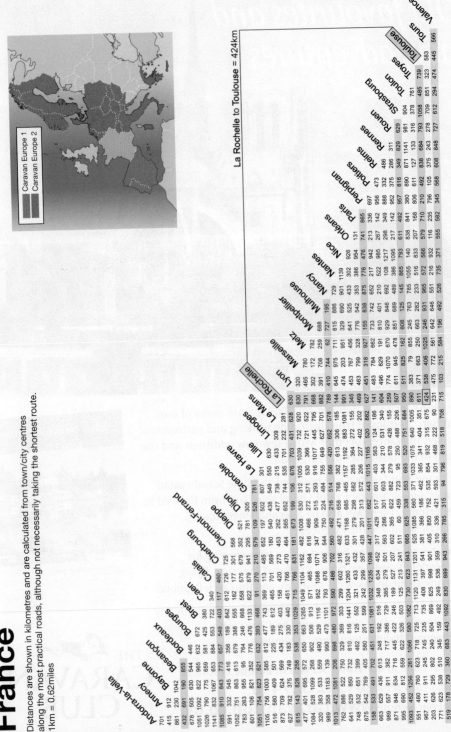

La Rochelle to Toulouse = 424km

Regions and Departments of France

ALSACE
67 Bas-Rhin
68 Haut-Rhin

AQUITAINE
24 Dordogne
33 Gironde
40 Landes
47 Lot-et-Garonne
64 Pyrénées-Atlantiques

AUVERGNE
03 Allier
15 Cantal
43 Haute-Loire
63 Puy-de-Dôme

BOURGOGNE
21 Côte-d'Or
58 Nièvre
71 Saône-et-Loire
89 Yonne

BRETAGNE
22 Côtes-d'Armor
29 Finistère
35 Ille-et-Vilaine
56 Morbihan

CENTRE
18 Cher
28 Eure-et-Loir
36 Indre
37 Indre-et-Loire
41 Loir-et-Cher
45 Loiret

CHAMPAGNE-ARDENNE
08 Ardennes
10 Aube
51 Marne
52 Haute-Marne

CORSE
02A Corse-du-Sud
02B Haute-Corse

FRANCHE-COMTE
25 Doubs
39 Jura
70 Haute-Saône
90 Territoire-de-Belfort

LANGUEDOC-ROUSSILLON
11 Aude
30 Gard
34 Hérault
48 Lozère
66 Pyrénées-Orientales

LIMOUSIN
19 Corrèze
23 Creuse
87 Haute-Vienne

LORRAINE
54 Meurthe-et-Moselle
55 Meuse
57 Moselle
88 Vosges

MIDI-PYRENEES
09 Ariège
12 Aveyron
31 Haute-Garonne
32 Gers
46 Lot
65 Hautes-Pyrénées
81 Tarn
82 Tarn-et-Garonne

NORD/PAS-DE-CALAIS
59 Nord
62 Pas-de-Calais

NORMANDIE
14 Calvados
27 Eure
50 Manche
61 Orne
76 Seine-Maritime

PARIS-ILE DE FRANCE
75 Paris
77 Seine-et-Marne
78 Yvelines
91 Essonne
92 Haut-de-Seine
93 Seine-St-Denis
94 Val-de-Marne
95 Val-d'Oise

PAYS DE LA LOIRE
44 Loire-Atlantique
49 Maine-et-Loire
53 Mayenne
72 Sarthe
85 Vendée

PICARDIE
02 Aisne
60 Oise
80 Somme

POITOU-CHARENTES
16 Charente
17 Charente-Maritime
79 Deux-Sèvres
86 Vienne

PROVENCE-COTE D'AZUR
04 Alpes-de-Haute-Provence
05 Hautes-Alpes
06 Alpes-Maritimes
13 Bouches-du-Rhône
83 Var
84 Vaucluse

RHONE-ALPS
01 Ain
07 Ardèche
26 Drôme
38 Isère
42 Loire
69 Rhône
73 Savoie
74 Haute-Savoie

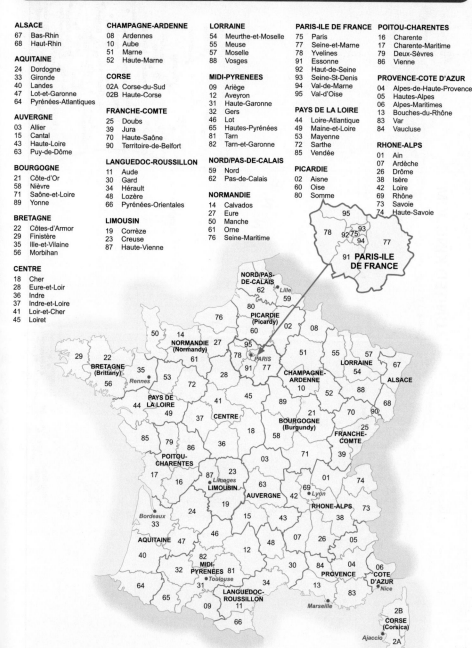

The first two digits of a French postcode correspond
to the number of the department in which that town or village is situated

Source : French Government Tourist Office

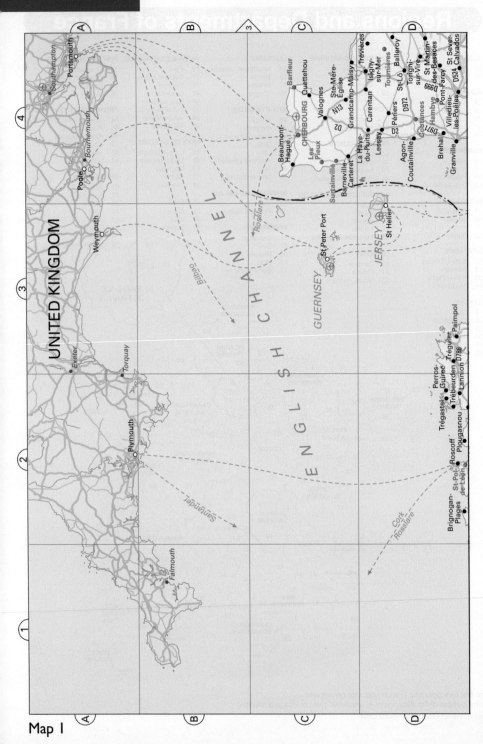

Map I

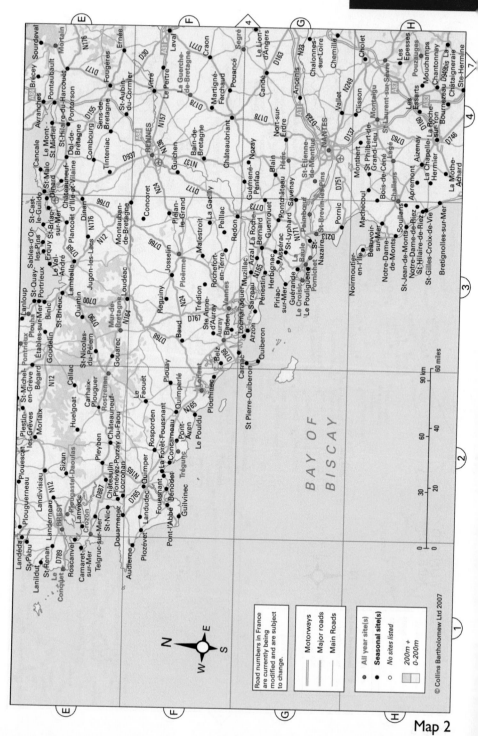

France

Map 2

Road numbers in France are currently being modified and are subject to change.

Motorways
Major roads
Main roads

● All year site(s)
● Seasonal site(s)
○ No sites listed

200m +
0–200m

BAY OF BISCAY

© Collins Bartholomew Ltd 2007

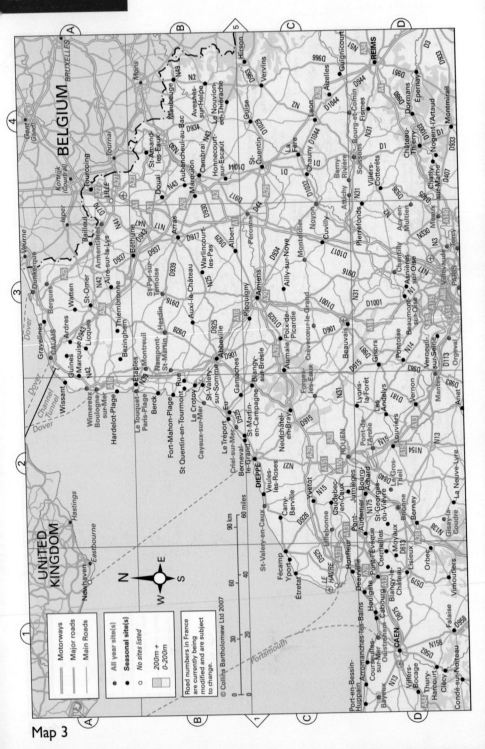

France

Map 3

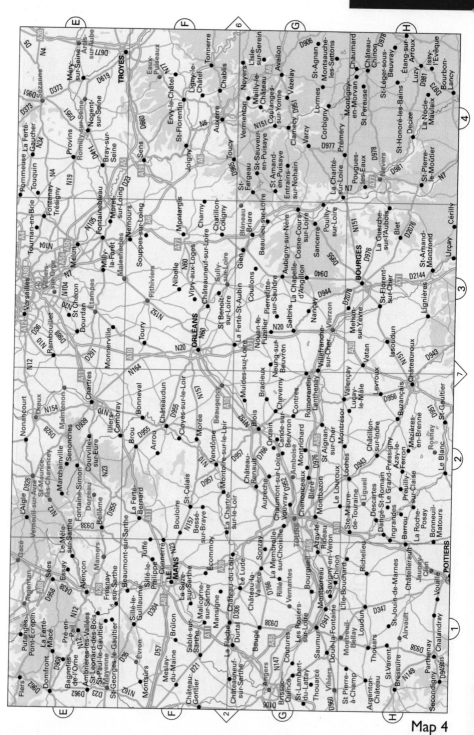

France

Map 4

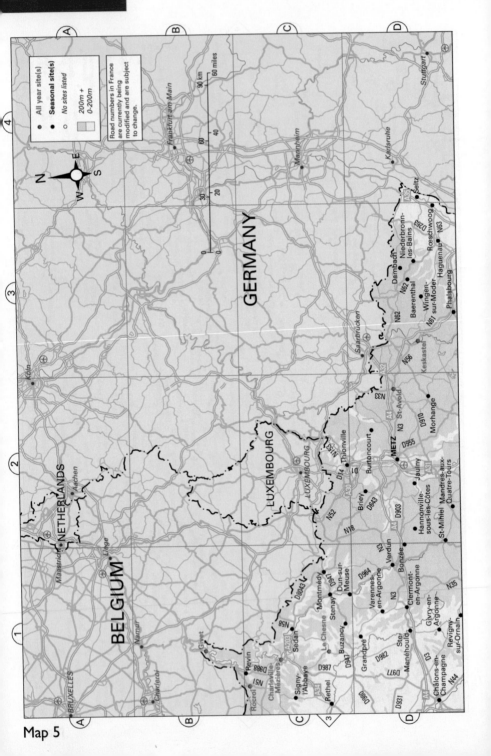

France

Map 5

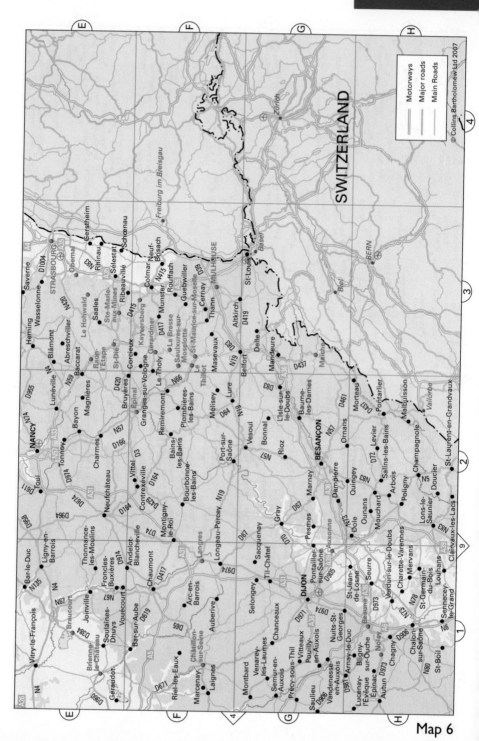

France

SWITZERLAND

Motorways
Major roads
Main Roads

© Collins Bartholomew Ltd 2007

Map 6

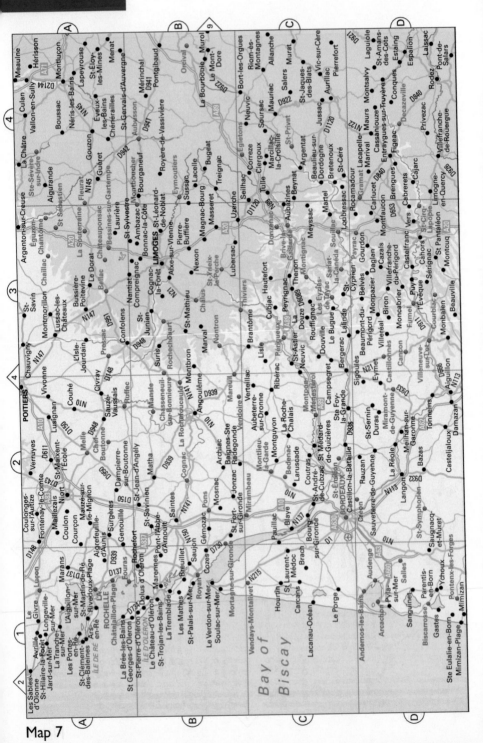

France

Map 7

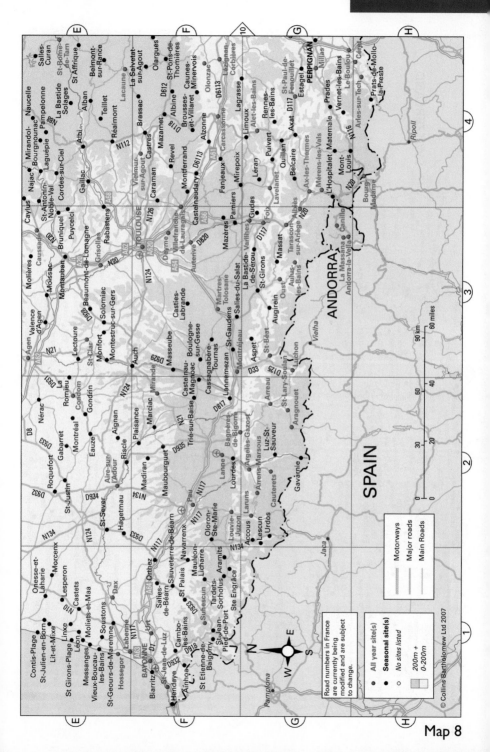

Map 8

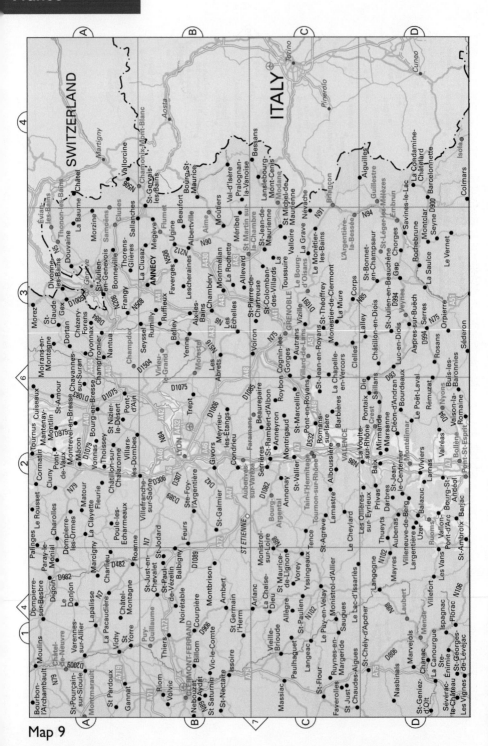

France

Map 9

SWITZERLAND

ITALY

Torino

Cuneo

Isola

Aosta

Marigny

Pinerolo

Éviatt-les-Bains
Thonon-les-Bains
La Baume
Douvaine
Morzine
Samoëns
Vallorcine
Châtel
Chamonix-Mont-Blanc
St-Gervais-les-Bains
Bourg-St-Maurice
Val-d'Isère
Pralognan-la-Vanoise
Bessans
Lanslebourg-Mont-Cenis
Modane
St-Michel-de-Maurienne
St-Jean-de-Maurienne
Aiguilles
La Condamine-Châtelard
Barcelonnette
Colmars

Morez
St-Claude
Gex
Divonne-les-Bains
Genève
St-Julien-en-Genevois
Bonneville
La Clusaz
Thorens-Glières
ANNECY
Megève
Ugine
Beaufort
Albertville
Flumet
Sallanches
Moûtiers
Méribel
St-Martin-sur-la-Chambre
Valloire
Névache
L'Argentière-la-Bessée
Guillestre
St-Léger-les-Mélèzes
Embrun
Savines-le-Lac
Montclar
Seyne
La Saulce
Le Vernet

Moirans-en-Montagne
St-Amour
Chavannes-sur-Suran
Oyonnax
Nantua
Champdor
Seyssel
Rumilly
Frangy
Faverges
Lescheraines
Chambéry
Montmélian
La Rochette
Allevard
Vizille
Le Bourg-d'Oisans
La Grave
Le Monêtier-les-Bains
Briançon
St-Bonnet-en-Champsaur
Gap
Rochebrune
Chorges

Cormatin
Tournus
Cuiseaux
Cluny
Montrevel-en-Bresse
Mâcon
Pont-de-Vaux
St-Nizier-le-Désert
Villars-les-Dombes
Bourg-en-Bresse
Thoissey
Vonnas
Châtillon-sur-Chalaronne
Pont-d'Ain
Ruffieux
Aix-les-Bains
Les Échelles
St-Pierre-de-Chartreuse
St-Colomban-des-Villards
La Toussuire
Villard-de-Lans
St-Théoffrey
La Mure
Corps
St-Julien-en-Beauchêne
Veynes
Serres
Orpierre
Séderon

Paray-le-Monial
Charolles
La Clayette
Matour
Poule-les-Écharmeaux
Villefranche-sur-Saône
Trept
Virieu-le-Grand
Belley
Yenne
Morestel
Les Abrets
Voiron
GRENOBLE
Autrans
Cognin-les-Gorges
Pont-en-Royans
St-Jean-en-Royans
La Chapelle-en-Vercors
Die
Châtillon-en-Diois
Luc-en-Diois
Aspres-sur-Buëch
Rosans
Buis-les-Baronnies

Palinges
Le Rousset
Digoin
Chauffailles
Marcigny
Chauffailles
Charlieu
Roanne
St-Just-en-Chevalet
St-Paul-de-Vézelin
Balbigny
Feurs
St-Galmier
Aubières-sur-Varèze
Givors
Condrieu
Serrières
St-Rambert-d'Albon
St-Vallier
Tain-l'Hermitage
Romans-sur-Isère
Beaurepaire
Meyrieu-les-Étangs
Faramans
Roybon
Annoyron
Montrigaud
Barbières
Bourdeaux
Le Poët-Laval
Remuzat
Nyons
Vaison-la-Romaine
Séderon

Dompierre-sur-Besbre
Paray-le-Monial
Le Donjon
Lapalisse
La Pacaudière
Chauffailles
Chârtieu
St-Martin-d'Estréaux
Noirétable
Montbrison
Courpière
St-Étienne
Bourg-Argental
Annonay
Tournon-sur-Rhône
VALENCE
Montélimar
Viviers
Bollène
Pont-St-Esprit

Moulins
Bourbon-l'Archambault
Châtel-de-Neuvre
Varennes-sur-Allier
Vichy
St-Yorre
Cusset
Thiers
Arlanc
Ambert
St-Germain-l'Herm
La Chaise-Dieu
Allègre
St-Paulien
Vorey
Yssingeaux
Monistrol-sur-Loire
St-Maurice-de-Lignon
Tence
St-Agrève
Le Cheylard
Privas
Baix
La Voulte-sur-Rhône
Crest
Mirmande
Marsanne
Cléon-d'Andran
Grâne
Saillans
Pontaix

Dompierre-sur-Besbre
Gannat
Riom
Volvic
CLERMONT-FERRAND
Aydat
St-Saturnin
Billom
Vic-le-Comte
Issoire
Vieille-Brioude
St-Germain
Paulhaguet
Langeac
Saugues
Le Puy-en-Velay
Langogne
Thueyts
Aubenas
Villeneuve-de-Berg
Uzer
Vallon-Pont-d'Arc
Les Vans
Barjac
Bourg-St-Andéol
Larnas

St-Pourçain-sur-Sioule
St-Pardoux
Montmarault
Puy-Guillaume
Nébouzat
St-Flour
Massiac
Ruynes-en-Margeride
Faverolles
St-Just
Chaudes-Aigues
St-Chély-d'Apcher
Le Lac-d'Issarlès
Mende
Florac
St-Georges-de-Lévéjac

Séverac-le-Château
St-Geniez-d'Olt
Sévérac
Ste-Enimie
Les Vignes
Marvejols
Chanac
La Canourgue
Ispagnac
Nasbinals
La Courgue
St-Ambroix

N79
N7
D982
D998
D2009
N79
A719
A71
N89
N88
A75
D906
N102
D996
N102
D906
A72
A75
N88
N102
N7
D42
A72
D1089
A47
A49
A6
A42
A391
A6
A40
A404
A40
D1084
A41
A410
A430
A43
A48
A51
A43
N75
D1075
D1006
D1075
D1006
D532
N7
N86
N86
N94
N91
D994
D994
D993
D94
N85
D900
D902
D1075
D306
D306
D389
D807
D1005
N5
N206
N206
N508
N508
N212
N90
D1090
A40
N504
A51

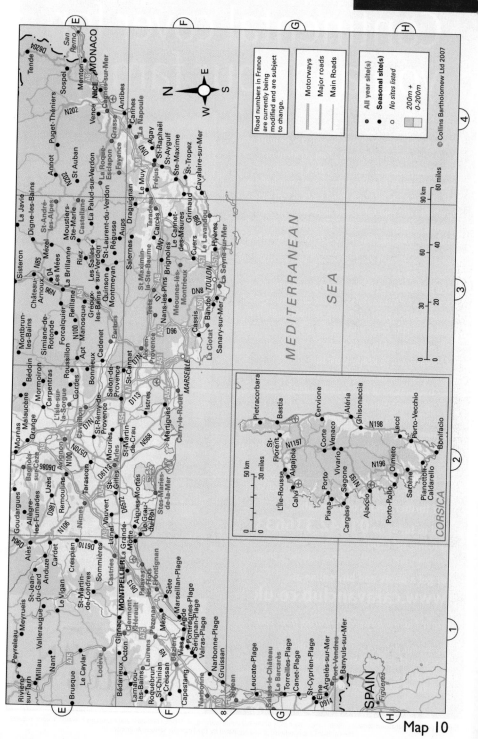

France

Map 10

Continental cover for you and your family!

Many travel insurance policies will pay to bring your car back home in the event of an accident or breakdown abroad, but would they provide the cover you need to protect the rest of your holiday, for instance car hire and hotel costs, if you were unable to use your car and/or caravan? Why risk having to return home after perhaps two days when you were looking forward to a relaxing two weeks?

With The Club's Red Pennant Insurance - you'll be covered all the way

Red Pennant is a holiday insurance specially designed for caravanners, motor caravanners and trailer tenters with Single-trip, Annual multi-trip and Long-stay cover options.

Cover can be taken to include:
- Breakdown roadside assistance
- Vehicle and passenger repatriation
- Continuation of holiday travel and/or accommodation
- Cancellation cover
- Medical cover
- Camping Card International including Personal Liability Cover
- Freephone 24-hour helpline, 7 days a week, manned by multi-lingual Caravan Club staff

For further details or a quotation

call us today on 01342 336633

quoting ref CE08

Lines are open Monday-Friday 9.00am-5.30pm

or get a quote and buy online at

www.caravanclub.co.uk

We're looking forward to hearing from you!

Sorry, our policies are only available to Caravan Club members. Why not join us? You could easily save the cost of your subscription. Call **0800 328 5535** quoting ref. INM08

THE
CARAVAN
CLUB

Portugal

One of the oldest nation-states in Europe and Britain's oldest ally, Portugal has a rich, seafaring history. It is now a modern, forward-looking country and is a founding member of NATO. The diversity of its geography and natural features, together with its mild climate, make Portugal a popular year-round holiday destination.

Essential Facts

Capital: Lisbon (population 2.6 million)

Area: 92,951 sq km (inc Azores and Madeira)

Bordered by: Spain

Terrain: Rolling plains in south; mountainous and forested north of River Tagus

Climate: Temperate climate with no extremes of temperature; wet winters in the north influenced by the gulf stream; elsewhere Mediterranean with hot, dry summers and short, mild winters

Coastline: 1,793 km

Highest Point (mainland Portugal): Monte Torre 1,993 m

Population: 10.5 million

Language: Portuguese

Religion: 94% Roman Catholic

Government: Parliamentary democracy

Local Time: GMT or BST, ie the same as the UK all year

Currency: Euro divided into 100 cents; £1 = €1.43, €1 = 70 pence*

Tourist Information

PORTUGUESE TOURIST OFFICE
11 BELGRAVE SQUARE
LONDON SW1X 8PP
Tel: 0845 3551212
www.visitportugal.com
info@visitportugal.com

Opening Hours

Banks — Mon-Fri 8.30am-3pm; some banks in city centres also open 6pm-11pm Mon-Sat.

Museums — Tue-Sun 10am-5pm; closed Monday.

Post Offices — Mon-Fri 9am-6pm; in main towns open on Saturday morning.

Shops — Mon-Fri 9am-1pm & 3pm-7pm, Sat 9am-1pm; food shops remain open Mon-Fri until 8pm & during the lunch hour; large supermarkets open Mon-Sat until 10pm & Sunday.

Public Holidays 2008

Jan 1; Feb 5 (Carnival); Mar 21, Apr 25 (Day of Liberty); May 1, 22; Jun 10 (Portugal Day); Aug 15; Oct 5 (Republic Day); Nov 1; Dec 1 (Independence Day), 8, 25. Other local holidays and saints' days are celebrated, according to region, eg Jun 13 in Lisbon (St Anthony), Jun 24 in Porto and Braga (St John the Baptist). School summer holidays run from the end of June to the end of August.

Telephoning and the Internet

From the UK dial 00351 for Portugal. All numbers have 9 digits, including the area code which starts with a 2. The area code must be dialled even for local calls. To call the UK from Portugal dial 0044, omitting the initial zero of the area code.

Mobile phones — use of hand-held phones is prohibited when driving.

Public phones — international calls from phone boxes with blue and white 'internacional' sign; phones operate with phone cards; some accept credit cards.

Internet — internet cafés in most towns; internet booths in post offices using pre-paid cards; some shopping centres, motorway service areas, hotels and restaurants offer public wifi access.

Emergency numbers — Police 112; Fire brigade 112; Ambulance 112.

* Exchange rates as at September 2007

Portugal

The following chapter should be read in conjunction with the important information contained in the Handbook chapters at the front of this guide.

Camping and Caravanning

There are approximately 170 campsites in Portugal, many of which are situated along the coast. Sites are rated from 1 to 4 stars. A Camping Card International (CCI) is essential in lieu of a passport at those sites belonging to the Portuguese Camping Federation, and may entitle the holder to a reduction in price.

There are 21 Orbitur sites which are privately owned. They are open to all and caravanners can join the Orbitur Camping Club to obtain generous discounts off current rates. Senior citizens may join this Club free, otherwise the cost is €15. Membership can be arranged via any Orbitur site or on the Orbitur website. Their head office is at:

RUA DIOGO DO COUTO 1-8° Fte
P-1149-042 LISBOA
Tel: 00351 21 8117000 Fax: 00351 21 8117034
www.orbitur.pt
info@orbitur.pt

Casual/wild camping is not permitted.

All place names used in the Site Entry listings which follow can be found in Michelin's Touring & Motoring Atlas for Spain & Portugal, scale 1:400,000 (1 cm = 4 km).

Affiliated National Clubs

FEDERAÇAO DE CAMPISMO E MONTANHISMO DE PORTUGAL
AVENIDA EDUARDO GALHARDO 24D
P-1199-007 LISBOA
Tel: 21 8126890 Fax: 21 8126918
www.fcmportugal.com
geral@fcmportugal.com

Country Information

Cycling — Transportation of Bicycles

Legislation stipulates that the exterior dimensions of a vehicle should not be exceeded and, in practice, this means that only caravans or motor caravans are allowed to carry bicycles/motorbikes at the rear of the vehicle. Bicycles may not extend beyond the width of the vehicle or more than 45 cms from the back. However, bicycles may be transported on the roof of ordinary cars provided that an overall height of 4 metres is not exceeded. Cars carrying bicycles/motorbikes on the back may be subject to a fine.

If you are planning to travel from Portugal to Spain please note that slightly different regulations apply and these are set out in the Spain Country Introduction.

Electricity and Gas

Usually current on campsites varies between 6 and 15 amps. Plugs have two round pins. CEE connections are commonplace.

The full range of Campingaz cylinders is available.

See **Electricity and Gas** in the section **PLANNING AND TRAVELLING**.

Entry Formalities

Holders of British and Irish passports may visit Portugal for up to 90 days without a visa. Registration formalities are carried out by campsite reception staff.

Regulations for Pets

See **Pet Travel Scheme** under **Documents** in the section **PLANNING AND TRAVELLING**.

Medical Services

For treatment of minor conditions go to a pharmacy (farmacia). Staff are generally well-trained and are qualified to dispense drugs which may only be available on prescription in Britain. In large towns there is usually at least one pharmacy whose staff speak English, and all have information posted on the door indicating the nearest pharmacy open at night.

All municipalities have a health centre. A doctor will charge you for treatment but basic emergency hospital treatment is free on production of your British passport. You will have to pay for prescribed medicines as well as dental treatment. Nationals of other EU countries resident in the UK will require a European Health Insurance Card (EHIC).

For serious illness you can obtain the name of an English-speaking doctor from the local police station or tourist office or from a British or American consulate. There is a British hospital in Rua Saraiva de Carvalho, Lisbon. Private treatment is expensive.

Normal precautions should be taken to avoid mosquito bites, including the use of insect repellents and mosquito nets, especially during the night.

You are strongly recommended to obtain comprehensive travel and medical insurance before travelling to Portugal, such as the Caravan Club's Red Pennant Motoring & Personal Holiday Insurance.

*See **Medical Matters** in the section **PLANNING AND TRAVELLING.***

Safety and Security

The crime rate is comparatively low but pickpocketing, bag-snatching and thefts from cars are increasingly common in major tourist areas. Be particularly vigilant on public transport, at crowded tourist sites and in public parks, where it is wise to go in pairs. Keep car windows closed and doors locked while driving in urban areas at night. Pedestrians, particularly the elderly, are advised not to wear valuable jewellery or watches in public areas.

Forest fires occasionally cause road and rail closures. You should be aware of this and be prepared for possible delays. Be extremely careful when visiting isolated areas in any affected regions and be guided by local fire service authorities at all times. No smoking is allowed in woodland areas and barbecues should be avoided. If you see the onset of a forest fire call the emergency services on 112 or 117. Don't waste water during your visit.

Death by drowning occurs every year on Portuguese beaches. Warning flags on beaches should be taken very seriously. A red flag indicates danger and you should not enter the water when it is flying. If a yellow flag is flying you may paddle at the water's edge, but you may not swim. A green flag indicates that it is safe to swim, and a chequered flag means that the lifeguard is temporarily absent. The police are entitled to fine bathers who disobey warning flags. Do not swim from beaches without lifeguards.

Take extra care when crossing busy roads, especially late at night. This warning also applies to zebra crossings which are often badly lit and poorly marked.

Portugal shares with the rest of Europe a threat from international terrorism. Attacks could be indiscriminate and against civilian targets in public places, including tourist sites.

*See **Safety and Security** in the section **DURING YOUR STAY.***

British Embassy

RUA DE SÃO BERNARDO 33, P-1249-082 LISBOA
Tel: 21 3924000
www.uk-embassy.pt
Consular@Lisbon.mail.fco.gov.uk

There are also British Consulates in Porto and Portimão.

Irish Embassy

RUA DA IMPRENSA A ESTRELA 1-4, -1200-684 LISBOA
Tel: 21 3929440
lisbon@dfa.ie

Customs Regulations

Caravans and Motor Caravans

Dimensions must not exceed 4 metres in height, 2.50 metres in width, 12 metres in length and combined length of car + caravan of 18 metres.

*See also **Customs Regulations** in the section **PLANNING AND TRAVELLING.***

Documents

The Portuguese authorities stipulate that proof of identity bearing the holder's photograph and signature (such as a passport, photocard driving licence or International Driving Permit) should be carried at all times. Failure to do so may incur a fine.

When driving you must carry your vehicle registration certificate, proof of insurance and MOT certificate (if appropriate). There are heavy on-the-spot fines for those who fail to do so.

*See **Documents** in the section **PLANNING AND TRAVELLING.***

Money

Travellers' cheques may be cashed in banks and are widely accepted as a means of payment in shops, hotels and restaurants displaying the appropriate logo or sign. Commission charges can be high.

The major credit cards are widely accepted and may be used to obtain cash from machines (Multibanco) throughout the country.

Cardholders are recommended to carry their credit card issuer/bank's 24-hour UK contact number in case of loss or theft.

Recent visitors report that small change appears to be in short supply and you may well be asked for it in shops.

Motoring

It is a fact that many Portuguese drive erratically and vigilance is advised. By comparison with the UK, the accident rate is very high. Particular blackspots are the N125 along the south coast, especially in the busy holiday season, and the coast road between

Portugal

Lisbon and Cascais. In rural areas you may encounter horse-drawn carts and flocks of sheep or goats. Otherwise there are no special difficulties in driving except in Lisbon and Porto, which are unlimited 'free-for-alls'.

Alcohol

The maximum legal level of alcohol in the blood is less than in the UK, at 0.05%. It is advisable to adopt the 'no drink and drive' rule at all times.

Breakdown Service

The Automovel Club de Portugal (ACP) operates a 24-hour breakdown service covering all roads in mainland Portugal. Its specially equipped vehicles are coloured red and white. Emergency telephones are located at 2 km intervals on main roads and motorways. Visiting motorists in need of assistance are advised to telephone the ACP breakdown service as follows:

- In Lisbon or the region south of Pombal: 21 9429103

- In Porto or north of Pombal: 22 8340001

In Aveiro, Braga, Coimbra, Faro, Grandola, Lisbon, Portimao, Porto, Setúbal and Santarém a special mobile breakdown service is in operation seven days a week.

This service is available to members of AIT and FIA affiliated clubs, such as the Caravan Club, and comprises on-the-spot repairs taking up to a maximum of 45 minutes and, if necessary, the towing of vehicles. The charges for breakdown assistance and towing vary according to distance, time of day and day of the week, plus motorway tolls if applicable. Payment by credit card is accepted.

Police patrols (GNR/Brigada de Transito) can assist motorists on some motorways.

Essential Equipment

Reflectorised Jackets

A driver whose vehicle is immobilised on the carriageway must wear a reflectorised jacket or waistcoat when getting out of the vehicle. Sensibly, any passenger who gets out to assist should also wear one. This rule does not apply to foreign-registered vehicles, but as you will need to buy a reflectorised jacket to comply with Spanish law while driving through Spain to Portugal, it would be sensible to observe the rule in Portugal.

Seat Belts

All passengers must wear a seat belt at all times. Children under 12 years and less than 1.5m (5 feet) in height are not allowed to travel in the front passenger seat.

Warning Triangles

Use a warning triangle if, for any reason, a stationary vehicle is not visible for at least 100 metres.

See **Motoring — Equipment** in the section **PLANNING AND TRAVELLING**.

Fuel

Unleaded petrol and diesel are readily available throughout the country. 'Super' petrol with a lead substitute has replaced leaded petrol. Credit cards are accepted at most filling stations but a small extra charge may be made. There are no automatic petrol pumps. LPG is widely available – see www.portugalmania.com/transports/gpl

See also **Fuel under Motoring — Advice** in the section **PLANNING AND TRAVELLING**.

Mountain Roads and Passes

There are no mountain passes or tunnels in Portugal. Roads through the Serra da Estrela near Guarda and Covilha may be temporarily obstructed for short periods after heavy snow; otherwise motorists will encounter no difficulties in winter.

Parking

There are no road markings indicating parking restrictions but parking is prohibited near intersections, pedestrian crossings, tram or bus stops. Vehicles must be parked facing in the direction of traffic. Blue zone parking areas operate in Lisbon and there are parking meters in the centre of main towns. Illegally parked vehicles may be towed away or clamped.

Parking for the Disabled

The leaflet 'European Parking Card for People with Disabilities' describes the concessions available under the Blue Badge scheme and gives advice on how to explain to police and parking attendants in their own language that, as a foreign visitor, you are entitled to the same parking concessions as disabled residents.

See also **Parking Facilities for the Disabled** under **Motoring — Advice** in the section **PLANNING AND TRAVELLING**.

Priority

In general, at intersections and road junctions, road users must give way to vehicles approaching from the right, unless signs indicate otherwise. At roundabouts vehicles already on the roundabout have right of way.

Do not pass stationary trams at a tram stop until you are certain that all passengers have finished entering or leaving the tram.

Roads

The national roads are surfaced with asphalt, concrete or stone setts. Main roads generally are well-surfaced but not always very wide. Roads in the south of the country are generally in good condition, but, despite recent extensive road improvement schemes, many sections in the north are still in a very poor state. All roads, with the exception of motorways, should be treated with care; even a good section may suddenly deteriorate and potholes may be a hazard. Roads in towns are often cobbled and rough.

Drivers entering Portugal from Zamora in Spain will notice an apparently shorter route on the CL527/N221 road via Mogadouro. Although this is actually the signposted route, the road surface is poor in places and this route is not recommended for trailer caravans. The recommended route is via the N122 to Bragança.

Road Signs and Markings

Road signs conform to international standards. Road markings are white or yellow.

You may incur an on-the-spot fine for crossing a continuous single or double white or yellow line in the centre of the road when overtaking or when executing a left turn into or off a main road, despite the lack of any other 'no left turn' signs. If necessary, drive on to a roundabout or junction to turn, or turn right as directed by arrows.

Speed Limits

See Speed Limits Table under Motoring — Advice in the section PLANNING AND TRAVELLING.

Exceptions

Drivers must maintain a speed between 40 km/h (25 mph) and 60 km/h (37 mph) on the 25th April Bridge over the Tagus. Speed is controlled by radar.

Motor caravans over 3,500 kg are restricted to 50 km/h (31 mph) in built-up areas, 70/80 km/h (44/50 mph) on the open road, and 90 km/h (56 mph) on motorways.

Visitors who have held a driving licence for less than one year must not exceed 90 km/h (56 mph) and must display a '90' disc on the rear of their vehicle. This can be obtained at the border.

It is prohibited to use a radar detector or to have one installed in a vehicle.

Towing

Motor caravans are permitted to tow a car on a four-wheel trailer, ie with all four wheels are off the ground. Towing a car on an A-frame (two back wheels on the ground) is not permitted.

Traffic Jams

Traffic jams are most likely to be encountered around the two major cities of Lisbon and Porto and on roads to the coast, such as the A1 Lisbon-Porto and the A2 Lisbon-Setúbal motorways, which are very busy on Friday evenings and Saturday mornings. The peak periods for holiday traffic are the last weekend in June and the first and last weekends in July and August.

Around Lisbon bottlenecks occur on the bridges across the River Tagus, the N6 to Cascais, the A1 and N10 to Vila Franca de Xira, the N8 to Loures and on the N10 road from Setúbal via Almada.

Around Porto you may encounter traffic jams on the Arribada Bridge on the A1, on the IC1 at Vila Nova de Gaia, the N13 from Póvoa de Varzim and near Vila de Conde, and on the N13, N14 and the N15.

Major motorways are equipped with suspended signs which indicate the recommended route to take when traffic is disrupted.

Violation of Traffic Regulations

Speeding, illegal parking and other infringements of traffic regulations are heavily penalised. The police are authorised to impose on-the-spot fines and a receipt must be given. Most police vehicles are now equipped with portable cash machines to facilitate immediate payment.

Portugal

Motorways

Portugal has more than 1,800 km of motorways (auto-estradas) and tolls (portagem) are payable on most sections. Take care not to use the 'Via Verde' green lanes reserved for motorists who subscribe to the automatic pay system.

It is permitted to spend the night on a motorway rest or service area with a caravan, although the Caravan Club does not recommend this practice for security reasons. It should be noted that toll tickets are only valid for 12 hours and fines are incurred if this period of time is exceeded.

Motorway Tolls

Class 1 Vehicle with or without trailer with height from front axle less than 1.10 m.

Class 2 Vehicle with or without trailer with height from front axle over 1.10 m.

Class 3 Vehicle or vehicle combination with 3 axles with height from front axle over 1.10 m.

Class 4* Vehicle or vehicle combination with 4 or more axles with height from front axle over 1.10 m.

* Drivers of high vehicles of the Range Rover/Jeep variety, together with some MPVs, and towing a twin-axle caravan pay Class 4 tolls.

Road No.	Route	km	Class 1	Class 2	Class 3	Class 4
A1	Lisbon to Porto	304	18.85	32.75	40.80	46.80
A2	Lisbon to Algarve	238	18.70	32.80	39.90	46.85
A3	Porto to Valenca	108	9.30	16.45	21.10	23.40
A4	Porto to Amarente	54	5.30	9.30	11.90	13.30
A5	Lisbon to Cascais	25	2.30	4.55	4.55	4.55
A6	A2 to A6 Caia (Spanish border)	156	11.50	20.05	25.75	28.55
A7	Povoa de Varzim (A28-IC1) to Vila Pouca de Aguiar	76	8.50	14.85	19.25	21.30
A8	Lisboa to Leiria	131	8.15	14.35	18.50	20.55
A9-A1-A5	Alverca to A5 (Estadio Nacional)	33	2.90	4.95	6.35	7.05
A10	A9 to junction A10/A13 Salvaterra de Magos	23	4.85	8.45	10.85	12.00
A11	Barcelos- A28 Braga (A3) to Guimaraes (A7) to A4	61	6.15	10.60	13.80	15.40
A12	Setúbal to Montijo (Vasco de Gama Bridge)	25	1.80	3.15	4.10	4.55
A13	Santa Estevão to Marateca	76	6.45	11.35	14.55	16.15
A14	Figueira da Foz to Coimbra (A1)	38	2.15	3.80	4.85	5.40
A15	Caldas da Rainhato Santarém (A1)	42	3.25	5.80	7.50	8.40
A17	Marina Grande Este (A8) to Louriçal	30	2.65	4.70	6.10	6.70
A21	Malveira (A80) to Mafra	6	0.55	1.00	1.25	1.35
	Vasco da Gama Bridge, Lisbon (S to N)	17	2.20	5.05	7.60	9.85
	25 April Bridge, Lisbon (S to N)	2	1.25	3.05	4.45	5.80

Toll charges (2007) in euros. Some exits have automatic toll booths. Credit cards accepted on the following motorways: A1, A2, A3, A4, A5, A6, A9, A10, A12, A13, A14, otherwise payment in cash.

Other stretches or motorway are toll-free, eg A17 Mira to Aveiro, A22 Lagos to Vila Real de Santo Antonio, A23/A1 Torres Novas to Guarda (IP5), A24 Castro Daire to Vila Real (IP4), A24/IP3 Castro Daire to A25 Viseu and Vila Verde de Raia (border), A25/IP5 Aveiro to Guarda (IP2) and Vilar Formosa (border), A27 Viana do Castelo to Ponte de Lima, A28 Porto to Carminha, A29 Estarreja (north of Aveiro) to Porto (A1), A41/IC24 Alfena to Ermida and A42/IC25 Seroa to Lousada (A11/IP9).

Toll Bridges

25th April Bridge and Vasco da Gama Bridge

The 2 km long 25th April Bridge in Lisbon crosses the Tagus River. Tolls are charged for vehicles travelling in a south-north direction only. Tolls also apply on the Vasco da Gama Bridge, north of Lisbon, but again only to vehicles travelling in a south-north direction.

In case of breakdown, or if you need assistance, you must keep as near to the right-hand side as possible and wait inside your vehicle until a patrol arrives. It is prohibited to carry out repairs, to push vehicles physically or to walk on the bridge. If you run out of petrol, you must wait for a patrol vehicle.

Touring

Some English is spoken in large cities and tourist areas. Elsewhere a knowledge of French could be useful.

A Lisboa Card entitles the holder to free unrestricted access to public transport, including trains to Cascais and Sintra, free entry to a number of museums, monuments and other places of interest in Lisbon and surrounding area, and discounts in shops and places offering services to tourists. It is obtainable from tourist information offices, travel agents, some hotels and Carris ticket booths, or from www.europeancitycards.com

Portuguese cuisine is rich and varied and makes the most of abundant, locally grown produce; seafood is particularly good. The national speciality is the bacalhau — dried, salted cod — for which there are 365 recipes, one for each day of the year. Aside from port, many excellent and inexpensive wines are produced, both red and white, including the famous vinho verde (verde means young and fresh, not green!) Do ensure when eating out that you understand exactly what you are

paying for; appetisers put on the table are not free. Service is included in the bill, but it is customary to tip 5 to 10% of the total if you have received good service.

Each town in Portugal devotes several days in the year to local celebrations which are invariably lively and colourful. Carnivals and festivals during the period before Lent, during Holy Week and at wine harvest can be particularly spectacular.

During the summer months bullfights are generally held each Sunday. In Portugal the bull is not killed.

Local Travel

A passenger and vehicle ferry crosses the River Sado estuary from Setúbal to Tróia and there are frequent ferry and catamaran services for cars and passengers across the River Tagus from Lisbon to Cacilhas, Barreiro, Montijo, Porto Brandão and Trafaria.

Throughout the country buses are cheap, regular and mostly on time, with every town connected. Both Lisbon and Porto have metro systems operating from 6am to 1am. In Lisbon the extensive bus and tram network is operated by Carris, together with one lift and three funiculars which tackle the steepest hills. Buy single journey tickets on board from bus drivers or buy a re-chargeable 'Sete Colinas' card for use on buses and the metro.

In Porto buy a 'Euro' bus ticket which can be charged with various amounts from metro stations and transport offices. Validate tickets for each journey at machines on the buses. Also available is an 'Andante' ticket which is valid on the metro and on buses. Porto also has a passenger lift and a funicular which allow you to avoid the steep walk to and from the riverside.

Portugal

Sites in Portugal

⊞ABRANTES *B3* (4km S Urban) **Clube de Campismo de Abrantes, Travessa do Cavaco, 2205-059 Rossio ao Sul do Tejo [(241) 331743; parquecampismoabrantes@iol.pt; www.parque campismoabrantes.pt]** Exit A23 sp Abrantes & foll sp Abrantes, then Rossio. Keep strt for 4km to rndabt with elaborate olive press in cent. Exit slightly L for 'Sul Ponte'. Keep strt & cross Rv Tejus on N2. At rndabt immed after bdge take exit sharp L down hill to rv. Site in 200m on R behind wall. Sm, pt shd; wc (own san rec); chem disp (wc); shwrs inc; el pnts (9A) €1.50; lndry rm; shop, rest, snacks, bar 200m; BBQ; playgrnd; pool 200m; rv sw adj; fishing; canoeing; entmnt high ssn; TV rm; no statics; bus 300m, rlwy stn 600m; poss cr; rd noise; CCI. "Friendly, helpful owners; unmkd pitches; renovated san facs 2006." € 8.00   2007*

ALANDROAL *C3* (13km S Rural) **Camping Rosário, Monte das Mimosas, Rosário, 7250-999 Alandroal [(268) 459566; info@campingrosario.com; www. campingrosario.com]** Fr E exit IP7/A6 at Elvas W junc 9; at 3rd rndabt take exit sp Espanha, immed 1st R dir Juromenha & Redondo. Onto N373 until exit Rosário. Fr W exit IP7/A6 junc 8 at Borba onto N255 to Alandroal, then N373 E sp Elvas. After 1.5km turn R to Rosário & foll sp to site. Sm, hdstg, pt sl, pt shd; wc; chem disp; shwrs inc; el pnts (6A) €2.15; gas 2km; lndtte; ice; shop 2km; tradsmn; rest; bar; playgrnd; pool; lake sw adj; boating; fishing; TV; no statics; dogs €1 (not acc Jul/Aug); Eng spkn; adv bkg; quiet; red long stay/low ssn; CCI. "Remote site being developed by enthusiastic young Dutch couple beside Alqueva Dam; excel touring base; ltd to 50 people max." 1 Mar-1 Oct. € 12.70   2005*

⊞ALBUFEIRA *B4* (1.5km NE Urban) **Camping Albufeira, Estrada de Ferreiras, 8200-555 Albufeira [(289) 587629 or 587630; fax (289) 587633; geral@campingalbufeira.net; www. campingalbufeira.net]** Exit IP1/E1 sp Albufeira onto N125. Turn R down slip rd sp Albufeira; camp on L approx 1km. V lge, some mkd pitch, pt shd; wc; chem disp; mv service pnt; shwrs inc; el pnts (10-12A) €2.90; gas; lndtte; ice; shop; supmkt; rest; snacks; bar; playgrnd; 3 pools; sand beach 1.5km; tennis; sports park; cycle hire; games area; games rm; disco (soundproofed); entmnt; TV; 20% statics; dogs; phone; bus adj; car wash; cash machine; security patrols; poss v cr; Eng spkn; no adv bkg; quiet; cc acc; red long stay/low/CCI. "Friendly, secure site; excel pool area/rest/bar; some pitches lge enough for US RVs; pitches on lower part of site prone to flooding in heavy rain; conv beach & town; poss lge rallies during Jan-Apr; camp bus to town high ssn." ♦ € 23.90   2007*

See advertisement opposite (top)

⊞ALBUFEIRA *B4* (10km W Rural) **Camping Canelas, Alcantarilha, 8365-908 Armação de Pêra [(282) 312612; fax (282) 314719; turismovel@ mail.telepac.pt; www.roteiro-campista.pt/Faro/ canelas.htm]** Fr Lagos take N125, turn R (S) at Alcantarilha twd Armação de Pêra, site in 1.5km on R. Fr IP1/A22 Algarve coastal m'way, take Alcantarilha exit & turn L on N125 into vill, turn R at traff lts. Site on R in 1.5km just bef 2nd rndabt. V lge, pt sl, pt shd; wc; chem disp; mv service pnt; shwrs €0.50; el pnts (5-12A) €2.75-3.50; gas; lndtte; ice; shop in ssn; rest; snacks; bar; playgrnd; 3 solar htd pools; sand beach 1.5km; tennis; entmnt; 5% statics; dogs; phone; poss cr; Eng spkn; cc not acc; red low ssn/long stay; CCI. "Spacious, shady, much improved site; v popular in winter; vg security at ent; excel cent for Algarve." ♦ € 17.00   2007*

See advertisement opposite (bottom)

⊞ *Site open all year*   734   *Help us to update this guide*

⊞**ALBUFEIRA** *B4* (10.5km W Coastal) **Parque de Campismo de Armação de Pêra, 8365-184 Armação de Pêra [(282) 312260; fax (282) 315379; camping_arm_pera@hotmail.com; www.roteiro-campista.pt/Faro/armpera.htm]** Fr Lagos take N125 coast rd E. At Alcantarilha turn S, sp Armação de Pêra & Campismo. Site at 3rd rndabt in 2km on L. V lge, pt sl, shd; wc; chem disp; mv service pnt; shwrs inc; el pnts (6-10A) €2.50-4; gas; lndtte; shop; rest; snacks; bar; playgrnd; pool & paddling pool; sand beach 1km; tennis; cycle hire; games area; entmnt; TV rm; 5% statics; phone; bus adj; car wash; poss cr; Eng spkn; adv bkg; quiet; red low ssn. "Friendly, popular & attractive site; min stay 3 days Oct-May; easy walk to town; interesting chapel of skulls at Alcantarilha." ♦ € 20.50   2007*

See advertisement on next page

> The opening dates and prices on this campsite have changed. I'll send a site report form to the editor for the next edition of the guide.

⊞**ALCACER DO SAL** *B3* (1km NW Rural) **Parque de Campismo Municipal de Alcácer do Sal, Olival do Outeiro, 7580-125 Alcácer do Sal [(265) 612303; fax (265) 610079; cmalcacer@mail.telepac.pt; www.m-alcacerdosal.pt]** Heading S on A2/IP1 turn L twd Alcácer do Sal on N5. Site on R 1km fr Alcácer do Sal. Sp at rndabt. Site behind supmkt. Sm, hdg/mkd pitch, pt sl, pt shd; wc; chem disp; mv service pnt; shwrs inc; el pnts (6-12A) €1.32; lndtte; shops 100m, rest, snacks & bar 50m; BBQ; playgrnd; pool, paddling pool adj; games area; rv sw 1km; sand beach 24km; dogs; phone; bus 50m; clsd mid-Dec to mid-Jan; poss cr; Eng spkn; quiet; red low ssn; cc acc; CCI. "Excel, clean facs; site manager not resident; site in rice growing area - major mosquito prob; spacious pitches." ♦ ltd. € 7.95   2007*

⊞**ALCOBACA** *B2* (N Urban) **Campismo Municipal de Alcobaça, Avda Joaquim V Natividade, 2460-071 Alcobaça [(262) 582265]** Turn W off A8/IC1at junc 21 onto N8 twd Alcobaça. Site on L on ent town, well sp. Med, hdg pitch, hdstg, pt sl, terr, shd; wc; chem disp; shwrs inc; el pnts (3-6A) €0.90-1.50; gas; lndtte; shop 100m, tradsmn; rest, snacks 200m; bar; playgrnd; pool 200m; TV; some statics; bus 250m; poss cr; Eng spkn; some noise fr rd & flats opp; quiet; red low ssn/CCI. "Well-run, clean, tidy site; friendly staff; vg facs; Batalha & monastery worth a visit; fascinating Mon mkt nrby; pleasant sm town with gd rests; bus service to Lisbon." ♦ € 9.30   2007*

Portugal

CAMPING ARMAÇÃO DE PÊRA

8365-184 Armação de Pêra   Tel: 351 282 312 260   Fax: 351 282 315 379

OPEN
ALL
YEAR

BUNGALOWS - SWIMMING POOL- SUPERMARKET - RESTAURANT

ALCOBACA *B2* (3km S Urban) **Camping Silveira, Capuchos, 2460-479 Alcobaça [(262) 509573; silveira.capuchos@clix.pt]** S fr Alcobaça on N 8-6 sp Evora de Alcobaça. Site on L in 3km after Capuchos. Med, hdg pitch, pt shd; wc; shwrs inc; el pnts (6A) €1.50; gas; lndtte; shops 1.5km; rest, snacks, bar 1km; pool 3km; sand beach 10km; games rm; no statics; Eng spkn; quiet; CCI. "Vg, wooded, CL-type site; friendly owner; gd views; excel facs; excel touring base." 1 Jun-30 Sep. € 12.00   2004*

Before we move on, I'm going to fill in some site report forms and post them off to the editor, otherwise they won't arrive in time for the deadline at the end of September.

⊞**ALJEZUR** *B4* (3.5km N Rural) **Camping Serrão, Herdade do Serrão, 8670-121 Aljezur [(282) 990220; fax (282) 990229; info@parque-campismo-serrao.com; www.parque-campismo-serrao.com]** Site off N120 sp Praia Amoreira & Campsite. Driving fr N 4km after Rogil turn by café on R on slight bend. Lge sp 200m bef turn. Driving fr S ignore 1st L turn sp Praia Amereira, 4km after Aljezur (camp sp 1.3km), turn on L by café. V lge, hdstg, shd; wc (some cont); chem disp; mv service pnt; shwrs inc; el pnts (6A) €2.60; lndtte; shop; tradsmn; rest; bar; playgrnd; pool; sand beach 3.5km; fishing; tennis; games area; cycle hire; internet; entmnt; TV; some statics; dogs; phone; quiet; no adv bkg; cc acc; red low ssn/long stay/CCI. "No mkd pitches, pitch between lines of trees; helpful owner; gd san facs; much quieter area than S coast; lovely beaches." ♦ € 20.00   2007*

ALVOR see Portimao *B4*

AMARANTE *C1* (1.5km NE Rural) **Camping Penedo da Rainha, Rua Pedro Alveollos, Gatão, 4600-099 Amarante [(255) 437630; fax (255) 437353; ccporto@sapo.pt]** Fr IP4 Vila Real to Porto foll sp to Amarante & N15. On N15 cross bdge for Porto & immed take R slip rd. Foll sp thro junc & up rv to site. Lge, some hdstg, pt sl, terr, shd; wc; chem disp; mv service pnt; shwrs inc; el pnts (4A) inc; gas 2km; lndtte; shop in ssn & 2km; rest; snacks 100m; bar; playgrnd; sm pool & 3km; rv adj; fishing; canoeing; cycling; games rm; entmnt; TV; dogs; phone; bus to Porto fr Amarante; some Eng spkn; adv bkg; quiet; red low ssn/CCI. "Well-run site in steep woodland/parkland - take advice or survey rte bef driving to pitch; excel facs but some pitches far fr facs; few touring pitches; friendly, helpful recep; plenty of shd; conv Amarante old town & Douro Valley; Sat mkt." ♦ 1 Feb-30 Nov. € 12.50   2007*

⊞**ARGANIL** *C2* (3km NE Rural) **Camp Municipal de Arganil, 3300-432 Sarzedo [(235) 205706; fax (235) 200134; camping@mail.telepac.pt; www.cm-arganil.pt]** Fr Coimbra on N17 twd Guarda; after 50km turn S sp Arganil on N342-4; site on L in 4km in o'skts of Sarzedo bef rv bdge; avoid Góis to Arganil rd fr SW. Med, terr, shd; wc (some cont); mv service pnt; shwrs inc; el pnts (5-15A) €2.40; gas; lndtte; ice; shop 100m; rest; snacks; bar; playgrnd; rv sw, fishing & canoeing adj; ski in Serra da Estrela 50km Dec/Jan; TV; phone; Eng spkn; quiet; red low ssn/long stay/snr citizens; cc acc; CCI. "Vg, well-run site; friendly owner; fine views; gd cent for touring." € 10.60   2007*

ARMACAO DE PERA see Albufeira *B4*

⊞**AVEIRO** *B2* (3km S Coastal) **Parque de Campismo Gafanha da Nazaré, Rua dos Balneários do G Desportivo, 3830-640 Gafanha da Nazaré [(234) 366565; fax (234) 365789; mail. gdg@clix.pt]** Exit Gafanha da Encarnacão, 3km S of Aveiro. Foll Campismo sp. Lge, hdstg, pt shd; wc; own san rec; shwrs inc; el pnts (4A) €1.05; gas; ice; shop 1km; rest; snacks; bar; playgrnd; pool 2km; sand beach 3km; fishing; canoeing; cycle hire; entmnt; TV; 90% statics; quiet; CCI. "Gd security; dated, shabby facs; NH only." ♦ ltd. € 6.82   2007*

Camping   Caravans   Apartments

PARQUE DE CAMPISMO ★★

Clube Náutico de Avis   Apartado 25   7480 - 999 Avis   PORTUGAL
E-mail: parque_campismo@cm-avis.pt   www.cm-avis.pt/parquecampismo
Tel.: (+351) 242 412 452   Fax: (+351) 242 412 369

albufeira do **MARANHÃO**

⊞**AVEIRO** *B2* (6km SW Coastal) **Camping Costa Nova, Estrada da Vagueira, Quinta dos Patos, 3830 Ílhavo [(234) 393220; fax (234) 394721; info@campingcostanova.com; www.camping costanova.com]** Site on Barra-Vagueira coast rd 1km on R after Costa Nova. V lge, mkd pitch, unshd; htd wc; chem disp; mv service pnt; shwrs inc; el pnts (2-6A) €2.30; gas; lndtte; shop & 1.5km; tradsmn; rest in ssn; snacks; bar; BBQ; playgrnd; pool 4km; sand beach; fishing; cycle hire; games area; games rm; entmnt; internet; TV rm; some statics; dogs €1.55; phone; site clsd 1st two weeks Jan; Eng spkn; adv bkg; quiet; cc acc; red long stay; CCI. "Peaceful, tidy site adj nature reserve; helpful staff; gd, modern facs; hot water to shwrs only; vg." ♦ € 17.25   2007*

> There aren't many sites open this early in the year. We'd better phone ahead to check that the one we're heading for is actually open.

AVEIRO *B2* (8km NW Coastal/Rural) **Camping ORBITUR, EN327, Km 20, 3800-901 São Jacinto [(234) 838284; fax (234) 838122; info@orbitur. pt; www.orbitur.com]** Fr Porto take A29/IC1 S & exit sp Ovar onto N327. (Note long detour fr Aveiro itself - 30+ km.) Site in trees to N of São Jacinto. Lge, mkd pitch, hdstg, terr, shd; wc; chem disp; mv service pnt; baby facs; shwrs inc; el pnts (5-15A) €2.50 (poss rev pol); gas; lndtte; ice; sm shop & 5km; tradsmn; rest; snacks; bar; BBQ; playgrnd; pool 5km; sand beach 2.5km; rv sw & fishing; TV; some statics; dogs €1.30; phone; bus; car wash; Eng spkn; adv bkg; quiet; red low ssn/long stay/snr citizens; cc acc; CCI. "Excel site; best in area; gd children's park; 15 min ferry (foot passengers only); gd, clean san facs." ♦ 1 Feb-31 Oct. € 17.50   2007*

⊞**AVIS** *C3* (1km SW Rural) **Parque de Campismo da Albufeira do Maranhão, Clube Náutico de Avis, Albufeira do Maranhão, 7480-999 Avis [(242) 412452; fax (242) 412369; parque_ campismo@cm-avis.pt; www.cm-avis.pt/ parquecampismo]** Fr N exit A23/IP6 at Abrantes onto N2 dir Ponte de Sor, then N244 to Avis. Fr S exit A6/IP7 N at junc 7 Estremoz or junc 4 Montemor onto N4 to Arraiolos, then onto N370 to Pavia & Avis. Site sp. V lge, terr, pt shd; wc; chem disp; mv service pnt; shwrs inc; el pnts (16A) €2.50; gas 1km; lndry rm; ice; shop 1km; rest adj; snacks; bar; playgrnd; pool complex adj; lake fishing & shgl beach adj; watersports; tennis; games area; games rm; TV; 40% statics; dogs €1; bus 1km; Eng spkn; adv bkg; quiet; CCI. "V pleasant site nr lakeside; v interesting historic town; gd walking area." ♦ € 12.50   2007*

See advertisement above

AVO see Oliveira do Hospital *C2*

⊞**BEJA** *C4* (500m S Urban) **Parque de Campismo Municipal de Beja, Avda Vasco da Gama, 7800-397 Beja [tel/fax (284) 311911; www.cm-beja. pt]** Fr S (N122) take 1st exit strt into Beja. In 600m turn R at island then L in 100m into Avda Vasco da Gama & foll sp for site on R in 300m - narr ent. Fr N on N122 take by-pass round town then 1st L after Intermarche supmkt, then as above. Lge, hdstg, shd, gravel pitches; wc; chem disp; shwrs inc; el pnts (6A) €1.75; supmkt 500m; rest 500m; snacks 200m; bar adj; pool, tennis & football stadium adj; bus 300m; rlwy stn 1.5km; Eng spkn; poss noisy in ssn; red low ssn; CCI. "C'van storage facs; helpful staff; san facs old but clean; NH only." ♦ € 8.65   2007*

Portugal

*Last year of report

⊞**BRAGA** *B1* (1km S Urban) **Parque Municipal da Ponte, São Lazaro, 4710 Braga [(253) 273355; fax (253) 613387]** Fr Porto N14 N to Braga, then fr ring rd exit junc 2 onto N101 dir Guimarães. After Guimarães bear L for underpass sp hospital & other rtes. Site by old football stadium 200m on R (do not confuse with new stadium). Fr N drive thro city, foll sp Guimarães, bear L for underpass (no max height shown) sp hospital & other rtes. Sm, hdstg, pt sl, terr, pt shd; chem disp; wc; own san rec; shwrs inc; el pnts (16A) €1.55; gas; shop 200m; playgrnd; pool adj; rd noise. "Not rec for disabled; terr pitches steep for vans, check site/pitch bef driving in; poss scruffy pitches & unclean shwrs; conv Porto, Gêres National Park; easy walk to city cent; NH only." € 11.35   2005*

BRAGANCA *D1* (6km N Rural) **Inatel Campismo de Bragança (formerly Municipal), Estrada Rabaçal, 5300-673 Bragança [tel/fax (273) 329409; pc.braganca@inatel.pt; www.inatel.pt]** Fr Bragança N for 6km on N103.7 twd Spanish border. Site on R, sp Inatel. Med, hdstg, pt sl, terr, pt shd; wc; chem disp; shwrs inc; el pnts (6A) inc; gas; lndry rm; ice; shop & 6km; tradsmn; rest in ssn; snacks; bar; playgrnd; rv sw; fishing; cycle hire; dogs; bus; poss cr; Eng spkn; quiet but barking dogs; CCI. "On S boundary of National Park; rv runs thro site; Bragança citadel worth visit." 1 May-30 Sep. € 8.80   2007*

BRAGANCA *D1* (10km W Rural) **Cepo Verde Camping, Gondesende, 5300-561 Bragança [(273) 999371; fax (273) 323577; cepoverde@bragancanet.pt; www.bragancanet.pt/cepoverde]** Fr IP4 fr W take N103 fr Bragança for 8km. Site sp fr IP4 ring rd. R off N103, foll lane & turn R at sp. NB Camping sp to rd 103-7 leads to different site (Sabor) N of city. Med, mkd pitch, hdstg, terr, pt shd; wc; chem disp; shwrs inc; el pnts (6A) €1.40 (poss rev pol & long lead poss req); lndtte; shop; rest; snacks; bar; playgrnd; pool; dogs; phone; bus 1km; Eng spkn; adv bkg; quiet; CCI. "Remote, friendly, v pleasant, scenic site adj Montesinho National Park; clean, modern facs; vg value." ♦ 1 Apr-30 Sep. € 10.20   2007*

BUDENS see Vila do Bispo *B4*

CABECEIRAS DE BASTO *C1* (4km N Rural) **Campismo Valsereno, 4860-431 Riodouro [(253) 664468; campismo-valsereno@sapo.pt; www.camping-valsereno.com]** Fr N206 or IC5 turn N onto N205 twd Cabeceiras. Site sp on N311. Sm, pt shd; wc; shwrs inc; el pnts (6A) €3; lndtte; shop 4km, rest, snacks 4km; bar; BBQ; playgrnd; pool; rv sw 300m; TV; some statics; dogs; carwash; quiet. "Friendly, welcoming owners; magnificent mountain setting; hiking trails." 15 Apr-1 Oct. € 15.50   2006*

CABRIL see Geres *C1*

⊞**CALDAS DA RAINHA** *B3* (8km W Rural) **Camping ORBITUR, Rua Maldonado Freitas, 2500-516 Foz do Arelho [(262) 978683; fax (262) 978685; info@orbitur.pt; www.orbitur.com]** Take N360 fr Caldas da Raina twds Foz do Arelho. Site on L; well sp. Lge, mkd pitch, terr, shd; wc; chem disp; mv service pnt; shwrs; el pnts (5-15A) €2.50; gas; lndtte; ice; shop; tradsmn; rest high ssn; snacks; bar; BBQ; playgrnd; htd pool high ssn; sand beach 2km; tennis; cycle hire; games rm; entmnt; cab/sat TV; 25% statics; dogs €1.30; car wash; Eng spkn; adv bkg; quiet; cc acc; red low ssn; CCI. "Lagoon Óbidos 2km; interesting walled town; attractive area; well-maintained, well-run site; excel san facs." ♦ € 20.90   2007*

⊞**CAMINHA** *B1* (4.5km NE) **Parque Natural, 4910 Vilar de Mouros [tel/fax (258) 727472; geral@casa-da-anta.com; www.casa-da-anta.com]** Fr Caminha take N13 NE twd Valença. In approx 5km, after Seixas, turn R onto rd sp Vilar de Mouros (Camping 1.5km). Foll camping sp, site on R. Lge, pt sl, terr, pt shd; wc; chem disp; shwrs inc; el pnts (10A) €2.30; lndtte; shop; rest; snacks; playgrnd; pool; fishing; tennis; entmnt; poss cr; 10% statics; phone; site clsd Dec; adv bkg; quiet; cc acc; CCI. "Excursion to mountains; mosquito repellant fr recep; site looking tired." € 14.50   2004*

⊞**CAMINHA** *B1* (2km SW Coastal) **Camping ORBITUR-Caminha, Mata do Camarido, N13, Km 90, 4910-180 Caminha [(258) 921295; fax (258) 921473; info@orbitur.pt; www.orbitur.pt]** Foll seafront rd N13/E1 fr Caminha dir Viana/Porto, at sp Foz do Minho turn R, site in approx 1km. Long o'fits take care at ent. Med, terr, shd; wc; mv service pnt; chem disp; shwrs inc; el pnts (5-15A) €2.50-3; gas; lndtte; ice; shop; tradsmn; rest; snacks; bar; playgrnd; pool 2.5km; sand beach 150m; rv sw; fishing; cycle hire; TV rm; 5% statics; dogs €1.30; Eng spkn; adv bkg; fairly quiet; cc acc; red low ssn/ long stay/snr citizens; CCI. "Pleasant, woodland site; care in shwrs - turn cold water on 1st as hot poss scalding; Gerês National Park & Viana do Castelo worth visit; poss to cycle to Caminha; vg site." ♦ € 19.20   2007*

⊞**CAMPO MAIOR** *C3* (4km W Rural) **Parque de Campismo de Campo Maior, Barragem do Caia, 7370 Campo Maior [(268) 689493; info@ parqueverde.pt; www.parqueverde.pt]** Fr Elvas on N373 or Badajoz on N371 turn L on edge of Campo Maior onto N243 sp Barragem do Caia. Site on R in 4km just bef reservoir, sp Faisão Rest. V lge, hdstg, terr, pt shd; wc; chem disp; shwrs inc; el pnts (6A) €1.95 (long lead poss req); lndtte; rest; snacks; bar; shop; pool 4km; lake sw adj; playgrnd; games area; boating; fishing; 98% statics; dogs; phone; poss cr/ noisy high ssn & w/e; CCI. "Gd welcome; superb views fr top terrs; poss muddy pitches or soft patches." ♦ € 13.75   2007*

CANDEMIL see Vila Nova de Cerveira *B1*

⊞**CASCAIS** *A3* (5km NW Coastal/Urban) **Camping ORBITUR-Guincho, N247-6, Lugar de Areia, Guincho, 2750-053 Cascais [(214) 870450 or 871014; fax (214) 872167; info@orbitur.pt; www. orbitur.com]** Fr Lisbon take A5 W, at end m'way foll sp twd Cascais. At 1st rndabt turn R sp Birre & Campismo. Foll sp for 2.5km. Steep traff calming hump - care needed. V lge, some hdg/mkd pitch, terr, shd; wc; chem disp; mv service pnt; baby facs; shwrs inc; el pnts (6A) €2.50; gas; lndtte; supmkt & 500m; rest; snacks; bar; BBQ; playgrnd; sand beach 800m; watersports & fishing 1km; tennis; cycle hire; horseriding 500m; golf 3km; entmnt in ssn; games rm; cab/sat TV; 50% statics; dogs on lead €1.30; phone; car wash; Eng spkn; adv bkg; some rd noise; red low ssn/long stay/snr citizens; cc acc; CCI. "Buses to Cascais for train to Lisbon; sandy, wooded site behind dunes; plenty of nice, open pitches with views; gd san facs; gd value rest; ltd facs in winter & poss itinerants; charge for awnings; v busy high ssn; vg low ssn but poss v windy." ♦ € 20.90 ABS - E10   2007*

CASTELO BRANCO *C2* (2.5km N Rural) **Camp Municipal Castelo Branco, 6000-113 Castelo Branco [(272) 322577; fax (272) 322578; albigec@ sm-castelobranco.pt]** Fr IP2 take Castelo Branco Norte, at 1st rndabt site sp. Turn L just bef Modelo supmkt, site 2km on L. Lge, pt sl, shd; wc; shwrs; chem disp; mv service pnt; el pnts (12A) €2.25; gas; lndtte; ice; shop, rest, bar 2km; playgrnd; pool 4km; lake 500m; bus 100m; Eng spkn; quiet but some rd noise; CCI. "Useful NH on little used x-ing to Portugal; gd site but rds to it poor." 2 Jan-15 Nov. € 8.75   2007*

CASTRO DAIRE *C2* (8km S Rural) **Camping Castro Daire, Termas do Carvalhal, 3600 Castro Daire [tel/fax (254) 613918; naturimont@oninet. pt; www.naturimont.com]** S fr Castro Daire or N fr Viseu on N2 at km 144, site clearly sp. Site on E of rd. Med, sl, terr, shd; wc; shwrs inc; el pnts (5-12A) €2; gas; lndry rm; shop; bar; playgrnd; pool adj; tennis; cycle hire; entmnt; TV; phone; adv bkg; some rd noise. "Thermal spa opp site." 1 Jun-30 Sep. € 11.50   2005*

⊞**CHAVES** *C1* (4km S Rural) **Camp Municipal Quinta do Rebentão, Vila Nova de Veiga, 5400-764 Chaves [tel/fax (276) 322733]** Fr o'skts Chaves take N2 S. After about 3km in vill of Vila Nova de Veiga turn E at sp thro new estate, site in about 500m. Med, hdstg, terr, pt shd; wc; chem disp; mv service pnt; shwrs inc; el pnts (6A) €1.20; gas 4km; lndry rm; shop 1km; rest; snacks; bar; BBQ; pool adj; rv sw & fishing 4km; cycle hire; dogs; phone; bus 800m; site clsd Dec; Eng spkn; adv bkg; red CCI. "Gd site in lovely valley but remote; v helpful staff; facs block quite a hike fr some terr pitches; Chaves interesting, historical Roman town." ♦ € 11.00   2006*

⊞**COIMBRA** *B2* (3km SE Urban) **Camp Municipal de Coimbra, Rua de Escola, Alto do Areeiro, Santo António dos Olivais, 3030-011 Coimbra [tel/fax (239) 086902; geral@campingcoimbra. com or geral@cacampings.com; www.camping coimbra.com or www.cacampings.com]** Fr S on AP1/IP1 at junc 11 turn twd Lousa & in 1km turn twd Coimbra on IC2. In 9.5km turn R at rndabt onto Ponte Rainha, strt on at 3 rndabts along Avda Mendes Silva. Then turn R along Estrada des Beiras & cross rndabt to Rua de Escola. Or fr N17 dir Beira foll sp sports stadium/campismo. Lge, terr, pt shd; htd wc (some cont); chem disp; mv service pnt; sauna; shwrs; el pnts (10A) €2.60; gas; lndtte; shop; tradsmn; rest; snacks; bar; BBQ; playgrnd; pool adj; sand beach 20km; rv sw 1km; health club; tennis; cycle hire; games area; games rm; internet; TV; 2% statics; dogs €2.15; bus 100m; poss cr; Eng spkn; adv bkg; red long stay/low ssn; CCI. "New site (2006) with vg facs; v interesting, lively university town." ♦ € 15.90   2007*

See advertisement

Portugal

⊞**COIMBRAO** *B2* (Rural) **Camping Coimbrão, 185 Travessa do Gomes, 2425-452 Coimbrão [tel/fax (244) 606007; campingcoimbrao@web.de]** Site down lane in vill cent. Care needed lge outfits, but site worth the effort. Sm, unshd; wc; chem disp; mv service pnt; shwrs inc; el pnts (6-10A) €2-3; lndry rm; tradsmn; shop & snacks 300m; playgrnd; pool; sw, fishing, canoeing 4km; TV; no dogs; bus 200m; Eng spkn; quiet; office open 0800-1200 & 1500-2200; red long stay. "Excel site; run by German couple, helpful & friendly; gd touring base." ◆ € 11.10   2006*

CORTEGACA see Espinho *B1*

COSTA DE CAPARICA see Lisboa *B3*

COVILHA *C2* (2km SW Urban) **Camping Parque Carlos Pinto, 6200-036 Covilhã** Well sp fr A23 off 1st island. Sm, terr, unshd; wc; chem disp; mv service pnt; baby facs; shwrs; el pnts (10A) inc; lndtte; rest; bar; playgrnd; quiet; CCI. ◆ 1 May-15 Oct. € 10.50   2005*

⊞**COVILHA** *C2* (4km NW Rural) **Clube de Campismo do Pião, 6200-036 Covilhã [tel/fax (275) 314312; campismopiao@hotmail.com; www.clubecampismocovilha.com]** App Covilhã, foll sp to cent, then sp to Penhas da Saúde; after 4km of gd but twisting climbing rd; site on L. Lge, terr, pt shd; wc; shwrs inc; el pnts (4A) €1.40; gas; shop; rest; snacks; bar; playgrnd; 2 pools; tennis; entmnt; many statics; phone; bus adj; poss cr; Eng spkn; CCI. "Gd walking fr site; few touring pitches." ◆ € 11.30   2006*

DARQUE see Viana do Castelo *B1*

ELVAS *C3* (1.5km W Urban) **Parque de Campismo da Piedade, 7350-901 Elvas [(268) 628997 or 622877; fax (268) 620729]** Exit IP7/E90 junc 9 or 12 & foll site sp dir Estremoz. Med, mkd pitch, hdstg, mostly sl, pt shd; wc; chem disp; shwrs inc; el pnts (16A) inc; gas; lndry rm; shop 200m; rest; snacks; bar; BBQ; playgrnd; dogs; phone; bus 500m; poss cr; CCI. "Attractive aqueduct & walls; Piedade church & relics adj; traditional shops; nice walk to town; v quiet site, even high ssn; excel san facs." 1 Apr-15 Sep. € 14.00   2007*

ENTRE AMBOS OS RIOS see Ponte da Barca *B1*

⊞**ERICEIRA** *B3* (1km N Coastal) **Camp Municipal Mil Regos, 2655-319 Ericeira [(261) 862706; fax (261) 866798; info@ericeiracamping.com; www.ericeiracamping.com]** On N247 coast rd, well sp N of Ericeira. V lge, pt sl, pt shd; wc (some cont); own san rec; shwrs inc; el pnts €2.65; gas; shop; rest; playgrnd; 2 pools adj; beach 200m; fishing; internet; entmnt; 50% statics; phone; bus adj; quiet. "Busy site with sea views; san facs basic; uneven, sl pitches." ◆ € 19.80   2007*

⊞**ESPINHO** *B1* (Urban) **Camp Municipal de Espinho, Rua Nova da Praia, 4500-083 Espinho [(227) 335871; fax (227) 322680; campismo@c.m-espinho.pt]** Foll N109 fr Porto to Espinho; on app town site sp at junc on R. V lge, sl, pt shd; wc; chem disp; mv service pnt; shwrs inc; el pnts (10A) €1.68; gas; shop; snacks; bar; playgrnd; pool; paddling pool; sand beach 800m; fishing; no dogs; bus 600m; poss cr; adv bkg; rd noise; red CCI. "Sep secure area for cars; if pitched at bottom of site must climb to get to facs; frequent trains to Porto 800m." € 14.07   2007*

⊞**ESPINHO** *B1* (11km S Coastal) **Camping Os Nortenhos, Praia de Cortegaça, 3885-278 Cortegaça [(256) 752199; fax (256) 755177; clube.nortenhos@netvisao.pt; http://cccosnortenhos.cidadevirtual.pt]** Fr Espinho foll rd thro Esmoriz twd Aveiro to Cortegaça vill. Turn R to beach (Praia), site on L at beach, sp fr vill. V lge, pt shd; wc (cont); shwrs; el pnts €2.25; gas; shop; snacks; bar; playgrnd; sand beach adj; entmnt; TV; 95% statics; no dogs; phone; bus 500m; poss cr; quiet; cc acc; CCI. "V helpful, friendly staff; v ltd tourer pitches & poss v cr high ssn; facs ltd at w/e; conv Porto; guarded at ent; sun shelters over pitches." ◆ € 12.40   2004*

ESTELA see Povoa De Varzim *B1*

⊞**EVORA** *C3* (2km SW Urban) **Camping ORBITUR, Estrada das Alcaçovas, Herdade Esparragosa, 7005-706 Évora [(266) 705190; fax (266) 709830; info@orbitur.pt; www.orbitur.com]** Fr N foll N18 & by-pass, then foll sps for Lisbon rd at each rndabt or traff lts. Fr town cent take N380 SW sp Alcaçovas, foll site sp, site in 2km. NB Narr gate to site. Med, mkd pitch, hdstg, pt sl, pt shd; wc; chem disp; mv service pnt; shwrs inc; el pnts (5-15A) €2.50 (long lead poss req); gas; lndtte; ice; shop; supmkt 500m; tradsmn; snacks; bar; playgrnd; pool; tennis; games area; TV rm; dogs €1.30; phone; car wash; bus; rlwy stn 2km; Eng spkn; adv bkg ess; quiet; cc acc; red low ssn/long stay/snr citizens; red CCI. "Conv town cent, Évora World Heritage site with wealth of monuments & prehistoric sites nrby; cycle path to town; free car parks just outside town walls; poss flooding some pitches after heavy rain; helpful staff; well-kept site." ◆ € 20.90   2007*

⊞**FAO** *B1* (1km S Urban/Coastal) **Parque de Campismo de Fão, Rua São João de Deus, 4740-380 Fão [(253) 981777; fax (253) 817786; contacto@cccbarcelos.com; www.cccbarcelos.com]** Exit A28/IC1 junc 8 fr S or junc 9 fr N onto N13 thro Fão twd coast. Site sp off rd M501. Sm, pt shd; wc; chem disp; mv service pnt; shwrs inc; el pnts (3A) €2.60; gas; shop, snacks, bar high ssn; playgrnd; pool 2km; sand beach 800m; entmnt; TV; many statics; no dogs; bus 800m; quiet. "Gd site; Barcelos mkt Thurs." € 15.40   2006*

⊞**FERNAO FERRO** *B3* (4km E Rural) **Camping Parque Verde, Rua da Escola 9, Fontainhas, Casal do Sapo, 2865-060 Fernão Ferro [(212) 108956; fax (212) 103263; info@ parqueverde.pt; www.parqueverde.pt]** Fr Sesimbra take N378 N, turn R at major junc Marco do Grilo. In approx 3km after rndabt turn R by factory, site on L in 1km in forest. Med, pt sl, pt shd; wc; chem disp; shwrs inc; el pnts (2A) €1.70 (long lead rec); gas; shop; rest; snacks; bar; playgrnd; pool; sand beach 13km; tennis; entmnt; some statics; phone; bus; poss cr; Eng spkn; quiet; cc acc. € 11.50   2006*

FERRAGUDO see Portimao *B4*

⊞**FIGUEIRA DA FOZ** *B2* (4km S Coastal/Urban) **Camping ORBITUR-Gala, N109, Km 4, Gala, 3090-458 Figueira da Foz [(233) 431492; fax (233) 431231; info@orbitur.pt; www.orbitur.com]** Fr Figueira da Foz on N109 dir Leiria for 3.5km. After Gala site on R in approx 400m. Ignore sp on R 'Campismo' after long bdge. Lge, mkd pitch, hdstg, terr, shd; wc; chem disp; mv service pnt; shwrs; el pnts (6-10A) €2.50-3; gas; lndtte; ice; shop; tradsmn; rest; snacks; bar; BBQ; htd pool; playgrnd; sand beach 400m; fishing 1km; tennis; games rm; entmnt; TV rm; 10% statics; dogs €1.30; phone; car wash; Eng spkn; adv bkg; red low ssn/long stay/snr citizens; cc acc; CCI. "Gd, renovated site adj busy rd; excel pool." ♦ € 20.90   2007*

FIGUEIRA DA FOZ *B2* (6km S Coastal) **Camping Foz do Mondego, Cabedelo-Gala, 3080-661 Figueira da Foz [(233) 402740/2; fax (233) 402749; foz.mondego@fcmportugal.com; www. fcmportugal.com]** Fr S on N109 turn L bef bdge sp Gala. Foll site sp. V lge, mkd pitch; htd wc; chem disp; mv service pnt; baby facs; shwrs inc; el pnts (2A) inc; gas; lndtte; shop 2km; rest; snacks; bar; BBQ; playgrnd; sand beach adj; fishing; surfing; TV; 40% statics; dogs €0.50; phone; bus 1km; CCI. "Wonderful sea views but indus est adj; NH only." ♦ 14 Jan-13 Nov. € 15.00   2006*

FOZ DO ARELHO see Caldas da Rainha *B3*

⊞**FUNDAO** *C2* (3km SW Urban) **Camping Quinta do Convento, 6234-909 Fundão [(275) 753118; fax (275) 771368]** Fr N thro town cent; when almost thro town take L fork at triangle dir Silvares; site 1km uphill on L - steep. Site well sp fr A23. Med, hdstg, terr, shd; wc (some cont); chem disp; mv service pnt; shwrs inc; el pnts (4-10A) €2; lndtte; shop; rest; snacks; bar; playgrnd; pool; entmnt; TV; bus 1.5km; adv bkg; quiet. "Guarded; no vehicle access after 2300; gd, friendly site with nice atmosphere; narr site rds & pitches diff to access - rec arr early for easy pitching." ♦ ltd. € 10.30   2007*

FUZETA see Olhao *C4*

GAFANHA DA BOA HORA see Vagos *B2*

GAFANHA DA NAZARE see Aveiro *B2*

⊞**GERES** *C1* (1km N Rural) **Parque de Campismo de Cerdeira, Campo do Gerês, 4840-030 Terras do Bouro [(253) 351005; fax (253) 353315; info@ parquecerdeira.com; www.parquecerdeira.com]** Fr N103 Braga-Chaves rd, 28km E of Braga turn N onto N304 at sp to Poussada. Cont N for 18km to Campo de Gerês. Site in 1km; well sp. V lge, shd; wc; chem disp; shwrs inc; el pnts (5-10A) €2.10-3.15; gas; lndry rm; rest; bar; shop; playgrnd; lake sw; TV rm; cycle hire; fishing 2km; canoeing; few statics; no dogs; bus 500m; entmnt; poss cr; quiet; adv bkg; Eng spkn; cc acc; CCI. "Beautiful scenery; unspoilt area; fascinating old vills nrby & gd walking; ltd facs low ssn." ♦ € 17.35   2005*

GERES *C1* (2km N Rural) **Vidoeiro Camping, Lugar do Vidoeiro, 4845-081 Gerês [(253) 391289; fax (258) 452450; aderepg@mail.telepac.pt; www. adere-pg.pt]** NE fr Braga take N103 twds Chaves for 25km. 1km past Cerdeirinhas turn L twds Gerês onto N308. Site on L 2km after Caldos do Gerês. Steep rds with hairpins. Cross bdge & reservoir, foll camp sps. Lge, mkd pitch, hdstg, terr, pt shd; wc; chem disp; shwrs inc; el pnts (12A) inc; lndry rm; tradsmn; rest, bar 500m; pool 500m, lake sw 500m; phone; quiet. "V attractive site in National Park; gd, clean facs; thermal spa in Gerês." ♦ 15 May-15 Oct. € 10.20   2005*

GERES *C1* (10km E Rural) **Camping Outeiro Alto, Eiredo-Cabril, 5470-013 Cabril [tel/fax (253) 659860; outeiro_alto@hotmail.com; www. geocities.com/campingouteiroalto]** Fr N103 turn N dir Ferral, Paradela & Cabril, site sp. App poss difficult. Med, terr, pt shd; wc; shwrs inc; el pnts (12A) €1.50; lndtte; shop 800m; rest 500m; snacks; bar; BBQ; rv sw; fishing; boating; entmnt; TV rm; dogs €1; Eng spkn; quiet. "A white knuckle app; spectacular scenery; sm area for tourers." 1 Mar-30 Oct. € 13.00   2006*

⊞**GOIS** *C2* (1km S Rural) **Camp Municipal do Castelo, Castelo, 3330-309 Góis [(235) 778585; fax (235) 770129; reservas@goistur.com; www. goistur.com]** Fr Coimbra take N17/N2 E to Góis, site sp to W of rv. Steep access rd. Med, terr, shd; wc (some cont); chem disp; baby facs; shwrs inc; el pnts (4-16A) €1.60-2.30; gas; lndry rm; ice; shop; tradsmn; rest 150m; snacks; bar; BBQ; playgrnd; sand beach 15km; rv sw 500m; fishing; canoeing; tennis; cycle hire; entmnt; some chalets; dogs €1.40; bus 100m; poss cr; Eng spkn; adv bkg; quiet; red low ssn/CCI. "Quiet, clean site in beautiful wooded countryside; ltd pitches for lge o'fits; helpful owners; highly rec." ♦ € 12.40   2007*

Portugal

⊞**GOUVEIA** *C2* (6km NE Rural) **Camping Quinta das Cegonhas, Nabaínhos, 6290-122 Melo [tel/ fax (238) 745886; cegonhas@cegonhas.com; www.cegonhas.com]** Turn S at 114km post on N17 Seia-Celorico da Beira. Site sp thro Melo vill. Sm, pt shd; wc; chem disp; mv service pnt; shwrs; el pnts (4A) €2.20; lndtte; shop 300m; rest; snacks; bar; playgrnd; pool; entmnt; TV; dogs €0.75; bus 400m; Eng spkn; adv bkg; quiet; 5-10% red 7+ days; CCI. "Vg, well-run, busy site in grounds of vill manor house; friendly Dutch owners; beautiful location conv Torre & Serra da Estrella; gd walks; highly rec." ♦ € 12.00   2007*

⊞**GUARDA** *C2* (500m SW Urban) **Camp Municipal da Guarda, Avda do Estádio Municipal, 6300-705 Guarda [(271) 221200; fax (271) 210025]** Exit A23 junc 35 onto N18 to Guarda. Foll sp cent & sports centre. Site adj sports cent off rndabt. Med, hdstg, sl, shd; wc (some cont, own san rec); chem disp (wc); shwrs inc; el pnts (15A) €1.40; gas; lndry rm; shop; rest, snacks, bar high ssn; BBQ; playgrnd; pool 2km; TV; phone; bus adj; Eng spkn; poss noise fr rd & nrby nightclub; CCI. "Access to some pitches diff for c'vans, OK for m'vans; poss run down facs & site poss neglected low/mid ssn; walking dist to interesting town - highest in Portugal & poss v cold at night; music festival 1st week Sep." ♦ € 9.15   2007*

GUIMARAES *B1* (6km SE Rural) **Camping Parque da Penha, Penha-Costa, 4800-026 Guimarães [tel/fax (253) 515912 or (253) 515085; geral@ turipenha.pt; www.turipenha.pt]** Take N101 SE fr Guimarães. Turn R at sp for Penha. Site sp. Lge, hdstg, pt sl, terr, shd; wc; shwrs inc; el pnts (6A) €1.80; gas; shop; rest adj; snacks; bar; playgrnd; pool; fishing; no statics; no dogs; phone; bus 200m, teleferic (cable car) 200m; car wash; poss cr; Eng spkn; adv bkg; poss noisy; CCI. "Excel staff; gd san facs; lower terrs not suitable lge o'fits; densely wooded hilltop site; conv Guimarães World Heritage site." ♦ ltd. 1 Apr-30 Sep. € 10.40   2007*

⊞**IDANHA A NOVA** *C2* (8km NE Rural) **Camping ORBITUR, EN354-1, Km 8, Barragem de Idanha-a-Nova, 6060 Idanha-a-Nova [(277) 202793; fax (277) 202945; info@orbitur.pt; www.orbitur.com]** Exit IP2 at junc 25 sp Lardosa & foll sp Idanha-a-Nova on N18, then N233, N353. Thro Idanha & cross Rv Ponsul onto N354 to site. Avoid rte fr Castelo Branco via Ladoeiro as rd narr, steep & winding in places. V lge, mkd pitch, hdstg, terr, shd; wc; chem disp; mv service pnt; shwrs inc; el pnts (6A) €2.50; gas; lndtte; ice; shop; tradsmn; rest; snacks; bar; BBQ; playgrnd; htd pool; lake sw, fishing; watersports 150m; tennis; games rm; entmnt; cab/sat TV; 10% statics; dogs €1.30; phone; car wash; Eng spkn; adv bkg; quiet; red long stay/low ssn/snr citizens; cc acc. "Uphill to town & supmkts; hot water to shwrs only; pitches poss diff - a mover req; excel." ♦ € 17.50   2007*

ILHAVO see Aveiro *B2*

Did you know you can fill in site report forms on the Club's website — www.caravanclub.co.uk?

⊞**LAGOS** *B4* (1km SW Urban/Coastal) **Parque de Campismo da Trinidade, Rossio da Trindade, 8601-908 Lagos [(282) 763893; fax (282) 762885; cfelagos@clix.pt; www.camingtrindade.com]** Fr Faro on N125 app Lagos, foll sp for Centro; drive 1.5km along front past BP stn, up hill to traff lts; turn L & foll Campismo sp to L. Cont to traff island & foll to bottom of hill, ent on R. Site adj football stadium Sm, hdstg, terr, pt shd; wc; own san facs; chem disp; shwrs inc; el pnts (12A) €3.50; gas; lndtte; shop; rest; snacks; bar; playgrnd; pool 500m; sand beach 500m; phone; poss cr; Eng spkn; rd noise; cc acc; red long stay; CCI. "Gd beaches & cliff walks; conv walk into Lagos." ♦ € 16.70   2007*

⊞**LAGOS** *B4* (4km W Rural) **Camping Turiscampo, N125 Espiche, 8600-109 Luz-Lagos [(282) 789265; fax (282) 788578; info@turiscampo.com or reservas@turiscampo.com; www.turiscampo.com]** Exit A22/IC4 junc 1 to Lagos then N125 fr Lagos dir Sagres, site 3km on R. Lge, mkd pitch, some hdstg, pt sl, terr, shd; htd wc; chem disp; mv service pnt; baby facs; shwrs inc; el pnts (6-10A) €2.90-€3.80; gas; lndtte; ice; supmkt; tradsmn; rest; snacks; bar; playgrnd; pool; paddling pool; solarium; sand beach 2km; fishing 2.5km; cycle hire; games rm; games area; archery; entmnt; child entmnt; wifi internet; TV rm; 16% statics; dogs €1.50; phone; bus 100m; Eng spkn; adv bkg; quiet; cc acc; red long stay/low ssn/ CCI. "Superb site; refurbished to high standards & excel for long winter stays; gd san facs; helpful staff; lovely vill, beach & views; varied & interesting area, Luz worth visit." ♦ € 24.50 (CChq acc)   2007*

See advertisement

⊞**LAGOS** *B4* (7km W Coastal/Urban) **Camping ORBITUR-Valverde, Estrada da Praia da Luz, Valverde, 8600-148 Lagos [(282) 789211 or 789212; fax (282) 789213; info@orbitur.pt; www.orbitur.com]** Foll coast rd N125 fr Lagos to Sagres for 3km. Turn L at traff lts sp Luz, site 2km on R, well sp. V lge, hdg/mkd pitch, hdstg, terr, pt shd; wc; chem disp; mv service pnt; baby facs; shwrs inc; el pnts (6A) €2.50; gas; lndtte; supmkt; tradsmn; rest; snacks; bar; BBQ: playgrnd; 2 pools; sand beach 3km; tennis; sports facs; games area; games rm; entmnt; cab/sat TV; some statics; dogs €1.30; bus; car wash; Eng spkn; adv bkg; quiet; red low ssn/long stay/snr citizens/Orbitur card; cc acc; CCI. "Well-run site; v friendly staff; gd, clean san facs; access to pitches tight due trees; disabled facs not suitable wheelchair users (steps); spacious low ssn; narr, busy rd to beach/town; lovely beach & town." ♦ € 22.80 ABS - E09   2007*

⊞**LAMAS DE MOURO** *C1* (1km S Rural) **Camping Lamas de Mouro, 4960-170 Lamas de Mouro [(251) 465129; info@versana.pt; www.versana.pt]** Fr N202 at Melgaco foll sp Peneda National Park, site sp in Lamas de Mouro. Med, pt shd; wc; chem disp; mv service pnt; shwrs inc; el pnts (10A) €2.30; lndry rm; shop; tradsmn; rest; snacks; bar; cooking facs; natural pool; phone; poss cr; quiet; CCI. "Ideal for walking in National Park; park ranger v helpful." € 13.20   2004*

LAMEGO *C1* (5km W Rural) **Parque de Campismo Dr João de Almeida, Serra das Meadas, 5100 Lamego [tel/fax (254) 613918; naturimont@oninet.pt; www.naturimont.com]** Fr Lamego, foll rd dir Resende. In 500m turn L sp 'Serra das Meadas, Complexo Turístico Turisserra.' Site in 4km uphill. Sm, pt sl, pt shd, wc; serviced pitch; shwrs inc; el pnts (12A) €1.50; gas; lndry rm; shop, rest, snacks, bar adj; playgrnd adj; pool 5km; lake sw 6km; fishing; canoeing; tennis; cycle hire; entmnt; TV rm; no statics; bus 4km; phone; Eng spkn; quiet. "Site situated at height of approx 1000m; spectacular views." 1 Jun-30 Sep. € 10.00   2007*

LAVRA see Porto *B1*

⊞**LISBOA** *B3* (10km SW Coastal) **Camping ORBITUR-Costa de Caparica, Ave Afonso de Albuquerque, Quinta de S. António, 2825-450 Costa de Caparica [(212) 901366 or 903894; fax (212) 900661; info@orbitur.pt; www.orbitur.com]** Take A2/IP7 S fr Lisbon; after Rv Tagus bdge turn W to Costa de Caparica. At end of rd turn N twd Trafaria, & site on L. Well sp fr a'strada. Lge, mkd pitch, terr, shd; wc; chem disp; mv service pnt; shwrs inc; el pnts (6A) €2.50; gas; lndtte; ice; shop; tradsmn; rest; snacks; bar; BBQ; playgrnd; pool 800m; sand beach 1km; fishing; tennis; games rm; entmnt; TV; 25% statics; dogs €1.30; phone; car wash; bus; Eng spkn; adv bkg; some rd noise; cc acc; red low ssn/long stay/snr citizens/Orbitur card; CCI. "Site fine but san facs need refurb; beach adequate, app on foot; heavy traff into city; rec use free parking at Monument to the Discoveries & tram to city cent; ferry to Belém; ltd facs low ssn; pleasant, helpful staff." ♦ € 20.90   2007*

This guide relies on site report forms submitted by caravanners like us; we'll do our bit and tell the editor what we think of the campsites we've visited.

⊞**LISBOA** *B3* (5km NW Urban) **Parque Municipal de Campismo de Monsanto, Estrada da Circunvalação, 1400-061 Lisboa [(217) 623100; fax (217) 623105; info@lisboacamping.com; www.roteiro-campista.pt/Lisboa/monsanto-moldura.htm]** Fr W on A5 foll sp Parque Florestal de Monsanto/Buraca. Fr S on A2, cross toll bdge & foll sp for Sintra; join expressway, foll up hill; site well sp; stay in RH lane. Fr N on A1 pass airport, take Benfica exit & foll sp under m'way to site. Site sp fr all major rds. Avoid rush hours! V lge, mkd pitch, hdstg, pt sl, terr, pt shd; htd wc (cont); chem disp; mv service pnt; 80% serviced pitches; baby facs; fam bthrm; shwrs inc; el pnts (6-16A) inc; gas; ice; lndtte; shop; tradsmn; rest; snacks; bar; playgrnd; pool; sand beach 10km; tennis; mini-golf; entmnt; bank; post office; car wash; TV rm; no statics; dogs; frequent bus to city; rlwy station 3km; poss cr; Eng spkn; adv bkg; some rd noise; red low ssn; cc acc; red CCI. "Well laid-out, spacious, guarded site in trees; ltd mv service pnt; take care hygiene at chem disp/clean water tap; facs poss badly maintained & stretched when site full; friendly, helpful staff; in high ssn some o'fits placed on sloping forest area (quiet); few pitches take awning; excel excursions booked at tourist office on site." ♦ € 26.00   2007*

Portugal

LOURICAL *B2* (4km SW Rural) **Campismo O Tamanco, Rua do Louriçal, Casas Brancas, 3105-158** Louriçal **[tel/fax (236) 952551; campismo.o.tamanco@mail.telepac.pt; www.campismo-o-tamanco.com]** S on N109 fr Figuera da Foz S twds Leiria foll sp at rndabt Matos do Corrico onto N342 to Louriçal. Site 800m on L. Med, hdg/mkd pitch, pt shd; wc; chem disp; shwrs inc; el pnts inc (6-16A) €2.25-3.50; gas; lndtte; shop; tradsmn; rest; snacks; bar; pool; sand beach 12km; lake sw adj; cycle hire; entmnt; TV; dogs €0.60; bus 500m; poss cr; Eng spkn; adv bkg; rd noise; 10% red low ssn 7+ days; CCI. "Excel; friendly Dutch owners; chickens & ducks roaming site; superb mkt on Sun at Louriçal; a bit of real Portugal; gd touring base." 1 Feb-31 Oct. € 13.15   2007*

⊞**LUSO** *B2* (1.5km S Rural) **Camping ORBITUR-Luso, N336, Pampilhosa, Quinta do Vale do Jorge, 3050-246 Luso [(231) 930916; fax (231) 930917; info@orbitur.pt; www.orbitur.com]** S fr Luso on N336, sp. Lge, hdstg, pt sl, pt shd; wc; chem disp; mv service pnt; shwrs inc; el pnts (5-15A) €2.50; gas; lndtte; shop; tradsmn; rest; snacks; bar; playgrnd; pool 1km; sand beach 35km; tennis; games rm; TV rm; some statics; dogs €1.30; car wash; adv bkg; Eng spkn; quiet; red low ssn/long stay/snr citizens; cc acc; CCI. "Excel site in wooded valley; vg san facs; some sm pitches unsuitable for c'vans + awnings; internet in vill; sh walk to vill." ♦ € 17.50   2007*

MEDAS GONDOMAR see Porto *B1*

MELO see Gouveia *C2*

MIRA *B2* (7km SW Coastal) **Camp Municipal de Mira, 3070-721 Praia de Mira [(231) 472173; fax (231) 458185]** S fr Aveiro on N109, turn R in Mira onto N334, sp Praia de Mira. Foll rd to seafront, turn L, foll rd S out of town, site in 300m. V lge, pt shd; wc; chem disp; shwrs €0.80; el pnts (6A) €1; shop; rest; snacks; bar; playgrnd; pool 300m; sand beach 500m; no dogs; phone; bus 1km. "Gd beach; Costa Nova & Aveiro worth a visit." ♦ 1 May-30 Sep. € 12.50   2004*

⊞**MIRA** *B2* (3km W Rural) **Camping Vila Caia, Lagoa de Mira, 3070-176 Mira [(231) 451524; fax (231) 451861; vlcaia@portugalmail.com; www.vilacaia.com]** S fr Aveiro on N109 for 29km; at Mira take N334 for 5km. Site sp on R 500m W of Lagoa de Mira. Lge, hdstg, pt shd; wc (some cont); chem disp; mv service pnt; shwrs inc; el pnts (4A) €2.50; gas; lndtte; shop; rest; snacks; bar; playgrnd; pool; paddling pool; sand beach 3km; fishing; tennis; cycle hire; entmnt; TV; some statics; no dogs; phone; bus adj; site clsd Dec; Eng spkn; no adv bkg; quiet, but poss noisy entmnt high ssn; cc acc; red low ssn; CCI. "Gd site." ♦ € 16.10   2006*

⊞**MIRA** *B2* (7km NW Coastal/Urban) **Camping ORBITUR-Mira, E Florestal 1, Km 2, Dunas de Mira, 3070-792 Praia de Mira [(231) 471234; fax (231) 472047; info@orbitur.pt; www.orbitur.com]** Fr N109 in Mira turn W to Praia de Mira, foll site sp. Lge, hdg pitch, hdstg, shd; wc; chem disp; mv service pnt; shwrs inc; el pnts (5-15A) €2.40-3; gas; lndtte; ice; shop (in ssn); tradsmn; rest, snacks, bar high ssn; playgrnd; pool 7km; sandy, surfing beach & dunes 800m; entmnt; fishing; boating; TV rm; 5% statics; dogs €1.20; phone; site clsd Dec; Eng spkn; adv bkg; poss noisy w/e; red low ssn/long stay/snr citizens; cc acc; CCI. "Friendly, helpful staff; excel surfing beach nr; suitable for cycling; nature reserve opp site." ♦ € 19.20   2007*

⊞**MIRANDA DO DOURO** *D1* (500m W Urban) **Campismo Municipal Santa Lúzia, Rua do Parque de Campismo, 5210-190 Miranda do Douro [(273) 431273 or 431216; fax (273) 431075; mirdouro@mail.telepac.pt; www.cm-mdouro.pt]** Fr Spain on ZA324/N221, cross dam & thro town, site well sp. Do not enter walled town. Lge, pt sl, terr, pt shd; wc; chem disp; shwrs inc; el pnts (5A) €1.25; shop, rest & 1km; snacks, bar; playgrnd; pool 100m; phone; bus 500m; Eng spkn; quiet; CCI. "Interesting ent into N Portugal; old walled town; spectacular rv gorge; boat trips." ♦ 1 Jun-30 Sep. € 9.50   2004*

⊞**MIRANDELA** *C1* (4km N Rural) **Camping Três Rios Maravilha, 5370-555 Mirandela [tel/ fax (278) 263177; clube.ccm@oninet.pt]** Fr IP4 take Mirandela N exit twd town. Foll camping sp at 1st rndabt. At 2nd rndabt take 1st exit, site on L in approx 2km, adj Rv Tuela. Site well sp. Lge, mkd pitch, pt shd; wc (some cont); chem disp; shwrs inc; el pnts (12-16A) €2 (poss rev pol); gas; lndtte; tradsmn; rest; snacks; bar; playgrnd; pool; canoeing; fishing; tennis; entmnt; TV; 60% statics; dogs; phone; bus; train 2km; Eng spkn; poss cr & noisy; red low ssn/CCI. "V pleasant situation by rv; busy site but v quiet low ssn; friendly owner; san facs need refurb & grubby (2006); attractive pool."
♦ € 14.00   2007*

As soon as we get home I'm going to post all these site report forms to the editor for inclusion in next year's guide. I don't want to miss the September deadline.

MOGADOURO *D1* (1km S Rural) **Camp Municipal Quinta da Agueira, Complexo Desportivo, 5200-244 Mogadouro [(279) 340231; fax (279) 341874; cameramogadouro@mail.telepac.pt]** Fr Miranda do Douro on N221 or fr Bragança on IP2 to Macedo then N216 to Mogadouro. Site sp adj sports complex. Lge, shd; wc; chem disp; mv service pnt; shwrs inc; el pnts (15A) €2; gas; lndry rm; ice; shop 1km; rest 200m; snacks; bar; BBQ; playgrnd; pool adj; waterslide; beach 15km; tennis; car wash; entmnt; internet; TV; dogs €1.50; phone; bus 300m; Eng spkn; adv bkg; quiet. "In lovely area; gd touring base." ♦ 1 Apr-30 Sep. € 11.50
                                                             2007*

See advertisement

MONCARAPACHO see Olhao *C4*

⊞**MONCHIQUE** *B4* (6km S Rural) **Parque Rural Caldas de Monchique, Barracão 190, 8550-213 Monchique [(282) 911502; fax (282) 911503; valedacarrasqueira@sapo.pt; www.valedacarrasqueira.com]** Fr S exit A22 N onto N266, site sp on R in 11km. Fr N on N266 dir Portimão, thru Monchique, site on L. Well sp. Sm, mkd pitch, hdstg, unshd; wc; chem disp; mv waste; all serviced pitches; shwrs inc; el pnts (16A) inc; lndtte; bar; BBQ; pool; dogs; m'vans only; no adv bkg; Eng spkn; quiet. "Excel, spotless new site (2005); peaceful with mountain views; excel san facs; helpful staff; poss taking c'vans in future."
€ 15.00   2006*

⊞**MONTARGIL** *B3* (5km N Rural) **Camping ORBITUR, EN2, 7425-017 Montargil [(242) 901207; fax (242) 901220; info@orbitur.pt; www.orbitur.com]** Fr N251 Coruche to Vimiero rd, turn N on N2, over dam at Barragem de Montargil. Fr Ponte de Sor S on N2 until 3km fr Montargil. Site clearly sp bet rd & lake. Med, mkd pitch, hdstg, terr, pt shd; wc; chem disp; mv service pnt; shwrs inc; el pnts (6-10A) €2.50-3; gas; lndtte; ice; shop & 3km; tradsmn; rest; snacks; bar; playgrnd; rv beach adj; boating; watersports; fishing; tennis; games rm; entmnt; cab/sat TV; 60% statics; dogs €1.30; phone; car wash; Eng spkn; adv bkg; some rd noise; cc acc; red low ssn/long stay/snr citizens; CCI. "Friendly site in area of natural beauty."
♦ € 19.20   2007*

⊞**NAZARE** *B2* (2km N Rural) **Camping Vale Paraíso, EN242, 2450-138 Nazaré [(262) 561800; fax (262) 561900; info@valeparaiso.com; www.valeparaiso.com]** Site thro pine reserve on N242 fr Nazaré to Leiria. V lge, mkd pitch, hdstg, terr, shd; wc (some cont); chem disp; mv service pnt; baby facs; shwrs inc; el pnts (4-10A) €2.50; gas; lndtte; ice; supmkt; rest; snacks & takeaway; bar; playgrnd; 2 pools; sand beach 2km; lake 1km; fishing; sports area; organised activities; games rm; cycle hire; child entmnt; internet; TV; 1% statics; dogs €2; bus; site clsd 18-26 Dec; Eng spkn; adv bkg; quiet; cc acc; red low ssn/long stay; CCI. "Gd security; pitches vary in size & price, & divided by concrete walls, poss not suitable lge o'fits."
♦ € 18.60 (CChq acc)   2006*

NAZARE *B2* (2km E Rural) **Camping ORBITUR-Valado, EN8, Km 5, Valado, 2450-148 Nazaré-Alcobaca [(262) 561609; fax (262) 561137; info@orbitur.pt; www.orbitur.com]** Site on N of rd to Alcobaça & Valado (N8-4), opp Monte de São Bartolomeu. Lge, mkd pitch, terr, sl, shd; wc; chem disp; mv service pnt; shwrs inc; el pnts (6A) €2.50; gas; lndtte; ice; shop & 2km; tradsmn; rest; snacks; bar; BBQ; playgrnd; pool 3km; sand beach 1.8km; tennis; TV rm; 10% statics; dogs €1.30; phone; car wash; Eng spkn; adv bkg; red low ssn/long stay/snr citizens; cc acc. "Pleasant site in pine trees; v soft sand - tractor avail; helpful manager; visits to Fátima, Alcobaça, Balhala rec." ♦ 1 Feb-31 Oct.
€ 17.50   2007*

⊞**ODECEIXE** *B4* (1km N Rural) **Camping São Miguel, 7630-592 Odeceixe [(282) 947145; fax (282) 947245; camping.sao.miguel@mail.telepac.pt; www.campingsaomiguel.com]** Fr N120 site ent 1km N of Odeceixe. V lge, pt sl, shd; wc; chem disp; mv service pnt; shwrs inc; el pnts (6A) €2.75; gas; lndtte; ice; shop, rest, snacks bar high ssn; BBQ; playgrnd; pool; paddling pool; sand beach 5km; tennis; games rm; TV; bus 500m; no dogs; phone; site clsd midnight-0800; adv bkg; quiet; red low ssn/long stay. "Gd, clean facs." ♦ € 25.50
                                                             2007*

Portugal

⊞**ODIVELAS** *B3* (3km NE Rural) **Camping Markádia, Barragem de Odivelas, 7920-999 Alvito [(284) 763141; fax (284) 763102]** Fr Ferreira do Alentejo on N2 N twd Torrão. After Odivelas turn R onto N257 twd Alvito & turn R twd Barragem de Odivels. Site in 7km, clearly sp. Med, hdstg, pt sl, pt shd; wc (some cont); chem disp; mv service pnt; shwrs inc; el pnts (10A) €2.50; gas; lndtte; ice; shop; tradsmn; rest; snacks; bar; playgrnd; pool 50m; sand beach, lake sw 500m; boating; fishing; horseriding; tennis; no dogs Jul-Aug; phone; car wash; adv bkg; v quiet; red low ssn/CCI. "Exceptionally beautiful, superb, secluded site on banks of reservoir; site lighting poor; excel walking, cycling, birdwatching." ♦ ltd. € 20.00   2007*

The opening dates and prices on this campsite have changed. I'll send a site report form to the editor for the next edition of the guide.

⊞**OLHAO** *C4* (10km NE Rural) **Camping Caravanas Algarve, Sitio da Cabeça Moncarapacho, 8700-623 Moncarapacho [(289) 791669]** Exit IP1/A22 sp Moncarapacho. In 2km turn L sp Fuzeta. At traff lts turn L & immed L opp supmkt in 1km. Turn R at site sp. Site on L. Sm, hdstg, pt sl, unshd; own san facs; chem disp; el pnts (10A) inc; lndtte; shop, rest, snacks, bar 1.5km; sand beach 4km; 10% statics; dogs; poss cr; Eng spkn; adv bkg (dep req); quiet; 10% red CCI. "Situated on a farm in orange groves; pitches ltd in wet conditions; Spanish border 35km; National Park Ria Formosa 4km." € 10.00   2007*

⊞**OLHAO** *C4* (10km NE Rural) **Campismo Casa Rosa, 8700 Moncarapacho [(289) 794400; fax (289) 792952; casarosa@sapo.pt; www.casarosa.com.pt]** Fr A22 (IP1) E twd Spain, leave at exit 15 Olhão/Moncarapacho. At rndabt take 2nd exit dir Moncarapacho. Cont past sp Moncarapacho Centro direction Olhão. In 1km at Lagoão, on L is Café Da Lagoão with its orange awning. Just past café is sp for Casa Rosa. Foll sp. Sm, hdstg, terr, unshd; htd wc; chem disp; shwrs inc; el pnts (6A) inc; gas 3km; lndtte; ice; rest & snacks 2km; pool; shgl beach 6km; rv sw 6km; sat TV; no dogs; Eng spkn; adv bkg (dep req); noise fr construction yard adj; CCI. "CL-type site adj holiday apartments; adults only; helpful, friendly owners; evening meals avail; access poss diff lge o'fits; ideal for touring E Algarve; conv Spanish border; rec." ♦ ltd. € 10.00   2006*

⊞**OLHAO** *C4* (1.5km E Rural) **Camping de Olhão, Pinheiros do Marim, 8700-912 Olhão [(289) 700300; fax (289) 700390 or 700391; parque.campismo@sbsi.pt;   www.roteiro-campista.pt/faro/olhao.htm]** Turn S twd coast fr N125 1.5km E of Olhão by filling stn. Clearly sp on S side of N125, adj Ria Formosa National Park. V lge, hdg/mkd pitch, pt sl, shd; wc; chem disp; mv service pnt; shwrs; el pnts (6A) €1.85; gas; lndtte; ice; supmkt; tradsmn; rest; bar; playgrnd; pool; paddling pool; beach 1.5km; tennis; games rm; games area; cycle hire; horseriding 1km; internet; TV; dogs €1.50; 40% statics; phone; bus adj; rlwy station 1.5km; sep car park for some pitches; car wash; security guard; Eng spkn; some rlwy noise; 50% red Oct-May & 30% red 30+ days; cc acc; CCI. "Pleasant, helpful staff; excel pool; v popular long stay low ssn; many sm sandy pitches, some diff access for lge o'fits; gd for cycling, bird-watching; ferry to islands." ♦ € 18.80   2007*

See advertisement

⊞ *Site open all year*   *Help us to update this guide*

⊞**OLHAO** *C4* (9km E Coastal/Urban) **Parque Campismo de Fuzeta, 2 Rua do Liberdade, 8700-019 Fuzeta [(289) 793459; fax (289) 794034; jf-fuseta@mail.pt]** Fr N125 Olhão-Tavira rd, turn S at traff lts at Alfandanga sp Fuzeta & foll sp to site. Lge, some hdstg, pt shd; wc; chem disp; shwrs €0.25; el pnts (6A) €1.30; gas; lndtte; shop & 1km; rest adj; snacks; bar; BBQ; playgrnd adj; sand beach adj; 5% statics; dogs; phone; Eng spkn; no adv bkg; noise fr rd & adj bars; red long stay. "Pleasant staff; popular with long-stay m'vanners; haphazard pitching; elec cables run across site rds; poss flooding after heavy rain; areas of soft sand; v clean san facs but hot water to shwrs only; gd security; gd value; gd shopping in town & train service to Algarve towns; attractive area." ♦ ltd. € 10.60   2005*

⊞**OLIVEIRA DE AZEMEIS** *B2* (1.5km E Urban) **Camping La Salette, 3720-222 Oliveira de Azeméis [(256) 674373]** Fr N1 turn E onto N224 to Vale de Cambra, foll sp Parque La Salette. Med, shd; wc; shwrs €0.75; el pnts (6A) €0.75; gas; lndtte; shop 100m; rest, snacks, bar adj; BBQ; playgrnd 300m; pool adj; TV; phone; bus 200m; Eng spkn; quiet. "Picturesque area; gd NH." ♦ € 8.50   2007*

⊞**OLIVEIRA DO HOSPITAL** *C2* (9km SE Rural) **Parque de São Gião, 3400-570 São Gião [(238) 691154; fax (238) 692451]** Fr N17 Guarda-Coimbra rd turn S almost opp N230 rd to Oliveira do Hospital, dir Sandomil. Site on R in about 3km over rv bdge. Lge, shd; wc; chem disp; shwrs; el pnts (6A) €1.50; gas; lndtte; shop; rest; snacks; bar; BBQ; playgrnd; pool 7km; rv sw; fishing; phone; 50% statics; no dogs; bus adj; quiet. "Facs basic but clean; working water mill; app/exit long, steep, narr, lane." € 10.50   2006*

⊞**OLIVEIRA DO HOSPITAL** *C2* (15km S Rural) **Parque de Campismo Ponte Das Três Entradas, Santa Ovaia, 3400-591 Avô [(238) 670050; fax (238) 670055; ponte3entradas@mail.telepac.pt]** On N17 Guarda-Coimbra rd after town of Oliveira do Hospital turn S at Pousada sp onto N230. Site sp by Rv Alva 4km bef Avô. Med, pt shd; wc; shwrs inc; el pnts (4A) €2.50; gas; lndtte; shop; rest; snacks; bar; BBQ; playgrnd; rv sw; fishing; tennis; games area; cycle hire; entmnt; TV; some statics; phone; quiet; cc acc; red low ssn/long stay; CCI. "Pretty site in mountains." ♦ € 9.00   2006*

⊞**OLIVEIRA DO HOSPITAL** *C2* (10km NW Rural) **Camping Quinta das Oliveiras (Naturist), Andorinha, 3405-498 Travanca de Lagos [(962) 621287; fax (235) 466007; campismo.nat@ sapo.pt; www.quinta-das-oliveiras.nl]** Fr Oliveira do Hospital foll N230 & N1314 to Travanca de Lagos. Then take N502 twd Midões. After 2km turn R on N1313 to Andorinha. Site on R 1.5km after Andorinha. Sm, pt sl, terr, pt shd; wc; chem disp; shwrs inc; el pnts (6A) €3.50; tradsmn; BBQ; playgrnd; pool; dogs €1.50; poss cr; Eng spkn; adv bkg; quiet; INF card. € 16.15   2006*

PENACOVA *B2* (3km N Rural) **Camp Municipal de Vila Nova, Rua dos Barqueiros, Vila Nova, 3360-204 Penacova [(239) 477946; fax (239) 474857; penaparque2@iol.pt]** IP3 fr Coimbra, cross Rv Mondego N of Penacova & foll sp R onto N2 to site. Med, pt shd; wc; shwrs inc; el pnts (6A) €1; shop 50m; rest 150m; snacks; bar; BBQ; playgrnd; rv sw 200m; fishing; cycle hire; TV; no dogs; phone; bus 150m; Eng spkn; red CCI. "Open, attractive site." 1 Apr-30 Sep. € 8.10   2006*

PENACOVA *B2* (1km S Rural) **Camping Penacova, Estrada da Carvoeira, 3360 Penacova [tel/fax (239) 477464; penacova@fcmportugal.com; www.fcmportugal.com]** On N2 S of Penacova on E bank of rv. Fairly steep app needing care. Lge, pt shd; wc; chem disp; shwrs inc; el pnts (6A) €2.20; gas 500m; shop; rest/snacks; bar; playgrnd; rv sw; fishing; canoeing; entmnt; 70% statics; dogs €0.60; phone; quiet but poss noisy w/e; red low ssn; CCI. "Impeccable; lovely site; friendly helpful owner; pretty, rural area; heavily wooded; strenuous trek up to Penacova." ♦ 14 Jan-13 Nov. € 12.15   2004*

PENELA *B2* (500m SE Rural) **Parque Municipal de Campismo de Panela, Rua de Coimbra, 3230-284 Penela [(239) 569256; fax (239) 569400]** Fr Coimbra S on IC2, L at Condeixa a Nova, IC3 dir Penela. Thro vill foll sp to site. Sm, hstg, pt sl, terr, pt shd; wc; chem disp; shwrs €0.50; el pnts (6A) €0.50; shop, rest, snacks, bar 200m pool 500m; some statics; no dogs; bus adj; some traff noise; CCI. "Attractive sm town; restful, clean, well-maintained site." ♦ ltd. 1 Jun-30 Sep. € 4.50   2006*

⊞**PENICHE** *B3* (3km E Coastal) **Camp Municipal de Peniche, Avda Monsenhor M Bastos, 2520-206 Peniche [(262) 789696; fax (262) 789529; www.cm-peniche.pt]** Site 2km E fr Lourinha after N114 (fr Obidos) joins N247; rd crosses bdge & site on R. V lge, terr, pt shd; wc; shwrs inc; el pnts (4A) €1.30; gas; lndtte; shop; rest; bar; playgrnd; pool adj; beach 200m; fishing; tennis; 40% statics; phone; bus 500m; red low ssn; v quiet; cc acc. "Friendly staff; interesting area; gd NH." ♦ € 10.00   2004*

Portugal

⊞**PENICHE** *B3* (1.5km NW Urban/Coastal) **Camping Peniche Praia, Estrada Marginal Norte, 2520 Peniche [(262) 783460; fax (262) 789447; penichepraia@hotmail.com; www.penichepraia. pt]** Travel S on IP6 then take N114 sp Peniche; fr Lisbon N on N247 then N114 sp Peniche. Site on R on N114 1km bef Peniche. Med, hdg/mkd pitch, hdstg, unshd; wc; chem disp; mv service pnt; shwrs inc; el pnts (6A) inc; lndtte; ice; shop 1.5km; tradsmn; rest, snacks, bar high ssn; BBQ; playgrnd; covrd pool; paddling pool; sand beach 1.5km; games rm; cycle hire; internet; entmnt; TV; 30% statics; phone; bus 2km; car wash; Eng spkn; adv bkg rec; quiet; red long stay/low ssn/CCI. "Vg site in lovely location; some sm pitches; rec." € 14.75   2007*

See advertisement

POCO REDONDO see Tomar *B2*

PONTE DA BARCA *B1* (4km N Rural) **Camping Travança, Lugar de Bouças Donas, 4970-094 Arcos de Valdevez [(258) 526105 or (258) 452280; fax (258) 452450; aderepg@mail.telepac.pt; www. adere-pg.pt]** Fr Arcos de Valdevez on N202 twd Mezio, turn L sp Bouças Donas. Foll sp National Park & site. Sm, hdstg, pt shd; wc (some cont); baby facs; showrs inc; el pnts (16A); shop; tradsmn; bar; BBQ; playgrnd; TV rm; no statics; quiet. "A new National Park site high up in glorious country; vg walking." 1 Jun-30 Aug. € 9.75   2004*

PONTE DA BARCA *B1* (11km E Rural) **Camping Entre-Ambos-os-Rios, Lugar da Igreja, Entre-Ambos-os-Rios, 4980-613 Ponte da Barca [(258) 588361 or 452250; fax (258) 452450; aderepg@mail.telepac.pt; www.adere-pg.pt]** N203 E fr Ponte da Barca, pass ent sp for vill. Site sp N twd Rv Lima, after 1st bdge. Lge, pt sl, shd; wc; shwrs inc; el pnts (12A) €1; gas; lndry rm; shop, rest 300m; snacks; bar; playgrnd; rv sw; canoeing; fishing; entmnt; TV; dogs €0.50; phone; bus 100m; adv bkg; CCI. "Beautiful, clean, well-run site in pine trees, well situated for National Park." 15 May-30 Sep. € 13.40   2007*

⊞**PORTIMAO** *B4* (3km SE Coastal) **Camping Ferragudo, 8400-280 Ferragudo [(282) 461121; fax (282) 461355; geral@clubecampismolisboa.pt]** Leave N125 at sp Ferraguda, turn L at traff lts at end of Parchal vill. Turn R over waterway in Ferraguda, foll sp. V lge, terr, pt shd; cont wc; shwrs inc; el pnts (4-6A) inc; gas; lndry rm; shop; rest; snacks; bar; playgrnd; pool; sw & fishing 800m; entmnt; TV; no dogs; phone; bus 100m; v cr Jul/Aug; CCI. "Helpful staff; bus to Portimão at ent; shop/recep 1.5km fr pitches; unsuitable lge m'vans; housing bet site & beach." € 26.40   2005*

⊞**PORTIMAO** *B4* (10km SW Urban) **Parque de Campismo da Dourada, 8500-053 Alvor [(282) 459178; fax (282) 458002]** Turn S at W end of N125 Portimão by-pass sp Alvor. Site on L in 4km bef ent town. V lge, pt sl, terr, pt shd; wc; chem disp; shwrs €0.50; el pnts (6A) €2.50; gas; lndtte; shop high ssn; rest; snacks; bar; playgrnd; pool; paddling pool; sand beach 1km; fishing; sports area; entmnt; TV rm; dogs €1.75; bus 50m; poss noisy; red long stay/low ssn. "Friendly & helpful family-run site; office frequently unattended in winter & ltd facs; excel rest; lovely town & beaches." ◆ € 15.75   2007*

⊞**PORTO** *B1* (11km N Coastal) **Camping ORBITUR-Angeiras, Rua de Angeiras, Matos-inhos, 4455-039 Lavra [(229) 270571 or 270634; fax (229) 271178; info@orbutur.pt; www.orbitur. com]** Fr ICI/A28 take turn-off sp Lavra, site sp at end of slip rd. Site in approx 3km - app rd potholed & cobbled. Lge, pt sl, shd; wc (some cont); chem disp; mv service pnt; shwrs inc; el pnts (6A) €2.50 (check earth); gas; lndtte; ice; shop; tradsmn; rest; snacks; bar; BBQ; playgrnd; pool; sand beach 400m; tennis; fishing; games area; games rm; cab/sat TV; 70% statics; dogs €1.30; phone; bus to Porto at site ent; car wash; Eng spkn; adv bkg; red low ssn/long stay/snr citizens; cc acc; CCI. "Friendly & helpful staff; clean, dated san facs; gd rest; gd pitches in trees at end of site but ltd space lge o'fits; fish & veg mkt in Matosinhos." ◆ € 20.90   2007*

⊞**PORTO** *B1* (16km SE Rural) **Campidouro Parque de Medas, Lugar do Gavinho, 4515-397 Medas-Gondomar [(224) 760162; fax (224) 769082; geral@campidouro.pt]** Take N12 dir Gondomar off A1. Almost immed take R exit sp Entre-os-Rios. At rndabt pick up N108 & in approx 14km. Sp for Medas on R, thro hamlet & forest for 3km & foll sp for site on R. Long, steep app. New concrete access/site rds. Lge, mkd pitch, hdstg, terr, pt shd; wc; chem disp; mv service pnt; serviced pitches; shwrs inc; el pnts (6A) €2.63; gas; lndtte; shop, rest (w/e only low ssn); bar; playgrnd; pool & paddling pool; rv sw, fishing, boating; tennis; games rm; entmnt; TV rm; 90% statics; phone; bus; poss cr; quiet; cc acc; 20% red CCI. "Beautiful site on Rv Douro; helpful owners; gd rest; v clean facs; hot water for shwrs only; sm level area (poss cr by rv) for tourers; some sm pitches, waterlogged after heavy rain; bus to Porto rec as parking diff (ltd buses at w/end); excel." € 16.20   2007*

⊞**PORTO** *B1* (6km SW Coastal) **Camping Marisol, Rua Alto das Chaquedas 82, Canidelo, 400-356 Vila Nova de Gaia [(227) 135942; fax (227) 126351]** Fr Porto ring rd IC1 take N109 exit sp Espinho. In 1km take exit Madalena. Site sp on coast rd. Med, hdg pitch, pt shd; wc; chem disp; mv service pnt; shwrs inc; el pnts (6A) inc; gas; lndry rm; shop; rest; bar; BBQ; playgrnd; pool 800m; sand beach adj; games area; car wash; TV; 50% statics; bus 150m; poss cr; Eng spkn. "Conv for Porto; gd." ♦ € 10.25   2004*

⊞**PORTO** *B1* (10km SW Coastal/Urban) **Camping ORBITUR-Madalena, Rua do Cerro 608, Praia da Madalena, 4405-736 Vila Nova de Gaia [(227) 122520 or 122524; fax (227) 122534; info@orbitur.pt; www.orbitur.com]** Fr Porto ring rd IC1/A44 take N109 exit dir Espinho. In 1km take exit sp Madalena opp Volvo agent. Watch for either 'Campismo' or 'Orbitur' sp to site along winding, cobbled rd. Lge, mkd pitch, terr, pt sl, pt shd; wc (some cont); chem disp; mv service pnt; baby facs; shwrs inc; el pnts (6A) €2.50; gas; lndtte; ice; shop; tradsmn; rest, snacks, bar in ssn; BBQ; playgrnd; pool; sand beach 250m; tennis; games area; entmnt; games rm; TV rm; 40% statics; dogs €1.30; phone; bus to Porto; car wash; Eng spkn; adv bkg; cc acc; red low ssn/long stay/snr citizens; CCI. "Vg site in forest; restricted area for tourers; slight aircraft noise; some uneven pitches; poss ltd facs low ssn; excel bus to Porto cent fr site ent - do not take c'van into Porto." ♦ € 20.90   2007*

PORTO COVO see Sines *B4*

⊞**PÓVOA DE VARZIM** *B1* (13km N Coastal) **Camping ORBITUR-Rio Alto, EN13, Km 13, Lugar do Rio Alto, Estela, 4470-275 Póvoa de Varzim [(252) 615699; fax (252) 615599; info@orbitur.pt; www.orbitur.com]** N on Póvoa by-pass, in 11km turn L 1km N of Estela at Golf sp, in 3km turn R to camp ent. V lge, some hdg/mkd pitch, shd; wc; chem disp; mv service pnt; baby facs; shwrs inc; el pnts (5-15A) €2.50; gas; lndtte; ice; shop; tradsmn; rest; snacks; bar; BBQ; playgrnd; pool; sand beach 150m; tennis; games area; games rm; golf adj; entmnt; cab/sat TV; 10% static/semi-statics; dogs €1.30; phone; bus 2km; car wash; Eng spkn; adv bkg; poss cr; red low ssn/long stay/snr citizens; cc acc; CCI. "Excel facs; vg rest on site; direct access to vg beach; strong NW prevailing wind; excel touring base." ♦ € 22.80   2007*

PRAIA DE MIRA see Mira *B2*

⊞**PRAIA DE QUIAIOS** *B2* (Coastal) **Camping ORBITUR, Praia de Quiaios, 3080-515 Quiaios [(233) 919995; fax (233) 919996; info@orbitur.pt; www.orbitur.com]** Fr N109 turn W onto N109-8 dir Quiaios, foll sp 3km to Praia de Quiaios & site. Lge, some mkd pitch, pt shd; wc; chem disp; mv service pnt; shwrs inc; el pnts (10A) €2.50; gas; lndtte; ice; supmkt; tradsmn; rest; snacks; bar; BBQ; playgrnd; pool 500m; sand beach 500m; tennis; cycle hire; games rm; TV; entmnt; 20% statics; dogs €1.30; phone; car wash; Eng spkn; adv bkg; quiet; cc acc; red low ssn/snr citizens/long stay; CCI. "Interesting historical area; vg touring base; peaceful site; hot water to shwrs only; care needed some pitches due soft sand." ♦ € 17.50   2007*

⊞**QUARTEIRA** *C4* (2km N Coastal/Urban) **Camping ORBITUR-Quarteira, Estrada da Fonte Santa, Ave Sá Carneira, 8125 Quarteira [(289) 302826 or 302821; fax (289) 302822; info@orbitur.pt; www.orbitur.com]** Fr E & IP1/A22 take exit junc 12 at Loulé onto N396 to Quarteira; in 8.5km at rndabt by g'ge L along dual c'way. In 1km at traff lts fork R into site. No advance sp to site. V lge, mkd pitch, pt sl, terr, pt shd; wc; chem disp; mv service pnt; shwrs inc; el pnts (6A) €2.50 (long lead req some pitches); gas; lndtte; ice; supmkt 200m; tradsmn; rest; snacks; bar; BBQ; playgrnd; pool; waterslide; sand beach 600m; tennis; games rm; entmnt; TV rm; 5% statics (tour ops); dogs €1.30; phone; bus 50m; car wash; Eng spkn; adv bkg; aircraft noise fr Faro; red low ssn/long stay/snr citizens; cc acc; CCI. "Lovely site; popular winter long stay; narr site rds & tight turns; some o'hanging trees; some pitches diff lge o'fits; gd san facs; caterpillar prob Jan-Mar; easy walk to town." ♦ € 24.00   2007*

ROSARIO see Alandroal *C3*

Portugal

⊞SAGRES *B4* (2km W Coastal) **Camping ORBITUR, Cerro das Moitas, 8650-998 Sagres [(282) 624371; fax (282) 624445; info@orbitur.pt; www.orbitur.com]** On N268 to Cape St Vincent; well sp. Lge, hdg/mkd pitch, hdstg, pt shd; wc; chem disp; mv service pnt; shwrs inc; el pnts (6-10A) €2.50-3; gas; lndtte; ice; shop; rest; snacks; bar; BBQ; playgrnd; sand beach 2km; cycle hire; games rm; TV rm; dogs €1.30; car wash; Eng spkn; adv bkg; quiet; red long stay/low ssn/snr citizens; cc acc. "Vg, clean, tidy site in pine trees; cliff walks." ♦ € 19.20   2007*

> Before we move on, I'm going to fill in some site report forms and post them off to the editor, otherwise they won't arrive in time for the deadline at the end of September.

⊞SANTO ANTONIO DAS AREIAS *C3* (3km SE Rural) Camping Asseiceira, Asseiceira, 7330-204 **Santo António das Areias [tel/fax (245) 992940; gary-campingasseiceira@hotmail.com; www. campingasseiceira.com]** Fr N246-1 turn off sp Marvão/Santo António das Areias. Turn L to Santo António das Areias then 1st R on ent town then immed R again, up sm hill to rndabt. At rndabt turn R then at next rndabt cont straight on. There is a petrol stn on R, cont down hill for 400m. Site on L. Sm, pt sl, pt shd; wc; chem disp; shwrs inc; el pnts (16A) €4; gas 500m; shop, rest, snacks, bar 3km; pool 500m; no statics; dogs €1; bus 1km; quiet; CCI. "Attractive area; peaceful, remote site among olive trees; clean, tidy; gd for walking, birdwatching; helpful, friendly owners; interesting vills; nr Spanish border; excel." ♦ ltd. € 12.00   2007*

⊞SAO MARTINHO DO PORTO *B2* (1.5km NE Coastal) **Parque de Campismo Colina do Sol, Serra dos Mangues, 2460-697 São Martinho do Porto [(262) 989764; fax (262) 989763; parque. colina.sol@clix.pt; www.colinadosol.com]** Leave A8/IC1 SW at junc 21 onto N242 W to São Martinho, by-pass town on N242 dir Nazaré. Site on L northside of São Martinho. V lge, mkd pitch, hdstg, terr, pt shd; wc; chem disp; mv service pnt; shwrs inc; el pnts (6A) €2.75; gas; lndtte; ice; shop high ssn; rest; snacks; bar; BBQ; playgrnd; pool; paddling pool; sand beach 2km; fishing; games rm; TV; mobile homes/c'vans for hire; dogs €1; phone; bus 2km; site clsd at Xmas; poss cr; Eng spkn; adv bkg; quiet; cc acc; CCI. "Gd touring base on attractive coastline; gd walking, cycling; excel site." ♦ € 18.00   2007*

See advertisement

⊞SAO PEDRO DE MOEL *B2* (N Urban/Coastal) **Camping ORBITUR, Rua Volta do Sete, São Pedro de Moel, 2430 Marinha Grande [(244) 599168; fax (244) 599148; info@orbitur. pt; www.orbitur.com]** Site at end of rd fr Marinha Grande to beach; turn R at 1st rndabt on ent vill. Site S of lighthouse. V lge, some hdg/mkd pitch, hdstg, pt terr, shd; wc; chem disp; mv service pnt; shwrs inc; el pnts (6A) €2.50; gas; lndtte; ice; shop; tradsmn; rest; snacks; bar; BBQ; playgrnd; htd pool; waterslide; sand beach 500m (heavy surf); fishing; tennis; cycle hire; games rm; entmnt; cab/sat TV; some statics; dogs €1.30; phone; car wash; poss cr; adv bkg; Eng spkn; quiet; red low ssn/long stay/ snr citizens; cc acc; CCI. "Friendly, well-run, clean site; easy walk to shops, rests; site in pinewoods; gd cycling to beaches; São Pedro smart resort; ltd facs low ssn." ♦ € 20.90   2007*

⊞SAO PEDRO DE MOEL *B2* (2km N Coastal) **Inatal Parque de Campismo, Avda do Farol, 2430-502 São Pedro de Moel [(244) 599289; fax (244) 599550; pc.spmoel@inatel.pt; www. inatel.pt]** Site 100m N of lighthouse on rd to Praia de Vieira. Lge, hdg/mkd pitch, hdstg, shd; wc (some cont); chem disp (wc); shwrs inc; el pnts (4A) inc; shop high ssn; rest, snacks, bar high ssn & 2km; playgrnd; pool 500m; sand beach adj; TV; 25% statics; no dogs; bus 300m; poss cr; quiet. "Tidy site; basic san facs." € 15.65   2007*

⊞SAO TEOTONIO *B4* (7km W Coastal) **Camping Monte Carvalhal da Rocha, Praia do Carvalhal, Brejão, 7630-569 São Teotónio [(282) 947293; fax (282) 947294; geral@montecarvalhalr-turismo. com; www.montecarvalhalr-turismo.com]** Turn W off N120 dir Brejão, Carvalhal. Site sp. Med, shd; wc; shwrs inc; el pnts (16A) €2.50; gas; lndry rm; shop, rest, snacks, bar high ssn; BBQ; playgrnd; sand beach 500m; fishing; cycle hire; TV; some statics; no dogs; phone; bus 2km; car wash; Eng spkn; adv bkg; quiet; cc acc; red low ssn. "Beautiful area; friendly, helpful staff." € 19.50   2005*

⊞SAO TEOTONIO *B4* (7km W Coastal) **Parque de Campismo da Zambujeira, Praia da Zambujeira, 7630-740 Zambujeira do Mar [(283) 961172; fax (283) 961320; www.campingzambujeira.com. sapo.pt]** S on N120 twd Lagos, turn W when level with São Teotónio on unclassified rd to Zambujeira. Site on L in 7km, bef vill. V lge, pt sl, pt shd; wc; chem disp; mv service pnt; shwrs inc; el pnts (6-10A) €3; gas; shop, rest, snacks & bar high ssn; playgrnd; sand beach 1km; tennis; TV; dogs €3; phone; bus adj; site clsd Nov; Eng spkn; some rd noise; red low ssn/long stay. "V welcoming, friendly owners; in pleasant rural setting; hot water to shwrs only; sh walk to unspoilt vill with some shops & rest; cliff walks; coastal scenery." € 20.00   2006*

SATAO *C2* (10km N Rural) **Camping Quinta Chave Grande, Casfreires, Ferreira d'Aves, 3560-043 Sátão [(232) 665552; fax (232) 665352; chave-grande@sapo.pt; www.chave-grande.com]** Leave IP5 Salamanca-Viseu rd onto N229 to Sátão, site sp in Satão. Med, terr, pt shd; wc; chem disp; mv service pnt; shwrs inc; el pnts (5A) €2.50; gas; lndtte; ice; shop 3km; tradsmn; rest 3km; snacks; bar; playgrnd; pool; tennis; TV; dogs €1.10; Eng spkn; quiet; red long stay. "Warm welcome fr friendly Dutch owners; gd facs; well organised BBQs - friendly atmosphere; gd touring base; gd walks fr site; excel." 15 Mar-31 Oct. € 15.60
2006*

SERPA *C4* (1km SE Urban) **Parque Municipal de Campismo Serpa, Largo de São Pedro, 7830-303 Serpa [(284) 544290; fax (284) 540109]** Fr N260 take 1st sp for town; site well sp fr most directions - opp sw pool. Do not ent walled town. Med, pt sl, pt shd; wc; chem disp; shwrs inc; el pnts (6A) €1.25; gas; lndtte; shop 100m; rest, snacks, bar 50m; BBQ; daily mkt 500m; supmkt nr; pool adj; rv sw 5km; 20% statics; dogs; phone; adv bkg; poss noise fr rd & barking dogs; no cc acc; CCI. "Popular site; simple, high quality facs; interesting town, developing rapidly; historic centre nrby." ♦ € 7.75   2007*

SESIMBRA *B3* (1.5km W Coastal) **Camp Municipal Forte do Cavalo, Porto de Abrigo, 2970 Sesimbra [(212) 288508; fax (212) 288265; decl_dtc_st@mun-sesimbra.pt; www.mun-sesimbra.pt]** Fr Lisbon S on A2/IP7 turn S onto N378 to Sesimbra. Turn R immed after town ent sp Campismo & Porto. Fork R again sp Porto; L downhill at traff lts to avoid town cent. Turn R at sea front to site by lighthouse. Steep uphill app. V lge, pt sl, terr, shd; wc; shwrs inc; el pnts (6A) €2.10; gas; ice; shop, rest 1km; snacks, bar 500m; BBQ; playgrnd; beach 800m; fishing; boating; no dogs; phone; bus 100m; poss cr; Eng spkn; no adv bkg; quiet; CCI. "Pitches ltd for tourers; gd views; lovely, unique fishing vill; castle worth visit; unreliable opening dates (poss not open until Jun) - phone ahead." € 11.50
2006*

SESIMBRA *B3* (12km W Coastal) **Parque Campismo Campimeco, Praia das Bicas, 2970-066 Aldeia do Meco [(212) 683374; fax (212) 683844]** Fr Sesimbra take N379 twd Azóia & Cabo Espichel. Turn R in Azóia, then L in Aldeia do Meco at x-rds, site sp. V lge, pt sl, pt shd; wc; chem disp (wc); shwrs inc; el pnts (5A) €1.90; lndry rm; shop; rest, snacks, bar 2km; playgrnd; pool; sand beach adj; tennis; 98% statics; dogs; bus 2km; poss cr; quiet; CCI. "Vg low ssn; steep descent to beach (dogs not allowed); ltd touring pitches." € 10.90
2007*

SETUBAL *B3* (4km W Coastal) **Parque de Campismo do Outão, Estrada de Rasca, 2900-182 Setúbal [(265) 238318; fax (265) 228098]** Fr Setúbal take coast rd W twd Outão, site on L. V lge, mkd pitch, hdstg, pt shd; wc (some cont); chem disp; shwrs inc; el pnts (5A) €2.40; gas; shop; rest; bar; playgrnd; sand beach adj; 90% statics; dogs €1.50; poss cr; Eng spkn; some rd noise; red low ssn; 10% red CCI. "Few pitches for tourers; hdstg not suitable for awning; vacant static pitches sm & have kerb; san facs poor & poss unclean low ssn ♦ € 14.00
2006*

SINES *B4* (15km SE Rural) **Parque de Campismo de Porto Covo, Estrada Municipal 554, 7250-437 Porto Covo [(269) 905136; fax (269) 905239; camping-portocovo@gmail.com]** S fr Sines on N120 twd Cercal, turn R after 13km dir Porto Covo & site 200m bef vill. V rough app rd to site. Med, hdstg, pt sl, unshd; wc (cont); chem disp; mv service pnt; shwrs inc; el pnts (4-10A) €3.05; gas; lndtte; shop; rest; snacks; bar; BBQ; playgrnd; pool; sand beach 400m; games area; cycle hire; boat trips; TV; mostly statics; dogs; phone; bus 300m; poss cr; adv bkg; poss noisy high ssn; red low ssn. "Not rec for tourers, few touring pitches & v sm, diff access; pleasant site; lovely vill." ♦ € 18.40
2007*

Portugal

TOMAR *B2* (7km NE Rural) **Camping Pelinos 77, 2300-093 Tomar [(249) 301814]** N fr Tomar on N110, turn R to Calçadas at traff lts opp g'ge, foll site sp. Steep descent to site. Sm, terr, pt shd; wc; shwrs inc; el pnts (12A) €2; Indtte; rest; snacks; bar; BBQ (winter only); playgrnd; pool; lake sw, watersports, fishing 7km; TV; dogs; phone; bus 100m; Eng spkn; adv bkg; quiet; red low ssn; CCI. "Owner will assist taking o'fits in/out; vg." 15 Jan-15 Nov. € 11.50   2006*

TOMAR *B2* (10km E Rural) **Camping Redondo, Rua do Casal Rei 6, 2300-035 Poço Redondo [tel/fax (249) 376421; hansfromme@hotmail. com; http://home.wanadoo.nl/edvols]** Fr N or S on N110, take IC3 for Tomar, then take 1st exit sp Albufeira do Castelo do Bode/Tomar. Foll site sp (red hearts) for 7km. Steep drop at site ent. Sm, pt sl, pt shd; wc; chem disp; mv service pnt; shwrs inc; el pnts (4-6A) €1.95-2.20; Indtte; shop 2km; rest; snacks; bar; playgrnd; pool; waterslide; lake beach 4.5km; TV rm; few statics; dogs €0.60; phone; bus; poss cr; Eng spkn; adv bkg; red low ssn; CCI. "Due steep drop at ent, site owner tows c'vans out." 15 Mar-30 Sep. € 12.50   2005*

TOMAR *B2* (10km SE Rural) **Camping Castelo do Bode, 2200 Martinchel [(241) 849262; fax (241) 849244; castelo.bode@fcmportugal.com]** S fr Tomar on N110, in approx 7km L onto N358-2 dir Barragem & Castelo do Bode. Site on L in 6km immed after dam; steep ent. Med, mkd pitch, hdstg, terr, pt shd; wc (some cont); chem disp; shwrs inc; el pnts (2A) inc; gas; ice; supmkt 6km; tradsmn; rest, snacks 2km; bar; playgrnd; lake sw adj; boating; fishing; dogs €0.60; phone; bus to Tomar 1km; no adv bkg; quiet; CCI. "Site on edge of 60km long lake with excel watersports; old san facs, but clean; helpful staff; lge free car park on ent Tomar - interesting town." ♦ 13 Jan-11 Nov. € 12.25   2007*

⊞**VAGOS** *B2* (8km W Coastal) **Camping Vagueira, Rua do Parque de Campismo, Vagueira, 3840-254 Gafanha da Boa-Hora [(234) 797526; fax (234) 797093; arlindo.lda@clix.pt; www.roteiro-campista.pt/Aveiro/vagueira.htm]** Fr Aveiro take N109 S twd Figuera da Foz. Turn R in Vagos vill. After 6km along narr poor rd, site on R bef reaching Vagueira vill. V lge, mkd pitch, shd; wc (some cont); chem disp; mv service pnt; shwrs inc; el pnts (6-16A) €2; gas; Indtte; ice; supmkt, rest, snacks, bar high ssn; playgrnd; pool 750m; sand beach 750m; fishing 1km; tennis; games area; cycle hire; entmnt; 90% statics; bus 500m; Eng spkn; adv bkg; quiet; cc acc; red CCI. "V pleasant & well-run; friendly staff; poss diff access to pitches for lge o'fits; areas soft sand; gd touring base; vg site." ♦ € 15.80   2007*

See advertisement

VALHELHAS *C2* (1km W Rural) **Camp Municipal Rossio de Valhelhas, 6300-235 Valhelhas [(275) 487160; fax (275) 487372; jfvalhelhas@clix. pt; www.valhelhas.com]** Fr Manteigas, site is on R of N232 on ent Valhelhas. Lge, shd; wc; shwrs inc; el pnts (5-10A) inc (long lead req); Indry rm; shop 150m; rest 300m; snacks; bar; playgrnd; rv sw adj; fishing; games area; few statics; no dogs; phone; bus 100m; poss cr; quiet; cc not acc; CCI. "Pleasant, woodland site; conv for touring Serra da Estrela; rv dammed to make natural sw pool; friendly, helpful staff." 1 May-30 Sep. € 9.30   2006*

⊞**VALPAÇOS** *C1* (6km E Rural) **Campismo Rabaçal-Valpaços, Rua Gago Coutinho 14, 5430 Valpaços [(278) 759354]** Fr E82/IP4 turn N onto N213 to Valpaços, turn R onto N206, site sp. Lge, pt shd; wc; mv service pnt; shwrs inc; el pnts (6A) €1.20; gas; Indtte; rest; bar; BBQ; playgrnd; rv sw & fishing adj; phone; quiet; red CCI. "Friendly staff; beautiful rvside setting." ♦ € 8.50   2006*

VALVERDE see Lagos *B4*

⊞**VIANA DO CASTELO** *B1* (3km S Coastal) **Parque de Campismo Inatel do Cabedelo, Avda dos Trabalhadores, Cabedelo, 4900-164 Darque [(258) 322042; fax (258) 331502; pc.cabedelo@ inatel.pt; www.inatel.pt]** Exit IC1 junc 11 to W sp Darque, Cabedelo, foll sp to site. Lge, mkd pitch, hdstg, pt sl, pt shd; wc (some cont); shwrs inc; el pnts (6A) inc; gas; lndtte; shop high ssn; tradsmn; snacks; bar; sand beach adj; entmnt; 30% statics; no dogs; phone; bus 100m; site clsd mid-Dec to mid-Jan; adv bkg; quiet; CCI. "V secure; gd for children; hourly ferry to Viana; spacious pitches under pines; poss poor facs low ssn & in need of refurb." ♦ € 12.50   2007*

⊞**VIANA DO CASTELO** *B1* (2km SW Coastal/ Urban) **Camping ORBITUR-Cabedelo, Rua Diogo Álvares, Cabedelo, 4900-161 Darque [(258) 322167; fax (258) 321946; info@orbitur.pt; www.orbitur.com]** Exit IC1 junc 11 to W sp Darque, Cabedelo, foll sp to site in park. Lge, mkd pitch, pt sl, shd; wc; chem disp; mv service pnt; shwrs inc; el pnts (5-15A) €2.50; gas; lndtte; ice; shop; tradsmn; rest; snacks; bar; BBQ; playgrnd; htd pool; lge sand beach adj; surfing; fishing; entmnt; TV; dogs €1.30; phone; car wash; Eng spkn; adv bkg; quiet; red low ssn/long stay/snr citizens; cc acc; CCI. "Site in pinewoods; friendly staff; gd facs; plenty of shade; major festival in Viana 3rd w/e in Aug; lge mkt in town Fri am; sm passenger ferry over Rv Lima to town high ssn; beach access fr site; Santa Luzia worth visit." ♦ € 20.90   2007*

> There aren't many sites open this early in the year. We'd better phone ahead to check that the one we're heading for is actually open.

VIEIRA DO MINHO *C1* (1.5km S Urban) **Parque de Campismo de Cabreira, Lugar de Entre os Rios, 4850 Vieira do Minho [(253) 648665; fax (253) 648667; bina.vc@mail.telepac.pt]** Take N103 E fr Braga for 30km; foll sp to Vieira Do Minho, site sp in Vieira at 1.5km. Lge, pt shd; wc; chem disp (wc); shwrs inc; el pnts (5A) €2.50; gas; lndtte; shop; rest; snacks; bar; playgrnd; 2 pools adj; rv sw adj; sports area; cycle hire; entmnt; phone; bus 1km; Eng spkn; quiet; CCI. "V friendly; gd, level grassy site; conv for Gerês National Park." ♦ ltd. 1 Feb-31 Oct. € 14.50   2005*

⊞**VILA DO BISPO** *B4* (8km SE Coastal/Rural) **Parque de Campismo Quinta dos Carriços (Part Naturist), Praia de Salema, 8650-196 Budens [(282) 695201; fax (282) 695122; quintacarrico@ oninet.pt; www.quintadoscarricos.com]** Take N125 out of Lagos twd Sagres. In approx 14km at sp Salema, turn L & again immed L twd Salema. Site on R 300m. V lge, pt terr (tractor avail), pt shd; wc; chem disp; mv service pnt; shwrs €0.65; el pnts (6A) €2.50 (metered for long stay); gas; lndtte; ice; shop; rest; snacks; bar; playgrnd; pool 1km; sand beach 1km; golf 1km; TV; 8% statics; dogs €2.10; phone; bus; Eng spkn; adv bkg (ess high ssn); quiet; cc acc; red long stay; CCI. "Naturist section in sep valley; apartments avail on site; friendly Dutch owners; tractor avail to tow to terr; area of wild flowers in spring; no music allowed; beach 30 mins walk; buses pass ent for Lagos, beach & Sagres; excel." ♦ € 20.30   2006*

⊞**VILA DO BISPO** *B4* (3km S Rural/Coastal) **Camping Praia da Ingrina, Raposeira, 8650 Vila do Bispo [tel/fax (282) 639242; camping.ingrina@ clix.pt; www.campingingrina.com]** Fr Vila do Bispo take N125 E to Raposeira. At traff lts turn R sp Ingrina. After 1km bear R & foll sp to site. Last km of access rd rough. Med, terr, pt shd; wc; chem disp (wc); shwrs inc; el pnts (6A) €2.50; gas; shop, rest, snacks, bar high ssn; BBQ; playgrnd; sand beach 600m; dogs €2.50; phone; bus 3km; red long stay; CCI. "Basic CL-type site; el pnts & facs ltd - long lead req; gd cliff walks to unspoilt beaches/ surfing beaches." € 17.20   2006*

⊞**VILA FLOR** *C1* (2.5km SW Rural) **Camp Municipal de Vila Flor, Barragem do Peneireiro, 5360-303 Vila Flor [(278) 512350; fax (278) 512380; cm.vila.flor@mail.telepac.pt; www.cm-vilaflor. espigueiro.pt]** Site is off N215, sp fr all dirs. V bumpy app rd - 12km. V lge, terr, pt shd; wc; chem disp (wc); shwrs inc; el pnts (16A) €1.50; gas; lndry rm; shop; snacks; bar; BBQ; playgrnd; pool adj; tennis adj; TV rm; 10% statics; dogs; phone; clsd 2300-0700 (1800-0800 low ssn); poss v cr; adv bkg; noisy high ssn; CCI. "Friendly staff; access to pitches diff." ♦ ltd. € 9.40   2006*

⊞**VILA FRANCA DE XIRA** *B3* (1km NE Rural) **Camp Municipal Vila Franca de Xira, 2600-125 Vila Franca de Xira [(263) 275258; fax (263) 271511; xiracamping@cm-vfxira.pt]** Fr A1/IP1 exit junc 3 onto N1 dir Vila Franca. Immed cobble stone rd to town seen, turn R & site well sp. Sm, hdstg, terr, pt shd; wc; chem disp (wc); shwrs inc; el pnts (12A) €0.90; shop 700m rest; snacks; bar; playgrnd; pool; fishing 800m; canoeing 400m; entmnt; 40% statics; bus adj; rlwy stn 800m; poss cr; Eng spkn; some rd noise; red long stay; CCI. "San facs need refurb/renovation but clean; many shabby statics (2007); conv trains to Lisbon; gd NH." € 10.80   2007*

VILA NOVA DE CACELA see Vila Real de Santo Antonio *C4*

VILA NOVA DE CERVEIRA *B1* (5km E Rural) **Parque de Campismo Convívio, Rua de Badão, 1 Bacelo, 4920-020 Candemil [(251) 794404; convivio@ vodafone.pt; http://convivio.planetaclix.pt]** Fr Vila Nova de Cerveira dir Candemil on N13/ N302, turn L at Bacelo, site sp 3m. Sm, terr, pt shd; wc; chem disp; shwrs inc; el pnts (6A) €2.50; lndtte; shop 2km; tradsmn; rest 4km; snacks; bar; BBQ; htd pool; games rm; no statics; dogs €0.85; phone; bus/train 5km; poss cr; Eng spkn; adv bkg (dep req); quiet; red long stay; CCI. "No twin-axle c'vans acc; site open Oct-Mar for adv bkgs only." 1 Apr-1 Oct. € 13.00   2007*

VILA NOVA DE GAIA see Porto *B1*

⊞**VILA NOVA DE MILFONTES** *B4* (Coastal) **Camping Campiférias, 7645-301 Vila Nova de Milfontes [(283) 996409; fax (283) 996581; novaferias@oninet.pt]** S fr Sines on N120/IC4 for 22km; turn R at Cercal on N390 SW for Milfontes on banks of Rio Mira; clearly sp on edge of town opp mkt. If driving thro Vila Nova twd coast, look out for site sp on R. App rds bumpy - care needed. Site well sp. V lge, pt shd; wc (cont); chem disp; mv service pnt; shwrs inc; el pnts (5A) €2.30; shop 50m; rest; snacks; bar; playgrnd; beach 800m; entmnt; TV; 50% statics; no dogs; bus 500m; phone; site clsd 3-25 Dec; adv bkg; quiet; red low ssn. "V clean site but san facs need upgrade; trees may make pitching diff; conv for beach & shops; mkt opp; leaving site poss diff - rec plan rte in advance." ♦ € 16.00   2007*

⊞**VILA NOVA DE MILFONTES** *B4* (1km N Coastal) **Camping Milfontes, 7645-300 Vila Nova de Milfontes [tel/fax (283) 996104; geral@parque milfontes.com; www.campingmilfontes.com]** S fr Sines on N120/IC4 for 22km; turn R at Cercal on N390 SW for Milfontes on banks of Rio Mira; clear sp. V lge, pt shd; wc; chem disp; mv service pnt; shwrs inc; el pnts (6A) €2.55 (long lead poss req); gas; lndtte; shop; supmkt & mkt 5 mins walk; rest, snacks, bar high ssn; playgrnd; sand beach 800m; TV; 10% statics; phone; bus 600m; poss cr; quiet; cc acc; 10% red CCI. "Pitching poss diff for lge o'fits due trees & static s; nr fishing vill at mouth Rv Mira with beaches & sailing on rv; nice site." ♦ € 18.00   2007*

⊞**VILA NOVA DE MILFONTES** *B4* (8km N Coastal) **Sitava Camping, Brejo da Zimbreira, 7645-017 Vila Nova de Milfontes [(283) 890100; fax (283) 890109; sitava@camping.sitave.pt; www. sitava.pt]** S fr Sines on N120/IC4. At Cercal take dir Vila Nova de Milfontes. At Brunheiras turn R at site sp; site in 4km on L. V lge, mkd pitch, pt sl, pt shd; wc; chem disp; shwrs inc; el pnts (6A) €2.15; gas; lndtte; ice; shop high ssn; tradsmn; rest; snacks; bar; BBQ; playgrnd; pool; sand beach 600m; tennis; games area; games rm; entmnt; TV; 60% statics; no dogs; phone; bus 100m; poss cr; Eng spkn; adv bkg; quiet; red low ssn/CCI. "Friendly staff; bus to beach; excel facs but ltd low ssn; vg security." ♦ € 13.60   2007*

VILA PRAIA DE ANCORA *B1* (7km S Coastal) **Parque de Campismo do Paço, 4910-024 Vila Praia de Âncora [tel/fax (258) 912697; geral@ campingpaco.com; www.campingpaco.com]** Fr N13 Caminha-Viana do Castelo, site sp 1km S of Âncora, km 81. Med, pt shd; wc; chem disp; mv service pnt; shwrs inc; el pnts (6A) €2.25; gas; lndtte; ice; shop; tradsmn; rest; snacks; bar; BBQ; playgrnd; pool 1.5km; rv sw; sand beach 1km; fishing; canoeing; games area; TV; phone; bus 600m; car wash; adv bkg (dep req); Eng spkn; quiet; cc acc; red CCI. "Pleasant staff; excel san facs; vg touring base; gd beaches nr." 15 Apr-30 Sep. € 14.70   2007*

VILA REAL *C1* (500m NE Urban) **Camping Vila Real, Rua Dr Manuel Cardona, 5000-558 Vila Real [(259) 324724]** On IP4/E82 take Vila Real N exit & head S into town. At Galp g'ge rndabt, turn L & in 30m turn L again Site at end of rd in 400m. Site sp fr all dirs. Lge, pt sl, terr, pt shd; wc; chem disp; baby facs; shwrs inc; el pnts (6A) inc; gas; sm shop adj; tradsmn; rest; snacks; bar; BBQ; playgrnd; pool complex adj; tennis; 10% statics; dogs; phone; bus 150m; site clsd mid-Dec to mid Jan; poss cr; 10% red CCI. "Conv upper Douro; old-fashioned facs ltd when site full; gd mkt in town." ♦ 1 Mar-30 Nov. € 16.15   2007*

⊞**VILA REAL DE SANTO ANTONIO** *C4* (3km W Coastal) **Parque Municipal de Campismo, 8900 Monte Gordo [(281) 510970; fax (281) 510003; cmvrsa@mail.telepac.pt]** Fr Faro on N125 turn R sp Monte Gordo. Site on sea front in 500m. Or fr Spain over bdge at border, exit junc 9 to Vila Real over rlwy line. Strt over rndabt & turn R at T-junc, site sp just bef ent town. V lge, pt sl, shd; wc (some cont); chem disp; shwrs inc; el pnts (10A) €1.60 (long cable poss req); gas; lndtte; lndry rm; ice; shop & 1km; tradsmn; rest; snacks; bar; BBQ; playgrnd; sand beach 100m; canoeing; TV; 10% statics; dogs; phone; bus; train to Faro 3km; v cr in ssn; Eng spkn; no adv bkg; quiet; cc acc; red low ssn/long stay/snr citizens; CCI. "V lge pitches but poss v overcr high ssn; many long stay c'vans; caution soft sand makes some pitches unreliable, esp in wet; ground poss too soft for lge o'fits; san facs poor & site unkempt; lovely area; gd birdwatching; gd security." ♦ € 16.85   2006*

⊞**VILA REAL DE SANTO ANTONIO** *C4* (10km W Rural) **Camping Caliço Park, Sitio do Caliço, 8900-907 Vila Nova de Cacela [(281) 951195; fax (281) 951977; transcampo@mail.telepac.pt]** On N side of N125 Vila Real to Faro rd. Sp on main rd & in Vila Nova de Cacela vill, visible fr rd. Rds have been re-surfaced for 95% of the way. Lge, pt sl, shd; wc; chem disp; shwrs inc; el pnts (6A) €2.60; gas; lndtte; shop; rest; snacks; bar; playgrnd; pool; sand beach 4km; cycle hire; many statics; dogs €1.30; phone; bus/train 2km; Eng spkn; adv bkg; noisy in ssn & rd noise; cc acc; red long stay/low ssn; CCI. "Friendly staff; gd NH." € 15.60   2007*

VILAR DE MOUROS see Caminha *B1*

VISEU *C2* (2km E Urban) **Camping Fontelo (formerly Orbitur), Rua do Fontelo, Barrio Santa Eugénia 3500-033 Viseu [(232) 436146; fax (232) 432076]** Take exit Viseu Este fr rd IP5, at 1st rndabt (approx 2km) foll sp to site. Steep rd access fr recep. Lge, sl, shd; wc; chem disp; mv service pnt; shwrs inc; el pnts (6A) €2.25; gas; lndtte; shop; rest 100m; snacks; bar; BBQ; playgrnd; pool 10km; TV; dogs €1.20; phone; adv bkg; quiet; cc acc; red low ssn/long stay/snr citizens; CCI. "V helpful & friendly; interesting cathedral, museum & art gallery nrby; excel san facs; surrounding country beautiful; poss diff to manoeuvre on site amongst trees; excel carnival 24 June annually." ♦ 15 Mar-15 Oct. € 17.20   2006*

⊞**VOUZELA** *C2* (3km E) **Parque Campismo Municipal Vouzela, Monte da Senhora do Castelo, 3670-250 Vouzela [(232) 740020; fax (232) 711513; parquecampismo@cm-vouzela.pt; www.cm-vouzela.pt]** Fr Vouzela foll N228; turn R sp Sra do Castelo. Site well sp fr town cent. Steep app. V lge, pt sl, terr, pt shd; wc; chem disp; mv service pnt; shwrs inc; el pnts (6-15A) €1.25; gas; lndry rm; shop; rest; snacks; bar; playgrnd; pool; tennis; cycle hire; entmnt; TV; 95% statics; dogs €1; phone; bus 3km; quiet except w/e; CCI. "Lovely location; poss diff to find pitch bet statics; access to higher terrs by steep hill." ♦ € 8.50   2005*

ZAMBUJEIRA DO MAR see Sao Teotonio *B4*

Portugal

Portugal

Distances are shown in kilometres and are calculated from town/city centres along the most practical roads, although not necessarily taking the shortest route.

1km = 0.62miles

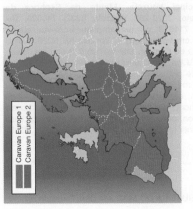

Legend:
- Caravan Europe 1
- Caravan Europe 2

Miranda do Douro to Vila Real de Santo António = 688km

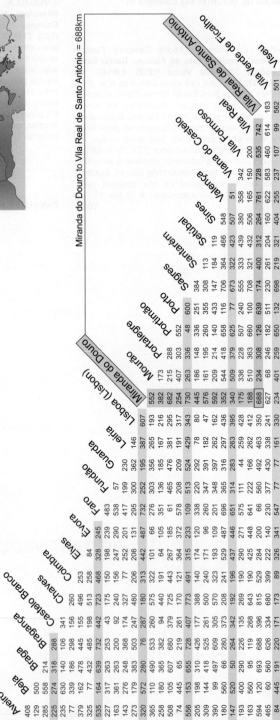

Distance chart (distances in km). Origin cities are listed as rows; figures give the distance to each destination city listed in the column heading.

From \ To	Aveiro	Beja	Bragança	Braga	Castelo Branco	Chaves	Coimbra	Elvas	Évora	Faro	Fundão	Guarda	Leiria	Lisboa (Lisbon)	Miranda do Douro	Mourão	Portalegre	Porto	Sagres	Santarém	Setúbal	Sines	Valença	Viana do Castelo	Vila Formoso	Vila Real	Vila Real de Santo António	Vila Verde de Ficalho
Beja	408																											
Bragança	129	500																										
Braga	285	558	288																									
Castelo Branco	235	214	341	106																								
Chaves	77	630	156	341	253																							
Coimbra	379	339	260	156	258	468																						
Elvas	325	162	298	253	84	723	175																					
Évora	535	77	260	92	328	150	43	263																				
Faro	227	164	732	200	239	247	200	253	253																			
Fundão	163	317	175	368	290	77	92	368	368	43																		
Guarda	143	361	253	174	201	417	174	180	174	327	200																	
Leiria	273	276	200	327	199	300	206	131	206	503	503	368																
Lisboa (Lisbon)	320	179	368	503	206	362	442	362	300	442	247	76	533															
Miranda do Douro	365	572	383	247	313	146	66	209	209	313	146	230	110	490														
Mourão	258	110	76	110	101	442	105	195	161	578	209	391	362	146	362													
Portalegre	508	180	533	490	191	313	185	214	214	391	347	262	182	347	391	161												
Porto	74	105	260	180	267	66	140	418	418	260	182	262	397	262	262	209	214											
Sagres	556	153	365	365	364	105	174	558	322	544	209	214	397	316	418	195	214	418										
Santarém	205	198	382	379	121	185	109	101	66	706	418	544	509	316	544	544	418	544	706									
Setúbal	309	144	379	680	491	364	529	96	185	575	186	195	509	340	509	195	209	186	658	575								
Sines	390	99	728	219	140	170	192	193	109	185	111	182	209	340	175	336	260	544	658	186	111							
Valença	180	560	426	310	174	773	269	487	446	487	222	166	263	44	336	195	214	209	706	544	509	509						
Viana do Castelo	147	120	310	418	109	388	190	437	575	651	314	283	111	283	228	336	140	116	673	379	336	336	234					
Vila Formoso	193	400	418	497	529	310	425	271	448	641	575	492	196	66	379	195	166	77	507	509	340	44	401	401				
Vila Real	163	560	497	99	261	323	284	425	140	560	222	166	560	350	509	44	379	264	174	322	507	509	116	116	234			
Vila Real de Santo António	594	445	99	50	170	570	815	284	230	66	166	430	284	492	234	111	126	639	312	423	439	506	264	77	230	259		
Vila Verde de Ficalho	465	191	50	119	261	192	399	222	341	230	204	338	430	182	401	509	660	100	174	400	312	432	182	204	511	68	650	
Viseu	84	—	220	171	170	268	190	341	321	547	377	338	241	330	259	132	650	132	698	219	321	404	237	183	107	246	132	501

Insurance Expertise at home and abroad!

All our insurance policies are designed with caravanners and motor caravanners in mind so, whether you're at home or away touring, you can rely on The Club to be sure you are fully covered.

Caravan Insurance

Our competitive policies offer comprehensive and flexible cover, based on more than 35 years' experience operating the UK's largest Caravan insurance scheme for our members.
Call on **01342 336610** or get a quote & buy online at **www.caravanclub.co.uk**

UK Breakdown & Recovery

The Club's Mayday UK vehicle rescue is provided in conjunction with Green Flag and offers fast and reliable rescue and recovery, whether you're towing or not.
Call on **0800 731 0112** or get a quote & buy online at **www.caravanclub.co.uk**

Car Insurance

Competitive Car insurance from a name you can trust, with a guarantee of a lower premium than your current insurer*.
Call on **0800 028 4809**

Home Insurance

Our Home insurance protects your buildings and/or contents against a wide range of risks and offers additional benefits.
Call on **0800 028 4815**

Pet Insurance

Be sure your pets are protected at home or when away touring in the UK or abroad, no matter how many trips you take.
Call on **0800 015 1396**

Motor Caravan Insurance

Another Club speciality, with wide cover at competitive rates and a guarantee to beat the renewal premium offered by your present insurer*.
Call on **0800 028 4809**

Overseas Holiday Insurance

When you travel abroad, take The Club's Red Pennant Holiday Insurance with you. Our own 24-hour emergency team helps you relax, knowing you're in experienced hands.
Call on **01342 336633** or get a quote & buy online at **www.caravanclub.co.uk**

To find out more, please call us stating reference CE08.
We look forward to hearing from you!

THE CARAVAN CLUB

Sorry, our policies are only available to Caravan Club members. Why not join us? You could easily save the cost of your subscription
Call **0800 328 5535** quoting ref. INM08

* Conditions apply

Spain

At the crossroads of Europe and Africa, and in western Europe second only in area to France, Spain has some of Europe's most popular holiday resorts and areas of outstanding natural beauty. Most visitors converge on the 'costas' but the mountains, national parks, towns and villages of the interior reflect a rich culture, history and artistic legacy combined with wonderful scenery.

Essential Facts

Capital: Madrid (population 3.3 million)

Area: 510,000 sq km (inc Balearic & Canary Islands)

Bordered by: Andorra, France, Portugal

Terrain: High, rugged central plateau, mountains to north and south

Climate: Temperate climate; hot summers, cold winters in the interior; more moderate summers and cool winters along the northern and eastern coasts; very hot summers and mild/warm winters along the southern coast; The best time to visit northern Spain is summer; the centre is best in autumn and the south best in winter and spring

Coastline: 4,964 km

Highest Point (mainland Spain): Mulhacén (Granada) 3,478 m

Population: 44 million

Languages: Castilian Spanish, Catalan, Galician, Basque

Religion: 97% Roman Catholic

Government: Parliamentary democracy and monarchy

Local Time: GMT or BST + 1, ie 1 hour ahead of the UK all year

Currency: Euro divided into 100 cents; £1 = €1.43, €1 = 70 pence *

Tourist Information

SPANISH TOURIST OFFICE
2ND FLOOR
79 NEW CAVENDISH STREET
LONDON W1W 6XB
P.O. BOX 4009, LONDON W1A 6NB
Tel: 0845 9400180 (brochure requests) or
020 7486 8077
(Visits by appointment only)
www.tourspain.co.uk or www.spain.info
info.londres@tourspain.es

Opening Hours

Banks – Mon-Fri 9am-2pm, Sat 9am-1pm.

Museums – Tue-Sat 10am-8pm, Sun 10am-2pm; closed Monday.

Post Offices – Mon-Fri 8.30am-2/2.30pm & 5pm-8pm, Sat 9am-1pm.

Shops – Mon-Sat 10am-1pm & 3pm-8pm; department stores and shopping centres do not close for lunch.

Public Holidays 2008

Jan 1, 6; Mar 20, 21, 24; May 1; Aug 15; Oct 12 (National Holiday); Nov 1; Dec 6 (Constitution Day), 8, 25. Several other dates for fiestas according to region. School summer holidays stretch from mid-June to mid-September.

Telephoning and the Internet

From the UK dial 0034 for Spain. All numbers have 9 digits, starting with 9, which incorporate the area code. Mobile phone numbers start with a 6. To call the UK from Spain dial 0044, omitting the initial zero of the area code. To call Gibraltar dial 00350.

Mobile phones – use of hand-held phones is prohibited when driving; mobile phones must not be used at all at petrol stations.

Public phones – operated with coins or cards.

Internet – access is widely available at cyber cafés and computer shops.

Emergency numbers – Police 112; Fire brigade 112; Ambulance 112; Civil Guard 062.

* Exchange rates as at September 2007

Spain

The following introduction to Spain should be read in conjunction with the important information contained in the Handbook chapters at the front of this guide.

Camping and Caravanning

Casual Camping

Before camping on private property it is necessary to obtain the owner's permission. In order to camp on municipal or communal land, permission must be obtained from the local authority or tourist office of the area. Camping is prohibited less than one kilometre from a campsite, near residential buildings and other populated centres or near a beach. 'Wild' camping is actively discouraged and is not recommended for security reasons. Police are frequently in evidence moving parked motor caravans on.

A number of local authorities now provide dedicated or short stay areas for motor caravanners called 'Áreas de Servicio'. For details see the websites www.lapaca.org (click on the motor caravan symbol) and www.viajarenautocaravana.com (click on 'Donde parar' under 'Preparando una salida' for a list of Spanish regions/towns which have at least one of these dedicated areas).

See **Parking** later in this chapter.

Organised Camping and Caravanning

There are more than 1,200 campsites in Spain with something to suit all tastes – from some of the best and biggest holiday parks in Europe, to a wealth of attractive small sites offering a personal, friendly welcome. Most campsites are located near the Mediterranean, especially on the Costa Brava and Costa del Sol, as well as in the Pyrenees and other areas of tourist interest. Spanish campsites are indicated by blue road signs. In general pitch sizes are small at about 80 square metres.

Recent visitors report that many popular, coastal sites favoured for long winter stays may contain tightly packed pitches whose long-term residents erect large awnings, umbrellas and other secondary structures. Many sites allow pitches to be reserved from year to year which can result in a tight knit community possibly biased to one nationality. As a result the availability of pitches to short term tourists may be restricted to the smaller or less favoured areas of the site. If planning

to stay on sites in the popular coastal areas between late spring and October, or in January and February, it is advisable to arrive early in the afternoon or to book in advance.

Although many sites claim to be open all year, this cannot always be relied on and if planning a visit out of season it is advisable to check first. Some 'all year' sites open only at the weekends during the winter and facilities may be very limited.

A Camping Card International (CCI), while not compulsory, is recommended and is increasingly required when checking into Spanish sites. Failing that, provide reception staff with a photocopy of your passport for registration purposes, rather than leave your passport for later collection. Senior citizens may be eligible for discounted prices at some sites on presentation of proof of age.

Affiliated National Club

FEDERACIÓN ESPAÑOLA DE CAMPING Y CARAVANING (FECC)
CALLE PIZARRO, 60 1° A
E-36204 VIGO
Tel/Fax: 986-47 22 73
www.guiacampingfecc.com/campistasfecc/
campistasfecc@yahoo.es

Country Information

Cycling

There are many dedicated cycle paths in Spain, many of which follow disused railway tracks. Known as 'Vias Verdes' (Green Ways) they can be found in northern Spain, in Andalucia, around Madrid and inland from the Costa Blanca. For more information see the website www.viasverdes.com or contact the Spanish Tourist Office.

It is compulsory for all cyclists, regardless of age, to wear a safety helmet on all roads outside built-up areas. The helmet may be removed on long hills or when the weather is extremely hot! At night, in tunnels or in bad weather, bicycles must have front and rear lights, together with reflectors at the rear and on wheels and pedals. Cyclists must also wear a reflecting device while riding at night on roads outside built-up areas (to be visible from a distance of 150 metres) or when visibility is bad.

Strictly speaking, cyclists have right of way when motor vehicles wish to cross their path to turn left or right, but great care should be taken. Do not proceed unless you are sure that a motorist is giving way.

Transportation of Bicycles

Spanish regulations stipulate that bicycles may be carried on the rear of a vehicle providing the rack to which the motorcycle or bicycle is fastened has been designed for the purpose. Lights, indicators, number plate and any signals made by the driver must not be obscured and the rack should not rest on the vehicle's tow bar or compromise the carrying vehicle's stability.

An overhanging load, such as bicycles, may exceed the length of the vehicle by up to 10% (up to 15% in the case of indivisible items) and the load must be indicated by a 50 cm square panel with reflectorised red and white diagonal stripes. These panels may be purchased in the UK from motor caravan or caravan dealers/accessory shops. There is currently no requirement for bicycle racks to be certified or pass a technical inspection.

If you are planning to travel from Spain to Portugal please note that slightly different official regulations apply which are set out in the Portugal Country Introduction.

Electricity and Gas

Usually the current on campsites is 4 amps or more. Plugs have two round pins. Most campsites do not yet have CEE connections.

Campingaz is widely available in 901 and 907 cylinders. The Cepsa Company sells butane gas cylinders and regulators, which are available in large stores and petrol stations, and the Repsol Company sells butane cylinders at their petrol stations throughout the country. It is understood that Repsol and Cepsa depots will refill cylinders, but the Caravan Club does not recommend this practice.

See *Electricity and Gas* in the section **DURING YOUR STAY.**

Entry Formalities

Holders of valid British and Irish passports are permitted to stay up to 90 days without a visa. EU residents planning to stay longer are required to register in person at the Oficina de Extranjeros (Foreigners' Office) in their province of residence or a designated police station. Residence cards are no longer supplied but you will be issued with a certificate confirming that the registration obligation has been fulfilled.

Regulations for Pets

See *Pet Travel Scheme* under **Documents** in the section **PLANNING AND TRAVELLING.**

Dogs must be kept on a lead in a public place and in a car they should be isolated from the driver by means of bars or netting.

Medical Services

Basic emergency health care is available free from practitioners in the Spanish National Health Service on production of a European Health Insurance Card (EHIC). In some parts of the country you may have to travel some distance to attend a surgery or health clinic operating within the health service. In any event, it is probably quicker and more convenient to use a private clinic, but the Spanish health service will not refund any private healthcare charges.

In an emergency go to the casualty department (urgencias) of any major hospital. Urgent treatment is free in a public ward at a public hospital on production of an EHIC; for other treatment you will have to pay 40% of the cost.

Medicines prescribed by health service practitioners can be obtained from any pharmacy (farmacia) and are free to EU pensioners. In all major towns there is a 24 hour pharmacy.

Dental treatment is not generally provided under the state system and you will have to pay for treatment.

RTFB Publishing produces a useful quick reference health guide for travellers entitled What Should I Do? priced £4.99, plus health phrase books in French and Spanish, priced £2.99 each. Telephone 023 8022 9041 or see www.whatshouldido.com for further details and orders.

You are strongly recommended to obtain comprehensive travel and medical insurance before travelling to Spain, such as the Caravan Club's Red Pennant Motoring & Personal Holiday Insurance.

See *Medical Matters* in the section **PLANNING AND TRAVELLING.**

Safety and Security

Street crime is common in many Spanish cities, towns and holiday resorts and is occasionally accompanied by violence. Avoid carrying passports, credit cards, travel tickets and money all together in handbags or

Spain

pockets and keep all valuable personal items, such as cameras or jewellery, out of sight. The authorities have stepped up the police presence in tourist areas but nevertheless, you should remain alert in all areas (including airports, train and bus stations, and even in supermarkets and their car parks).

In Madrid particular care should be taken in the Puerto de Sol and surrounding streets, including the Plaza Mayor, Retiro Park and Lavapies, and on the metro. This advice also applies to the Ramblas, Monjuic, Plaza Catalunya, Port Vell and Olympic Port areas of Barcelona. Be wary of approaches by strangers either asking directions or offering any kind of help. These approaches are sometimes ploys to distract attention while they or their accomplices make off with valuables and/or take note of credit card numbers for future illegal use. Beware muggers who use children or babies to distract your attention while you are being robbed.

The incidence of rape and sexual assault is very low; nevertheless attacks occur and are often carried out by other British nationals. Visitors are advised not to lower their personal security awareness because they are on holiday. You should also be alert to the availability and possible use of 'date rape' drugs. Purchase your own drinks and keep sight of them at all times to make sure they cannot be spiked.

Motorists travelling on motorways – particularly those north and south of Barcelona, on the M30 and M40 Madrid ring roads and on the A4 and A5– should be wary of approaches by bogus policemen in plain clothes travelling in unmarked cars. In all traffic-related matters police officers will be in uniform. Unmarked vehicles will have a flashing electronic sign on the rear window reading 'Policia' or 'Guardia Civil' and normally have blue flashing lights incorporated into the headlights, which are activated by the police when they stop you. In non-related traffic matters police officers may be in plain clothes but you have the right to ask to see identification. Genuine officers will ask you to show them your documents only and would not request that you hand over your bag or wallet. If in any doubt, drivers should converse through the car window and telephone the police on 112 or the Guardia Civil on 062 and ask them to confirm that the registration number of the vehicle corresponds to an official police vehicle.

On the A7 motorway between La Junquera and Tarragona toll stations be alert for 'highway pirates' who target foreign registered and hire cars (the latter have a distinctive number plate), especially those towing caravans. Motorists are sometimes targetted in service areas, followed and subsequently tricked into stopping on the hard shoulder. The usual ploy is for the driver or passenger in a passing vehicle, which may be 'official-looking', to suggest by gesture that there is something seriously wrong with a rear wheel or exhaust pipe (a tyre having been punctured earlier, for example, in a petrol station). The Club has received reports of the involvement of a second vehicle whose occupants also indicate a problem at the rear of your vehicle and gesture that you should pull over onto the hard shoulder. If flagged down by other motorists or a motorcyclist in this way, be extremely wary. The Spanish Tourist Office advises you not to pull over but to wait until you reach a service area or toll station. If you do get out of your car when flagged down, take care it is locked while you check outside, even if someone is left inside. Car keys should never be left in the ignition. Be suspicious when parked in lay-bys or picnic areas of approaches by other motorists asking for help.

A few incidents have been reported of visitors being approached by a bogus uniformed police officer asking to inspect wallets for fake euro notes or to check their identity by keying their credit card PIN into an official-looking piece of equipment carried by the officer. If in doubt ask to see a police officer's official indentification, refuse to comply with the request and offer instead to go to the nearest police station.

Spanish police have set up an emergency number with English-speaking staff for holidaymakers (902-10 21 12) offering round-the-clock assistance. An English-speaking operator will take a statement about the incident, translate it into Spanish and fax or email it to the nearest police station. Tourists still have to report to a police station if they have an accident, or have been robbed or swindled. They will be told on the phone where to find the nearest police station.

The Basque terrorist organisation, ETA, announced an end to their ceasefire with effect from June 2007. There is a very real threat of terrorism – real or hoax – in Spain and attacks could be indiscriminate and against civilian targets, including tourist sites. You should be vigilant and follow the instructions of local police and other authorities.

During the summer months stinging jellyfish frequent Mediterranean coastal waters. Coast guards operate a beach flag system to indicate the general safety of water: red – do not enter water; yellow – take precautions; green – all clear. Coast guards operate on most of the popular beaches, so if in doubt, ask.

There is a high risk of forest fires during the hottest months and you should avoid camping in areas with limited escape routes. It is possible that the Spanish government will introduce a total prohibition on the lighting of fires (including barbecues) in forest areas throughout Spain.

If you are planning a skiing holiday contact the Spanish Tourist Office before travelling for advice on safety and weather conditions. Information about Spanish ski resorts can be obtained from the website www.goski.com

Respect Spanish laws and customs. Parents should be aware that Spanish law defines anyone under the age of 18 to be a minor, subject to parental control or adult supervision. Any unaccompanied minor coming to the attention of the local authorities for whatever reason is deemed to be vulnerable under the law and faces being taken into a minors' centre for protection until a parent or suitable guardian can be found.

See **Safety and Security** in the section **DURING YOUR STAY.**

British Embassy

CALLE FERNANDO EL SANTO 16, E-28010 MADRID
Tel: 917-00 82 00
www.ukinspain.com
madridconsulate@ukinspain.com

British Consulates-General

EDIFICIO TORRE DE BARCELONA
AVDA DIAGONAL 477-13°, E-08036 BARCELONA
Tel: 933-66 62 00
barcelonaconsulate@fco.gov.uk

PASEO DE RECOLETOS 7/9, E-28004 MADRID
Tel: 915-24 97 00
madridconsulate@fco.gov.uk

There are also British Consulates in Alicante, Bilbao and Málaga, and Honorary Consulates in Benidorm (via the Consulate in Alicante), Cadiz, Seville and Vigo.

Irish Embassy

IRELAND HOUSE, PASEO DE LA CASTELLANA 46-4
E-28046 MADRID
Tel: 914-36 40 93
embajada@ireland.es

There are also Irish Honorary Consulates in Alicante, Barcelona, Bilbao, El Ferrol, Fuengirola and Seville.

Customs Regulations

Caravans and Motor Caravans

The maximum permitted height of a caravan or motor caravan is 4 metres, width 2.5 metres and length of motor vehicle, caravan or trailer, 12 metres. Maximum combined length of car + caravan 18.75 metres.

Duty-Free Imports

Duty-free shopping is permitted in Andorra, which is not a member of the EU, but there are strict limits on the amount of goods which can be imported into Spain, and Customs checks are frequently made. Each person is permitted to import the following items from Andorra free of duty or tax:

1.5 litres of spirits

5 litres of table wine

300 cigarettes or 150 cigarillos or 75 cigars or 400 gm of tobacco

75 gm of perfume and 375 ml of eau de toilette

Other items up to the value of €525

Alcohol and tobacco allowances apply only to persons aged 17 or over.

Tobacco

Under Spanish law the number of cigarettes which may be exported from Spain is set at eight hundred. Anything above this amount is regarded as a trade transaction which must be accompanied by the required documentation. If travellers are apprehended with more than 800 cigarettes but without the necessary paperwork, they face seizure of the cigarettes and a large fine.

See also **Customs Regulations** in the section **PLANNING AND TRAVELLING.**

Documents

Visitors must be able to show some form of identity if requested to do so by the police. Carry your passport, or other form of photographic ID, such as a photocard driving licence, at all times.

Spain

Although Spain's incorporation into the European Union has removed the need to provide bail cover, as a precautionary measure it will continue to be provided with the Caravan Club's Red Pennant Motoring & Personal Holiday Insurance.

The British EU-format pink driving licence is recognised in Spain. Holders of the old-style green driving licence are advised to apply for a photocard driving licence. Alternatively, the old-style licence may be accompanied by an International Driving Permit available from the AA, Green Flag or the RAC.

At all times when driving in Spain it is compulsory to carry your driving licence, vehicle registration certificate, insurance certificate and MOT certificate, if applicable. Vehicles imported by a person other than the owner must have a letter of authority from the owner.

*See also **Documents and Insurance** in the section **PLANNING AND TRAVELLING**.*

Money

- All bank branches offer foreign currency exchange, as do many hotels and travel agents. Travellers' cheques are widely accepted as a means of payment in hotels, shops and restaurants and can be changed at banks and bureaux de change. However, recent visitors continue to report difficulties cashing euro travellers' cheques and you should not rely on them for all your immediate cash needs.

- The major credit cards are widely accepted as a means of payment at shops, restaurants and petrol stations. Smaller retail outlets in non-commercial areas may not accept payments by credit card – check before buying. When shopping it is advisable to carry your passport or photocard driving licence if paying with a credit card as you will almost certainly be asked for photographic proof of identity.

- Cardholders are recommended to carry their credit card issuer/bank's 24-hour UK contact number in case of loss or theft.

- Keep a supply of loose change as you could frequently be asked for it in shops and at kiosks.

Motoring

Drivers should take particular care as driving standards can be erratic, eg excessive speed and dangerous overtaking. Pedestrians should take particular care when crossing roads (even at zebra crossings) or walking along unlit roads at night.

Alcohol

The maximum limit for the level of alcohol in the blood is 0.05%, ie less than in the UK and it reduces to 0.03% for drivers with less than two years' experience. After a traffic accident all road users have to undergo a breath test. Penalties for refusing a test or exceeding the legal limit are severe and may include immobilisation of vehicles, a heavy fine and three month's suspension of driving licence. This limit applies to cyclists as well as drivers of private vehicles.

Breakdown Service

The Real Automóvil Club de España (RACE) operates a breakdown service and assistance may be obtained 24 hours a day by telephoning the national centre in Madrid on 915-94 93 47. After hearing a message in Spanish press the number 1 to access the control room where English is spoken.

RACE's breakdown vehicles are blue and yellow and display the words 'RACE Asistencia' on the sides. There are assistance points throughout mainland and insular Spain and vehicles patrol the main roads and towns. This service provides on-the-spot minor repairs and towing to the nearest garage. Charges vary according to type of vehicle and time of day, but payment for road assistance must be made in cash.

Essential Equipment

Glasses

Spanish drivers requiring glasses to drive must carry a spare pair at all times when driving. Visiting motorists are advised to do the same in order to avoid any local difficulties.

Lights

Dipped headlights should be used in built-up areas, in tunnels and at night on motorways and fast roads, even if they are well lit. Spare bulbs and fuses should be carried, together with the tools to fit them.

Dipped headlights must be used at all times on 'special' roads, eg temporary routes created at the time of road works such as the hard shoulder, or in a lane travelling in the opposite of the normal direction.

Emergency flashing lights should be used if you are unable to reach the minimum required speed on a motorway – 60 km/h (37 mph) – or to alert drivers behind you to danger ahead.

Reflectorised Jackets

If your vehicle is immobilised on the carriageway outside a built-up area at night, or in poor visibility, you must wear a reflectorised jacket or waistcoat when getting out of your vehicle. This rule also applies to passengers who may leave the vehicle, for example, to assist with a repair.

Warning Triangles

Foreign-registered vehicles are recommended to carry two triangles – as required by Spanish drivers – in order to avoid any local difficulties which may arise. Warning triangles should be placed 50 metres behind and in front of broken-down vehicles.

See also **Motoring – Equipment** in the section **PLANNING AND TRAVELLING.**

Fuel

Credit cards are accepted at most service stations, but you should be prepared to pay cash if necessary in remote areas.

For diesel (gasoleo 'A' or gasoil) supplies in the Santurtzi/Bilbao area a visitor has advised using the fuel station at the Carrefour supermarket about halfway between Santurtzi and Bilbao. Follow the signs to Sestao from the adjacent motorway.

Leaded petrol is not available.

LPG (known as Autogas and formerly only available for public service vehicles) can now be purchased by private motorists from some Repsol filling stations. Details in English of approximately 30 sales outlets throughout mainland Spain can be found on www.spainautogas.com

See also **Fuel** under **Motoring – Advice** in the section **PLANNING AND TRAVELLING.**

Mountain Passes and Tunnels

Some passes are occasionally blocked in winter following heavy falls of snow. Check locally for information on road conditions.

See **Mountain Passes and Tunnels** in the section **PLANNING AND TRAVELLING.**

Parking

Yellow road markings indicate parking restrictions. Vehicles must be parked on the right-hand side of the carriageway except in one-way streets where parking is allowed on both sides. Illegally parked vehicles may be towed away or clamped but, despite this, you will frequently encounter double and triple parking.

In large cities there are parking meters and traffic wardens operate. Signs indicate blue zones (zona azul); the maximum period of parking is 90 minutes between 8am and 9pm. Parking discs are available from town halls, hotels and travel agents. In the centre of some towns there is a 'zona ORA' where parking is permitted for up to 90 minutes against tickets bought in tobacconists.

Recent visitors to tourist areas on Spain's Mediterranean coast report that the parking of motor caravans on public roads and, in some instances in public parking areas, may be prohibited in an effort to discourage 'wild camping'. The Club has been unable to obtain confirmation of such regulations which may vary according to region or province. Specific areas where visitors have encountered this problem include Alicante, Dénia and Palamós. It is understood that a number of owners of motor caravans have been fined for parking on sections of the beach belonging to the local authority.

See **Casual Camping** earlier in this chapter.

Parking for the Disabled

The leaflet 'European Parking Card for People with Disabilities' describes the concessions available under the Blue Badge scheme and gives advice on how to explain to police and parking attendants in their own language that, as a foreign visitor, you are entitled to the same parking concessions as disabled residents.

See also **Parking Facilities for the Disabled** under **Motoring – Advice** in the section **PLANNING AND TRAVELLING.**

Pedestrians

Jaywalking is not permitted. In main towns pedestrians may not cross a road unless a traffic light is at red against the traffic, or a policeman gives permission. Offenders may be fined on-the-spot.

Priority and Overtaking

As a general rule traffic coming from the right has priority at intersections but when entering

Spain

a main road from a secondary road drivers must give way to traffic from both directions. Traffic already on a roundabout has priority over traffic joining it. Trams and emergency vehicles have priority at all times over other road users and you must not pass trams which are stationary while letting passengers on or off.

Motorists must give way to cyclists on a cycle lane, cycle crossing or other specially designated cycle track. They must also give way to cyclists when turning left or right.

You must use your indicators when overtaking. If a vehicle comes up behind you signalling that it wants to overtake and if the road ahead is clear, you must use your right indicator to acknowledge the situation.

Roads

Roads marked AP (autopista) are toll roads and roads marked A (autovia) or N are dual carriageways with motorway characteristics (but not necessarily with a central reservation) and are toll-free. Autovias are often as fast as autopistas and are generally more scenic. Local roads are prefixed with the letter C. All national roads and roads of interest to tourists are in good condition and well-signposted, and driving is straightforward. Hills often tend to be longer and steeper than in parts of the UK and some of the coastal roads are very winding, so traffic flows at the speed of the slowest lorry.

As far as accidents are concerned the N340 coast road, especially between Málaga and Fuengirola, is notorious, as is the Madrid ring road, and special vigilance is necessary.

Road humps are making an appearance on Spanish roads and recent visitors report that they may be high, putting low stabilisers at risk.

Road Signs and Markings

Road signs conform to international standards. Lines and markings are white. Place names may appear both in standard (Castilian) Spanish and in a local form, eg Gerona/Girona, San Sebastián/Donostia, Jávea/Xàbio, and road atlases and maps usually show both. You may encounter the following signs:

| Turning permitted | Change direction only as shown | Use dipped headlights | Use of dipped headlights no longer required |

The following may also be seen:

Carretera de peaje – *Toll road*
Ceda el paso – *Give way*
Cuidado – *Caution*
Curva peligrosa – *Dangerous bend*
Despacio – *Slow*
Desviación – *Detour*
Dirección única – *One-way street*
Embotellamiento – *Traffic jam*
Estacionamiento prohibido – *No parking*
Estrechamiento – *Narrow lane*
Gravillas – *Loose chippings/gravel*
Inicio – *Start*
Obras – *Roadworks*
Paso prohibido – *No entry*
Peligro – *Danger*
Prioridad – *Right of way*
Salida – *Exit*
Todas direcciones – *All directions*

Many ordinary roads have a continuous white line on the near (verge) side of the carriageway. Any narrow lane between this line and the side of the carriageway is intended primarily for pedestrians and cyclists and not for use as a hard shoulder.

A continuous line also indicates 'no stopping'; even if it is possible to park entirely off the road, it should be treated as a double white line and not crossed except in a serious emergency. If your vehicle breaks down on a road where there is a continuous white line along the verge, it should not be left unattended as this is illegal and an on-the-spot fine may be levied.

Many road junctions have a continuous white centre line along the main road. This line must not be crossed to execute a left turn, despite the lack of any other 'no left turn' signs. If necessary, drive on to a 'cambio de sentido' (change of direction) sign to turn.

The Club has received reports that the traffic police are keen to enforce both the above regulations.

Watch out for traffic lights which may be mounted high above the road and hard to spot. Green, amber and red arrows are used on traffic lights at some intersections. Two red lights mean no entry.

Speed Limits

See Speed Limits Table under Motoring – Advice in the section **PLANNING AND TRAVELLING.**

In built-up areas, speed is limited to 50 km/h (31 mph) except where signs indicate a lower limit. Reduce your speed to 20 km/h (13 mph) in residential areas. On motorways and dual carriageways in built-up areas, speed is limited to 80 km/h (50 mph) except where indicated by signs.

Outside built-up areas motor caravans of any weight are limited to 90 km/h (56 mph) on motorways and dual carriageways, to 80 km/h (50 mph) on other main roads with more than one lane in each direction, and to 70 km/h (44 mph) on secondary roads.

It is prohibited to own, transport or use radar detectors. Drivers are not allowed to make signals to warn other drivers of the presence of police, eg headlight-flashing.

Towing

Motor caravans are prohibited from towing a car unless the car is on a special towing trailer with all four wheels off the ground.

Any towing combination in excess of 10 metres must keep at least 50 metres from the vehicle in front except in built-up areas, on roads where overtaking is prohibited or where there are several lanes in the same direction.

Traffic Jams

Roads around the large Spanish cities such as Madrid, Barcelona, Zaragoza, Valencia and Seville are extremely busy on Friday afternoons when residents leave for the mountains or coast, and again on Sunday evenings when they return. The coastal roads along the Costa Brava and the Costa Dorada may also be congested. The coast road south of Torrevieja is frequently heavily congested as a result of extensive holiday home construction.

Summer holidays extend from mid-June to mid-September and the busiest periods are the last weekend in July, the first weekend in August and the period around the Assumption holiday in mid-August.

Traffic jams occur on the busy AP7 from the French border to Barcelona during the peak summer holiday period. An alternative route now exists from Malgrat de Mar along the coast to Barcelona using the C2 where tolls are lower than on the AP7.

The Autovía de la Cataluña Central (C25) provides a rapid east-west link between Gerona and Lleida via Vic, Manresa and Cervera. There is fast access from La Coruña in the far north-west to Madrid via the A6/AP6.

Violation of Traffic Regulations

The police are empowered to impose on-the-spot fines. There is usually a 30% reduction for immediate settlement; an official receipt should be obtained. An appeal may be made within 15 days and there are instructions on the back of the form in English. RACE can provide legal advice – tel 902-40 45 45.

Accidents

The Central Traffic Department runs an assistance service for victims of traffic accidents linked to an SOS telephone network along motorways and some roads. Motorists in need of help should ask for 'auxilio en carretera' (road assistance). The special ambulances used are connected by radio to hospitals participating in the scheme.

Motorways

The Spanish motorway system has been subject to considerable expansion in recent years and there are now approximately 7,000 km of motorways (autopistas) and dual carriageways (autovias), with more under construction or planned. The main sections of motorway are along the Mediterranean coast, across the north of the country and around Madrid. Tolls are charged on most autopistas but many sections are toll-free, as are autovias. Exits on autopistas are numbered consecutively from Madrid. Exits on autovias are numbered according to the kilometre point from Madrid.

Many different companies operate within the motorway network, each setting their own tolls, which may vary according to the time of day, and classification of vehicles. For an overview of the motorway network (in English) see www.aseta.es. This website has links to the numerous motorway companies where you will be able to view routes and tolls (generally shown in Spanish only). Tolls are payable in cash or by credit card.

Rest areas with parking facilities, petrol stations and restaurants or cafés are strategically placed and are well-signposted. Emergency telephones are located on both sides of the carriageway at 2 km intervals.

Spain

Motorway signs near Barcelona are confusing. To avoid the city traffic when heading south, follow signs for Barcelona but the moment signs for Tarragona appear follow these and ignore Barcelona signs.

Touring

- One of Spain's greatest attractions is undoubtedly its cuisine. Spanish cooking is rich and varied with many regional specialities and traditional dishes which have achieved worldwide fame such as paella, gazpacho and tapas. Seafood in particular is excellent and plentiful. A fixed-price menu or 'menu del dia' invariably offers good value. Spain is one of the world's top wine producers, enjoying a great variety of high quality wines of which rioja and sherry are probably the best known. Local beer is low in alcohol content and is generally drunk as an aperitif to accompany tapas. Service is generally included in restaurant bills but a tip of approximately 50-60 cents per person up to 10% of the bill is appropriate if you have received good service. Smoking is not allowed in public places, including bars, restaurants and cafés. In small bars and restaurants smoking may be allowed at the owner's discretion in designated areas.

- Perhaps due to the benign climate and long hours of sunshine, Spaniards tend to get up later and stay out later at night than their European neighbours. Out of the main tourist season and in 'non-touristy' areas it may be difficult to find a restaurant open in the evening before 9pm. Taking a siesta is still common practice, although it is becoming more common for businesses to stay open during the traditional siesta hours.

- Spain's many different cultural and regional influences are responsible for the variety and originality of fiestas held each year. Over 200 have been classified as 'of interest to tourists' while others have gained international fame. A full list can be obtained from the Spanish Tourist Office in London, from Real Automóvil Club de Espana (RACE), or from provincial tourist offices.

- The Madrid Card, valid for one, two or three days, gives free use of public transport, free entry to various attractions and museums, including the Prado, Reina Sofia and Thyssen-Bornesmisza collection, as well as free tours and discounts at restaurants and shows. You can buy the card from www.madridcard.com, by telephoning 0034 915-24 13 70, or by visiting the City Tourist Office in Plaza Mayor, or on Madrid Visión tour buses. Similar generous discounts can be obtained with the Barcelona Card, valid from one to five days, which can be purchased from tourist offices and from El Corte Inglés department stores; see www.barcelonaturisme.com. Other tourist cards are available in Burgos, Córdoba, Seville and Zaragoza.

- Bullfighting is still a very popular entertainment in Spain and fights take place in the bullrings or plazas of main towns during the summer. In addition, every year each town celebrates its local Saint's Day which is always a very happy and colourful occasion.

- BBC World Service radio in English can be heard on the following local frequencies: Marbella 101.6 FM, Nerja 97.7 FM, Málaga 96.8 or 107 FM.

Local Travel

- Year-round ferry services from Spain to North Africa, the Balearic Islands and the Canary Islands are operated by Acciona Trasmediterranea. All enquiries should be made through their UK agent:

  SOUTHERN FERRIES
  30 CHURTON STREET
  LONDON SW1V 2LP
  Tel: 0870 4991305, Fax: 0870 4991304
  www.sncm.fr
  mail@southernferries.co.uk

- Madrid boasts an extensive and efficient public transport network including a metro system, suburban railways and bus routes. Tourist travel passes for use on all public transport are available from metro stations, tourist offices and travel agencies and are valid for one to seven days. Single tickets must be validated before travel.

Gibraltar

- For information on Gibraltar contact:

  GIBRALTAR GOVERNMENT TOURIST OFFICE
  ARUNDUL GREAT COURT
  178-179 STRAND
  LONDON WC2R 1EL
  Tel: 020 7836 0777
  www.gibraltar.gi or www.gibraltar.gov.uk
  info@gibraltar.gov.uk

- There are no campsites on the Rock, the nearest being at San Roque and La Linea de la Concepción in Spain. The only direct access to Gibraltar from Spain is via the border at La Línea which is open 24 hours a day. You may cross on foot and it is also possible to take cars or motor caravans to Gibraltar, but be prepared for long queues. As roads in the town are extremely narrow and bridges low, it is advisable to park on the outskirts. Visitors advise against leaving vehicles on the Spanish side of the border owing to the high risk of break-ins. There is currently no charge for visitors or cars to enter Gibraltar but Spanish border checks can cause delays. An attraction to taking the car into Gibraltar is an English-style supermarket and a wide variety of competitively priced goods free of VAT.

- Disabled visitors to Gibraltar may obtain a temporary parking permit from the police station on production of evidence confirming their disability. This permit allows parking for up to two hours (between 8am and 10pm) in parking places reserved for disabled people.

All place names used in the Site Entry listings which follow can be found in Michelin's Tourist & Motoring Atlas for Spain & Portugal, scale 1:400,000 (1 cm = 4 km).

Spain

Sites in Spain

ABEJAR *3C1* (800m NW Rural) **Camping El Concurso, Ctra de Molinos de Duero s/n, 42146 Abejar (Soria) [975-37 33 61; fax 975-37 33 96]** N234 W fr Soria to Abejar. Turn onto rd CL117 dir Molinos de Duero, site on L. Lge, mkd pitch, pt sl, pt shd; wc; chem disp; mv service pnt; shwrs inc; el pnts (5A) inc; gas; lndtte; shop & 500m; tradsmn; rest; snacks; bar; playgrnd; pool; lake 2km; dogs; phone; poss cr & noisy in ssn; cc acc; CCI. "Nr lake & National Park; v beautiful; gd san facs; not suitable m'van due slope." ♦ ltd. Easter-30 Sep. € 19.04   2006*

⊞ABIZANDA *3B2* (Rural) **Fundación Liguerré de Cinca, Ctra A138, Km 28, 22393 Abizanda (Huesca) [974-50 08 00; fax 974-50 08 30; icinca@ aragon.ugt.ore; www.liguerredecinca.com]** A138 N fr Barbastro, site sp at km 29 or S fr Ainsa, site sp at km 27, 18 km S of Ainsa. Med, mkd pitch, terr, shd; wc; chem disp; shwrs inc; baby rm; el pnts (10A) €4.60; gas; lndtte; shop, rest, snacks, bar high ssn; playgrnd; pool; lake sw 1km; watersports; tennis; games rm; horseriding; cycle hire; car wash; 10% statics; dogs; phone; poss cr; Eng spkn; adv bkg (dep & bkg fee); quiet; cc acc; red long stay; CCI. "Excel facs, ltd low ssn; v highly rec; site in 2 parts sep by ravine, bottom terr muddy in wet; trees may be diff for lge o'fits; v helpful staff & lovely site; few British; nearest shops at Ainsa; conv Ordesa & Monte Perdido National Park." € 19.90   2006*

⊞ADRA *2H4* (5km E Coastal) **Camping La Habana, Ctra N340 Motril-Almería, Km 64, Puente del Río, 04770 Adra (Almería) [950-52 21 27 or 619-45 41 34]** Exit N340 junc 391 to Puente del Rio, foll site sp. Med, pt shd; wc; shwrs; el pnts; gas; lndtte; shop; rest; bar; beach adj; horseriding; phone; bus 3km; CCI. "Narr app rd & ent; site rather tatty."   2004*

The opening dates and prices on this campsite have changed. I'll send a site report form to the editor for the next edition of the guide.

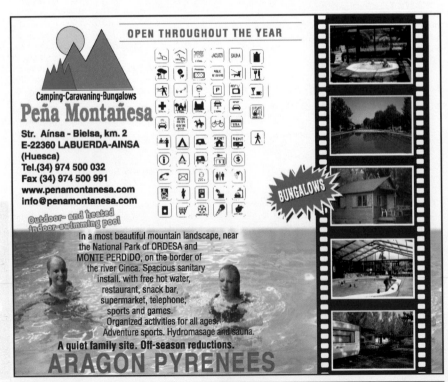

⊞AGUILAR DE CAMPOO *1B4* (3km W Rural) **Monte Royal Camping, Ave Virgen del Llano, s/n, 34800 Aguilar de Campóo (Palencia) [979-12 30 83]** App site fr S on N611 fr Palencia. At Aguilar de Campóo turn W at S end of rv bdge at S end of town. Site on L in 3km; sp at edge of reservoir. Fr N take 3rd exit fr rndabt on N611. Do not tow thro town. Lge, mkd pitch, pt sl, shd; wc; chem disp (wc); baby facs; shwrs €0.60; el pnts (2A) €3.30; gas; lndry rm; ice; shops 3km; rest in ssn; bar; playgrnd; sand beach nr lake; watersports; horseriding; fishing; TV; 20% statics; dogs; phone; cc acc; CCI. "Useful NH 2 hrs fr Santander; peaceful site in beautiful area but v ltd/basic facs low ssn & poss stretched high ssn; barking dogs poss problem; friendly staff; gd walking, cycling & birdwatching in National Park; unreliable opening dates low ssn." ♦ € 18.32   2007*

⊞AGUILAS *4G1* (4km NE Rural) **Camping Águilas, Ctra Cabo Cope, Los Geraneos, 30880 Águilas (Murcia) [968-41 92 05; fax 968-41 92 82; campingaquilas@hotmail.com]** Fr A7 N of Lorca take C3211 dir Águilas. On joining N332 turn L & foll sp L to Calabardina/Cabo Cope; site on L within 3km. Med, mkd pitch, hdstg, pt shd; wc; chem disp; shwrs inc; el pnts (10A) inc; gas; lndtte; shop high ssn; rest; snacks; bar; playgrnd; pool; sand beach 4km; tennis; 30% statics; phone; site clsd last 2 weeks May & Sep; Eng spkn; adv bkg; quiet; red low ssn/long stay; cc acc; CCI. "All pitches shaded with trees or netting; clean facs; v helpful warden; building works around site (2006); v popular winter long stay; excel." € 20.00   2006*

Before we move on, I'm going to fill in some site report forms and post them off to the editor, otherwise they won't arrive in time for the deadline at the end of September.

⊞AGUILAS *4G1* (3km SW Coastal) **Camping Bellavista, Ctra de Vera, Km 3, 30880 Águilas (Murcia) [968-44 91 51; fax 968-44 93 27; info@campingbellavista.com www.campingbellavista.com]** On N332 Águilas to Vera rd. Well marked by flags. Sm, hdg pitch, hdstg, pt sl, pt shd; wc; chem disp; shwrs inc; el pnts (10A) €4.40 or metered; gas; lndtte; shop 2km; tradsmn; rest adj; snacks; BBQ; playgrnd; sand beach 500m; cycle hire; dogs €0.85; poss cr; Eng spkn; adv bkg; quiet; cc acc; red long stay/low ssn; CCI. "Gd winter stay; clean, tidy, improving site with excel facs & rest; pitch access poss diff for lge o'fits - ltd pitches for lge vans; v helpful owner; fine views; rd noise at 1 end; 30 min walk to town; excel town & vg beaches." € 20.10   2006*

AINSA *3B2* (2.5km N Rural) **Camping Pena Montanesa, Ctra Ainsa-Bielsa, Km 2.3, 22360 Labuerda (Huesca) [974-50 00 32; fax 974-50 09 91; info@penamontanesa.com; www.penamontanesa.com]** E fr Huesca on N240 for approx 50km, turn N onto N123 just after Barbastro twd Ainsa. In 8km turn onto A138 N for Ainsa & Bielsa. Or S fr St Lary-Soulan on D929 to French/Spanish border, cross via Bielsa Tunnel to join A138 S to Ainsa & Bielsa. Site 2km N of Ainsa on this rd. NB: Bielsa Tunnel sometimes clsd bet Oct & Easter due to weather. Lge, mkd pitch, shd, htd wc; chem disp; mv service pnt; baby facs; sauna; shwrs inc; el pnts (6A) inc; gas; lndtte; supmkt; rest; snacks; bar; BBQ (gas/elec only); playgrnd; htd pools (1 covrd) + paddling pool; lake sw 2km; canoeing; tennis; cycle hire; horseriding; games area; entmnt child & adult; disco; TV; 20% statics; dogs €4 kept on lead; phone; recep 0800-0000; adv bkg (bkg fee, min 7 nights); quiet but poss noise fr late arrivals & at w/ends; red low ssn; cc acc; CCI. "Friendly staff; gd, clean facs; pitches poss tight due trees; site nr beautiful medieval town & Ordesa National Park; local map given at recep & info on excursions; excel." ♦ 1 Mar-10 Dec. € 45.00 ABS - E12   2007*

See advertisement

AINSA *3B2* (1km E Rural) **Camping Ainsa, Ctra Ainsa-Campo, 22330 Ainsa (Huesca) [tel/fax 974-50 02 60; info@campingainsa.com; www.campingainsa.com]** Fr Ainsa take N260 E dir Pueyo de Araguás, cross rv bdge, site sp L in 200m. Foll lane to site. Sm, terr, pt shd; wc; shwrs inc; el pnts €4.10; gas; lndtte; shop 1km; rest, snacks bar high ssn; playgrnd; pool; 50% statics; dogs €2; phone; poss cr; some indus noise mornings; cc acc; CCI. "Pleasant, welcoming, well-maintained site; fine view of old city & some pitches mountain views; not suitable lge o'fits; gd pool." Holy Week-30 Sep. € 19.40   2007*

⊞AINSA *3B2* (6km NW Rural) **Camping Boltaña, Ctra N260, Km 442, Ctra Margudgued, 22340 Boltaña (Huesca) [974-50 23 47; fax 974-50 20 23; info@campingboltana.com; www.campingboltana.com]** Fr Ainsa head into Boltaña, turn L over rv & foll sp. Site is 2km E of Boltaña, final 300m on single track rd. Med, mkd pitch, pt sl, terr, pt shd; htd wc; chem disp; baby facs; shwrs inc; el pnts (4-10A) €4.92-6.74; gas; lndtte; shop & 2km; tradsmn; rest; snacks; bar; playgrnd; pool; paddling pool; rv sw & fishing 600m; tennis 1km; horseriding 500m; games area; cycle hire; adventure sports; 50% statics; dogs €2.78; phone; clsd 21 Dec-12 Jan; poss cr; Eng spkn; adv bkg; poss noisy; cc acc. "Many activities avail; conv Ordesa National Park; poss diff for disabled travellers; san facs stretched high ssn; friendly, helpful staff; excel; Ainsa old town worth visit." ♦ ltd. € 24.07 (CChq acc)   2006*

Spain

ALBANYA 3B3 (W Rural) **Camping Bassegoda Park, Camí Camp de l'Illa, 17733 Albanyà (Gerona) [972-54 20 20; fax 972-54 20 21; info@ bassegodapark.com; www.bassegodapark.com]** Fr France exit AP7/E15 junc 3 onto GI510 to Albanyà. At end of rd turn R, site on rvside. Fr S exit AP7 junc 4 dir Terrades, then Albanyà. Med, hdg pitch, hdstg, pt shd; htd wc; chem disp; mv waste; baby facs; shwrs inc; el pnts (10A) €4.50; lndtte; ice; shop; rest; snacks; bar; playgrnd; pool; fishing; trekking; hill walking; mountain biking; games area; games rm; entmnt; 8% statics; dogs €3.60 (1 only); phone; Eng spkn; adv bkg; quiet; red snr citizens/ CCI. "Excel site in Pyrenees, surrounded by woods, rvs & streams." ♦ 1 Mar-4 Nov. € 21.75   2007*

ALBARRACIN 3D1 (1km E Rural) **Camp Municipal Ciudad de Albarracín, Casco Urbano, Junto Polideportivo, 44100 Albarracín (Teruel) [978- 71 01 97 or 978-71 01 07; fax 978-71 01 07]** Fr Teruel take A1512 to Albarracín. Go thro vill, foll camping sps. Med, pt sl, pt shd; wc; chem disp; baby facs; shwrs inc; el pnts (16A) €2.84; gas; lndtte; shop & adj; tradsmn; rest; snacks; bar; BBQ; playgrnd; pool in ssn; phone; poss cr; adv bkg; quiet; cc acc; CCI. "Excel site; immac san facs; sh walk to quaint town for shops & rests; sports cent adj; gd touring base; rec." 16 Mar-31 Oct. € 13.59
2007*

ALBERCA, LA 1D3 (2km N Rural) **Camping Al- Bereka, Ctra Salamanca-La Alberca, Km 75.6, 37624 La Alberca (Salamanca) [923-41 51 95]** Fr Salamanca S on N630/E803 take C515 to Mogarraz, then SA202 to La Alberca. Site on L at km 75.6 bef vill. Rte fr Ciudad Real OK but bumpy in places. Med, mkd pitch, terr, shd; wc; chem disp; shwrs inc; el pnts €2.50; lndry rm; ice; shop; rest 2km; snacks; bar; BBQ; playgrnd; pool; paddling pool; some statics; dogs; quiet; cc acc; CCI. "Nice, quiet site but run down low ssn; helpful owner; beautiful countryside; La Alberca is beautifully restored medieval vill with abbey - gem." ♦ 1 Mar- 30 Oct. € 21.40   2005*

ALBERCA, LA 1D3 (6km N Rural) **Camping Sierra de Francia, Ctra Salamanca-La Alberca, Km 73, El Caserito, 37623 Nava de Francia (Salamanca) [923-45 40 81; fax 923-45 40 01; www. campingsierradefrancia.com]** Fr Cuidad Rodrigo take C515. Turn R at El Cabaco, site on L in approx 2km. Med, shd; wc; shwrs; el pnts €3.75; gas; lndtte; shop; rest; bar; playgrnd; pool; horseriding; cycle hire; some statics; dogs; quiet; cc acc. "Conv 'living history' vill of La Alberca & Monasterio San Juan de la Peña; excel views." ♦ ltd. 1 Apr-30 Sep. € 18.88   2006*

ALBERCA, LA 1D3 (10km SE Rural) **Camping Vega de Francia, Ctra Sotoserrano-Béjar, Paraje Vega de Francia, 37657 Sotoserrano (Salamanca) [tel/ fax 923-16 11 04]** Fr Sotoserrano take Ctra de Béjar for 3km sp Lagunilla & El Cerro. Bef Roman bdge turn L onto rd sp Camping Vega de Francia for 500m to site. Single track in places. Sm, hdg pitch, hdstg, terr, shd; wc; chem disp; mv service pnt; baby facs; shwrs inc; el pnts (3A) €2.25; lndry rm; shop; tradsmn; rest; snacks; bar; BBQ; playgrnd; rv sw adj; TV rm; 50% statics; dogs; phone; Eng spkn; adv bkg dep req; quiet; 20% red 15+ days; cc acc. "V friendly, family-run site; excel bar-rest popular with locals; shop sells local produce; owner makes wine, olive oil & honey; gd walking & views; app poss not suitable for lge o'fits." ♦ 1 Mar-3 Oct. € 17.00   2004*

⊞**ALCALA DE GUADAIRA** 2G3 (1km SE Rural) **Camping Oromana, Camino de Maestre s/n, 41500 Alcalá de Guadaira [955-68 32 57; fax 955- 68 18 44; oromana@campingoromana.es; www. campingoromana.es]** Leave A92 at junc 12, foll sp to Alcalá & Utrera. Cross rv bdge; turn L into Utrera rd & L again at T-junc twd Hotel Oromana; turn R at fork to site; sp. Fr A376 take C432 to Alcalá, site sp on R on ent Alcalá at bottom of hill. Lge, mkd pitch, hdstg, pt sl, pt shd; wc; chem disp; shwrs inc; el pnts €3.75; lndtte; shop 2km; rest, snacks & bar high ssn; playgrnd; pool in ssn; 50% statics; phone; poss cr; Eng spkn; quiet; cc acc; red long stay; CCI. "Bus every 30 mins to Seville (12km), 2km walk fr site; lovely setting in pine park; friendly recep; poss itinerants & unclean/ltd facs low ssn & neglected vans; noise fr nrby shooting range & disco high ssn; muddy after rain." ♦ € 15.50   2007*

⊞**ALCALA DE LOS GAZULES** 2H3 (4km E Rural) **Camping Los Gazules, Ctra de Patrite, Km 4, 11180 Alcalá de los Gazules (Cádiz) [956- 42 04 86; fax 956-42 03 88; losgazules@hotmail. com; www.campinglosgazules.com]** Fr N exit A381 at 1st junc to Alcalá, proceed thro town to 1st rndabt & turn L onto A375/A2304 dir Ubriqu, site sp strt ahead in 1km onto CA2115 dir Patrite on v sharp L. Fr S exit A381 at 1st sp for Acalá. At rndabt turn R onto A375/A2304 dir Ubrique. Then as above. Med, mkd pitch, pt sl, pt shd; wc; chem disp (wc); mv service pnt; shwrs inc; el pnts (10A) €3.75 (poss rev pol); lndtte; shop; rest; bar; playgrnd; pool; cycle hire; TV rm; 90% statics; phone; adv bkg; red long stay; CCI. "Well- maintained site extended & upgraded; take care canopy frames; sm pitches & tight turns & kerbs on site; v friendly & helpful staff; attractive town with v narr streets, leave car in park at bottom & walk; gd walking, birdwatching; activities avail - hiking, cycling/mountain biking, canoeing; ltd facs low ssn; ltd touring pitches." € 17.60   2007*

ALCANAR *3D2* (3km N Coastal) **Camping Los Alfaques, 43530 Alcanar Platja (Tarragona) [977-74 05 61; fax 977-74 25 95; info@alfaques.com; www.alfaques.com]** Clearly sp on main rd N340, approx 2km S of San Carlos de la Rápita. Lge, pt sl, shd; wc; chem disp; shwrs €0.20; el pnts (5A) €3.50; gas; lndtte; ice; shop & 2km; rest; snacks; bar; playgrnd; pool 200m; steep, shgl beach adj; fishing; internet; entmnt; 50% statics; dogs free; phone; some rd noise. "Vg for boat-launching, fishing; seafront pitches rec; conv ancient town of Morella." 1 Apr-30 Sep. € 22.00   2007*

ALCANTARA *2E2* (4km NW Rural) **Camping Puente de Alcántara, Finca Los Cabezos, 10980 Alcántara (Cáceres) [927-39 09 47]** W fr Alcántara to Roman bdge over Rv Tagus. Turn R at camping sp over cattle grid. Med, pt sl, unshd; wc; chem disp; shwrs inc; el pnts (5A) €3.25; gas; lndtte; shop; snacks; bar; playgrnd; pool; watersports; tennis; adv bkg; quiet; cc acc; CCI. "Nice views; attractive vill with many storks; gd birdwatching area; friendly owner; ltd facs low ssn." ♦ 1 Apr-30 Sep. € 15.00   2004*

⊞**ALCARAZ** *4F1* (6km E Rural) **Camping Sierra de Peñascosa, Ctra Peñascosa-Bogarra, Km 1, 02313 Peñascosa (Albacete) [967-38 25 21; fax 967-21 10 13; informacion@campingpenascosa. com; www.campingpenascosa.com]** Fr N322 turn E bet km posts 279 & 280 sp Peñascosa. In vill foll site sp for 1km beyond vill. Gravel access track & narr ent. Sm, mkd pitch, hdstg, terr, shd; wc; chem disp; shwrs; el pnts (6A) €2.80; gas; lndtte; shop; rest high ssn; snacks; bar; playgrnd; pool; cycle hire; dogs; open w/e in winter; v quiet; cc acc; CCI. "Not suitable lge o'fits or faint-hearted; pitches sm, uneven & amongst trees - care needed when manoeuvring; gd for exploring Sierras; historical sites nr." ♦ € 17.50   2005*

ALCOSSEBRE *3D2* (3km NE Coastal/Rural) **Camping Ribamar, Partida Ribamar s/n, 12579 Alcossebre (Castellón) [964-76 11 63; fax 964-76 72 31; info@campingribamar.com; www. campingribamar.com]** Exit AP7 at junc 44 into N340 & foll sp to Alcossebre. Foll Las Fuentes sp, then site sp. Med, hdg/mkd pitch, hdstg, pt sl, terr, pt shd; wc; chem disp; mv service pnt; baby facs; shwrs inc; el pnts (10A) €4.12; gas; lndtte; shop; tradsmn; rest; bar; playgrnd; pool; sand beach 200m; paddling pool; tennis; games area; 25% statics; dogs €1.50; poss cr; adv bkg; quiet; red long stay/low ssn; CCI. "Excel, refurbished site in 'natural park'; realistic pitch size." 1 Jun-31 Dec. € 34.80   2007*

ALCOSSEBRE *3D2* (2.5km S Coastal) **Camping Playa Tropicana, 12579 Alcossebre (Castellón) [964-41 24 63; fax 964 41 28 05; info@ playatropicana.com; www.playatropicana.com]** Fr AP7 exit junc 44 onto N340 dir Barcelona. After 3km at km 1018 turn on CV142 twd Alcossebre. Just bef ent town turn R sp 'Platjes Capicorb', turn R at beach in 2.5km, site on R. Lge, mkd pitch, pt terr, pt shd; wc; chem disp; baby facs; serviced pitches (extra charge); shwrs inc; el pnts (6A) inc; gas; lndtte; shop; rest; snacks; bar; playgrnd; pool; sand beach adj; watersports; cycle hire; games area; TV; cinema rm; car wash; 10% statics; no dogs; poss cr; adv bkg rec high ssn; quiet; 50% red low ssn/long stay & special offers; variable pitch prices; cc acc. "Excel facs & security; superb well-run site; vg low ssn; poss rallies Jan-Apr; management v helpful; poss flooding after heavy rain; pitch access poss diff lge o'fits; take fly swat!" ♦ 1 May-31 Oct. € 49.22 (CChq acc)   2006*

There aren't many sites open this early in the year. We'd better phone ahead to check that the one we're heading for is actually open.

⊞**ALCOSSEBRE** *3D2* (500m W Coastal) **Camping Alcossebre, 12579 Alcossebre (Castellón) [964-41 28 89]** Turn off N340 twds Alcossebre. Site 500m bef town & sm beach; narr app rd. Sm, shd; wc; shwrs; el pnts €2.50; gas; snacks; bar; playgrnd; pools; watersports; fishing; CCI. € 18.90   2004*

⊞**ALHAMA DE MURCIA** *4F1* (6km NW Rural) **Camping Sierra Espuña, El Berro, 30848 Alhama de Murcia (Murcia) [968-66 80 38; fax 968-66 80 79; info@campingelberro.com; www. campingsierraespuna.com]** Exit A7 junc 627 or 631 to Alhama de Murcia & take C3315 sp Gebas & Mula. Ignore 1st sp to site & after Gebas foll sp to site sp El Berro, site on edge of vill. 15km by rd fr Alhama - narr, twisty & steep in parts, diff for lge o'fits. Med, hdstg, terr, pt shd; wc; chem disp; baby facs; shwrs; el pnts (6A) inc; gas; lndtte; shop 200m; rest in vill; snacks; bar; playgrnd; pool; tennis; minigolf; organised activities; wifi internet; 30% statics; dogs €2; phone; adv bkg; quiet but poss noise w/e; red long stay; cc acc; CCI. "In Sierra Espuña National Park on edge of unspoilt vill; gd walking, climbing, mountain biking area; v friendly staff; highly rec." ♦ € 15.00   2007*

Spain

CAMPING CABO DE GATA

Camping Cabo de Gata is situated in the south-east of the province of Almeria. It is a volcanic area wich offers the visitant beautiful beaches, incredible landscapes, traditional cooking and a lot of sun and calm places. From the camp site you can visit the natural park, the desert of Tabernas (the only desert all arround Europe), the sorbas caves (the most important gypsum karst in the world), the minihollywood (where you will be the wildest cowboy, for one day), and many more things. Come and enjoy it! • Bar-restaurant, supermarket, social hall, tennis, petanca & volley-ball, swimming pool • Beach situated at 900 mts. • English spoken. **OPEN THROUGHOUT THE YEAR**

PARQUE NATURAL
Cabo de Gata – Níjar

Costa de almería
Andalucía - Spain
Tel.: (34) 950 16 04 43
Fax: (34) 950 52 00 03
Ctra. Cabo de Gata, s/n. - Cortijo Ferrón
E-04150 CABO DE GATA (Almería)

SPECIAL OFFER AUTUMN-WINTER-SPRING
2 adults + car & caravan or camping-car + electricity (6 Amp.):
1.1./30.6.2008 and 1.9./31.12.2008
Stays above 8 nights – 16.15 €p. night
Stays above 16 nights – 14.81 €p. night } +7% VAT
Stays above 31 nights – 10.71 €p. night
Stays above 61 nights – 9.76 €p. night
Extra electr. 10 Amp. + 0,55 € p.day; 16 A.p. +0,91€p.day

Bungalows

Special offer in spring, winter and autumn for
Bungalows: 2 person

1 month: 525 €   2 months: 987€ } +7%
3 months: 1.344 €   4 months: 1.764€ } VAT

www.campingcabodegata.com
info@campingcabodegata.com

⊞ALICANTE *4F2* (8km NE Coastal) **Camping Costa Blanca, Calle Convento 143, 03560 El Campello (Alicante) [tel/fax 965-63 06 70; info@campingcostablanca.com; www.campingcosta blanca.com]** Exit AP7/E15 junc 67 onto N332, site visible on L at turn for El Campello. Med, hdg pitch, hdstg, shd; htd wc; chem disp; mv service pnt; shwrs inc; baby facs; el pnts (6A) €3.80; gas; lndtte; shop; rest; snacks; bar; playgrnd; pool; waterslides; sand beach 500m; watersports; tennis 800m; horseriding 1km; golf 3km; TV cab/sat; 80% statics; dogs; train 1km; sep car park; poss cr; adv bkg; some noise fr rlwy; red long stay; CCI. "Pleasant site nr archaeological site & fishmkt; modern facs; friendly, helpful staff; not suitable RVs & lge o'fits due narr access to pitches; pitches sm & low canvas awnings; gd security." ♦ € 36.50
2006*

⊞ALICANTE *4F2* (10km NE Coastal) **Camping Bon Sol, Camino Real de Villajoyosa 35, Playa Muchavista, 03560 El Campello (Alicante) [tel/fax 965-94 13 83; bonsol@infonegocio.com]** Exit AP7 N of Alicante at junc 67 onto N332 sp Playa San Juan; on reaching coast rd turn N twds El Campello; site sp. Sm, mkd pitch, hdstg, pt shd, all serviced pitches; wc; chem disp; shwrs; el pnts (4A) €4.50; lndtte; shop; rest; bar; sand beach; 50% statics; adv bkg; cc acc; red long stay/low ssn; CCI. "Diff ent for long o'fits; helpful staff; noisy w/e; poss cold shwrs; vg." ♦ € 25.00
2006*

⊞ALLARIZ *1B2* (1.5km W Rural) **Camping Os Invernadeiros, Crta Allariz-Celanova, Km 3, 32660 Allariz (Ourense) [988-44 01 26; fax 988-44 20 06]** Well sp off N525 Orense-Xinzo rd & fr A52. Sm, pt shd; wc; shwrs inc; el pnts €2.40; gas; lndtte; shop; snacks; bar; playgrnd; pool 1.5km; horseriding; cycle hire; quiet; red long stay; cc acc; CCI. "Vg; site combined with horseriding stable; rv walk adj." € 13.60
2004*

ALMAYATE see Torre del Mar *2H4*

⊞ALMERIA *4G1* (23km SE Coastal/Rural) **Camping Cabo de Gata, Ctra Cabo de Gata s/n, Cortijo Ferrón, 04150 Cabo de Gata (Almería) [950-16 04 43; fax 950-52 00 03; info@campingcabodegata.com; www.camping cabodegata.com]** Exit m'way N340/344/E15 junc 460 or 467 sp Cabo de Gata, foll sp to site. Lge, hdg/mkd pitch, shd; wc; chem disp; baby facs; shwrs inc; el pnts (6-16A) €4.05-4.65; gas; lndtte; ice; supmkt high ssn; tradsmn; rest; snacks; bar; playgrnd; pool; diving cent; sand beach 900m; tennis; games area; games rm; excursions; cycle hire; internet; TV; some statics; dogs €2.60; bus 1km; Eng spkn; adv bkg; quiet; cc acc; red long stay/low ssn/CCI. "M'vans with solar panels/TV aerials take care with metal framed sun shd; occasional power cuts & poss drinking water restricted supply; poss long walk to water point; exchange 2nd hand Eng books avail; gd for cycling, birdwatching esp flamingoes; popular at w/e; isolated, dry area of Spain with many interesting features; warm winters; excel." ♦ € 22.50 (CChq acc)
2007*

See advertisement

Did you know you can fill in site report forms on the Club's website — www.caravanclub.co.uk?

⊞ALMERIA *4G1* (4km W Coastal) **Camping La Garrofa, Ctra N340a, Km 435.4, 04002 Almería [tel/fax 950-23 57 70; info@lagarrofa.com; www. lagarrofa.com]** Site sp on coast rd bet Almería & Aguadulce. Med, some hdstg, pt sl, pt shd; wc; chem disp; mv service pnt; shwrs inc; el pnts €4.17; gas; lndtte; shop; rest; snacks; shgl beach adj; games area; 10% statics; dogs €1.80; phone; bus adj; sep car park; m'wy noise; CCI. "V pleasant site; helpful staff; clean facs; long haul to chem disp; sm pitches, not rec lge o'fits." ♦ € 19.80
2007*

⊞ Site open all year

774

Tell us about the sites you visit

⊞**ALMERIA** *4G1* (10km W Coastal) **Camping Roquetas, Ctra Los Parrales s/n, 04740 Roquetas de Mar (Almería) [950-34 38 09; fax 950-34 25 25; info@campingroquetas.com; www. campingroquetas.com]** Fr A7 take exit 429; at rndabt turn L twd Aguadulce, turn R in 500m nr pedestrian lts; foll sp to site. V lge, pt shd; wc; chem disp; mv service pnt; shwrs inc; el pnts (5-15A) €3.90-6.25; gas; lndtte; ice; shop; snacks; bar; 2 pools; paddling pool; shgl beach 400m; tennis; TV rm; 10% statics; dogs €2.09; phone; bus 1km; Eng spkn; adv bkg rec all year; quiet; cc acc; red low ssn/long stay/CCI. "Double-size pitches in winter; helpful staff; gd clean facs; poss dusty; artificial shade; many long term visitors in winter." ♦ € 23.50
2006*

⊞**AMETLLA DE MAR, L'** *3C2* (2.5km S Coastal) **Camping L'Ametlla Village Platja, Paratge Stes Creus s/n, 43860 L'Ametlla de Mar (Tarragona) [977-26 77 84; fax 977-26 78 68; info@ campingametlla.com; www.campingametlla. com]** Exit AP7 junc 39, fork R as soon as cross m'way. Foll site sp for 3km - 1 v sharp, steep bend. Lge, hdg/mkd pitch, hdstg, terr, pt shd; htd wc; chem disp; mv service pnt; baby facs; shwrs inc; el pnts (5A) inc; gas; lndtte; ice; shop high ssn; rest; snacks; bar; BBQ; playgrnd; pool; paddling pool; shgl beach 400m; diving cent; games area; games rm; fitness rm; cycle hire; wifi internet; entmnt; TV rm; some statics; dogs free; phone; Eng spkn; adv bkg; some rd & rlwy noise; cc acc; red low ssn/long stay; CCI. "Conv Port Aventura & Ebro Delta National Park; excel site & facs." ♦ € 31.47 2007*

This guide relies on site report forms submitted by caravanners like us; we'll do our bit and tell the editor what we think of the campsites we've visited.

⊞**ALMUNECAR** *2H4* (6km W Coastal) **Nuevo Camping La Herradura, Paseo Andrés Segovia (Peña Parda), 18690 La Herradura (Granada) [958-64 06 34; fax 958-64 06 42; campingnet@ hotmail.com; www.almunecar.com]** Turn S off N340 sp La Herradura & foll rd to seafront. Turn R to end of beach rd. Avoid town cent due narr rds. Med, mkd pitch, pt terr, pt shd; wc; chem disp; mv service pnt; serviced pitches; shwrs inc; el pnts (5A) €3.30; gas 500m; lndtte; shop; rest; snacks; bar; playgrnd; shgl beach adj; 20% statics; dogs €1; phone; bus 300m; poss v cr; adv bkg; quiet; cc acc; red low ssn/long stay; CCI. "Friendly site in avocado orchard; mountain views some pitches; height restriction lge m'vans; some sm pitches - v tight to manoeuvre; vg san facs but ltd low ssn; popular winter long stay." ♦ € 19.10 2006*

⊞**ALTEA** *4F2* (4km S Coastal) **Camping Cap-Blanch, Playa de Albir, 03530 Altea (Alicante) [965-84 59 46; fax 965-84 45 56; capblanch@ctv. es; www.camping-capblanch.com]** Exit AP7/E15 junc 64 Altea-Collosa onto N332, site bet Altea & Benidorm, dir Albir. 'No entry' sps on prom rd do not apply to access to site. Lge, pt shd, hdstg; wc; chem disp; mv service pnt; baby facs; shwrs inc; el pnts (5A) €5.35; gas; shop 100m; lndtte; rest; bar; playgrnd; shgl beach adj; watersports; tennis; golf 5km; TV; some statics; carwash; poss cr; Eng spkn; adv bkg; quiet; cc acc; red low ssn/long stay. "V cr in winter with long stay campers; Altea mkt Tues; buses to Benidorm & Altea; most pitches hdstg on pebbles." ♦ € 39.59 2006*

AMPOLLA, L' *3C2* (Coastal) **Camping Sant Jordi, Calle del Mar 5, 43895 L'Ampolla (Tarragona) [tel/fax 977-46 04 15; campingsantjord@teleline. es]** Turn off N340 for L'Ampolla at km stone 1098. Fr harbour 500m NE. 1st site reached. Med, terr, pt shd; wc (cont); own san rec; chem disp; shwrs inc; el pnts (6A) inc; gas; lndtte; ice; shop & 500m; rest; snacks; bar; playgrnd; sand beach adj; 10% statics; dogs; phone; Eng spkn; adv bkg; quiet; red long stay; cc acc; CCI. "V helpful manager/owner; unspoilt coast; poss itinerants on site; facs poss poor low ssn; gd." ♦ 20 Apr-15 Oct. € 28.80
2004*

⊞**ARANDA DE DUERO** *1C4* (3km N Urban) **Camping Costajan, Ctra A1/E5, Km 164-165, 09400 Aranda de Duero (Burgos) [947-50 20 70; fax 947-51 13 54; campingcostajan@camping-costajan.com]** Sp on N1 Madrid-Burgos rd, N'bound exit km 164 Aranda Norte, S'bound exit km 165 & foll sp to Aranda & site 500m on R. Med, pt sl, shd; htd wc; chem disp; mv service pnt; shwrs inc; el pnts (10A) €4.45 (poss no earth); gas; lndtte; shop; tradsmn; supmkt 1km; rest high ssn; snacks; bar; BBQ; playgrnd; pool high ssn; tennis; games area; 10% statics; dogs €2; phone; bus 2km; adv bkg; quiet, but some traff noise; red low ssn but ltd facs; CCI. "Lovely site under pine trees; poultry farm adj; diff pitch access due trees & sandy soil; v friendly, helpful owner; site poss clsd low ssn - phone ahead to check; low ssn recep opens 1830 - site yourself; many facs clsd low ssn & gate clsd o'night until 0800; excel facs for disabled; poss cold/tepid shwrs low ssn; gd winter NH but unhtd san facs." € 19.90 2007*

Spain

⊞ARANJUEZ *1D4* (1.5km NE Urban) **Camping International Aranjuez** (formerly Soto del Castillo), Calle Soto del Rebollo s/n, 28300 Aranjuez (Madrid) [918-91 13 95; fax 918-92 04 06; info@campingaranjuez.com; www.campingaranjuez.com] Fr N (Madrid) turn off A4 exit 37 onto M305. On ent town turn L bef rv, after petrol stn on R. Take L lane & watch for site sp on L, also mkd M305 Madrid. Site in 500m on R. (If missed cont around cobbled rndabt & back twd Madrid.) Fr S turn off A4 for Aranjuez & foll Palacio Real sp. Join M305 & foll sp for Madrid & camping site. Site on Rv Tajo. Warning: rd surface rolls, take it slowly on app to site. Med, mkd pitch, pt shd; wc; chem disp; some serviced pitches; shwrs inc; el pnts (16A) €3.50 (poss no earth, rev pol); gas; lndtte; shop; tradsmn; hypmkt 3km; rest; snacks; bar; playgrnd; pool & paddling pool; rv fishing; canoe & cycle hire; wifi internet; some statics; phone; cc acc; red low ssn; CCI. "Newly refurbished site 2006/2007 & new owners; some lge pitches; pleasant town - World Heritage site; conv Madrid by train; conv Royal Palace & gardens." ♦ € 27.00 (CChq acc)   2007*

See advertisement

ARBON *1A3* (S Rural) **Camping La Cascada**, 33718 Arbón (Asturias) [985-62 50 81; campinglacascada@hotmail.com] Approx 20km W of Luarca on N634, turn S onto AS25 for approx 10km. Immed bef town of Navia, site sp. Winding rd. Med, sl, pt shd; wc; chem disp (wc); shwrs inc; el pnts (3-4A) €2.15; gas; shop & 1km; snacks; bar; BBQ; playgrnd; pool; sand beach 12km; 15% statics; dogs; phone; bus 1km; Eng spkn; adv bkg; quiet; CCI. "V friendly, family-run site in beautiful area; excel info fr local tourist office." Easter-15 Sep. € 12.40   2007*

⊞ARCOS DE LA FRONTERA *2G3* (1km E Rural) **Camping Lago de Arcos**, 11630 Arcos de la Frontera (Cádiz) [956-70 83 33; fax 956-70 80 00; lagodearcos@campings.net] On A382 at Arcos turn E at sp El Bosque onto A372. Turn L at sp El Santiscal & site, site on R. (New rd being built 2006, directions may change.) Med, pt shd; wc; shwrs inc; el pnts (5A) €2.75; gas; lndtte; sm shop; snacks; bar; playgrnd; pool high ssn; dogs; phone; poss cr; quiet; cc acc; CCI. "Noisy at Easter due Running Bull Festival; unkempt low ssn & poss itinerants; tel to check open in low ssn; busy w/e; friendly staff; most pitches have canopy frames; sh walk to lake." ♦ ltd. € 15.73   2007*

⊞ARDALES *2G3* (6km N Rural) **Camping Parque Ardales**, Bda Los Embalses, s/n, 29550 Ardales (Málaga) [tel/fax 952-11 24 01; rey@campingparqueardales.com] Fr Antequera on A382 W to Campillos, then A357 S dir Ardales. Foll sp twd Embalse del Conde de Guadalhorce. V steep ent & exit not suitable towed c'vans. Sm, hdstg, pt sl, shd; wc; chem disp (wc); shwrs inc; el pnts (10A) €3.50; shop high ssn; poss cr; quiet; cc acc. "Forested site around lake with steep sl & sharp corners; stunning views; mainly for tenters; helpful owner; hot water only 2hrs am & pm; conv walk to Camino del Rey & drive to Bobastro." € 14.25   2005*

⊞ARENAS DE SAN PEDRO *1D3* (8km N Rural) **Camping Prados Abiertos**, Ctra Ávila-Talavera, N502, Km 72, 05410 Mombeltran (Ávila) [tel/fax 920-38 60 61; derivera@telepolis.com] N fr Arenas de San Pedro, site is 3km S of Mombeltran, 600m past junc with AV923, on R adj hotel. Med, mkd pitch, terr, shd; wc; chem disp; shwrs inc; el pnts (5A) inc; gas; lndtte; shop; rest; snacks; bar; playgrnd; pool; paddling pool; tennis; cycle hire; TV; 20% statics; phone; site clsd 19 Dec-6 Jan; poss cr; cc acc; CCI. "Ltd pitches accessible with c'van; in Gredos mountains." € 16.40   2005*

⊞ARENAS DEL REY *2G4* (Rural) **Camping Los Bermejales, Km 360, Embalse Los Bermejales, 18129 Arenas del Rey (Granada) [958-35 91 90; fax 958-35 93 36; camping@losbermejales. com; www.losbermejales.com]** On A44/E902 S fr Granada, exit at junc 139 dir La Malahá onto A385. In approx 10km, turn L onto A338 dir Alhama de Granada & foll sp for site. Fr A92 foll sp Alhama de Granada, then Embalse Los Bermejales. Med, mkd pitch, hdstg, terr, pt shd; wc; chem disp; mv service pnt; shwrs inc; el pnts (9A) €2.45; gas; lndtte; ice; shop; rest; snacks; bar; BBQ; playgrnd; pool; lake sw & sand/shgl beach adj; fishing (licence req); pedalos; tennis; TV rm; 50% statics; dogs; phone; poss cr high ssn; little Eng spkn; adv bkg; quiet. "Ideal base for touring Granada; Roman baths 12km at Alhama de Granada; vg disabled facs." ♦ € 14.70   2005*

ARENAS, LAS *1A4* (1km E Rural) **Camping Naranjo de Bulnes, Ctra Cangas de Onís-Panes, Km 32,6, 33554 Arenas de Cabrales (Asturias) [tel/fax 985-84 65 78]** Fr Unquera on N634, take N621 S to Panes, AS114 23km to Las Arenas. Site E of vill of Las Arenas de Cabrales, both sides of rd. V lge, mkd pitch, pt sl, pt shd; wc; chem disp; baby facs; shwrs inc; el pnts (10A) €3.25; gas; lndtte; ice; shop; rest; snacks; bar; playgrnd; rv sw; TV rm; poss cr; some Eng spkn; adv bkg; some rd noise; cc acc. "Beautifully situated site by rv; attractive, rustic-style san facs but no hot water at basins; rds thro site poor; poss poor security; excel value rest; conv Picos de Europa; mountain-climbing school; guides; excursions; walking." 2 Mar-4 Nov. € 23.24   2007*

ARENYS DE MAR *3C3* (3km NE Coastal) **Camping Globo Rojo, Ctra N11, Km 660.9, 08360 Canet de Mar (Barcelona) [tel/fax 937-94 11 43; camping@ globo-rojo.com; www.globo-rojo.com]** On N11 500m N of Canet de Mar. Site clearly sp on L. Gd access. Med, hdg/mkd pitch, hdstg, shd; wc; chem disp; baby facs; shwrs; el pnts (10A) €4.25; gas; lndtte; shop; tradsmn; rest; snacks; bar; BBQ; playgrnd; pool; paddling pool; shgl beach & watersports adj; games area; tennis 50m; horseriding 2km; cycle hire; child entmnt; internet; TV rm; 80% statics; dogs €5.35; phone; sep car park; Eng spkn; adv bkg (dep req); rd noise; cc acc; red low ssn/CCI. "Excel facs; friendly, family-run site; busy w/e; slightly run down area; conv Barcelona by train (40km)." ♦ 1 Apr-30 Sep. € 30.80   2007*

ARES see Ferrol *1A2*

⊞ARISTOT *3B3* (Rural) **Camping Pont d'Ardaix, N260, Km 210, El Pont de Bar, 25722 Aristot (Lleida) [973-38 40 98; fax 973-38 41 14; pontdardaix@clior.es; www.pontdardaix.com]** On Seo de Urgel-Puigcerdà rd, N260, at rear of bar/rest Pont d'Ardaix. Med, terr, pt shd; wc; mv service pnt; shwrs inc; el pnts (3-10A) €4.60-6.60; gas; lndtte; shop & 4km; rest; bar; playgrnd; pool; 80% statics; dogs €5; phone; Eng spkn; quiet; CCI. "In v pleasant valley on bank of Rv Segre; touring pitches on rv bank; site poss scruffy & unkempt low ssn; gd NH." ♦ € 18.40   2005*

⊞ARNES *3C2* (Rural) **Camping Els Ports, Ctra Arnes-Horta San Joan, Km 2, 43597 Arnes (Tarragona) [tel/fax 977-43 55 60]** Exit AP7 at junc Tortosa onto C12 sp Gandesa. Turn W onto T333 at El Pinell de Brai, then T330 to site. Med, pt shd; htd wc; shwrs inc; el pnts €3.85; lndtte; shop; rest; bar; pool; paddling pool; games area; cycle hire; horseriding 3km; entmnt; TV rm; some statics; phone; bus 1km; quiet; cc acc. "Nr nature reserve & many sports activities." ♦ ltd. € 17.20   2005*

AURITZ *3A1* (3km SW Rural) **Camping Urrobi, Ctra Pamplona-Valcarlos, Km 42, 31694 Aurizberri-Espinal (Navarra) [tel/fax 948-76 02 00; info@ campingurrobi.com; www.campingurrobi.com]** NE fr Pamplona on N135 twd Valcarlos thro Erro; 1.5km after Auritzberri (Espinal) turn R on N172. Site on N172 at junc with N135 opp picnic area. Med, pt shd; wc; chem disp; mv service pnt; shwrs inc; el pnts (5A) €4.35; gas; lndtte; shop; tradsmn; supmkt 1.5km; rest; snacks; bar; BBQ; playgrnd; pool; rv adj; tennis; mini-golf; cycle hire; horseriding; wifi internet; 20% statics; phone; Eng spkn; adv bkg; quiet; cc acc; CCI. "Excel site & facs; solar htd water - hot water to shwrs only; walks in surrounding hills; ltd facs low ssn." ♦ 1 Apr-31 Oct. € 17.85   2007*

AVIN see Cangas de Onis *1A3*

⊞AYERBE *3B2* (1km NE Rural) **Camping La Banera, Ctra Loarre Km.1, 22800 Ayerbe (Huesca) [tel/fax 974 38 02 42; labanera@ wanadoo.es; www.labanera.turincon.com]** Take A132 NW fr Huesca dir Pamplona. Turn R at 1st x-rds at ent to Ayerbe. Site 1km on R on A1206. Med, mkd pitch, terr, pt shd; wc; chem disp; baby facs; fam bthrm; shwrs inc; el pnts (6A) €2.67; gas; lndtte; ice; shop 1km; rest; snacks; bar; cooking facs; TV rm; dogs; some Eng spkn; adv bkg; quiet; cc acc; red long stay; CCI. "V friendly, well-maintained, family-run site; facs clean; excel peace & quiet; helpful owners; wonderful views; gd rest, vg value; close to Loarre - one of best positioned castles in Spain; care req by high o'fits as many low trees." ♦ € 11.34   2006*

Spain

AYERBE *3B2* (10km NE Rural) **Camping Castillo de Loarre, 22809 Loarre (Huesca) [974-38 27 23; fax 974-38 27 22; info@campingloarre.com; www.campingloarre.com]** NW on A132 fr Huesca, turn R at ent to Ayerbe to Loare sp Castillo de Loarre. Pass 1st site on R (La Banera) & foll sp to castle past Loarre vill on L; site on L. App rd steep & twisting. Med, pt sl, pt shd; wc; chem disp; shwrs inc; el pnts (6A) €3.50; gas; lndtte; ice; shop; tradsmn; rest; snacks; bar; playgrnd; sm pool; cycle hire; 10% statics; dogs; phone; poss cr; Eng spkn; quiet; cc acc; CCI. "Elevated site in almond grove beneath castle; superb scenery & views, esp fr pitches on far L of site; some pitches ltd el pnts; excel birdwatching - many vultures/ eagles at eye level; gd touring area; site open w/e in winter; v busy high ssn & weekends; pitching poss diff lge o'fits due low trees; worth the journey." 9 Apr-4 Nov. € 12.50   2007*

BAIONA *1B2* (2km NE Urban/Coastal) **Camping Playa América, Ctra Vigo-Baiona, Km 9.250, 36350 Nigrán (Pontevedra) [986-36 71 61; fax 986-36 54 04; oficina@campingplayaamerica. com; www.campingplayaamerica.com]** Sp on rd PO552 fr all dirs (Vigo/Baiona/La Guardia) nr beach. Med, mkd pitch, pt shd; wc; chem disp; mv service pnt; baby facs; shwrs inc; el pnts (6A) €3; gas; lndtte; shop; tradsmn; rest; snacks; bar; BBQ; playgrnd; pool; sand beach 500m; cycle hire; 60% statics; dogs; bus 500m; poss cr; Eng spkn; adv bkg; CCI. "Friendly staff; gd." ♦ 16 Mar-16 Oct. € 19.50   2004*

⊞**BAIONA** *1B2* (1km E Coastal) **Camping Bayona Playa, Ctra Vigo-Baiona, Km 19, Sabarís, 36393 Baiona (Pontevedra) [986-35 00 35; fax 986-35 29 52; campingbayona@bme.es; www. campingbayona.com]** Fr Vigo on PO552 sp Baiona. Or fr A57 exit Baiona & foll sp Vigo & site sp. Site clearly sp for 25km around. Lge, mkd pitch, pt shd; wc (some cont); chem disp; mv service pnt; shwrs inc; el pnts (3A) €3.53; gas; lndtte; ice; shop; rest; snacks; bar; playgrnd; pool; waterslide; sand beach adj; 50% statics; dogs; phone; poss cr; adv bkg (ess high ssn); quiet; red low ssn/long stay; CCI. "Area of o'stndg natural beauty with sea on 3 sides; gd cycle track to town; well-organised site; excel, clean san facs; avoid access w/e as v busy; ltd facs low ssn; sm pitches." ♦ € 23.84   2006*

BAIONA *1B2* (7km S Coastal) **Camping Mougás, As Mariñas s/n, Crta Baiona-A Guarda, Km 156, 36309 Mougás (Pontevedra) [986-38 50 11; fax 986-38 29 90; campingmougas@campingmougas. com; www.campingmougas.com]** Fr Baiona take coastal rd PO552 S; site sp. Med, pt shd; wc; chem disp; shwrs; el pnts inc; lndtte; supmkt; rest; snacks; bar; BBQ; playgrnd; pool; beach adj; fishing; tennis; horseriding; games rn; entmnt; some statics; phone; cc acc; red low ssn; CCI. "Excel staff; lovely site on rocky coast; gd for watching sunsets; gd NH." ♦ Holy Week-30 Sep. € 23.50   2006*

⊞**BALAGUER** *3C2* (8km N Rural) **Camping La Noguera, Partida de la Solana s/n, 25615 Sant Llorenç de Montgai (Lleida) [973-42 03 34; fax 973-42 02 12; jaume@campinglanoguera.com; www.campinglanoguera.com]** Fr Lleida, take N11 ring rd & exit at km 467 onto C13 NE dir Andorra & Balaguer. Head for Balaguer town cent, cross rv & turn R onto LV9047 dir Gerb. Site on L in 8km thro Gerb. App fr Camarasa not rec. Lge, mkd pitch, hdstg, terr, pt shd; wc; chem disp; mv service pnt; baby facs; shwrs inc; el pnts (6A) €4.60; gas; lndtte; ice; supmkt; tradsmn; rest; snacks; bar; BBQ; playgrnd; pool; games area; TV rm; 80% statics; dogs €3.10; phone; poss cr; Eng spkn; adv bkg; quiet; cc acc; red long stay; CCI. "Next to lake & nature reserve; gd cycling; poss diff lge o'fits." ♦ ltd. € 19.20   2006*

BANOS DE FORTUNA see Fortuna *4F1*

BANOS DE MONTEMAYOR see Béjar *1D3*

⊞**BANYOLES** *3B3* (2km W Rural) **Camping Caravaning El Llac, 17834 Porqueres (Gerona) [tel/fax 972-57 03 05; info@campingllac.com]** Exit AP7 junc 6 to Banyoles. Go strt thro town (do not use by-pass) & exit town at end of lake in 1.6km. Use R-hand layby to turn L sp Porqueres. Site on R in 2.5km. Lge, mkd pitch, pt shd; chem disp; wc; shwrs; el pnts €3.95; lndtte; shop; snacks; bar; pool; lake sw; 80% statics; dogs €2.30; bus 1km; site clsd mid-Dec to mid-Jan; poss cr; quiet but noisy rest/disco adj in high ssn; red long stay. "Museums & ancient churches; immac, ltd facs low ssn; facs stretched high ssn." ♦ € 19.10   2006*

BARBATE see Vejer de la Frontera *2H3*

BARCELONA See sites listed under El Masnou, Gavà and Sitges.

⊞**BECERREA** *1B2* (15km E Rural) **Camping Os Ancares, Ctra NV1, Liber, 27664 Mosteiro-Cervantes (Lugo) [tel/fax 982-36 45 56]** Fr A6 exit Becerreá S onto LU722 sp Navia de Suarna. After 10km in Liber turn R onto LU723 sp Doiras, site in 7km just beyond Mosteiro hamlet; site sp. Site ent poss diff lge o'fits & lge m'vans. Med, terr, shd; wc; shwrs inc; el pnts (6A) €3.60; gas; lndry rm; rest; snacks; bar; playgrnd; pool; fishing; horseriding; some statics; dogs €1; poss cr; quiet; CCI. "Isolated site; a little run down; gd rest & san facs; ltd facs low ssn; outstanding mountain scenery; gd walking." € 13.30   2006*

BEGUR *3B3* (2km N Coastal) **Camping El Maset, Playa Sa Riera, 17255 Begur (Gerona) [972-62 30 23; fax 972-62 39 01; info@campingelmaset. com; www.campingelmaset.com]** Fr Begur take rd N twd Sa Riera. Med, shd; wc; chem disp; mv service pnt; baby facs; shwrs inc; el pnts (4-6A) €3.40-4.50; gas; lndtte; shop; rest; snacks; bar; playgrnd; pool; sand beach 300m; games area; games rm; internet; phone; no dogs; cc acc; quiet. "Pleasant site in gd location." ♦ 10 Apr-24 Sep. € 26.30   2006*

BEGUR *3B3* (1.5km S Rural) **Camping Begur, Ctra d'Esclanya, Km 2, 17255 Begur (Gerona)** [972-62 32 01; fax 972-62 45 66; info@campingbegur. com; www.campingbegur.com] Exit AP7/E15 junc 6 Gerona onto C66 dir La Bisbal & Palamós. At x-rds to Pals turn L dir Begur then turn R twd Esclanya, site on R, clearly sp. Slope to site ent. Lge, mkd pitch, pt sl, shd; wc; chem disp; mv service pnt; baby facs; fam bthrm; serviced pitches; shwrs inc; el pnts (10A) inc; Indtte; ice; supmkt; rest; bar; BBQ; playgrnd; pool; paddling pool; sand beach 2km; tennis; games area; games rm; gym; wifi internet; 14% statics; dogs €3.40; phone; Eng spkn; adv bkg; cc not acc; red long stay/CCI. "Excel, peaceful site; narr site rds poss diff lge o'fits; adj castle & magnificent views; excursions arranged." ♦ 15 Apr-28 Sep. € 27.40 2007*

See advertisement

As soon as we get home I'm going to post all these site report forms to the editor for inclusion in next year's guide. I don't want to miss the September deadline.

BEJAR *1D3* (6km S Rural) **Camping Cinco Castaños, Ctra de la Sierra s/n, 37710 Candelario (Salamanca)** [923-41 32 04; fax 923-41 32 82; profetur@candelariohotel.com; www. candelariohotel.com] Fr Béjar foll sp Candelario on C515/SA220, site sp on N side of vill. Steep bends & narr app rd. Sm, mkd pitch, pt sl, pt shd; htd wc; chem disp (wc); baby facs; shwrs inc; el pnts (6A) €3.15; gas; Indtte; ice; shop 500m; rest; bar; playgrnd; pool high ssn; no dogs; bus 500m; phone; quiet; CCI. "Mountain vill; friendly owner; no facs in winter; no lge o'fits as steep site." ♦ Holy Week-15 Oct. € 18.50 2007*

⊞**BEJAR** *1D3* (15km SW Rural) **Camping Las Cañadas, Ctra N630, Km 432, 10750 Baños de Montemayor (Cáceres)** [927-48 11 26; fax 927-48 13 14; info@campinglascanadas.com; www.campinglascanadas.com] Fr S turn off A630 m'way at 437km stone to Heruns then take old N630 twd Béjar. Site at 432km stone, behind 'Hervas Peil' (leather goods shop). Fr N exit A66 junc 427 thro Baños for 3km to site at km432 on R. Lge, mkd pitch, pt sl; shd (net shdg); htd wc; chem disp; mv service pnt; baby facs; shwrs inc; el pnts (5A) €3.20; gas; Indtte; shop; rest; snacks; bar; playgrnd; pool in high ssn; paddling pool; fishing; tennis; games area; TV rm; 60% statics; dogs; poss cr; Eng spkn; quiet but rd noise; cc acc; 15% red long stay; CCI. "Gd san facs but poss cold shwrs; high vehicles take care overhanging trees; gd walking country; NH/sh stay." ♦ ltd. € 15.66 (CChq acc) 2007*

⊞**BELLVER DE CERDANYA** *3B3* (2km E Rural) **Camping Bellver, Ctra N260, Km 193.7, 17539 Isòvol (Gerona)** [973-51 02 39; fax 973-51 07 19; campingbellver@campingbellver.com; www. campingbellver.com] On N260 fr Puigcerdà to Bellver; site on L, well sp. Lge, mkd pitch, shd; htd wc; chem disp (wc); shwrs inc; el pnts (5A) €3.50; gas; Indtte; rest; snacks; bar; playgrnd; pool; 90% statics; dogs; phone; poss cr; Eng spkn; quiet; cc acc; CCI. "Friendly, helpful staff; lovely pitches along rv; san facs immac; v quiet low ssn; gd NH for Andorra." € 19.20 2007*

⊞**BELLVER DE CERDANYA** *3B3* (1km W Rural) **Camping La Cerdanya, Ctra N260, Km 200, 25727 Prullans (Lleida)** [973-51 02 62; fax 973-51 06 72; cerdanya@prullens.net; www.prullens. net/camping] Fr Andorra frontier on N260, site sp. Lge, mkd pitch, shd; wc; baby facs; mv service pnt; shwrs inc; el pnts (4A) €5; gas; Indtte; shop; rest; snacks; playgrnd; pool; paddling pool; games area; internet; entmnt; 80% statics; dogs €3.45; phone; bus 1km; poss cr; adv bkg; quiet; red long stay; cc acc. ♦ € 23.30 2007*

Spain

⊞**BELLVER DE CERDANYA** 3B3 (1km W Rural) Camping Solana del Segre, Ctra N260, Km 198, 25720 Bellver de Cerdanya (Lleida) [973-51 03 10; fax 973-51 06 98; info@solanadelsegre.com; www.solanadelsegre.com] Take N260 fr Puigcerdà to Seo de Urgell, site at km 198 after Bellver de Cerdanya on L. Lge, pt sl, pt shd; wc; chem disp; shwrs inc; baby facs; el pnts (5A) €4.20; lndtte; shop; rest (w/e only low ssn); snacks; bar; BBQ; playgrnd; pool; games area; games rm; internet; entmnt; 80% statics; dogs €4.50; phone; bus 500m; poss cr; adv bkg; quiet; cc acc; 10% red low ssn. "Steep exit fr site to main rd & steep hills on site; poss diff for cars under 2L; conv NH nr Cadí Tunnel; site poss clsd 15 Sep-14 Oct."
♦ € 33.60   2007*

BENABARRE 3B2 (500m Urban) Camping Benabarre, 22580 Benabarre (Huesca) [974-54 35 72; fax 974-54 34 32; aytobenabarre@aragon.es] Fr N230 S, turn L after 2nd camping sp over bdge & into vill. Ignore brown camping sp (part of riding cent). Med, pt shd; wc; shwrs inc; el pnts (10A) inc; shops 500m; bar; pool; tennis; no statics; bus 600m; phone; quiet. "Excel, friendly, simple site; gd facs; gd value for money; v quiet low ssn; warden calls 1700; mkt on Fri; lovely vill with excel chocolate shop; conv Graus & mountains - a real find." 1 Apr-30 Sep. € 13.50   2007*

BENAMAHOMA see Ubrique 2H3

⊞**BENASQUE** 3B2 (3km N Rural) Camping Aneto, 22440 Benasque (Huesca) [974-55 11 41; fax 974-55 16 63; info@campinganeto.com; www.campinganeto.com] Fr Vielha N230 then N260 to Castejón de Sos, foll sp to Benasque, site on L in 3km. Med, pt sl, pt shd; wc; chem disp; shwrs inc; el pnts (10A) €4.60; gas; ice; lndtte; shop in ssn & 3km; tradsmn; rest in ssn; snacks; bar; BBQ; playgrnd; sw 3km; trekking; poss cr; Eng spkn; 75% statics; site clsd Nov; phone; quiet; cc acc; CCI. "Friendly owners; access to pitches poss diff lge o'fits; unspoilt countryside; stunning app via gorges fr S; gd walking, wildflowers." € 19.20
                                                2005*

BENAVENTE 1B3 (11km SW Rural) Camping Rió Tera, Puente Mozar s/n, 49698 Mozar de Valverde (Zamora) [980-64 05 50; fax 980-64 05 73; campingriotera@terra.es; www.campingriotera.com] W fr Benavente on N525; in about 12km camp sp just bef Colinas de Trasmonte. Turn L & go thro Villanázar. Turn R at T-junc, cross rv. Site in 100m on R. Med, mkd pitch, pt shd; wc; chem disp; shwrs inc; el pnts (5A) €3; lndry rm; shop; rest; snacks; bar; playgrnd; tennis; 10% statics; dogs; quiet; cc acc; CCI. 1 Apr-30 Sep. € 15.50   2004*

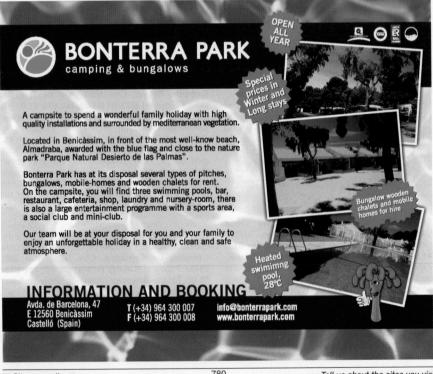

⊞**BENICARLO** *3D2* (2km NE Urban/Coastal) **Camping La Alegría del Mar, Ctra N340, Km 1046, Calle Playa Norte, 12580 Benicarló (Castellón) [964-47 08 71]** Sp off main N340 app Benicarló. Take slip rd mkd Service, go under underpass, turn R on exit & cont twd town, then turn at camp sp by Peugeot dealers. Sm, mkd pitch, pt shd; htd wc; shwrs; el pnts (4-6A) €3.80; gas; lndtte; shop 500m; rest; snacks; bar; playgrnd; sm pool; beach adj; games rm; phone; bus 800m; poss cr; quiet but rd noise at night; red long stay/ low ssn; cc acc. "British owners; access to pitches poss diff in ssn; vg san facs; Xmas & New Year packages; phone ahead to reserve pitch." € 19.60
2006*

The opening dates and prices on this campsite have changed. I'll send a site report form to the editor for the next edition of the guide.

⊞**BENICASIM** *3D2* (500m NE Coastal) **Camping Bonterra Park, Avda de Barcelona 47, 12560 Benicasim (Castellón) [964-30 00 07; fax 964 30 00 08; info@bonterrapark.com; www. bonterrapark.com]** Fr N exit AP7 junc 45 onto N340 dir Benicasim. In approx 7km turn R to Benicasim/ Centro Urba; strt ahead to traff lts, then turn L, site on L 500m after going under rlwy bdge. Fr S on AP7 exit junc 46 onto N340 dir Benicasim. In approx 8km turn R sp Benicasim (not Benicasim Playas), round rndabt into vill main street Calle Santo Tomas past rlwy bdge, site on L in 500m. Lge, mkd pitch, pt sl, shd; htd wc; chem disp; mv service pnt; baby facs; shwrs inc; el pnts (10A) inc; gas; lndtte; shop adj; rest; snacks; bar; BBQ; playgrnd; 2 pools (1 covrd & htd); paddling pool; sand beach 300m; tennis; cycle hire; entmnt (daytime only); games area; wifi internet; games/TV rm; 15% statics; dogs €0.80 (not acc Jul/Aug); phone; train; sep car park; Eng spkn; adv bkg; quiet; cc acc; red long stay/low ssn/ CCI. "Busy, popular site in gd location; clean & well-managed; excel walks; winter festival 3rd wk Jan; access to some pitches poss diff due trees; sun shades some pitches; dog baths provided; lovely beach; town in walking dist; highly rec." ♦ € 49.33
ABS - E19   2007*

See advertisement

⊞**BENICASIM** *3D2* (4.5km NW Coastal) **Camping Azahar, Ptda Villaroig s/n, 12560 Benicasim (Castellón) [964-30 31 96; fax 964-30 25 12; info@ campingazahar.net; www.campingazahar.net]** Fr AP7 junc 45 take N340 twd València; in 5km L at top of hill (do not turn R to go-karting); foll sp. Turn R under rlwy bdge opp Hotel Voramar. Lge, mkd pitch, pt sl, terr, unshd; htd wc; chem disp; mv service pnt; baby facs; shwrs inc; el pnts (4-6A) €2.90 (long leads poss req); gas; lndtte; rest; snacks; bar; playgrnd; pool; sand beach 300m across rd; tennis at hotel; cycle hire; 25% statics; dogs €3.85; phone; bus adj; poss cr high ssn; Eng spkn; bus adj; adv bkg; red long stay/low ssn/snr citizens; cc acc; CCI. "Popular site, esp in winter; poss noisy high ssn; access poss diff for m'vans & lge o'fits; poss uneven pitches; organised events; gd walking & cycling; gd touring base." ♦ ltd. € 25.80
2007*

⊞**BENIDORM** *4F2* (3km Coastal) **Camping La Torreta, Avda Dr Severo Ochoa s/n, 03500 Benidorm (Alicante) [965-85 46 68; fax 965-80 26 53]** Exit AP7/E15 junc 65 onto N332. Foll sp Playa Levante, site sp. Lge, mkd pitch, hdstg, pt sl, terr, pt shd (bamboo shades); wc (some cont); mv service pnt; shwrs inc; el pnts (10A) €3.30; gas; lndtte; ice; shop; rest; bar; playgrnd; pool & paddling pool; sand beach 1km; 10% statics; dogs; bus; no adv bkg; quiet; red 15+ days; CCI. "Take care siting if heavy rain; some pitches v sm; popular with long stay winter visitors." ♦ € 24.90   2006*

⊞**BENIDORM** *4F2* (1km N) **Camping Arena Blanca, Avda Dr Severo Ochoa 44, 03500 Benidorm (Alicante) [965-86 18 89; fax 86 11 07; info@camping-arenablanca.es; www. camping-arenablanca.es]** Fr AP7 exit junc 65 onto N332 dir Playa Levante. Site sp. Med, terr, pt shd; wc; chem disp; some serviced pitches; shwrs inc; el pnts (16A) €3; gas; lndtte; supmkt; rest; snacks; bar; playgrnd; pool; paddling pool; sand beach 1km; cash machine; sat TV conn all pitches; 30% statics; dogs; phone; bus 200m; adv bkg; quiet; red long stays; cc acc. ♦ € 32.50   2005*

⊞**BENIDORM** *4F2* (1.5km NE Urban) **Camping El Raco, Avda Dr Severo Ochoa s/n, Racó de Loix, 03500 Benidorm (Alicante) [965-86 85 52; fax 965-86 85 44; info@campingraco.com; www. campingraco.com]** Turn off A7 m'way at junc 65 then L onto A332; take turning sp Benidorm Levante Beach; ignore others; L at 1st traff lghts; strt on at next traff lts, El Raco 1km on R. Lge, hdg/ mkd pitch, hdstg, pt sl, pt shd; wc; chem disp; 50% serviced pitches; baby facs; shwrs inc; el pnts (10A) €3; gas; lndtte; shop; bar; BBQ; rest; playgrnd; 2 pools (1 htd, covrd); beach 1.5km; games area; TV (UK channels); 30% statics; bus; poss v cr in winter; quiet; red 15+ days low ssn; CCI. "Excel site; v popular winter long stay but strictly applied rules about leaving c'van unoccupied; easy 30 min walk to Benidorm; vg local sightseeing; el pnts metered for long stay." ♦ € 26.00   2006*

Spain

⊞**BENIDORM** *4F2* (3km NE Urban) **Camping Benisol, Avda de la Comunidad Valenciana s/n, 03500 Benidorm (Alicante)** [965-85 16 73; fax 965-86 08 95; campingbenisol@yahoo.es; www. campingbenisol.com] Exit AP7/E15 junc 65 onto N332. Foll sp Benidorm, Playa Levante (avoid bypass). Dangerous rd on ent to sit; site ent easy to miss. Lge, hdg pitch, hdstg, shd; wc; chem disp; serviced pitches; shwrs inc; el pnts (4-6A) €2.80; gas; lndtte; shop & rest (high ssn); snacks; bar; playgrnd; pool (hgh ssn); sand beach 4km; TV; 85% statics; dogs; phone; bus to Benidorm; poss cr; Eng spkn; adv bkg with dep; some rd noise; red long stay/low ssn; CCI. "Helpful staff; well-run, clean site; many permanent residents; poor facs low ssn." ♦ € 27.20   2007*

Before we move on, I'm going to fill in some site report forms and post them off to the editor, otherwise they won't arrive in time for the deadline at the end of September.

⊞**BENIDORM** *4F2* (1km E Coastal) **Camping Villasol, Avda Bernat de Sarriá 13, 03500 Benidorm (Alicante)** [965-85 04 22; fax 966-80 64 20; campingvillasol@dragonet.es; www.camping-villasol.com] Leave AP7 at junc 65 onto N332 dir Alicante; take exit into Benidorm sp Levante. Turn L at traff lts just past Camping Titus, then in 200m R at lts in Avda Albir. Site on R in 1km. Care - dip at ent, poss grounding. V lge, mkd pitch, hdstg, shd; htd wc; chem disp; baby facs; shwrs inc; el pnts (5A) €3.90; lndtte; supmkt; rest; snacks; bar; playgrnd; 2 pools (1 htd, covrd); sand beach 300m; games area; wifi internet; sat TV all pitches; medical service; currency exchange; 5% statics; no dogs; phone; adv bkg; Eng spkn; quiet; cc acc; red low ssn/long stay. "Excel - especially in winter - well-kept site; some sm pitches; friendly staff." ♦ € 31.40   2007*

See advertisement opposite

⊞**BERCEO** *1B4* (200m SE Rural) **Camping Berceo, El Molino s/n, 26327 Berceo (La Rioja)** [941-37 32 37; fax 941-37 32 01] Fr E on N120 foll sp Tricio, San Millan de la Cogolla on LR136/LR206. Fr W foll sp Villar de Torre & San Millan. In Berceo foll sp sw pools & site. Med, hdg/mkd pitch, hdstg, pt sl, shd; htd wc; chem disp; fam bthrm; shwrs inc; el pnts (7A) €3.20; lndtte; ice; shop; tradsmn; rest; snacks; bar; playgrnd; pool; paddling pool; cycle hire; TV; 50% statics; phone; bus 200m; adv bkg; quiet; red long stay; CCI. "Excel base for Rioja vineyards; gd site." ♦ € 24.00   2006*

BESALU *3B3* (2km E Rural) **Camping Masia Can Coromines, Ctra N260, Km 60, 17851 Maià del Montcal (Gerona)** [tel/fax 972-59 11 08; coromines@grn.es; www.cancoromines.com] NW fr Gerona on C66 to Besalú. Turn R sp Figueras (N260) for 2.5km. At 60km sp turn into driveway on L opp fountain for approx 300m. Narr app & ent. Site is 1km W of Maià. Sm, pt shd; wc; serviced pitch; shwrs inc; el pnts (10-15A) €3; gas; lndtte; ice; shop 2.5km; rest high ssn; snacks; bar; playgrnd; pool; cycle hire; internet; some statics; dogs €2.90; Eng spkn; adv bkg; quiet with some rd noise; cc acc; CCI. "Friendly, family-run site in beautiful area; gd walks." ♦ 1 Apr-1 Nov. € 20.40   2007*

BETANZOS *1A2* (6km NW Rural) **Camping Santa Marta-Coruna, Babio 23, 15165 Bergondo (La Coruña)** [tel/fax 981-79 58 26; info@campingsantamarta.com; www.camping santamarta.com] Fr AP/E19 exit junc sp Bergondo/Sada, foll sp to site. Lge, some hdg/mkd pitch, sl, pt shd; wc; chem disp; baby facs; shwrs inc; el pnts (10A) €3.60 (poss rev pol); gas; lndtte; ice; shop, tradsmn; rest high ssn; snacks; bar; BBQ; playgrnd; pool high ssn; sand beach 2km; tennis; games area; cycle hire; internet; TV; dogs; bus 300m; Eng spkn; adv bkg; quiet; CCI. "V peaceful, friendly, under-used site away fr cr beach sites; clean facs; req blocks for levelling; gd touring base." ♦ 15 Jun-15 Sep. € 20.25   2006*

BIELSA *3B2* (8km W Rural) **Camping Pineta, Ctra del Parador, Km 7, 22350 Bielsa (Huesca)** [974-50 10 89; fax 974-50 11 84; www.campingpineta. com] Fr A138 in Beilsa turn W & foll sp for Parador Monte Perdido & Valle de Pineta. Site on L after 8km (ignore previous campsite off rd). Lge, terr, pt sl, pt shd; wc; chem disp; baby facs; shwrs inc; el pnts (6A) €4.17 (poss rev pol); gas; lndtte; shop & 8km; rest; snacks; bar; BBQ; playgrnd; pool; games area; cycle hire; some statics; phone; cc acc; CCI. "Well-maintained site; clean facs; glorious location in National Park." Easter-10 Dec. € 17.48   2006*

⊞**BIESCAS** *3B2* (3km SE Rural) **Camping Gavín, Ctra N260, Km 503, 22639 Biescas (Huesca)** [974-48 50 90 or 659-47 95 51; fax 974-48 50 17; info@ campinggavin.com; www.campinggavin.com] Take N330/A23/E7 N fr Huesca twd Sabiñánigo then N260 twd Biescas & Valle de Tena. Bear R on N260 at Biescas & foll sp Gavín & site. Site is at km 503 fr Huesca, bet Biescas & Gavín. Lge, mkd pitch, terr, pt shd; htd wc; chem disp; mv service pnt; baby facs; fam bthrm; shwrs inc; el pnts (10A) €4.80; gas; lndtte; ice; shop; tradsmn; rest; snacks; bar; playgrnd; pool; tennis; cycle hire in National Park; wifi internet; TV rm; 20% statics; dogs €1; phone; bus 1km; adv bkg; quiet; CCI. "Wonderful site on edge of Ordesa National Park; poss diff access to pitches for lge o'fits & m'vans; super views; immac san facs; excel." ♦ € 22.40 (CChq acc)   2006*

⊞**BILBAO** *1A4* (14km N Coastal) **Camping Sopelana, Ctra Bilbao-Plentzia, Km 18, Playa Atxabiribil 30, 48600 Sopelana (Vizcaya)** [946-76 19 81; fax 944-21 50 10; recepcion@campingsopelana.com; www.campingsopelana.com] In Bilbao cross rv by m'way bdge sp to airport, foll 637/634 N twd & Plentzia. Cont thro Sopelana & foll sp on L. Med, hdg pitch, sl, terr; wc (some cont); own san; chem disp; mv service pnt; baby facs; shwrs; el pnts (10A) €3.50; gas; lndtte; shop, rest (w/e only low ssn); snacks; bar; playgrnd; pool; sand beach 200m; 70% statics; metro 1km; poss cr; Eng spkn; adv bkg ess high ssn; quiet but noise fr disco adj; red long stay; CCI. "Conv Bilbao & Guggenheim museum; poss stong sea winds; v ltd space for tourers; pitches sm, poss flooded after heavy rain & poss diff due narr, steep site access rds; ltd facs low ssn & poss v unclean; poss no hot water for shwrs; v helpful manager; used by local workers; poor security in city cent/Guggenheim car park; NH/sh stay only." ♦ € 26.20　　　2007*

BLANES *3C3* (1km S Coastal) **Camping Bella Terra, Avda Vila de Madrid 35-40, 17300 Blanes (Gerona)** [972-34 80 17 or 972-34 80 23; fax 972-34 82 75; info@campingbellaterra.com; www.campingbellaterra.com] Exit A7 junc 9 via Lloret or junc 10 via Tordera. On app Blanes, all campsites are sp at rndabts; all sites along same rd. V lge, mkd pitch, shd; wc; chem disp; mv service pnt; baby facs; shwrs inc; el pnts (5A) inc; gas; lndtte; ice; shop; tradsmn; rest; snacks; bar; BBQ; playgrnd; pools; sand beach adj; tennis; games area; games rm; cycle hire; entmnt; internet; TV; 50% statics; dogs €4.50; Eng spkn; quiet; cc acc; red long stay/CCI. "Split site - 1 side has pool, 1 side adj beach; some pitches poss diff for lge o'fits - pitches on pool side lger; vg site." ♦ 15 Mar-30 Sep. € 40.00　　　2007*

See advertisement on next page (bottom)

Spain

⊞BLANES *3C3* (1km S Coastal) **Camping Blanes, Avda Villa Madrid 33, 17300 Blanes (Gerona)** [972-33 15 91; fax 972-33 70 63; info@campingblanes.com; www.campingblanes.com] Fr N on AP7/E15 exit junc 9 onto NII dir Barcelona. In 15km at 1st traff lts turn L & foll sp Blanes. Fr S to end of C32, then NII dir Blanes. On app Blanes, foll camping sps & Playa S'Abanell - all campsites are sp at rndabts; all sites along same rd. Site adj Hotel Blau-Mar. Lge, mkd pitch, shd; htd wc; chem disp; mv service pnt; shwrs inc; shop; el pnts (5A) inc; gas; lndtte; supmkt; snacks high ssn; bar; playgrnd; pool; dir access to sand beach; watersports; cycle hire; games rm; wifi internet; entmnt; dogs; phone; bus; poss cr; Eng spkn; quiet; cc acc; red low ssn. "Some sm pitches with low-hanging trees; easy walk to town cent; trains to Barcelona & Gerona; excel." ♦ € 32.90   2007*

See advertisement above

BLANES *3C3* (1km S Coastal) **Camping El Pinar Beach, Calle Villa de Madrid s/n, 17300 Blanes (Gerona)** [972-331083; fax 972-331100; camping@elpinarbeach.com; www.elpinarbeach.com] Exit AP7/E15 junc 9 dir Malgrat. On app Blanes, all campsites are sp at rndabts; all sites along same rd. V lge, mkd pitch, shd; wc; chem disp; mv service pnt; baby facs; shwrs inc; el pnts (5A) inc; lndtte; ice; shop; rest; snacks; bar; BBQ; playgrnd; pool; sand beach adj; games area; entmnt; excursions; TV; 10% statics; dogs; phone; adv bkg; cc acc; red long stay/CCI. "V pleasant site; gd facs; lovely beach; lots to do." ♦ ltd 31 Mar-30 Sep. € 29.60   2007*

See advertisement opposite

⊞**BLANES** *3C3* (1km S Coastal) **Camping S'Abanell, Avda Villa de Madrid 7-9, 17300 Blanes (Gerona)** [972-33 18 09; fax 972-35 05 06; info@sabanell.com; www.sabanell.com] Take coast rd S fr cent Blanes. Site well sp on L in 1km. Lge, mkd pitch, pt sl, shd; wc; chem disp; serviced pitches; shwrs; el pnts (6A) €2.70; gas; lndtte; shop; rest; snacks; bar; sand beach adj; 5% statics; dogs €1; phone; site clsd 25 Dec-7 Jan; poss cr; adv bkg; rd noise; red low ssn/snr citizens; CCI. "Friendly, helpful staff; lge o'fits need manhandling due trees & pitch layout." € 29.80   2007*

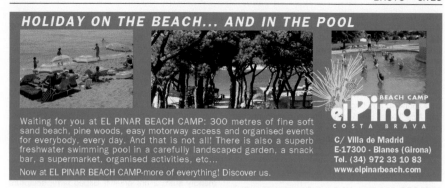

⊞**BLANES** *3C3* (1.5km SW Urban/Coastal) **Camping La Masia, Calle Colon 44, 17300 Blanes (Gerona) [972-33 10 13; fax 972-33 31 28; info@campinglamasia.com; www.campinglamasia.com]** Fr A7 exit junc 9 sp Lloret de Mar, then Blanes. At Blanes foll sp Blanes Sur & Campings, site immed past Camping S'Abanell. V lge, hdstg, pt shd; htd wc; chem disp; mv service pnt; 25% serviced pitches; sauna; steam rm; shwrs inc; el pnts (3-5A) inc; lndtte; shop; rest; snacks; bar; playgrnd; 2 pools (1 htd, covrd); sand beach nrby; watersports; tennis 500m; weights rm; entmnt; TV rm; 70% statics; dogs; poss cr; Eng spkn; adv bkg; poss noisy at w/ends; red long stay/low ssn; CCI. "Well-maintained site; excel, clean facs; helpful staff." ♦ € 38.50 (CChq acc)   2006*

BOCA DE HUERGANO see Riaño *1A3*

⊞**BOCAIRENT** *4F2* (9km E Rural) **Camping Mariola, Ctra Bocairent-Alcoi, Km 9, 46880 Bocairent (València) [962-13 51 60; fax 962-13 50 31; info@campingmariola.com; www.campingmariola.com]** Fr N330 turn E at Villena onto CV81. N of Banyeres & bef Bocairent turn E sp Alcoi up narr, steep hill with some diff turns & sheer drops; site sp. Lge, hdstg, pt shd; htd wc (cont); mv service pnt; shwrs inc; el pnts (6A) €4; lndtte; shop; rest; snacks; bar; BBQ; cooking facs; playgrnd; pool; paddling pool; games area; internet; child entmnt; 50% statics; phone; cc acc; CCI. "In Mariola mountains; gd walking." € 17.55 (CChq acc)   2007*

BOLTANA see Ainsa *3B2*

BONANSA see Pont de Suert *3B2*

⊞**BOSSOST** *3B2* (3km SE Rural) **Camping Prado Verde, 25551 Era Bordeta/La Bordeta de Vilamòs (Lleida) [973-64 71 72; fax 973-64 04 56; joseluisperise@hotmail.com; www.campingpradoverde.es]** On N230 at km 173 on banks of Rv Garona. Med, shd; wc; baby facs; mv service pnt; shwrs; el pnts €4.80; lndtte; shop & 3km; rest; snacks; bar; playgrnd; pool; fishing; cycle hire; TV; some statics; no dogs; bus 1km; quiet; cc acc; CCI. "V pleasant NH." € 20.40   2006*

BOSSOST *3B2* (4km S Rural) **Camping Bedura Park, Ctra N230, Km 174.5, 25551 Era Bordeta (Lleida) [973-64 82 93; fax 973-64 70 38; info@bedurapark.com; www.bedurapark.com]** Fr N on N230, R over rv behind Camping Forcanada. Fr S on N230, 10km fr Viela, L turn over rv. Site is 12km fr French border. Med, mkd pitch, terr, pt shd; wc; chem disp; baby facs; shwrs; el pnts (5A) €3.50; gas; lndtte; shop; rest; BBQ; playgrnd; htd pool; fishing; cycle hire; 20% statics; no dogs; phone; bus 200m; poss cr; Eng spkn; adv bkg (dep req); CCI. "Skiing, walking in area; excel." ♦ 1 Apr-30 Sep. € 21.50   2004*

BROTO *3B2* (3km N Rural) **Camping Rió Ara, Ctra Ordesa s/n, 22376 Torla (Huesca) [974-48 62 48; fax 974-48 63 52]** Leave N260 on bend approx 2km N of Broto sp Torla & Ordesa National Park. Drive thro Torla; as leaving vill turn R sp Rió Ara. Steep, narr rd down to & across narr bdge (worth it). Med, pt sl, pt shd; wc; chem disp (wc); baby facs; shwrs inc; el pnts (5A) €4.39; lndtte; shop; tradsmn; rest 500m; bar; no statics; phone; cc not acc; CCI. "Attractive, well-kept site; mainly tents; conv for Torla; bus to Ordesa National Park (high ssn); not rec for lge o'fits due to steep app; gd walking & birdwatching; excel." Easter-31 Oct. € 18.20   2006*

BROTO *3B2* (5km N Rural) **Camping Ordesa, 22376 Torla (Huesca) [974-48 61 25; fax 974-48 63 81]** Fr Ainsa on N260 twd Torla. Pass Torla turn R onto A135 (Valle de Ordesa twd Ordesa National Park. Site 2km N of Torla, adj Hotel Ordesa. Med, pt shd; wc; chem disp; serviced pitch; baby facs; shwrs; el pnts (6A) €3; gas 2km; lndtte; shop 2km, tradsmn; rest high ssn; bar; playgrnd; pool; tennis; some statics (sep area); phone; bus 1km; poss cr; Eng spkn; adv bkg (ess Jul/Aug); quiet; red low ssn; cc acc; CCI. "V scenic; recep in adj Hotel Ordesa; excel rest; v helpful staff; facs poss stretched w/e; long, narr pitches & lge trees on access rd poss diff lge o'fits; ltd facs low ssn; no access to National Park by car Jul/Aug, shuttlebus fr Torla." Holy Week-12 Oct. € 16.90   2005*

Spain

BROTO *3B2* (1.2km W Rural) **Camping Oto, Afueras s/n, 22370 Oto-Broto (Huesca) [974-48 60 75; fax 974-48 63 47; info@campingoto. com; www.campingoto.com]** On N260 foll camp sp on N o'skts of Broto. Diff app thro vill but poss. Lge, pt sl, pt shd; wc; chem disp; baby facs; shwrs inc; el pnts (10A) €3.30 (poss no earth); gas; lndtte; shop; snacks; bar; BBQ; playgrnd; pool; paddling pool; entmnt; adv bkg; quiet; cc acc. "Excel, clean san facs; excel bar & café; friendly owner; pitches below pool rec; some noise fr adj youth site; conv Ordesa National Park." 6 Mar-14 Oct. € 14.70
2005*

⊞**BROTO** *3B2* (6km W Rural) **Camping Viu, Ctra N260 Biescas-Ordesa, Km 484.2, 22378 Viu de Linás (Huesca) [974-48 63 01; fax 974-48 63 73; info@campingviu.com; www.campingviu.com]** Lies on N260, 4km W of Broto. Fr Broto, N for 2km on rd 135; turn W twd Biesca at junc with Torla rd; site approx 4km on R. Med, sl, pt shd; htd wc; chem disp; mv service pnt; shwrs inc; el pnts (5-8A) €4; gas; lndtte; shop; rest; BBQ; playgrnd; games rm; cycle hire; horseriding; walking, skiing & climbing adj; car wash; phone; adv bkg; quiet; cc acc; CCI. "Friendly owners; gd home cooking; fine views; highly rec; clean, modern san facs." € 16.50
2005*

BURGO DE OSMA, EL *1C4* (17km N Rural) **Camping Cañón del Rió Lobos, Ctra Burgo de Osma-San Leonardo, 42317 Ucero (Soria) [tel/ fax 975-36 35 65]** On SO 920 17km N fr El Burgo de Osma or S fr San Leonardo de Yagüe. Site 1km N of Ucero. Care needed over narr bdge in vill cent. Med, hdg/mkd pitch, hdstg & grass, shd; wc; chem disp; shwrs inc; el pnts (6A) €4.85; ice; lndtte; rest; snacks; bar; BBQ; playgrnd; pool; no dogs; quiet; no cc acc; CCI. "Sm pitches/tight turning; help avail; heart of canyon of Rv Lobos; v pretty location; gd base walking, cycling, climbing; bird watchers' paradise; poss w/e only until beginning Jun." Easter-30 Sep. € 22.50
2007*

⊞**BURGOS** *1B4* (4km NE Urban) **Camping Rió Vena, Km 245, Burgos-Irún, 09192 Villafría de Burgos (Burgos) [947-48 41 20]** Leave m'way AP1 at junc 2. Foll N1 twd city. On sight of 1st camp sp take service rd (parallel to N1) for 1km to site on R bet industrial units. Sp quite poor. Important to get into service rd early as no direct access fr N1 dual c'way to site. Sm, pt sl, pt shd; wc; shwrs inc; el pnts (10A) €4.20 (no earth); gas; lndtte; tradsmn; rest; bar; shop; bus to Burgos at gate; poss cr; rd noise; cc acc; CCI. "Clean facs; delightful owner; v helpful staff; sm uneven, dusty pitches; many trees - poss diff lge o'fits; conv Burgos cathedral; indus est nrby; heavy traffic noise; NH only; poss clsd low ssn." € 14.40
2005*

⊞**BURGOS** *1B4* (22km NE Rural) **Camping Picon del Conde, Ctra N1 Madrid-Irún, Km 263, 09292 Monasterio de Rodilla (Burgos) [tel/fax 947-59 43 55]** Fr Burgos, leave E80 at junc 3 & join N1 twd Burgos. Site is on L after passing under 2nd m'way bridge. Fr S or W head N on AP1/E80 & leave at junc 2, head N on N1 over pass (max gradient 12%). Site about 500m past Monasterio de Rodilla on R. Med, hdg/mkd pitch, shd; htd wc; chem disp; shwrs inc; el pnts (5A) €3.60; gas; lndry rm; shop; rest; snacks; bar; playgrnd; pool; 75% statics; dogs; phone; rd noise; cc acc; CCI. "Ltd facs low ssn; poss migrant workers; caution el pnts; awkward access to san facs & wash-up on 1st floor, shwrs on 2nd; site muddy in wet weather; friendly staff; 2 hrs drive fr Bilbao ferry; sculpture gallery adj worth a visit; fair NH only." ♦ € 14.34
2006*

⊞**BURGOS** *1B4* (3.5km E Rural) **Camping Fuentes Blancas, Ctra Cartuja Miraflores, Km 3.5, 09193 Burgos [tel/fax 947-48 60 16; info@ campingburgos.com; www.campingburgos.com]** Fr N foll sp for N1 Madrid S thro Burgos. After x-ing rv in cent of town take slip rd to R sp León; site sp. Fr W (easiest app) on A62 keep rv on L, site eventually sp. Fr m'way exit junc 238, 1st R sp Cortes then L sp Burgos; over rlwy x-ing, turn R onto S bank of rv, site sp. Lge, mkd pitch, shd; htd wc; chem disp; mv service pnt; baby facs; shwrs inc; el pnts (6A) inc; gas; ice; lndtte; shop high ssn & 3km; rest; snacks; bar; playgrnd; pool high ssn; games area; 10% statics; dogs €2; phone; bus at gate; poss cr; Eng spkn; quiet, some rd noise; cc acc. "V clean facs & plenty of hot water; neat, roomy site but some sm pitches; ltd facs low ssn & poss itinerants; poss v muddy in wet; recep open 0800-2200; gd bar/rest; easy access town car parks; Burgos lovely town with art gallery & cathedral; cycle paths & attractive walk into city; gd, improving NH en rte S." € 21.50
2007*

CABO DE GATA see Almería *4G1*

⊞**CABRERA, LA** *1D4* (4km S Rural) **Camping d'Oremor, Ctra Cabanillas-Bustarviejo, 28721 Cabanillas de la Sierra (Madrid) [918-43 90 34; fax 918-43 90 09; doremor@doremor.com; www. doremor.com]** Fr Madrid N on A1/E5 exit junc 50 onto M608; in 500m turn N parallel to E5/N1. Site clearly sp in 3km. Med, shd; htd wc; chem disp; mv service pnt; shwrs inc; el pnts €4.70; gas; lndtte; shop; rest; snacks; bar; playgrnd; pool; lake sw & fishing adj; tennis; mainly statics; dogs; bus 700m; poss cr; adv bkg; quiet; cc acc. "Ltd facs low ssn & site run down, untidy; dated facs; check el pnts carefully; windsurfing on lake & skiing in area in winter; take care marble floor tiles in shwrs - v slippery when wet; NH only." ♦ € 19.70
2007*

⊞**CABRERA, LA** *1D4* (1km SW Rural) **Camping Pico de la Miel, Ctra N1, Km 58, Finca Prado Nuevo, 28751 La Cabrera (Madrid) [918-68 80 82 or 918-68 81 20; fax 918-68 68 41; pico-miel@ sierranorte.com; www.picodelamiel.com]** Fr Madrid on A1/E5, exit junc 57 sp La Cabrera. Turn L at rndabt, site sp. Lge, mkd pitch, pt sl, pt shd; htd wc; chem disp; shwrs inc; el pnts (10A) €4; gas; lndtte; shop high ssn; supmkt 1km; rest, snacks, bar high ssn & w/e; playgrnd; Olympic-size pool; paddling pool; sailing; fishing; windsurfing; tennis; games area; squash; mountain-climbing; car wash; 75% statics; dogs; phone; v cr high ssn & w/e; some Eng spkn; adv bkg; quiet; cc acc; red long stay/CCI. "Attractive walking country; 30 mins fr Madrid; ltd touring area not v attractive; some pitches have low sun shades; interesting park adj; excel san facs; ltd facs low ssn." ♦ ltd. € 22.20
2007*

⊞**CABRERA, LA** *1D4* (15km SW Rural) **Camping Piscis, Ctra Guadalix de la Sierra a Navalafuente, Km 3, 28729 Navalafuente (Madrid) [918-43 22 68; fax 918-43 22 53; campiscis@campiscis.com; www.campiscis.com]** Fr A1/E5 exit junc 50 onto M608 dir Guidalix de la Sierra, foll sp to Navalafuente & site. Lge, hdg pitch, hdstg, pt sl, pt shd; wc; chem disp; shwrs €0.30; el pnts (5A) €3.40 (long lead req); gas; lndtte; shop 6km; rest; snacks; bar; playgrnd; pool; paddling pool; watersports 10km; tennis; games area; 75% statics; quiet; adv bkg; Eng spkn; 10% red 6+ days low ssn; cc acc; CCI. "Mountain views; walking; bus to Madrid daily outside gate, 1 hr ride; spacious pitches but uneven; rough site rds; v ltd facs, poss unclean low ssn & poss no hot water." ♦ € 21.40
2007*

⊞**CACERES** *2E3* (2km NW Urban) **Camp Municipal Ciudad de Cáceres, Ctra N630, Km 549.5, 10080 Cáceres [tel/fax 927-23 31 00; info@ campingcaceres.com; www.campingcaceres. com]** Fr Cáceres ring rd take N630 dir Salamanca. At 1st rndbt turn R sp Via de Servicio with camping symbol. Foll sp 500m to site. Or fr N exit A66 junc 545 onto N630 twd Cáceres. At 2nd rndabt turn L sp Via de Servicio, site on L adj football stadium. Med, mkd pitch, hdstg, terr, pt shd; wc; chem disp; mv service pnt; individ san facs each pitch; shwrs inc; el pnts (10-16A) €3; gas; lndtte; ice; shop; rest; snacks; bar; BBQ; playgrnd; pool; paddling pool; games area; wifi internet; TV; 15% statics; dogs; bus 100m over footbdge; Eng spkn; adv bkg; noise fr indus est nrby; cc acc; red CCI. "Vg site; excel facs; vg value rest; gd for disabled access." € 17.40
2007*

CADAQUES *3B3* (1km N Coastal) **Camping Cadaqués, Ctra Port Lligat 17, 17488 Cadaqués (Gerona) [972-25 81 26; fax 972-15 93 83; info@ campingcadaques.com]** At ent to town, turn L onto tarmac rd thro narr streets, site in about 1.5km on L. NB App to Cadaqués on busy, narr mountain rds, not suitable lge o'fits. If raining, roads only towable with 4x4. Lge, mkd pitch, hdstg, sl, pt shd; wc; chem disp; shwrs; el pnts (5A) €3.70; gas; lndtte; shop; rest; bar; playgrnd; pools; shgl beach 600m; no dogs; sep car park; poss cr; Eng spkn; no adv bkg; quiet; cc acc. "Cadaqués home of Salvador Dali; sm pitches; medical facs high ssn; san facs poss poor low ssn; fair." 10 Apr-30 Sep. € 22.15
2004*

CADAVEDO see Luarca *1A3*

> Did you know you can fill in site report forms on the Club's website — www.caravanclub.co.uk?

⊞**CALATAYUD** *3C1* (15km N Rural) **Camping Saviñan Parc, Ctra El Frasno-Illueca, Km 7, 50299 Saviñan (Zaragoza) [tel/fax 976-82 54 23]** Exit A2/E90 (Zaragoza-Madrid) at km 255 to T-junc. Turn R to Saviñan for 6km, foll sps to site 1km S. Lge, hdstg, terr, pt shd; wc; chem disp; mv service pnt; shwrs; el pnts (10A) €3.85 (adaptor req); gas; lndry rm; shop 1.5km; rest; snacks; bar; playgrnd; pool high ssn; tennis; horseriding; phone; some statics; dogs €2.70; cc acc; CCI. "Beautiful scenery; helpful, friendly staff; some sm narr pitches; rec identify pitch location to avoid stop/start on hill; terr pitches have steep, unfenced edges; many pitches with sunscreen frames & diff to manoeuvre long o'fits; all hot water on coin slots; modern facs block but cold in winter & poss stretched high ssn; site poss clsd Feb." € 17.12
2007*

⊞**CALATAYUD** *3C1* (3km E) **Camping Calatayud, Ctra Madrid-Barcelona, Km 239, 50300 Calatayud (Zaragoza) [976-88 05 92]** Fr W exit A2 sp Calatayud; site on S side of old N11 (parallel to new dual c'way) at km stone 239a. Med, pt shd; wc; chem disp; shwrs inc; el pnts (5-10A) €4 (rev pol); gas; lndtte; snacks; shop 2km; pool; dogs; some rd noise; cc acc; CCI. "Site area bleak; facs, inc pool, poorly maintained; run-down/dirty low ssn; interesting town, Moorish features; excel excursion to Monasterio de Piedra; NH only, not rec." 15 Mar-15 Oct. € 17.10
2006*

Spain

CALELLA *3C3* (2km NE Coastal) **Camping Caballo de Mar, Passeig Maritim s/n, 08397 Pineda de Mar (Barcelona) [937-67 17 06; fax 937-67 16 15; info@caballodemar.com; www.caballodemar.com]** Fr N exit AP7 junc 9 & immed turn R onto NII dir Barcelona. Foll sp Pineda de Mar & turn L twd Paseo Maritimo. Fr S on C32 exit 122 dir Pineda de Mar & foll dir Paseo Maritimo. Lge, mkd pitch, shd; wc; chem disp; baby facs; shwrs inc; el pnts (3-6A) €3.40-4.40; gas; lndtte; ice; shop; tradsmn; rest; snacks; bar; BBQ; playgrnd; pool; sand beach adj; games area; games rm; entmnt; internet; 10% statics; dogs €2.20; rlwy stn 2km (Barcelona 30 mins); Eng spkn; adv bkg; quiet; cc acc; red long stay/CCI. "Excursions arranged; gd touring base & conv Barcelona; gd, modern facs; excel." ♦ 31 Mar-30 Sep. € 25.60   2007*

⊞**CALELLA** *3C3* (1km S Coastal) **Camping Botànic Bona Vista Kim, Ctra N11, Km 665, 08370 Calella de la Costa (Barcelona) [937-69 24 88; fax 937-69 58 04; info@botanic-bonavista.net; www.botanic-bonavista.net]** A19/C32 exit sp Calella onto NII coast rd, site is sp S of Calella on R. Care needed on busy rd & sp almost on top of turning (adj Camp Roca Grossa). Lge, mkd pitch, hdstg, terr, pt shd; shwrs inc; wc; chem disp; mv service pnt; sauna; shwrs inc; el pnts (6A) €6.42 (rev pol); lndtte; supmkt; rest; snacks; bar; BBQ/picnic area; playgrnd; pool; sand beach adj; solarium; jacuzzi; TV; 20% statics; dogs €4.81; phone; poss cr; Eng spkn; adv bkg; some rd noise; CCI. "V steep access rd to site - owner prefers to tow c'vans with 4x4; poss diff v lge m'vans; all pitches have sea view; v friendly owner; spotless facs; train to Barcelona fr St Pol (2km)." ♦ € 25.46   2006*

CALELLA *3C3* (1km SW Coastal) **Camping Roca Grossa, Ctra N-11, Km 665, 08370 Calella (Barcelona) [937-69 12 97; fax 937-66 15 56; rocagrossa@rocagrossa.com; www.rocagrossa. com]** Situated off rd N11 at km stone 665, site sp. V steep access rd to site. Lge, sl, terr, shd; wc; chem disp; mv service pnt; shwrs inc; el pnts (6A) €4.75; gas; ice; lndtte; shop; rest; snacks; bar; games rm; TV rm; pool; playgrnd; beach adj; windsurfing; tennis; statics; phone; dogs €3.40; adv bkg; Eng spkn; cc acc. "V friendly, family-run site; steep site - tractor pull avail; modern facs; excel pool & playgrnd on top of hill; scenic drive to Tossa de Mar; conv for Barcelona." 1 Apr-30 Sep. € 25.80   2006*

CALONGE see Playa de Aro *3B3*

⊞**CALPE** *4F2* (1km N Urban/Coastal) **Camping La Merced, Ctra de la Cometa, 03710 Calpe (Alicante) [965-83 00 97]** Exit A7/E15 at junc 63 & foll sp Calpe Norte down hill to traff lts & turn L. Foll dual c'way round Calpe, past Peñón de Ifach. Pass Cmp Levante on L, at next rndabt turn L, site on R in 400m. Med, mkd pitch, hdstg, pt terr, shd; htd wc; chem disp; mv service pnt; shwrs inc; el pnts (10A) €3.20 (poss long cable req); gas; lndtte; shop; rest 150m; snacks; bar; BBQ; pool adj; sand beach 400m; TV rm; 10% statics; dogs; phone; bus 50m; poss cr; Eng spkn; adv bkg; poss noisy; red long stay/low ssn; CCI. "Gd san facs; improved site; log fire in bar in winter; fair site." ♦ € 23.10   2007*

⊞**CALPE** *4F2* (1km N Urban/Coastal) **Camping Levante, Avda de la Marina s/n, 03710 Calpe (Alicante) [tel/fax 965-83 22 72; info@campinglevantecalpe.com; www.campinglevantecalpe.com]** Fr N332 (Alicante-València) take slip rd sp Calpe. Foll dual c'way round Calpe past Peñón-de-Ifach . Pass site on L, cont to rndabt & back to site. Sm, hdstg, shd; wc; chem disp; shwrs inc; el pnts (6A) inc; lndtte; shop; rest; snacks; bar; sand beach 500m; 10% statics; dogs; quiet; adv bkg; cc acc; red long stay; CCI. "Site liable to flood after heavy rain; in need of improvement - new owner 2007; currently poor value." € 25.20   2007*

⊞**CAMARASA** *3B2* (23km N Rural) **Camping Zodiac, Ctra C13, Km 66, La Baronia de Sant Oïsme, 25615 Camarasa (Lleida) [tel/fax 973-45 50 03; zodiac@campingzodiac.com; www. campingzodiac.com]** Fr C13 Lleida to Balaguer. N of Balaguer take C13 & foll sp for Camarasa, then dir Tremp & site. Steep, winding but scenic app rd. Med, hdstg, pt sl, terr, pt shd; wc; chem disp; baby facs; shwrs; el pnts (5A) €4.60; shop; lndtte; rest; snacks; bar; playgrnd; pool; rv sw adj; tennis; TV; 90% statics; phone; Eng spkn; quiet; cc acc. "Site on reservoir; poss untidy, shabby low ssn; some sm pitches diff due trees; excel views & walks; Terradets Pass 2km." ♦ ltd. € 18.80   2007*

CAMBRILS See also Salou

⊞**CAMBRILS** *3C2* (1km N Coastal) **Camping Àmfora d'Arcs, Ctra N340, Km 1145, Vinyols i Els Arcs, 43850 Cambrils (Tarragona) [977-36 12 11; fax 977-79 50 75; campingamfora@amforadarcs. com; www.amforadarcs.com]** Exit A7 junc 37 onto N340 & watch for km sps, site bet 1145 & 1146km. Lge, hdg pitch, hdstg, pt shd; wc; chem disp; shwrs inc; el pnts (5A) inc; gas; lndtte; supmkt opp; rest high ssn; bar; playgrnd; pool; beach 1.5km; 60% statics; dogs €3.75; phone; site clsd Jan; poss cr; Eng spkn; adv bkg; noisy espec at w/e; cc acc; red 7+ days low ssn; CCI. "Sm pitches; high ssn elec mandatory; NH only." € 26.50

2005*

CAMBRILS *3C2* (1.5km N Urban/Coastal) **Camping Playa Cambrils Don Camilo, Ctra Salou-Cambrils, Km 1.5, 43850 Cambrils (Tarragona) [977-36 14 90; fax 977-36 49 88; camping@ playacambrils.com; www.playacambrils.com]** Exit A7 junc 37 dir Cambrils & N340. Turn L onto N340 then R dir Port then L onto coast rd N twd Salou on N340. Site sp on L after rv bdge 100m bef watch tower on R approx 2km fr port. Slow app req not to overshoot. V lge, hdg/mkd pitch, shd; wc; chem disp; baby facs; shwrs inc; el pnts (5A) inc; gas; lndtte; ice; supmkt; rest; snacks; bar; playgrnd; htd pool; sand beach adj; tennis; games rm; boat hire; cycle hire; watersports; entmnt; children's club; cinema; TV rm; 25% statics; bus to Port Aventura; cash machine; doctor; 24-hour security; dogs €4.20; Eng spkn; adv bkg ess high ssn; some rd & rlwy noise; cc acc; 25-45% red long stay/low ssn; 10% red CCI. "Excel site; lge pitches; helpful, friendly staff; sports activities avail; Port Aventura 5km." ♦ 15 Mar-12 Oct. € 37.20

2007*

See advertisement opposite

⊞**CAMBRILS** *3C2* (S Urban/Coastal) **Camping La Llosa, Ctra N340, Km 1143, 43850 Cambrils (Tarragona) [977-36 26 15; fax 977-79 11 80; camping-lallosa@telefonica.net; www.camping-lallosa.com]** Exit A7/E15 at junc 37 & join N340 S. Head S into Cambrils (ignore L turn to cent) & at traff lts turn R. Site sp on L within 100m. Fr N exit junc 35 onto N340. Strt over at x-rds, then L over rlwy bdge at end of rd, strt to site. V lge, hdstg, shd; wc; shwrs inc; el pnts (5A) €4; gas; lndtte; ice; shop; rest; snacks; bar; playgrnd; pool; sand beach; entmnt high ssn; car wash; 50% statics; dogs €2.20; phone; bus 500m; poss cr; Eng spkn; some rd & rlwy noise; cc acc; red long stay. "Interesting fishing port; v clean wc; excel pool; gd supmkt nrby; poss diff siting for m'vans due low trees; excel winter NH." ♦ € 23.10   2006*

This guide relies on site report forms submitted by caravanners like us; we'll do our bit and tell the editor what we think of the campsites we've visited.

CAMBRILS *3C2* (2km S Coastal) **Camping Joan, Calle Pedro III 14, 43850 Cambrils (Tarragona) [977-36 46 04 or 977-36 15 57; fax 977-36 46 04; info@campingjoan.com; www.campingjoan. com]** Exit AP7 junc 37 onto N340, S dir València. Turn off at km 1.141 & Hotel Daurada, foll site sp. Lge, hdg/mkd pitch, hdstg, terr, shd; htd wc; chem disp; mv service pnt; baby facs; shwrs inc; el pnts (5A) €4.17; gas; lndtte; supmkt; rest; snacks; bar; BBQ; playgrnd; pool & paddling pool; sand beach adj; watersports; fishing; games area; games rm; entmnt; internet; sat TV; 16% statics; dogs €2.35; phone; currency exchange; car wash; Eng spkn; adv bkg; quiet; red low ssn/long stay/CCI. "Conv Port Aventura; family site; v clean san facs; friendly welcome; some sm pitches; vg." ♦ 1 Mar-19 Oct. € 24.88   2007*

See advertisement on next page

CAMBRILS *3C2* (5km SW Coastal) **Camping Oasis Mar, Ctra de València, 43892 Montroig (Tarragona) [977-17 95 95; fax 977-17 95 16; info@oasismar.com; www.oasismar.com]** Fr A7 exit 37; N340 Tarragona-València rd, at Montroig, km 1139. Lge, mkd pitch, pt shd; wc; chem disp; shwrs inc; baby facs; el pnts (6A) €3.75; gas; lndtte; ice; shop; rest; snacks; bar; BBQ; playgrnd; pool; sand beach adj; watersports; 30% statics; dogs €4; Eng spkn; red long ssn/low ssn. "Helpful staff; busy at w/e when statics occupied; vg." 1 Mar-31 Oct. € 22.00   2004*

Spain

CAMBRILS *3C2* (7km SW Coastal) **Camping Els Prats**, Ctra N340, Km 1137, 43892 Miami Playa (Tarragona) [977-81 00 27; fax 977-17 09 01; info@campingelsprats.com; www.campingelsprats.com] Exit AP7 junc 37 onto N340 twds València. At km 1137 turn dir Camping Marius, under rlwy bdge & turn R to site. Lge, mkd pitch, shd; wc; chem disp; mv service pnt; baby facs; shwrs; el pnts (5A) €4.50; lndtte; shop; rest; snacks; bar; playgrnd; pool; sand beach adj; watersports; games area; tennis 100m; horseriding 3km; golf 6km; cycle hire; entmnt; TV; 20% statics; dogs €2.50 (not acc end Jun-mid Aug); adv bkg; quiet; cc acc. "Pleasant, family site." ♦ 9 Mar-14 Oct. € 32.00 (CChq acc)
2007*

CAMBRILS *3C2* (7km SW Coastal) **Camping Marius**, N-340km 1137, Miami Playa, 43892 Montroig (Tarragona) [977-81 06 84; fax 977-17 96 58; info@campingmarius.com; www.campingmarius.com] Exit AP7 junc 37 onto N340 twds València. At km 1137 turn dir Camping Marius under rlwy bdge to site. Lge, hdg/mkd pitch, shd; wc; baby facs; shwrs inc; el pnts (6A) €3; gas; lndtte; ice; shop; snacks; bar; playgrnd; shgl beach; dogs €3.50; phone; poss cr; adv bkg (ess Jul-Aug); overflow v cramped); cc acc; red low ssn/long stay/snr citizens. "Well-managed, friendly campsite; poss noise fr night club, rd & rlwy." ♦ Easter-15 Oct. € 32.00
2007*

CAMBRILS *3C2* (8km SW Coastal) **Playa Montroig Camping Resort**, N340, Km1.136, 43300 Montroig (Tarragona) [977-81 06 37; fax 977-81 14 11; info@playamontroig.com; www.playamontroig.com] Exit AP7 fr m'way 37, W onto N340. Site has own dir access onto N340 bet Cambrils & Hospitalet, well sp fr Cambrils. V lge, mkd pitch, pt sl, shd; htd wc; chem disp; mv service pnt; serviced pitches; baby facs; shwrs inc; el pnts (10A) inc; gas; lndtte; ice; supmkt; rest; snacks; bars; playgrnd; 3 htd pools; sand beach adj; tennis; games area; games rm; skateboard track; sports & child club; disco; mini-golf; cycle hire; golf 3km; cash machine; excursions; doctor; entmnt; child entmnt; internet; 30% statics; no dogs; phone; security guards; poss cr; Eng spkn; adv bkg (dep req); some rd & rlwy noise; cc acc; red snr citizens low ssn; CCI. "Magnificent site; unbelievably clean; private, swept beach; some sm pitches & low branches; 4 grades pitch/price; highly rec." ♦ 16 Mar-28 Oct. € 53.00
2007*

> As soon as we get home I'm going to post all these site report forms to the editor for inclusion in next year's guide. I don't want to miss the September deadline.

CAMBRILS *3C2* (8km W Coastal) **Camping La Torre del Sol**, Ctra N340, Km 1136, Miami-Playa, 43300 Montroig Del Camp (Tarragona) [977-81 04 86; fax 977-81 13 06; info@latorredelsol.com; www.latorredelsol.com] Leave A7 València/Barcelona m'way at junc 37 & foll sp Cambrils. After 1.5km join N340 coast rd S for 6km. Watch for site sp 4km bef Miami Playa. Fr S exit AP7 junc 38, foll sp Cambrils on N340. Site on R 4km after Miami Playa. Site ent narr, alt ent avail for lge o'fits. Lge, hdg/mkd pitch, shd; wc; chem disp; mv service pnt; baby facs; sauna; shwrs inc; el pnts (6A) inc (10A avail); gas; lndtte; ice; supmkt; tradsmn; rest; snacks; bar; BBQ; luxury playgrnd; 3 pools; whirlpool; private sand beach; tennis; squash; cycle hire; horseriding; gym; skateboard zone; golf 4km; cinema; disco; wifi internet; entmnt & child entmt; live shows high ssn; day-care cent for children; excursions; doctor; cash machine; hairdresser; TV; 40% statics; no dogs; poss v cr; Eng spkn; adv bkg; quiet, but some rd/rlwy noise & disco; red low ssn. "Well guarded; radios/TVs to be used inside vans only; conv Port Aventura, Aquaparc, Aquopolis; no c'vans over 7m high ssn; excel, attractive site for all ages." ♦ 15 Mar-22 Oct. € 48.50 (CChq acc) ABS - E14   2007*

See advertisement inside the back cover

The opening dates and prices on this campsite have changed. I'll send a site report form to the editor for the next edition of the guide.

CAMPELL *4E2* (1km S Rural) **Camping Vall de Laguar**, Carrer Sant Antoni 24, 03791 La Vall de Laguar (Alicante) [965-57 74 90 or 699-77 35 09; info@campinglaguar.com; www.campinglaguar.com] Exit A7 junc 62 sp Ondara. Turn L to Orba onto CV733 dir Benimaurell & foll sp to Vall de Laguar. In Campell vill (narr rds) fork L & foll site sp uphill (narr rd). Steep ent to site. Lge o'fits ignore sp in vill & turn R to Fleix vill. In Fleix turn L to main rd, downhill to site sp at hairpin. Med, mkd pitch, hdstg, terr, pt shd; htd wc; chem disp; shwrs inc; el pnts (5-10A) €2.72; gas; lndtte; ice; shop 500m; rest; snacks; bar; BBQ; pool; sand beach 18km; 50% statics; dogs €1.28; phone; Eng spkn; adv bkg; quiet; cc acc; red long stay; CCI. "Sm pitches diff for lge o'fits; m'vans 7.50m max; excel home-cooked food in rest; ideal site for walkers; mountain views; friendly owners live on site; excel but rec sm o'fits & m'vans only." ♦ ltd. € 20.16   2006*

CAMPELLO, EL see Alicante *4F2*

CAMPRODON *3B3* (2km S Rural) **Camping Vall de Camprodón**, Ctra Ripoll-Camprodón, C38, Km 7.5, 17867 Camprodón [972-74 05 07; fax 972-13 06 32; info@valldecamprodon.net; www.valldecamprodon.net] Fr Gerona W on C66/C26 to Sant Pau de Segúries. Turn N onto C38 to Camprodón, site sp. Lge, mkd pitch, pt shd; htd wc; mv service pnt; baby facs; shwrs; el pnts (4-10) €3-6; lndtte; shop; rest (w/end & public hols) & 2km; snacks; bar; playgrnd; pool; paddling pool; tennis; games area; horseriding; entmnt; TV; 20% statics; dogs €3.25; bus 200m; adv bkg; quiet. "Camprodón attractive vill; lovely scenery; peaceful." ♦ € 28.80 (CChq acc)   2006*

CANDELARIO see Béjar *1D3*

CANET DE MAR see Arenys de Mar *3C3*

CANGAS DE ONIS *1A3* (16km E Rural) **Camping Picos de Europa**, Ctra Cangas de Onis-Cabrales, Km 6, 33556 Avin (Asturias) [985-84 40 70; fax 985-84 42 40; info@picos-europa.com; www.picos-europa.com] N625 fr Arriondas to Cangas, then AS114 dir Panes for approx 15km. Go thro Avin vill, site on R. Med, terr, pt shd; wc; chem disp; baby facs; shwrs inc; el pnts (5A) €3.48; gas; lndtte; shop; rest; snacks; bar; pool; beach 20km; horseriding; canoeing on local rvs; some statics; phone; poss cr; Eng spkn; adv bkg; some rd noise & goat bells; cc acc; CCI. "Owners v helpful; beautiful, busy, well-run site; vg value rest; new san facs 2007; poss diff access due narr site rds & cr; some sm pitches - lge o'fits may need 2; conv local caves, mountains, National Park, beaches; vg rest." € 19.26   2007*

CANGAS DE ONIS *1A3* (3km SE Rural) **Camping Covadonga**, 33589 Soto de Cangas (Asturias) [tel/fax 985-94 00 97; info@camping-covadonga.com; www.camping-covadonga.com] N625 fr Arriondas to Cangas de Onis, then AS114 twds Covadonga & Panes, cont thro town sp Covadonga. At rndabt take 2nd exit sp Cabrales, site on R in 100m. Med, mkd pitch, pt shd; wc; chem disp; shwrs; el pnts (3A) €3.30 (no earth); shop; supmkt in town; rest; snacks; bar; poss cr; adv bkg; quiet, but slight rd noise; 10% red long stay; CCI. "V sm pitches (approx 5 x 6m); take care with access; site rds v narr; 17 uneven steps to san facs; conv for Picos de Europa; gd." Holy Week & 15 Jun-30 Sep. € 20.00   2006*

CAPMANY see Figueres *3B3*

CARAVIA ALTA see Colunga *1A3*

Spain

Special deals for Members...

The Club has negotiated special rates for members with most ferry operators and Eurotunnel, which give you significant savings over normal retail rates.

We also offer special combined 'Ferry plus Site' rates (minimum 7 nights) that show even greater savings than when booked separately. These 'package' arrangements are available on most ferry routes.

Find out more in our **Travel Service in Europe** brochure
For your copy phone **01342 327410**
or visit our website **www.caravanclub.co.uk**

It's a long way back without The Club's Holiday Insurance

When you travel abroad, don't leave home without The Club's Red Pennant Holiday Insurance, specially designed for caravanners, motor caravanners and trailer tenters.
There are single-trip, annual multi-trip and long-stay cover options, all backed by The Club's own 24-hour Emergency Team, so you can relax knowing you're in experienced hands.

To find out more about our Red Pennant Holiday Insurance call us today on **01342 336633** ref CE08

Get a quote and buy online at
www.caravanclub.co.uk

We're looking forward to hearing from you!

⊞**CARBALLO** *1A2* (6km N Coastal) **Camping Baldayo, Rebordelos, 15684 Carballo (La Coruña)** [981-73 95 29] On AC552 fr La Coruña dir Carballo, turn R approx 3km bef Carballo sp Noicela 8km. In Noicela fork R sp Caión, next L & site sp when app dunes. App fr Arteijo diff for lge vans. Sm, pt sl, terr, pt shd; wc; chem disp; shwrs; el pnts inc; lndtte; shop; snacks; bar; playgrnd; sand beach 500m; 95% statics; no dogs; phone; poss cr; quiet. "Sm pitches & narr camp rds poss diff lge o'fits; poss unkempt low ssn." € 14.80   2006*

CARBALLO *1A2* (10km N Coastal) **Camping As Nevedas, Ctra Carballo-Caión, Km.8.5, 15105 Noicela (La Coruña)** [tel/fax 981-73 95 52; info@ asnevedas.com; www.asnevedas.com] On AC552 fr La Coruña dir Carballo, turn R approx 3km bef Carballo sp Noicela 8km. Site on L in vill. Sm, hdg pitch, pt sl, pt shd; wc; chem disp (wc); serviced pitch; shwrs inc; el pnts (5A) €2.25; gas; lndtte; shop; tradsmn; rest; bar; BBQ; playgrnd; pool; sand beach 2km; golf 2km; 20% statics; dogs; bus fr ent; phone; poss cr; Eng spkn; adv bkg; quiet; red long stay; cc acc; CCI. "Santiago de Compostela 45km; water amusement park 15km; friendly staff; facs slightly run-down low ssn; mkt Sun Carballo; excel." 1 Apr-30 Sep. € 16.65
2007*

CARCHUNA see Motril *2H4*

CARIDAD, LA (EL FRANCO) *1A3* (1km SE Coastal) **Camping Playa de Castelló, Ctra N634, Santander-La Coruña, Km 532, 33758 La Caridad (El Franco) (Asturias)** [985-47 82 77; camping_castello@hotmail.com] On N634/E70 Santander dir La Coruña, turn N at km 532. Site in 200m fr N634, sp fr each direction. Sm, mkd pitch, pt shd; wc; chem disp; baby facs; shwrs inc; el pnts (2-5A) €2; gas; lndtte; shop, tradsmn, bar high ssn only; shgl beach 800m; internet; some statics; dogs €1; bus 200m; Eng spkn; adv bkg; quiet; red long stay/CCI. "A green oasis with character; gd." Holy Week & 1 Jun-30 Sep. € 13.00   2006*

⊞**CARLOTA, LA** *2G3* (1km NE Rural) **Camping Carlos III, Ctra de Madrid-Cádiz Km 430.5, 14100 La Carlota (Córdoba)** [957-30 03 38; fax 957-30 06 97; camping@campingcarlosiii.com; www.campingcarlosiii.com] Approx 25km SW of Córdoba on A4/E5, exit at km 432 turning L under autovia. Turn L at rndabt on main rd, site well sp on L in 800m. Lge, mkd pitch, hdstg, pt sl, pt shd; htd wc (some cont); chem disp; shwrs inc; el pnts (5-10A) €3.70; gas; lndtte; shop; rest; bar; BBQ; playgrnd; pool; horseriding; 30% statics; dogs; phone; Eng spkn; adv bkg; cc acc; red long stay; CCI. "V efficient, well-run site; less cr than Córdoba municipal site; excel pool; gd, clean facs; if pitched under mulberry trees, poss staining fr berries; bus to Córdoba every 2 hrs."♦ € 19.50   2007*

⊞**CAROLINA, LA** *2F4* (12km NE Rural) **Camping Despeñaperros, Calle Infanta Elena s/n, Junto a Autovia de Andulucia, Km 257, 23213 Santa Elena (Jaén)** [953-66 41 92; fax 953-66 19 93; info@ campingdespenaperros.com; www.camping despenaperros.com] Leave A4/E5 at junc 257 or 259, site well sp to N side of vill - municipal leisure complex. Med, mkd pitch, hdstg, pt shd; wc; chem disp; mv service pnt; all serviced pitches; shwrs inc; el pnts (10A) €3.74 (poss rev pol); gas; lndtte; sm shop; tradsmn; rest high ssn; snacks; bar; playgrnd; pool; TV & tel points all pitches; dogs; phone; bus 500m; adv bkg; poss noisy w/e high ssn; red long stay/CCI. "Gd winter NH; gd size pitches but muddy if wet; gd walking area; friendly, helpful staff; v clean san facs; disabled facs (wc only) only useable with manual wheelchair; pleasant wooded location; conv National Park de Despeñaperros & m'way; gd rest; sh walk to vill & shops (ltd opening hrs low ssn)." ♦ ltd. € 16.90   2007*

⊞**CARRION DE LOS CONDES** *1B4* (W Rural) **Camping El Edén, Ctra Vigo-Logroño, Km 200, 34120 Carrión de los Condes (Palencia)** [979-88 11 52] Exit A231 to Carrión. Site sp E & W ents to town off N120 adj Rv Carrión at El Plantio. App poorly sp down narr rds to rv. Suggest park nr Café España & check rte on foot. Med, mkd pitch, pt shd; wc; shwrs; el pnts (5A) €3.50; gas; lndtte; rest; bar; playgrnd; dogs; bus 500m; cc acc. "Pleasant walk to town; basic rvside site; recep in bar/rest; site open w/ends only low ssn; fair NH." ♦ € 14.00
2007*

CARRIZO DE LA RIBERA *1B3* (Urban) **Camping Órbigo, Paraje El Soto, 24270 Carrizo de la Ribera (León)** [987-35 82 50; fax 987-35 78 98] Fr León take LE441 W 20km thro Villanueva & cross bdge onto LE240. Immed after bdge turn R at traff lts, site in 300m. Med, pt shd; wc; shwrs €0.65; el pnts (6A) €1.60; shop; rest 300m; bar; playgrnd adj; pool 500m; fishing; 50% statics; no dogs; phone; bus 500m; poss cr w/e; some rd noise; CCI. "Pleasant, grassy, rvside site." ♦ ltd. 15 Jun-15 Sep. € 9.50   2005*

⊞**CARTAGENA** *4G1* (10km SW Coastal/Rural) **Camping Naturista El Portús (Naturist), 30393 Cartagena (Murcia)** [968-55 30 52; fax 968-55 30 53; elportus@elportus.com; www.elportus.com] Fr N332 Cartagena to Mazarrón rd take E20 to Canteras. In Canteras turn R onto E22 sp Isla Plana & in 500m turn L onto E21 sp Galifa/El Portús. In 2km at rndabt, site ent on L. Lge, mkd pitch; some hdstg, pt shd; wc; chem disp; mv service pnt; shwrs inc; el pnts (6A) inc; gas; lndtte; ice; shop; rest; snacks; bar; playgrnd; htd, covrd pool & paddling pool; shgl beach adj; tennis; games area; gym; spa; golf 15km; internet; entmnt; 30% statics; dogs €3.90; phone; poss cr; Eng spkn; cc acc; red low ssn/long stay; INF card req. "Restful low ssn; gd situation; many long-stay winter visitors; helpful staff; random pitching; Cartagena interesting old town." ♦ ltd. € 30.00 (CChq acc)   2005*

*Last year of report

CASPE *3C2* (12km NE Rural) **Lake Caspe Camping, Ctra N211, Km 286.7, 50700 Caspe (Zaragoza)** [976-63 41 74; fax 976-63 41 87; www.lakecaspe.com] E fr Zaragoza on N11. S at Bujaraloz onto C230. E thro Caspe on N211. In 16km on L at km 286.7, sp. Med, hdg/mkd pitch, hdstg, pt shd; wc; chem disp; baby facs; shwrs inc; el pnts (5A) €4.80; gas; ice; lndtte; shop; rest; snacks; bar; playgrnd; pool high ssn; rv fishing; sailing; 10% statics; dogs €3.35; phone; poss cr; Eng spkn; adv bkg; quiet; CCI. "Gd site but avoid on public hols; beautiful surroundings; sm pitches nr lake; gd water sports; mosquitoes." 18 Mar-5 Nov. € 18.66   2006*

CASTANARES DE LA RIOJA see Haro *1B4*

CASTELLBO see Seo de Urgel *3B3*

CASTELLO D'EMPURIES *3B3* (4km NE Urban) **Camping Mas Nou, Ctra Figueras-Rosas, Km 38, 17486 Castelló d'Empúries (Gerona)** [972-45 41 75; fax 972-45 43 58; info@campingmasnou.com; www.campingmasnou.com] On m'way A7 exit 3 if coming fr France & exit 4 fr Barcelona dir Rosas (E) C260. Site on L at ent to Empuriabrava - use rndabt to turn. Lge, shd, mkd pitch; wc; chem disp; baby facs; shwrs inc; el pnts (10A) €4.10; lndtte; ice; shops 200m; rest; snacks; bar; BBQ; playgrnd; pool; beach 2.5km; tennis; games area; mini-golf; entmnt; TV; car wash; 5% statics; dogs €1.90; phone; Eng spkn; red long stay/low ssn; cc acc; CCI. "Aqua Park 4km, Dali Museum 10km; Roman monastery; gd touring base; helpful staff; well-run site; excel, spotless san facs; sports activities & children's club; excel value site takeaway; gd cycling; excel." ♦ 31 Mar-30 Sep. € 34.30 (CChq acc)   2007*

See advertisement

CASTELLO D'EMPURIES *3B3* (4km SE Coastal) **Camping Nautic Almata, Aiguamolls de l'Empordà, 17486 Castelló d'Empúries (Gerona)** [972-45 44 77; fax 972-45 46 86; info@almata.com; www.almata.com] Fr A7 m'way exit 3; foll sp to Rosas. After 12km turn S ® for Santt Pere Pescador & site on L in 5km. Site clearly sp on rd Castelló d'Empúries-Sant Pere Pescador. Lge, pt shd; wc; chem disp; shwrs inc; el pnts (10A) inc; rest; gas; shop; lndtte; playgrnd; pool; sand beach adj; sailing school; tennis; games area; horseriding; cycle hire; TV; disco bar on beach; entmnt; dogs €5.67; poss cr; adv bkg; quiet; 50% red low ssn. "Excel, clean facs; boats & moorings avail; ample pitches; sports facs inc in price; helpful staff; direct access to nature reserve; waterside pitches rec." ♦ 12 May-23 Sep. € 49.32   2006*

> This guide relies on site report forms submitted by caravanners like us; we'll do our bit and tell the editor what we think of the campsites we've visited.

CASTELLO D'EMPURIES *3B3* (1km S Coastal) **Camping Castell Mar, Ctra Rosas-Figueres, Playa de la Rubina, 17486 Castelló d'Empúries (Gerona)** [972-45 08 22; fax 972-45 23 30; cmar@campingparks.com; www.campingparks.com] Exit A7 at junc 3 sp Figueres; turn L onto C260 sp Rosas, after traff lts cont twd Rosas, turn R down side of rest La Llar for 1.5km, foll sp Playa de la Rubina. Lge, hdg/mkd pitch, pt shd; wc; chem disp; serviced pitches; baby facs; shwrs inc; el pnts (6A) inc; gas; lndtte; shop; tradsmn; rest; snacks; bar; BBQ; playgrnd; pool; sand beach 100m; games rm; entmnt; excursions; TV; 30% statics; dogs; phone; Eng spkn; adv bkg; quiet; red low ssn; CCI. "Sm pitches, poss unsuitable lge o'fits; excel for families." ♦ 19 May-23 Sep. € 42.00   2006*

CASTELLO D'EMPURIES *3B3* (5km S Coastal) Camping-Caravaning Laguna, Platja Can Turias, 17486 Castelló d'Empúries (Gerona) [972-45 05 53 or 45 20 33; fax 972-45 07 99; info@campinglaguna.com or reservas@camping laguna.com; www.campinglaguna.com] Exit AP7 junc 4 dir Roses. After 12km at rndabt take 3rd exit, site sp. Site in 4km; rough app track. V lge, mkd pitch, pt shd; wc; chem disp; mv service pnt; some serviced pitches (inc gas); baby facs; shwrs inc; el pnts (5A) €3.50; gas; lndtte; ice; supmkt; rest; snacks; bar; playgrnd; htd pool; sand beach; sailing; watersports; tennis; games area; multisports area; cycle hire; mini-golf; horseriding; entmnt; child entmnt; wifi internet; 4% statics; dogs free; Eng spkn; adv bkg; quiet; red snr citizens/long stay; cc acc; CCI. "Spotless, modern san facs; site improving all the time; gd birdwatching; excel." ♦ 15 Mar-21 Oct. € 32.60   2006*

CASTRO URDIALES *1A4* (1km N Coastal) Camping de Castro, Barrio Campijo, 39700 Castro Urdiales (Cantabria) [942-86 74 23; fax 942-63 07 25; info@camping.castro.com] Fr Bilbao turn off A8 at 2nd Castro Urdiales sp, km 151. Camp sp on R by bullring. V narr, steep lanes to site - no passing places, great care req. Lge, pt sl, pt terr, unshd; wc; shwrs inc; el pnts (6A) €2.60; lndtte; ice; shop; rest; bar; playgrnd; pool; sand beach 1km; 90% statics; dogs; phone; bus; poss cr; Eng spkn; adv bkg; quiet; CCI. "Gd, clean facs; conv NH for ferries; ltd touring pitches." ♦ ltd. Easter & 1 Jun-30 Sep. € 19.50   2006*

CASTROPOL see Ribadeo *1A2*

CAZORLA *2F4* (6km E Rural) Camping Puente de las Herrerías, El Vadillo del Castril, 23470 Cazorla (Jaén) [953-72 70 90; puenteh@infonegocio.com; www.puentedelasherrerias.com] Fr Cazorla foll sp for Parador & then Puente de la Herrerías. Driving distance 25km fr Cazorla on narr rd with many bends & two passes - not rec trailer c'vans. Lge, pt shd; wc; shwrs; el pnts (16A) inc; gas; shop; rest; bar; playgrnd; pool; horseriding; cycle hire; phone; quiet. "Stunning scenery in National Park." Easter-9 Dec. € 21.20   2004*

CAZORLA *2F4* (2km SW Rural) Camping San Isicio, Camino de San Isicio s/n, 23470 Cazorla (Jaén) [tel/fax 953-72 12 80; campingcortijo@ hotmail.com] Fr W on A319, turn R bef Cazorla, foll sp. Sm, pt shd; wc; shwrs; el pnts €2.50; playgrnd; pool; no dogs; quiet. "Perched on steep hill; towing service for c'vans but really only suitable sm m'vans; ltd facs but a gem of a site." 1 Mar-1 Nov. € 15.30   2007*

CEE *1A1* (6km NW Coastal) Camping Ruta Finisterre, Ctra La Coruña-Finisterre, Km 6, Playa de Estorde, 15270 Cée (La Coruña) [tel/fax 981-74 63 02; estorde@finisterrae.com; www. rutafinisterre.com] Foll sp thro Cée & Corcubión on rd AC445 twd Finisterre; site easily seen on R of rd (no thro rd). Lge, mkd pitch, terr, shd; wc; chem disp; shwrs inc; el pnts (10A) €3; gas; lndtte; ice; shop & 1km; rest; snacks; bar; playgrnd; sand beach 100m; dogs €3.70; phone; poss cr; Eng spkn; adv bkg; some rd noise; cc acc; CCI. "Family-run site in pine trees - check access to pitch & el pnts bef positioning; gd, clean facs; 5km to Finisterre; clean beach adj; peaceful." ♦ Holy Week & 15 Jun-15 Sep. € 19.90   2006*

CERVERA DE PISUERGA *1B4* (500m W Rural) Camping Fuentes Carrionas, La Bárcena s/n, 34840 Cervera de Pisuerga (Palencia) [979-87 04 24; fax 979-12 30 76] Fr Aguilar de Campóo on CL626 pass thro Cervera foll sp CL627 Potes. Site sp on L bef rv bdge. Med, mkd pitch, pt shd; wc; chem disp; shwrs inc; el pnts €2.73; lndtte; shop 500m; rest 500m; bar; games area; 80% statics; bus 100m; quiet; CCI. "Gd walking in Reserva Nacional Fuentes Carrionas; conv for Casa del Osos bear info cent." ♦ ltd. 13 Apr-30 Sep. € 23.11   2006*

⊞**CHILCHES** *4E2* (1km S Coastal) Camping Mediterraneo, Avda Mare Nostrum s/n, 12592 Chilches (Castellón) [tel/fax 964-58 32 18; www. mediterraneocamping.com] Exit AP7 junc 49 onto N340, exit junc 947-948 twds Chilches. Site at extreme S end Chilches, sp. Lge, mkd pitch, hdstg, shd; wc; chem disp; shwrs inc; el pnts inc; gas; lndtte; ice; shop; tradsmn; rest; snacks; bar; playgrnd; pool; sand beach 500m; solarium; TV rm; some statics; dogs; phone; bus 1km; poss cr; adv bkg; cc acc; red long stay/CCI. ♦ ltd. € 21.40
                                           2005*

⊞**CHIPIONA** *2G3* (2km S Coastal) Camping El Pinar de Chipiona, Ctra Chipiona-Rota, Km 3.2, 11550 Chipiona (Cádiz) [956-37 23 21] Site on R on A491 to Rota. Lge, mkd pitch, hdstg, pt shd; wc; chem disp; shwrs inc; el pnts (5-10A) €2.70; gas; lndtte; shop; rest; snacks; bar; playgrnd; sand beach 1km; 20% statics; dogs; quiet but some rd noise; Eng spkn; red low stay; CCI. "Many pitches with perm awnings; some san facs clsd low ssn; gd." ♦ € 17.50   2004*

Spain

CIUDAD RODRIGO 1D3 (1km S Rural) **Camping La Pesquera, Ctra Cáceres-Arrabal, Km 424, 37500 Ciudad Rodrigo (Salamanca)** [923-48 13 48] Fr Salamanca on A62/E80. At W end of Ciudad Rodrigo, foll sp Portugal/Cáceras. Keep in L lane, site sp in 300m on L on rvside. Med, mkd pitch, pt shd; wc; shwrs inc; el pnts (3A) €3; lndtte; shop; snacks; rv sw, fishing adj; TV; phone; poss cr; no adv bkg; noisy; cc acc; CCI. "Medieval walled city worth visit; low ssn phone ahead to check open; facs dated but clean; recep open 1700-1900 low ssn - site yourself; NH only." ♦ 1 Apr-30 Sep. € 12.80   2007*

⊞**CLARIANA** 3B3 (4km NE Rural) **Camping La Ribera, Pantà de Sant Ponç, 25290 Clariana de Cardener (Lleida)** [tel/fax 973-48 25 52; info@ campinglaribera.com; www.campinglaribera.com] Fr Solsona S on C55, turn L onto C26 at km 71. Go 2.7km, site sp immed bef Sant Ponç Dam. Lge, mkd pitch, hdstg, pt shd; wc; chem disp; baby facs; shwrs; el pnts (4-10A) €3.10-6.20; lndtte; shop; snacks; bar; playgrnd; pool; paddling pool; lake sw & beach 500m; tennis; games area; TV; dogs €3.10; bus 2.5km; phone; quiet.. "Excel facs; gd site." ♦ € 24.50   2006*

COLERA see Llançà 3B3

COLOMBRES see Unquera 1A4

COLUNGA 1A3 (1km N Coastal) **Camping Costa Verde, Playa La Griega de Colunga, 33320 Colunga (Asturias)** [tel/fax 985-85 63 73] N632 coast rd, fr E turn R twd Lastres in cent of Colunga; site 1km on R. Med, mkd pitch, unshd; wc; chem disp; baby facs; shwrs; el pnts (5A) €3; gas; lndtte; shop; rest; bar; BBQ; playgrnd; sand beach 500m; games area; cycle hire; 50% statics; dogs €2.80; bus 500m; adv bkg; quiet but noisy campers w/ ends & high ssn; cc acc; CCI. "Beautiful sandy beach; lovely views to mountains & sea; some site access rds used for winter storage; gd, plentiful facs; ltd hot water low ssn." Easter & 1 Jun-30 Sep. € 18.40   2006*

COLUNGA 1A3 (8km E Coastal) **Camping Arenal de Moris, Ctra de la Playa s/n, 33344 Caravia Alta (Asturias)** [985-85 30 97; fax 985-85 31 37; moris@desdeasturias.com; www.arenaldemoris. com] Fr E70/A8 exit junc 337 onto N632 to Caravia Alta, site clearly sp. Lge, mkd pitch, terr, unshd; wc; chem disp; shwrs inc; el pnts (5A) inc; lndtte; shop; rest; snacks; bar; playgrnd; pool; sand beach 500m; tennis; adv bkg; quiet but rd noise; cc acc; CCI. "Lovely views to mountains & sea; excel, clean san facs." Holy Week & 1 Jun-15 Sep. € 19.00   2005*

COMA RUGA see Vendrell, El 3C3

COMILLAS 1A4 (1km E Coastal) **Camping Comillas, 39520 Comillas (Cantabria)** [942-72 00 74; fax 942-21 52 06; info@campingcomillas. com; www.campingcomillas.com] Site on coast rd C6316 at E end of Comillas by-pass. App fr Santillana or San Vicente avoids town cent & narr streets. Lge, mkd pitch, pt sl, unshd; wc; chem disp; shwrs inc; el pnts (3A) €3.25; lndtte; shop; rest 1km; snacks; bar; playgrnd; sand beach 100m; TV; dogs; phone; poss cr; adv bkg; quiet; CCI. "Clean, ltd facs low ssn (poss no hot water); vg site in gd position with views; easy walk to interesting town; gd beach across rd." Holy Week & 1 Jun-30 Sep. € 20.00   2006*

COMILLAS 1A4 (3km E Rural) **Camping El Helguero, 39527 Ruiloba (Cantabria)** [942-72 21 24; fax 942-72 10 20; elhelguero@ctv. es; www.campingelhelguero.com] Exit A8 junc 249 dir Comillas onto CA135 to km 7. Turn dir Ruiloba onto CA359 & thro Ruiloba & La Iglesia, fork R uphill. Site sp. Lge, mkd pitch, pt sl, pt shd; htd wc; chem disp; mv service pnt; shwrs inc; el pnts (6A) €3.45; lndtte; shop, rest, snacks, bar in ssn; playgrnd; pool; paddling pool; sand beach 3km; tennis 300m; cycle hire; many statics; dogs; night security; poss v cr high ssn; Eng spkn; poss noisy high ssn; cc acc; CCI. "Attractive site, gd touring cent; v clean facs; helpful staff; sm pitches poss muddy in wet." ♦ Easter-30 Sep. € 18.00 (CChq acc)   2007*

⊞**COMILLAS** 1A4 (3km W Rural/Coastal) **Camping Rodero, Ctra Comillas-St Vicente, Km 5, 39528 Oyambre (Cantabria)** [942-72 20 40; fax 942-72 26 29] Exit A8 dir San Vicente, cross bdge over estuary & take R fork. Foll sp Oyambre & site. Lge, mkd pitch, pt sl, terr, pt shd; wc; chem disp; shwrs inc; el pnts (6A) inc; gas; lndtte; ice; shop; tradsmn; rest; snacks; bar; playgrnd; sm pool; sand beach 200m; 10% statics; no dogs; phone; bus 200m; poss v cr; adv bkg; cc acc; CCI. "Lovely views; friendly owners; site noisy but happy - owner puts Dutch/British in quieter part; sm pitches; poss run down low ssn; Comillas & San Vicente de la Barquera worth visit." ♦ € 26.00   2006*

⊞**CONIL DE LA FRONTERA** 2H3 (3km N Coastal) **Camping Cala del Aceite (Naturist), Ctra del Puerto Pesquero, Km 4, 11140 Conil de la Frontera (Cádiz)** [956-44 29 50; fax 956-44 09 72; info@caladelaceite.com; www.caladelaceite.com] Sp fr N340 Cádiz to Algeciras in both dir. In Conil turn R to Fuente del Gallo, site on L. V lge, mkd pitch, pt shd; wc; fam bthrm; sauna; shwrs inc; el pnts (10A) €5; gas; lndtte; ice; supmkt; rest; snacks; bar; playgrnd; pool; sand beach 200m; 20% statics; dogs €2.50; phone; poss cr; Eng spkn; adv bkg; quiet; red long stay; CCI. "Friendly, helpful staff; interesting region; gd cliff-top walking; lge pitches; gd, modern san facs; site being improved (2007)." ♦ € 21.90   2007*

⊞ Site open all year   796   *Send in your site reports*

⊞**CONIL DE LA FRONTERA** *2H3* (3km NE Rural) Camping Roche, Carril Pilahito s/n, N340km 19.2, 11149 Conil de la Frontera (Cádiz) [956-44 22 16; fax 956-23 23 19; info@campingroche.com; www.campingroche.com] Exit A48 junc 15 Conil Norte. Site sp on N340 dir Algeciras. Last 600m on unmade rd. Lge, mkd pitch, pt shd; wc; chem disp; mv service pnt; el pnts (5A) €5; lndtte; shop; rest; snacks; bar; playgrnd; pool; paddling pool; sand beach 3km; tennis; games area; TV; 20% statics; dogs €3.75; adv bkg; quiet; red low ssn/long stay. "V pleasant, peaceful site in pine woods; friendly, helpful staff; superb beaches nr." ♦ € 26.00   2007*

See advertisement

⊞**CONIL DE LA FRONTERA** *2H3* (1.3km NW Rural/Coastal) Camping La Rosaleda, Ctra del Pradillo, Km 1.3, 11140 Conil de la Frontera (Cádiz) [956-44 33 27; fax 956-44 33 85; camping larosaleda.com; www.camping larosaleda.com] Fr N340 turn L onto C2131 sp Conil. Pass rndabt/1-way system with 'boat'. Turn R at next, rndabt then R at 3rd rndabt onto CA2308. Site on R; sp. Lge, mkd pitch, pt sl, terr, pt shd; wc; chem disp; mv service pnt; shwrs inc; el pnts (5-10A) inc; ice; gas; lndtte; shop & 1.3km; tradsmn; rest; snacks; bar; playgrnd; pool; sand beach 1.3km; entmnt; internet; 10% statics; no dogs 15 Jun-15 Sep, otherwise in sep area €5; phone; car wash; Eng spkn; adv bkg; quiet; red low ssn/long stay; CCI. "Friendly, helpful staff; gd social atmosphere; poss noisy w/e; sm pitches not suitable lge o'fits but double-length pitches avail; poss itinerants; pitches soft when wet; poss cold & windy in winter; lge rally on site in winter; gd walking & cycling; sea views; historical, interesting area; conv Seville, Cádiz, Jerez, ferries to Canaries & day trips Morocco etc." ♦ € 34.00   2007*

⊞**CORDOBA** *2F3* (8km N Rural) Camping Los Villares, Parque Periurbano, Avda de la Fuensanta 8, 14071 Córdoba (Córdoba) [957-33 01 45; fax 957-33 14 55; campingvillares@latinmail.com] Best app fr N on N432: turn W onto CP45 1km N of Cerro Muriano at km 254. Site on R after approx 7km shortly after golf club. Last 5-6km of app rd v narr & steep, but well-engineered. Badly sp, easy to miss. Or fr city cent foll sp for Parador until past municipal site on R. Shortly after, turn L onto CP45 & foll sp Parque Forestal Los Villares, then as above. Sm, hdstg, sl, shd; wc; chem disp; shwrs inc; el pnts (15A) €3 (poss rev pol); gas; lndry rm; shop; rest & bar (high ssn); quiet; red long stay; CCI. "In nature reserve; peaceful; cooler than Córdoba city with beautiful walks, views & wildlife; sm, close pitches; basic facs (ltd & poss unclean low ssn); mainly sl site in trees; strictly run; take care electrics; poss no drinking water/hot water." ♦ € 13.30   2007*

⊞**CORDOBA** *2F3* (1km NW Urban) Camp Municipal El Brillante, Avda del Brillante 50, 14012 Córdoba [957-40 38 36; fax 957-28 21 65; elbrillante@campings.net; www.campingelbrillante.com] Fr N1V take Badejoz turning N432. Take rd Córdoba N & foll sp to Parador. Turn R into Paseo del Brilliante which leads into Avda del Brilliante; white grilleblock wall surrounds site. Alt, foll sp for 'Macdonalds Brilliante.' Site on R 1km beyond Macdonalds on main rd going uphill away fr town cent. Site poorly sp. Med, hdg/mkd pitch, hdstg, pt shd; wc; chem disp; mv service pnt; serviced pitches; shwrs inc; el pnts (6-10A) €3.50 (poss no earth); gas; lndry rm; shop; tradsmn; hypmkt nrby; rest in ssn; snacks; bar; playgrnd; pool adj in ssn; dogs free; phone; bus; poss cr; Eng spkn; no adv bkg; quiet but traff noise & barking dogs off site; cc not acc; CCI. "Well-run, v busy, clean site; rec arr bef 1500; friendly staff; sun shades over pitches; san facs need refurb (2007); easy walk/gd bus service to town; poss cramped pitches - diff lge o'fits; poss itinerants low ssn (noisy); gd for wheelchair users; highly rec." ♦ € 19.80   2007*

CORUNA, A see Coruña, La *1A2*

CORUNA, LA *1A2* (5km E Coastal/Rural) **Camping Bastiagueiro, Playa Bastiagueiro, 15110 Oleiros (La Coruña)** [981-61 48 78; fax 981-26 60 08] Exit La Coruña by NVI twd Betanzos. After bdge, take LC173 sp Santa Cruz. At 3rd rndabt, take 3rd exit sp Camping. In 100m, turn R up narr rd. Site on R in 150m. Sm, pt shd; wc (some cont); chem disp; shwrs inc; el pnts (6A) €3; gas; lndtte; shop; snacks; bar; playgrnd; sand beach 500m; dogs; phone; bus 300m; poss cr; adv bkg; quiet; CCI. "Friendly owners; lovely views of beach; care req going thro narr ent gate; poss feral cats on site." Holy Week & 1 Jun-30 Sep. € 19.00   2005*

Before we move on, I'm going to fill in some site report forms and post them off to the editor, otherwise they won't arrive in time for the deadline at the end of September.

CORUNA, LA *1A2* (9km E Rural) **Camping Los Manzanos, Olieros, 15179 Santa Cruz (La Coruña)** [981-61 48 25; info@camping-losmanzanos.com; www.camping-losmanzanos.com] App La Coruña fr E on NVI, bef bdge take AC173 sp Santa Cruz. Turn R at traff lts in Santa Cruz cent, foll sp site, site on L. Fr AP9/E1 exit junc 3, turn R onto NVI dir Lugo. Take L fork dir Santa Cruz/La Coruña, then foll sp Meiras. Site sp. Lge, pt shd; wc; chem disp; shwrs; el pnts (6A) €3.75 gas; lndtte; shop; rest; snacks; playgrnd; pool; TV; 10% statics; dogs; phone; bus 100m; cc acc; CCI. "Lovely site, beautiful trees; steep slope into site; helpful owners; excel rest; hilly 1km walk to Santa Cruz for bus to La Coruña or park at Torre de Hércules (lighthouse); conv for Santiago de Compostela; excel." € 21.80   2007*

COTORIOS *4F1* (500m Rural) **Camping Chopera, Cazorla-Cotorios, Km 21, Santiago Pontones, 23478 Cotorios (Jaén)** [tel/fax 953-71 30 05] Fr Jaén-Albacete rd N322 turn onto A1305, nr Villanueva del Arzobispo, sp El Tranco. In 26km at app to El Tranco lake (sh distance after exit fr tunnel), turn R & cross over embankment. Cotorios at km 52-53, approx 25km on shore of lake & Río Guadalquivir. Warning, if towing c'van, do not app via Cazorla as rds are tortuous. Only app & return fr Villanueva as rd well surfaced, but still some steep sections. Med, shd; wc; shwrs; el pnts (16A); lndtte; gas; shop; snacks; bar; playgrnd; rv adj; dogs; phone; car wash; cc acc. "In cent of beautiful National Park; lots of wildlife." ♦   2005*

COTORIOS *4F1* (2km E Rural) **Camping Llanos de Arance, Ctra Sierra de Cazorla/Beas de Segura, Km 22, 23478 Cotorios (Jaén)** [953-71 31 39; fax 953-71 30 36; arancell@inicia.es; www.llanosdearance.com] Fr Jaén-Albecete rd N322 turn E onto A1305 N of Villanueva del Arzobispo sp El Tranco. In 26km to El Tranco lake, turn R & cross over embankment. Cotorios at km stone 53, approx 25km on shore of lake & Río Guadalquivir. App fr Cazorla or Beas definitely not rec if towing. Lge, shd; wc; shwrs; el pnts (5A) €2.95; gas; shops 1.5km; rest; snacks; bar; BBQ; playgrnd; pool; rv sw; 2% statics; no dogs; phone; poss cr; quiet; cc acc; red low ssn; CCI. "Lovely site; excel walks & bird life, boar & wild life in Cazorla National Park." € 16.00   2007*

COVARRUBIAS *1B4* (500m E Rural) **Camping Covarrubias, Ctra Hortigüela, 09346 Covarrubias (Burgos)** [947-40 64 17; fax 983-29 58 41; proatur@proatur.com; www.proatur.com] Take N1/E5 or N234 S fr Burgos, turn onto BU905 after approx 35km. Site sp on BU905. Med, mkd pitch, pt sl, pt shd; wc; shwrs; el pnts (12A) inc; gas; lndtte; shop 500m; rest; bar; playgrnd; pool & paddling pool; 50% statics; phone; poss cr; cc acc. "Ltd facs low ssn; pitches poss muddy after rain; charming vill; Santo Domingo de Silos monastery 18km; poss vultures." € 19.35   2007*

CREIXELL *3C3* (Coastal) **Camping La Plana, Ctra N340, Km 1182, 43839 Creixell (Tarragona)** [977-80 03 04; fax 977-66 36 63] Site sp at Creixell off N340. Med, hdstg, shd; wc; chem disp; shwrs inc; el pnts inc; gas; lndtte; ice; shop; rest; snacks; bar; sand beach adj; poss cr; Eng spkn; adv bkg; some rlwy noise. "Vg, v clean site; v helpful & pleasant owners." 1 May-30 Sep. € 21.00   2007*

CREIXELL *3C3* (Coastal) **Camping La Sirena Dorada, 43839 Creixell (Tarragona)** [977-80 13 03; fax 977-80 12 15; info@sirenadorada.com; www.sirenadorada.com] Fr N exit AP7 at junc 31, foll N340 sp Tarragona, site 200m past Roman arch on L. Fr S exit junc 32 onto N340 to Creixall. Lge, pt shd; wc; shwrs inc; el pnts (5A) €4.60; gas; lndtte; ice; shop; rest; bar; playgrnd; pool; sand beach 200m; games area; mini-golf; entmnt; 15% statics; poss cr; adv bkg; quiet; CCI. "Winter/low ssn phone to check site open." ♦ € 27.70   2006*

CREIXELL *3C3* (1km S Coastal) **Camping Gavina Platja, N340, Km 1181, Platja Creixell, 43839 Creixell de Mar (Tarragona) [977-80 15 03; fax 977-80 05 27; info@gavina.net; www.gavina. net]** Exit AP7 junc 31 (Coma-Ruga) onto N340 dir Tarragona. At km 1181 turn R twd Playa de Creixel via undergnd passage. Site 1km S of Creixell, adj beach - foll sp Creixell Platja. Lge, mkd pitch, pt shd; wc; chem disp; baby facs; fam bthrm; shwrs inc; el pnts (6A) €3.80; gas; lndtte; shop; rest; snacks; bar; playgrnd; sand beach adj; watersports; tennis; entmnt; wifi internet; car wash; 20% statics; dogs; poss cr; adv bkg rec Jul/Aug; some train noise; cc acc; red long stay; CCI. "Rest overlooks beach; Port Aventura 20km." ♦ 26 Mar-31 Oct. € 28.30 (CChq acc)   2007*

CREVILLENTE see Elche *4F2*

⊞**CUBILLAS DE SANTA MARTA** *1C4* (4km S Rural) **Camping Cubillas, Ctra N620, Km 102, 47290 Cubillas de Santa Marta (Valladolid) [983-58 50 02; fax 983-58 50 16; info@campingcubillas. com; www.campingcubillas.com]** A62 Valladolid-Palencia, turn W at km 102. Site on L. Lge, some hdg/mkd pitch, pt sl, unshd; wc; chem disp; mv service pnt; shwrs inc; el pnts (2-5A) €3.37; gas; lndtte; sm shop; tradsmn; rest; snacks & bar in ssn; BBQ; playgrnd; pool; entmnt; 50% statics; dogs; phone; site clsd 18 Dec-8 Jan; red long stay/ low ssn; cc acc; CCI. "Ltd space for tourers; conv visit Palencia & Valladolid; rd, rlwy & disco noise at w/e until v late; v ltd facs low ssn; NH only." ♦ ltd. € 21.24   2007*

CUDILLERO *1A3* (2km SE Rural) **Camping Cudillero, Ctra Playa de Aguilar, 33154 Cudillero-El Pito (Asturias) [tel/fax 985-59 06 63; info@ campingcudillero.com]** Fr E on N632 (E70) fr Aviles twd La Coruña, turn R at sp El Pito past km 120.8. Foll camping sp where rd bends to L, then turn R at camp sp on rd to Playa de Aguilar. Site on R in 1km. Do not app thro Cudillero; streets v narr & steep; much traffic. Med, hdg/mkd pitch, pt shd; wc; chem disp; baby facs; shwrs inc; el pnts (3-5A) €3.75; gas; lndtte; ice; shop; snacks high ssn; bar; playgrnd; sand beach 1.2km; games area; entmnt high ssn; TV; some statics; dogs €2.14; phone; bus 1km; adv bkg; quiet; CCI. "Busy rd; gd site." ♦ Easter & 1 Jun-15 Sep. € 19.52   2006*

CUDILLERO *1A3* (2km S Rural) **Camping L'Amuravela, El Pito, 33150 Cudillero (Asturias) [tel/fax 985-59 09 95; camping@lamuravela.com; www.lamuravela.com]** Fr E take N632 & turn R at junc El Pito-Cudillero. Foll sp to site for 500m, R turn to site then on R after bend. Do not app thro Cudillero as streets narr & steep; much traffic. Med, mkd pitch, pt sl, unshd; wc; chem disp; shwrs inc; el pnts €2.60; gas; shop; snacks; bar; pool; sand beach 2km; 50% statics (sep area); poss cr; cc acc high ssn. "Hillside walks into Cudillero, attractive fishing vill with gd fish rests; gd clean facs; red facs low ssn." Easter & 1 Jun-30 Sep. € 16.15   2004*

CUENCA *3D1* (6.5km N Rural) **Camping Cuenca, Ctra Cuenca-Tragacete, Km 8, 16147 Cuenca [tel/fax 969-23 16 56; info@campingcuenca. com]** Fr Madrid take N400/A40 dir Cuenca & exit sp 'Ciudad Encantada' & Valdecabras on CM2105. In 7km rd splits, take CM2105 to site in 1km on L. Lge, pt sl, pt terr, pt shd; wc; chem disp; shwrs inc; el pnts (6-10A) €2.90; gas; lndtte; ice; shop; snacks; bar; playgrnd; pool high ssn; jacuzzi; tennis; games area; dogs €1.07; phone; poss cr esp Easter w/e; Eng spkn; adv bkg; quiet; CCI. "Nice green site; gd touring cent in fascinating area; well-kept; friendly, helpful staff; excel san facs but ltd low ssn; mv service pnt by appointment; interesting rock formations at Ciudad Encantada." ♦ 17 Mar-13 Oct. € 21.18   2007*

CUEVAS DEL ALMANZORA see Garrucha *4G1*

CULLERA see Sueca *4E2*

DEBA *3A1* (6km E Coastal) **Camping Itxaspe, 20829 Itziar (Guipúzkoa) [tel/fax 943-19 93 77; itxaspe@campingitxaspe.com; www.camping itxaspe.com]** Exit A8 junc 13 dir Deba; in short dist turn L, sp on L. NB Do not go into Itziar vill. Sm, mkd pitch, pt sl, pt shd; wc; chem disp; shwrs; el pnts (5A) €2; gas; shop; rest, bar adj; BBQ; playgrnd; pool; solarium; shgl beach 4km; some statics; bus 2km; adv bkg; quiet; red low ssn; CCI. "Excel site; helpful owner; w/ends busy." ♦ ltd. 1 Apr-30 Sep. € 17.70   2006*

⊞**DEBA** *3A1* (5km W Coastal) **Camping Aitzeta, Ctra Deba-Guernica, Km. 3.5, C6212, 20930 Mutriku (Guipúzkoa) [943-60 33 56; fax 943-60 31 06; www.campingseuskadi.com/aitzeta]** On N634 San Sebastián-Bilbao rd thro Deba & on o'skts turn R over level x-ing & over rv sp Mutriku. Site on L after 3km on narr & winding rd up short steep climb. Med, mkd pitch, terr, pt shd; wc; chem disp (wc); shwrs inc; el pnts (4A) €3; gas; lndry rm; sm shop; rest 300m; snacks; bar; playgrnd; sand beach 1km; dogs; phone; quiet; CCI. "Easy reach of Bilbao ferry; gd views; gd, well-run, clean site; not suitable lge o'fits; ltd pitches for tourers; helpful staff." ♦ ltd. € 21.00   2007*

⊞**DEBA** *3A1* (7km W Rural) **Camping Santa Elena, 20830 Mutriku (Guipúzkoa) [tel/fax 943-60 39 82]** On N634 San Sebastián-Bilbao rd, thro Deba on o'skts turn R over rv bdge, thro Mutriku & at end of town slowly under narr bdge, 30m after turn R sp Galdonamendi, 2km up hill. Med, sl, terr, shd; wc; shwrs; el pnts inc; shop; rest; playgrnd; sand beach 4km; 80% statics; phone; poss cr w/e; adv bkg; quiet. "Blocks ess for levelling; gd views; cramped pitches & narr site rds; NH only." € 19.50   2005*

Spain

DELTEBRE *3D2* (8km E Coastal) **Camping L'Aube, Afores s/n, 43580 Deltebre (Tarragona) [tel/fax 977-26 70 66]** Exit A7 junc 40 or 41 onto N340 dir Deltebre. Fr Deltebre foll T340 sp Riumar for 8km. At info kiosk branch R, site sp 1km on R. Lge, mkd pitch, hdstg, pt shd; wc; chem disp; mv service pnt; shwrs inc; el pnts (3-10A) €2.30-5; lndtte; shop; rest; bar; snacks; pool; playgrnd; phone; sand beach adj; 40% statics; poss cr low ssn; red long stay; CCI. "At edge of Ebro Delta National Park; excel bird-watching; ltd facs in winter; san facs tired." ♦ ltd. 1 Mar-31 Oct. € 15.60   2005*

DELTEBRE *3D2* (10km SE Coastal) **Camping Eucaliptus, Playa Eucaliptus 43870 Amposta (Tarragona) [tel/fax 977-47 90 46; eucaliptus@campingeucaliptus.com; www. campingeucaliptus.com]** Exit AP7/E15 at junc 41. Foll sp to Amposta but do not go into town. Take sp for Els Muntells on TV3405 then Eucaliptus beach. Site on R 100m fr beach. Lge, mkd pitch, pt shd; wc; chem disp; shwrs; el pnts (5A) €3.60; gas; ice; lndtte; shops; rest; snacks; bar; BBQ area; playgrnd; pool; sand beach adj; watersports; cycling; fishing; 20% statics; dogs €1.90; poss cr; adv bkg; noisy w/e & high ssn; red long stay; CCI. "V quiet area in Parc Natural; excel birdwatching; poss mosquito problem; gd." Holy Week-30 Nov. € 18.50   2005*

⊞**DENIA** *4E2* (6km N Coastal) **Camping Diana I & II, Ctra Dénia por la Costa, Km 6, Llac Maracaibo 12, 03700 Dénia (Alicante) [966-47 41 85; fax 966-47 53 89; camping-diana@camping-diana.com; www.camping-diana.com]** N fr Dénia on coast rd, site on R in 6km. Med, mkd pitch, hdstg, pt shd; wc; chem disp; baby facs; shwrs inc; el pnts (6A) €3.65; lndtte; shop & 1km; rest high ssn; bar; sand beach adj; games area; 10% statics; dogs; phone; bus adj; adv bkg; cc acc; red low ssn/CCI. "Well-maintained site in 2 sections - old part adj beach with gd shade, new part back fr beach with young trees." € 26.35   2004*

DENIA *4E2* (2km SE Coastal) **Camping Tolosa, Camí d'Urios 32, Les Rotes, 03700 Dénia (Alicante) [965-78 72 94; info@campingtolosa. com; www.campingtolosa.com]** Fr E end of Dénia Harbour take Jávea/Les Rotes rd. In approx 2km keep L at fork exit Jávea rd on R. In approx 1km site app clearly sp on L; site 300m twd sea. Med, mkd pitch, hdstg, pt shd; wc; chem disp; shwrs inc; el pnts (6A) €3; gas; shop; supmkt adj; bar; BBQ; shgl beach adj; 40% statics; dogs; phone; bus 300m; poss cr; quiet; 10% red long stay. "Well-managed site; pleasant staff; sm pitches." Holy Week & 1 Apr-30 Sep. € 20.00   2005*

⊞**DENIA** *4E2* (3.5km SE Coastal) **Camping Los Pinos, Ctra Dénia-Les Rotes, Km 3, Les Rotes, 03700 Dénia (Alicante) [965-78 26 98]** Fr N332 foll sp to Dénia then dir Les Rotes/Jávea, site sp. Narr access rd poss diff lge o'fits. Med, mkd pitch, pt shd; wc; chem disp; shwrs inc; el pnts (6-10A) €3; gas; lndtte; shop adj; tradsmn; BBQ; cooking facs; playgrnd; shgl beach; TV rm; 25% statics; dogs; phone; bus 300m; poss cr; Eng spkn; adv bkg; quiet; red long stays/low ssn; CCI. "Friendly, well-run, clean, tidy site; excel value; access some pitches poss diff due trees - not suitable lge o'fits or m'vans; many long-stay winter residents; cycle path into Dénia; social rm with log fire; interesting area; naturist beach 1km, v private but rocky shore." ♦ € 22.50   2005*

⊞**DENIA** *4E2* (9km W Rural) **Camping Los Llanos, Vergel, 03700 Dénia (Alicante) [965-75 51 88; fax 965-75 54 25; losllanos@losllanos.net; www. losllanos.net]** Exit AP7 junc 62 dir Dénia onto CV7222. At x-rds foll sp to site. Med, pt shd; wc; chem disp; mv service pnt; shwrs inc; el pnts €3.50; lndtte; shop & 2km; rest 500m; snacks; bar; playgrnd; pool; paddling pool; sand beach 300m; 30% statics; dogs €2; phone; bus 100m; poss cr; adv bkg; quiet; cc acc. € 21.70   2007*

DOLORES see Guardamar del Segura *4F2*

⊞**DOS HERMANAS** *2G3* (1km W Urban) **Camping Villsom, Ctra Sevilla/Cádiz A4, Km 554.8, 41700 Dos Hermanas (Sevilla) [tel/fax 954-72 08 28; villsom@autovia.com]** Fr A4/E5 Sevilla-Cádiz, exit junc 553 or 555, site on L on ent Dos Hermanas. Lge, mkd pitch, hdstg, pt sl, pt shd; wc (some cont); chem disp; shwrs inc; el pnts (8A) €2.70; gas; lndtte; sm shop; hypmkt 1km; snacks in ssn; bar; playgrnd; pool in ssn; mini-golf; wifi internet; bus to Seville 1km (over bdge & rndabt); site clsd 23 Dec-8 Jan; poss cr; Eng spkn; adv bkg; rd noise & barking dogs adj (2007); cc acc; CCI. "Adv bkg rec Holy Week; sm pitches - diff access lge o'fits; helpful staff; clean, tidy, well-run site; poss v cr & noisy high ssn; height barrier at Carrefour hypmkt - ent via deliveries." € 12.50   2007*

⊞**ELCHE** *4F2* (10km SW Urban) **Camping Internacional Las Palmeras, Ctra Murcia-Alicante, Km 45.3, 03330 Crevillente (Alicante) [965-40 01 88; fax 966-68 06 64; laspalmeras@ laspalmeras-sl.com; www.laspalmeras-sl.com]** Exit A7 junc 77 onto N340 to Crevillente. Site on R well sp, access rd down side of hotel. Sm, mkd pitch, hdstg, pt shd; wc; chem disp; shwrs inc; el pnts (10A) inc; lndtte; supmkt adj; rest; snacks; bar; pool; paddling pool; 20% statics; dogs; cc acc; CCI. "Useful NH; report to recep in hotel; helpful staff; gd cent for touring Murcia; gd rest in hotel." € 16.00   2004*

ERRATZU *3A1* (E Rural) **Camping Baztan, Ctra Francia s/n, 31714 Erratzu (Navarra)** [948-45 31 33; fax 948-45 30 85; campingbaztan@ campingbaztan.com; www.campingbaztan.com] Fr N121B km 62 marker take NA2600 sp Erratzu. In vill strt on at staggered x-rds & foll sp dir France, site on R outside vill 100m after Y junc. App rd thro vill narr with tight turns. Med, hdg/mkd pitch, shd; wc; chem disp; shwrs inc; el pnts inc; lndtte; ice; shop; rest; playgrnd; pool; dogs €3.75; poss cr; adv bkg; quiet; cc acc. "Site manned w/e only low ssn; gd walking; lovely scenery." ♦ 1 Mar-31 Oct. € 25.70   2005*

⊞**ESCALA, L'** *3B3* (2km E Coastal) **Camping Cala Montgó, Avda Montgó s/n, 17130 L'Escala (Gerona)** [972-77 08 66; fax 972-77 43 40; calamontgo@betsa.es] On N11 thro Figueras approx 3km on L sp rd C252 L'Escala. Thro town & camp sp. V lge, pt sl, pt shd; wc; chem disp; baby facs; shwrs inc; el pnts (5A) €3.40; gas; lndtte; ice; shop; tradsmn; rest; bar; playgrnd; pool; sand beach 200m; fishing; sports area; cycle hire; minigolf; 30% statics; dogs; poss cr; adv bkg; quiet; cc not acc; red low ssn; CCI. "Nr trad fishing vill; excel rest; facs ltd/run down & v quiet low ssn; exposed, windy & dusty site." ♦ € 31.20   2005*

ESCALA, L' *3B3* (500m S Urban/Coastal) **Camping L'Escala, Camí Ample 21, 17130 L'Escala (Gerona)** [972-77 00 08; fax 972-55 00 46; info@ campinglescala.com; www.campinglescala.com] Fr exit 4 or 5 off A7 turn R outside L'Escala for L'Estartit. 1st turn L, 1st R, site sp, do not app thro L'Escala town. Lge, shd; wc; chem disp; all serviced pitches; shwrs inc; el pnts (6A) inc; gas; shop; rest; snacks; bar; playgrnd; beach 300m; some statics; dogs; phone; car wash; poss cr; quiet. "Access to sm pitches poss diff lge o'fits; helpful, friendly staff; excel sh stay/NH; Empúrias ruins 5km." Easter-30 Sep. € 20.20   2004*

ESCALA, L' *3B3* (1km S Coastal) **Camping Maite, Playa de Riells, 17130 L'Escala (Gerona)** [tel/ fax 972-77 05 44; rmaite@campings.net; www. campingmaite.com] Exit A7 junc 5 dir L'Escala. Thro town dir Riells to rndabt with supmkts on each corner, turn R to site. Lge, mkd pitch, some terr, shd; wc; chem disp; mv service pnt; shwrs inc; el pnts (6A) €4.30; gas; ice; shop adj; rest; bar; playgrnd; beach 200m; TV; bus 1km; adv bkg; red long stay; cc acc; CCI. "Well-run site; quiet oasis in busy resort; steep site rds; some pitches narr access." ♦ 1 Jun-15 Sep. € 20.80   2007*

ESCALA, L' *3B3* (2km S Coastal) **Camping Illa Mateua (formerly Camping Paradis), Ave Montgó 260, 17130 L'Escala (Gerona)** [972-77 02 00 or 77 17 95; fax 972-77 20 31; info@campingparadis. com; www.campingparadis.com] On N11 thro Figueras, approx 3km on L sp C31 L'Escala; in town foll sp for Montgó & Paradis. Lge, terr, pt shd; wc; chem disp; mv service pnt; baby facs; shwrs inc; el pnts (5A) €3.25; gas; lndtte; ice; shop; rest; bar; playgrnd; 2 pools; sand beach adj; watersports; tennis; games area; entmnt; 5% statics; dogs €3.05; Eng spkn; adv bkg ess high ssn; quiet; CCI. "V well-run site; spacious pitches; excel san facs; gd beach; no depth marking in pool." ♦ ltd. 18 Mar-15 Oct. € 32.20   2006*

ESCALA, L' *3B3* (3km S Coastal) **Camping Neus, Cala Montgó, 17130 L'Escala (Gerona)** [972-77 04 03 or 972-20 86 67; fax 972-77 27 51 or 972-22 24 09; info@campingneus.com; www. campingneus.cat] Exit AP7 junc 5 twd L'Escala then turn R twd Cala Montgó & foll sp. Med, mkd pitch, pt sl, pt terr, shd; wc; chem disp; shwrs inc; el pnts (6A) €3.50; gas; lndtte; ice; shop; snacks; bar; playgrnd; pool; paddling pool; sand beach 850m; fishing; tennis; car wash; TV rm; 15% statics; dogs €1.50; phone; bus 500m; Eng spkn; adv bkg; quiet; cc acc; red low ssn/long stay; CCI. "Pleasant, clean site in pine forest; gd san facs; lge pitches; vg." 30 May-14 Sep. € 35.00   2007*

See advertisement

Spain

⊞ESCARRILLA *3B2* (500m Rural) **Camping Escarra, Ctra Huesca-Francia, Km 85, 22660 Escarrilla (Huesca)** [974-48 71 28; fax 974-48 76 42; info@campingescarra.com; www. campingescarra.com] On A136 bet Sabiñánigo & Portalet Pass, sp in Escarrilla. Lge, pt sl, pt shd; wc; chem disp; shwrs inc; el pnts (6A) €4.45; gas; lndtte; shop; rest; snacks; bar; pool; games area; tennis; horseriding; phone; poss cr; adv bkg; 80% statics; quiet; cc acc. "Conv Ordesa National Park; mountain & adventure sports." € 20.70 2005*

⊞ESCORIAL, EL *1D4* (6km NE Rural) **Camping-Caravaning El Escorial, Crta Guadarrama a El Escorial, Km 3.5, 28280 El Escorial (Madrid)** [918-90 24 12; fax 918-96 10 62; info@campingelescorial.com; www.camping elescorial.com] Exit AP6 NW of Madrid junc 47 El Escorial/Guadarrama, onto M600 & foll sp to El Escorial, site on L at km stone 3,500. Fr S foll sp fr El Escorial to Guadarrama on M600, site on R in 5km. V lge, mkd pitch, some hdstg, pt shd; htd wc; chem disp; baby facs; shwrs inc; el pnts (5A) inc (long cable rec); gas; lndtte; shop; rest, bar in ssn & w/e; hypmkt 5km; snacks; BBQ; playgrnd; 3 pools high ssn; tennis; horseriding 7km; games rm; child entmnt; excursions; internet; TV; 25% statics (sep area); dogs; cash machine; adv bkg; some Eng spkn; poss cr & noisy at w/e; cc not acc. "Excel base for sightseeing; clean facs; helpful staff; gd security; sm pitches poss diff to access due trees but able to use 2 low ssn; facs ltd low ssn; overhead canopies, strong awning pegs rec; day trips to Segovia & Ávila (high ssn); trains & buses to Madrid nr; Valle de Los Caídos & Palace at El Escorial well worth visit; gd views of mountains; easy parking in town for m'vans if go in early; mkt Wed." ♦ € 31.25 ABS - E13 2007*

See advertisement opposite

ESPINAL see Auritz *3A1*

⊞ESPONELLA *3B3* (500m N Rural) **Camping Esponellà, Ctra Banyoles-Figueres, Km 8, 17832 Esponellà (Gerona)** [972-59 70 74; fax 972-59 71 32; informa@campingesponella.com; www.campingesponella.com] Heading S fr French frontier, turn R (W) at Figueras on C260. After 13km turn L at junc to Banyoles. Site 6.4km SW. Lge, pt shd; htd wc (some cont); chem disp; shwrs inc; rest; el pnts (5A) €4.33 (check earth); lndtte; ice; shop; rest; bar; BBQ; playgrnd; 2 htd covrd pools; tennis; games area; cycle hire; mini-golf; rv fishing; horseriding; entmnt; some statics; dogs €1.60; quiet; red long stay/CCI. "Banyoles Lake (boating) 10km; Costa Brava 50km, S side of Pyrenees 30km; gd walks; excel facs; v busy w/e; lovely site." € 27.39 2006*

ESPOT *3B2* (500m SE Rural) **Camping Sol I Neu, Ctra Sant Maurici s/n, 25597 Espot (Lleida)** [973-62 40 01; fax 973-62 41 07; camping@ solineu.com] Fr Sort on C13 turn L to Espot on rd LV5004, site on L in approx 6.5km by rvside. Med, mkd pitch, pt shd; wc; chem disp; baby facs; shwrs inc; el pnts (6-10A) €5; gas; lndtte; shop, bar high ssn; playgrnd; pool; paddling pool; TV; quiet; cc acc; CCI. "Excel facs; beatiful site 4km fr ent to National Park; Landrover taxis fr Espot take walkers into heart of park (no private vehicles allowed); suitable sm o'fits only." 15 Jun-15 Sep. € 23.00 2007*

ESPOT *3B2* (1km W Rural) **Camping Voraparc, Ctra Sant Maurici s/n, Prat del Vedat, 25597 Espot (Lleida)** [973-62 41 08 or 973-25 23 24; fax 973-62 41 43; info@voraparc.com; www. voraparc.com] Fr Sort N on C13 N. At sp turn L for Espot, go thro vill then turn R for National Park. Site in 1.5km on R. Well sp. Med, mkd pitch, pt sl, shd; wc; chem disp (wc); mv service pnt; baby facs; shwrs inc; el pnts (6A) €4.60 (poss rev pol); gas; lndtte; shop; tradsmn; snacks; bar; BBQ; playgrnd; htd pool; watersports nrby; walks; cycle hire; TV/ games rm; no statics; dogs; phone; bus 1km; Eng spkn; adv bkg; quiet; 10% red 15+ days; cc acc; CCI. "Friendly owners; v clean facs; access rd narr & needs care; conv for National Park in walking/ cycling distance; gd birdwatching; excel." ♦ Holy Week & 1 May-30 Sep. € 20.00 2006*

ESTARTIT L' *3B3* (Coastal) **Camping Rifort, Ctra de Torroella s/n, 17258 L'Estartit (Gerona)** [972-75 04 06; fax 972-75 17 22; campingrifort@ campingrifort.com; www.campingrifort.com] Site on rndabt at ent to L'Estartit. Med, hdg/mkd pitch, terr, pt shd; wc; chem disp; shwrs; baby facs; el pnts €3.10; gas; lndtte; shop 50m; snacks; bar; pool; sand beach 500m; tennis 150m; watersports; dogs €1.60; phone; bus adj; Eng spkn; adv bkg; noise fr adj main rd & entmnt; red low ssn; cc acc. "Family-run; excel, immac facs." ♦ 7 Apr-12 Oct. € 20.40 2005*

ESTARTIT, L' *3B3* (Coastal) **Camping Estartit, Calle Villa Primevera 12, 17258 L'Estartit (Gerona)** [972-75 19 09; fax 972-75 00 91; www. campingestartit.com] On N11 fr Figueras-Gerona turn L onto C66, then G642 dir Torroella de Montgri & L'Estartit; fork L on ent L'Estartit, foll site sps. Med, pt sl, shd; htd wc; chem disp; baby facs; shwrs inc; el pnts (2-6A) €2.20-3.10; gas; lndtte; ice; shop; rest adj; snacks; bar; playgrnd; htd pool; paddling pool; sand beach 400m; entmnt; child entmnt; 15% statics; no dogs 20/6-20/8; phone; poss cr; Eng spkn; red long stay. "Friendly staff; 100m fr vill cent; gd security; gd walks adj nature reserve; bar/rest & night club adj; facs poss stretched high ssn." 15 Mar-15 Oct. € 19.00 2005*

⊞ *Site open all year*

ESTARTIT, L' *3B3* (500m Urban/Coastal) **Camping La Sirena, Calle La Platera s/n, 17258 L'Estartit (Gerona) [972-75 15 42; fax 972-75 09 44; info@ camping-lasirena.com; www.camping-lasirena. com]** Fr Torroella foll sp to L'Estartit. On o'skts of vill turn R at Jocs Amusements, site on L 200m. Lge, pt shd; wc; chem disp; baby facs; shwrs inc; el pnts (6-10A) €3.30; gas; lndtte; shop; rest; snacks; bar; BBQ; playgrnd; htd pool; sand beach adj; scuba diving; TV; money exchange; car wash; 10% statics; dogs; Eng spkn; quiet; red long stay/low ssn; CCI. "V ltd facs low ssn; gd value boat trips; nature reserve adj." ♦ 18 Apr-12 Oct. € 19.20

2004*

ESTARTIT, L' *3B3* (1km S Coastal) **Camping El Molino, Camino del Ter, 17258 L'Estartit (Gerona) [tel/fax 972-75 06 29]** Fr N11 junc 5, take rd to L'Escala. Foll sp to Torroella de Montgri, then L'Estartit. Ent town & foll sp. V lge, hdg pitch, pt sl, pt shd; wc; mv service pnt; shwrs; el pnts (6A) €3.08; gas; ice; supmkt high ssn & 2km; rest; bar; playgrnd; sand beach 1km; games rm; internet; bus 1km; poss cr; adv bkg. "Site in 2 parts - 1 in shd, 1 at beach unshd; gd facs; quiet location outside busy town." 1 Apr-30 Sep. € 20.66

2006*

⊞**ESTARTIT, L'** *3B3* (2km S Coastal) **Camping Les Medes, Paratge Camp de l'Arbre s/n, 17258 L'Estartit (Gerona) [972-75 18 05; fax 972-75 04 13; info@campinglesmedes.com; www. campinglesmedes.com]** Fr Torroella foll sp to L'Estartit. In vill turn R at town name sp (sp Urb Estartit Oeste), foll rd for 1.5km, turn R, site well sp. Lge, mkd pitch, shd; htd wc; chem disp; mv service pnt; serviced pitches; baby facs; sauna; shwrs inc; el pnts (6A) €4.20 (poss no earth); gas; lndtte; ice; shop; rest; snacks; bar; playgrnd; htd indoor/ outdoor pools; sand beach 800m; watersports; solarium; tennis; games area; horseriding 400m; cycle hire; car wash; games rm; wifi internet; entmnt; TV; 7% statics; no dogs high ssn otherwise €2.30; phone; site clsd Nov; poss cr; Eng spkn; adv bkg; quiet; red long stay/low ssn (pay on arrival); cc not acc; CCI. "Excel, family-run & well organised site; welcome pack; gd clean facs & constant hot water; gd for children; no twin-axle vans high ssn - by arrangement low ssn; conv National Park; well mkd foot & cycle paths." ♦ € 37.90

2007*

See advertisement on next page

Spain

*Last year of report

■ Family campsite OPEN ALL YEAR ROUND in the heart of nature, and just 800 metres from the beach

■ in a superb natural and cultural setting

■ modern facilities: heated indoor swimming pool, solarium, sauna...

■ good times assured for all the family

■ water sports, bicycle hire...

G P S
42° 02' 33" N
3° 11' 00" E

Paratge Camp de l'Arbre
Apartat de Correus 140
17258 L'ESTARTIT – Girona
Catalunya – COSTA BRAVA – Spain
T. +34 972 751 805
F. +34 972 750 413
info@campinglesmedes.com

WWW.CAMPINGLESMEDES.COM

ESTARTIT, L' *3B3* (W Coastal) **Camping Castell Montgri**, Ctra de Torroella, Km 4.7, 17258 L'Estartit (Gerona) [972-75 16 30; fax 972-75 09 06; cmontgri@campingparks.com; www.campingparks.com] Exit A7 junc 5 onto GI 623 dir L'Escala. Foll sp on rd C252 fr Torroella de Montgri to L'Estartit. Site on L clearly sp. V lge, hdg pitch, terr, hdstg, shd; wc; mv service pnt; chem disp; baby facs; shwrs inc; el pnts (6A) inc; gas; lndtte; shop; rest; snacks; bar; playgrnd; 3 pools; waterslide; beach 1km; tennis; games area; watersports; entmnt; excursions; internet; TV; car wash; money exchange; 30% statics; dogs free; phone; poss cr; adv bkg; red long stay. "Gd views; help given to get to pitch; excel." ♦ 12 May-30 Sep. € 44.00   2006*

ESTARTIT, L' *3B3* (1km W Coastal) **Camping L'Empordà**, Ctra Torroella de Montgri, Km 4.8, 17258 L'Estartit (Gerona) [972-76 06 49; fax 972-75 14 30; info@campingemporda.com; www.campingemporda.com] Exit AP7 junc 5 onto GI623 dir L'Escala. Bef L'Escala turn S onto C31 dir Torroella de Montgri, then at Torroella take rd GI641 dir L'Estartit. Site bet L'Estartit & Torroella, opp Castell Montgri. Lge, pt shd; wc; chem disp; shwrs inc; baby facs; el pnts (6A) €4; gas; lndtte; ice; shop; snacks; bar; playgrnd; pool; paddling pool; sand beach 1km; tennis; entmnt; organised walks; TV; dogs €2.10; phone; bus 70m; car wash; poss cr; adv bkg; quiet; red low ssn/long stay; CCI. "Family-run, pleasant & helpful; easy walking dist town cent; lge pitches." ♦ 25 Mar-28 Sep. € 22.40   2007*

See advertisement opposite

There aren't many sites open this early in the year. We'd better phone ahead to check that the one we're heading for is actually open.

⊞ESTELLA *3B1* (2km S Rural) **Camping Lizarra, Ordoiz s/n, 31200 Estella (Navarra) [948-55 17 33; fax 948-55 47 55; info@campinglizarra.com; www.campinglizarra.com]** N111 Pamplona to Logroño. Leave N111 sp Estella, turn R at T-junc, bear R at traff lts & turn R immed after rd tunnel, site sp. Pass factory, site on L in 1.5km. Well sp thro town. Lge, mkd pitch, wide terr, pt sl, unshd; htd wc; chem disp; mv service pnt; baby facs; shwrs inc; el pnts (6A) inc; gas; lndtte; shop high ssn; rest; snacks; bar; BBQ; playgrnd; pool; 80% w/e statics; phone; bus at w/e; poss cr; Eng spkn; noisy; cc acc; CCI. "Poss school parties; no hdstg; poss muddy when wet; poss smell fr nrby factory; interesting old town; excel birdwatching in hills; on rte Camino de Compostella." ♦ € 20.20   2006*

⊞ESTEPAR *1B4* (2km NE Rural) **Camping Cabia, Ctra Burgos-Valladolid, Km 15.2, 09196 Cabia/ Cavia (Burgos) [947-41 20 78]** Site 15km SW of Burgos on N side of A62/E80, adj Hotel Rio Cabia. Ent via Campsa petrol stn, W'bound exit 17, E'bound exit 18, cross over & re-join m'way. Site sp fr A62 via service rd. Med, pt shd; wc; chem disp; shwrs inc; el pnts (6A) €2.35; shops 15km & basic supplies fr rest; rest; bar; playgrnd; few statics; constant rd noise; cc acc; CCI. "Friendly, helpful owner; gd rest; conv for m'way for Portugal but poorly sp fr W; ground poss v muddy in winter; poorly maintained san facs; vg NH." € 12.41   2007*

⊞ESTEPONA *2H3* (7km E Coastal) **Camping Parque Tropical, Ctra N340, Km 162, 29680 Estepona (Málaga) [tel/fax 952-79 36 18]** On N side of N340 at km 162, 200m off main rd. Med, hdg/mkd pitch, terr, pt shd; wc; chem disp; mv service pnt; serviced pitch; shwrs inc; el pnts (10A) €3.45; gas; lndtte; ice; shop; rest; snacks; bar; sm playgrnd; htd, covrd pool; sand/shgl beach 1km; golf, horseriding nrby; wildlife park 1km; 60% statics; dogs €2; phone; bus 400m; poss cr; Eng spkn; adv bkg; rd noise; red low ssn/long stay; CCI. "Regimented, but gd site." ♦ € 25.00   2007*

ETXARRI ARANATZ *3B1* (2km) **Camping Etxarri, 31820 Etxarri-Aranatz (Navarra) [tel/fax 948-46 05 37; info@campingetxarri.com; www.campingetxarri.com]** S on AP15, turn W at Irurtzun onto N240A/N1 dir Vitoria/Gasteiz. Go thro Etxarri vill, turn L & cross old bdge, then take new rd over rlwy. Turn L, site sp. Med, pt shd; wc; shwrs inc; el pnts €3.80; gas; lndtte; shop; rest; bar; BBQ; pool; playgrnd; sports area; archery; horseriding; cycling; hang-gliding; paragliding; entmnt; 50% statics; phone; poss cr; Eng spkn; cc acc; CCI. "Wooded site; gd walks; interesting area; helpful owner; conv NH to/fr Pyrenees; youth hostel on site." 1 Apr-12 Oct. € 16.80   2006*

Did you know you can fill in site report forms on the Club's website — www.caravanclub.co.uk?

EUSA see Pamplona *3B1*

FARGA DE MOLES, LA see Seo de Urgel *3B3*

FERROL *1A2* (5km S Coastal) **Camping El Raso, Ctra de Redes, 15624 Ares (La Coruña) [981-46 06 76; campingraso@caamouco.net; www.caamouco.net/raso]** Turn W off N651 Betanzos-El Ferrol N of Pontedeume, foll sp to Playa El Raso & site. Med, hdg pitch, pt sl, terr, pt shd; wc; serviced pitches; shwrs €0.70; el pnts (10A) €2.20 (check earth); gas; lndtte; shop in ssn & 1km; tradsmn; rest; bar; snacks; BBQ; sand beach adj; 5% statics; poss cr w/e; noisy (beach); Eng spkn; cc acc; CCI. "Rec inspect pitch bef accepting; access poss diff lge vans." ♦ ltd 1 Jun-31 Aug. € 14.30   2005*

Spain

⊞**FIGUERES** *3B3* (1km N Urban) **Camping Pous, Ctra N11, Km 763, 17600 Figueres (Gerona) [972-67 54 96; fax 972-67 50 57; info@androl. internet-park.net; www.androl.internet-park. net]** Fr S exit AP7/E15 S at junc 3 & join N11. Then foll N11A S twd Figueres. Site on L in 2km, ent adj Hostal Androl. From S exit junc 4 onto NII to N of town. At rndabt (access to AP7 junc 3) foll NII S, then as above. Site recep in hotel. No access to N11A fr junc 4. Med, mkd pitch, shd; wc; chem disp; shwrs inc; el pnts (10A) inc; shop 1km; rest; snacks; bar; playgrnd; few statics; dogs €2.50; Eng spkn; quiet with some rd noise; cc acc. "Gd, clean site but san facs slightly run down & ltd low ssn; easy access; pleasant owner; excel rest; sh walk to town & Dali museum; 18km fr Rosas on coast." ♦ € 24.00   2006*

⊞**FIGUERES** *3B3* (12km N Rural) **Camping Les Pedres, Calle Darnius, 15, 17750 Capmany (Gerona) [972-54 91 92; JanDenDaas@ CampingLesPedres.com; www.camping lespedres.com]** S fr French border on N11, turn L sp Capmany, L again in 2km at site sp & foll site sp. Med, mkd pitch, pt sl, pt shd; htd wc; chem disp; shwrs inc; el pnts (6A) €3.55; lndry rm; shop 1km; rest; snacks; bar; pool; sand beach 25km; 20% statics; dogs; Eng spkn; adv bkg; quiet; cc acc; red low ssn; CCI. "Helpful Dutch owner; lovely views; gd touring & walking cent." ♦ € 26.50   2007*

FIGUERES *3B3* (8km NE Rural) **Camping Vell Empordà, Ctra Rosas-La Jonquera s/n, 17780 Garriguella (Gerona) [972-53 02 00 or 972-57 06 31 (LS); fax 972-55 23 43; vellemporda@ vellemporda.com; www.vellemporda.com]** On A7/E11 exit junc 3 onto N260 NE dir Llançà. Nr km 26 marker, turn R sp Garriguella, then L at T-junc N twd Garriguella. Site on R shortly bef vill. Lge, hdg/mkd pitch, hdstg, terr, shd; htd wc; chem disp; mv service pnt; baby facs; shwrs inc; el pnts (10A) inc; gas; lndtte; ice; shop; rest; snacks; bar; BBQ; playgrnd; pool; paddling pool; sand beach 6km; games area; games rm; entmnt; internet; TV; 20% statics; dogs €3; phone; Eng spkn; adv bkg; quiet; cc acc; red long stay/low ssn; CCI. "Conv N Costa Brava away fr cr beaches & sites; 20 mins to sea, at Llançà; overhanging trees poss diff high vehicles; excel." ♦ 1 Feb-15 Dec. € 30.15   2007*

See advertisement

⊞**FIGUERES** *3B3* (15km NW Rural) **Camping La Fradera, 17732 Sant Llorenç de la Muga (Gerona) [tel/fax 972-54 20 54]** Fr cent Figueres take N260 W dir Olot. After 11km turn R at mini-rndabt (supmkt on L), pass police stn to rd junc, strt on & cross over A7 m'way & pass thro Llers & Terrades to Sant Llorenç. Site 1km past vill on L. Med, mkd pitch, pt shd; wc; chem disp; shwrs inc; el pnts (6A) inc; lndtte; shop 2km; tradsmn; snacks; rest in vill; playgrnd; htd pool; rv sw 1km; few statics; poss cr; adv bkg; quiet; red long stay. "Vg site in delightful vill in foothills of Pyrenees; fiesta 2nd w/e Aug; v pleasant staff." ♦ ltd. € 16.30   2005*

FORNELLS DE LA SELVA see Gerona *3B3*

⊞**FORTUNA** *4F1* (1.5km N Rural) **Castillejo Camping, 30709 Baños de Fortuna (Murcia) [629-07 70 52; jarrod.vigrass@virgin.net; www. elysiumcamping.com]** Exit A7 junc 83, 7km after Murcia onto C3223. Site sp on L. Sm, hdg/mkd pitch, hdstg, unshd; wc; chem disp; mv service pnt; el pnts (15A) €2; gas; lndry rm; shop 1km; tradsmn; rest; snacks; bar; playgrnd; htd pool; 10% statics; dogs free; adv bkg; quiet; red long stay; CCI. "Nr Fortuna natural hot springs & thermal treatment cent; flat site suitable disabled; gd bar, rest; British owners; excel." € 13.08   2006*

⊞**FORTUNA** *4F1* (3km N Rural) **Camping Fuente, Camino de la Bocamina s/n, 30709 Baños de Fortuna (Murcia) [tel/fax 968-68 51 25; info@ campingfuente.com; www.campingfuente.com]** Fr Murcia on A7/E15 turn L onto C3223 sp Fortuna, thro town dir Balneario to Baños de Fortuna. Site on R down narr rd, sp. Med, mkd pitch, hdstg, pt sl, unshd; htd wc; chem disp; serviced pitches; indiv san facs some pitches; shwrs; el pnts (10-16A) €1.60 or metered; gas; lndtte; tradsmn; rest; snacks; bar; BBQ; playgrnd; htd pool, spa, jacuzzi; internet; some statics; dogs €1.15; phone; adv bkg; cc acc; red long stay; CCI. "Gd san facs; excel pool; secure overflow parking area; gd rest; many long-stay winter visitors; ltd recep hrs low ssn; poss sulphurous smell fr thermal baths." ♦ € 18.50
                                                         2007*

⊞**FORTUNA** *4F1* (3km N Rural) **Camping Las Palmeras, 30709 Baños de Fortuna (Murcia) [tel/ fax 968-68 60 95]** Exit A7 junc 83 Fortuna; cont on C3223 thro Fortuna to Los Baños; turn R & foll sp. Concealed R turn on crest at beg of vill. Med, mkd pitch, pt shd; wc; chem disp; shwrs; el pnts (6A) €3; gas; lndtte; shops 300m; tradsmn; rest; snacks; bar; natural hot water mineral pool 200m; 5% statics; poss cr; quiet; adv bkg acc; 20% red long stay; cc acc; CCI. "Gd value, friendly site; new san facs planned 2007; lge pitches; thermal baths also at Archena (15km)." ♦ ltd. € 10.00   2007*

⊞FOZ *1A2* (2km E Coastal) **Camping Benquerencia, 27792 Benquerencia-Barreiros (Lugo) [tel/fax 982-12 44 50 or 679-15 87 88; manuel@campingbenquerencia.com; www. campingbenquerencia.com]** Fr junc of N642 & N634 S of Foz; E twd Ribadeo; in 1km past Barreiros at km stone 566 turn L at site sp. Site on R in 1.5km. Med, mkd pitch, pt sl, pt shd; wc; shwrs inc; el pnts (6A) €3; gas; lndtte; shop in ssn & 2km; rest; bar; playgrnd; sand beach 400m; tennis; games area; phone; quiet; cc acc; CCI. "Hot water to shwrs only; NH only." € 15.70   2005*

FOZ *1A2* (2.5km W Coastal) **Camping San Rafael, Playa de Peizas, 27789 Foz (Lugo) [tel/ fax 982-13 22 18; info@campingsanrafael.com]** Site sp. Med, unshd; wc; chem disp; shwrs inc; el pnts (5A) €3; gas; lndtte; shop; tradsmn; rest; snacks; bar; sand beach adj; games area; dogs; poss cr; adv bkg; quiet; 15% red long stay; cc acc; CCI. 1 Apr-30 Sep. € 14.00   2004*

⊞FRAGA *3C2* (1km SE Urban) **Camping Fraga, Ctra N11-Seros, Km 437, Ptda Vicanet s/n, 22520 Fraga (Huesca) [974-34 52 12; info@ campingfraga.com; www.campingfraga.com]** Fr W pass thro Fraga town on N11. After about 500m turn R into indus est just past petrol stn. Turn R again in indus est, foll site sp. Fr E turn L into indus est just bef petrol stn. Sm, mkd pitch, hdstg, terr, pt shd; wc; chem disp; mv service pnt; shwrs inc; el pnts (4A) inc (rev pol); lndtte; hypmkt 1km; tradsmn; rest; snacks; bar; playgrnd; pool; TV rm; some statics; dogs €2; phone; poss cr; adv bkg; red low ssn; CCI. "Conv NH bet Zaragoza & Tarragona; unspoilt town in beautiful area." ♦ € 21.00
                                                                    2005*

FRANCA, LA *1A4* (1km NW Coastal) **Camping Las Hortensias, Ctra N634, Km 286, 33590 Playa de la Franca (Asturias) [985-41 24 42; fax 985-41 21 53; lashortensias@campinglashortensias.com;www. campinglashortensias.com]** Fr N634 on leaving vill of La Franca, foll sp 'Playa de la Franca' & cont past 1st site & thro car park to end of rd. Med, mkd pitch, pt sl, pt terr, pt shd; wc; chem disp; baby facs; shwrs inc; el pnts (3-10A) €3.15; gas; lndtte; shop; rest, snacks, bar adj; playgrnd; sand beach adj; tennis; cycle hire; phone; dogs (but not on beach) €3; poss cr; Eng spkn; adv bkg; cc acc; red CCI. "Beautiful location nr scenic beach; sea views fr top terr pitches; vg." 1 Jun-15 Sep. € 19.70
                                                                    2005*

FRIAS *1B4* (1.5km NW Rural) **Camping Frias, 09211 Frias (Burgos) [947-35 71 98; fax 947-35 71 99; info@campingfrias.com; www. campingfrias.com]** Fr AP1 take N232 & N629 to Trespaderne. Turn sharp R (dir Miranda) & E for 10km. Turn R at Frias & camping sp. Site on R in 3km bef rv bdge. Med, mkd pitch, pt shd; wc; chem disp; mv service pnt; shwrs €0.60; el pnts €2.50; ice; shop; rest; bar; 3 pools; rv adj; fishing; archery; cycle hire; 95% statics; dogs €2.50; phone; poss cr w/e; quiet; cc acc. "Open w/e only in winter, but phone ahead to check; sh stay/NH only; interesting vill with castle & Roman bdge." 1 Apr-30 Sep. € 20.40   2004*

⊞FUENGIROLA *2H4* (2km SW Coastal) **Camping Fuengirola, Ctra Cádiz-Málaga Km 207, 29640 Fuengirola (Málaga) [tel/fax 952-47 41 08]** On R of N340 Málaga-Algeciras rd opp hotel immed at km stone 207. Go slowly down service stn exit (if missed, next rndabt is 2km). Lge, shd; wc; chem disp; serviced pitches; shwrs inc; el pnts (6A) inc; gas; lndtte; ice; shop; rest; bar; playgrnd; pool; sand beach adj; watersports; TV; adv bkg; Eng spkn; some rd noise; red long stay; cc acc; CCI. "Sea views; clean facs; helpful staff." € 27.00
                                                                    2007*

Spain

⊞FUENGIROLA *2H4* (9km W Coastal) **Camping Los Jarales, Ctra N340, Km 197 Calahonda, 29650 Mijas-Costa (Málaga) [tel/fax 952-93 00 03]** Fr Fuengirola take N340 W twd Marbella, turn at km 197 stone; site located to N of rd. Lge, mkd pitch, hdstg, pt sl, pt shd; wc; chem disp; serviced pitch; shwrs inc; el pnts (5A) €3.15; gas; ice; lndtte; shop adj; rest; snacks; bar; playgrnd; pool; sand beach 400m; tennis; TV; no dogs; bus adj; poss cr; Eng spkn; adv bkg; rd noise; red long stay/CCI. "Well-run site; buses to Marbella & Fuengirola." ♦ € 23.00
2007*

⊞FUENTE DE PIEDRA *2G4* (700m S Urban) **Camping Fuente de Pedra (formerly La Laguna), Camino de la Rábita, Km 132 N334, 29520 Fuente de Piedra (Málaga) [952-73 52 94; fax 952-73 54 61; info@camping-rural.com; www.camping-rural.com]** Turn off A92 at km 132 sp Fuente de Piedra. Sp fr vill cent. Or to avoid town turn N fr A384 just W of turn for Bobadilla Estación, sp Sierra de Yeguas. In 2km turn R into nature reserve, cont for approx 3km, site on L at end of town. Sm, mkd pitch, hdstg, pt sl, terr, pt shd; wc; shwrs inc; el pnts (10A) €4.28; gas; lndry rm; ice; shop; rest; snacks; bar; BBQ; playgrnd; pool in ssn; internet; 25% chalets; dogs €3.21; phone; bus 700m; Eng spkn; poss noise fr adj public pool; cc acc; red long stay/CCI. "Mostly v sm pitches, but some now avail for o'fits up to 7m; gd rest; san facs clean but dated & poss stretched; adj lge lake with many flamingoes; interesting visits in region." ♦ ltd. € 23.50
2007*

FUENTE DE SAN ESTEBAN, LA *1D3* (1km E Rural) **Camping El Cruce, Ctra A62, Km 291 (E80), 37200 La Fuente de San Esteban (Salamanca) [923-44 01 30; campingelcruce@yahoo.es]** On A62/E80 (Salamanca-Portugal) km stone 291 immed behind hotel on S side of rd. Fr E watch for sp 'Cambio de Sentido' to cross main rd. Med, pt shd; wc; chem disp; shwrs; el pnts (6A) €3 (poss no earth); rest adj; snacks; bar; playgrnd; Eng spkn; some rd noise; cc acc; CCI. "Conv NH/sh stay en rte Portugal; friendly." 15 Jun-30 Sep. € 14.00
2006*

⊞FUENTEHERIDOS *2F3* (600m SW Rural) **Camping El Madroñal, Ctra Fuenteheridos-Castaño del Robledo, Km 0.6, 21292 Fuenteheridos (Huelva) [959-50 12 01; castillo@campingelmadronal.com; www.campingelmadronal.com]** Fr Zafra S on N435n turn L onto N433 sp Aracena, ignore first R to Fuenteheridos vill, camp sp R at next x-rd 500m on R. Med, mkd pitch, pt sl, pt shd; wc; chem disp; shwrs; el pnts inc; gas; lndry rm; shop & 600m; snacks, bar high ssn; BBQ; 2 pools; cycle hire; horseriding; 5% statics; dogs; phone; bus 1km; carwash; quiet; CCI. "Tranquil site in National Park of Sierra de Aracena; lge pitches among chestnut trees; nrby vill streets diff for lge o'fits." € 15.00
2007*

GALENDE see Puebla de Sanabria *1B3*

⊞GALLARDOS, LOS *4G1* (4km N Rural) **Camping Los Gallardos, 04280 Los Gallardos (Almería) [950-52 83 24; fax 950-46 95 96; reception@campinglosgallardos.com; www.campinglosgallardos.com]** Fr N leave A7/E15 at junc 525; foll sp to Los Gallardos; pass under a'route after 800m; turn L into site ent. Med, mkd pitch, hdstg, pt shd; wc; chem disp; serviced pitch; mv service pnt; shwrs inc; el pnts (10A) €3; gas; lndtte; ice; supmkt; rest (clsd Thurs); snacks; bar; pool; sand beach 10km; 2 grass bowling greens; golf; tennis adj; dogs €2.25; 40% statics; poss v cr; m'way noise; adv bkg; reds long stay/low ssn; cc acc; CCI. "British owned; 90% British clientele low ssn; gd social atmosphere; sep drinking water supply nr recep; prone to flooding wet weather." ♦ € 17.60
2007*

⊞**GANDIA** *4E2* (2km N Coastal) **Camping L'Alqueria, Ctra Gandía-Grao de Gandía s/n; 46730 Grao de Gandía (València) [962-84 04 70; fax 962-84 10 63; info@campinggandia.es; www. lalqueria.com]** Fr N on A7/AP7 exit 60 onto N332 dir Grao de Gandía. Site sp on rd bet Gandía & seafront. Fr S exit junc 61 & foll sp to beaches. Lge, mkd pitch, hdstg, pt shd; htd wc; chem disp; mv service pnt; baby facs; shwrs inc; el pnts (6-10A) €3.30-5.50; gas; lndtte; shop; rest adj; snacks; bar; playgrnd; htd, covrd pool; jacuzzi; sand beach 800m; games area; cycle hire; wifi internet; entmnt; 30% statics; sm dogs (under 10kg) €1.80; phone; bus; adv bkg; quiet; cc acc; red long stay/snr citizens; CCI. "Excel clean, pleasant, well-managed site & facs; helpful family owners; lovely pool; easy walk to town & stn; excel beach nrby; bus & train to Valencia." ♦ € 35.60   2007*

See advertisement

⊞**GARGANTILLA DEL LOZOYA** *1C4* (2km Rural) **Camping Monte Holiday, 28739 Gargantilla del Lozoya (Madrid) [tel/fax 918-69 52 78; monteholiday@campings.net; www.sierranorte. com/holiday]** Fr N on N1/E5 Burgos-Madrid rd turn R on M604 at km stone 69 sp Rascafria; in 8km turn R immed after rlwy bdge & then L up track in 300m, foll site sp. Do not ent vill. Lge, terr, pt sl, pt shd; wc; chem disp; baby facs; shwrs inc; el pnts (7A) €3; lndtte; shop 6km; rest; bar; pool; rv sw; 80% statics; phone; little Eng spkn; adv bkg; quiet; cc acc; red CCI. "Interesting, friendly site; vg san facs; gd views; easy to find; some facs clsd low ssn; lovely area but site isolated in winter & poss heavy snow; conv NH fr m'way & for Madrid & Segovia." ♦ € 19.60   2006*

GARRIGUELLA see Figueres *3B3*

⊞**GARRUCHA** *4G1* (6km N Coastal) **Camping Cuevas Mar, Ctra Garrucha-Villaricos, 04618 Palomares-Cuevas de Almanzora (Almería) [tel/ fax 950-46 73 82; cuevasmar@arrakis.es; www. campingcuevasmar.com]** Exit A7 at junc 537 sp Cuevas del Almanzora & take A1200 sp Vera. In 2km turn L onto AL7101 (ALP118) sp Palomares & turn R at site sp at rndabt immed bef Palomares, site on L in 1.5km. Fr S exit A7 at junc 520, by-pass Garrucha, site on L in 6km. Med, hdg/mkd pitch, hdstg, pt shd; wc; chem disp; mv service pnt; baby facs; shwrs inc; el pnts (6A) €3.75; gas 3km; lndtte; ice; shop; tradsmn; rest 500m; bar; BBQ; playgrnd; pool; jacuzzi; sand/shgl beach 150m; wifi internet; 10% statics; dogs €1.90; bus; poss cr; adv bkg; red low ssn/long stay; CCI. "Immac, well-maintained site; lge pitches; friendly owner; vg san facs; only 1 tap for drinking water; cycle track adj; beautiful coastline; mosquito problems; Fri mkt Garrucha; popular long stay site." ♦ ltd. € 19.00   2007*

⊞**GARRUCHA** *4G1* (4km NE Coastal) **Camping Almanzora (Naturist), Ctra Garrucha-Palomares, 04620 Vera (Almería) [950-46 74 25; fax 950-46 73 82; www.campingalmanzora.com]** SE on N340 Murcia-Almería rd, exit Vera, foll sp Garrucha. In 5km L & foll site sp. At junc with Garrucha & Villaricos rd turn L, then R at Vera Playa Hotel. Site on L at rndabt on hotel access rd. Lge, pt shd, wc; chem disp; mv service pnt; shwrs inc; baby facs; el pnts (16A) inc (rec long lead); gas; lndtte; shop; tradsmn; rest; snacks; bar; playgrnd; pools; sand beach 300m; tennis; phone; quiet; poss cr; few statics; adv bkg rec; dogs; Eng spkn; cc acc; reds for long stay; CCI. "Excel site but part overlooked fr main rd; many long-stay winter visitors; naturist beach adj; adj hotel naturist until 8pm; many pitches have shade awnings but sm & poss diff for lge o'fits; Friday mkt at Garrucha." € 30.00

2005*

GATA *1D3* (4km W Rural) **Camping Sierra de Gata, Ctra EX109 a Gata, Km 4.100, 10860 Gata (Cáceres) [tel/fax 927-67 21 68; sierradegata@ campingsonline.com]** Foll sp Gata fr rd EX109/ C526, site sp on unmkd rd on rvside. Med, shd; wc; chem disp; shwrs; el pnts (5-10A); lndry rm; shop; rest 100m; snacks; playgrnd; pool; rv sw; fishing; paddling pool; tennis; games area; cycle hire; TV; quiet. "Peaceful, family-run site in beautiful area." ♦ ltd. 12 Mar-31 Oct.   2004*

As soon as we get home I'm going to post all these site report forms to the editor for inclusion in next year's guide. I don't want to miss the September deadline.

GAVA *3C3* (5km S Coastal) **Camping Tres Estrellas, C31, Km 186.2, 08850 Gavà (Barcelona) [936-33 06 37; fax 936-33 15 25; fina@ camping3estrellas.com;www.camping3estrellas. com]** Fr S take C31 (Castelldefels to Barcelona), exit 13. Site at km 186.2 300m past rd bdge. Fr N foll Barcelona airport sp, then C31 junc 13 Gavà-Mar slip rd immed under rd bdge. Cross m'way, turn R then R again to join m'way heading N for 400m. Lge, mkd pitch, pt sl, pt shd; htd wc; chem disp; mv service pnt; shwrs inc; el pnts (6A) €4.80 (poss rev pol &/or no earth); gas; lndtte; ice; shop; rest; snacks; bar; playgrnd; htd pool; sand beach adj; tennis; entmnt; internet; TV; 20% statics; dogs €3.95; phone; bus to Barcelona 400m; poss cr; Eng spkn; adv bkg; some aircraft & rd noise; cc acc; red snr citizens/CCI. "Excel site; 20 min by bus to Barcelona cent." ♦ 15 Mar-15 Oct. € 29.50 (CChq acc)   2007*

Spain

GERONA *3B3* (8km S Rural) **Camping Can Toni Manescal, Ctra Llambillas, Km 2, 17458 Fornells de la Selva (Gerona) [972-47 61 17; fax 972-47 67 35; campinggirona@campinggirona. com]** Fr N leave AP7 at junc 7 onto N11 dir Barcelona. In 2km turn L to Fornells de la Selva; in vill turn L at church (sp); over rv; in 1km bear R & site on L in 400m. Sm, mkd pitch, pt sl, pt shd; wc; chem disp; baby facs; shwrs inc; el pnts (5A) €2.70 (poss long lead req); gas; lndtte; shop, rest 2km; snacks, bar 4km; playgrnd; pool; sand beach 23km; dogs; phone; bus 1.5km; Eng spkn; adv bkg; quiet; cc acc; CCI. "V pleasant, open site; gd base for lovely medieval city Gerona - foll bus stn sp for gd, secure m'van parking; san facs poss dirty low ssn; welcoming & helpful owners; lge pitches; cold water only to washbasins; local rlwy stn; excel cycle path into Gerona, along old rlwy line; Gerona mid-May flower festival rec." 16 Jun-15 Sep. € 15.00
2005*

GETAFE see Madrid *1D4*

The opening dates and prices on this campsite have changed. I'll send a site report form to the editor for the next edition of the guide.

⊞**GIJON** *1A3* (4km E Rural) **Camping Deva-Gijón, Parroquia de Deva, 33394 Deva (Asturias) [985-13 38 48; fax 985-13 38 89; info@campingdeva-gijon.com; www.campingdeva-gijon.com]** Exit A8 junc 382 N. Site nr km marker 65 - foll sp carefully. Lge, mkd pitch; pt sl, terr, pt shd; serviced pitches; wc; chem disp; shwrs inc; el pnts (16A) €3.30; lndtte; ice; shop, rest, snacks in ssn; bar; pool & paddling pool; sand beach 4km; tennis; cycle hire; golf 3km; internet; 50% statics; bus; car wash; sep car park; poss cr; noisy visitors & nr rd; cc acc €40 min; CCI. "Gd touring base; facs ltd low ssn & v open san facs not rec winter." ♦ € 25.20
2007*

GIJON *1A3* (13km NW Coastal) **Camping Buenavista, Ctra Dormon-Perlora s/n, Carreño, 33491 Perlora (Asturias) [tel/fax 985-87 17 93; buenavista@campingbuenavista.com; www. campingbuenavista.com]** Fr Gijón take AS19 sp Tremañes & foll rd for approx 5km. On sharp L bend take exit on R (Avilés) & immed L onto AS239 sp Candás/Perlora, site sp. Med, terr, pt shd; wc; chem disp; shwrs; el pnts inc; gas; lndtte; shop; rest; snacks; bar; playgrnd; sand beach 500m; 70% statics; bus 200m; site open w/e only out of ssn & clsd Dec & Jan; poss cr; noisy; CCI. "Oviedo historic town worth a visit; quite steep pull-out, need gd power/weight ratio." 15 Jun-15 Sep. € 22.70
2007*

⊞**GIJON** *1A3* (13km NW Coastal) **Camping Perlora, Ctra Candás, Km 12, Perán, 33491 Candás (Asturias) [985-87 00 48]** Fr A8 take exit Candás & foll rd to seafront, site sp at end promenade in Candás. Med, pt sl, unshd; wc; chem disp; mv service pnt; some serviced pitches; shwrs €0.50; el pnts (5A) €2.88; gas; lndtte; ice; shop; rest; playgrnd; sand beach 1km; tennis; watersports; fishing; 80% statics; phone; poss cr; Eng spkn; quiet; no cc acc; red long stay; CCI. "Excel; v helpful staff; lovely, immac site on dramatic headland; ltd space for tourers; superb san facs, ltd low ssn." ♦ € 17.65
2005*

GIRONELLA *3B3* (500m S Rural) **Camping Gironella, Ctra C16/E9, Km 86.750 Entrada Sud Gironella, 08680 Gironella (Barcelona) [938-25 15 29; fax 938-22 97 37; informacio@ campinggironella.com; www.campinggironella. com]** Site is bet Berga & Puig-reig on C16/E9. Well sp. Med, hdg/mkd pitch, hdstg, pt shd; wc; chem disp; serviced pitch; baby facs; shwrs inc; el pnts (3-10A) €2.75-7; gas; lndtte; shop; tradsmn; rest; snacks; bar; playgrnd; htd pool; games rm; entmnt; TV rm; 90% statics; dogs €1; phone; bus 600m; poss cr; Eng spkn; adv bkg (dep req); quiet; CCI. "Pleasant site; friendly staff; ltd touring pitches (phone ahead); conv NH." ♦ Holy Week, 1 Jul-15 Sep & w/e low ssn. € 18.00
2007*

GORLIZ *1A4* (700m Coastal) **Camping Arrien, Uresarantze Bidea, 48630 Gorliz (Bizkaia) [946-77 19 11; fax 946-77 44 80; arrien@teleline.es; www.campingarrien.com]** Fr Bilbao foll m'way to Getxo, then 637/634 thro Sopelana & Plentzia to Gorliz. In Gorliz foll sp to site on L. Lge, pt sl, pt shd; wc; chem disp; shwrs inc; el pnts (3-5A) €3.75; lndtte; gas; shop; rest; snacks; bar; BBQ; playgrnd; sand beach 700m; 60% statics; dogs; phone; bus 150m; poss cr; Eng spkn; cc acc; 10% red CCI. "Useful base for Bilbao & ferry (approx 1hr); bus to Plentzia every 20 mins, fr there can get metro to Bilbao; friendly, v helpful staff." 1 Mar-31 Oct. € 21.70
2007*

GRANADA *2G4* (4km N Rural) **Camping Granada, Cerro de la Cruz s/n, 18210 Peligros (Granada) [tel/fax 958-34 05 48; pruizlopez1953@yahoo. es]** S on A44 fr Jaén twd Granada; take exit 121 & foll sp Peligros. Turn L at rndabt after 1km by Spar shop, site access rd 300m on R. Single track access 1km. Med, hdstg, terr, pt shd; wc; chem disp; shwrs inc; el pnts (10A) €3.21; gas; lndtte; shop; rest; bar; playgrnd; pool; tennis; dogs €1.30; bus 1km; poss cr; some Eng spkn; adv bkg; quiet; cc acc; CCI. "Friendly, helpful owners; well-run site in olive grove; vg facs; superb views; gd access for m'vans but poss diff for v lge o'fits; pitches poss uneven & muddy after rain; site rds & access steep; conv Alhambra - book tickets at recep." ♦ ltd. 15 Mar-30 Sep. € 20.54
2006*

GRANADA *2G4* (4km N) **Camping Motel Sierra Nevada**, Avda de Madrid 107, 18014 Granada [958-15 00 62; fax 958-15 09 54; campingmotel@ terra.es; www.campingsierranevada.com] App Granada S-bound on A44 & exit at junc 123, foll dir Granada. Site on R in 1.5km just beyond bus stn & opp El Campo supmkt, well sp. Lge, shd; wc; chem disp; mv service pnt; baby facs; shwrs inc; el pnts (6A) €3.60; gas; lndtte; ice; supmkt opp; rest; snacks; BBQ; playgrnd; 2 pools adj; sports facs; dogs; bus to city cent; poss cr (arr early); noisy at w/e; cc acc; CCI. "V helpful staff; excel san facs, but poss ltd low ssn; motel rms avail; can book Alhambra tickets at recep (24 hrs notice); vg & v conv 'city' site." ♦ 1 Mar-30 Oct. € 22.60   2006*

⊞**GRANADA** *2G4* (3km SE Urban) **Camping Reina Isabel**, Ctra de La Zubia, Km 4, 18140 La Zubia (Granada) [958-59 00 41; fax 958-59 11 91; info@ reinaisabelcamping.com; www.reinaisabel camping.com] Exit A44 nr Granada at junc sp Ronda Sur, dir Sierra Nevada, Alhambra, then exit 2 sp La Zubia. Foll site sp. Med, hdg pitch, hdstg, shd; htd wc; chem disp; mv service pnt; baby facs; shwrs inc; el pnts (5A) €2.90 (poss rev pol); gas; lndtte; ice; shop; supmkt 1km; tradsmn; rest; snacks; bar; pool high ssn; internet; TV; dogs; phone; bus; Eng spkn; poss cr; quiet except during festival in May; cc acc; 20% red 7+ days low ssn; red CCI. "Well-run, v busy site; gd rest; poss shwrs v hot/cold - warn children; easy to find; helpful staff; sm pitches; bus to Granada every 30 mins at w/e, every 20 mins fr 0700 in week; v busy; conv Sierra Nevada & Alhambra (order tickets at site to avoid queues peak periods)." ♦ € 21.00   2007*

See advertisement

⊞**GRANADA** *2G4* (13km E Rural) **Camping Las Lomas**, 11 Ctra de Güejar-Sierra, Km 6.5, 18160 Güejar-Sierra (Granada) [958-48 47 42; fax 958-48 40 00; laslomas@campings.net; www. campinglaslomas.com] Fr A44 exit onto by-pass 'Ronda Sur', then exit onto A395 sp Sierra Nevada. In approx 4km exit sp Cenes, turn under A395 to T-junc & turn R sp Güejar-Sierra, Embalse de Canales, site sp bef vill. Med, hdg/mkd pitch, terr, pt shd; htd wc; chem disp; mv service pnt; baby facs; fam bthrm; shwrs inc; el pnts (10A) €3.50 (poss no earth); gas; lndtte; shop; rest; snacks; bar; playgrnd; pool; waterskiing nrby; internet; dogs free; poss cr; Eng spkn; adv bkg ess; quiet; red long stay; cc acc; CCI. "Helpful, friendly site; conv Granada (bus at gate); access poss diff for lge o'fits; excel san facs; gd shop & rest; beautiful mountain scenery; excel site." ♦ ltd. € 23.00
                                              2006*

GRANADA *2G4* (11km S Rural) **Camping Suspiro del Moro**, 107 Avda de Madrid, 18630 Otura (Granada) [958-55 54 11; fax 958-55 51 05; info@campingsuspirodelmoro.com; www. campingsuspirodelmoro.com] On A44/E902 dir Motril, exit junc 139. Foll camp sp fr W side of rndabt; site visible at top of slight rise on W side of A44. Med, mkd pitch, hdstg, shd; wc; chem disp; mv service pnt; shwrs inc; el pnts (5A) €2.40 (poss no earth); gas; lndry rm; ice; shop; snacks & rest in ssn; bar; playgrnd; lge pool; tennis; games area; 10% statics; phone; bus; Eng spkn; rd noise & noisy rest at w/e; 35% red low ssn; cc acc; CCI. "Decent site; reasonable pitches; quiet low ssn; clean facs but inadequate for site this size; rest poss noisy; hourly bus to Granada." ♦ ltd. 1 Mar-1 Nov. € 15.00
                                              2004*

Spain

⊞**GRANADA** *2G4* (10km W Rural) **Camping Maria Eugenia, Avda Andalucia 190, Santa Fé, 18014 Granada [958-20 06 06; fax 958-20 63 17; campingmariaeugenia@gmail.com; www. campingmariaeugenia.com]** On A329/A92G fr Granada dir Antequera. Nr airport; site on main rd, well sp. Fr W exit A92 junc 230 dir Granada. Bypass Santa Fé, site on R in 3km. Sm, mkd pitch, pt shd; wc; chem disp; mv service pnt; shwrs inc; el pnts (5A) €3.20; lndtte; shop; rest; snacks; bar; BBQ; pool; TV; 30% statics; dogs; phone; bus fr site ent; poss cr; rd noise. "Friendly, family-run site; unkempt low ssn; conv Granada, bus adj; NH only." € 18.00
2007*

⊞**GRAUS** *3B2* (6km S Rural) **Camping Bellavista & Subenuix, Embalse de Barasona, Ctra Graus N123, Km 23, 22435 La Puebla de Castro (Huesca) [974-54 51 13; fax 974 34 70 71; info@ hotelcampingbellavista.com; www.hotelcamping bellavista.com]** Fr E on N230/N123 ignore 1st sp for Graus. Cont to 2nd sp 'El Grado/Graus' & turn R. Site on L in 1km adj hotel. Med, mkd pitch, terr, pt shd; htd wc; chem disp; shwrs inc; el pnts (10A) €3.50; gas; lndry rm; shop; rest; snacks; bar; playgrnd; pool; lake sw adj; watersports; fishing; tennis; horseriding; entmnt; internet; TV rm; 50% statics; dogs €1.50; phone; Eng spkn; adv bkg; noisy at w/e; red low ssn; cc acc; CCI. "V helpful staff; sm pitches; excel rest; beautiful position above lake; mountain views." € 17.90
2006*

GRAUS *3B2* (5km SW Rural) **Camping Lago Barasona, Ctra N123A, Km 25, 22435 La Puebla de Castro (Huesca) [974-54 51 48 or 974-24 69 06; fax 974-54 52 28; info@lagobarasona. com; www.lagobarasona.com]** Fr E on N123, ignore 1st sp for Graus. Cont to 2nd sp 'El Grado/ Graus/Benasque' & turn R. Site on L in 2km. Lge, hdg/mkd pitch, hdstg, sl, terr, shd; htd wc; chem disp; mv service pnt; shwrs inc; el pnts (6A) €3.70; gas; lndry rm; ice; shop; tradsmn; rest; snacks; bar; BBQ; playgrnd; 2 pools; lake beach & sw 100m; watersports; sailing; tennis; horseriding 1km; entmnt; TV rm; 15% statics; dogs; Eng spkn; adv bkg; quiet; cc acc; red long stay; CCI. "Excel, well-equipped site; lge pitches; v helpful staff; highly rec." ♦ 1 Mar-9 Dec. € 21.50 (CChq acc)
2005*

⊞**GUADALUPE** *2E3* (1.5km S Rural) **Camping Las Villuercas, Ctra Villanueva-Huerta del Río, Km 2, 10140 Guadalupe (Cáceres) [927-36 71 39; fax 927-36 70 28]** Exit A5/E90 at junc 178 onto EX118 to Guadalupe. Do not ent town. Site sp on R at rndabt at foot of hill. Med, shd; wc; shwrs; el pnts €2.50 (poss no earth/rev pol); lndtte; shop; rest; bar; playgrnd; pool; tennis; cc acc. "Vg; helpful owners; ltd facs low ssn; some pitches sm & poss not avail in wet weather; nr famous monastery." € 12.50
2007*

⊞**GUARDA, A** *1B2* (1km E Coastal) **Camping Santa Tecla, Salcidos, Ctra Tui-La Guardia, 36780 A Guarda (Pontevedra) [986-61 30 11; fax 986-61 30 63; campingstatecla@navegalia .com; www.campingsantatecla.com]** S fr Vigo on C550. Site well sp thro A Guarda. Lge, mkd pitch, pt shd; wc; chem disp; mv service pnt; shwrs; el pnts €3; gas; lndtte; shop; rest; bar; playgrnd; pool; rv sw adj; games area; dogs; bus 1km; Eng spkn; quiet. "Views across estuary to Portugal; 2km fr ferry; excel san facs; ltd facs low ssn." ♦ € 15.00
2004*

⊞**GUARDAMAR DEL SEGURA** *4F2* (2km N Rural/Coastal) **Camping Marjal, Ctra N332, Km 73.4, 03140 Guardamar de Segura (Alicante) [966-72 70 70 or 966-72 50 22; fax 966-72 66 95; camping@marjal.com; www.campingmarjal.com]** Fr N exit A7 junc 72 sp Aeropuerto/Santa Pola; in 5km turn R onto N332 sp Santa Pola/Cartagena, U-turn at km 73.4, site sp on R at km 73.5. Lge, hdg/mkd pitch, hdstg, pt shd; all serviced pitches; wc; chem disp; baby facs; sauna; shwrs inc; el pnts (16A) €3 or metered; gas; ice; lndtte; ice; supmkt; rest; snacks & bar; BBQ; playgrnd; 2 htd pools (1 covrd); sand beaches 1km (inc naturist); lake sw 15km; tennis; sports cent; cycle hire; entmnt; child entmnt; internet; TV rm; 18% statics; dogs €3; phone; recep 0800-2300; adv bkg rec; Eng spkn; quiet; red long stay/low ssn; cc acc; CCI. "Gd facs; friendly, helpful staff; excel family entmnt & activities; excel." ♦ € 51.00
2007*

See advertisement

GUARDAMAR DEL SEGURA *4F2* (1km S Coastal) **Camping Palm-Mar, 03140 Guardamar del Segura (Alicante) [tel/fax 965-72 88 56; campingplammar@hotmail.com; www.costa blanca.org/campingpalm-mar.asp]** Foll site sp fr N332 at x-rds, twds sea. Med, hdg/mkd pitch, pt shd; wc; chem disp; mv service pnt; baby facs; shwrs inc; el pnts (3A) €5; lndtte; ice; shop; rest; snacks; bar; BBQ; playgrnd; sand beach adj; internet; TV rm; 20% statics; dogs; bus adj; no adv bkg; quiet; red long stay." 15 May-30 Sep. € 27.00
2007*

GUARDAMAR DEL SEGURA *4F2* (3km S Urban) **Camping Mare Nostrum, Ctra N332 Cartagena-Alicante, Km 67, 03140 Guardamar del Segura (Alicante) [tel/fax 965-72 80 73; dymercuryhotmail.com]** Entrance to site immed off N332 on L fr Guardamar del Segura dir Torrevieja. Med, mkd pitch, hdstg, pt shd; htd wc; chem disp; baby facs; shwrs inc; el pnts (5A) €2.50; gas; lndtte; shop; snacks; bar; playgrnd; pool high ssn; sand beach 400m; 10% statics; dogs; phone; bus; some daytime rd noise; cc acc. "Rec sh stay/NH; dir access to beach thro pine woods." Holy Week-15 Sep. € 21.00
2005*

⊞**GUARDAMAR DEL SEGURA** *4F2* (12km W Rural) **Camping Sheppards Rest (formerly Quinta Mare), 99 Partida Cebades, Vereda Los Niguez, 03150 Dolores (Alicante) [965-99 89 12 or 617-00 34 92 (mob); jillanddaniel@myway. com]** A7 fr Alicante twd Murcia. At junc 724 take AP37 sp Cartagena/Torrevieja to junc 737 Dolores. At rndabt (Max) take 1st exit, at next rndabt go strt over two Dolores. At next rndabt take 2nd exit twd Catrel. Go thro 2 traff lts, past Repsol g'ge & green railings to sm x-rds with orange house on R. Turn R & travel approx 3km to yellow house on R. Vareda Los Niguez is 2nd rd on R, cont to last house at end. Sm, hdg pitch, hdstg, unshd; wc; chem disp; shwrs; el pnts (10A) inc; gas; lndtte; shops, snacks, bar 3km; BBQ; playgrnd; pool; sand beach 10km; dogs; phone 3km; adv bkg dep req; quiet; cc not acc; CCI. "14km fr historical cent (Elche); excel shopping malls in town; old Arab Quarter; El Hondo Nature Reserve (5km); gd birdwatching; gd cycling area." ♦ € 15.00   2006*

⊞**GUARDIOLA DE BERGUEDA** *3B3* (3.5km W Rural) **Camping El Bergueda, Ctra B400, Km 3.5, 08694 Guardiola de Bergueda (Barcelona) [938-22 74 32; campingbergueda@worldonline. es; www.campingbergueda.com]** On C16 S take B400 W dir Saldes. Site is approx 10km S of Cadí Tunnel. Med, mkd pitch, some hdstg, terr, pt shd; wc; chem disp; baby facs; shwrs; el pnts (6A) €3.90 (poss rev pol); gas; lndtte; ice; shop; tradsmn; rest; snacks; bar; BBQ; playgrnd; pool; paddling pool; games area; games rm; TV; some statics; phone; dogs; Eng spkn; quiet; CCI. "V helpful staff; vg san facs; beautiful situation with mountain views; gd walking; a gem of a site." ♦ € 18.20   2007*

GUEJAR SIERRA see Granada *2G4*

Before we move on, I'm going to fill in some site report forms and post them off to the editor, otherwise they won't arrive in time for the deadline at the end of September.

GUITIRIZ *1A2* (1km N Rural) **Camping El Mesón, Camino de Santiago, 27305 Guitiriz (Lugo) [982-37 32 88]** On A6 NW fr Lugo, exit km 535 sp Guitiriz, site sp. Sm, pt sl, pt shd; wc; chem disp (wc); shwrs inc; el pnts (6A) inc; gas; supmkt 1km; rest; bar; playgrnd; pool 6km; rv sw 500m; phone; bus adj; quiet. 15 Jun-15 Sep. € 11.80   2004*

⊞**HARO** *1B4* (500m N Urban) **Camping de Haro, Avda Miranda 1, 26200 Haro (La Rioja) [941-31 27 37; fax 941-31 20 68; campingdeharo@ fer.es; www.campingdeharo.com]** Fr N or S on N124 take exit sp Haro. In 500m at rndabt take 1st exit, under rlwy bdge, cont to site on R immed bef rv bdge. Fr AP68 exit junc 9. Fr W on N232 fr Pancorbo, at ent to town on LR111, bear L; down hill, over rv bdge; foll site sp. Avoid cont into town cent. Med, hdg/mkd pitch, pt shd; wc; chem disp; mv service pnt; shwrs inc (am only in winter); el pnts (3-5A) €3.60; gas; lndry rm; shop & 600m; snacks; bar; playgrnd; htd pool high ssn; 70% statics; dogs €2; phone; bus 800m; car wash; site clsd 11 Dec-9 Jan; poss cr; Eng spkn; adv bkg; quiet (not w/e), some rv noise; red low ssn; cc acc; CCI. "Clean, tidy site but dusty rds & poss untidy low ssn; friendly owner; some sm pitches & diff turns; excel facs; busy at w/ends; sh walk to v pleasant town nr vineyards & mountains; conv Rioja bodegas; 2 hrs to Bilbao ferry; conv NH." ♦ € 17.76 (CChq acc)
2007*

⊞**HARO** *1B4* (10km SW) **Camping De La Rioja, Ctra de Haro/Santo Domingo de la Calzada, Km 8.5, 26240 Castañares de la Rioja (La Rioja) [941-30 01 74; fax 941-30 01 56; info@ campingdelarioja.com]** Exit AP68 junc 9, take rd twd Santo Domingo de la Calzada. Foll by-pass round Casalarreina, site on R nr rvside just past vill on rd LR111. Lge, hdg pitch, pt shd; htd wc; chem disp; shwrs; el pnts (4A) €3.48 (poss rev pol); gas; lndtte; sm shop; rest; snacks; bar; pool high ssn; tennis; cycle hire; entmnt; dogs; clsd 10 Dec-8 Jan; 90% statics; dogs; site clsd 9 Dec-7 Jan; poss cr; adv bkg; noisy high ssn; cc acc. "Fair site; basic san facs but clean; ltd facs in winter; sm pitches; conv for Rioja wine cents; Bilbao ferry." € 24.50
2007*

⊞**HECHO** *3B1* (8km N Rural) **Camping Borda Bisaltico, Ctra Gabardito, Km 2, 22720 Hecho (Huesca) [974-37 53 88; bordabisaltico@staragon. com; www.staragon.com/bordabisaltico]** Fr Jaca W on N240 dir Pamplona, after 25km at Puente la Reina de Jaca turn R onto A176 then take HU210. Foll sp. Site in 8km. Take care, 1.5km narr, winding, potholed rd. Med, sl, terr, pt shd; wc; chem disp; mv service pnt; baby facs; shwrs inc; el pnts (6A) €4.82; gas; lndtte; tradsmn; rest; bar; no statics; dogs; site clsd Nov; phone; bus; quiet; CCI. "Well-organised site; friendly owners; camping area around mountain inn; beautiful views; excel san facs; gd walking, climbing, birdwatching; extensive improvements planned 2007-9 inc pool; excel." € 18.72   2006*

⊞**HECHO** *3B1* (1km S Rural) **Camping Valle de Hecho, Ctra Puente La Reina-Hecho s/n, 22720 Hecho (Huesca)** [974-37 53 61; fax 976-27 78 42; www.campinghecho.com] Leave Jaca W on N240. After 25km turn N on A176 at Puente La Reina de Jaca. Site on W of rd, o'skts of Hecho/Echo. Med, mkd pitch, pt sl, pt shd; htd wc; chem disp; mv service pnt; shwrs inc; el pnts (5-15A) €3.60; gas; lndtte; shop; rest; snacks; bar; playgrnd; pool; games area; 50% statics; dogs; phone; bus 200m; quiet; cc acc; CCI. "Pleasant site in foothills of Pyrenees; excel, spotless facs but poss inadequate hot water; gd birdwatching area; Hecho fascinating vill; shop & bar clsd low ssn except w/e; v ltd facs & poss neglected low ssn." € 16.00   2006*

HERRADURA, LA see Almuñécar *2H4*

HONDARRIBIA see Irun *3A1*

⊞**HORCAJO DE LOS MONTES** *2E4* (200m Rural) **Camping El Mirador de Cabañeros, Calle Cañada Real Segoviana s/n, 13110 Horcajo de los Montes (Ciudad Real)** [926-77 54 39; fax 926-77 50 03; camping-cabaneros@hortur.com; www.campingcabaneros.com] At km 53 off CM4103 Horcajo-Alcoba rd, 200m fr vill. CM4106 to Horcajo fr NW poor in parts. Med, mkd pitch, hdstg, terr, pt shd; htd wc; chem disp; mv service pnt; baby facs; shwrs; el pnts (6A) €2.50; gas; shop 500m; rest; bar; BBQ; playgrnd; pool; rv sw 12km; games area; games rm; tennis 500m; cycle hire; entmnt; TV; 10% statics; phone; adv bkg rec high ssn; quiet; red long stay; cc acc; CCI. "Beside Cabañeros National Park; beautiful views." ♦ € 15.90   2005*

HOSPITAL DE ORBIGO *1B3* (S Urban) **Camping Don Suero de Quiñones, 24286 Hospital de Órbigo (León)** [987-36 10 18; fax 987-38 82 36; camping@hospitaldeorbigo.com; www.hospitaldeorbigo.com] N120 rd fr León to Astorga, km 30. Site well sp fr N120. Narr streets in Hospital. Med, hdg pitch, pt shd; wc; shwrs; el pnts (6A) €1.90; lndtte; shop; bar; rest adj; BBQ; pool adj; bus to León nr; 50% statics; dogs; poss open w/e only mid Apr-May; phone; poss cr; Eng spkn; cc acc; CCI. "Statics v busy w/ends, facs stretched; poss noisy; phone ahead to check site open if travelling close to opening/closing dates." ♦ Holy Week-30 Sep. € 14.00   2007*

⊞**HOSPITALET DE L'INFANT, L'** *3C2* (2km S Coastal) **Camping Cala d'Oques, Via Augusta s/n, 43890 L'Hospitalet de l'Infant (Tarragona)** [977-82 32 54; fax 977-82 06 91; eroller@tinet.org; www.tinet.org/~eroller/] Exit AP7 junc 38 onto N340. Take rd sp L'Hospitalet de l'Infant at km 1123. Lge, terr, shd; htd wc; mv service pnt; baby facs; shwrs; el pnts (5A) €3.90; gas; lndtte; shop; rest; bar; playgrnd; sand/shgl beach adj (naturist beaches nr); entmnt; dogs €2.95; phone; poss cr; quiet; ltd facs low ssn; red snr citizens/long stay; CCI. "Excel, well-run, winter NH; friendly, relaxing; gd facs; vg rest; sea views; poss v windy; conv Aquapolis & Port Aventura." € 33.00   2006*

HOSPITALET DE L'INFANT, L' *3C2* (2km S Coastal) **Camping El Templo del Sol (Naturist), Playa del Torn, 43890 L'Hospitalet de l'Infant (Tarragona)** [977-82 34 34; fax 977-82 34 64; info@eltemplodelsol.com; www.eltemplodelsol.com] Leave A7 at exit 38 or N340 twds town cent. Turn R (S) along coast rd for 2km. Ignore 1st camp sp on L, site 200m further on L. Lge, hdg/mkd pitch, pt sl, pt shd; wc; chem disp; serviced pitch; shwrs; el pnts (6A) inc; gas; lndtte; ice; shop; rest; snacks; bar; playgrnd; pools; solar-energy park; jacuzzi; official naturist sand/shgl beach adj; cinema/theatre; TV rm; 5% statics; poss cr; Eng spkn; adv bkg (dep); some rlwy noise rear of site; 15% red 14+ days; cc acc. "Excel naturist site; no dogs, radios or TV on pitches; lge private wash/shwr rms; pitches v tight; conv Port Aventura; mosquitoes a problem; poss strong winds - take care with awnings." ♦ 1 Apr-22 Oct. € 40.45   2006*

> There aren't many sites open this early in the year. We'd better phone ahead to check that the one we're heading for is actually open.

⊞**HOSPITALET DE L'INFANT, L'** *3C2* (8km S Coastal) **Camping La Masia, Playa de l'Almadrava, Km 1121, N340, 43890 L'Hospitalet de l'Infant (Tarragona)** [977-82 31 02 or 82 05 88; fax 977-82 33 54; info@campinglamasia.com; www.campinglamasia.com] Site sp on sea side of N340 at km 1121. Med, hdstg, sl, terr, pt shd; wc; chem disp (wc); jaccuzi; baby facs; sauna; shwrs inc; el pnts (5A) inc; lndtte; shop; rest; bar; BBQ; playgrnd; pool; beach adj; gym; tennis; games area; squash; minigolf; cycle hire; horseriding 5km; golf 6km; entmnt; games/TV rm; internet; 80% statics; phone; poss cr; rlwy noise. "Not rec lge o'fits due poss diff access to pitches." ♦ € 32.35   2004*

HOYOS DEL ESPINO *1D3* (4km E) **Camping Navagredos, Ctra de Valdecasas, 05635 Navarredonda de Gredos (Ávila)** [920-20 74 76; fax 983-29 58 41; proatur@proatur.com] Fr N take N502 S. Then W on C500 twd El Barco. Site sp in Navarredonda on L in 2km, just bef petrol stn. Med, pt sl, pt shd; wc; chem disp; mv service pnt; baby facs; shwrs inc; el pnts (10A) €2.73; lndry rm; shops 2km; tradsmn; rest & snacks in ssn; bar; phone; quiet. "Excel walking in Gredos mountains; some facs poorly maintained low ssn; steep slope to san facs; rd app site steep with bends; site open w/ends until mid-Nov." ♦ Easter-12 Oct. € 12.65   2006*

Spain

HOYOS DEL ESPINO *1D3* (1.5km S Rural) **Camping Gredos, Ctra Plataforma, Km.1,8, 05634 Hoyos del Espino (Ávila) [920-20 75 85; campingredos@campingredos.com; www. campingredos.com]** Fr N110 turn E at El Barco onto AV941 for approx 41km; at Hoyos del Espino turn S twd Plataforma de Gredos. Site on R in 1.8km. Or fr N502 turn W dir Parador de Gredos to Hoyos del Espino, then as above. Sm, pt sl, pt shd; wc; chem disp; shwrs inc; el pnts €2.90; gas; lndtte; shop 1km; snacks; playgrnd; rv sw adj; cycle hire; horseriding; adv bkg; quiet; CCI. "Lovely mountain scenery." ♦ Holy Week & 1 May-1 Oct. € 12.20
2004*

⊞**HUELVA** *2G2* (8km SE Coastal) **Camping Playa de Mazagón, Calle Cuesta de la Barca, s/n, 21130 Mazagón [959-37 62 08; fax 959-53 62 56; info@campingplayamazagon.com; www. campingplayamazagon.com]** Best app fr A494 fr Matalascañas, site clearly sp. Of fr A49 ent Huelva & eventually pick up & foll sp twds indus zone. Head for coast, keep sea on R; over bdge & strt on twds Mazagón; site on R clearly sp off rd up hill. Lge, mkd pitch, pt shd; wc; chem disp; shwrs inc; el pnts (10A) €5.61; gas; lndry rm; ice; shop; rest; snacks; bar; playgrnd; pool; paddling pool; sand beach adj; 75% statics; dogs €3; phone; poss cr; quiet; cc acc; red CCI. "Close to Doñana National Park; poss exposed low ssn; poss unclean; some pitches v soft; more sites along coast; fair sh stay/ NH only." € 22.45
2007*

HUESCA *3B2* (1.5km SW Urban) **Camping San Jorge, Calle Ricardo del Arco s/n, 22004 Huesca [tel/fax 974-22 74 16; contacto@ campingsanjorge.com; www.campingsanjorge. com]** Exit A23 S of town at km 568 & head N twd town cent. Look for sp immed bef rlwy x-ing & turn L. Site ent strt ahead in municipal sports park, foll sp for pool. Med, shd; wc; chem disp (wc); shwrs inc; el pnts (10A) €3.53; lndtte; shop; snacks; bar; 2 pools; dogs; bus 300m; cc acc; CCI. "Grassy pitches poss flooded after heavy rain; san facs gd but poss stretched high ssn; superb pool; friendly; conv town cent; gd NH." 1 Apr-15 Oct. € 16.32
2007*

⊞**IRUN** *3A1* (2km N Rural) **Camping Jaizkibel, Ctra Guadalupe Km 22, 20280 Hondarribia (Guipúzcoa) [943-64 16 79; fax 943-64 26 53; jaizkibel@campingseuskadi.com; www. campingseuskadi.com/jaizkibel]** Fr Hondarribia/ Fuenterrabia inner ring rd foll sp to site below old town wall. Do not ent town. Med, hdg pitch, pt hdstg, terr, pt shd; wc; baby facs; shwrs; el pnts (2-6A) €3.62 (check earth); lndtte; tradsmn; rest; bar; BBQ; playgrnd; sand beach 1.5km; tennis; 90% statics; no dogs; phone; bus 1km; adv bkg; quiet; red low ssn; cc acc; CCI. "Easy 20 mins walk to historic town; v scenic area; gd walking; gd touring base but ltd space on site for tourers; clean facs; gd rest & bar." € 16.10
2007*

⊞**IRUN** *3A1* (3km S Rural) **Camping Oliden, Ctra NI Madrid-Irún, Km 470, 20180 Oiartzun (Guipúzcoa) [943-49 07 28; oliden@ campingseuskadi.com; www.campingseuskadi. com/oliden]** On S side of N1 at E end of vill. Lge, pt sl, pt shd; wc; chem disp; shwrs; el pnts (5A) €3.40; lndtte; shops adj; bar; playgrnd; pool in ssn; beach 10km; rlwy & factory noise; red CCI. "Steps to shwrs, diff access for disabled; san facs old but clean; grass pitches v wet low ssn; NH only." € 19.60
2006*

⊞**ISABA** *3B1* (13km E Rural) **Camping Zuriza, Ctra Anso-Zuriza, Km 14, 22728 Anso (Huesca) [974-37 01 96; www.lospirineos.info/campingzuriza]** On NA 137 N fr Isaba, turn R 4km onto NA 2000 to Zuriza. Foll sp to site. Fr Ansó, take HU 2024 N to Zuriza. Foll sp to site; narr, rough rd not rec for underpowered o'fits. Lge, pt sl, pt shd; wc; some serviced pitches; shwrs inc; el pnts €3.75; lndry rm; shop; tradsmn; rest; bar; playgrnd; 50% statics; phone; quiet; cc acc; CCI. "Beautiful, remote valley; no vill at Zuriza, nearest vills Isaba & Ansó; no direct route to France; superb location for walking." € 16.85
2006*

ISLA *1A4* (1km NW Coastal) **Camping Playa de Isla, Calle Ardanal 1, 39195 Isla (Cantabria) [tel/fax 942-67 93 61; consultas@playadeisla.com; www.playadeisla.com]** Turn off A8/E70 at km 185 Beranga sp Noja & Isla. Foll sp Isla. In town to beach, site sp to L. Then in 100m keep R along narr seafront lane (main rd bends L) for 1km (rd looks like dead end). Med, mkd pitch, pt sl, terr, pt shd; wc; chem disp; shwrs inc; el pnts (3A) €3.65; gas; lndtte; shop & 1km; snacks; bar; playgrnd; sand beach adj; 70% statics; no dogs; phone; bus 1km; poss cr; quiet; cc acc; CCI. "Beautiful situation; spotless san facs; busy w/e; gd shop." Easter-30 Sep. € 22.90
2006*

⊞**ISLA CRISTINA** *2G2* (1.5km E Coastal) **Camping Giralda, Ctra La Antilla, Km 1.5, 21410 Isla Cristina [959-34 33 18; fax 959-34 32 84; campinggiralda@infonegocia.com; www. campinggiralda.com]** Exit A49 sp Isla Cristina & go thro town heading E (speed bumps in town). Or exit A49 at km 117 sp Lepe. In Lepe turn S on H4116 to La Antilla, then R on coast rd to Isla Cristina & site. V lge, mkd/hdstg/sandy pitches; shd; wc; chem disp; mv service pnt; baby facs; shwrs inc; el pnts €5.62; gas; lndtte; shop; rest; snacks; bar; playgrnd; pool high ssn; paddling pool; sand beach nrby; windsurfing; TV rm; 20% statics; dogs €2.46; poss cr, even low ssn; Eng spkn; red long stay/low ssn; cc acc. "V helpful staff; some pitches uneven & muddy in wet weather; unkempt low ssn; san facs OK, irreg cleaning low ssn; diff for lge o'fits; narr site rds, some high kerbs; gd winter stay." € 24.12
2006*

⊞ISLA CRISTINA *2G2* (4km E Coastal) **Camping Playa Taray, Ctra La Antilla-Isla Cristina, Km 9, 21430 La Redondela (Huelva) [959-34 11 02; fax 959-34 11 96; www.campingtaray.com]** Fr W exit A49 sp Isla Cristina & go thro town heading E. Fr E exit A49 at km 117 sp Lepe. In Lepe turn S on H4116 to La Antilla, then R on coast rd to Isla Cristina & site. Lge, pt shd; wc; mv service pnt; shwrs; el pnts (10) €4.28; gas; lndtte; shop; bar; rest; playrnd; sand beach adj; some statics; phone; dogs; bus; quiet; cc acc; red long stay/low ssn; CCI. "Gd birdwatching, cycling; less cr than other sites in area in winter; poss untidy low ssn & ltd facs; poss diff for lge o'fits; friendly, helpful owner."
♦ € 19.10   2007*

⊞ISLA CRISTINA *2G2* (7km E Coastal) **Camping Luz, Ctra La Antilla-Isla Cristina, Km 5, 21410 Isla Cristina (Huelva) [959-34 11 42; fax 059-48 64 54]** Fr W exit A49 sp Isla Cristina & go thro town heading E. Fr E exit A49 at km 117 sp Lepe. In Lepe turn S on H4116 to La Antilla, then R on coast rd to Isla Cristina & site. Med, pt sl, pt shd; wc; shwrs inc; el pnts (5A) €4; gas; lndtte; shop & 3km; tradsmn; rest; snacks; bar; BBQ; playgrnd; pool; beach 200m; 40% statics; dogs; phone; bus 50m; poss cr; rd noise/noisy at w/e; red long stay; CCI. "V friendly staff, well-managed; vg shwrs; ltd facs low ssn; uneven pitches; poss diff for lge o'fits."
€ 31.20   2005*

ISLA PLANA see Puerto de Mazarrón *4G1*

ISLARES see Oriñón *1A4*

ITZIAR see Deba *3A1*

⊞IZNATE *2G4* (1km NE Rural) **Camping Rural, Ctra Iznate-Benamocarra s/n, 29792 Iznate (Málaga) [952-03 06 06; fax 952-55 61 93; info@ campingiznate.com; www.campingiznate.com]** Exit A7/E15 junc 265 dir Cajiz & Iznate. Med, mkd pitch, hdstg, unshd; wc; chem disp; shwrs; el pnts (15A) €3 (poss no earth); gas; lndtte; shop; rest, bar & pool (planned 2007); shgl beach 8km; no statics; dogs €2; bus adj; Eng spkn; quiet; red long stay. "Beautiful scenery & mountain villages; conv Vélez-Málaga & Torre del Mar; pleasant owners." € 17.30
                                                             2007*

JARANDILLA DE LA VERA *1D3* (2km W Rural) **Camping Yuste, N501, Km 47, 10440 Aldeaneuva de la Vera (Cáceres) [927-57 26 59]** Fr Plasencia head E on EX203 following sp for Parador, site at km stone 47 in Aldeaneuva de la Vera. Clearly sp down narr rd. Med, shd; wc; shwrs; el pnts €3.20; gas; snacks; bar; pool; tennis; bus 500m; phone; quiet. "Most attractive in mountain country; simple, well-maintained site." 1 Apr-30 Sep. € 12.90
                                                             2006*

JARANDILLA DE LA VERA *1D3* (1km NW Urban) **Camping Jaranda, Ctra EX 203, Km 47, 10450 Jarandilla de la Vera (Cáceres) [927-56 04 54; fax 927-56 05 87; campingjaranda@eresmas.com]** Site sp. Med, pt sl, terr, shd; wc; chem disp; mv service pnt; baby facs; shwrs; el pnts (5A) €3.60; gas; lndtte; ice; shop; rest; snacks; bar; playgrnd; pool; paddling pool; games area; cycle hire; 30% statics; dogs €1.60; poss cr; adv bkg; quiet; cc acc. ♦ 15 Mar-15 Sep. € 14.50   2005*

⊞JAVEA/XABIA *4E2* (1km S Rural) **Camping Jávea, Ctra Cabo de la Nao, Km 1, 03730 Jávea (Alicante) [965-79 10 70; fax 966-46 05 07; info@ camping-javea.com; www.camping-javea.com]** Exit N332 for Jávea on A132, cont in dir Port on CV734. At rndabt & Lidl supmkt, turn R sp Arenal Platjas & Cap de la Nau. Strt on at next rndabt to site sp & slip rd 100m sp Autocine. If you miss slip rd go back fr next rndabt. Lge, mkd pitch, pt shd; wc; chem disp; baby facs; shwrs inc; el pnts (8A) €3.50 (long lead rec); gas; lndtte; ice; shop 1km; tradsmn; rest; snacks; bar; BBQ; playgrnd; pool; paddling pool; sand beach 1.5km; tennis; games area; internet; 15% statics; dogs €2; adv bkg; quiet; red low ssn/long stay; cc acc; CCI. "Excel site; variable pitch sizes/prices; some lge pitches; mountain views; helpful staff; m'vans beware low trees." € 27.60   2007*

See advertisement

Spain

⊞ **JAVEA/XABIA** *4E2* (3km S Coastal) **Camping El Naranjal, Ctra Cabo de la Nao, Ptda dels Morers 15, 03730 Jávea (Alicante) [965-79 29 89; fax 966-46 02 56; naranjal@telelines.es; www.campingelnaranjal.com]** Exit A7 junc 62 or 63 onto N332 València/Alicante rd. Exit at Gata de Gorgos to Jávea. Foll sp Camping Jávea/Camping El Naranjal. Access rd by tennis club, foll sp. Med, mkd pitch, hdstg, pt shd; htd wc; chem disp; baby facs; shwrs inc; el pnts (10A) €3.20 (poss rev pol); gas; lndtte; ice; shop; tradsmn; rest; snacks; bar; BBQ; playgrnd; pool inc; paddling pool; sand beach 300m; tennis 300m; cycle hire; games rm; golf 3km; wifi internet; TV rm; 35% statics; dogs free; phone; bus 500m; adv bkg; Eng spkn; quiet; cc acc; red long stay/low ssn/CCI. "Gd scenery & beach; pitches poss tight lge o'fits; c'van storage; excel rest; tourist info - tickets sold; rec." ♦ € 24.00
2007*

See advertisement

⊞ **JIMENA DE LA FRONTERA** *2H3* (NW Rural) **Camping Los Alcornocales, Ctra CC3331/A369, 11330 Jimena de la Frontera (Cádiz) [956-64 00 60; fax 956-64 12 90; alcornocales@terra.es]** Site sp fr A369 Ronda to Algeciras rd. Rec app fr N onto C3331, turn L at camping sp at top of bank, site on R in 100m. Do not enter Jimena - narr rds. Med, hdg/mkd pitch, pt sl, terr, shd; wc; chem disp; shwrs inc; el pnts €3.37; gas; lndtte; shop; rest; bar; cycle hire; excursions; 90% statics; dogs; phone; adv bkg; quiet; cc acc; red CCI. "V friendly owner; poss unkempt & ltd facs low ssn; unsuitable lge o'fits; conv Gibraltar; 5 mins walk to attractive hill town; wonderful flora, fauna & scenery in National Park." ♦ ltd. € 16.80
2005*

LABUERDA see Ainsa *3B2*

LAREDO *1A4* (W Coastal) **Camping Laredo, Calle Rep de Filipinas s/n, 39770 Laredo (Cantabria) [942-60 50 35; fax 942-61 31 80; info@campinglaredo.com; www.campinglaredo. com]** Fr A8 exit junc 172 sp Laredo; cont N at rndabt into Laredo Playa, L at traff lts & foll site sp. Lge, mkd pitch, pt shd; wc; chem disp; mv service pnt; baby facs; shwrs; el pnts (5A) €2.80; gas; lndtte; shop (high ssn) snacks; bar; playgrnd; pool (caps essential); sand beach 500m; cycle hire; horseriding; TV; 20% statics; no dogs; phone; bus 300m; poss cr; noisy; adv bkg; 10% red CCI. 1 Jun-15 Sep. € 20.00
2005*

LAREDO *1A4* (500m W Urban/Coastal) **Camping Carlos V, Avnda Los Derechos Humanos 15, Ctra Residencial Playa, 39770 Laredo (Cantabria) [tel/fax 942-60 55 93]** Leave A8 at junc 172 to Laredo, foll yellow camping sp, site on W side of town. Med, mkd pitch, pt shd; wc; mv service pnt; baby facs; shwrs inc; el pnts €2.60; gas; lndtte; shop & 100m; rest; bar; playgrnd; sand beach 200m; dogs; bus 100m; poss cr; noisy; CCI. "Well sheltered & lively resort." Holy Week & 6 May-15 Sep. € 23.90
2007*

LAREDO *1A4* (2km W Coastal) **Camping Playa del Regatón, El Sable 8, 39770 Laredo (Cantabria) [tel/fax 942-60 69 95; info@campingplayaregaton. com; www.campingplayaregaton.com]** Fr W leave A8 junc 172, under m'way to rndabt & take exit sp Calle Rep Colombia. In 800m turn L at traff lts, in further 800m turn L onto tarmac rd to end, passing other sites. Fr E leave at junc 172, at 1st rndabt take 2nd exit sp Centro Comercial N634 Colindres. At next rndabt take exit Calle Rep Colombia, then as above. Lge, mkd pitch; pt shd; wc; chem disp; mv service pnt; shwrs inc; el pnts (4A) €2.70; gas; lndtte; shop; rest; bar; sand beach adj; 75% statics; no dogs; bus 600m; Eng spkn; adv bkg; quiet; cc acc; red long stay/CCI. "Clean site by beach; sep area for tourers; horseriding nrby; wash up facs every pitch; gd NH (check opening times of office for el pnt release)." ♦ 1 Apr-23 Sep. € 18.60
2007*

Did you know you can fill in site report forms on the Club's website — www.caravanclub.co.uk?

LASPAULES *3B2* (Rural) **Camping Laspaúles, Ctra N260, Km 369, 22471 Laspaúles (Huesca) [974-55 33 20; camping@laspaules.com; www. laspaules.com]** Approx 20km NW Pont de Suert, in cent of vill adj rv. Med, pt shd; wc; baby facs; shwrs; el pnts (6A) €3.85; gas; lndry rm; shop & in vill; tradsmn; snacks; bar; playgrnd; pool; paddling pool; TV; some statics; quiet; cc acc; red long stay/low ssn; CCI. "V pleasant; pitches well back fr rd." Holy Week-30 Sep. € 17.33
2006*

⊞ **LEKEITIO** *3A1* (3km S Coastal) **Camping Leagi, Calle Barrio Leagi s/n, 48289 Mendexa (Vizcaya) [tel/fax 946-84 23 52; leagi@campingleagi.com; www.campingleagi.com]** Fr San Sebastian leave A8/N634 at Deba twd Ondarroa. At Ondarroa do not turn into town, but cont on BI633 beyond Berriatua, then turn R onto BI3405 to Lekeitio. Fr Bilbao leave A8/N634 at Durango & foll BI633 twd Ondarroa. Turn L after Markina onto BI3405 to Lekeitio - do not go via Ondarroa. Steep climb to site & v steep tarmac ent to site. Only suitable for o'fits with v high power/weight ratio. Med, mkd pitch, pt sl, unshd; wc; chem disp; mv service pnt; serviced pitch; shwrs inc; el pnts (5A) €3.60 (rev pol); lndtte; shop; rest; snacks; bar; playgrnd; sand beach 1km; many statics; dogs; bus 1.5km; cr & noisy high ssn; cc acc (over €50); CCI. "Ltd facs low ssn; dogs roam (& foul) site (Aug 05); tractor tow avail up to site ent; beautiful scenery; excel local beach; lovely town; gd views; gd walking." € 22.80
2007*

LEKUNBERRI *3A1* (500m SE Rural) **Aralar Camping**, Plazaola 9, 31870 Lekunberri (Navarra) [tel/fax 948-50 40 11 or 948-50 40 49; info@campingaralar.com; www.campingaralar.com] Exit fr AP15 at junc 124 dir Lukunberri & foll sp for site. Site on R after v sharp downhill turn. Med, all hdstg, pt sl, terr, pt shd; htd wc; chem disp; shwrs inc; el pnts (5A) inc; gas; lndtte; shop; rest; snacks; bar; playgrnd; pool; cycle hire; horseriding; TV; dogs €2; 70% statics; phone; some Eng spkn; quiet; cc acc. "Beautiful scenery & mountain walks; only 14 touring pitches; v pleasantly arranged site; avoid Pamplona mid-Aug during bull-run; site also open at w/e & long w/e all year except Jan/Feb." Holy Week & 1 Jun-30 Sep. € 19.70   2006*

LEON *1B3* (3km SE Rural) **Camping Ciudad de León**, Ctra N601, 24195 Golpejar de la Sobarriba [tel/fax 987-26 90 86; camping_leon@yahoo.es; www.vivaleon.com/campingleon.htm] SE fr León on N601 twds Valladolid, L at top of hill at rndabt & Opel g'ge & foll site sp Golpejar de la Sobarriba; 500m after radio masts turn R at site sp. Sm, pt sl, shd; wc; chem disp; shwrs inc; el pnts inc (4A) €2.75; gas; lndry rm; shop; rest; snacks; bar; playgrnd; pool; paddling pool; tennis; cycle hire; dogs €1.50; bus 200m; quiet; adv bkg; poss cr; Eng spkn; CCI. "Clean, pleasant site; excel welcome; helpful staff; access some pitches poss diff; easy access to beautiful city" ♦ 1 Jun-25 Sep. € 15.75   2007*

LEON *1B3* (14km SE Rural) **Camp Municipal Esla**, N601, Km 310, 24210 Mansilla de las Mulas (León) [987-31 00 89; fax 987-31 18 10; info@ayto-mansilla.org; www.ayto-mansilla.org] N601 SE fr León, turn W onto N625 twd Mansilla. In 200m, turn L onto slip rd sp to site. Site in 1km. Heading N on N601 twd León, exit junc 21 sp León. Turn L into Mansilla & drive thro town. Site sp on R immed after bdge. Med, pt shd; wc; chem disp; shwrs inc; el pnts €1.90; lndtte; rest; bar; playgrnd; rv sw nrby; adv bkg; quiet; cc acc; CCI. "Gd base for León." 18 Jun-11 Sep. € 9.85   2007*

LEON *1B3* (12km SW Urban) **Camping Camino de Santiago**, Ctra N120, Km 324.4, 24392 Villadangos del Páramo (León) [tel/fax 987-68 02 53; campingcamino@yahoo.es] Access fr N120 to W of vill, site sp (take care fast, o'taking traff). Ent concealed fr E. Lge, mkd pitch, pt shd; wc; chem disp; mv service pnt; baby facs; shwrs inc; el pnts €3.50; gas; lndtte; shop; rest; snacks; bar; pool; 50% statics; phone; bus 300m; poss cr; adv bkg; rd noise; cc acc; 10% red 15+ days; CCI. "Conv for León; poss no hot water low ssn; pleasant, helpful staff; mosquitoes; vill church worth visit; gd NH." ♦ Easter-24 Sep. € 16.85   2007*

⊞**LINEA DE LA CONCEPCION, LA** *2H3* (S Urban/Coastal) **Camping Sureuropa**, Camino de Sobrevela s/n, 11300 La Línea de la Concepción (Cádiz) [956-64 35 87; fax 956-64 30 59; info@campingsureuropa.com; www.campingsureuropa.com] Fr S on E5/N340 onto N351 coast rd. Just bef Gibraltar turn R up lane, in 200m turn L into site. Fr N on AP7, exit junc 124 onto A383 dir La Línea; foll sp Santa Margarita thro to beach, site sp. Med, hdg/mkd pitch, hdstg, pt shd; wc; chem disp (wc); shwrs inc; el pnts €3; lndtte; bar; sand beach 500m; sports club adj; some statics; no dogs; phone; bus 1.5km; poss cr; Eng spkn; adv bkg; no cc acc; quiet; CCI. "Clean, flat, pretty site (gd for disabled); vg, modern san facs; sm pitches & tight site rds poss diff twin-axles & l'ge o'fits; ideal for Gibraltar 4km." ♦ € 13.00   2007*

LLAFRANC see Palafrugell *3B3*

⊞**LLANCA** *3B3* (500m N Coastal) **Camping L'Ombra**, Ctra Bisbal-Portbou, Km 13, 17490 Llançà (Gerona) [tel/fax 972-12 02 61; lombra@lycos.com] Fr Figueres on N260 dir Portbou, site on L 500m N of traff lts at Llançà turn off. Med, mkd pitch, pt sl, pt shd; wc; chem disp; shwrs inc; el pnts €4; lndtte; shop; supmkt 1km; bar; playgrnd; beach 1km; 75% statics; train 1km; quiet; red low ssn. "Useful winter base for coastal towns when other sites clsd." € 28.45   2004*

Spain

LLANCA *3B3* (2km N Coastal) **Camping Garbet,** 17469 Colera (Gerona) [972-38 90 01; fax 972-12 80 59] On L of main rd fr Portbou to Cadaqués (narr, twisting rd) 2km after vill of Colera. Easier app fr Llançà dir Portbou, site on R 2m bef Colera. Site easily seen on beach. Med, hdstg, pt shd; wc; shwrs; el pnts €3.20; gas; lndtte; ice; shop; rest; snacks; bar; shgl beach; TV; rlwy stn 100m; poss cr; adv bkg; quiet but rd & rlwy noise; cc acc. "Situated in v sheltered bay; fishing, boating & historical attractions." 1 Apr-15 Oct. € 20.00

2005*

LLANCA *3B3* (4km N Coastal) **Camping Caravaning Sant Miquel,** 17469 Colera (Gerona) [tel/fax 972-38 90 18; info@campingsantmiquel. com; www.campingsantmiquel.com]** Take main rd fr Portbou to Cadaqués. After 7km turn L into Colera vill, then 1st R over bdge, turn L into site in 200m, well sp. Lge, mkd pitch, pt shd; wc; chem disp; shwrs inc; el pnts (6-10A) €4.25; gas; lndtte; ice; shop; rest; snacks; bar; playgrnd; htd pool; shgl beach 1km; watersports; diving; cycle hire; entmnt; TV rm; 10% statics; dogs €2; poss cr; Eng spkn; adv bkg; quiet; cc acc; CCI. "Friendly site; gd rest & pool; v cr high ssn with students; conv local fishing ports & Dali Museum." ♦ 1 Mar-30 Sep. € 21.10 (CChq acc)

2005*

LLANES *1A4* (10km E Coastal) **Camping La Paz, Ctra N634, Km 292,** 33597 Playa de Vidiago (Asturias) [985-41 10 12; fax 985-41 12 35; delfin@campinglapaz.com; www.campinglapaz. com]** Take N634/E70 fr Unquera to Ribadesella. Turn R at sp to site bet km stone 292 & 293 bef Vidiago. If coming fr Santander, foll Way Out/Salida to m'way A67 for Torrelavega. Site access via narr 1km lane. Stop bef bdge & park on R, staff will tow to pitch. Narr site ent & steep to pitches. Lge, mkd pitch, terr, shd; wc; chem disp; mv service pnt; baby facs; shwrs inc; el pnts (9A) €3.37 (poss rev pol); gas; lndtte; ice; shop; rest; bar; BBQ; playgrnd; sand beach adj; fishing; watersports; horseriding; mountain sports; no statics; dogs €2.15; phone; poss cr w/e; Eng spkn; adv bkg; quiet; cc acc; CCI. "Exceptionally helpful owner & staff; excel views; superb beaches in area." ♦ Easter-15 Oct. € 21.10

2007*

See advertisement

LLANES *1A4* (1.5km W Coastal) **Camping Las Conchas de Póo, Ctra General,** 33509 Póo de Llanes (Asturias) [985-402 290] Exit A8/E70 at Llanes West junc 307 & foll sp. Med, sl, terr, pt shd; wc; chem disp; baby facs; shwrs; el pnts (5A) €2.50; lndtte; ice; shop; rest; bar; playgrnd; sand beach adj; 50% statics; no dogs; phone; bus; quiet. "Pleasant site; footpath to lovely beach." 1 Jun-30 Sep. € 15.00

2006*

LLANES *1A4* (5km W Coastal) **Camping Playa de Troenzo, Ctra de Celerio-Barro,** 33595 Celorio (Asturias) [985-40 16 72; fax 985-74 07 23; troenzo@telepolis.com]** Fr E take E70/A8 past Llanes & exit at junc 307 to Celorio. At T-junc with AS263 turn L dir Celorio & Llanes. Turn L on N9 (Celorio) thro vill & foll sp to Barro. Site on R after 500m (after Maria Elena site). Lge, terr, pt shd; wc; chem disp; mv service pnt; shwrs inc; el pnts (6A) €2.51; gas; lndtte; shop; rest; snacks; bar; playgrnd; sand beach 400m; 90% statics; dogs; phone; poss cr; Eng spkn; adv bkg; CCI. "Lovely, old town; for pitches with sea views go thro statics to end of site; gd, modern facs; gd rests in town; nr harbour." 16 Feb-19 Dec. € 19.10

2007*

LLAVORSI *3B2* (3km N Rural) **Camping Riberies, Ctra Vall d'Arau 55,** 25595 Llavorsí (Lleida) [973-62 21 51; fax 973-62 20 02; consulta@ campingriberies.com; www.campingriberies. com]** On C113 3km N of Llavorsí. Fr S site is immed bef rv bdge on ent Riberies. Med, shd; wc; shwrs; el pnts €4.20; lndtte; shop in vill; rest adj; bar; playgrnd; kayaking; rafting; phone; bus 500m; quiet but some rd noise. 15 Mar-30 Oct. € 17.20

2006*

LLAVORSI *3B2* (8km N Rural) **Camping Del Cardós,** 25570 Ribera de Cardós [973-62 31 12; fax 973-62 31 83; info@campingdelcardos. com; www.campingdelcardos.com]** Take L504 fr Llavorsí dir Ribera de Cardós for 8km; site on R on ent vill. Med, mkd pitch, pt shd; wc; chem disp; mv service pnt; shwrs; el pnts (4-6A) €3.90-4.60; gas; lndtte; shop; tradsmn; rest; playgrnd; pool; 2 paddling pools; fishing; games area; TV rm; 5% statics; dogs €3.20; Eng spkn; quiet; CCI. "By side of rv, v quiet low ssn; excel." 1 Apr-30 Sep. € 22.60

2006*

⊞**LLAVORSI** *3B2* (9km N Rural) **Camping La Borda del Pubill, Ctra de Tavescan, Km 9.5,** 25570 Ribera de Cardós (Lleida) [973-62 30 80; fax 973-62 30 28; info@campinglabordadelpubill. com; www.campinglabordadelpubill.com]** Fr France on A64 exit junc 17 at Montréjeau & head twd Spanish border. At Vielha turn E onto C28/ C1412 to Llavorsí, then L504 to Ribera. Fr S take N260 fr Tremp to Llavorsí, then L504 to site. Lge, pt shd; htd wc; baby facs; shwrs; el pnts €3.75; gas; lndtte; shop, rest high ssn; snacks; bar; playgrnd; htd pool; paddling pool; rv sw & fishing; kayaking; trekking; adventure sports; quad bike hire; horseriding; skiing 30km; games area; games rm; TV; 10% statics; dogs €3; phone; car wash; adv bkg; quiet; cc acc. "In beautiful area; excel walking; gd rest." ♦ € 21.70 (CChq acc)

2005*

LLORET DE MAR *3B3* (1km S Coastal) **Camping Tucan**, Ctra Blanes-Lloret, 17310 Lloret de Mar (Gerona) [972-36 99 65; fax 972-36 00 79; info@ campingtucan.com; www.campingtucan.com] Fr N exit AP7 junc 9 onto C35 twd Sant Feliu then C63 on R sp Lloret de Mar. At x-rds foll sp Blanes, site on R. Fr S take last exit fr C32 & foll sp Lloret de Mar, site on L, sp. Lge, mkd pitch, terr, shd; wc; chem disp; baby facs; shwrs inc; el pnts (3-6A) €3.40-4.40; gas; lndtte; ice; shop; rest; snacks; bar; BBQ; playgrnd; pool; paddling pool; sand beach 600m; games area; golf 500m; entmnt; internet; TV rm; 25% statics; dogs €2; phone; bus; car wash; Eng spkn; adv bkg; quiet; cc acc; red long stay/snr citizens/CCI. "Well-appointed site; friendly staff." ♦ 1 Apr-30 Sep. € 27.80   2007*

⊞**LLORET DE MAR** *3B3* (1km SW Coastal) **Camping Santa Elena-Ciutat**, Ctra Blanes/Lloret, 17310 Lloret de Mar (Gerona) [972-36 40 09; fax 972-36 79 54; santaelana@betsa.es; www.betsa. es] Exit A7 junc 9 dir Lloret. In Lloret take Blanes rd, site sp at km 10.5 on rd GI 682. V lge, pt sl; wc; baby facs; shwrs; el pnts €3.50; gas; lndtte; shop; rest; snacks; bar; playgrnd; pool; shgl beach 800m; games area; phone; cash machine; poss cr; Eng spkn; noisy disco & traffic on adj main rd; red facs low ssn; CCI. "Ideal for teenagers." ♦ € 29.50
                                        2004*

⊞**LOGRONO** *3B1* (500m N Urban) **Camping La Playa**, Avda de la Playa 6, 26006 Logroño (La Rioja) [tel/fax 941-25 22 53; info@campinglaplaya. com; www.campinglaplaya.com] N of Rv Ebro. Leave city by bdge 'Puente de Piedra', then turn L at traff lts. Site well sp in town & fr N111, adj sports cent Las Novias. Avoid old bdge as weight limit poss a prob for lge o'fits. Med, hdg pitch, shd; wc; shwrs inc; el pnts (5A) €3; gas; lndtte; ice; shop; snacks, bar in ssn; playgrnd; pool; rv sw adj; tennis; 80% statics; red CCI. "Sh walk to town cent; ltd facs low ssn & site poss clsd; vg." € 18.50   2007*

⊞**LOGRONO** *3B1* (10km W Rural) **Camping Navarrete**, Ctra La Navarrete-Entrena, Km I.5, 26370 Navarrete (La Rioja) [941-44 01 69; fax 941-44 06 39; campingnavarrete@fer.es] Fr AP68 exit junc 11, at end slip rd turn L. At x-rds in Navarette, go strt over into town (site sp), turn R for site & R again onto LR137 sp Entrena. Site 1km on R. Lge, mkd pitch, pt shd; wc; chem disp; mv service pnt; baby facs; shwrs inc; el pnts (5A) €3.85; gas; lndtte; shop; snacks; bar; BBQ; playgrnd; pool & paddling pool; tennis; horseriding; car wash; 95% statics; dogs €2.14; site clsd 12 Dec-13 Jan; Eng spkn; noisy at w/e; cc acc; red low ssn/long stay. "Professionally run, v clean & tidy site; excel san facs; helpful staff; some sm pitches; local wine sold at recep; Bilbao ferry 2 hrs via m'way; interesting area." € 20.30   2007*

As soon as we get home I'm going to post all these site report forms to the editor for inclusion in next year's guide. I don't want to miss the September deadline.

LORCA *4G1* (8km W Rural) **Camping La Torrecilla**, Ctra Granada-LaTorrecilla, 30817 Lorca (Murcia) [tel/fax 968-44 21 96; campinglatorrecilla@ alocom.net] Leave A7/E15 at junc 585. In 1km turn L, site well sp. Med, mkd pitch, hdstg, pt sl, pt shd; htd wc; chem disp; mv service pnt; shwrs inc; el pnts (6A) €3; gas; lndtte; shop 2km; tradsmn; rest; snacks; bar; BBQ; playgrnd; pool; tennis; games area; TV rm; 5% statics; dogs; phone; bus 1km; poss cr; Eng spkn; quiet; cc acc; red long stay. "Friendly, helpful staff; excel pool; vg san facs." ♦ 11 May-31 Dec. € 12.10   2006*

LOREDO see Santander *1A4*

Spain

⊞LUARCA 1A3 (1km NE Coastal) Camping Los Cantiles, Ctra N634, Km 502.7, 33700 Luarca (Asturias) [tel/fax 985-64 09 38; cantiles@campingloscantiles.com; www.campingloscantiles.com] Fr E leave N632 sp Luarca onto N634 S, then take exit to Barcia/Almuña onto rd 754 to sea; site sp (easily missed - look out for R turn with railings). Not rec to ent town fr W. Cont on N634/N632 to exit for Oviedo (N634) then take exit to Barcia/Almuña, then as for app fr E. On leaving site, retrace to main rd - do not tow thro Luarca. Med, hdg pitch, pt shd; wc; chem disp; baby facs; shwrs inc; el pnts inc (3-6A) €2-2.50; gas; Indtte; shop; tradsmn; rest high ssn; snacks; bar; pool 300m; shgl beach at foot of cliff; phone; poss cr; Eng spkn; adv bkg; quiet; 10% red long stay; CCI. "Beautiful, clean, guarded site on cliff top; superb views; facs ltd low ssn; some narr site rds; pitches soft after rain; access to beach diff due to steep climb down, but beach in next bay full rock pools." ♦ € 17.00   2007*

This guide relies on site report forms submitted by caravanners like us; we'll do our bit and tell the editor what we think of the campsites we've visited.

⊞LUARCA 1A3 (12km E Rural/Coastal) Camping La Regalina, Ctra de la Playa s/n, 33788 Cadavedo (Asturias) [tel/fax 985-64 50 14; info@laregalina.com] Fr N632 dir Cadavedo, km126. Site sp. Med, pt shd; wc; chem disp; shwrs inc; el pnts (5-8A) inc; gas; shop; rest; snacks; bar; pool; beach 1km; TV; 10% statics; phone; bus 600m; adv bkg; quiet; cc acc high ssn; red long stay. "Attractive mountain scenery by coast; pretty vill; ltd facs low ssn & some in need of renovation; gd." € 17.20   2005*

LUARCA 1A3 (2km W Coastal) Camping Playa de Taurán, 33700 Luarca (Asturias) [tel/fax 985-64 12 72; tauran@campingtauran.com; www.campingtauran.com] Fr Luarca, take N634 W & turn R at rndabt, sp El Chano. If missed, another sp in 1km. Cont 3.5km on long, narr, rough access rd. Rd thro Luarca unsuitable for c'vans. Med, some hdg pitch, pt sl, pt shd; wc; chem disp; mv service pnt; baby facs; shwrs inc; el pnts (6A) €3.21; gas; ice; Indtte; shop; tradsmn; rest; snacks; bar; BBQ; pool; paddling pool; shgl beach 200m; sand beach 2km; cycle hire; phone; dogs €1; quiet; red long stays; CCI. "Superb sea views & mountain views; off beaten track; conv fishing & hill vills; excel; v peaceful, restful, attractive, well-kept site; excel." Holy Week & 1 Apr-30 Sep. € 17.65   2006*

LUMBIER 3B1 (Rural) Camping Iturbero, Ctra N240 Pamplona-Huesca, 31440 Lumbier (Navarra) [948-88 04 05; fax 948-88 04 14; iturbero@campingiturbero.com; www.campingiturbero.com] SE fr Pamplona on N240 twds Yesa Reservoir. In 30km L on NA150 twds Lumbier. In 3.5km immed bef Lumbier turn R at rndabt then over single track bdge, 1st L to site, adj sw pool. Well sp fr N240. Med, hdg/mkd pitch, some hdstg, pt shd; wc; chem disp; mv service pnt; shwrs inc; el pnts (5A) €4; gas; Indtte; ice; shop 1km; rest; snacks; bar; BBQ; playgrnd; pool 100m; tennis; hang-gliding; 25% statics; dogs €2; bus 1km; quiet; CCI. "Beautiful, well-kept site; excel touring base; open w/e only Dec-Easter but clsd 19 Dec-19 Feb; eagles & vultures in gorge & seen fr site; v helpful staff; Lumbier lovely sm town." Holy Week-8 Dec. € 17.00   2007*

⊞MADRID 1D4 (8km NE Urban) Camping Osuna, Ruta el Aeropuerto (N11), Km 8, Avda de Logroño s/n, 28042 Madrid [917-41 05 10; fax 913-20 63 65] Fr M40, travelling S clockwise (anti-clockwise fr N or E) exit junc 8 at Canillejas sp 'Avda de Logroño'. Turn L under m'way, then R under rlwy, immed after turn R at traff lts. Site on L corner - white painted wall. Travelling N, leave M40 at junc 7 (no turn off at junc 8) sp Avda 25 Sep, U-turn at km 7, head S to junc 8, then as above. Med, hdg/mkd pitch, pt sl, pt shd; wc; chem disp; shwrs inc; el pnts (5A) €4.50 (long lead rec); Indtte; shop 600m; playgrnd; metro to town 600m; 10% statics; phone; poss cr; rd & aircraft noise; Eng spkn; red low ssn; CCI. "Sm pitches poss diff lge o'fits; helpful staff; conv city cent; clean site but poss neglected low ssn & facs tired; poss itinerants." ♦ ltd. € 25.00   2006*

⊞MADRID 1D4 (13km S Urban) Camping Alpha, Ctra de Andalucía N-IV, Km 12.4, 28906 Getafe (Madrid) [916-95 80 69; fax 916-83 16 59; info@campingalpha.com; www.campingalpha.com] Fr S on A4/E5 twd Madrid, leave at km 12.4 to W dir Ocaña & foll sp. Fr N on A4/E5 at km 13b to change dir back onto A4; then exit 12b sp 'Pol. Inc. Los Olivos' to site. Lge, hdstg, hdg pitch, pt shd; wc; chem disp; mv service pnt; shwrs inc; el pnts (15A) €5.90 (poss no earth); ice; Indtte; shop; rest; snacks; bar; playgrnd; pool high ssn; tennis; games area; 20% statics; dogs; phone; poss cr; Eng spkn; adv bkg; cc acc; 10% red CCI. "Lorry depot adj; poss vehicle movements 24 hrs but minimal noise; bus & metro to Madrid 30-40 mins; sm pitches poss tight for space; clean facs but need update; ltd hot water low ssn; v helpful staff; NH only." € 26.40   2007*

⊞**MADRIGAL DE LA VERA** *1D3* (500m E Rural) Camping Alardos, Ctra Madrigal-Candeleda, 10480 Madrigal de la Vera (Cáceres) [tel/fax 927-56 50 66; mirceavd@hotmail.com] Fr Jarandilla take EX203 E to Madrigal. Site sp in vill nr rv bdge. Med, mkd pitch, pt shd; wc; chem disp; shwrs inc; el pnts (6-10A) €3; ice; lndtte; shop & 1km; rest; snacks; bar; BBQ; playgrnd; pool; rv sw adj; TV; 10% statics; no dogs; phone; poss cr Jul/Aug; Eng spkn; adv bkg; cc not acc. "Friendly owners; superb site; ltd facs low ssn; beautiful scenery; excel touring area; ancient Celtic settlement at El Raso 5km." € 16.00   2005*

⊞**MALGRAT DE MAR** *3C3* (500m SW Coastal) Camping Bon Repós, Pg Maritim s/n, 08398 Santa Susanna (Barcelona) [937-67 84 75; fax 937-76 85 26; info@campingbonrepos.com; www.campingbonrepos.com] App fr Gerona on rd N11, site sp. Track leaves on L of N11; foll camp sp for 680m & turn R at sea-front T-junc. Cont thro Santa Susanna, down underpass & turn L in middle, rough app rd to site on beach behind rlwy stn; sp. NB Heavy rain may cause flooding of underpass; alt exit max 2.5m height. V lge, shd; wc; chem disp; baby facs; shwrs inc; el pnts (5A) €6; gas; lndtte; supmkt; rest; bar; playgrnd; 2 pools; beach adj; watersports; tennis; entmnt; 10% statics; dogs €2.50; poss cr; poss noisy; red low ssn; cc acc. "Conv rlwy stn - trains to Barcelona; site has pitches next to sea with el pnts; vg." ♦ € 29.00
2005*

⊞**MAMOLA, LA** *2H4* (500m Coastal) Camping Castillo de Baños, Castillo de Baños, 18750 La Mamola (Granada) [958-82 95 28; fax 958-82 97 68; info@campingcastillo.com; www.campingcastillo.com] On N340/A7 site sp at km 360, 500m fr vill of Castillo de Baños. Lge, mkd pitch, hdstg, pt shd; wc; chem disp; mv service pnt; shwrs inc; el pnts (5A) €2.80; gas; lndtte; shop; tradsmn; rest; snacks; bar; playgrnd; pool; private shgl beach adj; fishing; cycle hire; entmnt; internet; dogs; adv bkg; quiet; cc acc; quiet; red CCI. ♦ € 19.00 (CChq acc)   2005*

⊞**MANGA DEL MAR MENOR, LA** *4G2* (2km W Coastal) Camping La Manga, Ctra El Algar/Cabo de Palos, Km 12, 30370 La Manga del Mar Menor (Murcia) [968-56 30 14 or 56 30 19; fax 968-56 34 26; lamanga@caravaning.es; www.caravaning.es] Leave MU312 junc 11 sp Playa Honda; over dual c'way then turn R. Site sp fr La Manga. Ent visible beside dual c'way with flags flying. V lge, hdg/mkd pitch, hdstg, pt shd; htd wc; chem disp; mv service pnt; sauna; serviced pitches; shwrs inc; el pnts (10A) inc; gas; lndtte; ice; supmkt; rest; snacks; bar; BBQ; playgrnd; 2 pools - 1 htd, covrd Oct-Mar; paddling pool; sand beach adj; fishing; windsurfing; jacuzzi, gym (Oct-Mar); tennis; open-air cinema high ssn; mini-golf; games rm; internet; cab TV/TV rm; 30% statics; dogs €1.25; phone; recep 0700-2300; poss cr; Eng spkn; adv bkg ess (dep req & bkg fee); cc acc; red long stay/low ssn. "Busy, popular winter site; poss lge rallies on site Dec-Mar; Mar Menor shallow & warm lagoon; gd for families; 2 pitch sizes - sm ones unsuitable o'fits over 5m; some narr site rds & trees; additional area for m'vans; regional park 5km; gd walking; mountain biking; bird sanctuary; excel beaches; conv Roman ruins Cartagena, Murcia, Alicante; excel." ♦ € 28.00 (CChq acc) ABS - E16
2007*

See advertisement

⊞**MANZANARES EL REAL** *1D4* (8km NE Rural) Camping La Fresneda, Ctra 608, Km 19.5, 28791 Soto del Real (Madrid) [tel/fax 918-47 65 23] Fr AP6/NV1 turn NE at Collado-Villalba onto M608 to Cerceda & Manzanares el Real. Foll rd round lake to Soto del Real, site sp at km 19.5. Med, shd; wc; chem disp; baby facs; shwrs €0.15; el pnts (4-8A) inc; gas; lndtte; shop; snacks; bar; playgrnd; pool; tennis; phone; rd noise; cc acc. ♦ € 28.00   2005*

Spain

⊞**MANZANARES EL REAL** *1D4* (3km NW Rural) **Camping El Ortigal, Montañeros 19, La Pedriza, 28410 Manzanares el Real (Madrid) [918-53 01 20]** Fr AP6/NV1 turn NE at Collado-Villalba onto M608 to Cerceda & Manzanares el Real. In 6km take L sp to Manzanares, cross rv & immed L. Sp at this junc; site further 3km - speed humps. Not many sp to site or Pedriza. Lge, pt sl; wc; shwrs; el pnts (10A) €3.85 (poss rev pol); gas; shop; rest; bar; playgrnd; 99% statics/chalets; phone; red low ssn. "Sm area for tourers; arr early to ensure pitch; warm welcome; san facs dated; attractive country & views; excel walking in adj sm National Park - narr mountain tracks; old castle in Manzanares." ♦ ltd. € 27.50   2005*

> The opening dates and prices on this campsite have changed. I'll send a site report form to the editor for the next edition of the guide.

⊞**MANZANERA** *3D2* (1km NE Rural) **Camping Villa de Manzanera, Partida Las Bateas s/n, Ctra 1514, Km 10.5, 44420 Manzanera (Teruel) [978-78 17 48 or 978-78 19 21; fax 978-78 17 09]** Fr A23/N234 Teruel-Sagunto at Mora, onto A1514 at site sp. Site on L by petrol stn bef vill. Med, mkd pitch, unshd; htd wc; chem disp; shwrs inc; el pnts (10A) €2; gas; lndtte; shop 1km; rest; snacks; bar; playgrnd; pool; 80% statics; dogs; phone; bus 200m; poss cr; poss noisy; cc acc; CCI. "Site much enlarged but a little run down; popular with young tenters; nr wintersports area; obliging staff; excel san facs but poss stretched high ssn; some pitches worn & uneven; excel, gd value rest; site controlled fr adj filling stn - pay there 1700-1900; ltd facs in winter." ♦ ltd. € 17.00   2007*

⊞**MARBELLA** *2H3* (6km E Coastal) **Camping La Buganvilla, 29600 Marbella (Málaga) [952-83 19 73 or 952-83 19 74; fax 952-83 19 74; info@campingbuganvilla.com; www.camping buganvilla.com]** E fr Marbella for 6km on N340/E15 twds Málaga. Pass site & cross over m'way at Elviria & foll site sp. Fr Málaga exit R off autovia immed after 189km marker. Lge, terr, shd; wc; chem disp; shwrs; el pnts (10A) €3.20; gas; lndtte; ice; shop & 250m; rest; bar & sun terr; playgrnd; pool; sand beach 350m; games rm; internet; TV; phone; no dogs Jul-Aug; Eng spkn; adv bkg; poss noisy at w/e; 15% red 7+ days & 5% for snr citizens; cc acc; CCI. "Relaxed, conv site; helpful staff; excel beach." ♦ € 22.00   2005*

⊞**MARBELLA** *2H3* (10km E Coastal) **Camping Marbella Playa, Ctra N340, Km 192.8, 29600 Marbella (Málaga) [952-83 39 98; fax 952-83 39 99; recepcion@campingmarbella.com; www.campingmarbella.com]** Fr Marbella on A7/N340 coast rd (not AP7/E15 toll m'way) & site is on R bef 193 km stone & just bef pedestrian bdge over A7/N340, sp 'to beach'. Fr Málaga U-turn on m'way as follows: pass 192km mark & immed take R slip rd to Elviria to turn L over bdge, back onto A7/N340. Turn R bef next bdge. Lge, mkd pitch, hdstg, pt shd; wc; chem disp; mv service pnt; baby facs; shwrs; el pnts (10A) inc; gas; ice; supmkt; rest; snacks; bar; BBQ; playgrnd; pool; sand beach adj; watersports; tennis 50m; internet; TV; 30% statics; dogs; phone; bus nr; poss v cr; rd noise; cc acc; red long stay/snr citizens/CCI. "Pitches tight; friendly, helpful manager; gd base Costa del Sol; noisy peak ssn & w/ends, espec Sat nights." ♦ € 29.69 ABS - E07   2007*

⊞**MARBELLA** *2H3* (12km E Coastal) **Camping Cabopino, Ctra N340/A7, Km 194.7, 29600 Marbella (Málaga) [tel/fax 952-85 01 06; info@ campingcabopino.com; www.campingcabopino. com]** Fr E site is on N side of N340/A7; turn R at km 195 'Salida Cabopino' past petrol stn, site on R at rndabt. Fr W on A7 turn R at 'Salida Cabopino' km 194.7, go over bdge to rndabt, site strt over. NB Do not take sm exit fr A7 immed at 1st Cabopino sp. Lge, mkd pitch, pt sl, pt shd; wc; chem disp; mv service pnt; baby facs; shwrs inc; el pnts (10A) inc (poss long lead req); lndtte; shop; rest; snacks; bar; BBQ; playgrnd; 2 pools (1 covrd); sand beach/dunes 200m; watersports; marina 300m; games area; archery; golf driving range; internet; games/TV rm; 40% statics; dogs €1.50; bus 100m; Eng spkn; rd noise & lge groups w/enders; red low ssn; cc acc; CCI. "Popular low ssn; busy w/e; tourers ltd to lower half of site - flooding danger in heavy rain; access to some pitches diff due drops; blocks req some pitches; poss power cuts; excel rest at site ent; gd, clean san facs; v nice site." ♦ € 33.00 (CChq acc) ABS - E21   2007*

⊞**MARIA** *4G1* (8km W Rural) **Camping Sierra de María, Ctra María a Orce, Km 7, Paraje La Piza, 04838 María (Málaga) [950-16 70 45 or 660-26 64 74; fax 950-48 54 16; campingsierrademaria@cajamar.es; www. campingsierrademaria.com]** Exit A92 at junc 408 to Vélez Rubio, Vélez Blanco & María. Foll A317 to María & cont dir Huéscar & Orce. Site on R. Med, mkd pitch, pt sl, pt shd; wc; chem disp; shwrs; el pnts (6-10A) €3.50; shop high ssn; bar; cycle hire; horseriding; dogs; adv bkg; quiet; cc acc; CCI. "Lovely, peaceful, ecological site in mountains; much wildlife; variable pitch sizes; facs poss stretched high ssn; v cold in winter. ♦ € 14.20   2004*

⊞ Site open all year   824   *Send in your site reports*

⊞**MARINA, LA** *4F2* (2km S Coastal) **Camping Internacional La Marina, Ctra N332a, Km 76, 03194 La Marina (Alicante)** [965-41 92 00; fax 965-41 91 10; info@campinglamarina.com; www.campinglamarina.com] On N332 coast rd Alicante/Cartagena; app La Marina on edge of town turn L twd sea after lge g'ge, site sp in 1km. V lge, hdg/mkd pitch, hdstg, terr, shd; htd wc; chem disp; mv service pnt; 50% serviced pitches; baby facs; fam bthrm; sauna; solarium; shwrs inc; el pnts (10A) inc; gas; lndtte; ice; supmkt; rest; snacks; bars; playgrnd; 2 pools (1 htd/covrd); waterslides; sand beach 500m; fishing; watersports; tennis; games area; games rm; fitness cent; entmnt; child entmnt; wifi internet; TV rm; 10% statics; dogs €2; phone; bus 50m; car wash; security; Eng spkn; adv bkg; cc acc; 30-76% red long stay/varying pitch size & price; red low ssn; CCI. "Almost full late Feb; v busy w/e; spotless, high quality facs; popular winter site; bus fr gate; gd security; gd rest; excel family site; red if booking/paying on site's website." ♦ € 50.00
2007*

See advertisement

⊞**MASNOU, EL** *3C3* (Coastal) **Camping Masnou, Ctra NII, Km 633, Camil Fabra 33, 08320 El Masnou (Barcelona)** [tel/fax 935-55 15 03; masnou@campingsonline.es] App site fr N on N11. Pass El Masnou rlwy station on L & go strt on at traff lts. Site on R on N11 after km 633. Not clearly sp. Med, pt sl, shd; wc; mv service pnt; shwrs inc; el pnts €5.35; shop, snacks, bar high ssn; BBQ; playgrnd; pool high ssn; sand beach opp; internet; dogs; phone; bus 300m; train to Barcelona nr; poss v cr; Eng spkn; noise fr N11; cc not acc; CCI. "Gd pitches, no awnings; some sm pitches, poss shared; facs vg, though poss stretched when site busy; no restriction on NH vehicle movements; well-run, friendly site." ♦ ltd. € 25.70
2006*

Before we move on, I'm going to fill in some site report forms and post them off to the editor, otherwise they won't arrive in time for the deadline at the end of September.

Spain

MATARO 3C3 (3km E Coastal) **Camping Playa Sol, Ctra NII, Km 650, 08304 Mataró (Barcelona)** [937-90 47 20; fax 937-41 02 82; info@campingplayasol.com; www.campingplayasol.com] Exit AP7 onto C60 sp Mataró. Turn N onto NII dir Gerona, site sp on L after rndabt. Lge, mkd pitch, hdstg, shd; wc; chem disp; mv service pnt; shwrs inc; el pnts (6A) €4; gas; lndtte; ice; shop; rest; snacks; bar; playgrnd; pool; paddling pool; sand beach 1km; games area; games rm; animal farm; internet; TV; 5% statics; dogs €4; bus; Eng spkn; adv bkg; rd noise; cc acc; red long stay/low ssn; CCI. "Conv Barcelona 28km; pleasant site; friendly, welcoming staff." ♦ 23 Mar-26 Nov. € 34.00   2006*

MAZAGON see Huelva 2G2

⊞**MAZAGON** 2G2 (10km E Coastal) **Camping Doñana Playa, Ctra San Juan del Puerto-Matalascañas, Km 34.6, 21130 Mazagón (Huelva)** [959-53 62 81; fax 959-53 63 13; info@campingdonana.com; www.campingdonana.com] Fr A49 exit junc 48 at Bullullos del Condado onto A483 sp El Rocio, Matalascañas. At coast turn R sp Mazagón, site on L in 16km. V lge, mkd pitch, hdstg, pt shd; wc; chem disp; shwrs inc; el pnts (6A) inc; lndtte; shop; rest; snacks; bar; playgrnd; pool; sand beach 300m; watersports; tennis; games area; cycle hire; internet; entmnt; some statics; dogs €4; bus 500m; site clsd 14 Dec-14 Jan; adv bkg; quiet; red low ssn; CCI. "Pleasant site amongst pine trees." ♦ € 30.00   2007*

MENDEXA see Lekeitio 3A1

⊞**MENDIGORRIA** 3B1 (500m S Rural) **Camping El Molino, Ctra Larraga, 31150 Mendigorría (Navarra)** [948-34 06 04; fax 948-34 00 82; info@campingelmolino.com; www.campingelmolino.com] Fr Pamplona on N111 turn L at 25km in Puente la Reina onto NA601 sp Mendigorría. Site sp thro vill dir Larraga. App fr S feasible but requires towing thro Tafalla - congestion. Med, some mkd pitch, unshd; wc; chem disp; mv service pnt; serviced pitches; baby facs; shwrs inc; el pnts (6A) inc; gas; lndtte; ice; shop; tradsmn; rest; snacks; bar; playgrnd; pool; tennis; games area; child entmnt; TV; statics (sep area); dogs; phone; poss cr at w/e; clsd 24 Dec-6 Jan; adv bkg; poss v noisy at w/e; cc acc; CCI. "Gd clean facs; v ltd facs low ssn; for early am dep low ssn, pay night bef & obtain barrier key; Roman site 3km; excel." ♦ € 21.30 (CChq acc)   2007*

MEQUINENZA 3C2 (Urban) **Camping Octogesa, Ctra N211 s/n, Km 314, 50170 Mequinenza (Zaragoza)** [974-46 44 31; fax 974-46 50 31; rai@fuibol.e.telefonica.net] W fr Lerida on N11 for 29km; turn S 2km W of Fraga onto N211. On ent Mequinenza just past wooded area on L, turn L thro break in service rd, site well sp. Tight ent poss unsuitable lge o'fits. Med, hdg/mkd pitch, terr, pt shd; wc; chem disp (wc); shwrs inc; el pnts (6A) inc; lndry rm; shop 1km; rest; snacks; bar; BBQ; playgrnd; 2 pools high ssn; tennis; dogs; phone; Eng spkn; adv bkg; quiet but noise fr arr of fishing parties; cc acc; CCI. "Site part of complex on bank of Rv Segre surrounded by hills & used as base for fishing trips - site will supply equipment; sm pitches unsuitable lge o'fits; only bottled water avail, no supply to site; NH only." 15 Feb-15 Nov. € 20.00   2005*

> There aren't many sites open this early in the year. We'd better phone ahead to check that the one we're heading for is actually open.

⊞**MERIDA** 2E3 (2km SE Urban) **Camping Mérida, Avda de la Reina Sofia s/n, 06800 Mérida (Badajoz)** [924-30 34 53; fax 924-30 03 98; proexcam@jet.es; www.pagina.de/campingmerida] Fr E on A5/E90 exit junc 334 to Mérida, site on L in 2km. Fr W on A5/E90 exit junc 346, site sp. Fr N exit A66/E803 at junc 339 onto A5 E. Leave at junc 334, site on L in 1km twd Mérida. Fr S on A66-E803 app Mérida, foll Cáceres sp onto bypass to E; at lge rndabt turn R sp Madrid; site on R after 2km. Med, mkd pitch, pt sl, pt shd; wc; chem disp; shwrs inc; el pnts (6A) €3.35 (long lead poss req); gas; lndtte; ltd shop high ssn & 3km; hypmkt 6km; rest; snacks; bar; 2 free pools; TV; some statics; dogs; phone; no bus; quiet but some rd noise; CCI. "Roman remains & National Museum of Roman Art worth visit; poss diff lge o'fits manoeuvring onto pitch due trees & soft ground after rain; facs tired; gd seafood rest; ltd facs low ssn; conv NH fr A5 in rte Portugal." ♦ € 19.10   2007*

⊞**MIAJADAS** 2E3 (10km SW Rural) **Camping-Restaurant El 301, Ctra Madrid-Lisbon, Km 301, 10100 Miajadas (Cáceres)** [tel/fax 927-34 79 14] Leave A5/E90 just bef km stone 301 & foll sp 'Via de Servicio' with rest & camping symbols; site in 500m. Med, pt shd; wc; chem disp; shwrs inc; el pnts (5-10A) €2.70 (poss no earth); gas; lndtte; shop; rest; snacks; bar; playgrnd; pool; phone; m'way noise & dogs; cc acc; CCI. "Well-maintained, clean site; grass pitches; OK wheelchair users but steps to pool; gd NH." € 14.10   2005*

MIJAS COSTA see Fuengirola 2H4

MIRANDA DEL CASTANAR *1D3* (500m Rural) Camping El Burro Blanco, Camino de las Norias s/n, 37660 Miranda del Castañar (Salamanca) [tel/fax 923-16 11 00; elburroblanco@internet-rural.com; www.elburroblanco.internet-rural.com] Fr Ciudad Rodrigo take SA220 to El Cabaco then foll sp for 2km to Miranda del Castañar. In 2km turn L onto concrete/dirt rd for 700m. Site on R. Sm, mkd pitch, terr, pt shd; wc; chem disp; shwrs inc; el pnts (2-10A) €2.50-4.80; lndtte; shop, rest, snacks 1km; tradsmn; bar; pool; no statics; dogs; phone 1km; Eng spkn; quiet; 10% red 3+ days; CCI. "Nice scenery, set in oak wood; medieval hill-top town 500m; tight ent to some pitches, manhandling req; excel." 1 Apr-1 Oct. € 18.20   2004*

MIRANTES DE LUNA *1B3* (S Rural) Camping Mirantes de Luna, 24147 Mirantes de Luna (León) [987-58 13 03; fax 987-25 26 60] Fr N exit AP66 junc 93 & foll C623 & camping sp for 10km around E side of lake to Mirantes & Los Barrios de Luna Sm, mkd pitch, terr, pt shd; wc; chem disp; shwrs; el pnts €2.10; gas; lndtte; rest; bar; playgrnd; some statics; phone; quiet; CCI. "Pleasant, friendly site; conv for caves at Valporquero; helpful owner with gd knowledge of area." 15 Jun-15 Sep. € 13.00
                    2004*

MOANA *1B2* (3km W Coastal) Camping Tiran, Ctra Cangas-Moaña, Km 3, 36957 Moaña (Pontevedra) [986-31 01 50; fax 986-44 72 04] Exit AP9 junc 146 & foll sp Moaña/Cangas. Site beyond Moaña. Med, hdg pitch, terr, pt shd; wc; shwrs inc; el pnts (6A) inc; lndry rm; shop; tradsmn; rest; snacks; bar; playgrnd; beach adj; TV; 80% statics; no dogs; phone; adv bkg; quiet. "Site on v steep hill - only suitable m'vans & single-axle c'vans with powerful tow car; gd touring base S Galicia." Apr-Nov. € 23.00   2005*

MOIXENT *4E2* (12km N Rural) Camping Sierra Natura (Naturist), Finca El Tejarico, Ctra Moixent-Navalón, Km 11.5, 46810 Enguera (València) [962-25 30 26; fax 962-25 30 20; info@sierranatura.com; www.sierranatura.com] Exit A35 fr N exit junc 23 or junc 23 fr S onto CV589 sp Navalón. At 11.5km turn R sp Sierra Natura - gd rd surface but narr & some steep, tight hairpin bends (owners arrange convoys on request). Fr E on N340 exit junc 18 (do not take junc 14). Sm, pt sl, pt shd; wc; chem disp; baby facs; sauna; shwrs inc; el pnts (10A) €2.90; lndry rm; ice; shop & 12 km; rest; snacks; bar; playgrnd; pool; 10% statics; dogs €3; phone; poss cr; Eng spkn; adv bkg; quiet; red long stay. "Tranquil, family-run site in remote area; unusual architecture; stunning mountain scenery; nature walks on site; excel pool & rest complex."
♦ ltd. € 16.00   2006*

MOJACAR *4G1* (3.5km S Coastal) Camping El Cantal di Mojácar, Ctra Garrucha-Carboneras, 04638 Mojácar (Almería) [950-47 82 04; fax 950-47 83 34] Exit A7 junc 520 sp Mojácar Parador. Foll Parador sps by-passing Mojácar, to site. Med, hdstg, pt shd; wc; chem disp; mv service pnt; shwrs inc; el pnts (15A) €2.80; gas; lndry rm; shop 500m; tradsmn; shops adj; rest; snacks; bar adj; BBQ; sand beach adj; 5% statics; no dogs; phone; bus; poss v cr; some rd noise; red long stay/low ssn; CCI. "Pitches quite lge, not mkd; lge o'fits rec use pitches at front of site; gd location for beach & shops; v busy site; min 2 nights w/e." ♦ € 17.50
                    2006*

MOJACAR *4G1* (9km S Rural) Camping Sopalmo, Sopalmo, 04638 Mojácar (Almería) [950-47 84 13; fax 950-47 30 02] Exit N340/E15 at junc 520 onto AL152 sp Mojácar Playa. Foll coast rd S to Carboneras, site sp on W of rd about 1km S of Agua de Enmedio. Sm, mkd pitch, hdstg, pt shd; wc; chem disp (wc); shwrs; el pnts (15A) €2.50; ice; gas; lndtte; sm shop (high ssn); tradsmn; rest, snacks 6km; bar; shgl beach 1.7km; internet; 10% statics; dogs €1; Eng spkn; adv bkg; some rd noise; cc not acc; red low ssn; CCI. "V clean, pleasant, popular site - constantly improving; friendly young owner; gd walking; remote but intimate & peaceful; poss windy; poss busy in low ssn; nr National Park; patchy mobile phone signal."
♦ € 18.20   2005*

Did you know you can fill in site report forms on the Club's website — www.caravanclub.co.uk?

MOJACAR *4G1* (4km SW Coastal) Camping Cueva Negra, Camino Lotaza, 2, 04638 Mojácar (Almería) [950-47 58 55; fax 950-47 57 11; info@campingcuevanegra.es; www.camping cuevanegra.es] Leave N340/E15 at junc 520 for AL151 twd Mojácar Playa. Turn R onto coastal rd. Site 500m fr Hotel Marina on R. App rd diff lge o'fits.m'vans due grounding. Take care dip at site ent. Med, hdg/mkd pitch, all hdstg, terr, unshd; wc; chem disp; mv service pnt; shwrs inc; el pnts (22A) €3.30; gas; lndtte; shop; tradsmn; rest; snacks; bar; covrd pool; jacuzzi; sand beach adj; entmnt; TV; 5% statics; dogs €1.90; poss cr; adv bkg; quiet; red 30+ days; CCI. "Well-kept, beautifully laid-out site; v clean san facs but some v basic; pleasant atmosphere; gd touring base; facs stretched when site full." ♦ € 28.60   2007*

Spain

⊞MOJACAR 4G1 (1km W Rural) Camping El Quinto, Ctra Mojácar-Turre, 04638 Mojácar (Almería) [950-47 87 04; fax 950-47 21 48; campingelquinto@hotmail.com] Fr A7/E15 exit 520 sp Turre & Mojácar. Site on R in approx 13km at bottom of Mojácar vill. Sm, hdg/mkd pitch, hdstg, pt shd; wc; chem disp; mv service pnt; shwrs inc; el pnts (6-10A) €3.21; gas; Indtte; ice; shop; tradsmn; rest 3km; snacks; bar; BBQ; playgrnd; pool; sand beach 3km; dogs €1; phone; poss cr; Eng spkn; adv bkg (dep req); quiet but some rd noise; red long stay; CCI. "Neat, tidy site; easy walk to vill; gd mkt Wed; close National Park; excel beaches; metered 6A elect for long winter stay; popular in winter, poss cr & facs stretched; security barrier; poss mosquitoes; drinking water ltd to 5L a time." ♦ € 21.40   2007*

⊞MOJACAR 4G1 (5km W Rural) Canada Camping, 04639 Turre (Almería) [627-76 39 08; canadacampingmojacar@yahoo.co.uk] Exit A7/E15 at junc 525 & foll sp Los Gallardos on N340A. After approx 3km turn L at sp Turre & Garrucha on A370. In 3.5km slow down at green sp 'Kapunda' & turn R in 300m at sp 'Casa Bruns'. Site in 100m. Sm, hdg/mkd pitch, hdstg, unshd; wc (cont); chem disp; mv service pnt; shwrs inc; el pnts (6A) inc; Indry rm; no statics; adv bkg; quiet; CCI. "Vg adults-only site; friendly atmosphere." € 12.00   2007*

MOMBELTRAN see Arenas de San Pedro 1D3

MONASTERIO DE RODILLA see Burgos 1B4

⊞MONCOFA 3D2 (2km E Coastal/Urban) Camping Monmar, Camino Serratelles s/n, 12593 Platja de Moncófa (Castellón) [tel/fax 964-58 85 92; campingonmarmoncofa@wanadoo.es] Exit 49 fr A7 or N340, foll sp Moncófa Platja passing thro Moncófa & foll sp beach & tourist info thro 1-way system. Site sp, adj Aqua Park. Lge, hdg pitch, hdstg, pt shd; htd wc; chem disp; all serviced pitches; baby facs; shwrs inc; el pnts (6A) inc; gas; Indtte; shop & 1km; tradsmn; rest; snacks; bar; BBQ; playgrnd; pool; sand/shgl beach 200m; entmnt; internet; 10% statics; no dogs; phone; poss cr; Eng spkn; adv bkg; quiet; cc acc; red low ssn/long stay; CCI. "V helpful owner & staff; rallies on site Dec-Apr; poss v cr & dusty; mini-bus to stn & excursions; sunshades over pitches poss diff high o'fits; excel clean, tidy site." ♦ € 25.00   2007*

⊞MONCOFA 3D2 (2km S Coastal) Camping Los Naranjos, Camino Cabres, Km 950.8, 12953 Moncófa (Castellón) [964-58 03 37; fax 964-76 62 37; info@campinglosnaranjos.com] Fr N340 at km post 950.8 turn L at site sp, site 1km on R. Med, mkd pitch, hdstg, pt shd; wc; chem disp; mv service pnt; shwrs inc; el pnts (10A) inc; gas; Indtte; ice; shop; tradsmn; rest; snacks; bar; playgrnd; pool; paddling pool; beach 300m; games area; 20% statics; phone; bus 1km; poss cr; adv bkg; quiet; red long stay. "Gd." € 22.00   2004*

⊞MONTAGUT I OIX 3B3 (2km N Rural) Camping Montagut, Ctra de Montagut a Sadernes, Km 2, 17855 Montagut i Oix [972-28 72 02; fax 972-28 72 01; info@campingmontagut.com; www.campingmontagut.com] Exit AP7 junc 4 onto N260 W; join A26 & approx 10km past Besalú at Sant Jaume turn R twd Montagut i Oix on GIP5233. At end of vill turn L twd Sadernes on GIV5231, site in 2km, sp. Med, hdg/mkd pitch, terr; shd; wc; chem disp; mv service pnt; baby facs; shwrs inc; el pnts (6A) €3.80; gas; Indtte; shop; tradsmn; rest (w/e); bar; playgrnd; pool; paddling pool; no statics; quiet; red low ssn/long stay. "Excel, peaceful, scenic site; high standard san facs; gd walks nrby." ♦ 31 Mar-21 Oct. € 24.75   2007*

⊞MONTBLANC 3C2 (1.5km NE Rural) Camping Montblanc Park, Ctra Prenafeta, Km 1.8, 43400 Montblanc (Tarragona) [977-86 25 44; fax 977-86 05 39; info@montblancpark.com; www.montblancpark.com] Exit AP2 junc 9 sp Montblanc; foll sp Montblanc/Prenafeta/TV2421; site on L on TV2421. Med, hdg pitch, pt sl, terr, pt shd; htd wc; chem disp; mv service pnt; baby facs; shwrs inc; el pnts (10A) inc; Indtte; ice; shop; tradsmn; rest; snacks; bar; BBQ; playgrnd; pool; paddling pool; waterslide; entmnt; 50% statics; dogs €4; phone; Eng spkn; adv bkg (dep req); cc acc; red long stay/snr citizens; CCI. "Excel site; superb san facs; lovely area; Cistercian monestaries nrby; conv NH Andorra." ♦ ltd. € 32.00   2007*

MONTERROSO 1B2 (1km S Rural) Camp Municipal de Monterroso, A Pineda, 27569 Monterroso (Lugo) [982-37 75 01; fax 982-37 74 16; aged@cinsl.es; www.campingmonterroso.com] Fr N540 turn W onto N640 to Monterroso. Fr town cent turn S on LU212. In 100m turn sharp R then downhill for 1km; 2 sharp bends to site. Sm, hdg/mkd pitch, pt sl, pt shd; wc; chem disp; shwrs inc; el pnts (10A) €2.90; shop; tradsmn; rest, snacks, bar 500m; pool adj; games area; internet; dogs; Eng spkn; quiet; CCI. "Helpful staff; v quiet & ltd facs low ssn; vg." 1 Mar-30 Sep. € 15.00   2007*

MONTROIG see Cambrils 3C2

⊞MORAIRA 4F2 (1.5km SW Coastal) Camping Moraira, Camino del Paellero 50, 03724 Moraira-Teulada (Alicante) [965-74 52 49; fax 965-74 53 15; campingmoraira@campingmoraira.com; www.campingmoraira.com] Fr A7 exit junc 63. Foll sp Teulada & Moraira. Turn W 1km S of Moraira at km post 1.2, then site 500m up hill. Med, mkd pitch, hdstg, terr, shd; wc; chem disp; 15% serviced pitches; baby facs; shwrs inc; el pnts (6A) €3.50; Indtte; ice; shop & 650m; tradsmn; rest; snacks; bar; htd pool; sand beach 1km; internet; some statics; dogs; phone; bus 500m; Eng spkn; adv bkg; poss noisy w/e high ssn; red low ssn/long stay; cc acc; CCI. "Coastal town with harbour; modern site; relaxed informal atmosphere; gd touring base; ltd facs low ssn, san facs stretched high ssn; pitching poss diff for lge o'fits." ♦ ltd. € 24.00   2007*

⊞**MORATALLA** *4F1* (8km NW Rural) **Camping La Puerta, Ctra del Canal, Paraje de la Puerta, 30440 Moratalla (Murcia) [tel/fax 968-73 00 08; lapuerta@forodigital.es; www.campinglapuerta. com]** Fr Murcia take C415 dir Mula & Caravaca. Foll sp Moratalla & site. Lge, shd; htd wc; shwrs inc; el pnts (10A) €3.80; gas; lndtte; shop; rest; bar; BBQ; playgrnd; pool; rv sw; tennis; games area; internet; TV rm; statics; dogs; adv bkg; quiet; cc acc. ♦ € 14.30 (CChq acc)   2005*

MORELLA *3D2* (35km S Rural) **Camping El Llosar, Partida Vegas Tejería, 12150 Villafranca del Cid (Castellón) [964-44 14 09; www.campingllosar. com]** S fr Morella on CV125 to La Iglesuela del Cid, then rd CV15 to Vilafranca del Cid, site 800 W of Vilafranca on L. Med, hdstg, terr, pt shd; wc; shwrs, el pnts (10A) €3; gas; shop; rest; bar; playgrnd; pool; tennis; phone; adv bkg; quiet; cc acc. "Nr desert; rock climbing; phone ahead to check if open." ♦ Holy Week & 1 Jun-30 Sep. € 11.40
2004*

MOSTEIRO CERVANTES see Becerreá *1B2*

⊞**MOTRIL** *2H4* (12km SE Coastal) **Camping Don Cactus, N340, Km 343, 18730 Carchuna (Granada) [958-62 31 09; fax 958-62 42 94; camping@doncactus.com; www.doncactus.com]** On N340 SE fr Motril 1km W of Calahonda. Foll site sp. Lge, hdstg, shd; wc; chem disp; mv service pnt; shwrs; el pnts (5A) €3.75 (no earth); gas; lndtte; supmkt; rest; snacks; bar; BBQ; playgrnd; pool; shgl beach adj; tennis; archery; golf 6km; entmnt; wi-fi internet; TV rm; 60% statics; no dogs Jul & Aug; poss cr; no adv bkg; quiet; cc acc; red 30+ days; CCI. "Conv caves of Nerja, Calahonda, Motril, Granada & Sierra Nevada; many plastic greenhouses around site, but not obtrusive; some sm pitches not rec lge o'fits; dated but clean san facs; gd pool & rest; helpful staff; NH only." ♦ € 22.70 (CChq acc)   2007*

⊞**MOTRIL** *2H4* (3km W Urban/Coastal) **Camping Playa de Poniente de Motril, 18600 Motril (Granada) [958-82 03 03; fax 958-60 41 91; camplapo@infonegocio.com; www.infonegocio. com/camplapo]** Turn off coast rd N340 to port bef flyover; at rndabt take rd for Motril. Turn R in town, site sp. Lge, pt shd; htd wc; chem disp; baby facs; shwrs; el pnts €2.50; gas; lndtte; ice; shop; supmkt 4km; rest, bar in ssn; beach adj; pool; playgrnd; golf; tennis; horseriding; cycle hire; 70% statics; dogs €1.50; bus; Eng spkn; adv bkg; cc acc; red low ssn/long stay. "Well-appointed site but surrounded by flats; gd, clean facs; helpful recep; gd shop; access diff for lge o'fits; poss lge flying beetles; excel long stay winter." ♦ € 17.00
2004*

MOZAR DE VALVERDE see Benavente *1B3*

⊞**MUNDAKA** *3A1* (1km S Coastal) **Camping Portuondo, Ctra Amorebieta-Bermeo, Km 43, 48360 Mundaka (Bilbao) [946-87 77 01; fax 946-87 78 28; recepcion@campingportuondo. com; www.campingportuondo.com]** Leave E70 E of Bilbao onto B1631 to Bermeo. Keep on coast rd to Mundaka, site 1km on L. Ess to app fr Bermeo due to steep ent. Do not drive past recep until booked in due steep access. Med, terr, pt shd; wc; shwrs inc; el pnts (6A) €3.25; lndtte; rest; snacks; bar; playgrnd; pool; paddling pool; beach 500m; 30% statics; dogs; train 800m; poss v cr w/ends; adv bkg rec; cc acc. "Clean, modern facs; pitches tight; popular with surfers; conv Bilbao - walk to stn for train to Bilbao/connect to Guggenheim; site suitable sm m'vans only; unreliable opening low ssn." € 20.10   2005*

⊞**MURCIA** *4F1* (10km SW Rural) **Camping La Paz, Ctra 340 Murcia-Granada, Km 321, 30835 Sangonera La Seca (Murcia) [968-89 39 29; fax 968-80 13 37; horepa_@hotmail.com]** Tourist complex La Paz off A7 on W of junc 647; site sp visible both dirs. Med, hdg/mkd pitch, hdstg, unshd; htd wc; chem disp; serviced pitches; shwrs inc; el pnts inc (poss rev pol); lndtte; ice; sm shop adj; tradsmn; rest; snacks; bar; BBQ; playgrnd; pool; tennis; games area; TV; 95% statics; dogs; phone; cash machine; bus 600m; Eng spkn; adv bkg; rd noise; red long stay/low ssn; cc acc; CCI. "Gd NH but v ltd number touring pitches - rec walking to find pitch." ♦ € 17.36   2007*

MUROS *1B1* (500m W Coastal/Rural) **Camping San Francisco, Camino de Convento 21, 15291 Louro (La Coruña) [981-82 61 48; fax 981-57 19 16; ofmlouro@yahoo.es]** Fr Muros cont on C550 coast rd for 3km to San Francisco vill. Site sp to R up narr rd. Med, mkd pitch, pt shd; htd wc; chem disp; mv service pnt; shwrs; el pnts (5-8A) €3.60; gas; lndtte; ice; rest; snacks; bar; sand beach 400m; playgrnd; dogs; phone; bus 300m; Eng spkn; adv bkg; quiet; cc acc; CCI. "Pleasant site with gd facs; clean; lovely surroundings; vg sm rest; sh walk to lovely beach; excel security." ♦ 24 Jun-4 Sep. € 22.00
2006*

MUROS *1B1* (7km W Coastal) **Camping Ancoradoiro, Ctra Corcubión-Muros, Km.7.2, 15250 Louro (La Coruña) [981-87 88 97; fax 981-87 85 50]** Foll AC550 W fr Muros. Site on L (S) thro pine wood, well sp. Med, hdg/mkd pitch, terr, pt shd; wc; chem disp; shwrs inc; el pnts (6A) €3.60; lndtte; ice; shop adj; rest; snacks, bar adj; playgrnd; sand beach 500m; watersports; entmnt; no statics; no dogs; phone; poss cr; adv bkg; quiet; CCI. "Well-run site; excel rest; beautiful beaches; scenic area; vg." 15 Mar-15 Sep. € 18.00   2006*

MUTRIKU see Deba *3A1*

Spain

MUXIA *1A1* (10km E Coastal) **Camping Playa de Leis, Playa Berreira, Leis, 15124 Camariñas-Muxia (La Coruña) [tel/fax 981-73 03 04]** Fr Ponte do Porto turn L sp Muxia; foll camp sp. Site is 1st after Leis vill on R. Med, mkd pitch, terr, pt shd; wc; chem disp; shwrs inc; el pnts €1.70; lndtte; shop; rest; bar; BBQ; playgrnd; sand beach 100m; dogs; TV; quiet; cc acc; CCI. "Beautiful situation on wooded hillside; dir acces to gd beach; ltd facs low ssn; mkt in Muxia Thurs." 1 Mar-31 Dec. € 12.80   2005*

NAJERA *3B1* (500m S Urban) **Camping El Ruedo, San Julián 24, 26300 Nájera (La Rioja) [941-36 01 02; www.campingelruedo.es.vg]** Take Nájera town dirs off N120. In town turn L bef x-ing bdge. Site sp. Sm, pt shd; htd wc; chem disp; shwrs inc; el pnts (10-16A) inc (rev pol); gas; lndtte; shop; rest; snacks; bar; pool 1km; playgrnd; TV; entmnt; phone; bus 200m; poss cr; adv bkg; quiet; cc acc; CCI. "Pleasant site in quiet location, don't be put off by 1st impression of town; monastery worth visit." 1 Apr-10 Sep. € 16.60   2006*

⊞**NAVAJAS** *3D2* (1km W Rural) **Camping Altomira, Ctra Navajas/Pantano del Regajo, 12470 Navajas (Castellón) [964-71 32 11 or 964-71 09 46; fax 964-71 35 12; reservas@campingaltomira.com; www.campingaltomira.com]** Exit A23/N234 at km 33 to rndabt & take CV214 dir Navajas. In approx 2km turn L onto CV213, site on L just past R turn into vill, sp. Med, hdstg, terr, pt shd; htd wc; chem disp; mv service pnt; serviced pitches; baby facs; shwrs; el pnts (6A) €3.50; gas; lndtte; shop; tradsmn; rest; snacks; bar; playgrnd; pool; paddling pool; tennis; cycle hire; wifi internet; 70% statics; dogs; phone; bus 500m; adv bkg; poss noisy w/e & public hols; cc acc; red low ssn/CCI. "Superb welcome; friendly staff; panoramic views fr upper level; red squirrels on site; gd birdwatching; sh walk to vill; walking/cycling rte adj site; ltd facs low ssn; steep app to touring pitches on upper levels & kerbs to pitches; excel san facs; some sm pitches poss diff for lge o'fits without motor mover; poss clsd low ssn - phone ahead to check; excel." ♦ € 22.10 (CChq acc)   2007*

See advertisement opposite

NAVALAFUENTE see Cabrera, La *1D4*

NAVALENO *1C4* (Urban) **Camping Fuente del Botón, Ctra Sagunto-Burgos, 42149 Navaleno (Soria) [975-37 43 38; fax 975-22 55 55]** W fr Soria/Abejar on N234. Site on R side of rd on o'skts of Navaleno. Med, mkd pitch, pt sl, pt shd; wc; shwrs; el pnts €2; lndtte; shop; rest; bar; playgrnd; pool; paddling pool; tennis; some rd noise; cc acc. ♦ ltd. 15 Jun-15 Sep. € 14.50   2004*

NAVARREDONDA DE GREDOS see Hoyos del Espino *1D3*

NAVARRETE see Logroño *3B1*

⊞**NEGRAS, LAS** *4G1* (1km N Coastal) **Camping Náutico La Caleta, Parque Natural del Cabo de Gata, 04116 Las Negras (Almería) [tel/fax 950-52 52 37; campinglacaleta@arrakis.es]** Exit N344 at km stone 487 twd Las Negras. Site sp at ent to vill on R. Med, hdg pitch, hdstg, shd; wc; chem disp; mv service pnt; shwrs inc; el pnts (10A) €3.20; gas; lndtte; ice; shop & 1km; tradsmn; rest; snacks; bar; playgrnd; pool (high ssn); sand/shgl beach adj; cycle hire; dogs €1.60; phone; poss cr; quiet; red long stay/low ssn; 10% red for 8 days to 60% for 90 days; CCI. "Lge o'fits need care on steep app rd; vans over 2.5m take care sun shades on pitches; gd walking area; picturesque; excel rest in vill o'looking sea; vg." ♦ € 18.90   2005*

⊞**NERJA** *2H4* (4km E Rural) **Nerja Camping, Ctra Vieja Almeria, Km 296.5, Camp de Maro, 29787 Nerja (Málaga) [952-52 97 14; fax 952-52 96 96; nerjacamping5@hotmail.com]** On N340, cont past sp on L for 200m around RH corner, bef turning round over broken white line. Foll partly surfaced rd to site on hillside. Fr Almuñécar on N340, site on R approx 20km. Med, pt sl, terr, pt shd; wc; chem disp; shwrs inc; el pnts (5A) €3.75 (check earth); gas; lndry rm; ice; shops; tradsmn; rest; snacks; bar; playgrnd; sm pool; sand beach 2km; cycle hire; site clsd Oct; Eng spkn; adv bkg rec; rd noise; red long stay/low ssn/CCI. "5 mins to Nerja caves; mkt Tue; annual carnival 15 May; diff access lge o'fits; gd horseriding; site rds steep but gd surface; gd views; friendly owners." ♦ ltd. € 23.80   2007*

⊞**NERJA** *2H4* (8km W Urban) **Camping El Pino, N340, Km 285-3, Urbanización Torrox Park, 29793 Torrox Costa (Málaga) [tel/fax 952-53 25 78; info@campingelpino.com; www. campingelpino.com]** Exit N340 at km 285, at rndabt turn L & foll sp Torrox Costa N340a; in 1.5km at rndabt turn R to Torrox Costa, then L onto rndabt sp Nerja, site well sp in 4km. App rd steep with S bends. Lge, mkd pitch, hdstg, pt sl, terr, pt shd; wc; chem disp; shwrs inc; el pnts €3.20 (long lead req); lndtte; shop; rest, snacks adj; bar; playgrnd; 2 pools; 80% statics; dogs €2.50; phone; adv bkg; red low ssn/long stay; CCI. "Gd size pitches but high kerbs; narr, rough rd to beach in 2km; gd hill walks; conv Granada, Ronda; gd security." ♦ ltd. € 18.50   2006*

⊞**NIJAR** *4G1* (23km SE Coastal) **Camping Los Escullos San José, Paraje de los Escullos s/n, 04118 San José-Nijar (Almería)** [950-38 98 11 or 950-38 98 10; fax 950-38 98 10; info@ losescullossanjose.com; www.losescullos sanjose.com] Fr E15/N344 (dir Almería) exit junc 487 dir Campohermoso/San José. Then foll sp for El Pozo de los Frailes, Los Escullos & site; fr N on N340 exit 479 & foll sps. Lge, mkd pitch, hdstg, pt sl, shd; wc; chem disp; mv service pnt; baby facs; sauna; shwrs inc; el pnts (10A) €4.75; gas; lndtte; ice; shop; rest; snacks; bar; playgrnd; pool; beach 700m; watersports; diving; tennis; cycle hire; fitness rm; entmnt; excursions arranged; internet; TV rm; 40% statics; dogs €2.50; Eng spkn; adv bkg; cc acc; red long stay/CCI. "Set in National Park on coast; many secluded beaches & walks; excel for watersports; vg pool & rest; helpful staff; pitches poss flood in heavy rain." ♦ € 27.00   2007*

NOJA *1A4* (N Coastal) **Camping Los Molinos, Playa del Ris, 39180 Noja (Cantabria)** [942-63 04 26; fax 942-63 07 25; losmolinos@ ceoecant.es; www.campinglosmolinos.com] Exit A8 at km 185. Go N & foll sp to Noja, then L at Playa del Ris. Site sp. V lge, hdg pitch, pt shd; wc; chem disp; mv service pnt; shwrs; baby facs; el pnts (3A) €3; gas; lndtte; shop; rest; snacks; bar; BBQ; playgrnd; pool; paddling pool; sand beach 500m; tennis; car wash; entmnt; 75% statics; dogs; poss cr; Eng spkn; adv bkg (dep req); cc not acc; CCI. "Gd site; lovely beach; some noise fr karting circuit until late evening but noise levels strictly curtailed at midnight." ♦ Holy Week & 1 Jun-30 Sep. € 24.00
                                                          2007*

⊞**NOIA** *1B2* (5km SW Coastal) **Camping Punta Batuda, Playa Hornanda, 15970 Porto do Son (La Coruña)** [981-76 65 42; camping@puntabatuda. com; www.puntabatuda.com] Fr Santiago take C543 twd Noia, then AC550 5km SW to Porto do Son. Site on R approx 1km after Boa. Lge, mkd pitch, terr, pt shd; htd wc; chem disp; shwrs inc; el pnts (3A) €2.90 (poss rev pol); gas; lndtte; ice; shop; rest w/e only; snacks; bar; tradsmn; playgrnd; htd pool w/e only; sand beach adj; tennis; 50% statics; some Eng spkn; adv bkg; quiet; red 15 days; CCI. "Wonderful views; exposed to elements & poss windy; ltd facs low ssn; hot water to shwrs only; some pitches v steep &/or sm; gd facs for disabled; naturist beach 5km S." ♦ € 20.50   2006*

NOJA *1A4* (700m N Coastal) **Camping Playa Joyel, Playa del Ris, 39180 Noja (Cantabria)** [942-63 00 81; fax 942-63 12 94; playajoyel@telefonica. net; www.playajoyel.com] Fr Santander or Bilbao foll sp A8/E70 (toll-free). Approx 15km E of Solares exit m'way junc 185 at Beranga onto CA147 N twd Noja & coast. On o'skirts of Noja turn L sp Playa de Ris, foll rd approx 1.5km to rndabt, site sp to L, 500m fr rndabt. V lge, mkd pitch, pt sl, pt shd; wc; chem disp; mv service pnt; baby facs; shwrs inc; el pnts (6A) €4.20; gas; lndtte; ice; supmkt; tradsmn; rest; snacks; bar; BBQ (gas/charcoal); playgrnd; pool & paddling pool (high ssn & caps ess); jacuzzi; sand beach adj; windsurfing; sailing; tennis; entmnt; disco nightly high ssn but not noisy; hairdresser; car wash; cash dispenser; wifi internet; child entment; games/TV rm; 15% statics; no dogs; phone; recep 0800-2200; poss v cr w/e & high ssn; Eng spkn; adv bkg; red low ssn; cc not acc; CCI. "Well-organised; gd, spotless facs; pleasant staff; ltd facs low ssn & ltd site lighting; gd location; conv Santander, Santillana; lovely sheltered bay with coves; some narr site rds + kerbs; midnight silence enforced; highly rec." ♦ 15 Mar-30 Sep. € 38.52 (CChq acc) ABS - E05   2007*

Spain

See advertisement on bookmark

*Last year of report

EUROCAMPING lies directly on the fine, sandy beach of Oliva. Pitches with plenty of shade. Modern sanitary instalations with free hot water. Supermarket, Bar-Restaurant, children's playground. Special rates. OPEN ALL YEAR ROUND. BUNGALOWS.

Tel. +34 96 285 40 98 · Fax +34 96 285 17 53 Apartado n° 7 45780 OLIVA (Valencia) e-mail: eurocamping@interbook.net www.eurocamping-es.com

NUEVALOS *3C1* (N Rural) **Camping Lago Park, Ctra De Alhama de Aragón a Cillas, Km 39, 50210 Nuévalos (Zaragoza)** [tel/fax 976-84 90 38; info@campinglagopark.com; www.campinglagopark.com] Fr E on A2/E90 exit junc 231 to Nuévalos, turn R sp Madrid. Site 1.5km on L when ent Nuévalos. Fr W exit junc 204, site well sp. Steep ent fr rd. V lge, mkd pitch, terr, pt shd; wc; chem disp; child/baby facs; shwrs inc; el pnts (4A) €5; gas; lndtte; shop, rest, snacks high ssn; bar 500m; BBQ; playgrnd; pool; lake nrby; fishing; boating; some statics; dogs; bus 500m; poss cr; adv bkg; quiet but noisy w/e high ssn; red long stay; CCI. "Nr wonderful beauty spot of Monasterio de Piedra & Tranquera Lake; excel facs on top terr, but stretched high ssn & poss long, steepish walk; ltd facs low ssn; gd birdwatching; only site in area." 1 Apr-30 Sep. € 24.60   2007*

⊞**OCHAGAVIA** *3A1* (500m S Rural) **Camping Osate, Crta Salazar s/n, 31680 Ochagavia (Navarra)** [tel/fax 948-89 01 84; info@campingsnavarra.com; www.campingsnavarra.com] On N135 SE fr Auritz, turn L onto NA140 & cont for 24km bef turning L twd Ochagavia on NA140. Site sp in 2km on R, 500m bef vill. Lge, mkd pitch, pt shd; wc; chem disp; some serviced pitches; shwrs inc; el pnts €4.25; gas; shop; rest high ssn; snacks; bar; BBQ; 50% statics; dogs €2.90; quiet. "Attractive, remote vill; gd, well-maintained site; touring pitches under trees, sep fr statics; facs poss stretched high ssn; site clsd Dec & rec phone ahead low ssn." € 17.00   2007*

⊞**OLITE** *3B1* (2km S Urban) **Camping Ciudad de Olite, Ctra N115, Tafalla-Peralta, Km 2.3, 31390 Olite** [948-74 10 14; fax 948-74 06 04; campingdeolite@hotmail.com; www.campingsnavarra.com] Fr Pamplona S on AP15 exit 50 twd Olite. At rndabt turn L, then in 300m turn R onto N115, site sp on L past Netto in 2km. Lge, mkd pitch, pt shd; wc; chem disp; serviced pitches; baby facs; shwrs inc; el pnts (5A) inc; shop 2km; rest; bar; playgrnd; htd pool (caps ess); tennis; entmnt; games area; 90% statics; site clsd 22 Dec-7 Jan; poss cr; Eng spkn; phone; poss noisy at w/ends; cc acc; CCI. "Close to m'way; ltd space & facs for tourers; site mostly used by Spanish for w/e; narr site rds; Olite historic vill with fairytale castle; bleak in winter; take care electrics; NH only." ♦ ltd. € 17.50   2007*

> As soon as we get home I'm going to post all these site report forms to the editor for inclusion in next year's guide. I don't want to miss the September deadline.

⊞**OLIVA** *4E2* (2km E Coastal) **Camping Kiko Park, Calle Assagador de Carro 2, 46780 Playa de Oliva (València) [962-85 09 05; fax 962-85 43 20; kikopark@kikopark.com; www.kikopark.com]** Exit AP7/E15 junc 61; fr toll turn R at T-junc onto N332. Site sp on L (by iron monoliths) around seaboard side of town. Do not drive thro Oliva. Access poss diff on app rds due humps. Lge, hdg/mkd pitches, hdstg, shd; htd wc; chem disp; mv service pnt; some serviced pitches; baby facs; fam bthrm; shwrs inc; el pnts (16A) inc; gas; lndtte; ice; supmkt; rest; bar; BBQ; playgrnd; 2 pools (1 covrd); sand beach adj; watersports; windsurfing school; fishing; tennis 1km; games area; cycle hire; entmnt; child entmnt; games rm; internet; dogs €2.50; phone; pitch price variable; Eng spkn; adv bkg; quiet; cc acc; red snr cititzens/long stay/low ssn; red CCI. "Excel rest in Michelin Guide; v helpful staff; excel clean, family-run site; vg san facs; lots to do in area." ♦ € 43.55 ABS - E20
2007*

See advertisement on next page

The opening dates and prices on this campsite have changed. I'll send a site report form to the editor for the next edition of the guide.

⊞**OLIVA** *4E2* (4km E Coastal) **Camping Azul, 46780 Playa de Oliva (València) [962-85 41 06; fax 962-85 40 96; campingazul@ctv.es; www.campingazul.com]** Exit A7/E15 junc 61; fr toll turn R at T-junc onto N332. Drive S thro Oliva, site sp, turn twds sea at km 209.8. Poor app over unmade rd. Med, mkd pitch, pt shd; wc; mv service pnt; shwrs inc; el pnts (10A) €2.75; gas; lndtte; shop; rest; bar; playgrnd; cycle hire; games area; golf 1km; wifi internet; entmnt; 20% statics; no adv bkg; quiet; cc acc; red long stay/low ssn. "Gd site." ♦ € 22.40
2007*

⊞**OLIVA** *4E2* (3km SE Coastal) **Eurocamping, Ctra València-Oliva, Aptdo 7, Partida Rabdells s/n, 46780 Playa de Oliva (València) [962-85 17 53; info@eurocamping-es.com; www.eurocamping-es.com]** Exit A7/E15 junc 61; fr toll turn R at T-junc onto N332. Drive S thro Oliva, turn R at km 213; at 1st rndabt foll sp to València; at 2nd take 1st exit (site sp). Fr S by N332 turn R sp Urbanization, L at rndabt & foll camping sp to site. Lge, hdg/mkd pitch, hdstg, pt shd; htd wc; chem disp; mv service pnt; baby facs; shwrs inc; el pnts (6-10A) €3.58-5.60; gas; lndtte; ice; shop; tradsmn; rest; snacks; bar; BBQ; playgrnd; sand beach adj; cycle hire; wifi internet; entmnt; TV; dogs €1.90; phone; poss cr; quiet but some noise fr adj bar; cc acc; red long stay/low ssn/CCI. "Gd facs; busy, well-maintained, clean site adj housing development; helpful British owners; beautiful clean beach; gd beach walks; cycle rte thro orange groves to town; pitch far fr recep if poss, night noise fr generators 1700-2400; highly rec." ♦ € 37.85 (CChq acc)
2007*

See advertisement opposite

⊞**OLIVA** *4E2* (3km S Coastal) **Camping Olé, Partida Aigua Morta s/n, 46780 Playa de Oliva (València) [962-85 75 17; fax 962-85 75 16; campingole@hotmail.com; www.camping-ole.com]** Exit AP7/E15 junc 61 onto N332 dir Dénia. At km 209.9 turn twds coast sp Oliva Nova golf club, no site sp. Site bet golf club & coast. Lge, hdg/mkd pitch, hdstg, pt shd; htd wc; chem disp; baby facs; shwrs inc; el pnts (6-10A) €4.74; gas; lndtte; ice; supmkt; rest; snacks; bar; BBQ; playgrnd; pool; sand beach adj; fishing; tennis 600m; cycle hire; horseriding 2km; golf adj; internet; entmnt; 15% statics; dogs €2.59; phone; Eng spkn; adv bkg; quiet; cc acc; red long stay/low ssn; CCI. "Many sports & activities; direct access to beach; excel." ♦ € 31.00
2007*

See advertisement below

Spain

⊞⊞⊞ **OLIVA** *4E2* (5km S Coastal) **Camping Pepe, 46780 Playa de Oliva (València)** [962-85 75 19; fax 962-85 75 22; campingpepe@telefonica. net; www.campingpepe.com] Exit A7 junc 61; fr toll turn R at T-junc onto N332. Drive S thro Oliva & in 3.5km at km 210, move R to service rd sp 'Urbanización'. Cont past service stn & across flyover. At 1st rndabt, take 2nd exit past golf club ent, then 1st exit at next rndabt, turn L sp ' Camping Pepe' & others. Site down narr rd on L. Lge, hdg/ mkd pitch, hdstg, pt shd; wc; chem disp; baby facs; shwrs; el pnts (5A) inc; gas; lndtte; ice; shop & 1km; tradmn; rest high ssn; snacks; bar; BBQ; playgrnd; sand beach adj; golf club nr; 30% statics; dogs €1.90; phone; poss cr; Eng spkn; quiet; red long stay/low ssn; CCI. "Well-managed, friendly, busy site; 5 san facs blocks; hot water avail all day for all needs; high kerb to some pitches; barrier locked at night; beautiful beach; vg for winter stay." ♦ ltd. € 25.80   2004*

OLIVA *4E2* (7km S Coastal) **Camping Rió Mar, Ctra N332, Km 207, 46780 Playa de Oliva (València)** [962-85 40 97; fax 962-83 91 32; riomar@campingriomar.com; www.camping riomar.com] Exit A7/E15 junc 61; fr toll turn R at T-junc onto N332. Drive S thro Oliva, site sp at km 207. Med, hdstg, shd; wc; chem disp; shwrs; el pnts (6A) €3.95; gas; lndtte; supmkt high ssn; rest, bar high ssn; playgrnd; sand beach adj; 20% statics; dogs €1.80; phone; poss cr; adv bkg; quiet; cc acc; red low ssn/snr citizens; CCI. "Friendly, family-run site; facs in need of refurb; sm pitches but lge o'fits use sandy area bet site & beach; Fri mkt in Oliva; NH only." € 25.78   2007*

⊞ **OLOT** *3B3* (3km SE Rural) **Camping Fageda, Batet de la Serra, Ctra Olot-Santa Pau, Km 4, 17800 Olot (Gerona)** [tel/fax 972-27 12 39; info@ campinglafageda.com; www.campinglafageda. com] E fr Olot on GR524 to Banyoles, site on L of minor rd (C150) at 3.8km. Med, mkd pitch, pt sl, terr, pt shd; htd wc; chem disp; shwrs inc; el pnts (10A) €4.90; gas; lndtte; shop; snacks; rest & bar high ssn; playgrnd; htd pool high ssn; 90% statics (sep area); dogs; phone; adv bkg (dep); quiet; cc acc; CCI. "Situated in beautiful area with extinct volcanoes & forests; walks fr site; diff access to water pnts for m'vans; isolated, pretty site, few visitors low ssn; v friendly, helpful staff." ♦ € 19.35   2006*

Before we move on, I'm going to fill in some site report forms and post them off to the editor, otherwise they won't arrive in time for the deadline at the end of September.

⊞ Site open all year   834   *Help us to update this guide*

ORGANYA *3B2* (500m NW Rural) **Camping Organyà, Calle de les Piscines s/n, Partida Lloredes, 25794 Organyà (Lleida) [973-38 20 39; fax 973-38 35 36]** Site sp to E of C14 adj sports cent/football pitch. Sharp rise off rd & narr access, not rec for lge o'fits. Med, pt shd; wc; shwrs; el pnts (3A) €3; shop, rest 1km; bar; playgrnd; pools adj; tennis; paragliding tuition avail; mainly statics; dogs €2; phone; some rd noise; CCI. "Excel mountain scenery & interesting vill; gd, clean san facs; pleasant pools adj; NH only - phone ahead low ssn to check site open." Holy Week & 22 Jun-11 Sep. € 15.70   2004*

⊞**ORGIVA** *2G4* (2km S Rural) **Camping Órgiva, Ctra A348, Km 18.9, 18400 Órgiva (Granada) [tel/fax 958-78 43 07; campingorgiva@ descubrelaalpujarra.com; www.descubrela alpujarra.com]** Fr N or S on Granada-Motril rd suggest avoid A348 via Lanjarón (narr & congested). Fr N323/A44 turn E nr km 179, 1km S of lge dam sp Vélez de Benaudalla, over multi-arch bdge, turn L sp Órgiva. Foll rd (easy climb) turn L after sh tunnel over rv bdge; site 2nd building on R. Sm, pt sl, pt shd; wc; chem disp; serviced pitches; baby facs; shwrs inc; el pnts (10A) €2.70 (rev pol); gas; ice; lndtte; supmkt 2km; rest; snacks; bar; playgrnd; pool; shgl beach 30km; bus 2km; adv bkg; cc acc; some Eng spkn; red low ssn/long stay; cc acc; 10% red CCI. "Immac san facs; excel, friendly site; vg value rest open all yr; magnificent scenery; gd base for mountains & coast; Thurs mkt in town; fiesta 27 Sep-1 Oct; pleasant walk thro orange & almond groves to vill; area popular for new-age travellers - festival early Mar." ♦ € 17.50

2005*

⊞**ORGIVA** *2G4* (2km NW Rural) **Camping Puerta de la Alpujarra, Ctra Lanjarón-Órgiva (Las Barreras), 18418 Órgiva (Granada) [tel/fax 958-78 44 50; puertadelaalpujarra@campings. net; www.campingpuertadelaalpujarra.com]** Fr Órgiva take A348 to Lanjarón. Site on L in 2km. Lanjarón poss diff for long o'fits. Med, mkd pitch, hdstg, terr, pt shd; wc; chem disp; mv service pnt; shwrs inc; el pnts (16A) €3; gas 2km; lndtte; shop; rest; bar; playgrnd; pool; paddling pool high ssn; entmnt; few statics; dogs free; phone; bus adj; poss cr; Eng spkn; adv bkg; quiet; cc acc; 10% red 7+ days. "Scenic area with gd views fr site; steepish access to pitches; excel walking." ♦ € 18.80

2007*

ORIHUELA DEL TREMEDAL *3D1* (1km S) **Camping Caimodorro, Camino Fuente de los Colladillos s/n, 44366 Orihuela del Tremedal (Teruel) [978-71 43 55; caimodorro@suone.com; www. caimodorro.com]** Fr Albarracin on A1512 head twd Orihuela. Turn R twd vill & R after petrol stn, sp. Sm, unshd; wc; shwrs; el pnts €2.20; lndtte; shop; bar; pool; dogs; phone; bus 600m; Eng spkn; cc acc. "Elevated, breezy situation overlooking mountain vill; lovely scenery; gd touring base; friendly owner; v quiet low ssn." 1 Apr-31 Oct. € 11.60   2006*

ORINON *1A4* (Rural/Coastal) **Camping Oriñón, 39797 Oriñón (Cantabria) [tel/fax 942-87 86 30; info@campingorinon.com; www.campingorinon. com]** Exit A8/E70 at km 160 to Oriñón. Med, mkd pitch, pt sl, unshd; wc; chem disp; mv service pnt; shwrs inc; el pnts (4A) €3; gas; lndtte; shop; rest; snacks; bar; playgrnd; sand beach adj; internet; TV; 90% statics; dogs; phone; bus 1km; Eng spkn; quiet. "Excel surfing beach adj; v clean site; helpful staff; vg." ♦ ltd. 1 Apr-30 Sep. € 22.50   2007*

ORINON *1A4* (2km E Coastal) **Camping Playa Arenillas, Ctra Santander-Bilbao, Km 64, 39798 Islares (Cantabria) [tel/fax 942-86 31 52; cueva@ mundivia.es; www.cantabria.com/arenillas.asp]** Exit A8 at km 156 Islares. Turn W on N634. Site on R at W end of Islares. Steep ent. Lge, mkd pitch, pt shd; wc; chem disp; baby facs; shwrs inc; el pnts (5A) €3.60 (poss no earth); gas; lndtte; ice; shop; tradsmn; rest adj; snacks; bar; BBQ; playgrnd; sand beach 100m; horseriding; cycle hire; games area; TV; 40% statics; no dogs; phone; bus 500m; poss cr; Eng spkn; adv bkg rec Jul/Aug; some rd noise; cc acc; CCI. "Facs ltd low ssn & stretched in ssn; well-staffed; facs constantly cleaned; rec arr early for choice of own pitch; conv Guggenheim Museum; excel NH for Bilbao ferry." 1 Apr-30 Sep. € 19.20   2006*

ORIO see Zarautz *3A1*

⊞**OROPESA** *3D2* (3km NE Coastal) **Camping Torre La Sal 1, Cami L'Atall s/n, 12595 Ribera de Cabanes (Castellón) [964-31 95 96; fax 964-31 96 29; info@campingtorrelasal.com]** Leave AP7 at exit 45 & take N340 twd Tarragona. Foll camp sp fr km 1000 stone. Site next after Torre La Sal 2. Lge, hdg/mkd pitch, hdstg, pt shd; htd wc; chem disp; baby facs; shwrs inc; el pnts (10A) €4; gas; lndtte; shop adj; rest high ssn; BBQ; playgrnd; htd, covrd pool; sand/shgl beach adj; tennis; games area; internet; 10% statics; dogs (except Jul/Aug); phone; bus 1.5km; poss cr; Eng spkn; adv bkg; quiet; cc acc; red long stay/snr citizens; CCI. "Clean, well-maintained site; elec metered for long stays." ♦ ltd. € 21.70   2006*

⊞**OROPESA** *3D2* (3.5km NE Coastal) **Camping Oasis, Ctra La Tall s/n, 12594 Oropesa (Castellón) [964-31 96 77; fax 964-31 97 18; oasis@camping-oropesa.com; www.camping-oropesa.com]** Leave A7 at exit 45 & take N340 twds Tarragona. Turn R after km stone 999, site sp R at beach rd. Med, hdg pitch, hdstg, shd; wc; chem disp; shwrs; el pnts (5A) €3.15; gas; lndtte; shop & 500m; tradsmn; rest; snacks; bar; playgrnd; pool; sand beach 200m; entmnt; TV rm; 20% statics; phone; car wash; quiet but some rd/ rlwy noise; Eng spkn; red long stay & snr citizens; CCI. "Gd rest; friendly, helpful staff." ♦ € 25.20

2006*

Spain

⊞OROPESA *3D2* (3.5km NE Coastal) **Camping Torre La Sal 2, Cami L'Atall s/n, 12595 Ribera de Cabanes (Castellón) [964-31 97 77; fax 964-31 97 44; camping@torrelasal2.com; www. torrelasal2.com]** Leave AP7 at exit 45 & take N340 twd Tarragona. Foll camp sp fr km 1000 stone. Site adj Torre La Sal 'Maria'. Lge, hdg/mkd pitch, hdstg, pt shd; htd wc; chem disp; sauna; serviced pitch; shwrs inc; el pnts (10A) €5.25; gas; lndtte; shop; tradsmn; supmkt adj; rest; snacks; bar; playgrnd; shgl beach adj; 4 pools (2 htd & covrd); tennis; games area; entmnt; library; TV rm; some statics; Eng spkn; adv bkg; quiet; CCI. "Clean, peaceful site; lge pitches; more mature c'vanners v welcome; poss diff for lge o'fits & m'vans; water points few & far between." ♦ € 26.00   2006*

⊞OSSA DE MONTIEL *4E1* (10km SW Rural) **Camping Los Batanes, Ctra Lagunas de Ruidera, Km 8, 02611 Ossa de Montiel (Albacete) [926-69 90 76; fax 926-69 91 71; camping@ losbatanes.com;   www.losbatanes.com]** Fr Munera twd Ossa de Montiel on N430. In Ossa foll sp in vill to site in 10km. Fr Manzanares on N430 app to Ruidera, cross bdge; turn immed R alongside lagoon, camp at 12km. Lge, pt shd; htd wc; chem disp; mv service pnt; shwrs; el pnts (5A) €3.10; lndtte; ice; shops 10km; tradsmn; rest 200m; snacks; bar; playgrnd; pool, paddling pool high ssn; lake sw adj; cycle hire; TV; 10% statics; dogs €2; phone; site clsd 28 Dec-2 Jan; Eng spkn; adv bkg; noisy at w/e; cc acc; 10% red CCI. "Lovely area of natural lakes; excel birdwatching & walking; friendly owners; low ssn phone to check open." ♦ € 23.90 2007*

OTURA see Granada *2G4*

> There aren't many sites open this early in the year. We'd better phone ahead to check that the one we're heading for is actually open.

PALAFRUGELL *3B3* (5km E Coastal) **Camping Tamariu, Costa Rica 2, 17212 Tamariu (Gerona) [972-62 04 22; fax 972-62 05 92; campingtamariu@ teleline.es;   www.campingtamariu.com]** In Tamariu,app fr Palafrugell, turn L at bottom of hill on ent vill, site sp. Lge, pt sl, pt terr, shd; wc; chem disp; shwrs; el pnts €3.10; gas; lndtte; shop; snacks; bar; shgl beach 600m; pool; playgrnd; paddling pool; some statics; phone; poss cr; quiet. "On beautiful part of coast away fr main rds; gd shops & rests in vill; steep app to terr pitches; conv parking for vill & beach." 1 May-30 Sep. € 19.30 2005*

PALAFRUGELL *3B3* (5km E Coastal) **Kim's Camping, Calle Font d'en Xeco s/n, 17211 Llafranc (Gerona) [972-30 11 56; fax 972-61 08 94; info@campingkims.com;   www.camping kims.com]** Exit AP7 at junc 6 Gerona Nord if coming fr France, or junc 9 fr S dir Palamós. Foll sp for Palafrugell, Playa Llafranc. Site is 500m N of Llafranc. Lge, hdg/mkd pitches, hdstg, pl sl, terr, shd; wc; chem disp; baby facs; shwrs inc; el pnts (6A) inc; gas; lndtte; ice; shop; rest; snacks; bar; BBQ (gas only); playgrnd; 2 pools; sand beach 500m; watersports; tennis 500m; games rm; games area; cycle hire 500m; golf 10km; internet; entmnt; excursions; TV; 10% statics; dogs; phone; guarded; poss cr; Eng spkn; adv bkg; quiet; cc acc; red low ssn/long stay; red CCI. "Excel, beachside site; steep site rds; friendly, well-organised; high ssn w/e noise fr adj site; excel, modern san facs inc bthrm for disabled; ltd facs low ssn." ♦ 30 Mar-30 Sep. € 39.00   2007*

PALAFRUGELL *3B3* (5km SE Rural) **Camping La Siesta, Chopitea 110, 17210 Calella de Palafrugell (Gerona) [972-61 51 16; fax 972-61 44 16; info@ campinglasiesta.com;   www.campinglasiesta. com]** On main rd to Gerona-Palamós turn L (E) at rndabt onto GI654 & foll sp Calella. Site on R just bef Calella dir Llafranc. V lge, mkd pitch, pt sl, pt shd; wc; chem disp; shwrs inc; el pnts inc; gas; lndtte; shops; rest; snacks; 2 bars; no BBQ; playgrnd; 2 lge pools; beach 1.3km; tennis; horseriding; entmnt; statics; no dogs; bus; site open w/ends Nov-March & clsd Xmas to 8 Jan; Eng spkn; adv bkg (dep req); noisy at w/e; red low ssn. "Excel beaches at Llafranc & Calella de Palafrugell; mkt at Palafrugell; many beaches & coves adj; narr, winding paths thro pines to pitches; most vans have to be manhandled onto pitches; twin-axles acc; Eng newspapers same day." Easter-31 Oct. € 40.90 2006*

PALAFRUGELL *3B3* (5km S Coastal) **Camping Moby Dick, Costa Verda 16-28, 17210 Calella de Palafrugell (Gerona) [972-61 43 07; fax 972-61 49 40; info@campingmobydick.com; www. campingmobydick.com]** Fr Palafrugell foll sps to Calella. At rndabt just bef Calella turn R, then 4th L, site clearly sp on R. Med, hdstg, sl, terr, pt shd; wc; chem disp; baby facs; shwrs inc; el pnts (6-10A); €3.50; lndtte; shop; supmkt 100m; rest 100m; snacks; bar; playgrnd; shgl beach 150m; 15% statics; dogs; phone; bus 100m; poss cr; Eng spkn; adv bkg; quiet; CCI. ♦ 1 Apr-15 Oct. € 19.50 2005*

⊞ *Site open all year*   836   *Send in your site reports*

PALAMOS *3B3* (1km N Coastal) **Camping Benelux,** Paratge de Castell s/n, 17230 Palamós (Gerona) [972-31 55 75; fax 972-60 19 01; cbenelux@ cbenelux.com; www.cbenelux.com] Turn E off Palamós-La Bisbal rd (C66) at km stone 40.7. Site in 800m on minor metalled rd, to sea at Playa del Castell. Lge, hdstg, pt sl, pt shd; wc; chem disp; mv service pnt; shwrs inc; el pnts (6A) inc; gas; lndtte; ice; shop; tradsmn; supmkt; rest (w/e only low ssn); snacks; bar; playgrnd; pool; sand beach 1km; safe dep; car wash; currency exchange; TV; 50% statics; dogs; poss cr; Eng spkn; adv bkg; noisy at w/e; red low ssn/long stay; cc acc; CCI. "In pine woods; many long stay British/Dutch; gd shop on site; excel supmkt in town; gd rests nrby; v friendly owner; clean facs poss ltd low ssn; poss flooding in heavy rain; poss diff for disabled, rough ground." ♦ ltd. 1 Apr-30 Sep. € 23.00   2004*

PALAMOS *3B3* (1km N Coastal) **Camping Internacional de Palamós,** Cami Cap de Planes s/n, 17230 Palamós (Gerona) [972-31 47 36; fax 972-31 76 26; info@internacionalpalamos.com; www.internacionalpalamos.com] Fr N leave AP7 at junc 6 to Palamós on C66. Fr Palafrugell turn L 16m after o/head sp to Sant Feliu-Palamós at sm sp La Fosca & camp sites. Winding app thro La Fosca. Fr S, take exit 9 dir Sant Feliu & Lloret, then C65/C31 to Santa Christina-Palamós, then La Fosca. Lge, pt shd; wc (mainly cont); chem disp; mv service pnt; baby facs; serviced pitches; private bthrms avail; shwrs inc; el pnts; (5A) €4.90; lndtte; shop; rest; snacks; bar; playgrnd; pool; paddling pool; sand beach 600m; solarium; mini-golf 200m; windsurfing, sailing & diving 1km; golf 15km; TV rm; car wash; 20% statics; phone; bus 600m; quiet. "Attractive site; superb san facs; some sm pitches on steep access rds - check bef pitching; highly rec; lovely area." ♦ 1 Apr-30 Sep. € 33.80 (CChq acc)   2007*

PALAMOS *3B3* (1km N Coastal) **Camping Palamós,** Ctra La Fosca 12, 17230 Palamós (Gerona) [972-31 42 96; fax 972-60 11 00; campingpal@grn.es; www.campingpalamos.com] App Palamós on C66/C31 fr Gerona & Palafrugell turn L 16m after o/ head sp Sant Feliu-Palamós at sm sp La Fosca & campsites. Lge, pt sl, terr, pt shd; wc; shwrs; baby facs; el pnts (4A) €2.70; gas; lndtte; ice; shop; rest 400m; playgrnd; 2 htd pools; shgl/rocky beach adj; tennis; golf; internet; 30% statics; dogs €2; phone; cc acc. ♦ 1 Apr-30 Sep. € 31.90   2007*

PALAMOS *3B3* (3km N Coastal) **Camping Relax Ge,** Barrio Roqueta s/n, 17253 Mont-Ràs (Gerona) [972-30 08 18; fax 972-60 11 00; info@ campingrelaxnat.com; www.campingrelaxge. com] C31 Palafrugell-Palamós rd at km 329, site sp. Med, mkd pitch, pt shd; wc; chem disp; shwrs (5A) €2; gas; lndtte; ice; shop; rest; snacks; bar; playgrnd; htd pool & paddling pool; sand beach 1km; 10% statics; adv bkg (dep req); quiet; CCI. "Friendly, family-run site; exceptional beaches; conv Gerona, Barcelona." 1 Jun-31 Aug. € 26.75   2004*

PALAMOS *3B3* (5km N Rural) **Camping Relax-Nat (Naturist),** Barrio Roqueta s/n, 17253 Mont-Ràs (Gerona) [972-30 08 18; fax 972-60 11 00; info@ campingrelaxnat.com; www.campingrelaxnat. com] Fr C66 Palafrugell-Palamós rd, turn E after km stone 38. Site in 1.5km on metalled rd. Lge, pt shd; wc; chem disp; shwrs; el pnts (2A) €3; lndtte; shop; rest; snacks; bar; playgrnd; sand beach 4km; pool; playgrnd; tennis; games area; entmnt; some statics; no dogs; adv bkg; quiet. "Naturist families & mixed groups min 2 people; diff pitch access for lge o'fits." ♦ 1 Apr-30 Sep. € 31.50   2007*

PALAMOS *3B3* (3km SW Coastal) **Camping Costa Brava,** Avda Unió s/n, 17252 Sant Antoni de Calonge (Gerona) [tel/fax 972-65 02 22; campingcostabrava@campingcostabrava.net; www.campingcostabrava.net] Foll sp St Antoni de Calonge fr C31, site sp. Lge, mkd pitch, shd; wc; chem disp; baby facs; shwrs inc; el pnts (4A) €3.80; lndtte; ice; shop adj; rest; snacks; bar; BBQ; playgrnd; pool & child pool; sand beach 300m; watersports; games rm; entmnt; car wash; dogs; phone; bus; poss cr; adv bkg; quiet; cc acc. "Well-managed, family-run site; sm pitches; clean san facs; rec arr early high ssn to secure pitch; pleasant, helpful owners." ♦ 1 Jun-15 Sep. € 22.75   2007*

PALAMOS *3B3* (3km SW Coastal) **Eurocamping,** Ctra Palamós-Playa de Aro, Km 49.2, Avda Catalunya 15, 17252 Sant Antoni de Calonge (Gerona) [972-65 08 79; fax 972-66 19 87; info@ euro-camping.com; www.euro-camping.com] Exit A7 junc 6 dir Palamós on C66 & Sant Feliu C31. Take exit Sant Antoni; on ent Sant Antoni turn R at 1st rndabt. Visible fr main rd at cent of Sant Antoni. V lge, mkd pitch, shd; wc; chem disp; mv service pnt; 20% serviced pitches; baby facs; shwrs inc; el pnts (5A) inc; lndtte; ice; supmkt; rest; snacks; bar; BBQ; playgrnd; 2 pools & paddling pool; sand beach 300m; waterpark 5km; tennis; cycle hire 200m; golf 7km; games area; games rm; fitness rm; doctor Jul & Aug; car wash; entmnt high ssn; internet; TV rm; 15% statics; dogs €3.60; phone; Eng spkn; adv bkg; quiet; cc acc; red long stay/low ssn; CCI. "Excel facs for families; lots to do in area; excel." ♦ 26 Apr-21 Sep. € 43.30   2007*

See advertisement on next page

Spain

PALAMOS 3B3 (2.5km W Rural) **Camping Castell Park**, Ctra C31 Palamós-Gerona, Km 328, 17253 Vall-Llobrega (Gerona) [tel/fax 972-31 52 63; info@campingcastellpark.com; www.camping castellpark.com] Exit m'way at junc 6 & take C66/C31 to Palamós. Site on R sp after 40km marker. Lge, mkd pitch, terr, shd; wc (some cont); chem disp; baby facs; shwrs inc; el pnts (5A) inc; gas; lndtte; supmkt; rest; snacks; bar; BBQ; playgrnd; pool; paddling pool; sand beach 2.5km; golf 11km; games rm; internet; entmnt; TV rm; some statics; dogs free; bus 700m; Eng spkn; adv bkg; quiet; red long stay ssn/snr citizens; CCI. "Quiet family site with friendly atmosphere; rallies & single c'vanners welcome; c'van storage avail." ♦ 15 Mar-14 Sep. € 27.90   2007*

⊞**PALS** 3B3 (1km E Rural) **Camping Resort Mas Patoxas Bungalow Park**, Ctra Torroella-Palafrugell, Km 5, 17256 Pals (Gerona) [972-63 69 28; fax 972-66 73 49; info@campingmaspatoxas.com; www.camping maspatoxas.com] AP7 exit 6 onto C66 Palamós/La Bisbal, turn L via Torrent to Pals. Turn R & site on R almost opp old town of Pals on rd to Torroella de Montgri. Or fr Palafrugell on C31 turn at km 339. Lge, mkd pitch, terr, shd; htd wc; 30% serviced pitches; chem disp; mv service pnt; baby facs; shwrs inc; el pnts (5A) inc; gas; ice; lndtte; supmkt; tradsmn; rest; snacks; bar; playgrnd; pool; sand beach 4km; games area; entmnt; tennis; cycle hire; mini-golf; golf 4km; TV; dogs €3; phone; site clsd 18 Dec-12 Jan; recep clsd Monday low ssn; Eng spkn; adv bkg ess high ssn; quiet; red long stay/low ssn; gd security; cc acc; CCI. "Excel." ♦ € 39.00
                              2005*

PALS 3B3 (2km NE Coastal) **Camping Inter Pals**, Avda Mediterránea s/n, Km 45, 17256 Playa de Pals (Gerona) [972-63 61 79; fax 972-66 74 76; interpals@interpals.com; www.interpals.com] Exit A7 junc 6 dir Palamós onto C66. Turn N sp Pals & foll sp Playa/Platja de Pals, site clearly sp. Lge, pt sl, terr, shd; htd wc; chem disp; mv service pnt; baby facs; shwrs inc; el pnts (5-10A) inc; lndtte; rest; snacks; bar; playgrnd; pool; sand beach 300m (naturist beach 1km); watersports; tennis; games area; golf 1km; internet; TV; 5% statics; dogs €2.90; phone; adv bkg; quiet; 10% red CCI. "Lovely site in pine forest; poss diff lge o'fits; modern, well-maintained facs." ♦ 1 Apr-30 Sep. € 29.30 (CChq acc)   2006*

PALS 3B3 (4km E Rural) **Camping Cypsela**, Rodors 7, 17256 Playa de Pals (Gerona) [972-66 76 96; fax 972-66 73 00; info@cypsela.com; www.cypsela.com] Exit AP7 junc 6, rd C66 dir Palamós. 7km fr La Bisbal take dir Pals & foll sp Playa/Platja de Pals, site sp. V lge, hdg/mkd pitch, shd; wc; chem disp; mv service pnt; 25% serviced pitches; baby facs; private bthrms; shwrs inc; el pnts (6A) inc; gas; lndtte; ice; supmkt; rest; snacks; bar; playgrnd; pool; sand beach 1.5km; tennis; mini-golf & other sports; cycle hire; golf 1km; entmnt; child entmnt; internet; TV; free bus to beach; 30% statics; no dogs; Eng spkn; adv bkg; cc acc; red long stay/CCI. "Noise levels controlled after midnight; excel san facs; 4 grades of pitch/price." ♦ 15 May-21 Sep. € 43.60   2007*

⊞**PAMPLONA** *3B1* (7km N Rural) **Camping Ezcaba, Ctra N121, Km 7, 31194 Eusa (Navarre)** [948-33 03 15; fax 948-33 13 16; info@campingszcaba.com; www.campingezcaba.com] Fr N leave AP15 onto NA30 (N ring rd) to N121A sp Francia/Iruña. Pass Arre & Oricáin, turn L foll site sp 500m on R dir Berriosuso. Site on R in 500m - fairly steep ent. Or fr S leave AP15 onto NA32 (E by-pass) to N121A sp Francia/Iruña, then as above. Med, mkd pitch, pt sl, pt shd; wc; shwrs inc; el pnts €3.96; gas; lndtte; ice; shop; rest; snacks; bar; pool; horseriding; tennis; dogs €2.14; phone; bus 1km; poss cr; adv bkg; rd noise; red low ssn. "V helpful & friendly staff; sm pitches unsuitable lge o'fits & poss diff due trees, esp when site full; nice walks fr site; attractive setting with surrounding hills; gd pool, bar & rest; in winter use as NH only; should be open all yr but phone to check." ◆ € 17.66

2006*

⊞**PANCORBO** *1B4* (3km NE Rural) **Camping El Desfiladero, Ctra Madrid-Irún, Km.305, 09280 Pancorbo (Burgos)** [947-35 40 27; fax 947-35 42 35; hoeldesfiladero@teleline.es] Fr A1/E5 exit junc 4 onto N1 dir Vitoria/Gasteiz, site on L in 2km at hostal. Med, hdg pitch, some hdstg, terr, pt shd; wc; chem disp; shwrs; el pnts (8A) €3.40; lndtte; shop 3km; rest; snacks; bar; playgrnd; pool; tennis; 25% statics; dogs; train 3km; some rd & rlwy noise; cc acc; red CCI. "Access diff lge o'fits due steep ent; recep in hostal rest low ssn; friendly, helpful owner; facs tired; sh stay/NH only." ◆ € 16.00

2007

⊞**PANCORBO** *1B4* (7km NE Rural) **Camping Monumento Al Pastor, Ctra Madrid-Irún, Km 308, 09219 Ameyugo (Burgos)** [947-34 43 55; fax 947-35 42 90] Fr W on N1 take slip rd to R sp Ameyugo & rest area. Pass under AP1 & foll sp to rest area & site. Site is 500m beyond Ameyugo on N side of AP1 at km stone 308, easily seen by monument of shepherd & lamb. If app fr E, take R turn on climbing hill on A1. Recep is in rest, sp 'Monumento al Pastor' fr rd. Med, terr, unshd; wc; shwrs inc; el pnts (6-10A) €2.35; shop; rest; snacks; bar; playgrnd; tennis; 90% statics; dogs; phone; poss cr; quiet but some rd noise; cc acc. "V ltd spaces for tourers & no easy alternative if they are occupied; san facs fair, ltd low ssn; vg rest, bar; beautiful views; conv NH for Bilbao." € 14.00

2006*

PELIGROS see Granada *2G4*

⊞**PENAFIEL** *1C4* (Rural) **Camping Riberduero, Avda Polideportivo 51, 47300 Peñafiel** [tel/fax 983-88 16 37; camping@campingpenafiel.com; www.campingpenafiel.com] Fr Valladolid 56km or Aranda de Duero 38km on N122. In Peñafiel take VA223 dir Cuéllar, foll sp to sports cent/camping. Med, mkd pitch, hdstg, shd; htd wc; chem disp; mv service pnt; baby facs; fam bthrm; shwrs inc; el pnts (5A) €3.30; gas; lndtte; shop; rest; snacks; bar; playgrnd; pool; rv 1km; cycle hire; TV; 20% statics; dogs €1.50; phone; bus 1km; site open w/e only low ssn; poss cr; Eng spkn; adv bkg (50% dep req); quiet; cc acc; 10% red 15 days. "Excel, well-kept site; interesting, historical area; ideal for wheelchair users." ◆ Holy Week & 1 Apr-30 Sep. € 17.98

2006*

PENASCOSA see Alcaraz *4F1*

⊞**PENISCOLA** *3D2* (1km N Coastal) **Camping El Edén, Ctra CS501 Benicarló-Peñíscola Km 6, 12598 Peñíscola (Castellón)** [964-48 05 62; fax 964-48 98 28; camping@camping-eden.com; www.camping-eden.com] Exit AP7 junc 43 onto N340 & CV141 dir Peñíscola. Take 3rd exit off rndabt nr marina, L at mini-rndabt, L after Hotel del Mar. Lge, hdg/mkd pitch, pt shd; htd wc; chem disp; mv service pnt; baby facs; shwrs inc; el pnts (10A) €3.30; gas; lndry service; shop 300m; rest, snacks; bar; playgrnd; pool; paddling pool; sand/shgl beach adj; wifi internet; 40% statics; dogs; bus adj; cash dispenser; poss cr; rd noise in ssn; cc acc; red long stay/low ssn. "San facs refurbished & v clean; beach adj cleaned daily; gd security; excel pool; easy access to sandy/gravel pitches but many sm trees poss diff for awnings or high m'vans; poss vicious mosquitoes at dusk; easy walk/cycle to town; 4 diff sizes of pitch (some with tap, sink & drain) with different prices; ltd facs low ssn; excel." ◆ € 36.00

2007*

⊞**PENISCOLA** *3D2* (2km N) **Camping El Cid, Azagador de la Cruz s/n, 12598 Peñíscola** [964-48 03 80] Exit A7 at junc 43. Take N340 sp València for sh distance, turn L sp Peñíscola. Approx 2km look for yellow sp to site. Med, mkd pitch, shd; wc; chem disp; shwrs inc; el pnts (10A) €3.10; gas; lndtte; shop; supmkt 2km; rest; snacks; bar; playgrnd; pool; sand beach 3km; 50% statics; poss cr; cc acc; red long stay/low ssn; CCI. "Well-run site; popular with Spanish families; v friendly staff." € 16.75

2004*

⊞**PENISCOLA** *3D2* (2km W) **Camping Los Pinos, Calle Abellars s/n, 12598 Peñíscola (Castellón)** [tel/fax 964-48 03 79; info@campinglospinos.com; www.campinglospinos.com] Exit A7 junc 43 or N340 sp Peñíscola. Site sp on L. Med, pt shd; wc; chem disp; mv service pnt; baby facs; shwrs; el pnts €4.25; gas; lndtte; shop; rest; snacks; bar; BBQ; playgrnd; pool; phone; bus fr site. "Narr site rds, lots of trees; poss diff access some pitches." € 17.40

2005*

Spain

⊞**PENISCOLA** *3D2* (2km NW Rural) **Camping Azahar Residencial, Partida Villarroyos s/n, Playa Montana, 12598 Peñíscola-Benicarló (Castellón) [tel/fax 964-47 54 80; info@campingazahar. com; www.campingazahar.com]** Exit AP7 junc 43, within 50m of toll booths turn R immed then immed L & foll site sp twd Benicarló (NB R turn is on slip rd). Fr N340 take CV141 to Peñíscola. Cross m'way bdge & immed turn L opp go-kart track, site sp. Med, mkd pitch, hdstg, shd; htd wc; chem disp; mv service pnt; serviced pitches; sauna; baby facs; shwrs inc; el pnts (6A) inc; gas; lndtte; ice; shop; tradsmn; rest; snacks; bar; BBQ; playgrnd; htd pool; paddling pool; jacuzzi; sand beach 2.5km; cycle hire; gym; games area; games rm; entmnt; child entment; internet; TV rm; 50% statics; dogs; phone; bus 600m; c'van storage; car wash; Eng spkn; adv bkg; some rd noise; cc acc; red long stay/snr citizens; red CCI. "V helpful, enthusiastic staff & owners; improving site; gd cycling." ♦ € 44.94 ABS - E23   2007*

PINEDA DE MAR see Calella *3C3*

PINEDA, LA see Salou *3C2*

PITRES *2G4* (500m Rural) **Camping El Balcón de Pitres, Ctra Órgiva-Ugijar, Km 51, 18414 Pitres (Granada) [958-76 61 11; fax 958-80 44 53; info@ balcondepitres.com; www.balcondepitres.com]** S fr Granada on A44/E902, turn E onto A348 for 22km. At Órgiva take A4132 dir Trevélez to Pitres to site. Ask at rest in vill for dirs. Sm, terr, shd; wc; chem disp; el pnts (10A) €4.28; gas; lndtte; ice; shop; rest; snacks; bar; playgrnd; pool; cycle hire; some statics; bus 600m; poss cr Aug; adv bkg; quiet; red long stay; cc acc; CCI. "Site in unspoilt Alpujarras region of Sierra Nevada mountains; fine scenery & wildlife; site on steep hillside, poss diff lge o'fits; san facs at top of hill - own san facs saves climb." 1 Mar-31 Oct. € 32.10 (3 persons)
2007*

PLASENCIA *1D3* (4km NE Urban) **Camping La Chopera, Ctra N110, Km 401, Valle del Jerte, 10600 Plasencia (Caceres) [tel/fax 927-41 66 60]** In Plasencia on N630 turn E on N110 sp Ávila & foll sp indus est & sp to site. Med, shd; wc; serviced pitches; chem disp; baby facs; shwrs inc; el pnts (6A) inc; gas; lndtte; ice; shop; rest; bar; BBQ; playgrnd; 2 pools in ssn; tennis; cycle hire; dogs; quiet but w/e disco; cc acc; CCI. "Peaceful & spacious; much birdsong; conv Manfragüe National Park (breeding of black/Egyptian vultures, black storks, imperial eagles); excel pool & modern facs; helpful owners." ♦ 1 Mar-30 Sep. € 15.40
2006*

This guide relies on site report forms submitted by caravanners like us; we'll do our bit and tell the editor what we think of the campsites we've visited.

⊞**PLASENCIA** *1D3* (10km SE Rural) **Camping Parque Natural Monfragüe, Ctra Plasencia-Trujillo, Km 10, 10680 Malpartida de Plasencia (Cáceres) [tel/fax 927-45 92 33; contact@ campingmonfrague.com; www.camping monfrague.com]** Fr N on A66/N630 by-pass town, 5km S of town at lge rndabt take EXA1 (EX108) sp Navalmoral de la Mata. In 6km turn R onto EX208 dir Trujillo, site on L in 5km. Med, hdg pitch, pt sl, terr, pt shd; htd wc; chem disp; mv service pnt; baby facs; shwrs inc; el pnts (5-15A) €3; gas; lndtte; shop; tradsmn; rest; snacks; bar; BBQ; playgrnd; pool; tennis; games area; archery; cycle hire; rambling; 4x4 off-rd; horseriding; TV rm; 10% statics; dogs; phone; Eng spkn; no adv bkg; quiet; cc acc; red long stay/CCI. "Friendly staff; vg facs; poss full w/e & public hols; gd rest; clean, tidy site but poss dusty - hoses avail; 10km to National Park (with eagles, vultures, storks); excel winter base." ♦ € 14.70 (CChq acc)   2007*

PLAYA DE ARO *3B3* (1km N Coastal) **Camping Treumal**, Ctra Playa de Aro/Palamós, C253, Km 47.5, 17250 Playa de Arro (Gerona) [972-65 10 95; fax 972-65 16 71; info@campingtreumal.com; www.campingtreumal.com] Exit m'way at junc 6, 7 or 9 dir Sant Feliu de Guixols to Playa de Aro; site is sp at km 47.5 fr C253 coast rd S of Palamós. Lge, mkd pitch, terr, shd; wc; chem disp; mv service pnt; baby facs; shwrs inc; chem disp; mv service pnt; el pnts (6-10A) inc; gas; lndtte; ice; supmkt; tradsmn; rest; snacks; bar; playgrnd; sm pool; sand beach adj; fishing; tennis 1km; games rm; sports facs; cycle hire; golf 5km; wifi internet; entmnt; 25% statics; no dogs; phone; car wash; Eng spkn; adv bkg; quiet; cc acc; red low ssn; CCI. "Set in pine trees; beautifully planted; peaceful; excel san facs; manhandling poss req onto terr pitches." ♦ 15 Mar-30 Sep. € 43.40   2007*

See advertisement below

⊞**PLAYA DE ARO** *3B3* (2km N Coastal) **Camping Internacional de Calonge**, Avda d'Andorra s/n, Ctra 253, Km 47, 17251 Calonge (Gerona) [972-65 12 33 or 972-65 14 64; fax 972-65 25 07; info@intercalonge.com;   www.intercalonge.com] Fr A7 exit junc 6 onto C66 dir La Bisbal, Palamós & Playa de Aro; 3km bef Palamós foll sp St Antoni de Calonge. At 2nd rndbt bear R onto C253 dir Sant Feliu, site on R in 3km. V lge, mkd pitch, terr, shd; htd wc; chem disp; mv service pnt; some serviced pitches; baby facs; shwrs inc; el pnts (5A) inc; gas; lndtte; ice; supmkt; rest; snacks; bar; BBQ; playgrnd; 2 pools; sand/shgl beach adj; tennis; extensive sports facs; entmnt; internet; TV rm; 30% statics; phone; dogs €3.90; Eng spkn; adv bkg; poss noisy high ssn; red low ssn/long stay; cc acc; CCI. "On side of steep hill - parking poss diff at times; conv Dali Museum; Roman ruins; excel site; gd security." ♦ € 42.80   2007*

See advertisement on next page

PLAYA DE ARO *3B3* (2km N Coastal) **Camping Cala Gogo**, Ctra Sant Feliu-Palamós s/n, 17250 Platja d'Aro (Gerona) [972-65 15 64; fax 972-65 05 53; calagogo@calagogo.es; www.calagogo.es] Exit AP7 junc 6 dir Palamós/Sant Feliu. Fr Palamós take C253 coast rd S twd Sant Antoni, site on R 2km fr Playa de Aro, sp. Lge, pt sl, pt terr, pt shd; wc; chem disp; mv service pnt; serviced pitch; baby facs; shwrs inc; el pnts (10A) inc; gas; lndtte; ice; supmkt; rest; snacks; bar; BBQ; playgrnds; htd pool; paddling pool; sand beach adj; boat hire; diving school; games area; games rm; tennis; cycle hire; golf 4km; entmnt; child entmnt; internet; TV; no dogs 22/6-23/8 (otherwise €2); Eng spkn; adv bkg; quiet; red long stay. "Clean, airy facs; site terraced into pinewood on steep hillside; some manhandling may be req when siting; excel family site." 26 Apr-28 Sep. € 43.95   2007*

See advertisement opposite

PLAYA DE ARO *3B3* (2km N Rural) **Yelloh! Village Mas Sant Josep**, Ctra Santa Cristina-Playa de Aro, Km 2, 17246 Santa Cristina de Aro (Gerona) [972-83 51 08; fax 972-83 70 18; info@campingmassantjosep. com; www.campingmassantjosep.com or www. yellohvillage.com] Fr A7/E15 take exit 7 dir Sant Feliu de Guixols to Santa Christina town. Take old rd dir Playa de Aro, site in 2km. V lge, mkd pitch, shd; htd wc; chem disp; mv service pnt; baby facs; serviced pitches; sauna; shwrs inc; el pnts (10A) inc; gas; lndtte; lndry rm; ice; shop; rest; snacks; bar; BBQ; playgrnd; lge pools; sand beach 3.5km; tennis; games rm; games area; mini-golf & assorted sports; cycle hire; entmnt; golf 4km; internet; TV rm; 60% statics; dogs; Eng spkn; adv bkg; quiet; cc acc; red low ssn; CCI. "Generous pitches; excel." ♦ 26 May-12 Sep. € 34.00   2005*

PLAYA DE ARO *3B3* (1km S Coastal) **Camping Valldaro, Avda Castell d'Aro 63, 17250 Playa de Aro (Gerona) [972-81 75 15; fax 972-81 66 62; info@valldaro.com; www.valldaro.com]** Exit A7 junc 7 onto C65 dir Sant Feliu. Turn L onto C31 for Playa de Aro thro Castillo de Aro & site on R, 1km fr Playa at km 4.2. V lge, pt shd; wc; chem disp; mv service pnt; baby facs; shwrs inc; el pnts (5A) inc; gas; lndtte; shop; rest; snacks; bar; playgrnd; 2 pools; waterslides; beach 1km; watersports; tennis; horseriding 2km; golf 3km; games area; cycle hire; wifi internet; entmnt; 50% statics; dogs €2.35; (no Pitbulls, Rottweilers or similar); phone; adv bkg; red long stay. "Gd family site; some lge pitches in new area; many facs." ♦ 31 Mar-1 Oct. € 37.20 (CChq acc)   2006*

PLAYA DE ARO *3B3* (2km S Coastal) **Camping Riembau, Calle Santiage Russinyol s/n, 17250 Playa de Aro (Gerona) [972-81 71 23; fax 972-82 52 10; camping@riembau.com; www.riembau.com]** Fr Gerona take C250 thro Llagostera, turn for Playa de Aro. Fr Playa de Aro take C253 twd Sant Feliu. Site access rd 2km on R. V lge, pt shd; wc; chem disp; baby facs; shwrs inc; el pnts (5A) inc; gas; lndtte; rest; snacks; bar; shop; beach 800m; 2 pools (1 indoor); playgrnd; tennis; fitness cent; games area; games rm; hairdresser; entmnt; child entmnt; internet; 40% statics; phone; adv bkg; some rd noise. ♦ Easter-30 Sep. € 35.90   2007*

PLAYA DE ARO *3B3* (2km S Urban/Coastal) **Camping Vall d'Or, Avda Verona-Teruel s/n, 17250 Playa de Aro (Gerona) [972-81 75 85; fax 972-67 44 95; valldor@betsa.es; www.betsa.es]** Exit A7 junc 7 onto C65 dir Sant Feliu de Guixols, then C31 to Playa de Aro. V lge, pt shd; wc; chem disp; shwrs inc; el pnts (5A) €3.50; gas; lndtte; shop; rest; bar; playgrnd; sand beach adj; TV; 50% statics; dogs; phone; poss cr; adv bkg. "Gd family site." 6 Apr-31 Oct. € 24.80   2004*

As soon as we get home I'm going to post all these site report forms to the editor for inclusion in next year's guide. I don't want to miss the September deadline.

PLAYA DE OLIVA see Oliva *4E2*

PLAYA DE PALS see Pals *3B3*

PLAYA DE PINEDO see Valencia *4E2*

PLAYA DE VIDIAGO see Llanes *1A4*

PLAYA TAMARIT see Tarragona *3C3*

POBLA DE SEGUR, LA *3B2* (3km NE Rural) **Camping Collegats, Ctra N260, Km 306, 25500 La Pobla de Segur (Lleida) [973-68 07 14; fax 973-68 14 02; camping@collegats.com; www. collegats.com]** Fr Tremp N to La Pobla on N260. Site sp in town at traff lts, turn R onto N260 dir Sort. Ent by hairpin bend. Last section of rd narr & rough. Med, mkd pitch, shd; wc; chem disp; shwrs; el pnts €5; gas; lndtte; shop & 4km; tradsmn; snacks; bar; BBQ; playgrnd; pool; games area; some statics (sep area); dogs; poss cr; Eng spkn; quiet; CCI. "Clean facs; site not suitable lge o'fits; twin-axle vans not acc; conv NH." ♦ 1 Apr-31 Oct. € 20.00   2007*

⊞**POBOLEDA** *3C2* (Rural) **Camping Poboleda, Plaça les Casetes s/n, 43376 Poboleda (Tarragona) [tel/fax 977-82 71 97; poboleda@ campingsonline.com; www.campingpoboleda. com]** By-pass Reus W of Tarragona on T11/N420 then turn N onto C242 sp Les Borges del Camp. Go thro Alforja over Col d'Alforja & turn L onto T207 to Poboleda & foll camping sp in vill. Med, mkd pitch, terr, pt shd; htd wc; chem disp; baby facs; fam bthrm; el pnts (4A) inc; lndry rm; shop, rest, snacks, bar in vill; pool; lake sw 8km; tennis; wifi internet; TV; no statics; dogs; phone; Eng spkn; quiet; cc acc; CCI. "In heart of welcoming vill in lovely mountain setting; v friendly, helpful owner; not suitable lge o'fits as access thro vill." ♦ € 25.00
2007*

PONT D'ARROS see Vielha *3B2*

PONT DE SUERT *3B2* (4km N Rural) **Camping Can Roig, Ctra De Boí, Km 0.5, 25520 Pont de Suert (Lleida) [973-69 05 02; fax 973-69 12 06; info@ campingcanroig.com; www.campingcanroig. com]** N of Pont de Suert on N230 turn NE onto L500 dir Caldes de Boí. Site in 1km. App narr for 100m. Med, mkd pitch, hdstg, pt sl, pt shd; wc; chem disp; shwrs inc; el pnts (5A) €3.75; gas; lndtte; ice; shop & 3km; snacks; bar; playgrnd; paddling pool; 5% statics; dogs €1.95; adv bkg; quiet; cc acc; red low ssn. "NH en rte S; beautiful valley." 1 Mar-31 Oct. € 15.60   2007*

⊞**PONT DE SUERT** *3B2* (16km NE Rural) **Camping Taüll, Ctra Taüll s/n, 25528 Taüll (Lleida) [973 69 61 74; www.campingtaull.com]** Fr Pont de Suert 3km N on N230 then NE on L500 dir Caldes de Boí. In 13km turn R into Taüll. Site sp on R. Sm, pt sl, terr, pt shd; htd wc; chem disp; baby facs' shwrs inc; el pnts €6; lndry rm; shop, rest, bar 300m; statics; dogs €3; clsd 15 Oct-15 Nov; poss cr; quiet; CCI. "Excel facs; taxis into National Park avail; ltd touring pitches; suitable sm m'vans only." € 21.50   2007*

⊞**PONT DE SUERT** *3B2* (5km NW Rural) **Camping Baliera, Ctra N260, Km 355.5, Castejón de Sos, 22523 Bonansa (Huesca) [974-55 40 16; fax 974-55 40 99; info@baliera.com; www.baliera. com]** N fr Pont de Suert on N230 turn L opp petrol stn onto N260 sp Castejón de Sos. In 1km turn L onto A1605 sp Bonansa, site on L immed over rv bdge. Site sp fr N230. Lge, mkd pitch, pt sl, terr, shd; htd wc; chem disp; mv service pnt; baby facs; shwrs inc; el pnts (5-10A) €4; gas; lndtte; ice; shop; tradsmn; rest in ssn; snacks; bar; BBQ; playgrnd; pool (high ssn); lrv fishing; ake sw 10km; horseriding 4km; golf 4km; weights rm; internet; sat TV; 50% statics; dogs €2.30; phone; site clsd Nov & Xmas; poss cr; Eng spkn; quiet; cc acc; red low ssn; CCI. "Excel, well-run, peaceful site in parkland setting; walking in summer, skiing in winter; excel cent for touring; conv Vielha tunnel; gd mountain rds; all facs up steps; part of site v sl; helpful owner proud of his site; spotless facs." ♦ € 21.40 (CChq acc)
2006*

PONTEAREAS *1B2* (1.5km N Rural) **Camping A Freixa, 36866 Ribadetea (Pontevedra) [986-64 02 99; fax 986-66 00 60]** On N120 fr Vigo & Porriño, turn L at fountain bef bdge at ent to Ponteareas. In 1.5km at tall chimney on L, turn R & site in 200m adj Rv Tea. Med, sl, pt shd; wc; shwrs; el pnts €3; lndtte; shop; rest; bar; playgrnd; sand beach & rv sw; tennis; phone; bus 700m; quiet. Holy Week & 1 Jul-30 Aug. € 15.30   2004*

PORT DE LA SELVA, EL *3B3* (1km N Coastal) **Camping L'Arola, Ctra. Llança-El Port de la Selva, 17489 El Port de la Selva (Gerona) [972-38 70 05; fax 972-12 60 81]** Off N11 at Figueras, sp to Llançà on N260. In 20km turn R to El Port de la Selva. Site on L (N side of coast rd) bef town. Sm, hdstg, unshd; wc; chem disp; shwrs; el pnts (10A) €6.42; lndry rm; shops 1km; tradsmn; rest; bar; shgl beach adj; 5% statics; dogs €3.21; bus; poss cr; adv bkg; CCI. "Nr sm, pleasant town with gd shops, rests, harbour, amusements for all ages; scenic beauty; v friendly owner." 16 May-30 Sep. € 25.70
2006*

PORT DE LA SELVA, EL *3B3* (2km N Coastal) **Camping Port de la Vall, Ctra Port de Llançà, 17489 El Port de la Selva (Gerona) [972-38 71 86; fax 972-12 63 08; info@campingportdelavall. com; www.campingportdelavall.com]** On coast rd fr French border at Llançà take minor rd twd El Port de la Selva. Site 2km fr El Port de la Selva on L. Easily seen. Lge, pt shd; wc; shwrs; el pnts (3-5A) €4.87; gas; lndtte; ice; shop; rest; snacks; bar; playgrnd; shgl beach adj; internet; some statics; dogs €2.40; phone; poss cr; adv bkg; poss noisy; cc acc; red low ssn. "Easy walk to harbour; gd site but facs showing age; sm pitches & low branches poss diff - check bef siting; overpriced." 1 Apr-31 Oct. € 36.90 (4 persons)   2005*

Spain

POTES *1A4* (1.5km W Rural) **Camping La Viorna, Ctra Santo Toribio, Km 1, Mieses, 39570 Potes (Cantabria) [942-73 20 21; fax 942-73 21 01; campinglaviorna@hotmail. com; www.liebanaypicosdeeuropa.com/guia/ campinglaviorna.htm]** Fr Potes take rd to Fuente Dé sp Espinama; in 1km turn L sp Toribio. Site on R in 1km. Med, mkd pitch, terr, pt shd; wc; chem disp; shwrs inc; el pnts (6A) €2.50; lndtte; shop 2km; rest; snacks; bar; playgrnd; pool (caps ess) high ssn; cycle hire; Eng spkn; adv bkg; quiet; cc acc; CCI; "Lovely views; gd walks; friendly, family-run, v clean site; gd pool; ideal Picos de Europa area; conv cable car; 4x4 tours; trekking; mkt on Mon; festival mid-Sep v noisy; superb quality & clean facs; some pitches diff in wet & diff lge o'fits; excel." ♦ 1 Apr-31 Oct. € 17.60   2007*

POTES *1A4* (3km W Rural) **Camping La Isla-Picos de Europa, Ctra Potes-Fuente Dé, 39586 Turieno (Cantabria) [tel/fax 942-73 08 96; campicoseuropa@terra.es]** Take N521 W fr Potes twd Espinama, site on R in 3km thro vill of Turieno (app Potes fr N). Med, hdg/mkd pitch, pt sl, shd; wc; chem disp; mv service pnt; shwrs inc; el pnts (3-8A) €2.80 (rev pol); gas; lndtte; shop; tradsmn; rest; bar; BBQ; playgrnd; pool; walking; horseriding; cycling; 4x4 touring; hang-gliding; mountain treks in area; some statics; phone; poss cr; Eng spkn; adv bkg; poss noisy high ssn; cc acc; red long stay; CCI. "Delightful family-run site; friendly, helpful owners; superb san facs; conv cable car & mountain walks (map fr recep); many trees & low branches; highly rec." 1 Apr-30 Oct. € 18.50   2007*

POTES *1A4* (5km W Rural) **Camping San Pelayo, Ruta Potes-Fuente Dé, Km 5, 39587 San Pelayo (Cantabria) [tel/fax 942-73 30 87 or 942-73 31 64; www.campingsanpelayo.com]** Take CA185 W fr Potes twd Espinama, site on R in 5km, 2km past Camping La Isla. Med, mkd pitch, pt sl, pt shd; wc; chem disp; shwrs inc; el pnts (6A) inc; lndtte; shop; rest; snacks; bar; playgrnd; pool; cycle hire; games rm; poss cr; adv bkg; quiet, but noise fr bar; cc acc high ssn; 20% red 5+ days; CCI. "Friendly, helpful owner; some sm pitches; conv mountain walking; excel pool." Easter-15 Oct. € 16.00   2006*

POZO ALCON *2G4* (7km N Rural) **Camping Hoyo de Los Pinos, Ctra Castril, Km 8, Pantano Bolera, 23485 Pozo Alcón (Jaén) [953-73 90 05]** Fr Pozo Alcón take A326 N dir Castril. Site on L. Med, pt sl, pt shd; wc; chem disp; shwrs inc; el pnts (5A) €2.60; gas; shop; rest; bar; BBQ; playgrnd; quiet; cc acc; CCI. "Excel scenery & wildlife." 1 Feb-19 Dec. € 10.00   2005*

PRADES see Vilanova de Prades *3C2*

PUEBLA DE CASTRO, LA see Graus *3B2*

PUEBLA DE SANABRIA *1B3* (500m S Rural) **Camping Isla de Puebla, Pago de Barregas, 49300 Puebla de Sanabria (Zamora) [980-56 79 54; fax 980-56 79 55]** Fr Portugal border on C622, at ent to Puebla de Sanabria foll sp down short track twd rv. Fr N525 ent vill & foll sp Isla de Puebla. Med, mkd pitch, pt shd; wc; chem disp; shwrs inc; el pnts (10A) €2.73; gas; lndtte; ice; shop; rest; snacks; bar; playgrnd; pool; trout-fishing; adv bkg; quiet; red long stay; cc acc; CCI. "V clean, spacious facs but tired; interesting town; vg for nature lovers; friendly, helpful wardens; facs ltd low ssn; internet facs at stn (fr 1500)." 15 Apr-30 Sep. € 16.70   2006*

PUEBLA DE SANABRIA *1B3* (10km NW Rural) **Camping El Folgoso, Ctra Puebla de Sanabria-San Martin de Castañeda, Km 13, 49361 Vigo de Sanabria (Zamora) [980-62 67 74; fax 980-62 68 00; camping@elfolgoso.com]** Exit A52 sp Puebla de Sanabria & foll sp for Lago/Vigo de Sanabria thro Puente de Sanabria & Galende; site 2km beyond vill of Galende; sp. Med, pt sl, terr, shd; wc; chem disp; shwrs €1; el pnts (5A) €2.46; gas; lndtte; shop high ssn; rest high ssn; snacks; bar; playgrnd; cycle hire; statics; phone; cc acc. "Lovely setting beside lake; v cold in winter." ♦ ltd. 1 Apr-31 Oct. € 16.50   2005*

PUEBLA DE SANABRIA *1B3* (10km NW Rural) **Camping Peña Gullón, Ctra Puebla de Santabria-Ribadelago, Km 11.5, Lago de Sanabria, 49360 Galende (Zamora) [980-62 67 72]** Fr Puebla de Sanabria foll sp for Lago de Sanabria. Site 3km beyond vill of Galende clearly sp. Lge, pt shd; wc; shwrs inc; el pnts (15A) €2.51; gas; lndtte; shop in ssn; rest; playgrnd; lake adj; poss cr; quiet; red long stay; CCI. "Site in nature park 35km fr Portugal's Montesinho Park; rec arr by 1200; beautiful area; excel site." 28 Jun-31 Aug. € 17.00   2007*

PUEBLA DO CARAMINAL see Ribeira *1B2*

⊞**PUERTO DE MAZARRON** *4G1* (3km NE Rural/ Coastal) **Camping Las Torres, Ctra N332, Cartagena-Mazarrón, Km 29, 30860 Puerto de Mazarrón (Murcia) [tel/fax 968-59 52 25; info@ campinglastorres.com; www.campinglastorres. com]** Fr N on A7/E15 exit junc 627 onto MU602, then MU603 to Mazarrón. At junc with N322 turn L to Puerto de Mazarrón & foll Cartagena sp until site sps. Lge, hdg/mkd pitch, terr, hdstg, pt shd; wc; chem disp; mv service pnt; 40% serviced pitch (€1.80 extra); baby facs; shwrs inc; el pnts (6A) inc; gas; lndtte; rest (w/e only); snacks; bar; sm shop & 3km; playgrnd; htd, covrd pool; sand/shgl beach 2km; tennis; cycle hire; sat TV; 60% statics; dogs; phone; Eng spkn; adv bkg (dep req) rec in winter; poss noisy; cc acc; red low ssn/long stay; CCI. "Unspoilt coastline; busy at w/e; poss full winter months; well-managed, family site; excel pool; sm pitches." ♦ € 20.00   2006*

⊞**PUERTO DE MAZARRON** *4G1* (5km NE Coastal) **Camping Los Madriles, Ctra a la Azohía 60, Km 4.5, 30868 Isla Plana (Murcia) [968-15 21 51; fax 968-15 20 92; camplosmadriles@terra.es; www.campinglosmadriles.com]** Fr Cartegena on N332 dir Puerto de Mazarrón. Turn L at rd junc sp La Azohía (32km). Site in 4km sp. Fr Murcia on E15/N340 dir Lorca exit junc 627 onto MU603 to Mazarrón, then foll sp. (Do not use rd fr Cartegena unless powerful tow vehicle/gd weight differential - use rte fr m'way thro Mazarrón.) Lge, hdstg, pt sl, terr, pt shd; wc; chem disp; mv service pnt; serviced pitches; shwrs inc; el pnts (10A) €4; gas; lndtte; ice; shop; rest high ssn; bar; playgrnd; 2 htd pools; jacuzzi; shgl beach 500m; games area; wifi internet; no dogs; bus; poss cr; Eng spkn; adv bkg (fr Oct for min 2 months only); quiet; cc acc high ssn; red long stay/low ssn/CCI. "V clean, popular winter site; adv bkg ess fr Oct; some sm pitches; some pitches sea views; unspoilt coast; delightful countryside; may not be suitable for disabled due to sl between terr; Easter high ssn rates; 3 days min Jul/Aug; excel." ♦ € 36.00   2007*

⊞**PUERTO DE MAZARRON** *4G1* (2km E Rural/Coastal) **Camping Los Delfines, Ctra Isla Plana-Playa El Mojon, 30860 Puerto de Mazarrón (Murcia) [tel/fax 968-59 45 27; www.campinglosdelfines.com]** Fr N332 turn S sp La Azohía & Isla Plana. Site on L in 3km. Med, hdstg, mkd pitch, unshd; wc; chem disp; mv service pnt; serviced pitches; shwrs inc; el pnts (5A) €2.75; gas; lndtte; tradsmn; snacks & bar high ssn; playgrnd; shgl beach adj; TV; 5% statics; dogs; quiet; poss cr; Eng spkn; phone; red long stay; CCI. "Gd sized pitches; popular low ssn." ♦ € 17.20   2005*

⊞**PUERTO DE MAZARRON** *4G1* (5km SW Coastal) **Camping Playa de Mazarrón, Ctra Mazarrón-Bolnuevo, Bolnuevo, 30877 Mazarrón (Murcia) [968-15 06 60; fax 968-15 08 37; camping@ playamazarron.com; www.playamazarron.com]** Take Bolnuevo rd fr Mazarrón, at rndabt go strt, site immed on L. Lge, mkd pitch, hdstg, pt shd; wc; 90% serviced pitches; chem disp; mv service pnt; shwrs inc; el pnts (5A) €3.50; gas; lndtte; shop, rest (high ssn); snacks, bar; playgrnd; sand beach adj; tennis; games area; TV; bus; phone; poss v cr; adv bkg; red long stay/low ssn; cc acc. "Some lge pitches but tight turning for lge o'fits; friendly staff; metal-framed sunshades in ssn on most pitches but low for m'vans; poss poor daytime security; gd for wheelchair users; v popular & v cr in winter - many long stay visitors." ♦ € 24.75   2007*

⊞**PUERTO DE SANTA MARIA, EL** *2H3* (2km SW Coastal) **Camping Playa Las Dunas, Paseo Maritimo La Puntilla s/n, 11500 El Puerto de Santa María (Cádiz) [956-87 22 10; fax 956-86 01 17; info@lasdunascamping.com; www.lasdunascamping.com]** Fr N or S exit A4 at El Puerto de Sta María. Foll site sp carefully to avoid narr streets of town cent. Site 3km S of marina & leisure complex of Puerto Sherry. Alternatively, fr A4 take Rota rd & look for sp to site & Hotel Playa Las Dunas. Site better sp fr this dir & avoids town. Lge, pt sl, pt shd; wc; chem disp; mv service pnt; shwrs inc; el pnts (5-10A) €3.10-6.30; gas; lndtte; shop (high ssn); tradsmn; snacks; bar; playgrnd; pool adj; sand beach 50m; sports facs; 30% statics; phone; guarded; poss cr; adv bkg rec; poss noisy disco w/e; red facs low ssn; cc acc; red CCI. "Friendly staff; conv Cádiz & Jerez sherry region, birdwatching areas & beaches; conv ferry or catamaran to Cádiz; facs poss stretched high ssn; hot water to shwrs only; pitches quiet away fr rd; take care caterpillars in spring - poss dangerous to dogs." ♦ € 17.77   2007*

⊞**PUERTO DE SANTA MARIA, EL** *2H3* (10km W Coastal) **Camping Punta Candor, Ctra Chipiona-Rota, Km. 13, 11520 Rota (Cádiz) [956-813303; fax 956-813211]** Fr El Puerto on A491; in Rota turn onto CA604 sp Punta Candor & camping. Lge, mkd pitch; wc; shwrs inc; el pnts inc; gas; lndtte; rest; shop; playgrnd; beach nrby; phone; 40% statics; cc acc. "V helpful staff; all pitches covrd by 2.50m high sun blinds - m'vans beware!" € 25.50   2004*

⊞**PUERTO DE SANTA MARIA, EL** *2H3* (12km W Coastal) **Camping Playa Aguadulce, Ctra Rota-Chipiona, Km 21, Pago Aguadulce, 11520 Rota (Cádiz) [956-84 70 78; fax 956-84 71 94]** W fr El Puerto on A491, twd Chipiona. Ignore sp Rota & turn L at sp Costa Ballena. Foll site sp & track. Med, hdg pitch, hdstg, shd; wc; chem disp; mv service pnt; shwrs inc; el pnts (6A) inc; gas; lndtte; ice; shop & 7km; tradsmn; rest; snacks; bar; playgrnd; sand beach adj; dogs; 25% statics; noisy; adv bkg (dep req); Eng spkn; cc acc; CCI. "Well-kept, attractive site; adj to excel beach; noisy at w/e & school holidays; v helpful owners; sm pitches poss diff lge o'fits." € 24.60   2004*

⊞**PUERTO LUMBRERAS** *4G1* (1km E Urban) **Camping Los Ángeles, Ctra Cádiz-Barcelona, Km 256, 30890 Puerto Lumbreras (Murcia) [968-40 27 82]** Exit 580 fr new dual c'way section of N340 at rndabt dir Lorca. Site 200m on R, ent beside rest, at rear. Steep driveway. Sm, hdstg, pt shd; wc; shwrs inc; el pnts (6A) inc (poss no earth); gas; shop 1km; rest/bar adj high ssn; playgrnd; htd pool; phone; no adv bkg; quiet; CCI. "Site run down low ssn, but fair NH; site yourself." ♦ € 12.50
                           2004*

Spain

PUIGCERDA *3B3* (2km NE Rural) **Camping Stel, Ctra Llívia s/n, 17520 Puigcerdà (Gerona) [972-88 23 61; fax 972-14 04 19; puigcerda@ stel.es; www.stel.es]** Fr France head for Bourg-Madame on N20 or N116. Cross border dir Llívia on N154, site is 1km after rndabt on L. Lge, mkd pitch, terr, pt shd; htd wc; chem disp; mv service pnt; baby facs; shwrs; el pnts (7A) €3.75; lndtte; shop; rest; snacks; bar; playgrnd; htd pool; canoeing; watersports; archery; cycle hire; games area; golf 4km; internet; entmnt; TV rm; 10% statics; dogs; site open w/ends only in winter; Eng spkn; adv bkg; some rd noise; cc acc. "Pitches on upper terr quieter; superb scenery; sep area for campers with pets; gd walking, cycling." ♦ 1 Jun-30 Sep. € 31.00 (CChq acc)   2006*

PUIGCERDA *3B3* (2km W Rural) **Camping Pirineus, 17528 Guils de Cerdanya (Gerona) [972-88 10 62; fax 972-88 24 71; guils@stel.es; www.stel.es]** Fr Puigcerdà take N260 twd Seo de Urgel. In 1km take R twd Guils de Cerdanya. Site in 1km. Lge, mkd pitch, pt shd; wc; chem disp; baby facs; shwrs inc; el pnts (8A) €3.40; gas; lndtte; shop; rest; bar; playgrnd; pool; tennis; canoe hire; some statics; no dogs; quiet; some Eng spkn; cc acc; CCI. "Well-run site; beautiful scenery; conv Andorra, Barcelona 2 hrs by train." ♦ Holy Week & 18 Jun-12 Sep. € 28.00   2005*

QUEVEDA see Santillana del Mar *1A4*

RIANO *1A3* (7km E Rural) **Camping Alto Esla, Ctra León-Santander, 24911 Boca de Huérgano (León) [987-74 01 39]** SW on N621 fr Potes just past junc with LE241 at Boca de Huérgano. Site on L. (See Picos de Europa in Mountain Passes & Tunnels in the section Planning & Travelling at front of guide.) Sm, pt sl, pt shd; wc; chem disp; el pnts (10A) €2.14; lndtte; shops 500m; phone; quiet; cc acc; CCI. "Superb views." ♦ 18 Jun-8 Sep. € 13.40
                                        2005*

⊞ **RIAZA** *1C4* (1km W Rural) **Camping Riaza, Ctra de la Estación s/n, 40500 Riaza (Segovia) [tel/fax 921-55 05 80; info@camping-riaza.com; www. camping-riaza.com]** Fr N exit A1/E5 junc 104, fr S exit 103 onto N110 N. In 12km turn R at rndabt, site on L. Lge, hdg pitch, unshd; htd wc; chem disp; mv service pnt; baby facs; shwrs inc; el pnts (15A) €4; lndtte; ice; shop; rest; snacks; bar; BBQ; playgrnd; pool; games area; games rm; internet; no dogs; some statics; phone; Eng spkn; adv bkg; quiet. "Vg new site (2006); various pitch sizes - some lge; excel san facs; easy access to/fr Santander or Bilbao." ♦ € 23.40   2007*

RIBADEO *1A2* (4km E Coastal) **Camping Playa Peñarronda, Playa de Peñarronda-Barres, 33794 Castropol (Asturias) [tel/fax 985-62 30 22; campingplayapenarrondacb@hotmail.com]** Fr N634 turn S onto N640 dir Lugo. Immed take 1st R, then foll site sp for 2km. Take care due ongoing rd works. Med, mkd pitch, shd; wc; chem disp; mv service pnt; shwrs inc; el pnts (6A) €3.37 (poss rev pol); gas; lndtte; shop; rest; snacks; bar; BBQ; playgrnd; sand beach adj; games area; cycle hire; phone; Eng spkn; quiet; red long stay; CCI. "Beautifully-kept, friendly, family-run site on 'Blue Flag' beach; rec arr early to get pitch; facs clean; gd cycling along coastal paths & to Ribadeo; ltd facs low ssn, poss no hot water for shwrs." 15 Mar-25 Sep & w/ends. € 24.00   2007*

RIBADEO *1A2* (4km E Coastal) **Camping Vegamar, Ctra Playa de Peñarronda-Barres, 33794 Castropol (Asturias) [985-62 39 48]** Fr E on E70/N634 turn L at junc (rndabt) N640 & N634 dir Vegadeo. Immed take 1st R & immed R under main rd. Site sp 500m. Med, pt shd; wc; chem disp; mv service pnt; shwrs; el pnts €2.35; gas; lndtte; shop; rest; snacks; bar; playgrnd; pool; sand beach 400m; games are; 60% statics; dogs; bus 500m; adv bkg; quiet; CCI. "Excel facs; family-run site; unreliable opening low ssn; excel NH." ♦ Easter & 1 Jun-30 Sep. € 13.30   2005*

RIBADEO *1A2* (3km W Rural) **Camping Ribadeo, Ctra Ribadeo-La Coruña, Km 2, 27700 Ribadeo (Lugo) [982-13 11 68; fax 982-13 11 67; www. campingribadeo.com]** W fr Ribadeo on N634/ E70 twd La Coruña. In 2km pass sp Camping Ribadeo. Ignore 1st camping sp, take next L in 1.4km. Lge, mkd pitch, pt shd; wc; chem disp; mv service pnt; shwrs inc; el pnts (3A) €3.20 (rev pol); gas 4km; lndtte; shop; tradsmn; rest; snacks; bar; BBQ; playgrnd; pool; sand beach 3km; no dogs; bus 500m; quiet; red for 10+ days; CCI. "Gd NH; friendly, family owners; gd san facs; request hot water for shwrs; everything immac; highly rec; many interesting local features." Holy Week & 1 Jun-30 Sep. € 16.65   2007*

RIBADESELLA *1A3* (3km W Coastal) **Camping Los Sauces, 33560 Ribadesella (Asturias) [985-86 13 12]** Cross narr bdge fr town twd W. Turn R to Playa, site sp. Access via narr, single track bdge immed off main rd. Med, pt shd; wc; baby facs; shwrs; el pnts €6.50; lndtte; shop; snacks; bar; sand beach 1km; phone; quiet; cc acc. "Cave paintings on edge of town; excel facs." ♦ 25 Jun-11 Sep. € 16.50   2005*

RIBADESELLA *1A3* (4km W) **Camping Ribadesella, Sebreño s/n, 33560 Ribadesella (Asturias) [tel/fax 985-85 82 93; camping.reservas@fade.es; www. camping-ribadesella.com]** W fr Ribadesella take N632. After 2km fork L up hill. Site on L after 2km. Poss diff for lge o'fits & alternative rte fr Ribadesella vill to site to avoid steep uphill turn can be used. Lge, mkd pitch, pt sl, pt terr, pt shd; wc; chem disp; baby facs; shwrs inc; el pnts (5A) €3.20; gas; lndtte; shop, rest, snacks, bar; BBQ; playgrnd; pool high ssn; sand beach 4km; tennis; sports facs; poss cr; adv bkg; quiet; cc acc; red low ssn/long stay; CCI. "Clean san facs; some sm pitches; attractive fishing vill; prehistoric cave paintings nrby." ♦ Easter-14 Sep. € 21.61   2006*

RIBADESELLA *1A3* (8km W Coastal/Rural) **Camping Playa de Vega, Vega, 33345 Ribadesella (Asturias) [985-86 04 06; fax 985-85 76 62; campingplayadevega@hotmail.com]** Fr A8 exit junc 333 sp Ribadesella W, thro Bones. At rndabt cont W dir Caravia, turn R opp quarry sp Playa de Vega. Fr cent of Ribadesella W on N632. After passing sp to Camping Los Sauces on R cont for 5km passing turning to autovia. Turn R at sp Vega & site. Med, hdg pitch, pt terr, pt shd; wc; chem disp; serviced pitch; shwrs inc; el pnts €2.70; lndtte; ice; shop; snacks; bar; BBQ; sand beach 400m; TV; dogs; phone; quiet; cc acc; CCI. "Attractive site; sh walk to beach thro orchards; not suitable lge o'fits." 1 Jul-15 Sep. € 19.00   2004*

⊞**RIBEIRA** *1B2* (8km NE Coastal) **Camping Ría de Arosa I, Playa de Cabío s/n, 15940 Puebla (Pobra) do Caramiñal (La Coruña) [981-83 13 05; fax 981-83 32 93; info@camping.riadearosa. com; www.camping.riadearosa.com]** Exit AP9/E1 junc 93 at Padrón onto C550 along N side of Ría de Arosa into Puebla del Caramiñal. Site is 1.5km S of Puebla, sp fr town. Lge, pt shd; wc; chem disp; mv service pnt; shwrs; el pnts (5A) €3; gas; lndtte; shop; rest; bar; playgrnd; sand beach; cycle hire; TV; some statics; phone; poss cr; adv bkg; quiet; cc acc. € 17.70   2004*

RIBEIRA *1B2* (2km E Coastal) **Camping Coroso, Santa Eugeria (Uxía) de Ribeira, Playa de Coroso, 15950 Coroso (La Coruña) [981-83 80 02; fax 981-83 85 77; info@campingcoroso.com; www. campingcoroso.com]** Fr Padrón on N550 6km S of Santiago de Compostela take VRG11 (fast rd) to Ribeira, then foll sp to site. Lge, some hdg/mkd pitches, hdstg, pt sl, terr, pt shd; wc; chem disp; baby facs; fam bthrm; shwrs inc; el pnts (10A) inc; gas; lndtte; ice; shop in ssn; café in ssn; snacks; bar; BBQ; sandy beach; sailing; tennis; bus; Eng spkn; poss cr; adv bkg; fairly quiet; red 15+ days; cc acc; CCI. "Marvellous views; gd coastal walks; friendly staff; gd rest." 1 Apr-30 Sep. € 20.20
2004*

RIBERA DE CARDOS see Llavorsí *3B2*

⊞**RIBES DE FRESER** *3B3* (500m NE Rural) **Camping Vall de Ribes, Ctra de Pardines, Km 0.5, 17534 Ribes de Freser (Gerona) [tel/fax 972-72 88 20; info@campingvallderibes.com; www.campingvallderibes.com]** N fr Ripoll on N152; turn E at Ribes de Freser; site beyond town dir Pardines. Site nr town but 1km by rd. Some rds narr. Med, mkd pitch, terr, pt shd; htd wc; chem disp; shwrs inc; el pnts (6A) €4.10; lndry rm; shop 500m; rest; bar; playgrnd; pool; 50% statics; dogs €2.15; train 500m; quiet; CCI. "Gd, basic site; steep footpath fr site to town; 10-20 min walk to stn; cog rlwy train to Núria a 'must' - spectacular gorge, gd walking & interesting exhibitions; sm/med o'fits only." € 20.00   2007*

> The opening dates and prices on this campsite have changed. I'll send a site report form to the editor for the next edition of the guide.

⊞**RIPOLL** *3B3* (2km N Rural) **Camping Molí Serradell, 17530 Campdevànol [tel/fax 972-73 09 27; calrei@teleline.es]** Fr Ripoll N on N152; L onto Gl401 dir Gombrèn; site on L in 4km. NB 2nd site. Sm, pt shd; htd wc; chem disp; mv service pnt; shwrs inc; el pnts €3.75; lndtte; ice; shop; snacks; 5% statics; poss cr; quiet; red low ssn; CCI. "Family farm site, v friendly; Fri night meal low ssn; excel." € 22.60   2006*

⊞**RIPOLL** *3B3* (2km N Rural) **Camping Ripollés, Ctra Barcelona/Puigcerdà, Km 109.3, 17500 Ripoll (Gerona) [972-70 37 70; fax 972-70 35 54]** At km 109.3 up hill N fr town; well sp. Steep access rd. Med, mkd pitch, pt sl, pt shd; htd wc; chem disp; baby facs; shwrs inc; el pnts €3.60; lndtte; shop 2km; rest; snacks; bar; BBQ; playgrnd; pool; tennis; 20% statics; phone; adv bkg; quiet; cc acc; CCI. "V pleasant; gd bar/rest; not suitable med/lge o'fits." ♦ € 18.20   2004*

RIPOLL *3B3* (2km S Rural) **Camping Solana del Ter, Ctra Barcelona-Puigcerdà, C17, Km 92.5, 17500 Ripoll (Gerona) [972-70 10 62; fax 972-71 43 43; hotel@solanadelter.com; www. solanadelter.com]** Site sp S of Ripoll behind hotel & rest. Med, mkd pitch, hdstg, pt shd; htd wc; chem disp; baby facs; shwrs inc; el pnts (4A) €5; lndtte; ice; shop; rest; snacks; bar; playgrnd; pool; tennis; TV; Eng spkn; phone; some rd & rlwy noise; cc acc; CCI. "Historic monastery in town; scenic drives nr; expensive for standard of site." 1 Apr-30 Oct. € 23.10   2006*

Spain

⊞ROCIO, EL *2G3* (500m N Rural) Camping La Aldea, Ctra del Rocío, Km 25, 21750 El Rocío (Huelva) [tel/fax 959-44 26 77; info@ campinglaaldea.com;www.campinglaaldea.com] Fr A49 turn S at junc 48 onto rd 483 to Almonte, site sp just bef El Rocío rndabt. Fr W (Portugal) turn off at junc 60 to A484 to Almonte, then A483. Lge, hdg/mkd pitch, hdstg, pt shd; htd wc; chem disp; mv service pnt; 15% serviced pitches; shwrs inc; el pnts (10A) €4.20; gas; lndtte; ice; shop; tradsmn; rest; snacks; bar; BBQ; playgrnd; pool; sand beach 16km; horseriding nrby; van washing facs; 50% statics; dogs; phone; bus 500m; site clsd Xmas to 6 Jan but poss to stay if arr & pay bef 24/12; poss cr; Eng spkn; adv bkg (dep req); rd noise; red long stay; cc acc; CCI. "Well-appointed & maintained site; friendly, helpful staff; tight turns on site; most pitches have kerb or gully; site rds & pitches soft after rain; gd birdwatching (lagoon 1km) & cycling; unusual Spanish town; parades with horses most Sundays; safari in National Park; annual pilgrimage at Pentecost & w/e visits by religious brotherhoods; avoid time of main festival (end May - early Jun) when town cr & site charges much more; poss exposed to winds until hdges grow; excel." ♦ ltd. € 22.45   2007*

RODA DE BARA *3C3* (2km E Coastal) Camping Stel, Ctra N340, Km 1182, 43883 Roda de Barà (Tarragona) [977-80 20 02; fax 977-80 05 25; rodadebara@stel.es; www.stel.es] Exit AP7 junc 31, foll sps for Tarragona on N340. Site on L immed after Arco de Barà. Lge, mkd pitch, pt shd; wc; chem disp; baby facs; htd private bthrms avail; shwrs inc; el pnts (5A) inc; gas; lndtte; ice; shop; rest; snacks; bar; playgrnd; htd pool; waterslides; sand beach adj; watersports; tennis; sports & entmnt; golf 20km; internet; TV; 10% statics; no dogs; phone; poss cr; adv bkg; some rd/rlwy noise; red long stay/low ssn; CCI. "Some sm pitches, poss ltd access for parking. ♦ 1 Apr-30 Sep. € 35.80 (CChq acc)   2005*

⊞RODA DE BARA *3C3* (3km E Coastal/Rural) Camping Arc de Barà, N340, Km 1182, 43883 Roda de Barà (Tarragona) [977-80 09 02; fax 977-80 15 52; camping@campingarcdebara.com; www.campingarcdebara.com] Exit AP7 junc 31 or 32, foll sp Arc de Barà on N340 dir Tarragona. Site on L after 5km shortly after Camping Park Playa Barà. NB When app fr N ess to use 'Cambia de Sentido' just after Arc de Barà (old arch). Lge, shd; htd wc; chem disp; baby facs; shwrs inc; el pnts (5A) €3.40; gas; lndtte; shop high ssn; supmkt 200m; rest; snacks; bar; BBQ; pool; sand beach adj; 75% statics in sep area; dogs €2.50; phone; bus adj; site clsd Nov; poss cr; Eng spkn; rlwy noise; cc acc; CCI. "Ltd number sm touring pitches; gd, clean NH en rte Alicante; phone ahead winter/ low ssn to check open." ♦ € 28.40 (3 persons)   2006*

RODA DE BARA *3C3* (3km E Coastal) Camping Park Playa Barà, N340, Km 1.183, 43883 Roda de Barà (Tarragona) [977-80 27 01; fax 977-80 04 56; info@barapark.es; www.barapark.es] Exit AP7 junc 31 onto N340, cont to Barà Roman Arch. Turn halfway bet El Vendrell & Torredembarra at km 1183. V lge, hdg/mkd pitch, terr, shd; htd wc; 100% serviced pitches; chem disp; mv service pnt; baby facs; shwrs inc; el pnts (5A) €3.20; gas; lndtte; supmkt; rest; snacks; bar; playgrnd; htd pool; sand beach adj; watersports; jacuzzi; solarium; tennis; games area; cycle hire; horseriding; entmnt; wifi internet; sat TV; doctor; car wash; cash machine; 10% statics; dogs free; bus; adv bkg; Eng spkn; quiet; red long stay/low ssn/snr citizens; red CCI (only for min 10 nights' stay high ssn). "Vg bathing in beautiful surroundings; conv Port Aventura; excel site." ♦ 7 Mar-28 Sep. € 37.60   2007*

See advertisement

Before we move on, I'm going to fill in some site report forms and post them off to the editor, otherwise they won't arrive in time for the deadline at the end of September.

RONDA *2H3* (4km NE Rural) Camping El Cortijo, Ctra Campillos, Km 4.5, 29400 Ronda (Málaga) [952-87 07 46; fax 952-87 30 82; www. hermanosmacias.com] Fr Ronda by-pass take A367 twd Campillos. Site on L after 4.5km opp new development 'Hacienda Los Pinos'. Med, mkd pitch, pt shd; wc; chem disp; mv service pnt; serviced pitches; baby facs; shwrs inc; el pnts inc; lndtte; shop; rest; bar; playgrnd; pool; tennis; games area; cycle hire; 5% statics; dogs; phone; Eng spkn; some rd noise; CCI. "Friendly, helpful owner; conv NH." ♦ 1 Apr-15 Oct. € 16.00   2007*

⊞RONDA *2H3* (6km NE) Camping El Abogao, Ctra Ronda-Campillos Km 5, 29400 Ronda (Málaga) [952-87 58 44; fax 952 19 02 67] Fr Marbella take A376 NW twds Ronda (NB: This rte is v mountainous); turn R onto A367 twds Campillos; site on R in 6km. Sm, pt shd, mkd pitch; wc; chem disp; shwrs inc; el pnts (6A) inc; gas; lndry rm; shop 6km; rest; bar; pool; cycle hire; dogs; phone; adv bkg; quiet; cc acc; CCI. "V narr ent, tight corners; poss diff access to pitches for long o'fits; take care low level obstructions when manoeuvring; v sandy & soft after rain; gd for touring mountains; san facs gd but site a bit run down; vg when quiet but ltd facs." € 14.70   2005*

⊞**RONDA** 2H3 (1.5km S Rural) **Camping El Sur, Ctra Ronda-Algeciras Km 1.5, 29400 Ronda (Málaga)** [952-87 59 39; fax 952-87 70 54; info@campingelsur.com; www.campingelsur.com] Site on W side of A369 dir Algeciras. Do not tow thro Ronda. Med, mkd pitch, hdstg, terr, pt shd; htd wc; chem disp; mv service pnt; baby facs; shwrs inc; el pnts (5-10A) €3.50-5.35 (poss rev pol &/or no earth); lndtte; shop; rest adj; snacks; bar; playgrnd; pool high ssn; dogs €2.14; phone; internet; poss cr; Eng spkn; adv bkg; quiet; red long stay/low ssn; CCI. "Gd rd fr coast with spectacular views; long haul for lge o'fits; busy family-run site in lovely setting; strict rules about noise; conv National Parks & Pileta Caves; poss diff access some pitches due trees; hard, rocky ground; san facs poss stretched high ssn; easy walk to town; friendly staff; vg rest; excel." ♦ € 22.45   2007*

There aren't many sites open this early in the year. We'd better phone ahead to check that the one we're heading for is actually open.

ROQUETAS DE MAR see Almería 4G1

ROSAS 3B3 (2km N Coastal) **Camping Salatà, Port Reig s/n, 17480 Rosas (Gerona)** [972-25 60 86; fax 972-15 02 33; info@campingsalata.com; www.campingsalata.com] At Figueres take Rosas rd C260. On ent Rosas site on R, sp. Lge, mkd pitch, hdstg, pt shd; htd wc; chem disp; mv service pnt; baby facs; shwrs inc; el pnts (6-10A) inc; gas; lndtte; shop; tradsmn; rest; snacks; bar; playgrnd; htd pool high ssn; sand beach 500m; internet; 10% statics; dogs; phone; site clsd Jan; poss cr; Eng spkn; adv bkg (bkg fee); red long stay/low ssn; cc acc; CCI. "Vg area for sub-aqua sports; vg clean facs; red facs low ssn; pleasant walk/cycle to town; excel winter site." ♦ 1 Mar-31 Oct. € 35.55
                    2007*

ROSAS 3B3 (200m SW Coastal) **Camping Rodas, Calle Punta Falconera 62,17480 Rosas (Gerona)** [972-25 76 17; fax 972-15 24 66; info@campingrodas.com; www.campingrodas.com] On Figueras-Rosas rd, at o'skts of Rosas sp on R after supmkt. Lge, hdg/mkd pitch, pt shd; wc; chem disp; serviced pitches; shwrs inc; el pnts inc; gas; rest; snacks; bar; lndtte; ice; shop adj; tradsmn; sm playgrnd; htd pool; sand beach 600m; bus 1km; poss cr; Eng spkn; adv bkg; quiet; cc acc; CCI. "Gd pool & children's pool; site rds all tarmac; Rosas gd cent for region; well-run site; gates clsd at midnight." 1 Jun-30 Sep. € 28.00   2007*

Spain

ROSAS *3B3* (1km W Urban/Coastal) **Camping Joncar Mar, Ctra Figueres s/n, 17480 Rosas (Gerona) [tel/fax 972-25 67 02; joncarmar@ hotmail.com; www.joncarmar.com]** At Figueres take C260 W for Rosas. On ent Rosas turn sharp R at last rndabt at end of dual c'way. Lge, pt sl, pt shd; htd wc; chem disp; baby facs; shwrs; el pnts (10A) €3.55 (poss no earth); gas; lndtte; shop; rest; bar; playgrnd; pool; sand beach adj; golf 15km; entmnt; games rm; 15% statics; dogs €2.10; phone; bus 500m; poss cr; Eng spkn; adv bkg; rd noise; cc acc; red low ssn/long stay. "Conv walk into Rosas; poss cramped/tight pitches; narr rds; vg value low ssn." 1 Apr-31 Oct. € 23.00   2007*

ROTA see Puerto de Santa María, El *2H3*

RUILOBA see Comillas *1A4*

⊞**SABINANIGO** *3B2* (6km N Rural) **Camping Valle de Tena, Ctra N260, Km 512.6, 22600 Senegüe (Huesca). [974-48 09 77; fax 974-48 25 51; correo@campingvalledetena.com; www.camping valledetena.com]** Fr Jaca take N330, in 12km turn L onto N260 dir Biescas. In 5km turn L sp Sorripas, foll sp to site in 1km. Lge, mkd pitch, terr, pt shd; htd wc; chem disp; mv service pnt; serviced pitches; baby facs; shwrs inc; el pnts (6A) €3.91-4.60; lndtte; shop; rest; snacks; bar; playgrnd; pool; sports facs; hiking & rv rafting nr; entmnt; internet; TV rm; 60% statics; phone; Eng spkn; adv bkg (dep req); rd noise during day but quiet at night. "Helpful staff; excel NH to/fr France." € 18.02   2006*

⊞**SABINANIGO** *3B2* (1km E Urban) **Camping Aurín, Ctra C330, Circunvalación Sabiñánigo-Francia, s/n, 22600 Sabiñánigo (Huesca) [974-48 34 45; fax 974-48 32 80; trh@trhhoteles. com]** On Sabiñánigo by-pass (N330) 1km SE of junc with N260. Fr Jaca (S) site on L, go past to turning point in 800m. Sp Confortel. Site behind & beside Confortel. Lge, mkd pitch, pt shd; htd wc; mv service pnt; chem disp; baby facs; shwrs inc; el pnts (5A) €4.30; gas; lndtte; shop 2km; supmkt opp; rest, bar in hotel; snacks; playgrnd; 2 pools; tennis; watersports; car wash; 90% statics; no dogs; bus 400m; site clsd 1 Nov-19 Dec; poss cr; Eng spkn; quiet excl w/e; cc acc. "V sm, cr area for tourers; lge o'fits park adj pool low ssn; mountain walking; skiing; all hotel facs avail to campers; site in area of outstanding beauty; wide range of activities on offer." ♦ € 18.80   2006*

⊞**SACEDON** *3D1* (500m E Rural) **Camp Municipal Sacedón, Camino Sacedón 15, 19120 Sacedón (Guadalajara) [949-35 10 18; fax 949-35 10 73; ecomillans63@hotmail.com]** At km 115 on N320 E fr Sacedón. Site on L. Med, mkd pitch, hdstg, pt sl, shd; wc (cont); shwrs; el pnts €3.75; lndry rm; shop 500m; lake sw 1km; quiet. "NH only in area of few sites; sm pitches; low ssn phone to check open." ♦ € 13.70   2007*

⊞**SAGUNTO** *4E2* (7km NE Coastal) **Camping Malvarrosa de Corinto, Playa Malvarrosa de Corinto, 46500 Sagunto (València) [962-60 89 06; fax 962-60 89 43; camalva@ctv.es; www. malvacorinto.com]** Exit 49 fr A7 onto N340, foll dir Almenara-Casa Blanca. Turn E twd Port de Sagunto & Canet d'en Berenguer on CV320. Foll site sp. Lge, pt shd; wc; chem disp; sauna; shwrs inc; el pnts (10A) €3.50; gas; lndtte; ice; shop & 5km; rest; snacks; bar; BBQ; playgrnd; sand & shgl beach adj; tennis; horseriding; gym; 80% statics; dogs; phone; poss cr; Eng spkn; quiet; red long stay; CCI. "Friendly & helpful owners; gd facs; owners' dogs v noisy; excel pitches adj beach; plenty of touring pitches, but access to some poss diff; ltd facs & poss neglected low ssn; no local transport." € 14.90   2004*

SALAMANCA *1C3* (4km N Rural) **Camping La Capea, Ctra N630, Km 384, 37189 Aldeaseca de la Armuña (Salamanca) [923-25 10 66; campinglacapea@hotmail.com]** Close to km post 333 on N630. Site sp fr both dirs. Ent on brow of a hill on W side of rd. Med, hdg/mkd pitch, hdstg, shd; wc; chem disp; mv service pnt; shwrs inc; el pnts (10A) €3.45; lndtte; ice; shop; snacks; bar; playgrnd; pool; TV; 10% statics; dogs; some Eng spkn; some rd noise; CCI. "Friendly; variety of pitch sizes." 1 Apr-30 Sep. € 13.80   2007*

Did you know you can fill in site report forms on the Club's website — www.caravanclub.co.uk?

⊞**SALAMANCA** *1C3* (4.5km NE Rural) **Camping Don Quijote, Ctra Salamanca-Aldealengua. Km 4, 37193 Cabrerizos (Salamanca) [tel/fax 923-20 90 52; info@campingdonquijote.com; www.campingdonquijote.com]** Fr Madrid or fr S cross Rv Tormes by most easterly bdge to join inner ring rd. Foll Paseo de Canalejas for 800m to Plaza España. Turn R onto SA804 Avda de los Comuneros & strt on for 5km. Site ent 2km after town boundary sp. Fr other dirs, head into city & foll inner ring rd to Plaza España. Site well sp fr rv & ring rd. Med, hdg pitch, pt shd; wc; chem disp; baby facs; shwrs inc; el pnts (10A) €3.15; lndtte; shop; supmkt 3km; rest; snacks; bar; playgrnd; pool; paddling pool; rv fishing; 10% statics; dogs; phone; bus; poss cr w/e; adv bkg; quiet; red CCI. "Gd walks; conv city cent." ♦ € 13.60   2006*

⊞**SALAMANCA** *1C3* (4km E Urban) **Camping Regio, Ctra Ávila-Madrid, Km 4, 37900 Santa Marta de Tormes (Salamanca) [923-13 88 88; fax 923-13 80 44; recepcion@campingregio.com; www.campingregio.com]** Fr outer ring rd dir Ávila & Madrid, foll sp to Commercial Cent (Le Clerc) & then Sta Marta de Tormes & Salamanca, site directly behind Hotel Regio. Foll sp to hotel. Lge, mkd pitch, pt sl, pt shd; wc; chem disp; mv service pnt; baby facs; shwrs inc; el pnts (10A) €3.42 (poss no earth); gas; lndtte; shop & 1km; hypmkt 3km; rest, snacks in hotel; poss discount hotel meals for campers; bar; playgrnd; hotel pool; cycle hire; TV; 5% statics; dogs; phone; bus to Salamanca; car wash; poss cr; Eng spkn; quiet; cc acc; CCI. "In winter stop at 24hr hotel recep; poss v cold in winter; poss no hdstg in wet conditions; conv en rte Portugal; refurbished facs to excel standard; site poss untidy low ssn & itinerants; spacious pitches but some poss tight for lge o'fits; take care lge brick placement markers when reversing; excel pool; vg."
♦ € 18.80   2007*

⊞**SALAMANCA** *1C3* (2.5km NW Rural) **Camping Ruta de la Plata, Ctra de Villamayor, 37184 Villares de la Reina (Salamanca) [tel/fax 923-28 95 74; recepcion@campingrutadelaplata. com; www.campingrutadelaplata.com]** Fr N on N630 turn R, opp football stadium' Helmantico' two Villamayor. Site on R in 800m. Or fr junc A62 with SA300 (Salamanca-Ledesma) turn N sp Ledesma for 1km. Turn R at 1st rndabt & turn R at next rndabt. Go thro vill of Villamayor. Site at end of vill. Well sp. Med, some hdg/mkd pitch, terr, pt sl, pt shd; htd wc; chem disp; mv service pnt; shwrs inc; el pnts (6A) €3; gas; lndtte; ice; shop & 1km; tradsmn; snacks; bar; playgrnd; pool high ssn; golf 3km; TV rm; dogs €1.50; reg bus to city at gate; poss cr; quiet but some rd noise at night; CCI. "Clean, tidy, family-owned site; gd san facs; red facs low ssn; conv NH." ♦ ltd. € 13.20 (CChq acc)
                                                              2007*

⊞**SALDANA** *1B4* (250m S Urban) **Camping El Soto, Avda del Instituto, 34100 Saldaña (Palencia) [979-89 20 10; mordax@iespana.es]** Cross rv bdge S of Saldana twds Carrión de los Condes. Turn R immed & then immed R again, site not sp. Med, pt shd; wc; baby facs; shwrs; el pnts (10A) €1.80; lndtte; shop in vill; tradsmn; snacks; bar; 20% statics; dogs; phone; quiet; cc acc; CCI. "Gd base for Roman mosaics at Villa La Olmeda, Pedrosa de la Vega." € 11.70   2006*

⊞**SALDES** *3B3* (3.5km E Rural) **Camping Repos del Pedraforca, Ctra B400, Km 13.5, 08697 Saldes (Barcelona) [938-25 80 44; fax 938-25 80 61; pedra@campingpedraforca.com; www.campingpedraforca.com]** S fr Puigcerdà on C1411 for 35km, turn R at B400, site on L in 13.5km. Med, mkd pitch, pt sl, shd; htd wc; chem disp; mv service pnt; baby facs; sauna; shwrs inc; el pnts (5-10A) €3.80; lndtte; shop; tradsmn; rest, snacks high ssn; bar; playgrnd; 2 htd pools (1 covrd); cycle hire; gym; entmnt; TV rm; 50% statics; dogs €1.90; phone; Eng spkn; some rd noise; adv bkg; red 14+ days; cc acc; CCI. "Tow to pitches avail; vg walking; in heart of nature reserve; poss diff ent long o'fits; excel." € 20.49 (CChq acc)
                                                              2006*

This guide relies on site report forms submitted by caravanners like us; we'll do our bit and tell the editor what we think of the campsites we've visited.

SALOU *3C2* (Urban/Coastal) **Camping La Siesta, Calle Norte 37, 43840 Salou (Tarragona) [977-38 08 52; fax 977-38 31 91; info@camping-lasiesta.com; www.campinglasiesta.es]** Site in cent of town, well sp. Lge, mkd pitch, pt sl, shd; wc; chem closet; chem disp; baby facs; shwrs; el pnts €3.10; gas; lndtte; ice; shop; rest; bar; pool; sand beach 200m; cycle hire; sports area; 30% statics; poss cr; adv bkg ess; some rd noise & disco; adv bkg; cc acc; CCI. "Gd cycle path by beach to Cambrils; site guarded; conv for beach & Port Aventura." 14 Mar-3 Nov. € 30.00   2004*

⊞**SALOU** *3C2* (2km NE Coastal) **Camping La Pineda de Salou, Ctra Tarragona-Salou, Km 5, 43481 La Pineda-Vilaseca (Tarragona) [977-37 30 80; fax 977-37 30 81; info@ campinglapineda.com; www.campinglapineda. com]** Exit A7 junc 35 dir Salou, Vilaseca & Port Aventura. Foll sp Port Aventura then La Pineda/ Platjes on rd TV 3148. Med, mkd pitch, pt shd; wc; baby facs; chem disp; sauna; shwrs; el pnts (5A) €3.50; gas; lndtte; ice; shop; rest; snacks; bar; playgrnd; pool & paddling pool; spa cent; beach 400m; watersports; fishing; tennis; horseriding; cycle hire; mini club; tourist info; entmnt; TV; some statics; dogs €2.90; phone; cc acc; red low ssn. "Conv Port Aventura & Tarragona." € 32.20
                                                              2006*

Spain

SALOU *3C2* (1km S Urban/Coastal) **Camping Sangulí-Salou, Prolongació Carrer E s/n, 43840 Salou (Tarragona) [977-38 16 41; fax 977-38 46 16; mail@sanguli.es; www.sanguli.es]** Exit AP7/E15 junc 35. At 1st rndbt take dir to Salou (Plaça Europa), at 2nd rndabt foll site sp. V lge, mkd pitch, hdstg, pt sl, shd; htd wc; chem disp; mv service pnt; some serviced pitches; baby facs; shwrs inc; el pnts (10A) inc; gas; lndtte; ice; shop; 2 supmkts; rest; snacks; bar; BBQ; playgrnd; 3 pools & 3 paddling pools; waterslide; jacuzzi; sand beach 50m; games area; tennis; games rm; mini-golf; fitness rm; entmnt; excursions; cinema; youth club; mini-club; amphitheatre; internet; TV; dogs; 35% statics; phone; bus; car wash; Eng spkn; adv bkg rec Jul-Aug; some rlwy noise; red low ssn/long stay/snr citizens; cc acc; CCI. "Quiet end of Salou nr Cambrils & 3km Port Aventura; lge o'fits take care manoeuvring on some pitches & overhanging trees; excel, well-maintained site." ♦ 14 Mar-2 Nov. € 55.00 2007*

See advertisement opposite

As soon as we get home I'm going to post all these site report forms to the editor for inclusion in next year's guide. I don't want to miss the September deadline.

SALOU *3C2* (2km W Coastal) **Camping Cambrils Park, Avda Mas Clariana s/n, 43850 Cambrils (Tarragona) [977-35 10 31; fax 977-35 22 10; mail@cambrilspark.es; www.cambrilspark.es]** Exit AP7 junc 35 & foll sp Salou; at 1st rndabt foll sp Cambrils; after 2km site sp to L at rndabt. V lge, mkd pitch, hdstg, pt sl, shd; htd wc; chem disp; mv service pnt; baby facs; some serviced pitches; shwrs inc; el pnts (10A) inc; gas; lndtte; shop; rest; snacks; bar; BBQ; playgrnd; pools; sand beach 400m; tennis; child mini-club; entmnt; excursions; mini-golf; games rm; internet; TV rm; car wash; 30% statics; no dogs; phone; Eng spkn; adv bkg rec; quiet; cc acc; red low ssn/long stay/snr citizens; CCI. "Superb, busy site; excel, clean facs; helpful staff; access to some pitches poss diff long o'fits; walk along sea front to Salou or Cambrils; conv Port Aventura; bus to Tarragona nrby or walk to Salou for train; excel site rest." ♦ 14 Mar-28 Sep. € 57.00 (CChq acc) 2007*

See advertisement on next page

SAN JOSE see Níjar *4G1*

SAN MIGUEL DE SALINAS see Torrevieja *4F2*

⊞**SAN ROQUE** *2H3* (4km E) **Camping La Casita, Ctra N340, Km 126, 11360 San Roque (Cádiz) [tel/fax 956-78 00 31]** Site sp 'Via de Servicio' parallel to N340/E15. Access at km 119 fr S, km 127 fr N. Site visible fr rd. Med, pt sl, pt terr, pt shd, wc; chem disp; mv service pnt; shwrs; el pnts (10A) €3.74; ice; shop; rest; bar; playgrnd; pool; sand beach 3km; mini-golf; horseriding; disco; 90% statics; dogs €2.15; bus 100m; phone; poss cr; Eng spkn; adv bkg ess; noisy; 10% red 30+ days; cc acc; CCI. "Ltd touring pitches; shwrs solar htd - water temp depends on weather (poss cold); conv Gibraltar & Morocco; daily buses to La Línea & Algeciras; ferries to N Africa (secure parking at port)." ♦ € 23.50 2007*

⊞**SAN SEBASTIAN/DONOSTIA** *3A1* (5km NW Rural) **Camping Igueldo, Barrio de Igueldo, 20008 San Sebastián (Guipúzkoa) [943-21 45 02; fax 943-28 04 11; info@campingigueldo.com; www.campingigueldo.com]** Fr W on A8, leave m'way at junc 9 twd city cent, take 1st R & R at rndabt onto Avda de Tolosa sp Ondarreta. At sea front turn hard L at rndabt sp to site (Avda Satrústegui) & foll sp up steep hill 4km to site. Fr E exit junc 8 then as above. Site sp as Garoa Camping Bungalows. Lge, hdg/mkd pitches, terr, pt shd, 40% serviced pitches; wc; chem disp; baby facs; shwrs inc; el pnts (5A) inc; gas; lndtte; shop; rest, bar high ssn; playgrnd; pool 5km; sand beach 5km; TV; phone; bus to city adj; poss cr/noisy; Eng spkn; red long stay/low ssn; cc acc; CCI. "Gd, clean facs; spectacular views; steep app poss diff for lge o'fits; site poss unkempt low ssn; pitches muddy when wet." ♦ € 28.20 2007*

SAN VICENTE DE LA BARQUERA *1A4* (1km E Coastal) **Camping El Rosal, Ctra de la Playa s/n, 39540 San Vicente de la Barquera (Cantabria) [942-71 01 65; fax 942-71 00 11; info@campingelrosal.com; www.campingelrosal.com]** Fr A8 km 264, foll sp San Vicente. Turn R over bdge then 1st L (site sp) immed at end of bdge; keep L & foll sp to site. Med, mkd pitch, pt sl, pt shd; wc; chem disp; shwrs; el pnts (6A) €2.50; gas; lndtte; shop; rest 1km; snacks; bar; sand beach adj; phone; poss cr; Eng spkn; adv bkg; quiet; cc acc; CCI. "Excel site in pine wood o'looking bay; modern, v clean facs; helpful staff; easy walk or cycle ride to interesting town; Sat mkt; few petrol stns on autovias app San Vicente." ♦ 1 Apr-14 Oct. € 24.80 2007*

Spain

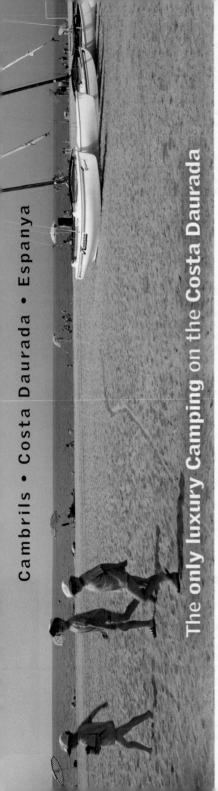
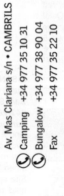

COSTA BRAVA CAMPING SANT POL

SAN VICENTE DE LA BARQUERA *1A4* (5km E Coastal) **Camping Playa de Oyambre, Playa de Oyambre, 39540 San Vicente de la Barquera (Cantabria) [942-71 14 61; fax 942-71 15 30; camping@oyambre.com; www.oyambre.com]** Fr N634 foll sp to La Revilla. Site on L in 3km. Lge, mkd pitch, terr, pt sl, pt shd; wc; chem disp; mv service pnt; shwrs inc; el pnts (10A) €4; gas; lndtte; shop; tradsmn; rest; snacks; bar; pool; beach 800m; 40% statics; bus 200m; Eng spkn; adv bkg; cc acc; CCI. "V well-kept site; v quiet week days low ssn; friendly staff; gd base for N coast & Pyrenees; 4x4 avail to tow to pitch if wet; some sm pitches & rd noise some pitches." 1 Apr-30 Sep. € 18.30

2007*

SANGONERA LA SECA see Murcia *4F1*

The opening dates and prices on this campsite have changed. I'll send a site report form to the editor for the next edition of the guide.

SANGUESA *3B1* (500m S Urban) **Camping Cantolagua, Camino de Cantolagua, 31400 Sangüesa (Navarra) [948-43 03 52; fax 948-87 13 13; camping.sanguesa@meganet.es]** Turn off N240 fr Pamplona onto N127 to Sangüesa. Turn into town over bdge, foll sp, 2nd R up thro town, R at Bull Ring then L, then 1st R. Site well sp in town. Med, hdg pitch, pt shd; wc; chem disp (wc); mv service pnt; some serviced pitches; shwrs inc; el pnts (8A) €3.40; lndtte; shops 1km; tradsmn; rest; snacks; bar; BBQ; htd pool adj; playgrnd; horseriding; tennis; cycle hire; TV rm; phone; poss cr; Eng spkn; 10% statics; quiet; cc acc; CCI. "Serviced pitches not suitable for m'vans; facs clean; lovely historic unspoilt town; adequate NH." ♦ ltd. 1 Feb-31 Oct. € 14.50

2006*

SANT ANTONI DE CALONGE see Palamós *3B3*

SANT FELIU DE GUIXOLS *3B3* (1km N Urban/Coastal) **Camping Sant Pol, Ctra Dr Fleming 1, 17220 Sant Feliu de Guixols (Gerona) [972-32 72 69 or 972-20 86 67; fax 972-32 72 11 or 972-22 24 09; info@campingsantpol.com; www.campingsantpol.com]** Exit AP7 junc 7 onto C31 dir S'Agaro; at km 312 take dir S'Agaro; at rndabt foll sp to site. Med, hdg/mkd pitch, terr, shd; htd wc; chem disp; mv service pnt; some serviced pitches; baby facs; shwrs inc; el pnts (10A) inc; lndtte; ice; shop; tradsmn; rest; bar; BBQ; playgrnd; htd 3 pools; sand beach 350m; games rm; cycle hire; child entmnt; internet; 30% statics; dogs €2; sep car park; Eng spkn; adv bkg; quiet - some rd noise; cc acc; red long stay/snr citizens/CCI. "Vg, well-run site; excel facs; lovely pool; cycle track to Gerona." ♦ 15 Mar-2 Nov. € 50.00

2007*

See advertisement above

SANT JOAN DE LES ABADESSES see Sant Pau de Segúries *3B3*

SANT LLORENC DE LA MUGA see Figueres *3B3*

⊞**SANT LLORENC DE MORUNYS** *3B3* (2km N Rural) **Camping Morunys, Ctra de la Coma s/n, Km.1,5, 25282 Sant Llorenç de Morunys (Lleida) [973-49 22 13; fax 973-49 21 03; jlab3@hotmail.com; www.valldelord.com]** Fr Solsona take rd N sp Sant Llorenç for approx 24km, site well sp. Lge, mkd pitch, hdstg, terr, pt shd; wc; chem disp; baby facs; shwrs; el pnts (6A) €3.30; gas; lndtte; shop; rest; bar; playgrnd; pool; phone; 80% statics; noisy; adv bkg; cc acc; red CCI. "Vg." € 16.40

2004*

Spain

Last year of report

LAS DUNAS
CAMPING BUNGALOW PARK

The holiday paradise for the whole family!

camping

bungalow park

Campsite and Bungalow pa...
located at an endless sand...
beach. A holiday paradise ...
the whole family. Immens...
variety of leisure activities a...
animation programme fo...
ages. State-of-the-art sani...
facilities and an outstand...
shopping centre.

Camping Las Dunas - E-17470 - Sant Pere Pescador - Costa Brava
Tel. (+34) 972 521 717 - Fax (+34) 972 550 046
E-mail: info@campinglasdunas.com
Your UK Agent: Derek & Jessica Callaway
Tel. 01205 366856 · callaway@campinglasdunas.com
www.campinglasdunas.com

GPS
N 42° 09'
E 03° 06'

⊞SANT PAU DE SEGURIES *3B3* (500m S Rural) Camping Els Roures, Avda del Mariner 34, 17864 Sant Pau de Segúries (Gerona) [972-74 70 00; fax 972-74 71 09; info@elsroures.com; www. elsroures.com] On C38/C26 Camprodón S twd Ripoll for 6km. In Sant Pau turn L 50m after traff lts. Site on R after 400m. Lge, mkd pitch, terr, shd; wc; mv service pnt; baby facs; shwrs inc; el pnts (4-8A) €3.20-6.50; gas; lndtte; shop; rest; bar; playgrnd; 2 pools; tennis; cinema; games rm; gym; internet; 80% statics; dogs €3.50; phone; bus 200m; poss cr; some noise; CCI. "Gd." ♦ € 26.00   2007*

⊞SANT PAU DE SEGURIES *3B3* (4km SW Rural) Camping Abadesses, Ctra Camprodón, Km 14.6, 17860 Sant Joan de les Abadesses (Gerona) [630-14 36 06; fax 972-70 20 69; info@ campingabadesses.com; www.camping abadesses.com] Fr Ripoll take C26 in dir Sant Joan, site approx 4km on R after vill. Steep access. Sm, mkd pitch, terr, unshd; htd wc; baby facs; shwrs; el pnts (6A) €2.88; gas; lndtte; shop; snacks; bar; playgrnd; pool; games area; wifi internet; 70% statics; dogs €3.21; bus 150m; quiet; cc acc. "Vg facs; gd views fr most pitches; steep access to recep; poss diff access around terraces." ♦ € 21.90   2007*

SANT PERE PESCADOR *3B3* (Coastal) Camping La Gaviota, Ctra de la Playa s/n, 17470 Sant Pere Pescador (Gerona) [972-52 05 69; fax 972-55 03 48; info@lagaviota.com; www.lagaviota. com] Exit 5 fr A7 dir Sant Martí d'Empúries, site at end of beach rd. Med, hdg/mkd pitch, pt shd; wc; chem disp; baby facs; shwrs inc; el pnts (5A) €2.85; gas; lndtte; ice; shop; rest; bar; playgrnd; direct access sand beach 50m; games rm; internet; 20% statics; phone; dogs €3.50; poss cr; Eng spkn; adv bkg; quiet; cc acc; CCI. "V friendly owners; clean site; excel facs & constant hot water; some sm pitches & narr site rds; poss ltd access for lge o'fits; take care overhanging trees; poss mosquito problem." ♦ 15 Mar-31 Oct. € 35.00   2006*

SANT PERE PESCADOR *3B3* (200m E Rural) Camping Riu, Ctra de la Playa s/n, 17470 Sant Pere Pescador (Gerona) [972-52 02 16; fax 972-55 04 69; info@campingriu.com; www. campingriu.com] Fr N exit AP7 junc 4 dir L'Escala & foll sp Sant Pere Pescador, then turn L twds coast, site on L. Fr S exit AP7 junc 5 dir L'Escala, then as above & turn R to beaches & site. Lge, mkd pitch, shd; wc; chem disp; baby facs; shwrs inc; el pnts (3A) €3.30; gas; lndtte; shop & 300m; rest; snacks; bar; BBQ; playgrnd; sand beach 2km; boat-launching on rv adj; fishing; kayak hire; games area; entmnt; child entmnt; internet; 5% statics; dogs €2.60; Eng spkn; adv bkg; quiet; cc acc; red long stay; CCI. "Excel boating facs & fishing on site; gd situation; site rec." ♦ 1 Apr-17 Sep. € 32.82   2005*

SANT PERE PESCADOR *3B3* (2km E Coastal) Camping Las Dunas, 17470 Sant Pere Pescador (Gerona)(PostalAddress:AptdoCorreos23,17130 L'Escala) [972-52 17 17 or 01205 366856 (UK); fax 972-52 00 46; info@campinglasdunas.com or callaway@campinglasdunas.com; www. campinglasdunas.com] Exit AP7 junc 5 dir Viladamat & L'Escala; 2km bef L'Escala turn L for Sant Martí d'Empúries, turn L bef ent vill for 2km, camp sp. V lge, mkd pitch, pt sl, pt shd; wc; chem disp; mv service pnt; baby facs; serviced pitches; shwrs inc; el pnts (10A) inc; gas; lndtte; ice; kiosk; supmkt; souvenir shop; rest; snacks; bar; BBQ; 2 pools; sand beach adj; playgrnd; tennis & sports; entmnt; TV; money exchange; cash machines; doctor; 5% statics; dogs €4.40; phone; quiet; adv bkg (ess high ssn); Eng spkn; red low ssn; CCI. "Greco-Roman ruins in Empúries; gd sized pitches - extra for serviced; excel facs." ♦ 9 May-19 Sep. € 51.00   2007*

See advertisement opposite

Before we move on, I'm going to fill in some site report forms and post them off to the editor, otherwise they won't arrive in time for the deadline at the end of September.

SANT PERE PESCADOR *3B3* (1km SE Coastal) Camping L'Àmfora, Avda Josep Tarradellas 2, 17470 Sant Pere Pescador (Gerona) [972-52 05 40 or 972-52 05 42; fax 972-52 05 39; info@ campingamfora.com; www.campingamfora. com] Fr N exit junc 3 fr AP7 onto N11 fro Figueres/ Roses. At junc with C260 foll sp Castelló d'Empúries & Roses. At Castelló turn R at rndabt sp Sant Pere Pescador then foll sp to L'Amfora. Fr S exit junc 5 fr AP7 onto GI 623/GI 624 to Sant Pere Pescador. V lge, hdg/mkd pitch, pt shd; htd wc; chem disp; mv service pnt; serviced pitches; baby facs; shwrs inc; el pnts (10A) inc; gas; lndtte; shop; supmkt; rest; snacks; bar; BBQ (charcoal/elec); playgrnd; 4 pools; waterslide; paddling pool; sand beach adj; windsurf school; fishing; tennis; horseriding 5km; cycle hire; mini-golf; entmnt; children's club; wifi internet; games/TV rm; 15% statics; dogs €1.30-4.80; phone; adv bkg; Eng spkn; quiet; red long stay/ low ssn/snr citizens/CCI. "Excel, v well-run, clean site; helpful staff; choice of 3 pitch sizes; lger pitches have own san facs & may be shared with another family to reduce cost; immac san facs; Parque Acuatico 18km." ♦ 5 Apr-30 Sep. € 48.60 (CChq acc) ABS - E22   2007*

See advertisement on next page

Spain

100% sol y playa

• Enjoy a real holiday on one of our unique pitches with private sanitary installations.
• Directly at a kilometre long, sandy beach under the Spanish sun, we offer you a wide variety of service and leisure activities for all ages : swimming pools, tennis, restaurant, self-service, beach bar, disco-bar,

supermarket and our mini-club for children. One of the sanitary building is heated.
• Pitches from 95 till 180 m2, bungalows and mobile-homes are waiting for you.
• We speak English.
• Open from 05/04 to 30/09

Special offers

Special Children

(05/04 - 20/06
28/08 - 30/09)

Children
under 10
free

Special senior citizens

(05/04 - 20/06
28/08 - 30/09)

10 days = 9 paying
14 days = 12 paying
18 days = 14 paying
22 days = 15 paying

10% discount on your stay CCI holders. Considerable discount on bungalows & mobile-homes.

L'Àmfora ★★★★
camping & bungalow park
Costa Brava-España

Av. Josep Tarradellas, 2 - E-17470 Sant Pere Pescador - Costa Brava (Girona) España
Information - Booking : +34 972 52 05 40 • +34 972 52 05 42 • Fax : +34 972 52 05 39
www.campingamfora.com - e-mail : info@campingamfora.com

SANT PERE PESCADOR *3B3* (3km SE Coastal) **Camping Aquarius, Camí Sant Martí d'Empúries, 17470 Sant Pere Pescador (Gerona) [972-52 00 03; fax 972-55 02 16; camping@ aquarius.es; www.aquarius.es]** Fr AP7 m'way exit 3, foll sp to Roses. Join C260, after 7km bear R to Sant Pere Pescador. Cross rv bdge in vill, take 1st L & foll camp sp. Turn R at next rndabt, site on R in 1.5km. Lge, pt shd; wc; chem disp; mv service pnt; serviced pitches; baby facs; fam bthrm; shwrs; el pnts (6A) €3.10; gas; lndtte; ice; supmkt; rest; snacks; bar; 2 playgrnds; sand beach adj; nursery in ssn; games rm; games area; car wash; some statics; phone; cash point in recep; dogs in designated area €3.53; poss cr; Eng spkn; adv bkg (ess Jul/Aug); quiet; red low ssn/long stay/ snr citizens (except Jul/Aug)/CCI. "Immac site, being extended for 2008; vg rest; windsurfing; vast beach; recycling facs; excel." ♦ ltd. 15 Mar-31 Oct. € 39.59 2007*

SANT PERE PESCADOR *3B3* (1.3km S Coastal) **Camping Las Palmeras, Ctra de la Platja 9, 17470 Sant Pere Pescador (Gerona) [972-52 05 06; fax 972-55 02 85; info@campinglaspalmeras.com; www.campinglaspalmeras.com]** Exit AP7 junc 3 or 4 at Figueras onto C260 dir Rosas/Cadaqués rd. After 8km at Castelló d'Empúries turn S for Sant Pere Pescador & cont twd beach. Site on R of rd. Lge, mkd pitch, shd; wc; chem disp; mv service pnt; some serviced pitches; baby facs; shwrs inc; el pnts (5-16A) €3.30 (check for earth); gas; lndtte; ice; shop; tradsmn; rest; snacks; bar; playgrnd; htd pool; paddling pool; sand beach 200m; tennis; cycle hire; games area; games rm; internet; entmnt; TV; 10% statics; dogs €4; phone; cash point; poss cr; Eng spkn; adv bkg; quiet; red CCI. "Pleasant site; helpful, friendly staff; superb, clean san facs; excel." ♦ 10 Mar-11 Oct. € 34.90 2007*

See advertisement opposite

There aren't many sites open this early in the year. We'd better phone ahead to check that the one we're heading for is actually open.

SANT PERE PESCADOR *3B3* (4km S Rural/ Coastal) **Camping La Ballena Alegre, Ctra Sant Martí d'Empúries, 17470 Sant Pere Pescador (Gerona)** [902-51 05 20; fax 902 51 05 21; infb2@ ballena-alegre.com; www.ballena-alegre.com] Fr A7 exit 5, dir L'Escala to rd GI 623, km 18.5. At 1st rndabt turn L dir Sant Martí d'Empúries, site on R in 1km. V lge, mkd pitch, hdstg, terr, pt shd; htd wc; chem disp; some serviced pitches; baby facs; shwrs inc; el pnts (10A) €4.30; gas; lndtte; supmkt; rest; snacks; bar; BBQ; playgrnd; 3 pools; sand beach adj; watersports; tennis; games area; games rm; fitness rm; cycle hire; money exchange; surf shop; entmnt; internet; TV rm; 10% statics; dogs €4.30; poss cr; Eng spkn; adv bkg; quiet; red low ssn/snr citizens/long stay; CCI. "Excel site; superb facs." ♦ 10 May-21 Sep. € 52.70   2007*

See advertisement on next page

⊞**SANT QUIRZE SAFAJA** *3C3* (2km E Rural) **Camping L'Illa, Ctra Sant Feliu de Codines-Centelles, Km 3.8, 08189 Sant Quirze Safaja (Barcelona)** [938-66 25 26; fax 935-72 96 21] N fr Sabadell on C1413 to Caldes de Montbui; then twds Moià on C59. Turn R at golf club, site 2km on R. Lge, mkd pitch, hdstg, terr, pt shd; wc; shwrs inc; el pnts (6A) €4.10; gas; lndtte; rest; sm shop; playgrnd; pool; paddling pool; 50% statics; dogs €4.50; bus 100m; site clsd mid-Dec to mid-Jan; adv bkg; CCI. "Easy drive to Barcelona; poss open w/e only low ssn." € 22.00   2007*

⊞**SANTA CILIA DE JACA** *3B2* (3km W Rural) **Camping Los Pirineos, Ctra Pamplona N240, Km 300, 22791 Santa Cilia de Jaca (Huesca)** [tel/fax 974-37 73 51; pirineos@pirinet.com; www.pirinet. com/pirineos] Fr Jaca on N240 twd Pamplona. Site on R after Santa Cilia de Jaca, clearly sp. Lge, hdg/ mkd pitch, hdstg, terr, pt shd; wc; chem disp; mv service pnt; baby facs; shwrs inc; el pnts (5A) €4.15 (check for earth); gas; lndtte; shop, rest high ssn; snacks; bar high ssn; playgrnd; pool in ssn; tennis; 90% statics; dogs; site clsd Nov; Eng spkn; adv bkg (dep req); some rd noise; cc acc; CCI. "Excel site in lovely area; ltd access for tourers; on Caminho de Santiago pilgrim rte; conv NH." ♦ € 23.41   2006*

SANTA CRISTINA DE ARO see Playa de Aro *3B3*

SANTA CRUZ see Coruña, La *1A2*

SANTA ELENA see Carolina, La *2F4*

SANTA MARINA DE VALDEON *1A3* (500m N Rural) **Camping El Cares, El Cardo, 24915 Santa Marina de Valdeón (León)** [tel/fax 987-74 26 76; cares@ elcares.com] Fr S take N621 to Portilla de la Reina. Turn L onto LE243 to Santa Marina. Turn L thro vill, just beyond vill turn L at camping sp. Vill street is narr & narr bdge 2.55m on app to site. Do not attempt to app fr N if towing - 4km of single track rd fr Posada. Med, terr, pt shd; wc; chem disp; shwrs; el pnts (5A) €3.20; lndtte; shop; tradsmn; rest; bar; 10% statics; dogs €2.10; phone; bus 1km; quiet; cc acc; CCI. "Site high in mountains; gd base for Cares Gorge; friendly, helpful staff; gd views; tight access." ♦ 1 Jun-30 Sep. € 18.85   2006*

SANTA MARTA DE TORMES see Salamanca *1C3*

⊞**SANTA PAU** *3B3* (2km E Rural) **Camping Ecológic Lava, Ctra Olot-Santa Pau, Km 7, 17811 Santa Pau (Gerona)** [972-68 03 58; fax 972-68 03 15; vacances@i-santapau.com; www.i-santapau.com] Take rd GI 524 fr Olot, site at top of hill, well sp & visible fr rd. Lge, mkd pitch, pt shd; wc; chem disp (wc); shwrs inc; baby facs; el pnts €4.20; gas; lndtte; shop 2km; tradsmn; rest; snacks; bar; playgrnd; pool; horseriding adj; dogs; phone; Eng spkn; adv bkg; quiet; cc acc. "V helpful staff; gd facs; v interesting, unspoilt area & town; in Garrotxa Parc Naturel volcanic region; v busy with tourists all ssn; walks sp fr site; Pyrenees museum in Olot; tourist train fr site to volcano; excel rests in medieval town." € 24.50   2007*

Spain

*Last year of report

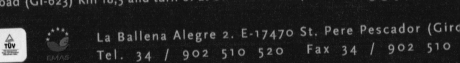

⊞**SANTA POLA** *4F2* (Urban/Coastal) **Camping Bahía de Santa Pola, Ctra de Elche s/n, Km 38, 03130 Santa Pola (Alicante)** [965-41 10 12; fax 965-41 67 90; campingbahia@santapola.com or web@santapola.com; www.santapola.com] Exit A7 junc 72. Site at junc bet N332 & CV865 or fr Elche take CV865 to Santa Pola. Lge, mkd pitch, hdstg, pt shd; wc; chem disp; mv service pnt; baby facs; shwrs inc; el pnts (6A) €2.50; gas; lndtte; shop; supmkt; rest; playgrnd; pool; sand beach 1km; sat TV; 50% statics; phone; bus adj; Eng spkn; adv bkg; rd noise; cc acc; red long stay/low ssn/CCI. "Helpful, friendly manager; well-organised site; excel san facs; site rds steep; attractive coastal cycle path." ♦ € 19.00   2007*

⊞**SANTAELLA** *2G3* (5km N Rural) **Camping La Campiña, La Guijarrosa-Santaella, 14547 Santaella (Córdoba)** [957-31 53 03; fax 957-31 51 58; info@campinglacampina.com; www.campinglacampina.com] Fr A4/E5 leave at km 441 onto A386 rd dir La Rambla to Santaella for 11km, turn L onto A379 for 5km & foll sp. Sm, mkd pitch, hdstg, pt sl, pt shd; wc; chem disp; baby facs; shwrs inc; el pnts (5A) €3.20; gas; lndtte; ice; shop & 6km; rest; snacks; bar; BBQ; playgrnd; pool; TV; dogs €2; bus at gate to Córdoba; Eng spkn; adv bkg; rd noise; cc acc; red long stay/low ssn; CCI. "Fine views; friendly, warm welcome; popular, family-run site; many pitches sm for lge o'fits; guided walks; poss clsd winter - phone to check." ♦ € 17.10   2006*

SANTANDER *1A4* (4km E Coastal) **Camping Latas, Barrio Arna, s/n, 39140 Somo (Cantabria)** [tel/fax 942-51 06 31] Exit A8 junc 11 dir Pedrena/Heres, thro Somo up hill; L at 2nd rndabt (sp Loredo NOT Laredo); turn L after camp sp; call at bar for access on R. Med, hdg pitch, pt sl, pt shd; wc; chem disp; baby facs; shwrs inc; el pnts (2-6A) €2.80; gas; lndtte; shop; rest; snacks; bar; pool; sand beach nr; watersports; tennis; 50% statics; phone; poss cr; adv bkg; poss noisy; no cc acc; CCI. "Noisy until midnight then strict silence." ♦ 15 Jun-15 Sep. € 17.50   2004*

SANTANDER *1A4* (8km E Coastal) **Camping Derby, Bajada a la Playa 6, 39140 Loredo (Cantabria)** [942-50 91 85; fax 942-50 92 52; info@campingderby.com; www.campingderby. com] Fr Santander exit A8 junc 7 onto CA141 twd Loredo. At 2nd rndabt after Somo take CA440 to Loredo, turn L at top of hill, site sp. Fr Bilbao exit A8 junc 11 onto CA145 sp Pedreña. At 1st rndabt turn R onto CA141, then as above. Lge, mkd pitch, pt sl, pt shd; wc; chem disp; shwrs inc; el pnts (3A) €2.25; gas; lndtte; ice; shop; tradsmn; rest; snacks; bar; BBQ; playgrnd; sm pool; sand beach adj; windsurfing school; child entmnt; 50% statics; dogs; phone; bus 2km; poss cr; Eng spkn; adv bkg; quiet; cc acc; CCI. "Vg." Easter-31 Oct. € 15.60   2004*

⊞**SANTANDER** *1A4* (12km E Rural) **Camping Somo Parque, Ctra Somo-Suesa s/n, 39150 Suesa-Ribamontán al Mar (Cantabria)** [tel/fax 942-51 03 09; somoparque@somoparque.com; www.somoparque.com] Fr car ferry foll sp Bilbao. After approx 8km turn L over bdge sp Pontejos & Somo. After Pedreña climb hill at Somo Playa & take 1st R sp Suesa. Foll site sp. Med, pt shd; wc; chem disp; shwrs & bath; el pnts inc; gas; ice; shop; snacks; bar; playgrnd; beach 1.5km; 75% statics; site clsd 16 Dec-14 Jan; some Eng spkn; quiet; CCI. "Fair NH; peaceful rural setting; sm ferry bet Somo & Santander." € 17.80   2005*

⊞**SANTANDER** *1A4* (6km W Coastal) **Camping Virgen del Mar, Ctra Santander-Liencres, San Román-Corbán s/n, 39000 Santander (Cantabria)** [942-34 24 25; fax 942-32 24 90; cvirdman@ ceoecant.es; www.ceoecant.es/aehc/virgenmar] Fr ferry turn R, then L up to football stadium, L again leads strt into San Román. If app fr W, take A67 (El Sardinero) then S20, leave at junc 2 dir Liencres, strt on. Site well sp. Lge, mkd pitch, pt shd; wc; chem disp; mv service pnt; shwrs; el pnts (6A) inc; lndtte; shop; supmkt 2km; rest; snacks; bar; playgrnd; pool; sand beach 300m; no dogs; adv bkg; quiet; cc acc; red long stay; CCI. "Some basic facs but gd hot water; some sm pitches not suitable lge o'fits; site adj cemetary; phone in low ssn to check site open; excel site but expensive low ssn." ♦ ltd. € 27.00   2005*

> Did you know you can fill in site report forms on the Club's website — www.caravanclub.co.uk?

SANTANDER *1A4* (6km NW Coastal) **Camping Cabo Mayor, Avda. del Faro s/n, 39012 Santander (Cantabria)** [tel/fax 942-39 15 42; info@cabomayor.com; www.cabomayor.com] Sp thro town but not v clearly. On waterfront (turn R if arr by ferry). At lge junc do not foll quayside, take uphill rd (resort type prom) & foll sp for Faro de Cabo Mayor. Site 200m bef lighthouse on L. Lge, mkd pitch, terr, unshd; wc; chem disp (wc); serviced pitches; baby facs; shwrs inc; el pnts (5A) inc; gas; lndtte; shop; rest; snacks; bar; playgrnd; pool high ssn; many beaches adj; tennis; TV; 10% statics; no dogs; phone; poss cr; Eng spkn; CCI. "San facs old but clean; v sm pitches; site popular with lge youth groups high ssn; shwrs clsd 2200-0800 & stretched in high ssn; NH only." ♦ 1 Apr-15 Oct. € 27.80   2007*

Spain

861   *Last year of report*

⊞SANTIAGO DE COMPOSTELA *1A2* (2km E Urban) **Camping As Cancelas, Rua 25 de Julio 35, 15704 Santiago de Compostela (La Coruña) [981-58 02 66 or 981-58 04 76; fax 981-57 55 53; info@campingascancelas.com; www.camping ascancelas.com]** Fr E on N634 or N547 cont across AP9 m'way to next rndabt. Turn L sp Santiago N. In 1km filter R to turn L sp Ourense & Lugo. Take immed L & foll site sp. Or app fr city & foll sp for Lugo until sp to site. Fr N or S leave A9 junc 67, at 1st rndabt take 2nd (sm) exit sp Santiago Historic City (not 3rd exit sp Ourense.) At next rndabt take 1st exit & site sp within 500m. Lge, mkd pitch, hdstg, terr, shd; htd wc; chem disp; baby facs; shwrs inc; el pnts (5-10A) €3.60 ; gas; lndtte; shop, rest, snacks & bar in ssn; BBQ; playgrnd; pool & paddling pool high ssn; internet; TV; dogs; phone; bus 100m; poss cr; Eng spkn; adv bkg ess high ssn; quiet; red low ssn; CCI. "Well-kept, busy site - conv for pilgrims; rec arr early high ssn; some sm pitches poss diff c'vans & steep ascent; spotless san facs but poss stretched when site busy; hot water avail all day low ssn; bus 100m fr gate avoids steep 15 min walk back fr town (low ssn adequate car parks in town); poss interference with car/c'van electrics fr local transmitter - if probs report to site recep; excel rest; in winter recep in bar." ♦ € 22.20   2007*

SANTIAGO DE COMPOSTELA *1A2* (4km E Urban) **Camping Monte do Gozo, Ctra Aeropuerto, Km 2, 15820 Santiago de Compostela (La Coruña) [981-55 89 42; fax 981-56 28 92; info@cvacaciones-montedogozo.com; www. montedogozo.com]** Site sp on 'old' rd N634 (not new autovia) into town fr E, nr San Marcos. Do not confuse with pilgrim site nr to city. Foll sp 'Ciudad de Vacaciones'. Lge, pt sl, shd; wc; chem disp; shwrs; el pnts €3.46 (poss rev pol); gas; lndtte; shop; rest; bar; playgrnd; 2 pools; tennis; cycle hire; 20% statics; no dogs; phone; bus 1km; cc acc. 1 Jul-31 Aug. € 16.40   2007*

SANTIAGO DE COMPOSTELA *1A2* (6km E Rural) **Camping San Marcos, 15704 Santiago de Compostela (La Coruña) [981-58 79 17; fax 981-58 74 30; info@camipngsanmarcos. com; www.campingsanmarcos.com]** Exit AP9 junc 67 onto A54 sp Aeropuerto. Exit junc 716 sp San Marcos, turn L in vill. After 800m turn R at sp Rotonda/TV Galicia, site sp in 500m. Or fr Santiago on N634 go thro San Marcos & 250m after vill turn R, sp Bando & site. Sm, pt shd; wc; chem disp; shwrs inc; el pnts (6-10A) €4.28; lndtte; shop; rest; snacks; bar; playgrnd; pool; TV rm; no statics; no dogs; phone; bus 800m; quiet; CCI. "Lovely, grassy site; excel san facs; gd touring base; unreliable opening dates low ssn." 1 Apr-31 Oct. € 18.80
                                                2007*

SANTILLANA DEL MAR *1A4* (3km E Rural) **Camping Altamira, Barrio Las Quintas s/n, 39314 Queveda (Cantabria) [942-84 01 81; fax 942-26 01 55; altamiracamping@yahoo.es; www. campingaltamira.com]** Clear sp to Santillana fr A67; site on R 3km bef vill. Med, mkd pitch, pt sl, terr, unshd; wc; shwrs; el pnts (3A) €3 (poss rev pol); gas; lndtte; sm shop; rest; bar; pool; sand beach 8km; horseriding; TV rm; 30% statics; bus 100m; poss cr; Eng spkn; adv bkg ess high ssn; cc acc in ssn; CCI. "Ltd facs low ssn; nr Altimira cave paintings; easy access Santander ferry on m'way; open w/e only Nov-Mar - rec phone ahead; excel." Easter-10 Nov. € 18.20   2006*

> As soon as we get home I'm going to post all these site report forms to the editor for inclusion in next year's guide. I don't want to miss the September deadline.

⊞SANTILLANA DEL MAR *1A4* (500m W Rural) **Camping Santillana del Mar, Ctra de Comillas s/n, 39330 Santillana del Mar (Cantabria) [942-81 82 50; fax 942-84 01 83; complejosantillana@cantabria.com; www. cantabria.com/complejosantillana]** Exit A8 junc 230 Santillana-Comillas, then foll sp Santillana & site on rd CA131. Lge, sl, terr, pt shd; htd wc; chem disp (wc); mv service pnt; baby facs; shwrs inc; el pnts (5A) €4; gas; lndtte; shop high ssn; rest; snacks; bar; playgrnd; pool & paddling pool; beach 5km; tennis; cycle hire; horseriding; golf 15km; entmnt; internet; car wash; cash machine; 20% statics; dogs; bus 300m; phone; poss cr; Eng spkn; some rd noise; CCI. "Gd facs but ltd low ssn - poss diff access to fresh water & grey water disposal; take care poss v hot shwrs; care needed to some pitches due narr, winding access rds; not rec after dark as movement restricted for turning & diff lge o'fits; poss muddy/v wet grass low ssn; poss itinerants; gd views; conv ferry & Altimira caves; vg." ♦ ltd. € 31.30 (CChq acc)   2007*

SANXENXO *1B2* (2km E Coastal) **Camping Airiños do Mar, Playa de Areas, O Grove, 36960 Sanxenxo (Pontevedra) [tel/fax 986-72 31 54]** Fr Pontevedra take P0308 W twd Sanxenxo & O Grove. Turn L at km junc 65; site sp on S side of rd. Access rd needs care in negotiation. Sm, mkd pitch, pt shd; wc; shwrs inc; el pnts (16A) €2.70; gas; lndtte; shop; rest; bar; beach adj; poss cr; Eng spkn; adv bkg; quiet. "Not suitable for m'vans over 2.5m high; c'vans over 6m long may need help of staff at ent; bar & rest overlook beach; lovely views; indiv pitches approx 6m wide." 1 Jun-30 Sep. € 18.20   2004*

Spain

*Last year of report

SANXENXO *1B2* (3km W Coastal) **Camping Paxariñas, Ctra C550, Km 2.3 Lanzada-Portonovo, 36960 Sanxenxo (Pontevedra) [tel/fax 986-72 30 55 or 986-69 07 49; info@ campingpaxarinas.com; www.sanxenxotur.com/paxarinas]** Fr Pontevedra W on P0308; 3km after Sanxenxo on coast rd. Site thro hotel on L at bend. Site poorly sp. Fr AP9 fr N exit junc 119 onto VRG41 & exit for Sanxenxo. Turn R at 3rd rndabt for Portonovo to site - do not ent Portonovo. Lge, mkd pitch, pt sl, terr, shd; wc (some cont); chem disp; mv service pnt; serviced pitches; baby facs; shwrs inc; el pnts (5A) €3.50; gas; lndtte; ice; shop & 2km; tradsmn; rest; snacks; bar; playgrnd; sand beach adj; TV; 40% statics; dogs; phone; Eng spkn; adv bkg; quiet; red long stay/CCI. "Vg site in development area; excel san facs; secluded beaches in area; views over estuary; take care high kerbs on pitches; v ltd facs low ssn & poss clsd." ♦ Easter-15 Oct. € 22.70   2007*

> This guide relies on site report forms submitted by caravanners like us; we'll do our bit and tell the editor what we think of the campsites we've visited.

SANXENXO *1B2* (4km W Rural/Coastal) **Camping Suavila, Playa de Montalvo 76-77, 36970 Portonovo (Pontevedra) [tel/fax 986-72 37 60; suavila@terra.es; www.suavila.com]** Fr Sanxenxo take P0308 W; at km 57.5 site sp on L. Med, mkd pitch, shd; wc; serviced pitches; baby facs; shwrs inc; el pnts (6A) €3.20; gas; lndtte; shop; tradsmn; rest; snacks; bar; BBQ; playgrnd; sand beach; TV rm; phone; adv bkg; cc acc; red long stay; quiet; CCI. "Warm welcome; v friendly owner; sm pitches in 1 part of site." ♦ ltd. Holy Week-30 Sep. € 16.05   2004*

⊞SANXENXO *1B2* (3km NW Coastal) **Camping Monte Cabo, Soutullo 174, 36990 Noalla (Pontevedra) [tel/fax 986-74 41 41; info@ montecabo.com; www.montecabo.com]** Fr AP9 exit junc 119 onto upgraded VRG4.1 dir Sanxenxo. Ignore sp for Sanxenxo until rndabt sp A Toxa/La Toja, where turn L onto P308. Cont to Fontenla supmkt on R - minor rd to site just bef supmkt. Rd P308 fr AP9 junc 129 best avoided. Sm, mkd pitch, terr, pt shd; wc; chem disp; shwrs inc; el pnts €3.40; lndtte; ice; shop & 500m; tradsmn; rest; snacks; bar; playgrnd; sand beach 250m; TV; 10% statics; phone; bus 700m; poss cr; Eng spkn; adv bkg; quiet; cc acc; red long stay/low ssn; CCI. "Peaceful, friendly site set above sm beach (access via steep path); beautiful coastline & interesting historical sites; vg." € 16.05   2007*

SAVINAN see Calatayud *3C1*

⊞SAX *4F2* (6km NW Rural) **Camping Gwen & Michael, Colonia de Santa Eulalia 1, 03630 Sax (Alicante) [965-47 44 19]** 700m fr km 191 on A31. Sm, hdg pitch, hdstg, unshd; wc; chem disp; fam bthrm; shwrs inc; el pnts (3A) €1; lndtte; no statics; dogs; quiet. "Vg CL-type site; friendly British owners; interesting town; gd NH." € 12.50   2007*

SEGOVIA *1C4* (2km SE Urban) **Camping El Acueducto, Avda Don Juan de Borbón 49, 40004 Segovia [tel/fax 921-42 50 00; campingsg@ navegalia.com; www.campingacueducto.com]** Turn off Segovia by-pass at La Granja exit, but head twd Segovia. Site in approx 500m off dual c'way just bef Restaurante Lago. If coming fr Madrid via N603 turn L twd Segovia onto N601 fr La Granja. Lge, mkd pitch, pt sl, pt shd; wc; chem disp; mv service pnt; shwrs inc; el pnts (10A) €4; gas; lndtte; sm shop; mkt 1km; rest adj; bar; BBQ; playgrnd; pool & paddling pool high ssn; cycle hire; dogs; phone; bus 150m; poss cr; m'way noise; CCI. "Excel; v helpful staff; lovely views; v clean facs; gates locked 0000-0800; city a 'must' to visit; gd bus service; some pitches sm & diff for lge o'fits." ♦ ltd. 1 Apr-30 Sep. € 20.50   2006*

SENEGUE see Sabiñánigo *3B2*

⊞**SEO DE URGEL** *3B3* (8km N Rural) **Camping Frontera, Ctra de Andorra, Km 8, 25799 La Farga de Moles (Lleida) [973-35 14 27; fax 973-35 33 40; info@fronterapark.com; www.fronterapark.com]** Sp on N145 about 300m fr Spanish Customs sheds. Access poss diff. Lge, mkd pitch, hdstg, pt sl, pt shd; htd wc; chem disp; mv service pnt; shwrs inc; el pnts (3-6A) €5; gas; Indtte; hypmkt 2km; tradsmn; rest; snacks; bar; playgrnd; 2 pools; rv sw; internet; child entmnt; TV rm; 12% statics; dogs; phone; car wash; poss cr; adv bkg; noisy; CCI. "Ideal for shopping in Andorra; winter skiing; beautiful situation but poss dusty; v helpful owners." ♦ € 20.00 (CChq acc)   2006*

⊞**SEO DE URGEL** *3B3* (3km SW Urban) **Camping Gran Sol, 25711 Montferrer (Lleida) [tel/fax 973-35 13 32; campgransol@jazzfree.com]** S fr Seo de Urgel on N260/C1313 twds Lerida/Lleida. Site approx 3km on L fr town. Med, pt shd; wc; chem disp (wc); shwrs inc; el pnts (2-6A) €3.90; gas; Indtte; ice; shop; rest; playgrnd; pool; dogs €3.10; bus 100m; some Eng spkn; adv bkg; some rd noise; CCI. "Gd site & facs (poss stretched if full); conv for Andorra; beautiful vills & mountain scenery; in low ssn phone to check site open; gd NH." ♦ € 19.20
                                                                        2006*

SEO DE URGEL *3B3* (9km W Rural) **Camping Buchaca, Ctra St Joan de l'Erm, 25712 Castellbò (Lleida) [973-35 21 55]** Leave Seo de Urgel on N260/1313 twd Lerida. In approx 3km turn N sp Castellbò. Site on L, well sp. Sm, mkd pitch, pt sl, pt shd; wc; chem disp (wc); shwrs inc; el pnts (5A) €5; Indtte; shop; snacks; playgrnd; pool; dogs €3.45; phone; poss cr; adv bkg; quiet. "CL-type site in beautiful surroundings; v friendly recep; poss diff access lge o'fits." 1 May-30 Sep. € 20.00
                                                                        2007*

SEVILLA See sites listed under Dos Hermanas and Alcalá de Guadaíra

SIGUES *3B1* (4km S Rural) **Camp Municipal Mar del Pirineo, Ctra Pamplona-Jaca, Km 337, Tiermas, 50682 Sigüés [948-39 80 74; fax 948-88 71 77]** On N240 approx 55km E of Pamplona by Yesa reservoir, site sp. Med, pt shd; wc; chem disp; shwrs €0.60; el pnts; gas; Indtte; shop; rest; snacks; bar; shop; beach/lake adj; watersports; 50% statics; poss cr; some noise; cc not acc; CCI. "Rec inspect pitch on foot bef booking; NH only." Holy Week & 13 Apr-29 Sep. € 15.00   2004*

⊞**SITGES** *3C3* (2km SW Urban/Coastal) **Camping El Garrofer, Ctra C246a, Km 39, 08870 Sitges (Barcelona) [938-94 17 80; fax 938-11 06 23; info@garroferpark.com; www.garroferpark.com]** Fr AP7 exit junc 29 dir Sitges. Thro Sitges twd Tarragona, site 1km on L, sp. V lge, hdg/mkd pitch, hdstg, pt shd; htd wc; chem disp; mv service pnt; baby facs; shwrs inc; serviced pitches; el pnts (5-16A) €3.20 (poss rev pol); gas; Indtte; ice; shop; rest; snacks; bar; playgrnd; pool; shgl beach 900m; windsurfing; tennis 800m; horseriding; cycle hire; sports ground; car wash; entmnt; internet; TV; 10% statics; dogs €3.25; phone; bus 300m (to Barcelona); recep open 0800-2100; site clsd 19 Dec-24 Jan to tourers; poss cr; Eng spkn; adv bkg; cc acc; red snr citizen/low ssn; CCI. "Gd location, conv Barcelona; sep area for m'vans with water & drainage." ♦ € 31.77   2007*

See advertisement

SITGES *3C3* (2km SW Urban/Coastal) **Camping Sitges, Ctra C31, Km 38, 08870 Sitges (Barcelona) [938-94 10 80; fax 938-94 98 52; info@campingsitges.com; www.campingsitges. com]** Fr A7/E15 exit junc 28 or 29 dir Sitges. Thro Sitges & under rlwy arch, then turn R twd Vilanova/ Tarragona. Site on L immed after x-ing rlwy bdges. Lge, mkd pitch, hdstg, pt shd; wc; chem disp; baby facs; shwrs inc; el pnts (6A) €4; gas; Indry rm; ice; shop; rest; snacks; bar; BBQ; playgrnd; pool high ssn; sand beach 800m; 30% statics; dogs; phone; bus to Barcelona; train 1.5km; poss cr; Eng spkn; quiet but some rlwy noise; cc acc; red CCI. "Friendly staff; excel, spotless san facs; well-maintained, clean site but poss dusty; some pitches not suitable lge o'fits; m'vans with trailers not acc; gd pool & shop; rec arr early as v popular." ♦ 1 Mar-20 Oct. € 22.00   2007*

⊞**SOLSONA** *3B3* (2km N Rural) **Camping El Solsonès, Ctra St Llorenç, Km 2, 25280 Solsona (Lleida) [973-48 28 61; fax 973-48 13 00; info@ campingsolsones.com; www.campingsolsones. com]** Fr Solsona to St Llorenç site on R in 2km well sp. Ignore new rd sp St Llorenç. Lge, mkd pitch, pt sl, pt shd; wc; chem disp; shwrs; el pnts (4-10A) €3.65-6.75; Indtte; shops & 2km; snacks; pool; 25% statics; no dogs; poss cr w/e; quiet off peak; cc acc; red CCI. "V helpful staff; v restful." € 21.60
                                                                        2007*

SOMO see Santander *1A4*

SOPELANA see Bilbao *1A4*

Spain

SORIA *3C1* (2km S Rural) **Camping Fuente de la Teja, Ctra Madrid-Soria, Km 223, 42004 Soria [tel/fax 975-22 29 67; www.fuentedelateja.com]** Fr N on N111 (Soria by-pass) 2km S of junc with N122 (500m S of Km 223) take exit for Quintana Redondo, site sp. Fr Soria on NIII dir Madrid sp just past km 223. V tight RH turn onto site app rd; poss diff lge o'fits - rough track cuts off sharp corner. Fr S on N111 site sp fr 2 exits. Med, mkd pitch, pt sl, pt shd; wc; chem disp; baby facs; shwrs inc; el pnts (6A) €2.46 (poss no earth); gas; lndtte; hypmkt 3km; tradsmn; rest; snacks; bar; playgrnd; pool high ssn; TV rm; many statics; dogs; bus 500m; phone; poss cr; adv bkg; some rd noise; cc acc; CCI. "Excel, busy NH bet France & Spain; vg refurbed san facs; interesting town, superb historical churches; phone ahead to check site open if travelling bet 1 Oct & Easter." ♦ ltd. Easter-30 Sep. € 21.76   2007*

⊞**SORT** *3B2* (200m N Rural) **Camping Noguera Pallaresa, Ctra Balaguer-Francia, Km 110, 25560 Sort (Lleida) [973-62 08 20; fax 973-62 12 04; info@noguera-pallaresa.com; www.noguera-pallaresa.com]** Leave C13 at km 110.9, site sp. Lge, pt sl, pt shd; wc; shwrs; el pnts (6A) €4.60; gas; lndtte; shop; rest; snacks; bar; playgrnd; pool; paddling pool; white watersports; games area; phone; quiet. "Popular canoeing resort close to Aigües Tortes National Park; exit via steep rough rd, may be diff for low power ratio o'fits; vg." ♦ € 18.40
2005*

SOTO DEL REAL see Manzanares el Real *1D4*

⊞**SUECA** *4E2* (5km NE Coastal) **Camping Les Barraquetes, Playa de Sueca, Mareny Barraquetes, 46410 Sueca (València) [961-76 07 23; fax 963-20 93 63; info@barraquetes.com; www.barraquetes.com]** Exit AP7 junc 58 dir Sueca onto N332. In Sueca take CV500 to Mareny Barraquetes. Or S fr València on CV500 coast rd. Foll sp for Cullera & Sueca. Site on L. Lge, mkd pitch, shd; wc; chem disp; mv service pnt; baby facs; shwrs inc; el pnts (10A) €5; gas; lndtte; ice; shop; bar; BBQ; playgrnd; pool; paddling pool; waterslide; sand beach 350m; windsurfing school; tennis; games area; entmnt; child entmnt; TV rm; 5% statics; dogs €3; phone; bus 500m; poss cr; Eng spkn; cc acc; red low ssn/long stay/snr citizens; CCI. "Quiet, family atmosphere; conv touring base & València." ♦ € 30.00   2006*

⊞**SUECA** *4E2* (6km SE Coastal) **Camping Santa Marta, Ctra Cullera-Faro, Km 2, Playa del Raço, 46400 Cullera (València) [961-72 14 40; fax 961-73 08 20; info@santamartacamping.com; www.santamartacamping.com]** On N332 ent Cullera & foll sp. Turn up steep lane beside bullring (white building). Lge, terr, pt sl, shd; wc; chem disp; baby facs; shwrs; el pnts (10A) €5.50; lndtte; shop; tradsmn; rest; bar; no BBQ; playgrnd; pool; sand beach 100m; windsurfing school; cycle hire; entmnt; 5% statics; dogs €4; phone; site clsd mid-Dec to mid-Jan; Eng spkn; quiet; cc acc; red long stay; CCI. "Pleasant site amongst pine trees; pitching poss diff on steep terrs; beach across busy rd; vg." ♦ € 26.50   2007*

⊞**TABERNAS** *4G1* (8km E Rural) **Camping Oro Verde, Piezas de Algarra s/n, 04200 Tabernas (Almería) [687-62 99 96 or 01434 320495 (UK); info@romanwallcamping.co.uk; www.oroverde.co.uk]** Fr N340A turn S onto ALP112 sp Turrillas. Turn R in 100m into narr tarmac lane bet villas, site on L in 600m. Sm, pt shd; wc; chem disp; shwrs inc; el pnts (6-10A) inc (poss long lead req); gas; lndtte; ice; shop 1km; rest, bar nrby in hotel; BBQ; pool; sand beach 40km; dogs; adv bkg; quiet; red long stay; CCI. "In sm olive grove; beautiful views; pitches muddy in wet; basic san facs; friendly British owners; 'Mini-Hollywood' 7km where many Westerns filmed; conv Sorbas & Guadix caves; excel." ♦ € 14.00   2007*

TALARN see Tremp *3B2*

TAMARIT see Tarragona *3C3*

TAMARIU see Palafrugell *3B3*

⊞**TAPIA DE CASARIEGO** *1A3* (2km W Rural) **Camping El Carbayin, La Penela-Serantes, 33740 Tapia de Casariego (Asturias) [tel/fax 985-62 37 09]** Foll N634/E70 E fr Ribadeo for 2km to Serantes. Site on R 400m fr rd, well sp. Sm, mkd pitch, pt sl, pt shd; wc; chem disp; baby facs; shwrs inc; el pnts (3A) €3; lndtte; shop; rest; bar; playgrnd; sand beach 1km; fishing; watersports; some statics; bus 400m; phone; adv bkg; quiet; cc acc; CCI. "Gd for coastal walks & trips to mountains; excel." ♦ € 16.50   2007*

TAPIA DE CASARIEGO *1A3* (3km W Coastal) **Camping Playa de Tapia, La Reburdia, 33740 Tapia de Casariego (Asturias) [985-47 27 21]** N634 fr Navia twd W go past 2 exits sp Tapia de Casariego; then 500m on R foll sp over x-rd to site on L. Med, hdg/mkd pitch, pt sl, pt shd; wc; chem disp; shwrs inc; el pnts (16A) inc; gas; lndtte; shop; rest; bar; sand beach 500m; bus 800m; phone; Eng spkn; adv bkg; quiet; CCI. "Gd access; well-maintained, friendly site; harbour & coastal views; walking dist to town." ♦ Holy Week & 1 Jun-15 Sep. € 18.30   2004*

TARAZONA *3B1* (8km SE Rural) **Camping Veruela Moncayo**, Ctra Vera-Veruela, 50580 Vera de Moncayo (Zaragoza) [976-64 91 54; fax 976-56 87 88] Fr Zaragoza, take AP68 or N232 twd Tudela/Logroño; after approx. 50km, turn L to join N122 (km stone 75) twd Tarazona; cont 30km & turn L twd Vera de Moncayo; go thro town cent; site on R; well sp. Lge, hdg pitch, pt sl, unshd; wc; shwrs inc; el pnts inc; gas; rest, snacks, bar & shop 300m; playgrnd adj; pool 500m; cycle hire; dogs; open w/e in winter; adv bkg; CCI. "Quiet site adj monastery; poss problem with elect at peak times; neglected; san facs in portakabins; gd birdwatching; NH only." ◆ ltd. Holy Week & 15 Jun-15 Oct. € 14.50

2005*

⊞**TARIFA** *2H3* (11km W Coastal) **Camping El Jardín de las Dunas**, Ctra N340, Km 74, Punta Paloma, 11380 Tarifa (Cádiz) [956-68 91 01; fax 956-69 91 06; recepcion@campingjdunas.com; www.campingjdunas.com] W on N340 fr Tarifa, L at sp Punta Paloma. Turn L 300m after Camping Paloma, site in 500m. Lge, hdg pitch, pt shd; wc; chem disp; serviced pitches; baby facs; shwrs inc; el pnts (6A) €3.37; lndtte; shop; rest; snacks; bar; playgrnd; beach 50m; entmnt; TV rm; no dogs; phone; noisy; cc acc; red low ssn. "Poss strong winds; unsuitable lge o'fits due tight turns & trees." ◆ € 28.20

2005*

⊞**TARIFA** *2H3* (3km NW Coastal) **Camping Rió Jara**, 11380 Tarifa (Cádiz) [tel/fax 956-68 05 70; campingriojara@terra.es] Site on S of N340 Cádiz-Algeciras rd at km post 81.2; 3km after Tarifa; clearly visible & sp. Med, mkd pitch, pt shd; wc (some cont); chem disp; mv service pnt; shwrs inc; el pnts (10A) €3; gas; lndtte; ice; shop; tradsmn; rest; snacks; bar; playgrnd; sand beach 200m; fishing; dogs; poss cr; adv bkg; rd noise; cc acc; CCI. "Clean, well-kept site; friendly recep; long, narr pitches diff for awnings; daily trips to N Africa; gd windsurfing nrby; poss strong winds; mosquitoes in summer." ◆ € 22.00

2005*

⊞**TARIFA** *2H3* (6km NW Coastal) **Camping Tarifa, N340, Km 78.87, Los Lances**, 11380 Tarifa (Cádiz) [tel/fax 956-68 47 78; camping-tarifa@camping-tarifa.com; www.camping-tarifa.com] Site on R of Cádiz-Málaga rd N340. Med, mkd pitch, hdstg, shd; wc; chem disp; mv service pnt; serviced pitch; baby facs; shwrs inc; el pnts (5A) €3.35; gas; lndtte; shop; rest; snacks; bar; playgrnd; pool; sand beach adj; no dogs; phone; car wash; Eng spkn; adv bkg; quiet; red long stay & low ssn; cc acc. "Vg; ideal for windsurfing; immed access to beach; lovely site with beautiful pool; v secure - fenced & locked at night; some pitches sm & poss diff access due bends, trees & kerbs; conv ferry to Morocco; poss strong winds." ◆ € 19.00 (CChq acc)

2006*

⊞**TARIFA** *2H3* (7km NW Coastal) **Camping Torre de la Peña 1**, Ctra Cádiz, 11380 Tarifa (Cádiz) [956-68 49 03; fax 956-68 14 73; informacion@campingtp.com; www.campingtp.com] Site at km 79 on both sides of N340, sp. Steep access fr fast main rd. Lge, terr, pt sl, pt shd; wc; shwrs; el pnts (5A) inc; gas; lndtte; shop; rest; bar; pool; sand beach adj (via tunnel under rd); dogs €2.50; few statics; poss cr; adv bkg; quiet; red long stay & low ssn. "Excel; upper level poss diff lge o'fits; helpful staff; superb views to Africa; conv for Gibraltar & Tangiers; poss strong winds." € 17.00

2006*

⊞**TARIFA** *2H3* (9km NW Coastal) **Camping Torre de la Peña II**, Ctra N340, Km 75.5, 11380 Tarifa (Cádiz) [956-68 41 74; fax 956-68 18 98; info@campingtp.com] Site on N340 at km 75.5, sp. Med, pt shd; wc; shwrs; el pnts (5A) €3; lndtte; shop; rest; bar; playgrnd; pool; sand beach 400m; tennis; adv bkg; quiet; cc acc. € 17.10

2004*

⊞**TARIFA** *2H3* (11km NW Coastal) **Camping Paloma**, Ctra Cádiz-Málaga, Km 74, Punta Paloma, 11380 Tarifa (Cádiz) [956-68 42 03; fax 956-68 18 80; info@campingpaloma.com; www.campingpaloma.com] Fr Tarifa on N340, site on L at 74km stone sp Punta Paloma, site on R. Lge, mkd pitch, hdstg, pt sl, terr, pt shd; wc (some cont); chem disp; mv service pnt; shwrs inc; el pnts (6A) €2.75; gas; lndtte; shop; rest; snacks; bar; playgrnd; pool high ssn; sand beach 1km; waterspsorts; windsurfing; horseriding; cycle hire; 20% statics; poss cr; Eng spkn; no adv bkg; quiet; cc acc; red long stay/low ssn; CCI. "Well-run site; vg facs; ideal for peace & quiet away fr busy rds; lge o'fits poss diff due low tree; trips to N Africa & whale-watching arranged; gd mountain views." ◆ ltd. € 22.80

2005*

TARRAGONA *3C3* (4km NE Coastal) **Camping Las Salinas**, Ctra N340, Km 1168, Playa Larga, 43007 Tarragona [977-20 76 28] Access via N340 bet km 1167 & 1168. Med, shd; wc; shwrs; el pnts €3.74; gas; lndtte; shop; snacks; bar; beach adj; some statics; bus 200m; poss cr; rlwy noise. Holy Week & 15 May-30 Sep. € 29.20

2007*

TARRAGONA *3C3* (5km NE Coastal) **Camping Las Palmeras, N340, Km 1168**, 43080 Tarragona [977-20 80 81; fax 977-20 78 17; laspalmeras@laspalmeras.com; www.laspalmeras.com] Exit AP7 at junc 32 (sp Altafulla). After about 5km on N340 twd Tarragona take sp L turn at crest of hill. Site sp. V lge, mkd pitch, shd; wc; chem disp; shwrs inc; el pnts (3-5A) inc; gas; lndtte; ice; shop; rest; snacks; bar; playgrnd; pool; sand beach adj; naturist beach 1km; tennis; games area; some statics; dogs €3; phone; poss cr; rlwy noise; cc acc; red long stay/low ssn; CCI. "Gd beach, ideal for families; poss mosquito prob; many sporting facs; friendly, helpful staff." ◆ 1 Apr-12 Oct. € 35.00 (CChq acc)

2006*

TARRAGONA *3C3* (7km NE Coastal) **Camping Torre de la Mora, Ctra N340, Km 1171, 43080 Tarragona-Tamarit [977-65 02 77; fax 977-65 28 58; info@torredelamora.com; www. torredelamora.com]** Fr AP7 exit junc 32 (sp Altafulla), at rndabt take La Mora rd. Then foll site sp. After approx 1km turn R, L at T-junc, site on R. Lge, hdstg, terr, pt shd; wc; chem disp; mv service pnt; baby facs; shwrs inc; el pnts (6A) €3.50; gas; lndtte; ice; shop & 1km; tradsmn; rest; snacks; bar; playgrnd; pool; sand beach adj; tennis; sports club adj; golf 2km; entmnt; internet; 50% statics; dogs €2.50; bus 200m; Eng spkn; adv bkg; quiet away fr rd & rlwy; cc acc; red long stay; CCI. "Improved, clean site set in attractive bay with fine beach; excel pool; conv Tarragona & Port Aventura; sports club adj; various pitch sizes, some v sm; private bthrms avail." ♦ 26 Mar-31 Oct. € 35.50   2007*

TARRAGONA *3C3* (7km NE Coastal) **Camping-Caravaning Tamarit Park, Playa Tamarit, Ctra N340, Km 1172, 43008 Playa Tamarit (Tarragona) [977-65 01 28; fax 977-65 04 51; tamaritpark@ tamarit.com; www.tamarit.com]** Fr A7/E15 exit junc 32 sp Altafulla/Torredembarra, at rndabt join N340 by-pass sp Tarragona. At rndabt foll sp Altafulla, turn sharp R to cross rlwy bdge to site in 1.2km, sp. V lge, hdg pitch, some hdstg, pt sl, shd; htd wc; chem disp; mv service pnt; serviced pitches; baby facs; fam bthrm; private bthrms avail; shwrs inc; el pnts (10A) inc; gas; lndtte; ice; supmkt; rest; snacks; bar; BBQ; playgrnd; htd pool; paddling pool; sand/shgl beach adj; watersports; tennis; games area; entmnt; internet; TV; 30% statics; dogs €3; phone; cash machine; car wash; adv bkg (rec Jul/Aug); Eng spkn; cc acc; red long stay/ snr citizens/low ssn; CCI. "Superb pool; well-maintained site; gets better & better; best site in area due to excel facs but poss noisy at night & w/e; variable pitch prices; beachside pitches avail; take care overhanging trees; excel." ♦ ltd. 30 Mar-14 Oct. € 51.36   2007*

TAULL see Pont de Suert *3B2*

TIEMBLO, EL *1D4* (8km W Rural) **Camping Valle de Iruelas, Las Cruceras, 05110 Barraco (Ávila) [920-28 72 50; fax 918-62 53 95; iruelas@ valledeiruelas.com; www.valledeiruelas.com]** Fr N403 turn off at sp Reserva Natural Valle de Iruelas. After x-ing dam foll sp Las Cruceras & camping. In 5km foll sp La Rinconada, site in 1km. Med, hdg/mkd pitch, terr, shd; wc; chem disp; baby facs; shwrs inc; el pnts inc; lndtte; supmkt; rest; bar; playgrnd; pool; canoeing; horseriding; bird hide; quiet; CCI. "Pleasant, woodland site with wildlife." ♦ Easter, 1 Jul-31 Aug & w/e 1 May-30 Jun. € 30.00   2006*

⊞**TOLEDO** *1D4* (2km W Rural) **Camping El Greco, Ctra CM-4000, Km.97, 45004 Toledo [tel/ fax 925-22 00 90; elgreco@retemail.es; www. campingelgreco.ya.st]** Site on CM4000 fr Toledo dir La Puebla de Montalbán & Talavera. When app, avoid town cent, keep to N outside of old town & watch for camping sp. Or use outer ring rd. Med, hdg/mkd pitch, pt sl, shd; htd wc; chem disp; mv service pnt; shwrs inc; el pnts (6A) €3.95 (poss rev pol); gas; lndtte; shop; tradsmn; bar; BBQ; playgrnd; pool; paddling pool; games area; dogs; bus to town; phone; Eng spkn; cc acc; CCI. "V clean & tidy; all pitches on gravel; gd rest; reg bus into town useful due to narr streets but easy parking on o'skts - adj Puerta de San Martín rec; some pitches poss tight; excel san facs but could be cleaner - stretched if site full; lovely situation, superb views; friendly, helpful owners; excel info on site; lge supermkt in town off Avda de Europa, 20 min walk into town." € 22.79   2007*

TORDESILLAS *1C3* (1km SW Urban) **Camping El Astral, Camino de Pollos 8, 47100 Tordesillas (Valladolid) [tel/fax 983-77 09 53; info@ campingelastral.com; www.campingelastral. com]** Fr NE on A62/E80 thro town turn L at rndabt over rv & immed after bdge turn R dir Salamanca & R again past Hostel Lorenzo & foll rd for 500m to ent to site; foll camping sp & Parador. Poorly sp. Fr A6 exit sp Tordesillas & take A62. Cross bdge out of town & foll site sp. Med, hdg/mkd pitch, hdstg, pt shd; wc; chem disp; mv service pnt; baby facs; shwrs inc; el pnts (5A) €3.50 (rev pol); gas; lndtte; shop; supmkt in town; tradsmn; rest; snacks; bar; playgrnd; pool in ssn; fishing; tennis; cycle hire; excursions; TV rm; 10% statics; dogs €2.35; phone; site open w/end Mar & Oct; Eng spkn; quiet, but some traff noise; cc acc; CCI. "Helpful owners; easy walk to interesting town; v nice site by rv; excel, poss tired facs." ♦ 31 Mar-30 Sep. € 23.00 (CChq acc)   2007*

TORLA see Broto *3B2*

⊞**TORRE DEL MAR** *2H4* (1km SW Coastal) **Camping Torre del Mar, Paseo Maritimo s/n, 29740 Torre del Mar (Málaga) [952-54 02 24; fax 952-54 04 31]** Clearly sp fr N340A at W end of town. Site on beach rd past lighthouse 200m E fr Mercadona supmkt. Lge, hdg/mkd pitch, hdstg, shd; wc; chem disp; mv service pnt; serviced pitches; shwrs inc; el pnts (10A) €2.30; gas; lndtte; shop & 500m; rest; snacks; bar in ssn; playgrnd; pool & paddling pool; sandy/shgl beach 50m; sat TV; tennis; few statics; no dogs; phone; poss cr all year; quiet but noise fr adj football pitch; red low ssn/long stay; CCI. "Tidy, clean, friendly, well-run site; sm pitches; gd san facs; popular low ssn." ♦ € 27.10   2005*

⊞**TORRE DEL MAR** *2H4* (1km W Coastal) **Camping Laguna Playa, Prolongación Paseo Maritimo s/n, 29740 Torre del Mar (Málaga) [952-54 06 31; fax 952-54 04 84; info@lagunaplaya.com; www. lagunaplaya.com]** Clearly sp fr N340A nr W end of town. Sp to site 400m along track past ent Camping Torre del Mar. Med, pt shd; wc; chem disp; mv service pnt; shwrs inc; el pnts (5-10A) €3.50; gas; lndtte; ice; shop; rest; snacks; bar; playgrnd; pool; sand beach 1km; 40% statics; dogs; poss cr; Eng spkn; adv bkg; quiet; red low ssn. "Popular low ssn; sm pitches; excel, clean san facs; gd location, easy walk to town." € 19.00   2007*

⊞**TORRE DEL MAR** *2H4* (2km W Coastal) **Camping Naturista Almanat (Naturist), Ctra de la Torre Alta, Km 269, 29749 Almayate (Málaga) [952-55 64 62; fax 952-55 62 71; director@almanat. de; www.almanat.de]** Exit E15/N340 junc 274 sp Vélez Málaga for Torre del Mar. Exit Torre del Mar on coast rd sp Málaga. In 2km bef lge black bull on R on hill & bef water tower turn L at sp. If rd not clear cont to next turning point & return in dir Torre del Mar & turn R to site at km 269. Site well sp. Lge, hdg/mkd pitch, hdstg (gravel), pt shd; htd wc; chem disp; mv service pnt (on request); sauna; shwrs inc; el pnts (10-16A) €3.50; gas; lndtte; ice; shop; rest; bar; BBQ; playgrnd; pool; jacuzzi; sand/shgl beach adj; tennis; entmnt; cinema; games area; gym; golf 10km; some statics; dogs €2.70; phone; bus 500m; poss cr; Eng spkn; adv bkg (dep req); quiet; cc acc; red long stay/low ssn/snr citizens up to 50%; INF card. "Superb facs; v popular; highly rec; reasonable dist Seville, Granada, Córdoba; easy walk/cycle to town; excel." ♦ € 20.00 (CChq acc)   2007*

TORRE DEL MAR *2H4* (3km W Coastal) **Camping Almayate Costa, Ctra N340, Km 267, 29749 Almayate Bajo (Málaga) [952-55 62 89; fax 952-55 63 10; almayatecosta@campings.net; www. campings.net/almayatecosta]** E fr Málaga on N340/E15 coast rd. Exit junc 258 dir Almería, site on R 3km bef Torre del Mar. Easy access. Lge, mkd pitch, hdstg, shd; wc; chem disp; mv service pnt; shwrs inc; el pnts (10A) inc; gas; lndtte; ice; supmkt; bar; BBQ; playgrnd; pool & paddling pool; sand beach adj; games rm; golf 7km; no dogs; car wash; phone; Eng spkn; adv bkg; quiet but some rd noise; cc acc; red long stay/low ssn; CCI. "Helpful manager; pitches nr beach tight for lge o'fits & access rds poss diff; vg resort." ♦ Easter-15 Oct. € 45.00 (4 persons)   2007*

⊞**TORREBLANCA** *3D2* (3km SE Coastal) **Camping Mon Rossi, Carrasa Mon Rossi, 12596 Torreblanca (Castellón) [964-42 50 96; fax 964-42 11 47; campingmonrossi@hotmail.com]** Exit A7 junc 44 & turn R to cross N340 & foll narr rd over rlwy bdge to Torrenostra, site on R in approx 3km, 150m bef beach. N'bound on N340 turn R immed bef access rd to A7; s'bound turn onto A7 access rd & immed L to cross N340. Med, hdg pitch, hdstg, pt shd; wc; chem disp; shwrs inc; el pnts €3; gas; lndtte; shop; tradsmn; snacks; bar; pool; shgl beach adj; cycle hire; TV; 10% statics; phone; poss cr; adv bkg; quiet; cc acc. "Friendly, family-run site; only 6 pitches suitable for lge o'fits." € 17.00
                    2004*

⊞**TORREMOLINOS** *2H4* (3km NE Coastal) **Camping Torremolinos, Loma del Paraíso 2, 29620 Torremolinos (Málaga) [952-38 26 02]** Fr Málaga by-pass heading W take exit sp 'aeropuerto' & foll sp Torremolinos & site. Med, hdstg; terr, pt sl, pt shd; wc (some cont); shwrs; el pnts (5A) €2.90; gas; lndtte; shop; rest 200m; snacks; bar; sand beach 700m; golf 500m; no dogs; buses & trains nrby; no adv bkg; noise fr rd, rlwy & aircraft; red CCI. "V helpful staff; v clean site; gd san facs." € 25.60   2004*

The opening dates and prices on this campsite have changed. I'll send a site report form to the editor for the next edition of the guide.

TORREVIEJA *4F2* (4km S Urban) **Camping La Campana, Ctra Torrevieja-Cartagena, Km 4.5, 03180 Torrevieja (Alicante) [965-71 21 52]** Take N332 S fr Torrevieja. Site ent dir off rndabt for Rocío del Mar at S end of Torrevieja by-pass. Med, mkd pitch, hdstg, pt shd; wc; chem disp; shwrs; el pnts (6A) €3.20; gas; 500m; lndtte; shop; rest; snacks; bar; playgrnd; pool; shngle beach 1km; 80% statics; dogs €2.15; phone adj; bus 50m; poss cr; Eng spkn; noisy; red up to 25% low ssn; 10% red CCI. ♦ 1 Apr-30 Sep. € 24.60   2006*

Spain

el delfin verde

Wi-Fi ZONE

bungalows and apartments for hire

One of the best and most beautiful holiday sites on the COSTA BRAVA

In quiet surroundings, by a magnificent wid and miles-long sand beach and with the large fresh-water swimmingpool of the Costa Brav By the way, we also have the most generousl sized pitches of the region. Many green area and groups of trees. Commercial centre. Fres water plant. 3 bars, 2 rest., 2 grills, pizzerk 2 snackbars and beach bar. SPORTS: larg sports area for hand, volley, basket and footb and badminton. 8 tennis courts, minigolf (300 m² - 18 holes), windsurfing school. ACTIVITIE Organised 'fiestas', disco 'light', dancin Excursions, organised sports competitions a movie/video shows. 8 Modern ablution bloc with hot water everywhere, money exchang safe, medical service, tel. Paddle and half pip Ciber café. Renting of barbecues.

OPEN: 15.03-30.03 / 26.04-28.0

Apartat de correus 43 • E-17257 TORROELLA DE MONTGRI
Tel. (34) 972 758 454 • Fax (34) 972 760 070 • www.eldelfinverde.com • info@eldelfinverde.co

⊞**TORREVIEJA** *4F2* (7km SW Rural) **Camping Florantilles, Ctra San Miguel de Salinas-Torrevieja, 03193 San Miguel de Salinas (Alicante) [965-72 04 56; fax 966-72 32 50; florantilles@terra.es]** Exit AP7 junc 758 onto CV95, sp Orihuela, Torrevieja Sud. Turn R at rndabt & after 300m turn R again, site immed on L. Or if travelling on N332 S past Alicante airport twd Torrevieja leave Torrevieja by-pass at its most S exit, sp Torrevieja, San Miguel. Turn R onto CV95 & foll for 3km over 4 rndabts thro urbanisation 'Los Balcones'. After leaving Los Balcones, cont for another 500m, under by-pass, round rndabt & up hill, site sp on R. Lge, hdg/mkd, hdstg, terr, pt shd; wc; chem disp; mv service pnt; shwrs inc; el pnts (10A) inc; gas; lndtte; ice; supmkt; tradsmn; snacks; bar; BBQ; pool & paddling pool (high ssn); sand beach 5km; horseriding 10km; fitness studio; games/TVrm; 80% statics; no dogs; recep clsd 1330-1630; poss cr in winter; adv bkg; rd noise; various red; cc acc; CCI. NB: Sm number of touring pitches ONLY avail if booked through The Caravan Club, remaining pitches avail for a 12-month rental period only. "Friendly staff; British-managed; popular site; many long stay visitors & all year vans; Spanish lessons, exercise sessions & walking clubs; own transport ess." ♦ € 25.17 ABS - E11   2007*

TORROELLA DE MONTGRI *3B3* (6km SE Coastal) **Camping El Delfin Verde, Ctra Torroella de Montgrí-Palafrugell, Km 4, 17257 Torroella de Montgrí (Gerona) [972-75 84 54; fax 972-76 00 70; info@eldelfinverde.com; www.eldelfinverde.com]** Fr N leave A7 at junc 5 dir L'Escala. At Viladamat turn R onto C31 sp La Bisbal. After a few km turn L twd Torroella de Montgrí. At rndabt foll sp for Pals (also sp El Delfin Verde). At the flags turn L sp Els Mas Pinell. Foll site sp for 5km. Lge, mkd pitch, pt sl, pt shd; wc; chem disp; mv service pnt; baby facs; shwrs inc; el pnts (6A) inc; gas; lndtte; ice; supmkt; rests; snacks; 3 bars; BBQ; playgrnd; pool; sand beach adj; fishing; tennis; horseriding 4km; cycle hire; windsurfing; sportsgrnd; mini-golf; hairdresser; money exchange; child entmnt; entmnt; disco; winter storage; games rm; wifi internet; TV/video; 40% statics (sep area); no dogs 11/7-14/8, at low ssn €4; poss cr; quiet; red low ssn; cc acc; CCI. "Superb, gd value site; excel pool; all water de-salinated fr fresh water production plant; bottled water rec for drinking & cooking; mkt Mon." ♦ 15 Mar-30 Mar & 26 Apr-28 Sep. € 53.00 ABS - E01   2007*

See advertisement

TOSSA DE MAR *3B3* (500m N Coastal) **Camping Can Martí, Avda Pau Casals s/n, 17320 Tossa de Mar (Gerona) [972-34 08 51; fax 972-34 24 61]** App fr Lloret, turn L at rndabt by Bahía de Tossa Hotel; strt at next rndabt, then L at Champion supmkt, site in 300m. Fr Llagostera turn L at rndabt , then L at Champion supmkt as above. Mountain rd fr Sant Feliu not rec. V lge, mkd pitch, pt shd; wc; chem disp; baby facs; shwrs inc; el pnts (10A) inc; gas; lndtte; ice; shop; rest; snacks; bar; playgrnd; pool & paddling pool; shgl beach 500m; fishing; tennis; horseriding; 10% statics; phone; car wash; sep car park; Eng spkn; no adv bkg; quiet; red long stay/ CCI. "Security guards; helpful, friendly staff; facs v clean; boat trips." ♦ 25 May-10 Sep. € 31.00   2005*

TOSSA DE MAR *3B3* (4km NE Coastal) **Camping Pola, Ctra Tossa-Sant Feliu, Km 4, 17320 Tossa de Mar (Gerona) [972-34 10 50; fax 972-34 10 83; campingpola@arrakis.es]** Fr Tossa on rd GE682 dir Sant Feliu. Narr, winding rd but gd. Site sp. Lge, pt sl, pt shd; wc; shwrs inc; el pnts (15A) inc; gas; shop; rest; bar; gas; playgrnd; pool; paddling pool; sand beach adj; tennis; games area; entmnt; dogs €3.10; sep car park high ssn; adv bkg; cc acc. 28 May-1 Oct. € 34.00   2005*

TOSSA DE MAR *3B3* (3km SW Coastal) **Camping Cala Llevado, Ctra Tossa-Lloret, Km 3, 17320 Tossa de Mar (Gerona) [972-34 03 14; fax 972-34 11 87; info@calallevado.com; www.calallevado.com]** Exit AP7 junc 9 dir Lloret. In Lloret take GI 682 dir Tossa de Mar. Site well sp. V lge, mkd pitch, terr, shd; wc; chem disp; mv service pnt; baby facs; shwrs inc; el pnts (5-10A) €3.50; gas; lndtte; ice; supmkt; rest; snacks; bar; playgrnd; 3 pools inc paddling pool; sand/shgl beach adj; waterskiing; windsurfing; diving; fishing; boat trips; tennis; games/sports facs; child entmnt Jul/Aug; internet; TV; 10% statics; no dogs; phone; Eng spkn; adv bkg; quiet; CCI. ♦ Holy Week & 1 May-30 Sep. € 28.85   2005*

⊞**TOTANA** *4G1* (2km SW Rural) **Camping Totana, Ctra N340, Km 614, 30850 Totana (Murcia) [tel/ fax 968-42 48 64; totana@intercamping.net; www.campingtotana.com]** Fr N340/E15 exit at km 612 fr N. Fr S exit km 609. Foll Totana rd, site 2km on R. Sl ent. Sm, mkd pitch, hdstg, terr, pt shd; wc; chem disp; shwrs inc; el pnts (6A) €2; shop & 4km; rest, bar high ssn; BBQ; playgrnd; pool high ssn; games rm; entmnt; 80% statics; dogs; Eng spkn; red long stay; CCI. "Conv mountains & Sierrra Espuña National Park; access to sm pitches tight due trees; helpful owners; tidy site; communal drying in shwr area; vg NH." € 13.00   2007*

Spain

TREMP 3B2 (4km N Rural) **Camping Gaset, Ctra C13, Km 91, 25630 Talarn (Lleida) [973-65 07 37; fax 973-65 01 02; campinggaset@pallarsjussa. net; www.pallarsjussa.net/gaset/]** Fr Tremp, take C13/N260 N sp Talarn. Site clearly visible on R by lake. Lge, pt sl, terr, pt shd; wc; shwrs; el pnts (4A) €3.90; lndtte; shop; rest 4km; snacks; bar; playgrnd; pool; paddling pool; sand beach for lake sw; tennis; 15% statics; dogs; phone; poss cr; quiet; cc acc. "Picturesque setting by San Antoni lake; gd fishing & boating on lake; some sm pitches." 1 Apr-15 Oct. € 19.20   2006*

⊞**TREVELEZ** 2G4 (1km Rural) **Camping Trevélez, Ctra Órgiva-Trevélez, Km 32.5, 18417 Trevélez (Granada) [tel/fax 958-85 87 35; info@ campingtrevelez.net; www.campingtrevelez.net]** Fr Granada on A44/E902 exit junc 164 onto A348 dir Lanjarón, Pampaneira. Cont for approx 50km to Trevélez, site sp. Med, mkd pitch, terr, shd; wc (cont); chem disp; mv service pnt; shwrs inc; el pnts (9A) €2.50; gas; lndtte; ice; shop; tradsmn; rest; snacks; bar; playgrnd; pool; rv sw 1km; entmnt; few statics; dogs; phone; bus adj; poss cr; Eng spkn; adv bkg (dep req); quiet; red long stay. "Excel site; access to Mulhacén (highest mountain mainland Spain); lots of hiking." ♦ € 19.00   2006*

TURIENO see Potes 1A4

UBRIQUE 2H3 (15km N Rural) **Camping Los Linares, Calle Nacimiento s/n, 11679 Benamahoma (Cádiz) [956-71 62 75; fax 956-71 64 73; parque@campingloslinares.com; www.campingloslinares.com]** N fr Ubrique to El Bosque, turn E dir Benamahoma & Grazalema. Site well sp in vill. To avoid narr streets ent fr El Bosque end of vill. Med, mkd pitch, unshd; wc; chem disp; shwrs inc; el pnts €4.20; shop 500m; rest; snacks; bar; playgrnd; pool; some statics; bus 300m; poss cr; CCI. "Gd walking/birdwatching area in National Park; narr vill streets poss diff lge o'fits; open w/e & public hols all year." ♦ ltd. 15 Jun-15 Sep. € 21.10   2007*

UNQUERA 1A4 (3km N Coastal) **Camping Las Arenas, Ctra Unquera-Pechón, Km. 2, 39594 Pechón (Cantabria) [tel/fax 942-71 71 88; lasarenas@ctv.es]** Exit A8/E70 at km 272 sp Unquera. At rndabt foll CA380 sp Pechón, climb narr winding rd to site ent at top on L. Lge, mkd pitch, pt sl, terr, pt shd; wc; chem disp; shwrs el pnts (8A) €2.80; gas; lndtte; rest; shop & 3km; bar; playgrnd; pool; shgl beach adj; fishing; cycle hire; internet; no statics; poss cr; Eng spkn; quiet; cc acc; CCI. "Magnificent position on terr cliffs; peaceful; well-kept & clean; immac san facs." 1 Jun-20 Sep. € 20.20   2006*

UNQUERA 1A4 (3km S Rural) **Camping El Mirador de Llavandes, Vegas Grandes, 33590 Colombres (Asturias) [tel/fax 985-41 22 44; campingmirador@campingmirador.com]** Fr N634 12km W of San Vicente de la Barquera turn at km 283/284 dir Noriega, site in 1.3km. Med, mkd pitch, terr, unshd; wc; chem disp; shwrs inc; el pnts (3A) €2.25; lndtte; shop & 3km; playgrnd; sand beach 1km; TV; phone; quiet; CCI. "Peaceful setting; excel for touring Picos." ♦ Holy Week & 15 Jun-15 Sep. € 17.30   2004*

VAL DE BIANYA, LA 3B3 (2km E Rural) **Camping La Vall de Bianya, Ctra C26, Km.215, 17813 La Vall de Bianya (Gerona) [972-29 00 57; fax 972-29 01 28; informacio@campingbianya. com; www.campingbianya.com]** Fr Olot N on C26, site sp. Med, mkd pitch, sl, pt shd; wc; chem disp; mv service pnt; baby facs; shwrs inc; el pnts (10A) €4.15; lndtte; gas; shop; rest; snacks; bar; playgrnd; pool; games rm; games area; entmnt; TV rm; 50% statics; dogs €2.40; phone; poss cr; quiet; cc acc. "Modern, clean facs; some pitches soft in wet." ♦ 1 Apr-31 Dec. € 16.80   2004*

⊞**VALDEAVELLANO DE TERA** 3B1 (1km NW Rural) **Camping Entrerrobles, 42165 Valdeavellano de Tera (Soria) [975-18 08 00; fax 975 -18 08 76; entrerobles@hotmail.com; www.entrerrobles. freeservers.com]** S fr Logroño on N111, after Almarza turn R onto S0-820 to Valdeavellano. In 10km turn R at site sp, site on R in 1km. Med, mkd pitch, pt sl, pt shd; htd wc; chem disp; baby facs; shwrs inc; el pnts (6A) €3; lndtte; sm shop; tradsmn; rest; snacks; bar; playgrnd; pool; games area; cycle hire; TV rm; 8% statics; dogs; phone; Eng spkn; adv bkg; quiet; cc acc; CCI. "Excel touring base Sierra de Urbión; attractive setting in valley; gd rest." ♦ € 18.00   2006*

VALDOVINO 1A2 (700m W Coastal) **Camping Valdoviño, Ctra Ferrol-Cedeira, Km 13, 15552 Valdoviño (La Coruña) [981-48 70 76; fax 981-48 61 31]** Fr Ortigueira on C642; turn W onto C646 sp Cadeira then Ferrol; turn R at camping sp, down hill R again, site on R almost on beach. Med, terr, pt shd; wc; chem disp; baby facs; shwrs inc; el pnts (15A) inc; gas; lndtte; ice; shop; rest; bar; snacks; playgrnd; sand beach adj; playgrnd; internet; TV; some statics; no dogs; bus adj; poss cr; quiet; Eng spkn; CCI. "Gd, busy site nr lge beach with lagoon & cliffs but poss windy; locality run down; vg rest." ♦ Easter & 1 Jun-30 Sep. € 25.70   2006*

VALENCIA *4E2* (9km S Coastal) **Camping Coll Vert, Ctra Nazaret-Oliva, Km 7.5, 46024 Playa de Pinedo (València)** [961-83 00 36; fax 961-83 00 40; info@collvertcamping.com; www. collvertcamping.com] Fr València on coast rd, foll sp El Saler. Site on R 1km bef El Saler. Med, hdg/ mkd pitch, shd; wc; shwrs inc; el pnts €4.50; gas; lndtte; ice; shop; bar; BBQ; playgrnd; pool; paddling pool; sand beach 500m; games area; entmnt; 5% statics; dogs €3; phone; bus to city & marine park; car wash; poss cr; Eng spkn; adv bkg; quiet; some rd noise; cc acc; red long stay. "Hourly bus service fr outside site to cent of València & marine park; helpful, friendly staff. ♦ 15 Feb-15 Dec. € 28.00   2006*

⊞**VALENCIA** *4E2* (16km S Rural) **Camping Devesa Gardens, Ctra El Saler, Km 13, 46012 València** [961-61 11 36; fax 961-61 11 05; www. devesagardens.com] S fr València on CV500, site well sp on R 4km S of El Saler. Med, mkd pitch, hdstg, pt shd; htd wc; chem disp; mv service pnt; baby facs; el pnts (7-15A) €4.50; gas; lndtte; ice; supmkt (high ssn) & 4km; rest; bar; BBQ; playgrnd; pool; beach 700m; tennis; lake canoeing; horseriding; 70% statics; no dogs; phone; bus to València; quiet; adv bkg; cc acc. "Friendly staff; warden needed to connect to el pt; site has own zoo; excel." ♦ € 31.00   2006*

VALENCIA DE DON JUAN see Villamañán *1B3*

VALL LLOBREGA see Palamós *3B3*

⊞**VALLE DE CABUERNIGA** *1A4* (1km NE Rural) **Camping El Molino de Cabuérniga, Sopeña, 39510 Cabuérniga (Cantabria)** [942-70 62 59; fax 942-70 62 78; cmcabuerniga@ campingcabuerniga.com; www.camping cabuerniga.com] SW on N634. At Cabezón de la Sal L onto C625. Site at km 42. Keep to R in vill, foll v sm green sp to site. Site clearly thro vill - v narr rds to site. Med, shd; wc; shwrs inc; el pnts (3A) €2.50 (check earth); gas; lndtte; shop; snacks; bar; playgrnd; rv sw 200m; fishing; tennis; phone; bus 500m; adv bkg; quiet; cc acc; CCI. "Excel site & facs on edge of vill; no shops in vicinity, but gd location." ♦ € 18.10   2006*

VEGUELLINA DE ORBIGO *1B3* (Rural) **Camping La Manga, Ctra LE421 Matalobos-Veguilla, Km 5, 24350 Veguellina de Órbigo (León)** [987-37 63 76; fax 987-37 61 35] Fr 1km S of Astorga fr A6, turn E onto N120 twds León; cont for 12km. At Hospital de Órbigo at LE421/420 turn S twds Veguellina de Órbigo; site sp fr vill. Med, pt shd; wc; chem disp; shwrs; el pnts €1.55; gas; lndtte; shop; snacks; bar; watersports adj; some statics; dogs; phone; quiet. Holy Week & 15 Jun-15 Sep. € 9.35   2004*

⊞**VEJER DE LA FRONTERA** *2H3* (4km SE) **Camping Vejer, 11150 Vejer de la Frontera (Cádiz)** [tel/fax 956-45 00 98; info@campingvejer. com; www.campingvejer.com] App fr Málaga dir on N340, at km stone 39.5, exit to L, bet 2 rests, site in 100m. Do not take o'fit into Vejer. Sm, pt sl, terr, pt shd; wc; chem disp; shwrs; el pnts (10A) €3; lndtte; shop; snacks; bar; playgrnd; pool; sand beach 9km; mini-golf; golf 2km; cycle hire; internet; 10% statics; dogs; phone; adv bkg; quiet; cc acc; CCI. "In wooded area away fr main rd; v ltd, neglected facs low ssn." € 20.00   2006*

⊞**VEJER DE LA FRONTERA** *2H3* (10km SE Coastal) **Camping Bahía de la Plata, Ctr. de Atlanterra s/n, 11399 Zahara de los Atunes (Cádiz)** [956-43 90 40; fax 956-43 90 87; info@campingbahiadelaplata.com; www. campingbahiadelaplata.com] Fr Vejer de la Frontera, take A393 twds Barbate; thro town & onto A5207 coastal rd twds Zahara de los Atunes; go thro Zahara, foll lorry rte to avoid narr streets & sharp corners of cent twds Atlanterra; site sp. Lge, mkd pitch, shd; wc; chem disp; shwrs inc; el pnts (16A) inc; lndtte; ice; shop; rest; snacks; bar; playgrnd; beach adj; cycle hire; entmnt; TV; some statics; no dogs; phone; cc acc. "Site opens onto beach; well-equipped & managed." ♦ ltd. € 21.10   2006*

VEJER DE LA FRONTERA *2H3* (10km S Coastal) **Camping Caños de Meca, Ctra de Vejer-Los Caños de Meca, Km 10, 11160 Barbate (Cádiz)** [956-43 71 20; fax 956-43 71 37; info@camping-canos-de-meca.com; www.camping-canos-de-meca.com] Fr N340 foll sp to Barbate then foll dir Los Caños de Meca. Turn R at seashore rd. Site on L 2km beyond town. Med, mkd pitch, shd; wc; chem disp; shwrs inc; el pnts (5A) €3.20; gas; lndtte; shop; rest; snacks; bar; playgrnd; pool; sand beach 600m; watersports; cycle hire; child entmnt; 20% statics; no dogs Jul/Aug; phone; poss cr; adv bkg; cc acc; CCI. "Vg." ♦ Easter-15 Oct. € 26.70   2005*

⊞**VELEZ BLANCO** *4G1* (1km S Rural) **Camping El Pinar del Rey, Paseo de los Sauces 5, 04830 Vélez Blanco (Almería)** [950-52 71 02; fax 950-34 92 76; info@pinardelrey.com] Fr A92N turn off at Vélez Rubio & foll sp Vélez Blanco. Site on R bef vill. Sm, hdstg, pt shd; htd wc; chem disp (wc); mv service pnt; shwrs inc; el pnts (6A) €3.20; rest; snacks; bar; playgrnd; pool; TV rm; no statics; site open w/e only low ssn; poss cr; adv bkg; CCI. "Beautiful area; clean mountain air; friendly staff." ♦ ltd. € 15.60   2007*

Spain

VENDRELL, EL *3C3* (2km S Coastal) **Camping Sant Salvador, Avda Palfuriana 68, 43880 Sant Salvador (Tarragona) [tel/fax 977-68 08 04; campingsantsalvador@troc.es; www. campingsantsalvador.com]** Exit A7 junc 31 onto N340, after 1km turn L. Site bet Calafell & Coma-Ruga. Lge, pt shd; wc; chem disp; baby facs; shwrs inc; el pnts (4A) €4; gas; lndtte; shop; rest; bar; playgrnd; beach; 75% statics; dogs €1.50; bus adj; poss cr; cc acc; red long stay/low ssn; CCI. "Secure site; not suitable lge o'fits; conv Safari Park & Port Aventura." ♦ 30 Mar-30 Sep. € 24.80   2007*

VENDRELL, EL *3C3* (7km SW Coastal) **Camping Francàs, Ctra N340, Km 1185.5, 43880 Coma-ruga (Tarragona) [977-68 07 25; fax 977-68 47 73; info@campingfrancas.net; www.campingfrancas. net]** Exit N340 at km stone 303 to Comarruga. Lge, mkd pitch, shd; wc; chem disp; baby facs; shwrs; el pnts €3.30; lndtte; shop; rest; snacks; bar; BBQ; playgrnd; sand beach adj; watersports; fishing; games area; entmnt; dogs; bus 100m; car wash; adv bkg; quiet. "Pleasant site." ♦ Easter-30 Sep. € 21.20   2007*

VERA see Garrucha *4G1*

VIELHA *3B2* (6km N Rural) **Camping Artigané, Ctra N230, Km 171, Val d'Arán, 25537 Pont d'Arròs (Lleida) [tel/fax 973-64 03 38; info@ campingartigane.com; www.campingartigane. com]** Fr French border head S on N230 for 15km. Fr Vielha head N to France & turn L at Pont d'Arròs. Site on main rd by rv. Lge, pt sl, pt shd; wc; chem disp; baby facs; shwrs inc; el pnts €4; gas; lndry rm; shop; rest, snacks, bar in high ssn; BBQ; playgrnd; htd pool; games area; golf; 5% statics; phone; poss cr; quiet; CCI. "V scenic area; excel for wild flowers, butterflies; friendly warden; low ssn site yourself - warden calls; simple facs, poss stretched when site full." ♦ Holy Week-15 Oct. € 17.50   2007*

VIELHA *3B2* (7km N Rural) **Camping Verneda, Ctra Francia N230, Km 171, 25537 Pont d'Arròs (Lleida) [973-64 10 24; fax 973-64 32 18; info@ campingverneda.com; www.campingverneda. com]** Fr Lerida N on N230 twd Spain/France border, site on R adj N230, 2km W of Pont d'Arròs on rvside, 1km after Camping Artigane. Med, pt shd; wc; chem disp; baby facs; shwrs inc; el pnts (4A) €3.90; gas; ice; lndtte; rest; snacks; bar; playgrnd; pool; horseriding; games rm; cycle hire; entmnt; TV; 10% statics; dogs €2.50; adv bkg; Eng spkn; cc acc; CCI. "Gd area for walking; site open w/e rest of year; well-run site; gd facs." 1 May-15 Oct. € 21.80   2007*

⊞**VIELHA** *3B2* (6km SE Rural) **Camping Era Yerla D'Arties, Ctra C142, Vielha-Baquiera s/n, 25599 Arties (Lleida) [973-64 16 02; fax 973-64 30 53; yerla@coac.net; www.aranweb.com/yerla]** Fr Vielha take C28 dir Baquiera, site sp. Turn R at rndabt into Arties, site in 30m on R. Med, shd; htd wc; chem disp; baby facs; shwrs inc; el pnts (4-10A) €4.10-7.60; gas; lndtte; shop & rest nrby; snacks; bar; pool; skiing nr; some statics; bus 200m; phone; quiet; cc acc; CCI. "Pleasant site; ideal for ski resort; v clean facs; gd shops, tapas bars & rests in vill; gd walking cent in summer." € 20.00   2007*

VILAFRANCA DEL CID see Morella *3D2*

Before we move on, I'm going to fill in some site report forms and post them off to the editor, otherwise they won't arrive in time for the deadline at the end of September.

⊞**VILALLONGA DE TER** *3B3* (Rural) **Camping Conca de Ter, Ctra Setcases s/n, 17869 Vilallonga de Ter (Gerona) [972-74 06 29; fax 972-13 01 71; concater@concater.com; www.concater.com]** Exit C38 at Camprodón; at Vilallonga de Ter do NOT turn off into vill but stay on main rd; site on L. Lge, mkd pitch, hdstg, pt shd; wc; chem disp; shwrs inc; el pnts (5-15A) €3.50-6.54; lndry rm; rest; pool; 95% statics; dogs €2; poss cr; Eng spkn; CCI. "Pitches sm & cr together; rest w/e only low ssn & then only after 2100; gd." € 24.00   2006*

⊞**VILANOVA DE PRADES** *3C2* (500m NE Rural) **Camping Serra de Prades, Calle Sant Antoni s/n, 43439 Vilanova de Prades (Tarragona) [tel/fax 977-86 90 50; info@serradeprades.com; www.serradeprades.com]** Fr AP2 take exit 8 (L'Albi) or 9 (Montblanc), foll C240 to Vimbodi. At km 47.5 take TV7004 for 10km to Vilanova de Prades. Site ent on R immed after rndabt at ent to vill. Lge, some hdg/mkd pitch, terr, pt shd; wc; chem disp; mv service pnt; baby facs; shwrs inc; el pnts (6A) €4.70 (poss long lead req) gas; lndtte; ice; basic shop & 8km; tradsmn; rest; snacks; bar; playgrnd; htd pool; lake sw 20km; tennis; games area; games rm; child entmnt; TV rm; many statics; dogs; phone; Eng spkn; adv bkg high ssn; quiet; red long stay/CCI. "Well-maintained, well-run, friendly site; sm pitches; access some pitches diff due steep, gravel site rds & storm gullies; facs spotless; gd walks fr site; mountain setting; wine rte; monasteries & musuems to visit; conv Barcelona; vg touring base/NH." ♦ € 22.00 (CChq acc)   2006*

⊞**VILANOVA DE PRADES** *3C2* (4km S Rural) **Camping Prades, Ctra T701, Km 6.850, 43364 Prades (Tarragona) [977-86 82 70; fax 977-86 82 79; camping@campingprades.com; www.campingprades.com]** Fr S take N420 W fr Reus, C242 N to Albarca, T701 E to Prades. Fr N exit AP2/E90 junc 9 Montblanc; N240 to Vimbodi; TV7004 to Vilanova de Prades; L at rndabt to Prades; go thro town, site on R in 500m. Narr rds & hairpins fr both dirs. Lge, mkd pitch, pt shd; wc; chem disp; mv service pnt; baby facs; shwrs; el pnts (3A) €4.40; gas; lndtte; shop; tradsmn; rest; snacks; bar; playgrnd; pool; cycle hire; wifi internet; 60% statics; phone; bus 200m; poss cr; adv bkg; cc acc; CCI. "Beautiful area; in walking dist of lovely, tranquil old town; excel." ♦ € 21.80   2006*

⊞**VILANOVA I LA GELTRU** *3C3* (3km Coastal) **Camping Vilanova Park, Ctra Arboç, Km 2.5, 08800 Vilanova i la Geltru (Barcelona) [938-93 34 02; fax 938-93 55 28; info@vilanovapark.es or reservas@vilanovapark.es; www.vilanovapark.es]** Fr N on AP7 exit junc 29 onto C15 dir Vilanova; then take C31 dir Cubelles. Leave at the 153km exit dir Vilanova Oeste/L'Arboç to site. Fr W on C32/A16 take the Vilanova-Sant Pere de Ribes exit. Take the C31 & at the 153km exit take BV2115 dir L'Arboc to site. Fr AP7 W leave at exit 31 onto the C32 (A16); take exit 16 (Vilanova-L'Arboc exit) onto BV2115 to site. Parked cars may block loop & obscure site sp. V lge, hdg/mkd pitch, hdstg, terr, pt shd; htd wc (some cont); chem disp; mv service pnt; serviced pitch; baby facs; fam bthrm; sauna; shwrs inc; el pnts (10A) inc (poss rev pol); gas; lndtte; ice; supmkt; tradsmn; rest; snacks; bar; BBQ (charcoal); playgrnd; 3 pools (1 htd covrd); jacuzzi; fitness centre; sand beach 3km; lake sw 2km; watersports 4km; fishing; cycle hire; tennis; gym; horseriding 500m; golf 1km; entmnt; child entmnt; excursions; games rm; wifi internet; TV; cash point; 40% statics; dogs €6.20; phone; bus/train; recep 0800-2300 high ssn; poss cr; Eng spkn; adv bkg ess (dep req+bkg fee); poss noisy nights & w/e high ssn; cc acc; red snr citizens/long stay; CCI. "Gd for children; excel san facs; v helpful staff; gd security; poss muddy in wet & some sm pitches with diff access due trees & high kerbs; poss diff pitch access on terr due ramps; gd rest & bar; nature walk with goats & deer in enclosures; conv Barcelona, Tarragona & Port Aventura; gd bus (with guide) & train service; gd sat TV; mkt Sat; excel site." ♦ € 41.00 (CChq acc) ABS - E08   2007*

See advertisement

VILANOVA I LA GELTRU *3C3* (5km SW Coastal) **Camping La Rueda**, Ctra C31, Km 146.2, 08880 Cubelles (Barcelona) [938-95 02 07; fax 938-95 03 47; larueda@la-rueda.com; www.la-rueda.com] Exit A7 junc 29 then take C15 dir Vilanova onto autopista C32 & take exit 13 dir Cunit. Site is 2.5km S of Cubelles on C31 at km stone 146.2. Lge, mkd pitch, shd; htd wc; chem disp; mv service pnt; shwrs inc; el pnts (4A) €5.86; gas; ice; lndtte; shop; rest; snacks; bar; sand beach 100m; playgrnd; pool; tennis; horseriding; watersports; fishing; entmnt; car wash; 12% statics; dogs €3.14; phone; bus; train; Eng spkn; adv bkg; quiet; red long stay/low ssn; cc acc; red CCI. "Conv Port Aventura & Barcelona; vg family site." 1 Apr-11 Sep. € 29.27   2005*

VILLADANGOS DEL PARAMO see León *1B3*

⊞**VILLAJOYOSA** *4F2* (3km NE Coastal) **Camping Playa del Torres**, Partida Torres Norte 11, 03570 Villajoyosa (Alicante) [966-81 00 31; fax 966-81 01 73; capto@ctv.es; www.playadeltorres.com] Exit A7/E15 at junc 65A onto N332. S fr Benidorm, exit L at km 140.5, site sp on main rd. Use traff lts/rndabt to turn round. Med, mkd pitch, hdstg, terr, pt shd; wc; chem disp; mv service pnt; 15% serviced pitches; shwrs inc; el pnts (16A) €4.37 ; gas; lndtte; sm shop; supmkt 5km; rest; snacks; bar; htd pool; shgl beach adj; internet; TV; 5% statics; dogs; phone; Eng spkn; cc acc; red long stay; CCI. "Diff access for disabled to shwrs/ wc due steep slope; excel facs." ♦ ltd. € 16.60   2006*

⊞**VILLAMANAN** *1B3* (1km SE) **Camping Palazuelo (formerly Covadonga)**, 24680 Villamañán (León) [987-76 80 64] Fr N630 Salamanca-León turn SE at Villamañán onto C621 dir Valencia de Don Juan. Site on R in 1km behind hotel. Med, pt shd; wc; shwrs inc; el pnts (10A) €2.40; shop 1km; rest; snacks; pool; quiet but some rd noise; cc acc. "NH only; neglected & run down low ssn; gd san facs but ltd privacy in shwrs." € 16.90   2006*

VILLAMANAN *1B3* (6km SE) **Camping Pico Verde**, Ctra C621, Km 27, 24200 Valencia de Don Juan (León) [tel/fax 987-75 05 25; campingpicoverd@terra.es] Fr N630 S, turn E at km 32.2 onto C621 sp Valencia de Don Juan. Site in 4km on R. Med, shd, mkd pitch; wc; shwrs inc; el pnts (6A) €2.20; lndtte; shop; rest; snacks 1km; playgrnd; 2 covrd pools; tennis; 25% statics; quiet; red CCI. "Friendly, helpful staff; conv León; picturesque vill; phone ahead to check site open if travelling close to opening/closing dates." 15 Jun-15 Sep. € 14.50   2004*

VILLAMANIN *1A3* (500m NW Rural) **Camping Ventosilla**, Ctra N630, Km 100, Calle del Camping s/n, 24680 Villamanín (León) [987-59 83 08] Fr N630 turn W over rv, site up thro vill of Villamanín, sp. Med, pt shd; wc (some cont); chem disp; baby facs; shwrs; el pnts (5-10A) €1.65; gas; lndtte; shop in vill; snacks; bar; playgrnd; cycle hire; TV; adv bkg; quiet; cc acc. "Superb caves; mountain walks; fishing." 1 Jul-31 Aug. € 12.00   2005*

> There aren't many sites open this early in the year. We'd better phone ahead to check that the one we're heading for is actually open.

VILLANANE *1B4* (3km S Rural) **Camping Angosto**, Ctra Villañañe-Angosto 2, 01425 Villañañe (Gipuzkoa) [945-35 32 71; fax 945-35 32 69; info@camping-angosto.com; www.camping-angosto.com] S fr Bilbao on AP68 exit at vill of Pobes & take rd to W sp Espejo. Site 1km N of Espejo on L. Med, pt shd; htd wc; chem disp; baby facs; shwrs inc; el pnts €4.15; lndtte; shop; rest; snacks; bar; BBQ; playgrnd; htd, covrd pool; entmnt; TV; 25% statics; dogs; phone; poss cr; Eng spkn; quiet. "Beautiful area; friendly staff; gd rest; conv NH fr Bilbao; vultures!" ♦ 15 Feb-30 Nov. € 18.50   2006*

⊞**VILLANUEVA DE TAPIA** *2G4* (2km S Rural) **Camping Cortijo La Alegria**, Cortijo La Alegria 36, 29315 Villanueva de Tapia (Málaga) [952-75 04 19] Exit A92 junc 175 onto A333 to Villanueva de Tapia. Turn L into layby at 63km opp Hotel/Rest La Paloma. Sm, pt sl, unshd; fam bthrm; lndtte; tradsmn; lake sw & beach 11km; Eng spkn; quiet. "CL-type site with superb mountain views." € 10.00   2005*

⊞**VILLARGORDO DEL CABRIEL** *4E1* (3km NW Rural) **Kiko Park Rural**, Ctra Embalse Contreras, Km 3, 46317 Villargordo del Cabriel (València) [tel/fax 962-13 90 82; kikoparkrural@kikopark.com; www.kikopark.com/rural] A3/E901 València-Madrid, exit junc 255 to Villargordo del Cabriel, foll sp to site. Med, mkd pitch, hdstg, terr, pt shd; wc; chem disp; mv service pnt; some serviced pitches; shwrs inc; el pnts (6A) €3.20; gas; lndtte; ice; shop; tradsmn; rest; snacks; bar; pool; lake sw 1km; canoeing; watersports; fishing; horseriding; white water rafting; cycle hire; TV; some statics; dogs €0.65; Eng spkn; adv bkg rec high ssn; quiet; cc acc; red long stay/low ssn; red CCI. "Beautiful location; gd walking; many activities; excel." ♦ € 25.35   2007*

See advertisement on page 834

VILLAVICIOSA *1A3* (8km NE Rural) **Camping La Rasa, Ctra La Busta-Selorio, 33316 Villaviciosa (Asturias) [985-89 15 29; info@campinglarase. com; www.campinglarasa.com]** Fr A8 exit km 353 sp Lastres/Venta del Pobre. In approx 500m foll site sp, cross bdge over m'way to site. Lge, hdg/ mkd pitch, sl, unshd; wc; chem disp; mv service pnt; serviced pitches; shwrs inc; el pnts (6A) €3.10; lndtte; sm shop; snacks; bar; playgrnd; pool; sand beach 7km; 60% statics; phone; site open w/e low ssn/winter; Eng spkn; CCI. "Pleasant, friendly site; beautiful countryside; conv m'way & coast; tight access rds to sm pitches." ♦ 15 Jun-15 Sep. € 18.50   2006*

VILLAVICIOSA *1A3* (15km W) **Camping Playa España, Playa de España, Quintes, 33300 Villaviciosa (Asturias) [tel/fax 985-89 42 73]** Sp on N632 approx 12km fr Villaviciosa & 10km fr Gijón. Last 3km of app rd narr & steep with sharp bends. Med, pt shd; wc; chem disp; shwrs; el pnts inc (pos rev pol); gas; shop; snacks; bar; beach 200m; phone; quiet; cc acc. "Gd site; lovely coast & scenery with mountains behind; clean; vg san facs." Holy Week & 14 May-17 Sep. € 17.00   2004*

⊞**VILLAVICIOSA DE CORDOBA** *2F3* (8km E Rural) **Camping Puente Nuevo, Ctra A3075, Km 8.5, 14300 Villaviciosa de Córdoba (Córdoba) [tel/fax 957-36 07 27; info@campingpuentenuevo.com; www.campingpuentenuevo.com]** Exit A4/E5 onto N432 dir Badajoz. In 32km turn L onto A3075, site in 8.5km. Med, hdg pitch, hdstg, sl, pt shd; wc; chem disp; shwrs inc; el pnts (16A) €4.17; lndtte; shop; tradsmn; rest; bar; BBQ; playgrnd; pool; lake sw 3km; games area; cycle hire; 40% statics; dogs €2; phone; bus 500m; poss cr; adv bkg; CCI. "Pitches poss tight lge o'fits; levellers needed all pitches; area well worth visit." ♦ ltd. € 17.70
                                                      2007*

⊞**VINAROS** *3D2* (5km N Coastal) **Camping Vinarós, Ctra N340, Km 1054, 12500 Vinarós (Castellón) [tel/fax 964-40 24 24; info@campingvinaros.com; www.campingvinaros.com]** Fr N exit AP7 junc 42 onto N238 dir Vinarós. At junc with N340 turn L dir Tarragona, site on R at km 1054. Fr S exit AP7 junc 43. Lge, hdg/mkd pitch, hdstg, pt shd; htd wc; chem disp; mv service pnt; 85% serviced pitches; baby facs; shwrs inc; el pnts (6A) €4; gas; lndtte; ice; shop 500m; tradsmn; rest adj; snacks; bar; playgrnd; pool; sand/shgl beach 1km; wifi internet; 15% statics; dogs €1; phone; bus adj; currency exchange; poss cr; Eng spkn; adv bkg; quiet but some rd noise; cc acc; red long stay/low ssn; CCI. "Excel gd value, busy, well-run site; many long-stay winter residents; spacious pitches; vg clean, modern san facs; gd rest; friendly, helpful staff; rec use bottled water; Peñíscola Castle & Morello worth a visit; site set amongst orange groves; easy cycle to town." ♦ ltd. € 26.40   2007*

VINUESA *3B1* (Rural) **Camping Cobijo, Ctra Laguna Negra Km 2, 42150 Vinuesa (Soria) [tel/ fax 975-37 83 31; www.campingcobijo.com]** Travelling W fr Soria to Burgos, at Abejar R on SO840. by-pass Abejar cont to Vinuesa. Well sp fr there. Lge, pt sl, pt shd; wc; chem disp; baby facs; shwrs inc; el pnts (3A) €3.75-5.40 (long lead poss req); gas; lndtte; shop; rest, snacks, bar high ssn; BBQ; playgrnd; pool; cycle hire; 10% statics; dogs; poss cr w/e; Eng spkn; phone; quiet; cc acc; CCI. "Friendly young management; v clean & attractive site; some pitches in wooded area poss diff lge o'fits; ltd bar & rest low ssn, excel rests in town 1.5km; gd walks." ♦ Holy Week-30 Sep. € 16.50   2005*

⊞**VITORIA/GASTEIZ** *3B1* (3km W Urban) **Camping Ibaya, Arbolado de Acacias en la N102, Km 346.5, 01195 Vitoria/Gasteiz (Alava) [945-14 76 20]** Fr A1 take exit 343 onto N102 W dir Vitoria/Gasteiz. Site sp fr N102 - site ent via rest gate adj Agip g'ge. Sm, mkd pitch, pt sl, pt shd; wc; chem disp; shwrs inc; el pnts (10A) €3.50; gas; lndry rm; sm shop; supmkt 2km; tradsmn; rest adj; bar; playgrnd; 5-10% statics; phone; poss cr; rd noise; CCI. "NH only; poss unkempt early ssn; gd, modern san facs; phone ahead to check open low ssn." € 17.00
                                                      2007*

VIU DE LINAS see Broto *3B2*

VIVEIRO *1A2* (500m NW Coastal) **Camping Viveiro, Cantarrana s/n, Covas, 27850 Viveiro (Lugo) [982-56 00 04; fax 982-56 00 84]** Fr E twd El Ferrol on rd LU862, turn R in town over rv bdge & bear R foll yellow camping sp. Site in 500m adj football stadium in Covas, sp. Fr W go into town on 1-way system & re-cross rv on parallel bdge to access rd to site. Foll stadium sp. Med, shd; wc; chem disp; shwrs inc; el pnts (10A) €4; lndtte; ice; shop & 1.5km; snacks; beach 500m; phone; bus adj; cc acc. "Gd clean site; uninspiring town." Easter & 1 Jun-30 Sep. € 16.00   2007*

VIVER *3D2* (3km W Rural) **Camping Villa de Viver, Camino Benaval s/n, 12460 Viver (Castellón) [964-14 13 34; info@campingviver.com; www. campingviver.com]** Fr Sagunto on A23 dir Terual, approx 10km fr Segorbe turn L sp Jérica, Viver. Thro vill dir Teresa, site sp W of Viver at end of single track lane (yellow sp). Med, hdg pitch, terr, pt shd; htd wc; chem disp; mv service pnt (planned for 2008); shwrs inc; el pnts (6A) €3.50; lndtte; ice; shop; tradsmn; rest; snacks; bar; playgrnd; pool; TV; 10% statics; dogs €2.75; phone; Eng spkn; adv bkg; quiet; red long stay; cc acc; CCI. "New owners 2007; many improvements planned for 2008; lovely situation." 1 Mar-1 Dec. € 12.00   2007*

ZAHARA DE LOS ATUNES see Vejer de la Frontera *2H3*

Spain

ZAMORA *1C3* (2.5km SE Urban) **Camping Ciudad de Zamora, Ctra Zamora-Fuentesaúco, Km 2.5, 49021 Zamora (Zamora) [980-53 72 95; fax 980-52 14 29; campingzamora@telefonica.net; www.campingzamora.com]** Fr N630 fr N or S, turn onto C605 dir Fuentesaúco, site sp. Med, mkd pitch, pt shd; wc; chem disp; mv service pnt; baby facs; shwrs inc; el pnts (6A) inc; gas; lndry service; ice; shop; tradsmn; rest; snacks; bar; BBQ; playgrnd; pool high ssn; rv sw - sand beach 3km; TV; dogs €1; phone; bus 2km; Eng spkn; adv bkg; quiet; cc acc; red long stay/low ssn; cc acc; red CCI. "Clean, well-run, conv site for town cent; excel san facs; friendly, helpful owners; gd cycling; excel." ♦ 30 Mar-15 Sep. € 20.60   2007*

⊞**ZARAUTZ** *3A1* (3km E Coastal) **Gran Camping Zarautz, Monte Talaimendi s/n, 20800 Zarautz (Guipúzkoa) [943-83 12 38; fax 943-13 24 86; info@grancampingzarautz.com; www.gran campingzarautz.com]** Exit A8 junc 11 Zarautz, turn R at 2nd rndbt onto N634 to site sp on L in 200m. On N634 fr San Sebastián to Zarautz, thro Orio & turn R 300m bef m'way exit foll sps. Long, steep app (approx 1km). Lge, hdg/mkd pitch, hdstg, pt sl, terr, pt shd; htd wc; chem disp; mv service pnt; shwrs inc; el pnts (6A) €3.50; gas; lndry rm; shop; tradsmn; rest; bar; BBQ; playgrnd; beach 1km (steep walk); games rm; golf 1km; TV rm; 50% statics; phone; train/bus to Bilbao & San Sebastian; poss cr; Eng spkn; no adv bkg; cc acc; CCI. "Site on cliff overlooking beautiful bay; excel beach at Zarautz, gd base for coast & mountains; fiesta in Jun; helpful staff; some pitches sm with steep access & overlooked fr terr above; old san facs block in need of upgrade - new OK; excel disabled facs; pitches poss muddy; NH for Bilbao ferry; rec arr early to secure pitch." ♦ € 28.70 (CChq acc)   2007*

ZARAUTZ *3A1* (4km E Coastal) **Camping Playa de Orio, 20810 Orio (Guipúzkoa) [943-83 48 01; fax 943-13 34 33; kanpina@terra.es; www.oriora. com]** Exit A8 m'way junc 11 at Zarautz & foll N634 to Orio, cross rv & turn L into town (v narr streets in town cent); sp fr town to site, about 1km. Or to avoid town cent cross bdge & foll N634 for 1km, turn L at sp Orio & camping, turn R at rndabt to site. Lge, mkd pitch, pt sl, pt shd; wc; chem disp; mv service pnt; baby facs; shwrs inc; el pnts (5A) inc; gas; lndtte; shop high ssn; tradsmn; rest adj; snacks; bar; playgrnd; pool high ssn; paddling pool; sand beach adj; tennis; 50% statics (sep area); no dogs; phone; car wash; poss cr at w/e; Eng spkn; adv bkg; quiet; red low ssn; cc acc; CCI. "Busy site; flats now built bet site & beach & new marina adj - now no sea views; walks; gd facs; friendly staff; useful NH bef leaving Spain." ♦ 1 Mar-1 Nov. € 27.00   2007*

ZUBIA, LA see Granada *2G4*

Take The Club with you when you go abroad!

Whether it's a short break or an extended tour, you can relax and enjoy your holiday protected by The Club's insurance.

For your **Caravan**
call **01342 336610**

With our **Standard** or **Super 5Cs** policies you'll have comprehensive insurance for your caravan, folding caravan or trailer tent, including 'new-for-old' cover until your caravan is either 3 or 10 years old, depending on which you choose. Both also include free Continental cover for up to 182 days in any policy year.

For your **Motor Caravan** or **Car**
call **0800 028 4809**

Our policies for motor caravans and cars offer wide-ranging cover with use in EU and Associated Countries for up to 180 days in any policy year. You choose how long each trip lasts within the annual limit.

For your **Holiday** cover
call **01342 336633**

The Club's Red Pennant Holiday Insurance offers several options including single trip and annual multi-trip policies. Whether you take motoring holidays, package flights or a combination of both, we can provide an insurance solution at a competitive price.

For further details or a quotation call today quoting ref CE08 or visit our website at

www.caravanclub.co.uk

We're looking forward to hearing from you!

Sorry, our policies are only available to Caravan Club members. Why not join us? You could easily save the cost of your subscription. Call **0800 328 5535** quoting ref. INM08

THE CARAVAN CLUB

Spain

Distances are shown in kilometres and are calculated from town/city centres along the most practical roads, although not necessarily taking the shortest route.

1km = 0.62miles

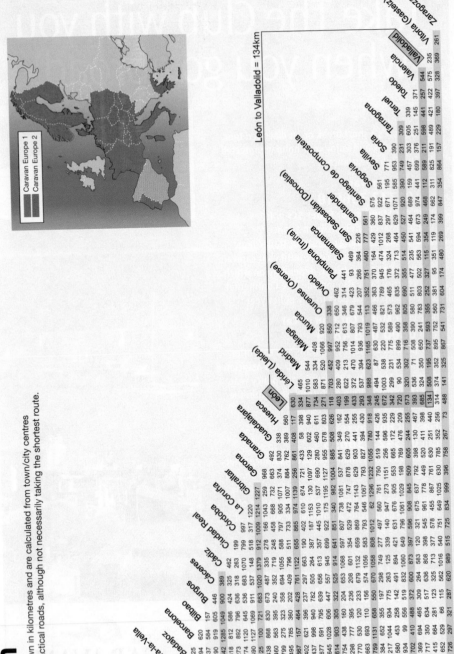

León to Valladolid = 134km

Regions and Provinces of Spain

ANDALUCIA
4   Alméria
11 Cádiz
14 Córdoba
18 Granada
21 Huelva
23 Jaén
29 Málaga
41 Sevilla

ARAGON
22 Huesca
44 Teruel
50 Zaragoza

ASTURIAS
33 Asturias

BALEARIC ISLANDS
7   Balearic Islands

CANARY ISLANDS
35 Las Palmas
38 Sta. Cruz de Tenerife

CANTABRIA
39 Cantabria

CASTILLA-LA MANCHA
2   Albacete
13 Cuidad Real
16 Cuenca
19 Guadalajara
45 Toledo

CASTILLA Y LEON
5   Ávila
9   Burgos
24 León
34 Palencia
37 Salamanca
40 Segovia
42 Soria
47 Valladolid
49 Zamora

CATALUÑA
8   Barcelona
17 Gerona
25 Lérida
43 Tarragona

COMUNIDAD VALENCIANA
3   Alicante
12 Castellón
46 Valencia

EXTREMADURA
6   Badajoz
10 Cáceres

GALICIA
15 La Coruña
27 Lugo
32 Ourense
36 Pontevedra

LA RIOJA
26 La Rioja

MADRID
28 Madrid

MURCIA
30 Murcia

NAVARRA
31 Navarra

PAIS VASCO
1   Álava
20 Guipúzcua
48 Vizcaya

SPANISH ENCLAVES
51 Ceuta
52 Melilla

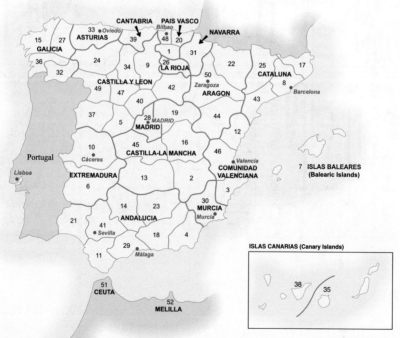

The first two digits of a Spanish postcode correspond to the number of the province in which that town or village is situated

Source : Spanish National Tourist Office

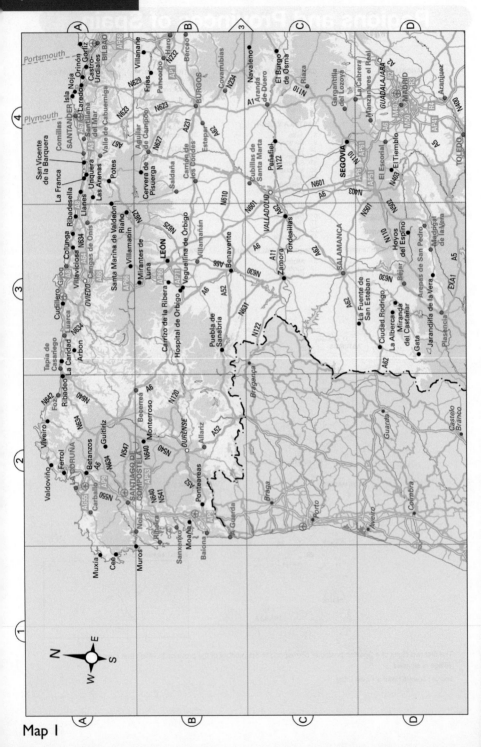

Map 1

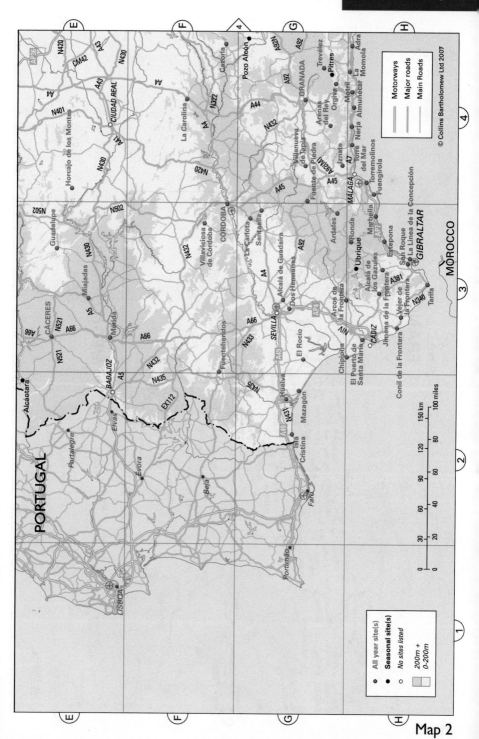

Spain

Map 2

© Collins Bartholomew Ltd 2007

Legend:
- Motorways
- Major roads
- Main Roads

- All year site(s)
- Seasonal site(s)
- No sites listed

200m +
0-200m

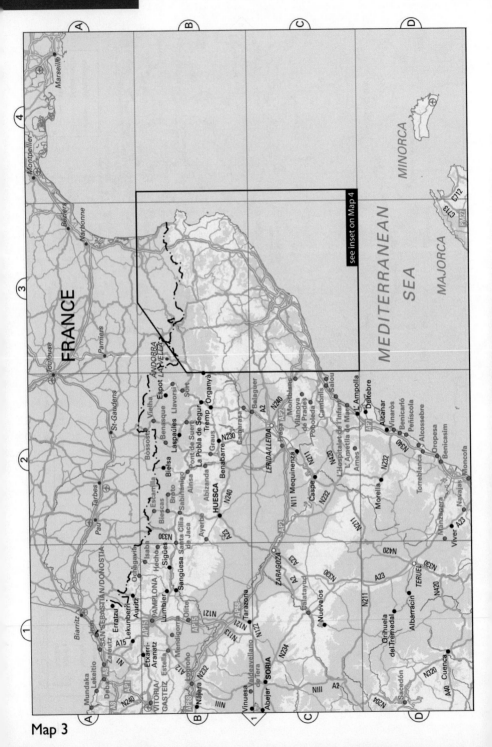

Map 3

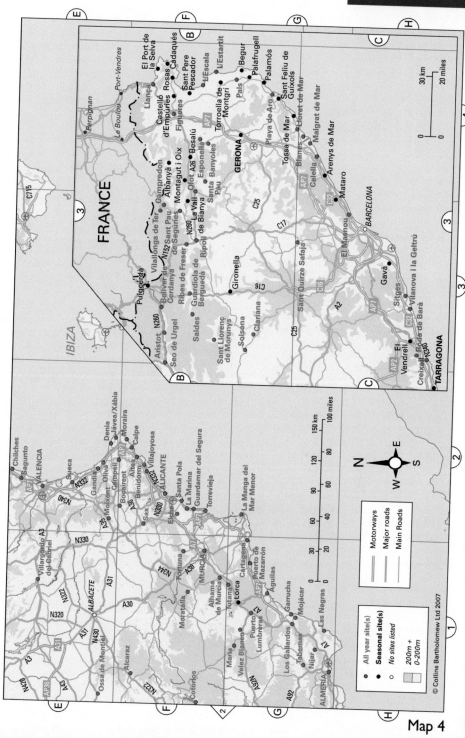

Map 4

© Collins Bartholomew Ltd 2007

●	All year site(s)
●	Seasonal site(s)
○	No sites listed

200m +
0–200m

Motorways
Major roads
Main Roads

FRANCE

IBIZA

GERONA

BARCELONA

TARRAGONA

VALENCIA

ALICANTE

MURCIA

ALBACETE

ALMERIA

El Port de la Selva
Port-Vendres
Perpignan
Le Boulou
Llançà
Castelló d'Empuries
Rosas
Cadaqués
Sant Pere Pescador
Figueres
L'Escala
L'Estartit
Begur
Palafrugell
Palamós
Sant Feliu de Guixols
Torroella de Montgrí
Pals
Lloret de Mar
Playa de Aro
Tossa de Mar
Blanes
Malgrat de Mar
Calella
Arenys de Mar
Mataro
El Masnou
Besalú
Esponellà
Santa Pau
Olot
Banyoles
La Vall de Bianya
Albanyà
Montagut i Oix
Camprodon
Vilallonga de Ter
Sant Pau de Séguries
Ripoll
Ribes de Freser
Guardiola de Berguedà
Bellver de Cerdanya
Puigcerdà
Aristot
Seo de Urgel
Saldes
Sant Llorenç de Morunys
Solsona
Clariana
Gironella
Sant Quirze Safaja
El Vendrell
Creixell
Roda de Barà
Vilanova i la Geltrú
Sitges
Gavà

Villargordo del Cabriel
Ossa de Montiel
Alcaraz
Chilches
Sagunto
Sueca
Gandia
Oliva
Denia
Jávea/Xábia
Moraira
Calpe
Altea
Benidorm
Campell
Bocairent
Moixent
Villajoyosa
Santa Pola
La Marina
Guardamar del Segura
Torrevieja
Elche
Sax
Moratalla
Fortuna
Alhama de Murcia
La Manga del Mar Menor
Cartagena
Puerto de Mazarrón
Aguilas
Garrucha
Mojácar
Los Gallardos
Jabanas
Nijar
Las Negras
Maria
Velez Blanco
Puerto Lumbreras
Totana
Lorca
Cotoros

N
W ——— E
S

0   30 km
0   20 miles

0 20 40 60 90 120 150 km
0   20   40   60   80   100 miles

Map 4

Caravan Europe Site Report

If campsite is already listed, complete only those sections of the form where changes apply

Please print, type or tick in the white areas

Sites not reported on for 5 years may be deleted from the guide

Year of guide used	200............	Is site listed?	Listed on page no.	Unlisted	Date of visit	........./........./.........

A - CAMPSITE NAME AND LOCATION

Country		Name of town/village site listed under (see Sites Location Maps)				
Distance & direction from centre of town site is listed under (in a straight line)		....................km	eg N, NE, S, SW	Urban	Rural	Coastal
Site open all year?	Y / N	Period site is open (if not all year)	................./................. to ..../.................			
Site name				Naturist site		Y / N
Site address						
Telephone			Fax			
E-mail			Website			

B - CAMPSITE CHARGES

	High season	Low season				
Charge for car, caravan + 2 adults per night in local currency			Electric hook up included in price quoted	Y / N		.........amps
			Price of electric hook-up (if not included)			.........amps

C - DIRECTIONS

Brief, specific directions to site (in km) To convert miles to kilometres multiply by 8 and divide by 5 or use Conversion Table in guide	
GPS	Latitude..(eg 12.34567) Longitude..(eg 1.23456 or -1.23456)

D - CAMPSITE DESCRIPTION

SITE size - number of pitches	Small Max 50	SM	Medium 51-150	MED	Large 151-500	LGE	Very large 500+	V LGE	Unchanged
PITCH size	eg small, medium, large, very large, various								Unchanged
Pitch features if NOT open-plan/grassy	Hedged	HDG PITCH	Marked or numbered	MKD PITCH	Hardstanding or gravel	HDSTG			Unchanged
If site is NOT level, is it	Part sloping	PT SL	Sloping	SL	Terraced	TERR			Unchanged
Is site shaded?	Shaded	SHD	Part shaded	PT SHD	Unshaded	UNSHD			Unchanged

E - CAMPSITE FACILITIES

WC	Heated	HTD WC	Continental		CONT	Own San recommended	OWN SAN REC
Chemical disposal point		CHEM DISP		Dedicated point			WC only
Motor caravan waste discharge and water refill point			MV SERVICE PNT				
Child / baby facilities (bathroom)		CHILD / BABY FACS	Family bathroom		FAM BTHRM		
Hot shower(s)		SHWR(S)	Inc in site fee?	Y / N	Price...................(if not inc)		
Mains electric hook-up		See 'B' above	Supplies of bottled gas	GAS	On site	or........km	
Launderette		LNDTTE	Laundry Room		LNDRY RM (if no launderette)		

F - FOOD & DRINK

Ice / freezer facilities	ICE	On site		and/or	.... kms	
Shop(s) / supermarket	SHOP(S) / SUPMKT	On site		and/or	.... kms	
Bread / milk delivered	TRADSMN					
Restaurant / cafeteria	REST	On site		and/or	.... kms	
Snack bar / take-away	SNACKS	On site		and/or	.... kms	
Bar	BAR	On site		and/or	.... kms	
Barbecue allowed	BBQ		Charcoal	Gas	Elec	Sep area
Cooking facilities	COOKING FACS					

G - LEISURE FACILITIES

Playground	PLAYGRND					
Swimming pool	POOL	On site		Or ....km	Heated	Covered
Beach	BEACH	Adj		Or ....km	Sand	Shingle
Alternative swimming (lake or river)	SW	Adj		Or ....km	Lake	River
Games /sports area / Games room	GAMES AREA	GAMES ROOM				
Entertainment in high season	ENTMNT	Child entertainment		CHILD ENTMNT		
Internet use by visitors	INTERNET	Wifi Internet		WIFI		
Television room	TV	Satellite / Cable to pitches		TV CAB / SAT		

G - OTHER INFORMATION

% Static caravans / mobile homes / chalets / cottages / fixed tents on site					........% STATICS
Dogs allowed	DOGS	Y / N	Price per night .... (if allowed)		
Phone	PHONE	On site	Adj		
Bus / tram / train	BUS / TRAM / TRAIN	Adj	Or .... km		
Twin axles caravans allowed?	TWIN AXLES Y / N	Possibly crowded in high season		POSS CR	
English spoken	ENG SPKN				
Advance bookings accepted	ADV BKG	Deposit required?		Y / N	
Noise levels on site in season	NOISY	QUIET	If noisy, why?		
Credit card accepted	CC ACC	Reduction low season		RED LOW SSN	
Camping Card International accepted in lieu of passport	CCI	INF card required (If naturist site)		Y / N	
Facilities for disabled	Full wheelchair facilities	♦	Limited disabled facilities	♦ ltd	

H - ADDITIONAL REMARKS AND/OR ITEMS OF INTEREST

Tourist attractions, unusual features or other facilities, eg waterslide, tennis, cycle hire, watersports, horseriding, separate car park, walking distance to shops etc	YOUR OPINION OF THE SITE:
	EXCEL
	VERY GOOD
	GOOD
	FAIR / POOR
	NIGHT HALT ONLY

Your comments & opinions may be used in future editions of the guide, if you do not wish them to be used please tick ....

I - MEMBER DETAILS

ARE YOU A:	Caravanner		Motor caravanner		Trailer-tenter?	
NAME:		CARAVAN CLUB MEMBERSHIP NO:				
		POST CODE:				
DO YOU NEED MORE BLANK SITE REPORT FORMS?			YES		NO	
Address (non-members only please complete this section)						

Please use a separate form for each campsite and do not send receipts. Owing to the large number of site reports received, it is not possible to enter into correspondence. Please return completed form to:

The Editor, Caravan Europe, The Caravan Club

FREEPOST PO Box 386, East Grinstead RH19 1UA

(This address to be used when mailing within the UK only)

Caravan Europe Site Report

If campsite is already listed, complete only those sections of the form where changes apply

Please print, type or tick in the white areas

Sites not reported on for 5 years may be deleted from the guide

Year of guide used	200..........	Is site listed?	Listed on page no.	Unlisted	Date of visit ..../......./........

A - CAMPSITE NAME AND LOCATION

Country		Name of town/village site listed under *(see Sites Location Maps)*			
Distance & direction from centre of town site is listed under *(in a striaght line)* ....km		eg N, NE, S, SW	Urban	Rural	Coastal
Site open all year?	Y / N	Period site is open *(if not all year)*	................./................. to ..../.................		
Site name				Naturist site	Y / N
Site address					
Telephone					
E-mail			Fax		
			Website		

B - CAMPSITE CHARGES

Charge for car, caravan + 2 adults per night in local currency	High season	Low season	Electric hook up included in price quoted	Y / N	.........amps
			Price of electric hook-up *(if not included)*		.........amps

C - DIRECTIONS

Brief, specific directions to site (in km) *To convert miles to kilometres multiply by 8 and divide by 5 or use Conversion Table in guide*	
GPS	Latitude...(eg 12.34567) Longitude...(eg 1.23456 or -1.23456)

D - CAMPSITE DESCRIPTION

SITE size - number of pitches	Small Max 50	SM	Medium 51-150	MED	Large 151-500	LGE	Very large 500+	V LGE	Unchanged
PITCH size	*eg small, medium, large, very large, various*								Unchanged
Pitch features if **NOT** open-plan/grassy	Hedged	HDG PITCH	Marked or numbered	MKD PITCH	Hardstanding or gravel	HDSTG			Unchanged
If site is **NOT** level, is it	Part sloping	PT SL	Sloping	SL	Terraced	TERR			Unchanged
Is site shaded?	Shaded	SHD	Part shaded	PT SHD	Unshaded	UNSHD			Unchanged

E - CAMPSITE FACILITIES

WC	Heated	HTD WC	Continental	CONT	Own San recommended	OWN SAN REC
Chemical disposal point		CHEM DISP		Dedicated point		WC only
Motor caravan waste discharge and water refill point			MV SERVICE PNT			
Child / baby facilities (bathroom)	CHILD / BABY FACS		Family bathroom		FAM BTHRM	
Hot shower(s)	SHWR(S)		Inc in site fee?	Y / N	Price...................*(if not inc)*	
Mains electric hook-up	See 'B' above		Supplies of bottled gas	GAS	On site	or........km
Launderette	LNDTTE		Laundry Room		LNDRY RM *(if no launderette)*	

F - FOOD & DRINK

Ice / freezer facilities	ICE	On site		and/or	.... kms
Shop(s) / supermarket	SHOP(S) / SUPMKT	On site		and/or	.... kms
Bread / milk delivered	TRADSMN				
Restaurant / cafeteria	REST	On site		and/or	.... kms
Snack bar / take-away	SNACKS	On site		and/or	.... kms
Bar	BAR	On site		and/or	.... kms
Barbecue allowed	BBQ		Charcoal	Gas	Elec	Sep area
Cooking facilities	COOKING FACS				

G - LEISURE FACILITIES

Playground	PLAYGRND					
Swimming pool	POOL	On site		Or ....km	Heated	Covered
Beach	BEACH	Adj		Or ....km	Sand	Shingle
Alternative swimming *(lake or river)*	SW	Adj		Or ....km	Lake	River
Games /sports area / Games room	GAMES AREA	GAMES ROOM				
Entertainment in high season	ENTMNT	Child entertainment	CHILD ENTMNT			
Internet use by visitors	INTERNET	Wifi Internet	WIFI			
Television room	TV	Satellite / Cable to pitches		TV CAB / SAT		

G - OTHER INFORMATION

% Static caravans / mobile homes / chalets / cottages / fixed tents on site				........% STATICS
Dogs allowed	DOGS	Y / N	Price per night .... *(if allowed)*	
Phone	PHONE	On site	Adj	
Bus / tram / train	BUS / TRAM / TRAIN	Adj	Or .... km	
Twin axles caravans allowed?	TWIN AXLES Y / N	Possibly crowded in high season		POSS CR
English spoken	ENG SPKN			
Advance bookings accepted	ADV BKG	Deposit required?		Y / N
Noise levels on site in season	NOISY	QUIET	If noisy, why?	
Credit card accepted	CC ACC	Reduction low season		RED LOW SSN
Camping Card International accepted in lieu of passport	CCI	INF card required *(If naturist site)*		Y / N
Facilities for disabled	Full wheelchair facilities	♦	Limited disabled facilities	♦ ltd

H - ADDITIONAL REMARKS AND/OR ITEMS OF INTEREST

Tourist attractions, unusual features or other facilities, eg waterslide, tennis, cycle hire, watersports, horseriding, separate car park, walking distance to shops etc

YOUR OPINION OF THE SITE:	
EXCEL	
VERY GOOD	
GOOD	
FAIR	POOR
NIGHT HALT ONLY	

Your comments & opinions may be used in future editions of the guide, if you do not wish them to be used please tick ....

I - MEMBER DETAILS

ARE YOU A:	Caravanner		Motor caravanner		Trailer-tenter?	
NAME:		CARAVAN CLUB MEMBERSHIP NO:				
		POST CODE:				
DO YOU NEED MORE BLANK SITE REPORT FORMS?			YES		NO	
Address *(non-members only please complete this section)*						

Please use a separate form for each campsite and do not send receipts. Owing to the large number of site reports received, it is not possible to enter into correspondence. Please return completed form to:

The Editor, Caravan Europe, The Caravan Club

FREEPOST PO Box 386, East Grinstead RH19 1UA

(This address to be used when mailing within the UK only)

Caravan Europe Site Report

If campsite is already listed, complete only those sections of the form where changes apply

Please print, type or tick in the white areas

Sites not reported on for 5 years may be deleted from the guide

Year of guide used	200............	Is site listed?	Listed on page no.	Unlisted	Date of visit	......../......../.........

A - CAMPSITE NAME AND LOCATION

Country		Name of town/village site listed under *(see Sites Location Maps)*				
Distance & direction from centre of town site is listed under *(in a striaght line)*		....................km	eg N, NE, S, SW	Urban	Rural	Coastal
Site open all year?	Y / N	Period site is open *(if not all year)*	................/.................. to ..../..................			
Site name				Naturist site	Y / N	
Site address						
Telephone			Fax			
E-mail			Website			

B - CAMPSITE CHARGES

Charge for car, caravan + 2 adults per night in local currency	High season	Low season	Electric hook up included in price quoted	Y / N	.........amps
			Price of electric hook-up *(if not included)*		.........amps

C - DIRECTIONS

Brief, specific directions to site (in km) *To convert miles to kilometres multiply by 8 and divide by 5 or use Conversion Table in guide*	
GPS	Latitude...(eg 12.34567) Longitude...(eg 1.23456 or -1.23456)

D - CAMPSITE DESCRIPTION

SITE size - number of pitches	Small Max 50	SM	Medium 51-150	MED	Large 151-500	LGE	Very large 500+	V LGE	Unchanged
PITCH size	eg small, medium, large, very large, various								Unchanged
Pitch features if NOT open-plan/grassy	Hedged	HDG PITCH	Marked or numbered	MKD PITCH	Hardstanding or gravel		HDSTG	Unchanged
If site is NOT level, is it	Part sloping	PT SL	Sloping	SL	Terraced		TERR	Unchanged
Is site shaded?	Shaded	SHD	Part shaded	PT SHD	Unshaded		UNSHD	Unchanged

E - CAMPSITE FACILITIES

WC	Heated	HTD WC	Continental		CONT	Own San recommended	OWN SAN REC
Chemical disposal point		CHEM DISP		Dedicated point			WC only
Motor caravan waste discharge and water refill point			MV SERVICE PNT				
Child / baby facilities (bathroom)		CHILD / BABY FACS	Family bathroom		FAM BTHRM		
Hot shower(s)		SHWR(S)	Inc in site fee?	Y / N	Price...................(if not inc)		
Mains electric hook-up		See 'B' above	Supplies of bottled gas	GAS	On site	or........km	
Launderette		LNDTTE	Laundry Room		LNDRY RM (if no launderette)		

F - FOOD & DRINK

Ice / freezer facilities	ICE	On site			and/or		.... kms
Shop(s) / supermarket	SHOP(S) / SUPMKT	On site			and/or		.... kms
Bread / milk delivered	TRADSMN						
Restaurant / cafeteria	REST	On site			and/or		.... kms
Snack bar / take-away	SNACKS	On site			and/or		.... kms
Bar	BAR	On site			and/or		.... kms
Barbecue allowed	BBQ		Charcoal	Gas	Elec	Sep area	
Cooking facilities	COOKING FACS						

G - LEISURE FACILITIES

Playground	PLAYGRND					
Swimming pool	POOL	On site		Or ....km	Heated	Covered
Beach	BEACH	Adj		Or ....km	Sand	Shingle
Alternative swimming *(lake or river)*	SW	Adj		Or ....km	Lake	River
Games /sports area / Games room	GAMES AREA	GAMES ROOM				
Entertainment in high season	ENTMNT	Child entertainment	CHILD ENTMNT			
Internet use by visitors	INTERNET	Wifi Internet	WIFI			
Television room	TV	Satellite / Cable to pitches		TV CAB / SAT		

G - OTHER INFORMATION

% Static caravans / mobile homes / chalets / cottages / fixed tents on site					........% STATICS
Dogs allowed	DOGS		Y / N	Price per night .... *(if allowed)*	
Phone	PHONE	On site		Adj	
Bus / tram / train	BUS / TRAM / TRAIN	Adj		Or .... km	
Twin axles caravans allowed?	TWIN AXLES Y / N	Possibly crowded in high season			POSS CR
English spoken	ENG SPKN				
Advance bookings accepted	ADV BKG	Deposit required?			Y / N
Noise levels on site in season	NOISY	QUIET	If noisy, why?		
Credit card accepted	CC ACC	Reduction low season			RED LOW SSN
Camping Card International accepted in lieu of passport	CCI	INF card required *(If naturist site)*			Y / N
Facilities for disabled	Full wheelchair facilities	♦	Limited disabled facilities		♦ ltd

H - ADDITIONAL REMARKS AND/OR ITEMS OF INTEREST

Tourist attractions, unusual features or other facilities, eg waterslide, tennis, cycle hire, watersports, horseriding, separate car park, walking distance to shops etc	YOUR OPINION OF THE SITE:
	EXCEL
	VERY GOOD
	GOOD
	FAIR / POOR
	NIGHT HALT ONLY

Your comments & opinions may be used in future editions of the guide, if you do not wish them to be used please tick ....

I - MEMBER DETAILS

ARE YOU A:	Caravanner		Motor caravanner		Trailer-tenter?	
NAME:		CARAVAN CLUB MEMBERSHIP NO:				
		POST CODE:				
DO YOU NEED MORE BLANK SITE REPORT FORMS?			YES		NO	
Address *(non-members only please complete this section)*						

Please use a separate form for each campsite and do not send receipts. Owing to the large number of site reports received, it is not possible to enter into correspondence. Please return completed form to:

The Editor, Caravan Europe, The Caravan Club

FREEPOST PO Box 386, East Grinstead RH19 1UA

(This address to be used when mailing within the UK only)

Caravan Europe Site Report

If campsite is already listed, complete only those sections of the form where changes apply

Please print, type or tick in the white areas

Sites not reported on for 5 years may be deleted from the guide

Year of guide used	200............	Is site listed?	Listed on page no.	Unlisted	Date of visit	......../......../.........

A - CAMPSITE NAME AND LOCATION

Country		Name of town/village site listed under *(see Sites Location Maps)*				
Distance & direction from centre of town site is listed under *(in a striaght line)*		....................km	eg N, NE, S, SW	Urban	Rural	Coastal
Site open all year?	Y / N	Period site is open *(if not all year)*	................../.................. to ..../..................			
Site name				Naturist site		Y / N
Site address						
Telephone			Fax			
E-mail			Website			

B - CAMPSITE CHARGES

	High season	Low season			
Charge for car, caravan + 2 adults per night in local currency			Electric hook up included in price quoted	Y / N	.........amps
			Price of electric hook-up *(if not included)*		.........amps

C - DIRECTIONS

Brief, specific directions to site (in km) *To convert miles to kilometres multiply by 8 and divide by 5 or use Conversion Table in guide*	
GPS	Latitude..(eg 12.34567) Longitude...(eg 1.23456 or -1.23456)

D - CAMPSITE DESCRIPTION

SITE size - number of pitches	Small Max 50	SM	Medium 51-150	MED	Large 151-500	LGE	Very large 500+	V LGE	Unchanged
PITCH size	*eg small, medium, large, very large, various*								Unchanged
Pitch features if **NOT** open-plan/grassy	Hedged	HDG PITCH	Marked or numbered	MKD PITCH	Hardstanding or gravel		HDSTG		Unchanged
If site is **NOT** level, is it	Part sloping	PT SL	Sloping		SL	Terraced		TERR	Unchanged
Is site shaded?	Shaded	SHD	Part shaded		PT SHD	Unshaded		UNSHD	Unchanged

E - CAMPSITE FACILITIES

WC	Heated	HTD WC	Continental		CONT	Own San recommended		OWN SAN REC
Chemical disposal point		CHEM DISP		Dedicated point			WC only	
Motor caravan waste discharge and water refill point			MV SERVICE PNT					
Child / baby facilities (bathroom)		CHILD / BABY FACS	Family bathroom			FAM BTHRM		
Hot shower(s)		SHWR(S)	Inc in site fee?		Y / N	Price....................*(if not inc)*		
Mains electric hook-up		See 'B' above	Supplies of bottled gas		GAS	On site	or........km	
Launderette		LNDTTE	Laundry Room			LNDRY RM *(if no launderette)*		

F - FOOD & DRINK

Ice / freezer facilities	ICE	On site		and/or	.... kms		
Shop(s) / supermarket	SHOP(S) / SUPMKT	On site		and/or	.... kms		
Bread / milk delivered	TRADSMN						
Restaurant / cafeteria	REST	On site		and/or	.... kms		
Snack bar / take-away	SNACKS	On site		and/or	.... kms		
Bar	BAR	On site		and/or	.... kms		
Barbecue allowed	BBQ		Charcoal	Gas	Elec	Sep area	
Cooking facilities	COOKING FACS						

G - LEISURE FACILITIES

Playground	PLAYGRND					
Swimming pool	POOL	On site		Or ....km	Heated	Covered
Beach	BEACH	Adj		Or ....km	Sand	Shingle
Alternative swimming *(lake or river)*	SW	Adj		Or ....km	Lake	River
Games /sports area / Games room	GAMES AREA	GAMES ROOM				
Entertainment in high season	ENTMNT	Child entertainment	CHILD ENTMNT			
Internet use by visitors	INTERNET	Wifi Internet	WIFI			
Television room	TV	Satellite / Cable to pitches		TV CAB / SAT		

G - OTHER INFORMATION

% Static caravans / mobile homes / chalets / cottages / fixed tents on site				........% STATICS
Dogs allowed	DOGS	Y / N	Price per night .... *(if allowed)*	
Phone	PHONE	On site	Adj	
Bus / tram / train	BUS / TRAM / TRAIN	Adj	Or .... km	
Twin axles caravans allowed?	TWIN AXLES Y / N	Possibly crowded in high season		POSS CR
English spoken	ENG SPKN			
Advance bookings accepted	ADV BKG	Deposit required?		Y / N
Noise levels on site in season	NOISY	QUIET	If noisy, why?	
Credit card accepted	CC ACC	Reduction low season		RED LOW SSN
Camping Card International accepted in lieu of passport	CCI	INF card required *(If naturist site)*		Y / N
Facilities for disabled	Full wheelchair facilities	♦	Limited disabled facilities	♦ ltd

H - ADDITIONAL REMARKS AND/OR ITEMS OF INTEREST

Tourist attractions, unusual features or other facilities, eg waterslide, tennis, cycle hire, watersports, horseriding, separate car park, walking distance to shops etc	YOUR OPINION OF THE SITE:	
	EXCEL	
	VERY GOOD	
	GOOD	
	FAIR	POOR
	NIGHT HALT ONLY	

Your comments & opinions may be used in future editions of the guide, if you do not wish them to be used please tick ....

I - MEMBER DETAILS

ARE YOU A:	Caravanner		Motor caravanner		Trailer-tenter?	
NAME:		CARAVAN CLUB MEMBERSHIP NO:				
		POST CODE:				
DO YOU NEED MORE BLANK SITE REPORT FORMS?			YES		NO	
Address *(non-members only please complete this section)*						

Please use a separate form for each campsite and do not send receipts. Owing to the large number of site reports received, it is not possible to enter into correspondence. Please return completed form to:

The Editor, Caravan Europe, The Caravan Club

FREEPOST PO Box 386, East Grinstead RH19 1UA

(This address to be used when mailing within the UK only)

Caravan Europe
Abbreviated Site Report Form

Use this abbreviated Site Report Form if you have visited a number of sites and there are no changes (or only insignificant changes) to their entries in the guide. If reporting on a new site, or reporting several changes, please use the full version of the report form. **If advising prices**, these should be for a car, caravan and 2 adults for one night's stay. **Please indicate high or low season prices and whether electricity is included.**

Remember, if you don't tell us about sites you have visited, they may eventually be deleted from the guide.

Year of guide used	200........	Page No.	....	Name of town/village site listed under		
Site Name					Date of visit	.... /....... /........

Site is in: Andorra / Austria / Belgium / Croatia / Czech Republic / Denmark / Finland / France / Germany / Greece / Hungary Italy / Luxembourg / Netherlands / Norway / Poland / Portugal / Slovakia / Slovenia / Spain / Sweden / Switzerland

Charge for car, caravan & 2 adults in local currency	High Season	Low Season	Elec inc in price?	Y / N	.............amps
			Price of elec (if not inc)		.............amps

Year of guide used	200........	Page No.	....	Name of town/village site listed under		
Site Name					Date of visit	.... /....... /........

Site is in: Andorra / Austria / Belgium / Croatia / Czech Republic / Denmark / Finland / France / Germany / Greece / Hungary Italy / Luxembourg / Netherlands / Norway / Poland / Portugal / Slovakia / Slovenia / Spain / Sweden / Switzerland

Charge for car, caravan & 2 adults in local currency	High Season	Low Season	Elec inc in price?	Y / N	.............amps
			Price of elec (if not inc)		.............amps

Year of guide used	200........	Page No.	....	Name of town/village site listed under		
Site Name					Date of visit	.... /....... /........

Site is in: Andorra / Austria / Belgium / Croatia / Czech Republic / Denmark / Finland / France / Germany / Greece / Hungary Italy / Luxembourg / Netherlands / Norway / Poland / Portugal / Slovakia / Slovenia / Spain / Sweden / Switzerland

Charge for car, caravan & 2 adults in local currency	High Season	Low Season	Elec inc in price?	Y / N	.............amps
			Price of elec (if not inc)		.............amps

Your comments & opinions may be used in future editions of the guide, if you do not wish them to be used please tick ....

Name..   Do you need more blank Site Report Forms?   Yes ☐   No ☐

Membership No...................................   Caravanner ☐   Motor caravanner ☐   Trailer-tenter ☐
or postcode

Please return completed form to:
The Caravan Club
Editor - Caravan Europe
FREEPOST PO Box 386
East Grinstead RH19 1UA
(This address to be used when mailing within UK only)

Year of guide used	200........	Page No.	....	Name of town/village site listed under		
Site Name					Date of visit	.... /....... /........

Site is in: Andorra / Austria / Belgium / Croatia / Czech Republic / Denmark / Finland / France / Germany / Greece / Hungary
Italy / Luxembourg / Netherlands / Norway / Poland / Portugal / Slovakia / Slovenia / Spain / Sweden / Switzerland

Charge for car, caravan & 2 adults in local currency	High Season	Low Season	Elec inc in price?	Y / N	.............amps
			Price of elec (if not inc)		.............amps

Year of guide used	200........	Page No.	....	Name of town/village site listed under		
Site Name					Date of visit	.... /....... /........

Site is in: Andorra / Austria / Belgium / Croatia / Czech Republic / Denmark / Finland / France / Germany / Greece / Hungary
Italy / Luxembourg / Netherlands / Norway / Poland / Portugal / Slovakia / Slovenia / Spain / Sweden / Switzerland

Charge for car, caravan & 2 adults in local currency	High Season	Low Season	Elec inc in price?	Y / N	.............amps
			Price of elec (if not inc)		.............amps

Year of guide used	200........	Page No.	....	Name of town/village site listed under		
Site Name					Date of visit	.... /....... /........

Site is in: Andorra / Austria / Belgium / Croatia / Czech Republic / Denmark / Finland / France / Germany / Greece / Hungary
Italy / Luxembourg / Netherlands / Norway / Poland / Portugal / Slovakia / Slovenia / Spain / Sweden / Switzerland

Charge for car, caravan & 2 adults in local currency	High Season	Low Season	Elec inc in price?	Y / N	.............amps
			Price of elec (if not inc)		.............amps

Year of guide used	200........	Page No.	....	Name of town/village site listed under		
Site Name					Date of visit	.... /....... /........

Site is in: Andorra / Austria / Belgium / Croatia / Czech Republic / Denmark / Finland / France / Germany / Greece / Hungary
Italy / Luxembourg / Netherlands / Norway / Poland / Portugal / Slovakia / Slovenia / Spain / Sweden / Switzerland

Charge for car, caravan & 2 adults in local currency	High Season	Low Season	Elec inc in price?	Y / N	.............amps
			Price of elec (if not inc)		.............amps

Caravan Europe
Abbreviated Site Report Form

Use this abbreviated Site Report Form if you have visited a number of sites and there are no changes (or only insignificant changes) to their entries in the guide. If reporting on a new site, or reporting several changes, please use the full version of the report form. **If advising prices**, these should be for a car, caravan and 2 adults for one night's stay. **Please indicate high or low season prices and whether electricity is included.**

Remember, if you don't tell us about sites you have visited, they may eventually be deleted from the guide.

Year of guide used	200........	Page No.	....	Name of town/village site listed under			
Site Name						Date of visit	.... /....... /........

Site is in: Andorra / Austria / Belgium / Croatia / Czech Republic / Denmark / Finland / France / Germany / Greece / Hungary Italy / Luxembourg / Netherlands / Norway / Poland / Portugal / Slovakia / Slovenia / Spain / Sweden / Switzerland

Charge for car, caravan & 2 adults in local currency	High Season	Low Season	Elec inc in price?		Y / N	............amps
			Price of elec (if not inc)			............amps

Year of guide used	200........	Page No.	....	Name of town/village site listed under			
Site Name						Date of visit	.... /....... /........

Site is in: Andorra / Austria / Belgium / Croatia / Czech Republic / Denmark / Finland / France / Germany / Greece / Hungary Italy / Luxembourg / Netherlands / Norway / Poland / Portugal / Slovakia / Slovenia / Spain / Sweden / Switzerland

Charge for car, caravan & 2 adults in local currency	High Season	Low Season	Elec inc in price?		Y / N	............amps
			Price of elec (if not inc)			............amps

Year of guide used	200........	Page No.	....	Name of town/village site listed under			
Site Name						Date of visit	.... /....... /........

Site is in: Andorra / Austria / Belgium / Croatia / Czech Republic / Denmark / Finland / France / Germany / Greece / Hungary Italy / Luxembourg / Netherlands / Norway / Poland / Portugal / Slovakia / Slovenia / Spain / Sweden / Switzerland

Charge for car, caravan & 2 adults in local currency	High Season	Low Season	Elec inc in price?		Y / N	............amps
			Price of elec (if not inc)			............amps

Your comments & opinions may be used in future editions of the guide, if you do not wish them to be used please tick ....

Name...   Do you need more blank Site Report Forms?   Yes ☐   No ☐

Membership No...................................   Caravanner ☐   Motor caravanner ☐   Trailer-tenter ☐
or postcode

Please return completed form to:
The Caravan Club
Editor - Caravan Europe
FREEPOST PO Box 386
East Grinstead RH19 1UA
(This address to be used when mailing within UK only)

Year of guide used 200........		Page No.		Name of town/village site listed under		
Site Name					Date of visit	.... /....... /........

Site is in: Andorra / Austria / Belgium / Croatia / Czech Republic / Denmark / Finland / France / Germany / Greece / Hungary Italy / Luxembourg / Netherlands / Norway / Poland / Portugal / Slovakia / Slovenia / Spain / Sweden / Switzerland

Charge for car, caravan & 2 adults in local currency	High Season	Low Season	Elec inc in price?	Y / N	.............amps
			Price of elec (if not inc)		.............amps

Year of guide used 200........		Page No.		Name of town/village site listed under		
Site Name					Date of visit	.... /....... /........

Site is in: Andorra / Austria / Belgium / Croatia / Czech Republic / Denmark / Finland / France / Germany / Greece / Hungary Italy / Luxembourg / Netherlands / Norway / Poland / Portugal / Slovakia / Slovenia / Spain / Sweden / Switzerland

Charge for car, caravan & 2 adults in local currency	High Season	Low Season	Elec inc in price?	Y / N	.............amps
			Price of elec (if not inc)		.............amps

Year of guide used 200........		Page No.		Name of town/village site listed under		
Site Name					Date of visit	.... /....... /........

Site is in: Andorra / Austria / Belgium / Croatia / Czech Republic / Denmark / Finland / France / Germany / Greece / Hungary Italy / Luxembourg / Netherlands / Norway / Poland / Portugal / Slovakia / Slovenia / Spain / Sweden / Switzerland

Charge for car, caravan & 2 adults in local currency	High Season	Low Season	Elec inc in price?	Y / N	.............amps
			Price of elec (if not inc)		.............amps

Year of guide used 200........		Page No.		Name of town/village site listed under		
Site Name					Date of visit	.... /....... /........

Site is in: Andorra / Austria / Belgium / Croatia / Czech Republic / Denmark / Finland / France / Germany / Greece / Hungary Italy / Luxembourg / Netherlands / Norway / Poland / Portugal / Slovakia / Slovenia / Spain / Sweden / Switzerland

Charge for car, caravan & 2 adults in local currency	High Season	Low Season	Elec inc in price?	Y / N	.............amps
			Price of elec (if not inc)		.............amps

Caravan Europe
Abbreviated Site Report Form

Use this abbreviated Site Report Form if you have visited a number of sites and there are no changes (or only insignificant changes) to their entries in the guide. If reporting on a new site, or reporting several changes, please use the full version of the report form. **If advising prices, these should be for a car, caravan and 2 adults for one night's stay. Please indicate high or low season prices and whether electricity is included.**

Remember, if you don't tell us about sites you have visited, they may eventually be deleted from the guide.

Year of guide used	200........	Page No.	....	Name of town/village site listed under			
Site Name						Date of visit	.... /....... /........

Site is in: Andorra / Austria / Belgium / Croatia / Czech Republic / Denmark / Finland / France / Germany / Greece / Hungary Italy / Luxembourg / Netherlands / Norway / Poland / Portugal / Slovakia / Slovenia / Spain / Sweden / Switzerland

Charge for car, caravan & 2 adults in local currency	High Season	Low Season	Elec inc in price?	Y / N	.............amps
			Price of elec (if not inc)		.............amps

Year of guide used	200........	Page No.	....	Name of town/village site listed under			
Site Name						Date of visit	.... /....... /........

Site is in: Andorra / Austria / Belgium / Croatia / Czech Republic / Denmark / Finland / France / Germany / Greece / Hungary Italy / Luxembourg / Netherlands / Norway / Poland / Portugal / Slovakia / Slovenia / Spain / Sweden / Switzerland

Charge for car, caravan & 2 adults in local currency	High Season	Low Season	Elec inc in price?	Y / N	.............amps
			Price of elec (if not inc)		.............amps

Year of guide used	200........	Page No.	....	Name of town/village site listed under			
Site Name						Date of visit	.... /....... /........

Site is in: Andorra / Austria / Belgium / Croatia / Czech Republic / Denmark / Finland / France / Germany / Greece / Hungary Italy / Luxembourg / Netherlands / Norway / Poland / Portugal / Slovakia / Slovenia / Spain / Sweden / Switzerland

Charge for car, caravan & 2 adults in local currency	High Season	Low Season	Elec inc in price?	Y / N	.............amps
			Price of elec (if not inc)		.............amps

Your comments & opinions may be used in future editions of the guide, if you do not wish them to be used please tick ....

Name..

Membership No...................................
or postcode

Do you need more blank Site Report Forms?   Yes ☐   No ☐

Caravanner ☐   Motor caravanner ☐   Trailer-tenter ☐

Please return completed form to:
The Caravan Club
Editor - Caravan Europe
FREEPOST PO Box 386
East Grinstead RH19 1UA
(This address to be used when mailing within UK only)

Year of guide used	200........	Page No.	....	Name of town/village site listed under		
Site Name					Date of visit	.... /....... /.......

Site is in: Andorra / Austria / Belgium / Croatia / Czech Republic / Denmark / Finland / France / Germany / Greece / Hungary
Italy / Luxembourg / Netherlands / Norway / Poland / Portugal / Slovakia / Slovenia / Spain / Sweden / Switzerland

Charge for car, caravan & 2 adults in local currency	High Season	Low Season	Elec inc in price?	Y / N	............amps
			Price of elec (if not inc)		............amps

Year of guide used	200........	Page No.	....	Name of town/village site listed under		
Site Name					Date of visit	.... /....... /.......

Site is in: Andorra / Austria / Belgium / Croatia / Czech Republic / Denmark / Finland / France / Germany / Greece / Hungary
Italy / Luxembourg / Netherlands / Norway / Poland / Portugal / Slovakia / Slovenia / Spain / Sweden / Switzerland

Charge for car, caravan & 2 adults in local currency	High Season	Low Season	Elec inc in price?	Y / N	............amps
			Price of elec (if not inc)		............amps

Year of guide used	200........	Page No.	....	Name of town/village site listed under		
Site Name					Date of visit	.... /....... /.......

Site is in: Andorra / Austria / Belgium / Croatia / Czech Republic / Denmark / Finland / France / Germany / Greece / Hungary
Italy / Luxembourg / Netherlands / Norway / Poland / Portugal / Slovakia / Slovenia / Spain / Sweden / Switzerland

Charge for car, caravan & 2 adults in local currency	High Season	Low Season	Elec inc in price?	Y / N	............amps
			Price of elec (if not inc)		............amps

Year of guide used	200........	Page No.	....	Name of town/village site listed under		
Site Name					Date of visit	.... /....... /.......

Site is in: Andorra / Austria / Belgium / Croatia / Czech Republic / Denmark / Finland / France / Germany / Greece / Hungary
Italy / Luxembourg / Netherlands / Norway / Poland / Portugal / Slovakia / Slovenia / Spain / Sweden / Switzerland

Charge for car, caravan & 2 adults in local currency	High Season	Low Season	Elec inc in price?	Y / N	............amps
			Price of elec (if not inc)		............amps

Index

Index